World
Masterpieces

VOLUME 2

REVISED

VOLUME 1

Masterpieces of the Ancient World · Knox
Masterpieces of the Middle Ages · McGalliard
Masterpieces of the Renaissance · Pasinetti

VOLUME 2

Masterpieces of Neoclassicism · Hugo
Masterpieces of Romanticism · Hugo
Masterpieces of Realism and Naturalism · Wellek
Masterpieces of Symbolism and the Modern
School · Douglas

A Companion Volume

Masterpieces of the Orient
Edited by G. L. Anderson

World Masterpieces

REVISED

Maynard Mack, *General Editor*
YALE UNIVERSITY

Bernard M. W. Knox
CENTER FOR HELLENIC STUDIES

John C. McGalliard
THE STATE UNIVERSITY OF IOWA

P. M. Pasinetti
UNIVERSITY OF CALIFORNIA, LOS ANGELES

Howard E. Hugo
UNIVERSITY OF CALIFORNIA

René Wellek
YALE UNIVERSITY

Kenneth Douglas
FORMERLY OF YALE UNIVERSITY

VOLUME
2
Literature of Western Culture since the Renaissance

W · W · NORTON & COMPANY · INC · *New York*

Cloth Edition SBN 393 09661 0
Paper Edition SBN 393 09547 9

Book design by John Woodlock

PRINTED IN THE UNITED STATES OF AMERICA

6 7 8 9

Contents

vi · *Contents*

Masterpieces of Realism and Naturalism

Masterpieces of Symbolism and the Modern School

Preface to the Revised Edition

After ten years in which this anthology has won reassuring approval from many quarters, there seems to be no need either to reiterate its principles here (they may, in any case, be consulted below, in the preface to the first edition) or to deviate from them. What we have sought in this revised edition of *World Masterpieces* is to widen very considerably the range of choice for teachers and of literary experience for students, while at the same time increasing the number of complete works and the quality of the translations.

Authors now represented for the first time include Aristophanes, the anonymous author of *Everyman*, Petrarch, Marlowe, Tirso de Molina, Calderón, Pascal, Pushkin, Turgenev, Henry James, Brecht, Sartre, and Camus. The "Ancient World" has been importantly enriched by the addition of *Lysistrata* and three books from the *Odyssey* and by supplementing *Agamemnon* with *Prometheus Bound*, *Oedipus Rex* with *Antigone* and *Oedipus at Colonus* (thus completing the Theban cycle), and *Medea* with *The Trojan Women*. For the "Middle Ages," Dante's *Inferno* is now complete, and *Everyman* has been added. The "Renaissance" gains by the addition of selections from Petrarch, Marlowe's *Dr. Faustus*, Tirso da Molina's *Trickster of Seville* (on the Don Juan theme), and Calderón's *Life Is a Dream*. "Neo-Classicism" and "Romanticism" are expanded and receive (we feel) a better balance from the addition of Pascal, the substitution of *Tartuffe* for *The Bourgeois Gentleman*, the addition of two selections from Wordsworth, the substitution of *Kubla Khan* and *Dejection: An Ode* for *The Rime of the Ancient Mariner*, and of *Billy Budd* for *Bartleby the Scrivener*, together with the addition of a long excerpt from Pushkin's *Eugene Onegin*. In the section on "Realism and Naturalism," Turgenev's *Fathers and Sons* and Henry James's *The Aspern Papers* replace an excerpt from Dickens' *Hard Times*. The range of works in the section "Symbolism and the Modern School" has been strikingly expanded by the addition of Brecht's *The Cauca-*

xi

sian Chalk Circle, Sartre's *No Exit*, and Camus' *The Renegade*, and the replacement of Kafka's *The Hunger Artist* by his *Metamorphosis*, a story that during the past decade has increasingly shown itself to be one of the true abstracts and brief chronicles of our time. Synge's *Playboy of the Western World*, delightful though it is, has a certain provinciality in this company and has been removed.

We hope that without immodesty we may again take special pride in our translations. Though every translation that we desired was not available to us, our effort to keep faith with our users and approvers may be seen in the reappearance here of Richard Lattimore, Louis MacNeice, Rex Warner, C. Day Lewis, Laurence Binyon, and Samuel Putnam; and in the appearance for the first time of Robert Fitzgerald (the *Odyssey* and *Oedipus at Colonus*), Edith Hamilton (*Prometheus Bound* and *The Trojan Women*), Richard Wilbur (*Tartuffe*), Robert Lowell (*Phaedra*), Edwin Muir (*Metamorphosis*), and several others of high distinction. Somewhat reluctantly, but recognizing that for all its virtues it is sometimes like an excerpt from the play than a translation, we have replaced William Butler Yeats' *Oedipus* with a more faithful version by T. H. Banks, whose unpretentious skill in getting things right will be appreciated by those who till now have felt obliged to spend class time pointing out that Yeats' play is magnificent but not the one that Sophocles wrote.

We would be less than candid if we did not remind our readers that the bounty they are afforded in these two volumes owes much to the traditions maintained by our publisher. The willingness of W. W. Norton & Company, Inc., to cooperate with the editors at all points in alleviating the burden of preparation, sharing the cost of permissions to reprint, and finding ways and means of making so much space available at a modest price is here gratefully acknowledged by all of us, and by none more heartily than the general editor.

The Editors

Preface

World Masterpieces is an anthology of Western literature, based on principles which we believe to be sound, but which have not always been sufficiently observed, we feel, in the existing anthologies in this field.

We have sought to make the range of readings in this collection unusually wide and varied. Its contents reach in time from Genesis and the *Iliad* to *Murder in the Cathedral*, and the literatures represented include English, Irish, American, Russian, German, Scandinavian, French, Italian, Spanish, Portuguese, Latin, Hebrew, and Greek. The literatures of the Far East have been omitted, on the ground that the principal aim of a course in world literature is to bring American students into living contact with their own Western tradition, and that this aim cannot be adequately realized in a single course if they must also be introduced to a very different tradition, one requiring extended treatment to be correctly understood. Twentieth-century literature has been represented with particular fullness, because we feel that it is important for students to grasp the continuity of literature.

World Masterpieces is predominantly an anthology of imaginative literature. We have not tried to cover the entire history of the West in print, and have avoided filling our pages with philosophy, political theory, theology, historiography, and the like. This principle was adopted not because we disapprove of coming at the history of an epoch by way of literature, but because imaginative literature, in our view, itself best defines the character of its epoch: great monuments of art, we would be inclined to say, furnish the *best* documents for history. They lead us deeper into the meaning of a past age than other modes of writing do, because they convey its unformulated aspirations and intuitions as well as its conscious theorems and ideals; and yet, being timeless, they have also an unmatched appeal to our own age. For this reason, we have admitted into *World Masterpieces* only works which have something important to say to modern readers, and we have made it a point to interpret them with reference not only to their time but to ours.

Teacher and student will find here a number of selections which they have not encountered before in a text of this kind.

We are convinced that effective understanding of any author depends upon studying an autonomous and substantial piece of his work: a whole drama, a whole story, at least a whole canto or book of a long poem. Our anthology therefore contains no snippets. Where it has been necessary to represent a long work by extracts, they are large extracts, forming a coherent whole. These considerations have also affected our treatment of lyric poems. Experience leads us to the conclusion that lyric poetry cannot be taught with full success in translation, and that very short poems, in whatever language, are nearly useless in a survey of these dimensions. We have accordingly excluded almost all *short* lyrics, and, with rare exceptions, all lyric poetry in foreign languages. We have preferred to represent the romantic movement, in which the lyric becomes a dominant form, with selections in English from the major English and American poets. This is not a flawless solution to the problem, but it seems to us better than printing many pages of inferior translations.

Since nothing has so deterred students from enjoying the great masterpieces of the classical and modern foreign languages as translations in an English idiom that is no longer alive, we have done our best to use translations which show a feeling for the English language as it is written and spoken today. Thus we offer here, with some pride, Richmond Lattimore's *Iliad*; Louis MacNeice's *Agamemnon* and his *Faust*; William Butler Yeats's *King Oedipus*; Rex Warner's *Medea*; C. Day Lewis' *Aeneid*; Lawrence Binyon's *Divine Comedy*; Samuel Putnam's *Don Quixote*; and many other renderings of equal quality.

Our introductions—in consonance with the scheme of the book —emphasize criticism rather than history. While providing all that seems to us necessary in the way of historical background (and supplying biographical summaries in the appendix following each introduction), we aim to give the student primarily a critical and analytical discussion of the works themselves. We try to suggest what these works have to say to us today, and why they should be valued now. In every instance, we seek to go beneath the usual generalizations about periods and philosophies, and to focus on men and books.

Our annotations of the texts are, we believe, exceptionally full and helpful. In a number of cases, these texts are annotated in this anthology for the first time. In one instance, we have been able to supply for a work the best-known notes on it in English, those of C. H. Grandgent to the *Divine Comedy*. Every care has been taken to furnish accurate and generous bibliographies as a guide to further reading.

In sum, we have sought to compile a new anthology, a text new in every sense—new in its emphasis on imaginative literature, on major authors, on wholes and large excerpts, on modern translations, on critical rather than historical treatment of texts, and, pervasively, on the tastes and values of our own time.

The Editors

World
Masterpieces

VOLUME 2

REVISED

Masterpieces of Neoclassicism

EDITED BY
HOWARD E. HUGO
Associate Professor of English, University of California, Berkeley

FROM PASCAL TO VOLTAIRE

Words such as "Reformation" and "Renaissance" are rich in connotations of drastic alteration, rebirth, and revolt—the new arising from the old and the old interpreted with sudden vigor and apparent heterodoxy. Not so are the names given at the time or by posterity to the last half of the seventeenth century and the first half of the eighteenth: the "neoclassical" period, the "Age of Reason," the "Enlightenment," the "Century of Light." Here are terms indicative of relative quiescence, the triumph of consolidation and harmony over innovation and disorder. There is some truth in these phrases, but not the whole truth.

For example, although the Renaissance and the Reformation appear to be at complementary opposite poles, by 1700 the tension between the two conceptions—of man in a state of nature and man in a state of grace—had softened. John Milton, writing *Paradise Regained* (1671) in his old age, portrays Christ raising a demurral about the moral worth of classical pagan writers—those extolled by the Renaissance. Satan's plea for their eminence is answered abruptly:

All our law and story strewed
With hymns, our Psalms with artful terms inscribed,
Our Hebrew songs and harps in Babylon,
That pleased so well our victor's ear, declare
That rather Greece from us these arts derived.

Almost two hundred years later Matthew Arnold was to descant

1

on this theme, when he opposed the Hebraic to the Hellenic strand in our culture. Most important for us is Milton's unceasing striving to realize the condition of Christian Humanism, to *unite* the values implicit in Renaissance and Reformation, the orders of nature and grace: those two worlds, to quote Maynard Mack, "whose reconciliation had exercised his imagination all his life." One has the impression that many of the thinkers after him found the task easier, possibly because they minimized or ignored the difficult polarity.

While men have never ceased to invigorate their thought by returning to the masterpieces of Greece and Rome, the special task of the Renaissance—to bring back to life a world bypassed or partly forgotten— seemed finished by the end of the seventeenth century. The "Quarrel of the Ancients and the Moderns" (to be referred to again later on) was fought with an acerbity that happily cost nobody's blood. Was modern man inferior, equal, or possibly superior to his glorious classical ancestors? Whatever their answer, the participants in the "Quarrel" recognized continuity with the great minds of classical antiquity. Similarly the religious strife occasioned by Protestant attacks on the institution of the Roman Catholic Church lost its acrimony. Conflicts henceforward were likely to be between nations, not sects, and to concern politics and the balance of power instead of the individual's private relation to God. True,

Louis XIV's revocation of the Edict of Nantes in 1685 upsets any easy picture of the gradual emergence of religious toleration, for the "Sun King" thereby denied to Protestants the right to practice their own variety of Christianity. Yet the French Regency repented that monarch's action some thirty years later, and in 1689 the English Toleration Acts set a broad pattern slowly emulated by most European commonwealths.

Political and economic wars, on the other hand, abounded: struggles about Spanish, Austrian, Polish, and Bavarian successions; various Silesian engagements; the war between Peter the Great and Charles XII of Sweden; ancillary combats in the New World and in the recently colonized East. Nationalistic marches and countermarches fill the years we now consider. The punctilio and formal splendor portrayed in Chapter 3 of Voltaire's *Candide* (in this volume) is that author's ironical commentary on his own best of all possible worlds from the point of view of man's organized inhumanity to man. Certainly it cannot be said that peace elected the Enlightenment as the moment to proclaim "olives of endless age." Yet fortunately the horrible slaughter of the Thirty Years' War (1618-1648) was not soon repeated. Europe had almost two hundred years from the start of that catastrophe before undergoing devastation on a similar scale. Then the battles of Napoleon's *Grande Armée* and his opponents involved hundreds, not merely tens, of thousands.

Classical Greece viewed its gods as residing serenely on Mount Olympus. Neoclassicism produced a pantheon of monarchs who enacted comparable roles within a more human, but also more elegant, environment. The modern state had arisen from its feudal antecedents; and kings, both absolute and enlightened, tended more and more to symbolize the aspirations of the countries they headed. At first glance the age seems to be dominated by the lengthening shadows of its rulers. What other epoch, for instance, could boast three political personalities of the order of Peter and Catherine of Russia, and Frederick II of Prussia—all called "the Great"? Add to them Maria Theresa of Austria and the Holy Roman Empire, with her forty-year reign; the radiant figure of Louis XIV; and the less spectacular but equally important English monarchs—Anne and her Hanoverian descendants, the first three Georges.

Nevertheless, the growth of certain theories about kingship made the condition of royalty less secure. Simpler medieval and Renaissance assumptions had invested earthly rulers with divine rights (even if the problem of Church and State, pope and emperor, persisted). When for example the English under Cromwell executed Charles I—to the horror of many contemporary Europeans—John Milton, in his *Tenure of Kings and Magistrates* (1649), attempted to justify the regicide by invoking precedents, history, common sense, and Holy Scripture. A true king, said Milton, enjoys his office by "the eminence of his wisdom and integrity." A tyrant, in contradistinction, "reigns only for himself and his faction." But his arguments for and against monarchy were slowly superseded by the notion that men live together by virtue of a social contract—the theme of such disparate thinkers as Hobbes, Locke, Rousseau, and many of the French *philosophes*. At the start of the eighteenth century a monarch, acting *in loco parentis*, was still generally considered necessary for the state, particularly if the royal prerogatives were circumscribed by custom or constitution. The age of neoclassicism and the Enlightenment accepted its rulers, but in good rationalist fashion attempted to define their station and duties within an orderly civil society. Future generations were to find more radical and violent solutions. Chapter 26 of *Candide* is strangely prophetic of the shape of things to come. Here the six indigent and dispossessed kings convening at the Carnival of Venice are portrayed as ultimately inferior to the commoner, Candide, who joins them: "Who is this fellow who is able to give a hundred times as much as any of us, and who gives it?"

These are broad cultural and political characteristics of the age. When we turn from them to the contributions of the philosophers of the period, generalization becomes more difficult: Descartes, Spinoza, Locke, Leibnitz, Berkeley, Hume, La Mettrie, D'Alembert, Holbach— what common denominator will reconcile such differing minds?

Yet most thinkers manifested two tendencies. First, they challenged traditional Christianity and classical philosophy by posing questions of a complex and problematic nature and thus helped to bring about what Paul Hazard has called a crisis in European thought. And second, they stressed that man's mind alone is the sole judge of the readings we make of the universe, of God, and of man; they assumed, as almost no earlier philosophers had done, that the cosmos conforms to what human experience and our judgments and abstractions seem to prove. They were, in short, *rationalists*, although many of them would be surprised at being so labeled.

In England, Sir Francis Bacon had earlier laid down a program for new scientific studies, although for him these were but dimly ascertained. Induction was to be the tool whereby we would derive "axioms from the senses and particulars, rising by a gradual and unbroken ascent, so that it [*i.e.*, the inductive method] arrives at the most general axioms last of all. This is the true way, but as yet untried." (*Novum organum*, 1620). His comment may seem relevant chiefly to the growth of the physical sciences, as indeed it was. Nevertheless, it also helped to determine the cast of thought in the subsequent century.

Descartes' *Discourse of Method* (*Discours de la méthode*, 1637) indicated that he was no Baconian worshiper of induction; yet he insisted on starting from one certain "truth" of observation—"I think, therefore I am"

—in building up a philosophical system. Perhaps most important, Descartes sharpened the distinction between mind and matter, spirit and body. After him philosophers tended to fall into one camp or the other: either asserting, as "idealists" (like Berkeley), that all reality is ultimately mind and spirit; or, as materialists (like Hobbes and many of the more extreme French *philosophes*), that reality is finally reduced to the world of matter. But whatever their beliefs, they all held one belief in common. To these thinkers the universe made *rational* sense; it possessed a discernible pattern; it moved according to fixed scientific and mathematical laws. And here the early scientists came to the aid of their more abstract-minded colleagues, with Newton making the greatest contribution; for it was he who synthesized the scientific work done from Copernicus to his own day, to produce a plausible and orderly picture of the material universe, the "Newtonian world-machine." At least two writers included in this portion of the anthology—Pope and Voltaire—wrote with full conviction of its existence.

TOWARD NEOCLASSICISM— PASCAL

We begin the neoclassic section of this anthology with Article III of Pascal's *Thoughts* (*Pensées*): *Concerning the Necessity of the Wager.* In terms of the preceding paragraphs the reader may be puzzled by this choice: a passionate defense of Christian belief, one of the greatest apologies for religion written since the Middle Ages. Where then is the "rationalism" evoked as one touchstone for the period? Where is the "quiescence, consolidation, harmony" alluded to above? Such substantives scarcely seem to apply to Pascal's mixture of pithy aphorisms, self-questions, and queries delivered to a mute and stubborn antagonist whom we feel to be listening on the other side of the page, or to the occasional moving emotional outbursts such as the famous *Thought* 206: "The eternal silence of these infinite spaces frightens me" (*Le silence éternel de ces espaces infinis m'effraie*).

Perhaps some explanation may be found if first we consider Pascal as natural scientist and mathematician. One of the greatest scientific geniuses of the age, he accepted the majestic edifice of the Newtonian world-machine; indeed, he contributed to further knowledge of its contours. Here was a "natural" universe that functioned with precise, discernible clarity, where quantitative measurement and empirical judgment were tools for observation, and where, to use his own phrase, the mathematical mind (*l'esprit de géometrie*) prevailed, rational and analytic. Many of his contemporaries (and their descendants still exist) were convinced that this discursive intellect was man's sole instrument for obtaining legitimate knowledge, and they rejoiced in the infinite brave new world of Galileo and Copernicus.

Yet for Pascal—as the *Thought* we have quoted indicates—the ever-widening physical and intellectual horizons showed vistas more disturbing than comforting. Neither the immensities of the universe nor the accumulation of scientific discoveries could guarantee what for him was the prime issue: the existence and dignity of the human being. This is not to say that he was antirational or that he concluded that his earlier scientific and mathematical activity was vain and foolish. As a creature of this world, man had a right—even an obligation—to comprehend its lineaments via his intellect. Two famous extracts from the *Pensées* demonstrate Pascal's vigorous validation of mind (Numbers 347 and 348).

Man is but a reed, the most feeble thing in nature; but he is a thinking reed. [*L'homme n'est qu'un roseau, le plus faible de la nature; mais c'est un roseau pensant.*] It is not necessary for the whole universe to take up arms to crush him: a puff of smoke, a drop of water, is enough to kill him. But even if the universe should crush him, man would still be more noble than that which killed him, because he knows that he dies and he realizes the advantage that the universe has over him: the universe knows nothing of this.

All our dignity, then, consists in thought. Upon this we must depend, not on space and time which we cannot fill. Let us labor then to think well: this is the foundation of morality.

The thinking reed. It is not in space that I should look to find my dignity, but in the ordering of my thought. I would gain nothing further by owning worlds: through space the universe encompasses me and swallows me up like a mere point; by thought, I embrace the universe

But "thought" might mean more than mathematical reasoning. In another *Pensée* (Number 253) Pascal spoke of "Two extremes: to exclude reason, to admit reason alone"; and he also added to *l'esprit géometrique* the more subtle *esprit de finesse*, the intuitive mind, which made its own claims on truth. Pure reason for him consorted with its own limitations. Like Montaigne—a thinker toward whom Pascal was curiously ambivalent—he felt increasingly the relativism of ideas, the impossibility that abstract reasoning should ever grasp the totality of ultimate truth. Yet unlike Montaigne, who could remain in a state of skepticism, Pascal found his answer in Christian faith.

The austerities of Jansenism had earlier appealed to him—that movement within the Catholic Church whose theological concerns were chiefly with Augustinian concepts of predestination and Divine Election. As far as we know, Pascal never actually contemplated entering the Jansenist order, as did his sister; but the high, puritanical standards of conduct observed at its Port-Royal headquarters were congenial to his disciplined mind, and were in sharp contrast to those of the fashionable world he frequented in Paris. His religiosity deepened as he grew older, culminating in what has been called his "second conversion." Pascal once spoke of the three "gates"—sensual, intellectual, emotional—through which we view the world. The "night of the fire," November 22, 1654, when he heard the call of the

"God of Abraham, Isaac, and Jacob," was the moment when he was vouchsafed that last portal. The note he made of this experience was always with him, and found sewed to the coat he wore when he died.

The *Thoughts*, edited after his death, were fragmentary comments sketching what was to have been a larger apology for Christianity. The nineteenth-century critic Saint-Beuve compared them to a tower, the stones laid without mortar, the entire edifice unfinished. Strictly speaking, they belong neither to the category of systematic theology nor to that of philosophy: Pascal does not attempt to render a comprehensive account of human nature, the natural universe, or the nature of God. His *Thoughts* use argument but do not remain, finally, *an* argument. One remembers them rather as insights, flashes of a vision, almost epiphanies. It is this that justifies their inclusion in this volume, where imaginative literature rather than philosophical abstraction is predominant, and it is this that makes them still cogent to the common reader, as the strictly philosophical works of the period seldom are. How then does Pascal proceed? And what are the modes of persuasion he employs?

In general his method is that of the traditional Christian believer; but Pascal's brilliance and power lie in his original expression of age-old themes and his psychological insights into human grandeur and human misery. "The Misery of Man without God" (*"Le misère de l'homme sans Dieu*"—the section immediately preceding "The Wager"—defines man as Pascal regards him: puny and weak, caught between two infinitudes, playing his infinitesimal role before a seemingly indifferent cosmic backdrop, happy at best when pleasure and frivolity distract him from thought. For Pascal conforming Christians too often represent superficial belief, or they shade off toward Deism, then to an outright materialistic denial of spiritual values. Deism he interpreted as ultimately negating the need for God.

I cannot forgive Descartes; he would have been quite willing, in all his philosophy, to do without God; but he couldn't refrain from letting Him give a tap to set the world in motion; beyond that, he had no further need of God. (*Thought* 77)

Pascal informs us that only a consciousness of the presence of God makes the human condition bearable, and that this is a truth beyond the capacity of human reason to establish. Finite knowledge can provide us with no reasonable certainty; no amount of sheer thought can kindle faith. Yet in the realization of our own insufficiency—and here Pascal foreshadows modern existentialist ideas of *angoisse* and *Angst* (or "anxiety")—we can discover our reliance on God. Hence the famous wager. Pascal asks the unbeliever to act as if Christianity were true, and at least give to religion an opportunity to prove its truth. Then he proceeds (here is the mathematician emerging) to a second stage. The image he employs is the player at the gaming table, weighing the odds. Surely there is more to gain in accepting faith than in rejecting it, despite the chance that Christianity may be in error; for there is the greater possibility that it represents ultimate truth. Love of God—that adherence of the heart which constitutes faith—has to be the sole explanation for the enigma that is mankind. Through the dark night of the soul, through skepticism and terrible doubt, Pascal was able to achieve a state of belief.

In a discriminating essay about Pascal, T.S. Eliot remarks that Voltaire—whom we meet later in this section, and who wrote attacking Pascal—presents "better than any one since, what is the unbelieving point of view; and in the end we must all choose for ourselves between one point of view and another." Even the most ardent secularist in this age of atomic fusion must be impressed by Pascal's description of the human situation, where the mind of man is simultaneously capable of vast intellectual power and equally vast moral, spiritual, and intellectual imperfection.

The seventeenth century had witnessed the apparent triumph of physics, mathematics, and philosophy over the residue of medieval thought. Pascal—a major contributor to this triumph in the physical and mathematical fields—was compelled nevertheless to look back to an apparently superannuated age of faith, as well as forward to an epoch describing itself as an Age of Reason, a Century of Light, an Enlightenment. The Renaissance had seemed to mean liberation from the limits of medieval scholastic thinking, a new spirit of inquiry, an awareness of the possibility of happiness on this earth, and a revaluation of the authors of classical, pagan antiquity. It had taken a point of view at once sensuous and rational, worldly and humanistic, with man neatly placed in the order of nature.

Yet for Pascal the liberation was largely illusion. At the end of all his research lay the discovery that the supernatural order of grace and salvation was primary. For him true spiritual knowledge meant, in the last analysis, that all mundane knowledge was vain, and the rational exploration of this world, exciting and temporarily valuable, merely one more episode in man's voyage home to God.

NEOCLASSICISM— MILTON

It is a critical commonplace that the Renaissance meant liberation from the limits of medieval Scholastic thought, a new spirit of inquiry, an awareness of the possibility of happiness on this earth, and a revaluation of the authors of classical, pagan antiquity. In one sense the Renaissance was a vindication of the natural as opposed to the spiritual order of existence. Once more the vision of unspoiled man, untroubled by any taint of original sin, appeared before the mind of the West.

Milton's writing expresses many of these tendencies. Indeed, the breadth of his learning qualifies him as one of the leading Renaissance scholars, and in spite of his affiliation with an established Protestant sect, his theological speculations often border on a daring heterodoxy. He is never content, like certain religious writers of earlier generations, merely to cite authority uncritically. This questioning attitude is evidence of the inquiring mind at work in the upper reaches of religious thought. Milton's debt to pagan antiquity is obvious even to the reader acquainted only with *Samson Agonistes* (1671) and unfamiliar with the tremendous body of his Greek and Latin reading. Classical literature stressed the humane and active virtues of prudence, courage, temperance, and justice. All these are exhibited by Samson. The play may even be understood entirely in terms of classical, non-Christian tragedy, in which the hero comes to see himself in relation to the world and to his own human limitations. Peace must be made with God, but the goal within this framework is self-realization and fulfillment. Here we have Milton the Humanist; for Samson, searching his own distressed soul, comes to find reconciliation with himself to some extent by dint of thought alone, on purely secular and rational terms. In this respect the play exemplifies not only Milton's closeness to the classical tradition but also his relationship to the coming Age of Reason. When man investigates his destiny in this way, unhampered by institutionalism and authority, the Enlightenment is not far off.

This is one side of the picture. On the other, in Milton's case, is Protestantism, and the Reformation as a reinterpretation of the Christian tradition. The early desire to *reform* the Catholic Church—the movement we associate with Luther—soon turned to active rebellion, and Milton's objection to the English Royalists was as much religious (anti-Anglican, since the Church of England leaned toward Rome) as it was political. The priest was no longer held the necessary mediator between an individual and his God. The vernacular Bible required no specialist to aid in its interpretation, and the Word of God plus a man's divinely given conscience were felt to be sufficient for the attainment of grace and eventual salvation. The burden of responsibility lay with each person and the new freedom brought with it a terrible seriousness in the re-emphasized doctrine of original sin; hence Milton's own youthful preparation for some remarkable act, yet undefined, and his preoccupation with the high office of poet-priest.

Samson's final tragic perception comes about when he accepts his limitations *qua* human being, in the style of a protagonist in Greek drama. But equally important, he attains a state of grace—or in strict Calvinist phraseology, he demonstrates himself as one of God's Elect—when he attunes himself to the inscrutable will of God. His "death so noble" 'synthesizes Renaissance and Reformation, Humanism and Christianity; and the struggle Samson undergoes with his conscience, marked by a bold spirit of inquiry and doubt, is illuminated by the clear radiance of an inner light.

By Milton and his coreligionists, the sacrifice and martyrdom of the Hebrew hero were seen as an Old Testament prefiguring of Christ's own trials and Crucifixion. That the writer should have turned to Greek tragedy as a vehicle for his treatment of this story is added testimony to the alliance of two partly opposed traditions. The play has many affinities with classical drama: it is confined by the unities of time and place; it treats a well-known legend at its climactic point, so that analytical exposition is unnecessary; its action is primarily psychological rather than physical; it supplies the same sense of foreboding and tragic irony that marks Greek tragedy; an oracular and sympathetic chorus makes riddling pronouncements both to us and to the perplexed hero; the entreaties of the individual characters produce a stylized, ritualistic effect. Finally, the device of the messenger reporting the off-stage events preserves classical decorum and objectivity.

Of all the classical tragedies, the *Prometheus Bound* of Aeschylus comes closest to *Samson Agonistes*; and the Greek hero, half divine, half human, gains added dimension, as the first *protestant*, after we read Milton's work. In each case the movement is from a state of angry rebellion to reconciliation. The focus of attention is upon the single leading figure who stands immobile before us, while advisers, choruses, and opponents appear, illuminating the state of mind of the protagonist. Almost more than any other Greek play, Aeschylus' work has as its chief concern the relation of man's destiny to the divine government of the cosmos, and the natural and spiritual levels of existence receive equal attention. That Milton's neoclassicism should be exhibited through his employment of Greek dramatic forms is not remarkable; the forms were conventional enough, and his use of them reflects his closeness to the Renaissance. But the affinities of *Samson* with this particular Greek play, in which Prometheus—like Samson—is a kind of proto-Christ, and the demands of man stand second to those of God, make the synthesis of Renaissance and Reformation more complete in Milton than in any other figure of his time.

TYPES OF NEOCLASSICISM— MOLIÈRE AND RACINE

Seventeenth-century religious conflicts created a strongly centralized Catholic France across the Channel, particularly after the revocation of the Edict of Nantes in 1685, which effectively ended French Protestantism. The emergence of a strongly centralized Catholic France may be viewed in one aspect as a triumph of the Counter Reformation—the various efforts taken by the Roman Catholic Church, in the face of the Protestant Reformation, to strengthen doctrine and dogma. Yet this monolithic new commonwealth had secular antecedents. Under Louis XIV Versailles and Paris were soon felt to be what Rome had been under Augustus Caesar, and the line from Greece and Rome to France was asserted to be direct and unbroken. Milton's neoclassicism expresses itself as a mixture of Renaissance and Reformation elements; Pascal's religious affiliations with Jansenism link him with the Counter Reformation; but Racine and Molière wrote in a milieu that united Renaissance and Counter Reformation. Whatever the precise ingredients may have been, seventeenth-century French neoclassicism emerges as a combination of these cultural forces, one religious and the other secular. Stated in other terms, two conceptions of the human condition were in opposition—man in a state of grace and man in a state of nature. Pascal shows how the lifetime of one individual could contain a gradual shift in allegiance from the latter to the former.

Even the famous "Quarrel of the Ancients and the Moderns," mentioned earlier, was symptomatic of the tension between these antithetical outlooks. The Renaissance had extolled classical, pagan antiquity and made it the model for human conduct and aspiration. But now the possibility gained credence that modern man might *excel* the Greeks and Romans and not merely emulate them in an effort to regain a lost golden age. Hence the birth of the idea of progress in history—a concept relatively new to mankind, and one hard to reconcile with the

Christian notion of man's fall from his pristine felicity. The "Moderns" were those who insisted that modern culture could equal or surpass that of the classical period; the "Ancients," those who joined literary modesty to something very like a Christian sense of imperfection. Yet while one side felt itself to be an inglorious heir and the other a superior son, *all* were convinced that they were neoclassic, a happy synthesis of the ancient and modern.

MOLIÈRE

Within this cultural environment of neoclassicism, France's two greatest dramatists, one in the comic and one in the tragic vein, wrote their plays. Molière, the comic dramatist, leaned heavily toward the pole of the natural, rational, and humanistic. His concern is not with metaphysics or with an eventual state of eternal salvation. He portrays man as a product of the social order. As Sainte-Beuve long ago pointed out, Molière's characters are untouched by any thought of Christian grace. Only one of his plays, the famous *Tartuffe* (1664), is concerned with a near-religious theme, and even this work is preoccupied more with an analysis of mundane hypocrisy than with the assessment of true belief. Each of Molière's plays is actually an *exemplum* and a critical study of the failure to conform to an ideal of urbanity, solid pragmatism, worldly common sense, good taste, and moderation—all the secular virtues of antiquity and Louis XIV's new state. Both Tartuffe and Orgon are ludi-

crous, for each fails to meet these criteria of behavior. Tartuffe is a rogue and a scoundrel, a hypocrite whose apparent religiosity and asceticism are eventually unmasked. Orgon is a dupe, in whom Molière satirizes the solid, middle-class citizen. Orgon's false values impel him to give his daughter a "good" marriage against her wishes, disinherit his son, sign over his property to Tartuffe, and himself be tricked by a fashionable rascal who uses pretended piety as an excuse for financial gain and amatory satisfaction.

Voltaire's description of true comedy as "the speaking picture of the follies and foibles of a nation" can readily be applied to Molière's plays. Actually Voltaire had the Greek comic playwright Aristophanes in mind; to compare Molière with Aristophanes is to see once more how close was the bond between neoclassicism and classical antiquity. Aristophanes' panorama of Athenian citizens displays the same infinite variety as Molière's collection taken from the Parisian scene. Stock characters were easily drawn from two societies where social stratification was menaced by a rising commercialism, and the resulting *parvenu* became material for the satirist's pen. Finally the problems of the day—political, religious, educational, ethical—served as subject matter for both Aristophanes and Molière. From the Greek playwright through the Latin authors Plautus and Terence and later the creators of the Italian Renaissance *commedia dell' arte*, the tradition of classical comedy moves to Molière. The topical issues may no longer interest us—arranged marriages, the excessive refinement of precious fops, and so on—but the classical vision of man in society rather than man the individual, the ideals of universality and rationality, these transcend the local and the temporary.

RACINE

When we move from the racy, realistic prose of comedy to Racine's lofty language of tragedy, more comprehension of the age and its conventions is required. It has always been difficult for the English reader, accustomed to the apparent looseness and gusto of Shakespearean drama, to savor the French playwright's decorous elegance. We are puzzled by the careful control and compression insisted on through adherence to the unities of time, place, and action; by the intrusion of long, distracted monologues, the alternating debatelike interchange between characters, and the operalike duets, and by the circumlocution of the vocabulary.

Racine's model for *Phaedra* (*Phèdre*, 1677) was the *Hippolytus* of Euripides. Racine assures us in his preface that he has retained all that is suitable from the Greek tragedy—and added to it ingredients which make it more pertinent to the audience of his own time. In Euripides' drama the protagonist is not Phaedra but Hippolytus, depicted as a follower of Artemis (Diana) and thus bound by vows of rigid chastity. This condition leads him into *hubris* (overweening human pride) toward Aphro-dite (Venus) and thus brings Nemesis (judgment) upon him —all according to the conventional Greek view of life. Phaedra appears in only two scenes, never face to face with Hippolytus; and her death occurs halfway through the play. No doubt the more thoughtful, discerning members of Euripides' audience caught a note of his own skepticism about the dubious ethics of the gods; but the action of the drama is satisfying on a human level alone, since the cause of Hippolytus' downfall is the pride implicit in his excessive, vehement denial of Phaedra. For the story of Theseus, Racine was indebted also to Plutarch's life of Theseus; and possibly, although he denied it, to the *Phaedra* (alternatively entitled *Hippolytus*) of the Roman Stoic Seneca. In Seneca's play Hippolytus is portrayed as a Stoic philosopher; Phaedra, not Hippolytus, suffers the wrath of Venus; and while he remains technically the protagonist, Phaedra is the focal figure, with her shameless love mixed with guilt. No divinities enter Seneca's declamatory, rhetorical drama, and Venus is the mere personification of passion.

Like his Greek predecessor and like Milton in *Samson Agonistes*, Racine deals with one terrible day—the culmination of previous events and states of feeling—and his technique is in keeping also with the tenets of French classical drama. He concentrates not on the pale Hippolytus, who even in Euripides' drama seems more a passive instrument of two rival goddesses than an active protagonist, but rather on the tormented, passion-racked Phaedra. She becomes a Greek woman with a Christian conscience, for the peculiar remorse Racine has his heroine exhibit when once she is aware of her illicit love is an emotion that was unknown to the ancient world.* Within her soul the fundamental conflict is between one overwhelming passion and the restraining power of reason. Her tragic flaw, to use the Aristotelian phrase, is her abnegation of rational responsibility for her moral conduct. The entire play is a slow unfolding, rather than a record of the development, of this fatal weakness. Only the most insensitive reader could be unaffected by Racine's skillfully conveyed, intricate psychological analysis—the cognizance of forces deep within the well of the unconscious that imperil the tenuously held supremacy of the intellect—and by the tone of majestic, dignified sadness.

TOWARD THE EN- LIGHTENMENT—POPE

In our day, or within the last twenty-five years, we have become accustomed to seeing our own cultural milieu, and that of our immediate predecessors, defined only in terms which are deprecatory, negative, or cynical —for example, "the Jazz Age," "the Lost Generation," "the Age of Anxiety," or "the Age of Longing." Hence, we are not well equipped to appreciate the eighteenth century, when for the first time in history men announced to each other and to posterity that theirs was an Age of Reason, an *Enlightenment*. Voltaire, in his *Last Remarks on the "Pensées of M. Pascal*," exclaimed with joy, "What a light has burst over Europe within the last few years! It first illuminated all the princes of the North; it has even come into the universities. It is the light of common sense!" Crane Brinton epitomizes the movement in *Ideas and Men* (1950) when he speaks of "the belief that all human beings can attain here on this earth a state of perfection hitherto in the West thought to be possible only for Christians in a state of grace, and for them only after death."

Traditional Christianity had been securely moored by a pair of anchors: *faith* ("the substance of things hoped for, and the evidence of things not seen") and *reason*. The two elements were always linked in an unstable combination. To watch the progress of thought in the late seventeenth century is to see the latter gradually usurp the position of the former. Biblical exegesis had succeeded in weakening the concept of the biblical God of miracles, and two popular books, one French and one Eng-

---

* So intense is her self-recrimination that some critics have attributed it to Racine's Jansenist background. The Jansenist order was a group within the Catholic Church concerned chiefly with the Augustinian concept of predistination and Divine Election. This preoccupation, as well as their general austerity and asceticism, links the Jansenists to Calvinism and the Puritan movement in England. The order was bitterly opposed by the Jesuits, and the Jansenist center at Port-Royal was destroyed in 1709-1710. Like the heroine of Euripides' tragedy, Racine's Phaedra implies that the gods have brought about her destruction. It is also possible to interpret her assertion in Jansenist-Christian terms as referring to a fall from grace.

lish, were Fontenelle's *History of Oracles* (*Histoire des oracles,* 1686) and Toland's *Christianity Not Mysterious* (1696). Of what practical use were the records of an obscure Hebrew tribe for the "modern" man who trusted in his subjective rational capabilities and for whom the wonders of an orderly universe were disclosed daily by contemporary scientists and philosophers? More and more the conviction arose that a superstitious, ignorant era had gone by. Reason, rapidly assuming a state of near deification, could show men how to control themselves and their environment. Furthermore this same environment—nature—began to seem increasingly benign as man explored its previously concealed workings. Small wonder that John Ray could say in 1691, "God has placed man in a spacious and well-furnished world."

The Renaissance had discovered that the cosmos was neither geocentric nor heliocentric. (Here was knowledge whose initial excitement could be offset by an equally real sentiment of terror, as in Pascal's statement, "The eternal silence of these infinite spaces frightens me.") The Protestant Reformation had made God comprehensible by emphasizing the Father, usually at the expense of the Son and the Holy Ghost. The Enlightenment progressed a step further. Some Deists, taking their point of departure from the traditional arguments of "first cause" and "design," which were used to demonstrate the existence of God, conceived of a Supreme Be-

ing—*Monsieur l'Étre*—who was an impersonal cosmic clockmaker the prime mover of Newton's vast mechanical machine, remote and abstract. In short, now one invented a God to whom one could not pray and from whom one could not expect forgiveness. (Voltaire once wrote an article describing the fallacy of prayer, finding it impious, superfluous, and ineffective.) The doctrinal handbook of the Middle Ages had been the *Summa theologica* of St. Thomas Aquinas; the Century of Light was to have its *Encyclopedia* (*Encyclopédie*), a joint effort published from 1751 to 1772 by the leading French philosophers (*les philosophes*), designed to popularize and disseminate the new doctrines. Both the classical *hubris* of pagan antiquity and the pride condemned by Christian theologians seem to have been forgotten or at least minimized by those who were complacent about the Enlightenment.

Deism attempted to reconcile Christianity with "modern" rationalism. In one sense this was nothing new. We must remember that from the very start, Christian thinkers—St. Paul and the early Church fathers—faced the task of amalgamating Hebraic ideas about a revealed Messiah, the Son of God, with Greek rationalist philosophy. Many centuries later it was inevitable that for intellectuals imbued with scientific attitudes, the revelatory aspects of Christianity—invoking that same God who spoke to Pascal—would retreat before more analytical approaches. The period when modern philosophy was formed can be placed between Galileo (1564-1642) and Leibnitz (1646-1716). While differences between interim thinkers such as Hobbes, Spinoza, and Descartes may seem to be more paramount than similarities, these men were unanimous in their rejection of medieval logic and in their insistence that the axioms of the new mathematical physics were consonant with the authentic workings of the universe. The omniscience and activity of God has to conform with the same laws He had established, and there could be no room for divine caprice and arbitrary conduct. The critical climate of the age is succinctly revealed in Alexander Pope's epitaph intended for Sir Isaac Newton's tomb in Westminster Abbey: "Nature and Nature's Laws lay hid in Night:/ God said, *Let Newton be!* and all was Light."

Hence Deistic thinkers constructed or adumbrated complicated philosophic abstractions such as the Great Chain of Being, plenitude, and the principle of sufficient reason. Gottfried Wilhelm Leibnitz, himself a respectable figure in the history of philosophy, was responsible for much of the dissemination of the new doctrine, mostly through the writings of his more superficial disciples. Leibnitz's hypothesis of "many possible worlds"—which in less capable hands became a theory of "the best of all possible worlds"—ran somewhat as follows. God considered an infinite number of possible worlds before the Creation; but His final decision was to make a world where good predominates over evil. A cosmos *without* evil would actually not have been as "good" as one where evil is a minor ingredient, since many "goods" are related to certain evils. (For example, by definition the existence of free will implies the possibility of sin, for there must be an alternative upon which to exercise the power of free choice. God therefore invented the forbidden apple, and Adam's fall ensued.) According to this view, the world contains a preponderance of good over evil in the long run, and the evil it does possess is no argument against God's benevolence. Reduced to finite, human terms, this philosophical outlook became known as *Optimism.* The student must be careful not to confuse it with our everyday use of the word.

Pope's *Essay on Man* (1733-1734)—the first epistle of which appears in the present volume—has often been interpreted as a poetic expression of the Deistic outlook we have just sketched, and even some present-day critics fall into this easy error. Pope was unusually aware of the intellectual currents of his age, and many of his turns of phrase do reflect the philosophical terminology we associate with the extreme exponents of the Enlightenment. Generally speaking, however, the *Essay* offers us arguments that stretch from Plato and the Stoics through the leading apologists for both Catholic and Protestant Christianity. Milton and Racine, each in his own way, synthesized a pagan, classical humanism with Christian ideology. Pope joins their company and speaks for his age by adding his voice to a chorus of his predecessors. His aim in the *Essay* is to bring home traditional wisdom by stating it superbly and to place Augustan man in a universal picture of mankind. He is concerned with a vision of common humanity transcending the idiosyncracies of place and personality.

The point of departure of the poem, as in *Paradise Lost* and *Samson Agonistes*, is individual man confronted by the problem of evil. The analogy with *Paradise Lost* is strengthened by the image of the garden—now extended to include the whole world in which man dwells. (We shall see Voltaire return to the same compelling metaphor at the conclusion of *Candide*.) The four epistles treat man in his relations to the universe, to himself as a sentient being, to society and finally to happiness and eventual salvation. The first epistle is our concern.

A logical progression in ideas marks the ten parts of this epistle. At the start it is rebellious man who questions the ways of God, and we are reminded of the opening querulous tone of *Samson Agonistes*. Man the microcosm sets out to assert himself against the macrocosm of the universe, and immediately confronts his finitude: ". . . can a part contain the whole?" We are but a portion of a universe, he has to learn—the mid-point in a Great Chain of Being, stretching from the smallest particle of inanimate matter to God Himself, and by definition we cannot envisage the grand scheme that the cosmic order embraces. Man's knowledge is "measured to his state and place"; to seek more is to exhibit classical *hubris,* Christian pride; not until Goethe's *Faust* will the problem be stated with added complications. The fallacy in our critique of the structure of the world at large, says Pope, is a too-rapid identification of the over-all pattern of divine providence with personal desire.

Pope then proceeds to examine the three causes of evil. First there are the catastrophes brought about by natural causes —the earthquakes and tempests that seem to defy human explanation, but are phenomena generated "not by partial, but by gen'ral laws." Next there are the limitations inherent in being "Man," a specific link of the Chain of Being: "The bliss of Man . . . / Is not to act or think beyond mankind." Finally, there is moral evil, man's misuse of the capabilities given him, capabilities which are summed up in the gift of reason bestowed upon man alone, while the lower orders—all equipped with their proper capabilities—do not share this ultimate, crowning dispensation. The triumphant final line of this epistle, "One truth is clear, WHATEVER IS, IS RIGHT," is an assertion about the rationale of the universe, and *not* a statement —though it has been often so misconstrued—that individual life is essentially rosy, blissful, or untroubled. Like his contemporary Swift, Pope was all too aware that man is merely *rationis capax*—a creature *capable* of reason, the attribute necessary if the individual is to harmonize his will with the cosmic framework.

But the modesty exhibited by Pope did not carry over to all his contemporaries and successors in the Enlightenment. As Pope saw it, the problem of evil was finally insoluble and humanity finally an enigma: "The glory, jest, and riddle of the world." Although outright revelation was minimized, faith and mystery were still present in Pope's vision. But when treated by lesser minds and lesser poets, the concepts he expounded became ridiculous. Moreover, complicated philosophical abstractions, such as the Great Chain of Being, plenitude, and the principle of sufficient reason, always tend to absurdity when oversimplified. The popularizers of the theories of the Enlightenment usually forgot, with rationalist zeal, that the identity of God's will with man's was an issue over which the best minds had *tentatively* speculated. Voltaire is the figure who has become the symbol of the Enlightenment. *Candide* is both the epitome of the age and its critique: the epitome, since Voltaire employs common-sensical, empirical methods to demonstrate abstract reason's limitations; the critique, since it is precisely the lack of *tentativeness* in the dogma of the extreme Enlightenment to which he objected.

VOLTAIRE AND THE ENLIGHTENMENT

The younger Voltaire began as an Optimist and embraced these ideas in his early *Discourse in Verse on Mankind* (*Discours en verse sur l'homme,* 1738). For a time it may have appeared to him, particularly since he participated in the writing of the *Encyclopédie,* that he and his fellow philosophers were leading the rest of humanity toward a revival of the golden age on earth by dint of unaided "reason." But the course of Voltaire's own life and the pattern of his intellectual development brought about inevitable disillusion.

Tragedy has been described as a pattern in which theory is destroyed by a fact. For Voltaire and many of his contemporaries, the stubborn fact that threatened to destroy the theories of the Century of Light was the Lisbon earthquake of November 1, 1755, when an estimated thirty to fifty thousand persons perished—ironically on All Saints' Day, when the churches were crowded. It was the greatest natural catastrophe in Western Europe since Pompeii disappeared under Vesuvius' lava. In 1756 Voltaire wrote his first bitter rebuttal of the Optimists, the *Poem on the Disaster of Lisbon* (*Poème sur le désastre de Lisbonne*). He revaluated the self-satisfied cosmic acceptance of these philosophers as complacent, negative fatalism. For him it was "an insult to the sadness of our existence"—we who are "Tormented atoms on this pile of mud/ Swallowed up by death, the mere playthings of Fate." Voltaire's concluding line in the poem expresses his *respect* for God and his *love* for humanity.

The major work that grew out of Voltaire's disgust with Optimistic metaphysics was *Candide*. Written with incredible speed in 1758 (he claimed in three days) and out of white-hot indignation, it was published in 1759 and ran to some forty editions within twenty years. Like Dante, Voltaire immortalized his enemies. Pangloss, Candide's mentor, is a caricature of the Optimistic philosophers Christian Wolf(f) and Leibnitz. Jean-Jacques Rousseau, Voltaire's intellectual enemy (he once remarked, "If Rousseau is dead, it's one scoundrel the less"), flattered himself into believing that the portrait was of him. But Voltaire's satiric concern with individual thinkers was peripheral, and the truth is that his main target was a system, a way of looking at the world. Here he joins the company of great French *moralistes* we have earlier discussed. The framework for *Candide* is one that was popular with seventeenth- and eighteenth-century writers—the exotic romance, the travel story. The romancer could use such a story to satisfy the age's desire for vicarious voyaging and knowledge of distant, strange lands. The satirist could use it to indulge in contemporary and often dangerous criticism without fear of persecution. The philosopher could use it to reinforce the rationalists' conviction that all men are basically alike—children of "reason."

But we must not ignore the subtle ingredient added by Voltaire, the element that gives the book its distinctive flavor. This is Voltaire's *parody* of his literary models. The tale is a satire, almost a burlesque, of the romance, the adventure story, and the pedagogical novel. Did a novel ever contain more ridiculous improbabilities? Within a rigid formal structure (ten chapters in the Old World, ten in the New World, and the last ten back in Europe and Asia Minor) we are presented with dozens of recognition scenes, most of them accompanied by appropriate flashbacks as the once-lost character tells his tale to the wondering Candide. "I am consoled by one thing," says the ingenuous young man. "We see that we often meet people we thought we should never meet again." The recognition device is an excellent way to impose a design upon what otherwise would be a series of loosely linked adventures. It is also Voltaire's ironical commentary on storybook life in comparison with our own sorry existence, where the lost stay lost and the dead remain dead. Several of the major "deaths" in the story fortunately turn out to be not permanent; but half of Lisbon, two entire armies, the inhabitants of one ship and two castles, and miscellaneous llamas, monkeys, and sheep are summarily dispatched. A dim view of this best of all possible worlds!

In a later tale, *The Simple Fellow* (*L'Ingenu*, 1767), Voltaire has a priest tell the wandering Huron hero that God must have great designs for him, since He moves the young man about so freely. To this the Indian retorts that more likely the devil plans his itinerary. Candide never descends to such pessimism, even when at last he recovers his beloved Cunégonde, now a haggard washerwoman on the shores of the Bosphorus. Perhaps it is the vision of Eldorado that saves Candide (and Voltaire) from complete despair. For a brief time the hero is allowed to dwell in a never-never land, a composite of all the utopian dreams of the Enlightenment.

The nineteenth-century writer Flaubert said that *Candide* was a book that made you want to gnash your teeth. Flaubert also commented that the conclusion of *Candide*, with its admonition to work, may be "serene and stu-pid, like life itself." Yet the garden must be cultivated. In a letter written in 1759, Voltaire remarked, "I have read a great deal; I have found nothing but uncertainties, lies, fanaticisms, and I am just about in the same certainty concerning our existence as I was when I was a suckling babe; I much prefer to plant, to sow, to build, and above all to be free." Voltaire seems to say that the answer is neither a complacent acceptance of existence —Optimism—nor an equally fatuous condemnation—pessimism —but rather an intermediate path which may be called *meliorism*.

LIVES, WRITINGS, AND CRITICISM
Biographical and critical works are listed only if they are available in English.

BLAISE PASCAL

LIFE. Born on June 19, 1623, at Clermont-Ferrand, son of the President of the Court of Assistance. In 1631 the family moved to Paris. Pascal's education was entirely undertaken by his father: chiefly in mathematics, where he displayed enough precocity at sixteen to elicit the attention of Descartes. In 1643 the father became associated with the Jansenists (a movement within the Catholic Church, begun by Cornelius Jansenius, Bishop of Ypres, stressing Augustine's teaching, emphasizing the need for divine grace, preaching puritanical austerity). Pascal became a Jansenist (his "first conversion"), but continued to live a worldly social life, and his mathematical and scientific studies flourished. He advanced the theory of mathematical probability, invented "Pascal's triangle"; described the properties of the cycloid, and developed theories in advanced differential calculus and other fields. His "second conversion" was "the night of the fire"—a mystical experience on November 22, 1654, when he heard, as he said, the call not of some abstract deity, but of the "God of Abraham, Isaac, and Jacob." Associated from then on till his death with Port-Royal, the Jansenist community of which his sister Jacqueline was a member. (Port-Royal was suppressed by the Catholic Church in 1704.)

CHIEF WRITINGS. Pascal's contributions to mathematics and experimental science appeared in various papers. *Letters to a Provincial* (1656-1657) and the *Thoughts of M. Pascal on Religion* ... (begun *ca.* 1660) were his philosophical and theological works.

BIOGRAPHY AND CRITICISM. R. H. Soltau, *Pascal* (1927); C. C. J. Webb, *Pascal's Philosophy of Religion* (1929); J. Mesnard, *Pascal* (1953); L. A. J. Chevalier, *Pascal* (1930); F. T. H. Fletcher, *Pascal and the Mystical Tradition* (1954); E. Mortimer, *Blaise Pascal* (1959). Two recent new translations of the *Pensées* have been done by J. M. Cohen (1961) and M. Turnell (1962).

JOHN MILTON

LIFE. Born on December 9, 1608, in London. Milton's father was an affluent Puritan banker and lawyer. From 1625 to 1632 the young man attended Cambridge University; in 1632 he retired to the family country house at Horton, Berkshire, and he remained there until 1638, pursuing an intensive and systematic course of study. Milton then spent nine months traveling in Italy. He had earlier abandoned his original plan to enter the ministry, and upon his return to England he took up an active career of pamphleteering in the Puritan cause. His marriage with Mary Powell, which was unsuccessful, took place in 1642. In 1649 he was appointed Latin secretary to the Council of State of the Commonwealth, and he served Cromwell in the same capacity under the Protectorate. He became totally blind in 1651, and retired from active life in 1660. The restoration of Charles II to the throne in that year meant the collapse of Milton's political hopes as well as a certain loss of property, since he had been one of the chief apologists for the execution of Charles I. He married twice more, surviving his first two wives, and his last years were spent in seclusion with his wife and his three daughters, to whom he dictated his last works. Milton died on November 8, 1674.

CHIEF WRITINGS. Milton's early poems in English, the works completed by the end of the Horton period, reflect the late Elizabethan and metaphysical traditions, and his Latin verse was modeled on Ovid and Virgil. The masque *Comus* (1634), and the long elegy *Lycidas* (1637), written in memory of Edward King, indicate his shift toward seriousness and away from lighter, bucolic poems such as *L'Allegro* and *Il Penseroso*, which were written between 1642 and 1645, are again examples of a traditionally lyric vehicle used for the presentation of profound ideas and feelings. His famous prose writings, published from 1641 (*Of Reformation Touching Church Discipline in England*) through 1654 (*Second Defence of the English People*, the *Defensio secunda*), include *Areopagitica* (1644), and two attempts to justify the deposition and regicide of Charles I: *The Tenure of Kings and Magistrates* (1649) and *John Milton, an Englishman, His Defence of the English People* (*Joannis Miltoni Angli pro populo Anglicano defensio*), the *Defensio prima* (1651). Greatest of all his works, the culmination and fulfillment of his life's ambition, was the epic poem *Paradise Lost* (1667), presenting the temptation and fall of Adam and Eve. *Paradise Regained*, which portrays the three temptations of Christ, was published in 1671. These two large poems show us Milton the Christian Humanist, in whom were merged the pagan Renaissance and the Protestant Reformation. His only tragedy was *Samson Agonistes* (1671), conceived along the lines of Greek drama, with its source in the Old Testament and its expression perhaps the most personal, subjective, and autobiographical of anything Milton ever wrote.

BIOGRAPHY AND CRITICISM. Many biographies are available: D. Masson, *The Life of John Milton,* 7 vols. (1859-1894); J. H. Hanford, *John Milton, Englishman* (1949); D. Saurat, *Milton: Man and Thinker* (1925, enlarged 1944); see also J. S. Diekhoff, *Milton on Himself* (1939). To these might be added more recent studies: *The Life Records of John Milton,* edited by J. Milton French (completed in 1948); Roy Daniells, *Milton, Mannerism and Baroque* (1963); A. B. Chambers, "Wisdom and Fortitude in *Samson Agonistes*," *Publications of the Modern Language Association,* LXXVIII (September, 1963). Don M. Wolfe, *Milton in the Puritan Revolu-*tion (1940); William Empson, *Milton's God* (1962); Harris F. Fletcher, *The Intellectual Development of John Milton* (1962); J. B. Broadbent, *Some Graver Subject* (1962); W. B. C. Watkins, *An Anatomy of Milton's Verse* (1956); Edward S. Le Comte, *Yet Once More: Verbal and Psychological Pattern in Milton* (1956); F. T. Prince, *The Italian Element in Milton's Verse* (1954). Excellent studies in the seventeenth-century background are B. Willey, *The Seventeenth Century Background* (1934); D. Bush, "English Literature in the Earlier Seventeenth Century," in the *Oxford History of English Literature*, Vol. V (1945). J. H. Hanford, *A Milton Handbook* (1939), is useful. Writings about *Samson Agonistes* include W. R. Parker, *Milton's Debt to Greek Tragedy* (1937); F. M. Krouse, *Milton's Samson and the Christian Tradition* (1949); J. H. Hanford, *Studies in Shakespeare, Milton, and Donne* (1925); Don C. Allen, *The Harmonious Vision* (1954). Cleanth Brooks and John E. Hardy have edited the 1645 edition of Milton's poems, with essays in analysis (1952).

JEAN-BAPTISTE POQUELIN MOLIÈRE

LIFE. Born in Paris in 1622 as Jean-Baptiste Poquelin. His father was upholsterer to the king. Molière attended the Jesuit school at Clermont and later studied under the famous "libertine" and Epicurean philosopher Gassendi. At about the age of twenty-five he joined the Illustrious Theater (Illustre Théâtre), a company of traveling players formed by the Béjart family. From 1646 to 1658 Molière and his troupe toured the provinces, playing mostly short pieces after the fashion of the Italian *commedia dell' arte*. In 1658 the players were ordered to perform before Louis XIV in Paris, and soon after their initial success they became the Troupe de Monsieur, enjoying royal patronage. Despite the intrigues of rival companies, particularly that of the Hôtel de Bourgogne, Molière's prestige increased; and when his theater of the Petit-Bourbon was demolished, the king gave him the Palais-Royal theater in 1661. Molière married Armande Béjart in 1662—an unfortunate match, since his enemies spread the scandal that she was his daughter by a former mistress, Madeleine Béjart, although in reality the women were sisters. *Tartuffe,* a study in religious hypocrisy, first produced in 1664, embroiled the playwright with certain groups in the Church. The king was forced to ban it, but Molière succeeded in having the play published and reperformed by 1669. In 1673, although ailing, the author-actor insisted on playing the lead role in his *Imaginary Invalid,* and he died a few hours after a performance on February 17, 1673. The Church refused him burial; but Louis XIV interceded at the pleas of his widow, and a compromise was effected.

CHIEF WRITINGS. Molière's first great success was *The High-Brow Ladies* (*Les Précieuses ridicules*, 1659), a satire on the intellectual pretensions of Parisian fashionable society. Approximately two dozen comedies can be definitely identified as his own. Among these are *The School for Husbands* (*L'École des maris*, 1661); *Don Juan* (1665)—a treatment of the legendary hero; *The Misanthrope* (*Le Misanthrope*, 1666); *Tartuffe*(1664-1669); *The Miser* (*L'Avare*, 1668); *The Bourgeois Gentleman* (*Le Bourgeois Gentilhomme*, 1670); *The Wise Ladies* (*Les Femmes savantes*, 1672); and his last play, *The Imaginary Invalid* (*Le Malade imaginaire*, 1673). The *Bourgeois Gentleman* was first performed at Chambord on November 14, 1670, and in Paris on November 29. Molière played the part of M. Jourdain. It is actually entitled a "comedy-ballet"; the court composer Lully (Lulli) wrote the incidental music for the play and sang the role of the Mufti. The part of Lucile was taken by Molière's wife.

BIOGRAPHY AND CRITICISM. Karl Mantzius, *Molière* (1908), is a good factual account of the author's life. C. H. C. Wright, *French Classicism* (1920), offers a brief survey of the period; Martin Turnell. *The Classical Moment* (1947), includes studies of Molière, Racine, and Corneille; W. G. Moore, *Molière: A New Criticism* (1950), is a recent study in English, as are J. D. Hubert, *Molière and the Comedy of Intellect* (1962) and D. B. Wyndham Lewis, *Molière: The Comic Mask* (1959). Recommended also are the chapter on Molière in E. Auerbach, *Mimesis* (1953), and L. Gossman, *Men and Masks: A Study of Molière* (1963).

JEAN RACINE

LIFE. Born in 1639 in the Valois district, eighty miles from Paris. His father was a government official. Racine attended the College de Beauvais, and from 1655 to 1659 studied at the Jansenist center of Port-Royal, when that institution was at its peak. (Pascal wrote his *Provincial Letters*, the *Provinciales*, dealing with Port-Royal, in 1656 and 1657.) Racine came to Paris in 1660, encouraged by a friend, the poet La Fontaine. His early plays were failures, and he went into seclusion at Uzès, in Provence—for an interval of retirement similar to Milton's Horton period. He returned to Paris early in 1663, received the patronage of the court and the nobility, and soon came to be one of the leading playwrights, along with Molière and Corneille. He left Paris in 1677, officially to write history; married Catherine de Romanet (after earlier liaisons with two of his actresses); and returned to Port-Royal—a move indicative of his increas-ing piety and interest in religious speculation. (Most of his seven children became nuns or priests.) He led the life of the affluent country gentleman, interrupted by occasional trips to Paris and by missions as historiographer on Louis XIV's campaigns during the period from 1678 to 1693. Racine died in 1699 and was buried at Port-Royal. His body was exhumed when the place was destroyed in 1711, and he was placed next to Pascal at the church of St. Étienne-du-Mont in Paris.

CHIEF WRITINGS. Racine's plays, twelve in all, consist of an early comedy, *The Suitors* (*Les Plaideurs*, 1668), based on Aristophanes; two tragedies, *The Thebaid* (*La Thébaïde*, 1664), and *Alexander the Great* (*Alexandre le Grand*, 1665), both imitative of Corneille; seven "profane" or secular tragedies; and two biblical dramas. His first major writing was *Andromache* (*Andromaque*, 1667), and this play enjoyed a success almost as great as that of the famous *Cid* of Corneille. *Britannicus* followed in 1669, *Bérénice* in 1670, *Mithridates* (*Mithridate*) in 1673—three tragedies whose sources were classical historians: Tacitus, Suetonius, and Plutarch. *Bajazet* (1672), marked an excursion into oriental *decor;* it is perhaps the most contemporary of Racine's plays, since despite the exotic locale, the plot—according to Racine—came from an adventure that had taken place only thirty years before. Both *Iphegenia* (*Iphigénie*, 1674), and *Phaedra* (*Phèdre*, 1677), were modeled on plays by Euripides. The latter was performed at the Hôtel de Bourgogne, the theater used by Molière's rivals; and it was after the play's success that Racine went into semiretirement. Twelve years later, at the request of Mme. de Maintenon, Racine wrote his first biblical drama, *Esther* (1689); this, like *Athalia* (*Athalie*, 1691), dealt with Old Testament material, and both plays were designed for performance at Mme. de Maintenon's school for girls at Saint-Cyr.

BIOGRAPHY AND CRITICISM. An excellent biography of the playwright, A. F. B. Clark, *Racine* (1939), may be supplemented by M. Duclaux, *The Life of Racine* (1925); K. Vossler, *Racine* (1926). C. H. C. Wright, *French Classicism* (1920), and Martin Turnell, *The Classical Moment* (1947), are recommended for background material. A recent and interesting study of Racine's plays is V. Orgel, *A New View of the Plays of Racine* (1948); a valuable edition of *Phèdre* has been prepared by R. C. Knight (1943); and translations by Lacy Lockert of several of Racine's plays—including *Phèdre*—in rhymed alexandrine couplets were published in

1936. E. Auerbach's chapter on Racine in *Mimesis* (1953) is excellent; and there is also G. Brereton, *Jean Racine: A Critical Biography* (1951); K. Wheatley, *Racine and English Classicism* (1956); M. Bowra, *The Simplicity of Racine* (1956); and the chapters on Racine in W. Sypher, *Four Stages of Renaissance Style* (1955) and in F. Fergusson, *The Idea of a Theater* (1949).

ALEXANDER POPE

LIFE. Born in May 21, 1688, in London, Pope was the son of a retired linen merchant. Because of his Roman Catholic parentage, Pope was excluded from an academic or political career; indeed, in 1700 the family was forced to move to Binfield in Windsor Forest to comply with the law forbidding Roman Catholics to live within ten miles of London. In the closing years of Queen Anne's reign he was closely associated with Whig journalists and pamphleteers, including Addison; later he joined literary forces with those Tories (Swift, Gay, Arbuthnot, and others) who styled themselves the Scriblerus Club. He was the first English poet to achieve financial independence through his writings, and in 1718 he bought a small estate at Twickenham, on the Thames outside of London. There he spent the rest of his life writing, entertaining his friends, and amusing himself with landscape gardening. He was never in good health—tiny in size, he later became afflicted with tubercular curvature of the spine—and he once referred to "this long disease, my life." He died of dropsy on May 30, 1744.

CHIEF WRITINGS. Pope devoted his youth to the study of Latin verse and of the technique of his predecessor John Dryden. His *Pastorals* were published when he was twenty-one, although he insisted that he had written them when he was sixteen. His translations of Homer's *Iliad* (1715-1720) and *Odyssey* (1725-1726), brought him fame and financial success: for the former he received over five thousand pounds, equal today to well above a hundred thousand dollars. The *Essay on Criticism* (1711), states the essential literary canons of the day, even as the *Essay on Man* (1733-1734) is the repository for much of the philosophic doctrine of Deism. The bulk of Pope's poetry, apart from the translations, is satiric; works of this type include *The Rape of the Lock* (1711-1714), the four *Moral Essays* (1731-1733), the *Epistle to Dr. Arbuthnot* (1735), and *The Dunciad* (1729-1743).

BIOGRAPHY AND CRITICISM. Biographies include the life by W. J. Courthope, in *The Works of Alexander Pope*, edited by W. Elwin and W. J. Courthope, Vol. V (1889); E. Sitwell, *Alexander Pope* (1930); G. Sherburn, *The Early Career of Alexander Pope* (1934); B. Dobrée, *Alexander Pope* (1951). For the background, A. O. Lovejoy, *The Great Chain of Being* (1933); J. Sutherland, *A Preface to Eighteenth Century Poetry* (1948); and B. Willey, *The Eighteenth Century Background* (1940), are recommended. Valuable general studies on Pope's poetry are F. R. Leavis, *Revaluations* (1936); G. Tillotson, *The Poetry of Pope* (1938); G. Sherburne, *The Best of Pope* (1931); R. A. Brower, *Alexander Pope: The Poetry of Allusion* (1959); and T. R. Edwards, *This Dark Estate: A Reading of Pope* (1963). For *An Essay on Man*, consult the introduction to the poem in the Twickenham edition, edited by M. Mack (1950), and Ernest Tuveson, "An Essay on Man and 'The Way of Ideas'", *Journal of English Literary History*, XXVI (September, 1959). There is also the *Correspondence*, edited by G. Sherburne (1957), and Bonamy Dobrée, *English Literature in the Early Eighteenth Century, 1700-1740* (1959).

FRANÇOIS-MARIE AROUET DE VOLTAIRE

LIFE. Born on November 21, 1694, in Paris, as François-Marie Arouet. His father was a minor treasury official, originally from Poitou. Voltaire attended a Jesuit school, and later undertook and abandoned the study of law. He spent eleven months in the Bastille (1717-1718), imprisoned by *lettre de cachet*, for writing satiric verses about the aristocracy. By 1718 he was using the name Voltaire. Literary and social success soon followed; speculations in the Compagnie des Indes made him wealthy by 1726. That same year the Chevalier de Rohan had him beaten and again sent to the Bastille, and 1726-1729 saw him in exile, mostly in England. From 1734 to 1749 he pursued philosophical, historical, and scientific studies, and became the companion of Mme. du Châtelet on her estate at Cirey. His election to the French Academy took place in 1746. From 1750 to 1753 he stayed with Frederick the Great of Prussia, at Potsdam, after Louis XV had failed to give him sufficient patronage. That unstable alliance broke in 1753. Soon after, Voltaire bought adjacent property in France and Switzerland, and settled first at his château, Les Délices, just outside Geneva, and then at nearby Ferney, on French soil. It was from there that he, as the foremost representative of the Enlightenment, directed his campaigns against intolerance and injustice. He made a triumphant return to Paris in 1778, and died there on May 30.

CHIEF WRITINGS. Voltaire's first serious work was a tragedy on Greek lines, *Oedipus* (*Oedipe*, 1715). His epic, *The Henriad* (*La Henriade*)—in praise of the tolerance of Henry IV—was published in 1728. His stay in England produced the *Letters on the English* (*Lettres sur les Anglais*, 1733); but before that, in 1731, appeared the *History of Charles XII* (*Histoire de Charles XII*) of Sweden—perhaps the first "modern" history. *Zadig* (1748), was his first famous philosophical tale, and *Candide* (1759), marked the summit of his achievement in this genre. Another major historical enterprice was *The Century of Louis XIV* (*Le Siècle de Louis XIV*, 1751). His *Philosophical Dictionary* (*Dictionnaire philosophique*, 1764) may be considered most typical both of Voltaire and of the Encyclopedists. In quantity, Voltaire's correspondence is almost unequaled, since he wrote to virtually every important intellectual, social, and political figure of his age.

BIOGRAPHY AND CRITICISM. Good biographies and studies of Voltaire are H. N. Brailsford, *Voltaire* (1935); R. Aldington, *Voltaire* (1934); G. Brandes, *The Life of Voltaire* (undated); and N. Torrey, *The Spirit of Voltaire* (1938). The best edition of *Candide*—to which this editor is greatly indebted—is by A. Morize, 1913. Also recommended are more recent studies: I. O. Wade, *Voltaire and "Candide"* (1959); P. Gay, *Voltaire's Politics: The Poet as Realist* (1961); and two articles by W. Bottiglia in *Publications of the Modern Language Association*, "Candide's Garden," LXVI (September, 1951), and "The Eldorado Episode in *Candide*," LXXIII (September, 1958).

BLAISE PASCAL
(1623–1662)
Thoughts (Les Pensées)*

Section III

OF THE NECESSITY OF THE WAGER

184

A Letter[1] to incite to the search after God.

And then to make people seek Him among the philosophers, sceptics, and dogmatists, who disquiet him who inquires of them.

185

The conduct of God, who disposes all things kindly, is to put religion into the mind by reason, and into the heart by grace. But to will to put it into the mind and heart by force and threats is not to put religion there, but terror, *terrorem potius quam religionem.*[2]

186

Nisi terrerentur et non docerentur, improba quasi dominatio videretur (Aug., Ep. 48 or 49), *Contra Mendacium ad Consentium.*[3]

187

Order.—Men despise religion; they hate it, and fear it is true. To remedy this, we must begin by showing that religion is not contrary to reason; that it is venerable, to inspire respect for it; then we must make it lovable, to make good men hope it is true; finally, we must prove it is true.

Venerable, because it has perfect knowledge of man; lovable, because it promises the true good.

188

In every dialogue and discourse, we must be able to say to those who take offence, "Of what do you complain?"

189

To begin by pitying unbelievers; they are wretched enough by

* From the book *Pensées* by Blaise Pascal, translated by W. F. Trotter. Everyman's Library edition. Published by E. P. Dutton & Co., Inc., and reprinted with their permission. Also by permission of J. M. Dent & Sons Ltd: Publishers. Pascal's earlier *Provincial Letters* (1656–1657) were a defense of Jansenism, ironic and polemical, partly aimed at the Jesuits. The success of their reception caused him to consider writing *An Apology for the Christian Religion.* The *Pensées* were the notes for this project, published in 1670 by a committee, with the title: *Thoughts of M. Pascal on Religion and Several Other Subjects.* Not until 1844 was a definitive text established. Section III, *The Wager*— perhaps most famous—is preceded by *The Misery of Man Without God* and followed by *Concerning the Means of Belief.*
1. *Letter:* This term, which occurs frequently throughout the *Thoughts*, seems to indicate that Pascal may have planned to edit them under the form of letters, following the pattern of the *Provincial Letters.*
2. *terrorem . . . religionem:* "terror rather than religion."
3. *Nisi . . . videretur:* "Lest they feel authority to be tyrannical, if they are led by fear, without being taught." [*Contra . . . Consentium:* Against Lying and Towards the Truth.]

their condition. We ought only to revile them where it is beneficial; but this does them harm.

190

To pity atheists who seek, for are they not unhappy enough? To inveigh against those who make a boast of it.

191

And will this one scoff at the other? Who ought to scoff? And yet, the latter does not scoff at the other, but pities him.

192

To reproach Miton[4] with not being troubled, since God will reproach him.

193

Quid fiet hominibus qui minima contemnunt, majora non credunt?[5]

194

. . . Let them at least learn what is the religion they attack, before attacking it. If this religion boasted of having a clear view of God, and of possessing it open and unveiled, it would be attacking it to say that we see nothing in the world which shows it with this clearness. But since, on the contrary, it says that men are in darkness and estranged from God, that He has hidden Himself from their knowledge, that this is in fact the name which He gives Himself in the Scriptures, *Deus absconditus*,[6] and finally, if it endeavours equally to establish these two things: that God has set up in the Church visible signs to make Himself known to those who should seek Him sincerely, and that He has nevertheless so disguised them that He will only be perceived by those who seek Him with all their heart; what advantage can they obtain, when, in the negligence with which they make profession of being in search of the truth, they cry out that nothing reveals it to them; and since that darkness in which they are, and with which they upbraid the Church, establishes only one of the things which she affirms, without touching the other, and, very far from destroying, proves her doctrine?

In order to attack it, they should have protested that they had made every effort to seek Him everywhere, and even in that which the Church proposes for their instruction, but without satisfaction. If they talked in this manner, they would in truth be attacking one of her pretensions. But I hope here to show that no reasonable person can speak thus, and I venture even to say that no one has ever done so. We know well enough how those who are of this mind

---

4. *Miton:* a fashionable Parisian gentleman, known to Pascal.

5. *Quid . . . credunt?:* "What shall we do with those men who scorn the tiniest evidence, and who do not believe in the greatest?"

6. *Deus absconditus:* "the withdrawn God; the God who stands off." Cf. Isaiah 45:15: "Truly Thou art the hidden God."

behave. They believe they have made great efforts for their instruction, when they have spent a few hours in reading some book of Scripture, and have questioned some priest on the truths of the faith. After that, they boast of having made vain search in books and among men. But, verily, I will tell them what I have often said, that this negligence is insufferable. We are not here concerned with the trifling interests of some stranger, that we should treat it in this fashion; the matter concerns ourselves and our all.

The immortality of the soul is a matter which is of so great consequence to us, and which touches us so profoundly, that we must have lost all feeling to be indifferent as to knowing what it is. All our actions and thoughts must take such different courses, according as there are or are not eternal joys to hope for, that it is impossible to take one step with sense and judgment, unless we regulate our course by our view of this point which ought to be our ultimate end.

Thus our first interest and our first duty is to enlighten ourselves on this subject, whereon depends all our conduct. Therefore among those who do not believe, I make a vast difference between those who strive with all their power to inform themselves, and those who live without troubling or thinking about it.

I can have only compassion for those who sincerely bewail their doubt, who regard it as the greatest of misfortunes, and who, sparing no effort to escape it, make of this inquiry their principal and most serious occupations.

But as for those who pass their life without thinking of this ultimate end of life, and who, for this sole reason that they do not find within themselves the lights which convince them of it, neglect to seek them elsewhere, and to examine thoroughly whether this opinion is one of those which people receive with credulous simplicity, or one of those which, although obscure in themselves, have nevertheless a solid and immovable foundation, I look upon them in a manner quite different.

This carelessness in a matter which concerns themselves, their eternity, their all, moves me more to anger than pity; it astonishes and shocks me; it is to me monstrous. I do not say this out of the pious zeal of a spiritual devotion. I expect, on the contrary, that we ought to have this feeling from principles of human interest and self-love; for this we need only see what the least enlightened persons see.

We do not require great education of the mind to understand that here is no real and lasting satisfaction; that our pleasures are only vanity; that our evils are infinite; and, lastly, that death, which threatens us every moment, must infallibly place us within a few years under the dreadful necessity of being for ever either annihilated or unhappy.

There is nothing more real than this, nothing more terrible. Be we as heroic as we like, that is the end which awaits the noblest life in the world. Let us reflect on this, and then say whether it is not beyond doubt that there is no good in this life but in the hope of another; that we are happy only in proportion as we draw near it; and that, as there are no more woes for those who have complete assurance of eternity, so there is no more happiness for those who have no insight into it.

Surely then it is a great evil thus to be in doubt, but it is at least an indispensable duty to seek when we are in such doubt; and thus the doubter who does not seek is altogether completely unhappy and completely wrong. And if besides this he is easy and content, professes to be so, and indeed boasts of it; if it is this state itself which is the subject of his joy and vanity, I have no words to describe so silly a creature.

How can people hold these opinions? What joy can we find in the expectation of nothing but hopeless misery? What reason for boasting that we are in impenetrable darkness? And how can it happen that the following argument occurs to a reasonable man?

"I know not who put me into the world, nor what the world is, nor what I myself am. I am in terrible ignorance of everything. I know not what my body is, nor my senses, nor my soul, not even that part of me which thinks what I say, which reflects on all and on itself, and knows itself no more than the rest. I see those frightful spaces of the universe which surround me, and I find myself tied to one corner of this vast expanse, without knowing why I am put in this place rather than in another, nor why the short time which is given me to live is assigned to me at this point rather than at another of the whole eternity which was before me or which shall come after me. I see nothing but infinites on all sides, which surround me as an atom, and as a shadow which endures only for an instant and returns no more. All I know is that I must soon die, but what I know least is this very death which I cannot escape.

"As I know not whence I come, so I know not whither I go. I know only that, in leaving this world, I fall for ever either into annihilation or into the hands of an angry God, without knowing to which of these two states I shall be for ever assigned. Such is my state, full of weakness and uncertainty. And from all this I conclude that I ought to spend all the days of my life without caring to inquire into what must happen to me. Perhaps I might find some solution to my doubts, but I will not take the trouble, nor take a step to seek it; and after treating with scorn those who are concerned with this care, I will go without foresight and without fear to try the great event, and let myself be led carelessly to death, uncertain of the eternity of my future state."

Who would desire to have for a friend a man who talks in this fashion? Who would choose him out from others to tell him of his affairs? Who would have recourse to him in affliction? And indeed to what use in life could one put him?

In truth, it is the glory of religion to have for enemies men so unreasonable: and their opposition to it so little dangerous that it serves on the contrary to establish its truths. For the Christian faith goes mainly to establish these two facts, the corruption of nature, and redemption by Jesus Christ. Now I contend that if these men do not serve to prove the truth of the redemption by the holiness of their behaviour, they at least serve admirably to show the corruption of nature by sentiments so unnatural.

Nothing is so important to man as his own state, nothing is so formidable to him as eternity; and thus it is not natural that there should be men indifferent to the loss of their existence, and to the perils of everlasting suffering. They are quite different with regard to all other things. They are afraid of mere trifles; they foresee them; they feel them. And this same man who spends so many days and nights in rage and despair for the loss of office, or for some imaginary insult to his honour, is the very one who knows without anxiety and without emotion that he will lose all by death. It is a monstrous thing to see in the same heart and at the same time this sensibility to trifles and this strange insensibility to the greatest objects. It is an incomprehensible enchantment, and a supernatural slumber, which indicates as its cause an all-powerful force.

There must be a strange confusion in the nature of man, that he should boast of being in that state in which it seems incredible that a single individual should be. However, experience has shown me so great a number of such persons that the fact would be surprising, if we did not know that the greater part of those who trouble themselves about the matter are disingenuous, and not in fact what they say. They are people who have heard it said that it is the fashion to be thus daring. It is what they call shaking off the yoke, and they try to imitate this. But it would not be difficult to make them understand how greatly they deceive themselves in thus seeking esteem. This is not the way to gain it, even I say among those men of the world who take a healthy view of things, and who know that the only way to succeed in this life is to make ourselves appear honourable, faithful, judicious, and capable of useful service to a friend; because naturally men love only what may be useful to them. Now, what do we gain by hearing it said of a man that he has now thrown off the yoke, that he does not believe there is a God who watches our actions, that he considers himself the sole master of his conduct, and that he thinks he is accountable for it only to himself? Does he think that he has thus brought us to have henceforth complete confidence in him, and to look to him for consolation, advice, and help in every need of life? Do they profess to have delighted us by telling us that they hold our soul to be only a little wind and smoke, especially by telling us this in a haughty and self-satisfied tone of voice? Is this a thing to say gaily? Is it not, on the contrary, a thing to say sadly, as the saddest thing in the world?

If they thought of it seriously, they would see that this is so bad a mistake, so contrary to good sense, so opposed to decency and so removed in every respect from that good breeding which they seek, that they would be more likely to correct than to pervert those who had an inclination to follow them. And indeed, make them give an account of their opinions, and of the reasons which they have for doubting religion, and they will say to you things so feeble and so petty, that they will persuade you of the contrary. The following is what a person one day said to such a one very appositely: "If you continue to talk in this manner, you will really make me religious." And he was right, for who would not have a horror of holding opinions in which he would have such contemptible persons as companions!

Thus those who only feign these opinions would be very unhappy, if they restrained their natural feelings in order to make themselves the most conceited of men. If, at the bottom of their heart, they are troubled at not having more light, let them not disguise the fact; this avowal will not be shameful. The only shame is to have none. Nothing reveals more an extreme weakness of mind than not to know the misery of a godless man. Nothing is more indicative of a bad disposition of heart than not to desire the truth of eternal promises. Nothing is more dastardly than to act with bravado before God. Let them then leave these impieties to those who are sufficiently ill-bred to be really capable of them. Let them at least be honest men, if they cannot be Christians. Finally, let them recognise that there are two kinds of people one can call reasonable; those who serve God with all their heart because they know Him, and those who seek Him with all their heart because they do not know Him.

But as for those who live without knowing Him and without seeking Him, they judge themselves so little worthy of their own care, that they are not worthy of the care of others; and it needs all the charity of the religion which they despise, not to despise them even to the point of leaving them to their folly. But because this religion obliges us always to regard them, so long as they are in this life, as capable of the grace which can enlighten them, and to believe that they may, in a little time, be more replenished with faith than we are, and that, on the other hand, we may fall into the blindness wherein they are, we must do for them what we would they should do for us if we were in their place, and call upon them to have pity upon themselves, and to take at least some steps in the endeavour to find light. Let them give to reading this some of the hours which they otherwise employ so uselessly; whatever aversion they may bring to the task, they will perhaps gain something, and at least will not lose much. But as for those who bring to the task perfect sincerity and a real desire to meet with truth, those I hope will be satisfied and convinced of the proofs of a religion so divine, which I have here collected, and in which I have followed somewhat after this order . . .

195

Before entering into the proofs of the Christian religion, I find it necessary to point out the sinfulness of those men who live in indifference to the search for truth in a matter which is so important to them, and which touches them so nearly.

Of all their errors, this doubtless is the one which most convicts them of foolishness and blindness, and in which it is easiest to confound them by the first glimmerings of common sense, and by natural feelings.

For it is not to be doubted that the duration of this life is but a moment; that the state of death is eternal, whatever may be its nature; and that thus all our actions and thoughts must take such different directions according to the state of that eternity, that it is impossible to take one step with sense and judgment, unless we regulate our course by the truth of that point which ought to be our ultimate end.

There is nothing clearer than this; and thus, according to the principles of reason, the conduct of men is wholly unreasonable, if they do not take another course.

On this point, therefore, we condemn those who live without thought of the ultimate end of life, who let themselves be guided by their own inclinations and their own pleasures without reflection and without concern, and, as if they could annihilate eternity by turning away their thought from it, think only of making themselves happy for the moment.

Yet this eternity exists, and death, which must open into it, and threatens them every hour, must in a little time infallibly put them under the dreadful necessity of being either annihilated or unhappy for ever, without knowing which of these eternities is for ever prepared for them.

This is a doubt of terrible consequence. They are in peril of eternal woe; and thereupon, as if the matter were not worth the trouble, they neglect to inquire whether this is one of those opinions which people receive with too credulous a facility, or one of those which, obscure in themselves, have a very firm, though hidden, foundation. Thus they know not whether there be truth or falsity in the matter, nor whether there be strength or weakness in the proofs. They have them before their eyes; they refuse to look at them; and in that ignorance they choose all that is necessary to fall into this misfortune if it exists, to await death to make trial of it, yet to be very content in this state, to make profession of it, and indeed to boast of it. Can we think seriously on the importance of this subject without being horrified at conduct so extravagant?

This resting in ignorance is a monstrous thing, and they who pass their life in it must be made to feel its extravagance and stupidity, by having it shown to them, so that they may be confounded by the sight of their folly. For this is how men reason, when they choose to live in such ignorance of what they are, and without seeking enlightenment. "I know not," they say . . .

196

Men lack heart; they would not make a friend of it.

197

To be insensible to the extent of despising interesting things, and to become insensible to the point which interests us most.

198

The sensibility of man to trifles, and his insensibility to great things, indicates a strange inversion.

199

Let us imagine a number of men in chains, and all condemned to death, where some are killed each day in the sight of the others, and those who remain see their own fate in that of their fellows, and wait their turn, looking at each other sorrowfully and without hope. It is an image of the condition of men.

200

A man in a dungeon, ignorant whether his sentence be pronounced, and having only one hour to learn it, but this hour enough, if he know that it is pronounced, to obtain its repeal, would act unnaturally in spending that hour, not in ascertaining his sentence, but in playing piquet. So it is against nature that man, etc. It is making heavy the hand of God.

Thus not only the zeal of those who seek Him proves God, but also the blindness of those who seek Him not.

201

All the objections of this one and that one only go against themselves, and not against religion. All that infidels say . . .

202

[From those who are in despair at being without faith, we see that God does not enlighten them; but as to the rest, we see there is a God who makes them blind.]

203

Fascinatio nugacitatis.[7]—That passion may not harm us, let us act as if we had only eight hours to live.

204

If we ought to devote eight hours of life, we ought to devote a hundred years.

205

When I consider the short duration of my life, swallowed up in the eternity before and after, the little space which I fill, and even can see, engulfed in the infinite immensity of spaces of which I am ignorant, and which know me not, I am frightened, and am astonished at being here rather than there; for there is no reason why here rather than there, why now rather than then. Who has put me here? By whose order and direction have this place and time been allotted to me? *Memoria hospitis unius diei praetereuntis.*[8]

206

The eternal silence of these infinite spaces frightens me.

207

How many kingdoms know us not!

208

Why is my knowledge limited? Why my stature? Why my life to one hundred years rather than to a thousand? What reason has nature had for giving me such, and for choosing this number rather than another in the infinity of those from which there is no more reason to choose one than another, trying nothing else?

209

Art thou less a slave by being loved and favoured by thy master? Thou art indeed well off, slave. Thy master favours thee; he will soon beat thee.

210

The last act is tragic, however happy all the rest of the play is; at the last a little earth is thrown upon our head, and that is the end for ever.

211

We are fools to depend upon the society of our fellow-men. Wretched as we are, powerless as we are, they will not aid us; we shall die alone. We should therefore act as if we were alone, and in

7. *Fascinatio nugacitatis: Book of Wisdom* iv, 12; "the fascination of mere bagatelles, trifles."

8. *Memoria . . . praetereuntis: Book of Wisdom* v, 15; ["The hope of the wicked is like the fluffy down blown away by the wind, like foam whipped up by the storm, like smoke dispersed by the wind, like] *the memory of the guest for a single fleeting day.*"

that case should we build fine houses, etc.? We should seek the truth without hesitation; and, if we refuse it, we show that we value the esteem of men more than the search for truth.

212

Instability.—It is a horrible thing to feel all that we possess slipping away.

213

Between us and heaven or hell there is only life, which is the frailest thing in the world.

214

Injustice.—That presumption should be joined to meanness is extreme injustice.

215

To fear death without danger, and not in danger, for one must be a man.

216

Sudden death alone is feared; hence confessors stay with lords.

217

An heir finds the title-deeds of his house. Will he say, "Perhaps they are forged?" and neglect to examine them?

218

Dungeon.—I approve of not examining the opinion of Copernicus;[9] but this . . . ! It concerns all our life to know whether the soul be mortal or immortal.

219

It is certain that the mortality or immortality of the soul must make an entire difference to morality. And yet philosophers have constructed their ethics independently of this: they discuss to pass an hour.

Plato, to incline to Christianity.

220

The fallacy of philosophers who have not discussed the immortality of the soul. The fallacy of their dilemma in Montaigne.[10]

221

Atheists ought to say what is perfectly evident; now it is not perfectly evident that the soul is material.

222

Atheists.—What reason have they for saying that we cannot rise from the dead? What is more difficult, to be born or to rise again; that what has never been should be, or that what has been should be again? Is it more difficult to come into existence than to return

---

9. *Copernicus:* Nicholas Copernicus (1473–1543), Polish astronomer whose *Concerning the Revolution of Celestial Bodies* (1543) described the sun as the center of the cosmos, with the earth re- volving about it—in contradistinction to older Ptolemaic cosmology.

10. *Montaigne:* Michel de Montaigne (1533–1592), whose *Essays* elaborate a philosophy of skepticism.

to it? Habit makes the one appear easy to us; want of habit makes the other impossible. A popular way of thinking!

Why cannot a virgin bear a child? Does a hen not lay eggs without a cock? What distinguishes these outwardly from others? And who has told us that the hen may not form the germ as well as the cock?

223

What have they to say against the resurrection, and against the child-bearing of the Virgin? Which is the more difficult, to produce a man or an animal, or to reproduce it? And if they had never seen any species of animals, could they have conjectured whether they were produced without connection with each other?

224

How I hate these follies of not believing in the Eucharist,[11] etc.! If the Gospel be true, if Jesus Christ be God, what difficulty is there?

225

Atheism shows strength of mind, but only to a certain degree.

226

Infidels, who profess to follow reason, ought to be exceedingly strong in reason. What say they then? "Do we not see," say they, "that the brutes live and die like men, and Turks like Christians? They have their ceremonies, their prophets, their doctors, their saints, their monks, like us," etc. (Is this contrary to Scripture? Does it not say all this?)

If you care but little to know the truth, here is enough of it to leave you in repose. But if you desire with all your heart to know it, it is not enough; look at it in detail. This would be sufficient for a question in philosophy; but not here, where it concerns your all. And yet, after a trifling reflection of this kind, we go to amuse ourselves, etc. Let us inquire of this same religion whether it does not give a reason for this obscurity; perhaps it will teach it to us.

227

Order by dialogues.—What ought I to do? I see only darkness everywhere. Shall I believe I am nothing? Shall I believe I am God?

"All things change and succeed each other." You are mistaken; there is . . .

228

Objection of atheists: "But we have no light."

229

This is what I see and what troubles me. I look on all sides, and I see only darkness everywhere. Nature presents to me nothing which is not matter of doubt and concern. If I saw nothing there

---

11. *Eucharist:* the Christian sacrament repeating Christ's distribution of bread and wine at the Last Supper.

which revealed a Divinity, I would come to a negative conclusion; if I saw everywhere the signs of a Creator, I would remain peacefully in faith. But, seeing too much to deny and too little to be sure, I am in a state to be pitied; wherefore I have a hundred times wished that if a God maintains nature, she should testify to Him unequivocally, and that, if the signs she gives are deceptive, she should suppress them altogether; that she should say everything or nothing, that I might see which cause I ought to follow. Whereas in my present state, ignorant of what I am or of what I ought to do, I know neither my condition nor my duty. My heart inclines wholly to know where is the true good, in order to follow it; nothing would be too dear to me for eternity.

I envy those whom I see living in the faith with such carelessness, and who make such a bad use of a gift of which it seems to me I would make such a different use.

230

It is incomprehensible that God should exist, and it is incomprehensible that He should not exist; that the soul should be joined to the body, and that we should have no soul; that the world should be created, and that it should not be created, etc.; that original sin should be, and that it should not be.

231

Do you believe it to be impossible that God is infinite, without parts?—Yes. I wish therefore to show you an infinite and indivisible thing. It is a point moving everywhere with an infinite velocity; for it is one in all places, and is all totality in every place.

Let this effect of nature, which previously seemed to you impossible, make you know that there may be others of which you are still ignorant. Do not draw this conclusion from your experiment, that there remains nothing for you to know; but rather that there remains an infinity for you to know.

232

Infinite movement, the point which fills everything, the moment of rest; infinite without quantity, indivisible and infinite.

233

Infinite—nothing.—Our soul is cast into a body, where it finds number, time, dimension. Thereupon it reasons, and calls this nature, necessity, and can believe nothing else.

Unity joined to infinity adds nothing to it, no more than one foot to an infinite measure. The finite is annihilated in the presence of the infinite, and becomes a pure nothing. So our spirit before God, so our justice before divine justice. There is not so great a disproportion between our justice and that of God, as between unity and infinity.

The justice of God must be vast like His compassion. Now justice to the outcast is less vast, and ought less to offend our feelings than mercy towards the elect.

We know that there is an infinite, and are ignorant of its nature. As we know it to be false that numbers are finite, it is therefore true that there is an infinity in number. But we do not know what it is. It is false that it is even, it is false that it is odd; for the addition of a unit can make no change in its nature. Yet it is a number, and every number is odd or even (this is certainly true of every finite number). So we may well know that there is a God without knowing what He is. Is there not one substantial truth, seeing there are so many things which are not the truth itself?

We know then the existence and nature of the finite, because we also are finite and have extension. We know the existence of the infinite, and are ignorant of its nature, because it has extension like us, but not limits like us. But we know neither the existence nor the nature of God, because He has neither extension nor limits.

But by faith we know His existence; in glory we shall know His nature. Now, I have already shown that we may well know the existence of a thing, without knowing its nature.

Let us now speak according to natural lights.

If there is a God, He is infinitely incomprehensible, since, having neither parts nor limits, He has no affinity to us. We are then incapable of knowing either what He is or if He is. This being so, who will dare to undertake the decision of the question? Not we, who have no affinity to Him.

Who then will blame Christians for not being able to give a reason for their belief, since they profess a religion for which they cannot give a reason? They declare, in expounding it to the world, that it is a foolishness, *stultitiam*; and then you complain that they do not prove it! If they proved it, they would not keep their word; it is in lacking proofs, that they are not lacking in sense. "Yes, but although this excuses those whose offer it as such, and takes away from them the blame of putting it forward without reason, it does not excuse those who receive it." Let us then examine this point, and say, "God is, or He is not." But to which side shall we incline? Reason can decide nothing here. There is an infinite chaos which separates us. A game is being played at the extremity of this infinite distance where heads or tails will turn up. What will you wager? According to reason, you can do neither the one thing nor the other; according to reason, you can defend neither of the propositions.

Do not then reprove for error those who have made a choice; for you know nothing about it. "No, but I blame them for having made, not this choice, but a choice; for again both he who chooses heads and he who chooses tails are equally at fault, they are both in the wrong. The true course is not to wager at all."

Yes; but you must wager. It is not optional. You are embarked. Which will you choose then? Let us see. Since you must choose, let us see which interests you least. You have two things to lose, the true and the good; and two things to stake, your reason and your will, your knowledge and your happiness; and your nature has two things to shun, error and misery. Your reason is no more shocked in choosing one rather than the other, since you must of necessity choose. This is one point settled. But your happiness? Let us weigh the gain and the loss in wagering that God is. Let us estimate these two chances. If you gain, you gain all; if you lose, you lose nothing. Wager, then, without hesitation that He is.—"That is very fine. Yes, I must wager; but I may perhaps wager too much."—Let us see. Since there is an equal risk of gain and of loss, if you had only to gain two lives, instead of one, you might still wager. But if there were three lives to gain, you would have to play (since you are under the necessity of playing), and you would be imprudent, when you are forced to play, not to chance your life to gain three at a game where there is an equal risk of loss and gain. But there is an eternity of life and happiness. And this being so, if there were an infinity of chances, of which one only would be for you, you would still be right in wagering one to win two, and you would act stupidly, being obliged to play, by refusing to stake one life against three at a game in which out of an infinity of chances there is one for you, if there were an infinity of an infinitely happy life to gain. But there is here an infinity of an infinitely happy life to gain, a chance of gain against a finite number of chances of loss, and what you stake is finite. It is all divided; wherever the infinite is and there is not an infinity of chances of loss against that of gain, there is no time to hesitate, you must give all. And thus, when one is forced to play, he must renounce reason to preserve his life, rather than risk it for infinite gain, as likely to happen as the loss of nothingness.

For it is no use to say it is uncertain if we will gain, and it is certain that we risk, and that the infinite distance between the *certainty* of what is staked and the *uncertainty* of what will be gained, equals the finite good which is certainly staked against the uncertain infinite. It is not so, as every player stakes a certainty to gain an uncertainty, and yet he stakes a finite certainty to gain a finite uncertainty, without transgressing against reason. There is not an infinite distance between the certainty staked and the uncertainty of the gain; that is untrue. In truth, there is an infinity between the certainty of gain and the certainty of loss. But the uncertainty of the gain is proportioned to the certainty of the stake according to the proportion of the chances of gain and loss. Hence it comes that, if there are as many risks on one side as on the other, the course is to play even; and then the certainty of the stake is equal to the uncertainty of the gain, so far is it from fact that there is an infinite distance between them. And so our proposition is of infinite force, when there is the finite to stake in a game where there are equal risks of gain and of loss, and the infinite to gain. This is demonstrable; and if men are capable of any truths, this is one.

"I confess it, I admit it. But, still, is there no means of seeing the faces of the cards?"—Yes, Scripture and the rest, etc. "Yes, but I have my hands tied and my mouth closed; I am forced to wager, and am not free. I am not released, and am so made that I cannot believe. What, then, would you have me do?"

True. But at least learn your inability to believe, since reason brings you to this, and yet you cannot believe. Endeavour then to convince yourself, not by increase of proofs of God, but by the abatement of your passions. You would like to attain faith, and do not know the way; you would like to cure yourself of unbelief, and ask the remedy for it. Learn of those who have been bound like you, and who now stake all their possessions. These are people who know the way which you would follow, and who are cured of an ill of which you would be cured. Follow the way by which they began; by acting as if they believed, taking the holy water, having masses said, etc. Even this will naturally make you believe, and deaden your acuteness.—"But this is what I am afraid of."—And why? What have you to lose?

But to show you that this leads you there, it is this which will lessen the passions, which are your stumbling-blocks.

The end of this discourse.—Now, what harm will befall you in taking this side? You will be faithful, honest, humble, grateful, generous, a sincere friend, truthful. Certainly you will not have those poisonous pleasures, glory and luxury; but will you not have others? I will tell you that you will thereby gain in this life, and that, at each step you take on this road, you will see so great certainty of gain, so much nothingness in what you risk, that you will at last recognise that you have wagered for something certain and infinite, for which you have given nothing.

"Ah! This discourse transports me, charms me," etc.

If this discourse pleases you and seems impressive, know that it is made by a man who has knelt, both before and after it, in prayer to that Being, infinite and without parts, before whom he lays all he has, for you also to lay before Him all you have for your own good and for His glory, that so strength may be given to lowliness.

234

If we must not act save on a certainty, we ought not to act on religion, for it is not certain. But how many things we do on an uncertainty, sea voyages, battles! I say then we must do nothing at all, for nothing is certain, and that there is more certainty in religion than there is as to whether we may see to-morrow; for it is not certain that we may see to-morrow, and it is certainly possible that we may not see it. We cannot say as much about religion. It is not certain that it is; but who will venture to say that it is certainly possible that it is not? Now when we work for to-morrow, and so on an uncertainty, we act reasonably; for we ought to work for an uncertainty according to the doctrine of chance which was demonstrated above.

Saint Augustine has seen that we work for an uncertainty, on sea, in battle, etc. But he has not seen the doctrine of chance which proves that we should do so. Montaigne has seen that we are shocked at a fool, and that habit is all-powerful; but he has not seen the reason of this effect.

All these persons have seen the effects, but they have not seen the causes. They are, in comparison with those who have discovered the causes, as those who have only eyes are in comparison with those who have intellect. For the effects are perceptible by sense, and the causes are visible only to the intellect. And although these effects are seen by the mind, this mind is, in comparison with the mind which sees the causes, as the bodily senses are in comparison with the intellect.

235

Rem viderunt, causam non viderunt.[12]

236

According to the doctrine of chance, you ought to put yourself to the trouble of searching for the truth; for if you die without worshipping the True Cause, you are lost.—"But," say you, "if He had wished me to worship Him, He would have left me signs of His will."—He has done so; but you neglect them. Seek them, therefore; it is well worth it.

237

Chances.—We must live differently in the world, according to these different assumptions: (1) that we could always remain in it; (2) that it is certain that we shall not remain here long, and uncertain if we shall remain here one hour. This last assumption is our condition.

12. *Rem . . . viderunt:* "They have seen the effect, but not the cause."

238

What do you then promise me, in addition to certain troubles, but ten years of self-love (for ten years is the chance), to try hard to please without success?

239

Objection.—Those who hope for salvation are so far happy; but they have as a counterpoise the fear of hell.

Reply.—Who has most reason to fear hell: he who is in ignorance whether there is a hell, and who is certain of damnation if there is; or he who certainly believes there is a hell, and hopes to be saved if there is?

240

"I would soon have renounced pleasure," say they, "had I faith." For my part I tell you, "You would soon have faith, if you renounced pleasure." Now, it is for you to begin. If I could, I would give you faith. I cannot do so, nor therefore test the truth of what you say. But you can well renounce pleasure, and test whether what I say is true.

241

Order.—I would have far more fear of being mistaken, and of finding that the Christian religion was true, than of not being mistaken in believing it true.

JOHN MILTON
(1608–1674)
Samson Agonistes*
A Dramatic Poem

THE ARGUMENT. Samson, made captive, blind, and now in the prison at Gaza, there to labour as in a common workhouse, on a festival day, in the general cessation from labour, comes forth into the open air, to a place nigh, somewhat retired, there to sit a while and bemoan his condition. Where he happens at length to be visited by certain friends and equals of his tribe, which make the Chorus, who seek to comfort him what they can; then by his old father, Manoa, who endeavours the like, and withal tells him his purpose to procure his liberty by ransom; lastly, that this feast was proclaimed by the Philistines as a day of thanksgiving for their deliverance from the hands of Samson—which yet more troubles him. Manoa then departs to prosecute his endeavour with the Philistian lords for Samson's redemption; who, in the meanwhile, is visited by other persons, and, lastly, by a public officer to require his coming to the feast before the lords and people, to play or show his strength in

* 1671. See Judges 13-16 for the biblical story of Samson.

their presence. He at first refuses, dismissing the public officer with absolute denial to come; at length persuaded inwardly that this was from God, he yields to go along with him, who came now the second time with great threatenings to fetch him. The Chorus yet remaining on the place, Manoa returns full of joyful hope to procure ere long his son's deliverance; in the midst of which discourse an Ebrew comes in haste, confusedly at first, and afterwards more distinctly, relating the catastrophe—What Samson had done to the Philistines, and by accident to himself; wherewith the Tragedy ends.

The Persons

SAMSON	HARAPHA *of Gath*
MANOA, *the father of Samson*	PUBLIC OFFICER
DALILA, *his wife*	MESSENGER

CHORUS OF DANITES

The SCENE, *before the Prison in Gaza.*

SAMSON. A little onward lend thy guiding hand
    To these dark steps, a little further on;
    For yonder bank hath choice of sun or shade.
    There I am wont to sit, when any chance
    Relieves me from my task of servile toil,   5
    Daily in the common prison else enjoined me,
    Where I, a prisoner chained, scarce freely draw
    The air, imprisoned also, close and damp,
    Unwholesome draught. But here I feel amends—
    The breath of heaven fresh blowing, pure and sweet,   10
    With day-spring born; here leave me to respire.
    This day a solemn feast the people hold
    To Dagon, their sea-idol, and forbid
    Laborious works. Unwillingly this rest
    Their superstition yields me; hence, with leave   15
    Retiring from the popular noise, I seek
    This unfrequented place, to find some ease—
    Ease to the body some, none to the mind
    From restless thoughts, that, like a deadly swarm
    Of hornets armed, no sooner found alone   20
    But rush upon me thronging, and present
    Times past, what once I was, and what am now.
    O, wherefore was my birth from Heaven foretold
    Twice by an Angel, who at last, in sight
    Of both my parents, all in flames ascended   25
    From off the altar where an offering burned,
    As in a fiery column charioting

11. *dayspring:* daybreak.
13. *Dagon:* Phoenician-Philistine idol.
24. *Twice:* An angel appeared twice
to Samson's mother before his birth.
See Judges 13.

His godlike presence, and from some great act
Or benefit revealed to Abraham's race?
Why was my breeding ordered and prescribed   30
As of a person separate to God,
Designed for great exploits, if I must die
Betrayed, captived, and both my eyes put out,
Made of my enemies the scorn and gaze,
To grind in brazen fetters under task   35
With this heaven-gifted strength? O glorious strength,
Put to the labour of a beast, debased
Lower than bond-slave! Promise was that I
Should Israel from Philistian yoke deliver!
Ask for this great deliverer now, and find him   40
Eyeless in Gaza, at the mill with slaves,
Himself in bonds under Philistian yoke.
Yet stay; let me not rashly call in doubt
Divine prediction. What if all foretold
Had been fulfilled but through mine own default?   45
Whom have I to complain of but myself,
Who this high gift of strength committed to me,
In what part lodged, how easily bereft me,
Under the seal of silence could not keep,
But weakly to a woman must reveal it,   50
O'ercome with importunity and tears?
O impotence of mind in body strong!
But what is strength without a double share
Of wisdom! Vast, unwieldy, burdensome,
Proudly secure, yet liable to fall   55
By weakest subtleties; not made to rule,
But to subserve where wisdom bears command.
God, when he gave me strength, to show withal,
How slight the gift was, hung it in my hair.
But peace! I must not quarrel with the will   60
Of highest dispensation, which herein
Haply had ends above my reach to know.
Suffices that to me strength is my bane,
And proves the source of all my miseries—
So many, and so huge, that each apart   65
Would ask a life to wail. But, chief of all,
O loss of sight, of thee I must complain!
Blind among enemies! O worse than chains,
Dungeon, or beggary, or decrepit age!
Light, the prime work of God, to me is extinct,   70
And all her various objects of delight

31. *person separate:* Samson was raised as a Nazarite—one dedicated to God's service.

Annulled, which might in part my grief have eased.
Inferior to the vilest now become
Of man or worm, the vilest here excel me:
They creep, yet see; I, dark in light, exposed   75
To daily fraud, contempt, abuse, and wrong,
Within doors, or without, still a a fool,
In power of others, never in my own—
Scarce half I seem to live, dead more than half.
O dark, dark, amid the blaze of noon,   80
Irrecoverably dark, total eclipse
Without all hope of day!
O first-created beam, and thou great Word,
"Let there be light, and light was over all,"
Why am I thus bereaved thy prime decree?   85
The Sun to me is dark
And silent as the Moon,
When she deserts the night,
Hid in her vacant interlunar cave.
Since light so necessary is to life,   90
And almost life itself, if it be true
That light is in the soul,
She all in every part, why was the sight
To such a tender ball as the eye confined,
So obvious and so easy to be quenched,   95
And not, as feeling, through all parts diffused,
That she might look at will through every pore?
Then had I not been thus exiled from light,
As in the land of darkness, yet in light,
To live a life half dead, a living death,   100
And buried; but, O yet more miserable!
Myself my sepulchre, a moving grave;
Buried, yet not exempt,
By privilege of death and burial,
From worst of other evils, pains, and wrongs;   105
But made hereby obnoxious more
To all the miseries of life,
Life in captivity
Among inhuman foes.
But who are these? for with joint pace I hear   110
The tread of many feet steering this way;
Perhaps my enemies, who come to stare
At my affliction, and perhaps to insult—
Their daily practice to afflict me more.

85. *Why . . . decree:* God's first act to create light; Samson queries why the effects of this divine deed should be denied him.

88-89. *When . . . cave:* i.e., during the dark of the moon.
106. *obnoxious:* liable to harm.
110. *with joint pace:* in step.

CHORUS. This, this is he; softly a while;   115
   Let us not break in upon him.
   O change beyond report, thought, or belief!
   See how he lies at random, carelessly diffused,
   With languished head unpropt,
   As one past hope, abandoned,   120
   And by himself given over,
   In slavish habit, ill-fitted weeds
   O'er-worn and soiled.
   Or do my eyes misrepresent? Can this be he,
   That heroic, that renowned,   125
   Irresistible Samson? whom, unarmed,
   No strength of man, or fiercest wild beast, could withstand;
   Who tore the lion as the lion tears the kid;
   Ran on embattled armies clad in iron,
   And, weaponless himself,   130
   Made arms ridiculous, useless the forgery
   Of brazen shield and spear, the hammered cuirass,
   Chalybean-tempered steel, and frock of mail
   Adamantean proof;
   But safest he who stood aloof,   135
   When insupportably his foot advanced,
   In scorn of their proud arms and warlike tools,
   Spurned them to death by troops. The bold Ascalonite
   Fled from his lion ramp; old warriors turned
   Their plated backs under his heel,   140
   Or grovelling soiled their crested helmets in the dust.
   Then with what trivial weapon came to hand,
   The jaw of a dead ass, his sword of bone,
   A thousand foreskins fell, the flower of Palestine,
   In Ramath-lechi, famous to this day: 145
   Then by main force pulled up, and on his shoulders bore,
   The gates of Azza, post and massy bar,
   Up to the hill by Hebron, seat of giants old—
   No journey of a sabbath-day, and loaded so—
   Like whom the Gentiles feign to bear up Heaven.   150
   Which shall I first bewail—
   Thy bondage or lost sight,
   Prison within prison
   Inseparably dark?
   Thou art become (O worst imprisonment!)   155

118. *diffused:* sprawled out.
122. *habit:* dress. *weeds:* clothes.
131. *forgery:* forging.
133. *Chalybean:* The Chalybes, an ancient peole of Asia Minor, were renowned for their work in iron.
138. *Ascalonite:* from Ascalon, or Askelon, a Philistine city.

144. *foreskins:* i.e., the uncircumcised Philistines.
147. *Azza:* Gaza.
149. *No journey:* The length of a trip on the Sabbath was limited by Mosaic law.
150. *whom:* Atlas.

The dungeon of thyself; thy soul,
(Which men enjoying sight oft without cause complain)
Imprisoned now indeed,
In real darkness of the body dwells,
Shut up from outward light   160
To incorporate with gloomy night;
For inward light, alas!
Puts forth no visual beam.
O mirror of our fickle state,
Since man on earth, unparalleled!   165
The rarer thy example stands,
By how much from the top of wondrous glory,
Strongest of mortal men,
To lowest pitch of abject fortune thou art fallen.
For him I reckon not in high estate   170
Whom long descent of birth,
Or the sphere of fortune, raises;
But thee, whose strength, while virtue was her mate,
Might have subdued the Earth,
Universally crowned with highest praises.   175

SAMS. I hear the sound of words; their sense the air
    Dissolves unjointed ere it reach my ear.

CHOR. He speaks: let us draw nigh. Matchless in night,
    The glory late of Israel, now the grief!
    We come, thy friends and neighbours not unknown,   180
    From Eshtaol and Zora's fruitful vale,
    To visit or bewail thee; or, if better,
    Counsel or consolation we may bring,
    Salve to thy sores: apt words have power to swage
    The tumours of a troubled mind,   185
    And are as balm to festered wounds.

SAMS. Your coming, friends, revives me; for I learn
    Now of my own experience, not by talk
    How counterfeit a coin they are who 'friends'
    Bear in their superscription (of the most   190
    I would be understood). In prosperous days
    They swarm, but in adverse withdraw their head,
    Not to be found, though sought. Ye see, O friends,
    How many evils have enclosed me round;
    Yet that which was the worst now least afflicts me,   195
    Blindness; or, had I sight, confused with shame,
    How could I once look up, or heave the head,
    Who, like a foolish pilot, have shipwrecked
    My vessel trusted to me from above,

181. *Eshtaol . . . Zora:* Eshtaol was   Samson's father.
near Zora, the native city of Manoa,   184. *swage:* assuage.

Gloriously rigged, and for a word, a tear, 200
Fool! have divulged the secret gift of God
To a deceitful woman? Tell me, friends,
Am I not sung and proverbed for a fool
In every street? Do they not say, 'How well
Are come upon him his deserts'? Yet why? 205
Immeasurable strength they might behold
In me; of wisdom nothing more than mean.
This with the other should at least have paired;
These two, proportioned ill, drove me transverse.

CHOR. Tax not divine disposal. Wisest men 210
Have erred, and by bad women been deceived;
And shall again, pretend they ne'er so wise.
Deject not, then, so overmuch thyself,
Who hast of sorrow thy full load besides.
Yet, truth to say, I oft have heard men wonder 215
Why thou should'st wed Philistian women rather
Than of thine own tribe fairer, or as fair,
At least of thy own nation, and as noble.

SAMS. The first I saw at Timna, and she pleased
Me, not my parents, that I sought to wed 220
The daughter of an infidel. They knew not
That what I motioned was of God; I knew
From intimate impulse, and therefore urged
The marriage on, that, by occasion hence,
I might begin Israel's deliverance— 225
The work to which I was divinely called.
She proving false, the next I took to wife
(O that I never had! fond wish too late!)
Was in the vale of Sorec, Dálila,
That specious monster, my accomplished snare. 230
I thought it lawful from my former act,
And the same end, still watching to oppress
Israel's oppressors. Of what now I suffer
She was not the prime cause, but I myself,
Who, vanquished with a peal of words (O weakness!), 235
Gave up my fort of silence to a woman.

CHOR. In seeking just occasion to provoke
The Philistine, thy country's enemy,
Thou never wast remiss, I bear thee witness;
Yet Israel still serves with all his sons. 240

SAMS. That fault I take not on me, but transfer
On Israel's governors and heads of tribes,

---

209. *transverse:* astray.
219. *Timna:* Timnath; a Philistine city.
231. *former act:* Samson's first marriage. See Judges 14–15.

Who, seeing those great acts which God had done
Singly by me against their conquerors,
Acknowledged not, or not at all considered,   245
Deliverance offered. I, on the other side,
Used no ambition to commend my deeds;
The deeds themselves, though mute, spoke loud the doer.
But they persisted deaf, and would not seem
To count them things worth notice, till at length   250
Their lords, the Philistines, with gathered powers,
Entered Judea, seeking me, who then
Safe to the rock of Etham was retired—
Not flying, but forecasting in what place
To set upon them, what advantaged best.   255
Meanwhile the men of Judah, to prevent
The harass of their land, beset me round;
I willingly on some conditions came
Into their hands, and they as gladly yield me
To the Uncircumcised a welcome prey,   260
Bound with two cords. But cords to me were threads
Touched with the flame: on their whole host I flew
Unarmed, and with a trivial weapon felled
Their choicest youth; they only lived who fled.
Had Judah that day joined, or one whole tribe,   265
They had by this possessed the towers of Gath,
And lorded over them whom now they serve.
But what more oft, in nations grown corrupt,
And by their vices brought to servitude,
Than to love bondage more than liberty—   270
Bondage with ease than strenuous liberty—
And to despise, or envy, or suspect,
Whom God hath of his special favour raised
As their deliverer? If he aught begin,
How frequent to desert him, and at last   275
To heap ingratitude on worthiest deeds!
CHOR. Thy words to my remembrance bring
How Succoth and the fort of Penuel
Their great deliverer contemned,
The matchless Gideon, in pursuit   280
Of Madian, and her vanquished kings;
And how ingrateful Ephraim
Had dealt with Jephtha, who by argument,

248. *doer:* i.e., God.
253. *Etham:* Etam; where Samson went after his first wife was killed.
263. *weapon:* See ll. 142 ff.
266. *Gath:* a city in Palestine; the word here denotes the whole sur-

rounding area as well.
278–285. *Succoth . . . Ammonite:* references to two instances where Hebrew tribes failed to aid each other. See Judges 8 and 12.

Not worse than by his shield and spear,
Defended Israel from the Ammonite,   285
Had not his prowess quelled their pride
In that sore battle when so many died
Without reprieve, adjudged to death
For want of well pronouncing *Shibboleth*.
SAMS. Of such examples add me to the roll.   290
Me easily indeed mine may neglect,
But God's proposed deliverance not so.
CHOR. Just are the ways of God,
And justifiable to men,
Unless there be who think not God at all.   295
If any be, they walk obscure;
For of such doctrine never was there school,
But the heart of the fool,
And no man therein doctor but himself.
    Yet more there be who doubt his ways not just,   300
As to his own edicts found contradicting;
Then give the reins to wandering thought,
Regardless of his glory's diminution,
Till, by their own perplexities involved,
They ravel more, still less resolved,   305
But never find self-satisfying solution.
    As if they would confine the Interminable,
And tie him to his own prescript,
Who made our laws to bind us, not himself,
And hath full right to exempt   310
Whomso it pleases him by choice
From national obstriction, without taint
Of sin, or legal debt;
For with his own laws he can best dispense.
    He would not else, who never wanted means,   315
Nor in respect of the enemy just cause,
To set his people free,
Have prompted this heroic Nazarite,
Against his vow of strictest purity,
To seek in marriage that fallacious bride,   320
Unclean, unchaste.
    Down, Reason, then; at least, vain reasonings down;
Though Reason here aver

289. *Shibboleth:* The Ephraimites were identified by their inability to pronounce this word. (Hence, it has now come to mean "test" or "distinguishing characteristic.") See Judges 12.
298. *fool:* See Psalms 14:1.

299. *doctor:* teacher, learned man.
305. *ravel:* complicate, confuse, entangle.
312: *obstriction:* the Mosaic prohibition of marriage with Gentiles, i.e., non-Hebrews.

That moral verdit quits her of unclean:
Unchaste was subsequent; her stain, not his.   325
  But see! here comes thy reverend sire,
With careful step, locks white as down,
Old Manoa; advise
Forthwith how thou ought'st to receive him.
SAMS. Ay me! another inward grief, awaked   330
  With mention of that name, renews the assault.
MANOA. Brethren and men of Dan (for such ye seem,
  Though in this uncouth place), if old respect,
  As I suppose, towards your once gloried friend,
  My son, now captive, hither hath informed   335
  Your younger feet, while mine, cast black with age,
  Came lagging after, say if he be here.
CHOR. As signal now in low dejected state
  As erst in highest, behold him where he lies.
MAN. O miserable change! Is this the man,   340
  That invincible Samson, far renowned,
  The dread of Israel's foes, who with a strength
  Equivalent to Angels' walked their streets,
  None offering fight; who, single combatant,
  Duelled their armies ranked in proud array,   345
  Himself an army—now unequal match
  To save himself against a coward armed
  At one spear's length? O ever-failing trust
  In mortal strength! and, oh, what not in man
  Deceivable and vain? Nay, what thing good   350
  Prayed for, but often proves our woe, our bane?
  I prayed for children, and thought barrenness
  In wedlock a reproach; I gained a son,
  And such a son as all men hailed me happy:
  Who would be now a father in my stead?   355
  Oh, wherefore did God grant me my request,
  And as a blessing with such pomp adorned?
  Why are his gifts desirable, to tempt
  Our earnest prayers, then, given with solemn hand
  As graces, draw a scorpion's tail behind?   360
  For this did the Angel twice descend? for this
  Ordained thy nurture holy, as of a plant
  Select and sacred? glorious for a while,
  The miracle of men; then in an hour
  Ensnared, assaulted, overcome, led bound,   365

324. *verdit:* verdict.   Manoa.
332. *Dan:* the tribe of Samson and   339. *erst:* formerly.

Thy foes' derision, captive, poor and blind,
Into a dungeon thrust, to work with slaves!
Alas! methinks whom God hath chosen once
To worthiest deeds, if he through frailty err,
He should not so o'erwhelm, and as a thrall   370
Subject him to so foul indignities,
Be it but for honour's sake of former deeds.
SAMS. Appoint not heavenly disposition, father.
Nothing of all these evils hath befallen me
But justly; I myself have brought them on;   375
Sole author I, sole cause. If aught seem vile,
As vile hath been my folly, who have profaned
The mystery of God, given me under pledge
Of vow, and have betrayed it to a woman,
A Canaanite, my faithless enemy.   380
This well I knew, nor was at all surprised,
But warned by oft experience. Did not she
Of Timna first betray me, and reveal
The secret wrested from me in her highth
Of nuptial love professed, carrying it straight   385
To them who had corrupted her, my spies
And rivals? In this other was there found
More faith, who, also in her prime of love,
Spousal embraces, vitiated with gold,
Though offered only, by the scent conceived,   390
Her spurious first-born, Treason against me?
Thrice she assayed, with flattering prayers and sighs,
And amorous reproaches, to win from me
My capital secret, in what part my strength
Lay stored, in what part summed, that she might know; 395
Thrice I deluded her, and turned to sport
Her importunity, each time perceiving
How openly and with what impudence
She purposed to betray me, and (which was worse
Than undissembled hate) with what contempt   400
She sought to make me traitor to myself.
Yet, the fourth time, when, mustering all her wiles,
With blandished parleys, feminine assaults,
Tongue-batteries, she surceased not day nor night
To storm me, over-watched and wearied out,   405

373. *Appoint not:* do not presume to limit.
380. *Canaanite:* Philistine dwelling in Canaan.
382–383. *she of Timna:* Samson's first wife.
390–391. *by the scent . . . spurious first-born, Treason:* The smell of gold
was enough to cause her to conceive her first "bastard," i.e., her treason against Samson.
394. *capital:* important, and having to do with the head; i.e., his hair.
405. *over-watched:* tired from lack of sleep.

At times when men seek most repose and rest,
I yielded, and unlocked her all my heart,
Who, with a grain of manhood well resolved,
Might easily have shook off all her snares;
But foul effeminacy held me yoked   410
Her bond-slave. O indignity, O blot
To honour and religion! servile mind
Rewarded well with servile punishment!
The base degree to which I now am fallen,
These rags, this grinding, is not yet so base   415
As was my former servitude, ignoble,
Unmanly, ignominious, infamous,
True slavery; and that blindness worse than this,
That saw not how degenerately I served.

MAN. I cannot praise thy marriage-choices, son—   420
Rather approved them not; but thou didst plead
Divine impulsion prompting how thou might'st
Find some occasion to infest our foes.
I state not that; this I am sure—our foes
Found soon occasion thereby to make thee   425
Their captive, and their triumph; thou the sooner
Temptation found'st, or over-potent charms,
To violate the sacred trust of silence
Deposited within thee—which to have kept
Tacit was in thy power. True; and thou bear'st   430
Enough, and more, the burden of that fault;
Bitterly hast thou paid, and still art paying,
That rigid score. A worse thing yet remains:—
This day the Philistines a popular feast
Here celebrate in Gaza, and proclaim   435
Great pomp, and sacrifice, and praises loud,
To Dagon, as their god who hath delivered
Thee, Samson, bound and blind, into their hands—
Them out of thine, who slew'st them many a slain.
So Dagon shall be magnified, and God,   440
Besides whom is no god, compared with idols,
Disglorified, blasphemed, and had in scorn
By the idolatrous rout amidst their wine;
Which to have come to pass by means of thee,
Samson, of all thy sufferings think the heaviest,   445
Of all reproach the most with shame that ever
Could have befallen thee and thy father's house.

SAMS. Father, I do acknowledge and confess
That I this honour, I this pomp, have brought
To Dagon, and advanced his praises high   450

Among the Heathen round—to God have brought
Dishonour, obloquy, and oped the mouths
Of idolists and atheists; have brought scandal
To Israel, diffidence of God, and doubt
In feeble hearts, propense enough before   455
To waver, or fall off and join with idols:
Which is my chief affliction, shame and sorrow,
The anguish of my soul, that suffers not
Mine eye to harbour sleep, or thoughts to rest.
This only hope relieves me, that the strife   460
With me hath end. All the contést is now
'Twixt God and Dagon. Dagon hath presumed,
Me overthrown, to enter lists with God,
His deity comparing and preferring
Before the God of Abraham. He, be sure,   465
Will not connive, or linger, thus provoked,
But will arise, and his great name assert.
Dagon must stoop, and shall ere long receive
Such a discomfit as shall quite despoil him
Of all these boasted trophies won on me,   470
And with confusion blank his worshippers.
MAN. With cause this hope relieves thee; and these words
I as a prophecy receive; for God
(Nothing more certain) will not long defer
To vindicate the glory of his name   475
Against all competition, nor will long
Endure it doubtful whether God be Lord
Or Dagon. But for thee what shall be done?
Thou must not in the meanwhile, here forgot,
Lie in this miserable loathsome plight   480
Neglected. I already have made way
To some Philistian lords, with whom to treat
About thy ransom. Well they may by this
Have satisfied their utmost revenge,
By pains and slaveries, worse than death, inflicted   485
On thee, who now no more canst do them harm.
SAMS. Spare that proposal, father; spare the trouble
Of that solicitation. Let me here,
As I deserve, pay on my punishment,
And expiate, if possible, my crime,   490
Shameful garrulity. To have revealed
Secrets of *men*, the secrets of a friend,
How heinous had the fact been, how deserving

454. *diffidence:* distrust, suspicion.   here the meaning is, "ignore," "con-
455. *propense:* inclined.   done."
466. *connive:* literally, "wink at";   471. *blank:* blot out, confound.

Contempt and scorn of all—to be excluded
All friendship, and avoided as a blab,   495
The mark of fool set on his front! But I
God's counsel have not kept, his holy secret
Presumptuously have published, impiously,
Weakly at least and shamefully—a sin
That Gentiles in their parables condemn   500
To their Abyss and horrid pains confined.
MAN. Be penitent, and for thy fault contrite;
But act not in thy own affliction, son.
Repent the sin; but, if the punishment
Thou canst avoid, self-preservation bids;   505
Or the execution leave to high disposal,
And let another hand, not thine, exact
Thy penal forfeit from thyself. Perhaps
God will relent, and quit thee all his debt;
Who ever more approves and more accepts   510
(Best pleased with humble and filial submission)
Him who, imploring mercy, sues for life,
Than who, self-rigorous, chooses death as due;
Which argues over-just, and self-displeased
For self-offence more than for God offended.   515
Reject not, then, what offered means who knows
But God hath set before us to return thee
Home to thy country and his sacred house,
Where thou may'st bring thy offerings, to avert
His further ire, with prayers and vows renewed.   520
SAMS. His pardon I implore; but, as for life,
To what end should I seek it? When in strength
All mortals I excelled, and great in hopes,
With youthful courage, and magnanimous thoughts
Of birth from Heaven foretold and high exploits,   525
Full of divine instinct, after some proof
Of acts indeed heroic, far beyond
The sons of Anak, famous now and blazed,
Fearless of danger, like a petty god
I walked about, admired of all, and dreaded   530
On hostile ground, none daring my affront—
Then, swoln with pride, into the snare I fell
Of fair fallacious looks, venereal trains,
Softened with pleasure and voluptuous life,

495. *blab:* foolish talker.
499–501. *a sin . . . confined:* Greek
mythology tells of Tantalus thus confined for revealing the gods' secrets.
509. *quit:* acquit.

515. *self-offence:* Suicide is here defined as an act of egotism.
533. *venereal trains:* sensual attraction (literally, "the lure of Venus").

At length to lay my head and hallowed pledge   535
Of all my strength in the lascivious lap
Of a deceitful concubine, who shore me,
Like a tame wether, all my precious fleece,
Then turned me out ridiculous, despoiled,
Shaven, and disarmed among my enemies.   540
CHOR. Desire of wine and all delicious drinks,
    Which many a famous warrior overturns,
    Thou could'st repress; nor did the dancing ruby,
    Sparkling out-poured, the flavour or the smell,
    Or taste, that cheers the heart of gods and men,   545
    Allure thee from the cool crystalline stream.
SAMS. Wherever fountain or fresh current flowed
    Against the eastern ray, translucent, pure
    With touch ethereal of Heaven's fiery rod,
    I drank, from the clear milky juice allaying   550
    Thirst, and refreshed; nor envied them the grape
    Whose heads that turbulent liquor fills with fumes.
CHOR. O madness! to think use of strongest wines
    And strongest drinks our chief support of health,
    When God with these forbidden made choice to rear   555
    His mighty champion, strong above compare,
    Whose drink was only from the liquid brook!
SAMS. But what availed this temperance, not complete
    Against another object more enticing?
    What boots it at one gate to make defence,   560
    And at another to let in the foe,
    Effeminately vanquished? by which means,
    Now blind, disheartened, shamed, dishonoured, quelled,
    To what can I be useful? wherein serve
    My nation, and the work from Heaven imposed?   565
    But to sit idle on the household hearth,
    A burdenous drone; to visitants a gaze,
    Or pitied object; these redundant locks,
    Robustious to no purpose, clustering down,
    Vain monument of strength; till length of years   570
    And sedentary numbness craze my limbs
    To a contemptible old age obscure.
    Here rather let me drudge, and earn my bread,
    Till vermin, or the draff of servile food,
    Consume me, and oft-invocated death   575
    Hasten the welcome end of all my pains.
MAN. Wilt thou then serve the Philistines with that gift
    Which was expressly given thee to annoy them?

538. *wether:* castrated ram.   574. *draff:* refuse, garbage.

Better at home lie bed-rid, not only idle,
Inglorious, unemployed, with age outworn.   580
But God, who caused a fountain at thy prayer
From the dry ground to spring, thy thirst to allay
After the brunt of battle, can as easy
Cause light again within thy eyes to spring,
Wherewith to serve him better than thou hast.   585
And I persuade me so. Why else his strength
Miraculous yet remaining in those locks?
His might continues in thee not for naught,
Nor shall his wondrous gifts be frustrate thus.

SAMS. All otherwise to me my thoughts portend,—   590
That these dark orbs no more shall treat with light,
Nor the other light of life continue long,
But yield to double darkness nigh at hand;
So much I feel my genial spirits droop,
My hopes all flat: Nature within me seems   595
In all her functions weary of herself;
My race of glory run, and race of shame,
And I shall shortly be with them that rest.

MAN. Believe not these suggestions, which proceed
From anguish of the mind, and humours black   600
That mingle with thy fancy. I, however,
Must not omit a father's timely care
To prosecute the means of thy deliverance
By ransom or how else: meanwhile be calm,
And healing words from these thy friends admit.   605

SAMS. Oh, that torment should not be confined
To the body's wounds and sores,
With maladies innumerable
In heart, head, breast, and reins,
But must secret passage find   610
To the inmost mind,
There exercise all his fierce accidents,
And on her purest spirits prey,
As on entrails, joints, and limbs,
With answerable pains, but more intense,   615
Though void of corporal sense!
    My griefs not only pain me
As a lingering disease,
But, finding no redress, ferment and rage;

581–582. *fountain . . . spring:*
Judges 15:18–19.
593. *double darkness:* blindness and
death.
600. *humours black:* black bile, in
Milton's day thought to make one

melancholy. It was assumed that one's
temperament was governed by four
body fluids, or "humours."
609. *reins:* kidneys.
612. *accidents:* symptoms.

Nor less than wounds immedicable   620
Rankle, and fester, and gangrene,
To black mortification,
Thoughts, my tormentors, armed with daily stings,
Mangle my apprehensive tenderest parts,
Exasperate, exulcerate, and raise   625
Dire inflammation, which no cooling herb
Or medicinal liquor can assuage,
Nor breath of vernal air from snowy Alp.
Sleep hath forsook and given me o'er
To death's benumbing opium as my only cure;   630
Thence faintings, swoonings of despair,
And sense of Heaven's desertion.
     I was his nursling once and choice delight,
His destined from the womb,
Promised by heavenly message twice descending.   635
Under his special eye
Abstemious I grew up and thrived amain;
He led me on to mightiest deeds,
Above the nerve of mortal arm,
Against the Uncircumcised, our enemies: 640
But now hath cast me off as never known,
And to those cruel enemies,
Whom I by his appointment had provoked,
Left me, all helpless with the irreparable loss
Of sight, reserved alive to be repeated   645
The subject of their cruelty or scorn.
Nor am I in the list of them that hope;
Hopeless are all my evils, all remediless.
This one prayer yet remains, might I be heard,
No long petition—speedy death,   650
The close of all my miseries and the balm.
CHOR. Many are the sayings of the wise,
     In ancient and in modern books enrolled,
     Extolling patience as the truest fortitude,
     And to the bearing well of all calamities,   655
     All chances incident to man's frail life,
     Consolatories writ
     With studied argument, and much persuasion sought,
     Lenient of grief and anxious thought.
     But with the afflicted in his pangs their sound   660
     Little prevails, or rather seems a tune
     Harsh, and of dissonant mood from his complaint

624. *apprehensive:* sensitive.   659. *Lenient of:* softening, allevi-
635. *twice descending:* see l. 24.   ating.
637. *amain:* mightily.

Unless he feel within
Some source of consolation from above,
Secret refreshings that repair his strength   665
And fainting spirits uphold.
    God of our fathers! what is Man,
That thou towards him with hand so various—
Or might I say contrarious?—
Temper'st thy providence through his short course: 670
Not evenly, as thou rul'st
The angelic orders, and inferior creatures mute,
Irrational and brute?
Nor do I name of men the common rout,
That, wandering loose about,   675
Grow up and perish as the summer fly,
Heads without name, no more remembered;
But such as thou hast solemnly elected,
With gifts and graces eminently adorned,
To some great work, thy glory,   680
And people's safety, which in part they effect.
Yet toward these, thus dignified, thou oft,
Amidst their highth of noon,
Changest thy countenance and thy hand, with no regard
Of highest favours past   685
From thee on them, or them to thee of service.
    Nor only dost degrade them, or remit
To life obscured, which were a fair dismission,
But throw'st them lower than thou didst exalt them high—
Unseemly falls in human eye,   690
Too grievous for the trespass or omission;
Oft leav'st them to the hostile sword
Of heathen and profane, their carcasses
To dogs and fowls a prey, or else captived,
Or to the unjust tribunals, under change of times,   695
And condemnation of the ungrateful multitude.
If these they scape, perhaps in poverty
With sickness and disease thou bow'st them down,
Painful diseases and deformed,
In crude old age;   700
Though not disordinate, yet causeless suffering
The punishment of dissolute days. In fine,
Just or unjust alike seem miserable,

---

672. *angelic orders:* the nine ranks in the angelic hierarchy.

693–700. *their carcasses . . . age:* possibly references to certain contemporary occurrences—the exhumation of Cromwell's body in 1661, Milton's loss of income during the Restoration, and his growing physical infirmities.

700. *crude:* immature, early.

58 · *John Milton*

For oft alike both come to evil end.
    So deal not with this once thy glorious champion,   705
The image of thy strength, and mighty minister.
What do I beg? how hast thou dealt already!
Behold him in this state calamitous, and turn
His labours, for thou canst, to peaceful end.
    But who is this? what thing of sea or land—   710
Female of sex it seems—
That, so bedecked, ornate, and gay,
Comes this way sailing,
Like a stately ship
Of Tarsus, bound for the isles   715
Of Javan or Gadire,
With all her bravery on, and tackle trim,
Sails filled, and streamers waving,
Courted by all the winds that hold them play;
An amber scent of odorous perfume   720
Her harbinger, a damsel train behind?
Some rich Philistian matron she may seem;
And now, at nearer view, no other certain
Than Dalila thy wife.
SAMS. My wife! my traitress! let her not come near me.   725
CHOR. Yet on she moves; now stands and eyes thee fixed,
  About to have spoke; but now, with head declined,
  Like a fair flower surcharged with dew, she weeps,
  And words addressed seem into tears dissolved,
  Wetting the borders of her silken veil.   730
  But now again she makes address to speak.
DALILA. With doubtful feet and wavering resolution
  I came, still dreading thy displeasure, Samson;
  Which to have merited, without excuse,
  I cannot but acknowledge. Yet, if tears   735
  May expiate (though the fact more evil drew
  In the perverse event than I foresaw),
  My penance hath not slackened, though my pardon
  No way assured. But conjugal affection,
  Prevailing over fear and timorous doubt,   740
  Hath led me on, desirous to behold
  Once more thy face, and know of thy estate,
  If aught in my ability may serve
  To lighten what thou suffer'st, and appease
  Thy mind with what amends is in my power—   745
  Though late, yet in some part to recompense

715. *Tarsus:* city in Asia Minor.   716. *Gadire:* Cadiz.
715–716. *the isles of Javan:* the 720. *amber:* ambergris, from the
Greek islands.   sperm whale; used in perfumes.

My rash but more unfortunate misdeed.

SAMS. Out, out, hyæna! These are thy wonted arts,
  And arts of every woman false like thee—
  To break all faith, all vows, deceive, betray; 750
  Then, as repentant, to submit, beseech,
  And reconcilement move with feigned remorse,
  Confess, and promise wonders in her change—
  Not truly penitent, but chief to try
  Her husband, how far urged his patience bears, 755
  His virtue or weakness which way to assail:
  Then, with more cautious and instructed skill,
  Again transgresses, and again submits;
  That wisest and best men, full oft beguiled,
  With goodness principled not to reject 760
  The penitent, but ever to forgive,
  Are drawn to wear out miserable days,
  Entangled with a poisonous bosom-snake,
  If not by quick destruction soon cut off,
  As I by thee, to ages an example. 765

DAL. Yet hear me, Samson; not that I endeavour
  To lessen or extenuate my offence,
  But that, on the other side, if it be weighed
  By itself, with aggravations not surcharged,
  Or else with just allowance counterpoised, 770
  I may, if possible, thy pardon find
  The easier towards me, or thy hatred less.
  First granting, as I do, it was a weakness
  In me, but incident to all our sex,
  Curiosity, inquisitive, importune 775
  Of secrets, then with like infirmity
  To publish them—both common female faults—
  Was it not weakness also to make known,
  For importunity, that is for naught,
  Wherein consisted all thy strength and safety? 780
  To what I did thou show'dst me first the way.
  But I to enemies revealed, and should not!
  Nor should'st thou have trusted that to woman's frailty:
  Ere I to thee, thou to thyself wast cruel.
  Let weakness, then, with weakness come to parle, 785
  So near related, or the same of kind;
  Thine forgive mine, that men may censure thine
  The gentler, if severely thou exact not
  More strength from me than in thyself was found.

760. *principled:* acting out of principle.

778–780. *Was . . . safety?* were you not also weak to yield to my entreaties and tell me all?

785. *parle:* parley, as in a truce.

And what if love, which thou interpret'st hate, 790
The jealousy of love, powerful to sway
In human hearts, nor less in mine towards thee,
Caused what I did? I saw thee mutable
Of fancy; feared lest one day thou would'st leave me,
As her at Timna; sought by all means, therefore, 795
How to endear, and hold thee to me firmest:
No better way I saw than by importuning
To learn thy secrets, get into my power
Thy key of strength and safety. Thou wilt say,
"Why, then, revealed?" I was assured by those 800
Who tempted me that nothing was desired
Against thee but safe custody and hold.
That made for me; I knew that liberty
Would draw thee forth to perilous enterprises,
While I at home sat full of cares and fears, 805
Wailing thy absence in my widowed bed;
Here I should still enjoy thee, day and night,
Mine and love's prisoner, not the Philistines',
Whole to myself, unhazarded abroad,
Fearless at home of partners in my love. 810
These reasons in Love's law have passed for good,
Though fond and reasonless to some perhaps;
And love hath oft, well meaning, wrought much woe,
Yet always pity or pardon hath obtained.
Be not unlike all others, not austere 815
As thou art strong, inflexible as steel.
If thou in strength all mortals dost exceed,
In uncompassionate anger do not so.

SAMS. How cunningly the sorceress displays
Her own transgressions, to upbraid me mine! 820
That malice, not repentance, brought thee hither,
By this appears. I gave, thou say'st, the example,
I led the way—bitter reproach, but true;
I to myself was false ere thou to me.
Such pardon, therefore, as I give my folly 825
Take to thy wicked deed; which when thou seest
Impartial, self-severe, inexorable,
Thou wilt renounce thy seeking, and much rather
Confess it feigned. Weakness is thy excuse,
And I believe it—weakness to resist 830
Philistian gold. If weakness may excuse,
What murtherer, what traitor, parricide,

795. *her:* Samson's first wife.
803. *That . . . me:* this protective custody was in my interest.
810. *Fearless . . . love:* Dalila could be sure of Samson's fidelity.

Incestuous, sacrilegious, but may plead it?
All wickedness is weakness; that plea, therefore,
With God or man will gain thee no remission.   835
But love constrained thee! Call it furious rage
To satisfy thy lust. Love seeks to have love;
My love how could'st thou hope, who took'st the way
To raise in me inexpiable hate,
Knowing, as needs I must, by thee betrayed?   840
In vain thou striv'st to cover shame with shame,
Or by evasions thy crime uncover'st more.

DAL. Since thou determin'st weakness for no plea
In man or woman, though to thy own condemning,
Hear what assaults I had, what snares besides,   845
What sieges girt me round, ere I consented;
Which might have awed the best-resolved of men,
The constantest, to have yielded without blame.
It was not gold, as to my charge thou lay'st,
That wrought with me. Thou knowest the magistrates   850
And princes of my country came in person,
Solicited, commanded, threatened, urged,
Adjured by all the bonds of civil duty
And of religion—pressed how just it was,
How honourable, how glorious, to entrap   855
A common enemy, who had destroyed
Such numbers of our nation: and the priest
Was not behind, but ever at my ear,
Preaching how meritorious with the gods
It would be to ensnare an irreligious   860
Dishonourer of Dagon. What had I
To oppose against such powerful arguments?
Only my love of thee held long debate,
And combated in silence all these reasons
With hard contest. At length, that grounded maxim,   865
So rife and celebrated in the mouths
Of wisest men, that to the public good
Private respects must yield, with grave authority
Took full possession of me, and prevailed;
Virtue, as I thought, truth, duty, so enjoining.   870

SAMS. I thought where all thy circling wiles would end—
In feigned religion, smooth hypocrisy!
But, had thy love, still odiously pretended,
Been, as it ought, sincere, it would have taught thee
Far other reasonings, brought forth other deeds.   875
I, before all the daughters of my tribe

840. *Knowing:* knowing myself.   850. *wrought with:* influenced.

And of my nation, chose thee from among
My enemies, loved thee, as too well thou knew'st;
Too well; unbosomed all my secrets to thee,
Not out of levity, but overpowered   880
By thy request, who could deny thee nothing;
Yet now am judged an enemy. Why, then,
Didst thou at first receive me for thy husband—
Then, as since then, thy country's foe professed?
Being once a wife, for me thou wast to leave   885
Parents and country; nor was I their subject,
Nor under their protection, but my own;
Thou mine, not theirs. If aught against my life
Thy country sought of thee, it sought unjustly,
Against the law of nature, law of nations;   890
No more thy country, but an impious crew
Of men conspiring to uphold their state
By worse than hostile deeds, violating the ends
For which our country is a name so dear;
Not therefore to be obeyed. But zeal moved thee;   895
To please thy gods thou didst it! Gods unable
To acquit themselves and prosecute their foes
But by ungodly deeds, the contradiction
Of their own deity, Gods cannot be—
Less therefore to be pleased, obeyed, or feared.   900
These false pretexts and varnished colours failing,
Bare in thy guilt, how foul must thou appear!
DAL. In argument with men a woman ever
    Goes by the worse, whatever be her cause.
SAMS. For want of words, no doubt, or lack of breath!   905
    Witness when I was worried with thy peals.
DAL. I was a fool, too rash, and quite mistaken
    In what I thought would have succeeded best.
    Let me obtain forgiveness of thee, Samson;
    Afford me place to show what recompense   910
    Towards thee I intend for what I have misdone,
    Misguided. Only what remains past cure
    Bear not too sensibly, nor still insist
    To afflict thyself in vain. Though sight be lost,
    Life yet hath many solaces, enjoyed   915
    Where other senses want not their delights—
    At home, in leisure and domestic ease,

891. *No . . . country:* Having married Samson, a non-Philistine, Dalila
is no longer bound to the Philistines.
Hence their acts against Samson are
doubly criminal if they try to evoke
her aid.
    906. *peals:* appeals; also, loud vol-
lies of words.
    913. *sensibly:* sensitively.
    916. *want:* lack.

Exempt from many a care and chance to which
Eyesight exposes, daily, men abroad.
I to the lords will intercede, not doubting   920
Their favourable ear, that I may fetch thee
From forth this loathsome prison-house, to abide
With me, where my redoubled love and care,
With nursing diligence, to me glad office,
May ever tend about thee to old age,   925
With all things grateful cheered, and so supplied
That what by me thou hast lost thou least shalt miss.

SAMS. No, no; of my condition take no care;
It fits not; thou and I long since are twain;
Nor think me so unwary or accursed   930
To bring my feet again into the snare
Where once I have been caught. I know thy trains,
Though dearly to my cost, thy gins, and toils.
Thy fair enchanted cup, and warbling charms,
No more on me have power; their force is nulled,   935
So much of adder's wisdom I have learned
To fence my ear against thy sorceries.
If in my flower of youth and strength, when all men
Loved, honoured, feared me, thou alone could hate me,
Thy husband, slight me, sell me, and forgo me,   940
How would'st thou use me now, blind, and thereby
Deceivable, in most things as a child
Helpless, thence easily contemned and scorned,
And last neglected! How would'st thou insult,
When I must live uxorious to thy will   945
In perfect thraldom! how again betray me,
Bearing my words and doings to the lords
To gloss upon, and, censuring, frown or smile!
This jail I count the house of liberty
To thine, whose doors my feet shall never enter.   950

DAL. Let me approach at least, and touch thy hand.

SAMS. Not for thy life, lest fierce remembrance wake
My sudden rage to tear thee joint by joint.
At distance I forgive thee; go with that;
Bewail thy falsehood, and the pious works   955
It hath brought forth to make thee memorable
Among illustrious women, faithful wives;
Cherish thy hastened widowhood with the gold

---

933. *gins, and toils:* fowling terms, meaning "nets, and snares."

934. *fair . . . charms:* Dalila is compared to Circe, who turned men into swine. Compare Milton's first Latin elegy.

936. *adder's wisdom:* This snake was thought to be deaf.

950. *To:* compared to.

Of matrimonial treason: so farewell.

DAL. I see thou art implacable, more deaf   960
To prayers than winds and seas. Yet winds to seas
Are reconciled at length, and sea to shore:
Thy anger, unappeasable, still rages,
Eternal tempest never to be calmed.
Why do I humble thus myself, and, suing   965
For peace, reap nothing but repulse and hate,
Bid go with evil omen, and the brand
Of infamy upon my name denounced?
To mix with thy concernments I desist
Henceforth, nor too much disapprove my own.   970
Fame, if not double-faced, is double-mouthed,
And with contráry blast proclaims most needs;
On both his wings, one black, the other white,
Bears greatest names in his wild aery flight.
My name, perhaps, among the Circumcised   975
In Dan, in Judah, and the bordering tribes,
To all posterity may stand defamed,
With malediction mentioned, and the blot
Of falsehood most unconjugal traduced.
But in my country, where I most desire,   980
In Ecron, Gaza, Asdod, and in Gath,
I shall be named among the famousest
Of women, sung at solemn festivals,
Living and dead recorded, who to save
Her country from a fierce destroyer chose   985
Above the faith of wedlock bands; my tomb
With odours visited and annual flowers;
Not less renowned than in Mount Ephraim
Jael, who, with inhospitable guile,
Smote Sisera sleeping, through the temples nailed.   990
Nor shall I count it heinous to enjoy
The public marks of honour and reward
Conferred upon me for the piety
Which to my country I was judged to have shown.
At this whoever envies or repines,   995
I leave him to his lot, and like my own.

CHOR. She's gone—a manifest serpent by her sting
Discovered in the end, till now concealed.

SAMS. So let her go. God sent her to debase me,
And aggravate my folly, who committed   1000
To such a viper his most sacred trust

981. *In Ecron . . . Gath:* through-   989. *Jael:* Jewish heroine. See Judges
out the chief cities of Palestine.   4–5.

Of secrecy, my safety, and my life.
CHOR. Yet beauty, though injurious, hath strange power,
    After offence returning, to regain
    Love once possessed, nor can be easily   1005
    Repulsed, without much inward passion felt,
    And secret sting of amorous remorse.
SAMS. Love-quarrels oft in pleasing concord end;
    Not wedlock-treachery, endangering life.
CHOR. It is not virtue, wisdom, valour, wit,   1010
    Strength, comeliness of shape, or amplest merit,
    That woman's love can win, or long inherit;
    But what it is hard is to say,
    Harder to hit,
    Which way soever men refer it   1015
    (Much like thy riddle, Samson), in one day
    Or seven though one should musing sit.
      If any of these, or all, the Timnian bride
    Had not so soon preferred
    Thy paranymph, worthless to thee compared,   1020
    Successor in thy bed,
    Nor both so loosely disallied
    Their nuptials, nor this last so treacherously
    Had shorn the fatal harvest of thy head.
    It is for that such outward ornament   1025
    Was lavished on their sex, that inward gifts
    Were left for haste unfinished, judgment scant,
    Capacity not raised to apprehend
    Or value what is best
    In choice, but oftest to affect the wrong?   1030
    Or was too much of self-love mixed,
    Of constancy no root infixed,
    That either they love nothing, or not long!
      Whate'er it be, to wisest men and best,
    Seeming at first all heavenly under virgin veil,   1035
    Soft, modest, meek, demure,
    Once joined, the contrary she proves—a thorn
    Intestine, far within defensive arms
    A cleaving mischief, in his way to virtue
    Adverse and turbulent; or by her charms   1040
    Draws him awry, enslaved
    With dotage, and his sense depraved
    To folly and shameful deeds, which ruin ends.

1018. *these:* See ll. 1010–1011.
1020. *paranymph:* Samson's "companion" (Judges 14:20), to whom the woman of Timnath was given by her father.
1022. *both:* Dalila and the first woman.
1038. *Intestine:* internal, domestic.

What pilot so expert but needs must wreck,
Embarked with such a steers-mate at the helm?   1045
    Favoured of Heaven who finds
One virtuous, rarely found,
That in domestic good combines!
Happy that house! his way to peace is smooth:
But virtue which breaks through all opposition,   1050
And all temptation can remove,
Most shines and most is acceptable above.
    Therefore God's universal law
Gave to the man despotic power
Over his female in due awe,   1055
Nor from that right to part an hour,
Smile she or lour:
So shall he least confusion draw
On his whole life, not swayed
By female usurpation, nor dismayed.   1060
    But had we best retire? I see a storm.
SAMS. Fair days have oft contracted wind and rain.
CHOR. But this another kind of tempest brings.
SAMS. Be less abstruse; my riddling days are past.
CHOR. Look now for no enchanting voice, nor fear   1065
    The bait of honeyed words; a rougher tongue
    Draws hitherward; I know him by his stride,
    The giant Harapha of Gath, his look
    Haughty, as is his pile high-built and proud.
    Comes he in peace? What wind hath blown him hither   1070
    I less conjecture than when first I saw
    The sumptuous Dalila floating this way:
    His habit carries peace, his brow defiance.
SAMS. Or peace or not, alike to me he comes.
CHOR. His fraught we soon shall know: he now arrives.   1075
HARAPHA. I come not, Samson, to condole thy chance,
    As these perhaps, yet wish it had not been,
    Though for no friendly intent. I am of Gath;
    Men call me Harapha, of stock renowned
    As Og, or Anak, and the Emims old   1080
    That Kiriathaim held. Thou know'st me now,
    If thou at all art known. Much I have heard
    Of thy prodigious might and feats performed,
    Incredible to me, in this displeased,—
    That I was never present on the place   1085
    Of those encounters, where we might have tried

1068. *Harapha:* in Hebrew, "giant."   1080. *Og . . . Emims:* biblical
1069. *pile:* frame.   giants.
1075. *fraught:* meaning, business.

Each other's force in camp or listed field;
And now am come to see of whom such noise
Hath walked about, and each limb to survey,
If thy appearance answer loud report.   1090

SAMS. The way to know were not to see, but taste.

HAR. Dost thou already single me? I thought
    Gyves and the mill had tamed thee. O that fortune
    Had brought me to the field where thou art famed
    To have wrought such wonders with an ass's jaw!   1095
    I should have forced thee soon with other arms,
    Or left thy carcass where the ass lay thrown;
    So had the glory of prowess been recovered
    To Palestine, won by a Philistine
    From the unforeskinned race, of whom thou bear'st   1100
    The highest name for valiant acts. That honour,
    Certain to have won by mortal duel from thee,
    I lose, prevented by thy eyes put out.

SAMS. Boast not of what thou would'st have done, but do
    What then thou would'st; thou seest it in thy hand. 1105

HAR. To combat with a blind man I disdain,
    And thou hast need much washing to be touched.

SAMS. Such usage as your honourable lords
    Afford me, assassinated and betrayed;
    Who durst not with their whole united powers   1110
    In fight withstand me single and unarmed,
    Nor in the house with chamber ambushes
    Close-banded durst attack me, no, not sleeping,
    Till they had hired a woman with their gold,
    Breaking her marriage-faith, to circumvent me.   1115
    Therefore, without feign'd shifts, let be assigned
    Some narrow place enclosed, where sight may give thee,
    Or rather flight, no great advantage on me;
    Then put on all thy gorgeous arms, thy helmet
    And brigandine of brass, thy broad habergeon,   1120
    Vant-brace and greaves and gauntlet; add thy spear,
    A weaver's beam, and seven-times-folded shield:
    I only with an oaken staff will meet thee,
    And raise such outcries on thy clattered iron,
    Which long shall not withhold me from thy head, 1125

1090: *answer loud report:* conform to popular opinion.
1092. *single:* challenge to single combat.
1093. *Gyves:* fetters.
1102. *mortal duel:* duel to the death.
1116. *feign'd shifts:* treacherous dodges.
1120. *brigandine:* flexible armor made of small metal plates. *habergeon:* sleeveless coat of mail.
1121. *Vant-brace:* armor for the forearm. *greaves:* armor for the leg below the knee.
1121–1122. *spear . . . beam:* spear thick as the beam of a loom.
1122. *seven-times-folded:* shield with seven layers or thicknesses.

That in a little time, while breath remains thee,
Thou oft shalt wish thyself at Gath, to boast
Again in safety what thou would'st have done
To Samson, but shalt never see Gath more.

HAR. Thou durst not thus disparage glorious arms,   1130
Which greatest heroes have in battle worn,
Their ornament and safety, had not spells
And black enchantments, some magician's art,
Armed thee or charmed thee strong, which thou from Heaven
Feign'dst at thy birth was given thee in thy hair,   1135
Where strength can least abide, though all thy hairs
Were bristles ranged like those that ridge the back
Of chafed wild boars or ruffled porcupines.

SAMS. I know no spells, use no forbidden arts;
My trust is in the Living God, who gave me,   1140
At my nativity, this strength, diffused
No less through all my sinews, joints, and bones,
Than thine, while I preserved these locks unshorn,
The pledge of my unviolated vow.
For proof hereof, if Dagon be thy god,   1145
Go to his temple, invocate his aid
With solemnest devotion, spread before him
How highly it concerns his glory now
To frustrate and dissolve these magic spells,
Which I to be the power of Israel's God   1150
Avow, and challenge Dagon to the test,
Offering to combat thee, his champion bold,
With the utmost of his godhead seconded:
Then thou shalt see, or rather to thy sorrow
Soon feel, whose God is strongest, thine or mine.   1155

HAR. Presume not on thy God. Whate'er he be,
Thee he regards not, owns not, hath cut off
Quite from his people, and delivered up
Into thy enemies' hand; permitted them
To put out both thine eyes, and fettered send thee   1160
Into the common prison, there to grind
Among the slaves and asses, thy comrádes,
As good for nothing else, no better service
With those thy boisterous locks; no worthy match
For valour to assail, nor by the sword   1165
Of noble warrior, so to stain his honour,
But by the barber's razor best subdued.

SAMS. All these indignities, for such they are
From thine, these evils I deserve and more,

1164. *boisterous:* thick and rough.   1169. *From thine:* from your race.

Acknowledge them from God inflicted on me   1170
Justly, yet despair not of his final pardon,
Whose ear is ever open, and his eye
Gracious to re-admit the suppliant;
In confidence whereof I once again
Defy thee to the trial of mortal fight,   1175
By combat to decide whose god is God,
Thine, or whom I with Israel's sons adore.

HAR. Fair honour that thou dost thy God, in trusting
He will accept thee to defend his cause,
A murtherer, a revolter, and a robber!   1180

SAMS. Tongue-doughty giant, how dost thou prove me these?

HAR. Is not thy nation subject to our lords?
Their magistrates confessed it when they took thee
As a league-breaker, and delivered bound
Into our hands; for hadst thou not committed   1185
Notorious murder on those thirty men
At Ascalon, who never did thee harm,
Then, like a robber, stripp'dst them of their robes?
The Philistines, when thou hadst broke the league,
Went up with armed powers thee only seeking,   1190
To others did no violence nor spoil.

SAMS. Among the daughters of the Philistines
I chose a wife, which argued me no foe,
And in your city held my nuptial feast;
But your ill-meaning politician lords,   1195
Under pretence of bridal friends and guests,
Appointed to await me thirty spies,
Who, threatening cruel death, constrained the bride
To wring from me, and tell to them, my secret,
That solved the riddle which I had proposed.   1200
When I perceived all set on enmity,
As on my enemies, wherever chanced,
I used hostility, and took their spoil,
To pay my underminers in their coin.
My nation was subjected to your lords!   1205
It was the force of conquest; force with force
Is well ejected when the conquered can.
But I, a private person, whom my country
As a league-breaker gave up bound, presumed
Single rebellion, and did hostile acts!   1210
I was no private, but a person raised,
With strength sufficient, and command from Heaven,
To free my country. If their servile minds

1195–1200. *But . . . proposed:* See Judges 14.

Me, their deliverer sent, would not receive,
But to their masters gave me up for nought,   1215
The unworthier they; whence to this day they serve.
I was to do my part from Heaven assigned,
And had performed it if my known offence
Had not disabled me, not all your force.
These shifts refuted, answer thy appellant,   1220
Though by his blindness maimed for high attempts,
Who now defies thee thrice to single fight,
As a petty enterprise of small enforce.

HAR. With thee, a man condemned, a slave enrolled,
Due by the law to capital punishment!   1225
To fight with thee no man of arms will deign.

SAMS. Cam'st thou for this, vain boaster, to survey me,
To descant on my strength, and give thy verdict?
Come nearer; part not hence so slight informed;
But take good heed my hand survey not thee.   1230

HAR. O Baal-zebub! can my ears unused
Hear these dishonours, and not render death?

SAMS. No man withholds thee; nothing from thy hand
Fear I incurable; bring up thy van;
My heels are fettered, but my fist is free.   1235

HAR. This insolence other kind of answer fits.

SAMS. Go, baffled coward, lest I run upon thee,
Though in these chains, bulk without spirit vast,
And with one buffet lay thy structure low,
Or swing thee in the air, then dash thee down,   1240
To the hazard of thy brains and shattered sides.

HAR. By Astaroth, ere long thou shalt lament
These braveries, in irons loaden on thee.

CHOR. His giantship is gone somewhat crestfallen,
Stalking with less unconscionable strides,   1245
And lower looks, but in a sultry chafe.

SAMS. I dread him not, nor all his giant brood,
Though fame divulge him father of five sons,
All of gigantic size, Goliath chief.

CHOR. He will directly to the lords, I fear,   1250
And with malicious counsel stir them up
Some way or other yet further to afflict thee.

1220. *shifts:* excuses. *appellant:* challenger.
1223. *enforce:* compulsion or magnitude.
1228. *descant:* comment (disparagingly).
1231. *Baal-zebub:* Beelzebub, the Philistine-Phoenician sun-god.

1234. *van:* vanguard, shock troops.
1245. *unconscionable:* ridiculous and arrogant.
1246. *chafe:* irritated frame of mind.
1248. *sons:* Milton makes Harapha the father of Goliath, and thus links the Samson and David stories.

SAMS. He must allege some cause, and offered fight
  Will not dare mention, lest a question rise
  Whether he durst accept the offer or not;   1255
  And that he durst not plain enough appeared.
  Much more affliction than already felt
  They cannot well impose, nor I sustain,
  If they intend advantage of my labours,
  The work of many hands, which earns my keeping,   1260
  With no small profit daily to my owners.
  But come what will; my deadliest foe will prove
  My speediest friend, by death to rid me hence;
  The worst that he can give to me the best.
  Yet so it may fall out, because their end   1265
  Is hate, not help to me, it may with mine
  Draw their own ruin who attempt the deed.
CHOR. O, how comely it is, and how reviving
  To the spirits of just men long oppressed,
  When God into the hands of their deliverer   1270
  Puts invincible might,
  To quell the mighty of the earth, the oppressor,
  The brute and boisterous force of violent men,
  Hardy and industrious to support
  Tyrannic power, but raging to pursue   1275
  The righteous, and all such as honour truth!
  He all their ammunition
  And feats of war defeats,
  With plain heroic magnitude of mind
  And celestial vigour armed;   1280
  Their armouries and magazines contemns,
  Renders them useless, while
  With winged expedition
  Swift as the lightning glance he executes
  His errand on the wicked, who, surprised,   1285
  Lose their defence, distracted and amazed.
    But patience is more oft the exercise
  Of saints, the trial of their fortitude,
  Making them each his own deliverer,
  And victor over all   1290
  That tyranny or fortune can inflict.
  Either of these is in thy lot,
  Samson, with might endued
  Above the sons of men; but sight bereaved
  May chance to number thee with those   1295
  Whom patience finally must crown.

1277. *He:* i.e., the deliverer (l. 1270).

This Idol's day hath been to thee no day of rest,
Labouring thy mind
More than the working day thy hands.
And yet, perhaps, more trouble is behind;   1300
For I descry this way
Some other tending; in his hand
A sceptre or quaint staff he bears,—
Comes on amain, speed in his look.
By his habit I discern him now   1305
A public officer, and now at hand.
His message will be short and voluble.

OFFICER. Ebrews, the prisoner Samson here I seek.

CHOR. His manacles remark him; there he sits.

OFF. Samson, to thee our lords thus bid me say: 1310
This day to Dagon is a solemn feast,
With sacrifices, triumph, pomp, and games;
Thy strength they know surpassing human rate,
And now some public proof thereof require
To honour this great feast, and great assembly.   1315
Rise, therefore, with all speed, and come along,
Where I will see thee heartened and fresh clad,
To appear as fits before the illustrious lords.

SAMS. Thou know'st I am an Ebrew; therefore tell them
Our law forbids at their religious rites   1320
My presence; for that cause I cannot come.

OFF. This answer, be assured, will not content them.

SAMS. Have they not sword-players, and every sort
Of gymnic artists, wrestlers, riders, runners,
Jugglers and dancers, antics, mummers, mimics,   1325
But they must pick me out, with shackles tired,
And over-laboured at their public mill,
To make them sport with blind activity?
Do they not seek occasion of new quarrels,
On my refusal, to distress me more,   1330
Or make a game of my calamities?
Return the way thou cam'st; I will not come.

OFF. Regard thyself; this will offend them highly.

SAMS. Myself! my conscience, and internal peace.
Can they think me so broken, so debased   1335
With corporal servitude, that my mind ever
Will condescend to such absurd commands?
Although their drudge, to be their fool or jester,
And, in my midst of sorrow and heart-grief,

1303. *quaint:* cunningly made.   1325. *antics:* clowns.   *mummers:*
1309. *remark:* indicate, designate.   dumb-show actors.

To show them feats, and play before their god—   1340
The worst of all indignities, yet on me
Joined with supreme contempt! I will not come.

OFF. My message was imposed on me with speed,
    Brooks no delay: is this thy resolution?

SAMS. So take it with what speed thy message needs.   1345

OFF. I am sorry what this stoutness will produce.

SAMS. Perhaps thou shalt have cause to sorrow indeed.

CHOR. Consider, Samson; matters now are strained
    Up to the highth, whether to hold or break.
    He's gone, and who knows how he may report   1350
    Thy words by adding fuel to the flame?
    Expect another message, more imperious,
    More lordly thundering than thou well wilt bear.

SAMS. Shall I abuse this consecrated gift
    Of strength, again returning with my hair   1355
    After my great transgression—so requite
    Favour renewed, and add a greater sin
    By prostituting holy things to idols,
    A Nazarite, in place abominable,
    Vaunting my strength in honour to their Dagon?   1360
    Besides how vile, contemptible, ridiculous,
    What act more execrably unclean, profane?

CHOR. Yet with this strength thou serv'st the Philistines,
    Idolatrous, uncircumcised, unclean.

SAMS. Not in their idol-worship, but by labour   1365
    Honest and lawful to deserve my food
    Of those who have me in their civil power.

CHOR. Where the heart joins not, outward acts defile not.

SAMS. Where outward force constrains, the sentence holds:
    But who constrains me to the temple of Dagon,   1370
    Not dragging? The Philistian lords command:
    Commands are no constraints. If I obey them,
    I do it freely, venturing to displease
    God for the fear of man, and man prefer,
    Set God behind; which, in his jealousy,   1375
    Shall never, unrepented, find forgiveness.
    Yet that he may dispense with me, or thee,
    Present in temples at idolatrous rites
    For some important cause, thou need'st not doubt.

CHOR. How thou wilt here come off surmounts my reach.   1380

SAMS. Be of good courage; I begin to feel

1342. *Joined:* enjoined, imposed.
1346. *stoutness:* pride.
1357. *Favour:* God's grace.
1369. *sentence:* the sentiment uttered
by the chorus in ll. 1363–1364 and
1368.
    1377. *dispense with me:* grant me
dispensation.

Some rousing motions in me, which dispose
To something extraordinary my thoughts.
I with this messenger will go along—
Nothing to do, be sure, that may dishonour   1385
Our Law, or stain my vow of Nazarite.
If there be aught of presage in the mind,
This day will be remarkable in my life
By some great act, or of my days the last.
CHOR. In time thou hast resolved: the man returns.   1390
OFF. Samson, this second message from our lords
To thee I am bid say: Art thou our slave,
Our captive, at the public mill our drudge,
And dar'st thou, at our sending and command,
Dispute thy coming? Come without delay;   1395
Or we shall find such engines to assail
And hamper thee, as thou shalt come of force,
Though thou wert firmlier fastened than a rock.
SAMS. I could be well content to try their art,
Which to no few of them would prove pernicious;   1400
Yet, knowing their advantages too many,
Because they shall not trail me through their streets
Like a wild beast, I am content to go.
Masters' commands come with a power resistless
To such as owe them absolute subjection;   1405
And for a life who will not change his purpose?
(So mutable are all the ways of men!)
Yet this be sure, in nothing to comply
Scandalous or forbidden in our Law.
OFF. I praise thy resolution. Doff these links: 1410
By this compliance thou wilt win the lords
To favour, and perhaps to set thee free.
SAMS. Brethren, farewell. Your company along
I will not wish, lest it perhaps offend them
To see me girt with friends; and how the sight   1415
Of me, as of a common enemy,
So dreaded once, may now exasperate them
I know not. Lords are lordliest in their wine;
And the well-feasted priest then soonest fired
With zeal, if aught religion seem concerned;   1420
No less the people, on their holy-days,
Impetuous, insolent, unquenchable.
Happen what may, of me expect to hear
Nothing dishonourable, impure, unworthy
Our God, our Law, my nation, or myself;   1425

The last of me or no I cannot warrant.
CHOR. Go, and the Holy One
    Of Israel be thy guide
    To what may serve his glory best, and spread his name
    Great among the Heathen round;   1430
    Send thee the Angel of thy birth, to stand
    Fast by thy side, who from thy father's field
    Rode up in flames after his message told
    Of thy conception, and be now a shield
    Of fire; that Spirit that first rushed on thee   1435
    In the camp of Dan,
    Be efficacious in thee now at need!
    For never was from Heaven imparted
    Measure of strength so great to mortal seed
    As in thy wondrous actions hath been seen.   1440
    But wherefore comes old Manoa in such haste
    With youthful steps? Much livelier than erewhile
    He seems: supposing here to find his son,
    Or of him bringing to us some glad news?
MAN. Peace with you, brethren! My inducement hither   1445
    Was not at present here to find my son,
    By order of the lords new parted hence
    To come and play before them at their feast.
    I heard all as I came; the city rings,
    And numbers thither flock: I had no will,   1450
    Lest I should see him forced to things unseemly.
    But that which moved my coming now was chiefly
    To give ye part with me what hope I have
    With good success to work his liberty.
CHOR. That hope would much rejoice us to partake   1455
    With thee. Say, reverend sire; we thirst to hear.
MAN. I have attempted, one by one, the lords,
    Either at home, or through the high street passing,
    With supplication prone and father's tears,
    To accept of ransom for my son, their prisoner.   1460
    Some much averse I found, and wondrous harsh,
    Contemptuous, proud, set on revenge and spite;
    That part most reverenced Dagon and his priests:
    Others more moderate seeming, but their aim
    Private reward, for which both God and State   1465
    They easily would set to sale: a third

1426. *The last . . . warrant:* I am
not sure whether you will ever see me
again.
   1435. *that Spirit:* See Judges 14:6.

1450. *will:* alternative.
1453. *part with me:* a share with
me in.

More generous far and civil, who confessed
They had enough revenged, having reduced
Their foe to misery beneath their fears;
The rest was magnanimity to remit,   1470
If some convenient ransom were proposed.
What noise or shout was that? It tore the sky.
CHOR. Doubtless the people shouting to behold
    Their once great dread, captive and blind before them,
    Or at some proof of strength before them shown.   1475
MAN. His ransom, if my whole inheritance
    May compass it, shall willingly be paid
    And numbered down. Much rather I shall choose
    To live the poorest in my tribe, than richest
    And he in that calamitous prison left.   1480
    No, I am fixed not to part hence without him.
    For his redemption all my patrimony,
    If need be, I am ready to forgo
    And quit. Not wanting him, I shall want nothing.
CHOR. Fathers are wont to lay up for their sons;   1485
    Thou for thy son art bent to lay out all:
    Sons wont to nurse their parents in old age;
    Thou in old age car'st how to nurse thy son,
    Made older than thy age through eye-sight lost.
MAN. It shall be my delight to tend his eyes,   1490
    And view him sitting in his house, ennobled
    With all those high exploits by him achieved,
    And on his shoulders waving down those locks
    That of a nation armed the strength contained.
    And I persuade me God hath not permitted   1495
    His strength again to grow up with his hair
    Garrisoned round about him like a camp
    Of faithful soldiery, were not his purpose
    To use him further yet in some great service—
    Not to sit idle with so great a gift   1500
    Useless, and thence ridiculous, about him.
    And, since his strength with eye-sight was not lost,
    God will restore him eye-sight to his strength.
CHOR. Thy hopes are not ill founded, nor seem vain,
    Of his delivery, and thy joy thereon   1505
    Conceived, agreeable to a father's love;
    In both which we, as next, participate.
MAN. I know your friendly minds, and . . . O, what noise!
    Mercy of Heaven! what hideous noise was that?
    Horribly loud, unlike the former shout.   1510

1507. *next:* next of kin.

CHOR. Noise call you it, or universal groan,
  As if the whole inhabitation perished?
  Blood, death, and deathful deeds, are in that noise,
  Ruin, destruction at the utmost point.
MAN. Of ruin indeed methought I heard the noise.   1515
  O! it continues; they have slain my son.
CHOR. Thy son is rather slaying them: that outcry
  From slaughter of one foe could not ascend.
MAN. Some dismal accident it needs must be.
  What shall we do—stay here, or run and see?   1520
CHOR. Best keep together here, lest, running thither,
  We unawares run into danger's mouth.
  This evil on the Philistines is fallen:
  From whom could else a general cry be heard?
  The sufferers then will scarce molest us here;   1525
  From other hands we need not much to fear.
  What if, his eye-sight (for to Israel's God
  Nothing is hard) by miracle restored,
  He now be dealing dole among his foes,
  And over heaps of slaughtered walk his way?   1530
MAN. That were a joy presumptuous to be thought.
CHOR. Yet God hath wrought things as incredible
  For his people of old; what hinders now?
MAN. He can, I know, but doubt to think he will;
  Yet hope would fain subscribe, and tempts belief.   1535
  A little stay will bring some notice hither.
CHOR. Of good or bad so great, of bad the sooner;
  For evil news rides post, while good news baits.
  And to our wish I see one hither speeding—
  An Ebrew, as I guess, and of our tribe.   1540
MESSENGER. O, whither shall I run, or which way fly
  The sight of this so horrid spectacle,
  Which erst my eyes beheld, and yet behold?
  For dire imagination still pursues me.
  But providence or instinct of nature seems,   1545
  Or reason, though disturbed and scarce consulted,
  To have guided me aright, I know not how,
  To thee first, reverend Manoa, and to these
  My countrymen, whom here I knew remaining,
  As at some distance from the place of horror,   1550
  So in the sad event too much concerned.
MAN. The accident was loud, and here before thee
  With rueful cry; yet what it was we hear not.
  No preface needs; thou seest we long to know.

1538. *baits:* moves slowly.   1543. *erst:* just recently.

MESS. It would burst forth; but I recover breath,   1555
 And sense distract, to know well what I utter.
MAN. Tell us the sum; the circumstance defer.
MESS. Gaza yet stands; but all her sons are fallen,
 All in a moment overwhelmed and fallen.
MAN. Sad! but thou know'st to Israelites not saddest   1560
 The desolation of a hostile city.
MESS. Feed on that first; there may in grief be surfeit.
MAN. Relate by whom.
MESS.   By Samson.
MAN.   That still lessens
 The sorrow, and converts it nigh to joy.
MESS. Ah! Manoa, I refrain too suddenly   1565
 To utter what will come at last too soon,
 Lest evil tidings, with too rude irruption
 Hitting thy aged ear, should pierce too deep.
MAN. Suspense in news is torture; speak them out.
MESS. Then take the worst in brief: Samson is dead.   1570
MAN. The worst indeed! O, all my hopes defeated
 To free him hence! but Death, who sets all free,
 Hath paid his ransom now and full discharge.
 What windy joy this day had I conceived,
 Hopeful of his delivery, which now proves   1575
 Abortive as the first-born bloom of spring
 Nipt with the lagging rear of winter's frost!
 Yet, ere I give the reins to grief, say first
 How died he; death to life is crown or shame.
 All by him fell, thou say'st; by whom fell he?   1580
 What glorious hand gave Samson his death's wound?
MESS. Unwounded of his enemies he fell.
MAN. Wearied with slaughter, then, or how? explain.
MESS. By his own hands.
MAN.   Self-violence! What cause
 Brought him so soon at variance with himself   1585
 Among his foes?
MESS.   Inevitable cause—
 At once both to destroy and be destroyed.
 The edifice, where all were met to see him,
 Upon their heads and on his own he pulled.
MAN. O lastly over-strong against thyself!   1590
 A dreadful way thou took'st to thy revenge.
 More than enough we know; but, while things yet
 Are in confusion, give us, if thou canst,
 Eye-witness of what first or last was done,

 1574. *windy:* empty, vain.

Relation more particular and distinct. 1595
MESS. Occasions drew me early to this city;
  And, as the gates I entered with sun-rise,
  The morning trumpets festival proclaimed
  Through each high street. Little I had dispatched,
  When all abroad was rumoured that this day 1600
  Samson should be brought forth, to show the people
  Proof of his mighty strength in feats and games.
  I sorrowed at his captive state, but minded
  Not to be absent at that spectacle.
  The building was a spacious theatre, 1605
  Half round on two main pillars vaulted high,
  With seats where all the lords, and each degree
  Of sort, might sit in order to behold;
  The other side was open, where the throng
  On banks and scaffolds under sky might stand: 1610
  I among these aloof obscurely stood.
  The feast and noon grew high, and sacrifice
  Had filled their hearts with mirth, high cheer, and wine,
  When to their sports they turned. Immediately
  Was Samson as a public servant brought, 1615
  In their state livery clad: before him pipes
  And timbrels; on each side went armed guards;
  Both horse and foot before him and behind,
  Archers and slingers, cataphracts and spears.
  At sight of him the people with a shout 1620
  Rifted the air, clamouring their god with praise,
  Who had made their dreadful enemy their thrall.
  He patient, but undaunted, where they led him,
  Came to the place; and what was set before him,
  Which without help of eye might be assayed, 1625
  To heave, pull, draw, or break, he still performed
  All with incredible, stupendous force,
  None daring to appear antagonist.
  At length, for intermission sake, they led him
  Between the pillars; he his guide requested 1630
  (For so from such as nearer stood we heard),
  As over-tired, to let him lean a while
  With both his arms on those two massy pillars,
  That to the arched roof gave main support.
  He unsuspicious led him; which when Samson 1635
  Felt in his arms, with head a while inclined,

1599. *dispatched*: accomplished.
1605–1610. *The building . . . stand*:
Milton may have been familiar with a
description of the ruins of a Philistine
palace in George Sandys' *Relation of
Foreign Travel* (1615).
1608. *sort*: rank.
1619. *cataphracts*: heavy cavalry.

And eyes fast fixed, he stood, as one who prayed,
Or some great matter in his mind revolved:
At last, with head erect, thus cried aloud:—
"Hitherto, Lords, what your commands imposed   1640
I have performed, as reason was, obeying,
Not without wonder or delight beheld;
Now, of my own accord, such other trial
I mean to show you of my strength yet greater
As with amaze shall strike all who behold."   1645
This uttered, straining all his nerves, he bowed;
As with the force of winds and waters pent
When mountains tremble, those two massy pillars
With horrible convulsion to and fro
He tugged, he shook, till down they came, and drew   1650
The whole roof after them with burst of thunder
Upon the heads of all who sat beneath,
Lords, ladies, captains, counsellors, or priests,
Their choice nobility and flower, not only
Of this, but each Philistian city round,   1655
Met from all parts to solemnise this feast.
Samson, with these immixed, inevitably
Pulled down the same destruction on himself;
The vulgar only scaped, who stood without.

CHOR. O dearly bought revenge, yet glorious!   1660
Living or dying thou hast fulfilled
The work for which thou wast foretold
To Israel, and now liest victorious
Among thy slain self-killed;
Not willingly, but tangled in the fold   1665
Of dire Necessity, whose law in death conjoined
Thee with thy slaughtered foes, in number more
Than all thy life had slain before.

SEMICHORUS. While their hearts were jocund and sublime,
Drunk with idolatry, drunk with wine   1670
And fat regorged of bulls and goats,
Chaunting their idol, and preferring
Before our living Dread, who dwells
In Silo, his bright sanctuary,
Among them he a spirit of phrenzy sent,   1675
Who hurt their minds,
And urged them on with mad desire

1659. *vulgar:* the crowd, or common people.
1665. *Not willingly:* Milton seems anxious to clear Samson from the imputation of suicide.

1669. *sublime:* uplifted.
1671. *regorged:* vomited up.
1672. *preferring:* preferring him.
1675. *he:* God.

To call in haste for their destroyer.
They, only set on sport and play,
Unweetingly importuned   1680
Their own destruction to come speedy upon them.
So fond are mortal men,
Fallen into wrath divine,
As their own ruin on themselves to invite,
Insensate left, or to sense reprobate,   1685
And with blindness internal struck.
SEMICHOR. But he, though blind of sight,
Despised, and thought extinguished quite,
With inward eyes illuminated,
His fiery virtue roused   1690
From under ashes into sudden flame,
And as an evening dragon came,
Assailant on the perched roosts
And nests in order ranged
Of tame villatic fowl, but as an eagle   1695
His cloudless thunder bolted on their heads.
So Virtue, given for lost,
Depressed and overthrown, as seemed
Like that self-begotten bird,
In the Arabian woods embost,   1700
That no second knows nor third,
And lay erewhile a holocaust,
From out her ashy womb how teemed,
Revives, reflourishes, then vigorous most
When most unactive deemed;   1705
And, though her body die, her fame survives,
A secular bird, ages of lives.
MAN. Come, come; no time for lamentation now,
Nor much more cause. Samson hath quit himself
Like Samson, and heroicly hath finished   1710
A life heroic, on his enemies
Fully revenged—hath left them years of mourning
And lamentation to the sons of Caphtor
Through all Philistian bounds; to Israel
Honour hath left and freedom, let but them   1715
Find courage to lay hold on this occasion;
To himself and father's house eternal fame;
And, which is best and happiest yet, all this

1680. *Unweetingly:* unwittingly.
1682. *fond:* foolish.
1695. *villatic:* domesticated.
1699–1707. *Like that self-begotten bird . . . lives.* Samson is here compared to the legendary phoenix, an

eaglelike bird with a five-hundred-year life span. It burned at death and then arose anew from its own ashes.
1713. *sons of Caphtor:* the Philistines.

With God not parted from him, as was feared,
But favouring and assisting to the end.   1720
Nothing is here for tears, nothing to wail
Or knock the breast; no weakness, no contempt,
Dispraise, or blame; nothing but well and fair,
And what may quiet us in a death so noble.
Let us go find the body where it lies   1725
Soaked in his enemies' blood, and from the stream
With lavers pure, and cleansing herbs, wash off
The clotted gore. I, with what speed the while
(Gaza is not in plight to say us nay),
Will send for all my kindred, all my friends,   1730
To fetch him hence, and solemnly attend,
With silent obsequy and funeral train,
Home to his father's house. There will I build him
A monument, and plant it round with shade
Of laurel ever green and branching palm,   1735
With all his trophies hung, and acts enrolled
In copious legend, or sweet lyric song.
Thither shall all the valiant youth resort,
And from his memory inflame their breasts
To matchless valour and adventures high;   1740
The virgins also shall, on feastful days,
Visit his tomb with flowers, only bewailing
His lot unfortunate in nuptial choice,
From whence captivity and loss of eyes.
CHOR. All is best, though we oft doubt   1745
What the unsearchable dispose
Of Highest Wisdom brings about,
And ever best found in the close.
Oft he seems to hide his face,
But unexpectedly returns,   1750
And to his faithful champion hath in place
Bore witness gloriously; whence Gaza mourns,
And all that band them to resist
His uncontrollable intent.
His servants he, with new acquist   1755
Of true experience from this great event,
With peace and consolation hath dismissed,
And calm of mind, all passion spent.

1746. *dispose:* disposal, ordering.   1755. *acquist:* acquisition or posses-
1748. *in the close:* at the end.   sion.
1751. *in place:* at this place.

JEAN-BAPTISTE POQUELIN MOLIÈRE
(1622–1673)

Tartuffe or The Imposter (Le Tartuffe ou L'Imposteur) *

Preface

Here is a comedy that has excited a good deal of discussion and that has been under attack for a long time; and the persons who are mocked by it have made it plain that they are more powerful in France than all whom my plays have satirized up to this time. Noblemen, ladies of fashion, cuckolds, and doctors all kindly consented to their presentation,[1] which they themselves seemed to enjoy along with everyone else; but hypocrites do not understand banter: they became angry at once, and found it strange that I was bold enough to represent their actions and to care to describe a profession shared by so many good men. This is a crime for which they cannot forgive me, and they have taken up arms against my comedy in a terrible rage. They were careful not to attack it at the point that had wounded them: they are too crafty for that and too clever to reveal their true character. In keeping with their lofty custom, they have used the cause of God to mask their private interests; and *Tartuffe*, they say, is a play that offends piety: it is filled with abominations from beginning to end, and nowhere is there a line that does not deserve to be burned. Every syllable is wicked, the very gestures are criminal, and the slightest glance, turn of the head, or step from right to left conceals mysteries that they are able to explain to my disadvantage. In vain did I submit the play to the criticism of my friends and the scrutiny of the public: all the corrections I could make, the judgment of the king and queen who saw the play,[2] the approval of great princes and ministers of state who honored it with their presence, the opinion of good men who found it worthwhile, all this did not help. They will not let go of their prey, and every day of the week they have pious zealots abusing me in public and damning me out of charity.

I would care very little about all they might say except that their devices make enemies of men whom I respect and gain the support of genuinely good men, whose faith they know and who, because of

* Molière's *Tartuffe* translated by Richard Wilbur. © 1961, 1962, 1963, by Richard Wilbur. Reprinted by permission of Harcourt, Brace & World. Inc. The preface and the three petitions are from Molière's *Tartuffe*, translated and edited by Haskell M. Block. Copyright © 1958, Appleton-Century-Crofts, Inc. Reprinted by permission of Appleton-Century-Crofts.

The first version of *Tartuffe* was performed in 1664 and the second in 1667.

The third and final version was published in March, 1669, accompanied by this preface. When a second edition of the third version was printed in June, 1669, Molière added his three petitions to Louis XIV; they follow the preface.

1. a reference to some of Molière's earlier plays, such as *Les Précieuses ridicules* and *L'Ecole des femmes*.

2. Louis XIV was married to Marie Thérèse of Austria.

the warmth of their piety, readily accept the impressions that others present to them. And it is this which forces me to defend myself. Especially to the truly devout do I wish to vindicate my play, and I beg of them with all my heart not to condemn it before seeing it, to rid themselves of preconceptions, and not aid the cause of men dishonored by their actions.

If one takes the trouble to examine my comedy in good faith, he will surely see that my intentions are innocent throughout, and tend in no way to make fun of what men revere; that I have presented the subject with all the precautions that its delicacy imposes; and that I have used all the art and skill that I could to distinguish clearly the character of the hypocrite from that of the truly devout man. For that purpose I used two whole acts to prepare the appearance of my scoundrel. Never is there a moment's doubt about his character; he is known at once from the qualities I have given him; and from one end of the play to the other, he does not say a word, he does not perform an action which does not depict to the audience the character of a wicked man, and which does not bring out in sharp relief the character of the truly good man which I oppose to it.

I know full well that by way of reply, these gentlemen try to insinuate that it is not the role of the theater to speak of these matters; but with their permission, I ask them on what do they base this fine doctrine. It is a proposition they advance as no more than a supposition, for which they offer not a shred of proof; and surely it would not be difficult to show them that comedy, for the ancients, had its origin in religion and constituted a part of its ceremonies; that our neighbors, the Spaniards, have hardly a single holiday celebration in which a comedy is not a part; and that even here in France, it owes its birth to the efforts of a religious brotherhood who still own the Hotel de Bourgogne, where the most important mystery plays of our faith were presented[3]; that you can still find comedies printed in gothic letters under the name of a learned doctor of the Sorbonne[4]; and without going so far, in our own day the religious dramas of Pierre Corneille[5] have been performed to the admiration of all France.

If the function of comedy is to correct men's vices, I do not see why any should be exempt. Such a condition in our society would be much more dangerous than the thing itself; and we have seen that the theater is admirably suited to provide correction. The most forceful lines of a serious moral statement are usually less powerful than

3. a reference to the *Confrérie de la Passion et Résurrection de Notre-Seigneur* (the Fraternity of the Passion and Resurrection of Our Saviour), founded in 1402. The Hôtel de Bourgogne was a rival theater of Molière.

4. probably Maitre Jehan Michel, a medical doctor who wrote mystery plays.

5. Pierre Corneille (1606–1684) and Racine were France's two greatest writers of classic tragedy. The two dramas Molière doubtlessly had in mind were *Polyeucte* (1643) and *Théodore, vierge et martyre* (1645).

those of satire; and nothing will reform most men better than the depiction of their faults. It is a vigorous blow to vices to expose them to public laughter. Criticism is taken lightly, but men will not tolerate satire. They are quite willing to be mean, but they never like to be ridiculed.

I have been attacked for having placed words of piety in the mouth of my impostor. Could I avoid doing so in order to represent properly the character of a hypocrite? It seemed to me sufficient to reveal the criminal motives which make him speak as he does, and I have eliminated all ceremonial phrases, which nonetheless he would not have been found using incorrectly. Yet some say that in the fourth act he sets forth a vicious morality; but is not this a morality which everyone has heard again and again? Does my comedy say anything new here? And is there any fear that ideas so thoroughly detested by everyone can make an impression on men's minds; that I make them dangerous by presenting them in the theater; that they acquire authority from the lips of a scoundrel? There is not the slightest suggestion of any of this; and one must either approve the comedy of *Tartuffe* or condemn all comedies in general.

This has indeed been done in a furious way for some time now, and never was the theater so much abused.[6] I cannot deny that there were Church Fathers who condemned comedy; but neither will it be denied me that there were some who looked on it somewhat more favorably. Thus authority, on which censure is supposed to depend, is destroyed by this disagreement; and the only conclusion that can be drawn from this difference of opinion among men enlightened by the same wisdom is that they viewed comedy in different ways, and that some considered it in its purity, while others regarded it in its corruption and confused it with all those wretched performances which have been rightly called performances of filth.

And in fact, since we should talk about things rather than words, and since most misunderstanding comes from including contrary notions in the same word, we need only to remove the veil of ambiguity and look at comedy in itself to see if it warrants condemnation. It will surely be recognized that as it is nothing more than a clever poem which corrects men's faults by means of agreeable lessons, it cannot be condemned without injustice. And if we listened to the voice of ancient times on this matter, it would tell us that its most famous philosophers have praised comedy—they who professed so austere a wisdom and who ceaselessly denounced the vices of their times. It would tell us that Aristotle spent his evenings at the theater[7] and took the trouble to reduce the art of making comedies to

6. Molière had in mind Nicole's two attacks on the theater: *Visionnaires* (1666) and *Traité de Comédie,* the Prince de Conti's *Traité de Comédie* (1666).

7. a reference to Aristotle's *Poetics* (composed between 335 and 322 B.C., the year of his death).

rules. It would tell us that some of its greatest and most honored men took pride in writing comedies themselves[8]; and that others did not disdain to recite them in public; that Greece expressed its admiration for this art by means of handsome prizes and magnificent theaters to honor it; and finally, that in Rome this same art also received extraordinary honors; I do not speak of Rome run riot under the license of the emperors, but of disciplined Rome, governed by the wisdom of the consuls, and in the age of the full vigor of Roman dignity.

I admit that there have been times when comedy became corrupt. And what do men not corrupt every day? There is nothing so innocent that men cannot turn it to crime; nothing so beneficial that its values cannot be reversed; nothing so good in itself that it cannot be put to bad uses. Medical knowledge benefits mankind and is revered as one of our most wonderful possessions; and yet there was a time when it fell into discredit, and was often used to poison men. Philosophy is a gift of Heaven; it has been given to us to bring us to the knowledge of a God by contemplating the wonders of nature; and yet we know that often it has been turned away from its function and has been used openly in support of impiety. Even the holiest of things are not immune from human corruption, and every day we see scoundrels who use and abuse piety, and wickedly make it serve the greatest of crimes. But this does not prevent one from making the necessary distinctions. We do not confuse in the same false inference the goodness of things that are corrupted with the wickedness of the corrupt. The function of an art is always distinguished from its misuse; and as medicine is not forbidden because it was banned in Rome,[9] nor philosophy because it was publicly condemned in Athens,[10] we should not suppress comedy simply because it has been condemned at certain times. This censure was justified then for reasons which no longer apply today; it was limited to what was then seen; and we should not seize on these limits, apply them more rigidly than is necessary, and include in our condemnation the innocent along with the guilty. The comedy that this censure attacked is in no way the comedy that we want to defend. We must be careful not to confuse the one with the other. There may be two persons whose morals may be completely different. They may have no resemblance to one another except in their names, and it would be a terrible injustice to want to condemn Olympia, who is a good woman, because there is also an Olympia who is lewd. Such procedures would make for great confusion everywhere. Everything under the sun

---

8. The Roman consul and general responsible for the final destruction of Carthage in 146 B.C., Scipio Africanus Minor (*ca.* 185-129 B.C.), collaborated with the writer of comedies, Terence (Publius Terentius Afer, *ca.* 195 or 185 -*ca.* 159 B.C.).

9. Pliny the Elder says that the Romans expelled their doctors at the same time that the Greeks did theirs.

10. an allusion to Socrates' condemnation to death.

would be condemned; now since this rigor is not applied to the count-less instances of abuse we see every day, the same should hold for comedy, and those plays should be approved in which instruction and virtue reign supreme.

I know there are some so delicate that they cannot tolerate a com-edy, who say that the most decent are the most dangerous, that the passions they present are all the more moving because they are vir-tuous, and that men's feelings are stirred by these presentations. I do not see what great crime it is to be affected by the sight of a generous passion; and this utter insensitivity to which they would lead us is indeed a high degree of virtue! I wonder if so great a perfection resides within the strength of human nature, and I wonder if it is not better to try to correct and moderate men's passions than to try to suppress them altogether. I grant that there are places better to visit than the theater; and if we want to condemn every single thing that does not bear directly on God and our salvation, it is right that comedy be included, and I should willingly grant that it be condemned along with everything else. But if we admit, as is in fact true, that the exercise of piety will permit interruptions, and that men need amusement, I maintain that there is none more innocent than comedy. I have dwelled too long on this matter. Let me finish with the words of a great prince on the comedy, *Tartuffe*.[11]

Eight days after it had been banned, a play called *Scaramouche the Hermit*[12] was performed before the court; and the king, on his way out, said to this great prince: "I should really like to know why the persons who make so much noise about Molière's comedy do not say a word about *Scaramouche*." To which the prince replied, "It is because the comedy of *Scaramouche* makes fun of Heaven and religion, which these gentlemen do not care about at all, but that of Molière makes fun of *them*, and that is what they cannot bear."

THE AUTHOR

First Petition[13]
(*presented to the King on the comedy of Tartuffe*)

Sire,

As the duty of comedy is to correct men by amusing them, I be-

11. One of Molière's benefactors who liked the play was the Prince de Condé; de Condé had *Tartuffe* read to him and also privately performed for him.

12. A troupe of Italian comedians had just performed the licentious farce, where a hermit dressed as a monk makes love to a married woman, announcing that *questo e per mortificar la carne* ("this is to mortify the flesh").

13. The first of the three *petitions* or *placets* to Louis XIV concerning the play. On May 12, 1664, *Tartuffe*—or at least the first three acts roughly as they now stand—was performed at Versailles. A cabal unfavorable to Molière, includ-ing the Archbishop of Paris, Hardouin de Péréfixe, Queen-Mother Anne of Austria, certain influential courtiers, and the Brotherhood or Company of the Holy Sacrament (formed in 1627 to enforce morality), arranged that the play be banned and Molière censured.

lieved that in my occupation I could do nothing better than attack the vices of my age by making them ridiculous; and as hypocrisy is undoubtedly one of the most common, most improper, and most dangerous, I thought, Sire, that I would perform a service for all good men of your kingdom if I wrote a comedy which denounced hypocrites and placed in proper view all of the contrived poses of these incredibly virtuous men, all of the concealed villainies of these counterfeit believers who would trap others with a fraudulent piety and a pretended virtue.

I have written this comedy, Sire, with all the care and caution that the delicacy of the subject demands; and so as to maintain all the more properly the admiration and respect due to truly devout men, I have delineated my character as sharply as I could; I have left no room for doubt; I have removed all that might confuse good with evil, and have used for this painting only the specific colors and essential lines that make one instantly recognize a true and brazen hypocrite.

Nevertheless, all my precautions have been to no avail. Others have taken advantage of the delicacy of your feelings on religious matters, and they have been able to deceive you on the only side of your character which lies open to deception: your respect for holy things. By underhanded means, the Tartuffes have skillfully gained Your Majesty's favor, and the models have succeeded in eliminating the copy, no matter how innocent it may have been and no matter what resemblance was found between them.

Although the suppression of this work was a serious blow for me, my misfortune was nonetheless softened by the way in which Your Majesty explained his attitude on the matter; and I believed, Sire, that Your Majesty removed any cause I had for complaint, as you were kind enough to declare that you found nothing in this comedy that you would forbid me to present in public.

Yet, despite this glorious declaration of the greatest and most enlightened king in the world, despite the approval of the Papal Legate[14] and of most of our churchmen, all of whom, at private readings of my work, agreed with the views of Your Majesty, despite all this, a book has appeared by a certain priest[15] which boldly contradicts all of these noble judgments. Your Majesty expressed himself in vain, and the Papal Legate and churchmen gave their opinion to no avail: sight unseen, my comedy is diabolical, and so is my brain; I am a devil garbed in flesh and disguised as a man,[16] a libertine, a disbeliever who deserves a punishment that will set an example. It is not

14. Cardinal Legate Chigi, nephew to Pope Alexander VII, heard a reading of *Tartuffe* at Fontainebleau on August 4, 1664.

15. Pierre Roullé, the curate of St.

Barthélémy, who wrote a scathing attack on the play and sent his book to the king.

16. Molière took some of these phrases from Roullé.

enough that fire expiate my crime in public, for that would be letting me off too easily: the generous piety of this good man will not stop there; he will not allow me to find any mercy in the sight of God; he demands that I be damned, and that will settle the matter.

This book, Sire, was presented to Your Majesty; and I am sure that you see for yourself how unpleasant it is for me to be exposed daily to the insults of these gentlemen, what harm these abuses will do my reputation if they must be tolerated, and finally, how important it is for me to clear myself of these false charges and let the public know that my comedy is nothing more than what they want it to be. I will not ask, Sire, for what I need for the sake of my reputation and the innocence of my work: enlightened kings such as you do not need to be told what is wished of them; like God, they see what we need and know better than we what they should give us. It is enough for me to place my interests in Your Majesty's hands, and I respectfully await whatever you may care to command.

(August, 1664)

Second Petition[17]

(presented to the King in his camp before the city of Lille, in Flanders)

Sire,

It is bold indeed for me to ask a favor of a great monarch in the midst of his glorious victories; but in my present situation, Sire, where will I find protection anywhere but where I seek it, and to whom can I appeal against the authority of the power that crushes me,[18] if not to the source of power and authority, the just dispenser of absolute law, the sovereign judge and master of all?

My comedy, Sire, has not enjoyed the kindnesses of Your Majesty. All to no avail, I produced it under the title of *The Hypocrite* and disguised the principal character as a man of the world; in vain I gave him a little hat, long hair, a wide collar, a sword, and lace clothing,[19] softened the action and carefully eliminated all that I thought might provide even the shadow of grounds for discontent on the part of the famous models of the portrait I wished to present; nothing did any good. The conspiracy of opposition revived even at mere conjecture of what the play would be like. They found a way

17. On August 5, 1667, *Tartuffe* was performed at the Palais-Royal. The opposition—headed by the First President of Parliament—brought in the police, and the play was stopped. Since Louis was campaigning in Flanders, friends of Molière brought the second *placet* to Lille. Louis had always been favorable toward the playwright; in August, 1665, Molière's company, the *Troupe de Mon-*sieur (nominally sponsored by Louis's brother Philippe, Duc d'Orléans) had become the *Troupe du Roi*.
18. President de Lanvignon, in charge of the Paris police.
19. There is evidence that in 1664 Tartuffe played his role dressed in a cassock, thus allying him more directly to the clergy.

of persuading those who in all other matters plainly insist that they are not to be deceived. No sooner did my comedy appear than it was struck down by the very power which should impose respect; and all that I could do to save myself from the fury of this tempest was to say that Your Majesty had given me permission to present the play and I did not think it was necessary to ask this permission of others, since only Your Majesty could have refused it.

I have no doubt, Sire, that the men whom I depict in my comedy will employ every means possible to influence Your Majesty, and will use, as they have used already, those truly good men who are all the more easily deceived because they judge of others by themselves.[20] They know how to display all of their aims in the most favorable light; yet, no matter how pious they may seem, it is surely not the interests of God which stir them; they have proven this often enough in the comedies they have allowed to be performed hundreds of times without making the least objection. Those plays attacked only piety and religion, for which they care very little; but this play attacks and makes fun of them, and that is what they cannot bear. They will never forgive me for unmasking their hypocrisy in the eyes of everyone. And I am sure that they will not neglect to tell Your Majesty that people are shocked by my comedy. But the simple truth, Sire, is that all Paris is shocked only by its ban, that the most scrupulous persons have found its presentation worthwhile, and men are astounded that individuals of such known integrity should show so great a deference to people whom everyone should abominate and who are so clearly opposed to the true piety which they profess.

I respectfully await the judgment that Your Majesty will deign to pronounce; but it is certain, Sire, that I need not think of writing comedies if the Tartuffes are triumphant, if they thereby seize the right to persecute me more than ever, and find fault with even the most innocent lines that flow from my pen.

Let your goodness, Sire, give me protection against their envenomed rage, and allow me, at your return from so glorious a campaign, to relieve Your Majesty from the fatigue of his conquests, give him innocent pleasures after such noble accomplishments, and make the monarch laugh who makes all Europe tremble!

(*August,* 1667)

20. Molière apparently did not know that de Lanvignon had been affiliated with the Company of the Holy Sacrament for the previous ten years.

Third Petition

(*presented to the King*)

Sire,

A very honest doctor[21] whose patient I have the honor to be, promises and will legally contract to make me live another thirty years if I can obtain a favor for him from Your Majesty. I told him of his promise that I do not deserve so much, and that I should be glad to help him if he will merely agree not to kill me. This favor, Sire, is a post of canon at your royal chapel of Vincennes, made vacant by death.

May I dare to ask for this favor from Your Majesty on the very day of the glorious resurrection of *Tartuffe*, brought back to life by your goodness? By this first favor I have been reconciled with the devout, and the second will reconcile me with the doctors.[22] Undoubtedly this would be too much grace for me at one time, but perhaps it would not be too much for Your Majesty, and I await your answer to my petition with respectful hope.

(*February, 1669*)

21. a physician friend, M. de Mauvillain, who helped Molière with some of the medical details of *Le Malade imaginaire*.

22. Doctors are ridiculed to varying degrees in earlier plays of Molière: *Dom Juan, L'Amour médecin,* and *Le Médecin malgré lui.*

Characters†

MME PERNELLE, *Orgon's mother*
ORGON, *Elmire's husband*
ELMIRE, *Orgon's wife*
DAMIS, *Orgon's son, Elmire's stepson*
MARIANE, *Orgon's daughter, Elmire's stepdaughter, in love with Valère*

† The name Tartuffe has been traced back to an older word associated with liar or charlatan: *truffer,* "to deceive" or "to cheat". Then there was also the Italian actor, Tartufo, physically deformed and truffle-shaped. Most of the other names are typical of this genre of court-comedy and possess rather elegant connotations of pastoral and *bergerie.*

Dorine would be a *demoiselle de compagne* and not a mere maid; that is, a female companion to Mariane of roughly the same social status. This in part accounts for the liberties she takes in conversation with Orgon, Madame Pernelle, and others. Her name is short for Théodorine.

VALERE, *in love with Mariane*

CLEANTE, *Organ's brother-in-law*

TARTUFFE, *a hypocrite*

DORINE, *Mariane's lady's-maid*

M. LOYAL, *a bailiff*

A POLICE OFFICER

FLIPOTE, *Mme Pernelle's maid*

The SCENE *throughout: Organ's house in Paris*

Act I

SCENE 1. *Madame Pernelle and Flipote, her maid, Elmire,*
Mariane, Dorine, Damis, Cleante

MADAME PERNELLE. Come, come, Flipote; it's time I left this place.

ELMIRE. I can't keep up, you walk at such a pace.

MADAME PERNELLE. Don't trouble, child; no need to show me out.
It's not your manners I'm concerned about.

ELMIRE. We merely pay you the respect we owe.   5
But, Mother, why this hurry? Must you go?

MADAME PERNELLE. I must. This house appals me. No one in it
Will pay attention for a single minute.
I offer good advice, but you won't hear it.
Children, I take my leave much vexed in spirit.   10
You all break in and chatter on and on.
It's like a madhouse with the keeper gone.

DORINE. If . . .

MADAME PERNELLE. Girl, you talk too much, and I'm afraid
You're far too saucy for a lady's-maid.
You push in everywhere and have your say.   15

DAMIS. But . . .

MADAME PERNELLE. You, boy, grow more foolish every day.
To think my grandson should be such a dunce!
I've said a hundred times, if I've said it once,
That if you keep the course on which you've started,
You'll leave your worthy father broken-hearted.   20

MARIANE. I think . . .

MADAME PERNELLE.   And you, his sister, seem so pure,
So shy, so innocent, and so demure.
But you know what they say about still waters.
I pity parents with secretive daughters.

ELMIRE. Now, Mother . . .

12. *Madhouse:* in the original, *la cour du roi Pétaud,* the Court of King Pétaud — where all are masters; a house of misrule.

MADAME PERNELLE.   And as for you, child, let me add
  That your behavior is extremely bad,   25
  And a poor example for these children, too.
  Their dear, dead mother did far better than you.
  You're much too free with money, and I'm distressed
  To see you so elaborately dressed.   30
  When it's one's husband that one aims to please,
  One has no need of costly fripperies.
CLEANTE. Oh, Madam, really . . .
MADAME PERNELLE.   You are her Brother, Sir,
  And I respect and love you; yet if I were
  My son, this lady's good and pious spouse,   35
  I wouldn't make you welcome in my house.
  You're full of worldly counsels which, I fear,
  Aren't suitable for decent folk to hear.
  I've spoken bluntly, Sir; but it behooves us
  Not to mince words when righteous fervor moves us.   40
DAMIS. Your man Tartuffe is full of holy speeches . . .
MADAME PERNELLE. And practises precisely what he preaches.
  He's a fine man, and should be listened to.
  I will not hear him mocked by fools like you.
DAMIS. Good God! Do you expect me to submit   45
  To the tyranny of that carping hypocrite?
  Must we forgo all joys and satisfactions
  Because that bigot censures all our actions?
DORINE. To hear him talk—and he talks all the time—
  There's nothing one can do that's not a crime.   50
  He rails at everything, your dear Tartuffe.
MADAME PERNELLE. Whatever he reproves deserves reproof.
  He's out to save your souls, and all of you
  Must love him, as my son would have you do.
DAMIS. Ah no, Grandmother, I could never take   55
  To such a rascal, even for my father's sake.
  That's how I feel, and I shall not dissemble.
  His every action makes me seethe and tremble,
  With helpless anger, and I have no doubt
  That he and I will shortly have it out.   60
DORINE. Surely it is a shame and a disgrace
  To see this man usurp the master's place—
  To see this beggar who, when first he came,
  Had not a shoe or shoestring to his name
  So far forget himself that he behaves   65
  As if the house were his, and we his slaves.
MADAME PERNELLE. Well, mark my words, your souls would fare
        far better

If you obeyed his precepts to the letter.

DORINE. You see him as a saint. I'm far less awed;
    In fact, I see right through him. He's a fraud.   70

MADAME PERNELLE. Nonsense!

DORINE.   His man Laurent's the same, or
        worse;
    I'd not trust either with a penny purse.

MADAME PERNELLE. I can't say what his servant's morals may be;
    His own great goodness I can guarantee.
    You all regard him with distaste and fear   75
    Because he tells you what you're loath to hear,
    Condemns your sins, points out your moral flaws,
    And humbly strives to further Heaven's cause.

DORINE. If sin is all that bothers him, why is it
    He's so upset when folk drop in to visit?   80
    Is Heaven so outraged by a social call
    That he must prophesy against us all?
    I'll tell you what I think: if you ask me,
    He's jealous of my mistress' company.

MADAME PERNELLE. Rubbish! [*To* ELMIRE] He's not alone, child,
      in complaining   85
    Of all of your promiscuous entertaining.
    Why, the whole neighborhood's upset, I know,
    By all these carriages that come and go,
    With crowds of guests parading in and out
    And noisy servants loitering about.   90
    In all of this, I'm sure there's nothing vicious;
    But why give people cause to be suspicious?

CLEANTE. They need no cause; they'll talk in any case.
    Madam, this world would be a joyless place
    If, fearing what malicious tongues might say,   95
    We locked our doors and turned our friends away.
    And even if one did so dreary a thing,
    D' you think those tongues would cease their chattering?
    One can't fight slander; it's a losing battle;
    Let us instead ignore their tittle-tattle.   100
    Let's strive to live by conscience' clear decrees,
    And let the gossips gossip as they please.

DORINE. If there is talk against us, I know the source:
    It's Daphne and her little husband, of course.
    Those who have greatest cause for guilt and shame   105
    Are quickest to besmirch a neighbor's name.
    When there's a chance for libel, they never miss it;
    When something can be made to seem illicit
    They're off at once to spread the joyous news,

Adding to fact what fantasies they choose.   110
By talking up their neighbor's indiscretions
They seek to camouflage their own transgressions,
Hoping that others' innocent affairs
Will lend a hue of innocence to theirs,
Or that their own black guilt will come to seem   115
Part of a general shady color-scheme.

MADAME PERNELLE. All that is quite irrelevant. I doubt
    That anyone's more virtuous and devout
    Than dear Orante; and I'm informed that she
    Condemns your mode of life most vehemently.   120

DORINE. Oh, yes, she's strict, devout, and has no taint
    Of worldliness; in short, she seems a saint.
    But it was time which taught her that disguise;
    She's thus because she can't be otherwise.
    So long as her attractions could enthrall,   125
    She flounced and flirted and enjoyed it all,
    But now that they're no longer what they were
    She quits a world which fast is quitting her,
    And wears a veil of virtue to conceal
    Her bankrupt beauty and her lost appeal.   130
    That's what becomes of old coquettes today:
    Distressed when all their lovers fall away,
    They see no recourse but to play the prude,
    And so confer a style on solitude.
    Thereafter, they're severe with everyone,   135
    Condemning all our actions, pardoning none,
    And claiming to be pure, austere, and zealous
    When, if the truth were known, they're merely jealous,
    And cannot bear to see another know
    The pleasures time has forced them to forgo.   140

MADAME PERNELLE. [*Initially to* ELMIRE] That sort of talk
        is what you like to hear;
    Therefore you'd have us all keep still, my dear,
    While Madam rattles on the livelong day.
    Nevertheless, I mean to have my say.
    I tell you that you're blest to have Tartuffe   145
    Dwelling, as my son's guest, beneath this roof;
    That Heaven has sent him to forestall its wrath
    By leading you, once more, to the true path;
    That all he reprehends is reprehensible,
    And that you'd better heed him, and be sensible.   150
    These visits, balls, and parties in which you revel

---

141. *That sort of talk:* in the original, chivalry found in *La Bibliothèque bleue*
a reference to a collection of novels about (*The Blue Library*), written for children.

Are nothing but inventions of the Devil.
One never hears a word that's edifying:
Nothing but chaff and foolishness and lying,
As well as vicious gossip in which one's neighbor   155
Is cut to bits with épée, foil, and saber.
People of sense are driven half-insane
At such affairs, where noise and folly reign
And reputations perish thick and fast.
As a wise preacher said on Sunday last,   160
Parties are Towers of Babylon, because
The guests all babble on with never a pause;
And then he told a story which, I think . . .
          [To CLEANTE] I heard that laugh, Sir, and I saw that wink!
Go find your silly friends and laugh some more!   165
Enough; I'm going; don't show me to the door.
I leave this household much dismayed and vexed;
I cannot say when I shall see you next.
          [Slapping FLIPOTE] Wake up, don't stand there gaping into
          space!
I'll slap some sense into that stupid face.   170
Move, move, you slut.

SCENE 2. Cléante, Dorine

CLEANTE.   I think I'll stay behind;
I want no further pieces of her mind.
How that old lady . . .

DORINE.   Oh, what wouldn't she say
If she could hear you speak of her that way!
She'd thank you for the *lady*, but I'm sure   5
She'd find the *old* a little premature.

CLEANTE. My, what a scene she made, and what a din!
And how this man Tartuffe has taken her in!

DORINE. Yes, but her son is even worse deceived;
His folly must be seen to be believed.   10
In the late troubles, he played an able part
And served his king with wise and loyal heart,
But he's quite lost his senses since he fell
Beneath Tartuffe's infatuating spell.
He calls him brother, and loves him as his life,   15
Preferring him to mother, child, or wife.
In him and him alone will he confide;
He's made him his confessor and his guide;

161. *Towers of Babylon:* i.e. Tower
of Babel. Mme. Pernelle's malapropism
is the cause of Cléante's laughter.

11. *the late troubles:* a series of political disturbances during the minority of
Louis XIV. Specifically these consisted

of the *Fronde* ("opposition") of the
Parlement (1648-1649) and the *Fronde*
of the Princes (1650-1653). Orgon is
depicted as supporting Louis XIV in
these outbreaks and their resolution.

He pets and pampers him with love more tender
Than any pretty maiden could engender, 20
Gives him the place of honor when they dine,
Delights to see him gorging like a swine,
Stuffs him with dainties till his guts distend,
And when he belches, cries "God bless you, friend!"
In short, he's mad; he worships him; he dotes; 25
His deeds he marvels at, his words, he quotes,
Thinking each act a miracle, each word
Oracular as those that Moses heard.
Tartuffe, much pleased to find so easy a victim,
Has in a hundred ways beguiled and tricked him, 30
Milked him of money, and with his permission
Established here a sort of Inquisition.
Even Laurent, his lackey, dares to give
Us arrogant advice on how to live;
He sermonizes us in thundering tones 35
And confiscates our ribbons and colognes.
Last week he tore a kerchief into pieces
Because he found it pressed in a *Life of Jesus:*
He said it was a sin to juxtapose
Unholy vanities and holy prose. 40

SCENE 3. *Elmire, Mariane, Damis, Cléante, Dorine*

ELMIRE. [*To* CLEANTE] You did well not to follow; she stood in
    the door
    And said *verbatim* all she'd said before.
    I saw my husband coming. I think I'd best
    Go upstairs now, and take a little rest.
CLEANTE. I'll wait and greet him here; then I must go. 5
    I've really only time to say hello.
DAMIS. Sound him about my sister's wedding, please.
    I think Tartuffe's against it, and that he's
    Been urging Father to withdraw his blessing.
    As you well know, I'd find that most distressing. 10
    Unless my sister and Valère can marry,
    My hopes to wed *his* sister will miscarry,
    And I'm determined . . .
DORINE.   He's coming.

SCENE 4. *Orgon, Cléante, Dorine*

ORGON.   Ah, Brother, good-day.
CLEANTE. Well, welcome back. I'm sorry I can't stay.

37. Laurent's act is more salacious
than the translation might suggest.

How was the country? Blooming, I trust, and green?
ORGON. Excuse me, Brother; just one moment.
      [*To* DORINE]   Dorine . . .
    [*To* CLEANTE] To put my mind at rest, I always learn   5
The household news the moment I return.
    [*To* DORINE] Has all been well, these two days I've been gone?
How are the family? What's been going on?
DORINE. Your wife, two days ago, had a bad fever,
    And a fierce headache which refused to leave her.   10
ORGON. Ah. And Tartuffe?
DORINE.   Tartuffe? Why, he's round and red,
    Bursting with health, and excellently fed.
ORGON. Poor fellow!
DORINE.   That night, the mistress was unable
    To take a single bite at the dinner-table.
    Her headache-pains, she said, were simply hellish.   15
ORGON. Ah. And Tartuffe?
DORINE.   He ate his meal with relish,
    And zealously devoured in her presence
    A leg of mutton and a brace of pheasants.
ORGON. Poor fellow!
DORINE.   Well, the pains continued strong,
    And so she tossed and tossed the whole night long,   20
    Now icy-cold, now burning like a flame.
    We sat beside her bed till morning came.
ORGON. Ah. And Tartuffe?
DORINE.   Why, having eaten, he rose
    And sought his room, already in a doze,
    Got into his warm bed, and snored away   25
    In perfect peace until the break of day.
ORGON. Poor fellow!
DORINE.   After much ado, we talked her
    Into dispatching someone for the doctor.
    He bled her, and the fever quickly fell.
ORGON. Ah. And Tartuffe?
DORINE.   He bore it very well.   30
    To keep his cheerfulness at any cost,
    And make up for the blood *Madame* had lost,
    He drank, at lunch, four beakers full of port.
ORGON. Poor fellow!
DORINE.   Both are doing well, in short.
    I'll go and tell *Madame* that you've expressed   35
    Keen sympathy and anxious interest.

SCENE 5. Orgon, Cléante

CLEANTE. That girl was laughing in your face, and though
    I've no wish to offend you, even so

I'm bound to say that she had some excuse.
How can you possibly be such a goose?
Are you so dazed by this man's hocus-pocus   5
That all the world, save him, is out of focus?
You've given him clothing, shelter, food, and care;
Why must you also . . .

ORGON.   Brother, stop right there.
You do not know the man of whom you speak.

CLEANTE. I grant you that. But my judgment's not so weak   10
That I can't tell, by his effect on others . . .

ORGON. Ah, when you meet him, you two will be like brothers!
There's been no loftier soul since time began.
He is a man who . . . a man who . . . an excellent man.
To keep his precepts is to be reborn,   15
And view this dunghill of a world with scorn.
Yes, thanks to him I'm a changed man indeed.
Under his tutelage my soul's been freed
From earthly loves, and every human tie:
My mother, children, brother, and wife could die,   20
And I'd not feel a single moment's pain.

CLEANTE. That's a fine sentiment, Brother; most humane.

ORGON. Oh, had you seen Tartuffe as I first knew him,
Your heart, like mine, would have surrendered to him.
He used to come into our church each day   25
And humbly kneel nearby, and start to pray.
He'd draw the eyes of everybody there
By the deep fervor of his heartfelt prayer;
He'd sigh and weep, and sometimes with a sound
Of rapture he would bend and kiss the ground;   30
And when I rose to go, he'd run before
To offer me holy-water at the door.
His serving-man, no less devout than he,
Informed me of his master's poverty;
I gave him gifts, but in his humbleness   35
He'd beg me every time to give him less.
"Oh, that's too much," he'd cry, "too much by twice!
I don't deserve it. The half, Sir, would suffice."
And when I wouldn't take it back, he'd share
Half of it with the poor, right then and there.   40
At length, Heaven prompted me to take him in
To dwell with us, and free our souls from sin.
He guides our lives, and to protect my honor
Stays by my wife, and keeps an eye upon her;
He tells me whom she sees, and all she does,   41
And seems more jealous than I ever was!
And how austere he is! Why, he can detect
A moral sin where you would least suspect;

In smallest trifles, he's extremely strict.
Last week, his conscience was severely pricked   50
Because, while praying, he had caught a flea
And killed it, so he felt, too wrathfully.

CLEANTE. Good God, man! Have you lost your common sense—
Or is this all some joke at my expense?
How can you stand there and in all sobriety . . .   55

ORGON. Brother, your language savors of impiety.
Too much free-thinking's made your faith unsteady,
And as I've warned you many times already,
'Twill get you into trouble before you're through.

CLEANTE. So I've been told before by dupes like you: 60
Being blind, you'd have all others blind as well;
The clear-eyed man you call an infidel,
And he who sees through humbug and pretense
Is charged, by you, with want of reverence.
Spare me your warnings, Brother; I have no fear   65
Of speaking out, for you and Heaven to hear,
Against affected zeal and pious knavery.
There's true and false in piety, as in bravery,
And just as those whose courage shines the most
In battle, are the least inclined to boast,   70
So those whose hearts are truly pure and lowly
Don't make a flashy show of being holy.
There's a vast difference, so it seems to me,
Between true piety and hypocrisy:
How do you fail to see it, may I ask?   75
Is not a face quite different from a mask?
Cannot sincerity and cunning art,
Realty and semblance, be told apart?
Are scarecrows just like men, and do you hold
That a false coin is just as good as gold?   80
Ah, Brother, man's a strangely fashioned creature
Who seldom is content to follow Nature,
But recklessly pursues his inclination
Beyond the narrow bounds of moderation,
And often, by transgressing Reason's laws,   85
Perverts, a lofty aim or noble cause.
A passing observation, but it applies.

ORGON. I see, dear Brother, that you're profoundly wise;
You harbor all the insight of the age.
You are our one clear mind, our only sage,   90

50-52. *Last week . . . wrathfully:* In the *Golden Legend* (*Legenda santorum*), a popular collection of the lives of the saints written in the thirteenth century, it is said of St. Marcarius the Elder (d. 390) that he dwelt naked in the desert for six months, a penance he felt appropriate for having killed a flea.

The era's oracle, its Cato too,
And all mankind are fools compared to you.
CLEANTE. Brother, I don't pretend to be a sage,
Nor have I all the wisdom of the age.
There's just one insight I would dare to claim: 95
I know that true and false are not the same;
And just as there is nothing I more revere
Than a soul whose faith is steadfast and sincere,
Nothing that I more cherish and admire
Than honest zeal and true religious fire,   100
So there is nothing that I find more base
Than specious piety's dishonest face—
Than these bold mountebanks, these histrios
Whose impious mummeries and hollow shows
Exploit our love of Heaven, and make a jest   105
Of all that men think holiest and best;
These calculating souls who offer prayers
Not to their Maker, but as public wares,
And seek to buy respect and reputation
With lifted eyes and sighs of exaltation;   110
These charlatans, I say, whose pilgrim souls
Proceed, by way of Heaven, toward earthly goals,
Who weep and pray and swindle and extort,
Who preach the monkish life, but haunt the court,
Who make their zeal the partner of their vice—   115
Such men are vengeful, sly, and cold as ice,
And when there is an enemy to defame
They cloak their spite in fair religion's name,
Their private spleen and malice being made
To seem a high and virtuous crusade,   120
Until, to mankind's reverent applause,
They crucify their foe in Heaven's cause.
Such knaves are all too common; yet, for the wise,
True piety isn't hard to recognize,
And, happily, these present times provide us   125
With bright examples to instruct and guide us.
Consider Ariston and Périandre;
Look at Oronte, Alcidamas, Clitandre;
Their virtue is acknowledged; who could doubt it?
But you won't hear them beat the drum about it.   130
They're never ostentatious, never vain,
And their religion's moderate and humane;
It's not their way to criticize and chide:

127-128. *Ariston . . . Clitandre:* vaguely Greek and Roman names derived
from the elegant literature of the day;
not names of actual persons.

They think censoriousness a mark of pride,
And therefore, letting others preach and rave,   135
They show, by deeds, how Christians should behave.
They think no evil of their fellow man,
But judge of him as kindly as they can.
They don't intrigue and wangle and conspire;
To lead a good life is their one desire;   140
The sinner wakes no rancorous hate in them;
It is the sin alone which they condemn;
Nor do they try to show a fiercer zeal
For Heaven's cause than Heaven itself could feel.
These men I honor, these men I advocate   145
As models for us all to emulate.
Your man is not their sort at all, I fear:
And, while your praise of him is quite sincere,
I think that you've been dreadfully deluded.

ORGON. Now then, dear Brother, is your speech concluded?   150

CLEANTE. Why, yes.

ORGON.   Your servant, Sir.   [*He turns to go.*]

CLEANTE.   No, Brother; wait.
There's one more matter. You agreed of late
That young Valère might have your daughter's hand.

ORGON. I did.

CLEANTE.   And set the date, I understand.

ORGON. Quite so.

CLEANTE.   You've now postponed it; is that true?   155

ORGON. No doubt.

CLEANTE.   The match no longer pleases you?

ORGON. Who knows?

CLEANTE.   D'you mean to go back on your word?

ORGON. I won't say that.

CLEANTE.   Has anything occurred
Which might entitle you to break your pledge?

ORGON. Perhaps.

CLEANTE.   Why must you hem, and haw, and hedge?
The boy asked me to sound you in this affair . . .   160

ORGON. It's been a pleasure.

CLEANTE.   But what shall I tell Valère?

ORGON. Whatever you like.

CLEANTE.   But what have you decided?
What are your plans?

ORGON.   I plan, Sir, to be guided
By Heaven's will.

CLEANTE.   Come, Brother, don't talk rot.   165
You've given Valère your word; will you keep it, or not?

ORGON. Good day.

CLEANTE. This looks like poor Valère's undoing;
I'll go and warn him that there's trouble brewing.

Act II

SCENE 1. *Orgon, Mariane*

ORGON. Mariane.

MARIANE. Yes, Father?

ORGON. A word with you; come here.

MARIANE. What are you looking for?

ORGON. [*Peering into a small closet*] Eavesdroppers, dear.
I'm making sure we shan't be overheard.
Someone in there could catch our every word.
Ah, good, we're safe. Now, Mariane, my child,   5
You're a sweet girl who's tractable and mild,
Whom I hold dear, and think most highly of.

MARIANE. I'm deeply grateful, Father, for your love.

ORGON. That's well said, Daughter; and you can repay me
If, in all things, you'll cheerfully obey me.   10

MARIANE. To please you, Sir, is what delights me best.

ORGON. Good, good. Now, what d'you think of Tartuffe, our guest?

MARIANE. I, Sir?

ORGON. Yes. Weigh your answer; think it through.

MARIANE. Oh, dear. I'll say whatever you wish me to.

ORGON. That's wisely said, my Daughter. Say of him, then,   15
That he's the very worthiest of men,
And that you're fond of him, and would rejoice
In being his wife, if that should be my choice.
Well?

MARIANE. What

ORGON. What's that?

MARIANE. I . . .

ORGON. Well?

MARIANE. Forgive me, pray.

ORGON. Did you not hear me?

MARIANE. Of *whom*, Sir, must I say   20
That I am fond of him, and would rejoice
In being his wife, if that should be your choice?

ORGON. Why, of Tartuffe.

MARIANE. But, Father, that's false, you know.
Why would you have me say what isn't so?

ORGON. Because I am resolved it shall be true.   25
That it's my wish should be enough for you.

MARIANE. You can't mean, Father . . .

ORGON.   Yes, Tartuffe shall be
   Allied by marriage to this family,
   And he's to be your husband, is that clear?
   It's a father's privilege . . .

SCENE 2. *Dorine, Orgon, Mariane*

ORGON. [*To* DORINE]   What are you doing in here?
   Is curiosity so fierce a passion
   With you, that you must eavesdrop in this fashion?
DORINE. There's lately been a rumor going about—
   Based on some hunch or chance remark, no doubt—   5
   That you mean Mariane to wed Tartuffe.
   I've laughed it off, of course, as just a spoof.
ORGON. You find it so incredible?
DORINE.   Yes, I do.
   I won't accept that story, even from you.
ORGON. Well, you'll believe it when the thing is done.   10
DORINE. Yes, yes, of course. Go on and have your fun.
ORGON. I've never been more serious in my life.
DORINE. Ha!
ORGON.   Daughter, I mean it; you're to be his wife.
DORINE. No, don't believe your father; it's all a hoax.
ORGON. See here, young woman . . .
DORINE.   Come, Sir, no more jokes;
   You can't fool us.   15
ORGON.   How dare you talk that way?
DORINE. All right, then: we believe you, sad to say.
   But how a man like you, who looks so wise
   And wears a moustache of such splendid size,
   Can be so foolish as to . . .
ORGON.   Silence, please!   20
   My girl, you take too many liberties.
   I'm master here, as you must not forget.
DORINE. Do let's discuss this calmly; don't be upset.
   You can't be serious, Sir, about this plan.
   What should that bigot want with Mariane?   25
   Praying and fasting ought to keep him busy.
   And then, in terms of wealth and rank, what is he?
   Why should a man of property like you
   Pick out a beggar son-in-law?
ORGON.   That will do.
   Speak of his poverty with reverence.   30

29. *Allied by marriage:* This assertion
is important and more than a mere device in the plot of the play. The second
placet or petition insists that Tartuffe be
costumed as a layman, and Orgon's plan
for him to marry again asserts Tartuffe's
position in the laity. In the 1664 version
of the play Tartuffe had been dressed in
a cassock suggestive of the priesthood,
and Molière was now anxious to avoid
any suggestion of this kind.

His is a pure and saintly indigence
Which far transcends all worldly pride and pelf.
He lost his fortune, as he says himself,
Because he cared for Heaven alone, and so
Was careless of his interests here below.   35
I mean to get him out of his present straits
And help him to recover his estates—
Which, in his part of the world, have no small fame.
Poor though he is, he's a gentleman just the same.

DORINE. Yes, so he tells us; and, Sir, it seems to me   40
Such pride goes very ill with piety.
A man whose spirit spurns this dungy earth
Ought not to brag of lands and noble birth;
Such worldly arrogance will hardly square
With meek devotion and the life of prayer.   45
. . . But this approach, I see, has drawn a blank;
Let's speak, then, of his person, not his rank.
Doesn't it seem to you a trifle grim
To give a girl like her to a man like him?
When two are so ill-suited, can't you see   50
What the sad consequence is bound to be?
A young girl's virtue is imperilled, Sir,
When such a marriage is imposed on her;
For if one's bridegroom isn't to one's taste,
It's hardly an inducement to be chaste,   55
And many a man with horns upon his brow
Has made his wife the thing that she is now.
It's hard to be a faithful wife, in short,
To certain husbands of a certain sort,
And he who gives his daughter to a man she hates   60
Must answer for her sins at Heaven's gates.
Think, Sir, before you play so risky a role.

ORGON. This servant-girl presumes to save my soul!

DORINE. You would do well to ponder what I've said.

ORGON. Daughter, we'll disregard this dunderhead.   65
Just trust your father's judgment. Oh, I'm aware
That I once promised you to young Valère;
But now I hear he gambles, which greatly shocks me;
What's more, I've doubts about his orthodoxy.
His visits to church, I note, are very few.   70

DORINE. Would you have him go at the same hours as you,
And kneel nearby, to be sure of being seen?

ORGON. I can dispense with such remarks, Dorine.
[*To* MARIANE] Tartuffe, however, is sure of Heaven's blessing.
And that's the only treasure worth possessing.   75
This match will bring you joys beyond all measure;
Your cup will overflow with every pleasure;

You two will interchange your faithful loves
Like two sweet cherubs, or two turtle-doves.
No harsh word shall be heard, no frown be seen,   80
And he shall make you happy as a queen.

DORINE. And she'll make him a cuckold, just wait and see.

ORGON. What language!

DORINE.   Oh, he's a man of destiny;
He's *made* for horns, and what the stars demand
Your daughter's virtue surely can't withstand.   85

ORGON. Don't interrupt me further. Why can't you learn
That certain things are none of your concern?

DORINE. It's for your own sake that I interfere.

[*She repeatedly interrupts* ORGON *just as he is turning to speak
to his daughter.*]

ORGON. Most kind of you. Now, hold your tongue, d'you hear?

DORINE. If I didn't love you . . .

ORGON.   Spare me your affection.   90

DORINE. I'll love you, Sir, in spite of your objection.

ORGON. Blast!

DORINE.   I can't bear, Sir, for your honor's sake,
To let you make this ludicrous mistake.

ORGON. You mean to go on talking?

DORINE.   If I didn't protest
This sinful marriage, my conscience couldn't rest.   95

ORGON. If you don't hold your tongue, you little shrew . . .

DORINE. What, lost your temper? A pious man like you?

ORGON. Yes! Yes! You talk and talk. I'm maddened by it.
Once and for all, I tell you to be quiet.

DORINE. Well, I'll be quiet. But I'll be thinking hard.   100

ORGON. Think all you like, but you had better guard
That saucy tongue of yours, or I'll . . .
[*Turning back to* MARIANE]   Now, child,
I've weighed this matter fully.

DORINE. [*Aside*]   It drives me wild
That I can't speak.
[ORGON *turns his head, and she is silent.*]

ORGON.   Tartuffe is no young dandy,
But, still, his person . . .

DORINE. [*Aside*]   Is as sweet as candy.   105

ORGON. Is such that, even if you shouldn't care
For his other merits . . .
[*He turns and stands facing* DORINE, *arms crossed.*]

DORINE. [*Aside*]   They'll make a lovely pair.
If I were she, no man would marry me
Against my inclination, and go scot-free.

He'd learn, before the wedding-day was over, **110**
How readily a wife can find a lover.

ORGON. [*To* DORINE] It seems you treat my orders as a joke.

DORINE. Why, what's the matter? 'Twas not to you I spoke.

ORGON. What *were* you doing?

DORINE.   Talking to myself, that's all.

ORGON. Ah! [*Aside*] One more bit of impudence and gall, **115**
And I shall give her a good slap in the face.

    [*He puts himself in position to slap her;* DORINE, *whenever*
    he glances at her, stands immobile and silent.]

Daughter, you shall accept, and with good grace,
The husband I've selected . . . Your wedding-day . . .
[*To* DORINE] Why don't you talk to yourself?

DORINE.   I've nothing to say.

ORGON. Come, just one word.

DORINE.   No thank you, Sir. I pass. **120**

ORGON. Come, speak; I'm waiting.

DORINE.   I'd not be such an ass.

ORGON. [*Turning to* MARIANE] In short, dear Daughter, I mean
    to be obeyed,
And you must bow to the sound choice I've made.

DORINE. [*Moving away*] I'd not wed such a monster, even in jest.
    [ORGON *attempts to slap her, but misses.*]

ORGON. Daughter, that maid of yours is a thorough pest; **125**
She makes me sinfully annoyed and nettled.
I can't speak further; my nerves are too unsettled.
She's so upset me by her insolent talk,
I'll calm myself by going for a walk.

SCENE 3. *Dorine, Mariane*

DORINE. [*Returning*] Well, have you lost your tongue, girl? Must
    I play
Your part, and say the lines you ought to say?
Faced with a fate so hideous and absurd,
Can you not utter one dissenting word?

MARIANE. What good would it do? A father's power is great. **5**

DORINE. Resist him now, or it will be too late.

MARIANE. But . . .

DORINE.   Tell him one cannot love at a father's whim;
That you shall marry for yourself, not him;
That since it's you who are to be the bride,
It's you, not he, who must be satisfied; **10**
And that if his Tartuffe is so sublime,
He's free to marry him at any time.

MARIANE. I've bowed so long to Father's strict control,

I couldn't oppose him now, to save my soul.   14

DORINE. Come, come, Mariane. Do listen to reason, won't you?
    Valère has asked your hand. Do you love him, or don't you?

MARIANE. Oh, how unjust of you! What can you mean
    By asking such a question, dear Dorine?
    You know the depth of my affection for him;
    I've told you a hundred times how I adore him.   20

DORINE. I don't believe in everything I hear;
    Who knows if your professions were sincere?

MARIANE. They were, Dorine, and you do me wrong to doubt it;
    Heaven knows that I've been all too frank about it.

DORINE. You love him, then?

MARIANE.   Oh, more than I can express.   25

DORINE. And he, I take it, cares for you no less?

MARIANE. I think so.

DORINE.   And you both, with equal fire,
    Burn to be married?

MARIANE.   That is our one desire.

DORINE. What of Tartuffe, then? What of your father's plan?

MARIANE. I'll kill myself, if I'm forced to wed that man.   30

DORINE. I hadn't thought of that recourse. How splendid!
    Just die, and all your troubles will be ended!
    A fine solution. Oh, it maddens me
    To hear you talk in that self-pitying key.

MARIANE. Dorine, how harsh you are! It's most unfair.   35
    You have no sympathy for my despair.

DORINE. I've none at all for people who talk drivel
    And, faced with difficulties, whine and snivel.

MARIANE. No doubt I'm timid, but it would be wrong . . .

DORINE. True love requires a heart that's firm and strong.   40

MARIANE. I'm strong in my affection for Valère,
    But coping with my father is his affair.

DORINE. But if your father's brain has grown so cracked
    Over his dear Tartuffe that he can retract
    His blessing, though your wedding-day was named,   45
    It's surely not Valère who's to be blamed.

MARIANE. If I defied my father, as you suggest,
    Would it not seem unmaidenly, at best?
    Shall I defend my love at the expense
    Of brazenness and disobedience?   50
    Shall I parade my heart's desires, and flaunt . . .

DORINE. No, I ask nothing of you. Clearly you want
    To be Madame Tartuffe, and I feel bound
    Not to oppose a wish so very sound.
    What right have I to criticize the match?   55

Indeed, my dear, the man's a brilliant catch.
Monsieur Tartuffe! Now, there's a man of weight!
Yes, yes, Monsieur Tartuffe, I'm bound to state,
Is quite a person; that's not to be denied;
'Twill be no little thing to be his bride.   60
The world already rings with his renown;
He's a great noble—in his native town;
His ears are red, he has a pink complexion,
And all in all, he'll suit you to perfection.

MARIANE. Dear God!

DORINE.   Oh, how triumphant you will feel   65
At having caught a husband so ideal!

MARIANE. Oh, do stop teasing, and use your cleverness
To get me out of this appalling mess.
Advise me, and I'll do whatever you say.

DORINE. Ah, no, a dutiful daughter must obey   70
Her father, even if he weds her to an ape.
You've a bright future; why struggle to escape?
Tartuffe will take you back where his family lives,
To a small town aswarm with relatives—
Uncles and cousins whom you'll be charmed to meet.   75
You'll be received at once by the elite,
Calling upon the bailiff's wife, no less—
Even, perhaps, upon the mayoress,
Who'll sit you down in the *best* kitchen chair.
Then, once a year, you'll dance at the village fair   80
To the drone of bagpipes—two of them, in fact—
And see a puppet-show, or an animal act.
Your husband . . .

MARIANE.   Oh, you turn my blood to ice!
Stop torturing me, and give me your advice.

DORINE. [*Threatening to go*] Your servant, Madam.

MARIANE.   Dorine, I
beg of you . . .   85

DORINE. No, you deserve it; this marriage must go through.

MARIANE. Dorine!

DORINE.   No.

MARIANE.   Not Tartuffe! You know I think him . . .

---

77. *bailiff:* a high-ranking official in the judiciary, not simply a sheriff's deputy as today.

78. *mayoress:* the wife of a tax collector (*élu*), an important official controlling imports, elected by the Estates General.

79. *the best chair:* In elegant society of Molière's day, there was a hierarchy of seats and the use of each was determined by rank. The seats descended from *fauteuils, chaises, perroquets, tabourets,* to *pliants.* Thus Mariane would get the lowest seat in the room.

82. *puppet-show . . . act:* in the original, *fagotin,* literally a monkey dressed up in a man's clothing.

DORINE. Tartuffe's your cup of tea, and you shall drink him.
MARIANE. I've always told you everything, and relied . . .
DORINE. No. You deserve to be tartuffified.   90
MARIANE. Well, since you mock me and refuse to care,
   I'll henceforth seek my solace in despair:
   Despair shall be my counsellor and friend,
   And help me bring my sorrows to an end. [*She starts to leave.*]
DORINE. There now, come back; my anger has subsided.   95
   You do deserve some pity, I've decided.
MARIANE. Dorine, if Father makes me undergo
   This dreadful martyrdom, I'll die, I know.
DORINE. Don't fret; it won't be difficult to discover
   Some plan of action . . . . But here's Valère, your lover.   100

SCENE 4. *Valère, Mariane, Dorine*

VALERE. Madam, I've just received some wondrous news
   Regarding which I'd like to hear your views.
MARIANE. What news?
VALERE.   You're marrying Tartuffe.
MARIANE.   I find
   That Father does have such a match in mind.
VALERE. Your father, Madam . . .
MARIANE.   . . . has just this minute said
   That it's Tartuffe he wishes me to wed.   5
VALERE. Can he be serious?
MARIANE.   Oh, indeed he can;
   He's clearly set his heart upon the plan.
VALERE. And what position do you propose to take,
   Madam?
MARIANE.   Why—I don't know.
VALERE.   For heaven's sake—   10
   You don't know?
MARIANE.   No.
VALERE.   Well, well!
MARIANE.   Advise me, do.
VALERE. Marry the man. That's my advice to you.
MARIANE. That's your advice?
VALERE.   Yes.
MARIANE.   Truly?
VALERE.   Oh, absolutely.
   You couldn't choose more wisely, more astutely.
MARIANE. Thanks for this counsel; I'll follow it, of course.   15
VALERE. Do, do; I'm sure 'twill cost you no remorse.
MARIANE. To give it didn't cause your heart to break.
VALERE. I gave it, Madam, only for your sake.
MARIANE. And it's for your sake that I take it, Sir.

DORINE. [*Withdrawing to the rear of the stage*]

    Let's see which fool will prove the stubborner.   **20**

VALERE. So! I am nothing to you, and it was flat

    Deception when you . . .

MARIANE.   Please, enough of that.

    You've told me plainly that I should agree

    To wed the man my father's chosen for me,

    And since you've deigned to counsel me so wisely,   **25**

    I promise, Sir, to do as you advise me.

VALERE. Ah, no, 'twas not by me that you were swayed.

    No, your decision was already made;

    Though now, to save appearances, you protest

    That you're betraying me at my behest.   **30**

MARIANE. Just as you say.

VALERE.   Quite so. And I now see

    That you were never truly in love with me.

MARIANE. Alas, you're free to think so if you choose.

VALERE. I choose to think so, and here's a bit of news:

    You've spurned my hand, but I know where to turn   **35**

    For kinder treatment, as you shall quickly learn.

MARIANE. I'm sure you do. Your noble qualities

    Inspire affection . . .

VALERE.   Forget my qualities, please.

    They don't inspire you overmuch, I find.

    But there's another lady I have in mind   **40**

    Whose sweet and generous nature will not scorn

    To compensate me for the loss I've borne.

MARIANE. I'm no great loss, and I'm sure that you'll transfer

    Your heart quite painlessly from me to her.

VALERE. I'll do my best to take it in my stride.   **45**

    The pain I feel at being cast aside

    Time and forgetfulness may put an end to.

    Or if I can't forget, I shall pretend to.

    No self-respecting person is expected

    To go on loving once he's been rejected.   **50**

MARIANE. Now, that's a fine, high-minded sentiment.

VALERE. One to which any sane man would assent.

    Would you prefer it if I pined away

    In hopeless passion till my dying day?

    Am I to yield you to a rival's arms   **55**

    And not console myself with other charms?

MARIANE. Go then; console yourself; don't hesitate.

    I wish you to; indeed, I cannot wait.

VALERE. You wish me to?

MARIANE.   Yes.

VALERE.   That's the final straw.

Madam, farewell. Your wish shall be my law.   60
    [*He starts to leave, and then returns: this repeatedly.*]
MARIANE. Splendid.
VALERE. [*Coming back again*]
                        This breach, remember, is of your
    making; It's you who've driven me to the step I'm taking.
MARIANE. Of course.
VALERE. [*Coming back again*] Remember, too, that I am merely
    Following your example.
MARIANE.   I see that clearly.
VALERE. Enough. I'll go and do your bidding, then.   65
MARIANE. Good.
VALERE. [*Coming back again*] You shall never see my face again.
MARIANE. Excellent.
VALERE. [*Walking to the door, then turning about*]
                        Yes?
MARIANE.   What?
VALERE.   What's that? What did you
    say?
MARIANE. Nothing. You're dreaming.
VALERE.   Ah. Well, I'm on my way.
    Farewell, *Madame*.   [*He moves slowly away.*]
MARIANE.   Farewell.
DORINE. [*To* MARIANE]   If you ask me,   70
    Both of you are as mad as mad can be.
    Do stop this nonsense, now. I've only let you
    Squabble so long to see where it would get you.
    Whoa there, Monsieur Valère!
        [*She goes and seizes* VALERE *by the arm; he makes a great
        show of resistance.*]
VALERE.   What's this, Dorine?
DORINE. Come here.
VALERE.   No, no, my heart's too full of spleen.
    Don't hold me back; her wish must be obeyed.   75
DORINE. Stop!
VALERE.   It's too late now; my decision's made.
DORINE. Oh, pooh!
MARIANE. [*Aside*]   He hates the sight of me, that's plain.
    I'll go, and so deliver him from pain.
DORINE. [*Leaving* VALERE, *running after* MARIANE]
    And now *you* run away! Come back.
MARIANE.   No, no.
    Nothing you say will keep me here. Let go!   80
VALERE. [*Aside*] She cannot bear my presence, I perceive.
    To spare her further torment, I shall leave.

DORINE. [*Leaving* MARIANE, *running after* VALERE]
  Again! You'll not escape, Sir; don't you try it.
  Come here, you two. Stop fussing and be quiet.
    [*She takes* VALERE *by the hand, then* MARIANE, *and draws*
    them together.]

VALERE. [*To* DORINE] What do you want of me?   85

MARIANE. [*To* DORINE] What is the point of this?

DORINE. We're going to have a little armistice.
  [*To* VALERE] Now, weren't you silly to get so overheated?

VALERE. Didn't you see how badly I was treated?

DORINE. [*To* MARIANE] Aren't you a simpleton, to have lost your head?

MARIANE. Didn't you hear the hateful things he said?   90

DORINE. [*To* VALERE] You're both great fools. Her sole desire, Valère,
  Is to be yours in marriage. To that I'll swear.
  [*To* MARIANE] He loves you only, and he wants no wife
  But you, Mariane. On that I'll stake my life.   95

MARIANE. [*To* VALERE] Then why you advised me so, I cannot see.

VALERE. [*To* MARIANE] On such a question, why ask advice of *me*?

DORINE. Oh, you're impossible. Give me your hands, you two.
  [*To* VALERE] Yours first.

VALERE. [*Giving* DORINE *his hand*] But why?

DORINE. [*To* MARIANE]   And now a hand from you.

MARIANE. [*Also giving* DORINE *her hand*]
  What are you doing?

DORINE.   There: a perfect fit.   100
  You suit each other better than you'll admit.
    [VALERE *and* MARIANE *hold hands for some time without*
    looking at each other.]

VALERE. [*Turning toward* MARIANE]
  Ah, come, don't be so haughty. Give a man
  A look of kindness, won't you, Mariane?
    [MARIANE *turns toward* VALERE *and smiles.*]

DORINE. I tell you, lovers are completely mad!

VALERE. [*To* MARIANE] Now come, confess that you were very bad
  To hurt my feelings as you did just now.   105
  I have a just complaint, you must allow.

MARIANE. *You* must allow that you were most unpleasant . . .

DORINE. Let's table that discussion for the present;
  Your father has a plan which must be stopped.   110

MARIANE. Advise us, then; what means must we adopt?

DORINE. We'll use all manner of means, and all at once.
  [*To* MARIANE] Your father's addled; he's acting like a dunce.
  Therefore you'd better humor the old fossil.
  Pretend to yield to him, be sweet and docile,   115
  And then postpone, as often as necessary,

The day on which you have agreed to marry.
You'll thus gain time, and time will turn the trick.
Sometimes, for instance, you'll be taken sick,
And that will seem good reason for delay;   120
Or some bad omen will make you change the day—
You'll dream of muddy water, or you'll pass
A dead man's hearse, or break a looking-glass.
If all else fails, no man can marry you
Unless you take his ring and say "I do."   125
But now, let's separate. If they should find
Us talking here, our plot might be divined.
[*To* VALERE]Go to your friends, and tell them what's occurred,
And have them urge her father to keep his word.
Meanwhile, we'll stir her brother into action,   130
And get Elmire, as well, to join our faction.
Good-bye.

VALERE. [*To* MARIANE] Though each of us will do his best,
   It's your true heart on which my hopes shall rest.

MARIANE. [*To* VALERE] Regardless of what Father may decide,
   None but Valère shall claim me as his bride.   135

VALERE. Oh, how those words content me! Come what will . . .

DORINE. Oh, lovers, lovers! Their tongues are never still.
   Be off, now.

VALERE. [*Turning to go, then turning back.*]
                    One last word . . .

DORINE.   No time to chat:
   You leave by this door; and you leave by that.
      [DORINE *pushes them, by the shoulders, toward opposing
      doors.*]

Act III

SCENE 1. *Damis, Dorine*

DAMIS. May lightning strike me even as I speak,
   May all men call me cowardly and weak,
   If any fear or scruple holds me back
   From settling things, at once, with that great quack!

DORINE. Now, don't give way to violent emotion.   5
   Your father's merely talked about this notion,
   And words and deeds are far from being one.
   Much that is talked about is never done.

DAMIS. No, I must stop that scoundrel's machinations;
   I'll go and tell him off; I'm out of patience.   10

130. *Elmire:* Orgon's second wife.

DORINE. Do calm down and be practical. I had rather
My mistress dealt with him—and with your father.
She has some influence with Tartuffe, I've noted.
He hangs upon her words, seems most devoted,
And may, indeed, be smitten by her charm.   15
Pray Heaven it's true! 'Twould do our cause no harm.
She sent for him, just now, to sound him out
On this affair you're so incensed about;
She'll find out where he stands, and tell him, too,
What dreadful strife and trouble will ensue   20
If he lends countenance to your father's plan.
I couldn't get in to see him, but his man
Says that he's almost finished with his prayers.
Go, now. I'll catch him when he comes downstairs.
DAMIS. I want to hear this conference, and I will.   25
DORINE. No, they must be alone.
DAMIS.   Oh, I'll keep still.
DORINE. Not you. I know your temper. You'd start a brawl,
And shout and stamp your foot and spoil it all.
Go on.
DAMIS.   I won't; I have a perfect right . . .   30
DORINE. Lord, you're a nuisance! He's coming; get out of sight.
        [DAMIS *conceals himself in a closet at the rear of the stage.*]

SCENE 2. *Tartuffe, Dorine*

TARTUFFE. [*Observing* DORINE, *and calling to his manservant off-
        stage*] Hang up my hair-shirt, put my scourge in place,
And pray, Laurent, for Heaven's perpetual grace.
I'm going to the prison now, to share
My last few coins with the poor wretches there.
DORINE. [*Aside*] Dear God, what affectation! What a fake!   5
TARTUFFE. You wished to see me?
DORINE.   Yes . . .
TARTUFFE. [*Taking a handkerchief from his pocket*]
                                    For mercy's sake,
Please take this handkerchief, before you speak.
DORINE. What?
TARTUFFE.   Cover that bosom, girl. The flesh is weak,
And unclean thoughts are difficult to control.
Such sights as that can undermine the soul.   10
DORINE. Your soul, it seems, has very poor defenses,

8. *Cover that bosom:* The Brotherhood of the Holy Sacrament (*cf.* note
13, p. 87) practiced almsgiving to prisoners and kept a careful, censorious
check on female wearing apparel if they
deemed it lascivious. Thus, Molière's
audience would have identified Tartuffe
as sympathetic—hypocritically—to the
aims of the organization.

And flesh makes quite an impact on your senses.
It's strange that you're so easily excited;
My own desires are not so soon ignited,
And if I saw you naked as a beast,   15
Not all your hide would tempt me in the least.

TARTUFFE. Girl, speak more modestly; unless you do,
I shall be forced to take my leave of you.

DORINE. Oh, no, it's I who must be on my way;
I've just one little message to convey.   20
Madame is coming down, and begs you, Sir,
To wait and have a word or two with her.

TARTUFFE. Gladly.

DORINE. [*Aside*]   *That* had a softening effect!
I think my guess about him was correct.

TARTUFFE. Will she be long?

DORINE.   No: that's her step I hear.   25
Ah, here she is, and I shall disappear.

SCENE 3. *Elmire, Tartuffe*

TARTUFFE. May Heaven, whose infinite goodness we adore,
Preserve your body and soul forevermore,
And bless your days, and answer thus the plea
Of one who is its humblest votary.

ELMIRE. I thank you for that pious wish. But please,   5
Do take a chair and let's be more at ease.
[*They sit down.*]

TARTUFFE. I trust that you are once more well and strong?

ELMIRE. Oh, yes: the fever didn't last for long.

TARTUFFE. My prayers are too unworthy, I am sure,
To have gained from Heaven this most gracious cure;   10
But lately, Madam, my every supplication
Has had for object your recuperation.

ELMIRE. You shouldn't have troubled so. I don't deserve it.

TARTUFFE. Your health is priceless, Madam, and to preserve it
I'd gladly give my own, in all sincerity.   15

ELMIRE. Sir, you outdo us all in Christian charity.
You've been most kind. I count myself your debtor.

TARTUFFE. 'Twas nothing, Madam. I long to serve you better.

ELMIRE. There's a private matter I'm anxious to discuss.
I'm glad there's no one here to hinder us.   20

TARTUFFE. I too am glad; it floods my heart with bliss
To find myself alone with you like this.
For just this chance I've prayed with all my power—
But prayed in vain, until this happy hour.

ELMIRE. This won't take long, Sir, and I hope you'll be   25

Entirely frank and unconstrained with me.
TARTUFFE. Indeed, there's nothing I had rather do
  Than bare my inmost heart and soul to you.
  First, let me say that what remarks I've made
  About the constant visits you are paid   **30**
  Were prompted not by any mean emotion,
  But rather by a pure and deep devotion,
  A fervent zeal . . .
ELMIRE.   No need for explanation.
  Your sole concern, I'm sure, was my salvation.
TARTUFFE. [*Taking* ELMIRE's *hand and pressing her fingertips*]
  Quite so; and such great fervor do I feel . . .   **35**
ELMIRE. Ooh! Please! You're pinching!
TARTUFFE.   'Twas from excess of zeal.
  I never meant to cause you pain, I swear.
  I'd rather . . .   [*He places his hand on* ELMIRE's *knee.*]
ELMIRE.   What can your hand be doing there?
TARTUFFE. Feeling your gown: what soft, fine-woven stuff!
ELMIRE. Please, I'm extremely ticklish. That's enough.   **40**
    [*She draws her chair away;* TARTUFFE *pulls his after her.*]
TARTUFFE. [*Fondling the lace collar of her gown*]
  My, my, what lovely lacework on your dress!
  The workmanship's miraculous, no less.
  I've not seen anything to equal it.
ELMIRE. Yes, quite. But let's talk business for a bit.
  They say my husband means to break his word   **45**
  And give his daughter to you, Sir. Had you heard?
TARTUFFE. He did once mention it. But I confess
  I dream of quite a different happiness.
  It's elsewhere, Madam, that my eyes discern
  The promise of that bliss for which I yearn.   **50**
ELMIRE. I see: you care for nothing here below.
TARTUFFE. Ah, well—my heart's not made of stone, you know.
ELMIRE. All your desires mount heavenward, I'm sure,
  In scorn of all that's earthly and impure.
TARTUFFE. A love of heavenly beauty does not preclude   **55**
  A proper love for earthly pulchritude;
  Our senses are quite rightly captivated
  By perfect works our Maker has created.
  Some glory clings to all that Heaven has made;
  In you, all Heaven's marvels are displayed.   **60**
  On that fair face, such beauties have been lavished,
  The eyes are dazzled and the heart is ravished;
  How could I look on you, O flawless creature,
  And not adore the Author of all Nature,

Feeling a love both passionate and pure   **65**
For you, his triumph of self-portraiture?
At first, I trembled lest that love should be
A subtle snare that Hell had laid for me;
I vowed to flee the sight of you, eschewing
A rapture that might prove my soul's undoing;   **70**
But soon, fair being, I became aware
That my deep passion could be made to square
With rectitude, and with my bounden duty,
I thereupon surrendered to your beauty.
It is, I know, presumptuous on my part   **75**
To bring you this poor offering of my heart,
And it is not my merit, Heaven knows,
But your compassion on which my hopes repose.
You are my peace, my solace, my salvation;
On you depends my bliss—or desolation;   **80**
I bide your judgment and, as you think best,
I shall be either miserable or blest.

ELMIRE. Your declaration is most gallant, Sir,
   But don't you think it's out of character?
   You'd have done better to restrain your passion   **85**
   And think before you spoke in such a fashion.
   It ill becomes a pious man like you . . .

TARTUFFE. I may be pious, but I'm human too:
   With your celestial charms before his eyes,
   A man has not the power to be wise.   **90**
   I know such words sound strangely, coming from me,
   But I'm no angel, nor was meant to be,
   And if you blame my passion, you must needs
   Reproach as well the charms on which it feeds.
   Your loveliness I had no sooner seen   **95**
   Than you became my soul's unrivalled queen;
   Before your seraph glance, divinely sweet,
   My heart's defenses crumbled in defeat,
   And nothing fasting, prayer, or tears might do
   Could stay my spirit from adoring you.   **100**
   My eyes, my sighs have told you in the past
   What now my lips make bold to say at last,
   And if, in your great goodness, you will deign
   To look upon your slave, and ease his pain,—
   If, in compassion for my soul's distress,   **105**
   You'll stoop to comfort my unworthiness,
   I'll raise to you, in thanks for that sweet manna,
   An endless hymn, an infinite hosanna.
   With me, of course, there need be no anxiety,

No fear of scandal or of notoriety. 110

These young court gallants, whom all the ladies fancy,

Are vain in speech, in action rash and chancy;

When they succeed in love, the world soon knows it;

No favor's granted them but they disclose it

And by the looseness of their tongues profane 115

The very altar where their hearts have lain.

Men of my sort, however, love discreetly,

And one may trust our reticence completely.

My keen concern for my good name insures

The absolute security of yours; 120

In short, I offer you, my dear Elmire,

Love without scandal, pleasure without fear.

ELMIRE. I've heard your well-turned speeches to the end,

And what you urge I clearly apprehend.

Aren't you afraid that I may take a notion 125

To tell my husband of your warm devotion,

And that, supposing he were duly told,

His feelings toward you might grow rather cold?

TARTUFFE. I know, dear lady, that your exceeding charity

Will lead your heart to pardon my temerity; 130

That you'll excuse my violent affection

As human weakness, human imperfection;

And that—O fairest!—you will bear in mind

That I'm but flesh and blood, and am not blind.

ELMIRE. Some women might do otherwise, perhaps, 135

But I shall be discreet about your lapse;

I'll tell my husband nothing of what's occurred

If, in return, you'll give your solemn word

To advocate as forcefully as you can

The marriage of Valère and Mariane, 140

Renouncing all desire to dispossess

Another of his rightful happiness,

And . . .

SCENE 4. *Damis, Elmire, Tartuffe*

DAMIS. [*Emerging from the closet where he has been hiding*]

        No! We'll not hush up this vile affair;

I heard it all inside that closet there,

Where Heaven, in order to confound the pride

Of this great rascal, prompted me to hide.

Ah, now I have my long-awaited chance 5

To punish his deceit and arrogance,

And give my father clear and shocking proof

Of the black character of his dear Tartuffe.

ELMIRE. Ah no, Damis; I'll be content if he
    Will study to deserve my leniency.   10
    I've promised silence—don't make me break my word;
    To make a scandal would be too absurd.
    Good wives laugh off such trifles, and forget them;
    Why should they tell their husbands, and upset them?
DAMIS. You have your reasons for taking such a course,   15
    And I have reasons, too, of equal force.
    To spare him now would be insanely wrong.
    I've swallowed my just wrath for far too long
    And watched this insolent bigot bringing strife
    And bitterness into our family life.   20
    Too long he's meddled in my father's affairs,
    Thwarting my marriage-hopes, and poor Valère's.
    It's high time that my father was undeceived,
    And now I've proof that can't be disbelieved—
    Proof that was furnished me by Heaven above.   25
    It's too good not to take advantage of.
    This is my chance, and I deserve to lose it
    If, for one moment, I hesitate to use it.
ELMIRE. Damis . . .
DAMIS.   No, I must do what I think right.
    Madam, my heart is bursting with delight,   30
    And, say whatever you will, I'll not consent
    To lose the sweet revenge on which I'm bent.
    I'll settle matters without more ado;
    And here, most opportunely, is my cue.

SCENE 5. *Orgon, Damis, Tartuffe, Elmire*

DAMIS. Father, I'm glad you've joined us. Let us advise you
    Of some fresh news which doubtless will surprise you.
    You've just now been repaid with interest
    For all your loving-kindness to our guest.
    He's proved his warm and grateful feelings toward you;   5
    It's with a pair of horns he would reward you.
    Yes, I surprised him with your wife, and heard
    His whole adulterous offer, every word.
    She, with her all too gentle disposition,
    Would not have told you of his proposition;   10
    But I shall not make terms with brazen lechery,
    And feel that not to tell you would be treachery.

34. *My cue:* In the original stage di-   lic Church, the book containing the
rections, Tartuffe now reads silently   Divine Office for each day, which those
from his breviary—in the Roman Catho-   in holy orders are required to recite.

ELMIRE. And I hold that one's husband's peace of mind
  Should not be spoilt by tattle of this kind.
  One's honor doesn't require it: to be proficient   15
  In keeping men at bay is quite sufficient.
  These are my sentiments, and I wish, Damis,
  That you had heeded me and held your peace.

SCENE 6. *Orgon, Damis, Tartuffe*

ORGON. Can it be true, this dreadful thing I hear?
TARTUFFE. Yes, Brother, I'm a wicked man, I fear:
  A wretched sinner, all depraved and twisted,
  The greatest villain that has ever existed.
  My life's one heap of crimes, which grows each minute;   5
  There's naught but foulness and corruption in it;
  And I perceive that Heaven, outraged by me,
  Has chosen this occasion to mortify me.
  Charge me with any deed you wish to name;
  I'll not defend myself, but take the blame.   10
  Believe what you are told, and drive Tartuffe
  Like some base criminal from beneath your roof;
  Yes, drive me hence, and with a parting curse:
  I shan't protest, for I deserve far worse.
ORGON. [*To* DAMIS] Ah, you deceitful boy, how dare you try   15
  To stain his purity with so foul a lie?
DAMIS. What! Are you taken in by such a bluff?
  Did you not hear . . . ?
ORGON.   Enough, you rogue, enough!
TARTUFFE. Ah, Brother, let him speak: you're being unjust.
  Believe his story; the boy deserves your trust.   20
  Why, after all, should you have faith in me?
  How can you know what I might do, or be?
  Is it on my good actions that you base
  Your favor? Do you trust my pious face?
  Ah, no, don't be deceived by hollow shows;   25
  I'm far, alas, from being what men suppose;
  Though the world takes me for a man of worth,
  I'm truly the most worthless man on earth.
      [*To* DAMIS]
  Yes, my dear son, speak out now: call me the chief
  Of sinners, a wretch, a murderer, a thief;   30
  Load me with all the names men most abhor;
  I'll not complain; I've earned them all, and more;
  I'll kneel here while you pour them on my head
  As a just punishment for the life I've led.

ORGON. [*To* TARTUFFE] This is too much, dear Brother.
  [*To* DAMIS]   Have you no heart?

DAMIS. Are you so hoodwinked by this rascal's art . . . ?   35

ORGON. Be still, you monster.
  [*To* TARTUFFE]   Brother, I pray you, rise.
  [*To* DAMIS] Villain!

DAMIS.   But . . .

ORGON.   Silence!

DAMIS.   Can't you realize . . . ?

ORGON. Just one word more, and I'll tear you limb from limb.

TARTUFFE. In God's name, Brother, don't be harsh with him.   40
  I'd rather far be tortured at the stake
  Than see him bear one scratch for my poor sake.

ORGON. [*To* DAMIS] Ingrate!

TARTUFFE   If I must beg you, on bended knee,
  To pardon him . . .

ORGON. [*Falling to his knees, addressing Tartuffe*]
                     Such goodness cannot be!
  [*To* DAMIS] *Now, there's* true charity!

DAMIS.   What, you . . . ?

ORGON. Villain, be still!   45
  I know your motives; I know you wish him ill:
  Yes, all of you—wife, children, servants, all—
  Conspire against him and desire his fall,
  Employing every shameful trick you can
  To alienate me from this saintly man.   50
  Ah, but the more you seek to drive him away,
  The more I'll do to keep him. Without delay,
  I'll spite this household and confound its pride
  By giving him my daughter as his bride.

DAMIS. You're going to force her to accept his hand?   55

ORGON. Yes, and this very night, d'you understand?
  I shall defy you all, and make it clear
  That I'm the one who gives the orders here.
  Come, wretch, kneel down and clasp his blessed feet,
  And ask his pardon for your black deceit.   60

DAMIS. I ask that swindler's pardon? Why, I'd rather . . .

ORGON. So! You insult him, and defy your father!
  A stick! A stick! [*To* TARTUFFE] No, no—release me, do.
  [*To* DAMIS.] Out of my house this minute! Be off with you,
  And never dare set foot in it again.   65

DAMIS. Well, I shall go, but . . .

ORGON.   Well, go quickly, then.
  I disinherit you; an empty purse
  Is all you'll get from me—except my curse!

SCENE 7. *Orgon, Tartuffe*

ORGON. How he blasphemed your goodness! What a son!

TARTUFFE. Forgive him, Lord, as I've already done.
  [*To* ORGON] You can't know how it hurts when someone tries
  To blacken me in my dear Brother's eyes.

ORGON. Ahh!

TARTUFFE.   The mere thought of such ingratitude   5
  Plunges my soul into so dark a mood . . .
  Such horror grips my heart . . . I gasp for breath,
  And cannot speak, and feel myself near death.

ORGON. [*He runs, in tears, to the door through which he has just
    driven his son.*]
  You blackguard! Why did I spare you? Why did I not
  Break you in little pieces on the spot?   10
  Compose yourself, and don't be hurt, dear friend.

TARTUFFE. These scenes, these dreadful quarrels, have got to end.
  I've much upset your household, and I perceive
  That the best thing will be for me to leave.

ORGON. What are you saying!

TARTUFFE.   They're all against me here;
  They'd have you think me false and insincere.   15

ORGON. Ah, what of that? Have I ceased believing in you?

TARTUFFE. Their adverse talk will certainly continue,
  And charges which you now repudiate
  You may find credible at a later date.   20

ORGON. No, Brother, never.

TARTUFFE.   Brother, a wife can sway
  Her husband's mind in many a subtle way.

ORGON. No, no.

TARTUFFE.   To leave at once is the solution;
  Thus only can I end their persecution.

ORGON. No, no, I'll not allow it; you shall remain.   25

TARTUFFE. Ah, well; 'twill mean much martyrdom and pain,
  But if you wish it . . .

ORGON.   Ah!

TARTUFFE.   Enough; so be it.
  But one thing must be settled, as I see it.
  For your dear honor, and for our friendship's sake,
  There's one precaution I feel bound to take.   30
  I shall avoid your wife, and keep away . . .

ORGON. No, you shall not, whatever they may say.
  It pleases me to vex them, and for spite
  I'd have them see you with her day and night.
  What's more, I'm going to drive them to despair   35

By making you my only son and heir;
This very day, I'll give to you alone
Clear deed and title to everything I own.
A dear, good friend and son-in-law-to-be
Is more than wife, or child, or kin to me.   40
Will you accept my offer, dearest son?
TARTUFFE. In all things, let the will of Heaven be done.
ORGON. Poor fellow! Come, we'll go draw up the deed.
Then let them burst with disappointed greed!

Act IV

SCENE 1. *Cleante, Tartuffe*

CLEANTE. Yes, all the town's discussing it, and truly,
Their comments do not flatter you unduly.
I'm glad we've met, Sir, and I'll give my view
Of this sad matter in a word or two.
As for who's guilty, that I shan't discuss;   5
Let's say it was Damis who caused the fuss;
Assuming, then, that you have been ill-used
By young Damis, and groundlessly accused,
Ought not a Christian to forgive, and ought
He not to stifle every vengeful thought?   10
Should you stand by and watch a father make
His only son an exile for your sake?
Again I tell you frankly, be advised:
The whole town, high and low, is scandalized;
This quarrel must be mended, and my advice is   15
Not to push matters to a further crisis.
No, sacrifice your wrath to God above,
And help Damis regain his father's love.
TARTUFFE. Alas, for my part I should take great joy
In doing so. I've nothing against the boy.   20
I pardon all, I harbor no resentment;
To serve him would afford me much contentment.
But Heaven's interest will not have it so:
If he comes back, then I shall have to go.
After his conduct—so extreme, so vicious—   25
Our further intercourse would look suspicious.
God knows what people would think! Why, they'd describe
My goodness to him as a sort of bribe;
They'd say that out of guilt I made pretense
Of loving-kindness and benevolence—   30
That, fearing my accuser's tongue, I strove

To buy his silence with a show of love.

CLEANTE. Your reasoning is badly warped and stretched,
    And these excuses, Sir, are most far-fetched.
    Why put yourself in charge of Heaven's cause?   35
    Does Heaven need our help to enforce its laws?
    Leave vengeance to the Lord Sir; while we live,
    Our duty's not to punish, but forgive;
    And what the Lord commands, we should obey
    Without regard to what the world may say.   40
    What! Shall the fear of being misunderstood
    Prevent our doing what is right and good?
    No, no: let's simply do what Heaven ordains,
    And let no other thoughts perplex our brains.

TARTUFFE. Again, Sir, let me say that I've forgiven   45
    Damis, and thus obeyed the laws of Heaven;
    But I am not commanded by the Bible
    To live with one who smears my name with libel.

CLEANTE. Were you commanded, Sir, to indulge the whim
    Of poor Orgon, and to encourage him   50
    In suddenly transferring to your name
    A large estate to which you have no claim?

TARTUFFE. 'Twould never occur to those who know me best
    To think I acted from self-interest.
    The treasures of this world I quite despise;   55
    Their specious glitter does not charm my eyes;
    And if I have resigned myself to taking
    The gift which my dear Brother insists on making,
    I do so only, as he well understands,
    Lest so much wealth fall into wicked hands,   60
    Lest those to whom it might descend in time
    Turn it to purposes of sin and crime,
    And not, as I shall do, make use of it
    For Heaven's glory and mankind's benefit.

CLEANTE. Forget these trumped-up fears. Your argument   65
    Is one the rightful heir might well resent;
    It *is* a moral burden to inherit
    Such wealth, but give Damis a chance to bear it.
    And would it not be worse to be accused
    Of swindling, than to see that wealth misused?   70
    I'm shocked that you allowed Orgon to broach
    This matter, and that you feel no self-reproach;
    Does true religion teach that lawful heirs
    May freely be deprived of what is theirs?
    And if the Lord has told you in your heart   75
    That you and young Damis must dwell apart,

Would it not be the decent thing to beat
A generous and honorable retreat,
Rather than let the son of the house be sent,
For your convenience, into banishment?   80
Sir, if you wish to prove the honesty
Of your intentions . . .

TARTUFFE.   Sir, it is a half past three.
  I've certain pious duties to attend to,
  And hope my prompt departure won't offend you.
CLEANTE. [*Alone*] Damn.

SCENE 2. *Elmire, Mariane, Cleante, Dorine*

DORINE. Stay, Sir, and help Mariane, for Heaven's sake!
  She's suffering so, I fear her heart will break.
  Her father's plan to marry her off tonight
  Has put the poor child in a desperate plight.
  I hear him coming. Let's stand together, now,   5
  And see if we can't change his mind, somehow,
  About this match we all deplore and fear.

SCENE 3. *Orgon, Elmire, Mariane, Cleante, Dorine*

ORGON. Hah! Glad to find you all assembled here.
  [*To* MARIANE] This contract, child, contains your happiness,
  And what it says I think your heart can guess.
MARIANE. [*Falling to her knees*]
  Sir, by that Heaven which sees me here distressed,
  And by whatever else can move your breast,   5
  Do not employ a father's power, I pray you,
  To crush my heart and force it to obey you,
  Nor by your harsh commands oppress me so
  That I'll begrudge the duty which I owe—
  And do not so embitter and enslave me   10
  That I shall hate the very life you gave me.
  If my sweet hopes must perish, if you refuse
  To give me to the one I've dared to choose,
  Spare me at least—I beg you, I implore—
  The pain of wedding one whom I abhor;   15
  And do not, by a heartless use of force,
  Drive me to contemplate some desperate course.
ORGON. [*Feeling himself touched by her*]
  Be firm, my soul. No human weakness, now.
MARIANE. I don't resent your love for him. Allow
  Your heart free rein, Sir; give him your property,   20
  And if that's not enough, take mine from me;
  He's welcome to my money; take it, do,

But don't, I pray, include my person too.
Spare me, I beg you; and let me end the tale
Of my sad days behind a convent veil.   25
ORGON. A convent! Hah! When crossed in their amours,
All lovesick girls have the same thought as yours.
Get up! The more you loathe the man, and dread him,
The more ennobling it will be to wed him.
Marry Tartuffe, and mortify your flesh!   30
Enough; don't start that whimpering afresh.
DORINE. But why . . . ?
ORGON.   Be still, there. Speak when you're spoken to.
Not one more bit of impudence out of you.
CLEANTE. If I may offer a word of counsel here . . .
ORGON. Brother, in counselling you have no peer;   35
All your advice is forceful, sound, and clever;
I don't propose to follow it, however.
ELMIRE. [*To* ORGON] I am amazed, and don't know what to say;
Your blindness simply takes my breath away.
You are indeed bewitched, to take no warning   40
From our account of what occurred this morning.
ORGON. Madam, I know a few plain facts, and one
Is that you're partial to my rascal son;
Hence, when he sought to make Tartuffe the victim
Of a base lie, you dared not contradict him.   45
Ah, but you underplayed your part, my pet;
You should have looked more angry, more upset.
ELMIRE. When men make overtures, must we reply
With righteous anger and a battle-cry?
Must we turn back their amorous advances   50
With sharp reproaches and with fiery glances?
Myself, I find such offers merely amusing,
And make no scenes and fusses in refusing;
My taste is for good-natured rectitude,
And I dislike the savage sort of prude   55
Who guards her virtue with her teeth and claws,
And tears men's eyes out for the slightest cause:
The Lord preserve me from such honor as that,
Which bites and scratches like an alley-cat!
I've found that a polite and cool rebuff   60
Discourages a lover quite enough.
ORGON. I know the facts, and I shall not be shaken.
ELMIRE. I marvel at your power to be mistaken.
Would it, I wonder, carry weight with you
If I could *show* you that our tale was true?   65
ORGON. Show me?

ELMIRE.   Yes.

ORGON.   Rot.

ELMIRE.   Come, what if I found a way
   To make you see the facts as plain as day?

ORGON. Nonsense.

ELMIRE.   Do answer me; don't be absurd.
   I'm not now asking you to trust our word.
   Suppose that from some hiding-place in here   70
   You learned the whole sad truth by eye and ear—
   What would you say of your good friend, after that?

ORGON. Why, I'd say . . . nothing, by Jehoshaphat!
   It can't be true.

ELMIRE.   You've been too long deceived,
   And I'm quite tired of being disbelieved.   75
   Come now: let's put my statements to the test,
   And you shall see the truth made manifest.

ORGON. I'll take that challenge. Now do your uttermost.
   We'll see how you make good your empty boast.

ELMIRE. [*To* DORINE] Send him to me.

DORINE.   He's crafty; it may be hard
   To catch the cunning scoundrel off his guard.   80

ELMIRE. No, amorous men are gullible. Their conceit
   So blinds them that they're never hard to cheat.
   Have him come down. [*To* CLEANTE *&* MARIANE] Please leave us,
      for a bit.

SCENE 4. *Elmire, Orgon*

ELMIRE. Pull up this table, and get under it.

ORGON. What?

ELMIRE.   It's essential that you be well-hidden.

ORGON. Why there?

ELMIRE.   Oh, Heavens! Just do as you are bidden.
   I have my plans; we'll soon see how they fare.
   Under the table, now; and once you're there,   5
   Take care that you are neither seen nor heard.

ORGON. Well, I'll indulge you, since I gave my word
   To see you through this infantile charade.

ELMIRE. Once it is over, you'll be glad we played.
      [*To her husband, who is now under the table*]
   I'm going to act quite strangely, now, and you   10
   Must not be shocked at anything I do.
   Whatever I may say, you must excuse
   As part of that deceit I'm forced to use.
   I shall employ sweet speeches in the task
   Of making that impostor drop his mask;   15

I'll give encouragement to his bold desires,
And furnish fuel to his amorous fires.
Since it's for your sake, and for his destruction,
That I shall seem to yield to his seduction,
I'll gladly stop whenever you decide   20
That all your doubts are fully satisfied.
I'll count on you, as soon as you have seen
What sort of man he is, to intervene,
And not expose me to his odious lust
One moment longer than you feel you must.   25
Remember: you're to save me from my plight
Whenever . . . He's coming! Hush! Keep out of sight!

SCENE 5. *Tartuffe, Elmire, Orgon*

TARTUFFE. You wish to have a word with me, I'm told.
ELMIRE. Yes, I've a little secret to unfold.
 Before I speak, however, it would be wise
 To close that door, and look about for spies.
  [TARTUFFE *goes to the door, closes it, and returns.*]
 The very last thing that must happen now   5
 Is a repetition of this morning's row.
 I've never been so badly caught off guard.
 Oh, how I feared for you! You saw how hard
 I tried to make that troublesome Damis
 Control his dreadful temper, and hold his peace.   10
 In my confusion, I didn't have the sense
 Simply to contradict his evidence;
 But as it happened, that was for the best,
 And all has worked out in our interest.
 This storm has only bettered your position;   15
 My husband doesn't have the least suspicion,
 And now, in mockery of those who do,
 He bids me be continually with you.
 And that is why, quite fearless of reproof,
 I now can be alone with my Tartuffe,   20
 And why my heart—perhaps too quick to yield—
 Feels free to let its passion be revealed.
TARTUFFE. Madam, your words confuse me. Not long ago,
 You spoke in quite a different style, you know.
ELMIRE. Ah, Sir, if that refusal made you smart,   25
 It's little that you know of woman's heart,
 Or what that heart is trying to convey
 When it resists in such a feeble way!
 Always, at first, our modesty prevents
 The frank avowal of tender sentiments: 30

However high the passion which inflames us,
Still, to confess its power somehow shames us.
Thus we reluct, at first, yet in a tone
Which tells you that our heart is overthrown,
That what our lips deny, our pulse confesses, 35
And that, in time, all noes will turn to yesses.
I fear my words are all too frank and free,
And a poor proof of woman's modesty;
But since I'm started, tell me, if you will—
Would I have tried to make Damis be still, 40
Would I have listened, calm and unoffended,
Until your lengthy offer of love was ended,
And been so very mild in my reaction,
Had your sweet words not given me satisfaction?
And when I tried to force you to undo 45
The marriage-plans my husband has in view,
What did my urgent pleading signify
If not that I admired you, and that I
Deplored the thought that someone else might own
Part of a heart I wished for mine alone? 50
TARTUFFE. Madam, no happiness is so complete
As when, from lips we love, come words so sweet;
Their nectar floods my every sense, and drains
In honeyed rivulets through all my veins.
To please you is my joy, my only goal; 55
Your love is the restorer of my soul;
And yet I must beg leave, now, to confess
Some lingering doubts as to my happiness.
Might this not be a trick? Might not the catch
Be that you wish me to break off the match 60
With Mariane, and so have feigned to love me?
I shan't quite trust your fond opinion of me
Until the feelings you've expressed so sweetly
Are demonstrated somewhat more concretely,
And you have shown, by certain kind concessions, 65
That I may put my faith in your professions.
ELMIRE. [*She coughs, to warn her husband.*] Why be in such a
    hurry? Must my heart
Exhaust its bounty at the very start?
To make that sweet admission cost me dear,
But you'll not be content, it would appear, 70
Unless my store of favors is disbursed
To the last farthing, and at the very first.
TARTUFFE. The less we merit, the less we dare to hope,
And with our doubts, mere words can never cope.

We trust no promised bliss till we receive it;   75
Not till a joy is ours can we believe it.
I, who so little merit your esteem,
Can't credit this fulfillment of my dream,
And shan't believe it, Madam, until I savor
Some palpable assurance of your favor.   80
ELMIRE. My, how tyrannical your love can be,
And how it flusters and perplexes me!
How furiously you take one's heart in hand,
And make your every wish a fierce command!
Come, must you hound and harry me to death?   85
Will you not give me time to catch my breath?
Can it be right to press me with such force,
Give me no quarter, show me no remorse,
And take advantage, by your stern insistence,
Of the fond feelings which weaken my resistance?   90
TARTUFFE. Well, if you look with favor upon my love,
Why, then, begrudge me some clear proof thereof?
ELMIRE. But how can I consent without offense
To Heaven, toward which you feel such reverence?
TARTUFFE. If Heaven is all that holds you back, don't worry.   95
I can remove that hindrance in a hurry.
Nothing of that sort need obstruct our path.
ELMIRE. Must one not be afraid of Heaven's wrath?
TARTUFFE. Madam, forget such fears, and be my pupil,
And I shall teach you how to conquer scruple.   100
Some joys, it's true, are wrong in Heaven's eyes;
Yet Heaven is not averse to compromise;
There is a science, lately formulated,
Whereby one's conscience may be liberated,
And any wrongful act you care to mention   105
May be redeemed by purity of intention.
I'll teach you, Madam, the secrets of that science;
Meanwhile, just place on me your full reliance.
Assuage my keen desires, and feel no dread:
The sin, if any, shall be on my head.   110
    [ELMIRE *coughs, this time more loudly.*]
You've a bad cough.
ELMIRE.   Yes, yes. It's bad indeed.
TARTUFFE. [*Producing a little paper bag*]
A bit of licorice may be what you need.
ELMIRE. No, I've a stubborn cold, it seems. I'm sure it
Will take much more than licorice to cure it.

---

104. *Whereby . . . liberated:* Molière appended his own footnote to this line: "It
is a scoundrel who speaks."

TARTUFFE. How aggravating.

ELMIRE.   Oh, more than I can say.   115

TARTUFFE. If you're still troubled, think of things this way:
   No one shall know our joys, save us alone,
   And there's no evil till the act is known;
   It's scandal, Madam, which makes it an offense,
   And it's no sin to sin in confidence.   120

ELMIRE. [*Having coughed once more*]
   Well, clearly I must do as you require,
   And yield to your importunate desire.
   It is apparent, now, that nothing less
   Will satisfy you, and so I acquiesce.
   To go so far is much against my will;   125
   I'm vexed that it should come to this; but still,
   Since you are so determined on it, since you
   Will not allow mere language to convince you,
   And since you ask for concrete evidence, I
   See nothing for it, now, but to comply.   130
   If this is sinful, if I'm wrong to do it,
   So much the worse for him who drove me to it.
   The fault can surely not be charged to me.

TARTUFFE. Madam, the fault is mine, if fault there be,
   And . . .

ELMIRE.   Open the door a little, and peek out;   135
   I wouldn't want my husband poking about.

TARTUFFE. Why worry about the man? Each day he grows
   More gullible; one can lead him by the nose.
   To find us here would fill him with delight,
   And if he saw the worst, he'd doubt his sight.   140

ELMIRE. Nevertheless, do step out for a minute
   Into the hall, and see that no one's in it.

SCENE 6. *Orgon, Elmire*

ORGON. [*Coming out from under the table*]
   That man's a perfect monster, I must admit!
   I'm simply stunned. I can't get over it.

ELMIRE. What, coming out so soon? How premature!
   Get back in hiding, and wait until you're sure.
   Stay till the end, and be convinced completely;   5
   We mustn't stop till things are proved concretely.

ORGON. Hell never harbored anything so vicious!

ELMIRE. Tut, don't be hasty. Try to be judicious.
   Wait, and be certain that there's no mistake.
   No jumping to conclusions, for Heaven's sake!   10
      [*She places* ORGON *behind her, as* TARTUFFE *re-enters.*]

SCENE 7. *Tartuffe, Elmire, Orgon*

TARTUFFE. [*Not seeing* ORGON]
  Madam, all things have worked out to perfection;
  I've given the neighboring rooms a full inspection;
  No one's about; and now I may at last . . .
ORGON. [*Intercepting him*] Hold on, my passionate fellow, **not so**
      fast!
  I should advise a little more restraint.   **5**
  Well, so you thought you'd fool me, my dear saint!
  How soon you wearied of the saintly life—
  Wedding my daughter, and coveting my wife!
  I've long suspected you, and had a feeling
  That soon I'd catch you at your double-dealing.   **10**
  Just now, you've given me evidence galore;
  It's quite enough; I have no wish for more.
ELMIRE. [*To* TARTUFFE] I'm sorry to have treated you so slyly,
  But circumstances forced me to be wily.
TARTUFFE. Brother, you can't think . . .
ORGON.   No more talk from you;
  Just leave this household, without more ado.   **15**
TARTUFFE. What I intended . . .
ORGON.   That seems fairly clear.
  Spare me your falsehoods and get out of here.
TARTUFFE. No, I'm the master, and you're the one to go!
  This house belongs to me, I'll have you know,   **20**
  And I shall show you that you can't hurt *me*
  By this contemptible conspiracy,
  That those who cross me know not what they **do,**
  And that I've means to expose and punish you,
  Avenge offended Heaven, and make you grieve   **25**
  That ever you dared order me to leave.

SCENE 8. *Elmire, Orgon*

ELMIRE. What was the point of all that angry chatter?
ORGON. Dear God, I'm worried. This is no laughing matter.
ELMIRE. How so?
ORGON.   I fear I understood his drift.
  I'm much disturbed about that deed of gift.
ELMIRE. You gave him . . . ?
ORGON.   Yes, it's all been drawn and signed.
  But one thing more is weighing on my mind.   **6**
ELMIRE. What's that?
ORGON.   I'll tell you; but first let's see if there's
  A certain strong-box in his room upstairs.

Act V

SCENE 1. *Orgon, Cleante*

CLEANTE. Where are you going so fast?

ORGON. God knows!

CLEANTE. Then wait;
Let's have a conference, and deliberate
On how this situation's to be met.

ORGON. That strong-box has me utterly upset;
This is the worst of many, many shocks.   5

CLEANTE. Is there some fearful mystery in that box?

ORGON. My poor friend Argas brought that box to me
With his own hands, in utmost secrecy;
'Twas on the very morning of his flight.
It's full of papers which, if they came to light,   10
Would ruin him—or such is my impression.

CLEANTE. Then why did you let it out of your possession?

ORGON. Those papers vexed my conscience, and it seemed best
To ask the counsel of my pious guest.
The cunning scoundrel got me to agree   15
To leave the strong-box in his custody,
So that, in case of an investigation,
I could employ a slight equivocation
And swear I didn't have it, and thereby,
At no expense to conscience, tell a lie.   20

CLEANTE. It looks to me as if you're out on a limb.
Trusting him with that box, and offering him
That deed of gift, were actions of a kind
Which scarcely indicate a prudent mind.
With two such weapons, he has the upper hand,   25
And since you're vulnerable, as matters stand,
You erred once more in bringing him to bay.
You should have acted in some subtler way.

ORGON. Just think of it: behind that fervent face,
A heart so wicked, and a soul so base!   30
I took him in, a hungry beggar, and then . . .
Enough, by God! I'm through with pious men:
Henceforth I'll hate the whole false brotherhood,
And persecute them worse than Satan could.

CLEANTE. Ah, there you go—extravagant as ever!   35
Why can you not be rational? You never
Manage to take the middle course, it seems,
But jump, instead, between absurd extremes.
You've recognized your recent grave mistake

In falling victim to a pious fake;   40
Now, to correct that error, must you embrace
An even greater error in its place,
And judge our worthy neighbors as a whole
By what you've learned of one corrupted soul?
Come, just because one rascal made you swallow   45
A show of zeal which turned out to be hollow,
Shall you conclude that all men are deceivers,
And that, today, there are no true believers?
Let atheists make that foolish inference;
Learn to distinguish virtue from pretense,   50
Be cautious in bestowing admiration,
And cultivate a sober moderation.
Don't humor fraud, but also don't asperse
True piety; the latter fault is worse,
And it is best to err, if err one must,   55
As you have done, upon the side of trust.

SCENE 2. *Damis, Orgon, Cléante*

DAMIS. Father, I hear that scoundrel's uttered threats
    Against you; that he pridefully forgets
    How, in his need, he was befriended by you,
    And means to use your gifts to crucify you.
ORGON. It's true, my boy. I'm too distressed for tears.   5
DAMIS. Leave it to me, Sir; let me trim his ears.
    Faced with such insolence, we must not waver.
    I shall rejoice in doing you the favor
    Of cutting short his life, and your distress.
CLEANTE. What a display of young hotheadedness!   10
    Do learn to moderate your fits of rage.
    In this just kingdom, this enlightened age,
    One does not settle things by violence.

SCENE 3. *Madame Pernelle, Mariane, Elmire, Dorine, Damis, Orgon, Cléante*

MADAME PERNELLE. I hear strange tales of very strange events.
ORGON. Yes, strange events which these two eyes beheld.
    The man's ingratitude is unparalleled.
    I save a wretched pauper from starvation,
    House him, and treat him like a blood relation,   5
    Shower him every day with my largesse,
    Give him my daughter, and all that I possess;
    And meanwhile the unconscionable knave
    Tries to induce my wife to misbehave;
    And not content with such extreme rascality,   10

Now threatens me with my own liberality,
And aims, by taking base advantage of
The gifts I gave him out of Christian love,
To drive me from my house, a ruined man,
And make me end a pauper, as he began.   15

DORINE. Poor fellow!

MADAME PERNELLE.   No, my son, I'll never bring
   Myself to think him guilty of such a thing.

ORGON. How's that?

MADAME PERNELLE.   The righteous always were maligned.

ORGON. Speak clearly, Mother. Say what's on your mind.

MADAME PERNELLE. I mean that I can smell a rat, my dear.
   You know how everybody hates him, here.   20

ORGON. That has no bearing on the case at all.

MADAME PERNELLE. I told you a hundred times, when you were
      small,
   That virtue in this world is hated ever;
   Malicious men may die, but malice never.   25

ORGON. No doubt that's true, but how does it apply?

MADAME PERNELLE. They've turned you against him by a clever lie.

ORGON. I've told you, I was there and saw it done.

MADAME PERNELLE. Ah, slanderers will stop at nothing, Son.

ORGON. Mother, I'll lose my temper . . . For the last time,   30
   I tell you I was witness to the crime.

MADAME PERNELLE. The tongues of spite are busy night and noon,
   And to their venom no man is immune.

ORGON. You're talking nonsense. Can't you realize
   I saw it; saw it; saw it with my eyes?   35
   Saw, do you understand me? Must I shout it
   Into your ears before you'll cease to doubt it?

MADAME PERNELLE. Appearances can deceive, my son. Dear me,
   We cannot always judge by what we see.

ORGON. Drat! Drat!

MADAME PERNELLE.   One often interprets things awry;   40
   Good can seem evil to a suspicious eye.

ORGON. Was I to see his pawing at Elmire
   As an act of charity?

MADAME PERNELLE.   Till his guilt is clear,
   A man deserves the benefit of the doubt.
   You should have waited, to see how things turned out.   45

ORGON. Great God in Heaven, what more proof did I need?
   Was I to sit there, watching, until he'd . . .
   You drive me to the brink of impropriety.

MADAME PERNELLE. No, no, a man of such surpassing piety

Could not do such a thing. You cannot shake me.   50
    I don't believe it, and you shall not make me.
ORGON. You vex me so that, if you weren't my mother,
    I'd say to you . . . some dreadful thing or other.
DORINE. It's your turn now, Sir, not to be listened to;
    You'd not trust us, and now she won't trust you.   55
CLEANTE. My friends, we're wasting time which should be spent
    In facing up to our predicament.
    I fear that scoundrel's threats weren't made in sport.
DAMIS. Do you think he'd have the nerve to go to court?
ELMIRE. I'm sure he won't: they'd find it all too crude   60
    A case of swindling and ingratitude.
CLEANTE. Don't be too sure. He won't be at a loss
    To give his claims a high and righteous gloss;
    And clever rogues with far less valid cause
    Have trapped their victims in a web of laws.   65
    I say again that to antagonize
    A man so strongly armed was most unwise.
ORGON. I know it; but the man's appalling cheek
    Outraged me so, I couldn't control my pique.
CLEANTE. I wish to Heaven that we could devise   70
    Some truce between you, or some compromise.
ELMIRE. If I had known what cards he held, I'd not
    Have roused his anger by my little plot.
ORGON. [*To* DORINE, *as* M. LOYAL *enters*] What is that fellow
        looking for? Who is he?
    Go talk to him—and tell him that I'm busy.   75

SCENE 4. *Monsieur Loyal, Madame Pernelle, Orgon, Damis,*
         Mariane, Dorine, Elmire, Cléante

MONSIEUR LOYAL. Good day, dear sister. Kindly let me see
    Your master.
DORINE.   He's involved with company,
    And cannot be disturbed just now, I fear.
MONSIEUR LOYAL. I hate to intrude; but what has brought me here
    Will not disturb your master, in any event.   5
    Indeed, my news will make him most content.
DORINE. Your name?
MONSIEUR LOYAL.   Just say that I bring greetings from
    Monsieur Tartuffe, on whose behalf I've come.
DORINE. [*To* ORGON] Sir, he's a very gracious man, and bears
    A message from Tartuffe, which, he declares,   10
    Will make you most content.

CLEANTE.   Upon my word,
I think this man had best be seen, and heard.

ORGON. Perhaps he has some settlement to suggest.
How shall I treat him? What manner would be best?

CLEANTE. Control your anger, and if he should mention   15
Some fair adjustment, give him your full attention.

MONSIEUR LOYAL. Good health to you, good Sir. May Heaven confound
Your enemies, and may your joys abound.

ORGON. [*Aside, to* CLEANTE] A gentle salutation: it confirms
My guess that he is here to offer terms.   20

MONSIEUR LOYAL. I've always held your family most dear;
I served your father, Sir, for many a year.

ORGON. Sir, I must ask your pardon; to my shame,
I cannot now recall your face or name.

MONSIEUR LOYAL. Loyal's my name; I come from Normandy,   25
And I'm a bailiff, in all modesty.
For forty years, praise God, it's been my boast
To serve with honor in that vital post,
And I am here, Sir, if you will permit
The liberty, to serve you with this writ . . .   30

ORGON. To—*what?*

MONSIEUR LOYAL.   Now, please, Sir, let us have no friction:
It's nothing but an order of eviction.
You are to move your goods and family out
And make way for new occupants, without
Deferment or delay, and give the keys . . .   35

ORGON. I? Leave this house?

MONSIEUR LOYAL.   Why yes, Sir, if you please.
This house, Sir, from the cellar to the roof,
Belongs now to the good Monsieur Tartuffe,
And he is lord and master of your estate
By virtue of a deed of present date,   40
Drawn in due form, with clearest legal phrasing . . .

DAMIS. Your insolence is utterly amazing!

MONSIEUR LOYAL. Young man, my business here is not with you,
But with your wise and temperate father, who,
Like every worthy citizen, stands in awe   45
Of justice, and would never obstruct the law.

ORGON. But . . .

MONSIEUR LOYAL. Not for a million, Sir, would you rebel
Against authority; I know that well.
You'll not make trouble, Sir, or interfere
With the execution of my duties here.   50

DAMIS. Someone may execute a smart tattoo

On that black jacket of yours, before you're through.
MONSIEUR LOYAL. Sir, bid your son be silent. I'd much regret
    Having to mention such a nasty threat
    Of violence, in writing my report.   55
DORINE. [*Aside*] This man Loyal's a most disloyal sort!
MONSIEUR LOYAL. I love all men of upright character,
    And when I agreed to serve these papers, Sir,
    It was your feelings that I had in mind.
    I couldn't bear to see the case assigned   60
    To someone else, who might esteem you less
    And so subject you to unpleasantness.
ORGON. What's more unpleasant than telling a man to leave
    His house and home?
MONSIEUR LOYAL.   You'd like a short reprieve?
    If you desire it, Sir, I shall not press you,   65
    But wait until tomorrow to dispossess you.
    Splendid. I'll come and spend the night here, then,
    Most quietly, with half a score of men.
    For form's sake, you might bring me, just before
    You go to bed, the keys to the front door.   70
    My men, I promise, will be on their best
    Behavior, and will not disturb your rest.
    But bright and early, Sir, you must be quick
    And move out all your furniture, every stick:
    The men I've chosen are both young and strong,   75
    And with their help it shouldn't take you long.
    In short, I'll make things pleasant and convenient,
    And since I'm being so extremely lenient,
    Please show me, Sir, a like consideration,
    And give me your entire cooperation.   80
ORGON. [*Aside*] I may be all but bankrupt, but I vow
    I'd give a hundred louis, here and now,
    Just for the pleasure of landing one good clout
    Right on the end of that complacent snout.
CLEANTE. Careful; don't make things worse.
DAMIS.   My bootsole itches
    To give that beggar a good kick in the breeches.   85
DORINE. Monsieur Loyal, I'd love to hear the whack
    Of a stout stick across your fine broad back.
MONSIEUR LOYAL. Take care: a woman too may go to jail if
    She uses threatening language to a bailiff.   90
CLEANTE. Enough, enough, Sir. This must not go on.
    Give me that paper, please, and then begone.

---

52. *black jacket:* in the original, *just-*   long black coat with skirts, the customa-
aucorps à longues basques, a close-fitting,   ry dress of a bailiff.

MONSIEUR LOYAL. Well, *au revoir.* God give you all good cheer!
ORGON. May God confound you, and him who sent you here!

SCENE 5. *Orgon, Cleante, Mariane, Elmire, Madame Pernelle,* *Dorine, Damis*

ORGON. Now, Mother, was I right or not? This writ
  Should change your notion of Tartuffe a bit.
  Do you perceive his villainy at last?
MADAME PERNELLE. I'm thunderstruck. I'm utterly aghast.
DORINE. Oh, come, be fair. You mustn't take offense   *5*
  At this new proof of his benevolence.
  He's acting out of selfless love, I know.
  Material things enslave the soul, and so
  He kindly has arranged your liberation
  From all that might endanger your salvation.   *10*
ORGON. Will you not ever hold your tongue, you dunce?
CLEANTE. Come, you must take some action, and at once.
ELMIRE. Go tell the world of the low trick he's tried.
  The deed of gift is surely nullified
  By such behavior, and public rage will not   *15*
  Permit the wretch to carry out his plot.

SCENE 6. *Valère, Orgon, Cléante, Elmire, Mariane, Madame* *Pernelle, Damis, Dorine*

VALERE. Sir, though I hate to bring you more bad news,
  Such is the danger that I cannot choose.
  A friend who is extremely close to me
  And knows my interest in your family
  Has, for my sake, presumed to violate   *5*
  The secrecy that's due to things of state,
  And sends me word that you are in a plight
  From which your one salvation lies in flight.
  That scoundrel who's imposed upon you so
  Denounced you to the King an hour ago   *10*
  And, as supporting evidence, displayed
  The strong-box of a certain renegade
  Whose secret papers, so he testified,
  You had disloyally agreed to hide.
  I don't know just what charges may be pressed,   *15*
  But there's a warrant out for your arrest;
  Tartuffe has been instructed, furthermore,
  To guide the arresting officer to your door.
CLEANTE. He's clearly done this to facilitate
  His seizure of your house and your estate.   *20*

ORGON. That man, I must say, is a vicious beast!

VALERE. You can't afford to delay, Sir, in the least.
  My carriage is outside, to take you hence;
  This thousand louis should cover all expense.
  Let's lose no time, or you shall be undone;   25
  The sole defense, in this case, is to run.
  I shall go with you all the way, and place you
  In a safe refuge to which they'll never trace you.

ORGON. Alas, dear boy, I wish that I could show you
  My gratitude for everything I owe you.   30
  But now is not the time; I pray the Lord
  That I may live to give you your reward.
  Farewell, my dears; be careful . . .

CLEANTE.   Brother, hurry.
  We shall take care of things; you needn't worry.

SCENE 7. *The Officer, Tartuffe, Valère, Orgon, Elmire, Mariane,*
  Madame Pernelle, Dorine, Cléante, Damis

TARTUFFE. Gently, Sir, Gently; stay right where you are.
  No need for haste; your lodging isn't far.
  You're off to prison, by order of the Prince.

ORGON. This is the crowning blow, you wretch; and since
  It means my total ruin and defeat,   5
  Your villainy is now at last complete.

TARTUFFE. You needn't try to provoke me; it's no use.
  Those who serve Heaven must expect abuse.

CLEANTE. You are indeed most patient, sweet, and blameless.

DORINE. How he exploits the name of Heaven! It's shameless.   10

TARTUFFE. Your taunts and mockeries are all for naught;
  To do my duty is my only thought.

MARIANE. Your love of duty is most meritorious,
  And what you've done is little short of glorious.

TARTUFFE. All deeds are glorious, Madam, which obey   15
  The sovereign prince who sent me here today.

ORGON. I rescued you when you were destitute;
  Have you forgotten that, you thankless brute?

TARTUFFE. No, no, I well remember everything;
  But my first duty is to serve my King.   20
  That obligation is so paramount
  That other claims, beside it, do not count;
  And for it I would sacrifice my wife,
  My family, my friend, or my own life.

ELMIRE. Hypocrite!

DORINE.   All that we most revere, he uses   25
  To cloak his plots and camouflage his ruses.

CLEANTE. If it is true that you are animated
　By pure and loyal zeal, as you have stated,
　Why was this zeal not roused until you'd sought
　To make Orgon a cuckold, and been caught? 30
　Why weren't you moved to give your evidence
　Until your outraged host had driven you hence?
　I shan't say that the gift of all his treasure
　Ought to have damped your zeal in any measure;
　But if he is a traitor, as you declare, 35
　How could you condescend to be his heir?
TARTUFFE. [*To the* OFFICER] Sir, spare me all this clamor; it's grow-
　　ing shrill.
　Please carry out your orders, if you will.
OFFICER. Yes, I've delayed too long, Sir. Thank you kindly.
　You're just the proper person to remind me. 40
　Come, you are off to join the other boarders
　In the King's prison, according to his orders.
TARTUFFE. Who? I, Sir?
OFFICER. 　　　　　Yes.
TARTUFFE. 　　　　　　　To prison? This can't be true!
OFFICER. I owe an explanation, but not to you.
　[*To* ORGON] Sir, all is well; rest easy, and be grateful. 45
　We serve a Prince to whom all sham is hateful,
　A Prince who sees into our inmost hearts,
　And can't be fooled by any trickster's arts.
　His royal soul, though generous and human,
　Views all things with discernment and acumen; 50
　His sovereign reason is not lightly swayed,
　And all his judgments are discreetly weighed.
　He honors righteous men of every kind,
　And yet his zeal for virtue is not blind,
　Nor does his love of piety numb his wits 55
　And make him tolerant of hypocrites.
　'Twas hardly likely that this man could cozen
　A King who's foiled such liars by the dozen.
　With one keen glance, the King perceived the whole
　Perverseness and corruption of his soul, 60
　And thus high Heaven's justice was displayed:
　Betraying you, the rogue stood self-betrayed.
　The King soon recognized Tartuffe as one
　Notorious by another name, who'd done
　So many vicious crimes that one could fill 65

<hr>

39. *police officer:* in the original, *un exempt.* He would actually have been a gentleman from the king's personal body- guard with the rank of lieutenant-colonel or "master of the camp."

Ten volumes with them, and be writing still.
But to be brief: our sovereign was appalled
By this man's treachery toward you, which he called
The last, worst villainy of a vile career,
And bade me follow the impostor here   70
To see how gross his impudence could be,
And force him to restore your property.
Your private papers, by the King's command,
I hereby seize and give into your hand.
The King, by royal order, invalidates   75
The deed which gave this rascal your estates,
And pardons, furthermore, your grave offense
In harboring an exile's documents.
By these decrees, our Prince rewards you for
Your loyal deeds in the late civil war,   80
And shows how heartfelt is his satisfaction
In recompensing any worthy action,
How much he prizes merit, and how he makes
More of men's virtues than of their mistakes.
DORINE. Heaven be praised!
MADAME PERNELLE.   I breathe again, at last.   85
ELMIRE. We're safe.
MARIANE.   I can't believe the danger's past.
ORGON. [*To* TARTUFFE]. Well, traitor, now you see . . .
CLEANTE. Ah, brother, please,
    Let's not descend to such indignities.
    Leave the poor wretch to his unhappy fate,
    And don't say anything to aggravate   90
    His present woes; but rather hope that he
    Will soon embrace an honest piety,
    And mend his ways, and by a true repentance
    Move our just King to moderate his sentence.
    Meanwhile, go kneel before your sovereign's throne 95
    And thank him for the mercies he has shown.
ORGON. Well said: let's go at once and, gladly kneeling,
    Express the gratitude which all are feeling.
    Then, when that first great duty has been done,
    We'll turn with pleasure to a second one,   100
    And give Valère, whose love has proven so true,
    The wedded happiness which is his due.

80. *late civil war*: a reference to Orgon's role in supporting the king during the Fronde (see note 17, p. 89).

JEAN RACINE
(1639–1699)
Phaedra (Phèdre) *

Preface †

Behold another tragedy whose theme is borrowed from Euripides! Although I have followed a rather different path than did this author for the course of the action, I have not failed to embellish my play with everything that seemed to me to be striking in his. While I took from him only the simple idea of the character of Phaedra, I might say that I owe to him perhaps the most logical elements of his stagecraft. I am not at all surprised that this character has had such a happy success since the days of Euripides, and that moreover it has been so successful in our own century, since the character has all the qualities required by Aristotle for the tragic hero that are proper for the raising of pity and terror. In all truth, Phaedra is neither completely guilty nor completely innocent. She is plunged by her fate, and by the anger of the gods, into an illegitimate passion for which she feels horror from the very start. She makes every attempt to surmount it. . . .

I have even taken care to make her a little less repellent than she is in classical tragedy, where she herself resolves to accuse Hippolytus. I believed that calumny was too low and too black to put in the mouth of a princess who otherwise showed such noble and virtuous feelings. This baseness seemed to me more fitting for a nurse, who could possess more servile inclinations, and who nevertheless only delivered this false accusation to save the life and honor of her mistress. . . .

Hippolytus, in Euripides and in Seneca, is accused of having in effect seduced his stepmother. . . . But here he is merely accused of planning to do it. I wished to spare Theseus a confusion in his character which might have made him less appealing to the audience.

Concerning the character of Hippolytus, I have noticed that among the Ancients Euripides was blamed for representing him as a philosopher free from any imperfection. The result was that the

---

* First produced in 1677; the original title, *Phèdre et Hippolyte,* was later shortened to *Phèdre.* Reprinted from *Phaedra & Figaro* by Robert Lowell, by permission of Farrar, Straus & Company, Inc. Copyright © 1960, 1961 by Robert Lowell, copyright © 1961 by Farrar, Straus & Cudahy, Inc. The original play was written in rhymed Alexandrine couplets. Mr. Lowell says the following about his own version: "My meter, with important differences, is based on Dryden and Pope. In his heroic plays, Dryden uses an end-stopped couplet, loaded with inversions, heavily alliterated, and varied by short unrhymed lines. My couplet is run on, avoids inversions and alliteration, and loosens its rhythm with shifted accents and occasional extra syllables. . . ."

† From the Preface published with the first edition in March, 1677. Translated by Howard E. Hugo.

death of the young prince caused more indignation than pity. I thought I should give him some weakness which would make him slightly culpable in his relations with his father, without however, robbing him of the magnanimity with which he spares Phaedra's honor, and let himself be charged without implicating her. I term "weakness" that passion that he bears for Aricia, in spite of himself: she who is the daughter and the sister of his father's mortal enemies. . . .

To conclude, I do not yet dare state that this play is my best tragedy. . . . What I can affirm is that I have never written one where virtue is brought more to light than in this. The slightest errors are severely punished here. The mere idea of crime is regarded with as much horror as the crime itself. . . . Passions are only revealed to the eyes to show all the disorder that they cause; and vice here is painted in colors so that one may recognize it and hate its hideousness. . . . This is what the first tragic poets always maintained. Their theater was a school where virtue was no less well taught than in the schools of philosophy. . . .

Characters

THESEUS (THÉSÉE), son of Ægeus and king of Athens

PHAEDRA (PHÈDRE), wife of Theseus and daughter of Minos and Pasiphaë

HIPPOLYTUS (HIPPOLYTE), son of Theseus and Antiope, queen of the Amazons

THERAMENES (THÉRAMÈNE), tutor of Theseus

ARICIA (ARICIE), princess of the blood royal of Athens

OENONE, Phaedra's nurse and confidante

ISMENE (ISMENE), Aricia's confidante

PANOPE, Phaedra's lady in waiting

GUARDS

The SCENE is laid at Troezen, a town in the Peloponnesus, on the south shore of the Saronic Gulf, opposite Athens.

Act 1

SCENE I. Hippolytus, Theramenes

HIPPOLYTUS. No, no, my friend, we're off! Six months have passed
since Father heard the ocean howl and cast
his galley on the Aegean's skull-white froth.
Listen! The blank sea calls us—off, off, off!
I'll follow Father to the fountainhead   5
and marsh of hell. We're off. Alive or dead,
I'll find him.
THERAMENES.   Where, my lord? I've sent a host of veteran seamen up and down the coast;

each village, creek and cove from here to Crete
has been ransacked and questioned by my fleet;   **10**
my flagship skirted Hades' rapids, furled
sail there a day, and scoured the underworld.
Have you fresh news? New hopes? One even doubts
if noble Theseus wants his whereabouts
discovered. Does he need helpers to share   **15**
the plunder of his latest love affair;
a shipload of spectators and his son
to watch him ruin his last Amazon—
some creature, taller than a man, whose tanned
and single bosom slithers from his hand,   **20**
when he leaps to crush her like a waterfall
of honeysuckle?

HIPPOLYTUS.   You are cynical,
my friend. Your insinuations wrong a king,
sick as myself of his philandering.
His heart is Phaedra's and no rivals dare   **25**
to challenge Phaedra's sole possession there.
I sail to find my father. The command
of duty calls me from this stifling land.

THERAMENES. This stifling land? Is that how you deride
this gentle province where you used to ride   **30**
the bridle-paths, pursuing happiness?
You cured your orphaned childhood's loneliness
and found a peace here you preferred to all
the blaze of Athens' brawling protocol.
A rage for exploits blinds you. Your disease is boredom.   **35**

HIPPOLYTUS. Friend, this kingdom lost its peace,
when Father left my mother for defiled
bull-serviced Pasiphaë's child. The child
of homicidal Minos is our queen!

THERAMENES. Yes, Phaedra reigns and rules here. I have seen   **40**
you crouch before her outbursts like a cur.
When she first met you, she refused to stir
until your father drove you out of court.
The news is better now; our friends report
the queen is dying. Will you cross the seas,   **45**
desert your party and abandon Greece?

---

11. *Hades' rapids:* The river Acheron
in Epirus was thought to flow into the
Underworld.
18. *Amazon:* that tribe of Greek
women who spent their time in warfare
and hunting.
20. *single bosom:* a reference to the
legend that the Amazons cut off the
right breast in order to draw their bows

further.
45. *queen:* i.e., Phaedra, daughter of
Minos of Crete and of Pasiphaë, sister to
Circe. Enamored of a white bull sent by
Poseidon, Pasiphaë consequently gave
birth to the Minotaur, the Cretan monster later slain by Theseus. Thus Phaedra
was half-sister to the Minotaur.

Why flee from Phaedra? Phaedra fears the night
less than she fears the day that strives to light
the universal ennui of her eye—
this dying woman, who desires to die!　　　　　　　　50

HIPPOLYTUS. No, I despise her Cretan vanity,
hysteria and idle cruelty.
I fear Aricia; she alone survives
the blood-feud that destroyed her brothers' lives.

THERAMENES. Prince, Prince, forgive my laughter. Must you fly　55
beyond the limits of the world and die,
floating in flotsam, friendless, far from help,
and clubbed to death by Tartars in the kelp?
Why arm the shrinking violet with a knife?
Do you hate Aricia, and fear for your life,　　　　　60
Prince?

HIPPOLYTUS. If I hated her, I'd trust myself and stay.

THERAMENES. Shall I explain you to yourself?
Prince, you have ceased to be that hard-mouthed, proud
and pure Hippolytus, who scorned the crowd
of common lovers once and rose above　　　　　　65
your wayward father by despising love.
Now you justify your father, and you feel
love's poison running through you, now you kneel
and breathe the heavy incense, and a god
possesses you and revels in your blood!　　　　　70
Are you in love?

HIPPOLYTUS. 　　　　Theramenes, when I call
and cry for help, you push me to the wall.
Why do you plague me, and try to make me fear
the qualities you taught me to revere?
I sucked in prudence with my mother's milk.　　　75
Antiope, no harlot draped in silk,
first hardened me. I was my mother's son
and not my father's. When the Amazon,
my mother, was dethroned, my mind approved
her lessons more than ever. I still loved　　　　　80
her bristling chastity. Later, you told
stories about my father's deeds that made me hold

53-54. *survives . . . lives:* According to one legend, Aegeus, father of Theseus, was the adopted son of Pandion. Pallas, Pandion's second son, had in turn fifty sons. These were the Pallantids and all brothers to Aricia; Theseus killed them because they threatened his own kingship of Athens.

76. *Antiope:* an Amazon, and sister to Hippolyta, the queen of the Amazons.

Antiope was beloved by Theseus, who carried her off to Athens. The Amazons then invaded Attica (Athens) in an effort to recover Antiope, but they were defeated in battle and Hippolyta lost her life. Antiope's son by Theseus was Hippolytus.

81. *chastity:* The Amazons were traditionally scornful of love.

back judgment—how he stood for Hercules,
a second Hercules who cleared the Cretan seas
of pirates, throttled Scirron, Cercyon,   85
Procrustes, Sinnis, and the giant man
of Epidaurus writhing in his gore.
He pierced the maze and killed the Minotaur.
Other things turned my stomach: that long list
of women, all refusing to resist.   90
Helen, caught up with all her honeyed flesh
from Sparta; Periboea, young and fresh,
already tired of Salinis. A hundred more,
their names forgotten by my father—whore
and virgin, child and mother, all deceived,   95
if their protestations can be believed!
Ariadne declaiming to the rocks,
her sister, Phaedra, kidnapped. Phaedra locks
the gate at last! You know how often I
would weary, fall to nodding and deny   100
the possiblity of hearing the whole
ignoble, dull, insipid boast unroll.
And now I too must fall. The gods have made me creep.
How can I be in love? I have no specious heap
of honors, friend. No mastered monsters drape   105
my shoulders—Theseus' excuse to rape
at will. Suppose I chose a woman. Why
choose an orphan? Aricia is eternally
cut off from marriage, lest she breed
successors to her fierce brothers, and seed   110
the land with treason. Father only grants
her life on one condition. This—he wants
no bridal torch to burn for her. Unwooed
and childless, she must answer for the blood
her brothers shed. How can I marry her,   115
gaily subvert our kingdom's character,
and sail on the high seas of love?

THERAMENES.   You'll prove
nothing by reason, for you are in love.
Theseus' injustice to Aricia throws
her in the light; your eyes he wished to close   120

91. *Helen:* famed as the most beautiful of women, daughter of Zeus and
Leda, sister of Castor and Pollux, later
the wife of Menelaus of Sparta. When
still a young girl, she was abducted by
Theseus and Pirithoüs (king of the Lapiths in Thessaly). Her brothers rescued
her and brought her back home to Leda
and Leda's husband, Tyndareus.

92. *Periboea:* mother of Ajax.
93. *Salinis:* Salamis, island in the
Gulf of Aegina on the eastern shore of
Greece, off which the Greeks later defeated the Persians in a naval battle, 480
B.C.
97. *Ariadne:* Phaedra's sister, deserted by Theseus after she rescued him
from the Minotaur.

are open. She dazzles you. Her pitiful
seclusion makes her doubly terrible.
Does this innocent passion freeze your blood?
There's sweetness in it. Is your only good
the dismal famine of your chastity?   125
You shun your father's path? Where would you be,
Prince, if Antiope had never burned
chastely for Theseus? Love, my lord, has turned
the head of Hercules, and thousands—fired
the forge of Vulcan! All your uninspired,   130
cold moralizing is nothing, Prince. You have changed!
Now no one sees you riding, half-deranged
along the sand-bars, where you drove your horse
and foaming chariot with all your force,
tilting and staggering upright through the surf—   135
far from their usual course across the turf.
The woods are quiet . . . How your eyes hang down!
You often murmur and forget to frown.
All's out, Prince. You're in love; you burn. Flames, flames,
Prince! A dissimulated sickness maims   140
The youthful quickness of your daring. Does
lovely Aricia haunt you?

HIPPOLYTUS.   Friend, spare us.
  I sail to find my father.

THERAMENES.   Will you see.
  Phaedra before you go?

HIPPOLYTUS.   I mean to be
here when she comes. Go, tell her. I will do   145
my duty. Wait, I see her nurse. What new
troubles torment her?

SCENE II. *Hippolytus, Theramenes, Oenone*

OENONE.   Who has griefs like mine,
  my lord? I cannot help the queen in her decline.
  Although I sit beside her day and night,
  she shuts her eyes and withers in my sight.   150
  An eternal tumult roisters through her head,
  panics her sleep, and drags her from her bed.
  Just now she fled me at the prime
  of day to see the sun for the last time.
  She's coming.

HIPPOLYTUS.   So! I'll steal away. My flight   155
  removes a hateful object from her sight.

127. *Antiope:* Hippolytus' mother.

SCENE III. *Phaedra, Oenone*

PHAEDRA. Dearest, we'll go no further. I must rest.
I'll sit here. My emotions shake my breast,
the sunlight throws black bars across my eyes.
My knees give. If I fall, why should I rise,   160
Nurse?

OENONE.   Heaven help us! Let me comfort you.

PHAEDRA. Tear off these gross, official rings, undo
these royal veils. They drag me to the ground.
Why have you frilled me, laced me, crowned me, and wound
my hair in turrets? All your skill torments   165
and chokes me. I am crushed by ornaments.
Everything hurts me, and drags me to my knees!

OENONE. Now this, now that, Madam. You never cease
commanding us, then cancelling your commands.
You feel your strength return, summon all hands   170
to dress you like a bride, then say you choke!
We open all the windows, fetch a cloak,
rush you outdoors. It's no use, you decide
that sunlight kills you, and only want to hide.

PHAEDRA. I feel the heavens' royal radiance cool   175
and fail, as if it feared my terrible
shame has destroyed its right to shine on men.
I'll never look upon the sun again.

OENONE. Renunciation or renunciation!
Now you slander the source of your creation.   180
Why do you run to death and tear your hair?

PHAEDRA. Oh God, take me to some sunless forest lair . . .
There hoof-beats raise a dust-cloud, and my eye
follows a horseman outlined on the sky!

OENONE. What's this, my lady?

PHAEDRA.   I have lost my mind.   185
Where am I? Oh forget my words! I find
I've lost the habit now of talking sense.
My face is red and guilty—evidence
of treason! I've betrayed my darkest fears,
Nurse, and my eyes, despite me, fill with tears.   190

OENONE. Lady, if you must weep, weep for your silence
that filled your days and mine with violence.
Ah deaf to argument and numb to care,
you have no mercy. Spare me, spare
yourself. Your blood is like polluted water,   195

---

178. *sun:* i.e., Helios, the sun-god,   184. *horseman:* Phaedra is thinking of
father of Pasiphaë, Phaedra's mother.   Hippolytus.

fouling a mind desiring its own slaughter.
The sun has died and shadows filled the skies
thrice now, since you have closed your eyes;
the day has broken through the night's content
thrice now, since you have tasted nourishment.   200
Is your salvation from your terrified
conscience this passive, servile suicide?
Lady, your madness harms the gods who gave
you life, betrays your husband. Who will save
your children? Your downfall will orphan them,   205
deprive them of their kingdom, and condemn
their lives and future to the discipline
of one who abhors you and all your kin,
a tyrant suckled by an amazon,
Hippolytus . . .

PHAEDRA.   Oh God!

OENONE.   You still hate someone;   210
thank heaven for that, Madam!

PHAEDRA.   You spoke his name!

OENONE. Hippolytus, Hippolytus! There's hope
in hatred, Lady. Give your anger rope.
I love your anger. If the winds of love
and fury stir you, you will live. Above   215
your children towers this foreigner, this child
of Scythian cannibals, now wild
to ruin the kingdom, master Greece, and choke
the children of the gods beneath his yoke.
Why dawdle? Why deliberate at length?   220
Oh, gather up your dissipated strength.

PHAEDRA. I've lived too long.

OENONE.   Always, always agonized!
Is your conscience still stunned and paralyzed?
Do you think you have washed your hands in blood?

PHAEDRA. Thank God, my hands are clean still. Would to God   225
my heart were innocent!

OENONE.   Your heart, your heart!
What have you done that tears your soul apart?

PHAEDRA. I've said too much. Oenone, let me die;
by dying I shall escape blasphemy.

OENONE. Search for another hand to close your eyes.   230
Oh cruel Queen, I see that you despise
my sorrow and devotion. I'll die first,

205. *children:* Phaedra's sons, Acamas and Demophoön.
217. *Scythian cannibals:* Scythia, the home of the Amazons, was for the ancient Greeks associated with barbarians.

and end the anguish of this service cursed
by your perversity. A thousand roads
always lie open to the killing gods.   235
I'll choose the nearest. Lady, tell me how
Oenone's love has failed you. Will you allow
your nurse to die, your nurse, who gave up all—
nation, parents, children, to serve in thrall.
I saved you from your mother, King Minos' wife!   240
Will your death pay me for giving up my life?

PHAEDRA. What I could tell you, I have told you. Nurse,
only my silence saves me from the curse
of heaven.

OENONE.   How could you tell me anything
worse than watching you dying?

PHAEDRA.   I would bring   245
my life and rank dishonor. What can I say
to save myself, or put off death a day.

OENONE. Ah Lady, I implore you by my tears
and by your suffering body. Heaven hears,
and knows the truth already. Let me see.   250

PHAEDRA. Stand up.

OENONE.   Your hesitation's killing me!

PHAEDRA. What can I tell you? How the gods reprove me!

OENONE. Speak!

PHAEDRA.   On Venus, murdering Venus! love
gored Pasiphaë with the bull.

OENONE.   Forget
your mother! When she died, she paid her debt.   255

PHAEDRA. Oh Ariadne, oh my Sister, lost
for love of Theseus on that rocky coast.

OENONE. Lady, what nervous languor makes you rave
against your family; they are in the grave.

PHAEDRA. Remorseless Aphrodite drives me. I,   260
my race's last and worst love-victim, die.

OENONE. Are you in love?

PHAEDRA.   I am insane with love!

OENONE.   Who is he?

PHAEDRA. I'll tell you. Nothing love can do could
equal . . . Nurse, I am in love. The shame
kills me. I love the . . . Do not ask his name.   265

OENONE. Who?

PHAEDRA.   Nurse, you know my old loathing for the son
of Theseus and the barbarous amazon?

---

257. *rocky coast:* Theseus abandoned
Ariadne on the island of Naxos, off the
southern coast of Greece in the Aegean
Sea.

OENONE. Hippolytus! My God, oh my God!

PHAEDRA.   You,
not I, have named him.

OENONE.   What can you do,
but die? Your words have turned my blood to ice.   270
Oh righteous heavens, must the blasphemies
of Pasiphaë fall upon her daughter?
Her Furies strike us down across the water.
Why did we come here?

PHAEDRA. My evil comes from farther off. In May,   275
in brilliant Athens, on my marriage day,
I turned aside for shelter from the smile
of Theseus. Death was frowning in an aisle—
Hippolytus! I saw his face, turned white!
My lost and dazzled eyes saw only night,   280
capricious burnings flickered through my bleak
abandoned flesh. I could not breathe or speak
I faced my flaming executioner,
Aphrodite, my mother's murderer!
I tried to calm her wrath by flowers and praise,   285
I built her a temple, fretted months and days
on decoration. I even hoped to find
symbols and stays for my distracted mind,
searching the guts of sacrificial steers.
Yet when my erring passions, mutineers   290
to virtue, offered incense at the shrine
of love, I failed to silence the malign
Goddess, Alas, my hungry open mouth,
thirsting with adoration, tasted drouth—
Venus resigned her altar to my new lord—   295
and even while I was praying, I adored
Hippolytus above the sacred flame,
now offered to his name I could not name.
I fled him, yet he stormed me in disguise,
and seemed to watch me from his father's eyes.   300
I even turned against myself, screwed up
my slack courage to fury, and would not stop
shrieking and raging, till half-dead with love
and the hatred of a stepmother, I drove
Hippolytus in exile from the rest   305
and strenuous wardship of his father's breast.
Then I could breathe, Oenone; he was gone;
my lazy, nerveless days meandered on
through dreams and daydreams, like a stately carriage
touring the level landscape of my marriage.   310

Yet nothing worked. My husband sent me here
to Troezen, far from Athens; once again the dear
face shattered me; I saw Hippolytus
each day, and felt my ancient, venomous
passion tear my body limb from limb;   313
naked Venus was clawing down her victim.
What could I do? Each moment, terrified
by loose diseased emotions, now I cried
for death to save my glory and expel
my gloomy frenzy from this world, my hell.   320
And yet your tears and words bewildered me,
and so endangered my tranquillity,
at last I spoke. Nurse, I shall not repent,
if you will leave me the passive content
of dry silence and solitude.   325

SCENE IV. Phaedra, Oenone, Panope

PANOPE. My heart breaks. Would to God, I could refuse
to tell your majesty my evil news.
The King is dead! Listen, the heavens ring
with shouts and lamentations for the King.
PHAEDRA. The King is dead? What's this?
PANOPE.   In vain   330
you beg the gods to send him back again.
Hippolytus has heard the true report,
he is already heading for the port.
PHAEDRA. Oh God!
PANOPE.   They've heard in Athens. Everyone
is joining factions—some salute your son,   335
others are calling for Hippolytus;
they want him to reform and harden us—
even Aricia claims the loyalty
of a fanatical minority.
The Prince's captains have recalled their men.   340
His flag is up and now he sails again
for Athens. Queen, if he appear there now,
he'll drag the people with him!
OENONE.   Stop, allow
the Queen a little respite for her grief.
She hears you, and will act for our relief.   345

SCENE V. Phaedra, Oenone

OENONE. I'd given up persuading you to live;
death was your refuge, only death could give

you peace and save your troubled glory. I
myself desired to follow you, and die.
But this catastrophe prescribes new laws: 350
the king is dead, and for the king who was,
fate offers you his kingdom. You have a son;
he should be king! If you abandon
him, he'll be a slave. The gods, his ancestors,
will curse and drive you on your fatal course.   355
Live! Who'll condemn you if you love and woo
the Prince? Your stepson is no kin to you,
now that your royal husband's death has cut
and freed you from the throttling marriage-knot.
Do not torment the Prince with persecution,   360
and give a leader to the revolution;
no, win his friendship, bind him to your side.
Give him this city and its countryside.
He will renounce the walls of Athens, piled
stone on stone by Minerva for your child.   365
Stand with Hippolytus, annihilate
Aricia's faction, and possess the state!

PHAEDRA. So be it! Your superior force has won.
I will live if compassion for my son,
devotion to the Prince, and love of power   370
can give me courage in this fearful hour.

Act 2

SCENE I. *Aricia, Ismene*

ARICIA. What's this? The Prince has sent a messenger?
The Prince begs me to wait and meet him here?
The Prince begs! Goose, you've lost your feeble wits!

ISMENE. Lady, be calm. These are the benefits
of Theseus' death: first Prince Hippolytus   5
comes courting favors; soon the populous
cities of Greece will follow—they will eat
out of your hand, Princess, and kiss your feet.

ARICIA. This felon's hand, this slave's! My dear, your news
is only frivolous gossip, I refuse   10
to hope.

ISMENE.   Ah Princess, the just powers of hell
have struck. Theseus has joined your brothers!

ARICIA.   Tell
me how he died.

---

365. *Minerva:* the Greek Goddess Athene, patroness of Athens.

ISMENE.   Princess, fearful tales
  are circulating. Sailors saw his sails,
  his infamous black sails, spin round and round   15
  in Charybdis' whirlpool; all hands were drowned.
  Yet others say on better evidence
  that Theseus and Pirithoüs passed the dense
  darkness of hell to rape Persephone.
  Pirithoüs was murdered by the hound;   20
  Theseus, still living, was buried in the ground.
ARICIA. This is an old wives' tale. Only the dead
  enter the underworld, and see the bed
  of Queen Persephone. What brought him there?
ISMENE. Princess, the King is dead—dead! Everywhere   25
  men know and mourn. Already our worshipping
  townsmen acclaim Hippolytus for their king;
  in her great palace, Phaedra, the self-styled
  regent, rages and trembles for her child.
ARICIA. What makes you think the puritanical   30
  son of Theseus is human. Will he recall
  my sentence and relent?
ISMENE.   I know he will.
ARICIA. You know nothing about him. He would kill
  a woman, rather than be kind to one.
  That wolf-cub of a fighting amazon   35
  hates me above all women. He would walk
  from here to hell, rather than hear me talk.
ISMENE. Do you know Hippolytus? Listen to me.
  His famous, blasphemous frigidity,
  what is it, when you've seen him close at hand?   40
  I've watched him like a hawk, and seen him stand
  shaking beside you—all his reputation
  for hating womenkind bears no relation
  to what I saw. He couldn't take his eyes
  off you! His eyes speak what his tongue denies.   45
ARICIA. I can't believe you. Your story's absurd!
  How greedily I listen to each word!
  Ismene, you know me, you know how my heart
  was reared on death, and always set apart
  from what it cherished—can this plaything of   50
  the gods and furies feel the peace of love?

16 *Charybdis:* in mythology, the destroying daughter of Poseidon and Gaea who lived beneath a large rock bearing her name, on the Sicilian side of the narrows between Sicily and Italy, and opposite Scylla—the cave at these same straits where the goddess-monster Scylla lived.

18-19. *Pirithoüs . . . Persephone:* Theseus went with Pirithoüs, king of the Lapiths, to Hades to help him steal Persephone. Hercules freed Theseus, whom Pluto had imprisoned, but could not free Pirithoüs, who was later killed.

What sights I've seen, Ismene! "Heads will roll,"
my brothers told me, "we will rule." I, the sole
survivor of those fabulous kings, who tilled
the soil of Greece, have seen my brothers killed,   55
six brothers murdered! In a single hour,
the tyrant, Theseus, lopped them in their flower.
The monster spared my life, and yet decreed
the torments of this childless life I lead
in exile, where no Greek can look on me;   60
my forced, perpetual virginity
preserves his crown; no son shall bear my name
or blow my brothers' ashes into flame.
Ismene, you know how well his tyranny
favors my temperament and strengthens me   65
to guard the honor of my reputation;
his rigor fortified my inclination.
How could I test his son's civilities?
I'd never even seen him with my eyes!
I'd never seen him. I'd restrained my eye,   70
that giddy nerve, from dwelling thoughtlessly
upon his outward grace and beauty—on mere
embellishments of nature, a veneer
the Prince himself despises and ignores.
My heart loves nobler virtues, and adores   75
in him his father's hard intelligence.
He has his father's daring and a sense
of honor his father lacks. Let me confess,
I love him for his lofty haughtiness
never submitted to a woman's yoke.   80
How could Phaedra's splendid marriage provoke
my jealousy? Have I so little pride,
I'd snatch at a rake's heart, a heart denied
to none—all riddled, opened up to let
thousands pass in like water through a net?   85
To carry sorrows to a heart, alone
untouched by passion, inflexible as stone,
to fasten my dominion on a force
as nervous as a never-harnessed horse—
this stirs me, this enflames me. Devilish Zeus   90
is easier mastered than Hippolytus;
heaven's love-infatuated emperor
confers less glory on his conqueror!
Ismene, I'm afraid. Why should I boast?
His very virtues I admire most   95
threaten to rise and throw me from the brink

of hope. What girlish folly made me think
Hippolytus could love Aricia?

ISMENE.   Here
he is. He loves you, Princess. Have no fear.

SCENE II. *Aricia, Ismene, Hippolytus*

HIPPOLYTUS. Princess, before   100
I leave here, I must tell you what's in store
for you in Greece. Alas, my father's dead.
The fierce forebodings that disquieted
my peace are true. Death, only death, could hide
his valor from this world he pacified.   105
The homicidal Fates will not release
the comrade, friend and peer of Hercules.
Princess, I trust your hate will not resent
honors whose justice is self-evident.
A single hope alleviates my grief,   110
Princess, I hope to offer you relief.
I now revoke a law whose cruelty
has pained my conscience. Princess, you are free
to marry. Oh enjoy this province, whose
honest, unhesitating subjects choose   115
Hippolytus for king. Live free as air,
here, free as I am, much more free!

ARICIA.   I dare
not hope. You are too gracious. Can you free
Aricia from your father's stern decree?

HIPPOLYTUS. Princess, the Athenian people, torn in two   120
between myself and Phaedra's son, want you.

ARICIA. Want me, my Lord!

HIPPOLYTUS.   I've no illusions. Lame
Athenian precedents condemn my claim,
because my mother was a foreigner.
But what is that? If my only rival were   125
my younger brother, his minority
would clear my legal disability.
However, a better claim than his or mine
now favors you, ennobled by the line
of great Erectheus. Your direct descent   130
sets you before my father; he was only lent

---

124. *foreigner:* In Euripides' time, Athenian law made the son of an Athenian and a non-Greek woman illegitimate. Hippolytus' mother was Antiope the Amazon. Yet in Racine, and in Euripides, it is not made clear why Phaedra's children do not suffer from the same liability.

130. *Erectheus:* son of Hephaestus and Gaea, brought up secretly by Athene in her temple. He subsequently became king of Athens, where he introduced her cult.

this kingdom by adoption. Once the common
Athenian, dazed by Theseus' superhuman
energies, had no longing to exhume
the rights that rushed your brothers to their doom.   135
Now Athens calls you home; the ancient feud
too long has stained the sacred olive wood;
blood festers in the furrows of our soil
to blight its fruits and scorch the farmer's toil.
This province suits me; let the vines of Crete   140
offer my brother a secure retreat.
The rest is yours. All Attica is yours;
I go to win you what your right assures.

ARICIA. Am I awake, my lord? Your sayings seem
like weird phantasmagoria in a dream.   145
How can your sparkling promises be true?
Some god, my lord, some god, has entered you!
How justly you are worshiped in this town;
oh how the truth surpasses your renown!
You wish to endow me with your heritage!   150
I only hoped you would not hate me. This rage
your father felt, how can you put it by
and treat me kindly?

HIPPOLYTUS.   Princess, is my eye
blind to beauty? Am I a bear, a bull, a boar,
some abortion fathered by the Minotaur?   155
Some one-eyed Cyclops, able to resist
Aricia's loveliness and still exist?
How can a man stand up against your grace?

ARICIA. My lord, my lord!

HIPPOLYTUS.   I cannot hide my face,
Princess! I'm driven. Why does my violence   160
so silence reason and intelligence?
Must I be still, and let my adoration
simmer away in silent resignation?
Princess, I've lost all power to restrain
myself. You see a madman, whose insane   165
pride hated love, and hoped to sit ashore,
watching the galleys founder in the war;
I was Diana's liegeman, dressed in steel.
I hoped to trample love beneath my heel—

156. *Cyclops:* one-eyed giants possessing vast strength, generally thought by
the Greeks to dwell in Sicily, where they
lived in a lawless and cannibalistic
fashion.
168-170. *Diana's liegeman . . . flaming*

Venus: In the original play by Euripides,
even more is made of Hippolytus worshipping Artemis (Diana), to the exclusion of Aphrodite (Venus), and the
latter goddess' jealousy brings about his
destruction.

alas, the flaming Venus burns me down,   170
I am the last dependent on her crown.
What left me charred and writhing in her clutch?
A single moment and a single touch.
Six months now, bounding like a wounded stag,
I've tried to shake this poisoned dart, and drag   175
myself to safety from your eyes that blind
when present, and when absent leave behind
volleys of burning arrows in my mind.
Ah Princess, shall I dive into the sea,
or steal the wings of Icarus to flee   180
love's Midas' touch that turns my world to gold?
Your image drives me stumbling through the cold,
floods my deserted forest caves with light,
darkens the day and dazzles through my night.
I'm grafted to your side by all I see;   185
all things unite us and imprison me.
I have no courage for the Spartan exercise
that trained my hand and steeled my energies.
Where are my horses? I forget their names.
My triumphs with my chariot at the games   190
no longer give me strength to mount a horse.
The ocean drives me shuddering from its shores.
Does such a savage conquest make you blush?
My boorish gestures, headlong cries that rush
at you like formless monsters from the sea?   195
Ah, Princess, hear me! Your serenity
must pardon the distortions of a weak
and new-born lover, forced by you to speak
love's foreign language, words that snarl and yelp . . .
I never could have spoken without your help.   200

SCENE III. *Aricia, Ismene, Hippolytus, Theramenes*

THERAMENES. I announce the Queen. She comes hurriedly,
    looking for you.
HIPPOLYTUS.   For me!
THERAMENES. Don't ask me why;
    she insisted. I promised I'd prevail
    on you to speak with her before you sail.   205
HIPPOLYTUS. What can she want to hear? What can I say?

---

180. *Icarus:* son of Daedalus. With his
father he escaped from Minos of Crete
by means of wings made from feathers
and wax. Despite Daedalus' warnings,
Icarus flew too high; the sun melted the
wax, and he fell into the sea.
181. *Midas:* King of Phrygia, to whom
the god Dionysus granted the wish that
all he touched might be changed to gold.

ARICIA. Wait for her, here! You cannot turn away.
  Forget her malice. Hating her will serve
  no purpose. Wait for her! Her tears deserve
  your pity.
HIPPOLYTUS.   You're going, Princess? And I must go   210
  to Athens, far from you. How shall I know
  if you accept my love.
ARICIA.   My lord, pursue
  your gracious promise. Do what you must do,
  make Athens tributary to my rule.
  Nothing you offer is unacceptable;   215
  yet this empire, so great, so glorious,
  is the least precious of your gifts to us.

SCENE IV. *Hippolytus, Theramenes*

HIPPOLYTUS. We're ready. Wait, the Queen's here. I need you.
  You must interrupt this tedious interview.
  Hurry down to the ship, then rush back, pale   220
  And breathless. Say the wind's up and we must sail.

SCENE V. *Hippolytus, Oenone, Phaedra*

PHAEDRA. He's here! Why does he scowl and look away
  from me? What shall I do? What shall I say?
OENONE. Speak for your son, he has no other patron.
PHAEDRA. Why are you so impatient to be gone   225
  from us, my lord? Stay! we will weep together.
  Pity my son; he too has lost his father.
  My own death's near. Rebellion, sick with wrongs,
  now like a sea-beast, lifts its slimey prongs,
  its muck, its jelly. You alone now stand   230
  to save the state. Who else can understand
  a mother? I forget. You will not hear
  me! An enemy deserves no pity. I fear
  your anger. Must my son, your brother, Prince,
  be punished for his cruel mother's sins?   235
HIPPOLYTUS. I've no such thoughts.
PHAEDRA.   I persecuted you
  blindly, and now you have good reason to
  return my impudence. How could you find
  the motivation of this heart and mind
  that scourged and tortured you, till you began   240
  to lose the calm composure of a man,
  and dwindle to a harsh and sullen boy,
  a thing of ice, unable to enjoy
  the charms of any civilized resource

except the heavy friendship of your horse,   245
that whirled you far from women, court and throne,
to course the savage woods for wolves alone?
You have good reason, yet if pain's a measure,
no one has less deserved your stern displeasure.
My lord, no one has more deserved compassion.   250

HIPPOLYTUS. Lady, I understand a mother's passion,
a mother jealous for her children's rights.
How can she spare a first wife's son? Long nights
of plotting, devious ways of quarrelling—
a madhouse! What else can remarriage bring?   255
Another would have shown equal hostility,
pushed her advantage more outrageously.

PHAEDRA. My lord, if you had known how far my love
and yearning have exalted me above
this usual weakness . . . Our afflicting kinship   260
is ending . . .

HIPPOLYTUS.   Madame, the precious minutes slip
by, I fatigue you. Fight against your fears.
Perhaps Poseidon has listened to our tears,
perhaps your husband's still alive. He hears
us, he is surging home—only a short   265
day's cruise conceals him, as he scuds for port.

PHAEDRA. That's folly, my lord. Who has twice visited
black Hades and the river of the dead
and returned? No, the poisonous Acheron
never lets go. Theseus drifts on and on,   270
a gutted galley on that clotted waste—
he woos, he wins Persephone, the chaste . . .
What am I saying? Theseus is not dead.
He lives in you. He speaks, he's taller by a head,
I see him, touch him, and my heart—a reef . . .   275
Ah Prince, I wander. Love betrays my grief . . .

HIPPOLYTUS. No, no, my father lives. Lady, the blind
furies release him; in your loyal mind,
love's fullness holds him, and he cannot die.

PHAEDRA. I hunger for Theseus. Always in my eye   280
he wanders, not as he appeared in hell,
lascivious eulogist of any belle
he found there, from the lowest to the Queen;
no, faithful, airy, just a little mean
through virtue, charming all, yet young and new,   285
as we would paint a god—as I now see you!
Your valiant shyness would have graced his speech,

263. *Poseidon:* Neptune, god of the sea, son of Cronus and Rhea.

he would have had your stature, eyes, and reach,
Prince, when he flashed across our Cretan waters,
the loved enslaver of King Minos' daughters.   290
Where were you? How could he conscript the flower
of Athens' youth against my father's power,
and ignore you? You were too young, they say;
you should have voyaged as a stowaway.
No dawdling bypath would have saved our bull,   295
when your just vengeance thundered through its skull.
There, light of foot, and certain of your goal,
you would have struck my brother's monstrous soul,
and pierced our maze's slow meanders, led
by Ariadne and her subtle thread.   300
By Ariadne? Prince I would have fought
for precedence; my every flaming thought,
love-quickened, would have shot you through the dark,
straight as an arrow to your quaking mark.
Could I have waited, panting, perishing,   305
entrusting your survival to a string,
like Ariadne, when she skulked behind,
there at the portal, to bemuse her mind
among the solemn cloisters of the porch?
No, Phaedra would have snatched your burning torch,   310
and lunged before you, reeling like a priest
of Dionysus to distract the beast.
I would have reached the final corridor
a lap before you, and killed the Minotaur!
Lost in the labyrinth, and at your side,   315
would it have mattered, if I lived or died?
HIPPOLYTUS. What are you saying, Madam? You forget
my father is your husband!
PHAEDRA.   I have let
you see my grief for Theseus! How could I
forget my honor and my majesty,
Prince?
HIPPOLYTUS. Madame, forgive me! My foolish youth   320
conjectured hideous untruths from your truth.
I cannot face my insolence. Farewell . . .
PHAEDRA. You monster! You understood me too well!
Why do you hang there, speechless, petrified,
polite! My mind whirls. What have I to hide?   325
Phaedra in all her madness stands before you.
I love you! Fool, I love you, I adore you!
Do not imagine that my mind approved
my first defection, Prince, or that I loved

your youth light-heartedly, and fed my treason   330
with cowardly compliance, till I lost my reason.
I wished to hate you, but the gods corrupt
us; though I never suffered their abrupt
seductions, shattering advances, I
too bear their sensual lightnings in my thigh.   335
I too am dying. I have felt the heat
that drove my mother through the fields of Crete,
the bride of Minos, dying for the full
magnetic April thunders of the bull.
I struggled with my sickness, but I found   340
no grace or magic to preserve my sound
intelligence and honor from this lust,
plowing my body with its horny thrust.
At first I fled you, and when this fell short
of safety, Prince, I exiled you from court.   345
Alas, my violence to resist you made
my face inhuman, hateful. I was afraid
to kiss my husband lest I love his son.
I made you fear me (this was easily done);
you loathed me more, I ached for you no less.   350
Misfortune magnified your loveliness.
I grew so wrung and wasted, men mistook
me for the Sibyl. If you could bear to look
your eyes would tell you. Do you believe my passion
is voluntary? That my obscene confession   355
is some dark trick, some oily artifice?
I came to beg you not to sacrifice
my son, already uncertain of his life.
Ridiculous, mad embassy, for a wife
who loves her stepson! Prince, I only spoke   360
about myself! Avenge yourself, invoke
your father; a worse monster threatens you
than any Theseus ever fought and slew.
The wife of Theseus loves Hippolytus!
See, Prince! Look, this monster, ravenous   365
for her execution, will not flinch.
I want your sword's spasmodic final inch.

OENONE. Madam, put down this weapon. Your distress
    attracts the people. Fly these witnesses.
    Hurry! Stop kneeling! What a time to pray!   370

---

353. *Sibyl*: originally the daughter of Dardanus and Neso, who had prophetic powers. Later the name was used about many old women who could foretell the future. Apollo granted the Cumaean Sibyl a lifetime of a thousand years, but not lasting youth.

SCENE VI. *Theramenes, Hippolytus*

THERAMENES. Is this Phaedra, fleeing, or rather dragged away
   sobbing? Where is your sword? Who tore
   this empty scabbard from your belt?
HIPPOLYTUS.   No more!
   Oh let me get away! I face disaster.
   Horrors unnerve me. Help! I cannot master   375
   my terror. Phaedra . . . No, I won't expose
   her. No! Something I do not dare disclose . . .
THERAMENES. Our ship is ready, but before you leave,
   listen! Prince, what we never would believe
   has happened: Athens has voted for your brother.   380
   The citizens have made him king. His mother
   is regent.
HIPPOLYTUS. Phaedra is in power!
THERAMENES. An envoy sent from Athens came this hour
   to place the scepter in her hands. Her son
   is king.
HIPPOLYTUS. Almighty gods, you know this woman!   385
   Is it her spotless virtue you reward?
THERAMENES. I've heard a rumor. Someone swam aboard
   a ship off Epirus. He claims the King
   is still alive. I've searched. I know the thing
   is nonsense.
HIPPOLYTUS.   Search! Nothing must be neglected.   390
   If the king's dead, I'll rouse the disaffected
   people, crown Aricia, and place our lands,
   our people, and our lives in worthy hands.

Act 3

SCENE I. *Phaedra, Oenone*

PHAEDRA. Why do my people rush to crown me queen?
   Who can even want to see me? They have seen
   my downfall. Will their praise deliver me?
   Oh bury me at the bottom of the sea!
   Nurse, I have said too much! Led on by you,   5
   I've said what no one should have listened to.
   He listened. How could he pretend my drift
   was hidden? Something held him, and made him shift
   his ground . . . He only wanted to depart
   and hide, while I was pouring out my heart.   10
   Oh how his blushing multiplied my shame!
   Why did you hold me back! You are to blame,

Oenone. But for you, I would have killed
myself. Would he have stood there, iron-willed
and merciless, while I fell upon his sword?   15
He would have snatched it, held me, and restored
my life. No! No!

OENONE.   Control yourself! No peace
comes from surrendering to your disease,
Madam. Oh daughter of the kings of Crete,
why are you weeping and fawning at the feet   20
of this barbarian, less afraid of fate
than of a woman? You must rule the state.

PHAEDRA. Can I, who have no courage to restrain
the insurrection of my passions, reign?
Will the Athenians trust their sovereignty   25
to me? Love's despotism is crushing me,
I am ruined.

OENONE.   Fly!

PHAEDRA.   How can I leave him?

OENONE. Lady, you have already banished him.
Can't you take flight?

PHAEDRA.   The time for flight has passed.   30
He knows me now. I rushed beyond the last
limits of modesty, when I confessed.
Hope was no longer blasting through my breast;
I was resigned to hopelessness and death,
and gasping out my last innocent breath,
Oenone, when you forced me back to life.   35
You thought I was no longer Theseus' wife,
and let me feel that I was free to love.

OENONE. I would have done anything to remove
your danger. Whether I'm guilty or innocent
is all the same to me. Your punishment   40
should fall on one who tried to kill you, not
on poor Oenone. Lady, you must plot
and sacrifice this monster, whose unjust
abhorence left you dying in the dust.
Oh humble him, undo him, oh despise   45
him! Lady, you must see him with my eyes.

PHAEDRA. Oenone, he was nourished in the woods;
he is all shyness and ungracious moods
because the forests left him half-inhuman.
He's never heard love spoken by a woman!   50
We've gone too far. Oenone, we're unwise;
perhaps the young man's silence was surprise.

OENONE. His mother, the amazon, was never moved
by men.

PHAEDRA.   The boy exists. She must have loved!
OENONE. He has a sullen hatred for our sex.   55
PHAEDRA. Oh, all the better; rivals will not vex
  my chances. Your advice is out of season;
  now you must serve my frenzy, not my reason!
  You tell me love has never touched his heart;
  we'll look, we'll find an undefended part.   60
  He's turned his bronze prows seaward; look, the wind
  already blows like a trumpeter behind
  his bulging canvas! The Acropolis
  of Athens and its empire shall be his!
  Hurry, Oenone, hunt the young man down,   65
  blind him with dazzling visions of the crown.
  Go tell him I relinquish my command,
  I only want the guidance of his hand.
  Let him assume these powers that weary me,
  he will instruct my son in sovereignty.   70
  Perhaps he will adopt my son, and be
  the son and mother's one divinity!
  Oenone, rush to him, use every means
  to bend and win him; if he fears the Queen's
  too proud, he'll listen to her slave. Plead, groan,   75
  insist, say I am giving him my throne . . .
  No, say I'm dying!

SCENE II. *Phaedra*

PHAEDRA.   Implacable Aphrodite, now you see
  the depths to which your tireless cruelty
  has driven Phaedra—here is my bosom;
  every thrust and arrow has struck home!   80
  Oh Goddess, if you hunger for renown,
  rise now, and shoot a worthier victim down!
  Conquer the barbarous Hippolytus,
  who mocks the graces and the power of Venus,
  and gazes on your godhead with disgust.   85
  Avenge me, Venus! See, my cause is just,
  my cause is yours. Oh bend him to my will! . . .
  You're back, Oenone? Does he hate me still?

SCENE III. *Phaedra, Oenone*

OENONE. Your love is folly, dash it from your soul,
  gather your scattered pride and self-control,   90
  Madam! I've seen the royal ship arrive.
  Theseus is back, Theseus is still alive!
  Thousands of voices thunder from the docks.
  People are waving flags and climbing rocks.

While I was looking for Hippolytus . . .   95

PHAEDRA. My husband's living! Must you trouble us
  by talking? What am I living for?
  He lives, Oenone, let me hear no more
  about it.

OENONE.   Why?

PHAEDRA.   I told you, but my fears
  were stilled, alas, and smothered by your tears.   100
  Had I died this morning, I might have faced
  the gods. I heeded you and die disgraced!

OENONE. You are disgraced!

PHAEDRA.   Oh Gods of wrath,
  how far I've travelled on my dangerous path!
  I go to meet my husband; at his side   105
  will stand Hippolytus. How shall I hide
  my thick adulterous passion for this youth,
  who has rejected me, and knows the truth?
  Will the stern Prince stand smiling and approve
  the labored histrionics of my love   110
  for Theseus, see my lips, still languishing
  for his, betray his father and his King?
  Will he not draw his sword and strike me dead?
  Suppose he spares me? What if nothing's said?
  Am I a gorgon, or Circe, or the infidel   115
  Medea, stifled by the flames of hell,
  yet rising like Aphrodite from the sea,
  refreshed and radiant with indecency?
  Can I kiss Theseus with dissembled poise?
  I think each stone and pillar has a voice.   120
  The very dust rises to disabuse
  my husband—to defame me and accuse!
  Oenone, I want to die. Death will give
  me freedom; oh it's nothing not to live;
  death to the unhappy's no catastrophe!   125
  I fear the name that must live after me,
  and crush my son until the end of time.
  Is his inheritance his mother's crime,
  his right to curse me, when my pollution stains

115-116. *gorgon . . . Medea:* The Gorgons were three sisters, the most famed being Medusa; they were frightful in appearance, with snakes in their hair, large mouths and irregular teeth, and flaming eyes; they were winged, and had claws. Circe, Pasiphaë's sister, was a magician who lived on the island of Aeaea. Her chief feat was changing Odysseus' men into swine. Medea, at one time beloved by Jason when he was questing for the Golden Fleece, had a notably bloodthirsty career: she strewed her brother's limbs on the sea, killed Jason's uncle by persuading his daughters to cut him up in small pieces and boil them in a cauldron, killed Jason's second wife with a poisoned bridal robe, and murdered the two children she had had by Jason.

the blood of heaven bubbling in his veins? 150
The day will come, alas, the day will come,
when nothing will be left to save him from
the voices of despair. If he should live
he'll flee his subjects like a fugitive.

OENONE. He has my pity. Who has ever built 135
firmer foundations to expose her guilt?
But why expose your son? Is your contribution
for his defense to serve the prosecution?
Suppose you kill yourself? The world will say
you fled your outraged husband in dismay. 140
Could there be stronger evidence and proof
than Phaedra crushed beneath the horse's hoof
of blasphemous self-destruction to convince
the crowds who'll dance attendance on the Prince?
The crowds will mob your children when they hear 145
their defamation by a foreigner!
Wouldn't you rather see earth bury us?
Tell me, do you still love Hippolytus?

PHAEDRA. I see him as a beast, who'd murder us.

OENONE. Madam, let the positions be reversed! 150
You fear the Prince; you must accuse him first.
Who'll dare assert your story is untrue,
if all the evidence shall speak for you:
your present grief, your past despair of mind,
the Prince's sword so luckily left behind? 155
Do you think Theseus will oppose his son's
second exile? He has consented once!

PHAEDRA. How dare I take this murderous, plunging course?

OENONE. I tremble, Lady, I too feel remorse.
If death could rescue you from infamy, 160
Madam, I too would follow you and die.
Help me by being silent. I will speak
in such a way the King will only seek
a bloodless exile to assert his rights.
A father is still a father when he smites, 165
You shudder at this evil sacrifice,
but nothing's evil or too high a price
to save your menaced honor from defeat.
Ah Minos, Minos, you defended Crete
by killing young men? Help us! If the cost 170
for saving Phaedra is a holocaust
of virtue, Minos, you must sanctify
our undertaking, or watch your daughter die.
I see the King.

PHAEDRA.   I see Hippolytus!

SCENE IV. *Phaedra, Theseus, Hippolytus, Oenone*

THESEUS. Fate's heard me, Phaedra, and removed the bar   175
that kept me from your arms.

PHAEDRA.   Theseus, stop where you are!
Your raptures and endearments are profane.
Your arm must never comfort me again.
You have been wronged, the gods who spared your life   180
have used your absence to disgrace your wife,
unworthy now to please you or come near.
My only refuge is to disappear.

SCENE V. *Theseus, Hippolytus*

THESEUS. What a strange welcome! This bewilders me.
My son, what's happened?

HIPPOLYTUS.   Phaedra holds the key.   185
Ask Phaedra. If you love me, let me leave
this kingdom. I'm determined to achieve
some action that will show my strength. I fear
Phaedra. I am afraid of living here,

THESEUS. My son, you want to leave me?

HIPPOLYTUS.   I never sought   190
her grace or favor. Your decision brought
her here from Athens. Your desires prevailed
against my judgment, Father, when you sailed
leaving Phaedra and Aricia in my care.
I've done my duty, now I must prepare   195
for sterner actions, I must test my skill
on monsters far more dangerous to kill
than any wolf or eagle in this wood.
Release me, I too must prove my manhood.
Oh Father, you were hardly half my age,   200
when herds of giants writhed before your rage—
you were already famous as the scourge
of insolence. Our people saw you purge
the pirates from the shores of Greece and Thrace,
the harmless merchantman was free to race   205
the winds, and weary Hercules could pause
from slaughter, knowing you upheld his cause.
The world revered you. I am still unknown;
even my mother's deeds surpass my own.
Some tyrants have escaped you; let me meet   210
with them and throw their bodies at your feet.

I'll drag them from their wolf-holes; if I die,
my death will show I struggled worthily.
Oh, Father, raise me from oblivion;
my deeds shall tell the universe I am your son.   215
THESEUS. What do I see? Oh gods, what horror drives
my queen and children fleeing for their lives
before me? If so little warmth remains,
oh why did you release me from my chains?
Why am I hated, and so little loved?   220
I had a friend, just one. His folly moved
me till I aided his conspiracy
to ravish Queen Persephone.
The gods, tormented by our blasphemous
designs, befogged our minds and blinded us—   225
we invaded Epirus instead of hell.
There a diseased and subtle tyrant fell
upon us as we slept, and while I stood
by, helpless, monsters crazed for human blood
consumed Pirithoüs. I myself was chained   230
fast in a death-deep dungeon. I remained
six months there, then the gods had pity,
and put me in possession of the city.
I killed the tyrant; now his body feasts
the famished, pampered bellies of his beasts.   235
At last, I voyaged home, cast anchor, furled
my sails. When I was rushing to my world—
what am I saying? When my heart and soul
were mine again, unable to control
themselves for longing—who receives me? All run   240
and shun me, as if I were a skeleton.
Now I myself begin to feel the fear
I inspire. I wish I were a prisoner
again or dead. Speak! Phaedra says my home
was outraged. Who betrayed me? Someone come   245
and tell me. I have fought for Greece. Will Greece,
sustained by Theseus, give my enemies
asylum in my household? Tell me why
I've no avenger? Is my son a spy?
You will not answer. I must know my fate.   250
Suspicion chokes me, while I hesitate
and stand here pleading. Wait, let no one stir.
Phaedra shall tell me what has troubled her.

221. *a friend:* Pirithoüs.
226. *Epirus:* a district in western Greece, on the Ionian Sea.

SCENE VI. *Hippolytus*

HIPPOLYTUS. What now? His anger turns my blood to ice.
    Will Phaedra, always uncertain, sacrifice   255
    herself? What will she tell the King? How hot
    the air's becoming here! I feel the rot
    of love seeping like poison through this house.
    I feel the pollution. I cannot rouse
    my former loyalties. When I try to gather   260
    the necessary strength to face my father,
    my mind spins with some dark presentiment . . .
    How can such terror touch the innocent?
    I LOVE ARICIA! Father, I confess
    my treason to you is my happiness!   265
    I LOVE ARICIA! Will this bring you joy,
    our love you have no power to destroy?

Act 4

SCENE I. *Theseus, Oenone*

THESEUS. What's this, you tell me he dishonors me,
    and has assaulted Phaedra's chastity?
    Oh heavy fortune, I no longer know
    who loves me, who I am, or where I go.
    Who has ever seen such disloyalty   5
    after such love? Such sly audacity!
    His youth made no impression on her soul,
    so he fell back on force to reach his goal!
    I recognize this perjured sword; I gave
    him this myself to teach him to be brave!   10
    Oh Zeus, are blood-ties no impediment?
    Phaedra tried to save him from punishment!
    Why did her silence spare this parricide?
OENONE. She hoped to spare a trusting father's pride.
    She felt so sickened by your son's attempt,   15
    his hot eyes leering at her with contempt,
    she had no wish to live. She read out her will
    to me, then lifted up her arm to kill
    herself. I struck the sword out of her hand.
    Fainting, she babbled the secret she had planned   20
    to bury with her in the grave. My ears
    unwillingly interpreted her tears.
THESEUS. Oh traitor! I know why he seemed to blanch
    and toss with terror like an aspen branch
    when Phaedra saw him. Now I know why he stood   25
    back, then embraced me so coldly he froze my blood.

Was Athens the first stage for his obscene
attentions? Did he dare attack the Queen
before our marriage?

OENONE.   Remember her disgust
and hate then? She already feared his lust.   30

THESEUS. And when I sailed, this started up again?

OENONE. I've hidden nothing. Do you want your pain
redoubled? Phaedra calls me. Let me go,
and save her. I have told you what I know.

SCENE II. *Theseus, Hippolytus*

THESEUS. My son returns! Oh God, reserved and cool,   35
dressed in a casual freedom that could fool
the sharpest. Is it right his brows should blaze
and dazzle me with virtue's sacred rays?
Are there not signs? Should not ADULTERER
in looping scarlet script be branded there?   40

HIPPOLYTUS. What cares becloud your kingly countenance,
Father! What is this irritated glance?
Tell me! Are you afraid to trust your son?

THESEUS. How dare you stand here? May the great Zeus stone
me, if I let my fondness and your birth   45
protect you! Is my strength which rid the earth
of brigands paralysed? Am I so sick
and senile, any coward with a stick
can strike me? Am I a schoolboy's target? Oh God,
am I food for vultures? Some carrion you must prod   50
and poke to see if it's alive or dead?
Your hands are moist and itching for my bed,
Coward! Wasn't begetting you enough
dishonor to destroy me? Must I snuff
your perjured life, my own son's life, and stain   55
a thousand glories? Let the gods restrain
my fury! Fly! live hated and alone—
there are places where my name may be unknown.
Go, find them, follow your disastrous star
through filth; if I discover where you are,   60
I'll add another body to the hill
of vermin I've extinguished by my skill.
Fly from me, let the grieving storm-winds bear
your contagion from me. You corrupt the air.
I call upon Poseidon. Help me, Lord   65
of Ocean, help your servant! Once my sword
heaped crucified assassins on your shore
and let them burn like beacons. God, you swore

my first request would be fulfilled. My first!
I never made it. Even through the worst   70
torments of Epirus I held my peace;
no threat or torture brought me to my knees
beseeching favors; even then I knew
some great project was reserved for you!
Poseidon, now I kneel. Avenge me, dash   75
my incestuous son against your rocks, and wash
his dishonor from my household; wave on wave
of roaring nothingness shall be his grave.

HIPPOLYTUS. Phaedra accuses me of lawless love!
Phaedra! My heart stops, I can hardly move   80
my lips and answer. I have no defense,
if you condemn me without evidence.

THESEUS. Oh coward, you were counting on the Queen
to hide your brutal insolence and screen
your outrage with her weakness! You forgot   85
something. You dropped your sword and spoiled your plot.
You should have kept it. Surely you had time
to kill the only witness to your crime!

HIPPOLYTUS. Why do I stand this, and forbear to clear
away these lies, and let the truth appear?   90
I could so easily. Where would you be,
if I spoke out? Respect my loyalty,
Father, respect your own intelligence.
Examine me. What am I? My defense
is my whole life. When have I wavered, when   95
have I pursued the vices of young men?
Father, you have no scaffolding to rig
your charges on. Small crimes precede the big.
Phaedra accused me of attempting rape!
Am I some Proteus, who can change his shape?   100
Nature despises such disparities.
Vice, like virtue, advances by degrees.
Bred by Antiope to manly arms,
I hate the fever of this lust that warms
the loins and rots the spirit. I was taught   105
uprightness by Theramenes. I fought
with wolves, tamed horses, gave my soul to sport,
and shunned the joys of women and the court.
I dislike praise, but those who know me best
grant me one virtue—it's that I detest   110
the very crimes of which I am accused.

100 *Proteus:* an old man of the ocean, keeper of Poseidon's seals, capable of assuming any form he wished.

How often you yourself have been amused
and puzzled by my love of purity,
pushed to the point of crudeness. By the sea
and in the forest, I have filled my heart   115
with freedom, far from women.

THESEUS.   When this part
was dropped, could only Phaedra violate
the cold abyss of your immaculate
reptilian soul. How could this funeral urn
contain a heart, a living heart, or burn   120
for any woman but my wife?

HIPPOLYTUS.   Ah no!
Father, I too have seen my passions blow
into a tempest. Why should I conceal
my true offense? I feel, Father, I feel
what other young men feel. I love, I love   125
Aricia. Father, I love the sister of
your worst enemies. I worship her!
I only feel and breathe and live for her!

THESEUS. You love Aricia? God! No, this is meant
to blind my eyes and throw me off the scent.   130

HIPPOLYTUS. Father, for six months I have done my worst
to kill this passion. You shall be the first
to know . . . You frown still. Nothing can remove
your dark obsession. Father, what will prove
my innocence? I swear by earth and sky,   135
and nature's solemn, shining majesty . . .

THESEUS. Oaths and religion are the common cant
of all betrayers. If you wish to taunt
me, find a better prop than blasphemy.

HIPPOLYTUS. All's blasphemy to eyes that cannot see.   140
Could even Phaedra bear me such ill will?

THESEUS. Phaedra, Phaedra! Name her again, I'll kill
you! My hand's already on my sword.

HIPPOLYTUS.   Explain
my terms of exile. What do you ordain?

THESEUS. Sail out across the ocean. Everywhere   145
on earth and under heaven is too near.

HIPPOLYTUS. Who'll take me in? Oh who will pity me,
and give me bread, if you abandon me?

THESEUS. You'll find fitting companions. Look for friends
who honor everything that most offends.   150
Pimps and jackals who praise adultery

---

116. *women:* In Euripides' play, much   temis (Diana), the "queen and huntress,
is made of Hippolytus' allegiance to Ar-   chaste and fair."

and incest will protect your purity!

HIPPOLYTUS. Adultery! Is it your privilege
to fling this word in my teeth? I've reached the edge
of madness . . . No, I'll say no more. Compare   155
my breeding with Phaedra's. Think and beware . . .
She had a mother . . . No, I must not speak.

THESEUS. You devil, you'll attack the queen still weak
from your assault. How can you stand and face
your father? Must I drive you from this place   160
with my own hand. Run off, or I will flog
you with the flat of my sword like a dog!

SCENE III. *Theseus*

THESEUS. You go to your inevitable fate,
Child—by the river immortals venerate.
Poseidon gave his word. You cannot fly: 165
death and the gods march on invisibly.
I loved you once; despite your perfidy,
my bowels writhe inside me. Must you die?
Yes; I am in too deep now to draw back.
What son has placed his father on such a rack?   170
What father groans for such a monstrous birth?
Oh gods, your thunder throws me to the earth.

SCENE IV. *Theseus, Phaedra*

PHAEDRA. Theseus, I heard the deluge of your voice,
and stand here trembling. If there's time for choice,
hold back your hand, still bloodless; spare your race!   175
I supplicate you, I kneel here for grace.
Oh, Theseus, Theseus, will you drench the earth
with your own blood? His virtue, youth and birth
cry out for him. Is he already slain
by you for me—spare me this incestuous pain!   180

THESEUS. Phaedra, my son's blood has not touched my hand;
and yet I'll be avenged. On sea and land,
spirits, the swift of foot, shall track him down
Poseidon owes me this. Why do you frown?

PHAEDRA. Poseidon owes you this? What have you done   185
in anger?

THESEUS.   What! You wish to help my son?
No, stir my anger, back me to the hilt,
call for blacker colors to paint his guilt.
Lash, strike and drive me on! You cannot guess

164. *river:* the Styx, the chief river in
Hades and sacred to the gods themselves,
so that their most binding oath was by
the Styx. If such an oath were broken,
the god would lie as one dead for a year.

the nerve and fury of his wickedness.   190
Phaedra, he slandered your sincerity,
he told me your accusation was a lie.
He swore he loved Aricia, he wants to wed
Aricia. . . .

PHAEDRA.   What, my lord!

THESEUS.   That's what he said.
Of course, I scorn his shallow artifice.   195
Help me, Poseidon, hear me, sacrifice
my son. I seek the altar. Come! Let us both
kneel down and beg the gods to keep their oath.

SCENE V. *Phaedra*

PHAEDRA. My husband's gone, still rumbling his own name
and fame. He has no inkling of the flame   200
his words have started. If he hadn't spoken,
I might have . . . I was on my feet, I'd broken
loose from Oenone, and had just begun
to say I know not what to save his son.
Who knows how far I would have gone? Remorse,   205
longing and anguish shook me with such force,
I might have told the truth and suffered death,
before this revelation stopped my breath:
Hippolytus is not insensible,
only insensible to me! His dull   210
heart chases shadows. He is glad to rest
upon Aricia's adolescent breast!
Oh thin abstraction! When I saw his firm
repugnance spurn my passion like a worm,
I thought he had some magic to withstand   215
the lure of any woman in the land,
and now I see a schoolgirl leads the boy,
as simply as her puppy or a toy.
Was I about to perish for this sham,
this panting hypocrite? Perhaps I am   220
the only woman that he could refuse!

SCENE VI. *Phaedra, Oenone*

PHAEDRA. Oenone, dearest, have you heard the news?

OENONE. No, I know nothing, but I am afraid.
How can I follow you? You have betrayed
your life and children. What have you revealed,   225
Madam?

PHAEDRA.   I have a rival in the field,
Oenone.

OENONE.   What?

PHAEDRA.   Oenone, he's in love—
  this howling monster, able to disprove
  my beauty, mock my passion, scorn each prayer,
  and face me like a tiger in its lair—   230
  he's tamed, the beast is harnessed to a cart;
  Aricia's found an entrance to his heart.
OENONE. Aricia?
PHAEDRA.   Nurse, my last calamity
  has come. This is the bottom of the sea.
  All that preceded this had little force—   235
  the flames of lust, the horrors of remorse,
  the prim refusal by my grim young master,
  were only feeble hints of this disaster.
  They love each other! Passion blinded me.
  I let them blind me, let them meet and see   240
  each other freely! Was such bounty wrong?
  Oenone, you have known this all along,
  you must have seen their meetings, watched them sneak
  off to their forest, playing hide-and-seek!
  Alas, such rendezvous are no offence: 245
  innocent nature smiles of innocence,
  for them each natural impulse was allowed,
  each day was summer and without a cloud.
  Oenone, nature hated me. I fled
  its light, as if a price were on my head.   250
  I shut my eyes and hungered for my end.
  Death was the only God my vows could bend.
  And even while my desolation served
  me gall and tears, I knew I was observed;
  I never had security or leisure   255
  for honest weeping, but must steal this pleasure.
  Oh hideous pomp; a monarch only wears
  the robes of majesty to hide her tears!
OENONE. How can their folly help them? They will never
  enjoy its fruit.   260
PHAEDRA.   Ugh, they will love forever—
  even while I am talking, they embrace,
  they scorn me, they are laughing in my face!
  In the teeth of exile, I hear them swear
  they will be true forever, everywhere.
  Oenone, have pity on my jealous rage;   265
  I'll kill this happiness that jeers at age.
  I'll summon Theseus; hate shall answer hate!
  I'll drive my husband to annihilate
  Aricia—let no trivial punishment,

her instant death, or bloodless banishment ...   270
What am I saying? Have I lost my mind?
I am jealous, and call my husband! Bind
me, gag me; I am frothing with desire.
My husband is alive, and I'm on fire!
For whom? Hippolytus. When I have said   275
his name, blood fills my eyes, my heart stops dead.
Imposture, incest, murder! I have passed
the limits of damnation; now at last,
my lover's lifeblood is my single good.
Nothing else cools my murderous thirst for blood.   280
Yet I live on! I live, looked down upon
by my progenitor, the sacred sun,
by Zeus, by Europa, by the universe
of gods and stars, my ancestors. They curse
their daughter. Let me die. In the great night   285
of Hades, I'll find shelter from their sight.
What am I saying? I've no place to turn:
Minos, my father, holds the judge's urn.
The gods have placed damnation in his hands,
the shades in Hades follow his commands.   290
Will he not shake and curse his fatal star
that brings his daughter trembling to his bar?
His child by Pasiphaë forced to tell
a thousand sins unclassified in hell?
Father, when you interpret what I speak,   295
I fear your fortitude will be too weak
to hold the urn. I see you fumbling for
new punishments for crimes unknown before.
You'll be your own child's executioner!
You cannot kill me; look, my murderer   300
is Venus, who destroyed our family;
Father, she has already murdered me.
I killed myself—and what is worse I wasted
my life for pleasures I have never tasted.
My lover flees me still, and my last gasp   305
is for the fleeting flesh I failed to clasp.

OENONE. Madam, Madam, cast off this groundless terror!
Is love now an unprecedented error?
You love! What then! You love! Accept your fate.
You're not the first to sail into this strait.   310

283. *Europa:* Carried off by Zeus in the form of a bull, Europa conceived three children by him, of whom one was Minos, Phaedra's father.
288. *judge's urn:* After his death, Minos of Crete became, along with his brother Rhadamanthus, one of the judges of souls in the Underworld. The urn held the lots which determined to what abode in the Underworld the souls of the dead were to be sent.

180 · *Jean Racine*

Will chaos overturn the earth and Jove,
because a mortal woman is in love?
Such accidents are easy, all too common.
A woman must submit to being woman.
You curse a failure in the source of things.   315
Venus has feasted on the hearts of kings;
even the gods, man's judges, feel desire,
Zeus learned to live with his adulterous fire.

PHAEDRA. Must I still listen and drink your poisoned breath?
My death's redoubled on the edge of death.   320
I'd fled Hippolytus and I was free
till your entreaties stabbed and blinded me,
and dragged me howling to the pit of lust.
Oenone, I was learning to be just.
You fed my malice. Attacking the young Prince   325
was not enough; you clothed him with my sins.
You wished to kill him; he is dying now,
because of you, and Theseus' brutal vow.
You watch my torture; I'm the last ungorged
scrap rooting in this trap your plots have forged.   330
What binds you to me? Leave me, go, and die,
may your punishment be to terrify
all those who ruin princes by their lies,
hints, acquiescence, filth, and blasphemies—
panders who grease the grooves of inclination,   335
and lure our willing bodies from salvation.
Go die, go frighten false flatterers, the worst
friends the gods can give to kings they've cursed!

OENONE. I have given all and left all for her service,
almighty gods! I have been paid my price!   340

Act 5

SCENE I. *Hippolytus, Aricia*

ARICIA. Take a stand, speak the truth, if you respect
your father's glory and your life. Protect
yourself! I'm nothing to you. You consent
without a struggle to your banishment.
If you are weary of Aricia, go;   5
at least do something to prevent the blow
that dooms your honor and existence—both
at a stroke! Your father must recall his oath;
there is time still, but if the truth's concealed,
you offer your accuser a free field.   10
Speak to your father!

HIPPOLYTUS.   I've already said

what's lawful. Shall I point to his soiled bed,
tell Athens how his marriage was foresworn,
make Theseus curse the day that he was born?
My aching heart recoils. I only want   15
God and Aricia for my confidants.
See how I love you; love makes me confide
in you this horror I have tried to hide
from my own heart. My faith must not be broken;
forget, if possible, what I have spoken.   20
Ah Princess, if even a whisper slips
past you, it will perjure your pure lips
God's justice is committed to the cause
of those who love him, and uphold his laws;
sooner or later, heaven itself will rise   25
in wrath and punish Phaedra's blasphemies.
I must not. If I rip away her mask,
I'll kill my father. Give me what I ask.
Do this! Then throw away your chains; it's right
for you to follow me, and share my flight.   30
Fly from this prison; here the vices seethe
and simmer, virtue has no air to breathe.
In the confusion of my exile, none
will even notice that Aricia's gone.
Banished and broken, Princess, I am still   35
a force in Greece. Your guards obey my will,
powerful intercessors wish us well:
our neighbors, Argos' citadel
is armed, and in Mycenae our allies
will shelter us, if lying Phaedra tries   40
to hurry us from our paternal throne,
and steal our sacred titles for her son.
The gods are ours, they urge us to attack.
Why do you tremble, falter and hold back?
Your interests drive me to this sacrifice.   45
While I'm on fire, your blood has changed to ice.
Princess, is exile more than you can face?
ARICIA. Exile with you, my lord? What sweeter place
is under heaven? Standing at your side,
I'd let the universe and heaven slide.   50
You're my one love, my king, but can I hope
for peace and honor, Prince, if I elope
unmarried? This . . . I wasn't questioning
the decency of flying from the King.
Is he my father? Only an abject   55

38. *Argos:* chief city in Argolis, in
the northeastern Peloponnesus.
39. *Mycenae:* also in Argolis, and
center of the Mycenaean civilization,
with close Cretan connections.

182 · *Jean Racine*

spirit honors tyrants with respect.
You say you love me. Prince, I am afraid.

HIPPOLYTUS. Aricia, you shall never be betrayed;
accept me! Let our love be sanctified,
then flee from your oppressor as my bride.   60
Bear witness, oh you gods, our love released
by danger, needs no temple or a priest.
It's faith, not ceremonial, that saves.
Here at the city gates, among these graves
the resting places of my ancient line,   65
there stands a sacred temple and a shrine.
Here, where no mortal ever swore in vain,
here in these shadows, where eternal pain
is ready to engulf the perjurer;
here heaven's scepter quivers to confer   70
its final sanction; here, my Love, we'll kneel,
and pray the gods to consecrate and seal
our love. Zeus, the father of the world will stand
here as your father and bestow your hand.
Only the pure shall be our witnesses: 75
Hera, the guarantor of marriages,
Demeter and the virgin Artemis.

ARICIA. The King is coming. Fly. I'll stay and meet
his anger here and cover your retreat.
Hurry. Be off, send me some friend to guide   80
my timid footsteps, husband, to your side.

SCENE II. *Theseus, Ismene, Aricia*

THESEUS. Oh God, illuminate my troubled mind.
Show me the answer I have failed to find.

ARICIA. Go, Ismene, be ready to escape.

SCENE III. *Theseus, Aricia*

THESEUS. Princess, you are disturbed. You twist your cape   85
and blush. The Prince was talking to you. Why
is he running?

ARICIA.   We've said our last goodbye,
my lord.

THESEUS.   I see the beauty of your eyes
moves even my son, and you have gained a prize
no woman hoped for.

ARICIA.   He hasn't taken on   90
your hatred for me, though he is your son.

---

76. *Hera . . . Demeter:* Hera was Zeus's wife, hence queen of the gods. She was closely associated with marriage. Demeter, the daughter of Cronus and Rhea, mother of Persephone, was also associated with marriage and fertility.

THESEUS. I follow. I can hear the oaths he swore.
He knelt, he wept. He has done this before
and worse. You are deceived.

RICIA.   Deceived, my lord?

THESEUS. Princess, are you so rich? Can you afford   95
to hunger for this lover that my queen
rejected? Your betrayer loves my wife.

RICIA. How can you bear to blacken his pure life?
Is kingship only for the blind and strong,
unable to distinguish right from wrong?   100
What insolent prerogative obscures
a light that shines in every eye but yours?
You have betrayed him to his enemies.
What more, my lord? Repent your blasphemies.
Are you not fearful lest the gods so loathe   105
and hate you they will gratify your oath?
Fear God, my lord, fear God. How many times
he grants men's wishes to expose their crimes.

THESEUS. Love blinds you, Princess, and beclouds your reason.
Your outburst cannot cover up his treason.   110
My trust's in witnesses that cannot lie.
I have seen Phaedra's tears. She tried to die.

RICIA. Take care, your Highness. When your killing hand
drove all the thieves and reptiles from the land,
you missed one monster, one was left alive,   115
one . . . No, I must not name her, Sire, or strive
to save your helpless son; he wants to spare
your reputation. Let me go. I dare
not stay here. If I stayed I'd be too weak
to keep my promise. I'd be forced to speak.   120

SCENE V. *Theseus*

THESEUS. What was she saying? I must try to reach
the meaning of her interrupted speech.
Is it a pitfall? A conspiracy?
Are they plotting together to torture me?
Why did I let the rash, wild girl depart?   125
What is this whisper crying in my heart?
A secret pity fills my soul with pain.
I must question Oenone once again.
My guards summon Oenone to the throne.
Quick, bring her. I must talk with her alone.   130

SCENE V. *Theseus, Panope*

PANOPE. The Queen's deranged, your Highness. Some accursed
madness is driving her; some fury stalks

behind her back, possesses her, and talks
its evil through her, and blasphemes the world.
She cursed Oenone. Now Oenone's hurled   13
herself into the ocean Sire, and drowned.
Why did she do it? No reason can be found.
THESEUS. Oenone's drowned?
PANOPE.   Her death has brought no peace
The cries of Phaedra's troubled soul increase.
Now driven by some sinister unrest,   14
she snatches up her children to her breast,
pets them and weeps, till something makes her scoff
at her affection and she drives them off.
Her glance is drunken and irregular,
she looks through us and wonders who we are;   14
thrice she has started letters to you, Sire,
thrice tossed the shredded fragments in the fire.
Oh call her to you. Help her!
THESEUS. The nurse is drowned? Phaedra wishes to die?
Oh gods! Summon my son. Let him defend   15
himself, tell him I'm ready to attend.
I want him!
        [*Exit* PANOPE.]
                    Neptune, hear me, spare my son!
My vengeance was too hastily begun.
Oh why was I so eager to believe
Oenone's accusation? The gods deceive   15
the victims they are ready to destroy!

SCENE VI. *Theseus, Theramenes*

THESEUS. Here is Theramenes. Where is my boy,
    my first-born? He was yours to guard and keep.
    Where is he? Answer me. What's this? You weep?
THERAMENES. Oh, tardy, futile grief, his blood is shed.   16
    My lord, your son, Hippolytus, is dead.
THESEUS. Oh gods, have mercy!
THERAMENES.   I saw him die. The most
    lovely and innocent of men is lost.
THESEUS. He's dead? The gods have hurried him away
    and killed him? . . . just as I began to pray . . .   165
    What sudden thunderbolt has struck him down?
THERAMENES. We'd started out, and hardly left the town.
    He held the reins; a few feet to his rear,
    a single, silent guard held up a spear.
    He followed the Mycenae highroad, deep   170
    in thought, reins dangling, as if half asleep;
    his famous horses, only he could hold,

trudged on with lowered heads, and sometimes rolled
their dull eyes slowly—they seemed to have caught
their master's melancholy, and aped his thought.   175
Then all at once winds struck us like a fist,
we heard a sudden roaring through the mist;
from underground a voice in agony
answered the prolonged groaning of the sea.
We shook, the horses' manes rose on their heads,   180
and now against a sky of blacks and reds,
we saw the flat waves hump into a mountain
of green-white water rising like a fountain,
as it reached land and crashed with a last roar
to shatter like a galley on the shore.   185
Out of its fragments rose a monster, half
dragon, half bull; a mouth that seemed to laugh
drooled venom on its dirty yellow scales
and python belly forking to three tails.
The shore was shaken like a tuning fork,   190
ships bounced on the stung sea like bits of cork,
the earth moved, and the sun spun round and round,
a sulphur-colored venom swept the ground.
We fled; each felt his useless courage falter,
and sought asylum at a nearby altar.   195
Only the Prince remained; he wheeled about,
and hurled a javelin through the monster's snout.
Each kept advancing. Flung from the Prince's arm,
dart after dart struck where the blood was warm.
The monster in its death-throes felt defeat,   200
and bounded howling to the horses' feet.
There its stretched gullet and its armor broke,
and drenched the chariot with blood and smoke,
and then the horses, terror-struck, stampeded.
Their master's whip and shouting went unheeded,   205
they dragged his breathless body to the spray.
Their red mouths bit the bloody surf, men say
Poseidon stood beside them, that the god
was stabbing at their bellies with a goad.
Their terror drove them crashing on a cliff,   210
the chariot crashed in two, they ran as if
the Furies screamed and crackled in their manes,
their fallen hero tangled in the reins,
jounced on the rocks behind them. The sweet light
of heaven never will expunge this sight: 215
the horses that Hippolytus had tamed,

212. *Furies:* Roman name *(Furiae)*
for the Greek Erinyes—the three winged
goddesses of vengeance, with snakes for
hair, named Alecto, Tisiphone, and Me-
gaera.

now dragged him headlong, and their mad hooves maimed
his face past recognition. When he tried
to call them, calling only terrified;
faster and ever faster moved their feet,   226
his body was a piece of bloody meat.
The cliffs and ocean trembled to our shout,
at last their panic failed, they turned about,
and stopped not far from where those hallowed graves,
the Prince's fathers, overlook the waves.   225
I ran on breathless, guards were at my back,
my master's blood had left a generous track.
The stones were red, each thistle in the mud
was stuck with bits of hair and skin and blood.
I came upon him, called; he stretched his right   230
hand to me, blinked his eyes, then closed them tight.
"I die," he whispered, "it's the gods' desire.
Friend, stand between Aricia and my sire—
some day enlightened, softened, disabused,
he will lament his son, falsely accused;   235
then when at last he wishes to appease
my soul, he'll treat my lover well, release
and honor Aricia. . . ." On this word, he died.
Only a broken body testified
he'd lived and loved once. On the sand now lies   240
something his father will not recognize.
THESEUS. My son, my son! Alas, I stand alone
before the gods. I never can atone.
THERAMENES. Meanwhile, Aricia, rushing down the path,
approached us. She was fleeing from your wrath,   245
my lord, and wished to make Hippolytus
her husband in God's eyes. Then nearing us,
she saw the signs of struggle in the waste,
she saw (oh what a sight) her love defaced,
her young love lying lifeless on the sand.   250
At first she hardly seemed to understand;
while staring at the body in the grass,
she kept on asking where her lover was.
At last the black and fearful truth broke through
her desolation! She seemed to curse the blue   255
and murdering ocean as she caught his head
up in her lap; then fainting lay half dead,
until Ismene somehow summoned back her breath,
restored the child to life—or rather death.
I come, great King, to urge my final task,   260
your dying son's last outcry was to ask
mercy for poor Aricia, for his bride.
Now Phaedra comes. She killed him. She has lied.

SCENE VII. *Theseus, Phaedra, Panope*

THESEUS. Ah Phaedra, you have won. He's dead. A man
  was killed. Were you watching? His horses ran   265
  him down, and tore his body limb from limb.
  Poseidon struck him, Theseus murdered him.
  I served you! Tell me why Oenone died?
  Was it to save you? Is her suicide
  A proof of your truth? No, since he's dead, I must   270
  accept your evidence, just or unjust.
  I must believe my faith has been abused;
  you have accused him; he shall stand accused.
  He's friendless even in the world below.
  There the shades fear him! Am I forced to know   275
  the truth? Truth cannot bring my son to life.
  If fathers murder, shall I kill my wife
  too? Leave me, Phaedra. Far from you, exiled
  from Greece, I will lament my murdered child.
  I am a murdered gladiator, whirled   280
  in black circles. I want to leave the world;
  my whole life rises to increase my guilt—
  all those dazzled, dazzling eyes, my glory built
  on killing killers. Less known, less magnified,
  I might escape, and find a place to hide.   285
  Stand back, Poseidon. I know the gods are hard
  to please. I pleased you. This is my reward:
  I killed my son. I killed him! Only a god
  spares enemies, and wants his servants' blood!

PHAEDRA. No, Theseus, I must disobey your prayer.   290
  Listen to me. I'm dying. I declare
  Hippolytus was innocent.

THESEUS. Ah Phaedra, on your evidence, I sent
  him to his death. Do you ask me to forgive
  my son's assassin? Can I let you live?   295

PHAEDRA. My time's too short, your highness. It was I,
  who lusted for your son with my hot eye.
  The flames of Aphrodite maddened me;
  I loathed myself, and yearned outrageously
  like a starved wolf to fall upon the sheep.   300
  I wished to hold him to me in my sleep
  and dreamt I had him. Then Oenone's tears,
  troubled my mind; she played upon my fears,
  until her pleading forced me to declare
  I loved your son. He scorned me. In despair,   305
  I plotted with my nurse, and our conspiracy
  made you believe your son assaulted me.
  Oenone's punished; fleeing from my wrath,
  she drowned herself, and found a too easy path

to death and hell. Perhaps you wonder why   310
I still survive her, and refuse to die?
Theseus, I stand before you to absolve
your noble son. Sire, only this resolve
upheld me, and made me throw down my knife.
I've chosen a slower way to end my life—   315
Medea's poison; chills already dart
along my boiling veins and squeeze my heart.
A cold composure I have never known
gives me a moment's poise. I stand alone
and seem to see my outraged husband fade   320
and waver into death's dissolving shade.
My eyes at last give up their light, and see
the day they've soiled resume its purity.

PANOPE. She's dead, my lord.

THESEUS.   Would God, all memory
of her and me had died with her! Now I   325
must live. This knowledge that has come too late
must give me strength and help me expiate
my sacrilegious vow. Let's go, I'll pay
my son the honors he has earned today.
His father's tears shall mingle with his blood.   330
My love that did my son so little good
asks mercy from his spirit. I declare
Aricia is my daughter and my heir.

324-325. *Would . . . her:* The performances of the *Comédie Française* traditionally end with this line, the remainder being regarded as anticlimactic.

ALEXANDER POPE
(1688–1744)
An Essay on Man*

TO HENRY ST. JOHN, LORD BOLINGBROKE

Epistle I

ARGUMENT OF THE NATURE AND STATE OF MAN, WITH RESPECT
TO THE UNIVERSE. Of man in the abstract—I. That we can judge
only with regard to our own system, being ignorant of the relations

---

* The four parts of the *Essay* were published separately and anonymously between February, 1733, and January, 1734. Pope probably started the poem in 1729 and finished it before 1732.

f systems and things, ver. 17, &c.—II. That man is not to be
eemed imperfect, but a being suited to his place and rank in the
reation, agreeable to the general order of things, and conformable
ɔ ends and relations to him unknown, ver. 35, &c.—III. That it
 partly upon his ignorance of future events, and partly upon the
ope of a future state, that all his happiness in the present depends,
er. 77, &c.—IV. The pride of aiming at more knowledge, and pre-
ending to more perfection, the cause of man's error and misery.
'he impiety of putting himself in the place of God, and judging
f the fitness or unfitness, perfection or imperfection, justice or
ijustice of his dispensations, ver. 113, &c.—V. The absurdity of
onceiting himself the final cause of the creation, or expecting that
erfection in the moral world which is not in the natural, ver. 131,
c.—VI. The unreasonableness of his complaints against Provi-
ence, while on the one hand he demands the perfections of the
ngels, and on the other the bodily qualifications of the brutes;
ιough, to possess any of the sensitive faculties in a higher degree,
ould render him miserable, ver. 173, &c.—VII. That throughout
ιe whole visible world, an universal order and gradation in the
ensual and mental faculties is observed, which causes a subordina-
on of creature to creature, and of all creatures to man. The grada-
ons of sense, instinct, thought, reflection, reason: that reason alone
ountervails all the other faculties, ver. 207.—VIII. How much
ιrther this order and subordination of living creatures may extend,
bove and below us; were any part of which broken, not that part
nly, but the whole connected creation must be destroyed, ver.
33—IX. The extravagance, madness, and pride of such a desire,
er. 259.—X. The consequence of all, the absolute submission due
ɔ Providence, both as to our present and future state, ver. 281, &c.,
ɔ the end.

> Awake, my St. John! leave all meaner things
> To low ambition, and the pride of Kings.
> Let us (since Life can little more supply
> Than just to look about us and to die)
> Expatiate free o'er all this scene of Man;   5
> A mighty maze! but not without a plan;
> A Wild, where weeds and flow'rs promiscuous shoot;
> Or Garden, tempting with forbidden fruit.
> Together let us beat this ample field,
> Try what the open, what the covert yield;   10
> The latent tracts, the giddy heights, explore
> Of all who blindly creep, or sightless soar;

1. *St. John:* Pope's friend, who had
us far neglected to keep his part of
eir friendly bargain: Pope was to
write his philosophical speculations in
verse, Bolingbroke was to write his in
prose.

Eye Nature's walks, shoot Folly **as** it flies,
And catch the Manners living as they rise;
Laugh where we must, be candid where we can;
But vindicate the ways of God to man.
    I. Say first, of God above, or Man below,
What can we reason, but from what we know?
Of Man, what see we but his station here,
From which to reason, or to which refer?
Through worlds unnumbered though the God be known,
'Tis ours to trace him only in our own.
He, who through vast immensity can pierce,
See worlds on worlds compose one universe,
Observe how system into system runs,
What other planets circle other suns,
What varied Being peoples ev'ry star,
May tell why Heav'n has made us as we are.
But of this frame the bearings, and the ties,
The strong connections, nice dependencies,
Gradations just, has thy pervading soul
Looked through? or can a part contain the whole?
    Is the great chain, that draws all to agree,
And drawn supports, upheld by God, or thee?
    II. Presumptuous Man! the reason wouldst thou find,
Why formed so weak, so little, and so blind?
First, if thou canst, the harder reason guess,
Why formed no weaker, blinder, and no less?
Ask of thy mother earth, why oaks are made
Taller or stronger than the weeds they shade?
Or ask of yonder argent fields above,
Why Jove's satellites are less than Jove?
    Of Systems possible, if 'tis confest.
That Wisdom infinite must form the best,
Where all must full or not coherent be,
And all that rises, rise in due degree;
Then, in the scale of reas'ning life, 'tis plain,
There must be, somewhere, such a rank as Man:
And all the question (wrangle e'er so long)
Is only this, if God has placed him wrong?
    Respecting Man, whatever wrong we call,

---

16. *vindicate . . . man:* compare
Milton's *Paradise Lost*, Book I, l. 26.
Pope's theme is essentially the same
as Milton's, and even the opening image
of the garden reminds us of the earlier
poet's "Paradise."
    33. *the great chain:* the popular
eighteenth-century notion of the Great

Chain of Being, in which elements
the universe took their places in
hierarchy ranging from the lowe
matter to God.
    45. *full:* According to the princi
of plenitude, there can be no gaps
the Chain.

May, must be right, as relative to all.
In human works, though laboured on with pain,
A thousand movements scarce one purpose gain;
In God's, one single can its end produce;   55
Yet serves to second too some other use.
So Man, who here seems principal alone,
Perhaps acts second to some sphere unknown,
Touches some wheel, or verges to some goal;
'Tis but a part we see, and not a whole.   60
　　When the proud steed shall know why Man restrains
His fiery course, or drives him o'er the plains;
When the dull Ox, why now he breaks the clod,
Is now a victim, and now Egypt's God:
Then shall Man's pride and dullness comprehend   65
His actions', passions', being's use and end;
Why doing, suff'ring, checked, impelled; and why
This hour a slave, the next a deity.
　　Then say not Man's imperfect, Heav'n in fault;
Say rather, Man's as perfect as he ought: 70
His knowledge measured to his state and place;
His time a moment, and a point his space.
If to be perfect in a certain sphere,
What matter, soon or late, or here or there?
The blest to-day is as completely so,   75
As who began a thousand years ago.
　　III. Heav'n from all creatures hides the book of Fate,
All but the page prescribed, their present state:
From brutes what men, from men what spirits know:
Or who could suffer Being here below?   80
The lamb thy riot dooms to bleed to-day,
Had he thy Reason, would he skip and play?
Pleased to the last, he crops the flow'ry food,
And licks the hand just raised to shed his blood.
Oh blindness to the future! kindly giv'n,   85
That each may fill the circle marked by Heav'n:
Who sees with equal eye, as God of all,
A hero perish, or a sparrow fall,
Atoms or systems into ruin hurled,
And now a bubble burst, and now a world.   90
　　Hope humbly then; with trembling pinions soar;
Wait the great teacher Death; and God adore.
What future bliss, he gives not thee to know,
But gives that Hope to be thy blessing now.
Hope springs eternal in the human breast: 95
Man never Is, but always To be blest:

The soul, uneasy and confined from home,
Rests and expatiates in a life to come.
  Lo, the poor Indian! whose untutored mind
Sees God in clouds, or hears him in the wind;   100
His soul, proud Science never taught to stray
Far as the solar walk, or milky way;
Yet simple Nature to his hope has giv'n,
Behind the cloud-topt hill, an humbler heav'n;
Some safer world in depth of woods embraced,   105
Some happier island in the wat'ry waste,
Where slaves once more their native land behold,
No fiends torment, no Christians thirst for gold.
To Be, contents his natural desire,
He asks no Angel's wing, no Seraph's fire;   110
But thinks, admitted to that equal sky,
His faithful dog shall bear him company.
  IV. Go, wiser thou! and, in thy scale of sense,
Weigh thy Opinion against Providence;
Call imperfection what thou fanciest such,   115
Say, here he gives too little, there too much:
Destroy all Creatures for thy sport or gust,
Yet cry, If Man's unhappy, God's unjust;
If Man alone engross not Heav'n's high care,
Alone made perfect here, immortal there: 120
Snatch from his hand the balance and the rod,
Re-judge his justice, be the GOD of GOD.
In Pride, in reas'ning Pride, our error lies;
All quit their sphere, and rush into the skies.
Pride still is aiming at the blest abodes,   125
Men would be Angels, Angels would be Gods.
Aspiring to be Gods, if Angels fell,
Aspiring to be Angels, Men rebel:
And who but wishes to invert the laws
Of ORDER, sins against th' Eternal Cause.   130
  V. Ask for what end the heav'nly bodies shine,
Earth for whose use? Pride answers, " 'Tis for mine:
For me kind Nature wakes her genial Pow'r,
Suckles each herb, and spreads out ev'ry flow'r;
Annual for me, the grape, the rose, renew,   135
The juice nectareous, and the balmy dew;
For me, the mine a thousand treasures brings;
For me, health gushes from a thousand springs;
Seas roll to waft me, suns to light me rise;
My footstool earth, my canopy the skies."   140
  But errs not Nature from this gracious end,

From burning suns when livid deaths descend,
When earthquakes swallow, or when tempests sweep
Towns to one grave, whole nations to the deep?
"No," 'tis replied, "the first Almighty Cause   145
Acts not by partial, but by gen'ral laws;
Th' exceptions few; some change since all began:
And what created perfect?"—Why then Man?
If the great end be human happiness,
Then Nature deviates; and can man do less?   150
As much that end a constant course requires
Of show'rs and sunshine, as of man's desires;
As much eternal springs and cloudless skies,
As Men forever temp'rate, calm, and wise.
If plagues or earthquakes break not Heav'n's design,   155
Why then a Borgia, or a Catiline?
Who knows but He whose hand the lightning forms,
Who heaves old Ocean, and who wings the storms;
Pours fierce Ambition in a Cæsar's mind,
Or turns young Ammon loose to scourge mankind?   160
From pride, from pride, our very reas'ning springs;
Account for moral, as for nat'ral things:
Why charge we Heav'n in those, in these acquit?
In both, to reason right is to submit.
    Better for Us, perhaps, it might appear,   165
Were there all harmony, all virtue here;
That never air or ocean felt the wind;
That never passion discomposed the mind.
But ALL subsists by elemental strife;
And Passions are the elements of Life.   170
The gen'ral ORDER, since the whole began,
Is kept in Nature, and is kept in Man.
    VI. What would this Man? Now upward will he soar,
And little less than Angel, would be more;
Now looking downwards, just as grieved appears   175
To want the strength of bulls, the fur of bears.
Made for his use all creatures if he call,
Say what their use, had he the pow'rs of all?
Nature to these, without profusion, kind,
The proper organs, proper pow'rs assigned;   180
Each seeming want compensated of course,
Here with degrees of swiftness, there of force;
All in exact proportion to the state;

156. *Borgia:* Cesare Borgia (1476–
507), Italian prince notorious for his
rimes. *Catiline:* Roman who conspired
gainst the state in 63 B.C.

160. *Ammon:* Alexander the Great,
who when he visited the oracle of Zeus
Ammon in Egypt was hailed by the
priest there as son of the god.

Nothing to add, and nothing to abate.
Each beast, each insect, happy in its own: 185
Is Heav'n unkind to Man, and Man alone?
Shall he alone, whom rational we call,
Be pleased with nothing, if not blessed with all?
    The bliss of Man (could Pride that blessing find)
Is not to act or think beyond mankind;   190
No pow'rs of body or of soul to share,
But what his nature and his state can bear.
Why has not Man a microscopic eye?
For this plain reason, Man is not a Fly.
Say what the use, were finer optics giv'n,   195
T' inspect a mite, not comprehend the heav'n?
Or touch, if tremblingly alive all o'er,
To smart and agonize at ev'ry pore?
Or quick effluvia darting through the brain,
Die of a rose in aromatic pain?   200
If nature thundered in his op'ning ears,
And stunned him with the music of the spheres,
How would he wish that Heav'n had left him still
The whisp'ring Zephyr, and the purling rill?
Who finds not Providence all good and wise,   205
Alike in what it gives, and what it denies?
    VII. Far as Creation's ample range extends,
The scale of sensual, mental pow'rs ascends:
Mark how it mounts, to Man's imperial race,
From the green myriads in the peopled grass: 210
What modes of sight betwixt each wide extreme,
The mole's dim curtain, and the lynx's beam:
Of smell, the headlong lioness between,
And hound sagacious on the tainted green:
Of hearing, from the life that fills the Flood,   215
To that which warbles through the vernal wood:
The spider's touch, how exquisitely fine!
Feels at each thread, and lives along the line:
In the nice bee, what sense so subtly true
From pois'nous herbs extracts the healing dew?   220
How Instinct varies in the grov'lling swine,
Compared, half-reas'ning elephant, with thine!
'Twixt that, and Reason, what a nice barrier,
For ever sep'rate, yet for ever near!
Remembrance and Reflection how allied;   225

195. *optics:* eyes.
199. *effluvia:* stream of minute particles.
202. *music . . . spheres:* the old notion that the movement of the planets created a "higher" music.

212. *dim curtain:* the mole's poor vision. *lynx's beam:* Legend made th. animal one of the keenest-sighted.
214. *sagacious:* here meaning "exceptionally quick of scent."

What thin partitions Sense from Thought divide:
And Middle natures, how they long to join,
Yet never pass th' insuperable line!
Without this just gradation, could they be
Subjected, these to those, or all to thee?   230
The pow'rs of all subdued by thee alone,
Is not thy Reason all these pow'rs in one?
 VIII. See, through this air, this ocean, and this earth,
All matter quick, and bursting into birth.
Above, how high, progressive life may go!   235
Around, how wide! how deep extend below!
Vast chain of Being! which from God began,
Natures ethereal, human, angel, man,
Beast, bird, fish, insect, what no eye can see,
No glass can reach; from Infinite to thee,   240
From thee to Nothing.—On superior pow'rs
Were we to press, inferior might on ours:
Or in the full creation leave a void,
Where, one step broken, the great scale's destroyed:
From Nature's chain whatever link you strike,   245
Tenth or ten thousandth, breaks the chain alike.
 And, if each system in gradation roll
Alike essential to th' amazing Whole,
The least confusion but in one, not all
That system only, but the Whole must fall.   250
Let Earth unbalanced from her orbit fly,
Planets and Suns run lawless through the sky;
Let ruling angels from their spheres be hurled,
Being on Being wrecked, and world on world;
Heav'n's whole foundations to their center nod,   255
And Nature trembles to the throne of God.
All this dread ORDER break—for whom? for thee?
Vile worm!—oh Madness! Pride! Impiety!
 IX. What if the foot, ordained the dust to tread,
Or hand, to toil, aspired to be the head?   260
What if the head, the eye, or ear repined
To serve mere engines to the ruling Mind?
Just as absurd for any part to claim
To be another, in this gen'ral frame:
Just as absurd, to mourn the tasks or pains,   265
The great directing MIND of ALL ordains.
 All are but parts of one stupendous whole,
Whose body Nature is, and God the soul;
That, changed through all, and yet in all the same;

227. *Middle natures:* animals that seem to share the characteristics of several different classes; for example, the duck-billed platypus.

Great in the earth, as in th' ethereal frame; 270
Warms in the sun, refreshes in the breeze,
Glows in the stars, and blossoms in the trees,
Lives through all life, extends through all extent,
Spreads undivided, operates unspent;
Breathes in our soul, informs our mortal part, 275
As full, as perfect, in a hair as heart;
As full, as perfect, in vile Man that mourns,
As the rapt Seraph that adores and burns:
To him no high, no low, no great, no small;
He fills, he bounds, connects, and equals all. 280
    X. Cease then, nor ORDER imperfection name:
Our proper bliss depends on what we blame.
Know thy own point: this kind, this due degree
Of blindness, weakness, Heav'n bestows on thee.
Submit.—In this, or any other sphere, 285
Secure to be as blest as thou canst bear:
Safe in the hand of one disposing Pow'r,
Or in the natal, or the mortal hour.
All Nature is but Art, unknown to thee;
All Chance, Direction, which thou canst not see; 290
All Discord, Harmony not understood;
All partial Evil, universal Good:
And, spite of Pride, in erring Reason's spite,
One truth is clear, WHATEVER IS, IS RIGHT.

294. Epistle II deals with "the Nature and State of Man with respect to himself, as an Individual"; Epistle III examines "the Nature and State of Man with respect to Society"; and the last Epistle concerns "the Nature and State of Man with respect to Happiness.")

FRANÇOIS-MARIE AROUET DE VOLTAIRE
(1694–1778)
Candide, or Optimism*

Chapter 1

How Candide was brought up in a noble castle and how he was expelled from the same

In the castle of the Baron Thunder-ten-tronckh in Westphalia[1] there lived a youth, endowed by Nature with the most gentle manners. His face proclaimed his soul. His judgment was quite honest

* Abridged. 1759. Our text is the anonymous standard English translation of 1779–1781, with some changes by the present editor to make more evident Voltaire's wit and the brilliance of his style.

1. German province east of the Dutch border. Voltaire was fond of referring to it as typical of the poverty of eighteenth-century Germany.

and he was extremely simple-minded; and this was the reason, I think, that he was named Candide. Old servants in the house suspected that he was the son of the Baron's sister and of a good honest gentleman in the neighborhood, whom this young lady would never marry because he could only prove seventy-one quarterings,[2] and the rest of his genealogical tree was lost, owing to the ravages of time.

The Baron was one of the most powerful lords in Westphalia, for his castle possessed a door and windows. His Great Hall was even decorated with a piece of tapestry. The dogs in his stable-yard made up a pack of hounds when necessary; his grooms were his huntsmen; the village curate was his Grand Almoner.[3] They all called him "My Lord," and laughed at his jokes.

The Baroness weighed about three hundred and fifty pounds, was therefore greatly respected, and did the honors of the house with a dignity which rendered her still more respectable. Her daughter Cunégonde, aged seventeen, was rosy-cheeked, fresh, plump and tempting. The Baron's son appeared in every respect worthy of his father. The tutor Pangloss was the oracle of the house, and little Candide followed his lessons with all the candor of his age and character.

Pangloss[4] taught metaphysico-theologo-cosmolonigology.[5] He proved admirably that there is no effect without a cause and that in this best of all possible worlds, My Lord the Baron's castle was the best of castles and his wife the best of all possible Baronesses.

" 'Tis demonstrated," said he, "that things cannot be otherwise; for, since everything is made for an end, everything is necessarily for the best end. Observe that noses were made to wear spectacles; and so we have spectacles. Legs were visibly instituted to be breeched, and we have breeches. Stones were formed to be quarried and to build castles; and My Lord has a very noble castle; the greatest Baron in the province should have the best house; and as pigs were made to be eaten, we eat pork all the year round; consequently, those who have asserted that all is well[6] talk nonsense; they ought to have said that all is for the best."

Candide listened attentively and believed innocently; for he thought Mademoiselle Cunégonde extremely beautiful, although he was never bold enough to tell her so. He decided that after the happiness of being born Baron of Thunder-ten-tronckh, the second degree of happiness was to be Mademoiselle Cunégonde; the third,

2. divisions on a coat of arms.
3. official alms-distributor at a royal court.
4. literally, "all-tongue."
5. Voltaire satirizes the pompous, heavily Germanic philosopher Christian Wolf(f) (1679–1754), popularizer of Leibnitz.
6. possible allusion to Pope's statement in the *Essay on Man:* "Whatever is, is right."

to see her every day; and the fourth to listen to Doctor Pangloss, the greatest philosopher of the province and consequently of the whole world.

One day when Cunégonde was walking near the castle, in a little wood they called The Park, she observed Doctor Pangloss in the bushes, giving a lesson in experimental physics to her mother's waiting maid, a very pretty and docile brunette. Mademoiselle Cunégonde had a great inclination for science and watched breathlessly the reiterated experiments she witnessed; she observed clearly the Doctor's sufficient reason,[7] the effects and the causes, and returned home very much excited, pensive, filled with the desire of learning, reflecting that she might be the sufficient reason of young Candide and that he might be her own.

On her way back to the castle she met Candide and blushed; Candide also blushed. She bade him good-morning in a hesitating voice; Candide replied without knowing what he was saying. Next day, when they left the table after dinner, Cunégonde and Candide found themselves behind a screen; Cunégonde dropped her handkerchief, Candide picked it up; she innocently held his hand; the young man innocently kissed the young lady's hand with remarkable vivacity, tenderness and grace; their lips met, their eyes sparkled, their knees trembled, their hands wandered. Baron Thunder-ten-tronckh passed near the screen, and, observing this cause and effect, expelled Candide from the castle by kicking him in the backside frequently and hard. Cunégonde swooned; to recover her senses, the Baroness slapped her in the face; and all was in consternation in the noblest and most agreeable of all possible castles.

Chapter 2

What happened to Candide among the Bulgarians

Candide, chased out of the earthly paradise, wandered for a long time without knowing where he was going, weeping, turning up his eyes to Heaven, gazing back frequently at the noblest of castles which held the most beautiful of young Baronesses; he lay down to sleep supperless between two furrows in the open fields; it snowed heavily in large flakes. The next morning the shivering Candide, penniless, dying of cold and exhaustion, dragged himself towards the neighboring town, which was called Waldberghoff-trarbk-dikdorff. He halted sadly at the door of an inn. Two men dressed in blue noticed him.

"Comrade," said one, "there's a well-built young man of the right

7. Wolf's chief concern was the proof of the philosophic principle of sufficient reason, previously propounded by his teacher Leibnitz.

height." They went up to Candide and very civilly invited him to
dinner.

"Gentlemen," said Candide with charming modesty, "you do me
a great honor, but I have no money to pay my share."

"Ah, sir," said one of the men in blue, "persons of your figure
and merit never pay anything; are you not five feet five tall?"

"Yes, gentlemen," said he, bowing, "that is my height."

"Ah, sir, come to table; we will not only pay your expenses, we
will never allow a man like you to be short of money; men were only
made to help each other."

"You are in the right," said Candide, "that is what Doctor Pangloss was always telling me, and I see that everything is for the best."

They begged him to accept a few crowns, he took them and
wished to give them an I O U; they refused to take it and all sat down
to table. "Do you not love tenderly . . ."

"Oh, yes," said he. "I love Mademoiselle Cunégonde tenderly."

"No," said one of the gentlemen. "We were asking if you do not
tenderly love the King of the Bulgarians."[8]

"Not a bit," said he, "for I have never seen him."

"What! He is the most charming of Kings, and you must drink
his health."

"Oh, gladly, gentlemen." And he drank.

"That is sufficient," he was told. "You are now the support, the
aid, the defender, the hero of the Bulgarians; your fortune is made
and your glory assured."

They immediately put irons on his legs and took him to a regiment. He was made to turn to the right and left, to raise the ramrod and return the ramrod, to aim, to fire, to double-time, and he
was given thirty strokes with a stick; the next day he drilled not quite
so badly, and received only twenty strokes; the day after, he only had
ten, and was looked on as a prodigy by his comrades.

Candide, completely mystified, could not yet make out how he
was a hero. One fine spring day he thought he would take a walk,
going straight ahead, in the belief that to use his legs as he pleased
was a privilege of the human species as well as of animals. He had
not gone two leagues when four other heroes, each six feet tall, fell
upon him, bound him and dragged him back to a cell. He was asked
by his judges whether he would rather be thrashed thirty-six times by
the whole regiment[9] or receive a dozen lead bullets at once in his
brain. Although he protested that men's wills are free and that he
wanted neither one nor the other, he had to make a choice; by

8. Actually, the king referred to is
Frederick the Great of Prussia, with
whom Voltaire stayed from 1750 to
1753.

9. Voltaire saw this punishment administered at Sans Souci, Frederick's
estate near Berlin, at Potsdam.

virtue of that gift of God which is called *liberty*, he determined to run the gauntlet thirty-six times and actually did so twice. There were two thousand men in the regiment. That made four thousand strokes, which laid bare the muscles and nerves from his neck to his backside. As they were about to proceed to a third turn, Candide, utterly exhausted, begged as a favor that they would be so kind as to smash his head; he obtained this favor; they bound his eyes and he was made to kneel. At that moment the King of the Bulgarians came by and inquired the culprit's crime; and as this King was possessed of a vast genius, he perceived from what he learned about Candide that he was a young metaphysician very ignorant in worldly matters, and therefore pardoned him with a clemency which will be praised in every newspaper and every age. An honest surgeon healed Candide in three weeks with the ointments recommended by Dioscorides.[10] He had already regained a little skin and could walk when the King of the Bulgarians joined battle with the King of the Abares.[11]

Chapter 3

How Candide escaped from the Bulgarians and what became of him

Nothing could have been smarter, more splendid, more brilliant, better drawn up than the two armies.[12] Trumpets, fifes, hautboys, drums, cannons, formed a harmony such as Hell has never heard. First the cannons laid flat about six thousand men on each side; then the musketry removed from the best of worlds some nine or ten thousand blackguards who infested its surface. The bayonet also was sufficient reason for the death of several thousand men. The whole might amount to thirty thousand souls. Candide, trembling like a philosopher, hid himself as well as he could during this heroic butchery.

At last, while the two Kings each commanded a *Te Deum*[13] sung in his camp, Candide decided to go elsewhere to reason about effects and causes. He clambered over heaps of dead and dying men and reached a neighboring village, which was in ashes; it was an Abare village which the Bulgarians had burned in accordance with international law. Here, old men crippled by blows watched the dying agonies of their murdered wives who clutched their children to their bleeding breasts; there, disembowelled girls made to satisfy the natural appetites of several heroes gasped their last sighs; others,

10. Greek physician of the first century A.D. Voltaire here satirizes backward medical practices.
11. or Avares; actually, the reference is to the French-Austrian coalition against Frederick in the Seven Years'
War (1756–1763).
12. Voltaire was probably thinking of the Battle of Fontenoy (1745), famous for its military precision.
13. hymn of thanks for victory.

half-burned, begged to be put to death. Brains were scattered on the ground among dismembered arms and legs.

Candide fled to another village as fast as he could; it belonged to the Bulgarians, and Abarian heroes had treated it in the same way. Candide, stumbling over quivering limbs or across ruins, at last escaped from the theatre of war, carrying a little food in his knapsack, and never forgetting Mademoiselle Cunégonde. His provisions were all gone when he reached Holland; but, having heard that everyone in that country was rich and Christian, he had no doubt at all but that he would be as well treated as he had been in the Baron's castle before he had been expelled on account of Mademoiselle Cunégonde's pretty eyes.

He asked alms of several grave persons, who all replied that if he continued that way he would be shut up in a house of correction to teach him how to live. He then addressed himself to a man who had been discoursing on charity in a large assembly for an hour on end. This orator, glancing at him askance, said: "What are you doing here? Are you for the good cause?"

"There is no effect without a cause," said Candide modestly. "Everything is necessarily linked up and arranged for the best. It was necessary that I should be expelled from the company of Mademoiselle Cunégonde, that I ran the gauntlet, and that I beg my bread until I can earn it; all this could not have happened differently."

"My friend," said the orator, "do you believe that the Pope is Anti-Christ?"

"I had never heard so before," said Candide, "but whether he is or isn't, I am starving."

"You don't deserve to eat," said the other. "Hence, rascal; hence, wretch; never come near me again."

The orator's wife thrust her head out of the window, and seeing a man who did not believe that the Pope was Anti-Christ, she poured on his head a full . . . O Heavens! To what excess religious zeal is carried by ladies!

A man who had not been baptized, an honest Anabaptist named Jacques, saw the cruel and ignominious treatment of one of his brothers, a featherless two-legged creature with a soul; he took him home, cleaned him up, gave him bread and beer, presented him with two florins, and even offered to apprentice him in the manufacture of Persian silks which are made in Holland. Candide almost threw himself at the man's feet, exclaiming: "Doctor Pangloss was right in telling me that all is for the best in this world, for I am vastly more touched by your extreme generosity than by the harshness of the gentleman in the black cloak and his good lady."

202 · François-Marie Arouet de Voltaire

The next day when he walked out he met a beggar covered with sores, dull-eyed, with the end of his nose rotted away, his mouth awry, his teeth black, who talked huskily, was tormented with a violent cough, and spat out a tooth at every coughing-spell.

[In Chapter 4, Candide discovers the beggar to be Pangloss, from whom he learns that the Bulgarians raped and disemboweled Cunégonde, treated the rest of the family in similar fashion, and destroyed the castle. Pangloss is suffering from a disease contracted from Paquette, the Baroness' maidservant. He traces the genealogy of his ailment: one of Columbus' companions brought it from the New World, and Pangloss insists that the malady is "indispensable in this best of worlds, a necessary ingredient." Without it "we should not have chocolate and cochineal."

Candide, Jacques, and Pangloss sail for Lisbon two months later, and arrive just as a tempest and an earthquake commence.]

Chapter 5

Storm, shipwreck, earthquake, and what happened to Dr. Pangloss, to Candide and the Anabaptist Jacques

Half the enfeebled passengers, suffering from that inconceivable anguish which the rolling of a ship causes in the nerves and in all the humors of bodies shaken in contrary directions, did not retain strength enough even to trouble about the danger. The other half screamed and prayed; the sails were ripped, the masts broken, the vessel leaking. Those worked who could, no one cooperated, no one commanded. The Anabaptist tried to help a little in the ship-handling; he was on the main deck; a furious sailor struck him violently and stretched him on the deck; but the blow he delivered gave him so violent a shock that he fell head-first out of the ship. He remained hanging and clinging to part of the broken mast. The good Jacques ran to his aid, helped him to climb back, and from the effort he made was flung into the sea in full view of the sailor, who allowed him to drown without condescending even to look at him. Candide came up, saw his benefactor reappear for a moment and then be engulfed for ever. He tried to throw himself after him into the sea; he was prevented by the philosopher Pangloss, who proved to him that the Lisbon roads had been expressly created for the Anabaptist to be drowned in them. While he was proving this *a priori*,[14] the vessel sank, and every one perished except Pangloss, Candide and the brutal sailor who had drowned the virtuous Anabaptist; the blackguard swam successfully to the shore and Pangloss and Candide were carried there on a plank.

14. by deductive rather than inductive reasoning.

When they had recovered a little, they walked toward Lisbon; they had a little money by which they hoped to be saved from hunger after having escaped the storm. Weeping the death of their benefactor, they had scarcely set foot in the town when they felt the earth tremble under their feet; the sea rose in foaming masses in the port and smashed the ships which rode at anchor. Whirlwinds of flame and ashes covered the streets and squares; the houses collapsed, the roofs were thrown upon the foundations, and the foundations were scattered; thirty thousand[15] inhabitants of every age and sex were crushed under the ruins. Whistling and swearing, the sailor said: "There'll be something to pick up here."

"What can be the sufficient reason for this phenomenon?" said Pangloss.

"It is the Last Day!" cried Candide.

The sailor immediately ran among the debris, dared death to find money, found it, seized it, got drunk, and having slept off his wine, bought the favors of the first woman of easy virtue he met on the ruins of the houses and among the dead and dying. Pangloss, however, pulled him by the sleeve. "My friend," said he, "this is not well, you are disregarding universal reason, you choose the wrong occasion."

"Bloody Hell!" he retorted, "I am a sailor and I was born in Batavia; four times have I stamped on the crucifix[16] during four voyages to Japan; you have found the right man for your universal reason!"

Candide had been hurt by some falling rocks; he lay in the street covered with debris. He said to Pangloss: "Alas! Get me a little wine and oil; I am dying."

"This earthquake is not a new thing," replied Pangloss. "The town of Lima[17] felt the same shocks in America last year; similar causes produce similar effects; there must certainly be a train of sulphur underground from Lima to Lisbon."

"Nothing is more probable," replied Candide; "but, for God's sake, a little oil and wine."

"What do you mean, probable?" replied the philosopher; "I maintain that it is proved."

Candide lost consciousness, and Pangloss brought him a little water from a neighboring fountain.

Next day they found a little food as they wandered among the ruins and regained a little strength. Afterwards they worked like others to help the inhabitants who had escaped death. Some citi-

---

15. Estimates of casualties in the Lisbon earthquake of November 1, 1755, ran from thirty to fifty thousand.

16. Dutch merchants had to perform this rite to prove they were not Portuguese Catholics, who had plotted against the Japanese in 1637.

17. The city in Peru had been partially destroyed in 1746.

zens they had assisted gave them as good a dinner as could be expected in such a disaster; true, it was a dreary meal; the hosts watered their bread with their tears, but Pangloss consoled them by assuring them that things could not be otherwise. "For," said he, "all this is for the best; for, if there is a volcano at Lisbon, it cannot be anywhere else; for it is impossible that things should not be where they are; for all is well."

A little man in black, a familiar[18] of the Inquisition, who sat beside him, politely took up the conversation, and said: "Apparently, you do not believe in original sin; for, if everything is for the best, there was neither fall nor punishment."

"I most humbly beg your excellency's pardon," replied Pangloss still more politely, "for the fall of man and the curse necessarily entered into the best of all possible worlds."

"Then you do not believe in free will?" said the familiar.

"Your excellency will pardon me," said Pangloss; "free will can exist with absolute necessity; for it was necessary that we should be free; for in short, limited will . . ."

Pangloss was in the middle of his phrase when the familiar nodded to his armed attendant who was pouring out port or Oporto wine for him.

Chapter 6

How a splendid auto-da-fé was held to prevent earthquakes, and how Candide was flogged

After the earthquake which destroyed three-quarters of Lisbon, the wise men of that country could discover no more efficacious way of preventing total ruin than by giving the people a splendid *auto-da-fé*.[19] It was decided by the university of Coimbre[20] that the sight of several persons being slowly burned in great ceremony is an infallible secret for preventing earthquakes. Consequently they had arrested a Biscayan convicted of having married his fellow-godmother, and two Portuguese who, when eating a chicken, had thrown away the bacon.[21] After dinner they came and bound Dr. Pangloss and his disciple Candide, one because he had spoken and the other because he had listened with an air of approbation. They were both carried separately to extremely cool apartments, where there was never any discomfort from the sun; a week afterwards each was dressed in a sanbenito[22] and their heads were ornamented with

18. police officer of the Inquisition or Holy Office—that branch of the Catholic Church which attempted to suppress heresies.

19. literally, "act of the faith" (Portuguese); the execution of a sentence imposed by the Holy Inquisition. Such a burning of heretics at the stake actually took place at Lisbon on June 26, 1756.

20. north of Lisbon.

21. and were therefore presumed to be Jewish.

22. a scapular-shaped penitential garment worn by a heretic.

paper mitres. Candide's mitre and sanbenito were painted with flames upside down and with devils who had neither tails nor claws; but Pangloss's devils had claws and tails, and his flames were upright.[23]

Dressed in this manner they marched in procession and listened to a most pathetic sermon, followed by lovely plain song music. Candide was flogged in time to the music, while the singing went on; the Biscayan and the two men who had not wanted to eat the bacon were burned, and Pangloss was hanged, although this is not the usual practice. The very same day, the earth shook again with a terrible clamor.

Candide, terrified, dumbfounded, bewildered, covered with blood, quivering from head to foot, said to himself: "If this is the best of all possible worlds, what are the others? Let it pass that I was flogged, for I was flogged by the Bulgarians, but, O my dear Pangloss! The greatest of philosophers! Must I see you hanged without knowing why! O my dear Anabaptist! The best of men! Was it necessary that you should be drowned in port! O Mademoiselle Cunégonde! The pearl of women! Was it necessary that they should disembowel you!"

He was staggering away, scarcely able to support himself, preached at, flogged, absolved and blessed, when an old woman accosted him and said: "Courage, my son, follow me."

[In Chapter 7, Candide is cared for by a mysterious old woman. She brings him to Cunégonde, whom he had thought dead; but Cunégonde informs him that the two mishaps of rape and disembowelment are not always fatal.]

Chapter 8

Cunégonde's story

"I was fast asleep in bed when it pleased Heaven to send the Bulgarians to our lovely castle of Thunder-ten-tronckh; they murdered my father and brother and cut my mother to bits. A large Bulgarian six feet tall, seeing that I had swooned at this spectacle, began to rape me; this brought me to, I recovered my senses, I screamed, I struggled, I bit, I scratched, I tried to tear out the big Bulgarian's eyes, not knowing that what was happening in my father's castle was a matter of custom; the brute stabbed me with a knife in the left side where I still have the scar."

"Alas! I hope I shall see it," said the naïf Candide.

"You shall see it," said Cunégonde, "but let me go on."

23. Candide's dress indicates repentance; Pangloss' shows he still remains in error. His costume is more correctly called a samarra.

"Go on," said Candide.

She took up thus the thread of her story: "A Bulgarian captain came in, saw me covered with blood, and the soldier did not disturb himself. The captain was angry at the brute's lack of respect to him, and killed him on my body. Afterwards, he had me bandaged and took me to his billet as a prisoner of war. I washed the few shirts he had and did the cooking; I must admit he thought me very pretty; and I will not deny that he was very well built and that his skin was white and soft; otherwise he had little wit, little philosophy; it was plain that he had not been brought up by Dr. Pangloss. At the end of three months he had lost all his money and was tired of me. He sold me to a Jew named Don Issachar, who traded in Holland and Portugal and had a passion for women. This Jew devoted himself to my person but he could not triumph over it. I resisted him more than I did the Bulgarian soldier; a lady of honor may be raped once, but it strengthens her virtue. In order to subdue me, the Jew brought me to the country house you now see. Up till then I believed there was nothing on earth so splendid as the castle of Thunder-ten-tronckh; I was mistaken.

"One day the Grand Inquisitor noticed me at Mass; he ogled me continually and sent a message that he wished to speak to me on secret affairs. I was taken to his palace; I informed him of my birth; he pointed out how much it was beneath my rank to belong to an Israelite. A proposition was made on his behalf to Don Issachar to give me up to His Lordship. Don Issachar, who is the court banker and a man of influence, would not agree. The Inquisitor threatened him with an *auto-da-fé*. At last the Jew was frightened and made a bargain whereby the house and I belong to both in common. The Jew has Mondays, Wednesdays and the Sabbath day, and the Inquisitor has the other days of the week. This arrangement has lasted for six months. It has not been without quarrels; for it has often been debated whether the night between Saturday and Sunday belonged to the old law or the new. For my part, I have hitherto resisted them both; and I think that is the reason they still love me.

"At last My Lord the Inquisitor was pleased to arrange an *auto-da-fé* to remove the scourge of earthquakes and to intimidate Don Issachar. He honored me with an invitation. I had an excellent seat; and refreshments were served to the ladies between the Mass and the execution. I was indeed horror stricken when I saw the burning of the two Jews and the honest Biscayan who had married his fellow-godmother; but what was my surprise, my terror, my anguish, when I saw in a sanbenito and under a mitre a face which resembled Pangloss's! I rubbed my eyes, I looked carefully, I saw him hanged; and I fainted. I had scarcely recovered my senses when I saw you stripped naked; that was the height of horror, of consternation, of grief and despair. I will frankly tell you that your skin is even whiter and of a more perfect tint than that of my Bulgarian captain. This spectacle redoubled all the feelings which crushed and devoured me. I exclaimed, I tried to say: 'Stop, Barbarians!' but my voice failed and my cries would have been useless. When you had been well flogged, I said to myself: 'How does it happen that the charming Candide and the wise Pangloss are in Lisbon, the one to receive a hundred lashes, and the other to be hanged, by order of My Lord the Inquisitor, whose beloved I am? Pangloss deceived me cruelly when he said that all is for the best in the world.'

"I was agitated, distracted, sometimes beside myself and sometimes ready to die of faintness, and my head was filled with the massacre of my father, of my mother, of my brother, the insolence of my horrid Bulgarian soldier, the gash he gave me, my slavery, my life as a kitchen wench, my Bulgarian captain, my horrid Don Issachar, my abominable Inquisitor, the hanging of Dr. Pangloss, that long plain song *miserere* during which you were flogged, and above all the kiss I gave you behind the screen that day when I saw you for the last time. I praised God for bringing you back to me through so many trials, I ordered my old woman to take care of you and to bring you here as soon as she could. She has carried out my commission very well; I have enjoyed the inexpressible pleasure of seeing you again, of listening to you, and of speaking to you. You must be very hungry; I have a good appetite; let's begin by having supper."

Both sat down to supper; and after supper they returned to the handsome sofa we have already mentioned; they were still there when Signor Don Issachar, one of the masters of the house, arrived. It was the day of the Sabbath. He came to enjoy his rights and to express his tender affection.

[In Chapter 9, Candide kills Don Issachar in self-defense. One hour later, early Sunday morning, the Inquisitor enters; and Candide is forced to kill him as well. Candide, Cunégonde, and the old woman flee on horseback to Avacena in the Sierra Morena.

In Chapter 10, Cunégonde is robbed of her remaining jewels; but the trio gets to Cadiz, where a fleet is being outfitted to attack the Jesuit community in Paraguay. Candide is given command of an infantry company, and they sail for the New World where they hope to find the best of all possible worlds. As Candide says, ". . . it must be admitted that one might lament a little over the physical and moral happenings in our own world." The old woman begins the story of her life to prove to the others that she is the most unfortunate of them all.]

Chapter 11

The old woman's story

"My eyes were not always bloodshot and red-rimmed; my nose did not always touch my chin and I was not always a servant. I am the daughter of Pope Urban X[24] and the Princess of Palestrina. Until I was fourteen I was brought up in a palace to which all the castles of your German Barons would not have served as stables; and any one of my dresses cost more than all the magnificence of Westphalia. I increased in beauty, in grace, in talents, among pleasures, respect and hopes; already I inspired love, my breasts were forming; and what breasts! White, firm, carved like those of the Venus de' Medici. And what eyes! What eyelids! What black eyebrows! What fire shone from my two eyeballs, and dimmed the glitter of the stars, as the local poets pointed out to me. The women who dressed and undressed me fell into ecstasy when they beheld me in front and behind; and all the men would have liked to be in their place.

"I was betrothed to a ruling prince of Massa-Carrara. What a prince! As beautiful as I was, formed of gentleness and charms, brilliantly witty and burning with love; I loved him with a first love, idolatrously and extravagantly. The marriage ceremonies were arranged with unheard of pomp and magnificence; there were continual fêtes, revels and comic operas; all Italy wrote sonnets for me and not a one was worth reading.

"I reached the moment of my happiness when an old marchioness who had been my prince's mistress invited him to take chocolate with her; less than two hours afterwards he died in horrible convulsions; but that is only a trifle. My mother was in despair, though less distressed than I, and wished to absent herself for a time from a place so disastrous. She had a most beautiful estate near Gaeta;[25] we embarked on a galley, gilded like the altar of St. Peter's at Rome. A Salle[26] pirate swooped down and boarded us; our soldiers defended us like soldiers of the Pope; they threw away their arms, fell on their knees and asked the pirates for absolution *in articulo mortis*.[27]

"They were immediately stripped as naked as monkeys, and my mother, our ladies-in-waiting and myself as well. The diligence with which these gentlemen strip people is truly admirable; but I was still more surprised by their inserting a finger in a place belonging to all of us where we women usually only admit the end of a syringe.

---

24. "Behold the extreme discretion of the author! Up to now there has never been a Pope called Urban X; the author hesitates to present an actual Pope with a bastard. Such circumspection! Such delicacy of conscience!" [Voltaire's note, first published posthumously.]

25. near Naples.

26. a Moroccan pirates' port.

27. at the point of death.

This appeared to me a very strange ceremony; but that is how we judge everything when we leave our own country. I soon learned that it was to find out if we had hidden any diamonds there; 'tis a custom established from time immemorial among the civilised nations who roam the seas. I have learned that the religious Knights of Malta[28] never fail in it when they capture Turks and Turkish women; this is an international law which has never been broken.

"I will not tell you how hard it is for a young princess to be taken with her mother as a slave to Morocco; you will also guess all we had to endure in the pirates' ship. My mother was still very beautiful; our ladies-in-waiting, even our maids possessed more charms than could be found in all Africa; and I was ravishing, I was beauty, grace itself, and I was a virgin. I did not remain so long; the flower which had been reserved for the handsome prince of Massa-Carrara was torn from me by a pirate captain; he was an abominable negro who thought he was doing me a great honor. The Princess of Palestrina and I must indeed have been strong to bear up against all we endured before our arrival in Morocco! But let that pass; these items are so common that they are not worth mentioning.

"Morocco was swimming in blood when we arrived. The fifty sons of the Emperor Muley Ismael had each a faction; and this produced fifty civil wars, of blacks against blacks, browns against browns, mulattoes against mulattoes. There was continual carnage throughout the whole extent of the empire.

"Scarcely had we landed when blacks of a party hostile to that of my pirate arrived with the purpose of depriving him of his booty. After the diamonds and the gold, we were the most valuable possessions. I witnessed a fight such as is never seen in your European climates. The blood of the northern races is not sufficiently ardent; their mania for women does not reach the point which is common in Africa. The Europeans seem to have milk in their veins; but vitriol and fire flow in the veins of the inhabitants of Mount Atlas and the neighboring countries. They fought with the fury of lions, tigers and serpents of the country to determine who should have us. A Moor grasped my mother by the right arm, my captain's lieutenant held her by the left arm; a Moorish soldier held one leg and one of our pirates seized the other. In a moment nearly all our women were seized in the same way by four soldiers. My captain kept me hidden behind him; he had a scimitar in his hand and killed everybody who opposed his fury. I saw my mother and all our Italian women torn in pieces, gashed, massacred by the monsters who disputed them. The prisoners, my companions, those who had cap-

28. originally known as Knights of St. John, or Hospitalers, they were given Malta in 1526.

tured them, soldiers, sailors, blacks, browns, whites, mulattoes and finally my captain were all killed and I lay expiring on a heap of corpses. As every one knows, such scenes go on in an area of more than three hundred square leagues and yet no one ever fails to recite the five daily prayers prescribed by Mahomet.

"With great difficulty I extricated myself from the bloody heaps of corpses and dragged myself to the foot of a large orange tree on the bank of a stream; there I fell down with terror, weariness, horror, despair and hunger. Soon afterwards, my exhausted senses fell into a sleep which was more like a swoon than repose. I was in this state of weakness and insensibility between life and death when I felt myself pressed by something stirring on my body. I opened my eyes and saw a white man of good appearance who was sighing and muttering between his teeth: *O che sciagura d'essere senza coglioni!*[29]

Chapter 12

Continuation of the old woman's misfortunes

"Amazed and delighted to hear my native language, and not less surprised at the words spoken by this man, I replied that there were greater misfortunes than that of which he complained. In a few words I informed him of the horrors I had undergone and then swooned again. He carried me to a neighboring house, had me put to bed, gave me food, waited on me, consoled me, flattered me, told me he had never seen anyone so beautiful as I, and that he had never so much regretted that which no one could give back to him.

" 'I was born at Naples,' he said, 'and every year they make two or three thousand children there into capons; some die of it, others acquire voices more beautiful than women's, and others become the governors of States.[30] This operation was performed upon me with very great success and I was a musician in the chapel of the Princess of Palestrina.'

" 'Of my mother,' I exclaimed.

" 'Of your mother!' cried he, weeping. 'What! Are you that young princess I brought up to the age of six and who even then gave promise of being as beautiful as you are?'

" 'I am! my mother is four hundred yards from here, cut into four pieces under a heap of corpses . . .'

"I related all that had happened to me; he also told me his adventures and informed me how he had been sent to the King of Morocco by a Christian power to make a treaty with that monarch whereby he was supplied with powder, cannons and ships to help

29. "What a pity to be a eunuch!" (Italian).
30. Voltaire had in mind the *cas-* *trato* Farinelli (1705–1782), who became peer of Spain and Chevalier of Calatrava.

to exterminate the commerce of other Christians. 'My mission is accomplished,' said this honest eunuch, 'I am about to embark at Ceuta and I will take you back to Italy. *O che sciagura d'essere senza coglioni!*'

"I thanked him with tears of gratitude; and instead of taking me back to Italy he conducted me to Algiers and sold me to the Dey.[31] I had scarcely been sold when the plague which had gone through Africa, Asia and Europe, broke out furiously in Algiers. You have seen earthquakes; but have you ever seen the plague?"

"Never," replied the Baroness.

"If you had," replied the old woman, "you would admit that it is much worse than an earthquake. It is very common in Africa; I caught it. Imagine the situation of a Pope's daughter aged fifteen, who in three months had undergone poverty and slavery, had been raped nearly every day, had seen her mother cut into four pieces, had undergone hunger and war, and was now dying of the plague in Algiers. However, I did not die; but my eunuch and the Dey and almost all the seraglio of Algiers perished.

"When the first ravages of this frightful plague were over, the Dey's slaves were sold. A merchant bought me and carried me to Tunis; he sold me to another merchant who re-sold me at Tripoli; from Tripoli I was re-sold to Alexandria, from Alexandria re-sold to Smyrna, from Smyrna to Constantinople. I was finally bought by an Aga of the Janizaries,[32] who was soon ordered to defend Azov against the Russians who were besieging it.

"The Aga,[33] who was a man of great gallantry, took his whole seraglio with him, and lodged us in a little fort on the Islands of Palus-Maeotis,[34] guarded by two black eunuchs and twenty soldiers. He killed a prodigious number of Russians but they returned the compliment as well. Azov[35] was given up to fire and blood, neither sex nor age was pardoned; only our little fort remained; and the enemy tried to reduce it by starving us. The twenty Janizaries had sworn never to surrender us. The extremities of hunger to which they were reduced forced them to eat our two eunuchs for fear of breaking their oath. Some days later they resolved to eat the women. We had with us a most pious and compassionate Imam[36] who delivered a fine sermon to them by which he persuaded them not to kill us outright. 'Cut,' said he, 'only one buttock from each of these ladies and you will make very good cheer; if you need more, there will still be as much left in a few days; Heaven will be pleased at so charitable an action and you will be saved.'

31. governor.
32. infantry bodyguards of the Turkish sultans.
33. literally, "master" (Turkish); a commander or chief officer of the Otto-

man Empire.
34. the Sea of Azov.
35. besieged in 1695–1696.
36. Mohammedan priest.

"He was very eloquent and persuaded them. This horrible operation was performed upon us; the Imam anointed us with the same balm that is used for children who have just been circumcised; we were all at the point of death.

"Scarcely had the Janizaries finished the meal we had supplied when the Russians arrived in flat-bottomed boats; not a Janizary escaped. The Russians paid no attention to the state we were in. There are French doctors everywhere; one of them who was very skilful, took care of us; he healed us and I shall remember all my life that, when my wounds were cured, he made propositions to me. For the rest, he told us all to cheer up; he told us that the same thing had happened in several sieges and that it was a law of war.

"As soon as my companions could walk they were sent to Moscow. I fell to the lot of a Boyar[37] who made me his gardener and gave me twenty lashes a day. But at the end of two years this lord was broken on the wheel with thirty other Boyars owing to some court disturbance,[38] and I profited by this adventure; I fled; I crossed all Russia; for a long time I was servant in an inn at Riga, then at Rostock, at Wismar, at Leipzig, at Cassel, at Utrecht, at Leyden, at the Hague, at Rotterdam; I have grown old in misery and in shame, with only half a backside, always remembering that I was the daughter of a Pope; a hundred times I wanted to kill myself but I still loved life. This ridiculous weakness is perhaps the most disastrous of our inclinations; for is there anything sillier than to desire to bear continually a burden one always wishes to throw on the ground; to look upon oneself with horror and yet to cling to oneself; in short, to caress the serpent which devours us until he has eaten our heart?

"In the countries it has been my fate to traverse and in the inns where I have served I have seen a prodigious number of people who hated their lives; but I have only seen twelve who voluntarily put an end to their misery: three negroes, four Englishmen, four Genevans[39] and a German professor named Robeck.[40] I ended up as servant to the Jew, Don Issachar; he placed me in your service, my fair young lady; I attached myself to your fate and have been more occupied with your adventures than with my own. I should never even have spoken of my misfortunes, if you had not piqued me a little and if it had not been the custom on board ship to tell stories to pass the time. In short, Mademoiselle, I have had experience, I know the world; provide yourself with an entertain-

37. Russian nobleman.
38. Peter the Great suppressed the revolt of the Strelitzes in 1698.
39. a touch of malice perhaps against Calvinism, or against Voltaire's literary enemy Rousseau, who was born in Geneva.
40. He wrote a book defending suicide and killed himself in 1739.

ment, make each passenger tell you his story; and if there is one who has not often cursed his life, who has not often said to himself that he was the most unfortunate of men, throw me headfirst into the sea."

[In Chapter 13, they arrive at Buenos Aires and call on the governor, who immediately proposes to Cunégonde. The old lady advises her to accept and counsels Candide to flee, since he has been identified as the murderer of the Inquisitor.]

Chapter 14

How Candide and Cacambo were received by the Jesuits in Paraguay

Candide had brought from Cadiz a valet of a sort which is very common on the coasts of Spain and in the colonies. He was one-quarter Spanish, the child of a half-breed in Tucuman;[41] he had been a choirboy, a sacristan, a sailor, a monk, a postman, a soldier and a lackey. His name was Cacambo and he loved his master because his master was a very good fellow. He saddled the two Andalusian horses with all speed. "Come, master, we must follow the old woman's advice; let us be off and ride without looking behind us."

Candide shed tears. "O my dear Cunégonde! Must I abandon you just when the governor was about to marry us! Cunégonde, brought here from such a distant land, what will become of you?"

"She will become what she can," said Cacambo. "Women can take care of themselves; God will see to her. Let us be off."

"Where are you taking me? Where are we going? What shall we do without Cunégonde?" said Candide.

"By St. James of Compostella,"[42] said Cacambo, "you were going to fight the Jesuits; let us go and fight for them; I know the roads, I will take you to their kingdom, they will be charmed to have a captain who can drill in the Bulgarian fashion; you will make a prodigious fortune; when a man fails in one world, he succeeds in another. 'Tis a very great pleasure to see and do new things."

"Then you have already been in Paraguay?" said Candide.

"Yes, indeed," said Cacambo. "I was janitor in the College of the Assumption, and I know the government of *Los Padres*[43] as well as I know the streets of Cadiz. Their government is a most admirable thing. The kingdom is already more than three hundred leagues in diameter and is divided into thirty provinces. *Los Padres* have everything and the people own nothing; 'tis the masterpiece

41. province in the Argentine.
42. patron saint of Spain.
43. i.e., the Jesuits.

of reason and justice. For my part, I know nothing so divine as *Los Padres* who here make war on the Kings of Spain and Portugal and in Europe act as their confessors; who here kill Spaniards and at Madrid send them to Heaven; all this delights me; come on; you will be the happiest of men. What a pleasure it will be to *Los Padres* when they know there is coming to them a captain who can drill in the Bulgarian manner!"[44]

As soon as they reached the first frontier post, Cacambo told the picket that a captain wished to speak to the Commandant. This information was carried to the main guard. A Paraguayan officer ran to the feet of the Commandant to tell him the news. Candide and Cacambo were disarmed and their two Andalusian horses were taken from them. The two strangers were brought in between two ranks of soldiers; the Commandant was at the end, with a biretta on his head, his gown tucked up, a sword at his side and a halberd in his hand. He made a sign and immediately the two newcomers were surrounded by twenty-four soldiers. A sergeant told them that they must wait, that the Commandant could not speak to them, that the Reverend Provincial Father did not allow any Spaniard to open his mouth in his presence or to remain more than three hours in the country.

"And where is the Reverend Provincial Father?" said Cacambo.

"He is on parade after having said Mass, and you will have to wait three hours before you will be allowed to kiss his spurs."

"But," said Cacambo, "the captain who is dying of hunger just as I am, is not a Spaniard but a German; can we not break our fast while we are waiting for his reverence?"

The sergeant went at once to inform the Commandant of this.

"Blessed be God!" said that lord. "Since he is a German I can speak to him; bring him to my arbor."

Candide was immediately taken to a leafy summerhouse decorated with a very pretty colonnade of green marble and gold, and lattices enclosing parrots, hummingbirds, colibris, guinea hens and many other rare birds. An excellent lunch stood ready in gold dishes; and while the Paraguayans were eating maize from wooden bowls, out of doors and in the heat of the sun, the Reverend Father Commandant entered the arbor.

He was a very handsome young man, with a full face, a fairly white skin, red cheeks, arched eyebrows, keen eyes, red ears, vermilion lips, a haughty air, but an arrogance which was neither that of a Spaniard nor of a Jesuit. Candide and Cacambo were given back the arms which had been taken from them and their two Andalusian horses; Cacambo fed them with oats near the arbor, and kept his eye on them for fear of a surprise. Candide first kissed

44. a reference to Prussian military excellence.

the hem of the Commandant's cassock and then they sat down to table. "So you are a German?" said the Jesuit in that language.

"Yes, Reverend Father," said Candide.

As they spoke these words they gazed at each other with extreme surprise and an emotion they could not control.

"And what part of Germany do you come from?" said the Jesuit.

"From the dirty province of Westphalia," said Candide; "I was born in the castle of Thunder-ten-tronckh."

"Heavens! Is it possible!" cried the Commandant.

"What a miracle!" cried Candide.

"Can it be you?" said the Commandant.

" 'Tis impossible!" said Candide. They both fell over backwards, embraced and shed rivers of tears.

"What! Can it be you, Reverend Father? You, the fair Cunégonde's brother! You, who were killed by the Bulgarians! You, the son of My Lord the Baron! You, a Jesuit in Paraguay! The world is indeed a strange place! O Pangloss! Pangloss! How happy you would have been if you had not been hanged!"

The Commandant dismissed the negro slaves and the Paraguayans who were serving wine in goblets of rock crystal. A thousand times did he thank God and St. Ignatius;[45] he clasped Candide in his arms; their faces were wet with tears.

"You would be still more surprised, more touched, more beside yourself," said Candide, "if I were to tell you that Mademoiselle Cunégonde, your sister, whom you thought disembowelled, is in the best of health."

"Where?"

"In your neighborhood, with the governor of Buenos Ayres; and I came to make war on you."

Every word they spoke in this long conversation piled marvel on marvel. Their whole souls flew from their tongues, listened in their ears and sparkled in their eyes. As they were Germans, they sat at table for a long time, waiting for the Reverend Father Provincial; and the Commandant spoke as follows to his dear Candide.

Chapter 15

How Candide killed his dear Cunégonde's brother

"I shall remember all my life the horrible day when I saw my father and mother killed and my sister raped. When the Bulgarians had gone, my adorable sister could not be found, and my mother, my father and I, two maidservants and three little murdered boys were placed in a cart to be buried in a Jesuit chapel two leagues from the castle of my fathers. A Jesuit sprinkled us with holy water;

45. St. Ignatius Loyola, who founded the Jesuit order in 1534.

it was horribly salt; a few drops fell in my eyes; the father noticed that my eyelids trembled, he put his hand on my heart and felt that it was still beating; I was attended to, and at the end of three weeks was as well as if nothing had happened. You know, my dear Candide, that I was a very pretty youth, and I became still prettier; and so the Reverend Father Croust,[46] the Superior of the house, was inspired with a most tender friendship for me; he gave me the dress of a novice and some time afterwards I was sent to Rome. The Father General wished to recruit some young German Jesuits. The sovereigns of Paraguay take as few Spanish Jesuits as they can; they prefer foreigners, whom they think they can control better. The Reverend Father General thought me apt to labor in his vineyard. I set off with a Pole and a Tyrolean. When I arrived I was honored with a subdeaconship and a lieutenancy; I am now colonel and priest. We shall give the King of Spain's troops a warm reception; I guarantee they will be excommunicated and beaten. Providence has sent you to help us. But is it really true that my dear sister Cunégonde is in the neighborhood staying with the governor of Buenos Ayres?"

Candide swore that nothing could be truer. Their tears began to flow once more. The Baron seemed never to grow tired of embracing Candide; he called him his brother, his savior.

"Ah! My dear Candide," said he, "perhaps we shall enter the town together as conquerors and regain my sister Cunégonde."

"I desire it above all things," said Candide, "for I meant to marry her and I still hope to do so."

"You, insolent wretch!" replied the Baron. "Would you have the impudence to marry my sister who has seventy-two quarterings! I consider you extremely impudent to dare to speak to me of such a presumptuous intention!"

Candide, petrified at this speech, replied: "Reverend Father, all the quarterings in the world are of no importance; I rescued your sister from the arms of a Jew and an Inquisitor; she is under considerable obligation to me and wishes to marry me. Dr. Pangloss always said that men are equal and I shall certainly marry her."

"We shall see about that, scoundrel!" said the Jesuit Baron of Thunder-ten-tronckh, at the same time hitting him violently in the face with the flat of his sword. Candide promptly drew his own and stuck it up to the hilt in the Jesuit Baron's belly; but, as he drew it forth dripping, he began to weep. "Alas! My God," said he, "I have killed my old master, my friend, my brother-in-law; I am the mildest man in the world and I have already killed three men, two of them priests."

46. an actual Jesuit priest from Colmar, much disliked by Voltaire.

Cacambo, who was acting as sentry at the door of the arbor, ran in.

"There is nothing left for us but to sell our lives dearly," said his master. "Somebody will certainly come into the arbor and we must die weapon in hand."

Cacambo, who had seen this sort of thing before, did not lose his head; he took off the Baron's Jesuit gown, put it on Candide, gave him the dead man's square hat, and made him mount a horse. All this was done in the twinkling of an eye. "Let us gallop, master; every one will take you for a Jesuit carrying despatches and we shall have passed the frontier before they can pursue us."

As he spoke these words he started off at full speed and shouted in Spanish: "Way, way for the Reverend Father Colonel . . ."

Chapter 16

What happened to the two travellers with two girls, two monkeys, and the savages called Oreillons

Candide and his valet were over the frontier before anybody in the camp knew of the death of the German Jesuit. The vigilant Cacambo had taken care to fill his saddlebag with bread, chocolate, ham, fruit, and several bottles of wine. On their Andalusian horses they plunged into an unknown country where they found no road. At last a beautiful plain traversed by streams met their eyes. Our two travellers put their horses to grass. Cacambo suggested to his master that they should eat and set the example.

"How can you expect me to eat ham," said Candide, "when I have killed the son of My Lord the Baron and find myself condemned never to see the fair Cunégonde again in my life? What is the use of prolonging my miserable days since I must drag them out far from her in remorse and despair? And what will the Journal de Trévoux[47] say?"

Speaking thus, he began to eat. The sun was setting. The two wanderers heard faint cries which seemed to be uttered by women. They could not tell whether these were cries of pain or of joy; but they rose hastily with that alarm and uneasiness caused by everything in an unknown country. These cries came from two completely naked girls who were tripping gently along the edge of the plain, while two monkeys pursued them and nibbled at their buttocks. Candide was moved to pity; he had learned to shoot among the Bulgarians and could have brought down a nut from a tree without touching the leaves. He raised his double-barrelled Spanish musket, fired, and killed the two monkeys.

47. the leading Jesuit journal in France, with which Voltaire quarreled.

"God be praised, my dear Cacambo, I have delivered these two poor creatures from a great danger; if I committed a sin by killing an Inquisitor and a Jesuit, I have atoned for it by saving the lives of these two girls. Perhaps they are young ladies of quality and this adventure may be of great advantage to us in this country."

He was going on, but his tongue clove to the roof of his mouth when he saw the two girls tenderly kissing the two monkeys, shedding tears on their bodies and filling the air with the most piteous cries.

"I did not expect so much human kindliness," he said at last to Cacambo, who replied: "You have performed a wonderful masterpiece; you have killed the two lovers of these young ladies."

"Their lovers! Can it be possible? You are laughing at me, Cacambo; how can I believe you?"

"My dear master," replied Cacambo, "you are always surprised by everything; why should you think it so strange that in some countries there should be monkeys who obtain ladies' favors? They are one-fourth man, as I am one-fourth Spaniard."

"Alas!" replied Candide, "I remember to have heard Dr. Pangloss say that similar accidents occurred in the past and that these mixtures produce Aigypans, fauns and satyrs; that several eminent persons of antiquity have seen them; but I thought they were fables."

"You ought now to be convinced that it is true," said Cacambo, "and you see how people behave when they have not received a proper education; the only thing I fear is that these ladies may get us into a scrape."

These wise reflections persuaded Candide to leave the plain and to plunge into the woods. He ate supper there with Cacambo and, after having cursed the Inquisitor of Portugal, the governor of Buenos Ayres and the Baron, they went to sleep on the moss. When they woke up they found they could not move; the reason was that during the night the Oreillons,[48] the inhabitants of the country, to whom they had been denounced by the two ladies, had bound them with ropes made of bark. They were surrounded by fifty naked Oreillons, armed with arrows, clubs and stone hatchets. Some were boiling a large cauldron, others were preparing spits and they were all shouting: "Here's a Jesuit, here's a Jesuit! We shall be revenged and have a good dinner; let us eat Jesuit, let us eat Jesuit!"

"I told you so, my dear master," said Cacambo sadly. "I knew those two girls would play us a dirty trick."

Candide perceived the cauldron and the spits and exclaimed:

48. in Spanish, *Orejones;* a tribe of Indians who distended their ear-lobes with ornaments.

"We are certainly going to be roasted or boiled. Ah! What would Dr. Pangloss say if he saw what the pure state of nature is? All is well, granted; but I confess it is very cruel to have lost Mademoiselle Cunégonde and to be skewered by the Oreillons."

Cacambo never lost his head. "Do not despair," he said to the wretched Candide. "I understand a little of their dialect and I will speak to them."

"Do not fail," said Candide, "to point out to them the dreadful inhumanity of cooking men and how very unchristian it is."

"Gentlemen," said Cacambo, "you mean to eat a Jesuit today? 'Tis a good deed; nothing could be more just than to treat one's enemies in this fashion. Indeed the law of nature teaches us to kill our neighbor and this is how people behave all over the world. If we do not exert the right of eating our neighbor, it is because we have other means of making good cheer; but you have not the same resources as we, and it is certainly better to eat our enemies than to abandon the fruits of victory to ravens and crows. But, gentlemen, you would not wish to eat your friends. You believe you are about to place a Jesuit on the skewer, and 'tis your defender, the enemy of your enemies you are about to roast. I was born in your country; the gentleman you see here is my master and, far from being a Jesuit, he has just killed a Jesuit and is wearing his clothes; which is the cause of your mistake. To verify what I say, take his gown, carry it to the first outpost of the kingdom of *Los Padres* and inquire whether my master has not killed a Jesuit officer. It will not take you long and you will have plenty of time to eat us if you find I have lied. But if I have told the truth, you are too well acquainted with the principles of public law, good morals and discipline, not to pardon us."

The Oreillons thought this a very reasonable speech; they appointed two of their notables to go with all diligence to find out the truth. The two deputies acquitted themselves of their task like intelligent men and soon returned with good news. The Oreillons untied their two prisoners, overwhelmed them with civilities, offered them girls, gave them refreshment, and accompanied them to the frontiers of their dominions, shouting joyfully: "He is no Jesuit, he is no Jesuit at all!"

Candide could not cease from wondering at the cause of his deliverance. "What a nation," said he. "What men! What manners! If I had not been so lucky as to stick my sword through the body of Mademoiselle Cunégonde's brother I should infallibly have been eaten. But, after all, there is something good in the pure state of nature, since these people, instead of eating me, offered me a thousand civilities as soon as they knew I was not a Jesuit."

Chapter 17

Arrival of Candide and his valet in the country of Eldorado and what they saw there

When they reached the Oreillon frontier, Cacambo said to Candide: "You see this hemisphere is no better than the other; take my advice, let us go back to Europe by the shortest road."

"How can we go back," said Candide, "and where can we go? If I go to my own country, the Bulgarians and the Abares are murdering everybody; if I return to Portugal I shall be burned; if we stay here, we run the risk of being skewered at any moment. But how can I make up my mind to leave that part of the world where Mademoiselle Cunégonde is living?"

"Let us go to Cayenne,"[49] said Cacambo, "we shall find Frenchmen there, for they go all over the world; they might help us. Perhaps God will have pity on us."

It was not easy to go to Cayenne. They knew roughly the direction to take, but mountains, rivers, precipices, brigands and savages were everywhere terrible obstacles. Their horses died of fatigue; their provisions were exhausted; for a whole month they lived on wild fruits and at last found themselves near a little river fringed with cocoanut-trees which supported their lives and their hopes.

Cacambo, who always gave advice as prudent as the old woman's, said to Candide: "We can go no farther, we have walked far enough; I can see an empty canoe in the bank, let us fill it with cocoanuts, get into the little boat and drift with the current; a river always leads to some inhabited place. If we do not find anything pleasant, we shall at least find something new."

"Come on then," said Candide, "and let us trust to Providence."

They drifted for some leagues between banks which were sometimes flowery, sometimes bare, sometimes flat, sometimes steep. The river continually became wider; finally it disappeared under an arch of frightful rocks which towered up to the very sky. The two travellers were bold enough to trust themselves to the current under this arch. The stream, narrowed between walls, carried them with horrible rapidity and noise. After twenty-four hours they saw daylight again; but their canoe was wrecked on reefs; they had to crawl from rock to rock for a whole league and at last they discovered an immense horizon, bordered by inaccessible mountains. The country was cultivated for pleasure as well as for necessity; everywhere the useful was agreeable. The roads were covered or rather ornamented with carriages of brilliant material and shape, carrying men and women of singular beauty, who were rapidly drawn along by

49. later capital of French Guiana.

huge red sheep whose swiftness surpassed that of the finest horses of Andalusia, Tetuan, and Mequinez.[50]

"This country," said Candide, "is better than Westphalia."

He landed with Cacambo near the first village he came to. Several children of the village, dressed in torn gold brocade, were playing quoits outside the village. Our two men from the other world amused themselves by looking on; their quoits were large round pieces, yellow, red and green which shone with peculiar lustre. The travellers were curious enough to pick up some of them; they were of gold, emeralds and rubies, the least of which would have been the greatest ornament in the Mogul's throne.

"No doubt," said Cacambo, "these children are the sons of the King of this country playing at quoits."

At that moment the village schoolmaster appeared to call them into school.

"This," said Candide, "is the tutor of the Royal Family."

The little urchins immediately left their game, abandoning their quoits and everything with which they had been playing. Candide picked them up, ran to the tutor, and presented them to him humbly, giving him to understand by signs that Their Royal Highnesses had forgotten their gold and their precious stones. The village schoolmaster smiled, threw them on the ground, gazed for a moment at Candide's face with much surprise, and continued on his way. The travellers did not fail to pick up the gold, the rubies and the emeralds.

"Where are we?" cried Candide. "The children of the King must be well brought up, since they are taught to despise gold and precious stones."

Cacambo was as much surprised as Candide. At last they reached the first house in the village, which was built like a European palace. There were crowds of people round the door and still more inside; very pleasant music could be heard and there was a delicious smell of cooking. Cacambo went up to the door and heard them speaking Peruvian; it was his maternal tongue, for everyone knows that Cacambo was born in a village of Tucuman where nothing else is spoken.

"I will act as your interpreter," he said to Candide, "this is an inn, let us enter."

Immediately two boys and two girls of the inn, dressed in cloth of gold, whose hair was bound up with ribbons, invited them to sit down at the table. They served four soups each garnished with two parrots, a boiled condor which weighed two hundred pounds, two roast monkeys of excellent flavor, three hundred colibris in one dish and six hundred hummingbirds in another, exquisite ragouts

50. *Tetuan, and Mequinez:* towns in Morocco, famous for horses.

and delicious pastries, all in dishes of a sort of rock crystal. The boys and girls brought several sorts of drinks made of sugarcane. Most of the guests were merchants and coachmen, all extremely polite, who asked Cacambo a few questions with the most delicate tact and answered his in a satisfactory manner.

When the meal was over, Cacambo, like Candide, thought he could pay the reckoning by throwing on the table two of the large pieces of gold he had picked up; the host and hostess laughed until they had to hold their sides. At last they recovered themselves.

"Gentlemen," said the host, "we perceive you are strangers; we are not accustomed to seeing them. Forgive us if we began to laugh when you offered us in payment the stones from our highways. No doubt you have none of the money of this country, but you do not need any to dine here. All the hotels established for the utility of commerce are subsidized by the government. You have been ill entertained here because this is a poor village; but everywhere else you will be received as you deserve to be."

Cacambo explained to Candide all that the host had said, and Candide listened in the same admiration and bewilderment with which his friend Cacambo interpreted. "What can this country be," they said to each other, "which is unknown to the rest of the world and where all nature is so different from ours? Probably it is the country where everything is for the best; for there must be one country of that sort. And, in spite of what Dr. Pangloss said, I often noticed that everything went very ill in Westphalia."

Chapter 18

What they saw in the land of Eldorado

Cacambo informed the host of his curiosity, and the host said: "I am a very ignorant man and am all the better for it; but we have here an old man who has retired from the Court and who is the most learned and most communicative man in the kingdom." And he at once took Cacambo to the old man. Candide now played only the second part and accompanied his valet. They entered a very simple house, for the door was only of silver and the panelling of the apartments in gold, but so tastefully carved that the richest decorations did not surpass it. The antechamber indeed was only encrusted with rubies and emeralds; but the order with which everything was arranged atoned for this extreme simplicity.

The old man received the two strangers on a sofa padded with hummingbird feathers, and presented them with drinks in diamond cups; after which he satisfied their curiosity in these words: "I am a hundred and seventy-two years old and I heard from my late father, the King's equerry, the astonishing revolutions of Peru of which he had been an eye-witness. The kingdom where we now are is the ancient country of the Incas, who most imprudently left it to conquer part of the world and were at last destroyed by the Spaniards. The princes of their family who remained in their native country had more wisdom; with the consent of the nation, they ordered that no inhabitants should ever leave our little kingdom, and this it is that has preserved our innocence and our felicity. The Spaniards had some vague knowledge of this country, which they called Eldorado,[51] and about a hundred years ago an Englishman named Raleigh came very near to it; but, since we are surrounded by inaccessible rocks and precipices, we have thus far been exempt from the rapacity of the nations of Europe who have an inconceivable lust for the pebbles and mud of our land and would kill us to the last man to get possession of them."

The conversation was long; it touched upon the form of the government, manners, women, public spectacles and the arts. Finally Candide, who was always interested in metaphysics, asked through Cacambo whether the country had a religion.

The old man blushed a little. "How can you doubt it?" said he. "Do you think we are ingrates?"

Cacambo humbly asked what was the religion of Eldorado.

The old man blushed again. "Can there be two religions?" said he. "We have, I think, the religion of every one else; we worship God from evening until morning."

"Do you worship only one God?" said Cacambo, who continued to act as the interpreter of Candide's doubts.

"Manifestly," said the old man, "there are not two or three or four. I must confess that the people of your world ask very extraordinary questions."

Candide continued to press the old man with questions; he wished to know how they prayed to God in Eldorado.

"We do not pray," said the good and respectable sage, "we have nothing to ask from Him; He has given us everything necessary and we continually give Him thanks."

Candide was curious to see the priests, and asked where they might be found.

The good old man smiled. "My friends," said he, "we are all priests; the King and all the heads of families solemnly sing praises every morning, accompanied by five or six thousand musicians."

"What! Have you no monks to teach, to dispute, to govern, to intrigue and to burn people who do not agree with them?"

51. the legendary "land of gold" that attracted so many explorers to the New World. Voltaire's sources are principally Sir Walter Raleigh, Garcilasso de la Vega, and Coréal—all seventeenth-century voyagers.

"For that, we should have to become fools," said the old man; "here we are all of the same opinion and do not understand what you mean with your monks."

At all this Candide was in an ecstasy and said to himself: "This is very different from Westphalia and the castle of His Lordship the Baron; if our friend Pangloss had seen Eldorado, he would not have said that the castle of Thunder-ten-tronckh was the best of all that exists on the earth; it shows that a man should travel."

After this long conversation the good old man ordered a carriage to be harnessed with six sheep and gave the two travellers twelve of his servants to take them to Court. "You will excuse me," he said, "if my age deprives me of the honor of accompanying you. The King will receive you in a manner which will not displease you and doubtless you will pardon the customs of the country if any of them disconcert you."

Candide and Cacambo entered the carriage; the six sheep galloped off and in less than four hours they reached the King's palace, situated at one end of the capital. The portico was two hundred and twenty feet high and a hundred feet wide; it is impossible to describe its material. Anyone can see the prodigious superiority it must have over the pebbles and sand we call *gold* and *gems.*

Twenty beautiful maidens of the guard received Candide and Cacambo as they alighted from the carriage, conducted them to the baths and dressed them in robes woven from the down of hummingbirds; after which the principal male and female officers of the Crown led them to His Majesty's apartment through two files of a thousand musicians each, according to the usual custom. As they approached the throneroom, Cacambo asked one of the chief officers how they should behave in His Majesty's presence; whether they should fall on their knees or flat on their faces, whether they should put their hands on their heads or on their backsides; whether they should lick the dust of the throneroom; in a word, what was the protocol?

"The custom," said the chief officer, "is to embrace the King and to kiss him on either cheek."

Candide and Cacambo threw their arms round His Majesty's neck; he received them with all imaginable graciousness and politely asked them to supper. Meanwhile they were carried to see the town, the public buildings rising to the very skies, the market-places ornamented with thousands of columns, the fountains of rose-water and of liqueurs distilled from sugarcane, which played continually in the public squares paved with precious stones which emitted a perfume like that of cloves and cinnamon.

Candide asked to see the law courts and the Court of Appeal; he was told there were none, and that nobody ever went to law. He asked if there were prisons and was told there were none. He was still more surprised and pleased by the palace of sciences, where he saw a gallery two thousand feet long, filled with instruments of mathematics and physics.

After they had explored all the afternoon about a thousandth part of the town, they were taken back to the King. Candide sat down to table with His Majesty, his valet Cacambo and several ladies. Never was better cheer, and never was anyone wittier at supper than His Majesty. Cacambo explained the King's witty remarks to Candide and even when translated they still appeared witty. Among all the things which amazed Candide, this did not amaze him the least.

They enjoyed this hospitality for a month. Candide repeatedly said to Cacambo: "Once again, my friend, it is quite true that the castle where I was born cannot be compared with this country; but then Mademoiselle Cunégonde is not here and you probably have a mistress in Europe. If we remain here, we shall only be like everyone else; but if we return to our own world with only twelve sheep laden with Eldorado pebbles, we shall be richer than all the kings put together; we shall have no more Inquisitors to fear and we can easily regain Mademoiselle Cunégonde."

Cacambo agreed with this; it is so pleasant to be on the move, to show off before friends, to boast of the things seen on one's travels, that these two happy men resolved to be so no longer and to ask His Majesty's permission to depart.

"You are doing a very foolish thing," said the King. "I know my country is small; but when we are comfortable anywhere we should stay there; I certainly have not the right to detain foreigners, that is a tyranny which does not exist either in our manners or our laws; all men are free, leave when you please, but the way out is very difficult. It is impossible to ascend the rapid river by which you miraculously came here and which flows under arches of rock. The mountains which surround the whole of my kingdom are ten thousand feet high and are perpendicular like walls; they are more than ten leagues broad, and you can only get down from them by way of precipices. However, since you must go, I will give orders to the directors of machinery to make a machine which will carry you comfortably. When you have been taken to the other side of the mountains, nobody can proceed any farther with you; for my subjects have sworn never to pass this boundary and they are too wise to break their oath. Ask anything else of me you wish."

"We ask nothing of Your Majesty," said Cacambo, "except a few sheep laden with provisions, pebbles and the mud of this country."

The King laughed. "I cannot understand," said he, "the taste you people of Europe have for our yellow mud; but take as much as you wish, and much good may it do you."

He immediately ordered his engineers to make a machine to hoist these two extraordinary men out of his kingdom. Three thousand learned scientists worked at it; it was ready in a fortnight and only cost about twenty million pounds sterling in the currency of that country. Candide and Cacambo were placed on the machine; there were two large red sheep saddled and bridled for them to ride on when they had passed the mountains, twenty pack-sheep laden with provisions, thirty carrying presents of the most curious productions of the country and fifty laden with gold, precious stones and diamonds. The King embraced the two wanderers tenderly. Their departure was a splendid sight and so was the ingenious manner in which they and their sheep were hoisted on to the top of the mountains. The scientists took leave of them after having landed them safely, and Candide's only desire and object was to go and present Mademoiselle Cunégonde with his sheep.

"We have sufficient to pay the governor of Buenos Ayres," said he, "if Mademoiselle Cunégonde can be bought. Let us go to Cayenne, and take ship, and then we will see what kingdom we will buy."

Chapter 19

What happened to them at Surinam and how Candide made the acquaintance of Martin

Our two travellers' first day was quite pleasant. They were encouraged by the idea of possessing more treasures than all Asia, Europe and Africa could collect. Candide in transport carved the name of Cunégonde on the trees. On the second day two of the sheep stuck in a swamp and were swallowed up with their loads; two other sheep died of fatigue a few days later; then seven or eight died of hunger in a desert; several days afterwards others fell off precipices. Finally, after they had travelled for a hundred days, they had only two sheep left.

Candide said to Cacambo: "My friend, you see how perishable are the riches of this world; nothing is steadfast but virtue and the happiness of seeing Mademoiselle Cunégonde again."

"I admit it," said Cacambo, "but we still have two sheep with more treasures than ever the King of Spain will have, and in the distance I see a town I suspect is Surinam,[52] which belongs to the Dutch. We are at the end of our troubles and the beginning of our happiness."

As they drew near the town they came upon a negro lying on the ground wearing only half his clothes, that is to say, a pair of blue

52. in Dutch Guiana.

cotton drawers; this poor man had no left leg and no right hand. "Good heavens!" said Candide to him in Dutch, "what are you doing there, my friend, in that horrible state?"

"I am waiting for my master, the famous merchant Monsieur Vanderdendur."

"Was it Monsieur Vanderdendur," said Candide, "who treated you in that way?"

"Yes, sir," said the negro, "it is the custom. We are given a pair of cotton drawers twice a year as clothing. When we work in the sugar mills and the grindstone catches our fingers, they cut off the hand; when we try to run away, they cut off a leg. Both these things happened to me. This is the price paid for the sugar you eat in Europe. But when my mother sold me for ten gold-edged crowns on the coast of Guinea, she said to me: 'My dear child, give thanks to our fetishes, always worship them, and they will make you happy; you have the honor to be a slave of our lords the white men and thereby you have made the fortune of your father and mother.' Alas! I do not know whether I made their fortune, but they certainly did not make mine. Dogs, monkeys and parrots are a thousand times less miserable than we are; the Dutch fetishes who converted me tell me that we are all of us, whites and blacks, the children of Adam. I am not a genealogist, but if these preachers tell the truth, we are all second cousins. Now, you will admit that no one could treat his relatives in a more horrible way."

"O Pangloss!" cried Candide. "This is an abomination you had not guessed; this is too much, in the end I shall have to renounce optimism."

"What is optimism?" said Cacambo.

"Alas!" said Candide, "it is the madness of maintaining that everything is well when we are wretched." And he shed tears as he looked at his negro; and he entered Surinam weeping.

The first thing they inquired was whether there was any ship in the port which could be sent to Buenos Ayres. The person they addressed happened to be a Spanish captain, who offered to strike an honest bargain with them. He arranged to meet them at an inn. Candide and the faithful Cacambo went and waited for him with their two sheep. Candide, who blurted everything out, told the Spaniard all his adventures and confessed that he wanted to elope with Mademoiselle Cunégonde.

"I shall certainly not take you to Buenos Ayres," said the captain. "I should be hanged and you would, too. The fair Cunégonde is his Lordship's favorite mistress."

Candide was thunderstruck; he sobbed for a long time; then he took Cacambo aside. "My dear friend," said he, "this is what you must do. We have each of us in our pockets five or six millions worth of diamonds; you are more skilful than I am; go to Buenos Ayres and get Mademoiselle Cunégonde. If the governor makes any difficulties give him a million; if he is still obstinate give him two; you have not killed an Inquisitor so they will not suspect you. I will fit out another ship, I will go and wait for you at Venice; it is a free country where there is nothing to fear from Bulgarians, Abares, Jews or Inquisitors."

Cacambo applauded this wise resolution; he was in despair at leaving a good master who had become his intimate friend; but the pleasure of being useful to him overcame the grief of leaving him. They embraced with tears. Candide urged him not to forget the good old woman. Cacambo set off that very same day; he was a very good fellow, this Cacambo.

Candide remained some time longer at Surinam waiting for another captain to take him to Italy with the two sheep he had left. He engaged servants and bought everything necessary for a long voyage. At last Monsieur Vanderdendur, the owner of a large ship, came to see him.

"How much do you want," he asked this man, "to take me straight to Venice with my servants, my baggage and these two sheep?"

The captain asked for ten thousand piastres. Candide did not hesitate. "Oh! Ho!" said the prudent Vanderdendur to himself, "this foreigner gives ten thousand piastres immediately! He must be very rich." He returned a moment afterwards and said he could not sail for less than twenty thousand.

"Very well, you shall have them," said Candide.

"Whew!" said the merchant to himself, "this man gives twenty thousand piastres as easily as ten thousand." He came back again, and said he could not take him to Venice for less than thirty thousand piastres.

"Then you shall have thirty thousand," replied Candide.

"Oho!" said the Dutch merchant to himself again, "thirty thousand piastres is nothing to this man; obviously the two sheep are laden with immense treasures; I will not insist any further; first let me make him pay the thirty thousand piastres, and then we will see."

Candide sold two little diamonds, the smaller of which was worth more than all the money the captain asked. He paid him in advance. The two sheep were taken on board. Candide followed in a small boat to join the ship which rode at anchor; the captain watched his time, set his sails and weighed anchor; the wind was favorable. Candide, bewildered and stupefied, soon lost sight of him. "Alas!" he cried, "this is a trick worthy of the old world."

He returned to shore, in grief; for he had lost enough to make the fortunes of twenty kings. He went to the Dutch judge; and, as he was rather disturbed, he knocked loudly at the door; he went in, related what had happened and talked a little louder than he ought to have done. The judge began by fining him ten thousand piastres for the noise he had made; he then listened patiently to him, promised to look into his affair as soon as the merchant returned, and charged him another ten thousand piastres for the expense of the hearing.

This behavior reduced Candide to despair; he had indeed endured misfortunes a thousand times more painful; but the calmness of the judge and of the captain who had robbed him, upset his spleen and plunged him into a black melancholy. The malevolence of men revealed itself to his mind in all its ugliness; he entertained only gloomy ideas.

At last a French ship was about to leave for Bordeaux and, since he no longer had any sheep laden with diamonds to put on board, he hired a cabin at a reasonable price and announced throughout the town that he would give the passage, food and two thousand piastres to an honest man who would make the journey with him, on condition that this man was the most unfortunate and the most disgusted with his condition in the whole province. Such a crowd of candidates arrived that a fleet would not have held them. Candide, wishing to choose among the most likely, picked out twenty persons who seemed reasonably sociable and who all claimed to deserve his preference. He collected them in a tavern and gave them supper, on condition that each took an oath to relate truthfully the story of his life, promising that he would choose the man who seemed to him the most deserving of pity and to have the most cause for being discontented with his condition, and that he would give the others a little money. The sitting lasted until four o'clock in the morning. As Candide listened to their adventures he remembered what the old woman had said on the voyage to Buenos Ayres and how she had wagered that there was nobody on the boat who had not experienced very great misfortunes. At each story which was told him, he thought of Pangloss.

"This Pangloss," said he, "would have some difficulty in supporting his system. I wish he were here. Certainly, if everything is well, it is only in Eldorado and not in the rest of the world."

He finally determined in favor of a poor man of letters who had worked ten years for the booksellers at Amsterdam.[53] He judged that there was no occupation in the world which could more disgust a man. This man of letters, who was also a good man, had been robbed by his wife, beaten by his son, and abandoned by his

---

53. Voltaire had a long career of unhappy dealings with these booksellers and attacked them on many occasions.

daughter, who had eloped with a Portuguese. He had just been deprived of a small post on which he depended and the preachers of Surinam were persecuting him because they thought he was a Socinian.[54] It must be admitted that the others were at least as unfortunate as he was; but Candide hoped that this learned man would help to pass the time during the voyage. All his other rivals considered that Candide was doing them a great injustice; but he soothed them down by giving each of them a hundred piastres.

Chapter 20

What happened to Candide and Martin at sea

Thus the old scholar, who was called Martin, embarked with Candide for Bordeaux. Both had seen and suffered much; and if the ship had been sailing from Surinam to Japan by way of the Cape of Good Hope they would have been able to discuss moral and physical evil during the whole voyage. However, Candide had one great advantage over Martin, because he still hoped to see Mademoiselle Cunégonde again, and Martin had nothing to hope for; moreover, he possessed gold and diamonds; and, although he had lost a hundred large red sheep laden with the greatest treasures on earth, although he was still enraged at being robbed by the Dutch captain, yet when he thought of what he still had left in his pockets and when he talked of Cunégonde, especially at the end of a meal, he still inclined towards the system of Pangloss.

"But what do you think of all this, Martin?" said he to the man of letters. "What is your view of moral and physical evil?"

"Sir," replied Martin, "my priests accused me of being a Socinian; but the truth is I am a Manichean."[55]

"You are poking fun at me," said Candide, "there are no Manicheans left in the world."

"I am one," said Martin. "I don't know what to do about it, but I am unable to think in any other fashion."

"You must be possessed by the devil," said Candide.

"He takes so great a share in the affairs of this world," said Martin, "that he might well be in me, as he is everywhere else; but I confess that when I consider this globe, or rather this globule, I think that God has abandoned it to some mischievous creature—always excepting Eldorado. I have never seen a town which did not desire the ruin of the next town, never a family which did not wish to exterminate some other family. Everywhere the weak loathe the powerful before whom they cower and the powerful treat them like

54. a believer in Socinianism—a doctrine resembling Unitarianism, founded in the sixteenth century. The Socinians denied original sin, the Trinity, salvation by grace, and so on.

55. one believing in the doctrine, Persian in origin, that good and evil are two forces equal in strength engaged in continual struggle.

flocks of sheep whose wool and flesh are to be sold. A million drilled assassins go from one end of Europe to the other murdering and robbing with discipline in order to earn their bread, because there is no honester occupation; and in the towns which seem to enjoy peace and where the arts flourish, men are devoured by more envy, troubles and worries than the afflictions of a besieged town. Secret griefs are even more cruel than public miseries. In a word, I have seen so much and endured so much that I have become a Manichean."

"Yet there is some good," replied Candide.

"There may be," said Martin, "but I have never met with it."

In the midst of this dispute they heard the sound of cannon. The noise increased every moment. Every one took his telescope. About three miles away they saw two ships engaged in battle; and the wind brought them so near the French ship that they had the pleasure of seeing the fight in comfort. At last one of the two ships fired a broadside so accurately and so low down that the other ship began to sink. Candide and Martin distinctly saw a hundred men on the main deck of the sinking ship; they raised their hands to Heaven and uttered frightful shrieks; in a moment all were engulfed.

"Well!" said Martin, "that is how men treat each other."

"It is certainly true," said Candide, "that there is something diabolical in this affair."

As he was speaking, he saw something bright red swimming near the ship. They launched a boat to see what it could be; it was one of his sheep. Candide felt more joy at recovering this sheep than grief at losing a hundred all laden with large diamonds from Eldorado.

The French captain soon perceived that the captain of the winning ship was a Spaniard and that the sunken ship was a Dutch pirate; the captain was the very same who had robbed Candide. The immense wealth this scoundrel had stolen was swallowed up with him in the sea and only one sheep was saved.

"You see," said Candide to Martin, "that crime is sometimes punished; this scoundrel of a Dutch captain has met the fate he deserved."

"Yes," said Martin, "but was it necessary that the other passengers on his ship should perish too? God punished the thief, and the devil drowned the others."

Meanwhile the French and Spanish ships continued on their way and Candide continued his conversation with Martin. They argued for a fortnight and at the end of the fortnight they had got no further than at the beginning. But after all, they talked, they exchanged ideas, they consoled each other. Candide stroked his sheep. "Since I have found you again," said he, "I may very likely find Cunégonde once more."

Chapter 21

Candide and Martin approach the coast of France and argue

At last they sighted the coast of France.

"Have you ever been to France, Monsieur Martin?" said Candide.

"Yes," said Martin, "I have gone through several provinces. In some half the inhabitants are crazy, in others they are too artful, in some they are usually quite gentle and stupid, and in others they think they are witty; in all of them the chief occupation is making love, the second scandal-mongering and the third talking nonsense."

"But, Monsieur Martin, have you seen Paris?"

"Yes, I have seen Paris; it is a mixture of all the species; it is a chaos, a throng where everybody hunts for pleasure and hardly anybody finds it, at least so far as I could see. I did not stay there long; when I arrived there I was robbed of everything I had by pickpockets at Saint-Germain's fair; they thought I was a thief and I spent a week in prison; after which I became a printer's reader to earn enough to return to Holland on foot. I met the scribbling rabble, the intriguing rabble and the fanatical rabble. We hear that there are very polite people in the town; I should like to think so."

"For my part, I have not the least curiosity to see France," said Candide. "You can easily guess that when a man has spent a month in Eldorado he cares to see nothing else in the world but Mademoiselle Cunégonde. I shall go and wait for her at Venice; we will go to Italy by way of France; will you come with me?"

"Willingly," said Martin. "They say that Venice is only for the Venetian nobles but that foreigners are nevertheless well received when they have plenty of money; I have none, you have plenty, I will follow you anywhere."

"By the way," said Candide, "do you think the earth was originally a sea, as we are assured by that large book[56] belonging to the captain?"

"I don't believe it in the least," said Martin, "any more than all the other whimsies we have been pestered with recently!"

"But to what end was this world formed?" said Candide.

"To drive us mad," replied Martin.

"Are you not very much surprised," continued Candide, "by the love those two girls of the country of the Oreillons had for those

---

56. possibly the naturalist Buffon's *Theory of the Earth* (*Théorie de la terre*, 1749). Voltaire engaged in a good- natured scholarly dispute with him over it.

two monkeys, whose adventure I told you?"

"Not in the least," said Martin. "I see nothing strange in their passion: I have seen so many extraordinary things that nothing seems extraordinary to me."

"Do you think," said Candide, "that men have always massacred each other, as they do today? Have they always been liars, cheats, traitors, brigands, weak, flighty, cowardly, envious, gluttonous, drunken, grasping, and vicious, bloody, backbiting, debauched, fanatical, hypocritical and silly?"

"Do you think," said Martin, "that sparrow-hawks have always eaten the pigeons they came across?"

"Yes, of course," said Candide.

"Well," said Martin, "if sparrow-hawks have always possessed the same character, why should you expect men to change theirs?"

"Oh!" said Candide, "there is a great difference; free will . . ." Arguing thus, they arrived at Bordeaux.

[In Chapter 22, Candide and Martin go to Paris, where Candide falls sick but recovers despite the ministrations of incompetent physicians. Describing an evening Candide spends at the theater in the company of an abbé, Voltaire engages in some vituperative criticism of contemporary drama. Candide loses fifty thousand francs at an elegant gambling house, and the owner—the Marquis de Parolignac—also robs him of two of his diamond rings.

The friendly abbé hears the tale of Cunégonde. He engages a female accomplice to play the rôle of Candide's fiancée. The police interrupt the plot, but not until Candide has filled her hands with diamonds. The police carry Candide and Martin off to prison as two suspicious foreigners. A bribe of three more jewels effects their release. They sail aboard a Dutch vessel from Dieppe to England.]

Chapter 23

*Candide and Martin reach the coast of England; and what they
saw there*

"Ah! Pangloss, Pangloss! Ah! Martin, Martin! Ah! my dear Cunégonde! What sort of a world is this?" said Candide on the Dutch ship.

"Something quite mad and quite abominable," replied Martin.

"You know England; are the people there as mad as they are in France?"

" 'Tis another sort of madness," said Martin. "You know these two nations are at war for a few acres of snow in Canada, and that they are spending more on this fine war[57] than all Canada is worth.

57. the French and Indian War (1754–1763), the New World counterpart of the Seven Years' War.

It is beyond my poor capacity to tell you whether there are more madmen in one country than in the other; all I know is that in general the people we are going to visit are extremely morose."

Talking thus, they arrived at Portsmouth. There were multitudes of people on the shore, looking attentively at a rather fat man[58] who was kneeling down with his eyes bandaged on the deck of one of the ships in the fleet; four soldiers placed opposite this man each shot three bullets into his brain in the calmest manner imaginable; and the whole crowd returned home with great satisfaction.

"What is all this?" said Candide. "And what Demon exercises his power everywhere?" He asked who was the fat man who had just been killed so ceremoniously.

"An admiral," was the reply.

"And why kill the admiral?"

"Because," he was told, "he did not kill enough people. He fought a battle with a French admiral[59] and it was established that the English admiral was not close enough to him."

"But," said Candide, "the French admiral was just as far from the English admiral!"

"That is indisputable," was the answer, "but in this country it is a good thing to kill an admiral from time to time to encourage the others."

Candide was so bewildered and so shocked by what he saw and heard that he would not even set foot on shore, but bargained with the Dutch captain (even if he had to pay him as much as the Surinam robber) to take him at once to Venice. The captain was ready in two days. They sailed down the coast of France; and passed in sight of Lisbon, at which Candide shuddered. They entered the Straits and the Mediterranean and at last reached Venice. "Praised be God!" said Candide, embracing Martin, "here I shall see the fair Cunégonde again. I trust Cacambo as I would myself. All is well, all goes well, all goes as well as it possibly could."

[In Chapter 24, Candide and Martin go to Venice to meet Cacambo, but do not find him. There Candide sees Paquette, former mistress of Pangloss, now in the company of Friar Giroflée, and befriends them both with money. Candide plans to visit Lord Pococurante, who is "supposed to be a man who has never known a grief."]

---

58. Admiral Byng was executed on March 14, 1757, for failing to prevent the French landing at Minorca. Voltaire had been active in Byng's defense.
59. La Gallissonnière.

Chapter 25

Visit to the noble Venetian, Lord Pococurante

Candide and Martin took a gondola and rowed to the noble Pococurante's palace. The gardens were extensive and ornamented with fine marble statues; the architecture of the palace was handsome. The master of this establishment, a very wealthy man of about sixty, received the two visitors very politely but with very little cordiality, which disconcerted Candide but did not displease Martin. Two pretty and neatly dressed girls served them with very frothy cups of chocolate. Candide could not refrain from praising their beauty, their grace and their skill.

"They are quite good creatures," said Senator Pococurante, "and I sometimes make them sleep in my bed, for I am very tired of the ladies of the town, with their coquetries, their jealousies, their quarrels, their humors, their meanness, their pride, their folly, and the sonnets one must write or have written for them; but I find that I am getting very tired of these two girls too."

After this refreshment, Candide walked in a long gallery and was surprised by the beauty of the pictures. He asked what master had painted the first two.

"They are by Raphael," said the Senator. "Some years ago I bought them at a very high price out of mere vanity; I am told they are the finest in Italy, but they give me no pleasure; the color has gone very dark, the faces are not sufficiently rounded and do not stand out enough; the draperies have not the least resemblance to material; in short, whatever they may say, I do not consider them a true imitation of nature. I shall only like a picture when it makes me think it is nature itself; and there are none of that kind. I have a great many pictures, but I never look at them now."

While they waited for dinner, Pococurante had a concerto performed for them. Candide thought the music delicious.

"This noise," said Pococurante, "is amusing for half an hour; but if it lasts any longer, it wearies everybody although nobody dares to say so. Music nowadays is merely the art of executing difficulties, and in the end that which is only difficult ceases to please. Perhaps I should like the opera more, if they had not made it a monster which revolts me. Those who please may go to see bad tragedies set to music, where the scenes are only composed to bring in clumsily two or three ridiculous songs which show off an actress's voice; those who will or can, may swoon with pleasure when they see an eunuch humming the part of Cæsar and Cato as he awkwardly treads the boards; for my part, I long ago abandoned such trivialities, which nowadays are the glory of Italy and for which monarchs pay so dearly."

Candide demurred a little, but discreetly. Martin entirely agreed with the Senator.

They sat down to table and after an excellent dinner went into the library. Candide saw a magnificently bound Homer and complimented the *Illustrissimo* on his good taste. "That is the book," said he, "which so much delighted the great Pangloss, the greatest philosopher of Germany."

"It does not delight me," said Pococurante coldly; "formerly I was made to believe that I took pleasure in reading it; but this continual repetition of battles which are all alike, these gods who are perpetually active and achieve nothing decisive, this Helen who is the cause of the war and yet scarcely an actor in the piece, this Troy which is always besieged and never taken—all bore me extremely. I have sometimes asked learned men if they were as bored as I am by reading it; all who were sincere confessed that the book dropped from their hands, but that it must be in every library, as a monument of antiquity, and like rusty coins which cannot be put into circulation."

"Your Excellency has a different opinion of Virgil?" said Candide.

"I admit," said Pococurante, "that the second, fourth and sixth books of his *Æneid* are excellent, but as for his pious Æneas and the strong Cloanthes and the faithful Achates and the little Ascanius and the imbecile king Latinus and the middle-class Amata and the insipid Lavinia, I think there could be nothing more frigid and disagreeable. I prefer Tasso and the fantastic tales of Ariosto."

"May I venture to ask you, sir," said Candide, "if you do not take great pleasure in reading Horace?"

"He has some maxims," said Pococurante, "which might be useful to a man of the world, and which, being expressed in powerful verses, are more easily impressed upon the memory; but I care very little for his Journey to Brundisium, and his description of a Bad Dinner, and the street brawlers' quarrel between—what is his name? —Pupilus,[60] whose words, he says, were full of pus, and another person whose words were all vinegar. I was extremely disgusted with his gross verses against old women and witches; and I cannot see there is any merit in his telling his friend Mæcenas that, if he is placed by him among the lyric poets, he will strike the stars with his lofty brow. Fools admire everything in a celebrated author. I only read to please myself, and I only like what suits me."

Candide, who had been taught never to judge anything for himself, was greatly surprised by what he heard; and Martin thought Pococurante's way of thinking quite reasonable.

60. actually "Rupilius" in Horace.

"Oh! There is Cicero," said Candide. "I suppose you are never tired of reading that great man?"

"I never read him," replied the Venetian. "What do I care that he pleaded for Rabirius or Cluentius. I have enough cases to try; I could better have endured his philosophical works; but when I saw that he doubted everything, I concluded I knew as much as he and did not need anybody else in order to be ignorant."

"Ah! There are eighty volumes of the Proceedings of an Academy of Sciences," exclaimed Martin, "there might be something good in them."

"There would be," said Pococurante, "if a single one of the authors of all that rubbish had invented even the art of making pins; but in all those books there is nothing but vain systems and not a single useful thing."

"What a lot of plays I see there," said Candide. "Italian, Spanish, and French!"

"Yes," said the Senator, "there are three thousand and not three dozen good ones. As for those collections of sermons, which all together are not worth a page of Seneca, and all those large volumes of theology you may well believe that they are never opened by me or anybody else."

Martin noticed some shelves filled with English books. "I should think," he said, "that a republican would enjoy most of those works written with so much freedom."

"Yes," replied Pococurante, "it is good to write as we think; it is the privilege of man. In all Italy, we only write what we do not think; those who inhabit the country of the Cæsars and the Antonines dare not have an idea without the permission of a Dominican monk. I should applaud the liberty which inspires Englishmen of genius if passion and party spirit did not corrupt everything estimable in that precious liberty."

Candide, in noticing a Milton, asked him if he did not consider that author to be a very great man.

"Who?" said Pococurante. "That barbarian who wrote a long commentary on the first chapter of Genesis in ten books[61] of harsh verses? That gross imitator of the Greeks, who disfigures the Creation, and who, while Moses represents the Eternal Being as producing the world by speech, makes the Messiah take a large compass from the heavenly cupboard in order to trace out his work? Should I esteem the man who spoiled Tasso's hell and devil; who disguises Lucifer sometimes as a toad, sometimes as a pigmy; who makes him repeat the same things a hundred times; makes him argue about

---

61. The first edition of *Paradise Lost* was in ten books; Milton divided the work into twelve books in the second edition (1674).

theology; and imitates seriously Ariosto's comical invention of fire-arms by making the devils fire a cannon in Heaven? Neither I nor anyone else in Italy could enjoy such wretched extravagances. The marriage of Sin and Death and the snakes which sin brings forth nauseate any man of delicate taste, and his long description of a hospital would only please a gravedigger. This obscure, bizarre and disgusting poem was despised at its birth; I treat it today as it was treated by its contemporaries in its own country. But then I say what I think, and care very little whether others think as I do."

Candide was distressed by these remarks; he respected Homer and rather liked Milton.

"Alas!" he whispered to Martin, "I am afraid this man would have supreme contempt for our German poets."

"There wouldn't be much harm in that," said Martin.

"Oh! What a superior man!" said Candide under his breath. "What a great genius this Pococurante is! Nothing can please him."

After they had thus reviewed all his books they went down into the garden. Candide praised all its beauties.

"I have never met anything more tasteless," said the owner. "We have nothing but knick-knacks; but tomorrow I shall begin to plant one on a nobler plan."

When the two visitors had taken farewell of His Excellency, Candide said to Martin: "Now will you admit that he is the happiest of men, for he is superior to everything he possesses."

"Do you not see," said Martin, "that he is disgusted with everything he possesses? Plato said long ago that the best stomachs are not those which refuse all food."

"But," said Candide, "is there not pleasure in criticising, in finding faults where other men think they see beauty?"

"That is to say," answered Martin, "that there is a pleasure in not being pleased."

"Oh! Well," said Candide, "then there is no one as happy as I will be—when I see Mademoiselle Cunégonde again."

"It is always good to hope," said Martin.

However, the days and weeks went by; Cacambo did not return and Candide was so much plunged in grief that he did not even notice that Paquette and Friar Giroflée had not once come to thank him.

Chapter 26

How Candide and Martin supped with six strangers and who they were

One evening while Candide and Martin were going to sit down to table with the strangers who lodged in the same hotel, a man with a face the color of soot came up to him from behind and, taking him by the arm, said: "Get ready to come with us, and do not fail."

He turned round and saw Cacambo. Only the sight of Cunégonde could have surprised and pleased him more. He was almost wild with joy. He embraced his dear friend.

"Cunégonde is here, of course? Where is she? Take me to her, let me die of joy with her."

"Cunégonde is not here," said Cacambo. "She is in Constantinople."

"Heavens! In Constantinople! But, were she in China, I would fly to her; let us start at once."

"We will start after supper," replied Cacambo. "I cannot tell you you any more; I am a slave, and my master is waiting for me; I must go and serve him at table! Do not say anything; eat your supper, and be in readiness."

Candide, torn between joy and grief, charmed to see his faithful agent again, amazed to see him a slave, filled with the idea of seeing his mistress again, with turmoil in his heart, agitation in his mind, sat down to table with Martin (who met every strange occurrence with the same calmness), and with six strangers, who had come to spend the Carnival at Venice.

Cacambo, who acted as butler to one of the strangers, bent down to his master's head towards the end of the meal and said: "Sire, Your Majesty can leave when you wish, the ship is ready." After saying this, Cacambo withdrew.

The guests looked at each other with surprise without saying a word, when another servant came up to his master and said: "Sire, Your Majesty's post chaise is at Padua, and the boat is ready." The master nodded and the servant departed.

Once more all the guests looked at each other, and the general surprise was increased twofold. A third servant went up to the third stranger and said: "Sire, believe me, Your Majesty cannot remain here any longer; I will prepare everything." And he immediately disappeared.

Candide and Martin had no doubt that this was a Carnival masquerade. A fourth servant said to the fourth master: "Your Majesty can leave when you wish." And he went out like the others. The fifth servant spoke similarly to the fifth master. But the sixth servant spoke differently to the sixth stranger who was next to Candide, and said: "Faith, sire, they will not give Your Majesty any more credit nor me either, and we may very likely be jailed tonight, both of us; I am going to look to my own affairs, good bye."

When the servants had all gone, the six strangers, Candide and Martin remained in profound silence. At last it was broken by Candide.

"Gentlemen," said he, "this is a curious jest. How is it you are all kings? I confess that neither Martin nor I are kings."

Cacambo's master then gravely spoke and said in Italian: "I am not jesting, my name is Achmet III.[62] For several years I was grand Sultan; I dethroned my brother; my nephew dethroned me; they cut off the heads of my viziers; I am ending my days in the old seraglio; my nephew, Sultan Mahmoud, sometimes allows me to travel for my health, and I have come to spend the Carnival at Venice."

A young man who sat next to Achmet spoke after him and said: "My name is Ivan;[63] I was Emperor of all the Russias; I was dethroned in my cradle; my father and mother were imprisoned and I was brought up in prison; I sometimes have permission to travel, accompanied by those who guard me, and I have come to spend the Carnival at Venice."

The third said: "I am Charles Edward,[64] King of England; my father gave up his rights to the throne to me and I fought a war to assert them; the hearts of eight hundred of my adherents were torn out and dashed in their faces. I have been in prison; I am going to Rome to visit the King, my father, who is dethroned like my grandfather and me; and I have come to spend the Carnival at Venice."

The fourth then spoke and said: "I am the King of Poland;[65] the chance of war deprived me of my hereditary states; my father endured the same reverse of fortune; I am resigned to Providence like the Sultan Achmet, the Emperor Ivan and King Charles Edward, to whom God grant long life; and I have come to spend the Carnival at Venice."

The fifth said: "I also am the King of Poland,[66] I have lost my kingdom twice; but Providence has given me another state in which I have been able to do more good than all the kings of the Sarmatians together have been ever able to do on the banks of the Vistula; I also am resigned to Providence and I have come to spend the Carnival at Venice."

It was now for the sixth monarch to speak. "Gentlemen," said he, "I am not so eminent as you; but I have been a king like anyone else. I am Theodore;[67] I was elected King of Corsica; I have been called Your Majesty and now I am barely called Sir. I have coined money and do not own a farthing; I have had two Secre-

62. He lived from 1673 to 1736, and ruled between 1703 and 1730.

63. Ivan VI (1740–1764), proclaimed emperor at the age of eight weeks, and dethroned in 1741.

64. the "Young Pretender" (1720–1788), son of James Stuart, beaten at Culloden in 1746.

65. Augustus III (1696–1763), elector of Saxony (1733–1763) and king of Poland (1736–1763). He was driven from Saxony during the Seven Years' War.

66. Stanislas Leczinsky (1677–1766), father-in-law of Louis XV; he was king of Poland from 1704 to 1709 and from 1733 to 1735.

67. Baron Neuhoff (1690–1756), king of Corsica for eight months in 1736.

taries of State and now have scarcely a valet; I have occupied a throne and for a long time lay on straw in a London prison. I am much afraid I shall be treated in the same way here, although I have come, like Your Majesties, to spend the Carnival at Venice."

The five other kings listened to this speech with a noble compassion. Each of them gave King Theodore twenty sequins to buy clothes and shirts; Candide presented him with a diamond worth two thousand sequins.

"Who is this fellow," said the five kings, "who is able to give a hundred times as much as any of us, and who gives it?"

As they left the table, there came to the same hotel four Serene Highnesses who had also lost their states in the chance of war, and who had come to spend the rest of the Carnival at Venice; but Candide did not even notice these newcomers, he could think of nothing but of going to Constantinople to find his dear Cunégonde.

Chapter 27

Candide's voyage to Constantinople

The faithful Cacambo had already spoken to the Turkish captain who was to take the Sultan Achmet back to Constantinople and had obtained permission for Candide and Martin to come on board. They both entered this ship after having prostrated themselves before His Miserable Highness.

On the way, Candide said to Martin: "So we have just supped with six dethroned kings! And among those six kings there was one to whom I gave charity. Perhaps there are many other princes still more unfortunate. Now, I have only lost a hundred sheep and I am hastening to Cunégonde's arms. My dear Martin, once more, Pangloss was right, all is well."

"I hope so," said Martin.

"But," said Candide, "this is a very singular experience we have just had at Venice. Nobody has ever seen or heard of six dethroned kings supping together in a tavern."

" 'Tis no more extraordinary," said Martin, "than most of the things which have happened to us. It is very common for kings to be dethroned; and as to the honor we have had of supping with them, 'tis a trifle not deserving our attention."

Scarcely had Candide entered the ship when he threw his arms round the neck of his old valet, of his friend Cacambo.

"Well!" said he, "what is Cunégonde doing? Is she still a marvel of beauty? Does she still love me? How is she? Of course you have bought her a palace in Constantinople?"

"My dear master," replied Cacambo, "Cunégonde is washing dishes on the banks of Propontis[68] for a prince who possesses very

68. the Sea of Marmora.

few dishes; she is a slave in the house of a former sovereign named Ragotski,[69] who receives as a refugee three crowns a day from the Grand Turk; but what is even more sad is that she has lost her beauty and has become horribly ugly."

"Ah! beautiful or ugly," said Candide, "I am a man of honor and my duty is to love her always. But how can she be reduced to so abject a condition with the five or six millions you carried off?"

"Ah!" said Cacambo, "did I not have to give two millions to Señor Don Fernando d'Ibaraa y Figueora y Mascarenes y Lampourdos y Souza, Governor of Buenos Ayres, for permission to bring away Mademoiselle Cunégonde? And did not a pirate bravely strip us of all the rest? And did not this pirate take us to Cape Matapan, to Milo, to Nicaria, to Samos, to Petra, to the Dardanelles, to Marmora, to Scutari? Cunégonde and the old woman are servants to the prince I mentioned, and I am slave to the dethroned Sultan."

"What a chain of terrible calamities!" said Candide. "But after all, I still have a few diamonds; I shall easily deliver Cunégonde. What a pity she has become so ugly."

Then, turning to Martin, he said: "Who do you think is the most to be pitied, Sultan Achmet, Emperor Ivan, King Charles Edward, or me?"

"I do not know at all," said Martin. "I should have to be in your hearts to know."

"Ah!" said Candide, "if Pangloss were here he would know and would tell us."

"I do not know," said Martin, "what scales your Pangloss would use to weigh the misfortunes of men and to estimate their sufferings. All I presume is that there are millions of men on the earth a hundred times more to be pitied than King Charles Edward, Emperor Ivan, and Sultan Achmet."

"That may very well be," said Candide.

In a few days they reached the Black Sea channel. Candide began by paying a high ransom for Cacambo and, without wasting time, he went on board a galley with his companions bound for the shores of Propontis, in order to find Cunégonde however ugly she might be. Among the galley slaves were two convicts who rowed very badly and from time to time the Levantine captain applied several strokes of a bull's pizzle to their naked shoulders. From a natural feeling of pity Candide watched them more attentively than the other galley slaves and went up to them. Some features of their disfigured faces appeared to him to have some resemblance to Pangloss and the wretched Jesuit, the Baron, Mademoiselle Cunégonde's brother. This idea disturbed and saddened him. He looked

69. king of Transylvania in 1707; he was later deposed, and died in 1735.

at them still more carefully. "Truly," said he to Cacambo, "if I had not seen Dr. Pangloss hanged, and if I had not been so unfortunate as to kill the Baron, I should think they were rowing in this galley."

At the words Baron and Pangloss, the two convicts gave a loud cry, stopped on their benches and dropped their oars. The Levantine captain ran up to them and the lashes with the bull's pizzle were redoubled.

"Stop! Stop, sir!" cried Candide. "I will give you as much money as you want."

"What! Is it Candide?" said one of the convicts.

"What! Is it Candide?" said the other.

"Is it a dream?" said Candide. "Am I awake! Am I in this galley? Is that my Lord the Baron whom I killed? Is that Dr. Pangloss whom I saw hanged?"

"It is, it is," they replied.

"What! Is that the great philosopher?" said Martin.

"Ah! sir," said Candide to the Levantine captain, "how much money do you want for My Lord Thunder-ten-tronckh, one of the first Barons of the Empire, and for Dr. Pangloss, the most profound metaphysician of Germany?"

"Dog of a Christian," replied the Levantine captain, "since these two dogs of Christian convicts are Barons and metaphysicians, which no doubt is a high rank in their country, you shall pay me fifty thousand sequins."

"You shall have them, sir. Row back to Constantinople like lightning and you shall be paid at once. But, no, take me to Mademoiselle Cunégonde."

The captain, at Candide's first offer had already turned the bow towards the town, and rowed there more swiftly than a bird cleaves the air.

Candide embraced the Baron and Pangloss a hundred times. "How was it I did not kill you, my dear Baron? And, my dear Pangloss, how do you happen to be alive after having been hanged? And why are you both in a Turkish galley?"

"Is it really true that my dear sister is in this country?" said the Baron.

"Yes," replied Cacambo.

"So once more I see my dear Candide!" cried Pangloss.

Candide introduced Martin and Cacambo. They all embraced and all talked at the same time. The galley flew; already they were in the harbor. They sent for a Jew, and Candide sold him for fifty thousand sequins a diamond worth a hundred thousand, for which he swore by Abraham he could not give any more. The ransom of the Baron and Pangloss was immediately paid. Pangloss threw himself at the feet of his liberator and bathed them with tears; the other thanked him with a nod and promised to repay the money at the first opportunity. "But is it possible that my sister is in Turkey?" said he.

"Nothing is so possible," replied Cacambo, "since she washes up the dishes of a Prince of Transylvania."

They immediately sent for two Jews; Candide sold some more diamonds; and they all set out in another galley to rescue Cunégonde.

Chapter 28

What happened to Candide, to Cunégonde, to Pangloss, to Martin, etc.

"Pardon once more," said Candide to the Baron, "pardon me, Reverend Father, for having thrust my sword through your body."

"Let us say no more about it," said the Baron. "I admit I was a little too hasty; but since you wish to know how it was you saw me in a galley, I must tell you that after my wound was healed by the brother apothecary of the college, I was attacked and carried off by a Spanish raiding party; I was imprisoned in Buenos Ayres at the time when my sister had just left. I asked to return to the Father-General in Rome. I was ordered to Constantinople to act as chaplain to the Ambassador of France. A week after I had taken up my office I met towards evening a very handsome young page of the Sultan. It was very hot; the young man wished to bathe; I took the opportunity to bathe also. I did not know that it was a most serious crime for a Christian to be found naked with a young Mahometan. A Cadi[70] sentenced me to a hundred strokes on the soles of my feet and condemned me to the galley. I do not think a more horrible injustice has ever been committed. But I should very much like to know why my sister is in the kitchen of a Transylvanian ruler living in exile among the Turks."

"But, my dear Pangloss," said Candide, "how does it happen that I see you once more?"

"It is true," said Pangloss, "that you saw me hanged; and in the natural course of events I should have been burned. But you remember, the rain poured when they were going to roast me; the storm was so violent that they despaired of lighting the fire; I was hanged because they could do nothing better; a surgeon bought my body, carried me home and dissected me. He first made a crucial incision in me from the navel to the collarbone. Nobody could have been more badly hanged than I was. The executioner of the holy Inquisition, who was a sub-deacon, was marvellously skilful in burning people, but he was not accustomed to hang them; the rope was wet and did not slide easily and it was knotted; in short, I still breathed.

70. Turkish judge.

The crucial incision caused me to utter so loud a scream that the surgeon fell over backwards and, thinking he was dissecting the devil, fled away in terror and fell down the staircase in his flight. His wife ran in from another room at the noise; she saw me stretched out on the table with my crucial incision; she was still more frightened than her husband, fled, and fell on top of him. When they had recovered themselves a little, I heard the surgeon's wife say to the surgeon: 'My dear, what were you thinking of, to dissect a heretic? Don't you know the devil always possesses them? I will go and get a priest at once to exorcise him.'

"At this I shuddered and collected the little strength I had left to shout: 'Have pity on me!' At last the Portuguese barber grew bolder; he sewed up my skin; his wife even took care of me, and at the end of a fortnight I was able to walk again. The barber found me a situation and made me lackey to a Knight of Malta who was going to Venice; but, as my master had no money to pay me, I entered the service of a Venetian merchant and followed him to Constantinople.

"One day I took it into my head to enter a mosque; there was nobody there except an old Imam[71] and a very pretty young devotee who was reciting her prayers; her breasts were entirely uncovered; between them she wore a bunch of tulips, roses, anemones, ranunculus, hyacinths and auriculas; she dropped her bunch of flowers; I picked it up and returned it to her with a most respectful alacrity. I was so long putting them back that the Imam grew angry and, seeing I was a Christian, called for help. I was taken to the Cadi, who sentenced me to receive a hundred strokes on the soles of my feet and sent me to the galleys. I was chained on the same seat and in the same galley as My Lord the Baron. In this galley there were four young men from Marseilles, five Neapolitan priests and two monks from Corfu, who assured us that similar accidents occurred every day. His Lordship the Baron claimed that he had suffered a greater injustice than I; and I claimed that it was much more permissible to replace a bunch of flowers between a woman's breasts than to be naked with one of the Sultan's pages. We argued continually, and every day received twenty strokes of the bull's pizzle, when the chain of events of this universe led you to our galley and you ransomed us."

"Well! my dear Pangloss," said Candide, "when you were hanged, dissected, stunned with blows and made to row in the galleys, did you always think that everything was for the best in this world?"

"I am still of my first opinion," replied Pangloss, "for after all I am a philosopher; and it would be unbecoming for me to recant,

71. Turkish priest.

since Leibnitz[72] could not be in the wrong and pre-established harmony is the finest thing imaginable like the plenum and subtle matter."

Chapter 29

How Candide found Cunégonde and the old woman again

While Candide, the Baron, Pangloss, Martin and Cacambo were relating their adventures, reasoning upon contingent or non-contingent events of the universe, arguing about effects and causes, moral and physical evil, free will and necessity, and the consolation to be found in the Turkish galleys, they came to the house of the Transylvanian prince on the shores of Propontis.

The first objects which met their sight were Cunégonde and the old woman hanging out towels to dry on the line. At this sight the Baron grew pale. Candide, that tender lover, seeing his fair Cunégonde sunburned, blear-eyed, flat-breasted, with wrinkles round her eyes and red, chapped arms, recoiled three paces in horror, and then advanced from mere politeness. She embraced Candide and her brother. They embraced the old woman; Candide bought them both.

In the neighborhood was a little farm; the old woman suggested that Candide should buy it, until some better fate befell the group. Cunégonde did not know that she had become ugly, for nobody had told her; she reminded Candide of his promises in so peremptory a tone that the good Candide dared not refuse her. He therefore informed the Baron that he was about to marry his sister.

"Never," said the Baron, "will I endure such baseness on her part and such insolence on yours; nobody shall ever reproach me with this infamy; my sister's children could never enter the best society of Germany. No, my sister shall never marry anyone but a Baron of the Holy Roman Empire."

Cunégonde threw herself at his feet and bathed them in tears; but he was inflexible.

"Madman," said Candide, "I rescued you from the galleys, I paid your ransom and your sister's; she was washing dishes here, she is ugly, I am so kind as to make her my wife, and you pretend to oppose me! I should re-kill you if I acceded to my anger."

"You may kill me again," said the Baron, "but you shall never marry my sister while I am alive."

Chapter 30

Conclusion

At the bottom of his heart Candide had not the least wish to marry Cunégonde. But the Baron's extreme impertinence deter-

72. This and the following terms are all borrowed from Leibnitz.

mined him to complete the marriage, and Cunégonde urged it so warmly that he could not retract. He consulted Pangloss, Martin and the faithful Cacambo. Pangloss wrote an excellent memorandum by which he proved that the Baron had no rights over his sister and that by all the laws of the empire she could make a left-handed marriage[73] with Candide. Martin recommended that the Baron should be thrown into the sea; Cacambo decided that he should be returned to the Levantine captain and sent back to the galleys, after which he would be returned by the first ship to the Father-General at Rome. This was thought to be very good advice; the old woman approved it; they said nothing to the sister; the plan was carried out with the aid of a little money and they had the pleasure of duping a Jesuit and punishing the pride of a German Baron.

It would be natural to suppose that when, after so many disasters, Candide was married to his mistress, and living with the philosopher Pangloss, the philosopher Martin, the prudent Cacambo and the old woman, having brought back so many diamonds from the country of the ancient Incas, he would lead the most pleasant life imaginable. But he was so cheated by the Jews that he had nothing left but his little farm; his wife, growing uglier every day, became shrewish and unendurable; the old woman was ailing and even more bad tempered than Cunégonde. Cacambo, who worked in the garden and then went to Constantinople to sell vegetables, was overworked and cursed his fate. Pangloss was in despair because he did not shine in some German university.

As for Martin, he was firmly convinced that people are equally uncomfortable everywhere; he accepted things patiently. Candide, Martin and Pangloss sometimes argued about metaphysics and morals. From the windows of the farm they often watched the ships going by, filled with Effendis,[74] Pashas,[75] and Cadis, who were being exiled to Lemnos, to Mitylene and Erzerum. They saw other Cadis, other Pashas and other Effendis coming back to take the place of the exiles and to be exiled in their turn. They saw the neatly impaled heads which were taken to the Sublime Porte.[76] These sights redoubled their discussions; and when they were not arguing, the boredom was so excessive that one day the old woman dared to say to them: "I should like to know which is worse, to be raped a hundred times by negro pirates, to have a buttock cut off, to run the gauntlet among the Bulgarians, to be whipped and flogged in an *auto-da-fé*, to be dissected, to row in a galley, in short, to endure all the miseries through which we have passed, or to remain here with nothing to do?"

" 'Tis a great question," said Candide.

73. i.e., a morganatic marriage—one in which Candide would not receive the rank held by his wife.
74. Turkish military officials.
75. district governors.
76. the gate of the sultan's palace, where justice was at one time administered.

These remarks led to new reflections, and Martin especially concluded that man was born to live in the convulsions of distress or in the lethargy of boredom. Candide did not agree, but he asserted nothing. Pangloss confessed that he had always suffered horribly; but, having once maintained that everything was for the best, he had continued to maintain it without believing it.

One thing confirmed Martin in his detestable principles, made Candide hesitate more than ever, and embarrassed Pangloss. And it was this. One day there came to their farm Paquette and Friar Giroflée, who were in the most extreme misery; they had soon wasted their three thousand piastres, had left each other, made it up, quarrelled again, been put in prison, escaped, and finally Friar Giroflée had turned Turk. Paquette continued her occupation everywhere but now earned nothing by it.

"I foresaw," said Martin to Candide, "that your gifts would soon be wasted and would only make them the more miserable. You and Cacambo were once bloated with millions of piastres and you are no happier than Friar Giroflée and Paquette."

"Ah! Ha!" said Pangloss to Paquette, "so Heaven brings you back to us, my dear child? Do you know that you cost me the end of my nose, an eye and an ear! What a plight you are in! Ah! What a world this is!"

This new occurrence caused them to philosophize more than ever. In the neighborhood there lived a very famous Dervish,[77] who was supposed to be the best philosopher in Turkey; they went to consult him; Pangloss was the spokesman and said: "Master, we have come to beg you to tell us why so strange an animal as man was ever created."

"What has it to do with you?" said the Dervish. "Is it your business?"

"But, reverend father," said Candide, "there is a horrible amount of evil in the world."

"What does it matter," said the Dervish, "whether there is evil or good? When His Highness sends a ship to Egypt, does he worry about the comfort or discomfort of the rats in the ship?"

"Then what should we do?" said Pangloss.

"Shut up," said the Dervish.

"I flattered myself," said Pangloss, "that I should discuss with you effects and causes, this best of all possible worlds, the origin of evil, the nature of the soul and pre-established harmony."

At these words the Dervish slammed the door in their faces.

During this conversation the news went round that at Constantinople two Viziers[78] and the Mufti[79] had been strangled and several

77. Mohammedan friar, vowed to poverty.
78. prime ministers.
79. an official expounder of Mohammedan law.

of their friends impaled. This catastrophe made a prodigious noise everywhere for several hours. As Pangloss, Candide and Martin were returning to their little farm, they came upon an old man who was taking the air under an arbor of orange trees at his door. Pangloss, who was as curious as he was argumentative, asked him what was the name of the Mufti who had just been strangled.

"I do not know," replied the old man. "I have never known the name of any Mufti or of any Vizier. I am entirely ignorant of the occurrence you mention; I presume that in general those who meddle with public affairs sometimes perish miserably and that they deserve it; but I never inquire what is going on in Constantinople; I content myself with sending there for sale the produce of the garden I cultivate."

Having spoken thus, he took the strangers into his house. His two daughters and his two sons presented them with several kinds of sherbert which they made themselves, caymac flavored with candied citron peel, oranges, lemons, limes, pineapples, dates, pistachios and Mocha coffee which had not been mixed with the bad coffee of Batavia and the Isles. After which this good Mussulman's two daughters perfumed the beards of Candide, Pangloss and Martin.

"You must have a vast and magnificent estate?" said Candide to the Turk.

"I have only twenty acres," replied the Turk. "I cultivate them with my children; and work keeps at bay three great evils: boredom, vice and need."

As Candide returned to his farm, he reflected deeply on the Turk's remarks. He said to Pangloss and Martin: "That good old man seems to me to have chosen an existence preferable by far to that of the six kings with whom we had the honor to sup."

"Exalted rank," said Pangloss, "is very dangerous, according to the testimony of all philosophers; for Eglon, King of Moab, was murdered by Ehud; Absalom was hanged by the hair and pierced by three darts; King Nadab, son of Jeroboam, was killed by Baasha; King Elah by Zimri; Ahaziah by Jehu; Athaliah by Jehoiada; the Kings Jehoiakim, Jeconiah and Zedekiah were made slaves. You know in what manner died Crœsus, Astyages, Darius, Dionysius of Syracuse, Pyrrhus, Perseus, Hannibal, Jugurtha, Ariovistus, Cæsar, Pompey, Nero, Otho, Vitellius, Domitian, Richard II of England, Edward II, Henry VI, Richard III, Mary Stuart, Charles I, the three Henrys of France, the Emperor Henry IV.[80] You know . . ."

"I also know," said Candide, "that we should cultivate our gardens."

"You are right," said Pangloss, "for, when man was placed in

---

80. The editor declines to enter the trap baited with potential footnotes laid for him by Voltaire.

the Garden of Eden, he was placed there *ut operaretur eum*, to dress it and to keep it; which proves that man was not born for idleness."

"Let us work without theorizing," said Martin; " 'tis the only way to make life endurable."

The whole small society entered into this praiseworthy plan, and each started to make use of his talents. The little farm yielded well. Cunégonde was indeed very ugly, but she became an excellent pastry cook; Paquette embroidered; the old woman took care of the linen. Even Friar Giroflée performed some service; he was a very good carpenter and even became an honest man; and Pangloss sometimes said to Candide: "All events are linked up in this best of all possible worlds; for, if you had not been expelled from the noble castle, by hard kicks on your behind for love of Mademoiselle Cunégonde, if you had not been clapped into the Inquisition, if you had not wandered about America on foot, if you had not stuck your sword in the Baron, if you had not lost all your sheep from the land of Eldorado, you would not be here eating candied citrons and pistachios."

" 'Tis well said," replied Candide, "but we must cultivate our gardens."[81]

---

81. This sentence marks the end of *Candide*. A second part—*not* by Voltaire—was published anonymously in 1761; it has been attributed to the hack writer Thorel de Campigneulles. This forgery is mentioned only to put the reader on his guard, since one of the popular American editions of *Candide* reprints the spurious sequel as if it were genuine.

Masterpieces of
Romanticism

EDITED BY
HOWARD E. HUGO

Associate Professor of English, University of California, Berkeley

FROM ROUSSEAU
TO MELVILLE

Only a little over a hundred years separate Rousseau's completion of his *Confessions* (1770) from Melville's *Billy Budd* (1891). Though there are broader chronological stretches in other sections of this anthology, one may venture to say that few periods offer more radical shifts in man's entire outlook than do these years. In fact one measure of the works we have selected is the awareness their authors show (often more implicit than explicit) of such mutations.

"Everything goes to the people and deserts the kings, even literary themes, which descend from royal misfortunes to private misfortunes, from Priam to Birotteau"—so lamented the Goncourt brothers in 1866. From Homer's great monarch of

Troy to Balzac's perfume manufacturer in Paris in the 1830's there is a vast movement, not only in time but also in the human spirit—a movement from the heroic hero that still interested Shakespeare and Racine to the unheroic hero of the nineteenth-century bourgeoisie. The dates 1775, 1789, 1830, and 1848 (all falling within the confines of this portion of the anthology) mark years of revolution when middle-class protests against the *status quo* emerged with various degrees of violence. Only one major monarch—Charles I of England—was deposed in the seventeenth century. By contrast, the reader will recall having met six kings in Chapter 26 of *Candide*, all impoverished and in exile. The nineteenth century was to see political alterations unanticipated by political theorists, as "the divinity [that] doth hedge a king" was examined with rational suspicion, and monarchical and aristocratic powers were curtailed or abolished. The firing of "the shot heard round the world" at Concord (1775) and the fall of the Bastille (1789) mark dramatic moments which made actual the abstract political thought of eighteenth-century philosophers (with their paper constitutions, social contracts, declarations of the rights of man, and plans for perpetual peace). By 1850, it seemed to many political liberals that the bourgeoisie was politically and socially canonized. Continental revolutions in 1830 and 1848 and legislative reforms in England (chiefly in 1832) may have disappointed a few radicals by their compromises; but on the whole, the ascendancy of the middle class was guaranteed.

The change just outlined was "horizontal," cutting across national boundaries. The Enlightenment had set the goal, for the rational man, of being a "citizen of the world"; later eighteenth-century thought and nineteenth-century romanticism moved from such universality toward the phenomenon known as nationalism. Rousseau's claim for personal uniqueness was expanded to apply to the individuality of the *Volk*, the nation, or the race. Nationalism was curiously intertwined with political liberalism from the French Revolution on. At times "vertical" national interests even superseded more generous ideas of man's brotherhood and the abolition of world-wide tyranny. The Year One, announced in Paris in September, 1792, was intended to inaugurate a new egalitarian millennium for the entire human race; yet twelve years later Napoleon was crowned Emperor of the French.

Whitman could combine both attitudes, the mystique of racial uniqueness and the ideal of an all-inclusive political democracy.

Come, I will make the continent indissoluble,
I will make the most splendid race the sun ever shone upon.
What we believe in waits latent forever through all the continents,
Invites no one, promises nothing, sits in calmness and light, is positive and composed, knows no discouragement,
Waiting patiently, waiting its time.

The amalgam of political liberalism and nationalism was not rare: many thinkers, the Italian liberal Mazzini, for example, regarded nationalism as a necessary stage before man reached true awareness of humanity as a whole. From 1815 to 1853 the comparative absence of all warfare save colonial engagements seemed to display the relative harmlessness of nationalism. We have had the dubious advantage of another hundred years of history, to watch nationalism flourishing in its full horror.

Political upheavals in this period had their counterpart in the Industrial Revolution, which indeed accentuated notions of "class" and "nation" and began the transformation of most of Western Europe from an agrarian to a primarily industrial culture. The Reformation had earlier underscored the dignity and necessity of individual labor, and had indicated a connection between spiritual and material prudence and enterprise. With the growth of wealth, industry, manufacturing, and colonies came a need for more comprehensive theories. Adam Smith's *Wealth of Nations* (1776) set the pattern for subsequent economic speculation and practice: the laissez-faire state, permitting free trade, free markets, and free competition, in keeping with what Smith termed the "obvious and simple system of natural liberty." The advocacy of economic liberalism places Smith and his followers squarely within the tradition of middle-class liberalism, broadly defined. The modern reader should note Smith's assumption that economic individualism, without any form of government regulation, will result in public benefit and ultimate harmony. This difference in viewpoint distinguishes the early liberal from his spiritual descendants, who enlarged, rather than circumscribed, the scope of governmental function.

The Industrial Revolution was made possible by the technological innovations of applied science. One thinks of the steam engine perfected by James Watt toward the end of the eighteenth century; George Stephenson's locomotive, built in 1814; the telegraph, in 1844, and so on. What theology had been to the Middle Ages, science was to become to the nineteenth century. While Milton could write *Paradise Lost* (1667) relatively untroubled by scientific investigations (and

only twenty years before Newton's *Principia*), Pope, in his *Essay on Man* (1733-1734), rejoiced in the wonders of the physical universe which scientists seemed daily to reveal, and writers after Pope found themselves situated in a world where science was increasingly important. To the already established abstract field of mathematics were slowly added the more empirical studies of astronomy, physics, geology, and chemistry. Shortly after 1800, biology became a recognized area of study, as scientists dealt more and more systematically with the organic as well as the inorganic. When Auguste Comte expounded his "Positive philosophy" in the 1820's, and spoke of the need of an additional "life science" (sociology), the definition of the scientific disciplines seemed complete. Comte divided human history into "religious-superstitious," "philosophical," and "scientific-positivistic" periods, and announced that the world was now enjoying the last of the three.

The trends we have just discussed inevitably gave rise to countertrends. The rise of the bourgeoisie and of democratic egalitarianism had opponents—not only defenders of privilege, and those who could say with Talleyrand, "No man not alive before 1789 knows the sweetness of life," but also those who anticipated the horrible potentialities implicit in "the revolt of the masses," later described by Ortega y Gasset. The "liberating" impulses of early nineteenth-century nationalism too frequently evolved into aggressive national pride or, worse, into rampant racism. The exponents of a free mercantile economy, assuming without justification that man's individual actions will naturally produce economic harmony, inspired economists like Karl Marx to correct the balance by elaborating theories according to which the independent capitalist would disappear altogether in the inexorable class struggle that (in Marx's view) he was helping to create. Finally, the faith in progress and the future which science apparently underwrote—the belief that man was destined to be biologically, materially, and morally better—was from its inception queried by those who feared the sin of pride, whether defined in Christian or in classical terms, and by those who resented the displacement of absolute truth by the relative, pragmatic truths which science asserted.

If some common direction is sought beneath these manifold tendencies, it may be found in the rise of secularity and in what the historian Lecky called "a declining sense of the miraculous." Medieval man knew that he lived in God's world, and Christianity had permeated every aspect of daily living. Whether the Reformation came as a symptom or a cause of weakened faith, the existence in the West of several hundred churches in 1700, in comparison with one Church in 1300, indicated doubts and questionings where once had been absolute doctrinal certainty. Politics and economics were increasingly shorn of theocratic presuppositions; and by the time of the Age of Reason, religious truth itself had to pass the tests of empirical and rational inquiry. Naturally there were individual thinkers, and even mass movements, who protested the departure from Christian orthodoxy; but, in general, during the first half of the nineteenth century, Christianity for the intellectual was absorbed into what Comte called vaguely "a religion of humanity." (Christianity for the average man often was summed up in a remark attributed to Lord Melbourne: "No man has more respect for the Christian religion than I have, but really, when it comes to intruding it into private life. . . .")

In 1859, Darwin published his *Origin of Species*. At first hailed with delight by many critics—for did not evolution make progress as *real* as the law of gravitation, and even coincide with ideas of Christian teleology?—Darwin's book was soon attacked by churchmen for destroying certain fundamentalist theses, and the fight between religion and science began in earnest. More important, as the century moved on, certain deeper minds were disturbed by the new conceptions of a universe from which mind and spirit seemed excluded, where chance determined change, where "survival of the fittest" and "natural selection" suggested that might and force won over right, and where moral laws were illusory fictions. Herbert Spencer's remark—"Nature's discipline is a little cruel that it may be very kind"—was then regarded either as small comfort or as downright erroneous. Many perplexed souls would have found Melville's lines in *Clarel* (1876) an expression of their own dubieties.

> Yea, ape and angel, strife and old debate—
> The harps of heaven and the dreary gongs of hell;
> Science the feud can only aggravate—
> No umpire she betwixt the chimes and knell;
> The running battle of the star and clod
> Shall run for ever—if there be no God.

It is within this climate of opinion that romanticism ends and realism begins.

ROMANTICISM—SENTIMENT AND NATURE

The preceding remarks range far ahead of the first works in this section. Let us return briefly to the mid-eighteenth century, when, in the period of transition from the Enlightenment to romanticism, certain philosophical, political, and cultural presuppositions at one time thought to be eternally true were discussed, then criticized, then finally abandoned. Once again we are faced with the fact that men very radically change their opinions within a relatively short span of history. Out of the mass of attitudes and ideas, we abstract two which seem particularly significant: the change in the concept of nature and the growing importance attributed to the senti-

ments, feelings, emotions, passions.

Frederick the Great, onetime patron of Voltaire, described *Candide* as "Job in modern dress," and it is good to remember that the Book of Job ends in mystery. In *Candide* the same mystery is posed en route, although the work itself ends with acceptance. Why does evil exist in the universe? Why does the good man suffer? What is the relation of God to mankind? Does the cosmos run according to some rational scheme comprehensible to the human mind? Eighteenth-century science and mathematics had seemed to confirm the mechanistic view that all parts of nature were intelligible. Yet an increasing number of dark spots on the once illuminated intellectual horizon puzzled and confused later thinkers. Nature was to remain the comforting talisman for romanticism that it had been for the Age of Reason, but we shall see that "nature" came to be redefined. The romantics were as anxious as their classical and neoclassical forbears to fathom the riddle of man in his world, but henceforth it was felt that perhaps the heart—the emotions—and not the head held the key to ultimate comprehension of the universe. To understand this change, we must examine the growing cult of sentiment in the eighteenth century.

It would be foolish to imagine that at a certain moment people stopped thinking and began feeling. The Enlightenment had made much of the "moral sense," and the early decades of the eighteenth century had enjoyed an honest tear with innumerable sentimental novels and plays. But on the whole the deliberate exploitation of the emotions had been held suspect; and if ultimate values—laws about the cosmos, the arts, society, end so on—were at stake, those areas of the psyche which related to the feelings were conceived to be irrelevant. Spinoza, in *Of Human Bondage, or The Power of the Affections* (1667) said, "In so far as men are subject to passions, they cannot be said to agree in nature." The idiosyncrasy resulting from adherence to personal emotion rather than to the generally accepted principles of reason was not considered ideal material for literature in a period unusually dedicated to ideas of universality, social man, communication between minds, and conformity to classical norms. Then, for reasons that are still not clear, philosophical introspection, reverie, the melancholy heart became fashionable. The brooding, solitary daydreamer came into his own, with varieties of "spleen," "the blue devils," *Weltschmerz* ("world sorrow"), *le mal du siècle* ("the sickness of the century"). Rousseau's *Confessions* (1781-1788), filled with this kind of passionate unrest, were hailed by a reading public already assured of the primacy of the emotions.

I am commencing [said Rousseau] an undertaking, hitherto without precedent, and which will never find an imitator. I desire to set before my fellow-men the likeness of a man in all the truth of nature, and that man is myself. Myself alone! I know the feelings of my heart, and I know men. I am not made like any of those I have seen; I venture to believe that I am not made like any of those who are in existence.

From the objective norms that were the delight of the Age of Reason, we turn to the subjective, innate, indefinable, and *unique* core of each individual. The "man of feeling" (the phrase forms the title of a popular novel by the Scottish writer, Henry MacKenzie, published in 1771) replaced the elegant conversationalist of the salon, coffee house, and boudoir. And his feelings were mostly mournful. Earlier eighteenth-century sentimental literature had displayed *both* pleasurable and painful experiences, enriched by laughter and tears. The romantics endeavored to show that sensibility was not equated with happiness, and romantic literature in general is rarely comical or amusing. Pushkin (met later in this section) does occasionally smile wryly, but after the manner of Byron, whom he so admired: "And if I laugh at any mortal thing, 'Tis that I may not weep." In Rousseau's novel, *Julie ou La Nouvelle Héloïse* (*Julia, or The New Héloïse*, 1761), the young hero Saint-Preux exclaims poignantly, "For me there is only a single way to be happy, but there are millions of ways to be miserable."

For the romantics, the so-called "tender passion"—love—gained pre-eminence among all the feelings. The modern colloquial usage of "romantic" with connotations of moon-June-spoon is in part a legacy from that period. With the exception of Racine's *Phèdre*, the preceding section of this anthology contains, significantly, no literature dealing with love. Candide voyages from continent to continent to find his elusive Cunégonde, but her chief virtue—physical indestructibility—scarcely qualifies her for the role of a *romantic* heroine. The eighteenth century —despite its finesse, social decorum, and elegance—abounds with works displaying the relations between the sexes as surprisingly lusty and earthy, or as a kind of psychological game with possession the assumed goal of the male partner. Against such amorous franchise the romantics rebelled. We shall watch Faust and Margaret, among other heroes and heroines, asserting that love is a genuine spiritual entity and a condition eagerly to be coveted—not for purposes of physical satisfaction but because unhappy as the condition may be, life is meaningless unless we exist in that state of morose delight.

Even as the age brought a revaluation of the less ratiocinative, more intuitive processes of the psyche, it also brought new colorings to the concept of nature. From classical antiquity through most of the eighteenth century, the word *nature* had meant the totality of existence, the entire cosmos—animate and inanimate—with its laws and activity, and when it meant anything less than this, it had usually meant the whole nature of man—common human nature.

But in the cult of nature inspired by the romantic movement, the term came to mean something much more limited: the physical world apart from man's achievements—that is, the landscape and countryside, the sea and mountains. In a sense this idealization of nature was no innovation. The Hebraic-Christian tradition had begun with a garden. Pagan antiquity in Greece and Rome had produced pastorals and bucolics, in which the vision of the simple life in close proximity to animals and the land was portrayed. But the cleavage that Rousseau and his heirs now felt to exist between the individual and his environment led to a redefinition of "nature." Neoclassical society, polished and polite, had been essentially urban, although the philosopher-gentleman could enjoy the country as a respite from strenuous city life with its Court and Parliament, salons and coffee houses, wit and conversation. The formal garden—like Voltaire's at Ferney, with two head gardeners and twenty laborers— may be taken as a symbol of what was held to be a happy compromise between the country's annoying miscellaneousness and civilized mankind's love of order. As Dr. Johnson, Voltaire's contemporary, put it: "Sir, they who are content to live in the country are fit for it."

In the passage above from Rousseau, he stated that he is psychologically unique and like no other man past or present. From this sense of acute individuality, it is only a short step to a feeling of being alien and misunderstood. If our insensitive contemporaries reject us, we can always find comfort in the great sympathetic soul of nature —nature who "never did betray/The heart that loved her."

The heroes of later eighteenth-century literature move out from the confines of city and drawing room to the seas and forests. By the early nineteenth century the new hero has become stereotyped and hostility to organized society a cliché. If any member of society gained the romantic's approbation, it was generally the simple rustic who—like the innocent child— was close to nature and therefore morally purer than his sophisticated fellows. Primitivism long had interested the rationalist thinkers, and the untutored mind afforded the *philosophes* fascinating material for their studies of general mankind, although for this purpose distant, exotic savages (Voltaire's *Oreillons*, for instance) were more pleasing and more conveniently remote than the local peasantry. Later eighteenth-century expansions of this concept marked a shift from mere interest in the Noble Savage to positive approval. Serious doubts were raised as to the validity of urbanity and cultivation and about the notion of progress itself. Perhaps the unspoiled savage partook of a Golden Age where hearts rather than purses were gold, where there was no *mine* or *thine*, no artificial legislation, no social hierarchy. Though Rousseau's "natural man" drew a shout of derision from Voltaire, who saw men once more getting down on all fours in abdication of their rational-human capabilities, Voltaire was fighting a rearguard action, and the success of a work he ridiculed proved it. Few literary productions have attained the popularity of the Ossian poems (1760-1763), ostensibly translated by James Macpherson. *Fingal* and *Temora*, two "epics" in the group, depicted early Scottish-Celtic-"Erse" days in an elegiac, melancholy tone. What critics seemed most to admire was the *goodness* of all the characters. The poems of Ossian, for example, were among the favorite reading of a most unprimitive figure—Napoleon. That Macpherson's work was later proved a forgery in no way diminished his incredible influence. Twenty-five years afterward, Bernardin de Saint-Pierre published *Paul and Virginia* (*Paul et Virginie*, 1788), in which the life of decadent Europe was contrasted unfavorably with life on an unspoiled, Eden-like island. "Here there is merely wooden furniture, but there you find serene faces and hearts of gold."

France had been the Continental fortress of the Age of Reason, as our selection of readings in the preceding section of the anthology indicates. The headquarters of the new ideology moved to the "misty" north and Germany. That country demonstrated conscious romantic symptoms during the 1770's with its "Storm and Stress" (*Sturm und Drang*) movement in literature —led by a coterie of young writers fired by naturalistic, anti-French, anticlassical feeling. In their twenties, they were impregnated with notions about "genius" that should transcend any fettering rules and standards, convinced of the primacy of the passions over the meddling intellect, desirous of writing simple folk poetry stemming directly from the heart of the race, anxious to identify the spirit of man with the spirit of the new "nature," and, finally, eager to use literature as a vehicle in the search for philosophic truth—the pursuit of the Absolute, the underlying reality of existence. This was one of the first *avant-garde* groups. Among those who contributed to the "Storm and Stress" movement was Johann Wolfgang von Goethe. His *Faust*, Part I, begun during these years, is an illustration of the fully developed romantic mood.

ROMANTICISM AND THE METAPHYSICAL QUEST— GOETHE'S *FAUST*

Goethe, speaking of *Faust* to his friend and amanuensis Eckermann, once commented, "I think that I have given them a bone to pick." Seldom in Western literature has a work been so provocative to its audience; yet many a critic has sunk deep in the morass of intellectualism when attempting to explicate the play. The average reader will find *Faust* difficult going. He will be aware that there is more to it than meets the eye, although perhaps his feeling of disquietude will overbalance any pleasure the reading has afforded. If he is honest with himself, however, he will be forced to one conclusion upon completing *Faust*: he has been in the presence of one of the greatest of the world's masterpieces. Such an experience *should* lead to healthy confusion, since the reader—with the artist—has just taken a plunge into the unknown.

The first part of *Faust* was published by Goethe in 1808. Many years had gone into its creation. His so-called *Ur-Faust* ("early" or "primitive" *Faust*) was written between 1770 and 1775, and *Faust, a Fragment*, appeared in 1790. Behind Goethe's extensive labors lay the whole legend of the Renaissance scholar, Dr. Faustus, who quested after universal knowledge by means of white magic—that is, orthodox science—and the more terrible instrument of black magic. A real Johannes Faustus lived from 1480 to 1540. His adventures, much embroidered, were related by Johannes Spies twenty-seven years later, and these became the subject for innumerable puppet shows and popular folk-dramas throughout the seventeenth and eighteenth centuries in Germany. Hence from childhood on, the Faust myth was familiar to Goethe; and from the time he was twenty until he died at eighty-two, the theme never left his imagination. To trace the slow genesis of *Faust*, Part I, and later *Faust*, Part II (the sequel published posthumously in 1833), is fascinating to the scholar, but dull for the student. The important fact to be grasped is simple. Once again, as in Greek tragedy, Milton's *Samson Agonistes*, and Racine's *Phèdre*, we have the playwright using traditional, legendary, even mythical material.

The "Prologue in Heaven" Benedetto Croce has called "the jest of a great artist . . . deliberately archaic, and slightly in the style of Voltaire." We should not be misled by its cosmic humor and high irony. It must be read with care, for the key to subsequent events is found in the dialogue between God and Mephistopheles. The paean of the Archangels in praise of the wonderful universe is succeeded by the nay-sayer's insouciant remarks. Like Satan in the Book of Job (the opening scene is obviously modeled on Job 1:6-12 and 2:1-6) Goethe's devil has just returned "from going to and fro in the earth, and from walking up and down on it." What he has seen has only increased his contempt for that silly grasshopper, man. The angels may place man a little lower than themselves. Mephistopheles finds restless mankind scarcely an improvement over primordial chaos. Already we note that Mephistopheles' quarrel is not with man or with Faust; his challenge is leveled at God and His fitness as a creator!

Then follows the *first* wager, which is between God and a fallen divinity. Faust is discontented, says Mephistopheles. That beautiful gift of reason has induced nothing but fatal curiosity. His bewilderment, answers God, is temporary; and He turns Faust over to this most cynical of devils for the rest of his life. No holds are barred for Mephistopheles. He is given *carte blanche* to lure Faust in any fashion. The cryptic language may obscure the real issue for the reader. Here is no simple temptation to be naughty. Mephistopheles' aim is to undermine Faust's whole *moral* sense, the awareness that values of good and evil do exist despite man's difficulties in defining them. A being of searchings and questionings, living a life of constant aspiration toward goals but dimly seen—this, as described by God, is the being He has created in His own image. We shall see shortly how the terms of the *second* pact between man and devil are an attempt on Mephistopheles' part to stop this vital activity, thus implicitly defeating God's description of life as an eternal Becoming.

Such a vitalistic and dynamic interpretation of the human condition is the essence of romantic philosophy. Christianity had posited a state of grace, and Christian thought is the history of attempts to determine how erring man might finally enjoy eternal bliss. The Enlightenment, ignoring the mystery of faith implicit in Christian doctrine, had expanded the element of reason to be an end in itself. Romanticism, suddenly aware of dynamic (even irrational) principles underlying both man and nature, took striving—tentative progression and development, and pure endeavor—and made it the defining quality of mankind. In the second part of *Faust* (about which we shall speak briefly later on), Goethe has a chorus of angels proclaim, "Should a man strive with all his heart/ Heaven can foil the devil." The paradox of *Faust* is that of a man finally redeemed by a God whose reality Faust doubts. Goethe has written a modern *Divine Comedy* paralleling Dante's, but it is "divine comedy" of the profoundest irony.

Following the prologue we move from heaven to earth—a shift in background reminiscent of the epic. The setting of the opening of the play is traditional: "a high-vaulted narrow *Gothic* room." It reminds us of Goethe's role in the "Storm and Stress" group, the young writers of Germany who were anxious to rescue the native scene, and also the Middle Ages, and also Shakespeare (their idol), from the undervaluations of the Enlightenment—by which they meant France and French neoclassicism. The late C. S. Lewis, in *The Screwtape Letters* (1942), pointed out how "the long, dull, monstrous years of middle-aged prosperity or middle-aged adversity are excellent campaigning weapons" for the devil, and Goethe's Heinrich Faust is in the full maturity of worldly success. He owns everything—and nothing. He as polymath has investigated the entire field of human knowledge to find a chaos of relativism. A simple three-meal-a-day life is impossible for him. He cherishes a passion for the Absolute which his pedantic assistant Wagner cannot comprehend. Black magic yields little save despair. Death is one road to possession of final truth, but a childhood memory of naïve faith averts suicide. At

this critical stage Mephistopheles enters (first in the guise of a poodle, and we remember that the Greek root of the word *cynic* means "dog"). The real action of the play begins.

The Prince of Darkness is a gentleman, and the devil soon abandons his earlier disguises for the elegant costume of the polished gallant and wit. He had minced no words when he said previously, "I am the Spirit which always denies" ("*Ich bin der Geist der stets verneint*"). Now he offers *his* wager to Faust. Their pact is a corollary of the one we witnessed in Heaven. An interesting point, however, is that Faust frames the terms. We have already indicated that God's picture of Mephistopheles does not coincide with the devil's view of himself. The relation of the tempter to Faust presents us with an additional facet to his character, for Mephistopheles never really understands the nature of his companion's problem. *If* Mephistopheles can destroy Faust's sense of aspiration, *if* Faust can say of any single moment in time that *this* is complete fulfillment of desire—then the devil wins, and God and man are defeated. Such repose and satiety would represent an end to striving. It would also—and here is the subtle touch—mean a cessation of Faust's moral awareness. By the achievement of a final "good" on earth, the whole conception of good and evil as being in a state of development would be denied. Faust examines existence in terms of a question that only modern man could conceive;

certainly it was unknown to the Greeks with their feeling for limitation. Is a life of tireless movement toward an undefined goal worth living? And the devil (orthodox conservative and traditionalist that he is) can hardly be expected to grasp such a radical query.

The varieties of pleasure that the devil parades before the hero are proffered in an effort to supply *the* moment of complete satisfaction, and thus obfuscate Faust's values. Mephistopheles almost wins with Margaret (Gretchen). But love is more complicated than mere sex, and Faust's love comes to mean the acme of human aspiration. From love he learns to break through the bonds of his individual ego and to see his state in humanity. Margaret's tragedy enhances rather than diminishes Faust's moral sensibility, and Mephistopheles is a puzzled, disappointed sensualist when he takes Faust back to Gretchen's dungeon for the last poignant scene in the play. It is essential that the reader comprehend how much the author stresses the nature of Faust's affection, how love is raised to the level of a high philosophical concept. Stendhal showed only his lack of perception when he remarked: "Goethe gives Faust the Devil for a friend; and with this powerful ally, Faust does what we have all done at the age of twenty—he seduces a seamstress."

Even before the first part of *Faust* was published, Goethe thought of writing a second drama where the hero would turn from individual to social concerns. From approximately 1800 to 1831 Goethe worked on *Faust*, Part II, a play designed principally to be read. To read it is, in the words of one critic, "a pilgrimage from which few have returned safe and sound." Few works in modern times present us with such a conglomeration of shifting symbols, and we move from mystery to mystery, carried forward by Goethe's incomparable verse and brilliant ideas. A "Classical Walpurgis Night" synthesizes ancient Greece and the Gothic north. Goethe returns to the older Faust legend to have his aging protagonist marry Helen of Troy, now a widow after the death of Menelaus. Their union begets Euphorion (the spirit of new humanity; it is said that Goethe had Byron in mind as his model). Faust also undertakes a military career to save a shaky kingdom from falling. The ultimate activity pursued by Faust consists in reclaiming land from the sea, and he sees the vision of a new, happy community composed of industrious mankind. *This* is at last the consummate moment for him, and Mephistopheles—a nearly exhausted tempter—wins the wager in a dubious victory. But Faust's satisfaction is potential rather than actual: the vision lies in the indeterminate future for which he strives. The angels rescue Faust's soul from the forces of evil and bear him in triumph to heaven. Goethe's God seems to say that Faust's errors are necessary imperfections of man's growth. Imperfections in time are perfections in eternity. Faust's has been a "good" life. The final lines of the great drama, declaimed by the *Chorus Mysticus* in heaven, sum up the author's profound affirmation of existence.

All that is past of us
Was but reflected;
All that was lost in us
Here is corrected;
All indescribables
Here we descry;
Eternal Womanhead
Leads us on high.
[*Das Ewig-Weibliche/
Zieht uns hinan*]

BYRON AND THE ROMANTIC HERO

No single figure served better to answer the demand for a romantic hero than did Byron. In 1812, as he said, he awoke to find himself famous when the public welcomed the first two cantos of *Childe Harold's Pilgrimage*. For the modern reader, one problem is to disentangle his life, his works, and the myth that arose about them both. Handsome, debonair, elegant— the English aristocrat rejected by the society he treated with contempt—he swaggered through his thirty-six years with the brilliance of a consummate actor. When he spoke of his poetry as the pageant of his bleeding heart, he satisfied the age's taste for the literary confession. The role he played as the satanic dandy, the fallen angel, extended his influence outside England to the Continent, where a young generation—already filled with sentiments of *taedium vitae*, melancholia, *accidia*, "spleen," *Weltschmerz*, and *mal du siècle*

—saw in him and in his writings the incarnation of their own feelings.

To understand *Don Juan* (1819-1824), it is necessary first to consider certain aspects of eighteenth-century poetry. The Augustan age had been concerned with social man, the general species rather than the peculiarities of the individual; Hence satire, as we have previously seen, was a favorite form, for it could serve to correct deviations from norms of attitude and behavior. By the same token, lyric poetry—typically intimate, personal, and written not to project some universal truth but rather to evoke a private, unique feeling—was generally considered least important in the hierarchy of poetic genres. But romanticism, stressing the imagination, the emotions, and the private instead of the public phase of life, naturally turned to lyric poetry for its medium.

Don Juan represents a peculiar amalgam of both attitudes. On the one hand, the haunting poignancy of the Juan-Haidée episode is an echo of Byron's own love affairs, the poetic statement of the man who could write the following lines to the Countess Guiccioli: "You, who are my only and my last love, who are my only joy, the delight of my life—you who are my only hope—you who were—at least for a moment—all mine—you have gone away—and I remain here alone and desolate." The love of Juan and Haidée, placed in the exotic setting so dear to the romantics eager to escape from the mediocrity of a hum drum existence, is transmitted to the reader in poetry expressive of excited passion in accordance with Byron's own definition of his art. The lovers personify the protest of innocent, natural goodness against the claims of a cynical, worldly, materialistic society; they fulfill the romantic dream of primitive man happy in a state of nature:

They were alone, but not alone as they
　Who shut in chambers think it loneliness;
The silent ocean, and the starlight bay,
　The twilight glow, which momently grew less,
The voiceless sands, and dropping caves, that lay
　Around them, made them to each other press . . .

On the other hand, we are faced with Byron's affection for eighteenth-century verse and the affinities between him and the Augustan poets, especially Pope. Despite his debt to other English romantic writers, he tended to be critical of them: he deplored the vulgarity of the so-called "cockney" style of Keats, the sentimental and formless effusions of Southey and Wordsworth, the metaphysical vagaries of Coleridge, the confused symbolism of Shelley. The earlier masters of the terse, sharp, concise heroic couplet were his ideal. Although he referred to Pope as "that bitter Queen Anne's man," it was from Pope that he learned the power of devices such as antithesis and deliberate anticlimax, calculated bathos produced by the "art of sinking," and the sudden intrusion of the critical intellect after a rhapsodic outpouring of the feelings. Other resemblances to the literature of the preceding century are easy to discern. Fielding had called his novel *Joseph Andrews* (1742) "a comic epic poem in prose." Byron too returns to the epic form: the heroic becomes mock-heroic, the epic machinery is burlesqued and parodied ("Hail, Muse! *et caetera*"), the once doughty deeds turn into a series of boudoir escapades and picaresque rogueries, and this satiric grand tour opens in the mood of French bedroom farce or Restoration comedy.

Yet it is impossible to define Byron's special complexity solely in terms of a synthesis of neoclassicism with romanticism. The explanation lies within his own personality, and to some extent within romanticism itself. The mixture of ardor and cynicism apparent in Canto II of *Don Juan*—the counterpoint of sympathy against cool detachment—is only one facet of the tensions within the poet: he is the impertinent skeptic and freethinker never able to suppress memories of a rigid Presbyterian childhood; the great lover of the autobiographical portrait and the real man eternally seeking fulfillment in love and too quick to discover boredom and satiety; the weary champion of liberty and egalitarianism dying at Missolonghi, and the aristocrat conscious of his station and title. Typical of the man who was ever posturing but always frank with himself is Byron's statement concerning *Don Juan:* "It

... is meant to be a little quietly facetious about everything." But we remember the lines within the poem that perhaps reveal more of the author than his explicit assertion would allow. "And if I laugh at any mortal thing,/ 'Tis that I may not weep." In short, Byron exhibits one facet of what we now call *romantic irony*. In verbal irony, a statement means something different from what it seems to say. But romantic irony results from the individual's compartmentalizing his personality, so that the "thinking ego" watches the "feeling ego" with objectivity and the human being, split between factor and spectator, experiences a desire to plunge into life and an equally strong urge to stand apart from it. An earlier writer, Horace Walpole, had said, "The world is a comedy to those that think, a tragedy to those that feel." It is almost as if certain romantics had discovered that the same person could do both and would consequently be doomed to remain in a state of unstable equilibrium.

ENGLISH ROMANTIC VERSE

WORDSWORTH

Although *Don Juan* caught the new romantic mood, Byron, as we have pointed out, looked to the eighteenth century for much of his technique. Some twenty years earlier there had appeared Wordsworth's Preface to the *Lyrical Ballads*—the first English romantic manifesto in the arts, in which the author was primarily concerned with a new poetics for a new era. The *Lyrical Ballads*, the work of both William Wordsworth and Samuel Taylor Coleridge, had originally been published in 1798. The Preface written by Wordsworth in 1800 for the second edition of the poems, stands as an apology for the techniques of both poets, although Wordsworth was chiefly interested in defending himself.

Included in the 1800 volume was "Tintern Abbey" ("Lines Composed a Few Miles above Tintern Abbey . . ."). This poem is a meditation in three parts: the description of the scene, the account of the poet's gradually maturing conception of nature and his relation to it, and finally the apostrophe to his sister Dorothy. To the modern reader the work seems innocent enough and scarcely revolutionary in thought or technique. Properly to estimate the poem's literary worth, we must remember the poetic tradition against which Wordsworth was rebelling and some of the doctrine presented in the Preface of 1800.

Wordsworth's aim (already outlined in the Advertisement to the 1798 *Lyrical Ballads*) was to write in "the language of conversation in the middle and lower classes of society," not in what seemed to him the flowery poetic diction which the Age of Reason ordinarily employed in pastoral and descriptive poetry. That he regarded "Tintern Abbey" as a departure from conventional forms is best illustrated by his own tentative feelings concerning its classification. "I have not ventured to call this

Poem an Ode; but it was written with the hope that in the transitions and the impassioned music of the versification, would be found the principal requisites, of this species of composition." The composition of the work, blending present sensations with past memories ("Five years have past"), exemplifies Wordsworth's definition of poetry as "emotion recollected in tranquility." Despite the simple vocabulary and the obvious effort to write in a blank-verse medium close to prose, critics have questioned how far the style of "Tintern Abbey" actually resembles the language of conversation in the middle and lower classes.

Perhaps most important in the poem is the pervading pantheistic sentiment, the notion of the world soul immanent in every part of nature. "Tintern Abbey" displays in miniature what Wordsworth's long poem, *The Prelude* (1798-1805), was to show on a grander scale. It traces the growth of the poet's mind from a naïve childhood association with nature based on mere physical sensations to a final vision where the individual soul and "the still, sad music of humanity" are made one with the outer world of external shapes and forms. For Wordsworth the "sense sublime / Of something far more deeply interfused" is not merely the occasion conducive to the poetic experience. It is also the credo of pantheism.

The "Ode on Intimations of Immortality" (1807) recapitulates much of Wordsworth's attitude in "Tintern Abbey"; yet the pattern of spiritual and artistic crisis, followed by explanation and finally consolation, gives the "Ode" an intensity modern readers may find lacking in the earlier poem. From the Platonic notion of an existence before birth, Wordsworth moves to the babe and to the child— each much closer than the adult (and the poet) to the pristine, visionary state where the soul was one with pure Being and God. The frequent use of images referring to light is significant. What he poignantly states is the problem of sustaining "the visionary gleam . . . the glory and the dream." For its loss, to Wordsworth and to many romantic poets, meant not merely a dearth of poetry but a loss of contact with the underlying spirit of the universe. By relating poetry to metaphysics—and exalting it to a quasi-religious, quasi-mystical level—the romantics were giving even the lyric new necessity and new dignity; but they also demonstrated how difficult it was to capture and to retain the moment of poetic inspiration.

COLERIDGE

The same belief in the high intent and lofty office of the poet was shared by Coleridge, but he approached his craft with a style and technique different, and in some ways diametrically opposed, to those of Wordsworth. Like Wordsworth he revolted against the artifice of eighteenth-century verse, but Coleridge was interested less in recreating the "real language of men" than in returning to the older poetry of humble people —the ballad and the folk song, Furthermore, he felt that the new poetry had to revive the ancient sense of awe and wonder that primitive men displayed toward the universe. While employing the strange and the supernatural, he attempted to forge a set of poetic symbols that might make poetry not mere entertainment but an instrument of metaphysical knowledge. Later studies in German Idealistic philosophers (Kant, Schelling, Fichte) were to intensify his temperamental bent toward intellectual speculation. Coleridge's belief in the power of the imagination to peer into the workings of the cosmos augmented his conviction that poetry was a form of truth, and that art was to mediate between man and nature. As it had been for his predecessor William Blake, the poetic symbol was for Coleridge a hieroglyphic of reality; and *Kubla Khan* (*ca.* 1800) displayed in practice what he later expanded into theory. Unlike Wordsworth, who could never squarely face the problem of rhyme and meter—are they part of the "real language of men?"—Coleridge found these aspects of verse necessary to raise language to its highest capacity, where poetry acts as verbal incantation—a conception anticipating the idea of "evocative magic" later introduced by the symbolist poet Baudelaire.

SHELLEY

Wordsworth and Coleridge proclaimed the new movement in the *Lyrical Ballads* of 1798-1800; Shelley and Keats estab-lished romantic verse as *the* poetic tradition of the period. In the poems by them offered here, we see the fulfillment of certain qualities associated with romantic poetry: the attempted musicalization of verse, with the emphasis on sound rather than on sense; a skillful metrical technique; a keen eye for the particularities of nature, and the employment of existing verse forms (combined with experimentation) to achieve special effects. In the "Ode to the West Wind" (1820), it may be said that Shelley takes his point of departure from Wordsworth. There is the same evocation of nature (although a wilder, more spectacular landscape than ever Wordsworth described); there is even a similar regret for powers possessed by the child and lost in maturity:

> If ...
> I were as in my boyhood, and could be
> The comrade of thy wanderings over heaven.

On the other hand, we see that already in Shelley a poetic diction has been developed—perhaps not that of the eighteenth century, but an equally stylized use of language. The imagery, the choice of words, the alternation of moods of fierce passion and abject despair are a far cry from Wordsworth's attempt to write in the speech of common men. Indeed, Shelley criticized his predecessor for "failing to distinguish between simplicity of intellect and silly foolishness," and he feared that an unexalted poetry approaching too close to prose would be no poetry at all.

Outweighing these differences is the fact that the attitude expressed in the "Ode to the West Wind" represents an intensification of Wordsworth's ideas. One feels that the wind, for example, is more than a convenient aspect of nature in which the author wishes to lose his identity. It becomes a symbol for the intuited perception Shelley believed the poet to possess—a power at once preserving and destroying, serene and terrible, joyful and sad. Hence the final section is the key both to Shelley's own reforming zeal and to the growing conviction on the part of romantic poets that they—to use his phrase—were the "unacknowledged legislators of the world." The thoughts that will be driven "over the universe/Like withered leaves to quicken a new birth!" will bring about "Spring"—the utopian dream of free, happy humanity. Whether Shelley was writing pamphlets to the Irish people pleading for moral reform as the necessary precondition for political and social change (addresses he then scattered by balloons and glass bottles!) or creating visions—by means of a complex of allegories and symbols—of the perfect future world in *Prometheus Unbound* (1820), this missionary zeal never left him.

KEATS

In the case of Keats and the "Ode to a Nightingale" (1820), again a brief reconsideration of the purpose of the earlier *Lyrical Ballads* is pertinent. While the aim of Wordsworth was primarily to recreate the "real language of men" (most of the Preface deals with *Wordsworth's* part in the program), Coleridge's poetic contributions and his later theorizing indicate that *his* intentions differed from those of his colleague. Coleridge was convinced that the new poetry had to revive the ancient sense of awe and wonder that primitive man displayed toward the universe. By employing the strange, the wonderful, and the supernatural he attempted to fashion a set of poetic symbols—"hieroglyphics of reality"—that might make poetry an instrument of metaphysical knowledge rather than mere entertainment.

This is the aspect of romantic tradition to which the "Ode to a Nightingale" belongs. The opening tone of despair and the desire to flee may seem simply to place the poem in the category of romantic escapist literature. But the curious spell, almost an enchantment, occasioned by the bird's song brings about an infinitely more complicated progression of ideas and emotions than any mere evasion-wish could prompt. The mutability of life, the sadness of an existence "where men sit and hear each other groan," the transiency of love, beauty, and the present, are contrasted with the eternal truth of myth and history— "The voice I hear this passing night was heard / In ancient days by emperor and clown"— and with the permanence of death itself. When the nightingale departs with the thrice-reiterated (and perhaps onomatopoetic) "Adieu!" we are left with a question. Which is the reality: the vision, the dream, or the "real" life to which the poet returns when the imaginative act is over? "Fled is that music:—do I wake or sleep?"

In short, the "Ode to a Nightingale" serves to embody two concepts essential for an understanding of Keats's verse and important for an adequate comprehension of what many romantic poets were trying to accomplish. Keats spoke of what he called "negative capability," describing it as the moment of artistic inspiration when the poet achieved a kind of self-annihilation—complete absorption in the object contemplated—and arrived "at that trembling, delicate, snail-horn perception of Beauty." Moreover, this instant was not only the occasion for poetic creation: for Keats it was then that the barrier between the individual ego and the world beyond this world dropped, and he partook of "fellowship with essence." Once more we are presented with the example of a romantic attempting to employ poetry—even the short lyric—as a means of exploring reality. If we perhaps cannot share the romantics' ultimate faith and grasp their curious convictions, at least we may sympathize with the boldness of their quest.

LATER ROMANTICISM AND THE VICTORIAN PERIOD

The earlier romantics had been conscious of living in an epoch of radical mutations and innovations in every sphere of activity. Dark voyages into the unknown such as the Ancient Mariner's were prerequisite for utopian visions such as Faust's at the end of the second part of Goethe's play. The poets felt with an intensity unequaled since the Renaissance that they were spearheading civilization. Hence Shelley could write in all conviction, "Poets are the unacknowledged legislators of the world." Perhaps the world had been callous to the exalted utterances of its prophets. A *new* society, a *new* golden age was about to be born, and there the artist-seer would come into his own. Earlier, William Blake could command his contemporaries to listen to the poet ("Hear the voice of the Bard! / Who Present, Past, & Future, sees").

Alas, the *new* society voted in its own legislation, without Shelley's aid, and it ignored a simple visionary like Blake. The marriage between life and art that in the romantic era had seemed eternal now dissolved; and the Victorian poets either tried unsuccessfully to effect a reunion or sang a sad elegiac strain. The future utopia that had gleamed so beautifully turned out to have smoke pouring from its ugly chimneys, and it was populated not by a pure, happy humanity but rather by a humanity mass-produced. The Industrial Revolution had slowly transformed England from an agrarian to a mechanized, urban nation. Romantic metaphysics gave way to scientific social theories; and Coleridge's high-flown speculations about life were matched by the cooler, more practical hypotheses of Jeremy Bentham and

John Stuart Mill, for whom the glow of reason shone brighter than it ever did in the Enlightenment. When the French thinker Auguste Comte described man's history in terms of religious-superstitious, philosophical, and scientific-positivistic periods, and announced that the world was now enjoying the emancipated last of these three epochs, he spoke for most of the intellectuals of his age. In such an era, the fruit of mechanical, scientific, materialistic progress, what was the role of the poet? Indeed, what was the place of poetry? If, as the critic Thomas Love Peacock said, perhaps ironically, "poetry was the mental rattle that awakened the attention of intellect in the infancy of civil society," then there could be little need for the ministrations of poetry in humanity's *adult* condition.

Victorian writers had several alternatives, and most of the authors vacillated among them. They could come to grips with the new "utilitarian" environment and extol its dubious virtues. A century before, Young had written, "Is 'Merchant' an inglorious name? / No! Fit for Pindar such a theme." Actually, the novel—the unique art form produced by middle-class, urban, liberal society—was better suited than the lyric for praising the entrepreneur, but scientific progress had its own poetic apologists. Tennyson himself, in his more optimistic moments, could speak of "the ringing grooves of change" (after a too-hasty glimpse of a railroad track), or write such twaddle as this:

Dash back that ocean with a pier,
Strew yonder mountain flat;
A railway there, a tunnel here—
Mix me this zone with that.

The modern gadgets had their fascination for the poet, ever anxious to extend the subject matter of his craft, and there was always the possibility that the new Iron Monster might be tamed.

Or the poets could return again to the dim, happy, idyllic past. Earlier romanticism had developed an awareness of distant periods and places which until then had been misunderstood or only vaguely comprehended: the medieval era, Greece, the East, primitive cultures. Victorian literature intensified interest in some of these. The cult of the Middle Ages, for example, was strengthened when in the 1830's and the 1840's aesthetic escapism was augmented by the religious hunger for dogma in the Oxford Movement and by the aristocratic, semifeudal conservatism of the Young England group. Or one could seek the solace of nature as an answer to trapped individualism. But Darwinian theory showed a nature "red in tooth and claw," and even beatific nature loses its powers of assuaging the hurt soul when one is forced to flee to it. To quote the modern poet Peter Viereck, there was soot on the ivory tower. The Victorian poets were uncomfortable, confused, baffled by necessary compromises, unsure of their function or of the world in which they lived.

TENNYSON

Tennyson has been hailed as

the spokesman for Victorian England. It would be safer to call him the spokesman for Victorian poets. A contemporary said that Tennyson "looked as if he might have written the *Iliad*." But the leonine, bearded face, the apparent gruff masculinity, the proto-Kiplingese heartiness found in "The Charge of the Light Brigade" (1854), were coupled with acute sensitivity, melancholia, and a capacity for pathos that had to answer as a capacity for passion. Such poems as "Locksley Hall" (1842) and "Ulysses" (1842), with their notes of courage, uplift, and praise of the active life, are counterbalanced—indeed outweighed—by the pessimistic tranquility of "The Passing of Arthur" (1842, 1869) and the quiet, sad contemplativeness of many of his short lyrics. Tennyson's material success (he became, to use the phrase of his friend Dickens, a "household word") in no way diminished his disquietude. He saw all too clearly the process he describes in the opening of "Tithonus" (1860):

The woods decay, the woods decay and fall,
The vapours weep their burthen to the ground,
Man comes and tills the field and lies beneath,
And after many a summer dies the swan.

This message was not likely to influence a generation interested in "muscular, jocular Christianity," the expansion of the Empire, investments at six per cent, and improved steam engines.

BROWNING

Browning is an example of a more vigorous Victorian writer, and one is tempted to speculate about how much his years in Italy contributed to his lustier, more robust outlook and expression. In any case he fulfilled the romantic myth of the Anglo-Saxon blossoming in the climate of the warm south. His early poems, from *Pauline* (1833) to *Sordello* (1840), exemplify a conception of poetry which had been intensified by the romantic movement—the view of poetry as the confessional, the place where the poet pours out his own intimate spiritual doubts, perhaps using the thin disguise of imaginary characters. Browning's inability to attain the slightest popular favor in this genre led him to try the drama. For almost ten years he devoted himself exclusively to the composition of a series of equally unsuccessful plays, in which he attempted to join Shakespearean effects with Bulwer-Lyttonian melodrama. The greatness of his later poems came from the union of what he had learned from these two failures, in the triumphant synthesis of the dramatic monologue. Here sensitive psychological analysis was conceived within the framework of the dramatic situation. Even Browning's shorter lyrics often share this quality, when the lyric catches the moment of sudden insight, but we are also keenly aware of narrative, atmosphere, and situation. "The Bishop Orders His Tomb" (1845) unites the private intensity of lyric self-expression with the objectivity of the dramatic form, and it may be regarded as one of

Browning's most impressive dramatic monologues.

Carlyle's contrast of Tennyson and Browning is the revealing comment of a keen contemporary: "Alfred knows how to jingle; Browning does not." Browning's ebullience is a cheerful contrast to Tennyson's tenderness. The Victorian writer, as we have suggested, could either grapple with the new ideas of his times or retreat; Browning certainly chose the first alternative. His philosophical point of view was a blend of conventional Christianity and Neoplatonism with the new scientific concepts of emergent, creative evolution. Yet Browning's roots were in the Italian Renaissance and the Elizabethan age. Consequently his love poetry, which came close to violating the Great Taboo of Grundyism, appeared daring and unconventional when held up against the "lollypoppism" (Carlyle's word) of Tennyson and Tennyson's imitators. Not since John Donne had love been anatomized with such incisions.

AMERICAN ROMANTICISM

The history of American literature is the story of the slow emergence of native elements and the gradual assimilation of foreign schools. It was simpler to throw off a political yoke in 1776 than it was to abandon a servile aping of English culture. Yet by the mid-nineteenth century, certain writers had demonstrated to all that the New World was no longer rude and unlettered. Cooper, Hawthorne, and Melville, in the novel, Emerson in philosophy, and Poe and Whitman were caught up in the general ambience of romanticism. To the movement, however, they added certain temperamental and national qualities—contributions which make American romanticism worthy of special attention.

POE

The loneliness of Edgar Allan Poe's curious verbal incantations and his preoccupation with the themes of death and decay seem odd when placed against the background of growing, optimistic young America. Baudelaire (the French translator of Poe, who saw in him one of the forerunners of the symbolist movement) said that America was Poe's prison, and explained the poet's tortured productions in terms of sick genius in an unsympathetic society. This is part of the answer; the rest dissolves into the inexplicable mystery of which Poe himself was so fond. The gloomy and macabre sensitivity of "The Fall of the House of Usher," "Ligeia," "The Masque of the Red Death," "The Raven," and "Ulalume" (all appearing during the dozen years preceding Poe's death in 1849) stems in part from the European Gothic novels of an earlier generation, from the bizarre tales of the German writer E. T. A. Hoffmann, and from the trends that the French have labeled "low" or "black" romanticism. The intense theatricality of his poems and tales has been often attributed to the fact that Poe's parents were actors (a doubtful hypothesis) and to his own interest in the drama.

Poe also belongs to the diversified group of authors who contributed to the evolution of the mystery or detective story so popular in our day. Like many of the romantics, he possessed a touch of the charlatan as well as the faded elegance of the aristocratic dandy. His verse and his poetic theory represent the essence of romantic word music, with the emphasis on sound rather than sense. Poe's insistence that a poem must be short, powerful, and fragmentary is again in keeping with the romantic stress on sudden insight rather than slower, logical comprehension. Few authors have provided the contemporary psychological critic with more material for a case study of neurosis. Poe's account of a strange voyage into a sea of polar ice, *The Narrative of Arthur Gordon Pym* (1838), has offered the Freudian interpreter as rich a field of study as Coleridge's *Ancient Mariner*. Indeed, the life and writings of Poe point to the Modern *Angst*— now reflected, for instance, in Kafka's hysterical characters driven into a claustrophobic little corner of the self, in the suffering and sadism of Graham Greene's guilty heroes, and even in the distorted, nightmarish landscapes of Salvador Dali.

WHITMAN

Poe typifies the dark side of American romanticism. Whitman stands for all the romantic aspirations toward brotherhood, humanity, freedom, and liberty. Once more we return to the notion of the bard-seer who would speak for the nation. "I will not descend among professors," cried the latter-day prophet who physically so resembled his Old Testament forebears; and his remark makes our comments seem presumptuous. The apparent artlessness of Whitman's prolix verse is apt to obscure its sources in the Bible, Shakespeare, "Ossian," nineteenth-century bombastic political oratory, Italian opera, and the traditional American love of unfettered liberty and hatred of restraint. In one sense, Whitman's free verse fulfills the romantic dream of a prose that would be poetry, and William James described *Leaves of Grass* as "thousands of images of patient, homely, American life." Like Wordsworth's milder departure from previous poetic diction, Whitman's rejection of the "genteel tradition" resulted from a determination to express the sentiments of the common, ordinary man—"and all the men that were born are also my brothers." Emerson had transplanted German idealism to domestic soil, where it became the major element in American transcendentalism. Whitman's ideas were often close to those of his philosopher-contemporary, and his "noiseless patient spider" might serve as an image for the Emersonian life process —spirit working through the natural phenomena of the universe. The grandeur and dignity of Whitman's writing is coupled with pagan sensuality, a lusty, hearty gusto for existence, and a constant contact with the earth. When he said, "Arnold gives me the feeling that he hates to touch the dirt," Whitman not only rendered a critique of his Victorian colleague but also revealed his own position. The entire—and in our time somewhat faded—hopes of a young agrarian country emerge from his lines. With Whitman we are always outside on the open road or amid the loving comradeship of the crowded city —never confined or disheartened, since implicit in the voice of the people is the romantic faith in an ideal community.

HAWTHORNE

At first glance the two tales with which this section on romantic literature concludes seem equally to be suitable for inclusion in the next section on realism. Their apparent similarities to the prose fiction of realism— chiefly their workaday backgrounds (the lime kiln and the ship of the line)—should not obscure the real differences. True, Hawthorne and Melville have abandoned such exotic settings as Poe's gloomy medieval abbey, Byron's Grecian isle, Browning's Rome, and Tennyson's Lyonesse. The firm shape of Mount Greylock in Massachusetts has replaced Shelley's ubiquitous west wind; the gun ports on Captain Vere's *Indomitable* open into no such vistas as Keats' Grecian urn. The puzzling voyages of Faust and other daring protagonists *seem* finished, and these questing romantic heroes have found their vocations as manual laborer and ordinary seaman. Nevertheless, the literary intent of Hawthorne and Melville, as revealed in the entire body of their writing (and more specifically in the stories offered here), gainsays

any attempt to place them within the later rather than the earlier tradition. The *New English Dictionary* tells us that their contemporary Emerson was the first in America to apply the term "realism" to literature, in 1856. His pejorative equation of the word with "materialism" would have met with their favor: neither artist was primarily occupied with the depiction of man in his physical setting—a concern of certain later realistic writers.

Three strains of thought conspired to give Hawthorne a bent for allegory and symbolism, the elements which introduce the mythic and poetic into the cool rationality of prose. First was seventeenth-century New England Puritanism, of which he was the nineteenth-century spiritual and physical heir. Had not an ancestor been a judge at the Salem witchcraft trials in 1692-1693? If Hawthorne could not literally accept the Calvinist dogma of Puritanism—the stress on original sin, natural depravity, total damnation, predestination, and divine election—its tenets, often strangely disguised, are always evident in his art. Second was the tradition of the Gothic novel and romance, in which horror and terror invested the world of ordinary shapes and forms with supernatural implications. Third, the intellectual climate of American transcendentalism induced its proponents to seek the realm of essence which they felt to exist behind the discrete phenomena of material nature. If Hawthorne could not share the self-reliant optimism of transcendentalism's foremost spokesman, Emerson, who proclaimed that "the first lesson of history is the good of evil," at least he partook of kindred sentiments about the substantial world of appearance concealing the true world of spirit. In this respect the current philosophy of the age resembled that of the Puritan, manifesting the same tendency to allegorize life and to regard events, both important and trivial, as signs of divine favor or displeasure. Whether consciously or unconsciously, Hawthorne therefore filled his novels and stories with complex symbols—the fountains and the marble faun, the poison flowers and the flaming furnace —by which, in keeping with the technique of European romantics a generation or two earlier, he attempted to decipher the hieroglyphs of nature.

That "Ethan Brand" (1851) is subtitled "A Chapter from an Abortive Romance" immediately indicates that it is no simple story of ordinary, daily existence. Against the innocence of the child, the practical indifference of Bartram the lime-burner, the jovial thoughtlessness of the guests, Hawthorne portrays the figure of Brand, burdened with his Unpardonable Sin. An earlier comment in Hawthorne's *Journal* appears to explain Brand's particular ethical transgression: "The Unpardonable Sin might consist in a want of love and reverence for the Human Soul" —where the investigator pries into the psyche out of "cold philosophic curiosity," with no interest in moral betterment.

The familiar romantic chastisement of the head, the "meddling intellect" of Wordsworth which destroys the richer sensibilities of the heart, was a favorite theme of Hawthorne's. The scientist in his story "Rappaccini's Daughter" (1846) uses his knowledge to create a garden of poisonous flowers; his perversion of the intellect ultimately culminates in the unwitting annihilation of his own child. But "Ethan Brand" actually transcends any easy conceptual explanation. As with Goethe's *Faust*, which it resembles, the reader is struck by the problematic details of the narrative. Overtones of the classical and Christian sin of pride, the fall of man and original sin, man's natural depravity and the absolute reality of evil, the irrational springs of conduct which impel us—all these emerge from an atmosphere of somber gloom, broken only by the bright glare of the miniature Inferno into which Brand hurls himself. Outcast and wanderer, spiritual cousin to the Ancient Mariner, Byron's Cain, Melville's Ahab in *Moby Dick*, Ethan Brand joins the desperate company of those impassioned figures, noble and guilt-laden overreachers, created by romanticism as symbols of man daring to aspire higher than human limitation permits.

MELVILLE

Many of the comments about Hawthorne can be applied to his close friend, Melville, if certain qualifications are added. Melville was raised in the theology of the Calvinist Dutch Reformed Church. What the Gothic romance was for Hawthorne, the sea stories of Smollett, Cooper (*Red Rover*, 1827), and Richard Henry Dana (*Two Years before the Mast*, 1840) were for the younger man. Melville was also well acquainted with the school of philosophic idealism in Europe (Hegel, Kant, Coleridge, Carlyle) and with transcendentalism on this side of the Atlantic. Hawthorne's early stories drew upon his scholarly research in New England history and legend; Melville's first literary efforts drew upon his experiences aboard ship and in the islands of the Pacific. The two authors met in the Berkshires in Massachusetts in 1850; their spiritual affinity is testimony that cultural history may subsume temperamental differences. The "darkness" of Hawthorne's art appealed most to Melville. He perceived in Hawthorne's writings a vision of "usable" and "unvarnished" truth, caught only in brief moments and then "cunningly and by snatches"—a truth which Melville felt only Shakespeare had fully expressed and which he himself also aspired to present.

Moby Dick (1851) is the summit of Melville's achievement. For forty more years he continued—to quote his own line— "to wrestle with the angel— Art," but he poignantly said in the early 1860's, "The work I was born to do is done." The modern reader of *Pierre* (1852), *The Confidence Man* (1857), and *Billy Budd* (finished shortly before his death in 1891) may disagree with Melville's modesty. In *Moby Dick* almost all the ro-

mantic themes are brought together and re-examined, often to their peril and ultimate rejection. The easy, happy pantheism of Wordsworth and Emerson and the cult of nature of Rousseau, Melville supplants with an insight more ambiguous, even terrible, where the inscrutable God revealed is the God of Blake's Tiger. The romantic utopian dream of an egalitarian democracy is brought up against the equally compelling notion of the role of the great man, the leader, in history. The romantic interpretation of science as the handmaid of human progress, the instrument by which man may discover final truths, is found suspect. The romantic vindication of Christianity in the face of what was construed to be eighteenth-century mechanism is likewise held inadequate.

Melville completed *Billy Budd* forty years after the publication of his monumental, but ill-received, *Moby Dick*. He probably began the tale in 1886. By 1888 the story as we read it had taken shape within his mind, but he kept revising it until the year he died. Mrs. Melville regarded the work as unfinished and made her own emendations. It was not published until 1924.

Billy Budd is set in the years immediately after the French Revolution, when romantic hopes for the beginning of a great new age ran highest. The special phenomenon of naval mutiny seems to have obsessed Melville. He had participated in a mutiny aboard the whaler *Lucy Ann* when he was a seaman not much older than his hero. In his writings he frequently alluded to the mutiny aboard the U.S. brig *Somers* in 1842, when his cousin Guert Gansevoort helped to condemn a rebellious mid-shipman to death by hanging. He also wrote about fictional muti-nies in *Benito Cereno* and in the interpolated narrative about the *Town-Ho* in *Moby Dick*. In all these instances, Melville's sym-pathy for this form of protest against constituted authority takes on certain romantic config-urations, if we identify the ro-mantic movement politically with the age of revolution.

The innocence of the passive protagonist, who goes down be-fore the demands of social and perhaps cosmic justice, places Billy Budd among those milder romantic heroes who share the traits of the unspoiled, unsophis-ticated primitive and the blame-less child trailing his Words-worthian clouds of glory, still un-touched by the corruption of adulthood and what Shelley called "the world's slow stain." Billy is also isolated, set apart from his fellows by his physical beauty—an outward sign of in-ner harmonies—and his speech impediment. Here he becomes a paler manifestation of Rous-seau's claim for extreme individ-ualism: "I venture to believe that I am not made like any of those [men] who are in existence."

As for the story, we know from Melville's sketches that Claggart was slowly developed as the an-tagonist, with overtones of some of Shakespeare's villains and of Milton's Satan. Similarly, Cap-tain Vere finally emerged as a kind of father-image, a perplex-ing figure of the older man torn between his respect for law and his humane and decent impulses. As in *Moby Dick*, Melville came back to the theme of good and evil that always occupied his mind.

As with his great novel, critical interpretations of *Billy Budd* have varied widely. Some critics, like the late John Middleton Murry, have seen it as Melville's "last will and spiritual testa-ment," and the author's final ac-ceptance of the universe. ("God bless Captain Vere," sings out Bill, at the very moment of his execution). But others have viewed *Billy Budd* as the last ex-pression of Melville's protest against the order of existence. Billy's sacrificial death has been construed to make him a Christ-figure; and it is at least true that the story, like many of Melville's is rich in Christian symbols and images . But Melville's lifelong ambivalence toward traditional Christianity makes this thesis problematical, although provoca-tive. In any case, Billy's death is occasioned at least in part by the inexorable demands of society, that key concept of the nine-teenth century.

RUSSIAN ROMANTICISM: PUSHKIN'S *EUGENE ONEGIN*

It has long been a critical com-monplace to say that all the cur-rents of the eighteenth century meet in Pushkin and all the rivers of the nineteenth flow from him. *Eugene Onegin* is acknowledged his masterpiece, the novel in verse that took him eight years to complete (1823-1830 with a few minor touches added in 1831). The initial idea came from Byron's immensely popular *Beppo*, his *Childe Harold*, and chiefly his *Don Juan*. From the latter Pushkin derived the notion of a long narrative poem in regular stanzaic pattern (fourteen lines of iambic tetrameter, with carefully alternating masculine and feminine endings); a subject taken from contemporary life in society (a departure from some of Pushkin's earlier works, with their exotic historical or geographical milieus); and a tone mixing wit with seriousness, irony with lyricism. Byronic too is the hero: handsome, debonair, elegant, a "child of his century" in his frequent fits of melancholy and ennui and his overriding contempt for the feelings of others which then fill him—as satanic dandy and fallen angel—with remorse and self-recrimination. The poem abounds in the same sort of digressions of which Byron was so fond—humorous, serious, lyrical, occasionally polemical. Even certain epic machinery is burlesqued and parodied (just as Byron opens Canto III of *Don Juan* with the invocation "Hail, Muse! *et caetera*").

But Pushkin's plot is far tighter, despite his admission that when he began he had no definite plan for the poem's conclusion, and there is a definite deepening of the emotions through the eight cantos. The young St. Petersburg dandy, rake, and cynic comes to know the meaning of tragedy when we arrive at what Prince D. S. Mir-sky has called "the unhappy, suggestively muffled ending." The moral stature attained by Tatyana in her final rejection of Onegin (she remains the virtuous wife despite the realization of her love for him) molds her into a most un-Byronic heroine. Yet, as noted earlier, both Don Juan and Onegin share a quality of mind caught up in two of Byron's lines: "And if I laugh at any mortal things, / 'Tis that I may not weep." This is *romantic irony*, or at least one aspect of that attitude.

Eugene Onegin is best understood if the reader is also cognizant of a larger cultural trend in Russian literature, the dichotomy between Slavophiles and Westerners. Onegin is a Europeanized aristocrat—typically from St. Petersburg, a "French" city, and not from Moscow—infected by Western intellectualism and skepticism, and a prototype for the "useless hero" who appears in so many Russian novels in the nineteenth century. Tatyana, on the other hand, was acclaimed by Dostoevsky, in a famous *Address on Pushkin* (1880), to be the embodiment of all the Russian and Slavophile virtues, untainted by Western decadence and spiritual corruption, existing in harmonious rapport with her environment. This pattern of East versus West was to be repeated with variations by most of the major Russian writers until the Revolution in 1917, and it is testimony to Pushkin's genius that he was one of the first to seize upon its larger implications.

LIVES, WRITINGS, AND CRITICISM

Biographical and critical works are listed only if they are available in English.

JEAN-JACQUES ROUSSEAU

LIFE. Born on June 28, 1712, in Geneva, son of a watchmaker. Unhappy as an engraver's apprentice, he left home while still in his teens, and for a time lived with Mme. de Warens—the first of many female protectors. He led a peripatetic existence and held many positions: as music teacher, secretary, footman, government official under the king of Sardinia, clerk in the Bureau of Taxes in Paris (where he settled in 1745). There he lived with Thérèse le Vasseur, with whom he had five children (all deposited at an orphanage). In 1756 Mme. d'Épinay invited him to live on her estate at Montmorency. Official criticism of his books several times forced Rousseau, like Voltaire, to leave France for Switzerland; in 1766 he traveled to England as guest of the philosopher David Hume. He was permitted to return to Paris in 1770 on condition that he write nothing against government or religion. Rousseau died on July 3, 1778, at Ermenonville. His body was brought to the Pantheon in Paris in 1794, during the Revolution.

CHIEF WRITINGS. His writings fall into four categories: Works involving music: *On Modern Music* (*Dissertation sur la musique moderne*, 1743); *Letter on French Music* (*Lettre sur la musique française*, 1752); *Musical Dictionary* (*Dictionnaire de musique*, 1767); and an opera, *The Village Soothsayer* (*Le Devin du village*, 1752). Political writings: *Concerning the Origin of Inequality among Men* (*Discours sur l'origine et les fondements de l'inégalité parmi les hommes*, 1754) and *The Social Contract* (*Le Contrat social*, 1762). A book, nominally a novel, on education: *Emile* (1762). Autobiographical productions: a novel, *Julie, or the New Heloise* (*Julie, ou La Nouvelle Héloïse*, 1761); the *Confessions*, composed between 1765 and 1770, published in 1781–1788; and *Musings of a Solitary Stroller* (*Les Rêveries du promeneur solitaire*), composed between 1776 and 1778, published in 1782.

BIOGRAPHY AND CRITICISM. J. Morley, *Rousseau* (1873, revised 1886); F. Macdonald, *Rousseau* (1906); I. Babbitt, *Rousseau and Romanticism* (1919); M. B. Ellis, *Julie: A Synthesis of Rousseau's Thought* (1949); E. Cassirer, "Rousseau," in *Rousseau, Kant, Goethe* (1945); H. Höffding, *Rousseau and His Philosophy* (1930); Frances Winwar, *Jean-Jacques Rousseau: Conscience of a Era* (1961); and the best recent study, F. C. Green, *Jean-Jacques Rousseau: A Critical Study of His Life and Writings* (1955). Excellent also is the series of essays about the author in *Yale French Studies*, No. 28 (1962).

JOHANN WOLFGANG VON GOETHE

LIFE. Born on August 28, 1749, in Frankfurt-am-Main, Germany. From 1765 to 1768 Goethe attended Leipzig University, then the center of French culture in Germany. It was at the end of that time that he met Suzanna von Klettenberg, eminent Pietist and mystic, who interested him in the theosophy of the period. At the University of Strassburg, in 1770–1771, he made the acquaintance of Gottfried Herder, leader of the new German literary movement later called the "Storm and Stress" (*Sturm und Drang*) movement. Herder showed the young writer the importance of Shakespeare (as opposed to the French neoclassic authors) and interested him in folk songs and in the need for an indigenous German literature. On a series of trips to Switzerland he began his scientific and philosophical studies. In 1775 Goethe moved to Weimar, and there his long friendship with the reigning duke, Karl August, began. He also received the first of several government appointments which guaranteed him financial independence. From 1786 to 1788 he took his famous Italian trip. He met the author Schiller in 1794, and their fruitful relationship was terminated only by the latter's death in 1805. Goethe married Christiane Vulpius in 1806 and subsequently legitimitized the son they had had some twelve years earlier. In 1808 occurred his meeting with Napoleon, an encounter mutually impressive; and four years later he met Beethoven. From 1823 to 1832 he was in the daily company of Johann Peter Eckermann, who was thus able to record, in his *Conversations with Goethe* (*Gespräche mit Goethe*, 1836–1848), all the commentary and criticism that Goethe's long life had accumulated. Goethe's presence made Weimar a cultural mecca for twenty years, and during that period there was scarcely a prominent European intellectual who did not come there to pay his respects. He died on March 22, 1832.

CHIEF WRITINGS. Goethe's earliest verse is in the rococo tradition of French and German eighteenth-century poetry. It was not until he was influenced by Herder—and until his many love affairs took on a more serious cast—that he achieved writing of high stature. His first great play, *Götz von Berlichingen*,1773), was a product of his Shakespeare studies and his enthusiasm for the preromantic "Storm and Stress" movement. About the same time, he started the first of many sketches for *Faust*, Part I. *The Sorrows of Young Werther* (*Die Leiden des jungen Werthers*), the short novel that inflamed the youth of Europe as did no other book before or after, was published in 1774. Goethe's increasing interest in classical literature led to the creation of such plays as *Iphigenie* (*Iphigenie auf Tauris*, 1787), and *Torquato Tasso* (1790) and the epic-idyll *Hermann and Dorothea* (*Hermann und Dorothea*, 1798). His two largest novels were *Wilhelm Meister's Apprenticeship* (*Wilhelm Meisters Lehrjahre*, 1795–1796), and *Wilhelm Meister's Travels* (*Wilhelm Meisters Wanderjahre*, 1821). *Faust*, Part I, appeared in 1808; *Faust*, Part II, completed in 1831, was published in 1833. Goethe's fame as a lyric poet rests on the many volumes of verse he wrote, from his first *Poems* (*Gedichte*, 1771) through the *Roman Elegies* (*Römische Elegien*, 1795); *Ballads* (*Balladen*, 1798); the enigmatic *West-East Divan* (*Westöstlicher Diwan*, 1819); and the last great *Marienbad Elegies* (*Marienbad Elegien*, 1823). His scientific writings fill several volumes. Most of Goethe's critical commentary is found in the penetrating *Truth and Poetry* (*Dichtung und Wahrheit*, 1811–1833).

BIOGRAPHY AND CRITICISM. Biographies and general studies of Goethe include A. Bielschowsky, *Life of Goethe* (1905–1908); K. Viëtor, *Goethe the Poet*(1949); E. Ludwig, *Goethe*(1928); B. Fairley, *A Study of Goethe* (1948); T. Mann, *Essays of Three Decades* (1947), and introduction to *The Permanent Goethe* (1948); A. Schweitzer, *Goethe* (1949); E. M. Wilkinson and L. A. Willoughby, *Goethe, Poet and Thinker* (1962); H. Hatfield, *Goethe* (1963); B. Croce, *Goethe* (1923); W. H. Bruford, *Culture and Society in Classical Weimar* (1962). For *Faust*, consult D. J. Enright, *Commentary on Goethe's Faust* (1949); F. M. Stawell and G. L. Dickinson, *Goethe and Faust* (1928); E. M. Butler, *The Myth of the Magus* (1948) and *The Fortunes of Faust* (1952); S. Atkins, *Goethe's Faust: A Literary Analysis* (1958); P. M. Palmer and R. P. More, *Sources of the Faust Tradition* (1910); G. Santayana, "Goethe," in *Three Philosophical Poets* (1910); A. Gillies, *Goethe's Faust: An Interpretation* (1957); and R. Peacock, *Goethe's Major Plays* (1959).

GEORGE GORDON, LORD BYRON

LIFE. Born on January 22, 1788, to Captain "Mad Jack" and Catherine Gordon Byron. He succeeded his great-uncle to the title and estate (Newstead Abbey) in 1798. He was educated at Harrow from 1801 to 1805 and at Trinity College, Cambridge, from 1805 to 1808. In 1809–1811 he traveled in Portugal, Spain, Albania, and the Near East. His life was marked by a series of love affairs: with Mary Chaworth, in 1803; with Lady Caroline Lamb, in 1812–1813; allegedly with his half sister Augusta; and later with Teresa, Countess Guiccioli. He married Anne Isabelle Milbanke, and they separated after the birth of their child late in 1815. His daughter Allegra was born of a liaison with Claire Clairmont. Byron left England permanently in 1816 to live in Italy. In 1823 he went to Greece to aid the fight against the Turks; he died of a fever at Missolonghi on April 19, 1824.

CHIEF WRITINGS. His first poems appeared in 1807; *Childe Harold's Pilgrimage* (1812–1818), an autobiographical travel poem, won him fame, which was further guaranteed by a series of verse dramas appearing between 1813 and 1821: *The Giaour, The Corsair, Lara, Manfred, Cain, Sardanapalus. English Bards and Scotch Reviewers* (1809); *A Vision of Judgment* (1822); and *Don Juan* (1819–1824) are the satires for which he is best known today.

BIOGRAPHY AND CRITICISM. E. C. Mayne, *Byron* (1912, revised 1924); P. Quennell, *Byron* (1934); W. J. Calvert, *Byron, Romantic Paradox* (1935). For criticism see C. M. Fuess, *Lord Byron as a Satirist in Verse* (1912); T. S. Eliot, "Byron," in *From Anne to Victoria*, edited by B. Dobree (1937), and Matthew Arnold, "Byron," in *Essays in Criticism, Second Series* (1888). Helpful studies of *Don Juan* are P. G. Trueblood, *The Flowering of Byron's Genius* (1945); J. Austen, *The Story of Don Juan* (1939), and L. Kronenberger, introduction to the Modern Library edition of *Don Juan* (1951). More recent studies of Byron include W. H. Marshall, *The Structure of Byron's Major Poems* (1963); P. Thorslev, *The Byronic Hero* (1962); A. Rutherford, *Byron: A Critical Study* (1961); P. West, *Byron and the Spoiler's Art* (1960); L. Marchand, *Byron* (1957); D. L. Moore, *The Late Lord Byron* (1961), a study of his posthumous fame and notoriety; E. J. Lovell, Jr., *Byron: The Record of a Quest* (1950); G. M. Ridenour, *The Style of "Don Juan"*. A variorum edition of *Don Juan*, edited by T. G. Steffan and W. W. Pratt, appeared in four volumes in 1957.

WILLIAM WORDSWORTH

LIFE. Born on April 7, 1770, at Cockermouth, Cumberland. His father was an attorney. Wordsworth had three brothers and a sister, Dorothy; she later played a large part in his intellectual development. He attended St. John's College, Cambridge, from 1787 to 1791, and spent the following year in France. There he met Annette Vallon, by whom he had a daughter. Like Coleridge, whom he met in 1795, he soon lost sympathy with the cause of the French Revolution, and like Coleridge, he was strongly influenced by the philosophical and social theories of William Godwin. In 1797 Wordsworth and Dorothy moved to Alfoxeden, close to Nether Stowey, where Coleridge lived. There he and Coleridge conceived the idea for collaborating on the *Lyrical Ballads;* these important poems appeared anonymously in 1798, commissioned by the publisher Cottle. In 1799 Wordsworth and his sister settled in the Lake District of northwest England. In 1802 he inherited his father's estate, and in the same year married Mary Hutchinson, who eventually bore him five children. In 1813 he was appointed to the office of stamp distributor, a comfortable sinecure. As he grew older, his earliest radicalism—both political and aesthetic—grew dimmer; it is significant that he opposed the Catholic Emancipation Bill, the Reform Bill of 1832, and the successive extensions of the ballot. In 1843 he succeeded Southey as poet laureate. He died on April 23, 1850.

CHIEF WRITINGS. Wordsworth's early work (verse composed up to 1791) reflects the dominant poetic taste of the late eighteenth century: it consists largely of conventional sonnets, Spenserian stanzas, "Gothic" verse, and folksong imitations. His acquaintance with Godwin seemed to deepen Wordsworth's seriousness and sensibilities, and this was evident in his new humanitarianism, his attitude toward nature, and his interest in psychology. As with Coleridge, the years of Wordsworth's greatest and richest productivity were from 1797 to 1807, the period not only of the *Lyrical Ballads* but also of *The Prelude,* composed between 1798 and 1805, and the "Ode on Intimations of Immortality," composed between 1802 and 1806. Except for the famous Preface to the *Lyrical Ballads,* Wordsworth—unlike Coleridge—wrote little prose. Much of his later verse (from 1807 until 1850) is occasional poetry.

BIOGRAPHY AND CRITICISM. For the author's life, see G. M. Harper, *Wordsworth* (1916-1929); *Letters of William and Dorothy Wordsworth,* edited by E. de Selincourt (1941); and M. Elwin, *The First Romantics* (1948). The following general studies of Wordsworth as a poet are recommended: J. W. Beach, *The Concept of Nature in Nineteenth Century English Poetry* (1936); C. M. Bowra, "Wordsworth," in *The Romantic Imagination* (1949); G. W. Knight, *The Starlit Dome* (1941); *Wordsworth and Coleridge Studies,* edited by E. L. Griggs (1939); S. Banerjee, *Critical Theories and Poetic Practice in the Lyrical Ballads* (1931); N. P. Stallknecht, *Strange Seas of Thought* (1945); M. Bowra, "Wordsworth," in *The Romantic Imagination* (1949); R. D. Ha-

vens, *The Mind of a Poet* (1950); Helen Darbishire, *The Poet Wordsworth* (1950); *Centenary Studies,* edited by G. T. Dunklin, (1951); F. Danby, *The Simple Wordsworth* (1960); D. Ferry, *The Limits of Mortality: An Essay on Wordsworth's Major Poems* (1960); J. C. Smith, *A Study of Wordsworth* (1961); and C. Clarke, *Romantic Paradox* (1962).

SAMUEL TAYLOR COLERIDGE

LIFE. Born on October 21, 1772, at Ottery St. Mary. His father was a clergyman. Coleridge attended Jesus College, Cambridge, from 1791 to 1793. In 1795 he married Sara Fricker, who bore him three children. Like Wordsworth and Southey, he did not long retain his initial enthusiasm for the French Revolution, and he also soon abandoned his plans, made with Southey, for founding a perfect society, or "pantisocracy," on the banks of the Susquehanna River, in America. He met Wordsworth in 1795, and they developed their idea for poetic collaboration in the *Lyrical Ballads,* published in 1798. Difficulties with his wife led to eventual separation, in 1810, and Coleridge became increasingly addicted to opium. He spent his last twenty years in lecturing, writing, and brilliant talk. He died on July 25, 1834.

CHIEF WRITINGS. Almost all of Coleridge's poetry dates from the period between 1797 and 1807, when he worked with Wordsworth, and it is a curious coincidence that both poets felt a distinct loss in poetic power after the latter year. His early philosophical studies had been among the works of the British empiricists thinkers, but a trip to Germany introduced Coleridge to the writings of Kant, Schelling, and Fichte. His own prose—including the *Biographia Literaria* (1817) and the posthumous *Table Talk and Anima Poetae*—reflects the outlook of German Idealism. The depth of his critical insights and his awareness of Continental ideas make Coleridge the leading theoretician for English romanticism, despite the cloudiness of his thinking and the opacity of his literary style.

BIOGRAPHY AND CRITICISM. Good biographies are E. K. Chambers, *Samuel Taylor Coleridge* (1938) and H. I. 'A. Fausset, *Samuel Taylor Coleridge* (1926). General studies of the poet's thought are found in C. M. Bowra, "Coleridge," in *The Romantic Imagination* (1949), and B. Willey, *Nineteenth Century Studies* (1950); M. Schulz, *The Poetic Voices of Coleridge* (1963); J. H. Muirhead, *Coleridge as Philosopher* (1930); M. H. Abrams, *The Mirror and the Lamp* (1953); I. A. Richards, *Coleridge on Imagination* (1934); M. Suther, *The Dark Night of Samuel Taylor Coleridge* (1960). For special studies of *Kubla Khan*, see J. L. Lowes, *The Road to Xanadu* (1927); J. Charpentier, *Coleridge the Sublime Somnambulist* (1929); G. W. Knight, *The Starlit Dome* (1941); R. C. Bald, "Coleridge," in *Nineteenth Century Studies*, edited by H. Davis (1940); J. V. Baker, *The Sacred River* (1957); E. L. Griggs, "Coleridge and Opium," *Huntington Library Quarterly*, XVII (1954); Dorothy F. Mercer, "The Symbolism of *Kubla Khan*," *Journal of Aesthetics*, XII (1953); and Elizabeth Schneider, *Coleridge, Opium, and Kubla Khan* (1953).

PERCY BYSSHE SHELLEY

LIFE. Born on August 4. 1792, in Sussex, to Timothy and Elizabeth Shelley; his father was a country squire, and his grandfather was Sir Bysshe Shelley. He attended Eton from 1804 to 1810 and Oxford in 1810-1811, until he was sent down for writing *The Necessity of Atheism*. In 1811 he married Harriet Westbrook; they had two children. During these early years he was interested in Irish emancipation and land reclamation. He ran away with Mary Wollstonecraft Godwin in 1814. Shortly after Harriet's suicide they married and had several children. He met Byron in 1816; Keats, Hunt, and Hazlitt in 1817. In 1816 he visited Switzerland, and in 1818 left England for Italy, where he saw much of Byron. He was drowned on July 8, 1822, while sailing from Livorno to Lerici.

CHIEF WRITINGS. Shelley's poems, which range from short personal lyrics to long philosophical, allegorical works, include the utopian *Queen Mab* (1813); the portrait of the poet-youth in *Alastor* (1816); the satiric *Witch of Atlas* (1820); the visionary-philosophical *Prometheus Unbound* (1820); the defense of free love. *Epipsychidion* (1821); the elegy *Adonais* (1821), written in memory of Keats; and lyrics such as "Lines Written among the Euganean Hills" (1818); the "Ode to the West Wind" (1820); "The Cloud" (1820); "To a Skylark" (1820). He also wrote a verse play, *The Cenci* (1819) and the essay "A Defence of Poetry" (first published in 1840).

BIOGRAPHY AND CRITICISM. N. I. White, *Shelley* (1940); K. N. Cameron, *The Young Shelley* (1950); F. E. Lea, *Shelley and the Romantic Revolution* (1945); J. W. Beach, "Shelley," in *The Concept of Nature in Nineteenth Century English Poetry* (1936); J. Barrell, *Shelley and the Thought of His Time* (1947); T. S. Eliot, "Shelley and Keats," in *The Use of Poetry and the Use of Criticism* (1933); Carlos Baker, *Shelley's Major Poetry: The Fabric of a Vision* (1948); C. S. Lewis, *Rehabilitations* (1939); C. M. Bowra,

"Shelley," in *The Romantic Imagination* (1949); A. M. D. Hughes, *The Nascent Mind of Shelley* (1947); E. Blunden, *Shelley: A Life Story* (1946); R. Fogle, *The Imagery of Keats and Shelley* (1949); P. Butler, *Shelley's Idols of the Cave* (1954); H. Bloom, *Shelley's Mythmaking* (1959); E. Wasserman, *The Subtler Language* (1959); Sylvia Norman, *Flight of the Skylark: The Development of Shelley's Reputation* (1955); M. Wilson, *Shelley's Later Poetry* (1959); and D. G. King-Hele, *Shelley: His Thought and Work* (1960).

JOHN KEATS

LIFE. Born on October 31, 1795. His father, Thomas Keats, was an hostler at the Swan and Hoop Inn in London. He attended school at Enfield, where his friend Charles Cowden Clarke, the headmaster's son, encouraged his literary inclinations. He was apprenticed to a druggist and surgeon from 1811 to 1814, and was licensed as an apothecary in 1816. His friends Haydon and Severn encouraged Keats' interest in the fine arts. He joined Leigh Hunt's literary circle in 1816, and there came to know Shelley, Hazlitt, and Lamb. Study, writing, several walking tours, and a love affair with Fanny Brawne (to whom he was engaged in 1819) made up his brief life. In 1820 he went to Italy, hoping to cure his tuberculosis, but he died in Rome on February 23, 1821.

CHIEF WRITINGS. His *Poems* (1817) evoked favorable comment and enjoyed a small sale. The long mythological poem *Endymion* (1818) was attacked by Tory reviews (*Blackwood's and the Quarterly*) for its "uncouth language" typical of the "Cockney School," with which Keats was associated because of his friendship with the liberal Leigh Hunt and his circle. *Lamia, Isabella, The Eve of St. Agnes and Other Poems*, the volume which included the great odes, was published in 1820, and met with better success from the critics. The unfinished *Fall of Hyperion*, a Miltonic poem in blank verse, appeared posthumously, in 1856-1857.

BIOGRAPHY AND CRITICISM. S. Colvin, *John Keats: His Life and Poetry* (1917); Amy Lowell, *John Keats* (1925); D. Hewlett, *A Life of John Keats* (1938); *Letters of John Keats*, edited by M. B. Forman (1935); *The Keats Circle: Letters and Papers*, edited by H. E. Rollins (1948). M. R. Ridley, *Keats's Craftsmanship* (1934); C. M. Bowra, "Keats," in *The Romantic Imagination* (1949); T. S. Eliot, "Shelley and Keats," in *The Use of Poetry and the Use of Criticism* (1933); W. J. Bate, *The Stylistic Development of Keats* (1945); G. W. Knight, *The Starlit Dome* (1941); B. I. Evans, *Keats* (1934); C. D. Thorpe, *The Mind of*

Keats (1926); R. H. Fogle, *The Imagery of Keats and Shelley* (1949); E. Wasserman, *The Finer Tone* (1953); Aileen Ward, *John Keats: The Making of a Poet* (1963); H. T. Lyon, *Keats's Well-Read Urn* (1958), a collection of comments about the "Ode on a Grecian Urn"; R. Gittings, *The Mask of Keats* (1956); E. C. Pettet, *On the Poetry of Keats* (1957); W. G. Bate, *John Keats* (1963); and B. Blackstone, *The Consecrated Urn* (1959).

ALFRED, LORD TENNYSON

LIFE. Born on August 6, 1809, in Somersby, into the family of an Anglican clergyman. An unhappy four years at school were succeeded by tutoring at home and finally by Trinity College, Cambridge, at nineteen. There he founded a literary society, The Apostles, with his friend Arthur Hallam, who died at sea in 1833. The poet became engaged to Emily Sellwood in 1836, but did not marry her till 1850. A pension, granted in 1845 and his appointment as poet laureate, in 1850 eased his financial difficulties. After 1850 he lived quietly at Twickenham (where Pope had once made his home), on the Isle of Wight, and at Aldworth. In 1884 Gladstone created him the first Baron Tennyson. He died on October 6, 1892.

CHIEF WRITINGS. In 1827, with his brother Charles, Tennyson published *Poems by Two Brothers*. The savage critical attack made on *Poems, Chiefly Lyrical* (1830) and *Poems* (1832) led to a nine-year silence. Hallam's death, the eventual subject of *In Memoriam* (1849), was also a great blow. The 1842 collection of *Poems* met with success, and from that date Tennyson became increasingly the poetic spokesman for Victorian England. *The Princess* (1847, revised 1855), *Maud* (1855), and *The Idylls of the King* (first published 1859, final version 1885) were among his most popular works.

BIOGRAPHY AND CRITICISM. The interesting biographies by Hallam Tennyson (1898) and Charles Tennyson (1949) reflect the point of view of the son and grandson respectively. Other biographical works are H. G. Nicholson, *Tennyson* (1923, 1925); and T. R. Lounsbury, *Life and Times of Tennyson* (1915). A standard critical study is W. J. Rolfe, *Poetic and Dramatic Works of Tennyson* (1898). Other commentary is available in F. L. Lucas, *Ten Victorian Poets* (1940); W. H. Auden, *Introduction to Selected Poems* (1944); P. Baum, *Tennyson Sixty Years After* (1948); and T. S. Eliot, "Tennyson," in *Essays Ancient and Modern* (1936). There is also J. Buckley, *Tennyson: The Growth of a Poet* (1961); *Critical Essays on the Poetry of Tennyson*, edited

by J. Kilham (1960); Valerie Pitt, *Tennyson Laureate* (1962); and Joanna Richardson, *The Pre-Eminent Victorian* (1962).

ROBERT BROWNING

LIFE. Born on May 7, 1812, in Camberwell, son of a clerk in the Bank of England who later became an affluent banker. He attended the University of London and traveled extensively on the Continent, visiting Italy for the first time in 1834. During the thirties and forties Browning moved in the literary circles of Wordsworth, Dickens, Carlyle, and Leigh Hunt. His marriage to Elizabeth Barrett in 1846 was one of the great "romantic" alliances of the century. For fifteen years they lived chiefly in Italy. After her death in 1861 Browning returned to London. He went back to the Continent frequently and died at his son's home in Venice on December 12, 1889.

CHIEF WRITINGS. Browning's early poems *Pauline* (1833), *Paracelsus*, (1835), and *Sordello* (1840), reflect a strong Shelleyan influence. Between 1841 and 1846 appeared a series of lyrics, dramatic monologues (the genre he made famous), and closet dramas which won him literary and popular acclaim. The poems in *Bells and Pomegranates* (1841-1846), *Men and Women* (1855), and *Dramatis Personae* (1864) all exemplify the dramatic cast he gave to lyric verse. Browning's largest, perhaps greatest work is *The Ring and the Book* (1868-1869), a series of monologues in blank verse based on a Renaissance murder trial.

BIOGRAPHY AND CRITICISM. There are biographies of value by A. Symons (1886, revised 1906); E. Dowden (1904); W. H. Griffin and H. C. Minchin (1910); F. M. Sim (1923), and O. Burdett (1933). F. Winwar, *The Immortal Lovers* (1950), is a fictionalized account of Browning's life with his poetess-wife. W. C. De Vane, *A Browning Handbook* (1935), is the single most important work for the student. A. A. Brockington, *Browning and the Twentieth Century* (1932); C. N. Wenger, *The Aesthetics of Browning* (1924); and F. L. Lucas, *Ten Victorian Poets* (1940), are provocative. To these might be added P. Honon, *Browning's Characters* (1962); R. A. King, Jr., *The Bow and the Lyre: The Art of Robert Browning* (1957); Betty Miller, *Robert Browning: A Portrait* (1952); and W. O. Raymond, *The Infinite Moment* (1950).

EDGAR ALLAN POE

LIFE. Born in Boston on January 19, 1809, to parents who were itinerant actors. He was later raised by the Allan family, whose name he adopted, in Richmond, Virginia, and attended schools in

Richmond and England. A nine-month stay at the University of Virginia was terminated in 1826 by excessive drinking and gambling debts. Poe subsequently served in the Coast Guard and spent a brief term at West Point. His dismissal from the Military Academy led his foster father to disown him. In 1836, he married his thirteen-year-old cousin Virginia Clemm. This invalid wife and his own alcoholism necessitated a peripatetic existence, with continual quests for jobs in Richmond, New York, and Philadelphia. Mrs. Poe died in 1847, and the poet fell into deeper poverty and dissipation. He died in Baltimore on October 7, 1849.

CHIEF WRITINGS. Poe's first poems were published in Boston in 1827, while he was in the Coast Guard. Another volume appeared in 1831, but not until the publication of "The Raven" (1844) did he gain fame. For short periods he was editor of the *Southern Literary Messenger, Graham's Magazine*, and the *Broadway Journal*, and he contributed the "Literati" sections to *Godey's Lady's Book* during 1846. *Tales of the Grotesque and Arabesque* was published in 1840, and the well-known "Gold Bug" in 1843.

BIOGRAPHY AND CRITICISM. Poe's letters were presented in an authoritative edition by J. W. Ostrom in 1948. There are good biographies by G. E. Woodberry (revised 1909); J. W. Krutch (1926); A. H. Quinn (1941); and N. B. Fagin (1949). Interested readers should also consult *The Centenary Poe*, edited by M. S. Slater (1949); K. Campbell, *The Mind of Poe* (1933); H. Allen, *Israfel* (1926); and Baudelaire's miscellaneous commentaries and translations of Poe into French. Provocative shorter pieces include P. V. D. Stern, "The Strange Death of Edgar Allan Poe," *Saturday Review*, October 15, 1949; W. Sansom, "Poe," in *Penguin New Writing*, No. 33 (1948); and D. H. Lawrence, "Poe," in *Studies in Classic American Literature* (1923). More recent larger studies include P. F. Quinn, *The French Face of Edgar Poe* (1957); H. Levin, *The Power of Blackness* (1958); E. Davidson, *Poe: A Critical Study* (1957); N. B. Fagin, *The Histrionic Mr. Poe* (1949); E. Wagenknecht, *Edgar Allan Poe: The Man Behind the Legend* (1963); W. Bittner, *Poe: A Biography* (1962); and P. Lindsay, *The Haunted Man* (1954).

WALT WHITMAN

LIFE. Born Walter Whitman (he shortened his name to distinguish it from his father's) on May 31, 1819, in Long Island. While he was still a child, his family moved to Brooklyn, New York. As a young man, Whitman was a schoolteacher and occasional author. In 1841 he became a journalist in New York City. After a varied life as a builder, bookstore proprietor, journalist, and poet, he went to Washington to work as a government clerk. There, as a volunteer nurse, he had firsthand experience with the Civil War wounded. Whitman settled in Camden, New Jersey, in 1873 —the year he suffered his inital attack of paralysis—and died there on March 26, 1892.

CHIEF WRITINGS. Whitman's earliest writings include much bad verse and one novel, a temperance tract. His journalistic efforts led to extensive reading, and by the 1840's he was an ardent admirer of Emerson and the New England Transcendentalist school, and a Jeffersonian Democrat. *Leaves of Grass* was first published in 1855, and Whitman continued to supplement and revise this important book of verse throughout his lifetime. *Drum Taps*—the result of his observations during the Civil War—appeared in 1865. *Democratic Vistas* (1871), a volume of essays, embodied his political and philosophical ideas about the future of America.

BIOGRAPHY AND CRITICISM. Whitman's *Complete Writings* were issued in 1902. Biographies include those by Whitman's friend John Burroughs, (1895); B. Perry (1906); J. Bailey (1926); and E. Holloway (1926). For critical interpretations see G. Santayana, "The Poetry of Barbarism," in *Interpretations of Poetry and Religion* (1900); N. Foerster, *American Criticism* (1928); V. L. Parrington, "The Culture of the Seventies," in *Main Currents of American Thought* (1927-1930); and F. O. Matthiessen, *American Renaissance* (1941). L. Untermeyer, *Poetry and Prose of Walt Whitman* (1948), contains a critical essay and bibliography. Other studies include R. Asselineau, *The Evolution of Walt Whitman* (1960); R. Chase, *Walt Whitman Reconsidered* (1955); R. H. Pearce, *The Continuity of American Poetry* (1961); J. E. Miller, Jr., *A Critical Guide to Leaves of Grass* (1957); and G. W. Allen, *The Solitary Singer: A Critical Biography of Walt Whitman* (1959) and *Walt Whitman as Man, Poet, and Legend* (1962), a collection of essays.

NATHANIEL HAWTHORNE

LIFE. Born in Salem, Massachusetts, on July 4, 1804. His sea-captain father died when Hawthorne was four. He graduated from Bowdoin College (Longfellow and Franklin Pierce were fellow students) in 1825, and for twelve years lived in Salem, writing stories. For a short time he was employed at the Boston Custom House, and later he joined the experimental community at Brook Farm. He married Sophia Peabody in 1842, moved to the Old Manse at Concord, and became acquainted with Emerson and Thoreau. From 1846 to 1849 Hawthorne was surveyor in the Salem Custom House, but he lost the position for political reasons. His friendship with Melville began in 1850 when they became neighbors in the Berkshires in western Massachusetts. From 1853 to 1857 he was consul at Liverpool, and from 1857 to 1860 he traveled in England and Italy. He returned to Concord in 1860, and died at Plymouth, New Hampshire, on May 10, 1864.

CHIEF WRITINGS. His stories were published anonymously until 1836. *Twice-Told Tales* appeared in 1837 and was followed by a second series in 1842. His first great book, *The Scarlet Letter*, was published in 1850, and his fame was secure when *The House of Seven Gables* followed in 1851. *The Blithedale Romance* was published in 1852. Other short stories are found in *Mosses from an Old Manse* (1846). Of interest are his *American Notebooks* (published posthumously in 1868, reedited in 1932), which cover the years 1835-1853, his most productive period; and *The Heart of Hawthorne's Journals*, edited by Newton Arvin (1929).

BIOGRAPHY AND CRITICISM. Biographies include those by R. Stewart (1948); R. Cantwell (1948); and M. Van Doren (1949). For critical interpretations, see H. James, *Hawthorne* (1880); F. O. Matthiessen, *American Renaissance* (1941); R. H. Fogle, *Hawthorne's Fiction* (1952); E. H. Davidson, *Hawthorne's Last Phase* (1949); W. B. Stein, *Hawthorne's Faust* (1953); and R. H. Fogle, "The Problem of Allegory in Hawthorne's 'Ethan Brand,'" *University of Toronto Quarterly*, January, 1948. To these may be added more recent studies: H. H. Waggoner, *Hawthorne: A Critical Study* (1955); A. Turner, *Nathaniel Hawthorne* (1962); H. H. Hoeltje, *Inward Sky: The Mind and Heart of Nathaniel Hawthorne* (1962); E. Wagenknecht, *Nathaniel Hawthorne: Man and Writer* (1961); R. R. Male, *Hawthorne's Tragic Vision* (1957); and the section about the writer in D. G. Hoffman, *Form and Fable in American Fiction* (1961).

HERMAN MELVILLE

LIFE. Born on August 1, 1819, in New York City, of New England and Hudson River Dutch stock. His father's death in 1832 left the family in reduced financial condition (a state from which Melville never escaped until his wife received an inheritance in 1878); and after teaching school, storekeeping, and clerking in a bank, he shipped aboard the Liverpool packet *St. Lawrence* in 1839-1840. He again taught school briefly upon his return, made a trip to the Midwest in 1840, and in January, 1841, sailed aboard the whaler *Acushnet* from New Bedford, bound for the South Seas. He jumped ship in the Marquesas in 1842, lived for a month among the Taipis (Typees), joined the Australian whaler *Lucy Ann*, where he participated in a mutiny, became a harpooner aboard the Nantucket whaler *Charles & Henry*, and after fourteen week in Hawaii enlisted as an ordinary seaman aboard the frigate *United States*, where he served from August, 1843, to October, 1844. Melville married Elizabeth Shaw, daughter of the Massachusetts chief justice, in 1847. By 1850 they had settled in Pittsfield, Massachusetts, where Melville concentrated on a career in letters. He made a brief trip to England in 1849. His attempts to obtain a foreign consulate failed, and his lecture tours were equally unsuccessful. He visited Hawthorne in England in 1856; toured Italy, Greece, the Near East, and the Holy Land in 1857; and in 1860 sailed for San Francisco aboard a clipper commanded by his brother Thomas. The Melville family, which included four children, moved to New York City in 1864, and in 1867 he took a position at the Custom House, which he held until 1885. Melville's last years were passed in relative obscurity. He died on September 28, 1891.

CHIEF WRITINGS. Melville's early novels, based on his seafaring experiences, achieved popularity; these are *Typee* (1846), *Omoo* (1847), *Redburn* (1849), and *White-Jacket* (1850). He moved toward allegory with *Mardi* (1849); and the mild reception the public gave *Moby Dick* (1851) indicated increasing puzzlement at his writing. In his remaining forty years he wrote novels, short stories, and poetry which met with small favor. The prose includes *Pierre* (1852); *Israel Potter* (1855); *The Piazza Tales* (1856), containing "Bartleby the Scrivener," "Benito Cereno," and other stories; *The Confidence Man* (1857); and *Billy Budd* (written 1888-1891, first published in 1924). *Battle-Pieces* (1866) is a volume of poems about the Civil War. The rest of Melville's verse consists of *Clarel*, (1876), a long narrative poem; *John Marr and Other Sailors* (1888); and *Timoleon* (1891). The last two were privately printed in editions of twenty-five copies.

BIOGRAPHY AND CRITICISM. Full-length studies of Melville begin with R. Weaver (1921); followed by J. Freeman (1926); L. Mumford (1929); W. E. Sedgwick (1944); C. Olson, *Call Me Ishmael* (1947); R. Chase (1949); G. Stone (1949); N. Arvin (1950); and L. Howard (1951). The interested reader should also consult F. O. Matthiessen, *American Renaissance* (1941); J. Leyda, *The Melville Log* (1951); L. Thompson, *Melville's Quarrel with God*

(1952); D. H. Lawrence, *Studies in Classic American Literature* (1923); C. Feidelson, *Symbolism and American Literature* (1953); R. W. B. Lewis, *The American Adam* (1955); E. Rosenberry, *Melville and the Comic Spirit* (1955); P. Miller, *The Raven and the Whale* (1956); and W. Berthoff, *The Example of Melville* (1962).

ALEXANDER PUSHKIN

LIFE. Born at Moscow, June 6, 1799 (May 26, Old Style). Pushkin was a member of an old boyar family; his maternal great-grandfather was an Abyssinian general ennobled by Peter the Great. He entered the Lyceum (at Tsarkoe Selo, near St. Petersburg) in 1811. Upon finishing his schooling (in 1817)he was attached to the Ministry of Foreign Affairs, in a nominal position enabling him to lead the life of a dandy and man of fashion. Suspected of political liberalism, he was exiled (in 1820) to southern Russia to aid in the administration of newly founded colonies. He made his first trip to the Caucasus; in 1823 he was transferred to Odessa. Suspected of atheistic tendencies and dismissed from the service (1824), Pushkin was ordered to stay on the family estate at Mikhailovskoye, near Pskov—an exile which unfortunately saved him from a more active involvement in the ill-fated Decembrist Revolution (1825). Pardoned by the new tsar, Nicholas I, he was allowed to return to Moscow. He married Natalie Goncharow (1831) and was reappointed to the Foreign Service in 1832. Pushkin was fatally wounded in a duel with Baron George Heckeren d'Anthes. He died February 10, 1837 (January 29, Old Style).

CHIEF WRITINGS. Pushkin was an avid reader of Byron, whose work many of his pieces resemble. Early works include the tales *The Captive of the Caucasus* and *The Fountain of Bakhchisarai* (1822) and a long poem, *The Gypsies* (1824). He wrote a Shakespearean drama, *Boris Godunov* (1825, published 1831), and the narrative poem *Poltava* (1829); he began his *History of Pugachev's Revolt in 1773* in 1834; he completed his one long novel, *The Captain's Daughter*, in 1836. His most famous short story is *The Queen of Spades* (1833). Pushkin completed *Eugene Onegin* in 1830 (it was published in 1833). This and *The Queen of Spades* were made into operas by Tchaikovsky, *Boris Godunov* by Moussorgsky, *Ruslan and Ludmilla* by Glinka, *The Golden Cockerel* by Rimsky-Korsakov.

BIOGRAPHY AND CRITICISM. B. L. Brasol, *The Mighty Three* (1934); D. S. Mirsky, *Pushkin* (1926); J. Lavrin. *Pushkin and Russian Literature* (1947); H. Troyat, *Pushkin* (1950); S. H. Cross and E. J. Simmons, *Pushkin* (1937).

JEAN-JACQUES ROUSSEAU
(1712–1778)
Confessions*

Part I

BOOK I

[The Years 1712–1719.] I am commencing an undertaking, hitherto without precedent, and which will never find an imitator. I desire to set before my fellows the likeness of a man in all the truth of nature, and that man myself.

Myself alone! I know the feelings of my heart, and I know men. I am not made like any of those I have seen; I venture to believe that I am not made like any of those who are in existence. If I am not better, at least I am different. Whether Nature has acted rightly or wrongly in destroying the mould in which she cast me, can only be decided after I have been read.

Let the trumpet of the Day of Judgment sound when it will, I will present myself before the Sovereign Judge with this book in my hand. I will say boldly: "This is what I have done, what I have thought, what I was. I have told the good and the bad with equal frankness. I have neither omitted anything bad, nor interpolated anything good. If I have occasionally made use of some immaterial embellishments, this has only been in order to fill a gap caused by lack of memory. I may have assumed the truth of that which I knew might have been true, never of that which I knew to be false. I have shown myself as I was: mean and contemptible, good, high-minded and sublime, according as I was one or the other. I have unveiled my inmost self even as Thou hast seen it, O Eternal Being. Gather round me the countless host of my fellow-men; let them hear my confessions, lament for my unworthiness, and blush for my imperfections. Then let each of them in turn reveal, with the same frankness, the secrets of his heart at the foot of the Throne, and say, if he dare, '*I was better than that man!*' " . . . .

I felt before I thought: this is the common lot of humanity. I experienced it more than others. I do not know what I did until I was five or six years old. I do not know how I learned to read; I only remember my earliest reading, and the effect it had upon me; from that time I date my uninterrupted self-consciousness. My mother had left some romances behind her, which my father and I began to read after supper. At first it was only a question of practising me

* Completed in 1770; published in 1781–1788. The selections reprinted here are from *The Confessions of Jean-Jacques Rousseau,* Everyman's Library, E. P. Dutton and Co., Inc., New York.

in reading by the aid of amusing books; but soon the interest became so lively, that we used to read in turns without stopping, and spent whole nights in this occupation. We were unable to leave off until the volume was finished. Sometimes, my father, hearing the swallows begin to twitter in the early morning, would say, quite ashamed, "Let us go to bed; I am more of a child than yourself."

In a short time I acquired, by this dangerous method, not only extreme facility in reading and understanding what I read, but a knowledge of the passions that was unique in a child of my age. I had no idea of things in themselves, although all the feelings of actual life were already known to me. I had conceived nothing, but felt everything. These confused emotions which I felt one after the other, certainly did not warp the reasoning powers which I did not as yet possess; but they shaped them in me of a peculiar stamp, and gave me odd and romantic notions of human life, of which experience and reflection have never been able wholly to cure me. . . .

How could I become wicked, when I had nothing but examples of gentleness before my eyes, and none around me but the best people in the world? My father, my aunt, my nurse, my relations, our friends, our neighbours, all who surrounded me, did not, it is true, obey me, but they loved me; and I loved them in return. My wishes were so little excited and so little opposed, that it did not occur to me to have any. I can swear that, until I served under a master, I never knew what a fancy was. Except during the time I spent in reading or writing in my father's company, or when my nurse took me for a walk, I was always with my aunt, sitting or standing by her side, watching her at her embroidery or listening to her singing; and I was content. Her cheerfulness, her gentleness and her pleasant face have stamped so deep and lively an impression on my mind that I can still see her manner, look, and attitude; I remember her affectionate language: I could describe what clothes she wore and how her head was dressed, not forgetting the two little curls of black hair on her temples, which she wore in accordance with the fashion of the time.

I am convinced that it is to her I owe the taste, or rather passion, for music, which only became fully developed in me a long time afterwards. She knew a prodigious number of tunes and songs which she used to sing in a very thin, gentle voice. This excellent woman's cheerfulness of soul banished dreaminess and melancholy from herself and all around her. The attraction which her singing possessed for me was so great, that not only have several of her songs always remained in my memory, but even now, when I have lost her, and as I grew older, many of them, totally forgotten since the days of my childhood, return to my mind with inexpressible charm. Would anyone believe that I, an old dotard, eaten up by cares and troubles, sometime find myself weeping like a child, when I mumble one of those little airs in a voice already broken and trembling?

. . . I have spent my life in idle longing, without saying a word, in the presence of those whom I loved most. Too bashful to declare my taste, I at least satisfied it in situations which had reference to it and kept up the idea of it. To lie at the feet of an imperious mistress, to obey her commands, to ask her forgiveness—this was for me a sweet enjoyment; and, the more my lively imagination heated my blood, the more I presented the appearance of a bashful lover. It may be easily imagined that this manner of making love does not lead to very speedy results, and is not very dangerous to the virtue of those who are its object. For this reason I have rarely possessed, but have none the less enjoyed myself in my own way —that is to say, in imagination. Thus it has happened that my senses, in harmony with my timid disposition and my romantic spirit, have kept my sentiments pure and my morals blameless, owing to the very tastes which, combined with a little more impudence, might have plunged me into the most brutal sensuality. . . .

I am a man of very strong passions, and, while I am stirred by them, nothing can equal my impetuosity; I forget all discretion, all feelings of respect, fear and decency; I am cynical, impudent, violent and fearless; no feeling of shame keeps me back, no danger frightens me; with the exception of the single object which occupies my thoughts, the universe is nothing to me. But all this lasts only for a moment, and the following moment plunges me into complete annihilation. In my calmer moments I am indolence and timidity itself; everything frightens and discourages me; a fly, buzzing past, alarms me; a word which I have to say, a gesture which I have to make, terrifies my idleness; fear and shame overpower me to such an extent that I would gladly hide myself from the sight of my fellow-creatures. If I have to act, I do not know what to do; if I have to speak, I do not know what to say; if anyone looks at me, I am put out of countenance. When I am strongly moved I sometimes know how to find the right words, but in ordinary conversation I can find absolutely nothing, and my condition is unbearable for the simple reason that I am obliged to speak.

Add to this, that none of my prevailing tastes centre in things that can be bought. I want nothing but unadulterated pleasures, and money poisons all. For instance, I am fond of the pleasures of the table; but, as I cannot endure either the constraint of good society or the drunkenness of the tavern, I can only enjoy them with a friend; alone, I cannot do so, for my imagination then occupies itself with other things, and eating affords me no pleasure. If my heated blood longs for women, my excited heart longs still more for affection. Women who could be bought for money would lose for me all their charms; I even doubt whether it would be in me to make use of them. I find it the same with all pleasures within my reach; unless they cost me nothing, I find them insipid. I only love those enjoyments which belong to no one but the first man who knows how to enjoy them.

. . . I worship freedom; I abhor restraint, trouble, dependence. As long as the money in my purse lasts, it assures my independence; it relieves me of the trouble of finding expedients to replenish it, a necessity which always inspired me with dread; but the fear of seeing it exhausted makes me hoard it carefully. The money which a man possesses is the instrument of freedom; that which we eagerly pursue is the instrument of slavery. Therefore I hold fast to that which I have, and desire nothing.

My disinterestedness is, therefore, nothing but idleness; the pleasure of possession is not worth the trouble of acquisition. In like manner, my extravagance is nothing but idleness; when the opportunity of spending agreeably presents itself, it cannot be too profitably employed. Money tempts me less than things, because between money and the possession of the desired object there is always an intermediary, whereas between the thing itself and the enjoyment of it there is none. If I see the thing, it tempts me; if I only see the means of gaining possession of it, it does not. For this reason I have committed thefts, and even now I sometimes pilfer trifles which tempt me, and which I prefer to take rather than to ask for; but neither when a child nor a grown-up man do I ever remember to have robbed anyone of a farthing, except on one occasion, fifteen years ago, when I stole seven *livres* ten *sous*. . . .

BOOK II

[The Years 1728–1731.] . . . I have drawn the great moral lesson, perhaps the only one of any practical value, to avoid those situations of life which bring our duties into conflict with our interests, and which show us our own advantage in the misfortunes of others; for it is certain that, in such situations, however sincere our love of virtue, we must, sooner or later, inevitably grow weak without perceiving it, and become unjust and wicked in act, without having ceased to be just and good in our hearts.

This principle, deeply imprinted on the bottom of my heart, which, although somewhat late, in practice guided my whole conduct, is one of those which have caused me to appear a very strange and foolish creature in the eyes of the world, and, above all, amongst my acquaintances. I have been reproached with wanting to pose as an original, and different from others. In reality, I have never troubled about acting like other people or differently from them. I sincerely desired to do what was right. I withdrew, as far as it lay in my power, from situations which opposed my interests to those of others, and might, consequently, inspire me with a secret, though involuntary, desire of injuring them.

. . . I loved too sincerely, too completely, I venture to say, to be able to be happy easily. Never have passions been at once more lively and purer than mine; never has love been tenderer, truer, more disinterested. I would have sacrificed my happiness a thousand times for that of the person whom I loved; her reputation was dearer to me than my life, and I would never have wished to endanger her repose for a single moment for all the pleasures of enjoyment. This feeling has made me employ such carefulness, such secrecy, and such precaution in my undertakings, that none of them have ever been successful. My want of success with women has always been caused by my excessive love for them. . . .

BOOK III

[The Years 1731–1732.] . . . I only felt the full strength of my attachment when I no longer saw her.[1] When I saw her, I was only content; but, during her absence, my restlessness became painful. The need of living with her caused me outbreaks of tenderness which often ended in tears. I shall never forget how, on the day of a great festival, while she was at vespers, I went for a walk outside the town, my heart full of her image and a burning desire to spend my life with her. I had sense enough to see that at present this was impossible, and that the happiness which I enjoyed so deeply could only be short. This gave to my reflections a tinge of melancholy, about which, however, there was nothing gloomy, and which was tempered by flattering hopes. The sound of the bells, which always singularly affects me, the song of the birds, the beauty of the daylight, the enchanting landscape, the scattered country dwellings in which my fancy placed our common home—all these produced upon me an impression so vivid, tender, melancholy and touching, that I saw myself transported, as it were, in ecstasy, into that happy time and place, wherein my heart, possessing all the happiness it could desire, tasted it with inexpressible rapture, without even a thought of sensual pleasure. I never remember to have plunged into the future with greater force and illusion than on that occasion; and what has struck me most in the recollection of this dream after it had been realised, is that I have found things again exactly as I had imagined them. If ever the dream of a man awake resembled a prophetic vision, it was assuredly that dream of mine. I was only deceived in the imaginary duration; for the days, the years, and our whole life were spent in serene and undisturbed tranquillity, whereas in reality it lasted only for a moment. Alas! my most lasting happiness belongs

1. Rousseau refers here to Mme. de Warens, whom he also calls "mamma."

to a dream, the fulfilment of which was almost immediately followed by the awakening. . . .

Two things, almost incompatible, are united in me in a manner which I am unable to understand: a very ardent temperament, lively and tumultuous passions, and, at the same time, slowly developed and confused ideas, which never present themselves until it is too late. One might say that my heart and my mind do not belong to the same person. Feeling takes possession of my soul more rapidly than a flash of lightning; but, instead of illuminating, inflames and dazzles me. I feel everything and see nothing. I am carried away by my passions, but stupid; in order to think, I must be cool. The astonishing thing is that, notwithstanding, I exhibit tolerably sound judgment, penetration, even finesse, if I am not hurried; with sufficient leisure I can compose excellent impromptus; but I have never said or done anything worthy of notice on the spur of the moment. I could carry on a very clever conversation through the post, as the Spaniards are said to carry on a game of chess. When I read of that Duke of Savoy, who turned round on his journey, in order to cry, "At your throat, Parisian huckster," I said, "There you have myself!"

This sluggishness of thought, combined with such liveliness of feeling, not only enters into my conversation, but I feel it even when alone and at work. My ideas arrange themselves in my head with almost incredible difficulty; they circulate in it with uncertain sound, and ferment till they excite and heat me, and make my heart beat fast; and, in the midst of this excitement, I see nothing clearly and am unable to write a single word—I am obliged to wait. Imperceptibly this great agitation subsides, the confusion clears up, everything takes its proper place, but slowly, and only after a period of long and confused agitation. . . .

BOOK IV

[The Years 1731–1732.] . . . I returned, not to Nyon, but to Lausanne. I wanted to sate myself with the sight of this beautiful lake, which is there seen in its greatest extent. Few of the secret motives which have determined me to act have been more rational. Things seen at a distance are rarely powerful enough to make me act. The uncertainty of the future has always made me look upon plans, which need considerable time to carry them out, as decoys for fools. I indulge in hopes like others, provided it costs me nothing to support them; but if they require continued attention, I have done with it. The least trifling pleasure which is within my reach tempts me more than the joys of Paradise. However, I make an exception of the pleasure which is followed by pain; this has no temptation for me, because I love only pure enjoyments, and these a man never has when he knows that he is preparing for himself repentance and regret. . . .

Why is it that, having found so many good people in my youth, I find so few in my later years? Is their race extinct? No; but the class in which I am obliged to look for them now, is no longer the same as that in which I found them. Among the people, where great passions only speak at intervals, the sentiments of nature make themselves more frequently heard; in the higher ranks they are absolutely stifled, and, under the mask of sentiment, it is only interest or vanity that speaks.

. . . Whenever I approach the Canton of Vaud, I am conscious of an impression in which the remembrance of Madame de Warens, who was born there, of my father who lived there, of Mademoiselle de Vulson who enjoyed the first fruits of my youthful love, of several pleasure trips which I made there when a child and, I believe, some other exciting cause, more mysterious and more powerful than all this, is combined. When the burning desire of this happy and peaceful life, which flees from me and for which I was born, inflames my imagination, it is always the Canton of Vaud, near the lake, in the midst of enchanting scenery, to which it draws me. I feel that I must have an orchard on the shore of this lake and no other, that I must have a loyal friend, a loving wife, a cow, and a little boat. I shall never enjoy perfect happiness on earth until I have all that. I laugh at the simplicity with which I have several times visited this country merely in search of this imaginary happiness. I was always surprised to find its inhabitants, especially the women, of quite a different character from that which I expected. How contradictory it appeared to me! The country and its inhabitants have never seemed to me made for each other.

During this journey to Vévay, walking along the beautiful shore, I abandoned myself to the sweetest melancholy. My heart eagerly flung itself into a thousand innocent raptures; I was filled with emotion, I sighed and wept like a child. How often have I stopped to weep to my heart's content, and, sitting on a large stone, amused myself with looking at my tears falling into the water! . . .

How greatly did the entrance into Paris belie the idea I had formed of it! The external decorations of Turin, the beauty of its streets, the symmetry and regularity of the houses, had made me look for something quite different in Paris. I had imagined to myself a city of most imposing aspect, as beautiful as it was large, where nothing was to be seen but splendid streets and palaces of gold and marble. Entering by the suburb of St. Marceau, I saw nothing but dirty and stinking little streets, ugly black houses, a general air of slovenliness and poverty, beggars, carters, menders of old clothes, criers of decoctions and old hats. All this, from the outset, struck me so forcibly, that all the real magnificence I have since seen in Paris has been unable to destroy this first impression, and I have always retained a secret dislike against residence in this capital. I may say that the whole time, during which I afterwards lived there, was employed solely in trying to find means to enable me to live away from it.

Such is the fruit of a too lively imagination, which exaggerates beyond human exaggeration, and is always ready to see more than it has been told to expect. I had heard Paris so much praised, that I had represented it to myself as the ancient Babylon, where, if I had ever visited it, I should, perhaps, have found as much to take off from the picture which I had drawn of it. The same thing happened to me at the Opera, whither I hastened to go the day after my arrival. The same thing happened to me later at Versailles; and again, when I saw the sea for the first time; and the same thing will always happen to me, when I see anything which has been too loudly announced; for it is impossible for men, and difficult for Nature herself, to surpass the exuberance of my imagination.

. . . The sight of the country, a succession of pleasant views, the open air, a good appetite, the sound health which walking gives me, the free life of the inns, the absence of all that makes me conscious of my dependent position, of all that reminds me of my condition— all this sets my soul free, gives me greater boldness of thought, throws me, so to speak, into the immensity of things, so that I can combine, select, and appropriate them at pleasure, without fear or restraint. I dispose of Nature in its entirety as its lord and master; my heart, roaming from object to object, mingles and identifies itself with those which soothe it, wraps itself up in charming fancies, and is intoxicated with delicious sensations. If, in order to render them permanent, I amuse myself by describing them by myself, what vigorous outlines, what fresh colouring, what power of expression I give them!

. . . At night I lay in the open air, and, stretched on the ground or on a bench, slept as calmly as upon a bed of roses. I remember, especially, that I spent a delightful night outside the city, on a road which ran by the side of the Rhône or Saône, I do not remember which. Raised gardens, with terraces, bordered the other side of the road. It had been very hot during the day; the evening was delightful; the dew moistened the parched grass; the night was calm, without a breath of wind; the air was fresh, without being cold; the sun, having gone down, had left in the sky red vapours, the reflection of which cast a rose-red tint upon the water; the trees on the terraces were full of nightingales answering one another. I walked on in a kind of ecstasy, abandoning my heart and senses to the enjoyment of all, only regretting, with a sigh, that I was obliged to enjoy it alone. Absorbed in my delightful reverie, I continued my walk late into the night, without noticing that I was tired. At last, I noticed it. I threw myself with a feeling of delight upon the shelf of a sort of niche or false door let into a terrace wall; the canopy of my bed was formed by the tops of trees; a nightingale was perched just over my head, and lulled me to sleep with his song; my slumbers were sweet, my awaking was still sweeter. . . .

In relating my journeys, as in making them, I do not know how to stop. My heart beat with joy when I drew near to my dear mamma, but I walked no faster. I like to walk at my ease, and to stop when I like. A wandering life is what I want. To walk through a beautiful country in fine weather, without being obliged to hurry, and with a pleasant prospect at the end, is of all kinds of life the one most suited to my taste. My idea of a beautiful country is already known. No flat country, however beautiful, has ever seemed so to my eyes. I must have mountain torrents, rocks, firs, dark forests, mountains, steep roads to climb or descend, precipices at my side to frighten me. . . .

BOOK V

[The Years 1732–1736.] . . . It is sometimes said that the sword wears out the scabbard. That is my history. My passions have made me live, and my passions have killed me. What passions? will be asked. Trifles, the most childish things in the world, which, however, excited me as much as if the possession of Helen or the throne of the universe had been at stake. In the first place—women. When I possessed one, my senses were calm; my heart, never. The needs of love devoured me in the midst of enjoyment; I had a tender mother, a dear friend; but I needed a mistress. I imagined one in her place; I represented her to myself in a thousand forms, in order to deceive myself. If I had thought that I held mamma in my arms when I embraced her, these embraces would have been no less lively, but all my desires would have been extinguished; I should have sobbed from affection, but I should never have felt any enjoyment. Enjoyment! Does this ever fall to the lot of man? If I had ever, a single time in my life, tasted all the delights of love in their fulness, I do not believe that my frail existence could have endured it; I should have died on the spot.

Thus I was burning with love, without an object; and it is this state, perhaps, that is most exhausting. I was restless, tormented by the hopeless condition of poor mamma's affairs, and her imprudent conduct, which were bound to ruin her completely at no distant date. My cruel imagination, which always anticipates misfortunes, exhibited this particular one to me continually, in all its extent and in all its results. I already saw myself compelled by want to separate from her to whom I had devoted my life, and without whom I could not enjoy it. Thus my soul was ever in a state of agitation; I was devoured alternately by desires and fears. . . .

BOOK VI

[The Year 1736.] . . . At this period commences the brief happiness of my life; here approach the peaceful, but rapid moments which have given me the right to say, *I have lived*. Precious and regretted moments! begin again for me your delightful course; and, if it be possible, pass more slowly in succession through my memory, than you did in your fugitive reality. What can I do, to prolong, as I should like, this touching and simple narrative, to repeat the same things over and over again, without wearying my readers by such repetition, any more than I was wearied of them myself, when I recommenced the life again and again? If all this consisted of facts, actions, and words, I could describe, and in a manner, give an idea of them; but how is it possible to describe what was neither said nor done, nor even thought, but enjoyed and felt, without being able to assign any other reason for my happiness than this simple feeling? I got up at sunrise, and was happy; I walked, and was happy; I saw mamma, and was happy; I left her, and was happy; I roamed the forests and hills, I wandered in the valleys, I read, I did nothing, I worked in the garden, I picked the fruit, I helped in the work of the house, and happiness followed me everywhere—happiness, which could not be referred to any definite object, but dwelt entirely within myself, and which never left me for a single instant. . . .

I should much like to know, whether the same childish ideas ever enter the hearts of other men as sometimes enter mine. In the midst of my studies, in the course of a life as blameless as a man could have led, the fear of hell still frequently troubled me. I asked myself: "In what state am I? If I were to die this moment, should I be damned?" According to my Jansenists, there was no doubt about the matter; but, according to my conscience, I thought differently. Always fearful, and a prey to cruel uncertainty, I had recourse to the most laughable expedients to escape from it, for which I would unhesitatingly have anyone locked up as a madman if I saw him doing as I did. One day, while musing upon this melancholy subject, I mechanically amused myself by throwing stones against the trunks of trees with my usual good aim, that is to say, without hardly hitting one. While engaged in this useful exercise, it occurred to me to draw a prognostic from it to calm my anxiety. I said to myself: "I will throw this stone at the tree opposite; if I hit it, I am saved; if I miss it, I am damned." While speaking, I threw my stone with a trembling hand and a terrible palpitation of the heart, but with so successful an aim that it hit the tree right in the middle, which, to tell the truth, was no very difficult feat, for I had been careful to choose a tree with a thick trunk close at hand. From that time I have never had any doubt about my salvation! When I recall this characteristic incident, I do not know whether to laugh or cry at myself. You great men, who are most certainly laughing, may congratulate yourselves; but do not mock my wretchedness, for I swear to you that I feel it deeply. . . .

Musings of a Solitary Stroller (Les Rêveries du promeneur solitaire)*

Fifth Promenade

. . . I found my existence so charming, and led a life so agreeable to my humor, that I resolved here to end my days. My only source of disquiet was whether I should be allowed to carry my project out. . . . In the midst of the presentiments that disturbed me, I would fain have had people make a perpetual prison of my refuge, to confine me in it for all the rest of my life. I longed for them to cut off all chance and all hope of leaving it; to forbid my holding any communication with the mainland, so that knowing nothing of what was going on in the world, I might have forgotten the world's existence, and people might have forgotten mine too.

They suffered me to pass only two months in the island,[1] but I could have passed two years, two centuries, and all eternity, without a moment's weariness; though I had not, with my companion,[2] any other society than that of the steward, his wife, and their servants. They were in truth honest souls and nothing more, but that was just what I wanted. . . .

Carried thither in a violent hurry, alone and without a thing, I afterwards sent for my housekeeper, my books, and my scanty possessions,—of which I had the delight of unpacking nothing,—leaving my boxes and chests just as they had come, and dwelling in the house where I counted on ending my days exactly as if it were an inn whence I must set forth on the morrow. All things went so well, just as they were, that to think of ordering them better were to spoil them. One of my greatest joys was to leave my books fastened up in their boxes, and to be without even a case for writing. When any luckless letter forced me to take up a pen for an answer,

* Written in 1776–1778; published in 1782. The passages reprinted here were written in 1777.

1. Rousseau had taken refuge in Switzerland in 1762, when the French government ordered his arrest for the publication of *Émile*. He lived on the Île de Saint-Pierre (St. Peter's Island), in the Lake of Bienne, Bern, from September through October, 1765.

2. Thérèse le Vasseur, with whom Rousseau had five children. All were raised in an orphanage.

I grumblingly borrowed the steward's inkstand, and hurried to give it back to him with all the haste I could, in the vain hope that I should never have need of the loan any more. Instead of meddling with those weary quires and reams and piles of old books, I filled my chamber with flowers and grasses; for I was then in my first fervor for botany. . . . Having given up employment that would be a task to me, I needed one that would be an amusement, nor cause me more pains than a sluggard might choose to take. I undertook to make the 'Flora Petrinsularis';[3] and to describe every single plant on the island, in detail enough to occupy me for the rest of my days. . . . In consequence of this fine scheme, every morning after breakfast, which we all took in company, I used to go with a magnifying-glass in my hand, and my 'Systema Naturae'[4] under my arm, to visit some district of the island. I had divided it for that purpose into small squares, meaning to go through them one after another in each season of the year. . . . At the end of two or three hours I used to return laden with an ample harvest,—a provision for amusing myself after dinner indoors, in case of rain. I spent the rest of the morning in going with the steward, his wife, and Thérèse, to see the laborers and the harvesting, and I generally set to work along with them: many a time when people from Berne came to see me, they found me perched on a high tree, with a bag fastened round my waist; I kept filling it with fruit, and then let it down to the ground with a rope. The exercise I had taken in the morning, and the good-humor that always comes from exercise, made the repose of dinner vastly pleasant to me. But if dinner was kept up too long, and fine weather invited me forth, I could not wait; but was speedily off to throw myself all alone into a boat, which, when the water was smooth enough, I used to pull out to the middle of the lake. There, stretched at full length in the boat's bottom, with my eyes turned up to the sky, I let myself float slowly hither and thither as the water listed, sometimes for hours together; plunged in a thousand confused delicious musings, which, though they had no fixed nor constant object, were not the less on that account a hundred times dearer to me than all that I had found sweetest in what they call the pleasures of life. Often warned by the going down of the sun that it was time to return, I found myself so far from the island that I was forced to row with all my might to get in before it was pitch dark. At other times, instead of losing myself in the midst of the waters, I had a fancy to coast along the green shores of the island, where the clear waters and cool shadows tempted me to bathe. But one of my most frequent expeditions was from the larger island to the smaller: there I disembarked and spent

3. i.e., a botanical guide to St. Peter's Island.   4. a work, published in 1735, by Linnaeus (Carl von Linné), 1708–1778, the great Swedish botanist.

my afternoon,—sometimes in limited rambles among wild elders, persicaries,[5] willows, and shrubs of every species; sometimes settling myself on the top of a sandy knoll, covered with turf, wild thyme, flowers, even sainfoin and trefoil that had most likely been sown there in old days, making excellent quarters for rabbits. They might multiply in peace without either fearing anything or harming anything. I spoke of this to the steward. He at once had male and female rabbits brought from Neuchâtel,[6] and we went in high state —his wife, one of his sisters, Thérèse, and I—to settle them in the little islet. . . . The foundation of our colony was a feast-day. The pilot of the Argonauts[7] was not prouder than I, as I bore my company and the rabbits in triumph from our island to the smaller one. . . .

When the lake was too rough for me to sail, I spent my afternoon in going up and down the island, gathering plants to right and left; seating myself now in smiling lonely nooks to dream at my ease, now on little terraces and knolls, to follow with my eyes the superb and ravishing prospect of the lake and its shores, crowned on one side by the neighboring hills, and on the other melting into rich and fertile plains up to the feet of the pale-blue mountains on their far-off edge.

As evening drew on, I used to come down from the high ground, and sit on the beach at the water's brink in some hidden sheltering-place. There the murmur of the waves and their agitation charmed all my senses, and drove every other movement away from my soul: they plunged it into delicious dreamings, in which I was often surprised by night. The flux and reflux of the water, its ceaseless stir, swelling and falling at intervals, striking on ear and sight, made up for the internal movements which my musings extinguished; they were enough to give me delight in mere existence, without taking any trouble of thinking. From time to time arose some passing thought of the instability of the things of this world, of which the face of the waters offered an image: but such light impressions were swiftly effaced in the uniformity of the ceaseless motion, which rocked me as in a cradle; it held me with such fascination that even when called at the hour and by the signal appointed, I could not tear myself away without summoning all my force.

After supper, when the evening was fine, we used to go all together for a saunter on the terrace, to breathe the freshness of the air from the lake. We sat down in the arbor,—laughing, chatting, or singing some old song,—and then we went home to bed, well pleased

5. of the genus *Persicaria;* a flowering shrub.

6. in Motiers-Travers, where Rousseau lived before coming to the Lake of Bienne. His neighbors—who looked at him as highly suspect—broke his windows, and he fled in fear of being stoned.

7. those accompanying Jason on the ship *Argo,* when that mythical Greek hero sought the Golden Fleece.

with the day, and only craving another that should be exactly like it on the morrow. . . .

All is a continual flux upon the earth. Nothing in it keeps a form constant and determinate; our affections—fastening on external things—necessarily change and pass just as they do. Ever in front of us or behind us, they recall the past that is gone, or anticipate a future that in many a case is destined never to be. There is nothing solid to which the heart can fix itself. Here we have little more than a pleasure that comes and passes away; as for the happiness that endures, I cannot tell if it be so much as known among men. There is hardly in the midst of our liveliest delights a single instant when the heart could tell us with real truth, *"I would this instant might last forever."*[8] And how can we give the name of happiness to a fleeting state that all the time leaves the heart unquiet and void,— that makes us regret something gone, or still long for something to come?

But if there is a state in which the soul finds a situation solid enough to comport with perfect repose, and with the expansion of its whole faculty, without need of calling back the past or pressing on towards the future; where time is nothing for it, and the present has no ending; with no mark for its own duration, and without a trace of succession; without a single other sense of privation or delight, of pleasure or pain, of desire or apprehension, than this single sense of existence,—so long as such a state endures, he who finds himself in it may talk of bliss, not with a poor, relative, and imperfect happiness such as people find in the pleasures of life, but with a happiness full, perfect, and sufficing, that leaves in the soul no conscious unfilled void. Such a state was many a day mine in my solitary musings in the isle of St. Peter, either lying in my boat as it floated on the water, or seated on the banks of the broad lake, or in other places than the little isle,—on the brink of some broad stream, or a rivulet murmuring over a gravel bed.

What is it that one enjoys in a situation like this? Nothing outside of one's self, nothing except one's self and one's own existence. . . . But most men, tossed as they are by unceasing passion, have little knowledge of such a state: they taste it imperfectly for a few moments, and then retain no more than an obscure confused idea of it, that is too weak to let them feel its charm. It would not even be good, in the present constitution of things, that in their eagerness for these gentle ecstasies, they should fall into a disgust for the active life in which their duty is prescribed to them by needs that are ever on the increase. But a wretch cut off from human society, who can do nothing here below that is useful and good

---

8. Rousseau's words foreshadow Faust's pact with Mephistopheles, in Goethe's *Faust*, Part I.

either for himself or for other people, may in such a state find for all lost human felicities many recompenses, of which neither fortune nor men can ever rob him.

It is true that these recompenses cannot be felt by all souls, nor in all situations. The heart must be in peace, nor any passion come to trouble its calm. There must be in the surrounding objects neither absolute repose nor excess of agitation; but a uniform and moderated movement, without shock, without interval. With no movement, life is only a lethargy. If the movement be unequal or too strong, it awakes us; by recalling us to the objects around, it destroys the charm of our musing, and plucks us from within ourselves, instantly to throw us back under the yoke of fortune and man, in a moment to restore us to all the consciousness of misery. Absolute stillness inclines one to gloom. It offers an image of death: then the help of a cheerful imagination is necessary, and presents itself naturally enough to those whom Heaven has endowed with such a gift. The movement which does not come from without then stirs within us. The repose is less complete, it is true; but it is also more agreeable when light and gentle ideas, without agitating the depths of the soul, only softly skim the surface. This sort of musing we may taste whenever there is tranquillity about us; and I have thought that in the Bastille,[9] and even in a dungeon where no object struck my sight, I could have dreamed away many a thrice pleasurable day.

But it must be said that all this came better and more happily in a fruitful and lonely island, where nothing presented itself to me save smiling pictures, where nothing recalled saddening memories, where the fellowship of the few dwellers there was gentle and obliging, without being exciting enough to busy me incessantly; where, in short, I was free to surrender myself all day long to the promptings of my taste or to the most luxurious indolence. . . . As I came out from a long and most sweet musing fit, seeing myself surrounded by verdure and flowers and birds, and letting my eyes wander far over romantic shores that fringed a wide expanse of water bright as crystal, I fitted all these attractive objects into my dreams; and when at last I slowly recovered myself, and recognized what was about me, I could not mark the point that cut off dream from reality, so equally did all things unite to endear to me the lonely retired life I led in this happy spot! Why can that life not come back to me again? Why can I not go finish my days in the beloved island, never to quit it, never again to see in it one dweller from the mainland, to bring back to me the memory of all the woes of every sort that they have delighted in heaping on my head for all these long years? . . . Freed from the earthly passions engendered by the tumult of social life, my soul would many a time lift itself above this atmosphere, and commune beforehand with the heavenly intelligences, into whose number it trusts to be ere long taken. . . .

JOHANN WOLFGANG VON GOETHE
(1749–1832)
Faust*

*Prologue in Heaven*ᵃ

The LORD. The HEAVENLY HOSTS. MEPHISTOPHELESᵇ *following.*

[*The* THREE ARCHANGELS *step forward.*]

RAPHAEL. The chanting sun, as ever, rivals
  The chanting of his brother spheres
  And marches round his destined circuit—
  A march that thunders in our ears.
  His aspect cheers the Hosts of Heaven   5
  Though what his essence none can say;
  These inconceivable creations
  Keep the high state of their first day.
GABRIEL. And swift, with inconceivable swiftness,
  The earth's full splendour rolls around,   10
  Celestial radiance alternating
  With a dread night too deep to sound;
  The sea against the rocks' deep bases
  Comes foaming up in far-flung force,
  And rock and sea go whirling onward   15
  In the swift spheres' eternal course.
MICHAEL. And storms in rivalry are raging
  From sea to land, from land to sea,
  In frenzy forge the world a girdle
  From which no inmost part is free.   20
  The blight of lightning flaming yonder
  Marks where the thunder-bolt will play;
  And yet Thine envoys, Lord, revere

---

* From *Goethe's Faust.* Parts I and II. An abridged edition translated by Louis MacNeice. Copyright 1951 by Louis MacNeice. Reprinted by permission of Oxford University Press, Inc. Part I was first published in 1808, and Part II in 1833. Goethe's Dedication and the Prologue at the Theater have not been included, since neither is part of the play itself. All of Part I, except for a few minor omissions made by the trans-

lator (indicated in the footnotes), and Act V of Part II are reprinted here.
  a. probably written in 1798. The scene is patterned on Job 1:6–12 and 2:1–6.
  b. The origin of the name is still debatable. It may come from Hebrew, Persian, or Greek, with such meanings as "destroyer-liar," "no friend of Faust," "no friend of light."

The gentle movement of Thy day.

CHOIR OF ANGELS. Thine aspect cheers the Hosts of Heaven   25
   Though what Thine essence none can say,
       And all Thy loftiest creations
       Keep the high state of their first day.
     [*Enter* MEPHISTOPHELES.]

MEPHISTOPHELES. Since you, O Lord, once more approach and ask
   If business down with us be light or heavy—   30
   And in the past you've usually welcomed me—
   That's why you see me also at your levee.
   Excuse me, I can't manage lofty words—
   Not though your whole court jeer and find me low;
   My pathos certainly would make you laugh   35
   Had you not left off laughing long ago.
   Your suns and worlds mean nothing much to me;
   How men torment themselves, that's all I see.
   The little god of the world, one can't reshape, reshade him;
   He is as strange to-day as that first day you made him.   40
   His life would be not so bad, not quite,
   Had you not granted him a gleam of Heaven's light;
   He calls it Reason, uses it not the least
   Except to be more beastly than any beast.
   He seems to me—if your Honour does not mind—   45
   Like a grasshopper—the long-legged kind—
   That's always in flight and leaps as it flies along
   And then in the grass strikes up its same old song.
   I could only wish he confined himself to the grass!
   He thrusts his nose into every filth, alas.   50

LORD. Mephistopheles, have you no other news?
   Do you always come here to accuse?
   Is nothing ever right in your eyes on earth?

MEPHISTOPHELES. No, Lord! I find things there as downright bad
    as ever.
   I am sorry for men's days of dread and dearth;   55
   Poor things, *my* wish to plague 'em isn't fervent.

LORD. Do you know Faust?

MEPHISTOPHELES.   The Doctor?

LORD.   Aye, my servant.

MEPHISTOPHELES. Indeed! He serves you oddly enough, I think.   60
   The fool has no earthly habits in meat and drink.
   The ferment in him drives him wide and far,
   That he is mad he too has almost guessed;
   He demands of heaven each fairest star

---

58. *Doctor:* i.e., doctor of philosophy.   stopheles shifts from *du* to *ihr*, indicat-
60. *you:* In the German text, Mephi-   ing his lack of respect for God.

And of earth each highest joy and best,   65
    And all that is new and all that is far
    Can bring no calm to the deep-sea swell of his breast.
LORD. Now he may serve me only gropingly,
    Soon I shall lead him into the light.
    The gardener knows when the sapling first turns green   70
    That flowers and fruit will make the future bright.
MEPHISTOPHELES. What do you wager? You will lose him yet,
    Provided *you* give *me* permission
    To steer him gently the course I set.
LORD. So long as he walks the earth alive,   75
    So long you may try what enters your head;
    Men make mistakes as long as they strive.
MEPHISTOPHELES. I thank you for that; as regards the dead,
    The dead have never taken my fancy.
    I favour cheeks that are full and rosy-red;   80
    No corpse is welcome to my house;
    I work as the cat does with the mouse.
LORD. Very well; you have my permission.
    Divert this soul from its primal source
    And carry it, if you can seize it,   85
    Down with you upon your course—
    And stand ashamed when you must needs admit:
    A good man with his groping intuitions
    Still knows the path that is true and fit.
MEPHISTOPHELES. All right—but it won't last for long.   90
    I'm not afraid my bet will turn out wrong.
    And, if my aim prove true and strong,
    Allow me to triumph wholeheartedly.
    Dust shall he eat—and greedily—
    Like my cousin the Snake renowned in tale and song.   95
LORD. That too you are free to give a trial;
    I have never hated the likes of you.
    Of all the spirits of denial
    The joker is the last that I eschew.
    Man finds relaxation too attractive—   100
    Too fond too soon of unconditional rest;
    Which is why I am pleased to give him a companion
    Who lures and thrusts and must, as devil, be active.
    But ye, true sons of Heaven, it is your duty
    To take your joy in the living wealth of beauty.   105
    The changing Essence which ever works and lives
    Wall you around with love, serene, secure!
    And that which floats in flickering appearance

95. *Snake:* the serpent in Genesis, who tempted Adam and Eve.

Fix ye it firm in thoughts that must endure.

CHOIR OF ANGELS. Thine aspect cheers the Hosts of Heaven   110
  Though what Thine essence none can say,
  And all Thy loftiest creations
  Keep the high state of their first day.
      [*Heaven closes.*]

MEPHISTOPHELES. [*Alone*] I like to see the Old One now and then
  And try to keep relations on the level.   115
  It's really decent of so great a person
  To talk so humanely even to the Devil.

The First Part of the Tragedy

NIGHT

In a high-vaulted narrow Gothic room FAUST, *restless, in a chair at his desk.*

FAUST. Here stand I, ach, Philosophy
  Behind me and Law and Medicine too
  And, to my cost, Theology—
  All these I have sweated through and through
  And now you see me a poor fool   5
  As wise as when I entered school!
  They call me Master, they call me Doctor,
  Ten years now I have dragged my college
  Along by the nose through zig and zag
  Through up and down and round and round   10
  And this is all that I have found—
  The impossibility of knowledge!
  It is this that burns away my heart;
  Of course I am cleverer than the quacks,
  Than master and doctor, than clerk and priest,   15
  I suffer no scruple or doubt in the least,
  I have no qualms about devil or burning,
  Which is just why all joy is torn from me,
  I cannot presume to make use of my learning,
  I cannot presume I could open my mind   20
  To proselytize and improve mankind.

  Besides, I have neither goods nor gold,
  Neither reputation nor rank in the world;
  No dog would choose to continue so!
  Which is why I have given myself to Magic   25
  To see if the Spirit may grant me to know
  Through its force and its voice full many a secret,

May spare the sour sweat that I used to pour out
In talking of what I know nothing about,
May grant me to learn what it is that girds   30
The world together in its inmost being,
That the seeing its whole germination, the seeing
Its workings, may end my traffic in words.

O couldst thou, light of the full moon,
Look now thy last upon my pain,   35
Thou for whom I have sat belated
So many midnights here and waited
Till, over books and papers, thou
Didst shine, sad friend, upon my brow!
O could I but walk to and fro   40
On mountain heights in thy dear glow
Or float with spirits round mountain eyries
Or weave through fields thy glances glean
And freed from all miasmal theories
Bathe in thy dew and wash me clean!   45

Oh! Am I still stuck in this jail?
This God-damned dreary hole in the wall
Where even the lovely light of heaven
Breaks wanly through the painted panes!
Cooped up among these heaps of books   50
Gnawed by worms, coated with dust,
Round which to the top of the Gothic vault
A smoke-stained paper forms a crust.
Retorts and canisters lie pell-mell
And pyramids of instruments,   55
The junk of centuries, dense and mat—
Your world, man! World? They call it that!

And yet you ask why your poor heart
Cramped in your breast should feel such fear,
Why an unspecified misery   60
Should throw your life so out of gear?
Instead of the living natural world
For which God made all men his sons
You hold a reeking mouldering court
Among assorted skeletons.   65

Away! There is a world outside!
And this one book of mystic art
Which Nostradamus wrote himself,

68. *Nostradamus:* Latin name of the French astrologer and physician Michel de Notredame, born in 1503. His col- lection of rhymed prophecies, *The Centuries*, appeared in 1555.

Is this not adequate guard and guide?
By this you can tell the course of the stars,   70
By this, once Nature gives the word,
The soul begins to stir and dawn,
A spirit by a spirit heard.
In vain your barren studies here
Construe the signs of sanctity.   75
You Spirits, you are hovering near;
If you can hear me, answer me!

    [*He opens the book and perceives the sign of the Mac-
rocosm.*[a]]

Ha! What a river of wonder at this vision
Bursts upon all my senses in one flood!
And I feel young, the holy joy of life   80
Glows new, flows fresh, through nerve and blood!
Was it a god designed this hieroglyph to calm
The storm which but now raged inside me,
To pour upon my heart such balm,
And by some secret urge to guide me   85
Where all the powers of Nature stand unveiled around me?
Am I a God? It grows so light!
And through the clear-cut symbol on this page
My soul comes face to face with all creating Nature.
At last I understand the dictum of the sage: 90
'The spiritual world is always open,
Your mind is closed, your heart is dead;
Rise, young man, and plunge undaunted
Your earthly breast in the morning red.'

    [*He contemplates the sign.*]

Into one Whole how all things blend,   95
Function and live within each other!
Passing gold buckets to each other
How heavenly powers ascend, descend!
The odour of grace upon their wings,
They thrust from heaven through earthly things   100
And as all sing so *the* All sings!

What a fine show! Aye, but only a show!
Infinite Nature, where can I tap thy veins?
Where are thy breasts, those well-springs of all life
On which hang heaven and earth,   105
Towards which my dry breast strains?
They well up, they give drink, but I feel drought and dearth.

a. literally, "the great world"; the universe as a whole.

[*He turns the pages and perceives the sign of the* EARTH
SPIRIT.]

How differently this new sign works upon me!
Thy sign, thou Spirit of the Earth, 'tis thine
And thou art nearer to me.   110
At once I feel my powers unfurled,
At once I glow as from new wine
And feel inspired to venture into the world,
To cope with the fortunes of earth benign or malign,
To enter the ring with the storm, to grapple and clinch, 115
To enter the jaws of the shipwreck and never flinch.
Over me comes a mist,
The moon muffles her light,
The lamp goes dark.
The air goes damp. Red beams flash   120
Around my head. There blows
A kind of a shudder down from the vault
And seizes on me.
It is thou must be hovering round me, come at my prayers!
Spirit, unveil thyself!   125
My heart, oh my heart, how it tears!
And how each and all of my senses
Seem burrowing upwards towards new light, new breath!
I feel my heart has surrendered, I have no more defences.
Come then! Come! Even if it prove my death!   130
        [*He seizes the book and solemnly pronounces the sign of the*
        EARTH SPIRIT. *There is a flash of red flame and the* SPIRIT
        appears in it.]
SPIRIT. Who calls upon me?
FAUST. Appalling vision!
SPIRIT. You have long been sucking at my sphere,
    Now by main force you have drawn me here
    And now—   135
FAUST. No! Not to be endured!
SPIRIT. With prayers and with pantings you have procured
    The sight of my face and the sound of my voice—
    Now I am here. What a pitiable shivering
    Seizes the Superman. Where is the call of your soul? 140
    Where the breast which created a world in itself
    And carried and fostered it, swelling up, joyfully quivering,
    Raising itself to a level with Us, the Spirits?
    Where are you, Faust, whose voice rang out to me,

109. *Spirit of the Earth:* The Macrocosm represented the ordered, harmonious universe in its totality; this
figure seems to be a symbol for the
energy of terrestrial nature—neither
good nor bad, merely powerful.

Who with every nerve so thrust yourself upon me? 145
Are you the thing that at a whiff of my breath
Trembles throughout its living frame,
A poor worm crawling off, askance, askew?

FAUST. Shall I yield to Thee, Thou shape of flame?
I am Faust, I can hold my own with Thee. 150

SPIRIT. In the floods of life, in the storm of work,
In ebb and flow,
In warp and weft,
Cradle and grave,
An eternal sea, 155
A changing patchwork,
A glowing life,
At the whirring loom of Time I weave
The living clothes of the Deity.

FAUST. Thou who dost rove the wide world round, 160
Busy Spirit, how near I feel to Thee!

SPIRIT. You are like that Spirit which you can grasp,
Not me!
[*The* SPIRIT *vanishes.*]

FAUST. Not Thee!
Whom then? 165
I who am Godhead's image,
Am I not even like Thee!
[*A knocking on the door.*]
Death! I know who that is. My assistant!
So ends my happiest, fairest hour.
The crawling pedant must interrupt 170
My visions at their fullest flower!
[WAGNER *enters in dressing-gown and nightcap, a lamp in his hand.*]

WAGNER. Excuse me but I heard your voice declaiming—
A passage doubtless from those old Greek plays.
That is an art from which I would gladly profit,
It has its advantages nowadays. 175
And I've often heard folks say it's true
A preacher can learn something from an actor.

FAUST. Yes, when the preacher is an actor too;
Which is a not uncommon factor.

WAGNER. Ah, when your study binds up your whole existence 180
And you scarcely can see the world on a holiday
Or through a spyglass—and always from a distance—
How can your rhetoric make it walk your way?

FAUST. Unless you feel it, you cannot gallop it down,
Unless it thrust up from your soul 185

Forcing the hearts of all your audience
With a primal joy beyond control.
Sit there for ever with scissors and paste!
Gather men's leavings for a rehash
And blow up a little paltry flicker   190
Out of your own little heap of ash!
It will win you claps from apes and toddlers—
Supposing your palate welcome such—
But heart can never awaken a spark in heart
Unless your own heart keep in touch.   195

WAGNER. However, it is the delivery wins all ears
    And I know that I am still far, too far, in arrears.

FAUST. Win your effects by honest means,
    Eschew the cap and bells of the fool!
    True insight and true sense will make   200
    Their point without the rhetoric school
    And, given a thought that must be heard,
    Is there such need to chase a word?
    Yes, your so glittering purple patches
    In which you make cat's cradles of humanity   205
    Are like the foggy wind which whispers in the autumn
    Through barren leaves—a fruitless vanity.

WAGNER. Ah God, we know that art
    Is long and short our life!
    Often enough my analytical labours   210
    Pester both brain and heart.
    How hard it is to attain the means
    By which one climbs to the fountain head;
    Before a poor devil can reach the halfway house,
    Like as not he is dead.   215

FAUST. Your manuscript, is that your holy well
    A draught of which for ever quenches thirst?
    You have achieved no true refreshment
    Unless you can tap your own soul first.

WAGNER. Excuse me—it is considerable gratification   220
    To transport oneself into the spirit of times past,
    To observe what a wise man thought before our days
    And how we now have brought his ideas to consummation.

FAUST. Oh yes, consummated in heaven!
    There is a book, my friend, and its seals are seven— 225
    The times that have been put on the shelf.
    Your so-called spirit of such times
    Is at bottom merely the spirit of the gentry

225. *its seals are seven:* See Revelation 5:1.

In whom each time reflects itself,
And at that it often makes one weep   230
And at the first glance run away,
A lumber-room and a rubbish heap,
At best an heroic puppet play
With excellent pragmatical Buts and Yets
Such as are suitable to marionettes.   235

WAGNER. And yet the world! The heart and spirit of men!
We all would wish to understand the same.

FAUST. Yes, what is known as understanding—
But who dare call the child by his real name?
The few who have known anything about it,   240
Whose hearts unwisely overbrimmed and spake,
Who showed the mob their feelings and their visions,
Have ended on the cross or at the stake.
My friend, I beg you, the night is now far gone;
We must break off for this occasion.   245

WAGNER. I'd have been happy sitting on and on
To continue such a learned conversation.
To-morrow however, as it is Easter Day,
I shall put you some further questions if I may.
Having given myself to knowledge heart and soul   250
I have a good share of it, now I would like the whole.
[*Exit* WAGNER.]

FAUST. [*Alone*] To think this head should still bring hope to
     birth
Sticking like glue to hackneyed rags and tags,
Delving with greedy hand for treasure
And glad when it finds an earthworm in the earth!   255

That such a human voice should here intrude
Where spiritual fulness only now enclosed me!
And yet, my God, you poorest of all the sons
Of earth, this time you have earned my gratitude.
For you have snatched me away from that despair   260
Which was ripe and ready to destroy my mind;
Beside that gigantic vision I could not find
My normal self; only a dwarf was there.

I, image of the Godhead, who deemed myself but now
On the brink of the mirror of eternal truth and seeing 265
My rapturous fill of the blaze of clearest Heaven,
Having stripped off my earthly being;
I, more than an angel, I whose boundless urge
To flow through Nature's veins and in the act of creation

To revel it like the gods—what a divination,   270
What an act of daring—and what an expiation!
One thundering word has swept me over the verge.

To boast myself thine equal I do not dare.
Granted I owned the power to draw thee down,
I lacked the power to hold thee there.   275
In that blest moment I felt myself,
Felt myself so small, so great;
Cruelly thou didst thrust me back
Into man's uncertain fate.
Who will teach me? What must I shun?   280
Or must I go where that impulse drives?
Alas, our very actions like our sufferings
Put a brake upon our lives.
Upon the highest concepts of the mind
There grows an alien and more alien mould;   285
When we have reached what in this world is good
That which is better is labelled a fraud, a blind.
What gave us life, feelings of highest worth,
Go dead amidst the madding crowds of earth.

Where once Imagination on daring wing   290
Reached out to the Eternal, full of hope,
Now, that the eddies of time have shipwrecked chance on chance,
She is contented with a narrow scope.
Care makes her nest forthwith in the heart's deep places,
And there contrives her secret sorrows,   295
Rocks herself restlessly, destroying rest and joy;
And always she is putting on new faces,
Will appear as your home, as those that you love within it,
As fire or water, poison or steel;
You tremble at every blow that you do not feel   300
And what you never lose you must weep for every minute.

I am not like the gods—that I too deeply feel—
No, I am like the worm that burrows through the dust
Which, as it keeps itself alive in the dust,
Is annulled and buried by some casual heel.   305

Is it not dust that on a thousand shelves
Narrows this high wall round me so?
The junk that with its thousandfold tawdriness
In this moth world keeps me so low?
Shall I find here what I require?   310
Read maybe in a thousand books how men
Have in the general run tortured themselves,

With but a lucky one now and then?
Why do you grin at me, you hollow skull?
To point out that your brain was once, like mine, confused   315
And looked for the easy day but in the difficult dusk,
Lusting for truth was led astray and abused?
You instruments, I know you are mocking me
With cog and crank and cylinder.
I stood at the door, you were to be the key;   320
A key with intricate wards—but the bolt declines to stir.
Mysterious in the light of day
Nature lets none unveil her; if she refuse
To make some revelation to your spirit
You cannot force her with levers and with screws.   325
You ancient gear I have never used, it is only
Because my father used you that I retain you.
You ancient scroll, you have been turning black
Since first the dim lamp smoked upon this desk to stain you.
Far better to have squandered the little I have   330
Than loaded with that little to stay sweating here.
Whatever legacy your fathers left you,
To own it you must earn it dear.
The thing that you fail to use is a load of lead;
The moment can only use what the moment itself has bred.   335

But why do my eyes fasten upon that spot?
Is that little bottle a magnet to my sight?
Why do I feel of a sudden this lovely illumination
As when the moon flows round us in a dark wood at night?

Bottle, unique little bottle, I salute you   340
As now I devoutly lift you down. In you
I honour human invention and human skill.
You, the quintessence of all sweet narcotics,
The extract of all rare and deadly powers,
I am your master—show me your good will!   345
I look on you, my sorrow is mitigated,
I hold you and my struggles are abated,
The flood-tide of my spirit ebbs away, away.
The mirroring waters glitter at my feet,
I am escorted forth on the high seas,   350
Allured towards new shores by a new day.
A fiery chariot floats on nimble wings
Down to me and I feel myself upbuoyed
To blaze a new trail through the upper air

326–327. *gear . . . father:* Later we find that Faust's father was a doctor of
medicine.

Into new spheres of energy unalloyed.   355
Oh this high life, this heavenly rapture! Do you
Merit this, you, a moment ago a worm?
Merit it? Aye—only turn your back on the sun
Which enchants the earth, turn your back and be firm!
And brace yourself to tear asunder the gates   360
Which everyone longs to shuffle past if he can;
Now is the time to act and acting prove
That God's height need not lower the merit of Man;
Nor tremble at that dark pit in which our fancy
Condemns itself to torments of its own framing,   365
But struggle on and upwards to that passage
At the narrow mouth of which all hell is flaming.
Be calm and take this step, though you should fall
Beyond it into nothing—nothing at all.

And you, you loving-cup of shining crystal—   370
I have not given a thought to you for years—
Down you come now out of your ancient chest!
You glittered at my ancestors' junketings
Enlivening the serious guest
When with you in his hand he proceeded to toast his neigh-
bour—   375
But to-day no neighbour will take you from my hand.
Here is a juice that makes one drunk in a wink;
It fills you full, you cup, with its brown flood.
It was I who made this, I who had it drawn;
So let my whole soul now make my last drink   380
A high and gala greeting, a toast to the dawn!
　　　[*He raises the cup to his mouth. There is an outburst of
　　　bells and choirs.*]
CHORUS OF ANGELS. Christ is arisen!
　　　　　　　　　Joy to mortality
　　　　　　　　　Whom its own fatally
　　　　　　　　　Earth-bound mortality   385
　　　　　　　　　Bound in a prison.
FAUST. What a deep booming, what a ringing tone
Pulls back the cup from my lips—and with such power!
So soon are you announcing, you deep bells,
Easter Day's first festive hour?   390
You choirs, do you raise so soon the solacing hymn
That once round the night of the grave rang out from the
seraphim

---

381. *dawn:* See l. 248.　　　　　an old medieval Easter hymn, freely
382. *Christ is arisen!:* first line of　adapted by Goethe.

As man's new covenant and dower?
CHORUS OF WOMEN. With balm and with spices
'Twas we laid him out,   395
We who tended him,
Faithful, devout;
We wound him in linen,
Made all clean where he lay,
Alas—to discover   400
Christ gone away.
CHORUS OF ANGELS. Christ is arisen!
The loving one! Blest
After enduring the
Grievous, the curing, the   405
Chastening test.
FAUST. You heavenly music, strong as you are kind,
Why do you search me out in the dust?
Better ring forth where men have open hearts!
I hear your message, my faith it is that lags behind;   410
And miracle is the favourite child of faith.
Those spheres whence peals the gospel of forgiving,
Those are beyond what I can dare,
And yet, so used am I from childhood to this sound,
It even now summons me back to living.   415
Once I could feel the kiss of heavenly love
Rain down through the calm and solemn Sabbath air,
Could find a prophecy in the full-toned bell,
A spasm of happiness in a prayer.
An ineffably sweet longing bound me   420
To quest at random through field and wood
Where among countless burning tears
I felt a world rise up around me.
This hymn announced the lively games of youth, the lovely
Freedom of Spring's own festival;   425
Now with its childlike feelings memory holds me back
From the last and gravest step of all.
But you, sweet songs of heaven, keep sounding forth!
My tears well up, I belong once more to earth.
CHORUS OF DISCIPLES. Now has the Buried One,   430
Lowliness ended,
Living in lordliness,
Lordly ascended;
He in the zest of birth

394–401. *With balm . . . away:* Goethe makes free use of the New Testament here. None of the Evangelists says that Christ was laid in the tomb by women. According to Mark and Luke, they came on the third day *intending* to anoint the body, but He was gone from the tomb.

316 of 1686 · *Johann Wolfgang von Goethe*

435

Near to creating light;
We on the breast of earth
Still in frustrating night!
He left us, his own ones,
Pining upon this spot,
Ah, and lamenting,
Master, thy lot.

CHORUS OF ANGELS. Christ is arisen
From the womb of decay!
Burst from your prison,
Rejoice in the day!
Praising him actively,
Practising charity,
Giving alms brotherly,
Preaching him wanderingly,
Promising sanctity,
You have your Master near,
You have him here!

435

440

445

450

EASTER HOLIDAY

Holidaymakers of all kinds come out through the city gate.[a]

FIRST STUDENT. Lord, these strapping wenches they go a lick!
    Hurry up, brother, we must give 'em an escort.
    My programme for to-day is a strong ale,
    A pipe of shag and a girl who's got up chic.
FIRST GIRL. Look! Will you look at the handsome boys!
    Really and truly its degrading;
    They could walk out with the best of us
    And they have to run round scullery-maiding!
SECOND STUDENT. Hold on, hold on! There are two coming up
        behind
    With a very pretty taste in dress;
    One of those girls is a neighbour of mine,
    She appeals to me, I must confess.
    You see how quietly they go
    And yet in the end they'll be taking *us* in tow.
BEGGAR. [*Singing*] Good gentlemen and lovely ladies,
            Rosy of cheek and neat of dress,
            Be kind enough to look upon me
            And see and comfort my distress.
            Leave me not here a hopeless busker!

5

10

15

a. It has been shown that Goethe had Frankfurt-am-Main in mind for this scene, and the "gate" referred to is the Sachsenhausen Tor, or Affenthor. The translator omits a few lines here which include other local references—to a hunting lodge, or *Forsthaus,* two miles southwest of the gate; to an inn called the Gerbermühle on the Main River; and to a village, probably Oberrad.

Only the giver can be gay.   20
A day when all the town rejoices,
Make it for me a harvest day.

FIRST BURGHER. I know nothing better on Sundays or on holidays
Than to have a chat about war and warlike pother
When far away, in Turkey say,   25
The peoples are socking one another.
One stands at the window, drinks one's half of mild,
And sees the painted ships glide down the waterways;
Then in the evening one goes happily home
And blesses peace and peaceful days.   30

SECOND BURGHER. Yes indeed, neighbour! That is all right with me.
They can break heads if they like it so
And churn up everything topsyturvy.
But at home let us keep the status quo.

OLD WOMAN. Eh, but how smart they look! Pretty young things!   35
Whoever saw you should adore you!
But not so haughty! It's all right—
Tell me your wish and I can get it for you.

FIRST GIRL. Come, Agatha! Such witches I avoid
In public places—it's much wiser really;   40
It's true, she helped me on St. Andrew's night
To see my future sweetheart clearly.

SECOND GIRL. Yes, mine she showed me in a crystal,
A soldier type with dashing chaps behind him;
I look around, I seek him everywhere   45
And yet—and yet I never find him.

SOLDIERS. [*Singing*] Castles with towering
                      Walls to maintain them,
                      Girls who have suitors
                      But to disdain them,   50
                      Would I could gain them!
                      Bold is the venture,
                      Lordly the pay.

                      Hark to the trumpets!
                      They may be crying   55
                      Summons to gladness,
                      Summons to dying.
                      Life is a storming!
                      Life is a splendour!
                      Maidens and castles   60
                      Have to surrender.

41. *St. Andrew's night:* Actually,   to consult fortunetellers about their
St. Andrew's eve, November 29. This   future lovers or husbands.
was the traditional time for young girls

Bold is the venture,
Lordly the pay;
Later the soldiers
Go marching away.   65

[FAUST *and* WAGNER *are now walking off on the road to the village.*]

FAUST. River and brook are freed from ice
By the lovely enlivening glance of spring
And hope grows green throughout the dale;
Ancient winter, weakening,
Has fallen back on the rugged mountains   70
And launches thence his Parthian shafts
Which are merely impotent showers of hail
Streaking over the greening mead;
But the sun who tolerates nothing white
Amidst all this shaping and stirring of seed,   75
Wants to enliven the world with colour
And, flowers being lacking, in their lieu
Takes colourful crowds to mend the view.
Turn round and look back from this rise
Towards the town. From the gloomy gate   80
Look, can you see them surging forth—
A harlequin-coloured crowd in fête!
Sunning themselves with one accord
In homage to the risen Lord
For they themselves to-day have risen: 85
Out of the dismal room in the slum,
Out of each shop and factory prison,
Out of the stuffiness of the garret,
Out of the squash of the narrow streets,
Out of the churches' reverend night—   90
One and all have been raised to light.
Look, only look, how quickly the gardens
And fields are sprinkled with the throng,
How the river all its length and breadth
Bears so many pleasure-boats along,   95
And almost sinking from its load
How this last dinghy moves away.
Even on the furthest mountain tracks
Gay rags continue to look gay.
Already I hear the hum of the village,   100
Here is the plain man's real heaven—
Great and small in a riot of fun;
Here I'm a man—and dare be one.

WAGNER. Doctor, to take a walk with you
 Is a profit and a privilege for me   105
 But I wouldn't lose my way alone round here,
 Sworn foe that I am of all vulgarity.
 This fiddling, screaming, skittle-playing,
 Are sounds I loathe beyond all measure;
 They run amuck as if the devil were in them   110
 And call it music, call it pleasure.
   [*They have now reached the village.*]
OLD PEASANT. Doctor, it is most good of you
 Not to look down on us to-day
 And, pillar of learning that you are,
 To mill around with folk at play.   115
 So take this most particular jug
 Which we have filled for you at the tap,
 This is a pledge and I pray aloud
 That it quench your thirst and more mayhap:
 As many drops as this can give,   120
 So many days extra may you live.
FAUST. Thank you for such a reviving beer
 And now—good health to all men here.
   [*The people collect round him.*]
OLD PEASANT. Of a truth, Doctor, you have done rightly
 To appear on this day when all are glad,   125
 Seeing how in times past you proved
 Our own good friend when days were bad.
 Many a man stands here alive
 Whom your father found in the grip
 Of a raging fever and tore him thence   130
 When he put paid to the pestilence.
 You too—you were a youngster then—
 Where any was ill you went your round,
 Right many a corpse left home feet first
 But you came out of it safe and sound,   135
 From many a gruelling trial—Aye,
 The helper got help from the Helper on high.
CROWD. Health to the trusty man. We pray
 He may live to help us many a day.
FAUST. Kneel to the One on high, our friend   140
 Who teaches us helpers, who help can send.
  [FAUST *and* WAGNER *leave the* CROWD *and move on.*]

129. *your father:* See l. 327 in the preceding scene. The old German Faust legend made Faust's father a peasant; but Nostradamus (see note to l. 68 in the preceding scene) and Paracelsus (1493–1541), two physician-astrologers closely linked to the Faust myth, were famous for their plague-curing remedies.

WAGNER. You great man, how your heart must leap
    To be so honoured by the masses!
    How happy is he who has such talents
    And from them such a crop can reap!   145
    The father points you out to his boy,
    They all ask questions, run and jostle,
    The fiddles and the dancers pause
    And, as you pass, they stand in rows
    And caps go hurtling in the sky;   150
    They almost kneel to you as though
    The eucharist were passing by.

FAUST. Only a few steps more up to that stone!
    Here, after our walk, we will take a rest.
    Here I have often sat, thoughtful, alone,   155
    Torturing myself with prayer and fast.
    Rich in hope and firm in faith,
    With tears and sighs to seven times seven
    I thought I could end that epidemic
    And force the hand of the Lord of Heaven.   160
    But now the crowd's applause sounds to me like derision.
    O could you only read in my inmost heart
    How little father and son
    Merited their great reputation!
    My father was a worthy man who worked in the dark,   165
    Who in good faith but on his own wise
    Brooded on Nature and her holy circles
    With laborious whimsicalities;
    Who used to collect the connoisseurs
    Into the kitchen and locked inside   170
    Its black walls pour together divers
    Ingredients of countless recipes;
    Such was our medicine, the patients died
    And no one counted the survivors.
    And thus we with our hellish powders   175
    Raged more perniciously than the plague
    Throughout this district—valley and town.
    Myself I have given the poison to thousands;
    They drooped away, *I* must live on to sample
    The brazen murderers' renown.   180

WAGNER. How can you let that weigh so heavily?
    Does not a good man do enough
    If he works at the art that he has received
    Conscientiously and scrupulously?
    As a young man you honour your father,   185
    What he can teach, you take with a will;

As a man you widen the range of knowledge
And your son's range may be wider still.

FAUST. Happy the man who swamped in this sea of Error
Still hopes to struggle up through the watery wall;   190
What we don't know is exactly what we need
And what we know fulfils no need at all.
But let us not with such sad thoughts
Make this good hour an hour undone!
Look how the cottages on the green   195
Shine in the glow of the evening sun!
He backs away, gives way, the day is overspent,
He hurries off to foster life elsewhere.
Would I could press on his trail, on his trail for ever—
Alas that I have no wings to raise me into the air!   200
Then I should see in an everlasting sunset
The quiet world before my feet unfold,
All of its peaks on fire, all of its vales becalmed,
And the silver brook dispersed in streams of gold.
Not the wild peaks with all their chasms   205
Could interrupt my godlike flight;
Already the bays of the sea that the sun has warmed
Unfurl upon my marvelling sight.
But in the end the sungod seems to sink away,
Yet the new impulse sets me again in motion,   210
I hasten on to drink his eternal light,
With night behind me and before me day,
Above me heaven and below me ocean.
A beautiful dream—yet the sun leaves me behind.
Alas, it is not so easy for earthly wing   215
To fly on level terms with the wings of the mind.
Yet born with each of us is the instinct
That struggles upwards and away
When over our heads, lost in the blue,
The lark pours out her vibrant lay;   220
When over rugged pine-clad ranges
The eagle hangs on outspread wings
And over lake and over plain
We see the homeward-struggling crane.

WAGNER. I myself have often had moments of fancifulness   225
But I never experienced yet an urge like this.
Woods and fields need only a quick look
And I shall never envy the bird its pinions.
How differently the joys of the mind's dominions
Draw us from page to page, from book to book.   230
That's what makes winter nights lovely and snug—

The blissful life that warms you through your body—
And, ah, should you unroll a worthwhile manuscript,
You bring all heaven down into your study.

FAUST. You are only conscious of one impulse. Never   235
    Seek an acquaintance with the other.
    Two souls, alas, cohabit in my breast,
    A contract one of them desires to sever.
    The one like a rough lover clings
    To the world with the tentacles of its senses;   240
    The other lifts itself to Elysian Fields
    Out of the mist on powerful wings.
    Oh, if there be spirits in the air,
    Princes that weave their way between heaven and earth,
    Come down to me from the golden atmosphere   245
    And carry me off to a new and colourful life.
    Aye, if I only had a magic mantle
    On which I could fly abroad, a-voyaging,
    I would not barter it for the costliest raiment,
    Not even for the mantle of a king.   250

WAGNER. Do not invoke the notorious host
    Deployed in streams upon the wind,
    Preparing danger in a thousand forms
    From every quarter for mankind.
    Thrusting upon you from the North   255
    Come fanged spirits with arrow tongues;
    From the lands of morning they come parching
    To feed themselves upon your lungs;
    The South despatches from the desert
    Incendiary hordes against your brain   260
    And the West a swarm which first refreshes,
    Then drowns both you and field and plain.
    They are glad to listen, adepts at doing harm,
    Glad to obey and so throw dust in our eyes;
    They make believe that they are sent from heaven   265
    And lisp like angels, telling lies.
    But let us move! The world has already gone grey,
    The air is beginning to cool and the mist to fall.
    It's in the evening one really values home—
    But why do you look so astonished, standing there, staring that
        way?   270
    What's there to see in the dusk that's worth the trouble?

FAUST. The black dog, do you mark him ranging through corn and
        stubble?

WAGNER. I noticed him long ago; he struck me as nothing much.

FAUST. Have a good look at the brute. What do you take him for?

WAGNER. For a poodle who, as is the way of such,   275
    Is trailing his master, worrying out the scent.
FAUST. But don't you perceive how in wide spirals around us
    He is getting nearer and nearer of set intent?
    And, unless I'm wrong, a running fire
    Eddies behind him in his wake.   280
WAGNER. I can see nothing but a black poodle;
    It must be your eyes have caused this mistake.
FAUST. He is casting, it seems to me, fine nooses of magic
    About our feet as a snare.
WAGNER. *I* see him leaping round us uncertainly, timidly,   285
    Finding instead of his master two strangers there.
FAUST. The circle narrows; now he is near.
WAGNER. Just a dog, you see; no phantoms here.
    He growls and hesitates, grovels on the green
    And wags his tail. Pure dog routine.   290
FAUST. Heel, sir, heel! Come, fellow, come!
WAGNER. He is a real poodle noodle.
    Stand still and he'll sit up and beg;
    Speak to him and he's all over you;
    Lose something and he'll fetch it quick,   295
    He'll jump in the water after your stick.
FAUST. I think you're right, I cannot find a trace
    Of a spirit here; it is all a matter of training.
WAGNER. If a dog is well brought up, a wise man even
    Can come to be fond of him in such a case.   300
    Yes, he fully deserves your name upon his collar,
    He whom the students have found so apt a scholar.

FAUST'S STUDY

He enters with the poodle.

FAUST. I have forsaken field and meadow
    Which night has laid in a deep bed,
    Night that wakes our better soul
    With a holy and foreboding dread.
    Now wild desires are wrapped in sleep   5
    And all the deeds that burn and break,
    The love of Man is waking now,
    The love of God begins to wake.

    Poodle! Quiet! Don't run hither and thither!
    Leave my threshold! Why are you snuffling there?   10
    Lie down behind the stove and rest.
    Here's a cushion; it's my best.
    Out of doors on the mountain paths

You kept us amused by running riot;
But as my protégé at home   15
You'll only be welcome if you're quiet.

    Ah, when in our narrow cell
    The lamp once more imparts good cheer,
    Then in our bosom—in the heart
    That knows itself—then things grow clear.   20
    Reason once more begins to speak
    And the blooms of hope once more to spread;
    One hankers for the brooks of life,
    Ah, and for life's fountain head.

Don't growl, you poodle! That animal sound   25
Is not in tune with the holy music
By which my soul is girdled round.
We are used to human beings who jeer
At what they do not understand,
Who grouse at the good and the beautiful   30
Which often causes them much ado;
But must a dog snarl at it too?

But, ah, already, for all my good intentions
I feel contentment ebbing away in my breast.
Why must the stream so soon run dry   35
And we be left once more athirst?
I have experienced this so often;
Yet this defect has its compensation,
We learn to prize the supernatural
And hanker after revelation,   40
Which burns most bright and wins assent
Most in the New Testament.
I feel impelled to open the master text
And this once, with true dedication,
Take the sacred original   45
And make in my mother tongue my own translation.
    [*He opens a Bible.*]
It is written: In the beginning was the Word.
Here I am stuck at once. Who will help me on?
I am unable to grant the Word such merit,
I must translate it differently   50
If I am truly illumined by the spirit.
It is written: In the beginning was the Mind.
But why should my pen scour

43. *master text:* i.e., the Greek.   47. *In the beginning . . . Word:* John 1:1.

So quickly ahead? Consider that first line well.
Is it the Mind that effects and creates all things?   55
It *should* read: In the beginning was the Power.
Yet, even as I am changing what I have writ,
Something warns me not to abide by it.
The spirit prompts me, I see in a flash what I need,
And write: In the beginning was the Deed!   60

Dog! If we two are to share this room,
Leave off your baying,
Leave off your barking!
I can't have such a fellow staying
Around me causing all this bother.   65
One of us or the other
Will have to leave the cell.
Well?
I don't really like to eject you so
But the door is open, you may go.   70

But what? What do I see?
Can this really happen naturally?
Is it a fact or is it a fraud?
My dog is growing so long and broad!
He raises himself mightily,   75
That is not a dog's anatomy!
What a phantom have I brought to my house!
He already looks like a river horse
With fiery eyes and frightful jaws—
Aha! But I can give you pause!   80
For such a hybrid out of hell
Solomon's Key is a good spell.
    [SPIRITS *are heard in the passage.*]
SPIRITS. Captured within there is one of us!
    Wait without, follow him none of us!
    Like a fox in a snare   85
    An old hell-cat's trembling there.
    But on the alert!
    Fly against and athwart,
    To starboard and port,
    And he's out with a spurt!   90
    If help you can take him,
    Do not forsake him!
    For often, to earn it, he

82. *Solomon's Key:* the *Clavicula Salomonis,* a standard work used by magicians for conjuring; in many medie-val legends, Solomon was noted as a great magician.

      Helped our fraternity.

FAUST. First, to confront the beast,   95
      Be the Spell of the Four released:
            Salamander shall glow,
            Undine shall coil,
            Sylph shall vanish
            And gnome shall toil.   100
      One without sense
      Of the elements,
      Of their force
      And proper course,
      The spirits would never   105
      Own him for master.
            Vanish in flames,
            Salamander!
            Commingle in babble of streams,
            Undine!   110
            Shine meteor-like and majestic,
            Sylph!
            Bring help domestic,
            Lubber-fiend! Lubber-fiend!
            Step out of him and make an end!   115
      None of the Four
      Is the creature's core.
      He lies quite quiet and grins at me,
      I have not yet worked him injury.
      To exercise you   120
      I'll have to chastise you.
            Are you, rapscallion,
            A displaced devil?
            This sign can level
            Each dark battalion;   125
            Look at this sign!
      He swells up already with bristling spine.
            You outcast! Heed it—
            This name! Can you read it?
            The unbegotten one,
            Unpronounceable,   130
            Poured throughout Paradise,
            Heinously wounded one?
      Behind the stove, bound by my spells,
      Look, like an elephant it swells,   135
      Filling up all the space and more,

---

96. *Spell of the Four:* Salamanders were spirits of fire; undines, of water; sylphs. of air; and gnomes, of earth.

It threatens to melt away in mist.
Down from the ceiling! Down before—!
Down at your master's feet! Desist!
You see, I have not proved a liar;   140
I can burn you up with holy fire!
Do not await
The triply glowing light!
Do not await
My strongest brand of necromancy!   145
[*The mist subsides and* MEPHISTOPHELES *comes forward from
behind the stove, dressed like a travelling scholar.*]
MEPHISTOPHELES. What is the noise about? What might the gentle-
man fancy?
FAUST. So that is what the poodle had inside him!
A travelling scholar? That casus makes me laugh.
MEPHISTOPHELES. My compliments to the learned gentleman.
You have put me a sweat—not half!   150
FAUST. What is your name?
MEPHISTOPHELES. The question strikes me as petty
For one who holds the Word in such low repute,
Who, far withdrawn from all mere surface,
Aims only at the Essential Root.   155
FAUST. With you, you gentry, what is essential
The name more often than not supplies,
As is indeed only too patent
When they call you Fly-God, Corrupter, Father of Lies.
All right, who are you then?   160
MEPHISTOPHELES. A part of that Power
Which always wills evil, always procures good.
FAUST. What do you mean by this conundrum?
MEPHISTOPHELES. I am the Spirit which always denies.
And quite rightly; whatever has a beginning   165
Deserves to have an undoing;
It would be better if nothing began at all.
Thus everything that you call
Sin, destruction, Evil in short,
Is my own element, my resort.   170
FAUST. You call yourself a part, yet you stand before me whole?
MEPHISTOPHELES. This is the unassuming truth.
Whereas mankind, that little world of fools,
Commonly takes itself for a whole—
I am a part of the Part which in the beginning was all,   175

143. *triply glowing light:* perhaps
the Trinity, or a triangle with divergent rays.
153. *Word:* See l. 47 in this scene.

159. *Fly-God:* an almost literal translation of the name of the Philistine
deity Beelzebub.

A part of the darkness which gave birth to light,
To that haughty light which is struggling now to usurp
The ancient rank and realm of its mother Night,
And yet has no success, try as it will,
Being bound and clamped by bodies still.   180
It streams from bodies, bodies it beautifies,
A body clogs it when it would run,
And so, I hope, it won't be long
Till, bodies and all, it is undone.

FAUST. Ah, now I know your honourable profession!   185
  You cannot destroy on a large scale,
  So you are trying it on a small.

MEPHISTOPHELES. And, candidly, not getting far at all.
  That which stands over against the Nothing,
  The Something, I mean this awkward world,   190
  For all my endeavours up to date
  I have failed to get it under foot
  With waves, with storms, with earthquakes, fire—
  Sea and land after all stay put.
  And this damned stuff, the brood of beasts and men,   195
  There is no coming to grips with them;
  I've already buried heaps of them!
  And always new blood, fresh blood, circulates again.
  So it goes on, it's enough to drive one crazy.
  A thousand embryos extricate themselves   200
  From air, from water and from earth
  In wet and dry and hot and cold.
  Had I not made a corner in fire
  I should find myself without a berth.

FAUST. So you when faced with the ever stirring,   205
  The creative force, the beneficent,
  Counter with your cold devil's fist
  Spitefully clenched but impotent.
  You curious son of Chaos, why
  Not turn your hand to something else?   210

MEPHISTOPHELES. We will give it our serious attention—
  But more on that subject by and by.
  Might I for this time take my leave?

FAUST. Why you ask I cannot see.
  I have already made your acquaintance;   215
  When you feel like it, call on me.
  Here is the window, here is the door—
  And a chimney too—if it comes to that.

176. *darkness:* Mephistopheles here speaks as the Prince of Darkness, the rôle in Christianity acquired by the devil from the Persian Manichaean deity Ahriman.

MEPHISTOPHELES. I must confess; there's a slight impediment
    That stops me making my exit pat,   220
    The pentagram upon your threshold—
FAUST. So the witch's foot is giving you trouble?
    Then tell me, since you're worried by that spell,
    How did you ever enter, child of Hell?
    How was a spirit like you betrayed?   225
MEPHISTOPHELES. You study that sign! It's not well made;
    One of its corners, do you see,
    The outside one's not quite intact.
FAUST. A happy accident in fact!
    Which means you're in my custody?   230
    I did not intend to set a gin.
MEPHISTOPHELES. The dog—he noticed nothing, jumping in;
    The case has now turned round about
    And I, the devil, can't get out.
FAUST. Then why not leave there by the window?   235
MEPHISTOPHELES. It is a law for devils and phantoms all:
    By the way that we slip in by the same we must take our
        leave.
    One's free in the first, in the second one's a thrall.
FAUST. So Hell itself has its regulations?
    That's excellent; a contract in that case   240
    Could be made with you, you gentry—and definite?
MEPHISTOPHELES. What we promise, you will enjoy with no reservations,
    Nothing will be nipped off from it.
    But all this needs a little explaining
    And will keep till our next heart-to-heart;   245
    But now I beg and doubly beg you:
    Let me, just for now, depart.
FAUST. But wait yet a minute and consent
    To tell me first some news of moment.
MEPHISTOPHELES. Let me go now! I'll soon be back   250
    To be questioned to your heart's content.
FAUST. It was not I laid a trap for you,
    You thrust your own head in the noose.
    A devil in the hand's worth two in hell!
    The second time he'll be longer loose.   255
MEPHISTOPHELES. If you so wish it, I'm prepared
    To keep you company and stay;
    Provided that by my arts the time
    Be to your betterment whiled away.

---

221. *pentagram:* a magic five-pointed   principally the female incubus **or** witch.
star designed to keep away evil spirits,   222. *witch's foot:* the pentagram.

FAUST. I am in favour, carry on— 260
    But let your art be a pleasing one.
MEPHISTOPHELES. My friend, your senses will have more
    Gratification in this hour
    Than in a year's monotony.
    What the delicate spirits sing to you 265
    And the beauties that they bring to you
    Are no empty, idle wizardry.
    You'll have your sense of smell delighted,
    Your palate in due course excited,
    Your feelings rapt enchantingly. 270
    Preparation? There's no need,
    We are all here. Strike up! Proceed!
        [*The* SPIRITS *sing.*]
SPIRITS. Vanish, you darkling
        Arches above him,
        That a more witching 275
        Blue and enriching
        Sky may look in!
        If only the darkling
        Clouds were unravelled!
        Small stars are sparkling, 280
        Suns are more gently
        Shining within!
        Spiritual beauty
        Of the children of Heaven
        Swaying and bowing 285
        Floats in the air,
        Leanings and longings
        Follow them there;
        And ribbons of raiment
        The breezes have caught 290
        Cover the country,
        Cover the arbour
        Where, drowning in thought,
        Lovers exchange their
        Pledges for life. 295
        Arbour on arbour!
        Creepers run rife!
        Grapes in great wreathing
        Clusters are poured into
        Vats that are seething, 300
        Wines that are foaming
        Pour out in rivulets
        Rippling and roaming

Through crystalline stones,
Leaving the sight of   305
The highlands behind them,
Widening to lakes
Amid the delight of
Green-growing foothills.
And the winged creatures   310
Sipping their ecstasy,
Sunwards they fly,
Fly to discover
The glittering islands
Which bob on the wave-tops   315
Deceiving the eye.
There we can hear
Huzzaing in chorus,
A landscape of dancers
Extending before us,   320
All in the open,
Free as the air.
Some of them climbing
Over the peaks,
Some of them swimming   325
Over the lakes,
Or floating in space—
All towards existence,
All towards the distance
Of stars that will love them,   330
The blessing of grace.

MEPHISTOPHELES. He is asleep. That's fine, you airy, dainty young-
    sters
You have sung him a real cradle song.
For this performance I am in your debt.
You are not yet the man to hold the devil for long.   335
Play round him with your sweet dream trickeries
And sink him in a sea of untruth!
But to break the spell upon this threshold
What I need now is a rat's tooth.
And I needn't bother to wave a wand,   340
I can hear one rustling already, he'll soon respond.
The lord of rats, the lord of mice,
Of flies, frogs, bugs and lice,
Commands you to come out of that
And gnaw away this threshold, rat,   345
While he takes oil and gives it a few—
So there you come hopping? Quick on your cue!

Now get on the job! The obstructing point
Is on the edge and right in front.
One bite more and the work's done.
Now, Faust, till we meet again, dream on!   350
FAUST. [*Waking*] Am I defrauded then once more?
Does the throng of spirits vanish away like fog
To prove that the devil appeared to me in a dream
But what escaped was only a dog?   355

FAUST'S STUDY

The same room. Later.

FAUST. Who's knocking? Come in! Now who wants to annoy me?
MEPHISTOPHELES. [*Outside door*] It's I.
FAUST.   Come in!
MEPHISTOPHELES. [*Outside door*]
                    You must say 'Come in' three times.
FAUST. Come in then!   5
MEPHISTOPHELES. [*Entering*] Thank you; you overjoy me.
We two, I hope, we shall be good friends;
To chase those megrims of yours away
I am here like a fine young squire to-day,
In a suit of scarlet trimmed with gold   10
And a little cape of stiff brocade,
With a cock's feather in my hat
And at my side a long sharp blade,
And the most succinct advice I can give
Is that you dress up just like me,   15
So that uninhibited and free
You may find out what it means to live.
FAUST. The pain of earth's constricted life, I fancy,
Will pierce me still, whatever my attire;
I am too old for mere amusement,   20
Too young to be without desire.
How can the world dispel my doubt?
You must do without, you must do without!
That is the everlasting song
Which rings in every ear, which rings,   25
And which to us our whole life long
Every hour hoarsely sings.
I wake in the morning only to feel appalled,
My eyes with bitter tears could run
To see the day which in its course   30
Will not fulfil a wish for me, not one;

9. *a fine young squire:* In the popular plays based on the Faust legend, the devil often appeared as a monk when the play catered to a Protestant audience, and as a cavalier when the audience was predominantly Catholic.

The day which whittles away with obstinate carping
All pleasures—even those of anticipation,
Which makes a thousand grimaces to obstruct
My heart when it is stirring in creation.   35
And again, when night comes down, in anguish
I must stretch out upon my bed
And again no rest is granted me,
For wild dreams fill my mind with dread.
The God who dwells within my bosom   40
Can make my inmost soul react;
The God who sways my every power
Is powerless with external fact.
And so existence weighs upon my breast
And I long for death and life—life I detest.   45

MEPHISTOPHELES. Yet death is never a wholly welcome guest.

FAUST. O happy is he whom death in the dazzle of victory
Crowns with the bloody laurel in the battling swirl!
Or he whom after the mad and breakneck dance
He comes upon in the arms of a girl!   50
O to have sunk away, delighted, deleted,
Before the Spirit of the Earth, before his might!

MEPHISTOPHELES. Yet I know someone who failed to drink
A brown juice on a certain night.

FAUST. Your hobby is espionage—is it not?   55

MEPHISTOPHELES. Oh I'm not omniscient—but I know a lot.

FAUST. Whereas that tumult in my soul
Was stilled by sweet familiar chimes
Which cozened the child that yet was in me
With echoes of more happy times,   60
I now curse all things that encompass
The soul with lures and jugglery
And bind it in this dungeon of grief
With trickery and flattery.
Cursed in advance be the high opinion   65
That serves our spirit for a cloak!
Cursed be the dazzle of appearance
Which bows our senses to its yoke!
Cursed be the lying dreams of glory,
The illusion that our name survives!   70
Cursed be the flattering things we own,
Servants and ploughs, children and wives!
Cursed be Mammon when with his treasures
He makes us play the adventurous man

73. *Mammon:* the Aramaic word for
"riches," used in the New Testament;
medieval writers interpreted the word
as a proper noun, the name of the
devil, as representing covetousness or
avarice.

Or when for our luxurious pleasures 75
He duly spreads the soft divan!
A curse on the balsam of the grape!
A curse on the love that rides for a fall!
A curse on hope! A curse on faith!
And a curse on patience most of all! 80

[*The invisible* SPIRITS *sing again.*]

SPIRITS.   Woe! Woe!
You have destroyed it,
The beautiful world;
By your violent hand
'Tis downward hurled! 85
A half-god has dashed it asunder!
From under
We bear off the rubble to nowhere
And ponder
Sadly the beauty departed. 90
Magnipotent
One among men,
Magnificent
Build it again,
Build it again in your breast! 95
Let a new course of life
Begin
With vision abounding
And new songs resounding
To welcome it in! 100

MEPHISTOPHELES. These are the juniors
Of my faction.
Hear how precociously they counsel
Pleasure and action.
Out and away 105
From your lonely day
Which dries your senses and your juices
Their melody seduces.

Stop playing with your grief which battens
Like a vulture on your life, your mind! 110
The worst of company would make you feel
That you are a man among mankind.
Not that it's really my proposition
To shove you among the common men:
Though I'm not one of the Upper Ten, 115
If you would like a coalition
With me for your career through life,

I am quite ready to fit in,
I'm yours before you can say knife.
I am your comrade;
If you so crave,
I am your servant, I am your slave.

FAUST. And what have I to undertake in return?

MEPHISTOPHELES. Oh it's early days to discuss what that is.

FAUST. No, no, the devil is an egoist
And ready to do nothing gratis
Which is to benefit a stranger.
Tell me your terms and don't prevaricate!
A servant like you in the house is a danger.

MEPHISTOPHELES. I will bind myself to your service in this
world,
To be at your beck and never rest nor slack;
When we meet again on the other side,
In the same coin you shall pay me back.

FAUST. The other side gives me little trouble;
First batter this present world to rubble,
Then the other may rise—if that's the plan.
This earth is where my springs of joy have started,
And this sun shines on me when broken-hearted;
If I can first from them be parted,
Then let happen what will and can!
I wish to hear no more about it—
Whether there too men hate and love
Or whether in those spheres too, in the future,
There is a Below or an Above.

MEPHISTOPHELES. With such an outlook you can risk it.
Sign on the line! In these next days you will get
Ravishing samples of my arts;
I am giving you what never man saw yet.

FAUST. Poor devil, can *you* give anything ever?
Was a human spirit in its high endeavour
Even once understood by one of your breed?
Have you got food which fails to feed?
Or red gold which, never at rest,
Like mercury runs away through the hand?
A game at which one never wins?
A girl who, even when on my breast,
Pledges herself to my neighbour with her eyes?
The divine and lovely delight of honour
Which falls like a falling star and dies?
Show me the fruits which, before they are plucked, decay
And the trees which day after day renew their green!

MEPHISTOPHELES. Such a commission doesn't alarm me,
  I have such treasures to purvey.
  But, my good friend, the time draws on when we
  Should be glad to feast at our ease on something good.   165
FAUST. If ever I stretch myself on a bed of ease,
  Then I am finished! Is that understood?
  If ever your flatteries can coax me
  To be pleased with myself, if ever you cast
  A spell of pleasure that can hoax me—   170
  Then let *that* day be my last!
  That's my wager!
MEPHISTOPHELES. Done!
FAUST.   Let's shake!
  If ever I say to the passing moment   175
  'Linger a while! Thou art so fair!'
  Then you may cast me into fetters,
  I will gladly perish then and there!
  Then you may set the death-bell tolling,
  Then from my service you are free,   180
  The clock may stop, its hand may fall,
  And that be the end of time for me!
MEPHISTOPHELES. Think what you're saying, we shall not forget it.
FAUST. And you are fully within your rights;
  I have made no mad or outrageous claim.   185
  If I stay as I am, I am a slave—
  Whether yours or another's, it's all the same.
MEPHISTOPHELES. I shall this very day at the College Banquet
  Enter your service with no more ado,
  But just one point—As a life-and-death insurance   190
  I must trouble you for a line or two.
FAUST. So you, you pedant, you too like things in writing?
  Have you never known a man? Or a man's word? Never?
  Is it not enough that my word of mouth
  Puts all my days in bond for ever?   195
  Does not the world rage on in all its streams
  And shall a promise hamper *me*?
  Yet this illusion reigns within our hearts
  And from it who would be gladly free?
  Happy the man who can inwardly keep his word;   200
  Whatever the cost, he will not be loath to pay!
  But a parchment, duly inscribed and sealed,
  Is a bogey from which all wince away.
  The word dies on the tip of the pen
  And wax and leather lord it then.   205

188. *College Banquet:* actually the *Doctorschmaus*, or dinner given by a successful candidate for a Ph.D. degree.

What do you, evil spirit, require?
Bronze, marble, parchment, paper?
Quill or chisel or pencil of slate?
You may choose whichever you desire.

MEPHISTOPHELES. How can you so exaggerate   210
With such a hectic rhetoric?
Any little snippet is quite good—
And you sign it with one little drop of blood.

FAUST. If that is enough and is some use,
One may as well pander to your fad.   215

MEPHISTOPHELES. Blood is a very special juice.

FAUST. Only do not fear that I shall break this contract.
What I promise is nothing more
Than what all my powers are striving for.
I have puffed myself up too much, it is only   220
Your sort that really fits my case.
The great Earth Spirit has despised me
And Nature shuts the door in my face.
The thread of thoughts is snapped asunder,
I have long loathed knowledge in all its fashions.   225
In the depths of sensuality
Let us now quench our glowing passions!
And at once make ready every wonder
Of unpenetrated sorcery!
Let us cast ourselves into the torrent of time,   230
Into the whirl of eventfulness,
Where disappointment and success,
Pleasure and pain may chop and change
As chop and change they will and can;
It is restless action makes the man.   235

MEPHISTOPHELES. No limit is fixed for you, no bound;
If you'd like to nibble at everything
Or to seize upon something flying round—
Well, may you have a run for your money!
But seize your chance and don't be funny!   240

FAUST. I've told you, it is no question of happiness.
The most painful joy, enamoured hate, enlivening
Disgust—I devote myself to all excess.
My breast, now cured of its appetite for knowledge,
From now is open to all and every smart,   245
And what is allotted to the whole of mankind
That will I sample in my inmost heart,
Grasping the highest and lowest with my spirit,

---

213. *blood:* This method of confirming an agreement with the devil is
older than the Faust legend—in which
it always appears—and is partly a
parody of the rôle of blood in the Christian Sacrament.

Piling men's weal and woe upon my neck,
To extend myself to embrace all human selves
And to founder in the end, like them, a wreck.

MEPHISTOPHELES. O believe *me*, who have been chewing
These iron rations many a thousand year,
No human being can digest
This stuff, from the cradle to the bier.
This universe—believe a devil—
Was made for no one but a god!
He exists in eternal light
But *us* he has brought into the darkness
While *your* sole portion is day and night.

FAUST. I will all the same!

MEPHISTOPHELES. That's very nice.
There's only one thing I find wrong;
Time is short, art is long.
You could do with a little artistic advice.
Confederate with one of the poets
And let him flog his imagination
To heap all virtues on your head,
A head with such a reputation:
Lion's bravery,
Stag's velocity,
Fire of Italy,
Northern tenacity.
Let *him* find out the secret art
Of combining craft with a noble heart
And of being in love like a young man,
Hotly, but working to a plan.
Such a person—*I'd* like to meet him;
'Mr. Microcosm' is how I'd greet him.

FAUST. What am I then if fate must bar
My efforts to reach that crown of humanity
After which all my senses strive?

MEPHISTOPHELES. You are in the end . . . what you are.
You can put on full-bottomed wigs with a million locks,
You can put on stilts instead of your socks,
You remain for ever what you are.

FAUST. I feel my endeavours have not been worth a pin
When I raked together the treasures of the human mind,
If at the end I but sit down to find
No new force welling up within.
I have not a hair's breadth more of height,

250

255

260

265

270

275

280

285

290

279. *Mr. Microcosm:* i.e., man viewed as the epitome of the universe.

I am no nearer the Infinite.

MEPHISTOPHELES. My very good sir, you look at things
  Just in the way that people do;
  We must be cleverer than that   295
  Or the joys of life will escape from you.
  Hell! You have surely hands and feet,
  Also a head and you-know-what;
  The pleasures I gather on the wing,
  Are they less mine? Of course they're not!   300
  Suppose I can afford six stallions,
  I can add that horse-power to my score
  And dash along and be a proper man
  As if my legs were twenty-four.
  So good-bye to thinking! On your toes!   305
  The world's before us. Quick! Here goes!
  I tell you, a chap who's intellectual
  Is like a beast on a blasted heath
  Driven in circles by a demon
  While a fine green meadow lies round beneath.   310

FAUST. How do we start?

MEPHISTOPHELES.   We just say go—and skip.
  But please get ready for this pleasure trip.
        [*Exit* FAUST.]
  Only look down on knowledge and reason,
  The highest gifts that men can prize,   315
  Only allow the spirit of lies
  To confirm you in magic and illusion,
  And then I have you body and soul.
  Fate has given this man a spirit
  Which is always pressing onwards, beyond control,   320
  And whose mad striving overleaps
  All joys of the earth between pole and pole.
  Him shall I drag through the wilds of life
  And through the flats of meaninglessness,
  I shall make him flounder and gape and stick   325
  And to tease his insatiableness
  Hang meat and drink in the air before his watering lips;
  In vain he will pray to slake his inner thirst,
  And even had he not sold himself to the devil
  He would be equally accursed.[a]   330
        [*Re-enter* FAUST.]

FAUST. And now, where are we going?

a. Between Faust's exit and entrance, the translator omits a scene in which Mephistopheles cynically interviews one of Faust's students.

MEPHISTOPHELES.   Wherever you please.
  The small world, then the great for us.
  With what pleasure and what profit
  You will roister through the syllabus!   335
FAUST. But I, with this long beard of mine,
  I lack the easy social touch,
  I know the experiment is doomed;
  Out in the world I never could fit in much.
  I feel so small in company   340
  I'll be embarrassed constantly.
MEPHISTOPHELES. My friend, it will solve itself, any such mis-
      giving;
  Just trust yourself and you'll learn the art of living.
FAUST. Well, then, how do we leave home?
  Where are your grooms? Your coach and horses?   345
MEPHISTOPHELES. We merely spread this mantle wide,
  It will bear us off on airy courses.
  But do not on this noble voyage
  Cumber yourself with heavy baggage.
  A little inflammable gas which I'll prepare   350
  Will lift us quickly into the air.
  If we travel light we shall cleave the sky like a knife.
  Congratulations on your new course of life![a]

THE WITCH'S KITCHEN[b]

Every sort of witch prop. A large cauldron hangs over the fire.
MONKEYS *sit around it, seen through the fumes.*

MEPHISTOPHELES. Look, what a pretty species of monkey!
  She is the kitchen-maid, he is the flunkey.
  It seems your mistress isn't at home?
MONKEYS. Out at a rout!
        Out and about!   5
        By the chimney spout!
MEPHISTOPHELES. How long does she keep it up at night?
MONKEYS. As long as we warm our paws at this fire.
MEPHISTOPHELES. How do you like these delicate animals?
FAUST. I never saw such an outré sight.   10
  I find it nauseating, this crazy witchcraft!

350. *gas:* indicative of Goethe's
scientific interests. The first hydrogen
balloon was sent aloft in Paris in
1783, and several letters by Goethe refer
to this new experiment.
  a. The translator omits the next
scene, in Auerbach's Cellar, where Faust
and Mephistopheles join a group of
genial drinking companions and Mephistopheles performs the trick—traditional
in early Faust stories—of making wine
flow from the table.
  b. Certain transpositions have been
made in this scene. [Translator's note.]
  11. *crazy witchcraft:* In composing
this scene, Goethe may have had in
mind certain paintings by the Flemish
artists David Teniers the Younger
(1610–1690) and Pieter Breughel the
Younger (1564?–1638).

Do you promise me that I shall improve
In this cesspit of insanity?
Do I need advice from an old hag?
And can this filthy brew remove   15
Thirty years from my age? O vanity,
If you know nothing better than this!
My hope has already vanished away.
Surely Nature, surely a noble spirit
Has brought some better balm to the light of day?   20
MEPHISTOPHELES. My friend, you once more talk to the point.
There is also a natural means of rejuvenation;
But that is written in another book
And is a chapter that needs some explanation.
FAUST. I want to know it.   25
MEPHISTOPHELES.   Right. There is a means requires
No money, no physician, and no witch:
Away with you this moment back to the land,
And there begin to dig and ditch,
Confine yourself, confine your mind,   30
In a narrow round, ever repeating,
Let your diet be of the simplest kind,
Live with the beasts like a beast and do not think it cheating
To use your own manure to insure your crops are weighty!
Believe me, that is the best means   35
To keep you young till you are eighty.
FAUST. I am not used to it, I cannot change
My nature and take the spade in hand.
The narrow life is not my style at all.
MEPHISTOPHELES. Then it's a job for the witch to arrange.   40
FAUST. The hag—but why do we need just her?
Can you yourself not brew the drink?
MEPHISTOPHELES. A pretty pastime! I'd prefer
To build a thousand bridges in that time.
It is not only art and science   45
That this work needs but patience too.
A quiet spirit is busy at it for years
And time but fortifies the subtle brew.
And the most wonderful ingredients
Go into it—you couldn't fake it!   50
The devil taught it her, I admit;
The devil, however, cannot make it.
Tell me, you monkeys, you damned puppets,
What are you doing with that great globe?

44. *bridges:* The folk legend existed that the devil built bridges at the request of men. As a reward, he caught either the first or the thirteenth soul to cross each new bridge.

HE-MONKEY. This is the world: 55
    It rises and falls
    And rolls every minute;
    It rings like glass—
    But how soon it breaks!
    And there's nothing in it.   60
    It glitters here
    And here still more:
    I am alive!
    O my son, my dear,
    Keep away, keep away!   65
    You are bound to die!
    The shards are sharp,
    It was made of clay.

  [FAUST *has meanwhile been gazing in a mirror.*]

FAUST. What do I see in this magic mirror?
 What a heavenly image to appear!   70
 O Love, lend me the swiftest of your wings
 And waft me away into her sphere!
 But, alas, when I do not keep this distance,
 If to go nearer I but dare
 I can see her only as if there were mist in the air—   75
 The fairest image of a woman!
 But can Woman be so fair?
 In that shape in the mirror must I see the quintessence
 Of all the heavens—reclining there?
 Can such a thing be found on earth?   80

MEPHISTOPHELES. Naturally, when a God works six days like a black
 And at the end of it slaps himself on the back,
 Something should come of it of some worth.
 For this occasion look your fill.
 I can smell you out a sweetheart as good as this,   85
 And happy the man who has the luck
 To bear her home to wedded bliss.

  [*The* WITCH *enters down the chimney—violently.*]

WITCH. What goes on here?
    Who are you two?
    What d'you want here?
    Who has sneaked through?   90
    May the fever of fire
    Harrow your marrow!

MEPHISTOPHELES. Don't you know me, you bag of bones? You
  monster, you!
 Don't you know your lord and master?   95
 What prevents me striking you

And your monkey spirits, smashing you up like plaster?
Has my red doublet no more claim to fame?
Can you not recognize the cock's feather?
Have I concealed my countenance?   100
Must I myself announce my name?

WITCH. My lord, excuse this rude reception.
  It is only I miss your cloven foot.
  And where is your usual brace of ravens?

MEPHISTOPHELES. I'll forgive you this once, as an exception;   105
  Admittedly some time has pass't
  Since we two saw each other last.
  Culture too, which is licking the whole world level,
  Has latterly even reached the devil.
  The Nordic spook no longer commands a sale;   110
  Where can you see horns, claws or tail?
  And as regards the foot, which is my *sine qua non*,
  It would prejudice me in the social sphere;
  Accordingly, as many young men have done,
  I have worn false calves this many a year.   115

WITCH. Really and truly I'm knocked flat
  To see Lord Satan here again!

MEPHISTOPHELES. Woman, you must not call me that!

WITCH. Why! What harm is there in the name?

MEPHISTOPHELES. Satan has long been a myth without sense or
    sinew;   120
  Not that it helps humanity all the same,
  They are quit of the Evil One but the evil ones continue.
  You may call me the Noble Baron, that should do;
  I am a cavalier among other cavaliers,
  You needn't doubt my blood is blue—   125
    [*He makes an indecent gesture.*]

WITCH. Ha! Ha! Always true to type!
  You still have the humour of a guttersnipe!

MEPHISTOPHELES. Observe my technique, my friend—not a single
    hitch;
  This is the way to get round a witch.

WITCH. Now tell me, gentlemen, what do you want?   130

MEPHISTOPHELES. A good glass of your well-known juice.
  And please let us have your oldest vintage;
  When it's been kept it's twice the use.

WITCH. Delighted! Why, there's some here on the shelf—
  I now and then take a nip myself—   135
  And, besides, this bottle no longer stinks;

---

104. *brace of ravens:* Perhaps Goethe was thinking of the Norse god Odin, who owned two such birds: Hugin (Thought) and Munin (Memory).

You're welcome while I've a drop to give.
[*Aside*] But, if this man is unprepared when he drinks,
You very well know he has not an hour to live.
MEPHISTOPHELES. He's a good friend and it should set him up;   140
I'd gladly grant him the best of your kitchen,
So draw your circle and do your witching
And give the man a decent cup.
    [*The* WITCH *begins her conjuration.*]
FAUST. But, tell me, how will this mend my status?
These lunatic gestures, this absurd apparatus,   145
This most distasteful conjuring trick—
I've known it all, it makes me sick.
MEPHISTOPHELES. Pooh, that's just fooling, get it in focus,
And don't be such a prig for goodness' sake!
As a doctor she must do her hocus-pocus   150
So that when you have drunk your medicine it will take.
WITCH. The lofty power
        That is wisdom's dower,
        Concealed from great and clever,
        Don't use your brain   155
        And that's your gain—
        No trouble whatsoever.
FAUST. What nonsense is she saying to us?
My head is splitting; I've the sensation
Of listening to a hundred thousand   160
Idiots giving a mass recitation.
MEPHISTOPHELES. Enough, enough, you excellent Sibyl!
Give us your drink and fill the cup
Full to the brim and don't delay!
This draught will do my friend no injury;   165
He is a man of more than one degree
And has drunk plenty in his day.
    [*The* WITCH *gives* FAUST *the cup.*]
Now lower it quickly. Bottoms up!
And your heart will begin to glow and perk.
Now out of the circle! You mustn't rest.   170
WITCH. I hope the little drink will work.
MEPHISTOPHELES. [*To* WITCH] And you, if there's anything you
        want, all right;
Just mention it to me on Walpurgis Night.
[*To* FAUST] Come now, follow me instantly!
You've got to perspire, it's necessary,   175
That the drug may pervade you inside and out.

173. *Walpurgis Night:* the eve of May Day (May 1), when witches are supposed to assemble on the Brocken, a peak in the Harz Mountains.

I can teach you later to value lordly leisure
And you soon will learn with intensest pleasure
How Cupid stirs within and bounds about.
FAUST. Just one more look, one quick look, in the mirror!   180
That woman was too fair to be true.
MEPHISTOPHELES. No, no! The paragon of womanhood
Will soon be revealed in the flesh to you.
[*Aside*] With a drink like this in you, take care—
You'll soon see Helens everywhere.   185

IN THE STREET

FAUST *accosts* GRETCHEN *as she passes.*

FAUST. My pretty young lady, might I venture
To offer you my arm and my escort too?
GRETCHEN. I'm not a young lady nor am I pretty
And I can get home without help from you.
        [*She releases herself and goes off.*]
FAUST. By Heaven, she's beautiful, this child!   5
I have never seen her parallel.
So decorous, so virtuous,
And just a little pert as well.
The light of her cheek, her lip so red,
I shall remember till I'm dead!   10
The way that she cast down her eye
Is stamped on my heart as with a die;
And the way that she got rid of me
Was a most ravishing thing to see!
        [*Enter* MEPHISTOPHELES.]
Listen to me! Get me that girl!   15
MEPHISTOPHELES. Which one?
FAUST.   The one that just went past.
MEPHISTOPHELES. She? She was coming from her priest,
Absolved from her sins one and all;
I'd crept up near the confessional.   20
An innocent thing. Innocent? Yes!
At church with nothing to confess!
Over that girl I have no power.
FAUST. Yet she's fourteen if she's an hour.
MEPHISTOPHELES. Why, you're talking like Randy Dick   25
Who covets every lovely flower
And all the favours, all the laurels,
He fancies are for him to pick;

185. *Helens:* Faust marries Helen
of Troy in the second part of *Faust*.
25. *Randy Dick:* in the original
German, "Hans Liederlich"—i.e., a
profligate, since *liederlich* means "careless" or "dissolute."

But it doesn't always work out like that.

FAUST. My dear Professor of Ancient Morals,　　30
　Spare me your trite morality!
　I tell you straight—and hear me right—
　Unless this object of delight
　Lies in my arms this very night,
　At midnight we part company.　　35

MEPHISTOPHELES. Haven't you heard: more haste less speed?
　A fortnight is the least I need
　Even to work up an occasion.

FAUST. If I had only seven hours clear,
　I should not need the devil here　　40
　To bring *this* quest to consummation.

MEPHISTOPHELES. It's almost French, your line of talk;
　I only ask you not to worry.
　Why make your conquest in a hurry?
　The pleasure is less by a long chalk　　45
　Than when you first by hook and by crook
　Have squeezed your doll and moulded her,
　Using all manner of poppycock
　That foreign novels keep in stock.

FAUST. I am keen enough without all that.　　50

MEPHISTOPHELES. Now, joking apart and without aspersion,
　You cannot expect, I tell you flat,
　This beautiful child in quick reversion.
　Immune to all direct attack—
　We must lay our plots behind her back.　　55

FAUST. Get me something of my angel's!
　Carry me to her place of rest!
　Get me a garter of my love's!
　Get me a kerchief from her breast!

MEPHISTOPHELES. That you may see the diligent fashion　　60
　In which I shall abet your passion,
　We won't let a moment waste away,
　I will take you to her room to-day.

FAUST. And shall I see her? Have her?

MEPHISTOPHELES.　　　　　　　　No!　　65
　She will be visiting a neighbour.
　But you in the meanwhile, quite alone,
　Can stay in her aura in her room
　And feast your fill on joys to come.

FAUST. Can we go now?　　70

MEPHISTOPHELES.　　　　　It is still too soon.

---

30. *Professor:* in the original German, Herr Magister Lobesan ("Master Worshipful")—stuffed shirt, or academic prig.

FAUST. Then a present for her! Get me one!
    [*Exit* FAUST.]
MEPHISTOPHELES. Presents already? Fine. A certain hit!
  I know plenty of pretty places
  And of long-buried jewel-cases;   75
  I must take stock of them a bit.

GRETCHEN'S ROOM

GRETCHEN. [*Alone, doing her hair*] I'd give a lot to be able to say
  Who the gentleman was to-day.
  He cut a fine figure certainly
  And is sprung from nobility;
  His face showed that—Besides, you see,   5
  He'd otherwise not have behaved so forwardly.
      [*She goes out; then* MEPHISTOPHELES *and* FAUST *enter.*]
MEPHISTOPHELES. Come in—very quietly—Only come in!
FAUST. [*After a silence*] I ask you: please leave me alone!
MEPHISTOPHELES. Not all girls keep their room so clean.
FAUST. [*Looking around*] Welcome, sweet gleaming of the
    gloaming   10
  That through this sanctuary falls aslope!
  Seize on my heart, sweet fever of love
  That lives and languishes on the dews of hope!
  What a feeling of quiet breathes around me,
  Of order, of contentedness!   15
  What fulness in this poverty,
  And in this cell what blessedness!

  Here I could while away hour after hour.
  It was here, O Nature, that your fleeting dreams
  Brought this born angel to full flower.   20
  Here lay the child and the warm life
  Filled and grew in her gentle breast,
  And here the pure and holy threads
  Wove a shape of the heavenliest.

  And you! What brought you here to-day?   25
  Why do I feel this deep dismay?
  What do you want here? Why is your heart so sore?
  Unhappy Faust! You are Faust no more.

  Is this an enchanted atmosphere?
  To have her at once was all my aim,   30
  Yet I feel my will dissolve in a lovesick dream.
  Are we the sport of every current of air?

And were she this moment to walk in,
You would pay for this outrage, how you would pay!
The big man, now, alas, so small,   35
Would lie at her feet melted away.
MEPHISTOPHELES. Quick! I can see her coming below.
FAUST. Out, yes out! I'll never come back!
MEPHISTOPHELES. Here is a casket, it's middling heavy,
I picked it up in a place I know.   40
Only put it at once here in the cupboard,
I swear she won't believe her eyes;
I put some nice little trinkets in it
In order to win a different prize.
Still child is child and a game's a game.   45
FAUST. I don't know; shall I?
MEPHISTOPHELES.   You ask? For shame!
Do you perhaps intend to keep the spoil?
Then I advise Your Lustfulness
To save these hours that are so precious   50
And save me any further toil.
I hope you aren't avaricious.
After scratching my head so much and twisting my hands—
    [*He puts the casket in the cupboard.*]
Now quick! We depart!
In order to sway the dear young thing   55
To meet the dearest wish of your heart;
And *you* assume
A look that belongs to the lecture room,
As if Physics and Metaphysics too
Stood grey as life in front of you!   60
Come on!
    [*They go out; then* GRETCHEN *reappears.*]
GRETCHEN. It is so sultry, so fusty here,
And it's not even so warm outside.
I feel as if I don't know what—
I wish my mother would appear.   65
I'm trembling all over from top to toe—
I'm a silly girl to get frightened so.
    [*She sings as she undresses.*]
    There was a king in Thule
    Was faithful to the grave,

---

68. *Thule:* the fabled *ultima Thule* of Latin literature—those distant lands just beyond the reach of every explorer. In Roman times, the phrase probably denoted the Shetland Islands. Goethe wrote this ballad in 1774; it was published and set to music in 1782. The poem also served as the inspiration for the slow movement of Mendelssohn's *Italian Symphony.*

To whom his dying lady   70
A golden winecup gave.

He drained it at every banquet—
A treasure none could buy;
Whenever he filled and drank it
The tears o'erflowed his eye.   75

And when his days were numbered
He numbered land and pelf;
He left his heir his kingdom,
The cup he kept himself.

He sat at the royal table   80
With his knights of high degree
In the lofty hall of his fathers
In the castle on the sea.

There stood the old man drinking
The last of the living glow,   85
Then threw the sacred winecup
Into the waves below.

He saw it fall and falter
And founder in the main;
His eyelids fell, thereafter   90
He never drank again.

    [*She opens the cupboard to put away her clothes and sees
    the casket.*]

How did this lovely casket get in here?
I locked the cupboard, I'm quite sure.
But what can be in it? It's very queer.
Perhaps someone left it here in pawn   95
And my mother gave him a loan on it.
Here's a little key tied on with tape—
I've a good mind to open it.
What is all this? My God! But see!
I have never come across such things.   100
Jewels—that would suit a countess
At a really grand festivity.
To whom can these splendid things belong?

    [*She tries on the jewels and looks in the looking-glass.*]

If only the ear-rings belonged to me!
They make one look quite differently.   105
What is the use of looks and youth?
That's all very well and fine in truth

But people leave it all alone,
They praise you and pity you in one;
Gold is their sole   110
Concern and goal.
Alas for us who have none!

A WALK

Elsewhere and later. MEPHISTOPHELES *joins* FAUST.

MEPHISTOPHELES. By every despised love! By the elements of hell!
  I wish I knew something worse to provide a curse as well!
FAUST. What's the trouble? What's biting you?
  I never saw such a face in my life.
MEPHISTOPHELES. I would sell myself to the devil this minute   5
  If only I weren't a devil too.
FAUST. What is it? Are you mad? Or sick?
  It suits you to rage like a lunatic!
MEPHISTOPHELES. Imagine! The jewels that Gretchen got,
  A priest has gone and scooped the lot!   10
  Her mother got wind of it and she
  At once had the horrors secretly.
  That woman has a nose beyond compare,
  She's always snuffling in the Book of Prayer,
  And can tell by how each object smells   15
  If it is sacred or something else;
  So the scent of the jewels tells her clear
  There's nothing very blessed here.
  'My child,' she cries, 'unrighteous wealth
  Invests the soul, infects the health.   20
  We'll dedicate it to the Virgin
  And *she'll* make heavenly manna burgeon!'
  Gretchen's face, you could see it fall;
  She thought: 'It's a gift-horse after all,
  And he *can't* be lacking in sanctity   25
  Who brought it here so handsomely!'
  The mother had a priest along
  And had hardly started up her song
  Before he thought things looked all right
  And said: 'Very proper and above board!   30
  Self-control is its own reward.
  The Church has an excellent appetite,
  She has swallowed whole countries and the question
  Has never arisen of indigestion.
  Only the Church, my dears, can take   35
  Ill-gotten goods without stomach-ache!'

FAUST. That is a custom the world through,
    A Jew and a king observe it too.
MEPHISTOPHELES. So brooch, ring, chain he swipes at speed
    As if they were merely chicken-feed,   40
    Thanks them no more and no less for the casket
    Than for a pound of nuts in a basket,
    Promises Heaven will provide
    And leaves them extremely edified.
FAUST. And Gretchen?   45
MEPHISTOPHELES.   Sits and worries there,
    Doesn't know what to do and doesn't care,
    Thinks day and night on gold and gem,
    Still more on the man who presented them.
FAUST. My sweetheart's grief distresses me.   50
    Get her more jewels instantly!
    The first lot barely deserved the name.
MEPHISTOPHELES. So the gentleman thinks it all a nursery game!
FAUST. Do what I tell you and get it right;
    Don't let her neighbour out of your sight.   55
    And don't be a sloppy devil; contrive
    A new set of jewels. Look alive!
        [*Exit* FAUST.]
MEPHISTOPHELES. Yes, my dear sir, with all my heart.
    This is the way that a fool in love
    Puffs away to amuse his lady   60
    Sun and moon and the stars above.

MARTHA'S HOUSE

MARTHA. [*Alone*] My dear husband, God forgive him,
    His behaviour has *not* been without a flaw!
    Careers away out into the world
    And leaves me alone to sleep on straw.
    And yet I never trod on his toes,   5
    I loved him with all my heart, God knows. [*Sobs.*]
    Perhaps he is even dead—O fate!
    If I'd only a death certificate!
        [GRETCHEN *enters.*]
GRETCHEN. Frau Martha!
MARTHA.   Gretelchen! What's up?   10
GRETCHEN. My legs are sinking under me,
    I've just discovered in my cupboard
    Another casket—of ebony,
    And things inside it, such a store,
    Far richer than the lot before.   15
MARTHA. You mustn't mention it to your mother;

She'd take it straight to the priest—like the other.
GRETCHEN. But only look! Just look at this!
MARTHA. O you lucky little Miss!
GRETCHEN. I daren't appear in the street, I'm afraid,   20
Or in church either, thus arrayed.
MARTHA. Just you visit me often here
And put on the jewels secretly!
Walk up and down for an hour in front of my glass
And that will be fun for you and me;   25
And then an occasion may offer, a holiday,
Where one can let them be seen in a gradual way;
A necklace to start with, then a pearl ear-ring; your mother
Most likely won't see; if she does one can think up something
    or other.
GRETCHEN. But who brought these two cases, who could it be?   30
It doesn't seem quite right to me.
    [*Knocking.*]
My God! My mother? Is that her?
MARTHA. It is a stranger. Come in, sir!
    [*Enter* MEPHISTOPHELES.]
MEPHISTOPHELES. I have made so free as to walk straight in;
The ladies will pardon me? May I begin   35
By inquiring for a Frau Martha Schwerdtlein?
MARTHA. That's me. What might the gentleman want?
MEPHISTOPHELES. [*Aside to* MARTHA] Now I know who you are,
    that's enough for me;
You have very distinguished company.
Forgive my bursting in so soon;   40
I will call again in the afternoon.
MARTHA. Imagine, child, in the name of Piety!
The gentleman takes you for society.
GRETCHEN. I'm a poor young thing, not at all refined;
My God, the gentleman is too kind.   45
These jewels and ornaments aren't my own.
MEPHISTOPHELES. Oh, it's not the jewellery alone;
She has a presence, a look so keen—
How delighted I am that I may remain.
MARTHA. What is your news? I cannot wait—   50
MEPHISTOPHELES. I wish I'd a better tale to relate.
I trust this will not earn me a beating:
Your husband is dead and sends his greeting.
MARTHA. Dead? The good soul? Oh why! Oh why!
My husband is dead! Oh I shall die!   55
GRETCHEN. Oh don't, dear woman, despair so.

36. *Schwerdtlein:* literally. "little sword." Her husband is a soldier.

MEPHISTOPHELES. Listen to my tale of woe!

GRETCHEN. Now, while I live, may I never love;
  Such a loss would bring me to my grave.

MEPHISTOPHELES. Joy must have grief, grief must have joy.   60

MARTHA. How was his end? Oh tell it me.

MEPHISTOPHELES. He lies buried in Padua
  At the church of Holy Anthony,
  In properly consecrated ground
  Where he sleeps for ever cool and sound.   65

MARTHA. Have you nothing else for me? Is that all?

MEPHISTOPHELES. Yes, a request; it's heavy and fat.
  You must have three hundred masses said for his soul.
  My pockets are empty apart from that.

MARTHA. What! Not a trinket? Not a token?   70
  What every prentice keeps at the bottom of his bag
  And saves it up as a souvenir
  And would sooner starve and sooner beg—

MEPHISTOPHELES. Madam, you make me quite heart-broken.
  But, really and truly, he didn't squander his money.   75
  And, besides, he repented his mistakes,
  Yes, and lamented still more his unlucky breaks.

GRETCHEN. Alas that men should be so unlucky!
  Be assured I shall often pray that he may find rest above.

MEPHISTOPHELES. *You* deserve to be taken straight to the altar;   80
  You are a child a man could love.

GRETCHEN. No, no, it's not yet time for that.

MEPHISTOPHELES. Then, if not a husband, a lover will do.
  It's one of the greatest gifts of Heaven
  To hold in one's arms a thing like you.   85

GRETCHEN. That is not the custom of our race.

MEPHISTOPHELES. Custom or not, it's what takes place.

MARTHA. But tell me!

MEPHISTOPHELES.   His deathbed, where I stood,
  Was something better than a dungheap—   90
  Half-rotten straw; however, he died like a Christian
  And found he had still a great many debts to make good.
  How thoroughly, he cried, I must hate myself
  To leave my job and my wife like that on the shelf!
  When I remember it, I die!   95
  If only she would forgive me here below!

MARTHA. Good man! I have forgiven him long ago.

MEPHISTOPHELES. All the same, God knows, she was more at fault
      than I.

63. *Anthony:* Mephistopheles' lie acquires added irony from the fact that
this is one of Padua's most famous
churches, its basilica holding the bones
of St. Anthony.

MARTHA. That's a lie! To think he lied at the point of death!

MEPHISTOPHELES. He certainly fibbed a bit with his last breath,   100
  If I'm half a judge of the situation.
  I had no need, said he, to gape for recreation;
  First getting children, then getting bread to feed 'em—
  And bread in the widest sense, you know—
  And I couldn't even eat my share in peace.   105

MARTHA. So all my love, my loyalty, went for naught,
  My toiling and moiling without cease!

MEPHISTOPHELES. Not at all; he gave it profoundest thought.
  When I left Malta—that was how he began—
  I prayed for my wife and children like one demented   110
  And Heaven heard me and consented
  To let us capture a Turkish merchantman,
  With a treasure for the Sultan himself on board.
  Well, bravery got its due reward
  And I myself, as was only fit,   115
  I got a decent cut of it.

MARTHA. Eh! Eh! How? Where? Has he perhaps buried it?

MEPHISTOPHELES. Who knows where the four winds now have
            carried it?
  As he lounged round Naples, quite unknown,
  A pretty lady made him her friend,   120
  She was so fond of him, so devoted,
  He wore her colours at his blessed end.

MARTHA. The crook! The robber of his children!
  Could no misery, no poverty,
  Check the scandalous life he led!   125

MEPHISTOPHELES. You see! That is just why he's dead.
  However, if I were placed like you,
  I would mourn him modestly for a year
  While looking round for someone new.

MARTHA. Ah God! My first one was so dear,   130
  His like in this world will be hard to discover.
  There could hardly be a more sweet little fool than mine.
  It was only he was too fond of playing the rover,
  And of foreign women and foreign wine,
  And of the God-damned gaming-table.   135

MEPHISTOPHELES. Now, now, he might have still got by
  If he on his part had been able
  To follow your suit and wink an eye.
  With that proviso, I swear, I too
  Would give an engagement ring to you.   140

MARTHA. The gentleman is pleased to be witty.

MEPHISTOPHELES. [*Aside*] I had better go while the going's good;

She'd hold the devil to his word, she would!
  And how is it with *your* heart, my pretty?
GRETCHEN. What does the gentleman mean?   145
MEPHISTOPHELES. [*Aside*]   Good, innocent child!
  Farewell, ladies!
GRETCHEN.   Farewell!
MARTHA.   O quickly! Tell me;
  I'd like to have the evidence filed   150
  Where, how and when my treasure died and was buried.
  I have always liked things orderly and decent
  And to read of his death in the weeklies would be pleasant.
MEPHISTOPHELES. Yes, Madam, when two witnesses are agreed,
  The truth, as we all know, is guaranteed;   155
  And I have a friend, an excellent sort,
  I'll get him to swear you this in court.
  I'll bring him here.
MARTHA.   O yes! Please do!
MEPHISTOPHELES. And the young lady will be here too?   160
  He's an honest lad. He's been around,
  His politeness to ladies is profound.
GRETCHEN. I'll be all blushes in his presence.
MEPHISTOPHELES. No king on earth should so affect you.
MARTHA. Behind the house there—in my garden—   165
  This evening—both of you—we'll expect you.

IN THE STREET

FAUST. How is it? Going ahead? Will it soon come right?
MEPHISTOPHELES. Excellent! Do I find you all on fire?
  Gretchen is yours before many days expire.
  You will see her at Martha's, her neighbour's house to-night
  And that's a woman with a special vocation,   5
  As it were, for the bawd-cum-gipsy occupation.
FAUST. Good!
MEPHISTOPHELES. But there is something *we* must do.
FAUST. One good turn deserves another. True.
MEPHISTOPHELES. It only means the legal attesting   10
  That her husband's played-out limbs are resting
  At Padua in consecrated ground.
FAUST. Very smart! I suppose we begin by going to Padua!
MEPHISTOPHELES. There's no need for that. What a simple lad
      you are!
  Only bear witness and don't ask questions.   15
FAUST. The scheme's at an end if you have no better suggestions.
MEPHISTOPHELES. Oh there you go! What sanctity!
  Is this the first time in your life

You have committed perjury?
God and the world and all that moves therein,   20
Man and the way his emotions and thoughts take place,
Have you not given downright definitions
Of these with an iron breast and a brazen face?
And if you will only look below the surface,
You must confess you knew as much of these   25
As you know to-day of Herr Schwerdtlein's late decease.

FAUST. You are and remain a sophist and a liar.

MEPHISTOPHELES. Quite so—if that is as deep as you'll inquire.
  Won't you to-morrow on your honour
  Befool poor Gretchen and swear before her   30
  That all your soul is set upon her?

FAUST. And from my heart.

MEPHISTOPHELES.   That's nice of you!
  And your talk of eternal faith and love,
  Of one single passion enthroned above   35
  All others—will that be heartfelt too?

FAUST. Stop! It will! If I have feeling, if I
  Feel this emotion, this commotion,
  And can find no name to call it by;
  If then I sweep the world with all my senses casting   40
  Around for words and all the highest titles
  And call this flame which burns my vitals
  Endless, everlasting, everlasting,
  Is that a devilish game of lies?

MEPHISTOPHELES. I'm right all the same.   45

FAUST.   Listen! Mark this well,
  I beg you, and spare me talking till I'm hoarse:
  The man who *will* be right, provided he has a tongue,
  Why, he'll be right of course.
  But come, I'm tired of listening to your voice;   50
  You're right, the more so since I have no choice.

MARTHA'S GARDEN

They are walking in pairs: MARTHA *with* MEPHISTOPHELES,
GRETCHEN *on* FAUST'S *arm.*

GRETCHEN. The gentleman's only indulging me, I feel,
  And condescending, to put me to shame.
  You travellers are all the same,
  You put up with things out of sheer good will.
  I know too well that my poor conversation   5
  Can't entertain a person of your station.

FAUST. One glance from you, one word, entertains me more

Than all this world's wisdom and lore.
    [*He kisses her hand.*]
GRETCHEN. Don't go to such inconvenience! How could you kiss
    my hand?
It is so ugly, it is so rough.   10
I have had to work at Heaven knows what!
My mother's exacting, true enough.
    [*They pass on.*]
MARTHA. And you, sir, do you always move round like this?
MEPHISTOPHELES. Oh, business and duty keep us up to the min-
    ute!
With what regret one often leaves a place   15
And yet one cannot ever linger in it.
MARTHA. That may go in one's salad days—
    To rush all over the world at random;
    But the evil time comes on apace
    And to drag oneself to the grave a lonely bachelor   20
    Is never much good in any case.
MEPHISTOPHELES. The prospect alarms me at a distant glance.
MARTHA. Then, worthy sir, be wise while you have the chance.
    [*They pass on.*]
GRETCHEN. Yes, out of sight, out of mind!
You are polite to your finger-ends   25
But you have lots of clever friends
Who must leave *me* so far behind.
FAUST. Believe me, dearest, what the world calls clever
More often is vanity and narrowness.
GRETCHEN.   What?   30
FAUST. Alas that simplicity, that innocence,
    Cannot assess itself and its sacred value ever!
    That humility, lowliness, the highest gifts
    That living Nature has shared out to men—
GRETCHEN. Only think of *me* one little minute,   35
I shall have time enough to think of you again.
FAUST. You are much alone, I suppose?
GRETCHEN. Yes, our household's only small
But it needs running after all.
We have no maid; I must cook and sweep and knit   40
And sew and be always on the run,
And my mother looks into every detail—
Each single one.
Not that she has such need to keep expenses down;
We could spread ourselves more than some others do;   45
My father left us a decent property,

14. *business:* Mephistopheles speaks as a traveling salesman.

A little house with a garden outside town.
However, my days at the present are pretty quiet;
My brother's in the army,
My little sister is dead.   50
The child indeed had worn me to a thread;
Still, all that trouble, I'd have it again, I'd try it,
I loved her so.

FAUST.   An angel, if she was like you!

GRETCHEN. I brought her up, she was very fond of me.   55
She was born after my father died,
We gave my mother up for lost,
Her life was at such a low, low tide,
And she only got better slowly, bit by bit;
The poor little creature, she could not even   60
Think for a minute of suckling it;
And so I brought her up quite alone
On milk and water; so she became my own.
On my own arm, on my own knee,
She smiled and kicked, grew fair to see.   65

FAUST. You felt, I am sure, the purest happiness.

GRETCHEN. Yes; and—be sure—many an hour of distress.
The little one's cradle stood at night
Beside my bed; she could hardly stir
But I was awake,   70
Now having to give her milk, now into my bed with her,
Now, if she went on crying, try to stop her
By getting up and dandling her up and down the room,
And then first thing in the morning stand at the copper;
Then off to the market and attend to the range,   75
And so on day after day, never a change.
Living like that, one can't always feel one's best;
But food tastes better for it, so does rest.

                    [*They pass on.*]

MARTHA. No, the poor women don't come out of it well,
A *vieux garçon* is a hard nut to crack.   80

MEPHISTOPHELES. It only rests with you and your like
To put me on a better tack.

MARTHA. Tell me, sir: have you never met someone you fancy?
Has your heart been nowhere involved among the girls?

MEPHISTOPHELES. The proverb says: A man's own fireside   85
And a good wife are gold and pearls.

MARTHA. I mean, have you never felt any inclination?

MEPHISTOPHELES. I've generally been received with all consideration.

MARTHA. What I wanted to say: has your heart never been serious?

MEPHISTOPHELES. To make a joke to a woman is always precarious.

MARTHA. Oh you don't understand me!

MEPHISTOPHELES. Now *that* I really mind!
But I do understand—that you are very kind.
  [*They pass on.*]

FAUST. You knew me again, you little angel,
  As soon as you saw me enter the garden?   95

GRETCHEN. Didn't you see me cast down my eyes?

FAUST. And the liberty that I took you pardon?
  The impudence that reared its head
  When you lately left the cathedral door.

GRETCHEN. I was upset; it had never happened before; 100
  No one could ever say anything bad of me—
  Oh can he, I thought, have seen in my behaviour
  Any cheekiness, any impropriety?
  The idea, it seemed, had come to you pat:
  'I can treat this woman just like that'.   105
  I must admit I did not know what it was
  In my heart that began to make me change my view,
  But indeed I was angry with myself because
  I could not be angrier with you.

FAUST. Sweet love!

GRETCHEN. Wait a moment!   110
  [*She plucks a flower and starts picking off the petals.*]

FAUST. What is that? A bouquet?

GRETCHEN. No, only a game.

FAUST. A what?

GRETCHEN. You will laugh at me. Go away!   115
  [GRETCHEN *murmurs.*]

FAUST. What are you murmuring?

GRETCHEN. Loves me—Loves me not—

FAUST. You flower from Heaven's garden plot!

GRETCHEN. Loves me—Not—Loves me—Not—
  Loves me!   120

FAUST. Yes, child. What this flower has told you
  Regard it as God's oracle. He loves you!
  Do you know the meaning of that? He loves you!
  [*He takes her hands.*]

GRETCHEN. Oh I feel so strange.

FAUST. Don't shudder. Let this look,   125
  Let this clasp of the hand tell you
  What mouth can never express:
  To give oneself up utterly and feel
  A rapture which must be everlasting.

Everlasting! Its end would be despair.   130
No; no end! No end!

> [*She breaks away from him and runs off. After a moment's
> thought he follows her.*]

MARTHA. [*Approaching*] The night's coming on.

MEPHISTOPHELES.   Yes—and we must go.

MARTHA. I would ask you to remain here longer
But this is a terrible place, you know.   135
It's as if no one were able to shape at
Any vocation or recreation
But must have his neighbour's comings and goings to gape at
And, whatever one does, the talk is unleashed, unfurled.
And our little couple?   140

MEPHISTOPHELES.   Carefree birds of summer!
Flown to the summerhouse.

MARTHA.   He seems to like her.

MEPHISTOPHELES. And vice versa. That is the way of the world.

A SUMMERHOUSE

GRETCHEN *runs in and hides behind the door.*

GRETCHEN. He comes!

FAUST. [*Entering*]   You rogue! Teasing me so!
I've caught you!

> [*He kisses her.*]

GRETCHEN.   Dearest! I love you so!

> [MEPHISTOPHELES *knocks.*]

FAUST. Who's there?

MEPHISTOPHELES.   A friend.   5

FAUST.   A brute!

MEPHISTOPHELES.   It is time to part, you know.

MARTHA. [*Joining them*] Yes, it is late, sir.

FAUST.   May I not see you home?   10

GRETCHEN. My mother would—Farewell!

FAUST.   I must go then?
Farewell!

MARTHA.   Adieu!

GRETCHEN.   Let us soon meet again!   15

> [FAUST *and* MEPHISTOPHELES *leave.*]

Dear God! A man of such a kind,
What things must go on in his mind!
I can only blush when he talks to me;
Whatever he says, I must agree.
Poor silly child, I cannot see   20
What it is he finds in me.

FOREST AND CAVERN

FAUST. [*Alone*] Exalted Spirit, you gave me, gave me all
    I prayed for. Aye, and it is not in vain
    That you have turned your face in fire upon me.
    You gave me glorious Nature for my kingdom
    With power to feel her and enjoy her. Nor   5
    Is it a mere cold wondering glance you grant me
    But you allow me to gaze into her depths
    Even as into the bosom of a friend.
    Aye, you parade the ranks of living things
    Before me and you teach me to know my brothers   10
    In the quiet copse, in the water, in the air.
    And when the storm growls and snarls in the forest
    And the giant pine falls headlong, bearing away
    And crushing its neighbours, bough and bole and all,
    With whose dull fall the hollow hill resounds,   15
    Then do you carry me off to a sheltered cave
    And show me myself, and wonders of my own breast
    Unveil themselves in their deep mystery.
    And now that the clear moon rises on my eyes
    To soften things, now floating up before me   20
    From walls of rocks and from the dripping covert
    Come silver forms of the past which soothe and temper
    The dour delight I find in contemplation.

    That nothing perfect falls to men, oh now
    I feel that true. In addition to the rapture   25
    Which brings me near and nearer to the gods
    You gave me that companion whom already
    I cannot do without, though cold and brazen
    He lowers me in my own eyes and with
    One whispered word can turn your gifts to nothing.   30
    He is always busily fanning in my breast
    A fire of longing for that lovely image.
    So do I stagger from desire to enjoyment
    And in enjoyment languish for desire.
        [MEPHISTOPHELES *enters.*]
MEPHISTOPHELES. Haven't you yet had enough of this kind of
    life?   35
    How can it still appeal to you?
    It is all very well to try it once,
    Then one should switch to something new.
FAUST. I wish you had something else to do
    On my better days than come plaguing me.   40
MEPHISTOPHELES. Now, now! I'd gladly leave you alone;

You needn't suggest it seriously.
So rude and farouche and mad a friend
Would certainly be little loss.
One has one's hands full without end! 45
One can never read in the gentleman's face
What he likes or what should be left alone.

FAUST. That is exactly the right tone!
He must be thanked for causing me ennui.

MEPHISTOPHELES. Poor son of earth, what sort of life 50
Would you have led were it not for me?
The flim-flams of imagination,
I have cured you of those for many a day.
But for me, this terrestrial ball
Would already have seen you flounce away. 55
Why behave as an owl behaves
Moping in rocky clefts and caves?
Why do you nourish yourself like a toad that sips
From moss that oozes, stone that drips?
A pretty pastime to contrive! 60
The doctor in you is still alive.

FAUST. Do you comprehend what a new and vital power
This wandering in the wilderness has given me?
Aye, with even an inkling of such joy,
You would be devil enough to grudge it me. 65

MEPHISTOPHELES. A supernatural gratification!
To lie on the mountain tops in the dark and dew
Rapturously embracing earth and heaven,
Swelling yourself to a godhead, ferreting through
The marrow of the earth with divination, 70
To feel in your breast the whole six days of creation,
To enjoy I know not what in arrogant might
And then, with the Old Adam discarded quite,
To overflow into all things in ecstasy;
After all which your lofty intuition 75
        [*He makes a gesture.*]
Will end—hm—unmentionably.

FAUST. Shame on you!

MEPHISTOPHELES.   Am I to blame?
You have the right to be moral and cry shame!
One must not mention to the modest ear 80
What the modest heart is ever agog to hear.
And, in a word, you are welcome to the pleasure
Of lying to yourself in measure;
But this deception will not last.

61. *Doctor:* i.e., the doctor of philosophy.

Already overdriven again, 85
If this goes on you must collapse,
Mad or tormented or aghast.
Enough of this! Back there your love is sitting
And all her world seems sad and small;
You are never absent from her mind, 90
Her love for you is more than all.
At first your passion came overflowing
Like a brook that the melted snows have bolstered high;
You have poured your passion into her heart
And now your brook once more is dry. 95
I think, instead of lording it here above
In the woods, the great man might think fit
In view of that poor ninny's love
To make her some return for it.
She finds the time wretchedly long; 100
She stands at the window, watches the clouds
As over the old town walls they roll away.
'If I had the wings of a dove'—so runs her song
Half the night and all the day.
Now she is cheerful, mostly low, 105
Now has spent all her tears,
Now calm again, it appears,
But always loves you so.

FAUST. You snake! You snake!
MEPHISTOPHELES. [*Aside*] Ha! It begins to take! 110
FAUST. You outcast! Take yourself away
And do not name that lovely woman.
Do not bring back the desire for her sweet body
Upon my senses that are half astray.
MEPHISTOPHELES. Where's this to end? She thinks you have run
off, 115
And so you have—about half and half.
FAUST. I am still near her, though far removed,
Her image must be always in my head;
I already envy the body of the Lord
When her lips rest upon the holy bread. 120
MEPHISTOPHELES. Very well, my friend. I have often envied you
Those two young roes that are twins, I mean her two—
FAUST. Pimp! Get away!
MEPHISTOPHELES.   Fine! So you scold? I must laugh.
The God who created girl and boy 125
Knew very well the high vocation
Which facilitates their joy.
But come, this is a fine excuse for gloom!

You should take the road to your sweetheart's room,
Rather than that to death, you know.   130

FAUST. What is the joy of heaven in her arms?
Even when I catch fire upon her breast
Do I not always sense her woe?
Am I not the runaway? The man without a home?
The monster restless and purposeless   135
Who roared like a waterfall from rock to rock in foam
Greedily raging towards the precipice?
And she on the bank in childlike innocence
In a little hut on the little alpine plot
And all her little household world   140
Concentrated in that spot.
And I, the loathed of God,
I was not satisfied
To seize and crush to powder
The rocks on the river side!   145
Her too, her peace, I must undermine as well!
This was the sacrifice I owed to Hell!
Help, Devil, to shorten my time of torment!
What must be, must be; hasten it!
Let her fate hurtle down with mine,   150
Let us go together to the pit!

MEPHISTOPHELES. How it glows again, how it boils again!
Go in and comfort her, my foolish friend!
When such a blockhead sees no outlet
He thinks at once it is the end.   155
Long live the man who does not flinch!
But you've a devil in you, somewhere there.
I know of nothing on earth more unattractive
Than your devil who feels despair.

GRETCHEN'S ROOM

GRETCHEN *is alone, singing at the spinning-wheel.*

GRETCHEN. My peace is gone,
My heart is sore,
I shall find it never
And never more.

He has left my room   5
An empty tomb,
He has gone and all
My world is gall.

My poor head

Is all astray, 10
My poor mind
Fallen away.

My peace is gone,
My heart is sore,
I shall find it never 15
And never more.

'Tis he that I look through
The window to see,
He that I open
The door for—he! 20

His gait, his figure,
So grand, so high!
The smile of his mouth,
The power of his eye,

And the magic stream 25
Of his words—what bliss!
The clasp of his hand
And, ah, his kiss!

My peace is gone,
My heart is sore, 30
I shall find it never
And never more.

My heart's desire
Is so strong, so vast;
Ah, could I seize him 35
And hold him fast

And kiss him for ever
Night and day—
And on his kisses
Pass away! 40

MARTHA'S GARDEN

GRETCHEN. Promise me, Heinrich!

FAUST.   If I can!

GRETCHEN. Tell me: how do you stand in regard to religion?
  You are indeed a good, good man
  But I think you give it scant attention. 5

FAUST. Leave that, my child! You feel what I feel for you;

---

1. *Heinrich:* i.e., Faust. In the legend, Faust's first name was generally Johann (John). Goethe changed it to Heinrich (Henry).

For those I love I would give my life and none
Will I deprive of his sentiments and his church.

GRETCHEN. That is not right; one must believe thereon.

FAUST. Must one? 10

GRETCHEN.   If only I had some influence!
Nor do you honour the holy sacraments.

FAUST. I honour them.

GRETCHEN.   Yes, but not with any zest.
When were you last at mass, when were you last confessed? 15
Do you believe in God?

FAUST.   My darling, who dare say:
I believe in God?
Ask professor or priest,
Their answers will make an odd 20
Mockery of you.

GRETCHEN.   You don't believe, you mean?

FAUST. Do not misunderstand me, my love, my queen!
Who can name him?
Admit on the spot: 25
I believe in him?
And who can dare
To perceive and declare:
I believe in him not?
The All-Embracing One, 30
All-Upholding One,
Does he not embrace, uphold,
You, me, Himself?
Does not the Heaven vault itself above us?
Is not the earth established fast below? 35
And with their friendly glances do not
Eternal stars rise over us?
Do not my eyes look into yours,
And all things thrust
Into your head, into your heart, 40
And weave in everlasting mystery
Invisibly, visibly, around you?
Fill your heart with *this*, great as it is,
And when this feeling grants you perfect bliss,
Then call it what you will— 45
Happiness! Heart! Love! God!
I have no name for it!
Feeling is all;
Name is mere sound and reek
Clouding Heaven's light. 50

GRETCHEN. That sounds quite good and right;

And much as the priest might speak,
Only not word for word.

FAUST. It is what all hearts have heard
In all the places heavenly day can reach,
Each in his own speech;
Why not I in mine?

GRETCHEN. I could almost accept it, you make it sound so fine,
Still there is something in it that shouldn't be;
For you have no Christianity.

FAUST. Dear child!

GRETCHEN.   It has long been a grief to me
To see you in such company.

FAUST. You mean?

GRETCHEN.   The man who goes about with you,
I hate him in my soul, right through and through.
And nothing has given my heart
In my whole life so keen a smart
As that man's face, so dire, so grim.

FAUST. Dear poppet, don't be afraid of him!

GRETCHEN. My blood is troubled by his presence.
All other people, I wish them well;
But much as I may long to see you,
He gives me a horror I cannot tell,
And I think he's a man too none can trust;
God forgive me if I'm unjust.

FAUST. Such queer fish too must have room to swim.

GRETCHEN. I wouldn't live with the like of him!
Whenever that man comes to the door,
He looks in so sarcastically,
Half angrily,
One can see he feels no sympathy;
It is written on his face so clear
There is not a soul he can hold dear.
I feel so cosy in your arms,
So warm and free from all restraint,
And his presence ties me up inside.

FAUST. You angel, with your wild alarms!

GRETCHEN. It makes me feel so ill, so faint,
That, if he merely happens to join us,
I even think I have no more love for you.
Besides, when he's there, I could never pray,
And that is eating my heart away;
You, Heinrich, you must feel it too.

FAUST. You suffer from an antipathy.

GRETCHEN. Now I must go.

FAUST.   Oh, can I never rest
  One little hour hanging upon your breast,
  Pressing both breast on breast and soul on soul?
GRETCHEN. Ah, if I only slept alone!   100
  I'd gladly leave the door unlatched for you to-night;
  My mother, however, sleeps so light
  And if she found us there, I own
  I should fall dead upon the spot.
FAUST. You angel, there is no fear of that.   105
  Here's a little flask. Three drops are all
  It needs—in her drink—to cover nature
  In a deep sleep, a gentle pall.
GRETCHEN. What would I not do for your sake!
  I hope it will do her no injury.   110
FAUST. My love, do you think that of me?
GRETCHEN. Dearest, I've only to look at you
  And I do not know what drives me to meet your will
  I have already done so much for you
  That little more is left me to fulfil.   115
      [*She goes out—and* MEPHISTOPHELES *enters.*]
MEPHISTOPHELES. The monkey! Is she gone?
FAUST.   Have you been spying again?
MEPHISTOPHELES. I have taken pretty good note of it,
  The doctor has been catechised—
  And much, I hope, to his benefit;   120
  The girls are really keen to be advised
  If a man belongs to the old simple-and-pious school.
  'If he stand that', they think, 'he'll stand *our* rule.'
FAUST. You, you monster, cannot see
  How this true and loving soul   125
  For whom faith is her whole
  Being and the only road
  To beatitude, must feel a holy horror
  Having to count her beloved lost for good.
MEPHISTOPHELES. You supersensual, sensual buck,   130
  Led by the nose by the girl you court!
FAUST. O you abortion of fire and muck!
MEPHISTOPHELES. And she also has skill in physiognomy;
  In my presence she feels she doesn't know what,
  She reads some hidden sense behind my little mask,   135
  She feels that I am assuredly a genius—
  Maybe the devil if she dared to ask.
  Now: to-night—
FAUST.   What is to-night to you?
MEPHISTOPHELES. I have my pleasure in it too.   140

AT THE WELL

GRETCHEN *and* LIESCHEN *with pitchers.*

LIESCHEN. Haven't you heard about Barbara? Not what's passed?
GRETCHEN. Not a word. I go out very little.
LIESCHEN. It's true, Sibylla told me to-day:
   She has made a fool of herself at last.
   So much for her fine airs!   5
GRETCHEN.   Why?
LIESCHEN.   It stinks!
   Now she feeds two when she eats and drinks.
GRETCHEN. Ah!
LIESCHEN. Yes; she has got her deserts in the end.   10
   What a time she's been hanging on her friend!
   Going the rounds
   To the dances and the amusement grounds,
   She had to be always the first in the line,
   He was always standing her cakes and wine;   15
   She thought her looks so mighty fine,
   She was so brazen she didn't waver
   To take the presents that he gave her.
   Such cuddlings and such carryings on—
   But now the pretty flower is gone.   20
GRETCHEN. Poor thing!
LIESCHEN.   Is that the way you feel?
   When we were at the spinning-wheel
   And mother kept us upstairs at night,
   She was below with her heart's delight;
   On the bench or in the shady alley   25
   They never had long enough to dally.
   But now she must grovel in the dirt,
   Do penance in church in a hair shirt.
GRETCHEN. But surely he will marry her.   30
LIESCHEN. He'd be a fool! A smart young chap
   Has plenty of other casks to tap.
   Besides he's gone.
GRETCHEN.   That's not right.
LIESCHEN. If she hooks him she won't get off light!   35
   The boys will tear her wreath in half
   And we shall strew her door with chaff.
   [LIESCHEN *goes off.*]

3. *Sibylla:* a friend of Gretchen's; not to be confused with the "Sibyl" named in l. 162 of the scene in the witch's kitchen.

37. *chaff:* in contrast to the bridal bouquet. In Germany this treatment was reserved for girls who had "fallen."

GRETCHEN. [*Going home*] What scorn I used to pour upon her
  When a poor maiden lost her honour!
  My tongue could never find a name
  Bad enough for another's shame!
  I thought it black and I blackened it,
  It was never black enough to fit,
  And I blessed myself and acted proud—
  And now I too am under a cloud.
  Yet, God! What drove me to this pass,
  It was all so good, so dear, alas!

RAMPARTS

In a niche in the wall is an image of the Mater Dolorosa.[a] *In front of it* GRETCHEN *is putting fresh flowers in the pots.*

GRETCHEN. Mary, bow down,
      Beneath thy woeful crown,
      Thy gracious face on me undone!

      The sword in thy heart,
      Smart upon smart,
      Thou lookest up to thy dear son;

      Sending up sighs
      To the Father which rise
      For his grief and for thine own.

      Who can gauge
      What torments rage
      Through the whole of me and how—
      How my poor heart is troubled in me,
      How fears and longings undermine me?
      Only thou knowest, only thou!

      Wherever I may go,
      What woe, what woe, what woe
      Is growing beneath my heart!
      Alas, I am hardly alone,
      I moan, I moan, I moan
      And my heart falls apart.

      The flower-pots in my window
      I watered with tears, ah me,
      When in the early morning
      I picked these flowers for thee.

a. literally, "sorrowful mother"; i.e., the Virgin Mary.

Not sooner in my bedroom
The sun's first rays were shed
Than I in deepest sorrow
Sat waking on my bed.

Save me from shame and death in one! **30**
Ah, bow down
Thou of the woeful crown,
Thy gracious face on me undone.

NIGHT SCENE AT GRETCHEN'S DOOR

VALENTINE. When I was at some drinking bout
Where big talk tends to blossom out,
And my companions raised their voice
To praise the maidens of their choice
And drowned their praises in their drink, **5**
Then I would sit and never blink,
Propped on my elbow listening
To all their brags and blustering.
Then smiling I would stroke my beard
And raise the bumper in my hand **10**
And say: 'Each fellow to his taste!
But is there one in all the land
To hold a candle to my own
Dear sister, Gretchen? No, there's none!'
Hear! Hear! Kling! Kling! It went around; **15**
Some cried: 'His judgment is quite sound,
She is the pearl of womanhood!'
That shut those boasters up for good.
And now! It would make one tear one's hair
And run up walls in one's despair! **20**
Each filthy fellow in the place
Can sneer and jeer at my disgrace!
And I, like a man who's deep in debt,
Every chance word must make me sweat.
I could smash their heads for them if I tried— **25**
I could not tell them that they lied.

[FAUST *and* MEPHISTOPHELES *enter*.]

VALENTINE. Who comes there, slinking? Who comes there?
If I mistake not, they're a pair.
If it's he, I'll scrag him on the spot;
He'll be dead before he knows what's what! **30**

FAUST. How from the window of the sacristy there
The undying lamp sends up its little flicker

Which glimmers sideways weak and weaker
And round it presses the dark air.
My heart too feels its night, its noose.   35

MEPHISTOPHELES. And I feel like a tom-cat on the loose,
　Brushing along the fire escape
　And round the walls, a stealthy shape;
　Moreover I feel quite virtuous,
　Just a bit burglarious, a bit lecherous.   40
　You see, I'm already haunted to the marrow
　By the glorious Walpurgis Night.
　It returns to us the day after to-morrow,
　Then one knows why one's awake all right.

FAUST. I'd like some ornament, some ring,   45
　For my dear mistress. I feel sad
　To visit her without anything.

MEPHISTOPHELES. It's really nothing to regret—
　That you needn't pay for what you get.
　Now that the stars are gems on heaven's brocade,   50
　You shall hear a real masterpiece.
　I will sing her a moral serenade
　That her folly may increase.

　　　　　　[*He sings to the guitar.*]

MEPHISTOPHELES. Catherine, my dear,
　　　　　　What? Waiting here   55
　　　　　　At your lover's door
　　　　　　When the stars of the night are fading?
　　　　　　Oh don't begin!
　　　　　　When he lifts the pin,
　　　　　　A maid goes in—   60
　　　　　　But she won't come out a maiden.

　　　　　　So think aright!
　　　　　　Grant him delight
　　　　　　And it's good night,
　　　　　　You poor, poor things—Don't linger!   65
　　　　　　A girl who's wise
　　　　　　Will hide her prize
　　　　　　From robber's eyes—
　　　　　　Unless she's a ring on her finger.

　　　　[VALENTINE *comes forward.*]

VALENTINE. Damn you! Who're you seducing here?   70
　You damned pied piper! You magician!
　First to the devil with your guitar!

54–69. *Catherine . . . finger:* adapted by Goethe from Shakespeare's *Hamlet,*
Act IV, Scene 5.

Then to the devil with the musician!

MEPHISTOPHELES. The guitar is finished. Look, it's broken in two.

VALENTINE. Now then, to break your heads for you!   75

MEPHISTOPHELES. Doctor! Courage! All you can muster!
  Stick by me and do as I say!
  Quick now, draw your feather duster!
  I'll parry his blows, so thrust away!

VALENTINE. Then parry that!   80

MEPHISTOPHELES.   Why not, why not?

VALENTINE. And that!

MEPHISTOPHELES.   Of course.

VALENTINE.   Is he the devil or what?
  What's this? My hand's already lamed.   85

MEPHISTOPHELES. Strike, you!

VALENTINE.   Oh!

  [VALENTINE *falls.*]

MEPHISTOPHELES.   Now the lout is tamed!
  But we must go! Vanish in the wink of an eye!
  They're already raising a murderous hue and cry.   90

MARTHA. [*At the window*] Come out! Come out!

GRETCHEN. [*At the window*]   Bring a light!

MARTHA. [*As before*] There's a row and a scuffle, they're having a
      fight.

MAN. Here's one on the ground; he's dead.

MARTHA. [*Coming out*] The murderers, have they gone?   95

GRETCHEN. [*Coming out*] Who's here?

MAN.   Your mother's son.

GRETCHEN. O God! What pain! O God!

VALENTINE. I am dying—that's soon said
  And sooner done, no doubt.
  Why do you women stand howling and wailing?   100
  Come round and hear me out.
      [*They all gather round him.*]
  Look, my Gretchen, you're young still,
  You have not yet sufficient skill,
  You bungle things a bit.
  Here is a tip—you need no more—   105
  Since you are once for all a whore,
  Then make a job of it!

GRETCHEN. My brother? O God! Is it I you blame!

VALENTINE. Leave our Lord God out of the game!
  What is done I'm afraid is done,   110
  As one starts one must carry on.
  You began with one man on the sly,

There will be more of them by and by,
And when a dozen have done with you
The whole town will have you too.   115

When Shame is born, she first appears
In this world in secrecy,
And the veil of night is drawn so tight
Over her head and ears;
Yes, people would kill her and forget her.   120
But she grows still more and more
And brazenly roams from door to door
And yet her appearance grows no better.
The more her face creates dismay,
The more she seeks the light of day.   125

Indeed I see the time draw on
When all good people in this town
Will turn aside from you, you tart,
As from a corpse in the plague cart.
Then your heart will sink within you,   130
When they look you in the eye!
It's good-bye to your golden chains!
And church-going and mass—good-bye!
No nice lace collars any more
To make you proud on the dancing floor!   135
No, in some dark and filthy nook
You'll hide with beggars and crippled folk
And, if God pardon you, he may;
You are cursed on earth till your dying day.
MARTHA. Commend your soul to the mercy of God!   140
Will you add slander to your load?
VALENTINE. If I could get at your withered body,
You bawd, you sinner born and hardened!
Then I should hope that all my sins
And in full measure might be pardoned.   145
GRETCHEN. My brother! O hell's misery!
VALENTINE. I tell you: let your weeping be.
When you and your honour came to part,
It was you that stabbed me to the heart.
I go to God through the sleep of death,   150
A soldier—brave to his last breath.
        [*He dies.*]

CATHEDRAL

Organ and anthem. GRETCHEN *in the congregation. An* EVIL
SPIRIT *whispers to her over her shoulder.*

EVIL SPIRIT. How different it all was
Gretchen, when you came here
All innocent to the altar,
Out of the worn-out little book
Lisping your prayers, 5
Half a child's game,
Half God in the heart!
Gretchen!
How is your head?
And your heart— 10
What are its crimes?
Do you pray for your mother's soul, who thanks to you
And your sleeping draught overslept into a long, long
pain?
And whose blood stains your threshold?
Yes, and already under your heart 15
Does it not grow and quicken
And torture itself and you
With its foreboding presence?

GRETCHEN. Alas! Alas!
If I could get rid of the thoughts 20
Which course through my head hither and thither
Despite me!

CHOIR. Dies irae, dies illa
Solvet saeclum in favilla.

[*The organ plays.*]

EVIL SPIRIT. Agony seizes you! 25
The trumpet sounds!
The graves tremble
And your heart
From its ashen rest
To fiery torment 30
Comes up recreated
Trembling too!

GRETCHEN. Oh to escape from here!
I feel as if the organ
Were stifling me, 35
And the music dissolving
My heart in its depths.

CHOIR. Judex ergo cum sedebit,
Quidquid latet adparebit,

23–24. *Dies . . . favilla:* Day of
wrath, that day that dissolves the world
into ashes. (The choir is singing the
famous thirteenth-century hymn by
Thomas Celano.)

38–40. *Judex . . . remanebit:* When
the judge shall be seated, what is hidden
shall appear, nothing shall remain un-
avenged.

Nil inultum remanebit.   40

GRETCHEN.   I cannot breathe!
The pillars of the walls
Are round my throat!
The vaulted roof
Chokes me!—Air!   45

EVIL SPIRIT.   Hide yourself! Nor sin nor shame
Remains hidden.
Air? Light?
Woe to you!

CHOIR.   Quid sum miser tunc dicturus?   50
Quem patronum rogaturus?
Cum vix justus sit securus.

EVIL SPIRIT.   The blessed turn
Their faces from you.
The pure shudder   55
To reach out their hands to you.
Woe!

CHOIR.   Quid sum miser tunc dicturus?

GRETCHEN.   Neighbour! Help! Your smelling bottle!
[*She faints.*]

WALPURGIS NIGHT

FAUST *and* MEPHISTOPHELES *making their way through the Hartz Mountains.*

MEPHISTOPHELES. A broomstick—don't you long for such a conveyance?
I'd find the coarsest he-goat some assistance.
Taking this road, our goal is still in the distance.
FAUST. No, so long as my legs are not in abeyance,
I can make do with this knotted stick.   5
What is the use of going too quick?
To creep along each labyrinthine valley,
Then climb this scarp, downwards from which
The bubbling spring makes its eternal sally,
This is the spice that makes such journeys rich.   10
Already the spring is weaving through the birches,
Even the pine already feels the spring;
Should not our bodies too give it some purchase?
MEPHISTOPHELES. Candidly—I don't feel a thing.
In my body all is winter,   15
I would prefer a route through frost and snow.
How sadly the imperfect disc

50–52. *Quid . . . securus:* What shall I say in my wretchedness? To whom shall I appeal when scarcely the righteous man is safe?

Of the red moon rises with belated glow
And the light it gives is bad, at every step
One runs into some rock or tree!   20
Permit me to ask a will o' the wisp.
I see one there, he's burning heartily.
Ahoy, my friend! Might I call on you to help us?
Why do you blaze away there to no purpose?
Be so good as to light us along our road.   25

WILL O' THE WISP. I only hope my sense of your mightiness
    Will control my natural flightiness;
    A zigzag course is our accustomed mode.

MEPHISTOPHELES. Ha! Ha! So it's men you want to imitate.
    In the name of the Devil you go straight   30
    Or I'll blow out your flickering, dickering light!

WILL O' THE WISP. You're the head of the house, I can see that all
      right,
    You are welcome to use me at your convenience.
    But remember, the mountain is magic-mad to-day
    And, if a will o' the wisp is to show you the way,   35
    You too must show a little lenience.

FAUST, MEPHISTOPHELES, WILL O' THE WISP. [*Singing successively*]
        Into realms of dreams and witchcraft
        We, it seems, have found an ingress.
        Lead us well and show your woodcraft,
        That we may make rapid progress   40
        Through these wide and desert spaces.

        Trees on trees—how each one races,
        Pushing past—how each one hastens!
        And the crags that make obeisance!
        And the rocks with long-nosed faces—   45
        Hear them snorting, hear them blowing!

        Through the stones and lawns are flowing
        Brook and brooklet, downward hustling.
        Is that song—or is it rustling?
        Sweet, sad notes of love—a relic—   50
        Voices from those days angelic?
        Thus we hope, we love—how vainly!
        Echo like an ancient rumour
        Calls again, yes, calls back plainly.

        Now—Tu-whit!—we near the purlieu   55
        Of—Tu-whoo!—owl, jay and curlew;
        Are they all in waking humour?

21. *will o' the wisp:* the Jack o' lantern, or ignis fatuus. In German folklore, this was thought of as leading travelers to their destruction.

In the bushes are those lizards—
Straggling legs and bloated gizzards?
And the roots like snakes around us   60
Coil from crag and sandy cranny,
Stretch their mad and strange antennae
Grasping at us to confound us;
Stretch from gnarled and living timber
Towards the passer-by their limber   65
Polyp-suckers!
      And in legions
Through these mossy, heathy regions
Mice, all colours, come cavorting!
And above, a serried cohort,   70
Fly the glow-worms as our escort—
More confusing than escorting.

Tell me what our real case is!
Are we stuck or are we going?
Rocks and trees, they all seem flying   75
Round and round and making faces,
And the will o' the wisps are blowing
Up so big and multiplying.

MEPHISTOPHELES. Hold my coat-tails, hold on tight!
Standing on this central height   80
Marvelling see how far and wide
Mammon lights the peaks inside.

FAUST. How strangely through the mountain hollows
A sad light gleams as of morning-red
And like a hound upon the scent   85
Probes the gorges' deepest bed!
Here fumes arise, there vapours float,
Here veils of mist catch sudden fire
Which creeps along, a flimsy thread,
Then fountains up, a towering spire.   90
Here a whole stretch it winds its way
With a hundred veins throughout the glen,
And here in the narrow neck of the pass
Is suddenly one strand again.
There, near by, are dancing sparks   95
Sprinkled around like golden sand.
But look! The conflagration climbs
The crags' full height, hand over hand.

MEPHISTOPHELES. Does not Sir Mammon light his palace

---

82. *Mammon:* See the note to l. 73
in the second scene titled FAUST'S STUDY.
Mammon is portrayed as the architect
of Satan's palace in Milton's *Paradise
Lost*, Book I, ll. 678 ff.

In splendid style for this occasion? 100
You are lucky to have seen it;
Already I sense the noisy guests' invasion.

FAUST. How the Wind Hag rages through the air!
What blows she rains upon the nape of my neck!

MEPHISTOPHELES. You must clamp yourself to the ancient ribs of
    the rock 105
Or she'll hurl you into this gorge, to find your grave down there.
A mist is thickening the night.
Hark to the crashing of the trees!
The owls are flying off in fright.
And the ever-green palaces— 110
Hark to their pillars sundering!
Branches moaning and breaking!
Tree-trunks mightily thundering!
Roots creaking and yawning!
Tree upon tree in appalling 115
Confusion crashing and falling,
And through the wreckage on the scarps
The winds are hissing and howling.
Do you hear those voices in the air?
Far-off voices? Voices near? 120
Aye, the whole length of the mountain side
The witch-song streams in a crazy tide.

WITCHES. [*In chorus*]. The witches enter the Brocken scene,
    The stubble is yellow, the corn is green.
    There assembles the mighty horde, 125
    Urian sits aloft as lord.
    So we go—over stock and stone—
    Farting witch on stinking goat.

A VOICE. But ancient Baubo comes alone,
    She rides on a mother sow—take note. 130

CHORUS. So honour to whom honour is due!
    Let Mother Baubo head the queue!
    A strapping sow and Mother on top
    And we'll come after, neck and crop.

    The way is broad, the way is long, 135
    How is this for a crazy throng?
    The pitchfork pricks, the broomstick pokes,
    The mother bursts and the child chokes.

VOICE FROM ABOVE. Come along, come along, from Felsensee!
VOICES FROM BELOW. We'd like to mount with you straight away.
    We wash ourselves clean behind and before 141

126. *Urian:* a name for the devil.   nurse of Demeter, noted for her ob-
129. *Baubo:* In Greek mythology, the   scenity and bestiality.

But we are barren for evermore.

CHORUS. The wind is silent, the star's in flight,
The sad moon hides herself from sight.
The soughing of the magic choir   145
Scatters a thousand sparks of fire.

VOICE FROM BELOW. Wait! Wait!

VOICE FROM ABOVE. Who calls there from the cleft in the rock?

VOICE FROM BELOW. Don't leave me behind! Don't leave me
behind!
Three hundred years I've been struggling up   150
And I can never reach the top;
I want to be with my own kind.

CHORUS. Ride on a broom or ride on a stick,
Ride on a fork or a goat—but quick!
Who cannot to-night achieve the climb   155
Is lost and damned till the end of time.

HALF-WITCH. So long, so long, I've been on the trot;
How far ahead the rest have got!
At home I have neither peace nor cheer
And yet I do not find it here.   160

CHORUS. Their ointment makes the witches hale,
A rag will make a decent sail
And any trough a ship for flight;
You'll never fly, if not to-night.
Once at the peak, you circle round   165
And then you sweep along the ground
And cover the heath far and wide—
Witchhood in swarms on every side.
[*The* WITCHES *land.*]

MEPHISTOPHELES. What a push and a crush and a rush and a
clatter!
How they sizzle and whisk, how they babble and batter!   170
Kindle and sparkle and blaze and stink!
A true witch-element, I think.
Only stick to me or we shall be swept apart!
Where are you?

FAUST.   Here!   175

MEPHISTOPHELES.   What! Carried so far already!
I must show myself the master on this ground.
Room! Here comes Voland! Room, sweet rabble! Steady!
Here, Doctor, catch hold of me. Let's make one bound
Out of this milling crowd and so get clear.   180
Even for the likes of me it's *too* mad here.

178. *Voland:* one of Mephistopheles' names for himself. *Voland,* or *Valand,* is an
old German word for "evil fiend."

There's something yonder casting a peculiar glare,
Something attracts me towards those bushes.
Come with me! We will slip in there.

FAUST. You spirit of contradiction! Go on though! I'll follow.   185
You have shown yourself a clever fellow. Quite!
We visit the Brocken on Walpurgis Night
To shut ourselves away in this lonely hollow!

MEPHISTOPHELES. Only look—what motley flames!
It's a little club for fun and games   190
One's not alone with a few, you know.

FAUST. I'd rather be above there though.
Already there's fire and whorls of smoke.
The Prince of Evil is drawing the folk;
Many a riddle must there be solved.   195

MEPHISTOPHELES. And many a new one too evolved.
Let the great world, if it likes, run riot;
We will set up here in quiet.
It is a custom of old date
To make one's own small worlds within the great.   200
I see young witches here, bare to the buff,
And old ones dressed—wisely enough.
If only for my sake, do come on;
It's little trouble and great fun.
I hear some music being let loose too.   205
What a damned clack! It's what one must get used to.
Come along! Come along! You have no choice.
I'll lead the way and sponsor you
And you'll be obliged to me anew.
What do you say? This milieu isn't small.   210
Just look! You can see no end to it at all.
A hundred fires are blazing in a row;
They dance and gossip and cook and drink and court—
Tell me where there is better sport!

FAUST. Do you intend, to introduce us here,   215
To play the devil or the sorcerer?

MEPHISTOPHELES. I am quite accustomed to go incognito
But one wears one's orders on gala days, you know.
I have no garter for identification
But my cloven foot has here some reputation.   220
See that snail? Creeping up slow and steady?
Her sensitive feelers have already
Sensed out something odd in me.
Here I could *not* hide my identity.

187. *Walpurgis Night:* the eve of May Day (May 1).

219. *garter:* i.e., he has no decoration of nobility, such as the Order of the Garter.

But come! Let us go the round of the fires   225
And I'll play go-between to your desires.

COSTER-WITCH. Gentlemen, don't pass me by!
Don't miss your opportunity!
Inspect my wares with careful eye;
I have a great variety.   230
And yet there is nothing on my stall
Whose like on earth you could not find,
That in its time has done no small
Harm to the world and to mankind.
No dagger which has not drunk of blood,   235
No goblet which has not poured its hot and searing
Poison into some healthy frame,
No gewgaw which has not ruined some endearing
Woman, no sword which has not been used to hack
A bond in two and stab a partner in the back.   240

MEPHISTOPHELES. Auntie! You are behind the times.
Past and done with! Past and done!
You must go in for novelties!
You'll lose our custom if you've none.

FAUST. I mustn't go crazy unawares!   245
This is a fair to end all fairs.

MEPHISTOPHELES. The whole crowd's forcing its way above;
You find you're shoved though you may think you shove.

FAUST. Who then is that?

MEPHISTOPHELES.   Look well at Madam;   250
That's Lilith.

FAUST.   Who?

MEPHISTOPHELES.   First wife of Adam.
Be on your guard against her lovely hair,
That shining ornament which has no match;   255
Any young man whom those fair toils can catch,
She will not quickly loose him from her snare.

FAUST. Look, an old and a young one, there they sit.
They have already frisked a bit.

MEPHISTOPHELES. No rest to-night for 'em, not a chance.   260
They're starting again. Come on! Let's join the dance.
        [FAUST *dances with a* YOUNG WITCH.]

FAUST.   A lovely dream once came to me
                In which I saw an apple tree,

227. *Coster-Witch:* The original, *Trödelhexe*, literally means "a witch (dealing in) old rags and clothes."
251. *Lilith:* According to an old rabbinical legend, Adam's first wife (the "female" mentioned in Genesis 1:27) was Lilith. After Eve was created, Lilith became a ghost who seduced men and inflicted evil upon children.

On which two lovely apples shine,
They beckon me, I start to climb.   265

YOUNG WITCH. Those little fruit you long for so
Just as in Eden long ago.
Joy runs through me, through and through;
My garden bears its apples too.

[FAUST *breaks away from the dance.*]

MEPHISTOPHELES. Why did you let that lovely maiden go   270
Who danced with you and so sweetly sang?

FAUST. Ugh, in the middle of it there sprang
Out of her mouth a little red mouse.

MEPHISTOPHELES. Why complain? That's nothing out of the way;
You should be thankful it wasn't grey.   275
In an hour of love! What a senseless grouse!

FAUST. And then I saw—

MEPHISTOPHELES.   What?

FAUST.   Mephisto, look over there!
Do you see a girl in the distance, pale and fair?   280
Who drags herself, only slowly, from the place?
And seems to walk with fetters on her feet?
I must tell you that I think I see
Something of dear Gretchen in her face.

MEPHISTOPHELES. That can do no good! Let it alone! Beware!   285
It is a lifeless phantom, an image of air.
It is a bad thing to behold;
Its cold look makes the blood of man run cold,
One turns to stone almost upon the spot;
You have heard of Medusa, have you not?   290

FAUST. Indeed, they are the eyes of one who is dead,
Unclosed by loving hands, left open, void.
That is the breast which Gretchen offered me,
And that is the sweet body I enjoyed.

MEPHISTOPHELES. That is mere magic, you gullible fool! She
can   295
Appear in the shape of his love to every man.

FAUST. What ravishment! What pain! Oh stay!
That look! I cannot turn away!
How strange that that adorable neck
In one red thread should be arrayed   300
As thin as the back of a knife-blade.

MEPHISTOPHELES. You are quite correct! I see it too.
She can also carry her head under her arm,

290. *Medusa:* the Gorgon, with hair made of serpents, whose glance turned men to stone. She was finally killed by Perseus, and her head was given to Athene.

Perseus has cut it off for her.
Always this love of things untrue!^a   305
[A CHOIR *is heard, pianissimo.*]
CHOIR. Drifting cloud and gauzy mist
    Brighten and dissever.
    Breeze on the leaf and wind in the reeds
    And all is gone for ever.

DREARY DAY—OPEN COUNTRY

FAUST. In misery! In despair! Long on the earth a wretched wanderer, now a prisoner! A criminal cooped in a dungeon for horrible
torments, that dear and luckless creature! To end so! So! Per-
fidious, worthless spirit—and this you have kept from me!
Stand, Just stand there! Roll your devilish eyes spitefully round
in your head! Stand and brave me with your unbearable presence!
A prisoner! In irremediable misery! Abandoned to evil spirits, to
judging, unfeeling man! And I in the meantime—you lull me
with stale diversions, you hide her worsening plight from me, you
abandon her to perdition!
MEPHISTOPHELES. She is not the first.
FAUST. Dog! Loathsome monster! Change him, Thou eternal Spirit!
Change this serpent back to his shape of a dog, in which he often
delighted to trot before me at night—to roll about at the feet of
the harmless wanderer and, as he tripped, to sink his teeth in his
shoulders. Change him back to his fancy-shape that he may
crouch in the sand on his belly before me, that I may trample
over his vileness!
    Not the first, you say! O the pity of it! What human soul can
grasp that more than one creature has sunk to the depth of this
misery, that the first did not pay off the guilt of all the rest,
writhing and racked in death before the eyes of the Ever-Pardon-
ing! It pierces me to my marrow and core, the torment of this
one girl—and you grin calmly at the fate of thousands!
MEPHISTOPHELES. Now we're already back at our wits' end—the
point where your human intelligence snaps. Why do you enter
our company, if you can't carry it through? So you want to fly—
and have no head for heights? Did we force ourselves on you—
or you on us?
FAUST. Do not bare at me so those greedy fangs of yours! You sicken
me! O great and glorious Spirit, Thou who didst deign to appear
to me, Thou who knowest my heart and my soul, why fetter me
to this odious partner who grazes on mischief and laps up destruction?

---

a. The Walpurgis Night's Dream, of *Faust,* is omitted. It occurs between
which is always cut from performances l. 305 and l. 306 of our text.

MEPHISTOPHELES. Have you finished?

FAUST. Save her! Or woe to you! The most withering curse upon you for thousands of years!

MEPHISTOPHELES. I cannot undo the avenger's bonds, his bolts I cannot open. Save her! Who was it plunged her into ruin? I or you?

    [FAUST *looks wildly around.*]

MEPHISTOPHELES. Are you snatching at the thunder? Luckily, that is forbidden you wretched mortals. To smash to pieces his innocent critic, that is the way the tyrant relieves himself when in difficulties.

FAUST. Bring me to her! She shall be free!

MEPHISTOPHELES. And what of the risk you will run? Let me tell you; the town is still tainted with blood-guilt from your hand. Over the site of the murder there float avenging spirits who await the returning murderer.

FAUST. That too from *you?* Murder and death of a world on your monstrous head! Take me to her, I tell you; set her free!

MEPHISTOPHELES. I will take you, and what I *can* do—listen! Am I omnipotent in heaven and earth? I will cast a cloud on the gaoler's senses; do you get hold of the keys and carry her out with your own human hands. I meanwhile wait, my magic horses are ready, I carry you off. That much I can manage.

FAUST. Away! Away!

NIGHT

FAUST *and* MEPHISTOPHELES *fly past on black horses.*

FAUST. What do they weave round the Gallows Rock?

MEPHISTOPHELES. Can't tell what they're cooking and hatching.

FAUST. Floating up, floating down, bending, descending.

MEPHISTOPHELES. A witch corporation.

FAUST. Black mass, black water.   5

MEPHISTOPHELES. Come on! Come on!

DUNGEON

FAUST *with a bunch of keys and a lamp, in front of an iron door.*

FAUST. A long unwonted trembling seizes me,
The woe of all mankind seizes me fast.
It is here she lives, behind these dripping walls,
Her crime was but a dream too good to last!
And *you*, Faust, waver at the door?   5
You fear to see your love once more?
Go in at once—or her hope of life is past.

---

1. *Gallows Rock:* the masonry supporting a gallows.

[*He tries the key.* GRETCHEN *starts singing inside.*]

GRETCHEN. My mother, the whore,
　　Who took my life!
　　My father, the rogue,
　　Who ate my flesh!　　　　　　　　　　　　10
　　My little sister
　　My bones did lay
　　In a cool, cool glen;
　　And there I turned to a pretty little wren;　　15
　　Fly away! Fly away!
　　　　[FAUST *opens the lock.*]

FAUST. She does not suspect that her lover is listening—
　　To the chains clanking, the straw rustling.
　　　　[*He enters.*]

GRETCHEN. Oh! They come! O death! It's hard! Hard!

FAUST. Quiet! I come to set you free.　　　　　　20
　　　　[*She throws herself at his feet.*]

GRETCHEN. If you are human, feel my misery.

FAUST. Do not cry out—you will wake the guard.
　　　　[*He takes hold of the chains to unlock them.*]

GRETCHEN. [*On her knees*] Who has given you this power,
　　Hangman, so to grieve me?
　　To fetch me at this midnight hour!　　　　　　25
　　Have pity! O reprieve me!
　　Will to-morrow not serve when the bells are rung?
　　　　[*She gets up.*]
　　I am still so young, I am still so young!
　　Is my death so near?
　　I was pretty too, that was what brought me here.　　30
　　My lover was by, he's far to-day;
　　My wreath lies torn, my flowers have been thrown away.
　　Don't seize on me so violently!
　　What have I done to you? Let me be!
　　Let me not vainly beg and implore;　　　　　　35
　　You know I have never seen you before.

FAUST. Can I survive this misery?

GRETCHEN. I am now completely in your power.
　　Only let me first suckle my child.
　　This night I cherished it, hour by hour;　　　　40
　　To torture me they took it away
　　And now I murdered it, so they say.
　　And I shall never be happy again.
　　People make ballads about me—the heartless crew!
　　An old story ends like this—　　　　　　　　45
　　Must mine too?

[FAUST *throws himself on the ground.*]

FAUST. Look! At your feet a lover lies
　　To loose you from your miseries.

　　　　[GRETCHEN *throws herself beside him.*]

GRETCHEN. O, let us call on the saints on bended knee!
　　Beneath these steps—but see—　　　　　　　　50
　　Beneath this sill
　　The cauldron of Hell!
　　And within,
　　The Evil One in his fury
　　Raising a din!　　　　　　　　　　　　　　55

FAUST. Gretchen! Gretchen!

GRETCHEN. That was my lover's voice!

　　　　[*She springs up: the chains fall off.*]

　　I heard him calling. Where can he be?
　　No one shall stop me. I am free!
　　Quick! My arms round his neck!　　　　　　60
　　And lie upon his bosom! Quick!
　　He called 'Gretchen!' He stood at the door.
　　Through the whole of Hell's racket and roar,
　　Through the threats and jeers and from far beyond
　　I heard that voice so sweet, so fond.　　　　65

FAUST. It is I!

GRETCHEN.　　　It's you? Oh say so once again!

　　　　[*She clasps him.*]

　　It is! It is! Where now is all my pain?
　　And where the anguish of my captivity?
　　It's you; you have come to rescue me!　　　　70
　　I am saved!
　　The street is back with me straight away
　　Where I saw you that first day,
　　And the happy garden too
　　Where Martha and I awaited you.　　　　　75

FAUST. Come! Come!

GRETCHEN.　　　　　　Oh stay with me, oh do!
　　Where *you* stay, I would like to, too.

FAUST. Hurry!
　　If you don't,　　　　　　　　　　　　　80
　　The penalty will be sore.

GRETCHEN. What! Can you kiss no more?
　　So short an absence, dear, as this
　　And you've forgotten how to kiss!
　　Why do I feel so afraid, clasping your neck?　　85
　　In the old days your words, your looks,
　　Were a heavenly flood I could not check

And you kissed me as if you would smother me—
Kiss me now!
Or I'll kiss you!   90
    [*She kisses him.*]
Oh your lips are cold as stone!
And dumb!
What has become
Of your love?
Who has robbed me of my own?   95
    [*She turns away from him.*]

FAUST. Come! Follow me, my love! Be bold!
    I will cherish you after a thousandfold.
    Only follow me now! That is all I ask of you.

GRETCHEN. And is it you then? Really? Is it true?

FAUST. It is! But come!   100

GRETCHEN.   You are undoing each chain,
    You take me to your arms again.
    How comes it you are not afraid of me?
    Do you know, my love, *whom* you are setting free?

FAUST. Come! The deep night is passing by and beyond.   105

GRETCHEN. My mother, I have murdered her;
    I drowned my child in the pond.
    Was it not a gift to you and me?
    To you too—You! Are you what you seem?
    Give me your hand! It is not a dream!   110
    Your dear hand—but, oh, it's wet!
    Wipe it off! I think
    There is blood on it.
    Oh God! What have you done?
    Put up your sword,   115
    I beg you to.

FAUST. Let what is gone be gone!
    You are killing me.

GRETCHEN. No! *You* must live on!
    I will tell you about the graves—   120
    You must get them put right
    At morning light;
    Give the best place to my mother,
    The one next door to my brother,
    Me a shade to the side—   125
    A gap, but not too wide.
    And the little one on my right breast.
    No one else shall share my rest.
    When it was you, when I could clasp you,
    That was a sweet, a lovely day!   130

But I no longer can attain it,
I feel I must use force to grasp you,
As if you were thrusting me away.
And yet it's you and you look so kind, so just.
FAUST. If you feel it's I, then come with me! You must!   135
GRETCHEN. Outside there?
FAUST. Into the air!
GRETCHEN.   If the grave is there
And death on the watch, then come!
Hence to the final rest of the tomb   140
And not a step beyond—
You are going now? O Heinrich, if *I* could too!
FAUST. You can! The door is open. Only respond!
GRETCHEN. I dare not go out; for me there is no more hope.
They are lying in wait for me; what use is flight?   145
To have to beg, it is so pitiable
And that with a conscience black as night!
So pitiable to tramp through foreign lands—
And in the end I must fall into their hands!
FAUST. I shall stay by you.   150
GRETCHEN. Be quick! Be quick!
Save your poor child!
Go! Straight up the path—
Along by the brook—
Over the bridge—   155
Into the wood—
Left where the plank is—
In the pond!
Catch hold of it quickly!
It's trying to rise,   160
It's kicking still!
Save it! Save it!
FAUST. Collect yourself!
One step—just one—and you are free.
GRETCHEN. If only we were past the hill!   165
There sits my mother on a stone—
My brain goes cold and dead—
There sits my mother on a stone—
And wags and wags her head.
No sign, no nod, her head is such a weight   170
She'll wake no more, she slept so late.
She slept that we might sport and play.
What a time that was of holiday!
FAUST. If prayer and argument are no resource,
I will risk saving you by force.   175

GRETCHEN. No! I will have no violence! Let me go!
  Don't seize me in that murderous grip!
  I have done everything else for you, you know.
FAUST. My love! My love! The day is dawning!
GRETCHEN. Day! Yes, it's growing day! The last day breaks on
  me!   180
  My wedding day it was to be!
  Tell no one you had been before with Gretchen.
  Alas for my garland!
  There's no more chance!
  We shall meet again—   185
  But not at the dance.
  The people are thronging—but silently;
  Street and square
  Cannot hold them there.
  The bell tolls—it tolls for *me*.   190
  How they seize me, bind me, like a slave!
  Already I'm swept away to the block.
  Already there jabs at every neck,
  The sharp blade which jabs at mine.
  The world lies mute as the grave.   195
FAUST. I wish I had never been born!
    [MEPHISTOPHELES *appears outside*.]
MEPHISTOPHELES. Away! Or you are lost.
  Futile wavering! Waiting and prating!
  My horses are shivering,
  The dawn's at the door.   200
GRETCHEN. What rises up from the floor?
  It's he! Send him away! It's he!
  What does he want in the holy place?
  It is I he wants!
FAUST.   You shall live!   205
GRETCHEN. Judgment of God! I have given myself to Thee!
MEPHISTOPHELES. [*To* FAUST] Come! Or I'll leave you both in the
    lurch.
GRETCHEN. O Father, save me! I am Thine!
  You angels! Hosts of the Heavenly Church,
  Guard me, stand round in serried line!   210
  Heinrich! I shudder to look at you.
MEPHISTOPHELES. She is condemned!
VOICE FROM ABOVE.   Redeemed!
MEPHISTOPHELES. Follow me!
    [*He vanishes with* FAUST.]
VOICE [*From within, dying away*] Heinrich! Heinrich!   215

The Second Part of the Tragedy

[In Part II of *Faust*, Goethe moves his hero through a series of practical and social activities. He saves a tottering kingdom from military and economic ruin; marries Helen of Troy, who bears him a son, Euphorion; and finally moves north again from Arcadia to Germany to accomplish his last endeavor, the reclamation of land from the sea.]

Act V

OPEN COUNTRY

WANDERER. Aye! It's they, the shady lindens
   Grown so old and yet so strong.
   And I chance again to find them
   After wandering so long!
   Aye, it is the old place, truly;   5
   There's the hut which sheltered me
   Tossed upon those sand-dunes yonder
   By the storm-distracted sea.
   Worthy couple, quick to help me,
   I would bless my hosts again.   10
   Talk of meeting me to-day!
   They were old already then.
   Ah, but they were pious people!
   Shall I knock? Or call? Well met,
   If to-day, still hospitable,   15
   They delight in good works yet!

BAUCIS. [A *very old woman*] O dear stranger! Softly! Softly!
   Quiet! For my husband's sake!
   Long sleep helps him to be active
   In the short time he's awake.   20

WANDERER. Mother, tell me, is it really
   You? At last can man and wife
   Now be thanked for what they once
   Did to save a young man's life?
   Are you Baucis, then so busy   25
   To fill a half-dead mouth with food?
     [*Her husband appears.*]

25. *Baucis:* The story of Philemon and Baucis is recounted by Ovid in *Metamorphoses*, Book VIII, ll. 620 ff. An old couple in Phrygia, they befriend Jupiter and Mercury; and as a reward, the gods save them and their hut from a flood and make them custodians of the temple erected on its site. They also ask the favor that neither die before the other. In *Faust* too they are shown living by the seaside, but their story is very different. Goethe said to his friend Eckermann: "I gave them [the couple] those names merely to elevate the characters." (June 6, 1831.)

Are *you* Philemon, then so sturdy
To save my treasures from the flood?
Yours the quickly kindled beacon,
Yours the silver-sounding bell,   30
The issue of that dread adventure
Was your trust—you bore it well.

And now let me walk out yonder,
Look upon the boundless sea—
There to kneel and pray; my heart   35
Feels so full, it troubles me.
    [*He walks forward on to the dunes.*]
PHILEMON. [*To* BAUCIS] Hurry now and lay the table
Where the garden flowers are bright.
Let him run and scare himself
When he can't believe his sight.   40
    [*Joining the* WANDERER.]
That which savaged you so fiercely—
Waves on waves in foaming spleen—
Here you see become a garden,
Altered to a heavenly scene.
Old by then, I could not lend   45
A helping hand as on a day,
And my powers had waned already
When the waves were far away.
Clever people's daring servants
Dug their dykes and dammed them high,   50
Whittling down the sea's dominion
To usurp its mastery.
Look! Green meadow after meadow,
Pasture, garden, village, wood.
But the sun is almost setting,   55
Come and eat—you'll find it good.
Aye, far off there sails are moving
Towards sure harbour for the night.
Birds, you know, they know their nest—
That is now the harbour site.   60
Gazing now into the distance
First you find the sea's blue seam—
All the spaces left and right
Thick with folk and houses teem.
BAUCIS. Aye, it *is* a marvel happened;   65
It still gives me qualms to-day.

40. *sight:* The following passages
are intended to reveal to the Wanderer
the extent to which Faust and his
workmen have reclaimed the land from
the sea. Thus, at the time of the shipwreck, the water lay close to the hill
where the hut stands. Now the ocean
is seen only at the horizon.

For the way it all was done—
It was not a proper way.

PHILEMON. Can the Emperor have sinned
    Granting him that fief of strand?   70
    Did a herald with a trumpet
    Not proclaim it round the land?
    Their first foothold it was planted
    Near our dunes, not far from here,
    Tents and huts—but soon a palace   75
    In green meadows must appear!

BAUCIS. In vain the workmen's daily racket—
    Pick and shovel, slog and slam;
    Where the flames by *night* were swarming,
    Stood next day a brand new dam.   80
    Human victims must have bled,
    Night resounded with such woe—
    Fireflakes flowing to the sea;
    Morning a canal would show.
    Godless man he is, he covets   85
    This our cabin and our wood;
    To this overweening neighbour
    Everyone must be subdued.

PHILEMON. All the same we have his offer—
    Fine new property elsewhere.   90

BAUCIS. Do not trust that water-surface;
    On your upland—stand you there!

PHILEMON. Let us move on to the chapel,
    There to watch the last of day.
    Trusting in our father's God   95
    Let us ring the bell and pray!

PALACE[a]

Extensive formal garden; broad canal, straight as a ruler. FAUST, *in the depths of old age, walking about and brooding.*

LYNCEUS THE WATCHMAN.[b] [*Through a megaphone*]
    The sun is sinking, the last ships
    Are sailing blithely into port.
    A fair-sized bark on the canal

68. *proper way:* Baucis' prejudice against her new lord, Faust, is so great that she believes that the actual work was done by evil spirits at night, not by the workmen by day, and that humans were sacrificed to the malignant deity who aided the task.
85. *Godless man:* i.e., Faust.
a. pictured as located away from the sea, but connected with it by a canal large enough to accommodate merchant ships. Goethe told Eckermann (June 6, 1831) that Faust was now a hundred years old. As the scene opens, his fleet of ships, commanded by Mephistopheles, is out at sea.
b. named after the "lynx-eyed" pilot aboard the *Argo*, the ship on which Jason sailed in search of the Golden Fleece.

Will reach us soon, its way is short.
Her coloured pennants flutter gaily,
Ready to dock her masts are bare;   5
On you the skipper rests his hopes
And luck now answers all your prayer.
    [*The little bell rings out on the dunes.*]
FAUST. [*With a start*] Oh that damned ringing! All too shameful
It wounds me like a stab in the back;   10
Before my eyes my realm is endless,
Behind—I'm vexed by what I lack,
Reminding me with spiteful ringing
My great possessions are not sound.
The linden plot, the wooden cabin,   15
The crumbling church are not my ground.
And, should I wish to rest me yonder,
Strange shadows fill my heart with fear—
Thorn in the eyes and thorn in the foot;
Oh were I far away from here!   20
LYNCEUS. [*As above*] The gay-rigged bark, how merrily
A sharp breeze bears it to the quay!
How, as it speeds, it towers on high—
Chests, crates and sacks to reach the sky!
    [*The ship docks, laden with foreign merchandise.* MEPHI-
    STOPHELES *and* THE THREE MIGHTY MEN *lead the chorus.*]
SAILORS' CHORUS. Here we land!   25
                Oh here we are!
            Luck to the owner
            From afar!
    [*They come ashore and the goods are unloaded.*]
MEPHISTOPHELES. You see how we have earned our bays!
Content to win the owner's praise.   30
We went out with two ships, no more,
And we're in harbour with a score.
Our cargo'll prove, to those who doubt,
What great things we have brought about.
The free sea makes the spirit free;   35
Who thinks of thinking on the sea?
The sea demands quick nerve and grip,
You catch a fish, you catch a ship,
And starting in command of three
You hook a fourth one presently.   40
Ill omen for the fifth ship? Quite.
Given the might, you have the right.

15–16. *The linden plot . . . church:* i.e., the land belonging to Philemon and
Baucis.

One asks the What and skips the How.
No need to know much navigation;
War, trade and piracy are one   45
Inseparable combination.

THE THREE MIGHTY MEN.   Not thank nor greet!
                         Not greet nor thank!
                         As if he found
                         Our cargo stank!   50
                         He makes a most
                         Offensive face;
                         Our royal freight
                         Is in disgrace.

MEPHISTOPHELES.   You need not wait for   55
                         More reward!
                         You had your share
                         While still on board.

THE THREE MIGHTY MEN.   Oh that was but
                         To lighten toil,   60
                         We all demand
                         An equal spoil.

MEPHISTOPHELES.   First, room by room.
                         Arrange up there
                         The precious cargo—   65
                         Nothing spare!
                         When Faust comes in
                         To such a sight
                         And reckons all,
                         Of it aright,   70
                         He'll surely not
                         Be stingy then,
                         He'll feast the fleet
                         And feast again.

                         To-morrow the painted birds are due,   75
                         I'll see the best results ensue.

[*The cargo is removed.*]

MEPHISTOPHELES. [*To* FAUST] With brow austere, with frowning
    glance
    You greet your latest vast advance.
    Crowning your high sagacity,
    Your shore is reconciled to sea;   80
    The sea agrees to take your ships
    Out from your shore on rapid trips;
    Admit then: from your palace here

_____

52. *face:* Faust winces at Mephi-   75. *painted birds:* probably the local
stopheles' defense of piracy.   town girls.

Your arms embrace the earthly sphere.
From here we started on this track, 85
Here stood your first poor wooden shack;
A little ditch was scratched in dirt
Where now the busy rudders spurt.
Your lofty mind, your navvies' worth,
Obtained for prize the sea and earth. 90
From here moreover—

FAUST.   This damned Here!
It's that which makes my spirits drear.
I must confess to you, the expert,
It sears my heart with flame on flame, 95
I find I can no more endure it!
And, while I say so, I feel shame.
That aged couple should have yielded,
I want the lindens in my grip,
Since these few trees that are denied me 100
Undo my world-wide ownership.
Yonder I planned a panorama,
A platform built from bough to bough,
To grant my eye a distant prospect
Of all that I have done till now, 105
Whence I could see at once aligned
The masterpiece of human mind,
Which energizes skilfully
The peoples' lands reclaimed from sea.

Hence is our soul upon the rack 110
Who feel, midst plenty, what we lack.
That clanging bell, that linden-scent,
Are like a tomb—I feel so pent.
The omnipotence of random will
Is broken on this sandy hill.
How to shake off this thing which binds me! 115
The bell rings out—and fury blinds me.

MEPHISTOPHELES. Naturally. Such a nagging pain
Must fill your life with gall, it's plain
To everyone. Your cultured ear 120
Must find this tinkling vile to hear.
And that damned ding-dong rising high
Befogs the happy evening sky,
Mingling in all things that befall
From baptism to burial, 125
As if between that ding and dong
Life were a dream that had gone wrong.

FAUST. That obstinacy, all-perverse,
    Makes all one's finest gains a curse,
    So that, though gnawed at heart, one must   130
    At last grow tired of being just.
MEPHISTOPHELES. Why then these scruples? Your vocation
    Has long meant shifts of population.
FAUST. Then go and shift them me at once!
    You know the pretty little place   135
    That I envisaged in their case.
MEPHISTOPHELES. One takes them out and dumps them—Why,
    Before one knows, they're up and spry;
    A fine new homestead, in due course,
    Atones them for our use of force.   140
        [*He whistles shrilly.* THE THREE *re-enter.*]
    The owner's orders! Come! Don't sorrow,
    For there's seamen's feast to-morrow.
THE THREE MIGHTY MEN. The old man welcomed us like beasts;
    It's what he owes us—he-men's feasts!
MEPHISTOPHELES. [*To the audience*] A tale long past is told
    again;   145
    There was a Naboth's vineyard then.

DEEP NIGHT

LYNCEUS. [*Singing on the water-tower*]
    For seeing begotten,
    My sight my employ,
    And sworn to the watch-tower,
    The world gives me joy.
    I gaze in the distance,   5
    I mark in the near
    The moon and the planets,
    The woods and the deer.
    So find I in all things
    Eternal delight,   10
    The more that they please me
    Am pleased to have sight.
    Oh eyes, what has reached you,
    So gladly aware,
    Whatever its outcome,   15
    At least it was fair.

  But not only to have pleasure
  Am I posted on this tower;

133. *population:* Mephistopheles suggests that Faust send the aged couple out as colonists.

146. *Naboth's vineyard:* See I Kings 21. The phrase is used figuratively to mean a possession that one will use any means to secure.

What a gruesome horror threatens
From the world at this dark hour!   20
Glancing sparks I see in fountains
Through the lindens' double night.
Burrowing onward, fanned by breezes,
Ever stronger glows the light.
Ah! The hut, once damp and mossy,   25
Flames within it pave and lave it;
There's a call for quick assistance,
No one is at hand to save it.
Ah, that aged decent couple,
Once so careful about fire,   30
Smothered now in smoke and cinders!
What an end! How strange! How dire!
Blaze on blaze and glowing red
Stands that black and lichened frame;
Could the good folk but escape   35
From that hell of crazy flame!
Little lightnings, tonguing, twisting,
Climb through leaf and bough, insisting;
Dried-up branches burn and flicker—
One quick flare and down they fall.   40
Must my eyes bear this? Must I be
So far-sighted after all?
Now the little church collapses
Under falling bough on bough.
In a swirl of pointed flames   45
The tree-tops are on fire by now.
To their roots the hollow tree-trunks
Glow, empurpled in their glow.
          [*Long pause. Chanting.*]
That which once enticed my vision—
Gone like ages long ago!   50
FAUST. [*On the balcony, towards the dunes*]
What is this whimpering above me?
Both words and burden are too late.
My watchman wails; my heart resents
An action so precipitate.
Yet, though the lindens' life be ended   55
In half-charred trunks, a thing to dread,
One soon can build there a gazebo
To gaze on the unlimited.
There I see too that fine new dwelling
Which will enfold that aged pair,

57. *gazebo:* a small structure from which a view can be seen—a belvedere, balcony, turret, or the like.

59. *dwelling:* Faust had no intention of killing the pair; he merely wanted to move them.

Who grateful for my generous forethought
Can spend their last days blithely there.

MEPHISTOPHELES AND THE THREE MIGHTY MEN. [*Below*]

At a full gallop, riding strong,
Excuse us if our task went wrong.
We knocked and beat upon the door   65
But no one opened it the more;
We went on knocking, rattled it,
The rotten door gave way and split;
We shouted angry threats at once
But still we met with no response.   70
And, as in such a case holds good
They could have heard us if they would;
But we refused to make delay,
We quickly dragged them both away.
The pain they felt was only slight,   75
They fell down dead at once from fright.
A stranger hidden in the hut,
Who wished to fight, we knocked him out.
And in that short but savage fight
The scattered fire-coals set alight   80
Some straw. And that unbridled fire
Now gives all three one funeral pyre.

FAUST. Did you then turn deaf ears to me?
I meant exchange, not robbery.
That random stroke, so wild, perverse—   85
I curse it; you can share the curse.

CHORUS. The word rings out, the ancient word:
When violence speaks, she's gladly heard.
Only be brave and tough, then take
House, goods—and self—and lay your stake.   90
[*They go out.*]

FAUST. [*On the balcony*] The stars conceal their light and now
The fire sinks down and glimmers low;
A shivery breeze still fanning it
Covers me here with smoke and grit.
Quickly required, too quickly done—   95
What shadowy shapes come drifting on?

MIDNIGHT

Four Grey Women approach.

WANT. They call me Want.

---

77. *stranger:* the Wanderer who appeared in the first scene of Act V.
96. *shapes:* The smoke from the
cottage assumes the shapes of the four
phantom hags who speak in the next
scene.
1–4. *Want . . . Need:* allegorical
personifications of four of life's chief
torments.

DEBT. They call me Debt.

CARE. They call me Care.

NEED. They call me Need.

DEBT. The door is locked and we cannot get in. 5

NEED. Nor do we want to, there's wealth within.

WANT. That makes me a shadow.

DEBT. That makes me naught.

NEED. The pampered spare me never a thought.

CARE. My sisters, you cannot and may not get in. 10
    But the keyhole there lets Care creep in.
        [CARE *vanishes*.]

WANT. Come, grey sisters, away from here!

DEBT. Debt at your side as close as fear.

NEED. And Need at your heels as close as breath.

THE THREE. Drifting cloud and vanishing star! 15
    Look yonder, look yonder!
        From far, from far,
    He's coming, our brother, he's coming . . .
        Death.

FAUST. [*In the palace*] Where four came hither, but three go hence;
    I heard them speak, I could not catch the sense. 21
    An echoing word resembling 'breath'—
    And a dark rhyme-word followed: 'Death'.
    A hollow, muffled, spectral sound to hear.
    Not yet have I fought my way out to the air. 25
    All magic—from my path if I could spurn it,
    All incantation—once for all unlearn it,
    To face you, Nature, as one man of men—
    It would be worth it to be human then.
    As I was once, before I probed the hidden, 30
    And cursed my world and self with words forbidden.
    But now such spectredom so throngs the air
    That none knows how to dodge it, none knows where.
    Though one day greet us with a rational gleam,
    The night entangles us in webs of dream. 35
    We come back happy from the fields of spring—
    And a bird croaks. Croaks what? Some evil thing.
    Enmeshed in superstition night and morn,
    It forms and shows itself and comes to warn.
    And we, so scared, stand without friend or kin, 40
    And the door creaks—and nobody comes in.
    Anyone here?

---

10. *cannot . . . get in:* Care ("Frau Sorge") alone can enter the rich man's house.
25–35. *Not yet . . . dream:* Despite age and experience, Faust cannot free himself from those superstitions which his rational mind tells him are false.

CARE.   The answer should be clear.

FAUST. And you, who *are* you then?

CARE.   I am just here.   45

FAUST. Take yourself off!

CARE.   This is where I belong.

[FAUST *is first angry, then recovers himself.*]

FAUST. [*To himself*] Take care, Faust, speak no magic spell, be
    strong.

CARE. Though to me no ear would hearken,
        Echoes through the heart must darken;   50
        Changing shape from hour to hour
        I employ my savage power.
        On the road or on the sea,
        Constant fearful company,
        Never looked for, always found,   55
        Cursed—but flattered by the sound.
    Care? Have you never met with Care?

FAUST. I have only galloped through the world
    And clutched each lust and longing by the hair;
    What did not please me, I let go,   60
    What flowed away, I let it flow.
    I have only felt, only fulfilled desire,
    And once again desired and thus with power
    Have stormed my way through life; first great and strong,
    Now moving sagely, prudently along.   65
    This earthly circle I know well enough.
    Towards the Beyond the view has been cut off;
    Fool—who directs that way his dazzled eye,
    Contrives himself a double in the sky!
    Let him look round him here, not stray beyond;   70
    To a sound man this world must needs respond.
    To roam into eternity is vain!
    What he perceives, he can attain.
    Thus let him walk along his earthlong day;
    Though phantoms haunt him, let him go his way,   75
    And, *moving on*, to weal and woe assent—
    He, at each moment ever discontent!

CARE. Whomsoever I possess,
        Finds the world but nothingness;
        Gloom descends on him for ever,   80
        Seeing sunrise, sunset, never;
        Though his senses are not wrong,
        Darknesses within him throng,

68–74. *Fool . . . day:* What is expressed here is less an agnostic disbelief in personal immortality than a refusal to admit that virtue in this life depends on faith in the existence of ultimate values in the next.

Who—of all that he may own—
Never owns himself alone. 85
Luck, ill luck, become but fancy;
Starving in the midst of plenty,
Be it rapture, be it sorrow,
He postpones it till to-morrow,
Fixed upon futurity, 90
Can never really come to be.

FAUST. Stop! You cannot touch me so!
Such nonsense I refuse to hear.
Away! Your evil tale of woe
Could fog a wise man's brain, however clear. 95

CARE. Let him come or go—he'll find
That he can't make up his mind;
Half-way down his destined way
Starts to stumble, grope and sway,
Ever deeper lost and thwarted, 100
Seeing all things more distorted,
Burden to himself and others,
Who takes breath and, breathing, smothers;
If not smothered, yet not living,
Not revolted, not self-giving. 105
Endless round—he must pursue it:
Painful Leave-it, hateful Do-it,
Freedom now, now harsh constraint,
Broken sleep that leaves him faint,
Bind him to his one position 110
And prepare him for perdition.

FAUST. You outcast phantoms! Thus a thousand times
You lead the human race into illusion;
Even indifferent days you thus transform
To nets of torment, nightmares of confusion. 115
Demons, I know, are hardly shaken off,
Their ghostly gripping bonds man cannot sever;
But you, O Care, your power that creeps and grows—
I shall not recognize it ever.

CARE. Then feel it now! As, leaving you, 120
This final curse on you I cast.
The human race are blind their whole life through;
Now, Faust, let *you* be blind at last.
[*She breathes upon him.*]

FAUST. [*Blindly*] The night seems pressing in more thickly, thickly,
Yet in my inmost heart a light shines clear; 125
What I have planned, I must complete it quickly;
Only the master's word is weighty here.

Up and to work, my men! Each man of you!
And bring my bold conception to full view.
Take up your tools and toil with pick and spade!   130
What has been outlined must at once be *made*.
Good order, active diligence,
Ensure the fairest recompense;
That this vast work completion find,
A thousand hands need but one mind.   135

GREAT FORECOURT OF THE PALACE

Torches.

MEPHISTOPHELES. [*Leading the way, as foreman*]
    Come on, come on! Come in, come in!
    You gangling gang of Lemurs,
    You half-alives patched up with thin
    Sinews and skulls and femurs.

LEMURS. [*In chorus*] You call us, here we are at hand;   5
    And, as we understand it,
    We stand to win a stretch of land
    Intended as our mandate.

    Our pointed staves we have them here,
    Our chain to measure sections,   10
    But why you called on us, we fear,
    Has slipped our recollections.

MEPHISTOPHELES. Artistic efforts we can spare;
    And just let each one's nature guide him!
    Let now the longest lie his length down there,   15
    You others prise away the turf beside him;
    As for your forebears long asleep,
    Dig you an oblong, long and deep.
    To narrow house from palace hall
    Is such a stupid way to end it all.   20

    [*The* LEMURS *begin to dig, with mocking gestures.*]

LEMURS. When I was young and lived and loved,
    Methought it was passing sweet;
    In the merry rout and roundabout
    There would I twirl my feet.

---

2. *Lemurs:* small mammals with pointed snouts, akin to monkeys. The word is related to the Latin *lemures*, denoting the spirits of the wicked dead. Goethe here depicts them as loose-jointed, shambling, semihuman skeletons, servants of the devil.
4. *femurs:* thighbones.
9–10. *staves . . . chain:* surveyor's tools.

12. *recollections:* Traditionally, lemurs were believed to have faulty and brief memories.
19. *narrow house:* the grave.
21–28. *When . . . there:* Goethe adapted these verses freely from the clown-gravedigger's song in *Hamlet*, Act V, Scene 1, when Ophelia's grave is being dug.

But sneaking Age has upped his crutch
And downed me unaware;
I stumbled over the door of the grave—
Why was it open *there*?

FAUST. [*Groping his way from the palace*] Oh how this clink of
spades rejoices me!
For that is my conscripted labour,   30
The earth is now her own good neighbour
And sets the waves a boundary—
Confinement strict and strenuous.

MEPHISTOPHELES. [*Aside*] And yet you've only toiled for *us*
With all your damming, all your dyking—   35
Spreading a feast to Neptune's liking
To glut that water-demon's maw.
In all respects you're lost and stranded,
The elements with us have banded—
Annihilation is the law.   40

FAUST. Foreman!

MEPHISTOPHELES. Here!

FAUST.   Use every means you can;
Bring all your gangs up and exhort them—
Threaten them if you like or court them—
But pay or woo or force each man!   45
And day by day send word to me, assessing
How my intended earthworks are progressing.

MEPHISTOPHELES. [*Half aloud*] The word to-day, from what I've
heard,
Is not 'intended' but 'interred'.   50

FAUST. A swamp along the mountains' flank
Makes all my previous gains contaminate;
My deeds, if I could drain this sink,
Would culminate as well as terminate:
To open to the millions living space,   55
Not danger-proof but free to run their race.
Green fields and fruitful; men and cattle hiving
Upon this newest earth at once and thriving,
Settled at once beneath this sheltering hill
Heaped by the masses' brave and busy skill.   60
With such a heavenly land behind this hedge,
The sea beyond may bluster to its edge
And, as it gnaws to swamp the work of masons,
To stop the gap one common impulse hastens.
Aye! Wedded to this concept like a wife,   65

29. *rejoices:* These noises, ironically, are actually the sound of his own grave being dug.
37. *water-demon:* Mephistopheles, following the fashion of early Christianity, makes Neptune (Poseidon), the Greek and Roman god of the sea, into a devil.

I find this wisdom's final form:
He only earns his freedom and his life
Who takes them every day by storm.
And so a man, beset by dangers here,
As child, man, old man, spends his manly year.   70
Oh to see such activity,
Treading free ground with people that are free!
Then could I bid the passing moment:
'Linger a while, thou art so fair!'
The traces of my earthly days can never   75
Sink in the aeons unaware.
And I, who feel ahead such heights of bliss,
At last enjoy my highest moment—this.

[FAUST *sinks back; the* LEMURS *seize him and lay him on the ground.*]

MEPHISTOPHELES. By no joy sated, filled by no success,
Still whoring after shapes that flutter past,   80
This last ill moment of sheer emptiness—
The poor man yearns to hold it fast.
He who withstood me with such strength,
Time masters him and here he lies his length.
The clock stands still—   85
CHORUS.   Stands still! Like midnight . . . silent . . . stilled.
Its hand drops down.
MEPHISTOPHELES.   Drops down; it is fulfilled.
LEMURS. It is gone by.
MEPHISTOPHELES.   Gone by! A stupid phrase.   90
Why say gone by?
Gone by—pure naught—complete monotony.
What use these cycles of creation!
Or snatching off the creatures to negation!
'It is gone by!'—and we can draw the inference: 95
If it had *not* been, it would make no difference;
The wheel revolves the same, no more, no less.
I should prefer eternal emptiness.

INTERMENT

LEMUR SOLO.   Oh who has built the house so ill
With spade and shovel rough?
LEMUR CHORUS.   For you, dull guest in hempen garb,

71–78. *Oh . . . this:* See the words
of the original pact, ll. 166–178 of the
second scene titled FAUST'S STUDY, in
Faust, Part I. By uttering them, Faust
loses to Mephistopheles; but the use
of the conditional ("Then could I
bid . . .") indicates that he is still
striving, and he can be saved by God.
His satisfaction is potential rather than
actual.

87–88. *Its hand . . . fulfilled:* It has
been suggested that this line refers to
the pointer on a medieval water clock,
which rose steadily for twenty-four
hours and then dropped back to its
starting point at the bottom when midnight was reached.

1–4. *Oh . . . enough:* another free

Yon house is fine enough.

LEMUR SOLO.   No chair or table in the hall—   5
Who's furnished it so meagre?

LEMUR CHORUS.   The loan was only for a time;
The creditors are eager.

MEPHISTOPHELES. Here lies the corpse and if the soul would flee
At once I show the bond, the blood-signed scroll;   10
Though now, alas, they have so many means
To cheat the devil of a soul.
Our old procedure gives offence,
Our new has not yet found endorsement;
Once I'd have managed it alone,   15
Now I must look for reinforcement.
Come up, you devils! Make it double quick!
You straight-horned peers and crooked-horned as well,
You old and sterling devil-stock,
Come up—and bring with you the jaws of Hell!   20
[*The Jaws of Hell open upon the left.*]
The eye-teeth gape; the throat's enormous vault
Spews forth a raging fiery flow
And through the smoking cyclone of the gullet
I see the infernal city's eternal glow.
You do right well to make the sinner quake;   25
And yet they think it all a dream, a fake.
Now, devils, watch this body! How does it seem?
See if you see a phosphorescent gleam.
That is the little soul, Psyche with wings—
Pull out her wings and it's a noisome worm;   30
With my own seal I'll set my stamp upon her,
Then forth with her into the fiery storm!
Come, claw and comb the air, strain every nerve
To catch her though she flutter, though she swerve.
To stay in her old lodging gives her pain;   35
The genius is about to leave the brain.
[*Glory, from above, on the right.*]

THE HOST OF HEAVEN. Fly, as directed,
Heaven's elected,
Serenely whereby
Sin shall have pardon,   40

adaptation by Goethe (as in ll. 21–28 of the preceding scene) from *Hamlet*, Act V, Scene 1; this time, of the third stanza of the gravedigger's song.

21–36. *The eye-teeth . . . the brain:* Mephistopheles' speech and description of hell may have been suggested to Goethe by Lasinio's reproductions of the Campo Santo frescoes at Pisa painted by an unknown follower of Lorenzetti.

29. *Psyche:* in Greek mythology, the beloved of Eros, god of love; she was represented with butterfly wings. The word also meant "life," "soul," or "breath."

Dust become garden;
Stay your progression,
Make intercession,
Trace for all natures
A path to the sky.   45

MEPHISTOPHELES. Discords I hear, a filthy strumming tumbling
Down from the sky with the unwelcome day;
That is the angels' boyish-girlish fumbling,
Their canting taste *likes* it to sound that way.
You know how we, in hours of deep damnation,   50
Have schemed annihilation for mankind;
Those angels use for adoration
The greatest stigma we could find.
They come so fawningly, the milksops!
They've kidnapped many souls before our eyes,   55
They fight us back with our own weapons;
They too are devils—in disguise.
Defeat to-day would mean disgrace eternal;
So stand around the grave and stand infernal!

CHORUS OF ANGELS. [*Scattering roses*]

    Roses, you glowing ones,   60
    Balsam-bestowing ones!
    Fluttering peaceably,
    Healing invisibly,
    Spraylets to glide upon,
    Budlets unspied upon,   65
    Hasten to bloom!

    Green and empurpled,
    Spring must have room;
    Carry your heaven
    Into the tomb!   70

MEPHISTOPHELES. [*To the Satans*] Why duck and squirm? Is that
    our wont in hell?
Stand fast and let them strew their roses!
Each gawk to his post and guard it well!
With such small flowers the enemy proposes
To snow up overheated devils;   75
Why, at your breath it melts and shrivels.
Now puff, you blow-fiends!

        . . . Here! Stop! Stop!
Your reek is bleaching the whole flight and crop.
Don't blow so hard! Muzzle your chops and noses!   80

---

74. *flowers:* In the Pisan frescoes the angels fight the devils with crosses, not
roses.

I'll swear you've *overblown* those roses!
You never know when you have passed the turn!
They're more than shrunk—they're browned, they're dry, they
    burn!
Bright flames of poison pelt on us already;
In close formation, devils! Steady! Steady!   85
What! All your valour gone! Your strength burns low!
The devils sense a strange insidious glow.
CHORUS OF ANGELS. Blooms of pure blessedness,
                Flames of pure joyfulness,
                Love is their ministry,   90
                Rapture their legacy,
                All we could pray.
                Hosts of eternity
                Find in such verity
                Heavens of clarity,   95
                Aeons of day!
MEPHISTOPHELES. A curse upon these louts! How scurvy!
My Satans are all topsy-turvy
And turning cartwheels in their path
And tumbling arse-up into Hell.   100
I hope you like your well-earned sulphur bath!
I stand my ground and wish you well.
      [*He beats off the roses falling around him.*]
CHORUS OF ANGELS. What is not right for you
                You must beware it,
                What does despite to you   105
                You may not bear it.
                Lightnings may dart on us,
                We must have heart in us.
                Lovers can only be
                Rescued by love.   110
MEPHISTOPHELES. My head's aflame! Liver and heart aflame!
A super-devilish element!
Hell's fires to this are damped and tame.
That's why you make such wild lament,
You luckless folk in love, despised alas,   115
Who sprain your necks to watch your sweethearts pass.

Me too! What draws my head in that direction?
I, their sworn enemy! Is this defection?
To see them once was agony or worse.
Has something alien entered me completely?   120
To see their flower of youth affects me now so sweetly;
I want to curse them—but what chokes the curse?

And, if I let them now befool me,
Whom can the future call a fool?
These dashing fellows, though I hate them,   125
Inspire a longing that I cannot rule.
Beautiful children, must I not infer
That you like me are kin to Lucifer?
With every look you seem more fair, more fair.
Oh come near, angels, glance on me! Come near!   130
ANGEL. See, we approach—why do you shrink away?
    We come; if you can face us—why, then, stay!
        [_The_ ANGELS, _closing in, occupy all the space._]
CHOIR OF ANGELS. Flames of dear feeling,
                Rise beyond seeing!
                Self-condemned being—   135
                Truth be its healing!
                Blessed transition
                Forth from perdition,
                Into Eternity,
                Into the One!   140
MEPHISTOPHELES. [_Collecting himself_]
    Look! The damned flames are out that caused my fall.
    Now I become myself and curse you one and all!
CHOIR OF ANGELS. Light of Creation!
                Whom it embraces
                Finds all the graces   145
                Found in salvation.
                Praising in unison
                Rise to your goal!
                Purged is the air now—
                Breathe now the soul!   150
        [_They soar up, carrying away the immortal part of_ FAUST.]
MEPHISTOPHELES. [_Looking around him_]
    But how is this? Where have they moved away to?
    You juveniles, to take me by surprise!
    Flying off heavenwards—and with my prey too;
    They nibbled at this grave to win this prize.
    Wresting from me a great and matchless treasure,   155
    That noble soul which gave me right of seizure
    They've filched by throwing rose-dust in my eyes.
    Who is there now to lend an ear to
    My wrong, restore my hard-earned right?
    You have been hoaxed—so late in your career too—   160
    It's your own fault, you're in a lurid plight.
    Such gross mismanagement—outrageous!
    Such a great outlay squandered! Oh the shame!

Erotic folly, vulgar lust, contagious
To an old devil at the game!   165
Experience has indulged its appetite
On such a childish-foolish level;
When all is said, the folly is not slight
Which in the end has seized the devil.

MOUNTAIN GORGES[a]

*Forest, Rock, Wilderness. Holy anchorites, disposed here and
there, at different heights among the chasms.*

CHORUS AND ECHO. Woods clamber tremblingly,
    Crags bear down weightily,
    Roots cling tenaciously,
    Trunks make a density;
    Spurting of wave on wave—   5
    Deep lies our hermits' cave.
    Lions around in dumb
    Friendliness gently come,
    Honour our sanctuary,
    Love's holy privacy.   10

PATER ECSTATICUS. [*Floating up and down*][b]
    Rapture which yearns ever,
    Love-bond which burns ever,
    Pain in me seething up,
    Love of God foaming up.
    Arrows, pierce through me and,   15
    Lances, subdue me and,
    Clubs, leave no form in me,
    Thunderstorms, storm in me!
    That now the Nothingness
    Drown all in emptiness,   20
    One constant star must shine,
    Kernel of love divine.

PATER PROFUNDUS.[c] [*From the depths*]
    As at my feet a craggy chasm
    Weighs on a deeper chasm's prop,
    As streams in thousands flow and sparkle   25
    Towards the dread rapids' foaming drop,
    As with its own strong urge the tree-trunk

a. The inspiration for this scene may
have come from what Goethe had read
of the Benedictine monastery of
Montserrat, near Barcelona, where the
holy mountain was covered by small
hermit cells accessible by ladders.

b. Several Christian mystics, such as
Philip of Neri, have been described
as achieving this saintly buoyancy,
where the flesh is so mortified as to
overcome gravity.
c. Originally this title was reserved
for Bernard of Clairvaux.

Climbs up the air, erect and tall,
Even so is that almighty love
Which all things forms and fosters all.   30

Around me here a frantic rushing
Makes wood and cleft a stormy sea,
Yet full of love the water's fullness
Roars as it plumbs the cavity,
Ordained to straightway feed the valley;   35
The thunderbolt which crashed in flame
To cleanse the air which bore within it
Poison and evil mists, these same

Are messengers of love, announcing
What round us ever moves and makes.   40
May that light kindle too within me
Where the cold spirit gropes and quakes,
Self-racked in body's bonds and dullness,
Riveted fast in chains that smart.
O God, have mercy on my thoughts,   45
Give light to my impoverished heart!

PATER SERAPHICUS.[d] [*At a middle height*]
    What a morning cloudlet hovers
    Through the pine-trees' waving hair!
    I divine what lives within it—
    Newborn souls are gathered there.   50

CHORUS OF BLESSED BOYS.[e] Tell us, Father, where we wander,
    Tell us, good one, who we are!
    All of us are happy, living
    In a state that naught can mar.

PATER SERAPHICUS. Innocents—who, born at midnight   55
    With half-opened soul and brain,
    Were at once your parents' loss,
    Were at once the angels' gain.
    That a living man is present,
    That you feel, so draw you near!   60
    Though earth's rugged ways are barred you,
    Alien to your happy sphere.
    Climb up then into my eyes—
    Organ matching world and earth;
    See this region, using mine   65
    For the eyes you lost at birth.
    [*He takes them into himself.*]

d. This name was given to St. Francis of Assisi.
e. Goethe elsewhere describes these as the spirits of children who have died at birth, before their senses develop, and who hence do not know sin.

Those are trees—and those are crags—
See that river plunging deep,
Which with its enormous welter
Delves a passage, short though deep.   70

BLESSED BOYS. [*From inside him*]
Yes, that is a mighty prospect—
But too sad this world below,
Shaking us with fear and horror.
Reverend father, let us go!

PATER SERAPHICUS. Aye. Ascend to higher circles,   75
Ever grow invisibly
As God's presence makes you stronger
Through eternal purity.
It is this which feeds the spirit,
Rules the heights of revelation: 80
Window into love eternal
Opening upon salvation.

BLESSED BOYS. [*Circling round the highest peak*]
Joyfully gyring
Dance ye in union,
Hands linked and choiring   85
Blessed communion!
Pattern before you,
Godly, to cheer you,
Whom you adore, you
Soon shall see near you.   90

ANGELS. [*Floating in the higher air, carrying the immortal part of
FAUST*]
Saved, saved now is that precious part
Of our spirit world from evil:
'Should a man strive with all his heart,
Heaven can foil the devil.'
And if love also from on high   95
Has helped him through his sorrow,
The hallowed legions of the sky
Will give him glad good morrow.

THE YOUNGER ANGELS. Ah those roses, *their* donation—
Loving-holy penitent women—   100
Helped us to defeat Apollyon,
Brought our work to consummation,
To this priceless spirit's capture.
Devils, as we scattered rapture,
Struck by roses, fled in panic,   105

---

83. *gyring:* ascending in a spiral.   101. *Apollyon:* the devil; from the
Greek word meaning "to destroy."

Feeling not their pains Satanic
But the pains of love's disaster;
Even that old Satan-master
Felt a torment arrowed, marrowed.
Alleluia! Hell is harrowed.   110

THE MORE PERFECT ANGELS. This scrap of earth, alas,
    We must convoy it;
    Were it asbestos, yet
    Earth would alloy it.
    When soul's dynamic force   115
    Has drawn up matter
    Into itself, then no
    Angel could shatter
    The bonds of that twoness—
    The oneness that tied it;   120
    Eternal love alone
    Knows to divide it.

THE YOUNGER ANGELS. Close, round the mountain top,
    To my perceiving
    Moves like a mist a   125
    Spiritual living.
    Those clouds are turning bright,
    I see a sainted flight:
    Children enmeshed from
    Meshes of earth, they   130
    Fly in a ring,
    Being refreshed from
    Heaven's rebirth they
    Bask in its spring.
    Faust, to begin to rise   135
    Towards highest Paradise,
    With them must wing.

THE BLESSED BOYS. Gladly receiving this
    Chrysalid entity,
    Now we achieve, in this,   140
    Angels' identity.
    Let the cocoon which is
    Round him be broken!
    Great! Fair! How soon he is
    Heaven-awoken!   145

DOCTOR MARIANUS.*f* [*In the highest, purest cell*]
    Here is the prospect free,

---

139. *Chrysalid:* Faust is figuratively in a transition stage between the mortal and the immortal.

f. the last of four saints present at the scene. The epithet "Marianus" indicates his special devotion to the Virgin Mary.

Spirit-uplifting.
Yonder go women's shapes
Over me drifting;
And, wreathed in her seven   150
Bright stars, they attend her—
The high queen of Heaven;
I gaze on her splendour.

[*Entranced.*]

Highest empress of the world,
Let these blue and sacred   155
Tents of heaven here unfurled
Show me now thy secret!
Sanction that which in man's breast
Soft and strong prepares him—
Love which joyful, love which blest   160
Towards thy presence bears him.

Thine august commands are such,
Nothing can subdue us—
Fires burn gentler at thy touch
Should thy peace imbue us.   165
Virgin, pure as none are pure,
Mother, pearl of honour,
Chosen as our queen, the sure
Godhead stamped upon her!

Light clouds enlacing   170
Circle her splendour—
These are the penitent
Women, a tender
Race. At thy knee,
Sipping the air, they   175
Call upon thee.

Thou, albeit immaculate,
It is of thy fashion
That the easily seduced
Sue to thy compassion.   180

Such whom frailty reft, are hard,
Hard to save, if ever;
Who can burst the bonds of lust
Through his own endeavour?
Do not sliding gradients cause   185
Sudden slips? What maiden

152. *high queen:* the Virgin Mary.

Is not fooled by flattering glance,
Tokens flattery-laden?

[*The* MATER GLORIOSA*ᵍ floats into vision.*]

CHORUS OF PENITENT WOMEN.*ʰ* Mary, in soaring
    To kingdoms eternal,   190
    Hear our imploring
    Thou beyond rival!
    Fount of survival!

MAGNA PECCATRIX. By my love which mingled tears with
    Balm to bathe His feet, revering   195
Him thy son, now God-transfigured,
When the Pharisees were jeering;
By that vessel which so sweetly
Spilt its perfumed wealth profusely,
By my hair which dried those holy   200
Limbs, around them falling loosely—

MULIER SAMARITANA. By the well where Father Abram
Watered once his flocks when marching,
By the bucket once allowed to
Touch and cool Christ's lips when parching;   205
By that pure and generous source which
Now extends its irrigation,
Overbrimming, ever-crystal,
Flowing through the whole creation—

MARIA AEGYPTIACA. By that more than sacred garden   210
Where they laid the Lord to rest,
By the arm which from the portal
Thrust me back with stern behest;
By my forty years' repentance
Served out in a desert land,   215
By the blessed word of parting
Which I copied in the sand—

THE THREE. Thou who to most sinning women
Thy dear presence ne'er deniest,
Raising us repentant women   220
To eternities the highest,
Make to *this* good soul concession—
Only once misled by pleasure
To a never-dreamt transgression;

g. the Virgin Mary.
h. Three famous penitents intercede for the fourth, Gretchen, Faust's former mistress. They are Mary Magdalene, the Woman of Samaria, and Mary of Egypt (described in the *Acta Sanctorum* as an infamous woman of Alexandria who later made a pilgrimage to Jerusalem).

197. *Pharisees:* members of an ancient Jewish sect noted for its strict observance of the law and its pretensions to sanctity.

202. *Abram:* Abraham.

Grant her pardon in her measure.   225

ONE OF THE PENITENTS. [*Formerly named* GRETCHEN]
     Uniquely tender,
     Thou queen of splendour,
     Thy visage render
     Benign towards my felicity!
     My love of old, he   230
     Is now consoled, he
     Comes back to me.

BLESSED BOYS. [*Approaching, flying in circles*]
     Passing beyond us
     So soon in resplendence,
     He will make ample   235
     Return for our tendance;
     Early we left the
     Terrestrial chorus;
     He will instruct us,
     Instructed before us.   240

THE SINGLE PENITENT. [*Formerly named* GRETCHEN]
  By choirs of noble souls surrounded
  This new one scarcely feels his soul,
  Can scarcely sense this life unbounded,
  Yet fills at once his heavenly role.
  See how he sheds the earthly leaven,   245
  Tears off each shroud of old untruth,
  And from apparel woven in heaven
  Shines forth his pristine power of youth!
  Mary, grant me to instruct him,
  Dazzled as yet by this new day.   250

MATER GLORIOSA. Come then! To higher spheres conduct him!
  Divining *you*, he knows the way.

DOCTOR MARIANUS. [*Bowing in adoration*]
     All you tender penitents,
     Gaze on her who saves you—
     Thus change your lineaments   255
     And salvation laves you.
     To her feet each virtue crawl,
     Let her will transcend us;
     Virgin, Mother, Queen of All,
     Goddess, still befriend us!   260

CHORUS MYSTICUS. All that is past of us
     Was but reflected;
     All that was lost in us
     Here is corrected;
     All indescribables   265

Here we descry;
Eternal Womanhead
Lead us on high.

GEORGE GORDON, LORD BYRON
(1788–1824)
Don Juan

Canto II*

I

Oh ye! who teach the ingenuous youth of nations,
    Holland, France, England, Germany, or Spain,
I pray ye flog them upon all occasions,
    It mends their morals, never mind the pain:
The best of mothers and of educations   5
    In Juan's case were but employed in vain,
Since, in a way that's rather of the oddest, he
Became divested of his native modesty.

II

Had he but been placed at a public school,
    In the third form, or even in the fourth,   10
His daily task had kept his fancy cool,
    At least, had he been nurtured in the north—
Spain may prove an exception to the rule,
    But then exceptions always prove its worth—
A lad of sixteen causing a divorce   15
Puzzled his tutors very much, of course.

III

I can't say that it puzzles me at all,
    If all things be considered; first, there was
His lady-mother, mathematical,
    A——never mind;—his tutor, an old ass;   20
A pretty woman—(that's quite natural,
    Or else the thing had hardly come to pass)
A husband rather old, not much in unity
With his young wife—a time, and opportunity.

* Written between December 13, 1818 and January 20, 1819; published on July 15, 1819.

6. *vain*: In Canto I Byron describes his hero Juan, born in Seville to a pedantic mother and an unfaithful father. Juan's mother, Donna Inez, is soon widowed; and despite Juan's careful education, he succumbs to the charms of the young Julia, married to a much older husband. A bedroom farce ensues, with Juan hiding under Julia's bedclothes. Juan escapes, but the scandal breaks. Don Alfonso, Julia's husband, sues for divorce, and Donna Inez orders her son to leave Spain by way of Cadiz.

IV

Well—well; the world must turn upon its axis,   25
　　And all mankind turn with it, heads or tails,
And live and die, make love and pay our taxes,
　　And as the veering wind shifts, shift our sails;
The king commands us, and the doctor quacks us,
　　The priest instructs, and so our life exhales,   30
A little breath, love, wine, ambition, fame,
Fighting, devotion, dust,—perhaps a name.

V

I said, that Juan had been sent to Cadiz—
　　A pretty town, I recollect it well—
'Tis where the mart of colonial trade is,   35
　　(Or was, before Peru learned to rebel,)
And such sweet girls—I mean, such graceful ladies,
　　Their very walk would make your bosom swell;
I can't describe it, though so much it strike,
Nor liken it—I never saw the like: 40

VI

An Arab horse, a stately stag, a barb
　　New broke, a cameleopard, a gazelle,
No—none of these will do;—and then their garb,
　　Their veil and petticoat—Alas! to dwell
Upon such things would very near absorb   45
　　A canto—then their feet and ankles,—well,
Thank Heaven I've got no metaphor quite ready,
(And so, my sober Muse—come, let's be steady—

VII

Chaste Muse!—well, if you must, you must)—the veil
　　Thrown back a moment with the glancing hand,   50
While the o'erpowering eye, that turns you pale,
　　Flashes into the heart:—All sunny land
Of love! when I forget you, may I fail
　　To——say my prayers—but never was there plann'd
A dress through which the eyes give such a volley,   55
Excepting the Venetian Fazzioli.

VIII

But to our tale: the Donna Inez sent
　　Her son to Cadiz only to embark;

36. *Peru:* Between 1810 and 1825 the Spanish and Portuguese colonies in South America were in a state of rebellion. Peru became an independent nation in 1821, two years after this canto was written.

41. *barb:* breed of horse imported from Barbary, in North Africa.
42. *cameleopard:* giraffe.
56. *Fazzioli:* "literally, the little handkerchiefs—the veils most availing of St. Mark." [Byron's note.]

To stay there had not answered her intent,
　　But why?—we leave the reader in the dark—　　60
'Twas for a voyage the young man was meant,
　　As if a Spanish ship were Noah's ark,
To wean him from the wickedness of earth,
And send him like a dove of promise forth.

IX

Don Juan bade his valet pack his things　　65
　　According to direction, then received
A lecture and some money: for four springs
　　He was to travel; and though Inez grieved
(As every kind of parting has its stings),
　　She hoped he would improve—perhaps believed:　　70
A letter, too, she gave (he never read it)
Of good advice—and two or three of credit.

X

In the mean time, to pass her hours away,
　　Brave Inez now set up a Sunday school
For naughty children, who would rather play　　75
　　(Like truant rogues) the devil, or the fool;
Infants of three years old were taught that day,
　　Dunces were whipt, or set upon a stool:
The great success of Juan's education
Spurred her to teach another generation.　　80

XI

Juan embarked—the ship got under way,
　　The wind was fair, the water passing rough;
A devil of a sea rolls in that bay,
　　As I, who've crossed it oft, know well enough;
And, standing upon deck, the dashing spray　　85
　　Flies in one's face, and makes it weather-tough:
And there he stood to take, and take again,
His first—perhaps his last—farewell of Spain.

XII

I can't but say it is an awkward sight
　　To see one's native land receding through　　90
The growing waters; it unmans one quite,
　　Especially when life is rather new:
I recollect Great Britain's coast looks white,
　　But almost every other country's blue,
When gazing on them, mystified by distance,　　95
We enter on our nautical existence.

XIII

So Juan stood, bewildered on the deck:
  The wind sung, cordage strained, and sailors swore,
And the ship creaked, the town became a speck,
  From which away so fair and fast they bore.   100
The best of remedies is a beef-steak
  Against sea-sickness: try it, sir, before
You sneer, and I assure you this is true,
For I have found it answer—so may you.

XIV

Don Juan stood, and, gazing from the stern,   105
  Beheld his native Spain receding far:
First partings form a lesson hard to learn,
  Even nations feel this when they go to war;
There is a sort of unexprest concern,
  A kind of shock that sets one's heart ajar: 110
At leaving even the most unpleasant people
And places, one keeps looking at the steeple.

XV

But Juan had got many things to leave,
  His mother, and a mistress, and no wife,
So that he had much better cause to grieve   115
  Than many persons more advanced in life;
And if we now and then a sigh must heave
  At quitting even those we quit in strife,
No doubt we weep for those the heart endears—
That is, till deeper griefs congeal our tears.   120

XVI

So Juan wept, as wept the captive Jews
  By Babel's waters, still remembering Sion:
I'd weep,—but mine is not a weeping Muse,
  And such light griefs are not a thing to die on;
Young men should travel, if but to amuse   125
  Themselves; and the next time their servants tie on
Behind their carriages their new portmanteau,
Perhaps it may be lined with this my canto.

XVII

And Juan wept, and much he sighed and thought,
  While his salt tears dropped into the salt sea,   130

121. *Jews:* a reference to the Babylonian captivity (586–538 B.C.), which
began when Nebuchadnezzar captured
and destroyed Jerusalem, and the Jews
were carried off in bondage. See
Psalm 137.

"Sweets to the sweet;" (I like so much to quote;
    You must excuse this extract—'tis where she,
The Queen of Denmark, for Ophelia brought
    Flowers to the grave;) and, sobbing often, he
Reflected on his present situation,   135
And seriously resolved on reformation.

XVIII

"Farewell, my Spain! a long farewell!" he cried,
    "Perhaps I may revisit thee no more,
But die, as many an exiled heart hath died,
    Of its own thirst to see again thy shore: 140
Farewell, where Guadalquivir's waters glide!
    Farewell, my mother! and, since all is o'er,
Farewell, too, dearest Julia—(here he drew
Her letter out again, and read it through.)

XIX

"And oh! if e'er I should forget, I swear—   145
    But that's impossible, and cannot be—
Sooner shall this blue ocean melt to air,
    Sooner shall earth resolve itself to sea,
Than I resign thine image, oh, my fair!
    Or think of anything, excepting thee;   150
A mind diseased no remedy can physic—
(Here the ship gave a lurch, and he grew sea-sick.)

XX

"Sooner shall heaven kiss earth—(here he fell sicker)
    Oh, Julia, what is every other woe?—
(For God's sake let me have a glass of liquor;   155
    Pedro, Battista, help me down below.)
Julia, my love—(you rascal, Pedro, quicker)—
    Oh, Julia!—(this curst vessel pitches so)—
Beloved Julia, hear me still beseeching!"
(Here he grew inarticulate with retching.)   160

XXI

He felt that chilling heaviness of heart,
    Or rather stomach, which, alas! attends,
Beyond the best apothecary's art,
    The loss of love, the treachery of friends,
Or death of those we dote on, when a part   165

131. *"Sweets to the sweet": Hamlet,*
Act V, Scene 1, l. 266 (l. 31 in our
text).

141. *Guadalquivir:* the river by
which Cadiz is situated.

Of us dies with them as each fond hope ends:
No doubt he would have been much more pathetic,
But the sea acted as a strong emetic.

XXII

Love's capricious power: I've known it hold
    Out through a fever caused by its own heat,   170
But be much puzzled by a cough and cold,
    And find a quinsy very hard to treat;
Against all noble maladies he's bold,
    But vulgar illnesses don't like to meet,
Nor that a sneeze should interrupt his sigh,   175
Nor inflammations redden his blind eye.

XXIII

But worse of all is nausea, or a pain
    About the lower region of the bowels;
Love, who heroically breathes a vein,
    Shrinks from the application of hot towels,   180
And purgatives are dangerous to his reign,
    Sea-sickness death: his love was perfect, how else
Could Juan's passion, while the billows roar,
Resist his stomach, ne'er at sea before?

XXIV

The ship, called the most holy *Trinidada*,   185
    Was steering duly for the port Leghorn;
For there the Spanish family Moncada
    Were settled long ere Juan's sire was born:
They were relations, and for them he had a
    Letter of introduction, which the morn   190
Of his departure had been sent him by
His Spanish friends for those in Italy.

XXV

His suite consisted of three servants and
    A tutor, the licentiate Pedrillo,
Who several languages did understand,   195
    But now lay sick and speechless on his pillow,
And, rocking in his hammock, longed for land,
    His headache being increased by every billow;

172. *quinsy:* inflammation of the throat.
179. *breathes:* lances.
185. *Trinidada:* Trinity.
186. *Leghorn:* Livorno, a port on the western coast of Italy, north of Rome.
194. *licentiate:* person holding a university degree, adjudged competent to teach.

And the waves oozing through the port-hole made
His berth a little damp, and him afraid.   200

XXVI

'Twas not without some reason, for the wind
    Increased at night, until it blew a gale;
And though 'twas not much to a naval mind,
    Some landsmen would have looked a little pale,
For sailors are, in fact, a different kind: 205
    At sunset they began to take in sail,
For the sky showed it would come on to blow,
And carry away, perhaps, a mast or so.

XXVII

At one o'clock the wind with sudden shift
    Threw the ship right into the trough of the sea,   210
Which struck her aft, and made an awkward rift,
    Started the stern-post, also shattered the
Whole of her stern-frame, and, ere she could lift
    Herself from out her present jeopardy,
The rudder tore away: 'twas time to sound   215
The pumps, and there were four feet water found.

XXVIII

One gang of people instantly was put
    Upon the pumps, and the remainder set
To get up part of the cargo, and what not;
    But they could not come at the leak as yet;   220
At last they did get at it really, but
    Still their salvation was an even bet:
The water rushed through in a way quite puzzling,
While they thrust sheets, shirts, jackets, bales of muslin,

XXIX

Into the opening; but all such ingredients   225
    Would have been in vain, and they must have gone down,
Despite of all their efforts and expedients,
    But for the pumps: I'm glad to make them known
To all the brother tars who may have need hence,
    For fifty tons of water were upthrown   230
By them per hour, and they all had been undone,
But for the maker, Mr. Mann, of London.

---

201. *wind:* Although Bryon maintained that all his sea descriptions came
from personal experience, it is now
known that he borrowed much from
Sir G. Dalzell's *Shipwrecks and Disasters at Sea* (1812).

XXX

As day advanced the weather seemed to abate,
    And then the leak they reckoned to reduce,
And keep the ship afloat, though three feet yet   235
    Kept two hand and one chain-pump still in use.
The wind blew fresh again: as it grew late
    A squall came on, and while some guns broke loose,
A gust—which all descriptive power transcends—
Laid with one blast the ship on her beam ends.   240

XXXI

There she lay, motionless, and seemed upset;
    The water left the hold, and washed the decks,
And made a scene men do not soon forget;
    For they remember battles, fires, and wrecks,
Or any other thing that brings regret,   245
    Or breaks their hopes, or hearts, or heads, or necks;
Thus drownings are much talked of by the divers,
And swimmers, who may chance to be survivors.

XXXII

Immediately the masts were cut away,
    Both main and mizen: first the mizen went,   250
The main-mast followed; but the ship still lay
    Like a mere log, and baffled our intent.
Foremast and bowsprit were cut down, and they
    Eased her at last (although we never meant
To part with all till every hope was blighted),   255
And then with violence the old ship righted.

XXXIII

It may be easily supposed, while this
    Was going on, some people were unquiet,
That passengers would find it much amiss
    To lose their lives, as well as spoil their diet;   260
That even the able seaman, deeming his
    Days nearly o'er, might be disposed to riot,
As upon such occasions tars will ask
For grog, and sometimes drink rum from the cask.

XXXIV

There's nought, no doubt, so much the spirit calms   265
    As rum and true religion: thus it was,
Some plundered, some drank spirits, some sung psalms,
    The high wind made the treble, and as bass

The hoarse harsh waves kept time; fright cured the qualms
  Of all the luckless landsmen's sea-sick maws: 270
Strange sounds of wailing, blasphemy, devotion,
Clamoured in chorus to the roaring ocean.

XXXV

Perhaps more mischief had been done, but for
  Our Juan, who, with sense beyond his years,
Got to the spirit-room, and stood before 275
  It with a pair of pistols; and their fears,
As if Death were more dreadful by his door
  Of fire than water, spite of oaths and tears,
Kept still aloof the crew, who, ere they sunk,
Thought it would be becoming to die drunk. 280

XXXVI

"Give us more grog," they cried, "for it will be
  All one an hour hence." Juan answered, "No!
'Tis true that death awaits both you and me,
  But let us die like men, not sink below
Like brutes:"—and thus his dangerous post kept he, 285
  And none liked to anticipate the blow;
And even Pedrillo, his most reverend tutor,
Was for some rum a disappointed suitor.

XXXVII

The good old gentleman was quite aghast,
  And made a loud and pious lamentation; 290
Repented all his sins, and made a last
  Irrevocable vow of reformation;
Nothing should tempt him more (this peril past)
  To quit his academic occupation,
In cloisters of the classic Salamanca, 295
To follow Juan's wake, like Sancho Panca.

XXXVIII

But now there came a flash of hope once more;
  Day broke, and the wind lulled: the masts were gone;
The leak increased; shoals round her, but no shore,
  The vessel swam, yet still she held her own. 300
They tried the pumps again, and though before
  Their desperate efforts seemed all useless grown,

295. *Salamanca:* city in eastern Spain, possessing the oldest university (founded 1230) on the Iberian peninsula.

296. *Sancho Panca:* Sancho Panza, the knight's servant in Cervantes' *Don Quixote.*

A glimpse of sunshine set some hands to bale—
The stronger pumped, the weaker thrummed a sail.

XXXIX

Under the vessel's keel the sail was passed,   305
    And for the moment it had some effect;
But with a leak, and not a stick of mast,
    Nor rag of canvas, what could they expect?
But still 'tis best to struggle to the last,
    'Tis never too late to be wholly wrecked: 310
And though 'tis true that man can only die once,
'Tis not so pleasant in the Gulf of Lyons.

XL

There winds and waves had hurled them, and from thence,
    Without their will, they carried them away;
For they were forced with steering to dispense,   315
    And never had as yet a quiet day
On which they might repose, or even commence
    A jurymast or rudder, or could say
The ship would swim an hour, which, by good luck,
Still swam—though not exactly like a duck.   320

XLI

The wind, in fact, perhaps, was rather less,
    But the ship laboured so, they scarce could hope
To weather out much longer; the distress
    Was also great with which they had to cope
For want of water, and their solid mess   325
    Was scant enough: in vain the telescope
Was used—nor sail nor shore appeared in sight,
Nought but the heavy sea, and coming night.

XLII

Again the weather threatened,—again blew
    A gale, and in the fore and after hold   330
Water appeared; yet, though the people knew
    All this, the most were patient, and some bold,
Until the chains and leathers were worn through
    Of all our pumps:—a wreck complete she rolled,

304. *thrummed:* To thrum a sail is to roughen its surface by sewing pieces of rope yarn to it. Such a sail, greased and tarred, would be passed under the hull of a leaking ship and heaved tight in an effort to stanch the leak.

312. *Gulf of Lyons:* off the southern coast of France, between Marseilles and the Spanish border.
318. *jurymast:* temporary mast in place of one broken or lost.

At mercy of the waves, whose mercies are   335
Like human beings during civil war.

XLIII

Then came the carpenter, at last, with tears
    In his rough eyes, and told the captain, he
Could do no more: he was a man in years,
    And long had voyaged through many a stormy sea,   340
And if he wept at length, they were not fears
    That made his eyelids as a woman's be,
But he, poor fellow, had a wife and children,
Two things for dying people quite bewildering.

XLIV

The ship was evidently settling now   345
    Fast by the head; and, all distinction gone,
Some went to prayers again, and made a vow
    Of candles to their saints—but there were none
To pay them with; and some looked o'er the bow;
    Some hoisted out the boats; and there was one   350
That begged Pedrillo for an absolution,
Who told him to be damned—in his confusion.

XLV

Some lashed them in their hammocks; some put on
    Their best clothes, as if going to a fair;
Some cursed the day on which they saw the sun,   355
    And gnashed their teeth, and howling, tore their hair;
And others went on as they had begun,
    Getting the boats out, being well aware
That a tight boat will live in a rough sea,
Unless with breakers close beneath her lee.   360

XLVI

The worst of all was, that in their condition,
    Having been several days in great distress,
'Twas difficult to get out such provision
    As now might render their long suffering less:
Men, even when dying, dislike inanition;   365
    Their stock was damaged by the weather's stress:
Two casks of biscuit, and a keg of butter,
Were all that could be thrown into the cutter.

XLVII

But in the long-boat they contrived to stow
    Some pounds of bread, though injured by the wet: 370

Water, a twenty-gallon cask or so;
  Six flasks of wine: and they contrived to get
A portion of their beef up from below,
  And with a piece of pork, moreover, met,
But scarce enough to serve them for a luncheon—   375
Then there was rum, eight gallons in a puncheon.

XLVIII

The other boats, the yawl and pinnace, had
  Been stove in the beginning of the gale;
And the long-boat's condition was but bad,
  As there were but two blankets for a sail,   380
And one for a mast, which a young lad
  Threw in by good luck over the ship's rail;
And two boats could not hold, far less be stored,
To save one half the people then on board.

XLIX

'Twas twilight, and the sunless day went down   385
  Over the waste of waters; like a veil,
Which, if withdrawn, would but disclose the frown
  Of one whose hate is masked but to assail.
Thus to their hopeless eyes the night was shown,
  And grimly darkled o'er the faces pale,   390
And the dim desolate deep: twelve days had Fear
Been their familiar, and now Death was here.

L

Some trial had been making at a raft,
  With little hope in such a rolling sea,
A sort of thing at which one would have laughed,   395
  If any laughter at such times could be,
Unless with people who too much have quaffed,
  And have a kind of wild and horrid glee,
Half epileptical, and half hysterical:—
Their preservation would have been a miracle.   400

LI

At half-past eight o'clock, booms, hencoops, spars,
  And all things, for a chance, had been cast loose
That still could keep afloat the struggling tars,
  For yet they strove, although of no great use:
There was no light in heaven but a few stars,   405
  The boats put off o'ercrowded with their crews;

376. *puncheon:* large cask, holding from 72 to 120 gallons.

She gave a heel, and then a lurch to port,
And, going down head foremost—sunk, in short.

LII

Then rose from sea to sky the wild farewell—
    Then shrieked the timid, and stood still the brave—   410
Then some leaped overboard with dreadful yell,
    As eager to anticipate their grave;
And the sea yawned around her like a hell,
    And down she sucked with her the whirling wave,
Like one who grapples with his enemy,   415
And strives to strangle him before he die.

LIII

And first one universal shriek there rushed,
    Louder than the loud ocean, like a crash
Of echoing thunder; and then all was hushed,
    Save the wild wind and the remorseless dash   420
Of billows; but at intervals there gushed,
    Accompanied with a convulsive splash,
A solitary shriek, the bubbling cry
Of some strong swimmer in his agony.

LIV

The boats, as stated, had got off before,   425
    And in them crowded several of the crew;
And yet their present hope was hardly more
    Than what it had been, for so strong it blew
There was slight chance of reaching any shore;
    And then they were too many, though so few—   430
Nine in the cutter, thirty in the boat,
Were counted in them when they got afloat.

LV

All the rest perished; near two hundred souls
    Had left their bodies; and what's worse, alas!
When over Catholics the ocean rolls,   435
    They must wait several weeks before a mass
Takes off one peck of purgatorial coals,
    Because, till people know what's come to pass,
They won't lay out their money on the dead—
It costs three francs for every mass that's said.   440

LVI

Juan got into the long-boat, and there
    Contrived to help Pedrillo to a place;

It seemed as if they had exchanged their care,
  For Juan wore the magisterial face
Which courage gives, while poor Pedrillo's pair   445
  Of eyes were crying for their owner's case:
Battista, though (a name called shortly Tita),
Was lost by getting at some aqua-vita.

LVII

Pedro, his valet, too, he tried to save,
  But the same cause, conducive to his loss,   450
Left him so drunk, he jumped into the wave,
  As o'er the cutter's edge he tried to cross,
And so he found a wine-and-watery grave;
  They could not rescue him although so close,
Because the sea ran higher every minute,   455
And for the boat—the crew kept crowding in it.

LVIII

A small old spaniel—which had been Don Jóse's,
  His father's, whom he loved, as ye may think,
For on such things the memory reposes
  With tenderness—stood howling on the brink,   460
Knowing, (dogs have such intellectual noses!)
  No doubt, the vessel was about to sink;
And Juan caught him up, and ere he stepped
Off threw him in, then after him he leaped.

LIX

He also stuffed his money where he could   465
  About his person, and Pedrillo's too,
Who let him do, in fact, whate'er he would,
  Not knowing what himself to say, or do,
As every rising wave his dread renewed;
  But Juan, trusting they might still get through,   470
And deeming there were remedies for any ill,
Thus re-embarked his tutor and his spaniel.

LX

'Twas a rough night, and blew so stiffly yet,
  That the sail was becalmed between the seas,
Though on the wave's high top too much to set,   475
  They dared not take it in for all the breeze:
Each sea curled o'er the stern, and kept them wet,
  And made them bale without a moment's ease,

448. *aqua-vita*: brandy.

So that themselves as well as hopes were damped,
And the poor little cutter quickly swamped.   480

LXI

Nine souls more went in her: the long-boat still
   Kept above water, with an oar for mast,
Two blankets stitched together, answering ill
   Instead of sail, were to the oar made fast:
Though every wave rolled menacing to fill,   485
   And present peril all before surpassed,
They grieved for those who perished with the cutter,
And also for the biscuit-casks and butter.

LXII

The sun rose red and fiery, a sure sign
   Of the continuance of the gale: to run   490
Before the sea until it should grow fine,
   Was all that for the present could be done:
A few tea-spoonfuls of their rum and wine
   Were served out to the people, who begun
To faint, and damaged bread wet through the bags,   495
And most of them had little clothes but rags.

LXIII

They counted thirty, crowded in a space
   Which left scarce room for motion or exertion;
They did their best to modify their case,
   One half sate up, though numbed with the immersion,   500
While t'other half were laid down in their place,
   At watch and watch; thus, shivering like the tertian
Ague in its cold fit, they filled their boat,
With nothing but the sky for a great coat.

LXIV

'Tis very certain the desire of life   505
   Prolongs it: this is obvious to physicians,
When patients, neither plagued with friends nor wife,
   Survive through very desperate conditions,
Because they still can hope, nor shines the knife
   Nor shears of Atropos before their visions: 510
Despair of all recovery spoils longevity,
And makes men's miseries of alarming brevity.

---

489. *fiery:* Compare the sailors' adage: "Red sky at night, sailors' delight; / Red sky at morning, sailors take warning."
502–503. *tertian ague:* a fever whose symptoms recur every third day, as in certain types of malaria.
510. *Atropos:* in Greek mythology the third of the three Fates, the one who cuts the thread of life.

LXV

'Tis said that persons living on annuities
    Are longer lived than others,—God knows why,
Unless to plague the grantors,—yet so true it is,
    That some, I really think, *do* never die;
Of any creditors the worst a Jew it is,
    And *that's* their mode of furnishing supply:
In my young days they lent me cash that way,
Which I found very troublesome to pay.   520

LXVI

'Tis thus with people in an open boat,
    They live upon the love of life, and bear
More than can be believed, or even thought,
    And stand like rocks the tempest's wear and tear;
And hardship still has been the sailor's lot,   525
    Since Noah's ark went cruising here and there;
She had a curious crew as well as cargo,
Like the first old Greek privateer, the Argo.

LXVII

But man is a carnivorous production,
    And must have meals, at least one meal a day;   530
He cannot live, like woodcocks, upon suction,
    But, like the shark and tiger, must have prey;
Although his anatomical construction
    Bears vegetables, in a grumbling way,
Your labouring people think beyond all question   535
Beef, veal, and mutton, better for digestion.

LXVIII

And thus it was with this our hapless crew;
    For on the third day there came on a calm,
And though at first their strength it might renew,
    And lying on their weariness like balm,   540
Lulled them like turtles sleeping on the blue
    Of ocean, when they woke they felt a qualm,
And fell all ravenously on their provision,
Instead of hoarding it with due precision.

LXIX

The consequence was easily foreseen—   545
    They ate up all they had, and drank their wine,

528. *Argo:* the ship—named after its builder, Argus—in which Jason and his followers sailed to find the Golden Fleece.

In spite of all remonstrances, and then
    On what, in fact, next day were they to dine?
They hoped the wind would rise, these foolish men!
    And carry them to shore; these hopes were fine,   550
But as they had but one oar, and that brittle,
It would have been more wise to save their victual.

LXX

The fourth day came, but not a breath of air,
    And Ocean slumbered like an unweaned child;
The fifth day, and their boat lay floating there,   555
    The sea and sky were blue, and clear, and mild—
With their one oar (I wish they had had a pair)
    What could they do? and hunger's rage grew wild:
So Juan's spaniel, spite of his entreating,
Was killed, and portioned out for present eating.   560

LXXI

On the sixth day they fed upon his hide,
    And Juan, who had still refused, because
The creature was his father's dog that died,
    Now feeling all the vulture in his jaws,
With some remorse received (though first denied)   565
    As a great favour one of the fore-paws,
Which he divided with Pedrillo, who
Devoured it, longing for the other too.

LXXII

The seventh day, and no wind—the burning sun
    Blistered and scorched, and, stagnant on the sea,
They lay like carcasses; and hope was none,   570
    Save in the breeze that came not: savagely
They glared upon each other—all was done,
    Water, and wine, and food,—and you might see
The longings of the cannibal arise   575
(Although they spoke not) in their wolfish eyes.

LXXIII

At length one whispered to his companion, who
    Whispered another, and thus it went round,
And then into a hoarser murmur grew,
    An ominous, and wild, and desperate sound;   580
And when his comrade's thought each sufferer knew,
    'Twas but his own, suppressed till now, he found:
And out they spoke of lots for flesh and blood,
And who should die to be his fellow's food.

LXXIV

But ere they came to this, they that day shared   585
   Some leathern caps, and what remained of shoes;
And then they looked around them, and despaired,
   And none to be the sacrifice would choose;
At length the lots were torn up, and prepared,
   But of materials that must shock the Muse—   590
Having no paper, for the want of better,
They took by force from Juan Julia's letter.

LXXV

Then lots were made, and marked, and mixed, and handed
   In silent horror, and their distribution
Lulled even the savage hunger which demanded,   595
   Like the Promethean vulture, this pollution;
None in particular had sought or planned it,
   'Twas nature gnawed them to this resolution,
By which none were permitted to be neuter—
And the lot fell on Juan's luckless tutor.   600

LXXVI

He but requested to be bled to death:
   The surgeon had his instruments, and bled
Pedrillo, and so gently ebbed his breath,
   You hardly could perceive when he was dead.
He died as born, a Catholic in faith,   605
   Like most in the belief in which they're bred,
And first a little crucifix he kissed,
And then held out his jugular and wrist.

LXXVII

The surgeon, as there was no other fee,
   Had his first choice of morsels for his pains;   610
But being thirstiest at the moment, he
   Preferred a draught from the fast-flowing veins:
Part was divided, part thrown in the sea,
   And such things as the entrails and the brains
Regaled two sharks, who followed o'er the billow—   615
The sailors ate the rest of poor Pedrillo.

LXXVIII

The sailors ate him, all save three or four,
   Who were not quite so fond of animal food;

596. *Promethean vulture:* According to Greek mythology (see Aeschylus, *Prometheus Bound*), Prometheus was chained to a rock on Mount Caucasus where vultures and eagles tore at him.

To these was added Juan, who, before
   Refusing his own spaniel, hardly could   620
Feel now his appetite increased much more;
   'Twas not to be expected that he should,
Even in extremity of their disaster,
Dine with them on his pastor and his master.

LXXIX

'Twas better that he did not; for, in fact,   625
   The consequence was awful in the extreme;
For they, who were most ravenous in the act,
   Went raging mad—Lord! how they did blaspheme!
And foam, and roll, with strange convulsions racked,
   Drinking salt-water like a mountain-stream;   630
Tearing, and grinning, howling, screeching, swearing,
And, with hyæna-laughter, died despairing.

LXXX

Their numbers were much thinned by this infliction
   And all the rest were thin enough, Heaven knows;
And some of them had lost their recollection,   635
   Happier than they who still perceived their woes;
But others pondered on a new dissection,
   As if not warned sufficiently by those
Who had already perished, suffering madly,
For having used their appetites so sadly.   640

LXXXI

And next they thought upon the master's mate,
   As fattest; but he saved himself, because,
Besides being much averse from such a fate,
   There were some other reasons: the first was,
He had been rather indisposed of late;   645
   And that which chiefly proved his saving clause,
Was a small present made to him at Cadiz,
By general subscription of the ladies.

LXXXII

Of poor Pedrillo something still remained,
   But was used sparingly,—some were afraid,   650
And others still their appetites constrained,
   Or but at times a little supper made;
All except Juan, who throughout abstained,

647. *present:* i.e., he had contracted a venereal disease.

Chewing a piece of bamboo, and some lead:
At length they caught two boobies, and a noddy,   655
And then they left off eating the dead body.

LXXXIII

And if Pedrillo's fate should shocking be,
    Remember Ugolino condescends
To eat the head of his arch-enemy
    The moment after he politely ends   660
His tale: if foes be food in hell, at sea
    'Tis surely fair to dine upon our friends,
When shipwreck's short allowance grows too scanty,
Without being much more horrible than Dante.

LXXXIV

And the same night there fell a shower of rain,   665
    For which their mouths gaped, like the cracks of earth
When dried to summer dust; till taught by pain,
    Men really know not what good water's worth;
If you had been in Turkey or in Spain,
    Or with a famished boat's-crew had your berth,   670
Or in the desert heard the camel's bell,
You'd wish yourself where Truth is—in a well.

LXXXV

It poured down torrents, but they were no richer,
    Until they found a ragged piece of sheet,
Which served them as a sort of spongy pitcher,   675
    And when they deemed its moisture was complete,
They wrung it out, and though a thirsty ditcher
    Might not have thought the scanty draught so sweet
As a full pot of porter, to their thinking
They ne'er till now had known the joys of drinking.   680

LXXXVI

And their baked lips, with many a bloody crack,
    Sucked in the moisture, which like nectar streamed;
Their throats were ovens, their swoln tongues were black
    As the rich man's in hell, who vainly screamed
To beg the beggar, who could not rain back   685
    A drop of dew, when every drop had seemed
To taste of heaven—If this be true, indeed,
Some Christians have a comfortable creed.

658. *Ugolino:* See Dante's *Inferno*,
Canto XXXIII. Ugolino, placed in the
circle of traitors, tells his story to
Dante and then returns to gnaw on the
skull of his enemy.
    683–686. *tongues . . . dew:* See the
episode of the rich man and Lazarus in
Luke 16:19–24.

LXXXVII

There were two fathers in this ghastly crew,
   And with them their two sons, of whom the one   690
Was more robust and hardy to the view,
   But he died early; and when he was gone,
His nearest messmate told his sire, who threw
   One glance at him, and said, "Heaven's will be done!
I can do nothing," and he saw him thrown   695
Into the deep without a tear or groan.

LXXXVIII

The other father had a weaklier child,
   Of a soft cheek, and aspect delicate;
But the boy bore up long, and with a mild
   And patient spirit held aloof his fate;   700
Little he said, and now and then he smiled,
   As if to win a part from off the weight
He saw increasing on his father's heart,
With the deep deadly thought, that they must part.

LXXXIX

And o'er him bent his sire, and never raised   705
   His eyes from off his face, but wiped the foam
From his pale lips, and ever on him gazed,
   And when the wished-for shower at length was come,
And the boy's eyes, which the dull film half glazed,
   Brightened, and for a moment seemed to roam,   710
He squeezed from out a rag some drops of rain
Into his dying child's mouth—but in vain.

XC

The boy expired—the father held the clay,
   And looked upon it long; and when at last
Death left no doubt, and the dead burthen lay   715
   Stiff on his heart, and pulse and hope were past,
He watched it wistfully, until away
   'Twas borne by the rude wave wherein 'twas cast;
Then he himself sunk down all dumb and shivering,
And gave no signs of life, save his limbs quivering.   720

XCI

Now overhead a rainbow, bursting through
   The scattering clouds, shone, spanning the dark sea,
Resting its bright base on the quivering blue;
   And all within its arch appeared to be

Clearer than that without, and its wide hue   725
    Waxed broad and waving, like a banner free,
Then changed like to a bow that's bent, and then
    Forsook the dim eyes of these shipwrecked men.

XCII

It changed, of course; a heavenly chameleon,
    The airy child of vapour and the sun,   730
Brought forth in purple, cradled in vermilion,
    Baptized in molten gold, and swathed in dun,
Glittering like crescents o'er a Turk's pavilion,
    And blending every colour into one,
Just like a black eye in a recent scuffle   735
(For sometimes we must box without the muffle).

XCIII

Our shipwrecked seamen thought it a good omen—
    It is as well to think so, now and then;
'Twas an old custom of the Greek and Roman,
    And may become of great advantage when   740
Folks are discouraged; and most surely no men
    Had greater need to nerve themselves again
Than these, and so this rainbow looked like hope—
Quite a celestial kaleidoscope.

XCIV

About this time a beautiful white bird,   745
    Web-footed, not unlike a dove in size
And plumage (probably it might have erred
    Upon its course), passed oft before their eyes,
And tried to perch, although it saw and heard
    The men within the boat, and in this guise   750
It came and went, and fluttered round them till
Night fell:—this seemed a better omen still.

XCV

But in this case I also must remark,
    'Twas well this bird of promise did not perch,
Because the tackle of our shattered bark   755
    Was not so safe for roosting as a church;
And had it been the dove from Noah's ark,
    Returning there from her successful search,
Which in their way that moment chanced to fall,
They would have eat her, olive-branch and all.   760

736. *muffle:* a boxing glove (originally, a leather restraining glove for lunatics).

XCVI

With twilight it again came on to blow,
  But not with violence; the stars shone out,
The boat made way; yet now they were so low,
  They knew not where nor what they were about;
Some fancied they saw land, and some said "No!"   765
  The frequent fog-banks gave them cause to doubt—
Some swore that they heard breakers, others guns,
And all mistook about the latter once.

XCVII

As morning broke, the light wind died away,
  When he who had the watch sung out and swore,   770
If 'twas not land that rose with the sun's ray,
  He wished that land he never might see more:
And the rest rubbed their eyes, and saw a bay,
  Or thought they saw, and shaped their course for shore;
For shore it was, and gradually grew   775
Distinct, and high, and palpable to view.

XCVIII

And then of these some part burst into tears,
  And others, looking with a stupid stare,
Could not yet separate their hopes from fears,
  And seemed as if they had no further care;   780
While a few prayed—(the first time for some years)—
  And at the bottom of the boat three were
Asleep: they shook them by the hand and head,
And tried to awaken them, but found them dead.

XCIX

The day before, fast sleeping on the water,   785
  They found a turtle of the hawk's-bill kind,
And by good fortune, gliding softly, caught her,
  Which yielded a day's life, and to their mind
Proved even still a more nutritious matter,
  Because it left encouragement behind: 790
They thought that in such perils, more than chance
Had sent them this for their deliverance.

C

The land appeared a high and rocky coast,
  And higher grew the mountains as they drew,
Set by a current, toward it: they were lost   795
  In various conjectures, for none knew

To what part of the earth they had been tost,
    So changeable had been the winds that blew;
Some thought it was Mount Etna, some the highlands
Of Candia, Cyprus, Rhodes, or other islands.   800

CI

Meantime the current, with a rising gale,
    Still set them onwards to the welcome shore,
Like Charon's bark of spectres, dull and pale:
    Their living freight was now reduced to four,
And three dead, whom their strength could not avail   805
    To heave into the deep with those before,
Though the two sharks still followed them, and dashed
The spray into their faces as they splashed.

CII

Famine, despair, cold, thirst, and heat, had done
    Their work on them by turns, and thinned them to   810
Such things a mother had not known her son
    Amidst the skeletons of that gaunt crew;
By night chilled, by day scorched, thus one by one
    They perished, until withered to these few,
But chiefly by a species of self-slaughter,   815
In washing down Pedrillo with salt water.

CIII

As they drew nigh the land, which now was seen
    Unequal in its aspect here and there,
They felt the freshness of its growing green,
    That waved in forest-tops, and smoothed the air,   820
And fell upon their glazed eyes like a screen
    From glistening waves—and skies so hot and bare—
Lovely seemed any object that should sweep
Away the vast, salt, dread, eternal deep.

CIV

The shore looked wild, without a trace of man,   825
    And girt by formidable waves; but they
Were mad for land, and thus their course they ran,
    Though right ahead the roaring breakers lay:
A reef between them also now began
    To show its boiling surf and bounding spray,   830

803. *Charon's bark:* In Greek myth-   Hades who rowed the dead across the
ology, Charon was the ferryman of   river Styx.

But finding no place for their landing better,
They ran the boat for shore,—and overset her.

CV

But in his native stream, the Guadalquivir,
  Juan to lave his youthful limbs was wont;
And having learnt to swim in that sweet river,   835
  Had often turned the art to some account:
A better swimmer you could scarce see ever,
  He could, perhaps, have passed the Hellespont,
As once (a feat on which ourselves we prided)
Leander, Mr. Ekenhead, and I did.   840

CVI

So here, though faint, emaciated, and stark,
  He buoyed his boyish limbs, and strove to ply
With the quick wave, and gain, ere it was dark,
  The beach which lay before him, high and dry:
The greatest danger here was from a shark,   845
  That carried off his neighbour by the thigh;
As for the other two, they could not swim,
So nobody arrived on shore but him.

CVII

Nor yet had he arrived but for the oar,
  Which, providentially for him, was washed   850
Just as his feeble arms could strike no more,
  And the hard wave o'erwhelm'd him as 'twas dashed
Within his grasp; he clung to it, and sore
  The waters beat while he thereto was lashed;
At last, with swimming, wading, scrambling, he   855
Rolled on the beach, half senseless, from the sea:

CVIII

There, breathless, with his digging nails he clung
  Fast to the sand, lest the returning wave,
From whose reluctant roar his life he wrung,
  Should suck him back to her insatiate grave: 860
And there he lay, full length, where he was flung,
  Before the entrance of a cliff-worn cave,
With just enough of life to feel its pain,
And deem that it was saved, perhaps in vain.

838–840. *Hellespont . . . I did:* On May 5, 1810, with a Mr. Ekenhead, Byron swam the Hellespont from Sestos to Abydos—a feat he never tired of mentioning. Leander, the lover of Hero (priestess of Aphrodite) was Byron's legendary predecessor.

CIX

With slow and staggering effort he arose,   865
   But sunk again upon his bleeding knee
And quivering hand; and then he looked for those
   Who long had been his mates upon the sea;
But none of them appeared to share his woes,
   Save one, a corpse, from out the famished three,   870
Who died two days before, and now had found
An unknown barren beach for burial-ground.

CX

And as he gazed, his dizzy brain spun fast,
   And down he sunk; and as he sunk, the sand
Swam round and round, and all his senses passed: 875
   He fell upon his side, and his stretched hand
Drooped dripping on the oar (their jury-mast),
   And, like a withered lily, on the land
His slender frame and pallid aspect lay,
As fair a thing as e'er was formed of clay.   880

CXI

How long in his damp trance young Juan lay
   He knew not, for the earth was gone for him,
And time had nothing more of night nor day
   For his congealing blood, and senses dim;
And how this heavy faintness passed away   885
   He knew not, till each painful pulse and limb,
And tingling vein, seemed throbbing back to life,
For Death, though vanquished, still retired with strife.

CXII

His eyes he opened, shut, again unclosed,
   For all was doubt and dizziness; he thought   890
He still was in the boat, and had but dozed,
   And felt again with his despair o'erwrought,
And wished it death in which he had reposed,
   And then once more his feelings back were brought,
And slowly by his swimming eyes was seen   895
A lovely female face of seventeen.

CXIII

'Twas bending close o'er his, and the small mouth
   Seemed almost prying into his for breath;

896 ff. *female face . . .* : In keeping with the mock-epic tone of the poem, Byron obviously borrows this scene from Homer's *Odyssey* (Book VI), where Odysseus is treated in similar fashion by Nausicaä—daughter of King Alcinous—in the land of the Phaeacians.

And chafing him, the soft warm hand of youth
    Recalled his answering spirits back from death; 900
And, bathing his chill temples, tried to soothe
    Each pulse to animation, till beneath
Its gentle touch and trembling care, a sigh
To these kind efforts made a low reply.

CXIV

Then was the cordial poured, and mantle flung 905
    Around his scarce-clad limbs; and the fair arm
Raised higher the faint head which o'er it hung;
    And her transparent cheek, all pure and warm,
Pillowed his death-like forehead; then she wrung
    His dewy curls, long drenched by every storm; 910
And watched with eagerness each throb that drew
A sigh from his heaved bosom—and hers, too.

CXV

And lifting him with care into the cave,
    The gentle girl, and her attendant,—one
Young, yet her elder, and of brow less grave, 915
    And more robust of figure—then begun
To kindle fire, and as the new flames gave
    Light to the rocks that roofed them, which the sun
Had never seen, the maid, or whatsoe'er
She was, appeared distinct, and tall, and fair. 920

CXVI

Her brow was overhung with coins of gold,
    That sparkled o'er the auburn of her hair,
Her clustering hair, whose longer locks were rolled
    In braids behind; and though her stature were
Even of the highest for a female mould, 925
    They nearly reached her heel; and in her air
There was a something which bespoke command,
As one who was a lady in the land.

CXVII

Her hair, I said, was auburn; but her eyes
    Were black as death, their lashes the same hue, 930
Of downcast length, in whose silk shadow lies
    Deepest attraction; for when to the view
Forth from its raven fringe the full glance flies,
    Ne'er with such force the swiftest arrow flew;
'Tis as the snake late coiled, who pours his length, 935
And hurls at once his venom and his strength.

CXVIII

Her brow was white and low, her cheek's pure dye
　Like twilight rosy still with the set sun;
Short upper lip—sweet lips! that make us sigh
　Ever to have seen such; for she was one　　　　　940
Fit for the model of a statuary
　(A race of mere impostors, when all's done—
I've seen much finer women, ripe and real,
Than all the nonsense of their stone ideal).

CXIX

I'll tell you why I say so, for 'tis just　　　　　945
　One should not rail without a decent cause:
There was an Irish lady, to whose bust
　I ne'er saw justice done, and yet she was
A frequent model; and if e'er she must
　Yield to stern Time and Nature's wrinkling laws,　950
They will destroy a face which mortal thought
Ne'er compassed, nor less mortal chisel wrought.

CXX

And such was she, the lady of the cave:
　Her dress was very different from the Spanish,
Simpler, and yet of colours not so grave;　　　　955
　For, as you know, the Spanish women banish
Bright hues when out of doors, and yet, while wave
　Around them (what I hope will never vanish)
The basquina and the mantilla, they
Seem at the same time mystical and gay.　　　　960

CXXI

But with our damsel this was not the case:
　Her dress was many-coloured, finely spun;
Her locks curled negligently round her face,
　But through them gold and gems profusely shone:
Her girdle sparkled, and the richest lace　　　　965
　Flowed in her veil, and many a precious stone
Flashed on her little hand; but, what was shocking,
Her small snow feet had slippers, but no stocking.

CXXII

The other female's dress was not unlike,
　But of inferior materials: she　　　　　　970

959. *basquina:* Spanish ornamented petticoat. *mantilla:* lace veil covering the head and shoulders.

Had not so many ornaments to strike
 Her hair had silver only, bound to be
Her dowry; and her veil, in form alike,
 Was coarser; and her air, though firm, less free;
Her hair was thicker, but less long; her eyes   975
As black, but quicker, and of smaller size.

CXXIII

And these two tended him, and cheered him both
 With food and raiment, and those soft attentions,
Which are—(as I must own)—of female growth,
 And have ten thousand delicate inventions: 980
They made a most superior mess of broth,
 A thing which poesy but seldom mentions,
But the best dish that e'er was cooked since Homer's
Achilles ordered dinner for new comers.

CXXIV

I'll tell you who they were, this female pair,   985
 Lest they should seem princesses in disguise;
Besides, I hate all mystery, and that air
 Of clap-trap, which your recent poets prize;
And so, in short, the girls they really were
 They shall appear before your curious eyes,   990
Mistress and maid; the first was only daughter
Of an old man, who lived upon the water.

CXXV

A fisherman he had been in his youth,
 And still a sort of fisherman was he;
But other speculations were, in sooth,   995
 Added to his connexion with the sea,
Perhaps not so respectable, in truth:
 A little smuggling, and some piracy,
Left him, at last, the sole of many masters
Of an ill-gotten million of piastres.   1000

CXXVI

A fisher, therefore, was he,—though of men,
 Like Peter the Apostle,—and he fished
For wandering merchant vessels, now and then,

---

984. *dinner:* a reference to the feast given by Achilles for Ajax, Odysseus, and Phoenix in Homer's *Iliad*, Book IX.
1000. *piastres:* Both a Spanish silver coin and a small Turkish coin were so called.
1001–1002. *of men . . . Peter the Apostle:* See Matthew 4:19 and Mark 1:17.

And sometimes caught as many as he wished;
The cargoes he confiscated, and gain 1005
 He sought in the slave-market, too, and dished
Full many a morsel for that Turkish trade,
 By which, no doubt, a good deal may be made.

CXXVII

He was a Greek, and on his isle had built
 (One of the wild and smaller Cyclades) 1010
A very handsome house from out his guilt,
 And there he lived exceedingly at ease;
Heaven knows what cash he got, or blood he spilt,
 A sad old fellow was he, if you please;
But this I know, it was a spacious building, 1015
Full of barbaric carving, paint, and gilding.

CXXVIII

He had an only daughter, called Haidée,
 The greatest heiress of the Eastern Isles;
Besides, so very beautiful was she,
 Her dowry was as nothing to her smiles: 1020
Still in her teens, and like a lovely tree
 She grew to womanhood, and between whiles
Rejected several suitors, just to learn
How to accept a better in his turn.

CXXIX

And walking out upon the beach, below 1025
 The cliff,—towards sunset, on that day she found,
Insensible,—not dead, but nearly so,—
 Don Juan, almost famished, and half drowned;
But being naked, she was shocked, you know,
 Yet deemed herself in common pity bound, 1030
As far as in her lay, "to take him in,
A stranger" dying, with so white a skin.

CXXX

But taking him into her father's house
 Was not exactly the best way to save,
But like conveying to the cat the mouse, 1035
 Or people in a trance into their grave;
Because the good old man had so much "νους,"
 Unlike the honest Arab thieves so brave,
He would have hospitably cured the stranger
And sold him instantly when out of danger. 1040

1037. *νους*: "mind" or "spirit" (Greek).

CXXXI

And therefore, with her maid, she thought it best
 (A virgin always on her maid relies)
To place him in the cave for present rest:
 And when, at last, he opened his black eyes,
Their charity increased about their guest;   1045
 And their compassion grew to such a size,
It opened half the turnpike gates to heaven—
(St. Paul says, 'tis the toll which must be given).

CXXXII

They made a fire,—but such a fire as they
 Upon the moment could contrive with such   1050
Materials as were cast up round the bay,—
 Some broken planks, and oars, that to the touch
Were nearly tinder, since so long they lay
 A mast was almost crumbled to a crutch;
But, by God's grace, here wrecks were in such plenty, 1055
That there was fuel to have furnished twenty.

CXXXIII

He had a bed of furs, and a pelisse,
 For Haidée stripped her sables off to make
His couch; and, that he might be more at ease,
 And warm, in case by chance he should awake, 1060
They also gave a petticoat apiece,
 She and her maid,—and promised by daybreak
To pay him a fresh visit, with a dish
For breakfast, of eggs, coffee, bread, and fish.

CXXXIV

And thus they left him to his lone repose: 1065
 Juan slept like a top, or like the dead,
Who sleep at last, perhaps (God only knows),
 Just for the present; and in his lulled head
Not even a vision of his former woes
 Throbbed in accursèd dreams, which sometimes spread 1070
Unwelcome visions of our former years,
Till the eye, cheated, opens thick with tears.

CXXXV

Young Juan slept all dreamless:—but the maid,
 Who smoothed his pillow, as she left the den
Looked back upon him, and a moment staid,   1075

1048. *St. Paul:* See I Corinthians 13:1–13.

And turned, believing that he called again.
He slumbered; yet she thought, at least she said
    (The heart will slip, even as the tongue and pen),
He had pronounced her name—but she forgot
That at this moment Juan knew it not.   1080

CXXXVI

And pensive to her father's house she went,
    Enjoining silence strict to Zoe, who
Better than her knew what, in fact, she meant,
    She being wiser by a year or two:
A year or two's an age when rightly spent,   1085
    And Zoe spent hers, as most women do,
In gaining all that useful sort of knowledge
Which is acquired in Nature's good old college.

CXXXVII

The morn broke, and found Juan slumbering still
    Fast in his cave, and nothing clashed upon   1090
His rest: the rushing of the neighbouring rill,
    And the young beams of the excluded sun,
Troubled him not, and he might sleep his fill;
    And need he had of slumber yet, for none
Had suffered more—his hardships were comparative   1095
To those related in my grand-dad's "Narrative."

CXXXVIII

Not so Haidée: she sadly tossed and tumbled,
    And started from her sleep, and turning o'er,
Dreamed of a thousand wrecks, o'er which she stumbled,
    And handsome corpses strewed upon the shore;   1100
And woke her maid so early that she grumbled,
    And called her father's old slaves up, who swore
In several oaths—Armenian, Turk, and Greek—
They knew not what to think of such a freak.

CXXXIX

But up she got, and up she made them get,   1105
    With some pretence about the sun, that makes
Sweet skies just when he rises, or is set;
    And 'tis, no doubt, a sight to see when breaks
Bright Phœbus, while the mountains still are wet

1096. *"Narrative"*: The poet drew upon his grandfather's *Narrative* . . . (1768), the tale of a shipwreck off the coast of Chile in 1741. John Byron (1723–1786) sailed as a midshipman aboard the *Wager,* one of Lord Anson's squadron in his famous voyage around the world.

With mist, and every bird with him awakes,
And night is flung off like a mourning suit
Worn for a husband,—or some other brute.   1110

CXL

I say, the sun is a most glorious sight:
    I've seen him rise full oft, indeed of late
I have sat up on purpose all the night,   1115
    Which hastens, as physicians say, one's fate;
And so all ye, who would be in the right
    In health and purse, begin your day to date
From daybreak, and when coffined at four-score
Engrave upon the plate, you rose at four.   1120

CXLI

And Haidée met the morning face to face;
    Her own was freshest, though a feverish flush
Had dyed it with the headlong blood, whose race
    From heart to cheek is curbed into a blush,
Like to a torrent which a mountain's base,   1125
    That overpowers some Alpine river's rush,
Checks to a lake, whose waves in circles spread;
Or the Red Sea—but the sea is not red.

CXLII

And down the cliff the island virgin came,
    And near the cave her quick light footsteps drew,   1130
While the sun smiled on her with his first flame,
    And young Aurora kissed her lips with dew,
Taking her for a sister; just the same
    Mistake you would have made on seeing the two,
Although the mortal, quite as fresh and fair,   1135
Had all the advantage, too, of not being air.

CXLIII

And when into the cavern Haidée stepped
    All timidly, yet rapidly, she saw
That like an infant Juan sweetly slept;
    And then she stopped, and stood as if in awe   1140
(For sleep is awful), and on tiptoe crept
    And wrapt him closer, lest the air, too raw,
Should reach his blood, then o'er him still as death
Bent, with hushed lips, that drank his scarce-drawn breath.

1132. *Aurora:* Roman name for Eos, goddess of the dawn.

CXLIV

And thus like to an angel o'er the dying   1145
  Who die in righteousness, she leaned; and there
All tranquilly the shipwrecked boy was lying,
  As o'er him lay the calm and stirless air:
But Zoe the meantime some eggs was frying,
  Since, after all, no doubt the youthful pair   1150
Must breakfast, and betimes—lest they should ask it,
She drew out her provision from the basket.

CXLV

She knew that the best feelings must have victual,
  And that a shipwrecked youth would hungry be;
Besides, being less in love, she yawned a little,   1155
  And felt her veins chilled by the neighbouring sea;
And so, she cooked their breakfast to a tittle;
  I can't say that she gave them any tea,
But there were eggs, fruit, coffee, bread, fish, honey,
With Scio wine,—and all for love, not money.   1160

CXLVI

And Zoe, when the eggs were ready, and
  The coffee made, would fain have wakened Juan;
But Haidée stopped her with her quick small hand,
  And without a word, a sign her finger drew on
Her lip, which Zoe needs must understand;   1165
  And, the first breakfast spoilt, prepared a new one,
Because her mistress would not let her break
That sleep which seemed as it would ne'er awake.

CXLVII

For still he lay, and on his thin worn cheek
  A purple hectic played like dying day   1170
On the snow-tops of distant hills; the streak
  Of sufferance yet upon his forehead lay,
Where the blue veins looked shadowy, shrunk, and weak;
  And his black curls were dewy with the spray,
Which weighed upon them yet, all damp and salt,   1175
Mixed with the stony vapours of the vault.

CXLVIII

And she bent o'er him, and he lay beneath,
  Hushed as the babe upon its mother's breast,
Drooped as the willow when no winds can breathe,
  Lulled like the depth of ocean when at rest,   1180

Fair as the crowning rose of the whole wreath,
    Soft as the callow cygnet in its nest;
In short, he was a very pretty fellow,
Although his woes had turned him rather yellow.

CXLIX

He woke and gazed, and would have slept again,   1185
    But the fair face which met his eyes forbade
Those eyes to close, though weariness and pain
    Had further sleep a further pleasure made;
For woman's face was never formed in vain
    For Juan, so that even when he prayed   1190
He turned from grisly saints, and martyrs hairy,
To the sweet portraits of the Virgin Mary.

CL

And thus upon his elbow he arose,
    And looked upon the lady, in whose cheek
The pale contended with the purple rose,   1195
    As with an effort she began to speak;
Her eyes were eloquent, her words would pose,
    Although she told him, in good modern Greek,
With an Ionian accent, low and sweet,
That he was faint, and must not talk, but eat.   1200

CLI

Now Juan could not understand a word,
    Being no Grecian; but he had an ear,
And her voice was the warble of a bird,
    So soft, so sweet, so delicately clear,
That finer, simpler, music ne'er was heard;   1205
    The sort of sound we echo with a tear,
Without knowing why—an overpowering tone,
Whence melody descends as from a throne.

CLII

And Juan gazed as one who is awoke
    By a distant organ, doubting if he be   1210
Not yet a dreamer, till the spell is broke
    By the watchman, or some such reality,
Or by one's early valet's cursèd knock;
    At least it is a heavy sound to me,
Who like a morning slumber—for the night   1215
Shows stars and women in a better light.

CLIII

And Juan, too, was helped out from his dream,
  Or sleep, or whatsoe'er it was, by feeling
A most prodigious appetite; the steam
  Of Zoe's cookery no doubt was stealing   1220
Upon his senses, and the kindling beam
  Of the new fire, which Zoe kept up, kneeling,
To stir her viands, made him quite awake
And long for food, but chiefly a beef-steak.

CLIV

But beef is rare within these oxless isles;   1225
  Goat's flesh there is, no doubt, and kid, and mutton,
And, when a holiday upon them smiles,
  A joint upon their barbarous spits they put on:
But this occurs but seldom, between whiles,
  For some of these are rocks with scarce a hut on;   1230
Others are fair and fertile, among which
This, though not large, was one of the most rich.

CLV

I say that beef is rare, and can't help thinking
  That the old fable of the Minotaur—
From which our modern rivals, rightly shrinking,   1235
  Condemn the royal lady's taste who wore
A cow's shape for a mask—was only (sinking
  The allegory) a mere type, no more,
That Pasiphae promoted breeding cattle,
To make the Cretans bloodier in battle.   1240

CLVI

For we all know that English people are
  Fed upon beef—I won't say much of beer,
Because 'tis liquor only, and being far
  From this my subject, has no business here;
We know, too, they are very fond of war,   1245
  A pleasure—like all pleasures—rather dear;
So were the Cretans—from which I infer
That beef and battles both were owing to her.

CLVII

But to resume. The languid Juan raised
  His head upon his elbow, and he saw   1250
A sight on which he had not lately gazed,

1234–1239. *Minotaur . . . Pasiphae:*   Crete. The beast was eventually slain
The Minotaur was the offspring of Pasi-   by Theseus.
phae and the bull sent to Minos, king of

As all his latter meals had been quite raw,
Three or four things, for which the Lord be praised,
  And, feeling still the famished vulture gnaw,
He fell upon whate'er was offered, like   1255
A priest, a shark, an alderman, or pike.

CLVIII

He ate, and he was well supplied; and she
  Who watched him like a mother, would have fed
Him past all bounds, because she smiled to see
  Such appetite in one she had deemed dead: 1260
But Zoe, being older than Haidée,
  Knew (by tradition, for she ne'er had read)
That famished people must be slowly nurst,
And fed by spoonfuls, else they always burst.

CLIX

And so she took the liberty to state,   1265
  Rather by deeds than words, because the case
Was urgent, that the gentleman, whose fate
  Had made her mistress quit her bed to trace
The sea-shore at this hour, must leave his plate,
  Unless he wished to die upon the place—   1270
She snatched it, and refused another morsel,
Saying, he had gorged enough to make a horse ill.

CLX

Next they—he being naked, save a tattered
  Pair of scarce decent trowsers—went to work,
And in the fire his recent rags they scattered,   1275
  And dressed him, for the present, like a Turk,
Or Greek—that is, although it not much mattered,
  Omitting turban, slippers, pistols, dirk,—
They furnished him, entire, except some stitches,
With a clean shirt, and very spacious britches.   1280

CLXI

And then fair Haidée tried her tongue at speaking,
  But not a word could Juan comprehend,
Although he listened so that the young Greek in
  Her earnestness would ne'er have made an end;
And, as he interrupted not, went eking   1285
  Her speech out to her protégé and friend,
Till pausing at the last her breath to take,
She saw he did not understand Romaic.

1288. *Romaic:* the vernacular language of modern Greece.

454 · *George Gordon, Lord Byron*

CLXII

And then she had recourse to nods, and signs,
   And smiles, and sparkles of the speaking eye,   1290
And read (the only book she could) the lines
   Of his fair face, and found, by sympathy,
The answer eloquent, where the soul shines
   And darts in one quick glance a long reply;
And thus in every look she saw exprest   1295
A world of words, and things at which she guessed.

CLXIII

And now, by dint of fingers and of eyes,
   And words repeated after her, he took
A lesson in her tongue; but by surmise,
   No doubt, less of her language than her look: 1300
As he who studies fervently the skies
   Turns oftener to the stars than to his book,
Thus Juan learned his alpha beta better
From Haidée's glance than any graven letter.

CLXIV

'Tis pleasing to be schooled in a strange tongue   1305
   By female lips and eyes—that is, I mean,
When both the teacher and the taught are young,
   As was the case, at least, where I have been;
They smile so when one's right, and when one's wrong
   They smile still more and then there intervene   1310
Pressure of hands, perhaps even a chaste kiss;—
I learned the little that I know by this:

CLXV

That is, some words of Spanish, Turk, and Greek,
   Italian not at all, having no teachers;
Much English I cannot pretend to speak,   1315
   Learning that language chiefly from its preachers,
Barrow, South, Tillotson, whom every week
   I study, also Blair, the highest reachers
Of eloquence in piety and prose—
I hate your poets, so read none of those.   1320

CLXVI

As for the ladies, I have nought to say,
   A wanderer from the British world of fashion,

1317–1318. *Barrow . . . Blair:* Isaac
Barrow (1630–1677), preacher and
professor of Greek at Cambridge; Robert South (1634–1716), court preacher
to Charles II; John Tillotson (1630–
1694), archbishop of Canterbury;
Hugh Blair (1699–1746), Scottish
preacher and professor of rhetoric.

Where I, like other "dogs, have had my day,"
   Like other men, too, may have had my passion—
But that, like other things, has passed away,   1325
   And all her fools whom I *could* lay the lash on:
Foes, friends, men, women, now are nought to me
But dreams of what has been, no more to be.

CLXVII

Return we to Don Juan. He begun
   To hear new words, and to repeat them; but   1330
Some feelings, universal as the sun,
   Were such as could not in his breast be shut
More than within the bosom of a nun:
   He was in love,—as you would be, no doubt,
With a young benefactress,—so was she,   1335
Just in the way we very often see.

CLXVIII

And every day by daybreak—rather early
   For Juan, who was somewhat fond of rest,—
She came into the cave, but it was merely
   To see her bird reposing in his nest;   1340
And she would softly stir his locks so curly,
   Without disturbing her yet slumbering guest,
Breathing all gently o'er his cheek and mouth,
As o'er a bed of roses the sweet south.

CLXIX

And every morn his colour freshlier came,   1345
   And every day helped on his convalescence;
'Twas well, because health in the human frame
   Is pleasant, besides being true love's essence,
For health and idleness to passion's flame
   Are oil and gunpowder; and some good lessons   1350
Are also learnt from Ceres and from Bacchus,
Without whom Venus will not long attack us.

CLXX

While Venus fills the heart (without heart really
   Love, though good always, is not quite so good),
Ceres presents a plate of vermicelli,—   1355
   For love must be sustained like flesh and blood,
While Bacchus pours out wine, or hands a jelly:

1351. *Ceres:* the Roman goddess of agriculture—here equivalent to foods made of grain.

Eggs, oysters, too, are amatory food;
But who is their purveyor from above
Heaven knows—it may be Neptune, Pan, or Jove.   1360

CLXXI

When Juan woke he found some good things ready,
  A bath, a breakfast, and the finest eyes
That ever made a youthful heart less steady,
  Besides her maid's, as pretty for their size;
But I have spoken of all this already—   1365
  And repetition's tiresome and unwise,—
Well—Juan, after bathing in the sea,
Came always back to coffee and Haidée.

CLXXII

Both were so young, and one so innocent,
  That bathing passed for nothing; Juan seemed   1370
To her, as 'twere, the kind of being sent,
  Of whom these two years she had nightly dreamed,
A something to be loved, a creature meant
  To be her happiness, and whom she deemed
To render happy: all who joy would win   1375
Must share it,—Happiness was born a twin.

CLXXIII

It was such a pleasure to behold him, such
  Enlargement of existence to partake
Nature with him, to thrill beneath his touch,
  To watch him slumbering, and to see him wake;   1380
To live with him for ever were too much;
  But then the thought of parting made her quake:
He was her own, her ocean-treasure, cast
Like a rich wreck—her first love, and her last.

CLXXIV

And thus a moon rolled on, and fair Haidée   1385
  Paid daily visits to her boy, and took
Such plentiful precautions, that still he
  Remained unknown within his craggy nook;
At last her father's prows put out to sea,
  For certain merchantmen upon the look,   1390
Not as of yore to carry off an Io,
But three Ragusan vessels bound for Scio.

1391. *Io:* beloved by Zeus, and
changed by him into a heifer to protect
her from his wife, Hera. See Aeschylus,
Prometheus Bound.

1392. *Ragusan:* from Ragusa, a port
in modern Yugoslavia, on the Adriatic.
Scio: an island in the Aegean, northeast
of Athens.

CLXXV

Then came her freedom, for she had no mother,
    So that, her father being at sea, she was
Free as a married woman, or such other   1395
    Female, as where she likes she may freely pass,
Without even the encumbrance of a brother,
    The freest she that ever gazed on glass:
I speak of Christian lands in this comparison,
Where wives, at least, are seldom kept in garrison.   1400

CLXXVI

Now she prolonged her visits and her talk
    (For they must talk), and he had learnt to say
So much as to propose to take a walk,—
    For little had he wandered since the day
On which, like a young flower snapped from the stalk,   1405
    Drooping and dewy on the beach he lay,—
And thus they walked out in the afternoon,
And saw the sun set opposite the moon.

CLXXVII

It was a wild and breaker-beaten coast,
    With cliffs above, and a broad sandy shore,   1410
Guarded by shoals and rocks as by an host,
    With here and there a creek, whose aspect wore
A better welcome to the tempest-tost;
    And rarely ceased the haughty billow's roar,
Save on the dead long summer days, which make   1415
The outstretched ocean glitter like a lake.

CLXXVIII

And the small ripple spilt upon the beach
    Scarcely o'erpassed the cream of your champagne,
When o'er the brim the sparkling bumpers reach,
    That spring-dew of the spirit! the heart's rain!   1420
Few things surpass old wine; and they may preach
    Who please,—the more because they preach in vain,—
Let us have wine and women, mirth and laughter,
Sermons and soda-water the day after.

CLXXIX

Man, being reasonable, must get drunk;   1425
    The best of life is but intoxication:
Glory, the grape, love, gold, in these are sunk
    The hopes of all men, and of every nation;

Without their sap, how branchless were the trunk
   Of life's strange tree, so fruitful on occasion!   1430
But to return,—Get very drunk; and when
You wake with headache, you shall see what then.

CLXXX

Ring for your valet—bid him quickly bring
   Some hock and soda-water, then you'll know
A pleasure worthy Xerxes the great king;   1435
   For not the blest sherbet, sublimed with snow,
Nor the first sparkle of the desert spring,
   Nor Burgundy in all its sunset glow,
After long travel, ennui, love, or slaughter,
Vie with that draught of hock and soda-water.   1440

CLXXXI

The coast—I think it was the coast that I
   Was just describing—Yes, it *was* the coast—
Lay at this period quiet as the sky,
   The sands untumbled, the blue waves untost,
And all was stillness, save the sea-birds' cry,   1445
   And dolphin's leap, and little billow crost
By some low rock or shelve, that made it fret
Against the boundary it scarcely wet.

CLXXXII

And forth they wandered, her sire being gone,
   As I have said, upon an expedition;   1450
And mother, brother, guardian, she had none,
   Save Zoe, who, although with due precision
She waited on her lady with the sun,
   Thought daily service was her only mission,
Bringing warm water, wreathing her long tresses,   1455
And asking now and then for cast-off dresses.

CLXXXIII

It was the cooling hour, just when the rounded
   Red sun sinks down behind the azure hill,
Which then seems as if the whole earth is bounded,
   Circling all nature, hushed, and dim, and still,   1460
With the far mountain-crescent half surrounded
   On one side, and the deep sea calm and chill,
Upon the other, and the rosy sky,
With one star sparkling through it like an eye.

1435. *Xerxes:* king of Persia and son of Darius. Xerxes (519–465 B.C.) bridged the Hellespont, invaded Greece, defeated the Spartans at Thermopylae, and was finally beaten by the Greeks at Salamis in 480 B.C.

CLXXXIV

And thus they wandered forth, hand in hand,   1465
  Over the shining pebbles and the shells,
Glided along the smooth and hardened sand,
  And in the worn and wild receptacles
Worked by the storms, yet worked as it were planned,
  In hollow halls, with sparry roofs and cells,   1470
They turned to rest; and, each clasped by an arm,
Yielded to the deep twilight's purple charm.

CLXXXV

They looked up to the sky, whose floating glow
  Spread like a rosy ocean, vast and bright;
They gazed upon the glittering sea below,   1475
  Whence the broad moon rose circling into sight;
They heard the waves splash, and the wind so low,
  And saw each other's dark eyes darting light
Into each other—and, beholding this,
Their lips drew near, and clung into a kiss;   1480

CLXXXVI

A long, long kiss, a kiss of youth, and love,
  And beauty, all concentrating like rays
Into one focus, kindled from above;
  Such kisses as belong to early days,
Where heart, and soul, and sense, in concert move,   1485
  And the blood's lava, and the pulse a blaze,
Each kiss a heart-quake,—for a kiss's strength,
I think it must be reckoned by its length.

CLXXXVII

By length I mean duration; theirs endured
  Heaven knows how long—no doubt they never reckoned;   1490
And if they had, they could not have secured
  The sum of their sensations to a second:
They had not spoken; but they felt allured,
  As if their souls and lips each other beckoned,
Which, being joined, like swarming bees they clung—   1495
Their hearts the flowers from whence the honey sprung.

CLXXXVIII

They were alone, but not alone as they
  Who shut in chambers think it loneliness;
The silent ocean, and the starlight bay,
  The twilight glow, which momently grew less,   1500

The voiceless sands, and dropping caves, that lay
    Around them, made them to each other press,
As if there were no life beneath the sky
Save theirs, and that their life could never die.

CLXXXIX

They feared no eyes nor ears on that lone beach,   1505
    They felt no terrors from the night; they were
All in all to each other; though their speech
    Was broken words, they *thought* a language there,—
And all the burning tongues the passions teach
    Found in one sigh the best interpreter   1510
Of nature's oracle—first love,—that all
Which Eve has left her daughters since her fall.

CXC

Haidée spoke not of scruples, asked no vows,
    Nor offered any; she had never heard
Of plight and promises to be a spouse,   1515
    Or perils by a loving maid incurred;
She was all which pure ignorance allows,
    And flew to her young mate like a young bird,
And never having dreamt of falsehood, she
Had not one word to say of constancy.   1520

CXCI

She loved, and was beloved—she adored,
    And she was worshipped; after nature's fashion,
Their intense souls, into each other poured,
    If souls could die, had perished in that passion,—
But by degrees their senses were restored,   1525
    Again to be o'ercome, again to dash on;
And, beating 'gainst *his* bosom, Haidée's heart
Felt as if never more to beat apart.

CXCII

Alas! they were so young, so beautiful,
    So lonely, loving, helpless, and the hour   1530
Was that in which the heart is always full,
    And, having o'er itself no further power,
Prompts deeds eternity cannot annul,
    But pays off moments in an endless shower
Of hell-fire—all prepared for people giving   1535
Pleasure or pain to one another living.

CXCIII

Alas; for Juan and Haidée! they were
   So loving and so lovely—till then never,
Excepting our first parents, such a pair
   Had run the risk of being damned for ever;   1540
And Haidée, being devout as well as fair,
   Had, doubtless, heard about the Stygian river,
And hell and purgatory—but forgot
Just in the very crisis she should not.

CXCIV

They look upon each other, and their eyes   1545
   Gleam in the moonlight; and her white arm clasps
Round Juan's head, and his around her lies
   Half buried in the tresses which it grasps;
She sits upon his knee, and drinks his sighs,
   He hers, until they end in broken gasps;   1550
And thus they form a group that's quite antique,
Half naked, loving, natural, and Greek.

CXCV

And when those deep and burning moments passed,
   And Juan sunk to sleep within her arms,
She slept not, but all tenderly, though fast,   1555
   Sustained his head upon her bosom's charms;
And now and then her eye to heaven is cast,
   And then on the pale cheek her breast now warms,
Pillowed on her o'erflowing heart, which pants
With all it granted, and with all it grants.   1560

CXCVI

An infant when it gazes on a light,
   A child the moment when it drains the breast,
A devotee when soars the Host in sight,
   An Arab with a stranger for a guest,
A sailor when the prize has struck in fight,   1565
   A miser filling his most hoarded chest,
Feel rapture; but not such true joy are reaping
As they who watch o'er what they love while sleeping.

CXCVII

For there it lies so tranquil, so beloved,
   All that it hath of life with us is living;   1570
So gentle, stirless, helpless, and unmoved,

And all unconscious of the joy 'tis giving;
All it hath felt, inflicted, passed, and proved,
   Hushed into depths beyond the watcher's diving;
There lies the thing we love with all its errors   1575
And all its charms, like death without its terrors.

CXCVIII

The lady watched her lover—and that hour
   Of Love's, and Night's, and Ocean's solitude,
O'erflowed her soul with their united power;
   Amidst the barren sand and rocks so rude   1580
She and her wave-born love had made their bower,
   Where nought upon their passion could intrude,
And all the stars that crowded the blue space
Saw nothing happier than her glowing face.

CXCIX

Alas! the love of women! it is known   1585
   To be a lovely and a fearful thing;
For all of theirs upon that die is thrown,
   And if 'tis lost, life hath no more to bring
To them but mockeries of the past alone,
   And their revenge is as the tiger's spring,   1590
Deadly, and quick, and crushing; yet, as real
Torture is theirs, what they inflict they feel.

CC

They are right; for man to man so oft unjust,
   Is always so to women; one sole bond
Awaits them, treachery is all their trust;   1595
   Taught to conceal, their bursting hearts despond
Over their idol, till some wealthier lust
   Buys them in marriage—and what rests beyond?
A thankless husband, next a faithless lover,
Then dressing, nursing, praying, and all's over.   1600

CCI

Some take a lover, some take drams or prayers,
   Some mind their household, others dissipation,
Some run away, and but exchange their cares,
   Losing the advantage of a virtuous station;
Few changes e'er can better their affairs,   1605
   Theirs being an unnatural situation,
From the dull palace to the dirty hovel:
Some play the devil, and then write a novel.

1608. *novel:* Lady Caroline Lamb
(1785–1828), infatuated with Byron,
wrote a thinly veiled autobiographical
novel about their affair after her

CCII

Haidée was Nature's bride, and knew not this:
   Haidée was Passion's child, born where the sun   1610
Showers triple light, and scorches even the kiss
   Of his gazelle-eyed daughters; she was one
Made to love, to feel that she was his
   Who was her chosen: what was said or done
Elsewhere was nothing. She had nought to fear,   1615
Hope, care, nor love beyond,—her heart beat *here*.

CCIII

And oh! that quickening of the heart, that beat!
   How much it costs us! yet each rising throb
Is in its cause as its effect so sweet,
   That Wisdom, ever on the watch to rob   1620
Joy of its alchemy, and to repeat
   Fine truths; even Conscience, too, has a tough job
To make us understand each good old maxim,
So good—I wonder Castlereagh don't tax 'em.

CCIV

And now 'twas done—on the lone shore were plighted   1625
   Their hearts; the stars, their nuptial torches, shed
Beauty upon the beautiful they lighted:
   Ocean their witness, and the cave their bed.
By their own feelings hallowed and united,
   Their priest was Solitude, and they were wed: 1630
And they were happy, for to their young eyes
Each was an angel, and earth paradise.

CCV

Oh, Love! of whom great Cæsar was the suitor,
   Titus the master, Anthony the slave,
Horace, Catullus, scholars, Ovid tutor,   1635
   Sappho the sage blue-stocking, in whose grave
All those may leap who rather would be neuter—
   (Leucadia's rock still overlooks the wave)—
Oh, Love! thou art the very god of evil,
For, after all, we cannot call thee devil.   1640

rupture with him. The book, *Glenarvon* (1816), was later republished as *The Fatal Passion* (1865). It was Lady Caroline who said of Byron that he was "mad, bad, and dangerous to know." The sight of his funeral in 1824 permanently deranged her mind.
1624. *Castlereagh:* Viscount Castlereagh (1769–1822), British foreign secretary between 1812 and 1822.

1634. *Titus:* Titus Flavius Vespasianus, Roman emperor from 79 to 81 A.D., called "the love and delight of the human race" for his virtues.
1638. *Leucadia's rock:* a promontory on the island of Leucadia, or Leucas, from which unhappy lovers—notably the poetess Sappho—were said to have leaped into the sea.

CCVI

Thou makest the chaste connubial state precarious,
    And jestest with the brows of mightiest men:
Cæsar and Pompey, Mahomet, Belisarius,
    Have much employed the muse of history's pen:
Their lives and fortunes were extremely various,   1645
    Such worthies Time will never see again;
Yet to these four in three things the same luck holds,
They all were heroes, conquerors, and cuckolds.

CCVII

Thou makest philosophers; there's Epicurus
    And Aristippus, a material crew!   1650
Who to immoral courses would allure us
    By theories quite practicable too;
If only from the devil they would insure us,
    How pleasant were the maxim (not quite new),
"Eat, drink, and love; what can the rest avail us?"   1655
So said the royal sage Sardanapalus.

CCVIII

But Juan! had he quite forgotten Julia?
    And should he have forgotten her so soon?
I can't but say it seems to me most truly a
    Perplexing question; but, no doubt, the moon   1660
Does these things for us, and whenever newly a
    Strong palpitation rises, 'tis her boon,
Else how the devil is it that fresh features
Have such a charm for us poor human creatures?

CCIX

I hate inconstancy—I loathe, detest,   1665
    Abhor, condemn, abjure the mortal made
Of such quicksilver clay that in his breast
    No permanent foundation can be laid;
Love, constant love, has been my constant guest,
    And yet last night, being at a masquerade,   1670
I saw the prettiest creature, fresh from Milan,
Which gave me some sensations like a villain.

1642. *brows:* alluding to the horns reputed to appear on the foreheads of cuckolds.
1643. *Belisarius:* military commander during the reign (527–565 A.D.) of the Roman emperor Justinian.
1650. *Aristippus:* born about 428 B.C., founder of the Cyrenaic (hedonistic) school of philosophy.
1656. *Sardanapalus:* last king of Assyria, according to legend notorious for effeminacy and love of luxury. He was the central character of Byron's play *Sardanapalus* (1821).

CCX

But soon Philosophy came to my aid,
   And whispered, "Think of every sacred tie!"
"I will, my dear Philosophy!" I said,   1675
   "But then her teeth, and then, oh, Heaven! her eye!
I'll just inquire if she be wife or maid,
   Or neither—out of curiosity."
"Stop!" cried Philosophy, with air so Grecian
(Though she was masqued then as a fair Venetian);   1680

CCXI

"Stop!" so I stopped.—But to return: that which
   Men call inconstancy is nothing more
Than admiration due where nature's rich
   Profusion with young beauty cover o'er
Some favoured object; and as in the niche   1685
   A lovely statue we almost adore,
This sort of adoration of the real
Is but a heightening of the "beau ideal."

CCXII

'Tis the perception of the beautiful,
   A fine extension of the faculties,   1690
Platonic, universal, wonderful,
   Drawn from the stars, and filtered through the skies,
Without which life would be extremely dull;
   In short, it is the use of our own eyes,
With one or two small senses added, just   1695
To hint that flesh is formed of fiery dust.

CCXIII

Yet 'tis a painful feeling, and unwilling,
   For surely if we always could perceive
In the same object graces quite as killing
   As when she rose upon us like an Eve,   1700
'Twould save us many a heart-ache, many a shilling
   (For we must get them any how, or grieve),
Whereas, if one sole lady pleased for ever,
How pleasant for the heart, as well as liver!

CCXIV

The heart is like the sky, a part of heaven,   1705
   But changes night and day, too, like the sky;
Now o'er it clouds and thunder must be driven,

And darkness and destruction as on high:
But when it hath been scorched, and pierced, and riven,
   Its storms expire in water-drops; the eye   1710
Pours forth at last the heart's blood turned to tears,
Which makes the English climate of our years.

CCXV

The liver is the lazaret of bile,
   But very rarely executes its function,
For the first passion stays there such a while,   1715
   That all the rest creep in and form a junction,
Like knots of vipers on a dunghill's soil,
   Rage, fear, hate, jealousy, revenge, compunction,
So that all mischiefs spring up from this entrail,
Like earthquakes from the hidden fire called "central."   1720

CCXVI

In the mean time, without proceeding more
   In this anatomy, I've finished now
Two hundred and odd stanzas as before,
   That being about the number I'll allow
Each canto of the twelve, or twenty-four;   1725
   And, laying down my pen, I make my bow,
Leaving Don Juan and Haidée to plead
For them and theirs with all who deign to read.

1726. *pen:* Cantos III through XVI were published between August, 1821, and March, 1824, and the fragmentary Canto XVII first appeared in 1903. The love affair is interrupted by the entrance of Haidée's father, Lambro; and Juan is sold as a slave, while Haidée dies of a broken heart. After a sojourn at the Sultan's court at Constantinople, where he becomes the lover of the Sultana Gulbeyaz and the concubine Dudú, Juan joins the Russian army besieging the Turks in Ismail. He later is the recipient of the affections of Catherine the Great, and eventually goes to England. Here he enters the elegant society of the day, and the poem breaks off with Juan's affair with the Duchess of Fitz-Fulke.

WILLIAM WORDSWORTH
(1770–1850)
Lines

COMPOSED A FEW MILES ABOVE TINTERN ABBEY, ON REVISITING THE BANKS OF THE WYE DURING A TOUR. JULY 13, 1798.*

Five years have past; five summers, with the length
   Of five long winters! and again I hear
   These waters, rolling from their mountain-springs

* First published in 1798 in *Lyrical Ballads*.

With a soft inland murmur.——Once again
Do I behold these steep and lofty cliffs,   5
That on a wild secluded scene impress
Thoughts of more deep seclusion; and connect
The landscape with the quiet of the sky.
The day is come when I again repose
Here, under this dark sycamore, and view   10
These plots of cottage-ground, these orchard-tufts,
Which at this season, with their unripe fruits,
Are clad in one green hue, and lose themselves
'Mid groves and copses. Once again I see
These hedge-rows, hardly hedge-rows, little lines   15
Of sportive wood run wild: these pastoral farms,
Green to the very door; and wreaths of smoke
Sent up, in silence, from among the trees!
With some uncertain notice, as might seem
Of vagrant dwellers in the houseless woods,   20
Or of some Hermit's cave, where by his fire
The Hermit sits alone.

                These beauteous forms,
Through a long absence, have not been to me
As is a landscape to a blind man's eye:
But oft, in lonely rooms, and 'mid the din   25
Of towns and cities, I have owed to them,
In hours of weariness, sensations sweet,
Felt in the blood, and felt along the heart;
And passing even into my purer mind,
With tranquil restoration:——feelings too   30
Of unremembered pleasure: such, perhaps,
As have no slight or trivial influence
On that best portion of a good man's life,
His little, nameless, unremembered, acts
Of kindness and of love. Nor less, I trust,   35
To them I may have owed another gift,
Of aspect more sublime; that blessed mood,
In which the burthen of the mystery,
In which the heavy and the weary weight
Of all this unintelligible world,   40
Is lightened:——that serene and blessed mood,
In which the affections gently lead us on,——
Until, the breath of this corporeal frame
And even the motion of our human blood
Almost suspended. we are laid asleep   45
In body, and become a living soul:

While with an eye made quiet by the power
Of harmony, and the deep power of joy,
We see into the life of things.

                            If this
Be but a vain belief, yet, oh! how oft—   50
In darkness and amid the many shapes
Of joyless daylight; when the fretful stir
Unprofitable, and the fever of the world,
Have hung upon the beatings of my heart—
How oft, in spirit, have I turned to thee,   55
O sylvan Wye! thou wanderer thro' the woods,
How often has my spirit turned to thee!

    And now, with gleams of half-extinguished thought
With many recognitions dim and faint,
And somewhat of a sad perplexity,   60
The picture of the mind revives again:
While here I stand, not only with the sense
Of present pleasure, but with pleasing thoughts
That in this moment there is life and food
For future years. And so I dare to hope,   65
Though changed, no doubt, from what I was when first
I came among these hills; when like a roe
I bounded o'er the mountains, by the sides
Of the deep rivers, and the lonely streams,
Wherever nature led: more like a man   70
Flying from something that he dreads than one
Who sought the thing he loved. For nature then
(The coarser pleasures of my boyish days,
And their glad animal movements all gone by)
To me was all in all.—I cannot paint   75
What then I was. The sounding cataract
Haunted me like a passion: the tall rock,
The mountain, and the deep and gloomy wood,
Their colours and their forms, were then to me
An appetite; a feeling and a love,   80
That had no need for a remoter charm,
By thought supplied, nor any interest
Unborrowed from the eye.—That time is past,
And all its aching joys are now no more,
And all its dizzy raptures. Not for this   85
Faint I, nor mourn nor murmur; other gifts
Have followed; for such loss, I would believe,
Abundant recompense. For I have learned

To look on nature, not as in the hour
Of thoughtless youth; but hearing oftentimes   90
The still, sad music of humanity,
Nor harsh nor grating, though of ample power
To chasten and subdue. And I have felt
A presence that disturbs me with the joy
Of elevated thoughts; a sense sublime   95
Of something far more deeply interfused,
Whose dwelling is the light of setting suns,
And the round ocean and the living air,
And the blue sky, and in the mind of man:
A motion and a spirit, that impels   100
All thinking things, all objects of all thought,
And rolls through all things. Therefore am I still
A lover of the meadows and the woods,
And mountains; and of all that we behold
From this green earth; of all the mighty world   105
Of eye, and ear,—both what they half create,
And what perceive; well pleased to recognise
In nature and the language of the sense
The anchor of my purest thoughts, the nurse,
The guide, the guardian of my heart, and soul   110
Of all my moral being.

                Nor perchance,
If I were not thus taught, should I the more
Suffer my genial spirits to decay:
For thou art with me here upon the banks
Of this fair river; thou my dearest Friend,   115
My dear, dear Friend; and in thy voice I catch
The language of my former heart, and read
My former pleasures in the shooting lights
Of thy wild eyes. Oh! yet a little while
May I behold in thee what I was once,   120
My dear, dear Sister! and this prayer I make,
Knowing that Nature never did betray
The heart that loved her; 'tis her privilege,
Through all the years of this our life, to lead
From joy to joy: for she can so inform   125
The mind that is within us, so impress
With quietness and beauty, and so feed
With lofty thoughts, that neither evil tongues,
Rash judgments, nor the sneers of selfish men,
Nor greetings where no kindness is, nor all   130
The dreary intercourse of daily life,

Shall e'er prevail against us, or disturb
Our cheerful faith, that all which we behold
Is full of blessings. Therefore let the moon
Shine on thee in thy solitary walk;   135
And let the misty mountain-winds be free
To blow against thee: and, in after years,
When these wild ecstasies shall be matured
Into a sober pleasure; when thy mind
Shall be a mansion for all lovely forms,   140
Thy memory be as a dwelling-place
For all sweet sounds and harmonies; oh! then,
If solitude, or fear, or pain, or grief
Should be thy portion, with what healing thoughts
Of tender joy wilt thou remember me,   145
And these my exhortations! Nor, perchance—
If I should be where I no more can hear
Thy voice, nor catch from thy wild eyes these gleams
Of past existence—wilt thou then forget
That on the banks of this delightful stream   150
We stood together; and that I, so long
A worshipper of Nature, hither came
Unwearied in that service: rather say
With warmer love—oh! with far deeper zeal
Of holier love. Nor wilt thou then forget   155
That after many wanderings, many years
Of absence, these steep woods and lofty cliffs,
And this green pastoral landscape, were to me
More dear, both for themselves and for thy sake!

Ode*

INTIMATIONS OF IMMORTALITY FROM RECOLLECTIONS OF EARLY CHILDHOOD

> The Child is father of the Man;
> And I could wish my days to be
> Bound each to each by natural piety.

I

There was a time when meadow, grove, and stream,
        The earth, and every common sight,
                To me did seem
              Apparelled in celestial light,
The glory and the freshness of a dream.
It is not now as it hath been of yore;—   5
              Turn wheresoe'er I may,

* Written between 1802 and 1806; published in 1807.

By night or day,
The things which I have seen I now can see no more.

II

The Rainbow comes and goes   10
And lovely is the Rose;
The Moon doth with delight
Look round her when the heavens are bare,
Waters on a starry night
Are beautiful and fair;   15
The sunshine is a glorious birth;
But yet I know, where'er I go,
That there hath past away a glory from the earth.

III

Now, while the birds thus sing a joyous song,
And while the young lambs bound   20
As to the tabor's sound,
To me alone there came a thought of grief:
A timely utterance gave that thought relief,
And I again am strong:
The cataracts blow their trumpets from the steep;   25
No more shall grief of mine the season wrong;
I hear the Echoes through the mountains throng,
The Winds come to me from the fields of sleep,
And all the earth is gay;
Land and sea   30
Give themselves up to jollity,
And with the heart of May
Doth every Beast keep holiday;—
Thou Child of Joy,
Shout round me, let me hear thy shouts, thou happy   35
Shepherd-boy!

IV

Ye blessèd Creatures, I have heard the call
Ye to each other make; I see
The heavens laugh with you in your jubilee;
My heart is at your festival,   40
My head hath its coronal,
The fulness of your bliss, I feel—I feel it all.
Oh evil day! if I were sullen
While Earth herself is adorning,
This sweet May-morning,   45
And the Children are culling
On every side,

In a thousand valleys far and wide,
    Fresh flowers; while the sun shines warm,
And the Babe leaps upon his Mother's arm:—   50
    I hear, I hear, with joy I hear!
    —But there's a Tree, of many, one,
A single Field which I have looked upon,
Both of them speak of something that is gone:
        The Pansy at my feet   55
        Doth the same tale repeat:
    Whither is fled the visionary gleam?
    Where is it now, the glory and the dream?

V

Our birth is but a sleep and a forgetting:
The Soul that rises with us, our life's Star,   60
        Hath had elsewhere its setting,
        And cometh from afar:
    Not in entire forgetfulness,
    And not in utter nakedness,
But trailing clouds of glory do we come   65
        From God, who is our home:
Heaven lies about us in our infancy!
Shades of the prison-house begin to close
        Upon the growing Boy,
But He beholds the light, and whence it flows,   70
        He sees it in his joy;
The Youth, who daily farther from the east
    Must travel, still is Nature's Priest,
        And by the vision splendid
        Is on his way attended;   75
At length the Man perceives it die away,
And fade into the light of common day.

VI

Earth fills her lap with pleasures of her own;
Yearnings she hath in her own natural kind,
And, even with something of a Mother's mind,   80
        And no unworthy aim,
    The homely Nurse doth all she can
To make her Foster-child, her Inmate, Man,
    Forget the glories he hath known,
And that imperial palace whence he came.   85

VII

Behold the Child among his new-born blisses,
A six years' Darling of a pigmy size!

See, where 'mid work of his own hand he lies,
Fretted by sallies of his mother's kisses,
With light upon him from his father's eyes! 90
See, at his feet, some little plan or chart,
Some fragment from his dream of human life,
Shaped by himself with newly-learned art;
    A wedding or a festival,
    A mourning or a funeral; 95
      And this hath now his heart,
      And unto this he frames his song
        Then will he fit his tongue
To dialogues of business, love, or strife;
      But it will not be long 100
      Ere this will be thrown aside,
      And with new joy and pride
The little Actor cons another part;
Filling from time to time his 'humorous stage'
With all the Persons, down to palsied Age, 105
That Life brings with her in her equipage;
      As if his whole vocation
      Were endless imitation.

        VIII

Thou, whose exterior semblance doth belie
      Thy Soul's immensity; 110
Thou best Philosopher, who yet dost keep
Thy heritage, thou Eye among the blind,
That, deaf and silent, read'st the eternal deep,
Haunted for ever by the eternal mind,—
      Mighty Prophet! Seer blest! 115
      On whom those truths do rest,
Which we are toiling all our lives to find,
In darkness lost, the darkness of the grave;
Thou, over whom thy Immortality
Broods like the Day, a Master o'er a Slave, 120
A presence which is not to be put by;
      [To whom the grave
Is but a lonely bed without the sense or sight
      Of day or the warm light
A place of thought where we in waiting lie;] 125
Thou little Child, yet glorious in the might
Of heaven-born freedom on thy being's height,

122–125. *To whom . . . lie:* These lines were included in the "Ode" in the 1807 and 1815 editions of Wordsworth's poems but were omitted in the 1820 and subsequent editions, as a result of Coleridge's severe censure of them.

Why with such earnest pains dost thou provoke
The years to bring the inevitable yoke,
Thus blindly with thy blessedness at strife?   130
Full soon thy Soul shall have her earthly freight,
And custom lie upon thee with a weight,
Heavy as frost, and deep almost as life!

                              IX

              O joy! that in our embers
              Is something that doth live,   135
              That nature yet remembers
              What was so fugitive!
The thought of our past years in me doth breed
Perpetual benediction: not indeed
For that which is most worthy to be blest;   140
Delight and liberty, the simple creed
Of Childhood, whether busy or at rest,
With new-fledged hope still fluttering in his breast—
              Not for these I raise
              The song of thanks and praise;   145
          But for those obstinate questionings
          Of sense and outward things,
          Fallings from us, vanishings;
          Blank misgivings of a Creature
Moving about in worlds not realized,   150
High instincts before which our mortal Nature
Did tremble like a guilty Thing surprised:
              But for those first affections,
              Those shadowy recollections,
          Which, be they what they may,   155
Are yet the fountain-light of all our day,
Are yet a master-light of all our seeing;
Uphold us, cherish, and have power to make
Our noisy years seem moments in the being
Of the eternal Silence: truths that wake,   160
              To perish never:
Which neither listlessness, nor mad endeavour,
              Nor Man nor Boy,
Nor all that is at enmity with joy,
Can utterly abolish or destroy!   165
          Hence in a season of calm weather
              Though inland far we be,
Our Souls have sight of that immortal sea
              Which brought us hither,

Can in a moment travel thither,   170
And see the Children sport upon the shore,
And hear the mighty waters rolling evermore.

                                        X

Then sing, ye Birds, sing, sing a joyous song!
          And let the young Lambs bound
          As to the tabor's sound!   175
We in thought will join your throng,
          Ye that pipe and ye that play,
          Ye that through your hearts to-day
          Feel the gladness of the May!
What though the radiance which was once so bright   180
Be now for ever taken from my sight,
          Though nothing can bring back the hour
Of splendour in the grass, of glory in the flower;
          We will grieve not, rather find
          Strength in what remains behind;   185
          In the primal sympathy
          Which having been must ever be;
          In the soothing thoughts that spring
          Out of human suffering;
          In the faith that looks through death,   190
In years that bring the philosophic mind.

                                        XI

And O, ye Fountains, Meadows, Hills, and Groves,
Forebode not any severing of our loves!
Yet in my heart of hearts I feel your might;
I only have relinquished one delight   195
To live beneath your more habitual sway.
I love the Brooks which down their channels fret,
Even more than when I tripped lightly as they;
The innocent brightness of a new-born Day
          Is lovely yet;   200
The Clouds that gather round the setting sun
Do take a sober colouring from an eye
That hath kept watch o'er man's mortality;
Another race hath been, and other palms are won.
Thanks to the human heart by which we live,   205
Thanks to its tenderness, its joys, and fears,
To me the meanest flower that blows can give
Thoughts that do often lie too deep for tears.

Composed upon Westminster Bridge,
September 3, 1802*

Earth has not anything to show more fair:
Dull would he be of soul who could pass by
A sight so touching in its majesty;
This City now doth, like a garment, wear
The beauty of the morning; silent, bare,   5
Ships, towers, domes, theatres, and temples lie
Open unto the fields, and to the sky;
All bright and glittering in the smokeless air.
Never did sun more beautifully steep
In his first splendour, valley, rock, or hill;   10
Ne'er saw I, never felt, a calm so deep!
The river glideth at his own sweet will:
Dear God! the very houses seem asleep;
And all that mighty heart is lying still!

The World Is Too Much with Us †

The world is too much with us; late and soon,
Getting and spending, we lay waste our powers
Little we see in Nature that is ours;
We have given our hearts away, a sordid boon!
This Sea that bares her bosom to the moon,   5
The winds that will be howling at all hours,
And are up-gathered now like sleeping flowers,
For this, for everything, we are out of tune;
It moves us not.—Great God! I'd rather be
A Pagan suckled in a creed outworn;   10
So might I, standing on this pleasant lea,
Have glimpses that would make me less forlorn;
Have sight of Proteus rising from the sea;
Or hear old Triton blow his wreathèd horn.

* Published in 1807. "Composed on the roof of a coach on my way to France" (Wordsworth), on July 31, not September 3. The conflict of feelings attending Wordsworth's brief return to France, where he had first gone in 1791-1792 sympathetic to the revolution and had been the lover of Annette Vallon and the father of her child, evoked a number of personal and political sonnets.

† Written in 1806; published in 1807.

4. *boon:* gift; *sordid* refers to the act of giving the heart away.

14. *Proteus:* an old man of the sea who, in the *Odyssey,* can assume a variety of shapes. *Triton:* a sea deity, usually represented as blowing on a conch shell.

SAMUEL TAYLOR COLERIDGE
(1772–1834)
Kubla Khan*

OR, A VISION IN A DREAM, A FRAGMENT

The following fragment is here published at the request of a poet of great and deserved celebrity [Lord Byron], and, as far as the Author's own opinions are concerned, rather as a psychological curiosity, than on the ground of any supposed poetic merits.

In the summer of the year 1797, the Author, then in ill health, had retired to a lonely farm-house between Porlock and Linton, on the Exmoore confines of Somerset and Devonshire.[1] In consequence of a slight indisposition, an anodyne had been prescribed, from the effects of which he fell asleep in his chair at the moment that he was reading the following sentence, or words of the same substance, in "Purchas's Pilgrimage"[2]: "Here the Khan Kubla commanded a palace to be built, and a stately garden thereunto. And thus ten miles of fertile ground were inclosed with a wall." The Author continued for about three hours in a profound sleep, at least of the external senses, during which time he has the most vivid confidence, that he could not have composed less than from two to three hundred lines; if that indeed can be called composition in which all the images rose up before him as things, with a parallel production of the correspondent expressions, without any sensation or consciousness of effort.[3] On awaking he appeared to himself to have a distinct recollection of the whole, and taking his pen, ink, and paper, instantly and eagerly wrote down the lines that are here preserved. At this moment he was unfortunately called out by a person on business from Porlock, and detained by him above an hour, and on his return to his room, found, to his no small surprise and mortification, that though he still retained some vague and dim recollection of the general purport of the vision yet, with the exception of some eight or ten scattered lines and images, all the rest had passed away

* The poem was first published together with *Christabel* and *The Pains of Sleep* in 1816. E. H. Coleridge dates the poem 1798; it may actually have been written in 1799 or as late as 1800.

1. A high moorland shared by the two southwestern counties in England of Devonshire and Somerset.

2. Samuel Purchas (1575?–1626) published *Purchas his Pilgrimage, or Relations of the World and the Religions observed in all Ages* in 1613. The passage in Purchas is slightly different: "In Xamdu did Cublai Can build a stately Palace, encompassing sixteene miles of plaine ground with a wall, wherein are fertile meddowes, pleasant Springs, delightfull Streames, and all sorts of beasts of chase and game, and in the middest thereof a sumptuous house of pleasure, which may be removed from place to place" (Book IV, Chap. 13).

3. Coleridge's statement that he dreamed the poem and wrote down what he could later remember *verbatim* has been queried, most recently by medical opinion. The belief that opium produces special dreams, or even any dreams at all, seems to lack confirmation.

like the images on the surface of a stream into which a stone has been cast, but, alas! without the after restoration of the latter!

> Then all the charm
> Is broken—all that phantom-world so fair
> Vanishes, and a thousand circlets spread,
> And each mis-shape['s] the other. Stay awhile,
> Poor youth! who scarcely dar'st lift up thine eyes—
> The stream will soon renew its smoothness, soon
> The visions will return! And lo, he stays,
> And soon the fragments dim of lovely forms
> Come trembling back, unite, and now once more
> The pool becomes a mirror.[4]

Yet from the still surviving recollections in his mind, the Author has frequently purposed to finish for himself what had been originally, as it were, given to him.

Σαμερον αδιον ασω:[5] but the to-morrow is yet to come.

> In Xanadu did Kubla Khan
> A stately pleasure-dome decree:
> Where Alph, the sacred river, ran
> Through caverns measureless to man
>   Down to a sunless sea.   5
> So twice five miles of fertile ground
> With walls and towers were girdled round:
> And there were gardens bright with sinuous rills,
> Where blossomed many an incense-bearing tree;
> And here were forests ancient as the hills,   10
> Enfolding sunny spots of greenery.
>
> But oh! that deep romantic chasm which slanted
> Down the green hill athwart a cedarn cover!
> A savage place! as holy and enchanted
> As e'er beneath a waning moon was haunted   15
> By woman wailing for her demon-lover!
> And from this chasm, with ceaseless turmoil seething,
> As if this earth in fast thick pants were breathing,
> A mighty fountain momently was forced:
> Amid whose swift half-intermitted burst   20
> Huge fragments vaulted like rebounding hail,
> Or chaffy grain beneath the thresher's flail:
> And 'mid these dancing rocks at once and ever

---

4. From Coleridge's poem *The Picture; or, the Lover's Resolution*, lines 91–100.

5. From Theocritus, *Idylls*, I, 132: "to sing a sweeter song tomorrow."

1. *Kubla Khan*: Mongol emperor (1215?–1294), visited by Marco Polo.

3. *Alph*: J. L. Lowes, in *The Road to Xanadu* (1927), thinks that Coleridge may have had in mind the river Alpheus —linked with the Nile—mentioned by Virgil.

It flung up momently the sacred river.
Five miles meandering with a mazy motion   25
Through wood and dale the sacred river ran,
Then reached the caverns measureless to man,
And sank in tumult to a lifeless ocean:
And 'mid this tumult Kubla heard from far
Ancestral voices prophesying war!   30

   The shadow of the dome of pleasure
   Floated midway on the waves;
   Where was heard the mingled measure
   From the fountain and the caves.
It was a miracle of rare device,   35
A sunny pleasure-dome with caves of ice!

   A damsel with a dulcimer
   In a vision once I saw:
   It was an Abyssinian maid,
   And on her dulcimer she played,   40
   Singing of Mount Abora.
   Could I revive within me
   Her symphony and song,
   To such a deep delight 'twould win me,
That with music loud and long,   45
I would build that dome in air,
That sunny dome! those caves of ice!
And all who heard should see them there,
And all should cry, Beware! Beware!
His flashing eyes, his floating hair!   50
Weave a circle round him thrice,
And close your eyes with holy dread,
For he on honey-dew hath fed,
And drunk the milk of Paradise.

Dejection: An Ode*

Late, late yestreen I saw the new Moon,
With the old Moon in her arms;
And I fear, I fear, my Master dear!
We shall have a deadly storm.
        Ballad of Sir Patrick Spence   5

41. *Mount Abora:* Lowes argues that this may have been "Mt. Amara," mentioned by Milton in *Paradise Lost* (IV, 28), or Amhara in Samuel Johnson's *Rasselas.*

* Written April 4, 1802. First published in the *Morning Post,* October 4, 1802. The first version was addressed to Sara Hutchinson, a close friend, and it is she who was originally meant in the opening of lines 25, 47, and 138. In later versions Colerdge changed the references to "William," "Edmund," and finally "Lady."

I

Well! If the Bard was weather-wise, who made
   The grand old ballad of Sir Patrick Spence,
   This night, so tranquil now, will not go hence
Unroused by winds, that ply a busier trade
Than those which mould yon cloud in lazy flakes,   10
Or the dull sobbing draft, that moans and rakes
Upon the strings of this Aeolian lute,
     Which better far were mute.
   For lo! the New-moon winter-bright!
   And overspread with phantom light,   15
   (With swimming phantom light o'erspread
   But rimmed and circled by a silver thread)
I see the old Moon in her lap, foretelling
   The coming-on of rain and squally blast.
And oh! that even now the gust were swelling,   20
   And the slant night-shower driving loud and fast!
Those sounds which oft have raised me, whilst they awed,
     And sent my soul abroad,
Might now perhaps their wonted impulse give,
Might startle this dull pain, and make it move and live! 25

II

A grief without a pang, void, dark, and drear,
   A stifled, drowsy, unimpassioned grief,
   Which finds no natural outlet, no relief,
     In word, or sigh, or tear—
O Lady! in this wan and heartless mood,   30
To other thoughts by yonder throstle woo'd,
   All this long eve, so balmy and serene,
Have I been gazing on the western sky,
   And its peculiar tint of yellow green:
And still I gaze—and with how blank an eye!   35
And those thin clouds above, in flakes and bars,
That give away their motion to the stars;
Those stars, that glide behind them or between,
Now sparkling, now bedimmed, but always seen:
Yon crescent Moon, as fixed as if it grew   40
In its own cloudless, starless lake of blue;
I see them all so excellently fair,
I see, not feel, how beautiful they are!

12. *Aeolian lute:* a frame fitted with
strings or wires which produce musical
tones when the wind hits them. Named
after Aeolus, god of the winds.
  24. *wonted:* accustomed.
  31. *throstle:* the song-thrush.

III

My genial spirits fail;
　　And what can these avail   45
To lift the smothering weight from off my breast?
　　　It were a vain endeavour,
　　　Though I should gaze for ever
On that green light that lingers in the west:
I may not hope from outward forms to win   50
The passion and the life, whose fountains are within.

IV

O Lady! we receive but what we give,
And in our life alone does Nature live:
Ours is her wedding garment, ours her shroud!
　　And would we aught behold, of higher worth,   55
Than that inanimate cold world allowed
To the poor loveless ever-anxious crowd,
　　Ah! from the soul itself must issue forth
A light, a glory, a fair luminous cloud
　　　Enveloping the Earth—   60
And from the soul itself must there be sent
　　A sweet and potent voice, of its own birth,
Of all sweet sounds the life and element!

V

O pure of heart! thou need'st not ask of me
What this strong music in the soul may be!   65
　　What, and wherein doth exist,
　　This light, this glory, this fair luminous mist,
　　This beautiful and beauty-making power.
　　Joy, virtuous Lady! Joy that ne'er was given,
Save to the pure, and in their purest hour,   70
Life, and Life's effluence, cloud at once and shower,
Joy, Lady! is the spirit and the power,
Which wedding Nature to us gives in dower
　　A new Earth and new Heaven,
Undreamt of by the sensual and the proud—   75
Joy is the sweet voice, Joy the luminous cloud—
　　　We in ourselves rejoice!
And thence flows all that charms or ear or sight,
　　All melodies the echoes of that voice,
All colours a suffusion from that light.   80

VI

There was a time when, though my path was rough,

---

44. *genial spirits:* Coleridge's genera-
tive spirits; in short, his creativity. The
first version was written soon after
Wordsworth had composed the first

four stanzas of the *Ode on Intimations
of Immortality,* and the themes are
similar.

This joy within me dallied with distress,
And all misfortunes were but as the stuff
   Whence Fancy made me dreams of happiness:
For hope grew round me, like the twining vine,   85
And fruits, and foliage, not my own, seemed mine.
But now afflictions bow me down to earth:
Nor care I that they rob me of my mirth;
   But oh! each visitation
Suspends what nature gave me at my birth,   90
   My shaping spirit of Imagination.
For not to think of what I needs must feel,
   But to be still and patient, all I can;
And haply by abstruse research to steal
   From my own nature all the natural man—   95
   This was my sole resource, my only plan:
Till that which suits a part infects the whole,
And now is almost grown the habit of my soul.

VII

Hence, viper thoughts, that coil around my mind,
   Reality's dark dream!   100
I turn from you, and listen to the wind,
   Which long has raved unnoticed. What a scream
Of agony by torture lengthened out
That lute sent forth! Thou Wind that rav'st without,
   Bare crag, or mountain-tairn, or blasted tree,   105
Or pine-grove whither woodman never clomb,
Or lonely house, long held the witches' home,
   Methinks were fitter instruments for thee,
Mad Lutanist! who in this month of showers,
Of dark-brown gardens, and of peeping flowers,   110
Mak'st Devils' yule with worse than wintry song,
The blossoms, buds, and timorous leaves among.
   Thou Actor, perfect in all tragic sounds!
Thou mighty Poet, e'en to frenzy bold!
   What tell'st thou now about?   115
   'Tis of the rushing of an host in rout,
   With groans, of trampled men, with smarting wounds—
At once they groan with pain, and shudder with the cold!
But hush! there is a pause of deepest silence!
   And all that noise, as of a rushing crowd,   120

84. *Fancy:* Coleridge made much of the distinction between "fancy" and the "imagination" (line 86). Fancy makes pleasant combinations of images (*cf.* lines 78–79); the Imagination is a higher faculty of the mind that combines images in such a way that they create a higher reality, a poetic "truth" more valid than that which is perceived by the ordinary senses.

89. *visitation:* of the misfortunes and afflictions in line 82.
105. *mountain-tairn:* tarn or small mountain lake.
109. *Mad Lutanist:* the storm wind in line 99.
111. *Devil's yule:* Originally, yule was a heathen feast.
116. *host:* an army.

With groans, and tremulous shudderings—all is over—
It tells another tale, with sounds less deep and loud!
 A tale of less affright,
 And tempered with delight,
As Otway's self had framed the tender lay,—   125
 'Tis of a little child
 Upon a lonesome wild,
Not far from home, but she hath lost her way:
And now moans low in bitter grief and fear,
And now screams loud, and hopes to make her mother hear. 130

VIII

'Tis midnight, but small thoughts have I of sleep.
Full seldom may my friend such vigils keep!
Visit her, gentle Sleep! with wings of healing,
 And may this storm be but a mountain-birth,
May all the stars hang bright above her dwelling, 135
 Silent as though they watched the sleeping Earth!
 With light heart may she rise,
 Gay fancy, cheerful eyes,
Joy lift her spirit, joy attune her voice;
To her may all things live, from pole to pole, 140
Their life the eddying of her living soul!
 O simple spirit, guided from above,
Dear Lady! friend devoutest of my choice,
Thus mayest thou ever, evermore rejoice.

PERCY BYSSHE SHELLEY
(1792–1822)
Ode to the West Wind*

I

O wild West Wind, thou breath of Autumn's being,
Thou, from whose unseen presence the leaves dead
Are driven, like ghosts from an enchanter fleeing,

Yellow, and black, and pale, and hectic red,
Pestilence-stricken multitudes: O thou,   5
Who chariotest to their dark wintry bed

The wingèd seeds, where they lie cold and low,
Each like a corpse within its grave, until
Thine azure sister of the spring shall blow

---

122. *another tale:* the story of Wordsworth's *Lucy Gray.*
 125. *Otway's self:* originally "William" (Wordsworth). Thomas Otway

(1652–1685) was a tragic dramatist.
 * Written in 1819–1820; published
in 1820.

Her clarion o'er the dreaming earth, and fill   10
(Driving sweet buds like flocks to feed in air)
With living hues and odours plain and hill:

Wild Spirit, which art moving everywhere;
Destroyer and preserver: hear, Oh hear!

II

Thou on whose stream, mid the steep sky's commotion,   15
Loose clouds like earth's decaying leaves are shed,
Shook from the tangled boughs of Heaven and Ocean,

Angels of rain and lightning; there are spread
On the blue surface of thine airy surge,
Like the bright hair uplifted from the head   20

Of some fierce Maenad, even from the dim verge
Of the horizon to the zenith's height
The locks of the approaching storm. Thou dirge

Of the dying year, to which this closing night
Will be the dome of a vast sepulchre,   25
Vaulted with all thy congregated might

Of vapours, from whose solid atmosphere
Black rain, and fire, and hail will burst; Oh hear!

III

Thou who didst waken from his summer dreams
The blue Mediterranean, where he lay,   30
Lulled by the coil of his crystalline streams,

Beside a pumice isle in Baiae's bay,
And saw in sleep old palaces and towers
Quivering within the wave's intenser day,

All overgrown with azure moss and flowers   35
So sweet, the sense faints picturing them! Thou
For whose path the Atlantic's level powers

Cleave themselves into chasms, while far below
The sea-blooms and the oozy woods which wear
The sapless foliage of the ocean, know   40

Thy voice, and suddenly grow gray with fear,
And tremble and despoil themselves: Oh hear!

21. *Maenad:* female devotee of   32. *Baiae:* suburb of Naples, in a
Dionysus (Bacchus).   bay west of the city

IV

If I were a dead leaf thou mightest bear;
If I were a swift cloud to fly with thee;
A wave to pant beneath thy power, and share   45

The impulse of thy strength, only less free
Than thou, O uncontrollable! If even
I were as in my boyhood, and could be

The comrade of thy wanderings over heaven,
As then when to outstrip thy skiey speed   50
Scarce seemed a vision; I would ne'er have striven

As thus with thee in prayer in my sore need.
Oh lift me as a wave, a leaf, a cloud!
I fall upon the thorns of life! I bleed!

A heavy weight of hours has chained and bowed   55
One too like thee: tameless, and swift, and proud.

V

Make me thy lyre, even as the forest is:
What if my leaves are falling like its own!
The tumult of thy mighty harmonies

Will take from both a deep, autumnal tone,   60
Sweet though in sadness. Be thou, spirit fierce,
My spirit! Be thou me, impetuous one!

Drive my dead thoughts over the universe
Like withered leaves to quicken a new birth!
And, by the incantation of this verse,   65

Scatter, as from an unextinguished hearth
Ashes and sparks, my words among mankind!
Be through my lips to unawakened earth

The trumpet of a prophecy! O, wind,
If Winter comes, can Spring be far behind?   70

A Defence of Poetry*

. . . Poetry is the record of the best and happiest moments of
the happiest and best minds. We are aware of evanescent visitations
of thought and feeling sometimes associated with place or person,

---

* Written in 1821; first published in 1840. Our selection is the conclusion of the
essay.

sometimes regarding our own mind alone, and always arising unforeseen and departing unbidden, but elevating and delightful beyond all expression: so that even in the desire and regret they leave,
there cannot but be pleasure, participating as it does in the nature
of its object. It is as it were the interpenetration of a diviner nature
through our own; but its footsteps are like those of a wind over the
sea, which the coming calm erases, and whose traces remain only,
as on the wrinkled sand which paves it. These and corresponding
conditions of being are experienced principally by those of the most
delicate sensibility and the most enlarged imagination; and the state
of mind produced by them is at war with every base desire. . . .
Poetry thus makes immortal all that is best and most beautiful in the
world; it arrests the vanishing apparitions which haunt the inter-
lunations of life, and veiling them, or in language or in form, sends
them forth among mankind, bearing sweet news of kindred joy to
those with whom their sisters abide—abide, because there is no
portal of expression from the caverns of the spirit which they inhabit into the universe of things. Poetry redeems from decay the
visitations of the divinity in man. . . .

The first part of these remarks has related to poetry in its elements
and principles; and it has been shown, as well as the narrow limits
assigned them would permit, that what is called poetry, in a restricted sense, has a common source with all other forms of order
and of beauty, according to which the materials of human life are
susceptible of being arranged, and which is poetry in a universal
sense.

The second part[1] will have for its object an application of these
principles to the present state of the cultivation of poetry, and a
defence of the attempt to idealize the modern forms of manners
and opinions, and compel them into a subordination to the imaginative and creative faculty. For the literature of England, an
energetic development of which has ever preceded or accompanied
a great and free development of the national will, has arisen as it
were from a new birth. In spite of the low-thoughted envy which
would undervalue contemporary merit, our own will be a memorable
age in intellectual achievements, and we live among such philosophers and poets as surpass beyond comparison any who have appeared since the last national struggle for civil and religious liberty.
The most unfailing herald, companion, and follower of the awakening of a great people to work a beneficial change in opinion or institution, is poetry. At such periods there is an accumulation of the
power of communicating and receiving intense and impassioned
conceptions respecting man and nature. The persons in whom this
power resides may often, as far as regards many portions of their

1. The second part was never written.

nature, have little apparent correspondence with that spirit of good of which they are the ministers. But even whilst they deny and abjure, they are yet compelled to serve, the power which is seated on the throne of their own soul. It is impossible to read the compositions of the most celebrated writers of the present day without being startled with the electric life which burns within their words. They measure the circumference and sound the depths of human nature with a comprehensive and all-penetrating spirit, and they are themselves perhaps the most sincerely astonished at its manifestations; for it is less their spirit than the spirit of the age. Poets are the hierophants of an unapprehended inspiration; the mirrors of the gigantic shadows which futurity casts upon the present; the words which express what they understand not; the trumpets which sing to battle, and feel not what they inspire; the influence which is moved not, but moves. Poets are the unacknowledged legislators of the world.

JOHN KEATS
(1795–1821)
Ode to a Nightingale*

I

My heart aches, and a drowsy numbness pains
  My sense, as though of hemlock I had drunk,
Or emptied some dull opiate to the drains
  One minute past, and Lethe-wards had sunk:
'Tis not through envy of thy happy lot,   5
  But being too happy in thy happiness,
    That thou, light-winged Dryad of the trees,
      In some melodious plot
Of beechen green, and shadows numberless,
    Singest of summer in full-throated ease.   10

II

O for a draught of vintage! that hath been
  Cooled a long age in the deep-delved earth,
Tasting of Flora and the country green,
  Dance, and Provençal song, and sunburnt mirth!
O for a beaker full of the warm South!   15
  Full of the true, the blushful Hippocrene,

---

* Written in 1819; published in 1820.
4. *Lethe-wards:* i.e., toward Lethe, the river of forgetfulness in Greek mythology.
7. *Dryad:* wood nymph.

14. *Provençal:* Provence was the district in France associated with the troubadours.
16. *Hippocrene:* the fountain on Mount Helicon, in Boeotia (a part of Greece), sacred to the Muse of poetry.

With beaded bubbles winking at the brim,
   And purple-stained mouth;
That I might drink, and leave the world unseen,
   And with thee fade away into the forest dim: 20

III

Fade far away, dissolve, and quite forget
   What thou among the leaves hast never known,
The weariness, the fever, and the fret
   Here, where men sit and hear each other groan;
Where palsy shakes a few, sad, last grey hairs,   25
   Where youth grows pale, and spectre-thin, and dies;
      Where but to think is to be full of sorrow
         And leaden-eyed despairs;
   Where beauty cannot keep her lustrous eyes,
      Or new love pine at them beyond tomorrow.   30

IV

Away! away! for I will fly to thee,
   Not charioted by Bacchus and his pards,
But on the viewless wings of Poesy,
   Though the dull brain perplexes and retards:
Already with thee! tender is the night,   35
   And haply the Queen-Moon is on her throne,
      Clustered around by all her starry Fays;
         But here there is no light,
   Save what from heaven is with the breezes blown
      Through verdurous glooms and winding mossy ways.   40

V

I cannot see what flowers are at my feet,
   Nor what soft incense hangs upon the boughs,
But, in embalmèd darkness, guess each sweet
   Wherewith the seasonable month endows
The grass, the thicket, and the fruit-tree wild;   45
   White hawthorn, and the pastoral eglantine;
      Fast-fading violets covered up in leaves;
         And mid-May's eldest child,
   The coming musk-rose, full of dewy wine,
      The murmurous haunt of flies on summer eves.   50

VI

Darkling I listen; and for many a time
   I have been half in love with easeful Death,
Called him soft names in many a mused rhyme,

---

32. *pards:* leopards. Bacchus (Dionysus) was traditionally supposed to be accompanied by leopards, lions, goats, and so on.

To take into the air my quiet breath;
Now more than ever seems it rich to die,   55
    To cease upon the midnight with no pain,
        While thou art pouring forth thy soul abroad
            In such an ecstasy!
    Still wouldst thou sing, and I have ears in vain—
        To thy high requiem become a sod.   60

VII

Thou wast not born for death, immortal Bird!
    No hungry generations tread thee down;
The voice I hear this passing night was heard
    In ancient days by emperor and clown:
Perhaps the self-same song that found a path   65
    Through the sad heart of Ruth, when, sick for home,
        She stood in tears amid the alien corn;
            The same that ofttimes hath
    Charmed magic casements, opening on the foam
        Of perilous seas, in faery lands forlorn.   70

VIII

Forlorn! the very word is like a bell
    To toll me back from thee to my sole self!
Adieu! the fancy cannot cheat so well
    As she is famed to do, deceiving elf.
Adieu! adieu! thy plaintive anthem fades   75
    Past the near meadows, over the still stream,
        Up the hill-side; and now 'tis buried deep
            In the next valley-glades:
    Was it a vision, or a waking dream?
        Fled is that music:—do I wake or sleep?   80

Ode on a Grecian Urn*

I

Thou still unravished bride of quietness,
    Thou foster-child of silence and slow time,
Sylvan historian, who canst thus express
    A flowery tale more sweetly than our rhyme:
What leaf-fringed legend haunts about thy shape   5
    Of deities or of mortals, or of both,

---

66. *Ruth:* See Ruth 1:16. After her Israelite husband died, she returned to his native land with her mother-in-law.
    * Written in 1819; published in 1820. Keats's Hellenism is nowhere more apparent than in this ode, which may have been inspired by his reading in Lemprière's *Classical Dictionary,* and by his acquaintance with various classical antiquities on exhibit in London.

In Tempe or the dales of Arcady?
What men or gods are these? What maidens loth?
What mad pursuit? What struggle to escape?
What pipes and timbrels? What wild ecstasy?   10

II

Heard melodies are sweet, but those unheard
Are sweeter; therefore, ye soft pipes, play on;
Not to the sensual ear, but, more endeared,
Pipe to the spirit ditties of no tone:
Fair youth, beneath the trees, thou canst not leave   15
Thy song, nor ever can those trees be bare;
Bold lover, never, never canst thou kiss,
Though winning near the goal—yet, do not grieve;
She cannot fade, though thou hast not thy bliss,
For ever wilt thou love, and she be fair!   20

III

Ah, happy, happy boughs! that cannot shed
Your leaves, nor ever bid the Spring adieu;
And, happy melodist, unwearièd,
For ever piping songs for ever new;
More happy love! more happy, happy love!   25
For ever warm and still to be enjoyed,
For ever panting, and for ever young;
All breathing human passion far above,
That leaves a heart high-sorrowful and cloyed,
A burning forehead, and a parching tongue.   30

IV

Who are these coming to the sacrifice?
To what green altar, O mysterious priest,
Lead'st thou that heifer lowing at the skies,
And all her silken flanks with garlands drest?
What little town by river or sea shore,   35
Or mountain-built with peaceful citadel,
Is emptied of this folk, this pious morn?
And, little town, thy streets for evermore
Will silent be; and not a soul to tell
Why thou art desolate, can e'er return.   40

V

O Attic shape! Fair attitude! with brede
Of marble men and maidens overwrought,

7. *Tempe* . . . *Arcady:* Tempe is a valley in Thessaly between Mount Olympus and Mount Ossa; Arcady is a mountainous region in the Peloponnese, traditionally regarded as the place of ideal rustic, bucolic contentment.
    41. *brede:* pattern.

With forest branches and the trodden weed;
    Thou, silent form, dost tease us out of thought
As doth eternity: Cold Pastoral!   45
    When old age shall this generation waste,
        Thou shalt remain, in midst of other woe
Than ours, a friend to man, to whom thou say'st,
    "Beauty is truth, truth beauty,"—that is all
        Ye know on earth, and all ye need to know.   50

Ode: To Autumn*

I

Season of mists and mellow fruitfulness,
    Close bosom-friend of the maturing sun;
Conspiring with him how to load and bless
    With fruit the vines that round the thatch-eves run;
To bend with apples the mossed cottage-trees,   5
    And fill all fruit with ripeness to the core;
        To swell the gourd, and plump the hazel shells
    With a sweet kernel; to set budding more,
And still more, later flowers for the bees,
Until they think warm days will never cease,   10
        For Summer has o'er-brimmed their clammy cells.

II

Who hath not seen thee oft amid thy store?
    Sometimes whoever seeks abroad may find
Thee sitting careless on a granary floor,
    Thy hair soft-lifted by the winnowing wind;   15
Or on a half-reaped furrow sound asleep,
    Drowsed with the fume of poppies, while thy hook
        Spares the next swath and all its twinèd flowers:
And sometimes like a gleaner thou dost keep
    Steady thy laden head across a brook;   20
    Or by a cyder-press, with patient look,
        Thou watchest the last oozings hours by hours.

III

Where are the songs of Spring? Ay, where are they?
    Think not of them, thou hast thy music too,—
While barrèd clouds bloom the soft-dying day,   25
    And touch the stubble-plains with rosy hue;
Then in a wailful choir the small gnats mourn
    Among the river sallows, borne aloft

* Written in 1819; published in 1820.

Or sinking as the light wind lives or dies;
And full-grown lambs loud bleat from hilly bourn;   30
Hedge-crickets sing; and now with treble soft
The red-breast whistles from a garden-croft;
And gathering swallows twitter in the skies.

ALFRED, LORD TENNYSON
(1809–1892)
Ulysses*

It little profits that an idle king,
By this still hearth, among these barren crags,
Matched with an agèd wife, I mete and dole
Unequal laws unto a savage race,
That hoard, and sleep, and feed, and know not me.   5
I cannot rest from travel. I will drink
Life to the lees. All time I have enjoyed
Greatly, have suffered greatly, both with those
That loved me, and alone; on shore, and when
Through scudding drifts the rainy Hyades   10
Vext the dim sea. I am become a name;
For always roaming with a hungry heart
Much have I seen and known,—cities of men
And manners, climates, councils, governments,
Myself not least, but honored of them all,—   15
And drunk delight of battle with my peers,
Far on the ringing plains of windy Troy.
I am a part of all that I have met;
Yet all experience is an arch where-through
Gleams that untravelled world whose margin fades   20
Forever and forever when I move.
How dull it is to pause, to make an end,
To rust unburnished, not to shine in use!
As though to breathe were life! Life piled on life
Were all too little, and of one to me   25
Little remains; but every hour is saved
From that eternal silence, something more,
A bringer of new things; and vile it were

---

* 1842.
3. *wife:* Penelope. Ulysses is pictured here long after his travels back from Troy.

10. *Hyades:* A cluster of seven stars in the constellation of Taurus. The ancients supposed that when they rose with the sun, rainy weather would follow.

For some three suns to store and hoard myself,
And this gray spirit yearning in desire   30
To follow knowledge like a sinking star,
Beyond the utmost bound of human thought.
    This is my son, mine own Telemachus,
To whom I leave the scepter and the isle—
Well-loved of me, discerning to fulfill   35
This labor, by slow prudence to make mild
A rugged people, and through soft degrees
Subdue them to the useful and the good.
Most blameless is he, centered in the sphere
Of common duties, decent not to fail   40
In offices of tenderness, and pay
Meet adoration to my household gods,
When I am gone. He works his work, I mine.
    There lies the port; the vessel puffs her sail;
There gloom the dark broad seas. My mariners,   45
Souls that have toiled, and wrought, and thought with me—
That ever with a frolic welcome took
The thunder and the sunshine, and opposed
Free hearts, free foreheads—you and I are old;
Old age hath yet his honor and his toil;   50
Death closes all. But something ere the end,
Some work of noble note, may yet be done,
Not unbecoming men that strove with gods.
The lights begin to twinkle from the rocks;
The long day wanes; the slow moon climbs; the deep   55
Moans round with many voices. Come, my friends,
'Tis not too late to seek a newer world.
Push off, and sitting well in order smite
The sounding furrows; for my purpose holds
To sail beyond the sunset, and the baths   60
Of all the western stars, until I die.
It may be that the gulfs will wash us down;
It may be we shall touch the Happy Isles,
And see the great Achilles, whom we knew.
Though much is taken, much abides; and though   65
We are not now that strength which in old days
Moved earth and heaven, that which we are, we are;
One equal temper of heroic hearts,
Made weak by time and fate, but strong in will
To strive, to seek, to find, and not to yield.   70

34. *isle:* Ithaca.   64. *Achilles:* comrade-in-arms of U-
63. *Happy Isles:* in Greek myth, the   lysses at Troy.
abode of the warriors after death.

The Passing of Arthur*

So all day long the noise of battle roll'd
Among the mountains by the winter sea;
Until King Arthur's table, man by man,
Had fall'n in Lyonnesse about their Lord,
King Arthur: then, because his wound was deep,   5
The bold Sir Bedivere uplifted him,
And bore him to a chapel nigh the field,
A broken chancel with a broken cross,
That stood on a dark strait of barren land.
On one side lay the Ocean, and on one   10
Lay a great water, and the moon was full.

  Then spake King Arthur to Sir Bedivere:
'The sequel of to-day unsolders all
The goodliest fellowship of famous knights
Whereof this world holds record. Such a sleep   15
They sleep—the men I loved. I think that we
Shall never more, at any future time,
Delight our souls with talk of knightly deeds,
Walking about the gardens and the halls
Of Camelot, as in the days that were.   20
I perish by this people which I made,—
Tho' Merlin sware that I should come again
To rule once more—but let what will be, be.
I am so deeply smitten thro' the helm
That without help I cannot last till morn.   25
Thou therefore take my brand Excalibur,
Which was my pride: for thou rememberest how

* The *Morte d'Arthur* (ll. 1–271 of
our text, with a short epilogue not reprinted here) was published in 1842. It
was the first composed of the twelve
connected poems later forming *The
Idylls of the King* (completed 1885).
In 1869, along with several other episodes of the *Idylls*, an expanded version of the *Morte d'Arthur* was published. Now called "The Passing of
Arthur," it included a description (not
reprinted here) of the battle in Lyonnesse with the traitor Mordred and a
new final passage (ll. 272–300 in our
text).
  3. *table:* the knights of the Round
Table.
  4. *Lyonnesse:* mythical area between
Land's End and the Scilly Isles, now
submerged.

  6. *Bedivere:* In Malory's *Morte
d'Arthur* (printed 1485), only Sir
Bedivere and his brother Sir Lucan survive the last battle. In the 1842 *Morte*,
Tennyson followed l. 6 with, "Sir Bedivere, the last of all his knights."
  8. *chancel:* the eastern part of a
church, reserved for the clergy, choir,
and so on.
  13. *sequel:* aftereffects.
  20. *Camelot:* seat of Arthur's court.
  22. *Merlin:* magician, bard, and
prophet in the Arthurian legends. In
Malory's *Morte*, Merlin builds the
Round Table.
  26. *Excalibur:* Arthur's sword, or
"brand." The legends make this either
the sword which he alone could pull
from the rock, or the one given him by
the Lady of the Lake. Tennyson uses
the latter story.

In those old days, one summer noon, an arm
Rose up from out the bosom of the lake,
Clothed in white samite, mystic, wonderful, 30
Holding the sword—and how I row'd across
And took it, and have worn it, like a king:
And, wheresoever I am sung or told
In aftertime, this also shall be known:
But now delay not: take Excalibur, 35
And fling him far into the middle mere:
Watch what thou seëst, and lightly bring me word.'

    To him replied the bold Sir Bedivere:
'It is not meet, Sir King, to leave thee thus,
Aidless, alone, and smitten thro' the helm. 40
A little thing may harm a wounded man.
Yet I thy hest will all perform at full,
Watch what I see, and lightly bring thee word.'

    So saying, from the ruin'd shrine he stept
And in the moon athwart the place of tombs, 45
Where lay the mighty bones of ancient men,
Old knights, and over them the sea-wind sang
Shrill, chill, with flakes of foam. He, stepping down
By zig-zag paths, and juts of pointed rock,
Came on the shining levels of the lake. 50

    There drew he forth the brand Excalibur,
And o'er him, drawing it, the winter moon,
Brightening the skirts of a long cloud, ran forth
And sparkled keen with frost against the hilt:
For all the haft twinkled with diamond sparks, 55
Myriads of topaz-lights, and jacinth-work
Of subtlest jewellery. He gazed so long
That both his eyes were dazzled, as he stood,
This way and that dividing the swift mind,
In act to throw: but at the last it seem'd 60
Better to leave Excalibur conceal'd
There in the many-knotted waterflags,
That whistled stiff and dry about the marge.
So strode he back slow to the wounded King.

    Then spake King Arthur to Sir Bedivere: 65
'Hast thou perform'd my mission which I gave?
What is it thou hast seen? or what hast heard?'
And answer made the bold Sir Bedivere:

---

30. *samite:* silk, sometimes inter-woven with gold.
36. *mere:* lake or pond.
40. *helm:* helmet.
42. *hest:* hehest.

56. *jacinth:* a reddish-orange gem, a type of zircon.
62. *waterflags:* The waterflag is a plant with bladed leaves.
63. *marge:* here, the water's edge.

'I heard the ripple washing in the reeds,
And the wild water lapping on the crag.'   70
   To whom replied King Arthur, faint and pale:
'Thou hast betray'd thy nature and thy name,
Not rendering true answer, as beseem'd
Thy fëalty, nor like a noble knight:
For surer sign had follow'd, either hand,   75
Or voice, or else a motion of the mere.
This is a shameful thing for men to lie.
Yet now, I charge thee, quickly go again
As thou art lief and dear, and do the thing
I bade thee, watch, and lightly bring me word.'   80
   Then went Sir Bedivere the second time
Across the ridge, and paced beside the mere,
Counting the dewy pebbles, fix'd in thought;
But when he saw the wonder of the hilt,
How curiously and strangely chased, he smote   85
His palms together, and he cried aloud,
   'And if indeed I cast the brand away,
Surely a precious thing, one worthy note,
Should thus be lost for ever from the earth,
Which might have pleased the eyes of many men.   90
What good should follow this, if this were done?
What harm, undone? deep harm to disobey,
Seeing obedience is the bond of rule.
Were it well to obey then, if a king demand
An act unprofitable, against himself?   95
The King is sick, and knows not what he does.
What record, or what relic of my lord
Should be to aftertime, but empty breath
And rumours of a doubt? but were this kept,
Stored in some treasure-house of mighty kings,   100
Some one might show it at a joust of arms,
Saying, "King Arthur's sword, Excalibur,
Wrought by the lonely maiden of the Lake,
Nine years she wrought it, sitting in the deeps
Upon the hidden bases of the hills."   105
So might some old man speak in the aftertime
To all the people, winning reverence.
But how much honour and much fame were lost.'
   So spake he, clouded with his own conceit,
And hid Excalibur the second time,   110
And so strode back slow to the wounded King.

---

74. *fëalty:* feudal fidelity to one's
lord.

79. *lief:* beloved.
85. *chased:* engraved.

Then spoke King Arthur, breathing heavily:
'What is it thou hast seen? or what hast heard?'
    And answer made the bold Sir Bedivere:
'I heard the water lapping on the crag,   115
And the long ripple washing in the reeds.'
    To whom replied King Arthur, much in wrath:
'Ah, miserable and unkind, untrue,
Unknightly, traitor-hearted! Woe is me!
Authority forgets a dying king,   120
Laid widow'd of the power in his eye
That bow'd the will. I see thee what thou art,
For thou, the latest-left of all my knights,
In whom should meet the offices of all,
Thou wouldst betray me for the precious hilt;   125
Either from lust of gold, or like a girl
Valuing the giddy pleasure of the eyes.
Yet, for a man may fail in duty twice,
And the third time may prosper, get thee hence:
But, if thou spare to fling Excalibur,   130
I will arise and slay thee with my hands.'
    Then quickly rose Sir Bedivere, and ran,
And, leaping down the ridges lightly, plunged
Among the bulrush-beds, and clutch'd the sword,
And strongly wheel'd and threw it. The great brand   135
Made lightnings in the splendour of the moon,
And flashing round and round, and whirl'd in an arch,
Shot like a streamer of the northern morn,
Seen where the moving isles of winter shock
By night, with noises of the Northern Sea.   140
So flash'd and fell the brand Excalibur:
But ere he dipt the surface, rose an arm
Clothed in white samite, mystic, wonderful,
And caught him by the hilt, and brandish'd him
Three times, and drew him under in the mere.   145
And lightly went the other to the King.
    Then spoke King Arthur, drawing thicker breath:
'Now see I by thine eyes that this is done.
Speak out: what is it thou hast heard, or seen?'
    And answer made the bold Sir Bedivere: 150
'Sir King, I closed mine eyelids, lest the gems
Should blind my purpose, for I never saw,
Nor shall see, here or elsewhere, till I die,
Not tho' I live three lives of mortal men,
So great a miracle as yonder hilt.   155
Then with both hands I flung him, wheeling him;

But when I look'd again, behold an arm,
Clothed in white samite, mystic, wonderful,
That caught him by the hilt, and brandish'd him
Three times, and drew him under in the mere.'   160
　　And answer made King Arthur, breathing hard:
'My end draws nigh: 'tis time that I were gone.
Make broad thy shoulders to receive my weight,
And bear me to the margin; yet I fear
My wound hath taken cold, and I shall die.'   165
　　So saying, from the pavement he half rose,
Slowly, with pain, reclining on his arm,
And looking wistfully with wide blue eyes
As in a picture. Him Sir Bedivere
Remorsefully regarded thro' his tears,   170
And would have spoken, but he found not words,
Then took with care, and kneeling on one knee,
O'er both his shoulders drew the languid hands,
And rising bore him thro' the place of tombs.
　　But, as he walk'd, King Arthur panted hard,   175
Like one that feels a nightmare on his bed
When all the house is mute. So sigh'd the King,
Muttering and murmuring at his ear, 'Quick, quick!
I fear it is too late, and I shall die.'
But the other swiftly strode from ridge to ridge,   180
Clothed with his breath, and looking, as he walk'd,
Larger than human on the frozen hills.
He heard the deep behind him, and a cry
Before. His own thought drove him like a goad.
Dry clash'd his harness in the icy caves   185
And barren chasms, and all to left and right
The bare black cliff clang'd round him, as he based
His feet on juts of slippery crag that rang
Sharp-smitten with the dint of armed heels—
And on a sudden, lo! the level lake,   190
And the long glories of the winter moon.
　　Then saw they how there hove a dusky barge,
Dark as a funeral scarf from stem to stern,
Beneath them; and descending they were ware
That all the decks were dense with stately forms   195
Black-stoled, black-hooded, like a dream—by these
Three Queens with crowns of gold—and from them rose
A cry that shiver'd to the tingling stars,
And, as it were one voice, an agony
Of lamentation, like a wind, that shrills   200

197. *Three Queens:* In Malory, Morgan le Fay is one of the three queens.

All night in a waste land, where no one comes,
Or hath come, since the making of the world.
    Then murmur'd Arthur, 'Place me in the barge,'
And to the barge they came. There those three Queens
Put forth their hands, and took the King, and wept.   205
But she, that rose the tallest of them all
And fairest, laid his head upon her lap,
And loosed the shatter'd casque, and chafed his hands,
And call'd him by his name, complaining loud,
And dropping bitter tears against his brow   210
Striped with dark blood: for all his face was white
And colourless, and like the wither'd moon
Smote by the fresh beam of the springing east;
And all his greaves and cuisses dash'd with drops
Of onset; and the light and lustrous curls—   215
That made his forehead like a rising sun
High from the daïs-throne—were parch'd with dust;
Or, clotted into points and hanging loose,
Mix'd with the knightly growth that fringed his lips.
So like a shatter'd column lay the King;   220
Not like that Arthur who, with lance in rest,
From spur to plume a star of tournament,
Shot thro' the lists at Camelot, and charged
Before the eyes of ladies and of kings.
    Then loudly cried the bold Sir Bedivere,   225
'Ah! my Lord Arthur, whither shall I go?
Where shall I hide my forehead and my eyes?
For now I see the true old times are dead,
When every morning brought a noble chance,
And every chance brought out a noble knight.   230
Such times have been not since the light that led
The holy Elders with the gift of myrrh.
But now the whole ROUND TABLE is dissolved
Which was an image of the mighty world;
And I, the last, go forth companionless,   235
And the days darken round me, and the years,
Among new men, strange faces, other minds.'
    And slowly answered Arthur from the barge:
'The old order changeth, yielding place to new,
And God fulfils Himself in many ways,   240
Lest one good custom should corrupt the world.
Comfort thyself: what comfort is in me?

208. *casque:* helmet.
214. *greaves and cuisses:* armor for
shin and thigh.
214–215. *drops of onset:* marks of
attack; i.e., blood.
   232. *holy Elders . . . myrrh:* the
Magi with their gift for the Christ
child.

I have lived my life, and that which I have done
May He within Himself make pure! but thou,
If thou shouldst never see my face again,   245
Pray for my soul. More things are wrought by prayer
Than this world dreams of. Wherefore, let thy voice
Rise like a fountain for me night and day.
For what are men better than sheep or goats
That nourish a blind life within the brain,   250
If, knowing God, they lift not hands of prayer
Both for themselves and those who call them friend?
For so the whole round earth is every way
Bound by gold chains about the feet of God.
But now farewell. I am going a long way   255
With these thou seëst—if indeed I go—
(For all my mind is clouded with a doubt)
To the island-valley of Avilion;
Where falls not hail, or rain, or any snow,
Nor ever wind blows loudly; but it lies   260
Deep-meadow'd, happy, fair with orchard-lawns
And bowery hollows crown'd with summer sea,
Where I will heal me of my grievous wound.'
    So said he, and the barge with oar and sail
Moved from the brink, like some full-breasted swan   265
That, fluting a wild carol ere her death,
Ruffles her pure cold plume, and takes the flood
With swarthy webs. Long stood Sir Bedivere
Revolving many memories, till the hull
Look'd one black dot against the verge of dawn,   270
And on the mere the wailing died away.
    But when that moan had passed for evermore,
The stillness of the dead world's winter dawn
Amazed him, and he groan'd, 'The King is gone.'
And therewithal came on him the weird rhyme,   275
'From the great deep to the great deep he goes.'
    Whereat he slowly turn'd and slowly clomb
The last hard footsteps of that iron crag;
Thence mark'd the black hull moving yet, and cried,
'He passes to be King among the dead,   280
And after healing of his grievous wound
He comes again; but—if he come no more—
O me, be yon dark Queens in yon black boat,
Who shriek'd and wail'd, the three whereat we gazed
On that high day, when, clothed with living light,   285

258. *Avilion:* Avalon or Avallon, a region in the mythical Isle of the Blessed of the Celts.

They stood before his throne in silence, friends
Of Arthur, who should help him at his need?'
   Then from the dawn it seem'd there came, but faint
As from beyond the limit of the world,
Like the last echo born of a great cry,   290
Sounds, as if some fair city were one voice
Around a king returning from his wars.
   Thereat once more he moved about, and clomb
Ev'n to the highest he could climb, and saw,
Straining his eyes beneath an arch of hand,   295
Or thought he saw, the speck that bare the King,
Down that long water opening on the deep
Somewhere far off, pass on and on, and go
From less to less and vanish into light.
And the new sun rose bringing the new year.*   300

* *The Idylls of the King* concludes with an epilogue, "To the Queen."

ROBERT BROWNING
(1812–1889)
The Bishop Orders His Tomb at Saint Praxed's Church†

ROME, 15—

Vanity, saith the preacher, vanity!
Draw round my bed: is Anselm keeping back?
Nephews—sons mine . . . ah God, I know not! Well—
She, men would have to be your mother once,
Old Gandolf envied me, so fair she was!   5
What's done is done, and she is dead beside,
Dead long ago, and I am Bishop since,
And as she died so must we die ourselves,
And thence ye may perceive the world's a dream.
Life, how and what is it? As here I lie   10
In this state-chamber, dying by degrees,
Hours and long hours in the dead night, I ask
'Do I live, am I dead?' Peace, peace seems all.
Saint Praxed's ever was the church for peace;
And so, about this tomb of mine. I fought   15
With tooth and nail to save my niche, ye know:

† Published in 1845. The Bishop, his tomb, and the character Gandolf are all fictional. Saint Praxed's church, seen by Browning in 1844, is named after a second-century Roman virgin.
1. *Vanity:* See Ecclesiastes 1:2. *preacher:* the author of Ecclesiastes.
5. *Gandolf:* the Bishop's predecessor.

—Old Gandolf cozened me, despite my care;
Shrewd was that snatch from out the corner South
He graced his carrion with, God curse the same!
Yet still my niche is not so cramped but thence   20
One sees the pulpit o' the epistle-side,
And somewhat of the choir, those silent seats,
And up into the aery dome where live
The angels, and a sunbeam's sure to lurk:
And I shall fill my slab of basalt there,   25
And 'neath my tabernacle take my rest,
With those nine columns round me, two and two,
The odd one at my feet where Anselm stands:
Peach-blossom marble all, the rare, the ripe
As fresh-poured red wine of a mighty pulse.   30
—Old Gandolf with his paltry onion-stone,
Put me where I may look at him! True peach,
Rosy and flawless: how I earned the prize!
Draw close: that conflagration of my church
—What then? So much was saved if aught were missed!   35
My sons, ye would not be my death? Go dig
The white-grape vineyard where the oil-press stood,
Drop water gently till the surface sink,
And if ye find . . . Ah God, I know not, I! . . .
Bedded in store of rotten fig-leaves soft,   40
And corded up in a tight olive-frail,
Some lump, ah God, of lapis lazuli,
Big as a Jew's head cut off at the nape,
Blue as a vein o'er the Madonna's breast . . .
Sons, all have I bequeathed you, villas, all,   45
That brave Frascati villa with its bath,
So, let the blue lump poise between my knees,
Like God the Father's globe on both his hands
Ye worship in the Jesu Church so gay,
For Gandolf shall not choose but see and burst!   50
Swift as a weaver's shuttle fleet our years:
Man goeth to the grave, and where is he?
Did I say basalt for my slab, sons? Black—
'Twas ever antique-black I meant! How else

21. *epistle-side:* i.e., the right side as the congregation faces the altar.
26. *tabernacle:* here, the canopy over his tomb.
31. *onion-stone:* a lesser grade of green marble.
41. *olive-frail:* basket made of rushes, for figs, raisins, olives, and so on.
42. *lapis lazuli:* a bright-blue semi-precious stone.
46. *Frascati:* a wealthy Roman suburb.
49. *Jesu Church:* the principal Jesuit church in Rome, off what came to be called the Corso Vittorio Emanuela.
51. *shuttle:* See Job 7:6.
54. *antique-black:* a grade of good marble.

Shall ye contrast my frieze to come beneath?   55
The bas-relief in bronze ye promised me,
Those Pans and Nymphs ye wot of, and perchance
Some tripod, thyrsus, with a vase or so,
The Saviour at his sermon on the mount,
Saint Praxed in a glory, and one Pan   60
Ready to twitch the Nymph's last garment off,
And Moses with the tables . . . but I know
Ye mark me not! What do they whisper thee,
Child of my bowels, Anselm? Ah, ye hope
To revel down my villas while I gasp   65
Bricked o'er with beggar's mouldy travertine
Which Gandolf from his tomb-top chuckles at!
Nay, boys, ye love me—all of jasper, then!
'Tis jasper ye stand pledged to, lest I grieve.
My bath must needs be left behind, alas!   70
One block, pure green as a pistachio-nut,
There's plenty jasper somewhere in the world—
And have I not Saint Praxed's ear to pray
Horses for ye, and brown Greek manuscripts,
And mistresses with great smooth marbly limbs?   75
—That's if ye carve my epitaph aright,
Choice Latin, picked phrase, Tully's every word,
No gaudy ware like Gandolf's second line—
Tully, my masters? Ulpian serves his need!
And then how I shall lie through centuries,   80
And hear the blessed mutter of the mass,
And see God made and eaten all day long,
And feel the steady candle-flame, and taste
Good strong thick stupefying incense-smoke!
For as I lie here, hours of the dead night,   85
Dying in state and by such slow degrees,
I fold my arms as if they clasped a crook,
And stretch my feet forth straight as stone can point,
And let the bedclothes, for a mortcloth, drop
Into great laps and folds of sculptor's-work: 90
And as yon tapers dwindle, and strange thoughts

56. *bas-relief:* a shallow carving or sculpture.

57. *Pans:* images of Greek nature deities.

58. *thyrsus:* a staff tipped with a pine cone, associated with the Greek god Bacchus.

62. *tables:* the stone tablets on which the Decalogue was inscribed.

66. *travertine:* a cheap, flaky Italian building stone.

68. *jasper:* reddish quartz.

77. *Tully:* Cicero.

79. *Ulpian:* Ulpianus Domitius (170–228 A.D.), lawyer, secretary to Emperor Alexander Severus, writer of nonclassical Latin.

82. *eaten:* a reference to the sacrament of Communion.

87. *crook:* the bishop's crosier.

89. *mortcloth:* funeral pall or winding sheet.

Grow, with a certain humming in my ears,
About the life before I lived this life.
And this life too, popes, cardinals and priests,
Saint Praxed at his sermon on the mount,   95
Your tall pale mother with her talking eyes,
And new-found agate urns as fresh as day,
And marble's language, Latin pure, discreet,
—Aha, *Elucescebat* quoth our friend?
No Tully, said I, Ulpian at the best!   100
Evil and brief hath been my pilgrimage.
All lapis, all, sons! Else I give the Pope
My villas! Will ye ever eat my heart?
Ever your eyes were as a lizard's quick,
They glitter like your mother's for my soul,   105
Or ye would heighten my impoverished frieze,
Piece out its starved design, and fill my vase
With grapes, and add a vizor and a Term,
And to the tripod ye would tie a lynx
That in his struggle throws the thyrsus down,   110
To comfort me on my entablature
Whereon I am to lie till I must ask
'Do I live, am I dead?' There, leave me, there!
For ye have stabbed me with ingratitude
To death—ye wish it—God, ye wish it! Stone—   115
Gritstone, a-crumble! Clammy squares which sweat
As if the corpse they keep were oozing through—
And no more lapis to delight the world!
Well go! I bless ye. Fewer tapers there,
But in a row: and, going, turn your backs   120
—Ay, like departing altar-ministrants,
And leave me in my church, the church for peace,
That I may watch at leisure if he leers—
Old Gandolf, at me, from his onion-stone,
As still he envied me, so fair she was!   125

95. *his sermon:* Browning's implication is evidently that the Bishop is unaware that St. Prassede was a woman.
99. *Elucescebat:* "He was illustrious," or "famous"; in classical Latin the word would be *elucebat. Elucescebat* is an example of the less elegant Latin associated with Ulpian's era.

108. *vizor:* mask. *Term:* a carved head atop a square pedestal.
111. *entablature:* in classical architecture, the wall resting upon the columns, consisting of the architrave, frieze, and cornice.
116. *Gritstone:* a coarse, poor-grade sandstone.

EDGAR ALLAN POE

(1809–1849)

Ligeia*

And the will therein lieth, which dieth not. Who knoweth the mysteries of the will, with its vigor? For God is but a great will pervading all things by nature of its intentness. Man doth not yield himself to the angels, nor unto death utterly, save only through the weakness of his feeble will.—JOSEPH GLANVILL[1]

I cannot, for my soul, remember how, when, or even precisely where, I first became acquainted with the lady Ligeia. Long years have since elapsed, and my memory is feeble through much suffering. Or, perhaps, I cannot *now* bring these points to mind, because, in truth, the character of my beloved, her rare learning, her singular yet placid cast of beauty, and the thrilling and enthralling eloquence of her low musical language, made their way into my heart by paces so steadily and stealthily progressive that they have been unnoticed and unknown. Yet I believe that I met her first and most frequently in some large, old, decaying city near the Rhine. Of her family—I have surely heard her speak. That it is of a remotely ancient date cannot be doubted. Ligeia! Ligeia! Buried in studies of a nature more than all else adapted to deaden impressions of the outward world, it is by that sweet word alone—by Ligeia—that I bring before mine eyes in fancy the image of her who is no more. And now, while I write, a recollection flashes upon me that I have *never known* the paternal name of her who was my friend and my betrothed, and who became the partner of my studies, and finally the wife of my bosom. Was it a playful charge on the part of my Ligeia? or was it a test of my strength of affection, that I should institute no inquiries upon this point? or was it rather a caprice of my own—a wildly romantic offering on the shrine of the most passionate devotion? I but indistinctly recall the fact itself—what wonder that I have utterly forgotten the circumstances which originated or attended it? And, indeed, if ever that spirit which is entitled *Romance*— if ever she, the wan and the misty-winged *Ashtophet*[2] of idolatrous Egypt, presided, as they tell, over marriages ill-omened, then most surely she presided over mine.

There is one dear topic, however, on which my memory fails

* First published in *The American Museum* for September, 1838; reprinted in 1840 in *Tales of the Grotesque and Arabesque*. G. E. Woodberry, one of Poe's biographers, says that he regarded "Ligeia" as his finest tale.
1. English scholar (1636–1680), author of *The Vanity of Dogmatizing*

(1661), a work on witchcraft, *Sadducismus triumphatus* (1661), and *Lux orientalis* (1662).
2. probably Ashtoreth or Ishtar, the Phoenician and Babylonian equivalents of the Greek Aphrodite, goddess of love.

me not. It is the *person* of Ligeia. In stature she was tall, somewhat slender, and, in her latter days, even emaciated. I would in
vain attempt to portray the majesty, the quiet ease of her demeanor,
or the incomprehensible lightness and elasticity of her footfall. She
came and departed as a shadow. I was never made aware of her
entrance into my closed study save by the dear music of her low
sweet voice, as she placed her marble hand upon my shoulder. In
beauty of face no maiden ever equalled her. It was the radiance of
an opium-dream—an airy and spirit-lifting vision more wildly divine
than the phantasies which hovered about the slumbering souls of
the daughters of Delos.[3] Yet her features were not of that regular
mould which we have been falsely taught to worship in the classical
labors of the heathen. "There is no exquisite beauty," says Bacon,
Lord Verulam,[4] speaking truly of all the forms and *genera* of beauty,
"without some *strangeness* in the proportion." Yet, although I saw
that the features of Ligeia were not of a classic regularity—although
I perceived that her loveliness was indeed "exquisite," and felt that
there was much of "strangeness" pervading it, yet I have tried in
vain to detect the irregularity and to trace home my own perception
of "the strange." I examined the contour of the lofty and pale forehead—it was faultless—how cold indeed that word when applied
to a majesty so divine!—the skin rivalling the purest ivory, the
commanding extent and repose, the gentle prominence of the regions
above the temples; and then the raven-black, the glossy, the luxuriant
and naturally-curling tresses, setting forth the full force of the
Homeric epithet, "hyacinthine!" I looked at the delicate outlines
of the nose—and nowhere but in the graceful medallions of the
Hebrews had I beheld a similar perfection. There were the same
luxurious smoothness of surface, the same scarcely perceptible
tendency to the aquiline, the same harmoniously curved nostrils
speaking the free spirit. I regarded the sweet mouth. Here was
indeed the triumph of all things heavenly—the magnificent turn
of the short upper lip—the soft, voluptuous slumber of the under
—the dimples which sported, and the color which spoke—the teeth
glancing back, with a brilliancy almost startling, every ray of the
holy light which fell upon them in her serene and placid yet most
exultingly radiant of all smiles. I scrutinized the formation of the
chin—and, here too, I found the gentleness of breadth, the softness
and the majesty, the fulness and the spirituality, of the Greek—
the contour which the god Apollo revealed but in a dream, to
Cleomenes, the son of the Athenian. And then I peered into the
large eyes of Ligeia.

3. an island in the Aegean, sacred to
the Greeks, containing temples of
Apollo and Leto (Latona).
4. Francis Bacon (1561–1626), English philosopher and statesman, author
of the *Advancement of Learning*, the
Novum Organum, the *New Atlantis*,
and other works.

For eyes we have no models in the remotely antique. It might have been, too, that in these eyes of my beloved lay the secret to which Lord Verulam alludes. They were, I must believe, far larger than the ordinary eyes of our own race. They were even fuller than the fullest of the gazelle eyes of the tribe of the valley of Nourjahad.[5] Yet it was only at intervals—in moments of intense excitement—that this peculiarity became more than slightly noticeable in Ligeia. And at such moments was her beauty—in my heated fancy thus it appeared perhaps—the beauty of beings either above or apart from the earth—the beauty of the fabulous Houri[6] of the Turk. The hue of the orbs was the most brilliant of black, and, far over them, hung jetty lashes of great length. The brows, slightly irregular in outline, had the same tint. The "strangeness," however, which I found in the eyes, was of a nature distinct from the formation, or the color, or the brilliancy of the features, and must, after all, be referred to the *expression*. Ah, word of no meaning! behind whose vast latitude of mere sound we intrench our ignorance of so much of the spiritual. The expression of the eyes of Ligeia! How for long hours have I pondered upon it! How have I, through the whole of a midsummer night, struggled to fathom it! What was it—that something more profound than the well of Democritus[7]— which lay far within the pupils of my beloved? What *was* it? I was possessed with a passion to discover. Those eyes! those large, those shining, those divine orbs! they became to me twin stars of Leda, and I to them devoutest of astrologers.

There is no point, among the many incomprehensible anomalies of the science of mind, more thrillingly exciting than the fact— never, I believe, noticed in the schools—that in our endeavors to recall to memory something long forgotten, we often find ourselves *upon the very verge* of remembrance, without being able, in the end, to remember. And thus how frequently, in my intense scrutiny of Ligeia's eyes, have I felt approaching the full knowledge of their expression—felt it approaching—yet not quite be mine—and so at length entirely depart! And (strange, oh strangest mystery of all!) I found, in the commonest objects of the universe, a circle of analogies to that expression. I mean to say that, subsequently to the period when Ligeia's beauty passed into my spirit, there dwelling as in a shrine, I derived, from many existences in the material world, a sentiment such as I felt always aroused, within me, by her large and luminous orbs. Yet not the more could I define that sentiment, or analyze, or even steadily view it. I recognized it,

5. Poe may have had in mind the *History of Nourjahad*, a tale by Mrs. Frances Sheridan (1724–1766), in which the hero awakens every fifty years.

6. a nymph in the Mohammedan paradise.

7. Greek philosopher of the fifth century B.C.

let me repeat, sometimes in the survey of a rapidly growing vine—
in the contemplation of a moth, a butterfly, a chrysalis, a stream of
running water. I have felt it in the ocean; in the falling of a meteor.
I have felt it in the glances of unusually aged people. And there
are one or two stars in heaven—(one especially, a star of the sixth
magnitude, double and changeable, to be found near the large star
in Lyra[8]) in a telescopic scrutiny of which I have been made aware
of the feeling. I have been filled with it by certain sounds from
stringed instruments, and not unfrequently by passages from books.
Among innumerable other instances, I well remember something in
a volume of Joseph Glanvill, which (perhaps merely from its quaint-
ness—who shall say?) never failed to inspire me with the sentiment;
—"And the will therein lieth, which dieth not. Who knoweth the
mysteries of the will, with its vigor? For God is but a great will
pervading all things by nature of its intentness. Man doth not yield
him to the angels, nor unto death utterly, save only through the
weakness of his feeble will."

Length of years and subsequent reflection, have enabled me to
trace, indeed, some remote connection between this passage in the
English moralist and a portion of the character of Ligeia. An *intensity* in thought, action, or speech, was possibly, in her, a result,
or at least an index, of that gigantic volition which, during our
long intercourse, failed to give other and more immediate evidence
of its existence. Of all the women whom I have ever known, she,
the outwardly calm, the ever-placid Ligeia, was the most violently
a prey to the tumultuous vultures of stern passion. And of such
passion I could form no estimate, save by the miraculous expansion of those eyes which at once so delighted and appalled me—
by the almost magical melody, modulation, distinctness, and placidity of her very low voice—and by the fierce energy (rendered
doubly effective by contrast with her manner of utterance) of the
wild words which she habitually uttered.

I have spoken of the learning of Ligeia: it was immense—such
as I have never known in woman. In the classical tongues was she
deeply proficient, and as far as my own acquaintance extended in
regard to the modern dialects of Europe, I have never known her
at fault. Indeed upon any theme of the most admired, because
simply the most abstruse of the boasted erudition of the academy,
have I *ever* found Ligeia at fault? How singularly—how thrillingly,
this one point in the nature of my wife has forced itself, at this
late period only, upon my attention! I said her knowledge was such
as I have never known in woman—but where breathes the man who
has traversed, and successfully, *all* the wide areas of moral, physical,
and mathematical science? I saw not then what I now clearly per-

8. a northern constellation.

ceive, that the acquisitions of Ligeia were gigantic, were astounding; yet I was sufficiently aware of her infinite supremacy to resign myself, with a child-like confidence, to her guidance through the chaotic world of metaphysical investigation at which I was most busily occupied during the earlier years of our marriage. With how vast a triumph—with how vivid a delight—with how much of all that is ethereal in hope—did I *feel*, as she bent over me in studies but little sought—but less known—that delicious vista by slow degrees expanding before me, down whose long, gorgeous, and all untrodden path, I might at length pass onward to the goal of a wisdom too divinely precious not to be forbidden!

How poignant, then, must have been the grief with which, after some years, I beheld my well-grounded expectations take wings to themselves and fly away! Without Ligeia I was but as a child groping benighted. Her presence, her readings alone, rendered vividly luminous the many mysteries of the transcendentalism in which we were immersed. Wanting the radiant lustre of her eyes, letters, lambent and golden, grew duller than Saturnian[9] lead. And now those eyes shone less and less frequently upon the pages over which I pored. Ligeia grew ill. The wild eyes blazed with a too—too glorious effulgence; the pale fingers became of the transparent waxen hue of the grave; and the blue veins upon the lofty forehead swelled and sank impetuously with the tides of the most gentle emotion. I saw that she must die—and I struggled desperately in spirit with the grim Azrael.[10] And the struggles of the passionate wife were, to my astonishment, even more energetic than my own. There had been much in her stern nature to impress me with the belief that, to her, death would have come without its terrors; but not so. Words are impotent to convey any just idea of the fierceness of resistance with which she wrestled with the Shadow. I groaned in anguish at the pitiable spectacle. I would have soothed—I would have reasoned; but, in the intensity of her wild desire for life,—for life—*but* for life—solace and reason were alike the uttermost of folly. Yet not until the last instance, amid the most convulsive writhings of her fierce spirit, was shaken the external placidity of her demeanor. Her voice grew more gentle—grew more low—yet I would not wish to dwell upon the wild meaning of the quietly uttered words. My brain reeled as I hearkened entranced, to a melody more than mortal —to assumptions and aspirations which mortality had never before known.

That she loved me I should not have doubted; and I might have been easily aware that, in a bosom such as hers, love would have reigned no ordinary passion. But in death only was I fully

9. In old chemistry, "Saturn" meant "lead."

10. In Jewish and Mohammedan mythology, the angel who severs the soul from the body after death.

impressed with the strength of her affection. For long hours, detaining my hand, would she pour out before me the overflowing
of a heart whose more than passionate devotion amounted to idolatry.
How had I deserved to be so blessed by such confessions?—how
had I deserved to be so cursed with the removal of my beloved in
the hour of my making them? But upon this subject I cannot bear
to dilate. Let me say only, that in Ligeia's more than womanly
abandonment to a love, alas! all unmerited, all unworthily bestowed,
I at length recognized the principle of her longing with so wildly
earnest a desire, for the life which was now fleeing so rapidly away.
It is this wild longing—it is this eager vehemence of desire for life
—*but* for life—that I have no power to portray—no utterance
capable of expressing.

At high noon of the night in which she departed, beckoning
me peremptorily, to her side, she bade me repeat certain verses
composed by herself not many days before. I obeyed her.—They
were these:—

> Lo! 'tis a gala night
>   Within the lonesome latter years!
> An angel throng, bewinged, bedight
>   In veils, and drowned in tears,
> Sit in a theatre, to see
>   A play of hopes and fears,
> While the orchestra breathes fitfully
>   The music of the spheres.
>
> Mimes, in the form of God on high,
>   Mutter and mumble low,
> And hither and thither fly;
>   Mere puppets they, who come and go
> At bidding of vast formless things
>   That shift the scenery to and fro,
> Flapping from out their Condor wings
>   Invisible Wo!
>
> That motley drama!—oh, be sure
>   It shall not be forgot!
> With its Phantom chased for evermore,
>   By a crowd that seize it not,
> Through a circle that ever returneth in
>   To the self-same spot,
> And much of Madness and more of Sin
>   And Horror the soul of the plot.
>
> But see, amid the mimic rout,
>   A crawling shape intrude!

> A blood-red thing that writhes from out
>   The scenic solitude!
> It writhes!—it writhes!—with mortal pangs
>   The mimes become its food,
> And the seraphs sob at vermin fangs
>   In human gore imbued.
>
> Out—out are the lights—out all!
>   And over each quivering form,
> The curtain, a funeral pall,
>   Comes down with the rush of a storm,
> And the angels, all pallid and wan,
>   Uprising, unveiling, affirm
> That the play is the tragedy, "Man,"
>   And its hero the Conqueror Worm.

"O God!" half shrieked Ligeia, leaping to her feet and extending her arms aloft with a spasmodic movement, as I made an end of these lines—"O God! O Divine Father—shall these things be undeviatingly so?—shall this Conqueror be not once conquered? Are we not part and parcel in Thee? Who—who knoweth the mysteries of the will with its vigor? Man doth not yield him to the angels, _nor unto death utterly_, save only through the weakness of his feeble will."

And now, as if exhausted with emotion, she suffered her white arms to fall, and returned solemnly to her bed of death. And as she breathed her last sighs, there came mingled with them a low murmur from her lips. I bent to them my ear, and distinguished, again, the concluding words of the passage in Glanvill—"_Man doth not yield him to the angels, nor unto death utterly, save only through the weakness of his feeble will._"

She died;—and I, crushed into the very dust with sorrow, could no longer endure the lonely desolation of my dwelling in the dim and decaying city by the Rhine. I had no lack of what the world calls wealth. Ligeia had brought me far more, very far more than ordinarily falls to the lot of mortals. After a few months, therefore, of weary and aimless wandering, I purchased, and put in some repair, an abbey, which I shall not name, in one of the wildest and least frequented portions of fair England. The gloomy and dreary grandeur of the building, the almost savage aspect of the domain, the many melancholy and time-honored memories connected with both, had much in unison with the feelings of utter abandonment which had driven me into that remote and unsocial region of the country. Yet although the external abbey, with its verdant decay hanging about it, suffered but little alteration, I gave way, with a child-like perversity, and perchance with a faint hope of alleviating

512 · *Edgar Allan Poe*

my sorrows, to a display of more than regal magnificence within.—
For such follies, even in childhood, I had imbibed a taste, and now
they came back to me as if in the dotage of grief. Alas, I feel how
much even of incipient madness might have been discovered in
the gorgeous and fantastic draperies, in the solemn carvings of
Egypt, in the wild cornices and furniture, in the Bedlam[11] patterns
of the carpets of tufted gold! I had become a bounden slave in the
trammels of opium, and my labors and orders had taken a coloring
from my dreams. But these absurdities I must not pause to detail.
Let me speak only of that one chamber, ever accursed, whither, in
a moment of mental alienation, I led from the altar as my bride—
as the successor of the unforgotten Ligeia—the fair-haired and blue-
eyed Lady Rowena Trevanion, of Tremaine.

There is no individual portion of the architecture and decoration
of that bridal chamber which is not now visibly before me. Where
were the souls of the haughty family of the bride, when, through
thirst of gold, they permitted to pass the threshold of an apartment
so bedecked, a maiden and a daughter so beloved? I have said that I
minutely remember the details of the chamber—yet I am sadly
forgetful on topics of deep moment—and here there was no system,
no keeping, in the fantastic display, to take hold upon the memory.
The room lay in a high turret of the castellated abbey, was pentagonal
in shape, and of capacious size. Occupying the whole southern face
of the pentagon was the sole window—an immense sheet of unbroken glass from Venice—a single pane, and tinted of a leaden
hue, so that the rays of either the sun or moon passing through
it, fell with a ghastly lustre on the objects within. Over the upper
portion of this huge window, extended the trellis-work of an aged
vine, which clambered up the massy walls of the turret. The ceiling,
of gloomy-looking oak, was excessively lofty, vaulted, and elaborately
fretted with the wildest and most grotesque specimens of a semi-
Gothic, semi-Druidical[12] device. From out the most central recess
of this melancholy vaulting, depended, by a single chain of gold
with long links, a huge censer of the same metal, Saracenic[13] in
pattern, and with many perforations so contrived that there writhed
in and out of them, as if endued with a serpent vitality, a continual
succession of parti-colored fires.

Some few ottomans and golden candelabra, of Eastern figure,
were in various stations about—and there was the couch, too—the
bridal couch—of an Indian model, and low, and sculptured of

11. a corruption of "Bethlehem"; the
hospital of St. Mary of Bethlehem, near
London, originally a priory, was serving
as a hospital for lunatics by 1402.
Here Poe uses the word to indicate
fantastic exoticism in design.
12. a reference to the religion of
the ancient Celts in Gaul and Britain.
13. Arabian.

solid ebony, with a pall-like canopy above. In each of the angles
of the chamber stood on end a gigantic sarcophagus[14] of black granite, from the tombs of the kings over against Luxor,[15] with their
aged lids full of immemorial sculpture. But in the draping of the
apartment lay, alas! the chief phantasy of all. The lofty walls,
gigantic in height—even unproportionably so—were hung from
summit to foot, in vast folds, with a heavy and massive-looking
tapestry—tapestry of a material which was found alike as a carpet
on the floor, as a covering for the ottomans and the ebony bed, as
a canopy for the bed and as the gorgeous volutes of the curtains
which partially shaded the window. The material was the richest
cloth of gold. It was spotted all over, at irregular intervals, with
arabesque figures, about a foot in diameter, and wrought upon
the cloth in patterns of the most jetty black. But these figures partook of the true character of the arabesque only when regarded
from a single point of view. By a contrivance now common, and
indeed traceable to a very remote period of antiquity, they were
made changeable in aspect. To one entering the room, they bore
the appearance of simple monstrosities; but upon a farther advance, this appearance gradually departed; and step by step, as the
visitor moved his station in the chamber, he saw himself surrounded
by an endless succession of the ghastly forms which belong to the
superstition of the Norman, or arise in the guilty slumbers of the
monk. The phantasmagoric effect was vastly heightened by the
artificial introduction of a strong continual current of wind behind
the draperies—giving a hideous and uneasy animation to the whole.

In halls such as these—in a bridal chamber such as this—I passed,
with the Lady of Tremaine, the unhallowed hours of the first month
of our marriage—passed them with but little disquietude. That my
wife dreaded the fierce moodiness of my temper—that she shunned
me and loved me but little—I could not help perceiving; but it
gave me rather pleasure than otherwise. I loathed her with a hatred
belonging more to demon than to man. My memory flew back,
(oh, what intensity of regret!) to Ligeia, the beloved, the august,
the beautiful, the entombed. I revelled in recollections of her purity,
of her wisdom, of her lofty, her ethereal nature, of her passionate,
her idolatrous love. Now, then, did my spirit fully and freely burn
with more than all the fires of her own. In the excitement of my
opium dreams (for I was habitually fettered in the shackles of the
drug) I would call aloud upon her name, during the silence of the
night, or among the sheltered recesses of the glens by day, as if,
through the wild eagerness, the solemn passion, the consuming

14. stone coffin.   15. city of ancient Egypt, on the
Nile.

ardor of my longing for the departed, I could restore her to the pathways she had abandoned—ah, *could* it be forever?—upon the earth.

About the commencement of the second month of the marriage, the Lady Rowena was attacked with sudden illness, from which her recovery was slow. The fever which consumed her rendered her nights uneasy; and in her perturbed state of half-slumber, she spoke of sounds, and of motions, in and about the chamber of the turret, which I concluded had no origin save in the distemper of her fancy, or perhaps in the phantasmagoric influences of the chamber itself. She became at length convalescent—finally well. Yet but a brief period elapsed, ere a second more violent disorder again threw her upon a bed of suffering; and from this attack her frame, at all times feeble, never altogether recovered. Her illnesses were, after this epoch, of alarming character, and of more alarming recurrence, defying alike the knowledge and the great exertions of her physicians. With the increase of the chronic disease which had thus, apparently, taken too sure hold upon her constitution to be eradicated by human means, I could not fail to observe a similar increase in the nervous irritation of her temperament, and in her excitability by trivial causes of fear. She spoke again, and now more frequently and pertinaciously, of the sounds—of the slight sounds—and of the unusual motions among the tapestries, to which she had formerly alluded.

One night, near the closing in of September, she pressed this distressing subject with more than usual emphasis upon my attention. She had just awakened from an unquiet slumber, and I had been watching, with feelings half of anxiety, half of vague terror, the workings of her emaciated countenance. I sat by the side of her ebony bed, upon one of the ottomans of India. She partly arose, and spoke, in an earnest low whisper, of sounds which she *then* heard, but which I could not hear—of motions which she *then* saw, but which I could not perceive. The wind was rushing hurriedly behind the tapestries, and I wished to show her (what, let me confess it, I could not *all* believe) that those almost inarticulate breathings, and those very gentle variations of the figures upon the wall, were but the natural effects of that customary rushing of the wind. But a deadly pallor, overspreading her face, had proved to me that my exertions to reassure her would be fruitless. She appeared to be fainting, and no attendants were within call. I remembered where was deposited a decanter of light wine which had been ordered by her physicians, and hastened across the chamber to procure it. But, as I stepped beneath the light of the censer, two circumstances of a startling nature attracted my attention. I had felt that some palpable although invisible object had passed lightly by my person;

and I saw that there lay upon the golden carpet, in the very middle of the rich lustre thrown from the censer, a shadow—a faint, indefinite shadow of angelic aspect—such as might be fancied for the shadow of a shade. But I was wild with the excitement of an immoderate dose of opium, and heeded these things but little, nor spoke of them to Rowena. Having found the wine, I recrossed the chamber, and poured out a gobletful, which I held to the lips of the fainting lady. She had now partially recovered, however, and took the vessel herself, while I sank upon an ottoman near me, with my eyes fastened upon her person. It was then that I became distinctly aware of a gentle foot-fall upon the carpet, and near the couch; and in a second thereafter, as Rowena was in the act of raising the wine to her lips, I saw, or may have dreamed that I saw, fall within the goblet, as if from some invisible spring in the atmosphere of the room, three or four large drops of a brilliant and ruby colored fluid. If this I saw—not so Rowena. She swallowed the wine unhesitatingly, and I forbore to speak to her of a circumstance which must, after all, I considered, have been but the suggestion of a vivid imagination, rendered morbidly active by the terror of the lady, by the opium, and by the hour.

Yet I cannot conceal it from my own perception that, immediately subsequent to the fall of the ruby-drops, a rapid change for the worse took place in the disorder of my wife; so that, on the third subsequent night, the hands of her menials prepared her for the tomb, and on the fourth, I sat alone, with her shrouded body, in that fantastic chamber which had received her as my bride.—Wild visions, opium-engendered, flitted, shadowlike, before me. I gazed with unquiet eye upon the sarcophagi in the angles of the room, upon the varying figures of the drapery, and upon the writhing of the parti-colored fires in the censer overhead. My eyes then fell, as I called to mind the circumstances of a former night, to the spot beneath the glare of the censer where I had seen the faint traces of the shadow. It was there, however, no longer; and breathing with greater freedom, I turned my glances to the pallid and rigid figure upon the bed. Then rushed upon me a thousand memories of Ligeia—and then came back upon my heart, with the turbulent violence of a flood, the whole of that unutterable woe with which I had regarded *her* thus enshrouded. The night waned; and still, with a bosom full of bitter thoughts of the one only and supremely beloved, I remained gazing upon the body of Rowena.

It might have been midnight, or perhaps earlier, or later, for I had taken no note of time, when a sob, low, gentle, but very distinct startled me from my revery.—I *felt* that it came from the bed of ebony—the bed of death. I listened in an agony of superstitious terror—but there was no repetition of the sound. I strained my vision to detect any motion in the corpse—but there was not the slightest perceptible. Yet I could not have been deceived. I *had* heard the noise, however faint, and my soul was awakened within me. I resolutely and perseveringly kept my attention riveted upon the body. Many minutes elapsed before any circumstance occurred tending to throw light upon the mystery. At length it became evident that a slight, a very feeble, and barely noticeable tinge of color had flushed up within the cheeks, and along the sunken small veins of the eyelids. Through a species of unutterable horror and awe, for which the language of mortality has no sufficiently energetic expression, I felt my heart cease to beat, my limbs grow rigid where I sat. Yet a sense of duty finally operated to restore my self-possession. I could no longer doubt that we had been precipitate in our preparations—that Rowena still lived. It was necessary that some immediate exertion be made; yet the turret was altogether apart from the portion of the abbey tenanted by the servants—there were none within call—I had no means of summoning them to my aid without leaving the room for many minutes—and this I could not venture to do. I therefore struggled alone in my endeavors to call back the spirit still hovering. In a short period it was certain, however, that a relapse had taken place; the color disappeared from both eyelid and cheek, leaving a wanness even more than that of marble; the lips became doubly shrivelled and pinched up in the ghastly expression of death; a repulsive clamminess and coldness overspread rapidly the surface of the body; and all the usual rigorous stiffness immediately supervened. I fell back with a shudder upon the couch from which I had been so startlingly aroused, and again gave myself up to passionate waking visions of Ligeia.

An hour thus elapsed when (could it be possible?) I was a second time aware of some vague sound issuing from the region of the bed. I listened—in extremity of horror. The sound came again—it was a sigh. Rushing to the corpse, I saw—distinctly saw—a tremor upon the lips. In a minute afterward they relaxed, disclosing a bright line of the pearly teeth. Amazement now struggled in my bosom with the profound awe which had hitherto reigned there alone. I felt that my vision grew dim, that my reason wandered; and it was only by a violent effort that I at length succeeded in nerving myself to the task which duty thus once more had pointed out. There was now a partial glow upon the forehead and upon the cheek and throat; a perceptible warmth pervaded the whole frame; there was even a slight pulsation at the heart. The lady *lived*; and with redoubled ardor I betook myself to the task of restoration. I chafed and bathed the temples and the hands, and used every exertion which experience, and no little medical reading, could suggest. But in vain. Suddenly, the color fled, the pulsation ceased, the lips resumed the expression of the dead, and, in an instant afterward, the whole body took upon itself the icy chilliness, the livid hue, the intense rigidity, the sunken outline, and all the loathsome peculiarities of that which has been, for many days, a tenant of the tomb.

And again I sunk into visions of Ligeia—and again, (what marvel that I shudder while I write?) *again* there reached my ears a low sob from the region of the ebony bed. But why shall I minutely detail the unspeakable horrors of that night? Why shall I pause to relate how, time after time, until near the period of the gray dawn, this hideous drama of revivification was repeated; how each terrific relapse was only into a sterner and apparently more irredeemable death; how each agony wore the aspect of a struggle with some invisible foe; and how each struggle was succeeded by I know not what of wild change in the personal appearance of the corpse? Let me hurry to a conclusion.

The greater part of the fearful night had worn away, and she who had been dead once again stirred—and now more vigorously than hitherto, although arousing from a dissolution more appalling in its utter hopelessness than any. I had long ceased to struggle or to move, and remained sitting rigidly upon the ottoman, a helpless prey to a whirl of violent emotions, of which extreme awe was perhaps the least terrible, the least consuming. The corpse, I repeat, stirred, and now more vigorously than before. The hues of life flushed up with unwonted energy into the countenance—the limbs relaxed—and, save that the eyelids were yet pressed heavily together, and that the bandages and draperies of the grave still imparted their charnel character to the figure, I might have dreamed that Rowena had indeed shaken off, utterly, the fetters of Death. But if this idea was not, even then, altogether adopted, I could at least doubt no longer, when, arising from the bed, tottering, with feeble steps, with closed eyes, and with the manner of one bewildered in a dream, the thing that was enshrouded advanced boldly and palpably into the middle of the apartment.

I trembled not—I stirred not—for a crowd of unutterable fancies connected with the air, the stature, the demeanor of the figure, rushing hurriedly through my brain, had paralyzed—had chilled me into stone. I stirred not—but gazed upon the apparition. There was a mad disorder in my thoughts—a tumult unappeasable. Could it, indeed, be the *living* Rowena who confronted me? Could it, indeed, be Rowena *at all*—the fair-haired, the blue-eyed Lady Rowena Trevanion of Tremaine? Why, *why* should I doubt it? The bandage lay heavily about the mouth—but then might it not be the mouth of the breathing Lady of Tremaine? And the cheeks—there were the roses as in her noon of life—yes, these might indeed be the fair cheeks of the living Lady of Tremaine. And the chin, with its dimples, as in health, might it not be hers?——but *had she then grown taller since her malady?* What inexpressible madness seized me with that thought? One bound, and I had reached her feet! Shrinking from my touch, she let fall from her head, unloosened, the ghastly cerements which had confined it, and there streamed forth into the rushing atmosphere of the chamber huge masses of long and dishevelled hair; *it was blacker than the raven wings of midnight!* And now slowly opened *the eyes* of the figure which stood before me. "Here then, at least," I shrieked aloud, "can I never——can I never be mistaken——these are the full, and the black, and the wild eyes——of my lost love——of the Lady——of the LADY LIGEIA."

WALT WHITMAN
(1819–1892)
Song of Myself*

1

I celebrate myself, and sing myself,
And what I assume you shall assume,
For every atom belonging to me as good belongs to you.

I loafe and invite my soul,
I lean and loafe at my ease observing a spear of summer grass.   5

My tongue, every atom of my blood, form'd from this soil, this air,
Born here of parents born here from parents the same, and their
    parents the same,
I, now thirty-seven years old in perfect health begin,
Hoping to cease not till death.

Creeds and schools in abeyance,   10
Retiring back a while sufficed at what they are, but never for-
    gotten,
I harbor for good or bad, I permit to speak at every hazard,
Nature without check with original energy.

4

Trippers and askers surround me,
People I meet, the effect upon me of my early life or the ward and
    city I live in, or the nation,   15
The latest dates, discoveries, inventions, societies, authors old and
    new,
My dinner, dress, associates, looks, compliments, dues,

* Selected sections. First published in 1855. Our text is from the 1891– 1892 edition of *Leaves of Grass*, the so-called Deathbed Edition.

The real or fancied indifference of some man or woman I love,
The sickness of one of my folks or of myself, or ill-doing or loss or
    lack of money, or depressions or exaltations,
Battles, the horrors of fratricidal war, the fever of doubtful news,
    the fitful events;   20
These come to me days and nights and go from me again,
But they are not the Me myself.

Apart from the pulling and hauling stands what I am,
Stands amused, complacent, compassionating, idle, unitary,
Looks down, is erect, or bends an arm on an impalpable certain rest,
Looking with side-curved head curious what will come next,   26
Both in and out of the game and watching and wondering at it.

Backward I see in my own days where I sweated through fog with
    linguists and contenders,
I have no mockings or arguments, I witness and wait.

7

Has any one supposed it lucky to be born?   30
I hasten to inform him or her it is just as lucky to die, and I know it.

I pass death with the dying and birth with the new-wash'd babe,
    and am not contain'd between my hat and boots,
And peruse manifold objects, no two alike and every one good,
The earth good and the stars good, and their adjuncts all good.

I am not an earth nor an adjunct of an earth,   35
I am the mate and companion of people, all just as immortal and
    fathomless as myself,
(They do not know how immortal, but I know.)

Every kind for itself and its own, for me mine male and female,
For me those that have been boys and that love women,
For me the man that is proud and feels how it stings to be slighted,
For me the sweet-heart and the old maid, for me mothers and the
    mothers of mothers,   41
For me lips that have smiled, eyes that have shed tears,
For me children and the begetters of children.

Undrape! you are not guilty to me, nor stale nor discarded,
I see through the broadcloth and gingham whether or no,   45
And am around, tenacious, acquisitive, tireless, and cannot be
    shaken away.

16

I am of old and young, of the foolish as much as the wise,
Regardless of others, ever regardful of others,
Maternal as well as paternal, a child as well as a man,

Stuff'd with the stuff that is coarse and stuff'd with the stuff that
 is fine,   50
One of the Nation of many nations, the smallest the same and the
 largest the same,
A Southerner soon as a Northerner, a planter nonchalant and hos-
 pitable down by the Oconee I live,
A Yankee bound my own was ready for trade, my joints the limberest
 joints on earth and the sternest joints on earth,
A Kentuckian walking the vale of the Elkhorn in my deer-skin
 leggings, a Louisianian or Georgian,
A boatman over lakes or bays or along coasts, a Hoosier, Badger,
 Buckeye;   55
At home on Kanadian snow-shoes or up in the bush, or with fisher-
 men off Newfoundland,
At home in the fleet of ice-boats, sailing with the rest and tacking,
At home on the hills of Vermont or in the woods of Maine, or the
 Texan ranch,
Comrade of Californians, comrade of free North-Westerners, (lov-
 ing their big proportions,)
Comrade of raftsmen and coalmen, comrade of all who shake hands
 and welcome to drink and meat,   60
A learner with the simplest, a teacher of the thoughtfullest,
A novice beginning yet experient of myriads of seasons,
Of every hue and caste am I, of every rank and religion,
A farmer, mechanic, artist, gentleman, sailor, quaker,
Prisoner, fancy-man, rowdy, lawyer, physician, priest.   65

I resist any thing better than my own diversity,
Breathe the air but leave plenty after me,
And am not stuck up, and am in my place.

(The moth and the fish-eggs are in their place,
The bright suns I see and the dark suns I cannot see are in their
 place,   70
The palpable is in its place and the impalpable is in its place.)

21

I am the poet of the Body and I am the poet of the Soul,
The pleasures of heaven are with me and the pains of hell are with
 me,
The first I graft and increase upon myself, the latter I translate into
 a new tongue.

I am the poet of the woman the same as the man,
And I say it is as great to be a woman as to be a man,
And I say there is nothing greater than the mother of men.

I chant the chant of dilation or pride,
We have had ducking and deprecating about enough,
I show that size is only development. 80

Have you outstript the rest? are you the President?
It is a trifle, they will more than arrive there every one, and still
pass on.

I am he that walks with the tender and growing night,
I call to the earth and sea half-held by the night.

Press close bare-bosom'd night—press close magnetic nourishing
night! 85
Night of south winds—night of the large few stars!
Still nodding night—mad naked summer night.

Smile O voluptuous cool-breath'd earth!
Earth of the slumbering and liquid trees!
Earth of departed sunset—earth of the mountains misty-topt! 90
Earth of the vitreous pour of the full moon just tinged with blue!
Earth of shine and dark mottling the tide of the river!
Earth of the limpid gray of clouds brighter and clearer for my sake!
Far-swooping elbow'd earth—rich apple-blossom'd earth!
Smile, for your lover comes. 95

Prodigal, you have given me love—therefore I to you give love!
O unspeakable passionate love.

24

Walt Whitman, a kosmos, of Manhattan the son,
Turbulent, fleshy, sensual, eating, drinking and breeding,
No sentimentalist, no stander above men and women or apart from
them, 100
No more modest than immodest.

Unscrew the locks from the doors!
Unscrew the doors themselves from their jambs!

Whoever degrades another degrades me,
And whatever is done or said returns at last to me. 105

Through me the afflatus surging and surging, through me the current and index.

I speak the pass-word primeval, I give the sign of democracy,
By God! I will accept nothing which all cannot have their counterpart of on the same terms.

. . .

32

I think I could turn and live with animals, they are so placid and
    self-contain'd,
I stand and look at them long and long.   110

They do not sweat and whine about their condition,
They do not lie awake in the dark and weep for their sins,
They do not make me sick discussing their duty to God,
Not one is dissatisfied, not one is demented with the mania of
    owning things,
Not one kneels to another, nor to his kind that lived thousands of
    years ago,   115
Not one is respectable or unhappy over the whole earth.
So they show their relations to me and I accept them,
They bring me tokens of myself, they evince them plainly in their
    possession.

I wonder where they get those tokens,
Did I pass that way huge times ago and negligently drop them?   120

Myself moving forward then and now and forever,
Gathering and showing more always and with velocity,
Infinite and omnigenous, and the like of these among them,
Not too exclusive toward the reachers of my remembrancers,
Picking out here one that I love, and now go with him on brotherly
    terms.   125

A gigantic beauty of a stallion, fresh and responsive to my caresses,
Head high in the forehead, wide between the ears,
Limbs glossy and supple, tail dusting the ground,
Eyes full of sparkling wickedness, ears finely cut, flexibly moving.

His nostrils dilate as my heels embrace him,   130
His well-built limbs tremble with pleasure as we race around and
    return.
I but use you a minute, then I resign you, stallion,
Why do I need your paces when I myself out-gallop them?
Even as I stand or sit passing faster than you.

46

I know I have the best of time and space, and was never measured
    and never will be measured.   135

I tramp a perpetual journey, (come listen all!)
My signs are a rain-proof coat, good shoes, and a staff cut from the
    woods,
No friend of mine takes his ease in my chair,
I have no chair, no church, no philosophy,

I lead no man to a dinner-table, library, exchange, 140
But each man and each woman of you I lead upon a knoll,
My left hand hooking you round the waist,
My right hand pointing to landscapes of continents and the public
    road.

Not I, not any one else can travel that road for you,
You must travel it for yourself. 145

It is not far, it is within reach,
Perhaps you have been on it since you were born and did not know,
Perhaps it is everywhere on water and on land.

Shoulder your duds dear son, and I will mine, and let us hasten
    forth,
Wonderful cities and free nations we shall fetch as we go. 150

. . .

51

The past and present wilt—I have fill'd them, emptied them,
And proceed to fill my next fold of the future.

Listener up there! what have you to confide to me?
Look in my face while I snuff the sidle of evening,
(Talk honestly, no one else hears you, and I stay only a minute
    longer.) 155

Do I contradict myself?
Very well then I contradict myself,
(I am large, I contain multitudes.)

I concentrate toward them that are nigh, I wait on the door-slab.

Who has done his day's work? who will soonest be through with
    his supper? 160
Who wishes to walk with me?

Will you speak before I am gone? will you prove already too late?

52

The spotted hawk swoops by and accuses me, he complains of my
    gab and my loitering.

I too am not a bit tamed, I too am untranslatable,
I sound my barbaric yawp over the roofs of the world. 165

The last scud of day holds back for me,
It flings my likeness after the rest and true as any on the shadow'd
    wilds,

It coaxes me to the vapor and the dusk.

I depart as air, I shake my white locks at the runaway sun,
I effuse my flesh in eddies, and drift it in lacy jags.   170

I bequeath myself to the dirt to grow from the grass I love,
If you want me again look for me under your boot-soles.

You will hardly know who I am or what I mean,
But I shall be good health to you nevertheless,
And filter and fibre your blood.   175

Failing to fetch me at first keep encouraged,
Missing me one place search another,
I stop somewhere waiting for you.

A Noiseless Patient Spider*

A noiseless patient spider,
I mark'd where on a little promontory it stood isolated,
Mark'd how to explore the vacant vast surrounding,
It launch'd forth filament, filament, filament, out of itself,
Ever unreeling them, ever tirelessly speeding them.   5

And you O my soul where you stand,
Surrounded, detached, in measureless oceans of space,
Ceaselessly musing, venturing, throwing, seeking the spheres to
   connect them,
Till the bridge you will need be form'd, till the ductile anchor hold,
Till the gossamer thread you fling catch somewhere, O my soul.   10

* First published 1862–1863; revised 1881.

NATHANIEL HAWTHORNE
(1804–1864)
Ethan Brand†

A *Chapter from an Abortive Romance*

Bartram the lime-burner, a rough, heavy-looking man, begrimed
with charcoal, sat watching his kiln at nightfall, while his little
son played at building houses with the scattered fragments of marble,
when, on the hill-side below them, they heard a roar of laughter,
not mirthful, but slow, and even solemn, like a wind shaking the
boughs of the forest.

† 1851. For sources, see passages in   the period from July 29 to September 9,
Hawthorne's *American Notebooks* for   1838.

"Father, what is that?" asked the little boy, leaving his play, and pressing betwixt his father's knees.

"Oh, some drunken man, I suppose," answered the lime-burner; "some merry fellow from the bar-room in the village, who dared not laugh loud enough within doors lest he should blow the roof of the house off. So here he is, shaking his jolly sides at the foot of Graylock."[1]

"But, father," said the child, more sensitive than the obtuse, middle-aged clown, "he does not laugh like a man that is glad. So the noise frightens me!"

"Don't be a fool, child!" cried his father, gruffly. "You will never make a man, I do believe; there is too much of your mother in you. I have known the rustling of a leaf startle you. Hark! Here comes the merry fellow now. You shall see that there is no harm in him."

Bartram and his little son, while they were talking thus, sat watching the same lime-kiln that had been the scene of Ethan Brand's solitary and meditative life, before he began his search for the Unpardonable Sin. Many years, as we have seen, had now elapsed, since that portentous night when the IDEA was first developed. The kiln, however, on the mountain-side, stood unimpaired, and was in nothing changed since he had thrown his dark thoughts into the intense glow of its furnace, and melted them, as it were, into the one thought that took possession of his life. It was a rude, round, tower-like structure about twenty feet high, heavily built of rough stones, and with a hillock of earth heaped about the larger part of its circumference; so that the blocks and fragments of marble might be drawn by cart-loads, and thrown in at the top. There was an opening at the bottom of the tower, like an oven-mouth, but large enough to admit a man in a stooping posture, and provided with a massive iron door. With the smoke and jets of flame issuing from the chinks and crevices of this door, which seemed to give admittance into the hill-side, it resembled nothing so much as the private entrance to the infernal regions, which the shepherds of the Delectable Mountains were accustomed to show to pilgrims.[2]

There are many such lime-kilns in that tract of country, for the purpose of burning the white marble which composes a large part of the substance of the hills. Some of them, built years ago, and long deserted, with weeds growing in the vacant round of the interior, which is open to the sky, and grass and wild-flowers root-

1. Mount Greylock, 3,505 feet high, the chief mountain of the Berkshire range, and the highest point in Massachusetts. Both Hawthorne (at Lenox) and Melville (at Pittsfield) lived nearby; and Melville's *Pierre* (1852) is dedicated to Greylock.

2. Hawthorne is referring to John Bunyan's *Pilgrim's Progress*, Part I (1678), in which there is a description of "a door in the side of a hill" through which Christian and his companions catch a glimpse of hell and hear "a rumbling noise as of fire, and a cry of some tormented."

ing themselves into the chinks of the stones, look already like relics of antiquity, and may yet be overspread with the lichens of centuries to come. Others, where the lime-burner still feeds his daily and night-long fire, afford points of interest to the wanderer among the hills, who seats himself on a log of wood or a fragment of marble, to hold a chat with the solitary man. It is a lonesome, and, when the character is inclined to thought, may be an intensely thoughtful occupation; as it proved in the case of Ethan Brand, who had mused to such strange purpose, in days gone by, while the fire in this very kiln was burning.

The man who now watched the fire was of a different order, and troubled himself with no thoughts save the very few that were requisite to his business. At frequent intervals, he flung back the clashing weight of the iron door, and, turning his face from the insufferable glare, thrust in huge logs of oak, or stirred the immense brands with a long pole. Within the furnace were seen the curling and riotous flames, and the burning marble, almost molten with the intensity of heat; while without, the reflection of the fire quivered on the dark intricacy of the surrounding forest, and showed in the foreground a bright and ruddy little picture of the hut, the spring beside its door, the athletic and coal-begrimed figure of the lime-burner, and the half-frightened child, shrinking into the protection of his father's shadow. And when, again, the iron door was closed, then reappeared the tender light of the half-full moon, which vainly strove to trace out the indistinct shapes of the neighboring mountains; and, in the upper sky, there was a flitting congregation of clouds, still faintly tinged with the rosy sunset, though thus far down into the valley the sunshine had vanished long and long ago.

The little boy now crept still closer to his father, as footsteps were heard ascending the hill-side, and a human form thrust aside the bushes that clustered beneath the trees.

"Halloo! who is it?" cried the lime-burner, vexed at his son's timidity, yet half infected by it. "Come forward, and show yourself, like a man, or I'll fling this chunk of marble at your head!"

"You offer me a rough welcome," said a gloomy voice, as the unknown man drew nigh. "Yet I neither claim nor desire a kinder one, even at my own fireside."

To obtain a distincter view, Bartram threw open the iron door of the kiln, whence immediately issued a gush of fierce light, that smote full upon the stranger's face and figure. To a careless eye there appeared nothing very remarkable in his aspect, which was that of a man in a coarse, brown, country-made suit of clothes, tall and thin, with the staff and heavy shoes of a wayfarer. As he advanced, he fixed his eyes—which were very bright—intently upon the brightness of the furnace, as if he beheld, or expected to behold, some object worthy of note within it.

"Good evening, stranger," said the lime-burner; "whence come you, so late in the day?"

"I come from my search," answered the wayfarer; "for, at last, it is finished."

"Drunk!—or crazy!" muttered Bartram to himself. "I shall have trouble with the fellow. The sooner I drive him away, the better."

The little boy, all in a tremble, whispered to his father, and begged him to shut the door of the kiln, so that there might not be so much light; for that there was something in the man's face which he was afraid to look at, yet could not look away from. And, indeed, even the lime-burner's dull and torpid sense began to be impressed by an indescribable something in that thin, rugged, thoughtful visage, with the grizzled hair hanging wildly about it, and those deeply sunken eyes, which gleamed like fires within the entrance of a mysterious cavern. But, as he closed the door, the stranger turned towards him, and spoke in a quiet, familiar way, that made Bartram feel as if he were a sane and sensible man, after all.

"Your task draws to an end, I see," said he. "This marble has already been burning three days. A few hours more will convert the stone to lime."

"Why, who are you?" exclaimed the lime-burner. "You seem as well acquainted with my business as I am myself."

"And well I may be," said the stranger; "for I followed the same craft many a long year, and here, too, on this very spot. But you are a new-comer in these parts. Did you never hear of Ethan Brand?"

"The man that went in search of the Unpardonable Sin?" asked Bartram, with a laugh.

"The same," answered the stranger. "He has found what he sought, and therefore he comes back again."

"What! then you are Ethan Brand himself?" cried the lime-burner, in amazement. "I am a new-comer here, as you say, and they call it eighteen years since you left the foot of Graylock. But, I can tell you, the good folks still talk about Ethan Brand, in the village yonder, and what a strange errand took him away from his lime-kiln. Well, and so you have found the Unpardonable Sin?"

"Even so!" said the stranger, calmly.

"If the question is a fair one," proceeded Bartram, "where might it be?"

Ethan Brand laid his finger on his own heart.

"Here!" replied he.

And then, without mirth in his countenance, but as if moved

by an involuntary recognition of the infinite absurdity of seeking throughout the world for what was the closest of all things to himself, and looking into every heart, save his own, for what was hidden in no other breast, he broke into a laugh of scorn. It was the same slow, heavy laugh, that had almost appalled the lime-burner when it heralded the wayfarer's approach.

The solitary mountain-side was made dismal by it. Laughter, when out of place, mistimed, or bursting forth from a disordered state of feeling, may be the most terrible modulation of the human voice. The laughter of one asleep, even if it be a little child,—the madman's laugh,—the wild, screaming laugh of a born idiot,—are sounds that we sometimes tremble to hear, and would always willingly forget. Poets have imagined no utterance of fiends or hobgoblins so fearfully appropriate as a laugh. And even the obtuse lime-burner felt his nerves shaken, as this strange man looked inward at his own heart, and burst into laughter that rolled away into the night, and was indistinctly reverberated among the hills.

"Joe," said he to his little son, "scamper down to the tavern in the village, and tell the jolly fellows there that Ethan Brand has come back, and that he has found the Unpardonable Sin!"

The boy darted away on his errand, to which Ethan Brand made no objection, nor seemed hardly to notice it. He sat on a log of wood, looking steadfastly at the iron door of the kiln. When the child was out of sight, and his swift and light footsteps ceased to be heard treading first on the fallen leaves and then on the rocky mountain-path, the lime-burner began to regret his departure. He felt that the little fellow's presence had been a barrier between his guest and himself, and that he must now deal, heart to heart, with a man who, on his own confession, had committed the one only crime for which Heaven could afford no mercy. That crime, in its indistinct blackness, seemed to overshadow him, and made his memory riotous with a throng of evil shapes that asserted their kindred with the Master Sin, whatever it might be, which it was within the scope of man's corrupted nature to conceive and cherish. They were all of one family; they went to and fro between his breast and Ethan Brand's, and carried dark greetings from one to the other.

Then Bartram remembered the stories which had grown traditionary in reference to this strange man, who had come upon him like a shadow of the night, and was making himself at home in his old place, after so long absence, that the dead people, dead and buried for years, would have had more right to be at home, in any familiar spot, than he. Ethan Brand, it was said, had conversed with Satan himself in the lurid blaze of this very kiln. The legend had been matter of mirth heretofore, but looked grisly now. According to this tale, before Ethan Brand departed on his search, he had been accustomed to evoke a fiend from the hot furnace of the lime-kiln, night after night, in order to confer with him about the Unpardonable Sin; the man and the fiend each laboring to frame the image of some mode of guilt which could neither be atoned for nor forgiven. And, with the first gleam of light upon the mountain-top, the fiend crept in at the iron door, there to abide the intensest element of fire until again summoned forth to share in the dreadful task of extending man's possible guilt beyond the scope of Heaven's else infinite mercy.

While the lime-burner was struggling with the horror of these thoughts, Ethan Brand rose from the log, and flung open the door of the kiln. The action was in such accordance with the idea in Bartram's mind, that he almost expected to see the Evil One issue forth, red-hot, from the raging furnace.

"Hold! hold!" cried he, with a tremulous attempt to laugh; for he was ashamed of his fears, although they overmastered him. "Don't, for mercy's sake, bring out your Devil now!"

"Man!" sternly replied Ethan Brand, "what need have I of the Devil? I have left him behind me, on my track. It is with such half-way sinners as you that he busies himself. Fear not, because I open the door. I do but act by old custom, and am going to trim your fire, like a lime-burner, as I was once."

He stirred the vast coals, thrust in more wood, and bent forward to gaze into the hollow prison-house of the fire, regardless of the fierce glow that reddened upon his face. The lime-burner sat watching him, and half suspected this strange guest of a purpose, if not to evoke a fiend, at least to plunge into the flames, and thus vanish from the sight of man. Ethan Brand, however, drew quietly back, and closed the door of the kiln.

"I have looked," said he, "into many a human heart that was seven times hotter with sinful passions than yonder furnace is with fire. But I found not there what I sought. No, not the Unpardonable Sin!"

"What is the Unpardonable Sin?" asked the lime-burner; and then he shrank farther from his companion, trembling lest his question should be answered.

"It is a sin that grew within my own breast," replied Ethan Brand, standing erect with a pride that distinguishes all enthusiasts of his stamp. "A sin that grew nowhere else! The sin of an intellect that triumphed over the sense of brotherhood with man and reverence for God, and sacrificed everything to its own mighty claims! The only sin that deserves a recompense of immortal agony! Freely, were it to do again, would I incur the guilt. Unshrinkingly I accept the retribution!"

"The man's head is turned," muttered the lime-burner to himself. "He may be a sinner like the rest of us,—nothing more likely,— but, I'll be sworn, he is a madman too."

Nevertheless, he felt uncomfortable at his situation, alone with Ethan Brand on the wild mountain-side, and was right glad to hear the rough murmur of tongues, and the footsteps of what seemed a pretty numerous party, stumbling over the stones and rustling through the underbrush. Soon appeared the whole lazy regiment that was wont to infest the village tavern, comprehending three or four individuals who had drunk flip beside the bar-room fire through all the winters, and smoked their pipes beneath the stoop through all the summers, since Ethan Brand's departure. Laughing boisterously, and mingling all their voices together in unceremonious talk, they now burst into the moonshine and narrow streaks of firelight that illuminated the open space before the lime-kiln. Bartram set the door ajar again, flooding the spot with light, that the whole company might get a fair view of Ethan Brand, and he of them.

There, among other old acquaintances, was a once ubiquitous man, now almost extinct, but whom we were formerly sure to encounter at the hotel of every thriving village throughout the country. It was the stage-agent. The present specimen of the genus was a wilted and smoke-dried man, wrinkled and red-nosed, in a smartly cut, brown, bobtailed coat, with brass buttons, who, for a length of time unknown, had kept his desk and corner in the bar-room, and was still puffing what seemed to be the same cigar that he had lighted twenty years before. He had great fame as a dry joker, though, perhaps, less on account of any intrinsic humor than from a certain flavor of brandy-toddy and tobacco-smoke, which impregnated all his ideas and expressions, as well as his person. Another well-remembered, though strangely altered, face was that of Lawyer Giles, as people still called him in courtesy; an elderly ragamuffin, in his soiled shirtsleeves and tow-cloth trousers. This poor fellow had been an attorney, in what he called his better days, a sharp practitioner, and in great vogue among the village litigants; but flip, and sling, and toddy, and cocktails, imbibed at all hours, morning, noon, and night, had caused him to slide from intellectual to various kinds and degrees of bodily labor, till at last, to adopt his own phrase, he slid into a soap-vat. In other words, Giles was now a soap-boiler, in a small way. He had come to be but the fragment of a human being, a part of one foot having been chopped off by an axe, and an entire hand torn away by the devilish grip of a steam-engine. Yet, though the corporeal hand was gone, a spiritual member remained; for, stretching forth the stump, Giles steadfastly averred that he felt an invisible thumb and fingers with as vivid a sensation as before the real ones were amputated. A maimed and miserable wretch he was; but one, nevertheless, whom the world could not trample on, and had no right to scorn, either in this or any previous stage of his misfortunes, since he had still kept up the courage and spirit of a man, asked nothing in charity, and with his one hand—and that the left one—fought a stern battle against want and hostile circumstances.

Among the throng, too, came another personage, who with certain points of similarity to Lawyer Giles, had many more of difference. It was the village doctor; a man of some fifty years, whom, at an earlier period of his life, we introduced as paying a professional visit to Ethan Brand during the latter's supposed insanity. He was now a purple-visaged, rude, and brutal, yet half-gentlemanly figure, with something wild, ruined, and desperate in his talk, and in all the details of his gesture and manners. Brandy possessed this man like an evil spirit, and made him as surly and savage as a wild beast, and as miserable as a lost soul; but there was supposed to be in him such wonderful skill, such native gifts of healing, beyond any which medical science could impart, that society caught hold of him, and would not let him sink out of its reach. So, swaying to and fro upon his horse, and grumbling thick accents at the bedside, he visited all the sick-chambers for miles about among the mountain towns, and sometimes raised a dying man, as it were, by miracle, or quite as often, no doubt, sent his patient to a grave that was dug many a year too soon. The doctor had an everlasting pipe in his mouth, and, as somebody said, in allusion to his habit of swearing, it was always alight with hell-fire.

These three worthies pressed forward, and greeted Ethan Brand each after his own fashion, earnestly inviting him to partake of the contents of a certain black bottle, in which, as they averred, he would find something far better worth seeking than the Unpardonable Sin. No mind, which has wrought itself by intense and solitary meditation into a high state of enthusiasm, can endure the kind of contact with low and vulgar modes of thought and feeling to which Ethan Brand was now subjected. It made him doubt—and, strange to say, it was a painful doubt—whether he had indeed found the Unpardonable Sin, and found it within himself. The whole question on which he had exhausted life, and more than life, looked like a delusion.

"Leave me," he said bitterly, "ye brute beasts, that have made yourselves so, shrivelling up your souls with fiery liquors! I have done with you. Years and years ago, I groped into your hearts and found nothing there for my purpose. Get ye gone!"

"Why, you uncivil scoundrel," cried the fierce doctor, "is that the way you respond to the kindness of your best friends? Then

let me tell you the truth. You have no more found the Unpardonable Sin than yonder boy Joe has. You are but a crazy fellow,—I
told you so twenty years ago,—neither better nor worse than a
crazy fellow, and the fit companion of old Humphrey, here!"

He pointed to an old man, shabbily dressed, with long white hair,
thin visage, and unsteady eyes. For some years past this aged person
had been wandering about among the hills, inquiring of all
travellers whom he met for his daughter. The girl, it seemed, had
gone off with a company of circus-performers, and occasionally
tidings of her came to the village, and fine stories were told of her
glittering appearance as she rode on horseback in the ring, or performed marvellous feats on the tight-rope.

The white-haired father now approached Ethan Brand, and
gazed unsteadily into his face.

"They tell me you have been all over the earth," said he, wringing his hands with earnestness. "You must have seen my daughter,
for she makes a grand figure in the world, and everybody goes to
see her. Did she send any word to her old father, or say when she
was coming back?"

Ethan Brand's eye quailed beneath the old man's. That daughter,
from whom he so earnestly desired a word of greeting, was the
Esther of our tale, the very girl whom, with such cold and remorseless purpose, Ethan Brand had made the subject of a psychological
experiment, and wasted, absorbed, and perhaps annihilated her
soul, in the process.

"Yes," he murmured, turning away from the hoary wanderer,
"it is no delusion. There is an Unpardonable Sin!"

While these things were passing, a merry scene was going forward in the area of cheerful light, beside the spring and before the
door of the hut. A number of the youth of the village, young men
and girls, had hurried up the hill-side, impelled by curiosity to see
Ethan Brand, the hero of so many a legend familiar to their childhood. Finding nothing, however, very remarkable in his aspect,—
nothing but a sunburnt wayfarer, in plain garb and dusty shoes,
who sat looking into the fire as if he fancied pictures among the
coals,—these young people speedily grew tired of observing him.
As it happened, there was other amusement at hand. An old
German Jew, travelling with a diorama[3] on his back, was passing
down the mountain-road towards the village just as the party turned
aside from it, and, in hopes of eking out the profits of the day, the
showman had kept them company to the lime-kiln.

3. a mechanical contrivance for exhibiting paintings. By manipulating
various devices (among them magnify-
ing glasses) and controlling the lighting, the operator could produce in the
pictures different scenic effects, such as
apparent sunsets.

"Come, old Dutchman," cried one of the young men, "let us see your pictures, if you can swear they are worth looking at!"

"Oh yes, Captain," answered the Jew,—whether as a matter of courtesy or craft, he styled everybody Captain,—"I shall show you, indeed, some very superb pictures!"

So, placing his box in a proper position, he invited the young men and girls to look through the glass orifices of the machine, and proceeded to exhibit a series of the most outrageous scratchings and daubings, as specimens of the fine arts, that ever an itinerant showman had the face to impose upon his circle of spectators. The pictures were worn out, moreover, tattered, full of cracks and wrinkles, dingy with tobacco-smoke, and otherwise in a most pitiable condition. Some purported to be cities, public edifices, and ruined castles in Europe; others represented Napoleon's battles and Nelson's sea-fights; and in the midst of these would be seen a gigantic, brown, hairy hand,—which might have been mistaken for the Hand of Destiny, though, in truth, it was only the show-man's,—pointing its forefinger to various scenes of the conflict, while its owner gave historical illustrations. When, with much merriment at its abominable deficiency of merit, the exhibition was concluded, the German bade little Joe put his head into the box. Viewed through the magnifying-glasses, the boy's round, rosy visage assumed the strangest imaginable aspect of an immense Titanic child, the mouth grinning broadly, and the eyes and every other feature overflowing with fun at the joke. Suddenly, however, that merry face turned pale, and its expression changed to horror, for this easily impressed and excitable child had become sensible that the eye of Ethan Brand was fixed upon him through the glass.

"You make the little man to be afraid, Captain," said the German Jew, turning up the dark and strong outline of his visage from his stooping posture. "But look again, and, by chance, I shall cause you to see somewhat that is very fine, upon my word!"

Ethan Brand gazed into the box for an instant, and then starting back, looked fixedly at the German. What had he seen? Nothing, apparently; for a curious youth, who had peeped in almost at the same moment, beheld only a vacant space of canvas.

"I remember you now," muttered Ethan Brand to the showman.

"Ah, Captain," whispered the Jew of Nuremberg, with a dark smile, "I find it to be a heavy matter in my show-box,—this Unpardonable Sin! By my faith, Captain, it has wearied my shoulders, this long day, to carry it over the mountain."

"Peace," answered Ethan Brand, sternly, "or get thee into the furnace yonder!"

The Jew's exhibition had scarcely concluded, when a great, elderly dog—who seemed to be his own master, as no person in the company laid claim to him—saw fit to render himself the object of public notice. Hitherto, he had shown himself a very quiet, well-disposed old dog, going round from one to another, and, by way of being sociable, offering his rough head to be patted by any kindly hand that would take so much trouble. But now, all of a sudden, this grave and venerable quadruped, of his own mere motion, and without the slightest suggestion from anybody else, began to run round after his tail, which, to heighten the absurdity of the proceeding, was a great deal shorter than it should have been. Never was seen such headlong eagerness in pursuit of an object that could not possibly be attained; never was heard such a tremendous outbreak of growling, snarling, barking, and snapping,—as if one end of the ridiculous brute's body were at deadly and most unforgivable enmity with the other. Faster and faster, round about went the cur; and faster and still faster fled the unapproachable brevity of his tail; and louder and fiercer grew his yells of rage and animosity; until, utterly exhausted, and as far from the goal as ever, the foolish old dog ceased his performance as suddenly as he had begun it. The next moment he was as mild, quiet, sensible, and respectable in his deportment, as when he first scraped acquaintance with the company.

As may be supposed, the exhibition was greeted with universal laughter, clapping of hands, and shouts of encore, to which the canine performer responded by wagging all that there was to wag of his tail, but appeared totally unable to repeat his very successful effort to amuse the spectators.

Meanwhile, Ethan Brand had resumed his seat upon the log, and moved, as it might be, by a perception of some remote analogy between his own case and that of this self-pursuing cur, he broke into the awful laugh, which, more than any other token, expressed the condition of his inward being. From that moment, the merriment of the party was at an end; they stood aghast, dreading lest the inauspicious sound should be reverberated around the horizon, and that mountain would thunder it to mountain, and so the horror be prolonged upon their ears. Then, whispering one to another that it was late,—that the moon was almost down,—that the August night was growing chill,—they hurried homewards, leaving the lime-burner and little Joe to deal as they might with their unwelcome guest. Save for these three human beings, the open space on the hill-side was a solitude, set in a vast gloom of forest. Beyond that darksome verge, the firelight glimmered on the stately trunks and almost black foliage of pines, intermixed with the lighter verdure of sapling oaks, maples, and poplars, while here and there lay the gigantic corpses of dead trees, decaying on the leaf-strewn soil. And it seemed to little Joe—a timorous and imaginative child—that the silent forest was holding its breath until some fearful thing should happen.

Ethan Brand thrust more wood into the fire, and closed the door of the kiln; then looking over his shoulder at the lime-burner and his son, he bade, rather than advised, them to retire to rest.

"For myself, I cannot sleep," said he. "I have matters that it concerns me to meditate upon. I will watch the fire, as I used to do in the old time."

"And call the Devil out of the furnace to keep you company, I suppose," muttered Bartram, who had been making intimate acquaintance with the black bottle above mentioned. "But watch, if you like, and call as many devils as you like! For my part, I shall be all the better for a snooze. Come, Joe!"

As the boy followed his father into the hut, he looked back at the wayfarer, and the tears came into his eyes, for his tender spirit had an intuition of the bleak and terrible loneliness in which this man had enveloped himself.

When they had gone, Ethan Brand sat listening to the crackling of the kindled wood, and looking at the little spirits of fire that issued through the chinks of the door. These trifles, however, once so familiar, had but the slightest hold of his attention, while deep within his mind he was reviewing the gradual but marvellous change that had been wrought upon him by the search to which he had devoted himself. He remembered how the night dew had fallen upon him,—how the dark forest had whispered to him,—how the stars had gleamed upon him,—a simple and loving man, watching his fire in the years gone by, and ever musing as it burned. He remembered with what tenderness, with what love and sympathy for mankind, and what pity for human guilt and woe, he had first begun to contemplate those ideas which afterwards became the inspiration of his life; with what reverence he had then looked into the heart of man, viewing it as a temple originally divine, and, however desecrated, still to be held sacred by a brother; with what awful fear he had deprecated the success of his pursuit, and prayed that the Unpardonable Sin might never be revealed to him. Then ensued that vast intellectual development, which, in its progress, disturbed the counterpoise between his mind and heart. The Idea that possessed his life had operated as a means of education; it had gone on cultivating his powers to the highest point of which they were susceptible; it had raised him from the level of an unlettered laborer to stand on a star-lit eminence, whither the philosophers of the earth, laden with the lore of universities, might vainly strive to clamber after him. So much for the intellect! But where was the heart? That, indeed, had withered,—had contracted,—had hardened,—had perished! It had ceased to partake of the universal throb. He had lost his hold of the magnetic chain of humanity. He was no longer a brother-man, opening the chambers or the dungeons of our common nature by the key of holy sympathy, which gave him a right to share in all its secrets; he was now a cold observer, looking on mankind as the subject of his experiment, and, at length, converting man and woman to be his puppets, and pulling the wires that moved them to such degrees of crime as were demanded for his study.

Thus Ethan Brand became a fiend. He began to be so from the moment that his moral nature had ceased to keep the pace of improvement with his intellect. And now, as his highest effort and inevitable development,—as the bright and gorgeous flower, and rich, delicious fruit of his life's labor,—he had produced the Unpardonable Sin!

"What more have I to seek? what more to achieve?" said Ethan Brand to himself. "My task is done, and well done!"

Starting from the log with a certain alacrity in his gait and ascending the hillock of earth that was raised against the stone circumference of the lime-kiln, he thus reached the top of the structure. It was a space of perhaps ten feet across, from edge to edge, presenting a view of the upper surface of the immense mass of broken marble with which the kiln was heaped. All these innumerable blocks and fragments of marble were red-hot and vividly on fire, sending up great spouts of blue flame, which quivered aloft and danced madly, as within a magic circle, and sank and rose again, with continual and multitudinous activity. As the lonely man bent forward over this terrible body of fire, the blasting heat smote up against his person with a breath that, it might be supposed, would have scorched and shrivelled him up in a moment.

Ethan Brand stood erect, and raised his arms on high. The blue flames played upon his face, and imparted the wild and ghastly light which alone could have suited its expression; it was that of a fiend on the verge of plunging into his gulf of intensest torment.

"O Mother Earth," cried he, "who art no more my Mother, and into whose bosom this frame shall never be resolved! O mankind, whose brotherhood I have cast off, and trampled thy great heart beneath my feet! O stars of heaven, that shone on me of old, as if to light me onward and upward!—farewell all, and forever. Come, deadly element of Fire,—henceforth my familiar friend! Embrace me, as I do thee!"

That night the sound of a fearful peal of laughter rolled heavily through the sleep of the lime-burner and his little son; dim shapes of horror and anguish haunted their dreams, and seemed still pres-

ent in the rude hovel, when they opened their eyes to the daylight.

"Up, boy, up!" cried the lime-burner, staring about him. "Thank
Heaven, the night is gone, at last; and rather than pass such another, I would watch my lime-kiln, wide awake, for a twelve-
month. This Ethan Brand, with his humbug of an Unpardonable
Sin, has done me no such mighty favor, in taking my place!"

He issued from the hut, followed by little Joe, who kept fast hold
of his father's hand. The early sunshine was already pouring its gold
upon the mountain-tops, and though the valleys were still in
shadow, they smiled cheerfully in the promise of the bright day
that was hastening onward. The village, completely shut in by hills,
which swelled away gently about it, looked as if it had rested peacefully in the hollow of the great hand of Providence. Every dwelling
was distinctly visible; the little spires of the two churches pointed
upwards, and caught a fore-glimmering of brightness from the
sun-gilt skies upon their gilded weather-cocks. The tavern was astir,
and the figure of the old, smoke-dried stage-agent, cigar in mouth,
was seen beneath the stoop. Old Graylock was glorified with a
golden cloud upon his head. Scattered likewise over the breasts of
the surrounding mountains, there were heaps of hoary mist, in
fantastic shapes, some of them far down into the valley, others high
up towards the summits, and still others, of the same family of
mist or cloud, hovering in the gold radiance of the upper atmosphere. Stepping from one to another of the clouds that rested on
the hills, and thence to the loftier brotherhood that sailed in air,
it seemed almost as if a mortal man might thus ascend into the
heavenly regions. Earth was so mingled with sky that it was a day-
dream to look at it.

To supply that charm of the familiar and homely, which Nature
so readily adopts into a scene like this, the stage-coach was rattling down the mountain-road, and the driver sounded his horn,
while Echo caught up the notes, and intertwined them into a rich
and varied and elaborate harmony, of which the original performer
could lay claim to little share. The great hills played a concert
among themselves, each contributing a strain of airy sweetness.

Little Joe's face brightened at once.

"Dear father," cried he, skipping cheerily to and fro, "that strange
man is gone, and the sky and the mountains all seem glad of it!"

"Yes," growled the lime-burner, with an oath, "but he has let
the fire go down, and no thanks to him if five hundred bushels of
lime are not spoiled. If I catch the fellow hereabouts again, I shall
feel like tossing him into the furnace!"

With his long pole in his hand, he ascended to the top of the kiln
After a moment's pause, he called to his son.

"Come up here, Joe!" said he.

So little Joe ran up the hillock, and stood by his father's side. The marble was all burnt into perfect, snow-white lime. But on its surface, in the midst of the circle,—snow-white too, and thoroughly converted into lime,—lay a human skeleton, in the attitude of a person who, after long toil, lies down to long repose. Within the ribs—strange to say—was the shape of a human heart.

"Was the fellow's heart made of marble?" cried Bartram, in some perplexity at this phenomenon. "At any rate, it is burnt into what looks like special good lime; and, taking all the bones together, my kiln is half a bushel the richer for him."

So saying, the rude lime-burner lifted his pole, and, letting it fall upon the skeleton, the relics of Ethan Brand were crumbled into fragments.

HERMAN MELVILLE
(1819–1891)

Billy Budd*

Preface[1]

The year 1797, the year of this narrative, belongs to a period which as every thinker now feels, involved a crisis for Christendom not exceeded in its undetermined momentousness at the time by any other era whereof there is record. The opening proposition made by the Spirit of that Age involved rectification of the Old World's hereditary wrongs. In France, to some extent, this was bloodily effected. But what then? Straightway the Revolution itself become a wrong-doer, one more oppressive than the kings. Under Napoleon it

* Reprinted by permission of the publishers from *Melville's Billy Budd*, edited by Frederick Barron Freeman and corrected by Elizabeth Treeman (Cambridge, Mass.: Harvard University Press). Copyright 1948, © 1956 by The President and Fellows of Harvard College.

The story was left as a semifinal draft by Melville at his death. It was posthumously published as *Billy Budd, Foretopman* in 1924, as a supplement to *The Works* *** (1922-1924). This was not strictly edited, but subsequent editions have been based on it. The text below represents a collation with the original manuscript in the Houghton Library of Harvard University by Miss Treeman, an assistant editor of Harvard University Press. Where additional punctuation is absolutely necessary for clarity, it has been inserted in square brackets. A few interpolated words and all words not entirely clear in the manuscript have also been placed in square brackets. A few important variant readings left standing in the manuscript are shown in footnotes. Melville's chapter divisions are different from those in the 1924 edition, and we have followed his manuscript in this matter also. Spelling is corrected.

In 1962 Harrison Hayford and Merton M. Sealts, Jr., published an edition that differs from the one printed here in several particulars of varying importance (they suggest, for example, that Melville's intended title was *Billy Budd / Sailor / An Inside Narrative*). As Lawrence Thompson has pointed out in *American Literature* (March, 1964), it will never be possible to determine Melville's precise intention in all its details. Consequently, major differences are mentioned in the footnotes, but no attempt has been made to record all minor disputed readings.

1. This preface appeared in the first publication of this work in 1924. Hayford and Sealts reject the preface.

enthroned upstart kings, and initiated that prolonged agony of continual war whose final throe was Waterloo. During those years not the wisest could have foreseen that the outcome of all would be what to some thinkers apparently it has since turned out to be—a political advance along nearly the whole line for Europeans.

Now, as elsewhere hinted, it was something caught from the Revolutionary Spirit that at Spithead emboldened the man-of-war's men to rise against real abuses, long-standing ones, and afterwards at the Nore to make inordinate and aggressive demands[2]—successful resistance to which was confirmed only when the ringleaders were hung for an admonitory spectacle to the anchored fleet. Yet in a way analogous to the operation of the Revolution at large—the Great Mutiny, though by Englishmen naturally deemed monstrous at the time, doubtless gave the first latent prompting to most important reforms in the British navy.

*

In the time before steamships, or then more frequently than now, a stroller along the docks of any considerable sea-port would occasionally have his attention arrested by a group of bronzed mariners, man-of-war's men or merchant-sailors in holiday attire ashore on liberty. In certain instances they would flank, or, like a body-guard quite surround some superior figure of their own class, moving along with them like Aldebaran among the lesser lights of his constellation.[3] That signal object was the "Handsome Sailor" of the less prosaic time alike of the military and merchant navies. With no perceptible trace of the vainglorious about him, rather with the off-hand unaffectedness of natural regality, he seemed to accept the spontaneous homage of his shipmates. A somewhat remarkable instance recurs to me. In Liverpool,[4] now half a century ago I saw under the shadow of the great dingy street-wall of Prince's Dock (an obstruction long since removed) a common sailor, so intensely black that he must needs have been a native African of the unadulterate blood of Ham.[5] A symmetric figure much above the average height. The two ends of a gay silk handkerchief thrown loose about the neck danced upon the displayed ebony of his chest; in his ears were big hoops of gold, and a Scotch Highland bonnet with a tartan band set off his shapely head.

2. There were a series of mutinies in the British fleet during the Napoleonic wars. The first, on April 15, 1797, was at the Spithead, the roadstead between Portsmouth and the Isle of Wight, and another was at a sandbank in the Thames estuary. The mutineers were all hanged.

3. a star of the first magnitude in the constellation of Taurus (the "Bull"), frequently used in navigation.

4. Melville served abroad the Liverpool packet *St. Lawrence* on his first sea voyage; his novel *Redburn* (1849) documents some of his experiences in Liverpool.

5. The word *Ham* derives from the Hebrew for "swarthy". Ham, the second son of Noah, was cursed by his father for mocking him. Later, it was thought that a black skin was the result of the curse. "Hamitic" languages include Somali, Berber, Tuareg, and Galla.

It was a hot noon in July; and his face, lustrous with persipiration, beamed with barbaric good humor. In jovial sallies right and left[,] his white teeth flashing into view, he rollicked along, the centre of a company of his shipmates. These were made up of such an assortment of tribes and complexions as would have well fitted them to be marched up by Anacharsis Cloots before the bar of the first French Assembly as Representatives of the Human Race.[6] At each spontaneous tribute rendered by the wayfarers to this black pagod[7] of a fellow—the tribute of a pause and stare, and less frequent an exclamation,—the motley retinue showed that they took that sort of pride in the evoker of it which the Assyrian priests doubtless showed for their grand sculptured Bull when the faithful prostrated themselves.[8]

To return.

If in some cases a bit of a nautical Murat[9] in setting forth his person ashore, the handsome sailor of the period in question evinced nothing of the dandified Billy-be-Damn, an amusing character all but extinct now, but occasionally to be encountered, and in a form yet more amusing than the original, at the tiller of the boats on the tempestuous Erie Canal or, more likely, vaporing in the groggeries along the tow-path. Invariably a proficient in his perilous calling, he was also more or less of a mighty boxer or wrestler. It was strength and beauty. Tales of his prowess were recited. Ashore he was the champion; afloat the spokesman; on every suitable occasion always foremost. Close-reefing topsails in a gale, there he was, astride the weather yard-arm-end foot in the Flemish horse as "stirrup," both hands tugging at the "earring" as at a bridle, in very much the attitude of young Alexander curbing the fiery Bucephalus.[10] A superb figure, tossed up as by the horns of Taurus[11] against the thunderous sky, cheerily hallooing to the strenuous file along the spar.

The moral nature was seldom out of keeping with the physical make. Indeed, except as toned by the former, the comeliness and power, always attractive in masculine conjunction, hardly could have drawn the sort of honest homage the Handsome Sailor in some examples received from his less gifted associates.

Such a cynosure, at least in aspect, and something such too in nature, though with important variations made apparent as the story

6. Jean Baptiste du Val-de-Grâce, Baron de Cloots (1755-1794) is mentioned in Carlyle's *French Revolution*. Cloots, or Clootz, assembled a crowd of assorted nationalities and introduced them at the French National Assembly during the Revolution. Cloots' zany idealism appealed to Melville, and he described the crew of the *Pequod* in *Moby Dick* as "an Anarcharsis Clootz deputation from all the isles of the sea."
7. pagoda.
8. In Assyrian bas-reliefs, the bull is prominent as a figure of worship.
9. Joachim Murat (1767-1815), Marshal of France and king of Naples, was Napoleon's brother-in-law and famous chiefly as a playboy and dandy.
10. Melville is alluding to one of the most hazardous activities engaged in by a sailor on a square-rigged ship. The "Flemish horse" was the footrope beneath the yard whose sail he was furling. Bucephalus (Greek: "ox-headed") was Alexander the Great's horse.
11. Cf. note 3.

proceeds, was welkin-eyed[12] Billy Budd, or Baby Budd as more familiarly under circumstances hereafter to be given he at last came to be called[,] aged twenty-one, a foretopman[13] of the British fleet toward the close of the last decade of the eighteenth century. It was not very long prior to the time of the narration that follows that he had entered the King's Service, having been impressed on the Narrow Seas from a homeward-bound English merchantman into a seventy-four outward-bound, H.M.S. *Indomitable*[14]; which ship, as was not unusual in those hurried days having been obliged to put to sea short of her proper complement of men. Plump upon Billy at first sight in the gangway the boarding officer Lieutenant Ratcliffe pounced, even before the merchantman's crew was formally mustered on the quarter-deck[15] for his deliberate inspection. And him only he elected. For whether it was because the other men when ranged before him showed to ill advantage after Billy, or whether he had some scruples in view of the merchantman being rather short-handed, however it might be, the officer contented himself with his first spontaneous choice. To the surprise of the ship's company, though much to the Lieutenant's satisfaction Billy made no demur. But, indeed, any demur would have been as idle as the protest of a goldfinch popped into a cage.

Noting this uncomplaining acquiescence, all but cheerful one might say, the shipmates turned a surprised glance of silent reproach at the sailor. The shipmaster was one of those worthy mortals found in every vocation even the humbler ones—the sort of person whom everybody agrees in calling "a respectable man." And—nor so strange to report as it may appear to be—though a ploughman of the troubled waters, life-long contending with the intractable elements, there was nothing this honest soul at heart loved better than simple peace and quiet. For the rest, he was fifty or thereabouts, a little inclined to corpulence, a prepossessing face unwhiskered, and of an agreeable color—a rather full face, humanely intelligent in expression. On a fair day with a fair wind and all going well, a certain musical chime in his voice seemed to be the veritable unobstructed outcome of the innermost man. He had much prudence, much conscientiousness, and there were occasions when these virtues were the cause of overmuch disquietude in him. On a passage, so long as his craft was in any proximity to land, no sleep for Captain Graveling. He took to heart those serious responsibilities not so heavily borne by some shipmasters.

12. eyes accustomed to looking at the vaulted heavens above.
13. junior to a maintopman like Jack Chase.
14. British naval commanders were then permitted by law to complete the complement of their crews by "impressing" (forcing into service aboard their own ships) foreign seamen. The Narrow Seas: the English Channel and the waters between England and Ireland. A *seventy-four* ship: a third-rate ship of the line, equivalent to a light cruiser today; the rating referred only to the number of guns.
15. the ceremonial part of the ship, near the stern.

Now while Billy Budd was down in the forecastle getting his kit together, the *Indomitable*'s lieutenant, burly and bluff, nowise disconcerted by Captain Graveling's omitting to proffer the customary hospitalities on an occassion so unwelcome to him, an omission simply caused by preoccupation of thought, unceremoniously invited himself into the cabin, and also to a flask from the spirit-locker, a receptacle which his experienced eye instantly discovered. In fact he was one of those sea-dogs in whom all the hardship and peril of naval life in the great prolonged wars of his time never impaired the natural instinct for sensuous enjoyment. His duty he always faithfully did; but duty is sometimes a dry obligation, and he was for irrigating its aridity, whensoever possible, with a fertilizing decoction of strong waters. For the cabin's proprietor there was nothing left but to play the part of the enforced host with whatever grace and alacrity were practicable. As necessary adjuncts to the flask, he silently placed tumbler and water-jug before the irrepressible guest. But excusing himself from partaking just then, [he] dismally watched the unembarrassed office deliberately diluting his grog a little, then tossing it off in three swallows, pushing the empty tumbler away, yet not so far as to be beyond easy reach, at the same [time] settling himself in his seat and smacking his lips with high satisfaction, looking straight at the host.

These proceedings over, the Master broke the silence; and there lurked a rueful reproach in the tone of his voice; "Lieutenant, you are going to take my best man from me, the jewel of 'em."

"Yes, I know" rejoined the other, immediately drawing back the tumbler preliminary to a replenishing; "Yes, I know. Sorry."

"Beg pardon, but you don't understand, Lieutenant. See here now. Before I shipped that young fellow, my forecastle[16] was a rat-pit of quarrels. It was black times, I tell you, aboard the 'Rights' here.[17] I was worried to that degree my pipe had no comfort for me. But Billy came; and it was like a Catholic priest striking peace in an Irish shindy.[18] Not that he preached to them or said or did anything in particular; but a virtue went out of him, sugaring the sour ones. They took to him like hornets to treacle; all but the buffer of the gang, the big shaggy chap with the fire-red whiskers. He indeed out of envy, perhaps, of the newcomer, and thinking such a 'sweet and pleasant fellow,' as he mockingly designated him to the others, could hardly have the spirit of a game-cock, must needs bestir himself in trying to get up an ugly row with him. Billy forebore with him and reasoned with him in a pleasant way—he is something like myself, lieutenant, to whom aught like a quarrel is hateful—but nothing

16. the forepart, or foc-sle, of a ship, where ordinary seamen lived.

17. Named for Thomas Paine's *The Rights of Man* (1791), a defense of the French Revolution. Melville may have chosen the name to underscore the political theme of the tale.

18. originally a spree, here associated with a row or a fight.

served. So, in the second dog-watch[19] one day the Red Whiskers in presence of the others, under pretence of showing Billy just whence a sirloin steak was cut—for the fellow had once been a butcher—insultingly gave him a dig under the ribs. Quick as lightning Billy let fly his arm. I dare say he never meant to do quite as much as he did, but anyhow he gave the burly fool a terrible drubbing. It took about half a minute, I should think. And, lord bless you, the lubber was astonished at the celerity. And will you believe it, Lieutenant, the Red Whiskers now really loves Billy—loves him, or is the biggest hypocrite that ever I heard of. But they all love him. Some of 'em do his washing, darn his old trousers for him; the carpenter is at odd times making a pretty little chest of drawers for him. Anybody will do anything for Billy Budd; and it's the happy family here. But now, Lieutenant, if that young fellow goes—I know how it will be aboard the '*Rights*.' Not again very soon shall I, coming up from dinner, lean over the capstan smoking a quiet pipe—no, not very soon again, I think. Ay, Lieutenant, you are going to take away the jewel of 'em; you are going to take away my peacemaker!" And with that the good soul had really some ado in checking a rising sob.

"Well," said the officer who had listened with amused interest to all this, and now waxing merry with his tipple; "Well, blessed are the peacemakers especially the fighting peacemakers! And such are the seventy-four beauties some of which you see poking their noses out of the port-holes of yonder war-ship lying-to for me" pointing thro' the cabin window at the *Indomitable*. "But courage! don't look so downhearted, man. Why, I pledge you in advance the royal approbation. Rest assured that His Majesty will be delighted to know that in a time when his hard tack[20] is not sought for by sailors with such avidity as should be; a time also when some shipmasters privily resent the borrowing from them a tar or two for the service; His Majesty, I say, will be delighted to learn that *one* shipmaster at least cheerfully surrenders to the King, the flower of his flock, a sailor who with equal loyalty makes no dissent.—But where's my beauty? Ah," looking through the cabin's open door "Here he comes; and by Jove—lugging along his chest—Apollo with his portmanteau!—My man," stepping out to him, "you can't take that big box aboard a warship. The boxes there are mostly shot-boxes. Put your duds in a bag, lad. Boot and saddle for the cavalryman, bag and hammock for the man-of-war's man."

The transfer from chest to bag was made. And, after seeing his man into the cutter and then following him down, the lieutenant pushed off from the *Rights-of-Man*. That was the merchant-ship's

19. At sea the day is divided into six four-hour watches. The 4 to 8 p.m. watch is further divided into two short or "dogged" watches of two hours each in order to rotate the time of day that any given crew member stands watch.
20. literally, a biscuit; often, all shipboard fare.

name; tho' by her master and crew abbreviated in sailor fashion into the *Rights*. The hard-headed Dundee[21] owner was a staunch admirer of Thomas Paine whose book in rejoinder to Burke's arraignment of the French Revolution had then been published for some time and had gone everywhere. In christening his vessel after the title of Paine's volume the man of Dundee was something like his contemporary shipowner, Stephen Girard[22] of Philadelphia, whose sympathies, alike with his native land and its liberal philosophers, he evinced by naming his ships after Voltaire, Diderot, and so forth.

But now, when the boat swept under the merchant-man's stern, and officer and oarsmen were noting—some bitterly and others with a grin,—the name emblazoned there; just then it was that the new recruit jumped up from the bow where the coxswain[23] had directed him to sit, and waving [his] hat to his silent shipmates sorrowfully looking over at him from the taffrail,[24] bade the lads a genial good-bye. Then, making a salutation as to the ship herself, "And good-bye to you too, old *Rights of Man*."

"Down, Sir!" roared the lieutenant, instantly assuming all the rigor of his rank, though with difficulty repressing a smile.

To be sure, Billy's action was a terrible breach of naval decorum. But in that decorum he had never been instructed; in consideration of which the lieutenant would hardly have been so energetic in reproof but for the concluding farewell to the ship. This he rather took as meant to convey a covert sally on the new recruit's part, a sly slur at impressment in general, and that of himself in especial. And yet, more likely, if satire it was in effect, it was hardly so by intention, for Billy tho' happily endowed with the gayety of high health, youth, and a free heart, was yet by no means of a satirical turn. The will to it and the sinister dexterity were alike wanting. To deal in double meanings and insinuations of any sort was quite foreign to his nature.

As to his enforced enlistment, that he seemed to take pretty much as he was wont to take any vicissitude of weather. Like the animals, though no philosopher, he was, without knowing it, practically a fatalist. And, it may be, that he rather liked his adventurous turn in his affairs, which promised an opening into novel scenes and martial excitements.

Aboard the *Indomitable* our merchant-sailor was forthwith rated as an able-seaman and assigned to the starboard watch of the foretop.[25] He was soon at home in the service, not at all disliked for

21. a port on the Firth of Tay in Scotland.
22. Girard (1750-1831), who emigrated from France when he was twenty-seven, became a wealthy banker and shipowner.
23. a petty-officer, the helmsman of a small boat.
24. at the stern of a ship.

25. The three ascending grades are ordinary, able, and leading seamen. Another grouping is: boys, able-bodied seamen, and ordinary seamen. A ship's crew is divided into port and starboard watches. The foretop watch assigned to Billy suggests his excellence as a seaman; according to Melville, this station was superior to a watch at the waist of

his unpretentious good looks and a sort of genial happy-go-lucky air. No merrier man in his mess; in marked contrast to certain other individuals included like himself among the impressed portion of the ship's company; for these when not actively employed were sometimes, and more particularly in the last dog-watch when the drawing near of twilight induced revery, apt to fall into a saddish mood which in some partook of sullenness. But they were not so young as our foretopman, and no few of them must have known a hearth of some sort, others may have had wives and children left, too probably, in uncertain circumstances, and hardly any but must have had acknowledged kith and kin, while for Billy, as will shortly be seen, his entire family was practically invested in himself.

2

Though our new-made foretopman was well received in the top and on the gun-decks, hardly here was he that cynosure he had previously been among those minor ship's companies of the merchant marine, with which companies only had he hitherto consorted

He was young; and despite his all but fully developed frame in aspect looked even younger than he really was, owing to a lingering adolescent expression in the as yet smooth face all but feminine in purity of natural complexion but where, thanks to his seagoing, the lily was quite suppressed and the rose had some ado visibly to flush through the tan.

To one essentially such a novice in the complexities of factitious life, the abrupt transition from his former and simpler sphere to the ampler and more knowing world of a great warship; this might well have abashed him had there been any conceit or vanity in his composition. Among her miscellaneous multitude, the *Indomitable* mustered several individuals who however inferior in grade were of no common natural stamp, sailors more signally susceptive of that air which continuous martial discipline and repeated presence in battle can in some degree impart even to the average man. As the *handsome sailor* Billy Budd's position aboard the seventy-four was something analogous to that of a rustic beauty transplanted from the provinces and brought into competition with the highborn dames of the court. But this change of circumstances he scarce noted. As little did he observe that something about him provoked an ambiguous smile in one or two harder faces among the blue-jackets. Nor less unaware was he of the peculiar favorable effect his person and demeanor had upon the more intelligent gentlemen of the quarter-deck.[26] Nor could this well have been otherwise. Cast in a mould peculiar to the finest physical examples of those Englishmen in whom the Saxon strain would seem not at all to partake of any Norman or other admixture, he showed in face that humane look

a ship or the afterguard, both of which   26. the officers.
entailed deck duties.

of reposeful good nature which the Greek sculptor in some instances
gave to his heroic strong man, Hercules. But this again was subtly
modified by another and pervasive quality. The ear, small and
shapely, the arch of the foot, the curve in mouth and nostril, even
the indurated hand dyed to the orange-tawny of the toucan's bill,[27]
a hand telling alike of the halyards[28] and tar-bucket; but, above all,
something in the mobile expression, and every chance attitude and
movement, something suggestive of a mother eminently favored by
Love and the Graces; all this strangely indicated a lineage in direct
contradiction to his lot. The mysteriousness here, became less mysterious through a matter-of-fact elicited when Billy at the capstan
was being formally mustered into the service. Asked by the officer,
a small brisk little gentleman as it chanced among other questions,
his place of birth, he replied, "Please, Sir, I don't know."

"Don't know where you were born?—Who was your father?"

"God knows, Sir."

Struck by the straightforward simplicity of these replies, the officer
next asked "Do you know anything about your beginning?"

"No, Sir. But I have heard that I was found in a pretty silk-lined
basket hanging one morning from the knocker of a good man's door
in Bristol[.]"[29]

"*Found* say you? Well," throwing back his head and looking up
and down the new recruit; "Well[,] it turns out to have been a pretty
good find. Hope they'll find some more like you, my man; the fleet
sadly needs them."

Yes, Billy Budd was a foundling, a presumable bye-blow,[30] and,
evidently, no ignoble one. Noble descent was as evident in him as in
a blood horse.

For the rest, with little or no sharpness of faculty or any trace of
the wisdom of the serpent, nor yet quite a dove,[31] he possessed that
kind and degree of intelligence going along with the unconventional
rectitude of a sound human creature, one to whom not yet has been
proffered the questionable apple of knowledge. He was illiterate; he
could not read, but he could sing, and like the illiterate nightingale
was sometimes the composer of his own song.

Of self-consciousness he seemed to have little or none, or about
as much as we may reasonably impute to a dog of Saint Bernard's
breed.

Habitually living with the elements and knowing little more of the
land than as a beach, or, rather, that portion of the terraqueous globe

---

27. *toucans:* birds, noted for their
large bill and striking coloration, inhabiting the tropical regions of South
and Central America.
28. ropes used to raise and lower or
to "haul the yards," the spars from
which the square sails are suspended.

29. a major English seaport.
30. Usually "by-blow," an illegitimate child.
31. *Cf.* Matthew 10:16: "Behold, I
send you forth as sheep in the midst of
wolves: be ye therefore as wise as serpents, and harmless as doves."

providentially set apart for dance-houses doxies and tapsters, in short what sailors call a "fiddlers' green,"[32] his simple nature remained unsophisticated by those moral obliquities which are not in every case incompatible with that manufacturable thing known as respectability. But are sailors, frequenters of "fiddlers'-greens," without vices? No; but less often than with landsmen do their vices, so called, partake of crookedness of heart, seeming less to proceed from viciousness than exuberance of vitality after long constraint; frank manifestations in accordance with natural law. By his original constitution aided by the cooperating influences of his lot, Billy in many respects was little more than a sort of upright barbarian, much such perhaps as Adam presumably might have been ere the urbane Serpent wriggled himself into his company.

And here be it submitted that apparently going to corroborate the doctrine of man's fall, a doctrine now popularly ignored, it is observable that where certain virtues pristine and unadulterate peculiarly characterize anybody in the external uniform of civilization, they will upon scrutiny seem not to be derived from custom or convention, but rather to be out of keeping with these, as if indeed exceptionally transmitted from a period prior to Cain's city[33] and citified man. The character marked by such qualities has to an unvitiated taste an untampered-with flavor like that of berries, while the man thoroughly civilized even in a fair specimen of the breed has to the same moral palate a questionable smack as of a compounded wine. To any stray inheritor of these primitive qualities found, like Caspar Hauser,[34] wandering dazed in any Christian capital of our time the good-natured poet's famous invocation, near two thousand years ago, of the good rustic out of his latitude in the Rome of the Cesars, still appropriately holds:—

"Honest and poor, faithful in word and thought
What has thee, Fabian, to the city brought."[35]

Though our Handsome Sailor had as much of masculine beauty as one can expect anywhere to see; nevertheless, like the beautiful woman in one of Hawthorne's minor tales,[36] there was just one thing amiss in him. No visible blemish indeed, as with the lady; no, but an occasional liability to a vocal defect. Though in the hour of elemental uproar or peril, he was everything that a sailor should be, yet under sudden provocation of strong heart-feeling his voice otherwise singularly musical, as if expressive of the harmony within, was apt to

32. *doxies:* prostitutes. *fiddler's green:* a sailor's utopia.
33. *i.e.,* in the time of the Garden of Eden. Cain "builded a city" in *Genesis* 4:16-17.
34. a German foundling (1817-1833) who claimed to have been brought up in a primitive wildness. In his autobiography (1828), he described his childhood as a prisoner.
35. Martial, *Epigrams,* I. iv. 1-2; Cowley's translation in the Bohn edition.
36. *The Birthmark.*

develop an organic hesitancy, in fact more or less of a stutter or even worse. In this particular Billy was a striking instance that the arch interferer, the envious marplot of Eden[37] still has more or less to do with every human consignment to this planet of earth. In every case, one way or another he is sure to slip in his little card, as much as to remind us—I too have a hand here.

The avowal of such an imperfection in the Handsome Sailor should be evidence not alone that he is not presented as a conventional hero, but also that the story in which he is the main figure is no romance.

3

At the time of Billy Budd's arbitrary enlistment into the *Indomitable* that ship was on her way to join the Mediterranean fleet. No long time elasped before the junction was effected. As one of that fleet the seventy-four participated in its movements, tho' at times on account of her superior sailing qualities, in the absence of frigates,[38] despatched on separate duty as a scout and at times on less temporary service. But with all this the story has little concernment, restricted as it is to the inner life of one particular ship and the career of an individual sailor.

It was the summer of 1797. In the April of that year had occurred the commotion at Spithead followed in May by a second and yet more serious outbreak in the fleet at the Nore. The latter is known, and without exaggeration in the epithet, as the Great Mutiny. It was indeed a demonstration more menacing to England than the contemporary manifestoes and conquering and proselyting armies of the French Directory.[39]

To the British Empire the Nore Mutiny was what a strike in the fire-brigade would be to London threatened by general arson. In a crisis when the kingdom might well have anticipated the famous signal that some years later published along the naval line of battle what it was that upon occasion England expected of Englishmen,[40] *that* was the time when at the mast-heads of the three-deckers and seventy-fours moored in her own roadstead—a fleet, the right arm of a Power then all but the sole free conservative one of the Old World, the blue-jackets, to be numbered by thousands[,] ran up with huzzas the British colors with the union and cross wiped out;[41] by that cancellation transmuting the flag of founded law and freedom defined, into the enemy's red meteor of unbridled and unbounded

37. *marplot:* one who destroys or defeats a plot or design; here, Satan.
38. ships mounting from 28 to 60 guns chiefly on the main deck, too small for line of battle.
39. the five directors who governed France from 1795 to 1799.
40. A reference to Lord Nelson's signal before the battle at Trafalgar (October 21, 1805): "England expects every man to do his duty!"
41. the British Union Jack, with the crosses of St. Andrew, St. George, and St. Patrick (the patron saints of Scotland, England, and Ireland).

revolt. Reasonable discontent growing out of practical grievances in the fleet had been ignited into irrational combustion as by live cinders blown across the Channel from France in flames.

The event converted into irony for a time those spirited strains of Dibdin[42]—as a song-writer no mean auxiliary to the English Government at the European conjuncture—strains celebrating, among other things, the patriotic devotion of the British tar:

> *"And as for my life, 'tis the Kings!"*

Such an episode in the Island's grand naval story her naval historians naturally abridge; one of them (G.P.R. James) candidly acknowledging that fain would he pass it over did not "impartiality forbid fastidiousness." And yet his mention is less a narration than a reference, having to do hardly at all with details. Nor are these readily to be found in the libraries. Like some other events in every age befalling states everywhere including America the Great Mutiny was of such character that national pride along with views of policy would fain shade it off into the historical background. Such events can not be ignored, but there is a considerate way of historically treating them. If a well-constituted individual refrains from blazoning aught amiss or calamitous in his family; a nation in the like circumstance may without reproach be equally discreet.

Though after parleyings between Government and the ringleaders, and concessions by the former as to some glaring abuses, the first uprising—that at Spithead—with difficulty was put down, or matters for the time pacified; yet at the Nore the unforeseen renewal of insurrection on a yet larger scale, and emphasized in the conferences that ensued by demands deemed by the authorities not only inadmissible but aggressively insolent, indicated—if the Red Flag did not sufficiently do so[—]what was the spirit animating the men. Final suppression, however, there was; but only made possible perhaps by the unswerving loyalty of the marine corps a[nd] voluntary resumption of loyalty among influential sections of the crews.

To some extent the Nore Mutiny may be regarded as analogous to the distempering irruption of contagious fever in a frame constitutionally sound, and which anon throws it off.

At all events, of these thousands of mutineers were some of the tars who not so very long afterwards—whether wholly prompted thereto by patriotism, or pugnacious instinct, or by both,—helped to win a coronet for Nelson at the Nile, and the naval crown of crowns for him at Trafalgar.[43] To the mutineers those battles and especially

42. Charles Dibdin (1745-1814), English dramatist, chiefly remembered for his sea chanteys.

43. A reference to Nelson's victory over the French (at Aboukir) in 1798, for which he was made a baronet; his victory at Trafalgar (1805) is considered one of the greatest in naval history.

Trafalgar were a plenary absolution and a grand one: For all that goes to make up scenic naval display, heroic magnificence in arms, those battles especially Trafalgar stand unmatched in human annals.

4

Concerning "The greatest sailor since the world began."

Tennyson?[44]

In this matter of writing, resolve as one may to keep to the main road, some by-paths have an enticement not readily to be withstood. I am going to err into such a by-path. If the reader will keep me company I shall be glad. At the least we can promise ourselves that pleasure which is wickedly said to be in sinning, for a literary sin the divergence will be.

Very likely it is no new remark that the inventions of our time have at last brought about a change in sea-warfare in degree corresponding to the revolution in all warfare effected by the original introduction from China into Europe of gunpowder. The first European fire-arm, a clumsy contrivance, was, as is well known, scouted by no few of the knights as a base implement, good enough peradventure for weavers too craven to stand up crossing steel with steel in frank fight. But as ashore knightly valor tho' shorn of its blazonry did not cease with the knights, neither on the seas though nowadays in encounters there a certain kind of displayed gallantry be fallen out of date as hardly applicable under changed circumstances, did the nobler qualities of such naval magnates as Don John of Austria, Doria, Van Tromp, Jean Bart, the long line of British Admirals and the American Decaturs of 1812 become obsolete with their wooden walls.[45]

Nevertheless, to anybody who can hold the Present at its worth without being inappreciative of the Past, it may be forgiven, if to such an one the solitary old hulk at Portsmouth, Nelson's *Victory*,[46] seems to float there, not alone as the decaying monument of a fame incorruptible, but also as a poetic reproach, softened by its picturesqueness, to the *Monitors*[47] and yet mightier hulls of the Euro-

44. The question mark inserted by Melville suggests that he intended to check it before publication. The quotation is line 7 in Tennyson's "Ode on the Death of the Duke of Wellington" (1852); it should read, "The greatest sailor since our world began."

45. Don Juan of Austria (1547-1578) commanded the fleet of the Holy League against the Turks at Lepanto in 1571, the last major sea battle where oared-ships predominated; Andrea Doria (1468-1560) liberated Genoa from the Turks; Maarten Van Tromp (1596-1653) was a Dutch admiral who fought successfully against the English under Charles II; Jean Bart (1651?-1702) was a French captain who battled the Dutch; Stephen Decatur (1779-1820) is best remembered for his victories over the Barbary Coast pirates at Tripoli and his over the British in the War of 1812. *wooden walls:* Iron-clad ships (see note 47) made all wooden ships obsolete.

46. Nelson's flagship at Trafalgar, still moored at Portsmouth.

47. John Ericsson's ironclad, launched in 1862 to fight the Confederate *Merrimac;* that battle effectively ended the era of wooden and sail-propelled battleships.

pean iron-clads. And this not altogether because such craft are unsightly, unavoidably lacking the symmetry and grand lines of the
old battle-ships, but equally for other reasons.

There are some, perhaps, who while not altogether inaccessible
to that poetic reproach just alluded to, may yet on behalf of the new
order, be disposed to parry it; and this to the extent of iconoclasm, if
need be. For example, prompted by the sight of the star inserted in
the *Victory's* quarter-deck designating the spot where the Great
Sailor fell, these martial utilitarians may suggest considerations implying that Nelson's ornate publication of his person in battle was
not only unnecessary, but not military, nay, savored of foolhardiness
and vanity. They may add, too, that at Trafalgar it was in effect
nothing less than a challenge to death; and death came; and that but
for his bravado the victorious Admiral might possibly have survived
the battle, and so, instead of having his sagacious dying injunctions
overruled by his immediate successor in command he himself when
the contest was decided might have brought his shattered fleet to
anchor, a proceeding which might have averted the deplorable loss
of life by shipwreck in the elemental tempest that followed the
martial one.

Well, should we set aside the more disputable point whether for
various reasons it was possible to anchor the fleet, then plausibly
enough the Benthamites[48] of war may urge the above.

But the *might-have-been* is but boggy ground to build on. And,
certainly, in foresight as to the larger issue of an encounter, and
anxious preparations for it—buoying the deadly way and mapping it
out, as at Copenhagen[49]—few commanders have been so painstak-
ingly circumspect as this same reckless declarer of his person in
fight.

Personal prudence even when dictated by quite other than selfish
considerations surely is no special virtue in a military man; while an
excessive love of glory, impassioning a less burning impulse, the
honest sense of duty, is the first. If the name *Wellington* is not so
much of a trumpet to the blood as the simpler name *Nelson*, the
reason for this may perhaps be inferred from the above. Alfred[50] in
his funeral ode on the victor of Waterloo ventures not to call him
the greatest soldier of all time, tho' in the same ode he invokes
Nelson as "the greatest sailor since the world began."

At Trafalgar Nelson on the brink of opening the fight sat down
and wrote his last brief will and testament. If under the presentiment of the most magnificent of all victories to be crowned by his

48. Utilitarian thinkers and followers
of Jeremy Bentham (1748-1832), famous for his theory that "the greatest
happiness of the greatest number is the
foundation of morals and legislation."

Melville uses the word derogatively.
49. another of Nelson's victories, in
(1801).
50. Tennyson; *cf.* note 44.

own glorious death, a sort of priestly motive led him to dress his person in the jewelled vouchers of his own shining deeds; if thus to have adorned himself for the altar and the sacrifice were indeed vainglory, then affection and fustian is each more heroic line in the great epics and dramas, since in such lines the poet but embodies in verse those exaltations of sentiment that a nature like Nelson, the opportunity being given, vitalizes into acts.

5

Yes, the outbreak at the Nore was put down. But not every grievance was redressed. If the contractors, for example, were no longer permitted to ply some practices peculiar to their tribe everywhere, such as providing shoddy cloth, rations not sound, or false in the measure, not the less impressment, for one thing, went on. By custom sanctioned for centuries, and judicially maintained by a Lord Chancellor as late as Mansfield,[51] that mode of manning the fleet, a mode now fallen into a sort of abeyance but never formally renounced, it was not practicable to give up in those years. Its abrogation would have crippled the indispensable fleet, one wholly under canvas, no steam-power, its innumerable sails and thousands of cannon, everything in short, worked by muscle alone; a fleet the more insatiate in demand for men, because then multiplying its ship[s] of all grades against contingencies present and to come of the convulsed Continent.

Discontent foreran the Two Mutinies, and more or less it lurkingly survived them. Hence it was not unreasonable to apprehend some return of trouble sporadic or general. One instance of such apprehensions: In the same year with this story, Nelson, then Vice Admiral Sir Horatio, being with the fleet off the Spanish coast, was directed by the Admiral in command to shift his pennant from the *Captain* to the *Theseus*; and for this reason: that the latter ship having newly arrived on the station from home where it had taken part in the Great Mutiny, danger was apprehended from the temper of the men; and it was thought that an officer like Nelson was the one, not indeed to terrorize the crew into base subjection, but to win them, by force of his mere presence back to an allegiance if not as enthusiatic as his own, yet as true. So it was that for a time on more than one quarter-deck anxiety did exist. At sea precautionary vigilance was strained against relapse. At short notice an engagement might come on. When it did, the lieutenants assigned to batteries felt it incumbent on them, in some instances, to stand with drawn swords behind the men working the guns.

51. William Murray, Baron Mansfield (1705-1793), Lord Chief Justice of Great Britain from 1756 and later a cabinet minister (1773-1788).

6

But on board the seventy-four in which Billy now swung his hammock, very little in the manner of the men and nothing obvious in the demeanor of the officers would have suggested to an ordinary observer that the Great Mutiny was a recent event. In their general bearing and conduct the commissioned officers of a war-ship naturally take their tone from the commander, that is if he have that ascendancy of character that ought to be his.

Captain the Honorable Edward Fairfax Vere, to give his full title, was a bachelor of forty or thereabouts, a sailor of distinction even in a time prolific of renowned seamen. Though allied to the higher nobility his advancement had not been altogether owing to influences connected with that circumstance. He had seen much service, been in various engagements, always acquitting himself as an officer mindful of the welfare of his men, but never tolerating an infraction of discipline; thoroughly versed in the science of his profession, and intrepid to the verge of temerity, though never injudiciously so. For his gallantry in the West Indian waters as flag-lieutenant under Rodney in that Admiral's crowning victory over De Grasse,[52] he was made a post-captain.

Ashore in the garb of a civilian scarce anyone would have taken him for a sailor, more especially that he never garnished unprofessional talk with nautical terms, and grave in his bearing, evinced little appreciation of mere humor. It was not out of keeping with these traits that on a passage when nothing demanded his paramount action, he was the most undemonstrative of men. Any landsmen observing this gentleman not conspicuous by his stature and wearing no pronounced insignia, emerging from his cabin to the open deck, and noting the silent deference of the officers retiring to leeward,[53] might have taken him for the King's guest, a civilian aboard the King's-ship[,] some highly honorable discreet envoy on his way to an important post. But in fact this unobtrusiveness of demeanor may have proceeded from a certain unaffected modesty of manhood sometimes accompanying a resolute nature, a modesty evinced at all times not calling for pronounced action, and which shown in any rank of life suggests a virtue aristocratic in kind.

As with some others engaged in various departments of the world's more heroic activities, Captain Vere though practical enough upon occasion would at times betray a certain dreaminess of mood. Standing alone on the weather-side of the quarter deck, one hand holding by the rigging he would absently gaze off at the blank sea. At the

52. The British admiral George Brydges, Baron Rodney (1719-1792) defeated the French Admiral De Grasse off Dominica, in the Leeward Islands, in 1782.

53. the side of the ship away from the direction of the wind, as opposed to "windward."

presentation to him then of some minor matter interrupting the current of his thoughts he would show more or less irascibility; but instantly he would control it.

In the navy he was popularly known by the appellation—Starry Vere. How such a designation happened to fall upon one who whatever his sturdy qualities was without any brilliant ones was in this wise: A favorite kinsman, Lord Denton, a free-hearted fellow, had been the first to meet and congratulate him upon his return to England from his West Indian cruise; and but the day previous turning over a copy of Andrew Marvell's[54] poems had lighted, not for the first time however, upon the lines entitled *Appleton House*, the name of one of the seats of their common ancestor, a hero in the German wars of the seventeenth century, in which poem occur the lines,

> "This 'tis to have been from the first
> In a domestic heaven nursed,
> Under the discipline severe
> Of Fairfax and the starry Vere[.]"

And so, upon embracing his cousin fresh from Rodney's great victory wherein he had played so gallant a part, brimming over with just family pride in the sailor of their house, he exuberantly exclaimed, "Give ye joy, Ed; give ye joy, my starry Vere!" This got currency, and the novel prefix serving in familiar parlance readily to distinguish the *Indomitable*'s Captain from another Vere his senior, a distant relative an officer of like rank in the navy, it remained permanently attached to the surname.

7

In view of the part that the commander of the *Indomitable* plays in scenes shortly to follow, it may be well to fill out that sketch of him outlined in the previous chapter.

Aside from his qualities as a sea-officer Captain Vere was an exceptional character. Unlike no few of England's renowned sailors, long and arduous service with signal devotion to it, had not resulted in absorbing and *salting* the entire man. He had a marked leaning toward everything intellectual. He loved books, never going to sea without a newly replenished library, compact but of the best. The isolated leisure, in some cases so wearisome, falling at intervals to commanders even during a war-cruise, never was tedious to Captain Vere. With nothing of that literary taste which less heeds the thing conveyed than the vehicle, his bias was towards those books to which every serious mind of superior order occupying any active post of authority in the world, naturally inclines: books treating of actual

54. English lyric poet (1621-1678).

men and events no matter of what era—history, biography and unconventional writers, who, free from cant and convention, like Montaigne, honestly and in the spirit of common sense philosophize upon realities.

In this line of reading he found confirmation of his own more reasoned thoughts—confirmation which he had vainly sought in social converse, so that as touching most fundamental topics, there had got to be established in him some positive convictions, which he forefelt would abide in him essentially unmodified so long as his intelligent part remained unimpaired. In view of the troubled period in which his lot was cast this was well for him. His settled convictions were as a dyke against those invading waters of novel opinion social political and otherwise, which carried away as in a torrent no few minds in those days, minds by nature not inferior to his own. While other members of that aristocracy to which by birth he belonged were incensed at the innovators mainly because their theories were inimical to the privileged classes, not alone Captain Vere disinterestedly opposed them because they seemed to him incapable of embodiment in lasting institutions, but at war with the peace of the world and the true welfare of mankind.

With minds less stored than his and less earnest, some officers of his rank, with whom at times he would necessarily consort, found him lacking in the companionable quality, a dry and bookish gentleman as they deemed. Upon any chance withdrawal from their company one would be apt to say to another, something like this: "Vere is a noble fellow, Starry Vere. Spite the gazettes,[55] Sir Horatio["] meaning him with the Lord title[56] ["]is at bottom scarce a better seaman or fighter. But between you and me now don't you think there is a queer streak of the pedantic running thro' him? Yes, like the King's yarn in a coil of navy-rope?["][57]

Some apparent ground there was for this sort of confidential criticism; since not only did the Captain's discourse never fall into the jocosely familiar, but in illustrating of any point touching the stirring personages and events of the time he would be as apt to cite some historic character or incident of antiquity as that he would cite from the moderns. He seemed unmindful of the circumstance that to his bluff company such remote allusions however pertinent they might really be were altogether alien to men whose reading was mainly confined to the journals. But considerateness in such matters is not easy to natures constituted like Captain Vere's. Their honesty prescribes to them directness, sometimes far-reaching like that of a migratory fowl that in its flight never heeds when it crosses a frontier.

---

55. the official gazettes that printed accounts of naval careers and honors.
56. Lord Nelson.

57. This may be a reference to the thread worked into hempen cable to mark it as belonging to the Royal Navy.

8

The lieutenants and other commissioned gentlemen forming Captain Vere's staff it is not necessary here to particularize, nor needs it to make any mention of any of the warrant-officers.[58] But among the petty-officers was one who having much to do with the story, may as well be forthwith introduced. His portrait I essay, but shall never hit it. This was John Claggart, the Master-at-arms.[59] But that sea-title may to landsmen seem somewhat equivocal. Originally doubtless that petty-officer's function was the instruction of the men in the use of arms, sword or cutlas. But very long ago, owing to the advance in gunnery making hand-to-hand encounters less frequent and giving to nitre and sulphur the preeminence over steel, that function ceased; the master-at-arms of a great war-ship becoming a sort of Chief of Police charged among other matters with the duty of preserving order on the populous lower gun-decks.

Claggart was a man about five and thirty, somewhat spare and tall, yet of no ill figure upon the whole. His hand was too small and shapely to have been accustomed to hard toil. The face was a notable one; the features all except the chin cleanly cut as those on a Greek medallion; yet the chin, beardless as Tecumseh's,[60] had something of strange protuberant heaviness in its make that recalled the prints of the Rev. Dr. Titus Oates, the historic deponent with the clerical drawl in the time of Charles II and the fraud of the alleged Popish Plot.[61] It served Claggart in his office that his eye could cast a tutoring glance. His brow was of the sort phrenologically [62] associated with more than average intellect; silken jet curls partly clustering over it, making a foil to the pallor below, a pallor tinged with a faint shade of amber akin to the hue of time-tinted marbles of old. This complexion, singularly contrasting with the red or deeply bronzed visages of the sailors, and in part the result of his official seclusion from the sunlight, tho it was not exactly displeasing, nevertheless seemed to hint of something defective or abnormal in the constitution and blood. But his general aspect and manner were so suggestive of an education and career incongruous with his naval function that when not actively engaged in it he looked like a man of high quality, social and moral, who for reasons of his own was keeping incog.[63] Nothing was known of his former life. It might be that he was an

58. officers midway in rank between commissioned and noncommissioned officers. Originally they held their rank by a warrant as distinct from a commission.

59. the principal police officer and small-arms instructor.

60. the Shawnee chief (1768?-1813) who attempted to unite the Indian tribes against the United States.

61. In 1678 Oates (1649-1705) in-vented a plot which accused Jesuits of planning to assassinate Charles II, burn London, and slaughter English Protestants. As a result many English Roman Catholics were persecuted and killed.

62. Phrenology is the study of the shape of the skull as indicative of mental faculties.

63. *incognito:* unrecognized.

Englishman; and yet there lurked a bit of accent in his speech suggesting that possibly he was not such by birth, but through naturalization in early childhood. Among certain grizzled sea-gossips of the gun-decks and forecastle went a rumor perdue that the master-at-arms was a *chevalier* who had volunteered into the King's navy by way of compounding for some mysterious swindle whereof he had been arraigned at the King's Bench.[64] The fact that nobody could substantiate this report was, of course, nothing against its secret currency. Such a rumor once started on the gun-decks in reference to almost anyone below the rank of a commissioned officer would, during the period assigned to this narrative, have seemed not altogether wanting in credibility to the tarry old wiseacres of a man-of-war crew. And indeed a man of Claggart's accomplishments, without prior nautical experience entering the navy at mature life, as he did, and necessarily allotted at the start to the lowest grade in it; a man too who never made allusion to his previous life ashore; these were circumstances which in the dearth of exact knowlege as to his true antecedents opened to the invidious a vague field for unfavorable surmise.

But the sailors' dog-watch gossip concerning him derived a vague plausibility from the fact that now for some period the British Navy could so little afford to be squeamish in the matter of keeping up the muster-rolls, that not only were press-gangs notoriously abroad both afloat and ashore, but there was little or no secret about another matter, namely that the London police were at liberty to capture any able-bodied suspect, any questionable fellow at large and summarily ship him to the dockyard or fleet. Furthermore, even among voluntary enlistments there were instances where the motive thereto partook neither of patriotic impulse nor yet of a random desire to experience a bit of sea-life and martial adventure. Insolvent debtors of minor grade, together with the promiscuous lame ducks of morality found in the Navy a convenient and secure refuge. Secure, because once enlisted aboard a King's-Ship, they were as much in sanctuary, as the transgressor of the Middle Ages harboring himself under the shadow of the altar. Such sanctioned irregularities, which for obvious reasons the Government would hardly think to parade at the time and which consequently, and as affecting the least influential class of mankind, have all but dropped into oblivion, lend color to something for the truth whereof I do not vouch, and hence have some scruple in stating; something I remember having seen in print though the book I can not recall; but the same thing was personally communicated to me now more than forty years ago by an old pensioner in a cocked hat with whom I had a most interesting talk on the terrace at Greenwich, a Baltimore negro, a Trafalgar

64. formerly the supreme court of common law in Great Britain.

man.[65] It was to this effect: In the case of a warship short of hands whose speedy sailing was imperative, the deficient quota in lack of any other way of making it good, would be eked out by draughts culled direct from the jails. For reasons previously suggested it would not perhaps be easy at the present day directly to prove or disprove the allegation. But allowed as a verity, how significant would it be of England's straits at the time confronted by those wars which like a flight of harpies rose shrieking from the din and dust of the fallen Bastille.[66] That era appears measurably clear to us who look back at it, and but read of it. But to the grandfathers of us graybeards, the more thoughtful of them, the genius of it presented an aspect like that of Camoen's Spirit of the Cape,[67] an eclipsing menace mysterious and prodigious. Not America was exempt from apprehension. At the height of Napoleon's unexampled conquests, there were Americans who had fought at Bunker Hill who looked forward to the possibility that the Atlantic might prove no barrier against the ultimate schemes of this French upstart from the revolutionary chaos who seemed in act of fulfilling judgment prefigured in the Apocalypse.

But the less credence was to be given to the gun-deck talk touching Claggart, seeing that no man holding his office in a man-of-war can ever hope to be popular with the crew. Besides, in derogatory comments upon anyone against whom they have a grudge, or for any reason or no reason mislike, sailors are much like landsmen, they are apt to exaggerate or romance it.

About as much was really known to the *Indomitable's* tars of the master-at-arms' career before entering the service as an astronomer knows about a comet's travels prior to its first observable appearance in the sky. The verdict of the sea quidnuncs[68] has been cited only by way of showing what sort of moral impression the man made upon rude uncultivated natures whose conceptions of human wickedness were necessarily of the narrowest, limited to ideas of vulgar rascality, —a thief among the swinging hammocks during a night-watch, or the man-brokers and land-sharks of the sea-ports.

It was no gossip, however, but fact, that though, as before hinted, Claggart upon his entrance into the navy was, as a novice, assigned to the least honorable section of a man-of-war's crew,[69] embracing the drudgery, he did not long remain there.

The superior capacity he immediately evinced, his constitutional

---

65. a Trafalgar veteran at Greenwich Hospital near London, a home for retired personnel.

66. figuratively the fall of the Bastille (July 14, 1789) signaling the beginning of the Napoleonic wars.

67. The Portuguese poet Luiz Vaz de Camoëns (Camões, 1524-1580), in his epic poem the *Lusiads*, has a monster named Adamastor who attempts to destroy Vasco de Gama and his crew.

68. Latin, "what now"; an inquisitive person, a gossip, a busybody.

69. the waist of the ship on the gun deck, where the duties included attending to the sewage and drainage.

sobriety, ingratiating deference to superiors, together with a peculiar
ferreting genius manifested on a singular occasion, all this capped by
a certain austere patriotism abruptly advanced him to the position of
master-at-arms.

Of this maritime Chief of Police the ship's-corporals, so called,
were the immediate subordinates, and compliant ones; and this, as is
to be noted in some business departments ashore, almost to a degree
inconsistent with entire moral volition. His place put various con-
verging wires of underground influence under the Chief's control,
capable when astutely worked thro his understrappers of operating to
the mysterious discomfort[,] if nothing worse, of any of the sea-
commonalty.

9

Life in the fore-top well agreed with Billy Budd. There, when not
actually engaged on the yards yet higher aloft, the topmen, who
as such had been picked out for youth and activity, constituted an
aerial club lounging at ease against the smaller stun'sails rolled up
into cushions, spinning yarns like the lazy gods, and frequently
amused with what was going on in the busy world of the decks below.
No wonder then that a young fellow of Billy's disposition was well
content in such society. Giving no cause of offence to anybody, he
was always alert at a call. So in the merchant service it had been with
him. But now such a punctiliousness in duty was shown that his topmates would sometimes good-naturedly laugh at him for it. This
heightened alacrity had its cause, namely, the impression made upon
him by the first formal gangway-punishment he had ever witnessed,
which befell the day following his impressment. It had been incurred by a little fellow, young, a novice[,]an after-guardsman absent
from his assigned post when the ship was being put about[70] a der-
eliction resulting in a rather serious hitch to that manœuvre, one
demanding instantaneous promptitude in letting go and making fast.
When Billy saw the culprit's naked back under the scourge gridironed
with red welts, and worse; when he marked the dire expression on the
liberated man's face as with his woolen shirt flung over him by the
executioner he rushed forward from the spot to bury himself in the
crowd, Billy was horrified. He resolved that never through remissness
would he make himself liable to such a visitation or do or omit aught
that might merit even verbal reproof. What then was his surprise and
concern when ultimately he found himself getting into petty trouble
occasionally about such matters as the stowage of his bag or something amiss in his hammock, matters under the police oversight of
the ship's-corporals of the lower decks, and which brought down on

70. The afterguard was responsible
for handling the braces and sheets of
the main and mizzen sails when the
ship was "put about" or headed up into
the wind making a 90-degree turn.

him a vague threat from one of them.

So heedful in all things as he was, how could this be? He could not understand it, and it more than vexed him. When he spoke to his young topmates about it they were either lightly incredulous or found something comical in his unconcealed anxiety. "Is it your bag, Billy?" said one "well, sew yourself up in it, bully boy, and then you'll be sure to know if anybody meddles with it."

Now there was a veteran aboard who because his years began to disqualify him for more active work had been recently assigned duty as main-mast-man in his watch, looking to the gear belayed at the rail roundabout that great spar near the deck. At off-times the fore-topman had picked up some acquaintance with him, and now in his trouble it occurred to him that he might be the sort of person to go to for wise counsel. He was an old Dansker[71] long anglicized in the service, of few words, many wrinkles and some honorable scars. His wizened face, time-tinted and weather-stained to the complexion of an antique parchment, was here and there peppered blue by the chance explosion of a gun-cartridge in action. He was an *Agamemnon*-man; some two years prior to the time of this story having served under Nelson when but Sir Horatio in that ship immortal in naval memory, and which[,] dismantled and in part broken up to her bare ribs[,] is seen a grand skeleton in Haydon's etching.[72] As one of a boarding-party from the *Agamemnon* he had received a cut slantwise along one temple and cheek leaving a long pale scar like a streak of dawn's light falling athwart the dark visage. It was on account of that scar and the affair in which it was known that he had received it, as well as from his blue-peppered complexion that the Dansker went among the *Indomitable*'s crew by the name of "Board-her-in-the-smoke."

Now the first time that his small weazel-eyes happened to light on Billy Budd, a certain grim internal merriment set all his ancient wrinkles into antic play. Was it that his eccentric unsentimental old sapience primitive in its kind saw or thought it saw something which in contrast with the war-ship's environment looked oddly incongruous in the handsome sailor? But after slyly studying him at intervals, the old Merlin's[73] equivocal merriment was modified; for now when the twain would meet, it would start in his face a quizzing sort of look, but it would be but momentary and sometimes replaced by an expression of speculative query as to what might eventually befall a nature like that, dropped into a world not without some man-traps and against whose subtleties simple courage lacking experience

71. Dane.

72. probably Sir Francis Seymour Haden (1818-1910), whose etching of the breaking-up of the *Agamemnon*, one of Lord Nelson's commands, was pub-lished in 1870. Benjamin Robert Haydon (1786-1846), a friend of Keats, was a popular historical painter.

73. King Arthur's court magician.

and address and without any touch of defensive ugliness, is of little avail; and where such innocence as man is capable of does yet in a moral emergency not always sharpen the faculties or enlighten the will.

However it was the Dansker in his ascetic way rather took to Billy. Nor was this only because of a certain philosophic interest in such a character. There was another cause. While the old man's eccentricities, sometimes bordering on the ursine,[74] repelled the juniors, Billy, undeterred thereby, revering him as a salt hero would make advances, never passing the old Agamemnon-man without a salutation marked by that respect which is seldom lost on the aged however crabbed at times or whatever their station in life.

There was a vein of dry humor, or what not, in the mast-man; and whether in freak of patriarchal irony touching Billy's youth and athletic frame, or for some other and more recondite reason, from the first in addressing him he always substituted Baby for Billy. The Dansker in fact being the originator of the name by which the foretopman eventually became known aboard ship.

Well then, in his mysterious little difficulty going in quest of the wrinkled one, Billy found him off duty in a dog-watch ruminating by himself seated on a shot-box of the upper gun-deck now and then surveying with a somewhat cynical regard certain of the more swaggering promenaders there. Billy recounted his trouble, again wondering how it all happened. The salt seer attentively listened, accompanying the foretopman's recital with queer twitchings of his wrinkles and problematical little sparkles of his small ferret eyes. Making an end of his story, the foretopman asked, "And now, Dansker, do tell me what you think of it."

The old man, shoving up the front of his tarpaulin and deliberately rubbing the long slant scar at the point where it entered the thin hair, laconically said, "Baby Budd, *Jemmy Legs*"[75] (meaning the master-at-arms) "is down on you[.]"

"*Jemmy Legs!*" ejaculated Billy his welkin eyes expanding, "what for? Why he calls me *the sweet and pleasant young fellow,* they tell me."

"Does he so?" grinned the grizzled one; then said "Ay[,] Baby Lad[,] a sweet voice has *Jemmy Legs.*"

"No, not always. But to me he has. I seldom pass him but there comes a pleasant word."

"And that's because he's down upon you, Baby Budd."

Such reiteration along with the manner of it, incomprehensible to a novice, disturbed Billy almost as much as the mystery for which he had sought explanation. Something less unpleasingly oracular he

74. bearlike.
75. "Jimmy Legs," a disparaging nickname for the master-at-arms, still used in the American navy.

tried to extract; but the old sea-Chiron[76] thinking perhaps that for the nonce he had sufficiently instructed his young Achilles, pursed his lips, gathered all his wrinkles together and would commit himself to nothing further.

Years, and those experiences which befall certain shrewder men subordinated life-long to the will of superiors, all this had developed in the Dansker the pithy guarded cynicism that was his leading characteristic.

10

The next day an incident served to confirm Billy Budd in his incredulity as to the Dansker's strange summing up of the case submitted. The ship at noon going large before the wind was rolling on her course, and he below at dinner and engaged in some sportful talk with the members of his mess, chanced in a sudden lurch to spill the entire contents of his soup-pan upon the new scrubbed deck. Claggart, the Master-at-arms, official rattan[77] in hand, happened to be passing along the battery in a bay of which the mess was lodged, and the greasy liquid streamed just across his path. Stepping over it, he was proceeding on his way without comment, since the matter was nothing to take notice of under the circumstances, when he happened to observe who it was that had done the spilling. His countenance changed. Pausing, he was about to ejaculate something hasty at the sailor, but checked himself, and pointing down to the streaming soup, playfull tapped him from behind with his rattan, saying in a low musical voice peculiar to him at times "Handsomely done, my lad! And handsome is as handsome did it too!" And with that passed on. Not noted by Bill as not coming within his view was the involuntary smile, or rather grimace, that accompanied Claggart's equivocal words. Aridly it drew down the thin corner of his shapely mouth. But everybody taking his remark as meant for humorous, and at which therefore as coming from a superior they were bound to laugh, "with counterfeited glee"[78] acted accordingly; and Billy tickled, it may be, by the allusion to his being the handsome sailor, merrily joined in; then addressing his messmates exclaimed "There now, who says that Jemmy Legs is down on me!" "And who said he was, Beauty?" demanded one Donald with some surprise. Whereat the foretopman looked a little foolish recalling that it was only one person. Board-her-in-the-smoke who had suggested what to him was the smoky idea that this master-at-arms was in any peculiar way hostile to him. Meantime that functionary resuming his path must have momentarily worn some expression less guarded than that of the bitter

76. Chiron the Centaur (half man and half horse), skilled in healing and the wisest of his species; the teacher of Achilles, Hercules, and Aesculapius.
77. swagger stick, light whip.

78. *Cf.* Oliver Goldsmith, "The Deserted Village," line 201. The reference is to the severe schoolmaster in the poem.

smile, and usurping the face from the heart, some distorting expression perhaps, for a drummer-boy heedlessly frolicking along from the opposite direction and chancing to come into light collision with his person was strangely disconcerted by his aspect. Nor was the impression lessened when the official impulsively giving him a sharp cut with the rattan, vehemently exclaimed "Look where you go!"

11

What was the matter with the master-at-arms? And, be the matter what it might, how could it have direct relation to Billy Budd with whom prior to the affair of the spilled soup he had never come into any special contact official or otherwise? What indeed could the trouble have to do with one so little inclined to give offence as the merchant-ship's *peacemaker*, even him who in Claggart's own phrase was "the sweet and pleasant young fellow? ["] Yes, why should *Jemmy Legs*, to borrow the Dansker's expression, be *down* on the Handsome Sailor? But, at heart and not for nothing, as the late chance encounter may indicate to the discerning, down on him, secretly down on him, he assuredly was.

Now to invent something touching the more private career of Claggart, something involving Billy Budd, of which something the latter should be wholly ignorant, some romantic incident implying that Claggart's knowledge of the young blue-jacket began at some period anterior to catching sight of him on board the seventy-four— all this, not so difficult to do, might avail in a way more or less interesting to account for whatever of enigma may appear to lurk in the case. But in fact there was nothing of the sort. And yet the cause, necessarily to be assumed as the sole one assignable, is in its very realism as much charged with that prime element of Radcliffian romance, *the mysterious,* as any that the ingenuity of the author of the *Mysteries of Udolpho* could devise.[79] For what can more partake of the mysterious than an antipathy spontaneous and profound such as is evoked in certain exceptional mortals by the mere aspect of some other mortal, however harmless he may be? if not called forth by this very harmlessness itself.

Now there can exist no irritating juxtaposition of dissimilar personalities comparable to that which is possible aboard a great war-ship fully manned and at sea. There, every day among all ranks almost every man comes into more or less of contact with almost every other man. Wholly there to avoid even the sight of an aggravating object one must needs give it Jonah's toss[80] or jump overboard himself. Imagine how all this might eventually operate on some peculiar

79. Mrs. Ann Radcliffe (1764-1823) was the author of this immensely popular Gothic novel.

80. Jonah 1:15: "So they took up Jonah, and cast him forth into the sea." A nautical expression, when an unlucky object or person is put overboard.

human creature the direct reverse of a saint?

But for the adequate comprehending of Claggart by a normal nature these hints are insufficient. To pass from a normal nature to him one must cross "the deadly space between." And this is best done by indirection.

Long ago an honest scholar my senior, said to me in reference to one who like himself is now no more, a man so unimpeachably respectable that against him nothing was ever openly said tho' among the few something was whispered, "Yes, X—— is a nut not to be cracked by the tap of a lady's fan. You are aware that I am the adherent of no organized religion much less of any philosophy built into a system. Well, for all that, I think that to try and get into X——, enter his labyrinth and get out again, without a clue derived from some source other than what is known as *knowledge of the world*—that were hardly possible, at least for me."

"Why" said I, "X——however singular a study to some, is yet human, and knowledge of the world assuredly implies the knowledge of human nature, and in most of its varieties."

"Yes, but a superficial knowledge of it, serving ordinary purposes. But for anything deeper, I am not certain whether to know the world and to know human nature be not two distinct branches of knowledge, which while they may coexist in the same heart, yet either may exist with little or nothing of the other. Nay, in an average man of the world, his constant rubbing with it blunts that fine spiritual insight indispensable to the understanding of the essential in certain exceptional characters, whether evil ones or good. In a matter of some importance I have seen a girl wind an old lawyer about her little finger. Nor was it the dotage of senile love. Nothing of the sort. But he knew law better than he knew the girl's heart. Coke and Blackstone[81] hardly shed so much light into obscure spiritual places as the Hebrew prophets. And who were they? Mostly recluses."

At the time my inexperience was such that I did not quite see the drift of all this. It may be that I see it now. And, indeed, if that lexicon which is based on Holy Writ were any longer popular, one might with less difficulty define and denominate certain phenomenal men. As it is, one must turn to some authority not liable to the charge of being tinctured with the Biblical element.

In a list of definitions included in the authentic translation of Plato, a list attributed to him, occurs this: "Natural Depravity: a depravity according to nature." A definition which tho' savoring of Calvinism, by no means involves Calvin's dogmas as to total mankind. Evidently its intent makes it applicable but to individuals.

---

81. Sir Edward Coke (1552-1634) and Sir William Blackstone (1723- 1780), famous British jurists and writers on the law.

Not many are the examples of this depravity which the gallows and jail supply. At any rate for notable instances, since these have no vulgar alloy of the brute in them, but invariably are dominated by intellectuality, one must go elsewhere. Civilization, especially if of the austerer sort, is auspicious to it. It folds itself in the mantle of respectability. It has its certain negative virtues serving as silent aux-iliaries. It never allows wine to get within its guard. It it not going too far to say that it is without vices or small sins. There is a phe-nomenal pride in it that excludes them from anything mercenary or avaricious. In short the depravity here meant partakes nothing of the sordid or sensual. It is serious, but free from acerbity. Though no flatterer of mankind it never speaks ill of it.

But the thing which in eminent instances signalizes so exceptional a nature is this: though the man's even temper and discreet bearing would seem to intimate a mind peculiarly subject to the law of rea-son, not the less in his heart he would seem to riot in complete exemption from that law[,] having apparently little to do with reason further than to employ it as an ambidexter implement for effecting the irrational. That is to say: Toward the accomplishment of an aim which in wantonness of malignity would seem to partake of the in-sane, he will direct a cool judgement sagacious and sound.

These men are true madmen, and of the most dangerous sort, for their lunacy is not continuous but occasional[,] evoked by some spe-cial object; it is probably secretive, which is as much to say it is self-contained, so that when moreover, most active[,] it is to the average mind not distinguishable from sanity, and for the reason above sug-gested that whatever its aims may be, and the aim is never declared —the method and the outward proceeding are always perfectly ra-tional.

Now something such an one was Claggart, in whom was the mania of an evil nature, not engendered by vicious training or corrupting books or licentious living, but born with him and innate, in short "a depravity according to nature."

12
Lawyers, Experts, Clergy: An Episode[82]

By the way, can it be the phenomenon, disowned or at least con-cealed, that in some criminal cases puzzles the courts? For this cause have our juries at times not only to endure the prolonged conten-tions of lawyers with their fees, but also the yet more perplexing strife of the medical experts with theirs?—But why leave it to them? why not subpoena as well the clerical proficients? Their vocation bringing them into peculiar contact with so many human beings, and sometimes in their least guarded hour, in interviews very much more confidential than those of physician and patient; this would

82. In their edition Hayford and Sealts reject this episode.

seem to qualify them to know something about those intricacies involved in the question of moral responsibility; whether in a given case, say, the crime proceeded from mania in the brain or rabies of the heart. As to any differences among themselves these clerical proficients might develop on the stand, these could hardly be greater than the direct contradictions exchanged between the remunerated medical experts.

Dark sayings are these, some will say. But why? Is it because they somewhat savor of Holy Writ in its phrase "mysteries of iniquity"?[83] If they do, such savor was far from being intended for little will it commend these pages to many a reader of to-day.

The point of the present story turning on the hidden nature of the master-at-arms has necessitated this chapter. With an added hint or two in connection with the incident at the mess, the resumed narrative must be left to vindicate, as it may, its own credibility.

13

Pale ire, envy and despair[84]

That Claggart's figure was not amiss, and his face, save the chin, well moulded, has already been said. Of these favorable points he seemed not insensible, for he was not only neat but careful in his dress. But the form of Billy Budd was heroic; and if his face was without the intellectual look of the pallid Claggart's, not the less was it lit, like his, from within, though from a different source. The bonfire in his heart made luminous the rose-tan in his cheek.

In view of the marked contrast between the persons of the twain, it is more than probable that when the master-at-arms in the scene last given applied to the sailor the proverb *Handsome is as handsome does*; he there let escape an ironic inkling, not caught by the young sailors who heard it, as to what it was that had first moved him against Billy, namely, his significant personal beauty.

Now envy and antipathy passions irreconcilable in reason, nevertheless in fact may spring conjoined like Chang and Eng[85] in one birth. Is Envy then such a monster? Well, though many an arraigned mortal has in hopes of mitigated penalty pleaded guilty to horrible actions, did ever anybody seriously confess to envy? Something there is in it universally felt to be more shameful than even felonious crime. And not only does everybody disown it but the better sort are inclined to incredulity when it is in earnest imputed to an intelligent man. But since its lodgement is in the heart not the brain, no degree of intellect supplies a guarantee against it. But Claggart's

83. II *Thessalonians,* ii:7: "For the mystery of iniquity doth already work * * *." The text is concerned with the principle of evil in nature.
84. In Milton's *Paradise Lost,* Book IV, 1. 115. As he approaches the Garden of Eden, Satan's face "thrice changed" with these emotions.
85. famous Siamese twins (1811-1874), who toured the United States.

was no vulgar form of the passion. Nor, as directed toward Billy Budd did it partake of that streak of apprehensive jealousy that marred Saul's visage perturbedly brooding on the comely young David.[86] Claggart's envy struck deeper. If askance he eyed the good looks, cheery health and frank enjoyment of young life in Billy Budd, it was because these [went] along with a nature that as Claggart magnetically felt, had in its simplicity never willed malice or experienced the reactionary bite of that serpent. To him, the spirit lodged within Billy, and looking out from his welkin eyes as from windows, that ineffability it was which made the dimple in his dyed cheek, suppled his joints, and dancing in his yellow curls made him preeminently the Handsome Sailor. One person excepted the master-at-arms was perhaps the only man in the ship intellectually capable of adequately appreciating the moral phenomenon presented in Billy Budd. And the insight but intensified his passion, which assuming various secret forms within him, at times assumed that of cynic disdain—disdain of innocence—To be nothing more than innocent! Yet in an aesthetic way he saw the charm of it, the courageous free-and-easy temper of it, and fain would have shared it, but he despaired of it.

With no power to annul the elemental evil in him, tho readily enough he could hide it; apprehending the good, but powerless to be it; a nature like Claggart's surcharged with energy as such natures almost invariably are, what recourse is left to it but to recoil upon itself and like the scorpion for which the Creator alone is responsible, act out to the end of the part allotted it.

14

Passion, and passion in its profoundest, is not a thing demanding a palatial stage whereon to play its part. Down among the groundlings,[87] among the beggars and rakers of the garbage, profound passion is enacted. And the circumstances that provoke it, however trivial or mean, are no measure of its power. In the present instance the stage is a scrubbed gun-deck, and one of the external provocations a man-of-war's-man's spilled soup.

Now when the Master-at-arms noticed whence came that greasy fluid streaming before his feet, he must have taken it—to some extent wilfully, perhaps—not for the mere accident it assuredly was, but for the sly escape of a spontaneous feeling on Billy's part more or less answering to the antipathy on his own. In effect a foolish demonstration he must have thought, and very harmless, like the futile kick of a heifer, which yet were the heifer a shod stallion, would not be so harmless. Even so was it that into the gall of

86. In I Samuel 16:18, 18:8ff., it is suggested that David's military successes, as well as his personal popularity with the Jews, brought about Saul's envy and dislike.
87. the part of the audience which stood on the ground in an Elizabethan theater; the poorest spectators.

Claggart's envy he infused the vitriol of his contempt. But the incident confirmed to him certain tell-tale reports purveyed to his ear by *Squeak,* one of his more cunning Corporals, a grizzled little man, so nicknamed by the sailors on account of his squeaky voice, and sharp visage ferreting about the dark corners of the lower decks after interlopers, satirically suggesting to them the idea of a rat in a cellar.

From his Chief's employing him as an implicit tool in laying little traps for the worriment of the Foretopman—for it was from the Master-at-arms that the petty persecutions heretofore adverted to had proceeded—the corporal having naturally enough concluded that his master could have no love for the sailor, made it his business, faithful understrapper that he was, to foment the ill blood by perverting to his Chief certain innocent frolics of the good natured Foretopman, besides inventing for his mouth sundry contumelious epithets he claimed to have overheard him let fall. The Master-at-arms never suspected the veracity of these reports, more especially as to the epithets, for he well knew how secretly unpopular may become a master-at-arms[,] at least a master-at-arms of those days zealous in his function, and how the blue-jackets shoot at him in private their raillery and wit; the nickname by which he goes among them (*Jemmy Legs*) implying under the form of merriment their cherished disrespect and dislike.

But in view of the greediness of hate for patrolmen it hardly needed a purveyor to feed Claggart's passion. An uncommon prudence is habitual with the subtler depravity, for it has everything to hide. And in case of an injury but suspected, its secretiveness voluntarily cuts if off from enlightenment or disillusion; and, not unreluctantly, action is taken upon surmise as upon certainty. And the retaliation is apt to be in monstrous disproportion to the supposed offence; for when in anybody was revenge in its exactions aught else but an inordinate usurer. But how with Claggart's conscience? For though consciences are unlike as foreheads, every intelligence, not excluding the Scriptural devils who "believe and tremble," has one. But Claggart's conscience being but the lawyer to his will, made ogres of trifles, probably arguing that the motive imputed to Billy in spilling the soup just when he did, together with the epithets alleged, these, if nothing more, made a strong case against him; nay, justified animosity into a sort of retributive righteousness. The Pharisee is the Guy Fawkes[88] prowling in the hid chambers underlying the Claggarts. And they can really form no conception of an unreciprocated malice. Probably, the master-at-arms' clandestine persecution of Billy was started to try the temper of the man; but it

88. *Pharisee*: a follower of a Jewish sect (*c.* 135 B.C.-A.D. 135) known for its strict observance of the Torah. The term has come to mean anyone of extremely rigid and dogmatic persuasion. *Guy Fawkes*: one of the instigators of the Gunpowder Plot, the plan to blow up the Houses of Parliament and King James I on November 5, 1605.

had not developed any quality in him that enmity could make official use of or even pervert into plausible self-justification; so that the occurrence at the mess, petty if it were, was a welcome one to that peculiar conscience assigned to be the private mentor of Claggart; And for the rest, not improbably it put him upon new experiments.

15

Not many days after the last incident narrated something befell Billy Budd that more gravelled him than aught that had previously occurred.

It was a warm night for the latitude; and the Foretopman, whose watch at the time was properly below, was dozing on the uppermost deck whither he had ascended from his hot hammock one of hundreds suspended so closely wedged together over a lower gun-deck that there was little or no swing to them. He lay as in the shadow of a hill-side, stretched under the lee of the booms, a piled ridge of spare spars amidships between foremast and mainmast and among which the ship's largest boat, the launch, was stowed. Alongside of three other slumberers from below, he lay near that end of the booms which approaches the foremast; his station aloft on duty as a foretopman being just over the deck-station of the forecastlemen, entitling him according to usage to make himself more or less at home in that neighborhood.

Presently he was stirred into semi-consciousness by somebody, who must have previously sounded the sleep of the others, touching his shoulder, and then as the Foretopman raised his head, breathing into his ear in a quick whisper, "Slip into the lee forechains,[89] Billy; there is something in the wind. Don't speak. Quick, I will meet you there;" and disappeared.

Now Billy like sundry other essentially good-natured ones had some of the weaknesses inseparable from essential good nature; and among these was a reluctance, almost an incapacity of plumply saying *no* to an abrupt proposition not obviously absurd, on the face of it, nor obviously unfriendly, nor iniquitous. And being of warm blood he had not the phlegm tacitly to negative any proposition by unresponsive inaction. Like his sense of fear, his apprehension as to aught outside of the honest and natural was seldom very quick. Besides, upon the present occasion, the drowse from his sleep still hung upon him.

However it was, he mechanically rose, and sleepily wondering what could be in the wind, betook himself to the designated place, a narrow platform, one of six, outside of the high bulwarks and screened by the great dead-eyes[90] and multiple columned lanyards of the shrouds and back-stays; and, in a great war-ship of that time, of

89. platforms near the bow, designed to carry the lower shrouds of the foremast out from the side of the ship.

90. wooden blocks through which lanyards (short lengths of line) are threaded.

dimensions commensurate [with the] hull's magnitude; a tarry balcony in short overhanging the sea, and so secluded that one mariner of the *Indomitable*, a non-conformist[91] old tar of a serious turn, made it even in daytime his private oratory.

In this retired nook the stranger soon joined Billy Budd. There was no moon as yet; a haze obscured the star-light. He could not distinctly see the stranger's face. Yet from something in the outline and carriage, Billy took him to be, and correctly, for one of the afterguard.[92]

"Hist! Billy," said the man in the same quick cautionary whisper as before; "You were impressed, weren't you? Well, so was I"; and he paused, as to mark the effect. But Billy not knowing exactly what to make of this said nothing. Then the other: "We are not the only impressed ones, Billy. There's a gang of us.—Couldn't you—help—at a pinch?["]

"What do you mean?["] demanded Billy here thoroughly shaking off his drowse.

"Hist, hist![''] the hurried whisper now growing husky, [''] see here"; and the man held up two small objects faintly twinkling in the nightlight; "see, they are yours, Billy, if you'll only—"

But Billy broke in, and in his resentful eagerness to deliver himself his vocal infirmity somewhat intruded: "D-D-Damme, I don't know what you are d-d-driving at, or what you mean, but you had better g-g-go where you belong!" For the moment the fellow, as confounded, did not stir; and Billy springing to his feet, said "If you d-don't start I'll t-t-toss you back over the r-rail!" There was no mistaking this and the mysterious emissary decamped disappearing in the direction of the mainmast in the shadow of the booms.

"Hallo, what's the matter?" here came growling from a forecastleman awakened from his deck-doze by Billy's raised voice. And as the foretopman reappeared and was recognized by him; "Ah, *Beauty*, is it you? Well, something must have been the matter for you st-st-stuttered."

"O," rejoined Billy, now mastering the impediment; "I found an afterguardsman in our part of the ship here and I bid him be off where he belongs."

"And is that all you did about it, foretopman?" gruffly demanded another, an irascible old fellow of brick-colored visage and hair, and who was known to his associate forecastlemen as *Red Pepper*; "Such sneaks I should like to marry to the gunner's daughter!" by that expression meaning that he would like to subject them to disciplinary castigation over a gun.

However, Billy's rendering of the matter satisfactorily accounted

91. a Protestant dissenter from the Church of England.
92. *cf.* note 70.

to these inquirers for the brief commotion, since of all the sections of a ship's company the forecastlemen, veterans for the most part and bigoted in their sea-prejudices, are the most jealous in resenting territorial encroachments, especially on the part of any of the after-guard, of whom they have but a sorry opinion, chiefly landsmen, never going aloft except to reef or furl the mainsail, and in no wise competent to handle a marlinspike[93] or turn in a *dead-eye*, say.

16

This incident sorely puzzled Billy Budd. It was an entirely new experience; the first time in his life that he had ever been personally approached in underhand intriguing fashion. Prior to this encounter he had known nothing of the afterguardsman, the two men being stationed wide apart, one forward and aloft during his watch, the other on deck and aft.

What could it mean? And could they reallly be guineas,[94] those two glittering objects the interloper had held up to his (Billy's)[95] eyes? Where could the fellow get guineas? Why even buttons spare buttons[96] are not so plentiful at sea. The more he turned the matter over, the more he was non-plussed, and made uneasy and discomforted. In his disgustful recoil from an overture which tho' he but ill comprehended he instinctively knew must involve evil of some sort, Billy Budd was like a young horse fresh from the pasture suddenly inhaling a vile whiff from some chemical factory and by repeated snortings tries to get it out of his nostrils and lungs. This frame of mind barred all desire of holding further parley with the fellow, even were it but for the purpose of gaining some enlightenment as to his design in approaching him. And yet he was not without natural curiosity to see how such a visitor in the dark would look in broad day.

He espied him the following afternoon in his first dog-watch be-low[,]one of the smokers on that forward part of the upper gun deck allotted to the pipe.[97] He recognized him by his general cut and build, more than by his round freckled face and glassy eyes of pale blue, veiled with lashes all but white. And yet Billy was a bit uncertain whether indeed it were he—yonder chap about his own age chatting and laughing in free-hearted way, leaning against a gun; a genial young fellow enough to look at, and something of a rattle-

---

93. an iron tool tapering to a point, used to separate the strands in a length of rope.

94. *guinea*: an English gold coin, not minted after 1813, worth about 21 shillings.

95. The parentheses around "Billy's" suggests that Melville may have intended to delete it.

96. *even buttons spare buttons:* Melville may have intended to delete the first "buttons."

97. Enlisted men were allowed to smoke on the galley on the forward upper gun deck. This ship had three decks in this order: lower gun deck, upper gun deck, and spar deck.

brain, to all appearance. Rather chubby too for a sailor even an afterguardsman. In short the last man in the world, one would think, to
be overburthened with thoughts, especially those perilous thoughts
that must needs belong to a conspirator in any serious project, or
even to the underling of such a conspirator.

Altho' Billy was not aware of it, the fellow, with a side-long watchful glance had perceived Billy first, and then noting that Billy was
looking at him, thereupon nodded a familiar sort of friendly recognition as to an old acquaintance, without interrupting the talk he was
engaged in with the group of smokers. A day or two afterwards
chancing in the evening promenade on a gun deck, to pass Billy, he
offered a flying word of good-fellowship as it were, which by its unexpectedness, and equivocalness under the circumstances so embarrassed Billy that he knew not how to respond to it, and let it go
unnoticed.

Billy was now left more at a loss than before. The ineffectual
speculation into which he was led was so disturbingly alien to him
that he did his bet to smother [it]. It never entered his mind that
here was a matter which from its extreme questionableness, it was his
duty as a loyal blue-jacket to report in the proper quarter. And,
probably, had such a step been suggested to him, he would have
been deterred from taking it by the thought, one of novice-mag-
nanimity, that it would savor overmuch of the dirty work of a tell-
tale. He kept the thing to himself. Yet upon one occasion, he could
not forbear a little disburthening himself to the old Dansker,
tempted thereto perhaps by the influence of a balmy night when the
ship lay becalmed; the twain, silent for the most part, sitting together on deck, their heads propped against the bulwarks. But it
was only a partial and anonymous account that Billy gave, the unfounded scruples above referred to preventing full disclosure to anybody. Upon hearing Billy's version, the sage Dansker seemed to divine more than he was told; and after a little meditation during
which his wrinkles were pursed as into a point, quite effacing for
the time that quizzing expression his face sometimes wore,—"Didn't
I say so, Baby Budd?"

"Say what?" demanded Billy.

"Why, *Jemmy Legs* is *down* on you."

"And what" rejoined Billy in amazement, "has *Jemmy Legs* to do
with that cracked afterguardsman?"

"Ho, it was an afterguardsman then. A cat's-paw, a cat's-paw!"
And with that exclamation, which, whether it had reference to a light
puff of air just then coming over the calm sea, or subtler relation to
the afterguardsman, there is no telling, the old Merlin gave a twisting
wrench with his black teeth at his plug of tobacco, vouchsafing no
reply to Billy's impetuous question, tho' now repeated, for it was his

wont to relapse into grim silence when interrogated in skeptical sort as to any of his sententious oracles, not always very clear ones, rather partaking of that obscurity which invests most Delphic deliverances[98] from any quarter.

Long experience had very likely brought this old man to that bitter prudence which never interferes in aught and never gives advice.

17

Yes, despite the Dansker's pithy insistence as to the Master-at-arms being at the bottom of these strange experiences of Billy on board the *Indomitable*, the young sailor was ready to ascribe them to almost anybody but the man who, to use Billy's own expression, "always had a pleasant word for him." This is to be wondered at. Yet not so much to be wondered at. In certain matters, some sailors even in mature life remain unsophisticated enough. But a young seafarer of the disposition of our athletic Foretopman, is much of a child-man. And yet a child's utter innocence is but its blank ignorance, and the innocence more or less wanes as intelligence waxes. But in Billy Budd intelligence, such as it was, had advanced, while yet his simple mindedness remained for the most part unaffected. Experience is a teacher indeed; yet did Billy's years make his experience small. Besides, he had none of that intuitive knowledge of the bad which in natures not good or incompletely so foreruns experience, and therefore may pertain, as in some instances it too clearly does pertain, even to youth.

And what could Billy know of man except of man as a mere sailor? And the old-fashioned sailor, the veritable man-before-the-mast, the sailor from boyhood up, he, tho' indeed of the same species as a landsman is in some respects singularly distinct from him. The sailor is frankness, the landsman is finesse. Life is not a game with the sailor, demanding the long head; no intricate game of chess where few moves are made in straightforwardness, and ends are attained by indirection; an oblique, tedious, barren game hardly worth that poor candle burnt out in playing it.[99]

Yes, as a class, sailors are in character a juvenile race. Even their deviations are marked by juvenility. And this more especially holding true with the sailors of Billy's time. Then, too, certain things which apply to all sailors, do more pointedly operate here and there, upon the junior one. Every sailor, too is accustomed to obey orders without debating them; his life afloat is externally ruled for him; he is not brought into that promiscuous commerce with mankind where unobstructed free agency on equal terms—equal superficially, at least—

98. a reference to the Pythian priestess, whose pronouncements in verse had to be interpreted by a priest. Her shrine was at Delphi.

99. *Cf.* Shakespeare, *Macbeth,* Act V, Scene 5, ll. 23–26: "* * * Out, out, brief candle! / Life's but a walking shadow, a poor player, / That struts and frets his hour upon the stage / And then is heard no more. * * *"

soon teaches one that unless upon occasion he exercise a distrust keen in proportion to the fairness of the appearance, some foul turn may be served him. A ruled undemonstrative distrustfulness is so habitual, not with business-men so much, as with men who know their kind in less shallow relations than business, namely, certain men-of-the-world, that they come at last to employ it all but unconsciously; and some of them would very likely feel real surprise at being charged with it as one of their general characteristics.

18

But after the little matter at the mess Billy Budd no more found himself in strange trouble at times about his hammock or his clothes-bag or what not. While, as to that smile that occasionally sunned him, and the pleasant passing word, these were if not more frequent, yet if anything more pronounced that before.

But for all that, there were certain other demonstrations now. When Claggart's unobserved glance happened to light on belted Billy rolling along the upper gun-deck in the leisure of the second dog-watch exchanging passing broadsides of fun with other young promenaders in the crowd; that glance would follow the cheerful sea-Hyperion[100] with a settled meditative and melancholy expression, his eyes strangely suffused with incipient feverish tears. Then would Claggart look like the man of sorrows.[101] Yes, and sometimes the melancholy expression would have in it a touch of soft yearning, as if Claggart could even have loved Billy but for fate and ban. But this was an evanescence, and quickly repented of, as it were, by an immitigable look, pinching and shrivelling the visage into the momentary semblance of a wrinkled walnut. But sometimes catching sight in advance of the foretopman coming in his direction, he would, upon their nearing, step aside a little to let him pass, dwelling upon Billy for the moment with the glittering dental satire of a Guise.[102] But upon any abrupt unforeseen encounter a red light would[flash] forth from his eye like a spark from an anvil in a dusk smithy. That quick fierce light was a strange one, darted from orbs which in repose were of a color nearest approaching a deeper violet, the softest of shades.

Tho' some of these caprices of the pit could not but be observed by their object, yet were they beyond the construing of such a nature. And the *thews* of Billy were hardly compatible with that sort of sensitive spiritual organisation which in some cases instinctively conveys to ignorant innocence an admonition of the proximity of the malign. He thought the Master-at-arms acted in a manner rather queer at

100. in Greek mythology, the Titan god who came to be identified with Apollo, the god of youth and beauty.

101. In *Isaiah* 53:3, the Lord's servant is described as "despised and rejected of men; a man of sorrows, and acquainted with grief."

102. Henri de Guise (1550-1588), remembered chiefly for his conspiratorial activities and his ability, like Claudius in *Hamlet*, to "smile, and smile, and be a villain."

times. That was all. But the occasional frank air and pleasant word went for what they purported to be, the young sailor never having heard as yet of the "too fair-spoken man."

Had the foretopman been conscious of having done or said anything to provoke the ill will of the official, it would have been different with him, and his sight might have been purged if not sharpened. As it was[,] innocence was his blinder.

So was it with him in yet another matter. Two minor officers—the Armorer and Captain of the Hold,[103] with whom he had never exchanged a word, his position in the ship not bringing him into contact with them; these men now for the first began to cast upon Billy when they chanced to encounter him, that peculiar glance which evidences that the man from whom it comes has been some way tampered with and to the prejudice of him upon whom the glance lights. Never did it occur to Billy as a thing to be noted or a thing suspicious, tho' he well knew the fact, that the Armorer and Captain of the Hold, with the ship's-yeoman,[104] apothecary, and others of that grade, were by naval usage, mess-mates of the master-at-arms, men with ears convenient to his confidential tongue.

But the general popularity that our *Handsome Sailor's* manly forwardness upon occasion, and[his] irresistible good nature[,] indicating no mental superiority tending to excite an invidious feeling; this good will on the part of most of his shipmates made him the less to concern himself about such mute aspects toward him as those whereto allusion has just been made.

As to the afterguardsman, tho' Billy for reasons already given necessarily saw little of him, yet when the two did happen to meet, invariably came the fellow's off-hand cheerful recognition, sometimes accompanied by a passing pleasant word or two. Whatever that equivocal young person's original design may really have been, or the design of which he might have been the deputy, certain it was from his manner upon these occasions, that he had wholly dropped it. It was as if his precocity of crookedness (and every vulgar villain is precocious) had for once deceived him, and the man he had sought to entrap as a simpleton had, through his very simplicity ignorantly baffled him.

But shrewd ones may opine that it was hardly possible for Billy to refrain from going up to the afterguardsman and bluntly demanding to know his purpose in the initial interview, so abruptly closed in the fore-chains. Shrewd ones may also think it but natural in Billy to set about sounding some of the other impressed men of the ship in order to discover what basis, if any, there was for the emissary's obscure suggestions as to plotting disaffection aboard. Yes, [the]

103. *Armorer:* the petty-officer in charge of the ship's arms, *Captain of the Hold:* the petty-officer in charge of stow- ing the hold.

104. the petty-officer in charge of stores.

shrewd may so think. But something more, or rather, something else than mere shrewdness is perhaps needful for the due understanding of such a character as Billy Budd's.

As to Claggart, the monomania in the man—if that indeed it were —as involuntarily disclosed by starts in the manifestations detailed, yet in general covered over by his self-contained and rational demeanor; this, like a subterranean fire was eating its way deeper and deeper in him. Something decisive must come of it.

19

After the mysterious interview in the fore-chains, the one so abruptly ended there by Billy, nothing especially German[105] to the story occurred until the events now about to be narrated.

Elsewhere it has been said that in the lack of frigates (of course better sailers than line-of-battle ships) in the English squadron up the Straits[106] at that period, the *Indomitable* was occasionally employed not only as an available substitute for a scout, but at times on detached service of more important kind. This was not alone because of her sailing qualities, not common in a ship of her rate, but quite as much, probably, that the character of her commander, it was thought, specially adapted him for any duty where under unforeseen difficulties a prompt initiative might have to be taken in some matter demanding knowledge and ability in addition to those qualities implied in good seamanship. It was on an expedition of the latter sort, a somewhat distant one, and when the *Indomitable* was almost at her furthest remove from the fleet that in the latter part of an afternoon-watch she unexpectedly came in sight of a ship of the enemy. It proved to be a frigate. The latter perceiving thro' the glass that the weight of men and metal would be heavily against her, invoking her light heels crowded sail to get away. After a chase urged almost against hope and lasting until about the middle of the first dog-watch, she signally succeeded in effecting her escape.

Not long after the pursuit had been given up, and ere the excite-ment incident thereto had altogether waned away, the Master-at-Arms ascending from his cavernous sphere made his appearance cap in hand by the mainmast respectfully waiting the notice of Captain Vere then solitary walking the weather-side of the quarter-deck, doubtless somewhat chafed at the failure of the pursuit. The spot where Claggart stood was the place allotted to men of lesser grades seeking some more particular interview either with the officer-of-the-deck or the Captain himself. But from the latter it was not often that a sailor or petty-officer of those days would seek a hearing; only some exceptional cause, would, according to established custom, have warranted that.

Presently, just as the Commander absorbed in his reflections was

105. *i.e.*, "germane" or "akin."
106. the British Mediterranean Fleet, sailing from the Straits of Gibraltar.

on the point of turning aft in his promenade, he became sensible of Claggart's presence, and saw the doffed cap held in deferential expectancy. Here be it said that Captain Vere's personal knowledge of this petty-officer had only begun at the time of the ship's last sailing from home, Claggart then for the first, in transfer from a ship detained for repairs, supplying on board the *Indomitable* the place of a previous master-at-arms disabled and ashore.

No sooner did the Commander observe who it was that now deferentially stood awaiting his notice, than a peculiar expression came over him. It was not unlike that which uncontrollably will flit across the countenance of one at unawares encountering a person who though known to him indeed has hardly been long enough known for thorough knowledge, but something in whose aspect nevertheless now for the first provokes a vaguely repellent distaste. But coming to a stand, and resuming much of his wonted official manner, save that a sort of impatience lurked in the intonation of the opening word, he said "Well? what is it, Master-at-Arms?"

With the air of a subordinate grieved at the necessity of being a messenger of ill tidings, and while conscientiously determined to be frank, yet equally resolved upon shunning overstatement, Claggart at this invitation or rather summons to disburthen, spoke up. What he said, conveyed in the language of no uneducated man, was to the effect following if not altogether in these words, namely, that during the chase and preparations for the possible encounter he had seen enough to convince him that at least one sailor aboard was a dangerous character in a ship mustering some who not only had taken a guilty part in the late serious troubles, but others also who, like the man in question, had entered His Majesty's service under another form than enlistment.

At this point Captain Vere with some impatience, interrupted him: "Be direct, man; say impressed men."

Claggart made a gesture of subservience, and proceeded.

Quite lately he (Claggart) had begun to suspect that on the gun-decks some sort of movement prompted by the sailor in question was covertly going on, but he had not thought himself warranted in reporting the suspicion so long as it remained indistinct. But from what he had that afternoon observed in the man referred to the suspicion of something clandestine going on had advanced to a point less removed from certainty. He deeply felt, he added, the serious responsibility assumed in making a report involving such possible consequences to the individual mainly concerned, besides tending to augment those natural anxieties which every naval commander must feel in view of extraordinary outbreaks so recent as those which, he sorrowfully said it, it needed not to name.

Now at the first broaching of the matter Captain Vere taken by surprise could not wholly dissemble his disquietude. But as Claggart went on, the former's aspect changed into restiveness under something in the witness' manner in giving his testimony. However, he refrained from interrupting him. And Claggart, continuing, concluded with this:

"God forbid, your honor, that the *Indomitable*'s should be the experience of the—"

"Never mind that!" here peremptorily broke in the superior, his face altering with anger, instinctively divining the ship that the other was about to name, one in which the Nore Mutiny had assumed a singularly tragical character that for a time jeopardized the life of its commander. Under the circumstances he was indignant at the purposed allusion. When the commissioned officers themselves were on all occasions very heedful how they referred to the recent events, for a petty-officer unnecessarily to allude to them in the presence of his Captain, this struck him as a most immodest presumption. Besides, to his quick sense of self-respect, it even looked under the circumstances something like an attempt to alarm him. Nor at first was he without some surprise that one who so far as he had hitherto come under his notice had shown considerable tact in his function should in this particular evince such lack of it.

But these thoughts and kindred dubious ones flitting across his mind were suddenly replaced by an intuitional surmise which though as yet obscure in form served practically to affect his reception of the ill tidings. Certain it is, that long versed in everything pertaining to the complicated gun-deck life, which like every other form of life, has its secret mines and dubious side, the side popularly disclaimed, Captain Vere did not permit himself to be unduly disturbed by the general tenor of his subordinate's report. Furthermore, if in view of recent events prompt action should be taken at the first palpable sign of recurring insubordination, for all that, not judicious would it be, he thought, to keep the idea of lingering disaffection alive by undue forwardness in crediting an informer even if his own subordinate and charged among other things with police surveillance of the crew. This feeling would not perhaps have so prevailed with him were it not that upon a prior occasion the patriotic zeal officially evinced by Claggart had somewhat irritated him as appearing rather supersensible and strained. Furthermore, something even in the official's self-possessed and somewhat ostentatious manner in making his specifications strangely reminded him of a bandsman, a perjurous witness in a capital case before a court-martial ashore of which when a lieutenant he Captain Vere had been a member.

Now the peremptory check given to Claggart in the matter of the arrested allusion was quickly followed up by this: "You say that there is at least one dangerous man aboard. Name him."

"William Budd. A foretopman, your honor—"

"William Budd" repeated Captain Vere with unfeigned astonishment; "and mean you the man that Lieutenant Ratcliffe took from the merchantman not very long ago— the young fellow who seems to be so popular with the men—Billy, the Handsome Sailor, as they call him?["]

"The same, your honor; but for all his youth and good looks, a deep one. Not for nothing does he insinuate himself into the good will of his shipmates, since at the least all hands will at a pinch say a good word for him at all hazards. Did Lieutenant Ratcliffe happen to tell your honor that adroit fling of Budd's, jumping up in the cutter's bow under the merchantman's stern when he was being taken off? It is even masqued by that sort of good humored air that at heart he resents his impressment. You have but noted his fair cheek. A man-trap may be under his ruddy-tipped daisies."

Now the *Handsome Sailor* as a signal figure among the crew had naturally enough attracted the Captain's attention from the first. Tho' in general not very demonstrative to his officers, he had congratulated Lieutenant Ratcliffe upon his good fortune in lighting on such a fine specimen of the genus homo, who in the nude might have posed for a statue of young Adam before the Fall.

As to Billy's adieu to the ship *Rights-of-Man*, which the boarding lieutenant had indeed reported to him but in a deferential way more as a good story than aught else, Captain Vere[,] tho mistakenly understanding it as a satiric sally, had but thought so much the better of the impressed man for it; as a military sailor, admiring the spirit that could take an arbitrary enlistment so merrily and sensibly. The foretopman's conduct, too, so far as it had fallen under the Captain's notice had confirmed the first happy augury, while the new recruit's qualities as a *sailor-man* seemed to be such that he had thought of recommending him to the executive officer for promotion to a place that would more frequently bring him under his own observation, namely, the captaincy of the mizzen-top, replacing there in the starboard watch a man not so young whom partly for that reason he deemed less fitted for the post. Be it parenthesized here that since the mizzen-top-men having not to handle such breadths of heavy canvas as the lower sails on the main-mast and fore-mast, a young man if of the right stuff not only seems best adapted to duty there, but in fact is generally selected for the captaincy of that top, and the company under him are light hands and often but striplings. In sum, Captain Vere had from the beginning deemed Billy Budd to be what in the naval parlance of the time was called a "King's *bargain*[,]" that is to say, for His Britannic Majesty's navy a capital investment at small outlay or none at all.

After a brief pause during which the reminiscences above mentioned passed vividly through his mind and he weighed the import of Claggart's last suggestion conveyed in the phrase "pitfall under the clover,"[107] and the more he weighed it the less reliance he felt in the informer's good faith. Suddenly[108] he turned upon him and in a low voice: "Do you come to me, master-at-arms[,] with so foggy a tale? As to Budd, cite me an act or spoken word of his confirmatory of what you in general charge against him. Stay," drawing nearer to him "heed what you speak. Just now, and in a case like this, there is a yard-arm-end for the false-witness."

"Ah, your honor!" sighed Claggart mildly shaking his shapely head as in sad deprecation of such unmerited severity of tone. Then, bridling—erecting himself as in virtuous self-assertion, he circumstantially alleged certain words and acts, which collectively, if credited, led to presumptions mortally inculpating Budd. And for some of these averments, he added, substantiating proof was not far.

With gray eyes impatient and distrustful essaying to fathom to the bottom Claggart's calm violet ones, Captain Vere again heard him out; then for the moment stood ruminating. The mood he evinced, Claggart—himself for the time liberated from the other's scrutiny—steadily regarded with a look difficult to render,—a look curious of the operation of his tactics, a look such as might have been that of the spokesman of the envious children of Jacob deceptively imposing upon the troubled patriarch the blood-dyed coat of young Joseph.[109]

Though something exceptional in the moral quality of Captain Vere made him, in earnest encounter with a fellow-man, a veritable touch-stone of that man's essential nature, yet now as to Claggart and what was really going on in him his feeling partook less of intuitional conviction than of strong suspicion clogged by strange dubieties. The perplexity he evinced proceeded less from aught touching the man informed against—as Claggart doubtless opined —than from considerations how best to act in regard to the informer. At first indeed he was naturally for summoning that substantiation of his allegations which Claggart said was at hand. But such a proceeding would result in the matter at once getting abroad, which in the present stage of it, he thought, might undesirably affect the ship's company. If Claggart was a false witness,—that closed the

---

107. *Cf.* "A man-trap * * * under his * * * daisies," ending the third paragraph above. There Melville had first written, then crossed out, "a pitfall under his ruddy clover," the words that Captain Vere remembers here. The discrepancy might have been corrected had Melville seen the manuscript through press.

108. The manuscript reads, "good faith, suddenly * * *," an obvious comma splice between two sentences. It was the first edition.

109. Genesis 37:31–32: "And they took Joseph's coat, and killed a kid of the goats, and dipped the coat in the blood; and they sent the coat of many colours, and they brought it to their father; and said, This have we found: know now whether it be thy son's coat or no."

affair. And therefore before trying the accusation, he would first practically test the accuser; and he thought this could be done in a quiet undemonstrative way.

The measure he determined upon involved a shifting of the scene, a transfer to a place less exposed to observation than the broad quarter-deck. For although the few gun-room officers there at the time had, in due observance of naval etiquette, withdrawn to leeward the moment Captain Vere had begun his promenade on the deck's weather-side; and tho' during the colloquy with Claggart they of course ventured not to diminish the distance; and though throughout the interview Captain Vere's voice was far from high, and Claggart's silvery and low; and the wind in the cordage and the wash of the sea helped the more to put them beyond ear-shot; nevertheless, the interview's continuance already had attracted observation from some topmen aloft and other sailors in the waist or further forward.

Having determined upon his measures, Captain Vere forthwith took action. Abruptly turning to Claggart he asked "Master-at-arms, is it now Budd's watch aloft?"

"No, your honor." Whereupon, "Mr. Wilkes!" summoning the nearest midshipman, "tell Albert to come to me." Albert was the Captain's hammock-boy, a sort of sea-valet in whose discretion and fidelity his master had much confidence. The lad appeared. "You know Budd the foretopman?"

"I do, Sir."

"Go find him. It is his watch off. Manage to tell him out of earshot that he is wanted aft. Contrive it that he speaks to nobody. Keep him in talk yourself. And not till you get well aft here, not till then let him know that the place where he is wanted is my cabin. You understand. Go.—Master-at-Arms, show yourself on the decks below, and when you think it time for Albert to be coming with his man, stand by quietly to follow the sailor in."

20

Now when the foretopman found himself closeted there, as it were, in the cabin with the Captain and Claggart, he was surprised enough. But it was a surprise unaccompanied by apprehension or distrust. To an immature nature essentially honest and humane, forewarning intimations of subtler danger from one's kind come tardily if at all. The only thing that took shape in the young sailor's mind was this: Yes, the Captain, I have always thought, looks kindly upon me. Wonder if he's going to make me his coxswain. I should like that. And maybe now he is going to ask the master-at-arms about me.

"Shut the door there, sentry," said the commander; "stand without, and let nobody come in.—Now, master-at-arms, tell this man to

his face what you told of him to me;" and stood prepared to scrutinize the mutually confronting visages.

With the measured step and calm collected air of an asylum-physician approaching in the public hall some patient beginning to show indications of a coming paroxysm, Claggart deliberately advanced within short range of Billy, and mesmerically looking him in the eye, briefly recapitulated the accusation.

Not at first did Billy take it in. When he did, the rose-tan of his cheek looked struck as by white leprosy. He stood like one impaled and gagged. Meanwhile the accuser's eyes removing not as yet from the blue dilated ones, underwent a phenomenal change, their wonted rich violet color blurring into a muddy purple. Those lights of human intelligence losing human expression, gelidly protruding like the alien eyes of certain uncatalogued creatures of the deep. The first mesmeric glance was one of serpent fascination; the last was as the hungry lurch of the torpedo-fish.

"Speak, man!" said Captain Vere to the transfixed one struck by his aspect even more than by Claggart's, "Speak! defend yourself." Which appeal caused but a strange dumb gesturing and gurgling in Billy; amazement at such an accusation to suddenly sprung on inexperienced nonage; this, and, it may be horror of the accuser, serving to bring out his lurking defect and in this instance for the time intensifying it into a convulsed tongue-tie; while the intent head and entire form straining forward in an agony of ineffectual eagerness to obey the injunction to speak and defend himself, gave an expression to the face like that of a condemned Vestal priestess in the moment of being buried alive, and in the first struggle against suffocation.[110]

Though at the time Captain Vere was quite ignorant of Billy's liability to vocal impediment, he now immediately divined it, since vividly Billy's aspect recalled to him that of a bright young schoolmate of his whom he had once seen struck by much the same startling impotence in the act of eagerly rising in the class to be foremost in response to a testing question put to it by the master. Going close up to the young sailor, and laying a soothing hand on his shoulder, he said[:] "There is no hurry, my boy. Take your time, take your time." Contrary to the effect intended, these words so fatherly in tone, doubtless touching Billy's heart to the quick, prompted yet more violent efforts at utterance—efforts soon ending for the time in confirming the paralysis, and bringing to his face an expression which was as a crucifixion to behold. The next instant, quick as the flame from a discharged cannon at night, his right arm shot out, and Claggart dropped to the deck. Whether intentionally or but owing to the young athlete's superior height, the blow had taken effect full upon the forehead, so shapely and intellectual-look-

110. the punishment given to Vestal Virgins in Rome if they violated their vows.

ing a feature in the master-at-arms; so that the body fell over length-wise, like a heavy plank tilted from erectness. A gasp or two, and he lay motionless.

"Fated boy," breathed Captain Vere in tone so low as to be almost a whisper, "what have you done! But here, help me."

The twain raised the felled one from the loins up into a sitting position. The spare form flexibly acquiesced, but inertly. It was like handling a dead snake. They lowered it back. Regaining erectness Captain Vere with one hand covering his face stood to all appearance as impassive as the object at his feet. Was he absorbed in taking in all the bearings of the event and what was best not only now at once to be done, but also in the sequel? Slowly he uncovered his face; and the effect was as if the moon emerging from eclipse should reappear with quite another aspect than that which had gone into hiding. The father in him, manifested towards Billy thus far in the scene, was replaced by the military disciplinarian. In his official tone he bade the foretopman retire to a state-room aft, (pointing it out) and there remain till thence summoned. This order Billy in silence mechanically obeyed. Then going to the cabin-door where it opened on the quarter-deck, Captain Vere said to the sentry without, "Tell somebody to send Albert here." When the lad appeared his master so contrived it that he should not catch sight of the prone one. "Albert," he said to him, "tell the Surgeon I wish to see him. You need not come back till called." When the Surgeon entered—a self-poised character of that grave sense and experience that hardly anything could take him aback,—Captain Vere advanced to meet him, thus unconsciously intercepting his view of Claggart and interrupting the other's wonted ceremonious salutation, said, "Nay, tell me how it is with yonder man," directing his attention to the prostrate one.

The Surgeon looked, and for all his self-command, somewhat started at the abrupt revelation. On Claggart's always pallid complexion, thick black blood was now oozing from nostril and ear. To the gazer's professional eye it was unmistakably no living man that he saw.

"Is it so then?["] said Captain Vere intently watching him. "I thought it. But verify it." Whereupon the customary tests confirmed the Surgeon's first glance, who now looking up in unfeigned concern, cast a look of intense inquisitiveness upon his superior. But Captain Vere, with one hand to his brow, was standing motionless. Suddenly, catching the Surgeon's arm convulsively, he exclaimed, pointing down to the body—"It is the divine judgment on Ananias![111] Look!"

Disturbed by the excited manner he had never before observed in

---

111. Acts 5: 3-5: "Peter said, Ananias * * * thou hast not lied unto men. but unto God. And Ananias hearing these words fell down, and gave up the ghost."

the *Indomitable*'s Captain, and as yet wholly ignorant of the affair, the prudent Surgeon nevertheless held his peace, only again looking an earnest interrogation as to what it was that had resulted in such a tragedy.

But Captain Vere was now again motionless standing absorbed in thought. But again starting, he vehemently exclaimed—"Struck dead by an angel of God! Yet the angel must hang!["]

At these passionate interjections, mere incoherences to the listener as yet unapprised of the antecedents, the Surgeon was profoundly discomposed. But now as recollecting himself, Captain Vere in less harsh tone briefly related the circumstances leading up to the event.

["]But come; we must despatch" he added. ["]Help me to remove him (meaning the body) to yonder compartment,["] designating one opposite that where the foretopman remained immured. Anew disturbed by a request that as implying a desire for secrecy, seemed unaccountably strange to him, there was nothing for the subordinate to do but comply.

"Go now" said Captain Vere with something of his wonted manner—["]Go now, I shall presently call a drum-head court.[112] Tell the lieutenants what has happened, and tell Mr. Mordant," meaning the captain of marines, "and charge them to keep the matter to themselves."

21

Full of disquietude and misgiving the Surgeon left the cabin. Was Captain Vere suddenly affected in his mind, or was it but a transient excitement, brought about by so strange and extraordinary a happening? As to the drum-head court, it struck the Surgeon as impolitic, if nothing more. The thing to do, he thought, was to place Billy Budd in confinement and in a way dictated by usage, and postpone further action in so extraordinary a case, to such time as they should rejoin the squadron, and then refer it to the Admiral. He recalled the unwonted agitation of Captain Vere and his excited exclamations so at variance with his normal manner. Was he unhinged? But assuming that he is, it is not so susceptible of proof. What then can he do? No more trying situation is conceivable than that of an officer subordinate under a Captain whom he suspects to be, not mad indeed, but yet not quite unaffected in his intellect. To argue his order to him would be insolence. To resist him would be mutiny.

In obedience to Captain Vere he communicated what had happened to the lieutenants & captain of marines; saying nothing as to the Captain's state. They fully shared his own surprise and concern.

---

112. a court-martial, originally held around an upturned drum, to try offenses committed during military operations.

Like him too they seemed to think that such a matter should be preferred to the Admiral.

22

Who in the rainbow can draw the line where the violet tint ends and the orange tint begins? Distinctly we see the difference of the colors, but where exactly does the one first blendingly enter into the other? So with sanity and insanity. In pronounced cases there is no question about them. But in some supposed cases, in various degrees supposedly less pronounced, to draw the exact line of demarkation few will undertake tho for a fee some professional experts will. There is nothing namable but that some men will undertake to do it for pay.

Whether Captain Vere, as the Surgeon professionally and privately surmised, was really the sudden victim of any degree of aberration, one must determine for himself by such light as this narrative may afford.

[That] the unhappy event which has been narrated could not have happened at a worse juncture was but too true. For it was close on the heel of the suppressed insurrections, an aftertime very critical to naval authority, demanding from every English sea-commander two qualities not readily interfusable—prudence and rigor. Moreover there was something crucial in the case.

In the jugglery of circumstances preceding and attending the event on board the *Indomitable* and in the light of that martial code whereby it was formally to be judged, innocence and guilt personified in Claggart and Budd in effect changed places. In a legal view the apparent victim of the tragedy was he who had sought to victimize a man blameless; and the indisputable deed of the latter, navally regarded, constituted the most heinous of military crimes. Yet more. The essential right and wrong involved in the matter, the clearer that might be, so much the worse for the responsibility of a loyal sea-commander inasmuch as he was not authorized to determine the matter on that primitive basis.

Small wonder then that the *Indomitable*'s Captain though in general a man of rapid decision, felt that circumspectness not less than promptitude was necessary. Until he could decide upon his course, and in each detail; and not only so, but until the concluding measure was upon the point of being enacted, he deemed it advisable, in view of all the circumstances to guard as much as possible against publicity. Here he may or may not have erred. Certain it is however that subsequently in the confidential talk of more than one or two gun-rooms and cabins he was not a little criticized by some officers, a fact imputed by his friends and vehemently by his cousin Jack Denton to professional jealousy of *Starry Vere*. Some imaginative ground for invidious comment there was. The maintenance of secrecy in the matter, the confining all knowledge of it for a time to the place where the homicide occurred, the quarter-deck cabin; in these particulars lurked some resemblance to the policy adopted in those tragedies of the palace which have occurred more than once in the capital founded by Peter the Barbarian.[113]

The case indeed was such that fain would the *Indomitable*'s captain have deferred taking any action whatever respecting it further than to keep the foretopman a close prisoner till the ship rejoined the squadron and then submitting the matter to the judgement of his Admiral.

But a true military officer is in one particular like a true monk. Not with more of self-abnegation will the latter keep his vows of monastic obedience than the former his vows of allegiance to martial duty.

Feeling that unless quick action was taken on it, the deed of the foretopman, so soon as it should be known on the gun-decks would tend to awaken any slumbering embers of the Nore among the crew, a sense of the urgency of the case overruled in Captain Vere every other consideration. But tho' a conscientious disciplinarian he was no lover of authority for mere authority's sake. Very far was he from embracing opportunities for monopolizing to himself the perils of moral responsibility[,] none at least that could properly be referred to an official superior or shared with him by his official equals or even subordinates. So thinking[,] he was glad it would not be at variance with usage to turn the matter over to a summary court of his own officers, reserving to himself as the one on whom the ultimate accountability would rest, the right of maintaining a supervision of it, or formally or informally interposing at need. Accordingly a drum-head court was summarily convened, he electing the individuals composing it, the First Lieutenant, the Captain of marines, and the Sailing Master.

In associating an officer of marines with the sea-lieutenants in a case having to do with a sailor the Commander perhaps deviated from general custom. He was prompted thereto by the circumstance that he took that soldier to be a judicious person, thoughtful, and not altogether incapable of grappling with a difficult case unprecedented in his prior experience. Yet even as to him he was not without some latent misgiving, for withal he was an extremely good-natured man, an enjoyer of his dinner, a sound sleeper, and inclined to obesity. [A] man who tho' he would always maintain his manhood in battle might not prove altogether reliable in a moral dilemma involving aught of the tragic. As to the First Lieutenant and the Sailing Master Captain Vere could not but be aware that though honest natures, of approved gallantry upon occasion[,] their intelligence was mostly confined to the matter of active seamanship and

113. St. Petersburg, founded by Peter the Great in 1703.

the fighting demands of their profession. The court was held in the same cabin where the unfortunate affair had taken place. This cabin, the Commander's, embraced the entire area under the poop-deck. Aft, and on either side[,] was a small state-room[;] the one room temporarily a jail & the other a dead-house[,] and a yet smaller compartment leaving a space between, expanding forward into a goodly oblong of length coinciding with the ship's beam. A skylight of moderate dimension was overhead and at each end of the oblong space were two sashed port-hole windows easily convertible back into embrasures for short carronades.

All being quickly in readiness, Billy Budd was arraigned, Captain Vere necessarily appearing as the sole witness in the case, and as such temporarily sinking his rank, though singularly maintaining it in a matter apparently trivial, namely, that he testified from the ship's weather-side[,] with that object having caused the court to sit on the lee-side. Concisely he narrated all that had led up to the catastrophe, omitting nothing in Claggart's accusation and deposing as to the manner in which the prisoner had received it. At his testimony the three officers glanced with no little surprise at Billy Budd, the last man they would have suspected either of the mutinous design alleged by Claggart or the undeniable deed he himself had done.

The First Lieutenant[,] taking judicial primacy and turning toward the prisoner, said, "Captain Vere has spoken. Is it or is it not as Captain Vere says?" In response came syllables not so much impeded in the utterance as might have been anticipated. They were these: "Captain Vere tells the truth. It is just as Captain Vere says, but it is not as the Master-at-Arms said. I have eaten the King's bread and I am true to the King."

"I believe you, my man" said the witness[,] his voice indicating a suppressed emotion not otherwise betrayed.

"God will bless you for that, Your Honor!" not without stammering said Billy, and all but broke down. But immediately was recalled to self-control by another question, to which with the same emotional difficulty of utterance he said "No, there was no malice between us. I never bore malice against the Master-at-arms. I am sorry that he is dead. I did not mean to kill him. Could I have used my tongue I would not have struck him. But he foully lied to my face and in presence of my Captain, and I had to say something, and I could only say it with a blow, God help me!"

In the impulsive above-board manner of the frank one[,] the court saw confirmed all that was implied in words that just previously had perplexed them[,] coming as they did from the testifier to the tragedy and promptly following Billy's impassioned disclaimer of mutinous intent—Captain Vere's words, "I believe you, my man."

Next it was asked of him whether he knew of or suspected aught savoring of incipient trouble (meaning mutiny, tho' the explicit term was avoided) going on in any section of the ship's company.

The reply lingered. This was naturally imputed by the court to the same vocal embarrassment which had retarded or obstructed previous answers. But in main it was otherwise here; the question immediately recalling to Billy's mind the interview with the after-guardsman in the fore-chains. But an innate repugnance to playing a part at all approaching that of an informer against one's own ship-mates—the same erring sense of uninstructed honor which had stood in the way of his reporting the matter at the time though as a loyal man-of-war-man it was incumbent on him[,] and failure so to do if charged against him and proven, would have subjected him to the heaviest of penalties; this, with the blind feeling now his, that nothing really was being hatched, prevailed with him. When the answer came it was a negative.

"One question more," said the officer of marines now first speaking and with a troubled earnestness, "You tell us that what the Master-at-arms said against you was a lie. Now why should he have so lied, so maliciously lied, since you declare there was no malice between you?"

At that question unintentionally touching on a spiritual sphere wholly obscure to Billy's thoughts, he was nonplussed, evincing a confusion indeed that some observers, such as can readily be imagined, would have construed into involuntary evidence of hidden guilt. Nevertheless he strove some way to answer, but all at once relinquished the vain endeavor, at the same time turning an appealing glance towards Captain Vere as deeming him his best helper and friend. Captain Vere who had been seated for a time rose to his feet, addressing the interrogator. "The question you put to him comes naturally enough. But how can he rightly answer it? or anybody else? unless indeed it be he who lies within there" designating the compartment where lay the corpse. "But the prone one there will not rise to our summons. In effect, tho', as it seems to me, the point you make is hardly material. Quite aside from any conceivable motive actuating the Master-at-arms, and irrespective of the provocation to the blow, a martial court must needs in the present case confine its attention to the blow's consequence, which consequence justly is to be deemed not otherwise than as the striker's deed."

This utterance the full significance of which it was not at all likely that Billy took in, nevertheless caused him to turn a wistful interrogative look toward the speaker, a look in its dumb expressiveness not unlike that which a dog of generous breed might turn upon his master seeking in his face some elucidation of a previous gesture ambiguous to the canine intelligence. Nor was the same utterance without marked effect upon the three officers, more especially the soldier. Couched in it seemed to them a meaning unanticipated, involving a prejudgement on the speaker's part. It served to augment a mental disturbance previously evident enough.

The soldier once more spoke; in a tone of suggestive dubiety addressing at once his associates and Captain Vere: "Nobody is present—none of the ship's company, I mean, who might shed lateral light, if any is to be had, upon what remains mysterious in this matter."

"That is thoughtfully put" said Captain Vere; "I see your drift. Ay, there is a mystery; but, to use a Scriptural phrase, it is 'a mystery of iniquity,' a matter for psychologic theologians to discuss. But what has a military court to do with it? Not to add that for us any possible investigation of it is cut off by the lasting tongue-tie of—him—in yonder," again designating the mortuary state-room ["]The prisoner's deed,—with that alone we have to do."

To this, and particularly the closing reiteration, the marine soldier knowing not how aptly to reply, sadly abstained from saying aught. The First Lieutenant who at the outset had not unnaturally assumed primacy in the court, now overrulingly instructed by a glance from Captain Vere, a glance more effective than words, resumed that primacy. Turning to the prisoner, "Budd," he said, and scarce in equable tones, "Budd, if you have aught further to say for yourself, say it now."

Upon this the young sailor turned another quick glance toward Captain Vere; then, as taking a hint from that aspect, a hint confirming his own instinct that silence was now best, replied to the Lieutenant "I have said all, Sir."

The marine—the same who had been the sentinel without the cabin-door at the time that the foretopman followed by the master-at-arms, entered it—he, standing by the sailor throughout these judicial proceedings, was now directed to take him back to the after compartment originally assigned to the prisoner and his custodian. As the twin disappeared from view, the three officers as partially liberated from some inward constraint associated with Billy's mere presence, simultaneously stirred in their seats. They exchanged looks of troubled indecision, yet feeling that decide they must and without long delay. As for Captain Vere, he for the time stood unconsciously with his back toward them, apparently in one of his absent fits, gazing out from a sashed port-hole to windward upon the monotonous blank of the twilight sea. But the court's silence continuing, broken only at moments by brief consultations in low earnest tones, this seemed to arm him and energize him. Turning, he to-and-fro paced the cabin athwart; in the returning ascent to windward, climbing the slant deck in the ship's lee roll; without knowing it symbolizing thus in his action a mind resolute to surmount difficulties even if against primitive instincts strong as the wind and the sea. Presently he came to a stand before the three. After scanning their faces he stood less as mustering his thoughts for expression, than as one only deliberating how best to put them to well-

meaning men not intellectually mature, men with whom it was necessary to demonstrate certain principles that were axioms to himself. Similar impatience as to talking is perhaps one reason that
deters some minds from addressing any popular assemblies.

When speak he did, something both in the substance of what he
said and his manner of saying it, showed the influence of unshared
studies modifying and tempering the practical training of an active
career. This, along with his phraseology now and then was suggestive
of the grounds whereon rested that imputation of a certain pedantry
socially alleged against him by certain naval men of wholly practical
cast, captains who nevertheless would frankly concede that His Majesty's navy mustered no more efficient officer of their grade than
Starry Vere.

What he said was to this effect: "Hitherto I have been but the
witness, little more; and I should hardly think now to take another
tone, that of your coadjutor, for the time, did I not perceive in you,
—at the crisis too—a troubled hesitancy, proceeding, I doubt not
from the clash of military duty with moral scruple—scruple vitalized
by compassion. For the compassion how can I otherwise than share
it. But, mindful of paramount obligations I strive against scruples
that may tend to enervate decision. Not, gentlemen, that I hide
from myself that the case is an exceptional one. Speculatively regarded, it well might be referred to a jury of casuists. But for us
here acting not as casuists or moralists, it is a case practical, and
under martial law practically to be dealt with.

"But your scruples: do they move as in a dusk? Challenge them.
Make them advance and declare themselves. Come now: do they
import something like this: If, mindless of palliating circumstances, we are bound to regard the death of the Master-at-arms as
the prisoner's deed, then does that deed constitute a capital crime
whereof the penalty is a mortal one. But in natural justice is nothing but the prisoner's overt act to be considered? How can we
adjudge to summary and shameful death a fellow-creature innocent before God, and whom we feel to be so?—Does that state it
aright? You sign sad assent. Well, I too feel that, the full force of
that. It is Nature. But do these buttons that we wear attest that
our allegiance is to Nature? No, to the King. Though the ocean,
which is inviolate Nature primeval, tho' this be the element where
we move and have our being as sailors, yet as the King's officers
lies our duty in a sphere correspondingly natural? So little is that
true, that in receiving our commissions we in the most important
regards ceased to be natural free-agents. When war is declared
are we the commissioned fighters previously consulted? We fight at
command. If our judgements approve the war, that is but coincidence. So in other particulars. So now. For suppose condemnation to follow these present proceedings. Would it be so much we
ourselves that would condemn as it would be martial law operating

through us? For that law and the rigour of it, we are not responsible. Our vowed responsibility is in this: That however pitilessly that law may operate, we nevertheless adhere to it and administer it.

["] But the exceptional in the matter moves the hearts within you. Even so too is mine moved. But let not warm hearts betray heads that should be cool. Ashore in a criminal case will an upright judge allow himself off the bench to be waylaid by some tender kinswoman of the accused seeking to touch him with her tearful plea? Well the heart here denotes the feminine in man[114] is as that piteous woman, and hard tho' it be[,] she must here be ruled out."

He paused, earnestly studying them for a moment; then resumed.

"But something in your aspect seems to urge that it is not solely the heart that moves in you, but also the conscience, the private conscience. But tell me whether or not, occupying the position we do, private conscience should not yield to that imperial one formulated in the code under which alone we officially proceed?"

Here the three men moved in their seats, less convinced than agitated by the course of an argument troubling but the more the spontaneous conflict within.

Perceiving which, the speaker paused for a moment; then abruptly changing his tone, went on.

"To steady us a bit, let us recur to the facts.—In war-time at sea a man-of-war's-man strikes his superior in grade, and the blow kills. Apart from its effect the blow itself is, according to the Articles of War,[115] a capital crime. Furthermore—"

"Ay, Sir," emotionally broke in the officer of marines, "in one sense it was. But surely Budd purposed neither mutiny nor homicide."

"Surely not, my good man. And before a court less arbitrary and more merciful than a martial one, that plea would largely extenuate. At the Last Assizes[116] it shall acquit. But how here? We proceed under the law of the Mutiny Act.[117] In feature no child can resemble his father more than that Act resembles in spirit the thing from which it derives—War. In His Majesty['s] service—in this ship indeed—there are Englishmen forced to fight for the King against their will. Against their conscience, for aught we know. Tho' as their fellow-creatures some of us may appreciate their position, yet as navy officers, what reck we of it? Still less recks the enemy. Our impressed men he would fain cut down in the same swath with our volunteers. As regards the enemy's naval conscripts, some of whom may even share our own abhorrence of the regicidal French Directory,[118] it is the same on our side. War looks but to the frontage,

114. the comma in the manuscript is deleted here.

115. regulations governing the behavior of military and naval forces.

116. Assizes are the highest courts of appeal in Great Britain. Here Melville means the Last Judgment.

117. The original Mutiny Act (1689) and successive acts passed by the British Parliaments applied only to the army; the navy followed the King's Regulations and Admiralty Instructions of 1772.

118. The governing body of France at the time of this story.

the appearance. And the Mutiny Act, War's child, takes after the father. Budd's intent or non-intent is nothing to the purpose.

["]But while, put to it by those anxieties in you which I can not but respect, I only repeat myself—while thus strangely we prolong proceedings that should be summary—the enemy may be sighted and an engagement result. We must do; and one of two things must we do—condemn or let go."

"Can we not convict and yet mitigate the penalty?" asked the junior Lieutenant here speaking, and falteringly, for the first.

"Lieutenant, were that clearly lawful for us under the circumstances consider the consequences of such clemency. The people" (meaning the ship's company) "have native-sense; most of them are familiar with our naval usage and tradition; and how would they take it? Even could you explain to them—which our official position forbids—they, long moulded by arbitrary discipline have not that kind of intelligent responsiveness that might qualify them to comprehend and discriminate. No, to the people the foretopman's deed however it be worded in the announcement will be plain homicide committed in a flagrant act of mutiny. What penalty for that should follow, they know. But it does not follow. Why? they will ruminate. You know what sailors are. Will they not revert to the recent outbreak at the Nore? Ay. They know the well-founded alarm—the panic it struck throughout England. Your clement sentence they would account pusillanimous. They would think that we flinch, that we are afraid of them—afraid of practising a lawful rigor singularly demanded at this juncture lest it should provoke new troubles. What shame to us such a conjecture on their part, and how deadly to discipline. You see then, whither prompted by duty and the law I steadfastly drive. But I beseech you, my friends, do not take me amiss. I feel as you do for this unfortunate boy. But did he know our hearts, I take him to be of that generous nature that he would feel even for us on whom in this military necessity so heavy a compulsion is laid."

With that, crossing the deck he resumed his place by the sashed port-hole tacitly leaving the three to come to a decision. On the cabin's opposite side the troubled court sat silent. Loyal lieges, plain and practical, though at bottom they dissented from some points Captain Vere had put to them, they were without the faculty, hardly had the inclination to gainsay one whom they felt to be an earnest man, one too not less their superior in mind than in naval rank. But it is not improbable that even such of his words as were not without influence over them, less came home to them than his closing appeal to their instinct as sea-officers in the forethought he threw out as to the practical consequences to discipline, considering the unconfirmed tone of the fleet at the time, should a man-of-war's-man['s] violent killing at sea of a superior in grade be allowed to pass for aught else than a capital crime demanding prompt infliction of the penalty.

Not unlikely they were brought to something more or less akin to that harassed frame of mind which in the year 1842 actuated the commander of the U.S. brig-of-war *Somers*[119] to resolve, under the so-called Articles of War, Articles modelled upon the English Mutiny Act, to resolve upon the execution at sea of a midshipman and two petty-officers as mutineers designing the seizure of the brig. Which resolution was carried out though in a time of peace and within not many days sail of home. An act vindicated by a naval court of inquiry subsequently convened ashore. History, and here cited without comment. True, the circumstances on board the *Somers* were different from those on board the *Indomitable*. But the urgency felt, well-warranted or otherwise, was much the same.

Says a writer whom few know, "Forty years after a battle it is easy for a non-combatant to reason about how it ought to have been fought. It is another thing personally and under fire to direct the fighting while involved in the obscuring smoke of it. Much so with respect to other emergencies involving considerations both practical and moral, and when it is imperative promptly to act. The greater the fog the more it imperils the steamer, and speed is put on tho' at the hazard of running somebody down. Little ween the snug card-players in the cabin of the responsibilities of the sleepless man on the bridge."

In brief, Billy Budd was formally convicted and sentenced to be hung at the yard-arm in the early morning-watch, it being now night. Otherwise, as is customary in such cases, the sentence would forthwith have been carried out. In war-time on the field or in the fleet, a mortal punishment decreed by a drum-head court—on the field sometimes decreed by but a nod from the General—follows without delay on the heel of conviction without appeal.

23

It was Captain Vere himself who of his own motion communicated the finding of the court to the prisoner; for that purpose going to the compartment where he was in custody and bidding the marine there to withdraw for the time.

Beyond the communication of the sentence what took place at this interview was never known. But in view of the character of the twain briefly closeted in that state-room, each radically sharing in the rarer qualities of our nature—so rare indeed as to be all but incredible to average minds however much cultivated—some conjectures may be ventured.

119. Melville's cousin, Guert Gansevoort, was first lieutenant of the *Somers* at the time of a mutiny. The incident seems to have impressed Melville, and perhaps it was in the back of his mind when he wrote *Billy Budd*.

It would have been in consonance with the spirit of Captain Vere should he on this occasion have concealed nothing from the condemned one—should he indeed have frankly disclosed to him the part he himself had played in bringing about the decision, at the same time revealing his actuating motives. On Billy's side it is not improbable that such a confession would have been received in much the same spirit that prompted it. Not without a sort of joy indeed he might have appreciated the brave opinion of him implied in his Captain making such a confidant of him. Nor, as to the sentence itself could he have been insensible that it was imparted to him as to one not afraid to die. Even more may have been. Captain Vere in [the] end may have developed the passion sometimes latent under a[n] exterior stoical or indifferent. He was old enough to have been Billy's father. The austere devotee of military duty letting himself melt back into what remains primeval in our formalized humanity may in [the] end have caught Billy to his heart even as Abraham may have caught young Isaac on the brink of resolutely offering him up in obedience to the exacting behest.[120] But there is no telling the sacrament, seldom if in any case revealed to the gadding world wherever under circumstances at all akin to those here attempted to be set forth two of great Nature's nobler order embrace. There is privacy at the time, inviolable to the survivor, and holy oblivion the sequel to each diviner magnanimity, providentially covers all at last.

The first to encounter Captain Vere in act of leaving the compartment was the senior Lieutenant. The face he beheld, for the moment one expressive of the agony of the strong, was to that officer, tho' a man of fifty, a startling revelation. That the condemned one suffered less than he who mainly had effected the condemnation was apparently indicated by the former's exclamation in the scene soon perforce to be touched upon.

24

Of a series of incidents within a brief term rapidly following each other, the adequate narration may take up a term less brief, especially if explanation or comment here and there seem requisite to the better understanding of such incidents. Between the entrance into the cabin of him who never left it alive, and him who when he did leave it left it as one condemned to die; between this and the closeted interview just given less than an hour and a half had elapsed. It was an interval long enough however to awaken speculations among no few of the ship's company as to what it was that could be detaining

120. Genesis 22: 1-18: "God did tempt Abraham, and said * * * Take now thy son, thine only son Isaac, whom thou lovest * * * and offer him * * * for a burnt offering * * * And Abraham bound Isaac his son, and laid him on the altar upon the wood. And Abraham stretched forth his hand, and took the knife to slay his son. And the angel of the Lord said, Lay not thine hand upon the lad, neither do thou anything unto him: for now I know that thou fearest God. And, saith the Lord, I will bless thee * * * because thou hast obeyed my voice."

in the cabin the master-at-arms and the sailor; for a rumor that both
of them had been seen to enter it and neither of them had been seen
to emerge, this rumor had got abroad upon the gun-decks and in the
tops; the people of a great warship being in one respect like villagers taking microscopic note of every outward movement or non-
movement going on. When therefore in weather not at all tempestuous all hands were called in the second dog-watch, a summons
under such circumstances not usual in those hours, the crew were
not wholly unprepared for some announcement extraordinary, one
having connection too with the continued absence of the two men
from their wonted haunts.

There was a moderate sea at the time; and the moon, newly risen
and near to being at its full, silvered the white spar-deck wherever not
blotted by the clear-cut shadows horizontally thrown of fixtures and
moving men. On either side the quarter-deck the marine guard
under arms was drawn up; and Captain Vere standing in his place
surrounded by all the ward-room officers, addressed his men. In so
doing his manner showed neither more nor less than that property
pertaining to his supreme position aboard his own ship. In clear
terms and concise he told them what had taken place in the cabin;
that the master-at-arms was dead; that he who had killed him had
been already tried by a summary court and condemned to death;
and that the execution would take place in the early morning
watch. The word *mutiny* was not named in what he said. He refrained too from making the occasion an opportunity for any preach-
ment as to the maintenance of discipline, thinking perhaps that under existing circumstances in the navy the consequence of violating
discipline should be made to speak for itself.

Their captain's announcement was listened to by the throng of
standing sailors in a dumbness like that of a seated congregation of
believers in hell listening to the clergyman's announcement of his
Calvinistic text.

At the close, however, a confused murmur went up. It began to
wax. All but instantly, then, at a sign, it was pierced and suppressed
by shrill whistles of the Boatswain and his Mates piping down one
watch.

To be prepared for burial Claggart's body was delivered to certain
petty-officers of his mess. And here, not to clog the sequel with
lateral matters, it may be added that at a suitable hour, the Master-
at-arms was committed to the sea with every funeral honor properly
belonging to his naval grade.

In this proceeding as in every public one growing out of the
tragedy strict adherence to usage was observed. Nor in any point could
it have been at all deviated from, either with respect to Claggart or
Billy Budd[,] without begetting undesirable speculations in the
ship's company, sailors, and more particularly men-of-war's men, be-

ing of all men the greatest sticklers for usage.

For similar cause, all communication between Captain Vere and the condemned one ended with the closeted interview already given, the latter being now surrendered to the ordinary routine preliminary to the end. This transfer under guard from the Captain's quarters was effected without unusual precautions—at least no visible ones.

If possible not to let the men so much as surmise that their officers anticipate aught amiss from them is the tacit rule in a military ship. And the more that some sort of trouble should really be apprehended the more do the officers keep that apprehension to themselves; tho' not the less unostentatious vigilance may be augmented.

In the present instance the sentry placed over the prisoner had strict orders to let no one have communication with him but the Chaplain. And certain unobtrusive measures were taken absolutely to insure this point.

25

In a seventy-four of the old order the deck known as the upper gun-deck was the one covered over by the spar-deck which last though not without its armament was for the most part exposed to the weather. In general it was at all hours free from hammocks; those of the crew swinging on the lower gun-deck, and berth-deck, the latter being not only a dormitory but also the place for the stowing of the sailors' bags, and on both sides lined with the large chests or movable pantries of the many messes of the men.

On the starboard side of the *Indomitable*'s upper gun-deck, behold Billy Budd under sentry lying prone in irons in one of the bays formed by the regular spacing of the guns comprising the batteries on either side. All these pieces were of the heavier calibre of that period. Mounted on lumbering wooden carriages they were hampered with cumbersome harness of breeching and strong side-tackles for running them out. Guns and carriages, together with the long rammers and shorter lintstocks lodged in loops overhead—all these, as customary, were painted black; and the heavy hempen breechings tarred to the same tint, wore the like livery of the undertakers. In contrast with the funeral hue of these surroundings the prone sailor's exterior apparel, white *jumper* and white duck trousers, each more or less soiled, dimly glimmered in the obscure light of the bay like a patch of discolored snow in early April lingering at some upland cave's black mouth. In effect he is already in his shroud or the garments that shall serve him in lieu of one. Over him but scarce illuminating him, two battle-lanterns swing from two massive beams of the deck above. Fed with the oil supplied by the war-contractors (whose gains, honest or otherwise, are in every land an anticipated portion of the harvest of death) with flickering splashes of dirty yellow light they pollute the pale moonshine[,] all but in-effectually struggling in obstructed flecks thro the open ports from which the tompioned[121] cannon protrude. Other lanterns at intervals serve but to bring out somewhat the obscurer bays which like small confessionals or side-chapels in a cathedral branch from the long dim-vistaed broad aisle between the two batteries of that covered tier.

Such was the deck where now lay the Handsome Sailor. Through the rose-tan of his complexion, no pallor could have shown. It would have taken days of sequestration from the winds and the sun to have brought about the effacement of that. But the skeleton in the cheekbone at the point of its angle was just beginning delicately to be defined under the warm-tinted skin. In fervid hearts self-contained some brief experiences devour our human tissue as secret fire in a ship's hold consumes cotton in the bale.

But now lying between the two guns, as nipped in the vice of fate, Billy's agony, mainly proceeding from a generous young heart's virgin experience of the diabolical incarnate and effective in some men—the tension of that agony was over now. It survived not the something healing in the closeted interview with Captain Vere. Without movement, he lay as in a trance. That adolescent expression previously noted as his, taking on something akin to the look of a slumbering child in the cradle when the warm hearth-glow of the still chamber at night plays on the dimples that at whiles mysteriously form in the cheek, silently coming and going there. For now and then in the gyved one's trance a serene happy light born of some wandering reminiscence or dream would diffuse itself over his face, and then wane away only anew to return.

The Chaplain coming to see him and finding him thus, and perceiving no sign that he was conscious of his presence, attentively regarded him for a space, then slipping aside, withdrew for the time, peradventure feeling that even he the minister of Christ tho' receiving his stipend from Mars had no consolation to proffer which could result in a peace transcending that which he beheld. But in the small hours he came again. And the prisoner now awake to his surroundings noticed his approach and civilly, all but cheerfully, welcomed him. But it was to little purpose that in the interview following the good man sought to bring Billy Budd to some godly understanding that he must die, and at dawn. True, Billy himself freely referred to his death as a thing close at hand; but it was something in the way that children will refer to death in general, who yet among their other sports will play a funeral with hearse and mourners.

Not that like children Billy was incapable of conceiving what death really is. No, but he was wholly without irrational fear of it, a fear more prevalent in highly civilized communities than those

121. usually "tampioned": plugged with a tampion, which fits into the muzzle of a gun not in use.

so-called barbarous ones which in all respects stand nearer to un-adulterate Nature. And, as elsewhere said, a barbarian Billy radically was; as much so, for all the costume, as his countrymen the British captives, living trophies, made to march in the Roman triumph of Germanicus.[122] Quite as much so as those later barbarians, young men probably, and picked specimens among the earlier British converts to Christianity, at least nominally such and taken to Rome (as today converts from lesser isles of the sea may be taken to London) of whom the Pope of that time, admiring the strangeness of their personal beauty so unlike the Italian stamp, their clear ruddy complexion and curled flaxen locks, exclaimed, "Angles" (meaning *English* the modern derivative) "Angles do you call them? And is it because they look so like angels?"[123] Had it been later in time one would think that the Pope had in mind Fra Angelico's seraphs some of whom, plucking apples in gardens of the Hesperides[124] have the faint rose-bud complexion of the more beautiful English girls.

If in vain the good Chaplain sought to impress the young barbarian with ideas of death akin to those conveyed in the skull, dial, and crossbones on old tombstones; equally futile to all appearance were his efforts to bring home the thought of salvation and a Saviour. Billy listened, but less out of awe or reverence perhaps than from a certain natural politeness; doubtless at bottom regarding all that in much the same way that most mariners of his class take any discourse abstract or out of the common one of the work-a-day world. And this sailor-way of taking clerical discourse is not wholly unlike the way in which the pioneer of Christianity full of transcendent miracles was received long ago on tropic isles by any superior *savage* so called—a Tahitian say of Captain Cook's time or shortly after that time.[125] Out of natural courtesy he received, but did not appropriate. It was like a gift placed in the palm of an outreached hand upon which the fingers do not close.

But the *Indomitable*'s Chaplain was a discreet man possessing the good sense of a good heart. So he insisted not in his vocation here. At the instance of Captain Vere, a lieutenant had apprised him of pretty much everything as to Billy; and since he felt that innocence was even a better thing than religion wherewith to go to Judgement, he reluctantly withdrew; but in his emotion not without first performing an act strange enough in an Englishman, and under the circumstances yet more so in any regular priest. Stooping over, he kissed on the fair cheek his fellow-man, a felon in martial law, one who though on the confines of death he felt he could never convert

---

122. Germanicus Caesar (15 B.C.–A.D. 19) was granted a triumph in Rome in A.D. 17.

123. The anecdote, told in Bede's *Ecclesiastical History of the English People,* is about Pope Gregory the Great (540?–604).

124. Fra Angelico, the Florentine painter Giovanni da Fiesole (1387–1455). Originally the Hesperides were nymphs, daughters of Atlas. They dwelled on an enchanted island in the western sea, guarding a tree bearing golden apples.

125. James Cook (1728–1779) was in Tahiti in 1769 and in 1772–1775.

to a dogma; nor for all that did he fear for his future.

Marvel not that having been made acquainted with the young sailor's essential innocence (an irruption of heretic thought hard to suppress) the worthy man lifted not a finger to avert the doom of such a martyr to martial discipline. So to do would not only have been as idle as invoking the desert, but would also have been an audacious transgression of the bounds of his function, one as exactly prescribed to him by military law as that of the boatswain or any other naval officer. Bluntly put, a chaplain is the minister of the Prince of Peace serving in the host of the God of War—Mars. As such, he is as incongruous as that musket of Blücher etc.[126] at Christmas. Why then is he there? Because he indirectly subserves the purpose attested by the cannon; because too he lends the sanction of the religion of the meek to that which practically is the abrogation of everything but brute Force.

26

The night so luminous on the spar-deck but otherwise on the cavernous ones below, levels so like the tiered galleries in a coal-mine —the luminous night passed away. But, like the prophet in the chariot disappearing in heaven and dropping his mantle to Elisha,[127] the withdrawing night transferred its pale robe to the breaking day. A meek shy light appeared in the East, where stretched a diaphanous fleece of white furrowed vapor. That light slowly waxed. Suddenly *eight bells*[128] was struck aft, responded to by one louder metallic stroke from forward. It was four o'clock in the morning. Instantly the silver whistles were heard summoning all hands to witness punishment. Up through the great hatchways rimmed with racks of heavy shot, the watch below came pouring overspreading with the watch already on deck the space between the mainmast and foremast including that occupied by the capacious *launch* and the black booms tiered on either side of it, boat and booms making a summit of observation for the powder-boys and younger tars. A different group comprising one watch of topmen leaned over the rail of that sea-balcony, no small one in a seventy-four, looking down on the crowd below. Man or boy none spake but in whisper, and few spake at all. Captain Vere—as before, the central figure among the assembled commissioned officers—stood nigh the break of the poop-deck facing forward. Just below him on the quarter-deck the marines in full equipment were drawn up much as at the scene of the promulgated sentence.

126. The manuscript is illegible, and "Blücher etc." is a conjectural reading. If the word is "Blücher," Melville was referring to the Prussian Field Marshal Blücher (1742-1819) who, with Wellington, defeated Napoleon at Waterloo. 127. *Cf.* II, *Kings* 2:11–13: "There appeared a chariot of fire, and horses of fire, and parted them both asunder; and Elijah went up by a whirlwind into heaven. And Elisha * * * took up * * * the mantle of Elijah that fell from him." 128. Aboard ship a bell is struck every half hour; thus eight bells are struck at the end of a four-hour watch. Here it is 4 A.M.

At sea in the old time, the execution by halter of a military sailor was generally from the fore-yard. In the present instance, for special reasons the main-yard was assigned. Under an arm of that lee yard[129] the prisoner was presently brought up, the Chaplain attending him. It was noted at the time and remarked upon afterwards, that in this final scene the good man evinced little or nothing of the perfunctory. Brief speech indeed he had with the condemned one, but the genuine Gospel was less on his tongue than in his aspect and manner towards him. The final preparations personal to the latter being speedily brought to an end by two boatswain's-mates, the consummation impended. Billy stood facing aft. At the penultimate moment, his words, his only ones, words wholly unobstructed in the utterance were these—"God bless Captain Vere!" Syllables so unanticipated coming from one with the ignominious hemp about his neck—a conventional felon's benediction directed aft towards the quarters of honor; syllables too delivered in the clear melody of a singing-bird on the point of launching from the twig, had a phenomenal effect, not unenhanced by the rare personal beauty of the young sailor spiritualized now thro' late experiences so poignantly profound.

Without volition as it were, as if indeed the ship's populace were but the vehicles of some vocal current electric, with one voice from alow and aloft came a resonant sympathetic echo—"God bless Captain Vere!" And yet at that instant Billy alone must have been in their hearts, even as he was in their eyes.

At the pronounced words and the spontaneous echo that voluminously rebounded them, Captain Vere, either thro stoic self-control or a sort of momentary paralysis induced by emotional shock, stood erectly rigid as a musket in the ship-armorer's rack.

The hull deliberately recovering from the periodic roll to leeward was just regaining an even keel, when the last signal[,] a preconcerted dumb one[,] was given. At the same moment it chanced that the vapory fleece hanging low in the East, was shot thro with a soft glory as of the fleece of the Lamb of God seen in mystical vision[,] and simultaneously therewith, watched by the wedged mass of upturned faces, Billy ascended; and, ascending, took the full rose of the dawn.

In the pinioned figure, arrived at the yard-end, to the wonder of all no motion was apparent[,] none save that created by the ship's motion, in moderate weather so majestic in a great ship ponderously cannoned.

End of Chapter

129. In the manuscript, Melville wrote both "weather" and "lee" above the word "yard." It is not clear why Captain Vere chooses the mainyard over the foreyard. The yards are the horizontal spars from which the square sails are suspended. Certain critics, who make Billy a Christ-figure, have suggested that the choice was dictated by the three masts, so that Billy would be raised to the central "cross," reminiscent of the Crucifixion.

27
A digression

When some days afterward in reference to the singularity just mentioned, the Purser a rather ruddy rotund person more accurate as an accountant than profound as a philosopher, said at mess to the Surgeon, "What testimony to the force lodged in will-power" the latter—saturnine spare and tall, one in whom a discreet causticity went along with a manner less genial than polite, replied, "Your pardon, Mr. Purser. In a hanging scientifically conducted—and under special orders I myself directed how Budd's was to be effected— any movement following the completed suspension and originating in the body suspended, such movement indicates mechanical spasm in the muscular system. Hence the absence of that is no more attributable to will-power as you call it than to horse-power—begging your pardon."

"But this muscular spasm you speak of, is not that in a degree more or less invariable in these cases?["]

"Assuredly so, Mr. Purser."

"How then, my good sir, do you account for its absence in this instance?"

"Mr. Purser, it is clear that your sense of the singularity in this matter equals not mine. You account for it by what you call will-power a term not yet included in the lexicon of science. For me I do not, with my present knowledge pretend to account for it at all. Even should we assume the hypothesis that at the first touch of the halyards the action of Budd's heart, intensified by extraordinary emotion at its climax, abruptly stopt—much like a watch when in carelessly winding it up you strain at the finish, thus snapping the chain—even under that hypothesis how account for the phenomenon that followed."

"You admit then that the absence of spasmodic movement was phenomenal."

["]It was phenomenal, Mr. Purser, in the sense that it was an appearance the cause of which is not immediately to be assigned."

["]But tell me, my dear Sir,["] pertinaciously continued the other, "was the man's death effected by the halter, or was it a species of euthanasia?["][130]

"*Euthanasia*, Mr. Purser, is something like your *will-power*: I doubt its authenticity as a scientific term—begging your pardon again. It is at once imaginative and metaphysical,—in short, Greek. But" abruptly changing his tone "there is a case in the sick-bay that I do not care to leave to my assistants. Beg your pardon, but excuse me." And rising from the mess he formally withdrew.

28

The silence at the moment of execution and for a moment or two

130. from the Greek, a quiet and easy death.

continuing thereafter, a silence but emphasized by the regular wash of the sea against the hull or the flutter of a sail caused by the helmsman's eyes being tempted astray, this emphasized silence was gradually disturbed by a sound not easily to be verbally rendered. Whoever has heard the freshet-wave of a torrent suddenly swelled by pouring showers in tropical mountains, showers not shared by the plain; whoever has heard the first muffled murmur of its sloping advance through precipitous woods, may form some conception of the sound now heard. The seeming remoteness of its source was because of its murmurous indistinctness since it came from close-by, even from the men massed on the ship's open deck. Being inarticulate, it was dubious in significance further than it seemed to indicate some capricious revulsion of thought or feeling such as mobs ashore are liable to, in the present instance possibly implying a sullen revocation on the men's part of their involuntary echoing of Billy's benediction. But ere the murmur had time to wax into clamor it was met by a strategic command, the more telling that it came with abrupt unexpectedness.

"Pipe down the starboard watch Boatswain, and see that they go."

Shrill as the shriek of the sea-hawk the whistles of the Boatswain and his Mates pierced that ominous low sound, dissipating it; and yielding to the mechanism of discipline the throng was thinned by one half. For the remainder most of them were set to temporary employments connected with trimming the yards and so forth, business readily to be got up to serve occasion by any officer-of-the-deck.

Now each proceeding that follows a mortal sentence pronounced at sea by a drum-head court is characterised by promptitude not perceptibly merging into hurry, tho bordering that. The hammock, the one which had been Billy's bed when alive, having already been ballasted with shot and otherwise prepared to serve for his canvas coffin, the last offices of the sea-undertakers, the Sail-Maker's Mates, were now speedily completed. When everything was in readiness a second call for all hands made necessary by the strategic movement before mentioned was sounded and now to witness burial.

The details of his closing formality it needs not to give. But when the tilted plank let slide its freight into the sea, a second strange human murmur was heard, blended now with another inarticulate sound proceeding from certain larger sea-fowl whose attention having been attracted by the peculiar commotion in the water resulting from the heavy sloped dive of the shotted hammock into the sea, flew screaming to the spot. So near the hull did they come, that the stridor[131] or bony creak of their gaunt double-jointed pinions was audible. As the ship under light airs passed on, leaving the burial-spot astern, they still kept circling it low down with the moving shadow of their outstretched wings and the croaked requiem of their cries.

131. a grating, harsh, high-pitched sound.

Upon sailors as superstitious as those of the age preceding ours, men-of-war's men too who had just beheld the prodigy of repose in the form suspended in air and now foundering in the deeps; to such mariners the action of the sea-fowl tho' dictated by mere animal greed for prey, was big with no prosaic significance. An uncertain movement began among them, in which some encroachment was made. It was tolerated but for a moment. For suddenly the drum beat to quarters, which familiar sound happening at least twice every day, had upon the present occasion a signal peremptoriness in it. True martial discipline long continued superinduces in average man a sort of impulse [of] docility whose operation at the official sound of command much resembles in its promptitude the effect of an instinct.

The drum-beat dissolved the multitude, distributing most of them along the batteries of the two covered gun-decks. There, as wont, the guns' crews stood by their respective cannon erect and silent. In due course the First Officer, sword under arm and standing in his place on the quarter-deck[,] formally received the successive reports of the sworded Lieutenants commanding the sections of batteries below; the last of which reports being made[,] the summed report he delivered with the customary salute to the Commander. All this occupied time, which in the present case, was the object of beating to quarters at an hour prior to the customary one. That such variance from usage was authorized by an officer like Captain Vere, a martinet as some deemed him, was evidence of the necessity for unusual action implied in what he deemed to be temporarily the mood of his men. "With mankind" he would say "forms, measured forms are everything; and that is the import couched in the story of Orpheus[132] with his lyre spell-binding the wild denizens of the wood." And this he once applied to the disruption of forms going on across the Channel and the consequences thereof.

At this unwonted muster at quarters, all proceeded as at the regular hour. The band on the quarter-deck played a sacred air. After which the Chaplain went thro' the customary morning service. That done, the drum beat the retreat, and toned by music and religious rites subserving the discipline & purpose of war, the men in their wonted orderly manner, dispersed to the places allotted them when not at the guns.

And now it was full day. The fleece of low-hanging vapor had vanished, licked up by the sun that late had so glorified it. And the circumambient air in the clearness of its serenity was like smooth white marble in the polished block not yet removed from the marbledealer's yard.

132. In Greek mythology, Orpheus was the son of Oeagrus and the Muse Calliope. When he played his lyre and sang, wild animals were charmed, trees and stones followed him, fish left the water in which they swam, and birds flew about his head.

29

The symmetry of form attainable in pure fiction can not so readily be achieved in a narration essentially having less to do with fable than with fact. Truth uncompromisingly told will always have its ragged edges; hence the conclusion of such a narration is apt to be less finished than an architectural finial.

How it fared with the Handsome Sailor during the year of the Great Mutiny has been faithfully given. But tho' properly the story ends with his life, something in way of sequel will not be amiss. Three brief chapters will suffice.

In the general re-christening under the Directory of the craft originally forming the navy of the French monarchy, the *St. Louis* line-of-battle ship was named the *Athéiste*. Such a name, like some other substituted ones in the Revolutionary fleet while proclaiming the infidel audacity of the ruling power was yet, tho' not so intended to be, the aptest name, if one consider it, ever given to a war-ship; far more so indeed than the *Devastation*, the *Erebus* (the *Hell*) and similar names bestowed upon fighting-ships.

On the return-passage to the English fleet from the detached cruise during which occurred the events already recorded, the *Indomitable* fell in with the *Athéiste*. An engagement ensued; during which Captain Vere in the act of putting his ship alongside the enemy with a view of throwing his boarders across her bulwarks, was hit by a musket-ball from a port-hole of the enemy's main cabin. More than disabled he dropped to the deck and was carried below to the same cock-pit[133] where some of his men already lay. The senior Lieutenant took command. Under him the enemy was finally captured and though much crippled was by rare good fortune successfully taken into Gibraltar, an English port not very distant from the scene of the fight. There, Captain Vere with the rest of the wounded was put ashore. He lingered for some days, but the end came. Unhappily he was cut off too early for the Nile and Trafalgar.[134] The spirit that spite its philosophic austerity may yet have indulged in the most secret of all passions, ambition, never attained to the fulness of fame.

Not long before death while lying under the influence of that magical drug which soothing the physical frame mysteriously operates on the subtler element in man, he was heard to murmur words inexplicable to his attendant—"Billy Budd, Billy Budd." That these were not the accents of remorse, would seem clear from what the attendant said to the *Indomitable*'s senior officer of marines who[,] as the most reluctant to condemn of the members of the drum-head court, too well knew[,] tho' here he kept the knowledge to himself, who Billy Budd was.

133. in the after-part of the deck below the lower gun deck; during battle it was converted into a sick bay.

134. Nelson's great victories over the French in 1798 and 1805.

30

Some few weeks after the execution, among other matters under the head of *News from the Mediterranean*, there appeared in a naval chronicle of the time, an authorized weekly publication, an account of the affair. It was doubtless for the most part written in good faith, tho' the medium, partly rumor, through which the facts must have reached the writer, served to deflect and in part falsify them. The account was as follows:—

"On the tenth of the last month a deplorable occurrence took place on board H.M.S. *Indomitable*. John Claggart, the ship's master-at-arms, discovering that some sort of plot was incipient among an inferior section of the ship's company, and that the ring-leader was one William Budd; he, Claggart in the act of arraigning the man before the Captain was vindictively stabbed to the heart by the suddenly drawn sheath-knife of Budd.

["]The deed and the implement employed, sufficiently suggest that tho' mustered into the service under an English name the assassin was no Englishman, but one of those aliens adopting English cognomens whom the present extraordinary necessities of the Service have caused to be admitted into it in considerable numbers.

["]The enormity of the crime and the extreme depravity of the criminal, appear the greater in view of the character of the victim, a middle-aged man respectable and discreet, belonging to that minor official grade, the petty-officers, upon whom, as none know better than the commissioned gentlemen, the efficiency of His Majesty's navy so largely depends. His function was a responsible one; at once onerous & thankless and his fidelity in it the greater because of his strong patriotic impulse. In this instance as in so many other instances in these days, the character of this unfortunate man signally refutes, if refutation were needed, that peevish saying attributed to the late Dr. Johnson, that patriotism is the last refuge of a scoundrel.[135]

["]The criminal paid the penalty of his crime. The promptitude of the punishment has proved salutary. Nothing amiss is now apprehended aboard H.M.S. *Indomitable*."

The above, appearing in a publication now long ago superannuated and forgotten[,] is all that hitherto has stood in human record to attest what manner of men respectively were John Claggart and Billy Budd[.]

31

Everything is for a term remarkable in navies. Any tangible object associated with some striking incident of the service is converted

135. Dr. Samuel Johnson (1709–1784), a noted English critic, man of letters, and lexicographer. The quotation about patriotism is in James Boswell's *Life of Johnson* (1791).

into a monument. The spar from which the Foretopman was suspended, was for some few years kept trace of by the bluejackets. Their knowledge followed it from ship to dock-yard and again from dock-yard to ship, still pursuing it even when at last reduced to a mere dock-yard boom. To them a chip of it was as a piece of the Cross. Ignorant tho' they were of the secret facts of the tragedy, and not thinking but that the penalty was somehow unavoidably inflicted from the naval point of view, for all that they instinctively felt that Billy was a sort of man as incapable of mutiny as of wilful murder. They recalled the fresh young image of the Handsome Sailor, that face never deformed by a sneer or subtler vile freak of the heart within. Their impression of him was doubtless deepened by the fact that he was gone, and in a measure mysteriously gone. At the time on the gun decks of the *Indomitable* the general estimate of his nature and its unconscious simplicity eventually found rude utterance from another foretopman[,] one of his own watch[,] gifted, as some sailors are, with an artless poetic temperament; the tarry hands made some lines which after circulating among the shipboard crew for a while, finally got rudely printed at Portsmouth as a ballad. The title given to it was the sailor's.

Billy in the Darbies[136]

Good of the Chaplain to enter Lone Bay
And down on his marrow-bones here and pray
For the likes just o' me, Billy Budd.—But look:
Through the port comes the moon-shine astray!
It tips the guard's cutlas and silvers this nook;
But 'twill die in the dawning of Billy's last day.
A jewel-block they'll make of me tomorrow,
Pendant pearl from the yard-arm-end
Like the ear-drop I gave to Bristol Molly—
O, 'tis me, not the sentence they'll suspend.
Ay, Ay, all is up; and I must up too
Early in the morning, aloft from alow.
On an empty stomach, now, never it would do.
They'll give me a nibble—bit o' biscuit ere I go.
Sure, a messmate will reach me the last parting cup;
But, turning heads away from the hoist and the belay,
Heaven knows who will have the running of me up!
No pipe to those halyards.—But aren't it all sham?
A blur's in my eyes; it is dreaming that I am.
A hatchet to my hawser? all adrift to go?
The drum roll to grog,[137] and Billy never know?

136. *darbies;* slang for handcuffs, irons, or fetters.
137. a mixture of rum diluted with water.

But Donald he has promised to stand by the plank;
So I'll shake a friendly hand ere I sink.
But—no! It is dead then I'll be, come to think.—
I remember Taff the Welshman when he sank.
And his cheek it was like the budding pink[.]
But me they'll lash me in hammock, drop me deep.
Fathoms down, fathoms down, how I'll dream fast asleep.
I feel it stealing now. Sentry, are you there?
Just ease this darbies at the wrist, and roll me over fair,
I am sleepy, and the oozy weeds about me twist.

END OF BOOK   April 19th 1891

ALEXANDER PUSHKIN
(1799–1837)
Eugene Onegin*

And he is in haste to live, and in a wild hurry to feel.—PRINCE VYAZEMSKY†

Canto I

1

"My uncle's life was always upright
And now that he has fallen ill
In earnest he makes one respect him:
He is a pattern for us still.
One really could not ask for more—   5
But heavens, what a fearful bore
To play the sick-nurse day and night
And never stir beyond his sight!
What petty, mean dissimulation
To entertain a man half dead   10
To poke his pillows up in bed,
And carry in some vile potation,
While all the time one's thinking, 'Why
The devil take so long to die?' "

2

So mused a youthful scapegrace flying   15
Along the post road thick in dust,
The only heir of all his kindred,
By the decree of Jove the Just.

* Cantos I and II, translated by Dorothea Prall Radin and George Z. Patrick, reprinted by permission of the University of California Press (Berkeley). Pushkin completed his verse-novel in 1830, made subsequent revisions until its publication in 1833.

† *Vyazemsky:* Pushkin's friend: poet, critic, satirist.
18. *Jove the Just:* i.e. Jupiter—Pushkin is being facetious about fate and chance.

Friends of Lyudmila and Ruslan,
Let me bring forward this young man   20
As hero of my tale without
More preamble or roundabout.
My friend Eugene Onegin, then,
Was born beside the Neva; you
May have been born there, reader, too,   25
Or lived as glittering denizen.
I also used to sojourn there,
But now I dread the northern air.

3

His father served with great distinction
And lived along on credit. He   30
Would give his three balls every season
And so went bankrupt finally.
The fates were gentle with Eugene:
At first a French *Madame* had been
His guardian—then *Monsieur*. The child   35
Was lovable though somewhat wild.
Monsieur l'Abbé, the needy tutor,
Taught him his lessons half in jest
And treated morals lightly, lest
He should appear the persecutor.   40
The Summer Garden saw the pair
Come frequently to take the air.

4

Now when Eugene had reached the season
Of ardent youth when passion soars
Or tender longing fills the bosom,   45
Monsieur was driven out of doors.
Behold our hero!—not a flaw;
Modeled on fashion's latest law;
A London dandy, combed and curled,
Prepared at last to see the world.   50
His French was perfect; he could write
And speak without a foreign taint;
His bow was free of all constraint,
His step in the mazurka light.

19. *Lyudmila and Ruslan:* characters in Pushkin's first narrative poem, published 1830.
24. *Neva:* river at Leningrad (formerly St. Petersburg) connecting Lake Ladoga with the Gulf of Finland.
34–7. *Madame . . . l'Abbé:* Eugene is raised first by a French governess, then a male tutor, then a priest.
41. *Summer Garden:* Summer Palace of Peter the Great, later a public garden.
54. *mazurka:* lively Polish dance resembling a polka.

The verdict was no more than truth: **55**
A charming, cultivated youth.

5

We all achieve a little learning
Somehow, somewhere, with the result
That dazzling by one's erudition
With us is never difficult.   **60**
And so Eugene, by those who grudged
Their praises often, was adjudged
Well read—almost to pedantry.
He could discourse most happily
Like an inspired amateur   **65**
On anything in Christendom,
And when the talk grew grave, become
The wise and silent connoisseur,
Then suddenly let fly a shaft
Of wit, till all the ladies laughed.   **70**

6

Latin of late is out of fashion,
And so our scholar, if I am
To tell the truth, could muster barely
Enough to read an epigram,
To mention Juvenal, and, better,   **75**
To add a *Vale* to his letter,
Or quote from Virgil without break
Two lines, though not without mistake.
He had no love for history's pages
Nor any antiquarian lust   **80**
For digging into ancient dust,
But anecdotes of other ages
From Romulus to us he'd find
And store away within his mind.

7

Of poetry, that lofty mistress,   **85**
He was no votary devout
Nor knew an iamb from a trochee
However one might count them out.

---

75. *Juvenal:* Decimus Junius Juvenalis
(ca. A.D. 60–130), Roman satirical poet.
76. *Vale:* Latin, "farewell."
77. *Virgil:* Cf. *The Ancient World* in
this volume.
83. *Romulus:* legendary founder of
Rome, eighth century B.C.
87. *iamb . . . trochee:* metrical feet
consisting respectively of an unaccented
syllable and an accented one (˘ ¯),
and an accented syllable and an unaccented one (¯ ˘).

Theocritus and Homer with
Their kind be damned, but Adam Smith   90
He read till he was a profound
Economist. He could expound
Wherein the wealth of nations lies
And what it lives on and how all
It needs is raw material,   95
Not gold. His father was less wise,
It seems, and could not understand
His son: he mortgaged all his land.

8

All the things Eugene had studied
I could not possibly impart,   100
But that wherein he was a genius,
Which was his own peculiar art,
That which from youth had been his pleasure
The toil and torment of his leisure,
Which filled his days of idleness   105
With melancholy, vague distress—
That was the art which Ovid sung,
The art of love, to which he died
A martyr in Moldavia's wide
And barren wilderness, among   110
Barbarian tribes, no more to see
His own far-distant Italy.

9

The fire of love torments us early,
Chateaubriand has said. Indeed,
Nature is not our guide, but rather   115
The first salacious book we read.
Beholding love in some romance
We seek to know it in advance
Of our own season, and meanwhile
All other joys seem puerile.   120
Intent on this foretaste of bliss
We spoil it by our very haste,
Our youthful fervor goes to waste
And all our lives are lived amiss.

89. *Theocritus:* Greek pastoral poet in the third century B.C., author of the *Idylls.*
Homer: Cf. *The Ancient World* in this volume.
90. *Adam Smith:* Scottish philosopher and economist (1723–1790), author of *The Wealth of Nations* (1776).
107. *Ovid:* Publius Ovidius Naso (43 B.C.–A.D. 18), author of *The Art of Love, Metamorphoses,* and much amatory verse; he spent his last years in exile in Moldavia on the Black Sea.

Such realizations came to vex   125
Eugene. But how he knew the sex!

10

How soon he learned to cloak his feelings,
To force his quarry to believe
Him true, to languish, dark and jealous,
To hide his hope—then undeceive;   130
To seem by turns subservient,
Proud, thoughtful, or indifferent,
With flaming eloquence to burn,
Or sit profoundly taciturn.
How in his notes of love unbounded   135
He threw discretion to the breeze,
Careless of all but how to please,
And how his glance, at once compounded
Of soft and keen, would then appear
To start with the obedient tear.   140

11

How skillfully he played the novice!
How well he knew the smiling ways
That startle an unpracticed maiden
And capture her with pleasant praise.
How he could seize the moment where,   145
Relenting at his feigned despair,
She yielded some half-meant caress
To his impassioned, shrewd address!
How ardently he then would sue
For an avowal! And at last,   150
When he perceived her heart beat fast,
Demand a secret rendezvous!
And then alone with her how he
Would tutor her in privacy!

12

How early he had learned to trouble   155
The heart of many a tried coquette;
And when he chose to crush his rivals,
What cunning pitfalls he could set!
With what malevolence he stung
Them with the poison of his tongue!   160
But you, you happy husbands, stayed
His friends: the married rake who made
A special point to pay him court,

Well versed in Faublas's strategy,   165
The old man prone to jealousy,
The cuckhold with the pompous port,
Completely satisfied with life,
Himself, his dinner, and his wife.

13–14^b

How from some meek and modest widow
He could attract a pious glance   170
And enter into conversation
With bashful, blushing countenance!
How, trifling with some ladylove,
He could discourse upon the worth
Of Plato's doctrines and could move   175
A pretty simpleton to mirth!
So from the forest's inmost heart
The savage starving wolf will creep
Upon the fold—all are asleep
And helpless; swifter than a dart   180
The cruel thief has snatched his prey
And in a flash is far away.

15

They bring his letters in the morning
Before he's thought of getting dressed;
Three houses ask him for the evening,   185
Requesting him to be their guest.
A children's name-day feast, a ball,
Which shall he start with of them all?
No matter, he will manage it!
Meantime, in raiment exquisite,   190
And hatted à la Bolivar,
The picture of a youthful spark,
Eugene is driven to the Park
To saunter in the open air
Until his watch with pleasant chime   195
Announces it is dinnertime.

16

Then to a sledge. The dark has fallen,
And to the driver's loud "Make way!"

---

164. *Faublas's strategy:* Faublas was the hero of the novel *The Adventures of Faublas* (1798), by Jean Baptiste Louvet de Couvray (1760–1797). His "adventures" are mainly amatory.

b. Stanzas with two numbers occur because either Pushkin or the Russian censor made deletions. Missing lines are also to be thus explained.

191. *hatted à la Bolivar:* the reference is to Simon Bolivar (1783–1830), leader of the revolution of Venezuela against Spain, later dictator of Chile. Bolivar's portraits indicate he favored broad-brimmed headgear.

He's whirled along; his beaver collar
Grows white beneath the frosty spray.   200
So to Talon's, for he's aware
His friend Kaverin waits him there.
He enters, and the pleasant pop
Of corks arises, and the plop
Of gurgling wine. The roast beef vies   205
With truffles, youth's delight,—the queen
And flower of the French cuisine,—
And the far-famous Strassburg pies.
Then Limburg cheese, mature and old,
And pineapple, all yellow gold.   210

17

The thirst that comes from eating cutlets
Still calls for wine, but the ballet,
His watch announces to Onegin,
Already must be under way.
And so the caustic arbiter   215
Of greenrooms and the theater,
The somewhat fickle appanage
Of lovely ladies of the stage,
Is driven off to view the play.
The stormy audience huzza,   220
Ready to clap the *entrechat*
And hiss Racine and boo Corneille,
Or call Moïna back because
They love to hear their own applause.

18

O magic country! There Fonvizin,   225
The friend of freedom, satire's bold
Old master, and the imitative
Knyazhnin shone forth in days of old.
There young Semyonova bore off

---

201. *Talon's:* famous restaurant in St. Petersburg.
202. *Kaverin:* dandy, sport, man-about-town, and friend of Pushkin, to whom the poet wrote several affectionate poems.
208. *Strassburg pies:* possibly made of goose-liver, for which Strasbourg—the capital of Alsace—is famous.
209. *Limburg cheese:* known for its odor; a product of the Belgian and Dutch provinces bearing the same name.
216. *greenrooms:* reception rooms in theaters and concert halls.
221. *entrechat:* a ballet step, where the feet are struck or crossed while the

dancer is in the air.
222. *Corneille:* Pierre Corneille (1606–1684), elder contemporary of Racine; author of *Le Cid* (1637), *Cinna* and *Horace* (1640), *Polyeucte* (1643).
223. *Moïna:* heroine in the play *Fingal* by Ozerov, based on James MacPherson's spurious epic of that name (cf. the notes to *René*).
225. *Fonvizin:* writer of comedies during the reign of Catherine the Great.
228. *Knyazhnin:* minor dramatist of the same period.
229. *Semyonova:* popular actress (1786–1849).

The palm of praise with Ozerov,   230
The idols of their countrymen.
Katenin brought to life again
The stately genius of Corneille;
And Shakhovskoy's tumultuous rout
Of biting farces were brought out   235
And Didelot was crowned with bay.
And in the shadow of the wings
I dreamed youth's sweet imaginings.

19

Dear goddesses of mine! Where are you?
Hear my unhappy voice and say,   240
Have other maidens filled your places
To triumph where you once held sway?
And shall I hear you sing once more?
Shall I behold you sweep and soar,
The spirits of the Russian dance?   245
Or shall my melancholy glance
View faces in a world unknown,
Turning upon them as they pass
My disenchanted opera glass,
Gazing at mirth I have outgrown!   250
Then shall I yawn and silently
Regret my past felicity?

20

The house is full, the boxes glitter,
The pit is like a seething cup,
The gallery claps with loud impatience,   255
The curtain rustles—and goes up.
There, half of air and all aglow,
Obedient to the magic bow,
Circled by nymphs in lovely bands,
Istomina, resplendent, stands.   260
Balanced on one toe, tremulous,
She slowly whirls the other round,
Then with a sudden leap and bound
Flies as if blown by Aeolus.
She winds, unwinds and, light as feather,   265
In mid-air beats her feet together.

230. *Ozerov:* Cf. note, line 223.
232. *Katenin:* translator of plays by
Corneille and Racine.
234. *Shakhovskoy's:* a prince, and patron of the theater.

236. *Didelot:* French ballet-master in
St. Petersburg.
261. *Istomina:* a dancer who died in
1848.
264. *Aeolus:* Greek god of the winds.

21

The house applauds. Onegin enters,
And, having trod on many a toe,
He studies through his opera glasses
The ladies whom he does not know.   270
His eye runs over every tier,
But gowns and faces all appear
To leave him far from satisfied.
He bows to men on every side,
Then carelessly begins to view   275
The stage and what is going on,
Averts his face and starts to yawn,
And mutters, "Time for something new!
The ballet pleased me once, but how
Didelot himself does bore me now!"   280

22

But still the cupids, snakes, and devils
Career about and scream and roar;
The tired lackeys in their sheepskins
Still doze before the entrance door;
And still they stamp and hiss and rap,   285
Or blow their noses, cough, and clap,
And still, outside and in, the night
Is all ablaze with lantern light.
The coach horse paws the ground or stands
Half frozen by the tedious wait,   290
And round the fires the cabbies rate
Their masters as they warm their hands;
But our Eugene, as you may guess,
Has long since left to change his dress.

23

Shall I depict in faithful colors   295
The private room where the mundane
Disciple of exacting fashion
Was dressed, undressed, and dressed again?
Everything London's nicest taste
Exports across the Baltic waste   300
To get, for gewgaws smart or strange,
Timber and tallow in exchange,
All that the workshop and the loom
Of greedy Paris could produce
Of luxuries as an excuse   305
For useful barter, in the room

Of our philosopher were seen—
The seer and sage just turned eighteen.

24

Pipes from Stamboul with stems of amber,
Bronzes and porcelain *en masse*,   310
And, that enjoyment of the pampered,
Perfumes in flagons of cut glass.
Steel files and combs elaborate
And scissors curved and scissors straight,
Brushes with thirty-odd details,   315
Some for the teeth, some for the nails.
(Rousseau could never understand,
They tell us, how the worthy Grimm
Could clean his nails in front of him,
The visionary firebrand: 320
The champion of natural rights
Here hardly followed his own lights.)

25

A man may see his nails are polished,
Yet be a useful citizen;
Why quarrel with one's generation?   325
Custom's a despot among men.
At any rate in our Eugene
A new Kaverin now was seen,
A dandy envied, watched, and thus
Forced to be most meticulous.   330
So when at last he sallied forth
After three hours before the glass,—
For so three hours at least would pass,—
'Twas like a Venus come to earth
Who thus in flighty mood essayed   335
The rôle of man in masquerade.

26

Now that I've drawn your kind attention
To fashion and the mode, you may
Expect me to describe more fully
My hero's elegant array;   340
A somewhat trying task, I fear,
Although description is my sphere,

---

309. *Stamboul:* Istanbul, Constantinople.
310. *en masse:* in a bulk.
318. *Grimm:* Friedrich Melchior,
Baron Grimm (1723–1807), friend of
Rousseau, Diderot, D'Alembert, etc.
321. *champion:* i.e., Rousseau.

For *pantaloons, frock coat,* and *vest*
No Russian wording can suggest,
And even now you must behold   845
How I have patched my halting style
With words of foreign domicile
Too lavishly. And yet of old,
To freshen my vocabulary,
I searched the Academy Dictionary.   850

27

But that is not the point at present:
Let's rather hurry to the ball
Where headlong in his cab Onegin
Has dashed already. On past tall
Dim houses where the horses' feet   855
Make echoes in the sleeping street
The carriage lamps, a double row,
Cast rainbow shadows on the snow.
Sown all around with firepots
A great house gleams; across the glass   860
Of lighted windows shadows pass,
Profiles of heads, and groups and knots
Of ladies with their cavaliers—
One moment, then each disappears.

28

Up drives our hero. Past the doorman   865
He darts and up the marble stair
Swift as an arrow; with one gesture
He brushes back a lock of hair—
And enters. Everywhere a crowd:
The orchestra is playing loud   870
And a mazurka fills the floor
While all about is crush and roar.
The spurs of many a guardsman clash
And tiny feet go flying by
And many a captivated eye   875
Flies after them. Then while the crash
Of violins drowns out the sound
A jealous whispering goes round.

29

In my gay days of youthful passion
Balls were my mad delight. Then, too,   380

350. *Academy Dictionary:* the French
Academy's conservative guide to correct French vocabulary, begun in the seventeenth century and not yet finished.

No better spot for an avowal
Or for delivering *billets-doux*.
You married folk, discreet and nice,
I offer you some sound advice:
  (I beg you, note my words with care)   885
For I would caution you, Beware!
And you, Mammas, had better bend
A stricter glance on those coquettes
Your daughters. Up with your lorgnettes!
For otherwise—Ah, Heaven forfend!   390
These secrets I instruct you in,
Since I myself long ceased to sin.

30

Alas! In my pursuit of pleasure
How many years have slipped away!
Yet were my morals not to suffer   395
I still should dote on balls today.
I love mad youth; I love the crowd,
Glitter and joy without a cloud,
The dresses, exquisite, complete,
And I adore the ladies' feet!   400
But you will hardly find, all told,
Six pretty feet in Russia. Yet
Two tiny feet I can't forget,
Although I've grown so sad and cold.
Their memory will not depart   405
And still in dreams they stir my heart.

31

Ah, little feet! To me, the madman,
What desert land will fail to bring
A vision of you! In what country
Do you now tread the flowers of spring?   410
Bred in the softness of the East,
Our sullen northern snow long ceased
To hold your imprint. You were such
As loved the soft luxurious touch
Of silky rugs—And are they past,   415
Those days when in you I forgot
Glory and country and my lot
As exile? Yes, they could not last,
And no more trace of them is seen
Than of your footfalls on the green.   420

382. *billets-doux*: little love-notes.

32

Diana's breast, the cheeks of Flora,
Are no doubt charming. But to me
Far lovelier and more enthralling
The fair feet of Terpsichore!
They promise us they will afford   425
An incomputable reward
And with their beauty light the fire
Of uncontrollable desire.
Elvina! I commemorate
Your feet! at all times: half concealed   430
Beneath the table; on the field
Of spring; in winter by the grate;
Upon the polished parquet floor;
Or granite rocks along the shore!

33

I can recall a stormy seashore: 435
The waves came rushing one above
Another in a fury, only
To lie before her feet in love.
I would have found it ah! how sweet,
As did the waves, to kiss her feet.   440
For never in my maddest days
When all my youth was yet ablaze
Did I so wildly long to press
The lips of Armida, or burn
To kiss her rosy cheeks or yearn   445
To touch her breast with a caress.
No, such a transport as then tore
My heart I never felt before.

34

And I remember one more picture—
In secret dreams again I stand   450
Holding for her the happy stirrup,
Her little foot within my hand.
Once more my fancy burns, once more
Her touch seems suddenly to pour
New streams of lifeblood through my heart,   455

421. *Diana's . . . Flora:* Latin goddess of the hunt; Latin goddess of flowers.
424. *Terpsichore:* Muse of dancing.
429. *Elvina:* Certain critics have suggested that Pushkin used the name as a conventional device; and in his lyrics, "Elvina" may represent three different females. Here she may be Maria Rajevsky, whom the poet knew when he was exiled to the Caucasus in 1820.
444. *Armida:* name of the enchantress in *Jerusalem Delivered*, epic by *Torquato Tasso* (1544–1595), perhaps used here to represent a love of Pushkin's youth.

Once more with love and pain I smart.
But sing no more, my noisy lyre,
These haughty damsels of the earth,
Enchantresses who are not worth
The love and songs that they inspire.   460
Their speeches and their glances cheat
As often as their little feet.

35

And our Onegin? He abandons
The ball for bed, half overcome
With sleep, as Petersburg the tireless   465
Is wakened by the noisy drum.
The cabman trudges to his stand,
Merchant and peddler are at hand,
An Ochta milkgirl hurries by,
The hard snow crunching frostily.   470
It is the pleasant morning stir:
The shutters open, in blue curls
The smoke from many a chimney whirls,
And, careful German manager,
The baker in his paper cap   475
Has answered many an early rap.

36

But wearied of the evening's turmoil,
Turning the morning into night,
The child of luxury and pleasure
Sleeps softly in the shaded light.   480
Then well past midday he awakes
To lead again, till morning breaks,
His life monotonous though gay,
Tomorrow like its yesterday.
But in this round of daily bliss   485
Was my Eugene quite satisfied?
To the proud victor in the pride
Of youth did nothing seem amiss?
In spite of all did he remain
At feasts and fêtes unspoiled and sane?   490

37

No, he had lost his freshness early
And wearied of society.
Beauties and belles no longer caused him

469. *Ochta:* a district in St. Petersburg.

A stronger passion than ennui.
He took no pleasure in intrigue,   495
His friendships only brought fatigue;
He could not sit the livelong day
Drinking champagne to wash away
The rare beefsteak and Strassburg pie;
Nor could he be prepared to make   500
Bright sallies with a bad headache;
And though a hothead, finally
He found his interest weakening
In pistols, swords, and dueling.

38

A sickness,—for its cure and treatment   505
We ought to find the formula,—
The thing they call the spleen in England,
Our Russian hypochondria,
Had mastered him by slow degrees;
And though, thank God, it did not please   510
The youth to blow his brains out, still
Life was a desert, dark and chill.
So, like Childe Harold, steeped in gloom,
Oblivious to the allure
Of gossip, Boston, sighs demure,   515
He would pass through a drawing room
Observing nothing that was there,
Nor altering his cheerless air.

42°

Fine ladies of the world of fashion,
You he abandoned first of all,   520
For at our age your upper circles
Undoubtedly begin to pall.
And though perhaps some lady may
Discourse on Bentham and on Say,
Their conversation as a rule   525
Is innocent but tedious drool.
Besides, they are so virtuous,
So lofty-minded and so clever,
So full of pious, pure endeavor,

513. *Childe Harold:* Byron's disenchanted hero in the peom by the same
name (1812–1818).
515. *Boston:* a game of cards resembling whist, in which the technical terms
refer to the British siege of Boston at
the start of the American Revolution.

c. Stanzas 39 through 41 are missing
from the original Russian text.
524. *Bentham . . . Say:* Jeremy Bentham (1748–1832), founder of the Utilitarian philosophy; Jean-Baptiste Say
(1767–1832), French economist who
popularized the ideas of Adam Smith.

So circumspect, so scrupulous,   530
So inaccessible of mien,
Their very sight brings on the spleen.

43

And you, young beauties of the evening,
Whom the wild droshkies dash along
The streets of Petersburg at midnight,   535
Eugene has left your boisterous throng.
Refusing all his visitors,
He had immured himself indoors
And shunned all riotous delight.
Yawning, he seized his pen to write—   540
But any stubborn work instilled
Disgust in him; no line would flow
From off his wavering pen, and so
He did not join that vexing guild
Of scribblers on whom I may pass   545
No judgment, being of their class.

44

Once more a prey to doing nothing,
His spirit sick with futile rage,
He sat down with the worthy purpose
Of mastering wisdom's heritage.   550
He filled a shelf with books and read—
But all to no avail. Instead,
One was a bore, one, mad pretense,
No conscience here, and there no sense;
Stale judgments everywhere he looks,   555
The old too old, the new all cast
In the old forms, and so at last,
Like women, he abandoned books,
And covered with a mourning-veil
The shelf of wisdom dead and stale.   560

45

Now I had likewise left the turmoil
And thrown convention's yoke aside,
And at this time we formed our friendship.
His traits and temper satisfied
My liking, the unique degree   565
To which he raised his oddity,
His dreams, his wit, that struck so close.

534. *droshkies:* low four-wheeled Russian carriages.

I was malicious, he morose.
We both had suffered passion's play
And we were weary of our parts,   570
The fire had died out in our hearts,
Though barely started on life's way,
And from blind fortune or from men
We hoped for nothing good again.

46

He who has lived and thought can hardly   575
Do otherwise than scorn his race;
He who has ever felt is troubled
With dreams of that which once took place,
No magic moments now will cause
Delight, the worm of memory gnaws   580
His heart and brings him vain regret;
But still it often does beget
A certain charm in conversation.
At first Onegin's sharp retorts
Put me a little out of sorts,   585
But later I felt no vexation
At his half-bilious sallies and
The sarcasm at his command.

47

How often in the summer evenings
When the night sky hung clear and bright   590
Above the waters of the Neva
Where yet there shone no mirrored light
From fair Diana's countenance,
We dreamed again of young romance
And thought of early love, again   595
Carefree and fond as we were then.
And the night air, so pure and good,
Without a word we breathed in deep;
Till like the prisoner whom sleep
Bears from his cell to some green wood.   600
Our reveries and musings bore
Us back to days of youth once more.

48

Eugene would stand in silence, leaning
Against the granite parapet,
Just as the poet did, he tells us,   605
Lost in old longing and regret.

No sound except a distant shout
When watchmen called the hours out
Or suddenly the rush and beat
Of cabs along a far-off street.   610
A lonely boat swept down the stream
And with the splash of oars were borne
A wild song and a fainter horn,
And we were spellbound in a dream.
But sweeter still than this delight   615
Are Tasso's octaves on the night.

49

O blue waves of the Adriatic,
O Brenta, river of my choice,
I yet shall look on you in rapture,
I yet shall hear your magic voice,   620
Sacred to all Apollo's sons
And known to me through Albion's
Proud lyre and ever dear to me.
The nights of golden Italy
I shall delight in to my fill!   625
Then in a dark mysterious boat
Some Venice maid with me will float
And now speak softly, now be still.
And she shall teach to me the tongue
Of Petrarch in which love is sung.   630

50

Oh, will it come, my hour of freedom?
For it is time to hear my cry.
I wait fair winds upon the seashore
And hail the vessels sailing by.
When shall I start my own free course?   635
When, under storm clouds, shall I force
My way across the battling sea
And leave a land so harsh to me?
And when at last I leave it, then
By the warm seas beneath the sky   640
Of sunny Africa I'll sigh

616. *Tasso's octaves:* the eight-line stanza (*ottava rima*) of Tasso's poetry.
618. *Brenta:* river near Venice, emptying into the Adriatic.
621. *Apollo's sons:* i.e., poets.
622-3. *Albion's proud lyre:* e.g., Byron's *Childe Harold.*
629-30. *tongue of Petrarch:* i.e., Italian, the language in which Francesco Petrarca (1304–1374), first and greatest of the Italian humanists, wrote his poems to Laura.
641. *Africa:* Pushkin's maternal great-grandfather may have been Hannibal, son of an Ethiopian king, brought to Constantinople as a hostage and taken by the Russian envoy to Russia; there he became a favorite of Peter the Great, who stood godfather to him, ennobled him, and married him off to one of the Court ladies.

For gloomy Russia once again,
Where I had learned to love and weep
And where my heart lies buried deep.

51

Onegin was about to travel   645
With me in foreign countries when
Fate cut the tie that bound our fortunes;
For years we did not meet again.
His father died. The creditors
Gathered before Onegin's doors   650
In greedy crowds, and each one came
Prepared to justify his claim.
Eugene, who hated legal traps
And law courts, took what came from chance,
Renouncing his inheritance   655
As no great forfeit. Or perhaps
Some vague presentiment, some breath
Spoke of his uncle's coming death.

52

And then a letter from the bailiff
Came suddenly, to notify   660
Him that his uncle now lay dying
And wished to bid his heir goodbye.
Eugene no sooner read the news
Than he was off, prepared to use
What speed he could along the way,   665
But yawning as he thought what lay
Ahead—what tedious hours he'd spend
Before he was a moneyed man.
(And at this point my tale began.)
But when he reached his journey's end   670
He found the body laid in state
And finished with its earthly fate.

53

The courtyard swarmed with neighbors' servants:
From north and south, from west and east,
The dead man's friends and foes had gathered,   675
All lovers of a funeral feast.
They buried him, and priest and guest
Refreshed themselves. Then, as if pressed
By weighty business matters, they
Took solemn leave and went away.   680

Behold Eugene, a country squire,
Owner of factory and river,
Of wood and field! The spendthrift liver
Of yesterday was all afire
To lead a life of order here   685
And end his former free career.

54

Two days the new enchantment lasted:
The fields with their deserted look,
The coolness of the shady forest,
The quiet murmuring of the brook.   690
But on the third, field, wood, and hill
No longer caused his heart to thrill
And later sent him fast asleep,
So that he could no longer keep
The knowledge from himself: he knew   695
That though here were no palace halls,
No cards, no verses, and no balls,
The spleen dwelt in the country, too,
And would attend him all his life
Like one's own shadow or one's wife.   700

55

Now, I was born for country quiet,
To be some peaceful villager,
For there my lyre's note grows louder,
My dreams and fancies livelier.
There, consecrated to the sway   705
Of *far niente*, every day
I wander round the lonely lake
And every morning I awake
To leisure, sweet and innocent.
I seldom read, but sleep, nor aim   710
To capture swiftly flying fame.
Was it not so my past was spent?
And then, obscure, unknown to praise,
Did I not live my happiest days?

56

A country house upon its acres,   715
Love, flowers, and utter idleness—
I love them all, unlike Onegin.
Indeed, I'm always glad to stress

706. *far niente:* "doing nothing."

The great dissimilarity
Between my friend Eugene and me,   720
So that no mocking reader nor
Malicious-tongued inquisitor,
Searching a likeness out, may sniff
And shamelessly asseverate
I've drawn myself upon the slate,   725
Like Byron in his pride. As if
No artist ever had been known
To paint a portrait not his own!

57

All poets, let me say, are dreamers,
The friends of love. And so of old   730
Sweet phantoms visited me sleeping
Whose images my heart would hold
Long after, till the Muse had brought
Life to these secret forms of thought.
Indifferently I have sung   735
An ideal mountain maid or young
Girl slave upon the Salhir's shore.
But you, my friends, keep asking me:
"Which of these jealous maids is she
Whom in your verses you adore?   740
Who is the loved one to inspire
The song that rises from your lyre?

58

"Whose glance has fired your inspiration?
Whose sweet caress was adequate
Reward for all your pensive music?   745
Whom do your verses celebrate?"
No one, my friends, no one, God knows.
The pangs of love, its senseless throes,
I suffered without recompense.
Happy the man who can condense   750
The heat of love to poetry!
So, following in Petrarch's ways,
His heart's hot torment he allays
And yet augments his ecstasy.
He tastes of glory and its fruit—   755
But love has always made me mute.

736. *mountain maid:* heroine of Push-kin's narrative, Byronic poem, *The Caucasian Prisoner,* written with similar works (*The Gypsies, The Brother Robbers*) between 1820 and 1824.

737. *girl slave:* character in *The Fountain of Bakhchisirai* (1824), which takes place in the Crimea.
Salhir: river in the Crimea.

59

Only when stormy love was over
Did my Muse enter. Then I found
My mind made free to seek the union
Between my dreams and magic sound.   760
I write, and my sad heart is eased,
My wandering pen no longer pleased
At each unfinished line to trace
Some tiny foot, some charming face.
The fire that was is burned to coal;   765
Now I, though sad, no longer weep,
And soon the storm will go to sleep
Forever in my quiet soul.
Then I may well begin a song
Some five-and-twenty cantos long.   770

60

Already I have planned my story
And named the hero, and meantime
I see that of my present novel
One chapter has been turned to rhyme.
I've looked it over carefully.   775
The contradictions that I see
I shall not alter now, but let
The censorship collect its debt.
And to the critics with my thanks
I send you, to be torn apart,   780
Newborn creation of my heart!
There on the Neva's well-known banks
To earn the tribute paid to fame:
Envy, abuse, and noisy blame.

Canto II

O Rus. O Rus!—Horace*

1

The place in which Onegin languished
Was a delightful country spot
Where lovers made for simpler pleasures
Would have been grateful for their lot.
The manor house itself was set   5
Apart beside a rivulet,
Cut off by hills from every storm.
Before it, flowery, golden-warm,
Meadows and cornfields stretched away,

* "O Russia!" Also a pun on *Horace*.

And cattle cropped the grassy land,   10
And hamlets shone; while near at hand
The great neglected gardens lay
Where wistful dryads came and made
Their refuge in the deep green shade.

2

The ancient and time-honored mansion   15
Was built, as mansions ought to be,
According to the bygone liking
For sober, wise solidity.
High-ceilinged chambers everywhere,
Silk tapestry on couch and chair,   20
Ancestral portraits in a style
Outworn, and stoves of colored tile.
To us all this seems antiquated,—
I can't say why,—but then, our friend
Most probably did not descend   25
To notice that they were outdated;
For fashion or antiquity
Produced in him the same ennui.

3

So in the room where the old landlord
Had forty years of exercise   30
In bickering with his woman servant
Or staring out and catching flies
Eugene took up his domicile.
No inkstain there that might defile
The plainness of the oaken floor: 35
Two cupboards, sofa, desk—no more.
Behind one cupboard door a great
Account book lay and close at hand
Bottles and jugs of cider and
A calendar of 1808.   40
Onegin's uncle would not look
At any other kind of book.

4

Alone on his ancestral acres,
Hard put to it for any scheme
To pass the time, Eugene decided   45
To introduce a new régime.
Here in the wilds the sage recluse
Declared forced labor an abuse

And changed it for a light quitrent.
His serfs thanked fate and were content.   50
Not so the neighboring landlords; some
Smiled mockingly, while others found
These innovations going round
Unsafe, and looked extremely glum.
But on one point they all were clear: 55
Eugene was dangerous and queer.

5

At first, indeed, they came to visit,
But presently, when they had found
He usually had his stallion
Led out and saddled and brought round   60
To the back porch, when he should hear
Their family coaches drawing near—
Affronted by such insolence,
They one and all took deep offense.
"Our neighbor's just a firebrand,   65
A freemason, a boor. They say
He sits and drinks red wine all day.
He will not kiss a lady's hand.
He won't say 'Sir,' just 'Yes' and 'No.' "
Their view of him was very low.   70

6

Just then another country squire
Had come to live on his estate
Who caused the same amount of gossip
And called forth censure just as great.
Vladimir Lensky was his name.   75
Direct from Göttingen he came,
A poet and a devotee
Of Kant. From misty Germany
He brought complete enlightenment:
High dreams of freedom democratic,   80
A spirit ardent if erratic,
A tongue forever eloquent.
A handsome youth, with fire and grace,
And black curls falling round his face.

---

49. *quitrent:* rent paid by a freeholder
in lieu of services which he might otherwise be bound to perform.
    67. *red wine:* i.e., a man of foreign
tastes. A "good" Russian would drink
vodka.
    75. *Lensky:* He becomes Onegin's
closest friend; they duel (Canto VI)
over Lensky's misconceived jealousy—he
thinks Onegin is flirting with Lensky's
beloved Olga—and Lensky is killed.
    76. *Göttingen:* university (founded
1737) popular with "Westernized" Russians in the early nineteenth century.
    78. *Kant:* Immanuel Kant (1724–
1804), professor at Königsberg, one of
the most influential philosophers of the
late eighteenth century.

7

Unblighted by the world's corruption   85
And by its cold perfidiousness,
His soul was set on fire by friendship
Or by a maiden's soft caress.
He was a charming innocent
In matters of the heart, intent   90
Upon the glamour and the noise
Of this new world of untried joys
Which hope held up to view. He lulled
His doubts with dreams. But still for him
The aim of life was strange and dim,   95
A riddle over which he mulled
And struggled, eager to divine
The miracle of its design.

8

He thought somewhere some kindred spirit
Was born for union with his own,   100
Some maiden waiting for him hourly
And longing to be his alone.
He thought the men he loved would spend
Their lives in prison to defend
His honor, and would not demur   105
To crush his venomous slanderer.
He thought there were some men appointed
By fate whose lot it was to be
A sort of friendly hierarchy,
A deathless band of the anointed,   110
Whose light would pierce our dark abyss
Some day and lead the world to bliss.

9

Pity and generous indignation,
A passion for the common good,
The torment caused by love of glory,   115
All worked together in his blood.
And so he wandered, lyre in hand,
His heart exalted, through the land
Where Goethe and where Schiller sung,
In air where still their genius clung.   120
Nor did he shame the lofty arts
Protected by the sacred Nine;

119. *Schiller:* Friedrich Schiller (1759–1805), close friend of Goethe in Weimar: dramatist, poet, historian, philosopher.

122. *sacred Nine:* the Muses, godesses presiding over the arts and the sciences.

His songs endeavored to enshrine
The noblest feelings of our hearts:
A maiden's dream of ecstasy,   125
The charm of grave simplicity.

10

The slave of love, he sang its praises
In stanzas like a limpid stream,
As simple as a maiden's fancies,
As artless as a childhood dream,   130
Clear as the moon in desert skies
That listens to a lover's sighs.
He sang of parting and of sorrow,
Of what-not and the misty morrow
And of the roses of romance.   135
He sang of countries far away
Where, weeping hotly, once he lay
Pillowed on silence' broad expanse.
He sang life's flowers dead and sere:
He then was in his eighteenth year.   140

11

Eugene alone could rightly value
Such talents in this arid waste,
And Lensky found the neighbors' dinners
Completely foreign to his taste.
He shunned their noisy conversations   145
About their dogs and their relations.
Indeed their sober talk of wine
And crops, though shrewd and genuine,
Did not exactly blaze with wit;
Nor was there any poet's fire   150
Nor brilliancy nor keen desire
Nor art nor social grace in it.
And certainly the ladies' words
Were quite as dull as were their lords'.

12   155

Both rich and personable, Lensky
Was thought an enviable match
And everyone who had a daughter—
Such was the custom—planned a match
With this half-Russian neighbor. They
Would manage, when he called, to say   160
How sad a single life must be

And ask the bachelor to tea
With Dunya at the samovar
To do the honors for their guest.
They'd whisper, "Dunya, do your best,"   165
And then they'd bring her her guitar,
And she would pipe as she was told,
Poor child, "Come to my halls of gold."

13

But Lensky had no inclination
For dalliance, it must be confessed;   170
While on the other hand Onegin
Aroused his deepest interest.
They met; and prose and poetry,
Cold ice and flame, firm rock and sea,
Were not so wholly different.   175
Quite bored at first, they underwent
A change of feeling to a state
Of liking in a certain way.
They met on horseback every day
And finally grew intimate.   180
So idleness achieved its end:
Each was the other's bosom friend.

14

But even such friendships are discarded
As prejudices of the past.
We rate ourselves alone as digits,   185
All others ciphers, to be classed
As vile by us, Napoleons
Among a million lesser ones
Created only for our tools,
And men of feeling we think fools.   190
Eugene was more forbearing. Though
Of course he knew and scorned mankind
As something very dull and blind,
All rules have their exceptions, so
Though alien to his intellect   195
He treated feeling with respect.

15

He listened with a smile to Lensky;
His bright and ardent conversation,

163. *samovar:* Russian tea-urn.

His unripe reasoning, and always
The poet's glance of inspiration,— 200
All this was novel to Eugene.
He struggled not to intervene
And chill such youthful ecstasy,
Thinking: "It is too bad of me
When bliss endures so short a space 205
To cloud this moment with regret.
His time will come; but meanwhile let
Him think the world a perfect place.
We must set down to youth's extremes
His youthful fire, his youthful dreams." 210

16

Between them everything was subject
For controversy and debate.
The treaty rights of ancient tribesmen,
Prejudices of antique date,
The fruits of learning, good and ill, 215
And life and fortune versatile,
And death, the mystery of ages,
Hung on the utterance of these sages.
Then, in the heat of argument,
Would Lensky eagerly rehearse 220
Fragments of northern poets' verse,
And our Eugene, the lenient,
Though missing an enormous deal
Would listen to his youthful zeal.

17

But oftener the tender passions 225
Engaged our youthful hermits' minds.
Onegin, freed from their dominion,
Discoursed of them as one who finds
Himself regretting quietly
The former tumult. Happy he 230
Who has outlived it. Happier still
The man who never felt that thrill,
Who conquered love by separation,
Hatred by lies—and yawned through life,
Bored by his friends and by his wife, 235
Untouched by jealous perturbation,
And never risked the ancestral hoard
Upon the treacherous gaming board.

18

When we enroll beneath the standard
Of safe and wise tranquillity,   **240**
And when love's passions are extinguished
And our wild whims and ecstasy
With their belated echoes seem
A foolish and outgrown extreme—
Then we, delivered from our spell,   **245**
May like to hear a stranger tell
His passionate and frenzied story
And feel our pulses stir again.
Just so some ancient veteran
Alone and shorn of former glory   **250**
Still loves to hear the young hussars
Recount their exploits in the wars.

19

And ardent youth is not secretive,
But always ready to impart
The love and hate, the joy and sorrow   **255**
Which animate its inmost heart.
Eugene, whose pride it was to be
The veteran lover, solemnly
Attended while his friend laid bare
His simple, fervent love affair,   **260**
Delighting in the utterance
Which artlessly disclosed his heart.
Thus without effort on his part
Onegin learned the youth's romance,
A tale of feeling it is true,   **265**
But long since anything but new.

20

He was indeed the sort of lover
Whose like we do not find today;
Only the mad soul of a poet
Is born to love in such a way.   **270**
At every time, in every place,
One single dream, one single face,
And one familiar sorrow still.
And neither distance bleak and chill,
Nor all the years of separation   **275**
Nor hours devoted to the arts
Nor lovely girls of foreign parts
Nor books nor scenes of animation

Could moderate his heart's desire
Still burning with its virgin fire.   280

21

Bewitched when still a boy by Olga,
Before he knew love's burning flames,
He used to watch the little maiden
With gentle pleasure at her games,
And in the shady wood he played   285
Alone with her. Their fathers made
Betrothal plans without demur,
Old friends and neighbors as they were.
Here in her peaceful country home
Beneath her parents' eyes she grew   290
As lilies of the valley do
That come at last to hidden bloom
Unnoticed in the clustering grass
By bees and butterflies that pass.

22

She gave the poet that first rapture   295
So poignant and so absolute.
Her image was the inspiration
Which first aroused his silent flute.
Farewell, you golden games of childhood,
For now he loved the deep-grown wildwood,   300
Silence and solitude and night,
The stars in heaven, the pale moon's light.
O Moon, the lamp of heaven! How
We used to walk in lonely grief
Until our tears would bring relief,   305
And vow the night to you—and now
You're but a makeshift, none too good,
For street-lamps in the neighborhood.

23

Olga was always good and modest,
Gay as the morning sun above,   310
As simple-hearted as the poet,
Sweet as the kiss of one's true love.
Her smile, her flaxen curls, her eyes
As blue as are the summer skies,
Her voice, her slimness, and her quick   315
And graceful movements—all.—But pick
Up any novel, you will see

Her portrait; it is charming, too,
And once it thrilled me through and through
But now it bores me utterly.   320
Her elder sister, in her turn,
Is now, dear reader, our concern.

24

Her sister had been called Tatyana—
We are the earliest to proclaim
Deliberately in a novel   325
A heroine by such a name.
Why not? It has a pleasant ring
Although, I know, around it cling
The odors of the servants' hall
Or of antiquity. We all   330
Must grant the names in poorest taste
With us have greatest currency
(I am not counting poetry):
Our education is a waste
From which we learn to set great store   335
On affectation—nothing more.

25

Her sister, then, was named Tatyana,
We've said, and she did not possess
The charm of Olga's rosy freshness
Nor of her winning prettiness.   340
Somber and silent and withdrawn,
As timid as a woodland fawn,
Even in her own family
She seemed some stranger child. For she
Had never learned the childish art   345
Of blandishment, so sure a way
To please one's parents. And for play
She never seemed to have the heart;
But often sat alone and still
All day beside the window sill.   350

26

She was a friend to meditation
And always had been so; the stream
Of quiet country days she colored
With the bright fancies of her dream.
Her tender fingers never held   355
A needle while the blossoms swelled

In silken fullness and became
A pattern on the embroidery frame.
It is a sign of love of power
Which little girls who like to play   360
With an obedient doll betray
When decorously by the hour
They solemnly repeat to it
Their mother's lessons, bit by bit.

27

But from her very little-girlhood   365
Tatyana never had been known
To touch a doll or tell it gossip
Or what the fashion was in town.
And childish naughtiness was quite
As strange to her; but when at night   370
In winter darkness they would start
Old grisly tales, it thrilled her heart.
And when the nursemaid would collect
All Olga's friends from round about
Upon the grass to run and shout   375
With laughter hearty and unchecked,
Tatyana never joined their game—
It seemed so boisterous yet so tame.

28

She loved to stand before the sunrise
Upon the balcony and watch   380
The galaxy of stars departing
From the pale sky, and the first blotch
Of faintest light where earth met sky,
And feel the little winds that sigh
In greeting to the risen dawn.   385
And long before the dark had gone
In winter or the shadows ceased
To lie on half the world, while still
The quiet moon, remote and chill,
Shone dimly on the lazy east,   390
This hour was still her favorite
And she got up by candlelight.

29

She took to novel-reading early,
And all her days became a glow
Of rapturous love for the creations   395

Of Richardson and of Rousseau.
Her father, who was good and kind,
Had long ago been left behind
By modern ways, but in the main,
Although he thought books light and vain,   400
He did not think them any harm.
And when a man has never read,
The books his daughter takes to bed
With her will cause him no alarm.
As for his wife, there was no one   405
So much in love with Richardson.

30

She worshiped Richardson not only
Because she read so much of him;
Nor because Lovelace suited better
Than Grandison her girlish whim.   410
But in old days Princess Aline,
Her Moscow cousin there, had been
His satellite. Then she was still
A girl, engaged against her will.
To him she later married, though   415
She sighed for one—unseen, unheard—
Whose mind and heart she much preferred.
Her Grandison was quite a beau,
A zealous devotee of cards,
And a young sergeant in the Guards.   420

31

Like his, her dress was always modish
And always most appropriate;
But, without asking her opinion,
They named the maiden's wedding date.
Her husband, in the wise belief   425
That he might thus divert her grief,
Moved to his country place where she
With God knows whom for company
Gave way to grief and was quite bent
On a divorce—then seemed to find   430
Her household duties claim her mind,

396. *Richardson . . . Rousseau:* for the latter, cf. notes in this volume; Samuel Richardson (1689–1761) was an English author of epistolary novels: *Pamela* (1740–1741), *Clarissa Harlowe* (1747–1748).

409. *Lovelace:* seducer of Clarissa.
410. *Grandison:* priggish hero of Richardson's *The History of Sir Charles Grandison.*
420. *Guards:* élite regiment attached to the ruling monarch.

Grew used to things, and then content.
For heaven-sent habit soothes distress
And takes the place of happiness.

32

So habit quieted a sorrow   435
Which nothing else could have allayed,
And soon her cure was quite completed
By a discovery she made.
In days now empty and now full
She learned the trick of how to rule   440
Her husband like an autocrat,
And all went smoothly after that.
She watched the field-work under way,
She salted mushrooms for the next
Long winter, beat her maids when vexed,   445
And took the baths on Saturday,
Kept books, sent off the new recruits—
All without marital disputes.

33

She had been wont to write in albums
Or girlish friends in blood, and call   450
Praskovya her Pauline, and lengthen
Each sentence to a genteel drawl.
She laced her corsets very tight
And said her Russian *n*'s in quite
The best French manner, through her nose.   455
But by degrees she dropped her pose:
Corsets and album and Pauline,
The notebook full of tender rhyme—
All were forgotten, and in time
Akulka had replaced Céline;   460
Till finally she went about
In cap and wrapper wadded out.

34

Her husband loved his wife sincerely
And never gave her cause to frown,
But spent his days, serene and trustful,   465
Attired in a dressing gown.
So life rolled placidly along:

451. *Praskovya . . . Pauline:* She preferred French to Russian names.

460. *Akulka . . . Céline:* She reverts
back to Russian.

Sometimes at night a little throng
Of friendly neighbors would arrive,
All intimates, and all alive   470
With gossip or with sympathy;
And they would laugh and chat and smile
And time would pass unnoticed, while
Olga was bid to make the tea.
Supper, the end of one more day—   475
And then the guests would drive away.

35

In this calm life, the good old customs
Were laws from which they never swerved;
When Shrovetide came and merrymaking,
Then Russian pancakes must be served.   480
They made confession twice a year;
They held a carrousel as dear
As bowl-songs and the circle-dance.
And when with yawning countenance
The peasants listened to the mass   485
On Trinity, they'd drop a tear
Upon a sprig of lovage; air
Was not more needful than was kvass;
And guests at dinner ate and drank
In strict accordance with their rank.   490

36

And so they lived for years together
Till for the husband, old and hoary,
Death drew aside the final curtain
And he received his crown of glory.
One afternoon he left this life,   495
Mourned by his children and his wife,
The neighborhood, and all his clan,
More truly than is many a man.
A simple squire without caprice,
Kindly to all—and on the stone   500
That marks his grave these verses run.

A HUMBLE SINNER, NOW AT PEACE,
GOD'S SERVANT AND A BRIGADIER,
'TIS DMITRI LARIN SLEEPETH HERE.

---

479. *Shrovetide:* Sunday through Tuesday preceding Ash Wednesday. Shrove Tuesday was once called "pancake day."

486. *Trinity:* Trinity Sunday, next after Whit Sunday: i.e., the eighth Sunday after Easter.

487. *lovage:* a medicinal herb.

488. *kvass:* a sour Russian beer, brewed from rye.

37

When he returned to his Penates,   505
Vladimir Lensky visited
His neighbor's unpretentious gravestone
And breathed a sigh above the dead.
He mourned him with sincerity.
"Poor Yorick!" he said mournfully,   510
"He used to hold me, as a child,
And many a moment I beguiled
With his Ochakov decoration.
He gave me Olga, and he'd say,
'Shall I be here to see the day?' "   515
And thereupon, his inspiration
Wakened by grief, Vladimir penned
An elegy upon his friend.

38

Then with another sad inscription
He paid the patriarchal dust   520
Of his own parents tearful tribute.
Alas! that generations must
By laws inscrutable and sealed
Like some brief harvest in the field
Rise up, mature, and die again,   525
Surrendering to other men!
So our ephemeral human race
Will wax and stew and seethe and boil
And finally, in great turmoil,
Themselves fill up their fathers' place.   530
And our own children, even so,
Will crowd us out, and we must go.

39

But meanwhile drink your fill of living,
Abortive as it is, my friends!
I know its emptiness and folly   535
And care but little how it ends.
I closed my eyes long since to dreams,
And yet one hope far distant seems
At times to agitate my heart:
I should be sorry to depart   540
And be entirely forgot.
I do not covet great renown,

505. *Penates:* household (from the Roman gods associated with the welfare of
one's house).
510. *"Poor Yorick!":* Hamlet's address
to the skull of the clown who once carried him about (V, i, 172 ff).
513. *Ochakov decoration:* medal awarded
by Catherine the Great, after the capture of Ochakov (on the Black Sea) from
the Turks in 1788.

Yet I am not averse, I own,
To singing of my mournful lot
So that one line of poetry,   545
Like a true friend, may speak of me.

40

Somewhere some heart may be affected,
And so the verses I create
May not be drowned at last in Lethe
But be preserved by fickle fate.   550
Perhaps—oh, flattering hope—some day
A future ignoramus may
Point to my picture and declare,
"You see a genuine poet there!"
Receive my grateful salutations,   555
You lover of the Grecian Nine,
Whose memory may yet enshrine
My brief and fugitive creations,
Whose reverent hands may yet caress
An old man's bays with tenderness!*   560

549. *Lethe:* i.e., oblivion (from the river in Hades of which the dead must drink).

560. *bays:* figuratively, the poet's laurel wreath.

* Six more cantos complete *Eugene Onegin.* Tatyana falls in love with Onegin, and writes him a letter stating her affection. The gloomy hero informs her of his fraternal love for her, but says that he could only make her miserable. Meanwhile Lensky courts Olga, Tatyana's younger sister. At her name-day ball, Onegin dances with Olga and arouses the jealousy of Lensky (Canto V), who is unaware of Tatyana's love for Onegin. Lensky challenges Onegin to a pistol duel, and is killed (Canto VI). Onegin leaves the village; Olga marries an Uhlan and departs. Tatyana visits Onegin's empty house, reads his volumes of Byron, and at last understands his melancholy. She and her mother move to Moscow, to enjoy the social life (Canto VII).

Several years later, Onegin (now twenty-six) attends a ball in Moscow; he inquires of a prince about a beautiful woman, to discover it is the prince's wife. Onegin calls upon her, and now realizes he loves Tatyana. On his last visit to her —when he finds her reading the last of his several unanswered letters—he falls before her feet, but she rejects him. They once might have been happy, she tells him, but now she will remain faithful to her husband.

Masterpieces of Realism and Naturalism

EDITED BY
RENÉ WELLEK

Sterling Professor of Comparative Literature, Yale University

As was indicated in the preceding introduction, the nineteenth century is the century of greatest change in the history of Western civilization. The upheavals following the French Revolution broke up the old order of Europe. The Holy Roman Empire and the Papal States were dissolved. Nationalism, nourished by the political and social aspirations of the middle classes, grew by leaps and bounds. "Liberty" became the main political slogan of the century. In different countries and different decades it meant different things: here liberation from the rule of the foreigner, there the emancipation of the serf; here the removal of economic restrictions on trade and manufacturing, there the introduction of a constitution, free speech, parliamentary institutions. Almost all over Europe, the middle classes established their effective rule, though monarchs often remained in more or less nominal power. Two large European countries, Germany and Italy, achieved their centuries-old dreams of political unification. The predominance of France, still marked at the beginning of the century, was broken, and England—or rather Great Britain—ruled the sea throughout the century. The smaller European nations, especially in the Balkans, began to emancipate themselves from foreign rule.

These major political changes were caused by, and in their turn caused, great social and economic changes. The Industrial Revolution which had begun in England in the eighteenth century spread over the Continent and transformed living conditions radically. The enormous increase in the speed and availability of transportation due to the development of railroads and steamships, the greatly increased urbanization following from the establishment of industries, changed the whole pattern of human life in most countries, and made possible, within a century, an unprecedented increase in the population (as much as threefold in most European countries), which was also fostered by the advances of medicine and hygiene. The increase of widespread wealth and prosperity is, in spite of the wretched living conditions and other hardships of the early factory workers, an undeniable fact. The barriers between the social classes diminished appreciably almost everywhere: both the social and the political power of the aristocracy declined. The industrial laborer began to be felt as a political force.

These social and economic changes were closely bound up with shifts in the prevailing outlooks and philosophies. Technological innovation is impossible without the discoveries of science. The scientific outlook, hitherto dominant only in a comparatively limited area, spread widely and permeated almost all fields of human thought and endeavor. It raised enormous hopes for the future betterment of man's condition on earth, especially when Darwin's evolutionary theories fortified the earlier, vaguer faith in unlimited progress. "Liberty," "science," "progress," "evolution" are the concepts which define the mental atmosphere of the nineteenth century.

But tendencies hostile to these were by no means absent. Feudal or Catholic conservatism succeeded, especially in Austria-Hungary, in Russia, and in much of the south of Europe, in preserving old regimes, and the philosophies of a conservative and religious society were reformulated in modern terms. At the same time, in England the very assumptions of the new industrial middle-class society were powerfully attacked by writers such as Carlyle and Ruskin who recommended a return to medieval forms of social co-operation and handicraft. The industrial civilization of the nineteenth century was also opposed by the fierce individualism of many artists and thinkers who were unhappy in the ugly commercial "Philistine" society of the age. The writings of Nietzsche, toward the end of the century, and the whole movement of "art for art's sake," which asserted the independence of the artist from society, are the most obvious symptoms of this revolt. The free-enterprise system and the liberalism of the ruling middle classes also early clashed with the rising proletariat, which was won over to diverse forms of socialism, preaching a new collectivism with the stress on equality. Socialism could have Christian or romantic motivations, or it could become "scientific" and revolutionary, as Marx's brand of socialism (a certain stage of which he called "communism") claimed to be.

While up through the eighteenth century religion was, at least in name, a major force in European civilization, in the nineteenth century there was a marked decrease in its influence on both the intellectual leaders and the masses. Local intense revivals of religious consciousness, such as the Oxford Movement in England, did occur, and the traditional religious institutions were preserved everywhere, but the impact of science on religion was such that many tenets of the old faiths crumbled. The discoveries of astronomy, geology, evolutionary biology, archaeology, and biblical criticism forced, almost everywhere, a restatement of the old creeds. Religion, especially in the Protestant countries, was frequently confined to an inner feeling of religiosity or to a system of morality which preserved the ancient Christian virtues. During the early nineteenth century, in Germany, Hegel and his predecessors and followers tried to interpret the world in spiritual terms outside the bounds of traditional religion. There were many attempts even late in the century to restate this view, but the methods and discoveries of science seemed to invalidate it, and various formulas which took science as their base in building new lay religions of hope in humanity gained popularity. French Positivism, English utilitarianism, the evolutionism of Herbert Spencer, are some of the best-known examples. Meanwhile, for the first time in history, at least in Europe, profoundly pessimistic and atheistic philosophies arose, of which Schopenhauer's was the most subtle, while a purely physical materialism was the most widespread. Thus the whole gamut

of views of the universe was represented during the century in new and impressive formulations.

The plastic arts did not show a similar vitality. For a long time, in most countries, painting and architecture floundered in a sterile eclecticism, in a bewildering variety of historical masquerades in which the neo-Gothic style was replaced by the neo-Renaissance and that by the neo-Baroque and other decorative revivals of past forms. Only in France, painting, with the impressionists, found a new style which was genuinely original. In music the highly romantic art of Richard Wagner attracted most attention, but the individual national schools either continued in their tradition, like Italian opera (Verdi) or founded an idiom of their own, often based on a revival of folklore, as in Russia (Tchaikovsky), Poland (Chopin), Bohemia (Dvořák), and Norway (Grieg).

But literature was the most representative and the most widely influential art of the nineteenth century. It found new forms and methods and expressed the social and intellectual situation of the time most fully and memorably.

After the great wave of the international romantic movement had spent its force in the fourth decade of the nineteenth century, European literature moved in the direction of what is usually called *realism*. Realism was not a coherent general movement which established itself unchallenged for a long period of time, as classicism had succeeded in doing during the eighteenth century. There were many authors in the nineteenth century who continued to practice a substantially romantic art (Tennyson and Hugo, for example); there were even movements which upheld a definitely romantic "escapist," antirealist program, such as that of the Pre-Raphaelites in England or the Parnassians in France. But, with whatever exceptions and reservations, in retrospect the nineteenth century appears as the period of the great realistic writers: Balzac and Flaubert in France, Dostoevsky and Tolstoy in Russia, Dickens in England, Ibsen in Norway.

What is meant by realism? The term, in literary use (there is a much older philosophical use), apparently dates back to the Germans at the turn of the century—to Schiller and the Schlegels. It cropped up in France as early as 1826 but became a commonly accepted literary and artistic slogan only in the 1850's. (A review called *Réalisme* began publication in 1856, and a critic, Champfleury, published a volume of critical articles with the title *Le Réalisme* in the following year.) Since then the word has been bandied about, discussed, analyzed, and abused as all slogans are. It is frequently confused with naturalism, a term which also has old philosophical uses, but seems, in France, at least, to have been applied first to painting and to have become a literary slogan only about 1880, when Émile Zola began to employ it to describe his art.

The program of the groups of writers and critics who used these terms can be easily summarized. The realists wanted a truthful representation in literature of reality—that is, of contemporary life and manners. They thought of their method as inductive, observational, and hence "objective." The personality of the author was to be suppressed, or was at least to recede into the background, since reality was to be seen "as it is." The naturalistic program, as formulated by Zola, was substantially the same except that Zola put greater stress on the analogies to science, considering the procedure of the novelist as identical with that of the experimenting scientist. He also more definitely and exclusively embraced the philosophy of scientific materialism, with its deterministic implications, its stress on heredity and environment, while the older realists were not always so clear in drawing the philosophical consequences. These French theories were anticipated, paralleled, or imitated all over the world of Western literature. In Germany, the movement called Young Germany, with which Heine was associated, had propounded a substantially antiromantic realistic program as early as the thirties, but versions of the French theories definitely triumphed there only in the 1880's. In Russia, as early as the forties, the most prominent critic of the time, Vissarion Belinsky, praised the "natural" school of Russian fiction, which described contemporary Russia with fidelity. Italy also, from the late seventies on, produced an analogous movement, which called itself *verismo*. The English-speaking countries were the last to adopt the critical programs and slogans of the Continent: George Moore and George Gissing brought the French theories to England in the late eighties, and in the United States William Dean Howells began his campaign for realism in 1886, when he became editor of *Harper's Magazine*. Realistic and naturalistic theories of literature have since been widely accepted in spite of many twentieth-century criticisms and the whole general trend of twentieth-century literature. Especially in the United States, the contemporary novel is usually considered naturalistic and judged by standards of nature and truth. The officially promoted doctrine in Russia is called "socialist Realism."

The slogans "realism" and "naturalism" were thus new in the nineteenth century. They served as effective formulas directed against the romantic creed. Truth, contemporaneity, and objectivity were the obvious counterparts of romantic imagination, of romantic historicism and its glorification of the past, and of romantic subjectivity, the exaltation of the ego and the individual. But, of course, the emphasis on truth and objectivity was not really new: these qualities had been demanded by many older, classical theories of imitation, and in the eighteenth century there were great writers such as Diderot who wanted a literal "imitation of life" even on the stage.

The practice of realism, it could be argued, is very old in-

deed. There are realistic scenes in the *Odyssey*, and there is plenty of realism in ancient comedy and satire, in medieval stories (fabliaux) like some of Chaucer's and Boccaccio's, in many Elizabethan plays, in the Spanish rogue novels, in the English eighteenth-century novel beginning with Defoe, and so on almost ad infinitum. But while it would be easy to find in early literature anticipations of almost every single element of modern realism, still the systematic description of contemporary society, with a serious purpose, often even with a tragic tone as well, and with sympathy for heroes drawn from the middle and lower classes, was a real innovation of the nineteenth century.

It is usually rash to explain a literary movement in social and political terms. But the new realistic art surely has something to do with the triumph of the middle classes in France after the July revolution in 1830, and in England after the passage of the Reform Bill in 1832, and with the increasing influence of the middle classes in almost every country. Russia is somewhat of an exception as no large middle class could develop there during the nineteenth century. An absolute feudal regime continued in power and the special character of most of Russian literature must be due to this distinction, but even in Russia there emerged an "intelligentsia" (the term comes from Russia) which was open to Western ideas and was highly critical of the czarist regime and its official "ideology." But while much nineteenth-century literature reflects the triumph of the middle classes, it would be an error to think of the great realistic writers as spokesmen or mouthpieces of the society they described. Balzac was politically a Catholic monarchist who applauded the Bourbon restoration after the fall of Napoleon, but he had an extraordinary imaginative insight into the processes leading to the victory of the middle classes. Flaubert despised the middle-class society of the Third Empire with an intense hatred and the pride of a self-conscious artist. Dickens became increasingly critical of the middle classes and the assumptions of industrial civilization. Dostoevsky, though he took part in a conspiracy against the Russian government early in his life and spent ten years in exile in Siberia, became the propounder of an extremely conservative nationalistic and religious creed which was definitely directed against the revolutionary forces in Russia. Tolstoy, himself a count and a landowner, was violent in his criticism of the czarist regime, especially later in his life, but he cannot be described as friendly to the middle classes, to the aims of the democratic movements in Western Europe, or to the science of the time. Ibsen's political attitude is that of a proud individualist who condemns the "compact majority" and its tyranny. Possibly all art is critical of its society, but in the nineteenth century this criticism became much more explicit, as social and political issues became much more urgent or, at least, were regarded as

more urgent by the writing groups. To a far greater degree than in earlier centuries, writers felt their isolation from society, viewed the structure and problems of the prevailing order as debatable and reformable, and in spite of all demands for objectivity became, in many cases, social propagandists and reformers in their own right.

The program of realism, while defensible enough as a reaction against romanticism, raises critical questions which were not answered theoretically by its defenders. What is meant by "truth" of representation? Photographic copying? This seems the implication of many famous pronouncements. "A novel is a mirror walking along the road," said Stendhal as early as 1830. But such statements can hardly be taken literally. All art must select and represent; it cannot be and has never been a simple transcript of reality. What such analogies are intended to convey is rather a claim for an all-inclusiveness of subject matter, a protest against the exclusion of themes which before were considered "low," "sordid," or "trivial" (like the puddles along the road the mirror walks). Chekhov formulated this protest with the usual parallel between the scientist and the writer: "To a chemist nothing on earth is unclean. A writer must be as objective as a chemist; he must abandon the subjective line: he must know that dungheaps play a very respectable part in a landscape, and that evil passions are as inherent in life as good ones." Thus the "truth" of realistic art includes the sordid, the low, the disgusting, and the evil; and, the implication is, the subject is treated objectively, without interference and falsification by the artist's personality and his own desires. But in practice, while the realistic artist succeeded in expanding the themes of art, he could not fulfill the demand for total objectivity. Works of art are written by human beings and inevitably express their personalities and their points of view. As Conrad admitted, "even the most artful of writers will give himself (and his morality) away in about every third sentence." Objectivity, in the sense which Zola had in mind when he proposed a scientific method in the writing of novels and conceived of the novelist as a sociologist collecting human documents, is impossible in practice. When it has been attempted, it has led only to bad art, to dullness and the display of inert materials, to the confusion between the art of the novel and reporting, "documentation." The demand for "objectivity" can be understood only as a demand for a specific method of narration, in which the author does not interfere explicitly, in his own name, and as a rejection of personal themes of introspection and reverie.

The realistic program, while it has made innumerable new subjects available to art, also implies a narrowing of its themes and methods—a condemnation of the fantastic, the historical, the remote, the idealized, the "unsullied," the idyllic. Realism professes to present us with a "slice of life." But one should recognize that it is an artistic

method and convention like any other. Romantic art could, without offending its readers, use coincidences, improbabilities, and even impossibilities, which were not, theoretically at least, tolerated in realistic art. Ibsen, for instance, avoided many older conventions of the stage: asides, soliloquies, eavesdropping, sudden unmotivated appearances of new characters, and so on; but his dramas have their own marked conventions, which seem today almost as "unnatural" as those of the romantics. Realistic theories of literature cannot be upheld in their literal sense; objective and impersonal truth is unobtainable, at least in art, since all art is a "making," a creating of a world of symbols which differs radically from the world which we call reality. The value of realism lies in its negation of the conventions of romanticism, its expansion of the themes of art, and its new demonstration (never forgotten by artists) that literature has to deal also with its time and society and has, at its best, an insight into reality (not only social reality) which is not necessarily identical with that of science. Many of the great writers make us "realize" the world of their time, evoke an imaginative picture of it which seems truer and will last longer than that of historians and sociologists. But this achievement is due to their imagination and their art, or craft, two requisites which realistic theory tended to forget or minimize.

When we observe the actual practice of the great realistic writers of the nineteenth century, we notice a sharp contradiction between theory and practice, and an independent evolution of the art of the novel which is obscured for us if we pay too much attention to the theories and slogans of the time, even those that the authors themselves propounded. Balzac, one of the originators of the realistic novel, who created a vast panorama of French society and thought of himself as its faithful chronicler, was, if we examine his actual works, a writer of powerful, almost visionary imagination, whose books are full of survivals of romanticism and an intricate occult view of the world. Flaubert, the high priest of a cult of "art for art's sake," the most consistent propounder of absolute objectivity, was actually, at least in a good half of his work, a writer of romantic fantasies of blood and gold, flesh and jewels. There is some truth in his saying that Madame Bovary is himself, for in the drab story of a provincial adulteress he castigated his own romanticism and romantic dreams.

So too with Dostoevsky. Although some of his settings resemble those of the "grime novel," he is actually a writer of high tragedy, of a drama of ideas in which ordinary reality is transformed into a symbol of the spiritual world. His technique is closely associated with Balzac's (it is significant that his first publication was a translation of Balzac's *Eugénie Grandet*) and thus with many devices of the sensational melodramatic novel of French romanticism. Tolstoy's art is more concretely real than that of any of the other great

masters mentioned, yet he is, at the same time, the most personal and even literally autobiographical author in the history of the novel—a writer, besides, who knows nothing of detachment toward social and religious problems, but frankly preaches his own very peculiar religion. And if we turn to Dickens and Ibsen, we find essentially the same situation. Dickens incorporated into his novels a variety of elements drawn from the fairy tale or the melodramatic stage. His method is frequently that of caricature and burlesque; his atmosphere that of a dream or a nightmare. Ibsen began as a writer of historical and fantastic dramas and slowly returned to a style which is fundamentally symbolist. All his later plays are organized by symbols, from the duck of *The Wild Duck* (1884) to the white horses in *Rosmersholm* (1886) and the tower in *The Master Builder* (1892). Even Zola, the propounder of the most scientific theory, was in practice a novelist who used the most extreme devices of melodrama and symbolism. In *Germinal* (1885), his novel of mining, the mine is the central symbol, alive as an animal, heaving, breathing. It would be an odd reader who could find literal truth in the final catastrophe of the cave-in or even in such "naturalistic" scenes as a dance where the beer oozes from the nostrils of the drinkers.

One could assert, in short, that all the great realists were at bottom romanticists, but it is probably wiser to conclude that they were simply artists who created worlds of imagination and knew (at least instinctively) that in art one can say something about reality only through symbols. The attempts at documentary art, at mere reporting and transcribing, are today forgotten.

BALZAC, "GOBSECK"

Balzac is the great conquistador, the Napoleon, of the modern novel. With a tremendous, almost unbelievable, energy and concentration he constructed the vast edifice of his series of novels, to which he gave the collective name of the *Human Comedy* (*Comédie humaine*), obviously in contrast to the *Divine Comedy* of Dante. Though the series was not conceived as a unified whole and though the position and order of the novels and stories within it were changed in different editions rather arbitrarily, the total effect of the *Human Comedy* is still that of a single enormous canvas, a comprehensive encyclopedia of society and humanity. Balzac came to think of his scheme as all-inclusive: he formulated ambitions similar to those of a social historian. "My plan," he said, "can be expressed in a sentence: a generation is a drama with four or five thousand prominent persons. This drama is my book" (and by "my book" he meant the whole cycle of his novels). Actually, the *Repertory of the Human Comedy* (*Répertoire de la Comédie humaine de H. de Balzac*, 1887) compiled by Anatole Cerfberr and Jules Christophe lists over two thousand characters, many of whom appear in several books and move from story to story under the watchful eye of the author, who kept careful track of their exact chronology and interrelationships in time and space.

Balzac impressed his own time with his power of creating the illusion of swarming life, of concrete social reality, by means of his accurate knowledge of people and of politics, of banking, law, medicine, journalism, industry, war—of everything which can be known in concrete circumstantiality. Balzac clearly knows his characters in this way too—their dress, their houses, their pockets, as well as their souls and bodies. In this important sense, as a recorder of social truth, Balzac is the first great realist. We can reconstruct from his novels the society of his time, or at least we can have the illusion that we reconstruct it: the decaying aristocracy, the rising middle classes, the artists and prostitutes on the fringes, the criminals of the underworld, and even, though more sketchily, the peasants in the provinces. But we miss the actual workmen and we may wonder at the large incidence of bandits, poets, and prostitutes. Reading more closely, we begin to see that Balzac is not a neutral depicter of a vanished society—if he were, his novels would be reduced to the dimensions of historical documents. Rather, at his best, Balzac is a visionary, a grandiose apocalyptic prophet of doom, who creates his superhuman and subhuman beings as Shakespeare created Lear and Caliban. At his worst, he is a bad romanticist, full of melodrama, sensationalism, romantic shudders, and pompous rhetoric.

There do exist, one must admit, sides of Balzac which seem, or are, scientific, "objective." He has an inexhaustible power of minute observation; he sees man in his environment, and even regards him as determined by and continuous with it. "Does not Society," he asks, "make, according to the environment in which its action develops, as many different men as there are varieties in zoology?" Man, in Balzac, seems primarily a product of nature. But this nature, we soon realize, is a special kind, fraught with mysteries, alive with queer relationships. It is the nature of Swedenborg, of occult philosophies, rather than of modern science. Each character in Balzac seems to be charged with energy, and this energy is channeled in only one direction, toward one end. Many of his most memorable characters are incarnations of lust, avarice, paternal love, the craving for power, and so on, almost like masks or the "humors"-dominated personages in a comedy by Ben Jonson. The ruling passion in Balzac begins to assume a mysterious air; the vital fluid is spread out beyond the individual throughout the universe. All is somehow one. "Everything," Balzac said, "is myth and figure."

Balzac's "Gobseck," which dates from 1830, is not merely a tiny fragment of the *Human Comedy*; it leads us straight into its very heart. The characters of the story told by Derville are central characters in other novels. In many points "Gobseck" is closely linked up with *Old Goriot* (*Le Père Goriot*, 1834). Mme. de Restaud, we are told,

is the younger daughter of Old Goriot, the miser who, devoured by love for his two beautiful daughters, was left by them to die in utter destitution. Mme. de Restaud, in *Old Goriot*, is married to a count and has a lover, the same handsome scoundrel, Maxime de Trailles, whom we meet in "Gobseck." Gobseck reappears prominently in other novels and stories, such as *The Rise and Fall of César Birotteau* (*Histoire de la grandeur et de la décadence de César Birotteau*, 1837). In our story Derville alludes to Gobseck's grandniece and to the great-grandniece to whom he leaves all his wealth: in *Splendors and Miseries of the Courtesans* (*Splendeurs et misères des courtisanes*, 1844–1847) we hear how Sarah van Gobseck was ruined by the same Maxime de Trailles and was assassinated by an officer. There also is the full story of her daughter, Esther van Gobseck. She becomes the great love of the poet Lucien de Rubempré, and dies of self-administered poison, just before she could have been saved by the inheritance of Gobseck's enormous wealth. Derville, the teller of our tale, is also the lawyer of Colonel Chabert, the hero of one of Balzac's most touching stories. And there is a story, "The Deputy of Arcis" ("Le Député d'Arcis," 1847), which tells us that Camille actually marries Ernest de Restaud. Thus our tale is enmeshed in the general scheme of the *Human Comedy*, and our sense of its reality is increased by an acquaintance with these figures and by the many references to actual historical events and personages. Reality and fiction interpenetrate as they did for Balzac, who, according to many witnesses, was apt to talk of his figures as personal acquaintances, and when ill was supposed to have called for the Dr. Bianchon of his novels.

But it is not only the persons that link this story closely with the *Human Comedy*. Its theme —money, gold, power—is also the same. The speech of Gobseck expounding the gospel of money as a symbol of power and life epitomizes the whole society Balzac evokes before us. The social picture sketched in the story presents the world of the *Human Comedy* in miniature: the conflict and the contrast between the decaying aristocracy, ridden with debts, and the rising money-hungry bourgeoisie to which both Gobseck and the narrator belong. Moral chaos and decay are reflected and symbolized in the chaos of the details vividly visualized in the settings of the three central scenes of the story: the bedroom of Mme. de Restaud; the bedroom of the dying and dead count; and the room of Gobseck, which at first is empty and stern, and at the end opens up into storerooms full of moldy edibles, bags of coffee, barrels of rum, heaps of books, pictures, and jewel cases. The legal transactions, the endorsing of bills, the taking of surety, the drawing of counterdeeds, form the one web (the cash nexus) which holds this society together; but it is also the web of destruction pulling its victims toward the great spider—Gobseck. He is a miser, somewhat of a traditional sort

appearing in humorous distortion in the comedies of Ben Jonson and Molière. But he is also something of a Faust: his desire for power is partly the desire for knowledge, knowledge of the human heart and its dark recesses. In a somewhat contradictory way, he is both an extortionist and a man of sterling honesty, he ruins but also helps; he is both Nemesis and Providence in the story. This element of the weird and superhuman which is only hinted at in the towering figure of Gobseck makes for the typical Balzacian mixture of details of finance, glimpses of depravity, and touches of sentiment. Derville, the storyteller, does not come off very well morally in his self-portrayal, though we are to believe in his happy marriage to his humble wife and his good intention in telling the story. But Camille is sent off to bed before she can hear its solution, as she must be spared the final horror of the degradation of Mme. de Restaud at the deathbed of her husband, and the dying scene of Gobseck. Within its small compass the story is almost a parable of the *Human Comedy*, of depravity caught in its own net, of power and wealth amassed to no end except to be taken by death.

FLAUBERT, "A SIMPLE HEART"

Flaubert's novel *Madame Bovary* (1856) is deservedly considered the showpiece of French realism. It would be impossible to find a novel, certainly before Flaubert, in which humble persons in a humble setting (the story concerns the adulteries and

final suicide of the wife of a simple country doctor) are treated
with such seriousness, restraint,
verisimilitude, and imaginative
clarity. There is nothing of Balzac's lurid melodrama, high-
pitched tone, and passionate eloquence in Flaubert's masterpiece. At first sight, *Madame
Bovary* is the prosaic description
of a prosaic life, set in its daily
surroundings, the French province of Normandy about the middle of the nineteenth century.
Everything is told soberly, objectively. The author hides his
feelings completely behind his
personages. All the light falls on
Emma Bovary, as we follow the
story of her romantic dreams,
disillusionment, despair. Every
scene is superbly realized, with
an extraordinary accuracy of observation, and details which at
times are based on scientific information. The topography of
the two villages, the interior of
the houses, great scenes—such
as those of the ball, the cattle
show, the operation for club-
foot, the opera in Rouen,
the arsenic poisoning—imprint
themselves vividly on our memory. Early readers were puzzled
by Flaubert's attitude toward
Emma Bovary, so accustomed
were they to the usual commentary of an author, approving
or condemning every action of
his characters. But today, when
we know the early unpublished
writings of Flaubert and his revealing correspondence, there
cannot be any doubt about the
tone of the book. Behind all the
detachment there is a victory
of art over temperament, a self-
imposed discipline and restraint.
It is, in part, the result of a

theory of the objectivity, the
complete impersonality of art.
According to this view, the artist
has to disappear behind his creation as God does behind his.
Future ages should hardly believe that he lived.

If we listen more carefully,
however, we become aware of
the author's savage satiric attitude toward the romantic illusions of poor Emma, his hatred
for the complacent freethinking
apothecary Homais, his contempt for the stupid husband
and the callous, weak lovers.
The pity of it all comes through
only because the author lets the
facts speak for themselves.

The story of the composition
of *Madame Bovary*, which we
know from Flaubert's letters, is
one of self-inflicted martyrdom,
of an artist perversely clinging to
an uncongenial and even repulsive subject because he believes
that the subject itself is of no
importance and that the artist
should, by his art, purge himself
of personal indulgences and
preferences. It is also the story
of a struggle for style, for the
"right word" (*mot juste*), for
which Flaubert worked with the
suppressed fury of a galley slave.

"A Simple Heart" ("Un
Cœur simple"), a late story
published in the collection
Three Tales (*Trois Contes*,
1877), is clearly related to *Madame Bovary*. It has the same setting of the Norman countryside,
the same houses and farms, some
of the same kind of people. And
it has the same theme of disillusionment. Félicité is anticipated in *Madame Bovary* by the
figure of Catherine Leroux, who
at the great agricultural show re-

ceives a silver medal, worth twenty-five francs, for fifty-four years of service at one farm. The little old woman, with the "monastic rigidity" of her face, the dumbness and calm of her animal look, has to be almost pushed by the audience to receive her prize. When she walks away with the medal, she is heard muttering, "I'll give it to our *curé* up home, to say some masses for me."

"A Simple Heart," like *Madame Bovary*, treats the life of a humble person with complete objectivity, with vivid concrete imagination, clear in every detail. We see and smell the interiors of the houses and farms, and can visualize the scenes of almost Dutch simplicity. But the story is also connected with the two other stories in the collection, "The Legend of St. Julian the Hospitaller" ("La Légende de Saint-Julien-l'Hospitalier") and "Hérodias." Like these it is a saint's legend: like a saint, Félicité undergoes a Calvary of suffering—the betrayal of her lover, the death of the little girl Virginie, the loss of her nephew, the loss of the parrot. Like a saint, too, she meets savage beasts (a bull in the fields), is lashed by a whip on the road, tends the running ulcer of a dying old man, and finally sees a beatific vision, during the Corpus Christi procession, in which the Holy Ghost and the parrot fuse into one.

But one would miss the implications of Flaubert's sophisticated art if one thought of the story merely as a realistic picture of a servant girl's plight or even as a serious legend of a modern saint. It is no doubt a combination of these two apparently very different types: we can see a social purpose in the picture of the poor oppressed woman, her devotion to a selfish mistress, her frustration, resignation, and final dying happiness; and we can sense the author's restraint as a device of simplicity to make the tone of the tale approach that of a legend. But such a reading would not capture all the undertones of Flaubert's style. There are disturbing elements in the story, which show that a simple interpretation is insufficient. We have glimpses, for instance, of Flaubert's predilection for the exotic and strange, for the deliberately decorative mosaic: the exotic pictures which constitute "the whole of [Félicité's] literary education," the curious color combinations of the scene at Virginie's deathbed (the spots of red of the candles, the white mist, the yellow face, the blue lips), and the gorgeous Corpus Christi wayside altar—all these clash with the otherwise sober and gray tone of the narrative. More disturbingly, there is an undertone of satire and contemptuous mockery of this humble world. In a letter to a woman correspondent (Mme. Roger de Genettes; June 19, 1876) Flaubert denied that "there is anything ironical as you suppose," and went on to declare that "on the contrary, it is very serious and very sad. I want to excite pity, I want to make sensitive souls weep, as I am one of them myself." But surely this professed intention (which could be interpreted as another instance of irony) cannot refute the evidence of the passages about the parrot, who is shown as grotesque and absurd. He is "almost a son and a lover" to the poor woman. The Holy Ghost on the stained-glass window seems to her to have something of the parrot in him, and Félicité reflects, somewhat surprisingly, that the Holy Ghost must have taken the form of one of her beloved Loulou's ancestors rather than of a dove. In saying her prayers she swerves a little from time to time from the picture of the Holy Ghost toward the stuffed parrot. It is both pathetic and grotesque, but also (though this would be difficult to prove with certainty) blasphemous and mocking, when Félicité dies thinking that "she saw an opening in the heavens, and a gigantic parrot hovering above her head." The Holy Ghost and the parrot are identified not only in the vision of the poor ignorant woman, but also in Flaubert's satire on religion as primitive magic, in his dark picture of ignorance and superstition illuminated only by the faint and futile glow of "a simple heart."

TURGENEV, *FATHERS AND SONS*

Turgenev was the first Russian author to gain recognition in the West. As late as 1884, Henry James, in his obituary, could write: "He seems to us impersonal, because it is from his writings almost alone that we of English, French and German speech have derived our notions—even yet, I fear, rather meagre and erroneous—of the Russian people. His genius for us is the Slav genius, his voice the voice of those vaguely imagined multitudes."

Today Turgenev is overshadowed by his younger contemporaries, Tolstoy and Dostoevsky. But he was the man who opened the doors for them. His success was due in part to the fact that he spent a great part of his life in Paris and knew and was liked by eminent French writers such as the Goncourts, Daudet, Flaubert, and Renan, and later by Henry James, who called on him in 1875. But Turgenev's success also has deeper reasons: he was a liberal, a "Westerner," who made his reputation first by *A Sportsman's Sketches* (1852), which gave a compassionate picture of the peasant serfs before the Emancipation. Turgenev's series of novels, *Rudin* (1856), *A Nest of Gentlefolk* (1858), *On the Eve* (1860), *Fathers and Sons* (1861), *Smoke* (1867), and *Virgin Soil* (1877), presented a gallery of Russian types in which a topical interest in social and political issues of the time was combined with a romantic love interest. The tone of brooding melancholy and the descriptions of the Russian forest and steppe landscape added to the impact of the well-composed and clearly told stories. Turgenev, we might say today, succeeded because he was not exotic or eccentric or passionately intense, as Tolstoy or Dostoevsky appeared to their first Western audiences, because he was in the mainstream of the European novel and nineteenth-century ideology. Turgenev could be extolled as an example of realism for the objective method of his narration, the apparent absence of the author, and the economy of his means. At the same time he was exempt from the usual charges against the French realists: he had no predilection for "low" subject matter, he was decently restrained in erotic scenes, and he refrained from cruelty and brutal violence. Henry James could rightly call him "a beautiful genius."

Fathers and Sons (1861) stands out among Turgenev's novels for many good reasons. It is free from the sentimentality and vague melancholy of several of the other books. Unobtrusively it achieves a balanced composition, while some of the later books seem to fall apart. It shows Turgenev's power of characterization at its best. He not only draws men and women vividly but he presents an ideological conflict in human terms, succeeding in that most difficult task of dramatizing ideas and social issues, while avoiding didacticism, preaching, and treatise-writing—succeeding, in short, in making a work of art.

In Russia *Fathers and Sons* stirred up an immense and acrimonious debate which centered around the figure of Bazarov, the nihilist who is the hero of the novel. Turgenev did not invent the word "nihilism": it was used in Germany early in the century in philosophical contexts and was imported into Russia by a satirical novelist, Vasily Narezhny (1780-1825). But Turgenev's novel gave it currency as a name for the young generation which did not recognize any authority. In reading the book we must dismiss from our minds the later connotation of the term, when it was affixed to the bomb-throwing revolutionaries who, in 1881, succeeded in killing the tsar. As Turgenev uses the word, however, and as Bazarov and his pupil Arkady explain it, "nihilism" means materialism, positivism, utilitarianism. It implies a rejection of religion and of the Russian class system of the time; it implies a trust in the spread of enlightenment and in science, conceived rather naively as purely empirical observation and investigation, symbolized by Bazarov's collecting of frogs and peering through the microscope at insects and infusoria. It implies a contempt for the conventions of society and romantic illusions, which for Bazarov include poetry and all art. But Bazarov is only potentially a revolutionary; he has no plan, no opportunity, and no time for political action. In debate he tells us that he wants to "make a clean sweep," that he wants to "change society," but he has no allies or even friends, except the doubtful Arkady. Although Bazarov comes from the people and gets along easily with them when he wants to do so, he despises their ignorance and at the end taunts the peasants for their superstition and subservience to their masters. Bazarov is entirely unattached; he is and remains an individualist, even though he tells us that all people are alike.

The figure of this rugged, uncouth, and even rude young man aroused at first the violent anger of the Russian radical intelligentsia. M. A. Antonovich, the critic of the main opposition journal, *The Contemporary*, denounced Bazarov as a "scarecrow" and "demon" and Turgenev for having written a pane-gyric of the fathers and a diatribe against the sons. A secret-police report ascribed to the novel "a beneficent influence on the public mind" because it "branded our underage revolutionaries with the biting name 'Nihilist' and shook the doctrine of materialism and its representatives." Turgenev was abused by the opposition, to which he himself belonged, and became so disgusted with the misinterpretation of the book that he defended and explained himself in letters and finally, in 1869, in a long article, "A propos of *Fathers and Sons*" (reprinted in *Literary Reminiscences*). Turgenev puts forth two arguments. He did not write about ideas, but he simply described an actual person whom he had met: a young doctor who had impressed him. And besides, "many of my readers will be surprised if I tell them that with the exception of Bazarov's views on art, I shared almost all his convictions." He put this even more strongly in an earlier letter (April 26, 1862, to Sluchevsky): "Bazarov dominates all the other characters of the novel. . . . I wished to make a tragic figure of him. . . . He is honest, truthful, and a democrat to the marrow of his bones. If he is called a 'nihilist,' you must read 'revolutionary.' My entire story is directed against the gentry as a leading class." Turgenev's defense was, surprisingly enough, accepted by the radicals: at least Dmitri Pisarev (1840-1868), who wrote a paper, "The Destruction of Aesthetics" (1865) and actually thought that a cobbler is more

important than Pushkin (or pretended to believe it), hailed Bazarov as the true image of the "new man" and elevated, in a genuine act of self-recognition, a fictional figure to a symbol quite independently of the intentions of the author. Soviet Russian criticism accepts this interpretation and consistently hails the novel as a forecast of the Revolution.

But surely this is a gross oversimplification, to which the critics and Turgenev himself were driven in the polemical situation of the time. The book is neither an anti-nihilist novel nor a glorification of the coming revolution. Its beauty is in the detachment, the objectivity, and even the ambivalence with which Turgenev treats his hero and his opinions and presents the conflict between his crude, arrogant, youthful nihilism and the conservative romanticism of his elders. We can delight in the delicate balance which Turgenev keeps and can admire the concrete social picture he presents: the very ancient provincials, father and mother Bazarov, devout, superstitious, kindhearted, intellectually belonging to a dead world; the finicky, aristocatic Pavel Kirsanov and his weak brother Nikolay, who represent the romantic 1840's; the sloppy, name-dropping, cigarette-smoking emancipated woman, Mme. Kukshin; and the elegant, frigid, landowning widow Mme. Odintsov.

Though the eternal conflict between the old and young is one of the main themes of the book, *Fathers and Sons* is not exhaustively described by the title. Even the preoccupation with nihilism is deceptive. The book goes beyond the temporal issues and enacts a far greater drama: man's deliverance to fate and chance, the defeat of man's calculating reason by the greater powers of love, honor, and death. It seems peculiarly imperceptive of some critics to dismiss Bazarov's death by complaining that Turgenev got weary of his hero. His accidental death is the necessary and logical conclusion: Bazarov, the man of reason, the man of hope, is defeated throughout the book. His pupil Arkady becomes unfaithful and reveals his commonplace mind. Bazarov had dismissed love as a matter of mere physiology, but fell in love himself. He is furiously angry at himself when he discovers what he feels to be an inexplicable weakness; he becomes depressed, tries to forget his love by work, and almost commits suicide when he neglects his wound. Bazarov is defeated even in the duel with Pavel, though he was the victor; he had jeered at chivalry as out of date and considered hatred irrational, but he did fight the duel after all. It was ridiculous and even grotesque, but he could not suffer humiliation or stand the charge of cowardice. He did love his parents, though he was embarrassed by their old-fashioned ways. He even consented to receive extreme unction. When death came, he took it as a cruel jest which he had to bear with Stoic endurance. He died like a man, though he knew that it made no difference to anyone how he died. He was not needed, as no individual is needed. We may feel that the moving deathbed scene is slightly marred by the rhetoric of his request to Mme. Odintsov, "Breathe on the dying lamp," and surely the very last paragraph of the book contradicts or tones down its main theme. Turgenev's reference to the "flowers" on the grave (when Bazarov himself had spoken of "weeds" before) and to "eternal reconciliation and life without end" seems a concession to the public, a gesture of vague piety which is refuted by all his other writings. Turgenev puts here "indifferent nature" in quotation marks, but as early as in *Sportsman's Sketches* he had said: "From the depths of the age-old forests, from the everlasting bosom of waters the same voice is heard: 'You are no concern of mine,' says nature to man." In the remarkable scene with Arkady on the haystack—the two friends almost come to blows—Bazarov had pronounced his disgust with "man's pettiness and insignificance beside the eternity where he has not been and will not be." There is no personal immortality, no God who cares for man; nature is indifferent, fate is blind and cruel, love is an affliction, even a disease beyond reason—this seems the message Turgenev wants to convey.

But *Fathers and Sons* is not a mere lesson or fable. It is a narrative, which with very simple means allows the author to move quietly from one location to the other—from the decaying farm of the Kirsanovs, to the provincial town, to the elegant estate of Mme. Odintsov, and from there to the small estate of the old Bazarovs, and back again—firmly situating each scene in its appropriate setting, building up each character by simple gestures, actions, or dialogue so clearly and vividly that we cannot forget him. Only rarely do we feel some lapse into satire, as in Mme. Kukshin's silly conversation. But on the whole, with little comment from the author, a unity of tone is achieved which links the Russian of 1859 with the eternally human and thus vindicates the universalizing power of all great art.

DOSTOEVSKY, *NOTES FROM UNDERGROUND*

Dostoevsky, like every great writer, can be approached in different ways and read on different levels. We can try to understand him as a religious philosopher, a political commentator, a psychologist, and a novelist, and if we know much about his fascinating and varied life, we can interpret his works as biographical.

The biographical interpretation is the one that has been pushed furthest. The lurid crimes of Dostoevsky's characters (such as the rape of a young girl) have been ascribed to him, and all his novels have been studied as if they constituted a great personal confession. Dostoevsky certainly did use many of his experiences in his books (as every writer does): he several times described the feelings of a man facing a firing squad as he himself faced it on December 22, 1849, only to be reprieved at the last moment. His writings also reflect his years in Siberia: four years working in a loghouse, in chains, as he describes it in an oddly impersonal book, *Memoirs from the House of the Dead* (1862), and six more years as a

common soldier on the borders of Mongolia, in a small, remote provincial town. Similarly, he used the experience of his disease (epilepsy), ascribing great spiritual significance to the ecstatic rapture preceding the actual seizure. He assigned his disease to both his most angelic "good" man, the "Idiot," Prince Myshkin, and his most diabolical, inhuman figure, the cold-blooded unsexed murderer of the old Karamazov, the flunky Smerdyakov. Dostoevsky also used something of his experiences in Germany, where in the 1860's he succumbed to a passion for gambling which he overcame only much later, during his second marriage. The short novel *The Gambler* (1866) gives an especially vivid account of this life and its moods.

There are other autobiographical elements in Dostoevsky's works, but it seems a gross misunderstanding of his methods and the procedures of art in general to conclude from his writings (as Thomas Mann has done) that he was a "saint and criminal" in one. Dostoevsky, after all, was an extremely hard worker who wrote and rewrote some twenty volumes. He was a novelist who employed the methods of the French sensational novel; he was constantly on the lookout for the most striking occurrences —the most shocking crimes and the most horrible disasters and scandals—because only in such fictional situations could he exalt his characters to their highest pitch, bringing out the clash of ideas and temperaments, revealing the deepest layers of their souls. But these fictions cannot be taken as literal transcripts **of** reality and actual experience.

Whole books have been written to explain Dostoevsky's religious philosophy and conception of man. The Russian philosopher Berdayev concludes his excellent study by saying, "So great is the value of Dostoevsky that to have produced him is by itself sufficient justification for the existence of the Russian people in the world." But there is no need for such extravagance. Dostoevsky's philosophy of religion is rather a personal version of extreme mystical Christianity, and assumes flesh and blood only in the context of the novels. Reduced to the bare bones of abstract propositions, it amounts to saying that man is fallen but is free to choose between evil and Christ. And choosing Christ means taking upon oneself the burden of humanity in love and pity, since "everybody is guilty for all and before all." Hence in Dostoevsky there is tremendous stress on personal freedom of choice, and his affirmation of the worth of every individual is combined, paradoxically, with an equal insistence on the substantial identity of all men, their equality before God, the bond of love which unites them.

Dostoevsky also develops a philosophy of history, with practical political implications, based upon this point of view. According to him, the West is in complete decay; only Russia has preserved Christianity in its original form. The West is either Catholic—and Catholicism is condemned by Dostoevsky as an attempt to force salvation by magic and authority—or bourgeois, and hence materialistic

and fallen away from Christ; or socialist, and socialism is to Dostoevsky identical with atheism, as it dreams of a utopia in which man would not be free to choose even at the expense of suffering. Dostoevsky—who himself had belonged to a revolutionary group and come into contact with Russian revolutionaries abroad—had an extraordinary insight into the mentality of the Russian underground. In *The Possessed* (1871-1872) he gave a lurid satiric picture of these would-be saviors of Russia and mankind. But while he was afraid of the revolution, Dostoevsky himself hoped and prophesied that Russia would save Europe from the dangers of communism, as Russia alone was the uncorrupted Christian land. Put in terms of political propositions (as Dostoevsky himself preached them in his journal, *The Diary of a Writer*, 1876-1881), what he propounds is a conservative Russian nationalism with messianic hopes for Russian Christianity. It is hard to imagine a political creed more remote from present-day realities.

When translated into abstractions, Dostoevsky's psychology is as unimpressive as his political theory. It is merely a derivative of theories propounded by German writers about the unconscious, the role of dreams, the ambivalence of human feelings. What makes it electric in the novels is his ability to dramatize it in scenes of sudden revulsions, in characters who in today's terminology would be called split personalities, in people twisted by isolation, lust, humiliation, and resentment. The dreams of Raskolnikov may be interpreted according to Freudian psychology, but to the reader without any knowledge of science they are comprehensible in their place in the novel and function as warnings and anticipations.

Dostoevsky is first of all an artist—a novelist who succeeded in using his ideas (many old and venerable, many new and fantastic) and psychological insights for the writing of stories of absorbing interest. As an artist, Dostoevsky treated the novel like a drama, constructing it in large, vivid scenes which end with a scandal or a crime or some act of violence, filling it with unforgettable "stagelike" figures torn by great passions and swayed by great ideas. Then he set this world in an environment of St. Petersburg slums, or of towns, monasteries, and country houses, all so vividly realized that we forget how the setting, the figures, and the ideas melt together into one cosmos of the imagination only remotely and obliquely related to any reality of nineteenth-century Russia. We take part in a great drama of pride and humility, good and evil, in a huge allegory of man's search for God and himself. We understand and share in this world because it is not merely Russia in the nineteenth century, where people could hardly have talked and behaved as Dostoevsky's people do, but a myth of humanity, universalized as all art is.

Notes from Underground (1864) precedes the four great novels, *Crime and Punishment* (1866), *The Idiot* (1868), *The Possessed*, and *The Brothers Karamazov* (1880). The *Notes* can be viewed as a prologue, an introduction to the cycle of the four great novels, an anticipation of the mature Dostoevsky's method and thought. Though it cannot compare in dramatic power and scope with these, the story has its own peculiar and original artistry. It is made up of two parts, at first glance seemingly independent: the monologue of the Underground man and the confession which he makes about himself, called "À Propos of the Wet Snow." The monologue, though it includes no action, is dramatic—a long address to an imaginary hostile reader, whom the Underground man ridicules, defies, jeers at, but also flatters. The confession is an autobiographical reminiscence of the Underground man. It describes events which occurred long before the delivery of the monologue, but it functions as a confirmation in concrete terms of the self-portrait drawn in the monologue and as an explanation of the isolation of the hero.

The narrative of the confession is a comic variation on the old theme of the rescue of a fallen woman from vice, a seesaw series of humiliations permitting Dostoevsky to display all the cruelty of his probing psychology. The hero, out of spite and craving for human company, forces himself into the company of former schoolfellows and is shamefully humiliated by them. He reasserts his ego (as he cannot revenge himself on them) in the company of a humble prostitute by impressing her with florid and moving speeches, which he knows to be insincere, about her horrible future. Ironically, he converts her, but when she comes to him and surprises him in a degrading scene with his servant, he humiliates her again. When, even then, she understands and forgives and thus shows her moral superiority, he crowns his spite by deliberately misunderstanding her and forcing money on her. She is the moral victor and the Underground man returns to his hideout to jeer at humanity. It is hard not to feel that we are shown a tortured and twisted soul almost too despicable to elicit our compassion.

Still it would be a complete misunderstanding of Dostoevsky's story to take the philosophy expounded jeeringly in the long monologue of the first part merely as the irrational railings of a sick soul. The Underground man, though abject and spiteful, represents not only a specific Russian type of the time —the intellectual divorced from the soil and his nation—but also modern humanity, even Everyman, and, strangely enough, even the author, who through the mouth of this despicable character, as through a mask, expresses his boldest and most intimate convictions. In spite of all the exaggerated pathos, wild paradox, and jeering irony used by the speaker, his self-criticism and his criticism of society and history must be taken seriously and interpreted patiently if we are to extract the meaning accepted by Dostoevsky.

The Underground man is the hyperconscious man who examines himself as if in a mirror, and sees himself with pitiless candor. His very self-consciousness cripples his will and poisons his feelings. He cannot escape from

his ego; he knows that he has acted badly toward the girl but at the same time he cannot help acting as he does. He knows that he is alone, that there is no bridge from him to humanity, that the world is hostile to him, and that he is being humiliated by everybody he meets. But though he resents the humiliation, he cannot help courting it, provoking it, and liking it in his perverse manner. He understands (and knows from his own experience) that man is not good but enjoys evil and destruction.

His self-criticism widens, then, into a criticism of the assumptions of modern civilization, of nineteenth-century optimism about human nature and progress, of utilitarianism, and of all kinds of utopias. It is possible to identify definite allusions to a contemporary novel by a radical socialist and revolutionary, Chernyshevsky, entitled *What Shall We Do?* (1863), but we do not need to know the exact target of Dostoevsky's satire to recognize what he attacks: the view that man is good, that he always seeks his enlightened self-interest, that science propounds immutable truths, and that a paradise on earth will be just around the corner once society is reformed along scientific lines. In a series of vivid symbols these assumptions are represented, parodied, exposed. Science says that "twice two makes four" but the Underground man laughs that "twice two makes five is sometimes a very charming thing too." Science means to him (and to Dostoevsky) the victory of the doctrine of fatality, of iron necessity, of determinism, and thus finally of death. Man would become an "organ-stop," a "piano-key," if deterministic science were valid.

Equally disastrous are the implications of the social philosophy of liberalism and of socialism (which Dostoevsky considers its necessary consequence). Man, in this view, need only follow his enlightened self-interest, need only be rational, and he will become noble and good and the earth will be a place of prosperity and peace. But the Underground man knows that this conception of man is entirely false. What if mankind does not follow, and never will follow, its own enlightened self-interest, is consciously and purposely irrational, even bloodthirsty and evil? History seems to the Underground man to speak a clear language: ". . . civilization has made mankind if not more bloodthirsty, at least more vilely, more loathsomely bloodthirsty." Man wills the irrational and evil because he does not want to become an organ-stop, a piano key, because he wants to be left with the freedom to choose between good and evil. This freedom of choice, even at the expense of chaos and destruction, is what makes him man.

Actually, man loves something other than his well-being and happiness, loves even suffering and pain, because he is a man and not an animal inhabiting some great organized rational "ant-heap." The ant-heap, the hen house, the block of tenements, and finally the Crystal Palace (then the newest wonder of architecture, a great hall of iron and glass erected for the Universal Exhibition in London) are the images used by the Underground man to represent his hated utopia. The heroine of *What Shall We Do?* had dreamed of a building, made of cast iron and glass and placed in the middle of a beautiful garden where there would be eternal spring and summer, eternal joy. Dostoevsky had recognized there the utopian dream of Fourier, the French socialist whom he had admired in his youth and whose ideals he had come to hate with a fierce revulsion. But we must realize that the Underground man, and Dostoevsky, despises this "ant heap," this perfectly organized society of robots, in the name of something higher, in the name of freedom. Dostoevsky does not believe that man can achieve freedom and happiness at the same time; he thinks that man can buy happiness only at the expense of freedom, and all utopian schemes seem to him devices to lure man into the yoke of slavery. This freedom is, of course, not political freedom but freedom of choice, indeterminism, even caprice and willfulness, in the paradoxical formulation of the Underground man.

There are hints at a positive solution only in the one section (Section X), which was mutilated by the censor. A letter by Dostoevsky to his brother about the "swine of a censor who let through the passages where I jeered at everything and blasphemed ostensibly" refers to the fact that he "suppressed everything where I drew the conclusion that faith in Christ is needed." In Section XI of the present text (and Dostoevsky never restored the suppressed passages) the Underground man says merely, "I am lying because I know myself that it is not underground that is better, but something different, quite different, for which I am thirsting, but which I cannot find!" This "something . . . quite different" all the other writings of Dostoevsky show to be the voluntary following of Christ even at the expense of suffering and pain.

In a paradoxical form, through the mouth of one of his vilest characters, Dostoevsky reveals in the story his view of man and history—of the evil in man's nature and of the blood and tragedy in history—and his criticism of the optimistic, utilitarian, utopian, progressive view of man which was spreading to Russia from the West during the nineteenth century and which found its most devoted adherents in the Russian revolutionaries. Preoccupied with criticism, Dostoevsky does not here suggest any positive remedy. But if we understand the *Notes* we can understand how Raskolnikov, the murderer out of intellect in *Crime and Punishment*, can find salvation at last, and how Dmitri, the guilty-guiltless parricide of *The Brothers Karamazov*, can sing his hymn to joy in the Siberian mines. We can even understand the legend of the Great Inquisitor told by Ivan Karamazov, in which we meet the same criticism of a utopia (this time that of Catholicism) and the same exaltation of human freedom even at the price of suffering.

TOLSTOY, *THE DEATH OF IVÁN ILYICH*

Tolstoy excited the interest of the West mainly as a public figure: a count owning large estates who decided to give up his wealth and live like a simple Russian peasant—to dress in a blouse, to eat peasant food, and even to plow the fields and make shoes with his own hands. Tragically, this renunciation involved him in a conflict with his wife and family; at the age of eighty-two he left his home and died in a stationmaster's house (at Astápovo, in 1910). By then he had become the leader of a religious cult, the propounder of a new religion. It was, in substance, a highly simplified primitive Christianity which he put into a few moral commands (such as, "Do not resist evil") and from which he drew, with radical consistency, a complete condemnation of modern civilization: the state, courts and law, war, patriotism, marriage, modern art and literature, science and medicine. In debating this Christian anarchism people have tended to forget that Tolstoy established his command of the public ear as a novelist, or they have exaggerated the contrast between the early worldly novelist and the later prophet.

In his youth, Tolstoy served as a Russian artillery officer in the little wars against the mountain tribes of the Caucasus and in the Crimean War against the English and French. His reputation in Russia was at first based on his war stories. In 1862 he married and settled down on his estate, Yásnaya Polyána, where he wrote his enormous novel *War and Peace* (1865-1869). The book made him famous in Russia but was not translated into English until long afterward. Superficially, *War and*

Peace is a historical novel about the Napoleonic invasion of Russia in 1812, a huge swarming epic of a nation's resistance to the foreigner. Tolstoy himself interprets history in general as a struggle of anonymous collective forces which are moved by unknown irrational impulses, waves of communal feeling. Heroes, great men, are actually not heroes but merely insignificant puppets; the best general is the one who does nothing to prevent the unknown course of Providence. But *War and Peace* is not only an impressive and vivid panorama of historical events but also the profound story—centered in two main characters, Pierre Bezúkhov and Prince Andrey Bolkónsky—of a search for the meaning of life. Andrey finds the meaning of life in love and forgiveness of his enemies. Pierre, at the end of a long groping struggle, an education by suffering, finds it in an acceptance of ordinary existence, its duties and pleasures, the family, the continuity of the race.

Tolstoy's next long novel, *Anna Karénina* (1875-1877), resumes this second thread of *War and Peace*. It is a novel of contemporary manners, a narrative of adultery and suicide. But this vivid story, told with incomparable concrete imagination, is counterpointed and framed by a second story, that of Levin, another seeker after the meaning of life, a figure who represents the author as Pierre did in the earlier book; the work ends with a promise of solution, with the ideal of a life in which we should "remember God." Thus *Anna Karénina* also anticipates the approaching crisis in Tolstoy's life. When it came, with the sudden revulsion he describes in *A Confession* (1879), he condemned his earlier books and spent the next years in writing pamphlets and tracts expounding his religion. Later, he returned to the writing of fiction, now regarded entirely as a means of presenting his creed. The earlier novels seemed to him unclear in their message, overdetailed in their method. Hence Tolstoy tried to simplify his art; he wrote plays with a thesis, stories which are like fables or parables, and one long, rather inferior novel, *The Resurrection* (1899), his most savage satire on Russian and modern institutions.

But surely if we look back on all of Tolstoy's work, we must recognize its complete continuity. From the very beginning Tolstoy was a Rousseauist. As early as 1851, when he was in the Caucasus, his diary announced his intention of founding a new, simplified religion. Even as a young man on his estate he had lived quite simply, like a peasant, except for occasional sprees and debauches. He had been horrified by war from the very beginning, though he admired the heroism of the individual soldier and had remnants of patriotic feeling. All his books concern the same theme, the good life, and they all say that the good life lies outside of civilization, near to the soil, in simplicity and humility, in love of one's neighbor. Power, the lust for power, luxury, are always evil.

As a novelist Tolstoy is rooted in the tradition of the older realism. He read and knew the

English writers of the eighteenth century, and also Thackeray and Trollope. He did not care for the recent French writers (he was strong in his disapproval of Flaubert) except for Maupassant, who struck him as truthful and useful in his struggle against hypocrisy. Tolstoy's long novels are loosely plotted, though they have large over-all designs. They work by little scenes vividly visualized, by an accumulation of exact detail. Each character is drawn by means of repeated emphasis on certain physical traits, like Pierre's shortsightedness and his hairy, clumsy hands, or Princess Marya's luminous eyes, the red patches on her face, and her shuffling gait. This concretely realized surface, however, everywhere recedes into depths: to the depiction of disease, delirium, and death and to glimpses into eternity. In *War and Peace* the blue sky is the recurrent symbol for the metaphysical relationships of man. Tolstoy is so robust, has his feet so firmly on the ground, presents what he sees with such clarity and objectivity, that one can be easily deluded into considering his dominating quality to be physical, sensual, antithetical to Dostoevsky's spirituality. The contrasts between the two greatest Russian novelists are indeed obvious. While Tolstoy's method can be called epic, Dostoevsky's is dramatic; while Tolstoy's view of man is Rousseauistic, Dostoevsky stresses the fall of man; while Tolstoy rejects history and status, Dostoevsky appeals to the past and wants a hierarchical society, and so on. But these profound differences should not obscure one basic similarity: the

deep spirituality of both, their rejection of the basic materialism and the conception of truth propounded by modern science and theorists of realism.

The Death of Iván Ilyich (1886) belongs to the period after Tolstoy's religious conversion when he slowly returned to fiction writing. It represents a happy medium between the early and late manner of Tolstoy. Its story and moral are simple and obvious, as always with Tolstoy (in contrast to Dostoevsky). And it says what almost all of his works are intended to convey—that man is leading the wrong kind of life, that he should return to essentials, to "nature." In *The Death of Iván Ilyich* Tolstoy combines a savage satire on the futility and hypocrisy of conventional life with a powerful symbolic presentation of man's isolation in the struggle with death and of man's hope for a final resurrection. Iván Ilyich is a Russian judge, an official, but he is also the average man of the prosperous middle classes of his time and ours, and he is also Everyman confronted with disease and dying and death. He is an ordinary person, neither virtuous nor particularly vicious, a "go-getter" in his profession, a "family man," as marriages go, who has children but has drifted apart from his wife. Through his disease, which comes about by a trivial accident in the trivial business of fixing a curtain, Iván Ilyich is slowly awakened to self-consciousness and a realization of the falsity of his life and ambitions. The isolation which disease imposes upon him, the wall of hypocrisy erected around him by his family and his doctors, his suffering and pain, drive him slowly to the recognition of *It*, to a knowledge, not merely theoretical but proved on his pulses, of his own mortality. At first he would like simply to return to his former pleasant and normal life—even in the last days of his illness, knowing he must die, he screams in his agony, "I won't!"—but at the end, struggling in the black sack into which he is being pushed, he sees the light at the bottom. " 'Death is finished,' he said to himself. 'It is no more!' "

All the people around him are egotists and hypocrites: his wife, who can remember only how she suffered during his agony; his daughter, who thinks only of the delay in her marriage; his colleagues, who speculate only about the room his death will make for promotions in the court; the doctors, who think only of the name of the disease and not of the patient; all except his shy and frightened son, Vásya, and the servant Gerásim. Gerásim is a healthy peasant lad, assistant to the butler, but because he is near to nature, he is free from hypocrisy, helps his master to be comfortable, and even mentions death, while all the others conceal the truth from him. The doctors, especially, are shown as mere specialists, inhuman and selfish. The first doctor is like a judge, like Iván himself when he sat in court, summing up and cutting off further questions of the patient (or is it the prisoner?). The satire at points appears ineffectively harsh in its violence, but it will not seem exceptional to those who know the older Tolstoy's general attitude toward

courts, medicine, marriage, and even modern literature. The cult of art is jeered at, in small touches, only incidentally; it belongs, according to Tolstoy, to the falsities of modern civilization, alongside marriage (which merely hides bestial sensuality), and science (which merely hides rapacity and ignorance).

The story is deliberately deprived of any element of suspense, not only by the announcement contained in the title but by the technique of the cutback. We first hear of Iván Ilyich's death and see the reaction of the widow and friends, and only then listen to the story of his life. The detail, as always in Tolstoy, is superbly concrete and realistic: he does not shy away from the smell of disease, the physical necessity of using a commode, or the sound of screaming. He can employ the creaking of a hassock as a recurrent motif to point up the comedy of hypocrisy played by the widow and her visitor. He can seriously and tragically use the humble image of a black sack or the illusion of the movement of a train.

But all this naturalistic detail serves the one purpose of making us realize, as Iván Ilyich realizes, that not only Caius is mortal but you and I also, and that the life of most of us civilized people is a great lie because it disguises and ignores its dark background, the metaphysical abyss, the reality of Death. While the presentation of *The Death of Iván Ilyich* approaches, at moments, the tone of a legend or fable ("Iván Ilyich's life had been most simple and most ordinary and therefore most terrible"), Tolstoy in this story manages to stay within the concrete situation of our society and to combine the aesthetic method of realism with the universalizing power of symbolic art.

CHEKHOV, "THE KISS"

Chekhov differs sharply from the two giants of Russian literature. His work is of smaller scope. With the exception of an immature, forgotten novel and a travel book, he never wrote anything but short stories and plays. He belongs, furthermore, to a very different moral and spiritual atmosphere. Chekhov had studied medicine, and practiced it for a time. He shared the scientific outlook of his age and had too skeptical a mind to believe in Christianity or in any metaphysical system. He confessed that an intelligent believer was a puzzle to him. His attitude toward his materials and characters is detached, "objective." He is thus much more in the stream of Western realism than either Tolstoy or Dostoevsky, and his affinities with Maupassant (to whom he is related also in technical matters) are obvious. But extended reading of Chekhov does convey an impression of his view of life. There is implied in his stories a philosophy of kindness and humanity, a sense of the unexplainable mystery of life, a sense, especially, of man's utter loneliness in this universe and among his fellow men. Chekhov's pessimism has nothing of the defiance of the universe or the horror at it which we meet in other writers with similar attitudes; it is somehow merely sad, pathetic, and yet also comforting and comfortable.

The Russia depicted in Chekhov's stories and plays is of a later period than that presented by Tolstoy and Dostoevsky. It seems to be nearing its end; there is a sense of decadence and frustration which heralds the approach of the catastrophe. The aristocracy still keeps up a beautiful front, but is losing its fight without much resistance, resignedly. Officialdom is stupid and venal. The Church is backward and narrow-minded. The intelligentsia are hopelessly ineffectual, futile, lost in the provinces or absorbed in their egos. The peasants live subject to the lowest degradations of poverty and drink, apparently rather aggravated than improved since the much-heralded emancipation of the serfs in 1861. There seems no hope for society except in a gradual spread of enlightenment, good sense, and hygiene, for Chekhov is skeptical of the revolution and revolutionaries as well as of Tolstoy's followers.

Chekhov's stories are frequently described as no stories at all. His many imitators, especially in the West, have reduced the art of short-story writing to the evocation of a mood, the sketching of a character or of the impression of a single situation, and have eliminated all plot and even all movement. This approach is comprehensible as a reaction to the surprise endings and contrived plots of such writers as O. Henry. But it would be a mistake to think of Chekhov's stories as formless or even static. "The Kiss" (1887), which is printed here, is actually constructed very ingeniously. Nothing much happens, it is true, in an outward sense; but the story has its movement and point. It succeeds in conveying its theme: the impossibility of communication between men, the human preference for dream over reality. All men are little islands; Ryabovich cannot describe what he has experienced (though the author can convey it to us very successfully). Ryabovich's little experience, the kiss in the dark room, is like a luminous point which broadens and assumes cosmic significance, keeping his soul warm and glowing while he knows that, in "reality," it is easily explainable and of no particular importance. Ryabovich's final action, or rather inaction, in refusing to pursue and renew his vision, is an act of self-defense, a final ironic recognition of the gulf between the ideal and the real. It is a logical and still surprising rounding off of the story—a genuine end, just as the episode of the kiss constitutes a middle. The atmosphere of a Russian country house, the contrast of Ryabovich's awkwardness and shy expectation with the crudity and vulgarity of the other officers, are conveyed with so much deft charm that this selection, at least, allows us to glimpse something of the gay and youthful author who had composed humorous sketches before he wrote his later stories and plays concerning the sadness of life, boredom, loneliness, and death.

IBSEN, *THE WILD DUCK*

Ibsen's plays can be viewed as the culmination point of the *bourgeois* drama which has flourished fitfully, in France and Germany particularly, since the eighteenth century, when Diderot advocated and wrote plays about the middle classes, their "conditions" and problems. But his works can also be seen as the fountainhead of much modern drama—of the plays of Shaw and Galsworthy, who discuss social problems, and of Maeterlinck and Chekhov, who have learned from the later "symbolist" Ibsen. After a long period of incubation and experimentation with romantic and historical themes, Ibsen wrote a series of "problem" plays, beginning with *The Pillars of Society* (1877), which in their time created a furor by their fearless criticism of the nineteenth-century social scene: the subjection of women, hypocrisy, hereditary disease, seamy politics, and corrupt journalism. He wrote these plays using naturalistic modes of presentation: ordinary colloquial speech, a simple setting in a drawing room or study, a natural way of introducing or dismissing characters. Ibsen had learned from the "well-made" Parisian play (typified by those of Scribe) how to confine his action to one climactic situation and how gradually to uncover the past by retrogressive exposition. But he went far beyond it in technical skill and intellectual honesty.

The success of Ibsen's problem plays was international. But we must not forget that he was a Norwegian, the first writer of his small nation (its population at that time was less than two million) to win a reputation outside of Norway. Ibsen more than anyone else widened the scope of world literature beyond the confines of the great modern nations, which had entered its community roughly in this order: Italy, Spain, France, England, Germany, Russia. Since the time of Ibsen, the other small nations have begun to play their part in the concert of European literature. Paradoxically, however, Ibsen rejected his own land. He had dreamed of becoming a great national poet, but in 1864 he left his country for voluntary exile in Italy, Germany, and Austria. In exile, he wrote the plays depicting Norwegian society—a stuffy, provincial middle class, redeemed, in Ibsen's eyes, by single upright, even fiery, individuals of initiative and courage.

Ibsen could hardly have survived his time if he had been merely a painter of society, a dialectician of social issues, and a magnificent technician of the theater. Many of his discussions are now dated. We smile at some of the doings in *A Doll's House* (1879) and *Ghosts* (1881). His stagecraft is not unusual, even on Broadway. But Ibsen stays with us because he has more to offer—because he was an artist who managed to create, at his best, works of poetry which, under their mask of sardonic humor, express his dream of humanity reborn by intelligence and self-sacrifice.

The Wild Duck (1884) surprised the "Ibsenites." The prophet and reformer who had torn the masks of hypocrisy from marriage, respectability, the rule of the "compact majority," seemed here to turn against his own teachings. Through the mouth of Dr. Relling, the *raisonneur* of the play, Ibsen recommends the "life-lie," an illusion which, however unfounded, keeps up the spirit and supports the morale. The meddling "idealist," Gregers Werle, de-

stroys the happiness of a family and causes, indirectly at least, the death of a young and innocent girl. The moral of the play seems to be: better happiness based on a lie than unhappiness based on truth. The ancient adage *Fiat justitia, pereat mundus,*[1] seems to be refuted and even savagely ridiculed here.

While there is this element of self-criticism in the play, the work does not, actually, constitute a break with the preceding "reformist" Ibsen. Gregers Werle, the "idealist," is too insensitive, too doctrinaire, even too stupid, to be a serious self-portrait of the mistaken reformer. At most, he is a caricature of the "idealist." Poor Hialmar Ekdal, whose life-illusion is destroyed, is no suffering hero. At the end, Dr. Relling predicts that even Hedvig's death will be nothing to him but a "pretty theme for declamation." He will, we are sure, recover his life-illusion, and he may even flourish on the tragedy of the girl. Idealism is really not abandoned in the play. Ibsen only criticizes wrongheaded, stubborn "idealism," the lack of human comprehension and insight in Werle, who makes a mess of everything, including his lodgings. Ibsen smiles with a new tolerance at people enmeshed in illusions, fancies, and even escapist vices. The one person of common sense in the play is Gina, who has her feet on the ground but is vulgar and narrow-minded. She, at least, knows that things bygone should be left bygone and that sins can be

1. "Justice must take its course even if the world should perish," supposedly the motto of Emperor Ferdinand I (1556-1564).

atoned by a life of love and sacrifice.

The tragedy in *The Wild Duck* (one cannot call the play as a whole a tragedy) is that of Hedvig, who, puzzled and grieved by her father's rejection, shoots herself in a gesture of self-sacrifice. Though hardly fully prepared for, the act is made psychologically comprehensible: she is a girl in her teens, in puberty, clinging in adoration to her charming father. She is prodded to shoot the duck by Gregers, who wants to destroy the symbol of escape and ineffectiveness. She thus conceives the whole idea of the need of sacrifice in order to conciliate her father. She is profoundly shocked by his histrionic aversion for her —her expulsion from a loving intimacy—for which she cannot conceive any proper reason. She overhears Hialmar's doubts about her love and readiness for sacrifice. But still her suicide comes as a shock, as a *coup de théâtre*, more surprising than the double suicide at the end of *Rosmersholm* (1886), the suicide of Hedda Gabler, or the accidental death (or suicide) of the Master Builder. Hedvig's tragedy is an episode, not quite central to the main theme of the play, which is carried by Hialmar and the older Ekdal.

Hialmar Ekdal is a charming but also absurd and hypocritical dreamer. He is supposed to be thinking out an invention, though he does not even cut the pages of his technical magazines. He pretends to be magnanimous and sturdily independent, but he carefully pastes together the pieces of the letter offering an income to his father, which he had torn into bits. He is supposed to be idealistic, unselfish, and unmaterialistic, but he loves his food and drink, his comfort, and, above all, his grandiose talk. He is a sham, but somehow an amusing and likeable sham. Old Ekdal is also comic, but pathos is the prevailing tone in his characterization. He lives in the past, in the illusion of former grandeur as an officer and a great hunter, though now he can only go shooting rabbits in his loft and put on his lieutenant's cap when no stranger is present. His gruff, pathetic senility sounds only a grim superstitious note when he comments on Hedvig's death that the "woods avenge themselves."

Gregers Werle is also made psychologically comprehensible. In modern terms, we would describe him as a victim of "mother fixation": he hates his overbearing father mainly for the sake of the memory of his injured mother. He adores Hialmar uncritically, refusing to see the shoddy reality behind the charming surface of his lackadaisical friend. He senses the failure of his own life, the position of being always "the thirteenth" at the table. But at times we feel that the author has ridiculed him too savagely. His scheme of putting the marriage of the Ekdals on a foundation of truth and honesty is too absurdly and improbably quixotic. Molvik, the drunken clergyman possessed by his "daemon," also verges at times, like Werle, on becoming a figure of farce; whereas Dr. Relling, in spite of his own drunkenness, is actually an impressive man of haughty disillusionment but fundamental kindness. The doctor voices the author's anger at the "idealism" of Werle, his compassion for the Ekdals, his insight into their characters, and he speaks the words about the "life-lie," which have become the most famous bit of the play.

In its first act, *The Wild Duck* seems simply a social comedy with tragic undertones; there is little hint of what is to come. The exposition slowly reveals the past, which is not fully explained till the last act. The basic realism of the first two acts is later modified by hints of symbolism, by the queer poetic world of the old lumber room, with its withered Christmas trees, its pigeons and rabbits, and the wild duck. It is still a real garret behind a studio, a little implausible in its size but not impossible. The duck is a real duck shot by old Werle. But it is also a symbol of the general defeat of these people, of old Ekdal's fate, of Hialmar's enmeshment in the "seaweed," and it belongs, by right, to Hedvig. As a true symbol it has many meanings and relationships. Old Werle, referring to Ekdal in the first act, long before we have heard of the wild duck, speaks of "people . . . who dive to the bottom the moment they get a couple of slugs in their body and never come to the surface again." Later, Ekdal takes up almost the same phrases: "They shoot to the bottom as deep as they can . . . and bite themselves fast in the tangle and seaweed. . . . And they never come up again." Hialmar—Gregers tells him twice—has something of the wild duck in him. Sacrificing herself instead of her wild duck, Hedvig identifies herself with the wounded and lame bird.

The many-sided symbol of the wild duck hovers over the play, always on the hither side of reality but lending a tone of unreality and poetry. Other such motifs seem less successfully carried out—the idea of "thirteen" at a table, which recurs in the last words of Gregers, appears trivial, and the motif of Hedvig's approaching blindness is somewhat overworked. It is used to make Hialmar's suspicion of his fatherhood plausible, but apparently on purpose the truth of the matter is left unclear. Hialmar's insinuations about Hedvig's plotting with Mrs. Sörby seem out of character with his easygoing nature.

Even if we feel that some details of the play are too farcical or too contrived in their tragic irony—like Hialmar's speech, presumably overheard by Hedvig just before her gun goes off backstage—*The Wild Duck* still represents Ibsen at his best and richest. It is a wonderful gallery of portraits. It allows actors even in the minor roles (such as that of the earthy Gina) a wide scope. It has action and excitement, provided by Ibsen's sense of theater. It brings into a successful blend humor and pathos, comedy and tragedy, realism and symbolism, prose and poetry. It fulfills the demand—made implicitly of all art—for richness and complexity, a demand which on today's stage is all too frequently disappointed.

JAMES, *THE ASPERN PAPERS*

The American novel began

676 · *Realism and Naturalism*

with the Gothic romances of
Charles Brockden Brown (1771-
1810), and one can argue that it
bears the imprint "Gothic romance" throughout its history
from Poe to Faulkner. As Leslie
Fiedler has said, "It is a literature of darkness and the grotesque in a land of light and affirmation." But in the 1860's two
young men, William Dean Howells (1837-1920) and Henry James
(1843-1916), set out to change
this. They imported the theory
and practice of realism from Europe, though, of course, close observation and local-color writing
had been widespread before.
Henry James, though less belligerent than Howells as a propaga-
tor of the slogan, became incomparably the subtlest theorist of
the new novel. To him we owe an
exposition (in several collections
of essays and in the prefaces to
the collected edition of his novels, the New York edition, 1907-
1909) of the principles of realism: it means creating the illusion of life, not only of its surface
but of the total inner life of man.
The illusion of reality can be
achieved by the complete objectivity of the author: the novel
must not appear to be a novel,
the author must not interfere.
With unparalleled ingenuity
James analyzed the technical
problems which face a novelist:
the choice between scene and
narration, dialogue and description; and the role of the "point
of view"—first-person narration,
omniscient author, or a narrator,
observer, "reflector" as a character in the book. James was the
first to state these problems
clearly and to discuss them with
the competence of a practicing
novelist.

Nobody can doubt James' importance as a critic of the novel.
He is, however, still a subject of
controversy as a novelist. James'
migration to England, which, in
the last year of his life, brought
him to accept British citizenship
as a profession of solidarity with
the nation at war with Germany,
aroused strong resentment in
this country. He has been judged
a "defector from America," and
all his failings as an artist have
been ascribed to his expatriation
and consequent isolation and
lack of roots. But James has to be
judged by his achievement. The
transplantation to Europe, "the
complex fate of being an American in Europe" gave him his
leading themes: the "international episode," the American in
Europe, the European in America. These themes are not merely
social or historical as the contrast
between Europe and America;
they become symbols to which
are attached his deepest concerns—the great moral issues of
innocence and experience, of
good and evil. Without the migration James would not be
James. The complaint that he is
writing about upper-class Americans and Europeans (sometimes
even princes, millionaires, and
lords) is pointless, as James (with
some exceptions, such as the
novel about anarchists, *The Princess Casamassima*) needs his lei-
sure-class people, his artists, ladies, and gentlemen in order to
probe into self-conscious reflec-
tive minds; he is concerned less
with society than with psychology and morality. One should
grant, however, that in his later
years, possibly because of his
age and his withdrawal into an
inner world, James seems to have

had a diminished grasp of reality; his last novels seem too finely spun, too elaborately drawn out to appeal to any but the most persistent Jamesians. One must discriminate among his huge output: the books written in the 1880's and 1890's when James was in his forties and fifties are the most perfect as works of art, and among them, the story, *The Aspern Papers* (1888), must be considered one of the very best.

The origin and background of the story is explained by an entry in James' *Notebooks*:

[Florence, January 12th, 1887] Hamilton [V. L.'s[2] brother] told me a curious thing of Capt. Silsbee —the Boston art-critic and Shelley-worshipper; that is of a curious adventure of his. Miss Claremont [Clairmont],[3] Byron's *ci-devant* mistress (the mother of Allegra), was living, until lately, here in Florence, at a great age, 80 or thereabouts, and with her lived her niece, a younger Miss Claremont—of about 50. Silsbee knew that they had interesting papers—letters of Shelley's and Byron's—he had known it for a long time and cherished the idea of getting hold of them. To this end he laid the plan of going to lodge with the Misses Claremont—hoping that the old lady in view of her great age and failing condition would die while he was there, so that he might then put his hand upon the documents, which she

hugged close in life. He carried out this scheme—and things *se passèrent* as he had expected. The old woman *did* die—and then he approached the younger one—the old maid of 50—on the subject of his desires. Her answer was—"I will give you all the letters if you marry me!" H. says that Silsbee *court encore*. Certainly there is a little subject there: the picture of the two faded, queer, poor and discredited old English women—living on into a strange generation, in their musty corner of a foreign town—with these illustrious letters their most precious possession. Then the plot of the Shelley fanatic—his watchings and waitings—the way he *couvers* the treasure. The denouement needn't be the one related of poor Silsbee; and at any rate the general situation is in itself a subject and a picture. It strikes me much. The interest would be in some price that the man has to pay—that the old woman —or the survivor—sets upon the papers. His hesitations—his struggle— for he really would give almost anything. —The Countess Gamba came in while I was there: her husband is a nephew of the Guiccioli[4] —and it was *à propos* of their having a lot of Byron's letters of which they are rather illiberal and dangerous guardians, that H. told me the above. They won't show them or publish any of them—and the Countess was very angry once on H.'s representing to her that it was her duty—especially to the English public!—to let them at least be seen. *Elle se fiche bien* of the English

2. *V. L.:* Vernon Lee (1865-1935), actually Violet Paget, an English authoress who wrote much on Italy and on aesthetics. She lived most of her life in Florence.

3. Clara Mary Jane Clairmont (1798-1879) was a daughter, by a former marriage, of the second wife of William Godwin. She accompanied her step-sister, Mary Godwin, in her elopement with Shelley in 1814. In 1816 she was briefly the mistress of Lord Byron and bore him a daughter, Allegra, who died in an Italian convent in 1822, aged 5. "Claire"

died in Florence, aged 81.

4. The Countess Teresa Guiccioli, née Gamba (1800-1873), was Byron's last love. At sixteen she had married a 60-year-old man. Byron met her in Venice in 1819, and they lived together in Ravenna, Pisa, and Genoa until Byron's departure for Greece in 1824. The Countess published hero-worshipping memoirs in French (*Lord Byron jugé par les témoins de sa vie*) in 1868. The letters then in danger were preserved and were published by Iris Origo in *The Last Attachment* (1949).

public. She says the letters—addressed in Italian to the Guiccioli—are discreditable to Byron; and H. elicited from her that she had *burned* one of them![5]

James, we see, kept the outline of the story but moved it from Florence to Venice and replaced Byron or Shelley by an imaginary American poet of their time. In the preface to the reprint of *The Aspern Papers* in the New York edition (1908), James comments at length on his "delight in a palpable imaginable *visitable* past." He argues elaborately that the writer has to find the exact time in the past with which he wants to establish intimate contact. The romantic period seems to James the right time as in it the past is neither too strange nor too familiar. James also defends the invention of an American poet, though he realizes that he is not "fully localized." The setting in the "mouldy rococo" of Venice increases the sense of verisimilitude: Miss Bordereau seems more probable as a survivor in decaying, disintegrating Venice, which is itself the monument of an even remoter history.

In the entry in the *Notebooks* and oddly enough in the late 1908 preface, James does not even touch on what is the leading theme of the story, the moral issue. The evocation of Venice is, no doubt, brilliant and convincing; it anticipates the Venice of Proust and Thomas Mann. The background figure of Jeffrey Aspern (the name is derived from the Austrian village near Vienna where, in 1809, Na-

poleon suffered his first serious defeat) is sufficiently sketched for the purposes of the story; he is a legend, and we must believe in his greatness and attraction. But all this is surely secondary. The story is at first sight that of a "cheater cheated." The persistent document-hunting scholar or would-be scholar is caught in his own trap. In three climactic scenes he is frustrated and humiliated: first, when he is surprised by the old woman in the act of inspecting her desk and called a "publishing scoundrel"; the next time, when he apparently has the letters in his reach but is confronted by the embarrassing proposal of marriage; and for the third time, when he is ready to accept the condition but is told by Tita that she has burned the papers. One could read the story as a defense of the rights of privacy, as an attack on the prying into the secrets of the past, and even as a satire on the collector's mania. We may feel that the failure serves the narrator right. The central device of the story is irony. The story is told by the target of the satire himself; it is a story of self-revelation, which is also self-exposure. It is the story of a cad who behaved badly partly out of cupidity, but also because he has raised hopes in an innocent soul which he has no intention of fulfilling. That James wanted us to think the unheroic hero a cad is particularly obvious from the revisions he made twenty years later. Most of them are only stylistic and quite trivial, but some make the giveaway of the narrator clearer and harsher. For

5. *The Notebooks of Henry James,* edited by F. C. Matthiessen and Kenneth B. Murdock (New York: Oxford University Press, 1947), pp. 71-72.

example, "I am sorry for it, but for Jeffrey Aspern's sake I would do worse still" (p. 1151) is changed to: "I am sorry for it, but there's no baseness I wouldn't commit for Jeffrey Aspern's sake." In the night scene when the narrator is caught by the old woman, James said of her eyes: "They glared at at me, they made me horribly ashamed" (p. 1203), while in the revision he inserted between the two clauses of the sentence the new sentence: "They were like the sudden drench, for a caught burglar, of a flood of gaslight."

Still, we may wonder whether the original version might not be preferred because it is less heavily ironical and less harshly satirical of the narrator. The insertions seem to upset the delicate balance of the story; surely the issue is not so simple as saying that the narrator is a base burglar. We must after all sympathize with the teller of the story: he really worships the memory of the poet who to him is a "god"; he really wants to establish a link with the past. He sacrifices money, time, and effort to his detective zeal. His victim is by no means innocent. Miss Bordereau is a greedy, cynical old woman who, in the years of her isolation, has lost all sense of proportion and is quite willing to extract as much money as possible from the narrator, if not for herself then for her niece's sake. She even lures him on by producing the miniature portrait of the poet and asking for the sum of £1000. Tita (or, as she is called in the revision, Tina) is, to be sure, entirely innocent. She is a pathetic woman of limited intelligence

who shows a calculating and scheming streak only in the scene in which she offers marriage as a condition for obtaining the papers. If we assume that the narrator is a youngish man of the world, his flight from what we must believe is a "plain, dingy, elderly person" is both natural and inevitable. The sudden resolution next day to go through with it (though dimly contemplating some escape) is a relapse for which the narrator is very properly punished by the destruction of the papers. The momentary transfiguration by which she ceases to be a "ridiculous old woman" is an improbable self-delusion. We feel the hurt which the rejection inflicted on poor Tita, but the narrator could hardly have acted differently. In the original version the story ends: "When I look at [the portrait] my chagrin at the loss of the letters becomes almost intolerable." In the revision this was changed to: "When I look at it I can scarcely bear my loss—I mean of the precious papers." The dash seems to indicate a hesitation on the narrator's part, whether the loss was not something else than that of the papers: a loss of self-respect or honor or even regret for the loss of Tita. But none of these is suggested in the body of the text. The narrator, with whom we cannot help sympathizing, as we do with every narrator except professed villains, is a sensitive man who revels in his appreciation of old Venice and shows a remarkable insight into what he is doing. We must believe him when he says that he did not make love to Tita, that he did not raise any hopes in her, and that he was genuinely shocked and surprised by her proposal, which he had, at first, some difficulty in understanding.

The possibility of debate on this moral issue—the ambiguity of all of the narrator's behavior for the reader—is of course due to the technique of the first-person narrative. The author does not tell us directly what we have to think. This technique is not a drawback, as has been argued, but a source of strength; the whole beauty of the story resides in it. If we were constantly instructed by an omniscient author commenting on each step with foresight and hindsight, the story would become flat and obvious. Even rewritten as a play (as it was in 1959 by Michael Redgrave), where the author is necessarily absent, the story becomes a recital of the disillusionment of two lonely women. But told by the protagonist himself, it preserves a delicate equilibrium. The two sides of the narrator can exist very well side by side; skill and sensitivity, love of poetry and art can go hand in hand with some moral obtuseness as he is carried away by the obsession of the collector hunting for a treasure. There seems to be no failure of technique or perception. James must have felt, however, that the self-exposure of the narrator was not perceived by readers of the first version, and in a few places he made it clearer in his revision. Recent commentators seem to lean heavily on the narrator's self-condemnation and to underplay the sympathy and ardor of the siege and the sensitivity of observation and evocation he displayed. James achieved his aim, common to most of his works: a delicate moral casuistry, a penetration into the depths of the human soul which puts him head and shoulders above the surface realists and has made him the initiator of the modern psychological novel.

LIVES, WRITINGS, AND CRITICISM
Biographical and critical works are listed only if they are available in English.

HONORÉ DE BALZAC
LIFE. Born at Tours on May 20, 1799. His father came from the south of France and was actually named Balsa. The "de" is the addition of the novelist. His father was a lawyer, and played a role in the local administration during and after the French Revolution. Balzac went to school in Tours and in 1816 went to Paris, where he studied law. In 1819 he took his baccalaureate, but he resisted his father's attempts to force him into a law office. He became instead a hack writer, living in poverty in a series of garrets. He wrote many gruesome, sensational, and sentimental novels before he achieved any literary success. He tried his hand at business, as a publisher and printer, but in 1829 went totally bankrupt.

Between 1822 and 1832 Balzac was the lover of Mme. de Berny, his elder by twenty-two years and the mother of eight. In 1832, he received an admiring letter signed *l'Étrangère*, "the foreigner," from a Polish lady, Mme. Hanska, with whom he entered into a prolonged correspondence. They met in 1833 and again later, at long intervals. Her husband died in 1841, but only in 1850 did Balzac marry her—on her estate in the Ukraine. Soon after their arrival in Paris, Balzac died, on August 18, 1850.

Balzac's life was a working life: between 1829 and 1848 he wrote four to five volumes, or about two thousand printed pages, a year. He worked through the nights, dressed in a white monk's robe, drinking enormous quantities of coffee. He also engaged in financial speculations, bought large collections of pictures and furniture, wrote five unsuccessful plays, was twice a candidate for the Chamber of Deputies, and so on. His tremendous energy was that of the heroes of his novels.

CHIEF WRITINGS. (All of the works listed are novels.) *The Wild Ass's Skin* (*La Peau de chagrin*, 1831); *Louis Lambert* (1832); *Eugénie Grandet*

(1833); *Old Goriot* (*Le Père Goriot,* 1834); *The Quest of the Absolute* (*La Recherche de l'absolu,* 1834); *The Rise and Fall of César Birotteau* (*Histoire de la grandeur et de da décadence de César Birotteau,* 1837); *Lost Illusions* (*Les Illusions perdues,* 1837-1843); *Cousin Betty* (*La Cousine Bette,* 1846).

BIOGRAPHY AND CRITICISM. Philippe Bertault, *Balzac and the Human Comedy,* trans. by Richard Monges (1963); Fedinand Brunetière, *Balzac,* trans. by R. L. Sanderson (1906); E. P. Dargan, *Studies in Balzac's Realism* (1932); Émile Faguet, *Balzac* (1914); Ramon Fernandez, "The Method of Balzac" in *Messages* (1926); Raymond D. Giraud, *The Unheroic Hero in the Novels of Stendhal, Balzac, and Flaubert* (1957); Herbert J. Hunt, *Honoré de Balzac: A Biography* (1957); Henry James, several essays called "Honoré de Balzac" in *French Poets and Novelists* (1878) and in *Notes on Novelists* (1916); Harry Levin, "Balzac" in *The Gates of Horn* (1963); Percy Lubbock, *The Craft of Fiction* (1921); Edward James Oliver, *Balzac, the European* (1960); Samuel Rogers, *Balzac and the Novel* (1953); and Stefan Zweig, *Balzac* (1946).

GUSTAVE FLAUBERT

LIFE. Born at Rouen, Normandy, on December 12, 1821, to the chief surgeon of the Hôtel Dieu. Flaubert was extremely precocious: by the age of sixteen he was writing stories in the romantic taste, which were published only after his death. In 1840 he went to Paris to study law (he had received his baccalaureate from the local *lycée*), but he failed in his examinations, and in 1843 suffered a sudden nervous breakdown which kept him at home. In 1846 he moved to Croisset, just outside of Rouen on the Seine, where he made his home for the rest of his life, devoting himself to writing. The same year, in Paris, Flaubert met Louise Colet, a minor poetess and lady about town, who became his mistress. In 1849-1851 he visited the Levant, traveling extensively in Greece, Syria, and Egypt. After his return he settled down to the writing of *Madame Bovary,* which took him five full years. *Madame Bovary* was a great popular success. An attempt was made to suppress it, however, and a lawsuit ensued, charging Flaubert with immorality. In 1857 he was acquitted of this charge. The remainder of his life was uneventful. He made occasional trips to Paris, and one trip, in 1860, to Tunisia to see the ruins of Carthage in preparation for the writing of his novel *Salammbô.* Flaubert died at Croisset on May 8, 1880.

CHIEF WRITINGS. *Madame Bovary* (1856); *Salammbô* (1862); *The Sentimental Education* (*L'Éducation sentimentale,* 1869); *The Temptation of St. Anthony* (*La Tentation de Saint Antoine,* 1874); *Three Tales* (*Trois Con-*

tes, 1877), including "A Simple Heart" ("Un Coeur simple"); *Bouvard and Pécuchet* (*Bouvard et Pécuchet,* a posthumous novel, unfinished, 1881).

BIOGRAPHY AND CRITICISM. Raymond D. Giraud, *The Unheroic Hero in the Novels of Stendhal, Balzac, and Flaubert* (1957); Harry Levin, *The Gates of Horn* (1963); Percy Lubbock, *The Craft of Fiction* (1921); L. P. Shanks, *Flaubert's Youth, 1821-45* (1927); Philip Spencer, *Flaubert: A Biography* (1952); Francis Steegmuller, *Flaubert and Madame Bovary* (1939, new edition 1950); John Charles Traver, *Gustave Flaubert as Seen in His Works and Correspondence* (1895); Margaret G. Tillett, *On Reading Flaubert* (1961); Anthony Thorlby, *Gustave Flaubert and the Art of Realism* (1957); and Martin Turnell, "Flaubert" in *The Novel in France* (1951).

IVAN TURGENEV

LIFE. Born at Orel, central Russia, on November 9, 1818. Turgenev's father was an impoverished nobleman, a cavalry officer who had married a rich heiress. His mother owned an estate, Spasskoye, with 5000 souls (male serfs). Turgenev's father died early. Young Turgenev attended the universities of Moscow and Petersburg, and in 1838-1841 studied philosophy at the University of Berlin. There he met the prominent revolutionary Bakunin. After his return to Russia, Turgenev took a master's degree in philosophy and considered a university career. But after a short stint in the civil service, he was drawn more and more into literary pursuits, met Belinsky, Dostoevsky, and others, and wrote romantic poetry. In 1843 Turgenev met the French opera singer Pauline Viardot, who was on a tour in Russia. He followed her to France in 1847, but returned in 1850 when his mother died, leaving him a large inheritance. Turgenev had trouble with the tsarist authorities; for a violation of censorship rules, he was arrested and jailed for a month in 1852 and then confined to his estate under police surveillance. After 1856 Turgenev lived abroad, mostly in Paris and later in Baden, in order to be near Mme. Viardot. He paid several prolonged visits to Russia, the last time in 1881. Turgenev also visited England several times (*Fathers and Sons* was begun on the Isle of Wight in 1860); in 1879 he received an honorary degree from Oxford. He died at Bougival near Paris, of a cancer, on September 3, 1883.

CHIEF WRITINGS. *A Sportsman's Sketches,* stories (1847-1851; as a book, 1852); *A Month in the Country,* play (1850); "Mumu," story (1852); *Rudin,* novel (1854); "Asya," story (1857); *A Nest of Gentlefolk,* novel (1858); *On the Eve,* novel (1859); "First Love," story (1860); "Hamlet and Don Quixote," essay (1860); *Fathers and Sons* (1861, in book form, 1862); *Smoke*, novel (1867); "King Lear of the Steppes," story (1870); *Torrents of the Spring*, short novel (1871); *Virgin Soil*, novel (1876); *Poems in Prose* (1822); and "Klara Milich," story (1883).

BIOGRAPHY AND CRITICISM. Richard Freeborn, *Turgenev: The Novelists' Novelist* (1960); Edward Garnett, *Turgenev, A Study* (1917); Royal A. Gettmann, *Turgenev in England and America* (1941); Harry Hershkowitz, *Democratic Ideas in Turgenev's Works* (1932); Irving Howe, "Turgenev: The Politics of Hesitation," in *Politics and the Novel* (1957); Henry James, "Ivan Turgénieff," in *French Poets and Novelists* (1884); "Ivan Turgénieff," in *Partial Portraits* (1888), and "Turgenev and Tolstoy," in *The Future of the Novel* (1956); David Magarshack, *Turgenev, A Life* (1954); Edmund Wilson, "Turgenev and the Life-giving Drop," in I. Turgenev, *Literary Reminiscences*, translated by D. Magarshack (1958); and Avrahm Yarmolinsky, *Turgenev: The Man, His Art and His Age* (1926; rev. ed., 1959).

FYODOR DOSTOEVSKY

LIFE. Fyodor Mikhailovich Dostoevsky, born in Moscow on October 30, 1821. His father was a staff doctor at the Hospital for the Poor. Later he acquired an estate and serfs. In 1839 he was killed by one of his peasants in a quarrel. Dostoevsky was sent to the Military Engineering Academy in St. Petersburg, from which he graduated in 1843. He became a civil servant, a draftsman in the St. Petersburg Engineering Corps, but resigned soon because he feared that he would be transferred to the provinces when his writing was discovered. His first novel, *Poor People* (1846), proved a great success with the critics; his second, *The Double* (1846), which followed immediately, was a failure.

Subsequently, Dostoevsky became involved in the Petrashevsky circle, a secret society of antigovernment and socialist tendencies. He was arrested on April 23, 1849, and condemned to be shot. On December 22 he was led to public execution, but he was reprieved at the last moment and sent to penal servitude in Siberia (near Omsk), where he worked for four years in a stockade, wearing fetters, completely cut off from communications with Russia. On his release in February, 1854, he was assigned as a common soldier to Semipalatinsk, a small town near the Mongolian frontier. There he received several promotions (eventually becoming an ensign); his rank of nobility, forfeited by his sentence, was restored; and he married the widow

of a customs official. In July, 1859, Dostoevsky was permitted to return to Russia, and finally, in December, 1859, to St. Petersburg—after ten years of his life had been spent in Siberia.

In the last year of his exile, Dostoevsky had resumed writing, and in 1861, shortly after his return, he founded a review, *Time (Vremya)*. This was suppressed in 1863, though Dostoevsky had changed his political opinions and was now strongly nationalistic and conservative in outlook. He made his first trip to France and England in 1862, and traveled in Europe again in 1863 and 1865, in order to follow a young woman friend, Apollinaria Suslova, and to indulge in gambling. After his wife's death in 1864, and another unsuccessful journalistic venture, *The Epoch (Epokha)*, 1864-1865, Dostoevsky was for a time almost crushed by gambling debts, emotional entanglements, and frequent epileptic seizures. He barely managed to return from Germany in 1865. In the winter of 1866 he wrote *Crime and Punishment*, and before he had finished it, dictated a shorter novel, *The Gambler*, to meet a deadline. He married his secretary, Anna Grigoryevna Snitkina, early in 1867 and left Russia with her to avoid his creditors. For years they wandered over Germany, Italy, and Switzerland, frequently in abject poverty. Their first child died. In 1871, when the initial chapters of *The Possessed* proved a popular success, Dostoevsky returned to St. Petersburg. He became the editor of a weekly, *The Citizen (Grazhdanin)*, for a short time and then published a periodical written by himself, *The Diary of a Writer* (1876-1881), which won great acclaim. Honors and some prosperity came to him. At a Pushkin anniversary celebrated in Moscow in 1880 he gave the main speech. But soon after his return to St. Petersburg he died, on January 28, 1881, not yet sixty years old.

CHIEF WRITINGS. *Memoirs from the House of the Dead* (1862); *Notes from Underground* (1864); *Crime and Punishment* (1866); *The Idiot* (1869); *The Possessed* (1871-1872); *The Raw Youth* (1875); *The Brothers Karamazov* (1880).

BIOGRAPHY AND CRITICISM. Monroe C. Beardsley, "Dostoyevsky's Metaphor of the 'Underground,'" *Journal of the History of Ideas*, III (June, 1942), 265-290; Maurice Beebe and Christopher Newton, "Dostoevsky in English: A Checklist of Criticism and Translations" in *Modern Fiction Studies* IV (1958); Nikolay N. Berdayev, *Dostoievsky: An Interpretation* (1934); E. H. Carr, *Dostoevsky* (1931); Richard Curle, *Characters of Dostoevsky: Studies from Four Novels* (1950);

Joseph Frank, "Nihilism and *Notes from Underground*," in *Sewanee Review* LXIX (1961); Sigmund Freud, "Dostoevski and Parricide," *Partisan Review* XIV (fall, 1945), 530-544; André Gide, *Dostoevski* (1926); Vyacheslav Ivanov, *Freedom and the Tragic Life, A Study in Dostoevsky* (1952); Robert L. Jackson, *The Underground Man in Russian Literature* (1958); Janko Lavrin, *Dostoevski: A Study* (1947); Thomas Mann, introduction to *The Short Novels of Dostoevsky* (1947); David Magarshack, *Dostoevsky* (1962); Helen Muchnic, *Dostoevsky's English Reputation, 1881-1936* (1939); Middleton Murry, *Fyodor Dostoevsky: A Critical Study* (1916); Ernest J. Simmons, *Dostoevski, The Making of a Novelist* (1940); George Steiner, *Tolstoy or Dostoevsky* (1959); René Wellek (ed.), *Dostoevsky: A Collection of Critical Essays* (1962); Avrahm Yarmolinsky, *Dostoievsky: A Study in His Ideology* (1921) and *Dostoevsky, A Life* (1934); L. A. Zander, *Dostoevsky*, trans. by N. Duddington (1948); and Stefan Zweig, *Three Masters: Balzac, Dickens, Dostoevsky* (1930).

LEO TOLSTOY

LIFE. Born at Yásnaya Polyána, his mother's estate near Tula (about 130 miles south of Moscow), on August 28, 1828. His father was a retired lieutenant colonel; one of his ancestors, the first count, had served Peter the Great as an ambassador. His mother's father was a Russian general in chief. Tolstoy lost both parents early in his life and was brought up by aunts. He went to the University of Kazan between 1844 and 1847, drifted along aimlessly for a few years more, and in 1851 became a cadet in the Caucasus. As an artillery officer he saw action in the wars with the mountain tribes and again, in 1854-1855, during the Crimean War against the French and English. Tolstoy had written fictional reminiscences of his childhood while he was in the Caucasus, and during the Crimean War he wrote war stories which established his literary reputation. For some years he lived on his estate, where he founded and himself taught an extremely "progressive" school for peasant children. He made two trips to western Europe, in 1857 and in 1860-1861. In 1862 he married the daughter of a physician, Sonya Bers, who bore him thirteen children. In the first years of his married life, between 1863 and 1869, he wrote *War and Peace*, and between 1873 and 1877 composed *Anna Karénina*. After this, a religious crisis came over him, which he described in 1879 in *A Confession*. The next years were devoted to the writing of tracts— attacks on orthodoxy, the government,

and the cult of art, and elaborations of his own religious creed. Only slowly did Tolstoy return to the writing of fiction. His longest later book was *The Resurrection*. In 1901 Tolstoy was excommunicated. A disagreement with his wife about the nature of the good life and about financial matters sharpened into a conflict over his last will, which finally led to a complete break: he left home in the company of a doctor friend. He caught cold on the train journey south and died in the house of the stationmaster of Astápovo, on November 20, 1910.

CHIEF WRITINGS. *The Cossacks* (1863); *War and Peace* (1865-1869); *Anna Karénina* (1875-1877); *A Confession* (1879); *The Death of Iván Ilyich* (1886); *The Power of Darkness* (1886); *The Kreutzer Sonata* (1889); *Master and Man* (1895); *What Is Art?* (1897); *The Resurrection* (1899); *Hadji Murad* (1896-1904).

BIOGRAPHY AND CRITICISM. Matthew Arnold, "Count Leo Tolstoy" in *Essays in Criticism*, Second Series (1888); Isaiah Berlin, *The Hedgehog and the Fox, An Essay on Tolstoy's View of History* (1953); P. I. Biryukov, *The Life of Tolstoy* (1911); R. F. Christian, *Tolstoy's "War and Peace," A Study* (1962); Maxim Gorky, *Reminiscences of Tolstoy* (1921); Janko Lavrin, *Tolstoy* (1946); Derrick Leon, *Tolstoy: His Life and Work* (1944); G. Lukács, in *Studies in European Realism*, trans. by E. Bone (1950); Thomas Mann, "Goethe and Tolstoy" in *Essays of Three Decades*, trans. by H. T. Lowe-Porter (1947); Aylmer Maude, *The Life of Tolstoy*, 2 vols. (1908-1910); D. S. Merezhkovsky, *Tolstoy as Man and Artist* (1902); G. R. Noyes, *Tolstoy* (1918); Philip Rahv, "Tolstoy: The Green Twig and the Black Trunk" and "The Death of Ivan Ilyich and Joseph K.," both in *Image and Idea* (1949); Theodore Redpath, *Tolstoy* (1960); Ernest J. Simmons, *Leo Tolstoy* (1946); George Steiner, *Tolstoy or Dostoevsky* (1959); and Stefan Zweig, *Adepts in Self-Portraiture (Casanova, Stendhal, Tolstoy)*, trans. by E. and C. Paul (1952).

ANTON CHEKHOV

LIFE. Anton Pavlovich Chekhov, born on January 17, 1860, at Taganrog, a small town on the Sea of Azov. His father was a grocer and haberdasher; his grandfather, a serf who had bought his freedom. Chekhov's father went bankrupt in 1876, and the family moved to Moscow, leaving Anton to finish school in his home town. After his graduation in 1879, he followed his family to Moscow, where he studied medicine. In order to earn additional money for his family and himself, he started to write humorous sketches and stories for magazines. In 1884 he became a doctor and published his first collection of stories, *Tales of Melpomene*. In the same year he had his first hemorrhage. All the rest of his life he struggled against tuberculosis. His first play, *Ivanov*, was performed in 1887. Three years later, he undertook an arduous journey through Siberia to the island of Sakhalin (north of Japan) and back by boat through the Suez Canal. He saw there the Russian penal settlements and wrote a moving account of his trip in *Sakhalin Island* (1892). In 1898 his play *The Sea Gull* was a great success at the Moscow Art Theater. The next year he moved to Yalta, in the Crimea, and in 1901 married the actress Olga Knipper. He died on July 2, 1904, at Badenweiler in the Black Forest.

CHIEF WRITINGS. Chekhov's stories, which first appeared in scattered magazines, have been collected in many variously titled volumes. The plays were performed in this order: *Ivanov* (1887); *The Sea Gull* (1896); *Uncle Vanya* (1899); *The Three Sisters* (1901); *The Cherry Orchard* (1904); they have been translated by Constance Garnett, 2 vols., 1924.

BIOGRAPHY AND CRITICISM. W. H. Bruford, *Chekhov and His Russia* (1948) and *Anton Chekhov* (1957); Korney Chukovsky, *Chekhov the Man*, trans. by Pauline Rose (1945); Thomas Adam Eekman, *A. Čechov, 1860-1960*. *Some Essays* (1960); Oliver Elton, "Chekhov" in *Essays and Addresses* (1939); Francis Fergusson, "*Ghosts* and *The Cherry Orchard*," in *The Idea of a Theater* (1949); Anna Heifetz (Sherman), *Chekhov in English: A List of Works by and about Him*, ed. by A. Yarmolinsky (1949); Ronald Hingley, *Chekhov, A Biographical and Critical Study* (1950); David Magarshack, *Chekhov the Dramatist* (1952) and *Chekhov, A Life* (1952); and Ernest J. Simmons, *Chekhov: A Biography* (1962).

HENRIK IBSEN

LIFE. Born at Skien, in Norway, on March 20, 1828. His family had sunk into poverty and finally complete bankruptcy. In 1844, at the age of sixteen, Ibsen was sent to Grimstad, another small coastal town, as an apothecary's apprentice. There he lived in almost complete isolation and cut himself off from his family, except for his sister Hedvig. In 1850 he managed to get to Oslo (then Christiana) and to enroll at the university. But he never passed his examinations and in the following year left for Bergen, where he had acquired the position of playwright and assistant stage manager at the newly founded Norwegian Theater. Ibsen supplied the small theater with several historical and romantic plays. In 1857 he was appointed artistic director at the Møllergate Theater in Christiana, and a year later he married Susannah Thoresen. *Love's Comedy* (1862) was his first major success on the stage. Ibsen was then deeply affected by Scandinavianism, the movement for the solidarity of the Northern nations, and when in 1864 Norway refused to do anything to support Denmark in her war with Prussia and Austria over Schleswig-Holstein, he was so disgusted with his country that he left it for what he thought would be permanent exile. After that, Ibsen led a life of wandering. He lived in Rome, in Dresden, in Munich, and in smaller summer resorts, and during this time wrote all his later plays. *The Wild Duck* was written in Gossensass, in the Austrian Alps, in 1884. He paid a visit to Norway in 1885, but returned again to Germany. Only in 1891, when he was sixty-three, did Ibsen return to Christiana for good. He was then famous and widely honored, but lived a very retired life. In 1900 he suffered a stroke which made him a complete invalid for the last years of his life. He died on May 23, 1906, at Christiana.

CHIEF WRITINGS. (All of the works listed are plays.) *A Doll's House* (1879); *Ghosts* (1881); *An Enemy of the People* (1882); *The Wild Duck* (1884); *Rosmersholm* (1886); *The Lady from the Sea* (1888); *Hedda Gabler* (1890); *The Master Builder* (1892).

BIOGRAPHY AND CRITICISM. Eric Bentley, *The Playwright as Thinker* (1947); M. C. Bradbrook, *Ibsen the Norwegian* (1946, 2nd ed., 1948); Georg Brandes, *Hendrik Ibsen*; *Björnstjerne Björnson: Critical Studies* (1899); Brian W. Downs, *Ibsen: The Intellectual Background* (1946) and *A Study of Six Plays by Ibsen* (1950); Theodore Jorgensen, *Henrik Ibsen: A Study in Art and Personality* (1945); Halvdan Koht, *Life of Ibsen*, 2 vols. (1931); Janko Lavrin, *Ibsen: An Approach* (1950); F. L. Lucas, *The Drama of Ibsen and Strindberg* (1962); James W. McFarlane, *Ibsen and the Temper of Norwegian Literature* (1960); Kenneth Muir, *Last Periods of Shakespeare, Racine, Ibsen* (1961); John Northam, *Ibsen's Dramatic Method: A Study of the Prose Dramas* (1953); George Bernard Shaw, *The Quintessence of Ibsenism* (1891, 3rd enlarged ed., 1913); Peter T. D. Tennant, *Ibsen's Dramatic Technique* (1948); Hermann J. Weigand, *The Modern Ibsen: A Reconsideration* (1925); and A. E. Zucker, *Henrik Ibsen, The Master Builder* (1927).

HENRY JAMES

LIFE. Henry James was born on April

15, 1843, in New York City. His father, Henry James, Sr., was an amateur religious philosopher who had inherited considerable wealth. His elder brother William James (1842-1910) became famous as a philosopher and psychologist. Henry James grew up in Albany and New York but in 1855-1858 attended schools in Geneva, London, and Paris, and in 1859 studied briefly at Bonn. In Newport, R. I., in 1860, James suffered an injury as a volunteer fireman which prevented him from taking part in the Civil War and apparently from ever marrying. In 1862-1863 he studied law at Harvard, but then began to write short stories and criticism. In 1869-1870 and in 1872-1874 he traveled again in Europe. When his first important novel, *Roderick Hudson*, was being published serially in 1875, he left for Paris, where he met Flaubert, Edmond de Goncourt, Zola, Daudet, and Turgenev. In 1876 James definitely settled in London. He revisited America in 1882-1883 when his parents died, and again as late as 1905. In 1887 he stayed in Italy, in Venice and Florence, where *The Aspern Papers* was written. In 1890-1891 James tried to score a success on the London stage with several plays, but failed. In 1897 he moved from London to Rye, Sussex. In 1915 James became a British subject. He died of a stroke on February 28, 1916, in London.

CHIEF WRITINGS. *Roderick Hudson* (1876); *The American* (1877); *French Poets and Novelists* (1878); *The Europeans* (1878); *Daisy Miller* (1879); *The Madonna of the Future and Other Tales* (1879); *Hawthorne* (1879); *Washington Square* (1881); *Portrait of a Lady* (1881); *The Bostonians* (1886); *The Princess Casamassima*

(1886); *Partial Portraits* (1888); *The Aspern Papers, Louisa Pallant,* and *The Modern Warning* (1888); *The Tragic Muse* (1890); *The Spoils of Poynton* (1897); *What Maisie Knew* (1897); *The Two Magics, The Turn of the Screw,* and *Covering End* (1898); *The Awkward Age* (1899); *The Wings of the Dove* (1902); *The Ambassadors* (1903); *The Golden Bowl* (1904); *The American Scene* (1907); *A Small Boy and Others* (1913); *Notes on Novelists* (1914); *The Middle Years* (1917).

BIOGRAPHY AND CRITICISM. Joseph Warren Beach, *The Method of Henry James* (1918); Van Wyck Brooks, *The Pilgrimage of Henry James* (1925); Oscar Cargill, *The Novels of Henry James* (1961); F. W. Dupee, *Henry James: His Life and Writings* (1956); Leon Edel, *Henry James: The Untried Years* (1953), *The Conquest of London* (1962), and *The Middle Years* (1962); Dorothea Krook, *The Ordeal of Consciousness in Henry James* (1962); F. O. Matthiessen, *Henry James: The Major Phase* (1944); René Wellek, "Henry James's Literary Theory and Criticism," in *American Literature,* XXX (1958).

On *The Aspern Papers,* besides pp. 213-226 in Edel's *Henry James: The Middle Years* (1962); Sam S. Baskett, "The Sense of the Present in *The Aspern Papers,*" in *Papers of the Michigan Academy of Science, Arts and Letters,* XLIV (1959), 381-388; Wayne C. Booth, *The Rhetoric of Fiction* (1961), pp. 354-364; Joseph Mg. Botkoll, "Introduction" to *The Europeans; The Europeans* (1950); William Bysshe Stein, "The Aspern Papers: A Comedy of Masks," in *Nineteenth Century Fiction,* XIV (1959), 172-178.

HONORÉ DE BALZAC

(1799–1850)

Gobseck*

At eleven o'clock one evening, during the winter of 1829–1830, two persons who were not members of the family were still seated

* 1830. Translated by Katharine Prescott Wormeley. From *The Works of Balzac,* Centenary Edition, Vol. XIV, Boston, Little, Brown & Company, 1899–1900.

ın the salon of the Vicomtesse de Grandlieu. One of them, a young and very good-looking man, took leave on hearing the clock strike the hour. When the sound of his carriage-wheels echoed from the courtyard, the viscountess, seeing no one present but her brother and a family friend who were finishing their game of piquet, went up to her daughter as she stood before the fireplace, apparently examining a fire-screen of shaded porcelain[1] while she listened to the sound of the same wheels in a manner to justify the mother's anxiety.

"Camille, if you continue to behave toward that young Comte de Restaud as you have done this evening, you will oblige me to close my doors to him. Listen to me, my child; if you have confidence in my affection, let me guide you in life. At seventeen years of age, a girl is unable to judge of either the future, or the past, or of certain social considerations. I shall make only one remark to you: Monsieur de Restaud has a mother who would squander millions—a woman ill-born, a Demoiselle Goriot,[2] who, in her youth, caused people to talk about her. She behaved so badly to her father that she does not deserve to have so good a son. The young count adores her, and stands by her with a filial piety which is worthy of all praise; he also takes the utmost care of his brother and sister. However admirable such conduct may be," continued the viscountess, in a pointed manner, "so long as the mother lives, all parents would fear to trust the future and the fortune of a daughter to young Restaud."

"I have overheard a few words which makes me desirous of intervening between you and Mademoiselle de Grandlieu," said the friend of the family, suddenly. "I've won, Monsieur le comte," he said, turning to his adversary. "I leave you now and rush to the succor of your niece."

"This is what is called having lawyer's ears," cried the viscountess. "My dear Derville, how could you overhear what I was saying in a low voice to Camille?"

"I knew it from your looks," replied Derville, sitting down on a sofa at the corner of the fireplace.

The uncle took a seat beside his niece, and Madame de Grandlieu placed herself on a low chair between her daughter and Derville.

"It is high time, Madame la vicomtesse, that I should tell you a little tale which will modify the opinion you have formed as to the fortunes of Comte Ernest de Restaud."

"A tale!" cried Camille. "Begin it, quick, monsieur."

1. The technique (then new and fashionable) of having a porcelain screen designed with figures which would stand out in the light of the fire was called *litophanie*.

2. Anastasie Goriot, who married the Comte de Restaud, was the younger daughter of the vermicelli (macaroni) merchant Goriot, who died in utter destitution (in Balzac's novel *Old Goriot*). *Demoiselle* is a term implying social inferiority.

Derville cast a look at Madame de Grandlieu which signified that the story he was about to tell would interest her.

The Vicomtesse de Grandlieu, by her fortune and the antiquity of her name, was one of the most distinguished women of the faubourg Saint-Germain,[3] and it may not seem natural that a Parisian lawyer should speak to her familiarly, and treat her in a manner so apparently cavalier; but the phenomenon is easily explained. Madame de Grandlieu, who returned to France with the royal family,[4] came to reside in Paris, where she lived, at first, on a stipend granted by Louis XVIII from the Civil List—a situation that was quite intolerable. Derville, the lawyer, chanced to discover certain legal blunders in the sale which the Republic had made of the hôtel de Grandlieu, and he asserted that it ought to be restored to the viscountess. He undertook the case for a certain fee, and won it. Encouraged by this success, he sued a fraternity of monks, and harassed them legally, until he obtained the restitution of the forest of Liceney. He also recovered a number of shares in the Orléans canal, and certain parcels of real estate with which the Emperor had endowed a few public institutions.

In this way the fortune of Madame de Grandlieu, restored to her by the care and ability of the young lawyer, amounted to an income of sixty thousand francs a year, before the law of indemnity (which restored to her enormous sums of money) had been passed. A man of the highest honor, well-informed, modest, and excellent company, he became, henceforth, the "friend of the family." Though his conduct to Madame de Grandlieu had won him the respect and the business of the best houses of the faubourg Saint-Germain, he never profited by that favor as a more ambitious man would have done. He resisted the proposals of the viscountess to sell his practice and enter the magistracy, a career in which, thanks to her influence, he would certainly have obtained a very rapid advancement. With the exception of the hôtel de Grandlieu, where he sometimes passed an evening, he never went into society unless to keep up his connections. It was fortunate for him that his talents had been brought to light by his devotion to the interests of Madame de Grandlieu, otherwise he would have run the risk of losing his practice altogether. Derville had not the soul of a pettifogger.

Ever since Comte Ernest de Restaud had been received in Madame de Grandlieu's salon and Derville had discovered Camille's sympathy for the young man, he had become as assiduous in his own visits as any dandy of the Chaussée-d'Antin newly admitted to the circles of the noble faubourg. A few days before the evening

3. the aristocratic quarter of Paris.
4. When, after the fall of Napoleon (1814), Louis XVIII (a younger brother of Louis XVI, who had been beheaded during the Revolution) came to the throne, many aristocrats returned from emigration and recovered their confiscated properties.

on which our story opens, he was standing near Camille at a ball when he said to her, motioning to the young count:

"Isn't it a pity that young fellow hasn't two or three millions?"

"Do you call it a pity? I don't think so," she answered. "Monsieur de Restaud has great talent, he is well-educated, and the minister with whom he is placed thinks highly of him. I have no doubt he will become a very remarkable man. Such a young fellow will find all the fortune he wants whenever he comes to power."

"Yes, but suppose he were rich now?"

"Suppose he were rich?" echoed Camille, coloring. "Oh! then all the girls in society would be quarrelling for him," she added, with a nod at the quadrilles.

"And then, perhaps," said the lawyer, slyly, "Mademoiselle de Grandlieu would not be the only one on whom his eyes would turn. Why do you blush? You have a liking for him, haven't you? Come, tell me."

Camille rose hastily.

"She loves him," thought Derville.

Since that evening Camille had shown the lawyer very unusual attentions, perceiving that he approved of her inclination for the young count. Until then, although she was not ignorant of the many obligations of her family to Derville, she had always shown him more courtesy than real friendship, more civility than feeling; her manners, and also the tone of her voice, had let him know the distance that conventions placed between them. Gratitude is a debt which children will not always accept as part of their inheritance.

"This affair," said Derville to the viscountess, on the evening when our story opens, "recalls to me the only romantic circumstances of my life—You are laughing already," he said, interrupting himself, "at the idea of a lawyer talking of romance. But I have been twenty-five years of age as well as others; and by that time of life I had already seen very strange things. I shall begin by telling you about a personage whom you can never know—a usurer. Imagine vividly that pale, wan visage, to which I wish the Academy would allow me to apply the word 'moon-faced';[5] it looked like tarnished silver. My usurer's hair was flat, carefully combed, and sandy-gray in color. The features of his face, impassible as that of Talleyrand,[6] had apparently been cast in iron. His little eyes, yellow as those of a weasel, had scarcely any lashes and seemed to fear the light; but the peak of an old cap protected them. His pointed nose was so pock-marked about the tip that you might have compared it to a

---

5. The French Academy publishes, at intervals, a dictionary of the French language, which lags far behind current usage. The adjective *lunaire* (literally, "lunar") was not yet allowed in its metaphorical sense.

6. Charles Maurice de Talleyrand (1754–1838) served Napoleon and the Bourbons as foreign minister and represented France at the Congress of Vienna (1814).

gimlet. He had the thin lips of those little old men and alchemists painted by Rembrandt or Metsu.[7] The man spoke low, in a gentle voice, and was never angry. His age was a problem: it was impossible to say whether he was old before his time, or whether he so spared his youth that it lasted him forever.

"All things in his room were clean and shabby, resembling, from the green cover of the desk to the bedside carpet, the frigid sanctum of old maids who spent their days in rubbing their furniture. In winter, the embers on his hearth, buried beneath a heap of ashes, smoked, but never blazed. His actions, from the hour of his rising to his evening fits of coughing, were subjected to the regularity of clock-work. He was in some respects an automaton, whom sleep wound up. If you touch a beetle crossing a piece of paper, it will stop and feign to be dead; just so this man would interrupt his speech if a carriage passed, in order not to force his voice. Imitating Fontenelle,[8] he economized the vital movement and concentrated all human sentiments upon the I. Consequently, his life flowed on without producing more noise than the sand of an ancient hour-glass. Occasionally, his victims made great outcries, and were furious; after which a dead silence fell, as in kitchens after a duck's neck is wrung.

"Towards evening the man-of-notes became an ordinary mortal; his metals were transformed into a human heart. If he was satisfied with his day he rubbed his hands, and from the chinks and wrinkles of his face a vapor of gayety exhaled—for it is impossible to otherwise describe the silent play of his muscles, where a sensation, like the noiseless laugh of Leather-Stocking, seemed to lie. In his moments of greatest joy his words were always monosyllabic, and the expression of his countenance invariably negative.

"Such was the neighbor whom chance bestowed upon me at a house where I was living, in the rue des Grès, when I was still a second clerk and had only just finished my third year in the Law school. This house, which has no courtyard, is damp and gloomy. The rooms get no light except from the street. The cloistral arrangement which divides the building into rooms of equal size, with no issue but a long corridor lighted from above, shows that the house was formerly part of a convent. At this sad aspect the gayety of even a dashing young blood would die away as he entered the usurer's abode. The man and his house resembled each other, like the rock and its barnacle.

"The only being with whom he held communication, socially speaking, was myself. He came to my room, sometimes, to ask for

7. Gabriel Metsu (1630?–1667), a Dutch painter.
8. Bernard Le Bovier, sieur de Fontenelle (1657–1757), popularizer of the Cartesian philosophy, and a centenarian, who had the reputation of guarding his strength and health most carefully.

tinder, or to borrow a book or a newspaper, and at night he allowed me to enter his cell, where we talked if he happened to be good-humored. These marks of confidence were the results of four years' vicinity and my virtuous conduct, which, for want of money, very closely resembled his own. Had he relations, or friends? Was he rich or poor? No one could have answered those questions. During these years I never saw any money in his possession. His wealth was no doubt in the cellars of the Bank of France. He collected his notes himself, racing through Paris on legs as sinewy as those of a deer. He was a martyr to his caution. One day, by accident, he showed a bit of gold: a double napoleon[9] made its escape, heaven knows how! through his waistcoat pocket; another tenant, who was following him up the staircase, picked it up and gave it to him.

" 'That is not mine,' he answered, with a gesture of surprise. 'Do you suppose that I have money? Should I live as I do if I were rich?'

"In the mornings he made his own coffee on a tin heater which always stood in the dingy corner of his fireplace. His dinner was brought from a cookshop. Our old portress went up at a fixed hour and put his room in order. And, to cap all, by a singularity which Sterne[10] would have called predestination, the man was named Gobseck.[11]

"Later, when I managed his affairs, I discovered that when we first knew each other he was sixty-six years old. He was born about 1740, in the suburbs of Antwerp, of a Dutchman and a Jewess; his name was Jean-Esther van Gobseck. You remember, of course, how all Paris was excited about the murder of a woman called *La belle Hollandaise?* When I chanced to speak of it to my neighbor, he said, without expressing the slightest interest or surprise:

" 'That was my great-niece.'

"He made no other comment on the death of his only known heir, the granddaughter of his sister. From the newspapers I learned that *La belle Hollandaise* was called Sarah van Gobseck. When I asked him by what strange chance his great-niece bore his name, he replied, with a smile:

" 'The women of our family never marry.'

"This singular man had always refused, through four generations, to know, or even see, a single female member of his family. He abhorred his heirs, and could not conceive that his wealth would ever be possessed by others, even after his death. His mother had despatched him as cabin-boy, when ten years old, to the Dutch possessions in India, where he had lived as he could for twenty

9. a gold coin worth about forty francs (about ten dollars in the nineteenth century).
10. Laurence Sterne (1713–1768), English novelist, author of *Tristram Shandy.* Walter Shandy, father of the hero, speculates much about the fatality of names and the misfortune of having bestowed the name Tristram on his son.
11. The name suggests the French words *gober,* "to gulp down," "to gobble," and *sec,* "lean," "dry."

years. The wrinkles of his yellow forehead covered the secrets of horrible events, awful terrors, unhoped-for luck, romantic disappointment, and infinite joys; also there were signs of hunger endured, love trodden underfoot, fortune compromised, lost, and refound, life many a time in danger, and saved, perhaps, by sudden decisions, the urgency for which excuses cruelty. He had known Monsieur de Lally,[12] Admiral Simeuse, Monsieur de Kergarouët, Monsieur d'Estaing, the Bailli de Suffren, Monsieur de Portenduère, Lord Cornwallis, Lord Hastings, the father of Tippu Sahib, and Tippu Sahib himself; for this Savoyard, who had served the King of Delhi, and contributed not a little to found the power of the Mahrattas,[13] had done business with him. He also had dealings with Victor Hughes,[14] and several other famous corsairs, for he lived for a long time on the island of Saint Thomas.[15] He had attempted so many things in quest of fortune that he even tried to discover the gold of that tribe of savages so celebrated near Buenos Ayres. He was not a stranger to any of the great events of the war of American Independence. But when he spoke of India or America, which he never did with others, and rarely with me, he seemed to think he had committed an indiscretion, and regretted it.

"If humanity, if social fellowship, are a religion, he must be considered an atheist. Though I set myself to examine him, I must admit, to my confusion, that up to the very last moment his heart was impenetrable to me. I sometimes asked myself to what sex he belonged. If all usurers resemble him, I believe they form a neutral species. Was he faithful to the religion of his mother, and did he look upon all Christians as his prey? Had he made himself a Catholic, a Mohammedan, a Brahman, a Lutheran? I never knew his religious opinions, but he seemed to me more indifferent than sceptical.

"One evening I entered the room of this man transmuted to gold, whom his victims (he called them clients) addressed either in jest

12. This list is a jumble of fictional and historical names. Monsieur de Kergarouët, Admiral Simeuse, and Monsieur de Portenduère appear in several other novels and stories of the *Human Comedy*. Thomas Arthur de Lally (1702–1766) was a French governor general in India, executed for treason. Charles Hector d' Estaing (1729–1794) was a French admiral who was beheaded during the Revolution. Pierre André de Suffren de Saint-Tropez (1726–1788) was another French naval officer who fought against the English in India. "Bailli," before his name, indicates a high rank in the Order of Maltese Knights. Charles Cornwallis (1738–1805) was the British general who surrendered at Yorktown. Later he commanded British troops against Tippu Sahib, the king of Mysore, in India. Warren Hastings (1732–1818) was the British governor of India impeached for his crimes and subsequently acquitted in spite of Burke's famous speeches for the prosecution. The "Savoyard" was a French adventurer, Claude Martin (1735–1800), who became a major general in the armies of the British East India Company. He actually came from Lyons, not the Savoy.

13. a tribe in India.

14. Apparently an error (suggested by the name Victor Hugo?) for Sir Edward Hughes (1720?–1794), a British admiral.

15. one of the Virgin Islands.

or satire as 'Papa Gobseck.' I found him in his armchair, motionless as a statue, his eyes fixed on the mantel of the fireplace, on which he seemed to be scanning memoranda of accounts. A smoky lamp cast out a gleam which, far from coloring his face, brought out its pallor. He looked at me silently, and pointed to the chair which awaited me. 'Of what is this strange being thinking?' I said to myself. 'Does he know that God exists? that there are feelings, women, happiness?' I pitied him as I pity a sick man, and yet I also understood that he possessed by thought the earth he had travelled over, dug into, weighed, sifted, and worked.

" 'Good-evening, papa Gobseck,' I said.

"He turned his head in my direction, his thick black eyebrows slightly contracting; in him that peculiar movement was equivalent to the gayest smile of a Southerner.

" 'You seem as gloomy,' I continued, 'as you were the day you heard of the bankruptcy of that publisher whose cleverness you have always admired, though you were made its victim.'

" 'Victim?' he said, in a surprised tone.

" 'Didn't he, in order to obtain his certificate of insolvency, pay up your account with notes subject to the settlement in bankruptcy, and when the business was re-established didn't those notes come under the reduction named in that settlement?'

" 'He was shrewd,' replied the old man, 'but I nipped him back.'

" 'Perhaps you hold a few protested notes?—this is the thirtieth of the month, you know.'

"I had never before mentioned money to him. He raised his eyes to me, satirically; then, in his softest voice, the tones of which were like the sounds a pupil draws from his flute when he has no mouthpiece, he said:

" 'I am amusing myself.'

" 'Then you *do* find amusement sometimes?'

" 'Do you think there are no poets but those who scribble verses?' he asked, shrugging his shoulders, and casting a look of pity on me.

" 'Poesy in that head!' I thought to myself; for at that time I knew nothing of his life.

" 'What existence is there as brilliant as mine?' he continued, and his eyes brightened. 'You are young; you have the ideas of your blood; you see faces of women in your embers, I see nothing but coals in mine. You believe in everything, I believe in nothing. Keep your illusions, if you can. I am going to reckon up life to you. Whether you travel about the world, or whether you stay in your chimney-corner with a wife, there comes an age when life is nothing more than a habit, practised in some preferred spot. Happiness then consists in the exercise of our faculties applied to real objects. Outside of those two precepts all else is false. My other principles have varied like those of other men; I have changed with each latitude in which I lived. What Europe admires, Asia punishes. A vice in Paris is a necessity after you pass the Azores. Nothing is a fixed fact here below; conventions alone exist, and those are modified by climate. To one who has flung himself forcibly into every social mold, convictions and moralities are nothing more than words without weight. There remains within us but the one true sentiment which Nature implanted there; namely, the instinct of preservation. In European societies this instinct is called *self-interest*. If you had lived as long as I have, you would know that there is but one material thing the value of which is sufficiently certain to be worth a man's while to care for it. That thing is—Gold. Gold represents all human forces. I have travelled; I have seen in all lands plains and mountains: plains are tiresome, mountains fatiguing; hence, places and regions signify nothing. As for customs and morals, man is the same everywhere; everywhere the struggle between wealth and poverty exists; everywhere it is inevitable. Better, therefore, to be the one to take advantage, than the one to be taken advantage of. Everywhere you will find muscular folk who work their way, and lymphatic folk who fret and worry. Everywhere pleasures are the same; for all emotions are exhausted, and nothing survives of them but the single sentiment of *vanity*. Vanity is always I. Vanity is never truly satisfied except by floods of gold. Desires need time, or physical means, or care. Well! gold contains all those things in the germ, and will give them in reality. None but fools or sick men can find pleasure in playing cards every night to see if they can win a few francs. None but fools can spend their time in asking each other what happens, and whether Madame So-and-so occupies her sofa alone or in company, or whether she has more blood than lymph, more ardor than virtue. None but dupes can think themselves useful to their fellow-men, by laying down political principles to govern events which are still unforeseen. None but ninnies can like to go through the same routine, pacing up and down like animals in a cage; dressing for others, eating for others, priding themselves on a horse or a carriage which their neighbor can't copy for at least three days! Isn't that the life of your Parisians, reduced to a few sentences? Let us look at life on a higher plane. There, happiness consists either in strong emotions which wear out life, or in regular occupations worked, as it were, by mechanism at stated times. Above these forms of happiness there exists the curiosity (said to be noble) of knowing the secrets of Nature, or of producing a certain imitation of her effects. Isn't that, in two words, art or knowledge, passion or tranquillity? Well! all human passions, heightened by the play of social interests, parade before me, who live in tranquillity. As for your scientific curiosity—a sort of combat in which man is always worsted!—I substitute for that a penetration into the secret springs that move humanity. In a word, I possess the world without fatigue, and the world has not the slightest hold upon me. Listen to me,' he continued. 'I will tell you the events of my morning, and you can judge by them of my pleasures.'

"He rose, went to the door and bolted it, drew a curtain of old tapestry, the brass rings grinding on the rod, and sat down again.

" 'This morning,' he said, 'I had only two notes to collect; the others I had given last evening to clients in place of ready money. So much made, you know! for in discounting them I deduct the cost of collection, taking forty sous for a street cab. A pretty thing it would be if a client made me cross all Paris for six francs discount—I, who am under bonds to no one!—I, who pay no more than seven francs in taxes! Well, the first note, for a thousand francs, presented by a young man, a dashing fellow, with a spangled waistcoat, eyeglass, tilbury, English horse, etc., was signed by one of the prettiest women in Paris, married to a rich man—a count. Why should this countess have signed that note (void in law[16] but excellent in fact)? For such poor women fear the scandal which a protested note would cause in their homes; they'll even sell themselves rather than not take up the note. I wanted to know the secret value of that paper. Was it folly, imprudence, love, or charity? The second note, also for a thousand francs, signed "Jenny Malvaut," was presented to me by a linen-draper in a fair way to be ruined. No person having credit at the Bank ever comes to me; the first step taken from my door to my desk means despair, bankruptcy on the verge of discovery, and, above all, the refusal of aid from many bankers. That's how it is that I see none but stags at bay, hunted by the pack of their creditors. The countess lived in the rue du Helder, and Jenny in the rue Montmartre. How many conjectures came into my mind as I went from here this morning! If those two women were not ready to pay, they would receive me with more respect than if I had been their own father. What grimaces that countess would play off upon me in place of her thousand francs! She'd pretend to be cordial, and speak in the coaxing voice such women reserve for holders of notes; she'd shower cajoling words upon me, perhaps implore me, and I—'

"Here the old man cast his eye upon me.

" 'and I—immovable!' he went on. 'I am there as an Avenger; I appear as Remorse. But enough of such fancies. I got there.

" ' "Madame la comtesse is still in bed," said the lady's-maid.

" ' "When will she be visible?"

" ' "At noon."

" ' "Is Madame la comtesse ill?"

16. because women needed the assent of their husbands.

" ' "No, monsieur, but she did not return from a ball till three in the morning."

" ' "My name is Gobseck; tell her my name, and say I shall return at noon."

" 'And off I went, signing my presence on the carpet that covered the stairs. I like to muddy the floors of rich men, not from petty meanness, but to let them feel the claws of necessity. Reached the rue Montmartre, found a shabby sort of house, pushed open the *porte-cochère*, and saw a damp, dark courtyard, where the sun never penetrates. The porter's lodge was dingy, the glass of the window looked like the sleeve of a wadded dressing-gown worn too long; it was greasy, cracked, and discolored.

" ' "Mademoiselle Jenny Malvaut?"

" ' "She's out; but if you have come about a note, the money is here."

" ' "I'll come back," I said.

" ' "The moment I heard the porter had the money I wanted to know that girl. I felt sure she was pretty. I spent the morning look-ing at the engravings displayed on the boulevard. Then, as twelve o'clock sounded, I entered the salon which adjoins the bedroom of Madame la comtesse.

" ' "Madame has just this moment rung for me," said the maid. "I don't think she will see you yet."

" ' "I'll wait," I answered, seating myself in an armchair.

" 'I heard the blinds open in madame's room; then the maid came hurrying in, and said to me:

" ' "Come in, monsieur."

" 'By the softness of her voice I knew very well her mistress was not ready to pay. What a beautiful woman I then saw! She had flung a camel's-hair shawl around her shoulders so hastily that her shape could be guessed in all its nudity. She wore a nightgown trimmed with frills as white as snow, which showed an annual ex-pense of over two thousand francs for washing. Her black hair fell in heavy curls from a silk handkerchief, carelessly knotted round her head after the Creole fashion. Her bed was the picture of dis-order, caused, no doubt, by troubled sleep. A painter would have paid a good deal to have stood a few moments in the midst of this scene. Under draperies voluptuously looped up were pillows on a down quilt of sky-blue silk, the lace of their trimming showing to advantage on that azure background. On a bear's skin, stretched between the carved lion's paws of the mahogany bedstead, lay white satin shoes, tossed off with the carelessness that comes of the fatigue of a ball. On a chair was a rumpled gown, the sleeves touch-ing the floor. Stockings which a breath of wind might have blown away were twisted round the legs of a chair. A fan of value, half-opened, glittered on the chimney-piece. The drawers of the bureau were open. Flowers, diamonds, gloves, a bouquet, a belt, were thrown here and there about the room. I breathed a vague odor of perfumes. All was luxury and disorder, beauty without harmony. Already for this woman, or for her lover, poverty, crouching beneath these riches, raised its head and made them feel its sharpened teeth. The tired face of the countess was in keeping with that room strewn with the fragments of a fête. Those scattered gew-gaws were pitiful; collected on her person the night before, they had brought her adoration. These vestiges of love, blasted by remorse, that image of a life of dissipation, of luxury, of tumult, betrayed the efforts of Tantalus to grasp eluding pleasures. A few red spots on the young woman's face showed the delicacy of her skin; but her features seemed swollen, and the brown circle beneath her eyes was more marked than was natural. Still, nature was too vigorous within her to let these indications of a life of folly injure her beauty. Her eyes sparkled. Like an Herodias[17] of Leonardo da Vinci[18] (I've sold those pictures), she was magnificent in life and vigor; there was nothing paltry in her form or in her features; she inspired love, and she seemed to me to be stronger than love. She pleased me. It is long since my heart has beaten. I was paid! I'd give a thousand francs any day for a sensation that recalled to me my youth.

" ' "Monsieur," she said, pointing to a chair, "will you have the kindness to wait for your money?"

" ' "Until to-morrow, at noon, madame," I replied, folding the note I had presented to her. "I have no legal right to protest until then." In my own mind, I was saying to myself: "Pay for your luxury, pay for your name, pay for your pleasures, pay for the monopoly you enjoy! To secure their property rights the rich have invented courts and judges and the guillotine—candles, in which poor ignorant creatures fly and singe themselves. But for you, who sleep in silk and satin, there's something else: there's remorse, grinding of teeth behind those smiles of yours, jaws of fantastic lions opening to crunch you!"

" ' "A protest!" she cried, looking me in the face. "You can't mean it! Would you have so little consideration for me?"

" ' "If the king himself owed me money, madame, and did not pay it, I'd summons him even quicker than another debtor."

" 'At this moment some one knocked at the door.

" ' "I am not visible," said the countess, imperiously.

---

17. should be, "a daughter of Herodias," i.e., Salome, who danced before Herod, her stepfather, and as she had demanded, received the head of John the Baptist on a platter. (See Matthew 14:6–11.)

18. the famous Italian Renaissance painter and inventor (1452–1519). No picture by him of Herod and Salome is known.

" ' "Anastasie, I want to see you very much."

" ' "Not just now, dear," she answered, in a milder voice, but not a kind one.

" ' "What nonsense! I hear you talking to someone," said a man, who could be, of course, none other than the count, as he entered the room.

" 'The countess looked at me; I understood her, and from that moment she became my slave. There was a time in my life, young man, when I might, perhaps, have been fool enough not to protest. In 1763, at Pondicherry,[19] I forgave a woman who swindled me finely. I deserved it; why did I ever trust her!

" ' "What does monsieur want?" said the count.

" 'I saw that woman tremble from head to foot; the white and satiny skin of her throat grew rough and turned, as they say, to goose-flesh. As for me, I laughed inwardly, without a muscle of my face quivering.

" ' "Monsieur is one of my tradesmen," she said.

" 'The count turned his back upon me. I pulled the note half out of my pocket. Seeing that inexorable action, the young woman came close up to me and offered me a diamond ring.

" ' "Take it, and go!" she said.

" 'That was simply an exchange of properties. I bowed, gave her the note, and left the room. The diamond was worth fully twelve hundred francs. In the courtyard I found a swarm of valets, brushing their liveries, blacking their boots, or cleaning the sumptuous equipages. "That," I said to myself, "is what brings these people to me. That's what drives them to steal millions decently, to betray their country. Not to soil his boots by going afoot, the great lord—or he who imitates the lord—takes, once for all, a bath of mud!" I was thinking all that, when the great gates opened, and in drove the cabriolet of the young man who had brought me the note.

" ' "Monsieur," I said to him as he got out, "here are two hundred francs, which I beg you to return to Madame la comtesse; and you will please say to her that I hold at her disposition the article she placed in my hands this morning."

" 'He took the two hundred francs with a sarcastic smile, which seemed to say: "Ha! she has paid! so much the better!" I read upon that young man's face the future of the countess. The pretty, fair youth, a gambler without emotion, will ruin himself, ruin her, ruin her husband, ruin her children, spend their dowries, and cause greater devastation through salons than a battery of grapeshot through a regiment. Then I went to the rue Montmartre to find Mademoiselle Jenny Malvaut. I climbed up a steep little staircase. When I reached the fifth floor, I entered a small apartment of

19. the capital of the French possessions in India.

two rooms only, where all was as clean and bright as a new ducat. I couldn't see the slightest trace of dust on the furniture of the first room, where I was received by Mademoiselle Jenny, a true Parisian young woman, very simply dressed; head fresh and elegant, prepossessing manner, chestnut hair, well-combed, raised in two puffs upon the temples, which gave a look of mischief to the eyes, that were clear as crystals. The daylight, coming through little curtains hanging at the windows, threw a soft reflection on her modest face. Round her were numerous bits of linen, cut in shapes which showed me her regular occupation; it was evidently that of a seamstress. She sat there like the genius of solitude. When I presented the note I said that I had not found her at home that morning.

" ' "But," she said, "the money was with the porter."

" 'I pretended not to hear.

" ' "Mademoiselle goes out early, it seems?"

" ' "I seldom go out at all; but if one works at night one must take a bath in the daytime."

" 'I looked at her. With one glance I could guess the truth about her. Here was a girl condemned to toil by poverty, belonging, no doubt, to a family of honest farmers; for I noticed a certain ruddiness in her face peculiar to those who are born in the country. I can't tell you what air of virtue it was that breathed from her features, but I seemed to have entered an atmosphere of sincerity and innocence; my lungs were freshened. Poor child! she believed in something! Her simple bedstead of painted wood was surmounted by a crucifix wreathed by two branches of box. I was half touched. I felt disposed to offer her money at twelve per cent, only to enable her to purchase some good business. "But," I said to myself, "I daresay there's some little cousin who would get money on her signature and eat up all she has." So I went away, being on my guard against such generous ideas, for I've often had occasion to notice that when benevolence does not injure the benefactor it is sure to destroy the person benefited. When you came in I was thinking what a good little wife Jenny Malvaut would make. I compared her pure and solitary life with that of the countess, who, with one foot over the precipice, is about to roll down into the gulf of vice!

" ' "Well!' he continued, after a moment of profound silence, during which I examined him, 'do you now think there is no enjoyment in penetrating thus to the inner folds of the human heart, in espousing the life of others, and seeing that life bared before me? Sights forever varied!—hideous sores, mortal sorrows, scenes of love, miseries which the waters of the Seine await, joys of youth leading to the scaffold, despairing laughter, sumptuous festivals! Yesterday, a tragedy—some good father of a family smothers himself with charcoal because he cannot feed his children. To-morrow, a comedy—a young man trying to play me the scene of Monsieur Dimanche,[20] varied to suit the times. You have heard the eloquence of our modern preachers vaunted; I've occasionally wasted my time listening to them; they have sometimes made me change my opinion, but my conduct—as some one, I forget who, says—never! Well, those good priests, and your Mirabeau[21] and Vergniaud[22] and others are stutterers compared with my orators. Often a young girl in love, an old merchant on the downhill to bankruptcy, a mother trying to hide her son's crime, an artist without food, a great man on the decline of his popularity, who, for want of money, is about to lose the fruit of his efforts—such beings have made me shudder by the power of their words. Those splendid actors play for me only, but they do not deceive me. My glance is like that of God; it enters the heart. Nothing is hidden from me. Nothing is denied to him who opens and closes the mouth of the sack. I am rich enough to buy the consciences of those who manage the ministers of the nation—be they ushers or mistresses: isn't that power? I can have beautiful women and tender caresses: isn't that love? Power and pleasure—don't those two things sum up the whole of your social order? There's a dozen of us such as that in Paris; silent, unknown kings, the arbiters of your destinies. Isn't life itself a machine to which money imparts motion? Know this: means are confounded with results; you will never attain to separating the soul from the senses, spirit from matter. Gold is the spirituality of your present social being. Bound by one and the same interest, we—that dozen men—meet together one day in every week, at the café Thémis, near the Pont Neuf.[23] There we reveal the mysteries of finance. No apparent wealth can mislead us; we possess the secrets of all families. We keep a species of *black book*, in which are recorded most important notes on the public credit, on the Bank, on commerce. Casuists of the Bourse,[24] we form an Inquisition where the most indifferent actions of men of any fortune are judged and analyzed, and our judgment is always true. One of us watches over the judiciary body; another, the financial body; a third, the administrative body; a fourth, the commercial body. As for me, I keep an eye on eldest sons, on artists, men of fashion, gamblers—the most stirring part of Paris. Every one whom we severally deal with tells us his neighbor's secrets: betrayed passions and bruised vanities are gar-

20. a character in Molière's comedy *Don Juan* (1665). In Act IV, Scene 3, this merchant tries to collect a debt from Don Juan, but is overwhelmed by his eloquence and finally shoved out of doors by Sganarelle, Don Juan's valet, without being able to say a word.
21. Honoré Gabriel de Mirabeau (1749–1791), the most famous of the French revolutionary orators.

22. Pierre Victurnien Vergniaud (1753–1793), a Girondist who was beheaded during the Terror.
23. in spite of its name, the oldest existing bridge over the Seine in Paris, connecting the Île de la Cité (the island on which Notre Dame is located) with the Louvre.
24. the stock exchange in Paris.

rulous; vices, vengeances, disappointments are the best police force in the world. My brethren, like myself, have enjoyed all things, are sated with all things, and have come to love power and money solely for power and money themselves. Here,' he added, pointing to his cold and barren room, 'the fiery lover, insulted by a look, and drawing his sabre at a word, kneels and prays to me with clasped hands. Here the proudest merchant, here the woman vain of her beauty, here the dashing soldier, pray one and all, with tears of rage or anguish in their eyes. Here the most celebrated artists, here the writer whose name is promised to posterity, pray, likewise. Here, too,' he added, laying his hand upon his forehead, 'are the scales in which are weighed the inheritances and the dividends of all Paris. Do you think *now* that there are no enjoyments beneath this livid mask whose immobility has so often amazed you?' he said, turning toward me his wan face, which seemed to smell of money.

"I returned home stupefied. That shrunken old man grew larger; he had changed, before my very eyes, into some fantastic image personifying the power of gold. Life, men, filled me with horror. 'Are all things to be measured by money?' I asked myself. I remember that I did not go to sleep that night till very late. Mounds of gold rose up around me. The beautiful countess filled my thoughts. I confess, to my shame, that her image completely eclipsed that of the simple and chaste creature doomed to toil and to obscurity. But on the morrow, through the mists of waking, the gentle Jenny appeared to me in all her beauty, and I thought of her alone."

"Will you have a glass of sugar water," said the viscountess, interrupting Derville.

"Gladly," he replied.

"But I don't see, in all this, anything that concerns us," said Madame de Grandlieu, ringing the bell.

"Sardanapalus!"[25] exclaimed Derville, launching his favorite oath. "I am going to wake up Mademoiselle Camille presently by showing her that her happiness has depended, until recently, on papa Gobseck. But the old man is now dead, at the age of eighty-nine, and the Comte de Restaud will soon come into possession of a noble fortune. This needs some explanation. As for Jenny Malvaut, you know her; she is now my wife."

"Poor boy!" exclaimed the viscountess, "he would tell that before a score of people, with his usual frankness."

"Yes, I'd shout it to the universe," said the lawyer.

"Drink your water, my poor Derville. You'll never be anything but the happiest and the best of men."

"I left you in the rue du Helder, with a countess," cried the

25. an ancient Assyrian king. Here, a jocular oath.

uncle, waking from a doze. "What did you do there?"

"A few days after my conversation with the old Dutchman," resumed Derville, "I took my licentiate's degree and became, soon after, a barrister. The confidence the old miser had in me increased greatly. He consulted me, gratuitously, on the ticklish affairs in which he embarked after obtaining certain data—affairs which, to practical minds, would have seemed very dangerous. That man, over whom no human being could have gained any power, listened to my counsels with a sort of respect. It is true that they usually helped him. At last, on the day when I was made head-clerk of the office in which I had worked three years, I left the house in the rue des Grès, and went to live with my patron, who gave me board and lodging, and one hundred and twenty francs a month. That was a fine day for me! When I said good-bye to the old usurer, he expressed neither friendship nor regret; he did not ask me to come and see him; he merely gave me one of those glances which seemed to reveal in him the gift of second-sight. At the end of a week, however, I received a visit from him; he brought me a rather difficult affair—a dispossession case—and he continued his gratuitous consultations with as much freedom as if he paid me. At the end of the second year, from 1818 to 1819, my patron—a man of pleasure, and very extravagant—became involved, and was forced to sell his practice. Although at that time a lawyer's practice had not acquired the exorbitant value it now possesses, my patron almost gave away his in asking no more than one hundred and fifty thousand francs for it. An active, intelligent, and well-trained lawyer might live respectably, pay the interest on that sum, and free himself of the debt in ten years, could he only inspire confidence in someone who would lend him the purchase-money. I, the seventh son of a small bourgeois of Noyon, did not possess one penny, and I knew but one capitalist; namely, papa Gobseck. A daring thought, and some strange gleam of hope, gave me courage to go to him. Accordingly, one evening, I slowly walked to the rue des Grès. My heart beat violently as I knocked at the door of that gloomy house. I remembered what the old miser had told me in former days, when I was far, indeed, from imagining the violence of the agony which began on the threshold of that door. I was now about to pray to him like the rest! 'No, no!' I said to myself, 'an honest man should keep his dignity under all circumstances; no fortune is worth a meanness; I'll make myself as stiff as he.' Since my departure, papa Gobseck had hired my room, in order to have no other neighbor; he had also put a little grated peep-hole into the middle of his door, which he did not open till he recognized my face.

" 'Well!' he said, in his fluty little voice, 'so your patron sells his practice.'

" 'How did you know that? He has not mentioned it to a soul but me.'

"The lips of the old man drew toward the corners of his mouth precisely like curtains, and that mute smile was accompanied by a frigid glance.

" 'It needed that fact to bring you here to me,' he said, in a dry tone, and after a pause, during which I remained somewhat confounded.

" 'Listen to me, Monsieur Gobseck,' I said, with as much calmness as I was able to muster in presence of that old man, who fixed upon me his impassible eyes, the clear flame of which disturbed me.

"He made a gesture as if to say, 'Speak.'

" 'I know how difficult it is to move you. I should waste my eloquence in trying to make you see the position of a clerk without a penny, whose only hope is in you, and who has no other heart in the world but yours in which his future is understood. Let us drop the question of heart; business is business, and not romance or sentimentality. Here are the facts: My patron's practice brings him about twenty thousand francs a year, but in my hands I think it would bring forty thousand. He wants to sell it for one hundred and fifty thousand. I feel, here,' I continued, striking my forehead, 'that if you will lend me the purchase-money I can pay it off in ten years.'

" 'That's talking,' replied papa Gobseck, stretching out his hand and pressing mine. 'Never, since I have been in business,' he went on, 'has any one declared more plainly the object of his visit. Security?' he said, looking me over from head to foot. 'None'— adding, after a pause, 'how old are you?'

" 'Twenty-five in a few days,' I replied. 'Except for that I couldn't purchase.'

" 'True.'

" 'Well?'

" 'Possibly I may do it.'

" 'There's no time to lose; I am likely to have competitors who will put up the price.'

" 'Bring me the certificate of your birth to-morrow morning, and we'll talk the matter over. I'll think of it.'

"The next day, by eight o'clock, I was in the old man's room. He took the official paper, put on his spectacles, coughed, spat, wrapped his big coat round him, and read the extracts from the register of the mayor's office carefully. Then he turned the paper and re-turned it, looked at me, coughed again, wriggled in his chair, and said, finally:

" 'This is a matter we will try to arrange.' I quivered. 'I get fifty per cent for my money,' he continued; 'sometimes one hundred, two hundred, even five hundred per cent.' I turned pale at these words. 'But, in consideration of our acquaintance, I shall content myself with twelve and a half per cent interest per—' He hesitated. 'Well, yes! for your sake I will be satisfied with thirteen per cent per annum. Will that suit you?'

" 'Yes,' I replied.

" 'But if it is too much,' he said, 'speak out, Grotius'[26] (he often called me Grotius in fun). 'In asking you thirteen per cent I ply my trade; consider whether you can pay it. I don't like a man who hobnobs to everything. Is it too much?'

" 'No,' I said, 'I can meet it by rather more privation.'

" '*Parbleu!*' he cried, casting his malicious, oblique glance upon me, 'make your clients pay it.'

" 'No, by all the devils!' I cried, 'it will be I who will pay it. I'd cut my hand off sooner than fleece others.'

" 'Fiddle!' said papa Gobseck.

" 'Besides, a lawyer's fees go by tariff,' I continued.

" 'They don't,' he said. 'Not for negotiations, suits for recovery of funds, compromises. You can make thousands of francs, according to the interests involved, out of your conferences, trips, drafts of deeds, memoranda, and other verbiage. You'll have to learn that sort of thing. I shall recommend you as the cleverest and most knowing of lawyers; I'll send you such a lot of such cases that all your brother-lawyers will burst with jealousy. Werbrust, Palma, Gigonnet, my friends, shall give you all their dispossession cases—and God knows how many they are! You'll thus have two practices—the one you buy, and the one I make for you. You ought to give me fifteen per cent, at least, for my hundred and fifty thousand francs.'

" 'So be it, but not a penny more,' I said, with the firmness of a man who will grant nothing further.

"Papa Gobseck relented at this, and seemed pleased with me.

" 'I'll pay the price to your patron myself,' he said, 'so as to secure myself a solid hold on the security.'

" 'Oh! yes, take all the security you want.'

" 'Also, you must give me fifteen bills of exchange, acceptances in blank, for ten thousand francs each.'

" 'Provided that double value[27] be distinctly recorded—'

" 'No!' cried Gobseck, interrupting me. 'Why do you want me to have more confidence in you than you have in me?' I kept si-

26. Hugo Grotius (1583–1645), the famous Dutch jurist who formulated international law for the first time.

27. Gobseck's aim is apparently to obtain a double security. He will formally buy the practice, paying the seller for it himself, and still keep Derville's promissory notes, with due dates left blank. Presumably he could dispose of both the practice and the promissory notes, thus collecting twice over.

lence. 'And also,' he went on, in a good-humored tone, 'you will do all my business without asking fees, as long as I live; is that agreed to?'

" 'Yes, provided there is no further demand made.'

" 'Right!' he said. '*Ah ça!*' added the little old man, after a momentary pause, his face taking, but with difficulty, an air of good-humor, 'you'll allow me to go and see you sometimes?'

" 'It will always give me pleasure.'

" 'Yes, but when? In the mornings it would be impossible; you have your business and I have mine.'

" 'Come in the evening.'

" 'Oh, no!' he said hastily; 'you ought to go into society and meet your clients; I, too, have my friends at the café.'

" 'His friends!' thought I. 'Well, then,' I said, 'why not take the dinner-hour?'

" 'That's it,' said Gobseck. 'After the Bourse, about five o'clock. You'll see me every Wednesday and Saturday. We talk of our affairs like a couple of friends. Ha! ha! I can be gay sometimes. Give me the wing of a partridge and a glass of champagne, and we'll *talk*. I know many things that can be told in these days; things which will teach you to know men and, above all, women.'

" 'So be it for the partridge and the champagne,' I said.

" 'Don't be extravagant, or you'll lose my confidence. Get an old woman-servant—only one, mind; don't set up an establishment. I shall come and see you to look after your health. I've capital invested on your head, he! he! and I ought to keep informed about you. Come back this evening, and bring your patron.'

" 'Might I be informed, if there is no indiscretion in asking,' I said to the old man when we reached the threshold of his door, 'of what possible importance the certificate of my birth could be in this affair?'

"Jean-Esther van Gobseck shrugged his shoulders, smiled maliciously, and replied: 'How foolish youth is! Know this, my learned barrister—you *must* know it to keep from being cheated—before the age of thirty honesty and talent are still a sort of mortgage to be taken on a man. After that age he is not to be trusted.'

"So saying, he shut the door.

"Three months later I became a barrister, and soon after I had the great good-fortune, madame, of being chosen to undertake the business concerning the restitution of your property. The winning of that suit made me known. In spite of the enormous interest I paid Gobseck, I was able, in five years, to pay off my indebtedness. I married Jenny Malvaut, whom I love sincerely. The likeness between our two lives, our toil, our successes, increased the tie between us. Jenny's uncle, a rich farmer, died, leaving her seventy thousand francs, which helped to pay off my debt. Since that day my life has been nothing but happiness and prosperity—no need, therefore, to say more about myself; nothing is so intolerably dull as a happy man. Let us go back to our personages. About a year after I bought my practice, I was enticed, almost against my will, to a bachelor's breakfast. The party was the result of a wager lost by one of my legal friends to a young man then much in vogue in the world of fashion. Monsieur Maxime de Trailles, the flower of dandyism in those days, enjoyed a great reputation—"

"And still enjoys it," said the Comte de Born, interrupting Derville. "No man wears a coat with more style or drives a tandem[28] better than he. Maxime has the art of playing cards, and eating and drinking with more grace than the rest of the world put together. He knows what is what in horses, hats, and pictures. The women dote upon him. He always spends a hundred thousand francs a year, though no one ever heard of his owning property or a single coupon of interest. A type of the knight-errant of salons, boudoirs, and the boulevards—an amphibious species, half-man, half-woman—Comte Maxime de Trailles is a singular being, good *at* everything and good *for* nothing, feared and despised, knowing most things, yet ignorant at bottom, just as capable of doing a benefit as of committing a crime, sometimes base, sometimes noble, more covered with mud than stained with blood, having anxieties but no remorse, caring more for digestion than for thought, feigning passions and feeling none. He's a brilliant ring that might connect the galleys with the highest society. Maxime de Trailles is a man who belongs to that eminently intelligent class from which sprang Mirabeau,[29] Pitt,[30] Richelieu,[31] but which more frequently supplies the world with Comtes de Horn,[32] Fouquier-Tinvilles,[33] and Coignards."[34]

"Well!" resumed Derville, after listening to these remarks of Madame de Grandlieu's brother. "I had heard a great deal of that personage from poor Père Goriot, who was one of my clients; but I had always avoided, when I met him in society, the dangerous honor of his acquaintance. However, my friend urged me so strongly to go to his breakfast that I could not escape doing so without being accused of austerity. You can hardly conceive of a bachelor's

28. a two-seated carriage with horses harnessed one before the other.

29. See footnote 21.

30. either William Pitt (1708–1778), the first earl of Chatham, or his son, also named William (1759–1806); both were British statesmen and leaders in the struggle against France.

31. Armand Jean du Plessis de Richelieu (1585–1642), cardinal and duke, leading French statesman of the seventeenth century.

32. the Count of Horn (Joseph Anthony, 1698–1720), of a noble Flemish family, killed a stockjobber and was executed for the murder in Paris.

33. Antoine Quentin Fouquier-Tinville (1746–1795), a public prosecutor during the Revolution. He was himself beheaded in 1795.

34. Pierre Coignard (1779–1831), also called Count Potis de Sainte-Hélène, a famous adventurer and highwayman who was condemned to life imprisonment in 1819. He was in the penitentiary at Brest when "Gobseck" was published, and died there a year later.

breakfast, madame. It is a magnificent show of the greatest rarities—
the luxury of a miser who is sumptuous for one day only. On entering, one is struck by the order that reigns on a table so dazzling
with silver and glass and damasked linen. Life is there in its flower;
the young men are so graceful, so smiling, they speak low, they resemble the newly wedded—all seems virgin about them. Two hours
later you would think that same room was a battlefield after the
battle. On all sides broken glasses, twisted and soiled napkins; dishes
half-eaten, and repugnant to the eye; shouts that split the ears, sarcastic toasts, a fire of epigrams, malignant jests, purple faces, eyes
inflamed, no longer capable of expression—involuntary confidences
which tell all! In the midst of this infernal racket, some break bottles, others troll songs, they challenge each other, they kiss or fight;
an odious smell arises of a hundred odors, shouts on a hundred
tones; no one knows what he eats, or what he drinks, or what he
says; some are sad, others garrulous; one man is monomaniacal, and
repeats the same word like a clock with the striker going; another
man wants to command the riot, and the wisest propose an orgy. If
any man entered the room in his senses he would think it a Bac-
chanalian revel. It was in the midst of such a tumult as this that
Monsieur de Trailles attempted to insinuate himself into my good
graces. I had preserved my senses pretty well, for I was on my guard.
As for him, though he affected to be decently drunk, he was perfectly cool, and full of his own projects. I can't say how it was done,
but by the time we left Grignon's that evening, at nine o'clock, he
had completely bewitched me, and I promised to take him, the next
day, to papa Gobseck. The words, honor, virtue, countess, honest
woman, adored woman, misery, despair, shone, thanks to his gilded
language, like magic through his talk. When I awoke the next morning, and tried to remember what I had done the day before, I had
much difficulty in putting my ideas together. However, it seemed to
me that the daughter of one of my clients was in danger of losing
her reputation and the respect and love of her husband, if she could
not obtain some fifty thousand francs that morning. She had debts:
losses at cards, coachmaker's bill, money lost I knew not how. My
fascinating friend had assured me that she was rich enough to
repair, by a few years of economy, the damage she was about to do
to her fortune. Not until morning did I perceive the insistency of
my new friend; and I certainly had no idea of the importance it was
for papa Gobseck to make peace with this dandy. Just as I was
getting out of bed Monsieur de Trailles came to see me.

" 'Monsieur le comte,' I said, after the usual compliments had
passed, 'I do not see that you need my introduction in presenting
yourself to van Gobseck, the most polite and harmless of all capi-

talists. He'll give you the money if he has it, or, rather, if you can present him with sufficient security.'

" 'Monsieur,' he replied, 'I have no wish whatever to force you into doing me a service, even though you may have promised it.'

" 'Sardanapalus!' I said to myself; 'shall I let this man think I go back on my word?'

" 'I had the honor to tell you yesterday,' he continued, 'that I have quarrelled, most inopportunely, with papa Gobseck. Now, as there is no other money-lender in Paris who can fork out at once, and the first of the month too, a hundred thousand francs, I begged you to make my peace with him. But let us say no more about it.'

"Monsieur de Trailles looked at me with an air that was politely insulting, and prepared to leave the room.

" 'I am ready to take you to him,' I said.

"When we reached the rue des Grès the dandy looked about him with an attention and an air of anxiety which surprised me. His face became livid, reddened and turned yellow in turn, and drops of sweat stood on his forehead as he saw the door of Gobseck's house. Just as we got out of his cabriolet, a hackney-coach entered the rue des Grès. The falcon eye of the young man enabled him, no doubt, to distinguish a woman in the depths of that vehicle. An expression of almost savage joy brightened his face; he called to a little urchin who was passing, and gave him his horse to hold. We went up at once to the money-lender.

" 'Monsieur Gobseck,' I said, 'I bring you one of my intimate friends' ('whom I distrust as I do the devil,' I added in his ear). 'To oblige me, I am sure you will restore him to your good graces (at the usual cost), and you will get him out of his present trouble (if you choose).'

"Monsieur de Trailles bowed to the usurer, sat down, and assumed, as if to listen to him, a courtier-like attitude, the graceful lowliness of which would have fascinated you. But my Gobseck sat still on his chair, at the corner of his fire, motionless, impassible. He looked like the statue of Voltaire[35] seen at night under the peristyle of the Théâtre-Français. He slightly lifted, by way of bow, the shabby cap with which he covered his head, and the small amount of yellow skull he thus exhibited completed his resemblance to that marble statue.

" 'I have no money except for my clients,' he said.

" 'That means that you are very angry with me for going elsewhere to ruin myself?' said the count, laughing.

" 'Ruin yourself!' said Gobseck, in a sarcastic tone.

35. famous statue of the old Voltaire by the sculptor Houdon. It is now in the foyer of the Comédie Française, in Paris.

" 'Do you mean that a man can't be ruined if he owns nothing? I defy you to find in all Paris a finer capital than *this*,' cried the dandy, rising, and twirling round upon his heels.

"This buffoonery, which was partly serious, had no power to move Gobseck.

" 'Am I not the intimate friend of Ronquerolles, de Marsay, Franchessini, the two Vandenesses, Ajuda-Pinto[36]—in short, all the young bloods in Paris? At cards I'm the ally of a prince and an ambassador whom you know. I have my revenues in London, at Carlsbad, Baden, Bath, Spa.[37] Don't you think *that* the most brilliant of industries?'

" 'Surely.'

" 'You make a sponge of me, *mordieu!* you encourage me to swell out in the great world only to squeeze me at a crisis. But all you money-lenders are sponges too, and death will squeeze you.'

" 'Possibly.'

" 'Without spendthrifts what would become of you? We are one, like body and soul.'

"True.'

" 'Come, shake hands, old papa Gobseck, and show your magnanimity.'

" 'You have come to me,' said Gobseck, coldly, 'because Girard, Palma, Werbrust, and Gigonnet have their bellies full of your notes, which they are offering everywhere at fifty per cent loss. Now as they probably only gave you one-half of their face value, those notes are not worth twenty-five francs on the hundred. No, I thank you! Could I, with any decency,' continued Gobseck, 'lend a single penny to a man who owes thirty thousand francs, and doesn't possess a farthing? You lost ten thousand francs night before last at Baron de Nucingen's[38] ball.'

" 'Monsieur,' replied the count, with rare impudence, looking at the old man haughtily, 'my doings are none of your business. He whose notes are not due owes nothing.'

" 'True.'

" 'My notes will be paid.'

" 'Possibly.'

" 'The question between us reduces itself, at this moment, to whether I present you sufficient security for the sum I wish to borrow.'

" 'Right.'

36. fictitious characters appearing in other novels by Balzac. Ajuda-Pinto was the wealthy Portuguese loved by Mme. de Beauséant, the great lady mentioned at the very end of this story.

37. watering places with gambling casinos. Carlsbad is in Bohemia; Spa,

near Brussels.

38. The Baron is a wealthy Alsatian banker and speculator who has married Delphine, the older of the two Goriot sisters. He appears in many of Balzac's novels.

"The noise of a carriage stopping before the door echoed through the room.

" 'I will now fetch something that will probably satisfy you,' said Monsieur de Trailles, rising, and turning to leave the room.

" 'O my son!' cried Gobseck, rising too, and stretching out his arms to me as soon as the young man had disappeared, 'if he only brings me good security, you have saved my life! I should have died! Werbrust and Gigonnet meant to play me a trick. Thanks to you, I shall have a good laugh to-night at their expense.'

"The old man's joy had something frightful about it. It was the sole moment of expansion or feeling I ever saw in him. Rapid and fleeting as it was, that joy will never pass from my memory.

" 'Do me the pleasure to stay here,' he said. 'Though I'm well-armed and sure of my shot, like a man who has hunted tigers and boarded ships to conquer or die, I distrust that elegant scoundrel.'

"He sat down again, this time in an armchair before his desk. His face was once more calm and livid.

" 'Ho! ho!' he said, suddenly turning round to me; 'you are no doubt going to see that handsome creature I once told you about. I hear an aristocratic step in the passage.'

"Sure enough, the young man now returned, leading a lady, in whom I recognized the countess whom Gobseck had once described to me—a daughter of Père Goriot. The countess did not at first see me, for I was standing back in the recess of a window, my face to the glass. As she entered the damp and gloomy room she cast a look of fear and distrust at Maxime. She was so beautiful that in spite of her faults I pitied her. Some terrible anguish shook her heart; her proud and noble features wore a convulsive expression, scarcely restrained. That young man must by this time have become to her an evil genius. I admired Gobseck, who, four years earlier, had foreseen the fate of these two beings at the time of their first note. 'Probably,' I said to myself, 'that monster with the face of an angel rules her in all possible ways, through vanity, jealousy, pleasure, the triumphs of society.' "

"But," cried Madame de Grandlieu, interrupting Derville, "the very virtues of this woman have been weapons for him; he has made her weep tears of devotion; he has roused in her soul the generosity of our sex; he has abused her tenderness, and sold to her, at a cruel price, her criminal joys."

"I confess to you," said Derville, who did not understand the signs that Madame de Grandlieu was making to him, "that I did not think of the fate of that unhappy creature, so brilliant to the eyes of the world, and so dreadful to those who could read her heart. No, I shuddered with horror as I looked at her slayer, that youth with a brow so pure, a mouth so fresh, a smile so gracious, teeth so white; a man in the semblance of an angel! They stood at this moment before a judge who examined them as an old Dominican of the sixteenth century might have watched the torturing of two Moors in the cellars of the Inquisition.

" 'Monsieur, is there any way of obtaining the value of these diamonds, reserving to myself the right to redeem them?' she said, in a trembling voice, holding out to him a casket.

" 'Yes, madame,' I replied, interposing, and coming forward.

"She looked at me, recognized me, gave a shudder, and then cast upon me that glance which says, in every country, 'Silence!'

" 'The matter you propose,' I continued, 'constitutes an act which we lawyers call sale with right of redemption—a transaction which consists in yielding and conveying property, either real or personal, for a given time, at the expiration of which the property can be taken back at a previously fixed price.'

"She breathed more easily. Comte Maxime frowned; he thought the usurer would give a smaller sum for the diamonds if subject to this condition. Gobseck, immovable, picked up his magnifier, and silently opened the casket. Were I to live a hundred years I could never forget the picture his face presented to our eyes. His pale cheeks colored; his eyes, in which the glitter of the stones seemed to be reflected, sparkled with unnatural fire. He rose, went to the light, held the diamonds close to his toothless mouth as if he wanted to devour them. He mumbled a few vague words, lifting, one after the other, the bracelets, necklaces, diadems, sprays—all of which he held to the light to judge of their water, their whiteness and cutting. He took them from the casket, and he laid them back, he played with them to make their fires sparkle, seeming more of a child than an old man—or, rather, a child and an old man combined.

" 'Fine! they must have been worth three hundred thousand francs before the Revolution. What water! True diamonds of Asia! from Golconda[39] or Visapur![40] Do you know their value? No, no, Gobseck is the only man in Paris who knows how to appraise them. Under the Empire it would still have cost two hundred thousand francs to collect that set, but now—' He made a gesture of disgust, and added, 'Now diamonds are losing value every day. Brazil is flooding us with stones—less white than those of India. Women no longer wear them, except at court. Does madame go to court?'

"While delivering this verdict he was still examining, with indescribable delight, each stone in the casket.

" 'No blemish!' he kept saying, 'one blemish! Here's a flaw— Beautiful stone!'

"His pallid face was so illumined by the light of these stones,

39. a city in southern India, now in ruins, where the Sultan of Deccan had supposedly accumulated immense treasures of diamonds.
40. also called Bijapur; another city in southern India.

that I compared it in my own mind to those old greenish mirrors we find in provincial inns, which receive the reflection of a light without returning it, and give an appearance of apoplexy to the traveller who is bold enough to look into them.

" 'Well?' said the count, striking Gobseck on the shoulder.

"The old child quivered; he laid his toys on the desk, sat down, and became once more a usurer, hard, cold, polished as a marble column.

" 'How much do you want?'

" 'One hundred thousand francs for three years,' replied the count. 'Can we have them?'

" 'Possibly,' answered Gobseck, taking from their mahogany box a pair of scales of inestimable worth for accuracy—his jewel-case, as it were! He weighed the stones, valuing, at a glance, Heaven knows how! the weight of the settings. During this time the expression on the money-lender's face wavered between joy and sternness. The countess was lost in a stupor, which I noted carefully; she seemed to be measuring the depth of the precipice down which she was falling. There was still some lingering remorse in the soul of that woman; it needed, perhaps, but a single effort, a hand stretched charitably out, to save her. I would try it.

" 'Are these diamonds yours, madame?' I asked, in a clear voice.

" 'Yes, monsieur,' she replied, giving me a haughty glance.

" 'Make out that redemption-deed, meddler,' said Gobseck to me, pointing to his seat at the desk.

" 'Madame is no doubt married?' I continued.

"She bowed her head quickly.

" 'I shall not make out the deed!' I exclaimed.

" 'Why not?' said Gobseck.

" 'Why not?' I echoed, drawing the old man to the window, and speaking in a low voice. 'Because, this woman being *feme covert*,[41] the deed of redemption would be null, and you could not claim ignorance of a fact proved by the deed itself. You would be obliged to produce the diamonds deposited in your hands, the weight, value, or cutting of which are described in the deed—'

"Gobseck interrupted me by a nod, and then turned to the two sinners.

" 'He is right,' he said. 'The terms are changed— Eighty thousand francs down, and you leave the diamonds with me,' adding, in a muffled tone, 'possession is nine-tenths of the law—'

" 'But—' interposed the young man.

" 'Take it, or leave it,' said Gobseck, giving the casket to the countess. 'I have too many risks to run.'

---

41. legal Old French, denoting a woman under her husband's control. She could not sell or borrow without her husband's consent.

" 'Madame,' I whispered in her ear, 'you would do better to throw yourself on your husband's mercy.'

"The usurer no doubt guessed my words from the movement of my lips, for he cast a severe look at me. The young man's face became livid. The hesitation of the countess was obvious. The count went closely up to her; and, though he spoke very low, I heard him say:

" 'Farewell, my Anastasie, be happy! As for me, my troubles will be over to-morrow.'

" 'Monsieur,' cried the young woman, addressing Gobseck, 'I accept your offer.'

" 'Well, well!' replied the old man, 'it takes a good deal to bring you to terms, fair lady.'

"He drew a check for fifty thousand francs on the Bank of France, and gave it to the countess.

" 'And now,' he said, with a smile like that of Voltaire, 'I shall complete the sum with notes for thirty thousand francs, the soundness of which cannot be questioned. They are as good as gold itself. Monsieur has just said to me: *My notes will be paid.*'

"So saying, he took out and handed to the countess the notes of the young man, protested the night before to several of his brother usurers, who had, no doubt, sold them to Gobseck at a low price, as comparatively worthless. The young man uttered a sort of roar, in the midst of which could be heard the words: 'Old scoundrel!'

"Papa Gobseck did not move one muscle of his face, but he took from a box a pair of pistols, and said, coldly:

" 'As the insulted party, I fire first.'

" 'Maxime, you owe monsieur an apology,' cried the trembling countess.

" 'I did not intend to offend you,' stammered the young man.

" 'I know that,' replied Gobseck, tranquilly. 'You merely intended not to pay your notes.'

"The countess rose, bowed, and left the room, apparently horrified. Monsieur de Trailles was forced to follow her; but before he did so he turned and said:

" 'If either of you betray one word of this, I shall have your blood, or you mine.'

" 'Amen!' replied Gobseck, putting away his pistols. 'To risk your blood, you must have some, my lad, and there's nothing but mud in your veins.'

"When the outer door was closed and the two carriages had driven away, Gobseck rose and began to dance about the room, crying out:

" 'I have the diamonds! I have the diamonds! the fine diamonds!

what diamonds! not dear! Ha! ha! ha! Werbrust and Gigonnet, you thought you'd catch old papa Gobseck! *Ego sum papa!*[42] I'm the master of all of you! Paid in full! paid in full! What fools they'll look to-night when I tell 'em the affair over the dominos!'

"This gloomy joy, this ferocity of a savage, excited by the possession of a few white pebbles, made me shudder. I was speechless and stupefied.

" 'Ha! ha! there you are, my boy! We'll dine together. We'll amuse ourselves at your house, for I haven't any home; and those eating-house fellows, with their gravies and sauces and wines, are fit to poison the devil!'

"The expression of my face seemed to bring him back to his usual cold impassibility.

" 'You can't conceive it, can you?' he said, sitting down by the hearth, and putting a tin sauce-pan full of milk on the hob. 'Will you breakfast with me? There may be enough for two.'

" 'Thank you, no,' I replied. 'I never breakfast till twelve o'clock.'

"At that instant hasty steps were heard in the corridor. Some one stopped before Gobseck's door, and rapped upon it several times, with a sort of fury. The usurer looked through the peep-hole before he opened the door, and admitted a man about thirty-five years of age, who had, no doubt, seemed to him inoffensive, in spite of his evident anger. The newcomer who was simply dressed, looked like the late Duc de Richelieu.[43] It was *the count*, whom you have often met, and who (if you will permit the remark) has the haughty bearing of the statesmen of your faubourg.

" 'Monsieur,' he said to Gobseck, 'my wife has just left this house.'

" 'Possibly.'

" 'Well, monsieur, don't you understand me?'

" 'I have not the honor to know your wife,' replied the usurer. 'Many persons have called here this morning: women, men, girls who looked like young men, and young men who looked like girls. It would be difficult for me to—'

" 'A truce to jesting, monsieur; I am talking of the woman who has just left this house.'

" 'How am I to know if she is your wife,' said the usurer, 'inasmuch as I have never before had the advantage of seeing you?'

" 'You are mistaken, Monsieur Gobseck,' said the count, in a tone of the deepest irony. 'We met one morning in my wife's bedroom. You came for the money of a note signed by her—a note for which she had not received the value.'

---

42. "I am the Pope," a saying ascribed to Pope Sixtus V at his election in 1585. He supposedly threw away his staff and cried triumphantly, *Ego sum Papa*. Gobseck puns on his own nick-name, Papa Gobseck.

43. Armand de La Porte de Richelieu (1696–1788), a French marshal, grandnephew of the famous cardinal.

" 'It is not my affair to know whether she received its value or not,' replied Gobseck, with a malicious glance at the count. 'I had discounted her note for one of my brethren in business. Besides, monsieur,' he added, not excited or hurried in speech, and slowly pouring some coffee into his pan of milk, 'you must permit me to remark, I see no proof that you have any right to make these remonstrances in my house. I came of age in the year sixty-one of the last century.'

" 'Monsieur, you have just bought family diamonds which do not belong to my wife.'

" 'Without considering myself obliged to let you into the secrets of my business, I must tell you, Monsieur le comte, that if your diamonds have been taken by Madame la comtesse, you should have notified all jewellers by circular letter not to buy them; otherwise, she may sell them piecemeal.'

" 'Monsieur,' cried the count, 'you know my wife.'

" 'Do I?'

" 'She is, in legal phrase, *feme covert*.'

" 'Possibly.'

" 'She has no legal right to dispose of those diamonds.'

" 'True.'

" 'Well, then, monsieur?'

" 'Well, monsieur, I know your wife; she is *feme covert*—that is, under your control; so be it, and she is under other controls as well; but—I—know nothing of—your diamonds. If Madame la comtesse signs notes of hand, she can, no doubt, do other business—buy diamonds, receive diamonds to sell again. That often happens.'

" 'Adieu, monsieur,' said the count, pale with anger. 'There are courts of justice.'

" 'True.'

" 'Monsieur here,' continued the count, pointing to me, 'must have witnessed the sale.'

" 'Possibly.'

"The count started to leave the room. Suddenly, aware of the seriousness of the affair, I interposed between the belligerent parties.

" 'Monsieur le comte,' I said, 'you are right, and Monsieur Gobseck is not wrong. You could not sue him without bringing your wife into court, and all the odium of this affair would fall on her. I am a barrister, but I owe it to myself, personally, even more than to my official character, to tell you that the diamonds of which you speak were bought by Monsieur Gobseck in my presence; I think, however, that you would do wrong to contest the validity of that sale, the articles of which are never easy to recognize. In equity, you would be right; legally, you would fail. Monsieur Gobseck is too honest a man to deny that this sale has been made to his profit, especially when my conscience and my duty oblige me to declare it. But suppose you bring a suit, Monsieur le comte, the issue would be very doubtful. I advise you, therefore, to compromise with Monsieur Gobseck, who might withdraw of his own good-will, but to whom you would, in any case, be obliged to return the purchase-money. Consent to a deed of redemption in six or eight months, a year even, a period of time which will enable you to pay the sum received by Madame la comtesse—unless, indeed, you would prefer to buy the diamonds back at once, giving security for the payment.'

"The usurer was sopping his bread in his coffee, and eating his breakfast with quiet indifference; but when I said the word compromise, he looked at me as if to say:

" 'The scamp! how he profits by my lessons!'

"I returned his look with a glance which he understood perfectly well. The whole affair was doubtful and base; it was necessary to compromise. Gobseck could not take refuge in denial, because I should tell the truth. The count thanked me with a friendly smile. After a discussion, in which Gobseck's cleverness and greed would have put to shame the diplomacy of a congress, I drew up a deed, by which the count admitted having received from the money-lender the sum of eighty-five thousand francs, including interest, on repayment of which sum Gobseck bound himself to return the diamonds.

" 'What hopeless extravagance!' cried the husband, as he signed the deed. 'How is it possible to bridge that yawning gulf?'

" 'Monsieur,' said Gobseck, gravely, 'have you many children?'

"That question made the count quiver as if, like an able surgeon, the usurer had laid his finger suddenly on the seat of a disease. The husband did not answer.

" 'Well!' resumed Gobseck, understanding that painful silence. 'I know your history by heart. That woman is a demon whom, perhaps, you still love; I am not surprised; she moves even me. But you may wish to save your fortune, and secure it to one, or, perhaps, two of your children. Well, cast yourself into the vortex of society, gamble, appear to lose your fortune, and come and see Gobseck frequently. The world will say that I am a Jew, a usurer, a pirate, and have ruined you. I don't care for that! If any one openly insults me I can shoot him; no one handles sword or pistol better than your humble servant; and everybody knows it. But find a friend, if you can, to whom you can make a fictitious sale of your property—don't you call that, in your legal tongue, making a trust?' he said, turning to me.

"The count seemed entirely absorbed by his own thoughts, and he left us, saying to Gobseck:

716 · *Honoré de Balzac*

" 'I shall bring you the money to-morrow; have the diamonds ready for me.'

" 'He looks to me as stupid as an honest man,' said Gobseck, when the count had gone.

" 'Say, rather, as stupid as a man who loves passionately.'

" 'The count is to pay you for drawing that deed,' said the old man, as I left him.

"Some days after these scenes, which had initiated me into the terrible mysteries in the lives of fashionable women, I was surprised to see the count enter my own office early one morning.

" 'Monsieur,' he said, 'I have come to consult you on very serious interests, assuring you that I feel the most entire confidence in your character—as I hope to prove to you. Your conduct towards Madame de Grandlieu is above praise.'

"Thus you see, Madame la vicomtesse," said Derville, interrupting his narrative, "that I have received from you a thousandfold the value of a very simple action. I bowed respectfully, and told him I had done no more than the duty of an honest man.

" 'Well, monsieur,' said the count, 'I have obtained much information about the singular personage to whom you owe your practice. From all I hear I judge that Gobseck belongs to the school of cynical philosophers. What do you think of his honesty?'

" 'Monsieur le comte,' I replied, 'Gobseck is my benefactor—at fifteen per cent,' I added, laughing. 'But that little avarice of his does not justify me in drawing a likeness of him for the benefit of strangers.'

" 'Speak out, monsieur; your frankness cannot injure either Gobseck or yourself. I don't expect to find an angel in a money-lender.'

" 'Papa Gobseck,' I then said, 'is profoundly convinced of one principle, which rules his conduct. According to him, money is merchandise which may, in all security of conscience, be sold cheap or dear, according to circumstances. A capitalist is, in his eyes, a man who enters, by the rate of interest which he claims for his money, as partner by anticipation in all enterprises and all lucrative speculations. Apart from these financial principles and his philosophical observations on human nature, which lead him to behave like a usurer, I am confidently persuaded that, outside of his own particular business, he is the most upright and the most scrupulous man in Paris. There are two men in that man: he is miserly and philosophical; great and petty. If I were to die, leaving children, I should make him their guardian. That, monsieur, is what experience has shown me of Gobseck. I know nothing of his past life. He may have been a pirate; he may have traversed the whole earth, trafficking in diamonds or men, women or state secrets; but I'll swear that no human soul was ever better tried or more powerfully tempered. The day on which I took him the sum which paid off a debt I had incurred to him at fifteen per cent interest, I asked him (not without some oratorical precautions) what motive had led him to make me pay such enormous interest, and why, wishing, as he did, to oblige me, his friend, he had not made the benefit complete. "My son," he replied, "I relieved you of all gratitude by giving you the right to think you owed me nothing; consequently, we are the best friends in the world." That speech, monsieur, will explain the man to you better than any possible words of mine.'

" 'My decision is irrevocably made,' said the count. 'Prepare the necessary deeds to transfer my whole property to Gobseck. I can rely on none but you, monsieur, to draw up the counter-deed, by which he declares that this sale is fictitious, and that he binds himself to place my fortune, administered as he knows how to administer it, in the hands of my eldest son when the lad attains his majority. Now, monsieur, I am compelled to make a statement to you. I dare not keep that deed in my own house. The attachment of my son to his mother makes me fear to tell him of that counter-deed. May I ask you to be its depositary? In case of his death, Gobseck is to make you legatee of my property. All is thus provided for.'

"The count was silent for a few moments, and seemed much agitated.

" 'Pardon me, monsieur,' he went on, 'I suffer terribly; my health causes me the greatest anxiety. Recent troubles have shaken my vital powers cruelly, and necessitate the great step I am now taking.'

" 'Monsieur,' I replied, 'allow me, in the first place, to thank you for the confidence you have in me. But I must justify it by pointing out to you that by this action you disinherit, utterly, your—other children. They bear your name. Were they only the children of a woman once loved, now fallen, they have a right to some means, at least, of existence. I declare to you that I cannot accept the duty with which you honor me, unless their future is secured.'

"These words made the count tremble violently. A few tears came to his eyes, and he pressed my hand.

" 'I did not wholly know you till this moment,' he said. 'You have just given me both pain and pleasure. We will fix the share of those children in the counter-deed.'

"I accompanied him to the door of my office, and it seemed to me that I saw his features relax with satisfaction at the sense that he was doing an act of justice. You see, now, Camille, how young women are led into fatal gulfs. Sometimes a mere dance, an air sung to a piano, a day spent in the country, lead to terrible disasters; vanity, pride, trust in a smile, folly, giddiness—all lead to it. Shame,

Remorse, and Misery are three Furies into whose hands all women fall, infallibly, the moment they pass the limits of—"

"My poor Camille is half-dead with sleep," said the viscountess, interrupting Derville. "Go to bed, my dear; your heart doesn't need such terrifying pictures to keep it pure and virtuous."

Camille de Grandlieu understood her mother, and left the room.

"You went a little too far, my dear Monsieur Derville," said the viscountess. "Lawyers are not mothers of families or preachers."

"But the newspapers tell—"

"My poor Derville!" said Madame de Grandlieu, interrupting him, "I don't know you! Do you suppose that my daughter reads the newspapers? Go on," she said, after a momentary pause.

"Three days later, the deeds were executed by the count, in favor of Gobseck—"

"You can call him the Comte de Restaud, now that my daughter is not here," said the viscountess.

"So be it," said the lawyer. "Well, a long time passed after that scene, and I had not received the counter-deed, which was to have been returned to me for safe-keeping. In Paris, barristers are so hurried along by the current of affairs that they cannot give to their clients' interests any greater attention than clients demand. Nevertheless, one day when Gobseck was dining with me, I remembered to ask him if he knew why I had not heard anything more from Monsieur de Restaud.

" 'There's a very good reason why,' he answered. 'That gentleman is dying. He is one of those tender souls who don't know how to kill grief, and so let grief kill them. Life is a toil, a trade, and people should take the trouble to learn it. When a man knows life, having experienced its pains, his fibre knits, and acquires a certain suppleness which enables him to command his feelings; he makes his nerves into steel springs which bend without breaking. If his stomach is good, a man can live as long as the cedars of Lebanon, which are famous trees.'

" 'Will the count die?'

" 'Possibly. You'll have a juicy affair in that legacy.'

"I looked at my man, and said, in order to sound him, 'Explain to me why the count and I are the only two beings in whom you have taken an interest.'

" 'Because you and he are the only ones who have trusted in me without reservations,' he replied.

"Although this answer induced me to suppose that Gobseck would not take advantage of his position in case the counter-deed was lost, I resolved to go and see the count. After parting from the old man, I went to the rue du Helder, and was shown into a salon where the countess was playing with her children. When she heard my name announced, she rose hastily and came to meet me; then she sat down without a word, and pointed to an armchair near the fire. She put upon her face that impenetrable mask beneath which women of the world know so well how to hide their passions. Griefs had already faded that face; the exquisite lines, which were always its chief merit, alone remained to tell of her beauty.

" 'It is essential, madame,' I said, 'that I should see Monsieur le comte.'

" 'Then you would be more favored than I am,' she said, interrupting me. 'Monsieur de Restaud will see no one; he will scarcely allow the doctor to visit him, and he rejects all attentions, even mine. Such men are so fanciful! they are like children; they don't know what they want.'

" 'Perhaps, like children, they know exactly what they want.'

"The countess colored. I was almost sorry for having made that speech, so worthy of Gobseck.

" 'But,' I continued, to change the conversation, 'Monsieur de Restaud cannot be always alone, I suppose.'

" 'His eldest son is with him,' she said.

"I looked at her; but this time she did not color; she seemed to have strengthened her resolution not to give way.

" 'Let me say, madame, that my request is not indiscreet,' I resumed. 'It is founded on important interests—' I bit my lips as I said the words, feeling, too late, that I had made a false move. The countess instantly took advantage of my heedlessness.

" 'My interests are not apart from those of my husband,' she said. 'Nothing hinders you from addressing yourself to me.'

" 'The affair which brings me here concerns Monsieur le comte only,' I replied firmly.

" 'I will have him informed of your wish to see him.'

"The polite tone and air she assumed, as she said those words, did not deceive me. I saw plainly she would never let me reach her husband. I talked for a time on indifferent matters, in order to observe her; but, like all women who have formed a plan, she could dissimulate with that rare perfection which, in persons of your sex, Madame la vicomtesse, is, in the highest degree, treacherous. Dare I say it? I began to apprehend the worst of her—even crime. This impression came from a glimpse into the future, revealed by her gestures, her glance, her manner, and even by the intonations of her voice. I left her—

"And now, madame," continued Derville, after a slight pause, "I must give you a narrative of the scenes which ended this affair, adding certain circumstances which time has revealed to me, and certain details which Gobseck's perspicacity, or my own, have enabled me to divine—

"As soon as the Comte de Restaud appeared to plunge into the pleasures of a gay life, and seemed to squander his money, scenes took place between husband and wife the secret of which was never divulged, although the count found reason to judge more unfavorably than ever of his wife's character. He fell ill from the effects of this shock, and took to his bed; it was then that his aversion to the countess and her two younger children showed itself. He forbade their entrance into his room, and when they attempted to elude this order, their disobedience brought on such dangerous excitement in Monsieur de Restaud that the doctor conjured the countess not to infringe her husband's orders. Madame de Restaud, who by this time had seen the landed estates, the family property, and even the house in which she lived made over, successively, to Gobseck, no doubt understood, in a measure, her husband's real intentions. Monsieur de Trailles, then rather hotly pursued by creditors, was travelling in England. He alone could have made her fully understand the secret precautions which Gobseck had suggested to the count against her. It is said that she resisted affixing her signature, as our laws require, to the sale of lands; nevertheless, the count obtained it in every instance. She appears to have thought that the count was capitalizing his fortune, and placing the total in the hands of some notary, or, possibly, in the Bank. According to her ideas, Monsieur de Restaud must possess a deed of some kind to enable her eldest son to recover a part at least of the landed estate, and this deed was probably now in the count's own custody. She therefore determined to establish a close watch upon her husband's room. Outside of that room she reigned despotically over the household, which she now subjected to the closest watching. She herself remained all day seated in the salon adjoining her husband's bedroom, where she could hear his every word and even his movements. At night, she had a bed made up in the same room; but for most of the time she slept little. The doctor was entirely in her interests. Such devotion seemed admirable. She knew, with the shrewdness natural to treacherous minds, how to explain the repugnance Monsieur de Restaud manifested for her; and she played grief so perfectly that her conduct attained to a sort of celebrity. A few prudes were heard to admit that she redeemed her faults by her present behavior. She herself had constantly before her eyes the property that awaited her at the count's death should she lose her presence of mind even for a moment. Consequently, repulsed as she was from the bed of pain on which her husband lay, she drew a magic ring around it. Far from him, but near to him, deprived of her functions, but all powerful, a devoted wife apparently, she sat there, watching for death and fortune, as that insect of the fields,[44] in the depths of the spiral mound he has laboriously thrown up, hearkens to every grain of dust that falls while awaiting his inevitable prey. The severest censors could not deny that the countess was carrying the sentiment of motherhood to an extreme. The death of her father had been, people said, a lesson to her. Adoring her children, she had given them the best and most brilliant of educations; they were too young to understand the immoralities of her life; she had been able to attain her end, and make herself adored by them. I admit that I cannot entirely avoid a sentiment of admiration for this woman, and a feeling of compassion about which Gobseck never ceased to joke. At this period, the countess, who had recognized, at last, the baseness of Maxime, was expiating, in tears of blood, the faults of her past life. I am sure of this. However odious were the measures which she took to obtain her husband's fortune, they were dictated by maternal affection, and the desire to repair the wrong she had done to her younger children. Each time that Ernest left his father's room, she subjected him to close inquiry on all the count had said and done. The boy lent himself willingly to his mother's wishes, which he attributed to tender feelings, and he often forestalled her questions. My visit was a flash of light to the countess, who believed she saw in me the agent of the count's vengeance; and she instantly determined not to let me see the dying man. I myself, under a strong presentiment of coming evil, was keenly desirous to obtain an interview with Monsieur de Restaud, for I was not without anxiety about the fate of the counter-deed; if it fell into the hands of the countess, she might raise money on it, and the result would be interminable lawsuits between herself and Gobseck. I knew the latter well enough to be certain he would never restore the property to the countess, and there were many elements of litigation in the construction of these deeds, the carrying out of which could only be done by me. Anxious to prevent misfortunes before it was too late, I determined to see the countess a second time.

"I have remarked, madame," said Derville to Madame de Grandlieu, in a confidential tone, "that certain moral phenomena exist to which we do not pay sufficient attention in social life. Being by nature an observer, I have carried into the various affairs of self-interest which come into my practice, and in which passions play so vehement a part, a spirit of involuntary analysis. Now, I have always noticed, with ever-recurring surprise, that the secret ideas and intentions of two adversaries are reciprocally divined. We sometimes find, in two enemies, the same lucidity of reasoning, the same power of

44. the larva of the ant lion (*Myrmeleon*), an insect similar to the dragon-fly.

intellectual sight as there is between two lovers who can read each other's souls. So, when the countess and I were once more in presence of each other, I suddenly understood the cause of her antipathy to me, although she disguised her feelings under the most gracious politeness and amenity. I was the confidant of her husband's affairs, and it was impossible that any woman could avoid hating a man before whom she was forced to blush. On her part, she guessed that, although I was the man to whom her husband gave his confidence, he had not yet given the charge of his property into my hands. Our conversation (which I will spare you) remains in my memory as one of the most perilous struggles in which I have ever been engaged. The countess, gifted by nature with the qualities necessary for the exercise of irresistible seduction, became, in turn, supple, haughty, caressing, confidential; she even went so far as to attempt to rouse my curiosity, and even to excite a sentiment of love in order to master me; but she failed. When I took leave of her I detected, in her eyes, an expression of hate and fury which made me tremble. We parted *enemies*. She would fain have annihilated me, while I felt pity for her—a feeling which, to certain natures, is the deepest of all insults. That feeling showed itself plainly in the last remarks I made to her. I left, as I believe, an awful terror in her soul, by assuring her that in whatever way she acted she would inevitably be ruined.

" 'If I could only see Monsieur le comte,' I said to her, 'the future of your children—'

" 'I should be at your mercy,' she said, interrupting me with a gesture of disgust.

"The questions between us being declared in so frank and positive a manner, I determined to go forward in my own way, and save that family from the ruin that awaited it. Resolving to commit even legal irregularities, if they were necessary to attain my ends, I made the following preparations: First, I sued the Comte de Restaud for a sum fictitiously due to Gobseck, and obtained a judgment against him. The countess concealed this proceeding; but it gave me the legal right to affix seals to the count's room on his death, which was, of course, my object. Next, I bribed one of the servants of the house, and made him promise to notify me the moment that his master appeared to be dying, were it even in the middle of the night; I did this, in order that I might reach the house suddenly, frighten the countess by threatening to affix the seals instantly, and so get possession of the counter-deed. I heard, afterwards, that this woman was studying the Code[45] while she listened to the moans of her dying husband. What frightful pictures might be made of the souls of those who surround some death-beds, if we could only paint ideas!

45. the Code Napoleon, enacted in 1804; the first great codification of French law.

And money is always the mover of the intrigues there elaborated, the plans there formed, the plots there laid! Let us now turn from these details, irksome, indeed, though they may have enabled you to see the wretchedness of this woman, that of her husband, and the secrets of other homes under like circumstances. For the last two months the Comte de Restaud, resigned to die, lay alone on his bed, in his own chamber. A mortal disease was slowly sapping both mind and body. A victim to those sick fancies the caprices of which appear inexplicable, he objected to the cleaning of his room, refused all personal cares, and even insisted that no one should make his bed. A sort of apathy took possession of him; the furniture was in disorder, dust and cobwebs lay thick on the delicate ornaments. Formerly choice and luxurious in his tastes, he now seemed to take pleasure in the melancholy spectacle of his room, where the chimney-piece and chairs and tables were encumbered with articles required by illness—phials, empty or full, and nearly all dirty, soiled linen, broken plates; a warming-pan was before the fire, and a tub, still full of some mineral water. The sentiment of *destruction* was expressed in every detail of this miserable chaos. Death loomed up in things before it invaded the person. The count had a horror of daylight; the outer blinds of the windows were closed, and this enforced darkness added to the gloom of the melancholy place. The sick man was shrunken, but his eyes, in which life appeared to have taken refuge, were still brilliant. The livid whiteness of his face had something horrible about it, increased by the extraordinary length of his hair, which he refused to have cut, so that it now hung in long, straight meshes beside his face. He bore some resemblance to the fanatical hermits of a desert. Grief had extinguished all other human feelings in this man, who was barely fifty years of age, and whom Paris had once known so brilliant and so happy. One morning, about the beginning of December, in the year 1824, he looked at his son Ernest, who was sitting at the foot of his bed, watching him sadly:

" 'Are you in pain, papa?' asked the lad.

" 'No,' he said, with a frightful smile, 'it is all *here* and *there*,'— he pointed first to his head, and then pressed his fleshless fingers on his heart, with a gesture that made Ernest weep.

" 'Why does not Monsieur Derville come to me?' he said to his valet, whom he thought attached to him, but who was really in collusion with the countess. 'Maurice,' cried the dying man, suddenly sitting up, and seeming to recover his presence of mind, 'I have sent you seven or eight times to my lawyer, within the last fortnight; why doesn't he come? Do you think some one is tricking me? Go and get him instantly, and bring him back with you. If you don't execute my orders, I'll get up myself and go—'

" 'Madame,' said the valet, going into the salon, 'you have heard Monsieur le comte; what am I to do?'

" 'Pretend to go to that lawyer, and then come back and say to Monsieur le comte that his man of business has gone a hundred miles into the country, to try an important case. You can add that he is expected back the last of the week. Sick men always deceive themselves about their state,' she thought. 'He will wait for the lawyer's return.'

"The doctor had that morning told her that the count could scarcely survive the day. When, two hours later, the valet brought back this discouraging message, the count was greatly agitated.

" 'My God! my God!' he repeated many times. 'I have no hope but in you!'

"He looked at his son for a long while, and said to him, at last, in a feeble voice:

" 'Ernest, my child, you are very young, but you have a good heart, and you will surely comprehend the sacredness of a promise made to a dying man—to a father. Do you feel capable of keeping a secret? of burying it in your own breast, so that even your mother shall not suspect it? My son, there is no one but you in this house whom I can trust. You will not betray my confidence?'

" 'No, father.'

" 'Then, Ernest, I shall give you, presently, a sealed package which belongs to Monsieur Derville; you must keep it in such a way that no one can know you have it; you must then manage to leave the house, and throw the package into the post-office box at the end of the street.'

" 'Yes, father.'

" 'Can I rely upon you?'

" 'Yes, father.'

" 'Then kiss me. You make my death less bitter, dear child. In six or seven years you will understand the importance of this secret— you will then be rewarded for your faithfulness and dexterity, and you will also know, my son, how much I have loved you. Leave me now, for a moment, and watch that no one enters this room.'

"Ernest went out, and found his mother standing in the salon.

" 'Ernest,' she said, 'come here.'

"She sat down, and held her son between her knees, pressing him to her heart, and kissing him.

" 'Ernest,' she said, 'your father has been talking to you.'

" 'Yes, mamma.'

" 'What did he say to you?'

" 'I cannot repeat it, mamma.'

" 'Oh! my dear child,' cried the countess, kissing him with enthusiasm, 'how much pleasure your discretion gives me. Tell the truth, and always be faithful to your word: those are two principles you must never forget.'

" 'Oh! how noble you are, mamma; you were never false, you!— of that I am sure.'

" 'Sometimes, Ernest, I have been false. Yes, I have broken my word under circumstances before which even laws must yield. Listen, my Ernest, you are now old enough and sensible enough to see that your father repulses me, and rejects my care; this is not natural, for you know, my son, how I love him.'

" 'Yes, mamma.'

" 'My poor child,' continued the countess, weeping, 'this misfortune is the result of treacherous insinuations. Wicked people have sought to separate me from your father, in order to satisfy their own cupidity. They want to deprive us of our propety and keep it themselves. If your father were well the separation now between us would cease; he would listen to me; you know how good and loving he is; he would recognize his error. But, as it is, his mind is weakened, the prejudice he has taken against me has become a fixed idea, a species of mania—the effect of his disease. The preference your father shows for you is another proof of the derangement of his faculties. You never noticed before his illness that he cared less for Pauline and Georges than for you. It is a mere caprice on his part. The tenderness he now feels for you may suggest to him to give you orders to execute. If you do not wish to ruin your family, my dear boy, if you would not see your mother begging her bread like a pauper, you must tell her everything—'

" 'Ah! ah!' cried the count, who, having opened the door, appeared to them suddenly, half naked, already as dry and fleshless as a skeleton. That hollow cry produced a terrible effect upon the countess, who remained motionless, rigid, and half stupefied. Her husband was so gaunt and pale, he looked as if issuing from a grave.

" 'You have steeped my life in misery, and now you seek to embitter my death, to pervert the mind of my son, and make him a vicious man!' cried the count, in a hoarse voice.

"The countess flung herself at the feet of the dying man, whom these last emotions of his waning life made almost hideous, and burst into a torrent of tears.

" 'Mercy! mercy!' she cried.

" 'Have you had pity for me?' he asked. 'I allowed you to squander your own fortune; would you now squander mine, and ruin my son?'

" 'Ah! yes, no pity for me! yes, be inflexible! but the children! Condemn your widow to a convent, and I will obey you; I will expiate my faults by doing all you order; but let the children prosper! the children! the children!'

" 'I have but one child,' replied the count, stretching his fleshless arm, with a despairing gesture, to his son.

" 'Pardon! I repent! I repent!' cried the countess, clasping the cold, damp feet of her husband. Sobs hindered her from speaking, only vague, incoherent words could force their way from her burning throat.

" 'After what you have just said to Ernest do you dare to talk of repentance?' said the dying man, freeing his feet, and throwing over the countess in doing so. 'You shock me,' he added, with an indifference in which there was something awful. 'You were a bad daughter, you have been a bad wife, you will be a bad mother.'

"The unhappy woman fainted as she lay there. The dying man returned to his bed, lay down, and lost consciousness soon after. The priests came to administer the sacraments. He died at midnight, the scene of the morning having exhausted his remaining strength. I reached the house, together with papa Gobseck, half an hour later. Thanks to the excitement that prevailed, we entered the little salon, next to the death-chamber, unnoticed. There we found the three children in tears, between two priests, who were to pass the night with the body. Ernest came to me, and said that his mother wished to be alone, in the count's chamber.

" 'Do not enter,' he said, with an exquisite expression of tone and gesture. 'She is praying.'

"Gobseck laughed, that silent laugh peculiar to him. I was far too moved by the feeling that shone on the boy's young face to share the old man's irony. When Ernest saw us going to the door, he ran to it, and called out:

" 'Mamma! here are some black men looking for you.'

"Gobseck lifted the child as if he were a feather, and opened the door. What a sight now met our eyes! Frightful disorder reigned in the room. Dishevelled by despair, her eyes flashing, the countess stood erect, speechless, in the midst of clothes, papers, articles of all kinds. Horrible confusion in the presence of death! Hardly had the count expired, before his wife had forced the drawers and the desk. Round her, on the carpet, lay fragments of all kinds, torn papers, portfolios broken open—all bearing the marks of her daring hands. If, at first, her search had been in vain, something in her attitude and the sort of agitation that possessed her made me think she had ended by discovering the mysterious papers. I turned my eyes to the bed, and, with the instinct that practice in our profession gives me, I divined what had happened. The count's body was rolled to the wall, and lay half across the bed, the nose to the mattress, disdainfully tossed aside, like the envelopes lying on the floor. His inflexible, stiffening limbs gave him an appearance grotesquely horrible. The dying man had no doubt hidden the counter-deed under his pillow, in order to preserve it from danger, while he lived. The countess, baffled in her search, must have divined her husband's thought at last; in fact, it seemed revealed by the convulsive form of his hooked fingers. The pillow was flung upon the ground; the imprint of the wife's foot was still upon it; beside it, and just before her, where she stood, I saw an envelope with many seals, bearing the count's arms. This I picked hastily up, and read a direction, showing that the contents of that envelope had been intended for me. I knew what they were! I looked fixedly at the countess, with the stern intelligence of a judge who examines a guilty person. A fire on the hearth was licking up the remains of the papers. When she saw us enter, the countess had doubtless flung the deed into it, believing (perhaps from its first formal words) that she was destroying a will that deprived her younger children of their property. A tortured conscience, and the involuntary fear inspired by the commission of a crime, had taken from her all power of reflection. Finding herself caught almost in the act, she may have fancied she already felt the branding iron of the galleys. The woman stood there, panting, as she awaited our first words, and looking at us with haggard eyes.

" 'Ah! madame,' I said, taking from the hearth a fragment which the fire had not wholly consumed, 'you have ruined your younger children! These papers secured their property to them.'

"Her mouth stirred, as if she were about to have a paralytic fit.

" 'He! he!' cried Gobseck, whose exclamation had the effect produced by the pushing of a brass candlestick on a bit of marble. After a slight pause, he said to me, calmly:

" 'Do you want to make Madame la comtesse believe that I am not the sole and legitimate possessor of the property sold to me by Monsieur le comte? This house belongs to me henceforth.'

"The blow of a club applied suddenly to my head could not have caused me greater pain or more surprise. The countess observed the puzzled glance which I cast on the old man.

" 'Monsieur! monsieur!' she said to him; but she could find no other words than those.

" 'Have you a deed of trust?' I said to him.

" 'Possibly.'

" 'Do you intend to take advantage of the crime which madame has committed?'

" 'Precisely.'

"I left the house, leaving the countess sitting by her husband's bedside, weeping hot tears. Gobseck followed me. When we reached the street I turned away from him; but he came to me, and gave me one of those piercing looks with which he sounded hearts, and said, with his fluty voice, in its sharpest tone:

" 'Do you pretend to judge me?'

"After that I saw but little of him. He let the count's house in Paris, and spent the summers on the Restaud estates in the country, where he played the lord, constructed farms, repaired mills, built roads, and planted trees. I met him one day in the Tuileries[46] gardens.

" 'The countess is living an heroic life,' I said. 'She devotes herself wholly to the education of her children, whom she is bringing up admirably. The eldest is a fine fellow.'

" 'Possibly.'

" 'But,' I said, 'don't you think you ought to help Ernest?'

" 'Help Ernest!' he cried. 'No! Misfortune is our greatest teacher. Misfortune will teach him the value of money, of men, and of women, too. Let him navigate the Parisian sea! When he has learned to be a good pilot it will be soon enough to give him a ship.'

"I left him without further explanation of the meaning of those words. Though Monsieur de Restaud, to whom his mother has no doubt imparted her own repugnance to me, is far, indeed, from taking me for his counsel, I went, two weeks ago, to Gobseck, and told him of Ernest's love for Mademoiselle Camille, and urged him to make ready to accomplish his trust, inasmuch as the young count has almost reached his majority. I found the old man had been confined for a long time to his bed, suffering from a disease which was about to carry him off. He declined to answer until he was able to get up and attend to business—unwilling, no doubt, to give up a penny while the breath of life was in him; his delay could have no other motive. Finding him very much worse than he thought himself, I stayed with him for some time, and was thus able to observe the progress of a passion which age had converted into a species of mania. In order to have no one in the house he occupied, he had become the sole tenant of it, leaving all the other apartments unoccupied. Nothing was changed in the room in which he lived. The furniture, which I had known so well for sixteen years, seemed to have been kept under glass, so exactly the same was it. His old and faithful portress, married to an old soldier who kept the lodge while she went up to do her master's work, was still his housekeeper, and was now fulfilling the functions of a nurse. Notwithstanding his weak condition, Gobseck still received his clients and his revenues; and he had so carefully simplified his business that a few messages sent by the old soldier were sufficient to regulate his external affairs. At the time of the treaty by which France recognized the republic of Haiti,[47] the knowledge possessed by Gobseck of the

46. a royal palace near the Louvre; burnt during the rule of the Commune in 1871.

47. during the eighteenth century, a French colony. In 1804 it revolted and a Negro republic was established. In 1825, France recognized Haitian independence in return for an indemnity of

former fortunes of San Domingo and the colonists, the assigns of whom were claiming indemnity, caused him to be appointed member of the commission instituted to determine these rights, and adjust the payments due from the Haitian government. Gobseck's genius led him to establish an agency for discounting the claims of the colonists and their heirs and assigns under the names of Werbrust and Gigonnet, with whom he shared all profits without advancing any money, his knowledge of these matters constituting his share in the enterprise. This agency was like a distillery, which threw out the claims of ignorant persons, distrustful persons, or those whose rights could be contested. As member of the commission, Gobseck negotiated with the large proprietors, who, either to get their claims valued at a high figure, or to have them speedily admitted, offered him gifts in proportion to the sums involved.

"These presents constituted a sort of discount on the sums he could not lay hands on himself; moreover, this agency gave him, at a low price, the claims of petty owners, or timid owners, who preferred an immediate payment, small as the sum might be, to the chance of uncertain payments from the republic. Gobseck was therefore the insatiable boa-constrictor of this great affair. Every morning he received his tribute, and looked it over as the minister of a pasha might have done before deciding to sign a pardon. Gobseck took all things—from the game-bag of some poor devil, and the pound of candles of a timorous soul, to the plate of the rich, and the gold snuff-boxes of speculators. No one knew what became of these presents made to the old usurer. All things went in to him, nothing came out:

" 'On the word of an honest woman,' the portress, an old acquaintance of mine, said to me, 'I believe he swallows 'em! But that don't make him fat, for he's as lank as the pendulum of my clock.'

"Last Monday Gobseck sent the old soldier to fetch me.

" 'Make haste, Monsieur Derville,' said the man as he entered my office; 'the master is going to give in his last account. He's as yellow as a lemon; and he's very impatient to see you. Death has got him; the last rattle growls in his throat.'

"When I entered the chamber of the dying man, I found him on his knees before the fireplace, where, though there was no fire, an enormous heap of ashes lay. Gobseck had crawled to it from his bed, but strength to return had failed him, also the voice with which to call for assistance.

" 'My old friend,' I said, lifting him, and helping him to regain his bed, 'you will take cold; why don't you have a fire?'

" 'I'm not cold,' he answered. 'No fire! no fire!—I'm going I

150,000,000 francs. By that time, the Haitian ruler, a mulatto, General Jean Pierre Boyer, had also conquered the Spanish portion of the island (Santo Domingo, today the Dominican republic).

don't know where, boy,' he went on, giving me his last blank, chilling look, 'but it is away from here! I've got the *carphology*,'[48] using a term which made me see how clear and precise his intellect still was. 'I thought my room was full of living gold, and I got up to get some. To whom will mine go? I won't let the government get it. I've made a will; find it, Grotius. The *belle Hollandaise* had a daughter that I saw somewhere; I don't know where—in the rue Vivienne, one evening. I think they call her "La Torpille"[49]—she's pretty; find her, Grotius. You are the executor of my will; take what you want; eat it; there's *pâtés de foie gras*, bags of coffee, sugar, gold spoons. Give the Odiot[50] service to your wife. But who's to have the diamonds? Do you care for them, boy? There's tobacco; sell it in Hamburg; it will bring half as much again. I've got *everything*! and I must leave it all! Come, come, papa Gobseck,' he said to himself, 'no weakness! be yourself.'

"He sat up in bed, his face clearly defined against the pillow like a piece of bronze; he stretched his withered arm and bony hand upon the coverlet, which he grasped as if to hold himself from going. He looked at his hearth, cold as his own metallic eye; and he died with his mind clear, presenting to his portress, the old soldier, and me, an image of those old Romans standing behind the Consuls, such as Lethière[51] has depicted them in his painting of the 'Death of the Sons of Brutus.'

" 'Hasn't he guts, that old Lascar!'[52] said the soldier, in barrack language.

"I still seemed to hear the fantastic enumeration that the dying man had made of his possessions, and my glance, which had followed his, again rested on that heap of ashes, the immense size of which suddenly struck me. I took the tongs, and when I thrust them into the mound, they struck upon a hoard of gold and silver—no doubt the fruit of his last receipts, which his weakness had prevented him from hiding elsewhere.

" 'Go for the justice-of-peace,' I said, 'and let the seals be put on at once.'

"Moved by Gobseck's last words, and by something the portress had told me, I took the keys of the other apartments in order to inspect them. In the first room I entered I found the explanation of words I had supposed delirious. Before my eyes were the effects of an avarice in which nothing remained but that illogical instinct of

48. the delirious fumbling with bed-clothes (i.e., restlessness).

49. "the Torpedo," a fish capable of giving electric shocks, the nickname of Esther van Gobseck. Her story is told in *Splendors and Miseries of the Courtesans*.

50. a famous Paris jeweler, Jean-Baptiste-Claude Odiot (1763–1850).

51. Guillaume Lethière (1760–1832) was a French painter. The picture, now in the Louvre, was painted in 1801. It showed Junius Brutus, Roman consul, ordering the execution of his own sons for their part in the Tarquin conspiracy (about 508 B.C.)

52. an East Indian sailor or pirate.

hoarding which we see in provincial misers. In the room adjoining that where Gobseck lay were moldy patties, a mass of eatables of all kinds, shell-fish, and other fish, now rotten, the various stenches of which almost asphyxiated me. Maggots and insects swarmed there. These presents, recently made, were lying among boxes of all shapes, chests of tea, bags of coffee. On the fireplace, in a silver soup tureen, were bills of lading of merchandise consigned to him at Havre: bales of cotton, hogsheads of sugar, barrels of rum, coffees, indigos, tobacco—an absolute bazaar of colonial products! The room was crowded with articles of furniture, silverware, lamps, pictures, vases, books, fine engravings, without frames or rolled up, and curiosities of various descriptions. Possibly this enormous mass of property of all kinds did not come wholly as gifts; part of it may have been taken in pledge for debts unpaid. I saw jewel-cases stamped with armorial bearings, sets of the finest damask, valuable weapons, but all without names. Opening a book, which seemed to me rather out of place, I found in it a number of thousand-franc notes. I resolved, therefore, to examine the most insignificant articles —to search the floors, the ceilings, the cornices, the walls, and find every fragment of that gold so passionately loved by the old Dutchman, who was worthy, indeed, of Rembrandt's pencil. I have never seen, throughout my legal life, such effects of avarice and originality. When I returned to his own chamber, I found, on his desk, the reason of this progressive heaping up of riches. Under a paper-weight was a correspondence between Gobseck and the merchants to whom, no doubt, he habitually sold his presents. Now whether it was that these dealers were the victims of his astuteness, or that Gobseck wanted too high a price for his provisions and manufactured articles, it was evident that each negotiation was suspended. He had not sold the comestibles to Chevet because Chevet would only take them at a reduction of thirty per cent. Gobseck haggled for a few extra francs, and meantime, the goods became damaged. As for the silver, he refused to pay the costs of transportation; neither would he make good the wastage on his coffees. In short, every article had given rise to squabbles which revealed in Gobseck the first symptoms of childishness, that incomprehensible obstinacy which old men fall into whenever a strong passion survives the vigor of their minds. I said to myself, as he had said:

" 'To whom will all this wealth go?'

"Thinking over the singular information he had given me about his only heiress, I saw that I should be compelled to ransack every questionable house in Paris, in order to cast this enormous fortune at the feet of a bad woman. But—what is of far more importance to us—let me now tell you, that, according to deeds drawn up in due form, Comte Ernest de Restaud will, in a few days, come into possession of a fortune which will enable him to marry Mademoiselle Camille, and also to give a sufficient dowry to his mother, and to portion his brother and sister suitably."

"Well, dear Monsieur Derville, we will think about it," replied Madame de Grandlieu. "Monsieur Ernest ought to be very rich to make a family like ours accept his mother. Remember that my son will one day be Duc de Grandlieu, and will unite the fortunes of the two Grandlieu houses. I wish him to have a brother-in-law to his taste."

"But," said the Comte de Born, "Restaud bears gules, a barre argent, with four escutcheons or, each charged with a cross sable.[53] It is a very old blazon."

"True," said the viscountess. "Besides, Camille need never see her mother-in-law, who turned the *Res tuta*[54]—the motto of that blazon, brother—to a lie."

"Madame de Beauséant[55] received Madame de Restaud," said the old uncle.

"Yes, but only at her routs," replied the viscountess.

53. heraldic terms, derived from Old French, describing the Restaud coat of arms.

54. "the safe thing"; a Latin motto.

55. a viscountess; a great and noble lady appearing in several of Balzac's novels, among them *Old Goriot*. The fact that she received Mme. de Restaud only at routs (big general receptions) shows that she excluded her from actual intimacy, either because of her tarnished reputation or because of her low social origin.

GUSTAVE FLAUBERT
(1821–1880)
A Simple Heart (Un Cœur simple)*

I

Madame Aubain's servant Félicité was the envy of the ladies of Pont-l'Évêque[1] for half a century.

She received a hundred francs a year. For that she was cook and general servant, and did the sewing, washing, and ironing; she could bridle a horse, fatten poultry, and churn butter—and she remained faithful to her mistress, unamiable as the latter was.

Mme. Aubain had married a gay bachelor without money who died at the beginning of 1809, leaving her with two small children and a quantity of debts. She then sold all her property except the farms of Toucques and Geffosses, which brought in five thousand francs a year at most, and left her house in Saint-Melaine for a less

* 1877. Reprinted from *Three Tales* by Gustave Flaubert, translated by Arthur McDowall, by permission of Alfred A. Knopf, Inc. Copyright 1924 by Alfred A. Knopf, Inc.

1. a village in Normandy, twenty-five miles from Caen.

expensive one that had belonged to her family and was situated behind the market.

This house had a slate roof and stood between an alley and a lane that went down to the river. There was an unevenness in the levels of the rooms which made you stumble. A narrow hall divided the kitchen from the "parlour" where Mme. Aubain spent her day, sitting in a wicker easy chair by the window. Against the panels, which were painted white, was a row of eight mahogany chairs. On an old piano under the barometer a heap of wooden and cardboard boxes rose like a pyramid. A stuffed armchair stood on either side of the Louis-Quinze chimney-piece, which was in yellow marble with a clock in the middle of it modelled like a temple of Vesta.[2] The whole room was a little musty, as the floor was lower than the garden.

The first floor began with "Madame's" room: very large, with a pale-flowered wall-paper and a portrait of "Monsieur" as a dandy of the period. It led to a smaller room, where there were two children's cots without mattresses. Next came the drawing-room, which was always shut up and full of furniture covered with sheets. Then there was a corridor leading to a study. The shelves of a large bookcase were respectably lined with books and papers, and its three wings surrounded a broad writing-table in darkwood. The two panels at the end of the room were covered with pen-drawings, water-colour landscapes, and engravings by Audran,[3] all relics of better days and vanished splendour. Félicité's room on the top floor got its light from a dormer-window, which looked over the meadows.

She rose at daybreak to be in time for Mass, and worked till evening without stopping. Then, when dinner was over, the plates and dishes in order, and the door shut fast, she thrust the log under the ashes and went to sleep in front of the hearth with her rosary in her hand. Félicité was the stubbornest of all bargainers; and as for cleanness, the polish on her saucepans was the despair of other servants. Thrifty in all things, she ate slowly, gathering off the table in her fingers the crumbs of her loaf—a twelve-pound loaf expressly baked for her, which lasted for three weeks.

At all times of year she wore a print handkerchief fastened with a pin behind, a bonnet that covered her hair, grey stockings, a red skirt, and a bibbed apron—such as hospital nurses wear—over her jacket.

Her face was thin and her voice sharp. At twenty-five she looked like forty. From fifty onwards she seemed of no particular age; and with her silence, straight figure, and precise movements she was like a woman made of wood, and going by clockwork.

2. temple of the Roman goddess of the hearth; it was round and enclosed by columns.

3. Gérard Audran (1640–1703) made engravings of many paintings by Poussin, Mignard, and others.

II

She had had her love-story like another.

Her father, a mason, had been killed by falling off some scaffolding. Then her mother died, her sisters scattered, and a farmer took her in and employed her, while she was still quite little, to herd the cows at pasture. She shivered in rags and would lie flat on the ground to drink water from the ponds; she was beaten for nothing, and finally turned out for the theft of thirty sous which she did not steal. She went to another farm, where she became dairy-maid; and as she was liked by her employers her companions were jealous of her.

One evening in August (she was then eighteen) they took her to the assembly at Colleville. She was dazed and stupefied in an instant by the noise of the fiddlers, the lights in the trees, the gay medley of dresses, the lace, the gold crosses, and the throng of people jigging all together. While she kept shyly apart a young man with a well-to-do air, who was leaning on the shaft of a cart and smoking his pipe, came up to ask her to dance. He treated her to cider, coffee, and cake, and bought her a silk handkerchief; and then, imagining she had guessed his meaning, offered to see her home. At the edge of a field of oats he pushed her roughly down. She was frightened and began to cry out; and he went off.

One evening later she was on the Beaumont road. A big hay-wagon was moving slowly along; she wanted to get in front of it, and as she brushed past the wheels she recognized Theodore. He greeted her quite calmly, saying she must excuse it all because it was "the fault of the drink." She could not think of any answer and wanted to run away.

He began at once to talk about the harvest and the worthies of the commune, for his father had left Colleville for the farm at Les Écots, so that now he and she were neighbours. "Ah!" she said. He added that they thought of settling him in life. Well, he was in no hurry; he was waiting for a wife to his fancy. She dropped her head; and then he asked her if she thought of marrying. She answered with a smile that it was mean to make fun of her.

"But I am not, I swear!"—and he passed his left hand round her waist. She walked in the support of his embrace; their steps grew slower. The wind was soft, the stars glittered, the huge wagon-load of hay swayed in front of them, and dust rose from the dragging steps of the four horses. Then, without a word of command, they turned to the right. He clasped her once more in his arms, and she disappeared into the shadow.

The week after Theodore secured some assignations with her.

They met at the end of farmyards, behind a wall, or under a solitary tree. She was not innocent as young ladies are—she had learned knowledge from the animals—but her reason and the instinct of her honour would not let her fall. Her resistance exasperated Theodore's passion; so much so that to satisfy it—or perhaps quite artlessly—he made her an offer of marriage. She was in doubt whether to trust him, but he swore great oaths of fidelity.

Soon he confessed to something troublesome; the year before his parents had bought him a substitute for the army, but any day he might be taken again, and the idea of serving was a terror to him. Félicité took this cowardice of his as a sign of affection, and it redoubled hers. She stole away at night to see him, and when she reached their meeting-place Theodore racked her with his anxieties and urgings.

At last he declared that he would go himself to the prefecture for information, and would tell her the result on the following Sunday, between eleven and midnight.

When the moment came she sped towards her lover. Instead of him she found one of his friends.

He told her that she would not see Theodore any more. To ensure himself against conscription he had married an old woman, Madame Lehoussais, of Toucques, who was very rich.

There was an uncontrollable burst of grief. She threw herself on the ground, screamed, called to the God of mercy, and moaned by herself in the fields till daylight came. Then she came back to the farm and announced that she was going to leave; and at the end of the month she received her wages, tied all her small belongings with a handkerchief, and went to Pont-l'Évêque.

In front of the inn there she made inquiries of a woman in a widow's cap, who, as it happened, was just looking for a cook. The girl did not know much, but her willingness seemed so great and her demands so small that Mme. Aubain ended by saying:

"Very well, then, I will take you."

A quarter of an hour afterwards Félicité was installed in her house.

She lived there at first in a tremble, as it were, at "the style of the house" and the memory of "Monsieur" floating over it all. Paul and Virginie, the first aged seven and the other hardly four, seemed to her beings of a precious substance; she carried them on her back like a horse; it was a sorrow to her that Mme. Aubain would not let her kiss them every minute. And yet she was happy there. Her grief had melted in the pleasantness of things all round.

Every Thursday regular visitors came in for a game of boston, and Félicité got the cards and foot-warmers ready beforehand. They arrived punctually at eight and left before the stroke of eleven.

On Monday mornings the dealer who lodged in the covered passage spread out all his old iron on the ground. Then a hum of voices began to fill the town, mingled with the neighing of horses, bleating of lambs, grunting of pigs, and the sharp rattle of carts along the street. About noon, when the market was at its height, you might see a tall, hook-nosed old countryman with his cap pushed back making his appearance at the door. It was Robelin, the farmer of Geffosses. A little later came Liébard, the farmer from Toucques—short, red, and corpulent—in a grey jacket and gaiters shod with spurs.

Both had poultry or cheese to offer their landlord. Félicité was invariably a match for their cunning, and they went away filled with respect for her.

At vague intervals Mme. Aubain had a visit from the Marquis de Gremanville, one of her uncles, who had ruined himself by debauchery and now lived at Falaise on his last remaining morsel of land. He invariably came at the luncheon hour, with a dreadful poodle whose paws left all the furniture in a mess. In spite of efforts to show his breeding, which he carried to the point of raising his hat every time he mentioned "my late father," habit was too strong for him; he poured himself out glass after glass and fired off improper remarks. Félicité edged him politely out of the house—"You have had enough, Monsieur de Gremanville! Another time!"—and she shut the door on him.

She opened it with pleasure to M. Bourais, who had been a lawyer. His baldness, his white stock, frilled shirt, and roomy brown coat, his way of rounding the arm as he took snuff—his whole person, in fact, created that disturbance of mind which overtakes us at the sight of extraordinary men.

As he looked after the property of "Madame" he remained shut up with her for hours in "Monsieur's" study, though all the time he was afraid of compromising himself. He respected the magistracy immensely, and had some pretensions to Latin.

To combine instruction and amusement he gave the children a geography book made up of a series of prints. They represented scenes in different parts of the world: cannibals with feathers on their heads, a monkey carrying off a young lady, Bedouins in the desert, the harpooning of a whale, and so on. Paul explained these engravings to Félicité; and that, in fact, was the whole of her literary education. The children's education was undertaken by Guyot, a poor creature employed at the town hall, who was famous for his beautiful hand and sharpened his penknife on his boots.

When the weather was bright the household set off early for a day at Geffosses Farm.

Its courtyard is on a slope, with the farmhouse in the middle, and the sea looks like a grey streak in the distance.

Félicité brought slices of cold meat out of her basket, and they breakfasted in a room adjoining the dairy. It was the only surviving fragment of a country house which was now no more. The wall-paper hung in tatters, and quivered in the draughts. Mme. Aubain sat with bowed head, overcome by her memories; the children became afraid to speak. "Why don't you play, then?" she would say, and off they went.

Paul climbed into the barn, caught birds, played at ducks and drakes over the pond, or hammered with his stick on the big casks which boomed like drums. Virginie fed the rabbits or dashed off to pick cornflowers, her quick legs showing their embroidered little drawers.

One autumn evening they went home by the fields. The moon was in its first quarter, lighting part of the sky; and mist floated like a scarf over the windings of the Toucques. Cattle, lying out in the middle of the grass, looked quietly at the four people as they passed. In the third meadow some of them got up and made a half-circle in front of the walkers. "There's nothing to be afraid of," said Félicité, as she stroked the nearest on the back with a kind of crooning song; he wheeled round and the others did the same. But when they crossed the next pasture there was a formidable bellow. It was a bull, hidden by the mist. Mme. Aubain was about to run. "No! no! don't go so fast!" They mended their pace, however, and heard a loud breathing behind them which came nearer. His hoofs thudded on the meadow grass like hammers; why, he was galloping now! Félicité turned round, and tore up clods of earth with both hands and threw them in his eyes. He lowered his muzzle, waved his horns, and quivered with fury, bellowing terribly. Mme. Aubain, now at the end of the pasture with her two little ones, was looking wildly for a place to get over the high bank. Félicité was retreating, still with her face to the bull, keeping up a shower of clods which blinded him, and crying all the time, "Be quick! be quick!"

Mme. Aubain went down into the ditch, pushed Virginie first and then Paul, fell several times as she tried to climb the bank, and managed it at last by dint of courage.

The bull had driven Félicité to bay against a rail-fence; his slaver was streaming into her face; another second, and he would have gored her. She had just time to slip between two of the rails, and the big animal stopped short in amazement.

This adventure was talked of at Pont-l'Évêque for many a year. Félicité did not pride herself on it in the least, not having the barest suspicion that she had done anything heroic.

Virginie was the sole object of her thoughts, for the child developed a nervous complaint as a result of her fright, and M. Poupart, the doctor, advised sea-bathing at Trouville. It was not a frequented place then. Mme. Aubain collected information, consulted Bourais, and made preparations as though for a long journey.

Her luggage started a day in advance, in Liébard's cart. The next day he brought round two horses, one of which had a lady's saddle with a velvet back to it, while a cloak was rolled up to make a kind of seat on the crupper of the other. Mme. Aubain rode on that, behind the farmer. Félicité took charge of Virginie, and Paul mounted M. Lechaptois' donkey, lent on condition that great care was taken of it.

The road was so bad that its five miles took two hours. The horses sank in the mud up to their pasterns, and their haunches jerked abruptly in the effort to get out; or else they stumbled in the ruts, and at other moments had to jump. In some places Liébard's mare came suddenly to a halt. He waited patiently until she went on again, talking about the people who had properties along the road, and adding moral reflections to their history. So it was that as they were in the middle of Toucques, and passed under some windows bowered with nasturtiums, he shrugged his shoulders and said: "There's a Mme. Lehoussais lives there; instead of taking a young man she . . ." Félicité did not hear the rest; the horses were trotting and the donkey galloping. They all turned down a bypath; a gate swung open and two boys appeared; and the party dismounted in front of a manure-heap at the very threshold of the farmhouse door.

When Mme. Liébard saw her mistress she gave lavish signs of joy. She served her a luncheon with a sirloin of beef, tripe, black-pudding, a fricassee of chicken, sparkling cider, a fruit tart, and brandied plums; seasoning it all with compliments to Madame, who seemed in better health; Mademoiselle, who was "splendid" now; and Monsieur Paul, who had "filled out" wonderfully. Nor did she forget their deceased grandparents, whom the Liébards had known, as they had been in the service of the family for several generations. The farm, like them, had the stamp of antiquity. The beams on the ceiling were worm-eaten, the walls blackened with smoke, and the window-panes grey with dust. There was an oak dresser laden with every sort of useful article—jugs, plates, pewter bowls, wolf-traps, and sheep-shears; and a huge syringe made the children laugh. There was not a tree in the three courtyards without mushrooms growing at the bottom of it or a tuft of mistletoe on its boughs. Several of them had been thrown down by the wind. They had taken root again at the middle; and all were bending under their wealth of apples. The thatched roofs, like brown velvet and of varying thickness, withstood the heaviest squalls. The cart-shed, however, was falling into ruin. Mme. Aubain said she would see about it, and ordered the animals to be saddled again.

It was another half-hour before they reached Trouville. The little caravan dismounted to pass Écores—it was an overhanging cliff with boats below it—and three minutes later they were at the end of the quay and entered the courtyard of the Golden Lamb, kept by good Mme. David.

From the first days of their stay Virginie began to feel less weak, thanks to the change of air and the effect of the sea-baths. These, for want of a bathing-dress, she took in her chemise; and her nurse dressed her afterwards in a coastguard's cabin which was used by the bathers.

In the afternoons they took the donkey and went off beyond the Black Rocks, in the direction of Hennequeville. The path climbed at first through ground with dells in it like the green sward of a park, and then reached a plateau where grass fields and arable lay side by side. Hollies rose stiffly out of the briary tangle at the edge of the road; and here and there a great withered tree made zigzags in the blue air with its branches.

They nearly always rested in a meadow, with Deauville on their left, Havre on their right, and the open sea in front. It glittered in the sunshine, smooth as a mirror and so quiet that its murmur was scarcely to be heard; sparrows chirped in hiding and the immense sky arched over it all. Mme. Aubain sat doing her needlework; Virginie plaited rushes by her side; Félicité pulled up lavender, and Paul was bored and anxious to start home.

Other days they crossed the Toucques in a boat and looked for shells. When the tide went out sea-urchins, starfish, and jelly-fish were left exposed; and the children ran in pursuit of the foam-flakes which scudded in the wind. The sleepy waves broke on the sand and unrolled all along the beach; it stretched away out of sight, bounded on the land-side by the dunes which parted it from the Marsh, a wide meadow shaped like an arena. As they came home that way, Trouville, on the hill-slope in the background, grew bigger at every step, and its miscellaneous throng of houses seemed to break into a gay disorder.

On days when it was too hot they did not leave their room. From the dazzling brilliance outside light fell in streaks between the laths of the blinds. There were no sounds in the village; and on the pavement below not a soul. This silence round them deepened the quietness of things. In the distance, where men were caulking, there was a tap of hammers as they plugged the hulls, and a sluggish breeze wafted up the smell of tar.

The chief amusement was the return of the fishing-boats. They began to tack as soon as they had passed the buoys. The sails came down on two of the three masts; and they drew on with the fore-sail swelling like a balloon, glided through the splash of the waves, and when they had reached the middle of the harbour suddenly dropped anchor. Then the boats drew up against the quay. The sailors threw quivering fish over the side; a row of carts was waiting, and women in cotton bonnets darted out to take the baskets and give their men a kiss.

One of them came up to Félicité one day, and she entered the lodgings a little later in a state of delight. She had found a sister again—and then Nastasie Barette, "wife of Leroux," appeared, holding an infant at her breast and another child with her right hand, while on her left was a little cabin boy with his hands on his hips and a cap over his ear.

After a quarter of an hour Mme. Aubain sent them off; but they were always to be found hanging about the kitchen, or encountered in the course of a walk. The husband never appeared.

Félicité was seized with affection for them. She bought them a blanket, some shirts, and a stove; it was clear that they were making a good thing out of her. Mme. Aubain was annoyed by this weakness of hers, and she did not like the liberties taken by the nephew, who said "thee" and "thou" to Paul. So as Virginie was coughing and the fine weather gone, she returned to Pont-l'Évêque.

There M. Bourais enlightened her on the choice of a boys' school. The one at Caen was reputed to be the best, and Paul was sent to it. He said his good-byes bravely, content enough at going to live in a house where he would have companions.

Mme. Aubain resigned herself to her son's absence as a thing that had to be. Virginie thought about it less and less. Félicité missed the noise he made. But she found an occupation to distract her; from Christmas onward she took the little girl to catechism every day.

III

After making a genuflexion at the door she walked up between the double rows of chairs under the lofty nave, opened Mme. Aubain's pew, sat down, and began to look about her. The choir stalls were filled with the boys on the right and the girls on the left, and the curé stood by the lectern. On a painted window in the apse the Holy Ghost looked down upon the Virgin. Another window showed her on her knees before the child Jesus, and a group carved in wood behind the altar-shrine represented St. Michael overthrowing the dragon.

The priest began with a sketch of sacred history. The Garden, the Flood, the Tower of Babel, cities in flames, dying nations, and overturned idols passed like a dream before her eyes; and the dizzying vision left her with reverence for the Most High and fear of his wrath. Then she wept at the story of the Passion. Why had they crucified Him, when He loved the children, fed the multitudes, healed the blind, and had willed, in His meekness, to be born among the poor, on the dung-heap of a stable? The sowings, harvests, wine-presses, all the familiar things that the Gospel speaks of, were a part of her life. They had been made holy by God's passing; and she loved the lambs more tenderly for her love of the Lamb, and the doves because of the Holy Ghost.

She found it hard to imagine Him in person, for He was not merely a bird, but a flame as well, and a breath at other times. It may be His light, she thought, which flits at night about the edge of the marshes, His breathing which drives on the clouds, His voice which gives harmony to the bells; and she would sit rapt in adoration, enjoying the cool walls and the quiet of the church.

Of doctrines she understood nothing—did not even try to understand. The curé discoursed, the children repeated their lesson, and finally she went to sleep, waking up with a start when their wooden shoes clattered on the flagstones as they went away.

It was thus that Félicité, whose religious education had been neglected in her youth, learned the catechism by dint of hearing it; and from that time she copied all Virginie's observances, fasting as she did and confessing with her. On Corpus Christi Day they made a festal altar together.

The first communion loomed distractingly ahead. She fussed over the shoes, the rosary, the book and gloves; and how she trembled as she helped Virginie's mother to dress her!

All through the mass she was racked with anxiety. She could not see one side of the choir because of M. Bourais but straight in front of her was the flock of maidens, with white crowns above their hanging veils, making the impression of a field of snow; and she knew her dear child at a distance by her dainty neck and thoughtful air. The bell tinkled. The heads bowed, and there was silence. As the organ pealed, singers and congregation took up the "Agnus Dei"; then the procession of the boys began, and after them the girls rose. Step by step, with their hands joined in prayer, they went towards the lighted altar, knelt on the first step, received the sacrament in turn, and came back in the same order to their places. When Virginie's turn came Félicité leaned forward to see her; and with the imaginativeness of deep and tender feeling it seemed to her that she actually was the child; Virginie's face became hers, she was dressed in her clothes, it was her heart beating in her breast. As the moment came to open her mouth she closed her eyes and nearly fainted.

She appeared early in the sacristy next morning for Monsieur the curé to give her the communion. She took it with devotion, but it did not give her the same exquisite delight.

Mme. Aubain wanted to make her daughter into an accomplished person; and as Guyot could not teach her music or English she decided to place her in the Ursuline Convent at Honfleur as a boarder.

The child made no objection. Félicité sighed and thought that Madame lacked feeling. Then she reflected that her mistress might be right; matters of this kind were beyond her.

So one day an old spring-van drew up at the door, and out of it stepped a nun to fetch the young lady. Félicité hoisted the luggage on to the top, admonished the driver, and put six pots of preserves, a dozen pears, and a bunch of violets under the seat.

At the last moment Virginie broke into a fit of sobbing; she threw her arms round her mother, who kissed her on the forehead, saying over and over "Come, be brave! be brave!" The step was raised, and the carriage drove off.

Then Mme. Aubain's strength gave way; and in the evening all her friends—the Lormeau family, Mme. Lechaptois, the Roche-feuille ladies, M. de Houppeville, and Bourais—came in to console her.

To be without her daughter was very painful for her at first. But she heard from Virginie three times a week, wrote to her on the other days, walked in the garden, and so filled up the empty hours.

From sheer habit Félicité went into Virginie's room in the mornings and gazed at the walls. It was boredom to her not to have to comb the child's hair now, lace up her boots, tuck her into bed—and not to see her charming face perpetually and hold her hand when they went out together. In this idle condition she tried making lace. But her fingers were too heavy and broke the threads; she could not attend to anything, she had lost her sleep, and was, in her own words, "destroyed."

To "divert herself" she asked leave to have visits from her nephew Victor.

He arrived on Sundays after mass, rosy-cheeked, bare-chested, with the scent of the country he had walked through still about him. She laid her table promptly and they had lunch, sitting opposite each other. She ate as little as possible herself to save expense, but stuffed him with food so generous that at last he went to sleep. At the first stroke of vespers she woke him up, brushed his trousers, fastened his tie, and went to church, leaning on his arm with maternal pride.

Victor was always instructed by his parents to get something out of her—a packet of moist sugar, it might be, a cake of soap, spirits, or even money at times. He brought his things for her to mend and she took over the task, only too glad to have a reason for making him come back.

In August his father took him off on a coasting voyage. It was holiday time, and she was consoled by the arrival of the children. Paul, however, was getting selfish, and Virginie was too old to be called "thou" any longer; this put a constraint and barrier between them.

Victor went to Morlaix, Dunkirk, and Brighton in succession and made Félicité a present on his return from each voyage. It was a box made of shells the first time, a coffee cup the next, and on the third occasion a large gingerbread man. Victor was growing handsome. He was well made, had a hint of a moustache, good honest eyes, and a small leather hat pushed backwards like a pilot's. He entertained her by telling stories embroidered with nautical terms.

On a Monday, July 14, 1819 (she never forgot the date), he told her that he had signed on for the big voyage and next night but one he would take the Honfleur boat and join his schooner, which was to weigh anchor from Havre before long. Perhaps he would be gone two years.

The prospect of this long absence threw Félicité into deep distress; one more good-bye she must have, and on the Wednesday evening, when Madame's dinner was finished, she put on her clogs and made short work of the twelve miles between Pont-l'Évêque and Honfleur.

When she arrived in front of the Calvary she took the turn to the right instead of the left, got lost in the timber-yards, and retraced her steps; some people to whom she spoke advised her to be quick. She went all round the harbour basin, full of ships, and knocked against hawsers; then the ground fell away, lights flashed across each other, and she thought her wits had left her, for she saw horses up in the sky.

Others were neighing by the quay-side, frightened at the sea. They were lifted by a tackle and deposited in a boat, where passengers jostled each other among cider casks, cheese baskets, and sacks of grain; fowls could be heard clucking, the captain swore; and a cabin-boy stood leaning over the bows, indifferent to it all. Félicité, who had not recognized him, called "Victor!" and he raised his head; all at once, as she was darting forwards, the gangway was drawn back.

The Honfleur packet, women singing as they hauled it, passed out of harbour. Its framework creaked and the heavy waves whipped its bows. The canvas had swung round, no one could be seen on board now; and on the moon-silvered sea the boat made a black speck which paled gradually, dipped, and vanished.

As Félicité passed by the Calvary she had a wish to commend to God what she cherished most, and she stood there praying a long time with her face bathed in tears and her eyes towards the clouds. The town was asleep, coastguards were walking to and fro; and water poured without cessation through the holes in the sluice, with the noise of a torrent. The clocks struck two.

The convent parlour would not be open before day. If Félicité were late Madame would most certainly be annoyed; and in spite of her desire to kiss the other child she turned home. The maids at the inn were waking up as she came in to Pont-l'Évêque.

So the poor slip of a boy was going to toss for months and months at sea! She had not been frightened by his previous voyages. From England or Brittany you came back safe enough; but America, the colonies, the islands—these were lost in a dim region at the other end of the world.

Félicité's thoughts from that moment ran entirely on her nephew. On sunny days she was harassed by the idea of thirst; when there was a storm she was afraid of the lightning on his account. As she listened to the wind growling in the chimney or carrying off the slates she pictured him lashed by that same tempest, at the top of a shattered mast, with his body thrown backwards under a sheet of foam; or else (with a reminiscence of the illustrated geography) he was being eaten by savages, captured in a wood by monkeys, or dying on a desert shore. And never did she mention her anxieties.

Mme. Aubain had anxieties of her own, about her daughter. The good sisters found her an affectionate but delicate child. The slightest emotion unnerved her. She had to give up the piano.

Her mother stipulated for regular letters from the convent. She lost patience one morning when the postman did not come, and walked to and fro in the parlour from her armchair to the window. It was really amazing; not a word for four days!

To console Mme. Aubain by her own example Félicité remarked: "As for me, Madame, it's six months since I heard . . ."

"From whom, pray?"

"Why . . . from my nephew," the servant answered gently.

"Oh! your nephew!" And Mme. Aubain resumed her walk with a shrug of the shoulders, as much as to say: "I was not thinking of him! And what is more, it's absurd! A scamp of a cabin-boy—what does he matter? . . . whereas my daughter . . . why, just think!"

Félicité, though she had been brought up on harshness, felt indignant with Madame—and then forgot. It seemed the simplest thing in the world to her to lose one's head over the little girl. For her the two children were equally important; a bond in her heart made them one, and their destinies must be the same.

She heard from the chemist that Victor's ship had arrived at Havana. He had read this piece of news in a gazette.

Cigars—they made her imagine Havana as a place where no one does anything but smoke, and there was Victor moving among the negroes in a cloud of tobacco. Could you, she wondered, "in case you needed," return by land? What was the distance from Pont-l'-Évêque? She questioned M. Bourais to find out.

He reached for his atlas and began explaining the longitudes; Félicité's consternation provoked a fine pedantic smile. Finally he marked with his pencil a black, imperceptible point in the indentations of an oval spot, and said as he did so, "Here it is." She bent over the map; the maze of coloured lines wearied her eyes without conveying anything; and on an invitation from Bourais to tell him her difficulty she begged him to show her the house where Victor was living. Bourais threw up his arms, sneezed, and laughed immensely: a simplicity like hers was a positive joy. And Félicité did not understand the reason; how could she when she expected, very likely, to see the actual image of her nephew—so stunted was her mind!

A fortnight afterwards Liébard came into the kitchen at market-time as usual and handed her a letter from her brother-in-law. As neither of them could read she took it to her mistress.

Mme. Aubain, who was counting the stitches in her knitting, put the work down by her side, broke the seal of the letter, started, and said in a low voice, with a look of meaning:

"It is bad news . . . that they have to tell you. Your nephew . . ."

He was dead. The letter said no more.

Félicité fell on to a chair, leaning her head against the wainscot; and she closed her eyelids, which suddenly flushed pink. Then with bent forehead, hands hanging, and fixed eyes, she said at intervals:

"Poor little lad! poor little lad!"

Liébard watched her and heaved sighs. Mme. Aubain trembled a little.

She suggested that Félicité should go to see her sister at Trouville.

Félicité answered by a gesture that she had no need.

There was a silence. The worthy Liébard thought it was time for them to withdraw.

Then Félicité said:

"They don't care, not they!"

Her head dropped again; and she took up mechanically, from time to time, the long needles on her work-table.

Women passed in the yard with a barrow of dripping linen.

As she saw them through the window-panes she remembered her washing; she had put it to soak the day before, to-day she must wring it out; and she left the room.

Her plank and tub were at the edge of the Toucques. She threw a pile of linen on the bank, rolled up her sleeves, and taking her wooden beater dealt lusty blows whose sound carried to the neighbouring gardens. The meadows were empty, the river stirred in the wind; and down below long grasses wavered, like the hair of corpses floating in the water. She kept her grief down and was very brave until the evening; but once in her room she surrendered to it utterly, lying stretched on the mattress with her face in the pillow and her hands clenched against her temples.

Much later she heard, from the captain himself, the circumstances of Victor's end. They had bled him too much at the hospital for yellow fever. Four doctors held him at once. He had died instantly, and the chief had said:

"Bah! there goes another!"

His parents had always been brutal to him. She preferred not to see them again; and they made no advances, either because they forgot her or from the callousness of the wretchedly poor.

Virginie began to grow weaker.

Tightness in her chest, coughing, continual fever, and veinings on her cheek-bones betrayed some deep-seated complaint. M. Poupart had advised a stay in Provence. Mme. Aubain determined on it, would have brought her daughter home at once but for the climate of Pont-l'Évêque.

She made an arrangement with a job-master, and he drove her to the convent every Tuesday. There is a terrace in the garden, with a view over the Seine. Virginie took walks there over the fallen vine-leaves, on her mother's arm. A shaft of sunlight through the clouds made her blink sometimes, as she gazed at the sails in the distance and the whole horizon from the castle of Tancarville to the light-houses at Havre. Afterwards they rested in the arbour. Her mother had secured a little cask of excellent Malaga; and Virginie, laughing at the idea of getting tipsy, drank a thimble-full of it, no more.

Her strength came back visibly. The autumn glided gently away. Félicité reassured Mme. Aubain. But one evening, when she had been out on a commission in the neighbourhood, she found M. Poupart's gig at the door. He was in the hall, and Mme. Aubain was tying her bonnet.

"Give me my foot-warmer, purse, gloves! Quicker, come!"

Virginie had inflammation of the lungs; perhaps it was hopeless.

"Not yet!" said the doctor, and they both got into the carriage under whirling flakes of snow. Night was coming on and it was very cold.

Félicité rushed into the church to light a taper. Then she ran after the gig, came up with it in an hour, and jumped lightly in behind. As she hung on by the fringes a thought came into her mind: "The courtyard has not been shut up; supposing burglars got in!" And she jumped down.

At dawn next day she presented herself at the doctor's. He had come in and started for the country again. Then she waited in the inn, thinking that a letter would come by some hand or other. Finally, when it was twilight, she took the Lisieux coach.

The convent was at the end of a steep lane. When she was about half-way up it she heard strange sounds—a death-bell tolling. "It is for someone else," thought Félicité, and she pulled the knocker violently.

After some minutes there was a sound of trailing slippers, the door opened ajar, and a nun appeared.

The good sister, with an air of compunction, said that "she had just passed away." On the instant the bell of St. Leonard's tolled twice as fast.

Félicité went up to the second floor.

From the doorway she saw Virginie stretched on her back, with her hands joined, her mouth open, and head thrown back under a black crucifix that leaned towards her, between curtains that hung stiffly, less pale than was her face. Mme. Aubain, at the foot of the bed which she clasped with her arms, was choking with sobs of agony. The mother superior stood on the right. Three candlesticks on the chest of drawers made spots of red, and the mist came whitely through the windows. Nuns came and took Mme. Aubain away.

For two nights Félicité never left the dead child. She repeated the same prayers, sprinkled holy water over the sheets, came and sat down again, and watched her. At the end of the first vigil she noticed that the face had grown yellow, the lips turned blue, the nose was sharper, and the eyes sunk in. She kissed them several times, and would not have been immensely surprised if Virginie had opened them again; to minds like hers the supernatural is quite simple. She made the girl's toilette, wrapped her in her shroud, lifted her down into her bier, put a garland on her head, and spread out her hair. It was fair, and extraordinarily long for her age. Félicité cut off a big lock and slipped half of it into her bosom, determined that she should never part with it.

The body was brought back to Pont-l'Évêque, as Mme. Aubain intended; she followed the hearse in a closed carriage.

It took another three-quarters of an hour after the mass to reach the cemetery. Paul walked in front, sobbing. M. Bourais was behind, and then came the chief residents, the women shrouded in black mantles, and Félicité. She thought of her nephew; and because she had not been able to pay these honours to him her grief was doubled, as though the one were being buried with the other.

Mme. Aubain's despair was boundless. It was against God that she first rebelled, thinking it unjust of Him to have taken her daughter from her—she had never done evil and her conscience was so clear! Ah, no!—she ought to have taken Virginie off to the south.

Other doctors would have saved her. She accused herself now, wanted to join her child, and broke into cries of distress in the middle of her dreams. One dream haunted her above all. Her husband, dressed as a sailor, was returning from a long voyage, and shedding tears he told her that he had been ordered to take Virginie away. Then they consulted how to hide her somewhere.

She came in once from the garden quite upset. A moment ago— and she pointed out the place—the father and daughter had appeared to her, standing side by side, and they did nothing, but they looked at her.

For several months after this she stayed inertly in her room. Félicité lectured her gently; she must live for her son's sake, and for the other, in remembrance of "her."

"Her?" answered Mme. Aubain, as though she were just waking up. "Ah, yes! . . . yes! . . . You do not forget her!" This was an allusion to the cemetery, where she was strictly forbidden to go.

Félicité went there every day.

Precisely at four she skirted the houses, climbed the hill, opened the gate, and came to Virginie's grave. It was a little column of pink marble with a stone underneath and a garden plot enclosed by chains. The beds were hidden under a coverlet of flowers. She watered their leaves, freshened the gravel, and knelt down to break up the earth better. When Mme. Aubain was able to come there she felt a relief and a sort of consolation.

Then years slipped away, one like another, and their only episodes were the great festivals as they recurred—Easter, the Assumption, All Saints' Day. Household occurrences marked dates that were referred to afterwards. In 1825, for instance, two glaziers white-washed the hall; in 1827 a piece of the roof fell into the courtyard and nearly killed a man. In the summer of 1828 it was Madame's turn to offer the consecrated bread; Bourais, about this time, mysteriously absented himself; and one by one the old acquaintances passed away: Guyot, Liébard, Mme. Lechaptois, Robelin, and Uncle Gremanville, who had been paralysed for a long time.

One night the driver of the mail-coach announced the Revolution of July[4] in Pont-l'Évêque. A new sub-prefect was appointed a few days later—Baron de Larsonnière, who had been consul in America, and brought with him, besides his wife, a sister-in-law and three young ladies, already growing up. They were to be seen about on their lawn, in loose blouses, and they had a negro and a parrot. They paid a call on Mme. Aubain which she did not fail to return. The moment they were seen in the distance Félicité ran to let her

4. In 1830 the Bourbons were driven out, and Louis-Philippe became king of France.

mistress know. But only one thing could really move her feelings
—the letters from her son.

He was swallowed up in a tavern life and could follow no career.
She paid his debts, he made new ones; and the sighs that Mme.
Aubain uttered as she sat knitting by the window reached Félicité
at her spinning-wheel in the kitchen.

They took walks together along the espaliered wall, always talking of Virginie and wondering if such and such a thing would have
pleased her and what, on some occasion, she would have been
likely to say.

All her small belongings filled a cupboard in the two-bedded
room. Mme. Aubain inspected them as seldom as she could. One
summer day she made up her mind to it—and some moths flew out
of the wardrobe.

Virginie's dresses were in a row underneath a shelf, on which
there were three dolls, some hoops, a set of toy pots and pans, and
the basin that she used. They took out her petticoats as well, and
the stockings and handkerchiefs, and laid them out on the two
beds before folding them up again. The sunshine lit up these poor
things, bringing out their stains and the creases made by the body's
movements. The air was warm and blue, a blackbird warbled, life
seemed bathed in a deep sweetness. They found a little plush hat
with thick, chestnut-coloured pile; but it was eaten all over by
moths. Félicité begged it for her own. Their eyes met fixedly and
filled with tears; at last the mistress opened her arms, the servant
threw herself into them, and they embraced each other, satisfying
their grief in a kiss that made them equal.

It was the first time in their lives, Mme. Aubain's nature not
being expansive. Félicité was as grateful as though she had received
a favour, and cherished her mistress from that moment with the
devotion of an animal and a religious worship.

The kindness of her heart unfolded.

When she heard the drums of a marching regiment in the street
she posted herself at the door with a pitcher of cider and asked the
soldiers to drink. She nursed cholera patients and protected the
Polish refugees;[5] one of these even declared that he wished to marry
her. They quarrelled, however; for when she came back from the
Angelus one morning she found that he had got into her kitchen
and made himself a vinegar salad which he was quietly eating.

After the Poles came father Colmiche, an old man who was supposed to have committed atrocities in '93.[6] He lived by the side of
the river in the ruins of a pigsty. The little boys watched him

5. After the Polish uprising against
Russia in 1831 was suppressed, many
Poles came to France.

6. In 1793 the Reign of Terror during the French Revolution began.

through the cracks in the wall, and threw pebbles at him which fell on the pallet where he lay constantly shaken by a catarrh; his hair was very long, his eyes inflamed, and there was a tumour on his arm bigger than his head. She got him some linen and tried to clean up his miserable hole; her dream was to establish him in the bake-house, without letting him annoy Madame. When the tumour burst she dressed it every day; sometimes she brought him cake, and would put him in the sunshine on a truss of straw. The poor old man, slobbering and trembling, thanked her in his worn-out voice, was terrified that he might lose her, and stretched out his hands when he saw her go away. He died; and she had a mass said for the repose of his soul.

That very day a great happiness befell her; just at dinner-time appeared Mme. de Larsonnière's negro, carrying the parrot in its cage, with perch, chain, and padlock. A note from the baroness informed Mme. Aubain that her husband had been raised to a prefecture and they were starting that evening; she begged her to accept the bird as a memento and mark of her regard.

For a long time he had absorbed Félicité's imagination, because he came from America; and that name reminded her of Victor, so much so that she made inquiries of the negro. She had once gone so far as to say "How Madame would enjoy having him!"

The negro repeated the remark to his mistress; and as she could not take the bird away with her she chose this way of getting rid of him.

IV

His name was Loulou. His body was green and the tips of his wings rose-pink; his forehead was blue and his throat golden.

But he had the tiresome habits of biting his perch, tearing out his feathers, sprinkling his dirt about, and spattering the water of his tub. He annoyed Mme. Aubain, and she gave him to Félicité for good.

She endeavoured to train him; soon he could repeat "Nice boy! Your servant, sir! Good morning, Marie!" He was placed by the side of the door, and astonished several people by not answering to the name Jacquot, for all parrots are called Jacquot. People compared him to a turkey and a log of wood, and stabbed Félicité to the heart each time. Strange obstinacy on Loulou's part!—directly you looked at him he refused to speak.

None the less he was eager for society; for on Sundays, while the Rochefeuille ladies, M. de Houppeville, and new familiars— Onfroy the apothecary, Monsieur Varin, and Captain Mathieu— were playing their game of cards, he beat the windows with his wings and threw himself about so frantically that they could not hear each other speak.

Bourais' face, undoubtedly, struck him as extremely droll. Directly he saw it he began to laugh—and laugh with all his might. His peals rang through the courtyard and were repeated by the echo; the neighbours came to their windows and laughed too; while M. Bourais, gliding along under the wall to escape the parrot's eye, and hiding his profile with his hat, got to the river and then entered by the garden gate. There was a lack of tenderness in the looks which he darted at the bird.

Loulou had been slapped by the butcher-boy for making so free as to plunge his head into his basket; and since then he was always trying to nip him through his shirt. Fabu threatened to wring his neck, although he was not cruel, for all his tattooed arms and large whiskers. Far from it; he really rather liked the parrot, and in a jovial humour even wanted to teach him to swear. Félicité, who was alarmed by such proceedings, put the bird in the kitchen. His little chain was taken off and he roamed about the house.

His way of going downstairs was to lean on each step with the curve of his beak, raise the right foot, and then the left; and Félicité was afraid that these gymnastics brought on fits of giddiness. He fell ill and could not talk or eat any longer. There was a growth under his tongue, such as fowls have sometimes. She cured him by tearing the pellicle off with her finger-nails. Mr. Paul was thoughtless enough one day to blow some cigar smoke into his nostrils, and another time when Mme. Lormeau was teasing him with the end of her umbrella he snapped at the ferrule. Finally he got lost.

Félicité had put him on the grass to refresh him, and gone away for a minute, and when she came back—no sign of the parrot! She began by looking for him in the shrubs, by the waterside, and over the roofs, without listening to her mistress's cries of "Take care, do! You are out of your wits!" Then she investigated all the gardens in Pont-l'Évêque, and stopped the passers-by. "You don't ever happen to have seen my parrot, by any chance, do you?" And she gave a description of the parrot to those who did not know him. Suddenly, behind the mills at the foot of the hill she thought she could make out something green that fluttered. But on the top of the hill there was nothing. A hawker assured her that he had come across the parrot just before, at Saint-Melaine, in Mère Simon's shop. She rushed there; they had no idea of what she meant. At last she came home exhausted, with her slippers in shreds and despair in her soul; and as she was sitting in the middle of the garden-seat at Madame's side, telling the whole story of her efforts, a light weight dropped on to her shoulder—it was Loulou! What on earth had he been doing? Taking a walk in the neighbourhood, perhaps!

She had some trouble in recovering from this, or rather never did recover. As the result of a chill she had an attack of quinsy, and soon afterwards an earache. Three years later she was deaf; and she spoke very loud, even in church. Though Félicité's sins might have been published in every corner of the diocese without dishonour to her or scandal to anybody, his Reverence the priest thought it right now to hear her confession in the sacristy only.

Imaginary noises in the head completed her upset. Her mistress often said to her, "Heavens! how stupid you are!" "Yes, Madame," she replied, and looked about for something.

Her little circle of ideas grew still narrower; the peal of church-bells and the lowing of cattle ceased to exist for her. All living beings moved as silently as ghosts. One sound only reached her ears now —the parrot's voice.

Loulou, as though to amuse her, reproduced the click-clack of the turn-spit, the shrill call of a man selling fish, and the noise of the saw in the joiner's house opposite; when the bell rang he imitated Mme. Aubain's "Félicité! the door! the door!"

They carried on conversations, he endlessly reciting the three phrases in his repertory, to which she replied with words that were just as disconnected but uttered what was in her heart. Loulou was almost a son and a lover to her in her isolated state. He climbed up her fingers, nibbled at her lips, and clung to her kerchief; and when she bent her forehead and shook her head gently to and fro, as nurses do, the great wings of her bonnet and the bird's wings quivered together.

When the clouds massed and the thunder rumbled Loulou broke into cries, perhaps remembering the downpours in his native forests. The streaming rain made him absolutely mad; he fluttered wildly about, dashed up to the ceiling, upset everything, and went out through the window to dabble in the garden; but he was back quickly to perch on one of the fire-dogs and hopped about to dry himself, exhibiting his tail and his beak in turn.

One morning in the terrible winter of 1837 she had put him in front of the fireplace because of the cold. She found him dead, in the middle of his cage: head downwards, with his claws in the wires. He had died from congestion, no doubt. But Félicité thought he had been poisoned with parsley, and though there was no proof of any kind her suspicions inclined to Fabu.

She wept so piteously that her mistress said to her, "Well, then, have him stuffed!"

She asked advice from the chemist, who had always been kind to the parrot. He wrote to Havre, and a person called Fellacher undertook the business. But as parcels sometimes got lost in the coach she decided to take the parrot as far as Honfleur herself.

Along the sides of the road were leafless apple-trees, one after the other. Ice covered the ditches. Dogs barked about the farms; and

Félicité, with her hands under her cloak, her little black sabots and her basket, walked briskly in the middle of the road.

She crossed the forest, passed High Oak, and reached St. Gatien.

A cloud of dust rose behind her, and in it a mail-coach, carried away by the steep hill, rushed down at full gallop like a hurricane. Seeing this woman who would not get out of the way, the driver stood up in front and the postilion shouted too. He could not hold in his four horses, which increased their pace, and the two leaders were grazing her when he threw them to one side with a jerk of the reins. But he was wild with rage, and lifting his arm as he passed at full speed, gave her such a lash from waist to neck with his big whip that she fell on her back.

Her first act, when she recovered consciousness, was to open her basket. Loulou was happily none the worse. She felt a burn in her right cheek, and when she put her hands against it they were red; the blood was flowing.

She sat down on a heap of stones and bound up her face with her handkerchief. Then she ate a crust of bread which she had put in the basket as a precaution, and found a consolation for her wound in gazing at the bird.

When she reached the crest of Ecquemauville she saw the Honfleur lights sparkling in the night sky like a company of stars; beyond, the sea stretched dimly. Then a faintness overtook her and she stopped; her wretched childhood, the disillusion of her first love, her nephew's going away, and Virginie's death all came back to her at once like the waves of an oncoming tide, rose to her throat, and choked her.

Afterwards, at the boat, she made a point of speaking to the captain, begging him to take care of the parcel, though she did not tell him what was in it.

Fellacher kept the parrot a long time. He was always promising it for the following week. After six months he announced that a packing-case had started, and then nothing more was heard of it. It really seemed as though Loulou was never coming back. "Ah, they have stolen him!" she thought.

He arrived at last, and looked superb. There he was, erect upon a branch which screwed into a mahogany socket, with a foot in the air and his head on one side, biting a nut which the bird-stuffer —with a taste for impressiveness—had gilded.

Félicité shut him up in her room. It was a place to which few people were admitted, and held so many religious objects and miscellaneous things that it looked like a chapel and bazaar in one.

A big cupboard impeded you as you opened the door. Opposite the window commanding the garden a little round one looked into the court; there was a table by the folding-bed with a water-jug, two

combs, and a cube of blue soap in a chipped plate. On the walls
hung rosaries, medals, several benign Virgins, and a holy water vessel made out of cocoa-nut; on the chest of drawers, which was
covered with a cloth like an altar, was the shell box that Victor had
given her, and after that a watering-can, a toy-balloon, exercise-
books, the illustrated geography, and a pair of young lady's boots;
and, fastened by its ribbons to the nail of the looking-glass, hung
the little plush hat! Félicité carried observances of this kind so far
as to keep one of Monsieur's frock-coats. All the old rubbish which
Mme. Aubain did not want any longer she laid hands on for her
room. That was why there were artificial flowers along the edge of
the chest of drawers and a portrait of the Comte d'Artois[7] in the
little window recess.

With the aid of a bracket Loulou was established over the chimney, which jutted into the room. Every morning when she woke up
she saw him there in the dawning light, and recalled old days and
the smallest details of insignificant acts in a deep quietness which
knew no pain.

Holding, as she did, no communication with anyone, Félicité
lived as insensibly as if she were walking in her sleep. The Corpus
Christi processions roused her to life again. Then she went round
begging mats and candlesticks from the neighbours to decorate the
altar they put up in the street.

In church she was always gazing at the Holy Ghost in the
window, and observed that there was something of the parrot in
him. The likeness was still clearer, she thought, on a crude colour-
print representing the baptism of Our Lord. With his purple wings
and emerald body he was the very image of Loulou.

She bought him, and hung him up instead of the Comte d'Artois,
so that she could see them both together in one glance. They were
linked in her thoughts; and the parrot was consecrated by his association with the Holy Ghost, which became more vivid to her eye
and more intelligible. The Father could not have chosen to express
Himself through a dove, for such creatures cannot speak; it must
have been one of Loulou's ancestors, surely. And though Félicité
looked at the picture while she said her prayers she swerved a little
from time to time towards the parrot.

She wanted to join the Ladies of the Virgin, but Mme. Aubain
dissuaded her.

And then a great event loomed up before them—Paul's marriage.

He had been a solicitor's clerk to begin with, and then tried business, the Customs, the Inland Revenue, and made efforts, even, to
get into the Rivers and Forests. By an inspiration from heaven he

7. title of Charles X, the last of the Bourbons, the youngest brother of Louis XVI and Louis XVIII. He was king between 1824 and 1830 and died in exile in 1836.

had suddenly, at thirty-six, discovered his real line—the Registrar's Office. And there he showed such marked capacity that an inspector had offered him his daughter's hand and promised him his influence.

So Paul, grown serious, brought the lady to see his mother.

She sniffed at the ways of Pont-l'Évêque, gave herself great airs, and wounded Félicité's feelings. Mme. Aubain was relieved at her departure.

The week after came news of M. Bourais' death in an inn in Lower Brittany. The rumour of suicide was confirmed, and doubts arose as to his honesty. Mme. Aubain studied his accounts, and soon found out the whole tale of his misdoings—embezzled arrears, secret sales of wood, forged receipts, etc. Besides that he had an illegitimate child, and "relations with a person at Dozulé."

These shameful facts distressed her greatly. In March 1853 she was seized with a pain in the chest; her tongue seemed to be covered with film, and leeches did not ease the difficult breathing. On the ninth evening of her illness she died, just at seventy-two.

She passed as being younger, owing to the bands of brown hair which framed her pale, pock-marked face. There were few friends to regret her, for she had a stiffness of manner which kept people at a distance.

But Félicité mourned for her as one seldom mourns for a master. It upset her ideas and seemed contrary to the order of things, impossible and monstrous, that Madame should die before her.

Ten days afterwards, which was the time it took to hurry there from Besançon, the heirs arrived. The daughter-in-law ransacked the drawers, chose some furniture, and sold the rest; and then they went back to their registering.

Madame's armchair, her small round table, her foot-warmer, and the eight chairs were gone! Yellow patches in the middle of the panels showed where the engravings had hung. They had carried off the two little beds and the mattresses, and all Virginie's belongings had disappeared from the cupboard. Félicité went from floor to floor dazed with sorrow.

The next day there was a notice on the door, and the apothecary shouted in her ear that the house was for sale.

She tottered, and was obliged to sit down. What distressed her most of all was to give up her room, so suitable as it was for poor Loulou. She enveloped him with a look of anguish when she was imploring the Holy Ghost, and formed the idolatrous habit of kneeling in front of the parrot to say her prayers. Sometimes the sun shone in at the attic window and caught his glass eye, and a great luminous ray shot out of it and put her in an ecstasy.

She had a pension of three hundred and eighty francs a year which her mistress had left her. The garden gave her a supply of vegetables. As for clothes, she had enough to last her to the end of her days, and she economized in candles by going to bed at dusk.

She hardly ever went out, as she did not like passing the dealer's shop, where some of the old furniture was exposed for sale. Since her fit of giddiness she dragged one leg; and as her strength was failing Mère Simon, whose grocery business had collapsed, came every morning to split the wood and pump water for her.

Her eyes grew feeble. The shutters ceased to be thrown open. Years and years passed, and the house was neither let nor sold.

Félicité never asked for repairs because she was afraid of being sent away. The boards on the roof rotted; her bolster was wet for a whole winter. After Easter she spat blood.

Then Mère Simon called in a doctor. Félicité wanted to know what was the matter with her. But she was too deaf to hear, and the only word which reached her was "pneumonia." It was a word she knew, and she answered softly "Ah! like Madame," thinking it natural that she should follow her mistress.

The time for the festal shrines was coming near. The first one was always at the bottom of the hill, the second in front of the post-office, and the third towards the middle of the street. There was some rivalry in the matter of this one, and the women of the parish ended by choosing Mme. Aubain's courtyard.

The hard breathing and fever increased. Félicité was vexed at doing nothing for the altar. If only she could at least have put something there! Then she thought of the parrot. The neighbours objected that it would not be decent. But the priest gave her permission, which so intensely delighted her that she begged him to accept Loulou, her sole possession, when she died.

From Tuesday to Saturday, the eve of the festival, she coughed more often. By the evening her face had shrivelled, her lips stuck to her gums, and she had vomitings; and at twilight next morning, feeling herself very low, she sent for a priest.

Three kindly women were round her during the extreme unction. Then she announced that she must speak to Fabu. He arrived in his Sunday clothes, by no means at his ease in the funereal atmosphere.

"Forgive me," she said, with an effort to stretch out her arm; "I thought it was you who had killed him."

What did she mean by such stories? She suspected him of murder—a man like him! He waxed indignant, and was on the point of making a row. "There," said the women, "she is no longer in her senses, you can see it well enough!"

Félicité spoke to shadows of her own from time to time. The women went away, and Mère Simon had breakfast. A little later she took Loulou and brought him close to Félicité with the words: "Come, now, say good-bye to him!"

Loulou was not a corpse, but the worms devoured him; one of his wings was broken, and the tow was coming out of his stomach. But she was blind now; she kissed him on the forehead and kept him close against her cheek. Mère Simon took him back from her to put him on the altar.

v

Summer scents came up from the meadows; flies buzzed; the sun made the river glitter and heated the slates. Mère Simon came back into the room and fell softly asleep.

She woke at the noise of bells; the people were coming out from vespers. Félicité's delirium subsided. She thought of the procession and saw it as if she had been there.

All the school children, the church-singers, and the firemen walked on the pavement, while in the middle of the road the verger armed with his hallebard and the beadle with a large cross advanced in front. Then came the schoolmaster, with an eye on the boys, and the sister, anxious about her little girls; three of the daintiest, with angelic curls, scattered rose-petals in the air; the deacon controlled the band with outstretched arms; and two censer-bearers turned back at every step towards the Holy Sacrament, which was borne by Monsieur the curé, wearing his beautiful chasuble, under a canopy of dark-red velvet held up by four churchwardens. A crowd of people pressed behind, between the white cloths covering the house walls, and they reached the bottom of the hill.

A cold sweat moistened Félicité's temples. Mère Simon sponged her with a piece of linen, saying to herself that one day she would have to go that way.

The hum of the crowd increased, was very loud for an instant, and then went further away.

A fusillade shook the window-panes. It was the postilions saluting the monstrance. Félicité rolled her eyes and said as audibly as she could: "Does he look well?" The parrot was weighing on her mind.

Her agony began. A death-rattle that grew more and more convulsed made her sides heave. Bubbles of froth came at the corners of her mouth and her whole body trembled.

Soon the booming of the ophicleides,[8] the high voices of the children, and the deep voices of the men were distinguishable. At intervals all was silent, and the tread of feet, deadened by the flowers they walked on, sounded like a flock pattering on grass.

The clergy appeared in the courtyard. Mère Simon clambered on to a chair to reach the attic window, and so looked down straight

8. an old large brass-wind instrument, now replaced by the tuba.

upon the shrine. Green garlands hung over the altar, which was decked with a flounce of English lace. In the middle was a small frame with relics in it; there were two orange-trees at the corners, and all along stood silver candlesticks and china vases, with sunflowers, lilies, peonies, foxgloves, and tufts of hortensia. This heap of blazing colour slanted from the level of the altar to the carpet which went on over the pavement; and some rare objects caught the eye. There was a silver-gilt sugar-basin with a crown of violets; pendants of Alençon stone glittered on the moss, and two Chinese screens displayed their landscapes. Loulou was hidden under roses, and showed nothing but his blue forehead, like a plaque of lapis lazuli.

The churchwardens, singers, and children took their places round the three sides of the court. The priest went slowly up the steps, and placed his great, radiant golden sun[9] upon the lace. Everyone knelt down. There was a deep silence; and the censers glided to and fro on the full swing of their chains.

An azure vapour rose up into Félicité's room. Her nostrils met it; she inhaled it sensuously, mystically; and then closed her eyes. Her lips smiled. The beats of her heart lessened one by one, vaguer each time and softer, as a fountain sinks, an echo disappears; and when she sighed her last breath she thought she saw an opening in the heavens, and a gigantic parrot hovering above her head.

9. the monstrance containing the consecrated Host.

IVAN TURGENEV
(1818–1883)
Fathers and Sons*

I

"Well, Piotr, any sign of them yet?" was the question asked on May the 20th, 1859, by a gentleman of a little over forty, in a dusty coat and checked trousers, who came out without his hat on to the low steps of the posting station at S——. He was addressing his servant, a chubby young fellow, with whitish down on his chin, and little, lack-lustre eyes.

The servant, in whom everything—the turquoise ring in his ear, the streaky hair plastered with grease, and the civility of his movements—indicated a man of the new, improved generation, glanced with an air of indulgence along the road, and made answer:

"No, sir; not a sign."

"Not a sign?" repeated his master.

"No, sir," responded the man a second time.

His master sighed, and sat down on a little bench. We will intro-

* 1861. Translated by Constance Garnett. Reprinted in full.

duce him to the reader while he sits, his feet tucked under him, gazing thoughtfully round.

His name was Nikolai Petrovitch Kirsanov. He had twelve miles from the posting station, a fine property of two hundred souls, or, as he expressed it—since he had arranged the division of his land with the peasants, and started a "farm"—of nearly five thousand acres. His father, a general in the army, who served in 1812, a coarse, half-educated, but not ill-natured man, a typical Russian, had been in harness all his life, first in command of a brigade, and then of a division, and lived constantly in the provinces, where, by virtue of his rank, he played a fairly important part. Nikolai Petrovitch was born in the south of Russia like his elder brother, Pavel, of whom more hereafter. He was educated at home till he was fourteen, surrounded by cheap tutors, free-and-easy but toadying adjutants, and all the usual regimental and staff set. His mother, one of the Kolyazin family, as a girl called Agathe, but as a general's wife Agathokleya Kuzminishna Kirsanov, was one of those military ladies who take their full share of the duties and dignities of office. She wore gorgeous caps and rustling silk dresses; in church she was the first to advance to the cross; she talked a great deal in a loud voice, let her children kiss her hand in the morning, and gave them her blessing at night—in fact, she got everything out of life she could. Nikolai Petrovitch, as a general's son—though so far from being distinguished by courage that he even deserved to be called "a funk"—was intended, like his brother Pavel, to enter the army; but he broke his leg on the very day when the news of his commission came, and, after being two months in bed, retained a slight limp to the end of his day. His father gave him up as a bad job, and let him go into the civil service. He took him to Petersburg directly he was eighteen, and placed him in the university. His brother happened about the same time to be made an officer in the Guards. The young men started living together in one set of rooms, under the remote supervision of a cousin on their mother's side, Ilya Kolyazin, an official of high rank. Their father returned to his division and his wife, and only rarely sent his sons large sheets of grey paper, scrawled over in a bold clerkly hand. At the bottom of these sheets stood in letters, enclosed carefully in scroll-work, the words, "Piotr Kirsanov, Major-General." In 1835 Nikolai Petrovitch left the university, a graduate, and in the same year General Kirsanov was put on the retired list after an unsuccessful review, and came to Petersburg with his wife to live. He was about to take a house in the Tavrichesky Gardens, and had joined the English club, but he died suddenly of an apoplectic fit. Agathokleya Kuzminishna soon followed him; she could not accustom herself to a dull life in the capital; she was consumed by the boredom of existence away from the regiment. Meanwhile Nikolai Petrovitch had already, in his parents' lifetime and to their no slight chagrin, had time to fall in love with the daughter of his landlord, a petty official, Prepolovensky. She was pretty, and, as it is called, an "advanced" girl; she used to read the serious articles in the "Science" column of the journals. He married her directly the term of mourning was over; and leaving the civil service in which his father had by favour procured him a post, was perfectly blissful with his Masha, first in a country villa near the Lyesny Institute, afterwards in town in a pretty little flat with a clean staircase and a draughty drawing-room, and then in the country, where he settled finally, and where in a short time a son, Arkady, was born to him. The young couple lived very happily and peacefully; they were scarcely ever apart; they read together, sung and played duets together on the piano; she tended her flowers and looked after the poultry-yard; he sometimes went hunting, and busied himself with the estate, while Arkady grew and grew in the same happy and peaceful way. Ten years passed like a dream. In 1847 Kirsanov's wife died. He almost succumbed to this blow; in a few weeks his hair was grey; he was getting ready to go abroad, if possible to distract his mind . . . but then came the year 1848. He returned unwillingly to the country, and, after a rather prolonged period of inactivity, began to take an interest in improvements in the management of his land. In 1855 he brought his son to the university; he spent three winters with him in Petersburg, hardly going out anywhere, and trying to make acquaintance with Arkady's young companions. The last winter he had not been able to go, and here we have seen him in the May of 1859, already quite grey, stoutish, and rather bent, waiting for his son, who had just taken his degree, as once he had taken it himself.

The servant, from a feeling of propriety, and perhaps, too, not anxious to remain under the master's eye, had gone to the gate, and was smoking a pipe. Nikolai Petrovitch bent his head, and began staring at the crumbling steps; a big mottled fowl walked sedately towards him, treading firmly with its great yellow legs; a muddy cat gave him an unfriendly look, twisting herself coyly round the railing. The sun was scorching; from the half-dark passage of the posting station came an odour of hot rye-bread. Nikolai Petrovitch fell to dreaming. "My son . . . a graduate . . . Arkasha . . ." were the ideas that continually came round again and again in his head; he tried to think of something else, and again the same thoughts returned. He remembered his dead wife. . . . "She did not live to see it!" he murmured sadly. A plump, dark-blue pigeon flew into the road, and hurriedly went to drink in a puddle near the well. Nikolai Petrovitch began looking at it, but his ear had already caught the sound of approaching wheels.

"It sounds as if they're coming, sir," announced the servant, popping in from the gateway.

Nikolai Petrovitch jumped up, and bent his eyes on the road. A carriage appeared with three posting-horses harnessed abreast; in the carriage he caught a glimpse of the blue band of a student's cap, the familiar outline of a dear face.

"Arkasha! Arkasha!" cried Kirsanov, and he ran waving his hands. . . . A few instants later, his lips were pressed to the beardless, sunburnt cheek of the youthful graduate.

II

"Let me shake myself first, daddy," said Arkady, in a voice tired from travelling, but boyish and clear as a bell, as he gaily responded to his father's caresses; "I am covering you with dust."

"Never mind, never mind," repeated Nikolai Petrovitch, smiling tenderly, and twice he struck the collar of his son's cloak and his own great-coat with his hand. "Let me have a look at you; let me have a look at you," he added, moving back from him, but immediately he went with hurried steps towards the yard of the station, calling, "This way, this way; and horses at once."

Nikolai Petrovitch seemed far more excited than his son; he seemed a little confused, a little timid. Arkady stopped him.

"Daddy," he said, "let me introduce you to my great friend, Bazarov, about whom I have so often written to you. He has been so good as to promise to stay with us."

Nikolai Petrovitch went back quickly, and going up to a tall man in a long, loose, rough coat with tassels, who had only just got out of the carriage, he warmly pressed the ungloved red hand, which the latter did not at once hold out to him.

"I am heartily glad," he began, "and very grateful for your kind intention of visiting us. . . . Let me know your name, and your father's."

"Yevgeny Vassilyev," answered Bazarov, in a lazy but manly voice; and turning back the collar of his rough coat, he showed Nikolai Petrovitch his whole face. It was long and lean, with a broad forehead, a nose flat at the base and sharper at the end, large greenish eyes, and drooping whiskers of a sandy colour; it was lighted up by a tranquil smile, and showed self-confidence and intelligence.

"I hope, dear Yevgeny Vassilyitch, you won't be dull with us," continued Nikolai Petrovitch.

Bazarov's thin lips moved just perceptibly, though he made no reply, but merely took off his cap. His long, thick hair did not hide the prominent bumps on his head.

"Then, Arkady," Nikolai Petrovitch began again, turning to his son, "shall the horses be put to at once, or would you like to rest?"

"We will rest at home, daddy; tell them to harness the horses."

"At once, at once," his father assented. "Hey, Piotr, do you hear? Get things ready, my good boy; look sharp."

Piotr, who as a modernised servant had not kissed the young master's hand, but only bowed to him from a distance, again vanished through the gateway.

"I came here with the carriage, but there are three horses for your coach too," said Nikolai Petrovitch fussily, while Arkady drank some water from an iron dipper brought him by the woman in charge of the station, and Bazarov began smoking a pipe and went up to the driver, who was taking out the horses; "there are only two seats in the carriage, and I don't know how our friend . . ."

"He will go in the coach," interposed Arkady in an undertone. "You must not stand on ceremony with him, please. He's a splendid fellow, so simple—you will see."

Nikolai Petrovitch's coachman brought the horses round.

"Come, hurry up, bushy beard!" said Bazarov, addressing the driver.

"Do you hear, Mityuha," put in another driver, standing by with his hands thrust behind him into the opening of his sheepskin coat, "what the gentleman called you? It's bushy beard you are too."

Mityuha only gave a jog to his hat and pulled the reins off the heated shaft-horse.

"Look sharp, look sharp, lads, lend a hand," cried Nikolai Petrovitch; "there'll be something for vodka."

In a few minutes the horses were harnessed; the father and son were installed in the carriage; Piotr climbed up on to the box; Bazarov jumped into the coach, and nestled his head down into the leather cushion; and both the vehicles rolled away.

III

"So here you are, a graduate at last, and come home again," said Nikolai Petrovitch, touching Arkady now on the shoulder, now on the knee. "At last!"

"And how is uncle, quite well?" asked Arkady who, in spite of the genuine, almost childish delight filling his heart, wanted as soon as possible to turn the conversation from the emotional into a commonplace channel.

"Quite well. He was thinking of coming with me to meet you, but for some reason or other he gave up the idea."

"And how long have you been waiting for me?" inquired Arkady.

"Oh, about five hours."

"Dear old dad!"

Arkady turned round quickly to his father, and gave him a sounding kiss on the cheek. Nikolai Petrovitch gave vent to a low chuckle.

"I have got such a capital horse for you!" he began. "You will see. And your room has been fresh papered."

"And is there a room for Bazarov?"

"We will find one for him too."

"Please, dad, make much of him. I can't tell you how I prize his friendship."

"Have you made friends with him lately?"

"Yes, quite lately."

"Ah, that's how it is I did not see him last winter. What does he study?"

"His chief subject is natural science. But he knows everything. Next year he wants to take his doctor's degree."

"Ah! he's in the medical faculty," observed Nikolai Petrovitch, and he was silent for a little. "Piotr," he went on, stretching out his hand, "aren't those our peasants driving along?"

Piotr looked where his master was pointing. Some carts harnessed with unbridled horses were moving rapidly along a narrow by-road. In each cart there were one or two peasants in sheepskin coats, unbuttoned.

"Yes, sir," replied Piotr.

"Where are they going,—to the town?"

"To the town, I suppose. To the gin-shop," he added contemptuously, turning slightly towards the coachman, as though he would appeal to him. But the latter did not stir a muscle; he was a man of the old stamp, and did not share the modern views of the younger generation.

"I have had a lot of bother with the peasants this year," pursued Nikolai Petrovitch, turning to his son. "They won't pay their rent. What is one to do?"

"But do you like your hired labourers?"

"Yes," said Nikolai Petrovitch between his teeth. "They are being set against me, that's the mischief; and they don't do their best. They spoil the tools. But they have tilled the land pretty fairly. When things have settled down a bit, it will be all right. Do you take an interest in farming now?"

"You've no shade; that's a pity," remarked Arkady, without answering the last question.

"I have had a great awning put up on the northside over the balcony," observed Nikolai Petrovitch; "now we can have dinner even in the open air."

"It'll be rather too like a summer villa. . . . Still, that's all nonsense. What air there is here! How delicious it smells! Really I fancy there's nowhere such fragrance in the world as in the meadows here! And the sky, too."

Arkady suddenly stopped short, cast a stealthy look behind him, and said no more.

"Of course," observed Nikolai Petrovitch, "you were born here, and so everything is bound to strike you in a special—"

"Come, dad, that makes no difference where a man is born."

"Still—"

"No; it makes absolutely no difference."

Nikolai Petrovitch gave a sidelong glance at his son, and the carriage went on half-a-mile further before the conversation was renewed between them.

"I don't recollect whether I wrote to you," began Nikolai Petrovitch, "your old nurse, Yegorovna, is dead."

"Really? Poor thing! Is Prokofitch still living?"

"Yes, and not a bit changed. As grumbling as ever. In fact, you won't find many changes in Maryino."

"Have you still the same bailiff?"

"Well, to be sure, there is a change there. I decided not to keep about me any freed serfs, who have been house servants, or, at least, not to entrust them with duties of any responsibility." (Arkady glanced towards Piotr.) "*Il est libre, en effet,*" observed Nikolai Petrovitch in an undertone; "but, you see, he's only a valet. Now I have a bailiff, a townsman; he seems a practical fellow. I pay him two hundred and fifty rubles a year. But," added Nikolai Petrovitch, rubbing his forehead and eyebrows with his hand, which was always an indication with him of inward embarrassment, "I told you just now that you would not find changes at Maryino. . . . That's not quite correct. I think it my duty to prepare you, though . . ."

He hesitated for an instant, and then went on in French.

"A severe moralist would regard my openness as improper; but, in the first place, it can't be concealed, and secondly, you are aware I have always had peculiar ideas as regards the relation of father and son. Though, of course, you would be right in blaming me. At my age . . . In short . . . that . . . that girl, about whom you have probably heard already . . ."

"Fenitchka?" asked Arkady easily.

Nikolai Petrovitch blushed. "Don't mention her name aloud, please. . . . Well . . . she is living with me now. I have installed her in the house . . . there were two little rooms there. But that can all be changed?"

"Goodness, daddy, what for?"

"Your friend is going to stay with us . . . it would be awkward . . ."

"Please, don't be uneasy on Bazarov's account. He's above all that."

"Well, but you, too," added Nikolai Petrovitch. "The little lodge is so horrid—that's the worst of it."

"Goodness, dad," interposed Arkady, "it's as if you were apologising; are you ashamed?"

"Of course, I ought to be ashamed," answered Nikolai Petrovitch, flushing more and more.

"Nonsense, dad, nonsense; please don't!" Arkady smiled affectionately. "What a thing to apologise for!" he thought to himself, and his heart was filled with a feeling of condescending tenderness for his kind, soft-hearted father, mixed with a sense of secret superiority. "Please stop," he repeated once more, instinctively revelling in a consciousness of his own advanced and emancipated condition.

Nikolai Petrovitch glanced at him from under the fingers of the hand with which he was still rubbing his forehead, and there was a pang in his heart. . . . But at once he blamed himself for it.

"Here are our meadows at last," he said, after a long silence.

"And that in front is our forest, isn't it?" asked Arkady.

"Yes. Only I have sold the timber. This year they will cut it down."

"Why did you sell it?"

"The money was needed; besides, that land is to go to the peasants."

"Who don't pay you their rent?"

"That's their affair; besides, they will pay it some day."

"I am sorry about the forest," observed Arkady, and he began to look about him.

The country through which they were driving could not be called picturesque. Fields upon fields stretched all along to the very horizon, now sloping gently upwards, then dropping down again; in some places woods were to be seen, and winding ravines, planted with low, scanty bushes, recalling vividly the representation of them on the old-fashioned maps of the times of Catherine. They came upon little streams too with hollow banks; and tiny lakes with narrow dykes; and little villages, with low hovels under dark and often tumble-down roofs, and slanting barns with walls woven of brushwood and gaping doorways beside neglected threshing-floors; and churches, some brick-built, with stucco peeling off in patches, others wooden, with crosses fallen askew, and overgrown graveyards. Slowly Arkady's heart sank. To complete the picture, the peasants they met were all in tatters and on the sorriest little nags; the willows, with their trunks stripped of bark, and broken branches, stood like ragged beggars along the roadside; cows lean and shaggy and looking pinched by hunger, were greedily tearing at the grass along the ditches. They looked as though they had just been snatched out of the murderous clutches of some threatening monster; and the piteous state of the weak, starved beasts in the midst of the lovely spring day, called up, like a white phantom, the endless, comfortless winter, with its storms, and frosts, and snows. . . . "No," thought Arkady, "this is not a rich country; it does not impress one by plenty or industry; it can't, it can't go on like this, reforms are absolutely necessary . . . but how is one to carry them out, how is one to begin?"

Such were Arkady's reflections; . . . but even as he reflected, the spring regained its sway. All around was golden green, all—trees, bushes, grass—shone and stirred gently in wide waves under the soft breath of the warm wind; from all sides flooded the endless trilling music of the larks; the peewits were calling as they hovered over the low-lying meadows, or noiselessly ran over the tussocks of grass; the rooks strutted along the half-grown spring-corn, standing out black against its tender green; they disappeared in the already whitening rye, only from to time their heads peeped out amid its grey waves. Arkady gazed and gazed, and his reflections grew slowly fainter and passed away. . . . He flung off his coat and turned to his father, with a face so bright and boyish, that the latter gave him another hug.

"We're not far off now," remarked Nikolai Petrovitch; "we have only to get us this hill, and the house will be in sight. We shall get on together splendidly, Arkasha; you shall help me in farming the estate, if it isn't a bore to you. We must draw close to one another now, and learn to know each other thoroughly, mustn't we?"

"Of course," said Arkady; "but what an exquisite day it is to-day!"

"To welcome you, my dear boy. Yes, it's spring in its full loveliness. Though I agree with Pushkin—do you remember in Yevgeny Onyegin[1]—

> 'To me how sad thy coming is,
> Spring, spring, sweet time of love!
> What . . .'

"Arkady!" called Bazarov's voice from the coach, "send me a match; I've nothing to light my pipe with."

Nikolai Petrovitch stopped, while Arkady, who had begun listening to him with some surprise, though with sympathy, too, made haste to pull a silver matchbox out of his pocket, and sent it to Bazarov by Piotr.

"Will you have a cigar?" shouted Bazarov again.

"Thanks," answered Arkady.

Piotr returned to the carriage, and handed him with the matchbox a thick black cigar, which Arkady began to smoke promptly, diffusing about him such a strong and pungent odour of cheap tobacco, that Nikolai Petrovitch, who had never been a smoker from his youth up, was forced to turn away his head, as imperceptibly as he could for fear of wounding his son.

A quarter of an hour later, the two carriages drew up before the steps of a new wooden house, painted grey, with a red iron roof. This was Maryino, also known as New-Wick, or as the peasants had nicknamed it, Poverty Farm.

IV

No crowd of house-serfs ran out on to the steps to meet the gentlemen; a little girl of twelve years old made her appearance alone. After her there came out of the house a young lad, very like Piotr, dressed in a coat of grey livery, with white armorial buttons, the servant of Pavel Petrovitch Kirsanov. Without speaking, he opened the door of the carriage, and unbuttoned the apron of

---

1. Nikolay Kirsanov quotes the second stanza of Canto VII of Pushkin's epic *Evgeny Onegin* (1828).

the coach. Nikolai Petrovitch with his son and Bazarov walked through a dark and almost empty hall, from behind the door of which they caught a glimpse of a young woman's face, into a drawing room furnished in the most modern style.

"Here we are at home," said Nikolai Petrovitch, taking off his cap, and shaking back his hair. "That's the great thing; now we must have supper and rest."

"A meal would not come amiss, certainly," observed Bazarov, stretching, and he dropped on to a sofa.

"Yes, yes, let us have supper, supper directly." Nikolai Petrovitch, with no apparent reason, stamped his foot. "And here just at the right moment comes Prokofitch."

A man about sixty entered, white-haired, thin, and swarthy, in a cinnamon-coloured dress-coat with brass buttons, and a pink neckerchief. He smirked, went up to kiss Arkady's hand, and bowing to the guest retreated to the door, and put his hands behind him.

"Here he is, Prokofitch," began Nikolai Petrovitch; "he's come back to us at last. . . . Well, how do you think him looking?"

"As well as could be," said the old man, and was grinning again, but he quickly knitted his bushy brows. "You wish supper to be served?" he said impressively.

"Yes, yes, please. But won't you like to go to your room first, Yevgeny Vassilyitch?"

"No, thanks; I don't care about it. Only give orders for my little box to be taken there, and this garment, too," he added, taking off his frieze overcoat.

"Certainly. Prokofitch, take the gentleman's coat." (Prokofitch, with an air of perplexity, picked up Bazarov's "garment" in both hands, and holding it high above his head, retreated on tiptoe.) "And you, Arkady, are you going to your room for a minute?"

"Yes, I must wash," answered Arkady, and was just moving towards the door, but at that instant there came into the drawing-room a man of medium height, dressed in a dark English suit, a fashionable low cravat, and kid shoes, Pavel Petrovitch Kirsanov. He looked about forty-five: his close-cropped grey hair shone with a dark lustre, like new silver; his face, yellow but free from wrinkles, was exceptionally regular and pure in line, as though carved by a light and delicate chisel, and showed traces of remarkable beauty; specially fine were his clear, black, almond-shaped eyes. The whole person of Arkady's uncle, with its aristocratic elegance, had preserved the gracefulness of youth and that air of striving upwards, away from earth, which for the most part is lost after the twenties are past.

Pavel Petrovitch took out of his trouser pocket his exquisite hand with its long tapering pink nails, a hand which seemed still more exquisite from the snowy whiteness of the cuff, buttoned with a single, big opal, and gave it to his nephew. After a preliminary handshake in the European style, he kissed him thrice after the Russian fashion, that is to say, he touched his cheek three times with his perfumed moustaches, and said "Welcome."

Nikolai Petrovitch presented him to Bazarov; Pavel Petrovitch greeted him with a slight inclination of his supple figure, and a slight smile, but he did not give him his hand, and even put it back into his pocket.

"I had begun to think you were not coming to-day," he began in a musical voice, with a genial swing and shrug of the shoulders, as he showed his splendid white teeth. "Did anything happen on the road?"

"Nothing happened," answered Arkady; "we were rather slow. But we're as hungry as wolves now. Hurry up Prokofitch, dad; and I'll be back directly."

"Stay, I'm coming with you," cried Bazarov, pulling himself up suddenly from the sofa. Both the young men went out.

"Who is he?" asked Pavel Petrovitch.

"A friend of Arkasha's; according to him a very clever fellow."

"Is he going to stay with us?"

"Yes."

"That unkempt creature?"

"Why, yes."

Pavel Petrovitch drummed with his finger-tips on the table. "I fancy Arkady *s'est dégourdi*,"[2] he remarked. "I'm glad he has come back."

At supper there was little conversation. Bazarov especially said nothing, but he ate a great deal. Nikolai Petrovitch related various incidents in what he called his career as a farmer, talked about the impending government measures, about committees, deputations, the necessity of introducing machinery, etc. Pavel Petrovitch paced slowly up and down the dining-room (he never ate supper), sometimes sipping at a wineglass of red wine, and less often uttering some remark or rather exclamation, of the nature of "Ah! aha! hm!" Arkady told some news from Petersburg, but he was conscious of a little awkwardness, that awkwardness which usually overtakes a youth when he has just ceased to be a child, and has come back to a place where they are accustomed to regard him and treat him as a child. He made his sentences quite unnecessarily long, avoided the word "daddy," and even sometimes replaced it by the word "father," mumbled, it is true, between his teeth; with an exaggerated carelessness he poured into his glass far more wine than he really wanted, and drank it all off. Prokofitch did not take his eyes off him, and kept chewing his lips. After supper they all separated at once.

2. "has lost his stiffness, has thawn up, awakened, ceased to be youthfully clumsy."

"Your uncle's a queer fish," Bazarov said to Arkady, as he sat in his dressing-gown by his bedside, smoking a short pipe. "Only fancy such style in the country! His nails, his nails—you ought to send them to an exhibition!"

"Why, of course, you don't know," replied Arkady. "He was a great swell in his own day, you know. I will tell you his story one day. He was very handsome, you know, used to turn all the women's heads."

"Oh, that's it, is it? So he keeps it up in the memory of the past. It's a pity there's no one for him to fascinate here, though. I kept staring at his exquisite collars. They're like marble, and his chin's shaved simply to perfection. Come, Arkady Nikolaitch, isn't that ridiculous?"

"Perhaps it is; but he's a splendid man, really."

"An antique survival! But your father's a capital fellow. He wastes his time reading poetry, and doesn't know much about farming, but he's a good-hearted fellow."

"My father's a man in a thousand."

"Did you notice how shy and nervous he is?"

Arkady shook his head as though he himself were not shy and nervous.

"It's something astonishing," pursued Bazarov, "these old idealists, they develop their nervous systems till they break down . . . so balance is lost. But good-night. In my room there's an English washstand, but the door won't fasten. Anyway that ought to be encouraged—an English washstand stands for progress!"

Bazarov went away, and a sense of great happiness came over Arkady. Sweet it is to fall asleep in one's own home, in the familiar bed, under the quilt worked by loving hands, perhaps a dear nurse's hands, those kind, tender, untiring hands. Arkady remembered Yegorovna, and sighed and wished her peace in heaven. . . . For himself he made no prayer.

Both he and Bazarov were soon asleep, but others in the house were awake long after. His son's return had agitated Nikolai Petrovitch. He lay down in bed, but did not put out the candles, and his head propped on his hand, he fell into long reveries. His brother was sitting long after midnight in his study, in a wide armchair before the fireplace, on which there smouldered some faintly glowing embers. Pavel Petrovitch was not undressed, only some red Chinese slippers had replaced the kid shoes on his feet. He held in his hand the last number of *Galignani*,[3] but he was not reading; he gazed fixedly into the grate, where a bluish flame flickered, dying

3. *Galignani:* refers to an English daily paper, *Galignani's Messenger*, published in Paris. It was founded by Giovanni Antonio Galignani (1752–1821), an Italian who had lived in England, in 1814 and after his death was carried on by his sons. It was discontinued in 1884.

down, then flaring up again. . . . God knows where his thoughts were rambling, but they were not rambling in the past only; the expression of his face was concentrated and surly, which is not the way when a man is absorbed solely in recollections. In a small back room there sat, on a large chest, a young woman in a blue dressing jacket with a white kerchief thrown over her dark hair, Fenitchka. She was half listening, half dozing, and often looked across towards the open door through which a child's cradle was visible, and the regular breathing of a sleeping baby could be heard.

v

The next morning Bazarov woke up earlier than any one and went out of the house. "Oh, my!" he thought, looking about him, "the little place isn't much to boast of!" When Nikolai Petrovitch had divided the land with his peasants, he had had to build his new manor-house on four acres of perfectly flat and barren land. He had built a house, offices, and farm buildings, laid out a garden, dug a pond, and sunk two wells; but the young trees had not done well, very little water had collected in the pond, and that in the wells tasted brackish. Only one arbour of lilac and acacia had grown fairly well; they sometimes had tea and dinner in it. In a few minutes Bazarov had traversed all the little paths of the garden; he went into the cattle-yard and the stable, routed out two farm-boys, with whom he made friends at once, and set off with them to a small swamp about a mile from the house to look for frogs.

"What do you want frogs for, sir?" one of the boys asked him.

"I'll tell you what for," answered Bazarov, who possessed the special faculty of inspiring confidence in people of a lower class, though he never tried to win them, and behaved very casually with them; "I shall cut the frog open, and see what's going on in his inside, and then, as you and I are much the same as frogs, only that we walk on legs, I shall know what's going on inside us, too."

"And what do you want to know that for?"

"So as not to make a mistake, if you're taken ill, and I have to cure you."

"Are you a doctor, then?"

"Yes."

"Vaska, do you hear, the gentleman says you and I are the same as frogs—that's funny!"

"I'm afraid of frogs," observed Vaska, a boy of seven, with a head as white as flax, and bare feet, dressed in a grey smock with a stand-up collar.

"What is there to be afraid of? Do they bite?"

"There, paddle into the water, philosophers," said Bazarov.

Meanwhile Nikolai Petrovitch, too, had waked up, and gone in to see Arkady, whom he found dressed. The father and son went out on to the terrace under the shelter of the awning; near the balustrade, on the table, among great bunches of lilac, the samovar was already boiling. A little girl came up, the same who had been the first to meet them at the steps on their arrival the evening before. In a shrill voice she said—

"Fedosya Nikolaevna is not quite well; she cannot come; she gave orders to ask you, will you please to pour out tea yourself, or should she send Dunyasha?"

"I will pour out myself, myself," interposed Nikolai Petrovitch hurriedly. "Arkady, how do you take your tea, with cream, or with lemon?"

"With cream," answered Arkady; and after a brief silence, he uttered interrogatively, "Daddy?"

Nikolai Petrovitch in confusion looked at his son.

"Well?" he said.

Arkady dropped his eyes.

"Forgive me, dad, if my question seems unsuitable to you," he began, "but you yourself, by your openness yesterday, encourage me to be open . . . you will not be angry . . . ?"

"Go on."

"You give me confidence to ask you. . . . Isn't the reason Fen . . . isn't the reason she will not come here to pour out tea, because I'm here?"

Nikolai Petrovitch turned slightly away.

"Perhaps," he said, at last, "she supposes . . . she is ashamed."

Arkady turned a rapid glance on his father.

"She has no need to be ashamed. In the first place, you are aware of my views" (it was very sweet of Arkady to utter that word); "and, secondly, could I be willing to hamper your life, your habits, in the least thing? Besides, I am sure you could not make a bad choice; if you have allowed her to live under the same roof with you, she must be worthy of it; in any case, a son cannot judge his father,—least of all, I, and least of all such a father who, like you, has never hampered my liberty in anything."

Arkady's voice had been shaky at the beginning; he felt himself magnanimous, though at the same time he realised he was delivering something of the nature of a lecture to his father; but the sound of one's own voice has a powerful effect on any man, and Arkady brought out his last words resolutely, even with emphasis.

"Thanks, Arkasha," said Nikolai Petrovitch thickly, and his fingers again strayed over his eyebrows and forehead. "Your suppositions are just in fact. Of course, if this girl had not deserved. . . . It is not a frivolous caprice. It's not easy for me to talk to you about this; but you will understand that it is difficult for her to come here, in your presence, especially the first day of your return."

"In that case I will go to her," cried Arkady, with a fresh rush of magnanimous feeling, and he jumped up from his seat. "I will explain to her that she has no need to be ashamed before me."

Nikolai Petrovitch, too, got up.

"Arkady," he began, "be so good . . . how can . . . there . . . I have not told you yet . . ."

But Arkady did not listen to him, and ran off the terrace. Nikolai Petrovitch looked after him, and sank into his chair overcome by confusion. His heart began to throb. Did he at that moment realise the inevitable strangeness of the future relations between him and his son? Was he conscious that Arkady would perhaps have shown him more respect if he had never touched on this subject at all? Did he reproach himself for weakness?—it is hard to say; all these feelings were within him, but in the state of sensations—and vague sensations—while the flush did not leave his face, and his heart throbbed.

There was the sound of hurrying footsteps, and Arkady came on to the terrace. "We have made friends, dad!" he cried, with an expression of a kind of affectionate and good-natured triumph on his face. "Fedosya Nikolaevna is not quite well to-day really, and she will come a little later. But why didn't you tell me I had a brother? I should have kissed him last night, as I have kissed him just now."

Nikolai Petrovitch tried to articulate something, tried to get up and open his arms. Arkady flung himself on his neck.

"What's this, embracing again?" sounded the voice of Pavel Petrovitch behind them.

Father and son were equally rejoiced at his appearance at that instant; there are positions, genuinely affecting, from which one longs to escape as soon as possible.

"Why should you be surprised at that?" said Nikolai Petrovitch gaily. "Think what ages I have been waiting for Arkasha. I've not had time to get a good look at him since yesterday."

"I'm not at all surprised," observed Pavel Petrovitch; "I feel not indisposed to be embracing him myself."

Arkady went up to his uncle, and again felt his cheeks caressed by his perfumed moustache. Pavel Petrovitch sat down at the table. He wore an elegant morning suit in the English style, and a gay little fez on his head. This fez and the carelessly tied little cravat carried a suggestion of the freedom of country life, but the stiff collars of his shirt—not white, it is true, but striped, as is correct in morning dress—stood up as inexorably as ever against his well-shaved chin.

"Where's your new friend?" he asked Arkady.

"He's not in the house; he usually gets up early and goes off somewhere. The great thing is, we mustn't pay any attention to him; he doesn't like ceremony."

"Yes, that's obvious." Pavel Petrovitch began deliberately spreading butter on his bread. "Is he going to stay long with us?"

"Perhaps. He came here on the way to his father's."

"And where does his father live?"

"In our province, sixty-four miles from here. He has a small property there. He was formerly an army doctor."

"Tut, tut, tut! To be sure, I kept asking myself, 'Where have I heard that name, Bazarov?' Nikolai, do you remember in our father's division there was a surgeon Bazarov?"

"I believe there was."

"Yes, yes, to be sure. So that surgeon was his father. Hm!" Pavel Petrovitch pulled his moustaches. "Well, and what is Mr. Bazarov himself?" he asked, deliberately.

"What is Bazarov?" Arkady smiled. "Would you like me, uncle, to tell you what he really is?"

"If you will be so good, nephew."

"He's a nihilist."

"Eh?" inquired Nikolai Petrovitch, while Pavel Petrovitch lifted a knife in the air with a small piece of butter on its tip, and remained motionless.

"He's a nihilist," repeated Arkady.

"A nihilist," said Nikolai Petrovitch. "That's from the Latin, *nihil, nothing*, as far as I can judge; the word must mean a man who . . . who accepts nothing?"

"Say, 'who respects nothing,'" put in Pavel Petrovitch, and he set to work on the butter again.

"Who regards everything from the critical point of view," observed Arkady.

"Isn't that just the same thing?" inquired Pavel Petrovitch.

"No, it's not the same thing. A nihilist is a man who does not bow down before any authority, who does not take any principle on faith, whatever reverence that principle may be enshrined in."

"Well, and is that good?" interrupted Pavel Petrovitch.

"That depends, uncle. Some people it will do good to, but some people will suffer for it."

"Indeed. Well, I see it's not in our line. We are old-fashioned people; we imagine that without principles, taken as you say on faith, there's no taking a step, no breathing. *Vous avez changé tout cela.*[4] God give you good health and the rank of a general, while we will be content to look on and admire, worthy . . . what was it?"

"Nihilists," Arkady said, speaking very distinctly.

"Yes. There used to be Hegelians, and now there are nihilists. We shall see how you will exist in void, in vacuum; and now ring, please, brother Nikolai Petrovitch; it's time I had my cocoa."

Nikolai Petrovitch rang the bell and called "Dunyasha!" But instead of Dunyasha, Fenitchka herself came on to the terrace. She was a young woman about three-and-twenty, with a white soft skin, dark hair and eyes, red, childishly-pouting lips, and little delicate

4. "You have changed this kind of thing."

hands. She wore a neat print dress; a new blue kerchief lay lightly on her plump shoulders. She carried a large cup of cocoa, and setting it down before Pavel Petrovitch, she was overwhelmed with confusion; the hot blood rushed in a wave of crimson over the delicate skin of her pretty face. She dropped her eyes, and stood at the table, leaning a little on the very tips of her fingers. It seemed as though she were ashamed of having come in, and at the same time felt she had a right to come.

Pavel Petrovitch knitted his brows severely while Nikolai Petrovitch looked embarrassed.

"Good morning, Fenitchka," he muttered through his teeth.

"Good morning," she replied in a voice not loud but resonant, and with a sidelong glance at Arkady, who gave her a friendly smile, she went gently away. She walked with a slightly rolling gait, but even that suited her.

For some minutes silence reigned on the terrace. Pavel Petrovitch sipped his cocoa; suddenly he raised his head. "Here is Sir Nihilist coming towards us," he said in an undertone.

Bazarov was in fact approaching through the garden, stepping over the flower-beds. His linen coat and trousers were besmeared with mud; clinging marsh weed was twined round the crown of his old round hat; in his right hand he held a small bag; in the bag something alive was moving. He quickly drew near the terrace, and said with a nod, "Good morning, gentlemen; sorry I was late for tea; I'll be back directly; I must just put these captives away."

"What have you there—leeches?" asked Pavel Petrovitch.

"No, frogs."

"Do you eat them—or keep them?"

"For experiment," said Bazarov indifferently, and he went off into the house.

"So he's going to cut them up," observed Pavel Petrovitch. "He has no faith in principles, but he has faith in frogs."

Arkady looked compassionately at his uncle; Nikolai Petrovitch shrugged his shoulders stealthily. Pavel Petrovitch himself felt that his epigram was unsuccessful, and began to talk about husbandry and the new bailiff, who had come to him the evening before to complain that a labourer, Foma, "was debauched," and quite unmanageable. "He's such an Æsop," he said among other things; "in all places he had protested himself a worthless fellow; he's not a man to keep his place; he'll walk off in a huff like a fool."

VI

Bazarov came back, sat down at the table, and began hastily drinking tea. The two brothers looked at him in silence, while Arkady stealthily watched first his father and then his uncle.

"Did you walk far from here?" Nikolai Petrovitch asked at last.

"Where you've a little swamp near the aspen wood. I started some half-dozen snipe; you might slaughter them, Arkady."

"Aren't you a sportsman, then?"

"No."

"Is your special study physics?" Pavel Petrovitch in his turn inquired.

"Physics, yes; and natural science in general."

"They say the Teutons of late have had great success in that line."

"Yes; the Germans are our teachers in it," Bazarov answered carelessly.

The word Teutons instead of Germans, Pavel Petrovitch had used with ironical intention; none noticed it, however.

"Have you such a high opinion of the Germans?" said Pavel Petrovitch, with exaggerated courtesy. He was beginning to feel a secret irritation. His aristocratic nature was revolted by Bazarov's absolute nonchalance. This surgeon's son was not only not overawed, he even gave abrupt and indifferent answers, and in the tone of his voice there was something churlish, almost insolent.

"The scientific men there are a clever lot."

"Ah, ah. To be sure, of Russian scientific men you have not such a flattering opinion, I dare say?"

"That's very likely."

"That's very praiseworthy self-abnegation," Pavel Petrovitch declared, drawing himself up, and throwing his head back. "But how is this? Arkady Nikolaitch was telling us just now that you accept no authorities? Don't you believe in *them*?"

"And how am I accepting them? And what am I to believe in? They tell me the truth, I agree, that's all."

"And do all Germans tell the truth?" said Pavel Petrovitch, and his face assumed an expression as unsympathetic, as remote, as if he had withdrawn to some cloudy height.

"Not all," replied Bazarov, with a short yawn. He obviously did not care to continue the discussion.

Pavel Petrovitch glanced at Arkady, as though he would say to him, "Your friend's polite, I must say." "For my own part," he began again, not without some effort, "I am so unregenerate as not to like Germans. Russian Germans I am not speaking of now; we all know what sort of creatures they are. But even German Germans are not to my liking. In former days there were some here and there; they had—well, Schiller, to be sure, Goethe . . . my brother— he takes a particularly favourable view of them. . . . But now they have all turned chemists and materialists. . . ."

"A good chemist is twenty times as useful as any poet," broke in Bazarov.

"Oh, indeed," commented Pavel Petrovitch, and, as though falling asleep, he faintly raised his eyebrows. "You don't acknowledge art then, I suppose?"

"The art of making money or of advertising pills!" cried Bazarov, with a contemptuous laugh.

"Ah, ah. You are pleased to jest, I see. You reject all that, no doubt? Granted. Then you believe in science only?"

"I have already explained to you that I don't believe in anything; and what is science—science in the abstract? There are sciences, as there are trades and crafts; but abstract science doesn't exist at all."

"Very good. Well, and in regard to the other traditions accepted in human conduct, do you maintain the same negative attitude?"

"What's this, an examination?" asked Bazarov.

Pavel Petrovitch turned slightly pale. . . . Nikolai Petrovitch thought it his duty to interpose in the conversation.

"We will converse on this subject with you more in detail some day, dear Yevgeny Vassilyitch; we will hear your views, and express our own. For my part, I am heartily glad you are studying the natural sciences. I have heard that Liebig[5] has made some wonderful discoveries in the amelioration of soils. You can be of assistance to me in my agricultural labours; you can give me some useful advice."

"I am at your service, Nikolai Petrovitch; but Liebig's miles over our heads! One has first to learn the a b c, and then begin to read, and we haven't set eyes on the alphabet yet."

"You are certainly a nihilist, I see that," thought Nikolai Petrovitch. "Still, you will allow me to apply to you on occasion," he added aloud. "And now I fancy, brother, it's time for us to be going to have a talk with the bailiff."

Pavel Petrovitch got up from his seat.

"Yes," he said, without looking at any one; "it's a misfortune to live five years in the country like this, far from mighty intellects! You turn into a fool directly. You may try not to forget what you've been taught, but—in a snap!—they'll prove all that's rubbish, and tell you that sensible men have nothing more to do with such foolishness, and that you, if you please, are an antiquated old fogey. What's to be done? Young people, of course, are cleverer than we are!"

Pavel Petrovitch turned slowly on his heels, and slowly walked away; Nikolai Petrovitch went after him.

"Is he always like that?" Bazarov coolly inquired of Arkady, directly the door had closed behind the two brothers.

"I must say, Yevgeny, you weren't nice to him," remarked Arkady. "You have hurt his feelings."

"Well, am I going to consider them, these provincial aristocrats! Why, it's all vanity, dandy habits, fatuity. He should have continued his career in Petersburg, if that's his bent. But there, enough of him! I've found a rather rare species of water-beetle, *Dytiscus marginatus*; do you know it? I will show you."

5. Justus von Liebig (1803–1873), a German chemist, was the first man to apply chemistry to agriculture and to develop artificial manures.

"I promised to tell you his story," began Arkady.

"The story of the beetle?"

"Come, don't, Yevgeny. The story of my uncle. You will see he's not the sort of man you fancy. He deserves pity rather than ridicule."

"I don't dispute it; but why are you worrying over him?"

"One ought to be just, Yevgeny."

"How does that follow?"

"No; listen. . . ."

And Arkady told him his uncle's story. The reader will find it in the following chapter.

VII

Pavel Petrovitch Kirsanov was educated first at home, like his younger brother, and afterwards in the Corps of Pages. From childhood he was distinguished by remarkable beauty; moreover he was self-confident, somewhat ironical, and had a rather biting humour; he could not fail to please. He began to be seen everywhere, directly he had received his commission as an officer. He was much admired in society, and he indulged every whim, even every caprice and every folly, and gave himself airs, but that too was attractive in him. Women went out of their senses over him; men called him a coxcomb, and were secretly jealous of him. He lived, as has been related already, in the same apartments as his brother, whom he loved sincerely, though he was not at all like him. Nikolai Petrovitch was a little lame, he had small, pleasing features of a rather melancholy cast, small, black eyes, and thin, soft hair; he liked being lazy, but he also liked reading, and was timid in society. Pavel Petrovitch did not spend a single evening at home, prided himself on his ease and audacity (he was just bringing gymnastics into fashion among young men in society), and had read in all some five or six French books. At twenty-eight he was already a captain; a brilliant career awaited him. Suddenly everything was changed.

At that time, there was sometimes seen in Petersburg society a woman who has even yet not been forgotten, Princess R——. She had a well-educated, well-bred, but rather stupid husband, and no children. She used suddenly to go abroad, and suddenly to return to Russia, and led an eccentric life in general. She had the reputation of being a frivolous coquette, abandoned herself eagerly to every sort of pleasure, danced to exhaustion, laughed and jested with young men, whom she received in the dim light of her drawing-room before dinner; while at night she wept and prayed, found no peace in anything, and often paced her room till morning, wringing her hands in anguish, or sat, pale and chill, over a psalter. Day came, and she was transformed again into a grand lady; again she went out, laughed, chattered, and simply flung herself headlong into anything which could afford her the slightest distraction. She was marvellously well-proportioned, her hair coloured like gold and heavy as gold hung

below her knees, but no one would have called her a beauty; in her
whole face the only good point was her eyes, and even her eyes were
not good—they were grey, and not large—but their glance was swift
and deep, unconcerned to the point of audacity, and thoughtful to
the point of melancholy—an enigmatic glance. There was a light of
something extraordinary in them, even while her tongue was lisping the emptiest of inanities. She dressed with elaborate care. Pavel
Petrovitch met her at a ball, danced a mazurka with her, in the
course of which she did not utter a single rational word, and fell
passionately in love with her. Being accustomed to make conquests,
in this instance, too, he soon attained his object, but his easy success
did not damp his ardour. On the contrary, he was in still more torturing, still closer bondage to this woman, in whom, even at the very
moment when she surrendered herself utterly, there seemed always
something still mysterious and unattainable, to which none could
penetrate. What was hidden in that soul—God knows! It seemed as
though she were in the power of mysterious forces, incomprehensible even to herself; they seemed to play on her at will; her intellect
was not powerful enough to master their caprices. Her whole behaviour presented a series of inconsistencies; the only letters which
could have awakened her husband's just suspicions, she wrote to a
man who was almost a stranger to her, whilst her love had always an
element of melancholy; with a man she had chosen as a lover, she
ceased to laugh and to jest, she listened to him, and gazed at him
with a look of bewilderment. Sometimes, for the most part suddenly,
this bewilderment passed into chill horror; her face took a wild,
death-like expression; she locked herself up in her bedroom, and
her maid, putting an ear to the keyhole, could hear her smothered
sobs. More than once, as he went home after a tender interview,
Kirsanov felt within him that heartrending, bitter vexation which
follows on a total failure.

"What more do I want?" he asked himself, while his heart was
heavy. He once gave her a ring with a sphinx engraved on the stone.

"What's that?" she asked; "a sphinx?"

"Yes," he answered, "and that sphinx is you."

"I?" she queried, and slowly raising her enigmatical glance upon
him. "Do you know that's awfully flattering?" she added with a
meaningless smile, while her eyes still kept the same strange look.

Pavel Petrovitch suffered even while Princess R— loved him;
but when she grew cold to him, and that happened rather quickly,
he almost went out of his mind. He was on the rack, and he was
jealous; he gave her no peace, followed her about everywhere; she
grew sick of his pursuit of her, and she went abroad. He resigned
his commission in spite of the entreaties of his friends and the
exhortations of his superiors, and followed the princess; four years
he spent in foreign countries, at one time pursuing her, at another

time intentionally losing sight of her. He was ashamed of himself, he was disgusted with his own lack of spirit . . . but nothing availed. Her image, that incomprehensible, almost meaningless, but bewitching image, was deeply rooted in his heart. At Baden he once more regained his old footing with her; it seemed as though she had never loved him so passionately . . . but in a month it was all at an end: the flame flickered up for the last time and went out forever. Foreseeing inevitable separation, he wanted at least to remain her friend, as though friendship with such a woman was possible. . . . She secretly left Baden, and from that time steadily avoided Kirsanov. He returned to Russia, and tried to live his former life again; but he could not get back into the old groove. He wandered from place to place like a man possessed; he still went into society; he still retained the habits of a man of the world; he could boast of two or three fresh conquests; but he no longer expected anything much of himself or of others, and he undertook nothing. He grew old and grey; spending all his evenings at the club, jaundiced and bored, and arguing in bachelor society became a necessity for him —a bad sign, as we all know. Marriage, of course, he did not even think of. Ten years passed in this way; they passed by colourless and fruitless—and quickly, fearfully quickly. Nowhere does time fly as fast as in Russia; in prison they say it flies even faster. One day at dinner at the club, Pavel Petrovitch heard of the death of the Princess R—. She had died at Paris in a state bordering on insanity. He got up from the table, and a long time he paced about the rooms of the club, or stood stockstill near the card-players, but he did not go home earlier than usual. Some time later he received a packet addressed to him; in it was the ring he had given the princess. She had drawn lines in the shape of a cross over the sphinx and sent him word that the solution of the enigma—was the cross.

This happened at the beginning of the year 1848, at the very time when Nikolai Petrovitch came to Petersburg, after the loss of his wife. Pavel Petrovitch had scarcely seen his brother since the latter had settled in the country; the marriage of Nikolai Petrovitch had coincided with the very first days of Pavel Petrovitch's acquaintance with the princess. When he came back from abroad, he had gone to him with the intention of staying a couple of months with him, in sympathetic enjoyment of his happiness, but he had only succeeded in standing a week of it. The difference in the positions of the two brothers was too great. In 1848, this difference had grown less; Nikolai Petrovitch had lost his wife, Pavel Petrovitch had lost his memories; after the death of the princess he tried not to think of her. But to Nikolai, there remained the sense of a well-spent life, his son was growing up under his eyes; Pavel, on the contrary, a solitary bachelor, was entering upon that indefinite twilight period of regrets that are akin to hopes, and hopes that are akin to regrets, when youth is over, while old age has not yet come.

This time was harder for Pavel Petrovitch than for another man; in losing his past, he lost everything.

"I will not invite you to Maryino now," Nikolai Petrovitch said to him one day, (he had called his property by that name in honour of his wife); "you were dull there in my dear wife's time, and now I think you would be bored to death."

"I was stupid and fidgety then," answered Pavel Petrovitch; "since then I have grown quieter, if not wiser. On the contrary, now, if you will let me, I am ready to settle with you for good."

For all answer Nikolai Petrovitch embraced him; but a year and a half passed after this conversation, before Pavel Petrovitch made up his mind to carry out his intention. When he was once settled in the country, however, he did not leave it, even during the three winters which Nikolai Petrovitch spent in Petersburg with his son. He began to read, chiefly English; he arranged his whole life, roughly speaking, in the English style, rarely saw the neighbours, and only went out to the election of marshals, where he was generally silent, only occasionally annoying and alarming land-owners of the old school by his liberal sallies, and not associating with the representatives of the younger generation. Both the latter and the former considered him "stuck up"; and both parties respected him for his fine aristocratic manners; for his reputation for successes in love; for the fact that he was very well dressed and always stayed in the best room in the best hotel; for the fact that he generally dined well, and had once even dined with Wellington at Louis Philippe's table; for the fact that he always took everywhere with him a real silver dressing-case and a portable bath; for the fact that he always smelt of some exceptionally "good form" scent; for the fact that he played whist in masterly fashion, and always lost; and lastly, they respected him also for his incorruptible honesty. Ladies considered him enchantingly romantic, but he did not cultivate ladies' acquaintance. . . .

"So you see, Yevgeny," observed Arkady, as he finished his story, "how unjustly you judge of my uncle! To say nothing of his having more than once helped my father out of difficulties, given him all his money—the property, perhaps you don't know, wasn't divided—he's glad to help any one, among other things he always sticks up for the peasants; it's true, when he talks to them he frowns and sniffs eau de cologne." . . .

"His nerves, no doubt," put in Bazarov.

"Perhaps; but his heart is very good. And he's far from being stupid. What useful advice he has given me especially . . . especially in regard to relations with women."

"Aha! a scalded dog fears cold water, we know that!"

"In short," continued Arkady, "he's profoundly unhappy, believe me; it's a sin to despise him."

"And who does despise him?" retorted Bazarov. "Still, I must say that a fellow who stakes his whole life on one card—a woman's love —and when that card fails, turns sour, and lets himself go till he's fit for nothing, is not a man, not a male. You say he's unhappy; you ought to know best; to be sure, he's not got rid of all his fads. I'm convinced that he solemnly imagines himself a superior creature because he reads that wretched *Galignani*, and once a month saves a peasant from a flogging."

"But remember his education, the age in which he grew up," observed Arkady.

"Education?" broke in Bazarov. "Every man must educate himself, just as I've done, for instance. . . . And as for the age, why should I depend on it? Let it rather depend on me. No, my dear fellow, that's all shallowness, want of backbone! And what stuff it all is, about these mysterious relations between a man and woman? We physiologists know what these relations are. You study the anatomy of the eye; where does the enigmatical glance you talk about come in there? That's all romantic, nonsensical, aesthetic rot. We had much better go and look at the beetle."

And the two friends went off to Bazarov's room, which was already pervaded by a sort of medico-surgical odour, mingled with the smell of cheap tobacco.

VIII

Pavel Petrovitch did not long remain present at his brother's interview with his bailiff, a tall, thin man with a sweet consumptive voice and knavish eyes, who to all Nikolai Petrovitch's remarks answered, "Certainly, sir," and tried to make the peasants out to be thieves and drunkards. The estate had only recently been put on to the new reformed system, and the new mechanism worked, creaking like an ungreased wheel, warping and cracking like home-made furniture of unseasoned wood. Nikolai Petrovitch did not lose heart, but often he sighed, and was gloomy; he felt that the thing could not go on without money, and his money was almot all spent. Arkady had spoken the truth; Pavel Petrovitch had more than once helped his brother; more than once, seeing him struggling and cudgelling his brains, at a loss which way to turn, Pavel Petrovitch moved deliberately to the window, and with his hands thrust into his pockets, muttered between his teeth, *"mais je puis vous donner de l'argent,"*[6] and gave him money; but to-day he had none himself, and he preferred to go away. The petty details of agricultural management worried him; besides, it constantly struck him that Nikolai Petrovitch, for all his zeal and industry, did not set about things in the right way, though he would not have been able to point out precisely where Nikolai Petrovitch's mistake lay. "My brother's not practical enough," he reasoned to himself; "they impose upon him." Nikolai

6. "but I can give you money."

Petrovitch, on the other hand, had the highest opinion of Pavel Petrovitch's practical ability, and always asked his advice. "I'm a soft, weak fellow, I've spent my life in the wilds," he used to say; "while you haven't seen so much of the world for nothing, you see through people; you have an eagle eye." In answer to which Pavel Petrovitch only turned away, but did not contradict his brother.

Leaving Nikolai Petrovitch in his study, he walked along the corridor, which separated the front part of the house from the back; when he had reached a low door, he stopped in hesitation, then pulling his moustaches, he knocked at it.

"Who's there? Come in," sounded Fenitchka's voice.

"It's I," said Pavel Petrovitch, and he opened the door.

Fenitchka jumped up from the chair on which she was sitting with her baby, and giving him into the arms of a girl, who at once carried him out of the room, she put straight her kerchief hastily.

"Pardon me, if I disturb you," began Pavel Petrovitch, not looking at her; "I only wanted to ask you . . . they are sending into the town to-day, I think . . . please let them buy me some green tea."

"Certainly," answered Fenitchka; "how much do you desire them to buy?"

"Oh, half a pound will be enough, I imagine. You have made a change here, I see," he added, with a rapid glance round him, which glided over Fenitchka's face too. "The curtains here," he explained, seeing she did not understand him.

"Oh, yes, the curtains; Nikolai Petrovitch was so good as to make me a present of them; but they have been put up a long while now."

"Yes, and it's a long while since I have been to see you. Now it is very nice here."

"Thanks to Nikolai Petrovitch's kindness," murmured Fenitchka.

"You are more comfortable here than in the little lodge you used to have?" inquired Pavel Petrovitch urbanely, but without the slightest smile.

"Certainly, it's more comfortable."

"Who has been put in your place now?"

"The laundry-maids are there now."

"Ah!"

Pavel Petrovitch was silent. "Now he is going," thought Fenitchka; but he did not go, and she stood before him motionless.

"What did you send your little one away for?" said Pavel Petrovitch at last. "I love children; let me see him."

Fenitchka blushed all over with confusion and delight. She was afraid of Pavel Petrovitch; he had scarcely ever spoken to her.

"Dunyasha," she called: "will you bring Mitya, please." (Fenitchka did not treat any one in the house familiarly.) "But wait a minute, he must have a frock on." Fenitchka was going towards the door.

"That doesn't matter," remarked Pavel Petrovitch.

"I will be back directly," answered Fenitchka, and she went out quickly.

Pavel Petrovitch was left alone, and he looked round this time with special attention. The small low-pitched room in which he found himself was very clean and snug. It smelt of the freshly painted floor and of camomile. Along the walls stood chairs with lyre-shaped backs, bought by the late general on his campaign in Poland; in one corner was a little bedstead under a muslin canopy beside an iron-clamped chest with a convex lid. In the opposite corner a little lamp was burning before a big dark picture of St. Nikolai, the wonder-worker; a tiny porcelain egg hung by a red ribbon from the protruding gold halo down to the saint's breast; by the windows greenish glass jars of last year's jam carefully tied down could be seen; on their paper covers Fenitchka herself had written in big letters "Gooseberry"; Nikolai Petrovitch was particularly fond of that preserve. On a long cord from the ceiling a cage hung with a short-tailed siskin in it; he was constantly chirping and hopping about, the cage was constantly shaking and swinging, while hempseeds fell with a light tap on to the floor. On the wall just above a small chest of drawers hung some rather bad photographs of Nikolai Petrovitch in various attitudes, taken by an itinerant photographer; there too hung a photograph of Fenitchka herself, which was an absolute failure; it was an eyeless face wearing a forced smile, in a dingy frame, nothing more could be made out; while above Fenitchka, General Yermolov, in a Circassian cloak, scowled menacingly upon the Caucasian mountains in the distance, from beneath a little silk shoe for pins which fell right onto his brows.

Five minutes passed; bustling and whispering could be heard in the next room. Pavel Petrovitch took up from the chest of drawers a greasy book, an odd volume of Masalsky's *Musketeers*,[7] and turned over a few pages . . . The door opened, and Fenitchka came in with Mitya in her arms. She had put on him a little red smock with embroidery on the collar, had combed his hair and washed his face; he was breathing heavily, his whole body working, and his little hands waving in the air, as is the way with all healthy babies; but his smart smock obviously impressed him, an expression of delight was reflected in every part of his little fat person. Fenitchka had put her own hair too in order, and had arranged her kerchief; but she might well have remained as she was. And really is there anything in the world more captivating than a beautiful young mother with a healthy baby in her arms?

"What a chubby fellow!" said Pavel Petrovitch graciously, and he tickled Mitya's little double chin with the tapering nail of his

7. an early nineteenth century novel about the Sharpshooters *(Streltsy)* organized by Peter the Great.

forefinger. The baby stared at the siskin, and chuckled.

"That's uncle," said Fenitchka, bending her face down to him and slightly rocking him, while Dunyasha quietly set in the window a smouldering, perfumed stick, putting a half-penny under it.

"How many months old is he?" asked Pavel Petrovitch.

"Six months; it will soon be seven, on the eleventh."

"Isn't it eight, Fedosya Nikolaevna?" put in Dunyasha, with some timidity.

"No, seven; what an idea!" The baby chuckled again, stared at the chest, and suddenly caught hold of his mother's nose and mouth with all his five little fingers. "You little mischief," said Fenitchka, not drawing her face away.

"He's like my brother," observed Pavel Petrovitch.

"Who else should he be like?" thought Fenitchka.

"Yes," continued Pavel Petrovitch, as though speaking to himself; "there's an unmistakable likeness." He looked attentively, almost mournfully, at Fenitchka.

"That's uncle," she repeated, in a whisper this time.

"Ah! Pavel! so you're here!" was heard suddenly the voice of Nikolai Petrovitch.

Pavel Petrovitch turned hurriedly round, frowning; but his brother looked at him with such delight, such gratitude that he could not help responding to his smile.

"You've a splendid little cherub," he said, and looking at his watch. "I came in here to speak about some tea."

And, assuming an expression of indifference, Pavel Petrovitch went out of the room.

"Did he come of himself?" Nikolai Petrovitch asked Fenitchka.

"Yes; he knocked and came in."

"Well, and has Arkasha been in to see you again?"

"No. Hadn't I better move into the lodge, Nikolai Petrovitch?"

"Why so?"

"I wonder whether it wouldn't be best just for the first."

"N—no," Nikolai Petrovitch brought out hesitatingly, rubbing his forehead. "We ought to have done it before. . . . How are you, fatty?" he said, suddenly brightening, and going up to the baby, he kissed him on the cheek; then he bent a little and pressed his lips to Fenitchka's hand, which lay white as milk upon Mitya's little red smock.

"Nikolai Petrovitch! what are you doing?" she whispered, dropping her eyes, then slowly raised them. Very charming was the expression of her eyes when she peeped, as it were, from under her lids, and smiled tenderly and a little foolishly.

Nikolai Petrovitch had made Fenitchka's acquaintance in the following manner. He had once happened three years before to stay a night at an inn in a remote district town. He was agreeably struck by the cleanness of the room assigned to him, the freshness of the bed-linen. Surely the woman of the house must be a German, was the idea that occurred to him; but she proved to be a Russian, a woman of about fifty, neatly dressed, of a good-looking, sensible countenance and discreet speech. He entered into conversation with her at tea; he liked her very much. Nikolai Petrovitch had at that time only just moved into his new home, and not wishing to keep serfs in the house, he was on the lookout for wage-servants; the woman of the inn on her side complained of the small number of visitors to the town, and the hard times; he proposed to her to come into his house in the capacity of housekeeper; she consented. Her husband had long been dead, leaving her an only daughter, Fenitchka. Within a fortnight Arina Savishna (that was the new housekeeper's name) arrived with her daughter at Maryino and installed herself in the little lodge. Nikolai Petrovitch's choice proved a successful one. Arina brought order into the household. As for Fenitchka, who was at that time seventeen, no one spoke of her, and scarcely any one saw her; she lived quietly and sedately, and only on Sundays Nikolai Petrovitch noticed in the church somewhere in a side place the delicate profile of her white face. More than a year passed thus.

One morning, Arina came into his study, and bowing low as usual, she asked him if he could do anything for her daughter, who had got a spark from the stove in her eye. Nikolai Petrovitch, like all stay-at-home people, had studied doctoring and even compiled a homoepathic guide. He at once told Arina to bring the patient to him. Fenitchka was much frightened when she heard the master had sent for her; however, she followed her mother. Nikolai Petrovitch led her to the window and took her head in his two hands. After thoroughly examining her red and swollen eye, he prescribed a fomentation, which he made up himself at once, and tearing his handkerchief in pieces, he showed her how it ought to be applied. Fenitchka listened to all he had to say, and then was going. "Kiss the master's hand, silly girl," said Arina. Nikolai Petrovitch did not give her his hand, and in confusion himself kissed her bent head on the parting of her hair. Fenitchka's eye was soon well again, but the impression she had made on Nikolai Petrovitch did not pass away so quickly. He was forever haunted by that pure, delicate, timidly raised face; he felt on the palms of his hands that soft hair, and saw those innocent, slightly parted lips, through which pearly teeth gleamed with moist brilliance in the sunshine. He began to watch her with great attention in church, and tried to get into conversation with her. At first she was shy of him, and one day meeting him at the approach of evening in a narrow footpath through a field of rye, she ran into the tall thick rye, overgrown with cornflowers and wormwood, so as not to meet him face to face. He caught sight of her little head through a golden network of ears of rye, from which she was peeping out like a little animal, and called affectionately to her:

"Good-evening, Fenitchka! I don't bite."

"Good-evening," she whispered, not coming out of her ambush.

By degrees she began to be more at home with him, but was still shy in his presence, when suddenly her mother, Arina, died of cholera. What was to become of Fenitchka? She inherited from her mother a love for order, regularity, and respectability; but she was so young, so alone. Nikolai Petrovitch was himself so good and considerate. . . . It's needless to relate the rest. . . .

"So my brother came in to see you?" Nikolai Petrovitch questioned her. "He knocked and came in?"

"Yes."

"Well, that's a good thing. Let me give Mitya a swing."

And Nikolai Petrovitch began tossing him almost up to the ceiling, to the huge delight of the baby, and to the considerable uneasiness of the mother, who every time he flew up stretched her arms up towards his little bare legs.

Pavel Petrovitch went back to his artistic study, with its walls covered with handsome bluish-grey hangings, with weapons hanging upon a variegated Persian rug nailed to the wall; with walnut furniture, upholstered in dark green velveteen, with a *renaissance* bookcase of old black oak, with bronze statuettes on the magnificent writing-table, with an open hearth. He threw himself on the sofa, clasped his hands behind his head, and remained without moving, looking with a face almost of despair at the ceiling. Whether he wanted to hide from the very walls that which was reflected in his face, or for some other reason, he got up, drew the heavy window curtains, and again threw himself on the sofa.

IX

On the same day Bazarov made acquaintance with Fenitchka. He was walking with Arkady in the garden, and explaining to him why some of the trees, especially the oaks, had not done well.

"You ought to have planted silver poplars here by preference, and spruce firs, and perhaps limes, giving them some loam. The arbour there has done well," he added, "because it's acacia and lilac; they're accommodating good fellows, those trees, they don't want much care. But there's some one in here."

In the arbour was sitting Fenitchka, with Dunyasha and Mitya. Bazarov stood still, while Arkady nodded to Fenitchka like an old friend.

"Who's that?" Bazarov asked him directly they passed by. "What a pretty girl!"

"Whom are you speaking of?"

"You know; only one of them was pretty."

Arkady, not without embarrassment, explained to him briefly who Fenitchka was.

"Aha!" commented Bazarov; "your father's got good taste, one can see. I like him, your father, ay, ay! He's a jolly fellow. We must make friends though," he added, and turned back towards the arbour.

"Yevgeny!" Arkady cried after him in dismay; "mind what you are about, for mercy's sake."

"Don't worry yourself," said Bazarov; "I know how to behave myself—I'm not a booby."

Going up to Fenitchka, he took off his cap.

"Allow me to introduce myself," he began, with a polite bow. "I'm a harmless person, and a friend of Arkady Nikolaevitch's."

Fenitchka got up from the garden seat and looked at him without speaking.

"What a splendid baby!" continued Bazarov; "don't be uneasy, my praises have never brought ill-luck yet. Why is it his cheeks are so flushed? Is he cutting his teeth?"

"Yes," said Fenitchka; "he has cut four teeth already, and now the gums are swollen again."

"Show me, and don't be afraid, I'm a doctor."

Bazarov took the baby up in his arms, and to the great astonishment both of Fenitchka and Dunyasha the child made no resistance, and was not frightened.

"I see, I see. . . . It's nothing, everything's as it should be; he will have a good set of teeth. If anything goes wrong, tell me. And are you quite well yourself?"

"Quite, thank God."

"Thank God, indeed—that's the great thing. And you?" he added, turning to Dunyasha.

Dunyasha, a girl very prim in the master's house, and a romp outside the gates, only giggled in answer.

"Well, that's all right. Here's your gallant fellow."

Fenitchka received the baby in her arms.

"How good he was with you!" she commented in an undertone.

"Children are always good with me," answered Bazarov; "I have a way with them."

"Children know who love them," remarked Dunyasha.

"Yes, they certainly do," Fenitchka said. "Why, Mitya will not go to some people for anything."

"Will he come to me?" asked Arkady, who, after standing in the distance for some time, had gone up to the arbour.

He tried to entice Mitya to come to him, but Mitya threw his head back and screamed. to Fenitchka's great confusion.

788 · *Ivan Turgenev*

"Another day, when he's had time to get used to me," said Arkady indulgently, and the two friends walked away.

"What's her name?" asked Bazarov.

"Fenitchka . . . Fedosya," answered Arkady.

"And her father's name? One must know that too."

"Nikolaevna."

"*Bene.* What I like in her is that she's not too embarrassed. Some people, I suppose, would think ill of her for it. What nonsense! What is there to embarrass her? She's a mother—she's all right."

"She's all right," observed Arkady,—"but my father."

"And he's right too," put in Bazarov.

"Well, no, I don't think so."

"I suppose an extra heir's not to your liking?"

"I wonder you're not ashamed to attribute such ideas to me!" retorted Arkady hotly; "I can't consider my father wrong from that point of view. I think he ought to marry her."

"Hoity-toity!" responded Bazarov tranquilly. "What magnanimous fellows we are! You still attach significance to marriage; I did not expect that of you."

The friends walked a few paces in silence.

"I have looked at all your father's establishment," Bazarov began again. "The cattle are inferior, the horses are broken down; the buildings aren't up to much, and the workmen look confirmed loafers; while the superintendent is either a fool, or a knave, I haven't quite found out which yet."

"You are rather hard on everything to-day, Yevgeny Vassilye-vitch."

"And the dear good peasants are taking your father in to a dead certainty. You know the Russian proverb, 'The Russian peasant will cheat God Himself.' "

"I begin to agree with my uncle," remarked Arkady; "you certainly have a poor opinion of Russians."

"As though that mattered! The only good point in a Russian is his having the lowest possible opinion of himself. What does matter is that two and two make four, and the rest is all foolery."

"And is nature foolery?" said Arkady, looking pensively at the bright-coloured fields in the distance, in the beautiful soft light of the sun, which was not yet high up in the sky.

"Nature, too, is foolery in the sense you understand it. Nature's not a temple, but a workshop, and man's the workman in it."

At that instant, the long drawn notes of a violoncello floated out to them from the house. Some one was playing Schubert's *Expectation* with much feeling though with an untrained hand, and the melody flowed with honey sweetness through the air.

"What's that?" cried Bazarov in amazement.

"It's my father."

"Your father plays the violoncello?"

"Yes."

"And how old is your father?"

"Forty-four."

Bazarov suddenly burst into a roar of laughter.

"What are you laughing at?"

"Upon my word, a man of forty-four, a *paterfamilias* in this out-of-the-way district, playing on the violoncello!"

Bazarov went on laughing; but much as he revered his master, this time Arkady did not even smile.

x

About a fortnight passed by. Life at Maryino went on its accustomed course, while Arkady was lazy and enjoyed himself, and Bazarov worked. Every one in the house had grown used to him, to his careless manners, and his curt and abrupt speeches. Fenitchka, in particular, was so far at home with him that one night she sent to wake him up; Mitya had had convulsions; and he had gone, and, half joking, half-yawning as usual, he stayed two hours with her and relieved the child. On the other hand Pavel Petrovitch had grown to detest Bazarov with all the strength of his soul; he regarded him as stuck-up, impudent, cynical, and vulgar; he suspected that Bazarov had no respect for him, that he had all but contempt for him—him, Pavel Kirsanov! Nikolai Petrovitch was rather afraid of the young "nihilist," and was doubtful whether his influence over Arkady was for the good; but he was glad to listen to him, and was glad to be present at his scientific and chemical experiments. Bazarov had brought with him a microscope, and busied himself for hours together with it. The servants, too, took to him, though he made fun of them; they felt, all the same, that he was one of themselves, not a master. Dunyasha was always ready to giggle with him, and used to cast significant and stealthy glances at him when she skipped by like a rabbit; Piotr, a man vain and stupid to the last degree, for ever wearing an affected frown on his brow, a man whose whole merit consisted in the fact that he looked civil, could spell out a page of reading, and was diligent in brushing his coat—even he smirked and brightened up directly Bazarov paid him any attention; the boys on the farm simply ran after the "doctor" like puppies. The old man Prokofitch was the only one who did not like him; he handed him the dishes at table with a surly face, called him a "butcher" and "an upstart," and declared that with his great whiskers he looked like a pig in a stye. Prokofitch in his own way was quite as much of an aristocrat as Pavel Petrovitch.

The best days of the year had come—the first days of June. The weather kept splendidly fine; in the distance, it is true, the cholera was threatening, but the inhabitants of that province had had time to get used to its visits. Bazarov used to get up very early and go out for two or three miles, not for a walk—he couldn't bear walking without an object—but to collect specimens of plants and insects. Sometimes he took Arkady with him. On the way home an argument usually sprang up, and Arkady was usually vanquished in it, though he said more than his companion.

One day they had lingered rather late; Nikolai Petrovitch went to meet them in the garden, and as he reached the arbour he suddenly heard the quick step and voices of the two young men. They were walking on the other side of the arbour, and could not see him.

"You don't know my father well enough," said Arkady.

"Your father's a nice chap," said Bazarov, "but he's behind the times; his day is done."

Nikolai Petrovitch listened intently. . . . Arkady made no answer.

The man whose day was done remained two minutes motionless, and stole slowly home.

"The day before yesterday I saw him reading Pushkin," Bazarov was continuing meanwhile. "Explain to him, please, that that's no earthly use. He's not a boy, you know; it's time to throw out that rubbish. And what an idea to be a romantic at this time of day! Give him something sensible to read."

"What ought I to give him?" asked Arkady.

"Oh, I think Büchner's *Stoff und Kraft*[8] to begin with."

"I think so, too," observed Arkady approvingly, "*Stoff und Kraft* is written in popular language. . . ."

"So it seems," Nikolai Petrovitch said the same day after dinner to his brother, as he sat in his study, "you and I are behind the times, our day's over. Well, well. Perhaps Bazarov is right; but one thing I confess, makes me feel sore; I did so hope, precisely now, to get on to such close, intimate terms with Arkady, and it turns out I'm left behind, and he has gone forward, and we can't understand one another."

"How has he gone forward? And in what way is he so superior to us already?" cried Pavel Petrovitch impatiently. "It's that high and mighty gentleman, that nihilist, who's knocked all that into his head. I hate that doctor fellow; in my opinion, he's simply a quack; I'm convinced, for all his tadpoles, he's not got very far even in medicine."

"No, brother, you mustn't say that; Bazarov is clever, and knows his subject."

"And his conceit's something revolting," Pavel Petrovitch broke in again.

"Yes," observed Nikolai Petrovitch, "he is conceited. But there's

8. Ludwig Büchner (1824–1899), a German physician, published *Kraft und Stoff* (Energy and Matter) in 1855. Büchner expounds materialism, the view that only matter and energy exist and that both are imperishable. Turgenev mistakenly reversed the words in the title.

no doing without that, it seems; only that's what I did not take into account. I thought I was doing everything to keep up with the times; I have started a model farm; I have done well by the peasants, so that I am positively called a "Red Radical" all over the province; I read, I study, I try in every way to keep abreast with the requirements of the day—and they say my day's over. And, brother, I begin to think that it is."

"Why so?"

"I'll tell you why. This morning I was sitting reading Pushkin. ...I remember, it happened to be *The Gipsies* ...all of a sudden Arkady came up to me, and, without speaking, with such a kindly compassion on his face, as gently as if I were a baby, took the book away from me, and laid another before me—a German book... smiled, and went away, carrying Pushkin off with him."

"Upon my word! What book did he give you?"

"This one here."

And Nikolai Petrovitch pulled the famous treatise of Büchner, in the ninth edition, out of his coat-tail pocket.

Pavel Petrovitch turned it over in his hands. "Hm!" he growled. "Arkady Nikolaevitch is taking your education in hand. Well, did you try reading it?"

"Yes, I tried it."

"Well, what did you think of it?"

"Either I'm stupid, or it's all—nonsense. I must be stupid, I suppose."

"Haven't you forgotten your German?" queried Pavel Petrovitch.

"Oh, I understand the German."

Pavel Petrovitch again turned the book over in his hands, and glanced from under his brows at his brother. Both were silent.

"Oh, by the way," began Nikolai Petrovitch, obviously wishing to change the subject, "I've got a letter from Kolyazin."

"Matvy Ilyitch?"

"Yes. He has come to—to inspect the province. He's quite a big-wig now; and writes to me that, as a relation, he should like to see us again, and invites you and me and Arkady to the town."

"Are you going?" asked Pavel Petrovitch.

"No; are you?"

"No, I shan't go either. Much object there would be in dragging oneself over forty miles on a wild-goose chase. *Mathieu* wants to show himself in all his glory. Damn him! he will have the whole province doing him homage; he can get on without the likes of us. A grand dignity, indeed, a privy councillor! If I had stayed in the service, if I had trudged on in official harness, I should have been a general-adjutant by now. Besides, you and I are behind the times, you know."

"Yes, brother; it's time, it seems, to order a coffin and cross one's arms on one's breast," remarked Nikolai Petrovitch, with a sigh.

"Well, I'm not going to give in quite so soon," muttered his brother. "I've got a tussle with that doctor fellow before me, I feel sure of that."

A tussle came off that same day at evening tea. Pavel Petrovitch came into the drawing-room, all ready for the fray, irritable and determined. He was only waiting for an excuse to fall upon the enemy; but for a long while an excuse did not present itself. As a rule, Bazarov said little in the presence of the "old Kirsanovs" (that was how he spoke of the brothers), and that evening he felt out of humour, and drank off cup after cup of tea without a word. Pavel Petrovitch was all aflame with impatience; his wishes were fulfilled at last.

The conversation turned on one of the neighbouring landowners. "Rotten aristocratic snob," observed Bazarov indifferently. He had met him in Petersburg.

"Allow me to ask you," began Pavel Petrovitch, and his lips were trembling, "according to your ideas, have the words 'rotten' and 'aristocrat' the same meaning?"

"I said 'aristocratic snob,' " replied Bazarov, lazily swallowing a sip of tea.

"Precisely so; but I imagine you have the same opinion of aristocrats as of aristocratic snobs. I think it my duty to inform you that I do not share that opinion. I venture to assert that every one knows me for a man of liberal ideas and devoted to progress; but, exactly for that reason, I respect aristocrats—real aristocrats. Kindly remember, sir" (at these words Bazarov lifted his eyes and looked at Pavel Petrovitch), "kindly remember, sir," he repeated, with acrimony— "the English aristocracy. They do not abate one iota of their rights, and for that reason they respect the rights of others; they demand the performance of what is due to them, and for that reason they perform their own duties. The aristocracy has given freedom to England, and maintains it for her."

"We've heard that story a good many times," replied Bazarov; "but what are you trying to prove by that?"

"I am tryin' to prove that, sir" (when Pavel Petrovitch was angry he intentionally clipped his words in this way, though, of course, he knew very well that such forms are not strictly grammatical. In this fashionable whim could be discerned a survival of the habits of the times of Alexander. The exquisites of those days, on the rare occasions when they spoke their own language, made use of such slipshod forms; as much as to say, "We, of course, are born Russians, at the same time we are great swells, who are at liberty to neglect the rules of scholars"); "I am tryin' to prove by that, sir, that without the sense of personal dignity, without self-respect—and these two sentiments are well developed in the aristocrat—there is no secure foundation for the social . . . *bien public* . . . the social fabric. Personal character, sir—that is the chief thing; a man's personal character must be firm as a rock, since everything is built on it. I am very well aware, for instance, that you are pleased to consider my habits, my dress, my refinements, in fact, ridiculous; but all that proceeds from a sense of self-respect, from a sense of duty— yes, indeed, of duty. I live in the country, in the wilds, but I will not lower myself. I respect the dignity of man in myself."

"Let me ask you, Pavel Petrovitch," commented Bazarov; "you respect yourself, and sit with your hands folded; what sort of benefit does that do to the *bien public*? If you didn't respect yourself, you'd do just the same."

Pavel Petrovitch turned white. "That's a different question. It's absolutely unnecessary for me to explain to you now why I sit with folded hands, as you are pleased to express yourself. I wish only to tell you that aristocracy is a principle, and in our days none but immoral or silly people can live without principles. I said that to Arkady the day after he came home, and I repeat it now. Isn't it so, Nikolai?"

Nikolai Petrovitch nodded his head. "Aristocracy, Liberalism, progress, principles," Bazarov was saying meanwhile; "if you think of it, what a lot of foreign . . . and useless words! To a Russian they're good for nothing."

"What is good for something according to you? If we listen to you, we shall find ourselves outside humanity, outside its laws. Come —the logic of history demands . . ."

"But what's that logic to us? We can get on without that too."

"How do you mean?"

"Why, this. You don't need logic, I hope, to put a bit of bread in your mouth when you're hungry. What's the object of these abstractions to us?"

Pavel Petrovitch raised his hands in horror.

"I don't understand you, after that. You insult the Russian people. I don't understand how it's possible not to acknowledge principles, rules! By virtue of what do you act then?"

"I've told you already, uncle, that we don't accept any authorities," put in Arkady.

"We act by virtue of what we recognise as beneficial," observed Bazarov. "At the present time, negation is the most beneficial of all—and we deny—"

"Everything?"

"Everything!"

"What, not only art and poetry . . . but even . . . horrible to say . . ."

"Everything," repeated Bazarov, with indescribable composure.

Pavel Petrovitch stared at him. He had not expected this; while

Arkady fairly blushed with delight.

"Allow me, though," began Nikolai Petrovitch. "You deny everything; or speaking more precisely, you destroy everything. . . . But one must construct too, you know."

"That's not our business now. . . . The ground wants clearing first."

"The present condition of the people requires it," added Arkady, with dignity; "we are bound to carry out these requirements, we have no right to yield to the satisfaction of our personal egoism."

This last phrase obviously displeased Bazarov; there was a flavour of philosophy, that is to say, romanticism about it, for Bazarov called philosophy, too, romanticism, but he did not think it necessary to correct his young disciple.

"No, no!" cried Pavel Petrovitch, with sudden energy. "I'm not willing to believe that you, young men, know the Russian people really, that you are the representatives of their requirements, their efforts! No; the Russian people is not what you imagine it. Tradition it holds sacred; it is a patriarchal people; it cannot live without faith . . ."

"I'm not going to dispute that," Bazarov interrupted. "I'm even ready to agree that in that you're right."

"But if I am right . . ."

"And, all the same, that proves nothing."

"It just proves nothing," repeated Arkady, with the confidence of a practised chess-player, who has foreseen an apparently dangerous move on the part of his adversary, and so is not at all taken aback by it.

"How does it prove nothing?" muttered Pavel Petrovitch, astounded. "You must be going against the people then?"

"And what if we are?" shouted Bazarov. "The people imagine that, when it thunders, the prophet Ilya's riding across the sky in his chariot. What then? Are we to agree with them? Besides, the people's Russian; but am I not Russian, too?"

"No, you are not Russian, after all you have just been saying! I can't acknowledge you as Russian."

"My grandfather ploughed the land," answered Bazarov with haughty pride. "Ask any one of your peasants which of us—you or me—he'd more readily acknowledge as a fellow-countryman. You don't even know how to talk to them."

"While you talk to him and despise him at the same time."

"Well, suppose he deserves contempt. You find fault with my attitude, but how do you know that I have got it by chance, that it's not a product of that very national spirit, in the name of which you wage war on it?"

"What an idea! Much use in nihilists!"

"Whether they're of use or not, is not for us to decide. Why, even suppose you're not a useless person."

"Gentlemen, gentlemen, no personalities, please!" cried Nikolai

Petrovitch, getting up.

Pavel Petrovitch smiled, and laying his hand on his brother's shoulder, forced him to sit down again.

"Don't be uneasy," he said; "I shall not forget myself, just through that sense of dignity which is made fun of so mercilessly by our friend—our friend, the doctor. Let me ask," he resumed, turning again to Bazarov; "you suppose, possibly that your doctrine is a novelty? That is quite a mistake. The materialism you advocate has been more than once in vogue already, and has always proved insufficient . . ."

"A foreign word again!" broke in Bazarov. He was beginning to feel vicious, and his face assumed a peculiar coarse coppery hue. "In the first place, we advocate nothing; that's not our way."

"What do you do, then?"

"I'll tell you what we do. Not long ago we used to say that our officials took bribes, that we had no roads, no commerce, no real justice . . ."

"Oh, I see, you are reformers—that's what that's called, I fancy. I too should agree to many of your reforms, but . . ."

"Then we suspected that talk, perpetual talk, and nothing but talk, about our social diseases, was not worth while, that it all led to nothing but superficiality and pedantry; we saw that our leading men, so-called advanced people and reformers, are no good; that we busy ourselves over foolery, talk rubbish about art, unconscious creativeness, parliamentarism, trial by jury, and the deuce knows what all; while, all the while, it's a question of getting bread to eat, while we're stifling under the grossest superstition, while all our enterprises come to grief, simply because there aren't honest men enough to carry them on, while the very emancipation our Government's busy upon will hardly come to any good, because peasants are glad to rob even themselves to get drunk at the gin-shop."

"Yes," interposed Pavel Petrovitch, "yes; you were convinced of all this, and decided not to undertake anything seriously, yourselves."

"We decided not to undertake anything," repeated Bazarov grimly. He suddenly felt vexed with himself for having, without reason, been so expansive before this gentleman.

"But to confine yourselves to abuse?"

"To confine ourselves to abuse."

"And that is called nihilism?"

"And that's called nihilism," Bazarov repeated again, this time with peculiar rudeness.

Pavel Petrovitch puckered up his face a little. "So that's it!" he observed in a strangely composed voice. "Nihilism is to cure all our woes, and you, you are our heroes and saviours. But why do you abuse others, those reformers even? Don't you do as much talking as every one else?"

"Whatever faults we have, we do not err in that way," Bazarov muttered between his teeth.

"What, then? Do you act, or what? Are you preparing for action?"

Bazarov made no answer. Something like a tremor passed over Pavel Petrovitch, but he at once regained control of himself.

"Hm! . . . Action, destruction . . ." he went on. "But how destroy without even knowing why?"

"We shall destroy, because we are a force," observed Arkady.

Pavel Petrovitch looked at his nephew and laughed.

"Yes, a force is not to be called to account," said Arkady, drawing himself up.

"Unhappy boy!" wailed Pavel Petrovitch, he was positively incapable of maintaining his firm demeanour any longer. "If you could only realise what it is you are doing to your country. No; it's enough to try the patience of an angel! Force! There's force in the savage Kalmuck, in the Mongolian; but what is it to us? What is precious to us is civilisation; yes, yes, sir, its fruits are precious to us. And don't tell me those fruits are worthless; the poorest dauber, *un barbouilleur*, the man who plays dance music for five kopeks an evening, is of more use than you, because they are the representatives of civilisation, and not of brute Mongolian force! You fancy yourselves advanced people, and all the while you are only fit for the Kalmuck's hovel! Force! And recollect, you forcible gentlemen, that you're only four men and a half, and the others are millions, who won't let you trample their sacred traditions under foot, who will crush you and walk over you!"

"If we're crushed, serves us right," observed Bazarov. "But that's an open question. We are not so few as you suppose."

"What? You seriously suppose you will come to terms with a whole people?"

"All Moscow was burnt down, you know, by a kopek candle," answered Bazarov.

"Yes, yes. First a pride almost Satanic, then ridicule—that, that's what it is attracts the young, that's what gains an ascendancy over the inexperienced hearts of boys! Here's one of them sitting beside you, ready to worship the ground under your feet. Look at him! (Arkady turned away and frowned.) And this plague has spread far already. I have been told that in Rome our artists never set foot in the Vatican. Raphael they regard as almost a fool, because, if you please, he's an authority; while they're all the while most disgustingly sterile and unsuccessful, men whose imagination does not soar beyond 'Girls at a Fountain,' however they try! And the girls even out of drawing. They are fine fellows to your mind, are they not?"

"To my mind," retorted Bazarov, "Raphael's not worth a brass farthing; and they're no better than he."

"Bravo! bravo! Listen, Arkady . . . that's how young men of to-day ought to express themselves! And if you come to think of it, how could they fail if they followed you! In old days, young men had to study; they didn't want to be called dunces, so they had to work hard whether they liked it or not. But now, they need only say, 'Everything in the world is foolery!' and the trick's done. Young men are delighted. And, to be sure, they were simply blockheads before, and now they have suddenly turned nihilists."

"Your praiseworthy sense of personal dignity has given way," remarked Bazarov phlegmatically, while Arkady was hot all over, and his eyes were flashing. "Our argument has gone too far; it's better to cut it short, I think. I shall be quite ready to agree with you," he added, getting up, "when you bring forward a single institution in our present mode of life, in family or in social life, which does not call for complete and unqualified destruction."

"I will bring forward millions of such institutions," cried Pavel Petrovitch—"millions! Well—the Mir, for instance."

A cold smile curved Bazarov's lips. "Well, as regards the Mir," he commented; "you had better talk to your brother. He has seen by now, I should fancy, what sort of thing the Mir is in fact—its common guarantee, its sobriety, and other features of the kind."

"The family, then, the family as it exists among our peasants!" cried Pavel Petrovitch.

"And that subject, too, I imagine, it will be better for yourselves not to go into in detail. Don't you realise all the advantages of the head of the family choosing his daughters in law? Take my advice, Pavel Petrovitch, allow yourself two days to think about it; you're not likely to find anything on the spot. Go through all our classes, and think well over each, while I and Arkady will . . ."

"Will go on turning everything into ridicule," broke in Pavel Petrovitch.

"No, will go on dissecting frogs. Come, Arkady; good-bye for the present, gentlemen!"

The two friends walked off. The brothers were left alone, and at first they only looked at one another.

"So that," began Pavel Petrovitch, "so that's what our young men of this generation are! They are like that—our successors!"

"Our successors!" repeated Nikolai Petrovitch, with a dejected smile. He had been sitting on thorns, all through the argument, and had done nothing but glance stealthily, with a sore heart, at Arkady. "Do you know what I was reminded of, brother? I once had a dispute with our poor mother; she stormed, and wouldn't listen to me. At last I said to her, 'Of course, you can't understand me; we belong,' I said, 'to two different generations.' She was dreadfully offended, while I thought, 'There's no help for it. It's a bitter pill, but she has to swallow it.' You see, now, our turn has come, and our successors can say to us, 'You are not of our generation;

swallow your pill.' "

"You are beyond everything in your generosity and modesty," replied Pavel Petrovitch. "I'm convinced, on the contrary, that you and I are far more in the right than these young gentlemen, though we do perhaps express ourselves in old-fashioned language, *vieilli*, and have not the same insolent conceit. . . . And the swagger of the young men nowadays! You ask one, 'Do you take red wine or white?' 'It is my custom to prefer red!' he answers, in a deep bass, with a face as solemn as if the whole universe had its eyes on him at that instant. . . ."

"Do you care for any more tea?" asked Fenitchka, putting her head in at the door; she had not been able to make up her mind to come into the drawing-room while there was the sound of voices in dispute there.

"No, you can tell them to take the samovar," answered Nikolai Petrovitch, and he got up to meet her. Pavel Petrovitch said "*bon soir*" to him abruptly, and went away to his study.

XI

Half an hour later Nikolai Petrovitch went into the garden to his favorite arbour. He was overtaken by melancholy thoughts. For the first time he realised clearly the distance between him and his son; he foresaw that every day it would grow wider and wider. In vain, then, had he spent whole days sometimes in the winter at Petersburg over the newest books; in vain had he listened to the talk of the young men; in vain had he rejoiced when he succeeded in putting in his word, too, in their heated discussions. "My brother says we are right," he thought, "and apart from all vanity, I do think myself that they are further from the truth than we are, though at the same time I feel there is something behind them we have not got, some superiority over us. . . . Is it youth? No; not only youth. Doesn't their superiority consist in there being fewer traces of the slave-owner in them than in us?"

Nikolai Petrovitch's head sank despondently, and he passed his hand over his face.

"But to renounce poetry?" he thought again; "to have no feeling for art, for nature . . ."

And he looked round, as though trying to understand how it was possible to have no feeling for nature. It was already evening; the sun was hidden behind a small copse of aspens which lay a quarter of a mile from the garden; its shadow stretched indefinitely across the still fields. A peasant on a white nag went at a trot along the dark, narrow path close beside the copse; his whole figure was clearly visible even to the patch on his shoulder, in spite of his being in the shade; the horse's hoofs flew along bravely. The sun's rays from the farther side fell full on the copse, and piercing through its thickets, threw such a warm light on the aspen trunks that they looked like pines, and their leaves were almost a dark blue, while above them rose a pale blue sky, faintly tinged by the glow of sunset. The swallows flew high; the wind had quite died away, belated bees hummed slowly and drowsily among the lilac blossoms; a swarm of midges hung like a cloud over a solitary branch which stood out against the sky. "How beautiful, my God!" thought Nikolai Petrovitch, and his favourite verses were almost on his lips; he remembered Arkady's *Stoff und Kraft*—and was silent, but still he sat there, still he gave himself up to the sorrowful consolation of solitary thought. He was fond of dreaming; his country life had developed the tendency in him. How short a time ago, he had been dreaming like this, waiting for his son at the posting station, and what a change already since that day; their relations that were then undefined, were defined now—and how defined! Again his dead wife came back to his imagination, but not as he had known her for many years, not as the good domestic housewife, but as a young girl with a slim figure, innocently inquiring eyes, and a tight twist of hair on her childish neck. He remembered how he had seen her for the first time. He was still a student then. He had met her on the staircase of his lodgings, and, jostling by accident against her, he tried to apologise, and could only mutter, "*Pardon, monsieur,*" while she bowed, smiled, and suddenly seemed frightened, and ran away, though at the bend of the staircase she had glanced rapidly at him, assumed a serious air, and blushed. Afterwards, the first timid visits, the half-words, the half-smiles, and embarrassment; and melancholy, and yearnings, and at last that breathing rapture.... Where had it all vanished? She had been his wife, he had been happy as few on earth are happy. ... "But," he mused, "these sweet first moments, why could not one live an eternal, undying life in them?"

He did not try to make his thought clear to himself; but he felt that he longed to keep that blissful time by something stronger than memory; he longed to feel his Marya near him again to have the sense of her warmth and breathing, and already he could fancy that over him. ...

"Nikolai Petrovitch," came the sound of Fenitchka's voice close by him; "where are you?"

He started. He felt no pang, no shame. He never even admitted the possibility of comparison between his wife and Fenitchka, but he was sorry she had thought of coming to look for him. Her voice had brought back to him at once his grey hairs, his age, his reality. ...

The enchanted world into which he was just stepping, which was just rising out of the dim mists of the past, was shaken—and vanished.

"I'm here," he answered; "I'm coming, run along." "There it is, the traces of the slave owner," flashed through his mind. Fenitchka peeped into the arbour at him without speaking, and disappeared; while he noticed with astonishment that the night had come on while he had been dreaming. Everything around was dark and hushed. Fenitchka's face had glimmered so pale and slight before him. He got up, and was about to go home; but the emotion stirred in his heart could not be soothed at once, and he began slowly walking about the garden, sometimes looking at the ground at his feet, and then raising his eyes towards the sky where swarms of stars were twinkling. He walked a great deal, till he was almost tired out, while the restlessness within him, a kind of yearning, vague, melancholy restlessness, still was not appeased. Oh, how Bazarov would have laughed at him, if he had known what was passing within him then! Arkady himself would have condemned him. He, a man forty-four years old, an agriculturist and a farmer, was shedding tears, causeless tears; this was a hundred times worse than the violoncello.

Nikolai Petrovitch continued walking, and could not make up his mind to go into the house, into the snug peaceful nest, which looked out at him so hospitably from all its lighted windows; he had not the force to tear himself away from the darkness, the garden, the sense of the fresh air in his face, from that melancholy, that restless craving.

At a turn in the path, he was met by Pavel Petrovitch. "What's the matter with you?" he asked Nikolai Petrovitch; "you are as white as a ghost; you are not well; why don't you go to bed?" Nikolai Petrovitch explained to him briefly his state of feeling and moved away. Pavel Petrovitch went to the end of the garden, and he too grew thoughtful, and he too raised his eyes toward the heavens. But in his beautiful dark eyes, nothing was reflected but the light of the stars. He was not born an idealist, and his fastidiously dry and sensuous soul, with its French tinge of cynicism was not capable of dreaming. . . .

"Do you know what?" Bazarov was saying to Arkady the same night. "I've got a splendid idea. Your father was saying to-day that he'd had an invitation from your illustrious relative. Your father's not going; let us be off to X—; you know the worthy man invites you too. You see what fine weather it is; we'll stroll about and look at the town. We'll have five or six days' outing, and enjoy ourselves."

"And you'll come back here again?"

"No; I must go to my father's. You know, he lives about twenty-five miles from X—. I've not seen him for a long while, and my mother too; I must cheer the old people up. They've been good to me, especially my father; he's awfully funny. I'm their only one too."

"And will you be long with them?"

"I don't suppose so. It will be dull, of course."

"And you'll come to us on your way back?"

"I don't know . . . I'll see. Well, what do you say? Shall we go?"

"If you like," observed Arkady languidly.

In his heart he was highly delighted with his friend's suggestion, but he thought it a duty to conceal his feeling. He was not a nihilist for nothing!

The next day he set off with Bazarov to X——. The younger part of the household at Maryino were sorry at their going; Dunyasha even cried . . . but the old folks breathed more easily.

XII

The town of X—— to which our friends set off was in the jurisdiction of a governor who was a young man, and at once a progressive and a despot, as often happens with Russians. Before the end of the first year of his government, he had managed to quarrel not only with the marshal of nobility, a retired officer of the guards, who kept open house and a stud of horses, but even with his own subordinates. The feuds arising from this cause assumed at last such proportions that the ministry in Petersburg had found it necessary to send down a trusted personage with a commission to investigate it all on the spot. The choice of the authorities fell upon Matvy Ilyitch Kolyazin, the son of the Kolyazin, under whose protection the brothers Kirsanov had once found themselves. He, too, was a "young man"; that is to say, he had not long passed forty, but he was already on the high road to becoming a statesman, and wore a star on each side of his breast—one, to be sure, a foreign star, not of the first magnitude. Like the governor, whom he had come down to pass judgment upon, he was reckoned a progressive; and though he was already a bigwig, he was not like the majority of bigwigs. He had the highest opinion of himself; his vanity knew no bounds, but he behaved simply, looked affably, listened condescendingly, and laughed so good-naturedly, that on a first acquaintance he might even be taken for "a jolly good fellow." On important occasions, however, he knew, as the saying is, how to make his authority felt. "Energy is essential," he used to say then, "*l'energie est la première qualité d'un homme d'état*"[9]; and for all that, he was usually taken in, and any moderately experienced official could turn him round his finger. Matvy Ilyitch used to speak with great respect of Guizot[10] and tried to impress every one with the idea that he did not belong to the class of *routiniers* and high-and-dry bureaucrats, that not a single phenomenon of social life passed unnoticed by him. . . . All such phrases were very familiar to him. He even followed, with dignified indifference, it is true, the development of contemporary literature; so a grown-up man who meets a procession of small boys in the street will sometimes walk after it. In reality, Matvy Ilyitch had not got

9. "energy is the first quality of a statesman."

10. François Guizot (1787–1874) was a famous French historian, orator, and statesman who served King Louis-Philippe (1830–1848) as Minister of Public Instruction, Ambassador to England, and Minister of Foreign Affairs. He was a vigorous defender of constitutional monarchy.

much beyond those political men of the days of Alexander, who used to prepare for an evening party at Madame Svyetchin's[11] by reading a page of Condillac[12]; only his methods were different, more modern. He was an adroit courtier, a great hypocrite, and nothing more; he had no special aptitude for affairs, and no intellect, but he knew how to manage his own business successfully; no one could get the better of him there, and, to be sure, that's the principal thing.

Matvy Ilyitch received Arkady with the good-nature, we might even call it playfulness, characteristic of the enlightened higher official. He was astonished, however, when he heard that the cousins he had invited had remained at home in the country. "Your father was always a queer fellow," he remarked, playing with the tassels of his magnificent velvet dressing-gown, and suddenly turning to a young official in a discreetly buttoned-up uniform, he cried, with an air of concentrated attention, "What?" The young man, whose lips were glued together from prolonged silence, got up and looked in perplexity at his chief. But, having nonplussed his subordinate, Matvy Ilyitch paid him no further attention. Our higher officials are fond as a rule of nonplussing their subordinates; the methods to which they have recourse to attain that end are rather various. The following means, among others, is in great vogue, "*is quite a favourite*," as the English say; a high official suddenly ceases to understand the simplest words, assuming total deafness. He will ask, for instance, "What's to-day?"

He is respectfully informed, "Today's Friday, your Ex-s-s-s-lency."

"Eh? What? What's that? What do you say?" the great man repeats with intense attention.

"Today's Friday, your Ex—s—s—lency."

"Eh? What? What's Friday? What Friday?"

"Friday, your Ex—s—s—s—lency, the day of the week."

"What, do you pretend to teach me, eh?"

Matvy Ilyitch was a higher official all the same, though he was reckoned a liberal.

"I advise you, my dear boy, to go and call on the Governor," he said to Arkady, "you understand, I don't advise you to do so because I adhere to old-fashioned ideas of the necessity of paying respect to authorities, but simply because the Governor's a very decent fellow; besides, you probably want to make acquaintance with the society here. . . . You're not a bear, I hope? And he's giving a great ball the day after to-morrow."

"Will you be at the ball?" inquired Arkady.

11. Anne Sophie Soymonov Svyechin (1715–1780) was a French philosopher later in Paris.
12. Étienne Bonnot de Condillac (1782–1857) was a Russian author who had a literary *salon* in St. Petersburg and who propounded a psychology based on sensation. Turgenev probably alludes to Condillac's many-volumed *Cours d'études* (Course of Studies), an elementary textbook written for the young Duke of Parma which the courtiers of Alexander read up in preparation for an evening party.

"He gives it in my honour," answered Matvy Ilyitch, almost pity-ingly. "Do you dance?"

"Yes; I dance, but not well."

"That's a pity! There are pretty girls here, and it's a disgrace for a young man not to dance. Again, I don't say that through any old-fashioned ideas; I don't in the least imagine that a man's wit lies in his feet, but Byronism is ridiculous, *il a fait son temps.*"[13]

"But, uncle, it's not through Byronism, I . . . ."

"I will introduce you to the ladies here; I will take you under my wing," interrupted Matvy Ilyitch, and he laughed complacently. "You'll find it warm, eh?"

A servant entered and announced the arrival of the superintendent of the Crown domains, a mild-eyed old man, with deep creases round his mouth, who was excessively fond of nature, especially on a sum-mer day, when, in his words, "every little busy bee takes a little bribe from every little flower." Arkady withdrew.

He found Bazarov at the tavern where they were staying, and was a long while persuading him to go with him to the Governor's. "Well, there's no help for it," said Bazarov at last. "It's no good doing things by halves. We came to look at the gentry; let's look at them!"

The Governor received the young men affably, but he did not ask them to sit down, nor did he sit down himself. He was in an everlasting fuss and hurry; in the morning he used to put on a tight uniform and an excessively stiff cravat; he never ate or drank enough; he was for ever making arrangements. He invited Kirsanov and Ba-zarov to his ball, and within a few minutes invited them a second time, regarding them as brothers, and calling them Kisarov.

They were on their way home from the Governor's, when sud-denly a short man, in a Slavophil national dress, leaped out of a trap that was passing them, and crying, "Yevgeny Vassilyitch!" dashed up to Bazarov.

"Ah! it's you, Herr Sitnikov," observed Bazarov, still stepping along on the pavement; "by what chance did you come here?"

"Fancy, absolutely by chance," he replied, and returning to the trap, he waved his hand several times, and shouted, "Follow, follow us! My father had business here," he went on, hopping across the gutter, "and so he asked me. . . . I heard to-day of your arrival, and have already been to see you. . . ." (The friends did, in fact, on returning to their room, find there a card, with the corners turned down, bearing the name of Sitnikov, on one side in French, on the other in Slavonic characters.) "I hope you are not coming from the Governor's?"

"It's no use to hope; we come straight from him."

"Ah! in that case I will call on him too. . . . Yevgeny Vassilyitch,

13. "he has had his time."

introduce me to your . . . to the . . ."

"Sitnikov, Kirsanov," mumbled Bazarov, not stopping.

"I am greatly flattered," began Sitnikov, walking sidewise, smirking, and hurriedly pulling off his really over-elegant gloves. "I have heard so much. . . . I am an old acquaintance of Yevgeny Vassilyitch, and, I may say—his disciple. I am indebted to him for my regeneration. . . ."

Arkady looked at Bazarov's disciple. There was an expression of excitement and dullness imprinted on the small but pleasant features of his well-groomed face; his small eyes, that seemed squeezed in, had a fixed and uneasy look, and his laugh, too, was uneasy—a sort of short, wooden laugh.

"Would you believe it," he pursued, "when Yevgeny Vassilyitch for the first time said before me that it was not right to accept any authorities, I felt such enthusiasm . . . as though my eyes were opened! Here, I thought, at last I have found a man! By the way, Yevgeny Vassilyitch, you positively must come to know a lady here, who is really capable of understanding you, and for whom your visit would be a real festival; you have heard of her, I suppose?"

"Who is it?" Bazarov brought out unwillingly.

"Kukshina, *Eudoxie*, Evdoksya Kukshin. She's a remarkable nature, *emancipée* in the true sense of the word, an advanced woman. Do you know what? We'll all go together to see her now. She lives only two steps from here. We will have lunch there. I suppose you have not lunched yet?"

"No; not yet."

"Well, that's capital. She has separated, you understand, from her husband; she is not dependent on any one."

"Is she pretty?" Bazarov cut in.

"N . . . no, one couldn't say that."

"Then, what the devil are you asking us to see her for?"

"Fie; you must have your joke. . . . She will give us a bottle of champagne."

"Oh, that's it. One can see the practical man at once. By the way, is your father still in the gin business?"

"Yes," said Sitnikov, hurriedly, and he gave a shrill spasmodic laugh. "Well? Will you come?"

"I don't really know."

"You wanted to see people, go along," said Arkady in an undertone.

"And what do you say to it, Mr. Kirsanov?" Sitnikov put in. "You must come too; we can't go without you."

"But how can we burst in upon her all at once?"

"That's no matter. Kukshina's a brick!"

"There will be a bottle of champagne?" asked Bazarov.

"Three!" cried Sitnikov; "that I answer for."

"What with?"

"My own head."

"Your father's purse would be better. However, we are coming."

The small gentleman's house in the Moscow style, in which Avdotya Nikitishna, otherwise Evdoksya, Kukshin, lived, was in one of the streets of X——, which had been lately burnt down; it is well known that our provincial towns are burnt down every five years. At the door, above a visiting card nailed on all askew, there was a bell-handle to be seen, and in the hall the visitors were met by some one, not exactly a servant, nor exactly a companion, in a cap—unmistakable tokens of the progressive tendencies of the lady of the house. Sitnikov inquired whether Avdotya Nikitishna was at home.

"Is that you, *Victor?*" sounded a shrill voice from the adjoining room. "Come in."

The woman in the cap disappeared at once.

"I'm not alone," observed Sitnikov, with a sharp look at Arkady and Bazarov as he briskly pulled off his overcoat, beneath which appeared something of the nature of a coachman's velvet jacket.

"No matter," answered the voice. "*Entrez.*"

The young men went in. The room into which they walked was more like a working study than a drawing-room. Papers, letters, fat numbers of Russian journals, for the most part uncut, lay at random on the dusty tables; white cigarette ends lay scattered in every direction. On a leather-covered sofa, a lady, still young, was reclining. Her fair hair was rather dishevelled; she wore a silk gown, not perfectly tidy, heavy bracelets on her short arms, and a lace handkerchief on her head. She got up from the sofa, and carelessly drawing a velvet cape trimmed with yellowish ermine over her shoulders, she said languidly, "Good-morning, *Victor,*" and pressed Sitnikov's hand.

"Bazarov, Kirsanov," he announced abruptly in imitation of Bazarov.

"Delighted," answered Madame Kukshin, and fixing on Bazarov a pair of round eyes, between which was a forlorn little turned-up red nose, "I know you," she added, and pressed his hand too.

Bazarov scowled. There was nothing repulsive in the little plain person of the emancipated woman; but the expression of her face produced a disagreeable effect on the spectator. One felt impelled to ask her, "What's the matter; are you hungry? or bored? Or shy? What are you in a fidget about?" Both she and Sitnikov had always the same uneasy air. She was extremely unconstrained, and at the same time awkward; she obviously regarded herself as a good-natured, simple creature, and all the while, whatever she did, it always struck one that it was not just what she wanted to do; everything with her seemed, as children say, done on purpose, that's to say, not simply, not naturally.

"Yes, yes, I know you, Bazarov," she repeated. (She had the habit —peculiar to many provincial and Moscow ladies—of calling men by their surnames from the first day of acquaintance with them.) "Will you have a cigar?"

"A cigar's all very well," put in Sitnikov, who by now was lolling in an armchair, his legs in the air; "but give us some lunch. We're awfully hungry; and tell them to bring us up a little bottle of champagne."

"Sybarite," commented Evdoksya, and she laughed. (When she laughed the gum showed above her upper teeth.) "Isn't it true, Bazarov; he's a Sybarite?"

"I like comfort in life," Sitnikov brought out, with dignity. "That does not prevent my being a Liberal."

"No, it does; it does prevent it!" cried Evdoksya. She gave directions, however, to her maid, both as regards the lunch and the champagne.

"What do you think about it?" she added, turning to Bazarov. "I'm persuaded you share my opinion."

"Well, no," retorted Bazarov; "a piece of meat's better than a piece of bread even from the chemical point of view."

"You are studying chemistry? That is my passion. I've even invented a new sort of composition myself."

"A composition? You?"

"Yes. And do you know for what purpose? To make dolls' heads so that they shouldn't break. I'm practical, too, you see. But everything's not quite ready yet. I've still to read Liebig. By the way, have you read Kislyakov's article on Female Labour, in the *Moscow Gazette*? Read it, please. You're interested in the woman question, I suppose? And in the schools too? What does your friend do? What is his name?"

Madame Kukshin shed her questions one after another with affected negligence, not waiting for an answer; spoilt children talk so to their nurses.

"My name's Arkady Nikolaitch Kirsanov," said Arkady, "and I'm doing nothing."

Evdoksya giggled. "How charming! What, don't you smoke? Victor, do you know, I'm very angry with you."

"What for?"

"They tell me you've begun singing the praises of George Sand[14] again. A retrograde woman, and nothing else? How can people compare her with Emerson? She hasn't an idea on education, nor physi-

<hr>

14. George Sand, the pseudonym of the French woman novelist Aurore Dupin (1804–1876), was most famous for her early novels defending woman's right to love and romantic passion.

ology, nor anything. She'd never, I'm persuaded, heard of embryology, and in these days—what can be done without that?" (Evdoksya even threw up her hands.) "Ah, what a wonderful article Elisyevitch has written on that subject! He's a gentleman of genius." (Evdoksya constantly made use of the word "gentleman" instead of the word "man.") "Bazarov, sit by me on the sofa. You don't know, perhaps, I'm awfully afraid of you."

"Why so? Allow me to ask."

"You're a dangerous gentleman; you're such a critic. Good God! yes! why, how absurd, I'm talking like some country lady. I really am a country lady, though. I manage my property myself; and only fancy, my bailiff Erofay's a wonderful type, quite like Cooper's Pathfinder; something in him so spontaneous! I've come to settle here finally; it's an intolerable town, isn't it? But what's one to do?"

"The town's like every town," Bazarov remarked coolly.

"All its interests are so petty, that's what's so awful! I used to spend the winters in Moscow . . . but now my lawful spouse, Monsieur Kukshin's residing there. And besides, Moscow nowadays . . . there, I don't know—it's not the same as it was. I'm thinking of going abroad; last year I was on the point of setting off."

"To Paris, I suppose?" queried Bazarov.

"To Paris and to Heidelberg."

"Why to Heidelberg?"

"How can you ask? Why, Bunsen's there![15]

To this Bazarov could find no reply.

"*Pierre* Sapozhnikov . . . do you know him?"

"No, I don't."

"Not know *Pierre* Sapozhnikov . . . he's always at Lidia Khestatov's."

"I don't know her either."

"Well, it was he undertook to escort me. Thank God, I'm independent; I've no children. . . . What was that I said: *thank God!* It's no matter though."

Evdoksya rolled a cigarette up between her fingers, which were brown with tobacco stains, put it to her tongue, licked it up, and began smoking. The maid came in with a tray.

"Ah, here's lunch! Will you have an appetiser first? Victor, open the bottle; that's in your line."

"Yes, it's in my line," muttered Sitnikov, and again he gave vent to the same convulsive laugh.

"Are there any pretty women here?" inquired Bazarov, as he drank off a third glass.

"Yes, there are," answered Evdoksya; "but they're all such empty-

15. Robert Wilhelm von Bunsen (1811–1899) was a German chemist and professor at Heidelberg who devised methods of measuring gaseous volumes, discovered spectrum analysis, etc. He invented the "Bunsen burner" in 1855.

headed creatures. *Mon amie*, Odintsova, for instance, is nice-looking.
It's a pity her reputation's rather doubtful. . . . That wouldn't matter, though, but she's no independence in her views, no width, nothing . . . of all that. The whole system of education wants changing.
I've thought a great deal about it; our women are very badly educated."

"There's no doing anything with them," put in Sitnikov; "one
ought to despise them, and I do despise them fully and completely!"
(The possibility of feeling and expressing contempt was the most
agreeable sensation to Sitnikov; he used to attack women in especial,
never suspecting that it was to be his fate a few months later to be
cringing before his wife merely because she had been born a princess
Durdoleosov.) "Not a single one of them would be capable of understanding our conversation; not a single one deserves to be spoken
of by serious men like us!"

"But there's not the least need for them to understand our conversation," observed Bazarov.

"Whom do you mean?" put in Evdoksya.

"Pretty women."

"What? Do you adopt Proudhon's[16] ideas then?"

Bazarov drew himself up haughtily. "I don't adopt any one's ideas;
I have my own."

"Damn all authorities!" shouted Sitnikov, delighted to have a
chance of expressing himself boldly before the man he slavishly admired.

"But even Macaulay,"[17] Madame Kukshin was beginning . . .

"Damn Macaulay," thundered Sitnikov. "Are you going to stand
up for the silly hussies?"

"For silly hussies, no, but for the rights of women, which I have
sworn to defend to the last drop of my blood."

"Damn!" but here Sitnikov stopped. "But I don't deny them,"
he said.

"No, I see you're a Slavophil."

"No, I'm not a Slavophil, though, of course . . ."

"No, no, no! You are a Slavophil. You're an advocate of patriarchal
despotism. You want to have the whip in your hand!"

"A whip's an excellent thing," remarked Bazarov; "but we've got
to the last drop."

"Of what?" interrupted Evdoksya.

"Of champagne, most honoured Avdotya Nikitishna, of champagne—not of your blood."

16. Pierre Joseph Proudhon (1809–
1865), a French socialist or rather anar-
chist, who propounded the thesis "Property is theft."

17. Thomas Babington Macaulay
(1800–1859), an English historian
whose *History of England* and *Critical
and Historical Essays* enjoyed a great
reputation. Macaulay was a political
liberal. The introduction of his name is
completely unmotivated.

"I can never listen calmly when women are attacked," pursued Evdoksya. "It's awful, awful. Instead of attacking them, you'd better read Michelet's book, *L'amour*.[18] That's exquisite! Gentlemen, let us talk of love," added Evdoksya, letting her arm fall languidly on the rumpled sofa cushion.

A sudden silence followed. "No, why should we talk of love," said Bazarov; "but you mentioned just now a Madame Odintsov . . . That was what you called her, I think? Who is that lady?"

"She's charming, charming!" piped Sitnikov. "I will introduce you. Clever, rich, a widow. It's a pity, she's not yet advanced enough; she ought to see more of our Evdoksya. I drink to your health, *Evdoxie!* Let us clink glasses! *Et toc, et toc, et tin-tin-tin! Et toc, et toc, et tin-tin-tin!!!*"

"Victor, you're a wretch."

The lunch dragged on a long while. The first bottle of champagne was followed by another, a third, and even a fourth. . . . Evdoksya chattered without pause; Sitnikov seconded her. They had much discussion upon the question whether marriage was a prejudice or a crime, and whether men were born equal or not, and precisely what individuality consists in. Things came at last to Evdoksya, flushed from the wine she had drunk, tapping with her flat finger-tips on the keys of a discordant piano, and beginning to sing in a hoarse voice, first gipsy songs, and then Seymour Schiff's song, "Granada lies slumbering"; while Sitnikov tied a scarf round his head, and represented the dying lover at the words—

> "And thy lips to mine
> In burning kiss entwine."

Arkady could not stand it at last. "Gentlemen, it's getting something like Bedlam," he remarked aloud. Bazarov, who had at rare intervals put in an ironical word in the conversation—he paid more attention to the champagne—gave a loud yawn, got up, and, without taking leave of their hostess, he walked off with Arkady. Sitnikov jumped up and followed them.

"Well, what do you think of her?" he inquired, skipping obsequiously from right to left of them. "I told you, you see, a remarkable personality! If we only had more women like that! She is, in her own way, an expression of the highest morality."

"And is that establishment of your father's an expression of the highest morality too?" observed Bazarov, pointing to a ginshop which they were passing at that instant.

Sitnikov again went off into a shrill laugh. He was greatly ashamed of his origin, and did not know whether to feel flattered or offended at Bazarov's unexpected familiarity.

18. Jules Michelet (1798–1874) was a French historian whose *Histoire de la France* was the great French history of the nineteenth century. Late in his life Michelet wrote *L'amour* (1858), a sentimental celebration of married love.

XIV

A few days later the ball at the Governor's took place. Matvy Ilyitch was the real "hero of the occasion." The marshal of nobility declared to all and each that he had come simply out of respect for him; while the Governor, even at the ball, even while he remained perfectly motionless, was still "making arrangements." The affability of Matvy Ilyitch's demeanour could only be equalled by its dignity. He was gracious to all, to some with a shade of disgust, to others with a shade of respect; he was all bows and smiles "*en vrai chevalier français*"[19] before the ladies, and was continually giving vent to a hearty, sonorous, unshared laugh, such as befits a high official. He slapped Arkady on the back, and called him loudly "nephew"; vouchsafed Bazarov—who was attired in a rather old evening coat— a sidelong glance in passing—absent but condescending—and an indistinct but affable grunt, in which nothing could be distinguished but "I . . ." and "very much"; gave Sitnikov a finger and a smile, though with his head already averted; even to Madame Kukshin, who made her appearance at the ball with dirty gloves, no crinoline, and a bird of Paradise in her hair, he said "*enchanté.*" There were crowds of people, and no lack of dancing men; the civilians were for the most part standing close along the walls, but the officers danced assiduously, especially one of them who had spent six weeks in Paris, where he had mastered various daring interjections of the kind of— "*zut,*" "Ah, *fichtr-re,*" "*pst, pst, mon bibi,*" and such. He pronounced them to perfection with genuine Parisian *chic* and at the same time he said "*si j'aurais*" for "*si j'avais,*" "*absolument*" in the sense of "absolutely," expressed himself, in fact, in that Great Russo- French jargon which the French ridicule so when they have no reason for assuring us that we speak French like angels, "*comme des anges.*"

Arkady, as we are aware, danced badly, while Bazarov did not dance at all; they both took up their position in a corner; Sitnikov joined himself on to them, with an expression of contemptuous scorn on his face, and giving vent to spiteful comments, he looked insolently about him, and seemed to be really enjoying himself. Suddenly his face changed, and turning to Arkady, he said, with some show of embarrassment it seemed, "Odintsova is here!"

Arkady looked round, and saw a tall woman in a black dress standing at the door of the room. He was struck by the dignity of her carriage. Her bare arms lay gracefully beside her slender waist; gracefully some light sprays of fuchsia drooped from her shining hair on to her sloping shoulders; her clear eyes looked out from under a rather overhanging white brow, with a tranquil and intelligent expression—tranquil it was precisely, not pensive—and on her lips was a scarcely perceptible smile. There was a kind of gracious and gentle force about her face.

19. "like a true French knight."

"Do you know her?" Arkady asked Sitnikov.

"Intimately. Would you like me to introduce you?"

"Please . . . after this quadrille."

Bazarov's attention, too, was directed to Madame Odintsov.

"That's a striking figure," he remarked. "Not like the other females."

After waiting till the end of the quadrille, Sitnikov led Arkady up to Madame Odintsov; but he hardly seemed to be intimately acquainted with her; he was embarrassed in his sentences, while she looked at him in some surprise. But her face assumed an expression of pleasure when she heard Arkady's surname. She asked him whether he was not the son of Nikolai Petrovitch.

"Yes."

"I have seen your father twice, and have heard a great deal about him," she went on; "I am glad to make your acquaintance."

At that instant some adjutant flew up to her and begged for a quadrille. She consented.

"Do you dance then?" asked Arkady respectfully.

"Yes, I dance. Why do you suppose I don't dance? Do you think I am too old?"

"Really, how could I possibly. . . . But in that case, let me ask you for a mazurka."

Madame Odintsov smiled graciously. "Certainly," she said, and she looked at Arkady, not exactly with an air of superiority, but as married sisters look at very young brothers. Madame Odintsov was a little older than Arkady—she was twenty-nine—but in her presence he felt himself a schoolboy, a little student, so that the difference in age between them seemed of more consequence. Matvy Ilyitch approached her with a majestic air and ingratiating speeches. Arkady moved away, but he still watched; he could not take his eyes off her even during the quadrille. She talked with equal ease to her partner and to the grand official, softly turned her head and eyes, and twice laughed softly. Her nose—like almost all Russian noses—was a little thick; and her complexion was not perfectly clear; Arkady made up his mind, for all that, that he had never before met such an attractive woman. He could not get the sound of her voice out of his ears; the very folds of her dress seemed to hang upon her differently from all the rest—more gracefully and amply—and her movements were distinguished by a peculiar smoothness and naturalness.

Arkady felt some timidity in his heart when at the first sounds of the mazurka he began to sit it out beside his partner; he had prepared to enter into a conversation with her, but he only passed his hand through his hair, and could not find a single word to say. But his timidity and agitation did not last long; Madame Odintsov's tranquillity gained upon him too; before a quarter of an hour had passed he was telling her freely about his father, his uncle, his life in Petersburg and in the country. Madame Odintsov listened to him with courteous sympathy, slightly opening and closing her fan; his talk was broken off when partners came for her; Sitnikov, among others, twice asked her. She came back, sat down again, took up her fan and her bosom did not even heave more rapidly, while Arkady fell to chattering again, filled through and through by the happiness of being near her, talking to her, looking at her eyes, her lovely brow, all her sweet dignified, clever face. She said little, but her words showed a knowledge of life; from some of her observations, Arkady gathered that this young woman had already felt and thought much. . . .

"Who is that you were standing with?" she asked him, "when Mr. Sitnikov brought you to me?"

"Did you notice him?" Arkady asked in his turn. "He has a splendid face, hasn't he? That's Bazarov, my friend."

Arkady fell to discussing "his friend." He spoke of him in such detail, and with such enthusiasm, that Madame Odintsov turned towards him and looked attentively at him. Meanwhile, the mazurka was drawing to a close. Arkady felt sorry to part from his partner; he had spent nearly an hour so happily with her! He had, it is true, during the whole time continually felt as though she were condescending to him, as though he ought to be grateful to her . . . but young hearts are not weighed down by that feeling.

The music stopped. "*Mercy*," said Madame Odintsov, getting up. "You promised to come and see me; bring your friend with you. I shall be very curious to see the man who has the courage to believe in nothing."

The Governor came up to Madame Odintsov, announced that supper was ready, and, with a careworn face, offered her his arm. As she went away, she turned to give a last smile and bow to Arkady. He bowed low, looked after her (how graceful her figure seemed to him, draped in the greyish lustre of the black silk!), and thinking, "This minute she has forgotten my existence," was conscious of an exquisite humility in his soul.

"Well?" Bazarov questioned him, directly he had gone back to him in the corner. "Did you have a good time? A gentleman has just been talking to me about that lady; he said, 'She's—oh, fie! fie!' but I fancy the fellow was a fool. What do you think, what is she!—oh, fie! fie!"

"I don't quite understand that definition," answered Arkady.

"Oh, my! What innocence!"

"In that case, I don't understand the gentleman you quote. Madame Odintsov is very sweet, no doubt, but she behaves so coldly and severely, that . . ."

"Still waters . . . you know!" put in Bazarov. "That's just what gives it piquancy. You like ices, I expect?"

"Perhaps," muttered Arkady. "I can't give an opinion about that. She wishes to make your acquaintance, and has asked me to bring you to see her."

"I can imagine how you've described me! But you did very well. Take me. Whatever she may be—whether she's simply a provincial lioness, or 'advanced' after Kukshina's fashion—any way she's got a pair of shoulders such as I've not set eyes on for a long while."

Arkady was wounded by Bazarov's cynicism, but—as often happens—he reproached his friend not precisely for what he did not like in him. . . .

"Why are you unwilling to allow freethinking in women?" he said in a low voice.

"Because, my boy, as far as my observations go, the only freethinkers among women are frights."

The conversation was cut short at this point. Both the young men went away immediately after supper. They were pursued by a nervously malicious, but somewhat fainthearted laugh from Madame Kukshin; her vanity had been deeply wounded by neither of them having paid any attention to her. She stayed later than any one at the ball, and at four o'clock in the morning she was dancing a polka-mazurka with Sitnikov in the Parisian style. This edifying spectacle was the final event of the Governor's ball.

xv

"Let's see what species of mammalia this specimen belongs to," Bazarov said to Arkady the following day, as they mounted the staircase of the hotel in which Madame Odintsov was staying. "I scent out something wrong here."

"I'm surprised at you!" cried Arkady. "What? You, you, Bazarov, clinging to the narrow morality, which . . ."

"What a funny fellow you are!" Bazarov cut him short, carelessly. "Don't you know that 'something wrong' means 'something right' in my dialect and for me? It's an advantage for me, of course. Didn't you tell me yourself this morning that she made a strange marriage, though, to my mind, to marry a rich old man is by no means a strange thing to do, but, on the contrary, very sensible. I don't believe the gossip of the town; but I should like to think, as our cultivated Governor says, that it's well-grounded."

Arkady made no answer, and knocked at the door of the apartments. A young servant in livery conducted the two friends into a large room, badly furnished, like all rooms in Russian hotels, but filled with flowers. Soon Madame Odintsov herself appeared in a simple morning dress. She seemed still younger by the light of the spring sunshine. Arkady presented Bazarov, and noticed with secret amazement that he seemed embarrassed, while Madame Odintsov remained perfectly tranquil, as she had been the previous day.

Bazarov himself was conscious of being embarrassed, and was irritated by it. "Here's a go!—frightened of a petticoat!" he thought, and lolling, quite like Sitnikov, in an easy-chair, he began talking with an exaggerated appearance of ease, while Madame Odintsov kept her clear eyes fixed on him.

Anna Sergyevna Odintsov was the daughter of Sergey Nikolaevitch Loktev, notorious for his personal beauty, his speculations, and his gambling propensities, who after cutting a figure and making a sensation for fifteen years in Petersburg and Moscow, finished by ruining himself completely at cards, and was forced to retire to the country, where, however, he soon after died, leaving a very small property to his two daughters—Anna, a girl of twenty, and Katya, a child of twelve. Their mother, who came of an impoverished line of princes —the H—s—had died at Petersburg when her husband was in his heyday. Anna's position after her father's death was very difficult. The brilliant education she had received in Petersburg had not fitted her for putting up with the cares of domestic life and economy,— for an obscure existence in the country. She knew positively no one in the whole neighbourhood, and there was no one she could consult. Her father had tried to avoid all contact with the neighbours; he despised them in his way, and they despised him in theirs. She did not lose her head, however, and promptly sent for a sister of her mother's, Princess Avdotya Stepanovna H—, a spiteful and arrogant old lady, who, on installing herself in the niece's house, appropriated all the best rooms for her own use, scolded and grumbled from morning till night, and would not go a walk even in the garden unattended by her one serf, a surly footman in a threadbare pea-green livery with light blue trimming and a three-cornered hat. Anna put up patiently with all her aunt's whims, gradually set to work on her sister's education, and was, it seemed, already getting reconciled to the idea of wasting her life in the wilds. . . . But destiny had decreed another fate of her. She chanced to be seen by Odintsov, a very wealthy man of forty-six, an eccentric hypochondriac, stout, heavy, and sour; but not stupid, and not ill-natured; he fell in love with her, and offered her his hand. She consented to become his wife, and he lived six years with her, and on his death settled all his property upon her. Anna Sergyevna remained in the country for nearly a year after his death; then she went abroad with her sister, but only stopped in Germany; she got tired of it and came back to live at her favourite Nikolskoe, which was nearly thirty miles from the town of X——. There she had a magnificent, splendidly furnished house and a beautiful garden, with conservatories; her late husband had spared no expense to gratify his fancies. Anna Sergyevna went very rarely to the town, generally only on business, and even then she did not stay long. She was not liked in the province; there had been a fearful outcry at her marriage with

Odintsov, all sorts of fictions were told about her; it was asserted that she had helped her father in his cardsharping tricks, and even that she had gone abroad for excellent reasons, that it had been necessary to conceal the lamentable consequences . . . "You understand?" the indignant gossips would wind up. "She has gone through the fire," was said of her; to which a noted provincial wit usually added: "And through all the other elements?" All this talk reached her; but she turned a deaf ear to it; there was much independence and a good deal of determination in her character.

Madame Odintsov sat leaning back in her easy-chair, and listened with folded hands to Bazarov. He, contrary to his habit, was talking a good deal, and obviously trying to interest her—again a surprise for Arkady. He could not make up his mind whether Bazarov was attaining his object. It was difficult to conjecture from Anna Sergyevna's face what impression was being made on her; it retained the same expression, gracious and refined; her beautiful eyes were lighted up by attention, but by quiet attention. Bazarov's bad manners had impressed her unpleasantly for the first minutes of the visit like a bad smell or a discordant sound; but she saw at once that he was nervous, and that even flattered her. Nothing was repulsive to her but vulgarity, and no one could have accused Bazarov of vulgarity. Arkady was fated to meet with surprises that day. He had expected that Bazarov would talk to a clever woman like Madame Odintsov about his opinions and his views; she had herself expressed a desire to listen to the man "who dares to have no belief in anything"; but, instead of that, Bazarov talked about medicine, about homeopathy, and about botany. It turned out that Madame Odintsov had not wasted her time in solitude; she had read a good many excellent books, and spoke herself in excellent Russian. She turned the conversation upon music; but noticing that Bazarov did not appreciate art, she quietly brought it back to botany, even though Arkady was just launching into a discourse upon the significance of national melodies. Madame Odintsov treated him as though he were a younger brother; she seemed to appreciate his good-nature and youthful simplicity and that was all. For over three hours, a lively conversation was kept up, ranging freely over various subjects.

The friends at last got up and began to take leave. Anna Sergyevna looked cordially at them, held out her beautiful, white hand to both, and, after a moment's thought, said with a doubtful but delightful smile, "If you are not afraid of being dull, gentlemen, come and see me at Nikolskoe."

"Oh, Anna Sergyevna," cried Arkady, "I shall think it the greatest happiness . . ."

"And you, Monsieur Bazarov?"

Bazarov only bowed, and a last surprise was in store for Arkady; he noticed that his friend was blushing.

"Well?" he said to him in the street; "are you still of the same opinion—that she's . . ."

"Who can tell? See how correct she is!" retorted Bazarov; and after a brief pause he added, "She's a perfect grand-duchess, a royal personage. She only needs a train on behind, and a crown on her head."

"Our grand-duchesses don't talk Russian like that," remarked Arkady

"She's seen ups and downs, my dear boy; she's known what it is to be hard up!"

"Any way, she's charming," observed Arkady.

"What a magnificent body," pursued Bazarov. "Shouldn't I like to see it on the dissecting-table."

"Hush, for mercy's sake, Yevgeny! that's beyond everything."

"Well, don't get angry, you baby. I meant it's first rate. We must go to stay with her."

"When?"

"Well, why not the day after to-morrow. What is there to do here? Drink champagne with Kukshina? Listen to your cousin, the Liberal dignitary? . . . Let's be off the day after to-morrow. By the way, too—my father's little place is not far from there. This Nikolskoe's on the S— road, isn't it?"

"Yes."

"*Optime*, why hesitate? Leave that to fools and prigs! I say, what a splendid body!"

Three days later the two friends were driving along the road to Nikolskoe. The day was bright, and not too hot, and the sleek post-ing-horses trotted smartly along, switching their tied and plaited tails. Arkady looked at the road, and not knowing why, he smiled.

"Congratulate me," cried Bazarov suddenly, "to-day's the 22nd of June, my guardian angel's day. Let's see how he will watch over me. To-day they expect me home," he added, dropping his voice. . . . "Well, they can go on expecting. . . . What does it matter!"

XVI

The country-house in which Anna Sergyevna lived stood on an exposed hill at no great distance from a yellow stone church with a green roof, white columns, and a fresco over the principal entrance representing the "Resurrection of Christ" in the "Italian" style. Sprawling in the foreground of the picture was a swarthy warrior in a helmet, specially conspicuous for his rotund contours. Behind the church a long village stretched in two rows, with chimneys peeping out here and there above the thatched roofs. The manor-house was built in the same style as the church, the style known among us as that of Alexander; the house, too, was painted yellow, and had a green roof, and white columns, and a pediment with an escutcheon on it. The architect had designed both buildings with the approval of the deceased Odintsov, who could not endure—as he expressed it—idle and arbitrary innovations. The house was enclosed on both sides by the dark trees of an old garden; an avenue of lopped pines led up to the entrance.

Our friends were met in the hall by two tall footmen in livery; one of them at once ran for the steward. The steward, a stout man in a black dress coat, promptly appeared and led the visitors by a staircase covered with rugs to a special room, in which two bedsteads were already prepared for them with all necessaries for the toilet. It was clear that order reigned supreme in the house; everything was clean, everywhere there was a peculiar delicate fragance, just as there is in the reception rooms of ministers.

"Anna Sergyevna asks you to come to her in half-an-hour," the steward announced; "will there be orders to give meanwhile?"

"No orders," answered Bazarov; "perhaps you will be so good as to trouble yourself to bring me a glass of vodka."

"Yes, sir," said the steward, looking in some perplexity, and he withdrew, his boots creaking as he walked.

"What *grand genre!*" remarked Bazarov. "That's what it's called in your set, isn't it? She's a grand-duchess, and that's all about it."

"A nice grand-duchess," retorted Arkady, "at the very first meeting she invited such great aristocrats as you and me to stay with her."

"Especially me, a future doctor, and a doctor's son, and a village sexton's grandson. . . . You know, I suppose, I'm the grandson of a sexton? Like the great Speransky,"[20] added Bazarov after a brief pause, contracting his lips. "At any rate she likes to be comfortable; oh, doesn't she, this lady! Oughtn't we to put on evening dress?"

Arkady only shrugged his shoulders . . . but he, too, was conscious of a little nervousness.

Half-an-hour later Bazarov and Arkady went together into the drawing-room. It was a large lofty room, furnished rather luxuriously but without particularly good taste. Heavy, expensive furniture stood in the ordinary stiff arrangement along the walls, which were covered with cinnamon-coloured paper with gold flowers on it; Odintsov had ordered the furniture from Moscow through a friend and agent of his, a spirit merchant. Over a sofa in the centre of one wall hung a portrait of a faded light-haired man—and it seemed to look with displeasure at the visitors. "It must be the late lamented," Bazarov whispered to Arkady, and turning up his nose, he added, "Hadn't we better bolt . . .?" But at that instant the lady of the house entered. She wore a light barège dress; her hair smoothy combed

20. Count Mikhail Speransky (1772–1839) was the son of a village priest who rose to become the all-powerful minister of Tsar Alexander I, but was dismissed just before Napoleon's invasion of Russia (1812). Later, however, he played a great role in the codification of Russian laws. He is a fictional character in Tolstoy's *War and Peace*.

back behind her ears gave a girlish expression to her pure and fresh face.

"Thank you for keeping your promise," she began. "You must stay a little while with me; it's really not bad here. I will introduce you to my sister; she plays the piano well. That is a matter of indifference to you, Monsieur Bazarov; but you, I think, Monsieur Kirsanov, are fond of music. Besides my sister I have an old aunt living with me, and one of our neighbours comes in sometimes to play cards; that makes up all our circle. And now let us sit down."

Madame Odintsov delivered all this little speech with peculiar precision, as though she had learned it by heart; then she turned to Arkady. It appeared that her mother had known Arkady's mother, and had even been her confidante in her love for Nikolai Petrovitch. Arkady began talking with great warmth of his dead mother; while Bazarov fell to turning over albums. "What a meek fellow I have become!" he was thinking to himself.

A beautiful greyhound with a blue collar on, ran into the drawing-room, tapping on the floor with his paws, and after him entered a girl of eighteen, black-haired and dark-skinned, with a rather round but pleasing face, and small dark eyes. In her hands she held a basket filled with flowers.

"This is my Katya," said Madame Odintsov, indicating her with a motion of her head. Katya made a slight curtsey, placed herself beside her sister, and began picking out flowers. The greyhound, whose name was Fifi, went up to both of the visitors, in turn wagging his tail, and thrusting his cold nose into their hands.

"Did you pick all that yourself?" asked Madame Odintsov.

"Yes," answered Katya.

"Is auntie coming to tea?"

"Yes."

When Katya spoke, she had a very charming smile, sweet, timid, and candid, and looked up from under her eyebrows with a sort of humorous severity. Everything about her was still young and undeveloped; the voice, and the bloom on her whole face, and the rosy hands, with white palms, and the rather narrow shoulders. . . . She was constantly blushing and getting out of breath.

Madame Odintsov turned to Bazarov. "You are looking at pictures from politeness, Yevgeny Vassilyitch," she began. "That does not interest you. You had better come nearer to us, and let us have a discussion about something."

Bazarov went closer. "What subject have you decided upon for discussion?" he said.

"What you like. I warn you, I am dreadfully argumentative."

"You?"

"Yes. That seems to surprise you. Why?"

"Because, as far as I can judge, you have a calm, cool character, and one must be impulsive to be argumentative."

"How can you have had time to understand me so soon? In the first place, I am impatient and obstinate—you should ask Katya; and secondly, I am very easily carried away."

Bazarov looked at Anna Sergyevna. "Perhaps; you must know best. And so you are inclined for a discussion—by all means. I was looking through the views of the Saxon mountains in your album, and you remarked that that couldn't interest me. You said so, because you suppose me to have no feeling for art, and as a fact I haven't any; but these views might be interesting to me from a geological standpoint, for the formation of the mountains, for instance."

"Excuse me; but as a geologist, you would sooner have recourse to a book, to a special work on the subject and not to a drawing."

"The drawing shows me at a glance what would be spread over ten pages in a book."

Anna Sergyevna was silent for a little.

"And so you haven't the least artistic feeling?" she observed, putting her elbow on the table, and by that very action bringing her face nearer to Bazarov. "How can you get on without it?"

"Why, what is it wanted for, may I ask?"

"Well, at least to enable one to study and understand men."

Bazarov smiled. "In the first place, experience of life does that; and in the second, I assure you, studying separate individuals is not worth the trouble. All people are like one another, in soul as in body; each of us has brain, spleen, heart, and lungs made alike; and the so-called moral qualities are the same in all; the slight variations are of no importance. A single human specimen is sufficient to judge all the others. People are like trees in a forest; no botanist would think of studying each individual birch-tree."

Katya, who was arranging the flowers, one at a time in a leisurely fashion, lifted her eyes to Bazarov with a puzzled look, and meeting his rapid and careless glance, she crimsoned up to her ears. Anna Sergyevna shook her head.

"The trees in a forest," she repeated. "Then according to you there is no difference between the stupid and the clever person, between the good-natured and ill-natured?"

"No, there is a difference, just as between the sick and the healthy. The lungs of a consumptive patient are not in the same condition as yours and mine, though they are made on the same plan. We know approximately what physical diseases come from; moral diseases come from bad education, from all the nonsense people's heads are stuffed with from childhood up, from the defective state of society; in short, reform society, and there will be no diseases."

Bazarov said all this with an air, as though he were all the while thinking to himself, "Believe me or not, as you like, it's all one to me!" He slowly passed his fingers over his whiskers, while his eyes strayed about the room.

"And you conclude," observed Anna Sergyevna, "that when society is reformed, there will be no stupid nor wicked people?"

"At any rate, in a proper organization of society, it will be absolutely the same whether a man is stupid or clever, wicked or good."

"Yes, I understand; they will all have the same spleen."

"Precisely so, madam."

Madame Odintsov turned to Arkady. "And what is your opinion, Arkady Nikolaevitch?"

"I agree with Yevgeny," he answered.

Katya looked up at him from under her eyelids.

"You amaze me, gentlemen," commented Madame Odintsov, "but we will have more talk together. But now I hear my aunt coming in to tea; we must spare her."

Anna Sergyevna's aunt, Princess H—, a thin little woman with a pinched-up face, drawn together like a fist, and staring ill-natured-looking eyes under a grey front, came in, and, scarcely bowing to the guests, she dropped into a wide velvet covered arm-chair, upon which no one but herself was privileged to sit. Katya put a footstool under her feet; the old lady did not thank her, did not even look at her, only her hands shook under the yellow shawl, which almost covered her feeble body. The Princess liked yellow; her cap, too, had bright yellow ribbons.

"How have you slept, aunt?" inquired Madame Odintsov, raising her voice.

"That dog in here again," the old lady muttered in reply, and noticing Fifi was making two hesitating steps in her direction, she cried, "Ss—ss!"

Katya called Fifi and opened the door for him.

Fifi rushed out delighted, in the expectation of being taken out for a walk; but when he was left alone outside the door, he began scratching and whining. The princess scowled. Katya was about to go out. . . .

"I expect tea is ready," said Madame Odintsov.

"Come, gentlemen; aunt, will you go in to tea?"

The princess got up from her chair without speaking and led the way out of the drawing-room. They all followed her into the dining-room. A little page in livery drew back, with a scraping sound, from the table, an arm-chair covered with cushions, devoted to the princess's use; she sank into it; Katya in pouring out the tea handed her first a cup emblazoned with a heraldic crest. The old lady put some honey in her cup (she considered it both sinful[21] and extravagant to

21. Devout Russians did not use sugar, particularly during Church fasts, because sugar used to be clarified with blood.

drink tea with sugar in it, though she never spent a kopek herself on anything), and suddenly asked in a hoarse voice, "And what does Prince Ivan write?"

No one made her any reply. Bazarov and Arkady soon guessed that they paid no attention to her, though they treated her respectfully. "Because of her grand family," thought Bazarov. . . .

After tea, Anna Sergyevna suggested they should go out for a walk; but it began to rain a little, and the whole party, with the exception of the princess, returned to the drawing-room. The neighbour, the devoted card-player, arrived; his name was Porfiry Platonitch, a stoutish, greyish man with short, spindly legs, very polite and ready to be amused. Anna Sergyevna, who still talked principally with Bazarov, asked him whether he'd like to try a contest with them in the old-fashioned way at preference? Bazarov assented, saying "that he ought to prepare himself beforehand for the duties awaiting him as a country doctor."

"You must be careful," observed Anna Sergyevna; "Porfiry Platonitch and I will beat you. And you, Katya," she added "play something to Arkady Nikolaevitch; he is fond of music, and we can listen, too."

Katya went unwillingly to the piano; and Arkady, though he certainly was fond of music, unwillingly followed her; it seemed to him that Madame Odintsov was sending him away, and already, like every young man at his age, he felt a vague and oppressive emotion surging up in his heart, like the forebodings of love. Katya raised the top of the piano, and not looking at Arkady, she said in a low voice:

"What am I to play you?"

"What you like," answered Arkady indifferently.

"What sort of music do you like best?" repeated Katya, without changing her attitude.

"Classical," Arkady answered in the same tone of voice.

"Do you like Mozart?"

"Yes, I like Mozart."

Katya pulled out Mozart's Sonata-Fantasia in C minor. She played very well, though rather over correctly and precisely. She sat upright and immovable, her eyes fixed on the notes, and her lips tightly compressed, only at the end of the sonata her face glowed, her hair came loose, and a little lock fell on to her dark brow.

Arkady was particularly struck by the last part of the sonata, the part in which, in the midst of the bewitching gaiety of the careless melody, the pangs of such mournful, almost tragic suffering, suddenly break in. . . . But the ideas stirred in him by Mozart's music had no reference to Katya. Looking at her he simply thought, "Well, that young lady doesn't play badly, and she's not bad-looking either."

When she had finished the sonata, Katya, without taking her hands from the keys, asked, "Is that enough?" Arkady declared that he could not venture to trouble her again, and began talking to her about Mozart; he asked her whether she had chosen that sonata herself, or some one had recommended it to her. But Katya answered him in monosyllables; she withdrew into herself, went back into her shell. When this happened to her, she did not very quickly come out again; her face even assumed at such times an obstinate, almost stupid expression. She was not exactly shy, but diffident, and rather overawed by her sister, who had educated her, and who had no suspicion of the fact. Arkady was reduced at last to calling Fifi to him, and with an affable smile patting him on the head to give himself an appearance of being at home.

Katya set to work again upon her flowers.

Bazarov meanwhile was losing and losing. Anna Sergyevna played cards in masterly fashion; Porfiry Platonitch, too, could hold his own in the game. Bazarov lost a sum which, though trifling in itself, was not altogether pleasant for him. At supper Anna Sergyevna again turned the conversation on botany.

"We will go for a walk to-morrow morning," she said to him. "I want you to teach me the Latin names of the wild flowers and their species."

"What use are the Latin names to you?" asked Bazarov.

"Order is needed in everything," she answered.

"What an exquisite woman Anna Sergyevna is!" cried Arkady, when he was alone with his friend in the room assigned to them.

"Yes," answered Bazarov, "a female with brains. Yes, and she's seen life too."

"In what sense do you mean that, Yevgeny Vassilitch?"

"In a good sense, a good sense, my dear friend, Arkady Nikolaeitch! I'm convinced she manages her estate capitally too. But what's splendid is not her, but her sister."

"What, that little dark thing?"

"Yes, that little dark thing. She now is fresh and untouched, and shy and silent, and anything you like. She's worth educating and developing. You might make something fine out of her; but the other's—a stale loaf."

Arkady made no reply to Bazarov, and each of them got into bed with rather singular thoughts in his head.

Anna Sergyevna, too, thought of her guests that evening. She liked Bazarov for the absence of gallantry in him, and even for his sharply defined views. She found in him something new, which she had not chanced to meet before, and she was curious.

Anna Sergyevna was a rather strange creature. Having no prejudices of any kind, having no strong convictions even, she never gave way or went out of her way for anything. She had seen many things very clearly; she had been interested in many things, but nothing had completely satisfied her; indeed, she hardly desired complete satisfaction. Her intellect was at the same time inquiring and indifferent; her doubts were never soothed to forgetfulness, and they never grew strong enough to distract her. Had she not been rich and independent, she would perhaps have thrown herself into the struggle, and have known passion. But life was easy for her, though she was bored at times, and she went on passing day after day with deliberation, never in a hurry, placid, and only rarely disturbed. Dreams sometimes danced in rainbow colours before her eyes even, but she breathed more freely when they died away, and did not regret them. Her imagination indeed overstepped the limits of what is reckoned permissible by conventional morality; but even then the blood flowed as quietly as ever in her fascinatingly graceful, tranquil body. Sometimes coming out of her fragrant bath all warm and enervated, she would fall to musing on the nothingness of life, the sorrow, the labour, the malice of it. . . . Her soul would be filled with sudden daring, and would flow with generous ardour, but a draught would blow from a half-closed window, and Anna Sergyevna would shrink into herself, and feel plaintive and almost angry, and there was only one thing she cared for at that instant—to get away from that horrid draught.

Like all women who have not succeeded in loving, she wanted something, without herself knowing what. Strictly speaking she wanted nothing; but it seemed to her that she wanted everything. She could hardly endure the late Odintsov (she had married him from prudential motives, though probably she would not have consented to become his wife if she had not considered him a good sort of man), and had conceived a secret repugnance for all men, whom she could only figure to herself as slovenly, heavy, drowsy, and feebly importunate creatures. Once, somewhere abroad, she had met a handsome young Swede, with a chivalrous expression, with honest blue eyes under an open brow; he had made a powerful impression on her, but it had not prevented her from going back to Russia.

"A strange man this doctor!" she thought as she lay in her luxurious bed, on lace pillows under a light silk coverlet. . . . Anna Sergyevna had inherited from her father a little of his inclination for splendour. She had fondly loved her sinful but good-natured father, and he had idolized her, used to joke with her in a friendly way as though she were an equal, and to confide in her fully, to ask her advice. Her mother she scarcely remembered.

"This doctor is a strange man!" she repeated to herself. She stretched, smiled, clasped her hands behind her head, then ran her eyes over two pages of a stupid French novel, dropped the book —and fell asleep, all pure and cold, in the pure and fragrant linen.

The following morning Anna Sergyevna went off botanizing with

Bazarov directly after lunch, and returned just before dinner; Arkady did not go off anywhere, and spent about an hour with Katya. He was not bored with her; she offered of herself to repeat the sonata of the day before; but when Madame Odintsov came back at last, when he caught sight of her, he felt an instantaneous pang at his heart. She came through the garden with a rather tired step; her cheeks were glowing and her eyes shining more brightly than usual under her round straw hat. She was twirling in her fingers the thin stalk of a wildflower, a light mantle had slipped down to her elbows, and the wide gray ribbons of her hat were clinging to her bosom. Bazarov walked behind her, self-confident and careless as usual, but the expression of his face, cheerful and even friendly as it was, did not please Arkady. Muttering between his teeth, "Good-morning!" Bazarov went away to his room, while Madame Odintsov shook Arkady's hand abstractedly, and also walked past him.

"Good-morning!" thought Arkady. . . . "As though we had not seen each other already to-day!"

XVII

Time, it is well known, sometimes flies like a bird, sometimes crawls like a worm; but man is wont to be particularly happy when he does not even notice whether it passes quickly or slowly. It was in that way Arkady and Bazarov spent a fortnight at Madame Odintsov's. The good order she had established in her house and in her life partly contributed to this result. She adhered strictly to this order herself, and forced others to submit to it. Everything during the day was done at a fixed time. In the morning, precisely at eight o'clock, all the party assembled for tea; from morning tea till lunch time every one did what he pleased, the hostess herself was engaged with her bailiff (the estate was on the rent system), her steward, and her head housekeeper. Before dinner the party met again for conversation or reading; the evening was devoted to walking, cards, and music; at half-past ten Anna Sergyevna retired to her own room, gave her orders for the following day, and went to bed. Bazarov did not like this measured, somewhat ostentatious punctuality in daily life, "like moving along rails," he pronounced it to be; the footmen in livery, the decorous stewards, offended his democratic sentiments. He declared that if one went so far, one might as well dine in the English style at once—in tail-coats and white ties. He once spoke plainly upon the subject to Anna Sergyevna. Her attitude was such that no one hesitated to speak his mind freely before her. She heard him out; and then her comment was, "From your point of view, you are right—and perhaps, in that respect, I am too much of a lady; but there's no living in the country without order, one would be devoured by ennui," and she continued to go her own way. Bazarov grumbled, but the very reason life was so easy for him and Arkady at Madame Odintsov's was that everything in the house "moved on rails." For all that, a change had taken place in both the young men since the first days of their stay at Nikolskoe. Bazarov, in whom Anna Serg-yevna was obviously interested, though she seldom agreed with him, began to show signs of an unrest, unprecedented in him; he was easily put out of temper, and unwilling to talk, he looked irritated, and could not sit still in one place, just as though he were possessed by some secret longing; while Arkady, who had made up his mind conclusively that he was in love with Madame Odintsov, had begun to yield to a gentle melancholy. This melancholy did not, however, prevent him from becoming friendly with Katya; it even impelled him to get into friendly, affectionate terms with her. "*She* does not appreciate me? So be it . . . But here is a good creature, who does not repulse me," he thought, and his heart again knew the sweet-ness of magnanimous emotions. Katya vaguely realized that he was seeking a sort of consolation in her company, and did not deny him or herself the innocent pleasure of a half-shy, half-confidential friend-ship. They did not talk to each other in Anna Sergyevna's presence; Katya always shrank into herself under her sister's sharp eyes; while Arkady, as befits a man in love, could pay attention to nothing else when near the object of his passion; but he was happy with Katya alone. He was conscious that he did not possess the power to in-terest Madame Odintsov; he was shy and at a loss when he was left alone with her, and she did not know what to say to him, he was too young for her. With Katya, on the other hand, Arkady felt at home; he treated her condescendingly, encouraged her to express the im-pressions made on her by music, reading novels, verses, and other such trifles, without noticing or realizing that these trifles were what interested him too. Katya, on her side, did not try to drive away melancholy. Arkady was at his ease with Katya, Madame Odintsov with Bazarov, and thus it usually came to pass that the two couples, after being a little while together, went off on their separate ways, especially during the walks. Katya adored nature, and Arkady loved it, though he did not dare to acknowledge it; Madame Odintsov was, like Bazarov, rather indifferent to the beauties of nature. The almost continual separation of the two friends was not without its conse-quences; the relations between them began to change. Bazarov gave up talking to Arkady about Madame Odintsov, gave up even abusing her "aristocratic ways"; Katya, it is true, he praised as before, and only advised him to restrain her sentimental tendencies, but his praises were hurried, his advice dry, and in general he talked less to Arkady than before . . . he seemed to avoid him, seemed ill at ease with him.

Arkady observed it all, but he kept his observations to himself.

The real cause of all this "newness" was the feeling inspired in Bazarov by Madame Odintsov, a feeling which tortured and mad-dened him, and which he would at once have denied, with scornful laughter and cynical abuse, if any one had ever so remotely hinted at the possibility of what was taking place in him. Bazarov had a great love for women and for feminine beauty; but love in the ideal, or, as he expressed it, romantic sense, he called lunacy, unpardonable imbecility; he regarded chivalrous sentiments as something of the nature of deformity or disease, and had more than once expressed his wonder that Toggenburg[22] and all the minnesingers and troubadours had not been put into a lunatic asylum. "If a woman takes your fancy," he used to say, "try and gain your end; but if you can't —well, turn your back on her—there are lots of good fish in the sea." Madame Odintsov had taken his fancy; the rumours about her, the freedom and independence of her ideas, her unmistakable liking for him, all seemed to be in his favour, but he soon saw that with her he would not "gain his ends," and to turn his back on her he found, to his own bewilderment, beyond his power. His blood was on fire directly if he merely thought of her; he could easily have mastered his blood, but something else was taking root in him, something he had never admitted, at which he had always jeered, at which all his pride revolted. In his conversations with Anna Sergyevna he expressed more strongly than ever his calm contempt for everything idealistic; but when he was alone, with indignation he recognized idealism in himself. Then he would set off to the forest and walk with long strides about it, smashing the twigs that came in his way, and cursing under his breath both her and himself; or he would get into the hay-loft in the barn, and, obstinately closing his eyes, try to force himself to sleep, in which, of course, he did not always succeed. Suddenly his fancy would bring before him those chaste hands twining one day about his neck, those proud lips responding to his kisses, those intellectual eyes dwelling with tenderness—yes, with tenderness—on his, and his head went round, and he forgot himself for an instant, till indignation boiled up in him again. He caught himself in all sorts of "shameful" thoughts as though he were driven on by a devil mocking him. Sometimes he fancied that there was a change taking place in Madame Odintsov too; that there were signs in the expression of her face of something special; that, perhaps . . . but at that point he would stamp, or grind his teeth, and clench his fists.

Meanwhile Bazarov was not altogether mistaken. He had struck Madame Odintsov's imagination; he interested her, she thought a great deal about him. In his absence, she was not dull, she was not impatient for his coming, but she always grew more lively on his appearance; she liked to be left alone with him, and she liked talking

---

22. Toggenburg, a medieval knight, was rejected by his beloved and he went on a crusade. The day he returned, his love took the veil; Toggenburg became a hermit and lived until his dying day in a hut near the nunnery, content to watch his love appear once a day at a distant window. The story is told in a well-known ballad, written in 1797, by the German poet Friedrich Schiller (1759–1805).

to him, even when he irritated her or offended her taste, her refined habits. She was, as it were, eager at once to sound him and to analyze herself.

One day walking in the garden with her, he suddenly announced, in a surly voice, that he intended going to his father's place very soon. . . . She turned white, as though something had given her a pang, and such a pang, that she wondered and pondered long after, what could be the meaning of it. Bazarov had spoken of his departure with no idea of putting her to the test, of seeing what would come of it; he never "fabricated." On the morning of that day he had an interview with his father's bailiff, who had taken care of him when he was a child, Timofeitch. This Timofeitch, a little old man of much experience and astuteness, with faded yellow hair, a weather-beaten red face, and tiny tear-drops in his shrunken eyes, unexpectedly appeared before Bazarov, in his shortish overcoat of stout greyish-blue cloth, girt with a strip of leather, and in tarred boots.

"Hullo, old man; how are you?" cried Bazarov.

"How do you do, Yevgeny Vassilyitch?" began the little old man, and he smiled with delight, so that his whole face was all at once covered with wrinkles.

"What have you come for? They sent for me, eh?"

"Upon my word, sir, how could we?" mumbled Timofeitch. (He remembered the strict injunctions he had received from his master on starting.) "We were sent to the town on business, and we'd heard news of your honour, so here we turned off on our way, that's to say—to have a look at your honour . . . as if we could think of disturbing you!"

"Come, don't tell lies!" Bazarov cut him short. "Is this the road to the town, do you mean to tell me?" Timofeitch hesitated, and made no answer. "Is my father well?"

"Thank God, yes."

"And my mother?"

"Anna Vlasyevna too, glory be to God."

"They are expecting me, I suppose?"

The little old man held his tiny head on one side.

"Ah, Yevgeny Vassilyitch, it makes one's heart ache to see them; it does really."

"Come, all right, all right, shut up! Tell them I'm coming soon."

"Yes, sir," answered Timofeitch, with a sigh.

As he went out of the house, he pulled his cap down on his head with both hands, clambered into a wretched-looking racing droshky, and went off at a trot, but not in the direction of the town.

On the evening of the same day, Madame Odintsov was sitting in her own room with Bazarov, while Arkady walked up and down the hall listening to Katya's playing. The princess had gone upstairs to her own room; she could not bear guests as a rule, and "especially this new riff-raff lot," as she called them. In the common rooms she only sulked; but she made up for it in her own room by breaking out into such abuse before her maid that the cap danced on her head, wig and all. Madame Odintsov was well aware of all this.

"How is it you are proposing to leave us?" she began; "how about your promise?"

Bazarov started. "What promise?"

"Have you forgotten? You meant to give me some lessons in chemistry."

"It can't be helped! My father expects me; I can't loiter any longer. However, you can read Pelouse et Frémy, *Notions générales de Chimie*; it's a good book, and clearly written. You will find everything you need in it."

"But do you remember; you assured me a book cannot take the place of . . . I've forgotten how you put it, but you know what I mean . . . do you remember?"

"It can't be helped!" repeated Bazarov.

"Why go away?" said Madame Odintsov, dropping her voice.

He glanced at her. Her head had fallen on to the back of her easy-chair, and her arms, bare to the elbows were folded on her bosom. She seemed paler in the light of the single lamp covered with a perforated paper shade. An ample white gown hid her completely in its soft folds; even the tips of her feet, also crossed, were hardly seen.

"And why stay?" answered Bazarov.

Madame Odintsov turned her head slightly. "You ask why? Have you not enjoyed yourself with me? Or do you suppose you will not be missed here?"

"I am sure of it."

Madame Odintsov was silent a minute. "You are wrong in thinking that. But I don't believe you. You could not say that seriously." Bazarov still sat immovable. "Yevgeny Vassilyitch, why don't you speak?"

"Why, what am I to say to you? People are not generally worth being missed, and I less than most."

"Why so?"

"I'm a practical, uninteresting person. I don't know how to talk."

"You are fishing, Yevgeny Vassilyitch."

"That's not a habit of mine. Don't you know yourself that I've nothing in common with the elegant side of life, the side you prize so much?"

Madame Odintsov bit the corner of her handkerchief.

"You may think what you like, but I shall be dull when you go away."

"Arkady will remain," remarked Bazorov. Madame Odintsov shrugged her shoulders slightly. "I shall be dull," she repeated.

"Really? In any case you will not feel dull for long."

"What makes you suppose that?"

"Because you told me yourself that you are only dull when your regular routine is broken in upon. You have ordered your existence with such unimpeachable regularity that there can be no place in it for dullness or sadness . . . for any unpleasant emotions."

"And do you consider I am so unimpeachable . . . that's to say, that I have ordered my life with such regularity?"

"I should think so. Here's an example: in a few minutes it will strike ten, and I know beforehand that you will drive me away."

"No; I'm not going to drive you away, Yevgeny Vassilyitch. You may stay. Open that window. . . . I feel half-stifled."

Bazarov got up and gave a push to the window. It flew up with a loud crash. . . . He had not expected it to open so easily; besides, his hands were shaking. The soft, dark night looked in to the room with its almost black sky, its faintly rustling trees, and the fresh fragrance of the pure open air.

"Draw the blind and sit down," said Madame Odintsov; "I want to have a talk with you before you go away. Tell me something about yourself, you never talk about yourself."

"I try to talk to you upon improving subjects, Anna Sergyevna."

"You are very modest. . . . But I should like to know something about you, about your family, about your father, for whom you are forsaking us."

"Why is she talking like that?" thought Bazarov.

"All that's not in the least interesting," he uttered aloud, "especially for you; we are obscure people. . . ."

"And you regard me as an aristocrat?"

Bazarov lifted his eyes to Madame Odintsov.

"Yes," he said, with exaggerated sharpness.

She smiled. "I see you know me very little, though you do maintain that all people are alike, and it's not worth while to study them. I will tell you my life some time or other . . . but first you tell me yours."

"I know you very little," repeated Bazarov. "Perhaps you are right; perhaps, really, every one is a riddle. You, for instance; you avoid society, you are oppressed by it, and you have invited two students to stay with you. What makes you, with your intellect, with your beauty, live in the country?"

"What? What was it you said?" Madame Odintsov interposed eagerly. "With my . . . beauty?"

Bazarov scowled. "Never mind that," he muttered; "I meant to say that I don't exactly understand why you have settled in the country."

"You don't understand it. . . . But you explain it to yourself in some way?"

"Yes . . . I assume that you remain continually in the same place because you indulge yourself, because you are very fond of comfort and ease, and very indifferent to everything else."

Madame Odintsov smiled again. "You would absolutely refuse to believe that I am capable of being carried away by anything?"

Bazarov glanced at her from under his brows.

"By curiosity, perhaps; but not otherwise."

"Really? Well, now I understand why we are such friends; you are just like me, you see."

"We are such friends . . ." Bazarov articulated in a choked voice.

Bazarov got up. The lamp burnt dimly in the middle of the dark, luxurious, isolated room; from time to time the blind was shaken, and there flowed in the freshness of the insidious night; there was heard its mysterious whisperings. Madame Odintsov did not move in a single limb; but she was gradually possessed by concealed emotion.

It communicated itself to Bazarov. He was suddenly conscious that he was alone with a young and lovely woman. . . .

"Where are you going?" she said slowly.

He answered nothing and sank into a chair.

"And so you consider me a placid, pampered, spoiled creature," she went on in the same voice, never taking her eyes off the window. "While I know so much about myself, that I am unhappy."

"You unhappy? What for? Surely you can't attach any importance to idle gossip?"

Madame Odintsov frowned. It annoyed her that he had given such a meaning to her words.

"Such gossip does not even affect me, Yevgeny Vassilyitch, and I am too proud to allow it to disturb me. I am unhappy because . . . I have no desires, no passion for life. You look at me incredulously; you think that's said by an 'aristocrat,' who is all in lace, and sitting in a velvet armchair. I don't conceal the fact: I love what you call comfort, and at the same time I have little desire to live. Explain that contradiction as best you can. But all that's romanticism in your eyes."

Bazarov shook his head. "You are in good health, independent, rich; what more would you have? What do you want?"

"What do I want?" echoed Madame Odintsov, and she sighed. "I am very tired, I am old, I feel as if I have had a very long life. Yes, I am old," she added softly drawing the ends of her lace over her bare arms. Her eyes met Bazarov's eyes, and she faintly blushed. "Behind me I have already so many memories: my life in Petersburg, wealth, then poverty, then my father's death, marriage, then the inevitable tour in due order. . . . So many memories, and nothing to remember, and before me, before me—a long, long road, and no goal. . . . I have no wish to go on."

"Are you disillusioned?" queried Bazarov.

"No, but I am dissatisfied," Madame Odintsov replied, dwelling on each syllable "I think if I could interest myself strongly in something. . . ."

"You want to fall in love," Bazarov interrupted her, "and you can't love; that's where your unhappiness lies."

Madame Odintsov began to examine the sleeve of her lace.

"Is it true I can't love?" she said.

"I should say not! Only I was wrong in calling that an unhappiness. On the contrary, any one's more to be pitied when such a mischance befalls him."

"Mischance, what?"

"Falling in love."

"And how do you come to know that?"

"By hearsay," answered Bazarov angrily.

"You're flirting," he thought; "you're bored, and teasing me for want of something to do, while I . . . ." His heart really seemed as though it were being torn to pieces.

"Besides, you are perhaps too exacting," he said, bending his whole frame forward and playing with the fringe of the chair.

"Perhaps. My idea is everything or nothing. A life for a life. Take mine, give up thine, and that without regret or turning back. Or else better have nothing."

"Well?" observed Bazarov; "that's fair terms, and I'm surprised that so far you . . . have not found what you wanted."

"And do you think it would be easy to give oneself up wholly to anything whatever?"

"Not easy, if you begin reflecting, waiting and attaching value to yourself, prizing yourself, I mean; but to give oneself up without reflection is very easy."

"How can one help prizing oneself? If I am of no value, who could need my devotion?"

"That's not my affair; that's the other's business to discover what is my value. The chief thing is to be able to devote oneself."

Madame Odintsov bent forward from the back of her chair. "You speak," she began, "as though you had experienced all that."

"It happened to come up, Anna Sergyevna; all that, as you know, is not in my line."

"But you could devote yourself?"

"I don't know. I shouldn't like to boast."

Madame Odintsov said nothing, and Bazarov was mute. The sounds of the piano floated up to them from the drawing-room.

"How is it Katya is playing so late?" observed Madame Odintsov.

Bazarov got up. "Yes, it is really late now; it's time for you to go to bed."

"Wait a little; why are you in a hurry? . . . I want to say one word to you."

"What is it?"

"Wait a little," whispered Madame Odintsov. Her eyes rested on Bazarov; it seemed as though she were examining him attentively. He walked across the room, then suddenly went up to her, hurriedly said, "Good-bye," squeezed her hand so that she almost screamed, and was gone. She raised her crushed fingers to her lips, breathed on them, and suddenly, impulsively getting up from her low chair, she moved with rapid steps towards the door, as though she wished to bring Bazarov back. . . . A maid came into the room with a decanter on a silver tray. Madame Odintsov stood still, told her she could go, and sat down again, and again sank into thought. Her hair slipped loose and fell in a dark coil down her shoulders. Long after the lamp was still burning in Anna Sergyevna's room, and for long she stayed without moving, only from time to time chafing her hands, which ached a little from the cold of the night.

Bazarov went back two hours later to his bedroom with his boots wet with dew, dishevelled and ill-humoured. He found Arkady at the writing table with a book in his hands, his coat buttoned up to the throat.

"You're not in bed yet?" he said, in a tone, it seemed, of annoyance.

"You stopped a long while with Anna Sergyevna this evening," remarked Arkady, not answering him.

"Yes, I stopped with her all the while you were playing the piano with Katya Sergyevna."

"I did not play . . ." Arkady began, and he stopped. He felt the tears were coming into his eyes, and he did not like to cry before his sarcastic friend.

XVIII

The following morning when Madame Odintsov came down to morning tea, Bazarov sat a long while bending over his cup, then suddenly he glanced up at her. . . . She turned to him as though he had struck her a blow, and he fancied that her face was a little paler since the night before. She quickly went off to her own room, and did not appear till lunch. It rained from early morning; there was no possibility of going for a walk. The whole company assembled in the drawing-room. Arkady took up the new number of a journal and began reading it aloud. The princess, as was her habit, tried to express her amazement in her face, as though he were doing something improper, then glared angrily at him; but he paid no attention to her.

"Yevgeny Vassilyitch," said Anna Sergyevna, "come to my room. . . . I want to ask you. . . . You mentioned a text-book yesterday. . . ."

She got up and went to the door. The princess looked round with an expression that seemed to say, "Look at me; see how shocked

I am!" and again glared at Arkady; but he raised his voice, and exchanging glances with Katya, near whom he was sitting, he went on reading.

Madame Odintsov went with rapid steps to her study. Bazarov followed her quickly, not raising his eyes, and only with his ears catching the delicate swish and rustle of her silk gown gliding before him. Madame Odintsov sank into the same easy-chair in which she had sat the previous evening, and Bazarov took up the same position as before.

"What was the name of that book?" she began, after a brief silence.

"Pelouse et Frémy, *Notions générales*," answered Bazarov. "I might though recommend you also Ganot, *Traité élémentaire de physique expérimentale*. In that book the illustrations are clearer, and in general it's a text-book."

Madame Odintsov stretched out her hand. "Yevgeny Vassilyitch, I beg your pardon, but I didn't invite you in here to discuss textbooks. I wanted to continue our conversation of last night. You went away so suddenly. . . . It will not bore you. . . ."

"I am at your service, Anna Sergyevna. But what were we talking about last night?"

Madame Odintsov flung a sidelong glance at Bazarov.

"We were talking of happiness, I believe. I told you about myself. By the way, I mentioned the word 'happiness.' Tell me why it is that even when we are enjoying music, for instance, or a fine evening, or a conversation with sympathetic people, it all seems an intimation of some measureless happiness existing apart somewhere rather than actual happiness—such, I mean, as we ourselves are in possession of? Why is it? Or perhaps you have no feeling like that?"

"You know the saying, "Happiness is where we are not,"[23] replied Bazarov; "besides, you told me yesterday you are discontented. I certainly never have such ideas come into my head."

"Perhaps they seem ridiculous to you?"

"No; but they don't come into my head."

"Really? Do you know, I should very much like to know what you think about?"

"What? I don't understand."

"Listen; I have long wanted to speak openly to you. There's no need to tell you—you are conscious of it yourself—that you are not an ordinary man; you are still young—all life is before you. What are you preparing yourself for? What future is awaiting you? I mean to say—what object do you want to attain? What are you going forward to? What is in your heart? In short, who are you, what are

---

23. A quotation from a German poem, "Der Wanderer" (The Wanderer) by Georg Phillip Schmidt (1766–1849) which became famous through its being set to music by Franz Schubert in 1816. The Wanderer asks where is the land of his desire, and a ghostly voice answers: *"Dort wo Du nicht bist, ist das Glück"* ("There where you are not, there is happiness").

you?"

"You surprise me, Anna Sergyevna. You are aware that I am studying natural science, and who I . . ."

"Well, who are you?"

"I have explained to you already that I am going to be a district doctor."

Anna Sergyevna made a movement of impatience.

"What do you say that for? You don't believe it yourself. Arkady might answer me in that way, but not you."

"Why, in what is Arkady . . ."

"Stop! Is it possible you could content yourself with such a humble career, and aren't you always maintaining yourself that you don't believe in medicine? You—with your ambition—a district doctor! You answer me like that to put me off, because you have no confidence in me. But, do you know, Yevgeny Vassilyitch, that I could understand you; I have been poor myself, and ambitious, like you; I have been perhaps through the same trials as you."

"That is all very well, Anna Sergyevna, but you must pardon me for . . . I am not in the habit of talking freely about myself at any time as a rule, and between you and me there is such a gulf. . . ."

"What sort of gulf? You mean to tell me again that I am an aristocrat? No more of that, Yevgeny Vassilyitch; I thought I had proved to you . . ."

"And even apart from that," broke in Bazarov, "what could induce one to talk and think about the future, which for the most part does not depend on us? If a chance turns up of doing something —so much the better; and if it doesn't turn up—at least one will be glad one didn't gossip idly about it beforehand."

"You call a friendly conversation idle gossip? . . . Or perhaps you consider me as a woman unworthy of your confidence? I know you despise us all."

"I don't despise you, Anna Sergyevna, and you know that."

"No, I don't know anything . . . but let us suppose so. I understand your disinclination to talk of your future career; but as to what is taking place within you now . . ."

"Taking place!" repeated Bazarov, "as though I were some sort of government or society! In any case, it is utterly uninteresting; and besides, can a man always speak of everything that 'takes place' in him?"

"Why, I don't see why you can't speak freely of everything you have in your heart."

"Can you?" asked Bazarov.

"Yes," answered Anna Sergyevna, after a brief hesitation.

Bazarov bowed his head. "You are more fortunate than I am."

Anna Sergevna looked at him questioningly. "As you please," she went on, "but still something tells me that we have not come together for nothing; that we shall be great friends. I am sure this—what should I say, constraint, reticence in you will vanish at last."

"So you have noticed reticence . . . as you expressed it . . . constraint?"

"Yes."

Bazarov got up and went to the window. "And would you like to know the reason of this reticence? Would you like to know what is passing within me?"

"Yes," repeated Madame Odintsov, with a sort of dread she did not at the time understand.

"And you will not be angry?"

"No."

"No?" Bazarov was standing with his back to her. "Let me tell you then that I love you like a fool, like a madman. . . . There, you've forced it out of me."

Madame Odintsov held both her hands out before her; but Bazarov was leaning with his forehead pressed against the window pane. He breathed hard; his whole body was visibly trembling. But it was not the tremor of youthful timidity, not the sweet alarm of the first declaration that possessed him; it was passion struggling in him, strong and painful—passion not unlike hatred, and perhaps akin to it . . . Madame Odintsov felt both afraid and sorry for him.

"Yevgeny Vassilyitch!" she said, and there was the ring of unconscious tenderness in her voice.

He turned quickly, flung a searching look on her, and snatching both her hands, he drew her suddenly to his breast.

She did not at once free herself from his embrace, but an instant later she was standing far away in a corner, and looking from there at Bazarov. He rushed at her. . . .

"You have misunderstood me," she whispered hurriedly, in alarm. It seemed as if he had made another step she would have screamed. . . . Bazarov bit his lips, and went out.

Half an hour after a maid gave Anna Sergyevna a note from Bazarov; it consisted simply of one line: "Am I to go to-day, or can I stop till to-morrow?"

"Why should you go? I did not understand you—you did not understand me," Anna Sergyevna answered him, but to herself she thought: "I did not understand myself either."

She did not show herself till dinner time and kept walking to and fro in her room, stopping sometimes at the window, sometimes at the looking-glass, and slowly rubbing her handkerchief over her neck, on which she still seemed to feel a burning spot. She asked herself what had induced her to "force" on Bazarov's words, his confidence, and whether she had suspected nothing. . . . "I am to blame," she decided aloud, "but I could not have foreseen this." She fell to musing, and blushed crimson, remembering Bazarov's almost animal face when he had rushed at her. . . .

"Or?" she uttered suddenly aloud, and she stopped short and shook back her curls. . . . She caught sight of herself in the glass; her head thrown back, with a mysterious smile on the half-closed, half-opened eyes and lips, told her, it seemed, in a flash something at which she herself was confused. . . .

"No," she made up her mind at last. "God knows what it would lead to; he couldn't be played with; peace is anyway the best thing in the world."

Her peace of mind was not shaken; but she felt gloomy, and even shed a few tears once, though she could not have said why—certainly not for the insult done her. She did not feel insulted; she was more inclined to feel guilty. Under the influence of various vague emotions, the sense of life passing by, the desire of novelty, she had forced herself to go up to a certain point, forced herself to look behind herself, and had seen behind her not even an abyss, but what was empty . . . or revolting.

XIX

Great as was Madame Odintsov's self-control, and superior as she was to every kind of prejudice, she felt awkward when she went into the dining-room to dinner. The meal went off fairly successfully, however. Porfiry Platonovitch made his appearance and told various anecdotes; he had just come back from the town. Among other things, he informed them that the governor had ordered his secretaries on special commissions to wear spurs, in case he might send them off anywhere for greater speed on horseback. Arkady talked in an undertone to Katya, and diplomatically attended to the princess's wants. Bazarov maintained a grim and obstinate silence. Madame Odintsov looked at him twice, not stealthily, but straight in the face, which was bilious and forbidding, with downcast eyes, and contemptuous determination stamped on every feature, and thought: "No . . . no . . . no." . . . After dinner, she went with the whole company into the garden, and seeing that Bazarov wanted to speak to her, she took a few steps to one side and stopped. He went up to her, but even then did not raise his eyes, and said hoarsely:

"I have to apologize to you, Anna Sergyevna. You must be in a fury with me."

"No, I'm not angry with you, Yevgeny Vassilyitch," answered Madame Odintsov; "but I am sorry."

"So much the worse. Anyway, I'm sufficiently punished. My position, you will certainly agree, is most foolish. You wrote to me, 'Why go away?' But I cannot stay, and don't wish to. To-morrow I shall be gone."

"Yevgeny Vassilyitch, why are you . . ."

"Why am I going away?"

"No; I didn't mean to say that."

"There's no recalling the past, Anna Sergyevna . . . and this was bound to come about sooner or later. Consequently I must go. I can only conceive of one condition upon which I could remain; but that condition will never be. Excuse my impertinence, but you don't love me, and you never will love me, I suppose?"

Bazarov's eyes glittered for an instant under their dark brows.

Anna Sergyevna did not answer him. "I'm afraid of this man," flashed through her brain.

"Good-bye, then," said Bazarov, as though he guessed her thought and he went back into the house.

Anna Sergyevna walked slowly after him, and calling Katya to her, she took her arm. She did not leave her side till quite evening. She did not play cards, and was constantly laughing, which did not at all accord with her pale and perplexed face. Arkady was bewildered, and looked on at her as all young people look on—that's to say, he was constantly asking himself, "What is the meaning of that?" Bazarov shut himself up in his room; he came back to tea, however. Anna Sergyevna longed to say some friendly word to him, but she did not know how to address him. . . .

An unexpected incident relieved her from her embarrassment; a steward announced the arrival of Sitnikov.

It is difficult to do justice in words to the strange figure cut by the young apostle of progress as he fluttered into the room. Though, with his characteristic impudence, he had made up his mind to go into the country to visit a woman whom he hardly knew, who had never invited him; but with whom, according to information he had gathered, such talented and intimate friends were staying, he was nevertheless trembling to the marrow of his bones; and instead of bringing out the apologies and compliments he had learned by heart beforehand, he muttered some absurdity about Evdoksya Kukshin having sent him to inquire after Anna Sergyevna's health, and Arkady Nicolaevitch's too, having always spoken to him in the highest terms. . . . At this point he faltered and lost his presence of mind so completely that he sat down on his own hat. However, since no one turned him out, and Anna Sergyevna even presented him to her aunt and her sister, he soon recovered himself and began to chatter volubly. The introduction of the commonplace is often an advantage in life; it relieves overstrained tension, and sobers too self-confident or self-sacrificing emotions by recalling its close kinship with them. With Sitnikov's appearance everything became somehow duller and simpler; they all even ate a more solid supper, and retired to bed half an hour earlier than usual.

"I might now repeat to you," said Arkady, as he lay down in bed, to Bazarov, who was also undressing, "what you once said to me, 'Why are you so melancholy? One would think you had fulfilled some sacred duty.'" For some time past a sort of pretence of free-

and-easy banter had sprung up between the two young men, which is always an unmistakable sign of secret displeasure or unexpressed suspicions.

"I'm going to my father's to-morrow," said Bazarov.

Arkady raised himself and leaned on his elbow. He felt both surprised, and for some reason or other pleased. "Ah!" he commented, "and is that why you're sad?"

Bazarov yawned. "You'll get old if you know too much."

"And Anna Sergyevna?" persisted Arkady.

"What about Anna Sergyevna?"

"I mean, will she let you go?"

"I am not her paid man."

Arkady grew thoughtful, while Bazarov lay down and turned his face to the wall.

Some minutes went by in silence. "Yevgeny?" cried Arkady suddenly.

"Well?"

"I will leave with you to-morrow, too."

Bazarov made no answer.

"Only I will go home," continued Arkady. "We will go together as far as Khokhlovsky, and there you can get horses at Fedot's. I should be delighted to make the acquaintance of your people, but I'm afraid of being in their way and yours. You are coming to us again, later, of course?"

"I've left all my things with you," Bazarov said, without turning round.

"Why doesn't he ask me why I am going, and just as suddenly as he?" thought Arkady. "In reality, why am I going, and why is he going?" he pursued his reflections. He could find no satisfactory answer to his own question, though his heart was filled with some bitter feeling. He felt it would be hard to part from this life to which he had grown so accustomed; but for him to remain alone would be rather odd. "Something has passed between them," he reasoned to himself; "what good would it be for me to hang on after he's gone? She's utterly sick of me; I'm losing the last that remained to me." He began to imagine Anna Sergyevna to himself, then other features gradually eclipsed the lovely young image of the young widow.

"I'm sorry to lose Katya too!" Arkady whispered to his pillow, on which a tear had already fallen. . . . All at once he shook back his hair and said aloud:

"What the devil made that fool of a Sitnikov turn up here?"

Bazarov at first stirred a little in his bed, then he uttered the following rejoinder: "You're still a fool, my boy, I see. Sitnikovs are indispensable to us. I—do you understand? I need dolts like him. It's not for the gods to bake bricks, in fact!" . . .

"Oho!" Arkady thought to himself, and then in a flash all the fathomless depths of Bazarov's conceit dawned upon him. "Are you and I gods then? At least, you're a god; am not I a dolt then?"

"Yes," repeated Bazarov; "you're still a fool."

Madame Odintsov expressed no special surprise when Arkady told her the next day that he was going with Bazarov; she seemed tired and absorbed. Katya looked at him silently and seriously; the princess went so far as to cross herself under her shawl so that he could not help noticing it. Sitnikov, on the other hand, was completely disconcerted. He had only just come in to lunch in a new and fashionable get-up, not on this occasion of a Slavophil cut; the evening before he had astonished the man told off to wait on him by the amount or linen he had brought with him, and now all of a sudden his comrades were deserting him! He took a few tiny steps, doubled back like a hunted hare at the edge of a copse, and abruptly, almost with dismay, almost with a wail, announced that he proposed going too. Madame Odintsov did not attempt to detain him.

"I have a very comfortable carriage," added the luckless young man, turning to Arkady; "I can take you, while Yevgeny Vassilyitch can take your coach, so it will be even more convenient."

"But, really, it's not at all in your way, and it's a long way to my place."

"That's nothing, nothing; I've plenty of time; besides, I have business in that direction."

"Gin-selling?" asked Arkady, rather too contemptuously.

But Sitnikov was reduced to such desperation that he did not even laugh as usual. "I assure you, my carriage is exceedingly comfortable," he muttered; "and there will be room for all."

"Don't wound Monsieur Sitnikov by a refusal," commented Anna Sergyevna.

Arkady glanced at her, and bowed his head significantly.

The visitors started off after lunch. As she said good-bye to Bazarov, Madame Odintsov held out her hand to him, and said, "We shall meet again, shan't we?"

"As you command," answered Bazarov.

"In that case, we shall."

Arkady was the first to descend the steps; he got into Sitnikov's carriage. A steward tucked him in respectfully, but he could have killed him with pleasure, or have burst into tears. Bazarov took his seat in the coach. When they reached Khokhlovsky, Arkady waited till Fedot, the keeper of the posting-station, had put in the horses, and going up to the coach he said, with his old smile, to Bazarov, "Yevgeny, take me with you; I want to come to you."

"Get in," Bazarov brought out through his teeth.

Sitnikov, who had been walking to and fro round the wheels of his carriage, whistling briskly, could only gape when he heard these words; while Arkady coolly pulled his luggage out of the carriage, took his seat beside Bazarov, and bowing politely to his former fellow-traveler, he called, "Whip up!" The coach rolled away, and was soon out of sight . . . Sitnikov, utterly confused, looked at his coachman, but the latter was flicking his whip about the tail of the off horse. Then Sitnikov jumped into the carriage, and growling at two passing peasants, "Put on your caps, idiots!" he drove to the town, where he arrived very late, and where, next day, at Madame Kukshin's, he dealt very severely with two "disgusting stuck-up churls."

When he was seated in the coach by Bazarov, Arkady pressed his hand warmly, and for a long while he said nothing. It seemed as though Bazarov understood and appreciated both the pressure and the silence. He had not slept all the previous night, and had not smoked, and had eaten scarcely anything for several days. His profile, already thinner, stood out darkly and sharply under his cap, which was pulled down to his eyebrows.

"Well, brother," he said at last, "give us a cigarette. But look, I say, is my tongue yellow?"

"Yes, it is," answered Arkady.

"Hm . . . and the cigarette's tasteless. The machine's out of gear."

"You look changed lately certainly," observed Arkady.

"It's nothing! We shall soon be all right. One thing's a bother—my mother's so tender-hearted; if you don't grow as round as a tub, and eat ten times a day, she's quite upset. My father's all right, he's known all sorts of ups and downs himself. No, I can't smoke," he added, and he flung the cigarette into the dust of the road.

"Do you think it's twenty miles?" asked Arkady.

"Yes. But ask this sage here." He indicated the peasant sitting on the box, a labourer of Fedot's.

But the sage only answered, "Who's to know—miles hereabout aren't measured," and went on swearing in an undertone at the shaft horse for "kicking with her head-piece," that is, shaking with her head down.

"Yes, yes," began Bazarov; "it's a lesson to you, my young friend, an instructive example. God knows, what rot it is. Every man hangs on a thread, the abyss may open under his feet any minute, and yet he must go and invent all sorts of discomforts for himself, and spoil his life."

"What are you alluding to?" asked Arkady.

"I'm not alluding to anything; I'm saying straight out that we've both behaved like fools. What's the use of talking about it! Still, I've noticed in hospital practice, the man who's furious at his illness —he's sure to get over it."

"I don't quite understand you," observed Arkady; "I should have thought you had nothing to complain of."

"And since you don't quite understand me, I'll tell you this—to

my mind, it's better to break stones on the highroad than to let a
woman have the mastery of even the end of one's little finger. That's
all ...." Bazarov was on the point of uttering his favourite word,
"romanticism," but he checked himself, and said, "rubbish. You
don't believe me now, but I tell you; you and I have been in feminine society, and very nice we found it; but to throw up society
like that is for all the world like a dip in cold water on a hot day.
A man hasn't time to attend to such trifles; a man ought not to be
tame, says an excellent Spanish proverb. Now, you, I suppose, my
sage friend," he added, turning to the peasant sitting on the box—
"you've a wife?"

The peasant showed both the friends his dull blear-eyed face.

"A wife? Yes. Every man has a wife."

"Do you beat her?"

"My wife? Everything happens sometimes. We don't beat her without good reason!"

"That's excellent. Well, and does she beat you?"

The peasant gave a tug at the reins. "That's a strange thing to
say, sir. You like your joke. . . ." He was obviously offended.

"You hear, Arkady Nikolaevitch! But we have taken a beating
. . . that's what comes of being educated people."

Arkady gave a forced laugh, while Bazarov turned away, and did
not open his mouth again the whole journey.

The twenty miles seemed to Arkady quite forty. But at last, on
the slope of some rising ground, appeared the small hamlet where
Bazarov's parents lived. Beside it, in a young birch copse, could be
seen a small house with a thatched roof. Two peasants stood with
their hats on at the first hut, abusing each other. "You're a great
sow," said one; "and worse than a little sucking pig."

"And your wife's a witch," retorted the other.

"From their unconstrained behaviour," Bazarov remarked to Arkady, "and the playfulness of their retorts, you can guess that my
father's peasants are not too much oppressed. Why, there he is himself coming out on the steps of his house. They must have heard
the bells. It's he; it's he—I know his figure. Ay, ay! how grey he's
grown though, poor chap!"

XX

Bazarov leaned out of the coach, while Arkady thrust his head out
behind his companion's back, and caught sight on the steps of the
little manor-house of a tall, thinnish man with dishevelled hair, and
thin hawk nose, dressed in an old military coat not buttoned up. He
was standing, his legs wide apart, smoking a long pipe and screwing
up his eyes to keep the sun out of them.

The horses stopped.

"Arrived at last," said Bazarov's father, still going on smoking
though the pipe was fairly dancing up and down between his fingers.

"Come, get out; get out; let me hug you."

He began embracing his son. . . . "Enyusha, Enyusha," was heard a trembling woman's voice. The door was flung open, and in the doorway was seen a plump, short, little old woman in a white cap and a short striped jacket. She moaned, staggered, and would certainly have fallen, had not Bazarov supported her. Her plump little hands were instantly twined round his neck, her head was pressed to his breast, and there was a complete hush. The only sound heard was her broken sobs.

Old Bazarov breathed hard and screwed his eyes up more than ever.

"There, that's enough, that's enough, Arisha! give over," he said, exchanging a glance with Arkady, who remained motionless in the coach, while the peasant on the box even turned his head away; "that's not at all necessary, please give over."

"Ah, Vassily Ivanovitch," faltered the old woman, "for what ages, my dear one, my darling, Enyusha," . . . and, not unclasping her hands, she drew her wrinkled face, wet with tears and working with tenderness, a little away from Bazarov, and gazed at him with blissful and comic-looking eyes, and again fell on his neck.

"Well, well, to be sure, that's all in the nature of things," commented Vassily Ivanovitch, "only we'd better come indoors. Here's a visitor come with Yevgeny. You must excuse it," he added, turning to Arkady, and scraping with his foot; "you understand, a woman's weakness; and well, a mother's heart . . ."

His lips and eyebrows, too, were twitching, and his beard was quivering . . . but he was obviously trying to control himself and appear almost indifferent.

"Let's come in, mother, really," said Bazarov, and he led the enfeebled old woman into the house. Putting her into a comfortable armchair, he once more hurriedly embraced his father and introduced Arkady to him.

"Heartily glad to make your acquaintance," said Vassily Ivanovitch, "but you mustn't expect great things; everything here in my house is done in a plain way, on a military footing. Arina Vlasyevna, calm yourself, pray; what weakness! The gentleman our guest will think ill of you."

"My dear sir," said the old lady through her tears, "your name and your father's I haven't the honour of knowing. . . ."

"Arkady Nikolaitch," put in Vassily Ivanovitch solemnly, in a low voice.

"You must excuse a silly old woman like me." The old woman blew her nose and bending her head to right and to left, carefully wiped one eye after the other. "You must excuse me. You see, I thought I should die, that I should not live to see my da . . arling."

"Well, here we have lived to see him, madam," put in Vassily

Ivanovitch. "Tanyushka," he turned to a barelegged little girl of thirteen in a bright red cotton dress, who was timidly peeping in at the door, "bring your mistress a glass of water—on a tray, do you hear?—and you, gentlemen," he added, with a kind of old-fashioned playfulness, "let me ask you into the study of a retired old veteran."

"Just once more let me embrace you, Enyusha," moaned Arina Vlasyevna. Bazarov bent down to her. "Why, what a handsome fellow you have grown!"

"Well, I don't know about being handsome," remarked Vassily Ivanovitch, "but he's a man, as the saying is, *ommfay*.[24] And now I hope, Arina Vlasyevna, that having satisfied your maternal heart, you will turn your thoughts to satisfying the appetites of our dear guests, because, as you're aware, even nightingales can't be fed on fairy tales."

The old lady got up from her chair. "This minute, Vassily Ivanovitch, the table shall be laid. I will run myself to the kitchen and order the samovar to be brought in; everything shall be ready, everything. Why, I have not seen him, not given him food or drink these three years; is that nothing?"

"There, mind, good mother, bustle about; don't put us to shame; while you, gentlemen, I beg you to follow me. Here's Timofeitch come to pay his respects to you, Yevgeny. He, too, I daresay, is delighted, the old dog. Eh, aren't you delighted, old dog? Be so good as to follow me."

And Vassily Ivanovitch went bustling forward, scraping and flapping with his slippers trodden down at heel.

His whole house consisted of six tiny rooms. One of them—the one to which he led our friends—was called the study. A thick-legged table, littered over with papers black with the accumulation of ancient dust as though they had been smoked, occupied all the space between the two windows; on the walls hung Turkish firearms, whips, a sabre, two maps, some anatomical diagrams, a portrait of Hufeland,[25] a monogram woven in hair in a blackened frame, and a diploma under glass; a leather sofa, torn and worn into hollows in parts, was placed between two huge cupboards of birchwood; on the shelves books, boxes, stuffed birds, jars, and phials were huddled together in confusion; in one corner stood a broken galvanic battery.

"I warned you, my dear Arkady Nikolaitch," began Vassily Ivanovitch, "that we live, so to say, bivouacking. . . ."

"There, stop that, what are you apologizing for?" Bazarov interrupted. "Kirsanov knows very well we're not Croesuses, and that you have no butler. Where are we going to put him, that's the question?"

---

24. *Ommfay* is a distorted spelling of *homme fait*, French for "grown-up man." Turgenev tries to suggest the poor French pronunciation of the old Bazarov.
25. Christoph Wilhelm Hufeland

(1762–1836) was a German physician who wrote a treatise *Makrobiotik or the Art of Prolonging Life* (1796). Turgenev connects the older Bazarov with a bygone prescientific stage of medicine.

"To be sure, Yevgeny; I have a capital room there in the little lodge; he will be very comfortable there."

"Have you had a lodge put up then?"

"Why, where the bath-house is," put in Timofeitch.

"That is next to the bathroom," Vassily Ivanovitch added hurriedly. "It's summer now. . . . I will run over there at once, and make arrangements; and you, Timofeitch, meanwhile bring in their things. You, Yevgeny, I shall of course offer my study. *Suum cuique.*"[26]

"There you have him! A comical old chap, and very good natured," remarked Bazarov, directly Vassily Ivanovitch had gone. "Just such a queer fish as yours, only in another way. He chatters too much."

"And your mother seems an awfully nice woman," observed Arkady.

"Yes, there's no humbug about her. You'll see what a dinner she'll give us."

"They didn't expect you to-day, sir; they've not brought any beef," observed Timofeitch, who was just dragging in Bazarov's box.

"We shall get on very well without beef. It's no use crying for the moon: Poverty, they say, is no vice."

"How many serfs has your father?" Arkady asked suddenly.

"The estate's not his, but mother's; there are fifteen serfs, if I remember."

"Twenty-two in all," Timofeitch added, with an air of displeasure.

The flapping of slippers was heard, and Vassily Ivanovitch reappeared. "In a few minutes your room will be ready to receive you," he cried triumphantly. "Arkady . . . Nikolaitch? I think that is right? And here is your attendant," he added, indicating a short-cropped boy, who had come in with him in a blue full-skirted coat with ragged elbows and a pair of boots which did not belong to him. "His name is Fedka. Again, I repeat, even though my son tells me not to, you mustn't expect great things. He knows how to fill a pipe, though. You smoke, of course?"

"I generally smoke cigars," answered Arkady.

"And you do very sensibly. I myself give the preference to cigars, but in these solitudes it is exceedingly difficult to obtain them."

"There, that's enough humble pie," Bazarov interrupted again. "You'd much better sit here on the sofa and let us have a look at you."

Vassily Ivanovitch laughed and sat down. He was very like his son in face, only his brow was lower and narrower, and his mouth rather wider, and he was forever restless, shrugging up his shoulder as though his coat cut him under the armpits, blinking, clearing his throat, and gesticulating with his fingers, while his son was distinguished by a kind of nonchalant immobility.

"Humble pie!" repeated Vassily Ivanovitch. "You must not

26. "to each his own." The expression is first found in Cicero.

imagine, Yevgeny, I want to appeal, so to speak, to our guest's sympathies by making out we live in such a wilderness. Quite the contrary, I maintain that for a thinking man nothing is a wilderness. At least, I try as far as possible not to get rusty, so to speak, not to fall behind the age."

Vassily Ivanovitch drew out of his pocket a new yellow silk handkerchief, which he had had time to snatch up on the way to Arkady's room, and flourishing it in the air, he proceeded: "I am not now alluding to the fact that, for example, at the cost of sacrifices not inconsiderable for me, I have put my peasants on the rent-system and given up my land to them on half profits. I regarded that as my duty; common sense itself enjoins such a proceeding, though other proprietors do not even dream of it; I am alluding to the sciences, to culture."

"Yes; I see you have here *The Friend of Health* for 1855," remarked Bazarov.

"It's sent me by an old comrade out of friendship," Vassily Ivanovitch made haste to answer; "but we have, for instance, some idea even of phrenology,"[27] he added, addressing himself principally, however, to Arkady, and pointing to a small plaster head on the cupboard, divided into numbered squares; "we are not unacquainted even with Schönlein[28] and Rademacher."[29]

"Why do people still believe in Rademacher in this province?" asked Bazarov.

Vassily Ivanovitch cleared his throat. "In this province. . . . Of course, gentlemen, you know best; how could we keep pace with you? You are here to take our places. In my day, too, there was some sort of a Humouralist school, Hoffmann, and Brown[30] too with his vitalism—they seemed very ridiculous to us, but, of course, they too had been great men at one time or other. Some one new has taken the place of Rademacher with you; you bow down to him, but in another twenty years it will be his turn to be laughed at."

"For your consolation I will tell you," observed Bazarov, "that nowadays we laugh at medicine altogether, and don't bow down to any one."

"How's that? Why, you're going to be a doctor, aren't you?"

27. Phrenology was a pseudo-science which was extremely popular and widely accepted in the early nineteenth century. It is actually a system of psychology which assumes that different mental faculties are located in specific regions of the brain and that by a study of the surface of the skull it is possible to ascertain the disposition and character of a man.

28. Johann Lukas Schönlein (1793–1864), a German physician who discovered the role of fungi in skin diseases.

29. Johann Gottfried Rademacher (1772–1850), another German physician who devised a scheme of "experimental" medicine in which diseases were diagnosed from the medicaments to which they reacted.

30. Friedrich Hoffmann (1660-1742) held a theory of medicine which was a revival of the ancient Greek system of four humors (blood, phlegm, and yellow and black bile), while the Scottish physician John Brown (1735–1788) considered the "life-force" to be the main principle of explanation (*Vitalism*). The elder Bazarov makes a pathetic display of out-dated medical authorities.

"Yes, but the one fact doesn't prevent the other."

Vassily Ivanovitch poked his third finger into his pipe, where a little smouldering ash was still left. "Well, perhaps—I am not going to dispute. What am I? A retired army-doctor, *volla-too*;[31] now fate has made me take to farming. I served in your grandfather's brigade," he addressed himself again to Arkady; "yes, yes, I have seen many sights in my day. And I was thrown into all kinds of society, brought into contact with all sorts of people! I myself, the man you see before you now, have felt the pulse of Prince Wittgenstein[32] and of Zhukovsky![33] They were in the southern army, in the fourteenth, you understand" (and here Vassily Ivanovitch pursed his mouth up significantly). "Well, well, but my business was on one side; stick to your lancet and let everything else go hang! Your grandfather was a very honourable man, a real soldier."

"Confess, now, he was rather a blockhead," remarked Bazarov, lazily.

"Ah, Yevgeny, how can you use such an expression! Do consider. ... Of course, General Kirsanov was not one of the ..."

"Come, drop him," broke in Bazarov; "I was pleased as I was driving along here to see your birch copse; it has shot up capitally."

Vassily Ivanovitch brightened up. "And you must see what a little garden I've got now! I planted every tree myself. I've fruit, and raspberries, and all kinds of medicinal herbs. However clever you young gentlemen may be, old Paracelsus spoke the holy truth: *in herbis, verbis et lapidibus*. . . .[34] I've retired from practice, you know, of course, but two or three times a week it will happen that I'm brought back to my old work. They come for advice—I can't drive them away. Sometimes the poor have recourse to me for help. And indeed there are no doctors here at all. There's one of the neighbours here, a retired major, only fancy, he doctors the people too. I asked the question, 'Has he studied medicine?' And they told me, 'No, he's not studied; he does it more from philanthropy.' . . . Ha! ha! ha! from philanthropy! What do you think of that? Ha! ha! ha!"

"Fedka, fill me a pipe!" said Bazarov rudely.

"And there's another doctor here who just got to a patient," Vassily Ivanovitch persisted in a kind of desperation, "when the patient had gone *ad patres*; the servant didn't let the doctor speak; 'you're no longer wanted,' he told him. He hadn't expected this, got confused, and asked, 'Why, did your master hiccup before his death?'

31. *voilà tout*— "that's all."
32. Prince Ludwig Adolf Peter Wittgenstein (1769–1843), Russian general who took command of the Russian armies against Napoleon after the death of Kutuzov in 1813. In 1828 he commanded the Russian army in the war against Turkey.
33. Vasily Zhukovsky (1783–1852), the most famous Russian romantic poet before Pushkin.
34. Paracelsus, actually Wilhelm Bombast von Hohenheim (ca. 1490–1541), was a Swiss physician and "natural philosopher" who believed in the healing power residing *"in herbis, verbis et lapidibus"* (Latin, "plants, words and stones").

'Yes.' 'Did he hiccup much?' 'Yes.' 'Ah, well, that's all right,' and off he set back again. Ha! ha! ha!"

The old man was alone in his laughter; Arkady forced a smile on his face. Bazarov simply stretched. The conversation went on in this way for about an hour; Arkady had time to go to his room, which turned out to be the anteroom attached to the bathroom, but was very snug and clean. At last Tanyusha came in and announced that dinner was ready.

Vassily Ivanovitch was the first to get up. "Come, gentlemen. You must be magnanimous and pardon me if I've bored you. I daresay my good wife will give you more satisfaction."

The dinner, though prepared in haste, turned out to be very good, even abundant; only the wine was not quite up to the mark; it was almost black sherry, bought by Timofeitch in the town at a well-known merchant's, and had a faint coppery, resinous taste, and the flies were a great nuisance. On ordinary days a serf-boy used to keep driving them away with a large green branch; but on this occasion Vassily Ivanovitch had sent him away through dread of the criticism of the younger generation. Arina Vlasyevna had had time to dress; she had put on a high cap with silk ribbons and a pale blue flowered shawl. She broke down again directly she caught sight of her Enyusha, but her husband had no need to admonish her; she made haste to wipe away her tears herself, for fear of spotting her shawl. Only the young men ate anything; the master and mistress of the house had dined long ago. Fedka waited at table, obviously encumbered by having boots on for the first time; he was assisted by a woman of a masculine cast of face and one eye, by name Anfisushka, who performed the duties of housekeeper, poultry-woman, and laundress. Vassily Ivanovitch walked up and down during the whole of dinner, and with a perfectly happy, positively beatific countenance, talked about the serious anxiety he felt at Napoleon's policy, and the intricacy of the Italian question.[35] Arina Vlasyevna took no notice of Arkady; leaning her round face, to which the full cherry-coloured lips and the little moles on the cheeks and over the eyebrows gave a very simple, good-natured expression, on her little closed fist, she did not take her eyes off her son, and kept constantly sighing; she was dying to know for how long he had come, but she was afraid to ask him.

"What if he says for two days," she thought, and her heart sank. After the roast Vassily Ivanovitch disappeared for an instant, and returned with an opened half-bottle of champagne. "Here," he cried, "though we do live in the wilds, we have something to make merry with on festive occasions!" He filled three champagne glasses and a

35. The allusion is to Napoleon III and to the Italian question in 1859: the French victory at the Battle of Solferino led to the liberation of Lombardy from Austrian occupation.

little wineglass, proposed the health of "our inestimable guests," and at once tossed off his glass in military fashion; while he made Arina Vlasyevna drink her wineglass to the last drop. When the time came in due course for preserves, Arkady, who could not bear anything sweet, thought it his duty, however, to taste four different kinds which had been freshly made, all the more as Bazarov flatly refused them and began at once smoking a cigarette. Then tea came on the scene with cream, butter, and biscuits; then Vassily Ivanovitch took them all into the garden to admire the beauty of the evening. As they passed a garden seat he whispered to Arkady—

"At this spot I love to meditate, as I watch the sunset; it suits a recluse like me. And there, a little farther off, I have planted some of the trees beloved of Horace."

"What trees?" asked Bazarov, overhearing.

"Oh . . . acacias."

Bazarov began to yawn.

"I imagine it's time our travellers were in the arms of Morpheus," observed Vassily Ivanovitch.

"That is, it's time for bed," Bazarov put in. "That's a correct idea. It is time, certainly."

As he said good-night to his mother, he kissed her on the forehead, while she embraced him, and stealthily behind his back she gave him her blessing three times. Vassily Ivanovitch conducted Arkady to his room, and wished him "as refreshing repose as I enjoyed at your happy years." And Arkady did as a fact sleep excellently in his bath-house; there was a smell of mint in it, and two crickets behind the stove rivalled each other in their drowsy chirping. Vassily Ivanovitch went from Arkady's room to his study, and perching on the sofa at his son's feet, he was looking forward to having a chat with him; but Bazarov at once sent him away, saying he was sleepy, and did not fall asleep till morning. With wide open eyes he stared vindictively into the darkness; the memories of childhood had no power over him; and besides, he had not yet had time to get rid of the impression of his recent bitter emotions. Arina Vlasyevna first prayed to her heart's content, then she had a long, long conversation with Anfisushka, who stood stockstill before her mistress, and fixing her solitary eye upon her, communicated in a mysterious whisper all her observations and conjectures in regard to Yevgeny Vassilyitch. The old lady's head was giddy with happiness and wine and tobacco smoke; her husband tried to talk to her, but with a wave of his hand gave it up in despair.

Arina Vlasyevna was a genuine Russian gentlewoman of the olden times; she ought to have lived two centuries before, in the old Moscow days. She was very devout and emotional; she believed in fortune-telling, charms, dreams, and omens of every possible kind; she believed in the prophecies of crazy people, in house-spirits, in

wood-spirits, in unlucky meetings, in the evil eye, in popular remedies, she ate specially prepared salt on Holy Thursday, and believed
that the end of the world was at hand; she believed that if on
Easter Sunday the lights did not go out at vespers, then there would
be a good crop of buckwheat, and that a mushroom will not grow
after it has been looked on by the eye of man; she believed that
the devil likes to be where there is water, and that every Jew has
a blood-stained patch on his breast; she was afraid of mice, of snakes,
of frogs, of sparrows, of leeches, of thunder, of cold water, of
draughts, of horses, of goats, of red-haired people, and black cats
and she regarded crickets and dogs as unclean beasts; she never ate
veal, doves, crayfishes, cheese, asparagus, artichokes, hares, nor water-
melons, because a cut water-melon suggested the head of John the
Baptist, and of oysters she could not speak without a shudder; she
was fond of eating—and fasted rigidly; she slept ten hours out of
the twenty-four—and never went to bed at all if Vassily Ivanovitch
had so much as a headache; she had never read a single book except
Alexis or the Cottage in the Forest; she wrote one, or at the most
two letters in a year, but was great in housewifery, preserving, and
jam-making, though with her own hands she never touched a thing,
and was generally disinclined to move from her place. Arina Vlasyevna was very kindhearted, and in her way not at all stupid. She
knew that the world is divided into masters whose duty it is to
command, and simple folk whose duty it is to serve them—and so
she felt no repugnance to servility and prostrations to the ground;
but she treated those in subjection to her kindly and gently, never
let a single beggar go away empty-handed, and never spoke ill of
any one, though she was fond of gossip. In her youth she had been
pretty, had played the clavichord, and spoken French a little; but in
the course of many years' wanderings with her husband, whom she
had married against her will, she had grown stout, and forgotten
music and French. Her son she loved and feared unutterably; she
had given up the management of the property to Vassily Ivanovitch
—and now did not interfere in anything; she used to groan, wave
her handkerchief, and raise her eyebrows higher and higher with
horror directly her old husband began to discuss the impending government reforms and his own plans. She was apprehensive, and constantly expecting some great misfortune, and began to weep directly
she remembered anything sorrowful. . . . Such women are not common
nowadays. God knows whether we ought to rejoice!

XXI

On getting up Arkady opened the window, and the first object
that met his view was Vassily Ivanovitch. In an Oriental dressing-
gown girt around the waist with a pocket-handkerchief he was in-
dustriously digging in his garden. He perceived his young visitor,
and leaning on his spade, he called, "The best of health to you!

How have you slept?"

"Capitally," answered Arkady.

"Here am I, as you see, like some Cincinnatus,[36] marking out a bed for late turnips. The time has come now—and thank God for it!—when every one ought to obtain his sustenance with his own hands; it's useless to reckon on others; one must labour oneself. And it turns out that Jean Jacques Rousseau is right. Half an hour ago, my dear young gentleman, you might have seen me in a totally different position. One peasant woman, who complained of looseness —that's how they express it, but in our language, dysentery—I . . . how can I express it best? I administered opium; and for another I extracted a tooth. I proposed an anaesthetic to her . . . but she would not consent. All that I do *gratis—anamatyer* (*en amateur*). I'm used to it, though; you see, I'm a plebeian, *homo novus*—not one of the old stock, not like my spouse. . . . Wouldn't you like to come this way into the shade, to breathe the morning freshness a little before tea?"

Arkady went out to him.

"Welcome once again," said Vassily Ivanovitch, raising his hand in a military salute to the greasy skull-cap which covered his head. "You, I know, are accustomed to luxury, to amusements, but even the great ones of this world do not disdain to spend a brief space under a cottage roof."

"Good heavens," protested Arkady, "as though I were one of the great ones of this world! And I'm not accustomed to luxury."

"Pardon me, pardon me," rejoined Vassily Ivanovitch with a polite simper. "Though I am laid on the shelf now, I have knocked about the world too—I can tell a bird by its flight. I am something of a psychologist, too, in my own way, and a physiognomist. If I had not, I will venture to say, been endowed with that gift, I should have come to grief long ago; I should have stood no chance, a poor man like me. I tell you without flattery, I am sincerely delighted at the friendship I observe between you and my son. I have just seen him; he got up as he usually does—no doubt you are aware of it— very early, and went a ramble about the neighbourhood. Permit me to inquire—have you known my son long?"

"Since last winter."

"Indeed. And permit me to question you further—but hadn't we better sit down? Permit me, as a father, to ask without reserve, What is your opinion of my Yevgeny?"

"Your son is one of the most remarkable men I have ever met," Arkady answered emphatically.

Vassily Ivanovitch's eyes suddenly grew round, and his cheeks

36. Lucius Quinctius Cincinnatus (born about 520 B.C.), a legendary hero of ancient Rome who, after defeating an enemy army, chose to return to his humble farm rather than to accept the dictatorship of Rome. The story is told in Livy's *History of Rome.*

were suffused with a faint flush. The spade fell out of his hand.

"And so you expect," he began . . .

"I'm convinced," Arkady put in, "that your son has a great future before him; that he will do honour to your name. I've been certain of that ever since I first met him."

"How . . . how was that?" Vassily Ivanovitch articulated with an effort. His wide mouth was relaxed in a triumphant smile, which would not leave it.

"Would you like me to tell you how we met?"

"Yes . . . and altogether. . . ."

Arkady began to tell his tale, and to talk of Bazarov with even greater warmth, even greater enthusiasm than he had done on the evening when he danced a mazurka with Madame Odintsov.

Vassily Ivanovitch listened and listened, blinked, and rolled his handkerchief up into a ball in both his hands, cleared his throat, ruffled up his hair, and at last could stand it no longer; he bent down to Arkady and kissed him on his shoulder. "You have made me perfectly happy," he said, never ceasing to smile. "I ought to tell you, I . . . idolise my son; my old wife I won't speak of—we all know what mothers are!—but I dare not show my feelings before him, because he doesn't like it. He is averse to every kind of demonstration of feeling; many people even find fault with him for such firmness of character, and regard it as a proof of pride or lack of feeling, but men like him ought not to be judged by the common standard, ought they? And here, for example, many another fellow in his place would have been a constant drag on his parents; but he, would you believe it, has never from the day he was born taken a kopek more than he could help, that's God's truth!"

"He is a disinterested, honest man," observed Arkady.

"Exactly so; he is disinterested. And I don't only idolise him, Arkady Nikolaitch, I am proud of him, and the height of my ambition is that some day there will be the following lines in his biography: 'The son of a simple army-doctor, who was, however, capable of divining his greatness betimes, and spared nothing for his education . . .'" The old man's voice broke.

Arkady pressed his hand.

"What do you think," inquired Vassily Ivanovitch, after a short silence, "will it be in the career of medicine that he will attain the celebrity you anticipate for him?"

"Of course, not in medicine, though even in that department he will be one of the leading scientific men."

"In what then, Arkady Nikolaitch?"

"It would be hard to say now, but he will be famous."

"He will be famous!" repeated the old man, and he sank into a reverie.

"Arina Vlasyevna sent me to call you in to tea," announced Anfisushka, coming by with an immense dish of ripe raspberries.

Vassily Ivanovitch started. "And will there be cooled cream for the raspberries?"

"Yes."

"Cold now, mind! Don't stand on ceremony, Arkady Nikolaitch; take some more. How is it Yevgeny doesn't come?"

"I'm here," was heard Bazarov's voice from Arkady's room.

Vassily Ivanovitch turned round quickly. "Aha! you wanted to pay a visit to your friend; but you were too late, *amice*, and we have already had a long conversation with him. Now we must go in to tea, mother summons us. By the way, I want to have a little talk with you."

"What about?"

"There's a peasant here; he's suffering from icterus. . . ."

"You mean jaundice?"

"Yes, a chronic and very obstinate case of icterus. I have prescribed him centaury and St. John's wort, ordered him to eat carrots, given him soda; but all that's merely palliative measures; we want some more decided treatment. Though you do laugh at medicine, I am certain you can give me practical advice. But we will talk of that later. Now come in to tea."

Vassily Ivanovitch jumped up briskly from the garden seat, and hummed from *Robert le Diable*[37]—

> "The rule, the rule we set ourselves,
> To live, to live for pleasure!"

"Singular vitality!" observed Bazarov, going away from the window.

It was midday. The sun was burning hot behind a thin veil of unbroken whitish clouds. Everything was hushed; there was no sound but the cocks crowing irritably at one another in the village, producing in every one who heard them a strange sense of drowsiness and ennui; and somewhere, high up in a tree-top, the incessant plaintive cheep of a young hawk. Arkady and Bazarov lay in the shade of a small haystack, putting under themselves two armfuls of dry and rustling but still greenish and fragrant grass.

"That aspen-tree," began Bazarov, "reminds me of my childhood; it grows at the edge of the clay-pits where the bricks were dug, and in those days I believed firmly that that clay-pit and aspen-tree possessed a peculiar talismanic power; I never felt dull near them. I did not understand then that I was not dull, because I was a child. Well, now I'm grown up, the talisman's lost its power."

"How long did you live here altogether?" asked Arkady.

37. Giacomo Meyerbeer (1791–1863) composed a grand opera to a French text, *Robert le Diable* (1831), which was an immense success.

"Two years on end; then we travelled about. We led a roving life, wandering from town to town for the most part."

"And has this house been standing long?"

"Yes. My grandfather built it—my mother's father."

"Who was he—your grandfather?"

"Devil knows. Some second-major. He served with Suvórov,[38] and was always telling stories about the crossing of the Alps—inventions probably."

"You have a portrait of Suvórov hanging in the drawing-room. I like these dear little houses like yours; they're so warm and old-fashioned; and there's always a special sort of scent about them."

"A smell of lamp-oil and clover," Bazarov remarked, yawning. "And the flies in those dear little houses. . . . Faugh!"

"Tell me," began Arkady, after a brief pause, "were they strict with you when you were a child?"

"You can see what my parents are like. They're not a severe sort."

"Are you fond of them, Yevgeny?"

"I am, Arkady."

"How fond they are of you!"

Bazarov was silent for a little. "Do you know what I'm thinking about?" he brought out at last, clasping his hands behind his head.

"No. What is it?"

"I'm thinking life is a happy thing for my parents. My father at sixty is fussing around, talking about 'palliative' measures, doctoring people, playing the bountiful master with the peasants—having a festive time, in fact; and my mother's happy too; her day's so chock-ful of duties of all sorts, and sighs and groans that she's no time even to think of herself; while I. . . ."

"While you?"

"I think; here I lie under a haystack. . . . The tiny space I occupy is so infinitely small in comparison with the rest of space, in which I am not, and which has nothing to do with me; and the period of time in which it is my lot to live is so petty beside the eternity in which I have not been, and shall not be. . . . And in this atom, this mathematical point, the blood is circulating, the brain is working and wanting something. . . . Isn't it loathsome? Isn't it petty?"

"Allow me to remark that what you're saying applies to men in general."

"You are right," Bazarov cut in. "I was going to say that they now—my parents, I mean—are absorbed and don't trouble them-

38. Count Alexander Suvórov (1729–1800) was the most prominent Russian general of the eighteenth century. He suppressed the peasant revolt of Pugachev, he subdued the Poles, and in 1790 he stormed Ismael in the war against the Turks. But he won his most famous victories against the French revolutionary armies in Italy and Switzerland in 1799–1800.

selves about their own nothingness; it doesn't sicken them . . . while I . . . I feel nothing but weariness and anger."

"Anger? Why anger?"

"Why? How can you ask why? Have you forgotten?"

"I remember everything, but still I don't admit that you have any right to be angry. You're unlucky, I'll allow, but . . ."

"Pooh! then you, Arkady Nikolaevitch, I can see, regard love like all modern young men; cluck, cluck, cluck you call to the hen, but if the hen comes near you, you run away. I'm not like that. But that's enough of that. What can't be helped, it's shameful to talk about." He turned over on his side. "Aha! there goes a valiant ant dragging off a dead fly. Take her, brother, take her! Don't pay attention to her resistance; it's your privilege as an animal to be free from the sentiment of pity—make the most of it—not like us conscientious self-destructive animals!"

"You shouldn't say that, Yevgeny! When have you destroyed yourself!"

Bazarov raised his head. "That's the only thing I pride myself on. I haven't crushed myself, so a woman can't crush me. Amen! It's all over! You shall not hear another word from me about it."

Both the friends lay for some time in silence.

"Yes," began Bazarov, "man's a strange animal. When one gets a side view from a distance of the dead-alive life our 'fathers' lead here, one thinks, What could be better? You eat and drink, and know you are acting in the most reasonable, most judicious manner. But if not, you're devoured by ennui. One wants to have to do with people if only to abuse them."

"One ought so to order one's life that every moment in it should be of significance," Arkady affirmed reflectively.

"I dare say! What's of significance is sweet, however mistaken; one could make up one's mind to what's insignificant even. But pettiness, pettiness, that's what's insufferable."

"Pettiness doesn't exist for a man so long as he refuses to recognise it."

"H'm . . . what you've just said is a commonplace reversed."

"What? What do you mean by that term?"

"I'll tell you: saying, for instance, that education is beneficial, that's a commonplace; but to say that education is injurious, that's a commonplace turned upside down. There's more style about it, so to say, but in reality it's one and the same."

"And the truth is—where, which side?"

"Where? Like an echo I answer, 'Where?'"

"You're in a melancholy mood to-day, Yevgeny."

"Really? The sun must have softened my brain, I suppose, and I can't stand so many raspberries either."

"In that case, a nap's not a bad thing," observed Arkady.

"Certainly; only don't look at me; every man's face is stupid when he's asleep."

"But isn't it all the same to you what people think of you?"

"I don't know what to say to you. A real man ought not to care; a real man is one whom it's no use thinking about, whom one must either obey or hate."

"It's funny! I don't hate anybody," observed Arkady, after a moment's thought.

"And I hate so many. You are a soft-hearted, mawkish creature; how could you hate any one? . . . You're timid; you don't rely on yourself much."

"And you," interrupted Arkady, "do you expect much of yourself? Have you a high opinion of yourself?"

Bazarov paused. "When I meet a man who can hold his own beside me," he said, dwelling on every syllable, "then I'll change my opinion of myself. Yes, hatred! You said, for instance, to-day as we passed our bailiff Philip's cottage—it's the one that's so nice and clean—well, you said, Russia will come to perfection when the poorest peasant has a house like that, and every one of us ought to work to bring it about. . . . And I felt such a hatred for this poorest peasant, this Philip or Sidor, for whom I'm to be ready to jump out of my skin, and who won't even thank me for it . . . and why should he thank me? Why, suppose he does live in a clean house, while the nettles are growing out of me,—well what do I gain by it?"

"Hush, Yevgeny . . . if one listened to you to-day one would be driven to agreeing with those who reproach us for want of principles."

"You talk like your uncle. There are no general principles—you've not made out that even yet! There are feelings. Everything depends on them."

"How so?"

"Why, I, for instance, take up a negative attitude, by virtue of my sensations; I like to deny—my brain's made on that plan, and that's all about it! Why do I like chemistry? Why do you like apples?—by virtue of our sensations. It's all the same thing. Deeper than that men will never penetrate. Not every one will tell you that, and, in fact, I shan't tell you so another time."

"What, and is honesty a matter of the senses?"

"I should rather think so."

"Yevgeny!" Arkady was beginning in a dejected voice . . .

"Well? What? Isn't it to your taste?" broke in Bazarov. "No, brother. If you've made up your mind to mow down everything, don't spare your own legs. But we've talked enough metaphysics.

856 • *Ivan Turgenev*

"Nature breathes the silence of sleep,' said Pushkin."

"He never said anything of the sort," protested Arkady.

"Well, if he didn't, as a poet he might have—and ought to have said it. By the way, he must have been a military man."

"Pushkin never was a military man!"

"Why, on every page of him there's, 'To arms! to arms! for Russia's honour!' "

"Why, what stories you invent! I declare, it's positive calumny."

"Calumny? That's a mighty matter! What a word he's found to frighten me with! Whatever charge you make against a man, you may be certain he deserves twenty times worse than that in reality."

"We had better go to sleep," said Arkady, in a tone of vexation.

"With the greatest pleasure," answered Bazarov. But neither of them slept. A feeling almost of hostility had come over both the young men. Five minutes later, they opened their eyes and glanced at one another in silence.

"Look," said Arkady suddenly, "a dry maple leaf has come off and is falling to the earth; its movement is exactly like a butterfly's flight. Isn't it strange? Gloom and decay—like brightness and life."

"Oh, my friend, Arkady Nikolaitch!" cried Bazarov, "one thing I entreat of you; no fine talk."

"I talk as best I can . . . And, I declare, it's perfect despotism. An idea came into my head; why shouldn't I utter it?"

"Yes; and why shouldn't I utter my ideas? I think that fine talk's positively indecent."

"And what is decent? Abuse?"

"Ha! ha! you really do intend, I see, to walk in your uncle's footsteps. How pleased that worthy imbecile would have been if he had heard you!"

"What did you call Pavel Petrovitch?"

"I called him, very justly, an imbecile."

"But this is unbearable!" cried Arkady.

"Aha! family feeling spoke there," Bazarov commented coolly. "I've noticed how obstinately it sticks to people. A man's ready to give up everything and break with every prejudice; but to admit that his brother, for instance, who steals handkerchiefs, is a thief—that's too much for him. And when one comes to think of it: my brother, mine—and no genius . . . that's an idea no one can swallow."

"It was a simple sense of justice spoke in me and not in the least family feeling," retorted Arkady passionately. "But since that's a sense you don't understand, since you haven't that sensation, you can't judge of it."

"In other words, Arkady Kirsanov is too exalted for my comprehension. I bow down before him and say no more."

"Don't, please, Yevgeny; we shall really quarrel at last."

"Ah, Arkady! do me a kindness. I entreat you, let us quarrel for once in earnest. . . ."

"But then perhaps we should end by . . ."

"Fighting?" put in Bazarov. "Well? Here, on the hay, in these idyllic surroundings, far from the world and the eyes of men, it wouldn't matter. But you'd be no match for me. I'd have you by the throat in a minute."

Bazarov spread out his long, cruel fingers. . . . Arkady turned round and prepared, as though in jest, to resist. . . . But his friend's face struck him as so vindictive—there was such menace in grim earnest in the smile that distorted his lips, and in his glittering eyes, that he felt instinctively afraid.

"Ah! so this is where you have got to!" the voice of Vassily Ivanovitch was heard saying at that instant, and the old army-doctor appeared before the young men, garbed in a home-made linen pea-jacket, with a straw hat, also home-made, on his head. "I've been looking everywhere for you. . . . Well, you've picked out a capital place, and you're excellently employed. Lying on the 'earth, gazing up to heaven.' Do you know, there's a special significance in that?"

"I never gaze up to heaven except when I want to sneeze," growled Bazarov, and turning to Arkady he added in an undertone. "Pity he interrupted us."

"I look at you, my youthful friends," Vassily Ivanovitch was saying meantime, shaking his head, and leaning his folded arms on a rather cunningly bent stick of his own carving, with a Turk's figure for a top,—"I look, and I cannot refrain from admiration. You have so much strength, such youth and bloom, such abilities, such talents! Positively, a Castor and Pollux."

"Get along with you—going off into mythology!" commented Bazarov. "You can see at once that he was a great Latinist in his day! Why, I seem to remember, you gained the silver medal for Latin prose—didn't you?"

"The Dioscuri, the Dioscuri!" repeated Vassily Ivanovitch.

"Come, shut up, father; don't show off."

"Once in a way it's surely permissible," murmured the old man. "However, I have not been seeking for you, gentlemen, to pay you compliments; but with the object, in the first place, of announcing to you that we shall soon be dining; and secondly, I wanted to prepare you, Yevgeny. . . . You are a sensible man, you know the world, and you know what women are, and consequently you will excuse. . . . Your mother wished to have a Te Deum sung on the occasion of your arrival. You must not imagine that I am inviting you to attend this thanksgiving—it is over indeed now; but Father Alexey . . ."

"The village priest?"

"Well, yes, the priest; he . . . is to dine . . . with us. . . . I did not anticipate this, and did not even approve of it . . . but it somehow came about . . . he did not understand me. . . . And, well . . . Arina Vlasyevna . . . Besides, he's a worthy, reasonable man."

"He won't eat my share at dinner, I suppose?" queried Bazarov.

Vassily Ivanovitch laughed. "How you talk!"

"Well, that's all I ask. I'm ready to sit down to table with any man."

Vassily Ivanovitch set his hat straight. "I was certain before I spoke," he said, "that you were above any kind of prejudice. Here am I, an old man at sixty-two, and I have none." (Vassily Ivanovitch did not dare to confess that he had himself desired the thanksgiving service. He was no less religious than his wife.) "And Father Alexey very much wanted to make your acquaintance. You will like him, you'll see. He's no objection even to cards, and he sometimes—but this is between ourselves . . . positively smokes a pipe."

"All right. We'll have a round of whist after dinner, and I'll clean him out."

"He! he! he! We shall see! That remains to be seen."

"I know you're an old hand," said Bazarov, with a peculiar emphasis.

Vassily Ivanovitch's bronzed cheeks were suffused with an uneasy flush.

"For shame, Yevgeny . . . Let bygones be bygones. Well, I'm ready to acknowledge before this gentleman I had that passion in my youth; and I have paid for it too! How hot it is, though! Let me sit down with you. I shan't be in your way, I hope?"

"Oh, not at all," answered Arkady.

Vassily Ivanovitch lowered himself, sighing, into the hay. "Your present quarters remind me, my dear sirs," he began, "of my military bivouacking existence, the ambulance halts, somewhere like this under a haystack, and even for that we were thankful." He sighed. "I have had many, many experiences in my life. For example, if you will allow me, I will tell you a curious episode of the plague in Bessarabia."

"For which you got the Vladimir cross?" put in Bazarov. "We know, we know. . . . By the way, why is it you're not wearing it?"

"Why, I told you that I have no prejudices," muttered Vassily Ivanovitch (he had only the evening before had the red ribbon unpicked off his coat), and he proceeded to relate the episode of the plague. "Why, he's fallen asleep," he whispered all at once to Arkady, pointing to Yevgeny, and winking good-naturedly. "Yevgeny! get up," he went on aloud. "Let's go in to dinner."

Father Alexey, a good-looking stout man with thick, carefully combed hair, with an embroidered girdle round his lilac silk cassock, appeared to be a man of much tact and adaptability. He made haste to be the first to offer his hand to Arkady and Bazarov, as though understanding beforehand that they did not want his blessing, and he behaved himself in general without constraint. He neither derogated from his own dignity, nor gave offence to others; he vouchsafed a passing smile at the seminary Latin, and stood up for his bishop; drank two small glasses of wine, but refused a third; accepted a cigar from Arkady, but did not proceed to smoke it, saying he would take it home with him. The only thing not quite agreeable about him was a way he had of constantly raising his hand with care and deliberation to catch the flies on his face, sometimes succeeding in smashing them. He took his seat at the green table, expressing his satisfaction at so doing in measured terms, and ended by winning from Bazarov two rubles and a half in paper money; they had no idea of even reckoning in silver in the house of Arina Vlasyevna. . . . She was sitting, as before, near her son (she did not play cards), her cheek, as before, propped on her little fist; she only got up to order some new dainty to be served. She was afraid to caress Bazarov, and he gave her no encouragement, he did not invite her caresses; and besides, Vassily Ivanovitch had advised her not to "worry" him too much. "Young men are not fond of that sort of thing," he declared to her. (It's needless to say what the dinner was like that day; Timofeitch in person had galloped off at early dawn for beef; the bailiff had gone off in another direction for turbot, gremille, and crayfish; for mushrooms alone forty-two farthings had been paid the peasant women in copper); but Arina Vlasyevna's eyes, bent steadfastly on Bazarov, did not express only devotion and tenderness; in them was to be seen sorrow also, mingled with awe and curiosity; there was to be seen too a sort of humble reproachfulness.

Bazarov, however, was not in a humour to analyse the exact expression of his mother's eyes; he seldom turned to her, and then only with some short question. Once he asked her for her hand "for luck"; she gently laid her soft, little hand on his rough, broad palm.

"Well," she asked, after waiting a little, "has it been any use?"

"Worse luck than ever," he answered, with a careless laugh.

"He plays too rashly," pronounced Father Alexey, as it were compassionately, and he stroked his beard.

"Napoleon's rule, good Father, Napoleon's rule," put in Vassily Ivanovitch, leading an ace.

"It brought him to St. Helena, though," observed Father Alexey, as he trumped the ace.

"Wouldn't you like some currant tea, Enyusha?" inquired Arina Vlasyevna.

Bazarov merely shrugged his shoulders.

"No!" he said to Arkady the next day, "I'm off from here tomorrow. I'm bored; I want to work, but I can't work here. I will come to your place again; I've left all my apparatus there, too. In your house one can at any rate shut oneself up. While here my father repeats to me, 'My study is at your disposal—nobody shall interfere with you,' and all the time he himself is never a yard away. And I'm ashamed somehow to shut myself away from him. It's the same thing, too, with mother. I hear her sighing the other side of the wall, and if one goes in to her, one's nothing to say to her."

"She will be very much grieved," observed Arkady, "and so will he."

"I shall come back again to them."

"When?"

"Why, when on my way to Petersburg."

"I feel sorry for your mother particularly."

"Why's that? Has she won your heart with strawberries, or what?"

Arkady dropped his eyes. "You don't understand your mother, Yevgeny. She's not only a very good woman, she's very clever really. This morning she talked to me for half-an-hour, and so sensibly, interestingly."

"I suppose she was expatiating upon me all the while?"

"We didn't talk only about you."

"Perhaps; lookers-on see most. If a woman can keep up half-an-hour's conversation, it's always a hopeful sign. But I'm going, all the same."

"It won't be very easy for you to break it to them."

"No, it won't be easy. Some demon drove me to tease my father to-day; he had one of his rent-paying peasants flogged the other day, and quite right too—yes, yes, you needn't look at me in such horror—he did quite right, because he's an awful thief and drunkard; only my father had no idea that I, as they say, was cognisant of the facts. He was greatly perturbed, and now I shall have to upset him more than ever. . . . Never mind! Never say die! He'll get over it!"

Bazarov said, "Never mind"; but the whole day passed before he could make up his mind to inform Vassily Ivanovitch of his intentions. At last, when he was just saying good-night to him in the study, he observed, with a feigned yawn—

"Oh . . . I was almost forgetting to tell you. . . . Send to Fedot's for our horses to-morrow."

Vassily Ivanovitch was dumfounded. "Is Mr. Kirsanov leaving us, then?"

"Yes; and I'm going with him."

Vassily Ivanovitch positively reeled. "You are going?"

"Yes . . . I must. Make the arrangements about the horses, please."

"Very good. . . ." faltered the old man; "to Fedot's . . . very good . . . only . . . only. . . . How is it?"

"I must go to stay with him for a little time. I will come back here again later."

"Ah! For a little time . . . very good." Vassily Ivanovitch drew out his handkerchief, and, blowing his nose, doubled up almost to the ground. "Well . . . everything shall be done. I had thought you were to be with us . . . a little longer. Three days. . . . After three years, it's rather little; rather little, Yevgeny!"

"But, I tell you, I'm coming back directly. It's necessary for me to go."

"Necessary. . . . Well! Duty before everything. So the horses shall be in readiness. Very good. Arina and I, of course, did not anticipate this. She has just begged some flowers from a neighbour; she meant to decorate the room for you." (Vassily Ivanovitch did not even mention that every morning almost at dawn he took counsel with Timofeitch, standing with his bare feet in his slippers, and pulling out with trembling fingers one dog's-eared ruble note after another, charged him with various purchases, with special reference to good things to eat, and to red wine, which, as far as he could observe, the young men liked extremely.) "Liberty . . . is the great thing; that's my rule. . . . I don't want to hamper you . . . not . . ."

He suddenly ceased, and made for the door.

"We shall soon see each other again, father, really."

But Vassily Ivanovitch, without turning round, merely waved his hand and was gone. When he got back to his bedroom he found his wife in bed, and began to say his prayers in a whisper, so as not to wake her up. She woke, however. "Is that you, Vassily Ivanovitch?" she asked.

"Yes, mother."

"Have you come from Enyusha? Do you know, I'm afraid of his not being comfortable on that sofa. I told Anfisushka to give him your travelling mattress and the new pillows; I should have given him our feather-bed, but I seem to remember he doesn't like too soft a bed. . . ."

"Never mind, mother; don't worry yourself. He's all right. Lord, have mercy on me, a sinner," he went on with his prayer in a low voice. Vassily Ivanovitch was sorry for his old wife; he did not mean to tell her over night what a sorrow there was in store for her.

Bazarov and Arkady set off the next day. From early morning all was dejection in the house; Anfisushka let the tray slip out of her hands; even Fedka was bewildered, and was reduced to taking off his boots. Vassily Ivanovitch was more fussy than ever; he was obviously trying to put a good face on it, talked loudly, and stamped with his feet, but his face looked haggard, and his eyes were continually avoiding his son. Arina Vlasyevna was crying quietly; she was utterly crushed, and could not have controlled herself at all if her husband had not spent two whole hours early in the morning exhorting her. When Bazarov, after repeated promises to come back certainly not later than in a month's time, tore himself at last from the embraces detaining him, and took his seat in the coach; when the horses had started, the bell was ringing, and the wheels were turning round, and when it was no longer any good to look after them, and the dust had settled, and Timofeitch, all bent and tottering as he walked, had crept back to his little room; when the old people were left alone in their little house, which seemed suddenly to have grown shrunken and decrepit too, Vassily Ivanovitch, after a few more moments of hearty waving of his handkerchief on the steps, sank into a chair, and his head dropped on to his breast. "He has cast us off; he has forsaken us," he faltered; "forsaken us; he was dull with us. Alone, alone!" he repeated several times. Then Arina Vlasyevna went up to him, and, leaning her grey head against his grey head, said, "There's no help for it, Vasya! A son is a separate piece cut off. He's like the falcon that flies home and flies away at his pleasure; while you and I are like funguses in the hollow of a tree, we sit side by side, and don't move from our place. Only I am left you unchanged forever, as you for me."

Vassily Ivanovitch took his hands from his face and clasped his wife, his friend, as firmly as he had never clasped in youth; she comforted him in his grief.

XXII

In silence, only rarely exchanging a few insignificant words, our friends travelled as far as Fedot's. Bazarov was not altogether pleased with himself. Arkady was displeased with him. He was feeling, too, that causeless melancholy which is only known to very young people. The coachman changed the horses, and getting up on to the box, inquired, "To the right or to the left?"

Arkady started. The road to the right led to the town, and from there home; the road to the left led to Madame Odintsov's.

He looked at Bazarov.

"Yevgeny," he queried; "to the left?"

Bazarov turned away. "What folly is this?" he muttered.

"I know it's folly," answered Arkady. . . . "But what does that matter? It's not the first time."

Bazarov pulled his cap down over his brows. "As you choose," he said at last. "Turn to the left," shouted Arkady.

The coach rolled away in the direction of Nikolskoe. But having resolved on the folly, the friends were even more obstinately silent than before, and seemed positively ill-humoured.

Directly the steward met them on the steps of Madame Odintov's house, the friends could perceive that they had acted injudiciously in giving way so suddenly to a passing impulse. They were obviously not expected. They sat rather a long while, looking rather foolish, in the drawing-room. Madame Odintsov came in to them at last. She greeted them with her customary politeness, but was surprised at their hasty return; and, so far as could be judged from the deliberation of her gestures and words, she was not over pleased at it. They made haste to announce that they had only called on their road, and must go on farther, to the town, within four hours. She confined herself to a slight exclamation, begged Arkady to remember her to his father, and sent for her aunt. The princess appeared very sleepy, which gave her wrinkled old face an even more ill-natured expression. Katya was not well; she did not leave her room. Arkady suddenly realised that he was at least as anxious to see Katya as Anna Sergyevna herself. The four hours were spent in insignificant discussion of one thing and another; Anna Sergyevna both listened and spoke without a smile. It was only quite at parting that her former friendliness seemed, as it were, to revive.

"I have an attack of spleen just now," she said; "but you must not pay attention to that, and come again—I say this to both of you—before long."

Both Bazarov and Arkady responded with a silent bow, took their seats in the coach, and without stopping again anywhere, went straight home to Maryino, where they arrived safely on the evening of the following day. During the whole course of the journey neither one nor the other even mentioned the name of Madame Odintsov; Bazarov, in particular, scarcely opened his mouth, and kept staring in a side direction away from the road, with a kind of exasperated intensity.

At Maryino every one was exceedingly delighted to see them. The prolonged absence of his son had begun to make Nikolai Petrovitch uneasy; he uttered a cry of joy, and bounced about on the sofa, dangling his legs, when Fenitchka ran to him with sparkling eyes, and informed him of the arrival of the "young gentlemen"; even Pavel Petrovitch was conscious of some degree of agreeable excitement, and smiled condescendingly as he shook hands with the returned wanderers. Talk, questions followed; Arkady talked most, especially at supper, which was prolonged long after midnight. Nikolai Petrovitch ordered up some bottles of porter which had only just been sent from Moscow, and partook of the festive beverage till his cheeks were crimson, and he kept laughing a half-childish, half-nervous little chuckle. Even the servants were infected by the general gaiety. Dunyasha ran up and down like one possessed, and was continually slamming doors; while Piotr was, at three o'clock in the morning, still attempting to strum a Cossack waltz on the guitar. The strings gave forth a sweet and plaintive sound in the still air; but with the exception of a small preliminary flourish, nothing came of the cultured valet's efforts; nature had given him no more musical talent than all the rest of the world.

But meanwhile things were not going over harmoniously at Maryino, and poor Nikolai Petrovitch was having a bad time of it. Difficulties on the farm sprang up every day—hired labourers had become insupportable. Some asked for their wages to be settled, or for an increase of wages, while others made off with the wages they had received in advance; the horses fell sick; the harness fell to pieces as though it were burnt; the work was carelessly done; a threshing machine that had been ordered from Moscow turned out to be useless from its great weight, another was ruined the first time it was used; half the cattle sheds were burnt down through an old blind woman on the farm going in windy weather with a burning brand to fumigate her cow . . . the old woman, it is true, maintained that the whole mischief could be traced to the master's plan of introducing new-fangled cheeses and milk-products. The overseer suddenly turned lazy, and began to grow fat, as every Russian grows fat when he gets a snug berth. When he caught sight of Nikolai Petrovitch in the distance, he would fling a stick at a passing pig, or threaten a half-naked urchin, to show his zeal, but the rest of the time he was generally asleep. The peasants who had been put on the rent system did not bring their money at the time due, and stole the forest-timber; almost every night the keepers caught peasants' horses in the meadows of the "farm," and sometimes forcibly bore them off. Nikolai Petrovitch would fix a money fine for damages, but the matter usually ended after the horses had been kept a day or two on the master's forage by their returning to their owners. To crown all, the peasants began quarrelling among themselves; brothers asked for a division of property, their wives could not get on together in one house; all of a sudden the squabble, as though at a given signal, came to a head, and at once the whole village came running to the counting-house steps, crawling to the master, often drunken and with battered face, demanding justice and judgment; then arose an uproar and clamour, the shrill wailing of the women mixed with the curses of the men. Then one had to examine the contending parties, and shout oneself hoarse, knowing all the while that one could never anyway arrive at a just decision. . . . There were not hands enough for the harvest; a neighbouring small owner, with the most benevolent countenance, contracted to supply him with reapers for a commission of two rubles an acre, and cheated him in the most shameless fashion; his peasant women demanded unheard-of sums, and the corn meanwhile went to waste; and here they were not getting on with the mowing, and there the Council of Guardians threatened and demanded prompt payment, in full, of interest due. . . .

"I can do nothing!" Nikolai Petrovitch cried more than once in despair. "I can't flog them myself; and as for calling in the police captain, my principles don't allow of it, while you can do nothing with them without the fear of punishment!"

"*Du calme, du calme,*" Pavel Petrovitch would remark upon this, but even he hummed to himself, knitted his brows, and tugged at his moustache.

Bazarov held aloof from these matters, and indeed as a guest it was not for him to meddle in other people's business. The day after his arrival at Maryino, he set to work on his frogs, his infusoria, and his chemical experiments, and was forever busy with them. Arkady, on the contrary, thought it his duty, if not to help his father, at least to make a show of being ready to help him. He gave him a patient hearing, and once offered him some advice, not with any idea of its being acted upon, but to show his interest. Farming details did not arouse any aversion in him; he used even to dream with pleasure of work on the land, but at this time his brain was swarming with other ideas. Arkady, to his own astonishment, thought incessantly of Nikolskoe; in former days he would simply have shrugged his shoulders if any one had told him that he could ever feel dull under the same roof as Bazarov—and that roof his father's! But he actually was dull and longed to get away. He tried going long walks till he was tired, but that was no use. In conversation with his father one day, he found out that Nikolai Petrovitch had in his possession rather interesting letters, written by Madame Odintsov's mother to his wife, and he gave him no rest till he got hold of the letters, for which Nikolai Petrovitch had to rummage in twenty drawers and boxes. Having gained possession of these half-crumbling papers, Arkady felt, as it were, soothed, just as though he had caught a glimpse of the goal towards which he ought now to go. "I mean that for both of you," he was constantly whispering—she had added that herself! "I'll go, I'll go, hang it all!" but he recalled the last visit, the cold reception, and his former embarrassment, and timidity got the better of him. The "go-ahead" feeling of youth, the secret desire to try his luck, to prove his worth in solitude, without the protection of any one whatever, gained the day at last. Before ten days had passed after his return to Maryino, on the pretext of studying the working of the Sunday schools,[39] he galloped off to the town again, and from there to Nikolskoe. Urging the driver on without intermission, he flew along, like a young officer riding to battle; and he felt both frightened and light-hearted, and was breathless with impatience. "The great thing is—one mustn't think," he kept repeating to himself. His driver happened to be a lad of spirit; he halted before every public house, saying, "A drink or not a drink?" but, to make up for it, when he had drunk he did not spare

39. not schools giving religious instruction, but schools teaching reading, writing, and arithmetic for those engaged in manual labor during the week.

his horses. At last the lofty roof of the familiar house came in sight.
. . . "What am I to do?" flashed through Arkady's head. "Well,
there's no turning back now!" The three horses galloped in unison;
the driver whooped and whistled at them. And now the bridge was
groaning under the hoofs and wheels, and now the avenue of lopped
pines seemed running to meet them. . . . There was a glimpse of
a woman's pink dress against the dark green, a young face peeped
out from under the light fringe of a parasol. . . . He recognised
Katya, and she recognised him. Arkady told the driver to stop the
galloping horses, leaped out of the carriage, and went up to her.
"It's you!" she cried, gradually flushing all over; "let us go to my
sister, she's here in the garden; she will be pleased to see you."

Katya led Arkady into the garden. His meeting with her struck
him as a particularly happy omen; he was delighted to see her, as
though she were of his own kindred. Everything had happened so
splendidly; no steward, no formal announcement. At a turn in the
path he caught sight of Anna Sergyevna. She was standing with her
back to him. Hearing footsteps, she turned slowly round.

Arkady felt confused again, but the first words she uttered soothed
him at once. "Welcome back, runaway!" she said in her even, caressing voice, and came to meet him, smiling and frowning to keep
the sun and wind out of her eyes. "Where did you pick him up,
Katya?"

"I have brought you something, Anna Sergyevna," he began,
"which you certainly don't expect."

"You have brought yourself; that's better than anything."

XXIII

Having seen Arkady off with ironical compassion, and given him
to understand that he was not in the least deceived as to the real
object of his journey, Bazarov shut himself up in complete solitude;
he was overtaken by a fever for work. He did not dispute now with
Pavel Petrovitch, especially as the latter assumed an excessively aristocratic demeanour in his presence, and expressed his opinions more
in inarticulate sounds than in words. Only on one occasion Pavel
Petrovitch fell into a controversy with the *nihilist* on the subject of
the question then much discussed of the rights of the nobles of the
Baltic province; but suddenly he stopped of his own accord, remarking with chilly politeness, "However, we cannot understand one
another; I, at least, have not the honour of understanding you."

"I should think not!" cried Bazarov. "A man's capable of understanding anything—how the aether vibrates, and what's going on in
the sun—but how any other man can blow his nose differently from
him, that he's incapable of understanding."

"What, is that an epigram?" observed Pavel Petrovitch inquiringly, and he walked away.

However, he sometimes asked permission to be present at Bazarov's experiments, and once even placed his perfumed face, washed with the very best soap, near the microscope to see how a transparent infusoria swallowed a green speck, and busily munched it with two very rapid sort of clappers which were in its throat. Nikolai Petrovitch visited Bazarov much oftener than his brother; he would have come every day, as he expressed it, to "study," if his worries on the farm had not taken off his attention. He did not hinder the young man in his scientific researches; he used to sit down somewhere in a corner of the room and look on attentively, occasionally permitting himself a discreet question. During dinner and supper-time he used to try to turn the conversation upon physics, geology, or chemistry, seeing that all other topics, even agriculture, to say nothing of politics might lead, if not to collisions, at least to mutual unpleasantness. Nikolai Petrovitch surmised that his brother's dislike for Bazarov was no less. An unimportant incident, among many others, confirmed his surmises. The cholera began to make its appearance in some places in the neighbourhood, and even "carried off" two persons from Maryino itself. In the night Pavel Petrovitch happened to have rather severe symptoms. He was in pain till the morning, but did not have recourse to Bazarov's skill. And when he met him the following day, in reply to his question, "Why he had not sent for him?" answered, still quite pale, but scrupulously brushed and shaved, "Why, I seem to recollect you said yourself you didn't believe in medicine." So the days went by. Bazarov went on obstinately and grimly working . . . and meanwhile there was in Nikolai Petrovitch's house one creature to whom, if he did not open his heart, he at least was glad to talk. . . . That creature was Fenitchka.

He used to meet her for the most part early in the morning, in the garden, or the farmyard; he never used to go to her room to see her, and she had only once been to his door to inquire—ought she to let Mitya have his bath or not? It was not only that she confided in him, that she was not afraid of him—she was positively freer and more at her ease in her behaviour with him than with Nikolai Petrovitch himself. It is hard to say how it came about; perhaps it was because she unconsciously felt the absence in Bazarov of all gentility, of all that superiority which at once attracts and overawes. In her eyes he was both an excellent doctor and a simple man. She looked after her baby without constraint in his presence; and once when she was suddenly attacked with giddiness and headache—she took a spoonful of medicine from his hand. Before Nikolai Petrovitch she kept, as it were, at a distance from Bazarov; she acted in this way not from hypocrisy, but from a kind of feeling of propriety. Pavel Petrovitch she was more afraid of than ever; for some time he had begun to watch her, and would suddenly make his appearance, as though he sprang out of the earth behind her back, in his English suit, with his immovable vigilant face, and his hands in his pockets. "It's like a bucket of cold water on one," Fenitchka complained to Dunyasha, and the latter sighed in response, and thought of another "heartless" man. Bazarov, without the least suspicion of the fact, had become the *cruel tyrant* of her heart.

Fenitchka liked Bazarov; but he liked her too. His face was positively transformed when he talked to her; it took a bright, almost kind expression, and his habitual nonchalance was replaced by a sort of jesting attentiveness. Fenitchka was growing prettier every day. There is a time in the life of young women when they suddenly begin to expand and blossom like summer roses; this time had come for Fenitchka. Dressed in a delicate white dress, she seemed herself slighter and whiter; she was not tanned by the sun; but the heat, from which she could not shield herself, spread a slight flush over her cheeks and ears, and, shedding a soft indolence over her whole body, was reflected in a dreamy languor in her pretty eyes. She was almost unable to work; her hands seemed to fall naturally into her lap. She scarcely walked at all, and was constantly sighing and complaining with comic helplessness.

"You should go oftener to bathe," Nikolai Petrovitch told her. He had made a large bath covered in with an awning in one of his ponds which had not yet quite disappeared.

"Oh, Nikolai Petrovitch! But by the time one gets to the pond, one's utterly dead, and, coming back, one's dead again. You see, there's no shade in the garden."

"That's true, there's no shade," replied Nikolai Petrovitch, rubbing his forehead.

One day at seven o'clock in the morning, Bazarov, returning from a walk, came upon Fenitchka in the lilac arbour, which was long past flowering, but was still thick and green. She was sitting on the garden seat, and had as usual thrown a white kerchief over her head; near her lay a whole heap of red and white roses still wet with dew. He said good morning to her.

"Ah! Yevgeny Vassilyitch!" she said, and lifted the edge of her kerchief a little to look at him, in doing which her arm was left bare to the elbow.

"What are you doing here?" said Bazarov, sitting down beside her. "Are you making a nosegay?"

"Yes, for the table at lunch. Nikolai Petrovitch likes it."

"But it's a long while yet to lunch time. What a heap of flowers!"

"I gathered them now, for it will be hot then, and one can't go out. One can only just breathe now. I feel quite weak with the heat. I'm really afraid whether I'm not going to be ill."

"What an idea! Let me feel your pulse." Bazarov took her hand, felt for the evenly-beating pulse, but did not even begin to count its throbs. "You'll live a hundred years!" he said, dropping her hand.

"Ah, God forbid!" she cried.

"Why? Don't you want a long life?"

"Well, but a hundred years! There was an old woman near us eighty-five years old—and what a martyr she was! Dirty and deaf and bent and coughing all the time; nothing but a burden to herself. That's a dreadful life!"

"So it's better to be young?"

"Well, isn't it?"

"But why is it better? Tell me!"

"How can you ask why? Why, here I now, while I'm young, I can do everything—go and come and carry, and needn't ask any one for anything. . . . What can be better?"

"And to me it's all the same whether I'm young or old."

"How do you mean—it's all the same? It's not possible what you say."

"Well, judge for yourself, Fedosya Nikolaevna, what good is my youth to me. I live alone, a poor lonely creature . . ."

"That always depends on you."

"It doesn't at all depend on me! At least, some one ought to take pity on me."

Fenitchka gave a sidelong look at Bazarov, but said nothing. "What's this book you have?" she asked after a short pause.

"That? That's a scientific book, very difficult."

"And are you still studying? And don't you find it dull? You know everything already, I should say."

"It seems not everything. You try to read a little."

"But I don't understand anything here. Is it Russian?" asked Fenitchka, taking the heavily bound book in both hands. "How thick it is!"

"Yes, it's Russian."

"All the same, I shan't understand anything."

"Well, I didn't give it you for you to understand it. I wanted to look at you while you were reading. When you read, the end of your little nose moves so nicely."

Fenitchka, who had set to work to spell out in a low voice the article on "Creosote" she had chanced upon, laughed and threw down the book . . . it slipped from the seat on to the ground.

"I like it, too, when you laugh," observed Bazarov.

"Nonsense!"

"I like it when you talk. It's just like a little brook babbling."

Fenitchka turned her head away. "What a person you are to talk!" she commented, picking the flowers over with her finger. "And how can you care to listen to me? You have talked with such clever ladies."

"Ah, Fedosya Nikolaevna, believe me; all the clever ladies in the world are not worth your little elbow."

"Come, there's another invention!" murmured Fenitchka, clasping her hands.

Bazarov picked the book up from the ground.

"That's a medical book; why do you throw it away?"

"Medical?" repeated Fenitchka, and she turned to him again. "Do you know, ever since you gave me those drops—do you remember? —Mitya has slept so well! I really can't think how to thank you; you are so good, really."

"But you have to pay doctors," observed Bazarov with a smile. "Doctors, you know yourself, are grasping people."

Fenitchka raised her eyes, which seemed still darker from the whitish reflection cast on the upper part of her face, and looked at Bazarov. She did not know whether he was joking or not.

"If you please, we shall be delighted. . . . I must ask Nikolai Petrovitch . . ."

"Why, do you think I want money?" Bazarov interposed. "No; I don't want money from you."

"What then?" asked Fenitchka.

"What?" repeated Bazarov. "Guess!"

"A likely person I am to guess!"

"Well, I will tell you; I want . . . one of those roses."

Fenitchka laughed again, and even clapped her hands, so amusing Bazarov's request seemed to her. She laughed, and at the same time felt flattered. Bazarov was looking intently at her.

"By all means," she said at last; and, bending down to the seat, she began picking over the roses. "Which will you have—a red or a white one?"

"Red—and not too large."

She sat up again. "Here, take it," she said, but at once drew back her outstretched hand, and, biting her lips, looked towards the entrance of the arbour, then listened.

"What is it?" asked Bazarov. "Nikolai Petrovitch?"

"No . . . Mr. Kirsanov has gone to the fields . . . besides, I'm not afraid of him . . . but Pavel Petrovitch . . . I fancied . . ."

"What?"

"I fancied he was coming here. No . . . it was no one. Take it." Fenitchka gave Bazarov the rose.

"On what grounds are you afraid of Pavel Petrovitch?"

"He always scares me. And I know you don't like him. Do you remember, you always used to quarrel with him? I don't know what your quarrel was about, but I can see you turn him about like this and like that."

Fenitchka showed with her hands how in her opinion Bazarov turned Pavel Petrovitch about.

Bazarov smiled. "But if he gave me a beating," he asked, "would you stand up for me?"

"How could I stand up for you? But no, no one will get the better of you."

"Do you think so? But I know a hand which could overcome me if it liked."

"What hand?"

"Why, don't you know, really? Smell, how delicious this rose smells you gave me."

Fenitchka stretched her little neck forward, and put her face close to the flower. . . . The kerchief slipped from her head on to her shoulders; her soft mass of dark, shining, slightly ruffled hair was visible.

"Wait a minute; I want to smell it with you," said Bazarov. He bent down and kissed her vigourously on her parted lips.

She started, pushed him back with both her hands on his breast, but pushed feebly, and he was able to renew and prolong his kiss.

A dry cough was heard behind the lilac bushes. Fenitchka instantly moved away to the other end of the seat. Pavel Petrovitch showed himself, made a slight bow, and saying with a sort of malicious mournfulness, "You are here," he retreated. Fenitchka at once gathered up all her roses and went out of the arbour. "It was wrong of you, Yevgeny Vassilyitch," she whispered as she went. There was a note of genuine reproach in her whisper.

Bazarov remembered another recent scene, and he felt both shame and contemptuous annoyance. But he shook his head directly, ironically congratulated himself "on his final assumption of the part of the gay Lothario,"[40] and went off to his own room.

Pavel Petrovitch went out of the garden, and made his way with deliberate steps to the copse. He stayed there rather a long while; and when he returned to lunch, Nikolai Petrovitch inquired anxiously whether he were quite well—his face looked so gloomy.

"You know, I sometimes suffer with my liver," Pavel Petrovitch answered tranquilly.

XXIV

Two hours later he knocked at Bazarov's door.

"I must apologise for hindering you in your scientific pursuits," he began, seating himself on a chair in the window, and leaning with both hands on a handsome walking-stick with an ivory knob (he usually walked without a stick), "But I am constrained to beg you to spare me five minutes of your time . . . no more."

"All my time is at your disposal," answered Bazarov, over whose face there passed a quick change of expression directly Pavel Petrovitch crossed the threshold.

"Five minutes will be enough for me: I have come to put a single question to you."

40. Lothario is a gay seducer of women in *The Fair Penitent* (1703), a play by Nicholas Rowe (1674-1718), the English playwright.

"A question? What is it about?"

"I will tell you, if you will kindly hear me out. At the commencement of your stay in my brother's house, before I had renounced the pleasure of conversing with you, it was my fortune to hear your opinions on many subjects; but so far as my memory serves, neither between us, nor in my presence, was the subject of single combats and duelling in general broached. Allow me to hear what are your views on that subject?"

Bazarov, who had risen to meet Pavel Petrovitch, sat down on the edge of the table and folded his arms.

"My view is," he said, "that from the theoretical standpoint, duelling is absurd; from the practical standpoint, now—it's quite a different matter."

"That is, you mean to say, if I understand you right, that whatever your theoretical views on duelling, you would not in practice allow yourself to be insulted without demanding satisfaction?"

"You have guessed my meaning absolutely."

"Very good. I am very glad to hear you say so. Your words relieve me from a state of incertitude."

"Of uncertainty, you mean to say."

"That is all the same; I express myself so as to be understood; I . . . am not a seminary rat. Your words save me from a rather deplorable necessity. I have made up my mind to fight you."

Bazarov opened his eyes wide. "Me?"

"Undoubtedly."

"But what for, pray?"

"I could explain the reason to you," began Pavel Petrovitch, "but I prefer to be silent about it. To my idea your presence here is superfluous; I cannot endure you; I despise you; and if that is not enough for you . . ."

Pavel Petrovitch's eyes glittered . . . Bazarov's, too, were flashing.

"Very good," he assented. "No need of further explanations. You've a whim to try your chivalrous spirit upon me. I might refuse you this pleasure, but—so be it!"

"I am sensible of my obligation to you," replied Pavel Petrovitch; "and may reckon then on your accepting my challenge without compelling me to resort to violent measures."

"That means, speaking without metaphor, to that stick?" Bazarov remarked coolly. "That is precisely correct. It's quite unnecessary for you to insult me. Indeed, it would not be a perfectly safe proceeding. You can remain a gentleman. . . . I accept your challenge, too, like a gentleman."

"That is excellent," observed Pavel Petrovitch, putting his stick in the corner. "We will say a few words directly about the conditions of our duel; but I should like first to know whether you think it necessary to resort to the formality of a trifling dispute, which might serve as a pretext for my challenge?"

"No; it's better without formalities."

"I think so myself. I presume it is also out of place to go into the real grounds of our difference. We cannot endure one another. What more is necessary?"

"What more, indeed?" repeated Bazarov ironically.

"As regards the conditions of the meeting itself, seeing that we shall have no seconds—for where could we get them?"

"Exactly so; where could we get them?"

"Then I have the honour to lay the following proposition before you: The combat to take place early to-morrow, at six, let us say, behind the copse, with pistols, at a distance of ten paces . . ."

"At ten paces? That will do; we hate one another at that distance."

"We might have it eight," remarked Pavel Petrovitch.

"We might."

"To fire twice; and, to be ready for any result, let each put a letter in his pocket, in which he accuses himself of his end."

"Now, that I don't approve of at all," observed Bazarov. "There's a slight flavour of the French novel about it, something not very plausible."

"Perhaps. You will agree, however, that it would be unpleasant to incur a suspicion of murder?"

"I agree as to that. But there is a means of avoiding that painful reproach. We shall have no seconds, but we can have a witness."

"And whom, allow me to inquire?"

"Why, Piotr."

"What Piotr?"

"Your brother's valet. He's a man who has attained to the acme of contemporary culture, and he will perform his part with all the *comilfo (comme il faut)* necessary in such cases."

"I think you are joking, sir."

"Not at all. If you think over my suggestion, you will be convinced that it's full of common sense and simplicity. You can't hide a candle under a bushel; but I'll undertake to prepare Piotr in a fitting manner, and bring him on to the field of battle."

"You persist in jesting still," Pavel Petrovitch declared, getting up from his chair. "But after the courteous readiness you have shown me, I have no right to pretend to lay down. . . . And so, everything is arranged. . . . By the way, perhaps you have no pistols?"

"How should I have pistols, Pavel Petrovitch? I'm not in the army."

"In that case, I offer you mine. You may rest assured that it's five years now since I shot with them."

"That's a very consoling piece of news."

Pavel Petrovitch took up his stick. . . . "And now, my dear sir, it only remains for me to thank you and to leave you to your studies.

I have the honour to take leave of you."

"Till we have the pleasure of meeting again, my dear sir," said Bazarov, conducting his visitor to the door.

Pavel Petrovitch went out, while Bazarov remained standing a minute before the door, and suddenly exclaimed, "Pish, well, I'm dashed! How fine and how foolish! A pretty farce we've been through! Like trained dogs dancing on their hind-paws. But to decline was out of the question; why I do believe he'd have struck me, and then . . ." (Bazarov turned white at the very thought; all his pride was up in arms at once)—"then it might have come to my strangling him like a cat." He went back to his microscope, but his heart was beating, and the composure necessary for taking observations had disappeared. "He caught sight of us to-day," he thought; "but would he really act like this on his brother's account? And what a mighty matter is it—a kiss? There must be something else in it. Bah! isn't he perhaps in love with her himself? To be sure, he's in love; it's as clear as day. What a complication! It's a nuisance!" he decided at last; "it's a bad job, look at it which way you will. In the first place, to risk a bullet through one's brains, and in any case to go away; and then Arkady . . . and that dear innocent pussy, Nikolai Petrovitch. It's a bad job, an awfully bad job."

The day passed in a kind of peculiar stillness and languor. Fenitchka gave no sign of her existence; she sat in her little room like a mouse in its hole. Nikolai Petrovitch had a careworn air. He had just heard that blight had begun to appear in his wheat, upon which he had in particular rested his hopes. Pavel Petrovitch overwhelmed every one, even Prokofitch, with his icy courtesy. Bazarov began a letter to his father, but tore it up, and threw it under the table.

"If I die," he thought, "they will find it out; but I'm not going to die. No, I shall struggle along in this world a good while yet." He gave Piotr orders to come to him on important business the next morning directly it was light. Piotr imagined that he wanted to take him to Petersburg with him. Bazarov went late to bed, and all night long he was harassed by disordered dreams . . . Madame Odintsov kept appearing in them, now she was his mother, and she was followed by a kitten with black whiskers, and this kitten seemed to be Fenitchka; then Pavel Petrovitch took the shape of a great wood, with which he had yet to fight. Piotr waked him at four o'clock; he dressed at once, and went out with him.

It was a lovely, fresh morning; tiny flecked clouds hovered overhead in little curls of foam on the pale clear blue; a fine dew lay in drops on the leaves and grass, and sparkled like silver on the spiders' webs; the damp, dark earth seemed still to keep traces of the rosy dawn; from the whole sky the songs of larks came pouring in showers. Bazarov walked as far as the copse, sat down in the shade at its edge, and only then disclosed to Piotr the nature of the service he expected of him. The refined valet was mortally alarmed; but Bazarov soothed him by the assurance that he would have nothing to do but stand at a distance and look on, and that he would not incur any sort of responsibility. "And meantime," he added, "only think what an important part you have to play!" Piotr threw up his hands, looked down, and leaned against a birch-tree, looking green with terror.

The road from Maryino skirted the copse; a light dust lay on it, untouched by wheel or foot since the previous day. Bazarov unconsciously stared along this road, picked and gnawed a blade of grass, while he kept repeating to himself, "What a piece of foolery!" The chill of the early morning made him shiver twice. . . . Piotr looked at him dejectedly, but Bazarov only smiled; he was not afraid.

The tramp of horses' hoofs was heard along the road. . . . A peasant came into sight from behind the trees. He was driving before him two horses hobbled together, and as he passed Bazarov he looked at him rather strangely, without touching his cap, which it was easy to see disturbed Piotr, as an unlucky omen. "There's some one else up early too," thought Bazarov; "but he at least has got up for work, while we . . ."

"Fancy the gentleman's coming," Piotr faltered suddenly.

Bazarov raised his head and saw Pavel Petrovitch. Dressed in a light check jacket and snow-white trousers, he was walking rapidly along the road; under his arm he carried a box wrapped up in green cloth.

"I beg your pardon, I believe I have kept you waiting," he observed bowing first to Bazarov, then to Piotr, whom he treated respectfully at that instant, as representing something in the nature of a second. "I was unwilling to wake my man."

"It doesn't matter," answered Bazarov; "we've only just arrived ourselves."

"Ah! so much the better!" Pavel Petrovitch took a look round. "There's no one in sight; no one hinders us. We can proceed?"

"Let us proceed."

"You do not, I presume, desire any fresh explanations?"

"No, I don't."

"Would you like to load?" inquired Pavel Petrovitch, taking the pistols out of the box.

"No; you load, and I will measure out the paces. My legs are longer," added Bazarov with a smile. "One, two, three."

"Yevgeny Vassilyitch," Piotr faltered with an effort (he was shaking as though he were in a fever), "say what you like, I am going farther off."

"Four . . . five . . . Good. Move away, my good fellow, move away; you may get behind a tree even, and stop up your ears, only don't shut your eyes; and if any one falls, run and pick him up. Six . . . seven . . . eight . . ." Bazarov stopped. "Is that enough?" he

said, turning to Pavel Petrovitch; "or shall I add two paces more?"*
"As you like," replied the latter, pressing down the second bullet.
"Well, we'll make it two paces more." Bazarov drew a line on
the ground with the toe of his boot. "There's the barrier then. By
the way, how many paces may each of us go back from the barrier?
That's an important question too. That point was not discussed yesterday."

"I imagine, ten," replied Pavel Petrovitch, handing Bazarov both
pistols. "Will you be so good as to choose?"

"I will be so good. But, Pavel Petrovitch, you must admit our
combat is singular to the point of absurdity. Only look at the countenance of our second."

"You are disposed to laugh at everything," answered Pavel
Petrovitch. "I acknowledge the strangeness of our duel, but I think
it my duty to warn you that I intend to fight seriously. *A bon en-
tendeur, salut!*"[41]

"Oh! I don't doubt that we've made up our minds to make
away with each other; but why not laugh too and unite *utile dulci*?[42]
You talk to me in French, while I talk to you in Latin."

"I am going to fight in earnest," repeated Pavel Petrovitch, and
he walked off to his place. Bazarov on his side counted off ten paces
from the barrier, and stood still.

"Are you ready?" asked Pavel Petrovitch.

"Perfectly."

"We can approach one another."

Bazarov moved slowly forward, and Pavel Petrovitch, his left hand
thrust in his pocket, walked towards him, gradually raising the muzzle
of his pistol. . . . "He's aiming straight at my nose," thought Bazarov,
"and doesn't he blink down it carefully, the ruffian! Not an agreeable sensation, though. I'm going to look at his watch chain."

Something whizzed sharply by his very ear, and at the same instant there was the sound of a shot. "I heard it, so it must be all
right," had time to flash through Bazarov's brain. He took one more
step, and without taking aim pressed the spring.

Pavel Petrovitch gave a slight start, and clutched at his thigh.
A stream of blood began to trickle down his white trousers.

Bazarov flung aside the pistol, and went up to his antagonist. "Are
you wounded?" he said.

"You had the right to call me up to the barrier," said Pavel
Petrovitch, "but that's of no consequence. According to our agreement, each of us has the right to one more shot."

"All right, but, excuse me, that'll do another time," answered
Bazarov, catching hold of Pavel Petrovitch, who was beginning to

41. "a word to the wise is enough."
42. a quotation from Horace's *Ars
poetica* (line 343), referring to the poet's
gaining recognition when he mixes "the
useful with pleasure."

turn pale. "Now, I'm not a duellist, but a doctor, and I must have a look at your wound before anything else. Piotr, come here, Piotr! where have you gone to?"

"That's all nonsense . . . I need no one's aid," Pavel Petrovitch declared jerkily, "and . . . we must . . . again . . ." He tried to pull at his moustaches, but his hand failed him, his eyes grew dim, and he lost consciousness.

"Here's a pretty pass! A fainting fit! What next!" Bazarov cried unconsciously, as he laid Pavel Petrovitch on the grass. "Let's have a look what's wrong." He pulled out a handkerchief, wiped away the blood, and began feeling round the wound. . . . "The bone's not touched," he muttered through his teeth; "the ball didn't go deep; one muscle, *vastus externus*, grazed. He'll be dancing about in three weeks! . . . And to faint! Oh, these nervous people, how I hate them! My word, what a delicate skin!"

"Is he killed?" the quaking voice of Piotr came rustling behind his back.

Bazarov looked round. "Go for some water as quick as you can, my good fellow, and he'll outlive us yet."

But the modern servant seemed not to understand his words, and he did not stir. Pavel Petrovitch slowly opened his eyes. "He will die!" whispered Piotr, and he began crossing himself.

"You are right. . . . What an imbecile countenance!" remarked the wounded gentleman with a forced smile.

"Well, go for the water, damn you!" shouted Bazarov.

"No need. . . . It was a momentary *vertigo*. . . . Help me to sit up. . . . there, that's right. . . . I only need something to bind up this scratch, and I can reach home on foot, or else you can send a droshky for me. The duel, if you are willing, shall not be renewed. You have behaved honourably . . . to-day, to-day—observe."

"There's no need to recall the past," rejoined Bazarov; "and as regards the future, it's not worth while for you to trouble your head about that either, for I intend being off without delay. Let me bind up your leg now; your wound's not serious, but it's always best to stop bleeding. But first I must bring this corpse to his senses."

Bazarov shook Piotr by the collar, and sent him for a droshky.

"Mind, you don't frighten my brother," Pavel Petrovitch said to him; "don't dream of informing him."

Piotr flew off; and while he was running for a droshky, the two antagonists sat on the ground and said nothing. Pavel Petrovitch tried not to look at Bazarov; he did not want to be reconciled to him in any case; he was ashamed of his own haughtiness, of his failure; he was ashamed of the whole position he had brought about, even while he felt it could not have ended in a more favourable manner. "At any rate, there will be no scandal," he consoled himself by re-flecting, "and for that I am thankful." The silence was prolonged, a silence distressing and awkward. Both of them were ill at ease. Each was conscious that the other understood him. That is pleasant to friends, and always very unpleasant to those who are not friends, especially when it is impossible either to have things out or to separate.

"Haven't I bound up your leg too tight?" inquired Bazarov at last.

"No, not at all; it's capital," answered Pavel Petrovitch; and after a brief pause, he added, "There's no deceiving my brother; we shall have to tell him we quarrelled over politics."

"Very good," assented Bazarov. "You can say I insulted all anglo-maniacs."

"That will do capitally. What do you imagine that man thinks of us now?" continued Pavel Petrovitch, pointing to the same peasant, who had driven the hobbled horses past Bazarov a few minutes before the duel, and going back again along the road, took off his cap at the sight of the "gentlefolk."

"Who can tell?" answered Bazarov. "It is quite likely he thinks nothing. The Russian peasant is that mysterious unknown about whom Mrs. Radcliffe[43] used to talk so much. Who is to understand him! He doesn't understand himself!"

"Ah! so that's your idea!" Pavel Petrovitch began; and suddenly he cried, "Look what your fool of a Piotr has done! Here's my brother galloping up to us!"

Bazarov turned round and saw the pale face of Nikolai Petrovitch, who was sitting in the droshky. He jumped out of it before it had stopped, and rushed up to his brother.

"What does this mean?" he said in an agitated voice. "Yevgeny Vassilyitch, pray, what is this?"

"Nothing," answered Pavel Petrovitch; "they have alarmed you for nothing. I had a little dispute with Mr. Bazarov, and I have had to pay for it a little."

"But what was it all about, mercy on us!"

"How can I tell you? Mr. Bazarov alluded disrespectfully to Sir Robert Peel.[44] I must hasten to add that I am the only person to blame in all this, while Mr. Bazarov has behaved most honourably. I called him out."

"But you're covered with blood, good heavens!"

"Well, did you suppose I had water in my veins? But this blood-letting is positively beneficial to me. Isn't that so, doctor? Help me to get into the droshky, and don't give way to melancholy. I shall be quite well to-morrow. That's it; capital. Drive on, coachman."

Nikolai Petrovitch walked after the droshky; Bazarov was remain-

<hr>

43. Mrs. Anne Radcliffe (1764–1823) was the popular author of many Gothic romances. *The Mysteries of Udolpho* (1794) is the best known of her horror stories.

44. Sir Robert Peel (1788–1850), British Prime Minister, a Conservative, who in 1846 brought about the repeal of the corn laws.

ing where he was. . . .

"I must ask you to look after my brother," Nikolai Petrovitch said to him, "till we get another doctor from the town."

Bazarov nodded his head without speaking. In an hour's time Pavel Petrovitch was already lying in bed with a skilfully bandaged leg. The whole house was alarmed; Fenitchka fainted. Nikolai Petrovitch kept stealthily wringing his hands, while Pavel Petrovitch laughed and joked, especially with Bazarov; he had put on a fine cambric night shirt, an elegant morning wrapper, and a fez, did not allow the blinds to be drawn down, and humourously complained of the necessity of being kept from food.

Towards night, however, he began to be feverish; his head ached. The doctor arrived from the town. (Nikolai Petrovitch would not listen to his brother, and indeed Bazarov himself did not wish him to; he sat the whole day in his room, looking yellow and vindictive, and only went in to the invalid for as brief a time as possible; twice he happened to meet Fenitchka, but she shrank away from him with horror.) The new doctor advised a cooling diet; he confirmed, however, Bazarov's assertion that there was no danger. Nikolai Petrovitch told him his brother had wounded himself by accident, to which the doctor responded, "Hm!" but having twenty-five silver rubles slipped into his hand on the spot, he observed, "You don't say so! Well, it's a thing that often happens, to be sure."

No one in the house went to bed or undressed. Nikolai Petrovitch kept going in to his brother on tiptoe, retreating on tiptoe again; the latter dozed, moaned a little, told him in French, *Couchez-vous*, and asked for drink. Nikolai Petrovitch sent Fenitchka twice to take him a glass of lemonade; Pavel Petrovitch gazed at her intently, and drank off the glass to the last drop. Towards morning the fever had increased a little; there was slight delirium. At first Pavel Petrovitch uttered incoherent words; then suddenly he opened his eyes, and seeing his brother near his bed bending anxiously over him, he said, "Don't you think, Nikolai, Fenitchka has something in common with Nellie?"

"What Nellie, Pavel dear?"

"How can you ask? Princess R——. Especially in the upper part of the face. *C'est de la même famille.*"

Nikolai Petrovitch made no answer, while inwardly he marveled at the persistence of old passions in man. "It's like this when it comes to the surface," he thought.

"Ah, how I love that light-headed creature!" moaned Pavel Petrovitch, clasping his hands mournfully behind his head. "I can't bear any insolent upstart to dare to touch . . ." he whispered a few minutes later.

Nikolai Petrovitch only sighed; he did not even suspect to whom these words referred.

Bazarov presented himself before him at eight o'clock the next day. He had already had time to pack, and to set free all his frogs, insects, and birds.

"You have come to say good-bye to me?" said Nikolai Petrovitch, getting up to meet him.

"Yes."

"I understand you, and approve of you fully. My poor brother, of course, is to blame; and he is punished for it. He told me himself that he made it impossible for you to act otherwise. I believe that you could not avoid this duel, which . . . which to some extent is explained by the almost constant antagonism of your respective views." (Nikolai Petrovitch began to get a little mixed up in his words.) "My brother is a man of the old school, hot-tempered and obstinate. . . . Thank God that it has ended as it has. I have taken every precaution to avoid publicity."

"I'm leaving you my address, in case there's any fuss," Bazarov remarked casually.

"I hope there will be no fuss, Yevgeny Vassilyitch. . . . I am very sorry your stay in my house should have such a . . . such an end. It is the more distressing to me through Arkady's . . ."

"I shall be seeing him, I expect," replied Bazarov, in whom "explanations" and "protestations" of every sort always aroused a feeling of impatience; "in case I don't, I beg you to say good-bye to him for me, and accept the expression of my regret."

"And I beg . . ." answered Nikolai Petrovitch. But Bazarov went off without waiting for the end of his sentence.

When he heard of Bazarov's going, Pavel Petrovitch expressed a desire to see him, and shook his hand. But even then he remained as cold as ice; he realized, that Pavel Petrovitch wanted to play the magnanimous. He did not succeed in saying good-bye to Fenitchka; he only exchanged glances with her at the window. Her face struck him as looking dejected. "She'll come to grief, perhaps," he said to himself. . . . "But who knows? she'll pull through somehow, I daresay!" Piotr, however, was so overcome that he wept on his shoulder, till Bazarov damped him by asking if he'd a constant supply laid on in his eyes; while Dunyasha was obliged to run away into the wood to hide her emotion. The originator of all this woe got into a light cart, smoked a cigar, and when at the third mile, at the bend in the road, the Kirsanovs' farm, with its new house, could be seen in a long line, he merely spat, and muttering, "Cursed snobs!" wrapped himself closer in his cloak.

Pavel Petrovitch was soon better; but he had to keep his bed about a week. He bore his captivity, as he called it, pretty patiently, though he took great pains over his toilette, and had everything scented with eau-de-cologne. Nikolai Petrovitch used to read him the journals; Fenitchka waited on him as before, brought him lemonade, soup,

boiled eggs, and tea; but she was overcome with secret dread whenever she went into his room. Pavel Petrovitch's unexpected action
had alarmed every one in the house, and her more than any one;
Prokofitch was the only person not agitated by it; he discoursed
upon how gentlemen in his day used to fight, but only with real
gentlemen; low curs like that they used to order a horsewhipping in
the stable for their insolence.

Fenitchka's conscience scarcely reproached her; but she was tormented at times by the thought of the real cause of the quarrel;
and Pavel Petrovitch, too, looked at her so strangely . . . that even
when her back was turned she felt his eyes upon her. She grew thinner from constant inward agitation, and, as is always the way, became
still more charming.

One day—the incident took place in the morning—Pavel Petrovitch
felt better, and moved from his bed to the sofa while Nikolai
Petrovitch, having satisfied himself he was better, went off to the
threshing floor. Fenitchka brought him a cup of tea, and setting it
down on a little table, was about to withdraw. Pavel Petrovitch detained her.

"Where are you going in such a hurry, Fedosya Nikolaevna?" he
began; "are you busy?"

"No . . . I have to pour out tea."

"Dunyasha will do that without you; sit a little while with a poor
invalid. By the way, I must have a little talk with you."

Fenitchka sat down on the edge of an easy-chair, without speaking.

"Listen," said Pavel Petrovitch, tugging at his moustaches; "I
have long wanted to ask you something; you seem somehow afraid
of me?"

"I?"

"Yes, you. You never look at me, as though your conscience were
not at rest."

Fenitchka crimsoned, but looked at Pavel Petrovitch. He impressed
her as looking strange, and her heart began throbbing slowly.

"Is your conscience at rest?" he questioned her.

"Why should it not be at rest?" she faltered.

"Goodness knows why! Besides, whom can you have wronged?
Me? That is not likely. Any other people in the house here? That,
too, is something incredible. Can it be my brother? But you love
him, don't you?"

"I love him."

"With your whole soul, with your whole heart?"

"I love Nikolai Petrovitch with my whole heart."

"Truly? Look at me, Fenitchka." (It was the first time he had
called her that name.) "You know, it's a great sin telling lies!"

"I am not telling lies, Pavel Petrovitch. Not love Nikolai Petrovitch
—I shouldn't care to live after that."

"And will you never give him up for any one?"

"For whom could I give him up?"

"For whom indeed! Well, how about that gentleman who has just gone away from here?"

Fenitchka got up. "My God, Pavel Petrovitch, what are you torturing me for? What have I done to you? How can such things be said?" . . .

"Fenitchka," said Pavel Petrovitch, in a sorrowful voice, "you know I saw . . ."

"What did you see?"

"Well, there . . . in the arbour."

Fenitchka crimsoned to her hair and to her ears. "How was I to blame for that?" she articulated with an effort.

Pavel Petrovitch raised himself up. "You were not to blame? No? Not at all?"

"I love Nikolai Petrovitch, and no one else in the world, and I shall always love him!" cried Fenitchka with sudden force, while her throat seemed fairly breaking with sobs. "As for what you saw, at the dreadful day of judgment I will say I'm not to blame, and wasn't to blame for it, and I would rather die at once if people can suspect me of such a thing against my benefactor, Nikolai Petrovitch."

But here her voice broke, and at the same time she felt that Pavel Petrovitch was snatching and pressing her hand. . . . She looked at him, and was fairly petrified. He had turned even paler than before; his eyes were shining, and what was most marvelous of all, one large solitary tear was rolling down his cheek.

"Fenitchka!" he was saying in a strange whisper; "love him, love my brother! Don't give him up for any one in the world; don't listen to any one else! Think what can be more terrible than to love and not be loved! Never leave my poor Nikolai!"

Fenitchka's eyes were dry, and her terror had passed away, so great was her amazement. But what were her feelings when Pavel Petrovitch, Pavel Petrovitch himself, put her hand to his lips and seemed to pierce into it without kissing it, and only heaving convulsive sighs from time to time. . . .

"Goodness," she thought, "isn't it some attack coming on him?" . . .

At that instant his whole ruined life was stirred up within him.

The staircase creaked under rapidly approaching footsteps. . . . He pushed her away from him, and let his head drop back on the pillow. The door opened, and Nikolai Petrovitch entered, cheerful, fresh, and ruddy. Mitya, as fresh and ruddy as his father, in nothing but his little shirt, was frisking on his shoulder, catching the big buttons of his rough country coat with his little bare toes.

Fenitchka simply flung herself upon him, and clasping him and her son together in her arms, dropped her head on his shoulder. Nikolai Petrovitch was surprised; Fenitchka, the reserved and staid

Fenitchka, had never given him a caress in the presence of a third person.

"What's the matter?" he said, and, glancing at his brother, he gave her Mitya. "You don't feel worse?" he inquired, going up to Pavel Petrovitch.

He buried his face in a cambric handkerchief. "No . . . not at all . . . on the contrary, I am much better."

"You were in too great a hurry to move on to the sofa. Where are you going?" added Nikolai Petrovitch, turning round to Fenitchka; but she had already closed the door behind her. "I was bringing in my young hero to show you; he's been crying for his uncle. Why has she carried him off? What's wrong with you, though? Has anything passed between you, eh?"

"Brother!" said Pavel Petrovitch solemnly.

Nikolai Petrovitch started. He felt dismayed, he could not have said why himself.

"Brother," repeated Pavel Petrovitch, "give me your word that you will carry out my one request."

"What request? Tell me."

"It is very important; the whole happiness of your life, to my idea, depends on it. I have been thinking a great deal all this time over what I want to say to you now. . . . Brother, do your duty, the duty of an honest and generous man; put an end to the scandal and bad example you are setting—you, the best of men!"

"What do you mean, Pavel?"

"Marry Fenitchka. . . . She loves you; she is the mother of your son."

Nikolai Petrovitch stepped back a pace, and flung up his hands. "Do you say that, Pavel? You whom I have always regarded as the most determined opponent of such marriages! You say that? Don't you know that it has simply been out of respect for you that I have not done what you so rightly call my duty?"

"You were wrong to respect me in that case," Pavel Petrovitch responded, with a weary smile. "I begin to think Bazarov was right in accusing me of snobbishness. No, dear brother, don't let us worry ourselves about appearances and the world's opinion any more; we are old folks and humble now; it's time we laid aside vanity of all kinds. Let us, just as you say, do our duty; and mind, we shall get happiness that way into the bargain."

Nikolai Petrovitch rushed to embrace his brother.

"You have opened my eyes completely!" he cried. "I was right in always declaring you the wisest and kindest-hearted fellow in the world, and now I see you are just as reasonable as you are noble-hearted."

"Quietly, quietly," Pavel Petrovitch interrupted him; "don't hurt the leg of your reasonable brother, who at close upon fifty has been fighting a duel like an ensign. So, then, it's a settled matter; Fenitchka is to be my . . . *belle soeur.*"[45]

"My dearest Pavel! But what will Arkady say?"

"Arkady? He'll be in ecstasies, you may depend upon it! Marriage is against his principles, but then the sentiment of equality in him will be gratified. And, after all, what sense have class distinctions *au dix-neuvième siècle?*"[46]

"Ah, Pavel, Pavel, let me kiss you once more! Don't be afraid, I'll be careful."

The brothers embraced each other.

"What do you think, should you not inform her of your intention now?" queried Pavel Petrovitch.

"Why be in a hurry?" responded Nikolai Petrovitch. "Has there been any conversation between you?"

"Conversation between us? *Quelle idée!*"

Well, that is all right then. First of all, you must get well, and meanwhile there's plenty of time. We must think it over well, and consider . . ."

"But your mind is made up, I suppose?"

"Of course, my mind is made up, and I thank you from the bottom of my heart. I will leave you now; you must rest; any excitement is bad for you. . . . But we will talk it over again. Sleep well, dear heart, and God bless you!"

"What is he thanking me like that for?" thought Pavel Petrovitch, when he was left alone. "As though it did not depend on him! I will go away directly he is married, somewhere a long way off—to Dresden or Florence, and will live there till——"

Pavel Petrovitch moistened his forehead with eau de cologne, and closed his eyes. His beautiful, emaciated head, the glaring daylight shining full upon it, lay on the white pillow like the head of a dead man. . . . And indeed he was a dead man.

XXV

At Nikolskoe Katya and Arkady were sitting in the garden on a turf seat in the shade of a tall ash tree; Fifi had placed himself on the ground near them, giving his slender body that graceful curve, which is known among dog fanciers as "the hare bend." Both Arkady and Katya were silent; he was holding a half-open book in his hands, while she was picking out of a basket the few crumbs of bread left in it, and throwing them to a small family of sparrows, who with the frightened impudence peculiar to them were hopping and chirping at her very feet. A faint breeze stirring in the ash leaves kept slowly moving pale-gold flecks of sunlight up and down over the path of Fifi's tawny back; a patch of unbroken shade fell upon Arkady and Katya; only from time to time a bright streak gleamed on her hair. Both were silent, but the very way in which they were silent, in which they were sitting together, was expressive of confidential intimacy; each of them seemed not even to be thinking of his companion, while secretly rejoicing in his presence. Their faces, too, had changed since we saw them last; Arkady looked more tranquil, Katya brighter and more daring.

"Don't you think," began Arkady, "that the ash has been very well named in Russian *yasen;* no other tree is so slightly and brightly transparent (*yasno*) against the air as it is."

Katya raised her eyes to look upward, and assented "Yes", while Arkady thought, "Well, she does not reproach me for *talking finely.*"

"I don't like Heine,"[47] said Katya, glancing towards the book which Arkady was holding in his hands, "either when he laughs or when he weeps; I like him when he's thoughtful and melancholy."

"And I like him when he laughs," remarked Arkady.

"That's the relics left in you of your old satirical tendencies." ("Relics!" thought Arkady—"if Bazarov had heard that?") "Wait a little; we shall transform you."

"Who will transform me? You?"

"Who?—my sister; Porfiry Platonovitch, whom you've given up quarrelling with; auntie, whom you escorted to church the day before yesterday."

"Well, I couldn't refuse! And as for Anna Sergyevna, she agreed with Yevgeny in a great many things, you remember?"

"My sister was under his influence then, just as you were."

"As I was? Do you discover, may I ask, that I've shaken off his influence now?"

Katya did not speak.

"I know," pursued Arkady, "you never liked him."

"I can have no opinion about him."

"Do you know, Katerina Sergyevna, every time I hear that answer I disbelieve it. . . . There is no man that every one of us could not have an opinion about! That's simply a way of getting out of it."

"Well, I'll say, then, I don't. . . . It's not exactly that I don't like him, but I feel that he's of a different order from me, and I am different from him . . . and you, too, are different from him."

"How's that?"

"How can I tell you? . . . He's a wild animal, and you and I are tame."

"Am I tame too?"

Katya nodded.

Arkady scratched his ear. "Let me tell you, Katerina Sergyevna, do you know, that's really an insult?"

"Why, would you like to be a wild—"

"Not wild, but strong, full of force."

47. The German poet Heinrich Heine (1797–1856) would be distasteful to a girl such as Katya because of his un- sentimental view of love and his mordant wit and irony.

"It's no good wishing for that. . . . Your friend, you see, doesn't wish for it, but he has it."

"Hm! So you imagine he had a great influence on Anna Sergyevna?"

"Yes. But no one can keep the upper hand of her for long," added Katya in a low voice.

"Why do you think that?"

"She's very proud. . . . I didn't mean that . . . she values her independence a great deal."

"Who doesn't value it?" asked Arkady, and the thought flashed through his mind, "What good is it?" "What good is it?" it occurred to Katya to wonder too. When young people are often together on friendly terms, they are constantly stumbling on the same ideas.

Arkady smiled, and coming slightly closer to Katya, he said in a whisper, "Confess that you are a little afraid of her."

"Of whom?"

"Her," repeated Arkady, significantly.

"And how about you?" Katya asked in her turn.

"I am too, observe I said I am, *too.*"

Katya threatened him with her finger. "I wonder at that," she began; "my sister has never felt so friendly to you as just now; much more so than when you first came."

"Really!"

"Why, haven't you noticed it? Aren't you glad of it?"

Arkady grew thoughtful.

"How have I succeeded in gaining Anna Sergyevna's good opinion? Wasn't it because I brought her your mother's letters?"

"Both that and other causes, which I shan't tell you."

"Why?"

"I shan't say."

"Oh! I know; you're very obstinate."

"Yes, I am."

"And observant."

Katya gave Arkady a sidelong look. "Perhaps so; does that irritate you? What are you thinking of?"

"I am wondering how you have come to be as observant as in fact you are. You are so shy, so reserved; you keep every one at a distance."

"I have lived a great deal alone; that drives one to reflection. But do I really keep every one at a distance?"

Arkady flung a grateful glance at Katya.

"That's all very well," he pursued; "but people in your position —I mean in your circumstances—don't often have that faculty; it is hard for them, as it is for sovereigns, to get at the truth."

"But, you see, I am not rich."

Arkady was taken aback, and did not at once understand Katya.

"Why, of course, the property's all her sister's!" struck him suddenly; the thought was not unpleasing to him. "How nicely you said that!" he commented.

"What?"

"You said it nicely, simply, without being ashamed or making a boast of it. By the way, I imagine there must always be something special, a kind of pride of a sort in the feeling of any man, who knows and says he is poor."

"I have never experienced anything of that sort, thanks to my sister. I only referred to my position just now because it happened to come up."

"Well; but you must own you have a share of that pride I spoke of just now."

"For instance?"

"For instance, you—forgive the question—you wouldn't marry a rich man, I fancy, would you?"

"If I loved him very much. . . . No, I think even then I wouldn't marry him."

"There! you see!" cried Arkady, and after a short pause he added, "And why wouldn't you marry him?"

"Because even in the ballads unequal matches are always unlucky."

"You want to rule, perhaps, or . . ."

"Oh, no! why should I? On the contrary, I am ready to obey; only inequality is intolerable. To respect one's self and obey, that I can understand, that's happiness; but a subordinate existence . . . No, I've had enough of that as it is."

"Enough of that as it is," Arkady repeated after Katya. "Yes, yes," he went on, "you're not Anna Sergyevna's sister for nothing; you're just as independent as she is; but you're more reserved. I'm certain you wouldn't be the first to give expression to your feeling, however strong and holy it might be . . ."

"Well, what would you expect?" asked Katya.

"You're equally clever; and you've as much, if not more, character than she."

"Don't compare me with my sister, please," interposed Katya hurriedly; "that's too much to my disadvantage. You seem to forget my sister's beautiful and clever, and . . . you in particular, Arkady Nikolaevitch, ought not to say such things, and with such a serious face, too."

"What do you mean by 'you in particular'—and what makes you suppose I am joking?"

"Of course, you are joking."

"You think so? But what if I'm persuaded of what I say? If I believe I have not put it strong enough even?"

"I don't understand you."

"Really? Well, now I see; I certainly took you to be more observant than you are."

"How?"

Arkady made no answer, and turned away, while Katya looked for a few more crumbs in the basket, and began throwing them to the sparrows; but she moved her arm too vigourously, and they flew away, without stopping to pick them up.

"Katerina Sergyevna!" began Arkady suddenly; "it's of no consequence to you, probably; but, let me tell you, I put you not only above your sister, but above every one in the world."

He got up and went quickly away, as though he were frightened at the words that had fallen from his lips.

Katya let her two hands drop together with the basket on to her lap, and with bent head she stared a long while after Arkady. Gradually a crimson flush came faintly out upon her cheeks; but her lips did not smile, and her dark eyes had a look of perplexity and some other, as yet undefined, feeling.

"Are you alone?" she heard the voice of Anna Sergyevna near her; "I thought you came into the garden with Arkady."

Katya slowly raised her eyes to her sister (elegantly, even elaborately dressed, she was standing in the path and tickling Fifi's ears with the tip of her open parasol), and slowly replied. "Yes, I'm alone."

"So I see," she answered with a smile; "I suppose he has gone to his room."

"Yes."

"Have you been reading together?"

"Yes."

Anna Sergyevna took Katya by the chin and lifted her face up. "You have not been quarrelling, I hope?"

"No," said Katya, and she quietly removed her sister's hand.

"How solemnly you answer! I expected to find him here, and meant to suggest his coming a walk with me. That's what he is always asking for. They have sent you some shoes from the town; go and try them on; I noticed only yesterday your old ones are quite shabby. You never think enough about it, and you have such charming little feet! Your hands are nice too . . . though they're large; so you must make the most of your little feet. But you're not vain."

Anna Sergyevna went farther along the path with a light rustle of her beautiful gown; Katya got up from the grass, and, taking Heine with her, went away too—but not to try on her shoes.

"Charming little feet!" she thought, as she slowly and lightly mounted the stone steps of the terrace, which were burning with the heat of the sun; "charming little feet you call them. . . . Well, he shall be at them."

But all at once a feeling of shame came upon her, and she ran swiftly upstairs.

Arkady had gone along the corridor to his room; a steward had overtaken him, and announced that Mr. Bazarov was in his room.

"Yevgeny!" murmured Arkady, almost with dismay; "has he been here long?"

"Mr. Bazarov arrived this minute, sir, and gave orders not to announce him to Anna Sergyevna, but to show him straight up to you."

"Can any misfortune have happened at home?" thought Arkady, and running hurriedly up the stairs, he at once opened the door. The sight of Bazarov at once reassured him, though a more experienced eye might very probably have discerned signs of inward agitation in the sunken, though still energetic face of the unexpected visitor. With a dusty cloak over his shoulders, with a cap on his head, he was sitting at the window; he did not even get up when Arkady flung himself with noisy exclamations on his neck.

"This is unexpected! What good luck brought you?" he kept repeating, bustling about the room like one who both imagines himself and wishes to show himself delighted. "I suppose everything's all right at home; every one's well, eh?"

"Everything's all right, but not every one's well," said Bazarov. "Don't be a chatterbox, but send for some kvass for me, sit down, and listen while I tell you all about it in a few, but, I hope, pretty vigourous sentences."

Arkady was quiet while Bazarov described his duel with Pavel Petrovitch. Arkady was very much surprised, and even grieved, but he did not think it necessary to show this; he only asked whether his uncle's wound was really not serious; and on receiving the reply that it was most interesting, but not from a medical point of view, he gave a forced smile, but at heart he felt both wounded and as it were ashamed. Bazarov seemed to understand him.

"Yes, my dear fellow," he commented, "you see what comes of living with feudal personages. You turn a feudal personage yourself, and find yourself taking part in knightly tournaments. Well, so I set off for my father's," Bazarov wound up, "and I've turned in here on the way . . . to tell you all this, I should say, if I didn't think a useless lie a piece of foolery. No, I turned in here—the devil only knows why. You see, it's sometimes a good thing for a man to take himself by the scruff of the neck and pull himself up, like a radish out of its bed; that's what I've been doing of late. . . . But I wanted to have one more look at what I'm giving up, at the bed where I've been planted."

"I hope those words don't refer to me," responded Arkady with some emotion; "I hope you don't think of giving me up?"

Bazarov turned an intent, amost piercing look upon him.

"Would that be such a grief to you? It strikes me *you* have given me up already, you look so fresh and smart. . . . Your affair with

Anna Sergyevna must be getting on successfully."

"What do you mean by my affair with Anna Sergyevna?"

"Why, didn't you come here from the town on her account, chicken? By the way, how are those Sunday schools getting on? Do you mean to tell me you're not in love with her? Or have you already reached the stage of discretion?"

"Yevgeny, you know I have always been open with you; I can assure you, I will swear to you, you're making a mistake."

"Hm! That's another story," remarked Bazarov in an undertone. "But you needn't be in a taking, it's a matter of absolute indifference to me. A sentimentalist would say, 'I feel that our paths are beginning to part,' but I will simply say that we're tired of each other."

"Yevgeny . . ."

"My dear soul, there's no great harm in that. One gets tired of much more than that in this life. And now I suppose we'd better say good-bye, hadn't we? Ever since I've been here I've had such a loathsome feeling, just as if I'd been reading Gogol's effusions to the governor of Kaluga's wife.[48] By the way, I didn't tell them to take the horses out."

"Upon my word, this is too much!"

"Why?"

"I'll say nothing of myself; but that would be discourteous to the last degree to Anna Sergyevna, who will certainly wish to see you."

"Oh, you're mistaken there."

"On the contrary, I am certain, I'm right," retorted Arkady. "And what are you pretending for? If it comes to that, haven't you come here on her account yourself?"

"That may be so, but you're mistaken any way."

But Arkady was right. Anna Sergyevna desired to see Bazarov, and sent a summons to him by a steward. Bazarov changed his clothes before going to her; it turned out that he had packed his new suit so as to be able to get it out easily.

Madame Odintsov received him not in the room where he had so unexpectedly declared his love to her, but in the drawing-room. She held her fingers tips out to him cordially, but her face betrayed an involuntary sense of tension.

"Anna Sergyevna," Bazarov hastened to say, "before everything else I must set your mind at rest. Before you is a poor mortal, who has come to his senses long ago, and hopes other people, too, have forgotten his follies. I am going away for a long while; and though, as you will allow, I'm by no means a very soft creature, it would be anything but cheerful for me to carry away with me the idea that

---

48. Nikolay Gogol (1809–1852), the author of *Dead Souls* and *The Inspector General*, wrote *Selected Passages from a Correspondence with Friends* (1847), which includes letters written to the wife of the Governor of Kaluga. They would be particularly distasteful to Bazarov for their social conservatism, unctuous tone, and sentimental religiosity.

you remember me with repugnance."

Anna Sergyevna gave a deep sigh like one who has just climbed up a high mountain, and her face was lighted up by a smile. She held out her hand a second time to Bazarov, and responded to his pressure.

"Let bygones be bygones," she said. "I am all the readier to do so because, speaking from my conscience, I was to blame then, too, for flirting or something. In a word, let us be friends as before. That was a dream, wasn't it? And who remembers dreams?"

"Who remembers them? And besides, love . . . you know, is a purely imaginary feeling."

"Really? I am very glad to hear that."

So Anna Sergyevna spoke, and so spoke Bazarov; they both supposed they were speaking the truth. Was the truth, the whole truth, to be found in their words? They could not themselves have said, and much less could the author. But a conversation followed between them precisely as though they completely believed one another.

Anna Sergyevna asked Bazarov, among other things, what he had been doing at the Kirsanovs'. He was on the point of telling her about his duel with Pavel Petrovitch, but he checked himself with the thought that she might imagine he was trying to make himself interesting and answered that he had been at work all the time.

"And I," observed Anna Sergyevna, "had a fit of depression at first, goodness knows why; I even made plans for going abroad, fancy! . . . Then it passed off, your friend Arkady Nikolaitch came, and I fell back into my old routine, and took up my real part again."

"What part is that, may I ask?"

"The character of aunt, guardian, mother—call it what you like. By the way, do you know I used not quite to understand your close friendship with Arkady Nikolaitch; I thought him rather insignificant. But now I have come to know him better, and to see that he is clever. . . . And he's young, he's young . . . that's the great thing . . . not like you and me, Yevgeny Vassilyitch."

"Is he still as shy in your company?" queried Bazarov.

"Why, was he?" . . . Anna Sergyevna began, and after a brief pause she went on: "He has grown more confiding now; he talks to me. He used to avoid me before. Though, indeed, I didn't seek his society either. He's more friends with Katya."

Bazarov felt irritated. "A woman can't help humbugging, of course!" he thought. "You say he used to avoid you," he said aloud, with a chilly smile; "but it is probably no secret to you that he was in love with you?"

"What! he too?" fell from Anna Sergyevna's lips.

"He too," repeated Bazarov, with a submissive bow. "Can it be you didn't know it, and I've told you something new?"

Anna Sergyevna dropped her eyes. "You are mistaken, Yevgeny

Vassilyitch."

"I don't think so. But perhaps I ought not to have mentioned it."

"And don't you try telling me lies again for the future," he added to himself.

"Why not? But I imagine that in this, too, you are attributing too much importance to a passing impression. I begin to suspect you are inclined to exaggeration."

"We had better not talk about it, Anna Sergyevna."

"Oh, why?" she retorted; but she herself led the conversation into another channel. She was still ill at ease with Bazarov, though she had told him and assured herself that everything was forgotten. While she was exchanging the simplest sentences with him, even while she was jesting with him, she was conscious of a faint spasm of dread. So people on a steamer at sea talk and laugh carelessly, for all the world as though they were on dry land; but let only the slighest hitch occur, let the least sign be seen of anything out of the common, and at once on every face there comes out an expression of peculiar alarm, betraying the constant consciousness of constant danger.

Anna Sergyevna's conversation with Bazarov did not last long. She began to seem absorbed in thought, answered abstractedly, and suggested at last that they should go into the hall, where they found the princess and Katya. "But where is Arkady Nikolaitch?" inquired the lady of the house; and on hearing that he had not shown himself for more than an hour, she sent for him. He was not very quickly found; he had hidden himself in the very thickest part of the garden, and with his chin propped on his folded hands, he was sitting lost in meditation. They were deep and serious meditations, but not mournful. He knew Anna Sergyevna was sitting alone with Bazarov, and he felt no jealousy, as once he had; on the contrary, his face slowly brightened; he seemed to be at once wondering and rejoicing, and resolving on something.

XXVI

The deceased Odintsov had not liked innovations, but he had tolerated "the fine arts within a certain sphere," and had in consequence put up in his garden, between the hothouse and the lake, an erection after the fashion of a Greek temple, made of Russian brick. Along the dark wall at the back of this temple or gallery were placed six niches for statues, which Odintsov had proceeded to order from abroad. These statues were to represent Solitude, Silence, Meditation, Melancholy, Modesty, and Sensibility. One of them, the goddess of Silence, with her finger on her lip, had been sent and put up; but on the very same day some boys on the farm had broken her nose; and though a plasterer of the neighbourhood undertook to make her a new nose "twice as good as the old one," Odintsov ordered her to be taken away, and she was still to be seen in the corner of the threshing barn, where she had stood many long years, a source of superstitious terror to the peasant women. The front part of the temple had long been overgrown with thick bushes; only the pediments of the columns could be seen above the dense green. In the temple itself it was cool even at mid-day. Anna Sergyevna had not liked visiting this place ever since she had seen a snake there; but Katya often came and sat on the wide stone seat under one of the niches. Here, in the midst of the shade and coolness, she used to read and work, or to give herself up to that sensation of perfect peace, known, doubtless, to each of us, the charm of which consists in the half-unconscious, silent listening to the vast current of life that flows forever both around us and within us.

The day after Bazarov's arrival Katya was sitting on her favourite stone seat, and beside her again was sitting Arkady. He had besought her to come with him to the "temple."

There was about an hour still to lunch time; the dewy morning had already given place to a sultry day. Arkady's face retained the expression of the preceding day; Katya had a preoccupied look. Her sister had, directly after their morning tea, called her into her room, and after some preliminary caresses, which always scared Katya a little, she had advised her to be more guarded in her behaviour with Arkady, and especially to avoid solitary talks with him, as likely to attract the notice of her aunt and all the household. Besides this, even the previous evening Anna Sergyevna had not been herself; and Katya herself had felt ill at ease, as though she were conscious of some fault in herself. As she yielded to Arkady's entreaties, she said to herself that it was for the last time.

"Katerina Sergyevna," he began with a sort of bashful easiness, "since I've had the happiness of living in the same house with you, I have discussed a great many things with you; but meanwhile there is one, very important . . . for me . . . one question, which I have not touched upon up till now. You remarked yesterday that I have been changed here," he went on, at once catching and avoiding the questioning glance Katya was turning upon him. "I have changed certainly a great deal, and you know that better than any one else—you to whom I really owe this change."

"I? . . . Me? . . ." said Katya.

"I am not now the conceited boy I was when I came here," Arkady went on. "I've not reached twenty-three for nothing; as before, I want to be useful, I want to devote all my powers to the truth; but I no longer look for my ideals where I did; they present themselves to me . . . much closer to hand. Up till now I did not understand myself; I set myself tasks which were beyond my powers. . . . My eyes have been opened lately, thanks to one feeling. . . . I'm not expressing myself quite clearly, but I hope you understand me."

Katya made no reply, but she ceased looking at Arkady.

"I suppose," he began again, this time in a more agitated voice, while above his head a chaffinch sang its song unheeding among the leaves of the birch—"I suppose it's the duty of every one to be open with those . . . with those people who . . . in fact, with those who are near to him, and so I . . . I resolved . . ."

But here Arkady's eloquence deserted him; he lost the thread, stammered, and was forced to be silent for a moment. Katya still did not raise her eyes. She seemed not to understand what he was leading up to in all this, and to be waiting for something.

"I foresee I shall surprise you," began Arkady, pulling himself together again with an effort, "especially since this feeling relates in a way . . . in a way, notice . . . to you. You reproached me, if you remember, yesterday with a want of seriousness," Arkady went on, with the air of a man who has got into a bog, feels that he is sinking further and further in at every step, and yet hurries onwards in the hope of crossing it as soon as possible; "that reproach is often aimed . . . often falls . . . on young men even when they cease to deserve it; and if I had more self-confidence . . ." ("Come, help me, do help me!" Arkady was thinking, in desperation; but, as before, Katya did not turn her head.) "If I could hope . . ."

"If I could feel sure of what you say," was heard at that instant the clear voice of Anna Sergyevna.

Arkady was still at once, while Katya turned pale. Close by the bushes that screened the temple ran a little path. Anna Sergyevna was walking along it escorted by Bazarov. Katya and Arkady could not see them, but they heard every word, the rustle of their clothes, their very breathing. They walked on a few steps, and, as though on purpose, stood still just opposite the temple.

"You see," pursued Anna Sergyevna, "you and I made a mistake; we are both past our first youth, I especially so; we have seen life, we are tired; we are both—why affect not to know it?—clever; at first we interested each other, curiosity was aroused . . . and then . . ."

"And then I grew stale," put in Bazarov.

"You know that was not the cause of our misunderstanding. But, however, it was to be, we had no need of one another, that's the chief point; there was too much . . . what shall I say? . . . that was alike in us. We did not realise it all at once. Now, Arkady . . ."

"Do you need him?" queried Bazarov.

"Hush, Yevgeny Vassilyitch. You tell me he is not indifferent to me, and it always seemed to me he liked me. I know that I might well be his aunt, but I don't wish to conceal from you that I have come to think more often of him. In such youthful, fresh feeling there is a special charm . . ."

"The word *fascination* is most usual in such cases," Bazarov interrupted; the effervescence of his spleen could be heard in his choked though steady voice. "Arkady was mysterious over something with me yesterday, and didn't talk either of you or of your sister.

. . . That's a serious symptom."

"He is just like a brother with Katya," commented Anna Sergyevna, "and I like that in him, though, perhaps, I ought not to have allowed such intimacy between them."

"That idea is prompted by . . . your feelings as a sister?" Bazarov brought out, drawling.

"Of course . . . but why are we standing still? Let us go on. What a strange talk we are having, aren't we? I could never have believed I should talk to you like this. You know, I am afraid of you . . . and at the same time I trust you, because in reality you are so good."

"In the first place, I am not in the least good; and in the second place, I have lost all significance for you, and you tell me I am good . . . It's like laying a wreath of flowers on the head of a corpse."

"Yevgeny Vassilyitch, we are not responsible . . ." Anna Sergyevna began; but a gust of wind blew across, set the leaves rustling, and carried away her words. "Of course, you are free . . ." Bazarov declared after a brief pause. Nothing more could be distinguished; the steps retreated . . . everything was still.

Arkady turned to Katya. She was sitting in the same position, but her head was bent still lower. "Katerina Sergyevna," he said with a shaking voice, and clasping his hands tightly together, "I love you forever and irrevocably, and I love no one but you. I wanted to tell you this, to find out your opinion of me, and to ask for your hand, since I am not rich, and I feel ready for any sacrifice. . . . You don't answer me? You don't believe me? Do you think I speak lightly? But remember these last days! Surely for a long time past you must have known that everything—understand me—everything else has vanished long ago and left no trace? Look at me, say one word to me . . . I love you . . . believe me!"

Katya glanced at Arkady with a bright and serious look, and after long hesitation, with the faintest smile, she said, "Yes."

Arkady leaped up from the stone seat. "Yes! You said Yes, Katerina Sergyevna! What does that word mean? Only that I do love you, that you believe me . . . or . . . or . . . I daren't go on . . ."

"Yes," repeated Katya, and this time he understood her. He snatched her large beautiful hands, and, breathless with rapture, pressed them to his heart. He could scarcely stand on his feet, and could only repeat, "Katya, Katya . . ." while she began weeping in a guileless way, smiling gently at her own tears. No one who has not seen those tears in the eyes of the beloved, knows yet to what a point, faint with shame and gratitude, a man may be happy on earth.

The next day, early in the morning, Anna Sergyevna sent to summon Bazarov to her boudoir, and with a forced laugh handed him a folded sheet of notepaper. It was a letter from Arkady; in it he asked for her sister's hand.

Bazarov quickly scanned the letter, and made an effort to control himself, that he might not show the malignant feeling which was instantaneously aflame in his breast.

"So that's how it is," he commented; "and you, I fancy, only yesterday imagined he loved Katerina Sergyevna as a brother. What are you intending to do now?"

"What do you advise me?" asked Anna Sergyevna, still laughing.

"Well, I suppose," answered Bazarov, also with a laugh, though he felt anything but cheerful, and had no more inclination to laugh than she had; "I suppose you ought to give the young people your blessing. It's a good match in every respect; Kirsanov's position is passable, he's the only son, and his father's a good-natured fellow, he won't try to thwart him."

Madame Odintsov walked up and down the room. By turns her face flushed and grew pale. "You think so," she said. "Well, I see no obstacles . . . I am glad for Katya . . . and for Arkady Nikolaevitch too. Of course, I will wait for his father's answer. I will send him in person to him. But it turns out, you see, that I was right yesterday when I told you we were both old people. . . . How was it I saw nothing? That's what amazes me!" Anna Sergyevna laughed again, and quickly turned her head away.

"The younger generation have grown awfully sly," remarked Bazarov, and he, too, laughed. "Good-bye," he began after a short silence. "I hope you will bring the matter to the most satisfactory conclusion; and I will rejoice from a distance."

Madame Odintsov turned quickly to him. "You are not going away? Why should you not stay *now?* Stay . . . it's exciting talking to you . . . one seems walking on the edge of a precipice. At first one feels timid, but one gains courage as one goes on. Do stay."

"Thanks for the suggestion, Anna Sergyevna, and for your flattering opinion of my conversational talents. But I think I have already been moving too long in a sphere which is not my own. Flying fishes can hold out for a time in the air, but soon they must splash back into the water; allow me, too, to paddle in my own element."

Madame Odintsov looked at Bazarov. His pale face was twitching with a bitter smile. "This man did love me!" she thought, and she felt pity for him, and held out her hand to him with sympathy.

But he, too, understood her. "No!" he said, stepping back a pace. "I'm a poor man, but I've never taken charity so far. Good-bye, and good luck to you."

"I am certain we are not seeing each other for the last time," Anna Sergyevna declared with an unconscious gesture.

"Anything may happen!" answered Bazarov, and he bowed and went away.

"So you are thinking of making yourself a nest?" he said the same day to Arkady, as he packed his box, crouching on the floor. "Well, it's a capital thing. But you needn't have been such a humbug. I expected something from you in quite another quarter. Perhaps, though, it took you by surprise yourself?"

"I certainly didn't expect this when I parted from you," answered Arkady; "but why are you, a humbug yourself, calling it 'a capital thing,' as though I didn't know your opinion of marriage."

"Ah, my dear fellow," said Bazarov, "how you talk! You see what I'm doing; there seems to be an empty space in the box, and I am putting hay in; that's how it is in the box of our life; we would stuff it up with anything rather than have a void. Don't be offended, please; you remember, no doubt, the opinion I have always had of Katerina Sergyevna. Many a young lady's called clever simply because she can sigh cleverly; but yours can hold her own, and, indeed, she'll hold it so well that she'll have you under her thumb—to be sure, though, that's quite as it ought to be." He slammed the lid to, and got up from the floor. "And now, I say again, good-bye, for it's useless to deceive ourselves—we are parting for good, and you know that yourself . . . you have acted sensibly; you're not made for our bitter, rough, lonely existence. There's no dash, no hate in you, but you've the daring of youth and the fire of youth. Your sort, you gentry, can never get beyond refined submission or refined indignation, and that's no good. You won't fight—and yet you fancy yourselves gallant chaps—but we mean to fight. Oh well! Our dust would get into your eyes, our mud would bespatter you, but yet you're not up to our level, you're admiring yourselves unconsciously; you like to abuse yourselves; but we're sick of that—we want something else! we want to smash other people! You're a capital fellow; but you're a sugary, liberal snob for all that—*ay volla-too*, as my parent is fond of saying."

"You are parting from me for ever, Yevgeny," responded Arkady mournfully; "and have you nothing else to say to me?"

Bazarov scratched the back of his head. "Yes, Arkady, yes, I have other things to say to you, but I'm not going to say them, because that's sentimentalism—that means, mawkishness. And you get married as soon as you can; and build your nest, and get children to your heart's content. They'll have the wit to be born in a better time than you and me. Aha! I see the horses are ready. Time's up! I've said good-bye to every one. . . . What now? embracing, eh?"

Arkady flung himself on the neck of his former leader and friend, and the tears fairly gushed from his eyes.

"That's what comes of being young!" Bazarov commented calmly. "But I rest my hopes on Katerina Sergyevna. You'll see how quickly she'll console you! Good-bye, brother!" he said to Arkady when he had got into the light cart, and, pointing to a pair of jackdaws sitting side by side on the stable roof, he added, "That's for you! follow that example."

"What does that mean?" asked Arkady.

"What? Are you so weak in natural history, or have you forgotten that the jackdaw is a most respectable family bird? An example to you! . . . Good-bye!"

The cart creaked and rolled away.

Bazarov had spoken truly. In talking that evening with Katya, Arkady completely forgot about his former teacher. He already began to follow her lead, and Katya was conscious of this, and not surprised at it. He was to set off the next day for Maryino, to see Nikolai Petrovitch. Anna Sergyevna was not disposed to put any constraint on the young people, and only on account of the proprieties did not leave them by themselves for too long together. She magnanimously kept the princess out of their way; the latter had been reduced to a state of tearful frenzy by the news of the proposed marriage. At first Anna Sergyevna was afraid the sight of their happiness might prove rather trying to herself, but it turned out quite the other way; this sight not only did not distress her, it interested her, it even softened her at last. Anna Sergyevna felt both glad and sorry at this. "It is clear that Bazarov was right," she thought; "it has been curiosity, nothing but curiosity, and love of ease, and egoism . . ."

"Children," she said aloud, "what do you say, is love a purely imaginary feeling?"

But neither Katya nor Arkady even understood her. They were shy with her; the fragment of conversation they had involuntarily overheard haunted their minds. But Anna Sergyevna soon set their minds at rest; and it was not difficult for her—she had set her own mind at rest.

<h3 style="text-align:center">XXVII</h3>

Bazarov's old parents were all the more overjoyed by their son's arrival, as it was quite unexpected. Arina Vlasyevna was greatly excited, and kept running backwards and forwards in the house, so that Vassily Ivanovitch compared her to a "hen partridge"; the short tail of her abbreviated jacket did, in fact, give her something of a birdlike appearance. He himself merely growled and gnawed the amber mouthpiece of his pipe, or, clutching his neck with his fingers, turned his head round, as though he were trying whether it were properly screwed on, then all at once he opened his wide mouth and went off into a perfectly noiseless chuckle. "I've come to you for six whole weeks, old man," Bazarov said to him. "I want to work, so please don't hinder me now."

"You shall forget my face completely, if you call that hindering you!" answered Vassily Ivanovitch.

He kept his promise. After installing his son as before in his study, he almost hid himself away from him, and kept his wife from all superfluous demonstrations of tenderness. "On Enyusha's first visit, my dear soul," he said to her, "we bothered him a little; we must be wiser this time." Arina Vlasyevna agreed with her husband, but that was small compensation since she saw her son only at meals, and was now absolutely afraid to address him. "Enyushen-ka," she would say sometimes—and before he had time to look round, she was nervously fingering the tassels of her reticule and faltering, "Never mind, never mind, I only—" and afterwards she would go to Vassily Ivanovitch and, her cheek in her hand, would consult him: "If you could only find out, darling, which Enyusha would like for dinner to-day—cabbage broth or beet-root soup?"— "But why didn't you ask him yourself?"—"Oh, he will get sick of me!" Bazarov, however, soon ceased to shut himself up; the fever of work fell away, and was replaced by dreary boredom or vague restlessness. A strange weariness began to show itself in all his movements; even his walk, firm, bold and strenuous, was changed. He gave up walking in solitude, and began to seek society; he drank tea in the drawing-room, strolled about the kitchen-garden with Vassily Ivanovitch, and smoked with him in silence; once even asked after Father Alexey. Vassily Ivanovitch at first rejoiced at this change, but his joy was not long-lived. "Enyusha's breaking my heart," he complained in secret to his wife: "it's not that he's discontented or angry—that would be nothing; he's sad, he's sorrowful—that's what's so terrible. He's always silent. If he'd only abuse us; he's growing thin, he's lost his colour."—"Mercy on us, mercy on us!" whispered the old woman; "I would put an amulet on his neck, but, of course, he won't allow it." Vassily Ivanovitch several times attempted in the most circumspect manner to question Bazarov about his work, about his health, and about Arkady. . . . But Bazarov's replies were reluctant and casual; and, once noticing that his father was trying gradually to lead up to something in conversation, he said to him in a tone of vexation: "Why do you always seem to be walking round me on tiptoe? That way's worse than the old one."—"There, there, I meant nothing!" poor Vassily Ivanovitch answered hurriedly. So his diplomatic hints remained fruitless. He hoped to awaken his son's sympathy one day by beginning *à propos* of the approaching emancipation of the peasantry, to talk about progress; but the latter responded indifferently: "Yesterday I was walking under the fence, and I heard the peasant boys here, instead of some old ballad, bawling a street song. That's what progress is."

Sometimes Bazarov went into the village, and in his usual bantering tone entered into conversation with some peasant: "Come," he would say to him, "expound your views on life to me, brother; you see, they say all the strength and future of Russia lies in your hands, a new epoch in history will be started by you—you give us our real language and our laws."

The peasant either made no reply, or articulated a few words of this sort, "Well, we'll try . . . because, you see, to be sure. . . ."

"You explain to me what your *mir*[49] is," Bazarov interrupted; "and is it the same *mir* that is said to rest on three fishes?"

"That, little father, is the earth that rests on three fishes," the peasant would declare soothingly, in a kind of patriarchal, simple-hearted sing-song; "and over against ours, that's to say, the *mir*, we know there's the master's will; wherefore you are our fathers. And the stricter the master's rule, the better for the peasant."

After listening to such a reply one day, Bazarov shrugged his shoulders contemptuously and turned away, while the peasant sauntered slowly homewards.

"What was he talking about?" inquired another peasant of middle age and surly aspect, who at a distance from the door of his hut had been following his conversation with Bazarov.—"Arrears? eh?"

"Arrears, no indeed, mate!" answered the first peasant, and now there was no trace of patriarchal singsong in his voice; on the contrary, there was a certain scornful gruffness to be heard in it: "Oh, he clacked away about something or other; wanted to stretch his tongue a bit. Of course, he's a gentleman; what does he understand?"

"What should he understand!" answered the other peasant, and jerking back their caps and pushing down their belts, they proceeded to deliberate upon their work and their wants. Alas! Bazarov, shrugging his shoulders contemptuously, Bazarov, who knew how to talk to peasants (as he had boasted in his dispute with Pavel Petrovitch), did not in his self-confidence even suspect that in their eyes he was all the while something of the nature of a buffooning clown.

He found employment for himself at last, however. One day Vassily Ivanovitch bound up a peasant's wounded leg before him, but the old man's hands trembled, and he could not manage the bandages; his son helped him, and from time to time began to take a share in his practice, though at the same time he was constantly sneering both at the remedies he himself advised and at his father, who hastened to make use of them. But Bazarov's jeers did not in the least perturb Vassily Ivanovitch; they were positively a comfort to him. Holding his greasy dressing-gown across his stomach with two fingers, and smoking his pipe, he used to listen with enjoyment to Bazarov; and the more malicious his sallies, the more good-humouredly did his delighted father chuckle, showing every one of his black teeth. He used even to repeat these sometimes flat or pointless retorts, and would, for instance, for several days constantly without rhyme or reason, reiterate, "Not a matter of the first importance!" simply because his son, on hearing he was going to matins, had made use of that expression. "Thank God! he has got over his

49. *mir:* in Russian, both the village commune (the village community holds the land in common and distributes it annually for cultivation to its members) and the universe or world. An old superstition holds that the world rests on three fishes.

melancholy!" he whispered to his wife; "how he gave it to me to-day, it was splendid!" Moreover, the idea of having such an assistant excited him to ecstasy, filled him with pride. "Yes, yes," he would say to some peasant woman in a man's cloak, and a cap shaped like a horn, as he handed her a bottle of Goulard's extract or a box of white ointment, "you ought to be thanking God, my good woman, every minute that my son is staying with me; you will be treated now by the most scientific, most modern method. Do you know what that means? The Emperor of the French, Napoleon, even, has no better doctor." And the peasant woman, who had come to complain that she felt so sort of queer all over (the exact meaning of these words she was not able, however, herself to explain), merely bowed low and rummaged in her bosom, where four eggs lay tied up in the corner of a towel.

Bazarov once even pulled out a tooth for a passing pedlar of cloth; and though this tooth was an average specimen, Vassily Ivanovitch preserved it as a curiosity, and incessantly repeated, as he showed it to Father Alexey, "Just look, what a fang! The force Yevgeny has! The pedlar seemed to leap into the air. If it had been an oak he'd have rooted it up!"

"Most promising!" Father Alexey would comment at last, not knowing what answer to make, and how to get rid of the ecstatic old man.

One day a peasant from a neighbouring village brought his brother to Vassily Ivanovitch, ill with typhus. The unhappy man, lying flat on a truss of straw, was dying; his body was covered with dark patches, he had long ago lost consciousness. Vassily Ivanovitch expressed his regret that no one had taken steps to procure medical aid sooner, and declared there was no hope. And, in fact, the peasant did not get his brother home again; he died in the cart.

Three days later Bazarov came into his father's room and asked him if he had any caustic.

"Yes; what do you want it for?"

"I must have some . . . to burn a cut."

"For whom?"

"For myself."

"What, yourself? Why is that? What sort of a cut? Where is it?"

"Look here, on my finger. I went to-day to the village, you know, where they brought that peasant with typhus fever. They were just going to open the body for some reason or other, and I've had no practice of that sort for a long while."

"Well?"

"Well, so I asked the district doctor about it; and so I dissected it."

Vassily Ivanovitch all at once turned quite white, and, without uttering a word, rushed to his study, from which he returned at once with a bit of caustic in his hand. Bazarov was about to take it and go away.

"For mercy's sake," said Vassily Ivanovitch, "let me do it myself."

Bazarov smiled. "What a devoted practitioner!"

"Don't laugh, please. Show me your finger. The cut is not a large one. Do I hurt?"

"Press harder; don't be afraid."

Vassily Ivanovitch stopped. "What do you think, Yevgeny; wouldn't it be better to burn it with hot iron?"

"That ought to have been done sooner; the caustic even is useless, really, now. If I've taken the infection, it's too late now."

"How . . . too late. . . ." Vassily Ivanovitch could scarcely articulate the words.

"I should think so! It's more than four hours ago."

Vassily Ivanovitch burnt the cut a little more. "But had the district doctor no caustic?"

"No."

"How was that, good Heavens? A doctor not have such an indispensable thing as that!"

"You should have seen his lancets," observed Bazarov as he walked away.

Up till late that evening, and all the following day, Vassily Ivanovitch kept catching at every possible excuse to go into his son's room; and though far from referring to the cut—he even tried to talk about the most irrelevant subjects—he looked so persistently into his face, and watched him in such trepidation, that Bazarov lost patience and threatened to go away. Vassily Ivanovitch gave him a promise not to bother him, the more readily as Arina Vlasyevna, from whom, of course, he kept it all secret, was beginning to worry him as to why he did not sleep, and what had come over him. For two whole days he held himself in, though he did not at all like the look of his son, whom he kept watching stealthily, . . . but on the third day, at dinner, he could bear it no longer. Bazarov sat with downcast looks, and had not touched a single dish.

"Why don't you eat, Yevgeny?" he inquired, putting on an expression of the most perfect carelessness. "The food, I think, is very nicely cooked."

"I don't want anything, so I don't eat."

"Have you no appetite? And your head," he added timidly; "does it ache?"

"Yes. Of course, it aches."

Arina Vlasyevna sat up and was all alert.

"Don't be angry, please, Yevgeny," continued Vassily Ivanovitch; "won't you let me feel your pulse?"

Bazarov got up. "I can tell you without feeling my pulse; I'm feverish."

"Has there been any shivering?"

"Yes, there has been shivering too. I'll go and lie down, and you can send me some lime-flower tea. I must have caught cold."

"To be sure, I heard you coughing last night," observed Arina Vlasyevna.

"I've caught cold," repeated Bazarov, and he went away.

Arina Vlasyevna busied herself about the preparation of the decoction of lime-flowers, while Vassily Ivanovitch went into the next room and clutched at his hair in silent desperation.

Bazarov did not get up again that day, and passed the whole night in heavy, half-unconscious torpor. At one o'clock in the morning, opening his eyes with an effort, he saw by the light of a lamp his father's pale face bending over him, and told him to go away. The old man begged his pardon, but he quickly came back on tiptoe, and half-hidden by the cupboard door, he gazed persistently at his son. Arina Vlasyevna did not go to bed either, and leaving the study door just open a very little, she kept coming up to it to listen "how Enyusha was breathing," and to look at Vassily Ivanovitch. She could see nothing but his motionless bent back, but even that afforded her some faint consolation. In the morning Bazarov tried to get up; he was seized with giddiness, his nose began to bleed; he lay down again. Vassily Ivanovitch waited on him in silence; Arina Vlasyevna went in to him and asked him how he was feeling. He answered, "Better," and turned to the wall. Vassily Ivanovitch gesticulated at his wife with both hands; she bit her lips so as not to cry, and went away. The whole house seemed suddenly darkened; every one looked gloomy; there was a strange hush; a shrill cock was carried away from the yard to the village, unable to comprehend why he should be treated so. Bazarov still lay, turned to the wall. Vassily Ivanovitch tried to address him with various questions, but they fatigued Bazarov, and the old man sank into his arm-chair, motionless, only cracking his finger-joints now and then. He went for a few minutes into the garden, stood there like a statue, as though overwhelmed with unutterable bewilderment (the expression of amazement never left his face all through), and went back again to his son, trying to avoid his wife's questions. She caught him by the arm at last, and passionately, almost menacingly, said, "What is wrong with him?" Then he came to himself, and forced himself to smile at her in reply; but to his own horror, instead of a smile, he found himself taken somehow by a fit of laughter. He had sent at daybreak for a doctor. He thought it necessary to inform his son of this, for fear he should be angry. Bazarov suddenly turned over on the sofa, bent a fixed dull look on his father, and asked for drink.

Vassily Ivanovitch gave him some water, and as he did so felt his forehead. It seemed on fire.

"Listen, old man," began Bazarov, in a slow, drowsy voice; "I'm in a bad way; I've got the infection, and in a few days you'll have to bury me."

Vassily Ivanovitch staggered back, as though some one had aimed a blow at his legs.

"Yevgeny!" he faltered; "what do you mean! . . . God have mercy on you! You've caught cold!"

"Hush!" Bazarov interposed deliberately. "A doctor can't be allowed to talk like that. There's every symptom of infection; you know yourself."

"Where are the symptoms . . . of infection, Yevgeny? . . . Good Heavens!"

"What's this?" said Bazarov, and, pulling up his shirtsleeve, he showed his father the ominous red patches coming out on his arm.

Vassily Ivanovitch was shaking and chill with terror.

"Supposing," he said at last, "even supposing . . . if even there's something like . . . infection . . ."

"Pyaemia," put in his son.

"Well, well . . . something of the epidemic . . ."

"Pyaemia," Bazarov repeated sharply and distinctly; "have you forgotten your text-books?"

"Well, well—as you like. . . . Anyway, we will cure you!"

"Come, that's humbug. But that's not the point. I didn't expect to die so soon; it's a most unpleasant incident, to tell the truth. You and mother ought to make the most of your strong religious belief; now's the time to put it to the test." He drank off a little water. "I want to ask you about one thing . . . while my head is still under my control. To-morrow or next day my brain, you know, will send in its resignation. I'm not quite certain even now whether I'm expressing myself clearly. While I've been lying here, I've kept fancying red dogs were running round me, while you were making them point at me, as if I were a woodcock. Just as if I were drunk. Do you understand me all right?"

"I assure you, Yevgeny, you are talking perfectly correctly."

"All the better. You told me you'd sent for the doctor. You did that to comfort yourself . . . comfort me too; send a messenger . . ."

"To Arkady Nikolaitch?" put in the old man.

"Who's Arkady Nikolaitch?" said Bazarov, as though in doubt. . . . "Oh, yes! that chicken! No, let him alone; he's turned jackdaw now. Don't be surprised; that's not delirium yet. You send a messenger to Madame Odintsov, Anna Sergyevna; she's a lady with an estate. . . . Do you know?" (Vassily Ivanovitch nodded). "Yevgeny Bazarov, say, sends his greetings, and sends word he is dying. Will you do that?"

"Yes, I will do it. . . . But is it a possible thing for you to die, Yevgeny? . . . Think only! Where would divine justice be after that?"

"I know nothing about that; only you send the messenger."

"I'll send this minute, and I'll write a letter myself."

"No, why? Say I send greetings; nothing more is necessary. And now I'll go back to my dogs. Strange! I want to fix my thoughts on death, and nothing comes of it. I see a kind of blur . . . and nothing more."

He turned painfully back to the wall again; while Vassily Ivanovitch went out of the study, and struggling as far as his wife's bedroom, simply dropped down on to his knees before the holy pictures.

"Pray, Arina, pray for us!" he moaned; "our son is dying."

The doctor, the same district doctor who had had no caustic, arrived, and after looking at the patient, advised them to persevere with a cooling treatment, and at that point said a few words of the chance of recovery.

"Have you ever chanced to see people in my state *not* set off for Elysium?" asked Bazarov, and suddenly snatching the leg of a heavy table that stood near his sofa, he swung it round, and pushed it away. "There's strength, there's strength," he murmured; "everything's here still, and I must die! . . . An old man at least has time to be weaned from life, but I . . . Well, go and try to disprove death. Death will disprove you, and that's all! Who's crying there?" he added, after a short pause.—"Mother? Poor thing! Whom will she feed now with her exquisite beet-root soup? You, Vassily Ivanovitch, whimpering too, I do believe! Why, if Christianity's no help to you, be a philosopher, a Stoic, or what not! Why, didn't you boast you were a philosopher?"

"Me a philosopher!" wailed Vassily Ivanovitch, while the tears fairly streamed down his cheeks.

Bazarov got worse every hour; the progress of the disease was rapid, as is usually the way in cases of surgical poisoning. He still had not lost consciousness, and understood what was said to him; he was still struggling. "I don't want to lose my wits," he muttered, clenching his fists; "what rot it all is!" And at once he would say, "Come, take ten from eight, what remains?" Vassily Ivanovitch wandered about like one possessed, proposed first one remedy, then another, and ended by doing nothing but cover up his son's feet. "Try cold pack . . . emetic . . . mustard plasters on the stomach . . . bleeding," he would murmur with an effort. The doctor, whom he had entreated to remain, agreed with him, ordered the patient lemonade to drink, and for himself asked for a pipe and something "warming and strengthening"—that's to say, brandy. Arina Vlasyevna sat on a low stool near the door, and only went out from time to time to pray. A few days before, a looking-glass had slipped out of her hands and been broken, and this she had always considered an omen of evil; even Anfisushka could say nothing to her. Timofeitch had gone off to Madame Odintsov's.

The night passed badly for Bazarov. . . . He was in the agonies of high fever. Towards morning he was a little easier. He asked for Arina Vlasyevna to comb his hair, kissed her hand, and swallowed two gulps of tea. Vassily Ivanovitch revived a little.

"Thank God!" he kept declaring; "the crisis is coming, the crisis is at hand!"

"There, to think now!" murmured Bazarov; "what a word can do! He's found it; he's said 'crisis,' and is comforted. It's an astounding thing how man believes in words. If he's told he's a fool, for instance, though he's not thrashed, he'll be wretched; call him a clever fellow, and he'll be delighted if you go off without paying him."

This little speech of Bazarov's, recalling his old retorts, moved Vassily Ivanovitch greatly.

"Bravo! well said, very good!" he cried, making as though he were clapping his hands.

Bazarov smiled mournfully.

"So what do you think," he said; "is the crisis over, or coming?"

"You are better, that's what I see, that's what rejoices me," answered Vassily Ivanovitch.

"Well, that's good; rejoicings never come amiss. And to her, do you remember, did you send?"

"To be sure I did."

The change for the better did not last long. The disease resumed its onslaughts. Vassily Ivanovitch was sitting by Bazarov. It seemed as though the old man were tormented by some special anguish. He was several times on the point of speaking—and could not.

"Yevgeny!" he brought out at last; "my son, my one, dear son!"

This unfamiliar mode of address produced an effect on Bazarov. He turned his head a little, and, obviously trying to fight against the load of oblivion weighing upon him, he articulated: "What is it, father?"

"Yevgeny," Vassily Ivanovitch went on, and he fell on his knees before Bazarov, though the latter had closed his eyes and could not see him. "Yevgeny, you are better now; please God, you will get well, but make use of this time, comfort your mother and me, perform the duty of a Christian! What it means for me to say this to you, it's awful; but still more awful . . . for ever and ever. Yevgeny . . . think a little, what . . ."

The old man's voice broke, and a strange look passed over his son's face, though he still lay with closed eyes.

"I won't refuse, if that can be any comfort to you," he brought out at last; "but it seems to me there's no need to be in a hurry. You say yourself I am better."

"Oh, yes, Yevgeny, better certainly; but who knows, it is all in God's hands, and in doing the duty . . ."

"No, I will wait a bit," broke in Bazarov. "I agree with you that the crisis has come. And if you're mistaken, well! they give the sacrament to men who are unconscious, you know."

"Yevgeny, I beg."

"I'll wait a little. And now I want to go to sleep. Don't disturb me." And he laid his head back on the pillow.

The old man rose from his knees, sat down in the armchair, and clutching his beard, began biting his own fingers . . .

The sound of a light carriage on springs, that sound which is peculiarly impressive in the wilds of the country, suddenly struck upon his hearing. Nearer and nearer rolled the light wheels; now even the neighing of the horses could be heard. . . . Vassily Ivanovitch jumped up and ran to the little window. There drove into the courtyard of his little house a carriage with seats for two, with four horses harnessed abreast. Without stopping to consider what it could mean, with a rush of a sort of senseless joy, he ran out on to the steps. . . . A groom in livery was opening the carriage doors; a lady in a black veil and a black mantle was getting out of it . . .

"I am Madame Odintsov," she said. "Yevgeny Vassilyitch is still living? You are his father? I have a doctor with me."

"Benefactress!" cried Vassily Ivanovitch, and snatching her hand, he pressed it convulsively to his lips, while the doctor brought by Anna Sergyevna, a little man in spectacles, of German physiognomy, stepped very deliberately out of the carriage. "Still living, my Yevgeny is living, and now he will be saved! Wife! wife! . . . An angel from heaven has come to us. . . ."

"What does it mean, good Lord!" faltered the old woman, running out of the drawing-room; and, comprehending nothing, she fell on the spot in the passage at Anna Sergyevna's feet, and began kissing her garments like a mad woman.

"What are you doing!" protested Anna Sergyevna; but Arina Vlasyevna did not heed her, while Vassily Ivanovitch could only repeat, "An angel! an angel!"

"*Wo ist der Kranke?* and where is the patient?" said the doctor at last, with some impatience.

Vassily Ivanovitch recovered himself. "Here, here, follow me, *würdigster Herr Collega*," he added through old associations.

"Ah!" articulated the German, grinning sourly.

Vassily Ivanovitch led him into the study. "The doctor from Anna Sergyevna Odintsov," he said, bending down quite to his son's ear, "and she herself is here."

Bazarov suddenly opened his eyes. "What did you say?"

"I say that Anna Sergyevna is here, and has brought this gentleman, a doctor, to you."

Bazarov moved his eyes about him. "She is here. . . . I want to see her."

"You shall see her, Yevgeny; but first we must have a little talk with the doctor. I will tell him the whole history of your illness since Sidor Sidoritch" (this was the name of the district doctor) "has gone, and we will have a little consultation."

Bazarov glanced at the German. "Well, talk away quickly, only not in Latin; you see, I know the meaning of *jam moritur*."[50]

"*Der Herr scheint des Deutschen mächtig zu sein*,"[51] began the new follower of Æsculapius, turning to Vassily Ivanovitch.

"*Ich . . . gabe. . . .*[52] We had better speak Russian," said the old man.

"Ah, ah! so that's how it is. . . . To be sure . . ." And the consultation began.

Half-an-hour later Anna Sergyevna, conducted by Vassily Ivanovitch, came into the study. The doctor had had time to whisper to her that it was hopeless even to think of the patient's recovery.

She looked at Bazarov . . . and stood still in the doorway, so greatly was she impressed by the inflamed, and at the same time deathly face, with its dim eyes fastened upon her. She felt simply dismayed, with a sort of cold and suffocating dismay; the thought that she would not have felt like that if she had really loved him flashed instantaneously through her brain.

"Thanks," he said painfully. "I did not expect this. It's a deed of mercy. So we have seen each other again, as you promised."

"Anna Sergyevna has been so kind," began Vassily Ivanovitch . . .

"Father, leave us alone. Anna Sergyevna, you will allow it, I fancy, now?"

With a motion of his head, he indicated his prostrate helpless frame.

Vassily Ivanovitch went out.

"Well, thanks," repeated Bazarov. "This is royally done. Monarchs, they say, visit the dying too."

"Yevgeny Vassilyitch, I hope—"

"Ah, Anna Sergyevna, let us speak the truth. It's all over with me. I'm under the wheel. So it turns out that it was useless to think of the future. Death's an old joke, but it comes fresh to every one. So far I'm not afraid . . . but there, unconsciousness is coming, and then it's all up!——" he waved his hand feebly. "Well, what had I to say to you . . . that I loved you? there was no sense in that even before, and less than ever now. Love is a form, and my own form is already breaking up. Better say how lovely you are! And now here you stand, so beautiful . . ."

Anna Sergyevna gave an involuntary shudder.

50. Latin, "he is dying."
51. "The gentleman seems to have a command of German."
52. "I have." *Gabe* should be *habe*, but Russians have trouble pronouncing *h* and must, e.g., transcribe *Hitler* as *Gitler*.

"Never mind, don't be uneasy. . . . Sit down there . . . Don't come close to me; you know, my illness is catching."

Anna Sergyevna swiftly crossed the room, and sat down in the armchair near the sofa on which Bazarov was lying.

"You are magnanimous!" he whispered. "Oh, how near, and how young, and fresh, and pure . . . in this loathsome room! . . . Well, good-bye! live long, that's the best of all, and make the most of it while there is time. You see what a hideous spectacle; the worm half crushed, but writhing still. And, you see, I thought too: I'd break down so many things, I wouldn't die, why should I, there were problems to solve, and I was a giant! And now all the problem for the giant is how to die decently, though that makes no difference to any one either . . . Never mind; I'm not going to turn tail."

Bazarov was silent, and began feeling with his hand for the glass. Anna Sergyevna gave him some drink, not taking off her glove, and drawing her breath timorously.

"You will forget me," he began again; "the dead's no companion for the living. My father will tell you what a man Russia is losing. . . . That's nonsense, but don't contradict the old man. Whatever toy will comfort the child . . . you know. And be kind to mother. People like them aren't to be found in your great world if you look by daylight with a candle. . . . I was needed by Russia. . . . No, it's clear, I wasn't needed. And who is needed? The shoemaker's needed, the tailor's needed, the butcher . . . give us meat . . . the butcher . . . wait a little, I'm getting mixed up. . . . There's a forest here . . ."

Bazarov put his hand to his brow.

Anna Sergyevna bent down to him. "Yevgeny Vassilyitch, I am here . . ."

He at once took his hand away, and raised himself.

"Good-bye," he said with sudden force, and his eyes gleamed with their last light. "Good-bye. . . . Listen . . . you know I didn't kiss you then. . . . Breathe on the dying lamp, and let it go out . . ."

Anna Sergyevna put her lips to his forehead.

"Enough!" he murmured, and dropped back on to the pillow. "Now . . . darkness . . ."

Anna Sergyevna went softly out. "Well?" Vassily Ivanovitch asked her in a whisper.

"He has fallen asleep," she answered, hardly audibly. Bazarov was not fated to awaken. Towards evening he sank into complete unconsciousness, and the following day he died. Father Alexey performed the last rites of religion over him. When they anointed him with the last unction, when the holy oil touched his breast, one eye opened, and it seemed as though at the sight of the priest in his vestments, the smoking censers, the light before the image, something like a shudder of horror passed over the death-stricken face. When at last he had breathed his last, and there arose a universal lamentation in the house, Vassily Ivanovitch was seized by a sudden frenzy. "I said I should rebel," he shrieked hoarsely, with his face inflamed and distorted, shaking his fist in the air, as though threatening some one; "and I rebel, I rebel!" But Arina Vlasyevna, all in tears, hung upon his neck, and both fell on their faces together. "Side by side," Anfisushka related afterwards in the servants' room, "they dropped their poor heads like lambs at noonday . . ."

But the heat of noonday passes, and evening comes and night, and then, too, the return to the kindly refuge, where sleep is sweet for the weary and heavy laden. . . .

XXVIII

Six months had passed by. White winter had come with the cruel stillness of unclouded frosts, the thick-lying, crunching snow, the rosy rime on the trees, the pale emerald sky, the wreaths of smoke above the chimneys, the clouds of steam rushing out of the doors when they are opened for an instant, with the fresh faces, that look stung by the cold, and the hurrying trot of the chilled horses. A January day was drawing to its close; the cold of evening was more keen than ever in the motionless air; and a lurid sunset was rapidly dying away. There were lights burning in the windows of the house at Maryino; Prokofitch in a black frock coat and white gloves, with a special solemnity, laid the table for seven. A week before in the small parish church two weddings had taken place quietly, and almost without witnesses—Arkady and Katya's, and Nikolai Petrovitch and Fenitchka's; and on this day Nikolai Petrovitch was giving a farewell dinner to his brother, who was going away to Moscow on business. Anna Sergyevna had gone there also directly after the ceremony was over, after making very handsome presents to the young people.

Precisely at three o'clock they all gathered about the table. Mitya was placed there too; with him appeared a nurse in a cap of glazed brocade. Pavel Petrovitch took his seat between Katya and Fenitchka; the "husbands" took their places beside their wives. Our friends had changed of late; they all seemed to have grown stronger and better looking; only Pavel Petrovitch was thinner, which gave even more of an elegant and "grand seigneur" air to his expressive features. . . . And Fenitchka, too, was different. In a new silk gown, with a wide velvet head-dress on her hair, with a gold chain round her neck, she sat with deprecating immobility, respectful towards herself and everything surrounding her, and smiled as though she would say, "I beg your pardon; I'm not to blame." And not she alone—all the others smiled, and also seemed apologetic; they were all a little awkward, a little sorry, and in reality very happy. They all helped one another with humourous attentiveness, as though they had all agreed to rehearse a sort of artless farce. Katya was the most composed of all; she looked confidently about her, and it could be seen that Nikolai Petrovitch was already devotedly fond of her. At the end of dinner he got up, and his glass in his hand, turned to Pavel Petrovitch.

"You are leaving us . . . you are leaving us, dear brother," he began; "not for long, to be sure; but still, I cannot help expressing what I . . . what we . . . how much I . . . how much we. . . . There, the worst of it is, we don't know how to make speeches. Arkady, you speak."

"No, daddy, I've not prepared anything."

"As though I were so well prepared! Well, brother, I will simply say, let us embrace you, wish you all good luck, and come back to us as quick as you can!"

Pavel Petrovitch exchanged kisses with every one, of course not excluding Mitya; in Fenitchka's case, he kissed also her hand, which she had not yet learned to offer properly, and drinking off the glass which had been filled again, he said with a deep sigh, "Be happy, my friends! *Farewell!*" This English finale passed unnoticed; but all were touched.

"To the memory of Bazarov," Katya whispered in her husband's ear, as she clinked glasses with him. Arkady pressed her hand warmly in response, but he did not venture to propose this toast aloud.

This would seem to be the end. But perhaps some one of our readers would care to know what each of the characters we have introduced is doing in the present, the actual present. We are ready to satisfy him.

Anna Sergyevna has recently made a marriage, not of love but of good sense, with one of the future leaders of Russia, a very clever man, a lawyer, possessed of vigorous practical sense, a strong will, and remarkable fluency—still young, good-natured, and cold as ice. They live in the greatest harmony together, and will live perhaps to attain complete happiness . . . perhaps love. The Princess K— is dead, forgotten the day of her death. The Kirsanovs, father and son, live at Maryino; their fortunes are beginning to mend. Arkady has become zealous in the management of the estate, and the "farm" now yields a fairly good income. Nikolai Petrovitch has been made one of the mediators appointed to carry out the emancipation reforms, and works with all his energies; he is forever driving about over his district; delivers long speeches (he maintains the opinion that the peasants ought to be "brought to comprehend things," that is to say, they ought to be reduced to a state of quiescence by the constant repetition of the same words); and yet, to tell the truth, he does not give complete satisfaction either to the refined gentry, who talk with *chic*, or depression of the *emancipation* (pronouncing it as though it were French), nor to the uncultivated gentry, who unceremoniously curse "the damned '*mancipation*.'" He is too soft-hearted for both sets. Katerina Sergyevna has a son, little Nikolai, while Mitya runs about merrily and talks fluently. Fenitchka, Fedosya Nikolaevna, after her husband and Mitya, adores no one so much as her daughter-in-law, and when the latter is at the piano, she would gladly spend the whole day at her side. A passing word of Piotr. He has grown perfectly rigid with stupidity and dignity, but he too is married, and received a respectable dowry with his bride, the daughter of a market-gardener of the town, who had refused two excellent suitors, only because they had no watch; while Piotr had not only a watch—he had a pair of patent-leather shoes.

In the Brühl Terrace in Dresden, between two and four o'clock—the most fashionable time for walking—you may meet a man about fifty, quite grey, and looking as though he suffered from gout, but still handsome, elegantly dressed, and with that special stamp, which is only gained by moving a long time in the higher strata of society. That is Pavel Petrovitch. From Moscow he went abroad for the sake of his health, and has settled for good at Dresden, where he associates most with English and Russian visitors. With English people he behaves simply, almost modestly, but with dignity; they find him rather a bore, but respect him for being, as they say, "*a perfect gentleman.*" With Russians he is more free and easy, gives vent to his spleen, and makes fun of himself and them, but that is done by him with great amiability, negligence, and propriety. He holds Slavophil views; it is well known that in the highest society this is regarded as *très distingué!* He reads nothing in Russian, but on his writing table there is a silver ashtray in the shape of a peasant's plaited shoe. He is much run after by our tourists. Matvy Ilyitch Kolyazin, happening to be in temporary opposition, paid him a majestic visit; while the natives, with whom, however, he is very little seen, positively grovel before him. No one can so readily and quickly obtain a ticket for the court chapel, for the theatre, and such things as *der Herr Baron von Kirsanoff*. He does everything good-naturedly that he can; he still makes some little noise in the world; it is not for nothing that he was once a great society lion;—but life is a burden to him . . . a heavier burden than he suspects himself. One need but glance at him in the Russian church, when, leaning against the wall on one side, he sinks into thought, and remains long without stirring, bitterly compressing his lips, then suddenly recollects himself, and begins almost imperceptibly crossing himself. . . .

Madame Kukshin, too, went abroad. She is in Heidelberg, and is now studying not natural science, but architecture, in which, according to her own account, she has discovered new laws. She still fraternises with students, especially with the young Russians study-ing natural science and chemistry, with whom Heidelberg is crowd-ed, and who, astounding the naïve German professors at first by the soundness of their views of things, astound the same professors no less in the sequel by their complete inefficiency and absolute idleness. In company with two or three such young chemists, who don't know oxygen from nitrogen, but are filled with scepticism and self-conceit, and, too, with the great Elisyevitch, Sitnikov roams about Peters-burg, also getting ready to be great, and in his own conviction con-tinues the "work" of Bazarov. There is a story that some one recently gave him a beating; but he was avenged upon him; in an obscure little article, hidden in an obscure little journal, he has hinted that the man who beat him was a coward. He calls this irony. His father bullies him as before, while his wife regards him as a fool . . . and a literary man.

There is a small village graveyard in one of the remote corners of Russia. Like almost all our graveyards, it presents a wretched appearance; the ditches surrounding it have long been overgrown; the grey wooden crosses lie fallen and rotting under their once painted gables; the stone slabs are all displaced, as though some one were pushing them up from below; two or three bare trees give a scanty shade; the sheep wander unchecked among the tombs . . . But among them is one untouched by man, untrampled by beast, only the birds perch upon it and sing at daybreak. An iron railing runs round it; two young fir-trees have been planted, one at each end. Yevgeny Bazarov is buried in this tomb. Often from the little village not far off, two quite feeble old people come to visit it—a husband and wife. Supporting one another, they move to it with heavy steps; they go up to the railing, fall down, and remain on their knees, and weep long and bitterly, and gaze long and intently at the mute stone, under which their son is lying; they exchange some brief word, wipe away the dust from the stone, set straight a branch of a fir-tree, and pray again, and cannot tear themselves from this place, where they seem to be nearer to their son, to their memories of him. . . . Can it be that their prayers, their tears are fruitless? Can it be that love, sacred, devoted love, is not all-powerful? Oh, no! However passionate, sinful, and rebellious the heart hidden in the tomb, the flowers growing over it look serenely at us with their innocent eyes; they tell us not of eternal peace alone, of that great peace of "in-different" nature; they tell us, too, of eternal reconciliation and of life without end. . . .

FYODOR DOSTOEVSKY
(1821–1881)
Notes from Underground* [1]

Part I

UNDERGROUND

I

I am a sick man. . . . I am a spiteful man. I am an unattractive
man. I believe my liver is diseased. However, I know nothing at all
about my disease, and do not know for certain what ails me. I don't
consult a doctor for it, and never have, though I have a respect for
medicine and doctors. Besides, I am extremely superstitious, sufficiently so to respect medicine, anyway (I am well-educated enough
not to be superstitious, but I am superstitious). No, I refuse to
consult a doctor from spite. That you probably will not understand.
Well, I understand it, though. Of course I can't explain who it is
precisely that I am mortifying in this case by my spite: I am perfectly well aware that I cannot "pay out" the doctors by not consulting them; I know better than any one that by all this I am
only injuring myself and no one else. But still, if I don't consult a
doctor it is from spite. My liver is bad, well—let it get worse!

I have been going on like that for a long time—twenty years.
Now I am forty. I used to be in the government service, but am
no longer. I was a spiteful official. I was rude and took pleasure in
being so. I did not take bribes, you see, so I was bound to find a
recompense in that, at least. (A poor jest, but I will not scratch it
out. I wrote it thinking it would sound very witty; but now that I
have seen myself that I only wanted to show off in a despicable
way, I will not scratch it out on purpose!)

When petitioners used to come for information to the table at
which I sat, I used to grind my teeth at them, and felt intense
enjoyment when I succeeded in making anybody unhappy. I almost
always did succeed. For the most part they were all timid people—

* 1864. Translated by Constance
Garnett. Reprinted in full. The punctuation ". . ." does not indicate omissions
from this text.

1. The author of the diary and the
diary itself are, of course, imaginary.
Nevertheless it is clear that such persons as the writer of these notes not
only may, but positively must, exist in
our society, when we consider the circumstances in the midst of which our
society is formed. I have tried to expose to the view of the public more
distinctly than is commonly done, one
of the characters of the recent past. He
is one of the representatives of a generation still living. In this fragment, entitled "Underground," this person intro-
duces himself and his views, and, as it
were, tries to explain the causes owing
to which he has made his appearance
and was bound to make his appearance
in our midst. In the second fragment
there are added the actual notes of this
person concerning certain events in his
life. [Author's note.]

of course, they were petitioners. But of the uppish ones there was one officer in particular I could not endure. He simply would not be humble, and clanked his sword in a disgusting way. I carried on a feud with him for eighteen months over that sword. At last I got the better of him. He left off clanking it. That happened in my youth, though.

But do you know, gentlemen, what was the chief point about my spite? Why, the whole point, the real sting of it lay in the fact that continually, even in the moment of the acutest spleen, I was inwardly conscious with shame that I was not only not a spiteful but not even an embittered man, that I was simply scaring sparrows at random and amusing myself by it. I might foam at the mouth, but bring me a doll to play with, give me a cup of tea with sugar in it, and maybe I should be appeased. I might even be genuinely touched, though probably I should grind my teeth at myself afterwards and lie awake at night with shame for months after. That was my way.

I was lying when I said just now that I was a spiteful official. I was lying from spite. I was simply amusing myself with the petitioners and with the officer, and in reality I never could become spiteful. I was conscious every moment in myself of many, very many elements absolutely opposite to that. I felt them positively swarming in me, these opposite elements. I knew that they had been swarming in me all my life and craving some outlet from me, but I would not let them, would not let them, purposely would not let them come out. They tormented me till I was ashamed: they drove me to convulsions and—sickened me, at last, how they sickened me! Now, are not you fancying, gentlemen, that I am expressing remorse for something now, that I am asking your forgiveness for something? I am sure you are fancying that . . . . However, I assure you I do not care if you are. . . .

It was not only that I could not become spiteful, I did not know how to become anything: neither spiteful nor kind, neither a rascal nor an honest man, neither a hero nor an insect. Now, I am living out my life in my corner, taunting myself with the spiteful and useless consolation that an intelligent man cannot become anything seriously, and it is only the fool who becomes anything. Yes, a man in the nineteenth century must and morally ought to be pre-eminently a characterless creature; a man of character, an active man is pre-eminently a limited creature. That is my conviction of forty years. I am forty years old now, and you know forty years is a whole lifetime; you know it is extreme old age. To live longer than forty years is bad manners, is vulgar, immoral. Who lives beyond forty? Answer that, sincerely and honestly. I will tell you who do: fools and worthless fellows. I tell all old men that to their face, all these venerable old men, all these silver-haired and reverend seniors! I tell the whole world that to its face! I have a right to say so, for I shall go on living to sixty myself. To seventy! To eighty! . . . Stay, let me take breath. . . .

You imagine no doubt, gentlemen, that I want to amuse you. You are mistaken in that, too. I am by no means such a mirthful person as you imagine, or as you may imagine; however, irritated by all this babble (and I feel that you are irritated) you think fit to ask me who am I—then my answer is, I am a collegiate assessor. I was in the service that I might have something to eat (and solely for that reason), and when last year a distant relation left me six thousand roubles in his will I immediately retired from the service and settled down in my corner. I used to live in this corner before, but now I have settled down in it. My room is a wretched, horrid one in the outskirts of the town. My servant is an old country-woman, ill-natured from stupidity, and, moreover, there is always a nasty smell about her. I am told that the Petersburg climate is bad for me, and that with my small means it is very expensive to live in Petersburg. I know all that better than all these sage and experienced counsellors and monitors. . . . But I am remaining in Petersburg; . . . I am not going away from Petersburg! I am not going away because . . . ech! Why, it is absolutely no matter whether I am going away or not going away.

But what can a decent man speak of with most pleasure?

Answer: Of himself.

Well, so I will talk about myself.

II

I want now to tell you, gentlemen, whether you care to hear it or not, why I could not even become an insect. I tell you solemnly, that I have many times tried to become an insect. But I was not equal even to that. I swear, gentlemen, that to be too conscious is an illness—a real thoroughgoing illness. For man's everyday needs, it would have been quite enough to have the ordinary human consciousness, that is, half or a quarter of the amount which falls to the lot of a cultivated man of our unhappy nineteenth century, especially one who has the fatal ill-luck to inhabit Petersburg, the most theoretical and intentional town on the whole terrestrial globe. (There are intentional and unintentional towns.) It would have been quite enough, for instance, to have the consciousness by which all so-called direct persons and men of action live. I bet you think I am writing all this from affectation, to be witty at the expense of men of action; and what is more, that from ill-bred affectation, I am clanking a sword like my officer. But, gentlemen, whoever can pride himself on his diseases and even swagger over them?

Though, after all, every one does do that; people do pride themselves on their diseases, and I do, may be, more than any one else. We will not dispute it; my contention was absurd. But yet I am firmly persuaded that a great deal of consciousness, every sort of consciousness, in fact, is a disease. I stick to that. Let us leave that, too, for a minute. Tell me this: why does it happen that at the very, yes, at the very moments when I am most capable of feeling every refinement of all that is "good and beautiful," as they used to say at one time, it would, as though of design, happen to me not only to feel but to do such ugly things, such that . . . Well, in short, actions that all, perhaps, commit; but which, as though purposely, occurred to me at the very time when I was most conscious that they ought not to be committed. The more conscious I was of goodness and of all that was "good and beautiful," the more deeply I sank into my mire and the more ready I was to sink in it altogether. But the chief point was that all this was, as it were, not accidental in me, but as though it were bound to be so. It was as though it were my most normal condition, and not in the least disease or depravity, so that at last all desire in me to struggle against this depravity passed. It ended by my almost believing (perhaps actually believing) that this was perhaps my normal condition. But at first, in the beginning, what agonies I endured in that struggle! I did not believe it was the same with other people, and all my life I hid this fact about myself as a secret. I was ashamed (even now, perhaps, I am ashamed): I got to the point of feeling a sort of secret abnormal, despicable enjoyment in returning home to my corner on some disgusting Petersburg night, acutely conscious that that day I had committed a loathsome action again, that what was done could never be undone, and secretly, inwardly gnawing, gnawing at myself for it, tearing and consuming myself till at last the bitterness turned into a sort of shameful accursed sweetness, and at last—into positive real enjoyment! Yes into enjoyment, into enjoyment! I insist upon that. I have spoken of this because I keep wanting to know for a fact whether other people feel such enjoyment? I will explain; the enjoyment was just from the too intense consciousness of one's own degradation; it was from feeling oneself that one had reached the last barrier, that it was horrible, but that it could not be otherwise; that there was no escape for you; that you never could become a different man; that even if time and faith were still left you to change into something different you would most likely not wish to change; or if you did wish to, even then you would do nothing; because perhaps in reality there was nothing for you to change into.

And the worst of it was, and the root of it all, that it was all in accord with the normal fundamental laws of over-acute consciousness, and with the inertia that was the direct result of those laws, and that consequently one was not only unable to change but could do absolutely nothing. Thus it would follow, as the result of acute consciousness, that one is not to blame in being a scoundrel; as though that were any consolation to the scoundrel once he has come to realize that he actually is a scoundrel. But enough. . . . Ech, I have talked a lot of nonsense, but what have I explained? How is enjoyment in this to be explained? But I will explain it. I will get to the bottom of it! That is why I have taken up my pen. . . .

I, for instance, have a great deal of *amour propre*. I am as suspicious and prone to take offence as a hunchback or a dwarf. But upon my word I sometimes have had moments when if I had happened to be slapped in the face I should, perhaps, have been positively glad of it. I say, in earnest, that I should probably have been able to discover even in that a peculiar sort of enjoyment—the enjoyment, of course, of despair; but in despair there are the most intense enjoyments, especially when one is very acutely conscious of the hopelessness of one's position. And when one is slapped in the face—why then the consciousness of being rubbed into a pulp would positively overwhelm one. The worst of it is, look at it which way one will, it still turns out that I was always the most to blame in everything. And what is most humiliating of all, to blame for no fault of my own but, so to say, through the laws of nature. In the first place, to blame because I am cleverer than any of the people surrounding me. (I have always considered myself cleverer than any of the people surrounding me, and sometimes, would you believe it, have been positively ashamed of it. At any rate, I have all my life, as it were, turned my eyes away and never could look people straight in the face.) To blame, finally, because even if I had had magnanimity, I should only have had more suffering from the sense of its uselessness. I should certainly have never been able to do anything from being magnanimous—neither to forgive, for my assailant would perhaps have slapped me from the laws of nature, and one cannot forgive the laws of nature; nor to forget, for even if it were owing to the laws of nature, it is insulting all the same. Finally, even if I had wanted to be anything but magnanimous, had desired on the contrary to revenge myself on my assailant, I could not have revenged myself on any one for anything because I should certainly never have made up my mind to do anything, even if I had been able to. Why should I not have made up my mind? About that in particular I want to say a few words.

III

With people who know how to revenge themselves and to stand up for themselves in general, how is it done? Why, when they are possessed, let us suppose, by the feeling of revenge, then for the time there is nothing else but that feeling left in their whole being. Such a gentleman simply dashes straight for his object like an infuriated bull with its horns down, and nothing but a wall will stop him. (By the way: facing the wall, such gentlemen—that is, the "direct" persons and men of action—are genuinely nonplussed. For them a wall is not an evasion, as for us people who think and consequently do nothing; it is not an excuse for turning aside, an excuse for which we are always very glad, though we scarcely believe in it ourselves, as a rule. No, they are nonplussed in all sincerity. The wall has for them something tranquillizing, morally soothing, final—maybe even something mysterious . . . but of the wall later.)

Well, such a direct person I regard as the real normal man, as his tender mother nature wished to see him when she graciously brought him into being on the earth. I envy such a man till I am green in the face. He is stupid. I am not disputing that, but perhaps the normal man should be stupid, how do you know? Perhaps it is very beautiful, in fact. And I am the more persuaded of that suspicion, if one can call it so, by the fact that if you take, for instance, the antithesis of the normal man, that is, the man of acute consciousness, who has come, of course, not out of the lap of nature but out of a retort (this is almost mysticism, gentlemen, but I suspect this, too), this retort-made man is sometimes so nonplussed in the presence of his antithesis that with all his exaggerated consciousness he genuinely thinks of himself as a mouse and not a man. It may be an acutely conscious mouse, yet it is a mouse, while the other is a man, and therefore, et cætera, et cætera. And the worst of it is, he himself, his very own self, looks on himself as a mouse; no one asks him to do so; and that is an important point. Now let us look at this mouse in action. Let us suppose, for instance, that it feels insulted, too (and it almost always does feel insulted), and wants to revenge itself, too. There may even be a greater accumulation of spite in it than in *l'homme de la nature et de la vérité*.[2] The base and nasty desire to vent that spite on its assailant rankles perhaps even more nastily in it than in *l'homme de la nature et de la vérité*. For through his innate stupidity the latter looks upon his revenge as justice pure and simple; while in consequence of his acute consciousness the mouse does not be-

2. "the man of nature and truth"; Rousseau's description of himself in the *Confessions* (1781–1788), which created an enormous stir because they professed to tell the whole truth about the author and were sometimes self-accusing.

lieve in the justice of it. To come at last to the deed itself, to the very act of revenge. Apart from the one fundamental nastiness the luckless mouse succeeds in creating around it so many other nastinesses in the form of doubts and questions, adds to the one question so many unsettled questions that there inevitably works up around it a sort of fatal brew, a stinking mess, made up of its doubts, emotions, and of the contempt spat upon it by the direct men of action who stand solemnly about it as judges and arbitrators, laughing at it till their healthy sides ache. Of course the only thing left for it is to dismiss all that with a wave of its paw, and, with a smile of assumed contempt in which it does not even itself believe, creep ignominiously into its mouse-hole. There in its nasty, stinking, underground home our insulted, crushed and ridiculed mouse promptly becomes absorbed in cold, malignant and, above all, everlasting spite. For forty years together it will remember its injury down to the smallest, most ignominious details, and every time will add, of itself, details still more ignominious, spitefully teasing and tormenting itself with its own imagination. It will itself be ashamed of its imaginings, but yet it will recall it all, it will go over and over every detail, it will invent unheard of things against itself, pretending that those things might happen, and will forgive nothing. Maybe it will begin to revenge itself, too, but, as it were, piecemeal, in trivial ways, from behind the stove, incognito, without believing either in its own right to vengeance, or in the success of its revenge knowing that from all its efforts at revenge it will suffer a hundred times more than he on whom it revenges itself, while he, I daresay, will not even scratch himself. On its deathbed it will recall it all over again, with interest accumulated over all the years and. . . .

But it is just in that cold, abominable half despair, half belief, in that conscious burying oneself alive for grief in the underworld for forty years, in that acutely recognized and yet partly doubtful hopelessness of one's position, in that hell of unsatisfied desires turned inward, in that fever of oscillations, or resolutions determined for ever and repented of again a minute later—that the savour of that strange enjoyment of which I have spoken lies. It is so subtle, so difficult of analysis, that persons who are a little limited, or even simply persons of strong nerves, will not understand a single atom of it. "Possibly," you will add on your own account with a grin, "people will not understand it either who have never received a slap in the face," and in that way you will politely hint to me that I, too, perhaps, have had the experience of a slap in the face in my life, and so I speak as one who knows. I bet that you are thinking that. But set your minds at rest, gentlemen, I have not received a slap in the face, though it is absolutely a matter of indifference to me what you may think about it. Possibly, I even regret, myself, that I have given so few slaps in the face during my life. But enough . . . not another word on that subject of such extreme interest to you.

I will continue calmly concerning persons with strong nerves who do not understand a certain refinement of enjoyment. Though in certain circumstances these gentlemen bellow their loudest like bulls, though this, let us suppose, does them the greatest credit, yet, as I have said already, confronted with the impossible they subside at once. The impossible means the stone wall! What stone wall? Why, of course, the laws of nature, the deductions of natural science, mathematics. As soon as they prove to you, for instance, that you are descended from a monkey, then it is no use scowling, accept it for a fact. When they prove to you that in reality one drop of your own fat must be dearer to you than a hundred thousand of your fellow-creatures, and that this conclusion is the final solution of all so-called virtues and duties and all such prejudices and fancies, then you have just to accept it, there is no help for it, for twice two is a law of mathematics. Just try refuting it.

"Upon my word," they will shout at you, "it is no use protesting: it is a case of twice two makes four! Nature does not ask your permission, she has nothing to do with your wishes, and whether you like her laws or dislike them, you are bound to accept her as she is, and consequently all her conclusions. A wall, you see, is a wall . . ." and so on, and so on.

Merciful Heavens! but what do I care for the laws of nature and arithmetic, when, for some reason I dislike those laws and the fact that twice two makes four? Of course I cannot break through the wall by battering my head against it if I really have not the strength to knock it down, but I am not going to be reconciled to it simply because it is a stone wall and I have not the strength.

As though such a stone wall really were a consolation, and really did contain some word of conciliation, simply because it is as true as twice two makes four. Oh, absurdity of absurdities! How much better it is to understand it all, to recognize it all, all the impossibilities and the stone wall; not to be reconciled to one of those impossibilities and stone walls if it disgusts you to be reconciled to it; by the way of the most inevitable, logical combinations to reach the most revolting conclusions on the everlasting theme, that even for the stone wall you are yourself somehow to blame, though again it is as clear as day you are not to blame in the least, and therefore grinding your teeth in silent impotence to sink into luxurious inertia, brooding on the fact that there is no one even for you to feel vindictive against, that you have not, and perhaps never will have, an object for your spite, that it is a sleight of hand, a bit of juggling, a card-sharper's trick, that it is simply a mess, no knowing what and no knowing who, but in spite of all these uncertainties and jugglings, still there is an ache in you, and the more you do not know, the worse the ache.

IV

"Ha, ha, ha! You will be finding enjoyment in toothache next," you cry, with a laugh.

"Well? Even in toothache there is enjoyment," I answer. I had toothache for a whole month and I know there is. In that case, of course, people are not spiteful in silence, but moan; but they are not candid moans, they are malignant moans, and the malignancy is the whole point. The enjoyment of the sufferer finds expression in those moans; if he did not feel enjoyment in them he would not moan. It is a good example, gentlemen, and I will develop it. Those moans express in the first place all the aimlessness of your pain, which is so humiliating to your consciousness; the whole legal system of nature on which you spit disdainfully, of course, but from which you suffer all the same while she does not. They express the consciousness that you have no enemy to punish, but that you have pain; the consciousness that in spite of all possible Wagenheims[3] you are in complete slavery to your teeth; that if some one wishes it, your teeth will leave off aching, and if he does not, they will go on aching another three months; and that finally if you are still contumacious and still protest, all that is left you for your own gratification is to thrash yourself or beat your wall with your fist as hard as you can, and absolutely nothing more. Well, these mortal insults, these jeers on the part of some one unknown, end at last in an enjoyment which sometimes reaches the highest degree of voluptuousness. I ask you, gentlemen, listen sometimes to the moans of an educated man of the nineteenth century suffering from toothache, on the second or third day of the attack, when he is beginning to moan, not as he moaned on the first day, that is, not simply because he has toothache, not just as any coarse peasant, but as a man affected by progress and European civilization, a man who is "divorced from the soil and the national elements," as they express it now-a-days. His moans become nasty, disgustingly malignant, and go on for whole days and nights. And of course he knows himself that he is doing himself no sort of good with his moans; he knows better than any one that he is only lacerating and harassing himself and others for nothing; he knows that even the audience before whom he is making his efforts, and his whole family, listen to him with loathing, do not put the

---

3. Wagenheim was apparently a German who advertised painless dentistry; he may have used hypnosis or auto-suggestion.

least faith in him, and inwardly understand that he might moan differently, more simply, without trills and flourishes, and that he is only amusing himself like that from ill-humour, from malignancy. Well, in all these recognitions and disgraces it is that there lies a voluptuous pleasure. As though he would say: "I am worrying you, I am lacerating your hearts, I am keeping every one in the house awake. Well, stay awake then, you, too, feel every minute that I have toothache. I am not a hero to you now, as I tried to seem before, but simply a nasty person, an impostor. Well, so be it, then! I am very glad that you see through me. It is nasty for you to hear my despicable moans: well, let it be nasty; here I will let you have a nastier flourish in a minute. . . . ." You do not understand even now, gentlemen? No, it seems our development and our consciousness must go further to understand all the intricacies of this pleasure. You laugh? Delighted. My jests, gentlemen, are of course in bad taste, jerky, involved, lacking self-confidence. But of course that is because I do not respect myself. Can a man of perception respect himself at all?

v

Come, can a man who attempts to find enjoyment in the very feeling of his own degradation possibly have a spark of respect for himself? I am not saying this now from any mawkish kind of remorse. And, indeed, I could never endure saying, "Forgive me, Papa, I won't do it again," not because I am incapable of saying that—on the contrary, perhaps just because I have been too capable of it, and in what a way, too! As though of design I used to get into trouble in cases when I was not to blame in any way. That was the nastiest part of it. At the same time I was genuinely touched and penitent, I used to shed tears and, of course, deceived myself, though I was not acting in the least and there was a sick feeling in my heart at the time. . . . For that one could not blame even the laws of nature, though the laws of nature have continually all my life offended me more than anything. It is loathsome to remember it all, but it was loathsome even then. Of course, a minute or so later I would realize wrathfully that is was all a lie, a revolting lie, an affected lie, that is, all this penitence, this emotion, these vows of reform. You will ask why did I worry myself with such antics: answer, because it was very dull to sit with one's hands folded, and so one began cutting capers. That is really it. Observe yourselves more carefully, gentlemen, then you will understand that it is so. I invented adventures for myself and made up a life, so as at least to live in some way. How many times it has happened to me—well, for instance, to take offence simply on purpose, for nothing; and one knows oneself, of course, that one is offended at nothing, that one is putting it on, but yet one brings oneself, at last to the point of being really offended. All my life I have had an impulse to play such pranks, so that in the end I could not control it in myself. Another time, twice, in fact, I tried hard to be in love. I suffered, too, gentlemen, I assure you. In the depth of my heart there was no faith in my suffering, only a faint stir of mockery, but yet I did suffer, and in the real, orthodox way; I was jealous, beside myself . . . and it was all from *ennui*, gentlemen, all from *ennui*; inertia overcame me. You know the direct, legitimate fruit of consciousness is inertia, that is, conscious sitting-with-the-hands-folded. I have referred to this already. I repeat, I repeat with emphasis: all "direct" persons and men of action are active just because they are stupid and limited. How explain that? I will tell you: in consequence of their limitation they take immediate and secondary causes for primary ones, and in that way persuade themselves more quickly and easily than other people do that they have found an infallible foundation for their activity, and their minds are at ease and you know that is the chief thing. To begin to act, you know, you must first have your mind completely at ease and no trace of doubt left in it. Why, how am I, for example to set my mind at rest? Where are the primary causes on which I am to build? Where are my foundations? Where am I to get them from? I exercise myself in reflection, and consequently with me every primary cause at once draws after itself another still more primary, and so on to infinity. That is just the essence of every sort of consciousness and reflection. It must be a case of the laws of nature again. What is the result of it in the end? Why, just the same. Remember I spoke just now of vengeance. (I am sure you did not take it in.) I said that a man revenges himself because he sees justice in it. Therefore he has found a primary cause, that is, justice. And so he is at rest on all sides, and consequently he carries out his revenge calmly and successfully, being persuaded that he is doing a just and honest thing. But I see no justice in it, I find no sort of virtue in it either, and consequently if I attempt to revenge myself, it is only out of spite. Spite, of course, might overcome everything, all my doubts, and so might serve quite successfully in place of a primary cause, precisely because it is not a cause. But what is to be done if I have not even spite (I began with that just now, you know). In consequence again of those accursed laws of consciousness, anger in me is subject to chemical disintegration. You look into it, the object flies off into air, your reasons evaporate, the criminal is not to be found, the wrong becomes not a wrong but a phantom, something like the toothache, for which no one is to blame, and consequently there is only the same outlet left again—that is, to beat the wall as hard as you can. So you give it up with a wave of the hand because you have not found a fundamental cause. And try letting yourself be carried away by your feelings, blindly, without reflection, without a primary cause, repelling consciousness at least for a time; hate or love, if only not to sit with your hands folded. The day after to-morrow, at the latest, you will begin despising yourself for having knowingly deceived yourself. Result: a soap-bubble and inertia. Oh, gentlemen, do you know, perhaps I consider myself an intelligent man, only because all my life I have been able neither to begin nor to finish anything. Granted I am a babbler, a harmless vexatious babbler, like all of us. But what is to be done if the direct and sole vocation of every intelligent man is babble, that is, the intentional pouring of water through a sieve?

VI

Oh, if I had done nothing simply from laziness! Heavens, how I should have respected myself, then. I should have respected myself because I should at least have been capable of being lazy; there would at least have been one quality, as it were, positive in me, in which I could have believed myself. Question: What is he? Answer: A sluggard; how very pleasant it would have been to hear that of oneself! It would mean that I was positively defined, it would mean that there was something to say about me. "Sluggard"—why, it is a calling and vocation, it is a career. Do not jest, it is so. I should then be a member of the best club by right, and should find my occupation in continually respecting myself. I knew a gentlemen who prided himself all his life on being a connoisseur of Lafitte. He considered this as his positive virtue, and never doubted himself. He died, not simply with a tranquil, but with a triumphant, conscience, and he was quite right, too. Then I should have chosen a career for myself, I should have been a sluggard and a glutton, not a simple one, but, for instance, one with sympathies for everything good and beautiful. How do you like that? I have long had visions of it. That "good and beautiful" weighs heavily on my mind at forty. But that is at forty; then—oh, then it would have been different! I should have found for myself a form of activity in keeping with it, to be precise, drinking to the health of everything "good and beautiful." I should have snatched at every opportunity to drop a tear into my glass and then to drain it to all that is "good and beautiful." I should then have turned everything into the good and the beautiful; in the nastiest, unquestionable trash, I should have sought out the good and the beautiful. I should have exuded tears like a wet sponge. An artist, for instance, paints a picture worthy of Gay.[4] At once I drink to the health of the artist who painted the picture worthy of Gay,

4. Nikolay Nikolaevich Gay (1831–1894), Russian painter of historical pictures who then had a great reputation. His father was a French emigrant.

because I love all that is "good and beautiful." An author has written *What you will*:[5] at once I drink to the health of "what you will" because I love all that is "good and beautiful."

I should claim respect for doing so. I should persecute any one who would not show me respect. I should live at ease, I should die with dignity, why, it is charming, perfectly charming! And what a good round belly I should have grown, what a triple chin I should have established, what a ruby nose I should have coloured for myself, so that every one would have said, looking at me: "Here is an asset! Here is something real and solid!" And, say what you like, it is very agreeable to hear such remarks about oneself in this negative age.

VII

But these are all golden dreams. Oh, tell me, who was it first announced, who was it first proclaimed, that man only does nasty things because he does not know his own interests; and that if he were enlightened, if his eyes were opened to his real normal interests, man would at once cease to do nasty things, would at once become good and noble because, being enlightened and understanding his real advantage, he would see his own advantage in the good and nothing else, and we all know that not one man can, consciously, act against his own interests, consequently, so to say, through necessity, he would begin doing good? Oh, the babe! Oh, the pure, innocent child! Why, in the first place, when in all these thousands of years has there been a time when man has acted only from his own interest? What is to be done with the millions of facts that bear witness that men, *consciously*, that is fully understanding their real interests, have left them in the background and have rushed headlong on another path, to meet peril and danger, compelled to this course by nobody and by nothing, but, as it were, simply disliking the beaten track, and have obstinately, wilfully, struck out another difficult, absurd way, seeking it almost in the darkness. So, I suppose, this obstinacy and perversity were pleasanter to them than any advantage. . . . Advantage! What is advantage? And will you take it upon yourself to define with perfect accuracy in what the advantage of man consists? And what if it so happens that a man's advantage, *sometimes*, not only may, but even must, consist in his desiring in certain cases what is harmful to himself and not advantageous. And if so, if there can be such a case, the whole principle falls into dust. What do you think—are there such cases? You laugh; laugh away, gentlemen, but only answer me: have man's advantages been reckoned up with perfect certainty? Are there not some which not only have

---

5. subtitle of Shakespeare's comedy *Twelfth Night*, generally used on the Continent instead of the main title, which is difficult to translate.

not been included but cannot possibly be included under any classification? You see, you gentlemen have, to the best of my knowledge, taken your whole register of human advantages from the averages of statistical figures and politico-economical formulas. Your advantages are prosperity, wealth, freedom, peace—and so on, and so on. So that the man who should, for instance, go openly and knowingly in opposition to all that list would, to your thinking, and indeed mine, too, of course, be an obscurantist or an absolute madman: would not he? But, you know, this is what is surprising: why does it so happen that all these statisticians, sages and lovers of humanity, when they reckon up human advantages invariably leave out one? They don't even take it into their reckoning in the form in which it should be taken, and the whole reckoning depends upon that. It would be no great matter, they would simply have to take it, this advantage, and add it to the list. But the trouble is, that this strange advantage does not fall under any classification and is not in place in any list. I have a friend for instance . . . Ech! gentlemen, but of course he is your friend, too; and indeed there is no one, no one, to whom he is not a friend! When he prepares for any undertaking this gentleman immediately explains to you, elegantly and clearly, exactly how he must act in accordance with the laws of reason and truth. What is more, he will talk to you with excitement and passion of the true normal interests of man; with irony he will upbraid the shortsighted fools who do not understand their own interests, nor the true significance of virtue; and, within a quarter of an hour, without any sudden outside provocation, but simply through something inside him which is stronger than all his interests, he will go off on quite a different tack—that is, act in direct opposition to what he has just been saying about himself, in opposition to the laws of reason, in opposition to his own advantage, in fact in opposition to everything . . . I warn you that my friend is a compound personality, and therefore it is difficult to blame him as an individual. The fact is, gentlemen, it seems there must really exist something that is dearer to almost every man than his greatest advantages, or (not to be illogical) there is a most advantageous advantage (the very one omitted of which we spoke just now) which is more important and more advantageous than all other advantages, for the sake of which a man if necessary is ready to act in opposition to all laws; that is, in opposition to reason, honour, peace, prosperity—in fact, in opposition to all those excellent and useful things if only he can attain that fundamental, most advantageous advantage which is dearer to him than all. "Yes, but it's advantage all the same" you will retort. But excuse me, I'll make the point clear, and it is not a case of playing upon words. What matters is, that this advantage is remarkable from the very fact that it breaks down all our classifications, and continually shatters every system constructed by lovers of mankind for the benefit of mankind. In fact, it upsets everything. But before I mention this advantage to you, I want to compromise myself personally, and therefore I boldly declare that all these fine systems, all these theories for explaining to mankind their real normal interests, in order that inevitably striving to pursue these interests they may at once become good and noble —are, in my opinion, so far, mere logical exercises! Yes, logical exercises. Why, to maintain this theory of the regeneration of mankind by means of the pursuit of his own advantage is to my mind almost the same thing as . . . as to affirm, for instance, following Buckle,[6] that through civilization mankind becomes softer, and consequently less bloodthirsty and less fitted for warfare. Logically it does seem to follow from his arguments. But man has such a predilection for systems and abstract deductions that he is ready to distort the truth intentionally, he is ready to deny the evidence of his senses only to justify his logic. I take this example because it is the most glaring instance of it. Only look about you: blood is being spilt in streams, and in the merriest way, as though it were champagne. Take the whole of the nineteenth century in which Buckle lived. Take Napoleon—the Great and also the present one. Take North America—the eternal union. Take the farce of Schleswig-Holstein.[7] . . . And what is it that civilization softens in us? The only gain of civilization for mankind is the greater capacity for variety of sensations—and absolutely nothing more. And through the development of this many-sidedness man may come to finding enjoyment in bloodshed. In fact, this has already happened to him. Have you noticed that it is the most civilized gentlemen who have been the subtlest slaughterers, to whom the Attilas[8] and Stenka Razins[9] could not hold a candle, and if they are not so conspicuous as the Attilas and Stenka Razins it is simply because they are so often met with, are so ordinary and have become so familiar to us. In any case civilization has made mankind if not more bloodthirsty, at least more vilely, more loathsomely bloodthirsty. In old days he saw justice in bloodshed and with his conscience at peace exterminated those he thought proper. Now we do think bloodshed abominable and yet we engage in this

6. Henry Thomas Buckle (1821–1862), the author of the *History of Civilization in England* (two volumes, 1857, 1861), which held that all progress is due to the march of mind. There is no moral progress except indirectly, as a result of intellectual enlightenment.

7. Austria and Prussia invaded Denmark and annexed its southernmost part, Schleswig-Holstein, in 1864.

8. Attila (406?–453 A.D.) was king of the Huns (433?–453). In 451 his armies penetrated as far as Orléans, in what today is France. He was defeated in the battle of Châlons on the Catalaunian plains and retired to Hungary. In 452 he led an expedition against Rome.

9. Stenka Razin was a Don Cossack leader who in 1670 conquered many cities along the Volga. He was finally defeated, captured, and executed in 1671.

abomination, and with more energy than ever. Which is worse? Decide that for yourselves. They say that Cleopatra (excuse an instance from Roman history) was fond of sticking gold pins into her slave-girls' breasts and derived gratification from their screams and writhings. You will say that that was in the comparatively barbarous times; that these are barbarous times too, because also, comparatively speaking, pins are stuck in even now; that though man has now learned to see more clearly than in barbarous ages, he is still far from having learnt to act as reason and science would dictate. But yet you are fully convinced that he will be sure to learn when he gets rid of certain old bad habits, and when common sense and science have completely re-educated human nature and turned it in a normal direction. You are confident that then man will cease from *intentional* error and will, so to say, be compelled not to want to set his will against his normal interests. That is not all; then, you say, science itself will teach man (though to my mind it's a superfluous luxury) that he never has really had any caprice or will of his own, and that he himself is something of the nature of a piano-key or the stop of an organ, and that there are, besides, things called the laws of nature; so that everything he does is not done by his willing it, but is done of itself, by the laws of nature. Consequently we have only to discover these laws of nature, and man will no longer have to answer for his actions and life will become exceedingly easy for him. All human actions will then, of course, be tabulated according to these laws, mathematically, like tables of logarithms up to 108,000, and entered in an index; or, better still, there would be published certain edifying works of the nature of encyclopædic lexicons, in which everything will be so clearly calculated and explained that there will be no more incidents or adventures in the world.

Then—this is all what you say—new economic relations will be established, all ready-made and worked out with mathematical exactitude, so that every possible question will vanish in the twinkling of any eye, simply because every possible answer to it will be provided. Then the "Crystal Palace"[10] will be built. Then . . . . In fact, those will be halcyon days. Of course there is no guaranteeing (this is my comment) that it will not be, for instance, frightfully dull then (for what will one have to do when everything will be calculated and tabulated), but on the other hand everything will be extraordinary rational. Of course boredom may lead you to anything. It is boredom sets one sticking golden pins into people, but all that would not matter. What is bad (this is my

10. Dostoevsky has in mind the London Crystal Palace, a structure of glass and iron built in 1851–1854, and at that time admired as the newest wonder of architecture. The nave was five hundred yards long. The building burned down in 1936.

comment again) is that I dare say people will be thankful for the gold pins then. Man is stupid, you know, phenomenally stupid; or rather he is not at all stupid, but he is so ungrateful that you could not find another like him in all creation. I, for instance, would not be in the least surprised if all of a sudden, *à propos* of nothing, in the midst of general prosperity a gentleman with an ignoble, or rather with a reactionary and ironical, countenance were to arise and, putting his arms akimbo, say to us all: "I say, gentlemen, hadn't we better kick over the whole show and scatter rationalism to the winds, simply to send these logarithms to the devil, and to enable us to live once more at our own sweet foolish will!" That again would not matter, but what is annoying is that he would be sure to find followers—such is the nature of man. And all that for the most foolish reason, which, one would think, was hardly worth mentioning: that is, that man everywhere and at all times, whoever he may be, has preferred to act as he chose and not in the least as his reason and advantage dictated. And one may choose what is contrary to one's own interests, and sometimes one *positively ought* (that is my idea). One's own free unfettered choice, one's own caprice, however wild it may be, one's own fancy worked up at times to frenzy—is that very "most advantageous advantage" which we have overlooked, which comes under no classification and against which all systems and theories are continually being shattered to atoms. And how do these wiseacres know that man wants a normal, a virtuous choice? What has made them conceive that man must want a rationally advantageous choice? What man wants is simply *independent* choice, whatever that independence may cost and wherever it may lead. And choice, of course, the devil only knows what choice.

VIII

"Ha! ha! ha! But you know there is no such thing as choice in reality, say what you like," you will interpose with a chuckle. "Science has succeeded in so far analysing man that we know already that choice and what is called freedom of will is nothing else than——"

Stay, gentlemen, I meant to begin with that myself. I confess, I was rather frightened. I was just going to say that the devil only knows what choice depends on, and that perhaps that was a very good thing, but I remembered the teaching of science . . . and pulled myself up. And here you have begun upon it. Indeed, if there really is some day discovered a formula for all our desires and caprices—that is, an explanation of what they depend upon, by what laws they arise, how they develop, what they are aiming at in one case and in another and so on, that is a real mathematical formula—then, most likely, man will at once cease to feel desire, indeed, he will be certain to. For who would want to choose by rule? Besides, he will at once be transformed from a human being into an organ-stop or something of the sort; for what is a man without desires, without freewill and without choice, if not a stop in an organ? What do you think? Let us reckon the chances—can such a thing happen or not?

"H'm!" you decide. "Our choice is usually mistaken from a false view of our advantage. We sometimes choose absolute nonsense because in our foolishness we see in that nonsense the easiest means for attaining a supposed advantage. But when all that is explained and worked out on paper (which is perfectly possible, for it is contemptible and senseless to suppose that some laws of nature man will never understand), then certainly so-called desires will no longer exist. For if a desire should come into conflict with reason we shall then reason and not desire, because it will be impossible retaining our reason to be *senseless* in our desires, and in that way knowingly act against reason and desire to injure ourselves. And as all choice and reasoning can be really calculated —because there will some day be discovered the laws of our so-called freewill—so, joking apart, there may one day be something like a table constructed of them, so that we really shall choose in accordance with it. If, for instance, some day they calculate and prove to me that I make a long nose at some one because I could not help making a long nose at him and that I had to do it in that particular way, what *freedom* is left me, especially if I am a learned man and have taken my degree somewhere? Then I should be able to calculate my whole life for thirty years beforehand. In short, if this could be arranged there would be nothing left for us to do; anyway, we should have to understand that. And, in fact, we ought unweariyingly to repeat to ourselves that at such and such a time and in such and such circumstances nature does not ask our leave; that we have got to take her as she is and not fashion her to suit our fancy, and if we really aspire to formulas and tables of rules, and well, even . . . to the chemical retort, there's no help for it, we must accept the retort too, or else it will be accepted without our consent. . . ."

Yes, but here I come to a stop! Gentlemen, you must excuse me for being over-philosophical; it's the result of forty years underground! Allow me to indulge my fancy. You see, gentlemen, reason is an excellent thing, there's no disputing that, but reason is nothing but reason and satisfies only the rational side of man's nature, while will is a manifestation of the whole life, that is, of the whole human life including reason and all the impulses. And although our life, in this manifestation of it, is often worthless, yet it is life and not simply extracting square roots. Here I, for instance, quite naturally want to live, in order to satisfy all my capacities for life, and not simply my capacity for reasoning, that is, not simply one twentieth of my capacity for life. What does reason know? Reason only knows what it has succeeded in learning (some things, perhaps, it will never learn; this is a poor comfort, but why not say so frankly?) and human nature acts as a whole, with everything that is in it, consciously or unconsciously, and, even if it goes wrong, it lives. I suspect, gentlemen, that you are looking at me with compassion; you tell me again that an enlightened and developed man, such, in short, as the future man will be, cannot consciously desire anything disadvantageous to himself, that that can be proved mathematically. I thoroughly agree, it can—by mathematics. But I repeat for the hundredth time, there is one case, one only, when man may consciously, purposely, desire what is injurious to himself, what is stupid, very stupid—simply in order to have the right to desire for himself even what is very stupid and not to be bound by an obligation to desire only what is sensible. Of course, this very stupid thing, this caprice of ours, may be in reality, gentlemen, more advantageous for us than anything else on earth, especially in certain cases. And in particular it may be more advantageous than any advantage even when it does us obvious harm, and contradicts the soundest conclusions of our reason concerning our advantage—for in any circumstances it preserves for us what is most precious and most important—that is, our personality, our individuality. Some, you see, maintain that this really is the most precious thing for mankind; choice can, of course, if it chooses, be in agreement with reason; and especially if this be not abused but kept within bounds. It is profitable and sometimes even praiseworthy. But very often, and even most often, choice is utterly and stubbornly opposed to reason . . . and . . . and . . . do you know that that, too, is profitable, sometimes even praiseworthy? Gentlemen, let us suppose that man is not stupid. (Indeed one cannot refuse to suppose that, if only from the one consideration, that, if man is stupid, then who is wise?) But if he is not stupid, he is monstrously ungrateful! Phenomenally ungrateful. In fact, I believe that the best definition of man is the ungrateful biped. But that is not all, that is not his worst defect; his worst defect is his perpetual moral obliquity, perpetual —from the days of the Flood to the Schleswig-Holstein period. Moral obliquity and consequently lack of good sense; for it has long been accepted that lack of good sense is due to no other cause than moral obliquity. Put it to the test and cast your eyes upon the history of mankind. What will you see? Is it a grand spectacle?

Grand, if you like. Take the Colossus of Rhodes,[11] for instance, that's worth something. With good reason Mr. Anaevsky testifies of it that some say that it is the work of man's hands, while others maintain that it has been created by nature herself. Is it many-coloured? May be it is many-coloured, too: if one takes the dress uniforms, military and civilian, of all peoples in all ages—that alone is worth something, and if you take the undress uniforms you will never get to the end of it; no historian would be equal to the job. Is it monotonous? May be it's monotonous too: it's fighting and fighting; they are fighting now, they fought first and they fought last—you will admit, that it is almost too monotonous. In short, one may say anything about the history of the world—anything that might enter the most disordered imagination. The only thing one can't say is that it's rational. The very word sticks in one's throat. And, indeed, this is the odd thing that is continually happening: there are continually turning up in life moral and rational persons, sages and lovers of humanity who make it their object to live all their lives as morally and rationally as possible, to be, so to speak, a light to their neighbours simply in order to show them that it is possible to live morally and rationally in this world. And yet we all know that those very people sooner or later have been false to themselves, playing some queer trick, often a most unseemly one. Now I ask you: what can be expected of man since he is a being endowed with such strange qualities? Shower upon him every earthly blessing, drown him in a sea of happiness, so that nothing but bubbles of bliss can be seen on the surface; give him economic prosperity, such that he should have nothing else to do but sleep, eat cakes and busy himself with the continuation of his species, and even then out of sheer ingratitude, sheer spite, man would play you some nasty trick. He would even risk his cakes and would deliberately desire the most fatal rubbish, the most uneconomical absurdity, simply to introduce into all this positive good sense his fatal fantastic element. It is just his fantastic dreams, his vulgar folly that he will desire to retain, simply in order to prove to himself—as though that were so necessary—that men still are men and not the keys of a piano, which the laws of nature threaten to control so completely that soon one will be able to desire nothing but by the calendar. And that is not all: even if man really were nothing but a piano-key, even if this were proved to him by natural science and mathematics, even then he would not become reasonable, but would purposely do something perverse out of simple ingratitude, simply to gain his point. And if he does not find means he will contrive

11. a statue of Helios (Apollo) at Rhodes (an island in the Aegean Sea), about a hundred feet high, which was considered one of the Seven Wonders of the World. It was erected about 290 B.C.

destruction and chaos, will contrive sufferings of all sorts, only to gain his point! He will launch a curse upon the world, and as only man can curse (it is his privilege, the primary distinction between him and other animals), may be by his curse alone he will attain his object—that is, convince himself that he is a man and not a piano-key! If you say that all this, too, can be calculated and tabulated—chaos and darkness and curses, so that the mere possibility of calculating it all beforehand would stop it all, and reason would reassert itself, then man would purposely go mad in order to be rid of reason and gain his point! I believe in it, I answer for it, for the whole work of man really seems to consist in nothing but proving to himself every minute that he is a man and not a piano-key! It may be at the cost of his skin, it may be by cannibalism! And this being so, can one help being tempted to rejoice that it has not yet come off, and that desire still depends on something we don't know?

You will scream at me (that is, if you condescend to do so) that no one is touching my free will, that all they are concerned with is that my will should of itself, of its own free will, coincide with my own normal interests, with the laws of nature and arithmetic.

Good Heavens, gentlemen, what sort of free will is left when we come to tabulation and arithmetic, when it will all be a case of twice two makes four? Twice two makes four without my will. As if free will meant that!

IX

Gentlemen, I am joking, and I know myself that my jokes are not brilliant, but you know one can't take everything as a joke. I am, perhaps, jesting against the grain. Gentlemen, I am tormented by questions; answer them for me. You, for instance, want to cure men of their old habits and reform their will in accordance with science and good sense. But how do you know, not only that it is possible, but also that it is *desirable*, to reform man in that way? And what leads you to the conclusion that man's inclinations *need* reforming? In short, how do you know that such a reformation will be a benefit to man? And to go to the root of the matter, why are you so positively convinced that not to act against his real normal interests guaranteed by the conclusions of reason and arithmetic is certainly always advantageous for man and must always be a law for mankind? So far, you know, this is only your supposition. It may be the law of logic, but not the law of humanity. You think, gentlemen, perhaps that I am mad? Allow me to defend myself. I agree that man is pre-eminently a creative animal, predestined to strive consciously for an object and to engage in engineering—that is, incessantly and eternally to make new

roads, *wherever they may lead*. But the reason why he wants sometimes to go off at a tangent may just be that he is *predestined* to
make the road, and perhaps, too, that however stupid the "direct"
practical man may be, the thought sometimes will occur to him
that the road almost always does lead *somewhere*, and that the
destination it leads to is less important than the process of making
it, and that the chief thing is to save the well-conducted child
from despising engineering, and so giving way to the fatal idleness,
which, as we all know, is the mother of all the vices. Man likes to
make roads and to create, that is a fact beyond dispute. But why
has he such a passionate love for destruction and chaos also? Tell
me that! But on that point I want to say a couple of words myself.
May it not be that he loves chaos and destruction (there can be
no disputing that he does sometimes love it) because he is instinctively afraid of attaining his object and completing the edifice
he is constructing? Who knows, perhaps he only loves that edifice
from a distance, and is by no means in love with it at close quarters;
perhaps he only loves building it and does not want to live in it,
but will leave it, when completed, for the use of *les animaux do-
mestiques*—such as the ants, the sheep, and so on. Now the ants
have quite a different taste. They have a marvellous edifice of
that pattern which endures for ever—the ant-heap.

With the ant-heap the respectable race of ants began and with
the ant-heap they will probably end, which does the greatest credit
to their perseverance and good sense. But man is a frivolous and
incongruous creature, and perhaps, like a chess player, loves the
process of the game, not the end of it. And who knows (there is
no saying with certainty), perhaps the only goal on earth to which
mankind is striving lies in this incessant process of attaining, in
other words, in life itself, and not in the thing to be attained,
which must always be expressed as a formula, as positive as twice
two makes four, and such positiveness is not life, gentlemen, but
is the beginning of death. Anyway, man has always been afraid
of this mathematical certainty, and I am afraid of it now. Granted
that man does nothing but seek that mathematical certainty, he
traverses oceans, sacrifices his life in the quest, but to succeed,
really to find it, he dreads, I assure you. He feels that when he
has found it there will be nothing for him to look for. When
workmen have finished their work they do at least receive their
pay, they go to the tavern, then they are taken to the police-
station—and there is occupation for a week. But where can man
go? Anyway, one can observe a certain awkwardness about him
when he has attained such objects. He loves the process of attaining, but does not quite like to have attained, and that, of course,
is very absurd. In fact, man is a comical creature; there seems to

936 · *Fyodor Dostoevsky*

be a kind of jest in it all. But yet mathematical certainty is, after all, something insufferable. Twice two makes four seems to me simply a piece of insolence. Twice two makes four is a pert cox-comb who stands with arms akimbo barring your path and spitting. I admit that twice two makes four is an excellent thing, but if we are to give everything its due, twice two makes five is sometimes a very charming thing too.

And why are you so firmly, so triumphantly, convinced that only the normal and the positive—in other words, only what is conducive to welfare—is for the advantage of man? Is not reason in error as regards advantage? Does not man, perhaps, love something besides well-being? Perhaps he is just as fond of suffering? Perhaps suffering is just as great a benefit to him as well-being? Man is sometimes extraordinarily, passionately, in love with suffering, and that is a fact. There is no need to appeal to universal history to prove that; only ask yourself, if you are a man and have lived at all. As far as my personal opinion is concerned, to care only for well-being seems to me positively ill-bred. Whether it's good or bad, it is sometimes very pleasant, too, to smash things. I hold no brief for suffering nor for well-being either. I am standing for . . . my caprice, and for its being guaranteed to me when neces-sary. Suffering would be out of place in vaudevilles, for instance; I know that. In the "Crystal Palace" it is unthinkable; suffering means doubt, negation, and what would be the good of a crystal palace if there could be any doubt about it? And yet I think man will never renounce real suffering, that is, destruction and chaos. Why, suffering is the sole origin of consciousness. Though I did lay it down at the beginning that consciousness is the greatest misfor-tune for man, yet I know man prizes it and would not give it up for any satisfaction. Consciousness, for instance, is infinitely superior to twice two makes four. Once you have mathematical certainty there is nothing left to do or to understand. There will be nothing left but to bottle up your five senses and plunge into contemplation. While if you stick to consciousness, even though the same result is at-tained, you can at least flog yourself at times, and that will, at any rate, liven you up. Reactionary as it is, corporal punishment is better than nothing.

X[12]

You believe in a crystal palace that can never be destroyed—a palace at which one will not be able to put out one's tongue or make a long nose on the sly. And perhaps that is just why I am afraid of this edifice, that it is of crystal and can never be destroyed and that one cannot put one's tongue out at it even on the sly.

12. Section X was badly mutilated by the censor, as Dostoevsky makes clear in the letter to his brother Mikhail, dated March 26, 1864, which is quoted in our introduction.

You see, if it were not a palace, but a hen-house, I might creep into it to avoid getting wet, and yet I would not call the hen-house a palace out of gratitude to it for keeping me dry. You laugh and say that in such circumstances a hen-house is as good as a mansion. Yes, I answer, if one had to live simply to keep out of the rain.

But what is to be done if I have taken it into my head that that is not the only object in life, and that if one must live one had better live in a mansion. That is my choice, my desire. You will only eradicate it when you have changed my preference. Well, do change it, allure me with something else, give me another ideal. But meanwhile I will not take a hen-house for a mansion. The crystal palace may be an idle dream, it may be that it is inconsistent with the laws of nature and that I have invented it only through my own stupidity, through the old-fashioned irrational habits of my generation. But what does it matter to me that it is inconsistent? That makes no difference since it exists in my desires, or rather exists as long as my desires exist. Perhaps you are laughing again? Laugh away; I will put up with any mockery rather than pretend that I am satisfied when I am hungry. I know, anyway, that I will not be put off with a compromise, with a recurring zero, simply because it is consistent with the laws of nature and actually exists. I will not accept as the crown of my desires a block of slum tenements on a lease of a thousand years, and perhaps with a sign-board of Wagenheim the dentist hanging out. Destroy my desires, eradicate my ideals, show me something better, and I will follow you. You will say, perhaps, that it is not worth your trouble; but in that case I can give you the same answer. We are discussing things seriously; but if you won't deign to give me your attention, I will drop your acquaintance. I can retreat into my underground hole.

But while I am alive and have desires I would rather my hand were withered off than bring one brick to such a building! Don't remind me that I have just rejected the crystal palace for the sole reason that one cannot put out one's tongue at it. I did not say because I am so fond of putting my tongue out. Perhaps the thing I resented was, that of all your edifices there has not been one at which one could not put out one's tongue. On the contrary, I would let my tongue be cut off out of gratitude if things could be so arranged that I should lose all desire to put it out. It is not my fault that things cannot be so arranged, and that one must be satisfied with model flats. Then why am I made with such desires? Can I have been constructed simply in order to come to the conclusion that all my construction is a cheat? Can this be my whole purpose? I do not believe it.

But do you know what: I am convinced that we underground folk ought to be kept on a curb. Though we may sit forty years under-

ground without speaking, when we do come out into the light of
day and break out we talk and talk and talk. . . .

XI

The long and the short of it is, gentlemen, that it is better to do
nothing! Better conscious inertia! And so hurrah for underground!
Though I have said that I envy the normal man to the last drop of
my bile, yet I should not care to be in his place such as he is now
(though I shall not cease envying him). No, no; anyway the underground life is more advantageous. There, at any rate, one can. . . .
Oh, but even now I am lying! I am lying because I know myself
that it is not underground that is better, but something different,
quite different, for which I am thirsting, but which I cannot find!
Damn underground!

I will tell you another thing that would be better, and that is,
if I myself believed in anything of what I have just written. I swear
to you, gentlemen, there is not one thing, not one word of what I
have written that I really believe. That is, I believe it, perhaps, but at
the same time I feel and suspect that I am lying like a cobbler.

"Then why have you written all this?" you will say to me. "I ought
to put you underground for forty years without anything to do and
then come to you in your cellar, to find out what stage you have
reached! How can a man be left with nothing to do for forty years?"

"Isn't that shameful, isn't that humiliating?" you will say, perhaps, wagging your heads contemptuously. "You thirst for life and
try to settle the problems of life by a logical tangle. And how persistent, how insolent are your sallies, and at the same time what a
scare you are in! You talk nonsense and are pleased with it; you say
impudent things and are in continual alarm and apologizing for
them. You declare that you are afraid of nothing and at the same
time try to ingratiate yourself in our good opinion. You declare that
you are gnashing your teeth and at the same time you try to be witty
so as to amuse us. You know that your witticisms are not witty, but
you are evidently well satisfied with their literary value. You may,
perhaps, have really suffered, but you have no respect for your own
suffering. You may have sincerity, but you have no modesty; out of
the pettiest vanity you expose your sincerity to publicity and ig-
nominy. You doubtlessly mean to say something, but hide your last
word through fear, because you have not the resolution to utter it,
and only have a cowardly impudence. You boast of consciousness,
but you are not sure of your ground, for though your mind works,
yet your heart is darkened and corrupt, and you cannot have a full,
genuine consciousness without a pure heart. And how intrusive you
are, how you insist and grimace! Lies, lies, lies!"

Of course I have myself made up all the things you say. That,
too, is from underground. I have been for forty years listening to

you through a crack under the floor. I have invented them myself, there was nothing else I could invent. It is no wonder that I have learned it by heart and it has taken a literary form. . .

But can you really be so credulous as to think that I will print all this and give it to you to read too? And another problem: why do I call you "gentlemen," why do I address you as though you really were my readers? Such confessions as I intend to make are never printed nor given to other people to read. Anyway, I am not strong-minded enough for that, and I don't see why I should be. But you see a fancy has occurred to me and I want to realize it at all costs. Let me explain.

Every man has reminiscences which he would not tell to every one, but only to his friends. He has other matters in his mind which he would not reveal even to his friends, but only to himself, and that in secret. But there are other things which a man is afraid to tell even to himself, and every decent man has a number of such things stored away in his mind. The more decent he is, the greater the number of such things in his mind. Anyway, I have only lately determined to remember some of my early adventures. Till now I have always avoided them, even with a certain uneasiness. Now, when I am not only recalling them, but have actually decided to write an account of them, I want to try the experiment whether one can, even with oneself, be perfectly open and not take fright at the whole truth. I will observe, in parenthesis, that Heine[13] says that a true autobiography is almost an impossibility, and that man is bound to lie about himself. He considers that Rousseau certainly told lies about himself in his *Confessions*, and even intentionally lied, out of vanity. I am convinced that Heine is right; I quite understand how sometimes one may, out of sheer vanity, attribute regular crimes to oneself, and indeed I can very well conceive that kind of vanity. But Heine judged of people who made their confessions to the public. I write only for myself, and I wish to declare once and for all that if I write as though I were addressing readers, that is simply because it is easier for me to write in that form. It is a form, an empty form—I shall never have readers. I have made this plain already. . .

I don't wish to be hampered by any restrictions in the compilation of my notes. I shall not attempt any system or method. I will jot things down as I remember them.

But here, perhaps, some one will catch at the word and ask me: if you really don't reckon on readers, why do you make such compacts with yourself—and on paper too—that is, that you won't at-

13. Dostoevsky alludes to *Confessions* (*Geständnisse*, 1854), fragmentary memoirs written by the German poet Heinrich Heine (1797–1856), in which on the very first page Heine speaks of Rousseau as lying and inventing disgraceful incidents about himself for his *Confessions*. (See footnote 2.)

tempt any system or method, that you jot things down as you remember them, and so on, and so on? Why are you explaining? Why do you apologize?

Well, there it is, I answer.

There is a whole psychology in all this, though. Perhaps it is simply that I am a coward. And perhaps that I purposely imagine an audience before me in order that I may be more dignified while I write. There are perhaps thousands of reasons. Again, what is my object precisely in writing? If it is not for the benefit of the public why should I not simply recall these incidents in my own mind without putting them on paper?

Quite so; but yet it is more imposing on paper. There is something more impressive in it; I shall be better able to criticize myself and improve my style. Besides, I shall perhaps obtain actual relief from writing. To-day, for instance, I am particularly oppressed by one memory of a distant past. It came back vividly to my mind a few days ago, and has remained haunting me like an annoying tune that one cannot get rid of. And yet I must get rid of it somehow. I have hundreds of such reminiscences; but at times some one stands out from the hundred and oppresses me. For some reason I believe that if I write it down I should get rid of it. Why not try?

Besides, I am bored, and I never have anything to do. Writing will be a sort of work. They say work makes man kind-hearted and honest. Well, here is a chance for me, anyway.

Snow is falling to-day, yellow and dingy. It fell yesterday, too, and a few days ago. I fancy it is the wet snow that has reminded me of that incident which I cannot shake off now. And so let it be a story *à propos* of the falling snow.

Part II

À PROPOS OF THE WET SNOW

When from dark error's subjugation
My words of passionate exhortation
   Had wrenched thy fainting spirit free;
And writhing prone in thine affliction
Thou didst recall with malediction
   The vice that had encompassed thee:
And when thy slumbering conscience, fretting
   By recollection's torturing flame,
Thou didst reveal the hideous setting
   Of thy life's current ere I came:
When suddenly I saw thee sicken,
   And weeping, hide thine anguished face,
Revolted, maddened, horror-stricken,
   At memories of foul disgrace, etc., etc., etc. . . .

NEKRASOV[14] (*translated by Juliet Soskice*)

14. Nikolay A. Nekrasov (1821–1878) was a famous Russian poet and editor of radical sympathies. The poem quoted dates from 1845, and is without title. The poem ends with the lines, "Into my house come bold and free, / Its rightful mistress there to be."

I

At that time I was only twenty-four. My life was even then gloomy, ill-regulated, and as solitary as that of a savage. I made friends with no one and positively avoided talking, and buried myself more and more in my hole. At work in the office I never looked at any one, and I was perfectly well aware that my companions looked upon me, not only as a queer fellow, but even looked upon me—I always fancied this—with a sort of loathing. I sometimes wondered why it was that nobody except me fancied that he was looked upon with aversion? One of the clerks had a most repulsive, pock-marked face, which looked positively villainous. I believe I should not have dared to look at any one with such an unsightly countenance. Another had such a very dirty old uniform that there was an unpleasant odor in his proximity. Yet not one of these gentlemen showed the slightest self-consciousness—either about their clothes or their countenance or their character in any way. Neither of them ever imagined that they were looked at with repulsion; if they had imagined it they would not have minded—so long as their superiors did not look at them in that way. It is clear to me now that, owing to my unbounded vanity and to the high standard I set for myself, I often looked at myself with furious discontent, which verged on loathing, and so I inwardly attributed the same feeling to every one. I hated my face, for instance: I thought it disgusting, and even suspected that there was something base in my expression, and so every day when I turned up at the office I tried to behave as independently as possible, and to assume a lofty expression, so that I might not be suspected of being abject. "My face may be ugly," I thought, "but let it be lofty, expressive, and, above all, *extremely* intelligent." But I was positively and painfully certain that it was impossible for my countenance ever to express those qualities. And what was worst of all, I thought it actually stupid looking, and I would have been quite satisfied if I could have looked intelligent. In fact, I would even have put up with looking base if, at the same time, my face could have been thought strikingly intelligent.

Of course, I hated my fellow clerks one and all, and I despised them all, yet at the same time I was, as it were, afraid of them. In fact, it happened at times that I thought more highly of them than of myself. It somehow happened quite suddenly that I alternated between despising them and thinking them superior to myself. A cultivated and decent man cannot be vain without setting a fearfully high standard for himself, and without despising and almost hating himself at certain moments. But whether I despised them or thought them superior I dropped my eyes almost every time I met any one. I even made experiments whether I could face so and so's looking at me, and I was always the first to drop my eyes. This worried me to distraction. I had a sickly dread, too, of being ridiculous, and so had a slavish passion for the conventional in everything external. I loved to fall into the common rut, and had a whole-hearted terror of any kind of eccentricity in myself. But how could I live up to it? I was morbidly sensitive, as a man of our age should be. They were all stupid, and as like one another as so many sheep. Perhaps I was the only one in the office who fancied that I was a coward and a slave, and I fancied it just because I was more highly developed. But it was not only that I fancied it, it really was so. I was a coward and a slave. I say this without the slightest embarrassment. Every decent man of our age must be a coward and a slave. That is his normal condition. Of that I am firmly persuaded. He is made and constructed to that very end. And not only at the present time owing to some casual circumstances, but always, at all times, a decent man is bound to be a coward and a slave. It is the law of nature for all decent people all over the earth. If any one of them happens to be valiant about something, he need not be comforted nor carried away by that; he would show the white feather just the same before something else. That is how it invariably and inevitably ends. Only donkeys and mules are valiant, and they only till they are pushed up to the wall. It is not worth while to pay attention to them for they really are of no consequence.

Another circumstance, too, worried me in those days: that there was no one like me and I was unlike any one else. "I am unique and they are all alike," I thought—and pondered.

From that it is evident that I was still a youngster.

The very opposite sometimes happened. It was loathsome sometimes to go to the office; things reached such a point that I often came home ill. But all at once, *à propos* of nothing, there would come a phase of scepticism and indifference (everything happened in phases to me), and I would laugh myself at my intolerance and fastidiousness, I would reproach myself with being *romantic*. At one time I was unwilling to speak to any one, while at other times I would not only talk, but go to the length of contemplating making friends with them. All my fastidiousness would suddenly, for no rhyme or reason, vanish. Who knows, perhaps I never had really had it, and it had simply been affected, and got out of books. I have not decided that question even now. Once I quite made friends with them, visited their homes, played preference, drank vodka, talked of promotions. . . . But here let me make a digression.

We Russians, speaking generally, have never had those foolish transcendental "romantics"—German, and still more French—on whom nothing produces any effect; if there were an earthquake, if all France perished at the barricades, they would still be the same, they would not even have the decency to affect a change, but would still go on singing their transcendental songs to the hour of their death, because they are fools. We, in Russia, have no fools; that is well known. That is what distinguishes us from foreign lands. Consequently these transcendental natures are not found amongst us in their pure form. The idea that they are is due to our "realistic" journalists and critics of that day, always on the look out for Kostanzhoglos[15] and Uncle Pyotr Ivanichs[16] and foolishly accepting them as our ideal; they have slandered our romantics, taking them for the same transcendental sort as in Germany or France. On the contrary, the characteristics of our "romantics" are absolutely and directly opposed to the transcendental European type, and no European standard can be applied to them. (Allow me to make use of this word "romantic"—an old-fashioned and much respected word which has done good service and is familiar to all). The characteristics of our romantic are to understand everything, *to see everything and to see it often incomparably more clearly than our most realistic minds see it*; to refuse to accept anyone or anything, but at the same time not to despise anything; to give way, to yield, from policy; never to lose sight of a useful practical object (such as rent-free quarters at the government expense, pensions, decorations), to keep their eye on that object through all the enthusiasms and volumes of lyrical poems, and at the same time to preserve "the good and the beautiful" inviolate within them to the hour of their death, and to preserve themselves also, incidentally, like some precious jewel wrapped in cotton wool if only for the benefit of "the good and the beautiful." Our "romantic" is a man of great breadth and the greatest rogue of all our rogues, I assure you. . . . I can assure you from experience, indeed. Of course, that is, if he is intelligent. But what am I saying! The romantic is always intelligent, and I only meant to observe that although we have had foolish romantics they don't count, and they were only so because in the flower of their youth they degenerated into Germans, and to preserve their precious jewel more comfortably, settled somewhere out there—by preference in Weimar or the Black Forest.

I, for instance, genuinely despised my official work and did not openly abuse it simply because I was in it myself and got a salary for it. Anyway, take note, I did not openly abuse it. Our romantic would rather go out of his mind—a thing, however, which very rarely happens—than take to open abuse, unless he had some other

---

15. Konstanzhoglo is the ideal efficient landowner in the second part of Gogol's novel *Dead Souls* (published posthumously in 1852).

16. Uncle Pyotr Ivanich, a character in Ivan Goncharov's novel *A Common Story* (1847), is a high bureaucrat, a factory owner who teaches lessons of sobriety and good sense to the romantic hero, Alexander Aduyev.

career in view; and he is never kicked out. At most, they would take him to the lunatic asylum as "the King of Spain"[17] if he should go very mad. But it is only the thin, fair people who go out of their minds in Russia. Innumerable "romantics" attain later in life to considerable rank in the service. Their many-sidedness is remarkable! And what a faculty they have for the most contradictory sensations! I was comforted by this thought even in those days, and I am of the same opinion now. That is why there are so many "broad natures" among us who never lose their ideal even in the depths of degradation; and though they never stir a finger for their ideal, though they are arrant thieves and knaves, yet they tearfully cherish their first ideal and are extraordinarily honest at heart. Yes, it is only among us that the most incorrigible rogue can be absolutely and loftily honest at heart without in the least ceasing to be a rogue. I repeat, our romantics, frequently, become such accomplished rascals (I use the term "rascals" affectionately), suddenly display such a sense of reality and practical knowledge that their bewildered superiors and the public generally can only ejaculate in amazement.

Their many-sidedness is really amazing, and goodness knows what it may develop into later on, and what the future has in store for us. It is not a poor material! I do not say this from any foolish or boastful patriotism. But I feel sure that you are again imagining that I am joking. Or perhaps it's just the contrary and you are convinced that I really think so. Anyway, gentlemen, I shall welcome both views as an honour and a special favour. And do forgive my digression.

I did not, of course, maintain friendly relations with my comrades and soon was at loggerheads with them, and in my youth and inexperience I even gave up bowing to them, as though I had cut off all relations. That, however, only happened to me once. As a rule, I was always alone.

In the first place I spent most of my time at home, reading. I tried to stifle all that was continually seething within me by means of external impressions. And the only external means I had was reading. Reading, of course, was a great help—exciting me, giving me pleasure and pain. But at times it bored me fearfully. One longed for movement in spite of everything, and I plunged all at once into dark, underground, loathsome vice of the pettiest kind. My wretched passions were acute, smarting, from my continual, sickly irritability. I had hysterical impulses, with tears and convulsions. I had no resource except reading, that is, there was nothing in my surroundings which I could respect and which attracted me. I was overwhelmed with depression, too; I had a hysterical craving for incongruity and

17. an allusion to Gogol's story "Memoirs of a Madman" (1835). The narrator imagines himself "the King of Spain" and is finally carried off to a lunatic asylum.

for contrast, and so I took to vice. I have not said all this to justify myself. . . . But, no! I am lying. I did want to justify myself. I make that little observation for my own benefit, gentlemen. I don't want to lie. I vowed to myself I would not.

And so, furtively, timidly, in solitude, at night, I indulged in filthy vice, with a feeling of shame which never deserted me, even at the most loathsome moments, and which at such moments nearly made me curse. Already even then I had my underground world in my soul. I was fearfully afraid of being seen, of being met, of being recognized. I visited various obscure haunts.

One night as I was passing a tavern I saw through a lighted window some gentlemen fighting with billiard cues, and saw one of them thrown out of a window. At other times I should have felt very much disgusted, but I was in such a mood at the time, that I actually envied the gentleman thrown out of a window—and I envied him so much that I even went into the tavern and into the billiard-room. "Perhaps," I thought, "I'll have a fight, too, and they'll throw me out of the window."

I was not drunk—but what is one to do—depression will drive a man to such a pitch of hysteria? But nothing happened. It seemed that I was not even equal to being thrown out of the window and I went away without having my fight.

An officer put me in my place from the first moment.

I was standing by the billiard-table and in my ignorance blocking up the way, and he wanted to pass; he took me by the shoulders and without a word—without a warning or explanation—moved me from where I was standing to another spot and passed by as though he had not noticed me. I could have forgiven blows, but I could not forgive his having moved me without noticing me.

Devil knows what I would have given for a real regular quarrel— a more decent, a more *literary* one, so to speak. I had been treated like a fly. This officer was over six foot, while I was a spindly little fellow. But the quarrel was in my hands. I had only to protest and I certainly would have been thrown out of the window. But I changed my mind and preferred to beat a resentful retreat.

I went out of the tavern straight home, confused and troubled, and the next night I went out again with the same lewd intentions, still more furtively, abjectly and miserably than before, as it were, with tears in my eyes—but still I did go out again. Don't imagine, though, it was cowardice made me slink away from the officer: I never have been a coward at heart, though I have always been a coward in action. Don't be in a hurry to laugh—I assure you I can explain it all.

Oh, if only that officer had been one of the sort who would consent to fight a duel! But no, he was one of those gentlemen (alas, long extinct!) who preferred fighting with cues or, like Gogol's Lieutenant Pirogov,[18] appealing to the police. They did not fight duels and would have thought a duel with a civilian like me an utterly unseemly procedure in any case—and they looked upon the duel altogether as something impossible, something free-thinking and French. But they were quite ready to bully, especially when they were over six foot.

I did not slink away through cowardice, but through an unbounded vanity. I was afraid not of his six foot, not of getting a sound thrashing and being thrown out of the window; I should have had physical courage enough, I assure you; but I had not the moral courage. What I was afraid of was that every one present, from the insolent marker down to the lowest little stinking, pimply clerk in a greasy collar, would jeer at me and fail to understand when I began to protest and to address them in literary language. For of the point of honour—not of honour, but of the point of honour (*point d'honneur*)—one cannot speak among us except in literary language. You can't allude to the "point of honour" in ordinary language. I was fully convinced (the sense of reality, in spite of all my romanticism!) that they would all simply split their sides with laughter, and that the officer would not simply beat me, that is, without insulting me, but would certainly prod me in the back with his knee, kick me round the billiard-table, and only then perhaps have pity and drop me out of the window.

Of course, this trivial incident could not with me end in that. I often met that officer afterwards in the street and noticed him very carefully. I am not quite sure whether he recognized me, I imagine not; I judge from certain signs. But I—I stared at him with spite and hatred and so it went on . . . for several years! My resentment grew even deeper with years. At first I began making stealthy inquiries about this officer. It was difficult for me to do so, for I knew no one. But one day I heard some one shout his surname in the street as I was following him at a distance, as though I were tied to him—and so I learnt his surname. Another time I followed him to his flat, and for ten kopecks learned from the porter where he lived, on which storey, whether he lived alone or with others, and so on—in fact, everything one could learn from a porter. One morning, though I had never tried my hand with the pen, it suddenly occurred to me to write a satire on this officer in the form of a novel which would unmask his villainy. I wrote the novel with relish. I did unmask his villainy, I even exaggerated it; at first I so altered his surname that it could easily be recognized, but on second thoughts

18. a character in Gogol's story "The Nevsky Prospekt" (1835). He pays violent court to the wife of a German tradesman and is thrown out by him and his friends. He does not actually call the police.

I changed it, and sent the story to the *Otechestvenniye Zapiski*.[19]
But at that time such attacks were not the fashion and my story was
not printed. That was a great vexation to me.

Sometimes I was positively choked with resentment. At last I determined to challenge my enemy to a duel. I composed a splendid,
charming letter to him, imploring him to apologize to me, and
hinting rather plainly at a duel in case of refusal. The letter was so
composed that if the officer had had the least understanding of the
good and the beautiful he would certainly have flung himself on my
neck and have offered me his friendship. And how fine that would
have been! How we should have got on together! "He could have
shielded me with his higher rank, while I could have improved his
mind with my culture, and, well . . . my ideas, and all sorts of
things might have happened." Only fancy, this was two years after
his insult to me, and my challenge would have been a ridiculous
anachronism, in spite of all the ingenuity of my letter in disguising
and explaining away the anachronism. But, thank God (to this day
I thank the Almighty with tears in my eyes) I did not send the
letter to him. Cold shivers run down my back when I think of what
might have happened if I had sent it.

And all at once I revenged myself in the simplest way, by a stroke
of genius! A brilliant thought suddenly dawned upon me. Sometimes on holidays I used to stroll along the sunny side of the
Nevsky[20] about four o'clock in the afternoon. Though it was hardly
a stroll so much as a series of innumerable miseries, humiliations
and resentments; but no doubt that was just what I wanted. I used
to wriggle along in a most unseemly fashion, like an eel, continually
moving aside to make way for generals, for officers of the guards and
the hussars, or for ladies. At such minutes there used to be a convulsive twinge at my heart, and I used to feel hot all down my back
at the mere thought of the wretchedness of my attire, of the
wretchedness and abjectness of my little scurrying figure. This was
a regular martyrdom, a continual, intolerable humiliation at the
thought, which passed into an incessant and direct sensation, that I
was a mere fly in the eyes of all this world, a nasty, disgusting fly—
more intelligent, more highly developed, more refined in feeling
than any of them, of course—but a fly that was continually making
way for every one, insulted and injured by every one. Why I inflicted this torture upon myself, why I went to the Nevsky, I don't
know. I felt simply drawn there at every possible opportunity.

Already then I began to experience a rush of the enjoyment of

19. *Notes of the Fatherland*, the most famous radical Russian journal, founded in 1839.

20. Nevsky Prospekt, the most ele-gant main street in St. Petersburg, about three miles long; now called "Prospekt of the 25th October."

which I spoke in the first chapter. After my affair with the officer I felt even more drawn there than before: it was on the Nevsky that I met him most frequently, there I could admire him. He, too, went there chiefly on holidays. He, too, turned out of his path for generals and persons of high rank, and he, too, wriggled between them like an eel; but people, like me, or even better dressed like me, he simply walked over; he made straight for them as though there was nothing but empty space before him, and never, under any circumstances, turned aside. I gloated over my resentment watching him and . . . always resentfully made way for him. It exasperated me that even in the street I could not be on an even footing with him.

"Why must you invariably be the first to move aside?" I kept asking myself in hysterical rage, waking up sometimes at three o'clock in the morning. "Why is it you and not he? There's no regulation about it; there's no written law. Let the making way be equal as it usually is when refined people meet: he moves half-way and you move half-way; you pass with mutual respect."

But that never happened, and I always moved aside, while he did not even notice my making way for him. And lo and behold a bright idea dawned upon me! "What," I thought, "if I meet him and don't move on one side? What if I don't move aside on purpose, even if I knock up against him? How would that be?" This audacious idea took such a hold on me that it gave me no peace. I was dreaming of it continually, horribly, and I purposely went more frequently to the Nevsky in order to picture more vividly how I should do it when I did do it. I was delighted. This intention seemed to me more and more practical and possible.

"Of course I shall not really push him," I thought, already more good-natured in my joy. "I will simply not turn aside, will run up against him, not very violently, but just shouldering each other—just as much as decency permits. I will push against him just as much as he pushes against me." At last I made up my mind completely. But my preparations took a great deal of time. To begin with, when I carried out my plan I should need to be looking rather more decent, and so I had to think of my get-up. "In case of emergency, if, for instance, there were any sort of public scandal (and the public there is of the most *recherché*: the Countess walks there; Prince D. walks there; all the literary world is there), I must be well dressed; that inspires respect and of itself puts us on an equal footing in the eyes of society."

With this object I asked for some of my salary in advance, and bought at Churkin's a pair of black gloves and a decent hat. Black gloves seemed to me both more dignified and *bon ton* than the lemon-coloured ones which I had contemplated at first. "The colour is too gaudy, it looks as though one were trying to be conspicuous," and I did not take the lemon-coloured ones. I had got ready long beforehand a good shirt, with white bone studs; my overcoat was the only thing that held me back. The coat in itself was a very good one, it kept me warm; but it was wadded and it had a raccoon collar which was the height of vulgarity. I had to change the collar at any sacrifice, and to have a beaver one like an officer's. For this purpose I began visiting the Gostiny Dvor[21] and after several attempts I pitched upon a piece of cheap German beaver. Though these German beavers soon grow shabby and look wretched, yet at first they look exceedingly well, and I only needed it for one occasion. I asked the price; even so, it was too expensive. After thinking it over thoroughly I decided to sell my raccoon collar. The rest of the money— a considerable sum for me, I decided to borrow from Anton Antonich Syetochkin, my immediate superior, an unassuming person, though grave and judicious. He never lent money to any one, but I had, on entering the service, been specially recommended to him by an important personage who had got me my berth. I was horribly worried. To borrow from Anton Antonich seemed to me monstrous and shameful. I did not sleep for two or three nights. Indeed, I did not sleep well at that time, I was in a fever; I had a vague sinking at my heart or else a sudden throbbing, throbbing, throbbing! Anton Antonich was surprised at first, then he frowned, then he reflected, and did after all lend me the money, receiving from me a written authorization to take from my salary a fortnight later the sum that he had lent me.

In this way everything was at last ready. The handsome beaver replaced the mean-looking raccoon, and I began by degrees to get to work. It would never have done to act off-hand, at random; the plan had to be carried out skilfully, by degrees. But I must confess that after many efforts I began to despair: we simply could not run into each other. I made every preparation, I was quite determined— it seemed as though we should run into one another directly—and before I knew what I was doing I had stepped aside for him again and he had passed without noticing me. I even prayed as I approached him that God would grant me determination. One time I had made up my mind thoroughly, but it ended in my stumbling and falling at his feet because at the very last instant when I was six inches from him my courage failed me. He very calmly stepped over me, while I flew on one side like a ball. That night I was ill again, feverish and delirious.

And suddenly it ended most happily. The night before I had made up my mind not to carry out my fatal plan and to abandon it all, and

---

21. originally a guesthouse for foreign merchants; later used for displaying their wares.

with that object I went to the Nevsky for the last time, just to see how I would abandon it all. Suddenly, three paces from my enemy, I unexpectedly made up my mind—I closed my eyes, and we ran full tilt, shoulder to shoulder, against one another! I did not budge an inch and passed him on a perfectly equal footing! He did not even look round and pretended not to notice it; but he was only pretending, I am convinced of that. I am convinced of that to this day! Of course, I got the worst of it—he was stronger, but that was not the point. The point was that I had attained my object, I had kept up my dignity, I had not yielded a step, and had put myself publicly on an equal social footing with him. I returned home feeling that I was fully avenged for everything. I was delighted. I was triumphant and sang Italian arias. Of course, I will not describe to you what happened to me three days later; if you have read my first chapter you can guess that for yourself. The officer was afterwards transferred; I have not seen him now for fourteen years. What is the dear fellow doing now? Whom is he walking over?

II

But the period of my dissipation would end and I always felt very sick afterwards. It was followed by remorse—I tried to drive it away: I felt too sick. By degrees, however, I grew used to that too. I grew used to everything, or rather I voluntarily resigned myself to enduring it. But I had a means of escape that reconciled everything—that was to find refuge in "the good and the beautiful," in dreams, of course. I was a terrible dreamer, I would dream for three months on end, tucked away in my corner, and you may believe me that at those moments I had no resemblance to the gentleman who, in the perturbation of his chicken heart, put a collar of German beaver on his great coat. I suddenly became a hero. I would not have admitted my six-foot lieutenant even if he had called on me. I could not even picture him before me then. What were my dreams and how I could satisfy myself with them—it is hard to say now, but at the time I was satisfied with them. Though, indeed, even now, I am to some extent satisfied with them. Dreams were particularly sweet and vivid after a spell of dissipation; they came with remorse and with tears, with curses and transports. There were moments of such positive intoxication, of such happiness, that there was not the faintest trace of irony within me, on my honour. I had faith, hope, love. I believed blindly at such times that by some miracle, by some external circumstance, all this would suddenly open out, expand; that suddenly a vista of suitable activity—beneficent, good, and, above all, *ready made* (what sort of activity I had no idea, but the great thing was that it should be all ready for me)—would rise up before me—and I should come out into the light of day, almost riding a white horse and crowned with laurel. Anything but the foremost place I could not conceive for myself, and for that very reason I quite content-edly occupied the lowest in reality. Either to be a hero or to grovel in the mud—there was nothing between. That was my ruin, for when I was in the mud I comforted myself with the thought that at other times I was a hero, and the hero was a cloak for the mud: for an ordinary man it was shameful to defile himself, but a hero was too lofty to be utterly defiled, and so he might defile himself. It is worth noting that these attacks of the "good and the beautiful" visited me even during the period of dissipation and just at the times when I was touching bottom. They came in separate spurts, as though re-minding me of themselves, but did not banish the dissipation by their appearance. On the contrary, they seemed to add a zest to it by contrast, and were only sufficiently present to serve as an ap-petizing sauce. That sauce was made up of contradictions and suf-ferings, of agonizing inward analysis, and all these pangs and pin-pricks gave a certain piquancy, even a significance to my dissipa-tion—in fact, completely answered the purpose of an appetizing sauce. There was a certain depth of meaning in it. And I could hardly have resigned myself to the simple, vulgar, direct debauchery of a clerk and have endured all the filthiness of it. What could have allured me about it then and have drawn me at night into the street? No, I had a lofty way of getting out of it all.

And what loving-kindness, oh Lord, what loving-kindness I felt at times in those dreams of mine! in those "flights into the good and the beautiful;" though it was fantastic love, though it was never applied to anything human in reality, yet there was so much of this love that one did not feel afterwards even the impulse to apply it in reality; that would have been superfluous. Everything, however, passed satisfactorily by a lazy and fascinating transition into the sphere of art, that is, into the beautiful forms of life, lying ready, largely stolen from the poets and novelists and adapted to all sorts of needs and uses. I, for instance, was triumphant over every one; every one, of course, was in dust and ashes, and was forced spontaneously to recognize my superiority, and I forgave them all. I was a poet and a grand gentleman, I fell in love; I came in for countless millions and immediately devoted them to humanity, and at the same time I confessed before all the people my shameful deeds, which, of course, were not merely shameful, but had in them much that was "good and beautiful" something in the Manfred[22] style. Every one would kiss me and weep (what idiots they would be if they did not), while I should go barefoot and hungry preaching new ideas and fighting a victorious Austerlitz[23] against the obscurantists. Then the

22. the hero of Lord Byron's verse drama *Manfred* (1817), who was op-pressed by a mysterious guilt.

23. a village near Brno, the capital of Moravia, now in Czechoslovakia, where Napoleon defeated the combined Austrian and Russian armies in 1805.

band would play a march, an amnesty would be declared, the Pope would agree to retire from Rome to Brazil; then there would be a ball for the whole of Italy at the Villa Borghese[24] on the shores of the Lake of Como,[25] the Lake of Como being for that purpose transferred to the neighbourhood of Rome; then would come a scene in the bushes, and so on, and so on—as though you did not know all about it? You will say that it is vulgar and contemptible to drag all this into public after all the tears and transports which I have myself confessed. But why is it contemptible? Can you imagine that I am ashamed of it all, and that it was stupider than anything in your life, gentlemen? And I can assure you that some of these fancies were by no means badly composed. . . . It did not all happen on the shores of Lake Como. And yet you are right—it really is vulgar and contemptible. And most contemptible of all it is that now I am attempting to justify myself to you. And even more contemptible than that is my making this remark now. But that's enough, or there will be no end to it: each step will be more contemptible than the last. . . .

I could never stand more than three months of dreaming at a time without feeling an irresistible desire to plunge into society. To plunge into society meant to visit my superior at the office, Anton Antonich Syetochkin. He was the only permanent acquaintance I have had in my life, and wonder at the fact myself now. But I only went to see him when that phase came over me, and when my dreams had reached such a point of bliss that it became essential at once to embrace my fellows and all mankind; and for that purpose I needed, at least, one human being, actually existing. I had to call on Anton Antonich, however, on Tuesday—his at-home day; so I had always to time my passionate desire to embrace humanity so that it might fall on a Tuesday.

This Anton Antonich lived on the fourth storey in a house in Five Corners, in four low-pitched rooms, one smaller than the other, of a particularly frugal and sallow appearance. He had two daughters and their aunt, who used to pour out the tea. Of the daughters one was thirteen and another fourteen, they both had snub noses, and I was awfully shy of them because they were always whispering and giggling together. The master of the house usually sat in his study on a leather couch in front of the table with some grey-headed gentleman, usually a colleague from our office or some other department. I never saw more than two or three visitors there, always the same. They talked about the excise duty; about business in the Senate,[26] about salaries, about promotions, about His Excellency, and the best means of pleasing him, and so on. I had the patience to sit like a fool beside these people for four hours at a stretch, lis-

24. in Rome.
25. on the border of Italy and Switzerland.

26. The Russian Senate was at that time not a parliamentary body, but a high court.

tening to them without knowing what to say to them or venturing to say a word. I became stupefied, several times I felt myself perspiring, I was overcome by a sort of paralysis; but this was pleasant and good for me. On returning home I deferred for a time my desire to embrace all mankind.

I had however one other acquaintance of a sort, Simonov, who was an old schoolfellow. I had a number of schoolfellows, indeed, in Petersburg, but I did not associate with them and had even given up nodding to them in the street. I believe I had transferred into the department I was in simply to avoid their company and to cut off all connection with my hateful childhood. Curses on that school and all those terrible years of penal servitude! In short, I parted from my schoolfellows as soon as I got out into the world. There were two or three left to whom I nodded in the street. One of them was Simonov, who had been in no way distinguished at school, was of a quiet and equable disposition; but I discovered in him a certain independence of character and even honesty. I don't even suppose that he was particularly stupid. I had at one time spent some rather soulful moments with him, but these had not lasted long and had somehow been suddenly clouded over. He was evidently uncomfortable at these reminiscences, and was, I fancy, always afraid that I might take up the same tone again. I suspected that he had an aversion for me, but still I went on going to see him, not being quite certain of it.

And so on one occasion, unable to endure my solitude and knowing that as it was Thursday Anton Antonich's door would be closed, I thought of Simonov. Climbing up to his fourth storey I was thinking that the man disliked me and that it was a mistake to go and see him. But as it always happened that such reflections impelled me, as though purposely, to put myself into a false position, I went in. It was almost a year since I had last seen Simonov.

III

I found two of my old schoolfellows with him. They seemed to be discussing an important matter. All of them took scarcely any notice of my entrance, which was strange, for I had not met them for years. Evidently they looked upon me as something on the level of a common fly. I had not been treated like that even at school, though they all hated me. I knew, of course, that they must despise me now for my lack of success in the service, and for my having let myself sink so low, going about badly dressed and so on—which seemed to them a sign of my incapacity and insignificance. But I had not expected such contempt. Simonov was positively surprised at my turning up. Even in old days he had always seemed surprised at my coming. All this disconcerted me: I sat down, feeling rather miserable, and began listening to what they were saying.

954 · *Fyodor Dostoevsky*

They were engaged in warm and earnest conversation about a farewell dinner which they wanted to arrange for the next day to a comrade of theirs called Zverkov, an officer in the army, who was going away to a distant province. This Zverkov had been all the time at school with me too. I had begun to hate him particularly in the upper grades. In the lower grades he had simply been a pretty, playful boy whom everybody liked. I had hated him, however, even in the lower grades, just because he was a pretty and playful boy. He was always bad at his lessons and got worse and worse as he went on; however, he left with a good certificate, as he had powerful interest. During his last year at school he came in for an estate of two hundred serfs, and as almost all of us were poor he took up a swaggering tone among us. He was vulgar in the extreme, but at the same time he was a good-natured fellow, even in his swaggering. In spite of superficial, fantastic and sham notions of honour and dignity, all but very few of us positively grovelled before Zverkov, and the more so the more he swaggered. And it was not from any interested motive that they grovelled, but simply because he had been favoured by the gifts of nature. Moreover, it was, as it were, an accepted idea among us that Zverkov was a specialist in regard to tact and the social graces. This last fact particularly infuriated me. I hated the abrupt self-confident tone of his voice, his admiration of his own witticisms, which were often frightfully stupid, though he was bold in his language; I hated his handsome, but stupid face (for which I would, however, have gladly exchanged my intelligent one), and the free-and-easy military manners in fashion in the 'forties. I hated the way in which he used to talk of his future conquests of women (he did not venture to begin his attack upon women until he had the epaulettes of an officer, and was looking forward to them with impatience), and boasted of the duels he would constantly be fighting. I remember how I, invariably so taciturn, suddenly fastened upon Zverkov, when one day talking at a leisure moment with his schoolfellows of his future relations with the fair sex, and growing as sportive as a puppy in the sun, he all at once declared that he would not leave a single village girl on his estate unnoticed, that that was his *droit de seigneur*,[27] and that if the peasants dared to protest he would have them all flogged and double the tax on them, the bearded rascals. Our servile rabble applauded, but I attacked him, not from compassion for the girls and their fathers, but simply because they were applauding such an insect. I got the better of him on that occasion, but though Zverkov was stupid he was lively and impudent, and so laughed it off, and in such a way that my victory was not really complete: the laugh was on his side. He got the better of me on several occasions afterwards, but without malice, jestingly,

27. "the right of the master," i.e., to all the women serfs.

casually. I remained angrily and contemptuously silent and would not answer him. When we left school he made advances to me; I did not rebuff them, for I was flattered, but we soon parted and quite naturally. Afterwards I heard of his barrack-room success as a lieutenant, and of the fast life he was leading. Then there came other rumours—of his successes in the service. By then he had taken to cutting me in the street, and I suspected that he was afraid of compromising himself by greeting a personage as insignificant as me. I saw him once in the theatre, in the third tier of boxes. By then he was wearing shoulder-straps. He was twisting and twirling about, ingratiating himself with the daughters of an ancient General. In three years he had gone off considerably, though he was still rather handsome and adroit. One could see that by the time he was thirty he would be corpulent. So it was to this Zverkov that my schoolfellows were going to give a dinner on his departure. They had kept up with him for those three years, though privately they did not consider themselves on an equal footing with him, I am convinced of that.

Of Simonov's two visitors, one was Ferfichkin, a Russianized German—a little fellow with the face of a monkey, a blockhead who was always deriding every one, a very bitter enemy of mine from our days in the lower grades—a vulgar, impudent, swaggering fellow, who affected a most sensitive feeling of personal honour, though, of course, he was a wretched little coward at heart. He was one of those worshippers of Zverkov who made up to the latter from interested motives, and often borrowed money from him. Simonov's other visitor, Trudolyubov, was a person in no way remarkable—a tall young fellow, in the army, with a cold face, fairly honest, though he worshipped success of every sort, and was only capable of thinking of promotion. He was some sort of distant relation of Zverkov's, and this, foolish as it seems, gave him a certain importance among us. He always thought me of no consequence whatever; his behaviour to me, though not quite courteous, was tolerable.

"Well, with seven roubles each," said Trudolyubov, "twenty-one roubles between the three of us, we ought to be able to get a good dinner. Zverkov, of course, won't pay."

"Of course not, since we are inviting him," Simonov decided.

"Can you imagine," Ferfichkin interrupted hotly and conceitedly, like some insolent flunkey boasting of his master the General's decorations, "can you imagine that Zverkov will let us pay alone? He will accept from delicacy, but he will order half a dozen bottles of champagne."

"Do we want half a dozen for the four of us?" observed Trudolyubov, taking notice only of the half dozen.

"So the three of us, with Zverkov for the fourth, twenty-one roubles, at the Hôtel de Paris at five o'clock to-morrow," Simonov, who had been asked to make the arrangements, concluded finally.

"How twenty-one roubles?" I asked in some agitation, with a show of being offended; "if you count me it will not be twenty-one, but twenty-eight roubles."

It seemed to me that to invite myself so suddenly and unexpectedly would be positively graceful, and that they would all be conquered at once and would look at me with respect.

"Do you want to join, too?" Simonov observed, with no appearance of pleasure, seeming to avoid looking at me. He knew me through and through.

It infuriated me that he knew me so thoroughly.

"Why not? I am an old schoolfellow of his, too, I believe, and I must own I feel hurt that you have left me out," I said, boiling over again.

"And where were we to find you?" Ferfichkin put in roughly.

"You never were on good terms with Zverkov," Trudolyubov added, frowning.

But I had already clutched at the idea and would not give it up.

"It seems to me that no one has a right to form an opinion upon that," I retorted in a shaking voice, as though something tremendous had happened. "Perhaps that is just my reason for wishing it now, that I have not always been on good terms with him."

"Oh, there's no making you out . . . with these refinements," Trudolyubov jeered.

"We'll put your name down," Simonov decided, addressing me. "To-morrow at five o'clock at the Hôtel de Paris."

"What about the money?" Ferfichkin began in an undertone, indicating me to Simonov, but he broke off, for even Simonov was embarrassed.

"That will do," said Trudolyubov, getting up. "If he wants to come so much, let him."

"But it's a private thing, between us friends," Ferfichkin said crossly, as he, too, picked up his hat. "It's not an official gathering."

"We do not want at all, perhaps . . ."

They went away. Ferfichkin did not greet me in any way as he went out, Trudolyubov barely nodded. Simonov, with whom I was left *tête-à-tête*, was in a state of vexation and perplexity, and looked at me queerly. He did not sit down and did not ask me to.

"H'm . . . yes . . . to-morrow, then. Will you pay your subscription now? I just ask so as to know," he muttered in embarrassment.

I flushed crimson, and as I did so I remembered that I had owed Simonov fifteen roubles for ages—which I had, indeed, never forgotten, though I had not paid it.

"You will understand, Simonov, that I could have no idea when I came here. . . . I am very much vexed that I have forgotten. . . ."

"All right, all right, that doesn't matter. You can pay to-morrow after the dinner. I simply wanted to know. . . . Please don't . . ."

He broke off and began pacing the room still more vexed. As he walked he began to stamp with his heels.

"Am I keeping you?" I asked, after two minutes of silence.

"Oh!" he said, starting, "that is—to be truthful—yes. I have to go and see some one . . . not far from here," he added in an apologetic voice, somewhat abashed.

"My goodness, why didn't you say so?" I cried, seizing my cap, with an astonishingly free-and-easy air, which was the last thing I should have expected of myself.

"It's close by . . . not two paces away," Simonov repeated, accompanying me to the front door with a fussy air which did not suit him at all. "So five o'clock, punctually, to-morrow," he called down the stairs after me. He was very glad to get rid of me. I was in a fury.

"What possessed me, what possessed me to force myself upon them?" I wondered, grinding my teeth as I strode along the street, "for a scoundrel, a pig like that Zverkov! Of course, I had better not go; of course, I must just snap my fingers at them. I am not bound in any way. I'll send Simonov a note by to-morrow's post. . . ."

But what made me furious was that I knew for certain that I should go, that I should make a point of going; and the more tactless, the more unseemly my going would be, the more certainly I would go.

And there was a positive obstacle to my going: I had no money. All I had was nine roubles, I had to give seven of that to my servant, Apollon, for his monthly wages. That was all I paid him—he had to keep himself.

Not to pay him was impossible, considering his character. But I will talk about that fellow, about that plague of mine, another time.

However, I knew I should go and should not pay him his wages.

That night I had the most hideous dreams. No wonder; all the evening I had been oppressed by memories of my miserable days at school, and I could not shake them off. I was sent to the school by distant relations, upon whom I was dependent and of whom I have heard nothing since—they sent me there a forlorn, silent boy, already crushed by their reproaches, already troubled by doubt, and looking with savage distrust at every one. My schoolfellows met me with spiteful and merciless jibes because I was not like any of them. But I could not endure their taunts; I could not give in to them with the ignoble readiness with which they gave in to one another. I hated them from the first, and shut myself away from every one in

timid, wounded and disproportionate pride. Their coarseness revolted me. They laughed cynically at my face, at my clumsy figure;
and yet what stupid faces they had themselves. In our school the
boys' faces seemed in a special way to degenerate and grow stupider.
How many fine-looking boys came to us! In a few years they became
repulsive. Even at sixteen I wondered at them morosely; even then
I was struck by the pettiness of their thoughts, the stupidity of their
pursuits, their games, their conversations. They had no understanding of such essential things, they took no interest in such striking,
impressive subjects, that I could not help considering them inferior
to myself. It was not wounded vanity that drove me to it, and for
God's sake do not thrust upon me your hackneyed remarks, repeated
to nausea, that "I was only a dreamer," while they even then had
an understanding of life. They understood nothing, they had no
idea of real life, and I swear that that was what made me most indignant with them. On the contrary, the most obvious, striking
reality they accepted with fantastic stupidity and even at that time
were accustomed to respect success. Everything that was just, but
oppressed and looked down upon, they laughed at heartlessly and
shamefully. They took rank for intelligence; even at sixteen they
were already talking about a snug berth. Of course, a great deal of
it was due to their stupidity, to the bad examples with which they
had always been surrounded in their childhood and boyhood. They
were monstrously depraved. Of course a great deal of that, too, was
superficial and an assumption of cynicism; of course there were
glimpses of youth and freshness even in their depravity; but even
that freshness was not attractive, and showed itself in a certain rak-
ishness. I hated them horribly, though perhaps I was worse than
any of them. They repaid me in the same way, and did not conceal
their aversion for me. But by then I did not desire their affection:
on the contrary I continually longed for their humiliation. To escape
from their derision I purposely began to make all the progress I
could with my studies and forced my way to the very top. This
impressed them. Moreover, they all began by degrees to grasp that
I had already read books none of them could read, and understood
things (not forming part of our school curriculum) of which they
had not even heard. They took a savage and sarcastic view of it, but
were morally impressed, especially as the teachers began to notice
me on those grounds. The mockery ceased, but the hostility remained, and cold and strained relations became permanent between
us. In the end I could not put up with it: with years a craving for
society, for friends, developed in me. I attempted to get on friendly
terms with some of my schoolfellows; but somehow or other my
intimacy with them was always strained and soon ended of itself.
Once, indeed, I did have a friend. But I was already a tyrant at

heart; I wanted to exercise unbounded sway over him; I tried to instil into him a contempt for his surroundings; I required of him a disdainful and complete break with those surroundings. I frightened him with my passionate affection; I reduced him to tears, to hysterics. He was a simple and devoted soul; but when he devoted himself to me entirely I began to hate him immediately and repulsed him—as though all I needed him for was to win a victory over him, to subjugate him and nothing else. But I could not subjugate all of them; my friend was not at all like them either, he was, in fact, a rare exception. The first thing I did on leaving school was to give up the special job for which I had been destined so as to break all ties, to curse my past and shake the dust from off my feet. . . . And goodness knows why, after all that, I should go trudging off to Simonov's!

Early next morning I roused myself and jumped out of bed with excitement, as though it were all about to happen at once. But I believed that some radical change in my life was coming, and would inevitably come that day. Owing to its rarity, perhaps, any external event, however trivial, always made me feel as though some radical change in my life were at hand. I went to the office, however, as usual, but sneaked away home two hours earlier to get ready. The great thing, I thought, is not to be the first to arrive, or they will think I am overjoyed at coming. But there were thousands of such great points to consider, and they all agitated and overwhelmed me. I polished my boots a second time with my own hands; nothing in the world would have induced Apollon to clean them twice a day, as he considered that it was more than his duties required of him. I stole the brushes to clean them from the passage, being careful he should not detect it, for fear of his contempt. Then I minutely examined my clothes and thought that everything looked old, worn and threadbare. I had let myself get too slovenly. My uniform, perhaps, was tidy, but I could not go out to dinner in my uniform. The worst of it was that on the knee of my trousers was a big yellow stain. I had a foreboding that that stain would deprive me of ninetenths of my personal dignity. I knew, too, that it was very bad to think so. "But this is no time for thinking: now I am in for the real thing," I thought, and my heart sank. I knew, too, perfectly well even then, that I was monstrously exaggerating the facts. But how could I help it? I could not control myself and was already shaking with fever. With despair I pictured to myself how coldly and disdainfully that "scoundrel" Zverkov would meet me; with what dullwitted, invincible contempt the blockhead Trudolyubov would look at me; with what impudent rudeness the insect Ferfichkin would snigger at me in order to curry favour with Zverkov; how completely Simonov would take it all in, and how he would despise me for the abjectness of my vanity and lack of spirit—and, worst of all, how paltry, *unliterary*, commonplace it would all be. Of course, the best thing would be not to go at all. But that was most impossible of all: if I feel impelled to do anything, I seem to be pitchforked into it. I should have jeered at myself ever afterwards: "So you funked it, you funked it, you funked the *real thing!*" On the contrary, I passionately longed to show all that "rabble" that I was by no means such a spiritless creature as I seemed to myself. What is more, even in the acutest paroxysm of this cowardly fever, I dreamed of getting the upper hand, of dominating them, carrying them away, making them like me—if only for my "elevation of thought and unmistakable wit." They would abandon Zverkov, he would sit on one side, silent and ashamed, while I should crush him. Then, perhaps, we would be reconciled and drink to our everlasting friendship; but what was most bitter and most humiliating for me was that I knew even then, knew fully and for certain, that I needed nothing of all this really, that I did not really want to crush, to subdue, to attract them, and that I did not care a straw really for the result, even if I did achieve it. Oh, how I prayed for the day to pass quickly! In unutterable anguish I went to the window, opened the movable pane and looked out into the troubled darkness of the thickly falling wet snow. At last my wretched little clock hissed out five. I seized my hat and trying not to look at Apollon, who had been all day expecting his month's wages, but in his foolishness was unwilling to be the first to speak about it, I slipt between him and the door and jumping into a high-class sledge, on which I spent my last half rouble, I drove up in grand style to the Hôtel de Paris.

IV

I had been certain the day before that I should be the first to arrive. But it was not a question of being the first to arrive. Not only were they not there, but I had difficulty in finding our room. The table was not laid even. What did it mean? After a good many questions I elicited from the waiters that the dinner had been ordered not for five, but for six o'clock. This was confirmed at the buffet too. I felt really ashamed to go on questioning them. It was only twenty-five minutes past five. If they changed the dinner hour they ought at least to have let me know—that is what the post is for, and not to have put me in an absurd position in my own eyes and . . . and even before the waiters. I sat down; the servant began laying the table; I felt even more humiliated when he was present. Towards six o'clock they brought in candles, though there were lamps burning in the room. It had not occurred to the waiter, however, to bring them in at once when I arrived. In the next room two gloomy, angry-looking persons were eating their dinners in silence at two different tables. There was a great deal of noise, even shouting, in a room further away; one could hear the laughter of a crowd of people, and nasty little shrieks in French: there were ladies at the dinner. It was sickening, in fact. I rarely passed more unpleasant moments, so much so that when they did arrive all together punctually at six I was overjoyed to see them, as though they were my deliverers, and even forgot that it was incumbent upon me to show resentment.

Zverkov walked in at the head of them; evidently he was the leading spirit. He and all of them were laughing; but, seeing me, Zverkov drew himself up a little, walked up to me deliberately with a slight, rather jaunty bend from the waist. He shook hands with me in a friendly, but not over-friendly, fashion, with a sort of circumspect courtesy like that of a General, as though in giving me his hand he were warding off something. I had imagined, on the contrary, that on coming in he would at once break into his habitual thin, shrill laugh and fall to making his insipid jokes and witticisms. I had been preparing for them ever since the previous day, but I had not expected such condescension, such high-official courtesy. So, then, he felt himself ineffably superior to me in every respect! If he only meant to insult me by that high-official tone, it would not matter, I thought—I could pay him back for it one way or another. But what if, in reality, without the least desire to be offensive, that sheepshead had a notion in earnest that he was superior to me and could only look at me in a patronizing way? The very supposition made me gasp.

"I was surprised to hear of your desire to join us," he began, lisping and drawling, which was something new. "You and I seem to have seen nothing of one another. You fight shy of us. You shouldn't. We are not such terrible people as you think. Well, anyway, I am glad to renew our acquaintance."

And he turned carelessly to put down his hat on the window.

"Have you been waiting long?" Trudolyubov inquired.

"I arrived at five o'clock as you told me yesterday," I answered aloud, with an irritability that threatened an explosion.

"Didn't you let him know that we had changed the hour?" said Trudolyubov to Simonov.

"No, I didn't. I forgot," the latter replied, with no sign of regret, and without even apologizing to me he went off to order the *hors d'œuvres*.

"So you've been here a whole hour? Oh, poor fellow!" Zverkov cried ironically, for to his notions this was bound to be extremely funny. That rascal Ferfichkin followed with his nasty little snigger like a puppy yapping. My position struck him, too, as exquisitely ludicrous and embarrassing.

"It isn't funny at all!" I cried to Ferfichkin, more and more irritated. "It wasn't my fault, but other people's. They neglected to let me know. It was . . . it was . . . it was simply absurd."

"It's not only absurd, but something else as well," muttered Trudolyubov, naïvely taking my part. "You are not hard enough upon it. It was simply rudeness—unintentional, of course. And how could Simonov . . . h'm!"

"If a trick like that had been played on me," observed Ferfichkin, "I should . . ."

"But you should have ordered something for yourself," Zverkov interrupted, "or simply asked for dinner without waiting for us."

"You will allow that I might have done that without your permission," I rapped out. "If I waited, it was . . ."

"Let us sit down, gentlemen," cried Simonov, coming in. "Everything is ready; I can answer for the champagne; it is capitally frozen. . . . You see, I did not know your address, where was I to look for you?" he suddenly turned to me, but again he seemed to avoid looking at me. Evidently he had something against me. It must have been what happened yesterday.

All sat down; I did the same. It was a round table. Trudolyubov was on my left, Simonov on my right. Zverkov was sitting opposite, Ferfichkin next to him, between him and Trudolyubov.

"Tell me, are you . . . in a government office?" Zverkov went on attending to me. Seeing that I was embarrassed he seriously thought that he ought to be friendly to me, and, so to speak, cheer me up.

"Does he want me to throw a bottle at his head?" I thought, in a fury. In my novel surroundings I was unnaturally ready to be irritated.

"In the N—— office," I answered jerkily, with my eyes on my plate.

"And ha-ave you a go-od berth? I say, what ma-a-de you leave your original job?"

"What ma-a-de me was that I wanted to leave my original job," I drawled more than he, hardly able to control myself. Ferfichkin went off into a guffaw. Simonov looked at me ironically. Trudolyubov left off eating and began looking at me with curiosity.

Zverkov winced, but he tried not to notice it.

"And the remuneration?"

"What remuneration?"

"I mean, your sa-a-lary?"

"Why are you cross-examining me?" However, I told him at once what my salary was. I turned horribly red.

"It is not very handsome," Zverkov observed majestically.

"Yes, you can't afford to dine at cafés on that," Ferfichkin added insolently.

"To my thinking it's very poor," Trudolyubov observed gravely.

"And how thin you have grown! How you have changed!" added Zverkov, with a shade of venom in his voice, scanning me and my attire with a sort of insolent compassion.

"Oh, spare his blushes," cried Ferfichkin, sniggering.

"My dear sir, allow me to tell you I am not blushing," I broke out at last; "do you hear? I am dining here, at this café, at my own expense, not at other people's—note that, Mr. Ferfichkin."

"Wha-at? Isn't every one here dining at his own expense? You would seem to be . . ." Ferfichkin flew out at me, turning as red as a lobster, and looking me in the face with fury.

"Tha-at," I answered, feeling I had gone too far, "and I imagine it would be better to talk of something more intelligent."

"You intend to show off your intelligence, I suppose?"

"Don't disturb yourself, that would be quite out of place here."

"Why are you clacking away like that, my good sir, eh? Have you gone out of your wits in your office?"

"Enough, gentlemen, enough!" Zverkov cried, authoritatively.

"How stupid it is!" muttered Simonov.

"It really is stupid. We have met here, a company of friends, for a farewell dinner to a comrade and you carry on an altercation," said Trudolyubov, rudely addressing himself to me alone. "You invited yourself to join us, so don't disturb the general harmony."

"Enough, enough!" cried Zverkov. "Give over, gentlemen, it's out of place. Better let me tell you how I nearly got married the day before yesterday. . . ."

And then followed a burlesque narrative of how this gentleman had almost been married two days before. There was not a word about the marriage, however, but the story was adorned with generals, colonels and gentlemen-in-waiting, while Zverkov almost took the lead among them. It was greeted with approving laughter; Ferfichkin positively squealed.

No one paid any attention to me, and I sat crushed and humiliated.

"Good Heavens, these are not the people for me!" I thought. "And what a fool I have made of myself before them! I let Ferfichkin go too far, though. The brutes imagine they are doing me an honour in letting me sit down with them. They don't understand that it's an honour to them and not to me! I've grown thinner! My clothes! Oh, damn my trousers! Zverkov noticed the yellow stain on the knee as soon as he came in. . . . But what's the use! I must get up at once, this very minute, take my hat and simply go without a word . . . with contempt! And to-morrow I can send a challenge. The scoundrels! As though I cared about the seven roubles. They may think. . . . Damn it! I don't care about the seven roubles. I'll go this minute!"

Of course I remained. I drank sherry and Lafitte by the glassful in my discomfiture. Being unaccustomed to it, I was quickly affected. My annoyance increased as the wine went to my head. I longed all at once to insult them all in a most flagrant manner and then go away. To seize the moment and show what I could do, so that they would say, "He's clever, though he is absurd," and . . . and . . . in fact, damn them all!

I scanned them all insolently with my drowsy eyes. But they seemed to have forgotten me altogether. They were noisy, vociferous, cheerful. Zverkov was talking all the time. I began listening. Zverkov was talking of some exuberant lady whom he had at last led on to declaring her love (of course, he was lying like a horse), and how he had been helped in this affair by an intimate friend of his, a Prince Kolya, an officer in the hussars, who had three thousand serfs.

"And yet this Kolya, who has three thousand serfs, has not put in an appearance here to-night to see you off," I cut in suddenly.

For a minute every one was silent. "You are drunk already." Trudolyubov deigned to notice me at last, glancing contemptuously in my direction. Zverkov, without a word, examined me as though I were an insect. I dropped my eyes. Simonov made haste to fill up the glasses with champagne.

Trudolyubov raised his glass, as did every one else but me.

"Your health and good luck on the journey!" he cried to Zverkov. "To old times, to our future, hurrah!"

They all tossed off their glasses, and crowded round Zverkov to kiss him. I did not move; my full glass stood untouched before me.

"Why, aren't you going to drink it?" roared Trudolyubov, losing patience and turning menacingly to me.

"I want to make a speech separately, on my own account . . . and then I'll drink it, Mr. Trudolyubov."

"Spiteful brute!" muttered Simonov. I drew myself up in my chair and feverishly seized my glass, prepared for something extraordinary, though I did not know myself precisely what I was going to say.

"*Silence!*" cried Ferfichkin. "Now for a display of wit!"

Zverkov waited very gravely, knowing what was coming.

"Mr. Lieutenant Zverkov," I began, "let me tell you that I hate phrases, phrasemongers and men in corsets . . . that's the first point, and there is a second one to follow it."

There was a general stir.

"The second point is: I hate ribaldry and ribald talkers. Especially ribald talkers! The third point: I love justice, truth and honesty." I went on almost mechanically, for I was beginning to shiver with horror myself and had no idea how I came to be talking like this. "I love thought, Monsieur Zverkov; I love true comradeship, on an equal footing and not . . . H'm . . . I love. . . . But, however, why not? I will drink your health, too, Mr. Zverkov. Seduce the Circassian girls, shoot the enemies of the fatherland and . . . and . . . to your health, Monsieur Zverkov!"

Zverkov got up from his seat, bowed to me and said:

"I am very much obliged to you." He was frightfully offended and turned pale.

"Damn the fellow!" roared Trudolyubov, bringing his fist down on the table.

"Well, he wants a punch in the face for that," squealed Ferfichkin.

"We ought to turn him out," muttered Simonov.

"Not a word, gentlemen, not a movement!" cried Zverkov solemnly, checking the general indignation. "I thank you all, but I can show him for myself how much value I attach to his words."

"Mr. Ferfichkin, you will give me satisfaction to-morrow for your words just now!" I said aloud, turning with dignity to Ferfichkin.

"A duel, you mean? Certainly," he answered. But probably I was so ridiculous as I challenged him and it was so out of keeping with my appearance that everyone, including Ferfichkin, was prostrate with laughter.

"Yes, let him alone, of course! He is quite drunk," Trudolyubov said with disgust.

"I shall never forgive myself for letting him join us," Simonov muttered again.

"Now is the time to throw a bottle at their heads," I thought to myself. I picked up the bottle . . . and filled my glass. . . . "No, I'd better sit on to the end," I went on thinking; "you would be pleased, my friends if I went away. Nothing will induce me to go. I'll go on sitting here and drinking to the end, on purpose, as a sign that I don't think you of the slightest consequence. I will go on sitting and drinking, because this is a public-house and I paid my entrance money. I'll sit here and drink, for I look upon you as so many pawns, as inanimate pawns. I'll sit here and drink . . . and sing if I want to, yes, sing, for I have the right to . . . to sing . . . H'm!"

But I did not sing. I simply tried not to look at any of them. I assumed most unconcerned attitudes and waited with impatience for them to speak *first*. But alas, they did not address me! And oh, how I wished, how I wished at that moment to be reconciled to them! It struck eight, at last nine. They moved from the table to the sofa. Zverkov stretched himself on a lounge and put one foot on a round table. Wine was brought there. He did, as a fact, order three bottles on his own account. I, of course, was not invited to join them. They all sat round him on the sofa. They listened to him, almost with reverence. It was evident that they were fond of him. "What for? What for?" I wondered. From time to time they were moved to drunken enthusiasm and kissed each other. They talked of the Caucasus, of the nature of true passion, of snug berths in the service, of the income of an hussar called Podkharzhevsky, whom none of them knew personally, and rejoiced in the largeness of it, of the extraordinary grace and beauty of a Princess D., whom none of them had ever seen; then it came to Shakespeare's being immortal.

I smiled contemptuously and walked up and down the other side of the room, opposite the sofa, from the table to the stove and back again. I tried my very utmost to show them that I could do without them, and yet I purposely made a noise with my boots, thumping with my heels. But it was all in vain. They paid no attention. I had the patience to walk up and down in front of them from eight o'clock till eleven, in the same place, from the table to the stove and back again. "I walk up and down to please myself and no one can prevent me." The waiter who came into the room stopped, from time to time, to look at me. I was somewhat giddy from turning round so often; at moments it seemed to me that I was in delirium. During those three hours I was three times soaked with sweat and dry again. At times, with an intense, acute pang I was stabbed to the heart by the thought that ten years, twenty years, forty years would pass, and that even in forty years I would remember with loathing and humiliation those filthiest, most ludicrous, and most awful moments of my life. No one could have gone out of his way to degrade himself more shamelessly, and I fully realized it, fully, and yet I went on pacing up and down from the table to the stove. "Oh, if you only knew what thoughts and feelings I am capable of, how cultured I am!" I thought at moments, mentally addressing the sofa on which my enemies were sitting. But my enemies behaved as though I were not in the room. Once —only once—they turned towards me, just when Zverkov was talking about Shakespeare, and I suddenly gave a contemptuous laugh. I laughed in such an affected and disgusting way that they all at once broke off their conversation, and silently and gravely for two minutes watched me walking up and down from the table to the stove, *taking no notice of them.* But nothing came of it: they said nothing, and two minutes later they ceased to notice me again. It struck eleven.

"Friends," cried Zverkov getting up from the sofa, "let us all be off now, *there!*"

"Of course, of course," the others assented. I turned sharply to Zverkov. I was so harassed, so exhausted, that I would have cut my throat to put an end to it. I was in a fever; my hair, soaked with perspiration, stuck to my forehead and temples.

"Zverkov, I beg your pardon," I said abruptly and resolutely. "Ferfichkin, yours too, and every one's, every one's: I have insulted you all!"

"Aha! A duel is not in your line, old man," Ferfichkin hissed venomously.

It sent a sharp pang to my heart.

"No, it's not the duel I am afraid of, Ferfichkin! I am ready to fight you to-morrow, after we are reconciled. I insist upon it, in fact, and you cannot refuse. I want to show you that I am not afraid of a duel. You shall fire first and I shall fire into the air."

"He is comforting himself," said Simonov.

"He's simply raving," said Trudolyubov.

"But let us pass. Why are you barring our way? What do you want?" Zverkov answered disdainfully.

They were all flushed, their eyes were bright: they had been drinking heavily.

"I ask for your friendship, Zverkov; I insulted you, but . . ."

"Insulted? *You* insulted *me*? Understand, sir, that you never, under any circumstances, could possibly insult *me*."

"And that's enough for you. Out of the way!" concluded Trudolyubov.

"Olympia is mine, friends, that's agreed!" cried Zverkov.

"We won't dispute your right, we won't dispute your right," the others answered, laughing.

I stood as though spat upon. The party went noisily out of the room. Trudolyubov struck up some stupid song. Simonov remained behind for a moment to tip the waiters. I suddenly went up to him.

"Simonov! give me six roubles!" I said, with desperate resolution.

He looked at me in extreme amazement, with vacant eyes. He, too, was drunk.

"You don't mean you are coming with us?"

"Yes."

"I've no money," he snapped out, and with a scornful laugh he went out of the room.

I clutched at his overcoat. It was a nightmare.

"Simonov, I saw you had money. Why do you refuse me? Am I a scoundrel? Beware of refusing me: if you knew, if you knew why I am asking! My whole future, my whole plans depend upon it!"

Simonov pulled out the money and almost flung it at me.

"Take it, if you have no sense of shame!" he pronounced pitilessly, and ran to overtake them.

I was left for a moment alone. Disorder, the remains of dinner, a broken wine-glass on the floor, spilt wine, cigarette ends, fumes of drink and delirium in my brain, an agonizing misery in my heart and finally the waiter, who had seen and heard all and was looking inquisitively into my face.

"I am going there!" I cried. "Either they shall all go down on their knees to beg for my friendship, or I will give Zverkov a slap in the face!"

v

"So this is it, this is it at last—contact with real life," I muttered as I ran headlong downstairs. "This is very different from the Pope's leaving Rome and going to Brazil, very different from the ball on Lake Como!"

"You are a scoundrel," a thought flashed through my mind, "if you laugh at this now."

"No matter!" I cried, answering myself. "Now everything is lost!"

There was no trace to be seen of them, but that made no difference—I knew where they had gone.

At the steps was standing a solitary night sledge-driver in a rough peasant coat, powdered over with the still falling, wet, and as it were warm, snow. It was hot and steamy. The little shaggy piebald horse was also covered with snow and coughing, I remember that very well. I made a rush for the roughly made sledge; but as soon as I raised my foot to get into it, the recollection of how Simonov had just given me six roubles seemed to double me up and I tumbled into the sledge like a sack.

"No, I must do a great deal to make up for all that," I cried. "But I will make up for it or perish on the spot this very night. Start!"

We set off. There was a perfect whirl in my head.

"They won't go down on their knees to beg for my friendship. That is a mirage, cheap mirage, revolting, romantic and fantastical —that's another ball on Lake Como. And so I am bound to slap Zverkov's face! It is my duty to. And so it is settled; I am flying to give him a slap in the face. Hurry up!"

The driver tugged at the reins.

"As soon as I go in I'll give it him. Ought I before giving him the slap to say a few words by way of preface? No. I'll simply go in and give it him. They will all be sitting in the drawing-room, and he with Olympia on the sofa. That damned Olympia! She laughed at my looks on one occasion and refused me. I'll pull Olympia's hair, pull Zverkov's ears! No, better one ear, and pull him by it round the room. Maybe they will all begin beating me and will kick me out. That's most likely, indeed. No matter! Anyway, I shall first slap him; the initiative will be mine; and by the laws of honour that is everything: he will be branded and cannot wipe off the slap by any blows, by nothing but a duel. He will be forced to fight. And let them beat me now. Let them, the ungrateful wretches! Trudolyubov will beat me hardest, he is so strong; Ferfichkin will be sure to catch hold sideways and tug at my hair. But no matter, no matter! That's what I am going for. The blockheads will be forced at last to see the tragedy of it all! When they drag me to the door I shall call out to them that in reality they are not worth my little finger. Get on, driver, get on!" I cried to the driver. He started and flicked his whip, I shouted so savagely.

"We shall fight at daybreak, that's a settled thing. I've done with the office. Ferfichkin made a joke about it just now. But where can I get pistols? Nonsense! I'll get my salary in advance and buy them. And powder, and bullets? That's the second's business. And how can it all be done by daybreak? And where am I to get a second? I have no friends. Nonsense!" I cried, lashing myself up more and more. "It's of no consequence! the first person I meet in the street is bound to be my second, just as he would be bound to pull a drowning man out of water. The most eccentric things may happen. Even if I were to ask the director himself to be my second to-morrow, he would be bound to consent, if only from a feeling of chivalry, and to keep the secret! Anton Antonich. . . ."

The fact is, that at that very minute the disgusting absurdity of my plan and the other side of the question was clearer and more vivid to my imagination than it could be to any one on earth. But. . . .

"Get on, driver, get on, you rascal, get on!"

"Ugh, sir!" said the son of toil.

Cold shivers suddenly ran down me.

Wouldn't it be better . . . to go straight home? My God, my God! Why did I invite myself to this dinner yesterday? But no, it's impossible. And my walking up and down for three hours from the table to the stove? No, they, they and no one else must pay for my walking up and down! They must wipe out this dishonour! Drive on!

And what if they give me into custody? They won't dare! They'll be afraid of the scandal. And what if Zverkov is so contemptuous that he refuses to fight a duel? He is sure to; but in that case I'll show them . . . I will turn up at the posting station when he is setting off to-morrow, I'll catch him by the leg, I'll pull off his coat when he gets into the carriage. I'll get my teeth into his hand, I'll bite him. "See what lengths you can drive a desperate man to!"

970 · Fyodor Dostoevsky

He may hit me on the head and they may belabour me from behind. I will shout to the assembled multitude: "Look at this young
puppy who is driving off to captivate the Circassian girls after letting me spit in his face!"

Of course, after that everything will be over! The office will have
vanished off the face of the earth. I shall be arrested, I shall be
tried, I shall be dismissed from the service, thrown in prison, sent to
Siberia. Never mind! In fifteen years when they let me out of prison
I will trudge off to him, a beggar, in rags. I shall find him in some
provincial town. He will be married and happy. He will have a
grown-up daughter. . . . I shall say to him: "Look, monster, at
my hollow cheeks and my rags! I've lost everything—my career, my
happiness, art, science, *the woman I loved*, and all through you.
Here are pistols. I have come to discharge my pistol and . . . and
I . . . forgive you. Then I shall fire into the air and he will hear
nothing more of me. . . ."

I was actually on the point of tears, though I knew perfectly
well at that moment that all this was out of Pushkin's *Silvio*[28] and
Lermontov's *Masquerade*.[29] And all at once I felt horribly ashamed,
so ashamed that I stopped the horse, got out of the sledge, and
stood still in the snow in the middle of the street. The driver gazed
at me, sighing and astonished.

What was I to do? I could not go on there—it was evidently
stupid, and I could not leave things as they were, because that
would seem as though . . . Heavens, how could I leave things!
And after such insults! "No!" I cried, throwing myself into the
sledge again. "It is ordained! It is fate! Drive on, drive on!"

And in my impatience I punched the sledge-driver on the back of
the neck.

"What are you up to? What are you hitting me for?" the peasant
shouted, but he whipped up his nag so that it began kicking.

The wet snow was falling in big flakes; I unbuttoned myself, regardless of it. I forgot everything else, for I had finally decided on
the slap, and felt with horror that it was going to happen *now, at
once*, and that *no force could stop it*. The deserted street lamps
gleamed sullenly in the snowy darkness like torches at a funeral.
The snow drifted under my great-coat, under my coat, under my
cravat, and melted there. I did not wrap myself up—all was lost,
anyway.

At last we arrived. I jumped out, almost unconscious, ran up the
steps and began knocking and kicking at the door. I felt fearfully
weak, particularly in my legs and my knees. The door was opened

28. actually "The Shot" (1830), by
the Russian Poet Alexander Pushkin
(1799–1837), a story in which the hero,
Silvio, finally gives up the idea of re-
venging himself for a slap in the face.
29. a verse play (1835) by the poet
Mikhail Y. Lermontov (1814–1841).

quickly as though they knew I was coming. As a fact, Simonov had warned them that perhaps another gentleman would arrive, and this was a place in which one had to give notice and to observe certain precautions. It was one of those "millinery establishments" which were abolished by the police a good time ago. By day it really was a shop; but at night, if one had an introduction, one might visit it for other purposes.

I walked rapidly through the dark shop into the familiar drawing-room, where there was only one candle burning, and stood still in amazement: there was no one there. "Where are they?" I asked somebody. But by now, of course, they had separated. Before me was standing a person with a stupid smile, the "madam" herself, who had seen me before. A minute later a door opened and another person came in.

Taking no notice of anything I strode about the room, and, I believe, I talked to myself. I felt as though I had been saved from death and was conscious of this, joyfully, all over: I should have given that slap, I should certainly, certainly have given it! But now they were not here and . . . everything had vanished and changed! I looked round. I could not realize my condition yet. I looked mechanically at the girl who had come in: and had a glimpse of a fresh, young, rather pale face, with straight, dark eyebrows, and with grave, as it were wondering, eyes that attracted me at once; I should have hated her if she had been smiling. I began looking at her more intently and, as it were, with effort. I had not fully collected my thoughts. There was something simple and good-natured in her face, but something strangely grave. I am sure that this stood in her way here, and no one of those fools had noticed her. She could not, however, have been called a beauty, though she was tall, strong-looking, and well built. She was very simply dressed. Something loathsome stirred within me. I went straight up to her.

I chanced to look into the glass. My harassed face struck me as revolting in the extreme, pale, angry, abject, with dishevelled hair. "No matter, I am glad of it," I thought; "I am glad that I shall seem repulsive to her; I like that."

VI

. . . Somewhere behind a screen a clock began wheezing, as though oppressed by something, as though some one were strangling it. After an unnaturally prolonged wheezing there followed a shrill, nasty, and as it were unexpectedly rapid, chime—as though some one were suddenly jumping forward. It struck two. I woke up, though I had indeed not been asleep but lying half conscious.

It was almost completely dark in the narrow, cramped, low-pitched room, cumbered up with an enormous wardrobe and piles of cardboard boxes and all sorts of frippery and litter. The candle end that had been burning on the table was going out and gave a faint flicker from time to time. In a few minutes there would be complete darkness.

I was not long in coming to myself; everything came back to my mind at once, without an effort, as though it had been in ambush to pounce upon me again. And, indeed, even while I was unconscious a point seemed continually to remain in my memory unforgotten, and round it my dreams moved drearily. But strange to say, everything that had happened to me in that day seemed to me now, on waking, to be in the far, far away past, as though I had long, long ago lived all that down.

My head was full of fumes. Something seemed to be hovering over me, rousing me, exciting me, and making me restless. Misery and spite seemed surging up in me again and seeking an outlet. Suddenly I saw beside me two wide open eyes scrutinizing me curiously and persistently. The look in those eyes was coldly detached, sullen, as it were utterly remote; it weighed upon me.

A grim idea came into my brain and passed all over my body, as a horrible sensation, such as one feels when one goes into a damp and mouldy cellar. There was something unnatural in those two eyes, beginning to look at me only now. I recalled, too, that during those two hours I had not said a single word to this creature, and had, in fact, considered it utterly superfluous; in fact, the silence had for some reason gratified me. Now I suddenly realized vividly the hideous idea—revolting as a spider—of vice, which, without love, grossly and shamelessly begins with that in which true love finds its consummation. For a long time we gazed at each other like that, but she did not drop her eyes before mine and her expression did not change, so that at last I felt uncomfortable.

"What is your name?" I asked abruptly, to put an end to it.

"Liza," she answered almost in a whisper, but somehow far from graciously, and she turned her eyes away.

I was silent.

"What weather! The snow . . . it's disgusting!" I said, almost to myself, putting my arm under my head despondently, and gazing at the ceiling.

She made no answer. This was horrible.

"Have you always lived in Petersburg?" I asked a minute later, almost angrily, turning my head slightly towards her.

"No."

"Where do you come from?"

"From Riga," she answered reluctantly.

"Are you a German?"

"No, Russian."

"Have you been here long?"

"Where?"

"In this house?"

"A fortnight."

She spoke more and more jerkily. The candle went out; I could no longer distinguish her face.

"Have you a father and mother?"

"Yes . . . no . . . I have."

"Where are they?"

"There . . . in Riga."

"What are they?"

"Oh, nothing."

"Nothing? Why, what class are they?"

"Tradespeople."

"Have you always lived with them?"

"Yes."

"How old are you?"

"Twenty."

"Why did you leave them?"

"Oh, for no reason."

That answer meant "Let me alone; I feel sick, sad."

We were silent.

God knows why I did not go away. I felt myself more and more sick and dreary. The images of the previous day began of themselves, apart from my will, flitting through my memory in confusion. I suddenly recalled something I had seen that morning when, full of anxious thoughts, I was hurrying to the office.

"I saw them carrying a coffin out yesterday and they nearly dropped it," I suddenly said aloud, not that I desired to open the conversation, but as it were by accident.

"A coffin?"

"Yes, in the Haymarket; they were bringing it up out of a cellar."

"From a cellar?"

"Not from a cellar, but from a basement. Oh, you know . . . down below . . . from a house of ill-fame. It was filthy all round . . . Egg-shells, litter . . . stench. It was loathsome."

Silence.

"A nasty day to be buried," I began, simply to avoid being silent.

"Nasty, in what way?"

"The snow, the wet." (I yawned.)

"It makes no difference," she said suddenly, after a brief silence.

"No, it's horrid." (I yawned again.) "The gravediggers must have sworn at getting drenched by the snow. And there must have been water in the grave."

"Why water in the grave?" she asked, with a sort of curiosity, but speaking even more harshly and abruptly than before.

I suddenly began to feel provoked.

"Why, there must have been water at the bottom a foot deep. You can't dig a dry grave in Volkovo Cemetery."

"Why?"

"Why? Why, the place is waterlogged. It's a regular marsh. So they bury them in water. I've seen it myself . . . many times."

(I had never seen it once, indeed I had never been in Volkovo, and had only heard stories of it.)

"Do you mean to say, you don't mind how you die?"

"But why should I die?" she answered, as though defending herself.

"Why, some day you will die, and you will die just the same as that dead woman. She was . . . a girl like you. She died of consumption."

"A wench would have died in a hospital . . ." (She knows all about it already: she said "wench," not "girl.")

"She was in debt to her madam," I retorted, more and more provoked by the discussion; "and went on earning money for her up to the end, though she was in consumption. Some sledge-drivers standing by were talking about her to some soldiers and telling them so. No doubt they knew her. They were laughing. They were going to meet in a pot-house to drink to her memory."

A great deal of this was my invention. Silence followed, profound silence. She did not stir.

"And is it better to die in a hospital?"

"Isn't it just the same? Besides, why should I die?" she added irritably.

"If not now, a little later."

"Why a little later?"

"Why, indeed? Now you are young, pretty, fresh, you fetch a high price. But after another year of this life you will be very different—you will go off."

"In a year?"

"Anyway, in a year you will be worth less," I continued malignantly. "You will go from here to something lower, another house; a year later—to a third, lower and lower, and in seven years you will come to a basement in the Haymarket. That will be if you were lucky. But it would be much worse if you got some disease, consumption, say . . . and caught a chill, or something or other. It's not easy to get over an illness in your way of life. If you catch anything you may not get rid of it. And so you would die."

"Oh, well, then I shall die," she answered, quite vindictively, and she made a quick movement.

"But one is sorry."

"Sorry for whom?"

"Sorry for life."

Silence.

"Have you been engaged to be married? Eh?"

"What's that to you?"

"Oh, I am not cross-examining you. It's nothing to me. Why are you so cross? Of course you may have had your own troubles. What is it to me? It's simply that I felt sorry."

"Sorry for whom?"

"Sorry for you."

"No need," she whispered hardly audibly, and again made a faint movement.

That incensed me at once. What! I was so gentle with her, and she. . . .

"Why, do you think that you are on the right path?"

"I don't think anything."

"That's what's wrong, that you don't think. Realize it while there is still time. There still is time. You are still young, good-looking; you might love, be married, be happy. . . ."

"Not all married women are happy," she snapped out in the rude abrupt tone she had used at first.

"Not all, of course, but anyway it is much better than the life here. Infinitely better. Besides, with love one can live even without happiness. Even in sorrow life is sweet; life is sweet, however one lives. But here what is there but . . . filth? Phew!"

I turned away with disgust; I was no longer reasoning coldly. I began to feel myself what I was saying and warmed to the subject. I was already longing to expound the cherished ideas I had brooded over in my corner. Something suddenly flared up in me. An object had appeared before me.

"Never mind my being here, I am not an example for you. I am, perhaps, worse than you are. I was drunk when I came here, though," I hastened, however, to say in self-defence. "Besides, a man is no example for a woman. It's a different thing. I may degrade and defile myself, but I am not any one's slave. I come and go, and that's an end of it. I shake it off, and I am a different man. But you are a slave from the start. Yes, a slave! You give up everything, your whole freedom. If you want to break your chains afterwards, you won't be able to: you will be more and more fast in the snares. It is an accursed bondage. I know it. I won't speak of anything else, maybe you won't understand, but tell me: no doubt you are in debt to your madam? There, you see," I added, though she made no answer, but only listened in silence, entirely absorbed, "that's a bondage for you! You will never buy your freedom. They will see to that. It's like selling your soul to the devil. . . . And besides . . . perhaps I, too, am just as unlucky—how do you know

—and wallow in the mud on purpose, out of misery? You know, men take to drink from grief; well, maybe I am here from grief. Come, tell me, what is there good here? Here you and I . . . came together . . . just now and did not say one word to one another all the time, and it was only afterwards you began staring at me like a wild creature, and I at you. Is that loving? Is that how one human being should meet another? It's hideous, that's what it is!"

"Yes!" she assented sharply and hurriedly.

I was positively astounded by the promptitude of this "Yes." So the same thought may have been straying through her mind when she was staring at me just before. So she, too, was capable of certain thoughts? "Damn it all, this was interesting, this was a point of likeness!" I thought, almost rubbing my hands. And indeed it's easy to turn a young soul like that!

It was the exercise of my power that attracted me most.

She turned her head nearer to me, and it seemed to me in the darkness that she propped herself on her arm. Perhaps she was scrutinizing me. How I regretted that I could not see her eyes. I heard her deep breathing.

"Why have you come here?" I asked her, with a note of authority already in my voice.

"Oh, I don't know."

"But how nice it would be to be living in your father's house! It's warm and free; and you have a home of your own."

"But what if it's worse than this?"

"I must take the right tone," flashed through my mind. "I may not get far with sentimentality." But it was only a momentary thought. I swear she really did interest me. Besides, I was exhausted and moody. And cunning so easily goes hand-in-hand with feeling.

"Who denies it!" I hastened to answer. "Anything may happen. I am convinced that some one has wronged you, and that you are more sinned against than sinning. Of course, I know nothing of your story, but it's not likely a girl like you has come here of her own inclination. . . ."

"A girl like me?" she whispered, hardly audibly; but I heard it.

Damn it all, I was flattering her. That was horrid. But perhaps it was a good thing. . . . She was silent.

"See, Liza, I will tell you about myself. If I had had a home from childhood, I shouldn't be what I am now. I often think that. However bad it may be at home, anyway they are your father and mother, and not enemies, strangers. Once a year at least, they'll show their love of you. Anyway, you know you are at home. I grew up without a home; and perhaps that's why I've turned so . . . unfeeling."

I waited again. "Perhaps she doesn't understand," I thought, "and, indeed, it is absurd—it's moralizing."

"If I were a father and had a daughter, I believe I should love my daughter more than my sons, really," I began indirectly, as though talking of something else, to distract her attention. I must confess I blushed.

"Why so?" she asked.

Ah! so she was listening!

"I don't know, Liza. I knew a father who was a stern, austere man, but used to go down on his knees to his daughter, used to kiss her hands, her feet, he couldn't make enough of her, really. When she danced at parties he used to stand for five hours at a stretch, gazing at her. He was mad over her: I understand that! She would fall asleep tired at night, and he would wake to kiss her in her sleep and make the sign of the cross over her. He would go about in a dirty old coat, he was stingy to every one else, but would spend his last penny for her, giving her expensive presents, and it was his greatest delight when she was pleased with what he gave her. Fathers always love their daughters more than the mothers do. Some girls live happily at home! And I believe I should never let my daughters marry."

"What next?" she said, with a faint smile.

"I should be jealous, I really should. To think that she should kiss any one else! That she should love a stranger more than her father! It's painful to imagine it. Of course, that's all nonsense, of course every father would be reasonable at last. But I believe before I should let her marry, I should worry myself to death; I should find fault with all her suitors. But I should end by letting her marry whom she herself loved. The one whom the daughter loves always seems the worst to the father, you know. That is always so. So many family troubles come from that."

"Some are glad to sell their daughters, rather than marrying them honourably."

Ah, so that was it!

"Such a thing, Liza, happens in those accursed families in which there is neither love nor God," I retorted warmly, "and where there is no love, there is no sense either. There are such families, it's true, but I am not speaking of them. You must have seen wickedness in your own family, if you talk like that. Truly, you must have been unlucky. H'm! . . . that sort of thing mostly comes about through poverty."

"And is it any better with the gentry? Even among the poor, honest people live happily."

"H'm . . . yes. Perhaps. Another thing, Liza, man is fond of reckoning up his troubles, but does not count his joys. If he counted them up as he ought, he would see that every lot has enough happiness provided for it. And what if all goes well with the family, if the blessing of God is upon it, if the husband is a good one, loves you, cherishes you, never leaves you! There is happiness in such a family! Even sometimes there is happiness in the midst of sorrow; and indeed sorrow is everywhere. If you marry *you will find out for yourself*. But think of the first years of married life with one you love: what happiness, what happiness there sometimes is in it! And indeed it's the ordinary thing. In those early days even quarrels with one's husband end happily. Some women get up quarrels with their husbands just because they love them. Indeed, I knew a woman like that: she seemed to say that because she loved him, she would torment him and make him feel it. You know that you may torment a man on purpose through love. Women are particularly given to that, thinking to themselves 'I will love him so, I will make so much of him afterwards, that it's no sin to torment him a little now.' And all in the house rejoice in the sight of you, and you are happy and gay and peaceful and honourable. . . . Then there are some women who are jealous. If he went off anywhere—I knew one such woman, she couldn't restrain herself, but would jump up at night and run off on the sly to find out where he was, whether he was with some other woman. That's a pity. And the woman knows herself it's wrong, and her heart fails her and she suffers, but she loves—it's all through love. And how sweet it is to make it up after quarrels, to own herself in the wrong or to forgive him! And they are both so happy all at once—as though they had met anew, been married over again; as though their love had begun afresh. And no one, no one should know what passes between husband and wife if they love one another. And whatever quarrels there may be between them they ought not to call in their own mother to judge between them and tell tales of one another. They are their own judges. Love is a holy mystery and ought to be hidden from all other eyes, whatever happens. That makes it holier and better. They respect one another more, and much is built on respect. And if once there has been love, if they have been married for love, why should love pass away? Surely one can keep it! It is rare that one cannot keep it. And if the husband is kind and straightforward, why should not love last? The first phase of married love will pass, it is true, but then there will come a love that is better still. Then there will be the union of souls, they will have everything in common, there will be no secrets between them. And once they have children, the most difficult times will seem to them happy, so long as there is love and courage. Even toil will be a joy, you may deny yourself bread for your children and even that will be a joy. They will love you for it afterwards; so you are laying by for your future. As the children grow up you feel that you are an example, a support for them; that even after you die your children will always keep your thoughts and feelings, because they have received them from you, they will take on your semblance and likeness. So you see this is a great duty. How can it fail to draw the father and mother nearer? People say it's a trial to have children. Who says that? It is heavenly happiness! Are you fond of little children, Liza? I am awfully fond of them. You know—a little rosy baby boy at your bosom, and what husband's heart is not touched, seeing his wife nursing his child! A plump little rosy baby, sprawling and snuggling, chubby little hands and feet, clean tiny little nails, so tiny that it makes one laugh to look at them; eyes that look as if they understand everything. And while it sucks it clutches at your bosom with its little hand, plays. When its father comes up, the child tears itself away from the bosom, flings itself back, looks at its father, laughs, as though it were fearfully funny and falls to sucking again. Or it will bite its mother's breast when its little teeth are coming, while it looks sideways at her with its little eyes as though to say, 'Look, I am biting!' Is not all that happiness when they are the three together, husband, wife and child? One can forgive a great deal for the sake of such moments. Yes, Liza, one must first learn to live oneself before one blames others!"

"It's by pictures, pictures like that one must get at you," I thought to myself, though I did speak with real feeling, and all at once I flushed crimson. "What if she were suddenly to burst out laughing, what should I do then?" That idea drove me to fury. Towards the end of my speech I really was excited, and now my vanity was somehow wounded. The silence continued. I almost nudged her.

"Why are you——" she began and stopped. But I understood: there was a quiver of something different in her voice, not abrupt, harsh and unyielding as before, but something soft and shamefaced, so shamefaced that I suddenly felt ashamed and guilty.

"What?" I asked, with tender curiosity.

"Why, you . . ."

"What?"

"Why, you . . . speak somehow like a book," she said, and again there was a note of irony in her voice.

That remark sent a pang to my heart. It was not what I was expecting.

I did not understand that she was hiding her feelings under irony, that this is usually the last refuge of modest and chaste-souled people when the privacy of their soul is coarsely and intrusively invaded, and that their pride makes them refuse to surrender till the last moment and shrink from giving expression to their feelings before you. I ought to have guessed the truth from the timidity with which she had repeatedly approached her sarcasm, only bringing herself to utter it at last with an effort. But I did not guess, and an evil feeling took possession of me.

"Wait a bit!" I thought.

VII

"Oh, hush, Liza! How can you talk about being like a book, when it makes even me, an outsider, feel sick? Though I don't look at it as an outsider, for, indeed, it touches me to the heart. . . . Is it possible, is it possible that you do not feel sick at being here yourself? Evidently habit does wonders! God knows what habit can do with any one. Can you seriously think that you will never grow old, that you will always be good-looking, and that they will keep you here for ever and ever? I say nothing of the loathsomeness of the life here. . . . Though let me tell you this about it—about your present life, I mean; here though you are young now, attractive, nice, with soul and feeling, yet you know as soon as I came to myself just now I felt at once sick at being here with you! One can only come here when one is drunk. But if you were anywhere else, living as good people live, I should perhaps be more than attracted by you, should fall in love with you, should be glad of a look from you, let alone a word; I should hang about your door, should go down on my knees to you, should look upon you as my betrothed and think it an honour to be allowed to. I should not dare to have an impure thought about you. But here, you see, I know that I have only to whistle and you have to come with me whether you like it or not. I don't consult your wishes, but you mine. The lowest labourer hires himself as a workman, but he doesn't make a slave of himself altogether; besides, he knows that he will be free again presently. But when are you free? Only think what you are giving up here? What is it you are making a slave of? It is your soul, together with your body; you are selling your soul which you have no right to dispose of! You give your love to be outraged by every drunkard! Love! But that's everything, you know, it's a priceless diamond, it's a maiden's treasure, love—why, a man would be ready to give his soul, to face death to gain that love. But how much is your love worth now? You are sold, all of you, body and soul, and there is no need to strive for love when you can have everything without love. And you know there is no greater insult to a girl than that, do you understand? To be sure, I have heard that they comfort you, poor fools, they let you have lovers of your own here. But you know that's simply a farce, that's simply a sham, it's just laughing at you, and you are taken in by it! Why, do you suppose he really loves you, that lover of yours? I don't believe it. How can he love you when he knows you may be called away from him any minute?

He would be a low fellow if he did! Will he have a grain of respect
for you? What have you in common with him? He laughs at you
and robs you—that is all his love amounts to! You are lucky if he
does not beat you. Very likely he does beat you, too. Ask him, if
you have got one, whether he will marry you. He will laugh in your
face, if he doesn't spit in it or give you a blow—though maybe he
is not worth a bad halfpenny himself. And for what have you ruined
your life, if you come to think of it? For the coffee they give you to
drink and the plentiful meals? But with what object are they feeding
you up? An honest girl couldn't swallow the food, for she would
know what she was being fed for. You are in debt here, and, of
course, you will always be in debt, and you will go on in debt to the
end, till the visitors here begin to scorn you. And that will soon
happen, don't rely upon your youth—all that flies by express train
here, you know. You will be kicked out. And not simply kicked out;
long before that she'll begin nagging at you, scolding you, abusing
you, as though you had not sacrificed your health for her, had not
thrown away your youth and your soul for her benefit, but as though
you had ruined her, beggared her, robbed her. And don't expect
any one to take your part: the others, your companions, will attack
you, too, to win her favour, for all are in slavery here, and have lost
all conscience and pity here long ago. They have become utterly
vile, and nothing on earth is viler, more loathsome, and more insulting than their abuse. And you are laying down everything here, unconditionally, youth and health and beauty and hope, and at twenty-
two you will look like a woman of five-and-thirty, and you will be
lucky if you are not diseased, pray to God for that! No doubt you
are thinking now that you have a gay time and no work to do! Yet
there is no work harder or more dreadful in the world or ever has
been. One would think that the heart alone would be worn out with
tears. And you won't dare to say a word, not half a word when they
drive you away from here; you will go away as though you were to
blame. You will change to another house, then to a third, then
somewhere else, till you come down at last to the Haymarket. There
you will be beaten at every turn; that is good manners there, the
visitors don't know how to be friendly without beating you. You
don't believe that it is so hateful there? Go and look for yourself
some time, you can see with your own eyes. Once, one New Year's
Day, I saw a woman at a door. They had turned her out as a joke,
to give her a taste of the frost because she had been crying so much,
and they shut the door behind her. At nine o'clock in the morning
she was already quite drunk, dishevelled, half-naked, covered with
bruises, her face was powdered, but she had a black-eye, blood was
trickling from her nose and her teeth; some cabman had just given
her a drubbing. She was sitting on the stone steps, a salt fish of some

sort was in her hand; she was crying, wailing something about her luck and beating with the fish on the steps, and cabmen and drunken soldiers were crowding in the doorway taunting her. You don't believe that you will ever be like that? I should be sorry to believe it, too, but how do you know; maybe ten years, eight years ago that very woman with the salt fish came here fresh as a cherub, innocent, pure, knowing no evil, blushing at every word. Perhaps she was like you, proud, ready to take offence, not like the others; perhaps she looked like a queen, and knew what happiness was in store for the man who should love her and whom she should love. Do you see how it ended? And what if at that very minute when she was beating on the filthy steps with that fish, drunken and dishevelled— what if at that very minute she recalled the pure early days in her father's house, when she used to go to school and the neighbour's son watched for her on the way, declaring that he would love her as long as he lived, that he would devote his life to her, and when they vowed to love one another for ever and be married as soon as they were grown up! No, Liza, it would be happy for you if you were to die soon of consumption in some corner, in some cellar like that woman just now. In the hospital, do you say? You will be lucky if they take you, but what if you are still of use to the madam here? Consumption is a queer disease, it is not like fever. The patient goes on hoping till the last minute and says he is all right. He deludes himself. And that just suits your madam. Don't doubt it, that's how it is; you have sold your soul, and what is more you owe money, so you daren't say a word. But when you are dying, all will abandon you, all will turn away from you, for then there will be nothing to get from you. What's more, they will reproach you for cumbering the place, for being so long over dying. However you beg you won't get a drink of water without abuse: 'Whenever are you going off, you nasty hussy, you won't let us sleep with your moaning, you make the gentlemen sick.' That's true, I have heard such things said myself. They will thrust you dying into the filthiest corner in the cellar—in the damp and darkness; what will your thoughts be, lying there alone? When you die, strange hands will lay you out, with grumbling and impatience; no one will bless you, no one will sigh for you, they only want to get rid of you as soon as may be; they will buy a coffin, take you to the grave as they did that poor woman to-day, and celebrate your memory at the tavern. In the gravest sleet, filth, wet snow—no need to put themselves out for you—'Let her down, Vanyukha; it's just like her luck—even here, she is head-foremost, the hussy. Shorten the cord, you rascal.' 'It's all right as it is.' 'All right, is it? Why, she's on her side! She was a fellow-creature, after all! But, never mind, throw the earth on her.' And they won't care to waste much time quarrelling over you. They will scatter the wet blue clay as quick as they can and go off to the tavern . . . and there your memory on earth will end; other women have children to go to their graves, fathers, husbands. While for you neither tear, nor sigh, nor remembrance; no one in the whole world will ever come to you, your name will vanish from the face of the earth —as though you had never existed, never been born at all! Nothing but filth and mud, however you knock at your coffin lid at night, when the dead arise, however you cry: 'Let me out, kind people, to live in the light of day! My life was no life at all; my life has been thrown away like a dish-clout; it was drunk away in the tavern at the Haymarket; let me out, kind people, to live in the world again.' "

And I worked myself up to such a pitch that I began to have a lump in my throat myself, and . . . and all at once I stopped, sat up in dismay, and bending over apprehensively, began to listen with a beating heart. I had reason to be troubled.

I had felt for some time that I was turning her soul upside down and rending her heart, and—and the more I was convinced of it, the more eagerly I desired to gain my object as quickly and as effectually as possible. It was the exercise of my skill that carried me away; yet it was not merely sport. . . .

I knew I was speaking stiffly, artificially, even bookishly, in fact, I could not speak except "like a book." But that did not trouble me: I knew, I felt that I should be understood and that this very bookishness might be an assistance. But now, having attained my effect, I was suddenly panic-stricken. Never before had I witnessed such despair! She was lying on her face, thrusting her face into the pillow and clutching it in both hands. Her heart was being torn. Her youthful body was shuddering all over as though in convulsions. Suppressed sobs rent her bosom and suddenly burst out in weeping and wailing, then she pressed closer into the pillow: she did not want any one here, not a living soul, to know of her anguish and her tears. She bit the pillow, bit her hand till it bled (I saw that afterwards), or, thrusting her fingers into her dishevelled hair seemed rigid with the effort of restraint, holding her breath and clenching her teeth. I began saying something, begging her to calm herself, but felt that I did not dare; and all at once, in a sort of cold shiver, almost in terror, began fumbling in the dark, trying hurriedly to get dressed to go. It was dark: though I tried my best I could not finish dressing quickly. Suddenly I felt a box of matches and a candlestick with a whole candle in it. As soon as the room was lighted up, Liza sprang up, sat up in bed, and with a contorted face, with a half insane smile, looked at me almost senselessly. I sat down beside her

and took her hands; she came to herself, made an impulsive movement towards me, would have caught hold of me, but did not dare,
and slowly bowed her head before me.

"Liza, my dear, I was wrong . . . forgive me, my dear," I began,
but she squeezed my hand in her fingers so tightly that I felt I was
saying the wrong thing and stopped.

"This is my address, Liza, come to me."

"I will come," she answered resolutely, her head still bowed.

"But now I am going, good-bye . . . till we meet again."

I got up; she, too, stood up and suddenly flushed all over, gave a
shudder, snatched up a shawl that was lying on a chair and muffled
herself in it to her chin. As she did this she gave another sickly
smile, blushed and looked at me strangely. I felt wretched; I was in
haste to get away—to disappear.

"Wait a minute," she said suddenly, in the passage just at the
doorway, stopping me with her hand on my overcoat. She put down
the candle in hot haste and ran off; evidently she had thought of
something or wanted to show me something. As she ran away she
flushed, her eyes shone, and there was a smile on her lips—what was
the meaning of it? Against my will I waited: she came back a minute
later with an expression that seemed to ask forgiveness for something. In fact, it was not the same face, not the same look as the
evening before: sullen, mistrustful and obstinate. Her eyes now were
imploring, soft, and at the same time trustful, caressing, timid. The
expression with which children look at people they are very fond of,
of whom they are asking a favour. Her eyes were a light hazel, they
were lovely eyes, full of life, and capable of expressing love as well as
sullen hatred.

Making no explanation, as though I, as a sort of higher being,
must understand everything without explanations, she held out a
piece of paper to me. Her whole face was positively beaming at that
instant with naïve, almost childish, triumph. I unfolded it. It was a
letter to her from a medical student or some one of that sort—a
very high-flown and flowery, but extremely respectful, love-letter.
I don't recall the words now, but I remember well that through the
high-flown phrases there was apparent a genuine feeling, which cannot be feigned. When I had finished reading it I met her glowing,
questioning, and childishly impatient eyes fixed upon me. She fastened her eyes upon my face and waited impatiently for what I
should say. In a few words, hurriedly, but with a sort of joy and
pride, she explained to me that she had been to a dance somewhere
in a private house, a family of "very nice people *who knew nothing,*
absolutely nothing, for she had only come here so lately and it had
all happened . . . and she hadn't made up her mind to stay and
was certainly going away as soon as she had paid her debt . . ."

and at that party there had been the student who had danced with her all the evening. He had talked to her, and it turned out that he had known her in old days at Riga when he was a child, they had played together, but a very long time ago—and he knew her parents, but *about this* he knew nothing, nothing whatever, and had no suspicion! And the day after the dance (three days ago) he had sent her that letter through the friend with whom she had gone to the party . . . and . . . well, that was all."

She dropped her shining eyes with a sort of bashfulness as she finished.

The poor girl was keeping that student's letter as a precious treasure, and had run to fetch it, her only treasure, because she did not want me to go away without knowing that she, too, was honestly and genuinely loved; that she, too, was addressed respectfully. No doubt that letter was destined to lie in her box and lead to nothing. But none the less, I am certain that she would keep it all her life as a precious treasure, as her pride and justification, and now at such a minute she had thought of that letter and brought it with naïve pride to raise herself in my eyes that I might see, that I, too, might think well of her. I said nothing, pressed her hand and went out. I so longed to get away. . . . I walked all the way home, in spite of the fact that the melting snow was still falling in heavy flakes. I was exhausted, shattered, in bewilderment. But behind the bewilderment the truth was already gleaming. The loathsome truth.

VIII

It was some time, however, before I consented to recognize that truth. Waking up in the morning after some hours of heavy, leaden sleep, and immediately realizing all that had happened on the previous day, I was positively amazed at my last night's *sentimentality* with Liza, at all those "outcries of horror and pity." "To think of having such an attack of womanish hysteria, pah!" I concluded. And what did I thrust my address upon her for? What if she comes? Let her come, though; it doesn't matter. . . . But *obviously*, that was not now the chief and the most important matter: I had to make haste and at all costs save my reputation in the eyes of Zverkov and Simonov as quickly as possible; that was the chief business. And I was so taken up that morning that I actually forgot all about Liza.

First of all I had at once to repay what I had borrowed the day before from Simonov. I resolved on a desperate measure: to borrow fifteen roubles straight off from Anton Antonich. As luck would have it he was in the best of humours that morning, and gave it to me at once, on the first asking. I was so delighted at this that, as I signed the I O U with a swaggering air, I told him casually that the night before "I had been keeping it up with some friends at the Hôtel de Paris; we were giving a farewell party to a comrade, in fact,

I might say a friend of my childhood, and you know—a desperate rake, fearfully spoilt—of course, he belongs to a good family, and has considerable means, a brilliant career; he is witty, charming, a regular Lovelace, you understand; we drank an extra 'half-dozen' and . . ."

And it went off all right; all this was uttered very easily, unconstrainedly and complacently.

On reaching home I promptly wrote to Simonov.

To this hour I am lost in admiration when I recall the truly gentlemanly, good-humoured, candid tone of my letter. With tact and good-breeding, and, above all, entirely without superfluous words, I blamed myself for all that had happened. I defended myself, "if I really may be allowed to defend myself," by alleging that being utterly unaccustomed to wine, I had been intoxicated with the first glass, which I said, I had drunk before they arrived, while I was waiting for them at the Hôtel de Paris between five and six o'clock. I begged Simonov's pardon especially; I asked him to convey my explanations to all the others, especially to Zverkov, whom "I seemed to remember as though in a dream" I had insulted. I added that I would have called upon all of them myself, but my head ached, and besides I had not the face to. I was particularly pleased with a certain lightness, almost carelessness (strictly within the bounds of politeness, however), which was apparent in my style, and better than any possible arguments, gave them at once to understand that I took rather an independent view of "all that unpleasantness last night;" that I was by no means so utterly crushed as you, my friends, probably imagine; but on the contrary, looked upon it as a gentleman serenely respecting himself should look upon it. "On a young hero's past no censure is cast!"

"There is actually an aristocratic playfulness about it!" I thought admiringly, as I read over the letter. And it's all because I am an intellectual and cultivated man! Another man in my place would not have known how to extricate himself, but here I have got out of it and am as jolly as ever again, and all because I am "a cultivated and educated man of our day." And, indeed, perhaps, everything was due to the wine yesterday. H'm! . . . no, it was not the wine. I did not drink anything at all between five and six when I was waiting for them. I had lied to Simonov; I had lied shamelessly; and indeed I wasn't ashamed now. . . . Hang it all though, the great thing was that I was rid of it.

I put six roubles in the letter, sealed it up, and asked Apollon to take it to Simonov. When he learned that there was money in the letter, Apollon became more respectful and agreed to take it. Towards evening I went out for a walk. My head was still aching and giddy after yesterday. But as evening came on and the twilight grew denser, my impressions and, following them, my thoughts, grew more and more different and confused. Something was not dead within me, in the depths of my heart and conscience it would not die, and it showed itself in acute depression. For the most part I jostled my way through the most crowded business streets, along Myeshchansky Street, along Sadovy Street and in Yusupov Garden. I always liked particularly sauntering along these streets in the dusk, just when there were crowds of working people of all sorts going home from their daily work, with faces looking cross with anxiety. What I liked was just that cheap bustle, that bare prose. On this occasion the jostling of the streets irritated me more than ever. I could not make out what was wrong with me, I could not find the clue, something seemed rising up continually in my soul, painfully, and refusing to be appeased. I returned home completely upset, it was just as though some crime were lying on my conscience.

The thought that Liza was coming worried me continually. It seemed queer to me that of all my recollections of yesterday this tormented me, as it were, especially, as it were, quite separately. Everything else I had quite succeeded in forgetting by the evening; I dismissed it all and was still perfectly satisfied with my letter to Simonov. But on this point I was not satisfied at all. It was as though I were worried only by Liza. "What if she comes," I thought incessantly, "well, it doesn't matter, let her come! H'm! it's horrid that she should see, for instance, how I live. Yesterday I seemed such a hero to her, while now, h'm! It's horrid, though, that I have let myself go so, the room looks like a beggar's. And I brought myself to go out to dinner in such a suit! And my American leather sofa with the stuffing sticking out. And my dressing-gown, which will not cover me, such tatters, and she will see all this and she will see Apollon. That beast is certain to insult her. He will fasten upon her in order to be rude to me. And I, of course, shall be panic-stricken as usual, I shall begin bowing and scraping before her and pulling my dressing-gown round me, I shall begin smiling, telling lies. Oh, the beastliness! And it isn't the beastliness of it that matters most! There is something more important, more loathsome, viler! Yes, viler! And to put on that dishonest lying mask again!" . . .

When I reached that thought I fired up all at once.

"Why dishonest? How dishonest? I was speaking sincerely last night. I remember there was real feeling in me, too. What I wanted was to excite an honourable feeling in her. . . . Her crying was a good thing, it will have a good effect."

Yet I could not feel at ease. All that evening, even when I had come back home, even after nine o'clock, when I calculated that Liza could not possibly come, she still haunted me, and what was worse, she came back to my mind always in the same position. One moment out of all that had happened last night stood vividly before my imagination; the moment when I struck a match and saw her pale, distorted face, with its look of torture. And what a pitiful, what an unnatural, what a distorted smile she had at that moment! But I did not know then, that fifteen years later I should still in my imagination see Liza, always with the pitiful, distorted, inappropriate smile which was on her face at that minute.

Next day I was ready again to look upon it all as nonsense, due to over-excited nerves, and, above all, as *exaggerated*. I was always conscious of that weak point of mine, and sometimes very much afraid of it. "I exaggerate everything, that is where I go wrong," I repeated to myself every hour. But, however, "Liza will very likely come all the same," was the refrain with which all my reflections ended. I was so uneasy that I sometimes flew into a fury: "She'll come, she is certain to come!" I cried, running about the room, "if not to-day, she will come to-morrow; she'll find me out! The damnable romanticism of these pure hearts! Oh, the vileness—oh, the silliness—oh, the stupidity of these 'wretched sentimental souls!' Why, how fail to understand? How could one fail to understand? . . ."

But at this point I stopped short, and in great confusion, indeed.

And how few, how few words, I thought, in passing, were needed; how little of the idyllic (and affectedly, bookishly, artificially idyllic too) had sufficed to turn a whole human life at once according to my will. That's virginity, to be sure! Freshness of soil!

At times a thought occurred to me, to go to her, "to tell her all," and beg her not to come to me. But this thought stirred such wrath in me that I believed I should have crushed that "damned" Liza if she had chanced to be near me at the time. I should have insulted her, have spat at her, have turned her out, have struck her!

One day passed, however, another and another; she did not come and I began to grow calmer. I felt particularly bold and cheerful after nine o'clock, I even sometimes began dreaming, and rather sweetly: I, for instance, became the salvation of Liza, simply through her coming to me and my talking to her. . . . I develop her, educate her. Finally, I notice that she loves me, loves me passionately. I pretend not to understand (I don't know, however, why I pretend, just for effect, perhaps). At last all confusion, transfigured, trembling and sobbing, she flings herself at my feet and says that I am her saviour, and that she loves me better than anything in the world. I am amazed, but. . . . "Liza," I say, "can you imagine that I have not noticed your love, I saw it all, I divined it, but I did not dare to approach you first, because I had an influence over you and was afraid that you would force yourself, from gratitude, to respond to my love, would try to rouse in your heart a

feeling which was perhaps absent, and I did not wish that . . . because it would be tyranny . . . it would be indelicate (in short, I
launch off at that point into European, inexplicably lofty subtleties à la George Sand[30]), but now, now you are mine, you are
my creation, you are pure, you are good, you are my noble wife.

> 'Into my house come bold and free,
> Its rightful mistress there to be.' "[31]

Then we begin living together, go abroad and so on, and so on.
In fact, in the end it seemed vulgar to me myself, and I began putting out my tongue at myself.

Besides, they won't let her out, "the hussy!" I thought. They
don't let them go out very readily, especially in the evening (for
some reason I fancied she would come in the evening, and at seven
o'clock precisely). Though she did say she was not altogether a
slave there yet, and had certain rights; so, h'm! Damn it all, she
will come, she is sure to come!

It was a good thing, in fact, that Apollon distracted my attention
at that time by his rudeness. He drove me beyond all patience! He
was the bane of my life, the curse laid upon me by Providence. We
had been squabbling continually for years, and I hated him. My
God, how I hated him! I believe I had never hated any one in my
life as I hated him, especially at some moments. He was an elderly,
dignified man, who worked part of his time as a tailor. But for some
unknown reason he despised me beyond all measure, and looked
down upon me insufferably. Though, indeed, he looked down upon
every one. Simply to glance at that flaxen, smoothly brushed head,
at the tuft of hair he combed up on his forehead and oiled with
sunflower oil, at that dignified mouth, compressed into the shape
of the letter V, made one feel one was confronting a man who never
doubted of himself. He was a pedant, to the most extreme point,
the greatest pedant I had met on earth, and with that had a vanity
only befitting Alexander of Macedon. He was in love with every button on his coat, every nail on his fingers—absolutely in love with
them, and he looked it! In his behaviour to me he was a perfect
tyrant, he spoke very little to me, and if he chanced to glance at me
he gave me a firm, majestically self-confident and invariably ironical
look that drove me sometimes to fury. He did his work with the air
of doing me the greatest favour. Though he did scarcely anything
for me, and did not, indeed, consider himself bound to do anything.
There could be no doubt that he looked upon me as the greatest
fool on earth, and that "he did not get rid of me" was simply that

30. pseudonym of the French woman
novelist Mme. Aurore Dudevant (1804–
1876), famous also as a promoter of
feminism.

31. the last lines of the poem by
Nekrasov used as the epigraph of Part
II of this story.

he could get wages from me every month. He consented to do nothing for me for seven roubles a month. Many sins should be forgiven me for what I suffered from him. My hatred reached such a point that sometimes his very step almost threw me into convulsions. What I loathed particularly was his lisp. His tongue must have been a little too long or something of that sort, for he continually lisped, and seemed to be very proud of it, imagining that it greatly added to his dignity. He spoke in a slow, measured tone, with his hands behind his back and his eyes fixed on the ground. He maddened me particularly when he read aloud the psalms to himself behind his partition. Many a battle I waged over that reading! But he was awfully fond of reading aloud in the evenings, in a slow, even, sing-song voice, as though over the dead. It is interesting that that is how he has ended: he hires himself out to read the psalms over the dead, and at the same time he kills rats and makes blacking. But at that time I could not get rid of him, it was as though he were chemically combined with my existence. Besides, nothing would have induced him to consent to leave me. I could not live in furnished lodgings: my lodging was my private solitude, my shell, my cave, in which I concealed myself from all mankind, and Apollon seemed to me, for some reason, an integral part of that flat, and for seven years I could not turn him away.

To be two or three days behind with his wages, for instance, was impossible. He would have made such a fuss, I should not have known where to hide my head. But I was so exasperated with every one during those days, that I made up my mind for some reason and with some object to *punish* Apollon and not to pay him for a fortnight the wages that were owing him. I had for a long time—for the last two years—been intending to do this, simply in order to teach him not to give himself airs with me, and to show him that if I liked I could withhold his wages. I purposed to say nothing to him about it, and was purposely silent indeed, in order to score off his pride and force him to be the first to speak of his wages. Then I would take the seven roubles out of a drawer, show him I have the money put aside on purpose, but that I won't, I won't, I simply won't pay him his wages, I won't just because that is "what I wish," because "I am master, and it is for me to decide," because he has been disrespectful, because he has been rude; but if he were to ask respectfully I might be softened and give it to him, otherwise he might wait another fortnight, another three weeks, a whole month. . . .

But angry as I was, yet he got the better of me. I could not hold out for four days. He began as he always did begin in such cases, for there had been such cases already, there had been attempts (and it may be observed I knew all this beforehand, I knew his nasty tactics by heart). He would begin by fixing upon me an exceedingly severe stare, keeping it up for several minutes at a time, particularly on meeting me or seeing me out of the house. If I held out and pretended not to notice these stares, he would, still in silence, proceed to further tortures. All at once, *à propos* of nothing, he would walk softly and smoothly into my room, when I was pacing up and down or reading, stand at the door, one hand behind his back and one foot behind the other, and fix upon me a stare more than severe, utterly contemptuous. If I suddenly asked him what he wanted, he would make me no answer, but continue staring at me persistently for some seconds, then, with a peculiar compression of his lips and a most significant air, deliberately turn round and deliberately go back to his room. Two hours later he would come out again and again present himself before me in the same way. It had happened that in my fury I did not even ask him what he wanted, but simply raised my head sharply and imperiously and began staring back at him. So we stared at one another for two minutes; at last he turned with deliberation and dignity and went back again for two hours.

If I were still not brought to reason by all this, but persisted in my revolt, he would suddenly begin sighing while he looked at me, long, deep sighs as though measuring by them the depths of my moral degradation, and, of course, it ended at last by his triumphing completely: I raged and shouted, but still was forced to do what he wanted.

This time the usual staring manœuvres had scarcely begun when I lost my temper and flew at him in a fury. I was irritated beyond endurance apart from him.

"Stay," I cried, in a frenzy, as he was slowly and silently turning, with one hand behind his back, to go to his room, "stay! Come back, come back, I tell you!" and I must have bawled so unnaturally, that he turned round and even looked at me with some wonder. However, he persisted in saying nothing, and that infuriated me.

"How dare you come and look at me like that without being sent for? Answer!"

After looking at me calmly for half a minute, he began turning round again.

"Stay!" I roared, running up to him, "don't stir! There. Answer, now: what did you come in to look at?"

"If you have any order to give me it's my duty to carry it out," he answered, after another silent pause, with a slow, measured lisp, raising his eyebrows and calmly twisting his head from one side to another, all this with exasperating composure.

"That's not what I am asking you about, you torturer!" I shouted, turning crimson with anger. "I'll tell you why you came here myself: you see, I don't give you your wages, you are so proud you don't want to bow down and ask for it, and so you come to punish me with your stupid stares, to worry me and you have no sus . . . pic . . . ion how stupid it is—stupid, stupid, stupid, stupid!" . . .

He would have turned round again without a word, but I seized him.

"Listen," I shouted to him. "Here's the money, do you see, here it is" (I took it out of the table drawer); "here's the seven roubles complete, but you are not going to have it, you . . . are . . . not . . . going . . . to . . . have it until you come respectfully with bowed head to beg my pardon. Do you hear?"

"That cannot be," he answered, with the most unnatural self-confidence.

"It shall be so," I said, "I give you my word of honour, it shall be!"

"And there's nothing for me to beg your pardon for," he went on, as though he had not noticed my exclamations at all. "Why, besides, you called me a 'torturer,' for which I can summon you at the police-station at any time for insulting behaviour."

"Go, summon me," I roared, "go at once, this very minute, this very second! You are a torturer all the same! a torturer!"

But he merely looked at me, then turned, and regardless of my loud calls to him, he walked to his room with an even step and without looking round.

"If it had not been for Liza nothing of this would have happened," I decided inwardly. Then, after waiting a minute, I went myself behind his screen with a dignified and solemn air, though my heart was beating slowly and violently.

"Apollon," I said quietly and emphatically, though I was breathless, "go at once without a minute's delay and fetch the police-officer."

He had meanwhile settled himself at his table, put on his spectacles and taken up some sewing. But, hearing my order, he burst into a guffaw.

"At once, go this minute! Go on, or else you can't imagine what will happen."

"You are certainly out of your mind," he observed, without even raising his head, lisping as deliberately as ever and threading his needle. "Whoever heard of a man sending for the police against himself? And as for being frightened—you are upsetting yourself about nothing, for nothing will come of it."

"Go!" I shrieked, clutching him by the shoulder. I felt I should strike him in a minute.

But I did not notice the door from the passage softly and slowly open at that instant and a figure come in, stop short, and begin staring at us in perplexity. I glanced, nearly swooned with shame, and rushed back to my room. There, clutching at my hair with both hands, I leaned my head against the wall and stood motionless in that position.

Two minutes later I heard Apollon's deliberate footsteps. "There is some woman asking for you," he said, looking at me with peculiar severity. Then he stood aside and let in Liza. He would not go away, but stared at us sarcastically.

"Go away, go away," I commanded in desperation. At that moment my clock began whirring and wheezing and struck seven.

IX

"Into my house come bold and free,
Its rightful mistress there to be."
(From the same poem)

I stood before her crushed, crestfallen, revoltingly confused, and I believe I smiled as I did my utmost to wrap myself in the skirts of my ragged wadded dressing-gown—exactly as I had imagined the scene not long before in a fit of depression. After standing over us for a couple of minutes Apollon went away, but that did not make me more at ease. What made it worse was that she, too, was overwhelmed with confusion, more so, in fact, than I should have expected. At the sight of me, of course.

"Sit down," I said mechanically, moving a chair up to the table, and I sat down on the sofa. She obediently sat down at once and gazed at me open-eyed, evidently expecting something from me at once. This naïveté of expectation drove me to fury, but I restrained myself.

She ought to have tried not to notice, as though everything had been as usual, while instead of that, she . . . and I dimly felt that I should make her pay dearly for *all this*.

"You have found me in a strange position, Liza," I began, stammering and knowing that this was the wrong way to begin. "No, no, don't imagine anything," I cried, seeing that she had suddenly flushed. "I am not ashamed of my poverty. . . . On the contrary I look with pride on my poverty. I am poor but honourable. . . . One can be poor and honourable," I muttered. "However . . . would you like tea?". . .

"No," she was beginning.

"Wait a minute."

I leapt up and ran to Apollon. I had to get out of the room somehow.

"Apollon," I whispered in feverish haste, flinging down before him the seven roubles which had remained all the time in my clenched fist, "here are your wages, you see I give them to you; but for that you must come to my rescue: bring me tea and a dozen rusks from the restaurant. If you won't go, you'll make me a miserable man! You don't know what this woman is. . . . This is—everything! You may be imagining something. . . . But you don't know what that woman is!" . . .

Apollon, who had already sat down to his work and put on his spectacles again, at first glanced askance at the money without speaking or putting down his needle; then, without paying the slightest attention to me or making any answer he went on busying himself with his needle, which he had not yet threaded. I waited before him for three minutes with my arms crossed *à la Napoléon*. My temples were moist with sweat. I was pale, I felt it. But, thank God, he must have been moved to pity, looking at me. Having threaded his needle he deliberately got up from his seat, deliberately moved back his chair, deliberately took off his spectacles, deliberately counted the money, and finally asking me over his shoulder: "Shall I get a whole portion?" deliberately walked out of the room. As I was going back to Liza, the thought occurred to me on the way: shouldn't I run away just as I was in my dressing-gown, no matter where, and then let happen what would.

I sat down again. She looked at me uneasily. For some minutes we were silent.

"I will kill him," I shouted suddenly, striking the table with my fist so that the ink spurted out of the inkstand.

"What are you saying!" she cried, starting.

"I will kill him! kill him!" I shrieked, suddenly striking the table in absolute frenzy, and at the same time fully understanding how stupid it was to be in such a frenzy. "You don't know, Liza, what that torturer is to me. He is my torturer. . . . He has gone now to fetch some rusks; he . . ."

And suddenly I burst into tears. It was an hysterical attack. How ashamed I felt in the midst of my sobs; but still I could not restrain them.

She was frightened.

"What is the matter? What is wrong?" she cried, fussing about me.

"Water, give me water, over there!" I muttered in a faint voice, though I was inwardly conscious that I could have got on very well without water and without muttering in a faint voice. But I was, what called, *putting it on*, to save appearances, though the attack was a genuine one.

She gave me water, looking at me in bewilderment. At that moment Apollon brought in the tea. It suddenly seemed to me that this commonplace, prosaic tea was horribly undignified and paltry after all that had happened, and I blushed crimson. Liza looked at Apollon with positive alarm. He went out without a glance at either of us.

"Liza, do you despise me?" I asked, looking at her fixedly, trembling with impatience to know what she was thinking.

She was confused, and did not know what to answer.

"Drink your tea," I said to her angrily. I was angry with myself, but, of course, it was she who would have to pay for it. A horrible spite against her suddenly surged up in my heart; I believe I could have killed her. To revenge myself on her I swore inwardly not to say a word to her all the time. "She is the cause of it all," I thought.

Our silence lasted for five minutes. The tea stood on the table; we did not touch it. I had got to the point of purposely refraining from beginning in order to embarrass her further; it was awkward for her to begin alone. Several times she glanced at me with mournful perplexity. I was obstinately silent. I was, of course, myself the chief sufferer, because I was fully conscious of the disgusting meanness of my spiteful stupidity, and yet at the same time I could not restrain myself.

"I want to . . . get away . . . from there altogether," she began, to break the silence in some way, but, poor girl, that was just what she ought not to have spoken about at such a stupid moment to a man so stupid as I was. My heart positively ached with pity for her tactless and unnecessary straightforwardness. But something hideous at once stifled all compassion in me; it even provoked me to greater venom. I did not care what happened. Another five minutes passed.

"Perhaps I am in your way," she began timidly, hardly audibly, and was getting up.

But as soon as I saw this first impulse of wounded dignity I positively trembled with spite, and at once burst out.

"Why have you come to me, tell me that, please?" I began, gasping for breath and regardless of logical connection in my words. I longed to have it all out at once, at one burst; I did not even trouble how to begin. "Why have you come? Answer, answer," I cried, hardly knowing what I was doing. "I'll tell you, my good girl, why you have come. You've come because I talked sentimental stuff to you then. So now you are soft as butter and longing for fine sentiments again. So you may as well know that I was laughing at you then. And I am laughing at you now. Why are you shuddering? Yes, I was laughing at you! I had been insulted just before, at dinner, by the fellows who came that evening before me. I came to you, meaning to thrash one of them, an officer; but I didn't succeed, I didn't find him; I had to avenge the insult on some one to get back my own again; you turned up, I vented my spleen on you and laughed at you. I had been humiliated, so I wanted to humiliate; I had been treated like a rag, so I wanted to show my power. . . . That's what it was, and you imagined I had come there on purpose to save you. Yes? You imagined that? You imagined that?"

I knew that she would perhaps be muddled and not take it all in exactly, but I knew, too, that she would grasp the gist of it, very well indeed. And so, indeed, she did. She turned white as a handkerchief, tried to say something, and her lips worked painfully; but she sank on a chair as though she had been felled by an axe. And all the time afterwards she listened to me with her lips parted and her eyes wide open, shuddering with awful terror. The cynicism, the cynicism of my words overwhelmed her. . . .

"Save you!" I went on, jumping up from my chair and running up and down the room before her. "Save you from what? But perhaps I am worse than you myself. Why didn't you throw it in my teeth when I was giving you that sermon: 'But what did you come here yourself for? was it to read us a sermon?' Power, power was what I wanted then, sport was what I wanted, I wanted to ring out your tears, your humiliation, your hysteria—that was what I wanted then! Of course, I couldn't keep it up then, because I am a wretched creature, I was frightened, and, the devil knows why, gave you my address in my folly. Afterwards, before I got home, I was cursing and swearing at you because of that address, I hated you already because of the lies I had told you. Because I only like playing with words, only dreaming, but, do you know, what I really want is that you should all go to hell. That is what I want. I want peace; yes, I'd sell the whole world for a farthing, straight off, so long as I was left in peace. Is the world to go to pot, or am I to go without my tea? I say that the world may go to pot for me so long as I always get my tea. Did you know that, or not? Well, anyway, I know that I am a blackguard, a scoundrel, an egoist, a sluggard. Here I have been shuddering for the last three days at the thought of your coming. And do you know what has worried me particularly for these three days? That I posed as such a hero to you, and now you would see me in a wretched torn dressing-gown, beggarly, loathsome. I told you just now that I was not ashamed of my poverty; so you may as well know that I am ashamed of it; I am more ashamed of it than of anything, more afraid of it than of being found out if I were a thief, because I am as vain as though I had been skinned and the very air blowing on me hurts. Surely by now you must realize that I shall never forgive you for having found me in this wretched dressing-gown, just as I was flying at Apollon like a spiteful cur. The saviour, the former hero, was flying like a mangy, unkempt sheep-dog at his lackey, and the lackey was jeering at him! And I shall never forgive you for the tears I could not help shedding before you just now, like some silly woman put to shame! And for what I am confessing to you now, I shall never forgive *you* either! Yes— you must answer for it all because you turned up like this, because

I am a blackguard, because I am the nastiest, stupidest, absurdest and most envious of all the worms on earth, who are not a bit better than I am, but, the devil knows why, are never put to confusion; while I shall always be insulted by every louse, that is my doom! And what is it to me that you don't understand a word of this! And what do I care, what do I care about you, and whether you go to ruin there or not? Do you understand? How I shall hate you now after saying this, for having been here and listening. Why, it's not once in a lifetime a man speaks out like this, and then it is in hysterics! . . . What more do you want? Why do you still stand confronting me, after all this? Why are you worrying me? Why don't you go?"

But at this point a strange thing happened. I was so accustomed to think and imagine everything from books, and to picture everything in the world to myself just as I had made it up in my dreams beforehand, that I could not all at once take in this strange circumstance. What happened was this: Liza, insulted and crushed by me, understood a great deal more than I imagined. She understood from all this what a woman understands first of all, if she feels genuine love, that is, that I was myself unhappy.

The frightened and wounded expression on her face was followed first by a look of sorrowful perplexity. When I began calling myself a scoundrel and a blackguard and my tears flowed (the tirade was accompanied throughout by tears) her whole face worked convulsively. She was on the point of getting up and stopping me; when I finished she took no notice of my shouting: "Why are you here, why don't you go away?" but realized only that it must have been very bitter to me to say all this. Besides, she was so crushed, poor girl; she considered herself infinitely beneath me; how could she feel anger or resentment? She suddenly leapt up from her chair with an irresistible impulse and held out her hands, yearning towards me, though still timid and not daring to stir. . . . At this point there was a revulsion in my heart, too. Then she suddenly rushed to me, threw her arms round me and burst into tears. I, too, could not restrain myself, and sobbed as I never had before.

"They won't let me . . . I can't be good!" I managed to articulate; then I went to the sofa, fell on it face downwards, and sobbed on it for a quarter of an hour in genuine hysterics. She came close to me, put her arms round me and stayed motionless in that position. But the trouble was that the hysterics could not go on for ever, and (I am writing the loathsome truth) lying face downwards on the sofa with my face thrust into my nasty leather pillow, I began by degrees to be aware of a far-away, involuntary but irresistible feeling that it would be awkward now for me to raise my head and look Liza straight in the face. Why was I ashamed? I don't know, but I was ashamed. The thought, too, came into my overwrought brain that our parts now were completely changed, that she was now the heroine, while I was just such a crushed and humiliated creature as she had been before me that night—four days before. . . . And all this came into my mind during the minutes I was lying on my face on the sofa.

My God! surely I was not envious of her then.

I don't know, to this day I cannot decide, and at the time, of course, I was still less able to understand what I was feeling than now. I cannot get on without domineering and tyrannizing over some one, but . . . there is no explaining anything by reasoning and so it is useless to reason.

I conquered myself, however, and raised my head; I had to do so sooner or later . . . and I am convinced to this day that it was just because I was ashamed to look at her that another feeling was suddenly kindled and flamed up in my heart . . . a feeling of mastery and possession. My eyes gleamed with passion, and I gripped her hands tightly. How I hated her and how I was drawn to her at that minute! The one feeling intensified the other. It was almost like an act of vengeance. At first there was a look of amazement, even of terror on her face, but only for one instant. She warmly and rapturously embraced me.

X

A quarter of an hour later I was rushing up and down the room in frenzied impatience, from minute to minute I went up to the screen and peeped through the crack at Liza. She was sitting on the ground with her head leaning against the bed, and must have been crying. But she did not go away, and that irritated me. This time she understood it all. I had insulted her finally, but . . . there's no need to describe it. She realized that my outburst of passion had been simply revenge, a fresh humiliation, and that to my earlier, almost causeless hatred was added a *personal hatred*, born of envy. . . . Though I do not maintain positively that she understood all this distinctly; but she certainly did fully understand that I was a despicable man, and what was worse, incapable of loving her.

I know I shall be told that this is incredible—but it is incredible to be as spiteful and stupid as I was; it may be added that it was strange I should not love her, or at any rate, appreciate her love. Why is it strange? In the first place, by then I was incapable of love, for I repeat, with me loving meant tyrannizing and showing my moral superiority. I have never in my life been able to imagine any other sort of love, and have nowadays come to the point of sometimes thinking that love really consists in the right—freely given by the beloved object—to tyrannize over her.

Even in my underground dreams I did not imagine love except as a struggle. I began it always with hatred and ended it with moral subjugation, and afterwards I never knew what to do with the sub-jugated object. And what is there to wonder at in that, since I had succeeded in so corrupting myself, since I was so out of touch with "real life," as to have actually thought of reproaching her, and put-ting her to shame for having come to me to hear "fine sentiments"; and did not even guess that she had come not to hear fine senti-ments, but to love me, because to a woman all reformation, all sal-vation from any sort of ruin, and all moral renewal is included in love and can only show itself in that form.

I did not hate her so much, however, when I was running about the room and peeping through the crack in the screen. I was only insufferably oppressed by her being here. I wanted her to disappear. I wanted "peace," to be left alone in my underground world. Real life oppressed me with its novelty so much that I could hardly breathe.

But several minutes passed and she still remained, without stir-ring, as though she were unconscious. I had the shamelessness to tap softly at the screen as though to remind her. . . . She started, sprang up, and flew to seek her kerchief, her hat, her coat, as though making her escape from me. . . . Two minutes later she came from behind the screen and looked with heavy eyes at me. I gave a spite-ful grin, which was forced, however, to *keep up appearances*, and I turned away from her eyes.

"Good-bye," she said, going towards the door.

I ran up to her, seized her hand, opened it, thrust something in it and closed it again. Then I turned at once and dashed away in haste to the other corner of the room to avoid seeing her, any-way. . . .

I did not mean a moment since to tell a lie—to write that I did this accidentally, not knowing what I was doing through foolishness, through losing my head. But I don't want to lie, and so I will say straight out that I opened her hand and put the money in it . . . from spite. It came into my head to do this while I was running up and down the room and she was sitting behind the screen. But this I can say for certain: though I did that cruel thing purposely, it was not an impulse from the heart, but came from my evil brain. This cruelty was so affected, so purposely made up, so completely a product of the brain, of books, that I could not even keep it up a minute—first I dashed away to avoid seeing her, and then in shame and despair rushed after Liza. I opened the door in the passage and began listening.

"Liza! Liza!" I cried on the stairs, but in a low voice, not boldly.

There was no answer, but I fancied I heard her footsteps, lower down on the stairs.

"Liza!" I cried, more loudly.

No answer. But at that minute I heard the stiff outer glass door open heavily with a creak and slam violently, the sound echoed up the stairs.

She had gone. I went back to my room in hesitation. I felt horribly oppressed.

I stood still at the table, beside the chair on which she had sat and looked aimlessly before me. A minute passed, suddenly I started; straight before me on the table I saw. . . . In short, I saw a crumpled blue five-rouble note, the one I had thrust into her hand a minute before. It was the same note; it could be no other, there was no other in the flat. So she had managed to fling it from her hand on the table at the moment when I had dashed into the further corner.

Well! I might have expected that she would do that. Might I have expected it? No, I was such an egoist, I was so lacking in respect for my fellow-creatures that I could not even imagine she would do so. I could not endure it. A minute later I flew like a madman to dress, flinging on what I could at random and ran headlong after her. She could not have got two hundred paces away when I ran out into the street.

It was a still night and the snow was coming down in masses and falling almost perpendicularly, covering the pavement and the empty street as though with a pillow. There was no one in the street, no sound was to be heard. The street lamps gave a disconsolate and useless glimmer. I ran two hundred paces to the cross-roads and stopped short.

Where had she gone? And why was I running after her?

Why? To fall down before her, to sob with remorse, to kiss her feet, to entreat her forgiveness! I longed for that, my whole breast was being rent to pieces, and never, never shall I recall that minute with indifference. But—what for? I thought. Should I not begin to hate her, perhaps, even to-morrow, just because I had kissed her feet to-day? Should I give her happiness? Had I not recognized that day, for the hundredth time, what I was worth? Should I not torture her?

I stood in the snow, gazing into the troubled darkness and pondered this.

"And will it not be better?" I mused fantastically, afterwards at home, stifling the living pang of my heart with fantastic dreams. "Will it not be better that she should keep the resentment of the insult for ever? Resentment—why, it is purification; it is a most stinging and painful consciousness! To-morrow I should have defiled her soul and have exhausted her heart, while now the feeling of insult will never die in her heart, and however loathsome the filth awaiting her—the feeling of insult will elevate and purify her . . .

by hatred . . . h'm! . . . perhaps, too, by forgiveness. . . . Will all that make things easier for her though? . . ."

And, indeed, I will ask on my own account here, an idle question: which is better—cheap happiness or exalted sufferings? Well, which is better?

So I dreamed as I sat at home that evening, almost dead with the pain in my soul. Never had I endured such suffering and remorse, yet could there have been the faintest doubt when I ran out from my lodging that I should turn back half-way? I never met Liza again and I have heard nothing of her. I will add, too, that I remained for a long time afterwards pleased with the phrase about the benefit from resentment and hatred in spite of the fact that I almost fell ill from misery.

Even now, so many years later, all this is somehow a very evil memory. I have many evil memories now, but . . . hadn't I better end my "Notes" here? I believe I made a mistake in beginning to write them, anyway I have felt ashamed all the time I've been writing this story; so it's hardly literature so much as a corrective punishment. Why, to tell long stories, showing how I have spoiled my life through morally rotting in my corner, through lack of fitting environment, through divorce from real life, and rankling spite in my underground world, would certainly not be interesting; a novel needs a hero, and all the traits for an anti-hero are *expressly* gathered together here, and what matters most, it all produces an unpleasant impression, for we are all divorced from life, we are all cripples, every one of us, more or less. We are so divorced from it that we feel at once a sort of loathing for real life, and so cannot bear to be reminded of it. Why, we have come almost to looking upon real life as an effort, almost as hard labour, and we are all privately agreed that it is better in books. And why do we fuss and fume sometimes? Why are we perverse and ask for something else? We don't know what ourselves. It would be the worse for us if our petulant prayers were answered. Come, try, give any one of us, for instance, a little more independence, untie our hands, widen the spheres of our activity, relax the control and we . . . yes, I assure you . . . we should be begging to be under control again at once. I know that you will very likely be angry with me for that, and will begin shouting and stamping. Speak for yourself, you will say, and for your miseries in your underground holes, and don't dare to say "all of us"—excuse me, gentlemen, I am not justifying myself with that "all of us." As for what concerns me in particular I have only in my life carried to an extreme what you have not dared to carry half-way, and what's more, you have taken your cowardice for good sense, and have found comfort in deceiving yourselves. So that per-

haps, after all, there is more life in me than in you. Look into it
more carefully! Why, we don't even know what living means now,
what it is, and what it is called? Leave us alone without books and
we shall be lost and in confusion at once. We shall not know what
to join on to, what to cling to, what to love and what to hate, what
to respect and what to despise. We are oppressed at being men—
men with a real individual flesh and blood, we are ashamed of it, we
think it a disgrace and try to contrive to be some sort of impossible
generalized man. We are stillborn, and for generations past have
been begotten, not by living fathers, and that suits us better and
better. We are developing a taste for it. Soon we shall contrive to be
born somehow from an idea. But enough; I don't want to write
more from "Underground."

(*The notes of this paradoxalist do not end here, however. He
could not refrain from going on with them, but it seems to us that
we may stop here.*)

LEO TOLSTOY
(1828–1910)
The Death of Iván Ilyich*

I

During an interval in the Melvínski trial in the large building of
the Law Courts the members and public prosecutor met in Iván
Egórovich Shébek's private room, where the conversation turned on
the celebrated Krasóvski case. Fëdor Vasílievich warmly maintained
that it was not subject to their jurisdiction, Iván Egórovich maintained the contrary, while Peter Ivánovich, not having entered into
the discussion at the start, took no part in it but looked through
the *Gazette* which had just been handed in.

"Gentlemen," he said, "Iván Ilyich has died!"

"You don't say!"

"Here, read it yourself," replied Peter Ivánovich, handing Fëdor
Vasílievich the paper still damp from the press. Surrounded by a
black border were the words: "Praskóvya Fëdorovna Golóviná,
with profound sorrow, informs relatives and friends of the demise
of her beloved husband Iván Ilyich Golóvin, Member of the Court
of Justice, which occurred on February the 4th of this year 1882.
The funeral will take place on Friday at one o'clock in the afternoon."

* 1886. Translated by Louise and   *Tolstoy,* Vol. XV, London, Oxford Uni-
Aylmer Maude. From *The Works of*   versity Press, 1934.

Iván Ilyich had been a colleague of the gentlemen present and was liked by them all. He had been ill for some weeks with an illness said to be incurable. His post had been kept open for him, but there had been conjectures that in case of his death Alexéev might receive his appointment, and that either Vínnikov or Shtábel would succeed Alexéev. So on receiving the news of Iván Ilyich's death the first thought of each of the gentlemen in that private room was of the changes and promotions it might occasion among themselves or their acquaintances.

"I shall be sure to get Shtábel's place or Vínnikov's," thought Fëdor Vasílievich. "I was promised that long ago, and the promotion means an extra eight hundred rubles a year for me besides the allowance."

"Now I must apply for my brother-in-law's transfer from Kalúga," thought Peter Ivánovich. "My wife will be very glad, and then she won't be able to say that I never do anything for her relations."

"I thought he would never leave his bed again," said Peter Ivánovich aloud. "It's very sad."

"But what really was the matter with him?"

"The doctors couldn't say—at least they could, but each of them said something different. When last I saw him I thought he was getting better."

"And I haven't been to see him since the holidays. I always meant to go."

"Had he any property?"

"I think his wife had a little—but something quite trifling."

"We shall have to go to see her, but they live so terribly far away."

"Far away from you, you mean. Everything's far away from your place."

"You see, he never can forgive my living on the other side of the river," said Peter Ivánovich, smiling at Shébek. Then, still talking of the distances between different parts of the city, they returned to the Court.

Besides considerations as to the possible transfers and promotions likely to result from Iván Ilyich's death, the mere fact of the death of a near acquaintance aroused, as usual, in all who heard of it the complacent feeling that, "it is he who is dead and not I."

Each one thought or felt, "Well, he's dead but I'm alive!" But the more intimate of Iván Ilyich's acquaintances, his so-called friends, could not help thinking also that they would now have to fulfil the very tiresome demands of propriety by attending the funeral service and paying a visit of condolence to the widow.

Fëdor Vasílievich and Peter Ivánovich had been his nearest acquaintances. Peter Ivánovich had studied law with Iván Ilyich and had considered himself to be under obligations to him.

Having told his wife at dinner-time of Iván Ilyich's death, and of his conjecture that it might be possible to get her brother transferred to their circuit, Peter Ivánovich sacrificed his usual nap, put on his evening clothes, and drove to Iván Ilyich's house.

At the entrance stood a carriage and two cabs. Leaning against the wall in the hall downstairs near the cloak-stand was a coffin-lid covered with cloth of gold, ornamented with gold cord and tassels, that had been polished up with metal powder. Two ladies in black were taking off their fur cloaks. Peter Ivánovich recognized one of them as Iván Ilyich's sister, but the other was a stranger to him. His colleague Schwartz was just coming downstairs, but on seeing Peter Ivánovich enter he stopped and winked at him, as if to say: "Iván Ilyich has made a mess of things—not like you and me."

Schwartz's face with his Piccadilly whiskers, and his slim figure in evening dress, had as usual an air of elegant solemnity which contrasted with the playfulness of his character and had a special piquancy here, or so it seemed to Peter Ivánovich.

Peter Ivánovich allowed the ladies to precede him and slowly followed them upstairs. Schwartz did not come down but remained where he was, and Peter Ivánovich understood that he wanted to arrange where they should play bridge that evening. The ladies went upstairs to the widow's room, and Schwartz with seriously compressed lips but a playful look in his eyes, indicated by a twist of his eyebrows the room to the right where the body lay.

Peter Ivánovich, like everyone else on such occasions, entered feeling uncertain what he would have to do. All he knew was that at such times it is always safe to cross oneself. But he was not quite sure whether one should make obeisances while doing so. He therefore adopted a middle course. On entering the room he began crossing himself and made a slight movement resembling a bow. At the same time, as far as the motion of his head and arm allowed, he surveyed the room. Two young men—apparently nephews, one of whom was a high-school pupil—were leaving the room, crossing themselves as they did so. An old woman was standing motionless, and a lady with strangely arched eyebrows was saying something to her in a whisper. A vigorous, resolute Church Reader, in a frock-coat, was reading something in a loud voice with an expression that precluded any contradiction. The butler's assistant, Gerásim, stepping lightly in front of Peter Ivánovich, was strewing something on the floor. Noticing this, Peter Ivánovich was immediately aware of a faint odour of a decomposing body.

The last time he had called on Iván Ilyich, Peter Ivánovich had seen Gerásim in the study. Iván Ilyich had been particularly fond of him and he was performing the duty of a sick nurse.

Peter Ivánovich continued to make the sign of the cross slightly inclining his head in an intermediate direction between the coffin, the Reader, and the icons on the table in a corner of the room. Afterwards, when it seemed to him that this movement of his arm in crossing himself had gone on too long, he stopped and began to look at the corpse.

The dead man lay, as dead men always lie, in a specially heavy way, his rigid limbs sunk in the soft cushions of the coffin, with the head forever bowed on the pillow. His yellow waxen brow with bald patches over his sunken temples was thrust up in the way peculiar to the dead, the protruding nose seeming to press on the upper lip. He was much changed and had grown even thinner since Peter Ivánovich had last seen him, but, as is always the case with the dead, his face was handsomer and above all more dignified than when he was alive. The expression on the face said that what was necessary had been accomplished, and accomplished rightly. Besides this there was in that expression a reproach and a warning to the living. This warning seemed to Peter Ivánovich out of place, or at least not applicable to him. He felt a certain discomfort and so he hurriedly crossed himself once more and turned and went out of the door—too hurriedly and too regardless of propriety, as he himself was aware.

Schwartz was waiting for him in the adjoining room with legs spread wide apart and both hands toying with his top-hat behind his back. The mere sight of that playful, well-groomed, and elegant figure refreshed Peter Ivánovich. He felt that Schwartz was above all these happenings and would not surrender to any depressing influences. His very look said that this incident of a church service for Iván Ilyich could not be a sufficient reason for infringing the order of the session—in other words, that it would certainly not prevent his unwrapping a new pack of cards and shuffling them that evening while a footman placed four fresh candles on the table: in fact, that there was no reason for supposing that this incident would hinder their spending the evening agreeably. Indeed he said this in a whisper as Peter Ivánovich passed him, proposing that they should meet for a game at Fëdor Vasílievich's. But apparently Peter Ivánovich was not destined to play bridge that evening. Praskóvya Fëdorovna (a short, fat woman who despite all efforts to the contrary had continued to broaden steadily from her shoulders downwards and who had the same extraordinary arched eyebrows as the lady who had been standing by the coffin), dressed all in black, her head covered with lace, came out of her own room with some other ladies, conducted them to the room where the dead body lay, and said: "The service will begin immediately. Please go in."

Schwartz, making an indefinite bow, stood still, evidently neither accepting nor declining this invitation. Praskóvya Fëdorovna recognizing Peter Ivánovich, sighed, went close up to him, took his hand, and said: "I know you were a true friend to Iván Ilyich . . ." and looked at him awaiting some suitable response. And Peter Ivánovich knew that, just as it had been the right thing to cross himself in that room, so what he had to do here was to press her hand, sigh, and say, "Believe me . . ." So he did all this and as he did it felt that the desired result had been achieved: that both he and she were touched.

"Come with me. I want to speak to you before it begins," said the widow. "Give me your arm."

Peter Ivánovich gave her his arm and they went to the inner rooms, passing Schwartz who winked at Peter Ivánovich compassionately.

"That does for our bridge! Don't object if we find another player. Perhaps you can cut in when you do escape," said his playful look.

Peter Ivánovich sighed still more deeply and despondently, and Praskóvya Fëdorovna pressed his arm gratefully. When they reached the drawing-room, upholstered in pink cretonne and lighted by a dim lamp, they sat down at the table—she on a sofa and Peter Ivánovich on a low hassock, the springs of which yielded spasmodically under his weight. Praskóvya Fëdorovna had been on the point of warning him to take another seat, but felt that such a warning was out of keeping with her present condition and so changed her mind. As he sat down on the hassock Peter Ivánovich recalled how Iván Ilyich had arranged this room and had consulted him regarding this pink cretonne with green leaves. The whole room was full of furniture and knick-knacks, and on her way to the sofa the lace of the widow's black shawl caught on the carved edge of the table. Peter Ivánovich rose to detach it, and the springs of the hassock, relieved of his weight, rose also and gave him a push. The widow began detaching her shawl herself, and Peter Ivánovich again sat down, suppressing the rebellious springs of the hassock under him. But the widow had not quite freed herself and Peter Ivánovich got up again, and again the hassock rebelled and even creaked. When this was all over she took out a clean cambric handkerchief and began to weep. The episode with the shawl and the struggle with the hassock had cooled Peter Ivánovich's emotions and he sat there with a sullen look on his face. This awkward situation was interrupted by Sokolóv, Iván Ilyich's butler, who came to report that the plot in the cemetery that Praskóvya Fëdorovna had chosen would cost two hundred rubles. She stopped weeping and, looking at Peter Ivánovich with the air of a victim, remarked in French that it was very hard for her. Peter Ivánovich made a silent gesture signifying his full conviction that it must indeed be so.

"Please smoke," she said in a magnanimous yet crushed voice, and turned to discuss with Sokolóv the price of the plot for the grave.

Peter Ivánovich while lighting his cigarette heard her inquiring very circumstantially into the prices of different plots in the cemetery and finally decide which she would take. When that was done she gave instructions about engaging the choir. Sokolóv then left the room.

"I look after everything myself," she told Peter Ivánovich, shifting the albums that lay on the table; and noticing that the table was endangered by his cigarette-ash, she immediately passed him an ash-tray, saying as she did so: "I consider it an affectation to say that my grief prevents my attending to practical affairs. On the contrary, if anything can—I won't say console me, but—distract me, it is seeing to everything concerning him." She again took out her handkerchief as if preparing to cry, but suddenly, as if mastering her feeling, she shook herself and began to speak calmly. "But there is something I want to talk to you about."

Peter Ivánovich bowed, keeping control of the springs of the hassock, which immediately began quivering under him.

"He suffered terribly the last few days."

"Did he?" said Peter Ivánovich.

"Oh, terribly! He screamed unceasingly, not for minutes but for hours. For the last three days he screamed incessantly. It was unendurable. I cannot understand how I bore it; you could hear him three rooms off. Oh, what I have suffered!"

"Is it possible that he was conscious all that time?" asked Peter Ivánovich.

"Yes," she whispered. "To the last moment. He took leave of us a quarter of an hour before he died, and asked us to take Volódya away."

The thought of the sufferings of this man he had known so intimately, first as a merry little boy, then as a school-mate, and later as a grown-up colleague, suddenly struck Peter Ivánovich with horror, despite an unpleasant consciousness of his own and this woman's dissimulation. He again saw that brow, and that nose pressing down on the lip, and felt afraid for himself.

"Three days of frightful suffering and then death! Why, that might suddenly, at any time, happen to me," he thought, and for a moment felt terrified. But—he did not himself know how—the customary reflection at once occurred to him that this had happened to Iván Ilyich and not to him, and that it should not and could

not happen to him, and that to think that it could would be yielding to depression which he ought not to do, as Schwartz's expression plainly showed. After which reflection Peter Ivánovich felt
reassured, and began to ask with interest about the details of Iván
Ilyich's death, as though death was an accident natural to Iván
Ilyich but certainly not to himself.

After many details of the really dreadful physical sufferings Iván
Ilyich had endured (which details he learnt only from the effect
those sufferings had produced on Praskóvya Fëdorovna's nerves)
the widow apparently found it necessary to get to business.

"Oh, Peter Ivánovich, how hard it is! How terribly, terribly
hard!" and she again began to weep.

Peter Ivánovich sighed and waited for her to finish blowing her
nose. When she had done so he said, "Believe me . . ." and she
again began talking and brought out what was evidently her chief
concern with him—namely, to question him as to how she could
obtain a grant of money from the government on the occasion of
her husband's death. She made it appear that she was asking Peter
Ivánovich's advice about her pension, but he soon saw that she already knew about that to the minutest detail, more even than he
did himself. She knew how much could be got out of the government in consequence of her husband's death, but wanted to find
out whether she could not possibly extract something more. Peter
Ivánovich tried to think of some means of doing so, but after reflecting for a while and, out of propriety, condemning the government for its niggardliness, he said he thought that nothing more
could be got. Then she sighed and evidently began to devise means
of getting rid of her visitor. Noticing this, he put out his cigarette,
rose, pressed her hand, and went out into the anteroom.

In the dining-room where the clock stood that Iván Ilyich had
liked so much and had bought at an antique shop, Peter Ivánovich
met a priest and a few acquaintances who had come to attend the
service, and he recognized Iván Ilyich's daughter, a handsome young
woman. She was in black and her slim figure appeared slimmer
than ever. She had a gloomy, determined, almost angry expression,
and bowed to Peter Ivánovich as though he were in some way to
blame. Behind her, with the same offended look, stood a wealthy
young man, an examining magistrate, whom Peter Ivánovich also
knew and who was her fiancé, as he had heard. He bowed mournfully to them and was about to pass into the death-chamber, when
from under the stairs appeared the figure of Iván Ilyich's schoolboy
son, who was extremely like his father. He seemed a little Iván
Ilyich, such as Peter Ivánovich remembered when they studied law
together. His tear-stained eyes had in them the look that is seen in
the eyes of boys of thirteen or fourteen who are not pure-minded.

When he saw Peter Ivánovich he scowled morosely and shame-facedly. Peter Ivánovich nodded to him and entered the death-chamber. The service began: candles, groans, incense, tears, and sobs. Peter Ivánovich stood looking gloomily down at his feet. He did not look once at the dead man, did not yield to any depressing influence, and was one of the first to leave the room. There was no one in the anteroom, but Gerásim darted out of the dead man's room, rummaged with his strong hands among the fur coats to find Peter Ivánovich's and helped him on with it.

"Well, friend Gerásim," said Peter Ivánovich, so as to say some-thing. "It's a sad affair, isn't it?"

"It's God's will. We shall all come to it some day," said Gerásim, displaying his teeth—the even, white teeth of a healthy peasant—and, like a man in the thick of urgent work, he briskly opened the front door, called the coachman, helped Peter Ivánovich into the sledge, and sprang back to the porch as if in readiness for what he had to do next.

Peter Ivánovich found the fresh air particularly pleasant after the smell of incense, the dead body, and carbolic acid.

"Where to, sir?" asked the coachman.

"It's not too late even now. . . . I'll call round on Fëdor Vasílie-vich."

He accordingly drove there and found them just finishing the first rubber, so that it was quite convenient for him to cut in.

II

Iván Ilyich's life had been most simple and most ordinary and therefore most terrible.

He had been a member of the Court of Justice, and died at the age of forty-five. His father had been an official who after serving in various ministries and departments in Petersburg had made the sort of career which brings men to positions from which by reason of their long service they cannot be dismissed, though they are obviously unfit to hold any responsible position, and for whom therefore posts are specially created, which though fictitious, carry salaries of from six to ten thousand rubles that are not fictitious, and in receipt of which they live on to a great age.

Such was the Privy Councillor and superfluous member of various superfluous institutions, Ilya Epímovich Golovín.

He had three sons, of whom Iván Ilyich was the second. The eldest son was following in his father's footsteps only in another department, and was already approaching that stage in the service at which a similar sinecure would be reached. The third son was a failure. He had ruined his prospects in a number of positions and was now serving in the railway department. His father and brothers, and still more their wives, not merely disliked meeting him, but avoided remembering his existence unless compelled to do so. His sister had married Baron Greff, a Petersburg official of her father's type. Iván Ilyich was *le phénix de la famille*[1] as people said. He was neither as cold and formal as his elder brother nor as wild as the younger, but was a happy mean between them—an intelligent, polished, lively and agreeable man. He had studied with his younger brother at the School of Law, but the latter had failed to complete the course and was expelled when he was in the fifth class. Iván Ilyich finished the course well. Even when he was at the School of Law he was just what he remained for the rest of his life: a capable, cheerful, good-natured, and sociable man, though strict in the fulfilment of what he considered to be his duty: and he considered his duty to be what was so considered by those in authority. Neither as a boy nor as a man was he a toady, but from early youth was by nature attracted to people of high station as a fly is drawn to the light, assimilating their ways and views of life and establishing friendly relations with them. All the enthusiasms of childhood and youth passed without leaving much trace on him; he succumbed to sensuality, to vanity, and latterly among the highest classes to liberalism, but always within limits which his instinct unfailingly indicated to him as correct.

At school he had done things which had formerly seemed to him very horrid and made him feel disgusted with himself when he did them; but when later on he saw that such actions were done by people of good position and that they did not regard them as wrong, he was able not exactly to regard them as right, but to forget about them entirely or not be at all troubled at remembering them.

Having graduated from the School of Law and qualified for the tenth rank of the civil service, and having received money from his father for his equipment, Iván Ilyich ordered himself clothes at Scharmer's, the fashionable tailor, hung a medallion inscribed *respice finem*[2] on his watch-chain, took leave of his professor and the prince who was patron of the school, had a farewell dinner with his comrades at Donon's first-class restaurant, and with his new and fashionable portmanteau, linen, clothes, shaving and other toilet appliances, and a travelling rug, all purchased at the best shops, he set off for one of the provinces where, through his father's influence, he had been attached to the governor as an official for special service.

In the province Iván Ilyich soon arranged as easy and agreeable a position for himself as he had had at the School of Law. He performed his official tasks, made his career, and at the same time amused himself pleasantly and decorously. Occasionally he paid

---

1. "the phoenix of the family." The word "phoenix" is used here to mean "rare bird," "prodigy."
2. "Regard the end" (a Latin motto).

official visits to country districts, where he behaved with dignity both to his superiors and inferiors, and performed the duties entrusted to him, which related chiefly to the sectarians,[3] with an exactness and incorruptible honesty of which he could not but feel proud.

In official matters, despite his youth and taste for frivolous gaiety, he was exceedingly reserved, punctilious, and even severe; but in society he was often amusing and witty, and always good-natured, correct in his manner, and *bon enfant*, as the governor and his wife —with whom he was like one of the family—used to say of him.

In the province he had an affair with a lady who made advances to the elegant young lawyer, and there was also a milliner; and there were carousals with aides-de-camp who visited the district, and after-supper visits to a certain outlying street of doubtful reputation; and there was too some obsequiousness to his chief and even to his chief's wife, but all this was done with such a tone of good breeding that no hard names could be applied to it. It all came under the heading of the French saying: *"Il faut que jeunesse se passe."*[4] It was all done with clean hands, in clean linen, with French phrases, and above all among people of the best society and consequently with the approval of people of rank.

So Iván Ilyich served for five years and then came a change in his official life. The new and reformed judicial institutions were introduced, and new men were needed. Iván Ilyich became such a new man. He was offered the post of Examining Magistrate, and he accepted it though the post was in another province and obliged him to give up the connexions he had formed and to make new ones. His friends met to give him a send-off; they had a group-photograph taken and presented him with a silver cigarette-case, and he set off to his new post.

As examining magistrate Iván Ilyich was just as *comme il faut* and decorous a man, inspiring general respect and capable of separating his official duties from his private life, as he had been when acting as an official on special service. His duties now as examining magistrate were far more interesting and attractive than before. In his former position it had been pleasant to wear an undress uniform made by Scharmer, and to pass through the crowd of petitioners and officials who were timorously awaiting an audience with the governor, and who envied him as with free and easy gait he went straight into his chief's private room to have a cup of tea and a cigarette with him. But not many people had then been directly dependent on him—only police officials and the sectarians

---

3. the Old Believers, a large group of Russians (about twenty-five million in 1900), members of a sect which originated in a break with the Orthodox Church in the seventeenth century; they were subject to many legal restrictions.
4. Youth must have its fling. [Translator's note.]

when he went on special missions—and he liked to treat them politely, almost as comrades, as if he were letting them feel that he who had the power to crush them was treating them in this simple, friendly way. There were then but few such people. But now, as an examining magistrate, Iván Ilyich felt that everyone without exception, even the most important and self-satisfied, was in his power, and that he need only write a few words on a sheet of paper with a certain heading, and this or that important, self-satisfied person would be brought before him in the role of an accused person or a witness, and if he did not choose to allow him to sit down, would have to stand before him and answer his questions. Iván Ilyich never abused his power; he tried on the contrary to soften its expression, but the consciousness of it and of the possibility of softening its effect, supplied the chief interest and attraction of his office. In his work itself, especially in his examinations, he very soon acquired a method of eliminating all considerations irrelevant to the legal aspect of the case, and reducing even the most complicated case to a form in which it would be presented on paper only in its externals, completely excluding his personal opinion of the matter, while above all observing every prescribed formality. The work was new and Iván Ilyich was one of the first men to apply the new Code of 1864.[5]

On taking up the post of examining magistrate in a new town, he made new acquaintances and connexions, placed himself on a new footing, and assumed a somewhat different tone. He took up an attitude of rather dignified aloofness towards the provincial authorities, but picked out the best circle of legal gentlemen and wealthy gentry living in the town and assumed a tone of slight dissatisfaction with the government, of moderate liberalism, and of enlightened citizenship. At the same time, without at all altering the elegance of his toilet, he ceased shaving his chin and allowed his beard to grow as it pleased.

Iván Ilyich settled down very pleasantly in this new town. The society there, which inclined towards opposition to the governor, was friendly, his salary was larger, and he began to play *vint* [a form of bridge], which he found added not a little to the pleasure of life, for he had a capacity for cards, played good-humouredly, and calculated rapidly and astutely, so that he usually won.

After living there for two years he met his future wife, Praskóvya Fëdorovna Míkhel, who was the most attractive, clever, and brilliant girl of the set in which he moved, and among other amusements and relaxations from his labours as examining magistrate, Iván Ilyich established light and playful relations with her.

While he had been an official on special service he had been ac-

5. The emancipation of the serfs in 1861 was followed by a thorough all-round reform of judicial proceedings. [Translator's note.]

customed to dance, but now as an examining magistrate it was exceptional for him to do so. If he danced now, he did it as if to show that though he served under the reformed order of things, and had reached the fifth official rank, yet when it came to dancing he could do it better than most people. So at the end of an evening he sometimes danced with Praskóvya Fëdorovna, and it was chiefly during these dances that he captivated her. She fell in love with him. Iván Ilyich had at first no definite intention of marrying, but when the girl fell in love with him he said to himself: "Really, why shouldn't I marry?"

Praskóvya Fëdorovna came of a good family, was not bad looking, and had some little property. Iván Ilyich might have aspired to a more brilliant match, but even this was good. He had his salary, and she, he hoped, would have an equal income. She was well connected, and was a sweet, pretty, and thoroughly correct young woman. To say that Iván Ilyich married because he fell in love with Praskóvya Fëdorovna and found that she sympathized with his views of life would be as incorrect as to say that he married because his social circle approved of the match. He was swayed by both these considerations: the marriage gave him personal satisfaction, and at the same time it was considered the right thing by the most highly placed of his associates.

So Iván Ilyich got married.

The preparations for marriage and the beginning of married life, with its conjugal caresses, the new furniture, new crockery, and new linen, were very pleasant until his wife became pregnant—so that Iván Ilyich had begun to think that marriage would not impair the easy, agreeable, gay, and always decorous character of his life, approved of by society and regarded by himself as natural, but would even improve it. But from the first months of his wife's pregnancy, something new, unpleasant, depressing, and unseemly, and from which there was no way of escape, unexpectedly showed itself.

His wife, without any reason—*de gaieté de coeur* as Iván Ilyich expressed it to himself—began to disturb the pleasure and propriety of their life. She began to be jealous without any cause, expected him to devote his whole attention to her, found fault with everything, and made coarse and ill-mannered scenes.

At first Iván Ilyich hoped to escape from the unpleasantness of this state of affairs by the same easy and decorous relation to life that had served him heretofore: he tried to ignore his wife's disagreeable moods, continued to live in his usual easy and pleasant way, invited friends to his house for a game of cards, and also tried going out to his club or spending his evenings with friends. But one day his wife began upbraiding him so vigorously, using such coarse words, and continued to abuse him every time he did not fulfil her

1014 · Leo Tolstoy

demands, so resolutely and with such evident determination not to give way till he submitted—that is, till he stayed at home and was bored just as she was—that he became alarmed. He now realized that matrimony—at any rate with Praskóvya Fëdorovna—was not always conducive to the pleasures and amenities of life, but on the contrary often infringed both comfort and propriety, and that he must therefore entrench himself against such infringement. And Iván Ilyich began to seek for means of doing so. His official duties were the one thing that imposed upon Praskóvya Fëdorovna, and by means of his official work and the duties attached to it he began struggling with his wife to secure his own independence.

With the birth of their child, the attempts to feed it and the various failures in doing so, and with the real and imaginary illnesses of mother and child, in which Iván Ilyich's sympathy was demanded but about which he understood nothing, the need of securing for himself an existence outside his family life became still more imperative.

As his wife grew more irritable and exacting and Iván Ilyich transferred the centre of gravity of his life more and more to his official work, so did he grow to like his work better and became more ambitious than before.

Very soon, within a year of his wedding, Iván Ilyich had realized that marriage, though it may add some comforts to life, is in fact a very intricate and difficult affair towards which in order to perform one's duty, that is, to lead a decorous life approved of by society, one must adopt a definite attitude just as towards one's official duties.

And Iván Ilyich evolved such an attitude towards married life. He only required of it those conveniences—dinner at home, house-wife, and bed—which it could give him, and above all that propriety of external forms required by public opinion. For the rest he looked for light-hearted pleasure and propriety, and was very thankful when he found them, but if he met with antagonism and querulousness he at once retired into his separate fenced-off world of official duties, where he found satisfaction.

Iván Ilyich was esteemed a good official, and after three years was made Assistant Public Prosecutor. His new duties, their importance, the possibility of indicting and imprisoning anyone he chose, the publicity his speeches received, and the success he had in all these things, made his work still more attractive.

More children came. His wife became more and more querulous and ill-tempered, but the attitude Iván Ilyich had adopted towards his home life rendered him almost impervious to her grumbling.

After seven years' service in that town he was transferred to another province as Public Prosecutor. They moved, but were short of money and his wife did not like the place they moved to. Though the salary was higher the cost of living was greater, besides which two of their children died and family life became still more unpleasant for him.

Praskóvya Fëdorovna blamed her husband for every inconvenience they encountered in their new home. Most of the conversations between husband and wife, especially as to the children's education, led to topics which recalled former disputes, and those disputes were apt to flare up again at any moment. There remained only those rare periods of amorousness which still came to them at times but did not last long. These were islets at which they anchored for a while and then again set out upon that ocean of veiled hostility which showed itself in their aloofness from one another. This aloofness might have grieved Iván Ilyich had he considered that it ought not to exist, but he now regarded the position as normal, and even made it the goal at which he aimed in family life. His aim was to free himself more and more from those unpleasantnesses and to give them a semblance of harmlessness and propriety. He attained this by spending less and less time with his family, and when obliged to be at home he tried to safeguard his position by the presence of outsiders. The chief thing however was that he had his official duties. The whole interest of his life now centered in the official world and that interest absorbed him. The consciousness of his power, being able to ruin anybody he wished to ruin, the importance, even the external dignity of his entry into court, or meetings with his subordinates, his success with superiors and inferiors, and above all his masterly handling of cases, of which he was conscious—all this gave him pleasure and filled his life, together with chats with his colleagues, dinners, and bridge. So that on the whole Iván Ilyich's life continued to flow as he considered it should do—pleasantly and properly.

So things continued for another seven years. His eldest daughter was already sixteen, another child had died, and only one son was left, a schoolboy and a subject of dissensions. Iván Ilyich wanted to put him in the School of Law, but to spite him Praskóvya Fëdorovna entered him at the High School. The daughter had been educated at home and had turned out well: the boy did not learn badly either.

III

So Iván Ilyich lived for seventeen years after his marriage. He was already a Public Prosecutor of long standing, and had declined several proposed transfers while awaiting a more desirable post, when an unanticipated and unpleasant occurrence quite upset the peaceful course of his life. He was expecting to be offered the post of presiding judge in a University town, but Hoppe somehow came to the front and obtained the appointment instead. Iván Ilyich became irritable, reproached Hoppe, and quarrelled both with him and with his immediate superiors—who became colder to him and again passed him over when other appointments were made.

This was in 1880, the hardest year of Iván Ilyich's life. It was then that it became evident on the one hand that his salary was insufficient for them to live on, and on the other that he had been forgotten, and not only this, but that what was for him the greatest and most cruel injustice appeared to others a quite ordinary occurrence. Even his father did not consider it his duty to help him. Iván Ilyich felt himself abandoned by everyone, and that they regarded his position with a salary of 3,500 rubles as quite normal and even fortunate. He alone knew that with the consciousness of the injustices done him, with his wife's incessant nagging, and with the debts he had contracted by living beyond his means, his position was far from normal.

In order to save money that summer he obtained leave of absence and went with his wife to live in the country at her brother's place.

In the country, without his work, he experienced *ennui* for the first time in his life, and not only *ennui* but intolerable depression, and he decided that it was impossible to go on living like that, and that it was necessary to take energetic measures.

Having passed a sleepless night pacing up and down the veranda, he decided to go to Petersburg and bestir himself, in order to punish those who had failed to appreciate him and to get transferred to another ministry.

Next day, despite many protests from his wife and her brother, he started for Petersburg with the sole object of obtaining a post with a salary of five thousand rubles a year. He was no longer bent on any particular department, or tendency, or kind of activity. All he now wanted was an appointment to another post with a salary of five thousand rubles, either in the administration, in the banks, with the railways, in one of the Empress Márya's Institutions,[6] or even in the customs—but it had to carry with it a salary of five thousand rubles and be in a ministry other than that in which they had failed to appreciate him.

And this quest of Iván Ilyich's was crowned with remarkable and unexpected success. At Kursk an acquaintance of his, F. I. Ilyín, got into the first-class carriage, sat down beside Iván Ilyich, and told him of a telegram just received by the governor of Kursk announcing that a change was about to take place in the ministry: Peter Ivánovich was to be superseded by Iván Semënovich.

The proposed change, apart from its significance for Russia, had

---

6. reference to the charitable organization founded by the Empress Márya, wife of Paul I, late in the eighteenth century.

a special significance for Iván Ilyich, because by bringing forward a new man, Peter Petróvich, and consequently his friend Zachár Ivánovich, it was highly favourable for Iván Ilyich, since Zachár Ivánovich was a friend and colleague of his.

In Moscow this news was confirmed, and on reaching Petersburg Iván Ilyich found Zachár Ivánovich and received a definite promise of an appointment in his former department of Justice.

A week later he telegraphed to his wife: "Zachár in Miller's place. I shall receive appointment on presentation of report."

Thanks to this change of personnel, Iván Ilyich had unexpectedly obtained an appointment in his former ministry which placed him two stages above his former colleagues besides giving him five thousand rubles salary and three thousand five hundred rubles for expenses connected with his removal. All his ill humour towards his former enemies and the whole department vanished, and Iván Ilyich was completely happy.

He returned to the country more cheerful and contented than he had been for a long time. Praskóvya Fëdorovna also cheered up and a truce was arranged between them. Iván Ilyich told of how he had been fêted by everybody in Petersburg, how all those who had been his enemies were put to shame and now fawned on him, how envious they were of his appointment, and how much everybody in Petersburg had liked him.

Praskóvya Fëdorovna listened to all this and appeared to believe it. She did not contradict anything, but only made plans for their life in the town to which they were going. Iván Ilyich saw with delight that these plans were his plans, that he and his wife agreed, and that, after a stumble, his life was regaining its due and natural character of pleasant lightheartedness and decorum.

Iván Ilyich had come back for a short time only, for he had to take up his new duties on the 10th of September. Moreover, he needed time to settle into the new place, to move all his belongings from the province, and to buy and order many additional things: in a word, to make such arrangements as he had resolved on, which were almost exactly what Praskóvya Fëdorovna too had decided on.

Now that everything had happened so fortunately, and that he and his wife were at one in their aims and moreover saw so little of one another they got on together better than they had done since the first years of marriage. Iván Ilyich had thought of taking his family away with him at once, but the insistence of his wife's brother and her sister-in-law, who had suddenly become particularly amiable and friendly to him and his family, induced him to depart alone.

So he departed, and the cheerful state of mind induced by his success and by the harmony between his wife and himself, the one intensifying the other, did not leave him. He found a delightful house, just the thing both he and his wife had dreamt of. Spacious, lofty reception rooms in the old style, a convenient and dignified study, rooms for his wife and daughter, a study for his son—it might have been specially built for them. Iván Ilyich himself superintended the arrangements, chose the wallpapers, supplemented the furniture (preferably with antiques which he considered particularly *comme il faut*), and supervised the upholstering. Everything progressed and progressed and approached the ideal he had set himself: even when things were only half completed they exceeded his expectations. He saw what a refined and elegant character, free from vulgarity, it would all have when it was ready. On falling asleep he pictured to himself how the reception-room would look. Looking at the yet unfinished drawing-room he could see the fireplace, the screen, the what-not, the little chairs dotted here and there, the dishes and plates on the walls, and the bronzes, as they would be when everything was in place. He was pleased by the thought of how his wife and daughter, who shared his taste in this matter, would be impressed by it. They were certainly not expecting as much. He had been particularly successful in finding, and buying cheaply, antiques which gave a particularly aristocratic character to the whole place. But in his letters he intentionally understated everything in order to be able to surprise them. All this so absorbed him that his new duties—though he liked his official work—interested him less than he had expected. Sometimes he even had moments of absent-mindedness during the Court Sessions, and would consider whether he should have straight or curved cornices for his curtains. He was so interested in it all that he often did things himself, rearranging the furniture, or rehanging the curtains. Once when mounting a step-ladder to show the upholsterer, who did not understand, how he wanted the hangings draped, he made a false step and slipped, but being a strong and agile man he clung on and only knocked his side against the knob of the window frame. The bruised place was painful but the pain soon passed, and he felt particularly bright and well just then. He wrote: "I feel fifteen years younger." He thought he would have everything ready by September, but it dragged on till mid-October. But the result was charming not only in his eyes but to everyone who saw it.

In reality it was just what is usually seen in the houses of people of moderate means who want to appear rich, and therefore succeed only in resembling others like themselves: there were damasks, dark wood, plants, rugs, and dull and polished bronzes—all the things people of a certain class have in order to resemble other people of that class. His house was so like the others that it would never have been noticed, but to him it all seemed to be quite ex-

ceptional. He was very happy when he met his family at the station and brought them to the newly furnished house all lit up,
where a footman in a white tie opened the door into the hall
decorated with plants, and when they went on into the drawing-
room and the study uttering exclamations of delight. He conducted
them everywhere, drank in their praises eagerly, and beamed with
pleasure. At tea that evening, when Praskóvya Fëdorovna among
other things asked him about his fall, he laughed, and showed them
how he had gone flying and had frightened the upholsterer.

"It's a good thing I'm a bit of an athlete. Another man might
have been killed, but I merely knocked myself, just here; it hurts
when it's touched, but it's passing off already—it's only a bruise."

So they began living in their new home—in which, as always
happens, when they got thoroughly settled in they found they were
just one room short—and with the increased income, which as always was just a little (some five hundred rubles) too little, but it
was all very nice.

Things went particularly well at first, before everything was
finally arranged and while something had still to be done: this
thing bought, that thing ordered, another thing moved, and something else adjusted. Though there were some disputes between
husband and wife, they were both so well satisfied and had so much
to do that it all passed off without any serious quarrels. When
nothing was left to arrange it became rather dull and something
seemed to be lacking, but they were then making acquaintances,
forming habits, and life was growing fuller.

Iván Ilyich spent his mornings at the law court and came home
to dinner, and at first he was generally in a good humour, though
he occasionally became irritable just on account of his house. (Every
spot on the tablecloth or the upholstery, and every broken window-
blind string, irritated him. He had devoted so much trouble to
arranging it all that every disturbance of it distressed him.) But on
the whole his life ran its course as he believed life should do:
easily, pleasantly, and decorously.

He got up at nine, drank his coffee, read the paper, and then
put on his undress uniform and went to the law courts. There the
harness in which he worked had already been stretched to fit him
and he donned it without a hitch: petitioners, inquiries at the
chancery, the chancery itself, and the sittings public and administrative. In all this the thing was to exclude everything fresh and vital,
which always disturbs the regular course of official business, and to
admit only official relations with people, and then only on official
grounds. A man would come, for instance, wanting some information. Iván Ilyich, as one in whose sphere the matter did not lie,
would have nothing to do with him: but if the man had some busi-

ness with him in his official capacity, something that could be expressed on officially stamped paper, he would do everything, positively everything he could within the limits of such relations, and in doing so would maintain the semblance of friendly human relations, that is, would observe the courtesies of life. As soon as the official relations ended, so did everything else. Iván Ilyich possessed this capacity to separate his real life from the official side of affairs and not mix the two, in the highest degree, and by long practice and natural aptitude had brought it to such a pitch that sometimes, in the manner of a virtuoso, he would even allow himself to let the human and official relations mingle. He let himself do this just because he felt that he could at any time he chose resume the strictly official attitude again and drop the human relation. And he did it all easily, pleasantly, correctly, and even artistically. In the intervals between the sessions he smoked, drank tea, chatted a little about politics, a little about general topics, a little about cards, but most of all about official appointments. Tired, but with the feelings of a virtuoso—one of the first violins who has played his part in an orchestra with precision—he would return home to find that his wife and daughter had been out paying calls, or had a visitor, and that his son had been to school, had done his homework with his tutor, and was duly learning what is taught at High Schools. Everything was as it should be. After dinner, if they had no visitors, Iván Ilyich sometimes read a book that was being much discussed at the time, and in the evening settled down to work, that is, read official papers, compared the depositions of witnesses, and noted paragraphs of the Code applying to them. This was neither dull nor amusing. It was dull when he might have been playing bridge, but if no bridge was available it was at any rate better than doing nothing or sitting with his wife. Iván Ilyich's chief pleasure was giving little dinners to which he invited men and women of good social position, and just as his drawing-room resembled all other drawing-rooms so did his enjoyable little parties resemble all other such parties.

Once they even gave a dance. Iván Ilyich enjoyed it and everything went off well, except that it led to a violent quarrel with his wife about the cakes and sweets. Praskóvya Fëdorovna had made her own plans, but Iván Ilyich insisted on getting everything from an expensive confectioner and ordered too many cakes, and the quarrel occurred because some of those cakes were left over and the confectioner's bill came to forty-five rubles. It was a great and disagreeable quarrel. Praskóvya Fëdorovna called him "a fool and an imbecile," and he clutched at his head and made angry allusions to divorce.

But the dance itself had been enjoyable. The best people were there, and Iván Ilyich had danced with Princess Trúfonova, a sister of the distinguished founder of the Society "Bear my Burden."

The pleasures connected with his work were pleasures of ambition; his social pleasures were those of vanity; but Iván Ilyich's greatest pleasure was playing bridge. He acknowledged that whatever disagreeable incident happened in his life, the pleasure that beamed like a ray of light above everything else was to sit down to bridge with good players, not noisy partners, and of course to four-handed bridge (with five players it was annoying to have to stand out, though one pretended not to mind), to play a clever and serious game (when the cards allowed it) and then to have supper and drink a glass of wine. After a game of bridge, especially if he had won a little (to win a large sum was unpleasant), Iván Ilyich went to bed in specially good humour.

So they lived. They formed a circle of acquaintances among the best people and were visited by people of importance and by young folk. In their views as to their acquaintances, husband, wife, and daughter were entirely agreed, and tacitly and unanimously kept at arm's length and shook off the various shabby friends and relations who, with much show of affection, gushed into the drawing-room with its Japanese plates on the walls. Soon these shabby friends ceased to obtrude themselves and only the best people remained in the Golovíns' set.

Young men made up to Lisa, and Petríshchev, an examining magistrate and Dmítri Ivánovich Petríshchev's son and sole heir, began to be so attentive to her that Iván Ilyich had already spoken to Praskóvya Fëdorovna about it, and considered whether they should not arrange a party for them, or get up some private theatricals.

So they lived, and all went well, without change, and life flowed pleasantly.

IV

They were all in good health. It could not be called ill health if Iván Ilyich sometimes said that he had a queer taste in his mouth and felt some discomfort in his left side.

But this discomfort increased and, though not exactly painful, grew into a sense of pressure in his side accompanied by ill humour. And his irritability became worse and worse and began to mar the agreeable, easy, and correct life that had established itself in the Golovín family. Quarrels between husband and wife became more and more frequent, and soon the ease and amenity disappeared and even the decorum was barely maintained. Scenes again became frequent, and very few of those islets remained on which husband and wife could meet without an explosion. Praskóvya Fëdorovna now had good reason to say that her husband's temper was trying. With characteristic exaggeration she said he had always had a dreadful temper, and that it had needed all her good nature to put up with it for twenty years. It was true that now the quarrels were started by him. His bursts of temper always came just before dinner, often just as he began to eat his soup. Sometimes he noticed that a plate or dish was chipped, or the food was not right, or his son put his elbow on the table, or his daughter's hair was not done as he liked it, and for all this he blamed Praskóvya Fëdorovna. At first she retorted and said disagreeable things to him, but once or twice he fell into such a rage at the beginning of dinner that she realized it was due to some physical derangement brought on by taking food, and so she restrained herself and did not answer, but only hurried to get the dinner over. She regarded this self-restraint as highly praiseworthy. Having come to the conclusion that her husband had a dreadful temper and made her life miserable, she began to feel sorry for herself, and the more she pitied herself the more she hated her husband. She began to wish he would die; yet she did not want him to die because then his salary would cease. And this irritated her against him still more. She considered herself dreadfully unhappy just because not even his death could save her, and though she concealed her exasperation, that hidden exasperation of hers increased his irritation also.

After one scene in which Iván Ilyich had been particularly unfair and after which he had said in explanation that he certainly was irritable but that it was due to his not being well, she said that if he was ill it should be attended to, and insisted on his going to see a celebrated doctor.

He went. Everything took place as he had expected and as it always does. There was the usual waiting and the important air assumed by the doctor, with which he was so familiar (resembling that which he himself assumed in court), and the sounding and listening, and the questions which called for answers that were foregone conclusions and were evidently unnecessary, and the look of importance which implied that "if only you put yourself in our hands we will arrange everything—we know indubitably how it has to be done, always in the same way for everybody alike." It was all just as it was in the law courts. The doctor put on just the same air towards him as he himself put on towards an accused person.

The doctor said that so-and-so indicated that there was so-and-so inside the patient, but if the investigation of so-and-so did not confirm this, then he must assume that and that. If he assumed that and that, then . . . and so on. To Iván Ilyich only one question was important: was his case serious or not? But the doctor ignored that inappropriate question. From his point of view it was not the one under consideration, the real question was to decide between a floating kidney, chronic catarrh, or appendicitis. It was not a question of Iván Ilyich's life or death, but one between a floating kidney and appendicitis. And that question the doctor solved brilliantly, as it seemed to Iván Ilyich, in favour of the appendix, with the reservation that should an examination of the urine give fresh indications the matter would be reconsidered. All this was just what Iván Ilyich had himself brilliantly accomplished a thousand times in dealing with men on trial. The doctor summed up just as brilliantly, looking over his spectacles triumphantly and even gaily at the accused. From the doctor's summing up Iván Ilyich concluded that things were bad, but that for the doctor, and perhaps for everybody else, it was a matter of indifference, though for him it was bad. And this conclusion struck him painfully, arousing in him a great feeling of pity for himself and of bitterness towards the doctor's indifference to a matter of such importance.

He said nothing of this, but rose, placed the doctor's fee on the table, and remarked with a sigh: "We sick people probably often put inappropriate questions. But tell me, in general, is this complaint dangerous, or not? . . ."

The doctor looked at him sternly over his spectacles with one eye, as if to say: "Prisoner, if you will not keep to the questions put to you, I shall be obliged to have you removed from the court."

"I have already told you what I consider necessary and proper. The analysis may show something more." And the doctor bowed.

Iván Ilyich went out slowly, seated himself disconsolately in his sledge, and drove home. All the way home he was going over what the doctor had said, trying to translate those complicated, obscure, scientific phrases into plain language and find in them an answer to the question: "Is my condition bad? Is it very bad? Or is there as yet nothing much wrong?" And it seemed to him that the meaning of what the doctor had said was that it was very bad. Everything in the streets seemed depressing. The cabmen, the houses, the passers-by, and the shops, were dismal. His ache, this dull gnawing ache that never ceased for a moment, seemed to have acquired a new and more serious significance from the doctor's dubious remarks. Iván Ilyich now watched it with a new and oppressive feeling.

He reached home and began to tell his wife about it. She listened, but in the middle of his account his daughter came in with her hat on, ready to go out with her mother. She sat down reluctantly to listen to this tedious story, but could not stand it long, and her mother too did not hear him to the end.

"Well, I am very glad," she said. "Mind now to take your medicine regularly. Give me the prescription and I'll send Gerásim to the chemist's." And she went to get ready to go out.

While she was in the room Iván Ilyich had hardly taken time to breathe, but he sighed deeply when she left it.

"Well," he thought, "perhaps it isn't so bad after all."

He began taking his medicine and following the doctor's directions, which had been altered after the examination of the urine. But then it happened that there was a contradiction between the indications drawn from the examination of the urine and the symptoms that showed themselves. It turned out that what was happening differed from what the doctor had told him, and that he had either forgotten, or blundered, or hidden something from him. He could not, however, be blamed for that, and Iván Ilyich still obeyed his orders implicitly and at first derived some comfort from doing so.

From the time of his visit to the doctor, Iván Ilyich's chief occupation was the exact fulfilment of the doctor's instructions regarding hygiene and the taking of medicine, and the observation of his pain and his excretions. His chief interests came to be people's ailments and people's health. When sickness, deaths, or recoveries were mentioned in his presence, especially when the illness resembled his own, he listened with agitation which he tried to hide, asked questions, and applied what he heard to his own case.

The pain did not grow less, but Iván Ilyich made efforts to force himself to think that he was better. And he could do this so long as nothing agitated him. But as soon as he had any unpleasantness with his wife, any lack of success in his official work, or held bad cards at bridge, he was at once acutely sensible of his disease. He had formerly borne such mischances, hoping soon to adjust what was wrong, to master it and attain success, or make a grand slam. But now every mischance upset him and plunged him into despair. He would say to himself. "There now, just as I was beginning to get better and the medicine had begun to take effect, comes this accursed misfortune, or unpleasantness . . ." And he was furious with the mishap, or with the people who were causing the unpleasantness and killing him, for he felt that this fury was killing him but could not restrain it. One would have thought that it should have been clear to him that this exasperation with circumstances and people aggravated his illness, and that he ought therefore to ignore unpleasant occurrences. But he drew the very opposite conclusion: he said that he needed peace, and he watched for everything that might disturb it and became irritable at the slightest infringement of it. His condition was rendered worse by the fact that he read medical books and consulted doctors. The progress of his disease was so gradual that he could deceive himself when comparing one day with another—the difference was so slight. But when he consulted the doctors it seemed to him that he was getting worse, and even very rapidly. Yet despite this he was continually consulting them.

That month he went to see another celebrity, who told him almost the same as the first had done but put his questions rather differently, and the interview with this celebrity only increased Iván Ilyich's doubts and fears. A friend of a friend of his, a very good doctor, diagnosed his illness again quite differently from the others, and though he predicted recovery, his questions and suppositions bewildered Iván Ilyich still more and increased his doubts. A homeopathist diagnosed the disease in yet another way, and prescribed medicine which Iván Ilyich took secretly for a week. But after a week, not feeling any improvement and having lost confidence both in the former doctor's treatment and in this one's, he became still more despondent. One day a lady acquaintance mentioned a cure effected by a wonder-working icon. Iván Ilyich caught himself listening attentively and beginning to believe that it had occurred. This incident alarmed him. "Has my mind really weakened to such an extent?" he asked himself. "Nonsense! It's all rubbish. I mustn't give way to nervous fears but having chosen a doctor must keep strictly to his treatment. That is what I will do. Now it's all settled. I won't think about it, but will follow the treatment seriously till summer, and then we shall see. From now there must be no more of this wavering!" This was easy to say but impossible to carry out. The pain in his side oppressed him and seemed to grow worse and more incessant, while the taste in his mouth grew stranger and stranger. It seemed to him that his breath had a disgusting smell, and he was conscious of a loss of appetite and strength. There was no deceiving himself: something terrible, new, and more important than anything before in his life, was taking place within him of which he alone was aware. Those about him did not understand or would not understand it, but thought everything in the world was going on as usual. That tormented Iván Ilyich more than anything. He saw that his household, especially his wife and daughter who were in a perfect whirl of visiting, did not understand anything of it and were annoyed that he was so depressed and so exacting, as if he were to blame for it. Though they tried to disguise it he saw that he was an obstacle in their path, and that his wife had adopted a definite line in regard to his illness and kept to it regardless of anything he said or did. Her attitude was this: "You know," she would say to her friends, "Iván Ilyich can't do as other people do, and keep to the treatment prescribed for him. One day he'll take his drops and keep strictly to his diet and go to bed in good time, but the next day unless I watch him he'll suddenly forget his medicine, eat sturgeon—which is forbidden—and sit up playing cards till one o'clock in the morning."

"Oh, come, when was that?" Iván Ilyich would ask in vexation. "Only once at Peter Ivánovich's."

"And yesterday with Shébek."

"Well, even if I hadn't stayed up, this pain would have kept me awake."

"Be that as it may you'll never get well like that, but will always make us wretched."

Praskóvya Fëdorovna's attitude to Iván Ilyich's illness, as she expressed it both to others and to him, was that it was his own fault and was another of the annoyances he caused her. Iván Ilyich felt that this opinion escaped her involuntarily—but that did not make it easier for him.

At the law courts too, Iván Ilyich noticed, or thought he noticed, a strange attitude towards himself. It sometimes seemed to him that people were watching him inquisitively as a man whose place might soon be vacant. Then again, his friends would suddenly begin to chaff him in a friendly way about his low spirits, as if the awful, horrible, and unheard-of thing that was going on within him, incessantly gnawing at him and irresistibly drawing him away, was a very agreeable subject for jests. Schwartz in particular irritated him by his jocularity, vivacity, and *savoir-faire*, which reminded him of what he himself had been ten years ago.

Friends came to make up a set and they sat down to cards. They dealt, bending the new cards to soften them, and he sorted the diamonds in his hand and found he had seven. His partner said "No trumps" and supported him with two diamonds. What more could be wished for? It ought to be jolly and lively. They would make a grand slam. But suddenly Iván Ilyich was conscious of that gnawing pain, that taste in his mouth, and it seemed ridiculous that in such circumstances he should be pleased to make a grand slam.

He looked at his partner Mikháil Mikháylovich, who rapped the table with his strong hand and instead of snatching up the tricks pushed the cards courteously and indulgently towards Iván Ilyich that he might have the pleasure of gathering them up without the trouble of stretching out his hand for them. "Does he think I am too weak to stretch out my arm?" thought Iván Ilyich, and forgetting what he was doing he over-trumped his partner, missing the grand slam by three tricks. And what was most awful of all was that he saw how upset Mikháil Mikháylovich was about it but did not himself care. And it was dreadful to realize why he did not care.

They all saw that he was suffering, and said: "We can stop if you are tired. Take a rest." Lie down? No, he was not at all tired, and he finished the rubber. All were gloomy and silent. Iván Ilyich felt that he had diffused this gloom over them and could not dispel it. They had supper and went away, and Iván Ilyich was left alone with the consciousness that his life was poisoned and was poisoning the lives of others, and that this poison did not weaken but penetrated more and more deeply into his whole being.

With this consciousness, and with physical pain besides the terror, he must go to bed, often to lie awake the greater part of the night. Next morning he had to get up again, dress, go to the law courts, speak, and write; or if he did not go out, spend at home those twenty-four hours a day each of which was a torture. And he had to live thus all alone on the brink of an abyss, with no one who understood or pitied him.

V

So one month passed and then another. Just before the New Year his brother-in-law came to town and stayed at their house. Iván Ilyich was at the law courts and Praskóvya Fëdorovna had gone shopping. When Iván Ilyich came home and entered his study he found his brother-in-law there—a healthy, florid man—unpacking his portmanteau himself. He raised his head on hearing Iván Ilyich's footsteps and looked up at him for a moment without a word. That stare told Iván everything. His brother-in-law opened his mouth to utter an exclamation of surprise but checked himself, and that action confirmed it all.

"I have changed, eh?"

"Yes, there is a change."

And after that, try as he would to get his brother-in-law to return to the subject of his looks, the latter would say nothing about it. Praskóvya Fëdorovna came home and her brother went out to her. Iván Ilyich locked the door and began to examine himself in the glass, first full face, then in profile. He took up a portrait of himself taken with his wife, and compared it with what he saw in the glass. The change in him was immense. Then he bared his arms to the elbow, looked at them, drew the sleeves down again, sat down on an ottoman, and grew blacker than night.

"No, no, this won't do!" he said to himself, and jumped up, went to the table, took up some law papers and began to read them, but could not continue. He unlocked the door and went into the reception-room. The door leading to the drawing-room was shut. He approached it on tiptoe and listened.

"No, you are exaggerating!" Praskóvya Fëdorovna was saying.

"Exaggerating! Don't you see it? Why, he's a dead man! Look at his eyes—there's no light in them. But what is it that is wrong with him?"

"No one knows. Nikoláevich [that was another doctor] said something, but I don't know what. And Leshchetítsky [this was the celebrated specialist] said quite the contrary . . ."

Iván Ilyich walked away, went to his own room, lay down and began musing: "The kidney, a floating kidney." He recalled all the doctors had told him of how it detached itself and swayed about. And by an effort of imagination he tried to catch that kidney and arrest it and support it. So little was needed for this, it seemed to him. "No, I'll go to see Peter Ivánovich again." [That was the friend whose friend was a doctor.] He rang, ordered the carriage, and got ready to go.

"Where are you going, *Jean?*" asked his wife, with a specially sad and exceptionally kind look.

This exceptionally kind look irritated him. He looked morosely at her.

"I must go to see Peter Ivánovich."

He went to see Peter Ivánovich, and together they went to see his friend, the doctor. He was in, and Iván Ilyich had a long talk with him.

Reviewing the anatomical and physiological details of what in the doctor's opinion was going on inside him, he understood it all.

There was something, a small thing, in the vermiform appendix. It might all come right. Only stimulate the energy of one organ and check the activity of another, then absorption would take place and everything would come right. He got home rather late for dinner, ate his dinner, and conversed cheerfully, but could not for a long time bring himself to go back to work in his room. At last, however, he went to his study and did what was necessary, but the consciousness that he had put something aside—an important, intimate matter which he would revert to when his work was done—never left him. When he had finished his work he remembered that this intimate matter was the thought of his vermiform appendix. But he did not give himself up to it, and went to the drawing-room for tea. There were callers there, including the examining magistrate who was a desirable match for his daughter, and they were conversing, playing the piano, and singing. Iván Ilyich, as Praskóvya Fëdorovna remarked, spent that evening more cheerfully than usual, but he never for a moment forgot that he had postponed the important matter of the appendix. At eleven o'clock he said goodnight and went to his bedroom. Since his illness he had slept alone in a small room next to his study. He undressed and took up a novel by Zola,[7] but instead of reading it he fell into thought, and in his imagination that desired improvement in the vermiform appendix occurred. There was the absorption and evacuation and the re-

7. Émile Zola (1840–1902), French novelist, author of the *Rougon-Macquart* novels (*Nana, Germinal,* and so on). Tolstoy condemned Zola for his naturalistic theories and considered his novels crude and gross.

establishment of normal activity. "Yes, that's it!" he said to himself. "One need only assist nature, that's all." He remembered his
medicine, rose, took it, and lay down on his back watching for the
beneficent action of the medicine and for it to lessen the pain. "I
need only take it regularly and avoid all injurious influences. I am
already feeling better, much better." He began touching his side:
it was not painful to the touch. "There, I really don't feel it. It's
much better already." He put out the light and turned on his
side . . . "The appendix is getting better, absorption is occurring."
Suddenly he felt the old, familiar, dull, gnawing pain, stubborn and
serious. There was the same familiar loathsome taste in his mouth.
His heart sank and he felt dazed. "My God! My God!" he muttered. "Again, again! And it will never cease." And suddenly the
matter presented itself in a quite different aspect. "Vermiform
appendix! Kidney!" he said to himself. "It's not a question of
appendix or kidney, but of life and . . . death. Yes, life was there
and now it is going, going and I cannot stop it. Yes. Why deceive
myself? Isn't it obvious to everyone but me that I'm dying, and that
it's only a question of weeks, days . . . it may happen this moment.
There was light and now there is darkness. I was here and now
I'm going there! Where?" A chill came over him, his breathing
ceased, and he felt only the throbbing of his heart.

"When I am not, what will there be? There will be nothing.
Then where shall I be when I am no more? Can this be dying? No,
I don't want to!" He jumped up and tried to light the candle, felt
for it with trembling hands, dropped candle and candlestick on the
floor, and fell back on his pillow.

"What's the use? It makes no difference," he said to himself,
staring with wide-open eyes into the darkness. "Death. Yes, death.
And none of them know or wish to know it, and they have no pity
for me. Now they are playing." (He heard through the door the
distant sound of a song and its accompaniment.) "It's all the same
to them, but they will die too! Fools! I first, and they later, but
it will be the same for them. And now they are merry . . . the
beasts!"

Anger choked him and he was agonizingly, unbearably miserable.
"It is impossible that all men have been doomed to suffer this
awful horror!" He raised himself.

"Something must be wrong. I must calm myself—must think it
all over from the beginning." And he again began thinking. "Yes,
the beginning of my illness: I knocked my side, but I was still quite
well that day and the next. It hurt a little, then rather more. I saw
the doctors, then followed despondency and anguish, more doctors,
and I drew nearer to the abyss. My strength grew less and I kept
coming nearer and nearer, and now I have wasted away and there

is no light in my eyes. I think of the appendix—but this is death! I think of mending the appendix, and all the while here is death! Can it really be death?" Again terror seized him and he gasped for breath. He leant down and began feeling for the matches, pressing with his elbow on the stand beside the bed. It was in his way and hurt him, he grew furious with it, pressed on it still harder, and upset it. Breathless and in despair he fell on his back, expecting death to come immediately.

Meanwhile the visitors were leaving. Praskóvya Fëdorovna was seeing them off. She heard something fall and came in.

"What has happened?"

"Nothing. I knocked it over accidentally."

She went out and returned with a candle. He lay there panting heavily, like a man who has run a thousand yards, and stared upwards at her with a fixed look.

"What is it, *Jean?*"

"No . . . o . . . thing. I upset it." ("Why speak of it? She won't understand," he thought.)

And in truth she did not understand. She picked up the stand, lit his candle, and hurried away to see another visitor off. When she came back he still lay on his back, looking upwards.

"What is it? Do you feel worse?"

"Yes."

She shook her head and sat down.

"Do you know, *Jean,* I think we must ask Leshchetísky to come and see you here."

This meant calling in the famous specialist, regardless of expense. He smiled malignantly and said "No." She remained a little longer and then went up to him and kissed his forehead.

While she was kissing him he hated her from the bottom of his soul and with difficulty refrained from pushing her away.

"Good-night. Please God you'll sleep."

"Yes."

VI

Iván Ilyich saw that he was dying, and he was in continual despair.

In the depth of his heart he knew he was dying, but not only was he not accustomed to the thought, he simply did not and could not grasp it.

The syllogism he had learned from Kiesewetter's *Logic*:[8] "Caius is a man, men are mortal, therefore Caius is mortal," had always seemed to him correct as applied to Caius, but certainly not as

8. Karl Kiesewetter (1766–1819) was a German popularizer of Kant's philosophy. His *Outline of Logic Ac-* *cording to Kantian Principles* (1796) was widely used in Russian adaptations as a schoolbook.

applied to himself. That Caius—man in the abstract—was mortal, was perfectly correct, but he was not Caius, not an abstract man, but a creature quite, quite separate from all others. He had been little Ványa, with a mamma and a papa, with Mítya and Volódya, with the toys, a coachman and a nurse, afterwards with Kátenka and with all the joys, griefs, and delights of childhood, boyhood, and youth. What did Caius know of the smell of that striped leather ball Ványa had been so fond of? Had Caius kissed his mother's hand like that, and did the silk of her dress rustle so for Caius? Had he rioted like that at school when the pastry was bad? Had Caius been in love like that? Could Caius preside at a session as he did? Caius really was mortal, and it was right for him to die; but for me, little Ványa, Iván Ilyich, with all my thoughts and emotions, it's altogether a different matter. It cannot be that I ought to die. That would be too terrible."

Such was his feeling.

"If I had to die like Caius I should have known it was so. An inner voice would have told me so, but there was nothing of the sort in me and I and all my friends felt that our case was quite different from that of Caius. And now here it is!" he said to himself. "It can't be. It's impossible! But here it is. How is this? How is one to understand it?"

He could not understand it, and tried to drive this false, incorrect, morbid thought away and to replace it by other proper and healthy thoughts. But that thought, and not the thought only but the reality itself, seemed to come and confront him.

And to replace that thought he called up a succession of others, hoping to find in them some support. He tried to get back into the former current of thoughts that had once screened the thought of death from him. But strange to say, all that had formerly shut off, hidden, and destroyed, his consciousness of death, no longer had that effect. Iván Ilyich now spent most of his time in attempting to re-establish that old current. He would say to himself: "I will take up my duties again—after all I used to live by them." And banishing all doubts he would go to the law courts, enter into conversation with his colleagues, and sit carelessly as was his wont, scanning the crowd with a thoughtful look and leaning both his emaciated arms on the arms of his oak chair; bending over as usual to a colleague and drawing his papers nearer he would interchange whispers with him, and then suddenly raising his eyes and sitting erect would pronounce certain words and open the proceedings. But suddenly in the midst of those proceedings the pain in his side, regardless of the stage the proceedings had reached, would begin its own gnawing work. Iván Ilyich would turn his attention to it and try to drive the thought of it away, but without success. *It* would come and stand before him and look at him, and he would be petrified and the light would die out of his eyes, and he would again begin asking himself whether *It* alone was true. And his colleagues and subordinates would see with surprise and distress that he, the brilliant and subtle judge, was becoming confused and making mistakes. He would shake himself, try to pull himself together, manage somehow to bring the sitting to a close, and return home with the sorrowful consciousness that his judicial labours could not as formerly hide from him what he wanted them to hide, and could not deliver him from *It*. And what was worst of all was that *It* drew his attention to itself not in order to make him take some action but only that he should look at *It*, look it straight in the face: look at it without doing anything, suffer inexpressibly.

And to save himself from this condition Iván Ilyich looked for consolations—new screens—and new screens were found and for a while seemed to save him, but then they immediately fell to pieces or rather became transparent, as if *It* penetrated them and nothing could veil *It*.

In these latter days he would go into the drawing-room he had arranged—that drawing-room where he had fallen and for the sake of which (how bitterly ridiculous it seemed) he had sacrificed his life—for he knew that his illness originated with that knock. He would enter and see that something had scratched the polished table. He would look for the cause of this and find that it was the bronze ornamentation of an album, that had got bent. He would take up the expensive album which he had lovingly arranged, and feel vexed with his daughter and her friends for their untidiness—for the album was torn here and there and some of the photographs turned upside down. He would put it carefully in order and bend the ornamentation back into position. Then it would occur to him to place all those things in another corner of the room, near the plants. He would call the footman, but his daughter or wife would come to help him. They would not agree, and his wife would contradict him, and he would dispute and grow angry. But that was all right, for then he did not think about *It*. *It* was invisible.

But then, when he was moving something himself, his wife would say: "Let the servants do it. You will hurt yourself again." And suddenly *It* would flash through the screen and he would see it. It was just a flash, and he hoped it would disappear, but he would involuntarily pay attention to his side. "It sits there as before, gnawing just the same!" And he could no longer forget *It*, but could distinctly see it looking at him from behind the flowers. "What is it all for?"

"It really is so! I lost my life over that curtain as I might have done when storming a fort. Is that possible? How terrible and how stupid. It can't be true! It can't, but it is."

He would go to his study, lie down, and again be alone with *It*: face to face with *It*. And nothing could be done with *It* except to look at it and shudder.

VII

How it happened it is impossible to say because it came about step by step, unnoticed, but in the third month of Iván Ilyich's illness, his wife, his daughter, his son, his acquaintances, the doctors, the servants, and above all he himself, were aware that the whole interest he had for other people was whether he would soon vacate his place, and at last release the living from the discomfort caused by his presence and be himself released from his sufferings.

He slept less and less. He was given opium and hypodermic injections of morphine, but this did not relieve him. The dull depression he experienced in a somnolent condition at first gave him a little relief, but only as something new, afterwards it became as distressing as the pain itself or even more so.

Special foods were prepared for him by the doctors' orders, but all those foods became increasingly distasteful and disgusting to him.

For his excretions also special arrangements had to be made, and this was a torment to him every time—a torment from the uncleanliness, the unseemliness, and the smell, and from knowing that another person had to take part in it.

But just through this most unpleasant matter, Iván Ilyich obtained comfort. Gerásim, the butler's young assistant, always came in to carry the things out. Gerásim was a clean, fresh peasant lad, grown stout on town food and always cheerful and bright. At first the sight of him, in his clean Russian peasant costume, engaged on that disgusting task embarrassed Iván Ilyich.

Once when he got up from the commode too weak to draw up his trousers, he dropped into a soft armchair and looked with horror at his bare, enfeebled thighs with the muscles so sharply marked on them.

Gerásim with a firm light tread, his heavy boots emitting a pleasant smell of tar and fresh winter air, came in wearing a clean Hessian apron, the sleeves of his print shirt tucked up over his strong bare young arms; and refraining from looking at his sick master out of consideration for his feelings, and restraining the joy of life that beamed from his face, he went up to the commode.

"Gerásim!" said Iván Ilyich in a weak voice.

Gerásim started, evidently afraid he might have committed some blunder, and with a rapid movement turned his fresh, kind, simple young face which just showed the first downy signs of a beard.

"Yes, sir?"

"That must be very unpleasant for you. You must forgive me. I am helpless."

"Oh, why, sir," and Gerásim's eyes beamed and he showed his glistening white teeth, "what's a little trouble? It's a case of illness with you, sir."

And his deft strong hands did their accustomed task, and he went out of the room stepping lightly. Five minutes later he as lightly returned.

Iván Ilyich was still sitting in the same position in the armchair.

"Gerásim," he said when the latter had replaced the freshly-washed utensil. "Please come here and help me." Gerásim went up to him. "Lift me up. It is hard for me to get up, and I have sent Dmítri away."

Gerásim went up to him, grasped his master with his strong arms deftly but gently, in the same way that he stepped—lifted him, supported him with one hand, and with the other drew up his trousers and would have set him down again, but Iván Ilyich asked to be led to the sofa. Gerásim, without an effort and without apparent pressure, led him, almost lifting him, to the sofa and placed him on it.

"Thank you. How easily and well you do it all!"

Gerásim smiled again and turned to leave the room. But Iván Ilyich felt his presence such a comfort that he did not want to let him go.

"One thing more, please move up that chair. No, the other one—under my feet. It is easier for me when my feet are raised."

Gerásim brought the chair, set it down gently in place, and raised Iván Ilyich's legs on to it. It seemed to Iván Ilyich that he felt better while Gerásim was holding up his legs.

"It's better when my legs are higher," he said. "Place that cushion under them."

Gerásim did so. He again lifted the legs and placed them, and again Iván Ilyich felt better while Gerásim held his legs. When he set them down Iván Ilyich fancied he felt worse.

"Gerásim," he said. "Are you busy now?"

"Not at all, sir," said Gerásim, who had learnt from the townsfolk how to speak to gentlefolk.

"What have you still to do?"

"What have I to do? I've done everything except chopping the logs for to-morrow."

"Then hold my legs up a bit higher, can you?"

"Of course I can. Why not?" And Gerásim raised his master's legs higher and Iván Ilyich thought that in that position he did not feel any pain at all.

"And how about the logs?"

"Don't trouble about that, sir. There's plenty of time."

Iván Ilyich told Gerásim to sit down and hold his legs, and began to talk to him. And strange to say it seemed to him that he felt better while Gerásim held his legs up.

After that Iván Ilyich would sometimes call Gerásim and get him to hold his legs on his shoulders, and he liked talking to him. Gerásim did it all easily, willingly, simply, and with a good nature that touched Iván Ilyich. Health, strength, and vitality in other people were offensive to him, but Gerásim's strength and vitality did not mortify but soothed him.

What tormented Iván Ilyich most was the deception, the lie, which for some reason they all accepted, that he was not dying but was simply ill, and that he only need keep quiet and undergo a treatment and then something very good would result. He however knew that do what they would nothing would come of it, only still more agonizing suffering and death. This deception tortured him—their not wishing to admit what they all knew and what he knew, but wanting to lie to him concerning his terrible condition, and wishing and forcing him to participate in that lie. Those lies —lies enacted over him on the eve of his death and destined to degrade this awful, solemn act to the level of their visitings, their curtains, their sturgeon for dinner—were a terrible agony for Iván Ilyich. And strangely enough, many times when they were going through their antics over him he had been within a hairbreadth of calling out to them: "Stop lying! You know and I know that I am dying. Then at least stop lying about it!" But he had never had the spirit to do it. The awful, terrible act of his dying was, he could see, reduced by those about him to the level of a casual, unpleasant, and almost indecorous incident (as if someone entered a drawing-room diffusing an unpleasant odour) and this was done by that very decorum which he had served all his life long. He saw that no one felt for him, because no one even wished to grasp his position. Only Gerásim recognized and pitied him. And so Iván Ilyich felt at ease only with him. He felt comforted when Gerásim supported his legs (sometimes all night long) and refused to go to bed, saying: "Don't you worry, Iván Ilyich. I'll get sleep enough later on," or when he suddenly became familiar and exclaimed: "If you weren't sick it would be another matter, but as it is, why should I grudge a little trouble?" Gerásim alone did not lie; everything showed that he alone understood the facts of the case and did not consider it necessary to disguise them, but simply felt sorry for his emaciated and enfeebled master. Once when Iván Ilyich was sending him away he even said straight out: "We shall all of us die, so why should I grudge a little trouble?"—expressing the fact that he did not think his work burdensome, because he was doing it for a dying man and hoped someone would do the same for him when his time came.

Apart from this lying, or because of it, what most tormented Iván Ilyich was that no one pitied him as he wished to be pitied. At certain moments after prolonged suffering he wished most of all (though he would have been ashamed to confess it) for someone to pity him as a sick child is pitied. He longed to be petted and comforted. He knew he was an important functionary, that he had a beard turning grey, and that therefore what he longed for was impossible, but still he longed for it. And in Gerásim's attitude towards him there was something akin to what he wished for, and so that attitude comforted him. Iván Ilyich wanted to weep, wanted to be petted and cried over, and then his colleague Shébek would come, and instead of weeping and being petted, Iván Ilyich would assume a serious, severe, and profound air, and by force of habit would express his opinion on a decision of the Court of Appeal and would stubbornly insist on that view. This falsity around him and within him did more than anything else to poison his last days.

VIII

It was morning. He knew it was morning because Gerásim had gone, and Peter the footman had come and put out the candles, drawn back one of the curtains, and begun quietly to tidy up. Whether it was morning or evening, Friday or Sunday, made no difference, it was all just the same: the gnawing, unmitigated, agonizing pain, never ceasing for an instant, the consciousness of life inexorably waning but not yet extinguished, the approach of that ever dreaded and hateful Death which was the only reality, and always the same falsity. What were days, weeks, hours, in such a case?

"Will you have some tea, sir?"

"He wants things to be regular, and wishes the gentlefolk to drink tea in the morning," thought Iván Ilyich, and only said "No."

"Wouldn't you like to move onto the sofa, sir?"

"He wants to tidy up the room, and I'm in the way. I am uncleanliness and disorder," he thought, and said only:

"No, leave me alone."

The man went on bustling about. Iván Ilyich stretched out his hand. Peter came up, ready to help.

"What is it, sir?"

"My watch."

Peter took the watch which was close at hand and gave it to his master.

"Half-past eight. Are they up?"

"No sir, except Vladímir Ivánich" (the son) "who has gone to school. Praskóvya Fëdorovna ordered me to wake her if you asked for her. Shall I do so?"

"No, there's no need to." "Perhaps I'd better have some tea," he thought, and added aloud: "Yes, bring me some tea."

Peter went to the door, but Iván Ilyich dreaded being left alone. "How can I keep him here? Oh yes, my medicine." "Peter, give me my medicine." "Why not? Perhaps it may still do me some good." He took a spoonful and swallowed it. "No, it won't help. It's all tomfoolery, all deception," he decided as soon as he became aware of the familiar, sickly, hopeless taste. "No, I can't believe in it any longer. But the pain, why this pain? If it would only cease just for a moment!" And he moaned. Peter turned towards him. "It's all right. Go and fetch me some tea."

Peter went out. Left alone Iván Ilyich groaned not so much with pain, terrible though that was, as from mental anguish. Always and forever the same, always these endless days and nights. If only it would come quicker! If only *what* would come quicker? Death, darkness? . . . No, no! Anything rather than death!

When Peter returned with the tea on a tray, Iván Ilyich stared at him for a time in perplexity, not realizing who and what he was. Peter was disconcerted by that look and his embarrassment brought Iván Ilyich to himself.

"Oh, tea! All right, put it down. Only help me to wash and put on a clean shirt."

And Iván Ilyich began to wash. With pauses for rest, he washed his hands and then his face, cleaned his teeth, brushed his hair, and looked in the glass. He was terrified by what he saw, especially by the limp way in which his hair clung to his pallid forehead.

While his shirt was being changed he knew that he would be still more frightened at the sight of his body, so he avoided looking at it. Finally he was ready. He drew on a dressing-gown, wrapped himself in a plaid, and sat down in the armchair to take his tea. For a moment he felt refreshed, but as soon as he began to drink the tea he was again aware of the same taste, and the pain also returned. He finished it with an effort, and then lay down stretching out his legs, and dismissed Peter.

Always the same. Now a spark of hope flashes up, then a sea of despair rages, and always pain; always pain, always despair, and always the same. When alone he had a dreadful and distressing desire to call someone, but he knew beforehand that with others present it would be still worse. "Another dose of morphine—to lose consciousness. I will tell him, the doctor, that he must think of something else. It's impossible, impossible, to go on like this."

An hour and another pass like that. But now there is a ring at the door bell. Perhaps it's the doctor? It is. He comes in fresh, hearty, plump, and cheerful, with that look on his face that seems to say: "There now, you're in a panic about something, but we'll arrange it all for you directly!" The doctor knows this expression is out of place here, but he has put it on once for all and can't take it off—like a man who has put on a frock-coat in the morning to pay a round of calls.

The doctor rubs his hands vigorously and reassuringly.

"Brr! How cold it is! There's such a sharp frost; just let me warm myself!" he says, as if it were only a matter of waiting till he was warm, and then he would put everything right.

"Well now, how are you?"

Iván Ilyich feels that the doctor would like to say: "Well, how are our affairs?" but that even he feels that this would not do, and says instead: "What sort of a night have you had?"

Iván Ilyich looks at him as much as to say: "Are you really never ashamed of lying?" But the doctor does not wish to understand this question, and Iván Ilyich says: "Just as terrible as ever. The pain never leaves me and never subsides. If only something . . ."

"Yes, you sick people are always like that. . . . There, now I think I'm warm enough. Even Praskóvya Fëdorovna, who is so particular, could find no fault with my temperature. Well, now I can say good-morning," and the doctor presses his patient's hand.

Then, dropping his former playfulness, he begins with a most serious face to examine the patient, feeling his pulse and taking his temperature, and then begins the sounding and auscultation.

Iván Ilyich knows quite well and definitely that all this is nonsense and pure deception, but when the doctor, getting down on his knee, leans over him, putting his ear first higher then lower, and performs various gymnastic movements over him with a significant expression on his face, Iván Ilyich submits to it all as he used to submit to the speeches of the lawyers, though he knew very well that they were all lying and why they were lying.

The doctor, kneeling on the sofa, is still sounding him when Praskóvya Fëdorovna's silk dress rustles at the door and she is heard scolding Peter for not having let her know of the doctor's arrival.

She comes in, kisses her husband, and at once proceeds to prove that she has been up a long time already, and only owing to a misunderstanding failed to be there when the doctor arrived.

Iván Ilyich looks at her, scans her all over, sets against her the whiteness and plumpness and cleanness of her hands and neck, the gloss of her hair, and the sparkle of her vivacious eyes. He hates her with his whole soul. And the thrill of hatred he feels for her makes him suffer from her touch.

Her attitude towards him and his disease is still the same. Just as the doctor had adopted a certain relation to his patient which he could not abandon, so had she formed one towards him—that he was not doing something he ought to do and was himself to blame, and that she reproached him lovingly for this—and she could not now change that attitude.

"You see he doesn't listen to me and doesn't take his medicine at the proper time. And above all he lies in a position that is no doubt bad for him—with his legs up."

She described how he made Gerásim hold his legs up.

The doctor smiled with a contemptuous affability that said: "What's to be done? These sick people do have foolish fancies of that kind, but we must forgive them."

When the examination was over the doctor looked at his watch, and then Praskóvya Fëdorovna announced to Iván Ilyich that it was of course as he pleased, but she had sent to-day for a celebrated specialist who would examine him and have a consultation with Michael Danílovich (their regular doctor).

"Please don't raise any objections. I am doing this for my own sake," she said ironically, letting it be felt that she was doing it all for his sake and only said this to leave him no right to refuse. He remained silent, knitting his brows. He felt that he was so surrounded and involved in a mesh of falsity that it was hard to unravel anything.

Everything she did for him was entirely for her own sake, and she told him she was doing for herself what she actually was doing for herself, as if that was so incredible that he must understand the opposite.

At half-past eleven the celebrated specialist arrived. Again the sounding began and the significant conversations in his presence and in another room, about the kidneys and the appendix, and the questions and answers, with such an air of importance that again, instead of the real question of life and death which now alone confronted him, the question arose of the kidney and the appendix which were not behaving as they ought to and would now be attacked by Michael Danílovich and the specialist and forced to amend their ways.

The celebrated specialist took leave of him with a serious though not hopeless look, and in reply to the timid question Iván Ilyich, with eyes glistening with fear and hope, put to him as to whether there was a chance of recovery, said that he could not vouch for it but there was a possibility. The look of hope with which Iván Ilyich watched the doctor out was so pathetic that Praskóvya Fëdorovna, seeing it, even wept as she left the room to hand the doctor his fee.

The gleam of hope kindled by the doctor's encouragement did not last long. The same room, the same pictures, curtains, wallpaper, medicine bottles, were all there, and the same aching suffering body, and Iván Ilyich began to moan. They gave him a subcutaneous injection and he sank into oblivion.

It was twilight when he came to. They brought him his dinner and he swallowed some beef tea with difficulty, and then everything was the same again and night was coming on.

After dinner, at seven o'clock, Praskóvya Fëdorovna came into the room in evening dress, her full bosom pushed up by her corset, and with traces of powder on her face. She had reminded him in the morning that they were going to the theatre. Sarah Bernhardt was visiting the town and they had a box, which he had insisted on their taking. Now he had forgotten about it and her toilet offended him, but he concealed his vexation when he remembered that he had himself insisted on their securing a box and going because it would be an instructive and aesthetic pleasure for the children.

Praskóvya Fëdorovna came in, self-satisfied but yet with a rather guilty air. She sat down and asked how he was, but, as he saw, only for the sake of asking and not in order to learn about it, knowing that there was nothing to learn—and then went on to what she really wanted to say: that she would not on any account have gone but that the box had been taken and Helen and their daughter were going, as well as Petríshchev (the examining magistrate, their daughter's fiancé) and that it was out of the question to let them go alone; but that she would have much preferred to sit with him for a while; and he must be sure to follow the doctor's orders while she was away.

"Oh, and Fëdor Petróvich" (the fiancé) "would like to come in. May he? And Lisa?"

"All right."

Their daughter came in in full evening dress, her fresh young flesh exposed (making a show of that very flesh which in his own case caused so much suffering), strong, healthy, evidently in love, and impatient with illness, suffering, and death, because they interfered with her happiness.

Fëdor Petróvich came in too, in evening dress, his hair curled *à la Capoul*, a tight stiff collar round his long sinewy neck, an enormous white shirt-front and narrow black trousers tightly stretched over his strong thighs. He had one white glove tightly drawn on, and was holding his opera hat in his hand.

Following him the schoolboy crept in unnoticed, in a new uniform, poor little fellow, and wearing gloves. Terribly dark shadows showed under his eyes, the meaning of which Iván Ilyich knew well.

His son had always seemed pathetic to him, and now it was dreadful to see the boy's frightened look of pity. It seemed to Iván Ilyich that Vásya was the only one besides Gerásim who understood and pitied him.

They all sat down and again asked how he was. A silence followed

Lisa asked her mother about the opera-glasses, and there was an altercation between mother and daughter as to who had taken them and where they had been put. This occasioned some unpleasantness.

Fëdor Petróvich inquired of Iván Ilyich whether he had ever seen Sarah Bernhardt. Iván Ilyich did not at first catch the question, but then replied: "No, have you seen her before?"

"Yes, in *Adrienne Lecouvreur.*"[9]

Praskóvya Fëdorovna mentioned some rôles in which Sarah Bernhardt was particularly good. Her daughter disagreed. Conversation sprang up as to the elegance and realism of her acting—the sort of conversation that is always repeated and is always the same.

In the midst of the conversation Fëdor Petróvich glanced at Iván Ilyich and became silent. The others also looked at him and grew silent. Iván Ilyich was staring with glittering eyes straight before him, evidently indignant with them. This had to be rectified, but it was impossible to do so. The silence had to be broken, but for a time no one dared to break it and they all became afraid that the conventional deception would suddenly become obvious and the truth become plain to all. Lisa was the first to pluck up courage and break that silence, but by trying to hide what everybody was feeling, she betrayed it.

"Well, if we are going it's time to start," she said, looking at her watch, a present from her father, and with a faint and significant smile at Fëdor Petróvich relating to something known only to them. She got up with a rustle of her dress.

They all rose, said good-night, and went away.

When they had gone it seemed to Iván Ilyich that he felt better; the falsity had gone with them. But the pain remained—that same pain and that same fear that made everything monotonously alike, nothing harder and nothing easier. Everything was worse.

Again minute followed minute and hour followed hour. Everything remained the same and there was no cessation. And the inevitable end of it all became more and more terrible.

"Yes, send Gerásim here," he replied to a question Peter asked.

IX

His wife returned late at night. She came in on tiptoe, but he heard her, opened his eyes, and made haste to close them again. She wished to send Gerásim away and to sit with him herself, but he opened his eyes and said: "No, go away."

"Are you in great pain?"

"Always the same."

"Take some opium."

9. a play (1849) by the French dramatist Eugène Scribe (1791–1861), in which the heroine was a famous actress of the eighteenth century. Tolstoy considered Scribe, who wrote over four hundred plays, a shoddy, commercial playwright.

He agreed and took some. She went away.

Till about three in the morning he was in a state of stupefied misery. It seemed to him that he and his pain were being thrust into a narrow, deep black sack, but though they were pushed further and further in they could not be pushed to the bottom. And this, terrible enough in itself, was accompanied by suffering. He was frightened yet wanted to fall through the sack, he struggled but yet co-operated. And suddenly he broke through, fell, and regained consciousness. Gerásim was sitting at the foot of the bed dozing quietly and patiently, while he himself lay with his emaciated stockinged legs resting on Gerásim's shoulders; the same shaded candle was there and the same unceasing pain.

"Go away, Gerásim," he whispered.

"It's all right, sir. I'll stay a while."

"No. Go away."

He removed his legs from Gerásim's shoulders, turned sideways onto his arm, and felt sorry for himself. He only waited till Gerásim had gone into the next room and then restrained himself no longer but wept like a child. He wept on account of his helplessness, his terrible loneliness, the cruelty of man, the cruelty of God, and the absence of God.

"Why hast Thou done all this? Why hast Thou brought me here? Why, dost Thou torment me so terribly?"

He did not expect an answer and yet wept because there was no answer and could be none. The pain again grew more acute, but he did not stir and did not call. He said to himself: "Go on! Strike me! But what is it for? What have I done to Thee? What is it for?"

Then he grew quiet and not only ceased weeping but even held his breath and became all attention. It was as though he were listening not to an audible voice but to a voice of his soul, to the current of thoughts arising within him.

"What is it you want?" was the first clear conception capable of expression in words, that he heard.

"What do you want? What do you want?" he repeated to himself.

"What do I want? To live and not to suffer," he answered.

And again he listened with such concentrated attention that even his pain did not distract him.

"To live? How?" asked his inner voice.

"Why, to live as I used to—well and pleasantly."

"As you lived before, well and pleasantly?" the voice repeated.

And in imagination he began to recall the best moments of his pleasant life. But strange to say none of those best moments of his pleasant life now seemed at all what they had then seemed—none of them except the first recollections of childhood. There, in childhood, there had been something really pleasant with which it would be possible to live if it could return. But the child who had experienced that happiness existed no longer, it was like a reminiscence of somebody else.

As soon as the period began which had produced the present Iván Ilyich, all that had then seemed joys now melted before his sight and turned into something trivial and often nasty.

And the further he departed from childhood and the nearer he came to the present the more worthless and doubtful were the joys. This began with the School of Law. A little that was really good was still found there—there was light-heartedness, friendship, and hope. But in the upper classes there had already been fewer of such good moments. Then during the first years of his official career, when he was in the service of the Governor, some pleasant moments again occurred: they were the memories of love for a woman. Then all became confused and there was still less of what was good; later on again there was still less that was good, and the further he went the less there was. His marriage, a mere accident, then the disenchantment that followed it, his wife's bad breath and the sensuality and hypocrisy: then that deadly official life and those preoccupations about money, a year of it, and two, and ten, and twenty, and always the same thing. And the longer it lasted the more deadly it became. "It is as if I had been going downhill while I imagined I was going up. And that is really what it was. I was going up in public opinion, but to the same extent life was ebbing away from me. And now it is all done and there is only death."

"Then what does it mean? Why? It can't be that life is so senseless and horrible. But if it really has been so horrible and senseless, why must I die and die in agony? There is something wrong!"

"Maybe I did not live as I ought to have done," it suddenly occurred to him. "But how could that be, when I did everything properly?" he replied, and immediately dismissed from his mind this, the sole solution of all the riddles of life and death, as something quite impossible.

"Then what do you want now? To live? Live how? Live as you lived in the law courts when the usher proclaimed 'The judge is coming!' The judge is coming, the judge!" he repeated to himself. "Here he is, the judge. But I am not guilty!" he exclaimed angrily. "What is it for?" And he ceased crying, but turning his face to the wall continued to ponder on the same question: Why, and for what purpose, is there all this horror? But however much he pondered he found no answer. And whenever the thought occurred to him, as it often did, that it all resulted from his not having lived as he ought to have done, he at once recalled the correctness of his whole life, and dismissed so strange an idea.

x

Another fortnight passed. Iván Ilyich now no longer left his sofa. He would not lie in bed but lay on the sofa, facing the wall nearly all the time. He suffered ever the same unceasing agonies and in his loneliness pondered always on the same insoluble question: "What is this? Can it be that it is Death?" And the inner voice answered: "Yes, it is Death."

"Why these sufferings?" And the voice answered, "For no reason —they just are so." Beyond and besides this there was nothing.

From the very beginning of his illness, ever since he had first been to see the doctor, Iván Ilyich's life had been divided between two contrary and alternating moods: now it was despair and the expectation of this uncomprehended and terrible death, and now hope and an intently interested observation of the functioning of his organs. Now before his eyes there was only a kidney or an intestine that temporarily evaded its duty, and now only that incomprehensible and dreadful death from which it was impossible to escape.

These two states of mind had alternated from the very beginning of his illness, but the further it progressed the more doubtful and fantastic became the conception of the kidney, and the more real the sense of impending death.

He had but to call to mind what he had been three months before and what he was now, to call to mind with what regularity he had been going downhill, for every possibility of hope to be shattered.

Latterly during that loneliness in which he found himself as he lay facing the back of the sofa, a loneliness in the midst of a populous town and surrounded by numerous acquaintances and relations but that yet could not have been more complete anywhere—either at the bottom of the sea or under the earth—during that terrible loneliness Iván Ilyich had lived only in memories of the past. Pictures of his past rose before him one after another. They always began with what was nearest in time and then went back to what was most remote—to his childhood—and rested there. If he thought of the stewed prunes that had been offered him that day, his mind went back to the raw shrivelled French plums of his childhood, their peculiar flavour and the flow of saliva when he sucked their stones, and along with the memory of that taste came a whole series of memories of those days: his nurse, his brother, and their toys. "No, I mustn't think of that. . . . It is too painful," Iván Ilyich said to himself, and brought himself back to the present—to the button on the back of the sofa and the creases in its morocco. "Morocco is expensive, but it does not wear well: there had been a quarrel about it. It was a different kind of quarrel and a different kind of morocco that time when we tore father's portfolio and were punished, and mamma brought us some tarts. . . ." And again his thoughts dwelt **on his** childhood, and again it was painful and he tried to banish them and fix his mind on something else.

Then again together with that chain of memories another series passed through his mind—of how his illness had progressed and grown worse. There also the further back he looked the more life there had been. There had been more of what was good in life and more of life itself. The two merged together. "Just as the pain went on getting worse and worse, so my life grew worse and worse," he thought. "There is one bright spot there at the back, at the beginning of life, and afterwards all becomes blacker and blacker and proceeds more and more rapidly—in inverse ratio to the square of the distance from death," thought Iván Ilyich. And the example of a stone falling downwards with increasing velocity entered his mind. Life, a series of increasing sufferings, flies further and further towards its end—the most terrible suffering. "I am flying. . . ." He shuddered, shifted himself, and tried to resist, but was already aware that resistance was impossible, and again with eyes weary of gazing but unable to cease seeing what was before them, he stared at the back of the sofa and waited—awaiting that dreadful fall and shock and destruction.

"Resistance is impossible!" he said to himself. "If I could only understand what it is all for! But that too is impossible. An explanation would be possible if it could be said that I have not lived as I ought to. But it is impossible to say that," and he remembered all the legality, correctitude, and propriety of his life. "That at any rate can certainly not be admitted," he thought, and his lips smiled ironically as if someone could see that smile and be taken in by it. "There is no explanation! Agony, death. . . . What for?"

XI

Another two weeks went by in this way and during that fortnight an event occurred that Iván Ilyich and his wife had desired. Petríshchev formally proposed. It happened in the evening. The next day Praskóvya Fëdorovna came into her husband's room considering how best to inform him of it, but that very night there had been a fresh change for the worse in his condition. She found him still lying on the sofa but in a different position. He lay on his back, groaning and staring fixedly straight in front of him.

She began to remind him of his medicines, but he turned his eyes towards her with such a look that she did not finish what she was saying; so great an animosity, to her in particular, did that look express.

"For Christ's sake let me die in peace!" he said.

She would have gone away, but just then their daughter came in and went up to say good morning. He looked at her as he had done at his wife, and in reply to her inquiry about his health said dryly that he would soon free them all of himself. They were both silent and after sitting with him for a while went away.

"Is it our fault?" Lisa said to her mother. "It's as if we were to blame! I am sorry for papa, but why should we be tortured?"

The doctor came at his usual time. Iván Ilyich answered "Yes" and "No," never taking his angry eyes from him, and at last said: "You know you can do nothing for me, so leave me alone."

"We can ease your sufferings."

"You can't even do that. Let me be."

The doctor went into the drawing-room and told Praskóvya Fëdorovna that the case was very serious and that the only resource left was opium to allay her husband's sufferings, which must be terrible.

It was true, as the doctor said, that Iván Ilyich's physical sufferings were terrible, but worse than the physical sufferings were his mental sufferings which were his chief torture.

His mental sufferings were due to the fact that that night, as he looked at Gerásim's sleepy, good-natured face with its prominent cheek-bones, the question suddenly occurred to him: "What if my whole life has really been wrong?"

It occurred to him that what had appeared perfectly impossible before, namely that he had not spent his life as he should have done, might after all be true. It occurred to him that his scarcely perceptible attempts to struggle against what was considered good by the most highly placed people, those scarcely noticeable impulses which he had immediately suppressed, might have been the real thing, and all the rest false. And his professional duties and the whole arrangement of his life and of his family, and all his social and official interests, might all have been false. He tried to defend all those things to himself and suddenly felt the weakness of what he was defending. There was nothing to defend.

"But if that is so," he said to himself, "and I am leaving this life with the consciousness that I have lost all that was given me and it is impossible to rectify it—what then?"

He lay on his back and began to pass his life in review in quite a new way. In the morning when he saw first his footman, then his wife, then his daughter, and then the doctor, their every word and movement confirmed to him the awful truth that had been revealed to him during the night. In them he saw himself—all that for which he had lived—and saw clearly that it was not real at all, but a terrible and huge deception which had hidden both life and death. This consciousness intensified his physical suffering tenfold. He groaned and tossed about, and pulled at his clothing which choked and stifled him. And he hated them on that account.

He was given a large dose of opium and became unconscious, but at noon his sufferings began again. He drove everybody away and tossed from side to side.

His wife came to him and said:

"*Jean*, my dear, do this for me. It can't do any harm and often helps. Healthy people often do it."

He opened his eyes wide.

"What? Take communion? Why? It's unnecessary! However . . ."

She began to cry.

"Yes, do, my dear. I'll send for our priest. He is such a nice man."

"All right. Very well," he muttered.

When the priest came and heard his confession, Iván Ilyich was softened and seemed to feel a relief from his doubts and consequently from his sufferings, and for a moment there came a ray of hope. He again began to think of the vermiform appendix and the possibility of correcting it. He received the sacrament with tears in his eyes.

When they laid him down again afterwards he felt a moment's ease, and the hope that he might live awoke in him again. He began to think of the operation that had been suggested to him. "To live! I want to live!" he said to himself.

His wife came in to congratulate him after his communion, and when uttering the usual conventional words she added:

"You feel better, don't you?"

Without looking at her he said "Yes."

Her dress, her figure, the expression of her face, the tone of her voice, all revealed the same thing. "This is wrong, it is not as it should be. All you have lived for and still live for is falsehood and deception, hiding life and death from you." And as soon as he admitted that thought, his hatred and his agonizing physical suffering again sprang up, and with that suffering a consciousness of the unavoidable, approaching end. And to this was added a new sensation of grinding shooting pain and a feeling of suffocation.

The expression of his face when he uttered that "yes" was dreadful. Having uttered it, he looked her straight in the eyes, turned on his face with a rapidity extraordinary in his weak state and shouted:

"Go away! Go away and leave me alone!"

XII

From that moment the screaming began that continued for three days, and was so terrible that one could not hear it through two closed doors without horror. At the moment he answered his wife he realized that he was lost, that there was no return, that the end had come, the very end, and his doubts were still unsolved and remained doubts.

"Oh! Oh! Oh!" he cried in various intonations. He had begun by screaming "I won't!" and continued screaming on the letter "o."

For three whole days, during which time did not exist for him, he struggled in that black sack into which he was being thrust by an invisible, resistless force. He struggled as a man condemned to death struggles in the hands of the executioner, knowing that he cannot save himself. And every moment he felt that despite all his efforts he was drawing nearer and nearer to what terrified him. He felt that his agony was due to his being thrust into that black hole and still more to his not being able to get right into it. He was hindered from getting into it by his conviction that his life had been a good one. That very justification of his life held him fast and prevented his moving forward, and it caused him most torment of all.

Suddenly some force struck him in the chest and side, making it still harder to breathe, and he fell through the hole and there at the bottom was a light. What had happened to him was like the sensation one sometimes experiences in a railway carriage when one thinks one is going backwards while one is really going forwards and suddenly becomes aware of the real direction.

"Yes, it was all not the right thing," he said to himself, "but that's no matter. It can be done. But what *is* the right thing?" he asked himself, and suddenly grew quiet.

This occurred at the end of the third day, two hours before his death. Just then his schoolboy son had crept softly in and gone up to the bedside. The dying man was still screaming desperately and waving his arms. His hand fell on the boy's head, and the boy caught it, pressed it to his lips, and began to cry.

At that very moment Iván Ilyich fell through and caught sight of the light, and it was revealed to him that though his life had not been what it should have been, this could still be rectified. He asked himself, "What *is* the right thing?" and grew still, listening. Then he felt that someone was kissing his hand. He opened his eyes, looked at his son, and felt sorry for him. His wife came up to him and he glanced at her. She was gazing at him open-mouthed, with undried tears on her nose and cheek and a despairing look on her face. He felt sorry for her too.

"Yes, I am making them wretched," he thought. "They are sorry, but it will be better for them when I die." He wished to say this but had not the strength to utter it. "Besides, why speak? I must act," he thought. With a look at his wife he indicated his son and said: "Take him away . . . sorry for him . . . sorry for you too. . . ." He tried to add, "forgive me," but said "forego" and waved his hand, knowing that He whose understanding mattered would understand.

And suddenly it grew clear to him that what had been oppressing him and would not leave him was all dropping away at once from two sides, from ten sides, and from all sides. He was sorry for them, he must act so as not to hurt them: release them and free himself from these sufferings. "How good and how simple!" he thought. "And the pain?" he asked himself. "What has become of it? Where are you, pain?"

He turned his attention to it.

"Yes, here it is. Well, what of it? Let the pain be."

"And death . . . where is it?"

He sought his former accustomed fear of death and did not find it. "Where is it? What death?" There was no fear because there was no death.

In place of death there was light.

"So that's what it is!" he suddenly exclaimed aloud. "What joy!"

To him all this happened in a single instant, and the meaning of that instant did not change. For those present his agony continued for another two hours. Something rattled in his throat, his emaciated body twitched, then the gasping and rattle became less and less frequent.

"It is finished!" said someone near him.

He heard these words and repeated them in his soul.

"Death is finished," he said to himself. "It is no more!"

He drew in a breath, stopped in the midst of a sigh, stretched out, and died.

ANTON CHEKHOV
(1860–1904)
The Kiss*

At eight o'clock on the evening of the twentieth of May all the six batteries of the N—— Reserve Artillery Brigade halted for the night in the village of Mestechki on their way to camp. At the height of the general commotion, while some officers were busily occupied around the guns, and others, gathered together in the square near the church enclosure, were receiving the reports of the quartermasters, a man in civilian dress, riding a queer horse, came into sight round the church. The little dun-colored horse with a fine neck and a short tail came, moving not straight forward, but as it were sideways, with a sort of dance step, as though it were being lashed about the legs. When he reached the officers the man on the horse took off his hat and said:

* 1887. Translated by Constance Garnett. Reprinted in full. The punctuation ". . ." does not indicate omissions from this text.

"His Excellency Lieutenant-General von Rabbeck, a local land-owner, invites the officers to have tea with him this minute. . . ."

The horse bowed, danced, and retired sideways; the rider raised his hat once more and in an instant disappeared with his strange horse behind the church.

"What the devil does it mean?" grumbled some of the officers, dispersing to their quarters. "One is sleepy, and here this von Rabbeck with his tea! We know what tea means."

The officers of all the six batteries remembered vividly an incident of the previous year, when during maneuvers they, together with the officers of a Cossack regiment, were in the same way invited to tea by a count who had an estate in the neighborhood and was a retired army officer; the hospitable and genial count made much of them, dined and wined them, refused to let them go to their quarters in the village, and made them stay the night. All that, of course, was very nice—nothing better could be desired, but the worst of it was, the old army officer was so carried away by the pleasure of the young men's company that till sunrise he was telling the officers anecdotes of his glorious past, taking them over the house, showing them expensive pictures, old engravings, rare guns, reading them autograph letters from great people, while the weary and exhausted officers looked and listened, longing for their beds and yawning in their sleeves; when at last their host let them go, it was too late for sleep.

Might not this von Rabbeck be just such another? Whether he were or not, there was no help for it. The officers changed their uniforms, brushed themselves, and went all together in search of the gentleman's house. In the square by the church they were told they could get to his Excellency's by the lower road—going down behind the church to the river, walking along the bank to the garden, and there the alleys would take them to the house; or by the upper way—straight from the church by the road which, half a mile from the village, led right up to his Excellency's barns. The officers decided to go by the upper road.

"Which von Rabbeck is it?" they wondered on the way. "Surely not the one who was in command of the N—— cavalry division at Plevna?"[1]

"No, that was not von Rabbeck, but simply Rabbe and no 'von.' "

"What lovely weather!"

At the first of the barns the road divided in two: one branch went straight on and vanished in the evening darkness, the other led to the owner's house on the right. The officers turned to the right and began to speak more softly. . . . On both sides of the road

1. a town in Bulgaria, defended by the Turks during the Russo-Turkish War. In 1877, the Russians finally captured it.

stretched stone barns with red roofs, heavy and sullen-looking, very much like barracks in a district town. Ahead of them gleamed the windows of the manor house.

"A good omen, gentlemen," said one of the officers. "Our setter leads the way; no doubt he scents game ahead of us! . . ."

Lieutenant Lobytko, who was walking in front, a tall and stalwart fellow, though entirely without mustache (he was over twenty-five, yet for some reason there was no sign of hair on his round, well-fed face), renowned in the brigade for his peculiar ability to divine the presence of women at a distance, turned round and said:

"Yes, there must be women here; I feel that by instinct."

On the threshold the officers were met by von Rabbeck himself, a comely looking man of sixty in civilian dress. Shaking hands with his guests, he said that he was very glad and happy to see them, but begged them earnestly for God's sake to excuse him for not asking them to stay the night; two sisters with their children, his brothers, and some neighbors, had come on a visit to him, so that he had not one spare room left.

The General shook hands with everyone, made his apologies, and smiled, but it was evident by his face that he was by no means so delighted as last year's count, and that he had invited the officers simply because, in his opinion, it was a social obligation. And the officers themselves, as they walked up the softly carpeted stairs, as they listened to him, felt that they had been invited to this house simply because it would have been awkward not to invite them; and at the sight of the footmen, who hastened to light the lamps at the entrance below and in the anteroom above, they began to feel as though they had brought uneasiness and discomfort into the house with them. In a house in which two sisters and their children, brothers, and neighbors were gathered together, probably on account of some family festivity or event, how could the presence of nineteen unknown officers possibly be welcome?

Upstairs at the entrance to the drawing room the officers were met by a tall, graceful old lady with black eyebrows and a long face, very much like the Empress Eugénie.[2] Smiling graciously and majestically, she said she was glad and happy to see her guests, and apologized that her husband and she were on this occasion unable to invite *messieurs les officiers* to stay the night. From her beautiful majestic smile, which instantly vanished from her face every time she turned away from her guests, it was evident that she had seen numbers of officers in her day, that she was in no humor for them now, and if she invited them to her house and apologized for not doing more, it was only because her breeding and position in society required it of her.

2. Empress Eugénie (1826–1920) was the wife of Emperor Napoleon III.

When the officers went into the big dining-room, there were about a dozen people, men and ladies, young and old, sitting at tea at the end of a long table. A group of men wrapped in a haze of cigar smoke was dimly visible behind their chairs; in the midst of them stood a lanky young man with red whiskers, talking loudly in English, with a burr. Through a door beyond the group could be seen a light room with pale blue furniture.

"Gentlemen, there are so many of you that it is impossible to introduce you all!" said the General in a loud voice, trying to sound very gay. "Make each other's acquaintance, gentlemen, without any ceremony!"

The officers—some with very serious and even stern faces, others with forced smiles, and all feeling extremely awkward—somehow made their bows and sat down to tea.

The most ill at ease of them all was Ryabovich—a short, somewhat stooped officer in spectacles, with whiskers like a lynx's. While some of his comrades assumed a serious expression, while others wore forced smiles, his face, his lynx-like whiskers, and spectacles seemed to say, "I am the shyest, most modest, and most undistinguished officer in the whole brigade!" At first, on going into the room and later, sitting down at table, he could not fix his attention on any one face or object. The faces, the dresses, the cut-glass decanters of brandy, the steam from the glasses, the molded cornices—all blended in one general impression that inspired in Ryabovich alarm and a desire to hide his head. Like a lecturer making his first appearance before the public, he saw everything that was before his eyes, but apparently only had a dim understanding of it (among physiologists this condition, when the subject sees but does not understand, is called "mental blindness"). After a little while, growing accustomed to his surroundings, Ryabovich regained his sight and began to observe. As a shy man, unused to society, what struck him first was that in which he had always been deficient—namely, the extraordinary boldness of his new acquaintances. Von Rabbeck, his wife, two elderly ladies, a young lady in a lilac dress, and the young man with the red whiskers, who was, it appeared, a younger son of von Rabbeck, very cleverly, as though they had rehearsed it beforehand, took seats among the officers, and at once got up a heated discussion in which the visitors could not help taking part. The lilac young lady hotly asserted that the artillery had a much better time than the cavalry and the infantry, while von Rabbeck and the elderly ladies maintained the opposite. A brisk interchange followed. Ryabovich looked at the lilac young lady who argued so hotly about what was unfamiliar and utterly uninteresting to her, and watched artificial smiles come and go on her face.

Von Rabbeck and his family skillfully drew the officers into the discussion, and meanwhile kept a sharp eye on their glasses and mouths, to see whether all of them were drinking, whether all had enough sugar, why someone was not eating cakes or not drinking brandy. And the longer Ryabovich watched and listened, the more he was attracted by this insincere but splendidly disciplined family.

After tea the officers went into the drawing room. Lieutenant Lobytko's instinct had not deceived him. There were a great many girls and young married ladies. The "setter" lieutenant was soon standing by a very young blonde in a black dress, and, bending over her jauntily, as though leaning on an unseen sword, smiled and twitched his shoulders coquettishly. He probably talked very interesting nonsense, for the blonde looked at his well-fed face condescendingly and asked indifferently, "Really?" And from that indifferent "Really?" the "setter," had he been intelligent, might have concluded that she would never call him to heel.

The piano struck up; the melancholy strains of a waltz floated out of the wide open windows, and everyone, for some reason, remembered that it was spring, a May evening. Everyone was conscious of the fragrance of roses, of lilac, and of the young leaves of the poplar. Ryabovich, who felt the brandy he had drunk, under the influence of the music stole a glance towards the window, smiled, and began watching the movements of the women, and it seemed to him that the smell of roses, of poplars, and lilac came not from the garden, but from the ladies' faces and dresses.

Von Rabbeck's son invited a scraggy-looking young lady to dance and waltzed round the room twice with her. Lobytko, gliding over the parquet floor, flew up to the lilac young lady and whirled her away. Dancing began. . . . Ryabovich stood near the door among those who were not dancing and looked on. He had never once danced in his whole life, and he had never once in his life put his arm round the waist of a respectable woman. He was highly delighted that a man should in the sight of all take a girl he did not know round the waist and offer her his shoulder to put her hand on, but he could not imagine himself in the position of such a man. There were times when he envied the boldness and swagger of his companions and was inwardly wretched; the knowledge that he was timid, round-shouldered, and uninteresting, that he had a long waist and lynx-like whiskers deeply mortified him, but with years he had grown used to this feeling, and now, looking at his comrades dancing or loudly talking, he no longer envied them, but only felt touched and mournful.

When the quadrille began, young von Rabbeck came up to those who were not dancing and invited two officers to have a game at billiards. The officers accepted and went with him out of the drawing room. Ryabovich, having nothing to do and wishing to take at least some part in the general movement, slouched after them. From the big drawing room they went into the little drawing room, then into a narrow corridor with a glass roof, and thence into a room in which on their entrance three sleepy-looking footmen jumped up quickly from couches. At last, after passing through a long succession of rooms, young von Rabbeck and the officers came into a small room where there was a billiard table. They began to play.

Ryabovich, who had never played any game but cards, stood near the billiard table and looked indifferently at the players, while they in unbuttoned coats, with cues in their hands, stepped about, made puns, and kept shouting out unintelligible words.

The players took no notice of him, and only now and then one of them, shoving him with his elbow or accidentally touching him with his cue, would turn round and say *"Pardon!"* Before the first game was over he was weary of it, and began to feel that he was not wanted and in the way. . . . He felt disposed to return to the drawing-room and he went out.

On his way back he met with a little adventure. When he had gone half-way he noticed that he had taken a wrong turning. He distinctly remembered that he ought to meet three sleepy footmen on his way, but he had passed five or six rooms, and those sleepy figures seemed to have been swallowed up by the earth. Noticing his mistake, he walked back a little way and turned to the right; he found himself in a little room which was in semidarkness and which he had not seen on his way to the billiard room. After standing there a little while, he resolutely opened the first door that met his eyes and walked into an absolutely dark room. Straight ahead could be seen the crack in the doorway through which came a gleam of vivid light; from the other side of the door came the muffled sound of a melancholy mazurka. Here, too, as in the drawing-room, the windows were wide open and there was a smell of poplars, lilac, and roses. . . .

Ryabovich stood still in hesitation. . . . At that moment, to his surprise, he heard hurried footsteps and the rustling of a dress, a breathless feminine voice whispered "At last!" and two soft, fragrant, unmistakably feminine arms were clasped about his neck; a warm cheek was pressed against his, and simultaneously there was the sound of a kiss. But at once the bestower of the kiss uttered a faint shriek and sprang away from him, as it seemed to Ryabovich, with disgust. He, too, almost shrieked and rushed towards the gleam of light at the door. . . .

When he returned to the drawing-room his heart was palpitating and his hands were trembling so noticeably that he made haste to hide them behind his back. At first he was tormented by shame and dread that the whole drawing-room knew that he had just been kissed and embraced by a woman. He shrank into himself and looked uneasily about him, but as he became convinced that people were dancing and talking as calmly as ever, he gave himself up entirely to the new sensation which he had never experienced before in his life. Something strange was happening to him. . . . His neck, round which soft, fragrant arms had so lately been clasped, seemed to him to be anointed with oil; on his left cheek near his mustache where the unknown had kissed him there was a faint chilly tingling sensation as from peppermint drops, and the more he rubbed the place the more distinct was the chilly sensation; all of him, from head to foot, was full of a strange new feeling which grew stronger and stronger. . . . He wanted to dance, to talk, to run into the garden, to laugh aloud. . . . He quite forgot that he was round-shouldered and uninteresting, that he had lynx-like whiskers and an "undistinguished appearance" (that was how his appearance had been described by some ladies whose conversation he had accidentally overheard). When von Rabbeck's wife happened to pass by him, he gave her such a broad and friendly smile that she stood still and looked at him inquiringly.

"I like your house immensely!" he said, setting his spectacles straight.

The General's wife smiled and said that the house had belonged to her father; then she asked whether his parents were living, whether he had long been in the army, why he was so thin, and so on. . . . After receiving answers to her questions, she went on, and after his conversation with her his smiles were more friendly than ever, and he thought he was surrounded by splendid people. . . .

At supper Ryabovich ate mechanically everything offered him, drank, and without listening to anything, tried to understand what had just happened to him. . . . The adventure was of a mysterious and romantic character, but it was not difficult to explain it. No doubt some girl or young married lady had arranged a tryst with some man in the dark room; had waited a long time, and being nervous and excited had taken Ryabovich for her hero; this was the more probable as Ryabovich had stood still hesitating in the dark room, so that he, too, had looked like a person waiting for something. . . . This was how Ryabovich explained to himself the kiss he had received.

"And who is she?" he wondered, looking round at the women's faces. "She must be young, for elderly ladies don't arrange rendezvous. That she was a lady, one could tell by the rustle of her dress, her perfume, her voice. . . ."

His eyes rested on the lilac young lady, and he thought her very attractive; she had beautiful shoulders and arms, a clever face, and a delightful voice. Ryabovich, looking at her, hoped that she and

no one else was his unknown. . . But she laughed somehow ar
tificially and wrinkled up her long nose, which seemed to him to
make her look old. Then he turned his eyes upon the blonde in a
black dress. She was younger, simpler, and more genuine, had a
charming brow, and drank very daintily out of her wineglass. Ryabovich now hoped that it was she. But soon he began to think her face
flat, and fixed his eyes upon the one next her.

"It's difficult to guess," he thought, musing. "If one were to take
only the shoulders and arms of the lilac girl, add the brow of the
blonde and the eyes of the one on the left of Lobytko, then . . ."

He made a combination of these things in his mind and so formed
the image of the girl who had kissed him, the image that he desired
but could not find at the table. . . .

After supper, replete and exhilarated, the officers began to take
leave and say thank you. Von Rabbeck and his wife began again
apologizing that they could not ask them to stay the night.

"Very, very glad to have met you, gentlemen," said von Rabbeck,
and this time sincerely (probably because people are far more sincere
and good-humored at speeding their parting guests than on meeting
them). "Delighted. Come again on your way back! Don't stand on
ceremony! Where are you going? Do you want to go by the upper
way? No, go across the garden; it's nearer by the lower road."

The officers went out into the garden. After the bright light
and the noise the garden seemed very dark and quiet. They walked
in silence all the way to the gate. They were a little drunk, in good
spirits, and contented, but the darkness and silence made them
thoughtful for a minute. Probaby the same idea occurred to each
one of them as to Ryabovich: would there ever come a time for
them when, like von Rabbeck, they would have a large house, a
family, a garden—when they, too, would be able to welcome people,
even though insincerely, feed them, make them drunk and contented?

Going out of the garden gate, they all began talking at once
and laughing loudly about nothing. They were walking now along
the little path that led down to the river and then ran along the
water's edge, winding round the bushes on the bank, the gulleys,
and the willows that overhung the water. The bank and the path
were scarcely visible, and the other bank was entirely plunged in
darkness. Stars were reflected here and there in the dark water;
they quivered and were broken up—and from that alone it could
be seen that the river was flowing rapidly. It was still. Drowsy sand-
pipers cried plaintively on the farther bank, and in one of the bushes
on the hither side a nightingale was trilling loudly, taking no notice
of the crowd of officers. The officers stood round the bush, touched
it, but the nightingale went on singing.

"What a fellow!" they exclaimed approvingly. "We stand beside him and he takes not a bit of notice! What a rascal!"

At the end of the way the path went uphill, and, skirting the church enclosure, led into the road. Here the officers, tired with walking uphill, sat down and lighted their cigarettes. On the farther bank of the river a murky red fire came into sight, and having nothing better to do, they spent a long time in discussing whether it was a camp fire or a light in a window, or something else. . . . Ryabovich, too, looked at the light, and he fancied that the light looked and winked at him, as though it knew about the kiss.

On reaching his quarters, Ryabovich undressed as quickly as possible and got into bed. Lobytko and Lieutenant Merzlyakov—a peaceable, silent fellow, who was considered in his own circle a highly educated officer, and was always, whenever it was possible, reading *The Messenger of Europe*,[3] which he carried about with him everywhere—were quartered in the same cottage with Ryabovich. Lobytko undressed, walked up and down the room for a long while with the air of a man who has not been satisfied, and sent his orderly for beer. Merzlyakov got into bed, put a candle by his pillow and plunged into *The Messenger of Europe*.

"Who was she?" Ryabovich wondered, looking at the sooty ceiling.

His neck still felt as though he had been anointed with oil, and there was still the chilly sensation near his mouth as though from peppermint drops. The shoulders and arms of the young lady in lilac, the brow and the candid eyes of the blonde in black, waists, dresses, and brooches, floated through his imagination. He tried to fix his attention on these images, but they danced about, broke up and flickered. When these images vanished altogether from the broad dark background which everyone sees when he closes his eyes, he began to hear hurried footsteps, the rustle of skirts, the sound of a kiss—and an intense baseless joy took possession of him. . . . Abandoning himself to this joy, he heard the orderly return and announce that there was no beer. Lobytko was terribly indignant, and began pacing up and down the room again.

"Well, isn't he an idiot?" he kept saying, stopping first before Ryabovich and then before Merzlyakov. "What a fool and a blockhead a man must be not to get hold of any beer! Eh? Isn't he a blackguard?"

"Of course you can't get beer here," said Merzlyakov, not removing his eyes from *The Messenger of Europe*.

"Oh! Is that your opinion?" Lobytko persisted. "Lord have mercy upon us, if you dropped me on the moon I'd find you beer and

3. *Vestnik Evropy*, a monthly magazine founded by the Russian historian Karamzin in 1802. It lasted until 1917.

women directly! I'll go and find some at once. . . . You may call me a rascal if I don't!"

He spent a long time in dressing and pulling on his high boots, then finished smoking his cigarette in silence and went out.

"Rabbeck, Grabbeck, Labbeck," he muttered, stopping in the outer room. "I don't care to go alone, damn it all! Ryabovich, wouldn't you like to go for a walk? Eh?"

Receiving no answer, he returned, slowly undressed, and got into bed. Merzlyakov sighed, put *The Messenger of Europe* away, and extinguished the light.

"H'm! . . . ." muttered Lobytko, lighting a cigarette in the dark.

Ryabovich pulled the bedclothes over his head, curled himself up in bed, and tried to gather together the flashing images in his mind and to combine them into a whole. But nothing came of it. He soon feel asleep, and his last thought was that someone had caressed him and made him happy—that something extraordinary, foolish, but joyful and delightful, had come into his life. The thought did not leave him even in his sleep.

When he woke up the sensations of oil on his neck and the chill of peppermint about his lips had gone, but joy flooded his heart just as the day before. He looked enthusiastically at the window-frames, gilded by the light of the rising sun, and listened to the movement of the passers-by in the street. People were talking loudly close to the window. Lebedetzky, the commander of Ryabovich's battery, who had only just overtaken the brigade, was talking to his sergeant at the top of his voice, having lost the habit of speaking in ordinary tones.

"What else?" shouted the commander.

"When they were shoeing the horses yesterday, your Honor, they injured Pigeon's hoof with a nail. The vet put on clay and vinegar; they are leading him apart now. Also, your Honor, Artemyev got drunk yesterday, and the lieutenant ordered him to be put in the limber of a spare gun-carriage."

The sergeant reported that Karpov had forgotten the new cords for the trumpets and the pegs for the tents, and that their Honors the officers had spent the previous evening visiting General von Rabbeck. In the middle of this conversation the red-bearded face of Lebedetzky appeared in the window. He screwed up his short-sighted eyes, looking at the sleepy faces of the officers, and greeted them.

"Is everything all right?" he asked.

"One of the horses has a sore neck from the new collar," answered Lobytko, yawning.

The commander sighed, thought a moment, and said in a loud voice:

"I am thinking of going to see Alexandra Yevgrafovna. I must call on her. Well, good-bye. I shall catch up with you in the evening."

A quarter of an hour later the brigade set off on its way. When it was moving along the road past the barns, Ryabovich looked at the house on the right. The blinds were down in all the windows. Evidently the household was still asleep. The one who had kissed Ryabovich the day before was asleep too. He tried to imagine her asleep. The wide-open window of the bedroom, the green branches peeping in, the morning freshness, the scent of the poplars, lilac, and roses, the bed, a chair, and on it the skirts that had rustled the day before, the little slippers, the little watch on the table—all this he pictured to himself clearly and distinctly, but the features of the face, the sweet sleepy smile, just what was characteristic and important, slipped through his imagination like quicksilver through the fingers. When he had ridden a third of a mile, he looked back: the yellow church, the house, and the river, were all bathed in light; the river with its bright green banks, with the blue sky reflected in it and glints of silver in the sunshine here and there, was very beautiful. Ryabovich gazed for the last time at Mestechki, and he felt as sad as though he were parting with something very near and dear to him.

And before him on the road were none but long familiar, uninteresting scenes. . . . To right and to left, fields of young rye and buckwheat with rooks hopping about in them; if one looked ahead, one saw dust and the backs of men's heads; if one looked back, one saw the same dust and faces. . . . Foremost of all marched four men with sabers—this was the vanguard. Next came the singers, and behind them the trumpeters on horseback. The vanguard and the singers, like torch-bearers in a funeral procession, often forgot to keep the regulation distance and pushed a long way ahead. . . . Ryabovich was with the first cannon of the fifth battery. He could see all the four batteries moving in front of him. To a civilian the long tedious procession which is a brigade on the move seems an intricate and unintelligible muddle; one cannot understand why there are so many people round one cannon, and why it is drawn by so many horses in such a strange network of harness, as though it really were so terrible and heavy. To Ryabovich it was all perfectly comprehensible and therefore uninteresting. He had known for ever so long why at the head of each battery beside the officer there rode a stalwart noncom, called bombardier; immediately behind him could be seen a horseman of the first and then of the middle units. Ryabovich knew that of the horses on which they rode, those on the left were called one name, while those on the right were called another—it was all extremely uninteresting. Behind the horsemen came two shaft-horses. On one of them sat a rider still covered with the dust of yesterday and with a clumsy and funny-looking wooden guard on his right leg. Ryabovich knew the object of this guard, and did not think it funny. All the riders waved their whips mechanically and shouted from time to time. The cannon itself was not presentable. On the limber lay sacks of oats covered with a tarpaulin, and the cannon itself was hung all over with kettles, soldiers' knapsacks, bags, and looked like some small harmless animal surrounded for some unknown reason by men and horses. To the leeward of it marched six men, the gunners, swinging their arms. After the cannon there came again more bombardiers, riders, shaft-horses, and behind them another cannon, as unpresentable and unimpressive as the first. After the second came a third, a fourth; near the fourth there was an officer, and so on. There were six batteries in all in the brigade, and four cannon in each battery. The procession covered a third of a mile; it ended in a string of wagons near which an extremely appealing creature—the ass, Magar, brought by a battery commander from Turkey—paced pensively, his long-eared head drooping.

Ryabovich looked indifferently ahead and behind him, at the backs of heads and at faces; at any other time he would have been half asleep, but now he was entirely absorbed in his new agreeable thoughts. At first when the brigade was setting off on the march he tried to persuade himself that the incident of the kiss could only be interesting as a mysterious little adventure, that it was in reality trivial, and to think of it seriously, to say the least, was stupid; but now he bade farewell to logic and gave himself up to dreams. . . . At one moment he imagined himself in von Rabbeck's drawing-room beside a girl who was like the young lady in lilac and the blonde in black; then he would close his eyes and see himself with another, entirely unknown girl, whose features were very vague. In his imagination he talked, caressed her, leaned over her shoulder, pictured war, separation, then meeting again, supper with his wife, children. . . .

"Brakes on!" The word of command rang out every time they went downhill.

He, too, shouted "Brakes on!" and was afraid this shout would disturb his reverie and bring him back to reality. . . .

As they passed by some landowner's estate Ryabovich looked over the fence into the garden. A long avenue, straight as a ruler, strewn with yellow sand and bordered with young birch-trees, met his eyes. . . . With the eagerness of a man who indulges in daydreaming, he pictured to himself little feminine feet tripping along yellow sand, and quite unexpectedly had a clear vision in his imagination of her who had kissed him and whom he had succeeded in picturing to himself the evening before at supper. This image remained in his brain and did not desert him again.

At midday there was a shout in the rear near the string of wagons: "Attention! Eyes to the left! Officers!"

The general of the brigade drove by in a carriage drawn by a pair of white horses. He stopped near the second battery, and shouted something which no one understood. Several officers, among them Ryabovich, galloped up to him.

"Well? How goes it?" asked the general, blinking his red eyes. "Are there any sick?"

Receiving an answer, the general, a little skinny man, chewed, thought for a moment and said, addressing one of the officers:

"One of your drivers of the third cannon has taken off his leg-guard and hung it on the fore part of the cannon, the rascal. Reprimand him."

He raised his eyes to Ryabovich and went on:

"It seems to me your breeching is too long."

Making a few other tedious remarks, the general looked at Lobytko and grinned.

"You look very melancholy today, Lieutenant Lobytko," he said. "Are you pining for Madame Lopukhova? Eh? Gentlemen, he is pining for Madame Lopukhova."

Madame Lopukhova was a very stout and very tall lady long past forty. The general, who had a predilection for large women, whatever their ages, suspected a similar taste in his officers. The officers smiled respectfully. The general, delighted at having said something very amusing and biting, laughed loudly, touched his coachman's back, and saluted. The carriage rolled on. . . .

"All I am dreaming about now which seems to me so impossible and unearthly is really quite an ordinary thing," thought Ryabovich, looking at the clouds of dust racing after the general's carriage. "It's all very ordinary, and everyone goes through it. . . . That general, for instance, was in love at one time; now he is married and has children. Captain Wachter, too, is married and loved, though the nape of his neck is very red and ugly and he has no waist. . . . Salmanov is coarse and too much of a Tartar, but he had a love affair that has ended in marriage. . . . I am the same as everyone else, and I, too, shall have the same experience as everyone else, sooner or later. . . ."

And the thought that he was an ordinary person and that his life was ordinary delighted him and gave him courage. He pictured *her* and his happiness boldly, just as he liked. . . .

When the brigade reached their halting-place in the evening, and the officers were resting in their tents, Ryabovich, Merzlyakov, and

Lobytko were sitting round a chest having supper. Merzlyakov ate
without haste, and, as he munched deliberately, read *The Messenger
of Europe*, which he held on his knees. Lobytko talked incessantly
and kept filling up his glass with beer, and Ryabovich, whose head
was confused from dreaming all day long, drank and said nothing.
After three glasses he got a little drunk, felt weak, and had an irresistible desire to relate his new sensations to his comrades.

"A strange thing happened to me at those von Rabbecks'," he
began, trying to impart an indifferent and ironical tone to his voice.
"You know I went into the billiard-room. . . ."

He began describing very minutely the incident of the kiss, and
a moment later relapsed into silence. . . . In the course of that
moment he had told everything, and it surprised him dreadfully to
find how short a time it took him to tell it. He had imagined that
he could have been telling the story of the kiss till next morning.
Listening to him, Lobytko, who was a great liar and consequently
believed no one, looked at him skeptically and laughed. Merzlyakov
twitched his eyebrows and, without removing his eyes from *The
Messenger of Europe*, said:

"That's an odd thing! How strange! . . . throws herself on a
man's neck, without addressing him by name. . . . She must have
been some sort of lunatic."

"Yes, she must," Ryabovich agreed.

"A similar thing once happened to me," said Lobytko, assuming
a scared expression. "I was going last year to Kovno. . . . I took a
second-class ticket. The train was crammed, and it was impossible
to sleep. I gave the guard half a ruble; he took my luggage and led
me to another compartment. . . . I lay down and covered myself
with a blanket. . . . It was dark, you understand. Suddenly I felt
someone touch me on the shoulder and breathe in my face. I made
a movement with my hand and felt somebody's elbow. . . . I
opened my eyes and only imagine—a woman. Black eyes, lips red
as a prime salmon, nostrils breathing passionately—a bosom like a
buffer. . . ."

"Excuse me," Merzlyakov interrupted calmly, "I understand
about the bosom, but how could you see the lips if it was dark?"

Lobytko began trying to put himself right and laughing at
Merzlyakov's being so dull-witted. It made Ryabovich wince. He
walked away from the chest, got into bed, and vowed never to confide again.

Camp life began. . . . The days flowed by, one very much like
another. All those days Ryabovich felt, thought, and behaved as
though he were in love. Every morning when his orderly handed
him what he needed for washing, and he sluiced his head with cold

water, he recalled that there was something warm and delightful in his life.

In the evenings when his comrades began talking of love and women, he would listen, and draw up closer; and he wore the expression of a soldier listening to the description of a battle in which he has taken part. And on the evenings when the officers, out on a spree with the setter Lobytko at their head, made Don-Juanesque raids on the neighboring "suburb," and Ryabovich took part in such excursions, he always was sad, felt profoundly guilty, and inwardly begged *her* forgiveness. . . . In hours of leisure or on sleepless nights when he felt moved to recall his childhood, his father and mother—everything near and dear, in fact, he invariably thought of Mestechki, the queer horse, von Rabbeck, his wife who resembled Empress Eugénie, the dark room, the light in the crack of the door. . . .

On the thirty-first of August he was returning from the camp, not with the whole brigade, but with only two batteries. He was dreamy and excited all the way, as though he were going home. He had an intense longing to see again the queer horse, the church, the insincere family of the von Rabbecks, the dark room. The "inner voice," which so often deceives lovers, whispered to him for some reason that he would surely see her . . . And he was tortured by the questions: How would he meet her? What would he talk to her about? Had she forgotten the kiss? If the worse came to the worst, he thought, even if he did not meet her, it would be a pleasure to him merely to go through the dark room and recall the past. . . .

Towards evening there appeared on the horizon the familiar church and white barns. Ryabovich's heart raced. . . . He did not hear the officer who was riding beside him and saying something to him, he forgot everything, and looked eagerly at the river shining in the distance, at the roof of the house, at the dovecote round which the pigeons were circling in the light of the setting sun.

When they reached the church and were listening to the quartermaster, he expected every second that a man on horseback would come round the church enclosure and invite the officers to tea, but . . . the quartermaster ended his report, the officers dismounted and strolled off to the village, and the man on horseback did not appear.

"Von Rabbeck will hear at once from the peasants that we have come and will send for us," thought Ryabovich, as he went into the peasant cottage, unable to understand why a comrade was lighting a candle and why the orderlies were hastening to get the samovars going.

A crushing uneasiness took possession of him. He lay down, then got up and looked out of the window to see whether the messenger were coming. But there was no sign of him.

He lay down again, but half an hour later he got up and, unable to restrain his uneasiness, went into the street and strode towards the church. It was dark and deserted in the square near the church enclosure. Three soldiers were standing silent in a row where the road began to go down-hill. Seeing Ryabovich, they roused themselves and saluted. He returned the salute and began to go down the familiar path.

On the farther bank of the river the whole sky was flooded with crimson: the moon was rising; two peasant women, talking loudly, were pulling cabbage leaves in the kitchen garden; beyond the kitchen garden there were some cottages that formed a dark mass. . . . Everything on the near side of the river was just as it had been in May: the path, the bushes, the willows overhanging the water . . . but there was no sound of the brave nightingale and no scent of poplar and young grass.

Reaching the garden, Ryabovich looked in at the gate. The garden was dark and still. . . . He could see nothing but the white stems of the nearest birch-trees and a little bit of the avenue; all the rest melted together into a dark mass. Ryabovich looked and listened eagerly, but after waiting for a quarter of an hour without hearing a sound or catching a glimpse of a light, he trudged back. . . .

He went down to the river. The General's bathing cabin and the bath-sheets on the rail of the little bridge showed white before him. . . . He walked up on the bridge, stood a little, and quite unnecessarily touched a sheet. It felt rough and cold. He looked down at the water. . . . The river ran rapidly and with a faintly audible gurgle round the piles of the bathing cabin. The red moon was reflected near the left bank; little ripples ran over the reflection, stretching it out, breaking it into bits, and seemed trying to carry it away. . . .

"How stupid, how stupid!" thought Ryabovich, looking at the running water. "How unintelligent it all is!"

Now that he expected nothing, the incident of the kiss, his impatience, his vague hopes and disappointment, presented themselves to him in a clear light. It no longer seemed to him strange that the General's messenger never came and that he would never see the girl who had accidentally kissed him instead of someone else; on the contrary, it would have been strange if he had seen her. . . .

The water was running, he knew not where or why, just as it did in May. At that time it had flowed into a great river, from the great river into the sea; then it had risen in vapor, turned into rain, and

perhaps the very same water was running now before Ryabovich's
eyes again. . . . What for? Why?

And the whole world, the whole of life, seemed to Ryabovich an
unintelligible, aimless jest. . . . And turning his eyes from the water
and looking at the sky, he remembered again how Fate in the person of an unknown woman had by chance caressed him, he recalled
his summer dreams and fancies, and his life struck him as extraordinarily meager, poverty-stricken, and drab. . . .

When he had returned to the cottage he did not find a single
comrade. The orderly informed him that they had all gone to
"General Fontryabkin, who had sent a messenger on horseback to
invite them. . . ."

For an instant there was a flash of joy in Ryabovich's heart, but
he quenched it at once, got into bed, and in his wrath with his
fate, as though to spite it, did not go to the General's.

HENRIK IBSEN
(1828–1906)
The Wild Duck*

Characters

WERLE, *a merchant, manufac-*
turer, etc.

GREGERS WERLE, *his son*

OLD EKDAL

HIALMAR EKDAL, *his son, a pho-*
tographer

GINA EKDAL, *Hialmar's wife*

HEDVIG, *their daughter, a girl of*
fourteen

MRS. SÖRBY, *Werle's housekeeper*

RELLING, *a doctor*

MOLVIK, *student of theology*

GRÅBERG, *Werle's bookkeeper*

PETTERSEN, *Werle's servant*

JENSEN, *a hired waiter*

FLABBY GENTLEMAN

THIN-HAIRED GENTLEMAN

SHORT-SIGHTED GENTLEMAN

SIX OTHER GENTLEMEN, *guests at*
Werle's dinner-party

SEVERAL HIRED WAITERS

The first act passes in WERLE'S *house, the remaining acts at*
HIALMAR EKDAL'S.

Act I

SCENE—*At* WERLE'S *house. A richly and comfortably furnished*
study; bookcases and upholstered furniture; a writing-table, with
papers and documents, in the centre of the room; lighted lamps
with green shades, giving a subdued light. At the back, open folding-
doors with curtains drawn back. Within is seen a large and hand-

* 1884. Translated by Frances Elizabeth Archer.

*some room, brilliantly lighted with lamps and branching candle-
sticks. In front, on the right (in the study), a small baize door leads
into* WERLE's *office. On the left, in front, a fireplace with a glowing
coal fire, and farther back a double door leading into the dining-
room.*

WERLE's *servant,* PETTERSEN, *in livery, and* JENSEN, *the hired
waiter, in black, are putting the study in order. In the large room,
two or three other hired waiters are moving about, arranging things
and lighting more candles. From the dining-room, the hum of
conversation and laughter of many voices are heard; a glass is tapped
with a knife; silence follows, and a toast is proposed; shouts of
"Bravo!" and then again a buzz of conversation.*

PETTERSEN. [*Lights a lamp on the chimney-place and places a shade
over it*] Listen to them, Jensen! Now the old man's on his legs
holding a long palaver about Mrs. Sörby.

JENSEN. [*Pushing forward an armchair*] Is it true, what folks say,
that they're—very good friends, eh?

PETTERSEN. Lord knows.

JENSEN. I've heard tell as he's been a lively customer in his day.

PETTERSEN. May be.

JENSEN. And he's giving this spread in honor of his son, they say.

PETTERSEN. Yes. His son came home yesterday.

JENSEN. This is the first time I ever heard as Mr. Werle had a son.

PETTERSEN. Oh, yes, he has a son, right enough. But he's a fixture,
as you might say, up at the Höidal works. He's never once come
to town all the years I've been in service here.

A WAITER. [*In the doorway of the other room*] Pettersen, here's an
old fellow wanting——

PETTERSEN. [*Mutters*] The devil—who's this now?

[OLD EKDAL *appears from the right, in the inner room. He
is dressed in a threadbare overcoat with a high collar; he
wears woollen mittens and carries in his hand a stick and a
fur cap. Under his arm, a brown paper parcel. Dirty red-
brown wig and small grey moustache.*]

PETTERSEN. [*Goes towards him*] Good Lord—what do you want
here?

EKDAL. [*In the doorway*] Must get into the office, Pettersen.

PETTERSEN. The office was closed an hour ago, and——

EKDAL. So they told me at the front door. But Gråberg's in there
still. Let me slip in this way, Pettersen; there's a good fellow.
[*Points towards the baize door*] It's not the first time I've come
this way.

PETTERSEN. Well, you may pass. [*Opens the door*] But mind you
go out again the proper way, for we've got company.

EKDAL. I know, I know—h'm! Thanks, Pettersen, good old friend! Thanks! [*Mutters softly*] Ass!

[*He goes into the office;* PETTERSEN *shuts the door after him.*]

JENSEN. Is he one of the office people?

PETTERSEN. No he's only an outside hand that does odd jobs of copying. But he's been a tip-topper in his day, has old Ekdal.

JENSEN. You can see he's been through a lot.

PETTERSEN. Yes; he was an army officer, you know.

JENSEN. You don't say so?

PETTERSEN. No mistake about it. But then he went into the timber trade or something of the sort. They say he once played Mr. Werle a very nasty trick. They were partners in the Höidal works at the time. Oh, I know old Ekdal well, I do. Many a nip of bitters and bottle of ale we two have drunk at Madame Eriksen's.

JENSEN. He don't look as if he'd much to stand treat with.

PETTERSEN. Why, bless you, Jensen, it's me that stands treat. I always think there's no harm in being a bit civil to folks that have seen better days.

JENSEN. Did he go bankrupt, then?

PETTERSEN. Worse than that. He went to prison.

JENSEN. To prison!

PETTERSEN. Or perhaps it was the Penitentiary. [*Listens*] Sh! They're leaving the table.

[*The dining-room door is thrown open from within by a couple of waiters.* MRS. SÖRBY *comes out conversing with two* GENTLEMEN. *Gradually the whole company follows, amongst them* WERLE. *Last come* HIALMAR EKDAL *and* GREGERS WERLE.]

MRS. SÖRBY. [*In passing, to the servant*] Tell them to serve the coffee in the music-room, Pettersen.

PETTERSEN. Very well, Madam.

[*She goes with the two* GENTLEMEN *into the inner room and thence out to the right.* PETTERSEN *and* JENSEN *go out the same way.*]

FLABBY GENTLEMAN. [*To* THIN-HAIRED GENTLEMAN] Whew! What a dinner!—It was no joke to do it justice!

THIN-HAIRED GENTLEMAN. Oh, with a little good-will one can get through a lot in three hours.

FLABBY GENTLEMAN. Yes, but afterwards, afterwards, my dear Chamberlain![1]

THIRD GENTLEMAN. I hear the coffee and maraschino are to be served in the music-room.

FLABBY GENTLEMAN. Bravo! Then perhaps Mrs. Sörby will play us something.

1. "Chamberlain" was the non-hereditary honorary title conferred by the King upon men of wealth and position. [Translator's note.]

THIN-HAIRED GENTLEMAN. [*In a low voice*] I hope Mrs. Sörby mayn't play us a tune we don't like, one of these days!

FLABBY GENTLEMAN. Oh, no, not she! Bertha will never turn against her old friends.

[*They laugh and pass into the inner room.*]

WERLE. [*In a low voice, dejectedly*] I don't think anybody noticed it, Gregers.

GREGERS. [*Looks at him*] Noticed what?

WERLE. Did you not notice it either?

GREGERS. What do you mean?

WERLE. We were thirteen at table.

GREGERS. Indeed? Were there thirteen of us?

WERLE. [*Glances towards* HIALMAR EKDAL] Our usual party is twelve. [*To the others*] This way, gentlemen!

[WERLE *and the others, all except* HIALMAR *and* GREGERS, *go out by the back, to the right.*]

HIALMAR. [*Who has overheard the conversation*] You ought not to have invited me, Gregers.

GREGERS. What! Not ask my best and only friend to a party supposed to be in my honor——?

HIALMAR. But I don't think your father likes it. You see I am quite outside his circle.

GREGERS. So I hear. But I wanted to see you and have a talk with you, and I certainly shan't be staying long.—Ah, we two old schoolfellows have drifted far apart from each other. It must be sixteen or seventeen years since we met.

HIALMAR. Is it so long?

GREGERS. It is indeed. Well, how goes it with you? You look well. You have put on flesh and grown almost stout.

HIALMAR. Well, "stout" is scarcely the word; but I daresay I look a little more of a man than I used to.

GREGERS. Yes, you do; your outer man is in first-rate condition.

HIALMAR. [*In a tone of gloom*] Ah, but the inner man! That is a very different matter, I can tell you! Of course you know of the terrible catastrophe that has befallen me and mine since last we met.

GREGERS. [*More softly*] How are things going with your father now?

HIALMAR. Don't let us talk of it, old fellow. Of course my poor unhappy father lives with me. He hasn't another soul in the world to care for him. But you can understand that this is a miserable subject for me.—Tell me, rather, how you have been getting on up at the works.

GREGERS. I have had a delightfully lonely time of it—plenty of leisure to think and think about things. Come over here; we may as well make ourselves comfortable.

[*He seats himself in an armchair by the fire and draws* HIALMAR *down into another alongside of it.*]

HIALMAR. [*Sentimentally*] After all, Gregers, I thank you for invit-ing me to your father's table, for I take it as a sign that you have got over your feeling against me.

GREGERS. [*Surprised*] How could you imagine I had any feeling against you?

HIALMAR. You had at first, you know.

GREGERS. How at first?

HIALMAR. After the great misfortune. It was natural enough that you should. Your father was within an ace of being drawn into that—well, that terrible business.

GREGERS. Why should that give me any feeling against you? Who can have put that into your head?

HIALMAR. I know it did, Gregers; your father told me so himself.

GREGERS. [*Starts*] My father! Oh, indeed. H'm.—Was that why you never let me hear from you?—not a single word.

HIALMAR. Yes.

GREGERS. Not even when you made up your mind to become a photographer?

HIALMAR. Your father said I had better not write to you at all, about anything.

GREGERS. [*Looking straight before him*] Well, well, perhaps he was right.—But tell me now, Hialmar: are you pretty well satisfied with your present position?

HIALMAR. [*With a little sigh*] Oh, yes, I am; I have really no cause to complain. At first, as you may guess, I felt it a little strange. It was such a totally new state of things for me. But of course my whole circumstances were totally changed. Father's utter, irre-trievable ruin,—the shame and disgrace of it, Gregers——

GREGERS. [*Affected*] Yes, yes; I understand.

HIALMAR. I couldn't think of remaining at college; there wasn't a shilling to spare; on the contrary, there were debts—mainly to your father, I believe——

GREGERS. H'm——

HIALMAR. In short, I thought it best to break, once for all, with my old surroundings and associations. It was your father that spe-cially urged me to it; and since he interested himself so much in me——

GREGERS. My father did?

HIALMAR. Yes, you surely knew that, didn't you? Where do you suppose I found the money to learn photography, and to furnish a studio and make a start? All that cost a pretty penny, I can tell you.

GREGERS. And my father provided the money?

HIALMAR. Yes, my dear fellow, didn't you know? I understood him to say he had written to you about it.

GREGERS. Not a word about his part in the business. He must have forgotten it. Our correspondence has always been purely a business one. So it was my father that——!

HIALMAR. Yes, certainly. He didn't wish it to be generally known; but he it was. And of course it was he, too, that put me in a position to marry. Don't you—don't you know about that either?

GREGERS. No, I haven't heard a word of it. [*Shakes him by the arm*] But, my dear Hialmar, I can't tell you what pleasure all this gives me—pleasure, and self-reproach. I have perhaps done my father injustice after all—in some things. This proves that he has a heart. It shows a sort of compunction——

HIALMAR. Compunction——?

GREGERS. Yes, yes—whatever you like to call it. Oh, I can't tell you how glad I am to hear this of father.—So you are a married man, Hialmar! That is further than I shall ever get. Well, I hope you are happy in your married life?

HIALMAR. Yes, thoroughly happy. She is as good and capable a wife as any man could wish for. And she is by no means without culture.

GREGERS. [*Rather surprised*] No, of course not.

HIALMAR. You see, life is itself an education. Her daily intercourse with me—— And then we know one or two rather remarkable men, who come a good deal about us. I assure you, you would hardly know Gina again.

GREGERS. Gina?

HIALMAR. Yes; had you forgotten that her name was Gina?

GREGERS. Whose name? I haven't the slightest idea——

HIALMAR. Don't you remember that she used to be in service here?

GREGERS. [*Looks at him*] Is it Gina Hansen——?

HIALMAR. Yes, of course it is Gina Hansen.

GREGERS. ——who kept house for us during the last year of my mother's illness?

HIALMAR. Yes, exactly. But, my dear friend, I'm quite sure your father told you that I was married.

GREGERS. [*Who has risen*] Oh, yes, he mentioned it; but not that—— [*Walking about the room*] Stay—perhaps he did—now that I think of it. My father always writes such short letters. [*Half seats himself on the arm of the chair*] Now tell me, Hialmar—this is interesting—how did you come to know Gina—your wife?

HIALMAR. The simplest thing in the world. You know Gina did not stay here long; everything was so much upset at that time, owing to your mother's illness and so forth, that Gina was not equal to it all; so she gave notice and left. That was the year before your mother died—or it may have been the same year.

GREGERS. It was the same year. I was up at the works then. But afterwards——?

HIALMAR. Well, Gina lived at home with her mother, Madame Hansen, an excellent hard-working woman, who kept a little eating-house. She had a room to let, too, a very nice comfortable room.

GREGERS. And I suppose you were lucky enough to secure it?

HIALMAR. Yes; in fact, it was your father that recommended it to me. So it was there, you see, that I really came to know Gina.

GREGERS. And then you got engaged?

HIALMAR Yes. It doesn't take young people long to fall in love——; h'm——

GREGERS. [*Rises and moves about a little*] Tell me: was it after your engagement—was it then that my father—I mean was it then that you began to take up photography?

HIALMAR. Yes, precisely. I wanted to make a start and to set up house as soon as possible; and your father and I agreed that this photography business was the readiest way. Gina thought so, too. Oh, and there was another thing in its favor, by-the-bye: it happened, luckily, that Gina had learnt to retouch.

GREGERS. That chimed in marvellously.

HIALMAR. [*Pleased, rises*] Yes, didn't it? Don't you think it was a marvellous piece of luck?

GREGERS. Oh, unquestionably. My father seems to have been almost a kind of providence for you.

HIALMAR. [*With emotion*] He did not forsake his old friend's son in the hour of his need. For he has a heart, you see.

MRS. SÖRBY [*Enters, arm-in-arm with* WERLE] Nonsense, my dear Mr. Werle; you mustn't stop there any longer staring at all the lights. It's very bad for you.

WERLE. [*Lets go her arm and passes his hand over his eyes*] I daresay you are right.

[PETTERSEN *and* JENSEN *carry round refreshment trays.*]

MRS. SÖRBY. [*To the guests in the other room*] This way, if you please, gentlemen. Whoever wants a glass of punch must be so good as to come in here.

FLABBY GENTLEMAN. [*Comes up to* MRS. SÖRBY] Surely, it isn't possible that you have suspended our cherished right to smoke?

MRS. SÖRBY. Yes. No smoking here, in Mr. Werle's sanctum, Chamberlain.

THIN-HAIRED GENTLEMAN. When did you enact these stringent amendments to the cigar law, Mrs. Sörby?

MRS. SÖRBY. After the last dinner, Chamberlain, when certain persons permitted themselves to overstep the mark.

THIN-HAIRED GENTLEMAN. And may one never overstep the mark a little bit, Madame Bertha? Not the least little bit?

MRS. SÖRBY. Not in any respect whatsoever, Mr. Balle.

[*Most of the guests have assembled in the study; servants hand round glasses of punch.*]

WERLE. [*To* HIALMAR, *who is standing beside a table*] What are you studying so intently, Ekdal?

HIALMAR. Only an album, Mr. Werle.

THIN-HAIRED GENTLEMAN. [*Who is wandering about*] Ah, photographs! They are quite in your line, of course.

FLABBY GENTLEMAN. [*In an armchair*] Haven't you brought any of your own with you?

HIALMAR. No, I haven't.

FLABBY GENTLEMAN. You ought to have; it's very good for the digestion to sit and look at pictures.

THIN-HAIRED GENTLEMAN. And it contributes to the entertainment, you know.

SHORT-SIGHTED GENTLEMAN. And all contributions are thankfully received.

MRS. SÖRBY. The Chamberlains think that when one is invited out to dinner, one ought to exert oneself a little in return, Mr. Ekdal.

FLABBY GENTLEMAN. Where one dines so well, that duty becomes a pleasure.

THIN-HAIRED GENTLEMAN. And when it's a case of the struggle for existence, you know——

MRS. SÖRBY. I quite agree with you!

[*They continue the conversation, with laughter and joking.*]

GREGERS. [*Softly*] You must join in, Hialmar.

HIALMAR. [*Writhing*] What am I to talk about?

FLABBY GENTLEMAN. Don't you think, Mr. Werle, that Tokay may be considered one of the more wholesome sorts of wine?

WERLE. [*By the fire*] I can answer for the Tokay you had today, at any rate; it's one of the very finest seasons. Of course you would notice that.

FLABBY GENTLEMAN. Yes, it had a remarkably delicate flavor.

HIALMAR. [*Shyly*] Is there any difference between the seasons?

FLABBY GENTLEMAN. [*Laughs*] Come! That's good!

WERLE. [*Smiles*] It really doesn't pay to set fine wine before you.

THIN-HAIRED GENTLEMAN. Tokay is like photographs, Mr. Ekdal: they both need sunshine. Am I not right?

HIALMAR. Yes, light is important, no doubt.

MRS. SÖRBY. And it's exactly the same with Chamberlains—they, too, depend very much on sunshine,[2] as the saying is.

2. The "sunshine" of court favor. [Translator's note.]

THIN-HAIRED GENTLEMAN. Oh, fie! That's a very threadbare sarcasm!

SHORT-SIGHTED GENTLEMAN. Mrs. Sörby is coming out——

FLABBY GENTLEMAN. ——and at our expense, too. [*Holds up his finger reprovingly*] Oh, Madame Bertha, Madame Bertha!

MRS. SÖRBY. Yes, and there's not the least doubt that the seasons differ greatly. The old vintages are the finest.

SHORT-SIGHTED GENTLEMAN. Do you reckon me among the old vintages?

MRS. SÖRBY. Oh, far from it.

THIN-HAIRED GENTLEMAN. There now! But me, dear Mrs. Sörby——?

FLABBY GENTLEMAN. Yes, and me? What vintage should you say that we belong to?

MRS. SÖRBY. Why, to the sweet vintages, gentlemen.

[*She sips a glass of punch. The* GENTLEMEN *laugh and flirt with her.*]

WERLE. Mrs. Sörby can always find a loop-hole—when she wants to. Fill your glasses, gentlemen! Pettersen, will you see to it—! Gregers, suppose we have a glass together. [GREGERS *does not move*] Won't you join us, Ekdal? I found no opportunity of drinking with you at table.

[GRÅBERG, *the bookkeeper, looks in at the baize door.*]

GRÅBERG. Excuse me, sir, but I can't get out.

WERLE. Have you been locked in again?

GRÅBERG. Yes, and Flakstad has carried off the keys.

WERLE. Well, you can pass out this way.

GRÅBERG. But there's some one else——

WERLE. All right; come through, both of you. Don't be afraid.

[GRÅBERG *and* OLD EKDAL *come out of the office.*]

WERLE. [*Involuntarily*] Ugh!

[*The laughter and talk among the guests cease.* HIALMAR *starts at the sight of his father, puts down his glass and turns towards the fireplace.*]

EKDAL. [*Does not look up, but makes little bows to both sides as he passes, murmuring*] Beg pardon, come the wrong way. Door locked—door locked. Beg pardon.

[*He and* GRÅBERG *go out by the back, to the right.*]

WERLE. [*Between his teeth*] That idiot Gråberg.

GREGERS. [*Opened-mouthed and staring, to* HIALMAR] Why surely that wasn't——!

FLABBY GENTLEMAN. What's the matter? Who was it?

GREGERS. Oh, nobody; only the bookkeeper and some one with him.

SHORT-SIGHTED GENTLEMAN. [*To* HIALMAR] Did you know that man?

HIALMAR. I don't know—I didn't notice——

FLABBY GENTLEMAN. What the deuce has come over every one? [*He joins another group who are talking softly.*]

MRS. SÖRBY. [*Whispers to the servant*] Give him something to take with him;—something good, mind.

PETTERSEN. [*Nods*] I'll see to it. [*Goes out.*]

GREGERS. [*Softly and with emotion, to* HIALMAR] So that was really he!

HIALMAR. Yes.

GREGERS. And you could stand there and deny that you knew him!

HIALMAR. [*Whispers vehemently*] But how could I——!

GREGERS. ——acknowledge your own father?

HIALMAR. [*With pain*] Oh, if you were in my place——

[*The conversation amongst the guests, which has been carried on in a low tone, now swells into constrained joviality.*]

THIN-HAIRED GENTLEMAN. [*Approaching* HIALMAR *and* GREGERS *in a friendly manner*] Aha! Reviving old college memories, eh? Don't you smoke, Mr. Ekdal? May I give you a light? Oh, by-the-bye, we mustn't——

HIALMAR. No, thank you, I won't——

FLABBY GENTLEMAN. Haven't you a nice little poem you could recite to us, Mr. Ekdal? You used to recite so charmingly.

HIALMAR. I am sorry I can't remember anything.

FLABBY GENTLEMAN. Oh, that's a pity. Well, what shall we do, Balle?

[*Both* GENTLEMEN *move away and pass into the other room.*]

HIALMAR. [*Gloomily*] Gregers—I am going! When a man has felt the crushing hand of Fate, you see—— Say good-bye to your father for me.

GREGERS. Yes, yes. Are you going straight home?

HIALMAR. Yes. Why?

GREGERS. Oh, because I may perhaps look in on you later.

HIALMAR. No, you mustn't do that. You must not come to my home. Mine is a melancholy abode, Gregers, especially after a splendid banquet like this. We can always arrange to meet somewhere in the town.

MRS. SÖRBY. [*Who has quietly approached*] Are you going, Ekdal?

HIALMAR. Yes.

MRS. SÖRBY. Remember me to Gina.

HIALMAR. Thanks.

MRS. SÖRBY. And say I am coming up to see her one of these days.

HIALMAR. Yes, thank you. [*To* GREGERS] Stay here; I will slip out unobserved.

[*He saunters away, then into the other room, and so out to the right.*]

MRS. SÖRBY. [*Softly to the servant, who has come back*] Well, did you give the old man something?

PETTERSEN. Yes; I sent him off with a bottle of cognac.

MRS. SÖRBY. Oh, you might have thought of something better than that.

PETTERSEN. Oh, no, Mrs. Sörby; cognac is what he likes best in the world.

FLABBY GENTLEMAN. [*In the doorway with a sheet of music in his hand*] Shall we play a duet, Mrs. Sörby?

MRS. SÖRBY. Yes, suppose we do.

THE GUESTS. Bravo, bravo!

> [*She goes with all the guests through the back room, out to the right.* GREGERS *remains standing by the fire.* WERLE *is looking for something on the writing-table and appears to wish that* GREGERS *would go; as* GREGERS *does not move,* WERLE *goes towards the door.*]

GREGERS. Father, won't you stay a moment?

WERLE. [*Stops*] What is it?

GREGERS. I must have a word with you.

WERLE. Can it not wait till we are alone?

GREGERS. No, it cannot; for perhaps we shall never be alone together.

WERLE. [*Drawing nearer*] What do you mean by that?

> [*During what follows, the pianoforte is faintly heard from the distant music-room.*]

GREGERS. How has that family been allowed to go so miserably to the wall?

WERLE. You mean the Ekdals, I suppose.

GREGERS. Yes, I mean the Ekdals. Lieutenant Ekdal was once so closely associated with you.

WERLE. Much too closely; I have felt that to my cost for many a year. It is thanks to him that I—yes I—have had a kind of slur cast upon my reputation.

GREGERS. [*Softly*] Are you sure that he alone was to blame?

WERLE. Who else do you suppose——?

GREGERS. You and he acted together in that affair of the forests——

WERLE. But was it not Ekdal that drew the map of the tracts we had bought—that fraudulent map! It was he who felled all that timber illegally on Government ground. In fact, the whole management was in his hands. I was quite in the dark as to what Lieutenant Ekdal was doing.

GREGERS. Lieutenant Ekdal himself seems to have been very much in the dark as to what he was doing.

WERLE. That may be. But the fact remains that he was found guilty and I acquitted.

GREGERS. Yes, I know that nothing was proved against you.

WERLE. Acquittal is acquittal. Why do you rake up these old miseries that turned my hair grey before its time? Is that the sort of thing you have been brooding over up there, all these years? I can assure you, Gregers, here in the town the whole story has been forgotten long ago—so far as *I* am concerned.

GREGERS. But that unhappy Ekdal family——

WERLE. What would you have had me do for the people? When Ekdal came out of prison he was a broken-down being, past all help. There are people in the world who dive to the bottom the moment they get a couple of slugs in their body and never come to the surface again. You may take my word for it, Gregers, I have done all I could without positively laying myself open to all sorts of suspicion and gossip——

GREGERS. Suspicion——? Oh, I see.

WERLE. I have given Ekdal copying to do for the office, and I pay him far, far more for it than his work is worth——

GREGERS. [*Without looking at him*] H'm; that I don't doubt.

WERLE. You laugh? Do you think I am not telling you the truth? Well, I certainly can't refer you to my books, for I never enter payments of that sort.

GREGERS. [*Smiles coldly*] No, there are certain payments it is best to keep no account of.

WERLE. [*Taken aback*] What do you mean by that?

GREGERS. [*Mustering up courage*] Have you entered what it cost you to have Hialmar Ekdal taught photography?

WERLE. I? How "entered" it?

GREGERS. I have learnt that it was you who paid for his training. And I have learnt, too, that it was you who enabled him to set up house so comfortably.

WERLE. Well, and yet you talk as though I had done nothing for the Ekdals! I can assure you these people have cost me enough in all conscience.

GREGERS. Have you entered any of these expenses in your books?

WERLE. Why do you ask?

GREGERS. Oh, I have my reasons. Now tell me: when you interested yourself so warmly in your old friend's son—it was just before his marriage, was it not?

WERLE. Why, deuce take it—after all these years, how can I——?

GREGERS. You wrote me a letter about that time—a business letter, of course; and in a postscript you mentioned—quite briefly—that Hialmar Ekdal had married a Miss Hansen.

WERLE. Yes, that was quite right. That was her name.

GREGERS. But you did not mention that this Miss Hansen was Gina Hansen—our former housekeeper.

WERLE. [*With a forced laugh of derision*] No; to tell the truth, it didn't occur to me that you were so particularly interested in our former housekeeper.

GREGERS. No more I was. But [*Lowers his voice*] there were others in this house who were particularly interested in her.

WERLE. What do you mean by that? [*Flaring up*] You are not alluding to me, I hope?

GREGERS. [*Softly but firmly*] Yes, I am alluding to you.

WERLE. And you dare——! You presume to——! How can that ungrateful hound—that photographer fellow—how dare he go making such insinuations!

GREGERS. Hialmar has never breathed a word about this. I don't believe he has the faintest suspicion of such a thing.

WERLE. Then where have you got it from? Who can have put such notions in your head?

GREGERS. My poor unhappy mother told me; and that the very last time I saw her.

WERLE. Your mother! I might have known as much! You and she— you always held together. It was she who turned you against me, from the first.

GREGERS. No, it was all that she had to suffer and submit to, until she broke down and came to such a pitiful end.

WERLE. Oh, she had nothing to suffer or submit to; not more than most people, at all events. But there's no getting on with morbid, overstrained creatures—that I have learnt to my cost.—And you could go on nursing such a suspicion—burrowing into all sorts of old rumors and slanders against your own father! I must say, Gregers, I really think that at your age you might find something more useful to do.

GREGERS. Yes, it is high time.

WERLE. Then perhaps your mind would be easier than it seems to be now. What can be your object in remaining up at the works, year out and year in, drudging away like a common clerk, and not drawing a farthing more than the ordinary monthly wage? It is downright folly.

GREGERS. Ah, if I were only sure of that.

WERLE. I understand you well enough. You want to be independent; you won't be beholden to me for anything. Well, now there happens to be an opportunity for you to become independent, your own master in everything.

GREGERS. Indeed? In what way——?

WERLE. When I wrote you insisting on your coming to town at once—h'm——

GREGERS. Yes, what is it you really want of me? I have been waiting all day to know.

WERLE. I want to propose that you should enter the firm, as partner.

GREGERS. I! Join your firm? As partner?

WERLE. Yes. It would not involve our being constantly together. You could take over the business here in town, and I should move up to the works.

GREGERS. You would?

WERLE. The fact is, I am not so fit for work as I once was. I am obliged to spare my eyes, Gregers; they have begun to trouble me.

GREGERS. They have always been weak.

WERLE. Not as they are now. And, besides, circumstances might possibly make it desirable for me to live up there—for a time, at any rate.

GREGERS. That is certainly quite a new idea to me.

WERLE. Listen, Gregers: there are many things that stand between us; but we are father and son after all. We ought surely to be able to come to some sort of understanding with each other.

GREGERS. Outwardly, you mean, of course?

WERLE. Well, even that would be something. Think it over, Gregers. Don't you think it ought to be possible? Eh?

GREGERS. [*Looking at him coldly*] There is something behind all this.

WERLE. How so?

GREGERS. You want to make use of me in some way.

WERLE. In such a close relationship as ours, the one can always be useful to the other.

GREGERS. Yes, so people say.

WERLE. I want very much to have you at home with me for a time. I am a lonely man, Gregers; I have always felt lonely, all my life through; but most of all now that I am getting up in years. I feel the need of some one about me——

GREGERS. You have Mrs. Sörby.

WERLE. Yes, I have her; and she has become, I may say, almost indispensable to me. She is lively and even-tempered; she brightens up the house; and that is a very great thing for me.

GREGERS. Well, then, you have everything just as you wish it.

WERLE. Yes, but I am afraid it can't last. A woman so situated may easily find herself in a false position, in the eyes of the world. For that matter it does a man no good, either.

GREGERS. Oh, when a man gives such dinners as you give, he can risk a great deal.

WERLE. Yes, but how about the woman, Gregers? I fear she won't accept the situation much longer; and even if she did—even if, out of attachment to me, she were to take her chance of gossip and scandal and all that——? Do you think, Gregers—you with your strong sense of justice——

GREGERS. [*Interrupts him*] Tell me in one word: are you thinking of marrying her?

WERLE. Suppose I were thinking of it? What then?

GREGERS. That's what I say: what then?

WERLE. Should you be inflexibly opposed to it!

GREGERS. Not at all. Not by any means.

WERLE. I was not sure whether your devotion to your mother's memory——

GREGERS. I am not overstrained.

WERLE. Well, whatever you may or may not be, at all events you have lifted a great weight from my mind. I am extremely pleased that I can reckon on your concurrence in this matter.

GREGERS. [*Looking intently at him*] Now I see the use you want to put me to.

WERLE. Use to put you to? What an expression!

GREGERS. Oh, don't let us be nice in our choice of words—not when we are alone together, at any rate. [*With a short laugh*] Well, well. So this is what made it absolutely essential that I should come to town in person. For the sake of Mrs. Sörby, we are to get up a pretence at family life in the house—a tableau of filial affection! That will be something new indeed.

WERLE. How dare you speak in that tone!

GREGERS. Was there ever any family life here? Never since I can remember. But now, forsooth, your plans demand something of the sort. No doubt it will have an excellent effect when it is reported that the son has hastened home, on the wings of filial piety, to the grey-haired father's wedding-feast. What will then remain of all the rumors as to the wrongs the poor dead mother had to submit to? Not a vestige. Her son annihilates them at one stroke.

WERLE. Gregers—I believe there is no one in the world you detest as you do me.

GREGERS. [*Softly*] I have seen you at too close quarters.

WERLE. You have seen me with your mother's eyes. [*Lowers his voice a little*] But you should remember that her eyes were—clouded now and then.

GREGERS [*Quivering*] I see what you are hinting at. But who was to blame for mother's unfortunate weakness? Why, you, and all those——! The last of them was this woman that you palmed off upon Hialmar Ekdal, when you were—— Ugh!

WERLE. [*Shrugs his shoulders*] Word for word as if it were your mother speaking!

GREGERS. [*Without heeding*] And there he is now, with his great, confiding, childlike mind, compassed about with all this treachery —living under the same roof with such a creature and never dreaming that what he calls his home is built upon a lie! [*Comes a step nearer*] When I look back upon your past, I seem to see a battle-field with shattered lives on every hand.

WERLE. I begin to think the chasm that divides us is too wide.

GREGERS. [*Bowing, with self-command*] So I have observed; and therefore I take my hat and go.

WERLE. You are going! Out of the house?

GREGERS. Yes. For at last I see my mission in life.

WERLE. What mission?

GREGERS. You would only laugh if I told you.

WERLE. A lonely man doesn't laugh so easily, Gregers.

GREGERS. [*Pointing towards the background*] Look, father,—the Chamberlains are playing blind-man's-buff with Mrs. Sörby.— Good-night and good-bye.

> [*He goes out by the back to the right. Sounds of laughter and merriment from the company, who are now visible in the outer room.*]

WERLE. [*Muttering contemptuously after* GREGERS] Ha——! Poor wretch—and he says he is not overstrained!

Act II

SCENE—HIALMAR EKDAL'S *studio, a good-sized room, evidently in the top story of the building. On the right, a sloping roof of large panes of glass, half-covered by a blue curtain. In the right-hand corner, at the back, the entrance door; farther forward, on the same side, a door leading to the sitting-room. Two doors on the opposite side, and between them an iron stove. At back, a wide double sliding-door. The studio is plainly but comfortably fitted up and furnished. Between the doors on the right, standing out a little from the wall, a sofa with a table and some chairs; on the table a lighted lamp with a shade; beside the stove an old arm-chair. Photographic instruments and apparatus of different kinds lying about the room. Against the back wall, to the left of the double door, stands a book-case containing a few books, boxes, and bottles of chemicals, instruments, tools, and other objects. Photographs and small articles, such as camel's-hair pencils, paper, and so forth, lie on the table.*

GINA EKDAL *sits on a chair by the table, sewing.* HEDVIG *is sitting on the sofa, with her hands shading her eyes and her thumbs in her ears, reading a book.*

GINA. [*Glances once or twice at* HEDVIG, *as if with secret anxiety; then says*] Hedvig!

> [HEDVIG *does not hear.*]

GINA. [*Repeats more loudly*] Hedvig!

HEDVIG. [*Takes away her hands and looks up*] Yes, mother?

GINA. Hedvig dear, you mustn't sit reading any longer now.

HEDVIG. Oh, mother, mayn't I read a little more? Just a little bit?

GINA. No, no, you must put away your book now. Father doesn't like it; he never reads hisself in the evening.

HEDVIG. [*Shuts the book*] No, father doesn't care much about reading.

GINA. [*Puts aside her sewing and takes up a lead pencil and a little account-book from the table*] Can you remember how much we paid for the butter today?

HEDVIG. It was one crown sixty-five.

GINA. That's right. [*Puts it down*] It's terrible what a lot of butter we get through in this house. Then there was the smoked sausage, and the cheese—let me see—[*Writes*]—and the ham—[*Adds up*] Yes, that makes just——

HEDVIG. And then the beer.

GINA. Yes, to be sure. [*Writes*] How it do mount up! But we can't manage with no less.

HEDVIG. And then you and I didn't need anything hot for dinner, as father was out.

GINA. No; that was so much to the good. And then I took eight crowns fifty for the photographs.

HEDVIG. Really! So much as that?

GINA. Exactly eight crowns fifty.

[*Silence.* GINA *takes up her sewing again;* HEDVIG *takes paper and pencil and begins to draw, shading her eyes with her left hand.*]

HEDVIG. Isn't it jolly to think that father is at Mr. Werle's big dinner-party?

GINA. You know he's not really Mr. Werle's guest. It was the son invited him. [*After a pause*] We have nothing to do with that Mr. Werle.

HEDVIG. I'm longing for father to come home. He promised to ask Mrs. Sörby for something nice for me.

GINA. Yes, there's plenty of good things in that house, I can tell you.

HEDVIG. [*Goes on drawing*] And I believe I'm a little hungry, too.

[OLD EKDAL, *with the paper parcel under his arm and another parcel in his coat pocket, comes in by the entrance door.*]

GINA. How late you are today, grandfather!

EKDAL. They had locked the office door. Had to wait in Gråberg's room. And then they let me through—h'm.

HEDVIG. Did you get some more copying to do, grandfather?

EKDAL. This whole packet. Just look.

GINA. That's capital.

HEDVIG. And you have another parcel in your pocket.

EKDAL. Eh? Oh, never mind, that's nothing. [*Puts his stick away in *a corner*] This work will keep me going a long time, Gina. [*Opens one of the sliding-doors in the back wall a little*] Hush! [*Peeps into the room for a moment, then pushes the door carefully to again*] Hee-hee! They're fast asleep, all the lot of them. And she's gone into the basket herself. Hee-hee!

HEDVIG. Are you sure she isn't cold in that basket, grandfather?

EKDAL. Not a bit of it! Cold? With all that straw? [*Goes towards the farther door on the left*] There are matches in here, I suppose.

GINA. The matches is on the drawers.

    [EKDAL *goes into his room.*]

HEDVIG. It's nice that grandfather has got all that copying.

GINA. Yes, poor old father; it means a bit of pocket-money for him.

HEDVIG. And he won't be able to sit the whole forenoon down at that horrid Madame Eriksen's.

GINA. No more he won't.   [*Short silence*]

HEDVIG. Do you suppose they are still at the dinner-table?

GINA. Goodness knows; as like as not.

HEDVIG. Think of all the delicious things father is having to eat! I'm certain he'll be in splendid spirits when he comes. Don't you think so, mother?

GINA. Yes; and if only we could tell him that we'd got the room let——

HEDVIG. But we don't need that this evening.

GINA. Oh, we'd be none the worst of it, I can tell you. It's no use to us as it is.

HEDVIG. I mean we don't need it this evening, for father will be in a good humor at any rate. It is best to keep the letting of the room for another time.

GINA. [*Looks across at her*] You like having some good news to tell father when he comes home in the evening?

HEDVIG. Yes; for then things are pleasanter somehow.

GINA. [*Thinking to herself*] Yes, yes, there's something in that.

    [OLD EKDAL *comes in again and is going out by the foremost door to the left.*]

GINA. [*Half turning in her chair*] Do you want something out of the kitchen, grandfather?

EKDAL. Yes, yes, I do. Don't you trouble.   [*Goes out*]

GINA. He's not poking away at the fire, is he? [*Waits a moment*] Hedvig, go and see what he's about.

    [EKDAL *comes in again with a small jug of steaming hot water.*]

HEDVIG. Have you been getting some hot water, grandfather?

EKDAL. Yes, hot water. Want it for something. Want to write, and the ink has got as thick as porridge—h'm.

GINA. But you'd best have your supper first, grandfather. It's laid in there.

EKDAL. Can't be bothered with supper, Gina. Very busy, I tell you. No one's to come to my room. No one—h'm.

[*He goes into his room;* GINA *and* HEDVIG *look at each other.*]

GINA. [*Softly*] Can you imagine where he's got money from?

HEDVIG. From Gråberg, perhaps.

GINA. Not a bit of it. Gråberg always sends the money to me.

HEDVIG. Then he must have got a bottle on credit somewhere.

GINA. Poor grandfather, who'd give him credit?

HIALMAR EKDAL, *in an overcoat and grey felt hat, comes in from the right.*]

GINA. [*Throws down her sewing and rises*] Why, Ekdal, is that you already?

HEDVIG. [*At the same time, jumping up*] Fancy your coming so soon, father!

HIALMAR. [*Taking off his hat*] Yes, most of the people were coming away.

HEDVIG. So early?

HIALMAR. Yes, it was a dinner-party, you know.

[*Taking off his overcoat*]

GINA. Let me help you.

HEDVIG. Me, too.

[*They draw off his coat;* GINA *hangs it up on the back wall.*]

HEDVIG. Were there many people there, father?

HIALMAR. Oh, no, not many. We were about twelve or fourteen at table.

GINA. And you had some talk with them all?

HIALMAR. Oh, yes, a little; but Gregers took up most of my time.

GINA. Is Gregers as ugly as ever?

HIALMAR. Well, he's not very much to look at. Hasn't the old man come home?

HEDVIG. Yes, grandfather is in his room, writing.

HIALMAR. Did he say anything?

GINA. No, what should he say?

HIALMAR. Didn't he say anything about——? I heard something about his having been with Gråberg. I'll go in and see him for a moment.

GINA. No, no, better not.

HIALMAR. Why not? Did he say he didn't want me to go in?

GINA. I don't think he wants to see nobody this evening——

HEDVIG. [*Making signs*] H'm—h'm!

GINA. [*Not noticing*]——he has been in to fetch hot water——

HIALMAR. Aha! Then he's——

GINA. Yes, I suppose so.

HIALMAR. Oh, God! my poor old white-haired father!—— Well, well; there let him sit and get all the enjoyment he can.

[OLD EKDAL, *in an indoor coat and with a lighted pipe, comes from his room.*]

EKDAL. Got home? Thought it was you I heard talking.

HIALMAR. Yes, I have just come.

EKDAL. You didn't see me, did you?

HIALMAR. No, but they told me you had passed through—so I thought I would follow you.

EKDAL. H'm, good of you, Hialmar.—Who were they, all those fellows?

HIALMAR.—Oh, all sorts of people. There was Chamberlain Flor, and Chamberlain Balle, and Chamberlain Kaspersen and Chamberlain—this, that, and the other—I don't know who all——

EKDAL. [*Nodding*] Hear that, Gina! Chamberlains every one of them!

GINA. Yes, I hear as they're terrible genteel in that house nowadays.

HEDVIG. Did the Chamberlains sing, father? Or did they read aloud?

HIALMAR. No, they only talked nonsense. They wanted me to recite something for them; but I knew better than that.

EKDAL. You weren't to be persuaded, eh?

GINA. Oh, you might have done it.

HIALMAR. No; one mustn't be at everybody's beck and call. [*Walks about the room*] That's not my way, at any rate.

EKDAL. No, no; Hialmar's not to be had for the asking, he isn't.

HIALMAR. I don't see why *I* should bother myself to entertain people on the rare occasions when I go into society. Let the others exert themselves. These fellows go from one great dinner-table to the next and gorge and guzzle day out and day in. It's for them to bestir themselves and do something in return for all the good feeding they get.

GINA. But you didn't say that?

HIALMAR. [*Humming*] Ho-ho-ho——; faith, I gave them a bit of my mind.

EKDAL. Not the Chamberlains?

HIALMAR. Oh, why not? [*Lightly*] After that, we had a little discussion about Tokay.

EKDAL. Tokay! There's a fine wine for you!

HIALMAR. [*Comes to a standstill*] It may be a fine wine. But of course you know the vintages differ; it all depends on how much sunshine the grapes have had.

GINA. Why, you know everything, Ekdal.

EKDAL. And did they dispute that?

HIALMAR. They tried to; but they were requested to observe that it was just the same with Chamberlains—that with them, too, different batches were of different qualities.

GINA. What things you do think of!

EKDAL. Hee-hee! So they got that in their pipes, too?

HIALMAR. Right in their teeth.

EKDAL. Do you hear that, Gina? He said it right in the very teeth of all the Chamberlains.

GINA. Fancy——! Right in their teeth!

HIALMAR. Yes, but I don't want it talked about. One doesn't speak of such things. The whole affair passed off quite amicably of course. They were nice, genial fellows; I didn't want to wound them—not I!

EKDAL. Right in their teeth, though——!

HEDVIG. [*Caressingly*] How nice it is to see you in a dress-coat! It suits you so well, father.

HIALMAR. Yes, don't you think so? And this one really sits to perfection. It fits almost as if it had been made for me;—a little tight in the arm-holes perhaps;—help me, Hedvig. [*Takes off the coat*] I think I'll put on my jacket. Where is my jacket, Gina?

GINA. Here it is.   [*Brings the jacket and helps him.*]

HIALMAR. That's it! Don't forget to send the coat back to Molvik first thing tomorrow morning.

GINA. [*Laying it away*] I'll be sure and see to it.

HIALMAR. [*Stretching himself*] After all, there's a more homely feeling about this. A free-and-easy indoor costume suits my whole personality better. Don't you think so, Hedvig?

HEDVIG. Yes, father.

HIALMAR. When I loosen my necktie into a pair of flowing ends— like this—eh?

HEDVIG. Yes, that goes so well with your moustache and the sweep of your curls.

HIALMAR. I should not call them curls exactly; I should rather say locks.

HEDVIG. Yes, there are too big for curls.

HIALMAR. Locks describes them better.

HEDVIG. [*After a pause, twitching his jacket*] Father!

HIALMAR. Well, what is it?

HEDVIG. Oh, you know very well.

HIALMAR. No, really I don't——

HEDVIG. [*Half laughing, half whispering*] Oh, yes, father; now don't tease me any longer!

HIALMAR. Why, what do you mean?

HEDVIG. [*Shaking him*] Oh, what nonsense; come, where are they, father? All the good things you promised me, you know?

HIALMAR. Oh—if I haven't forgotten all about them!

HEDVIG. Now you're only teasing me, father! Oh, it's too bad of you! Where have you put them?

HIALMAR. No, I positively forgot to get anything. But wait a little! I have something else for you, Hedvig.

[*Goes and searches in the pockets of the coat.*]

HEDVIG. [*Skipping and clapping her hands*] Oh, mother, mother!

GINA. There, you see; if you only give him time——

HIALMAR. [*With a paper*] Look, here it is.

HEDVIG. That? Why, that's only a paper.

HIALMAR. That is the bill of fare, my dear; the whole bill of fare. Here you see: "Menu"—that means bill of fare.

HEDVIG. Haven't you anything else?

HIALMAR. I forgot the other things, I tell you. But you may take my word for it, these dainties are very unsatisfying. Sit down at the table and read the bill of fare, and then I'll describe to you how the dishes taste. Here you are, Hedvig.

HEDVIG. [*Gulping down her tears*] Thank you. [*She seats herself, but does not read; GINA makes signs to her; HIALMAR notices it.*]

HIALMAR. [*Pacing up and down the room*] It's monstrous what absurd things the father of a family is expected to think of; and if he forgets the smallest trifle, he is treated to sour faces at once. Well, well, one gets used to that, too. [*Stops near the stove, by the old man's chair*] Have you peeped in there this evening, father?

EKDAL. Yes, to be sure I have. She's gone into the basket.

HIALMAR. Ah, she has gone into the basket. Then she's beginning to get used to it.

EKDAL. Yes; just as I prophesied. But you know there are still a few little things——

HIALMAR. A few improvements, yes.

EKDAL. They've got to be made, you know.

HIALMAR. Yes, let us have a talk about the improvements, father. Come, let us sit on the sofa.

EKDAL. All right. H'm—think I'll just fill my pipe first. Must clean it out, too. H'm.

[*He goes into his room.*]

GINA. [*Smiling to HIALMAR*] His pipe!

HIALMAR. Oh, yes, yes, Gina; let him alone—the poor shipwrecked old man.—Yes, these improvements—we had better get them out of hand tomorrow.

GINA. You'll hardly have time tomorrow, Ekdal.

HEDVIG. [*Interposing*] Oh, yes he will, mother!

GINA. ——for remember them prints that has to be retouched; they've sent for them time after time.

HIALMAR. There now! those prints again! I shall get them finished all right! Have any new orders come in?

GINA. No, worse luck; tomorrow I have nothing but those two sittings, you know.

HIALMAR. Nothing else? Oh, no, if people won't set about things with a will——

GINA. But what more can I do? Don't I advertise in the papers as much as we can afford?

HIALMAR. Yes, the papers, the papers; you see how much good they do. And I suppose no one has been to look at the room either?

GINA. No, not yet.

HIALMAR. That was only to be expected. If people won't keep their eyes open——. Nothing can be done without a real effort, Gina!

HEDVIG. [*Going towards him*] Shall I fetch you the flute, father?

HIALMAR. No; no flute for me; I want no pleasures in this world. [*Pacing about*] Yes, indeed I will work tomorrow; you shall see if I don't. You may be sure I shall work as long as my strength holds out.

GINA. But my dear, good Ekdal, I didn't mean it in that way.

HEDVIG. Father, mayn't I bring in a bottle of beer?

HIALMAR. No, certainly not. I require nothing, nothing——[*Comes to a standstill*] Beer? Was it beer you were talking about?

HEDVIG. [*Cheerfully*] Yes, father; beautiful, fresh beer.

HIALMAR. Well—since you insist upon it, you may bring in a bottle.

GINA. Yes, do; and we'll be nice and cosy.

[HEDVIG *runs towards the kitchen door.*]

HIALMAR. [*By the stove, stops her, looks at her, puts his arm round her neck and presses her to him*] Hedvig, Hedvig!

HEDVIG. [*With tears of joy*] My dear, kind father!

HIALMAR. No, don't call me that. Here have I been feasting at the rich man's table,—battening at the groaning board——! And I couldn't even——!

GINA. [*Sitting at the table*] Oh, nonsense, nonsense, Ekdal.

HIALMAR. It's not nonsense! And yet you mustn't be too hard upon me. You know that I love you for all that.

HEDVIG. [*Throwing her arms round him*] And we love you, oh, so dearly, father!

HIALMAR. And if I am unreasonable once in a while,—why then— you must remember that I am a man beset by a host of cares. There, there! [*Dries his eyes*] No beer at such a moment as this. Give me the flute.

[HEDVIG *runs to the bookcase and fetches it.*]

HIALMAR. Thanks! That's right. With my flute in my hand and you two at my side——ah——!

[HEDVIG *seats herself at the table near* GINA; HIALMAR *paces backwards and forwards, pipes up vigorously and plays a Bohemian peasant dance, but in a slow plaintive tempo, and with sentimental expression.*]

HIALMAR. [*Breaking off the melody, holds out his left hand to* GINA *and says with emotion*] Our roof may be poor and humble, Gina, but it is home. And with all my heart I say: here dwells my happiness.

[*He begins to play again; almost immediately after, a knocking is heard at the entrance door.*]

GINA. [*Rising*] Hush, Ekdal,—I think there's some one at the door.

HIALMAR. [*Laying the flute on the bookcase*] There! Again!

[GINA *goes and opens the door.*]

GREGERS WERLE. [*In the passage*] Excuse me——

GINA. [*Starting back slightly*] Oh!

GREGERS. ——does not Mr. Ekdal, the photographer, live here?

GINA. Yes, he does.

HIALMAR. [*Going towards the door*] Gregers! You here after all? Well, come in then.

GREGERS. [*Coming in*] I told you I would come and look you up.

HIALMAR. But this evening——? Have you left the party?

GREGERS. I have left both the party and my father's house.—Good evening, Mrs. Ekdal. I don't know whether you recognize me?

GINA. Oh, yes; it's not difficult to know young Mr. Werle again.

GREGERS. No, I am like my mother; and no doubt you remember her.

HIALMAR. Left your father's house, did you say?

GREGERS. Yes, I have gone to a hotel.

HIALMAR. Indeed. Well, since you're here, take off your coat and sit down.

GREGERS. Thanks.

[*He takes off his overcoat. He is now dressed in a plain grey suit of a countrified cut.*]

HIALMAR. Here, on the sofa. Make yourself comfortable.

[GREGERS *seats himself on the sofa;* HIALMAR *takes a chair at the table.*]

GREGERS. [*Looking around him*] So these are your quarters, Hialmar—this is your home.

HIALMAR. This is the studio, as you see——

GINA. But it's the largest of our rooms, so we generally sit here.

HIALMAR. We used to live in a better place; but this flat has one great advantage; there are such capital outer rooms——

GINA. And we have a room on the other side of the passage that we can let.

GREGERS. [*To* HIALMAR] Ah—so you have lodgers, too?

HIALMAR. No, not yet. They're not so easy to find, you see; you have

to keep your eyes open. [*To* HEDVIG] What about the beer, eh?
[HEDVIG *nods and goes out into the kitchen.*]

GREGERS. So that is your daughter?

HIALMAR. Yes, that is Hedvig.

GREGERS. And she is your only child?

HIALMAR. Yes, the only one. She is the joy of our lives, and—[*lowering his voice*]—at the same time our deepest sorrow, Gregers.

GREGERS. What do you mean?

HIALMAR. She is in serious danger of losing her eyesight.

GREGERS. Becoming blind?

HIALMAR. Yes. Only the first symptoms have appeared as yet, and she may not feel it much for some time. But the doctor has warned us. It is coming, inexorably.

GREGERS. What a terrible misfortune! How do you account for it?

HIALMAR. [*Sighs*] Hereditary, no doubt.

GREGERS. [*Starting*] Hereditary?

GINA. Ekdal's mother had weak eyes.

HIALMAR. Yes, so my father says; I can't remember her.

GREGERS. Poor child! And how does she take it?

HIALMAR. Oh, you can imagine we haven't the heart to tell her of it. She dreams of no danger. Gay and careless and chirping like a little bird, she flutters onward into a life of endless night. [*Overcome*] Oh, it is cruelly hard on me, Gregers.

[HEDVIG *brings a tray with beer and glasses, which she sets upon the table.*]

HIALMAR. [*Stroking her hair*] Thanks, thanks, Hedvig.

[HEDVIG *puts her arm around his neck and whispers in his ear.*]

HIALMAR. No, no bread and butter just now. [*Looks up*] But perhaps you would like some, Gregers.

GREGERS. [*With a gesture of refusal*] No, no, thank you.

HIALMAR. [*Still melancholy*] Well, you can bring in a little all the same. If you have a crust, that is all I want. And plenty of butter on it, mind.

[HEDVIG *nods gaily and goes out into the kitchen again.*]

GREGERS. [*Who has been following her with his eyes*] She seems quite strong and healthy otherwise.

GINA. Yes. In other ways there's nothing amiss with her, thank goodness.

GREGERS. She promises to be very like you, Mrs. Ekdal. How old is she now?

GINA. Hedvig is close on fourteen; her birthday is the day after tomorrow.

GREGERS. She is pretty tall for her age, then.

GINA. Yes, she's shot up wonderful this last year.

GREGERS. It makes one realize one's own age to see these young people growing up.——How long is it now since you were married?

GINA. We've been married—let me see—just on fifteen years.

GREGERS. Is it so long as that?

GINA. [*Becomes attentive; looks at him*] Yes, it is indeed.

HIALMAR. Yes, so it is. Fifteen years all but a few months. [*Changing his tone*] They must have been long years for you, up at the works, Gregers.

GREGERS. They seemed long while I was living them; now they are over, I hardly know how the time has gone.

[OLD EKDAL *comes from his room without his pipe, but with his old-fashioned uniform cap on his head; his gait is somewhat unsteady.*]

EKDAL. Come now, Hialmar, let's sit down and have a good talk about this—h'm—what was it again?

HIALMAR. [*Going towards him*] Father, we have a visitor here—Gregers Werle.—I don't know if you remember him.

EKDAL. [*Looking at* GREGERS, *who has risen*] Werle? Is that the son? What does he want with me?

HIALMAR. Nothing; it's me he has come to see.

EKDAL. Oh! Then there's nothing wrong?

HIALMAR. No, no, of course not.

EKDAL. [*With a large gesture*] Not that I'm afraid, you know; but——

GREGERS. [*Goes over to him*] I bring you a greeting from your old hunting-grounds, Lieutenant Ekdal.

EKDAL. Hunting-grounds?

GREGERS. Yes, up in Höidal, about the works, you know.

EKDAL. Oh, up there. Yes, I knew all those places well in the old days.

GREGERS. You were a great sportsman then.

EKDAL. So I was, I don't deny it. You're looking at my uniform cap. I don't ask anybody's leave to wear it in the house. So long as I don't go out in the streets with it——

[HEDVIG *brings a plate of bread and butter, which she puts upon the table.*]

HIALMAR. Sit down, father, and have a glass of beer. Help yourself, Gregers.

[EKDAL *mutters and stumbles over to the sofa.* GREGERS *seats himself on the chair nearest to him,* HIALMAR *on the other side of* GREGERS. GINA *sits a little way from the table, sewing;* HEDVIG *stands beside her father.*]

GREGERS. Can you remember, Lieutenant Ekdal, how Hialmar and I used to come up and visit you in the summer and at Christmas?

EKDAL. Did you? No, no, no; I don't remember it. But sure enough

I've been a tidy bit of a sportsman in my day. I've shots bears, too. I've shot nine of 'em, no less.

GREGERS. [*Looking sympathetically at him*] And now you never get any shooting?

EKDAL. Can't just say that, sir. Get a shot now and then perhaps. Of course not in the old way. For the woods, you see—the woods, the woods——! [*Drinks*] Are the woods fine up there now?

GREGERS. Not so fine as in your time. They have been thinned a good deal.

EKDAL. Thinned? [*More softly, and as if afraid*] It's dangerous work that. Bad things come of it. The woods revenge themselves.

HIALMAR. [*Filling up his glass*] Come—a little more, father.

GREGERS. How can a man like you—such a man for the open air —live in the midst of a stuffy town, boxed within four walls?

EKDAL. [*Laughs quietly and glances at* HIALMAR] Oh, it's not so bad here. Not at all so bad.

GREGERS. But don't you miss all the things that used to be a part of your very being—the cool sweeping breezes, the free life in the woods and on the uplands, among beasts and birds——?

EKDAL. [*Smiling*] Hialmar, shall we let him see it?

HIALMAR. [*Hastily and a little embarrassed*] Oh, no, no, father; not this evening.

GREGERS. What does he want to show me?

HIALMAR. Oh, it's only something—you can see it another time.

GREGERS. [*Continues, to the old man*] You see I have been thinking, Lieutenant Ekdal, that you should come up with me to the works; I am sure to be going back soon. No doubt you could get some copying there, too. And here, you have nothing on earth to interest you—nothing to liven you up.

EKDAL. [*Stares in astonishment at him*] Have *I* nothing on earth to——!

GREGERS. Of course you have Hialmar; but then he has his own family. And a man like you, who has always had such a passion for what is free and wild——

EKDAL. [*Thumps the table*] Hialmar, he shall see it!

HIALMAR. Oh, do you think it's worth while, father? It's all dark.

EKDAL. Nonsense; it's moonlight. [*Rises*] He shall see it, I tell you. Let me pass! Come and help me, Hialmar.

HEDVIG. Oh, yes, do, father!

HIALMAR. [*Rising*] Very well then.

GREGERS. [*To* GINA] What is it?

GINA. Oh, nothing so very wonderful, after all.

[EKDAL *and* HIALMAR *have gone to the back wall and are each pushing back a side of the sliding door;* HEDVIG *helps the old man;* GREGERS *remains standing by the sofa;* GINA

*sits still and sews. Through the open doorway a large, deep
irregular garret is seen with odd nooks and corners; a couple
of stove-pipes running through it, from rooms below. There
are skylights through which clear moonbeams shine in on
some parts of the great room; others lie in deep shadow.*]

EKDAL. [*To* GREGERS] You may come close up if you like.

GREGERS. [*Going over to them*] Why, what is it?

EKDAL. Look for yourself. H'm.

HIALMAR. [*Somewhat embarrassed*] This belongs to father, you
understand.

GREGERS. [*At the door, looks into the garret*] Why, you keep poultry,
Lieutenant Ekdal.

EKDAL. Should think we did keep poultry. They've gone to roost
now. But you should just see our fowls by daylight, sir!

HEDVIG. And there's a——

EKDAL. Sh—sh! don't say anything about it yet.

GREGERS. And you have pigeons, too, I see.

EKDAL. Oh, yes, haven't we just got pigeons! They have their nest-
boxes up there under the roof-tree; for pigeons like to roost high,
you see.

HIALMAR. They aren't all common pigeons.

EKDAL. Common! Should think not indeed! We have tumblers and
a pair of pouters, too. But come here! Can you see that hutch
down there by the wall?

GREGERS. Yes; what do you use it for?

EKDAL. That's where the rabbits sleep, sir.

GREGERS. Dear me; so you have rabbits, too?

EKDAL. Yes, you may take my word for it, we have rabbits! He wants
to know if we have rabbits, Hialmar! H'm! But now comes the
thing, let me tell you! Here we have it! Move away, Hedvig.
Stand here; that's right,—and now look down there.—Don't you
see a basket with straw in it?

GREGERS. Yes. And I can see a fowl lying in the basket.

EKDAL. H'm—"a fowl"——

GREGERS. Isn't it a duck?

EKDAL. [*Hurt*] Why, of course it's a duck.

HIALMAR. But what kind of duck, do you think?

HEDVIG. It's not just a common duck——

EKDAL. Sh!

GREGERS. And it's not a Muscovy duck either.

EKDAL. No, Mr.—Werle; it's not a Muscovy duck; for it's a wild
duck!

GREGERS. Is it really? A wild duck?

EKDAL. Yes, that's what it is. That "fowl" as you call it—is the wild
duck. It's our wild duck, sir.

HEDVIG. My wild duck. It belongs to me.

GREGERS. And can it live up here in the garret? Does it thrive?

EKDAL. Of course it has a trough of water to splash about in, you know.

HIALMAR. Fresh water every other day.

GINA. [*Turning towards* HIALMAR] But my dear Ekdal, it's getting icy cold here.

EKDAL. H'm, we had better shut up then. It's as well not to disturb their night's rest, too. Close up, Hedvig.

[HIALMAR *and* HEDVIG *push the garret doors together.*]

EKDAL. Another time you shall see her properly. [*Seats himself in the armchair by the stove*] Oh, they're curious things, these wild ducks, I can tell you.

GREGERS. How did you manage to catch it, Lieutenant Ekdal?

EKDAL. I didn't catch it. There's a certain man in this town whom we have to thank for it.

GREGERS. [*Starts slightly*] That man was not my father, was he?

EKDAL. You've hit it. Your father and no one else. H'm.

HIALMAR. Strange that you should guess that, Gregers.

GREGERS. You were telling me that you owed so many things to my father; and so I thought perhaps——

GINA. But we didn't get the duck from Mr. Werle himself——

EKDAL. It's Håkon Werle we have to thank for her, all the same, Gina. [*To* GREGERS] He was shooting from a boat, you see, and he brought her down. But your father's sight is not very good now. H'm; she was only wounded.

GREGERS. Ah! She got a couple of slugs in her body, I suppose.

HIALMAR. Yes, two or three.

HEDVIG. She was hit under the wing, so that she couldn't fly.

GREGERS. And I suppose she dived to the bottom, eh?

EKDAL. [*Sleepily, in a thick voice*] Of course. Always do that, wild ducks do. They shoot to the bottom as deep as they can get, sir —and bite themselves fast in the tangle and seaweed—and all the devil's own mess that grows down there. And they never come up again.

GREGERS. But your wild duck came up again, Lieutenant Ekdal.

EKDAL. He had such an amazingly clever dog, your father had. And that dog—he dived in after the duck and fetched her up again.

GREGERS. [*Who has turned to* HIALMAR] And then she was sent to you here?

HIALMAR. Not at once; at first your father took her home. But she wouldn't thrive there; so Pettersen was told to put an end to her——

EKDAL. [*Half asleep*] H'm—yes—Pettersen—that ass——

HIALMAR. [*Speaking more softly*] That was how we got her, you see;

for father knows Pettersen a little; and when he heard about the wild duck he got him to hand her over to us.

GREGERS. And now she thrives as well as possible in the garret there?

HIALMAR. Yes, wonderfully well. She has got fat. You see, she has lived in there so long now that she has forgotten her natural wild life; and it all depends on that.

GREGERS. You are right there, Hialmar. Be sure you never let her get a glimpse of the sky and the sea——. But I mustn't stay any longer; I think your father is asleep.

HIALMAR. Oh, as for that——

GREGERS. But, by-the-bye—you said you had a room to let—a spare room?

HIALMAR. Yes; what then? Do you know of anybody——?

GREGERS. Can *I* have that room?

HIALMAR. You?

GINA. Oh, no, Mr. Werle, you——

GREGERS. May I have the room? If so, I'll take possession first thing tomorrow morning.

HIALMAR. Yes, with the greatest pleasure——

GINA. But, Mr. Werle, I'm sure it's not at all the sort of room for you.

HIALMAR. Why, Gina! how can you say that?

GINA. Why, because the room's neither large enough nor light enough, and——

GREGERS. That really doesn't matter, Mrs. Ekdal.

HIALMAR. I call it quite a nice room, and not at all badly furnished either.

GINA. But remember the pair of them underneath.

GREGERS. What pair?

GINA. Well, there's one as has been a tutor——

HIALMAR. That's Molvik—Mr. Molvik, B.A.

GINA. And then there's a doctor, by the name of Relling.

GREGERS. Relling? I know him a little; he practised for a time up in Höidal.

GINA. They're a regular rackety pair, they are. As often as not, they're out on the loose in the evenings; and then they come home at all hours, and they're not always just——

GREGERS. One soon gets used to that sort of thing. I daresay I shall be like the wild duck——

GINA. H'm; I think you ought to sleep upon it first, anyway.

GREGERS. You seem very unwilling to have me in the house, Mrs. Ekdal.

GINA. Oh, no! What makes you think that?

HIALMAR. Well, you really behave strangely about it, Gina. [*To* GREGERS] Then I suppose you intend to remain in the town for the present?

GREGERS. [*Putting on his overcoat*] Yes, now I intend to remain here.

HIALMAR. And yet not at your father's? What do you propose to do, then?

GREGERS. Ah, if I only knew that, Hialmar, I shouldn't be so badly off! But when one has the misfortune to be called Gregers—! "Gregers"—and then "Werle" after it; did you ever hear anything so hideous?

HIALMAR. Oh, I don't think so at all.

GREGERS. Ugh! Bah! I feel I should like to spit upon the fellow that answers to such a name. But when a man is once for all doomed to be Gregers—Werle in this world, as I am——

HIALMAR. [*Laughs*] Ha, ha! If you weren't Gregers Werle, what would you like to be?

GREGERS. If I should choose, I should like best to be a clever dog.

GINA. A dog!

HEDVIG. [*Involuntarily*] Oh, no!

GREGERS. Yes, an amazingly clever dog; one that goes to the bottom after wild ducks when they dive and bite themselves fast in tangle and seaweed, down among the ooze.

HIALMAR. Upon my word now, Gregers—I don't in the least know what you're driving at.

GREGERS. Oh, well, you might not be much the wiser if you did. It's understood, then, that I move in early tomorrow morning. [*To* GINA] I won't give you any trouble; I do everything for myself. [*To* HIALMAR] We can talk about the rest tomorrow.—Goodnight, Mrs. Ekdal. [*Nods to* HEDVIG] Goodnight.

GINA. Goodnight, Mr. Werle.

HEDVIG. Goodnight.

HIALMAR. [*Who has lighted a candle*] Wait a moment; I must show you a light; the stairs are sure to be dark.

[GREGERS *and* HIALMAR *go out by the passage door.*]

GINA. [*Looking straight before her, with her sewing in her lap*] Wasn't that queer-like talk about wanting to be a dog?

HEDVIG. Do you know, mother—I believe he meant something quite different by that.

GINA. Why, what should he mean?

HEDVIG. Oh, I don't know; but it seemed to me he meant something different from what he said—all the time.

GINA. Do you think so? Yes, it was sort of queer.

HIALMAR. [*Comes back*] The lamp was still burning. [*Puts out the candle and sets it down*] Ah, now one can get a mouthful of food at last. [*Begins to eat the bread and butter*] Well, you see, Gina —if only you keep your eyes open——

GINA. How, keep your eyes open——?

HIALMAR. Why, haven't we at last had the luck to get the room let? And just think—to a person like Gregers—a good old friend.

GINA. Well, I don't know what to say about it.

HEDVIG. Oh, mother, you'll see; it'll be such fun!

HIALMAR. You're very strange. You were so bent upon getting the room let before; and now you don't like it.

GINA. Yes, I do, Ekdal; if it had only been to some one else—— But what do you suppose Mr. Werle will say?

HIALMAR. Old Werle? It doesn't concern him.

GINA. But surely you can see that there's something amiss between them again, or the young man wouldn't be leaving home. You know very well those two can't get on with each other.

HIALMAR. Very likely not, but——

GINA. And now Mr. Werle may fancy it's you that has egged him on——

HIALMAR. Let him fancy so, then! Mr. Werle has done a great deal for me; far be it from me to deny it. But that doesn't make me everlastingly dependent upon him.

GINA. But, my dear Ekdal, maybe grandfather'll suffer for it. He may lose the little bit of work he gets from Gråberg.

HIALMAR. I could almost say: so much the better! Is it not humiliating for a man like me to see his grey-haired father treated as a pariah? But now I believe the fulness of time is at hand. [*Takes a fresh piece of bread and butter*] As sure as I have a mission in life, I mean to fulfil it now!

HEDVIG. Oh, yes, father, do!

GINA. Hush! Don't wake him!

HIALMAR. [*More softly*] I will fulfil it, I say. The day shall come when—— And that is why I say it's a good thing we have let the room; for that makes me more independent. The man who has a mission in life must be independent. [*By the armchair, with emotion*] Poor old white-haired father! Rely on your Hialmar. He has broad shoulders—strong shoulders, at any rate. You shall yet wake up some fine day and—— [*To* GINA] Do you not believe it?

GINA. [*Rising*] Yes, of course I do; but in the meantime suppose we see about getting him to bed.

HIALMAR. Yes, come.

[*They take hold of the old man carefully.*]

Act III

SCENE—HIALMAR EKDAL'S *studio. It is morning: the daylight shines through the large window in the slanting roof; the curtain is drawn back.*

HIALMAR *is sitting at the table, busy retouching a photograph;*

several others lie before him. Presently GINA, *wearing her hat and cloak, enters by the passage door; she has a covered basket on her arm.*

HIALMAR. Back already, Gina?

GINA. Oh, yes, one can't let the grass grow under one's feet.
[*Sets her basket on a chair and takes off her things.*]

HIALMAR. Did you look in at Gregers' room?

GINA. Yes, that I did. It's a rare sight, I can tell you; he's made a pretty mess to start off with.

HIALMAR. How so?

GINA. He was determined to do everything for himself, he said; so he sets to work to light the stove, and what must he do but screw down the damper till the whole room is full of smoke. Ugh! There was a smell fit to——

HIALMAR. Well, really!

GINA. But that's not the worst of it; for then he thinks he'll put out the fire, and goes and empties his water-jug into the stove and so makes the whole floor one filthy puddle.

HIALMAR. How annoying!

GINA. I've got the porter's wife to clear up after him, pig that he is! But the room won't be fit to live in till the afternoon.

HIALMAR. What's he doing with himself in the meantime?

GINA. He said he was going out for a little while.

HIALMAR. I looked in upon him, too, for a moment—after you had gone.

GINA. So I heard. You've asked him to lunch.

HIALMAR. Just to a little bit of early lunch, you know. It's his first day—we can hardly do less. You've got something in the house, I suppose?

GINA. I shall have to find something or other.

HIALMAR. And don't cut it too fine, for I fancy Relling and Molvik are coming up, too. I just happened to meet Relling on the stairs, you see; so I had to——

GINA. Oh, are we to have those two as well?

HIALMAR. Good Lord—couple more or less can't make any difference.

OLD EKDAL. [*Opens his door and looks in*] I say, Hialmar—— [*Sees* GINA] Oh!

GINA. Do you want anything, grandfather?

EKDAL. Oh, no, it doesn't matter. H'm!   [*Retires again.*]

GINA. [*Takes up the basket*] Be sure you see that he doesn't go out.

HIALMAR. All right, all right. And, Gina, a little herring-salad wouldn't be a bad idea; Relling and Molvik were out on the loose again last night.

GINA. If only they don't come before I'm ready for them——

HIALMAR. No, of course they won't; take your own time.

GINA. Very well; and meanwhile you can be working a bit.

HIALMAR. Well, I am working! I am working as hard as I can!

GINA. Then you'll have that job off your hands, you see.

> [*She goes out to the kitchen with her basket.* HIALMAR *sits for a time penciling away at the photograph in an indolent and listless manner.*]

EKDAL. [*Peeps in, looks round the studio and says softly*] Are you busy?

HIALMAR. Yes, I'm toiling at these wretched pictures——

EKDAL. Well, well, never mind,—since you're so busy—h'm!

> [*He goes out again; the door stands open.*]

HIALMAR. [*Continues for some time in silence; then he lays down his brush and goes over to the door*] Are you busy, father?

EKDAL. [*In a grumbling tone, within*] If you're busy, I'm busy, too. H'm!

HIALMAR. Oh, very well, then.   [*Goes to his work again.*]

EKDAL. [*Presently, coming to the door again*] H'm; I say, Hialmar, I'm not so very busy, you know.

HIALMAR. I thought you were writing.

EKDAL. Oh, the devil take it! can't Gråberg wait a day or two? After all, it's not a matter of life and death.

HIALMAR. No; and you're not his slave either.

EKDAL. And about that other business in there——

HIALMAR. Just what I was thinking of. Do you want to go in? Shall I open the door for you?

EKDAL. Well, it wouldn't be a bad notion.

HIALMAR. [*Rises*] Then we'd have that off our hands.

EKDAL. Yes, exactly. It's got to be ready first thing tomorrow. It is tomorrow, isn't it? H'm?

HIALMAR. Yes, of course it's tomorrow.

> [HIALMAR *and* EKDAL *push aside each his half of the sliding door. The morning sun is shining in through the skylights; some doves are flying about; others sit cooing, upon the perches; the hens are heard clucking now and then, further back in the garret.*]

HIALMAR. There; now you can get to work, father.

EKDAL. [*Goes in*] Aren't you coming, too?

HIALMAR. Well, really, do you know——; I almost think—— [*Sees* GINA *at the kitchen door*] I? No; I haven't time; I must work.— But now for our new contrivance——

> [*He pulls a cord, a curtain slips down inside, the lower part consisting of a piece of old sailcloth, the upper part of a*

stretched fishing net. *The floor of the garret is thus no longer visible.*]

HIALMAR. [*Goes to the table*] So! Now, perhaps I can sit in peace for a little while.

GINA. Is he rampaging in there again?

HIALMAR. Would you rather have had him slip down to Madame Eriksen's? [*Seats himself*] Do you want anything? You know you said——

GINA. I only wanted to ask if you think we can lay the table for lunch here?

HIALMAR. Yes; we have no early appointment, I suppose?

GINA. No, I expect no one today except those two sweethearts that are to be taken together.

HIALMAR. Why the deuce couldn't they be taken together another day?

GINA. Don't you know I told them to come in the afternoon, when you are having your nap?

HIALMAR. Oh, that's capital. Very well, let us have lunch here then.

GINA. All right; but there's no hurry about laying the cloth; you can have the table for a good while yet.

HIALMAR. Do you think I am not sticking at my work? I'm at it as hard as I can!

GINA. Then you'll be free later on, you know.

[*Goes out into the kitchen again. Short pause.*]

EKDAL. [*In the garret doorway, behind the net*] Hialmar!

HIALMAR. Well?

EKDAL. Afraid we shall have to move the water-trough, after all.

HIALMAR. What else have I been saying all along?

EKDAL. H'm—h'm—h'm.

[*Goes away from the door again.* HIALMAR *goes on working a little; glances towards the garret and half rises.* HEDVIG *comes in from the kitchen.*]

HIALMAR. [*Sits down again hurriedly*] What do you want?

HEDVIG. I only wanted to come in beside you, father.

HIALMAR. [*After a pause*] What makes you go prying around like that? Perhaps you are told off to watch me?

HEDVIG. No, no.

HIALMAR. What is your mother doing out there?

HEDVIG. Oh, mother's in the middle of making the herring-salad. [*Goes to the table*] Isn't there any little thing I could help you with, father?

HIALMAR. Oh, no. It is right that I should bear the whole burden—so long as my strength holds out. Set your mind at rest, Hedvig; if only your father keeps his health——

HEDVIG. Oh, no, father! You mustn't talk in that horrid way.
[*She wanders about a little, stops by the doorway and looks into the garret.*]

HIALMAR. Tell me, what is he doing?

HEDVIG. I think he's making a new path to the water-trough.

HIALMAR. He can never manage that by himself! And here am I doomed to sit——!

HEDVIG. [*Goes to him*] Let me take the brush, father; I can do it, quite well.

HIALMAR. Oh, nonsense; you will only hurt your eyes.

HEDVIG. Not a bit. Give me the brush.

HIALMAR. [*Rising*] Well, it won't take more than a minute or two.

HEDVIG. Pooh, what harm can it do then? [*Takes the brush*] There! [*Seats herself*] I can begin upon this one.

HIALMAR. But mind you don't hurt your eyes! Do you hear? *I* won't be answerable; you do it on your own responsibility—understand that.

HEDVIG. [*Retouching*] Yes, yes, I understand.

HIALMAR. You are quite clever at it, Hedvig. Only a minute or two, you know.
[*He slips through by the edge of the curtain into the garret.* HEDVIG *sits at her work.* HIALMAR *and* EKDAL *are heard disputing inside.*]

HIALMAR. [*Appears behind the net*] I say, Hedvig—give me those pincers that are lying on the shelf. And the chisel. [*Turns away inside*] Now you shall see, father. Just let me show you first what I mean!
[HEDVIG *has fetched the required tools from the shelf and hands them to him through the net.*]

HIALMAR. Ah, thanks. I didn't come a moment too soon.
[*Goes back from the curtain again; they are heard carpentering and talking inside.* HEDVIG *stands looking in at them. A moment later there is a knock at the passage door; she does not notice it.*]

GREGERS WERLE. [*Bareheaded, in indoor dress, enters and stops near the door*] H'm——!

HEDVIG. [*Turns and goes towards him*] Good morning. Please come in.

GREGERS. Thank you. [*Looking towards the garret*] You seem to have workpeople in the house.

HEDVIG. No, it is only father and grandfather. I'll tell them you are here.

GREGERS. No, no, don't do that; I would rather wait a little.
[*Seats himself on the sofa.*]

HEDVIG. It looks so untidy here——

[*Begins to clear away the photographs.*]

GREGERS. Oh, don't take them away. Are those prints that have to be finished off?

HEDVIG. Yes, they are a few I was helping father with.

GREGERS. Please don't let me disturb you.

HEDVIG. Oh, no.

[*She gathers the things to her and sits down to work;* GREGERS *looks at her, meanwhile, in silence.*]

GREGERS. Did the wild duck sleep well last night?

HEDVIG. Yes, I think so, thanks.

GREGERS. [*Turning towards the garret*] It looks quite different by day from what it did last night in the moonlight.

HEDVIG. Yes, it changes ever so much. It looks different in the morning and in the afternoon; and it's different on rainy days from what it is in fine weather.

GREGERS. Have you noticed that?

HEDVIG. Yes, how could I help it?

GREGERS. Are you, too, fond of being in there with the wild duck?

HEDVIG. Yes, when I can manage it——

GREGERS. But I suppose you haven't much spare time; you go to school, no doubt.

HEDVIG. No, not now; father is afraid of my hurting my eyes.

GREGERS. Oh; then he reads with you himself?

HEDVIG. Father has promised to read with me; but he has never had time yet.

GREGERS. Then is there nobody else to give you a little help?

HEDVIG. Yes, there is Mr. Molvik; but he is not always exactly—quite——

GREGERS. Sober?

HEDVIG. Yes, I suppose that's it!

GREGERS. Why, then you must have any amount of time on your hands. And in there I suppose it is a sort of world by itself?

HEDVIG. Oh, yes, quite. And there are such lots of wonderful things.

GREGERS. Indeed?

HEDVIG. Yes, there are big cupboards full of books; and a great many of the books have pictures in them.

GREGERS. Aha!

HEDVIG. And there's an old bureau with drawers and flaps, and a big clock with figures that go out and in. But the clock isn't going now.

GREGERS. So time has come to a standstill in there—in the wild duck's domain.

HEDVIG. Yes. And then there's an old paint-box and things of that sort, and all the books.

GREGERS. And you read the books, I suppose?

HEDVIG. Oh, yes, when I get the chance. Most of them are English though, and I don't understand English. But then I look at the pictures.—There is one great big book called "Harrison's History of London."[3] It must be a hundred years old; and there are such heaps of pictures in it. At the beginning there is Death with an hour-glass and a woman. I think that is horrid. But then there are all the other pictures of churches, and castles, and streets, and great ships sailing on the sea.

GREGERS. But tell me, where did all those wonderful things come from?

HEDVIG. Oh, an old sea captain once lived here, and he brought them home with him. They used to call him "The Flying Dutchman." That was curious, because he wasn't a Dutchman at all.

GREGERS. Was he not?

HEDVIG. No. But at last he was drowned at sea, and so he left all those things behind him.

GREGERS. Tell me now—when you are sitting in there looking at the pictures, don't you wish you could travel and see the real world for yourself?

HEDVIG. Oh, no! I mean always to stay at home and help father and mother.

GREGERS. To retouch photographs?

HEDVIG. No, not only that. I should love above everything to learn to engrave pictures like those in the English books.

GREGERS. H'm. What does your father say to that?

HEDVIG. I don't think father likes it; father is strange about such things. Only think, he talks of my learning basket-making and straw-plaiting! But I don't think that would be much good.

GREGERS. Oh, no, I don't think so either.

HEDVIG. But father was right in saying that if I had learnt basket-making I could have made the new basket for the wild duck.

GREGERS. So you could; and it was you that ought to have done it, wasn't it?

HEDVIG. Yes, for it's my wild duck.

GREGERS. Of course it is.

HEDVIG. Yes, it belongs to me. But I lend it to father and grandfather as often as they please.

GREGERS. Indeed? What do they do with it?

HEDVIG. Oh, they look after it, and build places for it, and so on.

GREGERS. I see; for no doubt the wild duck is by far the most distinguished inhabitant of the garret?

HEDVIG. Yes, indeed she is; for she is a real wild fowl, you know.

3. *A New and Universal History of the Cities of London and Westminster,* by Walter Harrison, London, 1775, folio. [Translator's note.]

And then she is so much to be pitied; she has no one to care for, poor thing.

GREGERS. She has no family, as the rabbits have——

HEDVIG. No. The hens, too, many of them, were chickens together; but she has been taken right away from all her friends. And then there is so much that is strange about the wild duck. Nobody knows her, and nobody knows where she came from either.

GREGERS. And she has been down in the depths of the sea.

HEDVIG. [*With a quick glance at him, represses a smile and asks*] Why do you say "depths of the sea"?

GREGERS. What else should I say?

HEDVIG. You could say "the bottom of the sea." [4]

GREGERS. Oh, mayn't I just as well say the depths of the sea?

HEDVIG. Yes; but it sounds so strange to me when other people speak of the depths of the sea.

GREGERS. Why so? Tell me why?

HEDVIG. No, I won't; it's so stupid.

GREGERS. Oh, no, I am sure it's not. Do tell me why you smiled.

HEDVIG. Well, this is the reason: whenever I come to realize suddenly—in a flash—what is in there, it always seems to me that the whole room and everything in it should be called "the depths of the sea."—But that is so stupid.

GREGERS. You mustn't say that.

HEDVIG. Oh, yes, for you know it is only a garret.

GREGERS. [*Looks fixedly at her*] Are you so sure of that?

HEDVIG. [*Astonished*] That it's a garret?

GREGERS. Are you quite certain of it?

[HEDVIG *is silent, and looks at him open-mouthed.* GINA *comes in from the kitchen with the table things.*]

GREGERS. [*Rising*] I have come in upon you too early.

GINA. Oh, you must be somewhere; and we're nearly ready now, anyway. Clear the table, Hedvig.

[HEDVIG *clears away her things; she and* GINA *lay the cloth during what follows.* GREGERS *seats himself in the armchair and turns over an album.*]

GREGERS. I hear you can retouch, Mrs. Ekdal.

GINA. [*With a side glance*] Yes, I can.

GREGERS. That was exceedingly lucky.

GINA. How—lucky?

GREGERS. Since Ekdal took to photography, I mean.

HEDVIG. Mother can take photographs, too.

GINA. Oh, yes; I was bound to learn that.

4. Gregers here uses the old-fashioned expression "havsens bund," while Hedvig would have him use the more commonplace "havets bund" or "havbunden." [Translator's note.]

GREGERS. So it is really you that carry on the business, I suppose?

GINA. Yes, when Ekdal hasn't time himself——

GREGERS. He is a great deal taken up with his old father, I daresay.

GINA. Yes; and then you can't expect a man like Ekdal to do nothing but take pictures of Dick, Tom, and Harry.

GREGERS. I quite agree with you; but having once gone in for the thing——

GINA. You can surely understand, Mr. Werle, that Ekdal's not like one of your common photographers.

GREGERS. Of course not; but still——

[*A shot is fired within the garret.*]

GREGERS [*Starting up*] What's that?

GINA. Ugh! now they're firing again!

GREGERS. Have they firearms in there?

HEDVIG. They are out shooting.

GREGERS. What! [*At the door of the garret*] Are you shooting, Hialmar?

HIALMAR. [*Inside the net*] Are you there? I didn't know; I was so taken up—— [*To* HEDVIG] Why did you not let us know? [*Comes into the studio.*]

GREGERS. Do you go shooting in the garret?

HIALMAR. [*Showing a double-barrelled pistol*] Oh, only with this thing.

GINA. Yes, you and grandfather will do yourselves a mischief some day with that there pigstol.

HIALMAR. [*With irritation*] I believe I have told you that this kind of firearm is called a pistol.

GINA. Oh, that doesn't make it much better, that I can see.

GREGERS. So you have become a sportsman, too, Hialmar?

HIALMAR. Only a little rabbit-shooting now and then. Mostly to please father, you understand.

GINA. Men are strange beings; they must always have something to pervert theirselves with.

HIALMAR. [*Snappishly*] Just so; we must always have something to divert ourselves with.

GINA. Yes, that's just what I say.

HIALMAR. H'm. [*To* GREGERS] You see the garret is fortunately so situated that no one can hear us shooting. [*Lays the pistol on the top shelf of the bookcase*] Don't touch the pistol, Hedvig! One of the barrels is loaded; remember that.

GREGERS. [*Looking through the net*] You have a fowling-piece, too, I see.

HIALMAR. That is father's old gun. It's no use now; something has gone wrong with the lock. But it's fun to have it all the same; for we can take it to pieces now and then, and clean and grease it, and screw it together again.—Of course, it's mostly father that fiddle-faddles with all that sort of thing.

HEDVIG. [*Beside* GREGERS] Now you can see the wild duck properly.

GREGERS. I was just looking at her. One of her wings seems to me to droop a bit.

HEDVIG. Well, no wonder; her wing was broken, you know.

GREGERS. And she trails one foot a little. Isn't that so?

HIALMAR. Perhaps a very little bit.

HEDVIG. Yes, it was by that foot the dog took hold of her.

HIALMAR. But otherwise she hasn't the least thing the matter with her; and that is simply marvellous for a creature that has a charge of shot in her body and has been between a dog's teeth——

GREGERS. [*With a glance at* HEDVIG] ——and that has lain in the depths of the sea—so long.

HEDVIG. [*Smiling*] Yes.

GINA. [*Laying the table*] That blessed wild duck! What a lot of fuss you do make over her.

HIALMAR. H'm;—will lunch soon be ready?

GINA. Yes, directly. Hedvig, you must come and help me now.

[GINA *and* HEDVIG *go out into the kitchen.*]

HIALMAR. [*In a low voice*] I think you had better not stand there looking in at father; he doesn't like it. [GREGERS *moves away from the garret door.*] Besides, I may as well shut up before the others come. [*Claps his hands to drive the fowls back*] Shh—shh, in with you! [*Draws up the curtain and pulls the doors together*] All the contrivances are my own invention. It's really quite amusing to have things of this sort to potter with and to put to rights when they get out of order. And it's absolutely necessary, too; for Gina objects to having rabbits and fowls in the studio.

GREGERS. To be sure; and I suppose the studio is your wife's special department?

HIALMAR. As a rule, I leave the everyday details of business to her; for then I can take refuge in the parlor and give my mind to more important things.

GREGERS. What things may they be, Hialmar?

HIALMAR. I wonder you have not asked that question sooner. But perhaps you haven't heard of the invention?

GREGERS. The invention? No.

HIALMAR. Really? Have you not? Oh, no, out there in the wilds——

GREGERS. So you have invented something, have you?

HIALMAR. It is not quite completed yet; but I am working at it. You can easily imagine that when I resolved to devote myself to photography, it wasn't simply with the idea of taking likenesses of all sorts of commonplace people.

GREGERS. No; your wife was saying the same thing just now.

HIALMAR. I swore that if I consecrated my powers to this handicraft, I would so exalt it that it should become both an art and a science. And to that end I determined to make this great invention.

GREGERS. And what is the nature of the invention? What purpose does it serve?

HIALMAR. Oh, my dear fellow, you mustn't ask for details yet. It takes time, you see. And you must not think that my motive is vanity. It is not for my own sake that I am working. Oh, no; it is my life's mission that stands before me night and day.

GREGERS. What is your life's mission?

HIALMAR. Do you forget the old man with the silver hair?

GREGERS. Your poor father? Well, but what can you do for him?

HIALMAR. I can raise up his self-respect from the dead, by restoring the name of Ekdal to honor and dignity.

GREGERS. Then that is your life's mission?

HIALMAR. Yes. I will rescue the shipwrecked man. For shipwrecked he was, by the very first blast of the storm. Even while those terrible investigations were going on, he was no longer himself. That pistol there—the one we use to shoot rabbits with—has played its part in the tragedy of the house of Ekdal.

GREGERS. The pistol? Indeed?

HIALMAR. When the sentence of imprisonment was passed—he had the pistol in his hand——

GREGERS. Had he——?

HIALMAR. Yes; but he dared not use it. His courage failed him. So broken, so demoralized was he even then! Oh, can you understand it? He, a soldier; he, who had shot nine bears, and who was descended from two lieutenant-colonels—one after the other, of course. Can you understand it, Gregers?

GREGERS. Yes, I understand it well enough.

HIALMAR. I cannot. And once more the pistol played a part in the history of our house. When he had put on the grey clothes and was under lock and key—oh, that was a terrible time for me, I can tell you. I kept the blinds drawn down over both my windows. When I peeped out, I saw the sun shining as if nothing had happened. I could not understand it. I saw people going along the street, laughing and talking about indifferent things. I could not understand it. It seemed to me that the whole of existence must be at a standstill—as if under an eclipse.

GREGERS. I felt that, too, when my mother died.

HIALMAR. It was in such an hour that Hialmar Ekdal pointed the pistol at his own breast.

GREGERS. You, too, thought of——!

HIALMAR. Yes.

GREGERS. But you did not fire?

HIALMAR. No. At the decisive moment I won the victory over myself. I remained in life. But I can assure you it takes some courage to choose life under circumstances like those.

GREGERS. Well, that depends on how you look at it.

HIALMAR. Yes, indeed, it takes courage. But I am glad I was firm: for now I shall soon perfect my invention; and Dr. Relling thinks, as I do myself, that father may be allowed to wear his uniform again. I will demand that as my sole reward.

GREGERS. So that is what he meant about his uniform——?

HIALMAR. Yes, that is what he most yearns for. You can't think how my heart bleeds for him. Every time we celebrate any little family festival—Gina's and my wedding-day, or whatever it may be—in comes the old man in the lieutenant's uniform of happier days. But if he only hears a knock at the door—for he daren't show himself to strangers, you know—he hurries back to his room again as fast as his old legs can carry him. Oh, it's heart-rending for a son to see such things!

GREGERS. How long do you think it will take you to finish your invention?

HIALMAR. Come now, you mustn't expect me to enter into particulars like that. An invention is not a thing completely under one's own control. It depends largely on inspiration—on intuition—and it is almost impossible to predict when the inspiration may come.

GREGERS. But it's advancing?

HIALMAR. Yes, certainly, it is advancing. I turn it over in my mind every day; I am full of it. Every afternoon, when I have had my dinner, I shut myself up in the parlor, where I can ponder undisturbed. But I can't be goaded to it; it's not a bit of good; Relling says so, too.

GREGERS. And you don't think that all that business in the garret draws you off and distracts you too much?

HIALMAR. No, no, no; quite the contrary. You mustn't say that. I cannot be everlastingly absorbed in the same laborious train of thought. I must have something alongside of it to fill up the time of waiting. The inspiration, the intuition, you see—when it comes, it comes, and there's an end of it.

GREGERS. My dear Hialmar, I almost think you have something of the wild duck in you.

HIALMAR. Something of the wild duck? How do you mean?

GREGERS. You have dived down and bitten yourself fast in the undergrowth.

HIALMAR. Are you alluding to the well-nigh fatal shot that has broken my father's wing—and mine, too?

GREGERS. Not exactly to that. I don't say that your wing has been broken; but you have strayed into a poisonous marsh, Hialmar; an insidious disease has taken hold of you, and you have sunk down to die in the dark.

HIALMAR. I? To die in the dark? Look here, Gregers, you must really leave off talking such nonsense.

GREGERS. Don't be afraid; I shall find a way to help you up again. I, too, have a mission in life now; I found it yesterday.

HIALMAR. That's all very well; but you will please leave me out of it. I can assure you that—apart from my very natural melancholy, of course—I am as contented as any one can wish to be.

GREGERS. Your contentment is an effect of the marsh poison.

HIALMAR. Now, my dear Gregers, pray do not go on about disease and poison; I am not used to that sort of talk. In my house nobody ever speaks to me about unpleasant things.

GREGERS. Ah, that I can easily believe.

HIALMAR. It's not good for me, you see. And there are no marsh poisons here, as you express it. The poor photographer's roof is lowly, I know—and my circumstances are narrow. But I am an inventor, and I am the breadwinner of a family. That exalts me above my mean surroundings.—Ah, here comes lunch!

[GINA *and* HEDVIG *bring bottles of ale, a decanter of brandy, glasses, etc. At the same time,* RELLING *and* MOLVIK *enter from the passage; they are both without hat or overcoat.* MOLVIK *is dressed in black.*]

GINA. [*Placing the things upon the table*] Ah, you two have come in the nick of time.

RELLING. Molvik got it into his head that he could smell herring-salad, and then there was no holding him.—Good morning again, Ekdal.

HIALMAR. Gregers, let me introduce you to Mr. Molvik. Doctor—— Oh, you know Relling, don't you?

GREGERS. Yes, slightly.

RELLING. Oh, Mr. Werle, junior! Yes, we two have had one or two little skirmishes up at the Höidal works. You've just moved in?

GREGERS. I moved in this morning.

RELLING. Molvik and I live right under you, so you haven't far to go for the doctor and the clergyman, if you should need anything in that line.

GREGERS. Thanks, it's not quite unlikely, for yesterday we were thirteen at table.

HIALMAR. Oh, come now, don't let us get upon unpleasant subjects again!

RELLING. You may make your mind easy, Ekdal; I'll be hanged if the finger of fate points to you.

HIALMAR. I should hope not, for the sake of my family. But let us sit down now, and eat and drink and be merry.

GREGERS. Shall we not wait for your father?

HIALMAR. No, his lunch will be taken in to him later. Come along!

[*The men seat themselves at table, and eat and drink.* GINA *and* HEDVIG *go in and out and wait upon them.*]

RELLING. Molvik was frightfully stewed yesterday, Mrs. Ekdal.

GINA. Really? Yesterday again?

RELLING. Didn't you hear him when I brought him home last night?

GINA. No, I can't say I did.

RELLING. That was a good thing, for Molvik was disgusting last night.

GINA. Is that true, Molvik?

MOLVIK. Let us draw a veil over last night's proceedings. That sort of thing is totally foreign to my better self.

RELLING. [*To* GREGERS] It comes over him like a sort of possession, and then I have to go out on the loose with him. Mr. Molvik is dæmonic, you see.

GREGERS. Dæmonic?

RELLING. Molvik is dæmonic, yes.

GREGERS. H'm.

RELLING. And dæmonic natures are not made to walk straight through the world; they must meander a little now and then.— Well, so you still stick up there at those horrible grimy works?

GREGERS. I have stuck there until now.

RELLING. And did you ever manage to collect that claim you went about presenting?

GREGERS. Claim? [*Understands him*] Ah. I see.

HIALMAR. Have you been presenting claims, Gregers?

GREGERS. Oh, nonsense.

RELLING. Faith, but he has, though! He went around to all the cottars' cabins presenting something he called "the claim of the ideal."

GREGERS. I was young then.

RELLING. You're right; you were very young. And as for the claim of the ideal—you never got it honored while *I* was up there.

GREGERS. Nor since either.

RELLING. Ah, then you've learnt to knock a little discount off, I expect.

GREGERS. Never, when I have a true man to deal with.

HIALMAR. No, I should think not, indeed. A little butter, Gina.

RELLING. And a slice of bacon for Molvik.

MOLVIK. Ugh; not bacon!   [*A knock at the garret door.*]

HIALMAR. Open the door, Hedvig; father wants to come out.

[HEDVIG *goes over and opens the door a little way;* EKDAL *en-*

ters with a fresh rabbit-skin; she closes the door after him.]

EKDAL. Good morning, gentlemen! Good sport today. Shot a big one.

HIALMAR. And you've gone and skinned it without waiting for me——!

EKDAL. Salted it, too. It's good tender meat, is rabbit; it's sweet; it tastes like sugar. Good appetite to you, gentlemen!
  [*Goes into his room.*]

MOLVIK. [*Rising*] Excuse me——; I can't——; I must get downstairs immediately——

RELLING. Drink some soda water, man!

MOLVIK. [*Hurrying away*] Ugh—ugh!
  [*Goes out by the passage door.*]

RELLING. [*To* HIALMAR] Let us drain a glass to the old hunter.

HIALMAR. [*Clinks glasses with him*] To the undaunted sportsman who has looked death in the face!

RELLING. To the grey-haired—— [*Drinks*] By-the-bye, is his hair grey or white?

HIALMAR. Something between the two, I fancy; for that matter, he has very few hairs left of any color.

RELLING. Well, well, one can get through the world with a wig. After all, you are a happy man, Ekdal; you have your noble mission to labor for——

HIALMAR. And I do labor, I can tell you.

RELLING. And then you have your excellent wife, shuffling quietly in and out in her felt slippers, and that seesaw walk of hers, and making everything cosy and comfortable about you.

HIALMAR. Yes, Gina—[*Nods to her*]—you were a good helpmate on the path of life.

GINA. Oh, don't sit there cricketizing me.

RELLING. And your Hedvig, too, Ekdal!

HIALMAR. [*Affected*] The child, yes! The child before everything! Hedvig, come here to me. [*Strokes her hair*] What day is it tomorrow, eh?

HEDVIG. [*Shaking him*] Oh, no, you're not to say anything, father.

HIALMAR. It cuts me to the heart when I think what a poor affair it will be; only a little festivity in the garret——

HEDVIG. Oh, but that's just what I like!

RELLING. Just you wait till the wonderful invention sees the light, Hedvig!

HIALMAR. Yes, indeed—then you shall see——! Hedvig, I have resolved to make your future secure. You shall live in comfort all your days. I will demand—something or other—on your behalf. That shall be the poor inventor's sole reward.

HEDVIG. [*Whispering, with her arms round his neck*] Oh, you dear, kind father!

RELLING. [*To* GREGERS] Come now, don't you find it pleasant, for once in a way, to sit at a well-spread table in a happy family circle?

HIALMAR. Ah, yes, I really prize these social hours.

GREGERS. For my part, I don't thrive in marsh vapors.

RELLING. Marsh vapors?

HIALMAR. Oh, don't begin with that stuff again!

GINA. Goodness knows there's no vapors in this house, Mr. Werle; I give the place a good airing every blessed day.

GREGERS. [*Leaves the table*] No airing you can give will drive out the taint I mean.

HIALMAR. Taint!

GINA. Yes, what do you say to that, Ekdal?

RELLING. Excuse me—may it not be you yourself that have brought the taint from those mines up there?

GREGERS. It is like you to call what I bring into this house a taint.

RELLING. [*Goes up to him*] Look here, Mr. Werle, junior: I have a strong suspicion that you are still carrying about that "claim of the ideal," large as life, in your coat-tail pocket.

GREGERS. I carry it in my breast.

RELLING. Well, wherever you carry it, I advise you not to come dunning us with it here, so long as *I* am on the premises.

GREGERS. And if I do so nonetheless?

RELLING. Then you'll go head-foremost down the stairs; now I've warned you.

HIALMAR [*Rising*] Oh, but Relling——!

GREGERS. Yes, you may turn me out——

GINA. [*Interposing between them*] We can't have that, Relling. But I must say, Mr. Werle, it ill becomes you to talk about vapors and taints, after all the mess you made with your stove.

[*A knock at the passage door.*]

HEDVIG. Mother, there's somebody knocking.

HIALMAR. There now, we're going to have a whole lot of people!

GINA. I'll go—— [*Goes over and opens the door, starts, and draws back*] Oh—oh, dear!

[WERLE, *in a fur coat, advances one step into the room.*]

WERLE. Excuse me, but I think my son is staying here.

GINA. [*With a gulp*] Yes.

HIALMAR. [*Approaching him*] Won't you do us the honor to——?

WERLE. Thank you, I merely wish to speak to my son.

GREGERS. What is it? Here I am.

WERLE. I want a few words with you, in your room.

GREGERS. In my room? Very well——   [*About to go.*]

GINA. No, no, your room's not in a fit state——

WERLE. Well then, out in the passage here; I want to have a few words with you alone.

HIALMAR. You can have them here, sir. Come into the parlor, Relling.

[HIALMAR *and* RELLING *go off to the right.* GINA *takes* HEDVIG *with her into the kitchen.*]

GREGERS. [*After a short pause*] Well, now we are alone.

WERLE. From something you let fall last evening, and from your coming to lodge with the Ekdals, I can't help inferring that you intend to make yourself unpleasant to me in one way or another.

GREGERS. I intend to open Hialmar Ekdal's eyes. He shall see his position as it really is—that is all.

WERLE. Is that the mission in life you spoke of yesterday?

GREGERS. Yes. You have left me no other.

WERLE. Is it I, then, that have crippled your mind, Gregers?

GREGERS. You have crippled my whole life. I am not thinking of all that about mother—— But it's thanks to you that I am continually haunted and harassed by a guilty conscience.

WERLE. Indeed! It is your conscience that troubles you, is it?

GREGERS. I ought to have taken a stand against you when the trap was set for Lieutenant Ekdal. I ought to have cautioned him, for I had a misgiving as to what was in the wind.

WERLE. Yes, that was the time to have spoken.

GREGERS. I did not dare to, I was so cowed and spiritless. I was mortally afraid of you—not only then, but long afterwards.

WERLE. You have got over that fear now, it appears.

GREGERS. Yes, fortunately. The wrong done to old Ekdal, both by me and by—others, can never be undone; but Hialmar I can rescue from all the falsehood and deception that are bringing him to ruin.

WERLE. Do you think that will be doing him a kindness?

GREGERS. I have not the least doubt of it.

WERLE. You think our worthy photographer is the sort of man to appreciate such friendly offices?

GREGERS. Yes, I do.

WERLE. H'm—we shall see.

GREGERS. Besides, if I am to go on living, I must try to find some cure for my sick conscience.

WERLE. It will never be sound. Your conscience has been sickly from childhood. That is a legacy from your mother, Gregers— the only one she left you.

GREGERS. [*With a scornful half-smile*] Have you not yet forgiven her for the mistake you made in supposing she would bring you a fortune?

WERLE. Don't let us wander from the point.—Then you hold to your purpose of setting young Ekdal upon what you imagine to be the right scent?

GREGERS. Yes, that is my fixed resolve.

WERLE. Well, in that case I might have spared myself this visit; for, of course, it is useless to ask whether you will return home with me?

GREGERS. Quite useless.

WERLE. And I suppose you won't enter the firm either?

GREGERS. No.

WERLE. Very good. But as I am thinking of marrying again, your share in the property will fall to you at once.[5]

GREGERS. [*Quickly*] No, I do not want that.

WERLE. You don't want it?

GREGERS. No, I dare not take it, for conscience' sake.

WERLE. [*After a pause*] Are you going up to the works again?

GREGERS. No; I consider myself released from your service.

WERLE. But what are you going to do?

GREGERS. Only to fulfil my mission; nothing more.

WERLE. Well, but afterwards? What are you going to live upon?

GREGERS. I have laid by a little out of my salary.

WERLE. How long will that last?

GREGERS. I think it will last my time.

WERLE. What do you mean?

GREGERS. I shall answer no more questions.

WERLE. Good-bye then, Gregers.

GREGERS. Good-bye. [WERLE *goes.*]

HIALMAR. [*Peeping in*] He's gone, isn't he?

GREGERS. Yes.

[HIALMAR *and* RELLING *enter; also* GINA *and* HEDVIG *from the kitchen.*]

RELLING. That luncheon-party was a failure.

GREGERS. Put on your coat, Hialmar; I want you to come for a long walk with me.

HIALMAR. With pleasure. What was it your father wanted? Had it anything to do with me?

GREGERS. Come along. We must have a talk. I'll go and put on my overcoat.

[*Goes out by the passage door.*]

GINA. You shouldn't go out with him, Ekdal.

5. By Norwegian law, before a widower can marry again, a certain proportion of his property must be settled on his children by his former marriage. [Translator's note.]

RELLING. No, don't you do it. Stay where you are.

HIALMAR. [*Gets his hat and overcoat*] Oh, nonsense! When a friend of my youth feels impelled to open his mind to me in private——

RELLING. But devil take it—don't you see that the fellow's mad, cracked, demented?

GINA. There, what did I tell you? His mother before him had crazy fits like that sometimes.

HIALMAR. The more need for a friend's watchful eye. [*To* GINA] Be sure you have dinner ready in good time. Good-bye for the present.

[*Goes out by the passage door.*]

RELLING. It's a thousand pities the fellow didn't go to hell through one of the Höidal mines.

GINA. Good Lord! what makes you say that?

RELLING. [*Muttering*] Oh, I have my own reasons.

GINA. Do you think young Werle is really mad?

RELLING. No, worse luck; he's no madder than most other people. But one disease he has certainly got in his system.

GINA. What's the matter with him?

RELLING. Well, I'll tell you, Mrs. Ekdal. He is suffering from an acute attack of integrity.

GINA. Integrity?

HEDVIG. Is that a kind of disease?

RELLING. Yes, it's a national disease; but it only appears sporadically. [*Nods to* GINA] Thanks for your hospitality.

[*He goes out by the passage door.*]

GINA. [*Moving restlessly to and fro*] Ugh, that Gregers Werle—he was always a wretched creature.

HEDVIG. [*Standing by the table and looking searchingly at her*] I think all this is very strange.

Act IV

SCENE—HIALMAR EKDAL'S *studio. A photograph has just been taken; a camera with the cloth over it, a pedestal, two chairs, a folding table, etc., are standing out in the room. Afternoon light; the sun is going down; a little later it begins to grow dusk.*

GINA *stands in the passage doorway, with a little box and a wet glass plate in her hand, and is speaking to somebody outside.*

GINA. Yes, certainly. When I make a promise I keep it. The first dozen shall be ready on Monday. Good afternoon.

[*Someone is heard going downstairs.* GINA *shuts the door, slips the plate into the box and puts it into the covered camera.*]

HEDVIG. [*Comes in from the kitchen*] Are they gone?

GINA. [*Tidying up*] Yes, thank goodness, I've got rid of them at last.

HEDVIG. But can you imagine why father hasn't come home yet?

GINA. Are you sure he's not down in Relling's room?

HEDVIG. No, he's not; I ran down the kitchen stair just now and asked.

GINA. And his dinner standing and getting cold, too.

HEDVIG. Yes, I can't understand it. Father's always so careful to be home to dinner!

GINA. Oh, he'll be here directly, you'll see.

HEDVIG. I wish he would come; everything seems so queer today.

GINA. [*Calls out*] There he is!

[HIALMAR EKDAL *comes in at the passage door.*]

HEDVIG. [*Going to him*] Father! Oh, what a time we've been waiting for you!

GINA. [*Glancing sidelong at him*] You've been out a long time, Ekdal.

HIALMAR. [*Without looking at her*] Rather long, yes.

[*He takes off his overcoat;* GINA *and* HEDVIG *go to help him; he motions them away.*]

GINA. Perhaps you've had dinner with Werle?

HIALMAR. [*Hanging up his coat*] No.

GINA. [*Going towards the kitchen door*] Then I'll bring some in for you.

HIALMAR. No; let the dinner alone. I want nothing to eat.

HEDVIG. [*Going nearer to him*] Are you not well, father?

HIALMAR. Well? Oh, yes, well enough. We have had a tiring walk, Gregers and I.

GINA. You didn't ought to have gone so far, Ekdal; you're not used to it.

HIALMAR. H'm; there's many a thing a man must get used to in this world. [*Wanders about the room*] Has any one been here whilst I was out?

GINA. Nobody but the two sweethearts.

HIALMAR. No new orders?

GINA. No, not today.

HEDVIG. There will be some tomorrow, father; you'll see.

HIALMAR. I hope there will, for tomorrow I am going to set to work in real earnest.

HEDVIG. Tomorrow! Don't you remember what day it is tomorrow?

HIALMAR. Oh, yes, by-the-bye——. Well, the day after, then. Henceforth I mean to do everything myself; I shall take all the work into my own hands.

GINA. Why, what can be the good of that, Ekdal? It'll only make your life a burden to you. I can manage the photography all right, and you can go on working at your invention.

HEDVIG. And think of the wild duck, father,—and all the hens and rabbits and——!

HIALMAR. Don't talk to me of all that trash! From tomorrow I will never set foot in the garret again.

HEDVIG. Oh, but father, you promised that we should have a little party——

HIALMAR. H'm, true. Well, then, from the day after tomorrow. I should almost like to wring that cursed wild duck's neck!

HEDVIG. [*Shrieks*] The wild duck!

GINA. Well, I never!

HEDVIG. [*Shaking him*] Oh, no, father; you know it's my wild duck!

HIALMAR. That is why I don't do it. I haven't the heart to—for your sake, Hedvig. But in my inmost soul I feel that I ought to do it. I ought not to tolerate under my roof a creature that has been through those hands.

GINA. Why, good gracious, even if grandfather did get it from that poor creature, Pettersen——

HIALMAR. [*Wandering about*] There are certain claims—what shall I call them?—let me say claims of the ideal—certain obligations, which a man cannot disregard without injury to his soul.

HEDVIG. [*Going after him*] But think of the wild duck,—the poor wild duck!

HIALMAR. [*Stops*] I tell you I will spare it—for your sake. Not a hair of its head shall be—I mean, it shall be spared. There are greater problems than that to be dealt with. But you should go out a little now, Hedvig, as usual; it is getting dusk enough for you now.

HEDVIG. No, I don't care about going out now.

HIALMAR. Yes, do; it seems to me your eyes are blinking a great deal; all these vapors in here are bad for you. The air is heavy under this roof.

HEDVIG. Very well, then, I'll run down the kitchen stair and go for a little walk. My cloak and hat?—oh, they're in my own room. Father—be sure you don't do the wild duck any harm while I'm out.

HIALMAR. Not a feather of its head shall be touched. [*Draws her to him*] You and I, Hedvig—we two——! Well, go along.

[HEDVIG *nods to her parents and goes out through the kitchen.*]

HIALMAR. [*Walks about without looking up*] Gina.

GINA. Yes?

HIALMAR. From tomorrow—or, say, from the day after tomorrow—I should like to keep the household account-book myself.

GINA. Do you want to keep the accounts, too, now?

HIALMAR. Yes; or to check the receipts at any rate.

GINA. Lord help us! that's soon done.

HIALMAR. One would hardly think so; at any rate, you seem to make the money go a very long way. [*Stops and looks at her*] How do you manage it?

GINA. It's because me and Hedvig, we need so little.

HIALMAR. Is it the case that father is very liberally paid for the copying he does for Mr. Werle?

GINA. I don't know as he gets anything out of the way. I don't know the rates for that sort of work.

HIALMAR. Well, what does he get, about? Let me hear!

GINA. Oh, it varies; I daresay it'll come to about as much as he costs us, with a little pocket-money over.

HIALMAR. As much as he costs us! And you have never told me this before!

GINA. No, how could I tell you? It pleased you so much to think he got everything from you.

HIALMAR. And he gets it from Mr. Werle.

GINA. Oh, well, he has plenty and to spare, he has.

HIALMAR. Light the lamp for me, please!

GINA. [*Lighting the lamp*] And, of course, we don't know as it's Mr. Werle himself; it may be Gråberg——

HIALMAR. Why attempt such an evasion?

GINA. I don't know; I only thought——

HIALMAR. H'm.

GINA. It wasn't me that got grandfather that copying. It was Bertha, when she used to come about us.

HIALMAR. It seems to me your voice is trembling.

GINA. [*Putting the lamp-shade on*] Is it?

HIALMAR. And your hands are shaking, are they not?

GINA. [*Firmly*] Come right out with it, Ekdal. What has he been saying about me?

HIALMAR. Is it true—can it be true that—that there was an—an understanding between you and Mr. Werle, while you were in service there?

GINA. That's not true. Not at that time. Mr. Werle did come after me, that's a fact. And his wife thought there was something in it, and then she made such a hocus-pocus and hurly-burly, and she hustled me and bustled me about so that I left her service.

HIALMAR. But afterwards, then?

GINA. Well, then I went home. And mother—well, she wasn't the woman you took her for, Ekdal; she kept on worrying and worrying at me about one thing and another—for Mr. Werle was a widower by that time.

HIALMAR. Well, and then?

GINA. I suppose you've got to know it. He gave me no peace until he'd had his way.

HIALMAR. [*Striking his hands together*] And this is the mother of my child! How could you hide this from me?

GINA. Yes, it was wrong of me; I ought certainly to have told you long ago.

HIALMAR. You should have told me at the very first;—then I should have known the sort of woman you were.

GINA. But would you have married me all the same?

HIALMAR. How can you dream that I would?

GINA. That's just why I didn't dare tell you anything, then. For I'd come to care for you so much, you see; and I couldn't go and make myself utterly miserable——

HIALMAR. [*Walks about*] And this is my Hedvig's mother. And to know that all I see before me—[*Kicks a chair*]—all that I call my home——I owe to a favored predecessor! Oh, that scoundrel Werle!

GINA. Do you repent of the fourteen—the fifteen years we've lived together?

HIALMAR. [*Placing himself in front of her*] Have you not every day, every hour, repented of the spider's-web of deceit you have spun around me? Answer me that! How could you help writhing with penitence and remorse?

GINA. Oh, my dear Ekdal, I've had all I could do to look after the house and get through the day's work——

HIALMAR. Then you never think of reviewing your past?

GINA. No; Heaven knows I'd almost forgotten those old stories.

HIALMAR. Oh, this dull, callous contentment! To me there is something revolting about it. Think of it—never so much as a twinge of remorse!

GINA. But tell me, Ekdal—what would have become of you if you hadn't had a wife like me?

HIALMAR. Like you——!

GINA. Yes; for you know I've always been a bit more practical and wide-awake than you. Of course I'm a year or two older.

HIALMAR. What would have become of me!

GINA. You'd got into all sorts of bad ways when first you met me; that you can't deny.

HIALMAR. "Bad ways" do you call them? Little do you know what a man goes through when he is in grief and despair—especially a man of my fiery temperament.

GINA. Well, well, that may be so. And I've no reason to crow over you, neither; for you turned a moral of a husband, that you did, as soon as ever you had a house and home of your own.——And now we've got everything so nice and cosy about us; and me and Hedvig was just thinking we'd soon be able to let ourselves go a bit, in the way of both food and clothes.

HIALMAR. In the swamp of deceit, yes.

GINA. I wish to goodness that detestable thing had never set his foot inside our doors!

HIALMAR. And I, too, thought my home such a pleasant one. That was a delusion. Where shall I now find the elasticity of spirit to bring my invention into the world of reality? Perhaps it will die with me; and then it will be your past, Gina, that will have killed it.

GINA. [*Nearly crying*] You mustn't say such things, Ekdal. Me, that has only wanted to do the best I could for you, all my days!

HIALMAR. I ask you, what becomes of the breadwinner's dream? When I used to lie in there on the sofa and brood over my invention, I had a clear enough presentiment that it would sap my vitality to the last drop. I felt even then that the day when I held the patent in my hand—that day—would bring my—release. And then it was my dream that you should live on after me, the dead inventor's well-to-do widow.

GINA. [*Drying her tears*] No, you mustn't talk like that, Ekdal. May the Lord never let me see the day I am left a widow!

HIALMAR. Oh, the whole dream has vanished. It is all over now. All over!

[GREGERS WERLE *opens the passage door cautiously and looks in.*]

GREGERS. May I come in?

HIALMAR. Yes, come in.

GREGERS. [*Comes forward, his face beaming with satisfaction, and holds out both his hands to them*] Well, dear friends——! [*Looks from one to the other and whispers to* HIALMAR] Have you not done it yet?

HIALMAR. [*Aloud*] It is done.

GREGERS. It is?

HIALMAR. I have passed through the bitterest moments of my life.

GREGERS. But also, I trust, the most ennobling.

HIALMAR. Well, at any rate, we have got through it for the present.

GINA. God forgive you, Mr. Werle.

GREGERS. [*In great surprise*] But I don't understand this.

HIALMAR. What don't you understand?

GREGERS. After so great a crisis—a crisis that is to be the starting-point of an entirely new life—of a communion founded on truth, and free from all taint of deception——

HIALMAR. Yes, yes, I know; I know that quite well.

GREGERS. I confidently expected, when I entered the room, to find the light of transfiguration shining upon me from both husband and wife. And now I see nothing but dulness, oppression, gloom——

GINA. Oh, is that it? [*Takes off the lamp-shade.*]

GREGERS. You will not understand me, Mrs. Ekdal. Ah, well, you, I suppose, need time to——. But you, Hialmar? Surely you feel a new consecration after the great crisis.

HIALMAR. Yes, of course I do. That is—in a sort of way.

GREGERS. For surely nothing in the world can compare with the joy of forgiving one who has erred and raising her up to oneself in love.

HIALMAR. Do you think a man can so easily throw off the bitter cup I have drained?

GREGERS. No, not a common man, perhaps. But a man like you——!

HIALMAR. Good God! I know that well enough. But you must keep me up to it, Gregers. It takes time, you know.

GREGERS. You have much of the wild duck in you, Hialmar.

[RELLING *has come in at the passage door.*]

RELLING. Oho! is the wild duck to the fore again?

HIALMAR. Yes; Mr. Werle's wing-broken victim.

RELLING. Mr. Werle's——? So it's him you are talking about?

HIALMAR. Him and—ourselves.

RELLING. [*In an undertone to* GREGERS] May the devil fly away with you!

HIALMAR. What is that you are saying?

RELLING. Only uttering a heartfelt wish that this quack-salver would take himself off. If he stays here, he is quite equal to making an utter mess of life, for both of you.

GREGERS. These two will not make a mess of life, Mr. Relling. Of course I won't speak of Hialmar—him we know. But she, too, in her innermost heart, has certainly something loyal and sincere——

GINA. [*Almost crying*] You might have let me alone for what I was, then.

RELLING. [*To* GREGERS] Is it rude to ask what you really want in this house?

GREGERS. To lay the foundations of a true marriage.

RELLING. So you don't think Ekdal's marriage is good enough as it is?

GREGERS. No doubt it is as good a marriage as most others, worse luck. But a true marriage it has yet to become.

HIALMAR. You have never had eyes for the claims of the ideal, Relling.

RELLING. Rubbish, my boy!—but excuse me, Mr. Werle: how many

—in round numbers—how many true marriages have you seen in the course of your life?

GREGERS. Scarcely a single one.

RELLING. Nor I either.

GREGERS. But I have seen innumerable marriages of the opposite kind. And it has been my fate to see at close quarters what ruin such a marriage can work in two human souls.

HIALMAR. A man's whole moral basis may give away beneath his feet; that is the terrible part of it.

RELLING. Well, I can't say I've ever been exactly married, so I don't pretend to speak with authority. But this I know, that the child enters into the marriage problem. And you must leave the child in peace.

HIALMAR. Oh—Hedvig! my poor Hedvig!

RELLING. Yes, you must be good enough to keep Hedvig outside of all this. You two are grown-up people; you are free, in God's name, to make what mess and muddle you please of your life. But you must deal cautiously with Hedvig, I tell you; else you may do her a great injury.

HIALMAR. An injury!

RELLING. Yes, or she may do herself an injury—and perhaps others, too.

GINA. How can you know that, Relling?

HIALMAR. Her sight is in no immediate danger, is it?

RELLING. I am not talking about her sight. Hedvig is at a critical age. She may be getting all sorts of mischief into her head.

GINA. That's true—I've noticed it already! She's taken to carrying on with the fire, out in the kitchen. She calls it playing at house-on-fire. I'm often scared for fear she really sets fire to the house.

RELLING. You see; I thought as much.

GREGERS. [*To* RELLING] But how do you account for that?

RELLING. [*Sullenly*] Her constitution's changing, sir.

HIALMAR. So long as the child has me——! So long as *I* am above ground——!

[*A knock at the door.*]

GINA. Hush, Ekdal; there's some one in the passage. [*Calls out*] Come in!

[MRS. SÖRBY, *in walking dress, comes in.*]

MRS. SÖRBY. Good evening.

GINA. [*Going towards her*] Is it really you, Bertha?

MRS. SÖRBY. Yes, of course it is. But I'm disturbing you, I'm afraid?

HIALMAR. No, not at all; an emissary from that house——

MRS. SÖRBY. [*To* GINA] To tell the truth, I hoped your men-folk would be out at this time. I just ran up to have a little chat with you, and to say good-bye.

GINA. Good-bye? Are you going away, then?

MRS. SÖRBY. Yes, tomorrow morning,—up to Höidal. Mr. Werle started this afternoon. [*Lightly to* GREGERS] He asked me to say good-bye for him.

GINA. Only fancy——!

HIALMAR. So Mr. Werle has gone? And now you are going after him?

MRS. SÖRBY. Yes, what do you say to that, Ekdal?

HIALMAR. I say: beware!

GREGERS. I must explain the situation. My father and Mrs. Sörby are going to be married.

HIALMAR. Going to be married!

GINA. Oh, Bertha! So it's come to that at last!

RELLING. [*His voice quivering a little*] This is surely not true?

MRS. SÖRBY. Yes, my dear Relling, it's true enough.

RELLING. You are going to marry again?

MRS. SÖRBY. Yes, it looks like it. Werle has got a special licence, and we are going to be married quite quietly, up at the works.

GREGERS. Then I must wish you all happiness, like a dutiful stepson.

MRS. SÖRBY. Thank you very much—if you mean what you say. I certainly hope it will lead to happiness, both for Werle and for me.

RELLING. You have every reason to hope that. Mr. Werle never gets drunk—so far as I know; and I don't suppose he's in the habit of thrashing his wives, like the late lamented horse-doctor.

MRS. SÖRBY. Come now, let Sörby rest in peace. He had his good points, too.

RELLING. Mr. Werle has better ones, I have no doubt.

MRS. SÖRBY. He hasn't frittered away all that was good in him, at any rate. The man who does that must take the consequences.

RELLING. I shall go out with Molvik this evening.

MRS. SÖRBY. You mustn't do that, Relling. Don't do it—for my sake.

RELLING. There's nothing else for it. [*To* HIALMAR] If you're going with us, come along.

GINA. No, thank you. Ekdal doesn't go in for that sort of dissertation.

HIALMAR. [*Half aloud, in vexation*] Oh, do hold your tongue!

RELLING. Good-bye, Mrs.—Werle.

[*Goes out through the passage door.*]

GREGERS. [*To* MRS. SÖRBY] You seem to know Dr. Relling pretty intimately.

MRS. SÖRBY. Yes, we have known each other for many years. At one time it seemed as if things might have gone further between us.

GREGERS. It was surely lucky for you that they did not.

MRS. SÖRBY. You may well say that. But I have always been wary of acting on impulse. A woman can't afford absolutely to throw herself away.

GREGERS. Are you not in the least afraid that I may let my father know about this old friendship?

MRS. SÖRBY. Why, of course, I have told him all about it myself.

GREGERS. Indeed?

MRS. SÖRBY. Your father knows every single thing that can, with any truth, be said about me. I have told him all; it was the first thing I did when I saw what was in his mind.

GREGERS. Then you have been franker than most people, I think.

MRS. SÖRBY. I have always been frank. We women find that the best policy.

HIALMAR. What do you say to that, Gina?

GINA. Oh, we're not all alike, us women aren't. Some are made one way, some another.

MRS. SÖRBY. Well, for my part, Gina, I believe it's wisest to do as I've done. And Werle has no secrets either, on his side. That's really the great bond between us, you see. Now he can talk to me as openly as a child. He has never had the chance to do that before. Fancy a man like him, full of health and vigor, passing his whole youth and the best years of his life in listening to nothing but penitential sermons! And very often the sermons had for their text the most imaginary offences—at least so I understand.

GINA. That's true enough.

GREGERS. If you ladies are going to follow up this topic, I had better withdraw.

MRS. SÖRBY. You can stay as far as that's concerned. I shan't say a word more. But I wanted you to know that I had done nothing secretly or in an underhand way. I may seem to have come in for a great piece of luck; and so I have, in a sense. But after all, I don't think I am getting any more than I am giving. I shall stand by him always, and I can tend and care for him as no one else can, now that he is getting helpless.

HIALMAR. Getting helpless?

GREGERS. [*To* MRS. SÖRBY] Hush, don't speak of that here.

MRS. SÖRBY. There is no disguising it any longer, however much he would like to. He is going blind.

HIALMAR. [*Starts*] Going blind? That's strange. He, too, going blind!

GINA. Lots of people do.

MRS. SÖRBY. And you can imagine what that means to a business man. Well, I shall try as well as I can to make my eyes take the place of his. But I mustn't stay any longer; I have heaps of things to do.—Oh, by-the-bye, Ekdal, I was to tell you that if there is anything Werle can do for you, you must just apply to Gråberg.

GREGERS. That offer I am sure Hialmar Ekdal will decline with thanks.

MRS. SÖRBY. Indeed? I don't think he used to be so——

GINA. No, Bertha, Ekdal doesn't need anything from Mr. Werle now.

HIALMAR. [*Slowly, and with emphasis*] Will you present my compliments to your future husband and say that I intend very shortly to call upon Mr. Gråberg——

GREGERS. What! You don't really mean that?

HIALMAR. To call upon Mr. Gråberg, I say, and obtain an account of the sum I owe his principal. I will pay that debt of honor—ha ha ha! a debt of honor, let us call it! In any case, I will pay the whole with five per cent interest.

GINA. But, my dear Ekdal, God knows we haven't got the money to do it.

HIALMAR. Be good enough to tell your future husband that I am working assiduously at my invention. Please tell him that what sustains me in this laborious task is the wish to free myself from a torturing burden of debt. That is my reason for proceeding with the invention. The entire profits shall be devoted to releasing me from my pecuniary obligations to your future husband.

MRS. SÖRBY. Something has happened here.

HIALMAR. Yes, you are right.

MRS. SÖRBY. Well, good-bye. I had something else to speak to you about, Gina; but it must keep till another time. Good-bye.

[HIALMAR *and* GREGERS *bow silently.* GINA *follows* MRS. SÖRBY *to the door.*]

HIALMAR. Not beyond the threshold, Gina!

[MRS. SÖRBY *goes;* GINA *shuts the door after her.*]

HIALMAR. There now, Gregers; I have got that burden of debt off my mind.

GREGERS. You soon will, at all events.

HIALMAR. I think my attitude may be called correct.

GREGERS. You are the man I have always taken you for.

HIALMAR. In certain cases, it is impossible to disregard the claim of the ideal. Yet, as the breadwinner of a family, I cannot but writhe and groan under it. I can tell you it is no joke for a man without capital to attempt the repayment of a long-standing obligation, over which, so to speak, the dust of oblivion had gathered. But it cannot be helped: the Man in me demands his rights.

GREGERS. [*Laying his hand on* HIALMAR's *shoulder*] My dear Hialmar—was it not a good thing I came?

HIALMAR. Yes.

GREGERS. Are you not glad to have had your true position made clear to you?

HIALMAR. [*Somewhat impatiently*] Yes, of course I am. But there is one thing that is revolting to my sense of justice.

GREGERS. And what is that?

HIALMAR. It is that—but I don't know whether I ought to express myself so unreservedly about your father.

GREGERS. Say what you please, so far as I am concerned.

HIALMAR. Well, then, is it not exasperating to think that it is not I, but he, who will realize the true marriage?

GREGERS. How can you say such a thing?

HIALMAR. Because it is clearly the case. Isn't the marriage between your father and Mrs. Sörby founded upon complete confidence, upon entire and unreserved candor on both sides? They hide nothing from each other; they keep no secrets in the background; their relation is based, if I may put it so, on mutual confession and absolution.

GREGERS. Well, what then?

HIALMAR. Well, is not that the whole thing? Did you not yourself say this was precisely the difficulty that had to be overcome in order to found a true marriage?

GREGERS. But this is a totally different matter, Hialmar. You surely don't compare either yourself or your wife with those two——? Oh, you understand me well enough.

HIALMAR. Say what you like, there is something in all this that hurts and offends my sense of justice. It really looks as if there were no just providence to rule the world.

GINA. Oh, no, Ekdal; for God's sake don't say such things.

GREGERS. H'm; don't let us get upon those questions.

HIALMAR. And yet, after all, I cannot but recognize the guiding finger of fate. He is going blind.

GINA. Oh, you can't be sure of that.

HIALMAR. There is no doubt about it. At all events there ought not to be; for in that very fact lies the righteous retribution. He has hoodwinked a confiding fellow-creature in days gone by——

GREGERS. I fear he has hoodwinked many.

HIALMAR. And now comes inexorable, mysterious Fate and demands Werle's own eyes.

GINA. Oh, how dare you say such dreadful things! You make me quite scared.

HIALMAR. It is profitable, now and then, to plunge deep into the night side of existence.

[HEDVIG, *in her hat and cloak, comes in by the passage door. She is pleasurably excited and out of breath.*]

GINA. Are you back already?

HEDVIG. Yes, I didn't care to go any farther. It was a good thing, too; for I've just met some one at the door.

HIALMAR. It must have been that Mrs. Sörby.

HEDVIG. Yes.

HIALMAR. [*Walks up and down*] I hope you have seen her for the last time.

[*Silence.* HEDVIG, *discouraged, looks first at one and then at the other, trying to divine their frame of mind.*]

HEDVIG. [*Approaching, coaxingly*] Father.

HIALMAR. Well—what is it, Hedvig?

HEDVIG. Mrs. Sörby had something with her for me.

HIALMAR. [*Stops*] For you?

HEDVIG. Yes. Something for tomorrow.

GINA. Bertha has always given you some little thing on your birthday.

HIALMAR. What is it?

HEDVIG. Oh, you mustn't see it now. Mother is to give it to me tomorrow morning before I'm up.

HIALMAR. What is all this hocus-pocus that I am to be in the dark about?

HEDVIG. [*Quickly*] Oh, no, you may see it if you like. It's a big letter.

[*Takes the letter out of her cloak pocket.*]

HIALMAR. A letter, too?

HEDVIG. Yes, it is only a letter. The rest will come afterwards, I suppose. But fancy—a letter! I've never had a letter before. And there's "Miss" written upon it. [*Reads*] "Miss Hedvig Ekdal." Only fancy—that's me!

HIALMAR. Let me see that letter.

HEDVIG. [*Hands it to him*] There it is.

HIALMAR. That is Mr. Werle's hand.

GINA. Are you sure of that, Ekdal?

HIALMAR. Look for yourself.

GINA. Oh, what do *I* know about such-like things?

HIALMAR. Hedvig, may I open the letter—and read it?

HEDVIG. Yes, of course you may, if you want to.

GINA. No, not tonight, Ekdal; it's to be kept till tomorrow.

HEDVIG. [*Softly*] Oh, can't you let him read it? It's sure to be something good; and then father will be glad, and everything will be nice again.

HIALMAR. I may open it, then?

HEDVIG. Yes, do, father. I'm so anxious to know what it is.

HIALMAR. Well and good. [*Opens the letter, takes out a paper, reads it through and appears bewildered*] What is this——?

GINA. What does it say?

HEDVIG. Oh, yes, father—tell us!

HIALMAR. Be quiet. [*Reads it through again; he has turned pale, but says with self-control*] It is a deed of gift, Hedvig.

HEDVIG. Is it? What sort of gift am I to have?

HIALMAR. Read for yourself.

[HEDVIG *goes over and reads for a time by the lamp.*]

HIALMAR. [*Half-aloud, clenching his hands*] The eyes! The eyes—and then that letter!

HEDVIG. [*Leaves off reading*] Yes, but it seems to me that it's grand-father that's to have it.

HIALMAR. [*Takes letter from her*] Gina—can you understand this?

GINA. I know nothing whatever about it; tell me what's the matter.

HIALMAR. Mr. Werle writes to Hedvig that her old grandfather need not trouble himself any longer with the copying, but that he can henceforth draw on the office for a hundred crowns a month——

GREGERS. Aha!

HEDVIG. A hundred crowns, mother! I read that.

GINA. What a good thing for grandfather!

HIALMAR. ——a hundred crowns a month so long as he needs it—that means, of course, so long as he lives.

GINA. Well, so he's provided for, poor dear.

HIALMAR. But there is more to come. You didn't read that, Hedvig. Afterwards this gift is to pass on to you.

HEDVIG. To me! The whole of it?

HIALMAR. He says that the same amount is assured to you for the whole of your life. Do you hear that, Gina?

GINA. Yes, I hear.

HEDVIG. Fancy—all that money for me! [*Shakes him*] Father, father, aren't you glad——?

HIALMAR. [*Eluding her*] Glad! [*Walks about*] Oh, what vistas—what perspectives open up before me! It is Hedvig, Hedvig that he showers these benefactions upon!

GINA. Yes, because it's Hedvig's birthday——

HEDVIG. And you'll get it all the same, father! You know quite well I shall give all the money to you and mother.

HIALMAR. To mother, yes! There we have it.

GREGERS. Hialmar, this is a trap he is setting for you.

HIALMAR. Do you think it's another trap?

GREGERS. When he was here this morning he said: Hialmar Ekdal is not the man you imagine him to be.

HIALMAR. Not the man——!

GREGERS. That you shall see, he said.

HIALMAR. He meant you should see that I would let myself be bought off——!

HEDVIG. Oh, mother, what does all this mean?

GINA. Go and take off your things.

[HEDVIG *goes out by the kitchen door, half-crying.*]

GREGERS. Yes, Hialmar—now is the time to show who was right, he or I.

HIALMAR. [*Slowly tears the paper across, lays both pieces on the table and says*] Here is my answer.

GREGERS. Just what I expected.

HIALMAR. [*Goes over to* GINA, *who stands by the stove, and says in a low voice*] Now please make a clean breast of it. If the connection between you and him was quite over when you—came to care for me, as you call it—why did he place us in a position to marry?

GINA. I suppose he thought as he could come and go in our house.

HIALMAR. Only that? Was not he afraid of a possible contingency?

GINA. I don't know what you mean.

HIALMAR. I want to know whether—your child has the right to live under my roof.

GINA. [*Draws herself up; her eyes flash*] You ask that?

HIALMAR. You shall answer me this one question: Does Hedvig belong to me—or——? Well?

GINA. [*Looking at him with cold defiance*] I don't know.

HIALMAR. [*Quivering a little*] You don't know!

GINA. How should *I* know? A creature like me——

HIALMAR. [*Quietly turning away from her*] Then I have nothing more to do in this house.

GREGERS. Take care, Hialmar! Think what you are doing!

HIALMAR. [*Puts on his overcoat*] In this case, there is nothing for a man like me to think twice about.

GREGERS. Yes, indeed, there are endless things to be considered. You three must be together if you are to attain the true frame of mind for self-sacrifice and forgiveness.

HIALMAR. I don't want to attain it. Never, never! My hat! [*Takes his hat*] My home has fallen in ruins about me. [*Bursts into tears*] Gregers, I have no child!

HEDVIG. [*Who has opened the kitchen door*] What is that you're saying? [*Coming to him*] Father, father!

GINA. There, you see!

HIALMAR. Don't come near me, Hedvig! Keep far away. I cannot bear to see you! Oh! those eyes——! Good-bye.

[*Makes for the door.*]

HEDVIG. [*Clinging close to him and screaming loudly*] No! no! Don't leave me!

GINA [*Cries out*] Look at the child, Ekdal! Look at the child!

HIALMAR. I will not! I cannot! I must get out—away from all this!
[*He tears himself away from* HEDVIG *and goes out by the passage door.*]

HEDVIG. [*With despairing eyes*] He is going away from us, mother!
He is going away from us! He will never come back again!

GINA. Don't cry, Hedvig. Father's sure to come back again.

HEDVIG. [*Throws herself sobbing on the sofa*] No, no, he'll never
come home to us any more.

GREGERS. Do you believe I meant all for the best, Mrs. Ekdal?

GINA. Yes, I daresay you did; but God forgive you, all the same.

HEDVIG. [*Lying on the sofa*] Oh, this will kill me! What have I done
to him? Mother, you must fetch him home again!

GINA. Yes, yes, yes; only be quiet, and I'll go out and look for him.
[*Puts on her outdoor things*] Perhaps he's gone in to Relling's.
But you mustn't lie there and cry. Promise me!

HEDVIG. [*Weeping convulsively*] Yes, I'll stop, I'll stop; if only
father comes back!

GREGERS. [*To* GINA, *who is going*] After all, had you not better leave
him to fight out his bitter fight to the end?

GINA. Oh, he can do that afterwards. First of all, we must get the
child quieted.
[*Goes out by the passage door.*]

HEDVIG. [*Sits up and dries her tears*] Now you must tell me what
all this means? Why doesn't father want me any more?

GREGERS. You mustn't ask that till you are a big girl—quite
grown-up.

HEDVIG. [*Sobs*] But I can't go on being as miserable as this till I'm
grown-up.—I think I know what it is.—Perhaps I'm not really
father's child.

GREGERS. [*Uneasily*] How could that be?

HEDVIG. Mother might have found me. And perhaps father has just
got to know it; I've read of such things.

GREGERS. Well, but if it were so——

HEDVIG. I think he might be just as fond of me for all that. Yes,
fonder almost. We got the wild duck in a present, you know,
and I love it so dearly all the same.

GREGERS. [*Turning the conversation*] Ah, the wild duck, by-the-bye!
Let us talk about the wild duck a little, Hedvig.

HEDVIG. The poor wild duck! He doesn't want to see it any more
either. Only think, he wanted to wring its neck!

GREGERS. Oh, he won't do that.

HEDVIG. No; but he said he would like to. And I think it was horrid
of father to say it, for I pray for the wild duck every night and
ask that it may be preserved from death and all that is evil.

GREGERS. [*Looking at her*] Do you say your prayers every night?

HEDVIG. Yes.

GREGERS. Who taught you to do that?

HEDVIG. I myself, one time when father was very ill, and had leeches on his neck and said that death was staring him in the face.

GREGERS. Well?

HEDVIG. Then I prayed for him as I lay in bed, and since then I have always kept it up.

GREGERS. And now you pray for the wild duck, too?

HEDVIG. I thought it was best to bring in the wild duck, for she was so weakly at first.

GREGERS. Do you pray in the morning, too?

HEDVIG. No, of course not.

GREGERS. Why not in the morning as well?

HEDVIG. In the morning it's light, you know, and there's nothing in particular to be afraid of.

GREGERS. And your father was going to wring the neck of the wild duck that you love so dearly?

HEDVIG. No; he said he ought to wring its neck, but he would spare it for my sake; and that was kind of father.

GREGERS. [*Coming a little nearer*] But suppose you were to sacrifice the wild duck of your own free will for his sake.

HEDVIG. [*Rising*] The wild duck!

GREGERS. Suppose you were to make a free-will offering, for his sake, of the dearest treasure you have in the world!

HEDVIG. Do you think that would do any good?

GREGERS. Try it, Hedvig.

HEDVIG. [*Softly, with flashing eyes*] Yes, I will try it.

GREGERS. Have you really the courage for it, do you think?

HEDVIG. I'll ask grandfather to shoot the wild duck for me.

GREGERS. Yes, do. But not a word to your mother about it.

HEDVIG. Why not?

GREGERS. She doesn't understand us.

HEDVIG. The wild duck! I'll try it tomorrow morning.

[GINA *comes in by the passage door.*]

HEDVIG. [*Going towards her*] Did you find him, mother?

GINA. No, but I heard as he had called and taken Relling with him.

GREGERS. Are you sure of that?

GINA. Yes, the porter's wife said so. Molvik went with them, too, she said.

GREGERS. This evening, when his mind so sorely needs to wrestle in solitude——!

GINA. [*Takes off her things*] Yes, men are strange creatures, so they are. The Lord only knows where Relling has dragged him to! I ran over to Madame Eriksen's, but they weren't there.

HEDVIG. [*Struggling to keep back her tears*] Oh, if he should never come home any more!

GREGERS. He will come home again. I shall have news to give him tomorrow; and then you shall see how he comes home. You may rely upon that, Hedvig, and sleep in peace. Good-night.

[*He goes out by the passage door.*]

HEDVIG. [*Throws herself sobbing on* GINA's *neck*] Mother, mother!

GINA. [*Pats her shoulder and sighs*] Ah, yes; Relling was right, he was. That's what comes of it when crazy creatures go about presenting the claims of the—what-you-may-call-it.

Act V

SCENE—HIALMAR EKDAL's *studio. Cold, grey morning light. Wet snow lies upon the large panes of the sloping roof-window.*

GINA *comes from the kitchen with an apron and bib on, and carrying a dusting-brush and a duster; she goes towards the sitting-room door. At the same moment* HEDVIG *comes hurriedly in from the passage.*

GINA. [*Stops*] Well?

HEDVIG. Oh, mother, I almost think he's down at Relling's——

GINA. There, you see!

HEDVIG. ——because the porter's wife says she could hear that Relling had two people with him when he came home last night.

GINA. That's just what I thought.

HEDVIG. But it's no use his being there, if he won't come up to us.

GINA. I'll go down and speak to him at all events.

[OLD EKDAL, *in dressing-gown and slippers, and with a lighted pipe, appears at the door of his room.*]

EKDAL. Hialmar—— Isn't Hialmar at home?

GINA. No, he's gone out.

EKDAL. So early? And in such a tearing snowstorm? Well, well; just as he pleases; I can take my morning walk alone.

[*He slides the garret door aside;* HEDVIG *helps him; he goes in; she closes it after him.*]

HEDVIG. [*In an undertone*] Only think, mother, when poor grandfather hears that father is going to leave us.

GINA. Oh, nonsense; grandfather mustn't hear anything about it. It was a heaven's mercy he wasn't at home yesterday in all that hurly-burly.

HEDVIG. Yes, but——

[GREGERS *comes in by the passage door.*]

GREGERS. Well, have you any news of him?

GINA. They say he's down at Relling's.

GREGERS. At Relling's! Has he really been out with those creatures?

GINA. Yes, like enough.

GREGERS. When he ought to have been yearning for solitude, to collect and clear his thoughts——

GINA. Yes, you may well say so.

[RELLING *enters from the passage.*]

HEDVIG. [*Going to him*] Is father in your room?

GINA. [*At the same time*] Is he there?

RELLING. Yes, to be sure he is.

HEDVIG. And you never let us know!

RELLING. Yes, I'm a brute. But in the first place I had to look after the other brute; I mean our dæmonic friend, of course; and then I fell so dead asleep that——

GINA. What does Ekdal say today?

RELLING. He says nothing whatever.

HEDVIG. Doesn't he speak?

RELLING. Not a blessed word.

GREGERS. No, no; I can understand that very well.

GINA. But what's he doing then?

RELLING. He's lying on the sofa, snoring.

GINA. Oh, is he? Yes, Ekdal's a rare one to snore.

HEDVIG. Asleep? Can he sleep?

RELLING. Well, it certainly looks like it.

GREGERS. No wonder, after the spiritual conflict that has rent him——

GINA. And then he's never been used to gadding about out of doors at night.

HEDVIG. Perhaps it's a good thing that he's getting sleep, mother.

GINA. Of course it is; and we must take care we don't wake him up too early. Thank you, Relling. I must get the house cleaned up a bit now, and then—— Come and help me, Hedvig.

[GINA *and* HEDVIG *go into the sitting-room.*]

GREGERS. [*Turning to* RELLING] What is your explanation of the spiritual tumult that is now going on in Hialmar Ekdal?

RELLING. Devil a bit of a spiritual tumult have *I* noticed in him.

GREGERS. What! Not at such a crisis, when his whole life has been placed on a new foundation——? How can you think that such an individuality as Hialmar's——?

RELLING. Oh, individuality—he! If he ever had any tendency to the abnormal development you call individuality, I can assure you it was rooted out of him while he was still in his teens.

GREGERS. That would be strange indeed,—considering the loving care with which he was brought up.

RELLING. By those two high-flown, hysterical maiden aunts, you mean?

GREGERS. Let me tell you that they were women who never forgot the claim of the ideal—but of course you will only jeer at me again.

RELLING. No, I'm in no humor for that. I know all about those ladies; for he has ladled out no end of rhetoric on the subject of his "two soul-mothers." But I don't think he has much to thank them for. Ekdal's misfortune is that in his own circle he has always been looked upon as a shining light——

GREGERS. Not without reason, surely. Look at the depth of his mind!

RELLING. I have never discovered it. That his father believed in it I don't so much wonder; the old lieutenant has been an ass all his days.

GREGERS. He has had a child-like mind all his days; that is what you cannot understand.

RELLING. Well, so be it. But then, when our dear, sweet Hialmar went to college, he at once passed for the great light of the future amongst his comrades, too! He was handsome, the rascal—red and white—a shop-girl's dream of manly beauty; and with his superficially emotional temperament, and his sympathetic voice and his talent for declaiming other people's verses and other people's thoughts——

GREGERS. [*Indignantly*] Is it Hialmar Ekdal you are talking about in this strain?

RELLING. Yes, with your permission; I am simply giving you an inside view of the idol you are grovelling before.

GREGERS. I should hardly have thought I was quite stone blind.

RELLING. Yes, you are—or not far from it. You are a sick man, too, you see.

GREGERS. You are right there.

RELLING. Yes. Yours is a complicated case. First of all there is that plaguy integrity-fever; and then—what's worse—you are always in a delirium of hero-worship; you must always have something to adore, outside yourself.

GREGERS. Yes, I must certainly seek it outside myself.

RELLING. But you make such shocking mistakes about every new phœnix you think you have discovered. Here again you have come to a cottar's cabin with your claim of the ideal; and the people of the house are insolvent.

GREGERS. If you don't think better than that of Hialmar Ekdal, what pleasure can you find in being everlastingly with him?

RELLING. Well, you see, I'm supposed to be a sort of doctor—save the mark! I can't but give a hand to the poor sick folk who live under the same roof with me.

GREGERS. Oh, indeed! Hialmar Ekdal is sick, too, is he?

RELLING. Most people are, worse luck.

GREGERS And what remedy are you applying in Hialmar's case?

RELLING. My usual one. I am cultivating the life-illusion[6] in him.

GREGERS. Life-illusion? I didn't catch what you said.

RELLING. Yes, I said illusion. For illusion, you know, is the stimulating principle.

GREGERS. May I ask with what illusion Hialmar is inoculated?

RELLING. No, thank you; I don't betray professional secrets to quacksalvers. You would probably go and muddle his case still more than you have already. But my method is infallible. I have applied it to Molvik as well. I have made him "dæmonic." That's the blister I have to put on his neck.

GREGERS. Is he not really dæmonic, then?

RELLING. What the devil do you mean by dæmonic? It's only a piece of gibberish I've invented to keep up a spark of life in him. But for that, the poor harmless creature would have succumbed to self-contempt and despair many a long year ago. And then the old lieutenant! But he has hit upon his own cure, you see.

GREGERS. Lieutenant Ekdal? What of him?

RELLING. Just think of the old bear-hunter shutting himself up in that dark garret to shoot rabbits! I tell you there is not a happier sportsman in the world than that old man pottering about in there among all that rubbish. The four or five withered Christmas trees he has saved up are the same to him as the whole great fresh Höidal forest; the cock and the hens are big game-birds in the fir-tops; and the rabbits that flop about the garret floor are the bears he has to battle with—the mighty hunter of the mountains!

GREGERS. Poor unfortunate old man! Yes; he has indeed had to narrow the ideals of his youth.

RELLING. While I think of it, Mr. Werle, junior—don't use that foreign word: ideals. We have the excellent native word: lies.

GREGERS. Do you think the two things are related?

RELLING. Yes, just about as closely as typhus and putrid fever.

GREGERS. Dr. Relling, I shall not give up the struggle until I have rescued Hialmar from your clutches!

RELLING. So much the worse for him. Rob the average man of his life-illusion, and you rob him of his happiness at the same stroke. [*To* HEDVIG, *who comes in from the sitting-room*] Well, little wild-duck-mother, I'm just going down to see whether papa is still lying meditating upon that wonderful invention of his.

[*Goes out by passage door.*]

GREGERS. [*Approaches* HEDVIG] I can see by your face that you have not yet done it.

HEDVIG. What? Oh, that about the wild duck! No.

6. "Livslögnen," literally "the life-lie." [Translator's note.]

GREGERS. I suppose your courage failed when the time came.

HEDVIG. No, that wasn't it. But when I awoke this morning and remembered what we had been talking about, it seemed so strange.

GREGERS. Strange?

HEDVIG. Yes, I don't know—— Yesterday evening, at the moment, I thought there was something so delightful about it; but since I have slept and thought of it again, it somehow doesn't seem worth while.

GREGERS. Ah, I thought you could not have grown up quite unharmed in this house.

HEDVIG. I don't care about that, if only father would come up——

GREGERS. Oh, if only your eyes had been opened to that which gives life its value—if you possessed the true, joyous, fearless spirit of sacrifice, you would soon see how he would come up to you.—But I believe in you still, Hedvig.

[*He goes out by the passage door.* HEDVIG *wanders about the room for a time; she is on the point of going into the kitchen when a knock is heard at the garret door.* HEDVIG *goes over and opens it a little;* OLD EKDAL *comes out; she pushes the door to again.*]

EKDAL. H'm, it's not much fun to take one's morning walk alone.

HEDVIG. Wouldn't you like to go shooting, grandfather?

EKDAL. It's not the weather for it today. It's so dark there, you can scarcely see where you're going.

HEDVIG. Do you never want to shoot anything besides the rabbits?

EKDAL. Do you think the rabbits aren't good enough?

HEDVIG. Yes, but what about the wild duck?

EKDAL. Ho-ho! are you afraid I shall shoot your wild duck? Never in the world. Never.

HEDVIG. No, I suppose you couldn't; they say it's very difficult to shoot wild ducks.

EKDAL. Couldn't! Should rather think I could.

HEDVIG. How would you set about it, grandfather?—I don't mean with my wild duck, but with others?

EKDAL. I should take care to shoot them in the breast, you know; that's the surest place. And then you must shoot against the feathers, you see—not the way of the feathers.

HEDVIG. Do they die then, grandfather?

EKDAL. Yes, they die right enough—when you shoot properly. Well, I must go and brush up a bit. H'm—understand—h'm. [*Goes into his room*]

[HEDVIG *waits a little, glances towards the sitting-room door, goes over to the book-case, stands on tip-toe, takes the*

double-barrelled pistol down from the shelf and looks at it.
GINA, *with brush and duster, comes from the sitting-room.*
HEDVIG *hastily lays down the pistol, unobserved.*]

GINA. Don't stand raking amongst father's things, Hedvig.

HEDVIG. [*Goes away from the bookcase*] I was only going to tidy up a little.

GINA. You'd better go into the kitchen and see if the coffee's keeping hot; I'll take his breakfast on a tray, when I go down to him.

[HEDVIG *goes out.* GINA *begins to sweep and clean up the studio. Presently the passage door is opened with hesitation, and* HIALMAR EKDAL *looks in. He has on his overcoat, but not his hat; he is unwashed, and his hair is dishevelled and unkempt. His eyes are dull and heavy.*]

GINA. [*Standing with the brush in her hand and looking at him*] Oh, there now, Ekdal—so you've come after all!

HIALMAR. [*Comes in and answers in a toneless voice*] I come—only to depart again immediately.

GINA. Yes, yes, I suppose so. But, Lord help us! what a sight you are!

HIALMAR. A sight?

GINA. And your nice winter coat, too! Well, that's done for.

HEDVIG. [*At the kitchen door*] Mother, hadn't I better——? [*Sees* HIALMAR, *gives a loud scream of joy and runs to him*] Oh, father, father!

HIALMAR. [*Turns away and makes a gesture of repulsion*] Away, away, away! [*To* GINA] Keep her away from me, I say!

GINA. [*In a low tone*] Go into the sitting-room, Hedvig.

[HEDVIG *does so without a word.*]

HIALMAR. [*Fussily pulls out the table-drawer*] I must have my books with me. Where are my books?

GINA. Which books?

HIALMAR. My scientific books, of course; the technical magazines I require for my invention.

GINA. [*Searches in the bookcase*] Is it these here paper-covered ones?

HIALMAR. Yes, of course.

GINA. [*Lays a heap of magazines on the table*] Shan't I get Hedvig to cut them for you?

HIALMAR. I don't require to have them cut for me.

[*Short silence.*]

GINA. Then you're still set on leaving us, Ekdal?

HIALMAR. [*Rummaging amongst the books*] Yes, that is a matter of course, I should think.

GINA. Well, well.

HIALMAR. [*Vehemently*] How can I live here, to be stabbed to the heart every hour of the day?

GINA. God forgive you for thinking such vile things of me.

HIALMAR. Prove———!

GINA. I think it's you as has got to prove.

HIALMAR. After a past like yours? There are certain claims—I may almost call them claims of the ideal———

GINA. But what about grandfather? What's to become of him, poor dear?

HIALMAR. I know my duty; my helpless father will come with me. I am going out into the town to make arrangements——— H'm— [*Hesitatingly*]—has any one found my hat on the stairs?

GINA. No. Have you lost your hat?

HIALMAR. Of course I had it on when I came in last night; there's no doubt about that; but I couldn't find it this morning.

GINA. Lord help us! where have you been to with those two ne'er-do-wells?

HIALMAR. Oh, don't bother me about trifles. Do you suppose I am in the mood to remember details?

GINA. If only you haven't caught cold, Ekdal———
[*Goes out into the kitchen.*]

HIALMAR. [*Talks to himself in a low tone of irritation, while he empties the table-drawer*] You're a scoundrel, Relling!—You're a low fellow!—Ah, you shameless tempter!—I wish I could get some one to stick a knife into you!
[*He lays some old letters on one side, finds the torn document of yesterday, takes it up and looks at the pieces; puts it down hurriedly as* GINA *enters.*]

GINA. [*Sets a tray with coffee, etc., on the table*] Here's a drop of something hot, if you'd fancy it. And there's some bread and butter and a snack of salt meat.

HIALMAR. [*Glancing at the tray*] Salt meat? Never under this roof! It's true I have not had a mouthful of solid food for nearly twenty-four hours; but no matter.—My memoranda! The commencement of my autobiography! What has become of my diary, and all my important papers? [*Opens the sitting-room door but draws back*] She is there, too!

GINA. Good Lord! the child must be somewhere!

HIALMAR. Come out.
[*He makes room;* HEDVIG *comes, scared, into the studio.*]

HIALMAR. [*With his hand upon the door-handle, says to* GINA] In these, the last moments I spend in my former home, I wish to be spared from interlopers———
[*Goes into the room.*]

HEDVIG. [*With a bound towards her mother, asks softly, trembling*] Does that mean me?

GINA. Stay out in the kitchen, Hedvig; or, no—you'd best go into

your own room. [*Speaks to* HIALMAR *as she goes into him*] Wait
a bit, Ekdal; don't rummage so in the drawers; I know where
everything is.

HEDVIG. [*Stands a moment immovable, in terror and perplexity,
biting her lips to keep back the tears; then she clenches her hands
convulsively and says softly*] The wild duck.

> [*She steals over and takes the pistol from the shelf, opens
> the garret door a little way, creeps in and draws the door to
> after her.* HIALMAR *and* GINA *can be heard disputing in the
> sitting-room.*]

HIALMAR. [*Comes in with some manuscript books and old loose
papers, which he lays upon the table*] That portmanteau is of no
use! There are a thousand and one things I must drag with me.

GINA. [*Following with the portmanteau*] Why not leave all the rest
for the present and only take a shirt and a pair of woollen drawers
with you?

HIALMAR. Whew!—all these exhausting preparations——!

> [*Pulls off his overcoat and throws it upon the sofa.*]

GINA. And there's the coffee getting cold.

HIALMAR. H'm.

> [*Drinks a mouthful without thinking of it and then an-
> other.*]

GINA. [*Dusting the backs of the chairs*] A nice job you'll have to find
such another big garret for the rabbits.

HIALMAR. What! Am I to drag all those rabbits with me, too?

GINA. You don't suppose grandfather can get on without his rabbits.

HIALMAR. He must just get used to doing without them. Have not I
to sacrifice very much greater things than rabbits?

GINA. [*Dusting the bookcase*] Shall I put the flute in the portmanteau for you?

HIALMAR. No. No flute for me. But give me the pistol!

GINA. Do you want to take the pistol with you?

HIALMAR. Yes. My loaded pistol.

GINA. [*Searching for it*] It's gone. He must have taken it in with
him.

HIALMAR. Is he in the garret?

GINA. Yes, of course he's in the garret.

HIALMAR. H'm—poor lonely old man.

> [*He takes a piece of bread and butter, eats it, and finishes his
> cup of coffee.*]

GINA. If we hadn't have let that room, you could have moved in
there.

HIALMAR. And continued to live under the same roof with——!
Never,—never!

GINA. But couldn't you put up with the sitting-room for a day or two? You could have it all to yourself.

HIALMAR. Never within these walls!

GINA. Well, then, down with Relling and Molvik.

HIALMAR. Don't mention those wretches' names to me! The very thought of them almost takes away my appetite.—Oh, no, I must go out into the storm and the snow-drift,—go from house to house and seek shelter for my father and myself.

GINA. But you've got no hat, Ekdal! You've been and lost your hat, you know.

HIALMAR. Oh, those two brutes, those slaves of all the vices! A hat must be procured. [*Takes another piece of bread and butter*] Some arrangements must be made. For I have no mind to throw away my life, either.

[*Looks for something on the tray.*]

GINA. What are you looking for?

HIALMAR. Butter.

GINA. I'll get some at once.   [*Goes out into the kitchen.*]

HIALMAR. [*Calls after her*] Oh, it doesn't matter; dry bread is good enough for me.

GINA. [*Brings a dish of butter*] Look here; this is fresh churned.

[*She pours out another cup of coffee for him; he seats him-self on the sofa, spreads more butter on the already buttered bread and eats and drinks awhile in silence.*]

HIALMAR. Could I, without being subject to intrusion—intrusion of any sort—could I live in the sitting-room there for a day or two?

GINA. Yes, to be sure you could, if you only would.

HIALMAR. For I see no possibility of getting all father's things out in such a hurry.

GINA. And, besides, you've surely got to tell him first as you don't mean to live with us others no more.

HIALMAR. [*Pushes away his coffee cup*] Yes, there is that, too; I shall have to lay bare the whole tangled story to him—— I must turn matters over; I must have breathing-time; I cannot take all these burdens on my shoulders in a single day.

GINA. No, especially in such horrible weather as it is outside.

HIALMAR. [*Touching* WERLE'S *letter*] I see that paper is still lying about here.

GINA. Yes, I haven't touched it.

HIALMAR. So far as I am concerned it is mere waste paper——

GINA. Well, I have certainly no notion of making any use of it.

HIALMAR. ——but we had better not let it get lost all the same;— in all the upset when I move, it might easily——

GINA. I'll take good care of it, Ekdal.

HIALMAR. The donation is in the first instance made to father, and it rests with him to accept or decline it.

GINA. [*Sighs*] Yes, poor old father——

HIALMAR. To make quite safe—— Where shall I find some gum?

GINA. [*Goes to the bookcase*] Here's the gum-pot.

HIALMAR. And a brush?

GINA. The brush is here, too.   [*Brings him the things.*]

HIALMAR. [*Takes a pair of scissors*] Just a strip of paper at the back ——[*Clips and gums*] Far be it from me to lay hands upon what is not my own—and least of all upon what belongs to a destitute old man—and to—the other as well.—There now. Let it lie there for a time; and when it is dry, take it away. I wish never to see that document again. Never!

[GREGERS WERLE *enters from the passage.*]

GREGERS. [*Somewhat surprised*] What,—are you sitting here, Hialmar?

HIALMAR. [*Rises hurriedly*] I had sunk down from fatigue.

GREGERS. You have been having breakfast, I see.

HIALMAR. The body sometimes makes its claims felt, too.

GREGERS. What have you decided to do?

HIALMAR. For a man like me, there is only one course possible. I am just putting my most important things together. But it takes time, you know.

GINA. [*With a touch of impatience*] Am I to get the room ready for you, or am I to pack your portmanteau?

HIALMAR. [*After a glance of annoyance at* GREGERS] Pack—and get the room ready!

GINA. [*Takes the portmanteau*] Very well; then I'll put in the shirt and the other things.

[*Goes into the sitting-room and draws the door to after her.*]

GREGERS. [*After a short silence*] I never dreamed that this would be the end of it. Do you really feel it a necessity to leave house and home?

HIALMAR. [*Wanders about restlessly*] What would you have me do? —I am not fitted to bear unhappiness, Gregers. I must feel secure and at peace in my surroundings.

GREGERS. But can you not feel that here? Just try it. I should have thought you had firm ground to build upon now—if only you start afresh. And, remember, you have your invention to live for.

HIALMAR. Oh, don't talk about my invention. It's perhaps still in the dim distance.

GREGERS. Indeed!

HIALMAR. Why, great heavens, what would you have me invent? Other people have invented almost everything already. It becomes more and more difficult every day——

GREGERS. And you have devoted so much labor to it.

HIALMAR. It was that blackguard Relling that urged me to it.

GREGERS. Relling?

HIALMAR. Yes, it was he that first made me realize my aptitude for making some notable discovery in photography.

GREGERS. Aha—it was Relling!

HIALMAR. Oh, I have been so truly happy over it! Not so much for the sake of the invention itself, as because Hedvig believed in it —believed in it with a child's whole eagerness of faith.—At least, I have been fool enough to go and imagine that she believed in it.

GREGERS. Can you really think Hedvig has been false towards you?

HIALMAR. I can think anything now. It is Hedvig that stands in my way. She will blot out the sunlight from my whole life.

GREGERS. Hedvig! Is it Hedvig you are talking of? How should she blot out your sunlight?

HIALMAR. [*Without answering*] How unutterably I have loved that child! How unutterably happy I have felt every time I came home to my humble room, and she flew to meet me, with her sweet little blinking eyes. Oh, confiding fool that I have been! I loved her unutterably;—and I yielded myself up to the dream, the delusion, that she loved me unutterably in return.

GREGERS. Do you call that a delusion?

HIALMAR. How should I know? I can get nothing out of Gina; and besides, she is totally blind to the ideal side of these complications. But to you I feel impelled to open my mind, Gregers. I cannot shake off this frightful doubt—perhaps Hedvig has never really and honestly loved me.

GREGERS. What would you say if she were to give you a proof of her love? [*Listens*] What's that? I thought I heard the wild duck——?

HIALMAR. It's the wild duck quacking. Father's in the garret.

GREGERS. Is he? [*His face lights up with joy*] I say, you may yet have proof that your poor misunderstood Hedvig loves you!

HIALMAR. Oh, what proof can she give me? I dare not believe in any assurance from that quarter.

GREGERS. Hedvig does not know what deceit means.

HIALMAR. Oh, Gregers, that is just what I cannot be sure of. Who knows what Gina and that Mrs. Sörby may many a time have sat here whispering and tattling about? And Hedvig usually has her ears open, I can tell you. Perhaps the deed of gift was not such a surprise to her, after all. In fact, I'm not sure but that I noticed something of the sort.

GREGERS. What spirit is this that has taken possession of you?

HIALMAR. I have had my eyes opened. Just you notice;—you'll see, the deed of gift is only a beginning. Mrs. Sörby has always been a good deal taken up with Hedvig, and now she has the power to do whatever she likes for the child. They can take her from me whenever they please.

GREGERS. Hedvig will never, never leave you.

HIALMAR. Don't be so sure of that. If only they beckon to her and throw out a golden bait——! And, oh! I have loved her so unspeakably! I would have counted it my highest happiness to take her tenderly by the hand and lead her, as one leads a timid child through a great dark empty room!—I am cruelly certain now that the poor photographer in his humble attic has never really and truly been anything to her. She has only cunningly contrived to keep on a good footing with him until the time came.

GREGERS. You don't believe that yourself, Hialmar.

HIALMAR. That is just the terrible part of it—I don't know what to believe,—I never can know it. But can you really doubt that it must be as I say? Ho-ho, you have far too much faith in the claim of the ideal, my good Gregers! If those others came, with the glamour of wealth about them, and called to the child:—"Leave him: come to us: here life awaits you——!"

GREGERS. [*Quickly*] Well, what then?

HIALMAR. If I then asked her: Hedvig, are you willing to renounce that life for me? [*Laughs scornfully*] No thank you! You would soon hear what answer I should get.

[*A pistol shot is heard from within the garret.*]

GREGERS. [*Loudly and joyfully*] Hialmar!

HIALMAR. There now; he must needs go shooting, too.

GINA. [*Comes in*] Oh, Ekdal, I can hear grandfather blazing away in the garret by hisself.

HIALMAR. I'll look in——

GREGERS. [*Eagerly, with emotion*] Wait a moment! Do you know what that was?

HIALMAR. Yes, of course I know.

GREGERS. No, you don't know. But I do. That was the proof!

HIALMAR. What proof?

GREGERS. It was a child's free-will offering. She has got your father to shoot the wild duck.

HIALMAR. To shoot the wild duck!

GINA. Oh, think of that——!

HIALMAR. What was that for?

GREGERS. She wanted to sacrifice to you her most cherished possession; for then she thought you would surely come to love her again.

HIALMAR. [*Tenderly, with emotion*] Oh, poor child!

GINA. What things she does think of!

GREGERS. She only wanted your love again, Hialmar. She could not live without it.

GINA. [*Struggling with her tears*] There, you can see for yourself, Ekdal.

HIALMAR. Gina, where is she?

GINA. [*Sniffs*] Poor dear, she's sitting out in the kitchen, I dare say.

HIALMAR. [*Goes over, tears open the kitchen door and says*] Hedvig, come, come in to me! [*Looks around*] No, she's not here.

GINA. Then she must be in her own little room.

HIALMAR. [*Without*] No, she's not here either. [*Comes in*] She must have gone out.

GINA. Yes, you wouldn't have her anywheres in the house.

HIALMAR. Oh, if she would only come home quickly, so that I can tell her—— Everything will come right now, Gregers; now I believe we can begin life afresh.

GREGERS. [*Quietly*] I knew it; I knew the child would make amends.

[OLD EKDAL *appears at the door of his room; he is in full uniform and is busy buckling on his sword.*]

HIALMAR. [*Astonished*] Father! Are you there?

GINA. Have you been firing in your room?

EKDAL. [*Resentfully, approaching*] So you go shooting alone, do you, Hialmar?

HIALMAR. [*Excited and confused*] Then it wasn't you that fired that shot in the garret?

EKDAL. Me that fired? H'm.

GREGERS. [*Calls out to* HIALMAR] She has shot the wild duck herself!

HIALMAR. What can it mean? [*Hastens to the garret door, tears it aside, looks in and calls loudly*] Hedvig!

GINA. [*Runs to the door*] Good God, what's that?

HIALMAR. [*Goes in*] She's lying on the floor!

GREGERS. Hedvig! lying on the floor?

[*Goes in to* HIALMAR.]

GINA. [*At the same time*] Hedvig! [*Inside the garret*] No, no, no!

EKDAL. Ho-ho! does she go shooting, too, now?

[HIALMAR, GINA, *and* GREGERS *carry* HEDVIG *into the studio; in her dangling right hand she holds the pistol fast clasped in her fingers.*]

HIALMAR. [*Distracted*] The pistol has gone off. She has wounded herself. Call for help! Help!

GINA. [*Runs into the passage and calls down*] Relling! Relling! Doctor Relling; come up as quick as you can!

[HIALMAR *and* GREGERS *lay* HEDVIG *down on the sofa.*]

EKDAL. [*Quietly*] The woods avenge themselves.

HIALMAR. [*On his knees beside* HEDVIG] She'll soon come to now. She's coming to——; yes, yes, yes.

GINA. [*Who has come in again*] Where has she hurt herself? I can't see anything——

> [RELLING *comes hurriedly, and immediately after him* MOL-VIK; *the latter without his waistcoat and necktie, and with his coat open.*]

RELLING. What's the matter here?

GINA. They say Hedvig has shot herself.

HIALMAR. Come and help us!

RELLING. Shot herself!

> [*He pushes the table aside and begins to examine her.*]

HIALMAR. [*Kneeling and looking anxiously up at him*] It can't be dangerous? Speak, Relling! She is scarcely bleeding at all. It can't be dangerous?

RELLING. How did it happen?

HIALMAR. Oh, we don't know——

GINA. She wanted to shoot the wild duck.

RELLING. The wild duck?

HIALMAR. The pistol must have gone off.

RELLING. H'm. Indeed.

EKDAL. The woods avenge themselves. But I'm not afraid, all the same.

> [*Goes into the garret and closes the door after him.*]

HIALMAR. Well, Relling,—why don't you say something?

RELLING. The ball has entered the breast.

HIALMAR. Yes, but she's coming to!

RELLING. Surely you can see that Hedvig is dead.

GINA. [*Bursts into tears*] Oh, my child, my child——

GREGERS. [*Huskily*] In the depths of the sea——

HIALMAR. [*Jumps up*] No, no, she must live! Oh, for God's sake, Relling—only a moment—only just till I can tell her how unspeakably I loved her all the time!

RELLING. The bullet has gone through her heart. Internal hemorrhage. Death must have been instantaneous.

HIALMAR. And I! I hunted her from me like an animal! And she crept terrified into the garret and died for love of me! [*Sobbing*] I can never atone to her! I can never tell her——! [*Clenches his hands and cries, upwards*] O thou above——! If thou be indeed! Why hast thou done this thing to me?

GINA. Hush, hush, you mustn't go on that awful way. We had no right to keep her, I suppose.

MOLVIK. The child is not dead, but sleepeth.

RELLING. Bosh.

HIALMAR. [*Becomes calm, goes over to the sofa, folds his arms and looks at* HEDVIG] There she lies so stiff and still.

RELLING. [*Tries to loosen the pistol*] She's holding it so tight, so tight.

GINA. No, no, Relling, don't break her fingers; let the pistol be.

HIALMAR. She shall take it with her.

GINA. Yes, let her. But the child mustn't lie here for a show. She shall go to her own room, so she shall. Help me, Ekdal.

[HIALMAR *and* GINA *take* HEDVIG *between them.*]

HIALMAR. [*As they are carrying her*] Oh, Gina, Gina, can you survive this?

GINA. We must help each other to bear it. For now at least she belongs to both of us.

MOLVIK. [*Stretches out his arms and mumbles*] Blessed be the Lord; to earth thou shalt return; to earth thou shalt return——

RELLING. [*Whispers*] Hold your tongue, you fool; you're drunk.

[HIALMAR *and* GINA *carry the body out through the kitchen door.* RELLING *shuts it after them.* MOLVIK *slinks out into the passage.*]

RELLING. [*Goes over to* GREGERS *and says*] No one shall ever convince me that the pistol went off by accident.

GREGERS. [*Who has stood terrified, with convulsive twitchings*] Who can say how the dreadful thing happened?

RELLING. The powder has burnt the body of her dress. She must have pressed the pistol right against her breast and fired.

GREGERS. Hedvig has not died in vain. Did you not see how sorrow set free what is noble in him?

RELLING. Most people are ennobled by the actual presence of death. But how long do you suppose this nobility will last in him?

GREGERS. Why should it not endure and increase throughout his life?

RELLING. Before a year is over, little Hedvig will be nothing to him but a pretty theme for declamation.

GREGERS. How dare you say that of Hialmar Ekdal?

RELLING. We will talk of this again, when the grass has first withered on her grave. Then you'll hear him spouting about "the child too early torn from her father's heart;" then you'll see him steep himself in a syrup of sentiment and self-admiration and self-pity. Just you wait!

GREGERS. If you are right and I am wrong, then life is not worth living.

RELLING. Oh, life would be quite tolerable, after all, if only we could be rid of the confounded duns that keep on pestering us, in our poverty, with the claim of the ideal.

GREGERS. [*Looking straight before him*] In that case, I am glad that
my destiny is what it is.

RELLING. May I inquire,—what is your destiny?

GREGERS. [*Going*] To be the thirteenth at table.

RELLING. The devil it is.

HENRY JAMES
(1843–1916)
The Aspern Papers*

I

I had taken Mrs. Prest into my confidence; in truth without her
I should have made but little advance, for the fruitful idea in the
whole business dropped from her friendly lips. It was she who invented the short cut, who severed the Gordian knot. It is not supposed to be the nature of women to rise as a general thing to the
largest and most liberal view—I mean of a practical scheme; but it
has struck me that they sometimes throw off a bold conception—
such as a man would not have risen to—with singular serenity. "Simply ask them to take you in on the footing of a lodger"—I don't think
that unaided I should have risen to that. I was beating about the
bush, trying to be ingenious, wondering by what combination of
arts I might become an acquaintance, when she offered this happy
suggestion that the way to become an acquaintance was first to become an inmate. Her actual knowledge of the Misses Bordereau was
scarcely larger than mine, and indeed I had brought with me from
England some definite facts which were new to her. Their name had
been mixed up ages before with one of the greatest names of the
century, and they lived now in Venice in obscurity, on very small
means, unvisited, unapproachable, in a dilapidated old palace on an
out-of-the-way canal: this was the substance of my friend's impression
of them. She herself had been established in Venice for fifteen years
and had done a great deal of good there; but the circle of her
benevolence did not include the two shy, mysterious, and, as it was
somehow supposed, scarcely respectable Americans (they were believed to have lost in their long exile all national quality, besides
having had, as their name implied, some French strain in their origin), who asked no favours and desired no attention. In the early
years of her residence she had made an attempt to see them, but
this had been successful only as regards the little one, as Mrs. Prest
called the niece; though in reality, as I afterwards learned, she was
considerably the bigger of the two. She had heard Miss Bordereau
was ill and had a suspicion that she was in want; and she had gone

* 1888. The text of the London edition is here reprinted.

to the house to offer assistance, so that if there were suffering (and American suffering), she should at least not have it on her conscience. The "little one" received her in the great cold, tarnished Venetian *sala*, the central hall of the house, paved with marble and roofed with dim cross-beams, and did not even ask her to sit down. This was not encouraging for me, who wished to sit so fast, and I remarked as much to Mrs. Prest. She however replied with profundity, "Ah, but there's all the difference: I went to confer a favour and you will go to ask one. If they are proud you will be on the right side." And she offered to show me their house to begin with—to row me thither in her gondola. I let her know that I had already been to look at it half a dozen times; but I accepted her invitation, for it charmed me to hover about the place. I had made my way to it the day after my arrival in Venice (it had been described to me in advance by the friend in England to whom I owed definite information as to their possession of the papers), and I had besieged it with my eyes while I considered my plan of campaign. Jeffrey Aspern had never been in it that I knew of; but some note of his voice seemed to abide there by a roundabout implication, a faint reverberation.

Mrs. Prest knew nothing about the papers, but she was interested in my curiosity, as she was always interested in the joys and sorrows of her friends. As we went, however, in her gondola, gliding there under the sociable hood with the bright Venetian picture framed on either side by the movable window, I could see that she was amused by my infatuation, the way my interest in the papers had become a fixed idea. "One would think you expected to find in them the answer to the riddle of the universe," she said; and I denied the impeachment only by replying that if I had to choose between that precious solution and a bundle of Jeffrey Aspern's letters I knew indeed which would appear to me the greater boon. She pretended to make light of his genius and I took no pains to defend him. One doesn't defend one's god: one's god is in himself a defence. Besides, to-day, after his long comparative obscuration, he hangs high in the heaven of our literature, for all the world to see; he is a part of the light by which we walk. The most I said was that he was no doubt not a woman's poet: to which she rejoined aptly enough that he had been at least Miss Bordereau's. The strange thing had been for me to discover in England that she was still alive; it was as if I had been told Mrs. Siddons[1] was, or Queen Caroline,[2] or the famous Lady Hamilton,[3] for it seemed to me that she belonged to a generation as extinct. "Why, she must be tre-

1. Mrs. Sarah Siddons (1755–1831), *née* Kemble, was the most famous English actress.

2. Caroline of Brunswick-Wolfenbüttel (1768–1821) was the German-born Queen of George IV. The King's attempt to divorce her in 1820 caused an immense sensation.

3. Emma, Lady Hamilton (1761–1815), *née* Lyon, was the wife of Sir William Hamilton, the British Ambassador to the Court of Naples. Her affair with Admiral Nelson was notorious.

mendously old—at least a hundred," I had said; but on coming to consider dates I saw that it was not strictly necessary that she should have exceeded by very much the common span. None the less she was very far advanced in life and her relations with Jeffrey Aspern had occurred in her early womanhood. "That is her excuse," said Mrs. Prest, half sententiously and yet also somewhat as if she were ashamed of making a speech so little in the real tone of Venice. As if a woman needed an excuse for having loved the divine poet! He had been not only one of the most brilliant minds of his day (and in those years, when the century was young, there were, as every one knows, many), but one of the most genial men and one of the handsomest.

The niece, according to Mrs. Prest, was not so old, and she risked the conjecture that she was only a grand-niece. This was possible; I had nothing but my share in the very limited knowledge of my English fellow-worshipper John Cumnor, who had never seen the couple. The world, as I say, had recognised Jeffrey Aspern, but Cumnor and I had recognised him most. The multitude, to-day, flocked to his temple, but of that temple he and I regarded ourselves as the ministers. We held, justly, as I think, that we had done more for his memory than any one else, and we had done it by opening lights into his life. He had nothing to fear from us because he had nothing to fear from the truth, which alone at such a distance of time we could be interested in establishing. His early death had been the only dark spot in his life, unless the papers in Miss Bordereau's hands should perversely bring out others. There had been an impression about 1825 that he had "treated her badly," just as there had been an impression that he had "served," as the London populace says, several other ladies in the same way. Each of these cases Cumnor and I had been able to investigate, and we had never failed to acquit him conscientiously of shabby behavior. I judged him perhaps more indulgently than my friend; certainly, at any rate, it appeared to me that no man could have walked straighter in the given circumstances. These were almost always awkward. Half the women of his time, to speak liberally, had flung themselves at his head, and out of this pernicious fashion many complications, some of them grave, had not failed to arise. He was not a woman's poet, as I had said to Mrs. Prest, in the modern phase of his reputation; but the situation had been different when the man's own voice was mingled with his song. That voice, by every testimony, was one of the sweetest ever heard. "Orpheus and the Maenads!" was the exclamation that rose to my lips when I first turned over his correspondence. Almost all the Maenads were unreasonable and many of them insupportable; it struck me in short that he was kinder, more considerate than, in his place (if I could imagine myself in such a place!) I should have been.

It was certainly strange beyond all strangeness, and I shall not take up space with attempting to explain it, that whereas in all these other lines of research we had to deal with phantoms and dust, the mere echoes of echoes, the one living source of information that had lingered on into our time had been unheeded by us. Every one of Aspern's contemporaries had, according to our belief, passed away; we had not been able to look into a single pair of eyes into which his had looked or to feel a transmitted contact in any aged hand that his had touched. Most dead of all did poor Miss Bordereau appear, and yet she alone had survived. We exhausted in the course of months our wonder that we had not found her out sooner, and the substance of our explanation was that she had kept so quiet. The poor lady on the whole had had reason for doing so. But it was a revelation to us that it was possible to keep so quiet as that in the latter half of the nineteenth century—the age of newspapers and telegrams and photographs and interviewers. And she had taken no great trouble about it either: she had not hidden herself away in an undiscoverable hole; she had boldly settled down in a city of exhibition. The only secret of her safety that we could perceive was that Venice contained so many curiosities that were greater than she. And then accident had somehow favoured her, as was shown for example in the fact that Mrs. Prest had never happened to mention her to me, though I had spent three weeks in Venice—under her nose, as it were—five years before. Mrs. Prest had not mentioned this much to any one; she appeared almost to have forgotten she was there. Of course she had not the responsibilities of an editor. It was no explanation of the old woman's having eluded us to say that she lived abroad, for our researches had again and again taken us (not only by correspondence but by personal inquiry) to France, to Germany, to Italy, in which countries, not counting his important stay in England, so many of the too few years of Aspern's career were spent. We were glad to think at least that in all our publishings (some people consider I believe that we have overdone them), we had only touched in passing and in the most discreet manner on Miss Bordereau's connection. Oddly enough, even if we had had the material (and we often wondered what had become of it), it would have been the most difficult episode to handle.

The gondola stopped, the old palace was there; it was a house of the class which in Venice carries even in extreme dilapidation the dignified name. "How charming! It's gray and pink!" my companion exclaimed; and that is the most comprehensive description of it. It was not particularly old, only two or three centuries; and it had an air not so much of decay as of quiet discouragement, as if it had rather missed its career. But its wide front, with a stone balcony from end to end of the *piano nobile* or most important floor, was architectural enough, with the aid of various pilasters and arches; and the stucco with which in the intervals it had long ago been endued was rosy in the April afternoon. It overlooked a clean, melancholy, unfrequented canal, which had a narrow *riva* or convenient footway on either side. "I don't know why—there are no brick gables," said Mrs. Prest, "but this corner has seemed to me before more Dutch than Italian, more like Amsterdam, than like Venice. It's perversely clean, for reasons of its own; and though you can pass on foot scarcely any one ever thinks of doing so. It has the air of a Protestant Sunday. Perhaps, the people are afraid of the Misses Bordereau. I daresay they have the reputation of witches."

I forget what answer I made to this—I was given up to two other reflections. The first of these was that if the old lady lived in such a big, imposing house she could not be in any sort of misery and therefore would not be tempted by a chance to let a couple of rooms. I expressed this idea to Mrs. Prest, who gave me a very logical reply. "If she didn't live in a big house how could it be a question of her having rooms to spare? If she were not amply lodged herself you would lack ground to approach her. Besides, a big house here, and especially in this *quartier perdu*, proves nothing at all: it is perfectly compatible with a state of penury. Dilapidated old *palazzi*, if you will go out of the way for them, are to be had for five shillings a year. And as for the people who live in them—no, until you have explored Venice socially as much as I have you can form no idea of their domestic desolation. They live on nothing, for they have nothing to live on." The other idea that had come into my head was connected with a high blank wall which appeared to confine an expanse of ground on one side of the house. Blank I call it, but it was figured over with the patches that please a painter, repaired breaches, crumblings of plaster, extrusions of brick that had turned pink with time; and a few thin trees, with the poles of certain rickety trellises, were visible over the top. The place was a garden and apparently it belonged to the house. It suddenly occurred to me that if it did belong to the house I had my pretext.

I sat looking out on all this with Mrs. Prest (it was covered with the golden glow of Venice) from the shade of our *felze*,[4] and she asked me if I would go in then, while she waited for me, or come back another time. At first I could not decide—it was doubtless very weak of me. I wanted to still think I *might* get a footing, and I was afraid to meet failure, for it would leave me, as I remarked to my companion, without another arrow for my bow. "Why not another?" she inquired, as I sat there hesitating and thinking it over; and she wished to know why even now and before taking the trouble of becoming an inmate (which might be wretchedly uncomfortable after all, even if it succeeded), I had not the resource of simply offering them a sum of money down. In that way I might obtain the documents without bad nights.

"Dearest lady," I exclaimed, "excuse the impatience of my tone when I suggest that you must have forgotten the very fact (surely

4. the cabin of a gondola.

I communicated it to you) which pushed me to throw myself upon your ingenuity. The old woman won't have the documents spoken of; they are personal, delicate, intimate, and she hasn't modern notions, God bless her! If I should sound that note first I should certainly spoil the game. I can arrive at the papers only by putting her off her guard, and I can put her off her guard only by ingratiating diplomatic practices. Hypocrisy, duplicity are my only chance. I am sorry for it, but for Jeffrey Aspern's sake I would do worse still. First I must take tea with her; then tackle the main job." And I told over what had happened to John Cumnor when he wrote to her. No notice whatever had been taken of his first letter, and the second had been answered very sharply, in six lines, by the niece. "Miss Bordereau requested her to say that she could not imagine what he meant by troubling them. They had none of Mr. Aspern's papers, and if they had should never think of showing them to any one on any account whatever. She didn't know what he was talking about and begged he would let her alone." I certainly did not want to be met that way.

"Well," said Mrs. Prest, after a moment, provokingly, "perhaps after all they haven't any of his things. If they deny it flat how are you sure?"

"John Cumnor is sure, and it would take me long to tell you how his conviction, or his very strong presumption—strong enough to stand against the old lady's not unnatural fib—has built itself up. Besides, he makes much of the internal evidence of the niece's letter."

"The internal evidence?"

"Her calling him 'Mr. Aspern.'"

"I don't see what that proves."

"It proves familiarity, and familiarity implies the possession of mementoes, of relics. I can't tell you how that 'Mr.' touches me— how it bridges over the gulf of time and brings our hero near to me—nor what an edge it gives to my desire to see Juliana. You don't say 'Mr.' Shakespeare."

"Would I, any more, if I had a box full of his letters?"

"Yes, if he had been your lover and some one wanted them!" And I added that John Cumnor was so convinced, and so all the more convinced by Miss Bordereau's tone, that he would have come himself to Venice on the business were it not that for him there was the obstacle that it would be difficult to disprove his identity with the person who had written to them, which the old ladies would be sure to suspect in spite of dissimulation and a change of name. If they were to ask him point-blank if he were not their correspondent it would be too awkward for him to lie; whereas I was fortunately not tied in that way. I was a fresh hand and could say no without lying.

"But you will have to change your name," said Mrs. Prest. "Juliana lives out of the world as much as it is possible to live, but none the less she has probably heard of Mr. Aspern's editors; she perhaps possesses what you have published."

"I have thought of that," I returned; and I drew out of my pocket-book a visiting-card, neatly engraved with a name that was not my own.

"You are very extravagant; you might have written it," said my companion.

"This looks more genuine."

"Certainly, you are prepared to go far! But it will be awkward about your letters; they won't come to you in that mask."

"My banker will take them in, and I will go every day to fetch them. It will give me a little walk."

"Shall you only depend upon that?" asked Mrs. Prest. "Aren't you coming to see me?"

"Oh, you will have left Venice, for the hot months, long before there are any results. I am prepared to roast all summer—as well as hereafter, perhaps you'll say! Meanwhile, John Cumnor will bombard me with letters addressed, in my feigned name, to the care of the *padrona*."

"She will recognize his hand," my companion suggested.

"On the envelope he can disguise it."

"Well, you're a precious pair! Doesn't it occur to you that even if you are able to say you are not Mr. Cumnor in person they may still suspect you of being his emissary?"

"Certainly, and I see only one way to parry that."

"And what may that be?"

I hesitated a moment. "To make love to the niece."

"Ah," cried Mrs. Prest, "wait till you see her!"

II

"I must work the garden—I must work the garden," I said to my-self, five minutes later, as I waited, upstairs, in the long, dusky *sala*, where the bare scagliola[5] floor gleamed vaguely in a chink of the closed shutters. The place was impressive but it looked cold and cautious. Mrs. Prest had floated away, giving me a rendezvous at the end of half an hour by some neighbouring watersteps; and I had been let into the house, after pulling the rusty bell-wire, by a little red-headed, white-faced maid-servant, who was very young and not ugly and wore clicking pattens and a shawl in the fashion of a hood. She had not contented herself with opening the door from above by the usual arrangement of a creaking pulley, though she had looked down at me first from an upper window, dropping the inevitable challenge which in Italy precedes the hospitable act. As a general thing I was irritated by this survival of mediaeval manners, though as I liked the old I suppose I ought to have liked it; but I was so determined to be genial that I took my false card out of my pocket

5. plaster of Paris.

and held it up to her, smiling as if it were a magic token. It had the effect of one indeed, for it brought her, as I say, all the way down. I begged her to hand it to her mistress, having first written on it in Italian the words, "Could you very kindly see a gentleman, an American, for a moment?" The little maid was not hostile, and I reflected that even that was perhaps something gained. She coloured, she smiled and looked both frightened and pleased. I could see that my arrival was a great affair, that visits were rare in that house, and that she was a person who would have liked a sociable place. When she pushed forward the heavy door behind me I felt that I had a foot in the citadel. She pattered across the damp, stony lower hall and I followed her up the high staircase—stonier still, as it seemed—without an invitation. I think she had meant I should wait for her below, but such was not my idea, and I took up my station in the *sala*. She flitted, at the far end of it, into impenetrable regions, and I looked at the place with my heart beating as I had known it to do in the dentist's parlour. It was gloomy and stately, but it owed its character almost entirely to its noble shape and to the fine architectural doors—as high as the doors of houses—which, leading into the various rooms, repeated themselves on either side at intervals. They were surmounted with old faded painted escutcheons, and here and there, in the spaces between them, brown pictures, which I perceived to be bad, in battered frames, were suspended. With the exception of several straw-bottomed chairs with their backs to the wall, the grand obscure vista contained nothing else to minister to effect. It was evidently never used save as a passage, and little even as that. I may add that by the time the door opened again through which the maid-servant had escaped, my eyes had grown used to the want of light.

I had not meant by my private ejaculation that I must myself cultivate the soil of the tangled enclosure which lay beneath the windows, but the lady who came toward me from the distance over the hard, shining floor might have supposed as much from the way in which, as I went rapidly to meet her, I exclaimed, taking care to speak Italian: "The garden, the garden—do me the pleasure to tell me if it's yours!"

She stopped short, looking at me with wonder; and then, "Nothing here is mine," she answered in English, coldly and sadly.

"Oh, you are English; how delightful!" I remarked, ingenuously. "But surely the garden belongs to the house?"

"Yes, but the house doesn't belong to me." She was a long, lean, pale person, habited apparently in a dull-coloured dressing-gown, and she spoke with a kind of mild literalness. She did not ask me to sit down, any more than years before (if she were the niece) she had asked Mrs. Prest, and we stood face to face in the empty pompous hall.

"Well then, would you kindly tell me to whom I must address

myself? I'm afraid you'll think me odiously intrusive, but you know I *must* have a garden—upon my honour I must!"

Her face was not young, but it was simple; it was not fresh, but it was mild. She had large eyes which were not bright, and a great deal of hair which was not "dressed," and long fine hands which were—possibly—not clean. She clasped these members almost convulsively as, with a confused, alarmed look, she broke out, "Oh, don't take it away from us; we like it ourselves!"

"You have the use of it then?"

"Oh yes. If it wasn't for that!" And she gave a shy, melancholy smile.

"Isn't it a luxury, precisely? That's why, intending to be in Venice some weeks possibly all summer, and having some literary work, some reading and writing to do, so that I must be quiet, and yet if possible a great deal in the open air—that's why I have felt that a garden is really indispensable. I appeal to your own experience," I went on, smiling. "Now can't I look at yours?"

"I don't know, I don't understand," the poor woman murmured, planted there and letting her embarrassed eyes wander all over my strangeness.

"I mean only from one of those windows—such grand ones as you have here—if you will let me open the shutters." And I walked toward the back of the house. When I had advanced half-way I stopped and waited, as if I took it for granted she would accompany me. I had been of necessity very abrupt, but I strove at the same time to give her the impression of extreme courtesy. "I have been looking at furnished rooms all over the place, and it seems impossible to find any with a garden attached. Naturally in a place like Venice gardens are rare. It's absurd if you like, for a man, but I can't live without flowers."

"There are none to speak of down there." She came nearer to me, as if, though she mistrusted me, I had drawn her by an invisible thread. I went on again, and she continued as she followed me: "We have a few, but they are very common. It costs too much to cultivate them; one has to have a man."

"Why shouldn't I be the man?" I asked. "I'll work without wages; or rather I'll put in a gardener. You shall have the sweetest flowers in Venice."

She protested at this, with a queer little sigh which might also have been a gush of rapture at the picture I presented. Then she observed, "We don't know you—we don't know you."

"You know me as much as I know you; that is, much more, because you know my name. And if you are English I am almost a countryman."

"We are not English," said my companion, watching me helplessly while I threw open the shutters of one of the divisions of the wide high window.

"You speak the language so beautifully: might I ask what you **are?**" Seen from above the garden was certainly shabby; but I perceived at a glance that it had great capabilities. She made no rejoinder, she was so lost in staring at me, and I exclaimed, "You don't mean to say you are also by chance American?"

"I don't know; we used to be."

"Used to be? Surely you haven't changed?"

"It's so many years ago—we are nothing."

"So many years that you have been living here? Well, I don't wonder at that; it's a grand old house. I suppose you all use the garden," I went on, "but I assure you I shouldn't be in your way. I would be very quiet and stay in one corner."

"We all use it?" she repeated after me, vaguely, not coming close to the window, but looking at my shoes. She appeared to think me capable of throwing her out.

"I mean all your family, as many as you are."

"There is only one other; she is very old—she never goes down."

"Only one other, in all this great house!" I feigned to be not only amazed but almost scandalised. "Dear lady, you must have space then to spare!"

"To spare?" she repeated, in the same dazed way.

"Why, you surely don't live (two quiet women—I see *you* are quiet, at any rate) in fifty rooms!" Then with a burst of hope and cheer I demanded: "Couldn't you let me two or three? That would set me up!"

I had now struck the note that translated my purpose and I need not reproduce the whole of the tune I played. I ended by making my interlocutress believe that I was an honourable person, though of course I did not even attempt to persuade her that I was not an eccentric one. I repeated that I had studies to pursue; that I wanted quiet; that I delighted in a garden and had vainly sought one up and down the city; that I would undertake that before another month was over the dear old house should be smothered in flowers. I think it was the flowers that won my suit, for I afterwards found that Miss Tita (for such the name of this high tremulous spinster proved somewhat incongruously to be) had an insatiable appetite for them. When I speak of my suit as won I mean that before I left her she had promised that she would refer the question to her aunt. I inquired who her aunt might be and she answered, "Why, Miss Bordereau!" with an air of surprise, as if I might have been expected to know. There were contradictions like this in Tita Bordereau which, as I observed later, contributed to make her an odd and affecting person. It was the study of the two ladies to live so that the world should not touch them, and yet they had never altogether accepted the idea that it never heard of them. In Tita at any rate a grateful susceptibility to human contact had not died out, and contact of a limited order there would be if I should come to live in the house.

"We have never done anything of the sort; we have never had a lodger or any kind of inmate." So much as this she made a point of saying to me. "We are very poor, we live very badly. The rooms are very bare—that you might take; they have nothing in them. I don't know how you would sleep, how you would eat."

"With your permission, I could easily put in a bed and a few tables and chairs. *C'est la moindre des choses*[6] and the affair of an hour or two. I know a little man from whom I can hire what I should want for a few months, for a trifle, and my gondolier can bring the things round in his boat. Of course in this great house you must have a second kitchen, and my servant, who is a wonderfully handy fellow" (this personage was an evocation of the moment), "can easily cook me a chop there. My tastes and habits are of the simplest; I live on flowers!" And then I ventured to add that if they were very poor it was all the more reason they should let their rooms. They were bad economists—I had never heard of such a waste of material.

I saw in a moment that the good lady had never before been spoken to in that way, with a kind of humorous firmness which did not exclude sympathy but was on the contrary founded on it. She might easily have told me that my sympathy was impertinent, but this by good fortune did not occur to her. I left her with the understanding that she would consider the matter with her aunt and that I might come back the next day for their decision.

"The aunt will refuse; she will think the whole proceeding very *louche!*"[7] Mrs. Prest declared shortly after this, when I had resumed my place in her gondola. She had put the idea into my head and now (so little are women to be counted on) she appeared to take a despondent view of it. Her pessimism provoked me and I pretended to have the best hopes; I went so far as to say that I had a distinct presentiment that I should succeed. Upon this Mrs. Prest broke out, "Oh, I see what's in your head! You fancy you have made such an impression in a quarter of an hour that she is dying for you to come and can be depended upon to bring the old one round. If you do get in you'll count it as a triumph."

I did count it as a triumph, but only for the editor (in the last analysis), not for the man, who had not the tradition of personal conquest. When I went back on the morrow the little maid-servant conducted me straight through the long *sala* (it opened there as before in perfect perspective and was lighter now, which I thought a good omen) into the apartment from which the recipient of my former visit had emerged on that occasion. It was a large shabby parlour, with a fine old painted ceiling and a strange figure sitting alone at one of the windows. They come back to me now almost with the palpitation they caused, the successive feelings that ac-

6. "That's the least thing."   7. "shady, suspicious."

companied my consciousness that as the door of the room closed
behind me I was really face to face with the Juliana of some of
Aspern's most exquisite and most renowned lyrics. I grew used to
her afterwards, though never completely; but as she sat there before
me my heart beat as fast as if the miracle of resurrection had taken
place for my benefit. Her presence seemed somehow to contain his,
and I felt nearer to him at that first moment of seeing her than I
ever had been before or ever have been since. Yes, I remember my
emotions in their order, even including a curious little tremor that
took me when I saw that the niece was not there. With her, the
day before, I had become sufficiently familiar, but it almost exceeded
my courage (much as I had longed for the event) to be left alone
with such a terrible relic as the aunt. She was too strange, too literally
resurgent. Then came a check, with the perception that we were
not really face to face, inasmuch as she had over her eyes a horrible
green shade which, for her, served almost as a mask. I believed for
the instant that she had put it on expressly, so that from underneath it she might scrutinise me without being scrutinised herself.
At the same time it increased the presumption that there was a
ghastly death's-head lurking behind it. The divine Juliana as a grinning skull—the vision hung there until it passed. Then it came to
me that she was tremendously old—so old that death might take
her at any moment, before I had time to get what I wanted from
her. The next thought was a correction to that; it lighted up the
situation. She would die next week, she would die tomorrow—
then I could seize her papers. Meanwhile she sat there neither moving nor speaking. She was very small, and shrunken, bent forward,
with her hands in her lap. She was dressed in black and her head
was wrapped in a piece of old black lace which showed no hair.

My emotion keeping me silent she spoke first, and the remark
she made was exactly the most unexpected.

III

"Our house is very far from the centre, but the little canal is very
comme il faut."

"It's the sweetest corner of Venice and I can imagine nothing
more charming," I hastened to reply. The old lady's voice was very
thin and weak, but it had an agreeable, cultivated murmur and there
was wonder in the thought that that individual note had been in
Jeffrey Aspern's ear.

"Please to sit down there. I hear very well," she said quietly, as
if perhaps I had been shouting at her; and the chair she pointed to
was at a certain distance. I took possession of it, telling her that I
was perfectly aware that I had intruded, that I had not been properly
introduced and could only throw myself upon her indulgence. Perhaps the other lady, the one I had had the honour of seeing the
day before, would have explained to her about the garden. That was

literally what had given me courage to take a step so unconventional.
I had fallen in love at sight with the whole place (she herself
probably was so used to it that she did not know the impression
it was capable of making on a stranger), and I had felt it was really
a case to risk something. Was her own kindness in receiving me a
sign that I was not wholly out in my calculation? It would render
me extremely happy to think so. I could give her my word of
honour that I was a most respectable, inoffensive person and that as
an inmate they would be barely conscious of my existence. I would
conform to any regulations, any restrictions if they would only let
me enjoy the garden. Moreover I should be delighted to give her
references, guarantees; they would be of the very best, both in
Venice and in England as well as in America.

She listened to me in perfect stillness and I felt that she was
looking at me with great attention, though I could see only the lower
part of her bleached and shrivelled face. Independently of the re-
fining process of old age it had a delicacy which once must have been
great. She had been very fair, she had had a wonderful complexion.
She was silent a little after I had ceased speaking; then she inquired,
"If you are so fond of a garden why don't you go to *terra firma*,
where there are so many far better than this?"

"Oh, it's the combination!" I answered, smiling; and then, with
rather a flight of fancy, "It's the idea of a garden in the middle of
the sea."

"It's not in the middle of the sea; you can't see the water."

I stared a moment, wondering whether she wished to convict me
of fraud. "Can't see the water? Why, dear madam, I can come up
to the very gate in my boat."

She appeared inconsequent, for she said vaguely in reply to this,
"Yes, if you have got a boat. I haven't any; it's many years since I
have been in one of the gondolas." She uttered these words as if
the gondolas were a curious far-away craft which she knew only by
hearsay.

"Let me assure you of the pleasure with which I would put mine
at your service!" I exclaimed. I had scarcely said this however before
I became aware that the speech was in questionable taste and might
also do me the injury of making me appear too eager, too possessed
of a hidden motive. But the old woman remained impenetrable and
her attitude bothered me by suggesting that she had a fuller vision
of me than I had of her. She gave me no thanks for my somewhat
extravagant offer but remarked that the lady I had seen the day
before was her niece; she would presently come in. She had asked
her to stay away a little on purpose, because she herself wished to
see me at first alone. She relapsed into silence and I asked myself
why she had judged this necessary and what was coming yet; also
whether I might venture on some judicious remark in praise of her

companion. I went so far as to say that I should be delighted to see her again: she had been so very courteous to me, considering how odd she must have thought me—a declaration which drew from Miss Bordereau another of her whimsical speeches.

"She has very good manners; I bred her up myself!" I was on the point of saying that that accounted for the easy grace of the niece, but I arrested myself in time, and the next moment the old woman went on: "I don't care who you may be—I don't want to know; it signifies very little to-day." This had all the air of being a formula of dismissal, as if her next words would be that I might take myself off now that she had had the amusement of looking on the face of such a monster of indiscretion. Therefore I was all the more surprised when she added, with her soft, venerable quaver, "You may have as many rooms as you like—if you will pay a good deal of money."

I hesitated but for a single instant, long enough to ask myself what she meant in particular by this condition. First it struck me that she must have really a large sum in her mind; then I reasoned quickly that her idea of a large sum would probably not correspond to my own. My deliberation, I think, was not so visible as to diminish the promptitude with which I replied, "I will pay with pleasure and of course in advance whatever you may think it proper to ask me."

"Well then, a thousand francs a month," she rejoined instantly, while her baffling green shade continued to cover her attitude.

The figure, as they say, was startling and my logic had been at fault. The sum she had mentioned was, by the Venetian measure of such matters, exceedingly large; there was many an old palace in an out-of-the-way corner that I might on such terms have enjoyed by the year. But so far as my small means allowed I was prepared to spend money, and my decision was quickly taken. I would pay her with a smiling face what she asked, but in that case I would give myself the compensation of extracting the papers from her for nothing. Moreover if she had asked five times as much I should have risen to the occasion; so odious would it have appeared to me to stand chaffering with Aspern's Juliana. It was queer enough to have a question of money with her at all. I assured her that her views perfectly met my own and that on the morrow I should have the pleasure of putting three months' rent into her hand. She received this announcement with serenity and with no apparent sense that after all it would be becoming of her to say that I ought to see the rooms first. This did not occur to her and indeed her serenity was mainly what I wanted. Our little bargain was just concluded when the door opened and the younger lady appeared on the threshold. As soon as Miss Bordereau saw her niece she cried out almost gaily, "He will give three thousand—three thousand to-morrow!"

Miss Tita stood still, with her patient eyes turning from one of us to the other; then she inquired, scarcely above her breath, "Do you mean francs?"

"Did you mean francs or dollars?" the old woman asked of me at this.

"I think francs were what you said," I answered, smiling.

"That is very good," said Miss Tita, as if she had become conscious that her own question might have looked over-reaching.

"What do *you* know? You are ignorant," Miss Bordereau remarked; not with acerbity but with a strange, soft coldness.

"Yes, of money—certainly of money!" Miss Tita hastened to exclaim.

"I am sure you have your own branches of knowledge," I took the liberty of saying, genially. There was something painful to me, somehow, in the turn the conversation had taken, in the discussion of the rent.

"She had a very good education when she was young. I looked into that myself," said Miss Bordereau. Then she added, "But she has learned nothing since."

"I have always been with you," Miss Tita rejoined very mildly, and evidently with no intention of making an epigram.

"Yes, but for that!" her aunt declared, with more satirical force. She evidently meant that but for this her niece would never have got on at all; the point of the observation however being lost on Miss Tita, though she blushed at hearing her history revealed to a stranger. Miss Bordereau went on, addressing herself to me: "And what time will you come to-morrow with the money?"

"The sooner the better. If it suits you I will come at noon."

"I am always here but I have my hours," said the old woman, as if her convenience were not to be taken for granted.

"You mean the times when you receive?"

"I never receive. But I will see you at noon, when you come with the money."

"Very good, I shall be punctual;" and I added, "May I shake hands with you, on our contract?" I thought there ought to be some little form, it would make me really feel easier, for I foresaw that there would be no other. Besides, though Miss Bordereau could not to-day be called personally attractive and there was something even in her wasted antiquity that bade one stand at one's distance, I felt an irresistible desire to hold in my own for a moment the hand that Jeffrey Aspern had pressed.

For a minute she made no answer and I saw that my proposal failed to meet with her approbation. She indulged in no movement of withdrawal, which I half expected; she only said coldly, "I belong to a time when that was not the custom."

I felt rather snubbed but I exclaimed good-humouredly to Miss

Tita, "Oh, you will do as well!" I shook hands with her while she replied, with a small flutter, "Yes, yes, to show it's all arranged!"

"Shall you bring the money in gold?" Miss Bordereau demanded, as I was turning to the door.

I looked at her a moment. "Aren't you a little afraid, after all, of keeping such a sum as that in the house?" It was not that I was annoyed at her avidity but I was really struck with the disparity between such a treasure and such scanty means of guarding it.

"Whom should I be afraid of if I am not afraid of you?" she asked with her shrunken grimness.

"Ah well," said I, laughing, "I shall be in point of fact a protector and I will bring gold if you prefer."

"Thank you," the old woman returned with dignity and with an inclination of her head which evidently signified that I might depart. I passed out of the room, reflecting that it would not be easy to circumvent her. As I stood in the *sala* again I saw that Miss Tita had followed me and I supposed that as her aunt had neglected to suggest that I should take a look at my quarters it was her purpose to repair the omission. But she made no such suggestion; she only stood there with a dim, though not a languid smile, and with an effect of irresponsible, incompetent youth which was almost comically at variance with the faded facts of her person. She was not infirm, like her aunt, but she struck me as still more helpless, because her inefficiency was spiritual, which was not the case with Miss Bordereau's. I waited to see if she would offer to show me the rest of the house, but I did not precipitate the question, inasmuch as my plan was from this moment to spend as much of my time as possible in her society. I only observed at the end of a minute:

"I have had better fortune than I hoped. It was very kind of her to see me. Perhaps you said a good word for me."

"It was the idea of the money," said Miss Tita.

"And did you suggest that?"

"I told her that you would perhaps give a good deal."

"What made you think that?"

"I told her I thought you were rich."

"And what put that idea into your head?"

"I don't know; the way you talked."

"Dear me, I must talk differently now," I declared. "I'm sorry to say it's not the case."

"Well," said Miss Tita, "I think that in Venice the *forestieri*,[8] in general, often give a great deal for something that after all isn't much." She appeared to make this remark with a comforting intention, to wish to remind me that if I had been extravagant I was not really foolishly singular. We walked together along the *sala*, and as I took its magnificent measure I said to her that I was afraid it would

8. "foreigners."

not form a part of my *quartiere*. Were my rooms by chance to be among those that opened into it? "Not if you go above, on the second floor," she answered with a little startled air, as if she had rather taken for granted I would know my proper place.

"And I infer that that's where your aunt would like me to be."

"She said your apartments ought to be very distinct."

"That certainly would be best." And I listened with respect while she told me that up above I was free to take whatever I liked; that there was another staircase, but only from the floor in which we stood, and that to pass from it to the garden-story or to come up to my lodging I should have in effect to cross the great hall. This was an immense point gained; I foresaw that it would constitute my whole leverage in my relations with the two ladies. When I asked Miss Tita how I was to manage at present to find my way up she replied with an access of that sociable shyness which constantly marked her manner.

"Perhaps you can't. I don't see—unless I should go with you." She evidently had not thought of this before.

We ascended to the upper floor and visited a long succession of empty rooms. The best of them looked over the garden; some of the others had a view of the blue lagoon, above the opposite rough-tiled housetops. They were all dusty and even a little disfigured with long neglect, but I saw that by spending a few hundred francs I should be able to convert three or four of them into a convenient habitation. My experiment was turning out costly, yet now that I had all but taken possession I ceased to allow this to trouble me. I mentioned to my companion a few of the things that I should put in, but she replied rather more precipitately than usual that I might do exactly what I liked; she seemed to wish to notify me that the Misses Bordereau would take no overt interest in my proceedings. I guessed that her aunt had instructed her to adopt this tone, and I may as well say now that I came afterwards to distinguish perfectly (as I believed) between the speeches she made on her own responsibility and those the old lady imposed upon her. She took no notice of the unswept condition of the rooms and indulged in no explanations nor apologies. I said to myself that this was a sign that Juliana and her niece (disenchanting idea!) were untidy persons, with a low Italian standard; but I afterwards recognized that a lodger who had forced an entrance had no *locus standi* as a critic. We looked out of a good many windows, for there was nothing within the rooms to look at, and still I wanted to linger. I asked her what several different objects in the prospect might be, but in no case did she appear to know. She was evidently not familiar with the view—it was if she had not looked at it for years—and I presently saw that she was too preoccupied with something else to pretend to care for it. Suddenly she said—the remark was not suggested:

"I don't know whether it will make any difference to you, but the money is for me."

"The money?"

"The money you are going to bring."

"Why, you'll make me wish to stay here two or three years." I spoke as benevolently as possible, though it had begun to act on my nerves that with these women so associated with Aspern the pecuniary question should constantly come back.

"That would be very good for me," she replied, smiling.

"You put me on my honour!"

She looked as if she failed to understand this, but went on: "She wants me to have more. She thinks she is going to die."

"Ah, not soon, I hope!" I exclaimed, with genuine feeling. I had perfectly considered the possibility that she would destroy her papers on the day she should feel her end really approach. I believed that she would cling to them till then and I think I had an idea that she read Aspern's letters over every night or at least pressed them to her withered lips. I would have given a good deal to have a glimpse of the latter spectacle. I asked Miss Tita if the old lady were seriously ill and she replied that she was only very tired—she had lived so very, very long. That was what she said herself—she wanted to die for a change. Besides, all her friends were dead long ago; either they ought to have remained or she ought to have gone. That was another thing her aunt often said—she was not at all content.

"But people don't die when they like, do they?" Miss Tita inquired. I took the liberty of asking why, if there was actually enough money to maintain both of them, there would not be more than enough in case of her being left alone. She considered this difficult problem a moment and then she said, "Oh, well, you know, she takes care of me. She thinks that when I'm alone I shall be a great fool, I shall not know how to manage."

"I should have supposed rather that you took care of her. I'm afraid she is very proud."

"Why, have you discovered that already?" Miss Tita cried, with the glimmer of an illumination in her face.

"I was shut up with her there for a considerable time, and she struck me, she interested me extremely. It didn't take me long to make my discovery. She won't have much to say to me while I'm here."

"No, I don't think she will," my companion averred.

"Do you suppose she has some suspicion of me?"

Miss Tita's honest eyes gave me no sign that I had touched a mark. "I shouldn't think so—letting you in after all so easily."

"Oh, so easily! she has covered her risk. But where is it that one could take an advantage of her?"

"I oughtn't to tell you if I knew, ought I?" And Miss Tita added, before I had time to reply to this, smiling dolefully, "Do you think we have any weak points?"

"That's exactly what I'm asking. You would only have to mention them for me to respect them religiously."

She looked at me, at this, with that air of timid but candid and even gratified curiosity with which she had confronted me from the first; and then she said, "There is nothing to tell. We are terribly quiet. I don't know how the days pass. We have no life."

"I wish I might think that I should bring you a little."

"Oh, we know what we want," she went on. "It's all right."

There were various things I desired to ask her: how in the world they did live; whether they had any friends or visitors, any relations in America or in other countries. But I judged such an inquiry would be premature; I must leave it to a later chance. "Well, don't *you* be proud," I contented myself with saying. "Don't hide from me altogether."

"Oh, I must stay with my aunt," she returned, without looking at me. And at the same moment, abruptly, without any ceremony of parting, she quitted me and disappeared, leaving me to make my own way downstairs. I remained a while longer, wandering about the bright desert (the sun was pouring in) of the old house, thinking the situation over on the spot. Not even the pattering little *serva* came to look after me and I reflected that after all this treatment showed confidence.

IV

Perhaps it did, but all the same, six weeks later, towards the middle of June, the moment when Mrs. Prest undertook her annual migration, I had made no measurable advance. I was obliged to confess to her that I had no results to speak of. My first step had been unexpectedly rapid, but there was no appearance that it would be followed by a second. I was a thousand miles from taking tea with my hostesses—that privilege of which, as I reminded Mrs. Prest, we both had had a vision. She reproached me with wanting boldness and I answered that even to be bold you must have an opportunity: you may push on through a breach but you can't batter down a dead wall. She answered that the breach I had already made was big enough to admit an army and accused me of wasting precious hours in whimpering in her salon when I ought to have been carrying on the struggle in the field. It is true that I went to see her very often, on the theory that it would console me (I freely expressed my discouragement) for my want of success on my own premises. But I began to perceive that it did not console me to be perpetually chaffed for my scruples, especially when I was really so vigilant; and I was rather glad when my derisive friend closed her house for the summer. She had expected to gather amusement from the drama of my intercourse with the Misses Bordereau and she was disappointed that the intercourse, and consequently the drama, had not come off. "They'll lead you on to your ruin," she said before she left Venice. "They'll get all your money without showing you a scrap." I think I settled down to my business with more concentration after she had gone away.

It was a fact that up to that time I had not, save on a single brief occasion, had even a moment's contact with my queer hostesses. The exception had occurred when I carried them according to my promise the terrible three thousand francs. Then I found Miss Tita waiting for me in the hall, and she took the money from my hand so that I did not see her aunt. The old lady had promised to receive me, but she apparently thought nothing of breaking that vow. The money was contained in a bag of chamois leather, of respectable dimensions, which my banker had given me, and Miss Tita had to make a big fist to receive it. This she did with extreme solemnity, though I tried to treat the affair a little as a joke. It was in no jocular strain, yet it was with simplicity, that she inquired, weighing the money in her two palms: "Don't you think it's too much?" To which I replied that that would depend upon the amount of pleasure I should get for it. Hereupon she turned away from me quickly, as she had done the day before, murmuring on a tone different from any she had used hitherto: "Oh, pleasure, pleasure—there's no pleasure in this house!"

After this, for a long time, I never saw her, and I wondered that the common chances of the day should not have helped us to meet. It could only be evident that she was immensely on her guard against them; and in addition to this the house was so big that for each other we were lost in it. I used to look out for her hopefully as I crossed the *sala* in my comings and goings, but I was not rewarded with a glimpse of the tail of her dress. It was as if she never peeped out of her aunt's apartment. I used to wonder what she did there week after week and year after year. I had never encountered such a violent *parti pris* of seclusion; it was more than keeping quiet—it was like hunted creatures feigning death. The two ladies appeared to have no visitors whatever and no sort of contact with the world. I judged at least that people could not have come to the house and that Miss Tita could not have gone out without my having some observation of it. I did what I disliked myself for doing (reflecting that it was only once in a way): I questioned my servant about their habits and let him divine that I should be interested in any information he could pick up. But he picked up amazingly little for a knowing Venetian: it must be added that where there is a perpetual fast there are very few crumbs on the floor. His cleverness in other ways was sufficient, if it was not quite all that I had attributed to him on the occasion of my first interview with Miss Tita. He had helped my gondolier to bring me round a boat-load of furniture; and when these articles had been carried to the top of the palace and distributed according to our associated wisdom he organised my household with such promptitude as was consistent with the fact that it was composed exclusively of himself. He made me in short as comfortable as I could be with my indifferent prospects. I should have been glad if he had fallen in love with Miss Bordereau's maid or, failing this, had taken her in aversion; either event might have brought about some kind of catastrophe and a catastrophe might have led to some parley. It was my idea that she would have been sociable, and I myself on various occasions saw her flit to and fro on domestic errands, so that I was sure she was accessible. But I tasted of no gossip from that fountain, and I afterwards learned that Pasquale's affections were fixed upon an object that made him heedless of other women. This was a young lady with a powdered face, a yellow cotton gown and much leisure, who used often to come to see him. She practised, at her convenience, the art of a stringer of beads (these ornaments are made in Venice, in profusion; she had her pocket full of them and I used to find them on the floor of my apartment), and kept an eye on the maiden in the house. It was not for me of course to make the domestics tattle, and I never said a word to Miss Bordereau's cook.

It seemed to me a proof of the old lady's determination to have nothing to do with me that she should never have sent me a receipt for my three months' rent. For some days I looked out for it and then, when I had given it up, I wasted a good deal of time in wondering what her reason had been for neglecting so indispensable and familiar a form. At first I was tempted to send her a reminder, after which I relinquished the idea (against my judgment as to what was right in the particular case), on the general ground of wishing to keep quiet. If Miss Bordereau suspected me of ulterior aims she would suspect me less if I should be businesslike, and yet I consented not to be so. It was possible she intended her omission as an impertinence, a visible irony, to show how she could overreach people who attempted to overreach her. On that hypothesis it was well to let her see that one did not notice her little tricks. The real reading of the matter, I afterwards perceived, was simply the poor old woman's desire to emphasise the fact that I was in the enjoyment of a favour as rigidly limited as it had been liberally bestowed. She had given me part of her house and now she would not give me even a morsel of paper with her name on it. Let me say that even at first this did not make me too miserable, for the whole episode was essentially delightful to me. I foresaw that I should have a summer after my own literary heart, and the sense of holding my opportunity was much greater than the sense of losing it. There could be no Venetian business without patience, and since I adored the place I was much more in the spirit of it for having laid in a large provision. That spirit kept me perpetual company and seemed to look out at me from the revived immortal face—in which all his genius shone—of the great poet who was my prompter. I had invoked him and he had come; he hovered before me half the time; it was as if his bright ghost had returned to earth to tell me that he regarded the affair as his own no less than mine and that we should see it fraternally, cheerfully to a conclusion. It was as if he had said, "Poor dear, be easy with her; she has some natural prejudices; only give her time. Strange as it may appear to you she was very attractive in 1820. Meanwhile are we not in Venice together, and what better place is there for the meeting of dear friends? See how it glows with the advancing summer; how the sky and the sea and the rosy air and the marble of the palaces all shimmer and melt together." My eccentric private errand became a part of the general romance and the general glory—I felt even a mystic companionship, a moral fraternity with all those who in the past had been in the service of art. They had worked for beauty, for a devotion; and what else was I doing? That element was in everything that Jeffrey Aspern had written and I was only bringing it to the light.

I lingered in the *sala* when I went to and fro; I used to watch—as long as I thought decent—the door that led to Miss Bordereau's part of the house. A person observing me might have supposed I was trying to cast a spell upon it or attempting some odd experiment in hypnotism. But I was only praying it would open or thinking what treasure probably lurked behind it. I hold it singular, as I look back, that I should never have doubted for a moment that the sacred relics were there; never have failed to feel a certain joy at being under the same roof with them. After all they were under my hand—they had not escaped me yet; and they made my life continuous, in a fashion, with the illustrious life they had touched at the other end. I lost myself in this satisfaction to the point of assuming—in my quiet extravagance—that poor Miss Tita also went back, went back, as I used to phrase it. She did indeed, the gentle spinster, but not quite so far as Jeffrey Aspern, who was simple hearsay to her, quite as he was to me. Only she had lived for years with Juliana, she had seen and handled the papers and (even though she was stupid) some esoteric knowledge had rubbed off on her. That was what the old woman represented—esoteric knowledge; and this was the idea with which my editorial heart used to thrill. It literally beat faster often, of an evening, when I had been out, as I stopped with my candle in the re-echoing hall on my way up to bed. It was as if at such a moment as that, in the stillness, after the long contradiction of the day, Miss Bordereau's secrets were in the air, the wonder of her survival more palpable. These were the acute impressions. I had them in another form, with more of a certain sort of reciprocity, during the hours that

I sat in the garden looking up over the top of my book at the closed windows of my hostess. In these windows no sign of life ever appeared; it was as if, for fear of my catching a glimpse of them, the two ladies passed their days in the dark. But this only proved to me that they had something to conceal; which was what I had wished to demonstrate. Their motionless shutters became as expressive as eyes consciously closed, and I took comfort in thinking that at all events though invisible themselves they saw me between the lashes.

I made a point of spending as much time as possible in the garden, to justify the picture I had originally given of my horticultural passion. And I not only spent time, but (hang it! as I said) I spent money. As soon as I had got my rooms arranged and could give the proper thought to the matter I surveyed the place with a clever expert and made terms for having it put in order. I was sorry to do this, for personally I liked it better as it was, with its weeds and its wild, rough tangle, its sweet, characteristic Venetian shabbiness. I had to be consistent, to keep my promise that I would smother the house in flowers. Moreover I formed this graceful project that by flowers I would make my way—I would succeed by big nosegays. I would batter the old women with lilies—I would bombard their citadel with roses. Their door would have to yield to the pressure when a mountain of carnations should be piled up against it. The place in truth had been brutally neglected. The Venetian capacity for dawdling is of the largest, and for a good many days unlimited litter was all my gardener had to show for his ministrations. There was a great digging of holes and carting about of earth, and after a while I grew so impatient that I had thoughts of sending for my bouquets to the nearest stand. But I reflected that the ladies would see through the chinks of their shutters that they must have been bought and might make up their minds from this that I was a humbug. So I composed myself and finally, though the delay was long, perceived some appearances of bloom. This encouraged me and I waited serenely enough till they multiplied. Meanwhile the real summer days arrived and began to pass, and as I look back upon them they seem to me almost the happiest of my life. I took more and more care to be in the garden whenever it was not too hot. I had an arbour arranged and a low table and an armchair put into it; and I carried out books and portfolios (I had always some business of writing in hand), and worked and waited and mused and hoped, while the golden hours elapsed and the plants drank in the light and the inscrutable old palace turned pale and then, as the day waned, began to flush in it and my papers rustled in the wandering breeze of the Adriatic.

Considering how little satisfaction I got from it at first it is remarkable that I should not have grown more tired of wondering what mystic rites of ennui the Misses Bordereau celebrated in their darkened rooms; whether this had always been the tenor of their life and how in previous years they had escaped elbowing their neighbours. It was clear that they must have had other habits and other circumstances; that they must once have been young or at least middle-aged. There was no end to the questions it was possible to ask about them and no end to the answers it was not possible to frame. I had known many of my country-people in Europe and was familiar with the strange ways they were liable to take up there; but the Misses Bordereau formed altogether a new type of the American absentee. Indeed it was plain that the American name had ceased to have any application to them—I had seen this in the ten minutes I spent in the old woman's room. You could never have said whence they came, from the appearance of either of them; wherever it was they had long ago dropped the local accent and fashion. There was nothing in them that one recognised, and putting the question of speech aside they might have been Norwegians or Spaniards. Miss Bordereau, after all, had been in Europe nearly three-quarters of a century; it appeared by some verses addressed to her by Aspern on the occasion of his own second absence from America—verses of which Cumnor and I had after infinite conjecture established solidly enough the date—that she was even then, as a girl of twenty, on the foreign side of the sea. There was an implication in the poem (I hope not just for the phrase) that he had come back for her sake. We had no real light upon her circumstances at that moment, any more than we had upon her origin, which we believed to be of the sort usually spoken of as modest. Cumnor had a theory that she had been a governess in some family in which the poet visited and that, in consequence of her position, there was from the first something un-avowed, or rather something positively clandestine, in their relations. I on the other hand had hatched a little romance according to which she was the daughter of an artist, a painter or a sculptor, who had left the western world when the century was fresh, to study in the an-cient schools. It was essential to my hypothesis that this amiable man should have lost his wife, should have been poor and unsuccess-ful and should have had a second daughter, of a disposition quite different from Juliana's. It was also indispensable that he should have been accompanied to Europe by these young ladies and should have established himself there for the remainder of a struggling, saddened life. There was a further implication that Miss Bordereau had had in her youth a perverse and adventurous, albeit a generous and fas-cinating character, and that she had passed through some singular vicissitudes. By what passions had she been ravaged, by what suf-ferings had she been blanched, what store of memories had she laid away for the monotonous future?

I asked myself these things as I sat spinning theories about her in my arbour and the bees droned in the flowers. It was incontestable that, whether for right or for wrong, most readers of certain of

Aspern's poems (poems not as ambiguous as the sonnets—scarcely more divine, I think—of Shakespeare) had taken for granted that Juliana had not always adhered to the steep footway of renunciation. There hovered about her name a perfume of reckless passion, an intimation that she had not been exactly as the respectable young person in general. Was this a sign that her singer had betrayed her, had given her away, as we say nowadays, to posterity? Certain it is that it would have been difficult to put one's finger on the passage in which her fair fame suffered an imputation. Moreover was not any fame fair enough that was so sure of duration and was associated with works immortal through their beauty? It was a part of my idea that the young lady had had a foreign lover (and an unedifying tragical rupture) before her meeting with Jeffrey Aspern. She had lived with her father and sister in a queer old-fashioned, expatriated, artistic Bohemia, in the days when the æsthetic was only the academic and the painters who knew the best models for a *contadina* and *pifferaro*[9] wore peaked hats and long hair. It was a society less furnished than the coteries of to-day (in its ignorance of the wonderful chances, the opportunities of the early bird, with which its path was strewn), with tatters of old stuff and fragments of old crockery; so that Miss Bordereau appeared not to have picked up or have inherited many objects of importance. There was no enviable *bric-à-brac*, with its provoking legend of cheapness, in the room in which I had seen her. Such a fact as that suggested bareness, but none the less it worked happily into the sentimental interest I had always taken in the early movements of my countrymen as visitors to Europe. When Americans went abroad in 1820 there was something romantic, almost heroic in it, as compared with the perpetual ferryings of the present hour, when photography and other conveniences have annihilated surprise. Miss Bordereau sailed with her family on a tossing brig, in the days of long voyages and sharp differences; she had her emotions on the top of yellow diligences, passed the night at inns where she dreamed of travellers' tales, and was struck, on reaching the eternal city, with the elegance of Roman pearls and scarfs. There was something touching to me in all that and my imagination frequently went back to the period. If Miss Bordereau carried it there of course Jeffrey Aspern at other times had done so a great deal more. It was a much more important fact, if one were looking at his genius critically, that he had lived in the days before the general transfusion. It had happened to me to regret that he had known Europe at all; I should have liked to see what he would have written without that experience, by which he had incontestably been enriched. But as his fate had ordered otherwise I went with him—I tried to judge how the old world would have struck him. It was not only there, however, that I watched him; the relations he had entertained with

9. *contadina:* peasant woman; *pifferaro:* fife-player.

the new had even a livelier interest. His own country after all had had most of his life, and his muse, as they said at that time, was essentially American. That was originally what I had loved him for: that at a period when our native land was nude and crude and provincial, when the famous "atmosphere" it is supposed to lack was not even missed, when literature was lonely there and art and form almost impossible, he had found means to live and write like one of the first; to be free and general and not at all afraid; to feel, understand and express everything.

V

I was seldom at home in the evening, for when I attempted to occupy myself in my apartments the lamplight brought in a swarm of noxious insects, and it was too hot for closed windows. Accordingly I spent the late hours either on the water (the moonlight of Venice is famous), or in the splendid square which serves as a vast forecourt to the strange old basilica of Saint Mark. I sat in front of Florian's *café*, eating ices, listening to music, talking with acquaintances: the traveller will remember how the immense cluster of tables and little chairs stretches like a promontory into the smooth lake of the Piazza. The whole place, of a summer's evening, under the stars and with all the lamps, all the voices and light footsteps on marble (the only sounds of the arcades that enclose it), is like an open-air saloon dedicated to cooling drinks and to a still finer degustation—that of the exquisite impressions received during the day. When I did not prefer to keep mine to myself there was always a stray tourist, disencumbered of his Bädeker, to discuss them with, or some domesticated painter rejoicing in the return of the season of strong effects. The wonderful church, with its low domes and bristling embroideries, the mystery of its mosaic and sculpture, looked ghostly in the tempered gloom, and the sea-breeze passed between the twin columns of the Piazzetta,[10] the lintels of a door no longer guarded, as gently as if a rich curtain were swaying there. I used sometimes on these occasions to think of the Misses Bordereau and of the pity of their being shut up in apartments which in the Venetian July even Venetian vastness did not prevent from being stuffy. Their life seemed miles away from the life of the Piazza, and no doubt it was really too late to make the austere Juliana change her habits. But poor Miss Tita would have enjoyed one of Florian's ices, I was sure; sometimes I even had thoughts of carrying one home to her. Fortunately my patience bore fruit and I was not obliged to do anything so ridiculous.

One evening about the middle of July I came in earlier than usual

10. The center of Venice is the Square (Piazza) of Saint Mark surrounded on three sides by *palazzi* which are today lined with shops and coffee houses. On the east side is the basilica of San Marco; from there a smaller square (*piazzetta*) opens toward the Lagoon. Two large granite columns, one with the Lion of Saint Mark, the other with a statue of Saint Theodore, frame the view.

—I forget what chance had led to this—and instead of going up to my quarters made my way into the garden. The temperature was very high; it was such a night as one would gladly have spent in the open air and I was in no hurry to go to bed. I had floated home in my gondola, listening to the slow splash of the oar in the narrow dark canals, and now the only thought that solicited me was the vague reflection that it would be pleasant to recline at one's length in the fragrant darkness on a garden bench. The odour of the canal was doubtless at the bottom of that aspiration and the breath of the garden, as I entered it, gave consistency to my purpose. It was delicious—just such an air as must have trembled with Romeo's vows when he stood among the flowers and raised his arms to his mistress's balcony. I looked at the windows of the palace to see if by chance the example of Verona (Verona being not far off) had been followed; but everything was dim, as usual, and everything was still. Juliana, on summer nights in her youth, might have murmured down from open windows at Jeffrey Aspern, but Miss Tita was not a poet's mistress any more than I was a poet. This however did not prevent my gratification from being great as I became aware on reaching the end of the garden that Miss Tita was seated in my little bower. At first I only made out an indistinct figure, not in the least counting on such an overture from one of my hostesses; it even occurred to me that some sentimental maidservant had stolen in to keep a tryst with her sweetheart. I was going to turn away, not to frighten her, when the figure rose to its height and I recognised Miss Bordereau's niece. I must do myself the justice to say that I did not wish to frighten her either, and much as I had longed for some such accident I should have been capable of retreating. It was as if I had laid a trap for her by coming home earlier than usual and adding to that eccentricity by creeping into the garden. As she rose she spoke to me, and then I reflected that perhaps, secure in my almost inveterate absence, it was her nightly practice to take a lonely airing. There was no trap, in truth, because I had had no suspicion. At first I took for granted that the words she uttered expressed discomfiture at my arrival; but as she repeated them—I had not caught them clearly—I had the surprise of hearing her say, "Oh, dear, I'm so very glad you've come!" She and her aunt had in common the property of unexpected speeches. She came out of the arbour almost as if she were going to throw herself into my arms.

I hasten to add that she did nothing of the kind; she did not even shake hands with me. It was a gratification to her to see me and presently she told me why—because she was nervous when she was out-of-doors at night alone. The plants and bushes looked so strange in the dark, and there were all sorts of queer sounds—she could not tell what they were—like the noises of animals. She stood close to me, looking about her with an air of greater security but without any demonstration of interest in me as an individual. Then I guessed that nocturnal prowlings were not in the least her habit, and I was also reminded (I had been struck with the circumstance in talking with her before I took possession) that it was impossible to over-estimate her simplicity.

"You speak as if you were lost in the backwoods," I said, laughing. "How you manage to keep out of this charming place when you have only three steps to take to get into it, is more than I have yet been able to discover. You hide away mighty well so long as I am on the premises, I know; but I had a hope that you peeped out a little at other times. You and your poor aunt are worse off than Carmelite nuns in their cells. Should you mind telling me how you exist without air, without exercise, without any sort of human contact? I don't see how you carry on the common business of life."

She looked at me as if I were talking some strange tongue and her answer was so little of an answer that I was considerably irritated.

"We go to bed very early—earlier than you would believe." I was on the point of saying that this only deepened the mystery when she gave me some relief by adding, "Before you came we were not so private. But I never have been out at night."

"Never in these fragrant alleys, blooming here under your nose?"

"Ah," said Miss Tita, "they were never nice till now!" There was an unmistakable reference in this and a flattering comparison, so that it seemed to me I had gained a small advantage. As it would help me to follow it up to establish a sort of grievance I asked her why, since she thought my garden nice, she had never thanked me in any way for the flowers I had been sending up in such quantities for the previous three weeks. I had not been discouraged—there had been, as she would have observed, a daily armful; but I had been brought up in the common forms and a word of recognition now and then would have touched me in the right place.

"Why I didn't know they were for me!"

"They were for both of you. Why should I make a difference?"

Miss Tita reflected as if she might be thinking of a reason for that, but she failed to produce one. Instead of this she asked abruptly, "Why in the world do you want to know us?"

"I ought after all to make a difference," I replied. "That question is your aunt's; it isn't yours. You wouldn't ask it if you hadn't been put up to it."

"She didn't tell me to ask you," Miss Tita replied, without con-fusion; she was the oddest mixture of the shrinking and the direct.

"Well, she has often wondered about it herself and expressed her wonder to you. She has insisted on it, so that she has put the idea into your head that I am insufferably pushing. Upon my word I think I have been very discreet. And how completely your aunt must have lost every tradition of sociability, to see anything out of the way in the idea that respectable intelligent people, living as we do under the same roof, should occasionally exchange a remark! What could be more natural? We are of the same country and we have at least some of the same tastes, since, like you, I am intensely fond of Venice."

My interlocutress appeared incapable of grasping more than one clause in any proposition, and she declared quickly, eagerly, as if she were answering my whole speech: "I am not in the least fond of Venice. I should like to go far away!"

"Has she always kept you back so?" I went on, to show her that I could be as irrelevant as herself.

"She told me to come out to-night; she has told me very often," said Miss Tita. "It is I who wouldn't come. I don't like to leave her."

"Is she too weak, is she failing?" I demanded, with more emotion, I think, than I intended to show. I judged this by the way her eyes rested upon me in the darkness. It embarrassed me a little, and to turn the matter off I continued genially: "Do let us sit down together comfortably somewhere and you will tell me all about her."

Miss Tita made no resistance to this. We found a bench less secluded, less confidential, as it were, than the one in the arbour; and we were still sitting there when I heard midnight ring out from those clear bells of Venice which vibrate with a solemnity of their own over the lagoon and hold the air so much more than the chimes of other places. We were together more than an hour and our interview gave, as it struck me, a great lift to my undertaking. Miss Tita accepted the situation without a protest; she had avoided me for three months, yet now she treated me almost as if these three months had made me an old friend. If I had chosen I might have inferred from this that though she had avoided me she had given a good deal of consideration to doing so. She paid no attention to the flight of time—never worried at my keeping her so long away from her aunt. She talked freely, answering questions and asking them and not even taking advantage of certain longish pauses with which they inevitably alternated to say she thought she had better go in. It was almost as if she were waiting for something—something I might say to her—and intended to give me my opportunity. I was the more struck by this as she told me that her aunt had been less well for a good many days and in a way that was rather new. She was weaker; at moments it seemed as if she had no strength at all; yet more than ever before she wished to be left alone. That was why she had told her to come out—not even to remain in her own room, which was alongside; she said her niece irritated her, made her nervous. She sat still for hours together as if she were asleep; she had always done that, musing and dozing; but at such times formerly, she gave at intervals some small sign of life, of interest, liking her companion to be near her with her work. Miss Tita confided to me that at present her aunt was so motionless that she sometimes feared she was dead; moreover she took hardly any food—one couldn't see what she lived on. The great thing was that she still on most days got up; the serious job was to dress her, to wheel her out of her bedroom. She clung to as many of her old habits as possible and she had always, little company as they had received for years, made a point of sitting in the parlour.

I scarcely knew what to think of all this—of Miss Tita's sudden conversion to sociability and of the strange circumstance that the more the old lady appeared to decline toward her end the less she should desire to be looked after. The story did not hang together, and I even asked myself whether it were not a trap laid for me, the result of a design to make me show my hand. I could not have told why my companions (as they could only by courtesy be called) should have this purpose—why they should try to trip up so lucrative a lodger. At any rate I kept on my guard, so that Miss Tita should not have occasion again to ask me if I had an *arrière-pensée*.[11] Poor woman, before we parted for the night my mind was at rest as to *her* capacity for entertaining one.

She told me more about their affairs than I had hoped; there was no need to be prying, for it evidently drew her out simply to feel that I listened, that I cared. She ceased wondering why I cared, and at last, as she spoke of the brilliant life they had led years before, she almost chattered. It was Miss Tita who judged it brilliant; she said that when they first came to live in Venice, years and years before (I saw that her mind was essentially vague about dates and the order in which events had occurred), there was scarcely a week that they had not some visitor or did not make some delightful *passeggio* in the city. They had seen all the curiosities; had even been to the Lido[12] in a boat (she spoke as if I might think there was a way on foot); they had had a collation there, brought in three baskets and spread out on the grass. I asked her what people they had known and she said, Oh! very nice ones—the Cavaliere Bombicci and the Contessa Altemura, with whom they had had a great friendship. Also English people—the Churtons and the Goldies and Mrs. Stock-Stock, whom they had loved dearly; she was dead and gone, poor dear. That was the case with most of their pleasant circle (this expression was Miss Tita's own), though a few were left, which was a wonder considering how they had neglected them. She mentioned the names of two or three Venetian old women; of a certain doctor, very clever, who was so kind—he came as a friend, he had really given up practice; of the *avvocato* Pochintesta,[13] who wrote beautiful poems and had addressed one to her aunt. These

11. hidden motive, mental reservation.
12. the largest island, which shelters Venice from the open sea.
13. a grotesque name: "little in-the-head."

people came to see them without fail every year, usually at the *capo d'anno*,[14] and of old her aunt used to make them some little present— her aunt and she together: small things that she, Miss Tita, made herself, like paper lamp-shades or mats for the decanters of wine at dinner or those woollen things that in cold weather were worn on the wrists. The last few years there had not been many presents; she could not think what to make and her aunt had lost her interest and never suggested. But the people came all the same; if the Venetians liked you once they liked you for ever.

There was something affecting in the good faith of this sketch of former social glories; the picnic at the Lido had remained vivid through the ages and poor Miss Tita evidently was of the impression that she had had a brilliant youth. She had in fact had a glimpse of the Venetian world in its gossiping, home-keeping, parsimonious, professional walks; for I observed for the first time that she had acquired by contact something of the trick of the familiar, soft-sounding, almost infantile speech of the place. I judged that she had imbibed this invertebrate dialect, from the natural way the names of things and people—mostly purely local—rose to her lips. If she knew little of what they represented she knew still less of anything else. Her aunt had drawn in—her failing interest in the table-mats and lamp-shades was a sign of that—and she had not been able to mingle in society or to entertain it alone; so that the matter of her reminiscences struck one as an old world altogether. If she had not been so decent her references would have seemed to carry one back to the queer rococo Venice of Casanova.[15] I found myself falling into the error of thinking of her too as one of Jeffrey Aspern's contemporaries; this came from her having so little in common with my own. It was possible, I said to myself, that she had not even heard of him; it might very well be that Juliana had not cared to lift even for her the veil that covered the temple of her youth. In this case she perhaps would not know of the existence of the papers, and I welcomed that presumption—it made me feel more safe with her —until I remembered that we had believed the letter of disavowal received by Cumnor to be in the handwriting of the niece. If it had been dictated to her she had of course to know what it was about; yet after all the effect of it was to repudiate the idea of any connection with the poet. I held it probable at all events that Miss Tita had not read a word of his poetry. Moreover, if, with her companion, she had always escaped the interviewer there was little occasion for her having got it into her head that people were "after" the letters. People had not been after them, inasmuch as they had not heard of them; and Cumnor's fruitless feeler would have been

14. New Year. In Italy presents are or were exchanged on New Year's day rather than at Christmas.
15. Giovanni Jacopo Casanova (1725–

1798) was a Venetian adventurer whose *Memoirs* (in French, not published until 1826) established his reputation as a seducer of women.

a solitary accident.

When midnight sounded Miss Tita got up; but she stopped at the door of the house only after she had wandered two or three times with me round the garden. "When shall I see you again?" I asked, before she went in; to which she replied with promptness that she should like to come out the next night. She added however that she should not come—she was so far from doing everything she liked.

"You might do a few things that *I* like," I said with a sigh.

"Oh, you—I don't believe you!" she murmured, at this, looking at me with her simple solemnity.

"Why don't you believe me?"

"Because I don't understand you."

"That is just the sort of occasion to have faith." I could not say more, though I should have liked to, as I saw that I only mystified her; for I had no wish to have it on my conscience that I might pass for having made love to her. Nothing less should I have seemed to do had I continued to beg a lady to "believe in me" in an Italian garden on a mid-summer night. There was some merit in my scruples, for Miss Tita lingered and lingered: I perceived that she felt that she should not really soon come down again and wished therefore to protract the present. She insisted too on making the talk between us personal to ourselves; and altogether her behaviour was such as would have been possible only to a completely innocent woman.

"I shall like the flowers better now that I know they are also meant for me."

"How could you have doubted it? If you will tell me the kind you like best I will send a double lot of them."

"Oh, I like them all best!" Then she went on, familiarly: "Shall you study—shall you read and write—when you go up to your rooms?"

"I don't do that at night, at this season. The lamplight brings in the animals."

"You might have known that when you came."

"I did know it!"

"And in winter do you work at night?"

"I read a good deal, but I don't often write." She listened as if these details had a rare interest, and suddenly a temptation quite at variance with the prudence I had been teaching myself associated itself with her plain, mild face. Ah yes, she was safe and I could make her safer! It seemed to me from one moment to another that I could not wait longer—that I really must take a sounding. So I went on: "In general before I go to sleep—very often in bed (it's a bad habit, but I confess to it), I read some great poet. In nine cases out of ten it's a volume of Jeffrey Aspern."

I watched her well as I pronounced that name but I saw nothing wonderful. Why should I indeed—was not Jeffrey Aspern the property of the human race?

"Oh, we read him—we *have* read him," she quietly replied.

"He is my poet of poets—I know him almost by heart."

For an instant Miss Tita hesitated; then her sociability was too much for her.

"Oh, by heart—that's nothing!" she murmured, smiling. "My aunt used to know him—to know him"—she paused an instant and I wondered what she was going to say—"to know him as a visitor."

"As a visitor?" I repeated, staring.

"He used to call on her and take her out."

I continued to stare. "My dear lady, he died a hundred years ago!"

"Well," she said, mirthfully, "my aunt is a hundred and fifty."

"Mercy on us!" I exclaimed; "why didn't you tell me before? I should like so to ask her about him."

"She wouldn't care for that—she wouldn't tell you," Miss Tita replied.

"I don't care what she cares for! She must tell me—it's not a chance to be lost.'

"Oh, you should have come twenty years ago: then she still talked about him."

"And what did she say?" I asked, eagerly.

"I don't know—that he liked her immensely."

"And she—didn't she like him?"

"She said he was a god." Miss Tita gave me this information flatly, without expression; her tone might have made it a piece of trivial gossip. But it stirred me deeply as she dropped the words into the summer night; it seemed such a direct testimony.

"Fancy, fancy!" I murmured. And then, "Tell me this, please—has she got a portrait of him? They are distressingly rare."

"A portrait? I don't know," said Miss Tita; and now there was discomfiture in her face. "Well, good-night!" she added; and she turned into the house.

I accompanied her into the wide, dusky, stone-paved passage which on the ground floor corresponded with our grand *sala*. It opened at one end into the garden, at the other upon the canal, and was lighted now only by the small lamp that always left for me to take up as I went to bed. An extinguished candle which Miss Tita apparently had brought down with her stood on the same table with it. "Good-night, good-night!" I replied, keeping beside her as she went to get her light. "Surely you would know, shouldn't you, if she had one?"

"If she had what?" the poor lady asked, looking at me queerly over the flame of her candle.

"A portrait of the god. I don't know what I wouldn't give to see it."

"I don't know what she has got. She keeps her things locked up." And Miss Tita went away, toward the staircase, with the sense evidently that she had said too much.

I let her go—I wished not to frighten her—and I contented myself with remarking that Miss Bordereau would not have locked up such a glorious possession as that—a thing a person would be proud of and hang up in a prominent place on the parlour-wall. Therefore of course she had not any portrait. Miss Tita made no direct answer to this and candle in hand, with her back to me, ascended two or three stairs. Then she stopped short and turned round looking at me across the dusky space.

"Do you write—do you write?" There was a shake in her voice—she could scarcely bring out what she wanted to ask.

"Do I write? Oh, don't speak of my writing on the same day with Aspern's!"

"Do you write about *him*—do you pry into his life?"

"Ah, that's your aunt's question; it can't be yours!" I said, in a tone of slightly wounded sensibility.

"All the more reason then that you should answer it. Do you, please?"

I thought I had allowed for the falsehoods I should have to tell; but I found that in fact when it came to the point I had not. Besides, now that I had an opening there was a kind of relief in being frank. Lastly (it was perhaps fanciful, even fatuous), I guessed that Miss Tita personally would not in the last resort be less my friend. So after a moment's hesitation I answered, "Yes, I have written about him and I am looking for more material. In heaven's name have you got any?"

"*Santo Dio!*" she exclaimed, without heeding my question; and she hurried upstairs and out of sight. I might count upon her in the last resort, but for the present she was visibly alarmed. The proof of it was that she began to hide again, so that for a fortnight I never beheld her. I found my patience ebbing and after four or five days of this I told the gardener to stop the flowers.

VI

One afternoon, as I came down from my quarters to go out, I found Miss Tita in the *sala*: it was our first encounter on that ground since I had come to the house. She put on no air of being there by accident; there was an ignorance of such arts in her angular, diffident directness. That I might be quite sure she was waiting for me she informed me of the fact and told me that Miss Bordereau wished to see me: she would take me into the room at that moment if I had time. If I had been late for a love-tryst I would have stayed for this, and I quickly signified that I should be delighted to wait upon the old lady. "She wants to talk with you—to know you," Miss Tita said, smiling as if she herself appreciated that idea; and she led me to the door of her aunt's apartment. I stopped her a moment before she had opened it, looking at her with some curiosity. I told her that this was a great satisfaction to me and a great honour; but all the same I should like to ask what had made Miss Bordereau change so suddenly. It was only the other day that she wouldn't suffer me near her. Miss Tita was not embarrassed by my question; she had as many little unexpected serenities as if she told fibs, but the odd part of them was that they had on the contrary their source in her truthfulness. "Oh, my aunt changes," she answered; "it's so terribly dull—I suppose she's tired."

"But you told me that she wanted more and more to be alone."

Poor Miss Tita coloured, as if she found me overinsistent. "Well, if you don't believe she wants to see you—I haven't invented it! I think people often are capricious when they are very old."

"That's perfectly true. I only wanted to be clear as to whether you have repeated to her what I told you the other night."

"What you told me?"

"About Jeffrey Aspern—that I am looking for materials."

"If I had told her do you think she would have sent for you?"

"That's exactly what I want to know. If she wants to keep him to herself, she might have sent for me to tell me so."

"She won't speak of him," said Miss Tita. Then as she opened the door she added in a lower tone, "I have told her nothing."

The old woman was sitting in the same place in which I had seen her last, in the same position, with the same mystifying bandage over her eyes. Her welcome was to turn her almost invisible face to me and show me that while she sat silent she saw me clearly. I made no motion to shake hands with her; I felt too well on this occasion that that was out of place for ever. It had been sufficiently enjoined upon me that she was too sacred for that sort of reciprocity —too venerable to touch. There was something so grim in her aspect (it was partly the accident of her green shade), as I stood there to be measured, that I ceased on the spot to feel any doubt as to her knowing my secret, though I did not in the least suspect that Miss Tita had not just spoken the truth. She had not betrayed me, but the old woman's brooding instinct had served her; she had turned me over and over in the long, still hours and she had guessed. The worst of it was that she looked terribly like an old woman who at a pinch would burn her papers. Miss Tita pushed a chair forward, saying to me, "This will be a good place for you to sit." As I took possession of it I asked after Miss Bordereau's health; expressed the hope that in spite of the very hot weather it was satisfactory. She replied that it was good enough—good enough; that it was a great thing to be alive.

"Oh, as to that, it depends upon what you compare it with!" I exclaimed, laughing.

"I don't compare—I don't compare. If I did that I should have given everything up long ago."

I liked to think that this was a subtle allusion to the rapture she had known in the society of Jeffrey Aspern—though it was true that such an allusion would have accorded ill with the wish I imputed to her to keep him buried in her soul. What it accorded with was my constant conviction that no human being had ever had a more delightful social gift than his, and what it seemed to convey was that nothing in the world was worth speaking of if one pretended to speak of that. But one did not! Miss Tita sat down beside her aunt, looking as if she had reason to believe some very remarkable conversation would come off between us.

"It's about the beautiful flowers," said the old lady; "you sent us so many—I ought to have thanked you for them before. But I don't write letters and I receive only at long intervals."

She had not thanked me while the flowers continued to come, but she departed from her custom so far as to send for me as soon as she began to fear that they would not come any more. I noted this; I remembered what an acquisitive propensity she had shown when it was a question of extracting gold from me, and I privately rejoiced at the happy thought I had had in suspending my tribute. She had missed it and she was willing to make a concession to bring it back. At the first sign of this concession I could only go to meet her. "I am afraid you have not had many, of late, but they shall begin again immediately—to-morrow, to-night."

"Oh, do send us some to-night!" Miss Tita cried, as if it were an immense circumstance.

"What else should you do with them? It isn't a manly taste to make a bower of your room," the old woman remarked.

"I don't make a bower of my room, but I am exceedingly fond of growing flowers, of watching their ways. There is nothing unmanly in that: it has been the amusement of philosophers, of statesmen in retirement; even I think of great captains."

"I suppose you know you can sell them—those you don't use," Miss Bordereau went on. "I daresay they wouldn't give you much for them; still, you could make a bargain."

"Oh, I have never made a bargain, as you ought to know. My gardener disposes of them and I ask no questions."

"I would ask a few, I can promise you!" said Miss Bordereau; and it was the first time I had heard her laugh. I could not get used to the idea that this vision of pecuniary profit was what drew out the divine Juliana most.

"Come into the garden yourself and pick them; come as often as you like; come every day. They are all for you," I pursued, addressing Miss Tita and carrying off this veracious statement by treating it as an innocent joke. "I can't imagine why she doesn't come down," I added, for Miss Bordereau's benefit.

"You must make her come; you must come up and fetch her," said the old woman, to my stupefaction. "That odd thing you have made in the corner would be a capital place for her to sit."

The allusion to my arbour was irreverent; it confirmed the impression I had already received that there was a flicker of impertinence in Miss Bordereau's talk, a strange mocking lambency which must have been a part of her adventurous youth and which had outlived passions and faculties. None the less I asked, "Wouldn't it be possible for you to come down there yourself? Wouldn't it do you good to sit there in the shade, in the sweet air?"

"Oh, sir, when I move out of this it won't be to sit in the air, and I'm afraid that any that may be stirring around me won't be particularly sweet! It will be a very dark shade indeed. But that won't be just yet," Miss Bordereau continued, cannily, as if to correct any hopes that this courageous allusion to the last receptacle of her mortality might lead me to entertain. "I have sat here many a day and I have had enough of arbours in my time. But I'm not afraid to wait till I'm called."

Miss Tita had expected some interesting talk, but perhaps she found it less genial on her aunt's side (considering that I had been sent for with a civil intention) than she had hoped. As if to give the conversation a turn that would put our companion in a light more favourable she said to me, "Didn't I tell you the other night that she had sent me out? You see that I can do what I like!"

"Do you pity her—do you teach her to pity herself?" Miss Bordereau demanded, before I had time to answer this appeal. "She has a much easier life than I had when I was her age."

"You must remember that it has been quite open to me to think you rather inhuman."

"Inhuman? That's what the poets used to call the women a hundred years ago. Don't try that; you won't do as well as they!" Juliana declared. "There is no more poetry in the world—that I know of at least. But I won't bandy words with you," she pursued, and I well remember the old-fashioned artificial sound she gave to the speech. "You have made me talk, talk! It isn't good for me at all." I got up at this and told her I would take no more of her time; but she detained me to ask, "Do you remember, the day I saw you about the rooms, that you offered us the use of your gondola?" And when I assented, promptly, struck again with her disposition to make a "good thing" of my being there and wondering what she now had in her eye, she broke out, "Why don't you take that girl out in it and show her the place?"

"Oh dear aunt, what do you want to do with me?" cried the "girl," with a piteous quaver. "I know all about the place!"

"Well then, go with him as a cicerone!" said Miss Bordereau, with an effect of something like cruelty in her implacable power of retort—an incongruous suggestion that she was a sarcastic, profane, cynical old woman. "Haven't we heard that there have been all sort of changes in all these years? You ought to see them and at your age (I don't mean because you're so young), you ought to take the chances that come. You're old enough, my dear, and this gentleman won't hurt you. He will show you the famous sunsets, if they still go on—*do* they go on? The sun set for me so long ago. But that's not a reason. Besides, I shall never miss you; you think you are too important. Take her to the Piazza; it used to be very pretty," Miss Bordereau continued, addressing herself to me. "What have they done with the funny old church? I hope it hasn't tumbled down. Let her look at the shops; she may take some money, she may buy what she likes."

Poor Miss Tita had got up, discountenanced and helpless, and as we stood there before her aunt it would certainly have seemed to a spectator of the scene that the old woman was amusing herself at our expense. Miss Tita protested, in a confusion of exclamations and murmurs; but I lost no time in saying that if she would do me the honour to accept the hospitality of my boat I would engage that she should not be bored. Or if she did not want so much of my company the boat itself, with the gondolier, was at her service; he was a capital oar and she might have every confidence. Miss Tita, without definitely answering this speech, looked away from me, out of the window, as if she were going to cry; and I remarked that once we had Miss Bordereau's approval we could easily come to an understanding. We would take an hour, whichever she liked, one of the very next days. As I made my obeisance to the old lady I asked her if she would kindly permit me to see her again.

For a moment she said nothing; then she inquired, "Is it very necessary to your happiness?"

"It diverts me more than I can say."

"You are wonderfully civil. Don't you know it almost kills *me*?"

"How can I believe that when I see you more animated, more brilliant than when I came in?"

"That is very true, aunt," said Miss Tita. "I think it does you good."

"Isn't it touching the solicitude we each have that the other shall enjoy herself?" sneered Miss Bordereau. "If you think me brilliant to-day you don't know what you are talking about; you have never seen an agreeable woman. Don't try to pay me a compliment; I have been spoiled," she went on. "My door is shut, but you may sometimes knock."

With this she dismissed me and I left the room. The latch closed

behind me, but Miss Tita, contrary to my hope, had remained within. I passed slowly across the hall and before taking my way downstairs I waited a little. My hope was answered; after a minute Miss
Tita followed me. "That's a delightful idea about the Piazza," I said,
"When will you go—to-night, to-morrow?"

She had been disconcerted, as I have mentioned, but I had already perceived and I was to observe again that when Miss Tita was
embarrassed she did not (as most women would have done) turn
away from you and try to escape, but came closer, as it were, with a
deprecating, clinging appeal to be spared, to be protected. Her attitude was perpetually a sort of prayer for assistance, for explanation;
and yet no woman in the world could have been less of a comedian.
From the moment you were kind to her she depended on you absolutely; her self-consciousness dropped from her and she took the
greatest intimacy, the innocent intimacy which was the only thing
she could conceive, for granted. She told me she did not know what
had got into her aunt; she had changed so quickly, she had got some
idea. I replied that she must find out what the idea was and then
let me know; we would go and have an ice together at Florian's
and she should tell me while we listened to the band.

"Oh, it will take me a long time to find out!" she said, rather
ruefully; and she could promise me this satisfaction neither for that
night nor for the next. I was patient now, however, for I felt that
I had only to wait; and in fact at the end of the week, one lovely
evening after dinner, she stepped into my gondola, to which in honour
of the occasion I had attached a second oar.

We swept in the course of five minutes into the Grand Canal;
whereupon she uttered a murmur of ecstasy as fresh as if she had
been a tourist just arrived. She had forgotten how splendid the great
waterway looked on a clear, hot summer evening, and how the sense
of floating between marble palaces and reflected lights disclosed the
mind to sympathetic talk. We floated long and far, and though Miss
Tita gave no high-pitched voice to her satisfaction I felt that she
surrendered herself. She was more than pleased, she was transported;
the whole thing was an immense liberation. The gondola moved with
slow strokes, to give her time to enjoy it, and she listened to the
plash of the oars, which grew louder and more musically liquid as
we passed into narrow canals, as if it were a revelation of Venice.
When I asked her how long it was since she had been in a boat she
answered, "Oh, I don't know; a long time—not since my aunt began
to be ill." This was not the only example she gave me of her extreme
vagueness about the previous years and the line which marked off
the period when Miss Bordereau flourished. I was not at liberty to
keep her out too long, but we took a considerable *giro*[16] before going

16. circle, roundabout way.

to the Piazza. I asked her no questions, keeping the conversation on purpose away from her domestic situation and the things I wanted to know; I poured treasures of information about Venice into her ears, described Florence and Rome, discoursed to her on the charms and advantages of travel. She reclined, receptive, on the deep leather cushions, turned her eyes conscientiously to everything I pointed out to her, and never mentioned to me till some time afterwards that she might be supposed to know Florence better than I, as she had lived there for years with Miss Bordereau. At last she asked, with the shy impatience of a child, "Are we not really going to the Piazza? That's what I want to see!" I immediately gave the order that we should go straight; and then we sat silent with the expectation of arrival. As some time still passed, however, she said suddenly, of her own movement, "I have found out what is the matter with my aunt: she is afraid you will go!"

"What has put that into her head?"

"She has had an idea you have not been happy. That is why she is different now."

"You mean she wants to make me happier?"

"Well, she wants you not to go; she wants you to stay."

"I suppose you mean on account of the rent," I remarked candidly. Miss Tita's candour showed itself a match for my own. "Yes, you know; so that I shall have more."

"How much does she want you to have?" I asked, laughing. "She ought to fix the sum, so that I may stay till it's made up."

"Oh, that wouldn't please me," said Miss Tita. "It would be unheard of, your taking that trouble."

"But suppose I should have my own reasons for staying in Venice?"

"Then it would be better for you to stay in some other house."

"And what would your aunt say to that?"

"She wouldn't like it at all. But I should think you would do well to give up your reasons and go away altogether."

"Dear Miss Tita," I said, "it's not so easy to give them up!"

She made no immediate answer to this, but after a moment she broke out: "I think I know what your reasons are!"

"I daresay, because the other night I almost told you how I wish you would help me to make them good."

"I can't do that without being false to my aunt."

"What do you mean, being false to her?"

"Why, she would never consent to what you want. She has been asked, she has been written to. It made her fearfully angry."

"Then she *has* got papers of value?" I demanded, quickly.

"Oh, she has got everything!" sighed Miss Tita, with a curious weariness, a sudden lapse into gloom.

These words caused all my pulses to throb, for I regarded them as precious evidence. For some minutes I was too agitated to speak, and in the interval the gondola approached the Piazzetta. After we had disembarked I asked my companion whether she would rather walk round the square or go and sit at the door of the café; to which she replied that she would do whichever I liked best—I must only remember again how little time she had. I assured her there was plenty to do both, and we made the circuit of the long arcades. Her spirits revived at the sight of the bright shop-windows and she lingered and stopped, admiring or disapproving of their contents, asking me what I thought of things, theorising about prices. My attention wandered from her; her words of a while before, "Oh, she has got everything!" echoed so in my consciousness. We sat down at last in the crowded circle at Florian's, finding an unoccupied table among those that were ranged in the square. It was a splendid night and all the world was out-of-doors; Miss Tita could not have wished the elements more auspicious for her return to society. I saw that she enjoyed it even more than she told; she was agitated with the multitude of her impressions. She had forgotten what an attractive thing the world is, and it was coming over her that somehow she had for the best years of her life been cheated of it. This did not make her angry; but as she looked all over the charming scene her face had, in spite of its smile of appreciation, the flush of a sort of wounded surprise. She became silent, as if she were thinking with a secret sadness of opportunities, for ever lost, which ought to have been easy; and this gave me a chance to say to her, "Did you mean a while ago that your aunt has a plan of keeping me on by admitting me occasionally to her presence?"

"She thinks it will make a difference with you if you sometimes see her. She wants you so much to stay that she is willing to make that concession."

"And what good does she consider that I think it will do me to see her?"

"I don't know; she thinks it's interesting," said Miss Tita, simply. "You told her you found it so."

"So I did; but every one doesn't think so."

"No, of course not, or more people would try."

"Well, if she is capable of making that reflection she is capable also of making this further one," I went on: "that I must have a particular reason for not doing as others do, in spite of the interest she offers—for not leaving her alone." Miss Tita looked as if she failed to grasp this rather complicated proposition; so I continued, "If you have not told her what I said to you the other night may she not at least have guessed it?"

"I don't know; she is very suspicious."

"But she has not been made so by indiscreet curiosity, by persecution?"

"No, no; it isn't that," said Miss Tita, turning on me a somewhat troubled face. "I don't know how to say it: it's on account of something—ages ago, before I was born—in her life."

"Something? What sort of thing?" I asked, as if I myself could have no idea.

"Oh, she has never told me," Miss Tita answered; and I was sure she was speaking the truth.

Her extreme limpidity was almost provoking, and I felt for the moment that she would have been more satisfactory if she had been less ingenuous. "Do you suppose it's something to which Jeffrey Aspern's letters and papers—I mean the things in her possession —have reference?"

"I daresay it is!" my companion exclaimed, as if this were a very happy suggestion. "I have never looked at any of those things."

"None of them? Then how do you know what they are?"

"I don't," said Miss Tita, placidly. "I have never had them in my hands. But I have seen them when she has had them out."

"Does she have them out often?"

"Not now, but she used to. She is very fond of them."

"In spite of their being compromising?"

"Compromising?" Miss Tita repeated, as if she was ignorant of the meaning of the word. I felt almost as one who corrupts the innocence of youth.

"I mean their containing painful memories."

"Oh, I don't think they are painful."

"You mean you don't think they affect her reputation?"

At this a singular look came into the face of Miss Bordereau's niece —a kind of confession of helplessness, an appeal to me to deal fairly, generously with her. I had brought her to the Piazza, placed her among charming influences, paid her an attention she appreciated, and now I seemed to let her perceive that all this had been a bribe— a bribe to make her turn in some way against her aunt. She was of a yielding nature and capable of doing almost anything to please a person who was kind to her; but the greatest kindness of all would be not to presume too much on this. It was strange enough, as I afterwards thought, that she had not the least air of resenting my want of consideration for her aunt's character, which would have been in the worst possible taste if anything less vital (from my point of view) had been at stake. I don't think she really measured it. "Do you mean that she did something bad?" she asked in a moment.

"Heaven forbid I should say so, and it's none of my business. Besides, if she did," I added, laughing, "it was in other ages, in another world. But why should she not destroy her papers?"

"Oh, she loves them too much."

"Even now, when she may be near her end?"

"Perhaps when she's sure of that she will."

"Well, Miss Tita," I said, "it's just what I should like you to prevent."

"How can I prevent it?"

"Couldn't you get them away from her?"

"And give them to you?"

This put the case very crudely, though I am sure there was no irony in her intention. "Oh, I mean that you might let me see them and look them over. It isn't for myself; there is no personal avidity in my desire. It is simply that they would be of such immense interest to the public, such immeasurable importance as a contribution to Jeffrey Aspern's history."

She listened to me in her usual manner, as if my speech were full of reference to things she had never heard of, and I felt particularly like the reporter of a newspaper who forces his way into a house of mourning. This was especially the case when after a moment she said, "There was a gentleman who some time ago wrote to her in very much those words. He also wanted her papers."

"And did she answer him?" I asked, rather ashamed of myself for not having her rectitude.

"Only when he had written two or three times. He made her very angry."

"And what did she say?"

"She said he was a devil," Miss Tita replied, simply.

"She used that expression in her letter?"

"Oh no; she said it to me. She made me write to him."

"And what did you say?"

"I told him there were no papers at all."

"Ah, poor gentleman!" I exclaimed.

"I knew there were, but I wrote what she bade me."

"Of course you had to do that. But I hope I shall not pass for a devil."

"It will depend upon what you ask me to do for you," said Miss Tita, smiling.

"Oh, if there is a chance of *your* thinking so my affair is in a bad way! I sha'n't ask you to steal for me, nor even to fib—for you can't fib, unless on paper. But the principal thing is this—to prevent her from destroying the papers."

"Why, I have no control of her," said Miss Tita. "It's she who controls me."

"But she doesn't control her own arms and legs, does she? The way she would naturally destroy her letters would be to burn them. Now she can't burn them without fire, and she can't get fire unless you give it to her."

"I have always done everything she has asked," my companion rejoined. "Besides, there's Olimpia."

I was on the point of saying that Olimpia was probably corruptible, but I thought it best not to sound that note. So I simply inquired if that faithful domestic could not be managed.

"Every one can be managed by my aunt," said Miss Tita. And then she observed that her holiday was over; she must go home.

I laid my hand on her arm, across the table, to stay her a moment. "What I want of you is a general promise to help me."

"Oh, how can I—how can I?" she asked, wondering and troubled. She was half surprised, half frightened at my wishing to make her play an active part.

"This is the main thing: to watch her carefully and warn me in time, before she commits that horrible sacrilege."

"I can't watch her when she makes me go out."

"That's very true."

"And when you do too."

"Mercy on us; do you think she will have done anything to-night?"

"I don't know; she is very cunning."

"Are you trying to frighten me?" I asked.

I felt this inquiry sufficiently answered when my companion murmured in a musing, almost envious way, "Oh, but she loves them—she loves them!"

This reflection, repeated with such emphasis, gave me great comfort; but to obtain more of that balm I said, "If she shouldn't intend to destroy the objects we speak of before her death she will probably have made some disposition by will."

"By will?"

"Hasn't she made a will for your benefit?"

"Why, she has so little to leave. That's why she likes money," said Miss Tita.

"Might I ask, since we are really talking things over, what you and she live on?"

"On some money that comes from America, from a lawyer. He sends it every quarter. It isn't much!"

"And won't she have disposed of that?"

My companion hesitated—I saw she was blushing. "I believe it's mine," she said; and the look and tone which accompanied these words betrayed so the absence of the habit of thinking of herself that I almost thought her charming. The next instant she added, "But she had a lawyer once, ever so long ago. And some people came and signed something."

"They were probably witnesses. And you were not asked to sign? Well then," I argued, rapidly and hopefully, "it is because you are the legatee; she has left all her documents to you!"

"If she has it's with very strict conditions," Miss Tita responded, rising quickly, while the movement gave the words a little character of decision. They seemed to imply that the bequest would be accompanied with a command that the articles bequeathed should remain concealed from every inquisitive eye and that I was very much mistaken if I thought she was the person to depart from an injunction so solemn.

"Oh, of course you will have to abide by the terms," I said; and she uttered nothing to mitigate the severity of this conclusion. None the less, later, just before we disembarked at her own door, on our return, which had taken place almost in silence, she said to me abruptly, "I will do what I can to help you." I was grateful for this —it was very well so far as it went; but it did not keep me from remembering that night in a worried waking hour that I now had her word for it to reinforce my own impression that the old woman was very cunning.

VII

The fear of what this side of her character might have led her to do made me nervous for days afterwards. I waited for an intimation from Miss Tita; I almost figured to myself that it was her duty to keep me informed, to let me know definitely whether or no Miss Bordereau had sacrificed her treasures. But as she gave no sign I lost patience and determined to judge so far as was possible with my own senses. I sent late one afternoon to ask if I might pay the ladies a visit, and my servant came back with surprising news. Miss Bordereau could be approached without the least difficulty; she had been moved out into the *sala* and was sitting by the window that overlooked the garden. I descended and found this picture correct; the old lady had been wheeled forth into the world and had a certain air, which came mainly perhaps from some brighter element in her dress, of being prepared again to have converse with it. It had not yet, however, begun to flock about her; she was perfectly alone and, though the door leading to her own quarters stood open, I had at first no glimpse of Miss Tita. The window at which she sat had the afternoon shade and, one of the shutters having been pushed back, she could see the pleasant garden, where the summer sun had by this time dried up too many of the plants—she could see the yellow light and the long shadows.

"Have you come to tell me that you will take the rooms for six months more?" she asked, as I approached her, startling me by something coarse in her cupidity almost as much as if she had not already given me a specimen of it. Juliana's desire to make our acquaintance lucrative had been, as I have sufficiently indicated, a false note in my image of the woman who had inspired a great poet with immortal lines; but I may say here definitely that I recognised after all that it behoved me to make a large allowance for her. It was I who had kindled the unholy flame; it was I who had put into her head that she had the means of making money. She appeared never to have thought of that; she had been living wastefully for years, in a house five times too big for her, on a footing that I could explain only by the presumption that, excessive as it was, the space she enjoyed cost her next to nothing and that small as were her revenues they left her, for Venice, an appreciable margin. I had descended on her one day and taught her to calculate, and my almost extravagant comedy on the subject of the garden had presented me irresistibly in the light of a victim. Like all persons who achieve the miracle of changing their point of view when they are old she had been intensely converted; she had seized my hint with a desperate, tremulous clutch.

I invited myself to go and get one of the chairs that stood, at a distance, against the wall (she had given herself no concern as to whether I should sit or stand); and while I placed it near her I began, gaily, "Oh, dear madam, what an imagination you have, what an intellectual sweep! I am a poor devil of a man of letters who lives from day to day. How can I take palaces by the year? My existence is precarious. I don't know whether six months hence I shall have bread to put in my mouth. I have treated myself for once; it has been an immense luxury. But when it comes to going on——!"

"Are your rooms too dear? if they are you can have more for the same money," Juliana responded. "We can arrange, we can *combin-are*, as they say here."

"Well, yes, since you ask me, they are too dear," I said. "Evidently you suppose me richer than I am."

She looked at me in her barricaded way. "If you write books don't you sell them?"

"Do you mean don't people buy them? A little—not so much as I could wish. Writing books, unless one be a great genius—and even then!—is the last road to fortune. I think there is no more money to be made by literature."

"Perhaps you don't choose good subjects. What do you write about?" Miss Bordereau inquired.

"About the books of other people. I'm a critic, an historian, in a small way." I wondered what she was coming to.

"And what other people, now?"

"Oh, better ones than myself: the great writers mainly—the great philosophers and poets of the past; those who are dead and gone and can't speak for themselves."

"And what do you say about them?"

"I say they sometimes attached themselves to very clever women!" I answered, laughing. I spoke with great deliberation, but as my words fell upon the air they struck me as imprudent. However, I risked them and I was not sorry, for perhaps after all the old woman would be willing to treat. It seemed to be tolerably obvious that she knew my secret: why therefore drag the matter out? But she did not take what I had said as a confession; she only asked:

"Do you think its right to rake up the past?"

"I don't know that I know what you mean by raking it up; but how can we get at it unless we dig a little? The present has such a rough way of treading it down."

"Oh, I like the past, but I don't like critics," the old woman declared, with her fine tranquillity.

"Neither do I, but I like their discoveries."

"Aren't they mostly lies?"

"The lies are what they sometimes discover," I said, smiling at the quiet impertinence of this. "They often lay bare the truth."

"The truth is God's, it isn't man's; we had better leave it alone. Who can judge of it—who can say?"

"We are terribly in the dark, I know," I admitted; "but if we give up trying what becomes of all the fine things? What becomes of the work I just mentioned, that of the great philosophers and poets? It is all vain words if there is nothing to measure it by!"

"You talk as if you were a tailor," said Miss Bordereau, whimsically; and then she added quickly, in a different manner, "This house is very fine; the proportions are magnificent. To-day I wanted to look at this place again. I made them bring me out here. When your man came, just now, to learn if I would see you, I was on the point of sending for you, to ask if you didn't mean to go on. I wanted to judge what I'm letting you have. This *sala* is very grand," she pursued, like an auctioneer, moving a little, as I guessed, her invisible eyes. "I don't believe you often have lived in such a house, eh?"

"I can't often afford to!" I said.

"Well, then, how much will you give for six months?"

I was on the point of exclaiming—and the air of excruciation in my face would have denoted a moral fact—"Don't, Juliana; for *his* sake, don't!" But I controlled myself and asked less passionately: "Why should I remain so long as that?"

"I thought you liked it," said Miss Bordereau, with her shrivelled dignity.

"So I thought I should."

For a moment she said nothing more, and I left my own words to suggest to her what they might. I half expected her to say, coldly enough, that if I had been disappointed we need not continue the discussion, and this in spite of the fact that I believed her now to have in her mind (however it had come there), what would have told her that my disappointment was natural. But to my extreme surprise she ended by observing: "If you don't think we have treated you well enough perhaps we can discover some way of treating you better." This speech was somehow so incongruous that it made me laugh again, and I excused myself by saying that she talked as if I were a sulky boy, pouting in the corner, to be "brought round." I had not a grain of complaint to make; and could anything have exceeded Miss Tita's graciousness in accompanying me a few nights before to the Piazza? At this the old woman went on: "Well, you brought it on yourself!" And then in a different tone, "She is a very nice girl." I assented cordially to this proposition, and she expressed the hope that I did so not merely to be obliging, but that I really liked her. Meanwhile I wondered still more what Miss Bordereau was coming to. "Except for me, to-day," she said, "she has not a relation in the world." Did she by describing her niece as amiable and unencumbered wish to represent her as a *parti*?

It was perfectly true that I could not afford to go on with my rooms at a fancy price and that I had already devoted to my under-taking almost all the hard cash I had set apart for it. My patience and my time were by no means exhausted, but I should be able to draw upon them only on a more usual Venetian basis. I was willing to pay the venerable woman with whom my pecuniary deal-ings were such a discord twice as much as any other *padrona di casa*[17] would have asked, but I was not willing to pay her twenty times as much. I told her so plainly, and my plainness appeared to have some success, for she exclaimed, "Very good; you have done what I asked—you have made an offer!"

"Yes, but not for half a year. Only by the month."

"Oh, I must think of that then." She seemed disappointed that I would not tie myself to a period, and I guessed that she wished both to secure me and to discourage me; to say, severely, "Do you dream that you can get off with less than six months? Do you dream that even by the end of that time you will be appreciably nearer your victory?" What was more in my mind was that she had a fancy to play me the trick of making me engage myself when in fact she had an-nihilated the papers. There was a moment when my suspense on this point was so acute that I all but broke out with the question, and what kept it back was but a kind of instinctive recoil (lest it should be a mistake), from the last violence of self-exposure. She was such a subtle old witch that one could never tell where one stood with her. You may imagine whether it cleared up the puzzle when, just after she had said she would think of my proposal and without any formal transition, she drew out of her pocket with an embarrassed hand a small object wrapped in crumpled white paper. She held it there a moment and then she asked, "Do you know much about curiosities?"

"About curiosities?"

"About antiquities, the old gimcracks that people pay so much for to-day. Do you know the kind of price they bring?"

I thought I saw what was coming, but I said ingenuously, "Do

17. landlady.

you want to buy something?"

"No, I want to sell. What would an amateur give me for that?" She unfolded the white paper and made a motion for me to take from her a small oval portrait. I possessed myself of it with a hand of which I could only hope that she did not perceive the tremor, and she added, "I would part with it only for a good price."

At the first glance I recognised Jeffrey Aspern, and I was well aware that I flushed with the act. As she was watching me however I had the consistency to exclaim, "What a striking face! Do tell me who it is."

"It's an old friend of mine, a very distinguished man in his day. He gave it to me himself, but I'm afraid to mention his name, lest you never should have heard of him, critic and historian as you are. I know the world goes fast and one generation forgets another. He was all the fashion when I was young."

She was perhaps amazed at my assurance, but I was surprised at hers; at her having the energy, in her state of health and at her time of life, to wish to sport with me that way simply for her private entertainment—the humour to test me and practise on me. This, at least, was the interpretation that I put upon her production of the portrait, for I could not believe that she really desired to sell it or cared for any information I might give her. What she wished was to dangle it before my eyes and put a prohibitive price on it. "The face comes back to me, it torments me," I said, turning the object this way and that and looking at it very critically. It was a careful but not a supreme work of art, larger than the ordinary miniature and representing a young man with a remarkably handsome face, in a high-collared green coat and a buff waistcoat. I judged the picture to have a valuable quality of resemblance and to have been painted when the model was about twenty-five years old. There are, as all the world knows, three other portraits of the poet in existence, but none of them is of so early a date as this elegant production. "I have never seen the original but I have seen other likenesses," I went on. "You expressed doubt of this generation having heard of the gentleman, but he strikes me for all the world as a celebrity. Now who is he? I can't put my finger on him—I can't give him a label. Wasn't he a writer? Surely he's a poet." I was determined that it should be she, not I, who should first pronounce Jeffrey Aspern's name.

My resolution was taken in ignorance of Miss Bordereau's extremely resolute character, and her lips never formed in my hearing the syllables that meant so much for her. She neglected to answer my question but raised her hand to take back the picture, with a gesture which though ineffectual was in a high degree peremptory. "It's only a person who should know for himself that would give me my price," she said with a certain dryness.

"Oh, then, you have a price?" I did not restore the precious thing; not from any vindictive purpose but because I instinctively clung to it. We looked at each other hard while I retained it.

"I know the least I would take. What it occurred to me to ask you about is the most I shall be able to get."

She made a movement, drawing herself together as if, in a spasm of dread at having lost her treasure, she were going to attempt the immense effort of rising to snatch it from me. I instantly placed it in her hand again, saying as I did so, "I should like to have it myself, but with your ideas I could never afford it."

She turned the small oval plate over in her lap, with its face down, and I thought I saw her catch her breath a little, as if she had had a strain or an escape. This however did not prevent her saying in a moment, "You would buy a likeness of a person you don't know, by an artist who has no reputation?"

"The artist may have no reputation, but that thing is wonderfully well painted," I replied, to give myself a reason.

"It's lucky you thought of saying that, because the painter was my father."

"That makes the picture indeed precious!" I exclaimed, laughing; and I may add that a part of my laughter came from my satisfaction in finding that I had been right in my theory of Miss Bordereau's origin. Aspern had of course met the young lady when he went to her father's studio as a sitter. I observed to Miss Bordereau that if she would entrust me with her property for twenty-four hours I should be happy to take advice upon it; but she made no answer to this save to slip it in silence into her pocket. This convinced me still more that she had no sincere intention of selling it during her lifetime, though she may have desired to satisfy herself as to the sum her niece, should she leave it to her, might expect eventually to obtain for it. "Well, at any rate I hope you will not offer it without giving me notice," I said, as she remained irresponsive. "Remember that I am a possible purchaser."

"I should want your money first!" she returned, with unexpected rudeness; and then, as if she bethought herself that I had just cause to complain of such an insinuation and wished to turn the matter off, asked abruptly what I talked about with her niece when I went out with her that way in the evening.

"You speak as if we had set up the habit," I replied. "Certainly I should be very glad if it were to become a habit. But in that case I should feel a still greater scruple at betraying a lady's confidence."

"Her confidence? Has she got confidence?"

"Here she is—she can tell you herself," I said; for Miss Tita now appeared on the threshold of the old woman's parlour. "Have you got confidence, Miss Tita. Your aunt wants very much to know."

"Not in her, not in her!" the younger lady declared, shaking her head with a dolefulness that was neither jocular nor affected. "I don't know what to do with her; she has fits of horrid imprudence. She is so easily tired—and yet she has begun to roam—to drag herself about the house." And she stood looking down at her immemorial companion with a sort of helpless wonder, as if all their years of familiarity had not made her perversities, on occasion, any more easy to follow.

"I know what I'm about. I'm not losing my mind. I daresay you would like to think so," said Miss Bordereau, with a cynical little sigh.

"I don't suppose you came out here yourself. Miss Tita must have had to lend you a hand," I interposed, with a pacifying intention.

"Oh, she insisted that we should push her; and when she insists!" said Miss Tita, in the same tone of apprehension; as if there were no knowing what service that she disapproved of her aunt might force her next to render.

"I have always got most things done I wanted, thank God! The people I have lived with have humoured me," the old woman continued, speaking out of the gray ashes of her vanity.

"I suppose you mean that they have obeyed you."

"Well, whatever it is, when they like you."

"It's just because I like you that I want to resist," said Miss Tita, with a nervous laugh.

"Oh, I suspect you'll bring Miss Bordereau upstairs next, to pay me a visit," I went on; to which the old lady replied:

"Oh no; I can keep an eye on you from here!"

"You are very tired; you will certainly be ill to-night!" cried Miss Tita.

"Nonsense, my dear; I feel better at this moment than I have done for a month. To-morrow I shall come out again. I want to be where I can see this clever gentleman."

"Shouldn't you perhaps see me better in your sitting-room?" I inquired.

"Don't you mean shouldn't you have a better chance at me?" she returned, fixing me a moment with her green shade.

"Ah, I haven't that anywhere! I look at you but I don't see you."

"You excite her dreadfully—and that is not good," said Miss Tita, giving me a reproachful, appealing look.

"I want to watch you—I want to watch you!" the old lady went on.

"Well then, let us spend as much of our time together as possible—I don't care where—and that will give you every facility."

"Oh, I've seen you enough for to-day. I'm satisfied. Now I'll go home." Miss Tita laid her hands on the back of her aunt's chair and began to push, but I begged her to let me take her place. "Oh yes, you may move me this way—you sha'n't in any other!" Miss Bordereau exclaimed, as she felt herself propelled firmly and easily over the smooth, hard floor. Before we reached the door of her own apartment she commanded me to stop, and she took a long, last look up and down the noble *sala*. "Oh, it's a magnificent house!" she murmured; after which I pushed her forward. When we had entered the parlour Miss Tita told me that she should now be able to manage, and at the same moment the little red-haired *donna* came to meet her mistress. Miss Tita's idea was evidently to get her aunt immediately back to bed. I confess that in spite of this urgency I was guilty of the indiscretion of lingering; it held me there to think that I was nearer the documents I coveted—that they were probably put away somewhere in the faded, unsociable room. The place had indeed a bareness which did not suggest hidden treasures; there were no dusky nooks nor curtained corners, no massive cabinets nor chests with iron bands. Moreover it was possible, it was perhaps even probable that the old lady had consigned her relics to her bedroom, to some battered box that was shoved under the bed, to the drawer of some lame dressing-table, where they would be in the range of vision by the dim night-lamp. None the less I scrutinised every article of furniture, every conceivable cover for a hoard, and noticed that there were half a dozen things with drawers, and in particular a tall old secretary, with brass ornaments of the style of the Empire—a receptacle somewhat rickety but still capable of keeping a great many secrets. I don't know why this article fascinated me so, inasmuch as I certainly had no definite purpose of breaking into it; but I stared at it so hard that Miss Tita noticed me and changed colour. Her doing this made me think I was right and that wherever they might have been before, the Aspern papers at that moment languished behind the peevish little lock of the secretary. It was hard to remove my eyes from the dull mahogany front when I reflected that a simple panel divided me from the goal of my hopes; but I remembered my prudence and with an effort took leave of Miss Bordereau. To make the effort graceful I said to her that I should certainly bring her an opinion about the little picture.

"The little picture?" Miss Tita asked, surprised.

"What do *you* know about it, my dear?" the old woman demanded. "You needn't mind. I have fixed my price."

"And what may that be?"

"A thousand pounds."

"Oh Lord," cried poor Miss Tita, irrepressibly.

"Is that what she talks to you about?" said Miss Bordereau.

"Imagine your aunt's wanting to know!" I had to separate from Miss Tita with only those words, though I should have liked immensely to add, "For heaven's sake meet me to-night in the garden!"

VIII

As it turned out the precaution had not been needed, for three hours later, just as I had finished my dinner, Miss Bordereau's niece appeared, unannounced, in the open doorway of the room in which my simple repasts were served. I remember well that I felt no surprise at seeing her; which is not a proof that I did not believe in her timidity. It was immense, but in a case in which there was a particular reason for boldness it never would have prevented her from running up to my rooms. I saw that she was now quite full of a particular reason; it threw her forward—made her seize me, as I rose to meet her, by the arm.

"My aunt is very ill; I think she is dying!"

"Never in the world," I answered, bitterly. "Don't you be afraid!"

"Do go for a doctor—do, do! Olimpia is gone for the one we always have, but she doesn't come back; I don't know what has happened to her. I told her that if he was not at home she was to follow him where he had gone; but apparently she is following him all over Venice. I don't know what to do—she looks so as if she were sinking."

"May I see her, may I judge?" I asked. "Of course I shall be delighted to bring some one; but hadn't we better send my man instead, so that I may stay with you?"

Miss Tita assented to this and I despatched my servant for the best doctor in the neighbourhood. I hurried downstairs with her, and on the way she told me that an hour after I quitted them in the afternoon Miss Bordereau had had an attack of "oppression," a terrible difficulty in breathing. This had subsided but had left her so exhausted that she did not come up: she seemed all gone. I repeated that she was not gone, that she would not go yet; whereupon Miss Tita gave me a sharper sidelong glance than she had ever directed at me and said, "Really, what do you mean? I suppose you don't accuse her of making-believe!" I forget what reply I made to this, but I grant that in my heart I thought the old woman capable of any weird manœuvre. Miss Tita wanted to know what I had done to her; her aunt had told her that I had made her so angry. I declared I had done nothing—I had been exceedingly careful; to which my companion rejoined that Miss Bordereau had assured her she had had a scene with me—a scene which had upset her. I answered with some resentment that it was a scene of her own making—that I couldn't think what she was angry with me for unless for not seeing my way to give a thousand pounds for the portrait of Jeffrey Aspern. "And did she show you that? Oh gracious—oh deary me!" groaned Miss Tita, who appeared to feel that the situation was passing out of her control and that the elements of her fate were thickening around her. I said that I would give anything to possess it, yet that I had not a thousand pounds; but I stopped when we came to the door of Miss Bordereau's room. I had an immense curiosity to pass it, but I thought it my duty to represent to Miss Tita that if I made the invalid angry she ought perhaps to be spared the sight of me. "The sight of you? Do you think she can see?" my companion demanded, almost with indignation. I did think so but forbore to say it, and I softly followed my conductress.

I remember that what I said to her as I stood for a moment beside the old woman's bed was, "Does she never show you her eyes then? Have you never seen them?" Miss Bordereau had been divested of her green shade, but (it was not my fortune to behold Juliana in her nightcap) the upper half of her face was covered by the fall of a piece of dingy lacelike muslin, a sort of extemporised hood which, wound round her head, descended to the end of her nose, leaving nothing visible but her white withered cheeks and puckered mouth, closed tightly and, as it were, consciously. Miss Tita gave me a glance of surprise, evidently not seeing a reason for my impatience. "You mean that she always wears something? She does it to preserve them."

"Because they are so fine?"

"Oh, to-day, to-day!" And Miss Tita shook her head, speaking very low. "But they used to be magnificent!"

"Yes indeed, we have Aspern's word for that." And as I looked again at the old woman's wrappings I could imagine that she had not wished to allow people a reason to say that the great poet had overdone it. But I did not waste my time in considering Miss Bordereau, in whom the appearance of respiration was so slight as to suggest that no human attention could ever help her more. I turned my eyes all over the room, rummaging with them the closets, the chests of drawers, the tables. Miss Tita met them quickly and read, I think, what was in them; but she did not answer it, turning away restlessly, anxiously, so that I felt rebuked, with reason, for a preoccupation that was almost profane in the presence of our dying companion. All the same I took another look, endeavouring to pick out mentally the place to try first, for a person who should wish to put his hand on Miss Bordereau's papers directly after her death. The room was a dire confusion; it looked like the room of an old actress. There were clothes hanging over chairs, odd-looking, shabby bundles here and there, and various pasteboard boxes piled together, battered, bulging and discoloured, which might have been fifty years old. Miss Tita after a moment noticed the direction of my eyes again and, as if she guessed how I judged the air of the place (forgetting I had no business to judge it at all), said, perhaps to defend herself from the imputation of complicity in such untidiness:

"She likes it this way; we can't move things. There are old bandboxes she has had most of her life." Then she added, half taking

pity on my real thought, "Those things were *there*." And she
pointed to a small, low trunk which stood under a sofa where there
was just room for it. It appeared to be a queer, superannuated
coffer, of painted wood, with elaborate handles and shrivelled straps
and with the colour (it had last been endued with a coat of light
green) much rubbed off. It evidently had travelled with Juliana
in the olden time—in the days of her adventures, which it had
shared. It would have made a strange figure arriving at a modern
hotel.

"*Were* there—they aren't now?" I asked, startled by Miss Tita's
implication.

She was going to answer, but at that moment the doctor came
in—the doctor whom the little maid had been sent to fetch and
whom she had at last overtaken. My servant, going on his own
errand, had met her with her companion in tow, and in the sociable
Venetian spirit, retracing his steps with them, had also come up
to the threshold of Miss Bordereau's room, where I saw him peeping
over the doctor's shoulder. I motioned him away the more instantly
that the sight of his prying face reminded me that I myself had
almost as little to do there—an admonition confirmed by the sharp
way the little doctor looked at me, appearing to take me for a rival
who had the field before him. He was a short, fat, brisk gentleman
who wore the tall hat of his profession and seemed to look at
everything but his patient. He looked particularly at me, as if it
struck him that I should be better for a dose, so that I bowed to him
and left him with the women, going down to smoke a cigar in the
garden. I was nervous; I could not go further; I could not leave
the place. I don't know exactly what I thought might happen, but
it seemed to me important to be there. I wandered about in the
alleys—the warm night had come on—smoking cigar after cigar and
looking at the light in Miss Bordereau's windows. They were open
now, I could see; the situation was different. Sometimes the light
moved, but not quickly; it did not suggest the hurry of a crisis.
Was the old woman dying or was she already dead? Had the doctor
said that there was nothing to be done at her tremendous age but
to let her quietly pass away; or had he simply announced with a
look a little more conventional that the end of the end had come?
Were the other two women moving about to perform the offices
that follow in such a case? It made me uneasy not to be nearer, as
if I thought the doctor himself might carry away the papers with
him. I bit my cigar hard as it came over me again that perhaps there
were now no papers to carry!

I wandered about for an hour—for an hour and a half. I looked
out for Miss Tita at one of the windows, having a vague idea that
she might come there to give me some sign. Would she not see the
red tip of my cigar moving about in the dark and feel that I wanted

eminently to know what the doctor had said? I am afraid it is a proof my anxieties had made me gross that I should have taken in some degree for granted that at such an hour, in the midst of the greatest change that could take place in her life, they were uppermost also in poor Miss Tita's mind. My servant came down and spoke to me; he knew nothing save that the doctor had gone after a visit of half an hour. If he had stayed half an hour then Miss Bordereau was still alive: it could not have taken so much time as that to enunciate the contrary. I sent the man out of the house; there were moments when the sense of his curiosity annoyed me and this was one of them. *He* had been watching my cigar-tip from an upper-window, if Miss Tita had not; he could not know what I was after and I could not tell him, though I was conscious he had fantastic private theories about me which he thought fine and which I, had I known them, should have thought offensive.

I went upstairs at last but I ascended no higher than the *sala*. The door of Miss Bordereau's apartment was open, showing from the parlour the dimness of a poor candle. I went toward it with a light tread and at the same moment Miss Tita appeared and stood looking at me as I approached. "She's better—she's better," she said, even before I had asked. "The doctor has given her something; she woke up, came back to life while he was there. He says there is no immediate danger."

"No immediate danger? Surely he thinks her condition strange!"

"Yes, because she had been excited. That affects her dreadfully."

"It will do so again then, because she excited herself. She did so this afternoon."

"Yes; she mustn't come out any more," said Miss Tita, with one of her lapses into a deeper placidity.

"What is the use of making such a remark as that if you begin to rattle her about again the first time she bids you?"

"I won't—I won't do it any more."

"You must learn to resist her," I went on.

"Oh yes, I shall; I shall do so better if you tell me it's right."

"You mustn't do it for me; you must do it for yourself. It all comes back to you, if you are frightened."

"Well, I am not frightened now," said Miss Tita cheerfully. "She is very quiet."

"Is she conscious again—does she speak?"

"No, she doesn't speak, but she takes my hand. She holds it fast."

"Yes," I rejoined, "I can see what force she still has by the way she grabbed that picture this afternoon. But if she holds you fast how comes it that you are here?"

Miss Tita hesitated a moment; though her face was in deep shadow (she had her back to the light in the parlour and I had put down my own candle far off, near the door of the *sala*), I thought I saw her smile ingenuously. "I came on purpose—I heard your step."

"Why, I came on tiptoe, as inaudibly as possible."

"Well, I heard you," said Miss Tita.

"And is your aunt alone now?"

"Oh no; Olimpia is sitting there."

On my side I hesitated. "Shall we then step in there?" And I nodded at the parlour; I wanted more and more to be on the spot.

"We can't talk there—she will hear us."

I was on the point of replying that in that case we would sit silent, but I was too conscious that this would not do, as there was something I desired immensely to ask her. So I proposed that we should walk a little in the *sala*, keeping more at the other end, where we should not disturb the old lady. Miss Tita assented unconditionally; the doctor was coming again, she said, and she would be there to meet him at the door. We strolled through the fine superfluous hall, where on the marble floor—particularly as at first we said nothing—our footsteps were more audible than I had expected. When we reached the other end—the wide window, inveterately closed, connecting with the balcony that overhung the canal—I suggested that we should remain there, as she would see the doctor arrive still better. I opened the window and we passed out on the balcony. The air of the canal seemed even heavier, hotter, than that of the *sala*. The place was hushed and void; the quiet neighbourhood had gone to sleep. A lamp, here and there, over the narrow black water, glimmered in double; the voice of a man going homeward singing, with his jacket on his shoulder and his hat on his ear, came to us from a distance. This did not prevent the scene from being very *comme il faut*, as Miss Bordereau had called it the first time I saw her. Presently a gondola passed along the canal with its slow rhythmical plash, and as we listened we watched it in silence. It did not stop, it did not carry the doctor; and after it had gone on I said to Miss Tita:

"And where are they now—the things that were in the trunk?"

"In the trunk?"

"That green box you pointed out to me in her room. You said her papers had been there; you seemed to imply that she had transferred them."

"Oh yes; they are not in the trunk," said Miss Tita.

"May I ask if you have looked?"

"Yes, I have looked—for you."

"How for me, dear Miss Tita? Do you mean you would have given them to me if you had found them?" I asked, almost trembling.

She delayed to reply and I waited. Suddenly she broke out. "I don't know what I would do—what I wouldn't!"

"Would you look again—somewhere else?"

She had spoken with a strange, unexpected emotion, and she

went on in the same tone: "I can't—I can't—while she lies there. It isn't decent."

"No, it isn't decent," I replied, gravely. "Let the poor lady rest in peace." And the words, on my lips, were not hypocritical, for I felt reprimanded and shamed.

Miss Tita added in a moment, as if she had guessed this and were sorry for me, but at the same time wished to explain that I did drive her on or at least did insist too much: "I can't deceive her that way. I can't deceive her—perhaps on her deathbed."

"Heaven forbid I should ask you, though I have been guilty myself!"

"You have been guilty?"

"I have sailed under false colours." I felt now as if I must tell her that I had given her an invented name, on account of my fear that her aunt would have heard of me and would refuse to take me in. I explained this and also that I had really been a party to the letter written to them by John Cumnor months before.

She listened with great attention, looking at me with parted lips, and when I had made my confession she said, "Then your real name—what is it?" She repeated it over twice when I had told her, accompanying it with the exclamation "Gracious, gracious!" Then she added, "I like your own best."

"So do I," I said, laughing. "Ouf! it's a relief to get rid of the other."

"So it was a regular plot—a kind of conspiracy?"

"Oh, a conspiracy—we were only two," I replied, leaving out Mrs. Prest of course.

She hesitated; I thought she was perhaps going to say that we had been very base. But she remarked after a moment, in a candid, wondering way, "How much you must want them!"

"Oh, I do, passionately!" I conceded, smiling. And this chance made me go on, forgetting my compunctions of a moment before. "How can she possibly have changed their place herself? How can she walk? How can she arrive at that sort of muscular exertion? How can she lift and carry things?"

"Oh, when one wants and when one has so much will!" said Miss Tita, as if she had thought over my question already herself and had simply had no choice but that answer—the idea that in the dead of night, or at some moment when the coast was clear, the old woman had been capable of a miraculous effort.

"Have you questioned Olimpia? Hasn't she helped her—hasn't she done it for her?" I asked; to which Miss Tita replied promptly and positively that their servant had had nothing to do with the matter, though without admitting definitely that she had spoken to her. It was as if she were a little shy, a little ashamed now of letting me see how much she had entered into my uneasiness and had me on her mind. Suddenly she said to me, without any immediate relevance:

"I feel as if you were a new person, now that you have got a new name."

"It isn't a new one; it is a very good old one, thank heaven!"

She looked at me a moment. "I do like it better."

"Oh, if you didn't I would almost go on with the other!"

"Would you really?"

I laughed again, but for all answer to this inquiry I said, "Of course if she can rummage about that way she can perfectly have burnt them."

"You must wait—you must wait," Miss Tita moralised mournfully; and her tone ministered little to my patience, for it seemed after all to accept that wretched possibility. I would teach myself to wait, I declared nevertheless; because in the first place I could not do otherwise and in the second I had her promise, given me the other night, that she would help me.

"Of course if the papers are gone that's no use," she said; not as if she wished to recede, but only to be conscientious.

"Naturally! But if you could only find out!" I groaned, quivering again.

"I thought you said you would wait."

"Oh, you mean wait even for that?"

"For what then?"

"Oh, nothing," I replied, rather foolishly, being ashamed to tell her what had been implied in my submission to delay—the idea that she would do more than merely find out. I know not whether she guessed this; at all events she appeared to become aware of the necessity for being a little more rigid.

"I didn't promise to deceive, did I? I don't think I did."

"It doesn't much matter whether you did or not, for you couldn't!"

I don't think Miss Tita would have contested this even had she not been diverted by our seeing the doctor's gondola shoot into the little canal and approach the house. I noted that he came as fast as if he believed that Miss Bordereau was still in danger. We looked down at him while he disembarked and then went back into the *sala* to meet him. When he came up however I naturally left Miss Tita to go off with him alone, only asking her leave to come back later for news.

I went out of the house and took a long walk, as far as the Piazza, where my restlessness declined to quit me. I was unable to sit down (it was very late now but there were people still at the little tables in front of the cafés); I could only walk round and round, and I did so a half dozen times. I was uncomfortable, but it gave me a certain pleasure to have told Miss Tita who I really was. At last I took my way home again, slowly getting all but inextricably lost, as I did whenever I went out in Venice: so that it was considerably past midnight when I reached my door. The *sala* upstairs was as dark as usual and my lamp as I crossed it found nothing satisfactory to show me. I was disappointed, for I had notified Miss Tita that I would come back for a report, and I thought she might have left a light there as a sign. The door of the ladies' apartment was closed; which seemed an intimation that my faltering friend had gone to bed, tired of waiting for me. I stood in the middle of the place, considering, hoping she would hear me and perhaps peep out, saying to myself too that she would never go to bed with her aunt in a state so critical; she would sit up and watch—she would be in a chair, in her dressing-gown. I went nearer the door; I stopped there and listened. I heard nothing at all and at last I tapped gently. No answer came and after another minute I turned the handle. There was no light in the room; this ought to have prevented me from going in, but it had no such effect. If I have candidly narrated the importunities, the indelicacies, of which my desire to possess myself of Jeffrey Aspern's papers had rendered me capable I need not shrink from confessing this last indiscretion. I think it was the worst thing I did; yet there were extenuating circumstances. I was deeply though doubtless not disinterestedly anxious for more news of the old lady, and Miss Tita had accepted from me, as it were, a rendezvous which it might have been a point of honour with me to keep. It may be said that her leaving the place dark was a positive sign that she released me, and to this I can only reply that I desired not to be released.

The door of Miss Bordereau's room was open and I could see beyond it the faintness of a taper. There was no sound—my footstep caused no one to stir. I came further into the room; I lingered there with my lamp in my hand. I wanted to give Miss Tita a chance to come to me if she were with her aunt, as she must be. I made no noise to call her; I only waited to see if she would not notice my light. She did not, and I explained this (I found afterwards I was right) by the idea that she had fallen asleep. If she had fallen asleep her aunt was not on her mind, and my explanation ought to have led me to go out as I had come. I must repeat again that it did not, for I found myself at the same moment thinking of something else. I had no definite purpose, no bad intention, but I felt myself held to the spot by an acute, though absurd, sense of opportunity. For what I could not have said, inasmuch as it was not in my mind that I might commit a theft. Even if it had been I was confronted with the evident fact that Miss Bordereau did not leave her secretary, her cupboard and the drawers of her tables gaping. I had no keys, no tools and no ambition to smash her furniture. None the less it came to me that I was now, perhaps alone, unmolested, at the hour of temptation and secrecy, nearer to the tormenting treasure than I had ever been. I held up my lamp, let the light play on the different objects as if it could tell me something. Still there came no movement from the other room. If Miss Tita was sleeping she was sleeping sound. Was she doing so—generous creature—on purpose to leave me the field? Did she know I was there and was she just keeping quiet to see what I would do—what I *could* do? But what could I do, when it came to that? She herself knew even better than I how little.

I stopped in front of the secretary, looking at it very idiotically; for what had it to say to me after all? In the first place it was locked, and in the second it almost surely contained nothing in which I was interested. Ten to one the papers had been destroyed; and even if they had not been destroyed the old woman would not have put them in such a place as that after removing them from the green trunk—would not have transferred them, if she had the idea of their safety on her brain, from the better hiding-place to the worse. The secretary was more conspicuous, more accessible in a room in which she could no longer mount guard. It opened with a key, but there was a little brass handle, like a button, as well; I saw this as I played my lamp over it. I did something more than this at that moment: I caught a glimpse of the possibility that Miss Tita wished me really to understand. If she did not wish me to understand, if she wished me to keep away, why had she not locked the door of communication between the sitting-room and the *sala*? That would have been a definite sign that I was to leave them alone. If I did not leave them alone she meant me to come for a purpose—a purpose now indicated by the quick, fantastic idea that to oblige me she had unlocked the secretary. She had not left the key, but the lid would probably move if I touched the button. This theory fascinated me, and I bent over very close to judge. I did not propose to do anything, not even—not in the least—to let down the lid; I only wanted to test my theory, to see if the cover *would* move. I touched the button with my hand—a mere touch would tell me; and as I did so (it is embarrassing for me to relate it), I looked over my shoulder. It was a chance, an instinct, for I had not heard anything. I almost let my luminary drop and certainly I stepped back, straightening myself up at what I saw. Miss Bordereau stood there in her night-dress, in the doorway of her room, watching me; her hands were raised, she had lifted the everlasting curtain that covered half her face, and for the first, the last, the only time I beheld her extraordinary eyes. They glared at me, they made me horribly ashamed. I never shall forget her strange little bent white tottering figure, with its lifted head, her attitude, her expression; neither shall I forget the tone in which as I turned, looking at her, she hissed out passionately, furiously:

"Ah, you publishing scoundrel!"

I know not what I stammered, to excuse myself, to explain; but I went towards her, to tell her I meant no harm. She waved me off with her old hands, retreating before me in horror; and the next thing I knew she had fallen back with a quick spasm, as if death had descended on her, into Miss Tita's arms.

IX

I left Venice the next morning, as soon as I learnt that the old lady had not succumbed, as I feared at the moment, to the shock I had given her—the shock I may also say she had given me. How in the world could I have supposed her capable of getting out of bed by herself? I failed to see Miss Tita before going; I only saw the *donna*, whom I entrusted with a note for her younger mistress. In this note I mentioned that I should be absent but for a few days. I went to Treviso, to Bassano, to Castelfranco;[18] I took walks and drives and looked at musty old churches with ill-lighted pictures and spent hours seated smoking at the doors of cafés, where there were flies and yellow curtains, on the shady side of sleepy little squares. In spite of these pastimes, which were mechanical and perfunctory, I scantily enjoyed my journey: there was too strong a taste of the disagreeable in my life. It had been devilish awkward, as the young men say, to be found by Miss Bordereau in the dead of night examining the attachment of her bureau; and it had not been less so to have to believe for a good many hours afterward that it was highly probable I had killed her. In writing to Miss Tita I attempted to minimise these irregularities; but as she gave me no word of answer I could not know what impression I made upon her. It rankled in my mind that I had been called a publishing scoundrel, for certainly I did publish and certainly I had not been very delicate. There was a moment when I stood convinced that the only way to make up for this latter fault was to take myself away altogether on the instant; to sacrifice my hopes and relieve the two poor women for ever of the oppression of my intercourse. Then I reflected that I had better try a short absence first, for I must already have had a sense (unexpressed and dim) that in disappearing completely it would not be merely my own hopes that I should condemn to extinction. It would perhaps be sufficient if I stayed away long enough to give the elder lady time to think she was rid of me. That she would wish to be rid of me after this (if I was not rid of her) was now not to be doubted: that nocturnal scene would have cured her of the disposition to put up with my company for the sake of my dollars. I said to myself that after all I could not abandon Miss Tita, and I continued to say this even while I observed that she quite failed to comply with my earnest request (I had given her two or three addresses, at little towns, *poste restante*) that she would let me know how she was getting

18. Three cities northwest of Venice on the mainland.

on. I would have made my servant write to me but that he was unable to manage a pen. It struck me there was a kind of scorn in Miss Tita's silence (little disdainful as she had ever been), so that I was uncomfortable and sore. I had scruples about going back and yet I had others about not doing so, for I wanted to put myself on a better footing. The end of it was that I did return to Venice on the twelfth day; and as my gondola gently bumped against Miss Bordereau's steps a certain palpitation of suspense told me that I had done myself a violence in holding off so long.

I had faced about so abruptly that I had not telegraphed to my servant. He was therefore not at the station to meet me, but he poked out his head from an upper window when I reached the house. "They have put her into the earth, *la vecchia*,"[19] he said to me in the lower hall, while he shouldered my valise; and he grinned and almost winked, as if he knew I should be pleased at the news.

"She's dead!" I exclaimed, giving him a very different look.

"So it appears, since they have buried her."

"It's all over? When was the funeral?"

"The other yesterday. But a funeral you could scarcely call it, signore; it was a dull little *passeggio* of two gondolas. *Poveretta!*"[20] the man continued, referring apparently to Miss Tita. His conception of funerals was apparently that they were mainly to amuse the living.

I wanted to know about Miss Tita—how she was and where she was—but I asked him no more questions till we had got upstairs. Now that the fact had met me I took a bad view of it, especially of the idea that poor Miss Tita had had to manage by herself after the end. What did she know about arrangements, about the steps to take in such a case? *Poveretta* indeed! I could only hope that the doctor had given her assistance and that she had not been neglected by the old friends of whom she had told me, the little band of the faithful whose fidelity consisted in coming to the house once a year. I elicited from my servant that two old ladies and an old gentleman had in fact rallied round Miss Tita and had supported her (they had come for her in a gondola of their own) during the journey to the cemetery, the little red-walled island of tombs which lies to the north of the town, on the way to Murano. It appeared from these circumstances that the Misses Bordereau were Catholics, a discovery I had never made, as the old woman could not go to church and her niece, so far as I perceived, either did not or went only to early mass in the parish, before I was stirring. Certainly even the priests respected their seclusion; I had never caught the whisk of the curato's skirt. That evening, an hour later, I sent my servant down with five words written on a card, to ask Miss Tita

19. the old woman.
20. *passeggio:* procession; *poveretta:* poor thing.

if she would see me for a few moments. She was not in the house, where he had sought her, he told me when he came back, but in the garden walking about to refresh herself and gathering flowers. He had found her there and she would be very happy to see me.

I went down and passed half an hour with poor Miss Tita. She had always had a look of musty mourning (as if she were wearing out old robes of sorrow that would not come to an end), and in this respect there was no appreciable change in her appearance. But she evidently had been crying, crying a great deal—simply, satisfyingly, refreshingly, with a sort of primitive, retarded sense of loneliness and violence. But she had none of the formalism or the self-consciousness of grief, and I was almost surprised to see her standing there in the first dusk with her hands full of flowers, smiling at me with her reddened eyes. Her white face, in the frame of her mantilla, looked longer, leaner than usual. I had had an idea that she would be a good deal disgusted with me—would consider that I ought to have been on the spot to advise her, to help her; and, though I was sure there was no rancour in her composition and no great conviction of the importance of her affairs, I had prepared myself for a difference in her manner, for some little injured look, half familiar, half estranged, which should say to my conscience, "Well, you are a nice person to have professed things!" But historic truth compels me to declare that Tita Bordereau's countenance expressed unqualified pleasure in seeing her late aunt's lodger. That touched him extremely and he thought it simplified his situation until he found it did not. I was as kind to her that evening as I knew how to be, and I walked about the garden with her for half an hour. There was no explanation of any sort between us; I did not ask her why she had not answered my letter. Still less did I repeat what I had said to her in that communication; if she chose to let me suppose that she had forgotten the position in which Miss Bordereau surprised me that night and the effect of the discovery on the old woman I was quite willing to take it that way: I was grateful to her for not treating me as if I had killed her aunt.

We strolled and strolled and really not much passed between us save the recognition of her bereavement, conveyed in my manner and in a visible air that she had of depending on me now, since I let her see that I took an interest in her. Miss Tita had none of the pride that makes a person wish to preserve the look of independence; she did not in the least pretend that she knew at present what would become of her. I forbore to touch particularly on that however, for I certainly was not prepared to say that I would take charge of her. I was cautious; not ignobly, I think, for I felt that her knowledge of life was so small that in her unsophisticated vision there would be no reason why—since I seemed to pity her—I should not look after her. She told me how her aunt had died, very peacefully at the last, and how everything had been done afterwards by the care of her good friends (fortunately, thanks to me, she said, smiling, there was money in the house; and she repeated that when once the Italians like you they are your friends for life); and when we had gone into this she asked me about my *giro*, my impressions, the places I had seen. I told her what I could, making it up partly, I am afraid, as in my depression I had not seen much; and after she had heard me she exclaimed, quite as if she had forgotten her aunt and her sorrow, "Dear, dear, how much I should like to do such things—to take a little journey!" It came over me for the moment that I ought to propose some tour, say I would take her anywhere she liked; and I remarked at any rate that some excursion—to give her a change—might be managed: we would think of it, talk it over. I said never a word to her about the Aspern documents; asked no questions as to what she had ascertained or what had otherwise happened with regard to them before Miss Bordereau's death. It was not that I was not on pins and needles to know, but that I thought it more decent not to betray my anxiety so soon after the catastrophe. I hoped she herself would say something, but she never glanced that way, and I thought this natural at the time. Later however, that night, it occurred to me that her silence was somewhat strange; for if she had talked of my movements, of anything so detached as the Giorgione at Castelfranco,[21] she might have alluded to what she could easily remember was in my mind. It was not to be supposed that the emotion produced by her aunt's death had blotted out the recollection that I was interested in that lady's relics, and I fidgeted afterwards as it came to me that her reticence might very possibly mean simply that nothing had been found. We separated in the garden (it was she who said she must go in); now that she was alone in the rooms I felt that (judged, at any rate, by Venetian ideas) I was on rather a different footing in regard to visiting her there. As I shook hands with her for good-night I asked her if she had any general plan—had thought over what she had better do. "Oh yes, oh yes, but I haven't settled anything yet," she replied, quite cheerfully. Was her cheerfulness explained by the impression that I would settle for her?

I was glad the next morning that we had neglected practical questions, for this gave me a pretext for seeing her again immediately. There was a very practical question to be touched upon. I owed it to her to let her know formally that of course I did not expect her to keep me on as a lodger, and also to show some interest in her own tenure, what she might have on her hands in

21. The altarpiece in the Cathedral at Castelfranco by Giorgione (1477– 1510), a great painter who was born at Castelfranco.

the way of a lease. But I was not destined, as it happened, to converse with her for more than an instant on either of these points. I sent her no message; I simply went down to the *sala* and walked to and fro there. I knew she would come out; she would very soon discover I was there. Somehow I preferred not to be shut up with her; gardens and big halls seemed better places to talk. It was a splendid morning, with something in the air that told of the waning of the long Venetian summer; a freshness from the sea which stirred the flowers in the garden and made a pleasant draught in the house, less shuttered and darkened now than when the old woman was alive. It was the beginning of autumn, of the end of the golden months. With this it was the end of my experiment—or would be in the course of half an hour, when I should really have learned that the papers had been reduced to ashes. After that there would be nothing left for me but to go to the station; for seriously (and as it struck me in the morning light) I could not linger there to act as guardian to a piece of middle-aged female helplessness. If she had not saved the papers wherein should I be indebted to her? I think I winced a little as I asked myself how much, if she *had* saved them, I should have to recognise and, as it were, to reward such a courtesy. Might not that circumstance after all saddle me with a guardianship? If this idea did not make me more uncomfortable as I walked up and down it was because I was convinced I had nothing to look to. If the old woman had not destroyed everything before she pounced upon me in the parlour she had done so afterwards.

It took Miss Tita rather longer than I had expected to guess I was there; but when at last she came out she looked at me without surprise. I said to her that I had been waiting for her and she asked why I had not let her know. I was glad the next day that I had checked myself before remarking that I had wished to see if a friendly intuition would not tell her: it became a satisfaction to me that I had not indulged in that rather tender joke. What I did say was virtually the truth—that I was too nervous, since I expected her now to settle my fate.

"Your fate?" said Miss Tita, giving me a queer look; and as she spoke I noticed a rare change in her. She was different from what she had been the evening before—less natural, less quiet. She had been crying the day before and she was not crying now, and yet she struck me as less confident. It was as if something had happened to her during the night, or at least as if she had thought of something that troubled her—something in particular that affected her relations with me, made them more embarrassing and complicated. Had she simply perceived that her aunt's not being there now altered my position?

"I mean about our papers. *Are* there any? You must know now."

"Yes, there are a great many; more than I supposed." I was struck with the way her voice trembled as she told me this.

"Do you mean that you have got them in there—and that I may see them?"

"I don't think you can see them," said Miss Tita, with an extraordinary expression of entreaty in her eyes, as if the dearest hope she had in the world now was that I would not take them from her. But how could she expect me to make such a sacrifice as that after all that had passed between us? What had I come back to Venice for but to see them, to take them? My delight at learning they were still in existence was such that if the poor woman had gone down on her knees to beseech me never to mention them again I would have treated the proceeding as a bad joke. "I have got them but I can't show them," she added.

"Not even to me? Ah, Miss Tita!" I groaned, with a voice of infinite remonstrance and reproach.

She coloured and the tears came back to her eyes; I saw that it cost her a kind of anguish to take such a stand but that a dreadful sense of duty had descended upon her. It made me quite sick to find myself confronted with that particular obstacle; all the more that it appeared to me I had been extremely encouraged to leave it out of account. I almost considered that Miss Tita had assured me that if she had no greater hindrance than that——! "You don't mean to say you made her a deathbed promise? It was precisely against your doing anything of that sort that I thought I was safe. Oh, I would rather she had burned the papers outright than that!"

"No, it isn't a promise," said Miss Tita.

"Pray what is it then?"

She hesitated and then she said, "She tried to burn them, but I prevented it. She had hid them in her bed."

"In her bed?"

"Between the mattresses. That's where she put them when she took them out of the trunk. I can't understand how she did it, because Olimpia didn't help her. She tells me so and I believe her. My aunt only told her afterwards so that she shouldn't touch the bed—anything but the sheets. So it was badly made," added Miss Tita, simply.

"I should think so! And how did she try to burn them?"

"She didn't try much; she was too weak, those last days. But she told me—she charged me. Oh, it was terrible! She couldn't speak after that night; she could only make signs."

"And what did you do?"

"I took them away. I locked them up."

"In the secretary?"

"Yes, in the secretary," said Miss Tita, reddening again.

"Did you tell her you would burn them?"

"No, I didn't—on purpose."

"On purpose to gratify me?"

"Yes, only for that."

"And what good will you have done me if after all you won't show them?"

"Oh, none; I know that—I know that."

"And did she believe you had destroyed them?"

"I don't know what she believed at the last. I couldn't tell—she was too far gone."

"Then if there was no promise and no assurance I can't see what ties you."

"Oh, she hated it so—she hated it so! She was so jealous. But here's the portrait—you may have that," Miss Tita announced, taking the little picture, wrapped up in the same manner in which her aunt had wrapped it, out of her pocket.

"I may have it—do you mean you give it to me?" I questioned, staring, as it passed into my hand.

"Oh yes."

"But it's worth money—a large sum."

"Well!" said Miss Tita, still with her strange look.

I did not know what to make of it, for it could scarcely mean that she wanted to bargain like her aunt. She spoke as if she wished to make me a present. "I can't take it from you as a gift," I said, "and yet I can't afford to pay you for it according to the ideas Miss Bordereau had of its value. She rated it at a thousand pounds."

"Couldn't we sell it?" asked Miss Tita.

"God forbid! I prefer the picture to the money."

"Well then keep it."

"You are very generous."

"So are you."

"I don't know why you should think so," I replied; and this was a truthful speech, for the singular creature appeared to have some very fine reference in her mind, which I did not in the least seize.

"Well, you have made a great difference for me," said Miss Tita.

I looked at Jeffrey Aspern's face in the little picture, partly in order not to look at that of my interlocutress, which had begun to trouble me, even to frighten me a little—it was so self-conscious, so unnatural. I made no answer to this last declaration; I only privately consulted Jeffrey Aspern's delightful eyes with my own (they were so young and brilliant, and yet so wise, so full of vision); I asked him what on earth was the matter with Miss Tita. He seemed to smile at me with friendly mockery, as if he were amused at my case. I had got into a pickle for him—as if he needed it! He was unsatisfactory, for the only moment since I had known him. Nevertheless, now that I held the little picture in my hand I felt that it would be a precious possession. "Is this a bribe to make me give up the papers?" I demanded in a moment, perversely. "Much as I value it, if I were to be obliged to choose, the papers are what I should prefer. Ah, but ever so much!"

"How can you choose—how can you choose?" Miss Tita asked, slowly, lamentably.

"I see! Of course there is nothing to be said, if you regard the interdiction that rests upon you as quite insurmountable. In this case it must seem to you that to part with them would be an impiety of the worst kind, a simple sacrilege!"

Miss Tita shook her head, full of her dolefulness. "You would understand if you had known her. I'm afraid," she quavered suddenly—"I'm afraid! She was terrible when she was angry."

"Yes, I saw something of that, that night. She was terrible. Then I saw her eyes. Lord, they were fine!"

"I see them—they stare at me in the dark!" said Miss Tita.

"You are nervous, with all you have been through."

"Oh yes, very—very!"

"You mustn't mind; that will pass away," I said, kindly. Then I added, resignedly, for it really seemed to me that I must accept the situation, "Well, so it is, and it can't be helped. I must renounce." Miss Tita, at this, looking at me, gave a low, soft moan, and I went on: "I only wish to heaven she had destroyed them; then there would be nothing more to say. And I can't understand why, with her ideas, she didn't."

"Oh, she lived on them!" said Miss Tita.

"You can imagine whether that makes me want less to see them," I answered, smiling. "But don't let me stand here as if I had it in my soul to tempt you to do anything base. Naturally you will understand I give up my rooms. I leave Venice immediately." And I took up my hat, which I had placed on a chair. We were still there rather awkwardly, on our feet, in the middle of the *sala*. She had left the door of the apartments open behind her but she had not led me that way.

A kind of spasm came into her face as she saw me take my hat. "Immediately—do you mean to-day?" The tone of the words was tragical—they were a cry of desolation.

"Oh no; not so long as I can be of the least service to you."

"Well, just a day or two more—just two or three days," she panted. Then controlling herself she added in another manner, "She wanted to say something to me—the last day—something very particular, but she couldn't."

"Something very particular?"

"Something more about the papers."

"And did you guess—have you any idea?"

"No, I have thought—but I don't know. I thought all kinds

of things."

"And for instance?"

"Well, that if you were a relation it would be different."

"If I were a relation?"

"If you were not a stranger. Then it would be the same for you as for me. Anything that is mine—would be yours, and you could do what you like. I couldn't prevent you—and you would have no responsibility."

She brought out this droll explanation with a little nervous rush, as if she were speaking words she had got by heart. They gave me an impression of subtlety and at first I failed to follow. But after a moment her face helped me to see further, and then a light came into my mind. It was embarrassing, and I bent my head over Jeffrey Aspern's portrait. What an odd expression was in his face! "Get out of it as you can, my dear fellow!" I put the picture into the pocket of my coat and said to Miss Tita. "Yes, I'll sell it for you. I sha'n't get a thousand pounds by any means, but I shall get something good."

She looked at me with tears in her eyes, but she seemed to try to smile as she remarked, "We can divide the money."

"No, no, it shall be all yours." Then I went on, "I think I know what your poor aunt wanted to say. She wanted to give directions that her papers should be buried with her."

Miss Tita appeared to consider this suggestion for a moment; after which she declared, with striking decision, "Oh no, she wouldn't have thought that safe!"

"It seems to me nothing could be safer."

"She had an idea that when people want to publish they are capable—" And she paused, blushing.

"Of violating a tomb? Mercy on us, what must she have thought of me!"

"She was not just, she was not generous!" Miss Tita cried with sudden passion.

The light that had come into my mind a moment before increased. "Ah, don't say that, for we *are* a dreadful race." Then I pursued, "If she left a will, that may give you some idea."

"I have found nothing of the sort—she destroyed it. She was very fond of me," Miss Tita added, incongruously. "She wanted me to be happy. And if any person should be kind to me—she wanted to speak of that."

I was almost awestricken at the astuteness with which the good lady found herself inspired, transparent astuteness as it was and sewn, as the phrase is, with white thread. "Depend upon it she didn't want to make any provision that would be agreeable to me."

"No, not to you but to me. She knew I should like it if you could carry out your idea. Not because she cared for you but because she did think of me," Miss Tita went on, with her unexpected, persuasive volubility. "You could see them—you could use them." She stopped, seeing that I perceived the sense of that conditional —stopped long enough for me to give some sign which I did not give. She must have been conscious however that though my face showed the greatest embarrassment that was ever painted on a human countenance it was not set as a stone, it was also full of compassion. It was a comfort to me a long time afterwards to consider that she could not have seen in me the smallest symptom of disrespect. "I don't know what to do; I'm too tormented, I'm too ashamed!" she continued, with vehemence. Then turning away from me and burying her face in her hands she burst into a flood of tears. If she did not know what to do it may be imagined whether I did any better. I stood there dumb, watching her while her sobs resounded in the great empty hall. In a moment she was facing me again, with her streaming eyes. "I would give you everything —and she would understand, where she is—she would forgive me!"

"Ah, Miss Tita—ah, Miss Tita," I stammered, for all reply. I did not know what to do, as I say, but at a venture I made a wild, vague movement, in consequence of which I found myself at the door. I remember standing there and saying, "It wouldn't do—it wouldn't do!" pensively, awkwardly, grotesquely, while I looked away to the opposite end of the *sala* as if there were a beautiful view there. The next thing I remember is that I was downstairs and out of the house. My gondola was there and my gondolier, reclining on the cushions, sprang up as soon as he saw me. I jumped in and to his usual "*Dove commanda?*"[22] I replied, in a tone that made him stare, "Anywhere, anywhere; out into the lagoon!"

He rowed me away and I sat there prostrate, groaning softly to myself, with my hat pulled over my face. What in the name of the preposterous did she mean if she did not mean to offer me her hand? That was the price—that was the price! And did she think I wanted it, poor deluded, infatuated, extravagant lady? My gondolier, behind me, must have seen my ears red as I wondered, sitting there under the fluttering *tenda*,[23] with my hidden face, noticing nothing as we passed—wondered whether her delusion, her infatuation had been my own reckless work. Did she think I had made love to her, even to get the papers? I had not, I had not; I repeated that over to myself for an hour, for two hours, till I was wearied if not convinced. I don't know where my gondolier took me; we floated aimlessly about on the lagoon, with slow, rare strokes. At last I became conscious that we were near the Lido, far up, on the right hand, as you turn your back to Venice, and I made him put me ashore. I wanted to walk, to move, to shed some of my bewilderment. I crossed the

22. "Where do you want me to go?"   23. curtain or awning.

narrow strip and got to the sea-beach—I took my way toward Mala-mocco. But presently I flung myself down again on the warm sand, in the breeze, on the coarse dry grass. It took it out of me to think I had been so much at fault, that I had unwittingly but none the less deplorably trifled. But I had not given her cause—distinctly I had not. I had said to Mrs. Prest that I would make love to her; but it had been a joke without consequences and I had never said it to Tita Bordereau. I had been as kind as possible, because I really liked her; but since when had that become a crime where a woman of such an age and such an appearance was concerned? I am far from remembering clearly the succession of events and feelings during this long day of confusion, which I spent entirely in wandering about, without going home, until late at night; it only comes back to me that there were moments when I pacified my conscience and others when I lashed it into pain. I did not laugh all day—that I do recol-lect; the case, however it might have struck others, seemed to me so little amusing. It would have been better perhaps for me to feel the comic side of it. At any rate, whether I had given cause or not it went without saying that I could not pay the price. I could not accept. I could not, for a bundle of tattered papers, marry a ridicu-lous, pathetic, provincial old woman. It was a proof that she did not think the idea would come to me, her having determined to suggest it herself in that practical argumentative, heroic way, in which the timidity however had been so much more striking than the boldness that her reasons appeared to come first and her feelings afterward.

As the day went on I grew to wish that I had never heard of Aspern's relics, and I cursed the extravagant curiosity that had put John Cumnor on the scent of them. We had more than enough material without them and my predicament was the just punishment of that most fatal of human follies, our not having known when to stop. It was very well to say it was no predicament, that the way out was simple, that I had only to leave Venice by the first train in the morning, after writing a note to Miss Tita, to be placed in her hand as soon as I got clear of the house; for it was a strong sign that I was embarrassed that when I tried to make up the note in my mind in advance (I would put it on paper as soon as I got home, before going to bed), I could not think of anything but "How can I thank you for the rare confidence you have placed in me?" That would never do; it sounded exactly as if an acceptance were to follow. Of course I might go away without writing a word, but that would be brutal and my idea was still to exclude brutal solutions. As my confusion cooled I was lost in wonder at the importance I had at-tached to Miss Bordereau's crumpled scraps; the thought of them became odious to me and I was as vexed with the old witch for the superstition that had prevented her from destroying them as I was with myself for having already spent more money than I could afford in attempting to control their fate. I forget what I did, where I went after leaving the Lido and at what hour or with what recovery of composure I made my way back to my boat. I only know that in the afternoon, when the air was aglow with the sunset, I was standing before the church of Saints John and Paul and looking up at the small square-jawed face of Bartolommeo Colleoni,[24] the terrible *condottiere* who sits so sturdily astride of his huge bronze horse, on the high pedestal on which Venetian gratitude maintains him. The statue is incomparable, the finest of all mounted figures, unless that of Marcus Aurelius,[25] who rides benignant before the Roman Capitol, be finer: but I was not thinking of that; I only found myself staring at the triumphant captain as if he had an oracle on his lips. The western light shines into all his grimness at that hour and makes it wonderfully personal. But he continued to look far over my head, at the red immersion of another day—he had seen so many go down into the lagoon through the centuries—and if he were thinking of battles and stratagems they were of a different quality from any I had to tell him of. He could not direct me what to do, gaze up at him as I might. Was it before this or after that I wandered about for an hour in the small canals, to the continued stupefaction of my gondolier, who had never seen me so restless and yet so void of a purpose and could extract from me no order but "Go anywhere—everywhere—all over the place"? He reminded me that I had not lunched and expressed therefore respectfully the hope that I would dine earlier. He had had long periods of leisure during the day, when I had left the boat and rambled, so that I was not obliged to consider him, and I told him that that day, for a change, I would touch no meat. It was an effect of poor Miss Tita's proposal, not altogether auspicious, that I had quite lost my appetite. I don't know why it happened that on this occasion I was more than ever struck with that queer air of sociability, of cousinship and family life, which makes up half the expression of Venice. Without streets and vehicles, the uproar of wheels, the brutality of horses, and with its little winding ways where people crowd together, where voices sound as in the corridors of a house, where the human step circulates as if it skirted the angles of furniture and shoes never wear out, the place has the character of an immense collective apartment, in which Piazza San Marco is the most ornamented corner and palaces and churches, for the rest, play the part of great divans of repose, tables of entertainment, expanses of decoration. And somehow the splendid common domicile, familiar, domestic and resonant, also

24. The equestrian statue of the *condottiere* Bartolemmeo Colleoni (*ca.*1400–1475), a general who served the Venetian Republic, is the work of the Florentine sculptor Andrea Verrocchio (1436–1488). It was erected in 1496 after the death of the artist, in front of the Church of St. John and Paul.

25. The statue of the Roman Emperor Marcus Aurelius (A.D. 161–180) stands on the Capitol in Rome. It escaped destruction because it was erroneously considered to be a statue of Emperor Constantine.

resembles a theatre, with actors clicking over bridges and, in straggling processions, tripping along *fondamentas*.[26] As you sit in your gondola the footways that in certain parts edge the canals assume to the eye the importance of a stage, meeting it at the same angle, and the Venetian figures, moving to and fro against the battered scenery of their little houses of comedy, strike you as members of an endless dramatic troupe.

I went to bed that night very tired, without being able to compose a letter to Miss Tita. Was this failure the reason why I became conscious the next morning as soon as I awoke of a determination to see the poor lady again the first moment she would receive me? That had something to do with it, but what had still more was the fact that during my sleep a very odd revulsion had taken place in my spirit. I found myself aware of this almost as soon as I opened my eyes; it made me jump out of my bed with the movement of a man who remembers that he has left the house-door ajar or a candle burning under a shelf. Was I still in time to save my goods? That question was in my heart; for what had now come to pass was that in the unconscious cerebration of sleep I had swung back to a passionate appreciation of Miss Bordereau's papers. They were now more precious than ever and a kind of ferocity had come into my desire to possess them. The condition Miss Tita had attached to the possession of them no longer appeared an obstacle worth thinking of, and for an hour, that morning, my repentant imagination brushed it aside. It was absurd that I should be able to invent nothing; absurd to renounce so easily and turn away helpless from the idea that the only way to get hold of the papers was to unite myself to her for life. I would not unite myself and yet I would have them. I must add that by the time I sent down to ask if she would see me I had invented no alternative, though to do so I had had all the time that I was dressing. This failure was humiliating, yet what could the alternative be? Miss Tita sent back word that I might come; and as I descended the stairs and crossed the *sala* to her door—this time she received me in her aunt's forlorn parlour—I hoped she would not think my errand was to tell her I accepted her hand. She certainly would have made the day before the reflection that I declined it.

As soon as I came into the room I saw that she had drawn this inference, but I also saw something which had not been in my forecast. Poor Miss Tita's sense of her failure had produced an extraordinary alteration in her, but I had been too full of my literary concupiscence to think of that. Now I perceived it; I can scarcely tell how it startled me. She stood in the middle of the room with a face of mildness bent upon me, and her look of forgiveness, of absolution made her angelic. It beautified her; she was younger; she was not a ridiculous old woman. This optical trick gave her a sort

26. *fondamenta:* a Venetian term for the narrow footpaths along the canals

of phantasmagoric brightness, and while I was still the victim of it I heard a whisper somewhere in the depths of my conscience: "Why not, after all—why not?" It seemed to me I was ready to pay the price. Still more distinctly however than the whisper I heard Miss Tita's own voice. I was so struck with the different effect she made upon me that at first I was not clearly aware of what she was saying; then I perceived she had bade me good-bye—she said something about hoping I should be very happy.

"Good-bye—good-bye?" I repeated, with an inflection interrogative and probably foolish.

I saw she did not feel the interrogation, she only heard the words; she had strung herself up to accepting our separation and they fell upon her ear as a proof. "Are you going to-day?" she asked. "But it doesn't matter, for whenever you go I shall not see you again. I don't want to." And she smiled strangely, with an infinite gentleness. She had never doubted that I had left her the day before in horror. How could she, since I had not come back before night to contradict, even as a simple form, such an idea? And now she had the force of soul—Miss Tita with force of soul was a new conception—to smile at me in her humiliation.

"What shall you do—where shall you go?" I asked.

"Oh, I don't know. I have done the great thing. I have destroyed the papers."

"Destroyed them?" I faltered.

"Yes; what was I to keep them for? I burnt them last night, one by one, in the kitchen."

"One by one?" I repeated, mechanically.

"It took a long time—there were so many." The room seemed to go round me as she said this and a real darkness for a moment descended upon my eyes. When it passed Miss Tita was there still, but the transfiguration was over and she had changed back to a plain, dingy, elderly person. It was in this character she spoke as she said, "I can't stay with you longer, I can't;" and it was in this character that she turned her back upon me, as I had turned mine upon her twenty-four hours before, and moved to the door of her room. Here she did what I had not done when I quitted her—she paused long enough to give me one look. I have never forgotten it and I sometimes still suffer from it, though it was not resentful. No, there was no resentment, nothing hard or vindictive in poor Miss Tita; for when, later, I sent her in exchange for the portrait of Jeffrey Aspern a larger sum of money than I had hoped to be able to gather for her, writing to her that I had sold the picture, she kept it with thanks; she never sent it back. I wrote to her that I had sold the picture, but I admitted to Mrs. Prest, at the time (I met her in London, in the autumn), that it hangs above my writing-table. When I look at it my chagrin at the loss of the letters becomes almost intolerable.

Masterpieces of Symbolism and the Modern School

EDITED BY

KENNETH DOUGLAS

formerly of Yale University

Art, life, politics are inseparable and at the same time in conflict.—ALEXANDER BLOK

The incarnation of the word—is not that, perhaps, what we are seeking?—GEORGES BERNANOS

In the world of the twentieth century it is by no means sure that any still, small voice, whether the voice of conscience or of the poet, will continue to be heard. The present epoch, which from the individual standpoint has been called "the age of anxiety," politically viewed is an age of public uproar. Wars have followed upon wars, conflicts between nations have stimulated rather than diminished domestic broils, and new demands, both national and social, make a seething cauldron of many a region where, formerly, undernourished peoples accepted with resignation disease and early death.

The upheavals that have occurred, and currently threaten, are not accompanied by those obvious signs of a breakdown in human inventiveness and the will to overcome difficulties that Gibbon and later historians have so profusely documented for the Roman Empire. On the contrary, never have more men flung themselves so enthusiastically into co-operative ventures, some of which promise a healthier life and a higher standard of living for millions—or could it be all?—of the world's inhabitants. Western techniques and ideals enjoy unchallenged prestige in every corner of the globe. Every condition making possible the unification of mankind would appear to be on the point of fulfillment. Nevertheless, as we have noted, the integrity of existing nations is menaced not only from outside but also from within. And the integrity of the individuals that make up these nations is exposed to a similar double jeopardy of external pressure and internal chaos; the center of equilibrium does not lie in themselves. But where is any center?

Increase in knowledge is not restricted to the accumulation of facts about the physical world; the past, too, has been dredged up, the functioning of contemporary primitive societies has been closely observed, and on these impressive mountains of fact and their partial interpretations some bold speculators (Pareto, Spengler, Toynbee, for instance, and Hegel and Marx before them) have constructed theories concerning the general functioning of all human society. Parallel with this sharpened awareness of man in the mass, in his interconnections, has been exploration of another human dimension: the unconscious, the depths of the individual psyche. Here the name of Freud stands pre-eminent. Another investigator, the Swiss psychologist Carl Gustav Jung, believes that he has discovered a hitherto only dimly apprehended correspondence between the individual and the group, and between the living man and the generations that have passed away. Only probe deeply enough, he maintains, and beneath the individual unconscious you will come upon the collective unconscious. Or, to give a literary example, in James Joyce's *Finnegans Wake*,

the initials *H. C. E.* stand for both Humphrey Chimpden Earwicker, the dreaming hero, and "Here Cometh Everyman."

Just as material knowledge has speeded up the exploitation of material resources, so man's self-knowledge has been turned to account. It enables men to *use* other men, to manipulate and to exploit them. The process, in the view of those employing it, cannot begin too early: people who are caught young are unlikely to give trouble by offering resistance to what their "betters" are planning for them, and can therefore be smoothly integrated into the whole—to such a degree that they may cease to be human, at least as that word has been understood in the past; the individual, the man who stands out in a crowd, is then no more.

All this knowledge, and this welter of limitless possibilities (for those in control), have given rise to a particular gamut of attitudes, ranging from an ebullient, blinkered optimism to an alert and responsible participation, and then proceeding through various forms of cynical compliance with current trends, to skepticism, apathy, disgust, sterile revolt, and the preaching of a return to some less alarming social order or to a time-hallowed religious belief. But those who proclaim most loudly the merits of their own point of view or panacea are not necessarily most worthy of trust. Has the machinery man has invented grown so complex that he cannot hope to remain its master? Is any clinging to the past feasible? Or, in view of the *relativity* that now appears to characterize what once were looked on as rock-bottom certitudes—the relativity of Euclidean geometry to other possible geometries, for example; of matter to energy; of simultaneity to the situation of the observer—must we all, even in moral matters, acquire something like the increased flexibility of the pilot who, compared to the automobile driver, has to cope with an additional dimension of space? It is easier to raise than to answer such questions, and we should not too harshly blame the writer of our day if the most he can offer appears to be the poignant evocation of an unresolved dilemma, and if, even in favorable circumstances, his enthusiasm utters only two cheers for the modern world.

These, at all events, are some of the more prominent features of our fanatical and sophisticated, relativistic and neoprimitive, mass-minded and isolating twentieth century. Having enumerated them, and before commenting on each of the authors represented here, we shall turn back to the second half of the nineteenth century and briefly consider the tendencies in literature that then became manifest. From our latter-day viewpoint we may expect to find there techniques and outlooks that have since been applied to current problems, and perhaps enjoy the fleeting glimpse of some principle of unification or of order.

If during the first part of the nineteenth century Germans had provided the impetus behind the romantic ideas in literature and philosophy that spread over Europe, after 1850 the living pulse beat most strongly in France. The outstanding feature of the period was the prestige accorded science, and the attempt, on the part of men engaged in other activities, to share in that prestige. Philosophy, far from challenging the pretentions of the scientists, sought to build on them, Zola raised the claim of scientific validity for the novel, and even poetry, with the Parnassian school, clung to the visible, and recognized that Science had dispelled man's dream of his own importance, of a universe where his longings met with a response. Thus the objective presentation of things threatened to discredit the subjective viewpoint and, along with it, the individual—who was, however, constitutionally incapable of forgetting his own petty little worries and becoming the impassive scientific observer.

But that is only half the story, and the other half must be presented here. For this acceptance of scientific dogma aroused resentment and provoked counteraffirmations. In the literary domain, poets were the first to react—doubtless because the poem is less cumbersome and less firmly shackled to externals than the novel, and its publication requires much less capital than the staging of a play. Now poetry, it has been suggested, inevitably tends toward one or another sister art; it aspires if not to the condition of painting then to that of music. Reacting against the dominant visual bias, the new poets declared that it could not be poetry's central task to do what painting could achieve so much more easily: to depict. They sought after subtler relations in poetry than the description of objects and their spatial disposition could provide, relations that would hint at the totality and the meaningfulness of experience—which, unperceived, were slipping past the noses of the scientist and his more lowly ally, the plain, blunt man. The analogy with the suggestive power of music was unavoidable: in music each note, indifferent in itself, acquires its importance from the melodic line, and harmonies and harmonics surround that core of meaning with a fringe of significance that yet remains undefinable. But there is also an alternative way of leaving the everyday world of plain, blunt things behind. One may isolate the object entirely, transforming it as the photograph of an ash tray, when enlarged to fill a whole screen, transforms the ash tray. Loosed from all connection with its functions, imperiously commanding our attention, the object may exert on us an uncanny fascination, like some idol or totem. This focusing on the object is one aspect of Rimbaud's poetry, and it has been exploited most thoroughly by the surrealists of our century.

So, more self-consciously than in previous ages, literature set out to explore itself, to discover its own essence and to widen its boundaries. The naturalistic novelists enlarged them with respect to the social group. The symbolists added, not the already familiar domain of subjective fantasy, but that obscure zone where inner and outer worlds, in some mysterious fashion, at least seem to coincide.

But in art there are no recipes, except for failure. Like all others, this symbolist approach to literature was beset by pitfalls. The spirit sometimes chose to move elsewhere, leaving behind it merely the accessories of symbolism. In that case the symbolist literary work remained plunged in subjectivism (Ernest Renan called the symbolist poets "children sucking their thumbs") and appeared to be the ultimate in artificiality and willful obscurity. Once again the new writers—approximately at the dawning of the twentieth century—would have to find new paths, they would aim at a new simplicity, perhaps a greater humility, and strive vigorously to establish communication with others. Faithfulness to the spirit required unfaithfulness to established forms.

One tendency of the romantic period continued into the latter half of the nineteenth century and, indeed, persists today. That is the feeling, on the part of many writers, despite their own (usually) middle-class origins, that between themselves and the middle classes, or *bourgeoisie*, or Philistines, a great gulf is fixed. These writers feel that no part is allotted them in society as it is constituted, and that reigning values are fraudulent or trivial, while their own meet with nothing but incomprehension. The writers themselves, in turn, are accused of nihilism, of ingratitude, of loss of nerve, of decadence, and of many other sins. Nihilism, of course, there may be—and the rest. But the question should be raised whether literature and even language itself are not *inevitably* subversive. If something is to remain unchanged, it should not be mentioned—not even praised. For to praise is to focus attention upon it, to drag it into the light of consciousness. Once that has been done, it is fair game for blame as well as praise, for termites and despoiling. On the other hand, to cease to talk, to cease to conjure up imaginary worlds, possible and impossible, would mean, surely, to be no longer human. The only *status quo* for human beings is, in literature as in life, the questionableness of every *status quo*. The challenge, to use Arnold Toynbee's term, should be welcomed, for how, otherwise, could there be response?

THREE INITIATORS

CHARLES BAUDELAIRE
(1821–1867)

Baudelaire set out deliberately to startle the bourgeois. His collection of poems bears the gaudy title *Flowers of Evil* (*Les Fleurs du mal*), and includes litanies to Satan and several poems which in 1857, the year of the volume's publication, were banned as obscene. Yet Baudelaire's tactics, and his deep-rooted instinct, aimed far beyond mere sensationalism: the reader was to be startled so that he would be forced to realize his *involvement*. If one were to judge exclusively by the accusations of turpitude hurled in the poem-preface against his readers

and himself, Baudelaire would appear to reject utterly the notion of a literature for consumers only, for the uncommitted aesthete. His work would seem rather a literature for *sinners* only, for those who, like himself, were seriously involved, and recognized their guilt:

Obtuseness, error, sin, and niggardliness
Possess our minds and drive our bodies hard,
And we nourish our lovely moments of remorse,
As beggars give sustenance to their own vermin.

"Our," "we"—poet and reader are accomplices in vileness. And so it goes unrelentingly on to the famous last line, which T. S. Eliot adopted in *The Waste Land*:

Hypocritical reader,—my fellow, —and my brother!

This, then, is Baudelaire's equivalent of the Ancient Mariner's skinny hand; in this way he repels, yet holds, his reader. In the process, it will be seen, he has enlarged the subject matter of poetry. For one thing, the landscape has changed. The lakes and mountain settings dear to the French romantics, Baudelaire replaces with an urban scene: Paris. He knows the Paris of debauch and crime ("Enchanted evening falls, the criminal's friend"), of the poor ("How often have I followed these little old women"), of the frustrated passing encounter ("Oh, you whom I'd have loved, oh, you who knew!"). His poetry embraces the "utterly impossible" topic, notably in "A Carcass," a poem which many have found revolting, though it is only a more circumstantial version of the thoughts that occupy Shakespeare's Hamlet with the skull of Yorick in his hand. It was this poem that encouraged the painter Cézanne in his long toil; and that Rainer Maria Rilke, struggling to master though not to blunt his hypersensitivity, hailed as redemption, through art, of repugnant reality.

A Carcass (Une Charogne)*

Do you remember the thing we saw, dear soul, on that gentle summer morning? At a bend of the path a vile carcass on a pebbly river bed, its legs in the air like a lustful woman, consumed and exuding poisons, exposed in careless, shameless fashion, its belly filled with effluvia. The sun shone on this corruption, as though to cook it to a turn, and to give back to Nature all she had joined together. And the sky saw how the haughty carcass blossomed out like a flower. The stench was so overpowering, you thought that you would faint on the grass. The flies kept buzzing over the decaying belly from which there emerged black regiments of larvae that flowed like a dense liquid along these living rags.

All this sank and rose again like a wave, or shot upwards, crackling; the body might have been thought to live, swollen with an uncertain breath, and to multiply. And this world emitted a strange music, as of running water and of wind, or the grain that a winnower in a rhythmic motion shakes and turns in his sieve.

The shapes were dissolving and were no more than a dream, an outline that comes slowly on the forgotten canvas, and that the artist finishes only from memory.

Behind the rocks an uneasy bitch looked at us with an angry eye, waiting for the moment to seize once again the portion of the skeleton she had dropped.

And yet you too will come to be like this filth, this ghastly infection, star of my eyes, my nature's sun, you, my angel and my passion! Yes, such you will be, oh, queen of all graces, after the last rites, when you go, beneath grass and luxuriant vegetation, to molder amid the bones.

Then, my beauty! tell the vermin that will eat you with kisses that I have preserved the shape and the divine essence of my decayed loves!

This extension of poetry's domain was not toward the outside only. Baudelaire also probed within his own self, including its least flattering aspects, with a boldness and acumen that anticipated the discoveries of psychoanalysis. The fascination that Baudelaire has exerted of recent years over so many, both French and foreign, is connected with this self-unveiling: his readers are won over not alone by the incantation of his verses but by the fact that they are meeting a man who like themselves has

* 1857. The poem is translated in full.

sensed despair, and disgust and infantile urges, and who, also, has made a largely futile attempt to order his existence.

These fresh prospectings into the world outside and the world inside were felt as a unity by Baudelaire, both in actual fact and on the theoretical level. The enunciation of the theory is to be found in the poem "Correspondences"—and it would be difficult to name any other lines that so remarkably map out the aims of literature for a hundred years ahead.

Correspondences (Correspondances)*

Nature is a temple whose living pillars at times give out confused speech; there man traverses forests of symbols which watch him with a look of kinship.

Like long echoes which far off are blended into a deep and shadowy oneness, vast as the night and as light's regions, perfumes, colors and sounds give each other answer.

There are perfumes cool as children's flesh, tender as oboes, green as grasslands,—and others, corrupt, rich and triumphant, with the expansiveness of infinite things, like amber, musk, benjamin and incense, which sing the transports of the spirit and senses.

While the sestet of this sonnet treats of synesthesia (the rendering of an object so as to affect one of the five senses in terms of another), the theme of the first quatrain is of incomparably greater importance. Here Baudelaire asserts the interrelatedness of all things, the presence of universal analogy. Science, in those positivistic mid-century days, was coming to be accepted as a substitute for religion, as a religion in itself. Against this trend, Baudelaire reaffirmed that the individual consciousness is unique and irreplaceable, for the sciences do not and cannot concern themselves with the *total impact* of experience. And precisely this, Baudelaire insisted, is the artist's task: to evoke and clarify the experiences of the individual consciousness, with its wealth of overtones and gossamer cross-paths and its transcendence of time and space. He was inspired, beyond a doubt, by his readings in the occult, but he profoundly felt the truth that we, and the external world also, are "members one of another."

Thus opposites meet in Baudelaire—cruelty and tenderness, lofty flights and black despair, debauch and spiritual longing; and the note of foreboding is perhaps never entirely absent. But he represents even blasphemies and curses, transfigured in the work of great artists, as an appeal to the Eternal. This was his own endeavor, to ennoble by his art a pitiful existence:

Oh, wastrel monk! When shall I learn to make
Of my sad misery's living spectacle
The labor of my hands, the adoration of my eyes?

* 1857. The poem is translated in full.

1228 • Symbolism and the Modern School

Baudelaire's theory of artistic creation called for a cold-blooded mastery and calculation of effects, and at the same time for sensitivity to all those components of personality, demonic or ethereal, which the conventional social self represses or ignores. "Like a perfect chemist and like a hallowed soul" expresses the union of qualities he sought in his creative work; while "Spleen and Ideal" ("Spleen et Idéal"), the title of the opening section of *Flowers of Evil*, names the warring forces that made this union difficult of accomplishment. As he expressed it in prose: "In every man, at every moment, there are two simultaneous urges, one directed to God, the other to Satan."

Such was Baudelaire, predecessor and inspirer of the symbolist poets in France, Russia, Germany, and elsewhere; a blasphemer in whom some Catholics see a profoundly Catholic poet; a dandy who could assert that his poems concerned only the aesthetic sensibilities and yet confess, more privately, that in them he had placed his "entire heart."

STÉPHANE MALLARMÉ
(1842–1898)

This frail little man with the drooping moustache—whom in the mind's eye one sees enveloped in a haze of tobacco smoke, its convolutions outdone in subtlety and tenuous continuity by the ribbon of ideas his conversation unwinds—this modest figure, appreciated during his lifetime by a limited circle, looms ever larger, of recent years, as an ascetic of the literary life. He had the gift of facility as is shown by his numerous contributions to drawing-room albums, the hundreds of envelopes he addressed in verse (the letters arrived), his brief editorship of a ladies' fashion magazine, most of which, including puffs of advertisers and replies to correspondents, he wrote himself. Yet where his art was concerned, he chose to sacrifice facility to unremitting labor, and actual poetic achievement to the entire mastery of his artistic means. Only the gift of two lives could have enabled him to exercise, as well as to acquire, his skills.

To begin with, he came under the spell of Baudelaire. Some lines of his early poems might have been written by his predecessor ("And I fear to die when I go to bed alone"). But already in his early twenties Mallarmé, very different in temperament from Baudelaire, set out to find his own path. He was distressed, at this period, by a sense of irremediable sterility, which he sometimes attributed to youthful excesses, and which certainly was not alleviated by the shrieks of his baby daughter or by the hordes of unruly schoolboys whose English teacher he undertook to be. However, from a more literary viewpoint we may be tempted to attribute his difficulties to an overweening ambition. He was not satisfied with the prospect of adding, to the long series of Western masterpieces, his own productions, more or less obscurely conceived and hazardously elaborated. He wished, instead, to possess consciously all the resources of his art and, prior to that, to under-stand the essence, function, goal, of art. It is easy to see how even the greatest natural facility would be inhibited by such an ambition.

All poetry is difficult if not impossible to translate. Mallarmé's represents the supreme impossibility. For to a degree no other poet has equaled, he developed his conscious artistry, and correspondingly reduced the share played in the writing of his poems by the happy accident. Consequently, they are more indissolubly wedded to the French language than are any others; the content refuses to be wrenched away from the particular poetic form it has espoused. If Rimbaud, whom we next consider, may be taken to embody the poetizing faculty at its most primordial, at the stage of eruption and hurled lava, Mallarmé represents the consummate artist. Each of his poems is a delicate miracle, the complex and conscious equilibration of many factors of sound and meaning, and of their interplay. This description especially fits his best-known poems, "The Afternoon of a Faun" ("L' Après-midi d'un faune," 1876), A *Throw of the Dice* (*Un Coup de dés*, 1914), and the fragmentary "Hérodiade." His ambition was to transform everything into a living, functional part of the poetic organism, not excluding even the visual aspect, the black and white of the printed page.

Although his poems defy translation, it is possible to convey some notion of Mallarmé's ideals. The words in a line of poetry, he thought, should recip-rocally illuminate each other, causing the line to acquire the brilliance and density of a diamond and the unchallengeable rightness of a single dictionary word. Thus no word within the line would stand out on its own or attract undue attention. The line, similarly shunning all exhibitionism, should take its place in the poem's onward flow. In later poems by Mallarmé the highly subtle use of a sometimes ambiguous syntax contributes to the achievement of this aim, and to the sense of unity that pervades the whole. Again, like his words and lines, the poet's attitudes should be free of posturing, so that the elements of the poem may co-operate with each other undisturbed, like the instruments in an orchestra. The poem, as Mallarmé's disciple Paul Valéry was to express it, should be "Not so much someone's voice / As that of the waters and the wood." Mallarmé was alert, it can be seen, to musical analogies. But this interest did not primarily involve sound effects; it reflected rather his desire to capture for poetry something of music's infinitive suggestiveness, to hold up for adoration "a treasure of mystery and oblivion."

Mallarmé's mastery of language and poetry was a highly personal affair that could not be handed over to someone else—it could only be divined. And in actual fact relatively few adolescent poets published work that sedulously aped the master's style. Even the symbolists, whose leader he is supposed to have been, radically diverged from his practice by experimenting with free verse, of which he never wrote a line. What could be intuited and taken as a model was his attitude, that unmatched self-abnegation and devotion to art. Although he had not a scrap of religious belief ("This old and malicious plumage, overthrown, fortunately, God"), the sufferings of his early years and the illumination that came to him ("for more than a month I have been on the purest glaciers of Æsthetics . . . after finding *Nothingness* I have found *Beauty*") recall nothing so closely as the "dark night of the soul" known to St. John of the Cross and other mystics, and their subsequent union with the Divine. Like these mystics, too, Mallarmé may have felt torn between the fidelity of silence and the temptation and pitfalls of communication. He was too essentially the Poet to choose the former.

ARTHUR RIMBAUD
(1854–1891)

Rimbaud has perhaps outraged even more sensibilities than Baudelaire. They both offended the backers of the established order in letters and in life, but Rimbaud has been a stumbling block even for the esthetes of the *avant-garde*; his example unceasingly calls into question their values also. Those for whom nothing but literature matters must accommodate themselves to a youth of exceptional genius who scornfully tossed aside literature before he had reached the age of twenty. The subsequent silence of Rimbaud is as much a part of the meaning of his career as the explosion of his teens.

Like many adolescent boys, he combined refractoriness and sensitivity, both of which, with him, were pushed to the extreme. In one sense, it is correct to say that his work is extraordinarily mature, but his genius nevertheless bears the stamp of youth. Everything came to him so astonishingly early that, exempt from the usual slow processes of emotional and cultural maturation, it strikes us like some elemental force. Here is the image-making faculty at its rawest and most torrential.

Subjected during his childhood to the rule of a domineering and narrowly pious mother, whose influence he was never completely to shake off, he expresses himself in many of the earlier poems, still written in the usual syllabic meters of French, with an extreme exacerbation. He flouts all the decencies and taboos of respectable middle-class family life and reveals his kinship with wall-scribblers at the same stage of development. Yet even the most trivial infringements of the social code, as he presents them, have a quality of force, urgency—authenticity, it would not be too much to say—that is unique; and sometimes themes as unpromising as the satisfaction of bodily needs or the removal of head-lice yield magnificent poems. Yet not all is rebellion. He could escape, too, from a constricting environment—although to the end of his days he always found the way back to his home and people—and find balm, relatively speaking, in his cosmic sense.

His flight from the conditioning of school and family was but the first step in a voyage of discovery. "Drunken Boat" maps out the course. Its first two stanzas record the poet's liberation from utilitarian, commercial considerations. His journey is an abandonment to the currents of river and sea. The booty he seeks, like the speaker in Tennyson's "Ulysses," is experience, sensations, reality. Men can only hinder him, but the universe appears disposed to give him aid. As conscious control is progressively lost, with the "rudder and grappling-anchor" of the third paragraph, below, he bathes in "the Poem of the Sea," where genuine love is found. The torrent of hallucinatory images rises to a climax. Yet at last a note of surfeit can be heard, and of longing for Europe's "ancient parapets."

In the original French, this poem makes a startling impact.

The images—which are stated, never developed—jostle each other for room and disappear, as though shaken in a kaleidoscope. If we succeed in fixing on one of them for a moment, it may prove to have a lurid, disturbing quality that increases the sense of estrangement. Familiar landmarks are gone, the whole lexicon seethes uncontrollably around us. Yet, on the other hand, the author cannot be accused of mental derangement. Not only is each individual alexandrine of an impeccably classical cut; together they build a severe and simple structure. This lack of control is under control, this dementia is precociously planned, the ocean boils within a mind that has not lost its bearings. Rimbaud, as he himself had announced, *cultivated* insanity. The insane do not need to do so. He ran grave risks, but returned from the voyage—just as, throughout his life, he returned home from every journey.

Drunken Boat (*Le Bateau ivre*)*

As I descended the impassive Streams, I felt myself no longer guided by the haulers: screeching Redskins had taken them for targets, nailing them naked to the colored stakes. I was heedless of all the ships' crews, carriers of Flemish grains or English cottons. When all the uproar around my haulers had ended, the Streams let me descend wherever I would.

In the raging tide-rips of last winter, deafer than the minds of children, I sped on! And the unmoored Peninsulas never withstood more triumphant hullabaloos. The tempest blessed my maritime awakenings. Lighter than a cork I danced on the waters that are called eternal victim-spinners, for ten nights, without regretting the foolish eye of the beacons!

Sweeter than for children the flesh of sour apples, the green water penetrated my hull of pine-wood and stains of blue

* Written in 1871; published in 1883. The poem is translated in full.

wines and vomitings washed me, scattering rudder and grappling-anchor. And from that moment, I bathed myself in the Poem of the Sea, infused with stars, and latescent,[1] devouring the green azures where, pale and entranced flotsam, a pensive drowned man, sometimes, descends; where, dye-ing all of a sudden the blue-nesses, deliriums and slow rhythms beneath daylight's crimson glows, stronger than liquor, vaster than your lyres, ferment the bitter russet splotches of love!

I know the skies that burst into lightning flashes, and the waterspouts and the surf and the currents; I know the evening, the dawn exalted like a people of doves, and at times I have seen what man believed he saw. I have seen the low sun stained with mystic horrors lighting up with long purple coagulations, similar to actors in age-old dramas, the waters revolving far away their shutter-tremors.[2] I have dreamed the green night with dazzling snows, kisses that rise slowly to the eyes of the seas, the circulation of the un-imaginable saps and the yellow and blue awakening of the sing-ing phosphoruses. I have fol-lowed for months entire the surge, like hysterical cow-byres, in its assault of the reefs, with-out reflecting that the luminous feet of the Maries[3] could curb

the muzzle of the wheezy Oceans! I have collided, do you know? with unbelievable Flor-idas mixing, among the flowers, eyes of panthers with the skins of men, rainbows stretched like bridles, beneath the horizon of the seas, on glaucous[4] herds. I have seen marshes ferment, enor-mous weirs in which a whole Leviathan[5] rots among the reeds, cataracts of water in the midst of calm seas, and the distances plunging into the abysses! Gla-ciers, silvery suns, pearly waters, skies of embers, hideous strand-ings at the head of dusky gulfs where giant serpents devoured by bugs fall from tortuous trees with black perfumes!

I would have liked to show the children these dorados of the blue water, these goldfish, these singing fish. Foams of flow-ers have cradled my driftings, and ineffable winds have lent me wings, at moments. Sometimes, a martyr weary of the poles and zones, the sea, whose sob made my rocking gentle, raised to me its flowers of shade with yellow suckers and I remained like a woman on her knees, a penin-sula tossing on my shores the quarrels and the droppings of clamorous birds with light-colored eyes, and I was sailing on when across my frail bonds drowned men descended back-wards to sleep . . .[6]

Now I, a boat lost under the

---

1. not in French dictionaries. It may be derived from *latex*, a word denoting the milky juice of plants, or from *latere*, "to lurk"; or it may be intended for "lactescent."

2. caused by the wind blowing over the water.

3. perhaps a reference to Mary Mag-dalene, Mary of Cleophas, and Mary Salome, who according to Provençal

legend landed at the place on the Medi-terranean coast of France now called Les Saintes-Maries-de-la-Mer. It is the goal of an annual pilgrimage for Euro-pean gypsies.

4. sea-green.

5. a monster mentioned in the Book of Job, usually identified as the whale.

6. Rimbaud's punctuation. Nothing has been omitted at this point.

hair of the coves, thrown by the hurricane into the birdless ether, I whose carcass, intoxicated with water, the Monitors[7] and the Hanse[8] sailing ships would not have fished out, free, smoking, manned by purple mists, I who pierced the sky glowing red like a wall which bears, an exquisite jam for the good poets, lichens of sun and snots of azure; I who ran, spotted with electric crescents, a mad plank, escorted by the black sea-horses, when the Julies[9] with bludgeon strokes brought down in collapse the ultramarine skies with their ardent funnels; I who trembled, hearing whimper fifty leagues off the rut of Behemoths[10] and the dense Maelstroms,[11] eternal weaver of blue immobilities, I regret Europe with its ancient parapets! I have seen sidereal[12] archipelagoes! And islands whose delirious skies are open to him who sails: Is it in these bottomless nights that you sleep and are exiled, million birds of gold, oh future Vigor?

But, true, I have wept too much! The Dawns are harrowing. Every moon is atrocious and every sun is bitter: pungent love has swollen me with intoxicating torpors. Oh, may my keel shatter! May I go to the sea!

If I long for a water of Europe, it is the black, cold puddle where towards the balmy twilight a crouching child full of sorrows launches a boat frail as a May butterfly.

I can no longer, bathed in your languors, waves, cross the wake of the carriers of cottons, nor traverse the pride of the flags and pennants, nor swim beneath the horrible eyes of the prison-ships!

Typical again of Rimbaud's attitude are the last three stanzas, expressing first of all a revulsion: "The Dawns are harrowing. . . . every sun is bitter." He voices the ultimate Dionysian urge, he would escape utterly from the limits of self: "Oh, may my keel shatter! May I go to the sea!" Then he turns back once more to Europe, to his own childhood, and in the final stanza admits defeat. Commerce, nationhood, a utilitarian and restrictive society, have triumphed. As has often been pointed out, Rimbaud's own career is here prefigured: the return home, first from European wanderings, and later from the East and Africa, where he faced reality as he had come to see it, abandoning literature, which could not satisfy the demands he had made on it, and making a living through commerce. This was the "gnarled reality" on which he had to fasten his grip.

The literary distinction of Rimbaud lies in the visionary quality of his work. Some would classify him as one of the supreme demiurges, or creators of imaginary universes, in contrast

7. ironclad warships with one or more revolving turrets for large-caliber guns. Named after the first such vessel, which was used against the *Merrimac* in 1862 by the Union forces.
8. the medieval Hanseatic League, a mercantile federation of North German cities.
9. plural of "July."
10. Mentioned in the Book of Job, the Behemoth is usually identified as the hippopotamus.
11. whirlpools.
12. starry.

to those poets who celebrate the revealed truth of divine creation or who themselves struggle to perceive the truth. The surrealists, during the twentieth century, have found in him a predecessor who opened the floodgates of the subconscious and far transcended the limitations of the ordinary waking mind. They can find in him, too, an indifference to the reader's comfort and a subordination of the petty question, Is this comprehensible? to the untrammeled rights of free creativity. Rimbaud did not, however, adhere to the surrealist doctrine that writing must be automatic and uncontrolled. In his search for concision and force of expression, he revised with the greatest care.

Rimbaud attempted to use poetry as a way to truth. To the subjective imaginings of the romantic poets, he opposed his own kind of objective poetry—a record made, so-to-speak, impassively, of the extraordinary phantasmagoria invading the consciousness, particularly when the poet has made himself a "seer by a long, immense, and deliberate derangement of all the senses." This was to be hallucination not for its own sake, but as a means to knowledge. And the poet's knowledge was to benefit all men. For the poet is Prometheus; he is "responsible for all humanity, even for the *animals.*" Rimbaud's sympathy for the poor can be seen in the "Farewell" which ends his *Season in Hell* (*Une Saison en enfer,* 1873). He had based great hopes for revolution on the Paris Commune. The defeat

of this experiment was another factor that turned him away from pursuit of the ideal.

One of the few writers during Rimbaud's lifetime to be influenced by his work was Paul Claudel. Like the priest who administered the last rites to Rimbaud (as reported by Isabelle Rimbaud), Claudel was convinced that Rimbaud was profoundly religious and profoundly Catholic. Not everyone is willing to allow the latter claim, but a greater number may agree with Claudel that Rimbaud was *un mystique à l'état sauvage,* "a mystic in the wild state." One may feel reasonably sure that the ways of grace cut directly across the paths of propriety, on occasion. Rimbaud was perhaps one such occasion.

A POET AND RUSSIA— ALEXANDER BLOK

A commercial civilization may be indifferent to its critics; in a despotism all but the timeservers awaken suspicion. "Siberia" is a word that enters the biographies of Russian writers quite early in the nineteenth century, and for many who did not actually make the journey it remained a displeasing possibility. Thus even at the century's end, when the Russian poets Konstantin Balmont and Valery Bryusov were adapting and spreading the doctrines of French symbolism, when art was to be for art's sake or was associated with a mystical religiosity, the Russian writer's refusal to interest himself in political issues had a singular background of which he could never be entirely unaware.

This was the atmosphere of Blok's youth. He soon became a prominent figure in the literary world of St. Petersburg, hymning his "Lady Beautiful" and blending this vision with the flesh-and-blood reality of his young wife, Lyubov. Andrey Bely and other friends joined him in this cult, which Blok celebrated in verses of a mysterious impressiveness that evaporates in translation. But doubts rose to haunt him. His fears that the "Lady Beautiful" might abandon him foreshadowed the vision's end. In a remarkable lyric drama, *The Puppet Show* (1907), which greatly shocked his still-believing friends, he mocked at himself and the beliefs he had lost.

His later work translates more readily. It is no longer purely ethereal, for Blok's "Muse," as one of his poems states, appears to him as a demonic power pushing him onward and downward. As he treads these lower circles, his poetry is enriched with new dimensions of human significance. He refers contemptuously to the symbolist illusions of former years, which still retain their fascination in his friends' eyes, and like Rimbaud turns to seize a harsher reality. But unlike Rimbaud, who fell silent, he transposes it into verse of tremendous strength.

Blok was never a politician, and clearly affirmed that the poet has another task to fulfill, that of giving ear, and expression, to "the music of the future"—the term was doubtless suggested to him by Wagner's *Musik der Zukunft*, for he maintains not only that Wagner's music was the voice of mighty elemental forces, but that Wagner himself, who had mounted the Dresden barricades in 1849, was a revolutionary whom the old dying world had hastened to disguise, since he could not be suppressed. The abortive Russian revolt of 1905 left an indelible mark on Blok's thinking; and after the collapse of the imperial regime and then of Kerensky's provisional government he heard ever more intensely the future's music, until that January of 1918 which produced "The Twelve" and his last poem, "The Scythians."

"The Twelve" had an extraordinary reception. Twelve million copies found their way into print. For a while, Blok's actress wife helped to keep her husband and herself alive by reciting it night after night in a café. Condemnation and praise were equally vehement. The poem was called a Bolshevist tract—and also a mockery of the Revolution. The conservative and orthodox declared it blasphemous. Blok's friend the poet Sologub, and the later émigrés Dmitri Merezhkovsky and his wife the poetess Zinaida Hippius, expressed their displeasure. On the revolutionary side it had the approval of such leaders as Lunacharsky and Kamenev, for example, while Trotsky advised Blok to substitute Lenin for the figure of Jesus Christ. In more recent years, "The Twelve" has by some again been acclaimed as Blok's supreme achievement, but others consider that it has dated, a fate that does not remotely threaten his earlier work. But let Blok himself speak, about both the meaning of the poem and its reception in time to come. He wrote, in April, 1920:

> While I was writing "The Twelve," and for several days after finishing the poem, I felt, with my physical sense of hearing, a great enveloping sound, a mixed sound, the sound probably of the old world's collapse. That is why those who, in "The Twelve," see political verses either have their eyes closed to art, or are sitting up to the ears in the mud of politics, or, again, are possessed by a great fury, whether they are the friends or the enemies of my poems. At the same time, it would be false to deny all connection between "The Twelve" and politics. The truth is that the poem was written in the exceptional and always brief period when the revolutionary cyclone, passing like a lightning flash, raises a storm in all the seas of Nature, of Life, and of Art. . . . The seas of Nature, Life, and Art were unloosed, and the spray rose in a rainbow above our heads. I was looking at the rainbow when I wrote "The Twelve": that is why there remains a drop of politics in the poem. We shall see what time will make of that. Perhaps—all politics is so dirty!—a single one of its drops will be enough to tarnish and decompose all the rest; perhaps again it will not succeed in killing the meaning of the poem; perhaps, finally, who knows, it will turn out to be the leavening thanks to which "The Twelve" will be read in an age no longer ours.

This prophetic transport could not last. Already depressed, suffering ever more, physically, in those terrible first years of the new regime, undertaking every sort of literary and administrative activity in order to make a livelihood, perhaps disappointed also in the course the Revolution was taking (the attempt to evaluate the relative strength of these factors cannot go beyond hypotheses), Blok wrote no more poetry. The sounds which he had heard for so many years now deserted him. He said to Chukovsky: "All the sounds have become silent. Don't you hear that there are no more sounds?"

In "The Twelve," amid the bitter blast that is sweeping away the old order and past figures who typify the groups that made it up, twelve drunken Red Army soldiers march through the streets of Petrograd. They catch sight of a comrade, Vanka, who has gone over to the enemy, riding in a carriage with Katya, a girl they have known intimately. When they glimpse him again, they shoot. The girl is killed. Pyotr, who fired the fatal shot, is overcome with remorse. His comrades tell him that this is no time to mourn over such an incident, and he puts it behind him. On they march, the mongrel that symbolizes the old world following them nevertheless, since they are its only hope. At their head is Christ.

Blok, it can be seen, idealizes nothing. Nor does he worship the brutalities, often senseless, that accompanied the upheaval. But beneath the present crimes, and with the prospect of iron years ahead, he senses the stirring of elemental things.

LYRICISM AND A REFRACTORY REALITY

WILLIAM BUTLER YEATS

There is a certain resemblance in the situations of Yeats and of Blok. In Ireland, as in Russia, the nation's future had become a matter of grave moment; in both countries poverty and a sense of frustration had led to deeds of violence, including political murders, which opened up a prospect of more general violence to come. The two poets belonged to privileged castes, the Russian intelligentsia and the Protestant ruling class, and began as singers of a misty, otherworldly idealism. Yeats, like Blok, was to transcend the limitations of his class and of the poetic school that reigned during his youth, and to take a passionate interest in the strivings of his homeland toward a fuller nationhood. He too found an important, nonpolitical part for himself in a movement whose later political aspect appeared to swallow up the literary and cultural aims cherished by the poet. Yeats, again like Blok, extended his horizon by the writing of plays and by direct participation in the running of a theater. And he evolved, in his own pursuit of poetry, not by ever more lofty soarings into the empyrean, but by exploration of the actualities of politics and daily life, sometimes trivial, sometimes coarse, which he transmuted into the lasting reality of a shockingly immediate lyric utterance. The old poetic words grew rarer in his verse, and by a miracle the rhythms of ordinary Irish speech (or so it seems), with its rapid changes of tone and its elliptical contempt for the slow-witted, became intensest poetry.

Poets learn, as Robert Frost has told us, in their own way, which is not the method of systematic assimilation practiced by scholars. Many different strands went into the weaving of Yeats's poet's coat: Irish mythology; the separate strand of Irish folklore; the malicious tongues of some— and the visionary powers of other —illiterate Irish peasants; Irish ballads; the voices of the contemporary English poets with whom he associated in the Rhymers' Club (Ernest Dowson, Lionel Johnson); Eastern scriptures and the works of Eastern mystics; the Cabala and a wide variety of material on the occult; French symbolism, to some degree directly, to some degree as interpreted, and distorted, in the conversation and the translations of Arthur Symons; and later in life, works of the philosophers. Science remained a bugbear, and Yeats more than once indicated his distaste for the writings of Bertrand Russell and H. G. Wells. His own philosophy he attempted to express in the prose work *A Vision* (1937), on which he labored long, but which has found few admirers. The poetry of his last years is colored by these views, and cannot always be fully understood without reference to them. But it shuns the didactic. Each poem remains true to the impulse that inspired it, even if this is a quite deplorable "lust" or immoderate "rage."

Gone in this later work is that Irish variant of elaborate and mannered end-of-the-century decadence, the "Celtic twilight" atmosphere of his youthful poems. Yeats developed an inimitable personal idiom, rhythmically off key, it has been said, whose twists and abrupt "awkward" pauses and sudden rushes of syllables match the colloquial and at times earthy, less often esoteric or learned, nature of the words he uses. The rhymes, too, are sometimes imperfect, or they vigorously pinpoint a prosaic, nonpoetic term. These traits quite admirably incarnate the antithetical quality of his thought as well as the shifts of feeling, and just as his thought welds together pairs of opposites in a transcendent whole, so do the heterogeneous elements of rhythm and vocabulary fuse in the oneness of the poem. Behind it we seem to glimpse a man of passion and reflection, haughtily ambitious, who cannot be satisfied to arrange in pleasing patterns a few brightly colored pebbles: with verses taut as lassos he would seize and dominate reality's wild horses.

"The Tower" (1926) considers the bitter contrast of old age, with its physical ruin but heaven-storming imaginative violence. For Yeats the tower was itself a symbol of lonely struggle. In this poem, he tries to bring together many things—from his personal past; from the past of his surroundings and their departed inhabitants; from his short-of-saintly present, with its decrepitude and passion and longing for essential knowledge; from his ever-alive gift of verse-making; and from those men younger or as yet unborn whom he can admire, and whose ancestor he feels himself to be. For himself, only wisdom is left. Closely related are the theme, and the ghosts summoned from the past, in "Among School Children" (1928), but here the

gap that separates the aged "scarecrow" from the glow of youth is experienced even more poignantly. To find a balm, Yeats must altogether transcend the earthly plane and voice his belief in immortality, and his sense of the glory suffusing all creation. "Sailing to Byzantium," actually written some three months later although published earlier, in 1927, is a brief but densely meaningful poem that celebrates at once his own apotheosis, and that of every artist and of all men, caught up in the whole. It is a vision of perfection which we must adore but also strive to attain, for it is by the act of creation that we best worship the Creator.

Yeats is more flawed, perhaps, but also more human and so closer to us, for arousing the invincible feeling that a renewal of ordinary, animal, lusty youth— within four months of hearing of Steinach's treatment for rejuvenation he had the operation performed on himself—would have outweighed, on his value scale, all that the saints and sages had entrusted to his care.

FEDERICO GARCÍA LORCA

Whether or not "Africa begins at the Pyrenees," Spaniards often impress the foreigner as being imbued with a spontaneity and depth of passion rarely found elsewhere in the Western world. Correspondingly, the Spanish poet, even when most extravagantly baroque, does not lose contact with the wellsprings of popular lyricism. Thus the Renaissance poet Góngora, whose name is associated with the kind of preciosity which in other countries was baptized "euphuism" or "Marinism," was inspired in many of his finest lyrics by Spanish folk poetry. Here is no divorce between learning and life, between the poet and the traditions of his people.

The same union of the indigenous and the most modern cosmopolitan trends distinguishes the work of García Lorca. He steeped himself, first of all, in the poetry and music of his native Andalusia (reserving a special place in his affections for Gypsy lore and Gypsy music), and went on to embrace all Spain. So irremediably Spanish was he that months of residence in New York provided him with only the merest smattering of mispronounced English words. Yet wherever he was he could sense and be inspired by the life around him, and in literary matters his intuition proved an entirely adequate substitute for polyglot readings.

It would be pointless to force resemblances, where they do not exist, between the careers of García Lorca, Yeats, and Blok. His lyric expression went through no such period of disintoxication as that of Yeats, nor did he, like Yeats and Blok, experience a loss of enchantment with some youthful ideal. He was, furthermore, resolutely nonpolitical, and voiced his discomfort at the Spanish public's finding in his writings, especially his plays, a political appositeness he had never intended. But we can scarcely dismiss this reaction of the audience as purely fortuitous. García Lorca had his finger on the pulse of the Spanish people, and his works, inevitably,

were relevant to their malaise.

In his turning to the theater, at least, García Lorca may be compared with Yeats and Blok. He had always enjoyed reciting and singing poems composed by himself and others. It appears inevitable that he should have been interested in the theater and its public. And his dramatic works offer evidence of a turning away from lyricism—from surface lyricism, that is—for each succeeding play of the trilogy *Blood Wedding* (*Bodas de sangre*, 1935), *Yerma* (1937), *The House of Bernarda Alba* (*La casa de Bernarda Alba*, 1945) reveals an increasing renunciation of lyric forms and "poetic" situations. García Lorca is yet another poet who sought to grasp, *through* the medium of his art, the "gnarled reality" for which Rimbaud abandoned literature.

"Lament for the Matador" ("Llanto por Ignacio Sánchez Mejías," 1935) is often regarded as the poet's supreme achievement. He had been personally friendly with Ignacio Sánchez Mejías, bullfighter, student of literature, and poet. Sánchez Mejías, finding no satisfaction in retirement from the bull ring, and unwilling, suggests Arturo Barea, to await the "grey death" between blankets, made a successful comeback. Several months later he was killed. This "Lament" seeks no consolation beyond the grave; it is self-fulfilling. The first section expresses the hypnotic fascination which the dread happening exerts on the poet. Images of the bull ring, of the fighter's agony, of medical care, of death and funeral rites haunt his conscious-ness. In the second section, he revolts against, but cannot es-cape, this monstrous reality: Ignacio's blood stains all things. In the third part he contem-plates the dead body and its speedy decay; in the fourth, a world from which Ignacio is absent. Both in form and in sub-ject matter, this poem takes its place in the long tradition of Spanish poetry—yet images are used with a freedom, with what one feels is an instinctive right-ness, that situate it at the very origin of the mythmaking fac-ulty. From this point of view it can be regarded as a supreme example of the successful em-bodiment of surrealist doctrines. But since no poet was ever less doctrinaire than García Lorca, perhaps we had better say that it is simply the type of creative phenomenon which provides evidence in support of the views of the surrealists.

A MEANING INTERFUSED —RAINER MARIA RILKE

Rilke's life was an immense *task*. Endowed with a morbid sensitivity and a dubious gift of facility that might have led to disaster in life or in art, he con-quered both dangers. He lived, someone has said, the aesthetic life to the full. And so he did, but only in the sense that he sub-mitted himself to a rigorous dis-cipline, aiming at no ivory-tower or coterie art, but at the elucida-tion of man's rôle in the world.

This "aesthete," then, this wanderer, this lifelong accepter of hospitality from the titled and wealthy, this husband too re-spectful of his wife's individual-ity to share a hearth with her— how far too easy it is to mock at Rilke!—had the good fortune or the skill to insure himself the proper material conditions for the fulfillment of his task, in spite of his apparent drifting and his slight financial resources. Re-siding at different periods in Germany, France, and Switzer-land, with visits to Scandinavia, Italy, Spain, Russia, and his na-tive Austria-Hungary, he made himself a truly European poet. The first World War, shattering European unity, shattered his peace of mind also, and not un-til several years after the war's close did he succeed in finding once again release of his poetic powers, which then flooded out to complete the *Duino Elegies* (*Duineser Ele-gien*, 1923), fragmentarily given him ten years before, and to call into being their pendant, the *Sonnets to Orpheus* (*Die Son-nette an Orpheus*, 1923).

The *Duino Elegies*, as befits the name, form a lament, but of a very special kind. Their slow modulations conjure up a pic-ture of man ill at ease in the universe. "The sick animal," Nietzsche had called man, and the second elegy finds similarly that "Everything is agreed to re-main silent concerning us, in part / as shameful perhaps and in part as an unutterable hope." It is in order to throw some light on the latter possibility that the elegiac form has been adopted, for, says one of the Orpheus sonnets, "Rejoicing *knows*, and longing tells its story,— / only lament learns still . . ."

The ninth of the ten elegies represents the climax of Rilke's long search for the meaning of human life; now he is able to glimpse the goal. This *once* that we live on earth will never *not* have been—but we can neither retain it nor bequeath it to another. Yet, possessing language, we are the only beings who can transmute the material thing and the transitory event into an enduring immateriality. Man can fulfill the hope of the earth by allowing the earth to arise once more, "invisible." In his *Elegies* and *Sonnets to Orpheus,* Rilke joins those who voice the poet's confidence in the supreme importance of his strivings. Almost to the word, he concurs with Stéphane Mallarmé, for whom literature was "the Orphic explanation of the earth," and who maintained, both humorously and more than humorously, "with an ineradicable, doubtless, writer's prejudice," that all things were destined to lead to a book.

T. S. ELIOT

The synthesis of innovation and return to the past gives Eliot's work its validity and its living tension. As a very young man, he considered that English poetry had reached a dead end, but was uncertain about how the ghost of Swinburne could be successfully laid. The reading of Arthur Symons' book on the French symbolists, followed by enlivening contact with their work and with Ezra Pound's literary enthusiasms, combined with a total lack of interest in English prosody to start Eliot on his path. His suspicion that falseness too often lurked behind ready displays of emotion, his search for the strictly authentic in word and thought, produced a limited quantity of verse whose astringency and verbal asceticism proved disconcerting to many. (Since those days his work has come to have so profound an effect on the ideals and practice of younger poets that to talk of an "age of Eliot" in English and American poetry is simply to state a fact.) In the late 1920's, after *The Waste Land* (1922) and "The Hollow Men" (1925) had crowned his investigations into contemporary disillusionment and the meaninglessness of existence as it was being lived, he disappointed a goodly share of his admirers by announcing his acceptance of the Christian revelation. In reality, there were quite a few touches in his poetry that should have made this turning to Christianity seem less surprising.

Robert Frost returned from the San Francisco of his birth to reside in the New England of his ancestors. Eliot's return took him farther back—from his natal St. Louis to the family's New England habitat and thence to England, to the Church of England, and to English citizenship. In his poetry also, he simultaneously discarded the outworn and spurious, and attempted to absorb the past, to bring it to life. He made a fully conscious effort to situate his writing in the long tradition of English literature, and beyond that in the tradition of European literature from the time of the Greeks. At the same time, the Christian tradition, and that of the mystics both within Christianity and in Hinduism and Buddhism, came to play an important part in his work, notably in "Ash-Wednesday" (1930) and in the *Four Quartets* (1944), which appear to be its culmination.

Like the other poets examined here, Eliot found in the theater a valued medium for the exercise of his creative gifts, and he in return made a perhaps central contribution to the living theater. The fact no doubt was significant that he did not begin his theatrical apprenticeship with any genuflection to the idols of established routine—although more recently, with *The Cocktail Party* (1950) and *The Confidential Clerk* (1954), he has moved toward the accepted forms. Writing with a religious purpose works to be produced in a religious setting, in *The Rock* (1934) and then in *Murder in the Cathedral* (1935), Eliot was spared the obligation of learning the "tricks of the trade," of accepting conventions whose inner meaning, if any, he could not intuitively seize, even of working out what might pass as a "normal" dramatic structure.

Murder in the Cathedral takes for its subject a saint's life at its apogee and conclusion, at the moment he is preparing himself for martyrdom. With its combination of liturgical recollections and bold adaptations of the verse rhythms Eliot had developed in others contexts; with its satisfyingly clear contrasts between the humble, suffering folk, the priests and laymen both intent on the purely temporal aspects of what is more than a temporal problem, and the future saint himself, together with the projection of aspects of his personality in the four tempters, this play impressively welds complexity into unity, and demonstrates the multiple facets and different levels of a conflict at once divisive and unifying.

Superficially (and perhaps profoundly as well), *Murder in the Cathedral* recalls a Greek tragedy: the audience, and also the participants in the drama who function as the audience's delegates or representatives, know what is bound to happen. Other possibilities than martyrdom would have been open to Becket had he been another man, and three tempters make this plain to him. But fundamentally the dramatic interest does not focus upon the actual episode of the murder. Dramatic excitement is aroused rather by the question of meaning: not, simply, What sense can we find in this revolting, premeditated assassination? but rather, What sense can the main participant, who refuses to flee his destiny, discover in or impose on his death and life? This is no passive slaughter—or, as Becket declares, action and suffering are inseparable. The murderers are passive tools, and it is the murdered man who accepts and wills the divine purpose.

JAMES JOYCE

Et Tu, Healy! was the title of Joyce's first work. His father, a passionate adherent of Parnell in the controversy which split the Irish Parliamentary party and embittered Irish politics for many years to come, was so delighted by his nine-year-old son's essay attacking the virulent anti-Parnellite Timothy Healy that he arranged to have it printed. No copy is known to survive.

While Joyce certainly never renounced his Irish nationalism to become that contemner of things national, a "West Briton," his subsequent career diverged in almost every particular from the path he might have seemed destined to follow. In the language of the Church he announced his refusal to slide along the grooves of patriotic, cultural, and religious conformity: *Non serviam!* At the earliest possible moment he left Irish soil in favor of starvation in Paris, and he saw Ireland for the last time before the outbreak of World War I. The new Ireland, it is true, did nothing to indicate that Joyce would be *persona grata* within its boundaries. Mr. Timothy Healy, the old anti-Parnellite zealot, became the first governor general of the Irish Free State, and today in the Republic of Ireland it is still impossible to purchase freely all of Joyce's works.

Yet this renunciation of residence in Ireland was accompanied by an unflagging interest in the Irish and, more particularly, in the Dublin scene. Friends sent him, at his request, all sorts of information and documentary material that kept him in touch with daily life. From *Dubliners* (1914) through *A Portrait of the Artist as a Young Man* (1916), *Exiles* (1918), *Ulysses* (1922), and *Finnegans Wake* (1939), his works never cease to evoke his birthplace. And Joyce it is, however displeasing the fact may be to routine piety and shamrock nationalism, who has inscribed Dublin on the map of world literature.

Joyce attempted a supremely difficult task: to obtain the verdict of what has been called "contemporary posterity." He aimed, that is, at international acceptance, while yet loading his works with a wealth of topical and highly transitory allusions that might defeat—and frequently have defeated—the best-intentioned non-Irishmen. This approach has nothing in common with the method of the writer who seeks an entrée to the foreign market by exploiting the "picturesqueness" of his native land. Joyce made no concessions in order to attract an audience.

The homage paid to Ibsen by the young Joyce is often cited in order to establish his link with the naturalist school of writers, yet this admiration for the author of *Brand* (1866) and *Peer Gynt* (1867) is equally well fitted to show his kinship with the symbolists. By making that unwieldy and least naturally artistic art form, the novel, a miracle of controlled and infinitely rich and infinitely graduated echoes, Joyce proved himself the supreme symbolist. To attain his ends he did not scorn to use the humblest form of humor, of echo and suggestiveness—the pun; and he did so most liberally in his last work, *Finnegans Wake*. But the pun is not a mere conglomeration of sounds; it is an indissoluble unity of sound and significance. With Joyce it reached its apotheosis.

The symbolists in the main were poets, and to transfer their vision to the novel, that is to say, to pack every phrase of a lengthy tale with the wealth of meaning that each epithet of a brief lyric poem should convey, and more especially to relate coherently the larger blocks of this structure, was a formidable undertaking. To carry it out Joyce had recourse to the hierarchical sense found in medieval Catholicism, to its sense of pattern in human life and of kinship between macrocosm and microcosm. If the music of his work has a symbolist inspiration, its architecture is the gift of Mother Church.

Joyce certainly did not write to demonstrate the truth of revealed religion. Faithful, however, to his Catholic upbringing and his training in Thomistic Aristotelianism, he did aim at revealing the universal embodied in the particular. Thus in Joyce two traditions ran together: the symbolist "revival" of literature —a token of his attitude is his knowing Baudelaire's "Correspondences" by heart—and the Catholic conviction of an ordered and interpretable universe. Both, of course, are fundamentally at one in their affirmation of significance and their denial of all isolated "just-so-ness."

The opening of the *Portrait*, reproduced here, touches on Irish history and politics, the Church, and family relations, in the settings of school and home. All of Joyce's themes are here in a nutshell, in the seemingly artless and disconnected musings of the little Stephen. His father with the "hairy face" is, like God the Father, the first speaker. The story he tells serves to make the child aware of his separate identity: "He was baby tuckoo." Foreshadowing his vocation as a creative artist, Stephen makes the song he sings his own, pro-

phetically enough, by taking liberties with everyday fact and ordinary language: "O, the green wothe botheth." Then comes the theme of the mother, the first incarnation for the artist-to-be of the Eternal Feminine and of the Muse. She plays on the piano so that he may dance. But this state of primal innocence and intimacy cannot endure. He hides under the table, and his mother asks for an apology. The threat which follows ("if not, the eagles will come and pull out his eyes") reminds us of Joyce's later near blindness. It becomes an insistent refrain:

> Pull out his eyes,
> Apologise,
> Apologise,
> Pull out his eyes.

Conscience is awakened. Here is the central theme of the *Portrait*, one critic (Hugh Kenner) insists, that of Sin: "the development of Stephen Dedalus from a bundle of sensations to a matured, self-conscious, dedicated, fallen being." The two later works, *Ulysses* and *Finnegans Wake*, will take up the phases, subsequent to the fall, of struggle and redemption.

Joyce placed comedy above tragedy. In other words, rather than hymn the nobility of heroic and inevitable defeat, he chose to affirm. And what Joyce affirmed, as in the repeated *yes* of Molly Bloom which marks the end of *Ulysses*, was the totality of things; a priori he excluded nothing. The artist's vocation is to understand, and hence— should he judge that men have erred—to forgive and ultimately to redeem.

To whatever degree they may remain caviar to the general, the impact of Joyce's works on numerous writers has been tremendous. For these writers they are not desiccating and defeatist, but lively stimuli to personal literary creativity. We may attribute this effect to Joyce's holding in a living tension those polar opposites—freedom bordering on chaos and a rigorous and fully conscious pattern. His handling of language revealed possibilities of which only traces can be found in earlier writers; he aroused the feeling that he had unhobbled and spurred on language so that for the first time its uttermost limits were explored. At the same time he showed that to construct the novel architectonically, with the minute care that had seemed appropriate only to the short lyric poem, was no vain endeavor.

ANDRÉ GIDE

The serpent was the most subtle of the beasts of the field, we read in Genesis, and that is the guise under which André Gide has appeared to some. *An Evildoer* is the title of a book written by a father who accused Gide of having led to his son's ruin. There are obviously other things to be said about him, or he would scarcely have been awarded a Nobel prize in his old age. But even those favorably disposed to Gide will be ready to admit that the quality of deviousness distinguishes his character.

Gide was a distinguished, and much more than a distinguished, man of letters, and his writings and personal example have had an incalculable influence over many younger men for, at this date, something close to fifty years. In France his reputation is now somewhat overshadowed, an inevitable phenomenon after the death of a writer more than eighty years old. Rightly or wrongly, the fellow citizens of an octogenarian tend to assume that they have assimilated any lesson he may have had to offer, and bow to newer idols. But the increasing attention devoted to Gide in the United States, during the last few years only, suggests that for a small segment of educated Americans, he may have an important message to deliver: negatively, of resistance to social pressures, or at least the refusal to accept them unthinkingly, and positively, of the importance of authenticity —of carving out a personal code and way of life in the area between the well-worn and not too numerous ruts that the social mores allow for, and the extensive morasses in which the individualist or moral pioneer may too easily bog down. For the French, the situation is different. Gide appears to them as the representative of a past generation and easier days, when the luxury of a hypersensitive private scrupulosity (available to a favored few) resulted in the exclusion of any vulgar concern with the public interest. And this is their view of Gide in spite of his at least triple involvement in public issues. While we cannot attempt to dictate the verdicts of posterity, this generalization concerning Gide may perhaps be risked: he will always be regarded, not so much as a great creative writer, but as a man who molded his own existence and crystallized his inner battles in a series of scrupulously authentic, yet cunningly contrived, literary works. He was also one of the widest readers of all time.

Gide chose to see the warring factors in his personality as determined by his mixed Catholic-Protestant ancestry. And though his career seems startlingly divergent from any Protestant orthodoxy, his whole heretical progress through life was stamped by the patterns of that orthodoxy, in a pietistic French Calvinist version. In terms of Gide's own explanation, then, the Catholic strain must be supposed to have contributed his urge to embrace the whole of life and pronounce it good—a notion that more often would be regarded as pagan but which echoes, in a distorted form, the medieval Christian view that the natural world is a forest of symbols which reveal divinity, that human love is a pale reflection, but a reflection none the less, of divine love.

With Gide, to a much greater extent than with most authors, it is important to read all of the works, and in the order of their writing, if one is to arrive at an understanding of the man and of the individual book's significance. Each is a "fragment of a great confession" and may, in isolation, give rise to quite false assumptions. Hence it is an especially thorny problem to decide which one of his writings is most typical.

To cut the Gordian knot—and at the risk of appearing to emphasize Gide's cynicism—we have chosen a late work, clearly its author's *ave atque vale*, in which he looks back on his life and pronounces it, in the balance, good. This Theseus is very close to his creator, and the concluding dialogue with Oedipus once more offers for inspection the ways of life between which Gide had hesitated. But here, finally, the retrospective path of contrition and atonement is ruled out, and one man's unavoidably arbitrary, particular choice weighs the scales in favor of the road ahead, of unremitting trial and concomitant error. This judgment is, however, expressed only at the end of the journey; Gide had not always seen himself as a Theseus, and even this book more assuredly attests its author's *desire* to jettison the load of past guilt than his attainment of this goal. Theseus did not understand Oedipus, but Gide understood him very well, and more than once had seemed to totter on the brink of a Christian and Gidean equivalent to Oedipus' self-mutilation. The man who is torn throughout his life between irreconcilable opposites, has—at least in the imagination and therefore as a writer—embraced them.

THOMAS MANN

The painter Cézanne put such passion and tenacity into his lifelong struggle with the problems of painting technique that even the layman, as he moves through an exhibition of Cézanne's work, may be gripped by a modified access of this passion. A similar intensity characterizes Thomas Mann, but in his case the impelling force is the desire to comprehend. Though all writers surely possess it to some extent, there are few outside the ranks of the philosophers in whom it so triumphantly overrides other considerations. One may perfectly well grant a restricted validity to the view that Mann's writings are "boring," another way of saying that in his eagerness to get to the root of a matter, even if doing so means exploring every possible facet under every possible illumination, he often shows little regard for a frivolous and short-winded reader's expectation of entertainment. But this "boringness" largely loses its unfavorable aspects when made to take its place in the totality of Mann's aims and achievements.

Mann exhibits qualities which are not a necessary part of the imaginative writer's equipment. As the fine flower of the tradition of the German burgher, with its respect for learning and the things of the spirit, he made his own an awe-inspiring erudition, and at the same time became, in a nontrivial sense, a genuine sophisticate. Without relinquishing the German burgher's virtues, Mann grew to be a citizen of the world. Rooted in his milieu and origins, he is yet, somewhat like Joyce, outside them. The literatures of Germany and the rest of Europe, philosophy, history, music, psychology, all contributed to make of Mann a mirror of his age.

"Much study is a weariness of the flesh," and sophistication, a late stage in any culture, threatens to collapse in a loss of the vital urge. Mann was acutely conscious of this danger, partly because of his absorption in the pessimistic philosophy of Scho-

penhauer, in Nietzsche's analysis of the nineteenth century's "nihilism," and in the music of Wagner, which Nietzsche denounced as an enervating poison. But this cultural experience bore fruit on the soil of lived experience—it can flourish nowhere else—which for Mann included family tragedy.

At about the age of twenty-three, he started to write *Buddenbrooks* (1900), a two-volume novel that certainly stands on its own merits. The original bears the subtitle *Decay of a Family (Verfall einer Familie)*, and the novel inextricably incorporates elements of the history of his own family, which was established in business at the old Hanse town of Lübeck, close to the Baltic. The magnificent instinctive self-assurance and the mental health that had been the Voltairian grandfather's have yielded, in the grandson Thomas Buddenbrooks, to doubts and sickly hesitations. Schopenhauer's *The World as Will and Idea* has for him a morbid fascination. His brother Christian grows up to be a harmless but unemployable eccentric. Hanno, the son of Thomas Buddenbrooks and last of the whole line, has an aversion from life and longing for death that exceeds his father's. To this longing he abandons himself, improvising on the piano melodies that end in a repeated, structureless series of sounds, and dies before his schooldays are over.

This novel embodies the central problem of the earlier Thomas Mann, a problem which continued to put forth offshoots in later years. On the one side he sees *bourgeois* obtuseness, health, and adaptation to the coarse demands of everyday reality, on the other the sensitivity and insight of the artist, a precious gift indeed, but sickly, a menace to itself and the body public. Mann did not contemplate this unfortunate dichotomy from the outside; it was his intimate conflict, for he knew himself to be a burgher and an artist also. The short story "Tonio Kröger" (1903) gives perhaps the most direct expression to this dilemma, while "Death in Venice" ("Der Tod in Venedig," 1913) associates love of beauty and a genuine artistic accomplishment with morbidity, perversion, and death.

In this area of concern Mann's "Tristan" (1902) obviously belongs. Yet if it looks back to the piano-playing Hanno Buddenbrooks in its linking of music with morbidity and the death urge, it also looks forward. The setting, assuredly, and the element of caricature in the portrait of the aesthete, suggest the great panoramic novel *The Magic Mountain* (*Der Zauberberg*, 1924), which unfolds its action in a sanitarium, but is much more essentially a survey and critique of occidental civilization prior to the catastrophe of World War I, a regretful but definitive "goodbye to all that."

Mann, quite admirably and without repudiating his past and his roots, continued to grow throughout his career, and his sympathies embraced a great deal more than the sad lot of the artist in a Philistine society. After reviewing what had been his own world, in *The Magic Mountain*, he tried in the four novels taking the biblical Joseph for their hero to plunge into the mythical past, to conjure up and grasp a prerational world view. Politically, too, Mann grew with the years, neither clinging obstinately to a dead past nor riding, like an aging adolescent, some hollow "wave of the future." Viewing his record, and Rilke's, we may conclude that those who initially appear the frailest are not necessarily the least enduring.

FRANZ KAFKA

It is not unusual to introduce Kafka in such a fashion that all but the boldest are frightened away from his writings. For tactical reasons, therefore, but also because it is true, let us begin by saying that Kafka's works are meticulously detailed accounts of happenings within the three dimensions and the time element of everyday reality. To see in the mind's eye what is represented as occurring presents no problem at all.

The dialogue, also, follows strictly all the normal rules of syntax; the sentences do not even approach those of Thomas Mann in complexity, the vocabulary is much more restricted than his. A great deal of this discourse, however, is of the "he said and she said" variety; that is, it records statements previously made by characters not present, perhaps reporting actions of yet other characters, or of personages who do not appear at all, or even passing on rumors and conflicting rumors. And nothing, and no one, is ever pinned down, a circumstance which is bound to give rise to bafflement and frustration.

The narrative sections, too,

quite frequently expend their lucidity on the reporting of highly improbable or extremely curious incidents. Couples sink to the floor in loving embraces whose embarrassing interruption the circumstances make almost inevitable; mysterious agencies, inconclusively discussed by one or more characters, impinge on the hero decisively, yet in a way which leaves the purport of their intervention far from clear.

The result is that the reader tends to oscillate between the bafflement already alluded to and the search for, even the discovery of, a solution. But the very proponent of this solution may come to see that he has been unjustifiably dogmatic, while those who deny that any solution can be found slip all too easily, a little later, into some one-sided dogmatism of their own.

Most trenchantly characterizing this uneasy pendulum movement to which Kafka drives us is a phrase of Sartre's: "Kafka, or the impossibility of transcendence." For Kafka, unlike the positivists and the horizonless men of every age, saw this world of ours as a system incomplete in itself, traversed by fissures through which we glimpse something that for a moment seems to hold out the promise of a transcendent justification of all things and of ourselves. But then the vision disappears, and we fall back on the patchwork of immanence, of mundane reality. According to the religious interpretation of his work made by his biographer and friend Max Brod, Kafka depicts the world as it is—disconcerting, harsh, incurably ambiguous, the

site of our logically undemonstrable conviction that God is good, but not of direct acquaintanceship with God—and does not share the view that a spiritual explanation of reality should try to win recruits by depicting the world as it is not. Yet according to another interpreter, Kafka mocks at the claims of the mystics and of religion in general.

Kafka's career as a whole was powerfully affected by the fact that he was a Jew. To be a Jew is to experience the impact of society in a way concerning which too few non-Jews trouble to inform themselves. Sooner or later the Jewish child is impressed, possibly as the result of some jeering remark or abusive epithet, with the sense of his *difference* from others, a difference about which nothing can be done. It does not stop there. The child learns that in the eyes of others the Jews are to blame, for anything or everything, and that he himself is guilty with the rest. But when such accusations from outside are repeated often enough, they arouse a sense of guilt within, also. Thus are born the conflicting impulses to admit guilt, yet to rebel against the unspecified and unproven accusation, proudly to refuse the assimilation which is denied and yet to long for it and strive toward it.

It should be mentioned, too, that Kafka's sense of guilt derived not only from these social pressures but also from his emotional involvement with his father, of whom he stood in awe and whose magnificent competence (so Franz Kafka saw it) contrasted with his own unreadiness to shoulder the burdens of marriage and a career. His first short story, "The Judgment" ("Das Urteil," 1913) most directly reveals the ambivalence of his attitude toward his father. Rebellion and repentance are intermingled. The story was written without a moment's hesitation in the course of one night, and the writing of the last sentence, very significantly, as Kafka told Brod, was accompanied by a sense of powerful sexual release.

Kafka's work is a great deal more, however, than an ingenious veiled portrayal of what it means to be a Jew in Western society. It does not affect us solely as the reflection of the situation of a minority to which we may not ourselves belong. For the suggestion may be advanced that the Jew, or the Wandering Jew, has come to be the archetype of Western man. The Jewish diaspora, the scattering of a people over the face of the earth, can be taken as the symbol of two things: of the increased uprootedness of individuals and populations all over the world, and of the state of consciousness induced by this separation from old values, old places, and old beloved objects. "The Metamorphosis" ("Die Verwandlung," 1912) is the masterful and haunting expansion of a term of abuse. A human being is contemptuously called a louse, an insect. And usually that's all there is to it. Except that something remains—the wound, the sense of having been depreciated or degraded. Perhaps even an element of fear lurks in some crevice of the psyche, especially when the psyche is that of a child. Who knows, at what tender age, what dread transformations may sometimes occur!

Transformation is a common literary motif. Sometimes the fanciful and poetic predominated; sometimes the horrible. Here the horrible has the upper hand. It pounds at us all the more relentlessly because of the matter-of-fact tone used and the precise and circumstantial detailing of the embarrassments and physical difficulties that beset the transformed Gregor Samsa. Nor does he enjoy the privilege of suffering in isolation. The family is at once drawn in, and so is Gregor's employer, to whom the family is indebted. Gregor's uncomplaining readiness to support the entire family and the quiet sacrifice of his personal desires—all this goes unrecognized. The faults he attributes to himself and the sense of guilt they have instilled, built up to intolerable proportions by the massive disapproval of society and family —of his father, to be precise— set a gulf between him and human kind. Step by step, whatever is human recedes from him.

The peak of tension in this quietly told drama is reached when the father begins to pelt Gregor with apples. To this painful dilemma there can be only one solution. It happens, and at once. The family—sister, mother, and father—is bathed in light and joy; they experience a genuine renewal, for the monster is dead.

Few readers will fail to sense the persistent echo that this tale arouses in them. We were all once ten-year-olds; we still are a little. We do not have Kafka's gift for dredging up, in mythical form, the fears that afflicted us then, but we can recognize them when Kafka brings them to the light of day.

MARCEL PROUST

Apart from one or two early works and a handful of essays, Marcel Proust put all he had to say into one novel of immense length, whose final volumes did not appear until after his death. Naturally enough, the subject matter treated, rather than the fundamental aim, drew the attention of the first readers of Proust, and since the complete work was not available (nor indeed written), they can readily be forgiven their oversights. The basic theme and its subsidiaries are actually indicated in the opening pages of *Remembrance of Things Past* (À *la Recherche du temps perdu*, 1913-1927), as the whole is called, but only by a miracle of divination could anyone else have developed them.

Remembrance of Things Past is a chronicle of society; that is to say, of the fashionable world, with its rulers and climbers, and also the valets, coachmen, maidservants, and panders who enable it to revolve. For quite a while it was a favored sport, among fashionable people, to guess at the real salon hostess or elderly reprobate hidden behind the fictitious name—and Proust did of course make use of the many exotic personalities he had encountered during his extensive social peregrinations.

Yet as volume succeeded volume, it became apparent that Proust was evolving something very different from an entertaining exposure of high life. The dimensions of his undertaking made it, first of all, a valuable portrait of a whole segment of society, in the wider sense. And as his characters pirouetted and struck their poses, rose or declined in the social scale, it became clear, too, that here was no static tableau, but the history, over perhaps forty years, of the individuals making up a so-called elite and of the subgroups which battled for prestige—the history of their rise, triumphs, and decay. Here is the justification for the quite exceptional length of Proust's novel: being a work of art, it must not simply affirm that time is slipping by, and with it all things; the conviction of this evanescence must seize hold of us.

This sense of transitoriness extends also to Proust's characters; psychologically, they have no solid, integrating core of personality. Their desires crystallize for a while around some beloved person, but the crystals dissolve. However, in the game of love which has so great a role in these idle lives, one principle, "the intermissions of the heart," provides for an oscillating consistency that may extend over many years. "He" loves "her," but she is cold to his advances. One day she receives him more kindly. At once she is devalued in his eyes, having lost the unattainableness, the promise of an unrealizable bliss, which has perhaps constituted for him her only charm. So now it is his turn to become indifferent, while she as a consequence loves and suffers.

"Vanity of vanities; all is vanity." Proust echoes and expands this cry of the Preacher in Ecclesiastes. Or, to borrow the terminology of existentialist philosophy, he spreads before our eyes a dreadful panorama of "inauthentic existence," and those who search for traditional consolations will be tempted to denounce his pessimism. Any interpretation of the book, however, must take into account Marcel, the central character and the narrator of the whole. His presence and his quest give a unity to what otherwise, indeed, might appear as an unrelieved chronicle of dissolution.

Two strands woven together will eventually, we may assume, enable Marcel to bridge the gulf that separates him from salvation. One strand is his longing to become a writer, an ambition which for long years, because of lethargy and the failure to find his own road, he never seriously attempts to realize; the other is his longing to escape from the bondage of time (one might say "fear of death" instead, but Marcel never puts it that way), and his discovery of a key that opens the door to eternity. For him, that is. There is no record of anyone else even having bothered to try the key in whose efficacy Marcel has such unquestioning faith.

How does one escape from time? The answer involves an understanding of the two types of memory distinguished by Proust—voluntary and involuntary. Voluntary memory is the everyday kind. I can recall, for example, that at the age of twelve I spent the summer at the seaside. Far more intimately bound up with the root of things is involuntary memory, which may be aroused for ex-

ample by our smelling some scent which many years before was associated with some happening. These gusts of memory, thus unpredictably aroused, fill Marcel with a pure joy, such as he has never felt when living in the present. But they are only the first glimpse of light peeping through from behind the door to salvation, and hard work and mental discipline are needed if ever the door is to be forced open. Marcel often shrinks from the effort required to penetrate, by way of this first summons from the past, into the sunken, paradisiacal world of his own dead years. When success is attained, the result is like the Japanese paper flower, a tiny pellet which when placed in water unfolds until it covers the whole surface. The image, which is Proust's own, might well serve to characterize his sentences also, those gently unfolding, interminable sentences which so amazingly combine the relaxed, dreamy quality of reminiscence and the acute vision of a man intellectually disciplined and in deadly earnest.

Proust does not entirely abandon the present in favor of the past, for the only access to this past is through the present. The immateriality of the joy accompanying involuntary memory rests on the fact that it is experience of a relation whose two terms are the past and the present. There is a kind of metaphor, in which the past finds expression in the forms of the present. The same penchant for telescoping various periods in time explains why Proust devotes page after page to the etymology of place names, why he sees the villagers as living incarnations of the statues in the village's Romanesque church. Odette, similarly, has stepped out of a Botticelli painting, and a footman at Mme. de Saint-Euverte's "is" a Mantegna. The present is linked to and justified by the past, for in this way the fatuous or boorish, contingent and nonessential living person is taken up into a hierarchy of archetypes which are outside time, immune from change. In the same way the snobbery of Proust and of Marcel can be explained. The Duchesse de Guermantes is the living distillation of centuries of French history. How could Marcel fail to adore her!

The arts too are an attempt to escape from the accidental and to unveil essence, and Proust therefore has a great deal to say about literature, music, and painting. In the passage we print here, taken from the first volume of the work, *Swann's Way (Du Côté de chez Swann*, 1913), an initial attempt is made to record the effect produced by, or rather the truth of things as they stand revealed in, a little musical phrase. For Swann, this phrase embodies his love for Odette, but in itself it is not indifferent or fortuitous; he had been attracted to it for its own sake and had on numerous occasions persuaded Odette to play it for him. However, Swann, the central character of this first part of the novel, is only a man of the world, an aesthete and dilettante, and proves incapable of the persistent mental and moral effort which alone could enable him to approximate in words the message made known through the phrase of music. Swann must yield his place to Marcel, a man who has not sold his soul for "the pomps and vanities of this wicked world," before the ultimate in elucidation can be achieved. And behind Marcel is Proust himself, who accomplished the destiny that Marcel, at the novel's end, has only begun really to make his own.

D. H. LAWRENCE

Of all the authors included in this section of the anthology, D. H. Lawrence is the only representative of those social classes whose members the spread of free popular education and the granting of scholarships enabled, in the nineteenth century, to rise intellectually "above their station." He was the son of a miner, and spent his childhood in a small mining town in the English Midlands. Despite his education and his travels, which took him through Europe, to Ceylon, Australia, Mexico, and the United States, and the contempt for his rough father which had been instilled in him by his bitter, "superior" mother, Lawrence remained in certain essentials very much his father's son.

When a writer of modest talent emerges from the people, his literary productions are likely to be rather palely derivative. He is conscious of the richer background of his social "betters," and treats too respectfully the established forms and conventions. But a young man driven on by the untamed forces that possessed Lawrence has an excellent opportunity to exceed in intensity and originality any similarly endowed but initially more cultivated writer. Did not Rimbaud bitterly condemn the education he felt had warped him, and express envy of the unspoiled illiterate?

Lawrence, however, could be classified as an unspoiled illiterate no more than any other writer. He read widely in English and other literatures, wrote a school text on European history, and explored a considerable range of topics—religion, psychology, myth, and so on. Not that he was ever in danger of becoming a scholar; he was interested more in finding confirmation of his own views and promptings that would aid their further development. But he is marked in spite of all by the narrowness of his early environment. The refinements, the smoothness, the avoidance of eccentricity, that come so easily to the young man from a cultivated home are rarely acquired later, and certainly not by a turbulent man of genius. In his life as in his writings, Lawrence was full of quirks, and it can surely be said that his books and articles contain more entirely preposterous assertions than those of any other writer represented in this section. But just as his most sensible friends, among them Aldous Huxley and Richard Aldington, and—above all— his wife, were able to discount in the man the elements of lesser value, since these were far outranked by his sterling qualities, so the perceptive reader, aided by the passage of time, will realize what genuine insight and passion inspire his works.

Lawrence's father was a quarrelsome, passionate man who found in the emotional ceremonies and hymn singing of the Nonconformist chapel a satisfaction that the politer religion of his wife could not provide. He worked in the bowels of the earth, and mounted again to the surface with an inner burden which required violent release. The son, though close to a mother ambitious on his behalf and possessive to a degree that for a while inhibited his relations with other women, not only came to feel, later, that he had wronged his father, but employed in his writings a symbolism that is reminiscent of the actual working conditions of his father's life. "Dark" is an adjective which he uses even to excess, and his concern is with the primitive, with the instinctual irrational urges without which the ingenious fabrics of our reasoning or rationalizations would never have been woven. This burrowing to the roots is often associated with the desire for a return to the womb of the mother, and it may be that in Lawrence the strong tug of repulsion-attraction, experienced with respect to both his parents, is to some extent responsible for the unique qualities, the richness and suggestiveness of his writing. There are other indications too that Lawrence could express the sexual state of innocent ambivalence (or polymorphism, as Freud calls it) which less gifted folk lose contact with after the years of earliest childhood. If Lawrence's creative imagination wafts us back to those days which have, for the isolated and responsible individual, the glamor of a lost paradise, it is indeed little wonder that he should hold and move us.

The story reprinted in these

pages, "The Horse Dealer's Daughter" (1922), very well exemplifies much of what we have been saying. But, as we recognized in discussing Kafka, the presence of relationships between a work and its author's life does not exclude other kinds of interpretation. "The Horse Dealer's Daughter" has to do with the myth of death and resurrection, the death of the year and of the seed in the ground and the mysterious changes that will lead on to germination and to springtime— and, for man and woman, to death of the old life and promise of a new. The way to new life passes through death.

Love has not always been represented as a cupid. In one spot in ancient Greece a massive, unhewn rock was worshiped as the god Eros. The latter image conveys more adequately Lawrence's conception of love. In this story, coquetry and all conscious wooing are entirely absent. The girl, suddenly, is seized with the awareness that her mate confronts her. And the man struggles to remain free, and fails, yielding to a fascination that has as much dread as delight.

BERTOLT BRECHT

Brecht must be considered one of the most imaginative and powerful playwrights of our time. "Song of a Scribbler of Plays" ("Lied des Stückeschreibers") he tells us something of how he conceived his task. "I am a scribbler of plays," he declares. "I present what I have seen"—how human beings are sold and bartered; how men stand idly in the street and wait, sometimes hopeful, sometimes dejected; how people set traps for one another;

what they say to each other, mother to son, wife to husband, undertaker to dying man—"I report it all."

In calling himself a scribbler rather than a playwright, Brecht assumes an anti-intellectual, unsophisticated attitude that is somewhat deceptive. For in the same "Song" he admits that he adapted the plays of other countries and other times, testing their techniques and absorbing whatever he felt he could utilize.

It is one of the many paradoxes in Brecht's life that his very originality grew out of his ability to take not only life itself but also literature as a source of inspiration—adapting, adopting, parodying, or satirizing what he found. Villon's ballads, the chronicles of the Thirty Years' War, religious hymns, the German classical authors, Goethe and Schiller, Japanese Nō plays, the Bible, all served him and contributed to his work. But this "scribbler" made them his own, thanks to the admirable adroitness with which he handled the German language. With the might of his poetry—which fluctuated between moving lyricism and crude comedy, biting criticism and sheer delight in existence—he transcended his conscious didactic intentions to achieve, to the accompaniment of stirring biblical echoes, a forthright excoriation of the rich and exaltation of the poor.

Brecht's life and work are both filled with seemingly irreconcilable features. Perhaps they account for the intensity and ever-surprising liveliness of his writing. There is naïveté and sophistication; a glorification of individuality and the subordination of the individual to a common cause; skepticism and a deep trust in simple folk; acceptance of myth and an insistence on rationality, science, and progress; a world of light fantasy and another of crass realism. Though painfully concerned with the economic problems of the day, the playwright is equally aware of the insignificance of the moment, in a world where men are transients who leave few traces. "We know that we are provisional. And after us will come: nothing worth mentioning." In spite of his desire to be engagé, a socially and politically committed ("engaged") writer, at a time when that word was still unknown, and to be a good Communist militant, neither the poet nor his work ever proved entirely acceptable to the Communists. But it was, nevertheless, the Communist sector of postwar divided Germany that at last offered him a stage suited to his plays, such as he had never known during the years of his American exile from the Nazis. Here it was—with the Berliner Ensemble that his wife Helene Weigel founded in 1949—that he laid the foundations for a fame that the western world had previously denied him.

As a dramatic author, Brecht ranged from experimental expressionism to serious musicals, whose high-spirited rhythms were so deceptive and so alluring that even audiences antagonistic to their "messages" eagerly applauded them; from didactic plays repeating the "Party line" to serious drama. At first he composed his own tunes for the ballads with which his plays are interspersed, but soon he sought the help of Kurt Weill, Paul Hindemith, and Hanns Eissler.

Receptive to all that was new, he took his place in the vanguard time and again. The "epic" style of theater that was developed in Germany after World War I, with its insertion of narrative and film into dramatic dialogue and its defiance of the Aristotelian unities of time and action, so captivated him that he became its outstanding representative. Yet other plays foreshadow the recent "theatre of the Absurd."

The playwright's profound interest in technique led him not only to study the drama of other ages and countries but also to write theoretical essays that prescribed a non-Aristotelian theater and rejected such supposedly essential elements as empathy, catharsis, unity of action, and psychological motivation of character. But he was too skilled a playwright and too experienced a man of the theater to be guided exclusively by any theory. His book *Staging in Progress*, as we might call his *Theaterarbeit*, written in collaboration with the staff of the Berliner Ensemble, demonstrates how he submitted his theories to an unceasing revision. In practical terms, his main aim as a dramatist and director was to establish an aesthetic distance between the audience and what was happening on the stage. This distancing sought to bar any emotional involvement on the part of the spectator and to provoke instead his intellectual awareness and comprehension. The style of acting called for is in direct opposition to the "method acting" prevalent in the United States, and this may explain why Brecht's plays have been less successful in the States than in European countries.

While Brecht's openly didactic period is not without interest, on the whole we must judge it arid. The years of the playwright's maturity, which coincided with his exile (1933-1948), brought forth his greatest theatrical masterpieces, though the earlier *Threepenny Opera*, thanks in part to the beguiling music of Kurt Weill, had brought him international fame and recognition. *Galileo*, written in 1938 and 1939, *Mother Courage and Her Children* (1939), *The Good Woman of Sezuan* (1938–1940), *Herr Puntila and His Man Matti* (1940-1941), and *The Caucasian Chalk Circle* (1943-1945) assure him a place among the great playwrights.

In these plays of his maturity, Brecht abandoned both the rigid didacticism and the anarchical romantic characters of his youth in favor of universal man presented in his pathetic struggle against all the forces that crush him and deprive him of a fully human existence. These enemies include war and poverty, political irresponsibility and arbitrary decisions. Rousseau's theme of the basic goodness of man and his corruption by society seems to pervade all of Brecht's work. As he presents him, man wants to be good. Man finds it difficult to be bad but, confronting corruption and greed, deprivation and suffering, he uses in sheer self-defense the weapons of his oppressors and sometimes stifles his natural feeling of pity. Thus Mother Courage, underneath her crust of greed and shrewd opportunism, remains the unselfish, afflicted mother. Shen-Te, the good woman of Sezuan, is ruthless against her exploiters in order to secure her child's future.

Brecht's distaste for "psychological" drama and his belief in man's innate goodness, covered over though it be by the corruption of society, often led him to depict his characters as split personalities, veering between extreme kindness and extreme meanness, or even between two seemingly contradictory masks. In the early *Man Is Man*, the protagonist is tricked into assuming another's name. His entire personality is changed; trusting simplicity yields to domineering cruelty. Herr Puntila has antithetical attitudes, character, and beliefs, depending upon whether he is drunk or sober. The good woman of Sezuan repeatedly dons the mask of a "visiting cousin" who, in contrast to her own unselfish nature, is shrewd and calculating. With Galileo and Mother Courage one might be justified in speaking of schizoid personalities, were it not that Brecht's plays reflect rather the cleavage between the spirit —which desires the good—and the flesh—whose selfish desires conjure up the bad. This emerges most clearly, perhaps, in *Saint Joan of the Stockyards*. The King of the stockyards, parodying Goethe's Faust, refers to the two souls that rend his breast.

Only in *The Caucasian Chalk Circle* does the playwright separate these two warring souls and embody them in two women, the vain and totally selfish Governor's wife and Grusha the maid, unselfish, infinitely faithful and kind. The stage is set for one of the most enchanting fairy tales. The bad woman, fleeing the beleaguered city, spends her time choosing clothes and abandons her child. The good woman finds that "the seductive power of goodness" is "terrible." Yet she shuns no danger or hardship to protect the other woman's child, and is even ready to abandon her hope of reunion with the man she loves. After peace has been restored, the Governor's wife again seeks her child, but for purely selfish reasons.

In Brecht's world, the law usually favors the rich. One might expect that the Governor's wife, rich and corrupt and, also, the child's actual mother, would win her case. But in this fairy tale, with its wholly bad and wholly good characters, a good fairy in the person of Azdak appears to ensure that rightness and goodness shall triumph. Grusha the maid keeps the child and departs with the man she loves. Obviously, they will live happily ever after. In its moving simplicity the love of Grusha and her soldier stands out even more strongly against the background of war and political intrigue.

Viewed technically, this play is epic theater at its best, with the narrator seated at one side of the stage, with its songs and significant dialogues. The Prologue reveals that the original play was Chinese. The story is enacted to entertain the State Reconstruction Commission that has come to consider the rebuilding of a shattered Caucasian village community. The play must reflect the problems to be solved, and that is why the old legend is transformed. The narrator voices the hope that, in the shadow of the Soviet tractors, the old poet will hold his own. He is convinced that the old and the new wisdom will mix admirably. And this is Brecht's own view. His

greatness lies in the fact that he has been able to embody both the soul of reality and the soul of poetry.

JEAN-PAUL SARTRE

Sartre, one of those rare authors who have been highly successful in various literary genres, has excelled equally as a novelist, a writer of short stories, a playwright, an essayist and literary critic, and a philosopher. He has now added to these achievements the first volume of his autobiography, which has met with universal acclaim and earned him the 1964 Nobel Prize for Literature (which he declined). His trilogy of novels, published under the title of *Roads to Freedom* (1945-49), has shown him capable of a variety of novelistic styles and approaches, although his early novel *Nausea* will doubtless remain his greatest contribution to that form. Among his plays, *No Exit* (1944) has gained a high place among the world's theatrical classics. His prefaces and critical essays on such contemporaries as Francis Mauriac, Albert Camus, John Dos Passos, William Faulkner, and Jean Genet have proved him one of the most imaginative and perceptive critics of our time. And he has given wide currency to such central critical terms as *engagé* and *anti-roman* (anti-novel).

Sartre is generally referred to as an *existentialist*. One should keep in mind, however, that in his first comprehensive philosophical work, *Being and Nothingness* (1943), the terms "existentialist" and "existentialism" occur neither in the title nor in the body of the study. He was labeled "existentialist" by French journalists — especially Gabriel Marcel—at a time when this work was completed but not yet in print. It appears that he adopted the designation, since only a year or so later he used the term in the title of a talk which he published in form of an essay as *Existentialism Is a Humanism*. Today existentialism cannot be dissociated from Sartre. One might even go so far as to say that Sartre's philosophy *is* existentialism, since he is perhaps the only one of the so-called existentialist thinkers who has not repudiated the label. What particularly justifies the use of the epithet is the fact that Sartre's thinking, like that of Martin Heidegger, presupposes that man is himself a part of Being and therefore cannot be its objective or subjective observer. Philosophy cannot be detached from the experiencing agent. As a consequence, it cannot find expression in purely intellectual and theoretical systems. Like Sören Kierkegaard, Sartre would wish to see philosophy removed from the highly developed intellectual systems of such nineteenth-century philosophers as Hegel and placed instead in the midst of life. It is thus that literature can become closely associated with philosophy. By the same token, Sartre's philosophy distinguishes itself from the Anglo-American empirical or "analytic" school of philosophy with its prosaic concern for the precise significance of ordinary language.

At the same time, Sartre does not treat the experiencing agent in romantic fashion as a preciously unique individual. He thinks of him rather as the medium through which the world reveals itself. In oversimplified and popularized manner this conception of man has been expressed in the essay *Existentialism Is a Humanism* by the formula that, in man, existence precedes essence. Man projects himself into the future, and thus truly "makes" himself. This implies that man cannot have a ready-made character, and is responsible for what he is. This leads us to the concept— which Sartre shares with such existentialist thinkers as Kierkegaard and Heidegger—of "authenticity." Contemporary life as well as language have fallen into meaningless patterns; authenticity must be re-established. Otherwise, the world remains chaotic and meaningless.

In his early novel *Nausea* Sartre depicted the absurdity of the universe. Nausea assails Roquentin, the novel's protagonist, as he progressively realizes that nature has no inherent meaning. The gooeyness of organic matter, burgeoning, growing, and decaying with amazing abundance and wastefulness, takes place without aim, rhyme, or reason. All life seems *de trop*, "superfluous." Timidly, but in a determined manner, man has thought to shield himself from such a nauseating realization of absurdity by building towns, constructing well-ordered societies, and libraries whose neatly classified volumes seem to hold the answers. But in doing so, man has simply placed a thin layer of rationality and logic upon the fundamental absurdity of the world. He has thus—almost—concealed from himself the fact that he, too, is superfluous. But in the novelist's views, only stuffed shirts or scoundrels can be satisfied with such sham answers, which disregard the absurdity underlying everything.

Were he to live authentically, however, man would not so blind himself. He would seek rather to assume the burden of his freedom of choice. For, in this world, Sartre recognizes no higher guiding or judging intelligence than that of man. It is, therefore, the "terrible freedom" of which Ivan speaks in Dostoevsky's *The Brothers Karamasov*. Yet, unlike Ivan, Sartre does not conclude that in such a world all is *permitted*. It is rather that all choices are *possible*, and that man must relentlessly bear the consequences of his choice unguided by established codes of conduct.

In almost all his works, theoretical or fictional (and Sartre has preferred literature to express a philosophy he considers to be descriptive rather than theoretical), the writer has broached the problem of human freedom and responsibility. But in his short stories and his two earliest plays, *The Flies* and *No Exit*, he has given it perhaps its most captivating expression.

In *No Exit* none of the protagonists has lived authentically. Inès assumed that all was predestined because of her "nature." Garcin made all his actions— that is, those visible to the world at large—conform to his carefully cultivated image of himself as an idealist, intellectual, and courageous liberal. This imposed no restrictions on his private life, nor did it enable him to live up to his self-image and reputation in a moment of crisis. For Estelle, life was shaped exclusively by her unauthentic desire to be admired. To the mask of beauty and innocence, which she offered to the world, she sacrificed every other consideration. Like an actress, she assumed the roles assigned to her. It is because they have never made authentic decisions while alive that the three protagonists cannot decide to depart when the opportunity is offered them. Each becomes hell to the others, yet each needs the others, because none of the three can turn away from the past and confront an unknown future. Sartre has intensified this human drama of squandered human freedom by placing his characters in an Empire drawing room. It is this background of shabby gentility, a clinging to what is not, that symbolizes their outlook.

Sartre's own desire to live authentically led him to declare that a writer should be "engaged" and that his works should endeavor to change a reality he cannot condone. Writing, in his view, was a form of action, and at the end of World War II he set out to act by arousing people's consciences against every kind of oppression and suffering.

In recent years he has become if not more resigned then less confident that the man of letters *is* a man of action, that the transfer of words to the printed page can markedly change men's minds and deeds. The first volume of his autobiography, *The Words*, reveals a more disabused and a more modest man. He goes on writing, he states, because that is what he is able to do and has got into the habit of doing. His influence on political events has been nil and will continue to be nil. But this somewhat new Sartre is neither cynical nor despairing. He appears to have discovered—or at least he reveals—a great good humor and a fundamental health that too many superficial observers have too often denied him. He may yet, in the way that a writer can, entertain and influence and enlighten his fellow men.

ALBERT CAMUS

Camus' untimely death has robbed his work of another dimension: the possibilities of change and growth that set off the work of a contemporary writer from the works of writers in literary history. Camus is now a writer of our literary past, and his patterns of thought have acquired a finality.

The most striking aspect of his work perhaps is its Dostoevskian overtones. Unlike such existentialists as Kierkegaard and Karl Jaspers, Camus stressed the absurdity of the world not as something to be surpassed by man but as something inherent in the existence we must face and accept—and perhaps transcend by such an acceptance. He looked upon himself as a "philosopher of the absurd." For him, as for Dostoevsky, absurdity arose from the perpetual clash of man's rationality with his irrationality and the irrationality of the universe. Like the Russian, Camus was haunted by the suffering of innocent men, women, and children and by the question of the individual's possible complicity in inflicting this suffering.

Dostoevskian questions were posed in Camus' first novel, *The Stranger (L'Étranger)*, published in 1942. As in *The Brothers Karamazov*, a man is shot and an innocent man is absurdly convicted of the deed. Though innocent of his father's murder, Dimitrof was condemned because of a series of events that seemed to point to him as the culprit. Meursault, hero of *The Stranger*, did actually commit murder, but one might say that the deed was done "in all innocence." It was a reflex movement that, in the glaring heat of noon, made him reach for the revolver in his pocket when the Arab's knife flashed menacingly.

On legal grounds Meursault should have been acquitted, since he had acted in self-defense. But what rendered him suspect and intolerable was his general behavior, which threatened to expose the duplicity of accepted mores. The first slip had been his failure to weep during his mother's funeral. Society, acting as judge, could not understand this individual who did not pay homage to the forces of the universal cliché. Condemned to death for his strangeness, the stranger is turned in on himself and forced to reflect as he has never reflected before. He emerges from his anguished pondering still in rebellion against his fate but able to rejoice in the "tender indifference" of the natural world, with its stars, night odors, salty air.

The Myth of Sisyphus, also published in 1942, restates in a more theoretical way what *The Stranger* had expressed in novelistic terms. Sisyphus, condemned by the gods to a labor of utter futility, was for Camus the archetype of the "absurd hero." But his Sisyphus, in a sense, escapes his punishment. Knowing that his work is in vain, that the boulder, once he has pushed it to the mountain top, will inevitably roll to the bottom, Sisyphus joyously carries out his repetitive task. "One ought to be Sisyphus, and happy," that is the lesson to be drawn. Camus finds happiness in activity and in a full and sensuous union with the world. Yet one question continues to obtrude itself. In this godless universe, where "everything is permitted," that is, where man is not held back by fear of divine retribution, is everything, indeed, permitted? This Dostoevskian question pursues Camus through novels, essays, and plays until he reaches the conclusion that man, in relation to his fellow man, can sin.

The Fall (1957), which once more takes up this problem of man's guilt and the extent of his freedom, again reminds us of *The Brothers Karamazov*, especially of the chapter on the Grand Inquisitor. The narrator and protagonist identifies himself as a "judge-penitent" and confesses to a life filled with self-love and vanity: "I, I, I is the refrain of my whole life." Vanity has led to duplicity, for the self-created image of self established a role that must be maintained and that must be acknowledged by others. The more virtuous this image, in terms of what society expects, the greater the applause that will be won. Yet the individual, basking in the warmth of this applause, may be situated at a far remove from any reality corresponding to the image. But he continues to live his lie, to play the role assigned to him partly by himself and partly by others, until something occurs that shatters his complacency.

The "I" of this novel is not unique; it is really "we." And this is generally true of Camus' highly stylized characters. They remain lifelike, nevertheless; though we do not expect to meet any individual so generically simplified, like a clown or a personage from the *commedia dell'arte*, these characters nonetheless possess stark reality.

"The Renegade" is also a narrative in the first person. This is the most savage and the most impressive of the stories that make up *Exile and the Kingdom* (published in 1958). In it Camus has created a masklike living thing that is horrifyingly real. A slave speaks, and the story centers around the problem of man's freedom. In this "renegade," slavery seems to be innate. His changes of allegiance leave him ever both slave and prisoner. It matters little that one of his masters is the god of love and the other a god of hatred. His dedication to the god of love has led him to flee the confines of the seminary and to set himself up as a missionary among the most cruel savages. Eager to accept suffering and torture in the service of his lord, he believes that the faith radiating from him will conquer his oppressors. The actuality is very different.

In their harsh city of salt, these silent savages, dressed in black, are his undoubted masters. So he abandons the god of love (in actual fact, nothing of the sort but only the means by which he sought to establish his own domination) and pays homage to the Fetish, the god of hatred. Here, he believes, is "the principle of the world." Once more he is disappointed. The god of malice and hatred also turns out to be vulnerable. Soldiers arrive;

they punish the worshippers of the Fetish. The missionary-turned-slave can achieve no second apostasy that would place him on the side of the big batallions. His tongueless mouth is stuffed with salt, and he dies a slave. Free men cannot be renegades because they have no masters. He who wanted to enslave others with the power of his word remains tongueless and can express his pain only in animallike grunts and cries.

The technique used by Camus in telling this story is rather extraordinary. It is an interior monologue. There is not even the nameless interlocutor of *The Fall*. Part of the story is a flashback. As he lies in wait for the new missionary, whom he has decided to kill, the renegade recapitulates his life. But though the flashback ends when, seemingly, he shoots the new missionary, the story goes on. Ramblingly, and between grunts of pain, the renegade finally acknowledges that the power of the sorcerer has been vanquished by the power of the soldiers, who are in the service of the god of love. Power replaces power, and the renegade's feeble gesture of aid has changed nothing. He dies, his mouth filled with salt. It is a bleak and despairing tale that Camus relates. We might do well to look back to his Sisyphus, happy in the recognition of the futility of his labor, in no man's service and rewarded by none.

WILLIAM FAULKNER

Every line written by William Faulkner exudes a fascination akin to that exercised by the snake on the rabbit. At first, Faulkner himself is the rabbit,

motionless and glassy-eyed before the visions of doom and decay by which he is afflicted. But then a strange metamorphosis occurs: either the snake has swallowed the rabbit and then proceeds to fascinate us with the vision of horror which had been the rabbit's—or the rabbit, getting a grip on itself, turns into a serpent and proceeds to find at least temporary release by freezing us, his readers, in the same helpless rabbit-terror.

Every line that Faulkner wrote has the flavor of slow, southern speech. Old men, and rustic men, who have spent all their lives in one locality (we must except the horrid brood of the Snopeses), and whose hearers are familiar with the ins and outs of what they have to say and with the genealogies and intermarriages of the local families, talk on with no concern for the impatience of the eavesdropping stranger, or for the difficulty he may experience in deciding whether the marriage spoken of occurred recently or perhaps sixty years ago.

Out of lethargy or out of a sense that literary talk dries the well springs of inspiration (but certainly not in a spirit of coquetry), Faulkner presented himself to the inquisitive "literary boys" as a simple, unreflecting man who turned out his stories with the routine phlegm that a hired man exhibits when knocking together a chicken coop. This obviously will not do. Faulkner may not have wanted or even able to give an account of the deliberations that preceded and accompanied the writing of his novels, but *The Sound and the Fury* (1929), for example, is too odd a chicken coop to be accounted for in that fashion.

Although some of Faulkner's novels are regarded as extremely difficult of access, and none has ever sold by the hundred thousand in the original edition, the market for paperbacks has seen Faulkner's works eagerly purchased by a mass audience in drugstores throughout the land. Also, and without defilement, he made the risky journey to Hollywood and wrote dialogue for films. One commentator, in view of these facts, finds a parallel with that great and popular writer Charles Dickens.

Blood appeals to the popular taste. There is, or once was, a genre of "blood-and-thunder" stories, and the creators of productions like television's *The Defenders* continue to supply the seemingly inexhaustible demand for violence. But blood has flowed in other types of literature too, and Faulkner, with his savage murders and lynchings and rapes, brings to mind the tragedies of the Greeks and of Seneca. The validity of the comparison does not stop there. Faulkner saw his region of the Mississippi delta as a community whose sufferings are due to the load of past guilt, the guilt of men toward each other and also toward the land they have ruthlessly tamed and exploited. His characters brood on this past. They are, it has been suggested, like men facing backward as they are driven along a road, who see only the road that has already been traveled, and on whom each new event descends with the inevitability of a destiny.

Still, all is not evil in Faulkner's world. The evil is caused, overwhelmingly, by white men of an age to play a part in affairs. But his world is inhabited also by children, women, old men, Negroes, and Indians. It is among these people, whose interest in seeking power is slight or nonexistent, that Faulkner finds purity, kindliness, morality, hope, and a wisdom (in the old men) that sinks its taproots deep into the soil of their region and into the traditions of three races: white, black, and red.

Hopefulness, not a prominent quality of Faulkner's novels, was a little more in evidence in his last years. There is actually, it would seem, something to be done (see, for example, *Intruder in the Dust*, 1948). With our slight knowledge of Faulkner the man, it is not easy to say what brought about his more optimistic phase. Perhaps it was the mellowing that sometimes comes with the passing of time. Perhaps Faulkner followed the trail that so many American authors once harshly critical of the native scene trod before him. After having reviled, if not these United States, at least certain prominent and scarcely avoidable features of existence here, they repent and return to the fold, praising the country that has borne and molded them. In this they are much like the straying Catholic who late in life remembers his childhood upbringing and makes his peace with the Church. True, as Americans, they have been exempt from the pressures of a totalitarian central government, or even the pressures that an English or Swiss or Dutch citizen readily accepts from constituted authority. But these rebels yield, finally, to all those community pressures which so strike the educated immigrant but of which many Americans, no doubt because they lack a standard of comparison, become to a surprising degree only partly conscious. America, the most deliberately projected of all the great nations, is, despite the inevitable blemishes, a success. Success of an American sort came to Faulkner in his last years: he was awarded the Nobel Prize for Literature in 1949, and he was invited to address college commencements and to write for popular mass-circulation magazines. One of his responses to such recognition was to make statements about national problems, particularly racial segregation, which some critics have found at variance with the complexities of his earlier novels.

To decide on the validity of the message that Faulkner offers in "Delta Autumn" (1942) through old McCaslin would be a hazardous undertaking, and it would be even more hazardous to express an opinion on the problem of reconciling white and black, national and local mores, in this southern region. But it can scarcely be unfair to assert that the old man, and Faulkner also, threw up their hands in despair and confessed the limits of their wisdom when they contemplated those cities where "Chinese and African and Aryan and Jew, all breed and spawn together until no man has time to say which one is which nor cares." But this is the modern world, and McCaslin and Faulkner knew that the end of their very different world was in sight. In any case, some representatives of those same mixed breeds of

the cities do find, as they ponder over Faulkner's writings, something that "speaks unto their condition"—the love of nature, perhaps, or the sense of a morality transcending the individual life and the one generation.

MAN'S FATE—
RAUL BRANDÃO

Raul Brandão, author of "The Thief and His Little Daughter" (1908), was a close contemporary of André Gide. We have put his story last, for it contributes a most fitting final word to this survey of literary activity over three thousand years. Since the date of its composition, world events have endowed it with a significance neither the author nor anyone else could have more than dimly divined at that time.

Freud, in his later years, found himself impelled to posit a death instinct in the human psyche, parallel to the life instinct. Not all psychiatrists accept this particular formulation, but they all do assent to the truism that men experience destructive urges, which may also be turned against themselves. In Brandão's thief, an outcast from society, we encounter more than a blind impulse to destroy his offspring and so, symbolically, himself. He judges society, finds it wanting, and condemns it.

Recent happenings—the displacement by war and its consequences of hundreds of thousands if not millions, the calculated annihilation of whole ethnic groups (genocide), the suffering resulting from Hitler's final attitude toward the German people, which had failed him and was therefore condemned to weeks of useless fighting, and above all the fearful development of destructive weapons, including biological techniques that may wipe out the food supply and water supply of millions of human beings—raise the question of whether the whole human race, or at least occidental civilization together with the numerous orientals who have modeled themselves on the West, has not vowed its own destruction—like the lemmings, those small rodents which periodically, when their numbers have grown too great for the available food supply, swim out from the Norwegian shore to perish in the ocean. An ominous note has been sounded, too, by the German philosopher Karl Jaspers. In 1931 he wrote that if human beings possessed the means of making human life on earth impossible, sooner or later that means would be employed. Today such techniques actually exist, or shortly will.

Brandão's thief condemns society, condemns the world as he finds it. He resolves to annihilate it, as far as his daughter is concerned. But he is unable to carry through his plan, for beneath the dross of existence he becomes aware, as he regards the child, of the sacredness of life, of a fundamental mystery before which we must bow. Some men have more joyously proclaimed their adherence to life than Brandão, but no one with a more rock-bottom sincerity. And modern literature, although perhaps a few undisguised nihilists can be found among writers and there is great stress on the anguish, ambiguity, and incurable fragmentation of existence, pays homage nevertheless to the glory of what is and what might be, quests after the unity in reality's patchwork quilt, and itself demonstrates the unflagging creative energies of mankind.

LIVES, WRITINGS, AND CRITICISM
Biographical and critical works are listed only if they are available in English.

CHARLES BAUDELAIRE

LIFE. Born in Paris on April 9, 1821. In 1828 his widowed mother married Jacques Aupick, later to become a general and an ambassador. Throughout his life Baudelaire remained greatly attached to his mother and detested his stepfather. His independent behavior having caused alarm, in 1841 he was dispatched on a voyage to the tropics. The following year saw the beginning of his lifelong liaison with Jeanne Duval, a mulatto woman, and of his frequent changes of residence in Paris. Disturbed by his extravagance, the family in 1844 placed him under a financial tutelage which was never to be lifted. The revolutionary disturbances of 1848 awakened his enthusiasm, though later he expressed reactionary political views. The same year he published the first of his many translations from Edgar Allan Poe. His long-heralded collection of poems *Flowers of Evil (Les Fleurs du mal)*, which at last appeared in 1857, was judged to contain matter offensive to morals: author and publisher were fined, and obliged to omit six poems.

Baudelaire, who had probably acquired a venereal infection many years before, noted in 1862 that he had felt on his forehead "the breeze from imbecility's wing." Two years later he left Paris, and his creditors, for Brussels. There, in 1866, he was stricken with aphasia and hemiplegia, and he was brought back to Paris. After prolonged suffering he died in his mother's arms, on August 31, 1867. He was interred beside the body of General Aupick.

CHIEF WRITINGS. *Flowers of Evil (Les Fleurs du mal,* 1857), translated by Lewis Piaget Shanks (1931), George Dillon and Edna St. Vincent Millay (1936), C. F. McIntyre (1947), Geoffrey Wagner (1949), Roy Campbell (1952), and William Aggeler (1954); *Artificial Paradises (Les Paradis artificiels,* 1860); *Aesthetic Curiosities (Curiosités esthétiques,* 1868); *Little Poems in Prose (Petits Poèmes en prose,* 1869), translated by A. Crowley (1928) and James Huneker (1929); *Romantic Art (L'Art romantique,* 1869); *Posthumous Works and Unedited Correspondence (Œuvres posthumes et correspondences inédites,* 1887), including material translated by Christopher Isherwood as *Intimate Journals* (1930); *Baudelaire as a Literary Critic* (1964), translated and edited by Lois B. and Francis E. Hyslop, Jr.; *Painter of Modern Life and Other Writings on Art* (1964), edited by Jonathan Mayne.

BIOGRAPHY AND CRITICISM. François Porché, *Charles Baudelaire* (1928); Peter Quennell, *Baudelaire and the Symbolists* (1929); S. A. Rhodes, *The Cult of Beauty in Charles Baudelaire* (1929); Enid Starkie, *Baudelaire* (1933); Margaret Gilman, *Baudelaire the Critic* (1943); Joseph D. Bennett, *Baudelaire, a Criticism* (1944); Marcel Raymond, *From Baudelaire to Surrealism* (1949); Jean-Paul Sartre, *Baudelaire* (1950); P. M. Jones, *Baudelaire* (1952); Martin Turnell, *Baudelaire* (1954); D. J. Mossop, *Baudelaire's Tragic Hero* (1961); and Henri Peyre (ed.), *Baudelaire* (1962).

STÉPHANE MALLARMÉ

LIFE. Born in Paris on March 18, 1842. Early attracted to the poetry of Baudelaire, he learned through him of Edgar Allan Poe. After marrying a German girl, he spent some time in London between 1862 and 1864 in order to improve his English. He then taught in French *lycées* in the provinces and Paris until his retirement in 1893. He was obsessed by aesthetic problems, and his private life was devoid of obvious drama. His "Tuesdays" in the humble apartment of the rue de Rome brought together many French and foreign literary men and artists, among them James McNeill Whistler, Oscar Wilde, George Moore, and Stefan George. His death on September 9, 1898, mourned by his disciples, found him, nevertheless, still mainly a figure of curiosity for most of his countrymen, in whose eyes Mallarmé's "obscurity" was his only claim to renown. But in more recent years his reputation and the interest in his work have grown enormously. The number of studies published in English does not reflect even dimly the attention being devoted to him.

CHIEF WRITINGS. *Poems (Poésies,* 1887); *Album of Verse and Prose (Album de vers et de prose,* 1887); *Pages* (1891); *Divagations* (1897); *Poems (Poésies,* 1899); *A Throw of the Dice (Un Coup de dés,* 1914); *Complete Works (Œuvres complètes,* 1945); *Remarks on Poetry (Propos sur la poésie,* 1946). For translations see *Poems,* translated by Roger Fry (1936).

BIOGRAPHY AND CRITICISM. A. R. Chisholm, *Towards Hérodiade* (1934); R. G. Cohn, *Mallarmé's un Coup de Dés* (1949); Wallace Fowlie, *Mallarmé as Hamlet* (1949) and *Mallarmé* (1953); A. R. Chisholm *Mallarmé's Grand Œuvre* (1962); Haskell M. Block, *Mallarmé and the Symbolist Drama* (1963); and Charles Mauron, *Introduction to the Psychoanalysis of*

Mallarmé (1963).

ARTHUR RIMBAUD

LIFE. Jean Nicholas Arthur Rimbaud was born on October 20, 1854, in Charleville, a town of northeastern France. He proved to be an unusually gifted student, and was encouraged in his literary tastes and endeavors, and also in his revolutionary ardor, by Georges Izambard, his teacher. In 1870 he made the first of his flights from home, and spent ten days in jail as a vagrant. The following year, the poet Paul Verlaine invited Rimbaud to Paris. It was the beginning of a stormy relationship. Together they visited London and Brussels, where, in 1873, Verlaine shot Rimbaud through the wrist and was sentenced to two years' imprisonment. In the same year, at the age of nineteen, Rimbaud gave up the writing of poetry. He found his way to many parts of Europe, to Cyprus, to Java, and to Aden, where he worked for an exporting firm, later moving to Harar, in Abyssinia. As an independent trader he went on expeditions in Abyssinia, and engaged in gunrunning, but it cannot be definitely established that he trafficked in slaves. Falling ill in 1891, he returned to France, and his leg, which was in horrible condition, was amputated at Marseilles. He died on November 10, 1891.

CHIEF WRITINGS. *A Season in Hell (Une Saison en enfer,* 1873), translated by Louise Varèse (1945), Norman Cameron (1950); *Illuminations (Les Illuminations,* 1887), partially translated by Louise Varèse in *Prose Poems from The Illuminations* (1946); *Complete Poems (Poésies complètes,* 1895); *Complete Works (Œuvres complètes,* 1946); *Works (Œuvres,* 1950). Other translations are to be found in Lionel Abel, *Some Poems of Rimbaud* (1939); Norman Cameron, *Selected Verse Poems* (1942).

BIOGRAPHY AND CRITICISM. Peter Quennell, *Baudelaire and the Symbolists* (1929); Enid Starkie, *Arthur Rimbaud* (1939, revised and enlarged edition, 1947); Wallace Fowlie, *Rimbaud* (1946) and *Rimbaud's Illuminations* (1953); Konrad Bercovici, *Savage Prodigal* (1948); and Marcel Raymond, *From Baudelaire to Surrealism* (1949).

ALEXANDER BLOK

LIFE. Alexander Alexandrovich Blok, born on November 16, 1880. His father was professor of law at the University of Warsaw, but the parents separated while Blok was still an infant, and he was taken by the mother to live in St. Petersburg, where her father was rector of the university. Blok began to write prolifically at a very early age. From 1897 on he traveled extensively in Europe. In 1903 he married the actress daughter of the chemist Mendeleyev. The early loss of their only child greatly affected Blok. The poetry he wrote during the years preceding and immediately following his marriage celebrates "the

Lady Beautiful," but subsequently this figure becomes more carnal and demonic, and his poetry is characterized by ironic realism and a cultivation of the grotesque. He wrote numerous plays, the most remarkable perhaps being *The Rose and the Cross* (1913). The abortive political revolt of 1905 aroused in him an intense interest, and he began to develop a personal revolutionary vision of Russia. After the collapse of the czarist regime, he served on a committee that investigated the regime's last days, and wrote the report. His poem inspired by the Bolshevik Revolution, "The Twelve" (1918), had an extraordinary success. Thereafter he became a theater director, lectured, and undertook any type of writing activity that would help to keep his wife and himself alive. His health grew steadily worse, and although admirably cared for by his wife, he died in Petrograd on August 9, 1921, after much despondency and physical suffering. National honors were paid at the funeral.

CHIEF WRITINGS. *Poems on the Lady Beautiful* (1905); *The Stranger* (1906); *The Puppet Show* (1907); *The Rose and the Cross* (1913); "The Twelve" (1918); "The Scythians" (1918). Translations of his poetry are included in *Russian Poetry, An Anthology,* edited and translated by Babette Deutsch and Avrahm Yarmolinsky (1927); *Russian Poems,* translated by Charles F. Coxwell (1929); *Soviet Literature, An Anthology,* edited by George Reavey and Marc Slonim (1934); *A Treasury of Russian Verse,* edited by Avrahm Yarmolinsky (1949). Translations of Blok's essays are to be found in *The Spirit of Music,* translated by I. Freiman (1946).

BIOGRAPHY AND CRITICISM. C. M. Bowra, *The Heritage of Symbolism* (1943); Ernest J. Simmons, *An Outline of Modern Russian Literature, 1880–1940* (1943); D. P. Mirski, *History of Russian Literature* (1949); O. A. Maslenikov, *Frenzied Poets* (1952); Marc Slonim, *Modern Russian Literature* (1953); and Franklin D. Reeve, *Aleksandr Blok* (1962).

WILLIAM BUTLER YEATS

LIFE. Born on June 13, 1865, in Sandymount, a suburb of Dublin, Ireland, to a Protestant family which had settled in Ireland at the beginning of the eighteenth century. Yeats's father gave up the law for the study of painting, and moved to London, but the child spent much time also with relatives in Sligo, in the west of Ireland. The boy was not happy at school in England. The failure of rents compelled the family to return to Ireland in 1880; there Yeats attended first the High School, Dublin, and then the Dublin School of Art. In 1887, in London once more with his parents, he did ill-paid literary work. He founded the Rhymers' Club there, associated with William Morris, W. E.

Henley, Arthur Symons, Lionel Johnson, and others, and became interested in both French symbolism and Celtic myth. In 1900, with Lady Gregory and Synge, he founded the theatrical venture which was to become, a little later, the Abbey Theatre. His meeting with Maud Gonne was a turning point in his life. He fell hopelessly in love with her, but throughout the years she steadfastly refused his suit, devoting herself to the aims of revolutionary Irish nationalism. Yeats eventually married Georgie Hyde-Lees, formerly his secretary, on October 21, 1917. He served for six years in the Irish Free State Senate, his most prominent speech being one in favor of divorce. In 1923 he was awarded the Nobel prize. His death occurred on January 28, 1939.

CHIEF WRITINGS. Poetry: *The Wind among the Reeds* (1899); *The Wild Swans at Coole* (1919); *The Tower* (1928); *The Collected Poems* (1933, new enlarged edition, 1950). Plays: *The Countess Cathleen* (1892); *The Land of Heart's Desire* (1894); *Collected Plays* (1934, new enlarged edition 1952); *Last Poems and Plays* (1940). Prose: *Dramatis Personae* (1936); *A Vision* (1937); *Letters to Katharine Tynan* (1953).

BIOGRAPHY AND CRITICISM. Edith Sitwell, *Aspects of Modern Poetry* (1934); Louis MacNeice, *The Poetry of W. B. Yeats* (1941); Joseph Hone, *W. B. Yeats* (1943); C. M. Bowra, *The Heritage of Symbolism* (1943); Richard Ellmann, *Yeats, The Man and the Mask* (1948); A. N. Jeffares, *W. B. Yeats, Man and Poet* (1949); Donald Stauffer, *The Golden Nightingale* (1940); Graham Hough, *The Last Romantics* (1950); J. Hall and M. Steinmann (eds.), *The Permanence of Yeats* (1950); T. R. Henn, *The Lonely Tower* (1950); Vivienne Koch, *W. B. Yeats: The Tragic Phase* (1951); T. Parkinson, *W. B. Yeats, Self-Critic* (1951); Richard Ellmann, *The Identity of Yeats* (1954); John Bayley, *Romantic Survival* (1957); John Unterecker, *Reader's Guide to William Butler Yeats* (1959); Francis Wilson, *Yeats' Iconography* (1960); V. K. N. Menon, *Development of William Butler Yeats* (1961); Benjamin L. Reid, *Yeats: The Lyric of Tragedy* (1961); Amy G. Stock, *Yeats: His Poetry and Thought* (1961); A. Norman Jeffares, *W. B. Yeats: The Poems* (1962); Morton I. Seiden, *Yeats: The Poet as Mythmaker* (1962); Edward Engelberg, *Vast Design: Patterns in W. B. Yeats' Aesthetic* (1963); Frank Kermode, *Romantic Image* (1963); Thomas Parkinson, *W. B. Yeats: The Later Poetry* (1963); Jon Stallworthy, *Between the Lines: Yeats's Poetry in the Making* (1963); John E. Unterecker (ed.), *Yeats: A Collection of Critical Essays* (1963); David R. Clark, *W. B. Yeats and the Theatre of Desolate Reality* (1964);

and Priscilla Shaw, *Rilke, Valéry and Yeats: The Domain of the Self* (1964).

FEDERICO GARCÍA LORCA

LIFE. Born on June 6, 1899, in Fuentevaqueros, Granada, to parents in comfortable circumstances. His early childhood was marred by poor health. He revealed at an early age his creative vocation. In 1919 he went to live at the Residencia de Estudiantes of the University of Madrid, and he remained there until 1928, although he did not work for any degree. He showed great interest in popular poetry, and collaborated with the composer Manuel de Falla in collecting folk songs. While relatively indifferent, at this time, to publishing his writings, he became known through his recitations of his own work. The year 1929 was one of emotional crisis, and the poet left Spain for New York. He learned no English there, but was forcibly, even painfully, impressed by his surroundings, and was fascinated by Harlem. In 1930, after a happy stay in Cuba, he returned to Spain. He founded and worked with the Barraca, a traveling theatrical company that presented classical Spanish plays all over the country. Although García Lorca had always avoided political involvement, the Spanish Civil War cost him his life. One day in the month of August, 1936, he was taken out and shot by some local adherents of General Franco.

CHIEF WRITINGS. Poetry: *Libro de poemas* (sometimes called *First Poems,* 1921); *Songs* (*Canciones,* 1927); *Gipsy Ballads* (*Romancero gitano,* 1928, translated by Rolfe Humphries, 1953); "Lament for the Matador" ("Llanto por Ignacio Sánchez Mejías," 1935); *The Poet in New York* (*El poeta en Nueva York,* 1940), translated by Rolfe Humphries; *Complete Works* (*Obras completas,* 1954). Other poetry translations are by A. L. Lloyd (1937); Stephen Spender and J. L. Gili (1939). Plays: *Mariana Pineda* (1928); *The Shoemaker's Prodigious Wife* (*La zapatera prodigiosa,* 1930); *Blood Wedding* (*Bodas de sangre,* 1935); *Yerma* (1937); *The House of Bernarda Alba* (*La casa de Bernarda Alba,* 1945). For translations see G. Neiman, *Blood Wedding* (1939); J. Graham and R. O'Connell, *From Lorca's Theatre,* (1941).

BIOGRAPHY AND CRITICISM. Arturo Barea, *Lorca, the Poet and His People* (1944); Edwin Honig, *García Lorca* (1944); C. M. Bowra, *The Creative Experiment* (1949); Roy Campbell, *Lorça,* (1952); and Manuel Duran (ed.), *García Lorca* (1962).

RAINER MARIA RILKE

LIFE. Born in Prague, Austria-Hungary, on December 4, 1875, of Bohemian and Alsatian stock. The family had strong military traditions, and between 1886 and 1891 the sensitive boy spent utterly wretched years in the military academies of Sankt Pölten and Weiss-

kirchen. Abandoning the prospect of a military career, he attended the commercial school at Linz for a year, and then was allowed to study the humanities at the universities of Prague and Munich. From 1899 on, he traveled extensively. He made two trips to Russia, in 1899 and 1900, meeting Tolstoy and acquiring a lively interest in Russian language and literature. He next spent two years in an artists' colony at Worpswede, near Bremen, Germany, and there met Clara Westhoff, a sculptress, whom he married in 1901. A daughter was born in 1902, but henceforth Rilke and his wife never again lived for any long period together. Rilke was frequently a guest at the houses of titled and wealthy people, and for a while, in 1905–1906, he acted as secretary to the sculptor Rodin, whom he revered. In 1912, at the castle of Duino, which is situated overlooking the Adriatic not far from Trieste (then Austrian territory), Rilke first conceived his *Duino Elegies* (*Duineser Elegien*). But inspiration deserted him, the war of 1914–1918 numbed his spirit, and not until 1922, at Muzot, his residence in French Switzerland, did the *Elegies* "write themselves" in the space of eight days, preceded and followed by the totally unexpected gift of the *Sonnets to Orpheus* (*Die Sonnette an Orpheus*), first and second parts. On December 29, 1926, the poet died, after considerable suffering, of myeloid leukemia. Its first symptom was the improper healing of the scratch of a rose thorn. He had been plucking roses to give to a young girl whose visit he expected.

CHIEF WRITINGS. *Stories of God* (*Geschichten vom lieben Gott,* 1900), translated by M. D. Herter Norton and Nora Purtscher-Wydenbruck (1932); *The Book of Pictures* (*Das Buch der Bilder,* 1902, and enlarged edition, 1906); *Auguste Rodin* (1903); *The Book of Hours* (*Das Stundenbuch,* 1905), translated in part by Babette Deutsch in *Poems from the Book of Hours* (1941); *The Tale of the Love and Death of Cornet Christopher Rilke* (*Die Weise von Liebe und Tod des Cornets Christoph Rilke,* 1906), translated by M. D. Herter Norton (1932); *New Poems* (*Neue Gedichte*), 2 vols., 1907–1908; *The Notebooks of Malte Laurids Brigge* (*Die Aufzeichnungen des Malte Laurids Brigge,* 1910), translated by M. D. Herter Norton (1949); *Duino Elegies* (*Duineser Elegien,* 1923), translated by J. B. Leishman and Stephen Spender (1939); *Sonnets to Orpheus* (*Die Sonnette an Orpheus,* 1923), translated by M. D. Herter Norton (1942). See also *Sonnets to Orpheus* [and] *Duino Elegies,* translated by Jessie Lemont (1945). For other translations see Richard von Mises, *Rilke in English: A Tentative Bibliography* (1947).

BIOGRAPHY AND CRITICISM. F. Olivero, *Rainer Maria Rilke* (1931); E. C.

Mason, *Rilke's Apotheosis* (1938); W. Rose and C. G. Houston (eds.), *Rainer Maria Rilke: Aspects of His Mind and Poetry* (1938); E. M. Butler, *Rainer Maria Rilke* (1941); C. M. Bowra, *The Heritage of Symbolism* (1943); Nora Purtscher, *Rilke, Man and Poet* (1949); F. W. van Heerikhuizen, *Rainer Maria Rilke* (1952); H. E. Holthusen, *Rainer Maria Rilke* (1952); H. W. Belmore, *Rilke's Craftsmanship* (1954); Geoffrey H. Hartman, *The Unmediated Vision* (1954); H. W. Belmore, *Rilke's Craftsmanship* (1955); W. L. Graff, *Rainer Maria Rilke* (1956); H. Frederic Peters, *Rainer Maria Rilke* (1960); Romano Guardini, *Rilke's Duino Elegies* (1961); Eudo C. Mason, *Rilke, Europe and the English-speaking World* (1961); J. R. von Salis, *Rainer Maria Rilke: The Years in Switzerland* (1964); and Priscilla Shaw, *Rilke, Valéry and Yeats* (1964).

T. S. ELIOT

LIFE. Thomas Stearns Eliot, born on September 26, 1888, in St. Louis, Missouri, to an old New England family. He was educated at Milton Academy and Harvard, where he took the B. A. degree in 1909 and the M. A. in 1910. He studied in Paris in 1911, at Harvard again in 1911–1914, and at Merton College, Oxford, in 1914–1915. In 1915 he married Vivienne Haigh, an Englishwoman. After teaching in a London school and working for Lloyd's Bank, he entered the publishing house of Faber & Faber, of which he was a director. In 1922 he founded the literary review *The Criterion*. He became a British subject in 1927, and a year later proclaimed himself an Anglo-Catholic and a royalist. The Nobel Prize for Literature was awarded him in 1948. Among the writers who have influenced or attracted him he has named Dante; the French poets Jules Laforgue, Tristan Corbière, and Baudelaire; the Elizabethan dramatists, particularly Webster, Shakespeare, Middleton, and Chapman; Dryden and the metaphysical poets; and, among his contemporaries, Ezra Pound. He died on January 4, 1965.

CHIEF WRITINGS. Poetry: *Prufrock and Other Observations* (1917); *Ara Vos Prec* (1920); *The Waste Land* (1922); *Collected Poems, 1909–1935* (1936); *Four Quartets* (1944); *Collected Poems, 1909–1962* (1963). Verse Plays: *The Rock* (1934); *Murder in the Cathedral* (1935); *The Family Reunion* (1939); *The Cocktail Party* (1950); *Collected Poems and Plays* (1952); *The Confidential Clerk* (1954). Criticism: *The Sacred Wood* (1920); *Selected Essays* (1932); *The Use of Poetry and the Use of Criticism* (1933); *Elizabethan Essays* (1934); *Essays Ancient and Modern* (1936); *Poetry and Drama* (1950). General: *The Idea of a Christian Society* (1939); *Notes toward the Definition of Culture* (1949).

BIOGRAPHY AND CRITICISM. For biography see F. O. Matthiessen, *The Achievement of T. S. Eliot*, rev. ed. (1947); and R. March and Tambimuttu (eds.), *T. S. Eliot, A Symposium* (1948). For criticism see T. McGreevey, *Thomas Stearns Eliot, A Study* (1931); F. R. Leavis, *New Bearings in English Poetry* (1932); H. R. Williamson, *The Poetry of T. S. Eliot* (1932); R. Preston, *Four Quartets Rehearsed* (1946); F. O. Matthiessen, *The Achievement of T. S. Eliot*, rev. ed. (1947); B. Rajan (ed.), *T. S. Eliot, A Study of His Writings by Several Hands* (1947); L. Unger (ed.), *T. S. Eliot, A Selected Critique* (1948); F. C. A. Wilson, *Six Essays on the Development of T. S. Eliot* (1948); Victor H. Brombert, *The Criticism of T. S. Eliot* (1949); E. A. Drew, *T. S. Eliot, The Design of His Poetry* (1949); H. L. Gardner, *The Art of T. S. Eliot* (1949); D. E. S. Maxwell, *The Poetry of T. S. Eliot* (1952); G. Williamson, *Reader's Guide to T. S. Eliot* (1953); Grover Smith, Jr., *T. S. Eliot's Poetry and Plays* (1956); Carl A. Bodelsen, *T. S. Eliot's Four Quartets* (1958); Neville Braybrooke (ed.), *T. S. Eliot, A Symposium* (1958); R. L. Brett, *Reason and Imagination* (1959); David E. Jones, *The Plays of T. S. Eliot* (1960); Ethel Cornwell, *Still Point* (1962); Hugh Kenner (ed.), *T. S. Eliot, A Collection of Critical Essays* (1962); Carol H. Smith, *T. S. Eliot's Dramatic Theory and Practice* (1963); Eric Thompson, *T. S. Eliot: The Metaphysical Perspective* (1963); and Philip R. Headings, *T. S. Eliot* (1964).

JAMES JOYCE

LIFE. James Augustine Aloysius Joyce, born on February 2, 1882, in Dublin, Ireland. His father, John Stanislaus Joyce, had political connections, and earned his living in a variety of makeshift occupations. Because of monetary difficulties, his family had to change residence frequently. Joyce was educated first at Clongowes Wood College, Clane, where he was a boarder for three years, and then, starting in 1891, at Belvedere College, Dublin, which he attended as a day pupil. Both these schools are under Jesuit direction. At the age of fifteen, he won a prize for an essay on "My Favorite Hero," in which his hero was Ulysses. He entertained but rejected the notion of becoming a Jesuit, and in 1898 entered the University College, Dublin, receiving a B.A. degree four years later. In October, 1902, he set off for Paris, where he nearly starved. The following year, receiving the news that his mother was dying, he made a hasty return journey to Ireland. In 1904 he left home to teach at the Clifton School in the Dublin seaside suburb of Dalkey, and lived for a while in the Martello Tower at Sandycove. At about this time he met Norah Barnacle of Galway, and he soon left with her for the Continent, in the belief that he had a position at the Berlitz School in Zurich. This proved to be a mistake, but he found a place instead at the Berlitz School in Trieste. There he became friendly with and encouraged the much older Italian novelist Italo Svevo. His last visit to Dublin occurred in 1912. After the outbreak of war in 1914, the Austrian authorities, because of his wretched eyesight, allowed him to leave the country on parole, and he settled in Zurich. In 1919 he returned to Trieste, but the following year he moved to Paris. At about this time, Harriet Weaver, the editor of the *Egoist*, freed him of financial worries by making over to him a sum of money sufficient to provide a lifelong income. With the collapse of armed resistance in France in World War II, the Joyces made their way to Vichy, and from there to Zurich, where Joyce was operated upon for malignant duodenal ulcer. He died on January 13, 1941.

CHIEF WRITINGS. *Chamber Music* (1907), edited by W. Y. Tindall (1954); *Dubliners* (1914); *A Portrait of the Artist as a Young Man* (1916); *Exiles* (1918); *Ulysses* (1922); *Finnegans Wake* (1939); *Stephen Hero* (1944); Stuart Gilbert (ed.), *Letters of James Joyce* (1957); David Hayman (ed.), *First Draft of Finnegans Wake* (1962).

BIOGRAPHY AND CRITICISM. For biography see Frank Budgen, *James Joyce and the Making of Ulysses* (1934); Herbert Gorman, *James Joyce* (1939); Leon Edel, *James Joyce, the Last Journey* (1947); Stanislaus Joyce, *Recollections of James Joyce* (1950); J. F. Byrne, *The Silent Years* (1953); Richard Ellmann, *James Joyce* (1959); Stanislaus Joyce, *Dublin Diary* (1962). For criticism see Stuart Gilbert, *James Joyce's "Ulysses"* (1931, 2nd rev. ed., 1952); Edmund Wilson, *Axel's Castle* (1932); Samuel Beckett and others, *Examination ... of Work in Progress* (1936); Harry Levin, *James Joyce,* (1941); D. S. Savage, *The Withered Branch* (1950); W. Y. Tindall, *James Joyce* (1950); William T. Noon, *Joyce and Aquinas* (1957); Richard M. Kain, *Fabulous Voyager* (1959); J. Mitchell Morse, *Sympathetic Alien* (1959); William Y. Tindall, *Reader's Guide to James Joyce* (1959); S. L. Goldberg, *The Classical Temper* (1961); A. Walton Litz, *The Art of James Joyce* (1961); Robert M. Adams, *Surface and Symbol* (1962); Thomas E. Connolly, *Joyce's Portrait: Criticisms and Critiques* (1962); Hugh Kenner, *Dublin's Joyce* (1962); and Seon Givens (ed.), *James Joyce: Two Decades of Criticism,* rev. ed. (1962).

ANDRÉ GIDE

LIFE. Born on November 22, 1869, in Paris, to Protestant parents (his mother's family had recently been converted from Catholicism). His father died in 1880. He received an irregular education, attending the École Alsacienne for some time but also studying with private tutors. During the 1890's he frequented the gathering places of the symbolists, among them the salon of Stéphane Mallarmé, but felt ill at ease, owing to his piety, his awkwardness, and his slowness of speech. A trip to North Africa in the autumn of 1893 revolutionized his existence. He became seriously ill at Biskra, and during his convalescence fell in love with earthly delights—see his *Fruits of the Earth* (*Les Nourritures terrestres*), *The Immoralist* (*L'Immoraliste*), and the autobiographical *If It Die* (*Si le Grain ne meurt*). At this time he broke with symbolist literary ideals. On returning to Paris in 1895 he married his cousin Emmanuèle. Thereafter he divided his life between his two estates (in Normandy and in Paris) and extensive travels in Europe and North Africa. During World War I he spent some time working with Belgian refugees. A journey to the Congo led him to expose the abuses that occurred there, and in the early 1930's he announced his adherence to communism. But this new faith did not survive the test of a journey to Russia. A highly controversial career was crowned by the award of the Nobel prize in 1947. With his wide and penetrating reading, his sympathy for the young, his readiness to encourage budding talents, and his preaching of self-realization, Gide exercised a great influence in France and other European countries. Recently there has been increased interest in his writings in the United States. He died on February 19, 1951.

CHIEF WRITINGS. *Marshlands* (*Paludes*, 1895), translated by G. D. Painter in *Marshlands and Prometheus Misbound* (1953); *Fruits of the Earth* (*Les Nourritures terrestres*, 1897), translated by Dorothy Bussy (1949); *Prometheus Misbound* (*Le Prométhée mal enchainé*, 1899), translated by G. D. Painter in *Marshlands and Prometheus Misbound* (1953); *The Immoralist* (*L'Immoraliste*, 1902), translated by Dorothy Bussy (1930); *Saül* (1903), translated by Dorothy Bussy in *Return of the Prodigal . . . Saul* (1953); *Return of the Prodigal* (*Le Retour de l'enfant prodigue*, 1907), translated by Dorothy Bussy in *Return of the Prodigal . . . Saul* (1953); *Strait Is the Gate* (*La Porte étroite*, 1909), translated by Dorothy Bussy (1924); *Isabelle* (1911), translated by Dorothy Bussy in *Two Symphonies* (1931); *Corydon* (1911), translated by Hugh Gibb (1950); *The Vatican Swindle* (*Les Caves du Vatican*, 1914), translated by Dorothy Bussy as *Lafcadio's Adventures* (1927); *The Pastoral Symphony* (*La Symphonie pastorale*, 1919), translated by Dorothy Bussy in *Two Symphonies* (1931); *The Counterfeiters* (*Les Faux-monnayeurs*, 1925), translated by Dorothy Bussy

(1928), and in 1951 published in one volume with *Journal of the Counterfeiters* (*Journal des faux-monnayeurs*, 1926), translated by Justin O'Brien; *If It Die* (*Si le Grain ne meurt*, 1926), translated by Dorothy Bussy (1935); *The Journals, 1889–1949* (1939–1950), translated by Justin O'Brien, 4 vols. (1947–1951); *Theseus* (*Thésée*, 1946), translated by John Russell in *Two Legends: Œdipus and Theseus* (1950); *Et nunc manet in te* (1947), translated by Justin O'Brien as *Madeleine* (1952).

BIOGRAPHY AND CRITICISM. Montgomery Belgion, *Our Present Philosophy of Life* (1929); Léon Pierre-Quint, *André Gide: His Life and His Work* (1934); G. E. Lemaître, *Four French Novelists* (1938); Klaus Mann, *André Gide and the Crisis of Modern Thought* (1943); Van Meter Ames, *André Gide* (1947); A. J. Guérard, *André Gide* (1951); Harold March, *André Gide and the Hound of Heaven* (1951); G. D. Painter, *André Gide* (1952); L. Thomas, *André Gide* (1952); Justin O'Brien, *Portrait of André Gide* (1953); J. C. McLaren, *The Theatre of André Gide* (1953); R. Martin du Gard, *Recollections of André Gide* (1953); Germaine Brée, *André Gide* (1962); and Jean Delay, *The Youth ... * (1963).

THOMAS MANN

LIFE. Born on June 6, 1875, in the old Hanse town of Lubeck, where his father was a grain merchant. His mother was of German-Brazilian extraction. Upon the death of the father, the family moved to Munich. Here Mann worked for an insurance company, and for the satirical and literary weekly *Simplicissimus*, and attended the university without taking a degree. The writing of *Buddenbrooks* was begun during a stay in Rome. He continued to live in Munich until 1933, but after the Nazis came into power he settled in Switzerland, where he edited the periodical *Mass und Wert*. He moved to the United States in 1938, and became a citizen. At the time of his death, in 1955, he was living in Switzerland. He was awarded the Nobel prize in 1929.

CHIEF WRITINGS. *Buddenbrooks* (1900); "Tonio Kröger" (1903); *Royal Highness* (*Königliche Hoheit*, 1909); *Death in Venice* (*Der Tod in Venedig*, 1913); *The Reflections of a Non-Political Man* (*Betrachtungen eines Unpolitischen*, 1918); *Of the German Republic* (*Von deutscher Republik*, 1923); *The Magic Mountain* (*Der Zauberberg*, 1924); *Mario and the Magician* (*Mario und der Zauberer*, 1929); *Joseph and His Brethren* (*Joseph und seine Brüder*, 4 vols., 1933–1944); *Lotte in Weimar* (1939), translated as *The Beloved Returns* (1940); *Doctor Faustus* (*Doktor Faustus*, 1947); *The Holy Sinner* (*Der Erwählte*, 1951); *Confessions of Felix Krull, Confidence Man* (*Bekenntnisse des Hock-*

staplers Felix Krull, 1954). Other volumes of translations are *Stories of Three Decades* (1936); *Selected Essays* (1941); *Order of the Day* (1942); *Essays of Three Decades* (1946); *The Thomas Mann Reader*, edited by J. W. Angell (1950).

BIOGRAPHY AND CRITICISM. James Cleugh, *Thomas Mann: A Study* (1933); H. J. Weigand, *Thomas Mann's Novel Der Zauberberg* (1933); J. G. Brennan, *Thomas Mann's World* (1942); Charles Neider (ed.), *The Stature of Thomas Mann* (1947); Henry Hatfield, *Thomas Mann* (1951); John Maurice Lindsay, *Thomas Mann* (1954); Klaus W. Jonas, *Fifty Years of Thomas Mann Studies, A Bibliography of Criticism* (1955); R. H. Thomas, *Thomas Mann: The Mediation of Art* (1956); F. Kaufmann, *Thomas Mann: The World as Will and Representation* (1957); Thomas Mann, *A Sketch of My Life*, rev. ed. (1960); Erich Heller, *Thomas Mann, Ironic German* (1961); and Henry C. Hatfield (ed.), *Thomas Mann* (1961).

FRANZ KAFKA

LIFE. Born on July 3, 1883, in Prague, then an important town of the Austro-Hungarian Empire. The son of a well-to-do middle-class Jewish merchant, he studied at the German University in Prague, obtaining his law degree in 1906. He then worked for many years in the workmen's insurance division of an insurance company that had official state backing. He was much impressed by his father and his father's satisfactory adjustment to life in the role of breadwinner and head of a family, and was troubled by a sense of his own contrasting inadequacy. For several years he entertained the idea of marriage; and he became engaged, but the projected marriage did not take place. In 1923 he met Dora Dymant, descendant of a prominent Eastern Jewish family, an excellent Hebrew scholar and a gifted actress. At the end of July he left Prague and established himself with her in Berlin. "I found an idyll," writes Max Brod of his visits to him there. "At last I saw my friend in a happy frame of mind; his physical condition however had grown worse." He had had several attacks of tuberculosis, and died, after considerable suffering, on June 3, 1924.

CHIEF WRITINGS. "The Judgment" ("Das Urteil," 1913), and "In the Penal Colony" ("In der Strafkolonie," 1919), translated in *The Penal Colony* (1948); *The Trial* (*Der Prozess*, 1925); *The Castle* (*Das Schloss*, 1926); *America* (*Amerika*, 1927); *Collected Works* (*Gesammelte Schriften*, 1935–1937); *The Diaries* (*Tagebücher*, 1951), translated (from the unpublished manuscript) by Joseph Kresh, 2 vols. (1948–1949); *Letters to Milena* (*Briefe an Milena*, 1952). Other translations are available in *Parables in German and English* (1947); *Selected Short Stories,* translated by Willa and Edwin Muir (1952); *Wedding Preparations in the Country, and Other Posthumous Writings,* translated by Ernest Kaiser and Eithne Wilkins (1954).

BIOGRAPHY AND CRITICISM. For biography see Max Brod, *Franz Kafka* (1947); G. Janouch, *Conversations with Kafka* (1953). For criticism see Angel Flores (ed.), *The Kafka Problem* (1946); Paul Goodman, *Kafka's Prayer* (1947); Charles Neider, *Kafka: His Mind and Art* (1949); Antel Flores and Homer Swanda (eds.), *Franz Kafka Today* (1958); Heinz Politzer, *Franz Kafka : Parable and Paradox* (1962); Ronald D. Gray (ed.), *Kafka* (1963); and Mark Spilka, *Dickens and Kafka* (1963).

MARCEL PROUST

LIFE. Born on July 10, 1871, to a successful Parisian doctor and a Jewish mother. When Proust was nine years old, it became evident that he was asthmatic. Very much attached to his mother, he was thoroughly spoiled by both parents, since his doctor-father decided that this was the wisest course. He studied erratically and moved in the best of society, frequenting among other salons that of Mme. de Caillavet, where he met Anatole France and later found support for his zeal in the Dreyfus cause. He made many friends, with whom he later corresponded extensively. Summers were spent not far from Chartres at Illiers, the Combray of the novel, or at Cabourg, which he renamed Balbec, on the Normandy coast. In 1900 he paid a visit to Venice, and acquired a liking for Ruskin. The death of his father in 1904 and his mother in 1905, and the increasing severity of his asthma, led him to withdraw from society. Henceforth he lived in a cork-lined room, the windows tight shut to keep out the pollen of plants, and he wrote generally at night. Often he wrote in bed, lying flat on his back and holding the paper in the air. The first volume of his long novel was originally printed at his own expense, and initially attracted little attention. Before his death, which occurred on November 18, 1922, he was able to complete his immense project, though not to revise the final part.

CHIEF WRITINGS. *Pleasures and Regrets* (*Les Plaisirs et les jours,* 1896); *Remembrance of Things Past* (*À la Recherche du temps perdu,* 1913– 1927); *Sketches and Miscellanies* (*Pastiches et mélanges,* 1919); *Chronicles* (*Chroniques,* 1927); *Letters* (*Correspondance,* 6 vols., 1930–1936); *Jean Santeuil* (1952); *Contre Sainte-Beuve* (1954). Another volume of translations is *Marcel Proust: A Selection from His Miscellaneous Writings,* edited by Gerard Hopkins (1948).

BIOGRAPHY AND CRITICISM. Léon Pierre-Quint, *Marcel Proust, His Life and Work* (1927); J. W. Krutch, *Five Masters* (1930); G. E. Lemaître, *Four French Novelists* (1938); Derrick Leon, *Introduction to Proust* (1940); Harold March, *The Two Worlds of Marcel Proust* (1948); F. C. Green, *The Mind of Proust* (1949); André Maurois, *Proust, Portrait of a Genius* (1950); Charlotte Haldane, *Proust* (1951); P. A. Spalding, *A Reader's Handbook to Proust* (1951); Walter A. Strauss, *Proust and Literature* (1957); Richard H. Barker, *Marcel Proust: A Biography* (1958); Germaine Brée, *Marcel Proust and the Deliverance from Time* (1958); George D. Painter, *Proust, The Early Years* (1959); René Girard (ed.), *Proust: A Collection of Critical Essays* (1962); Milton Hindus, *Reader's Guide to Marcel Proust* (1962); Margaret Mein, *Proust's Challenge to Time* (1962); Howard Moss, *The Magic Lantern of Marcel Proust* (1962); William S. Bell, *Proust's Nocturnal Muse* (1963); and Roger Shattuck, *Proust's Binoculars* (1963).

D. H. LAWRENCE

LIFE. David Herbert Lawrence, born on September 11, 1885, in Eastwood, a mining village with rural surroundings not far from Nottingham, England. His father was a coal miner, unschooled and of a violent temperament. His mother, better educated and ambitious for her sons, encouraged in her children a sense of superiority to their father. Lawrence was a good student, and a scholarship enabled him to go to secondary school. Poor health made it impossible for him to be a miner, and after a short spell of commercial employment, also brought to an end by ill health, he turned to teaching, which occupied him for the next three years. Then a scholarship took him to Nottingham University, and he spent two years there. In 1911, following the death of his mother and the publication of his first novel, he gave up teaching. The following year he met a German woman of good family, Frieda von Richthofen, then the wife of Professor Ernest Weekley of Nottingham University, and eloped with her. Their marriage, which at last became possible in 1914, was marked by reciprocal devotion and almost incessant quarreling. *The Rainbow,* published in 1915, was the first of Lawrence's books to be suppressed by the British authorities as obscene. The Lawrences went to live in Cornwall, but came under suspicion as spies and were ordered to leave the region. Lawrence was glad to get out of England in 1919, and made his way through Europe, Ceylon, and Australia to New Mexico and Mexico. He returned to Europe in 1923, and again, after bouts of dysentery and malaria in Mexico, in 1925. He was suffering from tuberculosis, and died at Vence, in the south of France, on March 2, 1930.

CHIEF WRITINGS. *The White Peacock*

(1911); *Sons and Lovers* (1913); *The Rainbow* (1915); *Women in Love* (1920); *Kangaroo* (1923); *The Plumed Serpent* (1926); *Lady Chatterly's Lover* (1928); *Collected Poems* (1928); *Last Poems* (1932); *Letters* (1936); *Phoenix* (1936); *Tales* (1949); *The Later D. H. Lawrence* (1952); *Sex, Literature and Censorship* (1953).

BIOGRAPHY AND CRITICISM. E. D. McDonald, *A Bibliography of the Writings of D. H. Lawrence* (1925), and *A Bibliographical Supplement* (1931); Wyndham Lewis, *Paleface* (1929); F. R. Leavis, *D. H. Lawrence* (1930); Catherine Carswell, *Savage Pilgrimage* (1932); R. P. Blackmur, *The Double Agent* (1933); T. S. Eliot, *After Strange Gods* (1934); Earl and Achsah Brewster, *D. H. Lawrence, Reminiscences and Correspondence* (1934); Frieda Lawrence, *"Not I But the Wind . . ."* (1934); E. T. [Jessie Chambers], *D. H. Lawrence, A Personal Record* (1935); Diana Trilling (ed.), *The Portable Lawrence* (1947); J. M. Keynes, *Two Memoirs* (1949); Richard Aldington, *Portrait of a Genius but . . .* (1950); H. T. Moore, *The Life and Works of D. H. Lawrence* (1951); Anthony West, *D. H. Lawrence* (1951); Witter Bynner, *Journey with Genius* (1951); William Tiverton, *D. H. Lawrence and Human Existence* (1952); F. J. Hoffman and H. T. Moore (eds.), *The Achievement of D. H. Lawrence* (1953); Eliot Gilbert Fay, *Lorenzo in Search of the Sun* (1953); H. T. Moore, *The Intelligent Heart* (1954); H. T. Moore (ed.), *A D. H. Lawrence Miscellany* (1959); Eliseo Vivas, *D. H. Lawrence: The Triumph and Failure of Art* (1960); Eugene Goodheart, *The Utopian Vision of D. H. Lawrence* (1963); Julian Moynahan, *Deed of Life* (1963); Mark Spilka (ed.), *D. H. Lawrence: A Collection of Critical Essays* (1963); Daniel A. Weiss, *Oedipus in Nottingham* (1963); and Kingsley Widmer, *The Art of Perversity* (1963).

BERTOLT BRECHT

LIFE. Brecht was born in Augsburg, Germany, on February 10, 1898. His first literary efforts were published when he was 16. During World War I, his study of medicine in Munich was interrupted by service in a military hospital. With the return of peace he set out to make his way as a free-lance writer. An early play was performed in 1922, and was awarded a prize. Two years later he moved to Berlin, and at once plunged into the theatrical life of the capital. He wrote many plays and worked actively at embodying them on the stage. The Nazi accession to power meant exile for him, for his left-wing views were no secret and as a Jew his life was in danger. After eight years spent in various European countries he found his way to the United States in 1941. Few of his works were performed, and the name of Brecht remained gen-

erally unknown. He returned to Europe in 1947, adopted Austrian citizenship but settled in the German People's Republic (East Germany). He died in East Berlin on August 14, 1958.

CHIEF WRITINGS. Plays: *The Wedding* (1919); *Man Is Man* (1927); *Threepenny Opera* (1934); *Galileo* (1938–1939); *Mother Courage and Her Children* (1939); *The Good Woman of Sezuan* (1938–1940); *Herr Puntila and His Man Matti* (1940–1941); *The Caucasian Chalk Circle* (1943–1945); *Saint Joan of the Stockyards* (1932). Theatrical criticism: *Staging in Progress* (*Theaterarbeit*); *Brecht on Theatre* (1964). Poetry: *Selected Poems* (1959).

BIOGRAPHY AND CRITICISM. John Willett, *The Theatre of Bertolt Brecht* (1959); Martin Esslin, *Brecht: The Man and His Work* (1960); R. Gray, *Bertolt Brecht* (1961); Peter Demetz (ed.), *Brecht: A Collection of Critical Essays* (1962); David I. Grossvogel, *Four Playwrights and a Postscript* (1962); and Walter Weideli, *The Art of Bertolt Brecht* (1963).

JEAN-PAUL SARTRE

LIFE. Sartre was born in Paris on June 21, 1905. His father, an officer in the French Navy, died while Sartre was still an infant, and his mother took him to live with her family. Sartre's mother remarried in 1916. After two years in a provincial secondary school, Sartre spent the rest of his schooldays in Paris, going on to study at the University of Paris. He became a secondary-school teacher. He was able to spend one year's leave of absence in Berlin. Made prisoner by the Germans after the French collapse of 1940, Sartre was released fairly soon and returned to teaching. He took part in the Resistance as a writer, though not as an activist, and became famous in 1943 with the performance of *The Flies* (*Les Mouches*) and the extraordinary success of his massive philosophical work *Being and Nothingness* (*L'Être et le Néant*). He gave up teaching the following year, and in 1945 founded the periodical *Les Temps Modernes*. Since then he has continued to write on philosophical, psychological, political, and topical matters, and has written many plays. His one postwar novel, *Roads to Freedom* (*Les Chemins de la Liberté*, 1945 and following years) remains unfinished. In 1962 he published the first volume of his autobiography, *The Words* (*Les Mots*), which deals with his childhood in grandfather Schweitzer's household. In 1964 he was awarded but refused to accept the Nobel Prize.

CHIEF WRITINGS. *Nausea* (*La Nausée*, 1938), translated by Lloyd Alexander (1949); *The Wall* (*Le Mur*, 1939), translated also as *Intimacy and Other Stories* by Lloyd Alexander (1948); *Outline of a Theory of the Emotions* (*Esquisse d'une Théorie des Émotions*,

1940), translated by Bernard Frecht-man (1948); *The Flies* (*Les Mouches,* 1942), translated by Stuart Gilbert (1947); *Being and Nothingness* (*L'Être et le Néant,* 1943), translated by Hazel E. Barnes (1956); *No Exit* (*Huis-Clos,* 1944), translated by Stuart Gilbert (1947); *The Age of Reason, The Reprieve,* and *Troubled Sleep* (*L'Âge du Raison, Le Sursis,* and *La Mort dans l'Âme,* constituting three parts of *Les Chemins de la Liberté,* 1945–1949), translated by Eric Sutton (1947) and by Gerard Hopkins (1950); *Existentialism* (*L'Existentialisme est un Humanisme,* 1946), translated by Bernard Frechtman (1947); *Baudelaire* (1947), translated by Martin Turnell (1950); *Saint Genet, Actor and Martyr* (1952), translated by Bernard Frechtman (1962); and *The Words* (*Les Mots,* 1962), translated by Bernard Frechtman (1964).

ALBERT CAMUS

LIFE. Camus was born in Mondovi, Algeria, on November 7, 1913, to a working-class family. The father was killed early in World War I, and the mother, who was Spanish, moved to the city of Algiers. The boy grew up talking the mixed dialect—French, Spanish, Arabic—of the streets. A schoolteacher who took a special interest in Camus arranged for a scholarship to secondary school. After several years of university work, Camus turned to journalism, joined the Communist Party but stayed a member less than three years, and became very active in the theater. He moved to Paris in 1940. He first attracted wide attention as a writer in 1942 for the underground newspaper *Combat,* and after the war he continued to write editorials for it. His total work brought him the Nobel prize in 1957. He died on January 4, 1960, in a car accident.

BIOGRAPHY AND CRITICISM. Albert Maquet, *Albert Camus: An Invincible Summer* (1958); John Cruickshank, *Albert Camus and the Literature of Revolt* (1959); Philip Thody, *Albert Camus* (1959); Thomas Hanna, *The Thought and Art of Albert Camus* (1959); and *Lyrical Existentialists* (1962); Germaine Brée, *Albert Camus* (1961) and *Camus: A Collection of Critical Essays* (1961); Adele King, *Albert Camus* (1964).

CHIEF WRITINGS. *The Stranger* (*L'Étranger,* 1942); *The Myth of Sisyphus* (*Le mythe de sisyphe,* 1942); *The Plague* (*La Peste,* 1948); *The Rebel* (*L'homme revolté,* 1954); *The Fall* (*La chute,* 1957); *Exile and the Kingdom* (*L'exil et la royaume,* 1958); *Caligula and Other Plays* (1958); *Possessed* (1960); *Resistance, Rebellion, and Death* (1960); *Notebooks 1935-1942* (*Cahiers,* 1963).

WILLIAM FAULKNER

LIFE. Born on September 25, 1897, in New Albany, Mississippi, the oldest of four brothers. Since childhood he lived at Oxford, Mississippi, the seat of the University of Mississippi. His father, who owned a livery stable, was treasurer of the university. The family had lapsed into genteel poverty following the Civil War. After the fifth grade Faulkner enjoyed only desultory schooling, taking some high-school and university courses. He served with the Canadian Flying Corps in World War I, and in 1918 became a lieutenant in the British Royal Air Force. He attended the University of Mississippi, on and off, between 1919 and 1921. He also worked as a house painter, and later as the university postmaster from which job he was dismissed for lack of attentiveness. A meeting with Sherwood Anderson, in New Orleans, turned his attention to the possibilities of a career as a writer. A few months in New York, where he was employed as a clerk in a bookstore, left him with a dislike for that city. In 1925 he sailed for Europe on a freighter, remaining there for most of the year. Back in Oxford, Mississippi, he carpentered, farmed, and fished, and published two novels (*Soldiers' Pay* and *Mosquitoes*). The first version of *The Sound and the Fury* found no publisher. In 1929 he married Mrs. Estelle Franklin, a widow with two children. They had one daughter. While employed as night superintendent of a power plant he revised the rejected novel, using an upturned barrel as his desk, and wrote *Sanctuary,* which was intended to be a potboiler. This too had to be rewritten, but when it was finally published, in 1931, it brought him his earliest popularity. In 1950 he was awarded the Nobel Prize for Literature. He died in 1962.

CHIEF WRITINGS. *Soldiers' Pay* (1926); *Mosquitoes* (1927); *Sartoris* (1929); *The Sound and the Fury* (1929); *As I Lay Dying* (1930); *Sanctuary* (1931); *Idyll in the Desert* (1931); *Light in August* (1932); *Pylon* (1933); *Absalom, Absalom!* (1936); *Unvanquished* (1938); *Wild Palms* (1939); *The Hamlet* (1940); *Go Down, Moses, and Other Stories* (1942); *Intruder in the Dust* (1948); *Knight's Gambit* (1949); *Collected Stories* (1950); *Requiem for a Nun* (1951); *A Fable* (1954).

BIOGRAPHY AND CRITICISM. Malcolm Cowley, *The Portable Faulkner* (1946); H. M. Campbell and R. E. Foster, *William Faulkner* (1951); Irving Howe, *William Faulkner* (1952); William Van O'Connor, *The Tangled Fire of William Faulkner* (1954); Robert Coughlan, *The Private World of William Faulkner* (1954); Hyatt H. Waggoner, *William Faulkner* (1959); Frederick J. Hoffman and Olga W. Vickery (eds.), *William Faulkner: Three Decades of Criticism* (1960); Walter J. Slatoff, *Quest for Failure* (1960); Peter Swiggart, *The Art of Faulkner's Novels* (1962); John L. Longley, Jr., *Tragic Mask: A Study of Faulkner's Heroes* (1963); Cleanth Brooks, *William Faulkner: The Yoknapatawpha Country* (1963).

RAUL BRANDÃO

LIFE. Born on March 12, 1867 (or, according to one authority, 1869), in Foz do Douro, Portugal. He studied in Oporto and went from the secondary school there to the Army School. He founded the Oporto daily *Correio da Manhã*. In 1912 he retired from the army with the rank of major, and thereafter spent most of his time with his wife in his isolated country place at Nespereira, going to Lisbon for the winter. For many years he wrote for the Lisbon daily paper *Correio da Manhã*. He wrote novels, short stories, essays, reminiscences, and plays. He died on December 5, 1930.

CHIEF WRITINGS. *Impressões e paisagens* (1890); *Memória de um palhaço* (1896); *Os pobres* (1908); *El-Rei Junot* (1912); *Humus a farsa* (1918); *Memórias*, 3 vols. (1919–1933); *Os pescadores* (1923); *As ilhas desconhecidese* (1926).

BIOGRAPHY AND CRITICISM. There is no biography. For criticism see A. F. G. Bell, *Portuguese Literature* (1923).

ALEXANDER BLOK

(1880–1921)

The Twelve*

1

Black night.
White snow.
The wind, the wind!
It all but lays you low.
The wind, the wind,   5
Across God's world it blows!

The wind is weaving
The white snow.
There is ice below.
Stumbling and tumbling,   10
Folk slip and fall.
God pity all!

From house to house
A rope is strung,
A sagging placard on it hung: 15
"All power to the Constituent Assembly!"

A bent old woman, tearful, trembly,
Stares at the placard in despair.
Her blear eyes see
How many fine foot-clouts could be   20

---

* 1918. Translated by Babette Deutsch. The selection from Avrahm Yarmolinsky, editor, *A Treasury of Russian Verse*. Copyright 1949 by The Macmillan Company and used with the publisher's permission. Reprinted in full. The punctuation ". . ." does not indicate omissions from this text.

16. *Constituent Assembly:* The Bolsheviks had been pressing for the calling of this assembly, and elections were finally held on November 25, 1917.

Cut from the canvas wasted there,
  While the children's feet go bare. . . .

  Like a hen she picks her way
Across the snow-blocked thoroughfare.
  "Oh, Mother of God, look down and see—   25
  "Those Bolsheviks will be the death of me!"

  The wind lashes at the crossing
And the frost stings to the bone.
  With his nose stuck in his collar
  A *bourzhooy* stands all alone.   30

And who is this? He has long hair
And mutters with a wrathful air:
    "Renegades!
    Russia is dead!"
A writer chap, no doubt, who has   35
  A glib tongue in his head. . . .

And here, slinking through the snow
Comes a cassock, black and bulky. . . .
Comrade priest
    Why so sulky?   40

You used to strut—
Do you recall?
Your belly with its pendent cross
Shining on one and all.

A lady wrapped in caracul   45
    Turns to confide
To a companion: "Oh, we cried and cried . . ."
    She slips—and smack!
She's flat upon her back!

    Oh, oh, oh!   50
  Lift her up, so!

  The restive wind flirts,
  A gay, cruel clown,
  Wringing the skirts,
  Mowing men down.   55
Fierce-fisted, it kneads
The big placard that reads:
"All power to the Constituent Assembly!"
  A gust wafts the words:

---

30. *bourzhooy:* a form of "bour-   temptuously by proletarians for mem-
geois"; the word was used con-   bers of the middle classes.

. . . Sure, we had a meeting too . . .   60
. . . In that building just ahead . . .
. . . We were divided,
But we decided:
Ten for a spell, twenty-five for the night,
   A copeck less wouldn't be right . . .   65
     . . . Let's go to bed . . .

    It's getting late.
    An empty street.
    Only a poor dead beat
    Goes past with shuffling gait.   70
And the wind wails.

    Come here,
      Poor dear,
    Give us a kiss!

    Bread!   75
    What's ahead?
    Get along!

Darkness, darkness overhead.

Hate, sorrowful hate
    Bursts the heart . . .   80
Black, holy hate . . .

    Hey, comrade.
    Look sharp!

2

The wind is romping, the snowflakes dance,
In the night twelve men advance.   85

Black, narrow rifle straps,
Cigarettes, crumpled caps.

A convict's stripes would fit their backs,
Fires, fires mark their tracks. . . .

    Freedom, ho, freedom,   90
    Unhallowed, unblest!
    Rat-tat-tat!

It's freezing, comrades, freezing.

"Now Vanka's off with Katya, on a spree. . . ."
"The tart, her stocking's stuffed with *kerenki!*"   95

65. *copeck:* a small Russian coin (a hundred to the ruble).   95. *kerenki:* bills issued in 1917 while Kerensky was head of the Provisional Government.

"And Vanka's got into a game that pays."
"He's ditched us, he's in uniform these days."
"Well, Vanka, you bourzhooy bastard, you!"
"Just try and kiss my girl—you'll see who's who!"

  Freedom, ho, freedom,   10c
 Unhallowed, unblessed!
 Vanka's with Katya . . .
  You know the rest.
  Rat-tat-tat!

Fires, fires mark their track,   105
Their rifle straps are gleaming black.

March to the revolution's pace!
We've a grim enemy to face!

Comrades, show spunk, take aim, the lot!
At Holy Russia let's fire a shot,   110

  At hutted Russia,
  Fat-rumped and solid,

 Russia the stolid!

 Eh, eh, unhallowed, unblessed!

3

Our boys they marched away   115
To serve in the Red Army.
To serve in the Red Army—
It's do or die today!

Eh, what bitter sorrow!
 A sweet life we've won!   120
A ragged overcoat,
An Austrian gun!

It's all up with exploiters now.
We'll set the world on fire, we vow,
Flaming, flaming amid blood—   125
 Bless us, Lord God!

4

Whirling snow. "Halloo, my bloods!"
Vanka with his Katya scuds,
Two electric lanterns winking
 On the wagon shafts . . .   130
 Clear the way!

Uniformed, the dandy dashes,
Silly fool whom nothing fashes,
How he twirls his black moustaches,
    Twirls, and teases,
     Sure he pleases . . .   135
Look at Vanka: he's got shoulders!
Listen: Vanka knows the game!
He is grabbing hold of Katya,
Trying to get round the dame.   140

Now she lifts her face, the girl's
Parted lips show teeth like pearls.
"Ho, Katya, my Katya,
Chubby mug!"

5

"On your neck, my little Katya,   145
The knife scored a mark still fresh;
There are scratches on the flesh
Under your left breast, my Katya.

    Eh, eh, dance for me!
    You've a pair of legs, I see!   150

You used to go a pretty pace,
Wearing linen trimmed with lace;
You used to whore with the gold-braid crew—
Whore then, and get along with you!

    Eh, eh, whore all you wish—   155
    You make my heart leap like a fish!

Say, recall that officer,
Katya—how I knifed the cur?
Don't tell me your memory's vague,
Just refresh your wits, you plague.   160

    Eh, eh, refresh me, too,
    Come and let me sleep with you.

In gray gaiters you went 'round,
Gobbled chocolates by the pound,
Promenaded with cadets,   165
Now plain troopers are your pets.
    Eh, eh, little tart,
    Sin away and ease your heart."

6

. . . The stallion gallops past again,
The driver, shouting, gives him rein.   170

"Andrukha, stop them, hold the horse!"
"Run back, Petrukha! Cut their course!"

Crrack-crack-crack! Crrack-crack-crack!
The snow leaps up and eddies back.

The sleigh and Vanka are out of sight.   175
"Now cock the gun again, wheel right!"

Crrack! "You'd better watch your game:
.   .   .   .
Stealing another fellow's dame!"

"The rat is gone. But I know who
Tomorrow will be quits with you."   180

And where is Katya? "Dead. She's dead!
The pretty slut shot through the head!

Happy, Katya? Don't you crow?
You carrion, lie there in the snow. . . ."

March to the revolution's pace.   185
We've a grim enemy to face.

7

And again the twelve go marching,
Shoulders back and guns in place,
Only he, the poor assassin,
Marching, does not show his face.   190

Forward, forward, stepping faster,
Marching with a reckless tread,
Like a dog without a master,
Muffled up, he strides ahead.

"Comrade, what on earth has got you?   195
Why is it you act so dumb?"
"Spill it, Pyotr, is it Katya
Makes you look so God-dam' glum?"

"Well, comrades, you know the story.
Katya was my girl by rights.   200
Yes, I loved her. God, our roaring
Black and drunken summer nights!

Her bright eyes—they drove me to it—
How they dared you, black as coal!
And her shoulder, well I knew it   205
With its poppy-colored mole. . . ."

I, mad fool, I had to do it,
Went and killed her . . . damn my soul. . . ."

"Listen to the bastard's patter!
Pyotr, are you a woman? Pooh!   210
Is your spirit soft as batter?
Got no guts, you donkey, you?
Come, friend, cut this silly chatter.
Take yourself in hand, man, do!"

"Comrade, we cannot be nursing   215
You or anyone just now.
Quit your glooming and your cursing.
Stiffer loads won't make us bow!"

Pyotr moves at a slower pace
And he shows a careless face.   220

Once again he lifts his head,
And his eyes grow bright.

    Hi! Hi! What a din!
Sure, a bit of fun's no sin!

Lock your doors and windows tight!   225
There are looters out tonight!

Burst the cellars—wine is free!
Tonight the rabble's on the spree!

8

    Oh, the bitter sorrow!
        Dullness, wearying,   230
            Deadly!

My time
I will pass, I will pass.

My pate
I will scratch, I will scratch.   235

Sunflower seeds
I will crack.

With my knife
I will rip, I will rip.

Fly like a sparrow, bourzhooy.   240
I'll drink to my dead little dove,
To my black-browed love

In your blood . . .
God rest the soul of thy servant, Katerina . . .

Ugh! I'm fed up!   245

9

The city's roar has died away,
All's quiet on the Neva's brink.
No more police! We can be gay,
Fellows without a drop to drink.

A bourzhooy, standing at the crossing,   250
Nose in his collar, does not stir,
While, tail between his legs, beside him
Shivers a cringing, mangy cur.

The bourzhooy like a silent question
Stands there, starved: a dog that begs—   255
The old world like a kinless mongrel
Behind him, tail between its legs.

10

How it's blowing! How it's snowing!
    The flakes blind you as they fly.
You can't see where you are going   260
    Through the blizzard whistling by.
Funnel-shaped, the snow swirls high,
Pillar-like against the sky.

"Saviour, here's a blizzard!" "What!
Pyotr, you're a dunderhead—   265
Did your Saviour and His kin
Save you from committing sin?
Pyotr, you are talking rot!
Whose fault is it Katya's dead?
You're a murderer—understand?   270
There is blood upon your hand!"
March to the revolution's pace:
We've a grim enemy to face!

    On and on the steady beat
    Of the workers' marching feet!   275

11

 . . . And the twelve, unblessed, unhallowed,
Still go marching on,

246–247. The city's roar . . . Neva's brink: These two lines echo an old Russian song.

274–275. On and on . . . marching feet: a variant of the refrain of a revolutionary song popular early in the century.

> Ready for what chance may offer,
> Pitying none. . . .

On, with rifles lifted   280
At the unseen enemy.
Through dead alleys where the snow has sifted,
Where the blizzard tosses free.
Onward, where the snow has drifted
Clutching at the marcher's knee.   285

> The red flag
> Whips their faces.

> Creaking snow,
> Measured paces.

> The grim foe   290
> Marks their traces.

Day and night the blizzard flings
> Snow that stings
> In their faces.

> On, the steady beat   295
Of the workers' marching feet.

12

. . . Onward as a haughty host they march.
"Hey! Who else is there? Come out!"
Only wind, wind bellying the flag,
Tossing the red flag about.   300

Up ahead a snowdrift towers sheer.
"Who is hiding in the drift? Come out!"
A starved mongrel shambles in the rear,
Limping off as though he feared a clout.

"Skip! D'you want your mangy fur   305
Tickled by this bayonet?
The old world is a mongrel cur. . . .
Beatings are the best you'll get."

. . . Teeth bared, gleaming in a wolfish grin,
Furtively it follows on behind,
A chilled mongrel, without friend or kin. . . .   310
"Hey! Who goes there? Answer quickly, mind!"

"Who's waving the red flag?" "Just try and see.
Lord, what darkness! and what blinding snow!"

"Who are those that run there stealthily,   315
Clinging to the houses as they go?"

"We will get you and your comrades too!
Best surrender while you're breathing still."
"Comrade . . . it will be the worse for you.
Come out! or we'll shoot to kill."   320

Crack-crack-crack! A solitary
Echo answers, from the houses thrown,
While the blizzard, wild and merry,
Laughs among the snows alone.

    Crrack-crack-crack!   325
    Crrack-crack-crack!
. . . Forward as a haughty host they tread.
  A starved mongrel shambles in the rear.
Bearing high the banner, bloody red,
    That He holds in hands no bullets sear—   330
    Hidden as the flying snow veils veer,
Lightly walking on the wind, as though
He Himself were diamonded snow,
    With mist-white roses garlanded:
    Jesus Christ is marching at their head.   335

WILLIAM BUTLER YEATS
(1865–1939)
The Tower*

I

What shall I do with this absurdity—
O heart, O troubled heart—this caricature,
Decrepit age that has been tied to me
As to a dog's tail?
        Never had I more
Excited, passionate, fantastical   5
Imagination, nor an ear and eye
That more expected the impossible—
No, not in boyhood when with rod and fly,
Or the humbler worm, I climbed Ben Bulben's back

* 1926. The selection from William Butler Yeats, *Collected Poems.* Copyright 1928 by The Macmillan Company and used with the publisher's permission. Yeats explains that the poem was written at Thoor Ballylee (Ballylee Castle), which he had bought. He refers to this castle in other poems also.
  9. *Ben Bulben:* a mountain in County Sligo. The churchyard where the poet's

And had the livelong summer day to spend.   10
It seems that I must bid the Muse go pack,
Choose Plato and Plotinus for a friend
Until imagination, ear and eye,
Can be content with argument and deal
In abstract things; or be derided by   15
A sort of battered kettle at the heel.

II

I pace upon the battlements and stare
On the foundations of a house, or where
Tree, like a sooty finger, starts from the earth;
And send imagination forth   20
Under the day's declining beam, and call
Images and memories
From ruin or from ancient trees,
For I would ask a question of them all.

Beyond that ridge lived Mrs. French, and once   25
When every silver candlestick or sconce
Lit up the dark mahogany and the wine,
A serving man, that could divine
That most respected lady's every wish,
Ran and with the garden shears   30
Clipped an insolent farmer's ears
And brought them in a little covered dish.

Some few remembered still when I was young
A peasant girl commended by a song,
Who'd lived somewhere upon that rocky place,   35
And praised the colour of her face,
And had the greater joy in praising her,
Remembering that, if walked she there,
Farmers jostled at the fair
So great a glory did the song confer.   40

And certain men, being maddened by those rhymes,
Or else by toasting her a score of times,
Rose from the table and declared it right
To test their fancy by their sight;
But they mistook the brightness of the moon   45
For the prosaic light of day—

body now lies is in sight of it.
12. *Plotinus:* a Roman Neoplatonic
philosopher (died 270 A.D.). He believed that ideal forms were the true
reality. He is mentioned again in l. 146.

25. *Mrs. French:* an eighteenth-
century resident of Peterswell, in the
neighborhood of Thoor Ballylee.
34. *peasant girl:* Mary Hines. The
poet who praised her was Blind Raf-
tery (see l. 49).

Music had driven their wits astray—
And one was drowned in the great bog of Cloone.

Strange, but the man who made the song was blind;
Yet, now I have considered it, I find   50
That nothing strange; the tragedy began
With Homer that was a blind man,
And Helen has all living hearts betrayed.
O may the moon and sunlight seem
One inextricable beam,   55
For if I triumph I must make men mad.

And I myself created Hanrahan
And drove him drunk or sober through the dawn
From somewhere in the neighbouring cottages.
Caught by an old man's juggleries   60
He stumbled, tumbled, fumbled to and fro
And had but broken knees for hire
And horrible splendour of desire;
I thought it all out twenty years ago:

Good fellows shuffled cards in an old bawn;   65
And when that ancient ruffian's turn was on
He so bewitched the cards under his thumb
That all but the one card became
A pack of hounds and not a pack of cards,
And that he changed into a hare.   70
Hanrahan rose in a frenzy there
And followed up those baying creatures towards—

O towards I have forgotten what—enough!
I must recall a man that neither love
Nor music nor an enemy's clipped ear   75
Could, he was so harried, cheer;
A figure that has grown so fabulous
There's not a neighbour left to say
When he finished his dog's day:
An ancient bankrupt master of this house.   80

Before that ruin came, for centuries,
Rough men-at-arms, cross-gartered to the knees
Or shod in iron, climbed the narrow stair,

48. *Cloone:* See *The Celtic Twilight* (1893), by Yeats, where the story summarized in this stanza is told.
54. *moon and sunlight:* In Yeats's own philosophy (see *A Vision*), moon and sun represent, respectively, the subjective and the objective components in man. In actual reality they are blended in "one inextricable beam."
57. *Hanrahan:* folk hero in Yeats's *Stories of Red Hanrahan* (1904).
65. *bawn:* cow barn.
80. *ancient bankrupt master:* He had lived about one hundred years before

And certain men-at-arms there were
Whose images, in the Great Memory stored,   85
Come with loud cry and panting breast
To break upon a sleeper's rest
While their great wooden dice beat on the board.

As I would question all, come all who can;
Come old, necessitous, half-mounted man;   90
And bring beauty's blind rambling celebrant;
The red man the juggler sent
Through God-forsaken meadows; Mrs. French,
Gifted with so fine an ear;
The man drowned in a bog's mire,   95
When mocking Muses chose the country wench.

Did all old men and women, rich and poor,
Who trod upon these rocks or passed this door,
Whether in public or in secret rage
As I do now against old age?   100
But I have found an answer in those eyes
That are impatient to be gone;
Go therefore; but leave Hanrahan,
For I need all his mighty memories.

Old lecher with a love on every wind,   105
Bring up out of that deep considering mind
All that you have discovered in the grave,
For it is certain that you have
Reckoned up every unforeknown, unseeing
Plunge, lured by a softening eye,   110
Or by a touch or sigh,
Into the labyrinth of another's being;

Does the imagination dwell the most
Upon a woman won or a woman lost?
If on the lost, admit you turned aside   115
From a great labyrinth out of pride,
Cowardice, some silly over-subtle thought
Or anything called conscience once;
And that if memory recur, the sun's
Under eclipse and the day blotted out.   120

III

It is time that I wrote my will;
I choose upstanding men

92. *red man:* Hanrahan.　　　　105. *Old lecher:* Hanrahan in old
　　　　　　　　　　　　　　　　age.

That climb the streams until
The fountain leap, and at dawn
Drop their cast at the side   125
Of dripping stone; I declare
They shall inherit my pride,
The pride of people that were
Bound neither to Cause nor to State,
Neither to slaves that were spat on,   130
Nor to tyrants that spat,
The people of Burke and of Grattan
That gave, though free to refuse—
Pride, like that of the morn,
When the headlong light is loose,   135
Or that of the fabulous horn,
Or that of the sudden shower
When all the streams are dry,
Or that of the hour
When the swan must fix his eye   140
Upon a fading gleam,
Float out upon a long
Last reach of glittering stream
And there sing his last song.
And I declare my faith: 145
I mock Plotinus' thought
And cry in Plato's teeth,
Death and life were not
Till man made up the whole,
Made lock, stock and barrel   150
Out of his bitter soul,
Aye, sun and moon and star, all.
And further add to that
That, being dead, we rise,
Dream and so create   155
Translunar Paradise.
I have prepared my peace
With learned Italian things
And the proud stones of Greece,
Poet's imaginings   160
And memories of love,
Memories of the words of women,
All those things whereof

132. *Burke and Grattan:* Edmund
Burke (1729–1797) and Henry Grattan
(1746–1820); Yeats very much admired these Irish statesmen.
  136. *horn:* which Roland, leader of
Charlemagne's rear guard, refused to
blow, as the Christian army left Spain.
As a consequence, the Saracens who had
ambushed Roland were able to kill him
and his friend Olivier. See the *Song of
Roland,* in the section on the Middle
Ages.

Man makes a superhuman
Mirror-resembling dream.   165

As at the loophole there
The daws chatter and scream,
And drop twigs layer upon layer.
When they have mounted up,
The mother bird will rest   170
On their hollow top,
And so warm her wild nest.

I leave both faith and pride
To young upstanding men
Climbing the mountain-side,   175
That under bursting dawn
They may drop a fly;
Being of that metal made
Till it was broken by
This sedentary trade.   180

Now shall I make my soul,
Compelling it to study
In a learned school
Till the wreck of body,
Slow decay of blood,   185
Testy delirium
Or dull decreptitude,
Or what worse evil come—
The death of friends, or death
Of every brilliant eye   190
That made a catch in the breath—
Seem but the clouds of the sky
When the horizon fades;
Or a bird's sleepy cry
Among the deepening shades.   195

Sailing to Byzantium*

I

That is no country for old men. The young
In one another's arms, birds in the trees
—Those dying generations—at their song,

* 1927. The selection from William   and used with the publisher's per-
Butler Yeats, *Collected Poems*. Copy-   mission.
right 1928 by The Macmillan Company

The salmon-falls, the mackerel-crowded seas,
Fish, flesh, or fowl, commend all summer long   5
Whatever is begotten, born, and dies.
Caught in the sensual music all neglect
Monuments of unageing intellect.

II

An aged man is but a paltry thing,
A tattered coat upon a stick, unless   10
Soul clap its hands and sing, and louder sing
For every tatter in its mortal dress,
Nor is there singing school but studying
Monuments of its own magnificence;
And therefore I have sailed the seas and come   15
To the holy city of Byzantium.

III

O sages standing in God's holy fire
As in the gold mosaic of a wall,
Come from the holy fire, perne in a gyre,
And be the singing-masters of my soul.   20
Consume my heart away; sick with desire
And fastened to a dying animal
It knows not what it is; and gather me
Into the artifice of eternity.

IV

Once out of nature I shall never take   25
My bodily form from any natural thing,
But such a form as Grecian goldsmiths make
Of hammered gold and gold enamelling
To keep a drowsy Emperor awake;
Or set upon a golden bough to sing   30
To lords and ladies of Byzantium
Of what is past, or passing, or to come.

16. *Byzantium:* Yeats had been greatly impressed by the Byzantine mosaics he had seen in 1907 and 1924. The ancient city came to be for him a symbol of philosophical speculation allied with craftsmanship, a unique fusion of the spiritual and the aesthetic with practical skills.
17. *fire:* Fire symbolized for Yeats reconciliation in harmony and tranquility; the opposite pole was formed by terrestrial power, strain, and division.
19. *perne:* whirl. *gyre* (Yeats pronounced the *g* hard, as in "guile"): a whirling cone. The poet believed that historical epochs, in their characteristics and development, could be symbolized by two opposed, interpenetrating, revolving gyres.
29. *Emperor:* Yeats had read that a tree made of gold and silver stood in the palace at Byzantium, and that artificial birds sang on its branches.

Among School Children*

I

I walk through the long schoolroom questioning;
A kind old nun in a white hood replies;
The children learn to cipher and to sing,
To study reading-books and histories,
To cut and sew, be neat in everything   5
In the best modern way—the children's eyes
In momentary wonder stare upon
A sixty-year-old smiling public man.

II

I dream of a Ledaean body, bent
Above a sinking fire, a tale that she   10
Told of a harsh reproof, or trivial event
That changed some childish day to tragedy—
Told, and it seemed that our two natures blent
Into a sphere from youthful sympathy,
Or else, to alter Plato's parable,   15
Into the yolk and white of the one shell.

III

And thinking of that fit of grief or rage
I look upon one child or t'other there
And wonder if she stood so at that age—
For even daughters of the swan can share   20
Something of every paddler's heritage—
And had that colour upon cheek or hair,
And thereupon my heart is driven wild:
She stands before me as a living child.

IV

Her present image floats into the mind—   25
Did Quattrocento finger fashion it
Hollow of cheek as though it drank the wind

* 1928. The selection from William Butler Yeats, *Collected Poems.* Copyright 1928 by The Macmillan Company and used with the publisher's permission.

8. *public man:* Yeats was an Irish Free State senator. When he visited a convent school in Waterford, a pupil introduced him by repeating the information contained about him in *Who's Who.*

9. *Ledaean body:* a body as beautiful as that of Leda; she was beloved of Zeus, who visited her in the form of a swan. Her offspring were Castor and Pollux, Helen and Clytemnestra.

14. *sphere:* symbol of wholeness and tranquility.

15. *parable:* Zeus, in a rage against human beings, split them into two, and ever since, Plato suggested, the two halves have been trying to unite once more. Thus Yeats and the friend of his childhood had been united by their sympathy like the white and yolk of an undivided egg.

26. *Quattrocento:* fifteenth-century.

And took a mess of shadows for its meat?
And I though never of Ledaean kind
Had pretty plumage once—enough of that,   30
Better to smile on all that smile, and show
There is a comfortable kind of old scarecrow.

V

What youthful mother, a shape upon her lap
Honey of generation had betrayed,
And that must sleep, shriek, struggle to escape   35
As recollection or the drug decide,
Would think her son, did she but see that shape
With sixty or more winters on its head,
A compensation for the pang of his birth,
Or the uncertainty of his setting forth?   40

VI

Plato thought nature but a spume that plays
Upon a ghostly paradigm of things;
Solider Aristotle played the taws
Upon the bottom of a king of kings;
World-famous golden-thighed Pythagoras   45
Fingered upon a fiddle-stick or strings
What a star sang and careless Muses heard:
Old clothes upon old sticks to scare a bird.

VII

Both nuns and mothers worship images,
But those the candles light are not as those   50
That animate a mother's reveries,
But keep a marble or a bronze repose.
And yet they too break hearts—O Presences
That passion, piety or affection knows,
And that all heavenly glory symbolise—   55
O self-born mockers of man's enterprise;

VIII

Labour is blossoming or dancing where
The body is not bruised to pleasure soul,
Nor beauty born out of its own despair,

34. *Honey of generation:* The phrase is from *The Cave of the Nymphs,* by the Neoplatonic philosopher Porphyry (233?–306? A.D.), but the idea that this drug destroys our recollection of our prenatal condition is Yeats's own.
42. *paradigm:* pattern of the forms that alone constitute reality.
43. *Aristotle:* The philosopher was tutor to Alexander the Great. *played the taws:* thrashed.
45. *golden-thighed:* According to Diogenes Laertius, Pythagoras was once observed to have a thigh of gold.

Nor blear-eyed wisdom out of midnight oil.   60
O chestnut-tree, great-rooted blossomer,
Are you the leaf, the blossom or the bole?
O body swayed to music, O brightening glance,
How can we know the dancer from the dance?

FEDERICO GARCÍA LORCA
(1899–1936)
Lament for the Matador
(Llanto por Ignacio Sánchez Mejías)*

1. Goring and Death

At five in the afternoon.
It was exactly five in the afternoon.
A boy brought a white sheet
at five in the afternoon.
A frail of lime prepared already   5
at five in the afternoon.
All else was death and death alone
at five in the afternoon.

The wind blew away the cotton-wool
at five in the afternoon.   10
The oxide scattered glass and nickel
at five in the afternoon.
Now the dove and the leopard fight
at five in the afternoon.
And a thigh against a grievous horn   15
at five in the afternoon.
The sounds of the bass burden started
at five in the afternoon.
The bells of arsenic and the smoke
at five in the afternoon.   20
At the corners groups in silence
at five in the afternoon.

And only the bull with a high heart
at five in the afternoon.
When the snow-cold sweat was coming   25
at five in the afternoon.
When the arena was covered with iodine
at five in the afternoon.

* 1935. Translated by Mary and   of Editions Poetry London.
Roy Campbell. Reprinted by permission   5. *frail:* basket.

Death laid eggs inside the wound
at five in the afternoon.　　　　　　　　　　　30
At five in the afternoon.
It was exactly five in the afternoon.

A coffin on wheels is the bed
at five in the afternoon.
Bones and flutes sound in his ears　　　　　　35
at five in the afternoon.
The bull was bellowing through his forehead
at five in the afternoon.
The room was rainbowed with agony
at five in the afternoon.　　　　　　　　　　40
From far away the gangrene comes already
at five in the afternoon.
The trumpet of the lily through green groins
at five in the afternoon.
Like suns his wounds were burning　　　　　45
at five in the afternoon.
And the crowd was breaking the windows
at five in the afternoon.
At five in the afternoon.
Ay, what a terrible five in the afternoon!　　50
It was five by all the clocks!
It was five in the shade of the afternoon.

2. *The Spilt Blood*

I do not want to look at it!

Tell the moon it's time to rise,
I do not want to see his blood　　　　　　　55
Where spilt upon the sand it lies.

I do not want to look at it!

The moon in open spaces lit,
Horse of the quiet clouds, is showing,
And the grey bullring of a dream　　　　　　60
With willows in the barriers growing.
I do not want to look at it!
Let my remembrance burn away.
Inform the jasmine-flowers of it
Within their tiny stars of spray!　　　　　　65

I do not want to look at it!

The cow of this old world was licking,
With its sad tongue, a muzzle red

With all the blood that on the sand
Of the arena had been shed.   70
And the two bulls of Guisando
Half made of death, and half of granite,
Like centuries began to low
Grown tired of trampling on this planet,
No.   75
I do not want to look at it!

With all his death borne on his shoulders
Ignacio ascends the tiers.
He was looking for the daybreak
Where never break of day appears.   80
He sought for his accustomed profile
But the dream baffled him instead.
He looked to find his handsome body,
But found his blood was opened red.
Don't ask of me to look at it!   85
I do not wish to smell the source
That pumps each moment with less force,
The stream by which the tiers are lit,
The stream that spills its crimson course
Over the corduroy and leather   90
Of the huge crowds that thirsting sit.
Who shouts to me to have a look?
Don't tell me I should look at it!

He did not try to close his eyes
When he saw the horns so nigh,   95
But the terrible mothers
Lifted up their heads on high.
And through the ranching lands, a wind
Of secret voices started sighing
That to the azure bulls of heaven   100
Pale cowboys of the mist were crying.
In all Seville to match with him
Has never lived a prince so royal,
Nor any sword to match with his,
Nor any heart so staunch and loyal.   105
Like a torrent of lions, his
Incomparable strength was rolled:
And like a torso hewn in marble
His prudence carven and controlled.

Gold airs of Andalusian Rome   110
Circled his head and gilded it,
Whereon his laugh was like a lily

Of clear intelligence and wit.
How great a fighter in the ring!
How good a peasant in the shire!   115
How gentle with the ears of corn!
And, with the spurs, how hard and dire!
How soft and tender with the dew!
How bright our fair-days to illume!
How tremendous with the final   120
Banderillas of the gloom!

But now he sleeps without an end.
Now the wild mosses and the grass,
Opening the lily of his skull,
Their fingers may securely pass.   125
And now his blood comes singing as it flows,
Singing by swamps and fields beyond control,
Gliding around the stiff horns of the snows,
And wavering in the mist without a soul.
Like a long, dark, sad tongue it seems to slide   130
Meeting a thousand cloven hoofs, and flies
To form a pool of agony beside
The starry Guadalquivir of the skies.
Oh white wall of Spain!
Oh black bull of pain!   135
Oh hard blood of Ignacio!
Oh nightingale of his red vein!
No.
I do not want to look at it.
There is no cup to hold it fit,   140
There are no swallows fit to light on it,
There is no frost of light to whiten it,
There is no song, no shower of lilies over it,
Nor any glass with silver screen to cover it.
No.   145
I do not want to look at it.

3. *The Wake*

Stone is a brow wherein our dreams may grieve
Though no curved water sees, nor cypress hears.
Stone is a shoulder on whose strength to heave
Time, with its trees of ribbons, stars, and tears. 150

I've seen the grey showers rush towards the deep,
Stretching frail wounded arms out to the flood,
So to escape the stone laid out in sleep,
Which thaws their limbs, but will not soak their blood.

Of seeds and clouds, the stone makes its collection—   155
Of larks' bones and wolves' shades: yet where it sprawls,
Gives forth no fire, no echo, nor reflection,
But only endless bullrings without walls!

Ignacio, the well born, lies on the stone.
It's over. What's the matter? Watch his mien.   160
Death flecks him with pale sulphur; for his own
The dark head of a minotaur is seen.

It's over. Rains into his mouth will flow.
The air, as if gone mad, has left his chest,
And Love, soaked to the skin with tears of snow,   165
Warms his cold limbs high on the ranch's crest.

What do they say? A foetid silence trails.
We're with a laid-out corpse that's fading still;
With a clear shape that once had nightingales—
But now with endless holes we watch it fill.   170

Who creased his shroud there? What he says is lies;
Nobody sings, or in the corner cries,
Nobody plies the spurs, nor scares the snake;
Here I want nothing more but these round eyes,
To watch this body, sleepless and awake.   175

I wish none here but those whose voices ring.
Tamers of steeds and rivers, from the heath.
The men whose skeletons resound, who sing
With flint and sunlight flashing from their teeth.

I want to see them here. Before this stone—   180
This body with its snapped and trailing reins.
By them I want to see the exit shown
For this great Captain whom death leads in chains.

And like great rivers let them teach me dirges
That have soft mists and canyons steep and full   185
To bear Ignacio's body on their surges
Far from the double snort of any bull:

Till, lost in the arena of the moon,
That feigns itself a bull in childish play,
They leave him, where no mortal fish may croon,   190
In the white thickets of the frozen spray.

I would not have them hide his face with cloth
To wean him to the death in which he lies.

Ignacio, go! Though bellowing bulls may froth—
Sleep, fly, and rest. Even the Ocean dies!   195

4. Absent Soul

The bull does not know you, nor the figtree,
The horses, nor the ants inside your house,
The child and the afternoon do not know you
Because you've died for evermore.

The ridge of the rock does not know you,   200
Nor the black satin in which you crumble:
Your own dumb memory doesn't know you
Because you've died for evermore.

Autumn will come with conches sounding,
With grapes of mist, and huddled hills,   205
But nobody will look into your eyes
Because you've died for evermore.

Because you've died for ever,
Like all the dead of this earth:
All the dead who are being forgotten   210
In a heap of extinguished dogs.

Nobody knows you. No. But I sing of you.
For aftertimes I sing your profile and grace,
The notable maturity of your understanding,
Your appetite for death and the taste of her mouth,   215
The sorrow which your valiant gaiety concealed.

It will be a long time before there'll be born, if ever,
An Andalusian so clear and so rich in adventure.
I sing his elegance with words that groan
And remember a sad breeze through the olives.   220

RAINER MARIA RILKE
(1875–1926)
Duino Elegies (Duineser Elegien)*

Third Elegy

To sing the Belovèd is one thing. Another, alas! is
to celebrate that hidden, guilty river-god of the blood.

* 1923. From *Sonnets to Orpheus* [and] *Duino Elegies*, translated by Jessie Lemont, New York, The Fine Editions Press, copyright 1945 by Jessie Lemont. The third and ninth elegies are reprinted in their entirety. The punctuation ". ." does not indicate omissions from the text.

He, whom she knows from afar, her young lover, what does he know
of that Lord of Pleasure, who, before his love had stilled him,
often from loneliness, often as if she did not exist,
would uplift his god-head, O, from what unknown depths, dripping,   5
rousing the night with his interminable uproar.
O the Neptune within our blood, O his terrible trident!
O the dark blast of his breast from his curved conch-shell!
Listen, how the night grows fluted and hollow. You stars,   10
is it not from you that the lover's delight in the loved one's
face arises? Does not his innermost insight
in her pure face come from the purest star?

It was not you, alas, nor was it his mother
who bent his brows into an arch so expectant.   15
Not for you, maiden who loves him, not for you did
his lips begin to curve in that more fruitful contour.
Do you really believe your gentle approach could have so
convulsed him, you, who wander like the dawn-wind?
It was you who shook his heart; but more ancient terrors   20
rushed into him in that shattering contact.
Call him . . . You cannot wholly call him from those dark
    companions.
He *will* free himself, he escapes them; lightly he dwells in
the home of your heart and accepts it and begins again there.
But did he begin himself, ever?   25
Mother, to you who began his life, he was the little one;
To you he was new, you arched over those young eyes
the friendly world and averted the strange one.
Where, O where are the years when you, simply
with your slender figure, concealed the surging chaos?   30
You hid so much from him; the nightly-distrusted chamber
you made harmless, and in your heart's great refuge
there was more human space than the night-space around him.
Not in the darkness, no, in your nearer presence
you placed the night-light and it shone as though out of friend-
    ship.   35
Nowhere was there a creak you could not explain with a smile, as
though you had long known *when* the floor would behave thus . . .
And he listened to you and was quieted. So much it availed,
gently, your coming; his tall cloaked Fate stepped
behind the wardrobe and his restless future vanished   40
into the lightly shifting folds of the curtain.

And he himself was comforted, as he lay there
under drowsy eye-lids, your light figure,

sweetly releasing the feeling of coming sleep,
appeared to be guarding . . . But *within*, who could resist,   45
prevent, within him, the flood of origins?
Alas, there *was* no caution in that sleeper; sleeping,
but dreaming, and feverish: what he embarked on!
He, so young, so timid, how he was entangled
in the ever on-creeping tendrils of inner event,   50
already twisted into patterns, to throttle growths, to preying
forms of animals? How he gave himself up to it— Loved.
Loved his inner universe, his interior wilderness,
this jungle within him, among whose silent ruins
green-lit, his heart stood. Loved, left it, went into his   55
own roots, and out into violent beginning
where his tiny birth was already outlived. Descended
lovingly into the older blood, the crevasses
where Frightfulness lay, still gorged with his fathers.
And each terror knew him, winked, as if with understanding.   60
Yes, Horror smiled at him . . . Seldom did you,
Mother, smile so tenderly. How could he
not love that which smiled at him? He loved it
before you, for, even while you bore him, it was
dissolved in the water that makes the seed lighter.   65

See, we do not love like the flowers, for a single
season only: when we love, immemorial
sap mounts in our arms. O maiden, it is
this: that we have loved *within* us, not one, of the
future, but all the innumerable brewing;   70
not only the one child, but even the fathers, who like
mountain-ruins rest in our depths; even the dry
river-bed of former mothers—; even the whole
soundless landscape under its clouded
or cloudless destiny—: *this*, maiden, was before your existence.   75

And you yourself, what do you know,—you have conjured
long past times in your lover. What feelings
welled up from those bygone beings. What women
hated you there. What sinister men you
roused in his youthful veins? Dead children were   80
trying to reach you . . . O gently, gently,
show him daily a loving, dependable task done,—
guide him close to the garden, give him
transcendent nights . . .
                    Hold him   85

Ninth Elegy

Why when this span of life might drift away,
as laurel, a little darker than all
the surrounding green, with tiny waves on the edges
of every leaf (like the wind's smile)—: why then
must we be human, and shunning Fate,   5
long for Fate? . . . O, not because happiness *is*
the precipitate benefit of a near loss.
Not out of curiosity, not for the sake of the heart,
that also could be in the laurel . . .
But because to be here is so much, and because   10
all the world around us, so fleeting, seems to need us,
to strangely concern us. Us, the most fleeting.
Once everything, only once. Once and no more. And we also
once. Never again. But this
having been once, though once only,   15
to have been once on Earth,—can it ever be blotted out?

And so we press on, striving toward attainment,
striving to hold it within our mere hands,
in the overfilled sight, and in the speechless heart.
Striving to become it— To whom to give it? We would love   20
to hold it all forever . . . Alas, in the other event,
O, what can be taken Beyond? Not the perception
learned here so slowly, and nothing that occurs here: Nothing.
But the sorrow— But all the hardness of life,
the long experience of love,—also the more   25
inexpressible things. But later
under the stars, what then? *They* are *indeed* inexpressible.
For the wanderer does not bring from the mountain-slope
a handful of earth to the valley, inexpressible earth, but only
a word he has gathered—pure, the gold and blue   30
gentian. Are we, perhaps, *here*, only to say: House.
Bridge. Fountain. Gate. Jug. Fruit-tree. Window.—
at most: Pillar. Tower . . . But to *say*,—you understand,
O to *say*, with an intensity the things themselves never
hoped to achieve. Is it not the secret guile   35
of this silent earth, which urges lovers
in their passion to be enchanted by each other?
Threshold: how much it means
for two lovers, that they should be wearing their own
worn threshold a little, they too, after the many before,   40
and before the many to come . . . lightly.

Here is the time for the *Legend*. *Here* is its home.
Speak and understand. More than ever
the things that we live with are falling away,
are dispossessed and replaced by an act without plan.   45
A concealed act, that is readily disrupted as soon as
the inner energy awakes and takes a new form.
Between the beats our heart
lives on, as between the teeth,
the tongue nevertheless   50
still continues to praise.

Praise the world to the Angel, not the inexpressible: you
cannot impress him with the splendour you have felt in all the
    world,
where he profoundly feels, you are only a novice. Show him
some simple thing, remoulded by age after age   55
till it lives, in our hands and our eyes, as a part of ourselves.
Tell him these things. He would be more astounded than you were
by the rope-maker in Rome or by the potter on the Nile.
Show him how joyous a thing can be, how innocent, and ours;
how the wailing lament clearly unfolds into form,   60
serves as a thing, or dies in a thing,—and fades in the beyond
like the melody of a violin. And these living things
that are departing, understand when you praise them; fleeting,
they believe they will be saved by us, the most fleeting of all.
They wish us to wholly change them within our invisible hearts 65
into—O endlessly—into ourselves! Whosoever we are.

Earth, is not this what you wish: an *invisible*
rebirth in us? Is it not your dream
to be once invisible?—Earth! invisible!
What is your urgent command, if not transformation?   70
Earth, you belovèd. O, believe me, you need
your Springtime no longer to win me: one
O, one only, even one is too much for my blood.
I have been unutterably yours from time immemorial.
Ever, you were in the right, and your holiest inspiration   75
is friendly Death.
See, I live. Wherefore? Neither childhood nor future
are growing less . . . Overflowing existence
leaps within my heart.

52. *the Angel:* The angel of Rilke, in the *Elegies,* has little to do with the Christian conception, but is a being of immense power who moves freely between the visible and invisible worlds. Men could not support his immediate presence.

T. S. ELIOT
(1888–1965)
Murder in the Cathedral*

Part I

Characters

CHORUS OF WOMEN OF CANTER-BURY	HERALD
THREE PRIESTS OF THE CATHEDRAL	ARCHBISHOP THOMAS BECKET
	FOUR TEMPTERS
	ATTENDANTS

The SCENE *is the Archbishop's Hall, on December 2nd, 1170.*

CHORUS. Here let us stand, close by the cathedral. Here let us wait.
   Are we drawn by danger? Is it the knowledge of safety, that draws
      our feet
   Towards the cathedral? What danger can be
   For us, the poor, the poor women of Canterbury? What tribula-
      tion
   With which we are not already familiar? There is no danger   5
   For us, and there is no safety in the cathedral. Some presage of
      an act
   Which our eyes are compelled to witness, has forced our feet
   Towards the cathedral. We are forced to bear witness.

   Since golden October declined into sombre November
   And the apples were gathered and stored, and the land became
      brown sharp points of death in a waste of water and mud,   10
   The New Year waits, breathes, waits, whispers in darkness.
   While the labourer kicks off a muddy boot and stretches his hand
      to the fire,
   The New Year waits, destiny waits for the coming.
   Who has stretched out his hand to the fire, and remembered the
      Saints at All Hallows,
   Remembered the martyrs and saints who wait? and who shall   15
   Stretch out his hand to the fire, and deny his master? who shall
      be warm
   By the fire, and deny his master?

   Seven years and the summer is over
   Seven years since the Archbishop left us,

* 1935. *Murder in the Cathedral* by T. S. Eliot. Copyright, 1935, by Harcourt, Brace and Company, Inc.

He who was always kind to his people.   20
But it would not be well if he should return.
King rules or barons rule;
We have suffered various oppression,
But mostly we are left to our own devices,
And we are content if we are left alone.   25
We try to keep our households in order;
The merchant, shy and cautious, tries to compile a little fortune,
And the labourer bends to his piece of earth, earth-colour, his
     own colour,
Preferring to pass unobserved.
Now I fear disturbance of the quiet seasons: 30
Winter shall come bringing death from the sea,
Ruinous spring shall beat at our doors,
Root and shoot shall eat our eyes and our ears,
Disastrous summer burn up the beds of our streams
And the poor shall wait for another decaying October.   35
Why should the summer bring consolation
For autumn fires and winter fogs?
What shall we do in the heat of summer
But wait in barren orchards for another October?
Some malady is coming upon us. We wait, we wait,   40
And the saints and martyrs wait, for those who shall be martyrs
     and saints.
Destiny waits in the hand of God, shaping the still unshapen:
I have seen these things in a shaft of sunlight.
Destiny waits in the hand of God, not in the hands of statesmen
Who do, some well, some ill, planning and guessing,   45
Having their aims which turn in their hands in the pattern of time.
Come, happy December, who shall observe you, who shall preserve
     you?
Shall the Son of Man be born again in the litter of scorn?
For us, the poor, there is no action,
But only to wait and to witness.   50
     [*Enter* PRIESTS.]
FIRST PRIEST. Seven years and the summer is over.
     Seven years since the Archbishop left us.
SECOND PRIEST. What does the Archbishop do, and our Sovereign
     Lord the Pope
     With the stubborn King and the French King
     In ceaseless intrigue, combinations,   55
     In conference, meetings accepted, meetings refused,

Meetings unended or endless
At one place or another in France?
THIRD PRIEST. I see nothing quite conclusive in the art of temporal
  government,
But violence, duplicity and frequent malversation.   60
King rules or barons rule:
The strong man strongly and the weak man by caprice.
They have but one law, to seize the power and keep it,
And the steadfast can manipulate the greed and lust of others,
The feeble is devoured by his own.   65
1ST PR. Shall these things not end
Until the poor at the gate
Have forgotten their friend, their Father in God, have forgotten
That they had a friend?
                    [*Enter* HERALD.]
HERALD. Servants of God, and watchers of the temple,   70
I am here to inform you, without circumlocution:
The Archbishop is in England, and is close outside the city.
I was sent before in haste
To give you notice of his coming, as much as was possible,
That you may prepare to meet him.   75
1ST PR. What, is the exile ended, is our Lord Archbishop
Reunited with the King? what reconciliation
Of two proud men? what peace can be found
To grow between the hammer and the anvil? Tell us,
Are the old disputes at an end, is the wall of pride cast down   80
That divided them? Is it peace or war? Does he come
In full assurance, or only secure
In the power of Rome, the spiritual rule,
The assurance of right, and the love of the people,
Contemning the hatred and envy of barons?   85
HER. You are right to express a certain incredulity.
He comes in pride and sorrow, affirming all his claims,
Assured, beyond doubt, of the devotion of the people,
Who receive him with scenes of frenzied enthusiasm,
Lining the road and throwing down their capes,   90
Strewing the way with leaves and late flowers of the season.
The streets of the city will be packed to suffocation,
And I think that his horse will be deprived of its tail,
A single hair of which becomes a precious relic.
He is at one with the Pope, and with the King of France,   95
Who indeed would have liked to detain him in his kingdom:

85. *Contemning:* treating with disdain.

But as for our King, that is another matter.

1ST PR. But again, is it war or peace?

HER.   Peace, but not the kiss of peace.

A patched up affair, if you ask my opinion.

And if you ask me, I think the Lord Archbishop   100

Is not the man to cherish any illusions,

Or yet to diminish the least of his pretensions.

If you ask my opinion, I think that this peace

Is nothing like an end, or like a beginning.

It is common knowledge that when the Archbishop   105

Parted from the King, he said to the King,

My Lord, he said, I leave you as a man

Whom in this life I shall not see again.

I have this, I assure you, on the highest authority;

There are several opinions as to what he meant   110

But no one considers it a happy prognostic.   [*Exit.*]

1ST PR. I fear for the Archbishop, I fear for the Church,

I know that the pride bred of sudden prosperity

Was but confirmed by bitter adversity.

I saw him as Chancellor, flattered by the King,   115

Liked or feared by courtiers, in their overbearing fashion.

Despised and despising, always isolated,

Never one among them, always insecure;

His pride always feeding upon his own virtues,

Pride drawing sustenance from impartiality,   120

Pride drawing sustenance from generosity,

Loathing power given by temporal devolution,

Wishing subjection to God alone.

Had the King been greater, or had he been weaker

Things had perhaps been different for Thomas.   125

2ND PR. Yet our Lord is returned. Our Lord has come back to his
     own again.

We have had enough of waiting, from December to dismal De-
     cember.

The Archbishop shall be at our head, dispelling dismay and doubt.

He will tell us what we are to do, he will give us our orders, in-
     struct us.

Our Lord is at one with the Pope, and also the King of France.

We can lean on a rock, we can feel a firm foothold   131

Against the perpetual wash of tides of balance of forces of barons
     and landholders.

---

115. *Chancellor:* From 1155 until after he became archbishop in 1162, Thomas
held this post.

The rock of God is beneath our feet. Let us meet the Archbishop
    with cordial thanksgiving:
Our Lord, our Archbishop returns. And when the Archbishop
    returns
Our doubts are dispelled. Let us therefore rejoice,   135
I say rejoice, and show a glad face for his welcome.
I am the Archbishop's man. Let us give the Archbishop welcome!
3RD PR. For good or ill, let the wheel turn.
The wheel has been still, these seven years, and no good.
For ill or good, let the wheel turn.   140
For who knows the end of good or evil?
Until the grinders cease
And the door shall be shut in the street,
And all the daughters of music shall be brought low.
CHOR. Here is no continuing city, here is no abiding stay.   145
Ill the wind, ill the time, uncertain the profit, certain the danger.
O late late late, late is the time, late too late, and rotten the year;
Evil the wind, and bitter the sea, and grey the sky, grey grey grey.
O Thomas, return, Archbishop; return, return to France.
Return. Quickly. Quietly. Leave us to perish in quiet.   150
You come with applause, you come with rejoicing, but you come
    bringing death into Canterbury:
A doom on the house, a doom on yourself, a doom on the world.

We do not wish anything to happen.
Seven years we have lived quietly,
Succeeded in avoiding notice,   155
Living and partly living.
There have been oppression and luxury,
There have been poverty and licence,
There has been minor injustice.
Yet we have gone on living,   160
Living and partly living.
Sometimes the corn has failed us,
Sometimes the harvest is good,
One year is a year of rain,
Another a year of dryness,   165
One year the apples are abundant,
Another year the plums are lacking.
Yet we have gone on living,
Living and partly living.
We have kept the feasts, heard the masses,   170
We have brewed beer and cyder,
Gathered wood against the winter,

Talked at the corner of the fire,
Talked at the corners of streets,
Talked not always in whispers,   175
Living and partly living.
We have seen births, deaths and marriages,
We have had various scandals,
We have been afflicted with taxes,
We have had laughter and gossip,   180
Several girls have disappeared
Unaccountably, and some not able to.
We have all had our private terrors,
Our particular shadows, our secret fears.   184

But now a great fear is upon us, a fear not of one but of many,
A fear like birth and death, when we see birth and death alone
In a void apart. We   187
Are afraid in a fear which we cannot know, which we cannot face,
    which none understands,
And our hearts are torn from us, our brains unskinned like the
    layers of an onion, our selves are lost lost
In a final fear which none understands. O Thomas Archbishop,
O Thomas our Lord, leave us and leave us be, in our humble and
    tarnished frame of existence, leave us; do not ask us   191
To stand to the doom on the house, the doom on the Archbishop,
    the doom on the world.
Archbishop, secure and assured of your fate, unaffrayed among
    the shades, do you realise what you ask, do you realise what
    it means
To the small folk drawn into the pattern of fate, the small folk
    who live among small things,   195
The strain on the brain of the small folk who stand to the doom
    of the house, the doom of their Lord, the doom of the world?
O Thomas, Archbishop, leave us, leave us, leave sullen Dover, and
    set sail for France. Thomas our Archbishop still our Arch-
    bishop even in France. Thomas Archbishop, set the white
    sail between the grey sky and the bitter sea, leave us, leave us
    for France.
2ND PR. What a way to talk at such a juncture!
    You are foolish, immodest and babbling women.
    Do you not know that the good Archbishop
    Is likely to arrive at any moment?   200
    The crowds in the streets will be cheering and cheering,
    You go on croaking like frogs in the treetops:
    But frogs at least can be cooked and eaten.

Whatever you are afraid of, in your craven apprehension,
Let me ask you at the least to put on pleasant faces,   205
And give a hearty welcome to our good Archbishop.
    [*Enter* THOMAS.]
THOMAS. Peace. And let them be, in their exaltation.
   They speak better than they know, and beyond your understand-
     ing.
   They know and do not know, what it is to act or suffer.
   They know and do not know, that acting is suffering   210
   And suffering is action. Neither does the actor suffer
   Nor the patient act. But both are fixed
   In an eternal action, an eternal patience
   To which all must consent that it may be willed
   And which all must suffer that they may will it,   215
   That the pattern may subsist, for the pattern is the action
   And the suffering, that the wheel may turn and still
   Be forever still.
2ND PR. O my Lord, forgive me, I did not see you coming,
   Engrossed by the chatter of these foolish women.   220
   Forgive us, my Lord, you would have had a better welcome
   If we had been sooner prepared for the event.
   But your Lordship knows that seven years of waiting,
   Seven years of prayer, seven years of emptiness,
   Have better prepared our hearts for your coming,   225
   Than seven days could make ready Canterbury.
   However, I will have fires laid in all your rooms
   To take the chill off our English December,
   Your Lordship now being used to a better climate.
   Your Lordship will find your rooms in order as you left them.   230
THOM. And will try to leave them in order as I find them.
   I am more than grateful for all your kind attentions.
   These are small matters. Little rest in Canterbury
   With eager enemies restless about us.
   Rebellious bishops, York, London, Salisbury,   235
   Would have intercepted our letters,
   Filled the coast with spies and sent to meet me
   Some who hold me in bitterest hate.
   By God's grace aware of their prevision
   I sent my letters on another day.   240
   Had fair crossing, found at Sandwich
   Broc, Warenne, and the Sheriff of Kent,

---

242. *Broc:* Ranulf de Broc, who had   *enne:* Reginald of Warenne, another
been excommunicated by Thomas. *War-*   bitter enemy.

Those who had sworn to have my head from me.
Only John, the Dean of Salisbury,
Fearing for the King's name, warning against treason,   245
Made them hold their hands. So for the time
We are unmolested.

1ST PR.   But do they follow after?

THOM. For a little time the hungry hawk
Will only soar and hover, circling lower,
Waiting excuse, pretence, opportunity.   25c
End will be simple, sudden, God-given.
Meanwhile the substance of our first act
Will be shadows, and the strife with shadows.
Heavier the interval than the consummation.
All things prepare the event. Watch.   255

          [*Enter* FIRST TEMPTER.]

FIRST TEMPTER. You see, my Lord, I do not wait upon ceremony:
Here I have come, forgetting all acrimony,
Hoping that your present gravity
Will find excuse for my humble levity
Remembering all the good time past.   260
Your Lordship won't despise an old friend out of favour?
Old Tom, gay Tom, Becket of London,
Your Lordship won't forget that evening on the river
When the King, and you and I were all friends together?
Friendship should be more than biting Time can sever.   265
What, my Lord, now that you recover
Favour with the King, shall we say that summer's over
Or that the good time cannot last?
Fluting in the meadows, viols in the hall,
Laughter and apple-blossom floating on the water,   270
Singing at nightfall, whispering in chambers,
Fires devouring the winter season,
Eating up the darkness, with wit and wine and wisdom!
Now that the King and you are in amity,
Clergy and laity may return to gaiety,   275
Mirth and sportfulness need not walk warily.

THOM. You talk of seasons that are past. I remember
Not worth forgetting.

TEM.   And of the new season.
Spring has come in winter. Snow in the branches
Shall float as sweet as blossoms. Ice along the ditches   280
Mirror the sunlight. Love in the orchard

---

244. *John, the Dean of Salisbury:* Thomas' faithful friend.

Send the sap shooting. Mirth matches melancholy.

THOM. We do not know very much of the future
   Except that from generation to generation
   The same things happen again and again.   285
   Men learn little from others' experience.
   But in the life of one man, never
   The same time returns. Sever
   The cord, shed the scale. Only
   The fool, fixed in his folly, may think   290
   He can turn the wheel on which he turns.

TEM. My Lord, a nod is as good as a wink.
   A man will often love what he spurns.
   For the good times past, that are come again
   I am your man.

THOM.   Not in this train.   295
   Look to your behavior. You were safer
   Think of penitence and follow your master.

TEM. Not at this gait!
   If you go so fast, others may go faster.
   Your Lordship is too proud!   300
   The safest beast is not the one that roars most loud.
   This was not the way of the King our master!
   You were not used to be so hard upon sinners
   When they were your friends. Be easy, man!
   The easy man lives to eat the best dinners.   305
   Take a friend's advice. Leave well alone,
   Or your goose may be cooked and eaten to the bone.

THOM. You come twenty years too late.

TEM. Then I leave you to your fate.
   I leave you to the pleasures of your higher vices,   310
   Which will have to be paid for at higher prices.
   Farewell, my Lord, I do not wait upon ceremony,
   I leave as I came, forgetting all acrimony,
   Hoping that your present gravity
   Will find excuse for my humble levity.   315
   If you will remember me, my Lord, at your prayers,
   I'll remember you at kissing-time below the stairs.

THOM. Leave-well-alone, the springtime fancy,
   So one thought goes whistling down the wind.
   The impossible is still temptation.   320
   The impossible, the undesirable,
   Voices under sleep, waking a dead world,
   So that the mind may not be whole in the present.

[*Enter* SECOND TEMPTER.]

SECOND TEMPTER. Your Lordship has forgotten me, perhaps. I will
    remind you.
  We met at Clarendon, at Northampton,   325
  And last at Montmirail, in Maine. Now that I have recalled them,
  Let us but set these not too pleasant memories
  In balance against other, earlier
  And weightier ones: those of the Chancellorship.
  See how the late ones rise! The master of policy   330
  Whom all acknowledged, should guide the state again.
THOM. Your meaning?
TEM.   The Chancellorship that you resigned
  When you were made Archbishop—that was a mistake
  On your part—still may be regained. Think, my Lord,
  Power obtained grows to glory,   335
  Life lasting, a permanent possession,
  A templed tomb, monument of marble.
  Rule over men reckon no madness.
THOM. To the man of God what gladness?
TEM.   Sadness
  Only to those giving love to God alone.   340
  Fare forward, shun two files of shadows:
  Mirth merrymaking, melting strength in sweetness,
  Fiddling to feebleness, doomed to disdain;
  And godlovers' longings, lost in God.
  Shall he who held the solid substance   345
  Wander waking with deceitful shadows?
  Power is present. Holiness hereafter.
THOM. Who then?
TEM.   The Chancellor, King and Chancellor.
  King commands. Chancellor richly rules.
  This is a sentence not taught in the schools.   350
  To set down the great, protect the poor,
  Beneath the throne of God can man do more?
  Disarm the ruffian, strengthen the laws,
  Rule for the good of the better cause,
  Dispensing justice make all even,   355
  Is thrive on earth and perhaps in heaven.
THOM. What means?
TEM.   Real power
  Is purchased at price of a certain submission.
  Your spiritual power is earthly perdition.
  Power is present, for him who will wield.   360

тном. Whose was it?

тем.   His who is gone.

тном. Who shall have it?

тем.   He who will come.

тном. What shall be the month?

тем.   The last from the first.

тном. What shall we give for it?

тем.   Pretence of priestly power.

тном. Why should we give it?

тем.   For the power and the glory.   365

тном. No!

тем.   Yes! Or bravery will be broken,
    Cabined in Canterbury, realmless ruler,
    Self-bound servant of a powerless Pope,
    The old stag, circled with hounds.

тном. No!

тем.   Yes! men must manoeuvre. Monarchs also,   370
    Waging war abroad, need fast friends at home.
    Private policy is public profit;
    Dignity still shall be dressed with decorum.

тном. You forget the bishops
    Whom I have laid under excommunication.   375

тем. Hungry hatred
    Will not strive against intelligent self-interest.

тном. You forget the barons. Who will not forget
    Constant curbing of petty privilege.

тем. Against the barons   380
    Is King's cause, churl's cause, Chancellor's cause.

тном. No! shall I, who keep the keys
    Of heaven and hell, supreme alone in England,
    Who bind and loose, with power from the Pope,
    Descend to desire a punier power?   385
    Delegate to deal the doom of damnation,
    To condemn kings, not serve among their servants,
    Is my open office. No! Go.

тем. Then I leave you to your fate.
    Your sin soars sunward, covering kings' falcons.   390

тном. Temporal power, to build a good world,
    To keep order, as the world knows order.
    Those who put their faith in worldly order
    Not controlled by the order of God,
    In confident ignorance, but arrest disorder,   395

381. *churl's:* peasant's.

Make it fast, breed fatal disease,
Degrade what they exalt. Power with the King—
I *was* the King, his arm, his better reason.
But what was once exaltation
Would now be only mean descent.   400
      [*Enter* THIRD TEMPTER.]

THIRD TEMPTER. I am an unexpected visitor.

THOM.   I expected you.

TEM. But not in this guise, or for my present purpose.

THOM. No purpose brings surprise.

TEM.   Well, my Lord,
I am no trifler, and no politician.
To idle or intrigue at court   405
I have no skill. I am no courtier.
I know a horse, a dog, a wench;
I know how to hold my estates in order,
A country-keeping lord who minds his own business.
It is we country lords who know the country   410
And we who know what the country needs.
It is our country. We care for the country.
We are the backbone of the nation.
We, not the plotting parasites
About the King. Excuse my bluntness: 415
I am a rough straightforward Englishman.

THOM. Proceed straight forward.

TEM.   Purpose is plain.
Endurance of friendship does not depend
Upon ourselves, but upon circumstance.
But circumstance is not undetermined.   420
Unreal friendship may turn to real
But real friendship, once ended, cannot be mended.
Sooner shall enmity turn to alliance.
The enmity that never knew friendship
Can sooner know accord.

THOM.   For a countryman   425
You wrap your meaning in as dark generality
As any courtier.

TEM.   This is the simple fact!
You have no hope of reconciliation
With Henry the King. You look only
To blind assertion in isolation.   430
That is a mistake.

THOM.   O Henry, O my King!
TEM.   Other friends
 May be found in the present situation.
 King in England is not all-powerful;
 King is in France, squabbling in Anjou;
 Round him waiting hungry sons.   435
 We are for England. We are in England.
 You and I, my Lord, are Normans.
 England is a land for Norman
 Sovereignty. Let the Angevin
 Destroy himself, fighting in Anjou.   440
 He does not understand us, the English barons.
 We are the people.
THOM. To what does this lead?
TEM.   To a happy coalition
 Of intelligent interests.
THOM.   But what have you—
 If you do speak for barons—
TEM.   For a powerful party 445
 Which has turned its eyes in your direction—
 To gain from you, your Lordship asks.
 For us, Church favour would be an advantage,
 Blessing of Pope powerful protection
 In the fight for liberty. You, my Lord,   450
 In being with us, would fight a good stroke
 At once, for England and for Rome,
 Ending the tyrannous jurisdiction
 Of king's court over bishop's court,
 Of king's court over baron's court.   455
THOM. Which I helped to found.
TEM.   Which you helped to found.
 But time past is time forgotten.
 We expect the rise of a new constellation.
THOM. And if the Archbishop cannot trust the King,
 How can he trust those who work for King's undoing? 460
TEM. Kings will allow no power but their own;
 Church and people have good cause against the throne.
THOM. If the Archbishop cannot trust the Throne,
 He has good cause to trust none but God alone.
 It is not better to be thrown   465
 To a thousand hungry appetites than to one.
 At a future time this may be shown.
 I ruled once as Chancellor
 And men like you were glad to wait at my door.
 Not only in the court, but in the field   470

And in the tilt-yard I made many yield.
Shall I who ruled like an eagle over doves
Now take the shape of a wolf among wolves?
Pursue your treacheries as you have done before:
No one shall say that I betrayed a king.   475
TEM. Then, my Lord, I shall not wait at your door;
  And I well hope, before another spring
  The King will show his regard for your loyalty.
THOM. To make, then break, this thought has come before,
  The desperate exercise of failing power.   480
  Samson in Gaza did no more.
  But if I break, I must break myself alone.
        [*Enter* FOURTH TEMPTER]
FOURTH TEMPTER. Well done, Thomas, your will is hard to bend.
  And with me beside you, you shall not lack a friend.
THOM. Who are you? I expected   485
  Three visitors, not four.
TEM. Do not be surprised to receive one more.
  Had I been expected, I had been here before.
  I always precede expectation.
THOM.   Who are you?
TEM. As you do not know me, I do not need a name,   490
  And, as you know me, that is why I come.
  You know me, but have never seen my face.
  To meet before was never time or place.
THOM. Say what you come to say.
TEM.   It shall be said at last.
  Hooks have been baited with morsels of the past.   495
  Wantonness is weakness. As for the King,
  His hardened hatred shall have no end.
  You know truly, the King will never trust
  Twice, the man who has been his friend.
  Borrow use cautiously, employ   500
  Your services as long as you have to lend.
  You would wait for trap to snap
  Having served your turn, broken and crushed.
  As for barons, envy of lesser men
  Is still more stubborn than king's anger.   505
  Kings have public policy, barons private profit,
  Jealousy raging possession of the fiend.
  Barons are employable against each other;
  Greater enemies must kings destroy.

---

471. *tilt-yard:* a place for holding jousts.
481. *Samson in Gaza:* The blinded Samson pulled down the temple of the Philistines, destroying himself and them. See Milton's *Samson Agonistes,* in this anthology.

THOM. What is your counsel?

TEM.   Fare forward to the end.   510
All other ways are closed to you
Except the way already chosen.
But what is pleasure, kingly rule,
Or rule of men beneath a king,
With craft in corners, stealthy stratagem,   515
To general grasp of spiritual power?
Man oppressed by sin, since Adam fell—
You hold the keys of heaven and hell.
Power to bind and loose: bind, Thomas, bind,
King and bishop under your heel.   520
King, emperor, bishop, baron, king:
Uncertain mastery of melting armies,
War, plague, and revolution,
New conspiracies, broken pacts;
To be master or servant within an hour,   525
This is the course of temporal power.
The Old King shall know it, when at last breath,
No sons, no empire, he bites broken teeth.
You hold the skein: wind, Thomas, wind
The thread of eternal life and death.   530
You hold this power, hold it.

THOM.   Supreme, in this land?

TEM. Supreme, but for one.

THOM.   That I do not understand.

TEM. It is not for me to tell you how this may be so;
I am only here, Thomas, to tell you what you know.

THOM. How long shall this be?   535

TEM. Save what you know already, ask nothing of me.
But think, Thomas, think of glory after death.
When king is dead, there's another king,
And one more king is another reign.
King is forgotten, when another shall come: 540
Saint and Martyr rule from the tomb.
Think, Thomas, think of enemies dismayed,
Creeping in penance, frightened of a shade;
Think of pilgrims, standing in line
Before the glittering jewelled shrine,   545
From generation to generation
Bending the knee in supplication.
Think of the miracles, by God's grace,
And think of your enemies, in another place.

THOM. I have thought of these things.

TEM.   That is why I tell you.   550

Your thoughts have more power than kings to compel you.
You have also thought, sometimes at your prayers,
Sometimes hesitating at the angles of stairs,
And between sleep and waking, early in the morning,
When the bird cries, have thought of further scorning.   555
That nothing lasts, but the wheel turns,
The nest is rifled, and the bird mourns;
That the shrine shall be pillaged, and the gold spent,
The jewels gone for light ladies' ornament,
The sanctuary broken, and its stores   560
Swept into the laps of parasites and whores.
When miracles cease, and the faithful desert you,
And men shall only do their best to forget you.
And later is worse, when men will not hate you
Enough to defame or to execrate you,   565
But pondering the qualities that you lacked
Will only try to find the historical fact.
When men shall declare that there was no mystery
About this man who played a certain part in history.
THOM. But what is there to do? what is left to be done?   570
　Is there no enduring crown to be won?
TEM. Yes, Thomas, yes; you have thought of that too.
　What can compare with glory of Saints
　Dwelling forever in presence of God?
　What earthly glory, of king or emperor,   575
　What earthly pride, that is not poverty
　Compared with richness of heavenly grandeur?
　Seek the way of martyrdom, make yourself the lowest
　On earth, to be high in heaven.
　And see far off below you, where the gulf if fixed,   580
　Your persecutors, in timeless torment,
　Parched passion, beyond expiation.
THOM.　　　　　　　　　No!
　Who are you, tempting with my own desires?
　Others have come, temporal tempters,
　With pleasure and power at palpable price.   585
　What do you offer? what do you ask?
TEM. I offer you desire. I ask
　What you have to give. Is it too much
　For such a vision of eternal grandeur?
THOM. Others offered real goods, worthless   590
　But real. You only offer
　Dreams to damnation.
TEM.　　　　　　　You have often dreamt them.
THOM. Is there no way, in my soul's sickness,

Does not lead to damnation in pride?
I well know that these temptations   595
Mean present vanity and future torment.
Can sinful pride be driven out
Only by more sinful? Can I either act nor suffer
Without perdition?

TEM. You know and do not know, what it is to act or suffer.   600
You know and do not know, that acting is suffering,
And suffering action. Neither does the actor suffer
Nor the patient act. But both are fixed
In an eternal action, an eternal patience
To which all must consent that it may be willed   605
And which all must suffer that they may will it,
That the pattern may subsist, that the wheel may turn and still
Be forever still.

CHOR. There is no rest in the house. There is no rest in the street.
I hear restless movement of feet. And the air is heavy and thick.
Thick and heavy the sky. And the earth presses up beneath my
    feet   611
What is the sickly smell, the vapour? the dark green light from
    a cloud on a withered tree? The earth is heaving to parturi-
    tion of issue of hell. What is the sticky dew that forms on
    the back of my hand?

THE FOUR TEMPTERS.
Man's life is a cheat and a disappointment;
All things are unreal,
Unreal or disappointing: 615
The Catherine wheel, the pantomime cat,
The prizes given at the children's party,
The prize awarded for the English Essay,
The scholar's degree, the statesman's decoration.
All things become less real, man passes   620
From unreality to unreality.
This man is obstinate, blind, intent
On self-destruction,
Passing from deception to deception,
From grandeur to grandeur to final illusion,   625
Lost in the wonder of his own greatness,
The enemy of society, enemy of himself.

THE THREE PRIESTS.
O Thomas my Lord do not fight the intractable tide,
Do not sail the irresistible wind; in the storm,
Should we not wait for the sea to subside, in the night   630
Abide the coming of day, when the traveller may find his way,

616. *Catherine wheel:* a revolving piece of fireworks.

The sailor lay course by the sun?

[CHORUS, PRIESTS *and* TEMPTERS *alternately*.]

c. Is it the owl that calls, or a signal between the trees?

p. Is the window-bar made fast, is the door under lock and bolt?

t. Is it rain that taps at the window, is it wind that pokes at the
 door? 635

c. Does the torch flame in the hall, the candle in the room?

p. Does the watchman walk by the wall?

t. Does the mastiff prowl by the gate?

c. Death has a hundred hands and walks by a thousand ways. 639

p. He may come in the sight of all, he may pass unseen unheard.

t. Come whispering through the ear, or a sudden shock on the skull.

c. A man may walk with a lamp at night, and yet be drowned in a
 ditch.

p. A man may climb the stair in the day, and slip on a broken step.

t. A man may sit at meat, and feel the cold in his groin.

CHOR. We have not been happy, my Lord, we have not been too
 happy. 645

We are not ignorant women, we know what we must expect and
 not expect.

We know of oppression and torture,

We know of extortion and violence,

Destitution, disease,

The old without fire in winter, 650

The child without milk in summer,

Our labour taken away from us,

Our sins made heavier upon us.

We have seen the young man mutilated,

The torn girl trembling by the mill-stream. 655

And meanwhile we have gone on living,

Living and partly living,

Picking together the pieces,

Gathering faggots at nightfall,

Building a partial shelter, 660

For sleeping, and eating and drinking and laughter.

God gave us always some reason, some hope; but now a new
 terror has soiled us, which none can avert, none can avoid,
 flowing under our feet and over the sky;

Under doors and down chimneys, flowing in at the ear and the
 mouth and the eye.

God is leaving us, God is leaving us, more pang, more pain, than
 birth or death.

Sweet and cloying through the dark air 665

Falls the stifling scent of despair;

The forms take shape in the dark air:
Puss-purr of leopard, footfall of padding bear,
Palm-pat of nodding ape, square hyaena waiting
For laughter, laughter, laughter. The Lords of Hell are here. 670
They curl round you, lie at your feet, swing and wing through
    the dark air.
O Thomas Archbishop, save us, save us, save yourself that we
    may be saved;
Destroy yourself and we are destroyed.

THOM. Now is my way clear, now is the meaning plain:
Temptation shall not come in this kind again. 675
The last temptation is the greatest treason:
To do the right deed for the wrong reason.
The natural vigour in the venial sin
Is the way in which our lives begin.
Thirty years ago, I searched all the ways 680
That lead to pleasure, advancement and praise.
Delight in sense, in learning and in thought,
Music and philosophy, curiosity,
The purple bullfinch in the lilac tree,
The tiltyard skill, the strategy of chess, 685
Love in the garden, singing to the instrument,
Were all things equally desirable.
Ambition comes when early force is spent
And when we find no longer all things possible.
Ambition comes behind and unobservable. 690
Sin grows with doing good. When I imposed the King's law
In England, and waged war with him against Toulouse,
I beat the barons at their own game. I
Could then despise the men who thought me most contemptible,
The raw nobility, whose manners matched their fingernails. 695
While I ate out of the King's dish
To become servant of God was never my wish.
Servant of God has chance of greater sin
And sorrow, than the man who serves a king.
For those who serve the greater cause may make the cause serve
    them, 700
Still doing right: and striving with political men
May make that cause political, not by what they do
But by what they are. I know
What yet remains to show you of my history
Will seem to most of you at best futility, 705
Senseless self-slaughter of a lunatic,
Arrogant passion of a fanatic.
I know that history at all times draws

The strangest consequence from remotest cause.
But for every evil, every sacrilege, 710
Crime, wrong, oppression and the axe's edge,
Indifference, exploitation, you, and you,
And you, must all be punished. So must you.
I shall no longer act or suffer, to the sword's end.
Now my good Angel, whom God appoints 715
To be my guardian, hover over the swords' points.

Interlude

THE ARCHBISHOP. [*Preaches in the Cathedral on Christmas Morning,* 1170] "Glory to God in the highest, and on earth peace, good will toward men." *The fourteenth verse of the second chapter of the Gospel according to Saint Luke.* In the Name of the Father, and of the Son, and of the Holy Ghost. Amen.

Dear children of God, my sermon this morning will be a very short one. I wish only that you should ponder and meditate the deep meaning and mystery of our masses of Christmas Day. For whenever Mass is said, we re-enact the Passion and Death of Our Lord; and on this Christmas Day we do this in celebration of His Birth. So that at the same moment we rejoice in His coming for the salvation of men, and offer again to God His Body and Blood in sacrifice, oblation[a] and satisfaction for the sins of the whole world. It was in this same night that has just passed, that a multitude of the heavenly host appeared before the shepherds at Bethlehem, saying, "Glory to God in the highest, and on earth peace, good will toward men"; at this same time of all the year that we celebrate at once the Birth of Our Lord and His Passion and Death upon the Cross. Beloved, as the World sees, this is to behave in a strange fashion. For who in the World will both mourn and rejoice at once and for the same reason? For either joy will be overborne by mourning, or mourning will be cast out by joy; so it is only in these our Christian mysteries that we can rejoice and mourn at once for the same reason. But think for a while on the meaning of this word "peace." Does it seem strange to you that the angels should have announced Peace, when ceaselessly the world has been stricken with War and the fear of War? Does it seem to you that the angelic voices were mistaken, and that the promise was a disappointment and a cheat?

Reflect now, how Our Lord Himself spoke of Peace. He said to His disciples, "My peace I leave with you, my peace I give unto you." Did He mean peace as we think of it: the kingdom of England at peace with its neighbours, the barons at peace with the King, the householder counting over his peaceful gains, the swept hearth, his best wine for a friend at the table, his wife singing to the chil-

a. offering to God of the elements of bread and wine in the Eucharist.

dren? Those men His disciples knew no such things: they went forth to journey afar, to suffer by land and sea, to know torture, imprisonment, disappointment, to suffer death by martyrdom. What then did He mean? If you ask that, remember then that He said also, "Not as the world gives, give I unto you." So then, He gave to His disciples peace, but not peace as the world gives.

Consider also one thing of which you have probably never thought. Not only do we at the feast of Christmas celebrate at once Our Lord's Birth and His Death: but on the next day we celebrate the martyrdom of His first martyr, the blessed Stephen. Is it an accident, do you think, that the day of the first martyr follows immediately the day of the Birth of Christ? By no means. Just as we rejoice and mourn at once, in the Birth and in the Passion of Our Lord; so also, in a smaller figure, we both rejoice and mourn in the death of martyrs. We mourn, for the sins of the world that has martyred them; we rejoice, that another soul is numbered among the Saints in Heaven, for the glory of God and for the salvation of men.

Beloved, we do not think of a martyr simply as a good Christian who has been killed because he is a Christian: for that would be solely to mourn. We do not think of him simply as a good Christian who has been elevated to the company of the Saints: for that would be simply to rejoice: and neither our mourning nor our rejoicing is as the world's is. A Christian martyrdom is no accident. Saints are not made by accident. Still less is a Christian martyrdom the effect of a man's will to become a Saint, as a man by willing and contriving may become a ruler of men. Ambition fortifies the will of man to become ruler over other men: it operates with deception, cajolery, and violence, it is the action of impurity upon impurity. Not so in Heaven. A martyr, a saint, is always made by the design of God, for His love of men, to warn them and to lead them, to bring them back to His ways. A martyrdom is never the design of man; for the true martyr is he who has become the instrument of God, who has lost his will in the will of God, not lost it but found it, for he has found freedom in submission to God. The martyr no longer desires anything for himself, not even the glory of martyrdom. So thus as on earth the Church mourns and rejoices at once, in a fashion that the world cannot understand; so in Heaven the Saints are most high, having made themselves most low, seeing themselves not as we see them, but in the light of the Godhead from which they draw their being.

I have spoken to you today, dear children of God, of the martyrs of the past, asking you to remember especially our martyr of Canterbury, the blessed Archbishop Elphage;[b] because it is fitting, on

---

b. Archbishop of Canterbury from 1006 to 1012, when he was burned to death by the Danes.

Christ's birthday, to remember what is that Peace which He brought; and because, dear children, I do not think I shall ever preach to you again; and because it is possible that in a short time you may have yet another martyr, and that one perhaps not the last. I would have you keep in your hearts these words that I say, and think of them at another time. In the Name of the Father, and of the Son, and of the Holy Ghost. Amen.

Part II

Characters

THREE PRIESTS	ARCHBISHOP THOMAS BECKET
FOUR KNIGHTS	CHORUS OF WOMEN OF CANTERBURY
	ATTENDANTS

The first scene is in the Archbishop's Hall, the second scene is in the Cathedral, on December 29th, 1170.

CHORUS. Does the bird sing in the South?
    Only the sea-bird cries, driven inland by the storm.
    What sign of the spring of the year?
    Only the death of the old: not a stir, not a shoot, not a breath.
    Do the days begin to lengthen?   5
    Longer and darker the day, shorter and colder the night.
    Still and stifling the air: but a wind is stored up in the East.
    The starved crow sits in the field, attentive; and in the wood
    The owl rehearses the hollow note of death.
    What signs of a bitter spring?   10
    The wind stored up in the East.
    What, at the time of the birth of Our Lord, at Christmastide,
    Is there not peace upon earth, goodwill among men?
    The peace of this world is always uncertain, unless men keep the
        peace of God.
    And war among men defiles this world, but death in the Lord
        renews it,   15
    And the world must be cleaned in the winter, or we shall have
        only
    A sour spring, a parched summer, an empty harvest.
    Between Christmas and Easter what work shall be done?
    The ploughman shall go out in March and turn the same earth
    He has turned before, the bird shall sing the same song.   20
    When the leaf is out on the tree, when the elder and may
    Burst over the stream, and the air is clear and high,
    And voices trill at windows, and children tumble in front of the
        door,

What work shall have been done, what wrong
Shall the bird's song cover, the green tree cover, what wrong   25
Shall the fresh earth cover? We wait, and the time is short
But waiting is long.

    [*Enter the* FOUR KNIGHTS.]

FIRST KNIGHT. Servants of the King.

FIRST PRIEST.   And known to us.
You are welcome. Have you ridden far?

1ST KNI. Not far today, but matters urgent   30
Have brought us from France. We rode hard,
Took ship yesterday, landed last night,
Having business with the Archbishop.

SECOND KNIGHT. Urgent business.

THIRD KNIGHT.   From the King.

FOURTH KNIGHT. By the King's order.

1ST KNI.   Our men are outside.   35

1ST PR. You know the Archbishop's hospitality.
We are about to go to dinner.
The good Archbishop would be vexed
If we did not offer you entertainment
Before your business. Please dine with us.   40
Your men shall be looked after also.
Dinner before business. Do you like roast pork?

1ST KNI. Business before dinner. We will roast your pork
First, and dine upon it after.

2ND KNI. We must see the Archbishop.

3RD KNI.   Go, tell the Archbishop
We have no need of his hospitality.   46
We will find our own dinner.

1ST PR. [*To* ATTENDANT] Go, tell His Lordship.

4TH KNI.   How much longer will you keep us waiting?

    [*Enter* THOMAS.]

THOMAS. [*To* PRIESTS] However certain our expectation
The moment foreseen may be unexpected   50
When it arrives. It comes when we are
Engrossed with matters of other urgency.
On my table you will find
The papers in order, and the documents signed.
[*To* KNIGHTS]
You are welcome, whatever your business may be.   55
You say, from the King?

1ST KNI.   Most surely from the King.
We must speak with you alone.

THOM. [*To* PRIESTS]   Leave us then alone.
Now what is the matter?

1ST KNI.   This is the matter.

THE FOUR KNIGHTS.

You are the Archbishop in revolt against the King; in rebellion
    to the King and the law of the land;   60

You are the Archbishop who was made by the King; whom he set
    in your place to carry out his command.

You are his servant, his tool, and his jack,

You wore his favours on your back,

You had your honours all from his hand; from him you had the
    power, the seal and the ring.

This is the man who was the tradesman's son: the backstairs brat
    who was born in Cheapside;   65

This is the creature that crawled upon the King; swollen with
    blood and swollen with pride.

Creeping out of the London dirt,

Crawling up like a louse on your shirt,

The man who cheated, swindled, lied; broke his oath and betrayed
    his King.

THOM. This is not true.   70

Both before and after I received the ring

I have been a loyal vassal to the King.

Saving my order, I am at his command,

As his most faithful vassal in the land.

1ST KNI. Saving your order! let your order save you—   75

As I do not think it is like to do.

Saving your ambition is what you mean,

Saving your pride, envy and spleen.

2ND KNI. Saving your insolence and greed.

Won't you ask us to pray to God for you, in your need?   80

3RD KNI. Yes, we'll pray for you!

4TH KNI.   Yes, we'll pray for you!

THE FOUR KNIGHTS.

Yes, we'll pray that God may help you!

THOM. But, gentlemen, your business

Which you said was so urgent, is it only

Scolding and blaspheming?

1ST KNI.   That was only   85

Our indignation, as loyal subjects.

THOM. Loyal? To whom?

1ST KNI.   To the King!

2ND KNI.   The King!

3RD KNI. The King!

4TH KNI.   God bless him!

THOM. Then let your new coat of loyalty be worn

65. *Cheapside:* in the east of London.

Carefully, so it get not soiled or torn.   90
Have you something to say?
1ST KNI.   By the King's command.
Shall we say it now?
2ND KNI.   Without delay,
Before the old fox is off and away.
THOM.   What you have to say
By the King's command—if it be the King's command—
Should be said in public. If you make charges,   95
Then in public I will refute them.
1ST KNI.   No! here and now!
   [*They make to attack him, but the* PRIESTS *and* ATTENDANTS
   return and quietly interpose themselves.]
THOM. Now and here!
1ST KNI. Of your earlier misdeeds I shall make no mention.
They are too well known. But after dissension
Had ended, in France, and you were endued   100
With your former privilege, how did you show your gratitude?
You had fled from England, not exiled
Or threatened, mind you; but in the hope
Of stirring up trouble in the French dominions.
You sowed strife abroad, you reviled   105
The King to the King of France, to the Pope,
Raising up against him false opinions.
2ND KNI. Yet the King, out of his charity,
And urged by your friends, offered clemency,
Made a pact of peace, and all dispute ended   110
Sent you back to your See as you demanded.
3RD KNI. And burying the memory of your transgressions
Restored your honours and your possessions.
All was granted for which you sued:
Yet how, I repeat, did you show your gratitude?   115
4TH KNI. Suspending those who had crowned the young prince,
Denying the legality of his coronation;
Binding with the chains of anathema,
Using every means in your power to evince
The King's faithful servants, everyone who transacts   120
His business in his absence, the business of the nation.
1ST KNI. These are the facts.
Say therefore if you will be content
To answer in the King's presence. Therefore were we sent.
THOM. Never was it my wish   125
To uncrown the King's son, or to diminish
His honour and power. Why should he wish

111. *See:* the area of jurisdiction of a bishop.

To deprive my people of me and keep me from my own
  And bid me sit in Canterbury, alone?
  I would wish him three crowns rather than one,   130
  And as for the bishops, it is not my yoke
  That is laid upon them, or mine to revoke.
  Let them go to the Pope. It was he who condemned them.
1ST KNI. Through you they were suspended.
2ND KNI.   By you be this amended.
3RD KNI. Absolve them.
4TH KNI.   Absolve them.
THOM.   I do not deny   135
  That this was done through me. But it is not I
  Who can loose whom the Pope has bound.
  Let them go to him, upon whom redounds
  Their contempt towards me, their contempt towards the Church
      shown.
1ST KNI. Be that as it may, here is the King's command: 140
  That you and your servants depart from this land.
THOM. If that *is* the King's command, I will be bold
  To say: seven years were my people without
  My presence; seven years of misery and pain.
  Seven years a mendicant on foreign charity   145
  I lingered abroad: seven years is no brevity.
  I shall not get those seven years back again.
  Never again, you must make no doubt,
  Shall the sea run between the shepherd and his fold.
1ST KNI. The King's justice, the King's majesty,   150
  You insult with gross indignity;
  Insolent madman, whom nothing deters
  From attainting his servants and ministers.
THOM. It is not I who insult the King,
  And there is higher than I or the King.   155
  It is not I, Becket from Cheapside,
  It is not against me, Becket, that you strive.
  It is not Becket who pronounces doom,
  But the Law of Christ's Church, the judgement of Rome.
  Go then to Rome, or let Rome come   160
  Here, to you, in the person of her most unworthy son.
  Petty politicians in your endless adventure!
  Rome alone can absolve those who break Christ's indenture.
1ST KNI. Priest, you have spoken in peril of your life.
2ND KNI. Priest, you have spoken in danger of the knife.   165
3RD KNI. Priest, you have spoken treachery and treason.
4TH KNI. Priest! traitor confirmed in malfeasance.
THOM. I submit my cause to the judgement of Rome.

But if you kill me, I shall rise from my tomb
To submit my cause before God's throne.   170

KNIGHTS. Priest! monk! and servant! take, hold, detain,
  Restrain this man, in the King's name;
  Or answer with your bodies, if he escape before we come,
  We come for the King's justice, we come again.   [*Exeunt.*]

THOM. Pursue those who flee, track down those who evade;   175
  Come for arrest, come with the sword,
  Here, here, you shall find me ready, in the battle of the Lord.
  At whatsoever time you are ready to come,
  You will find me still more ready for martyrdom.

CHOR. I have smelt them, the death-bringers, senses are quickened
  By subtile forebodings; I have heard   181
  Fluting in the nighttime, fluting and owls, have seen at noon
  Scaly wings slanting over, huge and ridiculous. I have tasted
  The savour of putrid flesh in the spoon. I have felt   184
  The heaving of earth at nightfall, restless, absurd. I have heard
  Laughter in the noises of beasts that make strange noises: jackal,
      jackass, jackdaw; the scurrying noise of mouse and jerboa; the
      laugh of the loon, the lunatic bird. I have seen
  Grey necks twisting, rat tails twining, in the thick light of dawn.
      I have eaten
  Smooth creatures still living, with the strong salt taste of living
      things under sea; I have tasted
  The living lobster, the crab, the oyster, the whelk and the prawn;
      and they live and spawn in my bowels, and my bowels dis-
      solve in the light of dawn. I have smelt
  Death in the rose, death in the hollyhock, sweet pea, hyacinth,
      primrose and cowslip. I have seen   190
  Trunk and horn, tusk and hoof, in odd places;
  I have lain on the floor of the sea and breathed with the breathing
      of the sea-anemone, swallowed with ingurgitation of the
      sponge. I have lain in the soil and criticised the worm. In
      the air
  Flirted with the passage of the kite, I have plunged with the kite
      and cowered with the wren. I have felt
  The horn of the beetle, the scale of the viper, the mobile hard
      insensitive skin of the elephant, the evasive flank of the fish.
      I have smelt
  Corruption in the dish, incense in the latrine, the sewer in the
      incense, the smell of sweet soap in the woodpath, a hellish
      sweet scent in the woodpath, while the ground heaved. I
      have seen   195
  Rings of light coiling downwards, leading
  To the horror of the ape. Have I not known, not known

What was coming to be? It was here, in the kitchen, in the pas
    sage,
In the mews in the barn in the byre in the market place
In our veins our bowels our skulls as well   200
As well as in the plottings of potentates
As well as in the consultations of powers.
What is woven on the loom of fate
What is woven in the councils of princes
Is woven also in our veins, our brains,   205
Is woven like a pattern of living worms
In the guts of the women of Canterbury.

I have smelt them, the death-bringers; now is too late
For action, too soon for contrition.
Nothing is possible but the shamed swoon   210
Of those consenting to the last humiliation.
I have consented, Lord Archbishop, have consented,
Am torn away, subdued, violated,
United to the spiritual flesh of nature,
Mastered by the animal powers of spirit,   215
Dominated by the lust of self-demolition,
By the final utter uttermost death of spirit,
By the final ecstasy of waste and shame,
O Lord Archbishop, O Thomas Archbishop, forgive us, forgive us,
    pray for us that we may pray for you, out of our shame.
тном. Peace, and be at peace with your thoughts and visions.   220
    These things had to come to you and you to accept them.
    This is your share of the eternal burden,
    The perpetual glory. This is one moment,
    But know that another
    Shall pierce you with a sudden painful joy   225
    When the figure of God's purpose is made complete.
    You shall forget these things, toiling in the household,
    You shall remember them, droning by the fire,
    When age and forgetfulness sweeten memory
    Only like a dream that has often been told   230
    And often been changed in the telling. They will seem unreal.
    Human kind cannot bear very much reality.   232
PRIESTS. [*Severally*] My Lord, you must not stop here. To the min-
    ster.[a] Through the cloister. No time to waste. They are coming
    back, armed. To the altar, to the altar. They are here already. To
    the sanctuary. They are breaking in. We can barricade the min-
    ster doors. You cannot stay here. Force him to come. Seize him.

199. *mews:* stables set around a   a. church connected with a monas-
court or alley. *byre:* cow barn.   tery.

THOM. All my life they have been coming, these feet. All my life 233
I have waited. Death will come only when I am worthy,
And if I am worthy, there is no danger. 235
I have therefore only to make perfect my will.

PRIESTS. My Lord, they are coming. They will break through presently.
You will be killed. Come to the altar.

THOM. Peace! be quiet! remember where you are, and what is happening;
No life here is sought for but mine, 240
And I am not in danger: only near to death.

PRIESTS. Make haste, my Lord. Don't stop here talking. It is not
right.
What shall become of us, my Lord, if you are killed; what shall
become of us?

THOM. That again is another theme
To be developed and resolved in the pattern of time. 245
It is not for me to run from city to city;
To meet death gladly is only
The only way in which I can defend
The Law of God, the holy canons.

PRIESTS. My Lord, to vespers! You must not be absent from vespers.
You must not be absent from the divine office. To vespers.
Into the cathedral! 250

THOM. Go to vespers, remember me at your prayers.
They shall find the shepherd here; the flock shall be spared.
I have had a tremor of bliss, a wink of heaven, a whisper,
And I would no longer be denied; all things
Proceed to a joyful consummation. 255

PRIESTS. Seize him! force him! drag him!

THOM. Keep your hands off!

PRIESTS. To vespers! Take his feet! Up with him! Hurry.
[*They drag him off. While the* CHORUS *speak, the scene is
changed to the cathedral.*]

CHOR. [*While a* Dies Irae[b] *is sung in Latin by a choir in the distance*]
Numb the hand and dry the eyelid,
Still the horror, but more horror 260
Than when tearing in the belly.

Still the horror, but more horror
Than when twisting in the fingers,
Than when splitting in the skull.

b. a Latin hymn, of the thirteenth century, evoking the Day of Judgment.

More than footfall in the passage,   265
More than shadow in the doorway,
More than fury in the hall.

The agents of hell disappear, the human, they shrink and dissolve
Into dust on the wind, forgotten, unmemorable; only is here
The white flat face of Death, God's silent servant,   270
And behind the face of Death the Judgement
And behind the Judgement the Void, more horrid than active
     shapes of hell;
Emptiness, absence, separation from God;
The horror of the effortless journey, to the empty land
Which is no land, only emptiness, absence, the Void,   275
Where those who were men can no longer turn the mind
To distraction, delusion, escape into dream, pretence,
Where the soul is no longer deceived, for there are no objects, no
     tones,
No colours, no forms to distract, to divert the soul
From seeing itself, foully united forever, nothing with nothing,
Not what we call death, but what beyond death is not death,   281
We fear, we fear. Who shall then plead for me,
Who intercede for me, in my most need?

Dead upon the tree, my Saviour,
Let not be in vain Thy labour;   285
Help me, Lord, in my last fear.

Dust I am, to dust am bending,
From the final doom impending
Help me, Lord, for death is near.
     [*In the cathedral.* THOMAS *and* PRIESTS.]
PRIESTS. Bar the door. Bar the door.   290
     The door is barred.
     We are safe. We are safe.
     The enemy may rage outside, he will tire
     In vain. They cannot break in.
     They dare not break in.   295
     They cannot break in. They have not the force.
     We are safe. We are safe.
THOM. Unbar the doors! throw open the doors!
     I will not have the house of prayer, the church of Christ,
     The sanctuary, turned into a fortress.   300
     The Church shall protect her own, in her own way, not
     As oak and stone; stone and oak decay,
     Give no stay, but the Church shall endure.

The church shall be open, even to our enemies. Open the door!

PRIESTS. My Lord! these are not men, these come not as men come,
but 305
Like maddened beasts. They come not like men, who
Respect the sanctuary, who kneel to the Body of Christ,
But like beasts. You would bar the door
Against the lion, the leopard, the wolf or the boar,
Why not more 310
Against beasts with the souls of damned men, against men
Who would damn themselves to beasts. My Lord! My Lord!

THOM. Unbar the door!
You think me reckless, desperate and mad.
You argue by results, as this world does,
To settle if an act be good or bad. 315
You defer to the fact. For every life and every act
Consequence of good and evil can be shown.
And as in time results of many deeds are blended
So good and evil in the end become confounded.
It is not in time that my death shall be known; 320
It is out of time that my decision is taken
If you call that decision
To which my whole being gives entire consent.
I give my life 325
To the Law of God above the Law of Man.
Those who do not the same
How should they know what I do?
How should you know what I do? Yet how much more
Should you know than these madmen beating on the door. 330
Unbar the door! unbar the door!
We are not here to triumph by fighting, by stratagem, or by re-
sistance,
Not to fight with beasts as men. We have fought the beast
And have conquered. We have only to conquer
Now, by suffering. This is the easier victory. 335
Now is the triumph of the Cross, now
Open the door! I command it. OPEN THE DOOR!

[*The door is opened. The* KNIGHTS *enter, slightly tipsy.*]

PRIESTS. This way, my Lord! Quick. Up the stair. To the roof. To
the crypt. Quick. Come. Force him.

KNIGHTS. [*One line each*]
Where is Becket, the traitor to the King?
Where is Becket the meddling priest?
Come down Daniel to the lions' den, 340
Come down Daniel for the mark of the beast.

Are you washed in the blood of the Lamb?
　Are you marked with the mark of the beast?
Come down Daniel to the lions' den,　　　　　　　　345
　Come down Daniel and join in the feast.

Where is Becket the Cheapside brat?
　Where is Becket the faithless priest?
Come down Daniel to the lions' den,
　Come down Daniel and join the feast.　　　　　　350

THOM. It is the just man who
Like a bold lion, should be without fear.
I am here.
No traitor to the King, I am a priest,
A Christian, saved by the blood of Christ,　　　　　355
Ready to suffer with my blood.
This is the sign of the Church always,
The sign of blood. Blood for blood.
His blood given to buy my life,
My blood given to pay for His death,　　　　　　360
My death for His death.

KNIGHTS. Absolve all those you have excommunicated.
Resign the powers you have arrogated.
Restore to the King the money you appropriated.
Renew the obedience you have violated.　　　　　　365

THOM. For my Lord I am now ready to die,
That His Church may have peace and liberty.
Do with me as you will, to your hurt and shame;
But none of my people, in God's name,
Whether layman or clerk, shall you touch.　　　　　370
This I forbid.

KNIGHTS. Traitor! traitor! traitor! traitor!

THOM. You, Reginald, three times traitor you:
Traitor to me as my temporal vassal,
Traitor to me as your spiritual lord,　　　　　　375
Traitor to God in desecrating His Church.

1ST KNI. No faith do I owe to a renegade,
And what I owe shall now be paid.　　　　　　　378

THOM. Now to Almighty God, to the Blessed Mary ever Virgin, to
　　　the blessed John the Baptist, the holy apostles Peter and
　　　Paul, to the blessed martyr Denys, and to all the Saints, I
　　　commend my cause and that of the Church.
　　　[*While the* KNIGHTS *kill him, we hear the* CHORUS.]

CHOR. Clear the air! clean the sky! wash the wind! take stone from
　　　stone and wash them.　　　　　　　　　　　379

343. *Lamb:* Christ.

The land is foul, the water is foul, our beasts and ourselves defiled
with blood.
A rain of blood has blinded my eyes. Where is England? where is
Kent? where is Canterbury?
O far far far far in the past; and I wander in a land of barren
boughs: if I break them, they bleed; I wander in a land of
dry stones: if I touch them they bleed.
How how can I ever return, to the soft quiet seasons?
Night stay with us, stop sun, hold season, let the day not come,
let the spring not come.
Can I look again at the day and its common things, and see them
all smeared with blood, through a curtain of falling blood?
We did not wish anything to happen.   386
We understood the private catastrophe,
The personal loss, the general misery,
Living and partly living;
The terror by night ends in daily action,   390
The terror by day that ends in sleep;
But the talk in the market-place, the hand on the broom,
The nighttime heaping of the ashes,
The fuel laid on the fire at daybreak,
These acts marked a limit to our suffering.   395
Every horror had its definition,
Every sorrow had a kind of end:
In life there is not time to grieve long.
But this, this is out of life, this is out of time,
An instant eternity of evil and wrong.   400
We are soiled by a filth that we cannot clean, united to super-
natural vermin,
It is not we alone, it is not the house, it is not the city that is
defiled,
But the world that is wholly foul.   403
Clear the air! clean the sky! wash the wind! take the stone from
the stone, take the skin from the arm, take the muscle from
the bone, and wash them. Wash the stone, wash the bone,
wash the brain, wash the soul, wash them wash them!
[*The* KNIGHTS, *having completed the murder, advance to the
front of the stage and address the audience.*]

1ST KNI. We beg you to give us your attention for a few moments.
We know that you may be disposed to judge unfavourably of our
action. You are Englishmen, and therefore you believe in fair
play: and when you see one man being set upon by four, then
your sympathies are all with the under dog. I respect such feelings, I share them. Nevertheless, I appeal to your sense of honour.
You are Englishmen, and therefore will not judge anybody with-

out hearing both sides of the case. That is in accordance with our long established principle of Trial by Jury. I am not myself qualified to put our case to you. I am a man of action and not of words. For that reason I shall do no more than introduce the other speakers, who, with their various abilities, and different points of view, will be able to lay before you the merits of this extremely complex problem. I shall call upon our youngest member to speak first. William de Traci.[c]

2ND KNI. I am afraid I am not anything like such an experienced speaker as Reginald Fitz Urse would lead you to believe. But there is one thing I should like to say, and I might as well say it at once. It is this: in what we have done, and whatever you may think of it, we have been perfectly disinterested. [*The other* KNIGHTS: "Hear! hear!"] *We* are not getting anything out of this. We have much more to lose than to gain. We are four plain Englishmen who put our country first. I dare say that we didn't make a very good impression when we came in. The fact is that we knew we had taken on a pretty stiff job; I'll only speak for myself, but I had drunk a good deal—I am not a drinking man ordinarily—to brace myself up for it. When you come to the point, it does go against the grain to kill an Archbishop, especially when you have been brought up in good Church traditions. So if we seemed a bit rowdy, you will understand why it was; and for my part I am awfully sorry about it. We realised that this was our duty, but all the same we had to work ourselves up to it. And, as I said, *we* are not getting a penny out of this. We know perfectly well how things will turn out. King Henry—God bless him—will have to say, for reasons of state, that he never meant this to happen; and there is going to be an awful row; and at the best we shall have to spend the rest of our lives abroad. And even when reasonable people come to see that the Archbishop *had* to be put out of the way—and personally I had a tremendous admiration for him— you must have noticed what a good show he put up at the end— they won't give *us* any glory. No, we have done for ourselves, there's no mistake about that. So, as I said at the beginning, please give us at least the credit for being completely disinterested in this business. I think that is about all I have to say.

1ST KNI. I think we will all agree that William de Traci has spoken well and has made a very important point. The gist of his argument is this: that we have been completely disinterested. But our act itself needs more justification than that; and you must hear our other speakers. I shall next call upon Hugh de Morville.

3RD KNI. I should like first to recur to a point that was very well put

c. He died in France in 1173 of a disease that rotted away his flesh. He repented on his deathbed. The other three knights obeyed the papal order to go to the Holy Land, and died fighting there.

by our leader, Reginald Fitz Urse: that you are Englishmen, and therefore your sympathies are always with the under dog. It is the English spirit of fair play. Now the worthy Archbishop, whose good qualities I very much admired, has throughout been presented as the under dog. But is this really the case? I am going to appeal not to your emotions but to your reason. You are hardheaded sensible people, as I can see, and not to be taken in by emotional clap-trap. I therefore ask you to consider soberly: what were the Archbishop's aims? and what are King Henry's aims? In the answer to these questions lies the key to the problem.

The King's aim has been perfectly consistent. During the reign of the late Queen Matilda[d] and the irruption of the unhappy usurper Stephen,[e] the kingdom was very much divided. Our King saw that the one thing needful was to restore order: to curb the excessive powers of local government, which were usually exercised for selfish and often for seditious ends, and to systematise the judiciary. There was utter chaos: there were three kinds of justice and three kinds of court: that of the King, that of the Bishops, and that of the baronage. I must repeat one point that the last speaker has made. While the late Archbishop was Chancellor, he wholeheartedly supported the King's designs: this is an important point, which, if necessary, I can substantiate. Now the King intended that Becket, who had proved himself an extremely able administrator—no one denies that—should unite the offices of Chancellor and Archbishop. No one would have grudged him that; no one than he was better qualified to fill at once these two most important posts. Had Becket concurred with the King's wishes, we should have had an almost ideal State: a union of spiritual and temporal administration, under the central government. I knew Becket well, in various official relations; and I may say that I have never known a man so well qualified for the highest rank of Civil Service. And what happened? The moment that Becket, at the King's instance, had been made Archbishop, he resigned the office of Chancellor, he became more priestly than the priests, he ostentatiously and offensively adopted an ascetic manner of life, he openly abandoned every policy that he had heretofore supported; he affirmed immediately that there was a higher order than that which our King, and he as the King's servant, had for so many years striven to establish; and that—God knows why—the two orders were incompatible.

You will agree with me that such interference by an Archbishop offends the instincts of a people like ours. So far, I know that I have your approval: I read it in your faces. It is only with

---

d. mother of Henry II.   *e.* king of England from 1135 to 1154.

the measures we have had to adopt, in order to set matters to rights, that you take issue. No one regrets the necessity for violence more than we do. Unhappily, there are times when violence is the only way in which social justice can be secured. At another time, you would condemn an Archbishop by vote of Parliament and execute him formally as a traitor, and no one would have to bear the burden of being called murderer. And at a later time still, even such temperate measures as these would become unnecessary. But, if you have now arrived at a just subordination of the pretensions of the Church to the welfare of the State, remember that it is we who took the first step. We have been instrumental in bringing about the state of affairs that you approve. We have served your interest; we merit your applause; and if there is any guilt whatever in the matter, you must share it with us.

1ST KNI. Morville has given us a great deal to think about. It seems to me that he has said almost the last word, for those who have been able to follow his very subtle reasoning. We have, however, one more speaker, who has I think another point of view to express. If there are any who are still unconvinced, I think that Richard Brito will be able to convince them. Richard Brito.

4TH KNI. The speakers who have preceded me, to say nothing of our leader, Reginald Fitz Urse, have all spoken very much to the point. I have nothing to add along their particular lines of argument. What I have to say may be put in the form of a question: *Who killed the Archbishop?* As you have been eyewitnesses of this lamentable scene, you may feel some surprise at my putting it in this way. But consider the course of events. I am obliged, very briefly, to go over the ground traversed by the last speaker. While the late Archbishop was Chancellor, no one, under the King, did more to weld the country together, to give it the unity, the stability, order, tranquillity, and justice that it so badly needed. From the moment he became Archbishop, he completely reversed his policy; he showed himself to be utterly indifferent to the fate of the country, to be, in fact, a monster of egotism, a menace to society. This egotism grew upon him, until it became at last an undoubted mania. Every means that had been tried to conciliate him, to restore him to reason, had failed. Now I have unimpeachable evidence to the effect that before he left France he clearly prophesied, in the presence of numerous witnesses, that he had not long to live, and that he would be killed in England. He used every means of provocation; from his conduct, step by step, there can be no inference except that he had determined upon a death by martyrdom. This man, formerly a great public servant, had become a wrecker. Even at the last, he could have given us reason: you have seen how he evaded our questions.

And when he had deliberately exasperated us beyond human endurance, he could still have easily escaped; he could have kept himself from us long enough to allow our righteous anger to cool. That was just what he did not wish to happen; he insisted, while we were still inflamed with wrath, that the doors should be opened. Need I say more? I think, with these facts before you, you will unhesitatingly render a verdict of Suicide while of Unsound Mind. It is the only charitable verdict you can give, upon one who was, after all, a great man.

1ST KNI. Thank you, Brito. I think that there is no more to be said; and I suggest that you now disperse quietly to your homes. Please be careful not to loiter in groups at street corners, and do nothing that might provoke any public outbreak.

[*Exeunt* KNIGHTS.]

1ST PR. O father, father, gone from us, lost to us,   404
How shall we find you, from what far place
Do you look down on us? You now in Heaven,
Who shall now guide us, protect us, direct us?
After what journey through what further dread
Shall we recover your presence? when inherit
Your strength? The Church lies bereft,   410
Alone, desecrated, desolated, and the heathen shall build on the ruins,
Their world without God. I see it. I see it.

3RD PR. No. For the Church is stronger for this action,
Triumphant in adversity. It is fortified
By persecution: supreme, so long as men will die for it.   415
Go, weak sad men, lost erring souls, homeless in earth or heaven.
Go where the sunset reddens the last grey rock
Of Brittany, or the Gates of Hercules.
Go venture shipwreck on the sullen coasts
Where blackamoors make captive Christian men;   420
Go to the northern seas confined with ice
Where the dead breath makes numb the hand, makes dull the brain;
Find an oasis in the desert sun,
Go seek alliance with the heathen Saracen,
To share his filthy rites, and try to snatch   425
Forgetfulness in his libidinous courts,
Oblivion in the fountain by the date-tree;
Or sit and bite your nails in Aquitaine.
In the small circle of pain within the skull
You still shall tramp and tread one endless round   430
Of thought, to justify your action to yourselves,
Weaving a fiction which unravels as you weave,

Pacing forever in the hell of make-believe
Which never is belief: this is your fate on earth
And we must think no further of you. O my Lord   435
The glory of whose new state is hidden from us,
Pray for us of your charity; now in the sight of God
Conjoined with all the saints and martyrs gone before you,
Remember us. Let our thanks ascend
To God, who has given us another Saint in Canterbury.   440

CHOR. [*While a* Te Deum *is sung in Latin by a choir in the distance*]

We praise Thee, O God, for Thy glory displayed in all the creatures of the earth,

In the snow, in the rain, in the wind, in the storm; in all of Thy creatures, both the hunters and the hunted.

For all things exist only as seen by Thee, only as known by Thee, all things exist

Only in Thy light, and Thy glory is declared even in that which denies Thee; the darkness declares the glory of light.

Those who deny Thee could not deny, if Thou didst not exist; and their denial is never complete, for if it were so, they would not exist.   445

They affirm Thee in living; all things affirm Thee in living; the bird in the air, both the hawk and the finch; the beast on the earth, both the wolf and the lamb; the worm in the soil and the worm in the belly.

Therefore man, whom Thou hast made to be conscious of Thee, must consciously praise Thee, in thought and in word and in deed.

Even with the hand to the broom, the back bent in laying the fire, the knee bent in cleaning the hearth, we, the scrubbers and sweepers of Canterbury,

The back bent under toil, the knee bent under sin, the hands to the face under fear, the head bent under grief,

Even in us the voices of seasons, the snuffle of winter, the song of spring, the drone of summer, the voices of beasts and of birds, praise Thee.   450

We thank Thee for Thy mercies of blood, for Thy redemption by blood. For the blood of Thy martyrs and saints

Shall enrich the earth, shall create the holy places.

For wherever a saint has dwelt, wherever a martyr has given his blood for the blood of Christ,

There is holy ground, and the sanctity shall not depart from it

Though armies trample over it, though sightseers come with guide-books looking over it;   455

From where the western seas gnaw at the coast of Iona,

To the death in the desert, the prayer in forgotten places by the
   broken imperial column,
From such ground springs that which forever renews the earth
Though it is forever denied. Therefore, O God, we thank Thee
Who hast given such blessing to Canterbury.   460

Forgive us, O Lord, we acknowledge ourselves as type of the com-
   mon man,
Of the men and women who shut the door and sit by the fire;
Who fear the blessing of God, the loneliness of the night of God,
   the surrender required, the deprivation inflicted;
Who fear the injustice of men less than the justice of God;
Who fear the hand at the window, the fire in the thatch, the fist
   in the tavern, the push into the canal,   465
Less than we fear the love of God.
We acknowledge our trespass, our weakness, our fault; we ac-
   knowledge
That the sin of the world is upon our heads; that the blood of the
   martyrs and the agony of the saints
Is upon our heads.
Lord, have mercy upon us.
Christ, have mercy upon us.   470
Lord, have mercy upon us.
Blessed Thomas, pray for us.

JAMES JOYCE

(1882–1941)

A Portrait of the Artist as a Young Man*

Once upon a time and a very good time it was there was a moocow coming down along the road and this moocow that was down
along the road met a nicens little boy named baby tuckoo. . . .

His father told him that story: his father looked at him through
a glass: he had a hairy face.

He was baby tuckoo. The moocow came down the road where
Betty Byrne lived: she sold lemon platt.

O, the wild rose blossoms
On the little green place.

* From *A Portrait of the Artist as a Young Man* by James Joyce, included in *The Portable James Joyce*. Copyright 1946, 1947 by The Viking Press, Inc. Reprinted by permission of The Viking Press, Inc., New York. According to Joyce the book was begun in 1904, in Dublin, and finished in 1914, in Trieste. It was published in 1916. The first two parts of the first chapter are reprinted here. The punctuation ". . ." does not indicate omissions from this text.

He sang that song. That was his song.

> O, the green wothe botheth.

When you wet the bed, first it is warm then it gets cold. His mother put on the oilsheet. That had the queer smell.

His mother had a nicer smell than his father. She played on the piano the sailor's hornpipe for him to dance. He danced:

> Tralala, lala,
> Tralala tralaladdy,
> Tralala, lala,
> Tralala lala.

Uncle Charles and Dante clapped. They were older than his father and mother but Uncle Charles was older than Dante.

Dante had two brushes in her press. The brush with the maroon velvet back was for Michael Davitt[1] and the brush with the green velvet back was for Parnell.[2] Dante gave him a cachou every time he brought her a piece of tissue paper.

The Vances lived in number seven. They had a different father and mother. They were Eileen's father and mother. When they were grown up he was going to marry Eileen. He hid under the table. His mother said:

—O, Stephen will apologise.

Dante said:

—O, if not, the eagles will come and pull out his eyes—

> Pull out his eyes,
> Apologise,
> Apologise,
> Pull out his eyes.

> Apologise,
> Pull out his eyes,
> Pull out his eyes,
> Apologise.

*   *   *

The wide playgrounds were swarming with boys. All were shouting and the prefects urged them on with strong cries. The evening air was pale and chilly and after every charge and thud of the footballers the greasy leather orb flew like a heavy bird through the

---

1. Irish patriot (1846–1906) who, like the majority of the Irish nationalist politicians, broke with Parnell when the latter's adultery with Mrs. O'Shea became known.

2. Charles Parnell (1846–1891), the leader of the Irish Parliamentary Party in the British House of Commons. Party and country were split on the question of his suitability as leader after Captain O'Shea named him as corespondent in a divorce suit (1889) against Mrs. O'Shea.

grey light. He kept on the fringe of his line, out of sight of his prefect, out of the reach of the rude feet, feigning to run now and then. He felt his body small and weak amid the throng of players and his eyes were weak and watery. Rody Kickham was not like that: he would be captain of the third line all the fellows said.

Rody Kickham was a decent fellow but Nasty Roche was a stink. Rody Kickham had greaves in his number[3] and a hamper in the refectory. Nasty Roche had big hands. He called the Friday pudding dog-in-the-blanket. And one day he had asked:

—What is your name?

Stephen had answered: Stephen Dedalus.

Then Nasty Roche had said:

—What kind of a name is that?

And when Stephen had not been able to answer Nasty Roche had asked:

—What is your father?

Stephen had answered:

—A gentleman.

Then Nasty Roche had asked:

—Is he a magistrate?

He crept about from point to point on the fringe of his line, making little runs now and then. But his hands were bluish with cold. He kept his hands in the side pockets of his belted grey suit. That was a belt round his pocket. And belt was also to give a fellow a belt. One day a fellow had said to Cantwell:

—I'd give you such a belt in a second.

Cantwell had answered:

—Go and fight your match. Give Cecil Thunder a belt. I'd like to see you. He'd give you a toe in the rump for yourself.

That was not a nice expression. His mother had told him not to speak with the rough boys in the college. Nice mother! The first day in the hall of the castle[4] when she had said goodbye she had put up her veil double to her nose to kiss him: and her nose and eyes were red. But he had pretended not to see that she was going to cry. She was a nice mother but she was not so nice when she cried. And his father had given him two five-shilling pieces for pocket money. And his father had told him if he wanted anything to write home to him and, whatever he did, never to peach[5] on a fellow. Then at the door of the castle the rector had shaken hands with his father and mother, his soutane[6] fluttering in the breeze, and the car had driven off with his father and mother on it. They had cried to him from the car, waving their hands:

—Good-bye, Stephen, goodbye!

3. sediment of melted animal fat in his locker.
4. The Jesuit school of Clongowes is housed in an old castle.
5. tell, inform.
6. cassock.

—Good-bye, Stephen, goodbye!

He was caught in the whirl of a scrimmage and, fearful of the flashing eyes and muddy boots, bent down to look through the legs. The fellows were struggling and groaning and their legs were rubbing and kicking and stamping. Then Jack Lawton's yellow boots dodged out the ball and all the other boots and legs ran after. He ran after them a little way and then stopped. It was useless to run on. Soon they would be going home for the holidays. After supper in the study hall he would change the number pasted up inside his desk from seventyseven to seventysix.

It would be better to be in the study hall than out there in the cold. The sky was pale and cold but there were lights in the castle. He wondered from which window Hamilton Rowan had thrown his hat on the haha and had there been flowerbeds at that time under the windows. One day when he had been called to the castle the butler had shown him the marks of the soldiers' slugs in the wood of the door and had given him a piece of shortbread that the community ate. It was nice and warm to see the lights in the castle. It was like something in a book. Perhaps Leicester Abbey was like that. And there were nice sentences in Doctor Cornwell's Spelling Book. They were like poetry but they were only sentences to learn the spelling from.

> Wolsey died in Leicester Abbey
> Where the abbots buried him.
> Canker is a disease of plants,
> Cancer one of animals.

It would be nice to lie on the hearthrug before the fire, leaning his head upon his hands, and think on those sentences. He shivered as if he had cold slimy water next his skin. That was mean of Wells to shoulder him into the square ditch because he would not swop his little snuffbox for Wells's seasoned hacking chestnut, the conqueror of forty. How cold and slimy the water had been! A fellow had once seen a big rat jump into the scum. Mother was sitting at the fire with Dante waiting for Brigid to bring in the tea. She had her feet on the fender and her jewelly slippers were so hot and they had such a lovely warm smell. Dante knew a lot of things. She had taught him where the Mozambique Channel was and what was the longest river in America and what was the name of the highest mountain in the moon. Father Arnall knew more than Dante because he was a priest but both his father and Uncle Charles said that Dante was a clever woman and a wellread woman. And when Dante made that noise after dinner and then put up her hand to her mouth: that was heartburn.

A voice cried far out on the playground:

—All in!

Then other voices cried from the lower and third lines:

—All in! All in!

The players closed around, flushed and muddy, and he went among them, glad to go in. Rody Kickham held the ball by its greasy lace. A fellow asked him to give it one last: but he walked on without even answering the fellow. Simon Moonan told him not to because the prefect was looking. The fellow turned to Simon Moonan and said:

—We all know why you speak. You are McGlade's suck.

Suck was a queer word. The fellow called Simon Moonan that name because Simon Moonan used to tie the prefect's false sleeves behind his back and the prefect used to let on to be angry. But the sound was ugly. Once he had washed his hands in the lavatory of the Wicklow Hotel and his father pulled the stopper up by the chain after and the dirty water went down through the hole in the basin. And when it had all gone down slowly the hole in the basin had made a sound like that: suck. Only louder.

To remember that and the white look of the lavatory made him feel cold and then hot. There were two cocks that you turned and water came out: cold and hot. He felt cold and then a little hot: and he could see the names printed on the cocks. That was a very queer thing.

And the air in the corridor chilled him too. It was queer and wettish. But soon the gas would be lit and in burning it made a light noise like a little song. Always the same: and when the fellows stopped talking in the playroom you could hear it.

It was the hour for sums. Father Arnall wrote a hard sum on the board and then said:

—Now then, who will win? Go ahead, York! Go ahead, Lancaster![7]

Stephen tried his best but the sum was too hard and he felt confused. The little silk badge with the white rose on it that was pinned on the breast of his jacket began to flutter. He was no good at sums but he tried his best so that York might not lose. Father Arnall's face looked very black but he was not in a wax:[8] he was laughing. Then Jack Lawton cracked his fingers and Father Arnall looked at his copybook and said:

—Right. Bravo Lancaster! The red rose wins. Come on now, York! Forge ahead!

Jack Lawton looked over from his side. The little silk badge with the red rose on it looked very rich because he had a blue sailor top on. Stephen felt his own face red too, thinking of all the bets about

7. The two sections of the class were named after York and Lancaster, the opposing factions in the Wars of the Roses, the English civil wars of the fifteenth century.
8. bad temper.

who would get first place in Elements, Jack Lawton or he. Some weeks Jack Lawton got the card for first and some weeks he got the card for first. His white silk badge fluttered and fluttered as he worked at the next sum and heard Father Arnall's voice. Then all his eagerness passed away and he felt his face quite cool. He thought his face must be white because it felt so cool. He could not get out the answer for the sum but it did not matter. White roses and red roses: those were beautiful colours to think of. And the cards for first place and third place were beautiful colours too: pink and cream and lavender. Lavender and cream and pink roses were beautiful to think of. Perhaps a wild rose might be like those colours and he remembered the song about the wild rose blossoms on the little green place. But you could not have a green rose. But perhaps somewhere in the world you could.

The bell rang and then the classes began to file out of the rooms and along the corridors towards the refectory. He sat looking at the two prints of butter on his plate but could not eat the damp bread. The tablecloth was damp and limp. But he drank off the hot weak tea which the clumsy scullion,[9] girt with a white apron, poured into his cup. He wondered whether the scullion's apron was damp too or whether all white things were cold and damp. Nasty Roche and Saurin drank cocoa that their people sent them in tins. They said they could not drink the tea; that it was hogwash. Their fathers were magistrates, the fellows said.

All the boys seemed to him very strange. They had all fathers and mothers and different clothes and voices. He longed to be at home and lay his head on his mother's lap. But he could not: and so he longed for the play and study and prayers to be over and to be in bed.

He drank another cup of hot tea and Fleming said:

—What's up? Have you a pain or what's up with you?

—I don't know, Stephen said.

—Sick in your bread basket, Fleming said, because your face looks white. It will go away.

—O yes, Stephen said.

But he was not sick there. He thought that he was sick in his heart if you could be sick in that place. Fleming was very decent to ask him. He wanted to cry. He leaned his elbows on the table and shut and opened the flaps of his ears. Then he heard the noise of the refectory every time he opened the flaps of his ears. It made a roar like a train at night. And when he closed the flaps the roar was shut off like a train going into a tunnel. That night at Dalkey[10] the train had roared like that and then, when it went into the tunnel, the

---

9. kitchen boy.   10. on the coast. It could be reached from Dublin by train or streetcar.

roar stopped. He closed his eyes and the train went on, roaring and then stopping; roaring again, stopping. It was nice to hear it roar and stop and then roar out of the tunnel again and then stop.

Then the higher line fellows began to come down along the matting in the middle of the refectory, Paddy Rath and Jimmy Magee and the Spaniard who was allowed to smoke cigars and the little Portuguese who wore the woolly cap. And then the lower line tables and the tables of the third line. And every single fellow had a different way of walking.

He sat in a corner of the playroom pretending to watch a game of dominos and once or twice he was able to hear for an instant the little song of the gas. The prefect was at the door with some boys and Simon Moonan was knotting his false sleeves. He was telling them something about Tullabeg.

Then he went away from the door and Wells came over to Stephen and said:

—Tell us, Dedalus, do you kiss your mother before you go to bed?

Stephen answered:

—I do.

Wells turned to the other fellows and said:

—O, I say, here's a fellow says he kisses his mother every night before he goes to bed.

The other fellows stopped their game and turned round, laughing. Stephen blushed under their eyes and said:

—I do not.

Wells said:

—O, I say, here's a fellow says he doesn't kiss his mother before he goes to bed.

They all laughed again. Stephen tried to laugh with them. He felt his whole body hot and confused in a moment. What was the right answer to the question? He had given two and still Wells laughed. But Wells must know the right answer for he was in third of grammar. He tried to think of Wells's mother but he did not dare to raise his eyes to Wells's face. He did not like Wells's face. It was Wells who had shouldered him into the square ditch the day before because he would not swop his little snuffbox for Wells's seasoned hacking chestnut, the conqueror of forty. It was a mean thing to do; all the fellows said it was. And how cold and slimy the water had been! And a fellow had once seen a big rat jump plop into the scum.

The cold slime of the ditch covered his whole body; and, when the bell rang for study and the lines filed out of the playrooms, he felt the cold air of the corridor and staircase inside his clothes. He still tried to think what was the right answer. Was it right to kiss his mother or wrong to kiss his mother? What did that mean, to kiss? You put your face up like that to say goodnight and then his mother put her face down. That was to kiss. His mother put her lips on his cheek; her lips were soft and they wetted his cheek; and they made a tiny little noise: kiss. Why did people do that with their two faces?

Sitting in the study hall he opened the lid of his desk and changed the number pasted up inside from seventyseven to seventysix. But the Christmas vacation was very far away: but one time it would come because the earth moved round always.

There was a picture of the earth on the first page of his geography: a big ball in the middle of clouds. Fleming had a box of crayons and one night during free study he had coloured the earth green and the clouds maroon. That was like the two brushes in Dante's press, the brush with the green velvet back for Parnell and the brush with the maroon velvet back for Michael Davitt. But he had not told Fleming to colour them those colours. Fleming had done it himself.

He opened the geography to study the lesson; but he could not learn the names of places in America. Still they were all different places that had different names. They were all in different countries and the countries were in continents and the continents were in the world and the world was in the universe.

He turned to the flyleaf of the geography and read what he had written there: himself, his name and where he was.

> Stephen Dedalus
> Class of Elements
> Clongowes Wood College
> Sallins
> County Kildare
> Ireland
> Europe
> The World
> The Universe

That was in his writing: and Fleming one night for a cod[11] had written on the opposite page:

> Stephen Dedalus is my name,
> Ireland is my nation.
> Clongowes is my dwellingplace
> And heaven my expectation.

He read the verses backwards but then they were not poetry. Then he read the flyleaf from the bottom to the top till he came to

11. joke.

his own name. That was he: and he read down the page again. What was after the universe? Nothing. But was there anything round the universe to show where it stopped before the nothing place began? It could not be a wall but there could be a thin thin line there all round everything. It was very big to think about everything and everywhere. Only God could do that. He tried to think what a big thought that must be but he could think only of God. God was God's name just as his name was Stephen. *Dieu* was the French for God and that was God's name too; and when anyone prayed to God and said *Dieu* then God knew at once that it was a French person that was praying. But though there were different names for God in all the different languages in the world and God understood what all the people who prayed said in their different languages still God remained always the same God and God's real name was God.

It made him very tired to think that way. It made him feel his head very big. He turned over the flyleaf and looked wearily at the green round earth in the middle of the maroon clouds. He wondered which was right, to be for the green or for the maroon, because Dante had ripped the green velvet back off the brush that was for Parnell one day with her scissors and had told him that Parnell was a bad man. He wondered if they were arguing at home about that. That was called politics. There were two sides in it: Dante was on one side and his father and Mr. Casey were on the other side but his mother and Uncle Charles were on no side. Every day there was something in the paper about it.

It pained him that he did not know well what politics meant and that he did not know where the universe ended. He felt small and weak. When would he be like the fellows in Poetry and Rhetoric? They had big voices and big boots and they studied trigonometry. That was very far away. First came the vacation and then the next term and then vacation again and then again another term and then again the vacation. It was like a train going in and out of tunnels and that was like the noise of the boys eating in the refectory when you opened and closed the flaps of the ears. Term, vacation; tunnel, out; noise, stop. How far away it was! It was better to go to bed to sleep. Only prayers in the chapel and then bed. He shivered and yawned. It would be lovely in bed after the sheets got a bit hot. First they were so cold to get into. He shivered to think how cold they were first. But then they got hot and then he could sleep. It was lovely to be tired. He yawned again. Night prayers and then bed: he shivered and wanted to yawn. It would be lovely in a few minutes. He felt a warm glow creeping up from the cold shivering sheets, warmer and warmer till he felt warm all over, ever so warm and yet he shivered a little and still wanted to yawn.

The bell rang for night prayers and he filed out of the study hall after the others and down the staircase and along the corridors to the chapel. The corridors were darkly lit and the chapel was darkly lit. Soon all would be dark and sleeping. There was cold night air in the chapel and the marbles were the colour the sea was at night. The sea was cold day and night: but it was colder at night. It was cold and dark under the seawall beside his father's house. But the kettle would be on the hob to make punch.

The prefect of the chapel prayed above his head and his memory knew the responses:

> O Lord, open our lips
> And our mouths shall announce Thy praise.
> Incline unto our aid, O God!
> O Lord, make haste to help us!

There was a cold night smell in the chapel. But it was a holy smell. It was not like the smell of the old peasants who knelt at the back of the chapel at Sunday mass. That was a smell of air and rain and turf and corduroy. But they were very holy peasants. They breathed behind him on his neck and sighed as they prayed. They lived in Clane, a fellow said: there were little cottages there and he had seen a woman standing at the halfdoor of a cottage with a child in her arms, as the cars had come past from Sallins. It would be lovely to sleep for one night in that cottage before the fire of smoking turf, in the dark lit by the fire, in the warm dark, breathing the smell of the peasants, air and rain and turf and corduroy. But, O, the road there between the trees was dark! You would be lost in the dark. It made him afraid to think of how it was.

He heard the voice of the prefect of the chapel saying the last prayer. He prayed it too against the dark outside under the trees.

> Visit, we beseech Thee, O Lord, this habitation and drive away from it all the snares of the enemy. May Thy holy angels dwell herein to preserve us in peace and may Thy blessing be always upon us through Christ our Lord. Amen.

His fingers trembled as he undressed himself in the dormitory. He told his fingers to hurry up. He had to undress and then kneel and say his own prayers and be in bed before the gas was lowered so that he might not go to hell when he died. He rolled his stockings off and put on his nightshirt quickly and knelt trembling at his bedside and repeated his prayers quickly, fearing that the gas would go down. He felt his shoulders shaking as he murmured:

> God bless my father and my mother and spare them to me!
> God bless my little brothers and sisters and spare them to me!
> God bless Dante and Uncle Charles and spare them to me!

He blessed himself and climbed quickly into bed and, tucking the end of the nightshirt under his feet, curled himself together under the cold white sheets, shaking and trembling. But he would not go to hell when he died; and the shaking would stop. A voice bade the boys in the dormitory goodnight. He peered out for an instant over the coverlet and saw the yellow curtains round and before his bed that shut him off on all sides. The light was lowered quietly.

The prefect's shoes went away. Where? Down the staircase and along the corridors or to his room at the end? He saw the dark. Was it true about the black dog that walked there at night with eyes as big as carriagelamps? They said it was the ghost of a murderer. A long shiver of fear flowed over his body. He saw the dark entrance hall of the castle. Old servants in old dress were in the ironingroom above the staircase. It was long ago. The old servants were quiet. There was a fire there but the hall was still dark. A figure came up the staircase from the hall. He wore the white cloak of a marshal; his face was pale and strange; he held his hand pressed to his side. He looked out of strange eyes at the old servants. They looked at him and saw their master's face and cloak and knew that he had received his death wound. But only the dark was where they looked: only dark silent air. Their master had received his death wound on the battlefield of Prague far away over the sea. He was standing on the field; his hand was pressed to his side; his face was pale and strange and he wore the white cloak of a marshal.

O how cold and strange it was to think of that! All the dark was cold and strange. There were pale strange faces there, great eyes like carriagelamps. They were the ghosts of murderers, the figures of marshals who had received their deathwound on battlefields far away over the sea. What did they wish to say that their faces were so strange?

Visit, we beseech Thee, O Lord, this habitation and drive away from it all . . .

Going home for the holidays! That would be lovely: the fellows had told him. Getting up on the cars in the early wintry morning outside the door of the castle. The cars were rolling on the gravel. Cheers for the rector!

Hurray! Hurray! Hurray!

The cars drove past the chapel and all caps were raised. They drove merrily along the country roads. The drivers pointed with their whips to Bodenstown. The fellows cheered. They passed the farmhouse of the Jolly Farmer. Cheer after cheer after cheer. Through Clane they drove, cheering and cheered. The peasant women stood at the halfdoors, the men stood here and there. The lovely smell there was in the wintry air: the smell of Clane: rain and wintry air and turf smouldering and corduroy.

The train was full of fellows: a long long chocolate train with cream facings. The guards went to and fro opening, closing, locking, unlocking the doors. They were men in dark blue and silver; they had silvery whistles and their keys made a quick music: click, click: click, click.

And the train raced on over the flat lands and past the Hill of Allen. The telegraphpoles were passing, passing. The train went on and on. It knew. There were lanterns in the hall of his father's house and ropes of green branches. There were holly and ivy round the pierglass[12] and holly and ivy, green and red, twined round the chandeliers. There were red holly and green ivy round the old portraits on the walls. Holly and ivy for him and for Christmas.

Lovely . . .

All the people. Welcome home, Stephen! Noises of welcome. His mother kissed him. Was that right? His father was a marshal now: higher than a magistrate. Welcome home, Stephen!

Noises . . .

There was a noise of curtainrings running back along the rods, of water being splashed in the basins. There was a noise of rising and dressing and washing in the dormitory: a noise of clapping of hands as the prefect went up and down telling the fellows to look sharp. A pale sunlight showed the yellow curtains drawn back, the tossed beds. His bed was very hot and his face and body were very hot.

He got up and sat on the side of his bed. He was weak. He tried to pull on his stocking. It had a horrid rough feel. The sunlight was queer and cold.

Fleming said:

—Are you not well?

He did not know; and Fleming said:

—Get back into bed. I'll tell McGlade you're not well.

—He's sick.

—Who is?

—Tell McGlade.

—Get back into bed.

—Is he sick?

A fellow held his arms while he loosened the stocking clinging to his foot and climbed back into the hot bed.

He crouched down between the sheets, glad of their tepid glow. He heard the fellows talk among themselves about him as they dressed for mass. It was a mean thing to do, to shoulder him into the square ditch, they were saying.

12. a tall mirror.

Then their voices ceased; they had gone. A voice at his bed said:

—Dedalus, don't spy on us, sure you won't?

Wells's face was there. He looked at it and saw that Wells was afraid.

—I didn't mean to. Sure you won't?

His father had told him, whatever he did, never to peach on a fellow. He shook his head and answered no and felt glad.

Wells said:

—I didn't mean to, honour bright. It was only for cod. I'm sorry.

The face and the voice went away. Sorry because he was afraid. Afraid that it was some disease. Canker was a disease of plants and cancer one of animals: or another different. That was a long time ago then out on the playgrounds in the evening light, creeping from point to point on the fringe of his line, a heavy bird flying low through the grey light. Leicester Abbey lit up. Wolsey died there. The abbots buried him themselves.

It was not Wells's face, it was the prefect's. He was not foxing.[13] No, no: he was sick really. He was not foxing. And he felt the prefect's hand on his forehead; and he felt his forehead warm and damp against the prefect's cold damp hand. That was the way a rat felt, slimy and damp and cold. Every rat had two eyes to look out of. Sleek slimy coats, little little feet tucked up to jump, black slimy eyes to look out of. They could understand how to jump. But the minds of rats could not understand trigonometry. When they were dead they lay on their sides. Their coats dried then. They were only dead things.

The prefect was there again and it was his voice that was saying that he was to get up, that Father Minister had said he was to get up and dress and go to the infirmary. And while he was dressing himself as quickly as he could the prefect said:

—We must pack off to Brother Michael because we have the collywobbles!

He was very decent to say that. That was all to make him laugh. But he could not laugh because his cheeks and lips were all shivery. and then the prefect had to laugh by himself.

The prefect cried:

—Quick march! Hayfoot! Strawfoot!

They went together down the staircase and along the corridor and past the bath. As he passed the door he remembered with a vague fear the warm turf-coloured bogwater, the warm moist air, the noise of plunges, the smell of the towels, like medicine.

Brother Michael was standing at the door of the infirmary and from the door of the dark cabinet on his right came a smell like medicine. That came from the bottles on the shelves. The prefect

13. pretending.

spoke to Brother Michael and Brother Michael answered and called the prefect sir. He had reddish hair mixed with grey and a queer look. It was queer that he would always be a brother. It was queer too that you could not call him sir because he was a brother and had a different kind of look. Was he not holy enough or why could he not catch up on the others?

There were two beds in the room and in one bed there was a fellow: and when they went in he called out:

—Hello! It's young Dedalus! What's up?

—The sky is up, Brother Michael said.

He was a fellow out of the third of grammar and, while Stephen was undressing, he asked Brother Michael to bring him a round of buttered toast.

—Ah, do! he said.

—Butter you up! said Brother Michael. You'll get your walking papers in the morning when the doctor comes.

—Will I? the fellow said. I'm not well yet.

Brother Michael repeated:

—You'll get your walking papers. I tell you.

He bent down to rake the fire. He had a long back like the long back of a tramhorse. He shook the poker gravely and nodded his head at the fellow out of third of grammar.

Then Brother Michael went away and after a while the fellow out of third of grammar turned in towards the wall and fell asleep.

That was the infirmary. He was sick then. Had they written home to tell his mother and father? But it would be quicker for one of the priests to go himself to tell them. Or he would write a letter for the priest to bring.

Dear Mother,

I am sick. I want to go home. Please come and take me home. I am in the infirmary.

Your fond son,
Stephen.

How far away they were! There was cold sunlight outside the window. He wondered if he would die. You could die just the same on a sunny day. He might die before his mother came. Then he would have a dead mass in the chapel like the way the fellows had told him it was when Little had died. All the fellows would be at the mass, dressed in black, all with sad faces. Wells too would be there but no fellow would look at him. The rector would be there in a cope[14] of black and gold and there would be tall yellow candles on the altar and round the catafalque. And they would carry the coffin out of the chapel slowly and he would be buried in the little

14. a long mantle worn over the surplice in processions and the like.

graveyard of the community off the main avenue of limes.[15] And Wells would be sorry then for what he had done. And the bell would toll slowly.

He could hear the tolling. He said over to himself the song that Brigid had taught him.

> Dingdong! The castle bell!
> Farewell, my mother!
> Bury me in the old churchyard
> Beside my eldest brother.
> My coffin shall be black,
> Six angels at my back,
> Two to sing and two to pray
> And two to carry my soul away.

How beautiful and sad that was! How beautiful the words were where they said *Bury me in the old churchyard!* A tremor passed over his body. How sad and how beautiful! He wanted to cry quietly but not for himself: for the words, so beautiful and sad, like music. The bell! The bell! Farewell! O farewell!

The cold sunlight was weaker and Brother Michael was standing at his bedside with a bowl of beeftea. He was glad for his mouth was hot and dry. He could hear them playing in the playgrounds. And the day was going on in the college just as if he were there.

Then Brother Michael was going away and the fellow out of third of grammar told him to be sure and come back and tell him all the news in the paper. He told Stephen that his name was Athy and that his father kept a lot of racehorses that were spiffing[16] jumpers and that his father would give a good tip to Brother Michael any time he wanted it because Brother Michael was very decent and always told him the news out of the paper they got every day up in the castle. There was every kind of news in the paper: accidents, shipwrecks, sports and politics.

—Now it is all about politics in the papers, he said. Do your people talk about that too?

—Yes, Stephen said.

—Mine too, he said.

Then he thought for a moment and said:

—You have a queer name, Dedalus, and I have a queer name too, Athy. My name is the name of a town. Your name is like Latin.

Then he asked:

—Are you good at riddles?

Stephen answered:

—Not very good.

Then he said:

---

15. linden trees.   16. top-notch, excellent.

—Can you answer me this one? Why is the county of Kildare like the leg of a fellow's breeches?

Stephen thought what could be the answer and then said:

—I give it up.

—Because there is a thigh in it, he said. Do you see the joke? Athy[17] is the town in the county Kildare, and a thigh is the other thigh.

—O, I see, Stephen said.

—That's an old riddle, he said.

After a moment he said:

—I say!

—What? asked Stephen.

—You know, he said, you can ask that riddle another way.

—Can you? said Stephen.

—The same riddle, he said. Do you know the other way to ask it?

—No, said Stephen.

—Can you not think of the other way? he said.

He looked at Stephen over the bedclothes as he spoke. Then he lay back on the pillow and said:

—There is another way but I won't tell you what it is.

Why did he not tell it? His father, who kept the racehorses, must be a magistrate too like Saurin's father and Nasty Roche's father. He thought of his own father, of how he sang songs while his mother played and of how he always gave him a shilling when he asked for sixpence and he felt sorry for him that he was not a magistrate like the other boys' fathers. Then why was he sent to that place with them? But his father had told him that he would be no stranger there because his granduncle had presented an address to the Liberator[18] there fifty years before. You could know the people of that time by their old dress. It seemed to him a solemn time: and he wondered if that was the time when the fellows in Clongowes wore blue coats with brass buttons and yellow waistcoats and caps of rabbitskin and drank beer like grownup people and kept greyhounds of their own to course the hares with.

He looked at the window and saw that the daylight had grown weaker. There would be cloudy grey light over the playgrounds. There was no noise on the playgrounds. The class must be doing the themes or perhaps Father Arnall was reading out of the book.

It was queer that they had not given him any medicine. Perhaps Brother Michael would bring it back when he came. They said you got stinking stuff to drink when you were in the infirmary. But he felt better now than before. It would be nice getting better slowly. You could get a book then. There was a book in the library about

<hr>

17. pronounced "a thigh."   18. Daniel O'Connell (1775–1847), Irish political leader.

Holland. There were lovely foreign names in it and pictures of strange-looking cities and ships. It made you feel so happy.

How pale the light was at the window! But that was nice. The fire rose and fell on the wall. It was like waves. Someone had put coal on and he heard voices. They were talking. It was the noise of the waves. Or the waves were talking among themselves as they rose and fell.

He saw the sea of waves, long dark waves rising and falling, dark under the moonless night. A tiny light twinkled at the pierhead where the ship[19] was entering: and he saw a multitude of people gathered by the waters' edge to see the ship that was entering their harbour. A tall man stood on the deck, looking out towards the flat dark land: and by the light at the pierhead he saw his face, the sorrowful face of Brother Michael.

He saw him lift his hand towards the people and heard him say in a loud voice of sorrow over the waters:

—He is dead. We saw him lying upon the catafalque.

A wail of sorrow went up from the people.

—Parnell! Parnell! He is dead!

They fell upon their knees, moaning in sorrow.

And he saw Dante in a maroon velvet dress and with a green velvet mantle hanging from her shoulders walking proudly and silently past the people who knelt by the waters' edge.

A great fire, banked high and red, flamed in the grate and under the ivytwined branches of the chandelier the Christmas table was spread. They had come home a little late and still dinner was not ready: but it would be ready in a jiffy, his mother had said. They were waiting for the door to open and for the servants to come in, holding the big dishes covered with their heavy metal covers.

All were waiting: Uncle Charles, who sat far away in the shadow of the window, Dante and Mr Casey, who sat in the easychairs at either side of the hearth, Stephen, seated on a chair between them, his feet resting on the toasted boss.[20] Mr Dedalus looked at himself in the pierglass above the mantelpiece, waxed out his moustache ends and then, parting his coat tails, stood with his back to the glowing fire: and still from time to time he withdrew a hand from his coat tail to wax out one of his moustache ends. Mr Casey leaned his head to one side and, smiling, tapped the gland of his neck with his fingers. And Stephen smiled too for he knew now that it was not true that Mr Casey had a purse of silver in his throat. He smiled to think how the silvery noise which Mr Casey used to make had deceived him. And when he had tried to open Mr Casey's hand

19. Stephen in his semidelirium evokes what he has heard of the return of Parnell's body to Ireland on Sun- day, October 11, 1891. There were great popular demonstrations.
20. hassock.

to see if the purse of silver was hidden there he had seen that the fingers could not be straightened out: and Mr Casey had told him that he had got those three cramped fingers[21] making a birthday present for Queen Victoria.

Mr Casey tapped the gland of his neck and smiled at Stephen with sleepy eyes: and Mr Dedalus said to him:

—Yes. Well now, that's all right. O, we had a good walk, hadn't we, John? Yes . . . I wonder if there's any likelihood of dinner this evening. Yes. . . . O, well now, we got a good breath of ozone round the Head[22] today. Ay, bedad.

He turned to Dante and said:

—You didn't stir out at all, Mrs Riordan?

Dante frowned and said shortly:

—No.

Mr Dedalus dropped his coat tails and went over to the side-board. He brought forth a great stone jar of whisky from the locker and filled the decanter slowly, bending now and then to see how much he had poured in. Then replacing the jar in the locker he poured a little of the whisky into two glasses, added a little water and came back with them to the fireplace.

—A thimbleful, John, he said, just to whet your appetite.

Mr Casey took the glass, drank, and placed it near him on the mantelpiece. Then he said:

—Well, I can't help thinking of our friend Christopher manufacturing . . .

He broke into a fit of laughter and coughing and added:

—. . . manufacturing that champagne for those fellows.

Mr Dedalus laughed loudly.

—Is it Christy? he said. There's more cunning in one of those warts on his bald head than in a pack of jack foxes.

He inclined his head, closed his eyes, and, licking his lips profusely, began to speak with the voice of the hotel keeper.

—And he has such a soft mouth when he's speaking to you, don't you know. He's very moist and watery about the dewlaps, God bless him.

Mr Casey was still struggling through his fit of coughing and laughter. Stephen, seeing and hearing the hotel keeper through his father's face and voice, laughed.

Mr Dedalus put up his eyeglass and, staring down at him, said quietly and kindly:

—What are you laughing at, you little puppy, you?

The servants entered and placed the dishes on the table. Mrs Dedalus followed and the places were arranged.

21. perhaps due to some patriotic misadventure with explosives. Mr. Casey is an ardent nationalist.

22. Howth Head, the promontory forming the northern side of Dublin Bay.

—Sit over, she said.

Mr Dedalus went to the end of the table and said:

—Now, Mrs Riordan, sit over. John, sit you down, my hearty.

He looked round to where Uncle Charles sat and said:

—Now then, sir, there's a bird here waiting for you.

When all had taken their seats he laid his hand on the cover and then said quickly, withdrawing it:

—Now, Stephen.

Stephen stood up in his place to say the grace before meals:

Bless us, O Lord, and these Thy gifts which through Thy bounty we are about to receive through Christ our Lord. Amen.

All blessed themselves and Mr Dedalus with a sigh of pleasure lifted from the dish the heavy cover pearled around the edge with glistening drops.

Stephen looked at the plump turkey which had lain, trussed and skewered, on the kitchen table. He knew that his father had paid a guinea for it in Dunn's of D'Olier Street and that the man had prodded it often at the breastbone to show how good it was: and he remembered the man's voice when he had said:

—Take that one, sir. That's the real Ally Daly.

Why did Mr Barrett in Clongowes call his pandybat[23] a turkey? But Clongowes was far away: and the warm heavy smell of turkey and ham and celery rose from the plates and dishes and the great fire was banked high and red in the grate and the green ivy and red holly made you feel so happy and when dinner was ended the big plum pudding would be carried in, studded with peeled almonds and sprigs of holly, with bluish fire running around it and a little green flag flying from the top.

It was his first Christmas dinner and he thought of his little brothers and sisters who were waiting in the nursery, as he had often waited, till the pudding came. The deep low collar and the Eton jacket made him feel queer and oldish: and that morning when his mother had brought him down to the parlour, dressed for mass, his father had cried. That was because he was thinking of his own father. And Uncle Charles had said so too.

Mr Dedalus covered the dish and began to eat hungrily. Then he said:

—Poor old Christy, he's nearly lopsided now with roguery.

—Simon, said Mrs Dedalus, you haven't given Mrs Riordan any sauce.

Mr Dedalus seized the sauceboat.

23. for inflicting corporal punishment.

A *Portrait of the Artist* · 1361

—Haven't I? he cried. Mrs Riordan, pity the poor blind.

Dante covered her plate with her hands and said:

—No, thanks.

Mr Dedalus turned to Uncle Charles.

—How are you off, sir?

—Right as the mail, Simon.

—You, John?

—I'm all right. Go on yourself.

—Mary? Here, Stephen, here's something to make your hair curl.

He poured sauce freely over Stephen's plate and set the boat again on the table. Then he asked Uncle Charles was it tender. Uncle Charles could not speak because his mouth was full but he nodded that it was.

—That was a good answer our friend made to the canon. What? said Mr Dedalus.

—I didn't think he had that much in him, said Mr Casey.

—*I'll pay your dues, father, when you cease turning the house of God into a pollingbooth.*[24]

—A nice answer, said Dante, for any man calling himself a catholic to give to his priest.

—They have only themselves to blame, said Mr Dedalus suavely. If they took a fool's advice they would confine their attention to religion.

—It is religion, Dante said. They are doing their duty in warning the people.

—We go to the house of God, Mr Casey said, in all humility to pray to our Maker and not to hear election addresses.

—It is religion, Dante said again. They are right. They must direct their flocks.

—And preach politics from the altar, is it? asked Mr Dedalus.

—Certainly, said Dante. It is a question of public morality. A priest would not be a priest if he did not tell his flock what is right and what is wrong.

Mrs Dedalus laid down her knife and fork, saying:

—For pity sake and for pity sake let us have no political discussion on this day of all days in the year.

—Quite right, ma'am, said Uncle Charles. Now Simon, that's quite enough now. Not another word now.

—Yes, yes, said Mr Dedalus quickly.

He uncovered the dish boldly and said:

—Now then, who's for more turkey?

Nobody answered. Dante said:

24. There had been clerical opposition to the continued leadership of Parnell.

—Nice language for any catholic to use!

—Mrs Riordan, I appeal to you, said Mrs Dedalus, to let the matter drop now.

Dante turned on her and said:

—And am I to sit here and listen to the pastors of my church being flouted?

—Nobody is saying a word against them, said Mr Dedalus, so long as they don't meddle in politics.

—The bishops and priests of Ireland have spoken, said Dante, and they must be obeyed.

—Let them leave politics alone, said Mr Casey, or the people may leave their church alone.

—You hear? said Dante turning to Mrs Dedalus.

—Mr Casey! Simon! said Mrs Dedalus, let it end now.

—Too bad! Too bad! said Uncle Charles.

What? cried Mr Dedalus. Were we to desert him at the bidding of the English people?[25]

—He was no longer worthy to lead, said Dante. He was a public sinner.

—We are all sinners and black sinners, said Mr Casey coldly.

—*Woe be to the man by whom the scandal cometh!* said Mrs. Riordan. *It would be better for him that a millstone were tied about his neck and that he were cast into the depths of the sea rather than that he should scandalise one of these, my least little ones.*[26] That is the language of the Holy Ghost.

—And very bad language if you ask me, said Mr Dedalus coolly.

—Simon! Simon! said Uncle Charles. The boy.

—Yes, yes, said Mr Dedalus. I meant about the . . . I was thinking about the bad language of that railway porter. Well now, that's all right. Here, Stephen, show me your plate, old chap. Eat away now. Here.

He heaped up the food on Stephen's plate and served Uncle Charles and Mr Casey to large pieces of turkey and splashes of sauce. Mrs Dedalus was eating little and Dante sat with her hands in her lap. She was red in the face. Mr Dedalus rooted with the carvers at the end of the dish and said:

—There's a tasty bit here we call the pope's nose. If any lady or gentleman . . .

He held a piece of fowl up on the prong of the carvingfork. Nobody spoke. He put it on his own plate, saying:

—Well, you can't say but you were asked. I think I had better eat it myself because I'm not well in my health lately.

25. English Nonconformist disapproval of the adulterer Parnell had forced Prime Minister Gladstone to refuse all dealings with him.
26. See Luke 17:1–2.

He winked at Stephen and, replacing the dishcover, began to eat again.

There was a silence while he ate. Then he said:

—Well now, the day kept up fine after all. There were plenty of strangers down too.

Nobody spoke. He said again:

—I think there were more strangers down than last Christmas.

He looked round at the others whose faces were bent towards their plates and, receiving no reply, waited for a moment and said bitterly:

—Well, my Christmas dinner has been spoiled anyhow.

—There could be neither luck nor grace, Dante said, in a house where there is no respect for the pastors of the church.

Mr Dedalus threw his knife and fork noisily on his plate.

—Respect! he said. Is it for Billy with the lip[27] or for the tub of guts up in Armagh?[28] Respect!

—Princes of the church, said Mr Casey with slow scorn.

—Lord Leitrim's[29] coachman, yes, said Mr Dedalus.

—They are the Lord's anointed, Dante said. They are an honour to their country.

—Tub of guts, said Mr Dedalus coarsely. He has a handsome face, mind you, in repose. You should see that fellow lapping up his bacon and cabbage of a cold winter's day. O Johnny!

He twisted his features into a grimace of heavy bestiality and made a lapping noise with his lips.

—Really, Simon, you should not speak that way before Stephen. It's not right.

—O, he'll remember all this when he grows up, said Dante hotly —the language he heard against God and religion and priests in his own home.

—Let him remember too, cried Mr Casey to her from across the table, the language with which the priests and the priests' pawns broke Parnell's heart and hounded him into his grave. Let him remember that too when he grows up.

—Sons of bitches! cried Mr Dedalus. When he was down they turned on him to betray him and rend him like rats in a sewer. Lowlived dogs! And they look it! By Christ, they look it!

—They behaved rightly, cried Dante. They obeyed their bishops and their priests. Honour to them!

—Well, it is perfectly dreadful to say that not even for one day

---

27. presumably a reference to William J. Walsh (1841–1921), archbishop of Dublin from 1885.

28. Archbishop of Armagh at this time was Michael Logue (1840–1924), later cardinal.

29. Lord Leitrim was an Irish landlord.

in the year, said Mrs Dedalus, can we be free from these dreadful disputes!

Uncle Charles raised his hands mildly and said:

—Come now, come now, come now! Can we not have our opinions whatever they are without this bad temper and this bad language? It is too bad surely.

Mrs Dedalus spoke to Dante in a low voice but Dante said loudly:

—I will not say nothing. I will defend my church and my religion when it is insulted and spit on by renegade catholics.

Mr Casey pushed his plate rudely into the middle of the table and, resting his elbows before him, said in a hoarse voice to his host:

—Tell me, did I tell you that story about a very famous spit?

—You did not, John, said Mr Dedalus.

Why then, said Mr Casey, it is a most instructive story. It happened not long ago in the county Wicklow where we are now.

He broke off and, turning towards Dante, said with quiet indignation:

—And I may tell you, ma'am, that I, if you mean me, am no renegade catholic. I am a catholic as my father was and his father before him and his father before him again when we gave up our lives rather than sell our faith.

—The more shame to you now, Dante said, to speak as you do.

—The story, John, said Mr Dedalus smiling. Let us have the story anyhow.

—Catholic indeed! repeated Dante ironically. The blackest protestant in the land would not speak the language I have heard this evening.

Mr Dedalus began to sway his head to and fro, crooning like a country singer.

—I am no protestant, I tell you again, said Mr Casey flushing.

Mr Dedalus, still crooning and swaying his head, began to sing in a grunting nasal tone:

> O, come all you Roman catholics
> That never went to mass.

He took up his knife and fork again in good humour and set to eating, saying to Mr Casey:

—Let us have the story, John. It will help us to digest.

Stephen looked with affection at Mr Casey's face which stared across the table over his joined hands. He liked to sit near him at the fire, looking up at his dark fierce face. But his dark eyes were never fierce and his slow voice was good to listen to. But why was he then against the priests? Because Dante must be right then. But he had heard his father say that she was a spoiled nun and that she had come out of the convent in the Alleghanies when her brother had got the money from the savages for the trinkets and the chainies. Perhaps that made her severe against Parnell. And she did not like him to play with Eileen because Eileen was a protestant and when she was young she knew children that used to play with protestants and the protestants used to make fun of the litany of the Blessed Virgin. *Tower of Ivory,* they used to say, *House of Gold!* How could a woman be a tower of ivory or a house of gold? Who was right then? And he remembered the evening in the infirmary in Clongowes, the dark waters, the light at the pierhead and the moan of sorrow from the people when they had heard.

Eileen had long white hands. One evening when playing tig[30] she had put her hands over his eyes: long and white and thin and cold and soft. That was ivory: a cold white thing. That was the meaning of *Tower of Ivory.*

—The story is very short and sweet, Mr Casey said. It was one day down in Arklow, a cold bitter day, not long before the chief died. May God have mercy on him!

He closed his eyes wearily and paused. Mr Dedalus took a bone from his plate and tore some meat from it with his teeth, saying:

—Before he was killed, you mean.

Mr Casey opened his eyes, sighed and went on:

—He was down in Arklow one day. We were down there at a meeting and after the meeting was over we had to make our way to the railway station through the crowd. Such booing and baaing, man, you never heard. They called us all the names in the world. Well there was one old lady, and a drunken old harridan she was surely, that paid all her attention to me. She kept dancing along beside me in the mud bawling and screaming into my face: *Priesthunter! The Paris Funds![31] Mr Fox![32] Kitty O'Shea!*

—And what did you do, John? asked Mr Dedalus.

—I let her bawl away, said Mr Casey. It was a cold day and to keep up my heart I had (saving your presence, ma'am) a quid of Tullamore[33] in my mouth and sure I couldn't say a word in any case because my mouth was full of tobacco juice.

—Well, John?

—Well. I let her bawl away, to her heart's content, *Kitty O'Shea* and the rest of it till at last she called that lady a name that I won't sully this Christmas board nor your ears, ma'am, nor my own lips by repeating.

He paused. Mr Dedalus, lifting his head from the bone, asked:

30. the game of tag.
31. This money, contributed by Irish-Americans, had been held in Paris at Parnell's disposal. After his death, the use he had made of it became a bone of contention between Parnellite and anti-Parnellite factions.
32. Parnell had used this name when registering at boardinghouses with Mrs. O'Shea.
33. a chewing tobacco.

—And what did you do, John?

—Do! said Mr Casey. She stuck her ugly old face up at me when she said it and I had my mouth full of tobacco juice. I bent down to her and *Phth!* says I to her like that.

He turned aside and made the act of spitting.

—Phth! says I to her like that, right into her eye.

He clapped a hand to his eye and gave a hoarse scream of pain.

—*O Jesus, Mary and Joseph!* says she. *I'm blinded! I'm blinded and drownded!*

He stopped in a fit of coughing and laughter, repeating:

—*I'm blinded entirely.*

Mr Dedalus laughed loudly and lay back in his chair while Uncle Charles swayed his head to and fro.

Dante looked terribly angry and repeated while they laughed:

—Very nice! Ha! Very nice!

It was not nice about the spit in the woman's eye.

But what was the name the woman had called Kitty O'Shea that Mr Casey would not repeat? He thought of Mr Casey walking through the crowds of people and making speeches from a wagonette. That was what he had been in prison for and he remembered that one night Sergeant O'Neill had come to the house and had stood in the hall, talking in a low voice with his father and chewing nervously at the chinstrap of his cap. And that night Mr Casey had not gone to Dublin by train but a car had come to the door and he had heard his father say something about the Cabinteely road.

He was for Ireland and Parnell and so was his father: and so was Dante too for one night at the band on the esplanade she had hit a gentleman on the head with her umbrella because he had taken off his hat when the band played *God save the Queen* at the end.

Mr Dedalus gave a snort of contempt.

—Ah, John, he said. It is true for them. We are an unfortunate priestridden race and always were and always will be till the end of the chapter.

Uncle Charles shook his head, saying:

—A bad business! A bad business!

Mr Dedalus repeated:

—A priestridden Godforsaken race!

He pointed to the portrait of his gandfather on the wall to his right.

—Do you see that old chap up there, John? he said. He was a good Irishman when there was no money in the job. He was condemned to death as a whiteboy.[34] But he had a saying about our clerical friends, that he would never let one of them put his two feet under his mahogany.[35]

34. one of a group of peasants who, from 1761 onward, resisted paying tithes to the Anglican Church. On their nocturnal excursions they hid their faces under white shirts.
35. dining-room table.

Dante broke in angrily:

—If we are a priestridden race we ought to be proud of it! They are the apple of God's eye. *Touch them not,* says Christ, *for they are the apple of My eye.*

—And can we not love our country then? asked Mr Casey. Are we not to follow the man that was born to lead us?

—A traitor to his country! replied Dante. A traitor, an adulterer! The priests were right to abandon him. The priests were always the true friends of Ireland.

—Were they, faith? said Mr Casey.

He threw his fist on the table and, frowning angrily, protruded one finger after another.

—Didn't the bishops of Ireland betray us in the time of the union[36] when Bishop Lanigan presented an address of loyalty to the Marquess Cornwallis? Didn't the bishops and priests sell the aspirations of their country in 1829 in return for catholic emancipation?[37] Didn't they denounce the fenian movement[38] from the pulpit and in the confession box? And didn't they dishonour the ashes of Terence Bellew MacManus?[39]

His face was glowing with anger and Stephen felt the glow rise to his own cheek as the spoken words thrilled him. Mr Dedalus uttered a guffaw of coarse scorn.

—O, by God, he cried, I forgot little old Paul Cullen![40] Another apple of God's eye!

Dante bent across the table and cried to Mr Casey:

—Right! Right! They were always right! God and morality and religion come first.

Mrs Dedalus, seeing her excitement, said to her:

—Mrs Riordan, don't excite yourself answering them.

God and religion before everything! Dante cried. God and religion before the world!

Mr Casey raised his clenched fist and brought it down on the table with a crash.

—Very well, then, he shouted hoarsely, if it comes to that, no God for Ireland!

—John! John! cried Mr Dedalus, seizing his guest by the coat sleeve.

36. The Irish parliament, representing the Anglo-Irish gentry, was abolished in 1802, and thereafter members for Ireland sat in the British House of Commons.

37. the legislation which freed Catholics from civil disabilities.

38. a secret society whose aim was Irish independence. It was formed in New York about 1854.

39. Irish rebel (1823–1860). He escaped from penal servitude, to which the British had condemned him, and died in the United States. His body was returned to Ireland.

40. Irish prelate (1803–1878). His expression of disapproval of Irish nationalism, when he was papal legate, disappointed the nationalists. He was later archbishop of Dublin, and cardinal.

Dante started across the table, her cheeks shaking. Mr Casey struggled up from his chair and bent across the table towards her, scraping the air from before his eyes with one hand as though he were tearing aside a cobweb.

—No God for Ireland! he cried. We have had too much God in Ireland. Away with God!

—Blasphemer! Devil! screamed Dante, starting to her feet and almost spitting in his face.

Uncle Charles and Mr Dedalus pulled Mr Casey back into his chair again, talking to him from both sides reasonably. He stared before him out of his dark flaming eyes, repeating:

—Away with God, I say!

Dante shoved her chair violently aside and left the table, upsetting her napkinring which rolled slowly along the carpet and came to rest against the foot of an easychair. Mrs Dedalus rose quickly and followed her towards the door. At the door Dante turned round violently and shouted down the room, her cheeks flushed and quivering with rage:

—Devil out of hell! We won! We crushed him to death! Fiend!

The door slammed behind her.

Mr Casey, freeing his arms from his holders, suddenly bowed his head on his hands with a sob of pain.

—Poor Parnell! he cried loudly. My dead king!

He sobbed loudly and bitterly.

Stephen, raising his terrorstricken face, saw that his father's eyes were full of tears.

ANDRÉ GIDE
(1869–1951)
Theseus (Thésée)*

I

I wanted to tell the story of my life as a lesson for my son Hippolytus; but he is no more, and I am telling it all the same. For his sake I should not have dared to include, as I shall now do, certain passages of love; he was extraordinarily prudish, and in his company I never dared to speak of my attachments. Besides, these only mattered to me during the first part of my life; but at least they taught me to know myself, as did also the various monsters whom I subdued. For "the first thing is to know exactly who one is," I used

* 1946. Reprinted from *Two Legends: Œdipus and Theseus* by André Gide, translated by John Russell, by permission of Alfred A. Knopf, Inc.

to say to Hippolytus; "later comes the time to assess and adopt one's inheritance. Whether you wish it or not, you are, as I was myself, a king's son. Nothing to be done about it; it's a fact; it pins you down." But Hippolytus never took much notice; even less than I had taken at his age; and like myself at that time, he got on very nicely without it. Oh, early years, all innocently passed! Oh, careless growth of body and mind! I was wind; I was wave. I grew with the plant; I flew with the bird. My self knew no boundaries; every contact with an outer world did not so much teach me my own limits as awaken within me some new power of enjoyment. Fruit I caressed, and the bark of young trees, and smooth stones on the shore, and the coats of horses and dogs, before ever my hands were laid on a woman. Toward all the charming things that Pan, Zeus, or Thetis could offer, I rose.

One day my father said to me that things couldn't go on as they were. "Why not?" Because, good heavens, I was his son and must show myself worthy of the throne to which I should succeed. . . . Just when I was feeling so happy, sprawled naked among cool grasses or on some scorching beach. Still, I can't say that he was wrong. Certainly he was right in teaching me to rebel against myself. To this I owe all that I have achieved since that day; no longer to live at random—agreeable as such license might have been. He taught me that nothing great, nothing of value, and nothing that will last can be got without effort.

My first effort was made at his invitation. It was to overturn boulders in the hope of finding the weapons which Poseidon (so he told me) had hidden beneath one of them. He laughed to see how quickly my strength grew through this training. With the toughening of my body there came also a toughening of the will. After I had dislodged the heaviest rocks of the neighborhood and was about to continue my unfruitful search by attacking the flagstones of the palace gateway, my father stopped me. "Weapons," said he, "count for less than the arm that wields them, and the arm in its turn for less than the thinking will that directs it. Here are the weapons. Before giving them to you, I was waiting to see you deserve them. I can sense in you now the ambition to use them, and that longing for fame which will allow you to take up arms only in defense of noble causes and for the weal of all mankind. Your childhood is over. Be a man. Show your fellow men what one of their kind can be and what he means to become. There are great things to be done. Claim yourself."

II

Ægeus, my father, was an excellent person; all that could be wished. In point of fact, I suspect that I was his son only in name. That's what I've been told, and that great Poseidon begat me. In which case it's from this god that I inherit my inconstancy of temper. Where women are concerned, I have never known how to settle down. Ægeus sometimes stood rather in my way; but I am grateful to him for his guardianship, and for having restored the cult of Aphrodite to honor in Attica. I am sorry for the fateful slip by which I brought about his death—when I forgot, I mean, to run up white sails in place of black on the ship that carried me home from Crete. It had been agreed that I should do this if I were to return in triumph from my rash venture. One can't think of everything. But to tell the truth, and if I cross-question myself (a thing I never much care to do), I can't swear that it was really forgetfulness. Ægeus was in my way, as I told you, and particularly when, through the potions of the witch Medea, who found him (as, indeed, he found himself) a rather elderly bedfellow, he formed the exasperating idea that a second meridian of enjoyment was his for the asking—thus blocking my career, whereas, after all, it's every man in his turn. Anyway, when he saw those black sails . . . I learned, on returning to Athens, that he had thrown himself into the sea.

No one can deny it. I think I have performed some notable services; I've purged the earth once and for all of a host of tyrants, bandits, and monsters; I've cleaned up certain dangerous byroads on which even the bravest could not venture without a shiver; and I've cleared up the skies in such a way that man, his head less bowed, may be less fearful of their surprises.

One must own that in those days the look of the country was hardly reassuring. Between the scattered townships there were huge stretches of uncultivated waste, crossed only by unreliable tracks. There were the dense forests, the mountainous ravines. At the most dangerous points robber gangs had taken up their positions; these pillaged, killed, or at best held for ransom the traveler, and there were no police to stop them. These incidents combined with the purposeful ferocity of wild beasts and the evil power of the deceitful elements until one could hardly tell, when some foolhardy person came to grief, whether the malignity of the gods had struck him down or merely that of his fellow men. Nor, in the case of such monsters as the Sphinx or the Gorgon who fell to Œdipus or to Bellerophon, could one be sure whether the human strain or the divine was preponderant. Whatever was inexplicable was put on to the gods. Terror and religion were so nearly one that heroism often seemed an impiety. The first and principal victories that man had to win were over the gods.

In a fight, whether with man or with god, it is only by seizing one's adversary's own weapon and turning it against him (as I did with the club of Periphetes, the dark giant of Epidaurus) that one can be sure of final victory.

And as for the thunderbolts of Zeus, I can tell you that the day will come when man will possess himself of them, as Prometheus possessed himself of fire. Yes, those are decisive victories. But with women, at once my strength and my weakness, I was always having to begin again. I escaped from one, only to fall into the lap of some other; nor did I ever conquer a woman who had not first conquered me. Pirithoüs was right when he told me (ah, how well we used to get on!) that the important thing was never to be unmanned by a woman, as was Hercules in the arms of Omphale. And since I have never been able or wished to live without women, he would say to me, as I darted off on each amorous chase: "Go ahead, but don't get stuck." There was one woman who, ostensibly to safeguard my life, would have bound me to herself by a cord—a thin one, it is true, but a fixed rein none the less. This same woman—but of that, more in due time.

Of them all, Antiope came nearest to catching me. She was queen of the Amazons, and like all her subjects had only one breast; but this in no way impaired her beauty. An accomplished runner and wrestler, she had muscles as firm and sturdy as those of our athletes. I took her on in single combat. In my arms she struggled like a leopard. Disarmed, she brought her teeth and nails into play; enraged by my laughter (for I, too, had no weapons) and because she could not stop herself from loving me. I have never possessed anyone more virginal. And little did it matter to me that later she could only suckle my Hippolytus, her son, with one breast. It was this chaste and savage being whom I wished to make my heir. I shall speak, during the course of my story, of what has been the greatest grief of my life. For it is not enough to exist, and then to have existed: one must make one's legacy and act in such a way that one is not extinguished with oneself, so my grandfather had often told me. Pittheus and Ægeus were much more intelligent than I; so is Pirithoüs. But people give me credit for good sense; the rest is added with the determination to do well that has never left me. Mine, too, is the kind of courage that incites me to desperate enterprises. On top of all this I was ambitious. The great deeds of my cousin Hercules, which they used to report to me, exasperated my young blood, and when it was time to leave Troezen, where I had lived till then, and rejoin my so-called father in Athens, I refused altogether to accept the advice, sound though it was, to go by sea because the route was safer. Well I knew it; but it was the very hazards of the overland route, with its immense detour, that tempted me; a chance to prove my worth. Thieves of every sort were beginning once again to infest the country, and did so with impunity now that Hercules was squandering his manhood at the feet of Omphale. I was sixteen. All the cards were in my hand. My turn had come. In great leaps my heart was bounding toward the extremity of my happiness. "What have I to do with safety," I cried, "and a route that's set in order!" I despised comfort and idleness and unlaureled ease. So it was on the road to Athens by way of the isthmus of the Peloponnesus that I first put myself to the test, and my heart and my arm together taught me their full strength, when I cut down some well-known and well-hated robbers: Sinis, Periphetes, Procrustes, Geryon (no, that was Hercules; I meant to say Cercyon). By the way, I made a slight mistake at that time, when Sciron was concerned, for he turned out afterwards to have been a very worthy man, good-natured and most helpful to passing travelers. But as I had just done away with him, it was soon agreed that he had been a rascal.

Also on the road to Athens, in a thicket of asparagus, there smiled upon me the first of my conquests in love. Perigone was tall and supple. I had just killed her father, and by way of amends I got her a very handsome son: Menalippes. I have lost track of both of them—breaking free, as usual, and anxious never to lose any time. I have never allowed the past to involve or detain me; rather have I been drawn forward by what was still to be achieved; and the most important things seemed to me always to lie ahead.

So much so that I won't waste more time with these preliminary trifles, which, after all, meant only too little to me. Here I was on the threshold of an admirable adventure. Hercules himself never had one like it. I must tell it at length.

III

It's very complicated, this story. I must say first that the island of Crete was a power in those days. Minos reigned there. He held Attica responsible for the death of his son Androgeus; and by way of reprisal he had exacted from us an annual tribute: seven young men and seven young girls had to be handed over to satisfy, it was said, the appetites of the Minotaur, the monstrous child that Pasiphaë, the wife of Minos, had brought forth after intercourse with a bull. These victims were chosen by lot.

But in the year in question, I had just returned to Greece. Though the lot would normally have spared me (princes readily escape these things), I insisted that I should figure in the list, notwithstanding the opposition of the king, my father. I care nothing for privilege, and claim that merit alone distinguishes me from the herd. My plan was, in point of fact, to vanquish the Minotaur and thus at a blow to free Greece from this abominable exaction. Also I was most anxious to visit Crete, whence beautiful, costly, and unusual objects were constantly arriving in Attica. Therefore I set sail for the island; among my thirteen companions was my friend Pirithoüs.

We landed, one morning in March, at Amnisos, a little township that served as harbor to its neighbor Knossos, the capital of the

island, where Minos resided and had had his palace built. We should
have arrived the previous evening, but a violent storm had delayed
us. As we stepped ashore we were surrounded by armed guards, who
took away my sword and that of Pirithoüs. When they had searched
us for other weapons, they led us off to appear before the king, who
had come from Knossos, with his court, to meet us. A large crowd
of the common people pressed round to have a look at us. All the
men were naked to the waist except Minos, who, seated beneath
a dais, wore a long robe made from a single piece of dark-red cloth;
this fell in majestic folds from his shoulders to his ankles. His chest,
broad as that of Zeus himself, bore three tiers of necklaces. Many
Cretans wear these, but of a trumpery sort. Minos had necklaces
of rare stones, and plaques of wrought gold in the shape of fleurs-de-lis.
The double-head ax hung above his throne, and with his right hand
he stretched before him a golden scepter, as tall as himself. In the
other hand was a three-leaved flower, like those on his necklaces, and
also in gold, but larger. Above his golden crown was a gigantic
panache,[1] in which were mingled the feathers of peacock, ostrich,
and halcyon. He looked us over for some time and then bade us
welcome to the island, with a smile that may well have been ironical,
since we had come there, after all, under sentence of death. By his
side were standing the queen and the two princesses, her daughters.
I saw at once that the elder daughter had taken a fancy to me. As our
guards were making ready to take us away, I saw her lean toward
her father and say to him in Greek (she whispered, but my ears are
sharp): "Not that one, I beg you," and she pointed toward me with
her finger. Minos smiled once again and gave orders that I should
not be taken away with my companions. I was no sooner alone
before him than he began to question me.

Although I had promised myself to act with all possible prudence
and to let slip no hint either of my noble birth or of my audacious
project, it suddenly occurred to me that it would be better to put
my cards on the table, now that I had attracted the attention of
the princess. Nothing would be more likely to heighten her feeling
for me, or to win me the favor of the king, than to hear me say
frankly that I was the grandson of Pittheus. I even hinted that the
current rumor in Attica was that the great Poseidon had begot me.
To this Minos replied gravely that he would presently clear up that
point by submitting me to trial by water. In return I replied complacently that I had no doubt I should survive triumphantly any test
that he cared to impose. The ladies of the court, if not Minos
himself, were favorably affected by my self-confidence.

"And now," said Minos, "you must go and have something to eat.
Your companions are already at table and will be waiting for you.

1. plume.

After such a disturbed night you must be quite peckish, as they say here. Have a good rest. I shall expect you to be present toward the end of the day at the ceremonial games in honor of your visit. Then, Prince Theseus, we shall take you with us to Knossos. You will sleep at the palace, and tomorrow evening you will dine with us —a simple, family meal, where you will feel quite at home, and these ladies will be delighted to hear you tell of your first exploits. And now they are going to prepare themselves for the festivities. We shall meet again at the games, where you will sit, with your companions, immediately beneath the royal box. This courtesy we owe to your princely rank; and as I do not wish to distinguish you openly from your companions they shall, by contagion, rank with you."

The games were held in a vast semicircular arena, opening on the sea. Huge crowds, both of men and of women, had come to see them, from Knossos, from Lyttos, and even from Gortyna (a matter of two hundred stadia distant, I was told), from other towns and their neighboring villages, and from the thickly populated open country. All my senses were taken by surprise, and I cannot describe how foreign the Cretans appeared to me to be. As there was not room for them all on the tiers of the amphitheater, they pushed and jostled their way up the staircases and along the aisles. The women, no less numerous than the men, were for the most part naked to the waist. A very few wore a light bodice, but even this was generously cut away, in a fashion that I could not help thinking rather immodest, and exposed both breasts to the air. Men and women alike were tightly, even absurdly laced around the hips with belts and corselets, which gave to each the figure of an hourglass. The men were nearly all brown-skinned, and at their fingers, wrists, and throats wore almost as many rings, bracelets, and necklaces as the women, who, for their part, were perfectly white. All the men were clean-shaven, except for the king, Rhadamanthus, his brother, and his friend Dædalus. The ladies of the court sat on a platform just above our own, which dominated the arena from a considerable height. They had indulged a prodigious extravagance of dress and ornament. Each wore a flounced skirt; billowing out oddly below the hips, this fell in embroidered furbelows to their feet, which were shod in little boots of white leather. The fatuosity of the queen, who sat in the center of the dais, made her most conspicuous of all. Her arms and the front of her person were bare. Upon her magnificent breasts, pearls, emeralds, and precious stones were embanked. Long black curls fell on either side of her face, and smaller ringlets streaked her forehead. She had the lips of a glutton, an upturned nose, and huge empty eyes, whose expression one might have called bovine. A sort of golden diadem served her as a crown. It sat, not directly on her hair, but on a ridiculous hat of some dark material, which came up through the diadem and tapered into a sharp point, like a horn, which jutted far out in front of her forehead. Her corsage uncovered her to the waist in front, but rose high at the back and ended in an enormous cutaway collar. Her skirt was spread wide around her, and one could admire, upon their creamy ground, three rows of embroidery, one above the other—purple irises at the top, saffrons in the center, and below them violets with their leaves. As I was sitting immediately below, I had only to turn round to have all this, as one might say, under my very nose. I marveled as much at the sense of color and the beauty of the design as at the delicate perfection of the work.

Ariadne, the elder daughter, sat at her mother's right hand and presided over the corrida. She was less sumptuously dressed than the queen, and she wore different colors. Her skirt, like that of her sister, had only two circles of embroidery: on the upper one, dogs and hinds; on the lower, dogs and partridges. Phædra, perceptibly a much younger girl, sat on Pasiphaë's left. Her dress had a frieze of children running after hoops, and another of younger children squatting on their behinds and playing marbles. She took a childish pleasure in the spectacle. As for me, I could hardly follow what was going on, it was all so disconcertingly new; but I could not help being amazed by the suppleness, speed, and agility of the acrobats who took their chance in the arena after the singers, the dancers, and then the wrestlers had had their turn. Myself about to encounter the Minotaur, I learned a good deal from watching the feints and passes that might help me to baffle and tire the bull.

IV

After Ariadne had rewarded the last champion with the last prize, Minos declared the games closed. Escorted by his courtiers, he bade me come to him separately.

"I am going to take you now, Prince Theseus," he said to me, "to a place by the sea where I shall put you to the test, and we shall see if you are the true son of the god Poseidon, as you claimed to be just now."

He took me to a small promontory with waves beating at its foot. "I shall now," said the king, "throw my crown into the sea, as a mark of my confidence that you will be able to retrieve it from the bottom."

The queen and the two princesses were there to see what would come of the test; and so, emboldened by their presence, I protested:

"Am I a dog, to fetch and carry for my master, even if it be a crown? Let me dive in without bait and I shall bring back to you something or other that will attest and prove my case."

In my audacity I went still farther. A stiff breeze had sprung up, and it happened that a long scarf was dislodged from Ariadne's shoulders. A gust blew it toward me. I caught it with a smile, as if the princess or one of the gods had offered it to me. Then, stripping off my close-fitting corselet, I wrapped the scarf round my loins in its place, twisted it up between my thighs, and made it fast. It looked as if I did this from modesty, lest I should expose my manhood before these ladies; but in fact it allowed me to hide the leather belt that I was still wearing, to which was attached a small purse. In this I had, not metal coins, but some valuable stones that I had brought with me from Greece, knowing that they would keep their full value, no matter where I went.

Then I took a deep breath and dived.

A practiced swimmer, I dived deep, and did not come up to the surface until I had removed from my purse an onyx and two chrysoprases. Once back on dry land I offered, with my most chivalrous bow, the onyx to the queen and a chrysoprase to each of her daughters. I pretended to have gathered them on the bottom, or rather (since it was hardly plausible that the stones, so rare upon dry land, should have lain promiscuously at the bottom of the sea, or that I should have had time to pick them out) that Poseidon himself had handed them to me, in order that I could offer them to the ladies. Here was proof, better than any test, of my divine origin and my good standing with the god.

After this, Minos gave me back my sword.

Soon afterwards chariots bore us off on the road to Knossos.

V

I was so overwhelmed by fatigue that I could hardly feel due astonishment at the great courtyard of the palace, or at a monumental balustraded staircase and the winding corridors through which attentive servants, torch in hand, guided me to the second floor, where a room had been set apart for me. All but one of its many lamps were snuffed out after I arrived. The bed was scented and soft; when they left me, I fell at once into a heavy sleep, which lasted until the evening of the following day, although I had already slept during our long journey; for only at dawn, after traveling all night, had we arrived at Knossos.

I am by no means a cosmopolitan. At the court of Minos I realized for the first time that I was Greek, and I felt very far from home. All unfamiliar things took me by surprise—dress, customs, ways of behaving, furniture (in my father's house we were short of furniture), household objects, and the manner of their use. Among so much that was exquisite, I felt like a savage, and my awkwardness was redoubled when people began smiling at my conduct. I had been used to biting my way through my food, lifting it to my mouth in my fingers, and these delicate forks of metal or wrought gold, these knives they used for cutting meat, gave me more trouble than the heaviest weapons of war. People couldn't take their eyes off me; and when I had to talk, I appeared a still greater oaf. God! How out of place I felt! Only on my own have I ever been good for anything; now for the first time I was in society. It was no longer a question of fighting, or carrying a thing through by main force, but rather of giving pleasure; and of this I had strangely little experience.

I sat, at table, between the two princesses. A simple family meal, without formality, I was told. And in fact, apart from Minos and the queen, Rhadamanthus, the king's brother, the two princesses, and their young brother Glaucus, there was nobody except the tutor to the young prince, a Greek from Corinth, who was not even presented to me.

They asked me to describe in my own tongue (which everybody at the court understood very well and spoke fluently, though with a slight accent) what they were pleased to call my exploits. I was delighted to see that the young Phædra and Glaucus were seized with uncontrollable laughter at the story of the treatment that Procrustes imposed upon passers-by, which I made him endure in his turn—chopping off all those parts of him which exceeded his statutory measure. But they tactfully avoided any allusion to the cause of my visit to Crete, and affected to see me as merely a traveler.

Throughout the meal Ariadne pressed her knee against mine under the table; but it was the warmth of the young Phædra that really stirred me. Meanwhile, Pasiphaë, the queen, who sat opposite me, was fairly eating me with her enormous eyes, and Minos, by her side, wore an unvarying smile. Only Rhadamanthus, with his long, fair beard, seemed rather out of humor. Both he and the king left the room after the fourth course—"to sit on their thrones," they said. Only later did I realize what this meant.

I still felt some traces of my seasickness. I ate a great deal, and drank still more. I was so liberally plied with wines and liqueurs of every sort that before long I didn't know where I was. I was used to drinking only water or diluted wine. With everything reeling before me, but still just able to stand, I begged permission to leave the room. The queen at once led me into a small closet that adjoined her private apartments. After I had been thoroughly sick, I rejoined her on a sofa in her room, and it was then that she began to tackle me.

"My young friend—if I may call you so," she began, "we must make the most of these few moments alone together. I am not what you suppose, and have no designs upon your person, attractive as that may be." And, protesting the while that she was addressing herself only to my spirit, or to some undefined but interior zone of my being, she continually stroked my forehead; later she slipped her hands under my leather jerkin and fondled my pectorals, as if to convince herself that I was really there.

"I know what brings you here, and I want to warn you of a mistake. Your intentions are murderous. You are here to fight my son. I don't know what you may have heard about him, and I don't want to know. Ah, listen to the pleas of my heart! He whom they call the Minotaur may or may not be the monster of whom you have no doubt heard, but he is my son."

At this point I thought it only decent to interject that I had nothing against monsters in themselves; but she went on without listening.

"Please try to understand me. By temperament I am a mystic. Heavenly things alone excite my love. The difficulty, you see, is one never can tell exactly where the god begins and where he ends. I have seen a good deal of my cousin Leda. For her the god hid himself in the guise of a swan. Now, Minos always knew that I wanted to give him a Dioscuros[2] for his heir. But how can one distinguish the animal residue that may remain even in the seed of the gods? If I have since then deplored my mistake—and I realize that to talk of it in this way robs the affair of all grandeur—yet I assure you, Theseus, that it was a celestial moment. For you must understand that my bull was no ordinary beast. Poseidon had sent him. He should have been offered to him as a sacrifice, but he was so beautiful that Minos could not bring himself to do it. That is how I have been able ever since to pass off my desires as an instrument of the god's revenge. And you no doubt know that my mother-in-law, Europa, was carried off by a bull. Zeus was hiding inside him. Minos himself was the fruit of their union. That is why bulls have always been held in great honor in his family. And, if ever, after the birth of the Minotaur, I noticed the king knitting his brows, I had only to say: 'What about your mother?' He could only admit that it was a natural mistake. He is very wise. He believes that Zeus has nominated him judge, along with Rhadamanthus, his brother. He takes the view that one must have understood before one can pass judgment, and he thinks that he will not be a good judge until he has experienced everything, either in his own person or through his family. This is a great encouragement for us all. His children, and I myself, in our several ways, are working, by our individual errors of conduct, for the advancement of his career. The Minotaur too, though he doesn't know it. That is why I am begging you here and now, Theseus, not to try to do him any sort of injury, but rather to become intimate with him, and so to end a misunderstanding that has made Crete the enemy of Greece and done great harm to our two countries."

2. child of Jupiter.

So saying, she became even more attentive, and a point was reached at which I was seriously incommoded, while the exhalations of wine heightened and mingled with the powerful effluvium which, in company with her breasts, was escaping from her corsage.

"Let us return to celestial things," she went on, "as return we always must. You yourself, Theseus—surely you must feel that you are inhabited by one of the gods?"

What put the final touch to my embarrassment was that Ariadne, the elder daughter (and an exceptional beauty, though less attractive to me personally than Phædra), had made it quite plain to me, before I began to feel so sick—had made it quite plain, as I say, as much by signs as by a whisper, that as soon as I felt better I was to join her on the terrace.

VI

What a terrace! And what a palace! Trance-like under the moon, the gardens seemed to be suspended in readiness for one knew not what. It was the month of March, but I could sense already the delicious half-warmth of spring. Once in the open air, I began to feel quite well. Never an indoor man, I need to fill my lungs with fresh air. Ariadne came running toward me, and without a word clamped her warm lips to mine—so violently that we were both sent staggering.

"Follow me," she said. "Not that I mind if anyone sees us; but we can talk more freely under the terebinths." She led me down a few steps toward a more leafy part of the gardens, where huge trees obscured the moon, though not its reflection upon the sea. She had changed her clothes, and now wore, in place of her hooped skirt and tight surcoat, a sort of loose dress, beneath which she was palpably naked.

"I can guess what my mother's been telling you," she began. "She's mad, raving mad, and you can disregard everything she says. First of all, I must tell you this: you are in great danger here. You came here, as I well know, to fight my half-brother, the Minotaur. I'm telling you all this for your own good, so listen carefully. You will win—I'm sure of it. To see you is to banish doubt. (Don't you think that's rather a good line of poetry? But perhaps you have no ear.) But nobody to this day has ever managed to get out of the maze in which the monster lives; and you won't succeed either unless your sweetheart (that I am, or shall presently be) comes to your rescue. You can't begin to conceive how complicated it is, that maze. Tomorrow I shall introduce you to Dædalus, who will tell you about it. It was he who built it; but even he has already forgotten how to get out of it. You'll hear from him how his son Icarus, who once ventured inside, could only get out on wings, through the upper air. That I don't dare recommend to you; it's too risky. You'd better get it into your head at once that your only hope is to stick close to me. We shall be together, you and I—we *must* be together, from now on, in life and in death. Only thanks to me, by me, and in me will you be able to recapture yourself. You must take it or leave it. If you leave me, so much the worse for you. So begin by taking me." Whereupon she abandoned all restraint, gave herself freely to my embrace, and kept me in her arms till morning.

The hours passed slowly for me, I must admit. I have never been good at staying in one place, be it even in the very bosom of delight. I always aim to break free as soon as the novelty has worn off. Afterwards Ariadne used to say: "You promised." I never gave a promise of any kind. Liberty above all things! My duty is to myself.

Although my powers of observation were still to some extent clouded by drink, Ariadne appeared to me to yield her last reserves with such readiness that I could hardly suppose myself to have done the work of a pioneer. This disposed of any scruples that I might later have had about leaving her. Besides, her sentimentality soon became unendurable. Unendurable her protestations of eternal devotion, and the tender diminutives with which she ornamented me. I was alternately her only treasure, her canary, her puppy, her tercelet,[3] her guinea fowl. I loathe pet names. And then she had read too much. "Little heart," she would say, "the irises will wither fast and die." (In point of fact, they'd hardly began to flower.) I know quite well that nothing lasts forever; but the present is all that matters to me. And then she would say: "I couldn't exist without you." This made me think all the time of how to get rid of her.

"What will the king, your father, say to that?" I had asked her. And her reply: "Minos, sweet chuck, puts up with everything. He thinks it's wisest to allow what cannot be prevented. He didn't complain of my mother's adventure with the bull, but according to my mother he simply remarked: 'Here I have some difficulty in following you.' 'What's done is done, and nothing can undo it,' he added. When it comes to us, he'll do the same. At the most, he'll banish you from the court—and a lot of difference that'll make! Wherever you go, I shall follow."

That remains to be seen, I thought.

After we had taken a light breakfast, I asked her to be kind enough to lead me to Dædalus, and added that I wished to speak to him privately and alone. She agreed to this only after I had sworn by Poseidon that immediately our talk was over, I would rejoin her at the palace.

VII

Dædalus rose to welcome me. I had found him in a dim-lit room, bending over the tablets and working drawings that were spread

3. male hawk trained for falconry.

before him, and surrounded by a great many peculiar instruments. He was very tall, and perfectly erect in spite of his great age. His beard was silvery in color, and even longer than that of Minos, which was still quite black, or the fairer one of Rhadamanthus. His vast forehead was marked by deep wrinkles across the whole of its width. When he looked downwards, his eyes were half-hidden by the over-hanging brushwood of his eyebrows. He spoke slowly, and in a deep voice. His silences had the quality of thought.

He began by congratulating me on my prowess. The echo of this, he said, had penetrated even to him, who lived in retirement, remote from the tumult of the world. He added that I looked to him to be something of a booby; that he took little account of feats of arms, and did not consider that physical strength was the godhead of man.

"At one time I saw quite a lot of your predecessor Hercules. He was a stupid man, and I could never get anything out of him except heroics. But what I did appreciate in him, and what I appreciate in you, is a sort of absorption in the task in hand, an unrecoiling audacity, a temerity even, which thrusts you forward and destroys your opponent, after first having destroyed the coward whom each of us carries within himself. Hercules took greater pains than you do; was more anxious, also, to do well; rather melancholy, especially when he had just completed an adventure. But what I like in you is your enjoyment; that is where you differ from Hercules. I shall commend you for never letting your mind interfere. You can leave that to others who are not men of action, but are clever at inventing sound and good motives for those who are.

"Do you realize that we are cousins? I too (but don't repeat this to Minos, who knows nothing about it)—I too am Greek. I was forced regretfully to leave Attica after certain differences had arisen between myself and my nephew Talos, a sculptor like myself, and my rival. He became a popular favorite, and claimed to uphold the dignity of the gods by representing them with their lower limbs set fast in a hieratic posture, and thus incapable of movement; whereas I was for setting free their limbs and bringing the gods nearer to ourselves. Olympus, thanks to me, became once again a neighbor of the earth. By way of complement, I aspired, with the aid of science, to mold mankind in the likeness of the gods.

"At your age I longed above all to acquire knowledge. I soon decided that man's personal strength can effect little or nothing without instruments, and that the old saying 'Better a good tool than a strong forearm' was true. Assuredly you could never have sub-dued the bandits of Attica and the Peloponnese without the weapons your father had given you. So I thought I could not employ myself more usefully than by bringing these auxiliaries nearer to perfection, and that I could not do this without first mastering mathematics, mechanics, and geometry to the degree, at any rate, in which they were known in Egypt, where such things are put to great use; also that I must then pass from theory to practice by learning all that was known about the properties and qualities of every kind of material, even of those for which no immediate use was apparent, for in these (as happens also in the human sphere) one sometimes discovers extraordinary qualities one had never expected to find. And so I widened and entrenched my knowledge.

"To familiarize myself with other trades, other crafts and skills, other climates, and other living things, I set myself to visit distant countries, put myself to school with eminent foreigners, and remained with them until they had nothing more to teach me. But no matter where I went or how long I stayed, I remained a Greek. In the same way it is because I know and feel that you are a son of Greece that I am interested in you, my cousin.

"Once back in Crete, I told Minos all about my studies and my travels, and went on to tell him of a project I had cherished. This was to build and equip, not far from his palace (if he approved the plan and would provide the means to carry it out), a labyrinth like the one which I had admired in Egypt, on the shore of Lake Moeris; but mine would be different in plan. At the very moment Minos was in an awkward position. His queen had whelped a monster; not knowing how best to look after it, but judging it prudent to isolate it and keep it well away from the public gaze, he asked me to devise a building and a set of communicating gardens which, without precisely imprisoning the monster, would at least contain him and make it impossible for him to get loose. I lavished all my scholarship, all my best thoughts, on the task.

"But, believing that no prison can withstand a really obstinate intention to escape, and that there is no barrier, no ditch, that daring and resolution will not overcome, I thought that the best way of containing a prisoner in the labyrinth was to make it of such a kind, not that he couldn't get out (try to grasp my meaning here), but that he wouldn't want to get out. I therefore assembled in this one place the means to satisfy every kind of appetite. The Minotaur's tastes were neither many nor various; but we had to plan for everybody, whomsoever it might be, who would enter the labyrinth. Another and indeed the prime necessity was to fine down the visitor's will-power to the point of extinction. To this end I made up some electuaries[4] and had them mixed with the wines that were served. But that was not enough; I found a better way. I had noticed that certain plants, when thrown into the fire, gave off, as they burned, semi-narcotic vapors. These seemed admirably suited to my purpose, and indeed they played exactly the part for which I needed them.

4. medicines usually composed of a powder mixed with syrup or honey.

Accordingly I had them fed to the stoves, which are kept alight night and day. The heavy gases thus distributed not only act upon the will and put it to sleep; they induce a delicious intoxication, rich in flattering delusions, and provoke the mind, filled as this is with voluptuous mirages, to a certain pointless activity; 'pointless,' I say, because it has merely an imaginary outcome, in visions and speculations without order, logic, or substance. The effect of these gases is not the same for all of those who breathe them; each is led on by the complexities implicit in his own mind to lose himself, if I may so put it, in a labyrinth of his own devising. For my son Icarus, the complexities were metaphysical. For me, they take the form of enormous edifices, palatial buildings heaped upon themselves with an elaboration of corridors and staircases . . . in which (as with my son's speculations) everything leads to a blank wall, a mysterious 'keep out.' But the most surprising thing about these perfumes is that when one has inhaled them for a certain time, they are already indispensable; body and mind have formed a taste for this malicious insobriety; outside of it reality seems charmless and one no longer has any wish to return to it. And that—that above all—is what keeps one inside the labyrinth. Knowing that you want to enter it in order to fight the Minotaur, I give you fair warning; and if I have told you at length of this danger, it was to put you on your guard. You will never bring it off alone; Ariadne must go with you. But she must remain on the threshold and not so much as sniff the vapors. It is important that she should keep a clear head while you are being overcome by drunkenness. But even when drunk, you must keep control of yourself: everything depends on that. Your will alone may not suffice (for, as I told you, these emanations will weaken it), and so I have thought of this plan: to link you and Ariadne by a thread, the tangible symbol of duty. This thread will allow, indeed will compel you to rejoin her after you have been some time away. Be always determined not to break it, no matter what may be the charms of the labyrinth, the seduction of the unknown, or the headlong urging of your own courage. Go back to her, or all the rest, and the best with it, will be lost. This thread will be your link with the past. Go back to it. Go back to yourself. For nothing can begin from nothing, and it is from your past, and from what you are at this moment, that what you are going to be must spring.

"I should have spoken more briefly if I had not been so interested in you. But before you go out to meet your destiny, I want you to hear my son. You will realize more vividly, while listening to him, what danger you will presently run. Although he was able, thanks to me, to escape the witchcraft of the maze, his mind is still most pitiably a slave to its maleficence."

He walked over to a small door, lifted the arras that covered it, and said very loudly:

"Icarus, my dear son, come and tell us of your distress. Or, rather, go on thinking aloud, as if you were alone. Pay no attention to me or to my guest. Behave as if neither of us were here."

VIII

I saw coming in a young man of about my own age who seemed in the half-light to be of great beauty. His fair hair was worn very long and fell in ringlets to his shoulders. He stared fixedly, but seemed not to focus his gaze on anything in particular. Naked to the waist, he wore a tight metal belt and a loincloth, as it seemed to me, of leather and dark cloth; this swathed the top of his thighs, and was held in place by a curious and prominent knot. His white leather boots caught my eye, and seemed to suggest that he was making ready to go out; but his mind alone was on the move. Himself seemed not to see us. Proceeding no doubt with some unbroken chain of argument, he was saying:

"Who came first: man or woman? Can the Eternal One be female? From the womb of what great Mother have you come, all you myriad species? And by what engendering cause can that womb have been made great? Duality is inadmissible. In that case the god himself would be the son. My mind refuses to divide God. If once I allow division, strife begins. Where there are gods, there are wars. There are not gods, but a God. The kingdom of God is peace. All is absorbed, all is reconciled in the Unique Being."

He was silent for a moment and then went on:

"If man is to give a form to the gods, he must localize and reduce. God spreads where he will. The gods are divided. His extension is immense; theirs merely local."

He was silent again, before going on in a voice panting with anguish:

"But what is the reason for all this, O God who art lucidity itself? For so much trouble, so many struggles? And toward what? What is our purpose here? Why do we seek reasons for everything? Where are we to turn, if not toward God? How are we to direct our steps? Where are we to stop? When can we say: so be it; nothing more to be done? How can we reach God, after starting from man? And if I start from God, how can I reach across to myself? Yet if man is the creation of God, is not God the creation of man? It is the exact crossing-place of those roads, at the very heart of that cross, that my mind would fix itself."

As he spoke, the veins swelled on his forehead, and the sweat ran down his temples. At least, so it seemed to me, for I could not see him clearly in the half-light; but I heard him gasping, like a man putting forth an immense effort.

He was quiet for a moment, then went on:

"I don't know where God begins, and still less where He ends. I shall even express myself more exactly if I say that His beginning never ends. Ah, how sick I am of 'therefore,' and 'since,' and 'because'! Sick of inference, sick of deduction. I never learn anything from the finest of syllogisms that I haven't first put into it myself. If I put God in at the beginning, He comes out at the end. I don't find Him unless I do put Him in. I have tramped all the roads of logic. On their horizontal plane I have wandered all too often. I crawl, and I would rather take wings; to lose my shadow, to lose the filth of my body, to throw off the weight of the past! The infinite calls me! I have the sensation of being drawn upwards from a great height. O mind of man, I shall climb to your topmost point. My father, with his great knowledge of mechanics, will provide me with the means to go. I shall travel alone. I'm not afraid. I can pay my way. It's my only chance to escape. O noble mind, too long entangled in the confusion of my problems, an uncharted road is waiting for you now. I cannot define what it is that summons me; but I know that my journey can have only one end: in God."

Then he backed away from us as far as the arras, which he raised and afterwards let drop behind him.

"Poor dear boy," said Dædalus. "As he thought he could never escape from the labyrinth and did not understand that the labyrinth was within himself, at his request I made him a set of wings, with which he was able to fly away. He thought that he could only escape by way of the heavens, all terrestrial routes being blocked. I knew him to be of a mystical turn, so that his longing did not surprise me. A longing that has not been fulfilled, as you will have been able to judge for yourself while listening to him. In spite of my warnings, he tried to fly too high and overtaxed his strength. He fell into the sea. He is dead."

"How can that be?" I burst out. "I saw him alive only a moment ago."

"Yes," he answered, "you did see him, and he seemed to be alive. But he is dead. At this point, Theseus, I am afraid that your intelligence, although Greek, and as such subtle and open to all aspects of the truth, cannot follow me; for I myself, I must confess, was slow to grasp and concede this fact: those of us whose souls, when weighed in the supreme scale, are not judged of too little account, do not just live an ordinary life. In time, as we mortals measure it, we grow up, accomplish our destiny, and die. But there is another, truer, eternal plane on which time does not exist; on this plane the representative gestures of our race are inscribed, each according to its particular significance. Icarus was, before his birth, and remains after his death, the image of man's disquiet, of the impulse to discovery, the soaring flight of poetry—the things of which, during his short life, he was the incarnation. He played out his hand, as he owed it to himself to do; but he didn't end there. What happens, in the case of a hero, is this: his mark endures. Poetry and the arts reanimate it, and it becomes an enduring symbol. That is how it is that Orion, the hunter, is riding still, across Elysian fields of asphodel, in search of the prey that he has already killed during his life; and meanwhile the night sky bears the eternal, constellated image of him and his baldric.[5] That is how Tantalus' throat is parched to all eternity, and how Sisyphus still rolls upward toward an unattainable summit the heavy and ever rebounding weight of care that tormented him in the days when he was king of Corinth. For you must realize that in hell the only punishment is to begin over and over again the actions which, in life, one failed to complete.

"In the same way, in the animal kingdom, the death of each creature in no way impoverishes its species, for this retains its habitual shape and behavior; there are no individuals among the beasts. Whereas among men it is the individual alone who counts. That is why Minos is already leading at Knossos the life which will fit him for his career as a judge in hell. That is why Pasiphaë and Ariadne are yielding to their destiny in such exemplary fashion. And you yourself, Theseus, may appear carefree, and you may feel it, but you will not escape the destiny that is shaping you, any more than did Hercules, or Jason, or Perseus. But know this (because my eyes have learned the art of discerning the future through the present)— there remain great things for you to do, and in a sphere quite different from that of your previous exploits; things beside which these exploits will seem, in the future, to have been the amusements of a child. It remains for you to found the city of Athens, and there to situate the supremacy of the human mind.

"Do not linger, therefore, in the labyrinth, or in the embrace of Ariadne, after the hideous combat from which you will emerge triumphant. Keep on the move. Regard indolence as treachery. Seek no rest until, with your destiny completed, it is time to die. It is only thus that, on the farther side of what seems to be death, you will live, forever re-created by the gratitude of mankind. Keep on the move, keep well ahead, keep on your own road, O valiant gatherer of cities.

"And now listen carefully, Theseus, and remember what I say. No doubt you will have an easy victory over the Minotaur. Taken in the right way, he is not so redoubtable as people suppose. (They used to say that he lived on carrion; but since when has a bull eaten anything but grass?) Nothing is easier than to get into the labyrinth,

5. a belt which is worn diagonally from the shoulder to the hip, and supports the sword.

nothing less easy than to get out. Nobody finds his way in there without first he lose it. And for your return journey (for footsteps leave no trace in the labyrinth) you must attach yourself to Ariadne by a thread. I have prepared several reels of this, and you will take them away with you. Unwind them as you make your way inside, and when the reel is exhausted, tie the end of the thread to the beginning of the next, so as never to have a break in the chain. Then on your way back you must rewind the thread until you come to the end, which Ariadne will have in her hand. I don't know why I insist so much, when all that part is as easy as good-morning. The real difficulty is to preserve unbroken, to the last inch of the thread, the will to come back; for the perfumes will make you forgetful, as will also your natural curiosity, which will conspire to make you weaken. I have told you this already and have nothing to add. Here are the reels. Good-by."

I left Dædalus and made off to rejoin Ariadne.

IX

Those reels of thread were the occasion of the first dispute between Ariadne and myself. She wanted me to hand over to her, for safe keeping in her corsage, those same reels which Dædalus had entrusted to me, claiming that to wind and unwind such things was a woman's job (one, in fact, in which she was particularly expert) and that she wanted to spare me the bother of attending to it. But in reality she hoped in this way to remain the mistress of my fate, a thing to which I would not consent at any price. Moreover, I had another suspicion: Ariadne would be reluctant to unwind, where every turn of the reel allowed me to stray farther from herself; she might hold back the thread, or pull it toward her; in such a case I should be prevented from going in as far as I wanted. I therefore stood my ground, in the face even of that last argument of women, a flood of tears—knowing well that if one once begins to yield one's little finger, they are quick to snap up the whole arm, and the rest with it.

This thread was neither of linen nor of wool. Dædalus had made it from some unknown material, which even my sword, when I experimented with a little piece, was powerless to cut. I left the sword in Ariadne's care, being determined (after what Dædalus had said to me about the superiority that man owes wholly to his instruments, and the decisive role of these in my victories over the monsters)—being determined, as I say, to subdue the Minotaur with the strength of my bare hands. When, after all this, we arrive before the entrance to the labyrinth, a portal embellished with that double ax which one saw everywhere in Crete, I entreated Ariadne on no account to stir from the spot. She insisted that she should herself tie the end of the thread to my wrist, with a knot that she was pleased to call a lover's; she then glued her lips to my own and held them there for what seemed to me an interminable time. I was longing to get on.

My thirteen companions, both male and female, had gone on ahead, Pirithoüs among them; I found them in the first big room, already quite fuddled by the vapors. I should have mentioned that, together with the thread, Dædalus had given me a piece of rag drenched with a powerful specific against the gases, and had pressed me most particularly to employ it as a gag. (This also Ariadne had taken in hand, as we stood before the entrance to the labyrinth.) Thanks to it, and though hardly able to breathe, I was able in the midst of these intoxicating vapors to keep my head clear and my will taut. I was rather suffocated, all the same, because, as I've said before, I never feel really well when I'm not in the open air, and the artificial atmosphere of that place was oppressive to me.

Unreeling the thread, I penetrated into a second room, darker than the first; then into another, still darker; then into a fourth, where I could only grope my way. My hand, brushing along the wall, fell upon the handle of a door. I opened it, and stepped into brilliant sunshine. I was in a garden. Facing me, and stretched at length upon a flowery bed of buttercups, pansies, jonquils, tulips, and carnations, lay the Minotaur. As luck would have it, he was asleep. I ought to have hurried forward and taken advantage of this, but something held me back, arrested my arm: the monster was beautiful. As happens with centaurs also, there was in his person a harmonious blending of man and beast. On top of this, he was young, and his youthfulness gave an indefinable bloom to his good looks; and I am more vulnerable to such things than to any show of strength. When faced with them, I needed to call upon all my reserves of energy. For one never fights better than with the doubled strength of hatred; and I could not hate the Minotaur. I even stood still for some time and just looked at him. But he opened one eye. I saw then that he was completely witless, and that it was time for me to set about my task. . . .

What I did next, what happened, I cannot exactly recall. Tightly as I had been gagged, my mind had doubtless been benumbed by the gases in the first room; they affected my memory, and if in spite of this I vanquished the Minotaur, my recollection of the victory is confused, though on the whole somewhat voluptuous. That must be my last word, since I refuse to invent. I have also many dreamlike memories of the charms of that garden; it so went to my head that I thought I could never bear to leave it; and it was only reluctantly that, after settling with the Minotaur, I rewound my thread and went back to the first room, there to rejoin my companions.

They were seated at table. Before them a massive repast had been spread (how or by whom I cannot say). They were busy gormandizing, drinking heavily, making passes of love at one another, and braying like so many madmen or idiots. When I made as if to take them away, they replied that they were getting on very well and had no thought of leaving. I insisted, saying that I had come to deliver them. "Deliver us from what?" they shouted; and suddenly they all banded together and covered me with insults. I was very much distressed, because of Pirithoüs. He hardly recognized me, forswore virtue, made mock of his own good qualities, and told me roundly that not for all the glory in the world would he consent to give up his present enjoyments. All the same, I couldn't blame him for it, because I knew too well that, but for Dædalus' precautions, I should have foundered in the same way, and joined in the chorus with him and with the others. It was only by beating them up, it was only by punching them and kicking them hard on their behinds, that I got them to follow me; of course there was also the fact that they were so clogged by drink as to be incapable of resistance.

Once out of the labyrinth, how slowly and painfully they came back to their senses and reassumed their normal selves! This they did with great sadness. It appeared to them (so they told me afterwards) as if they were climbing down from some high peak of happiness into a dark and narrow valley. Each rebuilt for himself the prison in which every man is his own jailor and from which he could never again escape. Pirithoüs, however, soon showed himself aghast at his momentary degradation, and he promised to redeem himself, in his own eyes and in mine, by an excess of zeal. An occasion was offered to him, not long afterwards, to give me proof of his devotion.

x

I hid nothing from him; he knew my feelings for Ariadne, and their decline. I did not even hide from him that, child though she might still be, I was very much taken with Phædra. She used often at that time to play on a swing strung up between the trunks of two palm trees; and when I saw her at the top of her flight, with the wind lifting her short skirts, my heart would miss a beat. But when Ariadne appeared, I looked the other way and dissembled my feelings as best I could, for fear of arousing in her the jealousy of an elder sister. Still, thwarted desires are not healthy. But if I was to abduct her, and thus bring off the audacious project that was beginning to simmer in my heart, I should need to employ a ruse of some sort. Then it was that Pirithoüs was able to help me by devising a plan stamped with all his fertile ingenuity. Meanwhile our stay in the island was dragging on, though both Ariadne and myself were obsessed with the idea of getting away. But what Ariadne didn't know was that I was resolved not to leave without Phædra. Pirithoüs knew it, and this is how he helped me.

He had more freedom than I—Ariadne stuck to me like a ball-and-chain—and he passed his leisure in the study and observation of the customs of Crete. "I think," he said to me one morning, "that I've got just what we want. You know that Minos and Rhadamanthus, those two model legislators, have drawn up a code of morals for the island, paying particular attention to pederasty. As you know, too, the Cretans are especially prone to this, as is evident from their culture. So much so, in fact, that every adolescent who reaches manhood without having been chosen by some older admirer becomes ashamed and regards his neglect as dishonorable; for if he is good-looking, people generally conclude that some vice of heart or mind must be the cause. Young Glaucus, the son of Minos, who is Phædra's absolute double, confided to me his anxiety in this respect. His friendless state causes him much distress. I made the vain suggestion that no doubt his princely rank has discouraged admirers; he replied that this, though possible, did not make his position in any way less painful, and that people ought to realize that it was also a grief to Minos; and that Minos as a rule disregards all distinctions of rank and position. All the same, he would certainly be flattered if an eminent prince like yourself were to be kind enough to take an interest in his son. It occurred to me that Ariadne, who shows herself so importunately jealous of her sister, would have no such feelings about her brother. There is hardly a single instance of a woman taking serious notice of the love of a man for a boy; in any case, she would think it unbecoming to show resentment. You need have no fear on that score."

"What!" I shouted. "Can you think that fear would ever stop me? But though I am a Greek, I do not feel myself drawn in any way toward people of my own sex, however young and attractive they may be. In this I differ from Hercules, and would gladly let him keep his Hylas. Your Glaucus may be like my Phædra, but it is she whom I desire, not he."

"You haven't grasped what I mean," he resumed, "I'm not suggesting you should take Glaucus in her place, but simply that you should pretend to take him, in order to deceive Ariadne and let her believe, and everybody else, that Phædra, whom you are carrying off, is Glaucus. Now listen and follow me carefully. One of the customs of the island, and one that Minos himself instituted, is that the lover assumes complete charge of the child whom he covets, and takes him to live with him, under his roof, for two months; after which period the child must announce publicly whether or not his lover has given him satisfaction and treated him properly. To take the supposed Glaucus under your roof, you must put him aboard the ship that brought us here from Greece. Once we are all assembled, with the crypto-Phædra[6] safe in our hands, we must up-anchor; Ariadne will have to be there, since she assumes that she will be going with you; then we shall put out with all speed to the open sea. The Cretans have a large fleet, but their ships are not so fast as ours, and if they give chase we can easily outdistance them. Tell Minos about this project. You may be sure that he'll smile on it, provided you let him believe that Glaucus, and not Phædra, is involved; for, as for Glaucus, he could hardy hope to secure a better master and lover than yourself. But tell me: is Phædra willing?"

"I don't know as yet. Ariadne takes good care never to leave me alone with her, so that I've had no chance to sound her. . . . But I don't doubt that she will be ready to follow me, when she realizes that I prefer her to her sister."

It was Ariadne who had to be approached first. I took her into my confidence, but deceitfully of course, and according to our agreed procedure.

"What a wonderful plan!" she cried. "And how I shall enjoy traveling with my small brother! You've no idea how charming he can be. I get on very well with him and in spite of the difference in our ages I am still his favorite playmate. Nothing could be better for broadening his mind than to visit a foreign country. At Athens he can perfect his Greek, which he already speaks passably, though with a bad accent; that will soon be put right. You will set him the best of examples, and I only hope he will grow to be like you."

I let her talk. The wretched girl could not foresee what fate was in store for her.

Glaucus had also to be warned, lest any hitch should occur. Pirithoüs took charge of this, and told me later the boy was at first bitterly disappointed. Only after an appeal to his better sentiments did he decide to join in the game; or rather, I should say, to drop out of it and yield up his place to his sister. Phædra had also to be informed. She might have started screaming if we had tried to abduct her by force or surprise. But Pirithoüs exploited with great skill the malicious pleasure that both children would not fail to take in gulling their elders—Glaucus his parents, and Phædra her sister.

Phædra duly rigged herself out in Glaucus' everyday clothes. The two were of exactly the same build, and when she had bound up her hair and muffled the lower part of her face, it was impossible for Ariadne not to mistake her identity.

It was certainly disagreeable for me to have to deceive Minos, who had lavished upon me every mark of his confidence, and had told me of the good influence that he expected me, as an older per-

6. the hidden, or disguised, Phædra.

son, to have upon his son. And I was his guest, too. Of course I
was abusing my position. But it was not, and indeed it is never, a
part of my character to allow myself to be stopped by scruples. The
voices of gratitude and decency were shouted down by the voice of
desire. The end justifies the means. What must be must be.

Ariadne was first on board, in her anxiety to secure comfortable
quarters. As soon as Phædra arrived, we could make off. Her abduction took place not at nightfall, as had at first been agreed, but after
the family dinner, at which she had insisted on appearing. She
pleaded that as she had formed the habit of going to her room immediately after dinner, her absence could not, she thought, be remarked before the morning of the next day. So everything went off
without a hitch, and I was able to disembark with Phædra, a few
days later, in Attica, having meanwhile dropped off her sister, the
beautiful and tedious Ariadne, at Naxos.

I learned on arriving at our territory that when Ægeus, my father,
had seen in the distance the black sails (those sails which I had
omitted to change), he had hurled himself into the sea. I have
already touched on this in a few words; I dislike returning to it. I
shall add, however, that I had dreamed, that last night of our voyage, that I was already king of Attica. Be that as it may, or as it
might have been, this was, for the whole population and for myself,
a day of rejoicing for our happy return and my promotion to the
throne, and a day of mourning for the death of my father. I therefore gave orders that in the rites for the day lamentations should
alternate with songs of joy; and in these songs and dances we took
a prominent part—my companions, now so implausibly restored to
their homes, and myself. Joy and desolation: it was fitting that the
people should be made to explore, at once and the same time, these
two extremes of feeling.

XI

People sometimes reproached me afterwards for my conduct
toward Ariadne. They said I had behaved like a coward; that I should
not have abandoned her, or at any rate not on an island. Possibly; but
I wanted to put the sea between us. She was after me, hunting me
down, marking me for the kill. When she got wind of my ruse and
detected her sister beneath her brother's clothes, she set up the
devil's own noise, broke into a series of rhythmical screams, up-
braided me for my treachery; and when, in my exasperation, I told
her that I did not intend to take her farther than the first island at
which the wind, now suddenly risen, would allow or compel us to
make landfall, she threatened me with a long poem she proposed to
write on the subject of this infamous desertion. I told her at once
that she could not do better; the poem promised to be very good,
as far as I could judge from her frenzied and lyrical tones; moreover,

it would serve as a distraction, and she would undoubtedly soon find in it the best solace for her grief. But all this only vexed her the more. Such are women, when one tries to make them see reason. For my part, I always allow myself to be guided by an instinct in which, by reason of its greater simplicity, I have perfect confidence.

The island in question was Naxos. One story has it that, some time after we had abandoned her, Dionysus[7] went there to join her, and indeed married her; all of which may be a way of saying that she found consolation in drink. People say that on their wedding day the god made her a present of a crown, the work of Hephæstus,[8] which now forms one of the constellations; and that Zeus welcomed her on Olympus and made her immortal. She was even mistaken, they say, for Aphrodite. I let people talk, and myself, in order to cut short hostile rumors, did my best to confirm her divine rank by founding a cult in her honor. I also went out of my way to be the first to dance my reverences there. May I be allowed to remark that, but for my desertion, she would have enjoyed none of these great advantages?

Certain imaginary incidents have enriched the mythology of my person: the abduction of Helen, the descent into hell with Pirithoüs, the rape of Proserpine. I took care never to deny these rumors for they all enhanced my prestige. I even improved upon some of them, in order to confirm the people in beliefs that they are all too inclined, in Attica, to discard. Popular emancipation is a good thing; irreverence quite another.

The truth is that after my return to Athens I remained faithful to Phædra. I took both the woman and the city for my bride. I was a husband, and the son of a dead king: I was a king. My days of adventure are over, I used to repeat to myself; where I had sought to conquer, I now sought to rule.

This was not easy. Athens at that time really did not exist. In Attica a mass of petty townships disputed for predominance; whence continual brawling, besieging, and strife. The essential thing was to secure a strong central unit of government—a thing I obtained only with great difficulty. I brought both strength and cunning to the task.

Ægeus, my father, thought he could assure his own authority by perpetuating these quarrels. Considering, myself, that the well-being of the citizens is compromised by such discords, I traced the source of most of the evils to the general inequality of wealth and the desire to increase one's own fortune. Myself caring little for the acquisition of wealth, and preoccupied with the public good as much as, if not more than, with my own, I set an example of plain living. By an equal division of all properties, I abolished at one blow both

7. often identified with Bacchus.   8. Vulcan.

the fact of supremacy and the rivalries it had provoked. This was a drastic measure, which no doubt pleased the poor (the great majority, that is to say) but antagonized the rich, whom I had thereby dispossessed. These, though few in number, were clever men. I summoned the most important among them, and said:

"Personal merit is the only thing to which I attach any importance; I recognize no other scale of values. You have made yourselves rich by ingenuity, practical knowledge, and perseverance; but also, and more often, by injustice and abuse. Your private rivalries are compromising the security of a state that I intend to be a great power, beyond the reach of your intrigues. Only thus will it be able to resist foreign invasion, and prosper. The accursed love of money that torments you does not bring you happiness, for one can truly call it insatiable. The more people have, the more they want. I shall therefore curtail your fortunes; and by force (I possess it) if you do not submit peaceably to the curtailment. For myself I shall keep only the preservation of the laws and the command of the army. I care very little for the rest. I mean to live, now that I am king, just as simply as I have lived hitherto, and in the same style as the humblest of my subjects. I shall see that the laws are respected, and that I myself am respected, if not feared. I mean to have it said among our neighbors that Attica is ruled, not by a tyrant, but by a government of the people; for each citizen of the state shall have an equal right to sit on the council, irrespective of his birth. If you do not side willingly with all this, I shall find ways, as I said, to compel you.

"I shall raze and destroy utterly your little courts of local justice and your regional council chambers, and I shall assemble, beneath the Acropolis, the capital city which already bears the name of Athens. And it is this name of Athens that for the races of the future—and this I promise to the gods who show me favor—will be a name of wonders. I dedicate my city to Pallas. Now go, all of you, and take my words as meant."

Then, suiting my example to my words, I stripped myself of all royal authority, stepped back into the ranks, and was not afraid to show myself to the public without escort, like a simple citizen; but I gave my attention unceasingly to public affairs, maintaining peace and watching over the good order of the state.

Pirithoüs, after hearing me address the men of wealth, said to me that he thought my speech sublime, but ridiculous. Because, he argued: "Equality is not natural among men; I would go farther and say that it is not desirable. It is a good thing that the superior men should rise above the vulgar mass to the full height of their eminence. Without emulation, rivalry, and jealousy, that mob will be forever a formless, stagnant, wallowing mass. There must be some leaven to make it rise; take care that it doesn't rise against yourself. Whether you like it or not, and though you may succeed in your wish and achieve an initial leveling by which each man starts on the same plane and with an equal chance, yet differences of talent will soon bring about differences of station; in other words, a downtrodden people and an aristocracy."

"Good gods!" That set me off again. "I certainly expect that, and I hope it won't be long in coming. But in the first place I don't see why the people should be downtrodden if the new aristocracy, to which I shall give all the support in my power, is, as I would have it, an aristocracy not of wealth, but of intellect."

And then, in order to increase the power and importance of Athens, I made it known that there would be an impartial welcome for everyone, no matter whence he came, who might choose to come and settle here. And criers were sent throughout the neighboring countries to carry this message: "Peoples all, make haste to Athens!"

The news spread far and wide. And was it not through this that Œdipus, the fallen monarch, saddest and noblest of derelicts, made his way from Thebes to Attica, there to seek help and protection, there to die? Because of which I was able later to secure for Athens the blessing that the gods had conferred on his ashes. Of this I shall have more to say.

I promised to all newcomers indifferently the same rights as were enjoyed by those who were natives of Athens or who had settled there earlier; any necessary discrimination could await the proofs of experience. For good tools reveal their quality only after use, and I wished to judge nobody except according to his services.

So that if I was later obliged none the less to admit differences among the Athenians (and consequently to admit a hierarchy), I allowed this only in order to ensure that the state would in general function better. Thus it is that, thanks to me, the Athenians came to deserve, among all the other Greeks, the fine name of "people," which was commonly bestowed upon them and upon them only. There lies my fame, far surpassing that of my earlier feats; a fame to which neither Hercules attained, nor Jason, nor Bellerophon, nor Perseus.

Pirithoüs, alas! the companion of my youthful exuberances, later fell away from me. All those heroes whom I have named, and others too, like Meleager and Peleus, never prolonged their career beyond their first feats, or sometimes beyond a single one. For myself, I was not content with that. "There is a time for conquest," I used to say to Pirithoüs, "a time for cleansing the earth of its monsters, and then a time for husbandry and the harvesting of well-cherished land; a time to set men free from fear, and then a time in which to find employment for their liberty, in which to profit by the moment of ease and coax it into bloom." And that could not be achieved without discipline: I would not admit that, as with the Bœotians,[9] man should make himself his own boundary, or aim merely at a mediocre happiness. I thought that man was not and would never be free, and that it would not be a good thing if he were. But I couldn't urge him forward without his consent; nor could I obtain that consent without leaving him (leaving the people, at any rate) the illusion of liberty. I wanted to educate him. I would not allow him to become in any degree content with his lot, or to resign himself to furrow his brow in perpetuity. Humanity (such was always the cast of my thought) can do more and deserves better. I remembered the teaching of Dædalus, who wanted to enrich mankind with all the spoils of the gods. My great strength was that I believed in progress.

So Pirithoüs and I parted company. In my youth he had been my constant companion, and often an invaluable aide. But I realized that constancy in friendship can prevent a man from advancing—can even pull him backwards; after a certain point one can only go forward alone. As Pirithoüs was a man of sense, I still listened to what he said, but that was all. He himself was growing old, and whereas he had once been enterprise itself, he now allowed wisdom to degenerate into temperance. His advice was now always for restriction and restraint.

"Mankind isn't worth all this trouble," he would say. And I would reply: "Well, what else is there to think about, except mankind? Man has not yet said his last word."

"Don't get excited," he used to reply. "Haven't you done enough? Now that the prosperity of Athens is assured, it is time for you to rest on your laurels and savor the happiness of married life."

He urged me to pay more attention to Phædra and there for once he was right. For I must now tell of how the peace of my fireside was disturbed, and what a hideous price was expected by the gods in return for my successes and my self-conceit.

XII

I had unlimited confidence in Phædra. I had watched her grow more beautiful month by month. She was the very breath of virtue. I had withdrawn her at so early an age from the pernicious influence of her family that I never conceived she might carry within her a full dose of inherited poison. She obviously took after her mother, and when she later tried to excuse herself by saying that she was not responsible, or that she was foredoomed, I had to own that there

---

9. The inhabitants of Bœotia were notorious for their boorishness and their dull wits.

was something in it. But that was not all: I also believe that she had too great a disdain for Aphrodite. The gods avenge themselves, and it was in vain that Phædra later strove to appease the goddess with an added abundance of offerings and supplications. For Phædra was pious, in spite of everything. In my wife's family everyone was pious. But it was no doubt regrettable that not everyone addressed his devotions to the same god. With Pasiphaë, it was Zeus; with Ariadne, Dionysus. For my own part, I reverenced above all Pallas Athene, and next Poseidon, to whom I was bound by a secret tie, and who, unfortunately for me, had similarly bound himself always to answer my prayers, so that I should never beseech him in vain. My son whose mother had been the Amazon, and whom I set above all the others, devoted himself to Artemis the huntress. He was as chaste as she—as chaste as I, at his age, had been dissolute. He used to run naked through moonlit woods and thickets; detested the court, formal parties, and, above all, the society of women, and was only happy when, with his bearhounds, he could go hunting for wild beasts and follow them to the topmost mountain or the last recesses of a valley. Often, too, he broke in wild horses, tamed them on the seashore, or rode them at full gallop into the sea. How I loved him then! Proud, handsome, unruly; not to me, whom he held in veneration, nor to the laws: but he despised the conventions that prevent a man from asserting himself and wear out his merits in futility. He it was whom I wanted for my heir. I could have slept quietly, once the reins of state were in his unsullied hands; for I knew that he would be as inaccessible to threats as to flatteries.

That Phædra might fall in love with him I realized only too late. I should have foreseen it, for he was very like me. (I mean, like what I had been at his age.) But I was already growing old, and Phædra was still astonishingly young. She may still have loved me, but it was as a young girl loves her father. It is not good, as I have learned to my cost, that there should be such a difference of age between husband and wife. Yet what I could not forgive her was not her passion (natural enough, after all, though half-incestuous), but that, when she realized she could not satisfy her desire, she should have accused my Hippolytus and imputed to him the impure longings that were consuming her. I was a blind father, and a too trustful husband; I believed her. For once in my life I took a woman at her word! I called down the vengeance of the gods upon my innocent son. And my prayer was heard. Men do not realize, when they address themselves to the gods, that if their prayers are answered, it is most often for their misfortune. By a sudden, passionate, mindless impulse I had killed my son. And I am still inconsolable. That Phædra, awakened to her guilt, should at once afterwards have wrought justice upon herself, well and good. But now that I cannot count even upon the friendship of Pirithoüs, I feel lonely; and I am old.

Œdipus,[10] when I welcomed him at Colonus, had been driven from Thebes, his fatherland; without eyes, dishonored, and wretched as he was, he at least had his two daughters with him, and in their constant tenderness he found relief from his sufferings. He had failed in every part of what he had undertaken. I have succeeded. Even the enduring blessing that his ashes are to confer upon the country where they are laid—even this will rest, not upon his ungrateful Thebes, but upon Athens.

I am surprised that so little should have been said about this meeting of our destinies at Colonus, this moment at the crossroads when our two careers confronted each other. I take it to have been the summit and the crown of my glory. Till then I had forced all life to do obeisance to me, and had seen all my fellow men bow in their turn (excepting only Dædalus, but he was my senior by many years; besides, even Dædalus gave me best in the end). In Œdipus alone did I recognize a nobility equal to my own. His misfortunes could only enhance his grandeur in my eyes. No doubt I had triumphed everywhere and always; but on a level which, in comparison with Œdipus, seemed to me merely human—inferior, I might say. He had held his own with the Sphinx; had stood man upright before the riddle of life, and dared to oppose him to the gods. How then, and why, had he accepted defeat? By putting out his eyes, had he not even contributed to it? There was something, in this dreadful act of violence against himself, that I could not contrive to understand. I told him of my bewilderment. But his explanation, I must admit, hardly satisfied me—or else I did not fully understand it.

"True," he said, "I yielded to an impulse of rage—one that could only be directed against myself; against whom else could I have turned? In face of the immeasurable horror of the accusations I had just discovered, I felt an overwhelming desire to make a protest. And besides, what I wanted to destroy was not so much my eyes themselves as the canvas they held before me; the scenery before which I was struggling, the falsehood in which I no longer believed; and this so as to break through to reality.

"And yet, no! I was not really thinking of anything very clearly; I acted rather by instinct. I put out my eyes to punish them for having failed to see the evidence that had, as people say, been staring me in the face. But, to speak the truth—ah, how can I put it to

10. the central figure of two plays by Sophocles, *Oedipus Rex* (*King Oedipus* in this anthology) and *Oedipus at Colonus*.

you? . . . Nobody understood me when I suddenly cried out: 'O darkness, my light!' And you also, you don't understand it—I feel that distinctly. People heard it as a cry of grief; it was a statement of fact. It meant that in my darkness I had found a source of supernatural light, illuminating the world of the spirit. I meant: 'Darkness, thou art henceforth my light.' And at the moment when the blue of the sky went black before me, my inward firmament became bright with stars."

He was silent and for some moments remained deep in meditation. Then he went on:

"As a young man, I passed for one who could see the future. I believed it myself, too. Was I not the first, the only man, to solve the riddle of the Sphinx? Only since my eyes of flesh were torn with my own hand from the world of appearances have I begun, it seems to me, to see truly. Yes; at the moment when the outer world was hidden forever from the eyes of my body, a kind of new eyesight opened out within myself upon the infinite perspectives of an inner world, which the world of appearances (the only one which had existed for me until that time) had led me to disdain. And this imperceptible world (inaccessible, I mean, to our senses) is, I now know, the only true one. All the rest is an illusion, a deception, moreover, that disturbs our contemplation of what is divine. Tiresias, the blind sage, once said to me: 'Who wishes to see God must first cease to see the world'; and I didn't understand him then: just as you, yourself, O Theseus, do not understand me now."

"I shall not attempt to deny," I replied, "the importance of this world beyond temporal things of which your blindness has made you aware; but what I still cannot understand is why you oppose it to the outer world in which we live and act."

"Because," said Œdipus, "for the first time, when with my inward eye I perceived what was formerly hidden from me, I suddenly became aware of this fact: that I had based my earthly sovereignty upon a crime, and that everything which followed from this was in consequence tainted; not merely all my personal decisions, but even those of the two sons to whom I had abandoned my crown—for I at once stepped down from the slippery eminence to which my crime had raised me. You must know already to what new villainies my sons have allowed themselves to stoop, and what an ignominious doom hangs over all that our sinful humanity may engender; of this my unhappy sons are no more than a signal example. For, as the fruits of an incestuous union, they are no doubt doubly branded; but I believe that an original stain of some sort afflicts the whole human race, in such a way that even the best bear its stripe, and are vowed to evil and perdition; from all this man can never break free without divine aid of some sort, for that alone can wash away his original sin and grant him amnesty."

He was silent again for a few moments, as if preparing to plunge still deeper, and then went on:

"You are astonished that I should have put out my eyes. I am astonished myself. But in this gesture, inconsidered and cruel as it was, there may yet be something else: an indefinable secret longing to follow my fortunes to their farthest limit, to give the final turn of the screw to my anguish, and to bring to a close the destiny of a hero. Perhaps I dimly foresaw the grandeur of suffering and its power to redeem; that is why the true hero is ashamed to turn away from it. I think that it is in fact the crowning proof of his greatness, and that he is never worthier than when he falls a victim; then does he exact the gratitude of heaven, and disarm the vengeance of the gods. Be that as it may, and however deplorable my mistakes may have been, the state of unearthly beatitude that I have been able to reach is an ample reward for all the ills that I have had to suffer—but for them, indeed, I should doubtless never have achieved it."

"Dear Œdipus," I said, when it was plain that he had finished speaking, "I can only congratulate you on the kind of superhuman wisdom you profess. But my thoughts can never march with yours along that road. I remain a child of this world, and I believe that man, be he what he may, and with whatever blemishes you judge him to be stained, is in duty bound to play out his hand to the end. No doubt you have learned to make good use even of your misfortunes, and through them have drawn nearer to what you call the divine world. I can well believe, too, that a sort of benediction now attaches to your person, and that it will presently be laid, as the oracles have said, upon the land in which you will take your everlasting rest."

I did not add that what mattered to me was that this blessing should be laid upon Attica, and I congratulated myself that the god had made Thebes abut upon my country.

If I compare my lot with that of Œdipus, I am content: I have fulfilled my destiny. Behind me I leave the city of Athens. It has been dearer to me even than my wife and my son. My city stands. After I am gone, my thoughts will live on there forever. Lonely and consenting, I draw near to death. I have enjoyed the good things of the earth, and I am happy to think that after me, and thanks to me, men will recognize themselves as being happier, better, and more free. I have worked always for the good of those who are to come. I have lived.

THOMAS MANN
(1875–1955)
Tristan*

Einfried, the sanatorium. A long, white, rectilinear building with a side wing, set in a spacious garden pleasingly equipped with grottoes, bowers, and little bark pavilions. Behind its slate roofs the mountains tower heavenwards, evergreen, massy, cleft with wooded ravines.

Now as then Dr. Leander directs the establishment. He wears a two-pronged black beard as curly and wiry as horsehair stuffing; his spectacle-lenses are thick, and glitter; he has the look of a man whom science has cooled and hardened and filled with silent, forbearing pessimism. And with this beard, these lenses, this look, and in his short, reserved, preoccupied way, he holds his patients in his spell; holds those sufferers who, too weak to be laws unto themselves, put themselves into his hands that his severity may be a shield unto them.

As for Fräulein von Osterloh, hers it is to preside with unwearying zeal over the housekeeping. Ah, what activity! How she plies, now here, now there, now upstairs, now down, from one end of the building to the other! She is queen in kitchen and storerooms, she mounts the shelves of the linen-presses, she marshals the domestic staff; she ordains the bill of fare, to the end that the table shall be economical, hygienic, attractive, appetizing, and all these in the highest degree; she keeps house diligently, furiously; and her exceeding capacity conceals a constant reproach to the world of men, to no one of whom has it yet occurred to lead her to the altar. But ever on her cheeks there glows, in two round, carmine spots, the unquenchable hope of one day becoming Frau Dr. Leander.

Ozone, and stirless, stirless air! Einfried, whatever Dr. Leander's rivals and detractors may choose to say about it, can be most warmly recommended for lung patients. And not only these, but patients of all sorts, gentlemen, ladies, even children, come to stop here. Dr. Leander's skill is challenged in many different fields. Sufferers from gastric disorders come, like Frau Magistrate Spatz—she has ear trouble into the bargain—people with defective hearts, paralytics, rheumatics, nervous sufferers of all kinds and degrees. A diabetic general here consumes his daily bread amid continual grumblings. There are several gentlemen with gaunt, fleshless faces who fling

* 1902. Reprinted from *Stories of Three Decades* by Thomas Mann, translated by H. T. Lowe-Porter, by permission of Alfred A. Knopf, Inc. Copyright 1936 by Alfred A. Knopf, Inc. Reprinted in full. The punctuation ". . ." does not indicate omissions from this text.

their legs about in that uncontrollable way that bodes no good. There is an elderly lady, a Frau Pastor Höhlenrauch, who has brought fourteen children into the world and is now incapable of a single thought, yet has not thereby attained to any peace of mind, but must go roving spectre-like all day long up and down through the house, on the arm of her private attendant, as she has been doing this year past.

Sometimes a death takes place among the "severe cases," those who lie in their chambers, never appearing at meals or in the reception-rooms. When this happens no one knows of it, not even the person sleeping next door. In the silence of the night the waxen guest is put away and life at Einfried goes tranquilly on, with its massage, its electric treatment, douches, baths; with its exercises, its steaming and inhaling, in rooms especially equipped with all the triumphs of modern therapeutic.

Yes, a deal happens hereabouts—the institution is in a flourishing way. When new guests arrive, at the entrance to the side wing, the porter sounds the great gong; when there are departures, Dr. Leander, together with Fräulein von Osterloh, conducts the traveller in due form to the waiting carriage. All sorts and kinds of people have received hospitality at Einfried. Even an author is here stealing time from God Almighty—a queer sort of man, with a name like some kind of mineral or precious stone.

Lastly there is, besides Dr. Leander, another physician, who takes care of the slight cases and the hopeless ones. But he bears the name of Müller and is not worth mentioning.

At the beginning of January a business man named Klöterjahn—of the firm of A. C. Klöterjahn & Co.—brought his wife to Einfried. The porter rang the gong, and Fräulein von Osterloh received the guests from a distance in the drawing-room on the ground floor, which, like nearly all the fine old mansion, was furnished in wonderfully pure Empire style. Dr. Leander appeared straightway. He made his best bow, and a preliminary conversation ensued, for the better information of both sides.

Beyond the windows lay the wintry garden, the flower-beds covered with straw, the grottoes snowed under, the little temples forlorn. Two porters were dragging in the guests' trunks from the carriage drawn up before the wrought-iron gate—for there was no drive up to the house.

"Be careful, Gabriele, *doucement, doucement*,[1] my angel, keep your mouth closed," Herr Klöterjahn had said as he led his wife through the garden; and nobody could look at her without tender-

---

1. gently.

heartedly echoing the caution—though, to be sure, Herr Klöterjahn might quite as well have uttered it all in his own language.

The coachman who had driven the pair from the station to the sanatorium was an uncouth man, and insensitive; yet he sat with his tongue between his teeth as the husband lifted down his wife. The very horses, steaming in the frosty air, seemed to follow the procedure with their eyeballs rolled back in their heads out of sheer concern for so much tenderness and fragile charm.

The young wife's trouble was her trachea; it was expressly so set down in the letter Herr Klöterjahn had sent from the shores of the Baltic to announce their impending arrival to the director of Einfried—the trachea, and not the lungs, thank God! But it is a question whether, if it had been the lungs, the new patient could have looked any more pure and ethereal, any remoter from the concerns of this world, than she did now as she leaned back pale and weary in her chaste white-enamelled arm-chair, beside her robust husband, and listened to the conversation.

Her beautiful white hands, bare save for the simple wedding-ring, rested in her lap, among the folds of a dark, heavy cloth skirt; she wore a close-fitting waist of silver-grey with a stiff collar—it had an all-over pattern of arabesques in high-pile velvet. But these warm, heavy materials only served to bring out the unspeakable delicacy, sweetness, and languor of the little head, to make it look more than ever touching, exquisite, and unearthly. Her light-brown hair was drawn smoothly back and gathered in a knot low in her neck, but near the right temple a single lock fell loose and curling, not far from the place where an odd little vein branched across one well-marked eyebrow, pale blue and sickly amid all that pure, well-nigh transparent spotlessness. That little blue vein above the eye dominated quite painfully the whole fine oval of the face. When she spoke, it stood out still more; yes, even when she smiled—and lent her expression a touch of strain, if not actually of distress, that stirred vague fear in the beholder. And yet she spoke, and she smiled: spoke frankly and pleasantly in her rather husky voice, with a smile in her eyes—though they again were sometimes a little difficult and showed a tendency to avoid a direct gaze. And the corners of her eyes, both sides the base of the slender little nose, were deeply shadowed. She smiled with her mouth too, her beautiful wide mouth, whose lips were so pale and yet seemed to flash—perhaps because their contours were so exceedingly pure and well-cut. Sometimes she cleared her throat, then carried her handkerchief to her mouth and afterwards looked at it.

"Don't clear your throat like that, Gabriele," said Herr Klöterjahn. "You know, darling, Dr. Hinzpeter expressly forbade it, and what we have to do is to exercise self-control, my angel. As I said, it is the trachea," he repeated. "Honestly, when it began, I thought it was the lungs, and it gave me a scare, I do assure you. But it isn't the lungs—we don't mean to let ourselves in for that, do we, Gabriele, my love, eh? Ha ha!"

"Surely not," said Dr. Leander, and glittered at her with his eyeglasses.

Whereupon Herr Klöterjahn ordered coffee, coffee and rolls; and the speaking way he had of sounding the *c* far back in his throat and exploding the *b* in "butter" must have made any soul alive hungry to hear it.

His order was filled; and rooms were assigned to him and his wife, and they took possession with their things.

And Dr. Leander took over the case himself, without calling in Dr. Müller.

The population of Einfried took unusual interest in the fair new patient; Herr Klöterjahn, used as he was to see homage paid her, received it all with great satisfaction. The diabetic general, when he first saw her, stopped grumbling a minute; the gentlemen with the fleshless faces smiled and did their best to keep their legs in order; as for Frau Magistrate Spatz, she made her her oldest friend on the spot. Yes, she made an impression, this woman who bore Herr Klöterjahn's name! A writer who had been sojourning a few weeks in Einfried, a queer sort, he was, with a name like some precious stone or other, positively coloured up when she passed him in the corridor, stopped stock-still and stood there as though rooted to the ground, long after she had disappeared.

Before two days were out, the whole little population knew her history. She came originally from Bremen, as one could tell by certain pleasant small twists in her pronunciation; and it had been in Bremen that, two years gone by, she had bestowed her hand upon Herr Klöterjahn, a successful business man, and become his life-partner. She had followed him to his native town on the Baltic coast, where she had presented him, some ten months before the time of which we write, and under circumstances of the greatest difficulty and danger, with a child, a particularly well-formed and vigorous son and heir. But since that terrible hour she had never fully recovered her strength—granting, that is, that she had ever had any. She had not been long up, still extremely weak, with extremely impoverished vitality, when one day after coughing she brought up a little blood—oh, not much, an insignificant quantity in fact; but it would have been much better to be none at all; and the suspicious thing was, that the same trifling but disquieting incident recurred after another short while. Well, of course, there were things to be done, and Dr. Hinzpeter, the family physician, did them. Complete rest was ordered, little pieces of ice swallowed; morphine administered to check the cough, and other medicines to regulate the heart action. But recovery failed to set in; and while the child, Anton Klöterjahn, junior, a magnificent specimen of a baby, seized on his place in life and held it with prodigious energy and ruthlessness, a low, unobservable fever seemed to waste the young mother daily. It was, as we have heard, an affection of the trachea —a word that in Dr. Hinzpeter's mouth sounded so soothing, so consoling, so reassuring, that it raised their spirits to a surprising degree. But even though it was not the lungs, the doctor presently found that a milder climate and a stay in a sanatorium were imperative if the cure was to be hastened. The reputation enjoyed by Einfried and its director had done the rest.

Such was the state of affairs; Herr Klöterjahn himself related it to all and sundry. He talked with a slovenly pronunciation, in a loud, good-humoured voice, like a man whose digestion is in as capital order as his pocket-book; shovelling out the words pell-mell, in the broad accents of the northern coast-dweller; hurtling some of them forth so that each sound was a little explosion, at which he laughed as at a successful joke.

He was of medium height, broad, stout, and short-legged; his face full and red, with watery blue eyes shaded by very fair lashes; with wide nostrils and humid lips. He wore English side-whiskers and English clothes, and it enchanted him to discover at Einfried an entire English family, father, mother, and three pretty children with their nurse, who were stopping here for the simple and sufficient reason that they knew not where else to go. With this family he partook of a good English breakfast every morning. He set great store by good eating and drinking and proved to be a connoisseur both of food and wines, entertaining the other guests with the most exciting accounts of dinners given in his circle of aquaintance back home, with full descriptions of the choicer and rarer dishes; in the telling his eyes would narrow benignly, and his pronunciation take on certain palatal and nasal sounds, accompanied by smacking noises at the back of his throat. That he was not fundamentally averse to earthly joys of another sort was evinced upon an evening when a guest of the cure, an author by calling, saw him in the corridor trifling in not quite permissible fashion with a chambermaid—a humorous little passage at which the author in question made a laughably disgusted face.

As for Herr Klöterjahn's wife, it was plain to see that she was devotedly attached to her husband. She followed his words and movements with a smile: not the rather arrogant toleration the ailing sometimes bestow upon the well and sound, but the sympathetic participation of a well-disposed invalid in the manifestations of people who rejoice in the blessing of abounding health.

Herr Klöterjahn did not stop long in Einfried. He had brought his wife hither, but when a week had gone by and he knew she was in good hands and well looked after, he did not linger. Duties equally weighty—his flourishing child, his no less flourishing business—took him away; they compelled him to go, leaving her rejoicing in the best of care.

Spinell was the name of that author who had been stopping some weeks in Einfried—Detlev Spinell was his name, and his looks were quite out of the common. Imagine a dark man at the beginning of the thirties, impressively tall, with hair already distinctly grey at the temples, and a round, white, slightly bloated face, without a vestige of beard. Not that it was shaven—that you could have told; it was soft, smooth, boyish, with at most a downy hair here and there. And the effect was singular. His bright, doe-like brown eyes had a gentle expression, the nose was thick and rather too fleshy. Also, Herr Spinell had an upper lip like an ancient Roman's, swelling and full of pores; large, carious[2] teeth, and feet of uncommon size. One of the gentlemen with the rebellious legs, a cynic and ribald wit, had christened him "the dissipated baby"; but the epithet was malicious, and not very apt. Herr Spinell dressed well, in a long black coat and a waistcoat with coloured spots.

He was unsocial and sought no man's company. Only once in a while he might be overtaken by an affable, blithe, expansive mood; and this always happened when he was carried away by an æsthetic fit at the sight of beauty, the harmony of two colours, a vase nobly formed, or the range of mountains lighted by the setting sun. "How beautiful!" he would say, with his head on one side, his shoulders raised, his hands spread out, his lips and nostrils curled and distended. "My God! look, how beautiful!" And in such moment of ardour he was quite capable of flinging his arms blindly round the neck of anybody, high or low, male or female, that happened to be near.

On his table, for anybody to see who entered his room, there always lay the book he had written. It was a novel of medium length, with a perfectly bewildering drawing on the jacket, printed on a sort of filter-paper. Each letter of the type looked like a Gothic cathedral. Fräulein von Osterloh had read it once, in a spare quarter-hour, and found it "very cultured"—which was her circumlocution for inhumanly boresome. Its scenes were laid in fashionable salons, in luxurious boudoirs full of choice *objets d'art*, old furniture, gobelins, rare porcelains, priceless stuffs, and art treasures of all sorts and kinds. On the description of these things was expended

2. decayed.

the most loving care; as you read you constantly saw Herr Spinell, with distended nostrils, saying: "How beautiful! My God! look, how beautiful!" After all, it was strange he had not written more than this one book; he so obviously adored writing. He spent the greater part of the day doing it, in his room, and sent an extraordinary number of letters to the post, two or three nearly every day —and that made it more striking, even almost funny, that he very seldom received one in return.

Herr Spinell sat opposite Herr Klöterjahn's wife. At the first meal of which the new guests partook, he came rather late into the dining-room, on the ground floor of the side wing, bade good-day to the company generally in a soft voice, and betook himself to his own place, whereupon Dr. Leander perfunctorily presented him to the new-comers. He bowed, and self-consciously began to eat, using his knife and fork rather affectedly with the large, finely shaped white hands that came out from his very narrow coat-sleeves. After a little he grew more at ease and looked tranquilly first at Herr Klöterjahn and then at his wife, by turns. And in the course of the meal Herr Klöterjahn addressed to him sundry queries touching the general situation and climate of Einfried; his wife, in her charming way, added a word or two, and Herr Spinell gave courteous answers. His voice was mild, and really agreeable; but he had a halting way of speaking that almost amounted to an impediment—as though his teeth got in the way of his tongue.

After luncheon, when they had gone into the salon, Dr. Leander came up to the new arrivals to wish them *Mahlzeit*,[3] and Herr Klöterjahn's wife took occasion to ask about their *vis-à-vis*.

"What was the gentleman's name?" she asked. "I did not quite catch it. Spinelli?"

"Spinell, not Spinelli, madame. No, he is not an Italian; he only comes from Lemberg, I believe."

"And what was it you said? He is an author, or something of the sort?" asked Herr Klöterjahn. He had his hands in the pockets of his very easy-fitting English trousers, cocked his head towards the doctor, and opened his mouth, as some people do, to listen the better.

"Yes . . . I really don't know," answered Dr. Leander. "He writes. . . . I believe he has written a book, some sort of novel. I really don't know what."

By which Dr. Leander conveyed that he had no great opinion of the author and declined all responsibility on the score of him.

"But I find that most interesting," said Herr Klöterjahn's wife.

3. for *gesegnete Mahlzeit* ("may your meal be blessed"), a greeting used at the beginning or end of a meal.

Never before she had met an author face to face.

"Oh, yes," said Dr. Leander obligingly. "I understand he has a certain amount of reputation," which closed the conversation.

But a little later, when the new guests had retired and Dr. Leander himself was about to go, Herr Spinell detained him in talk to put a few questions for his own part.

"What was their name?" he asked. "I did not understand a syllable, of course."

"Klöterjahn," answered Dr. Leander, turning away.

"What's that?" asked Herr Spinell.

"*Klöterjahn* is their name," said Dr. Leander, and went his way. He set no great store by the author.

Have we got as far on as where Herr Klöterjahn went home? Yes, he was back on the shore of the Baltic once more, with his business and his babe, that ruthless and vigorous little being who had cost his mother great suffering and a slight weakness of the trachea; while she herself, the young wife, remained in Einfried and became the intimate friend of Frau Spatz. Which did not prevent Herr Klöterjahn's wife from being on friendly terms with the rest of the guests—for instance with Herr Spinell, who, to the astonishment of everybody, for he had up to now held communion with not a single soul, displayed from the very first an extraordinary devotion and courtesy, and with whom she enjoyed talking, whenever she had any time left over from the stern service of the cure.

He approached her with immense circumspection and reverence, and never spoke save with his voice so carefully subdued that Frau Spatz, with her bad hearing, seldom or never caught anything he said. He tiptoed on his great feet up to the arm-chair in which Herr Klöterjahn's wife leaned, fragilely smiling; stopped two paces off, with his body bent forward and one leg poised behind him, and talked in his halting way, as though he had an impediment in his speech; with ardour, yet prepared to retire at any moment and vanish at the first sign of fatigue or satiety. But he did not tire her; she begged him to sit down with her and the Rätin;[4] she asked him questions and listened with curious smiles, for he had a way of talking sometimes that was so odd and amusing, different from anything she had ever heard before.

"Why are you in Einfried, really?" she asked. "What cure are you taking, Herr Spinell?"

"Cure? Oh, I'm having myself electrified a bit. Nothing worth mentioning. I will tell you the real reason why I am here, madame. It is a feeling for style."

"Ah?" said Herr Klöterjahn's wife; supported her chin on her

4. magistrate's wife.

hand and turned to him with exaggerated eagerness, as one does to
a child who wants to tell a story.

"Yes, madame. Einfried is perfect Empire. It was once a castle,
a summer residence, I am told. This side wing is a later addition,
but the main building is old and genuine. There are times when I
cannot endure Empire, and then times when I simply must have
it in order to attain any sense of well-being. Obviously, people
feel one way among furniture that is soft and comfortable and
voluptuous, and quite another among the straight lines of these
tables, chairs, and draperies. This brightness and hardness, this cold,
austere simplicity and reserved strength, madame—it has upon me
the ultimate effect of an inward purification and rebirth. Beyond
a doubt, it is morally elevating."

"Yes, that is remarkable," she said. "And when I try I can understand what you mean."

Whereto he responded that it was not worth her taking any sort
of trouble, and they laughed together. Frau Spatz laughed too and
found it remarkable in her turn, though she did not say she understood it.

The reception-room was spacious and beautiful. The high, white
folding doors that led to the billiard-room were wide open, and
the gentlemen with the rebellious legs were disporting themselves
within, others as well. On the opposite side of the room a glass
door gave on the broad veranda and the garden. Near the door
stood a piano. At a green-covered folding table the diabetic general
was playing whist with some other gentlemen. Ladies sat reading
or embroidering. The rooms were heated by an iron stove, but the
chimney-piece, in the purest style, had coals pasted over with red
paper to simulate a fire, and chairs were drawn up invitingly.

"You are an early riser, Herr Spinell," said Herr Klöterjahn's
wife. "Two or three times already I have chanced to see you leaving the house at half past seven in the morning."

"An early riser? Ah, with a difference, madame, with a vast difference. The truth is, I rise early because I am such a late sleeper."

"You really must explain yourself, Herr Spinell." Frau Spatz
too said she demanded an explanation.

"Well, if one is an early riser, one does not need to get up so
early. Or so it seems to me. The conscience, madame, is a bad business. I, and other people like me, work hard all our lives to swindle
our consciences into feeling pleased and satisfied. We are feckless
creatures, and aside from a few good hours we go around weighted
down, sick and sore with the knowledge of our own futility. We
hate the useful; we know it is vulgar and unlovely, and we defend
this position, as a man defends something that is absolutely necessary to his existence. Yet all the while conscience is gnawing at us,

to such an extent that we are simply one wound. Added to that, our whole inner life, our view of the world, our way of working, is of a kind—its effect is frightfully unhealthy, undermining, irritating, and this only aggravates the situation. Well, then, there are certain little counter-irritants, without which we would most certainly not hold out. A kind of decorum, a hygienic regimen, for instance, becomes a necessity for some of us. To get up early, to get up ghastly early, take a cold bath, and go out walking in a snowstorm—that may give us a sense of self-satisfaction that lasts as much as an hour. If I were to act out my true character, I should be lying in bed late into the afternoon. My getting up early is all hypocrisy, believe me."

"Why do you say that, Herr Spinell? On the contrary, I call it self-abnegation." Frau Spatz, too, called it self-abnegation.

"Hypocrisy or self-abnegation—call it what you like, madame. I have such a hideously downright nature—"

"Yes, that's it. Surely you torment yourself far too much."

"Yes, madame, I torment myself a great deal."

The fine weather continued. Rigid and spotless white the region lay, the mountains, house and garden, in a windless air that was blinding clear and cast bluish shadows; and above it arched the spotless pale-blue sky, where myriads of bright particles of glittering crystals seemed to dance. Herr Klöterjahn's wife felt tolerably well these days: free of fever, with scarce any cough, and able to eat without too great distaste. Many days she sat taking her cure for hours on end in the sunny cold on the terrace. She sat in the snow, bundled in wraps and furs, and hopefully breathed in the pure icy air to do her trachea good. Sometimes she saw Herr Spinell, dressed like herself, and in fur boots that made his feet a fantastic size, taking an airing in the garden. He walked with tentative tread through the snow, holding his arms in a certain careful pose that was stiff yet not without grace; coming up to the terrace he would bow very respectfully and mount the first step or so to exchange a few words with her.

"Today on my morning walk I saw a beautiful woman—good Lord! how beautiful she was!" he said; laid his head on one side and spread out his hands.

"Really, Herr Spinell. Do describe her to me."

"That I cannot do. Or, rather, it would not be a fair picture. I only saw the lady as I glanced at her in passing, I did not actually see her at all. But that fleeting glimpse was enough to rouse my fancy and make me carry away a picture so beautiful that—good Lord! how beautiful it is!"

She laughed. "Is that the way you always look at beautiful women, Herr Spinell? Just a fleeting glance?"

"Yes, madame; it is a better way than if I were avid of actuality, stared them plump in the face, and carried away with me only a consciousness of the blemishes they in fact possess."

" 'Avid of actuality'—what a strange phrase, a regular literary phrase, Herr Spinell; no one but an author could have said that. It impresses me very much, I must say. There is a lot in it that I dimly understand; there is something free about it, and independent, that even seems to be looking down on reality though it is so very respectable—is respectability itself, as you might say. And it makes me comprehend, too, that there is something else besides the tangible, something more subtle—"

"I know only one face," he said suddenly, with a strange lift in his voice, carrying his closed hands to his shoulders as he spoke and showing his carious teeth in an almost hysterical smile, "I know only one face of such lofty nobility that the mere thought of enhancing it through my imagination would be blasphemous; at which I could wish to look, on which I could wish to dwell, not minutes and not hours, but my whole life long; losing myself utterly therein, forgotten to every earthly thought. . . ."

"Yes, indeed, Herr Spinell. And yet don't you find Fräulein von Osterloh has rather prominent ears?"

He replied only by a profound bow; then, standing erect, let his eyes rest with a look of embarrassment and pain on the strange little vein that branched pale-blue and sickly across her pure translucent brow.

An odd sort, a very odd sort. Herr Klöterjahn's wife thought about him sometimes; for she had much leisure for thought. Whether it was that the change of air began to lose its effect or some positively detrimental influence was at work, she began to go backward, the condition of her trachea left much to be desired, she had fever not infrequently, felt tired and exhausted, and could not eat. Dr. Leander most emphatically recommended rest, quiet, caution, care. So she sat, when indeed she was not forced to lie, quite motionless, in the society of Frau Spatz, holding some sort of sewing which she did not sew, and following one or another train of thought.

Yes, he gave her food for thought, this very odd Herr Spinell; and the strange thing was she thought not so much about him as about herself, for he had managed to rouse in her a quite novel interest in her own personality. One day he had said, in the course of conversation:

"No, they are positively the most enigmatic facts in nature—women, I mean. That is a truism, and yet one never ceases to marvel at it afresh. Take some wonderful creature, a sylph, an airy wraith, a fairy dream of a thing, and what does she do? Goes

and gives herself to a brawny Hercules at a country fair, or maybe
to a butcher's apprentice. Walks about on his arm, even leans her
head on his shoulder and looks round with an impish smile as if
so say: 'Look on this, if you like, and break your heads over it.'
And we break them."

With this speech Herr Klöterjahn's wife had occupied her leisure
again and again.

Another day, to the wonderment of Frau Spatz, the following
conversation took place:

"May I ask, madame—though you may very likely think me
prying—what your name really is?"

"Why, Herr Spinell, you know my name is Klöterjahn!"

"H'm. Yes, I know that—or, rather, I deny it. I mean your own
name, your maiden name, of course. You will in justice, madame,
admit that anybody who calls you Klöterjahn ought to be thrashed."

She laughed so hard that the little blue vein stood out alarmingly
on her brow and gave the pale sweet face a strained expression
most disquieting to see.

"Oh, no! Not at all, Herr Spinell! Thrashed, indeed! Is the
name Klöterjahn so horrible to you?"

"Yes, madame. I hate the name from the bottom of my heart.
I hated it the first time I heard it. It is the abandonment of ugliness;
it is grotesque to make you comply with the custom so far as to
fasten your husband's name upon you; is barbarous and vile."

"Well, and how about Eckhof? Is that any better? Eckhof is my
father's name."

"Ah, you see! Eckhof is quite another thing. There was a great
actor named Eckhof. Eckhof will do nicely. You spoke of your
father—Then is your mother—?"

"Yes, my mother died when I was little."

"Ah! Tell me a little more of yourself, pray. But not if it tires
you. When it tires you, stop, and I will go on talking about Paris,
as I did the other day. But you could speak very softly, or even
whisper—that would be more beautiful still. You were born in
Bremen?" He breathed, rather than uttered, the question with an
expression so awed, so heavy with import, as to suggest that Bremen
was a city like no other on earth, full of hidden beauties and nameless adventures, and ennobling in some mysterious way those born
within its walls.

"Yes, imagine," said she involuntarily. "I was born in Bremen."

"I was there once," he thoughtfully remarked.

"Goodness me, you have been there, too? Why, Herr Spinell,
it seems to me you must have been everywhere there is between
Spitzbergen and Tunis!"

"Yes, I was there once," he repeated. "A few hours, one evening.

I recall a narrow old street, with a strange, warped-looking moon above the gabled roofs. Then I was in a cellar that smelled of wine and mould. It is a poignant memory."

"Really? Where could that have been, I wonder? Yes, in just such a grey old gabled house I was born, one of the old merchant houses, with echoing wooden floor and white-painted gallery."

"Then your father is a business man?" he asked hesitatingly.

"Yes, but he is also, and in the first place, an artist."

"Ah! In what way?"

"He plays the violin. But just saying that does not mean much. It is *how* he plays, Herr Spinell—it is that that matters! Sometimes I cannot listen to some of the notes without the tears coming into my eyes and making them burn. Nothing else in the world makes me feel like that. You won't believe it—"

"But I do. Oh, very much I believe it! Tell me, madame, your family is old, is it not? Your family has been living for generations in the old gabled house—living and working and closing their eyes on time?"

"Yes. Tell me why you ask."

"Because it not infrequently happens that a race with sober, practical bourgeois traditions will towards the end of its days flare up in some form of art."

"Is that a fact?"

"Yes."

"It is true, my father is surely more of an artist than some that call themselves so and get the glory of it. I only play the piano a little. They have forbidden me now, but at home, in the old days, I still played. Father and I played together. Yes, I have precious memories of all those years; and especially of the garden, our garden, back of the house. It was dreadfully wild and overgrown, and shut in by crumbling mossy walls. But it was just that gave it such charm. In the middle was a fountain with a wide border of sword-lilies. In summer I spent long hours there with my friends. We all sat round the fountain on little camp-stools—"

"How beautiful!" said Herr Spinell, and flung up his shoulders. "You sat there and sang?"

"No, we mostly crocheted."

"But still—"

"Yes, we crocheted and chattered, my six friends and I—"

"How beautiful! Good Lord! think of it, *how beautiful!*" cried Herr Spinell again, his face quite distorted with emotion.

"Now, what is it you find so particularly beautiful about that, Herr Spinell?"

"Oh. there being six of them besides you, and your being not one of the six, but a queen among them . . . set apart from your six friends. A little gold crown showed in your hair—quite a modest, unostentatious little crown, still it was there—"

"Nonsense, there was nothing of the sort."

"Yes, there was; it shone unseen. But if I had been there, standing among the shrubbery, one of those times, I should have seen it."

"God knows what you would have seen. But you were not there. Instead of that, it was my husband who came out of the shrubbery one day, with my father. I was afraid they had been listening to our prattle—"

"So it was there, then, madame, that you first met your husband?"

"Yes, there it was I saw him first," she said, in quite a glad, strong voice; she smiled, and as she did so the little blue vein came out and gave her face a constrained and anxious expression. "He was calling on my father on business, you see. Next day he came to dinner, and three days later he proposed for my hand."

"Really? It all happened as fast as that?"

"Yes. Or, rather, it went a little slower after that. For my father was not very much inclined to it, you see, and consented on condition that we wait a long time first. He would rather I had stopped with him, and he had doubts in other ways too. But—"

"But?"

"But I had set my heart on it," she said, smiling; and once more the little vein dominated her whole face with its look of constraint and anxiety.

"Ah, so you set your heart on it."

"Yes, and I displayed great strength of purpose, as you see—"

"As I see. Yes."

"So that my father had to give way in the end."

"And so you forsook him and his fiddle and the old house with the overgrown garden, and the fountain and your six friends, and clave unto Herr Klöterjahn—"

"'And clave unto'—you have such a strange way of saying things, Herr Spinell. Positively biblical. Yes, I forsook all that; nature has arranged things that way."

"Yes, I suppose that is it."

"And it was a question of my happiness—"

"Of course. And happiness came to you?"

"It came, Herr Spinell, in the moment when they brought little Anton to me, our little Anton, and he screamed so lustily with his strong little lungs—he is very, very strong and healthy, you know—"

"This is not the first time, madame, that I have heard you speak of your little Anton's good health and great strength. He must be quite uncommonly healthy?"

"That he is. And looks so absurdly like my husband!"

"Ah! . . . So that was the way of it. And now you are no longer called by the name of Eckhof, but a different one, and you have your healthy little Anton, and are troubled with your trachea."

"Yes. And you are a perfectly enigmatic man, Herr Spinell, I do assure you."

"Yes. God knows you certainly are," said Frau Spatz, who was present on this occasion.

And that conversation, too, gave Herr Klöterjahn's wife food for reflection. Idle as it was, it contained much to nourish those secret thoughts of hers about herself. Was this the baleful influence which was at work? Her weakness increased and fever often supervened, a quiet glow in which she rested with a feeling of mild elevation, to which she yielded in a pensive mood that was a little affected, self-satisfied, even rather self-righteous. When she had not to keep her bed, Herr Spinell would approach her with immense caution, tiptoeing on his great feet; he would pause two paces off, with his body inclined and one leg behind him, and speak in a voice that was hushed with awe, as though he would lift her higher and higher on the tide of his devotion until she rested on billowy cushions of cloud where no shrill sound nor any earthly touch might reach her. And when he did this she would think of the way Herr Klöterjahn said: "Take care, my angel, keep your mouth closed, Gabriele," a way that made her feel as though he had struck her roughly though well-meaningly on the shoulder. Then as fast as she could she would put the memory away and rest in her weakness and elevation of spirit upon the clouds which Herr Spinell spread out for her.

One day she abruptly returned to the talk they had had about her early life. "Is it really true, Herr Spinell," she asked, "that you would have seen the little gold crown?"

Two weeks had passed since that conversation, yet he knew at once what she meant, and his voice shook as he assured her that he would have seen the little crown as she sat among her friends by the fountain—would have caught its fugitive gleam among her locks.

A few days later one of the guests chanced to make a polite inquiry after the health of little Anton. Herr Klöterjahn's wife gave a quick glance at Herr Spinell, who was standing near, and answered in a perfunctory voice:

"Thanks, how should he be? He and my husband are quite well, of course."

There came a day at the end of February, colder, purer, more brilliant than any that had come before it, and high spirits held sway at Einfried. The "heart cases" consulted in groups, flushed of cheek, the diabetic general carolled like a boy out of school, and the gentlemen of the rebellious legs cast aside all restraint. And the reason for all these things was that a sleighing party was in prospect, an excursion in sledges into the mountains, with cracking whips and sleighbells jingling. Dr. Leander had arranged this diversion for his patients.

The serious cases, of course, had to stop at home. Poor things! The other guests arranged to keep it from them; it did them good to practise this much sympathy and consideration. But a few of those remained at home who might very well have gone. Fräulein von Osterloh was of course excused, she had too much on her mind to permit her even to think of going. She was needed at home, and at home she remained. But the disappointment was general when Herr Klöterjahn's wife announced her intention of stopping away. Dr. Leander exhorted her to come and get the benefit of the fresh air—but in vain. She said she was not up to it, she had a headache, she felt too weak—they had to resign themselves. The cynical gentleman took occasion to say:

"You will see, the dissipated baby will stop at home too."

And he proved to be right, for Herr Spinell gave out that he intended to "work" that afternoon—he was prone thus to characterize his dubious activities. Anyhow, not a soul regretted his absence; nor did they take more to heart the news that Frau Magistrate Spatz had decided to keep her young friend company at home— sleighing made her feel sea-sick.

Luncheon on the great day was eaten as early as twelve o'clock, and immediately thereafter the sledges drew up in front of Einfried. The guests came through the garden in little groups, warmly wrapped, excited, full of eager anticipation. Herr Klöterjahn's wife stood with Frau Spatz at the glass door which gave on the terrace, while Herr Spinell watched the setting-forth from above, at the window of his room. They saw the little struggles that took place for the best seats, amid joking and laughter; and Fräulein von Osterloh, with a fur boa round her neck, running from one sleigh to the other and shoving baskets of provisions under the seats; they saw Dr. Leander, with his fur cap pulled low on his brow, marshalling the whole scene with his spectacle-lenses glittering, to make sure everything was ready. At last he took his own seat and gave the signal to drive off. The horses started up, a few of the ladies shrieked and collapsed, the bells jingled, the short-shafted whips cracked and their long lashes trailed across the snow; Fräulein von Osterloh stood at the gate waving her handkerchief until the train rounded a curve and disappeared; slowly the merry tinkling died away. Then she turned and hastened back through the garden in pursuit of her duties; the two ladies left the glass door, and almost at the same time Herr Spinell abandoned his post of observation above.

Quiet reigned at Einfried. The party would not return before evening. The serious cases lay in their rooms and suffered. Herr Klöterjahn's wife took a short turn with her friend, then they went to their respective chambers. Herr Spinell kept to his, occupied in his own way. Towards four o'clock the ladies were served with half a litre of milk apiece, and Herr Spinell with a light tea. Soon after, Herr Klöterjahn's wife tapped on the wall between her room and Frau Spatz's and called:

"Shan't we go down to the salon, Frau Spatz? I have nothing to do up here."

"In just a minute, my dear," answered she. "I'll just put on my shoes—if you will wait a minute. I have been lying down."

The salon, naturally, was empty. The ladies took seats by the fireplace. The Frau Magistrate embroidered flowers on a strip of canvas; Herr Klöterjahn's wife took a few stitches too, but soon let her work fall in her lap and, leaning on the arm of her chair, fell to dreaming. At length she made some remark, hardly worth the trouble of opening her lips for; the Frau Magistrate asked what she said, and she had to make the effort of saying it all over again, which quite wore her out. But just then steps were heard outside, the door opened, and Herr Spinell came in.

"Shall I be disturbing you?" he asked mildly from the threshold, addressing Herr Klöterjahn's wife and her alone; bending over her, as it were, from a distance, in the tender, hovering way he had.

The young wife answered:

"Why should you? The room is free to everybody—and besides, why would it be disturbing us? On the contrary, I am convinced that I am boring Frau Spatz."

He had no ready answer, merely smiled and showed his carious teeth, then went hesitatingly up to the glass door, the ladies watching him, and stood with his back to them looking out. Presently he half turned round, still gazing into the garden, and said:

"The sun has gone in. The sky clouded over without our seeing it. The dark is coming on already."

"Yes, it is all overcast," replied Herr Klöterjahn's wife. "It looks as though our sleighing party would have some snow after all. Yesterday at this hour it was still broad daylight, now it is already getting dark."

"Well," he said, "after all these brilliant weeks a little dullness is good for the eyes. The sun shines with the same penetrating clearness upon the lovely and the commonplace, and I for one am positively grateful to it for finally going under a cloud."

"Don't you like the sun, Herr Spinell?"

"Well, I am no painter . . . when there is no sun one becomes more profound. . . . It is a thick layer of greyish-white cloud. Perhaps it means thawing weather for tomorrow. But, madame, let me advise you not to sit there at the back of the room looking at your embroidery."

"Don't be alarmed; I am not looking at it. But what else is there to do?"

He had sat down on the piano-stool, resting one arm on the lid of the instrument.

"Music," he said. "If we could only have a little music here. The English children sing darky songs, and that is all."

"And yesterday afternoon Fräulein von Osterloh rendered 'Cloister Bells' at top speed," remarked Herr Klöterjahn's wife.

"But you play, madame!" said he, in an imploring tone. He stood up. "Once you used to play every day with your father."

"Yes, Herr Spinell, in those old days I did. In the time of the fountain, you know."

"Play to us today," he begged. "Just a few notes—this once. If you knew how I long for some music—"

"But our family physician, as well as Dr. Leander, expressly forbade it, Herr Spinell."

"But they aren't here—either of them. We are free agents. Just a few bars—"

"No, Herr Spinell, it would be no use. Goodness knows what marvels you expect of me—and I have forgotten everything I knew. Truly. I know scarcely anything by heart."

"Well, then, play that scarcely anything. But there are notes here too. On top of the piano. No, that is nothing. But here is some Chopin."

"Chopin?"

"Yes, the Nocturnes. All we have to do is to light the candles—"

"Pray don't ask me to play, Herr Spinell. I must not. Suppose it were to be bad for me—"

He was silent; standing there in the light of the two candles, with his great feet, in his long black tail-coat, with his beardless face and greying hair. His hands hung down at his sides.

"Then, madame, I will ask no more," he said at length, in a low voice. "If you are afraid it will do you harm, then we shall leave the beauty dead and dumb that might have come alive beneath your fingers. You were not always so sensible; at least not when it was the opposite question from what it is today, and you had to decide to take leave of beauty. Then you did not care about your bodily welfare; you showed a firm and unhesitating resolution when you left the fountain and laid aside the little gold crown. Listen," he said, after a pause, and his voice dropped still lower; "if you sit down and play as you used to play when your father stood behind you and brought tears to your eyes with the tones of his violin—

who knows but the little gold crown might glimmer once more in your hair. . . ."

"Really," said she, with a smile. Her voice happened to break on the word, it sounded husky and barely audible. She cleared her throat and went on:

"Are those really Chopin's Nocturnes you have there?"

"Yes, here they are open at the place; everything is ready."

"Well, then, in God's name, I will play one," said she. "But only one—do you hear? In any case, one will do you, I am sure."

With which she got up, laid aside her work, and went to the piano. She seated herself on the music-stool, on a few bound volumes, arranged the lights, and turned over the notes. Herr Spinell had drawn up a chair and sat beside her, like a music-master.

She played the Nocturne in E major, opus 9, number 2. If her playing had really lost very much then she must originally have been a consummate artist. The piano was mediocre, but after the first few notes she learned to control it. She displayed a nervous feeling for modulations of timbre and a joy in mobility of rhythm that amounted to the fantastic. Her attack was at once firm and soft. Under her hands the very last drop of sweetness was wrung from the melody; the embellishments seemed to cling with slow grace about her limbs.

She wore the same frock as on the day of her arrival, the dark, heavy bodice with the velvet arabesques in high relief, that gave her head and hands such an unearthly fragile look. Her face did not change as she played, but her lips seemed to become more clear-cut, the shadows deepened at the corners of her eyes. When she finished she laid her hands in her lap and went on looking at the notes. Herr Spinell sat motionless.

She played another Nocturne, and then a third. Then she stood up, but only to look on the top of the piano for more music.

It occurred to Herr Spinell to look at the black-bound volumes on the piano-stool. All at once he uttered an incoherent exclamation, his large white hands clutching at one of the books.

"Impossible! No, it cannot be," he said. "But yes, it is. Guess what this is—what was lying here! Guess what I have in my hands."

"What?" she asked.

Mutely he showed her the title-page. He was quite pale; he let the book sink and looked at her, his lips trembling.

"Really? How did that get here? Give it me," was all she said; set the notes on the piano and after a moment's silence began to play.

He sat beside her, bent forward, his hands between his knees, his head bowed. She played the beginning with exaggerated and tormenting slowness, with painfully long pauses between the single figures. The *Sehnsuchtsmotiv*,[5] roving lost and forlorn like a voice in the night, lifted its trembling question. Then silence, a waiting. And lo, an answer: the same timorous, lonely note, only clearer, only tenderer. Silence again. And then, with that marvellous muted *sforzando*,[6] like mounting passion, the love-motif came in; reared and soared and yearned ecstatically upward to its consummation, sank back, was resolved; the cellos taking up the melody to carry it on with their deep, heavy notes of rapture and despair.

Not unsuccessfully did the player seek to suggest the orchestral effects upon the poor instrument at her command. The violin runs of the great climax rang out with brilliant precision. She played with a fastidious reverence, lingering on each figure, bringing out each detail, with the self-forgotten concentration of the priest who lifts the Host above his head. Here two forces, two beings, strove towards each other, in transports of joy and pain; here they embraced and became one in delirious yearning after eternity and the absolute. . . . The prelude flamed up and died away. She stopped at the point where the curtains part, and sat speechless, staring at the keys.

But the boredom of Frau Spatz had by now reached that pitch where it distorts the countenance of man, makes the eyes protrude from the head, and lends the features a corpse-like and terrifying aspect. More than that, this music acted on the nerves that controlled her digestion, producing in her dyspeptic organism such *malaise* that she was really afraid she would have an attack.

"I shall have to go up to my room," she said weakly. "Good-bye; I will come back soon."

She went out. Twilight was far advanced. Outside the snow fell thick and soundlessly upon the terrace. The two tapers cast a flickering, circumscribed light.

"The Second Act," he whispered, and she turned the pages and began.

What was it dying away in the distance—the ring of a horn? The rustle of leaves? The rippling of a brook? Silence and night crept up over grove and house; the power of longing had full sway, no prayers or warnings could avail against it. The holy mystery was consummated. The light was quenched; with a strange clouding of the timbre the death-motif sank down: white-veiled desire, by passion driven, fluttered towards love as through the dark it groped to meet her.

Ah, boundless, unquenchable exultation of union in the eternal

5. literally, "motif of longing"; a theme from Wagner's *Tristan and Isolde* (1865).

6. literally, "forcing"; used in music to indicate that a note or chord is to be rendered with special emphasis.

beyond! Freed from torturing error, escaped from fettering space
and time, the Thou and the I, the Thine and the Mine at one
forever in a sublimity of bliss! The day might part them with de-
luding show; but when night fell, then by the power of the potion
they would see clear. To him who has looked upon the night of
death and known its secret sweets, to him day never can be aught
but vain, nor can he know a longing save for night, eternal, real,
in which he is made one with love.

O night of love, sink downwards and enfold them, grant them
the oblivion they crave, release them from this world of partings
and betrayals. Lo, the last light is quenched. Fancy and thought
alike are lost, merged in the mystic shade that spread its wings of
healing above their madness and despair. "Now, when deceitful
daylight pales, when my raptured eye grows dim, then all that from
which the light of day would shut my sight, seeking to blind me
with false show, to the stanchless torments of my longing soul—
then, ah, then, O wonder of fulfilment, even then I am the world!"
Followed Brangäna's dark notes of warning, and then those soaring
violins so higher than all reason.

"I cannot understand it all, Herr Spinell. Much of it I only
divine. What does it mean, this 'even then I am the world'?"

He explained, in a few low-toned words.

"Yes, yes. It means that. How is it you can understand it all so
well, yet cannot play it?"

Strangely enough, he was not proof against this simple question.
He coloured, twisted his hands together, shrank into his chair.

"The two things seldom happen together," he wrung from his
lips at last. "No, I cannot play. But go on."

And on they went, into the intoxicated music of the love-mystery.
Did love ever die? Tristan's love? The love of thy Isolde, and of
mine? Ah, no, death cannot touch that which can never die—and
what of him could die, save what distracts and tortures love and
severs united lovers? Love joined the two in sweet conjunction,
death was powerless to sever such a bond, save only when death
was given to one with the very life of the other. Their voices rose
in mystic unison, rapt in the wordless hope of that death-in-love,
of endless oneness in the wonder-kingdom of the night. Sweet
night! Eternal night of love! And all-encompassing land of rapture!
Once envisaged or divined, what eye could bear to open again on
desolate dawn? Forfend such fears, most gentle death! Release these
lovers quite from need of waking. Oh, tumultuous storm of
rhythms! Oh, glad chromatic upward surge of metaphysical perception! How find, how bind this bliss so far remote from parting's
torturing pangs? Ah, gentle glow of longing, soothing and kind, ah,

yielding sweet-sublime, ah, raptured sinking into the twilight of eternity! Thou Isolde, Tristan I, yet no more Tristan, no more Isolde. . . .

All at once something startling happened. The musician broke off and peered into the darkness with her hand above her eyes. Herr Spinell turned round quickly in his chair. The corridor door had opened, a sinister form appeared, leant on the arm of a second form. It was a guest of Einfried, one of those who, like themselves, had been in no state to undertake the sleigh-ride, but had passed this twilight hour in one of her pathetic, instinctive rounds of the house. It was that patient who had borne fourteen children and was no longer capable of a single thought; it was Frau Pastor Höhlenrauch, on the arm of her nurse. She did not look up; with groping step she paced the dim background of the room and vanished by the opposite door, rigid and still, like a lost and wandering soul. Stillness reigned once more.

"That was Frau Pastor Höhlenrauch," he said.

"Yes, that was poor Frau Höhlenrauch," she answered. Then she turned over some leaves and played the finale, played Isolde's song of love and death.

How colourless and clear were her lips, how deep the shadows lay beneath her eyes! The little pale-blue vein in her transparent brow showed fearfully plain and prominent. Beneath her flying fingers the music mounted to its unbelievable climax and was resolved in that ruthless, sudden *pianissimo* which is like having the ground glide from beneath one's feet, yet like a sinking too into the very deeps of desire. Followed the immeasurable plenitude of that vast redemption and fulfilment; it was repeated, swelled into a deafening, unquenchable tumult of immense appeasement that wove and welled and seemed about to die away, only to swell again and weave the *Sehnsuchtsmotiv* into its harmony; at length to breathe an outward breath and die, faint on the air, and soar away. Profound stillness.

They both listened, their heads on one side.

"Those are bells," she said.

"It is the sleighs," he said. "I will go now."

He rose and walked across the room. At the door he halted, then turned and shifted uneasily from one foot to the other. And then, some fifteen or twenty paces from her, it came to pass that he fell upon his knees, both knees, without a sound. His long black coat spread out on the floor. He held his hands clasped over his mouth, and his shoulders heaved.

She sat there with hands in her lap, leaning forward, turned away from the piano, and looked at him. Her face wore a distressed, uncertain smile, while her eyes searched the dimness at the back of the room, searched so painfully, so dreamily, she seemed hardly able to focus her gaze.

The jingling of sleigh-bells came nearer and nearer, there was the crack of whips, a babel of voices.

The sleighing party had taken place on the twenty-sixth of February, and was talked of for long afterwards. The next day, February twenty-seventh, a day of thaw, that set everything to melt ing and dripping, splashing and running, Herr Klöterjahn's wife was in capital health and spirits. On the twenty-eighth she brought up a little blood—not much, still it was blood, and accompanied by far greater loss of strength than ever before. She went to bed.

Dr. Leander examined her, stony-faced. He prescribed according to the dictates of science—morphia, little pieces of ice, absolute quiet. Next day, on account of pressure of work, he turned her case over to Dr. Müller, who took it on in humility and meekness of spirit and according to the letter of his contract—a quiet, pallid, insignificant little man, whose unadvertised activities were conse crated to the care of the slight cases and the hopeless ones.

Dr. Müller presently expressed the view that the separation be tween Frau Klöterjahn and her spouse had lasted overlong. It would be well if Herr Klöterjahn, in case his flourishing business per mitted, were to make another visit to Einfried. One might write him—or even wire. And surely it would benefit the young mother's health and spirits if he were to bring young Anton with him— quite aside from the pleasure it would give the physicians to behold with their own eyes this so healthy little Anton.

And Herr Klöterjahn came. He got Herr Müller's little wire and arrived from the Baltic coast. He got out of the carriage, ordered coffee and rolls, and looked considerably aggrieved.

"My dear sir," he asked, "what is the matter? Why have I been summoned?"

"Because it is desirable that you should be near your wife," Dr. Müller replied.

"Desirable! Desirable! But is it *necessary*? It is a question of ex pense with me—times are poor and railway journeys cost money. Was it imperative I should take this whole day's journey? If it were the lungs that are attacked, I should say nothing. But as it is only the trachea, thank God—"

"Herr Klöterjahn," said Dr. Müller mildly, "in the first place the trachea is an important organ. . . ." He ought not to have said "in the first place," because he did not go on to the second.

But there also arrived at Einfried, in Herr Klöterjahn's company, a full-figured personage arrayed all in red and gold and plaid, and she it was who carried on her arm Anton Klöterjahn, junior, that healthy little Anton. Yes, there he was, and nobody could deny that he was healthy even to excess. Pink and white and plump and fragrant, in fresh and immaculate attire, he rested heavily upon the bare red arm of his bebraided body-servant, consumed huge quantities of milk and chopped beef, shouted and screamed, and in every way surrendered himself to his instincts.

Our author from the window of his chamber had seen him arrive. With a peculiar gaze, both veiled and piercing, he fixed young Anton with his eye as he was carried from the carriage into the house. He stood there a long time with the same expression on his face.

Herr Spinell was sitting in his room "at work."

His room was like all the others at Einfried—old-fashioned, simple, and distinguished. The massive chest of drawers was mounted with brass lions' heads; the tall mirror on the wall was not a single surface, but made up of many little panes set in lead. There was no carpet on the polished blue paved floor, the stiff legs of the furniture prolonged themselves on it in clear-cut shadows. A spacious writing-table stood at the window, across whose panes the author had drawn the folds of a yellow curtain, in all probability that he might feel more retired.

In the yellow twilight he bent over the table and wrote—wrote one of those numerous letters which he sent weekly to the post and to which, quaintly enough, he seldom or never received an answer. A large, thick quire of paper lay before him, in whose upper left-hand corner was a curious involved drawing of a landscape and the name Detlev Spinell in the very latest thing in lettering. He was covering the page with a small, painfully neat, and punctiliously traced script.

"Sir:" he wrote, "I address the following lines to you because I cannot help it; because what I have to say so fills and shakes and tortures me, the words come in such a rush, that I should choke if I did not take this means to relieve myself."

If the truth were told, this about the rush of words was quite simply wide of the fact. And God knows what sort of vanity it was made Herr Spinell put it down. For his words did not come in a rush; they came with such pathetic slowness, considering the man was a writer by trade, you would have drawn the conclusion, watching him, that a writer is one to whom writing comes harder than to anybody else.

He held between two finger-tips one of those curious downy hairs he had on his cheek, and twirled it round and round, whole quarter-hours at a time, gazing into space and not coming forwards by a single line; then wrote a few words, daintily, and stuck again. Yet so much was true: that what had managed to get written sounded fluent and vigorous, though the matter was odd enough, even almost equivocal, and at times impossible to follow.

"I feel," the letter went on, "an imperative necessity to make you see what I see; to show you through my eyes, illuminated by the same power of language that clothes them for me, all the things which have stood before my inner eye for weeks, like an indelible vision. It is my habit to yield to the impulse which urges me to put my own experiences into flamingly right and unforgettable words and to give them to the world. And therefore hear me.

"I will do no more than relate what has been and what is: I will merely tell a story, a brief, unspeakably touching story, without comment, blame, or passing of judgment, simply in my own words. It is the story of Gabriele Eckhof, of the woman whom you, sir, call your wife—and mark you this: it is your story, it happened to you, yet it will be I who will for the first time lift it for you to the level of an experience.

"Do you remember the garden, the old, overgrown garden behind the grey patrician house? The moss was green in the crannies of its weather-beaten wall, and behind the wall dreams and neglect held sway. Do you remember the fountain in the centre? The pale mauve lilies leaned over its crumbling rim, the little stream prattled softly as it fell upon the riven paving. The summer day was drawing to its close.

"Seven maidens sat circlewise round the fountain; but the seventh, or rather the first and only one, was not like the others, for the sinking sun seemed to be weaving a queenly coronal[7] among her locks. Her eyes were like troubled dreams, and yet her pure lips wore a smile.

"They were singing. They lifted their little faces to the leaping streamlet and watched its charming curve droop earthward—their music hovered round it as it leaped and danced. Perhaps their slim hands were folded in their laps the while they sang.

"Can you, sir, recall the scene? Or did you ever see it? No, you saw it not. Your eyes were not formed to see it nor your ears to catch the chaste music of their song. You saw it not, or else you would have forbade your lungs to breathe, your heart to beat. You must have turned aside and gone back to your own life, taking with you what you had seen to preserve it in the depth of your soul to the end of your earthly life, a sacred and inviolable relic. But what did you do?

"That scene, sir, was an end and culmination. Why did you come to spoil it, to give it a sequel, to turn it into the channels of ugly and commonplace life? It was a peaceful apotheosis and a

7. garland.

moving, bathed in a sunset beauty of decadence, decay, and death. An ancient stock, too exhausted and refined for life and action, stood there at the end of its days; its latest manifestations were those of art: violin notes, full of that melancholy understanding which is ripeness for death. . . . Did you look into her eyes—those eyes where tears so often stood, lured by the dying sweetness of the violin? Her six friends may have had souls that belonged to life; but hers, the queen's and sister's, death and beauty had claimed for their own.

"You saw it, that deathly beauty; saw, and coveted. The sight of that touching purity moved you with no awe or trepidation. And it was not enough for you to see, you must possess, you must use, you must desecrate. . . . It was the refinement of a choice you made— you are a gourmand, sir, a plebeian gourmand, a peasant with taste.

"Once more let me say that I have no wish to offend you. What I have just said is not an affront; it is a statement, a simple, psychological statement of your simple personality—a personality which for literary purposes is entirely uninteresting. I make the statement solely because I feel an impulse to clarify for you your own thoughts and actions; because it is my inevitable task on this earth to call things by their right names, to make them speak, to illuminate the unconscious. The world is full of what I call the unconscious type, and I cannot endure it; I cannot endure all these unconscious types! I cannot bear all this dull, uncomprehending, unperceiving living and behaving, this world of maddening naïveté about me! It tortures me until I am driven irresistibly to set it all in relief, in the round, to explain, express, and make self-conscious everything in the world —so far as my powers will reach—quite unhampered by the result, whether it be for good or evil, whether it brings consolation and healing or piles grief on grief.

"You, sir, as I said, are a plebeian gourmand, a peasant with taste. You stand upon an extremely low evolutionary level; your own constitution is coarse-fibred. But wealth and a sedentary habit of life have brought about in you a corruption of the nervous system, as sudden as it is unhistoric; and this corruption has been accompanied by a lascivious refinement in your choice of gratifications. It is altogether possible that the muscles of your gullet began to contract, as at the sight of some particularly rare dish, when you conceived the idea of making Gabriele Eckhof your own.

"In short, you lead her idle will astray, you beguile her out of that moss-grown garden into the ugliness of life, you give her your own vulgar name and make of her a married woman, a housewife, a mother. You take that deathly beauty—spent, aloof, flowering in lofty unconcern of the uses of this world—and debase it to the service of common things, you sacrifice it to that stupid, contemptible, clumsy graven image we call 'nature'—and not the faintest suspicion of the vileness of your conduct visits your peasant soul.

"Again. What is the result? This being, whose eyes are like troubled dreams, she bears you a child; and so doing she endows the new life, a gross continuation of its author's own, with all the blood, all the physical energy she possesses—and she dies. She dies, sir! And if she does not go hence with your vulgarity upon her head; if at the very last she has lifted herself out of the depths of degradation, and passes in an ecstasy, with the deathly kiss of beauty on her brow—well, it is I, sir, who have seen to that! You, meanwhile, were probably spending your time with chambermaids in dark corners.

"But your son, Gabriele Eckhof's son, is alive; he is living and flourishing. Perhaps he will continue in the way of his father, become a well-fed, trading, tax-paying citizen; a capable, philistine pillar of society; in any case, a tone-deaf, normally functioning individual, responsible, sturdy, and stupid, troubled by not a doubt.

"Kindly permit me to tell you, sir, that I hate you. I hate you and your child, as I hate the life of which you are the representative: cheap, ridiculous, but yet triumphant life, the everlasting antipodes and deadly enemy of beauty. I cannot say I despise you—for I am honest. You are stronger than I. I have no armour for the struggle between us, I have only the Word, avenging weapon of the weak. Today I have availed myself of this weapon. This letter is nothing but an act of revenge—you see how honourable I am—and if any word of mine is sharp and bright and beautiful enough to strike home, to make you feel the presence of a power you do not know, to shake even a minute your robust equilibrium, I shall rejoice indeed.—DETLEV SPINELL."

And Herr Spinell put this screed into an envelope, applied a stamp and a many-flourished address, and committed it to the post.

Herr Klöterjahn knocked on Herr Spinell's door. He carried a sheet of paper in his hand covered with neat script, and he looked like a man bent on energetic action. The post office had done its duty, the letter had taken its appointed way: it had travelled from Einfried to Einfried and reached the hand for which it was meant. It was now four o'clock in the afternoon.

Herr Klöterjahn's entry found Herr Spinell sitting on the sofa reading his own novel with the appalling cover-design. He rose and gave his caller a surprised and inquiring look, though at the same time he distinctly flushed.

"Good afternoon," said Herr Klöterjahn. "Pardon the interruption. But may I ask if you wrote this?" He held up in his left hand the sheet inscribed with fine clear characters and struck it with the back of his right and made it crackle. Then he stuffed that hand into the pocket of his easy-fitting trousers, put his head on one side, and opened his mouth, in a way some people have, to listen.

Herr Spinell, curiously enough, smiled; he smiled engagingly, with a rather confused, apologetic air. He put his hand to his head as though trying to recollect himself, and said:

"Ah!—yes, quite right, I took the liberty—"

The fact was, he had given in to his natural man today and slept nearly up to midday, with the result that he was suffering from a bad conscience and a heavy head, was nervous and incapable of putting up a fight. And the spring air made him limp and good-for-nothing. So much we must say in extenuation of the utterly silly figure he cut in the interview which followed.

"Ah? Indeed! Very good!" said Herr Klöterjahn. He dug his chin into his chest, elevated his brows, stretched his arms, and indulged in various other antics by way of getting down to business after his introductory question. But unfortunately he so much enjoyed the figure he cut that he rather overshot the mark, and the rest of the scene hardly lived up to this preliminary pantomime. However, Herr Spinell went rather pale.

"Very good!" repeated Herr Klöterjahn. "Then permit me to give you an answer in person; it strikes me as idiotic to write pages of letter to a person when you can speak to him any hour of the day."

"Well, idiotic . . ." Herr Spinell said, with his apologetic smile. He sounded almost meek.

"Idiotic!" repeated Herr Klöterjahn, nodding violently in token of the soundness of his position. "And I should not demean myself to answer this scrawl; to tell the truth, I should have thrown it away at once if I had not found in it the explanation of certain changes —however, that is no affair of yours, and has nothing to do with the thing anyhow. I am a man of action, I have other things to do than to think about your unspeakable visions."

"I wrote 'indelible vision,'" said Herr Spinell, drawing himself up. This was the only moment at which he displayed a little self-respect.

"Indelible, unspeakable," responded Herr Klöterjahn, referring to the text. "You write a villainous hand, sir; you would not get a position in my office, let me tell you. It looks clear enough at first, but when you come to study it, it is full of shakes and quavers. But that is your affair, it's no business of mine. What I have come to say to you is that you are a tomfool—which you probably know already. Furthermore, you are a cowardly sneak; I don't suppose I have to give the evidence for that either. My wife wrote me once that when you meet a woman you don't look her square in the face, but just give her a side squint, so as to carry away a good impression, because you are afraid of the reality. I should probably have heard more of the same sort of stories about you, only unfortunately she stopped mentioning you. But this is the kind of thing you are: you talk so much about 'beauty'; you are all chicken-livered hypocrisy and cant—which is probably at the bottom of your impudent allusion to out-of-the-way corners too. That ought to crush me, of course, but it just makes me laugh—it doesn't do a thing but make me laugh! Understand? Have I clarified your thoughts and actions for you, you pitiable object, you? Though of course it is not my invariable calling—"

" '*Inevitable*' was the word I used," Herr Spinell said; but he did not insist on the point. He stood there, crestfallen, like a big, unhappy, chidden, grey-haired schoolboy.

"Invariable or inevitable, whichever you like—anyhow you are a contemptible cur, and that I tell you. You see me every day at table, you bow and smirk and say good-morning—and one fine day you send me a scrawl full of idiotic abuse. Yes, you've a lot of courage—on paper! And it's not only this ridiculous letter—you have been intriguing behind my back. I can see that now. Though you need not flatter yourself it did any good. If you imagine you put any ideas into my wife's head you never were more mistaken in your life. And if you think she behaved any different when we came from what she always does, then you just put the cap onto your own foolishness. She did not kiss the little chap, that's true, but it was only a precaution, because they have the idea now that the trouble is with her lungs, and in such cases you can't tell whether—though that still remains to be proved, no matter what you say with your 'She dies, sir,' you silly ass!"

Here Herr Klöterjahn paused for breath. He was in a furious passion; he kept stabbing the air with his right forefinger and crumpling the sheet of paper in his other hand. His face, between the blond English mutton-chops, was frightfully red and his dark brow was rent with swollen veins like lightnings of scorn.

"You hate me," he went on, "and you would despise me if I were not stronger than you. Yes, you're right there! I've got my heart in the right place, by God, and you've got yours mostly in the seat of your trousers. I would most certainly hack you into bits if it weren't against the law, you and your gabble about the 'Word,' you skulking fool! But I have no intention of putting up with your insults; and when I show this part about the vulgar name to my lawyer at home, you will very likely get a little surprise. My name, sir, is a first-rate name, and I have made it so by my own efforts. You know better than I do whether anybody would ever lend you a penny piece on yours, you lazy lout! The law defends people against the kind you are! You are a common danger, you are enough to drive a body crazy! But you're left this time, my master! I don't let individuals like you get the best of me so fast! I've got my heart in the right place—"

Herr Klöterjahn's excitement had really reached a pitch. He shrieked, he bellowed, over and over again, that his heart was in the right place.

" 'They were singing.' Exactly. Well, they weren't. They were knitting. And if I heard what they said, it was about a recipe for potato pancakes; and when I show my father-in-law that about the old decayed family you'll probably have a libel suit on your hands. 'Did you see the picture?' Yes, of course I saw it; only I don't see why that should make me hold my breath and run away. I don't leer at women out of the corner of my eye; I look at them square, and if I like their looks I go for them. I have my heart in the right place—"

Somebody knocked. Knocked eight or ten times, quite fast, one after the other—a sudden, alarming little commotion that made Herr Klöterjahn pause; and an unsteady voice that kept tripping over itself in its haste and distress said:

"Herr Klöterjahn, Herr Klöterjahn—oh, is Herr Klöterjahn there?"

"Stop outside," said Herr Klöterjahn, in a growl. . . . "What's the matter? I'm busy talking."

"Oh, Herr Klöterjahn," said the quaking, breaking voice, "you must come! The doctors are there too—oh, it is all so dreadfully sad—"

He took one step to the door and tore it open. Frau Magistrate Spatz was standing there. She had her handkerchief before her mouth, and great egg-shaped tears rolled into it, two by two.

"Herr Klöterjahn," she got out. "It is so frightfully sad. . . . She has brought up so much blood, such a horrible lot of blood. . . . She was sitting up quite quietly in bed and humming a little snatch of music . . . and there it came . . . my God, such a quantity you never saw. . . ."

"Is she dead?" yelled Herr Klöterjahn. As he spoke he clutched the Rätin by the arm and pulled her to and fro on the sill. "Not quite? Not dead; she can see me, can't she? Brought up a little blood again, from the lung, eh? Yes, I give in, it may be from the lung. Gabriele!" he suddenly cried out, and his eyes filled with tears; you could see what a burst of good, warm, honest human feeling came over him. "Yes, I'm coming," he said, and dragged the Rätin after him as he went with long strides down the corridor. You could still hear his voice, from quite a distance, sounding fainter and fainter: "Not quite, eh? From the lung?"

Herr Spinell stood still on the spot where he had stood during the whole of Herr Klöterjahn's rudely interrupted call and looked out the open door. At length he took a couple of steps and listened down the corridor. But all was quiet, so he closed the door and came back into the room.

He looked at himself awhile in the glass, then he went up to the writing-table, took a little flask and a glass out of a drawer, and drank a cognac—for which nobody can blame him. Then he stretched himself out on the sofa and closed his eyes.

The upper half of the window was down. Outside in the garden birds were twittering; those dainty, saucy little notes held all the spring, finely and penetratingly expressed. Herr Spinell spoke once: "*Invariable calling*," he said, and moved his head and drew in the air through his teeth as though his nerves pained him violently.

Impossible to recover any poise or tranquillity. Crude experiences like this were too much—he was not made for them. By a sequence of emotions, the analysis of which would lead us too far afield, Herr Spinell arrived at the decision that it would be well for him to have a little out-of-doors exercise. He took his hat and went downstairs.

As he left the house and issued into the mild, fragrant air, he turned his head and lifted his eyes, slowly, scanning the house until he reached one of the windows, a curtained window, on which his gaze rested awhile, fixed and sombre. Then he laid his hands on his back and moved away across the gravel path. He moved in deep thought.

The beds were still straw-covered, the trees and bushes bare; but the snow was gone, the path was only damp in spots. The large garden with its grottoes, bowers and little pavilions lay in the splendid colourful afternoon light, strong shadow and rich, golden sun, and the dark network of branches stood out sharp and articulate against the bright sky.

It was about that hour of the afternoon when the sun takes shape, and from being a formless volume of light turns to a visibly sinking disk, whose milder, more saturated glow the eye can tolerate. Herr Spinell did not see the sun, the direction the path took hid it from his view. He walked with bent head and hummed a strain of music, a short phrase, a figure that mounted wailingly and complainingly upward—the *Sehnsuchtsmotiv*. . . . But suddenly, with a start, a quick, jerky intake of breath, he stopped, as though rooted to the path, and gazed straight ahead of him, with brows fiercely gathered, staring eyes, and an expression of horrified repulsion.

The path had curved just here, he was facing the setting sun. It stood large and slantwise in the sky, crossed by two narrow strips of gold-rimmed cloud; it set the tree-tops aglow and poured its red-gold radiance across the garden. And there, erect in the path, in the midst of the glory, with the sun's mighty aureola[8] above her head, there confronted him an exuberant figure, all arrayed in red and gold and plaid. She had one hand on her swelling hip, with the other she moved to and fro the graceful little perambulator. And in this perambulator sat the child—sat Anton Klöterjahn, junior, Gabriele Eckhof's fat son.

There he sat among his cushions, in a woolly white jacket and large white hat, plump-cheeked, well cared for, and magnificent; and his blithe unerring gaze encountered Herr Spinell's. The novelist pulled himself together. Was he not a man, had he not the power to pass this unexpected, sun-kindled apparition there in the path and continue on his walk? But Anton Klöterjahn began to laugh and shout—most horrible to see. He squealed, he crowed with inconceivable delight—it was positively uncanny to hear him.

God knows what had taken him; perhaps the sight of Herr Spinell's long, black figure set him off; perhaps an attack of sheer animal spirits gave rise to his wild outburst of merriment. He had a bone teething-ring in one hand and a tin rattle in the other; and these two objects he flung aloft with shoutings, shook them to and fro, and clashed them together in the air, as though purposely to frighten Herr Spinell. His eyes were almost shut, his mouth gaped open till all the rosy gums were displayed; and as he shouted he rolled his head about in excess of mirth.

Herr Spinell turned round and went thence. Pursued by the youthful Klöterjahn's joyous screams, he went away across the gravel, walking stiffly, yet not without grace; his gait was the hesitating gait of one who would disguise the fact that, inwardly, he is running away.

8. radiance.

FRANZ KAFKA
(1883–1924)
The Metamorphosis (Die Verwandlung) *

As Gregor Samsa awoke one morning from uneasy dreams he found himself transformed in his bed into a gigantic insect. He was lying on his hard, as it were armor-plated, back and when he lifted his head a little he could see his dome-like brown belly divided into stiff arched segments on top of which the bed quilt could hardly

* 1916. Reprinted by permission of Schocken Books Inc. from *The Penal Colony* by Franz Kafka. Copyright © 1948 by Schocken Books Inc., New York. Translated by Willa and Edwin Muir.

keep in position and was about to slide off completely. His numerous legs, which were pitifully thin compared to the rest of his bulk, waved helplessly before his eyes.

What has happened to me? he thought. It was no dream. His room, a regular human bedroom, only rather too small, lay quiet between the four familiar walls. Above the table on which a collection of cloth samples was unpacked and spread out—Samsa was a commercial traveler—hung the picture which he had recently cut out of an illustrated magazine and put into a pretty gilt frame. It showed a lady, with a fur cap on and a fur stole, sitting upright and holding out to the spectator a huge fur muff into which the whole of her forearm had vanished!

Gregor's eyes turned next to the window, and the overcast sky—one could hear rain drops beating on the window gutter—made him quite melancholy. What about sleeping a little longer and forgetting all this nonsense, he thought, but it could not be done, for he was accustomed to sleep on his right side and in his present condition he could not turn himself over. However violently he forced himself towards his right side he always rolled on to his back again. He tried it at least a hundred times, shutting his eyes to keep from seeing his struggling legs, and only desisted when he began to feel in his side a faint dull ache he had never experienced before.

Oh God, he thought, what an exhausting job I've picked on! Traveling about day in, day out. It's much more irritating work than doing the actual business in the office, and on top of that there's the trouble of constant traveling, of worrying about train connections, the bed and irregular meals, casual acquaintances that are always new and never become intimate friends. The devil take it all! He felt a slight itching up on his belly; slowly pushed himself on his back nearer to the top of the bed so that he could lift his head more easily; identified the itching place which was surrounded by many small white spots the nature of which he could not understand and made to touch it with a leg, but drew the leg back immediately, for the contact made a cold shiver run through him.

He slid down again into his former position. This getting up early, he thought, makes one quite stupid. A man needs his sleep. Other commercials live like harem women. For instance, when I come back to the hotel of a morning to write up the orders I've got, these others are only sitting down to breakfast. Let me just try that with my chief; I'd be sacked on the spot. Anyhow, that might be quite a good thing for me, who can tell? If I didn't have to hold my hand because of my parents I'd have given notice long ago, I'd have gone to the chief and told him exactly what I think of him. That would knock him endways from his desk! It's a queer way of doing, too, this sitting on high at a desk and talking down to employees, especially when they have to come quite near because the chief is hard of hearing. Well, there's still hope; once I've saved enough money to pay back my parents' debts to him—that should take another five or six years—I'll do it without fail. I'll cut myself completely loose then. For the moment, though, I'd better get up, since my train goes at five.

He looked at the alarm clock ticking on the chest. Heavenly Father! he thought. It was half-past six o'clock and the hands were quietly moving on, it was even past the half-hour, it was getting on toward a quarter to seven. Had the alarm clock not gone off? From the bed one could see that it had been properly set for four o'clock; of course it must have gone off. Yes, but was it possible to sleep quietly through that ear-splitting noise? Well, he had not slept quietly, yet apparently all the more soundly for that. But what was he to do now? The next train went at seven o'clock; to catch that he would need to hurry like mad and his samples weren't even packed up, and he himself wasn't feeling particularly fresh and active. And even if he did catch the train he wouldn't avoid a row with the chief, since the firm's porter would have been waiting for the five o'clock train and would have long since reported his failure to turn up. The porter was a creature of the chief's, spineless and stupid. Well, supposing he were to say he was sick? But that would be most unpleasant and would look suspicious, since during his five years' employment he had not been ill once. The chief himself would be sure to come with the sick-insurance doctor, would reproach his parents with their son's laziness and would cut all excuses short by referring to the insurance doctor, who of course regarded all mankind as perfectly healthy malingerers. And would he be so far wrong on this occasion? Gregor really felt quite well, apart from a drowsiness that was utterly superfluous after such a long sleep, and he was even unusually hungry.

As all this was running through his mind at top speed without his being able to decide to leave his bed—the alarm clock had just struck a quarter to seven—there came a cautious tap at the door behind the head of his bed. "Gregor," said a voice—it was his mother's—"it's a quarter to seven. Hadn't you a train to catch?" That gentle voice! Gregor had a shock as he heard his own voice answering hers, unmistakably his own voice, it was true, but with a persistent horrible twittering squeak behind it like an undertone, that left the words in their clear shape only for the first moment and then rose up reverberating round them to destroy their sense, so that one could not be sure one had heard them rightly. Gregor wanted to answer at length and explain everything, but in the circumstances he confined himself to saying: "Yes, yes, thank you, Mother, I'm getting up now." The wooden door between them must have kept the change in his voice from being noticeable outside, for his mother contented herself with this statement and shuffled away. Yet this brief exchange of words had made the other members of the family aware that Gregor was still in the house, as they had not expected, and at one of the side doors his father was already knocking, gently, yet with his fist. "Gregor, Gregor," he called, "what's the matter with you?" And after a little while he called again in a deeper voice: "Gregor! Gregor!" At the other side door his sister was saying in a low, plaintive tone: "Gregor? Aren't you well? Are you needing anything?" He answered them both at once: "I'm just ready," and did his best to make his voice sound as normal as possible by enunciating the words very clearly and leaving long pauses between them. So his father went back to his breakfast, but his sister whispered: "Gregor, open the door, do." However, he was not thinking of opening the door, and felt thankful for the prudent habit he had acquired in traveling of locking all doors during the night, even at home.

His immediate intention was to get up quietly without being disturbed, to put on his clothes and above all eat his breakfast, and only then to consider what else was to be done, since in bed, he was well aware, his meditations would come to no sensible conclusion. He remembered that often enough in bed he had felt small aches and pains, probably caused by awkward postures, which had proved purely imaginary once he got up, and he looked forward eagerly to seeing this morning's delusions gradually fall away. That the change in his voice was nothing but the precursor of a severe chill, a standing ailment of commercial travelers, he had not the least possible doubt.

To get rid of the quilt was quite easy; he had only to inflate himself a little and it fell off by itself. But the next move was difficult, especially because he was so uncommonly broad. He would have needed arms and hands to hoist himself up; instead he had only the numerous little legs which never stopped waving in all directions and which he could not control in the least. When he tried to bend one of them it was the first to stretch itself straight; and did he succeed at last in making it do what he wanted, all the other legs meanwhile waved the more wildly in a high degree of unpleasant agitation. "But what's the use of lying idle in bed," said Gregor to himself.

He thought that he might get out of bed with the lower part of his body first, but this lower part, which he had not yet seen and of which he could form no clear conception, proved too difficult to move; it shifted so slowly; and when finally, almost wild with annoyance, he gathered his forces together and thrust out recklessly, he had miscalculated the direction and bumped heavily against the lower end of the bed, and the stinging pain he felt informed him that precisely this lower part of his body was at the moment probably the most sensitive.

So he tried to get the top part of himself out first, and cautiously moved his head towards the edge of the bed. That proved easy enough, and despite its breadth and mass the bulk of his body at last slowly followed the movement of his head. Still, when he finally got his head free over the edge of the bed he felt too scared to go on advancing, for after all if he let himself fall in this way it would take a miracle to keep his head from being injured. And at all costs he must not lose consciousness now, precisely now; he would rather stay in bed.

But when after a repetition of the same efforts he lay in his former position again, sighing, and watched his little legs struggling against each other more wildly than ever, if that were possible, and saw no way of bringing any order into this arbitrary confusion, he told himself again that it was impossible to stay in bed and that the most sensible course was to risk everything for the smallest hope of getting away from it. At the same time he did not forget meanwhile to remind himself that cool reflection, the coolest possible, was much better than desperate resolves. In such moments he focused his eyes as sharply as possible on the window, but, unfortunately, the prospect of the morning fog, which muffled even the other side of the narrow street, brought him little encouragement and comfort. "Seven o'clock already," he said to himself when the alarm clock chimed again, "seven o'clock already and still such a thick fog." And for a little while he lay quiet, breathing lightly, as if perhaps expecting such complete repose to restore all things to their real and normal condition.

But then he said to himself: "Before it strikes a quarter past seven I must be quite out of this bed, without fail. Anyhow, by that time someone will have come from the office to ask for me, since it opens before seven." And he set himself to rocking his whole body at once in a regular rhythm, with the idea of swinging it out of the bed. If he tipped himself out in that way he could keep his head from injury by lifting it at an acute angle when he fell. His back seemed to be hard and was not likely to suffer from a fall on the carpet. His biggest worry was the loud crash he would not be able to help making, which would probably cause anxiety, if not terror, behind all the doors. Still, he must take the risk.

When he was already half out of the bed—the new method was more a game than an effort, for he needed only to hitch himself across by rocking to and fro—it struck him how simple it would be if he could get help. Two strong people—he thought of his father and the servant girl—would be amply sufficient; they would only have to thrust their arms under his convex back, lever him out of the bed, bend down with their burden and then be patient enough to let him turn himself right over on the the floor, where it was to be hoped his legs would then find their proper function. Well, ignoring the fact that the doors were all locked, ought he really to call for help? In spite of his misery he could not suppress a smile at the very idea of it.

He had got so far that he could barely keep his equilibrium when he rocked himself strongly, and he would have to nerve himself very soon for the final decision since in five minutes' time it would be a quarter past seven—when the front door bell rang. "That's someone from the office," he said to himself, and grew almost rigid, while his little legs only jigged about all the faster. For a moment everything stayed quiet. "They're not going to open the door," said Gregor to himself, catching at some kind of irrational hope. But then of course the servant girl went as usual to the door with her heavy tread and opened it. Gregor needed only to hear the first good morning of the visitor to know immediately who it was—the chief clerk himself. What a fate, to be condemned to work for a firm where the smallest omission at once gave rise to the gravest suspicion! Were all employees in a body nothing but scoundrels, was there not among them one single loyal devoted man who, had he wasted only an hour or so of the firm's time in a morning, was so tormented by conscience as to be driven out of his mind and actually incapable of leaving his bed? Wouldn't it really have been sufficient to send an apprentice to inquire—if any inquiry were necessary at all—did the chief clerk himself have to come and thus indicate to the entire family, an innocent family, that this suspicious circumstance could be investigated by no one less versed in affairs than himself? And more through the agitation caused by these reflections than through any act of will Gregor swung himself out of bed with all his strength. There was a loud thump, but it was not really a crash. His fall was broken to some extent by the carpet, his back, too, was less stiff than he thought, and so there was merely a dull thud, not so very startling. Only he had not lifted his head carefully enough and had hit it; he turned it and rubbed it on the carpet in pain and irritation.

"That was something falling down in there," said the chief clerk in the next room to the left. Gregor tried to suppose to himself that something like what had happened to him today might some day happen to the chief clerk; one really could not deny that it was possible. But as if in brusque reply to this supposition the chief clerk took a couple of firm steps in the next-door room and his patent leather boots creaked. From the right-hand room his sister was whispering to inform him of the situation: "Gregor, the chief clerk's here." "I know," muttered Gregor to himself; but he didn't dare to make his voice loud enough for his sister to hear it.

"Gregor," said his father now from the left-hand room, "the chief clerk has come and wants to know why you didn't catch the early train. We don't know what to say to him. Besides, he wants to talk to you in person. So open the door, please. He will be good enough to excuse the untidiness of your room." "Good morning, Mr. Samsa," the chief clerk was calling amiably meanwhile. "He's not well," said his mother to the visitor, while his father was still speaking through the door, "he's not well, sir, believe me. What else would make him miss a train! The boy thinks about nothing but his work. It makes me almost cross the way he never goes out in the evenings; he's been here the last eight days and has stayed at home every single evening. He just sits there quietly at the table reading a newspaper or looking through railway timetables. The only amusement he gets is doing fretwork. For instance, he spent two or three evenings cutting out a little picture frame; you would be surprised to see how pretty it is; it's hanging in his room; you'll see it in a minute when Gregor opens the door. I must say I'm glad you've come, sir; we should never have got him to unlock the door by ourselves; he's so obstinate; and I'm sure he's unwell, though he wouldn't have it to be so this morning." "I'm just coming," said Gregor slowly and carefully, not moving an inch for fear of losing one word of the conversation. "I can't think of any other explanation, madam," said the chief clerk, "I hope it's nothing serious. Although on the other hand I must say that we men of business— fortunately or unfortunately—very often simply have to ignore any slight indisposition, since business must be attended to." "Well, can the chief clerk come in now?" asked Gregor's father impatiently, again knocking on the door. "No," said Gregor. In the left-hand room a painful silence followed this refusal, in the right-hand room his sister began to sob.

Why didn't his sister join the others? She was probably newly out of bed and hadn't even begun to put on her clothes yet. Well, why was she crying? Because he wouldn't get up and let the chief clerk in, because he was in danger of losing his job, and because the chief would begin dunning his parents again for the old debts? Surely these were things one didn't need to worry about for the present. Gregor was still at home and not in the least thinking of deserting the family. At the moment, true, he was lying on the carpet and no one who knew the condition he was in could seriously expect him to admit the chief clerk. But for such a small discourtesy, which could plausibly be explained away somehow later on, Gregor could hardly be dismissed on the spot. And it seemed to Gregor that it would be much more sensible to leave him in peace for the present than to trouble him with tears and entreaties. Still, of course, their uncertainty bewildered them all and excused their behavior.

"Mr. Samsa," the chief clerk called now in a louder voice, "what's the matter with you? Here you are, barricading yourself in your room, giving only 'yes' and 'no' for answers, causing your parents a lot of unnecessary trouble and neglecting—I mention this only in passing—neglecting your business duties in an incredible fashion. I am speaking here in the name of your parents and of your chief, and I beg you quite seriously to give me an immediate and precise explanation. You amaze me, you amaze me. I thought you were a quiet, dependable person, and now all at once you seem bent on making a disgraceful exhibition of yourself. The chief did hint to me early this morning a possible explanation for your disappearance —with reference to the cash payments that were entrusted to you recently—but I almost pledged my solemn word of honor that this could not be so. But now that I see how incredibly obstinate you are, I no longer have the slightest desire to take your part at all. And your position in the firm is not so unassailable. I came with the intention of telling you all this in private, but since you are wasting my time so needlessly I don't see why your parents shouldn't hear it too. For some time past your work has been most unsatisfactory; this is not the season of the year for a business boom, of course, we admit that, but a season of the year for doing no business at all, that does not exist, Mr. Samsa, must not exist."

"But, sir," cried Gregor, beside himself and in his agitation forgetting everything else, "I'm just going to open the door this very minute. A slight illness, an attack of giddiness, has kept me from getting up. I'm still lying in bed. But I feel all right again. I'm getting out of bed now. Just give me a moment or two longer! I'm not quite so well as I thought. But I'm all right, really. How a thing like that can suddenly strike one down! Only last night I was quite well, my parents can tell you, or rather I did have a slight presentiment. I must have showed some sign of it. Why didn't I report it at the office! But one always thinks that an indisposition can be got over without staying in the house. Oh sir, do spare my parents! All that you're reproaching me with now has no foundation; no one has ever said a word to me about it. Perhaps you haven't looked at the last orders I sent in. Anyhow, I can still catch the eight o'clock train, I'm much the better for my few hours' rest. Don't let me detain you here, sir; I'll be attending to business very soon, and do be good enough to tell the chief so and to make my excuses to him!"

And while all this was tumbling out pell-mell and Gregor hardly knew what he was saying, he had reached the chest quite easily, perhaps because of the practice he had had in bed, and was now trying to lever himself upright by means of it. He meant actually to open the door, actually to show himself and speak to the chief clerk; he was eager to find out what the others, after all their insistence, would say at the sight of him. If they were horrified then the responsibility was no longer his and he could stay quiet. But if they took it calmly, then he had no reason either to be upset, and could really get to the station for the eight o'clock train if he hurried. At first he slipped down a few times from the polished surface of the chest, but at length with a last heave he stood upright; he paid no more attention to the pains in the lower part of his body, however they smarted. Then he let himself fall against the back of a near-by chair, and clung with his little legs to the edges of it. That brought him into control of himself again and he stopped speaking, for now he could listen to what the chief clerk was saying.

"Did you understand a word of it?" the chief clerk was asking; "surely he can't be trying to make fools of us?" "Oh dear," cried his mother, in tears, "perhaps he's terribly ill and we're tormenting him. Grete! Grete!" she called out then. "Yes Mother?" called his sister from the other side. They were calling to each other across Gregor's room. "You must go this minute for the doctor. Gregor is ill. Go for the doctor, quick. Did you hear how he was speaking?" "That was no human voice," said the chief clerk in a voice noticeably low beside the shrillness of the mother's. "Anna! Anna!" his father was calling through the hall to the kitchen, clapping his hands, "get a locksmith at once!" And the two girls were already running through the hall with a swish of skirts—how could his sister have got dressed so quickly?—and were tearing the front door open. There was no sound of its closing again; they had evidently left it open, as one does in houses where some great misfortune has happened.

But Gregor was now much calmer. The words he uttered were no longer understandable, apparently, although they seemed clear enough to him, even clearer than before, perhaps because his ear had grown accustomed to the sound of them. Yet at any rate people now believed that something was wrong with him, and were ready to help him. The positive certainty with which these first measures had been taken comforted him. He felt himself drawn once more into the human circle and hoped for great and remarkable results from both the doctor and the locksmith, without really distinguishing precisely between them. To make his voice as clear as possible for the decisive conversation that was now imminent he coughed a little, as quietly as he could, of course, since this noise too might not sound like a human cough for all he was able to judge. In the next room meanwhile there was complete silence. Perhaps his parents were sitting at the table with the chief clerk, whispering, perhaps they were all leaning against the door and listening.

Slowly Gregor pushed the chair towards the door, then let go of it, caught hold of the door for support—the soles at the end of his little legs were somewhat sticky—and rested against it for a moment after his efforts. Then he set himself to turning the key in the lock with his mouth. It seemed, unhappily, that he hadn't really any teeth—what could he grip the key with?—but on the other hand his jaws were certainly very strong; with their help he did manage to set the key in motion, heedless of the fact that he was undoubtedly damaging them somewhere, since a brown fluid issued from his mouth, flowed over the key and dripped on the floor. "Just listen to that," said the chief clerk next door; "he's turning the key." That was a great encouragement to Gregor; but they should all have shouted encouragement to him, his father and mother too: "Go on, Gregor," they should have called out, "keep going, hold on to that key!" And in the belief that they were all following his efforts intently, he clenched his jaws recklessly on the key with all the force at his command. As the turning of the key progressed he circled round the lock, holding on now only with his mouth, pushing on the key, as required, or pulling it down again with all the weight of his body. The louder click of the finally yielding lock literally quickened Gregor. With a deep breath of relief he said to himself: "So I didn't need the locksmith," and laid his head on the handle to open the door wide.

Since he had to pull the door towards him, he was still invisible when it was really wide open. He had to edge himself slowly round the near half of the double door, and to do it very carefully if he was not to fall plump upon his back just on the threshold. He was still carrying out this difficult manoeuvre, with no time to observe anything else, when he heard the chief clerk utter a loud "Oh!"—it sounded like a gust of wind—and now he could see the man, standing as he was nearest to the door, clapping one hand before his open mouth and slowly backing away as if driven by some invisible steady pressure. His mother—in spite of the chief clerk's being there her hair was still undone and sticking up in all directions—first clasped her hands and looked at his father, then took two steps towards Gregor and fell on the floor among her outspread skirts, her face quite hidden on her breast. His father knotted his fist with a fierce expression on his face as if he meant to knock Gregor back into his room, then looked uncertainly round the living room, covered his eyes with his hands and wept till his great chest heaved.

Gregor did not go now into the living room, but leaned against the inside of the firmly shut wing of the door, so that only half his body was visible and his head above it bending sideways to look at the others. The light had meanwhile strengthened; on the other side of the street one could see clearly a section of the endlessly long, dark gray building opposite—it was a hospital—abruptly punctuated by its row of regular windows; the rain was still falling, but only in large singly discernible and literally singly splashing drops. The breakfast dishes were set out on the table lavishly, for breakfast was the most important meal of the day to Gregor's father, who lingered it out for hours over various newspapers. Right opposite Gregor on the wall hung a photograph of himself on military service, as a lieutenant, hand on sword, a carefree smile on his face, inviting one to respect his uniform and military bearing. The door leading to the hall was open, and one could see that the front door stood open too, showing the landing beyond and the beginning of the stairs going down.

"Well," said Gregor, knowing perfectly that he was the only one who had retained any composure, "I'll put my clothes on at once, pack up my samples and start off. Will you only let me go? You see, sir, I'm not obstinate, and I'm willing to work; traveling is a hard life, but I couldn't live without it. Where are you going, sir? To the office? Yes? Will you give a true account of all this? One can be temporarily incapacitated, but that's just the moment for remembering former services and bearing in mind that later on, when the incapacity has been got over, one will certainly work with all the more industry and concentration. I'm loyally bound to serve the chief, you know that very well. Besides, I have to provide for my parents and my sister. I'm in great difficulties, but I'll get out of them again. Don't make things any worse for me than they are. Stand up for me in the firm. Travelers are not popular there, I know. People think they earn sacks of money and just have a good time. A prejudice there's no particular reason for revising. But you, sir, have a more comprehensive view of affairs than the rest of the staff, yes, let me tell you in confidence, a more comprehensive view than the chief himself, who, being the owner, lets his judgment easily be swayed against one of his employees. And you know very well that the traveler, who is never seen in the office almost the whole year round, can so easily fall a victim to gossip and ill luck and unfounded complaints, which he mostly knows nothing about, except when he comes back exhausted from his rounds, and only then suffers in person from their evil consequences, which he can no longer trace back to the original causes. Sir, sir, don't go away without a word to me to show that you think me in the right at least to some extent!"

But at Gregor's very first words the chief clerk had already backed away and only stared at him with parted lips over one twitching shoulder. And while Gregor was speaking he did not stand still one moment but stole away towards the door, without taking his eyes off Gregor, yet only an inch at a time, as if obeying some secret injunction to leave the room. He was already at the hall, and the suddenness with which he took his last step out of the living room would have made one believe he had burned the sole of his foot. Once in the hall he stretched his right arm before him towards the staircase, as if some supernatural power were waiting there to deliver him.

Gregor perceived that the chief clerk must on no account be allowed to go away in this frame of mind if his position in the firm were not to be endangered to the utmost. His parents did not understand this so well; they had convinced themselves in the course of years that Gregor was settled for life in this firm, and besides they were so preoccupied with their immediate troubles that all foresight had forsaken them. Yet Gregor had this foresight. The chief clerk must be detained, soothed, persuaded and finally won over; the whole future of Gregor and his family depended on it! If only his sister had been there! She was intelligent; she had begun to cry while Gregor was still lying quietly on his back. And no doubt the chief clerk, so partial to ladies, would have been guided by her; she would have shut the door of the flat and in the hall talked him out of his horror. But she was not there, and Gregor would have to handle the situation himself. And without remembering that he was still unaware what powers of movement he possessed, without even remembering that his words in all possibility, indeed in all likelihood, would again be unintelligible, he let go the wing of the door, pushed himself through the opening, started to walk towards the chief clerk, who was already ridiculously clinging with both hands to the railing on the landing; but immediately, as he was feeling for a support, he fell down with a little cry upon all his numerous legs. Hardly was he down when he experienced for the first time this morning a sense of physical comfort; his legs had firm ground under them; they were completely obedient, as he noted with joy; they even strove to carry him forward in whatever direction he chose; and he was inclined to believe that a final relief from all his sufferings was at hand. But in the same moment as he found himself on the floor, rocking with suppressed eagerness to move, not far from his mother, indeed just in front of her, she, who had seemed so completely crushed, sprang all at once to her feet, her arms and fingers outspread, cried: "Help, for God's sake, help!" bent her head down as if to see Gregor better, yet on the contrary kept backing senselessly away; had quite forgotten that the laden table stood behind her; sat upon it hastily, as if in absence of mind, when she bumped into it; and seemed altogether unaware that the big coffee pot beside her was upset and pouring coffee in a flood over the carpet.

"Mother, Mother," said Gregor in a low voice, and looked up at her. The chief clerk, for the moment, had quite slipped from his mind; instead, he could not resist snapping his jaws together at the sight of the streaming coffee. That made his mother scream again, she fled from the table and fell into the arms of his father, who hastened to catch her. But Gregor had now no time to spare for his parents; the chief clerk was already on the stairs; with his chin on the banisters he was taking one last backward look. Gregor made a spring, to be as sure as possible of overtaking him; the chief clerk must have divined his intention, for he leaped down several steps and vanished; he was still yelling "Ugh!" and it echoed through the whole staircase.

Unfortunately, the flight of the chief clerk seemed completely to upset Gregor's father, who had remained relatively calm until now, for instead of running after the man himself, or at least not hindering Gregor in his pursuit, he seized in his right hand the walking stick which the chief clerk had left behind on a chair, together with a hat and greatcoat, snatched in his left hand a large newspaper from the table and began stamping his feet and flourishing the stick and the newspaper to drive Gregor back into his room. No entreaty of Gregor's availed, indeed no entreaty was even understood, however humbly he bent his head his father only stamped on the floor the more loudly. Behind his father his mother had torn open a window, despite the cold weather, and was leaning far out of it with her face in her hands. A strong draught set in from the street to the staircase, the window curtains blew in, the newspapers on the table fluttered, stray pages whisked over the floor. Pitilessly Gregor's father drove him back, hissing and crying "Shoo!" like a savage. But Gregor was quite unpracticed in walking backwards, it really was a slow business. If he only had a chance to turn round he could get back to his room at once, but he was afraid of exasperating his father by the slowness of such a rotation and at any moment the stick in his father's hand might hit him a fatal blow on the back or on the head. In the end, however, nothing else was left for him to do since to his horror he observed that in moving backwards he could not even control the direction he took; and so, keeping an anxious eye on his father all the time over his shoulder, he began to turn round as quickly as he could, which was in reality very slowly. Perhaps his father noted his good intentions, for he did not interfere except every now and then to help him in the manoeuvre from a distance with the point of the stick. If only he would have stopped making that unbearable hissing noise! It made Gregor quite lose his head. He had turned almost completely round when the hissing noise so distracted him that he even turned a little the wrong way again. But when at last his head was fortunately right in front of the doorway, it appeared that his body was too broad simply to get through the opening. His father, of course, in his present mood was far from thinking of such a thing as opening the other half of the door, to let Gregor have enough space. He had merely the fixed idea of driving Gregor back into his room as quickly as possible. He would never have suffered Gregor to make the circumstantial preparations for standing up on end and perhaps slipping his way through the door. Maybe he was now making more noise than ever to urge Gregor forward, as if no obstacle impeded him; to Gregor, anyhow, the noise in his rear sounded no longer like the voice of one single father; this was really no joke, and Gregor thrust himself —come what might—into the doorway. One side of his body rose up, he was tilted at an angle in the doorway, his flank was quite bruised, horrid blotches stained the white door, soon he was stuck fast and, left to himself, could not have moved at all, his legs on one side fluttered trembling in the air, those on the other were crushed painfully to the floor—when from behind his father gave him a strong push which was literally a deliverance and he flew far into the room, bleeding freely. The door was slammed behind him with the stick, and then at last there was silence.

II

Not until it was twilight did Gregor awake out of a deep sleep, more like a swoon than a sleep. He would certainly have waked up of his own accord not much later, for he felt himself sufficiently rested and well-slept, but it seemed to him as if a fleeting step and a cautious shutting of the door leading into the hall had aroused him. The electric lights in the street cast a pale sheen here and there on the ceiling and the upper surfaces of the furniture, but down below, where he lay, it was dark. Slowly, awkwardly trying out his feelers, which he now first learned to appreciate, he pushed his way to the door to see what had been happening there. His left side felt like one single long, unpleasantly tense scar, and he had actually to limp on his two rows of legs. One little leg, moreover, had been severely damaged in the course of that morning's events— it was almost a miracle that only one had been damaged—and trailed uselessly behind him.

He had reached the door before he discovered what had really drawn him to it: the smell of food. For there stood a basin filled with fresh milk in which floated little sops of white bread. He could almost have laughed with joy, since he was now still hungrier than in the morning, and he dipped his head almost over the eyes straight into the milk. But soon in disappointment he withdrew it again; not only did he find it difficult to feed because of his tender left side—and he could only feed with the palpitating collaboration of his whole body—he did not like the milk either, although milk had been his favorite drink and that was certainly why his sister had set it there for him, indeed it was almost with repulsion that he turned away from the basin and crawled back to the middle of the room.

He could see through the crack of the door that the gas was turned on in the living room, but while usually at this time his father made a habit of reading the afternoon newspaper in a loud voice to his mother and occasionally to his sister as well, not a sound was now to be heard. Well, perhaps his father had recently given up this habit of reading aloud, which his sister had mentioned so often in conversation and in her letters. But there was the same silence all around, although the flat was certainly not empty of occupants. "What a quiet life our family has been leading," said Gregor to himself, and as he sat there motionless staring into the darkness he felt great pride in the fact that he had been able to provide such a life for his parents and sister in such a fine flat. But what if all the quiet, the comfort, the contentment were now to end in horror? To keep himself from being lost in such thoughts Gregor took refuge in movement and crawled up and down the room.

Once during the long evening one of the side doors was opened a little and quickly shut again, later the other side door too; someone had apparently wanted to come in and then thought better of it. Gregor now stationed himself immediately before the living room door, determined to persuade any hesitating visitor to come in or at least to discover who it might be; but the door was not opened again and he waited in vain. In the early morning, when the doors were locked, they had all wanted to come in, now that he had opened one door and the other had apparently been opened during the day, no one came in and even the keys were on the other side of the doors.

It was late at night before the gas went out in the living room, and Gregor could easily tell that his parents and his sister had all stayed awake until then, for he could clearly hear the three of them stealing away on tiptoe. No one was likely to visit him, not until the morning, that was certain; so he had plenty of time to meditate at his leisure on how he was to arrange his life afresh. But the lofty, empty room in which he had to lie flat on the floor filled him with an apprehension he could not account for, since it had been his very own room for the past five years—and with a half-unconscious action, not without a slight feeling of shame, he scuttled under the sofa, where he felt comfortable at once, although his back was a little cramped and he could not lift his head up, and his only regret was that his body was too broad to get the whole of it under the sofa.

He stayed there all night, spending the time partly in a light slumber, from which his hunger kept waking him up with a start, and partly in worrying and sketching vague hopes, which all led to the same conclusion, that he must lie low for the present and, by exercising patience and the utmost consideration, help the family to bear the inconvenience he was bound to cause them in his present condition.

Very early in the morning, it was still almost night, Gregor had the chance to test the strength of his new resolutions, for his sister, nearly fully dressed, opened the door from the hall and peered in. She did not see him at once, yet when she caught sight of him under the sofa—well, he had to be somewhere, he couldn't have flown away, could he?—she was so startled that without being able to help it she slammed the door shut again. But as if regretting her behavior she opened the door again immediately and came in on tiptoe, as if she were visiting an invalid or even a stranger. Gregor had pushed his head forward to the very edge of the sofa and watched her. Would she notice that he had left the milk standing, and not for lack of hunger, and would she bring in some other kind of food more to his taste? If she did not do it of her own accord, he would rather starve than draw her attention to the fact, although he felt a wild impulse to dart out from under the sofa, throw himself at her feet and beg her for something to eat. But his sister at once noticed, with surprise, that the basin was still full, except for a little milk that had been spilt all around it, she lifted it immediately, not with her bare hands, true, but with a cloth and carried it away. Gregor was wildly curious to know what she would bring instead, and made various speculations about it. Yet what she actually did next, in the goodness of her heart, he could never have guessed at. To find out what he liked she brought him a whole selection of food, all set out on an old newspaper. There were old, half-decayed vegetables, bones from last night's supper covered with a white sauce that had thickened; some raisins and almonds; a piece of cheese that Gregor would have called uneatable two days ago; a dry roll of bread, a buttered roll, and a roll both buttered and salted. Besides all that, she set down again the same basin, into which she had poured some water, and which was apparently to be reserved for his exclusive use. And with fine tact, knowing that Gregor would not eat in her presence, she withdrew quickly and even turned the key, to let him understand that he could take his ease as much as he liked. Gregor's legs all whizzed towards the food. His wounds must have healed completely, moreover, for he felt no disability, which amazed him and made him reflect how more than a month ago he had cut one finger a little with a knife and had still suffered pain from the wound only the day before yesterday. Am I less sensitive now? he thought, and sucked greedily at the cheese, which above all the other edibles attracted him at once and strongly. One after another and with tears of satisfaction in his eyes he quickly devoured the cheese, the vegetables and the sauce; the fresh food, on the other hand, had no charms for him, he could not even stand the smell of it and actually dragged away to some little distance the things he could eat. He had long finished his meal and was only lying lazily on the same spot when his sister turned the key slowly as a sign for him to retreat. That roused him at once, although he was nearly asleep, and he hurried under the sofa again. But it took considerable self-control for him to stay under the sofa, even for the short time his sister was in the room, since the large meal had swollen his body somewhat and he was so cramped he could hardly breathe. Slight attacks of breathlessness afflicted him and his eyes were starting a little out of his head as he watched his unsuspecting sister sweeping together with a broom not only the remains of what he had eaten but even the things he had not touched, as if these were now of no use to anyone, and hastily shoveling it all into a bucket, which she covered with a wooden lid and carried away. Hardly had she turned her back when Gregor came from under the sofa and stretched and puffed himself out.

In this manner Gregor was fed, once in the early morning while his parents and the servant girl were still asleep, and a second time after they had all had their midday dinner, for then his parents took a short nap and the servant girl could be sent out on some errand or other by his sister. Not that they would have wanted him to starve, of course, but perhaps they could not have borne to know more about his feeding than from hearsay, perhaps too his sister wanted to spare them such little anxieties wherever possible, since they had quite enough to bear as it was.

Under what pretext the doctor and the locksmith had been got rid of on that first morning Gregor could not discover, for since what he said was not understood by the others it never struck any of them, not even his sister, that he could understand what they said, and so whenever his sister came into his room he had to content himself with hearing her utter only a sigh now and then and an occasional appeal to the saints. Later on, when she had got a little used to the situation—of course she could never get completely used to it—she sometimes threw out a remark which was kindly meant or could be so interpreted. "Well, he liked his dinner today," she would say when Gregor had made a good clearance of his food; and when he had not eaten, which gradually happened more and more often, she would say almost sadly: "Everything's been left standing again."

But although Gregor could get no news directly, he overheard a lot from the neighboring rooms, and as soon as voices were audible, he would run to the door of the room concerned and press his whole body against it. In the first few days especially there was no conversation that did not refer to him somehow, even if only indirectly. For two whole days there were family consultations at every mealtime about what should be done; but also between meals the same subject was discussed, for there were always at least two members of the family at home, since no one wanted to be alone in the flat and to leave it quite empty was unthinkable. And on the very first of these days the household cook—it was not quite clear what and how much she knew of the situation—went down on her knees to his mother and begged leave to go, and when she departed, a quarter of an hour later, gave thanks for her dismissal with tears in her eyes as if for the greatest benefit that could have been conferred on her, and without any prompting swore a solemn oath that she would never say a single word to anyone about what had happened.

Now Gregor's sister had to cook too, helping her mother; true, the cooking did not amount to much, for they ate scarcely anything. Gregor was always hearing one of the family vainly urging another to eat and getting no answer but: "Thanks, I've had all I want," or something similar. Perhaps they drank nothing either. Time and again his sister kept asking his father if he wouldn't like some beer and offered kindly to go and fetch it herself, and when he made no answer suggested that she could ask the concierge to fetch it, so that he need feel no sense of obligation, but then a round "No" came from his father and no more was said about it.

In the course of that very first day Gregor's father explained the family's financial position and prospects to both his mother and his sister. Now and then he rose from the table to get some voucher or memorandum out of the small safe he had rescued from the collapse of his business five years earlier. One could hear him opening the complicated lock and rustling papers out and shutting it again. This statement made by his father was the first cheerful information Gregor had heard since his imprisonment. He had been of the opinion that nothing at all was left over from his father's business, at least his father had never said anything to the contrary, and of course he had not asked him directly. At that time Gregor's sole desire was to do his utmost to help the family to forget as soon as possible the catastrophe which had overwhelmed the business and thrown them all into a state of complete despair. And so he had set to work with unusual ardor and almost overnight had become a commercial traveler instead of a little clerk, with of course much greater chances of earning money, and his success was immediately translated into good round coin which he could lay on the table for his amazed and happy family. These had been fine times, and they had never recurred, at least not with the same sense of glory, although later on Gregor had earned so much money that he was able to meet the expenses of the whole household and did so. They had simply got used to it, both the family and Gregor; the money was gratefully accepted and gladly given, but there was no special uprush of warm feeling. With his sister alone had he remained intimate, and it was a secret plan of his that she, who loved music, unlike himself, and could play movingly on the violin, should be sent next year to study at the Conservatorium, despite the great expense that would entail, which must be made up in some other way. During his brief visits home the Conservatorium was often mentioned in the talks he had with his sister, but always merely as a beautiful dream which could never come true, and his parents discouraged even these innocent references to it; yet Gregor had made up his mind firmly about it and meant to announce the fact with due solemnity on Christmas Day.

Such were the thoughts, completely futile in his present condition, that went through his head as he stood clinging upright to the door and listening. Sometimes out of sheer weariness he had to give up listening and let his head fall negligently against the door, but he always had to pull himself together again at once, for even the slight sound his head made was audible next door and brought all conversation to a stop. "What can he be doing now?" his father would say after a while, obviously turning towards the door, and only then would the interrupted conversation gradually be set going again.

Gregor was now informed as amply as he could wish—for his father tended to repeat himself in his explanations, partly because it was a long time since he had handled such matters and partly because his mother could not always grasp things at once—that a certain amount of investments, a very small amount it was true, had survived the wreck of their fortunes and had even increased a little because the dividends had not been touched meanwhile. And besides that, the money Gregor brought home every month—he had kept only a few dollars for himself—had never been quite used up and now amounted to a small capital sum. Behind the door Gregor nodded his head eagerly, rejoiced at this evidence of unexpected thrift and foresight. True, he could really have paid off some more of his father's debts to the chief with this extra money, and so brought much nearer the day on which he could quit his job, but doubtless it was better the way his father had arranged it.

Yet this capital was by no means sufficient to let the family live on the interest of it; for one year, perhaps, or at the most two, they could live on the principal, that was all. It was simply a sum that ought not to be touched and should be kept for a rainy day; money for living expenses would have to be earned. Now his father was still hale enough but an old man, and he had done no work for the past five years and could not be expected to do much; during these five years, the first years of leisure in his laborious though unsuccessful life, he had grown rather fat and become sluggish. And Gregor's old mother, how was she to earn a living with her asthma, which troubled her even when she walked through the flat and kept her lying on a sofa every other day panting for breath beside an open window? And was his sister to earn her bread, she who was still a child of seventeen and whose life hitherto had been so pleasant, consisting as it did in dressing herself nicely, sleeping long, helping in the housekeeping, going out to a few modest entertainments and above all playing the violin? At first whenever the need for earning money was mentioned Gregor let go his hold on the door and threw himself down on the cool leather sofa beside it, he felt so hot with shame and grief.

Often he just lay there the long nights through without sleeping at all, scrabbling for hours on the leather. Or he nerved himself to the great effort of pushing an armchair to the window, then crawled up over the window sill and, braced against the chair, leaned against the window panes, obviously in some recollection of the sense of freedom that looking out of a window always used to give him. For in reality day by day things that were even a little way off were growing dimmer to his sight; the hospital across the street, which he used to execrate for being all too often before his eyes, was now quite beyond his range of vision, and if he had not known that he lived in Charlotte Street, a quiet street but still a city street, he might have believed that his window gave on a desert waste where gray sky and gray land blended indistinguishably into each other. His quick-witted sister only needed to observe twice that the armchair stood by the window; after that whenever she had tidied the room she always pushed the chair back to the same place at the window and even left the inner casements open.

If he could have spoken to her and thanked her for all she had to do for him, he could have borne her ministrations better; as it was, they oppressed him. She certainly tried to make as light as possible of whatever was disagreeable in her task, and as time went on she succeeded, of course, more and more, but time brought more enlightenment to Gregor too. The very way she came in distressed him. Hardly was she in the room when she rushed to the window, without even taking time to shut the door, careful as she was usually to shield the sight of Gregor's room from the others, and as if she were almost suffocating tore the casements open with hasty fingers, standing then in the open draught for a while even in the bitterest cold and drawing deep breaths. This noisy scurry of hers upset Gregor twice a day; he would crouch trembling under the sofa all the time, knowing quite well that she would certainly have spared him such a disturbance had she found it at all possible to stay in his presence without opening the window.

On one occasion, about a month after Gregor's metamorphosis, when there was surely no reason for her to be still startled at his appearance, she came a little earlier than usual and found him gazing out of the window, quite motionless, and thus well placed to look like a bogey. Gregor would not have been surprised had she not come in at all, for she could not immediately open the window while he was there, but not only did she retreat, she jumped back as if in alarm and banged the door shut; a stranger might well have thought that he had been lying in wait for her there meaning to bite her. Of course he hid himself under the sofa at once, but he had to wait until midday before she came again, and she seemed more ill at ease than usual. This made him realize how repulsive the sight of him still was to her, and that it was bound to go on being repulsive, and what an effort it must cost her not to run away even from the sight of the small portion of his body that stuck out from under the sofa. In order to spare her that, therefore, one day he carried a sheet on his back to the sofa—it cost him four hours' labor—and arranged it there in such a way as to hide him completely, so that even if she were to bend down she could not see him. Had she considered the sheet unnecessary, she would certainly have stripped it off the sofa again, for it was clear enough that this curtaining and confining of himself was not likely to conduce to Gregor's comfort, but she left it where it was, and Gregor even fancied that he caught a thankful glance from her eye when he lifted the sheet carefully a very little with his head to see how she was taking the new arrangement.

For the first fortnight his parents could not bring themselves to the point of entering his room, and he often heard them expressing their appreciation of his sister's activities, whereas formerly they had frequently scolded her for being as they thought a somewhat useless daughter. But now, both of them often waited outside the door, his father and his mother, while his sister tidied his room, and as soon as she came out she had to tell them exactly how things were in the room, what Gregor had eaten, how he had conducted himself this time and whether there was not perhaps some slight improvement in his condition. His mother, moreover, began relatively soon to want to visit him, but his father and sister dissuaded her at first with arguments which Gregor listened to very attentively and altogether approved. Later, however, she had to be held back by main force, and when she cried out: "Do let me in to Gregor, he is my unfortunate son! Can't you understand that I must go to him?" Gregor thought that it might be well to have her come in, not every day, of course, but perhaps once a week; she understood things, after all, much better than his sister, who was only a child despite the efforts she was making and had perhaps taken on so difficult a task merely out of childish thoughtlessness.

Gregor's desire to see his mother was soon fulfilled. During the daytime he did not want to show himself at the window, out of consideration for his parents, but he could not crawl very far around the few square yards of floor space he had, nor could be bear lying quietly at rest all during the night, while he was fast losing any interest he had ever taken in food, so that for mere recreation he had formed the habit of crawling crisscross over the walls and ceiling. He especially enjoyed hanging suspended from the ceiling; it was much better than lying on the floor; one could breathe more freely; one's body swung and rocked lightly; and in the almost blissful absorption induced by this suspension it could happen to his own surprise that he let go and fell plump on the floor. Yet he now had his body much better under control than formerly, and even such a big fall did him no harm. His sister at once remarked the new distraction Gregor had found for himself—he left traces behind him of the sticky stuff on his soles wherever he crawled—and she got the idea in her head of giving him as wide a field as possible to crawl in and of removing the pieces of furniture that hindered him, above all the chest of drawers and the writing desk. But that was more than she could manage all by herself; she did not dare ask her father to help her; and as for the servant girl, a young creature of sixteen who had had the courage to stay on after the cook's departure, she could not be asked to help, for she had begged as an especial favor that she might keep the kitchen door locked and open it only on a definite summons; so there was nothing left but to apply to her mother at an hour when her father was out. And the old lady did come, with exclamations of joyful eagerness, which, however, died away at the door of Gregor's room. Gregor's sister, of course, went in first, to see that everything was in order before letting his mother enter. In great haste Gregor pulled the sheet lower and rucked it more in folds so that it really looked as if it had been thrown accidentally over the sofa. And this time he did not peer out from under it; he renounced the pleasure of seeing his mother on this occasion and was only glad that she had come at all. "Come in, he's out of sight," said his sister, obviously leading her mother in by the hand. Gregor could now hear the two women struggling to shift the heavy old chest from its place, and his sister claiming the greater part of the labor for herself, without listening to the admonitions of her mother who feared she might overstrain herself. It took a long time. After at least a quarter of an hour's tugging his mother objected that the chest had better be left where it was, for in the first place it was too heavy and could never be got out before his father came home, and standing in the middle of the room like that it would only hamper Gregor's movements, while in the second place it was not at all certain that removing the furniture would be doing a service to Gregor. She was inclined to think to the contrary; the sight of the naked walls made her own heart heavy, and why shouldn't Gregor have the same feeling, considering that he had been used to his furniture for so long and might feel forlorn without it. "And doesn't it look," she concluded in a low voice—in fact she had been almost whispering all the time as if to avoid letting Gregor, whose exact whereabouts she did not know, hear even the tones of her voice, for she was convinced that he could not understand her words—"doesn't it look as if we were showing him, by taking away his furniture, that we have given up hope of his ever getting better and are just leaving him coldly to himself? I think it would be best to keep his room exactly as it has always been, so that when he comes back to us he will find everything unchanged and be able all the more easily to forget what has happened in between."

On hearing these words from his mother Gregor realized that the lack of all direct human speech for the past two months together with the monotony of family life must have confused his mind, otherwise he could not account for the fact that he had quite earnestly looked forward to having his room emptied of furnishing. Did he really want his warm room, so comfortably fitted with old family furniture, to be turned into a naked den in which he would certainly be able to crawl unhampered in all directions but at the price of shedding simultaneously all recollection of his human background? He had indeed been so near the brink of forgetfulness that only the voice of his mother, which he had not heard for so long, had drawn him back from it. Nothing should be taken out of his room; everything must stay as it was; he could not dispense with the good influence of the furniture on his state of mind; and even if the furniture did hamper him in his senseless crawling round and round, that was no drawback but a great advantage.

Unfortunately his sister was of the contrary opinion; she had grown accustomed, and not without reason, to consider herself an expert in Gregor's affairs as against her parents, and so her mother's advice was now enough to make her determined on the removal not only of the chest and the writing desk, which had been her first intention, but of all the furniture except the indispensable sofa. This determination was not, of course, merely the outcome of childish recalcitrance and of the self-confidence she had recently developed so unexpectedly and at such cost; she had in fact perceived that Gregor needed a lot of space to crawl about in, while on the other hand he never used the furniture at all, so far as could be seen. Another factor might have been also the enthusiastic temperament of an adolescent girl, which seeks to indulge itself on every opportunity

and which now tempted Grete to exaggerate the horror of her brother's circumstances in order that she might do all the more for him.
In a room where Gregor lorded it all alone over empty walls no one
save herself was likely ever to set foot.

And so she was not to be moved from her resolve by her mother,
who seemed moreover to be ill at ease in Gregor's room and therefore unsure of herself, was soon reduced to silence and helped her
daughter as best she could to push the chest outside. Now, Gregor
could do without the chest, if need be, but the writing desk he must
retain. As soon as the two women had got the chest out of his room,
groaning as they pushed it, Gregor stuck his head out from under
the sofa to see how he might intervene as kindly and cautiously as
possible. But as bad luck would have it, his mother was the first to
return, leaving Grete clasping the chest in the room next door where
she was trying to shift it all by herself, without of course moving it
from the spot. His mother however was not accustomed to the sight
of him, it might sicken her and so in alarm Gregor backed quickly
to the other end of the sofa, yet could not prevent the sheet from
swaying a little in front. That was enough to put her on the alert.
She paused, stood still for a moment and then went back to Grete.

Although Gregor kept reassuring himself that nothing out of the
way was happening, but only a few bits of furniture were being
changed round, he soon had to admit that all this trotting to and
fro of the two women, their little ejaculations and the scraping of
furniture along the floor affected him like a vast disturbance coming
from all sides at once, and however much he tucked in his head and
legs and cowered to the very floor he was bound to confess that
he would not be able to stand it for long. They were clearing his
room out; taking away everything he loved; the chest in which he
kept his fret saw and other tools was already dragged off; they were
now loosening the writing desk which had almost sunk into the floor,
the desk at which he had done all his homework when he was at
the commercial academy, at the grammar school before that, and,
yes, even at the primary school—he had no more time to waste in
weighing the good intentions of the two women, whose existence he
had by now almost forgotten, for they were so exhausted that they
were laboring in silence and nothing could be heard but the heavy
scuffling of their feet.

And so he rushed out—the women were just leaning against the
writing desk in the next room to give themselves a breather—and
four times changed his direction, since he really did not know what
to rescue first, then on the wall opposite, which was already otherwise
cleared, he was struck by the picture of the lady muffled in so much
fur and quickly crawled up to it and pressed himself to the glass,
which was a good surface to hold on to and comforted his hot belly

This picture at least, which was entirely hidden beneath him, was going to be removed by nobody. He turned his head towards the door of the living room so as to observe the women when they came back.

They had not allowed themselves much of a rest and were already coming; Grete had twined her arm round her mother and was almost supporting her. "Well, what shall we take now?" said Grete, looking round. Her eyes met Gregor's from the wall. She kept her composure, presumably because of her mother, bent her head down to her mother, to keep her from looking up, and said, although in a fluttering, unpremeditated voice: "Come, hadn't we better go back to the living room for a moment?" Her intentions were clear enough to Gregor, she wanted to bestow her mother in safety and then chase him down from the wall. Well, just let her try it! He clung to his picture and would not give it up. He would rather fly in Grete's face.

But Grete's words had succeeded in disquieting her mother, who took a step to one side, caught sight of the huge brown mass on the flowered wallpaper, and before she was really conscious that what she saw was Gregor screamed in a loud, hoarse voice: "Oh God, oh God!" fell with outspread arms over the sofa as if giving up and did not move. "Gregor!" cried his sister, shaking her fist and glaring at him. This was the first time she had directly addressed him since his metamorphosis. She ran into the next room for some aromatic essence with which to rouse her mother from her fainting fit. Gregor wanted to help too—there was still time to rescue the picture—but he was stuck fast to the glass and had to tear himself loose; he then ran after his sister into the next room as if he could advise her, as he used to do; but then had to stand helplessly behind her; she meanwhile searched among various small bottles and when she turned round started in alarm at the sight of him; one bottle fell on the floor and broke; a splinter of glass cut Gregor's face and some kind of corrosive medicine splashed him; without pausing a moment longer Grete gathered up all the bottles she could carry and ran to her mother with them; she banged the door shut with her foot. Gregor was now cut off from his mother, who was perhaps nearly dying because of him; he dared not open the door for fear of frightening away his sister, who had to stay with her mother; there was nothing he could do but wait; and harassed by self-reproach and worry he began now to crawl to and fro, over everything, walls, furniture and ceiling, and finally in his despair, when the whole room seemed to be reeling round him, fell down on to the middle of the big table.

A little while elapsed, Gregor was still lying there feebly and all around was quiet, perhaps that was a good omen. Then the doorbell rang. The servant girl was of course locked in her kitchen, and Grete would have to open the door. It was his father. "What's been happening?" were his first words; Grete's face must have told him everything. Grete answered in a muffled voice, apparently hiding her head on his breast: "Mother has been fainting, but she's better now. Gregor's broken loose." "Just what I expected," said his father, "just what I've been telling you, but you women would never listen." It was clear to Gregor that his father had taken the worst interpretation of Grete's all too brief statement and was assuming that Gregor had been guilty of some violent act. Therefore Gregor must now try to propitiate his father, since he had neither time nor means for an explanation. And so he fled to the door of his own room and crouched against it, to let his father see as soon as he came in from the hall that his son had the good intention of getting back into his room immediately and that it was not necessary to drive him there, but that if only the door were opened he would disappear at once.

Yet his father was not in the mood to perceive such fine distinctions. "Ah!" he cried as soon as he appeared, in a tone which sounded at once angry and exultant. Gregor drew his head back from the door and lifted it to look at his father. Truly, this was not the father he had imagined to himself; admittedly he had been too absorbed of late in his new recreation of crawling over the ceiling to take the same interest as before in what was happening elsewhere in the flat, and he ought really to be prepared for some changes. And yet, and yet, could that be his father? The man who used to lie wearily sunk in bed whenever Gregor set out on a business journey; who welcomed him back of an evening lying in a long chair in a dressing gown; who could not really rise to his feet but only lifted his arms in greeting, and on the rare occasions when he did go out with his family, on one or two Sundays a year and on high holidays, walked between Gregor and his mother, who were slow walkers anyhow, even more slowly than they did, muffled in his old greatcoat, shuffling laboriously forward with the help of his crook-handled stick which he set down most cautiously at every step and, whenever he wanted to say anything, nearly always came to a full stop and gathered his escort around him? Now he was standing there in fine shape; dressed in a smart blue uniform with gold buttons, such as bank messengers wear; his strong double chin bulged over the stiff high collar of his jacket; from under his bushy eyebrows his black eyes darted fresh and penetrating glances; his onetime tangled white hair had been combed flat on either side of a shining and carefully exact parting. He pitched his cap, which bore a gold monogram, probably the badge of some bank, in a wide sweep across the whole room on to a sofa and with the tail-ends of his jacket thrown back, his hands in his trouser pockets, advanced with a grim visage towards Gregor. Likely enough he did not himself know what he meant to do, at any rate he lifted his

feet uncommonly high, and Gregor was dumbfounded at the enormous size of his shoe soles. But Gregor could not risk standing up to
him, aware as he had been from the very first day of his new life that
his father believed only the severest measures suitable for dealing
with him. And so he ran before his father, stopping when he stopped
and scuttling forward again when his father made any kind of move.
In this way they circled the room several times without anything
decisive happening, indeed the whole operation did not even look
like a pursuit because it was carried out so slowly. And so Gregor did
not leave the floor, for he feared that his father might take as a
piece of peculiar wickedness any excursion of his over the walls or
the ceiling. All the same, he could not stay this course much
longer, for while his father took one step he had to carry out a whole
series of movements. He was already beginning to feel breathless,
just as in his former life his lungs had not been very dependable. As
he was staggering along, trying to concentrate his energy on running, hardly keeping his eyes open; in his dazed state never even
thinking of any other escape than simply going forward; and having
almost forgotten that the walls were free to him, which in this room
were well provided with finely carved pieces of furniture full of knobs
and crevices—suddenly something lightly flung landed close behind
him and rolled before him. It was an apple; a second apple followed
immediately; Gregor came to a stop in alarm; there was no point in
running on, for his father was determined to bombard him. He had
filled his pockets with fruit from the dish on the sideboard and was
now shying apple after apple, without taking particularly good aim
for the moment. The small red apples rolled about the floor as if
magnetized and cannoned into each other. An apple thrown without
much force grazed Gregor's back and glanced off harmlessly. But
another following immediately landed right on his back and sank in;
Gregor wanted to drag himself forward, as if this startling, incredible pain could be left behind him; but he felt as if nailed to the
spot and flattened himself out in a complete derangement of all his
senses. With his last conscious look he saw the door of his room being torn open and his mother rushing out ahead of his screaming
sister, in her underbodice, for her daughter had loosened her clothing
to let her breathe more freely and recover from her swoon, he saw
his mother rushing towards his father, leaving one after another behind her on the floor her loosened petticoats, stumbling over her
petticoats straight to his father and embracing him, in complete union
with him—but here Gregor's sight began to fail—with her hands
clasped round his father's neck as she begged for her son's life.

III

The serious injury done to Gregor, which disabled him for more
than a month—the apple went on sticking in his body as a visible

reminder, since no one ventured to remove it—seemed to have made even his father recollect that Gregor was a member of the family, despite his present unfortunate and repulsive shape, and ought not to be treated as an enemy, that, on the contrary, family duty required the suppression of disgust and the exercise of patience, nothing but patience.

And although his injury had impaired, probably for ever, his powers of movement, and for the time being it took him long, long minutes to creep across his room like an old invalid—there was no question now of crawling up the wall—yet in his own opinion he was sufficiently compensated for this worsening of his condition by the fact that towards evening the living-room door, which he used to watch intently for an hour or two beforehand, was always thrown open, so that lying in the darkness of his room, invisible to the family, he could see them all at the lamp-lit table and listen to their talk, by general consent as it were, very different from his earlier eavesdropping.

True, their intercourse lacked the lively character of former times, which he had always called to mind with a certain wistfulness in the small hotel bedrooms where he had been wont to throw himself down, tired out, on damp bedding. They were now mostly very silent. Soon after supper his father would fall asleep in his armchair; his mother and sister would admonish each other to be silent; his mother, bending low over the lamp, stitched at fine sewing for an underwear firm; his sister, who had taken a job as a salesgirl, was learning shorthand and French in the evenings on the chance of bettering herself. Sometimes his father woke up, and as if quite unaware that he had been sleeping said to his mother: "What a lot of sewing you're doing today!" and at once fell asleep again, while the two women exchanged a tired smile.

With a kind of mulishness his father persisted in keeping his uniform on even in the house; his dressing gown hung uselessly on its peg and he slept fully dressed where he sat, as if he were ready for service at any moment and even here only at the beck and call of his superior. As a result, his uniform, which was not brand-new to start with, began to look dirty, despite all the loving care of the mother and sister to keep it clean, and Gregor often spent whole evenings gazing at the many greasy spots on the garment, gleaming with gold buttons always in a high state of polish, in which the old man sat sleeping in extreme discomfort and yet quite peacefully.

As soon as the clock struck ten his mother tried to rouse his father with gentle words and to persuade him after that to get into bed, for sitting there he could not have a proper sleep and that was what he needed most, since he had to go on duty at six. But with the mulishness that had obsessed him since he became a bank messenger he always insisted on staying longer at the table, although he regularly fell asleep again and in the end only with the greatest trouble could be got out of his armchair and into his bed. However insistently Gregor's mother and sister kept urging him with gentle reminders, he would go on slowly shaking his head for a quarter of an hour, keeping his eyes shut, and refuse to get to his feet. The mother plucked at his sleeve, whispering endearments in his ear, the sister left her lessons to come to her mother's help, but Gregor's father was not to be caught. He would only sink down deeper in his chair. Not until the two women hoisted him up by the armpits did he open his eyes and look at them both, one after the other, usually with the remark: "This is a life. This is the peace and quiet of my old age." And leaning on the two of them he would heave himself up, with difficulty, as if he were a great burden to himself, suffer them to lead him as far as the door and then wave them off and go on alone, while the mother abandoned her needlework and the sister her pen in order to run after him and help him farther.

Who could find time, in this overworked and tired-out family, to bother about Gregor more than was absolutely needful? The household was reduced more and more; the servant girl was turned off; a gigantic bony charwoman with white hair flying round her head came in morning and evening to do the rough work; everything else was done by Gregor's mother, as well as great piles of sewing. Even various family ornaments, which his mother and sister used to wear with pride at parties and celebrations, had to be sold, as Gregor discovered of an evening from hearing them all discuss the prices obtained. But what they lamented most was the fact that they could not leave the flat which was much too big for their present circumstances, because they could not think of any way to shift Gregor. Yet Gregor saw well enough that consideration for him was not the main difficulty preventing the removal, for they could have easily shifted him in some suitable box with a few air holes in it; what really kept them from moving into another flat was rather their own complete hopelessness and the belief that they had been singled out for a misfortune such as had never happened to any of their relations or acquaintances. They fulfilled to the uttermost all that the world demands of poor people, the father fetched breakfast for the small clerks in the bank, the mother devoted her energy to making underwear for strangers, the sister trotted to and fro behind the counter at the behest of customers, but more than this they had not the strength to do. And the wound in Gregor's back began to nag at him afresh when his mother and sister, after getting his father into bed, came back again, left their work lying, drew close to each other and sat cheek to cheek; when his mother, pointing towards his room, said: "Shut that door now, Grete," and he was left again in darkness, while next door the women mingled their tears or perhaps sat dry-eyed staring at the table.

Gregor hardly slept at all by night or by day. He was often haunted by the idea that next time the door opened he would take the family's affairs in hand again just as he used to do; once more, after this long interval, there appeared in his thoughts the figures of the chief and the chief clerk, the commercial travelers and the apprentices, the porter who was so dull-witted, two or three friends in other firms, a chambermaid in one of the rural hotels, a sweet and fleeting memory, a cashier in a milliner's shop, whom he had wooed earnestly but too slowly—they all appeared, together with strangers or people he had quite forgotten, but instead of helping him and his family they were one and all unapproachable and he was glad when they vanished. At other times he would not be in the mood to bother about his family, he was only filled with rage at the way they were neglecting him, and although he had no clear idea of what he might care to eat he would make plans for getting into the larder to take the food that was after all his due, even if he were not hungry. His sister no longer took thought to bring him what might especially please him, but in the morning and at noon before she went to business hurriedly pushed into his room with her foot any food that was available, and in the evening cleared it out again with one sweep of the broom, heedless of whether it had been merely tasted, or—as most frequently happened—left untouched. The cleaning of his room, which she now did always in the evenings, could not have been more hastily done. Streaks of dirt stretched along the walls, here and there lay balls of dust and filth. At first Gregor used to station himself in some particularly filthy corner when his sister arrived, in order to reproach her with it, so to speak. But he could have sat there for weeks without getting her to make any improvement; she could see the dirt as well as he did, but she had simply made up her mind to leave it alone. And yet, with a touchiness that was new to her, which seemed anyhow to have infected the whole family, she jealously guarded her claim to be the sole caretaker of Gregor's room. His mother once subjected his room to a thorough cleaning, which was achieved only by means of several buckets of water—all this dampness of course upset Gregor too and he lay widespread, sulky and motionless on the sofa—but she was well punished for it. Hardly had his sister noticed the changed aspect of his room that evening than she rushed in high dudgeon into the living room and, despite the imploringly raised hands of her mother, burst into a storm of weeping, while her parents—her father had of course been startled out of his chair—looked on at first in helpless amazement; then they too began to go into action; the father reproached the mother on his right for not having left the cleaning of Gregor's room to his sister; shrieked at the sister on his left that never again was she to be allowed to clean Gregor's room; while the mother tried to pull the father into his bedroom, since he was beyond himself with agitation; the sister, shaken with sobs, then beat upon the table with her small fists; and Gregor hissed loudly with rage because not one of them thought of shutting the door to spare him such a spectacle and so much noise.

Still, even if the sister, exhausted by her daily work, had grown tired of looking after Gregor as she did formerly, there was no need for his mother's intervention or for Gregor's being neglected at all. The charwoman was there. This old widow, whose strong bony frame had enabled her to survive the worst a long life could offer, by no means recoiled from Gregor. Without being in the least curious she had once by chance opened the door of his room and at the sight of Gregor, who, taken by surprise, began to rush to and fro although no one was chasing him, merely stood there with her arms folded. From that time she never failed to open his door a little for a moment, morning and evening, to have a look at him. At first she even used to call him to her, with words which apparently she took to be friendly, such as: "Come along, then, you old dung beetle!" or "Look at the old dung beetle, then!" To such allocutions Gregor made no answer, but stayed motionless where he was, as if the door had never been opened. Instead of being allowed to disturb him so senselessly whenever the whim took her, she should rather have been ordered to clean out his room daily, that charwoman! Once, early in the morning—heavy rain was lashing on the windowpanes, perhaps a sign that spring was on the way—Gregor was so exasperated when she began addressing him again that he ran at her, as if to attack her, although slowly and feebly enough. But the charwoman instead of showing fright merely lifted high a chair that happened to be beside the door, and as she stood there with her mouth wide open it was clear that she meant to shut it only when she brought the chair down on Gregor's back. "So you're not coming any nearer?" she asked, as Gregor turned away again, and quietly put the chair back into the corner.

Gregor was now eating hardly anything. Only when he happened to pass the food laid out for him did he take a bit of something in his mouth as a pastime, kept it there for an hour at a time and usually spat it out again. At first he thought it was chagrin over the state of his room that prevented him from eating, yet he soon got used to the various changes in his room. It had become a habit in the family to push into his room things there was no room for elsewhere, and there were plenty of these now, since one of the rooms had been let to three lodgers. These serious gentlemen—all three of them with full beards, as Gregor once observed through a crack in the door—had a passion for order, not only in their own room but,

since they were now members of the household, in all its arrangements, especially in the kitchen. Superfluous, not to say dirty, objects they could not bear. Besides, they had brought with them most
of the furnishings they needed. For this reason many things could
be dispensed with that it was no use trying to sell but that should
not be thrown away either. All of them found their way into Gregor's
room. The ash can likewise and the kitchen garbage can. Anything
that was not needed for the moment was simply flung into Gregor's
room by the charwoman, who did everything in a hurry; fortunately
Gregor usually saw only the object, whatever it was, and the hand
that held it. Perhaps she intended to take the things away again
as time and opportunity offered, or to collect them until she could
throw them all out in a heap, but in fact they just lay wherever
she happened to throw them, except when Gregor pushed his way
through the junk heap and shifted it somewhat, at first out of necessity, because he had not room enough to crawl, but later with increasing enjoyment, although after such excursions, being sad and
weary to death, he would lie motionless for hours. And since the
lodgers often ate their supper at home in the common living room,
the living-room door stayed shut many an evening, yet Gregor reconciled himself quite easily to the shutting of the door, for often
enough on evenings when it was opened he had disregarded it entirely and lain in the darkest corner of his room, quite unnoticed by
the family. But on one occasion the charwoman left the door open
a little and it stayed ajar even when the lodgers came in for supper
and the lamp was lit. They set themselves at the top end of the
table where formerly Gregor and his father and mother had eaten
their meals, unfolded their napkins and took knife and fork in hand.
At once his mother appeared in the other doorway with a dish of
meat and close behind her his sister with a dish of potatoes piled high.
The food steamed with a thick vapor. The lodgers bent over the food
set before them as if to scrutinize it before eating, in fact the man in
the middle, who seemed to pass for an authority with the other two,
cut a piece of meat as it lay on the dish, obviously to discover if it were
tender or should be sent back to the kitchen. He showed satisfaction,
and Gregor's mother and sister, who had been watching anxiously,
breathed freely and began to smile.

The family itself took its meals in the kitchen. None the less,
Gregor's father came into the living room before going into the kitch-
en and with one prolonged bow, cap in hand, made a round of the
table. The lodgers all stood up and murmured something in their
beards. When they were alone again they ate their food in almost
complete silence. It seemed remarkable to Gregor that among the
various noises coming from the table he could always distinguish the
sound of their masticating teeth, as if this were a sign to Gregor

that one needed teeth in order to eat, and that with toothless jaws even of the finest make one could do nothing. "I'm hungry enough," said Gregor sadly to himself, "but not for that kind of food. How these lodgers are stuffing themselves, and here am I dying of starvation!"

On that very evening—during the whole of his time there Gregor could not remember ever having heard the violin—the sound of violin-playing came from the kitchen. The lodgers had already finished their supper, the one in the middle had brought out a newspaper and given the other two a page apiece, and now they were leaning back at ease reading and smoking. When the violin began to play they pricked up their ears, got to their feet, and went on tiptoe to the hall door where they stood huddled together. Their movements must have been heard in the kitchen, for Gregor's father called out: "Is the violin-playing disturbing you, gentlemen? It can be stopped at once." "On the contrary," said the middle lodger, "could not Fräulein Samsa come and play in this room, beside us, where it is much more convenient and comfortable?" "Oh certainly," cried Gregor's father, as if he were the violin-player. The lodgers came back into the living room and waited. Presently Gregor's father arrived with the music stand, his mother carrying the music and his sister with the violin. His sister quietly made everything ready to start playing; his parents, who had never let rooms before and so had an exaggerated idea of the courtesy due to lodgers, did not venture to sit down on their own chairs; his father leaned against the door, the right hand thrust between two buttons of his livery coat, which was formally buttoned up; but his mother was offered a chair by one of the lodgers and, since she left the chair just where he had happened to put it, sat down in a corner to one side.

Gregor's sister began to play; the father and mother, from either side, intently watched the movements of her hands. Gregor, attracted by the playing, ventured to move forward a little until his head was actually inside the living room. He felt hardly any surprise at his growing lack of consideration for the others; there had been a time when he prided himself on being considerate. And yet just on this occasion he had more reason than ever to hide himself, since owing to the amount of dust which lay thick in his room and rose into the air at the slightest movement, he too was covered with dust; fluff and hair and remnants of food trailed with him, caught on his back and along his sides; his indifference to everything was much too great for him to turn on his back and scrape himself clean on the carpet, as once he had done several times a day. And in spite of his condition, no shame deterred him from advancing a little over the spotless floor of the living room.

To be sure, no one was aware of him. The family was entirely absorbed in the violin-playing; the lodgers, however, who first of all had stationed themselves, hands in pockets, much too close behind the music stand so that they could all have read the music, which must have bothered his sister, had soon retreated to the window, half-whispering with downbent heads, and stayed there while his father turned an anxious eye on them. Indeed, they were making it more than obvious that they had been disappointed in their ex-pectation of hearing good or enjoyable violin-playing, that they had had more than enough of the performance and only out of courtesy suffered a continued disturbance of their peace. From the way they all kept blowing the smoke of their cigars high in the air through nose and mouth one could divine their irritation. And yet Gregor's sister was playing so beautifully. Her face leaned sideways, intently and sadly her eyes followed the notes of music. Gregor crawled a little farther forward and lowered his head to the ground so that it might be possible for his eyes to meet hers. Was he an animal, that music had such an effect upon him? He felt as if the way were opening before him to the unknown nourishment he craved. He was deter-mined to push forward till he reached his sister, to pull at her skirt and so let her know that she was to come into his room with her violin, for no one here appreciated her playing as he would appreciate it. He would never let her out of his room, at least, not so long as he lived; his frightful appearance would become, for the first time, useful to him; he would watch all the doors of his room at once and spit at intruders; but his sister should need no constraint, she should stay with him of her own free will; she should sit beside him on the sofa, bend down her ear to him and hear him confide that he had had the firm intention of sending her to the Conservatorium, and that, but for his mishap, last Christmas—surely Christmas was long past?—he would have announced it to everybody without allowing a single objection. After this confession his sister would be so touched that she would burst into tears, and Gregor would then raise himself to her shoulder and kiss her on the neck, which, now that she went to business, she kept free of any ribbon or collar.

"Mr. Samsa!" cried the middle lodger, to Gregor's father, and pointed, without wasting any more words, at Gregor, now working himself slowly forwards. The violin fell silent, the middle lodger first smiled to his friends with a shake of the head and then looked at Gregor again. Instead of driving Gregor out, his father seemed to think it more needful to begin by soothing down the lodgers, although they were not at all agitated and apparently found Gregor more entertaining than the violin-playing. He hurried towards them and spreading out his arms, tried to urge them back into their own room and at the same time to block their view of Gregor. They now began to be really a little angry, one could not tell whether because of the old man's behavior or because it had just dawned on them that all unwittingly they had such a neighbor as Gregor next door. They demanded explanations of his father, they waved their arms like him, tugged uneasily at their beards, and only with reluctance backed towards their room. Meanwhile Gregor's sister, who stood there as if lost when her playing was so abruptly broken off, came to life again, pulled herself together all at once after standing for a while holding violin and bow in nervelessly hanging hands and staring at her music, pushed her violin into the lap of her mother, who was still sitting in her chair fighting asthmatically for breath, and ran into the lodgers' room to which they were now being shepherded by her father rather more quickly than before. One could see the pillows and blankets on the beds flying under her accustomed fingers and being laid in order. Before the lodgers had actually reached their room she had finished making the beds and slipped out.

The old man seemed once more to be so possessed by his mulish self-assertiveness that he was forgetting all the respect he should show to his lodgers. He kept driving them on and driving them on until in the very door of the bedroom the middle lodger stamped his foot loudly on the floor and so brought him to a halt. "I beg to announce," said the lodger, lifting one hand and looking also at Gregor's mother and sister, "that because of the disgusting conditions prevailing in this household and family"—here he spat on the floor with emphatic brevity—"I give you notice on the spot. Naturally I won't pay you a penny for the days I have lived here, on the contrary I shall consider bringing an action for damages against you, based on claims—believe me—that will be easily susceptible of proof." He ceased and stared straight in front of him, as if he expected something. In fact his two friends at once rushed into the breach with these words: "And we too give notice on the spot." On that he seized the door-handle and shut the door with a slam.

Gregor's father, groping with his hands, staggered forward and fell into his chair; it looked as if he were stretching himself there for his ordinary evening nap, but the marked jerkings of his head, which was as if uncontrollable, showed that he was far from asleep. Gregor had simply stayed quietly all the time on the spot where the lodgers had espied him. Disappointment at the failure of his plan, perhaps also the weakness arising from extreme hunger, made it impossible for him to move. He feared, with a fair degree of certainty, that at any moment the general tension would discharge itself in a combined attack upon him, and he lay waiting. He did not react even to the noise made by the violin as it fell off his mother's lap from under her trembling fingers and gave out a resonant note.

"My dear parents," said his sister, slapping her hand on the table by way of introduction, "things can't go on like this. Perhaps you don't realize that, but I do. I won't utter my brother's name in the presence of this creature, and so all I say is: we must try to get rid of it. We've tried to look after it and to put up with it as far as is humanly possible, and I don't think anyone could reproach us in the slightest."

"She is more than right," said Gregor's father to himself. His mother, who was still choking for lack of breath, began to cough hollowly into her hand with a wild look in her eyes.

His sister rushed over to her and held her forehead. His father's thoughts seemed to have lost their vagueness at Grete's words, he sat more upright, fingering his service cap that lay among the plates still lying on the table from the lodgers' supper, and from time to time looked at the still form of Gregor.

"We must try to get rid of it," his sister now said explicitly to her father, since her mother was coughing too much to hear a word, "it will be the death of both of you, I can see that coming. When one has to work as hard as we do, all of us, one can't stand this continual torment at home on top of it. At least I can't stand it any longer." And she burst into such a passion of sobbing that her tears dropped on her mother's face, where she wiped them off mechanically.

"My dear," said the old man sympathetically, and with evident understanding, "but what can we do?"

Gregor's sister merely shrugged her shoulders to indicate the feeling of helplessness that had now overmastered her during her weeping fit, in contrast to her former confidence.

"If he could understand us," said her father, half questioningly; Grete, still sobbing, vehemently waved a hand to show how unthinkable that was.

"If he could understand us," repeated the old man, shutting his eyes to consider his daughter's conviction that understanding was impossible, "then perhaps we might come to some agreement with him. But as it is——"

"He must go," cried Gregor's sister, "that's the only solution, Father. You must just try to get rid of the idea that this is Gregor. The fact that we've believed it for so long is the root of all our trouble. But how can it be Gregor? If this were Gregor, he would have realized long ago that human beings can't live with such a creature, and he'd have gone away on his own accord. Then we wouldn't have any brother, but we'd be able to go on living and keep his memory in honor. As it is, this creature persecutes us, drives away our lodgers, obviously wants the whole apartment to himself and would have us all sleep in the gutter. Just look, Father," she shrieked all at once, "he's at it again!" And in an access of panic that was quite incomprehensible to Gregor she even quitted her mother, literally thrusting the chair from her as if she would rather sacrifice her mother than stay so near to Gregor, and rushed behind her father, who also rose up, being simply upset by her agitation, and half-spread his arms out as if to protect her.

Yet Gregor had not the slightest intention of frightening anyone, far less his sister. He had only begun to turn round in order to crawl back to his room, but it was certainly a startling operation to watch, since because of his disabled condition he could not execute the difficult turning movements except by lifting his head and then bracing it against the floor over and over again. He paused and looked round. His good intentions seemed to have been recognized; the alarm had only been momentary. Now they were all watching him in melancholy silence. His mother lay in her chair, her legs stiffly outstretched and pressed together, her eyes almost closing for sheer weariness; his father and his sister were sitting beside each other, his sister's arm around the old man's neck.

Perhaps I can go on turning round now, thought Gregor, and began his labors again. He could not stop himself from panting with the effort, and had to pause now and then to take breath. Nor did anyone harass him, he was left entirely to himself. When he had completed the turn-round he began at once to crawl straight back. He was amazed at the distance separating him from his room and could not understand how in his weak state he had managed to accomplish the same journey so recently, almost without remarking it. Intent on crawling as fast as possible, he barely noticed that not a single word, not an ejaculation from his family, interfered with his progress. Only when he was already in the doorway did he turn his head round, not completely, for his neck muscles were getting stiff, but enough to see that nothing had changed behind him except that his sister had risen to her feet. His last glance fell on his mother, who was not quite overcome by sleep.

Hardly was he well inside his room when the door was hastily pushed shut, bolted and locked. The sudden noise in his rear startled him so much that his little legs gave beneath him. It was his sister who had shown such haste. She had been standing ready waiting and had made a light spring forward, Gregor had not even heard her coming, and she cried "At last!" to her parents as she turned the key in the lock.

"And what now?" said Gregor to himself, looking round in the darkness. Soon he made the discovery that he was now unable to stir a limb. This did not surprise him, rather it seemed unnatural that he should ever actually have been able to move on these feeble little legs. Otherwise he felt relatively comfortable. True, his whole body was aching, but it seemed that the pain was gradually growing less and would finally pass away. The rotting apple in his back and the inflamed area around it, all covered with soft dust, already hardly troubled him. He thought of his family with tenderness and love. The decision that he must disappear was one that he held to even more strongly than his sister, if that were possible. In this state of vacant and peaceful meditation he remained until the tower clock struck three in the morning. The first broadening of light in the world outside the window entered his consciousness once more. Then his head sank to the floor of its own accord and from his nostrils came the last faint flicker of his breath.

When the charwoman arrived early in the morning—what between her strength and her impatience she slammed all the doors so loudly, never mind how often she had been begged not to do so, that no one in the whole apartment could enjoy any quiet sleep after her arrival—she noticed nothing unusual as she took her customary peep into Gregor's room. She thought he was lying motionless on purpose, pretending to be in the sulks; she credited him with every kind of intelligence. Since she happened to have the long-handled broom in her hand she tried to tickle him up with it from the doorway. When that too produced no reaction she felt provoked and poked at him a little harder, and only when she had pushed him along the floor without meeting any resistance was her attention aroused. It did not take her long to establish the truth of the matter, and her eyes widened, she let out a whistle, yet did not waste much time over it but tore open the door of the Samsas' bedroom and yelled into the darkness at the top of her voice: "Just look at this, it's dead; it's lying here dead and done for!"

Mr. and Mrs. Samsa started up in their double bed and before they realized the nature of the charwoman's announcement had some difficulty in overcoming the shock of it. But then they got out of bed quickly, one on either side, Mr. Samsa throwing a blanket over his shoulders, Mrs. Samsa in nothing but her nightgown; in this array they entered Gregor's room. Meanwhile the door of the living room opened, too, where Grete had been sleeping since the advent of the lodgers; she was completely dressed as if she had not been to bed, which seemed to be confirmed also by the paleness of her face. "Dead?" said Mrs. Samsa, looking questioningly at the charwoman, although she could have investigated for herself, and the fact was obvious enough without investigation. "I should say so," said the charwoman, proving her words by pushing Gregor's corpse a long way to one side with her broomstick. Mrs. Samsa made a movement as if to stop her, but checked it. "Well," said Mr. Samsa, "now thanks be to God." He crossed himself, and the three women followed his example. Grete, whose eyes never left the corpse, said: "Just see how thin he was. It's such a long time since he's eaten anything. The food came out again just as it went in." Indeed,

Gregor's body was completely flat and dry, as could only now be seen when it was no longer supported by the legs and nothing prevented one from looking closely at it.

"Come in beside us, Grete, for a little while," said Mrs. Samsa with a tremulous smile, and Grete, not without looking back at the corpse, followed her parents into their bedroom. The charwoman shut the door and opened the window wide. Although it was so early in the morning a certain softness was perceptible in the fresh air. After all, it was already the end of March.

The three lodgers emerged from their room and were surprised to see no breakfast; they had been forgotten. "Where's our breakfast?" said the middle lodger peevishly to the charwoman. But she put her finger to her lips and hastily, without a word, indicated by gestures that they should go into Gregor's room. They did so and stood, their hands in the pockets of their somewhat shabby coats, around Gregor's corpse in the room where it was now fully light.

At that the door of the Samsas' bedroom opened and Mr. Samsa appeared in his uniform, his wife on one arm, his daughter on the other. They all looked a little as if they had been crying; from time to time Grete hid her face on her father's arm.

"Leave my house at once!" said Mr. Samsa, and pointed to the door without disengaging himself from the women. "What do you mean by that?" said the middle lodger, taken somewhat aback, with a feeble smile. The two others put their hands behind them and kept rubbing them together, as if in gleeful expectation of a fine set-to in which they were bound to come off the winners. "I mean just what I say," answered Mr. Samsa, and advanced in a straight line with his two companions towards the lodger. He stood his ground at first quietly, looking at the floor as if his thoughts were taking a new pattern in his head. "Then let us go, by all means," he said, and looked up at Mr. Samsa as if in a sudden access of humility he were expecting some renewed sanction for this decision. Mr. Samsa merely nodded briefly once or twice with meaning eyes. Upon that the lodger really did go with long strides into the hall, his two friends had been listening and had quite stopped rubbing their hands for some moments and now went scuttling after him as if afraid that Mr. Samsa might get into the hall before them and cut them off from their leader. In the hall they all three took their hats from the rack, their sticks from the umbrella stand, bowed in silence and quitted the apartment. With a suspiciousness which proved quite unfounded Mr. Samsa and the two women followed them out to the landing; leaning over the banister they watched the three figures slowly but surely going down the long stairs, vanishing from sight at a certain turn of the staircase on every floor and coming into view again after a moment or so; the more they dwindled, the more the Samsa family's interest in them dwindled, and when a butcher's boy met them and passed them on the stairs coming up proudly with a tray on his head, Mr. Samsa and the two women soon left the landing and as if a burden had been lifted from them went back into their apartment.

They decided to spend this day in resting and going for a stroll; they had not only deserved such a respite from work, but absolutely needed it. And so they sat down at the table and wrote three notes of excuse, Mr. Samsa to his board of management, Mrs. Samsa to her employer and Grete to the head of her firm. While they were writing, the charwoman came in to say that she was going now, since her morning's work was finished. At first they only nodded without looking up, but as she kept hovering there they eyed her irritably. "Well?" said Mr. Samsa. The charwoman stood grinning in the doorway as if she had good news to impart to the family but meant not to say a word unless properly questioned. The small ostrich feather standing upright on her hat, which had annoyed Mr. Samsa ever since she was engaged, was waving gaily in all directions. "Well, what is it then?" asked Mrs. Samsa, who obtained more respect from the charwoman than the others. "Oh," said the charwoman, giggling so amiably that she could not at once continue, "just this, you don't need to bother about how to get rid of the thing next door. It's been seen to already." Mrs. Samsa and Grete bent over their letters again, as if preoccupied; Mr. Samsa, who perceived that she was eager to begin describing it all in detail, stopped her with a decisive hand. But since she was not allowed to tell her story, she remembered the great hurry she was in, being obviously deeply huffed: "Bye, everybody," she said, whirling off violently, and departed with a frightful slamming of doors.

"She'll be given notice tonight," said Mr. Samsa, but neither from his wife nor his daughter did he get any answer, for the charwoman seemed to have shattered again the composure they had barely achieved. They rose, went to the window and stayed there, clasping each other tight. Mr. Samsa turned in his chair to look at them and quietly observed them for a little. Then he called out: "Come along, now, do. Let bygones by bygones. And you might have some consideration for me." The two of them complied at once, hastened to him, caressed him and quickly finished their letters.

Then they all three left the apartment together, which was more than they had done for months, and went by tram into the open country outside the town. The tram, in which they were the only passengers, was filled with warm sunshine. Leaning comfortably back in their seats they canvassed their prospects for the future, and it appeared on closer inspection that these were not at all bad, for the jobs they had got, which so far they had never really discussed with each other, were all three admirable and likely to lead to better things later on. The greatest immediate improvement in their condition would of course arise from moving to another house; they wanted to take a smaller and cheaper but also better situated and more easily run apartment than the one they had, which Gregor had selected. While they were thus conversing, it struck both Mr. and Mrs. Samsa, almost at the same moment, as they became aware of their daughter's increasing vivacity, that in spite of all the sorrow of recent times, which had made her cheeks pale, she had bloomed into a pretty girl with a good figure. They grew quieter and half unconsciously exchanged glances of complete agreement, having come to the conclusion that it would soon be time to find a good husband for her. And it was like a confirmation of their new dreams and excellent intentions that at the end of their journey their daughter sprang to her feet first and stretched her young body.

MARCEL PROUST
(1871–1922)
Remembrance of Things Past
(À la Recherche du temps perdu)*

It was at the Marquise de Saint-Euverte's, on the last, for that season, of the evenings on which she invited people to listen to the musicians who would serve, later on, for her charity concerts. Swann, who had intended to go to each of the previous evenings in turn, but had never been able to make up his mind, received, while he was dressing for this party, a visit from the Baron de Charlus, who came with an offer to go with him to the Marquise's, if his company could be of any use in helping Swann not to feel quite so bored when he got there, to be a little less unhappy. But Swann had thanked him with:

"You can't conceive how glad I should be of your company. But the greatest pleasure that you can give me will be if you will go instead to see Odette.[1] You know what a splendid influence you have over her. I don't suppose she'll be going anywhere this evening, unless she goes to see her old dressmaker, and I'm sure she would be de-

* 1913–1927. Translated by C. K. Scott Moncrieff. Reprinted by permission of Random House, Inc. Our selection is from *Swann's Way* (*Du Côté de chez Swann*, 1913), the first part of Proust's novel. The punctuation ". . ." does not indicate omissions from this text.

1. Charles Swann had paid court to Odette de Crécy, a woman of rather doubtful antecedents, and she had become his mistress. Not, however, until she showed indifference and avoided him did Swann, who hitherto had imagined his emotions to be in perfect control, fall hopelessly in love with her.

lighted if you went with her there. In any case, you'll find her at home before then. Try to keep her amused, and also to give her a little sound advice. If you could arrange something for tomorrow which would please her, something that we could all three do together. Try to put out a feeler, too, for the summer; see if there's anything she wants to do, a cruise that we might all three take; anything you can think of. I don't count upon seeing her tonight, myself; still if she would like me to come, or if you find a loophole, you've only to send me a line at Mme. de Saint-Euverte's up till midnight; after that I shall be here. Ever so many thanks for all you are doing for me—you know what I feel about you!"

His friend promised to go and do as Swann wished as soon as he had deposited him at the door of the Saint-Euverte house, where he arrived soothed by the thought that M. de Charlus would be spending the evening in the Rue La Pérouse,[2] but in a state of melancholy indifference to everything that did not involve Odette, and in particular to the details of fashionable life, a state which invested them with the charm that is to be found in anything which, being no longer an object of our desire, appears to us in its own guise. On alighting from his carriage, in the foreground of that fictitious summary of their domestic existence which hostesses are pleased to offer to their guests on ceremonial occasions, and in which they shew a great regard for accuracy of costume and setting, Swann was amused to discover the heirs and successors of Balzac's[3] 'tigers'[4] —now 'grooms'—who normally followed their mistress when she walked abroad, but now, hatted and booted, were posted out of doors, in front of the house on the gravelled drive, or outside the stables, as gardeners might be drawn up for inspection at the ends of their several flower-beds. The peculiar tendency which he had always had to look for analogies between living people and the portraits in galleries reasserted itself here, but in a more positive and more general form; it was society as a whole, now that he was detached from it, which presented itself to him in a series of pictures. In the cloak-room, into which, in the old days, when he was still a man of fashion, he would have gone in his overcoat, to emerge from it in evening dress, but without any impression of what had occurred there, his mind having been, during the minute or two that he had spent in it, either still at the party which he had just left, or already at the party into which he was just about to be ushered, he now noticed, for the first time, roused by the unexpected arrival of so belated a guest, the scattered pack of splendid effortless animals, the enormous footmen who were drowsing here and there upon

2. Odette lived on this street.
3. Honoré de Balzac (1799–1850), French novelist, whose novels are known collectively as the *Human Comedy*. See the section on realism.
4. grooms, footmen.

benches and chests, until, pointing their noble greyhound profiles, they towered upon their feet and gathered in a circle round about him.

One of them, of a particularly ferocious aspect, and not unlike the headsman in certain Renaissance pictures which represent executions, tortures, and the like, advanced upon him with an implacable air to take his 'things.' But the harshness of his steely glare was compensated by the softness of his cotton gloves, so effectively that, as he approached Swann, he seemed to be exhibiting at once an utter contempt for his person and the most tender regard for his hat. He took it with a care to which the precision of his movements imparted something that was almost overfastidious, and with a delicacy that was rendered almost touching by the evidence of his splendid strength. Then he passed it to one of his satellites, a novice and timid, who was expressing the panic that overpowered him by casting furious glances in every direction, and displayed all the dumb agitation of a wild animal in the first hours of its captivity.

A few feet away, a strapping great lad in livery stood musing, motionless, statuesque, useless, like that purely decorative warrior whom one sees in the most tumultuous of Mantegna's[5] paintings, lost in dreams, leaning upon his shield, while all around him are fighting and bloodshed and death; detached from the group of his companions who were thronging about Swann, he seemed as determined to remain unconcerned in the scene, which he followed vaguely with his cruel, greenish eyes, as if it had been the Massacre of the Innocents or the Martyrdom of Saint James. He seemed precisely to have sprung from that vanished race—if, indeed, it ever existed, save in the reredos of San Zeno[6] and the frescoes of the Eremitani,[7] where Swann had come in contact with it, and where it still dreams—fruit of the impregnation of a classical statue by some one of the Master's[8] Paduan models, or of Albert Dürer's[9] Saxons. And the locks of his reddish hair, crinkled by nature, but glued to his head by brilliantine, were treated broadly as they are in that Greek sculpture which the Mantuan painter never ceased to study, and which, if in its creator's purpose it represents but man, manages at least to extract from man's simple outlines such a variety of richness, borrowed, as it were, from the whole of animated nature, that a head of hair, by the glossy undulation and beak-like points of its curls, or in the overlaying of the florid triple diadem of its brushed tresses, can suggest at once a bunch of seaweed, a brood of fledgling doves, a bed of hyacinths and a serpent's writhing back. Others again, no less colossal, were dis-

5. Andrea Mantegna (1431–1506), Italian painter, died at Mantua. Such figures can be seen in the paintings named at the end of this sentence, which are among the frescoes the artist painted in the two churches mentioned in the following sentence.
6. a church in Verona.
7. the church of San Agostino degli Eremitani in Padua.
8. Mantegna's.
9. German painter (1471–1528).

posed upon the steps of a monumental staircase which, by their
decorative presence and marmorean immobility, was made worthy
to be named, like that god-crowned ascent in the Palace of the
Doges,[10] the 'Staircase of the Giants,' and on which Swann now set
foot, saddened by the thought that Odette had never climbed it.
Ah, with what joy would he, on the other hand, have raced up the
dark, evil-smelling, breakneck flights to the little dressmaker's, in
whose attic he would so gladly have paid the price of a weekly stage-
box at the Opera for the right to spend the evening there when
Odette came, and other days too, for the privilege of talking about
her, of living among people whom she was in the habit of seeing
when he was not there, and who, on that account, seemed to keep
secret among themselves some part of the life of his mistress more
real, more inaccessible and more mysterious than anything that he
knew. Whereas upon that pestilential, enviable staircase to the old
dressmaker's, since there was no other, no service stair in the building, one saw in the evening outside every door an empty, unwashed
milk-can set out, in readiness for the morning round, upon the door-
mat; on the despicable, enormous staircase which Swann was at that
moment climbing, on either side of him, at different levels, before
each anfractuosity[11] made in its walls by the window of the porter's
lodge or the entrance to a set of rooms, representing the departments of indoor service which they controlled, and doing homage
for them to the guests, a gate-keeper, a major-domo, a steward
(worthy men who spent the rest of the week in semi-independence
in their own domains, dined there by themselves like small shop-
keepers, and might tomorrow lapse to the plebeian service of some
successful doctor or industrial magnate), scrupulous in carrying out
to the letter all the instructions that had been heaped upon them
before they were allowed to don the brilliant livery which they wore
only at long intervals, and in which they did not feel altogether at
their ease, stood each in the arcade of his doorway, their splendid
pomp tempered by a democratic good-fellowship, like saints in their
niches, and a gigantic usher, dressed Swiss Guard fashion, like the
beadle in a church, struck the pavement with his staff as each fresh
arrival passed him. Coming to the top of the staircase, up which
he had been followed by a servant with a pallid countenance and
a small pigtail clubbed at the back of his head, like one of Goya's[12]
sacristans or a tabellion[13] in an old play, Swann passed by an office in
which the lackeys, seated like notaries before their massive registers,
rose solemnly to their feet and inscribed his name. He next crossed
a little hall which—just as certain rooms are arranged by their

10. The Doge was the elected ruler
of Venice (697–1797).
11. channel, crevice, or passage full
of windings and turnings.

12. Francisco Goya (1746–1828),
Spanish painter.
13. notary or scrivener.

owners to serve as the setting for a single work of art (from which they take their name), and, in their studied bareness, contain nothing else besides—displayed to him as he entered it, like some priceless effigy by Benvenuto Cellini[14] of an armed watchman, a young footman, his body slightly bent forward, rearing above his crimson gorget[15] an even more crimson face, from which seemed to burst forth torrents of fire, timidity and zeal, who, as he pierced the Aubusson tapestries[16] that screened the door of the room in which the music was being given with his impetuous, vigilant, desperate gaze, appeared, with a soldierly impassibility or a supernatural faith —an allegory of alarums, incarnation of alertness, commemoration of a riot—to be looking out, angel or sentinel, from the tower of dungeon or cathedral, for the approach of the enemy or for the hour of Judgment. Swann had now only to enter the concert-room, the doors of which were thrown open to him by an usher loaded with chains, who bowed low before him as though tendering to him the keys of a conquered city. But he thought of the house in which at that very moment he might have been, if Odette had but permitted, and the remembered glimpse of an empty milk-can upon a door-mat wrung his heart.

He speedily recovered his sense of the general ugliness of the human male when, on the other side of the tapestry curtain, the spectacle of the servants gave place to that of the guests. But even this ugliness of faces, which of course were mostly familiar to him, seemed something new and uncanny, now that their features,—instead of being to him symbols of practical utility in the identification of this or that man, who until then had represented merely so many pleasures to be sought-after, boredoms to be avoided, or courtesies to be acknowledged—were at rest, measurable by aesthetic co-ordinates alone, in the autonomy of their curves and angles. And in these men, in the thick of whom Swann now found himself packed, there was nothing (even to the monocle which many of them wore, and which, previously, would, at the most, have enabled Swann to say that so-and-so wore a monocle) which, no longer restricted to the general connotation of a habit, the same in all of them, did not now strike him with a sense of individuality in each. Perhaps because he did not regard General de Froberville and the Marquis de Bréauté, who were talking together just inside the door, as anything more than two figures in a picture, whereas they were the old and useful friends who had put him up for the Jockey Club[17] and had supported him in duels, the General's monocle, stuck like a shell-splinter in his common, scarred, victorious, overbearing face, in the middle of a

14. Florentine engraver, sculptor and goldsmith (1500–1571). See the section on the Renaissance.

15. a piece of armor for the throat.

16. woven at Aubusson, in the *département* of Creuse, France.

17. a highly exclusive club which organizes race meetings.

forehead which it left half-blinded, like the single-eyed flashing front of the Cyclops,[18] appeared to Swann as a monstrous wound which it might have been glorious to receive but which it was certainly not decent to expose, while that which M. de Bréauté wore, as a festive badge, with his pearl-grey gloves, his crush hat and white tie, substituting it for the familiar pair of glasses (as Swann himself did) when he went out to places, bore, glued to its other side, like a specimen prepared on a slide for the microscope, an infinitesimal gaze that swarmed with friendly feeling and never ceased to twinkle at the loftiness of ceilings, the delightfulness of parties, the interestingness of programmes and the excellence of refreshments.

"Hallo! you here! why, it's ages since I've seen you," the General greeted Swann and, noticing the look of strain on his face and concluding that it was perhaps a serious illness that had kept him away, went on, "You're looking well, old man!" while M. de Bréauté turned with, "My dear fellow, what on earth are you doing here?" to a 'society novelist' who had just fitted into the angle of eyebrow and cheek his own monocle, the sole instrument that he used in his psychological investigations and remorseless analyses of character, and who now replied, with an air of mystery and importance, rolling the 'r';—"I am observing!"

The Marquis de Forestelle's monocle was minute and rimless, and, by enforcing an incessant and painful contraction of the eye over which it was incrusted like a superfluous cartilage, the presence of which there was inexplicable and its substance unimaginable, it gave to his face a melancholy refinement, and led women to suppose him capable of suffering terribly when in love. But that of M. de Saint-Candé, girdled, like Saturn, with an enormous ring, was the centre of gravity of a face which composed itself afresh every moment in relation to the glass, while his thrusting red nose and swollen sarcastic lips endeavoured by their grimaces to rise to the level of the steady flame of wit that sparkled in the polished disk, and saw itself preferred to the most ravishing eyes in the world by the smart, depraved young women whom it set dreaming of artificial charms and a refinement of sensual bliss; and then, behind him, M. de Palancy, who with his huge carp's head and goggling eyes moved slowly up and down the stream of festive gatherings, unlocking his great mandibles[19] at every moment as though in search of his orientation, had the air of carrying about upon his person only an accidental and perhaps purely symbolical fragment of the glass wall of his aquarium, a part intended to suggest the whole which recalled to Swann, a fervent admirer of Giotto's[20] Vices and Virtues at Padua, that In-

---

18. in Homer's *Odyssey*, a giant with but one eye in the middle of his forehead.

19. here, the upper and lower jaws.

20. Giotto di Bondone (1266?–1336?), Florentine painter.

justice by whose side a leafy bough evokes the idea of the forests
that enshroud his secret lair.

Swann had gone forward into the room, under pressure from Mme.
de Saint-Euverte and in order to listen to an aria from *Orfeo*[21] which
was being rendered on the flute, and had taken up a position in a
corner from which, unfortunately, his horizon was bounded by two
ladies of 'uncertain' age, seated side by side, the Marquise de Cambremer and the Vicomtesse de Franquetot, who, because they were
cousins, used to spend their time at parties in wandering through
the rooms, each clutching her bag and followed by her daughter,
hunting for one another like people at a railway station, and could
never be at rest until they had reserved, by marking them with their
fans or handkerchiefs, two adjacent chairs; Mme. de Cambremer,
since she knew scarcely anyone, being all the more glad of a companion, while Mme. de Franquetot, who, on the contrary, was extremely
popular, thought it effective and original to shew all her fine friends
that she preferred to their company that of an obscure country
cousin with whom she had childish memories in common. Filled
with ironical melancholy, Swann watched them as they listened to
the pianoforte intermezzo (Liszt's[22] 'Saint Francis preaching to the
birds') which came after the flute, and followed the virtuoso in his
dizzy flight; Mme. de Franquetot anxiously, her eyes starting from
her head, as though the keys over which his fingers skipped with such
agility were a series of trapezes, from any one of which he might
come crashing, a hundred feet, to the ground, stealing now and then
a glance of astonishment and unbelief at her companion, as who
should say: "It isn't possible, I would never have believed that a
human being could do all that!"; Mme. de Cambremer, as a woman
who had received a sound musical education, beating time with her
head—transformed for the nonce into the pendulum of a metronome,
the sweep and rapidity of whose movements from one shoulder to
the other (performed with that look of wild abandonment in her eye
which a sufferer shews who is no longer able to analyse his pain, nor
anxious to master it, and says merely "I can't help it") so increased
that at every moment her diamond earrings caught in the trimming
of her bodice, and she was obliged to put straight the bunch of black
grapes which she had in her hair, though without any interruption
of her constantly accelerated motion. On the other side (and a little
way in front) of Mme. de Franquetot was the Marquise de Gallardon,
absorbed in her favourite meditation, namely, upon her own kinship
with the Guermantes family,[23] from which she derived both publicly
and in private a good deal of glory not unmingled with shame, the

21. an opera (1762) with music by
Christoph Willibald Gluck (1714–
1787).

22. Franz Liszt (1811–1886), Hun-
garian composer.
    23. in Proust's novel, an aristocratic
family of the greatest eminence.

most brilliant ornaments of that house remaining somewhat aloof from her, perhaps because she was just a tiresome old woman, or because she was a scandalous old woman, or because she came of an inferior branch of the family, or very possibly for no reason at all. When she found herself seated next to some one whom she did not know, as she was at this moment next to Mme. de Franquetot, she suffered acutely from the feeling that her own consciousness of her Guermantes connection could not be made externally manifest in visible characters, like those which, in the mosaics in Byzantine churches, placed one beneath another, inscribe in a vertical column by the side of some Sacred Personage the words which he is supposed to be uttering. At this moment she was pondering the fact that she had never received an invitation, or even a call, from her young cousin the Princesse des Laumes,[24] during the six years that had already elapsed since the latter's marriage. The thought filled her with anger—and with pride; for, by virtue of having told everyone who expressed surprise at never seeing her at Mme. des Laumes's, that it was because of the risk of meeting the Princesse Mathilde[25] there—a degradation which her own family, the truest and bluest of Legitimists,[26] would never have forgiven her, she had come gradually to believe that this actually was the reason for her not visiting her young cousin. She remembered, it is true, that she had several times inquired of Mme. des Laumes how they might contrive to meet, but she remembered it only in a confused way, and besides did more than neutralise this slightly humiliating reminiscence by murmuring, "After all, it isn't for me to take the first step; I am at least twenty years older than she is." And fortified by these unspoken words she flung her shoulders proudly back until they seemed to part company with her bust, while her head, which lay almost horizontally upon them, made one think of the 'stuck-on' head of a pheasant which is brought to the table regally adorned with its feathers. Not that she in the least degree resembled a pheasant, having been endowed by nature with a short and squat and masculine figure; but successive mortifications had given her a backward tilt, such as one may observe in trees which have taken root on the very edge of a precipice and are forced to grow backwards to preserve their balance. Since she was obliged, in order to console herself for not being quite on a level with the rest of the Guermantes, to repeat to herself incessantly that it was owing to the uncompromising rigidity of her principles and pride that she saw so little of them, the constant iteration had gradually remoulded her body, and had given her a sort of 'bearing' which was accepted by the plebeian as a sign of breeding,

24. later, on the death of her father-in-law, to be known as the Duchesse de Guermantes.

25. a Bonaparte princess. This real-life personage appears as a character in Proust's novel.

26. royalists.

and even kindled, at times, a momentary spark in the jaded eyes of old gentlemen in clubs. Had anyone subjected Mme. de Gallardon's conversation to that form of analysis which by noting the relative frequency of its several terms would furnish him with the key to a ciphered message, he would at once have remarked that no expression, not even the commonest forms of speech, occurred in it nearly so often as "at my cousins the Guermantes'," "at my aunt Guermantes's," "Elzéar de Guermantes's health," "my cousin Guermantes's box." If anyone spoke to her of a distinguished personage, she would reply that, although she was not personally acquainted with him, she had seen him hundreds of times at her aunt Guermantes's, but she would utter this reply in so icy a tone, with such a hollow sound, that it was at once quite clear that if she did not know the celebrity personally that was because of all the obstinate, ineradicable principles against which her arching shoulders were stretched back to rest, as on one of those ladders on which gymnastic instructors make us 'extend' so as to develop the expansion of our chests.

At this moment the Princesse des Laumes, who had not been expected to appear at Mme. de Saint-Euverte's that evening, did in fact arrive. To shew that she did not wish any special attention, in a house to which she had come by an act of condescension, to be paid to her superior rank, she had entered the room with her arms pressed close to her sides, even when there was no crowd to be squeezed through, no one attempting to get past her; staying purposely at the back, with the air of being in her proper place, like a king who stands in the waiting procession at the doors of a theatre where the management have not been warned of his coming; and strictly limiting her field of vision—so as not to seem to be advertising her presence and claiming the consideration that was her due—to the study of a pattern in the carpet or of her own skirt, she stood there on the spot which had struck her as the most modest (and from which, as she very well knew, a cry of rapture from Mme. de Saint-Euverte would extricate her as soon as her presence there was noticed), next to Mme. de Cambremer, whom, however, she did not know. She observed the dumb-show by which her neighbour was expressing her passion for music, but she refrained from copying it. This was not to say that, for once that she had consented to spend a few minutes in Mme. de Saint-Euverte's house, the Princesse des Laumes would not have wished (so that the act of politeness to her hostess which she had performed by coming might, so to speak, 'count double') to shew herself as friendly and obliging as possible. But she had a natural horror of what she called 'exaggerating,' and always made a point of letting people see that she 'simply must not' indulge in any display of emotion that was not in keeping with the tone of the circle in which she moved, although such displays never failed to make an impression upon her, by virtue of that spirit of imitation, akin to timidity, which is developed in the most self-confident persons, by contact with an unfamiliar environment, even though it be inferior to their own. She began to ask herself whether these gesticulations might not, perhaps, be a necessary concomitant of the piece of music that was being played, a piece which, it might be, was in a different category from all the music that she had ever heard before; and whether to abstain from them was not a sign of her own inability to understand the music, and of discourtesy towards the lady of the house; with the result that, in order to express by a compromise both of her contradictory inclinations in turn, at one moment she would merely straighten her shoulder-straps or feel in her golden hair for the little balls of coral or of pink enamel, frosted with tiny diamonds, which formed its simple but effective ornament, studying, with a cold interest, her impassioned neighbour, while at another she would beat time for a few bars with her fan, but, so as not to forfeit her independence, she would beat a different time from the pianist's. When he had finished the Liszt Intermezzo and had begun a Prelude by Chopin,[27] Mme. de Cambremer turned to Mme. de Franquetot with a tender smile, full of intimate reminiscence, as well as of satisfaction (that of a competent judge) with the performance. She had been taught in her girlhood to fondle and cherish those long-necked, sinuous creatures, the phrases of Chopin, so free, so flexible, so tactile, which begin by seeking their ultimate resting-place somewhere beyond and far wide of the direction in which they started, the point which one might have expected them to reach, phrases which divert themselves in those fantastic bypaths only to return more deliberately—with a more premeditated reaction, with more precision, as on a crystal bowl which, if you strike it, will ring and throb until you cry aloud in anguish—to clutch at one's heart.

Brought up in a provincial household with few friends or visitors, hardly ever invited to a ball, she had fuddled her mind, in the solitude of her old manor-house, over setting the pace, now crawling-slow, now passionate, whirling, breathless, for all those imaginary waltzing couples, gathering them like flowers, leaving the ball-room for a moment to listen, where the wind sighed among the pine-trees, on the shore of the lake, and seeing him of a sudden advancing towards her, more different from anything one had ever dreamed of than earthly lovers are, a slender young man, whose voice was resonant and strange and false, in white gloves. But nowadays the old-fashioned beauty of this music seemed to have become a trifle stale. Having forfeited, some years back, the esteem of 'really musical' people, it had lost its distinction and its charm, and even those whose

27. Frédéric Chopin (1810–1849), Polish composer.

taste was frankly bad had ceased to find in it more than a moderate pleasure to which they hardly liked to confess. Mme. de Cambremer cast a furtive glance behind her. She knew that her young daughter-in-law (full of respect for her new and noble family, except in such matters as related to the intellect, upon which, having 'got as far' as Harmony and the Greek alphabet, she was specially enlightened) despised Chopin, and fell quite ill when she heard him played. But finding herself free from the scrutiny of this Wagnerian, who was sitting, at some distance, in a group of her own contemporaries, Mme. de Cambremer let herself drift upon a stream of exquisite memories and sensations. The Princesse des Laumes was touched also. Though without any natural gift for music, she had received, some fifteen years earlier, the instruction which a music-mistress of the Faubourg Saint-Germain,[28] a woman of genius who had been, towards the end of her life, reduced to penury, had started, at seventy, to give to the daughters and granddaughters of her old pupils. This lady was now dead. But her method, an echo of her charming touch, came to life now and then in the fingers of her pupils, even of those who had been in other respects quite mediocre, had given up music, and hardly ever opened a piano. And so Mme. des Laumes could let her head sway to and fro, fully aware of the cause, with a perfect appreciation of the manner in which the pianist was rendering this Prelude, since she knew it by heart. The closing notes of the phrase that he had begun sounded already on her lips. And she murmured "How charming it is!" with a stress on the opening consonants of the adjective, a token of her refinement by which she felt her lips so romantically compressed, like the petals of a beautiful, budding flower, that she instinctively brought her eyes into harmony, illuminating them for a moment with a vague and sentimental gaze. Meanwhile Mme. de Gallardon had arrived at the point of saying to herself how annoying it was that she had so few opportunities of meeting the Princesse des Laumes, for she meant to teach her a lesson by not acknowledging her bow. She did not know that her cousin was in the room. A movement of Mme. de Franquetot's head disclosed the Princess. At once Mme. de Gallardon dashed towards her, upsetting all her neighbours; although determined to preserve a distant and glacial manner which should remind everyone present that she had no desire to remain on friendly terms with a person in whose house one might find oneself, any day, cheek by jowl with the Princesse Mathilde, and to whom it was not her duty to make advances since she was not 'of her generation,' she felt bound to modify this air of dignity and reserve by some non-committal remark which would justify her overture and would force the Princess to engage in conversation; and so, when she reached her cousin, Mme.

28. the aristocratic district of Paris.

de Gallardon, with a stern countenance and one hand thrust out as though she were trying to 'force' a card, began with "How is your husband?" in the same anxious tone that she would have used if the Prince had been seriously ill. The Princess, breaking into a laugh which was one of her characteristics, and was intended at once to shew the rest of an assembly that she was making fun of some one and also to enhance her own beauty by concentrating her features around her animated lips and sparkling eyes, answered: "Why, he's never been better in his life!" And she went on laughing.

Mme. de Gallardon then drew herself up and, chilling her expression still further, perhaps because she was still uneasy about the Prince's health, said to her cousin:

"Oriane" (at once Mme. des Laumes looked with amused astonishment towards an invisible third, whom she seemed to call to witness that she had never authorised Mme. de Gallardon to use her Christian name), "I should be so pleased if you would look in, just for a minute, tomorrow evening, to hear a quintet, with the clarinet, by Mozart. I should like to have your opinion of it."

She seemed not so much to be issuing an invitation as to be asking a favour, and to want the Princess's opinion of the Mozart quintet just as though it had been a dish invented by a new cook, whose talent it was most important that an epicure should come to judge.

"But I know that quintet quite well. I can tell you now—that I adore it."

"You know, my husband isn't at all well; it's his liver. He would like so much to see you," Mme. de Gallardon resumed, making it now a corporal work of charity for the Princess to appear at her party.

The Princess never liked to tell people that she would not go to their houses. Every day she would write to express her regret at having been kept away—by the sudden arrival of her husband's mother, by an invitation from his brother, by the Opera, by some excursion to the country—from some party to which she had never for a moment dreamed of going. In this way she gave many people the satisfaction of feeling that she was on intimate terms with them, that she would gladly have come to their houses, and that she had been prevented from doing so only by some princely occurrence which they were flattered to find competing with their own humble entertainment. And then, as she belonged to that witty 'Guermantes set' —in which there survived something of the alert mentality, stripped of all commonplace phrases and conventional sentiments, which dated from Mérimée,[29] and found its final expression in the plays of Meilhac and Halévy[30]—she adapted its formula so as to suit even

---

29. Prosper Mérimée (1803–1870), French writer and intimate of the Empress Eugénie.

30. Henry Meilhac (1831–1897) and Ludovic Halévy (1834–1884) collaborated in the writing of many comedies and operettas.

her social engagements, transposed it into the courtesy which was always struggling to be positive and precise, to approximate itself to the plain truth. She would never develop at any length to a hostess the expression of her anxiety to be present at her party; she found it more pleasant to disclose to her all the various little incidents on which it would depend whether it was or was not possible for her to come.

"Listen, and I'll explain," she began to Mme. de Gallardon. "Tomorrow evening I must go to a friend of mine, who has been pestering me to fix a day for ages. If she takes us to the theatre afterwards, then I can't possibly come to you, much as I should love to; but if we just stay in the house, I know there won't be anyone else there, so I can slip away."

"Tell me, have you seen your friend M. Swann?"

"No! my precious Charles! I never knew he was here. Where is he? I must catch his eye."

"It's a funny thing that he should come to old Saint-Euverte's," Mme. de Gallardon went on. "Oh, I know he's very clever," meaning by that 'very cunning,' "but that makes no difference; fancy a Jew here, and she the sister and sister-in-law of two Archbishops."

"I am ashamed to confess that I am not in the least shocked," said the Princesse des Laumes.

"I know he's a converted Jew, and all that, and his parents and grandparents before him. But they do say that the converted ones are worse about their religion than the practising ones, that it's all just a pretence; is that true, d'you think?"

"I can throw no light at all on the matter."

The pianist, who was 'down' to play two pieces by Chopin, after finishing the Prelude had at once attacked a Polonaise. But once Mme. de Gallardon had informed her cousin that Swann was in the room, Chopin himself might have risen from the grave and played all his works in turn without Mme. des Laumes's paying him the slightest attention. She belonged to that one of the two divisions of the human race in which the untiring curiosity which the other half feels about the people whom it does not know is replaced by an unfailing interest in the people whom it does. As with many women of the Faubourg Saint-Germain, the presence, in any room in which she might find herself, of another member of her set, even although she had nothing in particular to say to him, would occupy her mind to the exclusion of every other consideration. From that moment, in the hope that Swann would catch sight of her, the Princess could do nothing but (like a tame white mouse when a lump of sugar is put down before its nose and then taken away) turn her face, in which were crowded a thousand signs of intimate connivance, none of them with the least relevance to the sentiment underlying Chopin's music, in the direction where Swann was, and, if he moved, divert accordingly the course of her magnetic smile.

"Oriane, don't be angry with me," resumed Mme. de Gallardon, who could never restrain herself from sacrificing her highest social ambitions, and the hope that she might one day emerge into a light that would dazzle the world, to the immediate and secret satisfaction of saying something disagreeable, "people do say about your M. Swann that he's the sort of man one can't have in the house; is that true?"

"Why, you, of all people, ought to know that it's true," replied the Princesse des Laumes, "for you must have asked him a hundred times, and he's never been to your house once."

And leaving her cousin mortified afresh, she broke out again into a laugh which scandalised everyone who was trying to listen to the music, but attracted the attention of Mme. de Saint-Euverte, who had stayed, out of politeness, near the piano, and caught sight of the Princess now for the first time. Mme. de Saint-Euverte was all the more delighted to see Mme. des Laumes, as she imagined her to be still at Guermantes,[31] looking after her father-in-law, who was ill.

"My dear Princess, you here?"

"Yes, I tucked myself away in a corner, and I've been hearing such lovely things."

"What, you've been in the room quite a time?"

"Oh, yes, quite a long time, which seemed very short; it was only long because I couldn't see you."

Mme. de Saint-Euverte offered her own chair to the Princess, who declined it with:

"Oh, please, no! Why should you? It doesn't matter in the least where I sit." And deliberately picking out, so as the better to display the simplicity of a really great lady, a low seat without a back: "There now, that hassock, that's all I want. It will make me keep my back straight. Oh! Good heavens, I'm making a noise again; they'll be telling you to have me 'chucked out'."

Meanwhile, the pianist having doubled his speed, the emotion of the music-lovers was reaching its climax, a servant was handing refreshments about on a salver, and was making the spoons rattle, and, as on every other 'party-night,' Mme. de Saint-Euverte was making signs to him, which he never saw, to leave the room. A recent bride, who had been told that a young woman ought never to appear bored, was smiling vigorously, trying to catch her hostess's eye so as to flash a token of her gratitude for the other's having 'thought of her' in connection with so delightful an entertainment. And yet, although she remained more calm than Mme. de Franquetot,

31. country seat of the Guermantes family.

it was not without some uneasiness that she followed the flying fingers; what alarmed her being not the pianist's fate but the piano's, on which a lighted candle, jumping at each *fortissimo*, threatened, if not to set its shade on fire, at least to spill wax upon the ebony. At last she could contain herself no longer, and, running up the two steps of the platform on which the piano stood, flung herself on the candle to adjust its sconce. But scarcely had her hand come within reach of it when, on a final chord, the piece finished, and the pianist rose to his feet. Nevertheless the bold initiative shewn by this young woman and the moment of blushing confusion between her and the pianist which resulted from it, produced an impression that was favourable on the whole.

"Did you see what that girl did just now, Princess?" asked General de Froberville, who had come up to Mme. des Laumes as her hostess left her for a moment. "Odd, wasn't it? Is she one of the performers?"

"No, she's a little Mme. de Cambremer," replied the Princess carelessly, and then, with more animation: "I am only repeating what I heard just now, myself; I haven't the faintest notion who said it, it was some one behind me who said that they were neighbours of Mme. de Saint-Euverte in the country, but I don't believe anyone knows them, really. They must be 'country cousins'! By the way, I don't know whether you're particularly 'well-up' in the brilliant society which we see before us, because I've no idea who all these astonishing people can be. What do you suppose they do with themselves when they're not at Mme. de Saint-Euverte's parties? She must have ordered them in with the musicians and the chairs and the food. 'Universal providers,' you know. You must admit, they're rather splendid, General. But can she really have the courage to hire the same 'supers' every week? It isn't possible!"

"Oh, but Cambremer is quite a good name; old, too," protested the General.

"I see no objection to its being old," the Princess answered dryly, "but whatever else it is it's not euphonious," she went on, isolating the word euphonious as though between inverted commas, a little affectation to which the Guermantes set were addicted.

"You think not, eh! She's a regular little peach, though," said the General, whose eyes never strayed from Mme. de Cambremer. "Don't you agree with me, Princess?"

"She thrusts herself forward too much; I think, in so young a woman, that's not very nice—for I don't suppose she's my generation," replied Mme. des Laumes (the last word being common, it appeared, to Gallardon and Guermantes). And then, seeing that M. de Froberville was still gazing at Mme. de Cambremer, she added, half out of malice towards the lady, half wishing to oblige the

General. "Not very nice . . . for her husband! I am sorry that I do not know her, since she seems to attract you so much; I might have introduced you to her," said the Princess, who, if she had known the young woman, would most probably have done nothing of the sort. "And now I must say good night, because one of my friends is having a birthday party, and I must go and wish her many happy returns," she explained, modestly and with truth, reducing the fashionable gathering to which she was going to the simple proportions of a ceremony which would be boring in the extreme, but at which she was obliged to be present, and there would be something touching about her appearance. "Besides, I must pick up Basin.[32] While I've been here, he's gone to see those friends of his —you know them too, I'm sure—who are called after a bridge—oh, yes, the Iénas."[33]

"It was a battle before it was a bridge, Princess; it was a victory!" said the General. "I mean to say, to an old soldier like me," he went on, wiping his monocle and replacing it, as though he were laying a fresh dressing on the raw wound underneath, while the Princess instinctively looked away, "that Empire nobility, well, of course, it's not the same thing, but, after all, taking it as it is, it's very fine of its kind; they were people who really did fight like heroes."

"But I have the deepest respect for heroes," the Princess assented, though with a faint trace of irony. "If I don't go with Basin to see this Princesse d'Iéna, it isn't for that, at all; it's simply because I don't know them. Basin knows them; he worships them. Oh, no, it's not what you think; he's not in love with her. I've nothing to set my face against! Besides, what good has it ever done when I have set my face against them?" she queried sadly, for the whole world knew that, ever since the day upon which the Prince des Laumes had married his fascinating cousin, he had been consistently unfaithful to her. "Anyhow, it isn't that at all. They're people he has known for ever so long, they do him very well, and that suits me down to the ground. But I must tell you what he's told me about their house; it's quite enough. Can you imagine it, all their furniture is 'Empire'!"

"But, my dear Princess, that's only natural; it belonged to their grandparents."

"I don't quite say it didn't, but that doesn't make it any less ugly. I quite understand that people can't always have nice things, but at least they needn't have things that are merely grotesque. What do you say? I can think of nothing more devastating, more utterly smug than that hideous style—cabinets covered all over with swans' heads, like bath-taps!"

32. baptismal name of her husband, the Prince des Laumes, later Duc de Guermantes.

33. Titles dating from the Napoleonic epoch were scorned by the old aristocracy.

"But I believe, all the same, that they've got some lovely things; why, they must have that famous mosaic table on which the Treaty of . . ."

"Oh, I don't deny, they may have things that are interesting enough from the historic point of view. But things like that can't, ever, be beautiful . . . because they're simply horrible! I've got things like that myself, that came to Basin from the Montesquious.[34] Only, they're up in the attics at Guermantes, where nobody ever sees them. But, after all, that's not the point, I would fly to see them, with Basin; I would even go to see them among all their sphinxes and brasses, if I knew them, but—I don't know them! D'you know, I was always taught, when I was a little girl, that it was not polite to call on people one didn't know." She assumed a tone of childish gravity. "And so I am just doing what I was taught to do. Can't you see those good people, with a totally strange woman bursting into their house? Why, I might get a most hostile reception."

And she coquettishly enhanced the charm of the smile which the idea had brought to her lips, by giving to her blue eyes, which were fixed on the General, a gentle, dreamy expression.

"My dear Princess, you know that they'ld be simply wild with joy."

"No, why?" she inquired, with the utmost vivacity, either so as to seem unaware that it would be because she was one of the first ladies in France, or so as to have the pleasure of hearing the General tell her so. "Why? How can you tell? Perhaps they would think it the most unpleasant thing that could possibly happen. I know nothing about them, but if they're anything like me, I find it quite boring enough to see the people I do know; I'm sure if I had to see people I didn't know as well, even if they had 'fought like heroes,' I should go stark mad. Besides, except when it's an old friend like you, whom one knows quite apart from that, I'm not sure that 'heroism' takes one very far in society. It's often quite boring enough to have to give a dinner-party, but if one had to offer one's arm to Spartacus,[35] to let him take one down . . . ! Really, no; it would never be Vercingetorix[36] I should send for, to make a fourteenth. I feel sure, I should keep him for really big 'crushes.' And as I never give any . . ."

"Ah! Princess, it's easy to see you're not a Guermantes for nothing. You have your share of it, all right, the 'wit of the Guermantes'!"

"But people always talk about the wit of *the* Guermantes; I never could make out why. Do you really know any *others* who have it?" she rallied him, with a rippling flow of laughter, her features concentrated, yoked to the service of her animation, her eyes sparkling,

34. The noble family of Montesquiou actually exists.
35. killed in 71 A.D. after heading a revolt of slaves against the Roman authority.
36. executed 46 B.C. He led a confederation of Gallic tribes in resistance to Julius Caesar.

blazing with a radiant sunshine of gaiety which could be kindled only by such speeches—even if the Princess had to make them herself—as were in praise of her wit or of her beauty. "Look, there's Swann talking to your Cambremer woman; over there, beside old Saint-Euverte, don't you see him? Ask him to introduce you. But hurry up, he seems to be just going!"

"Did you notice how dreadfully ill he's looking?" asked the General.

"My precious Charles? Ah, he's coming at last; I was beginning to think he didn't want to see me!"

Swann was extremely fond of the Princesse des Laumes, and the sight of her recalled to him Guermantes, a property close to Combray,[37] and all that country which he so dearly loved and had ceased to visit, so as not to be separated from Odette. Slipping into the manner, half-artistic, half-amorous—with which he could always manage to amuse the Princess—a manner which came to him quite naturally whenever he dipped for a moment into the old social atmosphere, and wishing also to express in words, for his own satisfaction, the longing that he felt for the country:

"Ah!" he exclaimed, or rather intoned, in such a way as to be audible at once to Mme. de Saint-Euverte, to whom he spoke, and to Mme. des Laumes, for whom he was speaking, "Behold our charming Princess! See, she has came up on purpose from Guermantes to hear Saint Francis[38] preach to the birds, and has only just had time, like a dear little titmouse, to go and pick a few little hips and haws and put them in her hair; there are even some drops of dew upon them still, a little of the hoar-frost which must be making the Duchess, down there, shiver. It is very pretty indeed, my dear Princess."

"What! The Princess came up on purpose from Guermantes? But that's too wonderful! I never knew; I'm quite bewildered," Mme. de Saint-Euverte protested with quaint simplicity, being but little accustomed to Swann's way of speaking. And then, examining the Princess's headdress, "Why, you're quite right; it is copied from . . . what shall I say, not chestnuts, no—oh, it's a delightful idea, but how can the Princess have known what was going to be on my programme? The musicians didn't tell me, even."

Swann, who was accustomed, when he was with a woman whom he had kept up the habit of addressing in terms of gallantry, to pay her delicate compliments which most other people would not and need not understand, did not condescend to explain to Mme. de Saint-Euverte that he had been speaking metaphorically. As for the Princess, she was in fits of laughter, both because Swann's wit was highly

37. Swann's country estate was situated near this (fictitious) village.   38. St. Francis of Assisi (1182–1226), founder of the Franciscan order of monks.

appreciated by her set, and because she could never hear a compliment addressed to herself without finding it exquisitely subtle and irresistibly amusing.

"Indeed! I'm delighted, Charles, if my little hips and haws meet with your approval. But tell me, why did you bow to that Cambremer person, are you also her neighbour in the country?"

Mme. de Saint-Euverte, seeing that the Princess seemed quite happy talking to Swann, had drifted away.

"But you are, yourself, Princess!"

"I! Why, they must have 'countries' everywhere, those creatures! Don't I wish I had!"

"No, not the Cambremers; her own people. She was a Legrandin, and used to come to Combray. I don't know whether you are aware that you are Comtesse de Combray, and that the Chapter[39] owes you a due."

"I don't know what the Chapter owes me, but I do know that I'm 'touched' for a hundred francs every year, by the Curé,[40] which is a due that I could very well do without. But surely these Cambremers have rather a startling name. It ends just in time, but it ends badly!"[41] she said with a laugh.

"It begins no better."[42] Swann took the point.

"Yes; that double abbreviation!"

"Some one very angry and very proper who didn't dare to finish the first word."

"But since he couldn't stop himself beginning the second, he'd have done better to finish the first and be done with it. We are indulging in the most refined form of humour, my dear Charles, in the very best of taste—but how tiresome it is that I never see you now," she went on in a coaxing tone, "I do so love talking to you. Just imagine, I could not make that idiot Froberville see that there was anything funny about the name Cambremer. Do agree that life is a dreadful business. It's only when I see you that I stop feeling bored."

Which was probably not true. But Swann and the Princess had the same way of looking at the little things of life—the effect, if not the cause of which was a close analogy between their modes of expression and even of pronunciation. This similarity was not striking because no two things could have been more unlike than their voices. But if one took the trouble to imagine Swann's utterances divested of the sonority that enwrapped them, of the moustache from under which they emerged, one found that they were the same phrases,

---

39. of the church at Combray.
40. the parish priest.
41. The last syllable of the name is the beginning of the vulgar French word *merde*.

42. General Cambronne (1770–1842) uttered the same word (*merde*) when he refused to surrender to the English at Waterloo, so it is called "Cambronne's word."

the same inflexions, that they had the 'tone' of the Guermantes set. On important matters, Swann and the Princess had not an idea in common. But since Swann had become so melancholy, and was always in that trembling condition which precedes a flood of tears, he had the same need to speak about his grief that a murderer has to tell some one about his crime. And when he heard the Princess say that life was a dreadful business, he felt as much comforted as if she had spoken to him of Odette.

"Yes, life is a dreadful business! We must meet more often, my dear friend. What is so nice about you is that you are not cheerful. We could spend a most pleasant evening together."

"I'm sure we could; why not come down to Guermantes? My mother-in-law would be wild with joy. It's supposed to be very ugly down there, but I must say, I find the neighbourhood not at all unattractive; I have a horror of 'picturesque spots'."

"I know it well, it's delightful!" replied Swann. "It's almost too beautiful, too much alive for me just at present; it's a country to be happy in. It's perhaps because I have lived there, but things there speak to me so. As soon as a breath of wind gets up, and the cornfields begin to stir, I feel that some one is going to appear suddenly, that I am going to hear some news; and those little houses by the water's edge . . . I should be quite wretched!"

"Oh! my dearest Charles, do take care; there's that appalling Rampillon woman; she's seen me; hide me somewhere, do tell me again, quickly, what it was that happened to her: I get so mixed up; she's just married off her daughter, or her lover (I never can remember)—perhaps both—to each other! Oh, no, I remember now, she's been dropped by her Prince . . . Pretend to be talking, so that the poor old Berenice[43] sha'n't come and invite me to dinner. Anyhow, I'm going. Listen, my dearest Charles, now that I have seen you, once in a blue moon, won't you let me carry you off and take you to the Princesse de Parme's, who would be so pleased to see you (you know), and Basin too, for that matter, he's meeting me there. If one didn't get news of you, sometimes, from Mémé[44] . . . Remember, I never see you at all now!"

Swann declined. Having told M. de Charlus that, on leaving Mme. de Saint-Euverte's, he would go straight home, he did not care to run the risk, by going on now to the Princesse de Parme's, of missing a message which he had, all the time, been hoping to see brought in to him by one of the footmen, during the party, and which he was perhaps going to find left with his own porter, at home.

"Poor Swann," said Mme. des Laumes that night to her husband; "he is always charming, but he does look so dreadfully unhappy.

43. In Racine's play of that name (1670), Queen Berenice is rejected by the Emperor Titus.
44. nickname of M. de Charlus.

You will see for yourself, for he has promised to dine with us one of these days. I do feel that it's really absurd that a man of his intelligence should let himself be made to suffer by a creature of that kind, who isn't even interesting, for they tell me she's an absolute idiot!" she concluded with the wisdom invariably shewn by people who, not being in love themselves, feel that a clever man ought to be unhappy only about such persons as are worth his while; which is rather like being astonished that anyone should condescend to die of cholera at the bidding of so insignificant a creature as the common bacillus.

Swann now wished to go home, but, just as he was making his escape, General de Froberville caught him and asked for an introduction to Mme. de Cambremer, and he was obliged to go back into the room to look for her.

"I say, Swann, I'ld rather be married to that little woman than killed by savages, what do you say?"

The words 'killed by savages' pierced Swann's aching heart; and at once he felt the need of continuing the conversation. "Ah!" he began, "some fine lives have been lost in that way . . . There was, you remember, that explorer whose remains Dumont d'Urville[45] brought back, La Pérouse . . ." (and he was at once happy again, as though he had named Odette). "He was a fine character, and interests me very much, does La Pérouse," he ended sadly.

"Oh, yes, of course, La Pérouse," said the General. "It's quite a well known name. There's a street called that."

"Do you know anyone in the Rue La Pérouse?" asked Swann excitedly.

"Only Mme. de Chanlivault, the sister of that good fellow Chaussepierre. She gave a most amusing theatre-party the other evening. That's a house that will be really smart some day, you'll see!"

"Oh, so she lives in the Rue La Pérouse. It's attractive; I like that street; it's so sombre."

"Indeed it isn't. You can't have been in it for a long time; it's not at all sombre now; they're beginning to build all round there."

When Swann did finally introduce M. de Froberville to the young Mme. de Cambremer, since it was the first time that she had heard the General's name, she hastily outlined upon her lips the smile of joy and surprise with which she would have greeted him if she had never, in the whole of her life, heard anything else; for, as she did not yet know all the friends of her new family, whenever anyone was presented to her, she assumed that he must be one of them, and thinking that she would shew her tact by appearing to have heard 'such a lot about him' since her marriage, she would hold out

45. French navigator (1780–1842) who discovered the remains of Jean-François de La Pérouse (1741–1788), massacred by the natives of Vanikoro, in Polynesia.

her hand with an air of hesitation which was meant as a proof at once of the inculcated reserve which she had to overcome and of the spontaneous friendliness which successfully overcame it. And so her parents-in-law, whom she still regarded as the most eminent pair in France, declared that she was an angel; all the more that they preferred to appear, in marrying her to their son, to have yielded to the attraction rather of her natural charm than of her considerable fortune.

"It's easy to see that you're a musician heart and soul, Madame," said the General, alluding to the incident of the candle.

Meanwhile the concert had begun again, and Swann saw that he could not now go before the end of the new number. He suffered greatly from being shut up among all these people whose stupidity and absurdities wounded him all the more cruelly since, being ignorant of his love, incapable, had they known of it, of taking any interest, or of doing more than smile at it as at some childish joke, or deplore it as an act of insanity, they made it appear to him in the aspect of a subjective state which existed for himself alone, whose reality there was nothing external to confirm; he suffered overwhelmingly, to the point at which even the sound of the instruments made him want to cry, from having to prolong his exile in this place to which Odette would never come, in which no one, nothing, was aware of her existence, from which she was entirely absent.

But suddenly it was as though she had entered, and this apparition tore him with such anguish that his hand rose impulsively to his heart. What had happened was that the violin had risen to a series of high notes, on which it rested as though expecting something, an expectancy which it prolonged without ceasing to hold on to the notes, in the exaltation with which it already saw the expected object approaching, and with a desperate effort to continue until its arrival, to welcome it before itself expired, to keep the way open for a moment longer, with all its remaining strength, that the stranger might enter in, as one holds a door open that would otherwise automatically close. And before Swann had had time to understand what was happening, to think: "It is the little phrase from Vinteuil's sonata.[46] I mustn't listen!", all his memories of the days when Odette had been in love with him, which he had succeeded, up till that evening, in keeping invisible in the depths of his being, deceived by this sudden reflection of a season of love, whose sun, they supposed, had dawned again, had awakened from their slumber, had taken wing and risen to sing maddeningly in his ears, without pity for his present desolation, the forgotten strains of happiness.

In place of the abstract expressions "the time when I was happy,"

46. Swann had "fallen in love" with a phrase from this sonata (fictitious, Vinteuil is a character of the novel) and had come to make of it the leitmotif of his relationship with Odette.

"the time when I was loved," which he had often used until then, and without much suffering, for his intelligence had not embodied in them anything of the past save fictitious extracts which preserved none of the reality, he now recovered everything that had fixed un-alterably the peculiar, volatile essence of that lost happiness; he could see it all; the snowy, curled petals of the chrysanthemum which she had tossed after him into his carriage, which he had kept pressed to his lips—the address 'Maison Dorée,' embossed on the note-paper on which he had read "My hand trembles so as I write to you," the frowning contraction of her eyebrows when she said pleadingly: "You won't let it be very long before you send for me?"; he could smell the heated iron of the barber whom he used to have in to singe his hair while Loredan[47] went to fetch the little working girl;[48] could feel the torrents of rain which fell so often that spring, the ice-cold home-ward drive in his victoria, by moonlight; all the network of mental habits, of seasonable impressions, of sensory reactions, which had ex-tended over a series of weeks its uniform meshes, by which his body now found itself inextricably held. At that time he had been satisfy-ing a sensual curiosity to know what were the pleasures of those people who lived for love alone. He had supposed that he could stop there, that he would not be obliged to learn their sorrows also; how small a thing the actual charm of Odette was now in comparison with that formidable terror which extended it like a cloudy halo all around her, that enormous anguish of not knowing at every hour of the day and night what she had been doing, of not possessing her wholly, at all times and in all places! Alas, he recalled the accents in which she had exclaimed: "But I can see you at any time; I am always free!"—she, who was never free now; the interest, the curiosity that she had shewn in his life, her passionate desire that he should do her the favour—of which it was he who, then, had felt suspicious, as of a possibly tedious waste of his time and disturbance of his ar-rangements—of granting her access to his study; how she had been obliged to beg that he would let her take him to the Verdurins'; and, when he did allow her to come to him once a month, how she had first, before he would let himself be swayed, had to repeat what a joy it would be to her, that custom of their seeing each other daily, for which she had longed at a time when to him it had seemed only a tiresome distraction, for which, since that time, she had con-ceived a distaste and had definitely broken herself of it, while it had become for him so insatiable, so dolorous a need. Little had he suspected how truly he spoke when, on their third meeting, as she repeated: "But why don't you let me come to you oftener?" he had

---

47. Swann's coachman.
48. It had been Swann's practice to dally with her in the earlier part of the evening, before going on to see

Odette at the Verdurins', a wealthy and socially ambitious couple, in whose house Odette spent almost every eve-ning.

told her, laughing, and in a vein of gallantry, that it was for fear of forming a hopeless passion. Now, alas, it still happened at times that she wrote to him from a restaurant or hotel, on paper which bore a printed address, but printed in letters of fire that seared his heart. "Written from the Hôtel Vouillemont. What on earth can she have gone there for? With whom? What happened there?" He remembered the gas-jets that were being extinguished along the Boulevard des Italiens when he had met her, when all hope was gone,[49] among the errant shades upon that night which had seemed to him almost supernatural and which now (that night of a period when he had not even to ask himself whether he would be annoying her by looking for her and by finding her, so certain was he that she knew no greater happiness than to see him and to let him take her home) belonged indeed to a mysterious world to which one never may return again once its doors are closed. And Swann could distinguish, standing, motionless, before that scene of happiness in which it lived again, a wretched figure which filled him with such pity, because he did not at first recognise who it was, that he must lower his head, lest anyone should observe that his eyes were filled with tears. It was himself.

When he had realised this, his pity ceased; he was jealous, now, of that other self whom she had loved, he was jealous of those men of whom he had so often said, without much suffering: "Perhaps she's in love with them," now that he had exchanged the vague idea of loving, in which there is no love, for the petals of the chrysanthemum and the 'letter-heading' of the Maison d'Or; for they were full of love. And then, his anguish becoming too keen, he passed his hand over his forehead, let the monocle drop from his eye, and wiped its glass. And doubtless, if he had caught sight of himself at that moment, he would have added to the collection of the monocles which he had already identified, this one which he removed, like an importunate, worrying thought, from his head, while from its misty surface, with his handkerchief, he sought to obliterate his cares.

There are in the music of the violin—if one does not see the instrument itself, and so cannot relate what one hears to its form, which modifies the fullness of the sound—accents which are so closely akin to those of certain contralto voices, that one has the illusion that a singer has taken her place amid the orchestra. One raises one's eyes; one sees only the wooden case, magical as a Chinese box; but, at moments, one is still tricked by the deceiving appeal of the Siren; at times, too, one believes that one is listening to a captive spirit, struggling in the darkness of its masterful box, a box quivering with enchantment, like a devil immersed in a stoup of holy water; some-

49. Swann, having arrived too late to find Odette at the Verdurins', had sought her long and fruitlessly in cafés and restaurants.

times, again, it is in the air, at large, like a pure and supernatural creature that reveals to the ear, as it passes, its invisible message.

As though the musicians were not nearly so much playing the little phrase as performing the rites on which it insisted before it would consent to appear, as proceeding to utter the incantations necessary to procure, and to prolong for a few moments, the miracle of its apparition, Swann, who was no more able now to see it than if it had belonged to a world of ultra-violet light, who experienced something like the refreshing sense of a metamorphosis in the momentary blindness with which he had been struck as he approached it, Swann felt that it was present, like a protective goddess, a confidant of his love, who, so as to be able to come to him through the crowd, and to draw him aside to speak to him, had disguised herself in this sweeping cloak of sound. And as she passed him, light, soothing, as softly murmured as the perfume of a flower, telling him what she had to say, every word of which he closely scanned, sorry to see them fly away so fast, he made involuntarily with his lips the motion of kissing, as it went by him, the harmonious, fleeting form.

He felt that he was no longer in exile and alone since she, who addressed herself to him, spoke to him in a whisper of Odette. For he had no longer, as of old, the impression that Odette and he were not known to the little phrase. Had it not often been the witness of their joys? True that, as often, it had warned him of their frailty. And indeed, whereas, in that distant time, he had divined an element of suffering in its smile, in its limpid and disillusioned intonation, tonight he found there rather the charm of a resignation that was almost gay. Of those sorrows, of which the little phrase had spoken to him then, which he had seen it—without his being touched by them himself—carry past him, smiling, on its sinuous and rapid course, of those sorrows which were now become his own, without his having any hope of being, ever, delivered from them, it seemed to say to him, as once it had said of his happiness: "What does all that matter; it is all nothing." And Swann's thoughts were borne for the first time on a wave of pity and tenderness towards that Vinteuil, towards that unknown, exalted brother who also must have suffered so greatly; what could his life have been? From the depths of what well of sorrow could he have drawn that god-like strength, that unlimited power of creation?

When it was the little phrase that spoke to him of the vanity of his sufferings, Swann found a sweetness in that very wisdom which, but a little while back, had seemed to him intolerable when he thought that he could read it on the faces of indifferent strangers, who would regard his love as a digression that was without importance. 'Twas because the little phrase, unlike them, whatever opinion it might hold on the short duration of these states of the soul, saw in them something not, as everyone else saw, less serious than the events of everyday life, but, on the contrary, so far superior to everyday life as to be alone worthy of the trouble of expressing it. Those graces of an intimate sorrow, 'twas them that the phrase endeavoured to imitate, to create anew; and even their essence, for all that it consists in being incommunicable and in appearing trivial to everyone save him who has experience of them, the little phrase had captured, had rendered visible. So much so that it made their value be confessed, their divine sweetness be tasted by all those same onlookers—provided only that they were in any sense musical—who, the next moment, would ignore, would disown them in real life, in every individual love that came into being beneath their eyes. Doubtless the form in which it had codified those graces could not be analysed into any logical elements. But ever since, more than a year before, discovering to him many of the riches of his own soul, the love of music had been born, and for a time at least had dwelt in him, Swann had regarded musical *motifs* as actual ideas, of another world, of another order, ideas veiled in shadows, unknown, impenetrable by the human mind, which none the less were perfectly distinct one from another, unequal among themselves in value and in significance. When, after that first evening at the Verdurins', he had had the little phrase played over to him again, and had sought to disentangle from his confused impressions how it was that, like a perfume or a caress, it swept over and enveloped him, he had observed that it was to the closeness of the intervals between the five notes which composed it and to the constant repetition of two of them that was due that impression of a frigid, a contracted sweetness; but in reality he knew that he was basing this conclusion not upon the phrase itself, but merely upon certain equivalents, substituted (for his mind's convenience) for the mysterious entity of which he had become aware, before ever he knew the Verdurins, at the earlier party, when for the first time he had heard the sonata played. He knew that his memory of the piano falsified still further the perspective in which he saw the music, that the field open to the musician is not a miserable stave of seven notes, but an immeasurable keyboard (still, almost all of it, unknown), on which, here and there only, separated by the gross darkness of its unexplored tracts, some few among the millions of keys, keys of tenderness, of passion, of courage, of serenity, which compose it, each one differing from all the rest as one universe differs from another, have been discovered by certain great artists who do us the service, when they awaken in us the emotion corresponding to the theme which they have found, of shewing us what richness, what variety lies hidden, unknown to us, in that great black impenetrable night, discouraging exploration, of our soul, which we have been content to regard as valueless and waste and void. Vinteuil had been one of those musicians. In his little phrase, albeit it presented to the mind's eye a clouded surface, there was contained, one felt, a matter so consistent, so explicit, to which the phrase gave so new, so original a force, that those who had once heard it preserved the memory of it in the treasure-chamber of their minds. Swann would repair to it as to a conception of love and happiness, of which at once he knew as well in what respects it was peculiar as he would know of the *Princesse de Clèves*,[50] or of *René*,[51] should either of those titles occur to him. Even when he was not thinking of the little phrase, it existed, latent, in his mind, in the same way as certain other conceptions without material equivalent, such as our notions of light, of sound, of perspective, of bodily desire, the rich possessions wherewith our inner temple is diversified and adorned. Perhaps we shall lose them, perhaps they will be obliterated, if we return to nothing in the dust. But so long as we are alive, we can no more bring ourselves to a state in which we shall not have known them than we can with regard to any material object, than we can, for example, doubt the luminosity of a lamp that has just been lighted, in view of the changed aspect of everything in the room, from which has vanished even the memory of the darkness. In that way Vinteuil's phrase, like some theme, say, in *Tristan*,[52] which represents to us also a certain acquisition of sentiment, has espoused our mortal state, had endued a vesture of humanity that was affecting enough. Its destiny was linked, for the future, with that of the human soul, of which it was one of the special, the most distinctive ornaments. Perhaps it is not-being that is the true state, and all our dream of life is without existence; but, if so, we feel that it must be that these phrases of music, these conceptions which exist in relation to our dream, are nothing either. We shall perish, but we have for our hostages these divine captives who shall follow and share our fate. And death in their company is something less bitter, less inglorious, perhaps even less certain.

So Swann was not mistaken in believing that the phrase of the sonata did, really, exist. Human as it was from this point of view, it belonged, none the less, to an order of supernatural creatures whom we have never seen, but whom, in spite of that, we recognise and acclaim with rapture when some explorer of the unseen contrives to coax one forth, to bring it down from that divine world to which he has access to shine for a brief moment in the firmament of ours. This was what Vinteuil had done for the little phrase. Swann felt that the composer had been content (with the musical instruments at his disposal) to draw aside its veil, to make it visible, following

---

50. novel by Mme. de La Fayette (1634–1692).

51. short novel by François-René de Chateaubriand (1768–1848).

52. *Tristan and Isolde* (1865) by Richard Wagner (1813–1883). See Thomas Mann's "Tristan," in this section.

and respecting its outlines with a hand so loving, so prudent, so delicate and so sure, that the sound altered at every moment, blunting itself to indicate a shadow, springing back into life when it must follow the curve of some more bold projection. And one proof that Swann was not mistaken when he believed in the real existence of this phrase, was that anyone with an ear at all delicate for music would at once have detected the imposture had Vinteuil, endowed with less power to see and to render its forms, sought to dissemble (by adding a line, here and there, of his own invention) the dimness of his vision or the feebleness of his hand.

The phrase had disappeared. Swann knew that it would come again at the end of the last movement, after a long passage which Mme. Verdurin's pianist always 'skipped.' There were in this passage some admirable ideas which Swann had not distinguished on first hearing the sonata, and which he now perceived, as if they had, in the cloakroom of his memory, divested themselves of their uniform disguise of novelty. Swann listened to all the scattered themes which entered into the composition of the phrase, as its premises enter into the inevitable conclusion of a syllogism;[53] he was assisting at the mystery of its birth. "Audacity," he exclaimed to himself, "as inspired, perhaps, as a Lavoisier's[54] or an Ampère's,[55] the audacity of a Vinteuil making experiment, discovering the secret laws that govern an unknown force, driving across a region unexplored towards the one possible goal the invisible team in which he has placed his trust and which he never may discern!" How charming the dialogue which Swann now heard between piano and violin, at the beginning of the last passage. The suppression of human speech, so far from letting fancy reign there uncontrolled (as one might have thought), had eliminated it altogether. Never was spoken language of such inflexible necessity, never had it known questions so pertinent, such obvious replies. At first the piano complained alone, like a bird deserted by its mate; the violin heard and answered it, as from a neighbouring tree. It was as at the first beginning of the world, as if there were not yet but these twain upon the earth, or rather in this world closed against all the rest, so fashioned by the logic of its creator that in it there should never be any but themselves; the world of this sonata. Was it a bird, was it the soul, not yet made perfect, of the little phrase, was it a fairy, invisibly somewhere lamenting, whose plaint the piano heard and tenderly repeated? Its cries were so sudden that the violinist must snatch up his bow and race to catch them as they came. Marvellous bird! The violinist seemed to wish to charm,

---

53. in logic, a type of formal argument consisting of three propositions.
54. Antoine Lavoisier (1743–1794), French chemist who established the law of the conservation of matter.

55. André Marie Ampère (1775–1836), French mathematician and physicist who discovered the fundamental law of electrodynamics.

to tame, to woo, to win it. Already it had passed into his soul, already the little phrase which it evoked shook like a medium's the body of the violinist, 'possessed' indeed. Swann knew that the phrase was going to speak to him once again. And his personality was now so divided that the strain of waiting for the imminent moment when he would find himself face to face, once more with the phrase, convulsed him in one of those sobs which a fine line of poetry or a piece of alarming news will wring from us, not when we are alone, but when we repeat one or the other to a friend, in whom we see ourselves reflected, like a third person, whose probable emotion softens him. It reappeared, but this time to remain poised in the air, and to sport there for a moment only, as though immobile, and shortly to expire. And so Swann lost nothing of the precious time for which it lingered. It was still there, like an iridescent bubble that floats for a while unbroken. As a rainbow, when its brightness fades, seems to subside, then soars again and, before it is extinguished, is glorified with greater splendour than it has ever shewn; so to the two colours which the phrase had hitherto allowed to appear it added others now, chords shot with every hue in the prism, and made them sing. Swann dared not move, and would have liked to compel all the other people in the room to remain still also, as if the slightest movement might embarrass the magic presence, supernatural, delicious, frail, that would so easily vanish. But no one, as it happened, dreamed of speaking. The ineffable utterance of one solitary man, absent, perhaps dead (Swann did not know whether Vinteuil were still alive), breathed out above the rites of those two hierophants, sufficed to arrest the attention of three hundred minds, and made of that stage on which a soul was thus called into being one of the noblest altars on which a supernatural ceremony could be performed. It followed that, when the phrase at last was finished, and only its fragmentary echoes floated among the subsequent themes which had already taken its place, if Swann at first was annoyed to see the Comtesse de Monteriender, famed for her imbecilities, lean over towards him to confide in him her impressions, before even the sonata had come to an end; he could not refrain from smiling, and perhaps also found an underlying sense, which she was incapable of perceiving, in the words that she used. Dazzled by the virtuosity of the performers, the Comtesse exclaimed to Swann: "It's astonishing! I have never seen anything to beat it . . ." But a scrupulous regard for accuracy making her correct her first assertion, she added the reservation: "anything to beat it . . . since the table-turning!"

From that evening, Swann understood that the feeling which Odette had once had for him would never revive, that his hopes of happiness would not be realised now. And the days on which, by a lucky chance, she had once more shewn herself kind and loving to him, or if she had paid him any attention, he recorded those apparent and misleading signs of a slight movement on her part towards him with the same tender and sceptical solicitude, the desperate joy that people reveal who, when they are nursing a friend in the last days of an incurable malady, relate, as significant facts of infinite value: "Yesterday he went through his accounts himself, and actually corrected a mistake that we had made in adding them up; he ate an egg today and seemed quite to enjoy it, if he digests it properly we shall try him with a cutlet tomorrow"—although they themselves know that these things are meaningless on the eve of an inevitable death. No doubt Swann was assured that if he had now been living at a distance from Odette he would gradually have lost all interest in her, so that he would have been glad to learn that she was leaving Paris for ever; he would have had the courage to remain there; but he had not the courage to go.

D. H. LAWRENCE
(1885–1930)
The Horse Dealer's Daughter*

"Well, Mabel, and what are you going to do with yourself?" asked Joe, with foolish flippancy. He felt quite safe himself. Without listening for an answer, he turned aside, worked a grain of tobacco to the tip of his tongue, and spat it out. He did not care about anything, since he felt safe himself.

The three brothers and the sister sat round the desolate breakfast table, attempting some sort of desultory consultation. The morning's post had given the final tap to the family fortune, and all was over. The dreary dining-room itself, with its heavy mahogany furniture, looked as if it were waiting to be done away with.

But the consultation amounted to nothing. There was a strange air of ineffectuality about the three men, as they sprawled at table, smoking and reflecting vaguely on their own condition. The girl was alone, a rather short, sullen-looking young woman of twenty-seven. She did not share the same life as her brothers. She would have been good-looking, save for the impassive fixity of her face, "bull-dog," as her brothers called it.

There was a confused tramping of horses' feet outside. The three men all sprawled round in their chairs to watch. Beyond the dark holly-bushes that separated the strip of lawn from the highroad, they could see a cavalcade of shire horses swinging out of their own yard,

* 1922. From *England, My England* by D. H. Lawrence. Copyright 1922 by Thomas Seltzer, Inc., 1950 by Frieda Lawrence. Reprinted by permission of The Viking Press, Inc., New York.

being taken for exercise. This was the last time. These were the last horses that would go through their hands. The young men watched with critical, callous look. They were all frightened at the collapse of their lives, and the sense of disaster in which they were involved left them no inner freedom.

Yet they were three fine, well-set fellows enough. Joe, the eldest, was a man of thirty-three, broad and handsome in a hot, flushed way. His face was red, he twisted his black moustache over a thick finger, his eyes were shallow and restless. He had a sensual way of uncovering his teeth when he laughed, and his bearing was stupid. Now he watched the horses with a glazed look of helplessness in his eyes, a certain stupor of downfall.

The great draught-horses swung past. They were tied head to tail, four of them, and they heaved along to where a lane branched off from the highroad, planting their great hoofs floutingly in the fine black mud, swinging their great rounded haunches sumptuously, and trotting a few sudden steps as they were led into the lane, round the corner. Every movement showed a massive, slumbrous strength, and a stupidity which held them in subjection. The groom at the head looked back, jerking the leading rope. And the cavalcade moved out of sight up the lane, the tail of the last horse, bobbed up tight and stiff, held out taut from the swinging great haunches as they rocked behind the hedges in a motion-like sleep.

Joe watched with glazed hopeless eyes. The horses were almost like his own body to him. He felt he was done for now. Luckily he was engaged to a woman as old as himself, and therefore her father, who was steward of a neighbouring estate, would provide him with a job. He would marry and go into harness. His life was over, he would be a subject animal now.

He turned uneasily aside, the retreating steps of the horses echoing in his ears. Then, with foolish restlessness, he reached for the scraps of bacon-rind from the plates, and making a faint whistling sound, flung them to the terrier that lay against the fender. He watched the dog swallow them, and waited till the creature looked into his eyes. Then a faint grin came on his face, and in a high, foolish voice he said:

"You won't get much more bacon, shall you, you little bitch?"

The dog faintly and dismally wagged its tail, then lowered its haunches, circled round, and lay down again.

There was another helpless silence at the table. Joe sprawled uneasily in his seat, not willing to go till the family conclave was dissolved. Fred Henry, the second brother, was erect, clean-limbed, alert. He had watched the passing of the horses with more sang-froid. If he was an animal, like Joe, he was an animal which controls, not one which is controlled. He was master of any horse, and he carried himself with a well-tempered air of mastery. But he was not master of the situations of life. He pushed his coarse brown moustache upwards, off his lip, and glanced irritably at his sister, who sat impassive and inscrutable.

"You'll go and stop with Lucy for a bit, shan't you?" he asked. The girl did not answer.

"I don't see what else you can do," persisted Fred Henry.

"Go as a skivvy," Joe interpolated laconically.

The girl did not move a muscle.

"If I was her, I should go in for training for a nurse," said Malcolm, the youngest of them all. He was the baby of the family, a young man of twenty-two, with a fresh, jaunty *museau*.[1]

But Mabel did not take any notice of him. They had talked at her and round her for so many years, that she hardly heard them at all.

The marble clock on the mantelpiece softly chimed the half-hour, the dog rose uneasily from the hearthrug and looked at the party at the breakfast table. But still they sat on in ineffectual conclave.

"Oh, all right," said Joe suddenly, apropos of nothing. "I'll get a move on."

He pushed back his chair, straddled his knees with a downward jerk, to get them free, in horsey fashion, and went to the fire. Still he did not go out of the room; he was curious to know what the others would do or say. He began to charge his pipe, looking down at the dog and saying, in a high, affected voice:

"Going wi' me? Going wi' me are ter? Tha'rt goin' further than tha counts on just now, dost hear?"

The dog faintly wagged its tail, the man stuck out his jaw and covered his pipe with his hands, and puffed intently, losing himself in the tobacco, looking down all the while at the dog with an absent brown eye. The dog looked up at him in mournful distrust. Joe stood with his knees stuck out, in real horsey fashion.

"Have you had a letter from Lucy?" Fred Henry asked of his sister.

"Last week," came the neutral reply.

"And what does she say?"

There was no answer.

"Does she *ask* you to go and stop there?" persisted Fred Henry.

"She says I can if I like."

"Well, then, you'd better. Tell her you'll come on Monday."

This was received in silence.

"That's what you'll do then, is it?" said Fred Henry, in some exasperation.

But she made no answer. There was a silence of futility and irritation in the room. Malcolm grinned fatuously.

"You'll have to make up your mind between now and next Wednes-

1. Face (French Slang).

day," said Joe loudly, "or else find yourself lodgings on the kerb-stone."

The face of the young woman darkened, but she sat on immutable.

"Here's Jack Fergusson!" exclaimed Malcolm, who was looking aimlessly out of the window.

"Where?" exclaimed Joe, loudly.

"Just gone past."

"Coming in?"

Malcolm craned his neck to see the gate.

"Yes," he said.

There was a silence. Mabel sat on like one condemned, at the head of the table. Then a whistle was heard from the kitchen. The dog got up and barked sharply. Joe opened the door and shouted:

"Come on."

After a moment a young man entered. He was muffled up in over-coat and a purple woollen scarf, and his tweed cap, which he did not remove, was pulled down on his head. He was of medium height, his face was rather long and pale, his eyes looked tired.

"Hello, Jack! Well, Jack!" exclaimed Malcolm and Joe. Fred Henry merely said, "Jack."

"What's doing?" asked the newcomer, evidently addressing Fred Henry.

"Same. We've got to be out by Wednesday. Got a cold?"

"I have—got it bad, too."

"Why don't you stop in?"

"*Me* stop in? When I can't stand on my legs, perhaps I shall have a chance." The young man spoke huskily. He had a slight Scotch accent.

"It's a knock-out, isn't it," said Joe, boisterously, "if a doctor goes round croaking with a cold. Looks bad for the patients, doesn't it?"

The young doctor looked at him slowly.

"Anything the matter with *you*, then?" he asked sarcastically.

"Not as I know of. Damn your eyes, I hope not. Why?"

"I thought you were very concerned about the patients, wondered if you might be one yourself."

"Damn it, no, I've never been patient to no flaming doctor, and hope I never shall be," returned Joe.

At this point Mabel rose from the table, and they all seemed to become aware of her existence. She began putting the dishes together. The young doctor looked at her, but did not address her. He had not greeted her. She went out of the room with the tray, her face impassive and unchanged.

"When are you off then, all of you?" asked the doctor.

"I'm catching the eleven-forty," replied Malcolm. "Are you goin' down wi' th' trap, Joe?"

"Yes, I've told you I'm going down wi' th' trap, haven't I?"

"We'd better be getting her in then. So long, Jack, if I don't see you before I go," said Malcolm, shaking hands.

He went out, followed by Joe, who seemed to have his tail between his legs.

"Well, this is the devil's own," exclaimed the doctor, when he was left alone with Fred Henry. "Going before Wednesday, are you?"

"That's the orders," replied the other.

"Where, to Northampton?"

"That's it."

"The devil!" exclaimed Fergusson, with quiet chagrin.

And there was silence between the two.

"All settled up, are you?" asked Fergusson.

"About."

There was another pause.

"Well, I shall miss yer, Freddy, boy," said the young doctor.

"And I shall miss thee, Jack," returned the other.

"Miss you like hell," mused the doctor.

Fred Henry turned aside. There was nothing to say. Mabel came in again, to finish clearing the table.

"What are *you* going to do, then, Miss Pervin?" asked Fergusson. "Going to your sister's, are you?"

Mabel looked at him with her steady, dangerous eyes, that always made him uncomfortable, unsettling his superficial ease.

"No," she said.

"Well, what in the name of fortune *are* you going to do? Say what you mean to do," cried Fred Henry, with futile intensity.

But she only averted her head, and continued her work. She folded the white table-cloth, and put on the chenille cloth.

"The sulkiest bitch that ever trod!" muttered her brother.

But she finished her task with perfectly impassive face, the young doctor watching her interestedly all the while. Then she went out.

Fred Henry stared after her, clenching his lips, his blue eyes fixing in sharp antagonism, as he made a grimace of sour exasperation.

"You could bray her into bits, and that's all you'd get out of her," he said in a small, narrowed tone.

The doctor smiled faintly.

"What's she *going* to do, then?" he asked.

"Strike me if I know!" returned the other.

There was a pause. Then the doctor stirred.

"I'll be seeing you to-night, shall I?" he said to his friend.

"Ay—where's it to be? Are we going over to Jessdale?"

"I don't know. I've got such a cold on me. I'll come round to the Moon and Stars, anyway."

"Let Lizzie and May miss their night for once, eh?"

"That's it—if I feel as I do now."

"All's one—"

The two young men went through the passage and down to the back door together. The house was large, but it was servantless now, and desolate. At the back was a small bricked house-yard, and beyond that a big square, gravelled fine and red, and having stables on two sides. Sloping, dank, winter-dark fields stretched away on the open sides.

But the stables were empty. Joseph Pervin, the father of the family, had been a man of no education, who had become a fairly large horse dealer. The stables had been full of horses, there was a great turmoil and come-and-go of horses and of dealers and grooms. Then the kitchen was full of servants. But of late things had declined. The old man had married a second time, to retrieve his fortunes. Now he was dead and everything was gone to the dogs, there was nothing but debt and threatening.

For months, Mabel had been servantless in the big house, keeping the home together in penury for her ineffectual brothers. She had kept house for ten years. But previously it was with unstinted means. Then, however brutal and coarse everything was, the sense of money had kept her proud, confident. The men might be foul-mouthed, the women in the kitchen might have bad reputations, her brothers might have illegitimate children. But so long as there was money, the girl felt herself established, and brutally proud, reserved.

No company came to the house, save dealers and coarse men. Mabel had no associates of her own sex, after her sister went away. But she did not mind. She went regularly to church, she attended to her father. And she lived in the memory of her mother, who had died when she was fourteen, and whom she had loved. She had loved her father, too, in a different way, depending upon him, and feeling secure in him, until at the age of fifty-four he married again. And then she had set hard against him. Now he had died and left them all hopelessly in debt.

She had suffered badly during the period of poverty. Nothing, however, could shake the curious sullen, animal pride that dominated each member of the family. Now, for Mabel, the end had come. Still she would not cast about her. She would follow her own way just the same. She would always hold the keys of her own situation. Mindless and persistent, she endured from day to day. Why should she think? Why should she answer anybody? It was enough that this was the end, and there was no way out. She need not pass any more darkly along the main street of the small town, avoiding every eye. She need not demean herself any more, going into the shops and buying the cheapest food. This was at an end. She thought of nobody, not even of herself. Mindless and persistent, she seemed in a sort of ecstasy to be coming near to her fulfilment, her own glorification, approaching her dead mother, who was glorified.

In the afternoon she took a little bag, with shears and sponge and a small scrubbing brush, and went out. It was a grey, wintry day, with saddened, dark green fields and an atmosphere blackened by the smoke of foundries not far off. She went quickly, darkly along the causeway, heeding nobody, through the town to the church-yard.

There she always felt secure, as if no one could see her, although as a matter of fact she was exposed to the stare of every one who passed along under the churchyard wall. Nevertheless, once under the shadow of the great looming church, among the graves, she felt immune from the world, reserved within the thick churchyard wall as in another country.

Carefully she clipped the grass from the grave, and arranged the pinky white, small chrysanthemums in the tin cross. When this was done, she took an empty jar from a neighbouring grave, brought water, and carefully, most scrupulously sponged the marble head-stone and the coping-stone.

It gave her sincere satisfaction to do this. She felt in immediate contact with the world of her mother. She took minute pains, went through the park in a state bordering on pure happiness, as if in performing this task she came into a subtle, intimate connection with her mother. For the life she followed here in the world was far less real than the world of death she inherited from her mother.

The doctor's house was just by the church. Fergusson, being a mere hired assistant, was slave to the country-side. As he hurried now to attend to the outpatients in the surgery, glancing across the grave-yard with his quick eye, he saw the girl at her task at the grave. She seemed so intent and remote, it was like looking into another world. Some mystical element was touched in him. He slowed down as he walked, watching her as if spell-bound.

She lifted her eyes, feeling him looking. Their eyes met. And each looked away again at once, each feeling, in some way, found out by the other. He lifted his cap and passed on down the road. There remained distinct in his consciousness, like a vision, the memory of her face, lifted from the tombstone in the churchyard, and looking at him with slow, large, portentous eyes. It *was* portentous, her face. It seemed to mesmerize him. There was a heavy power in her eyes which laid hold of his whole being, as if he had drunk some powerful drug. He had been feeling weak and done before. Now the life came back into him, he felt delivered from his own fretted, daily self.

He finished his duties at the surgery as quickly as might be, hastily filling up the bottles of the waiting people with cheap drugs. Then, in perpetual haste, he set off again to visit several cases in another part of his round, before teatime. At all times he preferred to walk if he could, but particularly when he was not well. He fancied the motion restored him.

The afternoon was falling. It was grey, deadened, and wintry, with a slow, moist, heavy coldness sinking in and deadening all the faculties. But why should he think or notice? He hastily climbed the hill and turned across the dark green fields, following the black cinder-track. In the distance, across a shallow dip in the country, the small town was clustered like smouldering ash, a tower, a spire, a heap of low, raw, extinct houses. And on the nearest fringe of the town, sloping into the dip, was Oldmeadow, the Pervins' house. He could see the stables and the outbuildings distinctly, as they lay towards him on the slope. Well, he would not go there many more times! Another resource would be lost to him, another place gone: the only company he cared for in the alien, ugly little town he was losing. Nothing but work, drudgery, constant hastening from dwelling to dwelling among the colliers and the iron-workers. It wore him out, but at the same time he had a craving for it. It was a stimulant to him to be in the homes of the working people, moving as it were through the innermost body of their life. His nerves were excited and gratified. He could come so near, into the very lives of the rough, inarticulate, powerfully emotional men and women. He grumbled, he said he hated the hellish hole. But as a matter of fact it excited him, the contact with the rough, strongly-feeling people was a stimulant applied direct to his nerves.

Below Oldmeadow, in the green, shallow, soddened hollow of fields, lay a square, deep pond. Roving across the landscape, the doctor's quick eye detected a figure in black passing through the gate of the field, down towards the pond. He looked again. It would be Mabel Pervin. His mind suddenly became alive and attentive.

Why was she going down there? He pulled up on the path on the slope above, and stood staring. He could just make sure of the small black figure moving in the hollow of the failing day. He seemed to see her in the midst of such obscurity, that he was like a clairvoyant, seeing rather with the mind's eye than with ordinary sight. Yet he could see her positively enough, whilst he kept his eye attentive. He felt, if he looked away from her, in the thick, ugly falling dusk, he would lose her altogether.

He followed her minutely as she moved, direct and intent, like something transmitted rather than stirring in voluntary activity, straight down the field towards the pond. There she stood on the bank for a moment. She never raised her head. Then she waded slowly into the water.

He stood motionless as the small black figure walked slowly and deliberately towards the centre of the pond, very slowly, gradually moving deeper into the motionless water, and still moving forward as the water got up to her breast. Then he could see her no more in the dusk of the dead afternoon.

"There!" he exclaimed. "Would you believe it?"

And he hastened straight down, running over the wet, soddened fields, pushing through the hedges, down into the depression of callous wintry obscurity. It took him several minutes to come to the pond. He stood on the bank, breathing heavily. He could see nothing. His eyes seemed to penetrate the dead water. Yes, perhaps that was the dark shadow of her black clothing beneath the surface of the water.

He slowly ventured into the pond. The bottom was deep, soft clay, he sank in, and the water clasped dead cold round his legs. As he stirred he could smell the cold, rotten clay that fouled up into the water. It was objectionable in his lungs. Still, repelled and yet not heeding, he moved deeper into the pond. The cold water rose over his thighs, over his loins, upon his abdomen. The lower part of his body was all sunk in the hideous cold element. And the bottom was so deeply soft and uncertain, he was afraid of pitching with his mouth underneath. He could not swim, and was afraid.

He crouched a little, spreading his hands under the water and moving them round, trying to feel for her. The dead cold pond swayed upon his chest. He moved again, a little deeper, and again, with his hands underneath, he felt all around under the water. And he touched her clothing. But it evaded his fingers. He made a desperate effort to grasp it.

And so doing he lost his balance and went under, horribly, suffocating in the foul earthy water, struggling madly for a few moments. At last, after what seemed an eternity, he got his footing, rose again into the air and looked around. He gasped, and knew he was in the world. Then he looked at the water. She had risen near him. He grasped her clothing, and drawing her nearer, turned to take his way to land again.

He went very slowly, carefully, absorbed in the slow progress. He rose higher, climbing out of the pond. The water was now only about his legs; he was thankful, full of relief to be out of the clutches of the pond. He lifted her and staggered on to the bank, out of the horror of wet, grey clay.

He laid her down on the bank. She was quite unconscious and running with water. He made the water come from her mouth, he worked to restore her. He did not have to work very long before he could feel the breathing begin again in her; she was breathing naturally. He worked a little longer. He could feel her live beneath his hands; she was coming back. He wiped her face, wrapped her in his overcoat, looked round into the dim, dark grey world, then lifted her and staggered down the bank and across the fields.

It seemed an unthinkably long way, and his burden so heavy he felt he would never get to the house. But at last he was in the stable-yard, and then in the house-yard. He opened the door and went into the house. In the kitchen he laid her down on the hearthrug, and called. The house was empty. But the fire was burning in the grate.

Then again he kneeled to attend to her. She was breathing regularly, her eyes were wide open and as if conscious, but there seemed something missing in her look. She was conscious in herself, but unconscious of her surroundings.

He ran upstairs, took blankets from a bed, and put them before the fire to warm. Then he removed her saturated, earthy-smelling clothing, rubbed her dry with a towel, and wrapped her naked in the blankets. Then he went into the dining-room, to look for spirits. There was a little whisky. He drank a gulp himself, and put some into her mouth.

The effect was instantaneous. She looked full into his face, as if she had been seeing him for some time, and yet had only just become conscious of him.

"Dr. Fergusson?" she said.

"What?" he answered.

He was divesting himself of his coat, intending to find some dry clothing upstairs. He could not bear the smell of the dead, clayey water, and he was mortally afraid for his own health.

"What did I do?" she asked.

"Walked into the pond," he replied. He had begun to shudder like one sick, and could hardly attend to her. Her eyes remained full on him, he seemed to be going dark in his mind, looking back at her helplessly. The shuddering became quieter in him, his life came back in him, dark and unknowing, but strong again.

"Was I out of my mind?" she asked, while her eyes were fixed on him all the time.

"Maybe, for the moment," he replied. He felt quiet, bcause his strength had come back. The strange fretful strain had left him.

"Am I out of my mind now?" she asked.

"Are you?" he reflected a moment. "No," he answered truthfully, "I don't see that you are." He turned his face aside. He was afraid now, because he felt dazed, and felt dimly that her power was stronger than his, in this issue. And she continued to look at him fixedly all the time. "Can you tell me where I shall find some dry things to put on?" he asked.

"Did you dive into the pond for me?" she asked.

"No," he answered. "I walked in. But I went in overhead as well."

There was silence for a moment. He hesitated. He very much wanted to go upstairs to get into dry clothing. But there was another desire in him. And she seemed to hold him. His will seemed to have gone to sleep, and left him, standing there slack before her. But he felt warm inside himself. He did not shudder at all, though his clothes were sodden on him.

"Why did you?" she asked.

"Because I didn't want you to do such a foolish thing," he said.

"It wasn't foolish," she said, still gazing at him as she lay on the floor, with a sofa cushion under her head. "It was the right thing to do. *I* knew best, then."

"I'll go and shift these wet things," he said. But still he had not the power to move out of her presence, until she sent him. It was as if she had the life of his body in her hands, and he could not extricate himself. Or perhaps he did not want to.

Suddenly she sat up. Then she became aware of her own immediate condition. She felt the blankets about her, she knew her own limbs. For a moment it seemed as if her reason were going. She looked round, with wild eye, as if seeking something. He stood still with fear. She saw her clothing lying scattered.

"Who undressed me?" she asked, her eyes resting full and inevitable on his face.

"I did," he replied, "to bring you round."

For some moments she sat and gazed at him awfully, her lips parted.

"Do you love me, then?" she asked.

He only stood and stared at her, fascinated. His soul seemed to melt.

She shuffled forward on her knees, and put her arms round him, round his legs, as he stood there, pressing her breasts against his knees and thighs, clutching him with strange, convulsive certainty, pressing his thighs against her, drawing him to her face, her throat, as she looked up at him with flaring, humble eyes of transfiguration, triumphant in first possession.

"You love me," she murmured, in strange transport, yearning and triumphant and confident. "You love me. I know you love me, I know."

And she was passionately kissing his knees, through the wet clothing, passionately and indiscriminately kissing his knees, his legs, as if unaware of everything.

He looked down at the tangled wet hair, the wild, bare, animal shoulders. He was amazed, bewildered, and afraid. He had never thought of loving her. He had never wanted to love her. When he rescued her and restored her, he was a doctor, and she was a patient. He had had no single personal thought of her. Nay, this introduction of the personal element was very distasteful to him, a violation of his professional honour. It was horrible to have her there embracing his knees. It was horrible. He revolted from it, violently. And yet—and not—he had not the power to break away.

She looked at him again, with the same supplication of powerful love, and that same transcendent, frightening light of triumph. In view of the delicate flame which seemed to come from her face like a light, he was powerless. And yet he had never intended to love her. He had never intended. And something stubborn in him could not give way.

"You love me," she repeated, in a murmur of deep, rhapsodic assurance. "You love me."

Her hands were drawing him, drawing him down to her. He was afraid, even a little horrified. For he had, really, no intention of loving her. Yet her hands were drawing him towards her. He put out his hand quickly to steady himself, and grasped her bare shoulder. A flame seemed to burn the hand that grasped her soft shoulder. He had no intention of loving her: his whole will was against his yielding. It was horrible. And yet wonderful was the touch of her shoulders, beautiful the shining of her face. Was she perhaps mad? He had a horror of yielding to her. Yet something in him ached also.

He had been staring away at the door, away from her. But his hand remained on her shoulder. She had gone suddenly very still. He looked down at her. Her eyes were now wide with fear, with doubt, the light was dying from her face, a shadow of terrible greyness was returning. He could not bear the touch of her eyes' question upon him, and the look of death behind the question.

With an inward groan he gave way, and let his heart yield towards her. A sudden gentle smile came on his face. And her eyes, which never left his face, slowly, slowly filled with tears. He watched the strange water rise in her eyes, like some slow fountain coming up. And his heart seemed to burn and melt away in his breast.

He could not bear to look at her any more. He dropped on his knees and caught her head with his arms and pressed her face against his throat. She was very still. His heart, which seemed to have broken, was burning with a kind of agony in his breast. And he felt her slow, hot tears wetting his throat. But he could not move.

He felt the hot tears wet his neck and the hollows of his neck, and he remained motionless, suspended through one of man's eternities. Only now it had become indispensable to him to have her face pressed close to him; he could never let her go again. He could never let her head go away from the close clutch of his arm. He wanted to remain like that for ever, with his heart hurting him in a pain that was also life to him. Without knowing, he was looking down on her damp, soft brown hair.

Then, as it were suddenly, he smelt the horrid stagnant smell of that water. And at the same moment she drew away from him and looked at him. Her eyes were wistful and unfathomable. He was afraid of them, and he fell to kissing her, not knowing what he was doing. He wanted her eyes not to have that terrible, wistful, unfathomable look.

When she turned her face to him again, a faint delicate flush was glowing, and there was again dawning that terrible shining of joy in her eyes, which really terrified him, and yet which he now wanted to see, because he feared the look of doubt still more.

"You love me?" she said, rather faltering.

"Yes." The word cost him a painful effort. Not because it wasn't true. But because it was too newly true, the *saying* seemed to tear open again his newly-torn heart. And he hardly wanted it to be true, even now.

She lifted her face to him, and he bent forward and kissed her on the mouth, gently, with the one kiss that is an eternal pledge. And as he kissed her his heart strained again in his breast. He never intended to love her. But now it was over. He had crossed over the gulf to her, and all that he had left behind had shrivelled and become void.

After the kiss, her eyes again slowly filled with tears. She sat still, away from him, with her face drooped aside, and her hands folded in her lap. The tears fell very slowly. There was complete silence. He too sat there motionless and silent on the hearthrug. The strange pain of his heart that was broken seemed to consume him. That he should love her? That this was love! That he should be ripped open in this way! Him, a doctor! How they would all jeer if they knew! It was agony to him to think they might know.

In the curious naked pain of the thought he looked again to her. She was sitting there drooped into a muse. He saw a tear fall, and his heart flared hot. He saw for the first time that one of her shoulders was quite uncovered, one arm bare, he could see one of her small breasts; dimly, because it had become almost dark in the room.

"Why are you crying?" he asked, in an altered voice.

She looked up at him, and behind her tears the consciousness of her situation for the first time brought a dark look of shame to her eyes.

"I'm not crying, really," she said, watching him half frightened.

He reached his hand, and softly closed it on her bare arm.

"I love you! I love you!" he said in a soft, low vibrating voice, unlike himself.

She shrank, and dropped her head. The soft, penetrating grip of his hand on her arm distressed her. She looked up at him.

"I want to go," she said. "I want to go and get you some dry things."

"Why?" he said. "I'm all right."

"But I want to go," she said. "And I want you to change your things."

He released her arm, and she wrapped herself in the blanket, looking at him rather frightened. And still she did not rise.

"Kiss me," she said wistfully.

He kissed her, but briefly, half in anger.

Then, after a second, she rose nervously, all mixed up in the blanket. He watched her in her confusion, as she tried to extricate herself and wrap herself up so that she could walk. He watched her relentlessly, as she knew. And as she went, the blanket trailing, and as he saw a glimpse of her feet and her white leg, he tried to remember her as she was when he had wrapped her in the blanket. But then he didn't want to remember, because she had been nothing to him then, and his nature revolted from remembering her as she was when she was nothing to him.

A tumbling, muffled noise from within the dark house startled him. Then he heard her voice:—"There are clothes." He rose and went to the foot of the stairs, and gathered up the garments she had thrown down. Then he came back to the fire, to rub himself down and dress. He grinned at his own appearance when he had finished.

The fire was sinking, so he put on coal. The house was now quite dark, save for the light of a street-lamp that shone in faintly from beyond the holly trees. He lit the gas with matches he found on the mantelpiece. Then he emptied the pockets of his own clothes, and threw all his wet things in a heap into the scullery. After which he gathered up her sodden clothes, gently, and put them in a separate heap on the copper-top in the scullery.

It was six o'clock on the clock. His own watch had stopped. He ought to go back to the surgery. He waited, and still she did not come down. So he went to the foot of the stairs and called:

"I shall have to go."

Almost immediately he heard her coming down. She had on her best dress of black voile, and her hair was tidy, but still damp. She looked at him—and in spite of herself, smiled.

"I don't like you in those clothes," she said.

"Do I look a sight?" he answered.

They were shy of one another.

"I'll make you some tea," she said.

"No, I must go."

"Must you?" And she looked at him again with the wide, strained, doubtful eyes. And again, from the pain of his breast, he knew how he loved her. He went and bent to kiss her, gently, passionately, with his heart's painful kiss.

"And my hair smells so horrible," she murmured in distraction. "And I'm so awful, I'm so awful! Oh, no, I'm too awful." And she broke into bitter, heart-broken sobbing. "You can't want to love me, I'm horrible."

"Don't be silly, don't be silly," he said, trying to comfort her, kissing her, holding her in his arms. "I want you, I want to marry you, we're going to be married, quickly, quickly—tomorrow if I can."

But she only sobbed terribly, and cried:

"I feel awful. I feel awful. I feel I'm horrible to you."

"No, I want you, I want you," was all he answered, blindly, with that terrible intonation which frightened her almost more than her horror lest he should *not* want her.

BERTOLT BRECHT
(1898–1956)

The Caucasian Chalk Circle*

English version by Eric Bentley

Characters

OLD MAN, *on the right*	GEORGI ABASHWILL, the Governor
PEASANT WOMAN, *on the right*	NATELLA, *the Governor's wife*
YOUNG PEASANT	MICHAEL, *their son*
A VERY YOUNG WORKER	SHALVA, *an Adjutant*
OLD MAN, *on the left*	ARSEN KAZBEKA, *a fat prince*
PEASANT WOMAN, *on the left*	MESSENGER, *from the Capital*
AGRICULTURIST KATO	NIKO MIKADZE and
GIRL TRACTORIST	MIKA LOLADZE, *Doctors*
WOUNDED SOLDIER	SIMON SHASHAVA, *a soldier*
THE DELEGATE *from the capital*	GRUSHA VASHNADZE,
THE STORY TELLER	*a kitchen maid*

* Written in 1944-1945.

Copyright © 1947, 1948, 1961, 1963 by Eric Bentley, Prologue Copyright © 1959 by Eric Bentley. Reprinted by permission of the University of Minnesota Press.

This adaptation, commissioned and approved by Bertolt Brecht, is based on the German MS of 1946. A German version very close to this MS was published in a supplement to *Sinn und Form*, 1949. My English text has now appeared in three versions. Maja Apelman collaborated on the first one (copyrighted 1947, 1948). The second and third were respectively copyrighted in 1961 and 1963.

—E.B., New York, 1963

1516 · Bertolt Brecht

OLD PEASANT, *with the milk*
CORPORAL *and* PRIVATE
PEASANT *and his wife*
LAVRENTI VASHNADZE,
    Grusha's brother
ANIKO, *his wife*
PEASANT WOMAN, *for a while*
    Grusha's mother-in-law
JUSSUP, *her son*
MONK
AZDAK, *village recorder*
SHAUWA, *a policeman*
GRAND DUKE
DOCTOR

INVALID
LIMPING MAN
BLACKMAILER
LUDOVICA
INNKEEPER, *her father-in-law*
STABLEBOY
POOR OLD PEASANT WOMAN
IRAKLI, *her brother-in-law,*
    a bandit
THREE WEALTHY FARMERS
ILLO SHUBOLADZE *and*
    SANDRO OBOLADZE, *lawyers*
OLD MARRIED COUPLE

SOLDIERS, SERVANTS, PEASANTS, BEGGARS, MUSICIANS, MERCHANTS,
    NOBLES, ARCHITECTS

Prologue

[*Among the ruins of a war-ravaged Caucasian village the
members of two Kolkhoz[1] villages, mostly women and older
men, are sitting in a circle, smoking and drinking wine. With
them is a* DELEGATE *of the state Reconstruction Commission
from Nuka, the capital.*]

PEASANT WOMAN, *left.* [*Pointing*] In those hills over there we stopped
three Nazi tanks, but the apple orchard was already destroyed.

OLD MAN, *right.* Our beautiful dairy farm: a ruin.

GIRL TRACTORIST. I laid the fire, Comrade.

    [*Pause*]

DELEGATE. Now listen to the report. Delegates from the goat-breed-
ing Kolkhoz "Rosa Luxemburg" have been to Nuka. When Hitler's armies approached, the Kolkhoz had moved its goat-herds
further east on orders from the authorities. They are now thinking of returning. Their delegates have investigated the village and
the land and found a lot of it destroyed.

    [DELEGATES *on right nod.*]

The neighboring fruit-culture Kolkhoz [*To the left*] "Galinsk" is
proposing to use the former grazing land of Kolkhoz "Rosa Luxemburg," a valley with scanty growth of grass, for orchards and
vineyards. As a delegate of the Reconstruction Commission, I
request that the two Kolkhoz villages decide between themselves whether Kolkhoz "Rosa Luxemburg" shall return here or
not.

OLD MAN, *right.* First of all, I want to protest against the restriction

1. *Kolkhoz:* a collective farm in the Soviet Union.

of time for discussion. We of Kolkhoz "Rosa Luxemburg"[2] have spent three days and three nights getting here. And now discussion is limited to half a day.

WOUNDED SOLDIER, *left.* Comrade, we haven't as many villages as we used to have. We haven't as many hands. We haven't as much time.

GIRL TRACTORIST. All pleasures have to be rationed. Tobacco is rationed, and wine. Discussion should be rationed.

OLD MAN, *right.* [*Sighing*] Death to the fascist! But I will come to the point and explain why we want our valley back. There are a great many reasons, but I'll begin with one of the simplest. Makina Abakidze, unpack the goat cheese.

[*A* PEASANT WOMAN *from right takes from a basket an enormous cheese wrapped in a cloth. Applause and laughter.*]

Help yourselves, Comrades, start in!

OLD MAN, *left.* [*Suspiciously*] Is this a way of influencing us?

OLD MAN, *right.* [*Amid laughter*] How could it be a way of influencing you, Surab, you valley-thief? Everyone knows you will take the cheese and the valley, too. [*Laughter*] All I expect from you is an honest answer. Do you like the cheese?

OLD MAN, *left.* The answer is: yes.

OLD MAN, *right.* Really. [*Bitterly*] I ought to have known you know nothing about cheese.

OLD MAN, *left.* Why not? When I tell you I like it?

OLD MAN, *right.* Because you can't like it. Because it's not what it was in the old days. And why not? Because our goats don't like the new grass as they did the old. Cheese is not cheese because grass is not grass, that's the thing. Please put that in your report.

OLD MAN, *left.* But your cheese is excellent.

OLD MAN, *right.* It isn't excellent. It's just passable. The new grazing land is no good, whatever the young people may say. One can't live there. It doesn't even smell of morning in the morning.

[*Several people laugh.*]

DELEGATE. Don't mind their laughing: they understand you. Comrades, why does one love one's country? Because the bread tastes better there, the air smells better, voices sound stronger, the sky is higher, the ground is easier to walk on. Isn't that so?

OLD MAN, *right.* The valley has belonged to us from all eternity.

SOLDIER, *left.* What does *that* mean—from all eternity? Nothing belongs to anyone from all eternity. When you were young you didn't even belong to yourself. You belonged to the Kazbeki[3] princes.

---

2. Rosa Luxemburg (1870–1919), member of the German Socialist movement, for whom one of the Kolkhozes is named. She protested against World War I and, with Karl Liebknecht, was responsible for the 1919 revolution in Berlin.

3. *Kazbeki:* Kazbek is a mountain peak in the Central Caucasus.

OLD MAN, *right*. Doesn't it make a difference, though, what kind of trees stand next to the house you are born in? Or what kind of neighbors you have? Doesn't that make a difference? We want to go back just to have you as our neighbors, valley-thieves! Now you can all laugh again.

OLD MAN, *left*. [*Laughing*] Then why don't you listen to what your neighbor, Kato Wachtang, our agriculturist, has to say about the valley?

PEASANT WOMAN, *right*. We've not said all there is to be said about our valley. By no means. Not all the houses are destroyed. As for the dairy farm, at least the foundation wall is still standing.

DELEGATE. You can claim State support—here and there—you know that. I have suggestions here in my pocket.

PEASANT WOMAN, *right*. Comrade Specialist, we haven't come here to bargain. I can't take your cap and hand you another, and say "This one's better." The other one might *be* better; but you *like* yours better.

GIRL TRACTORIST. A piece of land is not a cap—not in our country, Comrade.

DELEGATE. Don't get angry. It's true we have to consider a piece of land as a tool to produce something useful, but it's also true that we must recognize love for a particular piece of land. As far as I'm concerned. I'd like to find out more exactly what you [*to those on the left*] want to do with the valley.

OTHERS. Yes, let Kato speak.

DELEGATE. Comrade Agriculturist!

KATO. [*Rising; she's in military uniform.*] Comrades, last winter, while we were fighting in these hills here as Partisans, we discussed how, after the expulsion of the Germans, we could build up our fruit culture to ten times its original size. I've prepared a plan for an irrigation project. By means of a cofferdam on our mountain lake, 300 hectares[4] of unfertile land can be irrigated. Our Kolkhoz could not only cultivate more fruit, but also have vineyards. The project, however, would pay only if the disputed valley of Kolkhoz "Galinsk" were also included. Here are the calculations. [*She hands the* DELEGATE *a briefcase.*]

OLD MAN, *right*. Write into a report that our Kolkhoz plans to start a new stud farm.

GIRL TRACTORIST. Comrades, the project was conceived during days and nights when we had to take cover in the mountains. We were often without ammunition for our half-dozen rifles. Even getting a pencil was difficult.

[*Applause from both sides*]

OLD MAN, *right*. Our thanks to the Comrades of Kolkhoz "Galinsk" and all who have defended our country!

[*They shake hands and embrace.*]

---

4. A hectare is not quite two and one half acres.

PEASANT WOMAN, *left.* In doing this our thought was that our soldiers—both your men and our men—should return to a still more productive homeland.

GIRL TRACTORIST. As the poet Mayakovsky said: "The home of the Soviet people shall also be the home of Reason!"[5]

[*The* DELEGATES *including the* OLD MAN *have got up, and with the* DELEGATE *specified proceed to study the Agriculturist's drawings . . . exclamations such as:* "Why is the altitude of all 22 meters?"—"This rock must be blown up"—"Actually, all they need is cement and dynamite"—"They force the water to come down here, that's clever!"]

VERY YOUNG WORKER, *right.* [*To* OLD MAN, *right*] They're going to irrigate all the fields between the hills, look at that, Aleko!

OLD MAN, *right.* I'm not going to look. I knew the project would be good. I won't have a revolver aimed at my chest.

DELEGATE. But they only want to aim a pencil at your chest.

[*Laughter*]

OLD MAN, *right.* [*Gets up gloomily, and walks over to look at the drawings.*] These valley-thieves know only too well that we can't resist machines and projects in this country

PEASANT WOMAN, *right.* Aleko Bereshwili, you have a weakness for new projects. That's well known.

DELEGATE. What about my report? May I write that you will all support the cession of your old valley in the interests of this project when you get back to your Kolkhoz?

PEASANT WOMAN, *right.* I will. What about you, Aleko?

OLD MAN, *right.* [*Bent over drawings*] I suggest that you give us copies of the drawings to take along.

PEASANT WOMAN, *right.* Then we can sit down and eat. Once he has the drawings and he's ready to discuss them, the matter is settled. I know him. And it will be the same with the rest of us.

[DELEGATES *laughingly embrace again.*]

OLD MAN, *left.* Long live the Kolkhoz "Rosa Luxemburg" and much luck to your horse-breeding project!

PEASANT WOMAN, *left.* In honor of the visit of the delegates from Kolkhoz "Rosa Luxemburg" and of the Specialist, the plan is that we all hear a presentation of the Story Teller Arkadi Tscheidse.

[*Applause.* GIRL TRACTORIST *has gone off to bring the* STORY TELLER.]

PEASANT WOMAN, *right.* Comrades, your entertainment had better be good. We're going to pay for it with a valley.

PEASANT WOMAN, *left.* Arkadi Tscheidse knows about our discussion. He's promised to perform something that has a bearing on the problem.

KATO. We wired to Tiflis three times. The whole thing nearly fell

5. Mayakovsky (1894-1930) was a prominent avant garde, revolutionary writer who committed suicide.

through at the last minute because his driver had a cold.

PEASANT WOMAN, *left*. Arkadi Tscheidse knows 21,000 lines of verse.

OLD MAN, *left*. It's very difficult to get him. You and the Planning Commission should see to it that you get him to come North more often, Comrade.

DELEGATE. We are more interested in economics, I'm afraid.

OLD MAN, *left*. [*Smiling*] You arrange the redistribution of vines and tractors, why not of songs?

> [*Enter the* STORY TELLER *Arkadi Tscheidse, led by* GIRL TRAC-TORIST. *He is a well-built man of simple manners, accompanied by four* MUSICIANS *with their instruments. The* ARTISTS *are greeted with applause*.]

GIRL TRACTORIST. This is the Comrade Specialist, Arkadi.

> [*The* STORY TELLER *greets them all*.]

DELEGATE. I'm honored to make your acquaintance. I heard about your songs when I was a boy at school. Will it be one of the old legends?

THE STORY TELLER. A very old one. It's called The Chalk Circle and comes from the Chinese. But we'll do it, of course, in a changed version. Comrades, it's an honor for me to entertain you after a difficult debate. We hope you will find that the voice of the old poet also sounds well in the shadow of Soviet tractors. It may be a mistake to mix different wines, but old and new wisdom mix admirably. Now I hope we'll get something to eat before the performance begins—it would certainly help.

VOICES. Surely. Everyone into the Club House!

> [*While everyone begins to move, the* DELEGATE *turns to the* GIRL TRACTORIST.]

DELEGATE. I hope it won't take long. I've got to get back tonight.

GIRL TRACTORIST. How long will it last, Arkadi? The Comrade Specialist must get back to Tiflis tonight.

THE STORY TELLER. [*Casually*] It's actually two stories. An hour or two.

GIRL TRACTORIST. [*Confidentially*] Couldn't you make it shorter?

THE STORY TELLER. No.

VOICE. Arkadi Tscheidse's performance will take place here in the square after the meal.

> [*And they all go happily to eat*.]

1. *The Noble Child*

> [*As the lights go up, the* STORY TELLER *is seen sitting on the floor, a black sheepskin cloak round his shoulders, and a little well-thumbed notebook in his hand. A small group of listeners —the chorus—sits with him. The manner of his recitation makes it clear that he has told his story over and over again.*

*He mechanically fingers the pages, seldom looking at them.
With appropriate gestures, he gives the signal for each scene
to begin.*]

THE STORY TELLER. In olden times, in a bloody time,
There ruled in a Caucasian city—
Men called it City of the Damned—
A governor.
His name was Georgi Abashwili.
He was rich as Croesus[6]
He had a beautiful wife
He had a healthy baby.
No other governor in Grusinia[7]
Had so many horses in his stable
So many beggars in his doorstep
So many soldiers in his service
So many petitioners in his courtyard.
Georgi Abashwili—how shall I describe him to you?
He enjoyed his life.
On the morning of Easter Sunday
The governor and his family went to church.

[*At the left a large doorway, at the right an even larger gateway.* BEGGARS *and* PETITIONERS *pour from the gateway, holding up thin children, crutches, and petitions. They are followed by* IRONSHIRTS, *and then, expensively dressed, the*
GOVERNOR'S FAMILY.]

BEGGARS AND PETITIONERS. Mercy! Mercy, Your Grace! The taxes
are too high.
—I lost my leg in the Persian War, where can I get ...
—My brother is innocent, Your Grace, a misunderstanding . . .
—The child is starving in my arms!
—Our petition is for our son's discharge from the army, our last
remaining son!
—Please, Your Grace, the water inspector takes bribes.

[*One* SERVANT *collects the petitions, another distributes coins
from a purse.* SOLDIERS *push the* CROWD *back, lashing at them
with thick leather whips.*]

THE SOLDIER. Get back! Clear the church door!

[*Behind the* GOVERNOR, *his* WIFE, *and the* ADJUTANT, *the* GOV-
ERNOR'S CHILD *is brought through the gateway in an ornate
carriage.*]

THE CROWD.
—The baby!

6. Croesus, whose wealth is prover-
bial, was the last king of Lydia in Asia
Minor, in the sixth century B.C.

7. Grusinia is a name used variously
for Georgia and for a province in eastern Georgia.

—I can't see it, don't shove so hard!

—God bless the child, Your Grace!

THE STORY TELLER. [*While the* CROWD *is driven back with whips*]
For the first time on that Easter Sunday, the people saw the
Governor's heir.

Two doctors never moved from the noble child, apple of the
Governor's eye.

Even the mighty Prince Kazbeki bows before him at the church
door.

[*A* FAT PRINCE *steps forward and greets the family.*]

THE FAT PRINCE. Happy Easter, Natella Abashwili! What a day!
When it was raining last night, I thought to myself, gloomy
holidays! But this morning the sky was gay. I love a gay sky, a
simple heart, Natella Abaswili. And little Michael is a governor
from head to foot! Tititi! [*He tickles the child.*]

THE GOVERNOR'S WIFE. What do you think, Arsen, at last Georgi
has decided to start building the wing on the east side. All those
wretched slums are to be torn down to make room for the garden.

THE FAT PRINCE. Good news after so much bad! What's the latest
on the war, Brother Georgi?

[*The* GOVERNOR *indicates a lack of interest.*]

THE FAT PRINCE. Strategical retreat, I hear. Well, minor reverses are
to be expected. Sometimes things go well, sometimes not. Such
is war. Doesn't mean a thing, does it?

THE GOVERNOR'S WIFE. He's coughing. Georgi, did you hear?

[*She speaks sharply to the* DOCTORS, *two dignified men standing close to the little carriage.*]

He's coughing!

THE FIRST DOCTOR. [*To the* SECOND] May I remind you, Niko
Mikadze, that I was against the lukewarm bath? [*To the* GOVER-
NOR'S WIFE] There's been a little error over warming the bath
water, Your Grace.

THE SECOND DOCTOR. [*Equally polite*] Mika Loladze, I'm afraid I
can't agree with you. The temperture of the bath water was
exactly what our great, beloved Mishiko Oboladze prescribed.
More likely a slight draft during the night, Your Grace.

THE GOVERNOR'S WIFE. But do pay more attention to him. He looks
feverish, Georgi.

THE FIRST DOCTOR. [*Bending over the child*] No cause for alarm,
Your Grace. The bath water will be warmer. It won't occur again.

THE SECOND DOCTOR. [*With a venomous glance at the* FIRST] I won't
forget that, my dear Mika Loladze. No cause for concern, Your
Grace.

THE FAT PRINCE. Well, well, well! I always say: "A pain in my
liver? Then the doctor gets fifty strokes on the soles of his feet."
We live in a decadent age. In the old days one said: "Off with

his head!"

THE GOVERNOR'S WIFE. Let's go into church. Very likely it's the draft here.

[*The procession of* FAMILY *and* SERVANTS *turns into the doorway. The* FAT PRINCE *follows, but the* GOVERNOR *is kept back by the* ADJUTANT, *a handsome young man. When the* CROWD *of* PETITIONERS *has been driven off, a young dust-stained* RIDER, *his arm in a sling, remains behind.*]

THE ADJUTANT. [*Pointing at the* RIDER, *who steps forward*] Won't you hear the messenger from the capital, Your Excellency? He arrived this morning. With confidential papers.

THE GOVERNOR. Not before Service, Shalva. But did you hear Brother Kazbeki wish me a happy Easter? Which is all very well, but I don't believe it did rain last night.

THE ADJUTANT. [*Nodding*] We must investigate.

THE GOVERNOR. Yes, at once. Tomorrow.

[*They pass through the doorway. The* RIDER, *who has waited in vain for an audience, turns sharply round and, muttering a curse, goes off. Only one of the palace guards—*SIMON SHASHAVA*—remains at the door.*]

THE STORY TELLER.

The city is still.

Pigeons strut in the church square.

A soldier of the Palace Guard

Is joking with a kitchen maid

As she comes up from the river with a bundle.

[*With a bundle made of large green leaves under her arm.*]

SIMON. What, the young lady is not in church? Shirking?

GRUSHA. I was dressed to go. But they needed another goose for the banquet. And they asked me to get it. I know about geese.

SIMON. A goose? [*He feigns suspicion.*] I'd like to see that goose. [GRUSHA *does not understand.*] One has to be on one's guard with women. "I only went for a fish," they tell you, but it turns out to be something else.

GRUSHA. [*Walking resolutely toward him and showing him the goose*] There! If it isn't a fifteen-pound goose stuffed full of corn, I'll eat the feathers.

SIMON. A queen of a goose! The Governor himself will eat it. So the young lady has been down to the river again?

GRUSHA. Yes, at the poultry farm.

SIMON. Really? At the poultry farm, down by the river . . . not higher up maybe? Near those willows?

GRUSHA. I only go to the willows to wash the linen.

SIMON. [*Insinuatingly*] Exactly.

GRUSHA. Exactly what?

SIMON. [*Winking*] Exactly that.

GRUSHA. Why shouldn't I wash the linen by the willows?

SIMON. [*With exaggerated laughter*] "Why shouldn't I wash the linen by the willows!" That's good, really good!

GRUSHA. I don't understand the soldier. What's so good about it?

SIMON. [*Slyly*] "If something I know someone learns, she'll grow hot and cold by turns!"

GRUSHA. I don't know what I could learn about those willows.

SIMON. Not even if there was a bush opposite? That one could see everything from? Everything that goes on there when a certain person is—"washing linen"

GRUSHA. What does go on? Won't the soldier say what he means and have done?

SIMON. Something goes on. And something can be seen.

GRUSHA. Could the soldier mean I dip my toes in the water when it is hot? There is nothing else.

SIMON. More. Your toes. And more.

GRUSHA. More what? At most my foot?

SIMON. Your foot. And a little more. [*He laughs heartily.*]

GRUSHA. [*Angrily*] Simon Shashava, you ought to be ashamed of yourself! To sit in a bush on a hot day and wait till someone comes and dips her leg in the river! And I bet you bring a friend along too! [*She runs off.*]

SIMON. [*Shouting after her*] I didn't bring any friend along!

[*As the* STORY TELLER *resumes his tale, the* SOLDIER *steps into the doorway as though to listen to the service.*]

STORY TELLER. The city lies still
But why are there armed men?
The Governor's palace is at peace
But why is it a fortress?
And the Governor returned to his palace
And the fortress was a trap
And the goose was plucked and roasted
But the goose was not eaten this time
And noon was no longer the hour to eat:
Noon was the hour to die.

[*From the doorway at the left the* FAT PRINCE *quickly appears, stands still, looks around. Before the gateway at the right two* IRONSHIRTS *are squatting and playing dice. The* FAT PRINCE *sees them, walks slowly past, making a sign to them. They rise: one goes through the gateway, the other goes off at the right. Muffled voices are heard from various directions in the rear: "To your posts!" The palace is surrounded. The* FAT PRINCE *quickly goes off. Church bells in the distance. Enter, through the doorway, the* GOVERNOR'S FAMILY *and* PROCESSION, *returning from church.*]

THE GOVERNOR'S WIFE. [*Passing the* ADJUTANT] It's impossible to live in such a slum. But Georgi, of course, will only build for his little Michael. Never for me! Michael is all! All for Michael!

[*The* PROCESSION *turns into the gateway. Again the* ADJUTANT *lingers behind. He waits. Enter the* WOUNDED RIDER *from the doorway. Two* IRONSHIRTS *of the palace guard have taken up positions by the gateway.*]

THE ADJUTANT. [*To the* RIDER] The Governor does not wish to receive military reports before dinner—especially if they're depressing, as I assume. In the afternoon His Excellency will confer with prominent architects. They're coming to dinner too. And here they are!

[*Enter* THREE GENTLEMEN *through the doorway.*]

Go in the kitchen and get yourself something to eat, my friend.

[*As the* RIDER *goes, the* ADJUTANT *greets the* ARCHITECTS.]

Gentlemen, His Excellency expects you at dinner. He will devote all his time to you and your great new plans. Come!

ONE OF THE ARCHITECTS. We marvel that His Excellency intends to build. There are disquieting rumors that the war in Persia has taken a turn for the worse.

THE ADJUTANT. All the more reason to build! There's nothing to those rumors anyway. Persia is a long way off, and the garrison here would let itself be hacked to bits for its Governor.

[*Noise from the palace. The shrill scream of a woman. Someone is shouting orders. Dumbfounded, the* ADJUTANT *moves toward the gateway. An* IRONSHIRT *steps out, points his lance at him.*]

What's this? Put down that lance, you dog.

ONE OF THE ARCHITECTS. It's the Princes! Don't you know the Princes met last night in the capital? And they're against the Grand Duke and his Governors? Gentlemen, we'd better make ourselves scarce.

[*They rush off. The* ADJUTANT *remains helplessly behind.*]

THE ADJUTANT. [*Furiously to the* PALACE GUARD] Down with those lances! Don't you see the Governor's life is threatened?

[*The* IRONSHIRTS *of the Palace Guard refuse to obey. They stare coldly and indifferently at the* ADJUTANT *and follow the next events without interest.*]

THE STORY TELLER. O blindness of the great!
They go their way like gods,
Great over bent backs,
Sure of hired fists,
Trusting in the power
Which has lasted so long.
But long is not forever.
O change from age to age!
Thou hope of the people!

[*Enter the* GOVERNOR, *through the gateway, between two* SOL-
DIERS *armed to the teeth. He is in chains. His face is gray.*]

Up, great sir, deign to walk upright!
From your palace, the eyes of many foes follow you!
And now you don't need an architect, a carpenter will do.
You won't be moving into a new palace
But into a little hole in the ground.
Look about you once more, blind man!

[*The arrested man looks round.*]

Does all you had please you?
Between the Easter mass and the Easter meal
You are walking to a place whence no one returns.

[*The* GOVERNOR *is led off. A horn sounds an alarm. Noise
behind the gateway.*]

When the house of a great one collapses
Many little ones are slain.
Those who had no share in the *good* fortunes of the mighty
Often have a share in their *mis*fortunes.
The plunging wagon
Drags the sweating oxen down with it
Into the abyss.

[*The* SERVANTS *come rushing through the gateway in panic.*]

THE SERVANTS. [*Among themselves*]
—The baskets!
—Take them all into the third courtyard! Food for five days!
—The mistress has fainted! Someone must carry her down.
—She must get away.
—What about us? We'll be slaughtered like chickens, as always.
—Goodness, what'll happen? There's bloodshed already in the
city, they say.
—Nonsense, the Governor has just been asked to appear at a
Princes' meeting. All very correct. Everything'll be ironed out. I
heard this on the best authority. . . .

[*The two* DOCTORS *rush into the courtyard.*]

THE FIRST DOCTOR. [*Trying to restrain the other*] Niko Mikadze, it
is your duty as a doctor to attend Natella Abashwili.
THE SECOND DOCTOR. My duty! It's yours!
THE FIRST DOCTOR. Whose turn is it to look after the child today,
Niko Mikadze, yours or mine?
THE SECOND DOCTOR. Do you really think, Nika Loladze, I'm going
to stay a minute longer in this accursed house on that little brat's
account?

[*They start fighting. All one hears is:* "You neglect your duty!"
and "Duty, my foot!" *Then the* SECOND DOCTOR *knocks the
FIRST down.*]

Go to hell! [*Exit.*]

[*Enter the* SOLDIER, SIMON SHASHAVA. *He searches in the crowd for* GRUSHA.]

SIMON. Grusha! There you are at last! What are you going to do?

GRUSHA. Nothing. If worst comes to worst, I've a brother in the mountains. How about you?

SIMON. Forget about me. [*Formally again*] Grusha Vashnadze, your wish to know my plans fills me with satisfaction. I've been ordered to accompany Madam Natella Abashwili as her guard.

GRUSHA. But hasn't the Palace Guard mutinied?

SIMON. [*Seriously*] That's a fact.

GRUSHA. Isn't it dangerous to go with her?

SIMON. In Tiflis, they say: Isn't the stabbing dangerous for the knife?

GRUSHA. You're not a knife, you're a man, Simon Shashava, what has that woman to do with you?

SIMON. That woman has nothing to do with me. I have my orders, and I go.

GRUSHA. The soldier is pigheaded: he is getting himself into danger for nothing—nothing at all. I must get into the third courtyard, I'm in a hurry.

SIMON. Since we're both in a hurry we shouldn't quarrel. You need time for a good quarrel. May I ask if the young lady still has parents?

GRUSHA. No, just a brother.

SIMON. As time is short—my second question is this: Is the young lady as healthy as a fish in water?

GRUSHA. I may have a pain in the right shoulder once in a while. Otherwise I'm strong enough for my job. No one has complained. So far.

SIMON. That's well known. When it's Easter Sunday, and the question arises who'll run for the goose all the same, she'll be the one. My third question is this: Is the young lady impatient? Does she want apples in winter?

GRUSHA. Impatient? No. But if a man goes to war without any reason and then no message comes—that's bad.

SIMON. A message will come. And now my final question . . .

GRUSHA. Simon Shashava, I must get to the third courtyard at once. My answer is yes.

SIMON. [*Very embarrassed*] Haste, they say, is the wind that blows down the scaffolding. But they also say: The rich don't know what haste is. I'm from . . .

GRUSHA. Kutsk . . .

SIMON. So the young lady has been inquiring about me? I'm healthy, I have no dependents. I make ten piasters a month, as paymaster twenty piasters, and I'm asking—very sincerely—for your hand.

GRUSHA. Simon Shashava, it suits me well.

SIMON. [*Taking from his neck a thin chain with a little cross on it*]
My mother gave me this cross, Grusha Vashnadze. The chain is
is silver. Please wear it.

GRUSHA. Many thanks, Simon.

SIMON. [*Hangs it round her neck*] It would be better for the young
lady to go to the third courtyard now. Or there'll be difficulties.
Anyway, I must harness the horses. The young lady will understand?

GRUSHA. Yes, Simon.

[*They stand undecided.*]

SIMON. I'll just take the mistress to the troops that have stayed loyal.
When the war's over, I'll be back. In two weeks. Or three. I hope
my intended won't get tired, awaiting my return.

GRUSHA. Simon Shashava, I shall wait for you.
Go calmly into battle, soldier
The bloody battle, the bitter battle
From which not everyone returns:
When you return I shall be there.
I shall be waiting for you under the green elm
I shall be waiting for you under the bare elm
I shall wait until the last soldier has returned
And longer.
When you come back from the battle
No boots will stand at my door
The pillow beside mine will be empty
And my mouth will be unkissed.
When you return, when you return
You will be able to say: It is just as it was.

SIMON. I thank you, Grusha Vashnadze. And goodbye!

[*He bows low before her. She does the same before him.
Then she runs quickly off without looking round. Enter the
ADJUTANT from the gateway.*]

THE ADJUTANT. [*Harshly*] Harness the horses to the carriage! Don't
stand there doing nothing, louse!

[*SIMON SHASHAVA stands to attention and goes off. Two SERV-
ANTS crowd from the gateway, bent low under huge trunks.
Behind them, supported by her WOMEN, stumbles NATELLA
ABASHWILI. She is followed by a WOMAN carrying the CHILD.*]

THE GOVERNOR'S WIFE. I hardly know if my head's still on. Where's
Michael? Don't hold him so clumsily. Pile the trunks onto the
carriage. Shalva, is there no news from the city?

THE ADJUTANT. None. All's quiet so far, but there's not a minute
to lose. No room for all these trunks in the carriage. Pick out what
you need. [*Exit quickly.*]

THE GOVERNOR'S WIFE. Only essentials! Quick, open the trunks!
I'll tell you what I need. [*The trunks are lowered and opened.*

She points at some brocade dresses.] The green one! And, of course, the one with the fur trimming. Where are Niko Mikadze and Mika Loladze? I've suddenly got the most terrible migraine again. It always starts in the temples.

[*Enter* GRUSHA.]

Taking your time, eh? Go at once and get the hot water bottles! [GRUSHA *runs off, returns later with hot water bottles; the* GOVERNOR'S WIFE *orders her about by signs.*] Don't tear the sleeves.

A YOUNG WOMAN. Pardon, madam, no harm has come to the dress.

THE GOVERNOR'S WIFE. Because I stopped you. I've been watching you for a long time. Nothing in your head but making eyes at Shalva Tzereteli. I'll kill you, you bitch! [*She beats the woman.*]

THE ADJUTANT. [*appearing in the gateway*] Please make haste. Natella Abashwili. Firing has broken out in the city. [*Exit.*]

THE GOVERNOR'S WIFE. [*Letting go of the* YOUNG WOMAN] Oh dear, do you think they'll lay hands on us? Why should they? Why? [*She herself begins to rummage in the trunks.*] How's Michael? Asleep?

THE WOMAN WITH THE CHILD. Yes, madam.

THE GOVERNOR'S WIFE. Then put him down a moment and get my little saffron-colored boots from the bedroom. I need them for the green dress.

[*The* WOMAN *puts down the* CHILD *and goes off.*]

Just look how these things have been packed! No love! No understanding! If you don't give them every order yourself . . . At such moments you realize what kind of servants you have! They gorge themselves at your expense, and never a word of gratitude! I'll remember this.

THE ADJUTANT. [*Entering, very excited*] Natella, you must leave at once!

THE GOVERNOR'S WIFE. Why? I've got to take this silver dress—it cost a thousand piasters. And that one there, and where's the wine-colored one?

THE ADJUTANT. [*Trying to pull her away*] Riots have broken out! We must leave at once. Where's the baby?

THE GOVERNOR'S WIFE. [*Calling to the* YOUNG WOMAN *who was holding the baby*] Maro, get the baby ready! Where on earth are you?

THE ADJUTANT. [*Leaving*] We'll probably have to leave the carriage behind and go ahead on horseback.

[*The* GOVERNOR'S WIFE *rummages again among her dresses, throws some onto the heap of chosen clothes, then takes them off again. Noises, drums are heard. The* YOUNG WOMAN *who was beaten creeps away. The sky begins to grow red.*]

THE GOVERNOR'S WIFE. [*Rummaging desperately*] I simply cannot find the wine-colored dress. Take the whole pile to the carriage.

Where's Asja? And why hasn't Maro come back? Have you all gone crazy?

THE ADJUTANT. [*Returning*] Quick! Quick!

THE GOVERNOR'S WIFE. [*To the* FIRST WOMAN] Run! Just throw them into the carriage!

THE ADJUTANT. We're not taking the carriage. And if you don't come now, I'll ride off on my own.

THE GOVERNOR'S WIFE. [*As the* FIRST WOMAN *can't carry everything*] Where's that bitch Asja? [*The* ADJUTANT *pulls her away.*] Maro, bring the baby! [*To the* FIRST WOMAN] Go and look for Masha. No, first take the dresses to the carriage. Such nonsense! I wouldn't dream of going on horseback!

> [*Turning round, she sees the red sky, and starts back rigid. The fire burns. She is pulled out by the* ADJUTANT. *Shaking, the* FIRST WOMAN *follows with the dresses.*]

MARO. [*From the doorway, with the boots*] Madam! [*She sees the trunks and dresses and runs toward the baby, picks it up, and holds it a moment.*] They left it behind, the beasts. [*She hands it to* GRUSHA.] Hold it a moment. [*She runs off, following the* GOVERNOR'S WIFE.]

> [*Enter* SERVANTS *from the gateway.*]

THE COOK. Well, so they've actually gone. Without the food wagons, and not a minute too early. It's time for us to clear out.

A GROOM. This'll be an unhealthy neighborhood for quite a while. [*To one of the* WOMEN] Suliko, take a few blankets and wait for me in the foal stables.

GRUSHA. What have they done with the governor?

THE GROOM. [*Gesturing throat cutting*] Ffffft.

A FAT WOMAN. [*Seeing the gesture and becoming hysterical*] Oh dear, oh dear, oh dear, oh dear! Our master Georgi Abashwili! A picture of health he was, at the Morning Mass—and now! Oh, take me away, we're all lost, we must die in sin like our master, Georgi Abashwili!

THE OTHER WOMAN. [*Soothing her*] Calm down, Nina! You'll be taken to safety. You've never hurt a fly.

THE FAT WOMAN. [*Being led out*] Oh dear, oh dear, oh dear! Quick! Let's all get out before they come, before they come!

A YOUNG WOMAN. Nina takes it more to heart than the mistress, that's a fact. They even have to have their weeping done for them.

THE COOK. We'd better get out, all of us.

ANOTHER WOMAN. [*Glancing back*] That must be the East Gate burning.

THE YOUNG WOMAN. [*Seeing the* CHILD *in* GRUSHA's *arms*] The baby! What are you doing with it?

GRUSHA. It got left behind.

THE YOUNG WOMAN. She simply left it there. Michael, who was kept out of all the drafts!

[*The* SERVANTS *gather round the* CHILD.]

GRUSHA. He's waking up.

THE GROOM. Better put him down, I tell you. I'd rather not think what'd happen to anybody who was found with that baby.

THE COOK. That's right. Once they get started, they'll kill each other off, whole families at a time. Let's go.

[*Exeunt all but* GRUSHA, *with the* CHILD *on her arm, and two* WOMEN.]

THE TWO WOMEN. Didn't you hear? Better put him down.

GRUSHA. The nurse asked me to hold him a moment.

THE OLDER WOMAN. She's not coming back, you simpleton.

THE YOUNGER WOMAN. Keep your hands off it.

THE OLDER WOMAN. [*Amiably*] Grusha, you're a good soul, but you're not very bright, and you know it. I tell you, if he had the plague he couldn't be more dangerous.

GRUSHA. [*stubbornly*] He hasn't got the plague. He looks at me! He's human!

THE OLDER WOMAN. Don't look at *him*. You're a fool—the kind that always gets put upon. A person need only say, "Run for the salad, you have the longest legs," and you run. My husband has an ox cart—you can come with us if you hurry! Lord, by now the whole neighborhood must be in flames.

[*Both* WOMEN *leave, sighing. After some hesitation,* GRUSHA *puts the sleeping* CHILD *down, looks at it for a moment, then takes a brocade blanket from the heap of clothes and covers it. Then both* WOMEN *return, dragging bundles.* GRUSHA *starts guiltily away from the* CHILD *and walks a few steps to one side.*]

THE YOUNGER WOMAN. Haven't you packed anything yet? There isn't much time, you know. The Ironshirts will be here from the barracks.

GRUSHA. Coming.

[*She runs through the doorway. Both* WOMEN *go to the gateway and wait. The sound of horses is heard. They flee, screaming. Enter the* FAT PRINCE *with drunken* IRONSHIRTS. *One of them carries the governor's head on a lance.*]

THE FAT PRINCE. Here! In the middle!

[*One* SOLDIER *climbs onto the other's back, takes the head, holds it tentatively over the door.*]

That's not the middle. Farther to the right. That's it. What I do, my friends, I do well.

[*While, with hammer and nail, the* SOLDIER *fastens the head to the wall by its hair.*]

This morning at the church door I said to Georgi Abashwili: "I love a clear sky." Actually, I prefer the lightning that comes out of

a clear sky. Yes, indeed. It's a pity they took the brat along,
though, I need him, urgently.

[*Exit with* IRONSHIRTS *through the gateway. Trampling of
horses again. Enter* GRUSHA *through the doorway looking cautiously about her. Clearly she has waited for the* IRONSHIRTS
*to go. Carrying a bundle, she walks toward the gateway. At
the last moment, she turns to see if the* CHILD *is still there.
Catching sight of the head over the doorway, she screams.
Horrified, she picks up her bundle again, and is about to leave
when the* STORY TELLER *starts to speak. She stands rooted to
the spot.*]

THE STORY TELLER. As she was standing between courtyard and gate,
She heard or she thought she heard a low voice calling.
The child called to her,
Not whining, but calling quite sensibly,
Or so it seemed to her.
"Woman," it said, "help me."
And it went on, not whining, but saying quite sensibly:
"Know, woman, he who hears not a cry for help
But passes by with troubled ears will never hear
The gentle call of a lover nor the blackbird at dawn
Nor the happy sigh of the tired grape-picker as the Angelus rings."

[*She walks a few steps toward the* CHILD *and bends over it.*]

Hearing this she went back for one more look at the child:
Only to sit with him for a moment or two,
Only till someone should come,
His mother, or anyone.

[*Leaning on a trunk, she sits facing the* CHILD.]

Only till she would have to leave, for the danger was too great,
The city was full of flame and crying.

[*The light grows dimmer, as though evening and night were
coming on.*]

Fearful is the seductive power of goodness!

[GRUSHA *now settles down to watch over the* CHILD *through
the night. Once, she lights a small lamp to look at it. Once,
she tucks it in with a coat. From time to time she listens and
looks to see whether someone is coming.*]

And she sat with the child a long time,
Till evening came, till night came, till dawn came.
She sat too long, too long she saw
The soft breathing, the small clenched fists,
Till toward morning the seduction was complete
And she rose, and bent down and, sighing, took the child
And carried it away.

[*She does what the* STORY TELLER *says as he describes it.*]

As if it was stolen goods she picked it up.

As if she was a thief she crept away.

2. *The Flight into the Northern Mountains*

THE STORY TELLER. When Grusha Vashnadze left the city
On the Grusinian highway
On the way to the Northern Mountains
She sang a song, she bought some milk.

THE CHORUS. How will this human child escape
The bloodhounds, the trap-setters?
Into the deserted mountains she journeyed
Along the Grusinian highway he journeyed
She sang a song, she bought some milk.

[GRUSHA VASHNADZE *walks on. On her back she carries the* CHILD *in a sack, in one hand is a large stick, in the other a bundle. She sings.*]

The Song of the Four Generals

Four generals
Set out for Iran.
With the first one, war did not agree.
The second never won a victory.
For the third the weather never was right.
For the fourth the men would never fight.
Four generals
And not a single man!

Sosso Robakidse
Went marching to Iran
With him the war did so agree
He soon had won a victory.
For him the weather was always right.
For him the men would always fight.
Sosso Robakidse,
He is our man!

[*A peasant's cottage appears.*]

GRUSHA. [*To the* CHILD] Noontime is meal time. Now we'll sit hopefully in the grass, while the good Grusha goes and buys a little pitcher of milk.

[*She lays the* CHILD *down and knocks at the cottage door. An* OLD MAN *opens it.*]

Grandfather, could I have a little pitcher of milk? And a corn cake, maybe?

THE OLD MAN. Milk? We have no milk. The soldiers from the city have our goats. Go to the soldiers if you want milk.

GRUSHA. But grandfather, you must have a little pitcher of milk for a baby?

THE OLD MAN. And for a God-bless-you, eh?

GRUSHA. Who said anything about a God-bless-you? [*She shows he purse*]. We'll pay like princes. "Head in the clouds, backside in the water."

[*The* PEASANT *goes off, grumbling, for milk.*]

How much for the milk?

THE OLD MAN. Three piasters. Milk has gone up.

GRUSHA. Three piasters for this little drop?

[*Without a word the* OLD MAN *shuts the door in her face.*] Michael, did you hear that? Three piasters! We can't afford it. [*She goes back, sits down again, and gives the* CHILD *her breast.*] Suck. Think of the three piasters. There's nothing there, but you think you're drinking, and that's something. [*Shaking her head she sees that the child isn't sucking any more. She gets up, walks back to the door, and knocks again.*]

Open, grandfather, we'll pay. [*Softly*] May lightning strike you!

[*When the* OLD MAN *appears.*]

I thought it would be half a piaster. But the baby must be fed. How about one piaster for that little drop?

THE OLD MAN. Two.

GRUSHA. Don't shut the door again.

[*She fishes a long time in her bag.*]

Here are two piasters. The milk better be good. I still have two days' journey ahead of me. It's a murderous business you have here—and sinful, too!

THE OLD MAN. Kill the soldiers if you want milk.

GRUSHA. [*Giving the* CHILD *some milk*] This is an expensive joke. Take a sip, Michael, it's a week's pay. Around here they think we earned our money just sitting around. Oh, Michael, Michael, you're a nice little load for a girl to take on!

[*Uneasy, she gets up, puts the* CHILD *on her back, and walks on. The* OLD MAN, *grumbling, picks up the pitcher and looks after her unmoved.*]

THE STORY TELLER. As Grusha Vashnadze went northward

The Princes' Ironshirts went after her.

THE CHORUS. How will the barefoot girl escape the Ironshirts,

The bloodhounds, the trap-setters?

They hunt even by night.

Pursuers never tire.

Butchers sleep little.

[*Two* IRONSHIRTS *are trudging along the highway.*]

THE CORPORAL. You'll never amount to anything, blockhead, your heart's not in it. Your senior officer sees this in little things. Yesterday, when I made the fat gal, yes, you grabbed her husband as commanded, and you did kick him in the stomach, at my request, but did you *enjoy* it, like a loyal Private, or were you just doing your duty? I've kept an eye on you, blockhead, you're a hollow reed and a tinkling cymbal, you won't get promoted.

[*They walk a while in silence.*]

Don't think I've forgotten how insubordinate you are, either. Stop limping! I forbid you to limp! You limp because I sold the horses, and I sold the horses because I'd never have got that price again. You limp to show me you don't like marching. I know you. It won't help. You wait. Sing!

THE TWO IRONSHIRTS. [*Singing*] Sadly to war I went my way
Leaving my loved one at her door.
My friends will keep her honor safe
Till from the war I'm back once more.

THE CORPORAL. Louder!

THE TWO IRONSHIRTS. [*Singing*] When 'neath a headstone I shall be
My love a little earth will bring:
"Here rest the feet that oft would run to me
And here the arms that oft to me would cling."

[*They begin to walk again in silence.*]

THE CORPORAL. A good soldier has his heart and soul in it. When he receives an order, he gets a hard on, and when he drives his lance into the enemy's guts, he comes. [*He shouts for joy.*] He lets himself be torn to bits for is superior officer, and as he lies dying he takes note that his corporal is nodding approval, and that is reward enough, it's his dearest wish. You won't get any nod of approval, but you'll croak all right. Christ, how'm I to get my hands on the Governor's bastard with the help of a fool like you!

[*They stay on stage behind.*]

THE STORY TELLER. When Grusha Vashnadze came to the river Sirra
Flight grew too much for her, the helpless child too heavy.
In the cornfields the rosy dawn
Is cold to the sleepless one, only cold.
The gay clatter of the milk cans in the farmyard where the smoke rises
Is only a threat to the fugitive.
She who carries the child feels its weight and little more.

[GRUSHA *stops in front of a farm. A* FAT PEASANT WOMAN *is carrying a milk can through the door.* GRUSHA *waits until she has gone in, then approaches the house cautiously.*]

GRUSHA. [*To the* CHILD] Now you've wet yourself again, and you know I've no linen. Michael, this is where we part company. It's far enough from the city. They wouldn't want you so much that they'd follow you all *this* way, little good-for-nothing. The peasant woman is kind, and can't you just smell the milk? [*She bends down to lay the* CHILD *on the threshold.*] So farewell, Michael, I'll forget how you kicked me in the back all night to make me walk faster. And you can forget the meager fare—it was meant well. I'd like to have kept you—your nose is so tiny—but it can't be. I'd have shown you your first rabbit, I'd have trained you to keep dry, but now I must turn around. My sweetheart the soldier might be back soon, and suppose he didn't find me? You can't ask that, can you?

> [*She creeps up to the door and lays the* CHILD *on the threshold. Then, hiding behind a tree, she waits until the* PEASANT WOMAN *opens the door and sees the bundle.*]

THE PEASANT WOMAN. Good heavens, what's this? Husband!

THE PEASANT. What is it? Let me finish my soup.

THE PEASANT WOMAN. [*To the* CHILD] Where's your mother then? Haven't you got one? It's a boy. Fine linen. He's from a good family, you can see that. And they just leave him on our doorstep. Oh, these are times!

THE PEASANT. If they think we're going to feed it, they're wrong. You can take it to the priest in the village. That's the best we can do.

THE PEASANT WOMAN. What'll the priest do with him? He needs a mother. There, he's waking up. Don't you think we could keep him, though?

THE PEASANT. [*Shouting*] No!

THE PEASANT WOMAN. I could lay him in the corner by the armchair. All I need is a crib. I can take him into the fields with me. See him laughing? Husband, we have a roof over our heads. We can do it. Not another word out of you!

> [*She carries the* CHILD *into the house. The* PEASANT *follows protesting.* GRUSHA *steps out from behind the tree, laughs, and hurries off in the opposite direction.*]

THE STORY TELLER. Why so cheerful, making for home?

THE CHORUS. Because the child has won new parents with a laugh, Because I'm rid of the little one, I'm cheerful.

THE STORY TELLER. And why so sad?

THE CHORUS. Because I'm single and free, I'm sad
Like someone who's been robbed
Someone who's newly poor.

> [*She walks for a short while, then meets the* TWO IRONSHIRTS, *who point their lances at her.*]

THE CORPORAL. Lady, you are running straight into the arms of the Armed Forces. Where are you coming from? And when? Are you having illicit relations with the enemy? Where is he hiding? What movements is he making in your rear? How about the hills? How about the valleys? How are your stockings secured?

> [GRUSHA *stands there frightened.*]

Don't be scared, we always withdraw if necessary . . . what, blockhead? I always withdraw. In that respect at least, I can be relied on. Why are you staring like that at my lance? In the field no soldier drops his lance, that's a rule. Learn it by heart, blockhead. Now, lady, where are you headed?

GRUSHA. To meet my intended, one Simon Shashava, of the Palace Guard in Nuka.

THE CORPORAL. Simon Shashava? Sure, I know him. He gave me the key so I could look you up once in a while. Blockhead, we are getting to be unpopular. We must make her realize we have honorable intentions. Lady, behind apparent frivolity I conceal a serious nature, so let me tell you officially: I want a child from you.

[GRUSHA *utters a little scream.*]

Blockhead, she understood me. Uh-huh, isn't it a sweet shock? "Then first I must take the noodles out of the oven, Officer. Then first I must change my torn shirt, Colonel." But away with jokes, away with my lance! We are looking for a baby. A baby from a good family. Have you heard of such a baby, from the city, dressed in fine linen, and suddenly turning up here?

GRUSHA. No, I haven't heard a thing. [*Suddenly she turns round and runs back, panic-stricken. The* IRONSHIRTS *glance at each other, then follow her, cursing.*]

THE STORY TELLER. Run, kind girl! The killers are coming!
Help the helpless babe, helpless girl!
And so she runs!

THE CHORUS. In the bloodiest times
There are kind people.

[*As* GRUSHA *rushes into the cottage, the* PEASANT WOMAN *is bending over the* CHILD's *crib.*]

GRUSHA. Hide him. Quick! The Ironshirts are coming! I laid him on your doorstep. But he isn't mine. He's from a good family.

THE PEASANT WOMAN. Who's coming? What Ironshirts?

GRUSHA. Don't ask questions. The Ironshirts that are looking for it.

THE PEASANT WOMAN. They've no business in my house. But I must have a little talk with you, it seems.

GRUSHA. Take off the fine linen. It'll give us away.

THE PEASANT WOMAN. Linen, my foot! In this house I make the decisions! "You can't vomit in *my* room!" Why did you abandon it? It's a sin.

GRUSHA. [*Looking out of the window*] Look, they're coming out from behind those trees! I shouldn't have run away, it made them angry. Oh, what shall I do?

THE PEASANT WOMAN. [*Looking out of the window and suddenly starting with fear*] Gracious! Ironshirts!

GRUSHA. They're after the baby.

THE PEASANT WOMAN. Suppose they come in!

GRUSHA. You mustn't give him to them. Say he's yours.

THE PEASANT WOMAN. Yes.

GRUSHA. They'll run him through if you hand him over.

THE PEASANT WOMAN. But suppose they ask for it? The silver for the harvest is in the house.

GRUSHA. If you let them have him, they'll run him through, right here in this room! You've got to say he's yours!

THE PEASANT WOMAN. Yes. But what if they don't believe me?

GRUSHA. You must be firm.

THE PEASANT WOMAN. They'll burn the roof over our heads.

GRUSHA. That's why you must say he's yours. His name's Michael. But I shouldn't have told you.

[*The* PEASANT WOMAN *nods.*]

Don't nod like that. And don't tremble—they'll notice.

THE PEASANT WOMAN. Yes.

GRUSHA. And stop saying yes, I can't stand it. [*She shakes the* WOMAN.] Don't you have any children?

THE PEASANT WOMAN. [*Muttering*] He's in the war.

GRUSHA. Then maybe *he's* an Ironshirt? Do you want *him* to run children through with a lance? You'd bawl him out. "No fooling with lances in *my* house!" you'd shout, "is that what I've reared you for? Wash your neck before you speak to your mother!"

THE PEASANT WOMAN. That's true, he couldn't get away with anything around here!

GRUSHA. So you'll say he's yours?

THE PEASANT WOMAN. Yes.

GRUSHA. Look! They're coming!

[*There is a knocking at the door. The women don't answer. Enter* IRONSHIRTS. *The* PEASANT WOMAN *bows low.*]

THE CORPORAL. Well, here she is. What did I tell you? What a nose I have! I *smelt* her. Lady, I have a question for you. Why did you run away? What did you think I would do to you? I'll bet it was something dirty. Confess!

GRUSHA. [*While the* PEASANT WOMAN *bows again and again*] I'd left some milk on the stove, and I suddenly remembered it.

THE CORPORAL. Or maybe you imagined I looked at you in a dirty way? Like there could be something between us? A lewd sort of look, know what I mean?

GRUSHA. I didn't see it.

THE CORPORAL. But it's possible, huh? You admit that much. After all, I might be a pig. I'll be frank with you: I could think of all sorts of things if we were alone. [*To the* PEASANT WOMAN] Shouldn't you be busy in the yard? Feeding the hens?

THE PEASANT WOMAN. [*Falling suddenly to her knees*] Soldier, I didn't know a thing about it. Please don't burn the roof over our heads.

THE CORPORAL. What are you talking about?

THE PEASANT WOMAN. I had nothing to do with it. She left it on my doorstep, I swear it!

THE CORPORAL. [*Suddenly seeing the* CHILD *and whistling*] Ah, **so** there's a little something in the crib! Blockhead, I smell a thousand piasters. Take the old girl outside and hold on to her. It looks like I have a little cross-examining to do.

    [*The* PEASANT WOMAN *lets herself be led out by the* PRIVATE *without a word.*]

So, you've got the child I wanted from you! [*He walks toward the crib.*]

GRUSHA. Officer, he's mine. He's not the one you're after.

THE CORPORAL. I'll just take a look. [*He bends over the crib.* GRUSHA *looks round in despair.*]

GRUSHA. He's mine! He's mine!

THE CORPORAL. Fine linen!

    [GRUSHA *dashes at him to pull him away. He throws her off and again bends over the crib. Again looking round in despair, she sees a log of wood, seizes it, and hits the* CORPORAL *over the head from behind. The* CORPORAL *collapses. She quickly picks up the* CHILD *and rushes off.*]

THE STORY TELLER. And in her flight from the Ironshirts
  After twenty-two days of journeying
  At the foot of the Janga-Tu Glacier
  Grusha Vashnadze decided to adopt the child.

THE CHORUS. The helpless girl adopted the helpless child.

    [GRUSHA *squats over a half-frozen stream to get the* CHILD *water in the hollow of her hand.*]

GRUSHA. Since no one else will take you, son,
  I must take you.
  Since no one else will take you, son,
  You must take me.
  O black day in a lean, lean year,
  The trip was long, the milk was dear,
  My legs are tired, my feet are sore:
  But I wouldn't be without you any more.
  I'll throw your silken shirt away.
  And dress you in rags and tatters.
  I'll wash you, son, and christen you in glacier water.
  We'll see it through together.

    [*She has taken off the* CHILD's *fine linen and wrapped it in a rag.*]

THE STORY TELLER. When Grusha Vashnadze
  Pursued by the Ironshirts
  Came to the bridge on the glacier
  Leading to the villages of the Eastern Slope
  She sang the Song of the Rotten Bridge
  And risked two lives.

[A *wind has risen. The bridge on the glacier is visible in the dark. One rope is broken and half the bridge is hanging down the abyss.* MERCHANTS, *two* MEN, *and a* WOMAN, *stand undecided before the bridge as* GRUSHA *and the* CHILD *arrive. One* MAN *is trying to catch the hanging rope with a stick.*]

THE FIRST MAN. Take your time, young woman. You won't get across here anyway.

GRUSHA. But I *have* to get the baby to the east side. To my brother's place.

THE MERCHANT WOMAN. Have to? How d'you mean, "have to"? I have to get there, too—because I have to buy carpets in Atum—carpets a woman had to sell because her husband had to die. But can *I* do what I have to? Can she? Andrei's been fishing for that rope for hours. And I ask you, how are we going to fasten it, even if he gets it up?

THE FIRST MAN. [*Listening*] Hush, I think I hear something.

GRUSHA. The bridge isn't quite rotted through. I think I'll try it.

THE MERCHANT WOMAN. *I* wouldn't—if the devil himself were after me. It's suicide.

THE FIRST MAN. [*Shouting*] Hi!

GRUSHA. Don't shout! [*To the* MERCHANT WOMAN] Tell him not to shout.

THE FIRST MAN. But there's someone down there calling. Maybe they've lost their way.

THE MERCHANT WOMAN. Why shouldn't he shout? Is there something funny about you? Are they after you?

GRUSHA. All right, I'll tell. The Ironshirts are after me. I knocked one down.

THE SECOND MAN. Hide our merchandise!

[*The* WOMAN *hides a sack behind a rock.*]

THE FIRST MAN. Why didn't you say so right away? [*To the others*] If they catch her they'll make mincemeat out of her!

GRUSHA. Get out of my way. I've got to cross that bridge.

THE SECOND MAN. You can't. The precipice is two thousand feet deep.

THE FIRST MAN. Even with the rope it'd be no use. We could hold it up with our hands. But then we'd have to do the same for the Ironshirts.

GRUSHA. Go away.

[*There are calls from the distance:* "Hi, up there!"]

THE MERCHANT WOMAN. They're getting near. But you can't take the child on that bridge. It's sure to break. And look!

[GRUSHA *looks down into the abyss. The* IRONSHIRTS *are heard calling again from below.*]

THE SECOND MAN. Two thousand feet!

GRUSHA. But those men are worse.

THE FIRST MAN. You can't do it. Think of the baby. Risk your life but not a child's.

THE SECOND MAN. With the child she's that much heavier!

THE MERCHANT WOMAN. Maybe she's *really* got to get across. Give *me* the baby. I'll hide it. Cross the bridge alone!

GRUSHA. I won't. We belong together. [*To the* CHILD] "Live together, die together." [*She sings.*]

> The Song of the Rotten Bridge
>
> Deep is the abyss, son,
> I see the weak bridge sway
> But it's not for us, son,
> To choose the way.
>
> The way I know
> Is the one you must tread,
> And all you will eat
> Is my bit of bread.
>
> Of every four pieces
> You shall have three.
> Would that I knew
> How big they will be!

Get out of my way, I'll try it without the rope.

THE MERCHANT WOMAN. You are tempting God!

[*There are shouts from below.*]

GRUSHA. Please, throw that stick away, or they'll get the rope and follow me. [*Pressing the* CHILD *to her, she steps onto the swaying bridge. The* MERCHANT WOMAN *screams when it looks as though the bridge is about to collapse. But* GRUSHA *walks on and reaches the far side.*]

THE FIRST MAN. She made it!

THE MERCHANT WOMAN. [*Who has fallen on her knees and begun to pray, angrily*] I still think it was a sin.

[*The* IRONSHIRTS *appear; the* CORPORAL'S *head is bandaged.*]

THE CORPORAL. Seen a woman with a child?

THE FIRST MAN. [*While the* SECOND MAN *throws the stick into the abyss*] Yes, there! But the bridge won't carry you!

THE CORPORAL. You'll pay for this, blockhead!

> GRUSHA, *from the far bank laughs and shows the* CHILD *to the* IRONSHIRTS. *She walks on. The wind blows.*]

GRUSHA. [*Turning to the* CHILD] You mustn't be afraid of the wind. He's a poor thing too. He has to push the clouds along and he gets quite cold doing it.

[*Snow starts falling.*]

And the snow isn't so bad, either, Michael. It covers the little fir trees so they won't die in winter. Let me sing you a little song. [*She sings.*]

The Song of the Child

Your father is a bandit
A harlot the mother who bore you.
Yet honorable men
Shall kneel down before you.

Food to the baby horses
The tiger's son will take.
The mothers will get milk
From the son of the snake.

3. *In the Northern Mountains*

THE STORY TELLER. Seven days the sister, Grusha Vashnadze,
Journeyed across the glacier
And down the slopes she journeyed.
"When I enter my brother's house," she thought
"He will rise and embrace me."
"Is that you, sister?" he will say,
"I have long expected you.
This is my dear wife,
And this is my farm, come to me by marriage,
With eleven horses and thirty-one cows. Sit down.
Sit down with your child at our table and eat."
The brother's house was in a lovely valley.
When the sister came to the brother,
She was ill from walking.
The brother rose from the table.

[A FAT PEASANT COUPLE *rise from the table.* LAVRENTI VASH-
NADZE *still has a napkin round his neck, as* GRUSHA, *pale and
supported by a* SERVANT, *enters with the* CHILD.]

LAVRENTI. Where've you come from, Grusha?
GRUSHA. [*Feebly*] Across the Janga-Tu Pass, Lavrenti.
THE SERVANT. I found her in front of the hay barn. She has a baby with her.
THE SISTER-IN-LAW. Go and groom the mare.

[*Exit the* SERVANT.]

LAVRENTI. This is my wife Aniko.
THE SISTER-IN-LAW. I thought you were in service in Nuka.
GRUSHA. [*Barely able to stand*] Yes, I was.
THE SISTER-IN-LAW. Wasn't it a good job? We were told it was.
GRUSHA. The Governor got killed.

LAVRENTI. Yes, we heard there were riots. Your aunt told us. Remember, Aniko?

THE SISTER-IN-LAW. Here with us, it's very quiet. City people always want something going on. [*She walks toward the door, calling.*] Sosso, Sosso, don't take the cake out of the oven yet, d'you hear? Where on earth are you? [*Exit, calling.*]

LAVRENTI. [*Quietly, quickly*] Is there a father? [*As she shakes her head*] I thought not. We must think up something. She's religious.

THE SISTER-IN-LAW. [*Returning*] Those servants! [*To* GRUSHA] You have a child.

GRUSHA. It's mine. [*She collapses.* LAVRENTI *rushes to her assistance.*]

THE SISTER-IN-LAW. Heavens, she's ill—what are we going to do?

LAVRENTI. [*Escorting her to a bench near the stove*] Sit down, sit. I think it's just weakness, Aniko.

THE SISTER-IN-LAW. As long as it's not scarlet fever!

LAVRENTI. She'd have spots if it was. It's only weakness. Don't worry, Aniko. [*To* GRUSHA] Better, sitting down?

THE SISTER-IN-LAW. Is the child hers?

GRUSHA. Yes, mine.

LAVRENTI. She's on her way to her husband.

THE SISTER-IN-LAW. I see. Your meat's getting cold.

[LAVRENTI *sits down and begins to eat.*]

Cold food's not good for you, the fat mustn't get cold, you know your stomach's your weak spot. [*To* GRUSHA] If your husband's not in the city, where is he?

LIVRENTI. She got married on the other side of the mountain, she says.

THE SISTER-IN-LAW. On the other side of the mountain. I see. [*She also sits down to eat.*]

GRUSHA. I think I should lie down somewhere, Lavrenti.

THE SISTER-IN-LAW. If it's consumption we'll all get it. [*She goes on cross-examining her.*] Has your husband got a farm?

GRUSHA. He's a soldier.

LAVRENTI. But he's coming into a farm—a small one—from his father.

THE SISTER-IN-LAW. Isn't he in the war? Why not?

GRUSHA. [*With effort*] Yes, he's in the war.

THE SISTER-IN-LAW. Then why d'you want to go to the farm?

LAVRENTI. When he comes back from the war, he'll return to his farm.

THE SISTER-IN-LAW. But you're going there now?

LAVRENTI. Yes, to wait for him.

THE SISTER-IN-LAW. [*Calling shrilly*] Sosso, the cake!

GRUSHA. [*Murmuring feverishly*] A farm—a soldier—waiting—sit down, eat.

THE SISTER-IN-LAW. It's scarlet fever.

GRUSHA. [*Starting up*] Yes, he's got a farm!

LAVRENTI. I think it's just weakness, Aniko. Would you look after the cake yourself, dear?

THE SISTER-IN-LAW. But when will he come back if war's broken out again as people say? [*She waddles off, shouting.*] Sosso! Where on earth are you? Sosso!

LAVRENTI. [*Getting up quickly and going to* GRUSHA] You'll get a bed in a minute. She has a good heart. But wait till after supper.

GRUSHA. [*Holding out the* CHILD *to him*] Take him.

LAVRENTI. [*Taking it and looking around*] But you can't stay here long with the child. She's religious, you see.

[GRUSHA *collapses.* LAVRENTI *catches her.*]

THE STORY TELLER. The sister was so ill,
The cowardly brother had to give her shelter.
Summer departed, winter came.
The winter was long, the winter was short

People mustn't know anything,
Rats mustn't bite,
Spring mustn't come.

[GRUSHA *sits over the weaving loom in a workroom. She and the* CHILD, *who is squatting on the floor, are wrapped in blankets. She sings.*]

The Song of the Center

GRUSHA. [*Sings*]
And the lover started to leave
And his betrothed ran pleading after him
Pleading and weeping, weeping and teaching:
"Dearest mine, dearest mine
When you go to war as now you do
When you fight the foe as soon you will
Don't lead with the front line
And don't push with the rear line
At the front is red fire
In the rear is red smoke
Stay in the war's center
Stay near the standard bearer
The first always die
The last are also hit
Those in the center come home."

Michael, we must be clever. If we make ourselves as small as cockroaches, the sister-in-law will forget we're in the house, and then we can stay till the snow melts.

[*Enter* LAVRENTI. *He sits down beside his sister.*]

LAVRENTI. Why are you sitting there muffled up like coachmen, you two? Is it too cold in the room?

GRUSHA. [*Hastily removing one shawl*] It's not too cold, Lavrenti.

LAVRENTI. If it's too cold, you shouldn't be sitting here with the child. Aniko would never forgive herself! [*Pause*] I hope our priest didn't question you about the child?

GRUSHA. He did, but I didn't tell him anything.

LAVRENTI. That's good. I wanted to speak to you about Aniko. She has a good heart but she's very, very sensitive. People need only mention our farm and she's worried. She takes everything hard, you see. One time our milkmaid went to church with a hole in her stocking. Ever since, Aniko has worn two pairs of stockings in church. It's the old family in her. [*He listens.*] Are you sure there are no rats around? If there are rats, you couldn't live here. [*There are sounds as of dripping from the roof.*] What's that dripping?

GRUSHA. It must be a barrel leaking.

LAVRENTI. Yes, it must be a barrel. You've been here six months, haven't you? Was I talking about Aniko? [*They listen again to the snow melting.*] You can't imagine how worried she gets about your soldier-husband. "Suppose he comes back and can't find her!" she says and lies awake. "He can't come before the spring," I tell her. The dear woman! [*The drops begin to fall faster.*] When d'you think he'll come? What do you think? [GRUSHA *is silent.*] Not before the spring, you agree? [GRUSHA *is silent.*] You don't believe he'll come at all? [GRUSHA *is silent.*] But when the spring comes and the snow melts here and on the passes, you can't stay on. They may come and look for you. There's already talk of an illegitimate child. [*The "glockenspiel" of the falling drops has grown faster and steadier.*] Grusha, the snow is melting on the roof. Spring is here.

GRUSHA. Yes.

LAVRENTI. [*Eagerly*] I'll tell you what we'll do. You need a place to go, and, because of the child [*He sighs.*], you have to have a husband, so people won't talk. Now I've made cautious inquiries to see if we can find you a husband. Grusha, I *have* one. I talked to a peasant woman who has a son. Just the other side of the mountain. A small farm. And she's willing.

GRUSHA. But I *can't* marry! I must wait for Simon Shashava.

LAVRENTI. Of course. That's all been taken care of. You don't need a man in bed—you need a man on paper. And I've found you one. The son of this peasant woman is going to die. Isn't that wonderful? He's at his last gasp. And all in line with our story—a husband from the other side of the mountain! And when you met him he was at the last gasp. So you're a widow. What do you say?

GRUSHA. It's true I could use a document with stamps on it for Michael.

LAVRENTI. Stamps make all the difference. Without something in writing the Shah couldn't prove he's a Shah. And you'll have a place to live.

GRUSHA. How much does the peasant woman want?

LAVRENTI. Four hundred piasters.

GRUSHA. Where will you find it?

LAVRENTI. [Guiltily] Aniko's milk money.

GRUSHA. No one would know us there. I'll do it.

LAVRENTI. [Getting up] I'll let the peasant woman know. [Quick exit.]

GRUSHA. Michael, you cause a lot of fuss. I came to you as the pear tree comes to the sparrows. And because a Christian bends down and picks up a crust of bread so nothing will go to waste. Michael, it would have been better had I walked quickly away on that Easter Sunday in Nuka in the second courtyard. Now I am a fool.

THE STORY TELLER.

The bridegroom was lying on his deathbed when the bride arrived.

The bridegroom's mother was waiting at the door, telling her to hurry.

The bride brought a child along.

The witness hid it during the wedding.

[On one side the bed. Under the mosquito net lies a very sick MAN. GRUSHA is pulled in at a run by her future MOTHER-IN-LAW. They are followed by LAVRENTI and the CHILD.]

THE MOTHER-IN-LAW. Quick! Quick! Or he'll die on us before the wedding. [To LAVRENTI] I was never told she had a child already.

LAVRENTI. What difference does it make? [Pointing toward the dying man] It can't matter to him—in his condition.

THE MOTHER-IN-LAW. To him? But I'll never survive the shame! We are honest people. [She begins to weep.] My Jussup doesn't have to marry a girl with a child!

LAVRENTI. All right, make it another two hundred piasters. You'll have it in writing that the farm will go to you: but she'll have the right to live here for two years.

THE MOTHER-IN-LAW. [Drying her tears] It'll hardly cover the funeral expenses. I hope she'll really lend a hand with the work. And what's happened to the monk? He must have slipped out through the kitchen window. We'll have the whole village round our necks when they hear Jussup's end is come! Oh dear! I'll run and get the monk. But he mustn't see the child!

LAVRENTI. I'll take care he doesn't. But why only a monk? Why not a priest?

THE MOTHER-IN-LAW. Oh, he's just as good. I only made one mistake:

I paid half his fee in advance. Enough to send him to the tavern. I only hope . . . [*She runs off.*]

LAVRENTI. She saved on the priest, the wretch! Hired a cheap monk.

GRUSHA. You *will* send Simon Shashava over to see me if he turns up after all?

LAVRENTI. Yes. [*Pointing at the* SICK MAN] Won't you take a look at him? [GRUSHA, *taking* MICHAEL *to her, shakes her head.*] He's not moving an eyelid. I hope we aren't too late.

[*They listen. On the opposite side enter* NEIGHBORS *who look around and take up positions against the walls, thus forming another wall near the bed, yet leaving an opening so that the bed can be seen. They start murmuring prayers. Enter the* MOTHER-IN-LAW *with a* MONK. *Showing some annoyance and surprise, she bows to the* GUESTS.]

THE MOTHER-IN-LAW. I hope you won't mind waiting a few moments? My son's bride has just arrived from the city. An emergency wedding is about to be celebrated. [*To the* MONK *in the bedroom.*] I might have known you couldn't keep your trap shut. [*To* GRUSHA.] The wedding can take place at once. Here's the license. I myself and the bride's brother,

[LAVRENTI *tries to hide in the background, after having quietly taken* MICHAEL *back from* GRUSHA. *The* MOTHER-IN-LAW *waves him away.*]

who will be here in a moment, are the witnesses.

[GRUSHA *has bowed to the* MONK. *They go to the bed. The* MOTHER-IN-LAW *lifts the mosquito net. The* MONK *starts reeling off the marriage ceremony in Latin. Meanwhile, the* MOTHER-IN-LAW *beckons to* LAVRENTI *to get rid of the* CHILD, *but fearing that it will cry he draws its attention to the ceremony.* GRUSHA *glances once at the* CHILD, *and* LAVRENTI *waves the* CHILD's *hand in a greeting.*]

THE MONK. Are you prepared to be a faithful, obedient, and good wife to this man, and to cleave to him until death you do part?

GRUSHA. [*Looking at the* CHILD] I am.

THE MONK. [*To the* SICK PEASANT] And are you prepared to be a good and loving husband to your wife until death you do part? [*As the* SICK PEASANT *does not answer, the* MONK *looks inquiringly around.*]

THE MOTHER-IN-LAW. Of course he is! Didn't you hear him say yes?

THE MONK. All right. We declare the marriage contracted! How about extreme unction?

THE MOTHER-IN-LAW. Nothing doing! The wedding cost quite enough. Now I must take care of the mourners. [*To* LAVRENTI] Did we say seven hundred?

LAVRENTI. Six hundred. [*He pays.*] Now I don't want to sit with the guests and get to know people. So farewell, Grusha, and if my widowed sister comes to visit me, she'll get a welcome from my wife, or I'll show my teeth. [*Nods, gives the* CHILD *to* GRUSHA, *and leaves. The* MOURNERS *glance after him without interest.*]

THE MONK. May one ask where this child comes from?

THE MOTHER-IN-LAW. Is there a child? I don't see a child. And you don't see a child either—you understand? Or it may turn out I saw all sorts of things in the tavern! Now come on.

[*After* GRUSHA *has put the* CHILD *down and told him to be quiet, they move over left;* GRUSHA *is introduced to the* NEIGHBORS.]

This is my daughter-in-law. She arrived just in time fo find dear Jussup still alive.

ONE WOMAN. He's been ill now a whole year, hasn't he? When our Vassili was drafted he was there to say goodbye.

ANOTHER WOMAN. Such things are terrible for a farm. The corn all ripe and the farmer in bed! It'll really be a blessing if he doesn't suffer too long, I say.

THE FIRST WOMAN. [*Confidentially*] You know why we thought he'd taken to his bed? Because of the draft! And now his end is come!

THE MOTHER-IN-LAW. Sit yourselves down, please! And have some cakes!

[*She beckons to* GRUSHA *and both women go into the bedroom, where they pick up the cake pans off the floor. The* GUESTS, *among them the* MONK, *sit on the floor and begin conversing in subdued voices.*]

ONE PEASANT. [*To whom the* MONK *has handed the bottle which he has taken from his soutane*] There's a child, you say! How can that have happened to Jussup?

A WOMAN. She was certainly lucky to get herself hitched, with him so sick!

THE MOTHER-IN-LAW. They're gossiping already. And gorging themselves on the funeral cakes at the same time! If he doesn't die today, I'll have to bake some more tomorrow!

GRUSHA. I'll bake them for you.

THE MOTHER-IN-LAW. Yesterday some horsemen rode by, and I went out to see who it was. When I came in again he was lying there like a corpse! So I sent for you. It can't take much longer. [*She listens.*]

THE MONK. Dear wedding and funeral guests! Deeply touched, we stand before a bed of death and marriage. The bride gets a veil; the groom, a shroud: how varied, my children, are the fates of men! Alas! One man dies and has a roof over his head, and the other is married and the flesh turns to dust from which it was made. Amen.

THE MOTHER-IN-LAW. He's getting his own back. I shouldn't have hired such a cheap one. It's what you'd expect. A more expensive monk would behave himself. In Sura there's one with a real air of sanctity about him, but of course he charges a fortune. A fifty-piaster monk like that has no dignity, and as for piety, just fifty piasters' worth and no more! When I came to get him in the tavern he'd just made a speech, and he was shouting: "The war is over, beware of the peace!" We must go in.

GRUSHA. [*Giving* MICHAEL *a cake*] Eat this cake, and keep nice and still, Michael.

[*The two women offer cakes to the* GUESTS. *The* DYING MAN *sits up in bed. He puts his head out from under the mosquito net, stares at the two women, then sinks back again. The* MONK *takes two bottles from his soutane and offers them to the* PEASANT *beside him. Enter three* MUSICIANS *who are greeted with a sly wink by the monk.*]

THE MOTHER-IN-LAW. [*To the* MUSICIANS] What are you doing here? With instruments?

ONE MUSICIAN. Brother Anastasius here [*Pointing at the* MONK] told us there was a wedding on.

THE MOTHER-IN-LAW. What? You brought them? Three more on my neck! Don't you know there's a dying man in the next room?

THE MONK. A very tempting assignment for a musician: something that could be either a subdued Wedding March or a spirited Funeral Dance.

THE MOTHER-IN-LAW. Well, you might as well play. Nobody can stop you eating in any case.

[*The* MUSICIANS *play a potpourri. The women serve cakes.*]

THE MONK. The trumpet sounds like a whining baby. And you, little drum, what have you got to tell the world?

THE DRUNKEN PEASANT. [*Beside the* MONK, *sings*]
Miss Roundass took the old old man
And said that marriage was the thing
To everyone who met'er.
She later withdrew from the contract because
Candles are better.

[*The* MOTHER-IN-LAW *throws the* DRUNKEN PEASANT *out. The music stops. The* GUESTS *are embarrassed.*]

THE GUESTS. [*Loudly*]
—Have you heard? The Grand Duke is back! But the Princes are against him.
—They say the Shah of Persia has lent him a great army to restore order in Grusinia.
—But how is that possible? The Shah of Persia is the enemy . . .
—The enemy of Grusinia, you donkey, not the enemy of the Grand Duke!
—In any case, the war's over, so our soldiers are coming back.

[GRUSHA *drops a cake pan.* GUESTS *help her pick up the cake.*]

AN OLD WOMAN. [*To* GRUSHA] Are you feeling bad? It's just excite-

ment about dear Jussup. Sit down and rest a while, my dear.
[GRUSHA *staggers*.]

THE GUESTS. Now everything'll be the way it was. Only the taxes'll
go up because now we'll have to pay for the war.

GRUSHA. [*Weakly*] Did someone say the soldiers are back?

A MAN. I did.

GRUSHA. It can't be true.

THE FIRST MAN. [*To a* WOMAN] Show her the shawl. We bought it
from a soldier. It's from Persia.

GRUSHA. [*Looking at the shawl*] They are here. [*She gets up, takes a
step, kneels down in prayer, takes the silver cross and chain out of
her blouse, and kisses it.*]

THE MOTHER-IN-LAW. [*While the* GUESTS *silently watch* GRUSHA]
What's the matter with you? Aren't you going to look after our
guests? What's all this city nonsense got to do with us?

THE GUESTS. [*Resuming conversation while* GRUSHA *remains in prayer*]
—You can buy Persian saddles from the soldiers too. Though
many want crutches in exchange for them.
—The big shots on one side can win a war, the soldiers on both
sides lose it.
—Anyway, the war's over. It's something they can't draft you any
more.
[*The* DYING MAN *sits bolt upright in bed. He listens.*]
—What we need is two weeks of good weather.
—Our pear trees are hardly bearing a thing this year.

THE MOTHER-IN-LAW. [*Offering cakes*] Have some more cakes and
welcome! There are more!
[*The* MOTHER-IN-LAW *goes to the bedroom with the empty
cake pans. Unaware of the* DYING MAN, *she is bending down
to pick up another tray when he begins to talk in a hoarse
voice.*]

THE PEASANT. How many more cakes are you going to stuff down
their throats? Think I'm a goldmine?
[*The* MOTHER-IN-LAW *starts, stares at him aghast, while he
climbs out from behind the mosquito net.*]

THE FIRST WOMAN. [*Talking kindly to* GRUSHA *in the next room*]
Has the young wife got someone at the front?

A MAN. It's good news that they're on their way home, huh?

THE PEASANT. Don't stare at me like that! Where's this wife you've
hung round my neck?
[*Receiving no answer, he climbs out of bed and in his nightshirt staggers into the other room. Trembling, she follows him
with the cake pan.*]

THE GUESTS. [*Seeing him and shrieking*] Good God! Jussup!
[*Everyone leaps up in alarm. The women rush to the door.
GRUSHA, still on her knees, turns round and stares at the* MAN.]

THE PEASANT. A funeral supper! You'd enjoy that, wouldn't you? Get out before I throw you out! [*As the* GUESTS *stampede from the house, gloomily to* GRUSHA] I've upset the apple cart, huh? [*Receiving no answer, he turns round and takes a cake from the pan which his mother is holding.*]

THE STORY TELLER. O confusion! The wife discovers she has a husband. By day there's the child, by night there's the husband. The lover is on his way both day and night. Husband and wife look at each other. The bedroom is small.

[*Near the bed the* PEASANT *is sitting in a high wooden bathtub, naked; the* MOTHER-IN-LAW *is pouring water from a pitcher. Opposite,* GRUSHA *cowers with* MICHAEL, *who is playing at mending straw mats.*]

THE PEASANT. [*To his mother*] That's her work, not yours. Where's she hiding out now?

THE MOTHER-IN-LAW. [*Calling*] Grusha! The peasant wants you!

GRUSHA. [*To* MICHAEL] There are still two holes to mend.

THE PEASANT. [*When* GRUSHA *approaches*] Scrub my back!

GRUSHA. Can't the peasant do it himself?

THE PEASANT. "Can't the peasant do it himself?" Get the brush! To hell with you! Are you the wife here? Or are you a visitor? [*To the* MOTHER-IN-LAW] It's too cold!

THE MOTHER-IN-LAW. I'll run for hot water.

GRUSHA. Let me go.

THE PEASANT. You stay here.

[*The* MOTHER-IN-LAW *exits.*]

Rub harder. And no shirking. You've seen a naked fellow before. That child didn't come out of thin air.

GRUSHA. The child was not conceived in joy, if that's what the peasant means.

THE PEASANT. [*Turning and grinning*] You don't look the type. [GRUSHA *stops scrubbing him, starts back. Enter the* MOTHER-IN-LAW.]

THE PEASANT. A nice thing you've hung around my neck! A simpleton for a wife!

THE MOTHER-IN-LAW. She just isn't co-operative.

THE PEASANT. Pour—but go easy! Ow! Go easy, I said. [*To* GRUSHA] Maybe you did something wrong in the city . . . I wouldn't be surprised. Why else should you be here? But I won't talk about that. I've not said a word about the illegitimate object you brought into my house either. But my patience has limits! It's against nature. [*To the* MOTHER-IN-LAW] More! [*To* GRUSHA] And even if your soldier does come back, you're married.

GRUSHA. Yes.

THE PEASANT. But your soldier won't come back. Don't you believe it.

GRUSHA. No.

THE PEASANT. You're cheating me. You're my wife and you're not my wife. Where you lie, nothing lies, and yet no other woman can lie there. When I go to work in the morning I'm tired—when I lie down at night I'm awake as the devil. God has given you sex—and what d'you do? I don't have ten piasters to buy myself a woman in the city. Besides, it's a long way. Woman weeds the fields and opens up her legs, that's what our calendar says. D'you hear?

GRUSHA. [*Quietly*] Yes. I didn't mean to cheat you out of it.

THE PEASANT. She didn't mean to cheat me out of it! Pour some more water! [*The* MOTHER-IN-LAW *pours.*] Ow!

THE STORY TELLER. As she sat by the stream to wash the linen
She saw his image in the water
And his face grew dimmer with the passing moons.
As she raised herself to wring the linen
She heard his voice from the murmuring maple
And his voice grew fainter with the passing moons.
Evasions and sighs grew more numerous,
Tears and sweat flowed.
With the passing moons the child grew up.

[GRUSHA *sits by a stream, dipping linen into the water. In the rear, a few* CHILDREN *are standing.*]

GRUSHA. [*To* MICHAEL] You can play with them, Michael, but don't let them boss you around just because you're the littlest. [MICHAEL *nods and joins the* CHILDREN. *They start playing.*]

THE BIGGEST BOY. Today it's the Heads-Off Game. [*To a* FAT BOY] You're the Prince and you laugh. [*To* MICHAEL] You're the Governor. [*To a* GIRL] You're the Governor's wife and you cry when his head's cut off. And I do the cutting. [*He shows his wooden sword.*] With this. First, they lead the Governor into the yard. The Prince walks in front. The Governor's wife comes last.

[*They form a procession. The* FAT BOY *is first and laughs. Then comes* MICHAEL, *then the* BIGGEST BOY, *and then the* GIRL, *who weeps.*]

MICHAEL. [*Standing still*] Me cut off head!

THE BIGGEST BOY. That's my job. You're the littlest. The Governor's the easy part. All you do is kneel down and get your head cut off—simple.

MICHAEL. Me want sword!

THE BIGGEST BOY. It's mine! [*He gives him a kick.*]

THE GIRL. [*Shouting to* GRUSHA] He won't play his part!

GRUSHA. [*Laughing*] Even the little duck is a swimmer, they say.

THE BIGGEST BOY. You can be the Prince if you can laugh. [MICHAEL *shakes his head.*]

THE FAT BOY. I laugh best. Let him cut off the head just once. Then you do it, then me.

[*Reluctantly, the* BIGGEST BOY *hands* MICHAEL *the wooden sword and kneels down. The* FAT BOY *sits down, slaps his thigh, and laughs with all his might. The* GIRL *weeps loudly.* MICHAEL *swings the big sword and "cuts off" the head. In doing so, he topples over.*]

THE BIGGEST BOY. Hey! I'll show you how to cut heads off!

[MICHAEL *runs away. The* CHILDREN *run after him.* GRUSHA *laughs, following them with her eyes. On looking back she sees* SIMON SHASHAVA *standing on the opposite bank. He wears a shabby uniform.*]

GRUSHA. Simon!

SIMON. Is that Grusha Vashnadze?

GRUSHA. Simon!

SIMON. [*Formally*] A good morning to the young lady. I hope she is well.

GRUSHA. [*Getting up gaily and bowing low*] A good morning to the soldier. God be thanked he has returned in good health.

SIMON. They found better fish, so they didn't eat me, said the haddock.

GRUSHA. Courage, said the kitchen boy. Good luck, said the hero.

SIMON. How are things here? Was the winter bearable? The neighbor considerate?

GRUSHA. The winter was a trifle rough, the neighbor as usual, Simon.

SIMON. May one ask if a certain person still dips her foot in the water when rinsing the linen?

GRUSHA. The answer is no. Because of the eyes in the bushes.

SIMON. The young lady is speaking of soldiers. Here stands a paymaster.

GRUSHA. A job worth twenty piasters?

SIMON. And lodgings.

GRUSHA. [*With tears in her eyes*] Behind the barracks under the date trees.

SIMON. Yes, there. A certain person has kept her eyes open.

GRUSHA. She has, Simon.

SIMON. And has not forgotten?

[GRUSHA *shakes her head.*]

So the door is still on its hinges as they say?

[GRUSHA *looks at him in silence and shakes her head again.*]

What's this? Is something not as it should be?

GRUSHA. Simon Shashava, I can never return to Nuka. Something has happened.

SIMON. What can have happened?

GRUSHA. For one thing, I knocked an Ironshirt down.

SIMON. Grusha Vashnadze must have had her reasons for that.

GRUSHA. Simon Shashava, I am no longer called what I used to be called.

SIMON. [*After a pause*] I do not understand.

GRUSHA. When do women change their names, Simon? Let me explain. Nothing stands between us. Everything is just as it was. You must believe that.

SIMON. Nothing stands between us and yet there's something?

GRUSHA. How can I explain it so fast and with the stream between us? Couldn't you cross the bridge there?

SIMON. Maybe it's no longer necessary.

GRUSHA. It's very necessary. Come over on this side, Simon. Quick!

SIMON. Does the young lady wish to say someone has come too late?

[GRUSHA *looks up at him in despair, her face streaming with tears.* SIMON *stares before him. He picks up a piece of wood and starts cutting it.*]

THE STORY TELLER. So many words are said, so many left unsaid.
The soldier has come
Where he comes from, he does not say.
Hear what he thought and did not say:
"The battle began, gray at dawn, grew bloody at noon.
The first man fell in front of me, the second behind me, the third at my side.
I trod on the first, left the second behind, the third was run through by the captain.
One of my brothers died by steel, the other by smoke.
My neck caught fire, my hands froze in my gloves, my toes in my socks.
I fed on aspen buds, I drank maple juice, I slept on stone, in water."

SIMON. I see a cap in the grass. Is there a little one already?

GRUSHA. There is, Simon. How could I conceal the fact? But please don't worry, it is not mine.

SIMON. When the wind once starts to blow, they say, it blows through every cranny. The wife need say no more.

[GRUSHA *looks into her lap and is silent.*]

THE STORY TELLER. There was yearning but there was no waiting.
The oath is broken. Neither could say why.
Hear what she thought but did not say:
"While you fought in the battle, soldier,
The bloody battle, the bitter battle
I found a helpless infant
I had not the heart to destroy him
I had to care for a creature that was lost
I had to stoop for breadcrumbs on the floor
I had to break myself for that which was not mine
That which was other people's.
Someone must help!
For the little tree needs water

The lamb loses its way when the shepherd is asleep
And its cry is unheard!"

SIMON. Give me back the cross I gave you. Better still, throw it in the
stream. [*He turns to go.*]

GRUSHA. [*Getting up*] Simon Shashava, don't go away! He isn't mine!
He isn't mine! [*She hears the* CHILDREN *calling.*] What's the matter, children?

VOICES. Soldiers! And they're taking Michael away!

[GRUSHA *stands aghast as two* IRONSHIRTS, *with* MICHAEL *between them, come toward her.*]

ONE OF THE IRONSHIRTS. Are you Grusha?

[*She nods.*]

Is this your child?

GRUSHA. Yes.

[SIMON *goes.*]

Simon!

THE IRONSHIRT. We have orders, in the name of the law, to take this
child, found in your custody, back to the city. It is suspected that
the child is Michael Abashwili, son and heir of the late Governor
Georgi Abashwili, and his wife, Natella Abashwili. Here is the
document and the seal. [*They lead the* CHILD *away.*]

GRUSHA. [*Running after them, shouting*] Leave him here. Please! He's
mine!

THE STORY TELLER. The ironshirts took the child, the beloved child.
The unhappy girl followed them to the city, the dreaded city.
She who had borne him demanded the child.
She who had raised him faced trial.
Who will decide the case?
To whom will the child be assigned?
Who will the judge be? A good judge? A bad?
The city was in flames.
In the judge's seat sat Azdak.[9]

4. *The Story of the Judge*

THE STORY TELLER. Hear the story of the judge
How he turned judge, how he passed judgment, what kind of judge
he was.
On that Easter Sunday of the great revolt, when the Grand Duke
was overthrown
And his Governor Abashwili, father of our child, lost his head
The Village Scrivener Azdak found a fugitive in the woods and hid
him in his hut.

[AZDAK, *in rags and slightly drunk, is helping an* OLD BEGGAR
into his cottage.]

9. The name AZDAK should be accented on the second syllable [Bentley's note].

AZDAK. Stop snorting, you're not a horse. And it won't do you any good with the police, to run like a snotty nose in April. Stand still, I say. [*He catches the* OLD MAN, *who has marched into the cottage as if he'd like to go through the wall.*] Sit down. Feed. Here's a hunk of cheese. [*From under some rags, in a chest, he fishes out some cheese, and the* OLD MAN *greedily begins to eat.*] Haven't eaten in a long time, huh? [*The* OLD MAN *growls.*] Why were you running like that, asshole? The cop wouldn't even have seen you.

THE OLD MAN. Had to! Had to!

AZDAK. Blue Funk? [*The* OLD MAN *stares, uncomprehending.*] Cold feet? Panic? Don't lick your chops like a Grand Duke. Or an old sow. I can't stand it. We have to accept respectable stinkers as God made them, but not you! I once heard of a senior judge who farted at a public dinner to show an independent spirit! Watching you eat like that gives me the most awful ideas. Why don't you say something? [*Sharply*] Show me your hand. Can't you hear? [*The* OLD MAN *slowly puts out his hand.*] White! So you're not a beggar at all! A fraud, a walking swindle! And I'm hiding you from the cops as though you were an honest man! Why were you running like that if you're a landowner? For that's what you are. Don't deny it! I see it in your guilty face! [*He gets up.*] Get out! [*The* OLD MAN *looks at him uncertainly.*] What are you waiting for, peasant-flogger?

THE OLD MAN. Pursued. Need undivided attention. Make proposition . . .

AZDAK. Make what? A proposition? Well, if that isn't the height of insolence. He's making me a proposition! The bitten man scratches his fingers bloody, and the leech that's biting him makes him a proposition! Get out, I tell you!

THE OLD MAN. Understand point of view! Persuasion! Pay hundred thousand piasters one night! Yes?

AZDAK. What, you think you can buy me? For a hundred thousand piasters? Let's say a hundred and fifty thousand. Where are they?

THE OLD MAN. Have not them here. Of course. Will be sent. Hope do not doubt.

AZDAK. Doubt very much. Get out!

    [*The* OLD MAN *gets up, waddles to the door. A* VOICE *is heard off stage.*]

A VOICE. Azdak!

    [*The* OLD MAN *turns, waddles to the opposite corner, stands still.*]

AZDAK. [*Calling out*] I'm not in! [*He walks to door.*] So you're sniffing around here again, Shauwa?

POLICEMAN SHAUWA. [*Reproachfully*] You've caught another rabbit, Azdak. And you promised me it wouldn't happen again!

AZDAK. [*Severely*] Shauwa, don't talk about things you don't understand. The rabbit is a dangerous and destructive beast. It feeds on plants, especially on the species of plants known as weeds. It must therefore be exterminated.

SHAUWA. Azdak, don't be so hard on me. I'll lose my job if I don't arrest you. I know you have a good heart.

AZDAK. I do not have a good heart! How often must I tell you I'm a man of intellect?

SHAUWA. [*Slyly*] I know, Azdak. You're a superior person. You say so yourself. I'm just a Christian and an ignoramus. So I ask you: When one of the Prince's rabbits is stolen, and I'm a policeman, what should I do with the offending party?

AZDAK. Shauwa, Shauwa, shame on you. You stand and ask me a question, than which nothing could be more seductive. It's like you were a woman—let's say that bad girl Nunowna, and you showed me your thigh—Nunowna's thigh, that would be—and asked me: "What shall I do with my thigh, it itches?" Is she as innocent as she pretends? Of course not. I catch a rabbit, but you catch a man. Man is made in God's image. Not so a rabbit, you know that. I'm a rabbit-eater, but you're a man-eater, Shauwa. And God will pass judgment on you. Shauwa, go home and repent. No, stop, there's something . . . [*He looks at the* OLD MAN *who stands trembling in the corner.*] No, it's nothing. Go home and repent. [*He slams the door behind* SHAUWA.] Now you're surprised, huh? Surprised I didn't hand you over? I couldn't hand over a bedbug to that animal. It goes against the grain. Now don't tremble because of a cop! So old and still so scared? Finish your cheese, but eat it like a poor man, or else they'll still catch you. Must I even explain how a poor man behaves? [*He pushes him down, and then gives him back the cheese.*] That box is the table. Lay your elbows on the table. Now, encircle the cheese on the plate like it might be snatched from you at any moment—what right have you to be safe, huh?—now, hold your knife like an undersized sickle, and give your cheese a troubled look because, like all beautiful things, it's already fading away. [AZDAK *watches him.*] They're after you, which speaks in your favor, but how can we be sure they're not mistaken about you? In Tiflis one time they hanged a landowner, a Turk, who could prove he quartered his peasants instead of merely cutting them in half, as is the custom, and he squeezed twice the usual amount of taxes out of them, his zeal was above suspicion. And yet they hanged him like a common criminal—because he was a Turk—a thing he couldn't do much about. What injustice! He got onto the gallows by a sheer fluke. In short, I don't trust you.

THE STORY TELLER. Thus Azdak gave the old beggar a bed,
  And learned that old beggar was the old butcher, the Grand Duke himself,

1558 · *Bertolt Brecht*

And was ashamed.

He denounced himself and ordered the policeman to take him to Nuka, to court, to be judged.

[*In the court of justice three* IRONSHIRTS *sit drinking. From a beam hangs a man in judge's robes. Enter* AZDAK, *in chains, dragging* SHAUWA *behind him.*]

AZDAK. [*Shouting*] I've helped the Grand Duke, the Grand Thief, the Grand Butcher, to escape! In the name of justice I ask to be severely judged in public trial!

THE FIRST IRONSHIRT. Who's this queer bird?

SHAUWA. That's our Village Scrivener, Azdak.

AZDAK. I am contemptible! I am a traitor! A branded criminal! Tell them, flat-foot, how I insisted on being chained up and brought to the capital. Because I sheltered the Grand Duke, the Grand Swindler, by mistake. And how I found out afterwards. See the marked man denounce himself! Tell them how I forced you to walk with me half the night to clear the whole thing up.

SHAUWA. And all by threats. That wasn't nice of you, Azdak.

AZDAK. Shut your mouth, Shauwa. You don't understand. A new age is upon us! It'll go thundering over you. You're finished. The police will be wiped out—poof! Everything will be gone into, everything will be brought into the open. The guilty will give themselves up. Why? They couldn't escape the people in any case. [*To* SHAUWA] Tell them how I shouted all along Shoemaker Street: [*With big gestures, looking at the* IRONSHIRTS] "In my ignorance I let the Grand Swindler escape! So tear me to pieces, brothers!" I wanted to get it in first.

THE FIRST IRONSHIRT. And what did your brothers answer?

SHAUWA. They comforted him in Butcher Street, and they laughed themselves sick in Shoemaker Street. That's all.

AZDAK. But with you it's different. I can see you're men of iron. Brothers, where's the judge? I must be tried.

THE FIRST IRONSHIRT. [*Pointing at the hanged man*] There's the judge. And please stop "brothering" us. It's rather a sore spot this evening.

AZDAK. "There's the judge." An answer never heard in Grusinia before. Townsman, where's His Excellency the Governor? [*Pointing to the floor*] There's His Excellency, stranger. Where's the Chief Tax Collector? Where's the official Recruiting officer? The Patriarch? The Chief of Police? There, there, there—all there. Brothers I expected no less of you.

THE SECOND IRONSHIRT. What? *What* was it you expected, funny man?

AZDAK. What happened in Persia, brother, what happened in Persia?

THE SECOND IRONSHIRT. What did happen in Persia?

AZDAK. Everybody was hanged. Viziers, tax collectors. Everybody.

Forty years ago now. My grandfather, a remarkable man by the way, saw it all. For three whole days. Everywhere.

THE SECOND IRONSHIRT. And who ruled when the Vizier was hanged?

AZDAK. A peasant ruled when the Vizier was hanged.

THE SECOND IRONSHIRT. And who commanded the army?

AZDAK. A soldier, a soldier.

THE SECOND IRONSHIRT. And who paid the wages?

AZDAK. A dyer. A dyer paid the wages.

THE SECOND IRONSHIRT. Wasn't it a weaver, maybe?

THE FIRST IRONSHIRT. And why did all this happen, Persian?

AZDAK. Why did all this happen? Must there be a special reason? Why do you scratch yourself, brother? War! Too long a war! And no justice! My grandfather brought back a song that tells how it was. I will sing it for you. With my friend the policeman. [*To* SHAUWA] And hold the rope tight. It's very suitable. [*He sings, with* SHAUWA *holding the rope tight around him.*]

The Song of Injustice in Persia

Why don't our sons bleed any more? Why don't our daughters weep?

Why do only the slaughter-house cattle have blood in their veins?

Why do only the willows shed tears on Lake Urmi?

The king must have a new province, the peasant must give up his savings.

That the roof of the world might be conquered, the roof of the cottage is torn down.

Our men are carried to the ends of the earth, so that great ones can eat at home.

The soldiers kill each other, the marshals salute each other.

They bite the widow's tax money to see if it's good, their swords break.

The battle was lost, the helmets were paid for.

[*Refrain*] Is it so? Is it so?

SHAUWA. [*Refrain*] Yes, yes, yes, yes, yes it's so.

AZDAK. Do you want to hear the rest of it?

[*The* FIRST IRONSHIRT *nods.*]

THE SECOND IRONSHIRT. [*To* SHAUWA] Did he teach you that song?

SHAUWA. Yes, only my voice isn't very good.

THE SECOND IRONSHIRT. No. [*To* AZDAK] Go on singing.

AZDAK. The second verse is about the peace. [*He sings.*]

The offices are packed, the streets overflow with officials.

The rivers jump their banks and ravage the fields.

Those who cannot let down their own trousers rule countries.

They can't count up to four, but they devour eight courses.

The corn farmers, looking round for buyers, see only the starving.

The weavers go home from their looms in rags.

[*Refrain*] Is it so? Is it so?

SHAUWA. [*Refrain*] Yes, yes, yes, yes, yes it's so.

AZDAK. That's why our sons don't bleed any more, that's why our
daughters don't weep.

That's why only the slaughter-house cattle have blood in their
veins,

And only the willows shed tears by Lake Urmi toward morning.

THE FIRST IRONSHIRT. Are you going to sing that song here in town?

AZDAK. Sure. What's wrong with it?

THE FIRST IRONSHIRT. Have you noticed that the sky's getting red?

[*Turning round,* AZDAK *sees the sky red with fire.*]

It's the people's quarters. On the outskirts of town. The carpet
weavers have caught the "Persian Sickness," too. And they've been
asking if Prince Kazbeki isn't eating too many courses. This morning they strung up the city judge. As for us we beat them to pulp.
We were paid one hundred piasters per man, you understand?

AZDAK. [*After a pause*] I understand. [*He glances shyly round and,
creeping away, sits down in a corner, his head in his hands.*]

THE IRONSHIRTS. [*To each other*]—If there ever was a trouble-maker
it's him.

—He must've come to the capital to fish in the troubled waters.

SHAUWA. Oh, I don't think he's a really bad character, gentlemen.
Steals a few chickens here and there. And maybe a rabbit.

THE SECOND IRONSHIRT. [*Approaching* AZDAK] Came to fish in the
troubled waters, huh?

AZDAK. [*Looking up*] I don't know why I came.

THE SECOND IRONSHIRT. Are you in with the carpet weavers maybe?

[AZDAK *shakes his head.*]

How about that song?

AZDAK. From my grandfather. A silly and ignorant man.

THE SECOND IRONSHIRT. Right. And how about the dyer who paid
the wages?

AZDAK. [*Muttering*] That was in Persia.

THE FIRST IRONSHIRT. And this denouncing of yourself? Because you
didn't hang the Grand Duke with your own hands?

AZDAK. Didn't I tell you I let him run? [*He creeps farther away and
sits on the floor.*]

SHAUWA. I can swear to that: he let him run.

[*The* IRONSHIRTS *burst out laughing and slap* SHAUWA *on the
back.* AZDAK *laughs loudest. They slap* AZDAK *too, and unchain
him. They all start drinking as the* FAT PRANCE *enters with a
YOUNG MAN.*]

THE FIRST IRONSHIRT. [*To* AZDAK, *pointing at the* FAT PRINCE] There's
your "new age" for you!

[*More laughter*]

THE FAT PRINCE. Well, my friends, what is there to laugh about?

Permit me a serious word. Yesterday morning the Princes of Grusinia overthrew the war-mongering government of the Grand Duke and did away with his Governors. Unfortunately the Grand Duke himself escaped. In this fateful hour our carpet weavers, those eternal trouble-makers, had the effrontery to stir up a rebellion and hang the universally loved city judge, our dear Illo Orbeliani. Ts—ts—ts. My friends, we need peace, peace, peace in Grusinia! And justice! So I've brought along my dear nephew Bizergan Kazbeki. He'll be the new judge, hm? A very gifted fellow. What do you say? I want your opinion. Let the people decide!

THE SECOND IRONSHIRT. Does this mean *we* elect the judge?

THE FAT PRINCE. Precisely. Let the people propose some very gifted fellow! Confer among yourselves, my friends.

[*The* IRONSHIRTS *confer.*]

Don't worry, my little fox. The job's yours. And when we catch the Grand Duke we won't have to kiss this rabble's ass any longer.

THE IRONSHIRTS. [*Between themselves*]—Very funny: they're wetting their pants because they haven't caught the Grand Duke.
—When the outlook isn't so bright, they say: "My friends!" and "Let the people decide!"
—Now he even wants justice for Grusinia! But fun is fun as long as it lasts!

[*Pointing at* AZDAK] —He knows all about justice. Hey, rascal, would you like this nephew fellow to be the judge?

AZDAK. Are you asking me? You're not asking *me*?!

THE FIRST IRONSHIRT. Why not? Anything for a laugh!

AZDAK. You'd like to test him to the marrow, correct? Have you a criminal on hand? An experienced one? So the candidate can show what he knows?

THE SECOND IRONSHIRT. Let's see. We do have a couple of doctors downstairs. Let's use them.

AZDAK. Oh, no, that's no good, we can't take real criminals till we're sure the judge will be appointed. He may be dumb, but he must be appointed, or the Law is violated. And the Law is a sensitive organ. I's like the spleen, you mustn't hit it—that would be fatal. Of course you can hang those two without violating the Law, because there was no judge in the vicinity. But Judgment, when pronounced, must be pronounced with absolute gravity—it's all such nonsense. Suppose, for instance, a judge jails a woman—let's say she's stolen a corn cake to feed her child—and this judge isn't wearing his robes—or maybe he's scratching himself while passing sentence and half his body is uncovered—a man's thigh *will* itch once in a while—the sentence this judge passes is a disgrace and the Law is violated. In short it would be easier for a judge's robe and a judge's hat to pass judgment than for a man with no robe and no hat. If you don't treat it with respect, the Law just dis-

1562 · *Bertolt Brecht*

appears on you. Now you don't try out a bottle of wine by offering it to a dog; you'd only lose your wine.

THE FIRST IRONSHIRT. Then what do you suggest, hair-splitter?

AZDAK. I'll be the defendant.

THE FIRST IRONSHIRT. You? [*He bursts out laughing.*]

THE FAT PRINCE. What have you decided?

THE FIRST IRONSHIRT. We've decided to stage a rehearsal. Our friend here will be the defendant. Let the candidate be the judge and sit there.

THE FAT PRINCE. It isn't customary, but why not? [*To the* NEPHEW.] A mere formality, my little fox. What have I taught you? Who got there first—the slow runner or the fast?

THE NEPHEW. The silent runner, Uncle Arsen.

> [*The* NEPHEW *takes the chair. The* IRONSHIRTS *and the* FAT PRINCE *sit on the steps. Enter* AZDAK, *mimicking the gait of the Grand Duke.*]

AZDAK. [*In the Grand Duke's accent*] Is any here knows me? Am Grand Duke.

THE IRONSHIRTS.

—*What* is he?

—The Grand Duke. He knows him, too.

—Fine. So get on with the trial.

AZDAK. Listen! Am accused instigating war? Ridiculous! Am saying ridiculous! That enough? If not, have brought lawyers. Believe five hundred. [*He points behind him, pretending to be surrounded by lawyers.*] Requisition all available seats for lawyers! [*The* IRON-SHIRTS *laugh; the* FAT PRINCE *joins in.*]

THE NEPHEW. [*To the* IRONSHIRTS] You really wish me to try this case?

I find it rather unusual. From the taste angle, I mean.

THE FIRST IRONSHIRT. Let's go!

THE FAT PRINCE. [*Smiling*] Let him have it, my little fox!

THE NEPHEW. All right. People of Grusinia versus Grand Duke. Defendant, what have you got to say for yourself?

AZDAK. Plenty. Naturally, have read war lost. Only started on the advice of patriots. Like Uncle Arsen Kazbeki. Call Uncle Arsen as witness.

THE FAT PRINCE. [*To the* IRONSHIRTS, *delightedly*] What a screwball!

THE NEPHEW. Motion rejected. One cannot be arraigned for declaring a war, which every ruler has to do once in a while, but only for running a war badly.

AZDAK. Rubbish! Did not run it at all! Had it run! Had it run by Princes! Naturally, they messed it up.

THE NEPHEW. Do you by any chance deny having been commander-in-chief?

AZDAK. Not at all! Always *was* commander-in-chief. At birth shouted

The Caucasian Chalk Circle · 1563

at wet nurse. Was trained drop turds in toilet, grew accustomed to command. Always commanded officials rob my cash box. Officers flog soldiers only on command. Landowners sleep with peasants' wives only on strictest command. Uncle Arsen here grew his belly at *my* command!

THE IRONSHIRTS. [*Clapping*] He's good! Long live the Grand Duke!

THE FAT PRINCE. Answer him, my little fox. I'm with you.

THE NEPHEW. I shall answer him according to the dignity of the law. Defendant, preserve the dignity of the law!

AZDAK. Agreed. Command you to proceed with the trial!

THE NEPHEW. It is not your place to command me. You claim that the Princes forced you to declare war. How can you claim, then, that they—er—"messed it up"?

AZDAK. Did not send enough people. Embezzled funds. Sent sick horses. During attack, drinking in whore house. Call Uncle Arsen as witness.

THE NEPHEW. Are you making the outrageous suggestion that the Princes of this country did not fight?

AZDAK. No. Princes fought. Fought for war contracts.

THE FAT PRINCE. [*Jumping up*] That's too much! This man talks like a carpet weaver!

AZDAK. Really? I told nothing but the truth.

THE FAT PRINCE. Hang him! Hang him!

THE FIRST IRONSHIRT. [*Pulling the PRINCE down*] Keep quiet! Go on, Excellency!

THE NEPHEW. Quiet! I now render a verdict: You must be hanged! By the neck! Having lost war!

AZDAK. Young man, seriously advise not fall publicly into jerky clipped manner of speech. Cannot be employed as watchdog if howl like wolf. Got it? If people realize Princes speak same language as Grand Duke, may hang Grand Duke *and* Princes, huh? By the way, must overrule verdict. Reason? War lost, but not for Princes. Princes won their war. Got 3,863,000 piasters for horses not delivered, 8,240,000 piasters for food supplies not produced. Are therefore victors. War lost only for Grusinia, which as such is not present in this court.

THE FAT PRINCE. I think that will do, my friends. [*To AZDAK*] You can withdraw, funny man. [*To the IRONSHIRTS*] You may now ratify the new judge's appointment, my friends.

THE FIRST IRONSHIRT. Yes, we can. Take down the judge's gown.

[*One IRONSHIRT climbs on the back of the other, pulls the gown off the hanged man.*]

[*To the NEPHEW*] Now you run away so the right ass can get on the right chair. [*To AZDAK*] Step forward! Go to the judge's seat! now sit in it [*AZDAK steps up, bows, and sits down.*] The judge was always a rascal! Now the rascal shall be a judge! [*The judge's gown is placed round his shoulders, the hat on his head.*] And what a judge!

THE STORY TELLER. And there was civil war in the land.
The mighty were not safe.
And Azdak was made a judge by the Ironshirts.
And Azdak remained a judge for two years.

THE STORY TELLER AND CHORUS. When the towns were set afire
And rivers of blood rose higher and higher,
Cockroaches crawled out of every crack.
And the court was full of schemers
And the church of foul blasphemers.
In the judge's cassock sat Azdak.

[AZDAK *sits in the judge's chair, peeling an apple.* SHAUWA *is sweeping out the hall. On one side an* INVALID *in a wheelchair. Opposite, a* YOUNG MAN *accused of blackmail. An* IRONSHIRT *stands guard, holding the* IRONSHIRT'S *banner.*]

AZDAK. In consideration of the large number of cases, the Court today will hear two cases at a time. Before I open the proceedings, a short announcement—I accept. [*He stretches out his hand. The* BLACKMAILER *is the only one to produce any money. He hands it to* AZDAK.] I reserve the right to punish one of the parties for contempt of court. [*He glances at the* INVALID.] You [*To the* DOCTOR] are a doctor, and you [*To the* INVALID] are bringing a complaint against him. Is the doctor responsible for your condition?

THE INVALID. Yes. I had a stroke on his account.

AZDAK. That would be professional negligence.

THE INVALID. Worse than negligence. I gave this man money for his studies. So far, he hasn't paid me back a cent. It was when I heard he was treating a patient free that I had my stroke.

AZDAK. Rightly. [*To a* LIMPING MAN] And what are you doing here?

THE LIMPING MAN. I'm the patient, your honor.

AZDAK. He treated your leg for nothing?

THE LIMPING MAN. The wrong leg! My rheumatism was in the left leg, and he operated on the right. That's why I limp now.

AZDAK. And you were treated free?

THE INVALID. A five-hundred-piaster operation free! For nothing! For God-bless-you! And I paid for this man's studies! [*To the* DOCTOR] Did they teach you to operate free?

THE DOCTOR. Your Honor, it is actually the custom to demand the fee before the operation, as the patient is more willing to pay before an operation than after. Which is only human. In the case in question I was convinced, when I started the operation, that my servant had already received the fee. In this I was mistaken.

THE INVALID. He was mistaken! A good doctor doesn't make mistakes! He examines before he operates!

AZDAK. That's right. [*To* SHAUWA] Public Prosecutor, what's the other case about?

SHAUWA. [*Busily sweeping*] Blackmail.

THE BLACKMAILER. High Court of Justice, I'm innocent. I only wanted to find out from the landowner concerned if he really *had* raped his niece. He informed me very politely that this was not the case, and gave me the money only so I could pay for my uncle's studies.

AZDAK. Hm. [*To the* DOCTOR] You, on the other hand, can cite no extenuating circumstances for your offense, huh?

THE DOCTOR. Except that to err is human.

AZDAK. And you are aware that in money matters a good doctor is a highly responsible person? I once heard of a doctor who got a thousand piasters for a sprained finger by remarking that sprains have something to do with blood circulation, which after all a less good doctor might have overlooked, and who, on another occasion made a real gold mine out of a somewhat disordered gall bladder, he treated it with such loving care. You have no excuse, Doctor. The corn merchant, Uxu, had his son study medicine to get some knowledge of trade, our medical schools are so good. [*To the* BLACKMAILER] What's the landowner's name?

SHAUWA. He doesn't want it mentioned.

AZDAK. In that case I will pass judgment. The Court considers the blackmail proved. And you [*To the* INVALID] are sentenced to a fine of one thousand piasters. If you have a second stroke, the doctor will have to treat you free. Even if he has to amputate. [*To the* LIMPING MAN.] As compensation, you will receive a bottle of rubbing alcohol. [*To the* BLACKMAILER] You are sentenced to hand over half the proceeds of your deal to the Public Prosecutor to keep the landowner's name secret. You are advised, moreover, to study medicine—you seem well suited to that calling. [*To the* DOCTOR] You have perpetrated an unpardonable error in the practice of your profession: you are acquitted. Next cases!

THE STORY TELLER AND CHORUS. Men won't do much for a shilling.
For a pound they may be willing.
For 20 pounds the verdict's in the sack.
As for the many, all too many,
Those who've only got a penny—
They've one single, sole recourse: Azdak.

> [*Enter* AZDAK *from the caravansary on the highroad, followed by an old bearded* INNKEEPER. *The judge's chair is carried by a* STABLEMAN *and* SHAUWA. *An* IRONSHIRT, *with a banner, takes up his position.*]

AZDAK. Put me down. Then we'll get some air, maybe even a good stiff breeze from the lemon grove there. It does justice good to be done in the open: the wind blows her skirts up and you can see what she's got. Shauwa, we've been eating too much. These official journeys are exhausting. [*To the* INNKEEPER] It's a question of your daughter-in-law?

THE INNKEEPER. Your Worship, it's a question of the family honor. I wish to bring an action on behalf of my son, who's on business on the other side of the mountain. This is the offending stableman, and here's my daughter-in-law.

[*Enter the* DAUGHTER-IN-LAW, *a voluptuous wench. She is veiled.*]

AZDAK. [*Sitting down*] I accept. [*Sighing, the* INNKEEPER *hands him some money.*] Good. Now the formalities are disposed of. This is a case of rape?

THE INNKEEPER. Your Honor, I caught the fellow in the act. Ludovica was in the straw on the stable floor.

AZDAK. Quite right, the stable. Lovely horses! I specially liked the little roan.

THE INNKEEPER. The first thing I did, of course, was to question Ludovica. On my son's behalf.

AZDAK. [*Seriously*] I said I specially liked the little roan.

THE INNKEEPER. [*Coldly*] Really? Ludovica confessed the stableman took her against her will.

AZDAK. Take your veil off, Ludovica.

[*She does so.*]

Ludovica, you please the Court. Tell us how it happened.

LUDOVICA. [*Well-schooled*] When I entered the stable to see the new foal the stableman said to me on his own accord: "It's hot today!" and laid his hand on my left breast. I said to him: "Don't do that!" But he continued to handle me indecently, which provoked my anger. Before I realized his sinful intentions, he got much closer. It was all over when my father-in-law entered and accidentally trod on me.

THE INNKEEPER. [*Explaining*] On my son's behalf.

AZDAK. [*To the* STABLEMAN] You admit you started it?

THE STABLEMAN. Yes.

AZDAK. Ludovica, you like to eat sweet things?

LUDOVICA. Yes, sunflower seeds!

AZDAK. You like to lie a long time in the bathtub?

LUDOVICA. Half an hour or so.

AZDAK. Public Prosecutor, drop your knife—there—on the ground.

[SHAUWA *does so.*]

Ludovica, pick up that knife.

[LUDOVICA, *swaying her hips, does so.*]

See that? [*He points at her.*] The way it moves? The rape is now proven. By eating too much—sweet things, especially—by lying too long in warm water, by laziness and too soft a skin, you have

raped that unfortunate man. Think you can run around with a behind like that and get away with it in court? This is a case of
intentional assault with a dangerous weapon! You are sentenced to
hand over to the Court the little roan which your father liked to
ride "on his son's behalf." And now, come with me to the stables,
so the Court may inspect the scene of the crime, Ludovica.
THE STORY TELLER AND CHORUS. When the sharks the sharks devour
    Little fishes have their hour.
    For a while the load is off their back.
    On Grusinia's highways faring
    Fixed-up scales of justice bearing
    Strode the poor man's magistrate: Azdak.

    And he gave to the forsaken
    All that from the rich he'd taken.
    And a bodyguard of roughnecks was Azdak's.
    And our good and evil man, he
    Smiled upon Grusinia's Granny.
    His emblem was a tear in sealing wax.

    All mankind should love each other
    But when visiting your brother
    Take an ax along and hold it fast.
    Not in theory but in practice
    Miracles are wrought with axes
    And the age of miracles is not past.
        [AZDAK's *judge's chair is in a tavern. Three* RICH FARMERS
        stand before AZDAK. SHAUWA *brings him wine. In a corner
        stands an* OLD PEASANT WOMAN. *In the open doorway, and
        outside, stand* VILLAGERS *looking on. An* IRONSHIRT *stands
        guard with a banner.*]
AZDAK. The Public Prosecutor has the floor.
SHAUWA. It concerns a cow. For five weeks the defendant has had a
    cow in her stable, the property of the farmer Suru. She was also
    found to be in possession of a stolen ham, and a number of cows
    belonging to Shutoff were killed after he asked the defendant to
    pay the rent on a piece of land.
THE FARMERS.
    —It's a matter of my ham, Your Honor.
    —It's a matter of my cow, Your Honor.
    —It's a matter of my land, Your Honor.
AZDAK. Well, Granny, what have *you* got to say to all this?
THE OLD WOMAN. Your Honor, one night toward morning, five weeks
    ago, there was a knock at my door, and outside stood a bearded
    man with a cow. "My dear woman," he said, "I am the miracle-
    working Saint Banditus and because your son has been killed in

the war, I bring you this cow as a souvenir. Take good care of it."

THE FARMERS.

—The robber, Irakli, Your Honor!

—Her brother-in-law, Your Honor!

—The cow-thief!

—The incendiary!

—He must be beheaded!

[*Outside, a* WOMAN *screams. The* CROWD *grows restless, retreats. Enter the* BANDIT IRAKLI *with a huge ax.*]

THE BANDIT. A very good evening, dear friends! A glass of vodka!

THE FARMERS. [*Crossing themselves*] Irakli!

AZDAK. Public Prosecutor, a glass of vodka for our guest. And who are you?

THE BANDIT. I'm a wandering hermit, Your Honor. Thanks for the gracious gift. [*He empties the glass which* SHAUWA *has brought.*] Another!

AZDAK. I am Azdak. [*He gets up and bows. The* BANDIT *also bows.*] The Court welcomes the foreign hermit. Go on with your story, Granny.

THE OLD WOMAN. Your Honor, that first night I didn't yet know Saint Banditus could work miracles, it was only the cow. But one night, a few days later, the farmer's servants came to take the cow away again. Then they turned round in front of my door and went off without the cow. And bumps as big as a fist sprouted on their heads. So I knew that Saint Banditus had changed their hearts and turned them into friendly people.

[*The* BANDIT *roars with laughter.*]

THE FIRST FARMER. I know what changed them.

AZDAK. That's fine. You can tell us later. Continue.

THE OLD WOMAN. Your Honor, the next one to become a good man was the farmer Shutoff—a devil, as everyone knows. But Saint Banditus arranged it so he let me off the rent on the little piece of land.

THE SECOND FARMER. Because my cows were killed in the field.

[*The* BANDIT *laughs.*]

THE OLD WOMAN. [*Answering* AZDAK's *sign to continue*] Then one morning the ham came flying in at my window. It hit me in the small of the back. I'm still lame, Your Honor, look. [*She limps a few steps.*]

[*The* BANDIT *laughs.*]

Your Honor, was there ever a time when a poor old woman could get a ham *without* a miracle?

[*The* BANDIT *starts sobbing.*]

AZDAK. [*Rising from his chair*] Granny, that's a question that strikes straight at the Court's heart. Be so kind as to sit here.

[*The* OLD WOMAN, *hesitating, sits in the judge's chair.*]

AZDAK. [*Sits on the floor, glass in hand, reciting*] Granny
   We could almost call you Granny Grusinia
   The Woebegone
   The Bereaved Mother
   Whose sons have gone to war
   Receiving the present of a cow
   She bursts out crying.
   When she is beaten
   She remains hopeful.
   When she's not beaten
   She's surprised.
   On us
   Who are already damned
   May you render a merciful verdict
   Granny Grusinia!

   [*Bellowing at* THE FARMERS] Admit you don't believe in miracles,
   you atheists! Each of you is sentenced to pay five hundred piasters!
   For godlessness! Get out!
      [*The* FARMERS *slink out.*]
   And you Granny, and you [*To the* BANDIT] pious man, *empty a*
   pitcher of wine with the Public Prosecutor and Azdak!

THE STORY TELLER AND CHORUS. And he broke the rules to save them.
   Broken law like bread he gave them,
   Brought them to shore upon his crooked back.
   At long last the poor and lowly
   Had someone who was not too holy
   To be bribed by empty hands: Azdak.

   For two years it was his pleasure
   To give the beasts of prey short measure:
   He became a wolf to fight the pack.
   From All Hallows to All Hallows[10]
   On his chair beside the gallows
   Dispensing justice in his fashion sat Azdak.

THE STORY TELLER. But the era of disorder came to an end.
   The Grand Duke returned.
   The Governor's wife returned.
   A trial was held.
   Many died.
   The people's quarters burned anew.
   And fear seized Azdak.

      [AZDAK'S *judge's chair stands again in the court of justice.*
      AZDAK *sits on the floor, shaving and talking to* SHAUWA. *Noises*
      outside. In the rear the FAT PRINCE's *head is carried by on a*
      lance.]

10. *All Hallows:* All Souls' Day, November 1.

AZDAK. Shauwa, the days of your slavery are numbered, maybe even the minutes. For a long time now I have held you in the iron curb of reason, and it has torn your mouth till it bleeds. I have lashed you with reasonable arguments, I have manhandled you with logic. You are by nature a weak man, and if one slyly throws an argument in your path, you *have* to snap it up, you can't resist. It is your nature to lick the hand of some superior being. But superior beings can be of very different kinds. And now, with your liberation, you will soon be able to follow your natural inclinations, which are low. You will be able to follow your infallible instinct, which teaches you to plant your fat heel on the faces of men. Gone is the era of confusion and disorder, which I find described in the Song of Chaos. Let us now sing that song together in memory of those terrible days. Sit down and don't do violence to the music. Don't be afraid. It sounds all right. And it has a fine refrain. [*He sings.*]

The Song of Chaos

Sister, hide your face! Brother, take your knife!
The times are out of joint!
Big men are full of complaint
And small men full of joy.
The city says:
"Let us drive the strong ones from our midst!"
Offices are raided. Lists of serfs are destroyed.
They have set Master's nose to the grindstone.
They who lived in the dark have seen the light.
The ebony poor box is broken.
Sesnem wood is sawed up for beds.
Who had no bread have barns full.
Who begged for alms of corn now mete it out.

SHAUWA. [*Refrain*] Oh, oh, oh, oh.

AZDAK. [*Refrain*] Where are you, General, where are you?
Please, please, please, restore order!
The nobleman's son can no longer be recognized;
The lady's child becomes the son of her slave.
The councilors meet in a shed.
Once, this man was barely allowed to sleep on the wall;
Now, he stretches his limbs in a bed.
Once, this man rowed a boat; now, he owns ships.
Their owner looks for them, but they're his no longer.
Five men are sent on a journey by their master.
"Go yourself," they say, "we have arrived."

SHAUWA. [*Refrain*] Oh, oh, oh, oh.

AZDAK. [*Refrain*] Where are you, General, where are you?
Please, please, please, restore order!
Yes, so it might have been, had order been neglected much longer.

But now the Grand Duke has returned to the capital, and the Persians have lent him an army to restore order with. The suburbs are already aflame. Go and get me the big book I always sit on.

[SHAUWA *brings the big book from the judge's chair.* AZDAK *opens it.*]

This is the Statute Book and I've always used it, as you can testify. Now I'd better look in this book and see what they can do to me. I've let the down-and-outs get away with murder, and I'll have to pay for it. I helped poverty onto its skinny legs, so they'll hang me for drunkenness. I peeped into the rich man's pocket, which is bad taste. And I can't hide anywhere—everybody knows me because I've helped everybody.

SHAUWA. Someone's coming!

AZDAK. [*In panic, he walks trembling to the chair.*] It's the end. And now they'd enjoy seeing what a Great Man I am. I'll deprive them of that pleasure. I'll beg on my knees for mercy. Spittle will slobber down my chin. The fear of death is in me.

[*Enter* NATELLA ABASHWILI, *the* GOVERNOR'S WIFE, *followed by the* ADJUTANT *and an* IRONSHIRT.]

THE GOVERNOR'S WIFE. What sort of a creature is that, Shalva?

AZDAK. A willing one, Your Highness, a man ready to oblige.

THE ADJUTANT. Natella Abashwili, wife of the late Governor, has just returned. She is looking for her two-year-old son, Michael. She has been informed that the child was carried off to the mountains by a former servant.

AZDAK. The child will be brought back, Your Highness, at your service.

THE ADJUTANT. They say that the person in question is passing it off as her own.

AZDAK. She will be beheaded, Your Highness, at your service.

THE ADJUTANT. That is all.

THE GOVERNOR'S WIFE. [*Leaving*] I don't like that man.

AZDAK. [*Following her to door, bowing*] At your service, Your Highness, it will all be arranged.

5. The Chalk Circle

THE STORY TELLER. Hear now the story of the trial
Concerning Governor Abashwili's child
And the establishing of the true mother
By the famous test of the Chalk Circle.

[*The court of justice in Nuka.* IRONSHIRTS *lead* MICHAEL *across stage and out at the back.* IRONSHIRTS *hold* GRUSHA *back with their lances under the gateway until the* CHILD *has been led through. Then she is admitted. She is accompanied by the former governor's* COOK. *Distant noises and a fire-red sky.*]

GRUSHA. [*Trying to hide*] He's brave, he can wash himself now.

THE COOK. You're lucky. It's not a real judge. It's Azdak, a drunk who doesn't know what he's doing. The biggest thieves have got by through him. Because he gets everything mixed up and the rich never offer him big enough bribes, the likes of us sometimes do pretty well.

GRUSHA. I *need* luck right now.

THE COOK. Touch wood. [*She crosses herself.*] I'd better offer up another prayer that the judge may be drunk. [*She prays with motionless lips, while* GRUSHA *looks around, in vain, for the child.*] Why must you hold on to him at any price if he isn't yours? In days like these?

GRUSHA. He's mine. I brought him up.

THE COOK. Have you never thought what'd happen when she came back?

GRUSHA. At first I thought I'd give him to her. Then I thought she wouldn't come back.

THE COOK. And even a borrowed coat keeps a man warm, hm?

[GRUSHA *nods.*]

I'll swear to anything for you. You're a decent girl. [*She sees the soldier* SIMON SHASHAVA *approaching.*] You've done wrong by Simon, though. I've been talking with him. He just can't understand.

GRUSHA. [*Unaware of* SIMON'S *presence*] Right now I can't be bothered whether he understands or not!

THE COOK. He knows the child isn't yours, but you married and not free "till death you do part"—he can't understand *that.*

[GRUSHA *sees* SIMON *and greets him.*]

SIMON. [*Gloomily*] I wish the lady to know I will swear I am the father of the child.

GRUSHA. [*Low*] Thank you, Simon.

SIMON. At the same time I wish the lady to know my hands are not tied—nor are hers.

THE COOK. You needn't have said that. You know she's married.

SIMON. And it needs no rubbing in.

[*Enter an* IRONSHIRT.]

THE IRONSHIRT. Where's the judge? Has anyone seen the judge?

ANOTHER IRONSHIRT. [*Stepping forward*] The judge isn't here yet. Nothing but a bed and a pitcher in the whole house!

[*Exeunt* IRONSHIRTS.]

THE COOK. I hope nothing has happened to him. With any other judge you'd have about as much chance as a chicken has teeth.

GRUSHA. [*Who has turned away and covered her face*] Stand in front of me. I shouldn't have come to Nuka. If I run into the Ironshirt, the one I hit over the head . . .

[*She screams. An* IRONSHIRT *had stopped and, turning his back, had been listening to her. He now wheels around. It is the* CORPORAL, *and he has a huge scar across his face.*]

THE IRONSHIRT. [*In the gateway*] What's the matter, Shotta? Do you know her?

THE CORPORAL. [*After staring for some time*] No.

THE IRONSHIRT. She's the one who stole the Abashwili child, or so they say. If you know anything about it you can make some money, Shotta.

[*Exit the* CORPORAL, *cursing.*]

THE COOK. Was it him? [GRUSHA *nods.*] I think he'll keep his mouth shut, or he'd be admitting he was after the child.

GRUSHA. I'd almost forgotten him.

[*Enter the* GOVERNOR'S WIFE, *followed by the* ADJUTANT *and two* LAWYERS.]

THE GOVERNOR'S WIFE. At least there are no common people here, thank God. I can't stand their smell. It always gives me migraine.

THE FIRST LAWYER. Madam, I must ask you to be careful what you say until we have another judge.

THE GOVERNOR'S WIFE. But I didn't say anything, Illo Shuboladze. I love the people with their simple straightforward minds. It's only that their smell brings on my migraine.

THE SECOND LAWYER. There won't be many spectators. The whole population is sitting at home behind locked doors because of the riots on the outskirts of town.

THE GOVERNOR'S WIFE. [*Looking at* GRUSHA] Is that the creature?

THE FIRST LAWYER. Please, most gracious Natella Abashwili, abstain from invective until it is certain the Grand Duke has appointed a new judge and we're rid of the present one, who's about the lowest fellow ever seen in judge's gown. Things are all set to move, you see.

[*Enter* IRONSHIRTS *from the courtyard.*]

THE COOK. Her Grace would pull your hair out on the spot if she didn't know Azdak is for the poor. He goes by the face.

[IRONSHIRTS *begin fastening a rope to a beam.* AZDAK, *in chains, is led in, followed by* SHAUWA, *also in chains. The three* FARMERS *bring up the rear.*]

AN IRONSHIRT. Trying to run away, were you? [*He strikes* AZDAK.]

ONE FARMER. Off with his judge's gown before we string him up!

[IRONSHIRTS *and* FARMERS *tear off* AZDAK's *gown. His torn underwear is visible. Then someone kicks him.*]

AN IRONSHIRT. [*Pushing him into someone else*] If you want a heap of justice, here it is!

[*Accompanied by shouts of* "You take it!" *and* "Let me have him, Brother!" *they throw* AZDAK *back and forth until he collapses. Then he is lifted up and dragged under the noose.*]

THE GOVERNOR'S WIFE. [*Who, during this* "Ball-game" *has clapped her hands hysterically*] I disliked that man from the moment I first saw him.

AZDAK. [*Covered with blood, panting*] I can't see. Give me a rag.

AN IRONSHIRT. What is it you want to see?

AZDAK. You, you dogs! [*He wipes the blood out of his eyes with his shirt.*] Good morning, dogs! How goes it, dogs! How's the dog world? Does it smell good? Got another boot for me to lick? Are you back at each other's throats, dogs?

[*Accompanied by a* CORPORAL, *a dust-covered* RIDER *enters. He takes some documents from a leather case, looks at them, then interrupts.*]

THE RIDER. Stop! I bring a dispatch from the Grand Duke, containing the latest appointments.

THE CORPORAL. [*Bellowing*] Atten-shun!

THE RIDER. Of the new judge it says: "We appoint a man whom we have to thank for saving a life indispensable to the country's welfare—a certain Azdak of Nuka." Which is he?

SHAUWA. [*Pointing*] That's him, Your Excellency.

THE CORPORAL. [*Bellowing*] What's going on here?

AN IRONSHIRT. I beg to report that His Honor Azdak was already His Honor Azdak, but on these farmer's denunciation was pronounced the Grand Duke's enemy.

THE CORPORAL. [*Pointing at the* FARMERS] March them off! [*They are marched off. They bow all the time.*] See to it that His Honor Azdak is exposed to no more violence.

[*Exeunt* RIDER *and* CORPORAL.]

THE COOK. [*To* SHAUWA] She clapped her hands! I hope he saw it!

THE FIRST LAWYER. It's a catastrophe.

[AZDAK *has fainted. Coming to, he is dressed again in judge's robes. He walks, swaying, toward the* IRONSHIRTS.]

AN IRONSHIRT. What does Your Honor desire?

AZDAK. Nothing, fellow dogs, or just an occasional boot to lick. [*To* SHAUWA] I pardon you. [*He is unchained.*] Get me some red wine, the sweet kind. [SHAUWA *stumbles off.*] Get out of here, I've got to judge a case.

[*Exeunt* IRONSHIRTS. SHAUWA *returns with a pitcher of wine.* AZDAK *gulps it down.*]

Something for my backside. [SHAUWA *brings the Statute Book, puts it on the judge's chair.* AZDAK *sits on it.*] I accept.

[*The* PROSECUTORS, *among whom a worried council has been held, smile with relief. They whisper.*]

THE COOK. Oh dear!

SIMON. A well can't be filled with dew, they say.

THE LAWYERS. [*Approaching* AZDAK, *who stands up, expectantly*] A quite ridiculous case, Your Honor. The accused has abducted a child and refuses to hand it over.

AZDAK. [*Stretching out his hand, glancing at* GRUSHA] A most attractive person. [*He fingers the money, then sits down, satisfied.*] I declare the proceedings open and demand the whole truth. [*To* GRUSHA] Especially from you.

THE FIRST LAWYER. High Court of Justice! Blood, as the popular saying goes, is thicker than water. This old adage . . .

AZDAK. [*Interrupting*] The Court wants to know the lawyers' fee.

THE FIRST LAWYER. [*Surprised*] I beg your pardon?

[AZDAK, *smiling, rubs his thumb and index finger.*]

Oh, I see. Five hundred piasters, Your Honor, to answer the Court's somewhat unusual question.

AZDAK. Did you hear? The question is unusual. I ask it because I listen in quite a different way when I know you're good.

THE FIRST LAWYER. [*Bowing*] Thank you, Your Honor. High Court of Justice, of all ties the ties of blood are strongest. Mother and child—is there a more intimate relationship? Can one tear a child from its mother? High Court of Justice, she has conceived it in the holy ecstasies of love. She has carried it in her womb. She has fed it with her blood. She has borne it with pain. High Court of Justice, it has been observed that even the wild tigress, robbed of her young, roams restless through the mountains, shrunk to a shadow. Nature herself . . .

AZDAK. [*Interrupting, to* GRUSHA] What's your answer to all this and anything else that lawyer might have to say?

GRUSHA. He's mine.

AZDAK. Is that all? I hope you can prove it. Why should I assign the child to you in any case?

GRUSHA. I brought him up like the priest says "according to my best knowledge and conscience." I always found him something to eat. Most of the time he had a roof over his head. And I went to such trouble for him. I had expenses too. I didn't look out for my own comfort. I brought the child up to be friendly with everyone, and from the beginning taught him to work. As well as he could, that is. He's still very little.

THE FIRST LAWYER. Your Honor, it is significant that the girl herself doesn't claim any tie of blood between her and the child.

AZDAK. The Court takes note of that.

THE FIRST LAWYER. Thank you, Your Honor. And now permit a woman bowed in sorrow—who has already lost her husband and now has also to fear the loss of her child—to address a few words to you. The gracious Natella Abashwili is . . .

THE GOVERNOR'S WIFE. [*Quietly*] A most cruel fate, Sir, forces me to describe to you the tortures of a bereaved mother's soul, the anxiety, the sleepless nights, the . . .

THE SECOND LAWYER. [*Bursting out*] It's outrageous the way this woman is being treated! Her husband's palace is closed to her! The revenue of her estates is blocked, and she is cold-bloodedly told that it's tied to the heir. She can't do a thing without that child. She can't even pay her lawyers! [*To the* FIRST LAWYER, *who, desperate about this outburst, makes frantic gestures to keep him from speaking.*] Dear Illo Shuboladze, surely it can be divulged now that the Abashwili estates are at stake?

THE FIRST LAWYER. Please, Honored Sandro Oboladze! We agreed ... [*To* AZDAK] Of course it is correct that the trial will also decide if our noble client can dispose of the Abashwili estates, which are rather extensive. I say "also" advisedly, for in the foreground stands the human tragedy of a mother, as Natella Abashwili very properly explained in the first words of her moving statement. Even if Michael Abashwili were not heir to the estates, he would still be the dearly beloved child of my client.

AZDAK. Stop! The Court is touched by the mention of estates. It's a proof of human feeling.

THE SECOND LAWYER. Thanks, Your Honor. Dear Illo Shuboladze, we can prove in any case that the woman who took the child is not the child's mother. Permit me to lay before the Court the bare facts. High Court of Justice, by an unfortunate chain of circumstances, Michael Abashwili was left behind on that Easter Sunday while his mother was making her escape. Grusha, a palace kitchen maid, was seen with the baby . . .

THE COOK. All her mistress was thinking of was what dresses she'd take along!

THE SECOND LAWYER. [*Unmoved*] Nearly a year later Grusha turned up in a mountain village with a baby and there entered into the state of matrimony with . . .

AZDAK. How did you get to that mountain village?

GRUSHA. On foot, Your Honor. And it was mine.

SIMON. I am the father, Your Honor.

THE COOK. I used to look after it for them, Your Honor. For five piasters.

THE SECOND LAWYER. This man is engaged to Grusha, High Court of Justice: his testimony is not trustworthy.

AZDAK. Are you the man she married in the mountain village?

SIMON. No, Your Honor, she married a peasant.

AZDAK. [*To* GRUSHA] Why? [*Pointing at* SIMON] Is he no good in bed? Tell the truth.

GRUSHA. We didn't get that far. I married because of the baby. So it'd have a roof over his head. [*Pointing at* SIMON] He was in the war, Your Honor.

AZDAK. And now he wants you back again, huh?

SIMON. I wish to state in evidence . . .

GRUSHA. [*Angrily*] I am no longer free, Your Honor.

AZDAK. And the child, you claim, comes from whoring?

[GRUSHA *doesn't answer.*]

I'm going to ask you a question: What kind of child is it? Is it a ragged little bastard or from a well-to-do family?

GRUSHA. [*Angrily*] He's just an ordinary child.

AZDAK. I mean—did he have refined features from the beginning?

GRUSHA. He had a nose on his face.

AZDAK. A very significant comment! It has been said of me that I went out one time and sniffed at a rosebush before rendering a verdict —tricks like that are needed nowadays. Well, I'll make it short, and not listen to any more lies. [*To* GRUSHA] Especially not yours. [*To all the accused*] I can imagine what you've cooked up to cheat me! I know you people. You're swindlers.

GRUSHA. [*Suddenly*] I can understand your wanting to cut it short, now I've seen what you accepted!

AZDAK. Shut up! Did I accept anything from you?

GRUSHA. [*While the* COOK *tries to restrain her*] I haven't got anything.

AZDAK. True. Quite true. From starvelings I never get a thing. I might just as well starve, myself. You want justice, but do you want to pay for it, hm? When you go to a butcher you know you have to pay, but you people go to a judge as if you were going to a funeral supper.

SIMON. [*Loudly*] When the horse was shod, the horse-fly held out its leg, as the saying is.

AZDAK. [*Eagerly accepting the challenge*] Better a treasure in manure than a stone in a mountain stream.

SIMON. A fine day. Let's go fishing, said the angler to the worm.

AZDAK. I'm my own master, said the servant, and cut off his foot.

SIMON. I love you as a father, said the Czar to the peasants, and had the Czarevitch's head chopped off.

AZDAK. A fool's worst enemy is himself.

SIMON. However, a fart has no nose.

AZDAK. Fined ten piasters for indecent language in court! That'll teach you what justice is.

GRUSHA. [*Furiously*] A fine kind of justice! You play fast and loose with us because we don't talk as refined as that crowd with their lawyers!

AZDAK. That's true. You people are too dumb. It's only right you should get it in the neck.

GRUSHA. You want to hand the child over to her, and she wouldn't even know how to keep it dry, she's so "refined"! You know about as much about justice as I do!

AZDAK. There's something in that. I'm an ignorant man. Haven't even a decent pair of pants on under this gown. Look! With me, every-thing goes for food and drink—I was educated at a convent. Incidentally, I'll fine you ten piasters for contempt of court. And you're a very silly girl, to turn me against you, instead of making eyes at me and wiggling your backside a little to keep me in a good temper. Twenty piasters!

GRUSHA. Even if it was thirty, I'd tell you what I think of your justice, you drunken onion! [*Incoherently*] How dare you talk to me
like the cracked Isaiah on the church window? As if you were somebody? For you weren't born to this. You weren't born to rap your
own mother on the knuckles if she swipes a little bowl of salt
someplace. Aren't you ashamed of yourself when you see how I
tremble before you? You've made yourself their servant so no one
will take their houses from them—houses they had stolen! Since
when have houses belonged to the bedbugs? But you're on the
watch, or they couldn't drag our men into their wars! You bribe-
taker!

> [AZDAK *half gets up, starts beaming. With his little hammer
> he half-heartedly knocks on the table as if to get silence. As
> GRUSHA's scolding continues, he only beats time with his
> hammer.*]

I've no respect for you. No more than for a thief or a bandit with
a knife! You can do what you want. You can take the child away
from me, a hundred against one, but I tell you one thing: only
extortioners should be chosen for a profession like yours, and men
who rape children! As punishment! Yes, let *them* sit in judgment
on their fellow creatures. It is worse than to hang from the gallows.

AZDAK. [*Sitting down*] Now it'll be thirty! And I won't go on squabbling with you—we're not in a tavern. What'd happen to my dignity as a judge? Anyway, I've lost interest in your case. Where's
the couple who wanted a divorce? [*To* SHAUWA] Bring 'em in.
This case is adjourned for fifteen minutes.

THE FIRST LAWYER. [*To the* GOVERNOR'S WIFE] Even without using
the rest of the evidence, Madam, we have the verdict in the bag.

THE COOK. [*To* GRUSHA] You've gone and spoiled your chances with
him. You won't get the child now.

THE GOVERNOR'S WIFE. Shalva, my smelling salts!

> [*Enter a* VERY OLD COUPLE.]

AZDAK. I accept.

> [*The* OLD COUPLE *don't understand.*]

I hear you want to be divorced. How long have you been together?

THE OLD WOMAN. Forty years, Your Honor.

AZDAK. And why do you want a divorce?

THE OLD MAN. We don't like each other, Your Honor.

AZDAK. Since when?

THE OLD WOMAN. Oh, from the very beginning, Your Honor.

AZDAK. I'll think about your request and render my verdict when I'm
through with the other case.

> [SHAUWA *leads them back.*]

I need the child. [*He beckons* GRUSHA *to and bends not unkindly
toward her.*] I've noticed you have a soft spot for justice. I don't
believe he's your child, but if he *were* yours, woman, wouldn't you

want him to be rich? You'd only have to say he wasn't yours, and he'd have a palace and many horses in his stable and many beggars on his doorstep and many soldiers in his service and many petitioners in his courtyard, wouldn't he? What do you say—don't you want him to be rich?

[GRUSHA *is silent.*]

THE STORY TELLER. Hear now what the angry girl thought but did not say:

Had he golden shoes to wear
He'd be cruel as a bear.
Evil would his life disgrace.
He'd laugh in my face.
Carrying a heart of flint
Is too troublesome a stint.
Being powerful and bad
Is hard on a lad.

Then let hunger be his foe!
Hungry men and women, no.
Let him fear the darksome night
But not daylight!

AZDAK. I think I understand you, woman.

GRUSHA. [*Suddenly and loudly*] I won't give him up. I've raised him, and he knows me.

[*Enter* SHAUWA *with the* CHILD.]

THE GOVERNOR'S WIFE. It's in rags!

GRUSHA. That's not true. But I wasn't given time to put his good shirt on.

THE GOVERNOR'S WIFE. It must have been in a pigsty.

GRUSHA. [*Furiously*] I'm not a pig, but there are some who are! Where did you leave your baby?

THE GOVERNOR'S WIFE. I'll show you, you vulgar creature! [*She is about to throw herself on* GRUSHA, *but is restrained by her* LAWYERS.] She's a criminal, she must be whipped. Immediately!

THE SECOND LAWYER. [*Holding his hand over her mouth*] Natella Abashwili, you promised . . . Your Honor, the plaintiff's nerves.

AZDAK. Plaintiff and defendant! The Court has listened to your case, and has come to no decision as to who the real mother is, therefore, I, the judge, am obliged to *choose* a mother for the child. I'll make a test. Shauwa, get a piece of chalk and draw a circle on the floor.

[SHAUWA *does so.*]

Now place the child in the center.

[SHAUWA *puts* MICHAEL, *who smiles at* GRUSHA, *in the center of the circle.*]

Stand near the circle, both of you.

[*The* GOVERNOR'S WIFE *and* GRUSHA *step up to the circle.* Now each of you take the child by one hand.

[*They do so.*]

The true mother is she who can pull the child out of the circle.

THE SECOND LAWYER. [*Quickly*] High Court of Justice, I object! The fate of the great Abashwili estates, which are tied to the child, as the heir, should not be made dependent on such a doubtful duel. In addition, my client does not command the strength of this person, who is accustomed to physical work.

AZDAK. She looks pretty well fed to me. Pull!

[*The* GOVERNOR'S WIFE *pulls the* CHILD *out of the circle on her side;* GRUSHA *has let go and stands aghast.*]

What's the matter with you? You didn't pull!

GRUSHA. I didn't hold on to him.

THE FIRST LAWYER. [*Congratulating the* GOVERNOR'S WIFE] What did I say! The ties of blood!

GRUSHA. [*Running to* AZDAK] Your Honor, I take back everything I said against you. I ask your forgiveness. But could I keep him till he can speak all the words? He knows a few.

AZDAK. Don't influence the Court. I bet you only know about twenty words yourself. All right, I'll make the test once more, just be to certain.

[*The two women take up their positions again.*] Pull!

[*Again* GRUSHA *lets go of the* CHILD.]

GRUSHA. [*In despair*] I brought him up! Shall I also tear him to pieces? I can't!

AZDAK. [*Rising*] And in this manner the Court has established the true mother. [*To* GRUSHA] Take your child and be off. I advise you not to stay in the city with him. [*To the* GOVERNOR'S WIFE] And you disappear before I fine you for fraud. Your estates fall to the city. They'll be converted into a playground for the children. They need one, and I've decided it shall be called after me: Azdak's Garden.

[*The* GOVERNOR'S WIFE *has fainted and is carried out by the* LAWYERS *and the* ADJUTANT. GRUSHA *stands motionless.* SHAUWA *leads the* CHILD *toward her.*]

Now I'll take off this judge's gown—it's grown too hot for me. I'm not cut out for a hero. In token of farewell I invite you all to a little dance outside on the meadow. Oh, I'd almost forgotten something in my excitement . . . to sign the divorce decree.

[*Using the judge's chair as a table, he writes something on a piece of paper, and prepares to leave. Dance music has started.*]

SHAUWA. [*Having read what is on the paper*] But that's not right. You've not divorced the old people. You've divorced Grusha!

AZDAK. Have I divorced the wrong couple? What a pity! And I never retract! If I did, how could we keep order in the land? [*To the* OLD COUPLE] I'll invite you to my party instead. You don't mind dancing with each other, do you? [*To* GRUSHA *and* SIMON] I've got forty piasters coming from you.

SIMON. [*Pulling out his purse*] Cheap at the price, Your Honor. And many thanks.

AZDAK. [*Pocketing the cash*] I'll be needing this.

GRUSHA. [*To* MICHAEL] So we'd better leave the city tonight, Michael? [*To* SIMON] You like him?

SIMON. With my respects, I like him.

GRUSHA. Now I can tell you: I took him because on that Easter Sunday I got engaged to you. So he's a child of love. Michael, let's dance.

> [*She dances with* MICHAEL, SIMON *dances with the* COOK, *the* OLD COUPLE *with each other.* AZDAK *stands lost in thought. The dancers soon hide him from view. Occasionally he is seen, but less and less as more couples join the dance.*]

THE STORY TELLER. And after that evening Azdak vanished and was never seen again.

The people of Grusinia did not forget him but long remembered
The period of his judging as a brief golden age,
Almost an age of justice.

> [*All the couples dance off.* AZDAK *has disappeared.*]

But you, you who have listened to the Story of the Chalk Circle,
Take note what men of old concluded:
That what there is shall go to those who are good for it,
Children to the motherly, that they prosper,
Carts to good drivers, that they be driven well,
The valley to the waterers, that it yield fruit.

JEAN-PAUL SARTRE
(born 1905)
No Exit (Huis Clos) *
A Play in One Act

Characters in the Play

VALET	ESTELLE
GARCIN	INEZ

Huis Clos (No Exit) was presented for the first time at the Théâtre du Vieux-Colombier, Paris, in May 1944.

SCENE—*A drawing-room in Second Empire style. A massive bronze ornament stands on the mantelpiece.*

GARCIN. [*Enters accompanied by the* ROOM-VALET, *and glances around him*] Hm! So here we are?

VALET. Yes, Mr. Garcin.

GARCIN. And this is what it looks like?

VALET. Yes.

GARCIN. Second Empire furniture, I observe. . . . Well, well, I dare say one gets used to it in time.

VALET. Some do. Some don't.

GARCIN. Are all the other rooms like this one?

VALET. How could they be? We cater for all sorts: Chinamen and Indians, for instance. What use would they have for a Second Empire chair?

GARCIN. And what use do you suppose *I* have for one? Do you know who I was? . . . Oh, well, it's no great matter. And, to tell the truth, I had quite a habit of living among furniture that I didn't relish, and in false positions. I'd even come to like it. A false position in a Louis-Philippe dining-room—you know the style?—well, that had its points, you know. Bogus in bogus, so to speak.

VALET. And you'll find that living in a Second Empire drawing-room has its points.

GARCIN. Really? . . . Yes, yes, I dare say. . . . [*He takes another look around.*] Still, I certainly didn't expect—this! You know what they tell us down there?

VALET. What about?

GARCIN. About [*Makes a sweeping gesture*] this—er—residence.

VALET. Really, sir, how could you belive such cock-and-bull stories? Told by people who'd never set foot here. For, of course, if they had—

* 1945. Copyright, 1946 by Stuart Gilbert. Reprinted from *No Exit and The Flies* by Jean-Paul Sartre, translated by Stuart Gilbert, by permission of Alfred A. Knopf. The punctuation "..." does not indicate omissions from this text.

GARCIN. Quite so. [*Both laugh. Abruptly the laugh dies from* GARCIN'S *face.*] But, I say, where are the instruments of torture?

VALET. The what?

GARCIN. The racks and red-hot pincers and all the other paraphernalia?

VALET. Ah, you must have your little joke, sir!

GARCIN. My little joke? Oh, I see. No, I wasn't joking. [*A short silence. He strolls around the room.*] No mirrors, I notice. No windows. Only to be expected. And nothing breakable. [*Bursts out angrily.*] But, damn it all, they might have left me my toothbrush!

VALET. That's good! So you haven't yet got over your—what-do-you-call-it?—sense of human dignity? Excuse me smiling.

GARCIN. [*Thumping ragefully the arm of an armchair*] I'll ask you to be more polite. I quite realize the position I'm in, but I won't tolerate . . .

VALET. Sorry, sir. No offense meant. But all our guests ask me the same questions. Silly questions, if you'll pardon me saying so. Where's the torture-chamber? That's the first thing they ask, all of them. They don't bother their heads about the bathroom requisites, that I can assure you. But after a bit, when they've got their nerve back, they start in about their toothbrushes and whatnot. Good heavens, Mr. Garcin, can't you use your brains? What, I ask you, would be the point of brushing your teeth?

GARCIN. [*More calmly*] Yes, of course you're right. [*He looks around again.*] And why should one want to see oneself in a looking-glass? But that bronze contraption on the mantelpiece, that's another story. I suppose there will be times when I stare my eyes out at it. Stare my eyes out—see what I mean? . . . All right, let's put our cards on the table. I assure you I'm quite conscious of my position. Shall I tell you what it feels like? A man's drowning, choking, sinking by inches, till only his eyes are just above water. And what does he see? A bronze atrocity by—what's the fellow's name? —Barbedienne. A collector's piece. As in a nightmare. That's their idea, isn't it? . . . No, I suppose you're under orders not to answer questions; and I won't insist. But don't forget, my man, I've a good notion of what's coming to me, so don't you boast you've caught me off my guard. I'm facing the situation, facing it. [*He starts pacing the room again.*] So that's that; no toothbrush. And no bed, either. One never sleeps, I take it?

VALET. That's so.

GARCIN. Just as I expected. Why should one sleep? A sort of drowsiness steals on you, tickles you behind the ears, and you feel your eyes closing—but why sleep? You lie down on the sofa and—in a flash, sleep flies away. Miles and miles away. So you rub your eyes, get up, and it starts all over again.

VALET. Romantic, that's what you are.

GARCIN. Will you keep quiet, please! . . . I won't make a scene, I shan't be sorry for myself, I'll face the situation, as I said just now. Face it fairly and squarely. I won't have it springing at me from behind, before I've time to size it up. And you call that being "romantic"! . . . So it comes to this; one doesn't need rest. Why bother about sleep if one isn't sleepy? That stands to reason, doesn't it? Wait a minute, there's a snag somewhere; something disagreeable. Why, now, should it be disagreeable? . . . Ah, I see; it's life without a break.

VALET. What do you mean by that?

GARCIN. What do I mean? [*Eyes the* VALET *suspiciously.*] I thought as much. That's why there's something so beastly, so damn bad-mannered, in the way you stare at me. They're paralyzed.

VALET. What are you talking about?

GARCIN. Your eyelids. We move ours up and down. Blinking, we call it. It's like a small black shutter that clicks down and makes a break. Everything goes black; one's eyes are moistened. You can't imagine how restful, refreshing, it is. Four thousand little rests per hour. Four thousand little respites—just think! . . . So that's the idea. I'm to live without eyelids. Don't act the fool, you know what I mean. No eyelids, no sleep; it follows, doesn't it? I shall never sleep again. But then—how shall I endure my own company? Try to understand. You see, I'm fond of teasing, it's a second nature with me—and I'm used to teasing myself. Plaguing myself, if you prefer; I don't tease nicely. But I can't go on doing that without a break. Down there I had my nights. I slept. I always had good nights. By way of compensation, I suppose. And happy little dreams. There was a green field. Just an ordinary field. I used to stroll in it. . . . Is it daytime now?

VALET. Can't you see? The lights are on.

GARCIN. Ah yes, I've got it. It's *your* daytime. And outside?

VALET. Outside?

GARCIN. Damn it, you know what I mean. Beyond that wall.

VALET. There's a passage.

GARCIN. And at the end of the passage?

VALET. There's more rooms, more passages, and stairs.

GARCIN. And what lies beyond them?

VALET. That's all.

GARCIN. But surely you have a day off sometimes. Where do you go?

VALET. To my uncle's place. He's the head valet here. He has a room on the third floor.

GARCIN. I should have guessed as much. Where's the light-switch?

VALET. There isn't any.

GARCIN. What? Can't one turn off the light?

VALET. Oh, the management can cut off the current if they want to. But I can't remember their having done so on this floor. We have all the electricity we want.

GARCIN. So one has to live with one's eyes open all the time?

VALET. To *live*, did you say?

GARCIN. Don't let's quibble over words. With one's eyes open. Forever. Always broad daylight in my eyes—and in my head. [*Short silence.*] And suppose I took that contraption on the mantelpiece and dropped it on the lamp—wouldn't it go out?

VALET. You can't move it. It's too heavy.

GARCIN. [*Seizing the bronze ornament and trying to lift it*] You're right. It's too heavy.

[*A short silence follows.*]

VALET. Very well, sir, if you don't need me any more, I'll be off.

GARCIN. What? You're going? [*The VALET goes up to the door.*] Wait. [*VALET looks round.*] That's a bell, isn't it? [*VALET nods.*] And if I ring, you're bound to come?

VALET. Well, yes, that's so—in a way. But you can never be sure about that bell. There's something wrong with the wiring, and it doesn't always work. [*GARCIN goes to the bell-push and presses the button. A bell purrs outside.*]

GARCIN. It's working all right.

VALET. [*Looking surprised*] So it is. [*He, too, presses the button.*] But I shouldn't count on it too much if I were you. It's—capricious. Well, I really must go now. [*GARCIN makes a gesture to detain him.*] Yes, sir?

GARCIN. No, never mind. [*He goes to the mantelpiece and picks up a paper-knife.*] What's this?

VALET. Can't you see? An ordinary paper-knife.

GARCIN. Are there books here?

VALET. No.

GARCIN. Then what's the use of this? [*VALET shrugs his shoulders.*] Very well. You can go. [*VALET goes out.*]

[*GARCIN is by himself. He goes to the bronze ornament and strokes it reflectively. He sits down; then gets up, goes to the bell-push, and presses the button. The bell remains silent. He tries two or three times, without success. Then he tries to open the door, also without success. He calls the VALET several times, but gets no result. He beats the door with his fists, still calling. Suddenly he grows calm and sits down again. At the moment the door opens and INEZ enters, followed by the VALET.*]

VALET. Did you call sir?

GARCIN. [*On the point of answering "Yes"—but then his eyes fall on INEZ.*] No.

VALET. [*Turning to INEZ*] This is your room, madam, [*INEZ says nothing.*] If there's any information you require—? [*INEZ still keeps silent, and the VALET looks slightly huffed.*] Most of our guests have quite a lot to ask me. But I won't insist. Anyhow, as regards the toothbrush, and the electric bell, and that thing on the mantel-shelf, this gentleman can tell you anything you want to know as well as I could. We've had a little chat, him and me. [VALET *goes out.*]

[GARCIN *refrains from looking at* INEZ, *who is inspecting the room. Abruptly she turns to* GARCIN.]

INEZ. Where's Florence? [*Garcin does not reply.*] Didn't you hear? I asked you about Florence. Where is she?

GARCIN. I haven't an idea.

INEZ. Ah, that's the way it works, is it? Torture by separation. Well, as far as I'm concerned, you won't get anywhere. Florence was a tiresome little fool, and I shan't miss her in the least.

GARCIN. I beg your pardon. Who do you suppose I am?

INEZ. You? Why, the torturer, of course.

GARCIN. [*Looks startled, then bursts out laughing*] Well, that's a good one! Too comic for words. I the torturer! So you came in, had a look at me, and thought I was—er—one of the staff. Of course, it's that silly fellow's fault; he should have introduced us. A torturer indeed! I'm Joseph Garcin, journalist and man of letters by profession. And as we're both in the same boat, so to speak, might I ask you, Mrs.—?

INEZ. [*Testily*] Not "Mrs." I'm unmarried.

GARCIN. Right. That's a start, anyway. Well, now that we've broken the ice, do you *really* think I look like a torturer? And, by the way, how does one recognize torturers when one sees them? Evidently you've ideas on the subject.

INEZ. They look frightened.

GARCIN. Frightened! But how ridiculous! Of whom should they be frightened? Of their victims?

INEZ. Laugh away, but I know what I'm talking about. I've often watched my face in the glass.

GARCIN. In the glass? [*He looks around him.*] How beastly of them! They've removed everything in the least resembling a glass. [*Short silence*] Anyhow, I can assure you I'm not frightened. Not that I take my position lightly; I realize its gravity only too well. But I'm not afraid.

INEZ. [*Shrugging her shoulders*] That's your affair. [*Silence*] Must you be here all the time, or do you take a stroll outside, now and then?

GARCIN. The door's locked.

INEZ. Oh! . . . . That's too bad.

GARCIN. I can quite understand that it bores you having me here. And I, too—well, quite frankly, I'd rather be alone. I want to think things out, you know; to set my life in order, and one does that better by oneself. But I'm sure we'll manage to pull along together somehow. I'm no talker, I don't move much; in fact I'm a peaceful sort of fellow. Only, if I may venture on a suggestion, we should make a point of being extremely courteous to each other. That will ease the situation for us both.

INEZ. I'm not polite.

GARCIN. Then I must be polite for two.

[*A longish silence.* GARCIN *is sitting on a sofa, while* INEZ *paces up and down the room.*]

INEZ. [*Fixing her eyes on him*] Your mouth!

GARCIN. [*As if waking from a dream*] I beg your pardon.

INEZ. Can't you keep your mouth still? You keep twisting it about all the time. It's grotesque.

GARCIN. So sorry. I wasn't aware of it.

INEZ. That's just what I reproach you with. [GARCIN'S *mouth twitches.*] There you are! You talk about politeness, and you don't even try to control your face. Remember you're not alone; you've no right to inflict the sight of your fear on me.

GARCIN. [*Getting up and going towards her*] How about you? Aren't you afraid?

INEZ. What would be the use? There was some point in being afraid *before*; while one still had hope.

GARCIN. [*In a low voice*] There's no more hope—but it's still "before." We haven't yet begun to suffer.

INEZ. That's so. [*A short silence*] Well? What's going to happen?

GARCIN. I don't know. I'm waiting.

[*Silence again.* GARCIN *sits down and* INEZ *resumes her pacing up and down the room.* GARCIN'S *mouth twitches; after a glance at* INEZ *he buries his face in his hands. Enter* ESTELLE *with the* VALET. ESTELLE *looks at* GARCIN, *whose face is still hidden by his hands.*]

ESTELLE. [*To* GARCIN] No! Don't look up. I know what you're hiding with your hands. I know you've no face left. [GARCIN *removes his hands.*] What! [*A short pause. Then, in a tone of surprise*] But I don't know you!

GARCIN. I'm not the torturer, madam.

ESTELLE. I never thought you were. I—I thought someone was trying to play a rather nasty trick on me. [*To the* VALET] Is anyone else coming?

VALET. No, madam. No one else is coming.

ESTELLE. Oh! Then we're to stay by ourselves, the three of us, this gentleman, this lady, and myself. [*She starts laughing.*]

GARCIN. [*Angrily*] There's nothing to laugh about.

ESTELLE. [*Still laughing*] It's those sofas. They're so hideous. And just look how they've been arranged. It makes me think of New Year's Day—when I used to visit that boring old aunt of mine, Aunt Mary. Her house is full of horrors like that.... I suppose each of us has a sofa of his own. Is that one mine? [*To the* VALET] But you can't expect me to sit on that one. It would be too horrible for words. I'm in pale blue and it's vivid green.

INEZ. Would you prefer mine?

ESTELLE. That claret-colored one, you mean? That's very sweet of you, but really—no, I don't think it'd be so much better. What's the good of worrying, anyhow? We've got to take what comes to us, and I'll stick to the green one. [*Pauses*] The only one which might do, at a pinch, is that gentleman's. [*Another pause*]

INEZ. Did you hear, Mr. Garcin?

GARCIN. [*With a slight start*] Oh—the sofa, you mean. So sorry. [*He rises.*] Please take it, madam.

ESTELLE. Thanks. [*She takes off her coat and drops it on the sofa. A short silence.*] Well, as we're to live together, I suppose we'd better introduce ourselves. My name's Rigault. Estelle Rigault. [GARCIN *bows and is going to announce his name, but* INEZ *steps in front of him.*]

INEZ. And I'm Inez Serrano. Very pleased to meet you.

GARCIN. [*Bowing again*] Joseph Garcin.

VALET. Do you require me any longer?

ESTELLE. No, you can go. I'll ring when I want you.

[*Exit* VALET, *with polite bows to everyone.*]

INEZ. You're very pretty. I wish we'd had some flowers to welcome you with.

ESTELLE. Flowers? Yes, I loved flowers. Only they'd fade so quickly here, wouldn't they? It's so stuffy. Oh, well, the great thing is to keep as cheerful as we can, don't you agree? Of course, you, too, are—[1]

INEZ. Yes. Last week. What about you?

ESTELLE. I'm—quite recent. Yesterday. As a matter of fact, the ceremony's not quite over. [*Her tone is natural enough, but she seems to be seeing what she describes.*] The wind's blowing my sister's veil all over the place. She's trying her best to cry. Come, dear! Make another effort. That's better. Two tears, two little tears are twinkling under the black veil. Oh dear! What a sight Olga looks this morning! She's holding my sister's arm, helping her along. She's not crying, and I don't blame her; tears always mess one's face up, don't they? Olga was my bosom friend, you know.

INEZ. Did you suffer much?

ESTELLE. No. I was only half conscious, mostly.

INEZ. What was it?

ESTELLE. Pneumonia. [*In the same tone as before*] It's over now, they're leaving the cemetery. Good-by. Good-by. Quite a crowd they are. My husband's stayed at home. Prostrated with grief, poor man. [*To* INEZ] How about you?

---

1. The word left unuttered is "dead."

INEZ. The gas stove.

ESTELLE. And you, Mr. Garcin?

GARCIN. Twelve bullets through my chest. [ESTELLE *makes a horrified gesture.*] Sorry! I fear I'm not good company among the dead.

ESTELLE. Please, please don't use that word. It's so—so crude. In terribly bad taste, really. It doesn't mean much anyhow. Somehow I feel we've never been so much alive as now. If we've absolutely got to mention this—this state of things, I suggest we call ourselves—wait!—absentees. Have you been—been absent for long?

GARCIN. About a month.

ESTELLE. Where do you come from?

GARCIN. From Rio.

ESTELLE. I'm from Paris. Have you anyone left down there?

GARCIN. Yes, my wife. [*In the same tone as* ESTELLE *has been using*] She's waiting at the entrance of the barracks. She comes there every day. But they won't let her in. Now she's trying to peep between the bars. She doesn't yet know I'm—absent, but she suspects it. Now she's going away. She's wearing her black dress. So much the better, she won't need to change. She isn't crying, but she never did cry, anyhow. It's a bright sunny day and she's like a black shadow creeping down the empty street. Those big tragic eyes of hers—with that martyred look they always had. Oh, how she got on my nerves!

[*A short silence.* GARCIN *sits on the central sofa and buries his head in his hands.*]

INEZ. Estelle!

ESTELLE. Please, Mr. Garcin!

GARCIN. What is it?

ESTELLE. You're sitting on my sofa.

GARCIN. I beg your pardon. [*He gets up.*]

ESTELLE. You looked so—so far away. Sorry I disturbed you.

GARCIN. I was setting my life in order. [INEZ *starts laughing.*] You may laugh, but you'd do better to follow my example.

INEZ. No need. My life's in perfect order. It tidied itself up nicely of its own accord. So I needn't bother about it now.

GARCIN. Really? You imagine it's so simple as that. [*He runs his hand over his forehead.*] Whew! How hot it is here! Do you mind if—? [*He begins taking off his coat.*]

ESTELLE. How dare you! [*More gently*] No, please don't. I loathe men in their shirt sleeves.

GARCIN. [*Putting on his coat again*] All right. [*A short pause*] Of course, I used to spend my nights in the newspaper office, and it was a regular Black Hole, so we never kept our coats on. Stiflingly hot it could be. [*Short pause. In the same tone as previously*] Stiffling, that it *is*. It's night now.

ESTELLE. That's so. Olga's undressing; it must be after midnight.

How quickly the time passes, on earth!

INEZ. Yes, after midnight. They've sealed up my room. It's dark, pitch-dark, and empty.

GARCIN. They've slung their coats on the backs of the chairs and rolled up their shirt-sleeves above the elbow. The air stinks of men and cigar-smoke. [*A short silence*] I used to like living among men in their shirt-sleeves.

ESTELLE. [*Aggressively*] Well, in that case our tastes differ. That's all it proves. [*Turning to* INEZ] What about you? Do you like men in their shirt-sleeves?

INEZ. Oh, I don't care much for men any way.

ESTELLE. [*Looking at the other two with a puzzled air*] Really I can't imagine why they put us three together. It doesn't make sense.

INEZ. [*Stifling a laugh*] What's that you said?

ESTELLE. I'm looking at you two and thinking that we're going to live together. . . . It's so absurd. I expected to meet old friends, or relatives.

INEZ. Yes, a charming old friend—with a hole in the middle of his face.

ESTELLE. Yes, him too. He danced the tango so divinely. Like a professional. . . . But why, why should we of all people be put together?

GARCIN. A pure fluke, I should say. They lodge folks as they can, in the order of their coming. [*To* INEZ] Why are you laughing?

INEZ. Because you amuse me, with your "flukes." As if they left anything to chance! But I suppose you've got to reassure yourself somehow.

ESTELLE. [*Hesitantly*] I wonder, now. Don't you think we may have met each other at some time in our lives?

INEZ. Never. I shouldn't have forgotten you.

ESTELLE. Or perhaps we have friends in common. I wonder if you know the Dubois-Seymours?

INEZ. Not likely.

ESTELLE. But *everyone* went to their parties.

INEZ. What's their job?

ESTELLE. Oh, they don't do anything. But they have a lovely house in the country, and hosts of people visit them.

INEZ. I didn't. I was a post-office clerk.

ESTELLE. [*Recoiling a little*] Ah, yes. . . . Of course, in that case— [*A pause*] And you, Mr. Garcin?

GARCIN. We've never met. I always lived in Rio.

ESTELLE. Then you must be right. It's mere chance that has brought us together.

INEZ. Mere chance? Then it's by chance this room is furnished as we see it. It's an accident that the sofa on the right is a livid green, and that one on the left's wine-red. Mere chance? Well, just try to shift the sofas and you'll see the difference quick enough. And that statue on the mantelpiece, do you think it's there by accident? And what about the heat here? How about that? [*A short silence*] I tell you they've thought it all out. Down to the last detail. Nothing was left to chance. This room was all set for us.

ESTELLE. But really! Everything here's so hideous; all in angles, so uncomfortable. I always loathed angles.

INEZ. [*Shrugging her shoulders*] And do you think I lived in a Second Empire drawing-room?

ESTELLE. So it was all fixed up beforehand?

INEZ. Yes. And they've put us together deliberately.

ESTELLE. Then it's not mere chance that *you* precisely are sitting opposite *me*? But what can be the idea behind it?

INEZ. Ask me another! I only know they're waiting.

ESTELLE. I never could bear the idea of anyone's expecting something from me. It always made me want to do just the opposite.

INEZ. Well, do it. Do it if you can. You don't even know what they expect.

ESTELLE. [*Stamping her foot*] It's outrageous! So something's coming to me from you two? [*She eyes each in turn.*] Something nasty, I suppose. There are some faces that tell me everything at once. Yours don't convey anything.

GARCIN. [*Turning abruptly towards* INEZ] Look here! Why are we together? You've given us quite enough hints, you may as well come out with it.

INEZ. [*In a surprised tone*] But I know nothing, absolutely nothing about it. I'm as much in the dark as you are.

GARCIN. We've got to know. [*Ponders for a while*]

INEZ. If only each of us had the guts to tell—

GARCIN. Tell what?

INEZ. Estelle!

ESTELLE. Yes?

INEZ. What have you done? I mean, why have they sent you here?

ESTELLE. [*Quickly*] That's just it. I haven't a notion, not the foggiest. In fact, I'm wondering if there hasn't been some ghastly mistake. [*To* INEZ] Don't smile. Just think of the number of people who—who become absentees every day. There must be thousands and thousands, and probably they're sorted out by—by understrappers, you know what I mean. Stupid employees who don't know their job. So they're bound to make mistakes sometimes. . . . Do stop smiling. [*To* GARCIN] Why don't you speak? If they made a mistake in my case, they may have done the same about you. [*To* INEZ] And you, too. Anyhow, isn't it better to think we've got here by mistake?

INEZ. Is that all you have to tell us?

ESTELLE. What else should I tell? I've nothing to hide. I lost my
parents when I was a kid, and I had my young brother to bring
up. We were terribly poor and when an old friend of my people
asked me to marry him I said yes. He was very well off, and quite
nice. My brother was a very delicate child and needed all sorts
of attention, so really that was the right thing for me to do,
don't you agree? My husband was old enough to be my father,
but for six years we had a happy married life. Then two years
ago I met the man I was fated to love. We knew it the moment
we set eyes on each other. He asked me to run away with him,
and I refused. Then I got pneumonia and it finished me. That's
the whole story. No doubt, by certain standards, I did wrong
to sacrifice my youth to a man nearly three times my age. [*To*
GARCIN] Do *you* think that could be called a sin?

GARCIN. Certainly not. [*A short silence*] And now, tell me, do you
think it's a crime to stand by one's principles?

ESTELLE. Of course not. Surely no one could blame a man for
that!

GARCIN. Wait a bit! I ran a pacifist newspaper. Then war broke
out. What was I to do? Everyone was watching me, wondering:
"Will he dare?" Well, I dared. I folded my arms and they shot
me. Had I done anything wrong?

ESTELLE. [*Laying her hand on his arm*] Wrong? On the contrary. You
were—

INEZ. [*Breaks in ironically*]—a hero! And how about your wife, Mr.
Garcin?

GARCIN. That's simple. I'd rescued her from—from the gutter.

ESTELLE. [*To* INEZ] You see! You see!

INEZ. Yes, I see. [*A pause*] Look here! What's the point of play-act-
ing, trying to throw dust in each other's eyes? We're all tarred
with the same brush.

ESTELLE. [*Indignantly*] How dare you!

INEZ. Yes, we are criminals—murderers—all three of us. We're in
hell, my pets; they never make mistakes, and people aren't damned
for nothing.

ESTELLE. Stop! For heaven's sake—

INEZ. In hell! Damned souls—that's us, all three!

ESTELLE. Keep quiet! I forbid you to use such disgusting words.

INEZ. A damned soul—that's you, my little plaster saint. And ditto
our friend there, the noble pacifist. We've had our hour of pleasure,
haven't we? There have been people who burned their lives out
for our sakes—and we chuckled over it. So now we have to pay the
reckoning.

GARCIN. [*Raising his fist*] Will you keep your mouth shut, damn it!

INEZ. [*Confronting him fearlessly, but with a look of vast surprise*]

Well, well! [*A pause*] Ah, I understand now. I know why they've put us three together.

GARCIN. I advise you to—to think twice before you say any more.

INEZ. Wait! You'll see how simple it is. Childishly simple. Obviously there aren't any physical torments—you agree, don't you? And yet we're in hell. And no one else will come here. We'll stay in this room together, the three of us, for ever and ever. . . . In short, there's someone absent here, the official torturer.

GARCIN. [*Sotto voce*] I'd noticed that.

INEZ. It's obvious what they're after—an economy of man-power—or devil-power, if you prefer. The same idea as in the cafeteria, where customers serve themselves.

ESTELLE. What ever do you mean?

INEZ. I mean that each of us will act as torturer of the two others.

[*There is a short silence while they digest this information.*]

GARCIN. [*Gently*] No, I shall never be your torturer. I wish neither of you any harm, and I've no concern with you. None at all. So the solution's easy enough, each of us stays put in his or her corner and takes no notice of the others. You here, you here, and I there. Like soldiers at our posts. Also, we mustn't speak. Not one word. That won't be difficult; each of us has plenty of material for self-communings. I think I could stay ten thousand years with only my thoughts for company.

ESTELLE. Have I got to keep silent, too?

GARCIN. Yes. And that way we—we'll work out our salvation. Looking into ourselves, never raising our heads. Agreed?

INEZ. Agreed.

ESTELLE. [*After some hesitation*] I agree.

GARCIN. Then—good-by.

[*He goes to his sofa and buries his head in his hands. There is a long silence; then* INEZ *begins singing to herself.*]

INEZ. [*Singing*]

What a crowd in Whitefriars Lane!
They've set trestles in a row,
With a scaffold and the knife,
And a pail of bran below.
Come, good folks, to Whitefriars Lane,
Come to see the merry show!

The headsman rose at crack of dawn,
He'd a long day's work in hand,
Chopping heads off generals,
Priests and peers and admirals,
All the highest in the land.
What a crowd in Whitefriars Lane!

> See them standing in a line,
> Ladies all dressed up so fine.
> But their heads have got to go,
> Heads and hats roll down below.
> Come, good folks, to Whitefriars Lane,
> Come to see the merry show!

[*Meanwhile* ESTELLE *has been plying her powder-puff and lipstick. She looks round for a mirror, fumbles in her bag, then turns towards* GARCIN.]

ESTELLE. Excuse me, have you a glass? [GARCIN *does not answer.*] Any sort of glass, a pocket-mirror will do. [GARCIN *remains silent.*] Even if you won't speak to me, you might lend me a glass.

[*His head still buried in his hands,* GARCIN *ignores her.*]

INEZ. [*Eagerly*] Don't worry. I've a glass in my bag. [*She opens her bag. Angrily*] It's gone! They must have taken it from me at the entrance.

ESTELLE. How tiresome!

[*A short silence.* ESTELLE *shuts her eyes and sways, as if about to faint.* INEZ *turns forward and holds her up.*]

INEZ. What's the matter?

ESTELLE. [*Opens her eyes and smiles*] I feel so queer. [*She pats herself.*] Don't you ever get taken that way? When I can't see myself I begin to wonder if I really and truly exist. I pat myself just to make sure, but it doesn't help much.

INEZ. You're lucky. I'm always conscious of myself—in my mind. Painfully conscious.

ESTELLE. Ah yes, in your mind. But everything that goes on in one's head is so vague, isn't it? It makes one want to sleep. [*She is silent for a while.*] I've six big mirrors in my bedroom. There they are. I can see them. But they don't see me. They're reflecting the carpet, the settee, the window—but how empty it is, a glass in which I'm absent! When I talked to people I always made sure there was one near by in which I could see myself. I watched myself talking. And somehow it kept me alert, seeing myself as the others saw me. . . . Oh dear! My lipstick! I'm sure I've put it on all crooked. No, I can't do without a looking-glass for ever and ever, I simply can't.

INEZ. Suppose I try to be your glass? Come and pay me a visit, dear. Here's a place for you on my sofa.

ESTELLE. But—[*Points to* GARCIN]

INEZ. Oh, he doesn't count.

ESTELLE. But we're going to—to hurt each other. You said it youself.

INEZ. Do I look as if I wanted to hurt you?

ESTELLE. One never can tell.

INEZ. Much more likely *you'll* hurt *me*. Still, what does it matter?

If I've got to suffer, it may as well be at your hands, your pretty hands. Sit down. Come closer. Closer. Look into my eyes. What do you see?

ESTELLE. Oh, I'm there! But so tiny I can't see myself properly.

INEZ. But I can. Every inch of you. Now ask me questions. I'll be as candid as any looking-glass.

[ESTELLE *seems rather embarrassed and turns to* GARCIN, *as if appealing to him for help.*]

ESTELLE. Please, Mr. Garcin. Sure our chatter isn't boring you?

[GARCIN *makes no reply.*]

INEZ. Don't worry about him. As I said, he doesn't count. We're by ourselves. . . . Ask away.

ESTELLE. Are my lips all right?

INEZ. Show! No, they're a bit smudgy.

ESTELLE. I thought as much. Luckily [*Throws a quick glance at* GARCIN] no one's seen me. I'll try again.

INEZ. That's better. No. Follow the line of your lips. Wait! I'll guide your hand. There. That's quite good.

ESTELLE. As good as when I came in?

INEZ. Far better. Crueler. Your mouth looks quite diabolical that way.

ESTELLE. Good gracious! And you say you like it! How maddening, not being able to see for myself! You're quite sure, Miss Serrano, that it's all right now?

INEZ. Won't you call me Inez?

ESTELLE. Are you sure it looks all right?

INEZ. You're lovely, Estelle.

ESTELLE. But how can I rely upon your taste? Is it the same as *my* taste? Oh, how sickening it all is, enough to drive one crazy!

INEZ. I *have* your taste, my dear, because I like you so much. Look at me. No, straight. Now smile. I'm not so ugly, either. Am I not nicer than your glass?

ESTELLE. Oh, I don't know. You scare me rather. My reflection in the glass never did that; of course, I knew it so well. Like something I had tamed. . . . I'm going to smile, and my smile will sink down into your pupils, and heaven knows what it will become.

INEZ. And why shouldn't you "tame" *me*? [*The women gaze at each other,* ESTELLE *with a sort of fearful fascination.*] Listen! I want you to call me Inez. We must be great friends.

ESTELLE. I don't make friends with women very easily.

INEZ. Not with postal clerks, you mean? Hullo, what's that—that nasty red spot at the bottom of your cheek? A pimple?

ESTELLE. A pimple? Oh, how simply foul! Where?

INEZ. There. . . . You know the way they catch larks—with a mirror? I'm your lark-mirror, my dear, and you can't escape me. . . . There isn't any pimple, not a trace of one. So what about it?

Suppose the mirror started telling lies? Or suppose I covered my eyes—as he is doing—and refused to look at you, all that loveliness of yours would be wasted on the desert air. No, don't be afraid, I can't help looking at you, I shan't turn my eyes away. And I'll be nice to you, ever so nice. Only you must be nice to me, too.

[*A short silence*]

ESTELLE. Are you really—attracted by me?

INEZ. Very much indeed.

[*Another short silence*]

ESTELLE. [*Indicating* GARCIN *by a slight movement of her head*] But I wish he'd notice me, too.

INEZ. Of course! Because he's a Man! [*To* GARCIN] You've won. [GARCIN *says nothing.*] But look at her, damn it! [*Still no reply from* GARCIN] Don't pretend. You haven't missed a word of what we've said.

GARCIN. Quite so; not a word. I stuck my fingers in my ears, but your voices thudded in my brain. Silly chatter. Now will you leave me in peace, you two? I'm not interested in you.

INEZ. Not in me, perhaps—but how about this child? Aren't you interested in her? Oh, I saw through your game; you got on your high horse just to impress her.

GARCIN. I asked you to leave me in peace. There's someone talking about me in the newspaper office and I want to listen. And, if it'll make you any happier, let me tell you that I've no use for the "child," as you call her.

ESTELLE. Thanks.

GARCIN. Oh, I didn't mean it rudely.

ESTELLE. You cad!

[*They confront each other in silence for some moments.*]

GARCIN. So's that's that. [*Pause*] You know I begged you not to speak.

ESTELLE. It's *her* fault; she started. I didn't ask anything of her and she came and offered me her—her glass.

INEZ. So you say. But all the time you were making up to him, trying every trick to catch his attention.

ESTELLE. Well, why shouldn't I?

GARCIN. You're crazy, both of you. Don't you see where this is leading us? For pity's sake, keep your mouths shut. [*Pause*] Now let's all sit down again quite quietly; we'll look at the floor and each must try to forget the others are there.

[*A longish silence.* GARCIN *sits down. The women return hesitantly to their places. Suddenly* INEZ *swings round on him.*]

INEZ. To forget about the others? How utterly absurd! I *feel* you there, in every pore. Your silence clamors in my ears. You can nail up your mouth, cut your tongue out—but you can't prevent your *being there.* Can you stop your thoughts? I hear them ticking away like a clock, tick-tock, tick-tock, and I'm certain you hear mine. It's all very well skulking on your sofa, but you're everywhere, and every sound comes to me soiled, because you've intercepted it on its way. Why, you've even stolen my face; you know it and I don't! And what about her, about Estelle? You've stolen her from me, too; if she and I were alone do you suppose she'd treat me as she does? No, take your hands from your face, I won't leave you in peace—that would suit your book too well. You'd go on sitting there, in a sort of trance, like a yogi, and even if I didn't see her I'd feel it in my bones—that she was making every sound, even the rustle of her dress, for your benefit, throwing you smiles you didn't see. . . . Well, I won't stand for that, I prefer to choose my hell; I prefer to look you in the eyes and fight it out face to face.

GARCIN. Have it your own way. I suppose we were bound to come to this; they knew what they were about, and we're easy game. If they'd put me in a room with men—men can keep their mouths shut. But it's no use wanting the impossible. [*He goes to* ESTELLE *and lightly fondles her neck.*] So I attract you, little girl? It seems you were making eyes at me?

ESTELLE. Don't touch me.

GARCIN. Why not? We might, anyhow, be natural. . . . Do you know, I used to be mad about women? And some were fond of me. So we may as well stop posing, we've nothing to lose. Why trouble about politeness, and decorum, and the rest of it? We're between ourselves. And presently we shall be naked as—as new-born babes.

ESTELLE. Oh, let me be!

GARCIN. As new-born babes. Well, I'd warned you, anyhow. I asked so little of you, nothing but peace and a little silence. I'd put my fingers in my ears. Gomez was spouting away as usual, standing in the center of the room, with all the pressmen listening. In their shirtsleeves. I tried to hear, but it wasn't too easy. Things on earth move so quickly, you know. Couldn't you have held your tongues? Now it's over, he's stopped talking, and what he thinks of me has gone back into his head. Well, we've got to see it through somehow. . . . Naked as we were born. So much the better; I want to know whom I have to deal with.

INEZ. You know already. There's nothing more to learn.

GARCIN. You're wrong. So long as each of us hasn't made a clean breast of it—why they've damned him or her—we know nothing. Nothing that counts. You, young lady, you shall begin. Why? Tell us why. If you are frank, if we bring our specters into the open, it may save us from disaster. So—out with it! Why?

ESTELLE. I tell you I haven't a notion. They wouldn't tell me why.

GARCIN. That's so. They wouldn't tell me, either. But I've a pretty

1598 · Jean-Paul Sartre

good idea. . . . Perhaps you're shy of speaking first? Right. I'll
lead off. [*A short silence*] I'm not a very estimable person.

INEZ. No need to tell us that. We know you were a deserter.

GARCIN. Let that be. It's only a side-issue. I'm here because I treated
my wife abominably. That's all. For five years. Naturally, she's
suffering still. There she is: the moment I mention her, I see
her. It's Gomez who interests me, and it's she I see. Where's
Gomez got to? For five years. There! They've given her back my
things; she's sitting by the window, with my coat on her knees.
The coat with the twelve bullet-holes. The blood's like rust; a brown
ring round each hole. It's quite a museum-piece, that coat; scarred
with history. And I used to wear it, fancy! . . . Now, can't you
shed a tear, my love? Surely you'll squeeze one out—at last?
No? You can't manage it? . . . Night after night I came home
blind drunk, stinking of wine and women. She'd sat up for me,
of course. But she never cried, never uttered a word of reproach.
Only her eyes spoke. Big, tragic eyes. I don't regret anything. I
must pay the price, but I shan't whine. . . . It's snowing in the
street. Won't you cry, confound you? That woman was a born
martyr, you know; a victim by vocation.

INEZ. [*Almost tenderly*] Why did you hurt her like that?

GARCIN. It was so easy. A word was enough to make her flinch. Like
a sensitive-plant. But never, never a reproach. I'm fond of teasing.
I watched and waited. But no, not a tear, not a protest. I'd picked
her up out of the gutter, you understand. . . . Now she's stroking
the coat. Her eyes are shut and she's feeling with her fingers for
the bullet-holes. What are you after? What do you expect? I tell
you I regret nothing. The truth is, she admired me too much.
Does that mean anything to you?

INEZ. No. Nobody admired *me*.

GARCIN. So much the better. So much the better for you. I suppose
all this strikes you as very vague. Well, here's something you can
get your teeth into. I brought a half-caste girl to stay in our house.
My wife slept upstairs; she must have heard—everything. She was
an early riser and, as I and the girl stayed in bed late, she served
us our morning coffee.

INEZ. You brute!

GARCIN. Yes, a brute, if you like. But a well-beloved brute. [*A far-
away look comes to his eyes*] No, it's nothing. Only Gomez, and
he's not talking about *me*. . . . What were you saying? Yes, a brute.
Certainly. Else why should I be here? [*To* INEZ] Your turn.

INEZ. Well, I was what some people down there called "a damned
bitch." Damned already. So it's no surprise, being here.

GARCIN. Is that all you have to say?

INEZ. No. There was that affair with Florence. A dead men's tale.

With three corpses to it. He to start with; then she and I. So there's no one left, I've nothing to worry about; it was a clean sweep. Only that room. I see it now and then. Empty, with the doors locked. . . . No, they've just unlocked them. "To Let." It's to let; there's a notice on the door. That's—too ridiculous.

GARCIN. Three. Three deaths, you said?

INEZ. Three.

GARCIN. One man and two women?

INEZ. Yes.

GARCIN. Well, well. [*A pause*] Did he kill himself?

INEZ. He? No, he hadn't the guts for that. Still, he'd every reason; we led him a dog's life. As a matter of fact, he was run over by a tram. A silly sort of end. . . . I was living with them; he was my cousin.

GARCIN. Was Florence fair?

INEZ. Fair? [*Glances at* ESTELLE] You know, I don't regret a thing; still, I'm not so very keen on telling you the story.

GARCIN. That's all right. . . . So you got sick of him?

INEZ. Quite gradually. All sorts of little things got on my nerves. For instance, he made a noise when he was drinking—a sort of gurgle. Trifles like that. He was rather pathetic really. Vulnerable. Why are you smiling?

GARCIN. Because I, anyhow, am *not* vulnerable.

INEZ. Don't be too sure. . . . I crept inside her skin, she saw the world through my eyes. When she left him, I had her on my hands. We shared a bed-sitting-room at the other end of the town.

GARCIN. And then?

INEZ. Then that tram did its job. I used to remind her every day: "Yes, my pet, we killed him between us." [*A pause*] I'm rather cruel, really.

GARCIN. So am I.

INEZ. No, you're not cruel. It's something else.

GARCIN. What?

INEZ. I'll tell you later. When I say I'm cruel, I mean I can't get on without making people suffer. Like a live coal. A live coal in others' hearts. When I'm alone I flicker out. For six months I flamed away in her heart, till there was nothing but a cinder. One night she got up and turned on the gas while I was asleep. Then she crept back into bed. So now you know.

GARCIN. Well! Well!

INEZ. Yes? What's in your mind?

GARCIN. Nothing. Only that it's not a pretty story.

INEZ. Obviously. But what matter?

GARCIN. As you say, what matter? [*To* ESTELLE] Your turn. What have you done?

ESTELLE. As I told you, I haven't a notion. I rack my brain, but it' no use.

GARCIN. Right. Then we'll give you a hand. That fellow with the smashed face, who was he?

ESTELLE. Who—who do you mean?

INEZ. You know quite well. The man you were so scared of seeing when you came in.

ESTELLE. Oh, him! A friend of mine.

GARCIN. Why were you afraid of him?

ESTELLE. That's my business, Mr. Garcin.

INEZ. Did he shoot himself on your account?

ESTELLE. Of course not. How absurd you are!

GARCIN. Then why should you have been so scared? He blew his brains out, didn't he? That's how his face got smashed.

ESTELLE. Don't! Please don't go on.

GARCIN. Because of you. Because of you.

INEZ. He shot himself because of you.

ESTELLE. Leave me alone! It's—it's not fair, bullying me like that. I want to go! I want to go!

[*She runs to the door and shakes it.*]

GARCIN. Go if you can. Personally, I ask for nothing better. Unfortunately, the door's locked.

[ESTELLE *presses the bell-push, but the bell does not ring. INEZ and GARCIN laugh. ESTELLE swings round on them, her back to the door.*]

ESTELLE. [*In a muffled voice*] You're hateful, both of you.

INEZ. Hateful? Yes, that's the word. Now get on with it. That fellow who killed himself on your account—you were his mistress, eh?

GARCIN. Of course she was. And he wanted her to have her to himself alone. That's so, isn't it?

INEZ. He danced the tango like a professional, but he was poor as a church mouse—that's right, isn't it?

[*A short silence*]

GARCIN. Was he poor or not? Give a straight answer.

ESTELLE. Yes, he was poor.

GARCIN. And then you had your reputation to keep up. One day he came and implored you to run away with him, and you laughed in his face.

INEZ. That's it. You laughed at him. And so he killed himself.

ESTELLE. Did you use to look at Florence in that way?

INEZ. Yes.

[*A short pause, then* ESTELLE *bursts out laughing.*]

ESTELLE. You've got it all wrong, you two. [*She stiffens her shoulders, still leaning against the door, and faces them. Her voice grows shrill, truculent.*] He wanted me to have a baby. So there!

GARCIN. And you didn't want one?

STELLE. I certainly didn't. But the baby came, worse luck. I went to Switzerland for five months. No one knew anything. It was a girl. Roger was with me when she was born. It pleased him no end, having a daughter. It didn't please *me!*

GARCIN. And then?

STELLE. There was a balcony overlooking the lake. I brought a big stone. He could see what I was up to and he kept on shouting: "Estelle, for God's sake, don't!" I hated him then. He saw it all. He was leaning over the balcony and he saw the rings spreading on the water—

GARCIN. Yes? And then?

STELLE. That's all. I came back to Paris—and he did as he wished.

GARCIN. You mean he blew his brains out?

STELLE. It was absurd of him, really, my husband never suspected anything. [*A pause*] Oh, how I loathe you! [*She sobs tearlessly.*]

GARCIN. Nothing doing. Tears don't flow in this place.

STELLE. I'm a coward. A coward! [*Pause*] If you knew how I hate you!

INEZ. [*Taking her in her arms*] Poor child! [*To* GARCIN] So the hearing's over. But there's no need to look like a hanging judge.

GARCIN. A hanging judge? [*He glances around him.*] I'd give a lot to be able to see myself in a glass. [*Pause*] How hot it is! [*Unthinkingly he takes off his coat.*] Oh, sorry! [*He starts putting it on again.*]

ESTELLE. Don't bother. You can stay in your shirt-sleeves. As things are—

GARCIN. Just so. [*He drops his coat on the sofa.*] You mustn't be angry with me, Estelle.

ESTELLE. I'm not angry with you.

INEZ. And what about me? Are you angry with me?

ESTELLE. Yes.

[*A short silence*]

INEZ. Well, Mr. Garcin, now you have us in the nude all right. Do you understand things any better for that?

GARCIN. I wonder. Yes, perhaps a trifle better. [*Timidly*] And now suppose we start trying to help each other.

INEZ. I don't need help.

GARCIN. Inez, they've laid their snare damned cunningly—like a cobweb. If you make any movement, if you raise your hand to fan yourself, Estelle and I feel a little tug. Alone, none of us can save himself or herself; we're linked together inextricably. So you can take your choice. [*A pause*] Hullo? What's happening?

INEZ. They've let it. The windows are wide open, a man is sitting on my bed. *My* bed, if you please! They've let it, let it! Step in, step in, make yourself at home, you brute! Ah, there's a woman too. She's going up to him, putting her hands on his shoulder ... Damn it, why don't they turn the lights on? It's getting dark. Now he's going to kiss her. But that's my room, *my* room. Pitch dark now. I can't see anything, but I hear them whispering, whispering. Is he going to make love to her on *my* bed? What's that she said? That it's noon and the sun is shining? I must be going blind. [*A pause*] Blacked out. I can't see or hear a thing. So I'm done with the earth, it seems. No more alibis for me! [*She shudders*] I feel so empty, desiccated—really dead at last. All of me's here in this room. [*A pause*] What were you saying? Something about helping me, wasn't it?

GARCIN. Yes.

INEZ. Helping me to do what?

GARCIN. To defeat their devilish tricks.

INEZ. And what do you expect me to do, in return?

GARCIN. To help *me*. It only needs a little effort, Inez; just a spark of human feeling.

INEZ. Human feeling. That's beyond my range. I'm rotten to the core.

GARCIN. And how about me? [*A pause*] All the same, suppose we try.

INEZ. It's no use. I'm all dried up. I can't give and I can't receive. How could I help you? A dead twig, ready for the burning. [*She falls silent, gazing at* ESTELLE, *who has buried her head in her hands.*] Florence was fair, a natural blonde.

GARCIN. Do you realize that this young woman's fated to be your torturer?

INEZ. Perhaps I've guessed it.

GARCIN. It's through her they'll get you. I, of course, I'm different—aloof. I take no notice of her. Suppose you had a try—

INEZ. Yes?

GARCIN. It's a trap. They're watching you, to see if you'll fall into it.

INEZ. I know. And you're another trap. Do you think they haven't foreknown every word you say? And of course there's a whole nest of pitfalls that we can't see. Everything here's a booby-trap. But what do I care? I'm a pitfall, too. For her, obviously. And perhaps I'll catch her.

GARCIN. You won't catch anything. We're chasing after each other, round and round in a vicious circle, like the horses on a roundabout. That's part of their plan, of course. . . . Drop it, Inez. Open your hands and let go of everything. Or else you'll bring disaster on all three of us.

INEZ. Do I look the sort of person who lets go? I know what's coming to me. I'm going to burn, and it's to last forever. Yes, I *know* everything. But do you think I'll let go? I'll catch her, she'll see you through my eyes, as Florence saw that other man. What's the good of trying to enlist my sympathy? I assure you I know everything, and I can't feel sorry even for myself. A trap! Don't I know it, and that I'm in a trap myself, up to the neck, and there's nothing to be done about it? And if it suits their book, so much the better!

GARCIN. [*Gripping her shoulders*] Well, I, anyhow, can feel sorry for you, too. Look at me, we're naked, naked right through, and I can see into your heart. That's one link between us. Do you think I'd want to hurt you? I don't regret anything, I'm dried up, too. But for you I can still feel pity.

INEZ. [*Who has let him keep his hands on her shoulders until now, shakes herself loose*] Don't. I hate being pawed about. And keep your pity for yourself. Don't forget, Garcin, that there are traps for you, too, in this room. All nicely set for you. You'd do better to watch your own interests. [*A pause.*] But, if you will leave us in peace, this child and me, I'll see I don't do you any harm.

GARCIN. [*Gazes at her for a moment, then shrugs his shoulders*] Very well.

ESTELLE. [*Raising her head*] Please, Garcin.

GARCIN. What do you want of me?

ESTELLE. [*Rises and goes up to him*] You can help *me*, anyhow.

GARCIN. If you want help, apply to her.

[INEZ *has come up and is standing behind* ESTELLE, *but without touching her. During the dialogue that follows she speaks almost in her ear. But* ESTELLE *keeps her eyes on* GARCIN, *who observes her without speaking, and she addresses her answers to him, as if it were he who is questioning her.*]

ESTELLE. I implore you, Garcin—you gave me your promise, didn't you? Help me quick. I don't want to be left alone. Olga's taken him to a cabaret.

INEZ. Taken whom?

ESTELLE. Peter. . . . Oh, now they're dancing together.

INEZ. Who's Peter?

ESTELLE. Such a silly boy. He called me his glancing stream—just fancy! He was terribly in love with me. . . . She's persuaded him to come out with her tonight.

INEZ. Do you love him?

ESTELLE. They're sitting down now. She's puffing like a grampus. What a fool the girl is to insist on dancing! But I dare say she does it to reduce. . . . No, of course I don't love him; he's only eighteen, and I'm not a baby-snatcher.

INEZ. Then why bother about them? What difference can it make?

ESTELLE. He belonged to me.

INEZ. Nothing on earth belongs to you any more.

ESTELLE. I tell you he was mine. All mine.

INEZ. Yes, he was yours—once. But now— Try to make him hear, try to touch him. Olga can touch him, talk to him as much as she likes. That's so, isn't it? She can squeeze his hands, rub herself against him—

ESTELLE. Yes, look! She's pressing her great fat chest against him, puffing and blowing in his face. But, my poor little lamb, can't you see how ridiculous she is? Why don't you laugh at her? Oh, once I'd have only had to glance at them and she'd have slunk away. Is there really nothing, nothing left of me?

INEZ. Nothing whatever. Nothing of you's left on earth—not even a shadow. All you own is here. Would you like that paper-knife? Or that ornament on the mantelpiece? That blue sofa's yours. And I, my dear, am yours forever.

ESTELLE. You mine! That's good! Well, which of you two would dare to call me his glancing stream, his crystal girl? You know too much about me, you know I'm rotten through and through. . . . Peter dear, think of me, fix your thoughts on me, and save me. All the time you're thinking "my glancing stream, my crystal girl," I'm only half here, I'm only half wicked, and half of me is down there with you, clean and bright and crystal-clear as running water. . . . Oh, just look at her face, all scarlet, like a tomato. No, it's absurd, we've laughed at her together, you and I, often and often. . . . What's that tune?—I always loved it. Yes, the *St. Louis Blues.* . . . All right, dance away, dance away. Garcin, I wish you could see her, you'd die of laughing. Only—she'll never know I see her. Yes, I see you Olga, with your hair all anyhow, and you do look a dope, my dear. Oh, now you're treading on his toes. It's a scream! Hurry up! Quicker! Quicker! He's dragging her along, bundling her round and round—it's too ghastly! He always said I was so light, he loved to dance with me. [*She is dancing as she speaks.*] I tell you, Olga, I can see you. No, she doesn't care, she's dancing through my gaze. What's that? What's that you said? "Our poor dear Estelle"? Oh, don't be such a humbug! You didn't even shed a tear at the funeral. . . . And she has the nerve to talk to him about her poor dear friend Estelle! How dare she discuss me with Peter? Now then, keep time. She never could dance and talk at once. Oh, what's that? No, no. Don't tell him. Please, please don't tell him. You can keep him, do what you like with him, but please don't tell him about—that! [*She has stopped dancing.*] All right. You can have him now. Isn't it foul, Garcin? She's told him everything, about Roger, my trip to Switzerland, the baby. "Poor Estelle wasn't exactly—" No, I wasn't exactly— True enough. He's looking grave, shaking his head, but he doesn't seem so very much surprised, not what one would expect. Keep him, then—I won't haggle with you over his long eyelashes, his pretty girlish face. They're yours for the asking. His glancing stream, his crystal. Well, the crystal's shattered into bits. "Poor Estelle!" Dance, dance, dance. On with it. But do keep time. One, two. One, two. How I'd love to go down to earth for just a moment, and dance with him again. [*She dances again for some moments.*] The music's growing fainter. They've turned down the lights, as they do for a tango. Why are they playing so softly? Louder, please. I can't hear. It's so far away, so far away. I—I can't hear a sound. [*She stops dancing.*] All over. It's the end. The earth has left me. [*To* GARCIN] Don't turn from me—please. Take me in your arms. [*Behind* ESTELLE's *back,* INEZ *signs to* GARCIN *to move away.*]

INEZ. [*Commandingly*] Now then, Garcin!

[GARCIN *moves back a step, and, glancing at* ESTELLE, *points to* INEZ.]

GARCIN. It's to her you should say that.

ESTELLE. [*Clinging to him*] Don't turn away. You're a man, aren't you, and surely I'm not such a fright as all that! Everyone says I've lovely hair and, after all, a man killed himself on my account. You have to look at something, and there's nothing here to see except the sofas and that awful ornament and the table. Surely I'm better to look at than a lot of stupid furniture. Listen! I've dropped out of their hearts like a little sparrow fallen from its nest. So gather me up, dear, fold me to your heart—and you'll see how nice I can be.

GARCIN. [*Freeing himself from her, after a short struggle*] I tell you it's to that lady you should speak.

ESTELLE. To her? But she doesn't count, she's a woman.

INEZ. Oh, I don't count? Is that what you think? But, my poor little fallen nestling, you've been sheltering in my heart for ages, though you didn't realize it. Don't be afraid; I'll keep looking at you for ever and ever, without a flutter of my eyelids, and you'll live in my gaze like a mote in a sunbeam.

ESTELLE. A sunbeam indeed! Don't talk such rubbish! You've tried that trick already, and you should know it doesn't work.

INEZ. Estelle! My glancing stream! My crystal!

ESTELLE. *Your* crystal? It's grotesque. Do you think you can fool me with that sort of talk? Everyone knows by now what I did to my baby. The crystal's shattered, but I don't care. I'm just a hollow dummy, all that's left of me is the outside—but it's not for you.

INEZ. Come to me, Estelle. You shall be whatever you like: a glancing stream, a muddy stream. And deep down in my eyes you'll see yourself just as you want to be.

ESTELLE. Oh, leave me in peace. You haven't any eyes. Oh, damn

it, isn't there anything I can do to get rid of you? I've an idea.
[*She spits in* INEZ's *face.*] There!

INEZ. Garcin, you shall pay for this.

[*A pause,* GARCIN *shrugs his shoulders and goes to* ESTELLE.]

GARCIN. So it's a man you need?

ESTELLE. Not *any* man. You.

GARCIN. No humbug now. Any man would do your business. As I happen to be here, you want me. Right!—[*He grips her shoulders.*] Mind, I'm not your sort at all, really; I'm not a young nincompoop and I don't dance the tango.

ESTELLE. I'll take you as you are. And perhaps I shall change you.

GARCIN. I doubt it. I shan't pay much attention; I've other things to think about.

ESTELLE. What things?

GARCIN. They wouldn't interest you.

ESTELLE. I'll sit on your sofa and wait for you to take some notice of me. I promise not to bother you at all.

INEZ. [*With a shrill laugh*] That's right, fawn on him, like the silly bitch you are. Grovel and cringe! And he hasn't even good looks to commend him!

ESTELLE. [*To* GARCIN] Don't listen to her. She has no eyes, no ears. She's—nothing.

GARCIN. I'll give you what I can. It doesn't amount to much. I shan't love you; I know you too well.

ESTELLE. Do you want me, anyhow?

GARCIN. Yes.

ESTELLE. I ask no more.

GARCIN. In that case—[*He bends over her.*]

INEZ. Estelle! Garcin! You must be going crazy. You're not alone. I'm here too.

GARCIN. Of course—but what does it matter?

INEZ. Under my eyes? You couldn't—couldn't do it.

ESTELLE. Why not? I often undressed with my maid looking on.

INEZ. [*Gripping* GARCIN's *arm*] Let her alone. Don't paw her with your dirty man's hands.

GARCIN. [*Thrusting her away roughly*] Take care. I'm no gentleman, and I'd have no compunction about striking a woman.

INEZ. But you promised me; you promised. I'm only asking you to keep your word.

GARCIN. Why should I, considering you were the first to break our agreement?

[INEZ *turns her back on him and retreats to the far end of the room.*]

INEZ. Very well, have it your own way. I'm the weaker party, one against two. But don't forget I'm here, and watching. I shan't take

my eyes off you, Garcin; when you're kissing her, you'll feel them
boring into you. Yes, have it your own way, make love and get
it over. We're in hell; my turn will come.

[*During the following scene she watches them without speaking.*]

GARCIN. [*Coming back to* ESTELLE *and grasping her shoulders*] Now
then. Your lips. Give me your lips.

[*A pause. He bends to kiss her, then abruptly straightens up.*]

ESTELLE. [*Indignantly*] Really! [*A pause*] Didn't I tell you not to pay
any attention to her?

GARCIN. You've got it wrong. [*Short silence*] It's Gomez; he's back
in the press-room. They've shut the windows; it must be winter
down there. Six months since I—Well, I warned you I'd be ab-
sent-minded sometimes, didn't I? They're shivering, they've kept
their coats on. Funny they should feel the cold like that, when I'm
feeling so hot. Ah, this time he's talking about me.

ESTELLE. Is it going to last long? [*Short silence*] You might at least
tell me what he's saying.

GARCIN. Nothing. Nothing worth repeating. He's a swine, that's all.
[*He listens attentively.*] A god-damned bloody swine. [*He turns to*
ESTELLE.] Let's come back to—to ourselves. Are you going to love
me?

ESTELLE. [*Smiling*] I wonder now!

GARCIN. Will you trust me?

ESTELLE. What a quaint thing to ask! Considering you'll be under
my eyes all the time, and I don't think I've much to fear from
Inez, so far as you're concerned.

GARCIN. Obviously. [*A pause. He takes his hands off* ESTELLE'S *shoulders.*] I was thinking of another kind of trust. [*Listens*] Talk away,
talk away, you swine. I'm not there to defend myself. [*To* ESTELLE]
Estelle, you must give me your trust.

ESTELLE. Oh, what a nuisance you are! I'm giving you my mouth,
my arms, my whole body—and everything could be so simple.
. . . My trust! I haven't any to give, I'm afraid, and you're making me terribly embarrassed. You must have something pretty
ghastly on your conscience to make such a fuss about my trusting
you.

GARCIN. They shot me.

ESTELLE. I know. Because you refused to fight. Well, why shouldn't
you?

GARCIN. I—I didn't exactly refuse. [*In a far-away voice*] I must say
he talks well, he makes out a good case against me, but he never
says what I should have done instead. Should I have gone to the
general and said: "General, I decline to fight"? A mug's game;
they'd have promptly locked me up. But I wanted to show my

colors, my true colors, do you understand? I wasn't going to be silenced. [*To* ESTELLE] So I—I took the train. . . . They caught me at the frontier.

ESTELLE. Where were you trying to go?

GARCIN. To Mexico. I meant to launch a pacifist newspaper down there. [*A short silence*] Well, why don't you speak?

ESTELLE. What could I say? You acted quite rightly, as you didn't want to fight. [GARCIN *makes a fretful gesture.*] But, darling, how on earth can I guess what you want me to answer?

INEZ. Can't you guess? Well, *I* can. He wants you to tell him that he bolted like a lion. For "bolt" he did, and that's what's biting him.

GARCIN. "Bolted," "went away"—we won't quarrel over words.

ESTELLE. But you *had* to run away. If you'd stayed they'd have sent you to jail, wouldn't they?

GARCIN. Of course. [*A pause*] Well, Estelle, am I a coward?

ESTELLE. How can I say? Don't be so unreasonable, darling. I can't put myself in your skin. You must decide that for yourself.

GARCIN. [*Wearily*] I can't decide.

ESTELLE. Anyhow, you must remember. You must have had reasons for acting as you did.

GARCIN. I had.

ESTELLE. Well?

GARCIN. But were they the *real* reasons?

ESTELLE. You've a twisted mind, that's your trouble. Plaguing yourself over such trifles!

GARCIN. I'd thought it all out, and I wanted to make a stand. But was that my real motive?

INEZ. Exactly. That's the question. Was that your real motive? No doubt you argued it out with yourself, you weighed the pros and cons, you found good reasons for what you did. But fear and hatred and all the dirty little instincts one keeps dark—they're motives too. So carry on, Mr. Garcin, and try to be honest with yourself—for once.

GARCIN. Do I need you to tell me that? Day and night I paced my cell, from the window to the door, from the door to the window. I pried into my heart, I sleuthed myself like a detective. By the end of it I felt as if I'd given my whole life to introspection. But always I harked back to the one thing certain—that I had acted as I did, I'd taken that train to the frontier. But why? Why? Finally I thought: My death will settle it. If I face death courageously, I'll prove I am no coward.

INEZ. And how did you face death?

GARCIN. Miserably. Rottenly. [INEZ *laughs.*] Oh, it was only a physical lapse—that might happen to anyone; I'm not ashamed of it.

Only everything's been left in suspense, forever. [*To* ESTELLE] Come here, Estelle. Look at me. I want to feel someone looking at me while they're talking about me on earth. . . . I like green eyes.

INEZ. Green eyes! Just hark to him! And you, Estelle, do you like cowards?

ESTELLE. If you knew how little I care! Coward or hero, it's all one—provided he kisses well.

GARCIN. There they are, slumped in their chairs, sucking at their cigars. Bored they look. Half-asleep. They're thinking: "Garcin's a coward." But only vaguely, dreamily. One's got to think of something. "That chap Garcin was a coward." That's what they've decided, those dear friends of mine. In six months' time they'll be saying: "Cowardly as that skunk Garcin." You're lucky, you two; no one on earth is giving you another thought. But I—I'm long in dying.

INEZ. What about your wife, Garcin?

GARCIN. Oh, didn't I tell you? She's dead.

INEZ. Dead?

GARCIN. Yes, she died just now. About two months ago.

INEZ. Of grief?

GARCIN. What else should she die of? So all is for the best, you see; the war's over, my wife's dead, and I've carved out my place in history.

[*He gives a choking sob and passes his hand over his face.* ESTELLE *catches his arm.*]

ESTELLE. My poor darling! Look at me. Please look. Touch me. Touch me. [*She takes his hand and puts it on her neck.*] There! Keep your hand there. [GARCIN *makes a fretful movement.*] No, don't move. Why trouble what those men are thinking? They'll die off one by one. Forget them. There's only me, now.

GARCIN. But *they* won't forget *me*, not they! They'll die, but others will come after them to carry on the legend. I've left my fate in their hands.

ESTELLE. You think too much, that's your trouble.

GARCIN. What else is there to do now? I was a man of action once. . . . Oh, if only I could be with them again, for just one day— I'd fling their lie in their teeth. But I'm locked out; they're passing judgment on my life without troubling about me, and they're right, because I'm dead. Dead and done with. [*Laughs*] A back number.

[*A short pause*]

ESTELLE. [*Gently*] GARCIN.

GARCIN. Still there? Now listen! I want you to do me a service. No, don't shrink away. I know it must seem strange to you, having someone asking you for help; you're not used to that. But if you'll make the effort, if you'll only *will* it hard enough, I dare say we can really love each other. Look at it this way. A thousand of them are proclaiming I'm a coward; but what do numbers matter? If there's someone, just one person, to say quite positively I did not run away, that I'm not the sort who runs away, that I'm brave and decent and the rest of it—well, that one person's faith would save me. Will you have that faith in me? Then I shall love you and cherish you for ever. Estelle—will you?

ESTELLE. [*Laughing*] Oh, you dear silly man, do you think I could love a coward?

GARCIN. But just now you said—

ESTELLE. I was only teasing you. I like men, my dear, who're real men, with tough skin and strong hands. You haven't a coward's chin, or a coward's mouth, or a coward's voice, or a coward's hair. And it's for your mouth, your hair, your voice, I love you.

GARCIN. Do you mean this? *Really* mean it?

ESTELLE. Shall I swear it?

GARCIN. Then I snap my fingers at them all, those below and those in here. Estelle, we shall climb out of hell. [INEZ *gives a shrill laugh. He breaks off and stares at her.*] What's that?

INEZ. [*Still laughing*] But she doesn't mean a word of what she says. How can you be such a simpleton? "Estelle, am I a coward?" As if she cared a damn either way.

ESTELLE. Inez, how dare you? [*To* GARCIN] Don't listen to her. If you want me to have faith in you, you must begin by trusting me.

INEZ. That's right! That's right! Trust away! She wants a man—that far you can trust her—she wants a man's arm round her waist, a man's smell, a man's eyes glowing with desire. And that's all she wants. She'd assure you you were God Almighty if she thought it would give you pleasure.

GARCIN. Estelle, is this true? Answer me. Is it true?

ESTELLE. What do you expect me to say? Don't you realize how maddening it is to have to answer questions one can't make head or tail of? [*She stamps her foot.*] You do make things difficult. . . . Anyhow, I'd love you just the same, even if you were a coward. Isn't that enough?

[*A short pause*]

GARCIN. [*To the two women*] You disgust me, both of you. [*He goes towards the door.*]

ESTELLE. What are you up to?

GARCIN. I'm going.

INEZ. [*Quickly*] You won't get far. The door is locked.

GARCIN. I'll make them open it. [*He presses the bell-push. The bell does not ring.*]

ESTELLE. Please! Please!

INEZ. [*To* ESTELLE] Don't worry, my pet. The bell doesn't work.

GARCIN. I tell you they shall open. [*Drums on the door*] I can't endure it any longer, I'm through with you both. [ESTELLE *runs to him; he pushes her away.*] Go away. You're even fouler than she. I won't let myself get bogged in your eyes. You're soft and slimy. Ugh! [*Bangs on the door again*] Like an octopus. Like a quagmire.

ESTELLE. I beg you, oh, I beg you not to leave me. I'll promise not to speak again, I won't trouble you in any way—but don't go. I daren't be left alone with Inez, now she's shown her claws.

GARCIN. Look after yourself. I never asked you to come here.

ESTELLE. Oh, how mean you are! Yes, it's quite true you're a coward.

INEZ. [*Going up to* ESTELLE] Well, my little sparrow fallen from the nest, I hope you're satisfied now. You spat in my face—playing up to him, of course—and we had a tiff on his account. But he's going, and a good riddance it will be. We two women will have the place to ourselves.

ESTELLE. You won't gain anything. If that door opens, I'm going, too.

INEZ. Where?

ESTELLE. I don't care where. As far from you as I can.

[GARCIN *has been drumming on the door while they talk.*]

GARCIN. Open the door! Open, blast you! I'll endure anything, your red-hot tongs and molten lead, your racks and prongs and garrotes—all your fiendish gadgets, everything that burns and flays and tears—I'll put up with any torture you impose. Anything, anything would be better than this agony of mind, this creeping pain that gnaws and fumbles and caresses one and never hurts quite enough. [*He grips the door-knob and rattles it.*] Now will you open? [*The door flies open with a jerk, and he just avoids falling.*] Ah! [*A long silence*]

INEZ. Well, Garcin? You're free to go.

GARCIN. [*Meditatively*] Now I wonder why that door opened.

INEZ. What are you waiting for? Hurry up and go.

GARCIN. I shall not go.

INEZ. And you, Estelle? [ESTELLE *does not move.* INEZ *bursts out laughing.*] So what? Which shall it be? Which of the three of us will leave? The barrier's down, why are we waiting? . . . But what a situation! It's a scream! We're—inseparables!

[ESTELLE *springs at her from behind.*]

ESTELLE. Inseparables? Garcin, come and lend a hand. Quickly. We'll push her out and slam the door on her. That'll teach her a lesson.

INEZ. [*Struggling with* ESTELLE] Estelle! I beg you, let me stay. I won't go, I won't go! Not into the passage.

GARCIN. Let go of her.

ESTELLE. You're crazy. She hates you.

GARCIN. It's because of her I'm staying here.

[ESTELLE *releases* INEZ *and stares dumbfoundedly at* GARCIN.]

INEZ. Because of me? [*Pause*] All right, shut the door. It's ten times hotter here since it opened. [GARCIN *goes to the door and shuts it.*] Because of me, you said?

GARCIN. Yes. *You*, anyhow, know what it means to be a coward.

INEZ. Yes, I know.

GARCIN. And you know what wickedness is, and shame, and fear. There were days when you peered into yourself, into the secret places of your heart, and what you saw there made you faint with horror. And then, next day, you didn't know what to make of it, you couldn't interpret the horror you had glimpsed the day before. Yes, you know what evil *costs*. And when you say I'm a coward, you know from experience what that means. Is that so?

INEZ. Yes.

GARCIN. So it's you whom I have to convince; you are of my kind. Did you suppose I meant to go? No, I couldn't leave you here, gloating over my defeat, with all those thoughts about me running in your head.

INEZ. Do you really wish to convince me?

GARCIN. That's the one and only thing I wish for now. I can't hear them any longer, you know. Probably that means they're through with me. For good and all. The curtain's down, nothing of me is left on earth—not even the name of coward. So, Inez, we're alone. Only you two remain to give a thought to me. She—she doesn't count. It's you who matter; you who hate me. If you'll have faith in me I'm saved.

INEZ. It won't be easy. Have a look at me. I'm a hard-headed woman.

GARCIN. I'll give you all the time that's needed.

INEZ. Yes, we've lots of time in hand. *All* time.

GARCIN. [*Putting his hands on her shoulders*] Listen! Each man has an aim in life, a leading motive; that's so, isn't it? Well, I didn't give a damn for wealth, or for love. I aimed at being a real man. A tough, as they say. I staked everything on the same horse. . . . Can one possibly be a coward when one's deliberately courted danger at every turn? And can one judge a life by a single action?

INEZ. Why not? For thirty years you dreamt you were a hero, and condoned a thousand petty lapses—because a hero, of course, can do no wrong. An easy method, obviously. Then a day came when you were up against it, the red light of real danger—and you took the train to Mexico.

GARCIN. I "dreamt," you say. It was no dream. When I chose the hardest path, I made my choice deliberately. A man is what he wills himself to be.

INEZ. Prove it. Prove it was no dream. It's what one does, and nothing else, that shows the stuff one's made of.

GARCIN. I died too soon. I wasn't allowed time to—to do my deeds.

INEZ. One always dies too soon—or too late. And yet one's whole life is complete at that moment, with a line drawn neatly under it, ready for the summing up. You are—your life, and nothing else.

GARCIN. What a poisonous woman you are! With an answer for everything.

INEZ. Now then! Don't lose heart. It shouldn't be so hard, convincing me. Pull yourself together, man, rake up some arguments. [GARCIN *shrugs his shoulders.*] Ah, wasn't I right when I said you were vulnerable? Now you're going to pay the price, and what a price! You're a coward, Garcin, because I wish it. I wish it—do you hear? —I wish it. And yet, just look at me, see how weak I am, a mere breath on the air, a gaze observing you, a formless thought that thinks you. [*He walks towards her, opening his hands.*] Ah, they're open now, those big hands, those coarse, man's hands! But what do you hope to do? You can't throttle thoughts with hands. So you've no choice, you must convince me, and you're at my mercy.

ESTELLE. Garcin!

GARCIN. What?

ESTELLE. Revenge yourself.

GARCIN. How?

ESTELLE. Kiss me, darling—then you'll hear her squeal.

GARCIN. That's true, Inez. I'm at your mercy, but you're at mine as well. [*He bends over* ESTELLE. INEZ *gives a little cry.*]

INEZ. Oh, you coward, you weakling, running to women to console you!

ESTELLE. That's right, Inez. Squeal away.

INEZ. What a lovely pair you make! If you could see his big paw splayed out on your back, rucking up your skin and creasing the silk. Be careful, though! He's perspiring, his hand will leave a blue stain on your dress.

ESTELLE. Squeal away, Inez, squeal away! . . . Hug me tight, darling; tighter still—that'll finish her off, and a good thing too!

INEZ. Yes, Garcin, she's right. Carry on with it, press her to you till you feel your bodies melting into each other; a lump of warm, throbbing flesh. . . . Love's a grand solace, isn't it, my friend? Deep and dark as sleep. But I'll see you don't sleep.

[GARCIN *makes a slight movement.*]

ESTELLE. Don't listen to her. Press your lips to my mouth. Oh, I'm yours, yours, yours.

INEZ. Well, what are you waiting for? Do as you're told. What a lovely scene: coward Garcin holding baby-killer Estelle in his man-

ly arms! Make your stakes, everyone. Will coward Garcin kiss
the lady, or won't he dare? What's the betting? I'm watching you,
everybody's watching, I'm a crowd all by myself. Do you hear
the crowd? Do you hear them muttering, Garcin? Mumbling and
muttering. "Coward! Coward! Coward! Coward!"—that's what
they're saying. . . . It's no use trying to escape, I'll never let you
go. What do you hope to get from her silly lips? Forgetfulness?
But I shan't forget you, not I! "It's I you must convince." So
come to me. I'm waiting. Come along, now. . . . Look how obedient he is, like a well-trained dog who comes when his mistress
calls. You can't hold him, and you never will.

GARCIN. Will night never come?

INEZ. Never.

GARCIN. You will always see me?

INEZ. Always.

[GARCIN *moves away from* ESTELLE *and takes some steps across
the room. He goes to the bronze ornament.*]

GARCIN. This bronze. [*Strokes it thoughtfully*] Yes, now's the moment; I'm looking at this thing on the mantelpiece, and I understand that I'm in hell. I tell you, everything's been thought out
beforehand. They knew I'd stand at the fireplace stroking this
thing of bronze, with all those eyes intent on me. Devouring me.
[*He swings round abruptly.*] What? Only two of you? I thought
there were more; many more. [*Laughs*] So this is hell. I'd never
have believed it. You remember all we were told about the torture-
chambers, the fire and brimstone, the "burning marl."[2] Old wives'
tales! There's no need for red-hot pokers. Hell is—other people!

ESTELLE. My darling! Please—

GARCIN. [*Thrusting her away*] No, let me be. She is between us. I
cannot love you when she's watching.

ESTELLE. Right! In that case, I'll stop her watching. [*She picks up
the paper-knife from the table, rushes at* INEZ, *and stabs her several
times.*]

INEZ. [*Struggling and laughing*] But, you crazy creature, what do
you think you're doing? You know quite well I'm dead.

ESTELLE. Dead?

[*She drops the knife. A pause.* INEZ *picks up the knife and
jabs herself with it regretfully.*]

INEZ. Dead! Dead! Dead! Knives, poison, ropes—all useless. It has
happened already, do you understand? Once and for all. So here
we are, forever. [*Laughs*]

ESTELLE. [*With a peal of laughter*] Forever. My God, how funny!
Forever.

GARCIN. [*Looks at the two women, and joins in the laughter*] For

2. earth.

ever, and ever, and ever.

[*They slump onto their respective sofas. A long silence. Their
laughter dies away and they gaze at each other.*]

GARCIN. Well, well, let's get on with it. . . .

CURTAIN

ALBERT CAMUS

(1913–1960)

The Renegade (Le Renégat)*

"What a jumble! What a jumble! I must tidy up my mind. Since
they cut out my tongue, another tongue, it seems, has been constantly wagging somewhere in my skull, something has been talking,
or someone, that suddenly falls silent and then it all begins again—
oh, I hear too many things I never utter, what a jumble, and if I
open my mouth it's like pebbles rattling together. Order and method, the tongue says, and then goes on talking of other matters
simultaneously—yes, I always longed for order. At least one thing
is certain, I am waiting for the missionary who is to come and take
my place. Here I am on the trail, an hour away from Taghâsa,
hidden in a pile of rocks, sitting on my old rifle. Day is breaking over
the desert, it's still very cold, soon it will be too hot, this country
drives men mad and I've been here I don't know how many years.
. . . No, just a little longer. The missionary is to come this morning,
or this evening. I've heard he'll come with a guide, perhaps they'll
have but one camel between them. I'll wait, I am waiting, it's only
the cold making me shiver. Just be patient a little longer, lousy
slave!

But I have been patient for so long. When I was home on that
high plateau of the Massif Central,[1] my coarse father, my boorish
mother, the wine, the pork soup every day, the wine above all, sour
and cold, and the long winter, the frigid wind, the snowdrifts, the
revolting bracken—oh, I wanted to get away, leave them all at once
and begin to live at last, in the sunlight, with fresh water. I believed
the priest, he spoke to me of the seminary, he tutored me daily, he
had plenty of time in that Protestant region, where he used to hug
the walls as he crossed the village. He told me of the future and of
the sun, Catholicism is the sun, he used to say, and he would get

* 1957. Copyright 1958 by Alfred A.
Knopf, Inc. Reprinted from *Exile and
the Kingdom* by Albert Camus, translated by Justin O'Brien, by permission
of Alfred A. Knopf, Inc.

1. the mountainous region that covers
one fifth of the area of France.

me to read, he beat Latin into my hard head ('The kid's bright but he's pig-headed'), my head was so hard that, despite all my falls, it has never once bled in my life: 'Bull-headed,' my pig of a father used to say. At the seminary they were proud as punch, a recruit from the Protestant region was a victory, they greeted me like the sun at Austerlitz.[2] The sun was pale and feeble, to be sure, because of the alcohol, they have drunk sour wine and the children's teeth are set on edge, *gra gra*,[3] one really ought to kill one's father, but after all there's no danger that *he*'ll hurl himself into missionary work since he's now long dead, the tart wine eventually cut through his stomach, so there's nothing left but to kill the missionary.

I have something to settle with him and with his teachers, with my teachers who deceived me, with the whole of lousy Europe, everybody deceived me. Missionary work, that's all they could say, go out to the savages and tell them: 'Here is my Lord, just look at him, he never strikes or kills, he issues his orders in a low voice, he turns the other cheek, he's the greatest of masters, choose him, just see how much better he's made me, offend me and you will see.' Yes, I believed, *gra gra*, and I felt better, I had put on weight, I was almost handsome, I wanted to be offended. When we would walk out in tight black rows, in summer, under Grenoble's hot sun and would meet girls in cotton dresses, *I* didn't look away, I despised them, I waited for them to offend me, and sometimes they would laugh. At such times I would think: 'Let them strike me and spit in my face,' but their laughter, to tell the truth, came to the same thing, bristling with teeth and quips that tore me to shreds, the offense and the suffering were sweet to me! My confessor couldn't understand when I used to heap accusations on myself: 'No, no, there's good in you!' Good! There was nothing but sour wine in me, and that was all for the best, how can a man become better if he's not bad, I had grasped that in everything they taught me. That's the only thing I did grasp, a single idea, and, pig-headed bright boy, I carried it to its logical conclusion, I went out of my way for punishments, I groused at the normal, in short I too wanted to be an example in order to be noticed and so that after noticing me people would give credit to what had made me better, through me praise my Lord.

Fierce sun! It's rising, the desert is changing, it has lost its mountain-cyclamen color, O my mountain, and the snow, the soft enveloping snow, no, it's a rather grayish yellow, the ugly moment before the great resplendence. Nothing, still nothing from here to the horizon over yonder where the plateau disappears in a circle of

2. Here, in 1805, Napoleon defeated the Austrians and Russians.
3. an inarticulate sound.

still soft colors. Behind me, the trail climbs to the dune hiding Taghâsa, whose iron name has been beating in my head for so many years. The first to mention it to me was the half-blind old priest who had retired to our monastery, but why do I say the first, he was the only one, and it wasn't the city of salt, the white walls under the blinding sun, that struck me in his account but the cruelty of the savage inhabitants and the town closed to all outsiders, only one of those who had tried to get in, one alone, to his knowledge, had lived to relate what he had seen. They had whipped him and driven him out into the desert after having put salt on his wounds and in his mouth, he had met nomads who for once were compassionate, a stroke of luck, and since then I had been dreaming about his tale, about the fire of the salt and the sky, about the House of the Fetish and his slaves, could anything more barbarous, more exciting be imagined, yes, that was my mission and I had to go and reveal to them my Lord.

They all expatiated on the subject at the seminary to discourage me, pointing out the necessity of waiting, that it was not missionary country, that I wasn't ready yet, I had to prepare myself specially, know who I was, and even then I had to go through tests, then they would see! But go on waiting, ah, no!—yes, if they insisted, for the special preparation and the tryouts because they took place at Algiers and brought me closer, but for all the rest I shook my pig-head and repeated the same thing, to get among the most barbarous and live as they did, to show them at home, and even in the House of the Fetish, through example, that my Lord's truth would prevail. They would offend me, of course, but I was not afraid of offenses, they were essential to the demonstration, and as a result of the way I endured them I'd get the upper hand of those savages like a strong sun. Strong, yes, that was the word I constantly had on the tip of my tongue, I dreamed of absolute power, the kind that makes people kneel down, that forces the adversary to capitulate, converts him in short, and the blinder, the crueler he is, the more he's sure of himself, mired in his own conviction, the more his consent establishes the royalty of whoever brought about his collapse. Converting good folk who had strayed somewhat was the shabby ideal of our priests, I despised them for daring so little when they could do so much, they lacked faith and I had it, I wanted to be acknowledged by the torturers themselves, to fling them on their knees and make them say: 'O Lord, here is thy victory,' to rule in short by the sheer force of words over an army of the wicked. Oh, I was sure of reasoning logically on that subject, never quite sure of myself otherwise, but once I get an idea I don't let go of it, that's my strong point, yes the strong point of the fellow they all pitied!

The sun has risen higher, my forehead is beginning to burn. Around me the stones are beginning to crack open with a dull sound, the only cool thing is the rifle's barrel, cool as the fields, as the evening rain long ago when the soup was simmering, they would wait for me, my father and mother who would occasionally smile at me, perhaps I loved them. But that's all in the past, a film of heat is beginning to rise from the trail, come on, missionary, I'm waiting for you, now I know how to answer the message, my new masters taught me, and I know they are right, you have to settle accounts with that question of love. When I fled the seminary in Algiers I had a different idea of the savages and only one detail of my imaginings was true, they are cruel. I had robbed the treasurer's office, cast off my habit, crossed the Atlas,[4] the upper plateaus and the desert, the bus-driver of the Trans-Sahara line made fun of me: 'Don't go there,' he too, what had got into them all, and the gusts of sand for hundreds of wind-blown kilometers, progressing and backing in the face of the wind, then the mountains again made up of black peaks and ridges sharp as steel, and after them it took a guide to go out on the endless sea of brown pebbles, screaming with heat, burning with the fires of a thousand mirrors, to the spot on the confines of the white country and the land of the blacks where stands the city of salt. And the money the guide stole from me, ever naïve I had shown it to him, but he left me on the trail—just about here, it so happens —after having struck me: 'Dog, there's the way, the honor's all mine, go ahead, go on, they'll show you,' and they did show me, oh yes, they're like the sun that never stops, except at night, beating sharply and proudly, that is beating me hard at this moment, too hard, with a multitude of lances burst from the ground, oh shelter, yes shelter, under the big rock, before everything gets muddled.

The shade here is good. How can anyone live in the city of salt, in the hollow of that basin full of dazzling heat? On each of the sharp right-angle walls cut out with a pickax and coarsely planed, the gashes left by the pickax bristle with blinding scales, pale scattered sand yellows them somewhat except when the wind dusts the upright walls and terraces, then everything shines with dazzling whiteness under a sky likewise dusted even to its blue rind. I was going blind during those days when the stationary fire would crackle for hours on the surface of the white terraces that all seemed to meet as if, in the remote past, they had all together tackled a mountain of salt, flattened it first, and then had hollowed out streets, the insides of houses and windows directly in the mass, or as if—yes, this is more like it, they had cut out their white, burning hell with a powerful jet of boiling water just to show that they could

4. a range of mountains in Morocco, Algeria, and Tunisia.

live where no one ever could, thirty days' travel from any living thing, in this hollow in the middle of the desert where the heat of day prevents any contact among creatures, separates them by a portcullis of invisible flames and of searing crystals, where without transition the cold of night congeals them individually in their rock-salt shells, nocturnal dwellers in a dried-up icefloe, black Eskimoes suddenly shivering in their cubical igloos. Black because they wear long black garments, and the salt that collects even under their nails, that they continue tasting bitterly and swallowing during the sleep of those polar nights, the salt they drink in the water from the only spring in the hollow of a dazzling groove, often spots their dark garments with something like the trail of snails after a rain.

Rain, O Lord, just one real rain, long and hard, rain from your heaven! Then at last the hideous city, gradually eaten away, would slowly and irresistibly cave in and, utterly melted in a slimy torrent, would carry off its savage inhabitants toward the sands. Just one rain, Lord! But what do I mean, what Lord, they are the lords and masters! They rule over their sterile homes, over their black slaves that they work to death in the mines and each slab of salt that is cut out is worth a man in the region to the south, they pass by, silent, wearing their mourning veils in the mineral whiteness of the streets, and at night, when the whole town looks like a milky phantom, they stoop down and enter the shade of their homes, where the salt walls shine dimly. They sleep with a weightless sleep and, as soon as they wake, they give orders, they strike, they say they are a united people, that their god is the true god, and that one must obey. They are my masters, they are ignorant of pity and, like masters, they want to be alone, to progress alone, to rule alone, because they alone had the daring to build in the salt and the sands a cold torrid city. And I . . .

What a jumble when the heat rises, I'm sweating, they never do, now the shade itself is heating up, I feel the sun on the stone above me, it's striking, striking like a hammer on all the stones and it's the music, the vast music of noon, air and stones vibrating over hundreds of kilometers, *gra*, I hear the silence as I did once before. Yes, it was the same silence, years ago, that greeted me when the guards led me to them, in the sunlight, in the center of the square, whence the concentric terraces rose gradually toward the lid of hard blue sky sitting on the edge of the basin. There I was, thrown on my knees in the hollow of that white shield, my eyes corroded by the swords of salt and fire issuing from all the walls, pale with fatigue, my ear bleeding from the blow given by my guide, and they, tall and black, looked at me without saying a word. The day was at its midcourse. Under the blows of the iron sun the sky resounded at length, a sheet of white-hot tin, it was the same silence, and they stared at me, time passed, they kept on staring at me, and I couldn't face their stares, I panted more and more violently, eventually I wept, and suddenly they turned their backs on me in silence and all together went off in the same direction. On my knees, all I could see, in the red-and-black sandals, was their feet sparkling with salt as they raised the long black gowns, the tip rising somewhat, the heel striking the ground lightly, and when the square was empty I was dragged to the House of the Fetish.

Squatting, as I am today in the shelter of the rock and the fire above my head pierces the rock's thickness, I spent several days within the dark of the House of the Fetish, somewhat higher than the others, surrounded by a wall of salt, but without windows, full of a sparkling night. Several days, and I was given a basin of brackish water and some grain that was thrown before me the way chickens are fed, I picked it up. By day the door remained closed and yet the darkness became less oppressive, as if the irresistible sun managed to flow through the masses of salt. No lamp, but by feeling my way along the walls I touched garlands of dried palms decorating the walls and, at the end, a small door, coarsely fitted, of which I could make out the bolt with my fingertips. Several days, long after—I couldn't count the days or the hours, but my handful of grain had been thrown me some ten times and I had dug out a hole for my excrements that I covered up in vain, the stench of an animal den hung on anyway—long after, yes, the door opened wide and they came in.

One of them came toward me where I was squatting in a corner. I felt the burning salt against my cheek, I smelled the dusty scent of the palms, I watched him approach. He stopped a yard away from me, he stared at me in silence, a signal, and I stood up, he stared at me with his metallic eyes that shone without expression in his brown horse-face, then he raised his hand. Still impassive, he seized me by the lower lip, which he twisted slowly until he tore my flesh and, without letting go, made me turn around and back up to the center of the room, he pulled on my lip to make me fall on my knees there, mad with pain and my mouth bleeding, then he turned away to join the others standing against the walls. They watched me moaning in the unbearable heat of the unbroken daylight that came in the wide-open door, and in that light suddenly appeared the Sorcerer with his raffia hair, his chest covered with a breastplate of pearls, his legs bare under a straw skirt, wearing a mask of reeds and wire with two square openings for the eyes. He was followed by musicians and women wearing heavy motley gowns that revealed nothing of their bodies. They danced in front of the door at the end, but a coarse, scarcely rhythmical dance, they just barely moved, and finally the Sorcerer opened the little door behind me, the masters did not stir, they were watching me, I turned around and saw the Fetish, his double ax-head, his iron nose twisted like a snake.

I was carried before him, to the foot of the pedestal, I was made to drink a black, bitter, bitter water, and at once my head began to burn, I was laughing, that's the offense, I have been offended. They undressed me, shaved my head and body, washed me in oil, beat my face with cords dipped in water and salt, and I laughed and turned my head away, but each time two women would take me by the ears and offer my face to the Sorcerer's blows while I could see only his square eyes, I was still laughing, covered with blood. They stopped, no one spoke but me, the jumble was beginning in my head, then they lifted me up and forced me to raise my eyes toward the Fetish, I had ceased laughing. I knew that I was now consecrated to him to serve him, adore him, no, I was not laughing any more, fear and pain stifled me. And there, in that white house, between those walls that the sun was assiduously burning on the outside, my face taut, my memory exhausted, yes, I tried to pray to the Fetish, he was all there was and even his horrible face was less horrible than the rest of the world. Then it was that my ankles were tied with a cord that permitted just one step, they danced again, but this time in front of the Fetish, the masters went out one by one.

The door once closed behind them, the music again, and the Sorcerer lighted a bark fire around which he pranced, his long silhouette broke on the angles of the white walls, fluttered on the flat surfaces, filled the room with dancing shadows. He traced a rectangle in a corner to which the women dragged me, I felt their dry and gentle hands, they set before me a bowl of water and a little pile of grain and pointed to the Fetish, I grasped that I was to keep my eyes fixed on him. Then the Sorcerer called them one after the other over to the fire, he beat some of them who moaned and who then went and prostrated themselves before the Fetish my god, while the Sorcerer kept on dancing and he made them all leave the room until only one was left, quite young, squatting near the musicians and not yet beaten. He held her by a shock of hair which he kept twisting around his wrist, she dropped backward with eyes popping until she finally fell on her back. Dropping her, the Sorcerer screamed, the musicians turned to the wall, while behind the square-eyed mask the scream rose to an impossible pitch, and the woman rolled on the ground in a sort of fit and, at last on all fours, her head hidden in her locked arms, she too screamed, but with a hollow, muffled sound, and in this position, without ceasing to scream and to look at the Fetish, the Sorcerer took her nimbly and nastily, without the woman's face being visible, for it was covered with the heavy folds of her garment. And, wild as a result of the solitude, I screamed too, yes, howled with fright toward the Fetish until a kick hurled me against the wall, biting the salt as I am biting this rock today with my tongueless mouth, while waiting for the man I must kill.

Now the sun has gone a little beyond the middle of the sky. Through the breaks in the rock I can see the hole it makes in the white-hot metal of the sky, a mouth voluble as mine, constantly vomiting rivers of flame over the colorless desert. On the trail in front of me, nothing, no cloud of dust on the horizon, behind me they must be looking for me, no, not yet, it's only in the late afternoon that they opened the door and I could go out a little, after having spent the day cleaning the House of the Fetish, set out fresh offerings, and in the evening the ceremony would begin, in which I was sometimes beaten, at others not, but always I served the Fetish, the Fetish whose image is engraved in iron in my memory and now in my hope also. Never had a god so possessed or enslaved me, my whole life day and night was devoted to him, and pain and the absence of pain, wasn't that joy, were due him and even, yes, desire, as a result of being present, almost every day, at that impersonal and nasty act which I heard without seeing it inasmuch as I now had to face the wall or else be beaten. But, my face up against the salt, obsessed by the bestial shadows moving on the wall, I listened to the long scream, my throat was dry, a burning sexless desire squeezed my temples and my belly as in a vise. Thus the days followed one another, I barely distinguished them as if they had liquefied in the torrid heat and the treacherous reverberation from the walls of salt, time had become merely a vague lapping of waves in which there would burst out, at regular intervals, screams of pain or possession, a long ageless day in which the Fetish ruled as this fierce sun does over my house of rocks, and now, as I did then, I weep with unhappiness and longing, a wicked hope consumes me, I want to betray, I lick the barrel of my gun and its soul inside, its soul, only guns have souls—oh, yes! the day they cut out my tongue, I learned to adore the immortal soul of hatred!

What a jumble, what a rage, *gra gra*, drunk with heat and wrath, lying prostrate on my gun. Who's panting here? I can't endure this endless heat, this waiting, I must kill him. Not a bird, not a blade of grass, stone, an arid desire, their screams, this tongue within me talking, and since they mutilated me, the long, flat, deserted suffering deprived even of the water of night, the night of which I would dream, when locked in with the god, in my den of salt. Night alone with its cool stars and dark fountains could save me, carry me off at last from the wicked gods of mankind, but ever locked up I could not contemplate it. If the newcomer tarries more, I shall see it at least rise from the desert and sweep over the sky, a cold golden vine that will hang from the dark zenith and from which I can drink at length, moisten this black dried hole that no muscle of live flexible flesh revives now, forget at last that day when madness took away my tongue.

How hot it was, really hot, the salt was melting or so it seemed to me, the air was corroding my eyes, and the Sorcerer came in without his mask. Almost naked under grayish tatters, a new woman followed him and her face, covered with a tattoo reproducing the mask of the Fetish, expressed only an idol's ugly stupor. The only thing alive about her was her thin flat body that flopped at the foot of the god when the Sorcerer opened the door of the niche. Then he went out without looking at me, the heat rose, I didn't stir, the Fetish looked at me over that motionless body whose muscles stirred gently and the woman's idol-face didn't change when I approached. Only her eyes enlarged as she stared at me, my feet touched hers, the heat then began to shriek, and the idol, without a word, still staring at me with her dilated eyes, gradually slipped onto her back, slowly drew her legs up and raised them as she gently spread her knees. But, immediately afterward, *gra*, the Sorcerer was lying in wait for me, they all entered and tore me from the woman, beat me dreadfully on the sinful place, what sin, I'm laughing, where is it and where is virtue, they clapped me against a wall, a hand of steel gripped my jaws, another opened my mouth, pulled on my tongue until it bled, was it I screaming with that bestial scream, a cool cutting caress, yes cool at last, went over my tongue. When I came to, I was alone in the night, glued to the wall, covered with hardened blood, a gag of strange-smelling dry grasses filled my mouth, it had stopped bleeding, but it was vacant and in that absence the only living thing was a tormenting pain. I wanted to rise, I fell back, happy, desperately happy to die at last, death too is cool and its shadow hides no god.

I did not die, a new feeling of hatred stood up one day, at the same time I did, walked toward the door of the niche, opened it, closed it behind me, I hated my people, the Fetish was there and from the depth of the hole in which I was I did more than pray to him, I believed in him and denied all I had believed up to then. Hail! he was strength and power, he could be destroyed but not converted, he stared over my head with his empty, rusty eyes. Hail! he was the master, the only lord, whose indisputable attribute was malice, there are no good masters. For the first time, as a result of offenses, my whole body crying out a single pain, I surrendered to him and approved his maleficent order, I adored in him the evil principle of the world. A prisoner of his kingdom—the sterile city carved out of a mountain of salt, divorced from nature, deprived of those rare and fleeting flowerings of the desert, preserved from those strokes of chance or marks of affection such as an unexpected cloud or a brief violent downpour that are familiar even to the sun or the sands, the city of order in short, right angles, square rooms, rigid men—I freely became its tortured, hate-filled citizen, I repudiated the long history that had been taught me. I had been misled, solely the reign of malice was devoid of defects, I had been misled, truth is square, heavy, thick, it does not admit distinctions, gold is an idle dream, an intention constantly postponed and pursued with exhausting effort, a limit never reached, its reign is impossible. Only evil can reach its limits and reign absolutely, it must be served to establish its visible kingdom, then we shall see, but what does 'then' mean, only evil is present, down with Europe, reason, honor, and the cross. Yes, I was to be converted to the religion of my masters, yes indeed, I was a slave, but if I too become vicious I cease to be a slave, despite my shackled feet and my mute mouth. Oh, this heat is driving me crazy, the desert cries out everywhere under the unbearable light, and he, the Lord of kindness, whose very name revolts me, I disown him, for I know him now. He dreamed and wanted to lie, his tongue was cut out so that his word would no longer be able to deceive the world, he was pierced with nails even in his head, his poor head, like mine now, what a jumble, how weak I am, and the earth didn't tremble, I am sure, it was not a righteous man they had killed, I refuse to believe it, there are no righteous men but only evil masters who bring about the reign of relentless truth. Yes, the Fetish alone has power, he is the sole god of this world, hatred is his commandment, the source of all life, the cool water, cool like mint that chills the mouth and burns the stomach.

Then it was that I changed, they realized it, I would kiss their hands when I met them, I was on their side, never wearying of admiring them, I trusted them, I hoped they would mutilate my people as they had mutilated me. And when I learned that the missionary was to come, I knew what I was to do. That day like all the others, the same blinding daylight that had been going on so long! Late in the afternoon a guard was suddenly seen running along the edge of the basin, and, a few minutes later, I was dragged to the House of the Fetish and the door closed. One of them held me on the ground in the dark, under threat of his cross-shaped sword, and the silence lasted for a long time until a strange sound filled the ordinarily peaceful town, voices that it took me some time to recognize because they were speaking my language, but as soon as they rang out the point of the sword was lowered toward **my** eyes, my guard stared at me in silence. Then two voices came closer and I can still hear them, one asking why that house was guarded and whether they should break in the door, Lieutenant, the other said: 'No' sharply, then added, after a moment, that an agreement had been reached, that the town accepted a garrison of twenty men on condition that they would camp outside the walls and respect the customs. The private laughed, 'They're knuckling under,' but the officer didn't know, for the first time in any case they were willing to receive someone to take care of the children and that would be the chaplain, later on they would see about the territory. The other said they would cut off the chaplain's you know what if the soldiers were not there. 'Oh, no!' the officer answered. 'In fact, Father Beffort will come before the garrison; he'll be here in two days.' That was all I heard, motionless, lying under the sword, I was in pain, a wheel of needles and knives was whirling in me. They were crazy, they were crazy, they were allowing a hand to be laid on the city, on their invincible power, on the true god, and the fellow who was to come would not have his tongue cut out, he would show off his insolent goodness without paying for it, without enduring any offense. The reign of evil would be postponed, there would be doubt again, again time would be wasted dreaming of the impossible good, wearing oneself out in fruitless efforts instead of hastening the realization of the only possible kingdom and I looked at the sword threatening me, O sole power to rule over the world! O power, and the city gradually emptied of its sounds, the door finally opened, I remained alone, burned and bitter, with the Fetish, and I swore to him to save my new faith, my true masters, my despotic God, to betray well, whatever it might cost me.

Gra, the heat is abating a little, the stone has ceased to vibrate, I can go out of my hole, watch the desert gradually take on yellow and ocher tints that will soon be mauve. Last night I waited until they were asleep, I had blocked the lock on the door, I went out with the same step as usual, measured by the cord, I knew the streets, I knew where to get the old rifle, what gate wasn't guarded, and I reached here just as the night was beginning to fade around a handful of stars while the desert was getting a little darker. And now it seems days and days that I have been crouching in these rocks. Soon, soon, I hope he comes soon! In a moment they'll begin to look for me, they'll speed over the trails in all directions, they won't know that I left for them and to serve them better, my legs are weak, drunk with hunger and hate. Oh! over there, *gra*, at the end of the trail, two camels are growing bigger, ambling along, already multiplied by short shadows, they are running with that lively and dreamy gait they always have. Here they are, here at last!

Quick, the rifle, and I load it quickly. O Fetish, my god over yonder, may your power be preserved, may the offense be multipled, may hate rule pitilessly over a world of the damned, may the wicked forever be masters, may the kingdom come, where in a single city of salt and iron black tyrants will enslave and possess without pity! And now, *gra gra*, fire on pity, fire on impotence and its charity, fire on all that postpones the coming of evil, fire twice, and there they are toppling over, falling, and the camels flee toward the horizon, where a geyser of black birds has just risen in the unchanged sky. I laugh, I laugh, the fellow is writhing in his detested habit, he is raising his head a little, he sees me—me his all-powerful shackled master, why does he smile at me, I'll crush that smile! How pleasant is the sound of a rifle butt on the face of goodness, today, today at last, all is consummated and everywhere in the desert, even hours away from here, jackals sniff the nonexistent wind, then set out in a patient trot toward the feast of carrion awaiting them. Victory! I raise my arms to a heaven moved to pity, a lavender shadow is just barely suggested on the opposite side, O nights of Europe, home, childhood, why must I weep in the moment of triumph?

He stirred, no the sound comes from somewhere else, and from the other direction here they come rushing like a flight of of dark birds, my masters, who fall upon me, seize me, ah yes! strike, they fear their city sacked and howling, they fear the avenging soldiers I called forth, and this is only right, upon the sacred city. Defend yourselves now, strike! strike me first, you possess the truth! O my masters, they will then conquer the soldiers, they'll conquer the word and love, they'll spread over the deserts, cross the seas, fill the light of Europe with their black veils—strike the belly, yes, strike the eyes —sow their salt on the continent, all vegetation, all youth will die out, and dumb crowds with shackled feet will plod beside me in the world-wide desert under the cruel sun of the true faith, I'll not be alone. Ah! the pain, the pain they cause me, their rage is good and on this cross-shaped war-saddle where they are now quartering me, pity! I'm laughing, I love the blow that nails me down crucified.

* * *

How silent the desert is! Already night and I am alone, I'm thirsty. Still waiting, where is the city, those sounds in the distance, and the soldiers perhaps the victors, no, it can't be, even if the soldiers are victorious, they're not wicked enough, they won't be able to rule, they'll still say one must become better, and still millions of men between evil and good, torn, bewildered, O Fetish, why hast thou forsaken me? All is over, I'm thirsty, my body is burning, a darker night fills my eyes.

This long, this long dream, I'm awaking, no, I'm going to die, dawn is breaking, the first light, daylight for the living, and for me the inexorable sun, the flies. Who is speaking, no one, the sky is not opening up, no, no, God doesn't speak in the desert, yet whence comes that voice saying: 'If you consent to die for hate and power, who will forgive us?' Is it another tongue in me or still that other fellow refusing to die, at my feet, and repeating: 'Courage! courage! courage!'? Ah! supposing I were wrong again! Once fraternal men, sole recourse, O solitude, forsake me not! Here, here who are you, torn, with bleeding mouth, is it you, Sorcerer, the soldiers defeated you, the salt is burning over there, it's you my beloved master! Cast off that hate-ridden face, be good now, we were mistaken, we'll begin all over again, we'll rebuild the city of mercy, I want to go back home. Yes, help me, that's right, give me your hand. . . ."

A handful of salt fills the mouth of the garrulous slave.

WILLIAM FAULKNER
(1897–1962)
Delta Autumn*

Soon now they would enter the Delta. The sensation was familiar to him. It had been renewed like this each last week in November for more than fifty years—the last hill, at the foot of which the rich unbroken alluvial flatness began as the sea began at the base of its cliffs, dissolving away beneath the unhurried November rain as the sea itself would dissolve away.

At first they had come in wagons: the guns, the bedding, the dogs, the food, the whisky, the keen heart-lifting anticipation of hunting; the young men who could drive all night and all the following day in the cold rain and pitch a camp in the rain and sleep in the wet blankets and rise at daylight the next morning and hunt. There had been bear then. A man shot a doe or a fawn as quickly as he did a buck, and in the afternoons they shot wild turkey with pistols to test their stalking skill and markmanship, feeding all but the breast to the dogs. But that time was gone now. Now they went in cars, driving faster and faster each year because the roads were better and they had farther and farther to drive, the territory in which game still existed drawing yearly inward as his life was drawing inward, until now he was the last of those who had once made the

* 1942. From *Go Down, Moses, and Other Stories*, New York, Random House. Copyright 1942 by William Faulkner.

journey in wagons without feeling it and now those who accompanied him were the sons and grandsons of the men who had ridden for twenty-four hours in the rain or sleet behind the steaming mules. They called him 'Uncle Ike' now, and he no longer told anyone how near eighty he actually was because he knew as well as they did that he no longer had any business making such expeditions, even by car.

In fact, each time now, on that first night in camp, lying aching and sleepless in the harsh blankets, his blood only faintly warmed by the single thin whisky-and-water which he allowed himself, he would tell himself that this would be his last. But he would stand that trip—he still shot almost as well as he ever had, still killed almost as much of the game he saw as he ever killed; he no longer even knew how many deer had fallen before his gun—and the fierce long heat of the next summer would renew him. Then November would come again, and again in the car with two of the sons of his old companions, whom he had taught not only how to distinguish between the prints left by a buck or a doe but between the sound they made in moving, he would look ahead past the jerking arc of the windshield wiper and see the land flatten suddenly and swoop, dissolving away beneath the rain as the sea itself would dissolve, and he would say, "Well, boys, there it is again."

This time though, he didn't have time to speak. The driver of the car stopped it, slamming it to a skidding halt on the greasy pavement without warning, actually flinging the two passengers forward until they caught themselves with their braced hands against the dash. "What the hell, Roth!" the man in the middle said. "Cant you whistle first when you do that? Hurt you, Uncle Ike?"

"No," the old man said. "What's the matter?" The driver didn't answer. Still leaning forward, the old man looked sharply past the face of the man between them, at the face of his kinsman. It was the youngest face of them all, aquiline, saturnine, a little ruthless, the face of his ancestor too, tempered a little, altered a little, staring sombrely through the streaming windshield across which the twin wipers flicked and flicked.

"I didn't intend to come back in here this time," he said suddenly and harshly.

"You said that back in Jefferson last week," the old man said. "Then you changed your mind. Have you changed it again? This aint a very good time to——"

"Oh, Roth's coming," the man in the middle said. His name was Legate. He seemed to be speaking to no one, as he was looking at neither of them. "If it was just a buck he was coming all this distance for, now. But he's got a doe in here. Of course a old man like Uncle Ike cant be interested in no doe, not one that walks on two legs—when she's standing up, that is. Pretty light-colored, too. The one he was after them nights last fall when he said he was coon-hunting, Uncle Ike. The one I figured maybe he was still running when he was gone all that month last January. But of course a old man like Uncle Ike aint got no interest in nothing like that." He chortled, still looking at no one, not completely jeering.

"What?" the old man said. "What's that?" But he had not even so much as glanced at Legate. He was still watching his kinsman's face. The eyes behind the spectacles were the blurred eyes of an old man, but they were quite sharp too; eyes which could still see a gun-barrel and what ran beyond it as well as any of them could. He was remembering himself now: how last year, during the final stage by motor boat in to where they camped, a box of food had been lost overboard and how on the next day his kinsman had gone back to the nearest town for supplies and had been gone overnight. And when he did return, something had happened to him. He would go into the woods with his rifle each dawn when the others went, but the old man, watching him, knew that he was not hunting. "All right," he said. "Take me and Will on to shelter where we can wait for the truck, and you can go on back."

"I'm going in," the other said harshly, "Dont worry. Because this will be the last of it."

"The last of deer hunting, or of doe hunting?" Legate said. This time the old man paid no attention to him even by speech. He still watched the young man's savage and brooding face.

"Why?" he said.

"After Hitler gets through with it? Or Smith or Jones or Roosevelt or Willkie or whatever he will call himself in this country?"

"We'll stop him in this country," Legate said. "Even if he calls himself George Washington."

"How?" Edmonds said. "By singing God bless America in bars at midnight and wearing dime-store flags in our lapels?"

"So that's what's worrying you," the old man said. "I aint noticed this country being short of defenders yet, when it needed them. You did some of it yourself twenty-odd years ago, before you were a grown man even. This country is a little mite stronger than any one man or group of men, outside of it or even inside of it either. I reckon, when the time comes and some of you have done got tired of hollering we are whipped if we dont go to war and some more are hollering we are whipped if we do, it will cope with one Austrian paper-hanger,[1] no matter what he will be calling himself. My pappy and some other better men than any of them you named tried once to tear it in two with a war, and they failed."

---

1. Adolf Hitler (1889–1945). He later took up politics in Germany and was chancellor, with dictatorial power, from 1933 to 1945.

"And what have you got left?" the other said. "Half the people without jobs and half the factories closed by strikes. Half the people on public dole that wont work and half that couldn't work even if they would. Too much cotton and corn and hogs, and not enough for people to eat and wear. The country full of people to tell a man how he cant raise his own cotton whether he will or wont, and Sally Rand[2] with a sergeant's stripes and not even the fan couldn't fill the army rolls. Too much not-butter and not even the guns——"

"We got a deer camp—if we ever get to it," Legate said. "Not to mention does."

"It's a good time to mention does," the old man said. "Does and fawns both. The only fighting anywhere that ever had anything of God's blessing on it has been when men fought to protect does and fawns. If it's going to come to fighting, that's a good thing to mention and remember too."

"Haven't you discovered in—how many years more than seventy is it?—that women and children are one thing there's never any scarcity of?" Edmonds said.

"Maybe that's why all I am worrying about right now is that ten miles of river we still have got to run before we can make camp," the old man said. "So let's get on."

They went on. Soon they were going fast again, as Edmonds always drove, consulting neither of them about the speed just as he had given neither of them any warning when he slammed the car to stop. The old man relaxed again. He watched, as he did each recurrent November while more than sixty of them passed, the land which he had seen change. At first there had been only the old towns along the River and the old towns along the hills, from each of which the planters with their gangs of slaves and then of hired laborers had wrested from the impenetrable jungle of water-standing cane and cypress, gum and holly and oak and ash, cotton patches which as the years passed became fields and then plantations. The paths made by deer and bear became roads and then highways, with towns in turn springing up along them and along the rivers Tallahatchie and Sunflower which joined and became the Yazoo, the River of the Dead of the Choctaws—the thick, slow, black, unsunned streams almost without current, which once each year ceased to flow at all and then reversed, spreading, drowning the rich land and subsiding again, leaving it still richer.

Most of that was gone now. Now a man drove two hundred miles from Jefferson before he found wilderness to hunt in. Now the land lay open from the cradling hills on the East to the rampart of levee on the West, standing horseman-tall with cotton for the world's looms —the rich black land, imponderable and vast, fecund up to the very

2. a well-known fan dancer.

doorsteps of the negroes who worked it and of the white men who owned it; which exhausted the hunting life of a dog in one year, the working life of a mule in five and of a man in twenty—the land in which neon flashed past them from the little countless towns and countless shining this-year's automobiles sped past them on the broad plumb-ruled highways, yet in which the only permanent mark of man's occupation seemed to be the tremendous gins, constructed in sections of sheet iron and in a week's time though they were, since no man, millionaire though he be, would build more than a roof and walls to shelter the camping equipment he lived from when he knew that once each ten years or so his house would be flooded to the second storey and all within it ruined;—the land across which there came now no scream of panther but instead the long hooting of locomotives: trains of incredible length and drawn by a single engine, since there was no gradient anywhere and no elevation save those raised by forgotten aboriginal hands as refuges from the yearly water and used by their Indian successors to sepulchre their fathers' bones, and all that remained of that old time were the Indian names on the little towns and usually pertaining to water—Aluschaskuna, Tillatoba, Homochitto, Yazoo.

By early afternoon, they were on water. At the last little Indian-named town at the end of pavement they waited until the other car and the two trucks—the one carrying the bedding and tents and food, the other the horses—overtook them. They left the concrete and, after another mile or so, the gravel too. In caravan they ground on through the ceaselessly dissolving afternoon, with skid-chains on the wheels now, lurching and splashing and sliding among the ruts, until presently it seemed to him that the retrograde of his remember-ing had gained an inverse velocity from their own slow progress, that the land had retreated not in minutes from the last spread of gravel but in years, decades, back toward what it had been when he first knew it: the road they now followed once more the ancient pathway of bear and deer, the diminishing fields they now passed once more scooped punily and terrifically by axe and saw and mule-drawn plow from the wilderness' flank, out of the brooding and immemorial tangle, in place of ruthless mile-wide parallelograms wrought by ditching the dyking machinery.

They reached the river landing and unloaded, the horses to go overland down stream to a point opposite the camp and swim the river, themselves and the bedding and food and dogs and guns in the motor launch. It was himself, though no horseman, no farmer, not even a countryman save by his distant birth and boyhood, who coaxed and soothed the two horses, drawing them by his own single frail hand until, backing, filling, trembling a little, they surged, halted, then sprang scrambling down from the truck, possessing no affinity for them as creatures, beasts, but being merely insulated by his years and time from the corruption of steel and oiled moving parts which tainted the others.

Then, his old hammer double gun which was only twelve years younger than he standing between his knees, he watched even the last puny marks of man—cabin, clearing, the small and irregular fields which a year ago were jungle and in which the skeleton stalks of this year's cotton stood almost as tall and rank as the old cane had stood, as if man had had to marry his planting to the wilderness in order to conquer it—fall away and vanish. The twin banks marched with wilderness as he remembered it—the tangle of brier and cane impenetrable even to sight twenty feet away, the tall tremendous soaring of oak and gum and ash and hickory which had rung to no axe save the hunter's, had echoed to no machinery save the beat of oldtime steam boats traversing it or to the snarling of launches like their own of people going into it to dwell for a week or two weeks because it was still wilderness. There was some of it left, although now it was two hundred miles from Jefferson when once it had been thirty. He had watched it, not being conquered, destroyed, so much as retreating since its purpose was served now and its time an outmoded time, retreating southward through this inverted-apex, this ▽-shaped section of earth between hills and River until what was left of it seemed now to be gathered and for the time arrested in one tremendous density of brooding and inscrutable impenetrability at the ultimate funnelling tip.

They reached the site of their last-year's camp with still two hours left of light. "You go on over under that driest tree and set down," Legate told him. "—if you can find it. Me and these other young boys will do this." He did neither. He was not tired yet. That would come later. *Maybe it wont come at all this time*, he thought, as he had thought at this point each November for the last five or six of them. *Maybe I will go out on stand in the morning too*; knowing that he would not, not even if he took the advice and sat down under the driest shelter and did nothing until camp was made and supper cooked. Because it would not be the fatigue. It would be because he would not sleep tonight but would lie instead wakeful and peaceful on the cot amid the tent-filling snoring and the rain's whisper as he always did on the first night in camp; peaceful, without regret or fretting, telling himself that was all right too, who didn't have so many of them left as to waste one sleeping.

In his slicker he directed the unloading of the boat—the tents, the stove, the bedding, the food for themselves and the dogs until there should be meat in camp. He sent two of the negroes to cut firewood; he had the cook-tent raised and the stove up and a fire going and supper cooking while the big tent was still being staked down. Then in the beginning of dusk he crossed in the boat to where the horses waited, backing and snorting at the water. He took the lead-ropes and with no more weight than that and his voice, he drew them down into the water and held them beside the boat with only their heads above the surface, as though they actually were suspended from his frail and strengthless old man's hands, while the boat recrossed and each horse in turn lay prone in the shallows, panting and trembling, its eyes rolling in the dusk, until the same weightless hand and unraised voice gathered it surging upward, splashing and thrashing up the bank.

Then the meal was ready. The last of light was gone now save the thin stain of it snared somewhere between the river's surface and the rain. He had the single glass of thin whisky-and-water, then, standing in the churned mud beneath the stretched tarpaulin, he said grace over the fried slabs of pork, the hot soft shapeless bread, the canned beans and molasses and coffee in iron plates and cups,— the town food, brought along with them—then covered himself again, the others following. "Eat," he said. "Eat it all up. I dont want a piece of town meat in camp after breakfast tomorrow. Then you boys will hunt. You'll have to. When I first started hunting in this bottom sixty years ago with old General Compson and Major de Spain and Roth's grandfather and Will Legate's too, Major de Spain wouldn't allow but two pieces of foreign grub in his camp. That was one side of pork and one ham of beef. And not to eat for the first supper and breakfast neither. It was to save until along toward the end of camp when everybody was so sick of bear meat and coon and venison that we couldn't even look at it."

"I thought Uncle Ike was going to say the pork and beef was for the dogs," Legate said, chewing. "But that's right; I remember. You just shot the dogs a mess of wild turkey every evening when they got tired of deer guts."

"Times are different now," another said. "There was game here then."

"Yes," the old man said quietly. "There was game here then."

"Besides, they shot does then too," Legate said. "As it is now, we aint got but one doe-hunter in——"

"And better men hunted it," Edmonds said. He stood at the end of the rough plank table, eating rapidly and steadily as the others ate. But again the old man looked sharply across at the sullen, handsome, brooding face which appeared now darker and more sullen still in the light of the smoky lantern. "Go on. Say it."

"I didn't say that," the old man said. "There are good men everywhere, at all times. Most men are. Some are just unlucky, because most men are a little better than their circumstances give them a chance to be. And I've known some that even the circumstances couldn't stop."

"Well, I wouldn't say——" Legate said.

"So you've lived almost eighty years," Edmonds said. "And that's what you finally learned about the other animals you lived among. I suppose the question to ask you is, where have you been all the time you were dead?"

There was a silence; for the instant even Legate's jaw stopped chewing while he gaped at Edmonds. "Well, by God, Roth——" the third speaker said. But it was the old man who spoke, his voice still peaceful and untroubled and merely grave:

"Maybe so," he said. "But if being what you call alive would have learned me any different, I reckon I'm satisfied, wherever it was I've been."

"Well, I wouldn't say that Roth——" Legate said.

The third speaker was still leaning forward a little over the table, looking at Edmonds. "Meaning that it's only because folks happen to be watching him that a man behaves at all," he said. "Is that it?"

"Yes," Edmonds said. "A man in a blue coat, with a badge on it watching him. Maybe just the badge."

"I deny that," the old man said. "I dont——"

The other two paid no attention to him. Even Legate was listening to them for the moment, his mouth still full of food and still open a little, his knife with another lump of something balanced on the tip of the blade arrested halfway to his mouth. "I'm glad I dont have your opinion of folks," the third speaker said. "I take it you include yourself."

"I see," Edmonds said. "You prefer Uncle Ike's opinion of circumstances. All right. Who makes the circumstances?"

"Luck," the third said. "Chance. Happen-so. I see what you are getting at. But that's just what Uncle Ike said: that now and then, maybe most of the time, man is a little better than the net result of his and his neighbors' doings, when he gets the chance to be."

This time Legate swallowed first. He was not to be stopped this time. "Well, I wouldn't say that Roth Edmonds can hunt one doe every day and night for two weeks and was a poor hunter or a unlucky one neither. A man that still have the same doe left to hunt on again next year——"

"Have some meat," the man next to him said.

"——aint no unlucky—— What?" Legate said.

"Have some meat." The other offered the dish.

"I got some," Legate said.

"Have some more," the third speaker said. "You and Roth Edmonds both. Have a heap of it. Clapping your jaws together that way with nothing to break the shock." Someone chortled. Then they all laughed, with relief, the tension broken. But the old man was speaking, even into the laughter, in that peaceful and still untroubled voice:

"I still believe. I see proof everywhere. I grant that man made a heap of his circumstances, him and his living neighbors between them. He even inherited some of them already made, already almost ruined even. A while ago Henry Wyatt there said how there used to be more game here. There was. So much that we even killed does. I seem to remember Will Legate mentioning that too—" Someone laughed, a single guffaw, stillborn. It ceased and they all listened, gravely, looking down at their plates. Edmonds was drinking his coffee, sullen, brooding, inattentive.

"Some folks still kill does," Wyatt said. "There wont be just one buck hanging in this bottom tomorrow night without any head to fit it."

"I didn't say all men," the old man said. "I said most men. And not just because there is a man with a badge to watch us. We probably wont even see him unless maybe he will stop here about noon tomorrow and eat dinner with us and check our licenses——"

"We dont kill does because if we did kill does in a few years there wouldn't even be any bucks left to kill, Uncle Ike," Wyatt said.

"According to Roth yonder, that's one thing we wont never have to worry about," the old man said. "He said on the way here this morning that does and fawns—I believe he said women and children—are two things this world aint ever lacked. But that aint all of it," he said. "That's just the mind's reason a man has to give himself because the heart dont always have time to bother with thinking up words that fit together. God created man and He created the world for him to live in and I reckon He created the kind of world He would have wanted to live in if He had been a man—the ground to walk on, the big woods, the trees and the water, and the game to live in it. And maybe He didn't put the desire to hunt and kill game in man but I reckon He knew it was going to be there, that man was going to teach it to himself, since he wasn't quite God himself yet——"

"When will he be?" Wyatt said.

"I think that every man and woman, at the instant when it dont even matter whether they marry or not, I think that whether they marry then or afterward or dont never, at that instant the two of them together were God."

"Then there are some Gods in this world I wouldn't want to touch, and with a damn long stick," Edmonds said. He set his coffee cup down and looked at Wyatt. "And that includes myself, if that's what you want to know. I'm going to bed." He was gone. There was a general movement among the others. But it ceased and they stood again about the table, not looking at the old man, apparently held there yet by his quiet and peaceful voice as the heads of the swimming horses had been held above the water by his weightless hand. The three negroes—the cook and his helper and old Isham— were sitting quietly in the entrance of the kitchen tent, listening too, the three faces dark and motionless and musing.

"He put them both here: man, and the game he would follow and kill, foreknowing it. I believe He said, 'So be it.' I reckon He even foreknew the end. But He said, 'I will give him his chance. I will give him warning and foreknowledge too, along with the desire to follow and the power to slay. The woods and fields he ravages and the game he devastates will be the consequence and signature of his crime and guilt, and his punishment.'—Bed time," he said. His voice and inflection did not change at all. "Breakfast at four oclock, Isham. We want meat on the ground by sunup time."

There was a good fire in the sheet-iron heater; the tent was warm and was beginning to dry out, except for the mud underfoot. Edmonds was already rolled into his blankets, motionless, his face to the wall. Isham had made up his bed too—the strong, battered iron cot, the stained mattress which was not quite soft enough, the worn, often-washed blankets which as the years passed were less and less warm enough. But the tent was warm; presently, when the kitchen was cleaned up and readied for breakfast, the young negro would come in to lie down before the heater, where he could be roused to put fresh wood into it from time to time. And then, he knew now he would not sleep tonight anyway; he no longer needed to tell himself that perhaps he would. But it was all right now. The day was ended now and night faced him, but alarmless, empty of fret. *Maybe I came for this,* he thought: *Not to hunt, but for this. I would come anyway, even if only to go back home tomorrow.* Wearing only his bagging woolen underwear, his spectacles folded away in the worn case beneath the pillow where he could reach them readily and his lean body fitted easily into the old worn groove of mattress and blankets, he lay on his back, his hands crossed on his breast and his eyes closed while the others undressed and went to bed and the last of the sporadic talking died into snoring. Then he opened his eyes and lay peaceful and quiet as a child, looking up at the motionless belly of rain-murmured canvas upon which the glow of the heater was dying slowly away and would fade still further until the young negro, lying on two planks before it, would sit up and stoke it and lie back down again.

They had a house once. That was sixty years ago, when the Big Bottom was only thirty miles from Jefferson and old Major de Spain, who had been his father's cavalry commander in '61 and '2 and '3 and '4, and his cousin (his older brother; his father too) had taken him into the woods for the first time. Old Sam Fathers was alive then, born in slavery, son of a Negro slave and a Chickasaw chief, who had taught him how to shoot, not only when to shoot but when not to; such a November dawn as tomorrow would be and the old man led him straight to the great cypress and he had known the buck would pass exactly there because there was something running in Sam Fathers' veins which ran in the veins of the buck too, and they stood there against the tremendous trunk, the old man of seventy and the boy of twelve, and there was nothing save the dawn until suddenly the buck was there, smoke-colored out of nothing, magnificent with speed: and Sam Fathers said, 'Now. Shoot quick and shoot slow:' and the gun levelled rapidly without haste and crashed and he walked to the buck lying still intact and still in the shape of that magnificent speed and bled it with Sam's knife and Sam dipped his hands into the hot blood and marked his face forever while he stood trying not to tremble, humbly and with pride too though the boy of twelve had been unable to phrase it then: *I slew you; my bearing must not shame your quitting life. My conduct forever onward must become your death*; marking him for that and for more than that: that day and himself and Mc-Caslin juxtaposed not against the wilderness but against the tamed land, the old wrong and shame itself, in repudiation and denial at least of the land and the wrong and shame even if he couldn't cure the wrong and eradicate the shame, who at fourteen when he learned of it had believed he could do both when he became competent and when at twenty-one he became competent he knew that he could do neither but at least he could repudiate the wrong and shame, at least in principle, and at least the land itself in fact, for his son at least: and did, thought he had: then (married then) in a rented cubicle in a back-street stock-traders' boarding-house, the first and last time he ever saw her naked body, himself and his wife juxtaposed in their turn against that same land, that same wrong and shame from whose regret and grief he would at least save and free his son and, saving and freeing his son, lost him. They had the house then. That roof, the two weeks of each November which they spent under it, had become his home. Although since that time they had lived during the two fall weeks in tents and not always in the same place two years in succession and now his companions were the sons and even the grandsons of them with whom he had lived in the house and for almost fifty years now the house itself had not even existed, the conviction, the sense and feeling of home, had been merely transferred into the canvas. He owned a house in Jefferson, a good house though small, where he had had a wife and lived with her and lost her, ay, lost her even though he had lost her in the rented cubicle before he and his old clever dipsomaniac partner had finished the house for them to move into it: but lost her, because she loved him. But women hope for so much. They never live too long to still believe that anything within the scope of their passionate wanting is likewise within the range of their passionate hope: and it was still kept for him by his dead wife's widowed niece and her children and he was comfortable in it, his wants and needs and even the small trying harmless crochets of an old man looked after by blood at least related to the blood which he had elected out of all the earth to cherish. But he spent the time within those walls waiting for November, because even this tent with its muddy floor and the bed which was not wide enough nor soft enough nor even warm enough, was his home and these men, some of whom he only saw during these two November weeks and not one of whom even bore any name he used to know—De Spain and Compson and Ewell and Hogganbeck—were more his kin than any. Because this was his land——

The shadow of the youngest negro loomed. It soared, blotting the heater's dying glow from the ceiling, the wood billets thumping into the iron maw until the glow, the flame, leaped high and bright across the canvas. But the negro's shadow still remained, by its length and breadth, standing, since it covered most of the ceiling, until after a moment he raised himself on one elbow to look. It was not the negro, it was his kinsman; when he spoke the other turned sharp against the red firelight the sullen and ruthless profile. "Nothing," Edmonds said. "Go on back to sleep."

"Since Will Legate mentioned it," McCaslin said, "I remember you had some trouble sleeping in here last fall too. Only you called it coon-hunting then. Or was it Will Legate called it that?" The other didn't answer. Then he turned and went back to his bed. McCaslin, still propped on his elbow, watched until the other's shadow sank down the wall and vanished, became one with the mass of sleeping shadows. "That's right," he said. "Try to get some sleep. We must have meat in camp tomorrow. You can do all the setting up you want to after that." He lay down again, his hands crossed again on his breast, watching the glow of the heater on the canvas ceiling. It was steady again now, the fresh wood accepted, being assimilated; soon it would begin to fade again, taking with it the last echo of that sudden upflare of a young man's passion and unrest. Let him lie awake for a little while, he thought; He will lie still some day for a long time without even dissatisfaction to disturb him. And lying awake here, in these surroundings, would soothe him if anything could, if anything could soothe a man just forty years old. Yes, he thought; Forty years old or thirty, or even the trembling and sleepless ardor of a boy; already the tent, the rain-murmured canvas globe, was once more filled with it. He lay on his back, his eyes closed, his breathing quiet and peaceful as a child's, listening to it—that silence which was never silence but was myriad. He could almost see it, tremendous, primeval, looming, musing downward upon this puny evanescent clutter of human sojourn which after a single brief week would vanish and in another week would be completely healed, traceless in the unmarked solitude. Because it was his land, although he had never owned a foot of it. He had never wanted to, not even after he saw plain its ultimate doom, watching it retreat year by year before the onslaught of axe and saw and log-lines and then dynamite and tractor plows, because it belonged to no man. It belonged to all; they had only to use it well, humbly and with pride. Then suddenly he knew why he had never wanted to own any of it, arrest at least that much of what people called progress, measure his longevity at least against that much of its ultimate fate. It was because there was just exactly enough of it. He seemed to see the two of them—himself and the wilderness—as coevals,[3] his own span as a hunter, a woodsman, not contemporary with his first breath but transmitted to him, assumed by him gladly, humbly, with joy and pride, from that old Major de Spain and that old Sam Fathers who had taught him to hunt, the two spans running out together, not toward oblivion, nothingness, but into a dimension free of both time and space where once more the untreed land warped and wrung to mathematical squares of rank cotton for the frantic old-world people to turn into shells to shoot at one another, would find ample room for both—the names, the faces of the old men he had known and loved and for a little while outlived, moving again among the shades of tall unaxed trees and sightless brakes where the wild strong immortal game ran forever before the tireless belling immortal hounds, falling and rising phoenix-like to the soundless guns.

He had been asleep. The lantern was lighted now. Outside in the darkness the oldest negro, Isham, was beating a spoon against the bottom of a tin pan and crying, "Raise up and get yo foa clock coffy. Raise up and get yo foa clock coffy," and the tent was full of low talk and of men dressing, and Legate's voice, repeating: "Get out of here now and let Uncle Ike sleep. If you wake him up, he'll go out with us. And he aint got any business in the woods this morning."

So he didn't move. He lay with his eyes closed, his breathing gentle and peaceful, and heard them one by one leave the tent. He listened to the breakfast sounds from the table beneath the tarpaulin and heard them depart—the horses, the dogs, the last voice until it died away and there was only the sounds of the negroes

---

3. contemporaries.

clearing breakfast away. After a while he might possibly even hear the first faint clear cry of the first hound ring through the wet woods from where the buck had bedded, then he would go back to sleep again—The tent-flap swung in and fell. Something jarred sharply against the end of the cot and a hand grasped his knee through the blanket before he could open his eyes. It was Edmonds, carrying a shotgun in place of his rifle. He spoke in a harsh, rapid voice:

"Sorry to wake you. There will be a——"

"I was awake," McCaslin said. "Are you going to shoot that shotgun today?"

"You just told me last night you want meat," Edmonds said. "There will be a——"

"Since when did you start having trouble getting meat with your rifle?"

"All right," the other said, with that harsh, restrained, furious impatience. Then McCaslin saw in his hand a thick oblong: an envelope. "There will be a message here some time this morning, looking for me. Maybe it wont come. If it does, give the messenger this and tell h— say I said No."

"A what?" McCaslin said. "Tell who?" He half rose onto his elbow as Edmonds jerked the envelope onto the blanket, already turning toward the entrance, the envelope striking solid and heavy and without noise and already sliding from the bed until McCaslin caught it, divining by feel through the paper as instantaneously and conclusively as if he had opened the envelope and looked, the thick sheaf of banknotes. "Wait," he said. "Wait:"—more than the blood kinsman, more even than the senior in years, so that the other paused, the canvas lifted, looking back, and McCaslin saw that outside it was already day. "Tell her No," he said. "Tell her." They stared at one another—the old face, wan, sleep-raddled above the tumbled bed, the dark and sullen younger one at once furious and cold. "Will Legate was right. This is what you called coon-hunting. And now this." He didn't raise the envelope. He made no motion, no gesture to indicate it. "What did you promise her that you haven't the courage to face her and retract?"

"Nothing!" the other said. "Nothing! This is all of it. Tell her I said No." He was gone. The tent flap lifted on an in-waft of faint light and the constant murmur of rain, and fell again, leaving the old man still half-raised onto one elbow, the envelope clutched in the other shaking hand. Afterward it seemed to him that he had begun to hear the approaching boat almost immediately, before the other could have got out of sight even. It seemed to him that there had been no interval whatever: the tent flap falling on the same out-waft of faint and rain-filled light like the suspiration and expiration of the same breath and then in the next second lifted again—the mounting snarl of the outboard engine, increasing, nearer and nearer and louder and louder then cut short off, ceasing with the absolute instantaneity of a blown-out candle, into the lap and plop of water under the bows as the skiff slid in to the bank, the youngest negro, the youth, raising the tent flap beyond which for that instant he saw the boat—a small skiff with a negro man sitting in the stern beside the up-slanted motor—then the woman entering, in a man's hat and a man's slicker and rubber boots, carry-ing the blanket-swaddled bundle on one arm and holding the edge of the unbuttoned raincoat over it with the other hand: and bring-ing something else, something intangible, an effluvium which he knew he would recognise in a moment because Isham had already told him, warned him, by sending the young negro to the tent to announce the visitor instead of coming himself, the flap falling at last on the young negro and they were alone—the face indistinct and as yet only young and with dark eyes, queerly colorless but not ill and not that of a country woman despite the garments she wore, looking down at him where he sat upright on the cot now, clutch-ing the envelope, the soiled undergarment bagging about him and the twisted blankets huddled about his hips.

"Is that his?" he cried. "Dont lie to me!"

"Yes," she said. "He's gone."

"Yes. He's gone. You wont jump him here. Not this time. I dont reckon even you expected that. He left you this. Here." He fumbled at the envelope. It was not to pick it up, because it was still in his hand; he had never put it down. It was as if he had to fumble somehow to co-ordinate physically his heretofore obedient hand with what his brain was commanding of it, as if he had never performed such an action before, extending the envelope at last, saying again, "Here. Take it. Take it:" until he became aware of her eyes, or not the eyes so much as the look, the regard fixed now on his face with that immersed contemplation, that bottomless and intent candor, of a child. If she had ever seen either the envelope or his movement to extend it, she did not show it.

"You're Uncle Isaac," she said.

"Yes," he said. "But never mind that. Here. Take it. He said to tell you No." She looked at the envelope, then she took it. It was sealed and bore no superscription. Nevertheless, even after she glanced at the front of it, he watched her hold it in the one free hand and tear the corner off with her teeth and manage to rip it open and tilt the neat sheaf of bound notes onto the blanket with-out even glancing at them and look into the empty envelope and take the edge between her teeth and tear it completely open before she crumpled and dropped it.

"That's just money," she said.

"What did you expect? What else did you expect? You have known him long enough or at least often enough to have got that child, and you dont know him any better than that?"

"Not very often. Not very long. Just that week here last fall, and in January he sent for me and we went West, to New Mexico. We were there six weeks, where I could at least sleep in the same apartment where I cooked for him and looked after his clothes——"

"But not marriage," he said. "Not marriage. He didn't promise you that. Dont lie to me. He didn't have to."

"No. He didn't have to. I didn't ask him to. I knew what I was doing. I knew that to begin with, long before honor I imagine he called it told him the time had come to tell me in so many words what his code I suppose he would call it would forbid him forever to do. And we agreed. Then we agreed again before he left New Mexico, to make sure. That that would be all of it. I believed him. No, I dont mean that; I mean I believed myself. I wasn't even listening to him anymore by then because by that time it had been a long time since he had had anything else to tell me for me to have to hear. By then I wasn't even listening enough to ask him to please stop talking. I was listening to myself. And I believed it. I must have believed it. I dont see how I could have helped but believe it, because he was gone then as we had agreed and he didn't write as we had agreed, just the money came to the bank in Vicksburg in my name but coming from nobody as we had agreed. So I must have believed it. I even wrote him last month to make sure again and the letter came back unopened and I was sure. So I left the hospital and rented myself a room to live in until the deer season opened so I could make sure myself and I was waiting beside the road yesterday when your car passed and he saw me and so I was sure."

"Then what do you want?" he said. "What do you want? What do you expect?"

"Yes," she said. And while he glared at her, his white hair awry from the pillow and his eyes, lacking the spectacles to focus them, blurred and irisless and apparently pupilless, he saw again that grave, intent, speculative and detached fixity like a child watching him. "His great great—Wait a minute.—great great *great* grandfather was your grandfather. McCaslin. Only it got to be Edmonds. Only it got to be more than that. Your cousin McCaslin was there that day when your father and Uncle Buddy won Tennie from Mr. Beauchamp for the one that had no name but Terrel so you called him Tomey's Terrel, to marry. But after that it got to be Edmonds." She regarded him, almost peacefully, with that unwinking and heatless fixity—the dark wide bottomless eyes in the face's dead and toneless pallor which to the old man looked anything but dead, but young and incredibly and even ineradicably alive—as though she were not only looking at anything, she was not even speaking to anyone but herself. "I would have made a man of him. He's not a man yet. You spoiled him. You, and Uncle Lucas and Aunt Mollie. But mostly you."

"Me?" he said. "Me?"

"Yes. When you gave to his grandfather that land which didn't belong to him, not even half of it by will or even law."

"And never mind that too," he said. "Never mind that too. You," he said. "You sound like you have been to college even. You sound almost like a Northerner even, not like the draggle-tailed women of these Delta peckerwoods. Yet you meet a man on the street one afternoon just because a box of groceries happened to fall out of a boat. And a month later you go off with him and live with him until he got a child on you: and then, by your own statement, you sat there while he took his hat and said goodbye and walked out. Even a Delta peckerwood would look after even a draggle-tail better than that. Haven't you got any folks at all?"

"Yes," she said. "I was living with one of them. My aunt, in Vicksburg. I came to live with her two years ago when my father died; we lived in Indianapolis then. But I got a job, teaching school here in Aluschaskuna, because my aunt was a widow, with a big family, taking in washing to sup——"

"Took in what?" he said. "Took in washing?" He sprang, still seated even, flinging himself backward onto one arm, awry-haired, glaring. Now he understood what it was she had brought into the tent with her, what old Isham had already told him by sending the youth to bring her in to him—the pale lips, the skin pallid and dead-looking yet not ill, the dark and tragic and foreknowing eyes. *Maybe in a thousand or two thousand years in America*, he thought. *But not now! Not now!* He cried, not loud, in a voice of amazement, pity, and outrage: "You're a nigger!"

"Yes," she said. "James Beauchamp—you called him Tennie's Jim though he had a name—was my grandfather. I said you were Uncle Isaac."

"And he knows?"

"No," she said. "What good would that have done?"

"But you did," he cried. "But you did. Then what do you expect here?"

"Nothing."

"Then why did you come here? You said you were waiting in Aluschaskuna yesterday and he saw you. Why did you come this morning?"

"I'm going back North. Back home. My cousin brought me up

the day before yesterday in his boat. He's going to take me on to Leland to get the train."

"Then go," he said. Then he cried again in that thin not loud and grieving voice: "Get out of here! I can do nothing for you! Cant nobody do nothing for you!" She moved; she was not looking at him again, toward the entrance. "Wait," he said. She paused again, obediently still, turning. He took up the sheaf of banknotes and laid it on the blanket at the foot of the cot and drew his hand back beneath the blanket. "There," he said.

Now she looked at the money, for the first time, one brief blank glance, then away again. "I dont need it. He gave me money last winter. Besides the money he sent to Vicksburg. Provided. Honor and code too. That was all arranged."

"Take it," he said. His voice began to rise again, but he stopped it. "Take it out of my tent." She came back to the cot and took up the money; whereupon once more he said, "Wait:" although she had not turned, still stooping, and he put out his hand. But, sitting, he could not complete the reach until she moved her hand, the single hand which held the money, until she touched it. He didn't grasp it, he merely touched it—the gnarled, bloodless, bone-light bone-dry old man's fingers touching for a second the smooth young flesh where the strong old blood ran after its long lost journey back to home. "Tennie's Jim," he said. "Tennie's Jim." He drew the hand back beneath the blanket again: he said harshly now: "It's a boy, I reckon. They usually are, except that one that was its own mother too."

"Yes," she said. "It's a boy." She stood for a moment longer, looking at him. Just for an instant her free hand moved as though she were about to lift the edge of the raincoat away from the child's face. But she did not. She turned again when once more he said Wait and moved beneath the blanket.

"Turn your back," he said. "I am going to get up. I aint got my pants on." Then he could not get up. He sat in the huddled blanket, shaking, while again she turned and looked down at him in dark interrogation. "There," he said harshly, in the thin and shaking old man's voice. "On the nail there. The tent-pole."

"What?" she said.

"The horn!" he said harshly. "The horn." She went and got it, thrust the money into the slicker's side pocket as if it were a rag, a soiled handkerchief, and lifted down the horn, the one which General Compson had left him in his will, covered with the unbroken skin from a buck's shank and bound with silver.

"What?" she said.

"It's his. Take it."

"Oh," she said. "Yes. Thank you."

"Yes," he said, harshly, rapidly, but not so harsh now and soon not harsh at all but just rapid, urgent, until he knew that his voice was running away with him and he had neither intended it nor could stop it: "That's right. Go back North. Marry: a man in your own race. That's the only salvation for you—for a while yet, maybe a long while yet. We will have to wait. Marry a black man. You are young, handsome, almost white; you could find a black man who would see in you what it was you saw in him, who would ask nothing of you and expect less and get even still less than that, if it's revenge you want. Then you will forget all this, forget it ever happened, that he ever existed—" until he could stop it at last and did, sitting there in his huddle of blankets during the instant when, without moving at all, she blazed silently down at him. Then that was gone too. She stood in the gleaming and still dripping slicker, looking quietly down at him from under the sodden hat.

"Old man," she said, "have you lived so long and forgotten so much that you dont remember anything you ever knew or felt or even heard about love?"

Then she was gone too. The waft of light and the murmur of the constant rain flowed into the tent and then out again as the flap fell. Lying back once more, trembling, panting, the blanket huddled to his chin and his hands crossed on his breast, he listened to the pop and snarl, the mounting then fading whine of the motor until it died away and once again the tent held only silence and the sound of rain. And cold too: he lay shaking faintly and steadily in it, rigid save for the shaking. This Delta, he thought: This Delta. *This land which man has deswamped and denuded and derivered in two generations so that white men can own plantations and commute every night to Memphis and black men own plantations and ride in jim crow cars to Chicago to live in millionaires' mansions on Lakeshore Drive, where white men rent farms and live like niggers and niggers crop on shares and live like animals, where cotton is planted and grows man-tall in the very cracks of the sidewalks, and usury and mortgage and bankruptcy and measureless wealth, Chinese and African and Aryan and Jew, all breed and spawn together until no man has time to say which one is which nor cares. . . .* No wonder the ruined woods I used to know dont cry for retribution! he thought: The people who have destroyed it will accomplish its revenge.

The tent flap jerked rapidly in and fell. He did not move save to turn his head and open his eyes. It was Legate. He went quickly to Edmonds' bed and stooped, rummaging hurriedly among the still-tumbled blankets.

"What is it?" he said.

"Looking for Roth's knife," Legate said. "I come back to get a horse We got a deer on the ground." He rose, the knife in his hand, and hurried toward the entrance.

"Who killed it?" McCaslin said. "Was it Roth?"

"Yes," Legate said, raising the flap.

"Wait," McCaslin said. He moved, suddenly, onto his elbow. "What was it?" Legate paused for an instant beneath the lifted flap. He did not look back.

"Just a deer, Uncle Ike," he said impatiently. "Nothing extra." He was gone; again the flap fell behind him, wafting out of the tent again the faint light and the constant and grieving rain. McCaslin lay back down, the blanket once more drawn to his chin, his crossed hands once more weightless on his breast in the empty tent.

"It was a doe," he said.

RAUL BRANDÃO
(1867?–1930)
The Thief and His Little Daughter*

The daughter of Death's-Head and the Orphanage Girl grew up in the alley amid the screams of prostitutes and the obscene jests of soldiers and thieves. She was four years old, and she slept in corners or in the arms of the Fat Girl or the Deaf Girl. The Old Man, who had been a ditch-digger, would set her on his knee, and to amuse her would open his enormous mouth that had not a tooth inside it. The Landlady was very good to her, and the "girls" would shower her with frenzied kisses; and then for days at a time she would see nothing of them; they would forget all about her, and she would cry herself to sleep in the beds or on the doorsteps. Her mother was the only one who avoided her always.

"I can't bear the sight of her!"

Yet she grew up. She grew up as chance would have it, in that realm of hallucination in which human beings are transformed as in a dream into figures of truth which, at certain hours only, come to the surface, from out of that world of pain and tragedy to which we all belong. . . .

Death's-Head, the thief, said to his sweetheart:

"Why can't you bear the sight of the child?"

"I can't! That's all . . ."

"You're worse than the nanny-goats!"

*1908. Translated from the Portuguese by Samuel Putnam for *Heart of Europe*, an anthology of European creative writing edited by Klaus Mann and Hermann Kesten. Copyright 1943 by A. A. Wyn, Inc. (formerly L. B. Fischer Publishing Corp.), New York. Reprinted in full. The punctuation ". . ." does not indicate omissions from this text.

And then he would beat her. She would be silent, her eyes full of malice and of fear.

"You may beat me if you like, but I can't bear to look at her. Take her out of my sight. Leave me alone!"

The thief would cover the child with old rags and draw her to his bosom, and in winter would give her an old overcoat to keep her warm.

"The brat isn't dead yet?" the Orphanage Girl would ask, thinking possibly that Death's-Head would give her a beating.

The brat did not die. With her eyes ever on her father, she would clasp his legs and want to follow him when he left. And so she continued to grow up in that dark alleyway, amid the screams and the insults and the sad little songs that the women sang.

"But why do you beat the little one?" the other women would ask.

"I don't know! I don't know!"

At the beginning of winter, the Orphanage Girl was taken to the hospital, and before she went, she embraced her daughter, weeping desperately. It was all they could do to wrest the child from her arms. The "girls" had to take care of the little one now, and she slept either with them or with the thief. One morning, they said to the latter:

"It's all up with your sweetie now; they are burying her today."

For hours Death's-Head remained alone, lost in thought. Then he heard laughter outside. Lifting the door-curtain, he went directly up to the old ditch-digger, who was sitting there with the little girl on his knees. All the others were silent as he snatched her roughly from the old man's arms, looking him fiercely in the face as the old fellow laughed back with his great toothless mouth, which was like that of a wild beast. Death's-Head left with the child and did not return until afternoon, when he turned her over to the Fat Girl.

"Keep her for me until night."

When night came, he called his daughter and held her closely for a long time. At that moment, it may be, he understood the horror which the Orphanage Girl had felt for her offspring, and the tenderness she displayed just before they took her to the hospital—she had, perhaps, seen the Old Man with the child in his arms and that monstrous gaping mouth of his.

"Come with me."

"Where are we going, Daddy? For a walk?"

"For a walk."

The little one laughed.

"Now?"

"Now."

And taking her by her little hand, he led her down to the river.

to the exact spot where he had met the Orphanage Girl for the first time. Climbing into a boat with her, he unmoored it and began rowing.

"Where are we going, Daddy?"

"You'll see. Go to sleep."

The thief now felt the same unconscious horror that had gripped the mother. He did not reason it out. It was not hatred for the alley, which was the only life that awaited the child; it was not seeing her in the ditch-digger's brutal hands or those of the squint-eyed soldier who gazed at her with silent ferocity. There was something that pained him, made it hard for him to breathe. That thing could not go on existing at his side—he had to put an end to it. He felt this, to the very depths of his being, as the mother had felt it without being able to explain it. In the thief's soul was a savage horror at the thought of inflicting all this upon the child. It was necessary to kill her, absolutely necessary.

"Now—"

But the child looked up at him and laughed—and he was afraid.

"Go to sleep!"

The little one began stammering—"O Daddy! Daddy!"—began uttering those disconnected and extraordinary words that children are in the habit of speaking, and along with them, the obscenities which she had heard from the Old Man in the alley as she clung to his neck. The thief was shaken by the profundities of life.

"O Daddy! Daddy!" she cried suddenly, "what is that up there?" And the little one, who had never had a glimpse of stars in that tragic alleyway, pointed to the sky.

"Stars."

"Ah, stars! stars!"— And the childish monologue was resumed. Charming words, words so often repeated, yet always new and fresh on lips the color of roses; it was as if life were always awakening for the first time when a child spoke. Terrible words as well, words that belonged to the tragic life of the alley and which she unconsciously mingled with the others.

At last she fell asleep in the bottom of the boat, gazing up at the sky. But sleeping she inspired as much fear in him as when awake. . . . Very slowly, he put out his hands and fastened a rope about her waist. The little one stirred, awoke, smiled up at him, opened her mouth to say "Daddy," and then dropped back into innocent slumber. The thief for a long time gazed at her quietly. The child could not go on living. Before his eyes always was the toothless mouth of the Old Man, and the women with their obscenities. He knew what fate was in store for her. The child was the thing that was troubling him. He would have peace on this earth only when he had thrown her into the river and had seen her going down there, down, down to the very bottom, far from this life of pain and tragedy.

For the first time he felt that he was committing a crime against something immense and extraordinary, something huge and invisible —felt with horror that he was poisoning the wellsprings of life. It was necessary to kill her. . . . Yet even now there came over him another fear, without real existence. . . . Noiselessly, holding his breath, he tried to steal forward, to sink his nails into her throat and strangle her. He could not. . . . He had a mission to fulfill, and he could not fulfill it.

"Am I going to be afraid? Am I going to be afraid?" And he wrung his hands, his enormous hands, his hands that were so cold.

He had come up against a living wall of tenderness. His soul was writhing in the tremendous silence of the night, crushed between two contradictory forces that weighed upon him like mountains. He glanced up at the sky—to the stars of no avail. The child was sleeping in the bottom of the boat. And those two forces, he could almost see them advancing upon him, looming larger all the while. The drama took place in the silence of the night, without his being able to separate his feeling of tenderness from the fierce and necessary act that he meditated.

Finally, he laid his hands upon her and she awoke.

"Daddy! Daddy!"

Thinking that he was playing, she nestled her head against him and exclaimed:

"The stars! The stars! . . . O Rosa! O Rosa! O Rosa! O Rosa! . . . Daddy, you are my friend, yes, you are. . . . How pretty it is up there! . . . Daddy! . . .

Through that pure and innocent mouth the world to which we all belong, we and the thieves of the streets, was speaking. It was too much for him. He could not go through with it. He was paralyzed with pain and horror as he listened to her and felt that little hand in his enormous ones. The thief tried to speak but the words would not come. What he had thought would be easy was impossible. It was better to kill her, but he could not. There was nothing to do but accept her fate: the squint-eyed soldier, the Old Man who waited for her with the joy of the wild beast that scents its prey near at hand and opens its frightful jaws. Slowly, he undid the cord, rowed the boat back to land, and, leaving it adrift, with the child in his arms he returned to deliver her to the life of the alley.

A Note on Translation

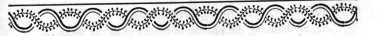

Reading literature in translation is a pleasure on which it is fruitless to frown. The purist may insist that we ought always read in the original languages, and we know ideally that he is right. But his counsel is a counsel of perfection, quite impractical even for him, since no man in one lifetime can master all the languages whose literatures he might wish to explore. Master languages as fast as we may, we shall always have to read to some extent in translation, and this means we must be alert to what we are about: if in reading a work of literature in translation we are not reading the "original," what precisely are we reading? This is a question of great complexity, to which justice cannot be done in a brief note. Nevertheless, the following sketch of some of the considerations that a mature answer would involve may be helpful to those who are coming into a self-conscious relation with literature in translation for the first time.

One of the memorable scenes of ancient literature is the meeting of Hector and Andromache in Book VI of Homer's *Iliad*. Hector, leader and mainstay of the armies defending Troy, is implored by his wife Andromache to withdraw within the city walls and carry on the defense from there, where his life will not be constantly at hazard. In Homer's text her opening words to him are these: δαιμόνιε, φθίσει σε τὸ σὸν μένος. How should they be translated into English?

Here is how they have actually been translated into English by capable translators, at various periods, in verse and prose.

1. George Chapman, 1598

O noblest in desire,
Thy mind, inflamed with others' good, will set thy self on fire.

2. John Dryden, 1693

Thy dauntless heart (which I foresee too late),
Too daring man, will urge thee to thy fate.

3. Alexander Pope, 1715

Too daring Prince! ...
For sure such courage length of life denies,
And thou must fall, thy virtue's sacrifice.

1651

4. William Cowper, 1791

> Thy own great courage will cut short thy days,
> My noble Hector....

5. Lang, Leaf, and Myers, 1883 (prose)

> Dear my lord, this thy hardihood will undo thee....

6. A. T. Murray, 1924 (prose, Loeb Library)

> Ah, my husband, this prowess of thine will be thy doom....

7. E. V. Rieu, 1950 (prose)

> "Hector," she said, "you are possessed. This bravery of yours will be your end."

8. I. A. Richards, 1950 (prose)

> "Strange man," she said, "your courage will be your destruction."

9. Richmond Lattimore, 1951

> Dearest,
> Your own great strength will be your death....

From these strikingly different renderings of the same six words, certain facts about the nature of translation begin to emerge. We notice, for one thing, that Homer's word μένος is diversified by the translators into "mind," "dauntless heart," "such courage," "great courage," "hardihood," "prowess," "bravery," "courage," "great strength." The word has in fact all these possibilities. Used of things, it normally means "force"; of animals, "fierceness" or "brute strength" or (in the case of horses) "mettle"; of men, "passion" or "spirit" or even "purpose." Homer's application of it in the present case points our attention equally—whatever particular sense we may imagine Andromache to have uppermost—to Hector's force, strength, fierceness in battle, spirited heart and mind. But since English has no matching term of like inclusiveness, the passage as the translators give it to us reflects this lack and we find one attribute singled out to the exclusion of the rest.

Here then is the first and most crucial fact about any work of literature read in translation. It cannot escape the linguistic characteristics of the language into which it is turned: the grammatical, syntactical, lexical, and phonetic boundaries which constitute collectively the individuality or "genius" of that language. A Greek play or a Russian novel in English will be governed first of all by the resources of the English language, resources which are certain to be in every instance very different, as the efforts with μένος show, from those of the original.

Turning from μένος to δαιμόνιε in Homer's clause, we encounter a second crucial fact about translations. Nobody knows exactly what shade of meaning δαιμόνιε had for Homer. In later writers the word normally suggests divinity, something miraculous, wondrous; but in Homer it appears as a vocative of address for both chieftain and commoner, man and wife. The coloring one gives it must therefore be determined either by the way one thinks a Greek wife of Homer's era might actually address her husband (a subject on which we have no information whatever), or in the way one thinks it suitable for a hero's wife to address her husband in an epic poem, that is to say, a highly stylized and formal work. In general, the translators of our century will be seen to have eschewed formality in order to stress the intimacy, the wifeliness, and, especially in Lattimore's case, the tenderness of Andromache's appeal: (6) "Ah, my husband," (7) "Hector" (with perhaps a hint, in "you are possessed," of the alarmed distaste with which wives have so often viewed their husbands' bellicose moods), (8) "Strange man," (9) "Dearest." On the other hand, the older translators have obviously removed Andromache to a certain epic or heroic distance from her beloved, whence she sees and kindles to his selfless courage, acknowledging, even in the moment of pleading with him to be otherwise, his moral grandeur and the tragic destiny this too certainly implies: (1) "O noblest in desire, . . . inflamed by others' good"; (2) "Thy dauntless heart (which I foresee too late), / Too daring man"; (3) "Too daring Prince! . . . / And thou must fall, thy virtue's sacrifice"; (4) "My noble Hector." Even the less specific "Dear my lord" of Lang, Leaf, and Myers looks in the same direction because of its echo of the speech of countless Shakespearean men and women who have shared this powerful moral sense: "Dear my lord, make me acquainted with your cause of grief"; "Perseverance, dear my lord, keeps honor bright"; etc.

The fact about translation which emerges from all this is that just as the translated work reflects the individuality of the language it is turned into, so it reflects the individuality of the age in which it is done, and the age will permeate it everywhere like yeast in dough. We think of one kind of permeation when we think of the governing verse forms and attitudes toward verse at a given epoch. In Chapman's time, experiments seeking an "heroic" verse form for English were widespread, and accordingly he tries a "fourteener" couplet (two rhymed lines of seven stresses each) in his *Iliad* and a pentameter couplet in his *Odyssey*. When Dryden and Pope wrote, a closed pentameter couplet had become established as the heroic form *par excellence*. By Cowper's day, thanks largely to the prestige of *Paradise Lost*, the couplet had gone out of fashion for narrative poetry in favor of blank verse. Our age, inclining to prose and in verse to proselike informalities and relaxations, has predictably produced half a dozen excellent prose translations of the *Iliad*, but only one in verse, and that one in swirling loose hexameters which are much of the time closer to the verse of William Carlos Williams and some of the prose of novelists like Faulkner than to the swift firm tread of Homer's Greek. For if it is true that what we translate from a given work is what, wearing the spectacles of our time, we see in it, it is also true that we see in it what we have the power to translate.

Of course there are other effects of the translator's epoch on his translation besides those exercised by contemporary taste in verse and verse forms. Chapman writes in a great age of poetic metaphor and therefore almost instinctively translates his understanding of Homer's verb φθίσει ("to cause to wane, consume, waste, pine") into metaphorical terms of flame, presenting his Hector to us as a man of burning generosity who will be consumed by this very ardor. This is a conception rooted in large part in the psychology of the Elizabethans, who had the habit of speaking of the soul as "fire," of one of the four temperaments as "fiery," of even the more material bodily processes, like digestion, as if they were carried on by the heat of fire ("concoction," "decoction"). It is rooted too in that characteristic Renaissance élan so unforgettably expressed in characters like Tamburlaine and Dr. Faustus, the former of whom exclaims to the stars above:

> ... I, the chiefest lamp of all the earth,
> First rising in the East with mild aspect,
> But fixèd now in the meridian line,
> Will send up fire to your turning spheres,
> And cause the sun to borrow light of you. ...

Pope and Dryden, by contrast, write to audiences for whom strong metaphor has become suspect. They therefore reject the fire image (which we must recall is not present in the Greek) in favor of a form of speech more congenial to their age, the *sententia* or aphorism, and give it extra vitality by making it the scene of a miniature drama: in Dryden's case, the hero's dauntless heart "urges" him (in the double sense of physical as well as moral pressure) to his fate; in Pope's, the hero's courage, like a judge, "denies" continuance of life, with the consequence that he "falls"—and here Pope's second line suggests analogy to the sacrificial animal—the victim of his own essential nature, of what he is.

To pose even more graphically the pressures that a translator's period brings, consider the following lines from Hector's reply to Andromache's appeal that he withdraw, first in Chapman's Elizabethan version, then in Lattimore's twentieth-century one:

Chapman, 1598:
> The spirit I did first breathe
> Did never teach me that—much less since the contempt of death
> Was settled in me, and my mind knew what a Worthy was,
> Whose office is to lead in fight and give no danger pass
> Without improvement. In this fire must Hector's trial shine.
> Here must his country, father, friends be in him made divine.

Lattimore, 1951:
> ...the spirit would not let me, since I have learned to be valiant
> and to fight always among the foremost rank of the Trojans,
> winning for myself great glory, and for my father.

If one may exaggerate to make a necessary point, the world of *Henry V* and *Othello* suddenly gives way here to the world of Willie Loman; we are still reading the *Iliad*, but we have obviously come home.

Besides the two factors so far mentioned, language and period, as affecting the character of a translation, there is inevitably a third—the translator himself, with his particular degree of talent, his personal way of regarding the work to be translated, his own special hierarchy of values, moral, esthetic, metaphysical (which may or may not be summed up in a "world view"), his unique style or lack of it. But this influence all readers are likely to bear in mind, and it needs no laboring here. That, for example, two translators of Hamlet, one a Freudian, the other an Existentialist, will produce impressively different translations is obvious from the fact that when Freudian and Existentialist argue about the play in English they often seem to have different plays in mind.

We can now return to the question from which we started. After all allowances have been made for language, age, and individual translator, is anything of the original left? What, in short, does the reader of translations read? Let it be said at once that in utility prose —prose whose function is mainly referential—he reads everything that matters. "*Nicht Rauchen*," "*Défense de Fumer*," and "*No Smoking*," posted in a railway car, make their point, and the differences between them in sound and form have no significance for us in that context. Since the prose of a treatise and of most fiction is preponderantly referential, we rightly feel, when we have paid close attention to Cervantes or Montaigne or Machiavelli or Tolstoy in a good English translation, that we have had roughly the same experience as a native Spaniard, Frenchman, Italian, or Russian. But "roughly" is the correct word; for good prose points iconically *to* itself as well as referentially beyond itself, and everything that it points to in itself in the original (rhythms, sounds, idioms, word play, etc.) must alter radically in being translated. The best analogy is to imagine a Van Gogh painting reproduced in the medium of tempera, etching, or engraving: the "picture" remains, but the intricate interanimation of volumes with colorings with brushstrokes has disappeared.

When we move on to poetry, even in its longer narrative and dramatic forms—plays like *Oedipus*, poems like the *Iliad* or the *Divine Comedy*—our situation as English readers worsens appreciably, as the many unlike versions of Andromache's appeal to Hector make very clear. But, again, only appreciably. True, this is the point at which the fact that a translation is *always* an interpretation explodes irresistibly on our attention; but if it is a good translation, the result will be a sensitive interpretation and also a work with intrinsic interest in its own right—at very best, a true work of art, a new poem. It is only when the shorter, primarily lyrical forms of poetry are presented that the reader of translations faces insuperable disadvantage. In these forms, the referential aspect of language has a tendency to disappear into, or, more often, draw its real meaning and accreditation from, the iconic aspect. Let us look for just a moment at a brief poem by Federico García Lorca and its English translation (by Stephen Spender and J. L. Gili):

> *¡Alto pinar!*
> *Cuatro palomas por el aire van.*
>
> *Cuatro palomas*
> *vuelan y tornan.*
> *Llevan heridas*
> *sus cuatro sombras.*
>
> *¡Bajo pinar!*
> *Cuatro palomas en la tierra están.*

> Above the pine trees:
> Four pigeons go through the air.
>
> Four pigeons
> fly and turn round.
> They carry wounded
> their four shadows.
>
> Below the pine trees:
> Four pigeons lie on the earth.

In this translation the referential sense of the English words follows with remarkable exactness the referential sense of the Spanish words they replace. But the life of Lorca's poem does not lie in that sense. It lies in such matters as the abruptness, like an intake of breath at a sudden revelation, of the two exclamatory lines (1 and 5), which then exhale musically in images of flight and death; or as the echoings of *palomas* in *heridas* and *sombras*, bringing together (as in fact the hunter's gun has done) these unrelated nouns and the unrelated experiences they stand for in a sequence that seems, momentarily, to have all the logic of a tragic action, in which *doves* become *wounds* become *shadows;* or as the external and internal rhyming among the five verbs, as though all motion must (as in fact it must) end with *están.*

Since none of this can be brought over into another tongue (least of all Lorca's rhythms), the translator must decide between leaving his reader to wonder why Lorca is a poet to be bothered about at all, and making a new but true poem of his own, whose merit will almost certainly be in inverse ratio to its likeness to the original. Samuel Johnson made such a poem in translating Horace's famous *Diffugere nives,* and so did A. E. Housman. If we juxtapose the last two stanzas of each translation, and the corresponding Latin, we can see at a glance that each has the consistency and inner life of a genuine poem, and that neither of them (even if we consider only what is obvious to the eye, the line-lengths) is very close to Horace.

> *Cum semel occideris, et de te splendida Minos*
> *fecerit arbitria,*
> *non, Torquate, genus, non te facundia, non te*
> *restituet pietas.*
>
> *Infernis neque enim tenebris Diana pudicum*
> *liberat Hippolytum*
> *nec Lethaea valet Theseus abrumpere caro*
> *vincula Pirithoo.*

Johnson:

> Not you, Torquatus, boast of Rome,
> When Minos once has fixed your doom,
> Or eloquence, or splendid birth,
> Or virtue, shall restore to earth.
> Hippolytus, unjustly slain,
> Diana calls to life in vain;
> Nor can the might of Theseus rend
> The chains of hell that hold his friend.

Housman:

> When thou descendest once the shades among,
>   The stern assize and equal judgment o'er,
> Not thy long lineage nor thy golden tongue,
>   No, nor thy righteousness, shall friend thee more.
>
> Night holds Hippolytus the pure of stain,
>   Diana steads him nothing, he must stay;
> And Theseus leaves Pirithous in the chain
>   The love of comrades cannot take away.

The truth of the matter is that when the translator of short poems chooses to be literal, he loses most or all of the poetry; and when he chooses to make his own poetry, he loses most or all of the author. There is no way out of this dilemma, and in our own selection of short poems for this edition we have acknowledged the problem by excluding translations in favor of short poems written originally in English.

We may assure ourselves, then, that the reading of literature in translation is not the disaster it has sometimes been represented. It is true that, however good the translation, we remain at a remove from the original, the remove becoming closest to impassable in the genre of the lyric poem. But with this exception, it is obvious that translation brings us closer by far to the work than we could be if we did not read it at all, or read it with a defective knowledge of the language. "To a thousand cavils," said Samuel Johnson, "one answer is sufficient; the purpose of a writer is to be read, and the criticism which would destroy the power of pleasing must be blown aside." Johnson was defending Pope's Homer for those marks of its own time and place that make it the great interpretation it is; but Johnson's exhilarating common sense applies equally to the problem we are considering here. Literature is to be read, and the criticism that would destroy the reader's power to make some form of contact with much of the world's great writing must indeed be blown aside.

MAYNARD MACK

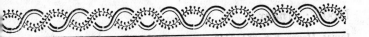

Index

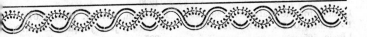